LEVITICUS
1–16

VOLUME 3

THE ANCHOR BIBLE is a fresh approach to the world's greatest classic. Its object is to make the Bible accessible to the modern reader; its method is to arrive at the meaning of biblical literature through exact translation and extended exposition, and to reconstruct the ancient setting of the biblical story, as well as the circumstances of its transcription and the characteristics of its transcribers.

THE ANCHOR BIBLE is a project of international and interfaith scope. Protestant, Catholic, and Jewish scholars from many countries contribute individual volumes. The project is not sponsored by any ecclesiastical organization and is not intended to reflect any particular theological doctrine. Prepared under our joint supervision, THE ANCHOR BIBLE is an effort to make available all the significant historical and linguistic knowledge which bears on the interpretation of the biblical record.

THE ANCHOR BIBLE is aimed at the general reader with no special formal training in biblical studies; yet, it is written with the most exacting standards of scholarship, reflecting the highest technical accomplishment.

This project marks the beginning of a new era of cooperation among scholars in biblical research, thus forming a common body of knowledge to be shared by all.

William Foxwell Albright
David Noel Freedman
GENERAL EDITORS

THE ANCHOR BIBLE

LEVITICUS
1–16

♦

A New Translation
with
Introduction and Commentary

JACOB MILGROM

THE ANCHOR BIBLE

Doubleday

New York   London   Toronto   Sydney   Auckland

For my students of the Graduate Seminar Hebrew 201:
I have learned much from my teachers, more from my colleagues, but from
my students more than all.

—Taʿanit 7a

THE ANCHOR BIBLE
Published by Doubleday
a division of Bantam Doubleday Dell Publishing Group, Inc.
666 Fifth Avenue, New York, New York 10103

THE ANCHOR BIBLE, DOUBLEDAY, and the portrayal of an anchor
with the letters AB are trademarks of Doubleday, a division of
Bantam Doubleday Dell Publishing Group, Inc.

LIBRARY OF CONGRESS CATALOGING-IN-PUBLICATION DATA

Bible. O.T. Leviticus I–XVI. English. Milgrom. 1991.
    Leviticus 1–16 : a new translation with introduction and commentary /
by Jacob Milgrom. — 1st ed.
        p.   cm. — (The Anchor Bible; v. 3)
    Includes bibliographical references and index.
    1. Bible. O.T. Leviticus I–XVI—Commentaries. I. Milgrom, Jacob, 1923– .
II. Title. III. Series: Bible. English. Anchor Bible. 1964 ; v. 3.
BS192.2.A1 1964.G3 vol. 3.
[BS1253]
220.7′7 s—dc20
[222′.13077]   90-37069
                                                                    CIP

ISBN 0-385-11434-6

Copyright © 1991 by Doubleday, a division of Bantam Doubleday Dell Publishing Group, Inc.

Printed in the United States of America
November 1991

10 9 8 7 6 5 4 3 2 1

First Edition

CONTENTS

◆

Abbreviations   xi

Introduction   1

  A. Name, Scope, Text, and Methodology   1
  B. The Antiquity of P   3
  C. On the Parameters, Date, and Provenience of P   13
  D. On Vocabulary, Style, and Structure   35
  E. The Priestly Theology   42
  F. The Priest   52
  G. Anthropomorphism and Revelation   58
  H. The Composition of Lev 1–16   61
  I. The Commentators   63

Bibliography   69

Translation, Notes, and Comments   129

I. The Sacrificial System (Chapters 1–7)   131
Sacrificial Instructions Directed to the Laity (1:1–5:26)   133
  Introduction (1:1–2)   133
  The Burnt Offering (1:3–17)   133
    From the Herd (1:3–9)   133
    From the Flock (1:10–13)   133
    From Birds (1:14–17)   133
    Comment: The Burnt Offering: Name, Antiquity, and Function   172
  The Cereal Offering (2:1–16)   177
    Raw Flour (2:1–3)   177
    Cooked: Baked, Toasted, Fried (2:4–10)   177
    Injunctions Concerning Leaven, Honey, and Salt (2:11–13)   178
    Natural Grain (2:14–16)   178

CONTENTS

Comment: The Cereal Offering: Function, Name, Types,
  and Development 195
The Well-Being Offering (3:1–17) 202
  From the Herd (3:1–5) 202
  From the Flock (3:6–16a) 203
  The Law of Suet and Blood (3:16b–17) 203
  Comment: The Well-Being Offering: Name, Motivation,
    Rendering, and Function 217
The Purification Offering (4:1–35) 226
  Introduction (4:1–2) 226
  Of the High Priest (4:3–12) 226
  Of the Community (4:13–21) 226
  Of the Chieftain (4:22–26) 227
  Of the Commoner (4:27–35) 227
  Comment: The Purification Offering 253
    A. The Name 253
    B. The Function 254
    C. The Theology 258
    D. The Two Kinds 261
    E. The *ḥaṭṭāʾt* of Num 15:22–26 264
    F. Genital Discharges 269
    G. Corpse Contamination 270
    H. The Levites' Induction 278
    I. The Consecration of the Altar 278
    J. The Nazirite 279
    K. The Public Cult 281
    L. Ezekiel's Temple and Priest 281
    M. The Remaining Instances 284
    N. The Provenience 288
    O. The Function of the *ḥaṭṭāʾt* (and *ʿōlā*): A New Proposal ... 289
The Graduated Purification Offering (5:1–13) 292
  The Four Cases (5:1–4) 292
  Resolution: Confession and Sacrifice (5:5–13) 293
  Comment: The Graduated Purification Offering:
    The Reduction of the Force of Impurity 307
The Reparation Offering (5:14–26) 319
  For Sacrilege Against Sancta (5:14–16) 319
  For Suspected Sacrilege Against Sancta (5:17–19) 319
  For Sacrilege Against Oaths (5:20–26) 319
  Comments: The Reparation Offering 339
    A. Etymology 339
    B. Sacrilege 345
    C. Additional Cases of Sancta Desecration 356

CONTENTS

D. Unwitting Sin in the Ancient Near East   361
E. The *'āšām* of the *měṣōrāʿ*   363
F. Sacrilege Against Oaths   365
G. The Priestly Doctrine of Repentance   373
Sacrifices: The Administrative Order (6:1–7:38)   378
Introduction (6:1–2a)   378
The Burnt Offering (6:2b–6)   378
The Cereal Offering (6:7–11)   379
The High Priest's Daily Cereal Offering (6:12–16)   379
The Purification Offering (6:17–23)   379
The Reparation Offering (7:1–6)   380
The Priestly Prebends from the Most
Holy Offerings (7:7–10)   380
The Well-Being Offering (7:11–21)   380
No Suet or Blood May Be Eaten (7:22–27)   381
The Priestly Prebends from the
Well-Being Offering (7:28–36)   381
Summary (7:37–38)   381
Comments: On Sacrifices   440
A. On the Theory of Sacrifice   440
B. Sancta Contagion   443
C. The *Tāmîd*   456
D. *Kārēt*   457
E. The *Těnûpâ*   461
F. The *Šôq Hattěrûmâ*   473
G. The Prophets and the Cult   482
H. Neusner on Holy Things   485
I. The Order of Sacrifices in a Cultic Rite   488

II. The Inauguration of the Cult (Chapters 8–10)   491

The Consecration of the Priests (8:1–36)   493
Introduction   494
Comments: The Consecration of the Priests   542
A. The Structure of Chapter 8   542
B. Leviticus 8 and Exodus 29   545
C. The Samsuiluna B Inscription   549
D. The Purpose of Anointing   553
E. Moses as Priest   555
F. The Priestly Consecration According to
the Temple Scroll   558
G. The Priestly Consecration: A Rite of Passage   566

CONTENTS

The Inaugural Service (9:1–24)	569
The Sacrificial Procedure (9:1–21)	569
Blessing and Theophany (9:22–24)	570
Comment: The Eighth Day, Meaning and Paradigm	592
The Tragic Aftermath of the Inaugural Service (10:1–20)	595
Nadab and Abihu (10:1–7)	595
The Conduct and Function of the Priests (10:8–11)	595
On Eating the Priestly Portions (10:12–20)	596
Comments: The Tragic Aftermath of the Inaugural Service	628
A. What Lies Behind the Nadab and Abihu Incident?	628
B. Nadab and Abihu in the History of Exegesis	633
C. What Lies Behind the Squabble over the Purification Offering?	635

III. The Impurity System (Chapters 11–16) — **641**

Diet Laws (11:1–47)	643
Introduction (11:1–2a)	643
Quadrupeds (11:2b–8)	643
Fish (11:9–12)	643
Birds (11:13–19)	643
Flying Insects (11:20–23)	644
Purification Procedures (11:24–40)	644
Land Swarmers (11:41–45)	645
Summary (11:46–47)	645
Comments: Diet Laws	691
A. The Composition of Lev 11	691
B. Deut 14:4–21, An Abridgment of Lev 11	698
C. The Ethical Foundations of the Dietary System: 1. The Blood Prohibition	704
D. The Ethical Foundations of the Dietary System: 2. Ritual Slaughter	713
E. The Ethical Foundations of the Dietary System: 3. The Prohibited Animals	718
F. The Ethical Foundations of the Dietary System: 4. The Kid Prohibition	737
Childbirth (12:1–8)	742
Comments: Childbirth	763
A. The Impurity of Genital Discharges: A Comparative Survey	763
B. The Impurity of Bodily Discharges: A Rationale	766

CONTENTS

Scale Disease (13:1–59) 768
  Introduction (13:1) 768
  Shiny Marks (13:2–8) 768
  Discolorations (13:9–17) 769
  Boils (13:18–23) 769
  Burns (13:24–28) 769
  Scalls (13:29–37) 770
  Tetters (13:38–39) 770
  Baldness (13:40–44) 770
  The Comportment of a Certified Carrier (13:45–46) 771
  Fabrics (13:47–59) 771
  Comments: Scale Disease 816
    A. The Nature of *Ṣāraʿat* and Its Rationale 816
    B. The Causes of *Ṣāraʿat* 820
    C. Symptomatology and Diagnosis of *Ṣāraʿat* in Humans,
      by David P. Wright 825
Purification After Scale Disease (14:1–57) 827
  Rite of Passage (14:1–9) 827
  Purification Sacrifices (14:10–20) 827
  Purification Sacrifices for the Poor (14:21–32) 828
  Fungous Houses: Diagnosis and Purification (14:33–53) 828
  Summary of Chapters 13–14 (14:54–57) 829
  Comments: Purification After Scale Disease 886
    A. The Composition of Chapters 13–14 886
    B. The Priest and the Ritual 887
    C. The Biblical Measures of Capacity, by Susan Rattray 890
Genital Discharges (15:1–33) 902
  Introduction (15:1–2a) 902
  Abnormal Male Discharges (15:2b–15) 902
  Normal Male Discharges (15:16–17) 902
  Marital Intercourse (15:18) 903
  Normal Female Discharges (15:19–24) 903
  Abnormal Female Discharges (15:25–30) 903
  Consequences for the Sanctuary and for Israel (15:31) 903
  Summary (15:32–33) 904
  Comments: Genital Discharges 948
    A. The Menstruant 948
    B. The Communicability of Impurity,
      by David P. Wright 953
    C. Ablutions 957
    D. First-Day Ablutions in Qumran 968
    E. The Priestly Laws of Sancta Contamination 976
    F. The Table of Purification Procedures and Effects 986

CONTENTS

G. The Rationale for Biblical Impurity (Continued) 1000
H. Neusner on Purities 1004
The Day of Purgation *(Yôm Kippûr)* (16:1–34) 1009
Introduction (16:1) 1009
Precautions and Provisions (16:2–5) 1009
The Purgation Ritual (16:6–19) 1009
The Scapegoat Ritual (16:20–22a) 1010
The Altar Sacrifices (16:22b–25) 1010
The Purification of the High Priest's Assistants (16:26–28) 1010
The Date: An Appendix (16:29–34a) 1011
Summary (16:34b) 1011
Comments: The Day of Purgation 1059
A. The Structure of Chapter 16 1059
B. The Public Fast 1065
C. Temple Purgation in Babylon 1067
D. The Date of Yom Kippur 1070
E. Azazel and Elimination Rites in
the Ancient Near East 1071
F. *Kippēr* 1079

Indexes **1085**

ABBREVIATIONS

◆

AAA	*Annals of Archaeology and Anthropology*
AASOR	Annual of the American Schools of Oriental Research
AB	Anchor Bible
ABL	R. F. Harper, *Assyrian and Babylonian Letters* (Chicago, 1892–1914)
ʿ*Abod. Zar.*	ʿ*Aboda Zara*
ʾ*Abot R. Nat.*	ʾ*Abot Rabbi Nathan*
AfO	*Archiv für Orientforschung*
ʾ*Ag.*	ʾ*Aggadah/*ʾ*Aggadic*
AHw	W. von Soden, *Akkadisches Handwörterbuch* (Wiesbaden, 1965–81)
Aistl.	Aistleitner
Akk.	Akkadian
AMT	R. C. Thompson, *Assyrian Medical Texts from the Originals in the British Museum* (London, 1923)
AnBib	Analecta Biblica
ANET[3]	J. B. Pritchard, ed., *Ancient Near Eastern Texts Relating to the Old Testament* (Princeton, 1969)
AnOr	*Analecta orientalia*
AOAT	Alter Orient und Altes Testament
Arab.	Arabic
ʿ*Arak.*	ʿ*Arakin*
Arıstotle, *Hist. anim.*	Aristotle, *Historia animalium*
ARM	Archives royales de Mari
ASTI	*Annual of the Swedish Theological Institute*
b.	Babylonian Talmud
B. Bat.	*Baba Batra*
B. Meṣ.	*Baba Meṣiʿa*
B. Qam.	*Baba Qamma*
BA	*Biblical Archaeologist*

BAM	F. Köcher, *Die babylonisch-assyrische Medizin* (Berlin, 1963)
BAR	*Biblical Archaeologist Reader*
Bar.	*Baraita*
BASOR	*Bulletin of the American Schools of Oriental Research*
BBR	H. Zimmern, *Beiträge zur Kenntnis der babylonischen Religion* (Leipzig, 1901)
B.C.E.	Before the Common Era; corresponds to B.C.
BDB	F. Brown, S. R. Driver, and C. A. Briggs, *Hebrew and English Lexicon of the Old Testament* (Oxford, orig. 1907; I cite the 1953 ed.)
Bek.	*Bekorot*
Ber.	*Berakot*
Beṣ ˙	*Beṣah*
BH	biblical Hebrew
BibOr	*Biblica et orientalia*
Bik.	*Bikkurim*
BJRL	*Bulletin of the John Rylands University Library of Manchester*
BL	G. R. Driver and J. C. Miles, *The Babylonian Laws* (Oxford, 1955–56)
BM	*Beth Mikra*
BN	*Biblische Notizen*
BRM	Babylonian Records in the Library of J. Pierpont Morgan
BZ	*Biblische Zeitschrift*
CAD	*The Assyrian Dictionary of the Oriental Institute of the University of Chicago*
CBQ	*Catholic Biblical Quarterly*
CD	Damascus Document
cf.	compare
CH	Code of Hammurabi
chap(s).	chapter(s)
CIH	*Corpus inscriptionum himyariticarum*
CIS	*Corpus inscriptionum semiticarum*
Clem. Alex. *Strom.*	Clement of Alexandria, *Stromateis*
col(s).	column(s)
CT	*Cuneiform Texts from Babylonian Tablets*
CTA	A. Herdner, *Corpus des tablettes en cunéiformes alphabétiques découvertes à Ras Shamra-Ugarit de 1929 à 1939* (Paris, 1963)
CTH	designation of compositions after Laroche 1971

cyl.	cylinder
D	Deuteronomist
DDS	M. Weinfeld, *Deuteronomy and the Deuteronomic School* (Oxford, 1972)
Diog. Laertius *Pythag.*	Diogenes Laertius, *Pythagoras,* in *Lives of Eminent Philosophers*
DISO	C.-F. Jean and J. Hoftijzer, *Dictionnaire des inscriptions sémitiques de l'ouest* (Leiden, 1965)
DJD	J. T. Milik et al., eds., *Discoveries in the Judaean Desert* (Oxford, 1955–62)
E	Elohist Source
EA	El-Amarna
EA	J. A. Knudtzon, *Die El-Amarna-Tafeln* (Aalen, 1964)
ʿEd.	*ʿEduyyot*
EI	*Eretz-Israel*
EM	*Encyclopaedia Miqraʾit*
Enc Jud	*Encyclopedia Judaica*
Eng.	English
ERE	J. Hastings, ed., *Encyclopedia of Religion and Ethics*
ʿErub.	*ʿErubin*
esp.	especially
ET	*The Expository Times*
EvQ	*The Evangelical Quarterly*
fig(s).	figure(s)
FRLANT	Forschungen zur Religion und Literatur des Alten und Neuen Testaments
Giṭ.	*Giṭṭin*
GKC	W. Gesenius, ed. E. Kautsch, trans. A. Cowley, *Gesenius' Hebrew Grammar* (Oxford, 1983)
H	Holiness Code
Ḥag.	*Ḥagiga*
Hagg.	*See* ʾAg.
HAR	*Hebrew Annual Review*
HAT	Handbuch zum Alten Testament
HBR	G. M. Beckman, *Hittite Birth Rituals,* 2d ed. (Wiesbaden, 1983; 1st ed. Malibu, 1978)
Heliod.	Heliodorus, *Aethiopica*
Herod.	Herodotus
HL	Hittite Laws
Homer, *Ody.*	Homer, *The Odyssey*
Hor.	*Horayot*

ABBREVIATIONS

HTR	*Harvard Theological Review*
HUCA	*Hebrew Union College Annual*
Ḥul.	*Ḥullin*
ICC	International Critical Commentary
IDB	G. A. Buttrick, ed., *Interpreter's Dictionary of the Bible*
IEJ	*Israel Exploration Journal*
J. M.	Jacob Milgrom
JA	*Journal asiatique*
JAAR	*Journal of the American Academy of Religion*
JANESCU	*Journal of the Ancient Near Eastern Society of Columbia University*
JAOS	*Journal of the American Oriental Society*
JB	*Jerusalem Bible*
JBL	*Journal of Biblical Literature*
JCS	*Journal of Cuneiform Studies*
J	Yahwist Source
JEA	*Journal of Egyptian Archaeology*
JEn	*Jewish Encyclopaedia*
JJS	*Journal of Jewish Studies*
JNES	*Journal of Near Eastern Studies*
JNSL	*Journal of Northwest Semitic Languages*
Jos.	Josephus (Loeb Classical Library editions)
Ant.	*Antiquities of the Jews*
Con. Ap.	*Contra Apion*
Wars	*The Jewish Wars*
JPOS	*Journal of the Palestine Oriental Society*
JQR	*Jewish Quarterly Review*
JRAS	*Journal of the Royal Asiatic Society*
JSOT	*Journal for the Study of the Old Testament*
JSS	*Journal of Semitic Studies*
JTS	*Journal of Theological Studies*
Jub.	*Jubilees*
K./Q.	Ketib/Qri'
KAH	*Keilschrifttexte aus Assur historischen Inhalts*
KAI	H. Donner and W. Röllig, *Kanaanäische und aramäische Inschriften* (Wiesbaden, 1968–71)
KAR	*Keilschrifttexte aus Assur religiösen Inhalts*
KB	L. Koehler and W. Baumgartner, *Lexicon in Veteris Testamenti libros* (Leiden, 1958)
KBo	*Keilschrifttexte aus Boghazkoy*
Kel. B. M.	*Kelim Baba Meṣiʿa*
Kel. B. Q.	*Kelim Baba Qamma*

ABBREVIATIONS

Ker.	Keritot
Ketub.	Ketubot
Kh.	tablets from Khafadje in the collections of the Oriental Institute, University of Chicago
Kil.	Kil'ayim
KTU	Die keilalphabetischen Texte aus Ugarit
KUB	Keilschrifturkunden aus Boghazkoy
LBH	late biblical Hebrew
LE	Laws of Eshnunna
lit.	literally
LKA	E. Ebeling, Literarische Keilschrifttexte aus Assur (Berlin, 1953)
LSC	F. Sokolowski, Lois sacrées des cités grecques (Paris, 1969)
Luc.	Lucian, De Syria Dea
LXX	Septuagint
LXXAB	Septuagint, Codices Alexandrinus and Vaticanus
m.	Mishna
Ma'aś.	Ma'aśerot
Maim.	Maimonides
Mak.	Makkot
Makš.	Makširin
MAL	Middle Assyrian Laws
MAOG	Mitteilungen der Altorientalischen Gesellschaft
MDP	Mémoires de la Délégation en Perse
Meg.	Megilla/construct Megillat (e.g., Megillat Ta'anit)
Me'il.	Me'ila
Mek.	Mekilta
Menaḥ.	Menaḥot
Mid.	Middot
Midr.	Midrash
Midr. 'Ag.	'Aggadic Midrash
Midr. Exod. Rab.	Midrash Exodus Rabbah
Midr. Gen. Rab.	Midrash Genesis Rabbah
Midr. Lev. Rab.	Midrash Leviticus Rabbah
Midr. Num. Rab.	Midrash Numbers Rabbah
Midr. Tanḥ.	Midrash Tanḥuma
Midr. Tanḥ. B	Midrash Tanḥuma, ed. M. Buber (New York, 1946)
MIOF	Mitteilungen des Instituts für Orientforschung
Miqw.	Miqwa'ot
MMT	Ma'āśê Miqṣat Hattôrâ, Qumran Cave 4, 394–99
Mo'ed Qaṭ.	Mo'ed Qaṭan

ABBREVIATIONS

MS(S)	manuscript(s)
MT	Masoretic Text
MVÄG	*Mitteilungen der vorderasiatisch-ägyptischen Gesellschaft*
Naz.	*Nazir*
NEB	*New English Bible*
Ned.	*Nedarim*
Neg.	*Negaʿim*
Nid.	*Niddah*
NJPS	*New Jewish Publication Society Bible*
NT	New Testament
OECT	Oxford Editions of Cuneiform Texts
Ohol.	*Oholot*
Or	*Orientalia* (Rome)
OTS	*Oudtestamentische Studiën*
P	Priestly Source
PAAJR	*Proceedings of the American Academy of Jewish Research*
par(s).	paragraph(s)
Paus.	Pausanias
PEQ	*Palestine Exploration Quarterly*
Pesaḥ.	*Pesaḥim*
Pesh.	Peshitta
Pesiq. R.	*Pesiqta Rabbati*
Pesiq. Rab Kah.	*Pesiqta de Rab Kahana*
Philo	Philo
Dec.	*De Decalogo*
Fug.	*De fuga et inventione*
Her.	*Quis rerum divinarum Heres*
Plant.	*De plantatione*
Som.	*De somniis*
Virt.	*De virtutibus*
Vit. Mos.	*De vitae Mose*
Pirqe R. El.	*Pirqe Rabbi Eleazar*
pl.	plural
Pliny, *H.N.*	Pliny, *Historia naturalis*
Plutarch, *Quaest. Rom.*	Plutarch, *Quaestiones Romanae*
PRU	C. F.-A. Schaeffer and J. Nougayrol, eds., *Le Palais royal d'Ugarit* (Paris, 1955–65)
1QH	Qumran, *Thanksgiving Psalms*, Cave 1
Qidd.	*Qiddušin*
1QM	Qumran, *War Scroll*, Cave 1
1QS	Qumran, *Manual of Discipline*, Cave 1

1QSa	Qumran, *Rule of the Congregation*, Cave 1
4QD	Qumran fragment on scale disease, Cave 4
4QOrd	Qumran, *Ordinances*, Cave 4
4QSam^a	Qumran, 1 Sam 1:22b–2:6; 2:16–25, Cave 4
4QtgLev	Qumran, *Targum to Leviticus*, Cave 4
4QThr	Qumran fragments on Purities, Cave 4
11QT	Qumran, Temple Scroll, Cave 11
R. Acc.	F. Thureau-Dangin, *Rituels accadiens* (Paris, 1921)
RA	*Revue d'assyriologie et d'archéologie orientale*
RB	*Revue biblique*
REJ	*Revue des études juives*
rev.	reverse
RHA	*Revue hittite et asianique*
RIDA	*Revue internationale des droits de l'antiquité*
Roš Haš.	*Roš Haššana*
RS	Ras Shamra, field numbers of tablets
RSV	*Revised Standard Version*
Šabb.	*Šabbat*
Sam.	Samaritan Pentateuch
Sanh.	*Sanhedrin*
SANT	Studien zum Alten und Neuen Testament
SBL	Studies in Biblical Literature
SBT	Studies in Biblical Theology
Schol. ad Aristoph. *Pac.*	Scholium to Arilstophanes, *Peace*
SDB	*Supplément, Dictionnaire de la Bible*
Šebu.	*Šebuʿot*
Šeqal.	*Šeqalim*
sing.	singular
Sop.	*Soperim*
StBoT	*Studien zu den Boghazkoy-Texten*
Sukk.	*Sukka*
SVT	*Supplements to Vetus Testamentum*
t.	Tosefta
T. Gad	*Testament of Gad*
T. Levi	*Testament of Levi*
Ṭ. Yom	*Ṭebul Yom*
Taʿan.	*Taʿanit*
TDNT	G. Kittel and G. Friedrich, eds., *Theological Dictionary of the New Testament*
TDOT	G. J. Botterweck and H. Ringgren, eds., *Theological Dictionary of the Old Testament*
Tem.	*Temura*

Ter.	*Terumot*
tg(s).	targum(s)
Tg. Neof.	*Targum Neofiti*
Tg. Onq.	*Targum Onqelos*
Tg. Ps.-J.	*Targum Pseudo-Jonathan*
Tg. Yer.	*Targum Yerušalmi*
ThLZ	*Theologische Literaturzeitung*
ThWAT	G. J. Botterweck and H. Ringgren, eds., *Theologisches Wörterbuch zum Alten Testament*
TLB	S. E. Loewenstamm and J. Blau, *Thesaurus of the Language of the Bible*, vol. 1 (Jerusalem, 1957)
Ṭohar.	*Ṭoharot*
Tos.	*Tosafot*
TZ	*Theologische Zeitschrift*
UF	*Ugaritische Forschungen*
Ug.	Ugaritic
Ugaritica	*Ugaritica*, C. F. A. Schaeffer, ed., 7 vols. (Paris, 1939–78)
UT	C. H. Gordon, *Ugaritic Textbook* (Rome, 1965)
v(v)	verse(s)
Vas.	Vasiṣṭha-dharma-sūtra
VAT	Vorderasiatische tablets in the collections of the Staatliche Museen, Berlin
VBW	B. Mazar, ed., *Views of the Biblical World* (Jerusalem, 1958–61)
VF	*Verkündigung und Forschung*
Vg	Vulgate
VT	*Vetus Testamentum*
WMANT	Wissenschaftliche Monographien zum Alten und Neuen Testaments
Y.	Talmud Yerušalmi = Jerusalem Talmud
Yad.	*Yadayim*
Yal.	*Yalquṭ*
Yebam.	*Yebamot*
ZA	*Zeitschrift für Assyriologie*
ZAW	*Zeitschrift für die alttestamentliche Wissenschaft*
YOS	Yale Oriental Series
Zebaḥ.	*Zebaḥim*
ZSTh	*Zeitschrift für systematische Theologie*

LEVITICUS
1–16

INTRODUCTION

♦

A. NAME, SCOPE, TEXT, AND METHODOLOGY

Leviticus, the name of the third book of the Pentateuch, has nothing to do with Levites. In Hellenistic times, the term "Levites" meant priests, and this is what the Septuagint (Greek) and Vulgate (Latin) title *Levitikon* 'Leviticus' means. It is equivalent to the rabbinic title *tôrat kōhănîm* 'the manual of the Priests' (*m. Meg.* 3:5; *m. Menaḥ.* 4:3) and that of the Peshitta (Syriac) *siprā' děkăhanā'* 'The Book of the Priests'. The Levites, however, are mentioned only in one small passage of Leviticus (25:32–34), almost as an afterthought and in a noncultic context. Thematically, the absence of the Levites makes sense. In Exodus, the Priestly texts describe the construction of the cultic implements (Tabernacle and priestly vestments). In Leviticus this static picture is converted into scenes from the living cult. Numbers follows with the cultic laws of the camp in motion, for example, the transport of the sancta and their protection against encroachment. Because these activities form the main function of the Levites, it is no accident that all of the cultic laws pertaining to the Levites are in Numbers, and none are in Leviticus.

Although the focus of the book is on the priests, only a few laws are reserved for them alone (i.e., 6:1–7:21; 10:8–15; 16:2–28). The reason is made apparent by the context. Leviticus includes such diverse matters as sacrifices, dietary regulations, ritual impurity, sexual relations, ethical precepts, the festival calendar, blasphemy, and the sabbatical and jubilee years. Because these subjects concern all of Israel, it is hardly surprising that their laws are mainly addressed to Israel.

Leviticus comprises two Priestly sources, P and H. They are not homogeneous; each exhibits the work of schools. For example, two P strata are discernible in chap. 11 (P_2 in vv 24–38, 47) and two H strata in chap. 23 (H_2 in vv 2aβ–3, 39–43). Most of P in Leviticus is found in chaps. 1–16, with only a few interpolations attributable to H (see §H, below). The reverse situation obtains in the latter part of Leviticus (chaps. 17–27), most of which stems from the school of H with only a few verses (mainly in chap. 23) ascribable to P. For this reason

1

—as well as concerns about bulk—my commentary is divided into two volumes. The first deals with the text of chaps. 1–16, and its introduction focuses on the language, style, theology, institutions, and composition of P.

Lev 1–16 and P in general are characterized by the term *tôrâ* 'rituals, instructions'. The term refers to documents, probably stored in sanctuary archives, that constitute the special lore of the priesthood. Ten *tôrôt* are recorded in Lev 1–16, as follows: five *tôrôt* of sacrifice—the burnt offering (6:2–6), the cereal offering (6:7–16), the purification offering (6:17–23), the reparation offering (7:1–7), the well-being offering (7:11–21)—and five *tôrôt* of impurity— animal carcasses (11:1–23, 41–42; see the NOTE on 11:46), the parturient (12:1–8), scale disease (13:1–59); purification from scale disease (14:1–57), genital discharges (15:1–32). Four more *tôrôt* are found in Numbers: the suspected adulteress (5:12–31), the Nazirite (6:1–21), corpse contamination (19:12), purification rites for booty (31:21–24)—all P. It is clear that these pericopes deal with priestly concerns, for they are either addressed to the priests (chaps. 6–7, 13–14, 16) or involve sacrificial rites, the domain of the priests (chaps. 12, 15). Even chap. 11, the remaining impurity pericope, though addressed to the laity, is a concern for the priests, for it is their responsibility to distinguish between "the pure and the impure" (10:10). Aside from the narrative portions (chaps. 8–10), the only material unaccounted for is chaps. 1–5. The absence of the term *tôrâ* from this unit is explicable on the grounds that it deals with the lay person's role in the preliminary rites of the sacrifices (see the NOTES on 1:2; 6:2).

The text of Leviticus is in an excellent state of preservation. The variations in the MT are few and nearly always insignificant. The rare meritorious variant in the LXX and Sam. is duly noted in this commentary. The LXX and Sam. additions to 15:3 are supported by 11QLev (see the NOTE). The few interesting variations in 4QLev[b] and 4QLev[d] (photocopies courtesy of E. Ulrich) are also reported.

The methodology employed in this work belongs, in the main, to the school of redaction criticism. It is characterized by synchronic rather than diachronic analysis. It refrains from dissecting the whole into parts. Rather, it studies each literary unit as a whole and attempts first to demonstrate the interaction of its parts. This approach is hardly new. The medieval Jewish exegetes (§I), for whom the unity of the Torah was an axiom of belief, were pressed into finding associated terms and themes that link together the material, even if that material is heterogeneous and disjunctive. Their insights have illumined almost every page of this commentary. I differ with them only in this respect: the MT is but the final redaction. There are many places in which editorial sutures are clearly visible, thereby exposing a penultimate (or, occasionally, earlier) stage in the development of the text. Stylistic, grammatical, and terminological anomalies by themselves, and even in concert, do not warrant the assumption of more than one source. These variations must be supplemented by jarring and irreconcilable inconsistencies and contradictions before the hypothesis of multiple strata is considered. In a word, source criticism is a last resort.

From earliest rabbinic times, Leviticus was the curricular foundation of the Jewish primary school: "Why do young children commence with the Priests' manual (i.e., Leviticus) and not with Genesis?—Surely, it is because young children are pure and sacrifices are pure; so let the pure come and engage in the study of the pure" (*Midr. Lev. Rab.* 7:2).

B. THE ANTIQUITY OF P

Today there is consensus that P is the repository of ancient materials, but debate still rages concerning the date of its composition. It must readily be admitted that many arguments for the antiquity of P are rife with logical errors. Historical studies, such as the formidable works of Dillmann (1886: 644–71), Kaufmann (1937–56 [English 1960]), and Haran (1978), fall victim to the objection that historical reconstruction never leaves the realm of speculation except when confirmation is available from a precisely dated outside source. For example, Isaiah's prophecy that Jerusalem will suffer the fate of Carchemish (Isa 10:9) can be given an exact *terminus a quo* because Assyrian annals inform us that in the year 717 Sargon II destroyed Carchemish. Unfortunately, P's historical referents are totally confined to the patriarchal and wilderness periods for which we have no extrabiblical sources.

To be sure, the mounting evidence culled from the study of comparative institutions in the ancient Near East has demolished the hitherto regnant theory that P's institutions are a late Israelite creation (cf. esp. Weinfeld 1980; 1983). This approach, however, also fails methodologically. A Priestly institution attested in neighboring cultures anterior to Israel (e.g., Hattia, Mesopotamia, Egypt, Ugarit) may have continued its existence for a long time and, hence, might have been introduced into Israel at a relatively late date. Thus, in my commentary on Numbers, I cited thirteen Priestly terms and ten Priestly institutions that originated in the earliest period of—or prior to—Israel's national existence. Yet I felt compelled to add that these "thirteen terms (and ten institutions), though attested in anterior Mesopotamian literature, could have survived in late Biblical Hebrew" (1990a:XXXII).

Thus, the desideratum is to find controls—datable standards that can counter the chronological fallacy. These controls, I submit, obtain in the area of terminology. Thus far, the chief investigator of Priestly terminology has been Avi Hurvitz. Using the book of Ezekiel as a standard against which to measure the lifespan of Priestly terms, Hurvitz finds ten such terms that are absent from Ezekiel in contexts in which one should expect to find them. Thus (God + *hērîah*) *rēah nîhôah* (26:31–32; Num 28:3–6, 11–13, 16–24) is missing in

YHWH contexts (cf. Ezek 6:6; 46:13–15; 46:6–7; 45:21–24, respectively), but instead is confined to descriptions of pagan worship (Ezek 6:13; 16:17–19; 20:28) except for its metaphoric use in Ezek 20:41 (1982: 53–58); *ʿāmît* (18:19– 20; 19:11–13) is wanting in Ezek 8:6 and 18:18, respectively (1982: 74–78); and *šēkār* (10:9) is absent in Ezek 44:21 (1982: 116–19; however, see Y. Hoffman's strictures, 1986: 21). The same holds true regarding the omission of *ʿēdâ* (Exod 16:2; Num 16:8–9) in Ezek 20:13 and 44:10–11 (1982: 65–69); *ʿammîm* (19:16; 21:1–4, 14) in Ezek 22:9, 44:25, and 44:22 (1982: 67–71); *šĕʾēr* (21:1–3) in Ezek 44:25 (1982: 71–74; Hoffman's objection that P/H's figurative *šĕʾēr* 'relative' is a later development from "flesh" [1986: 20–21] is refuted by the Akk. cognate *šīru*, which carries both meanings coevally [cf. *AHw* 1249b, no. 7; Lambert 1960: 34, line 92]); *lĕdōrōtēkem* (Exod 31:13; Lev 10:9; Num 15:21, 23) in Ezek 20:2, 48:21, 44:30, and 39:22 (1982: 98–101); God and *hithallēk* (26:11–12) in Ezek 37:26–27 (1982: 102–3); God and *gāʾal* (26:11–12, 30, 43) in Ezek 37:26– 27, 6:3–5, and 5:6; and *ʾiššeh* (23:37; Num 28:3–6, 12–13, 17–19) in Ezek 45:7, 46:13, 46:7, and 45:21–23, respectively (1982: 59–63). What makes these terms significant is that they are missing not only in Ezekiel but also in all postexilic Hebrew thereafter. Either they became obsolete or—in the case of God + *rēaḥ nîḥôaḥ*, God + *gāʾal*, and God + *hithallēk*—they were dropped by later generations, who found their anthropormorphisms offensive. Yet on the basis of this evidence alone it would be foolhardy to conclude that these P terms are anterior to Ezekiel. The biblical corpus is too limited and the given citations are too few; the *é silencio* weakness still holds.

Hurvitz strengthens his position, however, by adducing another set of data: P terms that are replaced by synonyms in postexilic Hebrew. If we limit ourselves once more to P passages reflected in *similar* contexts in Ezekiel, the following transformations emerge: *rābûaʿ* (Exod 27:1; 28:15–16) → *mĕrûbāʿ* (Ezek 40:47; 45:1–2 [1982: 27–30]); *ʾammātayim* (Exod 30:1–2; 40:8–9) → *štê ʾammôt* (Ezek 41:22; 41:31 [1982: 30–32]); *hēqîm* (26:9) → *qiyyēm* (Ezek 13:6, but in a different context [1982: 32–35]); *gezel, gĕzēlâ* (5:21, 23) → *gĕzēlôt* (Ezek 18:12 [1982: 43–46]); *ḥay* (18:5) → *ḥāyâ* (Ezek 18:23 [1982: 46–48]); *rāḥaṣ* (1:9) → *hēdîaḥ* (Ezek 40:38 [1982: 63–65; 1988: 97–99]); *tabnît* (Exod 35:8–9) → *ṣûrâ* (Ezek 43:11 [1982: 82–84]); *sābîb* (Exod 27:17; 30:3; Lev 25:31) → *sābîb sābîb* (Ezek 40:17; 8:10; 40:5 [1982: 84–87]); *mizzeh [û]mizzeh* (Exod 26:12–13; 25:19; 38:14–15) → *mippōh [û]mippōh* (Ezek 40:12; 41:18–19; 41:2 [1982: 87–91]); *mi . . . wāmaʿălâ* (Num 3:15) → *mi . . . ûlĕma ʿălâ* (Ezek 1:27 [1982: 107–9]); *šākēn be* (26:1–12) → *šākēn ʿal* (Ezek 37:26–27 [1982: 109–13]); *bên . . . bên* (10:10) → *bên . . . le* (Ezek 22:26 [1982: 113–15]); and *kaʿas* (10:6) → *qeṣep* (Ezek 16:42 [1982: 115–16]).

Hurvitz also adduces evidence of the demise of P's vocabulary in postexilic books: *pqd* (Num 26:62–64), *šph* (Josh 19:7–8), and *yld* (Num 1:18; Gen 5:1) → *yḥś/s* (1 Chr 7:6–7; 1 Chr 4:32–33; *Tg. Onq.*; Neh 7:5 [1974: 26–29]); *šēš* (Exod 36:35) → *bûṣ* (2 Chr 3:14; [1967: 117–21; 1974: 33–35]); *lāqaḥ + dam*

4

(8:15) → *qibbēl* + *dam* (2 Chr 29:22 [1974: 43–45]; *qādôš* (23:2; 27:32) → *mĕquddāš* (Ezra 3:5; 2 Chr 31:6 [1982: 35–39]). Hurvitz's stockpile has been augmented by M. Paran: *ḥallâ* (only in 2 Sam 6:19 and P) → *kikkār* (2 Chr 16:3 [1983: 199]); *bad* (6:3) → *baddîm* (Ezek 9:2 [1983: 197]); *'abnēṭ* (8:7) → *'ēzôr* (Ezek 23:15 and Jer 13 [1983: 196]); and *leḥem pānîm* (24:6–7) → *ma'āreket* (2 Chr 2:3 [1983: 201]).

The examples adduced above can be supplemented by the key terms of Israel's sociopolitical structure. This area is more decisive, as these terms describe living institutions. Thus the early (and P's) technical term for the national assembly, *'ēdâ*, is not only absent in postexilic Hebrew (Hurvitz 1971–72) but is replaced by *qāhāl* (e.g., Ezra 10:12; Neh 8:2; 2 Chr 23:1–3). Especially noteworthy is the Chronicler's use of pentateuchal passages that demonstrate this change (cf. Exod 35:4, 20 with 2 Chr 24:6) and Ezekiel's exclusive use of *qāhāl* in legal passages in which P/H calls for the *'ēdâ* (cf. Lev 24:16; Num 15:35 with Ezek 16:40; 23:46–47). Moreover, *'ēdâ* is no longer attested after the ninth century; even Deuteronomy uses *qāhāl* exclusively. Strikingly, the other P terms for Israel's societal order—*maṭṭeh* 'tribe', *'elep* 'clan', and *nāśî'* 'chieftain'—also fall out of use (except for Ezekiel's artificial resurrection of *nāśî'*, by which he means Israel's king) beginning with the eighth century (details in Milgrom 1978a; 1990a: XXXII–XXXV).

The terminology for the doctrine of repentance also exhibits this diachronic transformation. P clearly posits repentance not by the prophetic (and postbiblical) root *šwb* but by its unique verb *'āšam* (Milgrom 1976f: 3–12). As I have said before, "The respective distribution of covenantal *šwb* and *'šm* can lead to only one conclusion: P devised its terminology at a time when *šwb* had not become the standard idiom for repentance. However, under the influence of the prophets, especially Jeremiah and Ezekiel, the root *šwb* overwhelmed all of its competitors, including *'šm*. The inference is clear: the Priestly legislation on sacrificial expiation is preexilic" (ibid.: 122). Indeed, it may even be preprophetic in accord with the findings of the study of Israel's sociopolitical institutions (1978a; cf. above) that the Priestly material (except for tangential additions; see below) must date no later than the eighth century. This time the argument from silence is virtually silenced. The replacement of P terms by others indicates not only that the former belong to an earlier age but also that their cumulative effect—twenty-two attestations in all—makes it unlikely that their absence in late Hebrew is purely an accident.

The terminological argument for the antiquity of P would be irreparably damaged if it could be shown that its key terms are demonstrably postexilic. Such has been the contention of B. A. Levine, who argues for the lateness of *mišḥâ/mošḥâ* and *degel* (1982b) and *'āḥuzzâ* (1983). These terms, however, can point to the opposite conclusion.

It is true that Akk. *mašāḥu*, designating measures of quantity, is only attested in neo-Babylonian and Achaemenid times, whereas previously it denoted the measurement of areas and distances. It should be noted, however, that terms for volume and length occasionally interchange. For example, the dimensions of land can be measured by the amount of seed needed to plant it (27:6). As for the argument that the use of *mišḥâ* (7:35) instead of the more common *mānâ* and *ḥōq*, attested in the previous two verses (vv 33, 34), betrays the hand of a later (hence, postexilic) editor, it is parried by the counterargument noted that two of these synonymous terms, *moshâ* and *ḥōq*, occur in a single, indisputably organic verse, Num 18:8b.

The view that *degel* is necessarily a borrowed Aramaism must be challenged. Outside the Bible *degel* occurs only in Elephantine and Arad. But the Elephantine papyri contain many Hebraisms; *ʿēdâ*, for example, is surely not Aramaic. Thus it is entirely possible that *degel* was part of the lexical baggage brought down by the founders of Elephantine from Judea. Moreover, because the community was probably founded by Judean mercenaries serving in imperial Assyrian forces in the seventh century, the term may have been used by the mercenaries in referring to themselves (it means "military unit") and, hence, a strong case can be made that the term is preexilic (see also Hurvitz 1983b: 91–93). The same linguistic argument holds for the Arad ostraca. To be sure, *degel* is frequently juxtaposed with its synonym *maḥăneh* (Num 2:3, 10, 18, 25; 10:14, 18, 22, 25), indicating that an editor may have glossed *maḥăneh* with his contemporary term *degel*. But who was this editor? If, as I maintain, P was redacted by the school of H, which flourished prior to the exile, then the term is preexilic. One might even grant, for the sake of argument, that *degel* is a postexilic term. Then all that might be inferred is that this word is late. But because its insertion is due to a redactor, it bears no significance whatever for the body of P.

ʾăḥuzzâ is another late term, according to Levine, because it is a gloss for an alleged synonym *naḥălâ* and, moreover, outside of P it occurs mainly in postexilic Ezra, Nehemiah, and Chronicles. First, the two terms are not interchangeable. As demonstrated by my student S. Rattray in a seminar paper, *ʾăḥuzzâ* is a technical term denoting inalienable property received (or seized) from a sovereign, in distinction to *naḥălâ*, inalienable property transmitted by inheritance. The land seized by the Israelites *(ʾăḥuzzâ)* becomes their inheritance *(naḥălâ)*. Thus the conflated expressions *ʾaḥuzzat naḥălâ* 'inherited holding' (Num 27:7; 32:35) and *naḥălat ʾaḥuzzātām* 'holdings apportioned to them' (Num 35:2) make sense. Furthermore, Paran has shown (1983: 218–19) that whereas *ʾăḥuzzâ* has an agricultural connotation in P (e.g., 27:16, 24), in Nehemiah and Chronicles *ʾăḥuzzâ* is linked with *ʿîr*, both terms being preceded by the prepositions *lamed* or *beth* (Neh 11:3; 1 Chr 9:2; 2 Chr 31:1). Thus Hurvitz is assuredly correct in concluding "that the lexical similarity is superficial and even misleading since both in form (use of prepositions) and meaning (semantic range) P and Neh–Chr represent entirely different linguistic milieux" (1988: 97).

Only one argument remains in the opposition arsenal: P is guilty of archaizing. So writes Wellhausen: "It [P] tries hard to imitate the costume of the

Mosaic period . . . to disguise its own" (1885: 9). In our day F. M. Cross echoes a similar view (1973: 322–23; see also Hoffman 1986). Hurvitz counters this argument by maintaining that archaizing is discernible only if "one can furnish positive evidence proving the existence of *late* linguistic elements in the same work" (1982: 163). That is, an author, particularly one represented by such an extensive corpus as the Priestly writings, would surely betray himself by some anachronistic slip. Nonetheless, the possibility must be granted that the Priestly redaction may have succeeded in concealing its true (late) period. Another control, however, is at hand that can vitiate the charge of anachronism. What if a term undergoes a change of meaning and there are ample attestations of this term in the early and late biblical literature, so that the change can be accurately charted? Moreover, what if the new meaning is incompatible with, and even contradictory to, its predecessor, so that it is inconceivable that both meanings could have existed simultaneously? The term *mišmeret* exemplifies the first case and *ʿăbōdâ*, the second.

The term *mišmeret* occurs seventy-six times in Scripture, chiefly in P. In connection with the Tabernacle it means "guard duty" *and nothing else* (cf. Abravanel on Num 3:5). When *mišmeret* is in construct with YHWH, the context involves proscriptions and taboos, so that "guarding" against the violation of the Lord's commandments is always meant (details in Milgrom 1970a: 8–12). The evolution of *mišmeret* from "guard duty" to postbiblical "service unit" is barely detectable in Scripture. This later meaning is found only in Nehemiah (Neh 12:9, 24; 13:30 [correcting 1970a: 12 n. 41]) and Chronicles (1 Chr 25:8 [Paran 1983: 205 n. 42]). But it is not even adumbrated in any of P's forty-three attestations (details in 1970a: 12–16).

The second term, *ʿăbōdâ*, is of weightier import. In P it occurs some seventy times and always denotes "physical labor" (Milgrom 1970a: 60–82). By contrast, in postexilic cultic texts (even when they cite pentateuchal passages) it means "cultic service" (1970a: 82–87). These two meanings are, of course, semantically related and are found within the same linguistic ambience in the cognate languages. For example, Akk. *dullu* and Aram. *pĕlaḥ* (cf. Akk. *palāḥu*) both denote "work" and "cultic service" (Latin *cultus* exhibits the same duality). In P, however, these two meanings clearly contradict each other and therefore cannot coexist. Levites on pain of death are forbidden to officiate in the cult (Num 18:3b) and, hence, their *ʿăbōdâ* is confined to the physical job of removing the Tabernacle. But in postexilic texts the contrary is true. Priests alone may perform *ʿăbōdâ*, for this term now means "cultic service." This change is still not reflected in Ezekiel, to judge by its absence from the detailed description of the cult in his visionary Temple (chaps. 40–48). The term, indeed, does appear once in these chapters (Ezek 44:14), and its context is most revealing: *wĕnātattî ʾōtām šōmĕrê mišmeret habbāyit lĕkōl ʿăbōdātô ûlĕkōl ʾăšer yēʿāśeh bô* 'I have assigned them the guarding function of the Temple, including all its labor *and everything that has to be done in it*'. This verse is clearly a recasting of Num

7

18:4a, and it demonstrates "that Ezekiel knew only too well the restricted meaning of ʿăbōdâ in P, and he therefore found it necessary to gloss his quotation with the explication that the Levites shall be liable for all labor on the Temple grounds" (Milgrom 1970a: 85). That is, whereas the pentateuchal Levites were responsible for the transport of the Tabernacle, the Ezekielian Levites are responsible for the maintenance of the stationary Temple.

Ezekiel's gloss on ʿăbōdâ falls within a passage (Ezek 44:8–16) that itself is a more extensive gloss on P's conception of the Levites' cultic duties, especially as they are delineated in Num 18 (acknowledged by Duke 1988). Ezekiel accuses the Levites of neglecting their guarding responsibilities (mišmeret, v 8; Num 18:3 [Milgrom 1970a: 8–16, esp. n. 41]), and he reappoints them to this task (vv 11a, 14a; for pĕquddôt cf. 2 Kgs 11:8; Ezek 9:1, and Milgrom 1970a: 84). They must pay the penalty for Israel's cultic defection (wĕnāśáʾ ʿăwōnām) as ordained in Num 18:1, 23 (cf. 1970a: 22–33). They will assist the lay offerers wĕhēmmâ yaʿ-amdû lipnêhem lĕšārĕtām (v 11; cf. Num 16:9) by slaughtering their burnt and well-being offerings (v 11 [cf. 1970a: 84]). But they dare not usurp priestly functions (v 13aα; cf. Num 18:4b–5) by encroaching (qārab, nāgaš) on the sancta (Num 18:3b [1970a: 16–22; cf. Duke 1988: 70]), be they holy or most holy (v 13aβ). Rather, the Levites shall continue to be responsible for guarding the sanctuary and its physical labor (not for its transport but for its maintenance, v 14; Num 18:4a, and see above). Indeed, it is only the (Zadokite) priests who are qualified (permissive qārab, 1970a: 33–37) to officiate (šērēt, cf. Exod 28:43; Ezek 44:27 [1970a: 67 n. 245]). Thus, the entire passage Ezek 44:8–16 is a quotation and amplification of corresponding elements in P. (Quotation and amplification are the hallmarks of Ezekiel's style. It is strikingly evident in his use of Lev 26; see the discussion in vol. 2.)

In sum, my terminological study of Ezek 44, supplemented by the studies of Hurvitz and Paran of the twenty-two Ezekielian passages adduced above, demonstrates that Ezekiel is the chronological watershed of Israel's cultic terminology. His book confirms the conclusions derived from P's central vocabulary in the area of cult (mišmeret, ʿăbōdâ), theology (absence of šwb), and sociopolitical institutions (ʿēdâ, maṭṭeh, ʾelep. nāśîʾ) that P is a product of the preexilic age (cf. also Grintz 1974–75; 1975; Polzin 1976; Guenther 1977; Rendsburg 1980). Furthermore, not a single Priestly term has been shown to be of postexilic coinage. Finally, the allegation that P is archaizing has proved baseless. No postexilic writer could have used ʿăbōdâ in its earlier sense of "physical labor" when it flatly contradicted the meaning it had in his own time. His readers would have been confused, nay shocked, to learn that "cultic service," exclusively the prerogative of priests and fatal to nonpriests, had been assigned to the Levites.

The antiquity of P is further buttressed by comparing it chronologically with D. If we assume that the pentateuchal sources are the products of schools that probably overlapped each other, it can still be demonstrated that in some places one source is dependent on another so that a relative chronology between the two is discernible. This clearly holds true for P and D. There is not one demonstrable case in which P shows the influence of D (Kaufmann 1937–56: 1.61–65). The reverse situation, however—that D is dependent on P (and H)— is manifest in many instances.

It has been shown that the expression *ka'ăšer ṣiwwâ/nišba'/dibbēr* is D's unique formula for indicating its sources (Milgrom 1976e). In three cases it points to P:

1. *Scale disease.* "In cases of a scaly affection be most careful to do exactly as the Levitical priests instruct you. Take care to do *as I have commanded them (ka' ăšer ṣiwwîtīm)*" (Deut 24:8; unless otherwise indicated, all English versions of biblical passages are my own translation or that of the AB). The instruction to the priests concerning scale disease is found in Lev 13–14.

2. *The covenantal relationship.* "To the end that he may establish you this day as his people and be your God *as he promised you (ka'ăšer dibber-lāk)* and *as he swore (wĕka'ăšer nišba')* to your fathers Abraham, Isaac, and Jacob" (Deut 29:12). The reciprocal relation of God and Israel is found again in Gen 17:7–8; Exod 6:7; Lev 26:12; and partially in Exod 29:45; Lev 11:45; 22:33; 25:28; 26:45; and Num 15:41—all P and H. (I. Knohl [1988: 54–81] claims that all stem from H but because, as will be maintained, H comprehends P, this argument is unaffected.)

3. *The levitic prebends.* "The Levites have received no hereditary state along with their kinsmen: the Lord is their portion *as the Lord your God promised them (ka'ăšer dibber YHWH ' ĕlōhekā lô)*" (Deut 10:9); "The Levitical priests, the whole tribe of Levi, . . . shall have no portion among their brother tribes: the Lord is their portion, *as he promised them (ka'ăšer dibber-lô)*" (Deut 18:1–2). D polemicizes with P: God has declared "I am your portion" (Num 18:20) not only to the priests but to "the whole tribe of Levi" (Deut 18:1).

To be sure, this evidence only proves that "D is certainly cognizant of the *content* of P, but not necessarily of the *language* of P. . . . (Nonetheless,) that D indicates its sources by a formula means that it takes for granted that they are well known to the reader. Though, it may be argued, God's commands, promises, and oaths could have been handed down orally, it is more likely that the accuracy of God's *ipsissima verba*, particularly his laws, would not have been left to the vagaries of memory, but would have been written down" (Milgrom 1976e: 10).

It can also be demonstrated that D draws heavily from the dietary laws of Leviticus, as follows:

1. D permits nonsacrificial slaughter (Deut 12:15, 21), as does P (see §C below). Thus D overturns the Priestly law (H) that all meat for the table must first be offered up on the altar (17:3–7). The same radical alteration can be deduced from the animal's suet. Whereas D continues to prohibit the consumption of the animal's blood (Deut 12:16, 23–25) it is silent concerning its suet,

implying that it may be eaten and thereby overturning the Priestly law (H) that prohibits the consumption of both the blood and the suet of sacrificial animals (Lev 3:16b; 7:23).

2. Lev 11 deals with nonsacrificial animals; hence, it does not enumerate the sacrificial ones (see the NOTE on 11:3). D lists them (Deut 14:4–5) because they no longer need to be sacrificed and must, therefore, be incorporated into P's diet list.

3. The kid prohibition is found three times, twice in the epic source (JE), where it is a cultic rite (Exod 23:19; 34:26), and once in D, where it is incorporated into its diet list (Deut 14:21). It is missing, however, in P's diet list (Lev 11), for it had not yet made the transition between cultic rite and dietary law (see the discussion in chap. 11, COMMENTS B and F).

4. Finally, all eighteen verses of D's diet laws can be shown to be a borrowing from and alteration of Lev 11 (chap. 11, COMMENT B), which proves that D had before it the present MT of Lev 11. A similar conclusion is derived from a comparison of the spy narratives in D and P, which shows that D relied on the Priestly strand of Numbers (McEvenue 1969; 1971: 91–92; Loewenstamm 1972–73; Zevit 1982).

Thus, the fact that P shows no signs of D, whereas whole sections of D evidence the very language of P, further buttresses the conclusion that P stems from preexilic times.

There are other indications of P's antiquity. They follow herewith in summary form. Fuller discussion is found in this commentary and in my commentary on Numbers (1990a).

(1) P's Tabernacle is based on a Canaanite (mythic) model (NOTE on 1:1).

(2) The details of the form and manufacture of the Tabernacle lampstand do not correspond to those of the lampstands in Solomon's Temple or in later periods. They most closely resemble the design of lampstands of the late Bronze Age (1990a: Excursus 17).

(3) The custody of the Tabernacle is shared by the priests guarding the sacred precincts within and the Levites guarding without, a tradition found solely in the anterior Hittite cult. In the texts dealing with Solomon's Temple, however, the Levites do not appear at all (1990a: Excursuses 4, 5, 40).

(4) In P, the private burnt-offering is expiatory; in H it is joyous. This shift is best explained by the theory that the Jerusalem Temple, not later than the eighth century, created the purification and reparation offerings with exclusive expiatory functions, leaving the burnt offering for occasions of private rejoicing (COMMENT on chap. 1).

(5) The purification offering required of the Nazirite who successfully completes his vow serves to desanctify him, a function that is more characteristic of the reparation offering. This function probably reflects a more ancient usage of the purification offering, before it became differentiated from the reparation offering (chap. 4, COMMENT J).

(6) The boiled shoulder of the Nazirite ram (Num 6:19) is at odds with the Israelite sacrificial system, which never requires the shoulder as a priestly prebend. Nor does the Israelite system require the lay offerer to cook his sacrificial portion inside the sacred precincts. The language of the thanksgiving offering (7:11–15) indicates that it too was cooked on the sanctuary grounds (NOTE on 7:15). Both sacrificial practices are attested in pre-Israelite Lachish and pre-Temple Shiloh, however, an indication that the rites of the local sanctuary, *bāmâ*, are incorporated into P (see below).

(7) The right thigh (7:32–33), the cooked cereal offering (2:4–10), and the meat of the purification offering (6:19) and of the reparation offering (7:4) probably reflect the practice of the small sanctuary, the local *bāmâ*, before they were incorporated into the Temple ritual and distributed to all priests (chap. 7, COMMENT F; NOTES to 6:22 and 7:9; and see below).

(8) Israel's camp in the wilderness is square-shaped; in later Israel the war camp was round. The wilderness camp most resembles the war camp of Rameses II, possibly the Pharaoh of the Exodus. Not only is the latter camp square in shape, but its tent sanctuary is in its center, surrounded by thick walls as protection against defilement, a function filled in Israel's camp by the Levitical cordon (1990a: Excursus 3).

(9) The rebellions that are conflated in the Korah passage (Num 16) are redolent of high antiquity. They all reflect events that took place long before the Temple was destroyed (Milgrom 1981d; 1988b; 1990a: Excursus 39).

(10) The account of the war against the Midianites (Num 31) bears many hallmarks of antiquity, chief of which is the absence of camels from the spoil. By contrast, camels predominate in the inventory of booty taken from the Midianites in Gideon's war (Judg 6:5; 8:27). Although the MT is later, the account must have originated before the eleventh century, when the Midianites developed a camel cavalry (1990a: Excursus 67).

(11) Moses permits his soldiers to marry their Midianite captive women (Num 31:18; cf. Deut 21:10–14), a precedent set by Moses himself (Exod 2:16–21) but which was anathema to the postexilic age (e.g., Ezra 9).

(12) The boundaries of the promised land (Num 34) do not conform to any historical situation in Israel's national existence but are congruent with Egypt's Asiatic province during the period of the New Empire (fifteenth through thirteenth centuries). Transjordan, notably, lies outside the promised land (and the Egyptian province), though it is occupied by Reuben and Gad during the period of conquest and settlement. Deuteronomy, by contrast, adjusts to historical reality by making the conquest of all of Transjordan a divine command (1990a: Excursus 73).

(13) As Y. Kaufmann has argued (1937–56: 1.113–42), the absence of priestly sancta such as the Ark, the Urim and Thummim (NOTE on 8:8), and the anointing oil (chap. 7, COMMENT D) in the postexilic age speaks eloquently for their antiquity.

(14) Similarly, the twelve-to-one ratio of priests to Levites in postexilic times (Ezra 2:36–42; 8:15) cannot be reconciled with the one-to-ten ratio presupposed by the tithe laws (Num 18:26) unless the latter stem from a much earlier period.

(15) The rare word for "tribe," *'ummâ* (Gen 25:16; Num 25:15), attested in the Akkadian of ancient Mari, is replaced in later literature, except for archaizing poetry, by *lĕ'ōm* (Malamat 1979).

In addition, there are many other institutions, literary forms, historical allusions, and realia reflected in the Priestly text of Numbers that are demonstrably old, as follows: (16) the census (Num 1:2, 3, 49), whose close model is that of ancient Mari (Milgrom 1990a: Excursus 2); (17) the golden libation bowls inside the Tent, which may reflect a pre-Mosaic usage (Milgrom 1990a at 4:8; 28:7; see below); (18) the antiquity of the temple tithe in general, and the levitic tithe (Num 18:25–32) in particular (1990a: Excursus 46); (19) the term *maśśā'*, which designates levitic "porterage" in the Tabernacle (Num 4:27, 32, 49), becomes levitic "song" in Chronicles (cf. *'Arak.* 11a), and *śar hammaśśā'* denotes "the choirleader" (1 Chr 15:22; cf. Gertner 1960). The transformation of *maśśā'* corresponds to that of two other levitic roles, *'ăbōdâ* and *mišmeret* (above), which also changed their meaning as the Levites moved from portable Tabernacle to fixed Temple; (20) the Priestly tradition that Balaam seduced Israel to engage in the idolatrous rites at Baal-peor (Num 31:16) may be reflected in the eighth-century Deir 'Alla inscription (1990a: Excursus 60); (21) the second census (Num 26) of Israel's clans (not its tribes) probably belongs to the premonarchic age (1990a: 219–20); (22) the Manassite clans (Num 26:29–34) are shown by the eighth-century Samarian ostraca to bear the names of districts, indicating that the Manassites settled there in a much earlier period (1990a: 224); (23) the master itinerary of the wilderness march (Num 33) most closely resembles, in form, ninth-century Assyrian itineraries (1990a: Excursus 71); (24) the original plan for the levitical and asylum towns (Num 35:1–15) is most likely found in Priestly (rather than Deuteronomic) texts (1990a: Excursuses 74 and 75); (25) the postexilic meaning of *rāsâ* 'desire', found for the first time in Mal 1:10, 13, is totally absent in P, in which only the older meaning "be accepted" is attested (Paran 1983: 210–11; see the NOTE on 1:3); (26) The term *'ašmâ* in postexilic texts denotes a sin against God (Ezra 9:6, 7, 13, 15; 10:10; 1 Chr 24:18), close to the meaning of *ma'al*, and may therefore be rendered "sacrilege." This late usage is absent in P (and H), where *'ašmâ* is *qal* inf. (e.g., 4:3; 5:24, 26) or possibly a nominal form like *'āšām*, conveying the consequential meaning of "penalty" (4:3) or "reparation" (22:16). Here, then, is another cultic term in P that is preexilic.

Thus the diachronic study of Priestly terminology, the comparison between P and D, and the variety of data culled from realia, institutions, literary forms, and historical allusions lead inexorably to one conclusion: the Priestly texts are preexilic. At most, one may allow the very last strand of the school of H (e.g., the framework of chap. 23, see below) and the final redactional touches to be the product of the exile. Otherwise, H and, all the more so, P were composed by the priests of Israel, in the land of Israel, during the days of the First Temple.

C. ON THE PARAMETERS, DATE, AND PROVENIENCE OF P

It has long been recognized that laws attributable to the Holiness Source can be found outside H (Lev 17–26), not only in Leviticus itself (e.g., 11:43–45) but in Exodus (e.g., 31:12–17) and Numbers (e.g., 15:37–41). Moreover, because these passages appear either at the end of a pericope or as links between pericopes, I had come to the conclusion that they constituted the final layers in the composition. Who, then, was responsible for their insertion? The evidence clearly pointed to their authors, the H tradents themselves. The implication was obvious: the school of H is later than P; indeed, H is P's redactor.

I am fortunate that my conclusion concerning P's redaction by H occurred independently to Israel Knohl, a doctoral student at the Hebrew University, Jerusalem. We discussed it intensively during four consecutive summers (1984–87). Subsequently he completed his doctoral thesis (1988), the first chapter of which has been published (Hebrew, 1983–84; English, 1987). In the course of our fruitful *Auseinandersetzung* a few differences emerged, some of which will be mentioned below. I wish to declare, however, that his thesis is brilliantly argued and his major findings are both persuasive and decisive. In summarizing them, I shall limit myself to their impact on the purview of this commentary, Lev 1–16.

Knohl has demonstrated masterfully that on the basis of style, idiom, and ideology, H can be separated from P and that a comparison of the two resultant blocks proves conclusively that H is later than P and indeed has redacted P. Among Knohl's many proofs is that Lev 23 seems to have been constructed on Num 28–29, attributed to P (Knohl 1987). Num 15:22–25 is clearly dependent on Lev 4:13–21 (Toeg 1974; Milgrom 1983f), Num 5:5–8 on Lev 5:20–26 (Milgrom 1976f: 104–6), and both Numbers pericopes are possibly the work of H (Knohl 1988: 76–77, 149). All arguments from Numbers are precarious, however; they rest on the assumption that certain of its pericopes are indisputably P and others H. Another argument for the chronological lateness of H, as will be expounded in volume 2 of this commentary, is that H takes for granted many of the laws of P, for example, the impurity laws (20:25 assumes chap. 11; 22:4 assumes chaps. 13–15). Here again, however, it can only be argued that the dependency rests on H's knowledge of the laws of P but not necessarily of its text. Nonetheless, an incontrovertible demonstration of H's dependency on P is possible if the two passages being compared are clearly and incontestably attributable to their respective sources. This demonstration is reserved for volume 2. Here, I shall present the highlights of one such instance: 7:18 and 19:7–8. The main differences between the two are bracketed.

7:18 (P)	*19:7–8 (H)*
1. *wĕ'im hē'ākōl yē'ākēl*	1. *wĕ'im hē'ākōl yē'ākēl*
2. *bayôm haššĕlîšî*	2. *bayyôm haššĕlîšî*
3. *lō' yērāṣeh [hammaqrîb 'ōtô lō' yēḥāšēb lô]*	3. *piggûl hû'*
4. *piggûl yihyeh*	4. *lō' yērāṣeh*
5. *wĕhannepeš hā'ōkelet mimmennû 'āwōnāh tiśśā'*	5. *wĕ'ōklāyw 'āwônô yiśśā'*
	6. *[kî-'et-qōdeš YHWH ḥillēl*
	7. *wĕnikrĕtâ hannepeš hahi(w)' me'ammêhā]*

1. If [any of the flesh of his sacrifice of well-being] is eaten	1. If (it) is eaten
2. on the third day,	2. on the third day,
3. it shall not be acceptable; [it shall not be accredited to him who offered it].	3. it is desecrated meat
4. It is desecrated meat,	4. it shall not be acceptable;
5. and the person who eats of it shall bear his punishment	5. and whoever eats it shall bear his punishment
	6. for he has profaned the sanctum of the Lord;
	7. that person shall be cut off from his kin].

The main points are as follows: (1) H abbreviates P, thereby removing the ambiguity regarding the antecedent of lines 3–5 (it must be *hannôtār* 'the remainder', 7:17; 19:6) and regarding the syntax of *hammaqrîb* (line 3), which might be taken as the subject of the previous sentence, in other words, "He who offered it shall not be acceptable" (see the NOTE on 7:18). (2) Because H needs *nepeš* for the *kārēt* formula (line 7), it therefore changes the subject of lines 5 and 6 to the masc. (3) Chapter 19 (H) opens in the second person (vv 2–4) and even begins this law of desecrated meat in the second person (v 5) but suddenly, in the middle of the law, switches to the third person (vv 6–7). There is only one plausible explanation: it follows the text of 7:16–17 (P), which is voiced in the third person. (4) H, as is its custom (e.g., 19:13, 20), adds a motive clause (line

6). (5) H also adds the *kārēt* formula (line 7), thereby clarifying that what P stated in general terms—that the violator "shall bear his punishment," that is, he shall be punished by divine agency (see the NOTES to 5:1, 17)—means that God will punish the violator with *kārēt* (for the meaning, see chap. 7, COMMENT D). (6) H acknowledges his dependence on P by creating a chiasm in lines 3–4, a stylistic device locking two parallel panels (e.g., Gen 1:6–8, 20–23; Num 20:7–13; 21:6–9, 16–18; see Milgrom 1990a: Excursus 55).

In the fuller discussion of this H pericope in volume 2, it will be shown that the entire law, including 19:5–6, is constructed on P (7:16–17), for example: (7) H specifies that the *nôtār* must be burned *before* the third day *('ad-yôm)* not *on* the third day *(bayyôm)*, and (8) H deliberately changes P's terms *neder 'ô nĕdābâ* 'votive or freewill offering' (7:16) to *zebaḥ šĕlāmîm* 'sacrifice of well-being' (19:5) because, in distinction from P (7:13–14), H refuses to subsume the *tôdâ* 'thanksgiving offering' under the *šĕlāmîm* rubric (see 22:21, 29), thereby reserving the term *šĕlāmîm* exclusively for the *neder* and *nĕdābâ*. In brief, H has composed a halakhic midrash on P, proving—at least in this instance—that the H tradent had the present text (MT) of P before him.

According to Knohl, P's style (1988: 95–97) is characterized by linguistic precision (1988: 226 n. 161), incipits and subscripts (1988: 214 n. 28; 219 n. 87), and the absence of motivational or exhortatory clauses (1988: 226 n. 162), whereas H is imprecise and abounds in motive clauses and exhortations (1988: 226 nn. 162, 165, 166). Lev 11:43–45 is paradigmatic of H in this regard. My analysis confirms that H blurs P's distinction between *šiqqeṣ* and *ṭimme'* and can be distinguished from P by its motival and exhortatory clause (see the NOTE on 11:10). Knohl also observes that in P, God's contact with man is direct and unmediated prior to the revelation of the Tetragrammaton (Exod 6:2). Afterward, however (Exod 7ff.), his address to man is no longer in the first person (not even to Moses) but is distant, indirect, and mediated (e.g., "and the Glory of the Lord appeared to all of the people. Fire came forth from before the Lord," Lev 9:23b–24a). H, by contrast, continues the Genesis pattern: God's revelation is direct and anthropomorphic (e.g., "I shall set My face against that man and his family and I shall excise him . . . ," 20:5). These terminological and stylistic distinctions lead Knohl to transfer many hitherto P-ascribed passages to the authorship of H. For example, he attributes most of the Priestly material in Numbers to H. In Lev 1–16, he assigns to H the following: 3:17; 6:10–11; 7:22–36; 9:17b; 10:6–11; 11:43–45; 14:34; 15:31; and 16:29–33.

These last observations suffice to illustrate the special strength of Knohl's thesis. The determination of P's terminology becomes not an end in itself but the means of probing and clarifying P's theology. Thus Knohl concludes, "The commandments given in this [Mosaic] period and the cultic system found in accord with them are also detached from morality and the needs of human existence . . . reflected in the absence of any real expression of an anticipation of salvation or of a wish to obtain well-being through the cult in PT's [the

Priestly Torah's] 'sanctuary of silence' " (1988: V). The priesthood is therefore a closed, elite circle isolated from the people, inimical to the folk religion, concerned solely with the holiness of the sanctuary and obsessed by the fear of its pollution. In brief, Knohl's terminological study reveals a gaping ideological chasm that divides P from H far beyond what has been proposed by any prior critic. Knohl, I submit, is in the main correct. I must, however, record several reservations.

I am not sure that all of his terminological distinctions (1988: 97–100) are valid. For example, he assigns the idiom *ḥuqqat ʿōlām* to P but *ḥuqqat ʿōlām lĕdōrōtām* to H (1987: 107–15; 1988: 40–49), though the one-word difference *lĕdōrōtām* carries no ideological weight. Moreover, I find that this distinction does not always hold. Let two examples suffice.

1. Exod 30:21, containing the clause *ḥoq-ʿōlām lô ûlĕzarʿô lĕdōrōtām*, belongs to P, not H. If the objection is raised that this verse is not an example in that it reads *ḥōq* and not *ḥuqqat*, one can reply that the meaning "due" for *ḥōq* (see the Note on 10:13) is nonsensical in this context and that the Sam. *ḥuqqat* must be preferred. Even if the Sam. reading were ignored and this verse dismissed from consideration, however, it would still be pertinent to ask: is it conceivable that P, which uses *ḥuqqat ʿōlām* (Exod 28:43; Num 19:10, 21) and *lĕdōrōtām* (Gen 9:12; 17:9, 12) separately, would be incapable of combining the two into a single phrase?

2. According to Knohl, H employs the full formula *ḥuqqat ʿōlām lĕdōrōtām* in 7:36 as a means of anchoring the preceding passage (vv 28–36) in the domain of H (1987: 111; 1988: 45). He finds two additional pieces of evidence of H's authorship: the occurrence of the ostensibly late word *mišḥa* (v 35) and the use of the first person by the deity *wāʾettēn* (v 34). First, however, it must be denied that the term *mišḥâ* is late (see the Note on 7:35). Second, that P is theologically incapable of having the deity address Moses in the first person must be questioned (see below). Third, there is a contradiction between this pericope, which awards the thigh to the officiating priest (v 33), and the texts of 9:21 and 10:15, which award the thigh to the entire priestly cadre (see chap. 7, Comment F). Knohl resolves this contradiction by postulating that 7:21–36 was inserted by a late H tradent who wanted to preserve the older pre-Temple rite prevailing at local sanctuaries of giving the thigh to the officiating priest (1987: 111–12; 1988: 208 n. 11). Knohl's thesis is illogical. Would an H tradent, a member of the priestly establishment of the Temple, introduce a practice of the banned local altars (cf. 17:3–4)? Moreover, would he reinstitute in the Temple the very abuses of favoritism and rivalry that the reform, reflected in the interpolations of 9:21 and 10:15, had striven to eliminate (cf. chap 7, Comment F)? Finally, the very existence of the formula in 7:36 must be questioned. Once again, the Sam. testifies to a better variant. It reads here not *ḥuqqat* but *ḥōq* 'due', and considering its context, namely, the priestly dues from the well-being offering, as well as the occurrence of *ḥoq-ʿōlām* just two verses later (v 34), the

Sam. reading is clearly preferable. If it is adopted, then the main prop supporting Knohl's claim that this pericope belongs to H is removed.

Rather, it must be assumed that Lev 7:28–36 belongs to the same early
stratum of P as the uninterpolated 9:21 and 10:15 (minus the thigh). That is,
the three passages together represent the older (Shiloh) tradition, which calls for
the thigh to be awarded to the officiant. In contrast, the interpolated 9:21 and
10:15 represent a later stratum (P_2), which calls for the equitable distribution of
the thigh to the entire priestly staff (see also below). The thigh interpolation was
not inserted into the pericope of 7:28–36 because it would have flatly contradicted the pericope's own explicit statement that the thigh belonged to the
officiant (v 33). Thus it was left to the two interpolated texts (9:21; 10:15) to
overrule the uninterpolated one (7:33). This juridical procedure is attested elsewhere in the pentateuchal codes: the tithe, heretofore the perquisite of the
priests (27:30), is transferred to the Levites (Num 18:21); communal expiation,
requiring a ḥaṭṭāʾt bull, henceforth calls for an ʿōlâ bull and a ḥaṭṭāʾt goat (Num
15:24; cf. chap. 4, COMMENT E). New cultic laws are introduced, but the ones
they replace are not excised. They may be glossed, but their texts are not
tampered with. Representing the expressed will of God, they are sacred and
must be preserved.

There can be no doubt that Knohl is correct in contrasting the impersonal,
indirect address of God in P with the first-person address in H. For this reason
he (following Dillmann) declares 6:10 (and 6:11) a reworked passage because it
twice carries the divine first person (nāttatî and mēʾiššāy) (1988: 234 n. 7). Here,
however, one is left to wonder: Why did the alleged H tradent fail to rework the
rest of this pericope (i.e., change mēʾiššê YHWH, v 12, to mēʾiššāy)? Besides, H
never rewrites but, as mentioned above, only interpolates and supplements (cf.
Knohl 1987: 109). Furthermore, this verse carries no ideological freight identifiable with H. To the contrary, it contains the essential information that the
offering is "most sacred," information that is included in other P pericopes in
chaps. 6–7 (6:18, 22; 7:1, 6). Besides, P has God address Moses (and Aaron!) in
direct discourse (e.g., 11:1–20; 15:1–2a). Perhaps, then, P is not averse to having
the deity speak in the first person and, hence, Knohl's use of this criterion,
especially in the book of Numbers, should be reevaluated. (See the NOTE on
14:34 for an explicable exception.)

Knohl objects to my claim that the niphʿal wĕnislaḥ for the ḥaṭṭāʾt implies
that the offering is not inherently efficacious but is dependent on the grace of
God (see the NOTE in 4:20). He, in turn, claims that P's niphʿal is in keeping
with its impersonal God and that on the contrary it denotes that divine forgiveness is assured and automatic (1988: 238 n. 42). But P's use of the niphʿal of the
verb sālaḥ in Lev 4 must be compared with its use of the qal in Num 30.
Precisely because the woman's vow was abrogated by her father or husband she
is not responsible for not fulfilling it, hence waYHWH yislaḥ-lāh 'the Lord will
(surely) forgive her' (vv 6, 9, 13). Here, then, P is unhesitant in stating that

divine forgiveness is assured. That P did not do the same in the *ḥaṭṭāʾt* pericope, but instead resorted to the *niphʿal*, can only mean that sacrificial expiation is not *ex opere operato* but rests with the ultimate decision of God.

Knohl also writes, "In the [P] complex of cultic commandments there is not even one gesture *(nîmûs)* whose aim is the abundance of blessing or salvation or is a direct request for the fulfillment of a human expectation. Especially prominent . . . is P's refraining from rites that symbolize hope for the blessing of the produce" (1988: 126; 1987: 102–3, following Kaufmann 1937–56: 2.473–76; 1960: 302). This entire statement must be rejected categorically. While it is true that there is no *explicit* statement in the P corpus concerning the hope for "blessing and salvation" there is scarcely a rite that does not take it for granted. Individual sacrifices, all of which are sanctioned by P, surely have personal gain in mind. Expiatory offerings (chaps. 4–5) are clearly brought for the shriving of sin. Well-being offerings are brought out of personal concerns: the thanksgiving and votive offerings for being rescued from danger (Ps 107; 2 Sam 15:7b–8), and the freewill offering for the spontaneous expression of joy (see the COMMENT on chap. 3). True, the sacrifices are brought for *past* blessings, but it is inconceivable that they are not also motivated by the hope that God's blessing will continue into the future.

After all, what was the function of the priestly blessing that accompanied and probably concluded the sacrifice (9:23)? Even if, for argument's sake, we discount, with Knohl, the priestly blessing (Num 6:22–24) because it may stem from the hand of H (1988: 78), we still must concede that P sanctions *a* priestly blessing as evidenced by the paradigmatic inaugural rites for the Tabernacle (9:23). And what would be the function of a blessing incorporated into the ritual if not the collective material and spiritual well-being of all Israel?

The claim that P lacks rites for abundant produce is equally in error. Again, there is no *explicit* statement in P. But here we must reckon with the Priestly style and manner (so acutely observed by Knohl), which refrains from motive clauses (see above). Knohl cites P's firstfruit prescriptions *wĕ'im-taqrîb minḥat bikkûrîm* (2:14) and *ûbĕyôm habbikkûrîm bĕhaqrîbkem minḥa ḥădāšâ* (Num 28:26) as evidence that the firstfruits offering was voluntary (1987: 83; 1988: 21). As explained in the NOTE on 2:14, however, *wĕ'im* must be rendered "when," not "if" (despite Ibn Ezra and the Karaites); it refers to the first-ripe fruits of the barley and therefore anticipates the *ʿōmer* offering prescribed by H (23:10). Moreover, that P calls the first-ripe wheat offering a *new* cereal offering (Num 28:26) also implies that it mandates an earlier one, namely, the barley offering. Even if one would grant Knohl's contention that the form *bĕhaqrîbkem* (Num 28:26) implies a voluntary offering—which I deny—P calls the day itself *yôm habbikkûrîm* 'the day of the firstfruits offering' (ibid.), which denotes a fixed date on the calendar for offering prescribed public sacrifices on the occasion of bringing the firstfruits (of the wheat) to the Temple. Now the purpose of the firstfruits ritual for both the barley and the wheat is made explicit elsewhere:

"to gain acceptance for yourselves" (23:11); "that a blessing may rest on your household" (Ezek 44:30); "then your bins will be filled with grain and your vats will overflow with wine" (Prov 3:10). A similar motivation for P's *mandatory* firstfruits prescription cannot be denied.

The main fault that recurs in Knohl's reasoning is that it is frequently based on the argument from silence. Thus the ostensible absence of music and prayer from P's prescriptions need not mean that it had no use for them or that it tolerated them in other sanctuaries but not in the Temple (1988: 132). Because P represents for Knohl the pre-Hezekian rite of the Jerusalem Temple (see below), is it conceivable that music and prayer were banned from it? Even if one would question the Chronicler's claim that the Temple's musical guilds were a Davidic innovation (2 Chr 7), it is difficult to believe that Solomon instituted a lavish Temple cult that did not make provision for music and prayer. To be sure, sacrificial rites may have been conducted in silence, as Kaufmann has brilliantly argued (1937–47: 2.476–80; 1960: 303–4) but, to judge by the prevalence of music and prayer in the contemporary temples of the ancient Near East, music and prayer would at least have played an ancillary but essential role in the service (for prayer compositions, see the temple hymns in *ANET*[3] 325–41; for music in Egypt: 371b, lines 2–3; 373a, XIV.3; cf. Sauneron 1960: 67–68; Mesopotamia: 331b, line 41; 332b, line 279; 33b, line 337; 335a, lines II, 14; 338b, line 33; 339b, lines 6, 13; 340b, line 6, etc.; Hattia: 352a, line 32; 358b, lines 39–44; 360a, lines 36–40; 361b, lines 29–30; Gurney 1952: 154). Finally, the fact that Amos rails against the music of the temples (Amos 5:23) is indicative of the existence of temple music in Israel; even if one attributes Amos's statement to his diatribe against northern Israelite sanctuaries (but see Amos 5:5), how could one possibly deny that the great Temple of Jerusalem was bereft of such a cultic installation?

Knohl also deduces from the fact that in two identifiably P passages (Gen 1:2–3; Num 28:7–10) the Sabbath is neither a *miqrā᾽ qōdeš* nor a day on which work is forbidden, that P does not consider the Sabbath a holy day and that "P does not forbid labor on the Sabbath" (1987: 76; modified in 1988: 250 n. 155) —again, an *é silencio* argument. That the Sabbath was sanctified by the Lord, *wayeqaddēš ᾽ōtô* (Gen 2:3), can only mean that it is *qōdeš* 'holy' and that this verse says nothing about the work prohibition is due to the obvious reason that it was enjoined not upon humankind (Adam) but only upon Israel (Exod 20·10) Its absence from Num 28 is also logical, but its demonstration entails a lengthier exposition, which follows.

Knohl shows convincingly that the Sabbath prescription in 23:2aβ–3 is an H interpolation into an original P list of festivals. That is, in this passage, H innovates the notion that the Sabbath is a *miqrā᾽ qōdeš* and a day of rest (1987: 72–77). What Knohl fails to notice is that H's innovation also consists in labeling the Sabbath a *mô῾ēd*. Whereas the original P list subsumed all of the festivals under the heading *᾽elleh mô῾ădê YHWH* 'these are the set times of the

Lord' (v 4), H inserted into the beginning of the list a prescription on the Sabbath containing the word *môʿēd* twice (v 2aβ, b) in order to make sure that the Sabbath would also be included. The question that therefore must be asked is: Why was the Sabbath not included in the original (P) list? A further question arises regarding the New Moon, which is totally missing in Lev 23. If it was present in the original P list (as in Num 28:11–15), why did H omit it?

The answer to both questions is the same: neither the Sabbath nor the New Moon is a *môʿēd*. All of Scripture affirms this. Isaiah distinguishes between New Moon and *môʿădêkem* (Isa 1:14). Ezekiel differentiates between the Sabbath and *môʿēd* in one context (Ezek 44:24) and between the Sabbath, the New Moon, and the *môʿădîm* in another (Ezek 46:1–9). Lamentations also does not confuse the Sabbath with *môʿēd* (Lam 2:6), and even the postexilic books meticulously maintain the distinction among all three (Neh 10:34; 1 Chr 23:1; 2 Chr 8:13; 31:3). Finally, let it be noted that P itself excludes the Sabbath from the *môʿădîm* (23:37–38). Lest the objection be raised that in Num 28–29 (P) Sabbath and New Moon are subsumed under the term *môʿēd*, it need only be observed that this term occurs solely in the superscript and subscript (Num 28:2; 29:39), which betray the hand of H (note the first-person *qorbānî laḥmî lĕʾ iššāy rēaḥ nîḥōḥî* in 28:2 [Knohl 1987: 88]). Just as in Lev 23:1–3, H uses this device to incorporate the Sabbath as a *môʿēd*. As to why H retained the New Moon in Num 28 but omitted it in Lev 23, it had no choice. Num 28–29 contain P's complete list of the fixed public sacrifices of the calendar year; hence the New Moon had to be included there. Besides, H had an additional reason for excluding the New Moon from Lev 23; it was neither a *miqrāʾ qōdeš* nor bound by *mĕleʾket ʿăbōdâ* as the other festivals of chap. 23 (Dillmann and Ryssel 1897: 639).

Thus, one must conclude that neither the Sabbath nor the New Moon was present in the original (P) list of Lev 23; not being *môʿădîm* they did not belong there. H's innovation, then, was to break this pattern. It deliberately designated the Sabbath a *môʿēd*, and did so uniquely, for the later literature continued to distinguish between them. H, however, did not do the same for the New Moon. Apparently, the same motivation that impelled H to call the Sabbath a *môʿēd* (which will be discussed below) did not apply to the New Moon. As proved by Num 10:10, which Knohl correctly assigns to H (1988: 46–47), H itself differentiates between New Moon and *môʿēd*, and for that reason it omitted P's New Moon pericope from its list of *môʿădîm* in Lev 23.

The discussion can now shift back to the question posed at the outset: Why are the Sabbath and New Moon not designated as *miqrāʾ qōdeš* and days of work stoppage in Num 28 (P)? The answer rests in the same Isaianic passage cited above: *ḥōdeš wĕšabbāt qĕrōʾ miqrāʾ* (Isa 1:13a). Just as the Sabbath and New Moon are not a *môʿēd*, neither are they a *miqrāʾ qōdeš!* A precise definition of the term *môʿēd* and *miqrāʾ qōdeš* would be of further help in distinguishing them from the Sabbath and New Moon. This task, however, would be long and diversionary; hence it is reserved for the discussion of chap. 23, in volume 2.

Here let it suffice to state my conclusion that *miqrā' qōdeš* is a "proclamation of (a day's) holiness" on which work is either forbidden (*kol-mĕlā'kâ*, e.g., Yom Kippur) or limited (*mĕle'ket 'ăbōdâ*, e.g., Pentecost). This term is omitted from P's New Moon pericope (Num 28:11–15) because, even granted that its arrival was officially announced (as in later days, cf. *m. Roš. Haš.* 1–2), it was not *qōdeš*, for work was permitted. This term was also omitted from the Sabbath pericope (Num 28:9–10), but for the reverse reason. Although it was *qōdeš* (Exod 31:14: 35:2), it was not a *miqrā'*. Occurring every seventh day, hence independent of the imprecise lunar calendar, it required no advance proclamation. Nevertheless, to conclude, with Knohl, that P (in Num 28) may have permitted work on the Sabbath is ridiculous. (Indeed, the rationale for the work prohibition in the Sabbath commandment of the Decalogue, Exod 20:11—in contrast to that of Deut 5:15—may very well be P!) Rather, its omission is simply due to style. The term *miqrā' qōdeš* is always coupled with a work prohibition (Exod 12:16; Lev 23:3, 8, 21, 24–25, 27–28, 35, 36; Num 28:18, 25, 26; 29:1, 7, 12). Thus, because the Sabbath fails to qualify as a *miqrā' qōdeš*, the second part of the paired expression, the work prohibition, is also omitted.

Knohl also deduces from the absence of ethical prescriptions in P that its cultic system is "detached from morality" (1988: V, cf. 125–26, 133–34, 138, 243 n. 94, 245 n. 114). As his conclusion impinges on my basic assumptions concerning the nature of the sacrificial cult as prescribed in Lev 1–16, I must deal with it at some length.

Knohl states categorically that the phrase *mikkōl miṣwōt YHWH 'ăšer lō' tē'āśênâ* 'all of the Lord's prohibitive commandments' found in the headings of the *ḥaṭṭā't* pericope (4:2, 13, 22) refers solely to ritual prohibitions (1988: 239 n. 55) such as the interdiction to concoct or use the sacred incense and oil or to contact the sacred in an impure state (Exod 30:32, 37; Lev 7:19; 12:4). In view of the limited number of cultic prohibitions in P, do they really warrant the designation *"all* of the Lord's prohibitive commandments"?

The issue of ethics and the cult can be illumined by brief excerpts from the Mesopotamian "Lipšur" Litanies and Šurpu: "If NN, son of NN, has sinned . . . if he committed an assault, if he committed murder . . . if he had intercourse with a wife of his friend . . . if he talked to a sinner . . . if he interceded for a sinner, if he committed grievous sin, if he sinned against his father, if he sinned against his mother . . ." (Reiner 1956: 137, lines 81–90).

Tablet II

1. [Incantation. Be it released], great gods,
2. [god and] goddess, lords of absolution.

3. [NN, son of] NN, whose god is NN, whose goddess is NN,

4. [who is . . .], sick, in danger (of death), distraught, troubled,

5. who has eaten what is tab[oo] to his god, who has eaten what is taboo to his goddess,

6. who said "no" for "yes," who said "yes" for "no,"

7. who pointed (his) finger (accusingly) [behind the back of]his [fellow-man],

8. [who calumniated], spoke what is not allowed to speak,

9. [who . . . . (. . . .)] gossip,

10. [who . . . . (. . . .)] . . . . . . crooked,

11. [who scorned his god], despised his goddess,

12. [who . . . . (. . . .)], spoke evil things,

13. [who . . . .], spoke [u]nseemly things,

14. [who, as a witness,] caused wicked things to be spoken,

15. who caused the judge to (pronounce) [incorrec]t (judgement),

16. who is always present [. . . . . . (. .)] . . . . . .

17. [who] says [. . . .], always says (and) exaggerates,

18. [who . . . .], has oppressed the weak woman,

19. who turned [a . . . woman] away from her city,

20. who estranged son [from] [father],

21. who estranged father [from] son,

22. who estranged daughter [from] mother,

23. who estranged mother [from] daughter,

24. who estranged daughter-in-law [from] mother-in-law,

25. who estranged mother-in-law [from] daughter-in-law,

26. who estranged brother from brother,

27. who estranged friend from friend,

28. who estranged companion from companion,

29. who did not free a captive, did not release a man in bonds,

30. who did not let the prisoner see the light (of day),

31. who said to the captive: "leave him captive!", to the man in bonds: "bind him tighter!"

32. He does not know what is a crime against god, he does not know what is a sin against the goddess.

33. He scorned the god, despised the goddess,

34.   his sins are against his god, his crimes are against his goddess,

35.   He is full of contempt [against] his father, full of hatred against his elder brother.

36.   He despised his parents, offended the elder sister,

37.   gave with small (measure) and received with big (measure),

38.   he said "there is," when there was not,

39.   he said "there is n[ot]," when there was,

40.   s[poke] unseemly things, [he spo]ke [. . .]

42.   he us[ed] an untrue balance, (but) [did not us]e [the true balance],

43.   he took money that was not due to him, (but) [did not ta]ke mo[ney due to him],

44.   he disinherited the legitimated son (and) [did not est]ablish (in his rights) the le[gitimated] son,

45.   he set up an untrue boundary, (but) did not set up the [tr]ue bound[ary],

46.   he removed mark, frontier and boundary.

47.   He entered his neighbor's house,

48.   had intercourse with his neighbor's wife,

49.   shed his neighbor's blood,

50.   put on (var.: took away) his neighbor's clothes,

51.   (and) did not clothe a young man when he was naked,

52.   He ousted a well-to-do young man from his family,

53.   scattered a gathered clan,

54.   used to stand by the . . . . . .

55.   His mouth is straight, (but) his heart is untrue,

56.   (when) his mouth (says) "yes," his heart (says) "no,"

57.   altogether he speaks untrue words,

58.   He who is . . . . shakes and trembles (of rage),

59.   destroys, expels, drives to flight,

60.   accuses and convicts, spreads gossip,

61.   wrongs, robs and incites to rob,

62.   sets his hand to evil,

63.   his mouth is . . . . , lying, his lips confused and violent,

(Reiner 1958: 2.13–14)

The refinement and sensitivity of the ethical violations listed above are truly amazing. What then shall we say concerning the silences of the biblical text? On the basis of these texts and others, a noted Assyriologist concludes, "there was no distinction such as we tend to make between morally right and ritually proper. The god was just as angry with the eating of ritually impure food as with oppressing the widow and orphan" (Lambert 1959: 194).

A recent comparative study of Mesopotamian and Israelite religion reaches this conclusion: "It is not true that the Babylonians restricted the notion of sin to cultic negligence or ritual errors. . . . The moral code remained materially co-terminous with the moral views held by neighboring civilizations. . . . We must conclude that the protection of the moral order . . . relied heavily on the involvement of the gods for its efficacy. . . . Most of the ethical demands are strikingly similar in Mesopotamia and Israel" (van der Toorn 1985: 39, 54, 113). This statement holds equally true for the religions of Egypt and Hattia (for the references see the NOTE on 4:2). Can it therefore be doubted that the violations listed in Mesopotamian documents that date at least a half a millennium earlier than P are embraced by the generalization, "all of the Lord's prohibitive commandments" (4:2)? What, then, shall we say about the silences of the Priestly texts?

Nevertheless, even the Priestly "silences" can be pierced. It has been noted, for example, that this very generalization which heads the *ḥaṭṭāʾt* pericope (4:2) is interpolated into the protasis of the "suspended" *ʾāšām* (and awkwardly at that) so that it reads, literally, "And if—when a person does wrong in regard to one of the Lord's prohibitive commandments—he does not know it . . ." (5:17). The omission of the key term *maʿal* from this *ʾāšām* case is telling. The term *maʿal* denotes either the desecration of sancta (5:14–16) or the desecration of an oath (5:20–26, COMMENT B). Its omission from the case in which a person is not aware of his wrong (5:17–19) and the insertion of the *ḥaṭṭāʾt* protasis can only mean that in this instance the suppliant's apprehension that he has offended God is not limited to the area of desecration but embraces the entire gamut of sins subsumed under the rubric of "the Lord's prohibitive commandments" (4:2). This situation is entirely congruent with the suppliant of the Šurpu and Lipšur who similarly is unaware of the cause of his plight and therefore recites the full range of possible offenses to his deity—offenses, as we have seen, comprising ethical as well as cultic violations.

This still small voice begins to rumble when we turn to the Day of Purgation (chap 16). It can be shown that whereas the sacrificial *ḥaṭṭāʾt* animals purge the sanctuary of Israel's impurities (*ṭumʾōt*, 16:16a), the live goat atones for Israel's sins (*ʿăwōnōt;* see the NOTE on "iniquities" v 21a). These sins the high priest confesses as he leans both of his hands on the head of the live goat (16:21a). But what are they? A clue is provided by the *ḥaṭṭāʾt* ritual of chap. 4. This passage prescribes the ritual for the purgation of the sanctuary by the sacrificial animals, but neither confession nor live goat is required. The reason is clear: the sins have been committed inadvertently *(bišĕgāgâ)* and the offerers have experienced remorse *(wĕ'āšēm)*; no further expiation is required. Both terms, inadvertence and remorse, however, are absent from the text of Lev 16. They are replaced by one word, *pĕšā'îm* 'transgressions' (vv 16, 21). It refers to brazen, presumptuous sins (see the NOTE to 16:16), which generate the most powerful of all impurities that penetrates into the adytum and pollutes it, requiring its purgation by the high priest on Yom Kippur. Thus, the high priest's confessional is directed mainly at Israel's premeditated, intentional sins.

The range of these sins is further elucidated by examining the word that describes them, *'ăwōnōt* (16:24). Limiting ourselves exclusively to indisputable P passages, we note in addition to cultic prohibitions (Exod 28:38, 43; Lev 7:18) the following cases: one who withholds testimony (5:1), one who is unaware of his sin (5:17; see above), the suspected adulteress and her accusing husband (Num 5:15, 31), and the husband who belatedly cancels his wife's vow (Num 30:16). Thus we have moved outside the circumscribed cultic area and entered the ethical sphere. Elsewhere in Scripture the ethical import of *'āwōn* is predominant (e.g., see the early pentateuchal strata: Gen 4:13; 15:16; 19:15; Exod 20:5; 34:9; Num 14:34). Clearly, this is precisely the reason that the Priestly legist chose this term in Lev 16 (and in 10:17: see the NOTE), in order to incorporate the totality of the offenses against the deity that the high priest then transfers to the scapegoat (provided the people fast in penitence, 16:29; Num 29:7).

It is not without significance that a comparable confession is recorded for the annual New Year Festival in Babylon, in which Marduk's temple, Esagila, is also purged. Here, however, it is the king and not the high priest, the *šešgallu*, who recites the confession, and it is for his own sins, not those of his people. The confession reads as follows: "I did [not] sin, lord of the countries. [I did not] destroy Babylon, I did not forget its rites. [I did not]rain blows on the cheek of a *kidinnu*. . . . I did not humiliate them. [I watched out] for Babylon; I did not smash its walls. (Five lines are missing)" *(ANET*[3] 334). True, the context of the king's confession differs sharply from that of Israel's high priest. The king speaks from a political standpoint: he has been a faithful custodian of the god's temple and has not violated the political rights of the *kidinnu* (a specially protected group). In other words, the king focuses on his own conduct, whereas in Israel the high priest expiates the sins of his people (for details see chap. 16, COMMENT C). Yet, if the respective contexts differ, the content is largely the same. Unfortunately, some key lines are missing in the Babylonian text. Nonetheless, it is clear that the king claims that he has fulfilled his responsibility as king, namely, to dispense justice in his realm and to prevent the exploitation of the weak and the downtrodden (e.g., see also the prologue and epilogue to CH 5.11–21; reverse 24.1–61; *ANET*[3] 165, 168). Hence, can there remain any doubt that when Israel's high priest recites not his own but his people's sins, he is making a complete inventory of all possible sins so that they may be carried off by the live goat into the wilderness?

To be sure, Knohl admits that P espouses a moral code, but it is universalistic in scope, incumbent on all humanity, and is not refined or supplemented in any way for Israel (1988: 130–31, 243 n. 93). What are the contents of this code? To judge by the book of Genesis, "the fear of God" includes such matters as murder (20:11), adultery (39:8), breach of faith (39:8–9), and benevolence (42:18; see Kaufmann 1937–56: 2.438–41; 1960: 297). Limiting ourselves again to incontestable P passages, we find that humanity is destroyed because of the prevalence of violence (ḥāmās, Gen 6:11). Whatever the specific nature of this "violence," it must be ethical in character. Because the antediluvians had no cultic commandments (outside of the blood prohibition, Gen 9:4), their only crimes could be those committed against each other. When Nineveh is threatened with destruction because of its ḥāmās, the Ninevites avert this fate by repenting of their evil ways and by altering their deeds (maʿāśêhem, Jonah 3:8–10). Noah, the progenitor of a new human race, is portrayed as ṣaddîq 'righteous', the antonym of rāšāʿ 'evil', and he is awarded the supreme epithet tāmîm (Gen 6:9), a term that is employed only once more by P in a charge to a human being—Abram (Gen 17:1). Now tāmîm is a bona fide Priestly term meaning "unblemished," an indispensable prerequisite for sacrificial animals (e.g., 1:3, 10; 3:1, 6; etc.). For Noah, then (and for Abram) the term must mean "blameless, morally blameless." Thus, even if we accept Knohl's restriction of P's moral code to a minimal universal ethic incumbent on all human beings, we must still admit that this ethic is subsumed under the phrase "all of the Lord's prohibitive commandments" (4:2), which are expiable, if committed inadvertently, by a ḥaṭṭāʾt sacrifice.

My critique of Knohl must be put into perspective. I disagree with some of the implications of his thesis but not with the thesis itself. Knohl's thesis stands, and it reaches its zenith in the search for the Sitz im Leben, the provenience and date of H. Although a full discussion of H must be postponed to volume 2, it is crucial at least to summarize his argument here, for whatever is determined for H automatically affects the provenience and date of P.

Following a suggestion of Menahem Haran (1968b: 1098; 1981) that H's interdiction of the Molech and the ʾōb and yiddĕ ʿōnî corresponds to the proliferation of these cults into the royal court during the second half of the eighth century, Knohl postulates that H must be a product of that period (1988: 178, 263 n. 19, 264 n. 22); here Knohl has been anticipated by Eerdmans (1912: 101), who added to the Molech factor the occurrence of ʾelîlīm in H (19:4; 26:1) and in the First Isaiah (nine out of a total of sixteen times: 2:8, 18, 21; 10:10, 11; 19:11; 31:7; see also Heinisch 1935: 11–13; Elliot-Binns 1955: 38; and Feucht 1964: 166–67). Knohl differs from all of them in that he alone postulates the priority of P, whereas the others hold with the consensus that H is earlier than and is absorbed by P. The new issues that concern H are idolatry, social injustice, the gap between ethics and the cult, and the gēr (1988: 176–77, 188–89). "HS's (the Holiness School's) writings become clear against the background of the socio-economic polarization and the religious crisis that developed in that period. The crisis led to the attacks by classical prophecy on the ritual and Temple institutions . . . HS expresses the attempt by priestly circles in Jerusalem to contend with the prophet's criticism. In reaction . . . HS created the broader concept of holiness that integrates morality and cult and drew up a comprehensive program for social rehabilitation formulated in sacral terms" (1988: IX; cf. 178–87). The Priestly answer to this crisis eventuated in the composition of H, and its tradents continued to amplify and supplement it through the exile and into the Second Commonwealth (1988: 173–76).

As can be seen from this capsule summary, Knohl's study mainly concentrates on H: its parameters, literary characteristics, provenience, and date. Its evaluation, which deserves and is given lengthy treatment, is reserved for volume 2. Here I wish only to mention that although I accept fully his argumentation for setting H's *terminus a quo* in the days of Hezekiah (end of the eighth century), I reject his *terminus ad quem* in the early Persian period. His only tangible evidence is the attestation of two alleged Persian words in H—*mišḥâ* and *degel*—which, however, can be refuted (on *mišḥâ* see the NOTE on 7:35, and on *degel* see Milgrom 1983d: X n. 5; Hurvitz 1983b: 91–93). I cannot find any statement by H that postdates the exile. On the contrary, I wish to demonstrate that what may be the very last layer of the H school, namely, the framework of Lev 23, has to be set in the exilic period.

The question can now be asked: why was the H legist so eager to label the Sabbath a *môʿēd?* The only logical answer, I submit, is that he lived among the exiles in Babylonia, where the Temple and its sacrificial system and all of the *môʿădîm* of Lev 23:4–38 and Num 28–29 were inoperative. He therefore composed the supplements Lev 23:2aβ–3 and Num 29:39 to indicate that the Sabbath is also one of the *môʿădê YHWH* 'the fixed times of the Lord' (23:2a, 4a) and should be scrupulously observed (v 3). Further supporting my claim is the fact that the reference to the Sabbath sacrifice (Num 28:7–10) is omitted in Lev 23 (noted by Abravanel) as distinct from the other festivals (vv 8, 12–13, 18–19, 25, 27, 36, 37). This striking omission has one plausible explanation—Israel is in exile.

The exilic provenience of 23:2aβ–3 can also explain the motivation behind the composition of the concluding supplement, vv 39–44. In contrast to the Temple-anchored, sacrifice-laden Sukkot festival (23:33–36; contrast Num 29:12–34), this supplement prescribes that Israelites must dwell in *sukkôt* all seven days of the festival (23:42; cf. Knohl 1987: 96). Thus this H tradent effectively resuscitates the Sukkot festival for his fellow exiles and, subsequently, for Jews everywhere. (Note also the rabbinic tradition that the use of the willow [23:40] originated in Babylonia; cf. *y. Sukk.* 4:1.) Previously, booths were erected by festival pilgrims in and near Jerusalem in response to their housing needs (on the model of the Greek *kupídes:* Nilsson 1940: 100–101; Licht 1968: 1042; cf. Ehrlich 1908–14 on 23:43). This would explain Ezra's innovation following his reading of this H passage in the Torah (Neh 8:13–18). Ezra transferred what had become common practice in the exile to Jerusalem. For the first time *all* Israelites had to erect *sukkôt,* not just in the Temple environs but on the roofs of their homes.

Thus the establishment of the Sabbath as a sacred *(miqrā᾿ qōdeš)* fixed time *(mô῾ēd)* with emphasis on its work prohibition (23:2aβ–3) and the limitation of the Feast of Tabernacles to the erection of *sukkôt* (23:39–43) represent the only remnant of the cultic calendar that could be observed in the exile and must therefore be the product of an H tradent in residence there.

What can unquestionably be accepted from Knohl's study is that H arose from the socioeconomic crisis at the end of the eighth century. And as H also includes the redaction of P, this can only mean that H is the *terminus ad quem* of P and, hence, that P—not just its teachings but its very texts—was composed not later than the middle of the eighth century (ca. 750 B.C.E.).

Having concluded that P is earlier than H and was incorporated into it at the time of its composition at the end of the eighth century, we can turn to the more difficult question concerning the provenience, the veritable *Sitz im Leben* of P. I state my initial thesis at the outset: P presumes the existence and the legitimacy of common slaughter. Or, to be more accurate, P espouses a modified form of common slaughter, one evidenced in Saul's battle against the Philistines (1 Sam 14:31–35).

I begin my argument with H's apodictic statement *kol-ḥēleb laYHWH* 'All suet is the Lord's' (3:16b). Though embedded in the P stratum, 3:16b–17 is clearly an interpolation inserted by H (see the NOTE on 3:17). This categorical pronouncement implies that heretofore not all suet of sacrificial animals was offered up on the altar. This occurred in only one circumstance: when meat was wanted for the table. In such a case, the animal victim was not brought to the altar but was slaughtered in a common way.

This deduction from 3:16b meshes perfectly with H's main statement on the subject in 17:3–7. In this pericope we learn that H forbids nonsacrificial slaughter "in order that the Israelites may bring *the sacrifices that they have been making in the open—that they may bring them* before the Lord, to the priest, at the entrance to the Tent of Meeting, and offer them as a sacrifice of well-being to the Lord . . . and that they may offer their sacrifice no more to the *goat demons (śĕ῾îrîm)* after whom they stray" (17:5, 7a; emphasis mine). This text avers that when Israelites desire to eat meat (see chap. 11, COMMENT C) they are wont to slaughter their animals in the open field and offer them to goat demons. Y. M. Grintz (1966 [1970–71]) has astutely recognized that this text is directed against chthonic worship. (His ancillary claim that Lev 17 stems from the wilderness period is to be rejected.) This, I submit, is the ideational back-drop for both P and H. P permits common slaughter but H rejects it on the grounds that it may lead to satyr worship. (P presumably would have endorsed Saul's method of slaughtering on a rock. The rock, however, should not be taken as an improvised altar for sacrifice, which would have required that the animal's suet be offered up as well; cf. Kaufmann 1937–47: 1.128–29, Brichto 1976: 39; Aloni 1983–84: 33 n. 64. Its purpose was to prevent the slaughter of the animals in a trench—a quintessential requirement for chthonic worship.)

Thus H is not the innovator of centralization; it has inherited P's explicit demand that all sacrifice take place at the Tabernacle. H is after something else —the banning of common slaughter. It claims that "all suet is the Lord's" and therefore demands that all animal flesh should first be offered as a well-being offering. If H is to be associated with Hezekiah's reform (see above), which was operative solely in the Land of Judah, then the edict of Lev 17, though idealistic, is still feasible. D's centralization, however, takes place under different historical circumstances. The expanded borders of Josiah's kingdom had made common slaughter an absolute necessity (Deut 12:15–16, 21–25). Even at the risk of chthonic worship, D ordains that "(the blood) shall be spilled on the ground like water" (Deut 12:16, 23). This prescription may reflect D's fear that the example of Saul's stone ultimately turning into an altar (1 Sam 14:35) might subvert D's centralization imperative by leading to the consecration of other slaughtering stones as altars.

P, then, presumes common slaughter. In arriving at this conclusion I revert to a view promulgated by the fathers of biblical criticism (cf. Kuenen 1886: 90; Wellhausen 1885: 51; cf. Paton 1897: 32–33; etc.), though their prooftext (7:25) is invalid (see the NOTE on 7:25). Furthermore, the absence of a prohibition against common slaughter in P's extensive treatment of the well-being offering (3:1ff. and 7:11–36)—the very place one would expect to find it—and, conversely, the restriction of the well-being offering to specific joyous occasions, the psychologically and religiously motivated tôdâ and nĕdābâ, further strengthen my conviction that in P the slaughter of animals for food is totally divorced from the rituals of sacrifices. Finally, the very fact that H's absolute ban on common slaughter is presented as an innovation (17:3–7) proves that hitherto—namely, in the time of P—common slaughter was both practiced and permitted.

If my conclusion proves correct, then D's reputed innovation of common slaughter has a legal precedent. In fact, it is not even an innovation. D has based itself on the earlier law of P that countenances common slaughter except in the case of sacrifices. D's polemic is directed, therefore, not at P but at H, which has banned common slaughter. By the same token, D's concession (by its silence) regarding suet is also grounded in P (3:16b–17 and 7:22–27 stem from H; see the NOTES).

What is P's locus of sacrifice? P along with H speaks of the Tent of Meeting as the only legitimate sanctuary. H clearly has the Jerusalem Temple in mind. But what of P? As will be demonstrated below, there are only two possibilities. Being anterior to H, P's reference could be the pre-Hezekian Temple (Knohl 1988: 189–91). Or P may advert to an anterior institution—the sanctuary at Shiloh (Haran 1962b; 1978: 175–204).

Knohl's choice of the Temple is based on one assumption: the Tabernacle is an anachronism because it follows the design of Solomon's Temple (1988: 269 n. 72). As evidence he cites the sanctuary of Arad, which, like the Tabernacle, is a one-room structure. But because the Arad sanctuary is broad, while the Tabernacle is long, Knohl concludes that the Arad sanctuary must have been designed to conform to the Temple's long dimensions (following Aharoni 1973). Furthermore, in details such as the floor plan, the forms of the altar and lampstand, and in its graded holiness, the Tabernacle is also modeled after the Jerusalem Temple (with Haran 1978: 189–92).

These points can be rebutted. First, the Arad evidence is flimsy; all that it evinces is that the Temple as a one-room structure is validated, but nothing more. Second, the dissimilarities between the Temple and Tabernacle structures should not be overlooked. For example, the cubic dimensions of the adytum in the Temple are 60/20/30, and those of the adytum in the Tabernacle are 30/10/10. The ratio of the respective lengths and widths is two to one, but that of the heights is three to one (Scott 1965). Third, the data concerning the cultic furniture are also subject to challenge. The design of the Tabernacle lampstand conforms to that attested in the late Bronze Age, never to be repeated (Meyers 1976: 39). Haran's assertion that the Tabernacle's bronze altar could not have been built before the time of Solomon is refuted by his own admission that "the bronze mines and refineries of the Arabah are now defined as pre-Israelite" (1978: 199 n. 4); and "that Solomon's bronze was produced in the plain of the Jordan (1 Kgs 7:46), not in the Arabah" (ibid.), only means that Solomon *cast* the bronze in the Jordan valley (probably because he depended on the skill of Philistine craftsmen) but the ore itself came from the Arabah mines. To prove that these mines were worked in antiquity one could cite, among other metallic artifacts, the discovery of a copper image of a snake at Timnah in the Arabah dating from between 1200 and 900 B.C.E.—originating in the same locale and from approximately the same time as the copper snake attributed to Moses (Num 21:8–9; cf. Rothenberg 1970). I choose Timnah deliberately because there is reason to believe that the contemporaneous Midianite sanctuary at Timnah took the form of a tent (Rothenberg 1972: 184; 1975). Finally, Hittite and Ugaritic mythological texts speak of the cultic tents of the gods (cf. Weinfeld 1983: 103–5). In sum, the Tabernacle tradition is rooted deep in antiquity and, conversely, cannot in even a single significant detail be positively linked to Solomon's Temple.

P's own history ends with the Tabernacle settled at Shiloh at the end of Joshua's days (Josh 18:1). This tradition finds confirmation in the independent text of 2 Sam 7:6–7 (= 1 Chr 17:5–6), generally conceded to be historically reliable, which relates contemporary opposition to the building of Jerusalem's Temple on the grounds that Israel's God had heretofore neither dwelt in a temple nor requested one. Rather, "I continued to move about in a Tabernacle-Tent. All the time I moved about among the Israelites." According to this ancient tradition, the Tabernacle was a viable, operative institution in the set-tled land. No wonder, then, that David housed the Ark in a tent when he brought it to Jerusalem (2 Sam 6:17); he was returning to the living wilderness tradition suspended only two generations earlier with the destruction of Shiloh. Indeed, the lavish furnishings of the Tabernacle (Exod 25–27) may only be a reflection of the very last Tabernacle, David's sacred tent in Jerusalem (Cross 1947).

The testimony of 2 Sam 7 (also Ps 78:60, 67) has been discredited by the flat contradiction of 1 Sam 1–3 (also Judg 18:31), which speaks of a temple at Shiloh rather than a tent. Haran, who vigorously defends the Tabernacle tradi-tion at Shiloh, labels the notices of a solid structure at Shiloh an anachronism (1978: 202; but see now Finkelstein 1985: 170). It is possible, however, that both traditions are correct. At Shiloh, the Tabernacle may have existed along-side the temple or even within it (Friedman 1980: 241–47).

The intensive excavations at the site of Shiloh and the survey explorations throughout the central hill-country have yielded valuable information concern-ing Shiloh's regional role during Iron Age I of the premonarchic period (Finkel-stein 1985: 164–74; 1988). The pertinent results can be summarized as follows: At the beginning of Iron Age I (end of the twelfth century) there was a dra-matic increase in the number of permanent settlements in the central hill-country. In the tribal territories of Ephraim and Manasseh, 27 sites during the late Bronze Age grew to 211 sites, nearly an eightfold increase. Most of the growth was registered in Ephraim (23 times to 4.4 times in Manasseh), espe-cially around Shiloh (22 sites within a five- or six-kilometer radius). The Shiloh Temple located in the heart of this population must have served as the regional center for the entire area before it was destroyed in the middle of the eleventh century. Expansion southward took place later, after the destruction of Shiloh. This meant that Shiloh probably was the first and only interregional, transtribal religious center before the Jerusalem Temple. Other important sanctuaries, such as Benjaminite Bethel and Gilgal (of Samuel and Saul), could not have borne regional significance while the Shiloh sanctuary existed.

Support for the prominence of Shiloh stems from the historical books of the Bible. They testify that the Tent of Meeting, that is to say, the Tabernacle, was set up at Shiloh (Josh 18:1a; 19:51a), and that it housed the Ark (1 Sam 4:3b) and offered oracular decisions (Josh 18:10a; 19:50–51; 21:2–4; 1 Sam 14:3 [N.B. the Ephod]). Shiloh also served as an administrative center and military base (Josh 18:9b; 22:12b; Judg 21:13). These sources, however, intimate that the influence of Shiloh was regional, limited in the main to the Josephite tribes of Ephraim and Manasseh (1 Sam 1:1–3; Ps 78:67). This can be inferred not only from the existence of the contemporary sanctuaries of Mizpah (Judg 11:11; 20:1; 21:5, 8; 1 Sam 7:5–6) and Bethel (Judg 20:18, 23, 26, 27) but also from the fact that the Benjaminites (who had their own sanctuary of Bethel) needed to be given detailed directions of how to reach Shiloh (Judg 21:19), implying that few of them, if any, had been there before.

Furthermore, the basic presuppositions of P fit the archaeological data of Shiloh to perfection. P prescribes a central sanctuary containing the Tabernacle with its Ark and other cultic paraphernalia. It also presupposes common slaughter at home (see above), so that households would journey to Shiloh only for the annual pilgrimage (1 Sam 1:3; 2:19) or festival (Judg 21:19). At the same time, P does not claim that the Tabernacle is the only legitimate sanctuary. There is neither admonition nor ban against worshiping at other altars—unlike H (Lev 19) and D (Deut 12). This fact automatically limits P's Tabernacle to either the temple of Shiloh or that of Jerusalem before Hezekiah's edict of centralization (2 Kgs 18:4).

To decide which option is correct we seek help from the P text itself. Three sacrificial procedures provide the necessary clues.

1. The *zāb*—one afflicted with chronic genital discharges—must undergo a week of purificatory rites ending with sacrifices on the eighth day (15:13–15). He cannot, however, journey to the sanctuary on the seventh day while he is still contagious by touch to persons and objects and even more so to sancta (see chap. 15, COMMENT F). Because he may begin his travel only with daybreak of the eighth day, it stands to reason that the sanctuary is not far away (already noted by Eerdmans 1912: 73). The same consideration holds for the other severe impurity bearers. On the day before the healed *mĕṣōrāʿ* (scale-diseased person) must bring his prescribed sacrifices (14:10–11, 21–22), he is contagious to persons and objects by touch and to sancta by overhang (i.e., if under the same roof). Similarly, the corpse-contaminated priest (Ezek 46:26–27; chap. 4, COMMENT L), the Nazirite (Num 6:9–12; chap. 4, COMMENT J), and the one whose impurity is accidentally prolonged (COMMENT on 5:1–13) contaminate objects and persons on the day before they bring their purification offering (details in chap. 15, COMMENT F), so that they too can only set out for the sanctuary on the day their sacrifice is due. Now, the distance to Shiloh from any point in the central hill-country of Benjamin, Ephraim, and Manasseh is just a one-day's journey. By contrast, there are many localities in the United Kingdom, and even in Judah of the divided kingdom, from which more than one day is needed to reach Jerusalem. Thus the sacrificial requirements for the *zāb* and other severe impurity bearers are better understood against the background of the central and regional sanctuary of Shiloh.

2. There is textual evidence that indicates that originally the thanksgiving offering (7:11–15) was cooked and eaten by its offerers on the sanctuary grounds (see the NOTE on 7:15). The resemblance of the thanksgiving offering to that of the priestly ordination, which was cooked and eaten within the sanctuary precincts (8:26–31), strengthens this assumption. Moreover, the same eating procedure is prescribed for the Nazirite (Num 6:18–19) and for all worshipers in Ezekiel's futuristic Temple (Ezek 46:24). Indeed, its actual practice is recorded

for the Shiloh sanctuary (1 Sam 2:13–14) and verified archaeologically by the discovery of cooked animal bones near the Lachish altar (NOTE on 10:14). When P insists that as long as the offerers are pure they may eat their sacrifice at "any pure place" (10:14; cf. 7:19), it is clearly polemicizing against the older practice. P's opposition is further in evidence when it subsumes the thanksgiving offering under the artificially and awkwardly constructed rubric *zebaḥ tôdat šĕlāmayw* 'thanksgiving sacrifice of well-being' (7:13–15), thereby subjecting the older thanksgiving offering to the rules and procedures of the well-being offering (details in the NOTE on 7:15). Thus, a sacrificial procedure actually attested at Shiloh has been reworked by Priestly editors to conform to the newer regulation of the Temple. The older practice survives in the deuteronomic regulation that sacrifices must be eaten at the sanctuary site (Deut 12:7, 12) and in the later rabbinic regulation that they must be eaten inside the city walls of Jerusalem (*m. Pesaḥ.* 3:8; 7:8, 9).

3. The priestly prebends from the sacrifices are awarded to the officiating priest (6:19; 7:7–9, 33). There are two exceptions to this rule. In the case of the well-being offering, the prebends are split: the right thigh to the officiating priest (7:33) and the breast to the entire priestly cadre (7:31). Nevertheless, interpolations inserted into two verses (9:21; 10:15) assign the thigh to all of the priests. The cereal offering is subject to a similar division: the cooked offering to the officiant (7:9) but the raw offering to all of the priests (7:10); but this division is contradicted by another passage, which prescribes that the prebends of all cereal offerings, cooked and raw alike, belong to the entire priesthood (2:3, 10). The only possible deduction from the prebend medley is that the text has experienced growth. The prescription that the prebends go to the officiating priest is geared to a sanctuary staffed by a single priestly family. Such was the case at Shiloh, where Eli and his sons officiated (1 Sam 1–3, especially 3:13). At the Temple, however, especially as its priestly core expanded to embrace many families, pressure began to build within the priesthood to distribute the sacrificial prebends equitably among all of the priests. The Josianic reform (Deut 18:6–8; 2 Kgs 23:8–9) bears witness to a similar situation (details in the NOTE on 2:10).

Thus, we have three sacrificial pericopes that must have originated in a sanctuary that existed prior to the Jerusalem Temple. Each pericope, however, experienced a different development. The text on the *zāb* (15:14) was untouched; he had to journey to the sanctuary the day his sacrifice was due. The text on the thanksgiving offering (7:11–15), which shows signs that originally the consumption of the sacrifice took place at the sanctuary, was reworked so as to incorporate the thanksgiving offering into the well-being offering, which could be eaten outside the sanctuary by any pure person in any pure place (7:19; cf, 10:14). Finally, the texts on the cereal and well-being offerings, which originally prescribed that portions of their prebends would be awarded to the officiant, were supplemented by notices that all of the prebends are to be distributed equitably among the entire priestly corps.

If the pericopes on the thanksgiving, cereal, and well-being offerings betray signs of revision and supplementation, why is there no such indication in the text of the *zāb* (15:14)? Did the priests of Jerusalem really expect him to journey to the Temple on the very day his sacrifices were due, regardless of how far away he lived? The most likely answer is that instead of altering the text, they altered the physical circumstances so that the *zāb* could fulfill the text. Namely, they would have constructed facilities outside the Temple and Jerusalem where the ritually impure person could reside while undergoing his purificatory ablutions. Such facilities are indeed prescribed by the Dead Sea sectarians (11Q Temple 46:16–18). Far from being utopian legislation, the likelihood is that Lev 15:14 was actually fulfilled in the Jerusalem of the late Second Temple. Josephus reports that the *zāb* was banished from the city (*Ant.* 3.261; *Wars* 5.227). Surely, because his banishment lasted as long as he was impure, there must have been facilities outside the city wall for his purification.

We are now in a position to answer the question posed at the outset. Granted that P's Tabernacle presumes a central but not a single sanctuary, which one is it: the precentralized (Hezekian) Jerusalem Temple or the regional Temple of Shiloh? The answer is—both. The sacrificial procedures attested in P probably had their origin at Shiloh. Some texts, like the thanksgiving offering pericope, were reworked by the Jerusalem priesthood so thoroughly that even where the seams are visible it is no longer possible to recover the original text. Others, like the cereal and well-being offerings, received interpolations or supplementary verses (P_2), which, when removed, reveal the original text (P_1). These additions are the work of subsequent generations of Jerusalem priests, but still from the time prior to Hezekiah. In substance these additions are not significant; they probably reflect the in-house adjustments of the priests regarding their sacrificial income as the one-family sanctuary gave way to the multi-family Temple. It would take the momentous events at the end of the eighth century, which led to an infusion of refugees from northern Israel and the prophetic rebuke concerning the social and economic injustices gripping the land, to provoke a major Priestly response, which resulted in the creation of the radically new vistas and ideology of H (see Knohl 1988: 146–93).

The final word concerns Aaron. Scholarly consensus holds that the figure of Aaron and his genealogy are ahistorical. If, however, my view prevails that P is traceable to the Shilonite sanctuary, then P's linkage to Aaron is not unreasonable, for Eli, the priest of Shiloh, was the direct descendant of a line dating back to the Egyptian exodus (1 Sam 2:27–28) and whose ancestor, according to one tradition, was Ithamar the son of Aaron (1 Chr 24:3). The descendants of Eli were subsequently displaced from the hierarchy of the Solomonic Temple by the Zadokites (22:9; 1 Kgs 2:26–27), justification for which is ascribed to Eli's sins (1 Sam 2:27–36) and, conversely, to the virtues of Zadok's ancestor, Phineas

(Num 25:10–13; cf. Milgrom 1990a: Excursus 61). Thus, there is neither need nor warrant to hypothesize with the consensus (cf. Noth 1965: 20) that originally P spoke of the officiant as an anonymous priest and only subsequently was the text rewritten to include Aaron.

D. On Vocabulary, Style, and Structure

The vocabulary of the Priestly writings is so markedly different from the other pentateuchal sources (JE, D) that introductions to the Bible or Pentateuch generally take pains to supply lists of their distinctive words and idioms (e.g., S. R. Driver 1913b: 131–35). The problem with these lists is that they do not distinguish between P and H. The reluctance of their compilers to do so is understandable. Because P and H are both Priestly schools they obviously share the same vocabulary. Thus the absence of, let us say, a P term in H would not (and probably does not) mean that H was unaware of it. The argument from silence, precarious at best (see above), would be totally fallacious in this instance. There exists, however, a more acceptable way to gauge the differences between P and H: identifying words or idioms in one source that are consistently altered or synonymized in the other.

This is precisely what Knohl has done in his study of the Priestly texts (1988: 97–99). He enumerates forty-four Priestly terms, nine of which are worded differently in P and in H. They are as follows:

P	H
wěnôʿadtî lěkā, ʾiwwāʿēd lěkā	wěnôʿadtî libnê yiśrāʾēl, ʾiwwāʿēd lākem
hakkōhēn hammāšîaḥ	hakkōhēn ʾāšer yimšaḥ ʾōtô, hakkōhēn haggādôl
kěhunnâ lěḥuqqat ʿôlām	kěhunnat ʿôlām
bigdê qōdeš lěʾahărōn	bigdê haśśěrād lěšārēt baqqōdeš
lirṣōnô, lěrāṣôn lāhem	lirṣōněkem, yērāṣû lāhem
kol-měleket ʿăbōdâ lōʾ taʿăśû	šabbātôn, šabbat šabbātôn
ḥiṭṭēʾ	hithaṭṭēʾ
qěhal yiśrāʾēl	qěhal YHWH
śāṭâ	zānâ

This list (to be examined in volume 2) can be supplemented by employing another criterion: terms carrying a precise meaning in P that lose their precision in H. In Lev 1–16 the following terms fall into this category:

1. In P, *ma'al* is a technical term denoting the specific sacrilege of "sancta desecration" (chap. 4, COMMENT B). In H, however, it reflects the abstract notion of "rebellion, treachery" not only against God (26:40) but also against man (Num 5:12). This instance provides us with a parade example of this terminological shift because in actual contexts of sacrilege, instead of *ma'al*, H resorts to the expression *ḥillēl 'et-šēm 'ĕlōhîm* (compare 5:15 with 9:12; Milgrom 1976f: 86–89), thereby allowing *ma'al* to take on figurative overtones.

2. As demonstrated (NOTE on 11:10), P distinguishes punctiliously between *šiqqēṣ* and *ṭimmē'*, whereby the former denotes "forbidden to ingest" and the latter "defile by touch." H, however, invariably confuses the two categories (20:25b, and see the NOTE on 11:43).

3. Chapter 16 provides a rich source for this terminological shift. The P stratum (vv 1–28) has reworked an older source that uses *qōdeš* and *'ōhel mô'ēd* altogether differently from P and H, the former term meaning "adytum" (vv 3, 16, 27) and the latter "shrine" (vv 16, 17). P, by contrast, claims that they denote the "shrine" and the entire "Tent of Meeting," respectively (e.g., Exod 26:33; Lev 1:1), and refers to the adytum as *qōdeš haqqodāšîm* (e.g., Exod 26:33); whereas H calls it, in this chapter, *miqdaš haqqōdeš* (v 33; for details, see chap. 16, COMMENT A).

4. P consistently uses the term *miškān* to refer to the sancta, the Tabernacle structure, or the *inner* tent curtains—all of which were anointed and rendered holy (8:10). It thereby distinguishes between the *miškān* and the *'ōhel*, the *upper*, nonsacred tent curtains (e.g., Exod 26:7; 35:11; 36:14; 40:1; Num 4:25). When P refers to the entire structure it uses the full term *'ōhel mô'ēd*. Even where it designates the entire tent as the *miškān* (Exod 26:30; 27:9; 40:22, 24), P is often referring to its sacred part (minus the upper curtains). Thus, the Lord's *kābôd* covers the *'ōhel mô'ēd*, the entire tent, but it also envelops the *miškān*, the inner sacred space (Exod 40:35). Indeed, the *miškān* in its technical usage is at times clearly distinguished from the entire tent complex by the expression *miškān 'ōhel mô'ēd* (Exod 39:32; 40:2, 6, 29), which must be rendered "the Tabernacle (portion) of the Tent of Meeting." In fact, in the account of the erection of the sanctuary, headed by this latter designation (Exod 40:2), the upper tent curtains, of goat's hair, reddened rams' skins, and yellow-orange skins (Exod 26:7–14; on the latter see Tadmor 1982), are not even mentioned.

Knohl (1988: 59–60) claims that Exod 35:4–40:38—and hence the expression *miškān 'ōhel mô'ēd*, which falls within its compass—was composed by H. His theory, however, cannot stand in view of the evidence of the building inscriptions of the ancient Near East, which invariably give both the divine (oracular) prescription to construct a temple and the description of its actual erection. As for the stylistic variations palpably evident between the account of the Tabernacle prescription (Exod 25–30) and that of its construction (Exod 35–40), A. Hurowitz (1985) has demonstrated that ancient Near Eastern building inscriptions also exhibit a variation in style between the prescriptive and descriptive accounts even though early inscriptions are usually the work of a single author (see also chap. 8, COMMENT C). H, however, refers to the sanctuary by the anthropomorphic expression *miškānî* 'my Tabernacle' (15:31), which in another context takes on the more figurative, abstract notion of "my divine presence" (26:11, and note its reflex in Ezek 37:27). Thus, for external reasons (building inscriptions) and internal ones (style), Exod 35:4–40:38 should be ascribed to P.

5. P meticulously distinguishes between fem. *ḥuqqâ/ḥuqqôt* 'statute, law' and masc. *ḥōq/ḥuqqîm* 'due, assigned portion' (see the NOTE on 10:13), whereas H blurs the two (e.g., 11:11; 26:46).

6. The term *ṭāmēʾ* in P strictly denotes "ritually impure," referring to the three sources of impurity—corpse or carcass, scale disease *(ṣāraʿat)*, and genital discharges *(zāb/zābâ)*—and their derivatives, while H employs this term metaphorically in nonritualistic contexts, such as adultery (18:20), other sexual violations (18:24), idolatry (19:31), and Israel's land (18:25–28).

7. Likewise in P, *ṭāhôr*, the antonym of *ṭāmēʾ*, denotes "ritually pure," that is, the purity one achieves through ablutions and sacrifices (chaps. 11–15). It suffices, however, to cite one verse from a pericope that, on other grounds, clearly stems from H (16:29–34a; see chap. 16, COMMENT A) in order to project into stark relief an entirely different usage: "For on this day shall purgation be effected on your behalf to purify *(lĕṭahēr)* you of all your sins; you shall become pure *(tiṭhārû)* before the Lord" (v 30). Manifestly, by means of the scapegoat rite, Israel is purified of its *moral* impurity (see the NOTE on 16:21). P, conversely, in prescribing the sacrificial means of expiating for Israel's moral wrongs, speaks of God's forgiveness *(wĕnislaḥ,* 4:20, 26, 31, 35; 5:10, 13, 16, 18, 26) but never of God's purification.

8. H fuses and confuses the terms *ḥillēl* 'desecrate' and *ṭimmēʾ* 'contaminate'. The high priest who is contaminated by a corpse obviously contaminates the sanctuary, a far more grievous sin than desecration (21:12). Similarly, the priest who eats sacred food in a state of impurity becomes contaminated thereby, not desecrated (22:9). Yet in both cases, H uses the verb *ḥillēl*.

9. P scrupulously distinguishes between the divine punishments *mût* 'death' and *kārēt* 'excision' (see chap. 7, COMMENT D). H, however, interchanges them indiscriminately. For example, H prescribes *mût* for the case in which an impure priest partakes of sacred food (22:9; cf. vv 4–8), whereas P prescribes *kārēt* for the lay person who does the same (7:20). Because *kārēt* is the severer penalty it is inconceivable that H would designate *mût*, a lesser penalty, for the priest. Furthermore, H actually prescribes *kārēt* for sancta desecration by a lay person (19:8; contrast 7:18). Would H, then, prescribe only *mût*, the lesser penalty, for

the same sin if committed by a priest? Hence, just as in the same verse (22:9), H writes *hillēl* when it has P's *timmē'* in mind (above), so we must assume that H's *mût*, at least in this verse, really implies *kārēt* (contrast Num 18:32, where *hillēl* and *mût* in the case of sancta *desecration* are appropriate terms). Another example of H's confusion of *mût* and *kārēt* is *yāmūtû bĕṭum'ātām bĕṭammĕ'ām 'et-miškānî* (15:31), where again *mût* really connotes *kārēt*, P's penalty for *polluting* the sancta.

One must carefully distinguish, however, between H's imprecision regarding *yāmût (qal)* and *kārēt* and its precise terminological distinction between *yûmāt (hoph'al)* and *kārēt*. For example, if the community does not put to death the violator of the prohibitions against working on the Sabbath (Exod 31:14[H]) or worshiping the Molech (20:2–3), then God will punish him (and his family, 20:4–5) with *kārēt* (contra Knohl 1987: 74).

10. As shown by Knohl (1988: 76–77), P distinguishes meticulously between *nepeš* and *'îš 'ô 'iššâ*, the former reserved for the sacrificial laws (2:1; 4:2, 27; 5:1, 2, 4, 15, 17, 21; 7:18, 20, 21) and the latter for the impurity laws (13:29, 38; and cf. 15:5 with 7:21). H, however, mixes the two indiscriminately in the same law (17:3, 8; 22:3; 22:4–6).

11. In P the word *niddâ* is a technical term for menstrual discharge (12:2, 5; 15:19, 24, 25, 26, 33). In H (20:21), however, and in derivative literature (e.g., Ezek 7:19, 20; Lam 1:8, 17; Ezra 9:11) it becomes a metaphor for impurity, indecency, or disgrace that stems from moral rather than physical causes.

Thus, these eleven examples demonstrate that H consistently blurs the rigid distinctions in P's terminology. They prove of even greater value in that they point to the chronological priority of P. Surely, there is no difficulty in presuming that H tradents had the text of P before them. Because their legislation, replete with motivations and exhortations, goes beyond cultic concerns to address ethical and national issues (details in volume 2), they would not have cared less that they were using Temple vocabulary imprecisely. Consider now the reverse. Would P have tolerated a text (H) that did not distinguish between the divine punishment of *mût* or *kārēt* (example 9) or that extended the term for ritual impurity *ṭāmē'* to adultery, idolatry, and the land (example 6)—items for which there were no corresponding purificatory measures—or applied its antonym *ṭāhôr*, a term P reserved for purification from physical impurity, to Israel's moral impurity (example 7)? Indeed, P would have found H not only inaccurate but misleading! If P had incorporated H it would have insisted on thoroughly overhauling it so that it would be consistent with P's vocabulary. The conclusion is therefore inescapable: H is the redactor of P.

The study of the Priestly style has also been immeasurably advanced by the finely honed investigation of M. Paran (1983), who—like his predecessor and probable pioneer, S. E. McEvenue (1971)—unfortunately fails to distinguish between P and H. Paran singles out the following Priestly literary devices: circular inclusions, poetic elements, refrains, and closing deviations (1983: 28–173).

All of these, however, are shared in common by P and H. Where they occur in chaps. 1–16 they are dutifully noted (e.g., the NOTES to 1:9; 4:12, 17; 6:9; 8:15, 17; 9:13, 21; 14:9; 16:10).

There exists, I submit, yet another literary artifice that holds better promise of yielding a distinction between P and H. I refer to structure, in particular, the chiastic form, alternately called introversion (Kikawada 1974) or palistrophe (McEvenue 1971: 29 n. 18). On occasion, P employs this device, but always as a straightforward introversion, A B C . . . X . . . C′ B′ A′, where each element after the central pivot X faithfully repeats its corresponding member. In chaps. 1–16, the introversions attributable to P are chap. 8 (see COMMENT A); 14:11–20, 21–32 (see the NOTES ad loc.); and chap. 15 (see its introductory NOTE). Other P examples outside Leviticus are Exod 25:31–37; 28:6–12; and 30:12–15 (Paran 1983: 112–20). But H is especially fond of this simple type of introversion (Exod 31:13–17; Lev 17:10–14; 23:27–32; 24:14–23) and is further characterized by an intricacy and artfulness of construction. Let us focus on the two indisputable H passages in chaps. 1–16: 11:43–44 and 16:29–31.

11:43–44

A. *'al-tešaqqĕṣû 'et-napšōtêkem bĕkol-haššereṣ haššōrēṣ ['al-hā'āreṣ]*

B₁. *wĕlō' tiṭṭamĕ'û bāhem weniṭmētem bām*

B₂. *kî 'ănî YHWH 'ĕlōhêkem*

B₁′. *wĕhitqaddištem wihĕyîtem qĕdōšîm*

B₂′. *kî qādôš 'ănî ['ĕlōhêkem]*

A′. *wĕlō' tĕṭammĕ'û 'et-napšōtêkem bĕkol-haššereṣ hārōmēś 'al-hā'āreṣ*

A. You shall not defile your throats with any creature that swarms [upon the earth].

B₁. You shall not make yourselves impure therewith and thus become impure,

B₂. for I the Lord am your God.

B₁′. You shall sanctify yourselves and be holy,

B₂′. for I [your God] am holy.

A′. You shall not contaminate your throats with any swarming creature that moves upon the earth.

16:29–31

A. *wĕhāyĕtā lākem lĕḥuqqat 'ôlām*

B. *tĕ'annû 'et-napšōtêkem . . .*

C.   wĕkol-mĕlākâ lōʾ taʿăśû. . . .

   X.   kî bayyôm hazzeh yĕkapper ʿălêkem lĕṭahēr ʾetkem mikkōl
ḥaṭṭōʾtēkem lipnê YHWH tiṭhārû

   C'.   šabbat šabbātôn hîʾ lākem

B'.   wĕʿinnîtem ʾet-napšōtêkem

A'.   ḥuqqat ʿôlām

A.   And this shall be for you a law for all time:

   B.   . . . you shall practice self-denial

   C.   and you shall do no manner of work. . . .

      X.   For on this day shall purgation be effected on your behalf
to purify you of all your sins; you shall become pure before
the Lord.

   C'.   It shall be a sabbath of complete rest for you,

   B'.   and you shall practice self-denial;

A'.   It is a law for all time.

The reconstructions and exegetical details are discussed in the NOTES. Both
pericopes ostensibly exhibit a simple introverted structure. A closer look, however, reveals that the chiastic symmetry is more complex. Lines B_1 and B_1' in
11:43–44 and lines C and C' in 16:29–31 are equivalent not in sameness but in
opposition, employing the antonyms ṭāmēʾ 'impure' and qādôš 'holy' in the
former and kol-mĕlākâ 'all manner of work' and šabbat šabbātôn 'complete rest'
in the latter. It is hardly an accident that this binary opposition is found solely in
the introverted structures of the only two verifiable H pericopes in Lev 1–16.

Another characteristic of H is that it builds its introverted scheme around
an older piece of legislation. Thus, as recognized by Paran (1983: 115–18), Exod
31:13–17 plays on the fourth commandment (Exod 20:8–11) while mentioning
the Sabbath seven times. Lev 24:14–23 is constructed on the law of talion
(which occupies the pivot, v 20a). In Lev 25:3, the sabbatical law is an expansion
of Exod 23:10 (Paran 1983: 16). But what Paran did not realize is that all of his
examples actually stem from H. They display a greater sophisticated artistry
than those evidenced in P and thereby form a viable criterion to distinguish
between the Priestly schools. As a "state-of-the-art" example from H's vast
portfolio, I would cite the following pericope:

21:17b–21

A.a.   ʾîš mizzarʿăkā lĕdōrōtām

   x.   ʾăšer yihyeh bô mûm

b.   *lōʾ yiqrab lĕhaqrîb leḥem ʾĕlōhāyw*

a₁.   *kî kol-ʾîš*

    x.   *ʾăšer bô-mûm*

b₁.   *lōʾ yiqrab [lĕhaqrîb ʾet-ʾiššê YHWH]*

    X.   twelve cases (vv 18b–20)

A′.a₁′.   *kol-ʾîš*

    x.   *ʾăšer bô-mûm*

a′.   *mizzeraʿ ʾahărōn hakkōhēn*

b₁′.   *lōʾ yiggaš lĕhaqrîb ʾet-ʾiššê YHWH*

    x.   *mûm bô*

b′.   *ʾēt leḥem ʾĕlōhāyw lōʾ yiggaš lĕhaqrîb*

A.a.   A man of your offspring throughout the ages

    x.   *who has a defect*

b.   shall not be qualified to offer the food of his God;

a₁.   indeed, a man

    x.   *who has a defect*

b₁.   shall not be qualified [to offer the food gifts of the Lord]

    X.   twelve cases (vv 18b–20)

A′.a₁′.   Every man

    x.   *who has a defect*

a′.   among the offspring of Aaron the priest

b₁′.   shall not be qualified to offer the food gifts of the Lord.

    x.   *He has a defect;*

b′.   the food of his God he shall not be qualified to offer.

The detailed discussion of this elaborate introversion is left for the commentary on this passage in volume 2. Here it will suffice to outline its major points. The larger chiasm A X A′ consists of twelve clauses (A A′) that balance twelve cases of defects (X). A breaks down into two parallel panels, whereas A′ subdivides into two chiastic units, yielding the structure

$$a \quad a_1 \quad a_1' \quad b_1'$$
$$x \quad x \quad x \quad x$$
$$b \quad b_1 \quad a' \quad b'$$

Note that $a + a_1 = a_1' + a'$ and that $b + b_1 = b_1' + b'$, which involves a subtle introversion of a and b in the second half (a_1 and b_1 preceding a and b). Above all, the word (or examples) of *mûm* 'defect' occupies every center: the twelve cases of *mûm* being the pivot of the entire introversion (A X A') and the word *mûm* being the pivot of the four smaller units (a x b; a_1 x b_1; a_1' x a'; b_1' x b'), the first two of which form panels and the last two, chiasms. The final unit (b_1' x b') is itself chiastically constructed, a neat finishing touch to the pericope.

The remarkable thing about the structure is that it accounts for every single word. The alleged redundancies, which have been the despair of critics (see the commentaries), make perfect sense once it is realized that they fulfill an aesthetic purpose. The full implications of this structural device will be drawn in the commentary to this chapter in volume 2. Here it needs only to be noted that such literary artistry is patently beyond the capacity of P. It demonstrates an advance in compositional technique, and it adds further evidence to my general theory that H is later than P. Moreover, it generates even more significant implications concerning the extent of the H stratum in the Pentateuch. In my commentary on Numbers (1990a: XXII–XXXI), I have made it a point to emphasize the structured sophistication of much of the book's content. Whether its composition or—the more likely prospect—its redaction is due to H will be discussed in volume 2.

E. THE PRIESTLY THEOLOGY

Theology is what Leviticus is all about. It pervades every chapter and almost every verse. It is not expressed in pronouncements but embedded in rituals. Indeed, every act, whether movement, manipulation, or gesticulation, is pregnant with meaning: "at their deepest level rituals reveal values which are sociological facts" (Turner 1967: 44). In describing the Priestly theology I shall not distinguish between the two main strands P and H, except when they clearly differ from each other. Most of the time, they form a single continuum: H articulates and develops what is incipient and even latent in P.

The basic premises of pagan religion are (1) that its deities are themselves dependent on and influenced by a metadivine realm, (2) that this realm spawns a multitude of malevolent and benevolent entities, and (3) that if humans can tap into this realm they can acquire the magical power to coerce the gods to do their will (Kaufmann 1937–56: 1.297–350; 1960: 21–59). An eminent Assyriologist has stated, "The impression is gained that everyday religion [in Mesopotamia] was dominated by fear of evil powers and black magic rather than a positive worship of the gods . . . the world was conceived to be full of evil demons who might cause trouble in any sphere of life. If they had attacked, the right ritual should effect the cure. . . . Humans, as well as devils, might work evil against a person by the black arts, and here too the appropriate ritual was required" (Lambert 1959: 194).

The Priestly theology negates these premises. It posits the existence of one supreme God who contends neither with a higher realm nor with competing peers. The world of demons is abolished; there is no struggle with autonomous foes because there are none. With the demise of the demons, only one creature remains with "demonic" power—the human being. Endowed with free will, his power is greater than any attributed to him by pagan society. Not only can he defy God but, in Priestly imagery, he can drive God out of his sanctuary. In this respect, humans have replaced the demons.

The pagans secured the perpetual aid of a benevolent deity by building him a temple-residence in which he was housed, fed, and worshiped in exchange for his protective care. Above all, his temple had to be inoculated by apotropaic rites—utilizing magic drawn from the metadivine realm—against incursions by malevolent forces from the supernal and infernal worlds. The Priestly theologians make use of the same imagery, except that the demons are replaced by humans. Humans can drive God out of the sanctuary by polluting it with their moral and ritual sins. All that the priests can do is periodically purge the sanctuary of its impurities and influence the people to atone for their wrongs.

This thoroughgoing evisceration of the demonic also transformed the concept of impurity. In Israel, impurity was harmless. It retained potency only with regard to sancta. Lay persons—but not priests—might contract impurity with impunity; they must not, however, delay their purificatory rites lest their impurity affect the sanctuary (COMMENT on 5:1–13). The retention of impurity's dynamic (but not demonic) power in regard to sancta served a theological function. The sanctuary symbolized the presence of God; impurity represented the wrongdoing of persons. If persons unremittingly polluted the sanctuary they forced God out of his sanctuary and out of their lives.

The Priestly texts on scale disease (chaps. 13–14) and chronic genital flows (chap. 15) give ample witness to the Priestly polemic against the idea that physical impurity arises from the activity of demons who must be either exorcised or appeased. Purification is neither healing nor theurgy. The afflicted person undergoes purification only after he is cured. Ablutions are wordless rites; they are unaccompanied by incantation or gesticulation—the quintessential ingredients in pagan healing rites. The adjective *ṭāher* means "purified," not "cured"; the verb *rāpaʾ* 'cure' never appears in the ritual. A moldy garment or a fungous house (13:47–58; 14:33–53) does not reflect on the character of its owner, for he brings no sacrifice and performs no rite that might indicate his culpability. Even though the scale-diseased person does bring sacrifices for possible wrongdoing, the only determinable "wrong" is that his impurity has polluted the sanctuary. Especially noteworthy is the bird rite at the beginning of his purification process, which, in spite of its clear exorcistic origins, has solely a symbolic function in Israel (see the NOTES on 14:4 and 5). Above all, it seems likely that most, if not all, of the varieties of scale disease described in chap. 13 are not even contagious (chap. 13, COMMENT A), which supports my conclusion that scale disease is only a part of a larger symbolic system (explained below and in chap. 15, COMMENT G).

Another example of the way the Priestly legists excised the demonic from impurity is the case of the person afflicted with chronic genital flux (15:1–15, 25–30). It is the discharge that contaminates, not the person. Hence, objects that are underneath him—bed, seat, saddle—but no others are considered impure. In Mesopotamia, however, his table and cup transmit impurity. The difference is that in Israel the afflicted person does not contaminate by touch as long as he washes his hands (see the NOTE on 15:11). As a result, he was not banished or isolated but was allowed to remain at home. The same concessions were extended to the menstruant, who was otherwise universally ostracized (chap. 15, COMMENT A). She, too, defiled only that which was beneath her. Touching such objects, however, incurred greater impurity than touching her directly (15:19b, 21–22). As illogical as it seems, it makes perfect sense when viewed from the larger perspective of the primary Priestly objective to root out the prevalent notion that the menstruant was possessed by demonic powers.

The parade example of the evisceration of the demonic from Israel's cult is provided by Azazel (16:10). Although Azazel seems to have been the name of a demon, the goat sent to him is not a sacrifice requiring slaughter and blood manipulation; nor does it have the effect of a sacrifice in providing purification, expiation, and the like. The goat is simply the symbolic vehicle for dispatching Israel's sins to the wilderness (16:21–22). The analogous elimination rites in the pagan world stand in sharp contrast (see chap. 16, COMMENT E). The purification of the corpse-contaminated person with the lustral ashes of the Red Cow (Num 19) can also claim pride of place among Israel's victories over pagan beliefs. The hitherto demonic impurity of the corpse has been devitalized, first by denying its autonomous power to pollute the sanctuary and then by denying that the corpse-contaminated person must be banished from his community during his purificatory period (chap. 4, COMMENT G).

Israel's battle against demonic beliefs was not won in one stroke. Scripture indicates that it was a gradual process. The cultic sphere attests a progressive reduction of contagious impurity in all three primary human sources: scale disease, pathological flux, and corpse contamination. The earliest Priestly tradition calls for their banishment (Num 5:2–4) because the presence of God is coextensive with the entire camp, but later strata show that banishment is prescribed only for scale disease (13:46). The fact that genital flux and corpse contamination permit their bearers to remain at home indicates that the divine presence is now viewed as confined to the sanctuary. Henceforth in P, the only fear evoked by impurity is its potential impact on the sanctuary. (The H school, which extends God's presence over the entire land of Israel, also innovates a nonritual and nonexpiable impurity, but this matter is reserved for volume 2 of this commentary.) The driving force behind this impurity reduction is Israel's monotheism. The baneful still inheres in things, but it spreads only under special conditions, for example, carrion when consumed and genital discharges when contacted. But note that impurity springs to life, resuming its virulent character, only in regard to the sphere of the sacred (COMMENT on 5:1–13), and that these impurities are not to be confused with evils.

A similar gradation in the contagion of holiness is also exhibited in Scripture, but for different reasons. In the earliest traditions of the Bible, the sancta communicate holiness to persons, the sanctuary's inner sancta more powerfully so—directly by sight (if uncovered) and indirectly by touch (if covered), even when the contact is accidental. According to the early narratives, this power can be deadly; note the stories about the Ark (1 Sam 6:19; 2 Sam 6:6–7), Mount Sinai (Exod 19:12–13), and the divine fire (Lev 10:1–2). In P a major change has occurred. This fatal power is restricted to the rare moment in which the Tabernacle is dismantled (Num 4:15, 20), but otherwise the sancta can no longer infect persons, even if touched (chap. 7, COMMENT B). Clearly, this drastic reduction in the contagious power of the sancta was not accepted by all Priestly schools. Ezekiel holds out for the older view that sancta (in his example, the priestly clothing, 44:19; 46:20) are contagious to persons (contrary to P; see the NOTE on 10:5).

The texts are silent concerning the motivation behind this priestly reform. Undoubtedly, the priests were disturbed by the superstitious fears of the fatal power of the sancta that might keep the masses away from the sanctuary (cf. Num 17:27–28). To the contrary, they taught the people that God's holiness stood for the forces of life (see below) and that only when approached in an unauthorized way (e.g., 10:1–2) would it bring death. Contact with the sancta would be fatal to the encroacher, that is, the nonpriest who dared officiate with the sancta (e.g., Num 16:35; 18:3), but not to the Israelites who worshiped God in their midst. There is also a more realistic, historically grounded reason that would have moved the priests in this direction—the anarchic institution of altar asylum. Precisely because the altar sanctified those who touched it, it thereby automatically gave them asylum regardless of whether they were murderers, bandits, or other assorted criminals. By taking the radical step of declaring that the sancta, in particular the altar, were no longer contagious to persons, the priests ended, once and for all, the institution of altar asylum. In this matter they were undoubtedly abetted by the king and his bureaucracy, who earnestly wanted to terminate the veto power of the sanctuary over their jurisdiction (details in chap. 7, COMMENT B; and in Milgrom 1981b).

It can be seen from the preceding discussion that the ritual complexes of Lev 1–16 make sense only as aspects of a symbolic system. As noted, only a few types of scale disease (many clearly noncontagious) were declared impure. Yet, to judge by the plethora of Mesopotamian texts dealing with the diagnosis and treatment of virulent diseases, it is fair to assume that Israel knew them as well (chap. 13, COMMENT A) but did not classify them as impure. The same situation obtains with genital discharges. Why are secretions from other orifices of the body not impure: mucus, perspiration, and, above all, urine and feces? This leads to a larger question: why are there only these three sources of impurity—corpse/carcass, scale disease, and genital discharges? There must be a comprehensive theory that can explain all of the cases. Moreover, because the phenomena declared impure are the precipitates of a filtering process initiated by the priests, the "filter" must be their invention. In other words, the impurity laws form a system governed by a priestly rationale.

This rationale comes to light once it is perceived that there is a common denominator to the three above-mentioned sources of impurity—death. Genital discharge from the male is semen and from the female, blood. They represent the life force; their loss represents death (chap. 12, COMMENT B). The case of scale disease also becomes comprehensible with the realization that the Priestly legists have not focused on disease per se but only on the *appearance* of disease. Moldy fabrics and fungous houses (13:47–58; 14:35–53) are singled out not because they are struck with scale disease but because they give that appearance. So too the few varieties of scale disease afflicting the human body: their appearance is that of approaching death. When Miriam is stricken with scale disease, Moses prays, "Let her not be like a corpse" (Num 12:12; cf. also Job 16:13 and chap. 13, COMMENT A). The wasting of the body, the common characteristic of the highly visible, biblically impure scale disease, symbolizes the death process as much as the loss of vaginal blood and semen.

It is of no small significance that the dietary laws (chap. 11), which are contiguous to and form a continuum with the bodily impurities (chaps. 12–15), are also governed by criteria such as cud-chewing and split hoofs, which are equally arbitrary and meaningless in themselves but serve a larger, extrinsic purpose. This purpose can be deduced both from the explicit rationale of holiness (11:43–45; cf. chap. 11, COMMENT E) and the implicit assumption of relevant texts (Gen 9:4; Lev 17:3–5, 10–14; cf. chap. 11, COMMENT C), to wit: animal life is inviolable except for a few edible animals, provided they are slaughtered properly (i.e., painlessly, chap. 11, COMMENT D) and their blood (i.e., their life) is drained and thereby returned to God (chap. 11, COMMENT C). To be sure, the rationale of holiness and the equation of blood and life are first articulated in H (11:43–45; 17:10–14), but they are already adumbrated in P (e.g., Gen 9:4).

Because impurity and holiness are antonyms, the identification of impurity with death must mean that holiness stands for life. No wonder that reddish substances, the surrogates of blood, are among the ingredients of the purificatory rites for scale-diseased and corpse-contaminated persons (14:4; Num 19:6). They symbolize the victory of the forces of life over death. A further example: the blood of the purification offering symbolically purges the sanctuary by symbolically absorbing its impurities (see below)—another victory of life over death.

Moreover, the priest is commanded to eat the flesh of the purification offering (6:19, 22; 10:17; chap. 10, COMMENT C), and the high priest dispatches the sanctuary's impurities together with the people's sins (16:21). In neither case is the priest affected. Again, holiness-life has triumphed over impurity-death. Impurity does not pollute the priest *as long as he serves God in his sanctuary* (see also the NOTE on 16:26). Israel, too, as long as it serves God by obeying his commandments, can overcome the forces of impurity-death.

Because the quintessential source of holiness resides with God, Israel is enjoined to control the occurrence of impurity lest it impinge on his realm (see below). The forces pitted against each other in a cosmic struggle are no longer the benevolent and the demonic deities who populate the mythologies of Israel's neighbors, but the forces of life and death set loose by man himself through his obedience to or defiance of God's commandments. Despite all of the changes that are manifested in the evolution of Israel's impurity laws, the objective remains the same: to sever impurity from the demonic and to reinterpret it as a symbolic system reminding Israel of the divine imperative to reject death and choose life.

In the NOTE on 11:11, it will be shown that the distinction between animals that are *šeqeṣ* and those that are *ṭāmēʾ* is, according to Gen 1 (P), that the former were created from the sea and the latter from the land. The fact that Lev 11 is rooted in Gen 1 is of deeper theological import. It signifies that, from the Priestly point of view, God's revelation is twofold: to Israel via Sinai and the Tabernacle and to humankind via nature. The refrain of P's account of creation is "God saw that it was good." In common with Israel's contemporaries, P holds that God punishes humankind through flood (Gen 6:19–22), plague (Exod 7:8–13; 8:12–15; 9:8–12), sickness (chap. 13, COMMENT B), and death. It is, however, P's distinctive teaching that nature maintains a balance between the forces of life and those of death, and it is incumbent on the human being, by dint of his intelligence, to discern the difference between them and to act accordingly. Israel, moreover, is charged with the additional obligation to distinguish between pure and impure, thereby providing it with a larger database for distinguishing between the forces of life and those of death. With P, therefore, we can detect the earliest gropings toward an ecological position (for details, see Milgrom forthcoming A).

It would be well to point out that the blood prohibition is an index of P's concern for the welfare of humanity. In Leviticus, to be sure, all of P is directed toward Israel. But one need only turn to the P stratum in Genesis to realize that it has not neglected the rest of mankind. P's blood prohibition in Genesis appears in the bipartite Noachide law, which states that human society is viable only if it desists from the shedding of human blood and the ingestion of animal blood (Gen 9:4–6). Thus it declares its fundamental premise that human beings can curb their violent nature through ritual means, specifically, a dietary discipline that will necessarily drive home the point that all life *(nepeš)*, shared also by animals, is inviolable, except—in the case of meat—when conceded by God (further, chap. 11, COMMENT C).

The P strand in Genesis also indicts the human race for its *ḥāmās* (Gen 6:11). Because the Noachide law of Gen 9 is the legal remedy for *ḥāmās* (Frymer-Kensky 1977), it probably denotes murder (as in Ezek 7:23), though in subsequent usage, especially under prophetic influence, it takes on a wide range of ethical violations (Haag 1980). Thus, the blood prohibition proves that P is of the opinion that a universal God imposed a basic ritual code upon humanity in general. Israel, nonetheless—bound by its covenantal relationship with the deity —is enjoined to follow a stricter code of conduct.

One would expect a sharp cleavage separating the theology of P from the non-Priestly strands of the Pentateuch. Still, it may come as a shock to realize that even the two Priestly sources, P and H, sharply diverge on many theological fundamentals. A comprehensive discussion of these differences must await volume 2 of this commentary. Here let it suffice to present my provisional conclusions in summary form.

The most important ideological distinction between P and H rests in their contrasting concepts of holiness. For P, spatial holiness is limited to the sanctuary; for H, it is coextensive with the promised land. Holiness of persons is restricted in P to priests and Nazirites (Num 6:5–8); H extends it to all Israel (see chap. 11, COMMENT E). This expansion follows logically from H's doctrine of spatial holiness: as the land is holy, all who reside in it are to keep it that way. Every adult Israelite is enjoined to attain holiness by observing the Lord's commandments, and even the *gēr*, the resident alien, must heed the prohibitive commandments, for their violation pollutes the land (e.g., 18:26).

P's doctrine of holiness is static; H's is dynamic. On the one hand, P constricts holiness to the sanctuary and its priests. P assiduously avoids the term *qādôš* 'holy' even in describing the Levites (compare their induction rites, Num 8:5–22, with the priestly consecration, Lev 8). H, on the other hand, though it concedes that only priests are innately holy (21:7), repeatedly calls on Israel to strive for holiness. The dynamic quality of H's concept is highlighted by its resort to the same participial construction *měqaddēš* 'sanctifying' in describing the holiness of both the laity and the priesthood. Sanctification is an ongoing process for priests (21:8, 15, 23; 22:9, 16) as well as for all Israelites (21:8; 22:32). No different from the Israelites, the priests bear a holiness that expands or contracts in proportion to their adherence to God's commandments.

The converse doctrine of pollution also varies sharply. P holds that the sanctuary is polluted by Israel's moral and ritual violations (4:2) committed anywhere in the camp (but not outside) and that this pollution can and must be effaced by the violator's purification offering and, if committed deliberately, by the high priest's sacrifice and confession (16:3–22). H, however, concentrates on the polluting force of Israel's violation of the covenant (26:15), for example, incest (18; 20:11–24), idolatry (20:1–6), or depriving the land of its sabbatical

48

rest (26:34–35). Pollution for H is nonritualistic, as shown by the metaphoric use of *ṭāmēʾ* (e.g., 18:21, 24; 19:31) and by the fact that the polluted land cannot be expiated by ritual, and, hence, the expulsion of its inhabitants is inevitable (18:24–29; 20:2). The underlying reason for these substantive changes will be thoroughly investigated in volume 2 (provisionally see Knohl 1988: 146–93).

The sacrificial system is intimately connected with the impurity system. Nonetheless, it possesses a distinctive theology (rather, theologies) of its own. No single theory embraces the entire complex of sacrifices (chap. 7, COMMENT A). All that can be said by way of generalization is that the sacrifices cover the gamut of the psychological, emotional, and religious needs of the people. We therefore adopt the more promising approach of seeking the specific rationale that underlies each kind of sacrifice. Even with this limited aim in mind, the texts are not always helpful. Nevertheless, hints gleaned from the terminology and the descriptions of the rites themselves will occasionally illumine our path. As of now, I believe, the comprehensive rationales for two sacrifices, the burnt and cereal offerings, still elude us (COMMENTS on chaps. 1 and 2), whereas the three remaining sacrifices—the well-being, purification, and reparation offerings —can be satisfactorily explained.

I begin with the well-being offering because of its connection with the blood prohibition (COMMENT on chap. 3; chap. 11, COMMENT C). This connection, however, was not present from the beginning. In the P stratum, the well-being offering is brought solely out of joyous motivations: thanksgiving, vow fulfillment, or spontaneous free-will (7:11–17). The meat of the offering is shared by the offerer with his family and invited guests (1 Sam 1:4; 9:21–24). The advent of H brought another dimension to this sacrifice. H's ban on non-sacrificial slaughter meant that all meat for the table had initially to be sanctified on the altar as a well-being offering (17:3–7). To be sure, the prohibition to ingest blood had existed before (Gen 9:4; cf. 1 Sam 14:32–35), implying that although man was conceded meat, its blood, which belongs to God, had to be drained (chap. 11, COMMENT C). Now that the blood had to be dashed on the altar (3:2, 8, 13), however, it served an additional function—to ransom the life of the offerer for taking the life of the animal (17:11; chap. 11, COMMENT C). Thus the principle of the inviolability of life was sharpened by this new provision: killing an animal was equivalent to murder (17:3–4) unless expiated by the well-being offering.

The rationale for the purification offering has been alluded to above. The violation of a prohibitive commandment generates impurity (NOTE on 4:2) and, if severe enough, pollutes the sanctuary from afar. This imagery portrays the Priestly theodicy that I have called the Priestly *Picture of Dorian Gray*. It declares that while sin may not scar the face of the sinner it does scar the face of the sanctuary. This image graphically illustrates the Priestly version of the old doctrine of collective responsibility: when the evildoers are punished they bring down the righteous with them. Those who perish with the wicked are not entirely blameless, however. They are inadvertent sinners who, by having allowed the wicked to flourish, have also contributed to the pollution of the sanctuary. In particular, the high priest and the tribal chieftain, the leaders of the people, bring special sacrifices (4:9, 23), for their errors cause harm to their people (see the NOTES on 4:3 and 10:6). Thus, in the Priestly scheme, the sanctuary is polluted (read: society is corrupted) by brazen sins (read: the rapacity of the leaders) and also by inadvertent sins (read: the acquiescence of the "silent majority"), with the result that God is driven out of his sanctuary (read: the nation is destroyed). In the theology of the purification offering Israel is close to the beliefs of its neighbors and yet so far from them. Both hold that the sanctuary stands in need of constant purification lest it be abandoned by its resident god. But whereas the pagans hold that the source of impurity is demonic, Israel, having expunged the demonic, attributes impurity to the rebellious and inadvertent sins of man instead (details in chap. 4, COMMENT C).

The reparation offering (5:14–26) seems at first glance to be restricted to offenses against the property of God, either his sancta or his name. It reflects, however, wider theological implications. The noun 'āšām 'reparation, reparation offering' is related to the verb 'āšam 'feel guilt', which predominates in this offering (5:17, 23, 26) and in the purification offering as well (4:13, 22, 27; 5:4, 5). This fact bears ethical consequences. Expiation by sacrifice depends on two factors: the remorse of the worshiper (verb 'āšam) and the reparation (noun 'āšām) he brings to both man and God to rectify his wrong. This sacrifice, however, strikes even deeper ethical roots. If someone falsely denies under oath having defrauded his fellow, subsequently feels guilt and restores the embezzled property and pays a 20-percent fine, he is then eligible to request of his deity that his reparation offering serve to expiate his false oath (5:20–26). Here we see the Priestly legists in action, bending the sacrificial rules in order to foster the growth of individual conscience. They permit sacrificial expiation for a deliberate crime against God (knowingly taking a false oath) provided the person repents before he is apprehended. Thus they ordain that repentance converts an intentional sin into an unintentional one, thereby making it eligible for sacrificial expiation (discussion in 5:14–16, COMMENT G).

It should already be clear that the Priestly polemic against pagan practice was also informed by ethical postulates. The impurity system pits the forces of life against the forces of death, reaching an ethical summit in the blood prohibition. Not only is blood identified with life; it is also declared inviolable. If the unauthorized taking of animal life is equated with murder, how much more so is the illegal taking of human life? And if the long list of prohibited animals has as its aim the restriction of meat to three domestic quadrupeds, whose blood (according to H) must be offered up on the altar of the central sanctuary, what else could the compliant Israelite derive from this arduous discipline except that all life must be treated with reverence?

INTRODUCTION

The reduction of sancta contagion may have been motivated by the desire to wean Israel from the universally attested morbid fear of approaching the sancta. But, as indicated above, there coexisted the more practical goal of breaking the equally current belief that the sanctuary gave asylum even to the criminal. As also noted already, the ethical current also ran strong in the rationale for the sacrifices. The purification offering taught the ecology of morality, that the sins of the individual adversely affect his society even when committed inadvertently, and the reparation offering became the vehicle for an incipient doctrine of repentance. The ethical thrust of these two expiatory sacrifices can be shown to be evident in other respects as well. The Priestly legists did not prescribe the purification offering just for cultic violations but extended the meaning of the term *miṣwâ* to embrace the broader area of ethical violations (see the NOTE on 4:2). And the texts on the reparation offering make it absolutely clear that in matters of expiation man takes precedence over God; only after rectification has been made with man can it be sought with God (5:24b–25).

A leitmotif of the sacrificial texts is their concern for the poor: everyone, regardless of means, should be able to bring an acceptable offering to the Lord. Thus, birds were added to the roster of burnt offerings (see the NOTE on 1:14–17), and the pericope on the cereal offering (chap. 2) was deliberately inserted after the burnt offering, implying that if a person could not afford birds he could bring a cereal offering (COMMENT on chap. 2). Indeed, this compassion for the poor is responsible for the prescribed sequence of the graduated purification offering: flock animal, bird, cereal (5:6–13). This concession of a cereal offering, however, was not allowed for severe impurity cases (12:8; 14:21–32; 15:14) because of the need for sacrificial blood to purge the contaminated altar (NOTE on 12:8).

The ethical impulse attains its zenith in the great Day of Purgation, Yom Kippur. What originally was only a rite to purge the sanctuary has been expanded to include a rite to purge the people. To begin with, as mentioned above, the pagan notion of demonic impurity was eviscerated by insisting that the accumulated pollution of the sanctuary was caused by human sin. Moreover, another dimension was introduced that represented a more radical alteration. The scapegoat, which initially eliminated the sanctuary's impurities, now became the vehicle of purging their source—the human heart. Provided that the people purge themselves through rites of penitence (16:29; 23:27, 29; Num 29:7), the high priest would confess their released sins upon the head of the scapegoat and then dispatch it and its load of sins into the wilderness (see the NOTE on 16:21; chap. 16, COMMENTS B and E). Thus, an initial widely attested purgation rite of the temple was broadened and transformed into an annual day for the collective catharsis of Israel. God would continue to reside with Israel because his temple and people were once again pure.

F. THE PRIEST

The role of Israel's priest cannot be fully appreciated without first contrasting him with his counterpart in the ancient Near East. Let us take as an example the roster of an Assyrian temple. It lists the following cultic functionaries (ērīb bīti): šangu high priest, kalû lamentation priest, nâru/nârtu (male/female) musician, āšipu/mašmaššu exorcist, and four kinds of diviners: baru extispicist, šāʾilu/šāʾiltu (male/female) necromancer, dream interpreter, maḫḫû ecstatic, and dāgil iṣṣūrē observer of birds (Saggs 1984: 201–24). The organization of the Babylonian temple was equally complex and perhaps included even more personnel (Renger 1967–69).

Israel had only the kōhēn priest (P's Levites had no cultic function), but he performed neither incantation, exorcism, divination, nor healing. What then were his functions? Let the texts speak for themselves: tummêkā wĕʾūrêkā . . . yôrû mišpāṭêkā lĕyaʿaqōb wĕtôrātĕkā lĕyiśrāʾēl yāśîmû qĕṭôrâ bĕappêkā wĕkālîl ʿal-mizbĕḥêkā "Your Thummim and your Urim . . . ; they (the priests) shall teach your laws to Jacob and your instructions to Israel. They shall offer your incense to savor (lit., 'in your nostrils') and burnt offerings on your altar" (Deut 33:10); laʿalôt ʿal-mizbĕḥî lĕhaqṭîr qĕṭōret lāśēʾt ʾēpôd lĕpānay "to ascend my altar, to burn incense, to carry an ephod before me" (1 Sam 2:28a).

These two old non-Priestly texts mention in common three cultic functions: sacrifices, incense, and oracles. Deuteronomy adds the teaching of God's laws (see also Deut 24:8), a function that is stressed in the later literature (2 Kgs 17:27b; Ezek 22:26; 44:23; Hag 2:11; Mal 2:7). It is also emphasized in H: ûlĕhôrōt ʾet-bĕnê yiśrāʾēl ʾēt kol-haḥuqqim ʾăšer dibber YHWH ʾălêhem bĕyad-mōšeh 'and you must teach the Israelites all of the laws that the Lord has imparted to them through Moses' (10:11). Because this pedagogic duty is not explicitly stated in P, Knohl concludes that "In the laws of PT (the Priestly Torah) the priests appear as a closed elite circle engaged in the traditional rites of the cult, which are conducted in *the sacred cultic enclosure from which persons who are not priests are barred*" (1988: V–VI; emphasis mine). Knohl's statement can be justified for Mesopotamia (Oppenheim 1964: 186) and Egypt (Sauneron 1960: 90)—not Hattia (cf. ANET³ 209, III, lines 21–24)—but for P, the evidence points in the opposite direction.

First, it should be noted that the householder and his guests are present at the sacrifice. Indeed, he is permitted to perform preliminary, nonaltar rites (NOTES on 1:4, 5, 6, 9); and for one of these rites, the hand-leaning, his presence is required (NOTE on 1:4). This means that he takes his stand inside the sacred enclosure. In fact, he has access to the entire court; he may circle the altar (NOTE on 1:3) and even touch it (chap. 7, COMMENT B). Only the tent shrine itself is off limits. In essence, then, all cultic acts are visible to the laity except the daily lampstand lighting and incense offering, performed by the high priest.

Furthermore, the recurring refrain in P is *wayyō'mer YHWH 'el-mōšeh lē'mōr dabbēr 'el-běnê yiśrā'ēl* 'The Lord spoke to Moses, saying: Speak to the Israelites' (e.g., 1:1–2; 4:1; 7:22; 11:1; 12:1; 15:1). The torah of the Lord is, therefore, not an esoteric doctrine, stored in the Temple archives and available solely to the elite priesthood (see also the NOTE on "to them," 1:11). Hence, the Lord's commandments compose the curriculum of the priest-teachers, so to speak, in Israel's schoolhouse. Its purpose is to reduce the incidence of impurity in Israel so that holiness, the sphere of God, can expand beyond the sanctuary. But because the source of this dynamic aspect of Priestly pedagogy is attributed to H (see the NOTES on 10:10–11), its discussion is postponed to volume 2. Let this pedagogic role of Israel's priest be contrasted with his Mesopotamian counterpart: "the ritual which you perform, (only) the *qualified* person shall view. An outsider who has nothing to do with the ritual shall not view (it); if he does, may his remaining days be few! The informed person may show (this tablet) to the informed person. The uninformed shall not see (it)—it is among the forbidden things of Anu, Enlil, and Ea, the great gods" (*ANET*[3] 336a; for the Egyptian equivalent, see the NOTE on 1:2).

A claim has been made that as the "Temple Program for the New Year Festival at Babylon" (*ANET*[3] 331–34) shares with P such matters as a call for artisans (lines 190–95; Exod 36:2–3), instructions for fashioning sacred objects (lines 201–8; Exod 25:17–21), and rituals for the purgation *(kuppuru; kipper)* of the sanctuary (lines 353–63; Lev 16:15–16, 27–28), therefore the colophon of the former—"secrets of Esagil. Whoever is for Bel must not show (them to anyone) but the *šešgallu* priest of the Temple Etusa" (lines 33–35)—must have existed in a similar form in P (Cohen 1969). But this is precisely my point: the very absence of such a colophon in P and the frequent incipits attesting to the contrary—that the priests must teach their lore to the Israelites—only underscore my claim that P is engaging in a polemic against standard priestly practice in Israel's environment.

There is one elitist aspect of P's priesthood that cannot be gainsaid: its strict hereditary character. Even non-Priestly sources indicate that everywhere in Israel a member of the levitic tribe was the preferred priest (cf. Judg 17:7–18:20). The alternative, a lay priesthood, did not work very well, to judge by the example of Egypt. "Because of its lay character and the ever recurring 'rotation' in the life of the priest, the Egyptian clergy was open to committing abuses of every sort" (Sauneron 1960: 23). To be sure, Israel's priests were on occasion guilty of corruption, venality, and assorted human failings (e.g., 1 Sam 2:22, Ezek 22:26; Hos 4:6–8). Still, a consecrated class of individuals who from childhood could be trained according to the high standards demanded by the Priestly texts stood the best chance of resisting abuses that flourished outside the sanctuary.

P confirms the other functions of the priest mentioned in the verses cited above. All priests were qualified to officiate at the altar. The incense offering, however, was reserved exclusively for the high priest (Exod 30:7–8) because it was performed inside the shrine. A possible reason for concentrating the total cult of the shrine into the hands of the high priest was the fear that ministrations with the lampstand (light), table (bread), and altar (incense) by all of the priests (not to speak of lay access to them) might lead to the belief that the purpose of these rites was the "care and feeding" of the God of Israel (see above). Perhaps this fear of anthropomorphism accounts also for P's sequestering of the Urim and Thummim in the breastpiece of the high priest (8:8), out of view even to his fellow priests, in contrast to earlier periods, when all priests consulted the oracle ephod (e.g., Judg 17:5; 18:17–20). To be sure, P tells us nothing concerning the actual use of the Urim and Thummim and, indeed, we never hear of their employment in the Solomonic Temple. Once again, silence must not be equated with disappearance. In any event, P concentrates on the rites involving the sancta of the Tabernacle. Just as we barely learn of the priestly blessing (9:23; cf. Num 6:22–27; Deut 10:5; 21:5) and the priestly trumpets (Num 10:1–10; 31:6), elements that are distinct from the sanctuary ritual, so we must presume that the single mention of the use of the Urim and Thummim in P (Num 27:21) is evidence for their actual use in the early history of Israel.

Deuteronomy also assigns a judicial role to the priest (Deut 17:8–13; 21:5), which the Chronicler attributes to the judicial reform of Jehoshaphat (2 Chr 19:8, 11; cf. Albright 1950b: 61–82). On this matter P is silent, a matter that Kaufmann ascribes to "a literary accident." This time, however, the silence is pregnant. True, P may have been reluctant to discuss any priestly activity dissociated from the sanctuary. Note that D assumes that priests sit on the national court of appeals located in the Temple city to adjudicate cases of tôrâ/dĕbar YHWH, in other words, religious law, fas, as opposed to mišpāṭ/dĕbar hammelek, that is to say, civil law, jus (Deut 17:11; 2 Chr 19:11). If P and H had known and accepted such a court they would have made some reference to it. Ezekiel, by contrast, who frequently fuses the Deuteronomic and Priestly traditions, does not hesitate to add this judicial function to the priestly portfolio (Ezek 44:24).

The high priest assumes responsibility for all Israel. The twelve tribes are inscribed on the two lazuli stones worn on his shoulders and on the twelve stones "before the Lord at all times" (Exod 28:29). Furthermore, "Inside the breastpiece of decision you [Moses] shall place the Urim and Thummim, so that they are over Aaron's heart when he comes *before the Lord*. Thus Aaron shall carry the (instrument of) decision over his heart *before the Lord at all times*" (Exod 28:30). Thus, both the stones and the Urim and Thummim function for Israel: the former for remembrance (lĕzikkārôn) and the latter for decision (mišpāṭ). The emphasis on the exclusive use of these materials inside the shrine *(haqqādoš)*, into which a nonpriest has no access, is clearly an open polemic against the practice attributed to the first kings, Saul and David, of consulting the Urim and Thummim outside the sanctuary (e.g., 1 Sam 10:22; 1 Sam 14:41 LXX; 2 Sam 2:1; 5:23–24), a practice that hardly differed in form from the mantic use of idols widely attested among the people (cf. Hos 4:12; Hab 2:18–19; Zech 10:2; and see the NOTE on 8:8).

The *ṣîṣ* 'plate' worn on the high priest's forehead was prophylactic in purpose: to expiate any imperfection inadvertently offered by the people (Exod 28:38; see the NOTE on 8:9). The high priest was required to purge the shrine of its impurities caused by Israel's collective inadvertent violations (4:13–21). His fellow priests purged the outer altar of Israel's individual inadvertencies (4:22–35). On each Yom Kippur, the high priest purged the entire sanctuary, including the adytum, of Israel's presumptuous wrongs (16:16) while, in the scapegoat rite, he purged a penitent Israel of all its sins (16:21). The purgative rites aimed not only to persuade the divine presence to remain in the sanctuary (i.e., with Israel) but also to repair the strained relations between a now repentant Israel and its God.

Penalty is a function of responsibility: the greater the latter, the more severe the former. Nadab and Abihu, the elder sons of Aaron—from whom his successor presumably would have been chosen—are struck down by God for their illicit incense offering (10:1–2). The penalty is precisely the same for all priestly (and levitic) encroachment upon the sancta. The duty of the clergy is to prevent the profanation of the sancta. All of its members are responsible for one another; the encroachment of one is the guilt of all. The penalty—death by divine agency. Thus, the collective responsibility of all Israel not to pollute the sanctuary (chap. 4, COMMENTS B and C) is matched here by the collective responsibility of all of the priests (and levites; cf. Num 18:2–3) to prevent encroachment by one of their own (see the NOTE on 10:3).

In times of war, the priests blew trumpets so that "you shall be remembered before the Lord your God and be saved from your enemies" (Num 10:9), and they would accompany Israel into battle bearing the *kĕlê haqqōdeš* 'sacred utensils' (Num 31:6). What these utensils were is moot. The term must refer to anointed (hence "sacred") cult objects, probably including the Ark (Milgrom 1970a: 49 n. 186). Whatever these utensils were, their being carried into battle clearly proves that the priests involved themselves in the welfare of their people, leaving the sanctuary so as to join them in distant and dangerous battlefields.

The responsibility of the priesthood for the welfare of all Israel is nowhere better exemplified than in P's conception of the relationship of priests and laity in the sacrificial service. The preliminary rites with the sacrificial animal are performed by the offerer: hand-leaning, slaughtering, flaying, quartering, and washing (NOTES on 1:1–9). The priest takes over at the altar and continues the sacrificial ritual in silence (see above). This means that the offerer commissions the priest to be his agent at the altar. In other words, the priest, by virtue of his sacred status, acts as the offerer's (silent) intermediary before God. He is more than a mere technician. In effect, he is the cultic counterpart of the prophet. Both represent the Israelites before God. Both intercede on their behalf, one through ritual, the other through prayer (though silence plays a role in the prophetic office [Milgrom 1983c: 258–62] and prayer is not absent from the priestly ministrations [see above]). The welfare of Israel depends on both a Moses and an Aaron.

There is also a tendency detectable in P to allocate increased responsibility in the cult to the laity. The priests enjoy a supervisory role in the lay preliminary rites, for example, ensuring that the slaughter be done correctly (NOTE on 1:5) and that the thanksgiving offering be eaten within the required one-day period (NOTE on 7:11). Even in such cases, God's instructions are addressed not to the priests but to the laity (1:2; 7:11–21, tacitly; 7:22–36, expressly). It is true that the well-being sacrifice was originally (in the Shilonite sanctuary) eaten by its offerer and his guests inside the sanctuary precincts, under priestly supervision (NOTE on 7:15); however, P mandates that it may be eaten anywhere, provided that place and persons are pure (7:19; 10:14), signifying that P has shifted the responsibility of supervision from the priest to the offerer. P thereby manifests faith in the piety and integrity of the individual Israelite.

In essence, what is predicated here is a partnership of trust between the priest and the layman. This hardly corresponds to the current view of biblicists that the Israelite priesthood is a closed, elitist group that relentlessly barred the laity from access to the sanctuary and its lore (most recently Knohl, above). Also vitiated is the current view of rabbinic scholars, who share a negative view of the biblical priests in view of the reforms introduced by the early rabbis. The following is a recent example:

> (In the Mishnah) it is the householder who commissions the priest to perform the sacrifice. Consequently, a priest performs a valid sacrifice only by faithfully carrying out the wishes of the householder. In effect, therefore, the Mishnah has turned Scripture's theory of the priesthood on its head . . . the Mishnah has demoted the priest and given house-holders a more central role in the sacrificial system. . . . It is the intentions of the householder which define the classification of the animal. . . . As agents of householders, therefore, priests are merely cogs in a machine which a householder sets in motion and ultimately controls. (Eilberg-Schwartz 1986: 172)

Substitute P for Mishna and this statement is virtually correct.

A word is in order concerning P's attitude regarding Israel's civil leaders. In the purification-offering pericope the tribal chieftain is singled out from the rest of the people by his distinct sacrifice (4:22–26), which tells us only that his authority is recognized by P, but nothing more. More informative is P's attitude to Moses. First, however, the notion that Moses himself was a high priest or functioned as one must be discounted. While it is true that he inducted Aaron and his sons into the priesthood in a week-long consecration service, Moses was only acting in his "royal" capacity, following an ancient Near Eastern tradition whereby kings installed their chief priests into office (see chap. 7, COMMENT E). Moreover, P makes the point of identifying Moses as a nonpriest by denying him the priestly prebend of the right thigh and by declaring that the theophany took place not during Moses' ministration but on the eighth day, when Aaron and his sons began to officiate. Also, in the aftermath of the deaths of Aaron's sons, Nadab and Abihu, Moses and Aaron differ on a sacrificial procedure and, at the end, Moses has to concede that Aaron is correct (10:20).

This last argument, however, actually proves Moses' superiority for, according to P, Moses had the right to question Aaron and, in spite of the fact that the issue was purely cultic—and a fine point at that—Aaron had to have Moses' approval. While P is perhaps expressing satisfaction that Aaron is more knowledgeable in the minutiae of cultic law, it is at the same time acknowledging that Aaron, the high priest, must answer to Moses, the prophet.

Indeed, it is Moses' prophetic role as the mediator between God and the people, including the priests, that is the specific teaching of P. There are only two passages in which God speaks solely to Aaron (10:8–11; and Num 18:1–24, which may be H!), a conspicuous paucity that serves to accentuate Moses' domination. What greater proof is there of Moses' supremacy than that Aaron's most important task—purging the sanctuary of its impurity and Israel of its sins —is mediated by Moses (16:1) and that when faithfully executed by Aaron, P notes that "he did as the Lord had commanded Moses" (16:34b)?

Above all, Aaron is powerless—even in P—in comparison to Moses. It is most instructive to compare the two with Samuel, the one individual in whom both the priestly and the prophetic jurisdictions were fused. Samuel was the chief priest of his time; his clash with Saul verifies this (1 Sam 13:9–14; cf. 9:12–13). In his valedictory to the people, however, it is his civil authority that comes to the fore: "Whose bull have I taken? Whose ass have I taken? Whom have I wronged? Whom have I abused? From whom have I taken a bribe [or a pair of shoes (LXX)]?" (1 Sam 12:3). It is hardly an accident that Samuel is elaborating on Moses' statement made under similar circumstances—"I have not taken the ass of any of them, nor have I wronged any of them" (Num 16:15)—both speakers apparently utilizing a stereotyped negative confession expected of ancient Near Eastern officials when called upon to prove that they exercised their powers justly (cf. EA 280:25–29). In sum, P admits that Aaron's authority is confined to the sanctuary, and even there, as noted, he is still subject to the higher authority of Moses.

G. ANTHROPOMORPHISM AND REVELATION

The Lord appears to Moses and Israel as his *kābôd* 'glory', whose form resembles fire (Exod 24:17a; Num 9:15; 2 Chr 7:3a). The *kābôd* fire is encased in a cloud (Exod 24:16a; 40:38). During the day only the cloud is visible, for presumably the fire is dimmed by the sunlight. The night renders the cloud invisible, but the luminous fire can be seen. Thus the deity is visibly present to Israel day and night.

In its first appearance, the Lord's fire cloud descends atop Mount Sinai (Exod 24:16–17). In its second appearance, it descends on the newly constructed Tabernacle (Exod 40:36). Just as the *kābôd* fire makes itself visible to Israel at Sinai (Exod 24:17) so it appears before the assembled Israelites at the Tabernacle's inauguration (9:6b, 23b, 24a). Thus the P tradition stakes out its claim that the Tabernacle is equivalent to Sinai—indeed, is a portable Sinai—assuring Israel of God's permanent presence in its midst. Moreover, the Tabernacle theophany is arguably even more important, for the *kābôd* fire separates itself from its nebulous encasement to consume the altar sacrifices in the sight of all Israel (9:23–24). Thereafter, according to P, the ascending and descending fire cloud becomes the signal to Israel indicating whether it should move or encamp (Num 9:18). (For the contrast with Mesopotamian theophanies and late biblical manifestations of the divine fire, see the NOTES on 9:4, 23, and 24.)

The *kābôd* fire presumably brightens in intensity as a sign to Moses that the Lord initiates or concedes an audience with him (Num 17:7–8; 20:6–7). It then condenses between the outstretched wings of the Cherubim in the adytum (Exod 25:22; 30:6). Yet Moses never enters the adytum itself but rather takes his stand before the veil in the outer shrine so that he may hear the voice of God (Num 7:89). Furthermore, when the Lord's *kābôd* condescends upon the newly erected Tabernacle, it fills the entire tent so that Moses must hear God's instructions concerning the sacrificial system (chaps. 1–7) while standing in the courtyard (Exod 40:34–35; Lev 1:1). Clearly, the Priestly narrator is indicating that Moses' experience at Sinai is never again to be repeated. At Sinai he was admitted into the divine cloud (Exod 24:18a), but henceforth he must never penetrate the divine cloud, condensed into the adytum. That is to say, he must never *see* God but may only *hear* him in the outer shrine, his view blocked by the veil. The same restrictions apply to the priests. When they dismantle the Tabernacle, they must shield their eyes from viewing the Ark by holding up the veil (Milgrom 1990a: 25–26), and the high priest who is commanded to purge the adytum annually is explicitly warned that he must block his vision by a smoke screen of incense lest his entry prove fatal to him (for details, see the NOTES on 1:1 and 16:13).

P makes a concerted effort to avoid anthropomorphisms. This holds true not only in its *kābôd* theology but also in its abstention from any expression that might imply that God is bound to material things on earth, such as *miškan YHWH* (17:4), *miqdāšî* (20:3), *miškānî* (15:31), and *laḥmî* and *rēaḥ nîḥōḥî* (Num 28:2), all of which are attributable to H (Knohl 1988: 120–22). It is not true, however, that P even avoids the notion of the Lord's residing *(škn*, lit., "tenting") in the Tabernacle by giving priority to the root *y*ᶜ*d* 'meet' (Knohl 1988: 120). On the contrary, P uses the verb *šākan* freely, for example, in Exod 24:16; 40:34–35 (P, not H, versus Knohl 1988: 235 n. 19, for these verses link with Lev 1:1), Lev 16:16, Num 9:17–23; 10:12. Besides, *šākan* implies an impermanent dwelling (Cross 1947: 65–68) and, no different from *nôᶜad*, signifies a rejection of, and perhaps a polemic against, the notion that the Lord actually dwells in the Tabernacle.

There can be no doubt that the Priestly legists have succeeded in eliminating even the slightest suspicion that the purpose of the Tabernacle is—in A. L. Oppenheim's succinct characterization of Mesopotamian religion—"the care and feeding" of Israel's God (1964: 183–97; for Egypt, see Sauneron 1960: 83–90). The terms *leḥem* 'food' and *rēaḥ nîḥōaḥ* 'pleasing aroma' are linguistic fossils, and yet P assiduously avoids these terms where one would most expect them, namely, in the expiatory sacrifices that function to placate the deity (Gray 1925: 79–81; but see the NOTE on 4:31). Even more significant is the apodictic command, "You shall not offer alien incense on it (the inner altar) or a burnt offering or a cereal offering; neither shall you pour a libation on it" (Exod 30:9). All sacrifices are to be offered on the outer altar in the open courtyard, visible to all worshipers and removed from the Tent, the Lord's purported domicile. Moreover, because pagans regularly set food and drink on the god's table, Israel banned all food rites inside the shrine. Exod 30:9 specifically prohibits the burnt offering (flesh), the cereal offering (bread), and all libations (drink) on the inner altar. Further, the frankincense of the bread of the presence is not placed upon the bread, as is the case with other cereal offerings (2:1, 15; 6:8), but is uniquely set apart from it, so that the bread could be eaten in its entirety by the priests (24:9; though H, it probably preserves P's practice), while the frankincense alone is burned on the inner altar. Of special importance are the libation jugs associated with the table of the bread of presence set inside the shrine (Exod 25:29; 37:16). Because they were made of gold they could be used only inside the shrine, nowhere else (Haran 1978: 158–65). Thus, the golden libation jugs may have been vestiges of an original libation rite (of ale, Num 28:7b; cf. the NOTE on Lev 10:9) on the inner altar, which was later rejected as a gross anthropomorphism. The jugs were probably empty (contra Haran 1978: 217), a hallowed fossil; no text prescribes otherwise (for the rabbinic view and other details, see Milgrom 1990a: 26, 240).

The polemic that P wages against anthropomorphism is best illustrated by the worship service of the Tabernacle, which Y. Kaufmann aptly labels "the sanctuary of silence" (1937–56; 2.476–77; 1960: 303–4). That the entire sacrificial ritual was conducted in silence can best be explained as the concerted attempt of P to distance the rites of Israel's priest from the magical incantations that necessarily accompanied and, indeed, empowered the ritual acts of his pagan counterpart. Kaufmann's insight can be supplemented and confirmed by the parallel phenomenon of Moses, the putative father of Israelite prophecy, who is also constrained to silence during his performance of a miracle. In the instance of the plagues, Moses not only acts without speech, but on four occasions, when he accedes to Pharaoh's plea to request their cessation, he leaves Pharaoh's presence and prays to God in private—so that he would not be taken to be a heathen magician (Exod 8:8, 25–26; 9:29, 33; 10:18–all JE). Likewise, Moses' intercessory prayers for Israel are always in private, again in order to dissociate him from his pagan counterpart (e.g., Exod 5:22; 32:11–13, 30–31; 33:7–11—again, all JE). Thus, all of the pentateuchal narratives on Moses and Aaron are in agreement that, in the initial stages of the formation of Israelite cult and prophecy, the gesticulation of the divine representative, whether in sacrifice or in miracle, was performed in total silence (details in Milgrom 1983c: 258–61).

Knohl takes issue with Kaufmann's explanation of this phenomenon (and hence mine) and claims that the sanctuary's silence is evoked by the awe and dread of standing before the ineffable majesty of the divine presence (1988: 132–42). Here Knohl is clearly influenced by Rudolph Otto's concept of the "numinous" reaction generated by the *mysterium tremendum,* in other words, the terror and stupor evoked by the confrontation with the "wholly other" (Otto 1958: 5–40). Knohl cites the expiatory force of the burnt offering (1:4) as proof that entering the sanctuary generated feelings of inadequacy and sin that required sacrificial expiation (1988: 134). But the private burnt offering of chap. 1 is voluntary, not mandatory. In fact, offerers could just bring a well-being offering of joy without the slightest feeling of dread or inadequacy. Further, as argued above (and in the COMMENT on chap. 1), the wholly expiatory nature of P's burnt offering may only be a reflection of this sacrifice's original function before the rise of the two exclusive expiatory sacrifices, the purification and reparation offerings, and the subsequent conversion of the burnt offering (by H) into a joyous sacrifice for the individual.

As a consequence of his view of the sacrificial service as a solemn affair, Knohl claims that it could countenance neither music nor prayer (1988: 132). He cannot be right. That total silence reigned in Solomon's Temple (which Knohl believes to be the *Sitz im Leben* for P) is not only contrary to what we know of temple services elsewhere in the ancient Near East but also in conflict with the biblical evidence itself. Even if we disallow the Chronicler's attribution of Temple music to the initiative of King David, it cannot be gainsaid that the Temple's musical guilds were old, probably Canaanite in origin (Albright 1942: 126–27) and, hence, must have been an integral part of Temple worship from its inception. In addition to the many psalms that were probably employed in the Temple liturgy, one cannot deny the primacy of the priestly benediction sanctioned by P itself (9:23, and see above). If, however, P's origins are ascribed to the Shiloh temple/tabernacle (see above), then one need only recall Hannah's prayer: the priest Eli is enraged not by the prayer itself but by Hannah's presumed inebriation (1 Sam 1:12–17). Kaufmann is not guilty of Knohl's mistake; he correctly limits his "sanctuary of silence" to the action of the priests during the execution of the sacrifices. This leaves ample room for lay (and levitic) vocal and musical participation, as well as for the priestly benediction at the conclusion of the service.

H. The Composition of Lev 1–16

The analysis of the first sixteen chapters of Leviticus as spread over the pages of this commentary affirms that Lev 1–16 is in its entirety the work of Israel's priesthood. It is, however, not of one hue. To be sure, the bulk of it can be assigned to a single author. But there are also clear signs of editorial arranging and supplementation. These have been identified and classified. Nevertheless, the reader should keep in mind that the task of separating out the purported strata is hazardous and that the results are, at best, tentative.

One would expect the account of the building of the Tabernacle (Exod 35–40) to be followed by the account of its dedication (Lev 8). This expectation is reinforced by the observation that Exod 39, Exod 40:17–33, and Lev 8 reveal the same septenary structure (see chap. 8, Comment A). Thus, Lev 1–7 is an insertion, but one that makes sense because the dedicatory and inaugural sacrifices that follow (8:14–29; 9:1–21) cannot be understood without it. The closing verses of Exodus (Exod 40:36–38), however, are clearly intrusive; the information that the divine cloud will lead Israel in its wilderness trek belongs in the book of Numbers. In fact, the same information is repeated, but in greater detail, just before Israel begins its march (Num 9:15–23). This repetition, however, instead of creating a problem, provides an answer, and a significant one at that: the Exodus passage is a proleptic summary of its Numbers counterpart and serves with it to bracket the intervening material, Lev 1:1–Num 9:14, which comprises all of the laws revealed to Moses at Sinai. These laws occupy the center of the Pentateuch. They must, therefore, be the foundation of Israel's life.

The laws themselves are the work of Priestly legists, but they do not all stem from the same Priestly school. It has long been recognized that Lev 17–27 is the product of a distinct school (H), the only exception being some P material in chap. 23 (see the commentaries). The situation in Lev 1–16 is more complex. This complexity can easily be shown by analyzing the composition of Lev 11.

My results (chap. 11, COMMENT A) lead to the following dissection: P₁ (vv 1–23, 41–42, 46), P₂ (vv 24–38, 47), H (vv 43–45), P₃ (vv 39–40).

Chapter 11, it turns out, is mainly composed of two Priestly strata (P₁ and P₂), each with its own conclusion (vv 46 and 47, respectively). It contains two interpolations, one each from the Holiness (H) and Priestly (P₃) schools. Because the author of P₂ has added his own subscript (v 47) to that of P₁ (v 46), he must be the redactor responsible for the fusion of P₁ and P₂ (vv 1–38, 41–42, 46–47). H (vv 43–45), inserted at the end of the combined material just before the closing subscripts, is an interpolation; so is P₃ (vv 39–40), but its placement is awkward (details in chap. 11, COMMENT A). The fact that H was inserted after the P material was in place leads to the suspicion that H is a later stratum than P—a conclusion that counters the scholarly consensus. The relative chronology of H and P₃ cannot be determined with certainty. Nevertheless, because P₃ uniquely prohibits touching the carcass of a pure animal, whereas P₁, P₂, and H (22:5a, 8) do not (see chap. 11, COMMENT A), the likelihood exists that the P₃ interpolation is later than H—in which case Knohl's claim that H is the final stratum in Leviticus may have to be abandoned.

Another example of complex composition is chap. 16. It is clearly the work of a redactor who united chap. 16 with chap. 10 (chaps. 11–15 being inserted later); vv 29–34a betray the handiwork of H. The preponderant part (vv 2–28), originally an emergency rite for purging the sanctuary, stems from P; but its use of such basic terms as ʾōhel môʿēd and qōdeš and the unique word pĕšaʿîm does not correspond to P. Most likely, an older pre-Temple document has been reworked by P and made to conform to its theology. Here too the H stratum comes at the end, indicating that it probably is the last stratum in the composition (details in chap. 11, COMMENT A). One implication is especially significant: the total purgation of the sanctuary was not fixed as an annual event on the tenth of Tishri until the time of H.

Other units that may be considered to be supplements to the basic P stratum are the burnt-offering birds (1:14–17), the firstfruits cereal offering (2:14–16), the sacrificial blood and suet prohibitions (3:16b–17), the high priest's cereal offering (6:12–16), the nonsacrificial blood and suet prohibitions (7:22–27), the assembling of the ʿēdâ and anointing of the Tabernacle (8:3–5, 10–11), the priests' pedagogic function (10:10–11), the reduced offering of the parturient, the moldy garment (13:47–59), the fungous house (14:33–53), and the subscript to the scale-disease laws (14:54–57), aside from interpolated verses (e.g., 15:31), clauses and phrases (e.g., 7:38b; 8:26bβ; 9:21aβ; 10:15a), and joins (e.g., 6:17–18a).

These supplemental units subdivide into two strands: the extension of the Priestly stratum, in which the older terminology and ideology continue unchanged; and the Holiness strand, marked by distinctive vocabulary and viewpoint. Thus, the H passages are detected by such telltale indicators, among others, as the absolute prohibition against common slaughter (3:16b–17), the emphasis on the holiness of Israel (11:43–45), and the inclusion of the alien (16:29–34a).

For the sake of simplicity, the supplemental passages will be designated P_2 and H, bearing in mind that some of them may stem from different hands. In other words, P_2 and H may represent the work of several tradents of each school. (Assumed is that the basic Priestly text, not represented here, is to be designated as P_1.) The resulting tabulation is as follows:

The Redaction of the Basic Text of Lev 1–16 (P_1)

P_2 1:14–17; 2:3, 10, 14–16; 7:8–10; 8:3–5, 10–11, 26bβ; 9:21aβ; 10:15aβ; 11:24–38, 47; 13:47–59; 15:33aβ; 16:1

H 3:16b–17; 6:12–18aα; 7:22–29a; 7:38b(?); 9:17b; 11:43–45; 12:8; 14:34–53(?), 54–57(?); 15:31; 16:2bβ, 29–34a

P_2 is solely a supplementation (e.g., 11:24–38). H as the redactor of P is responsible for both supplementation (e.g., 3:16b–17) and the present arrangement of Lev 1–16, that is, the insertion of the large blocs, the sacrificial laws (chaps. 1–7) and the impurity laws (chaps. 11–15)—which may have existed as independent and discrete scrolls—in their present places. Uncertainty persists regarding whether 7:38b and 14:35–53, 54–57 are to be assigned to P_2 or H, though the evidence points to H. Unaccounted for is the interpolation 11:39–40, which is, therefore, assigned to P_3.

I. THE COMMENTATORS

A. Medieval

My commentary is selective in citing other interpretations. It grapples only with differing views that, in my opinion, are important, but it acknowledges all with which I agree. In the latter category, the reader will find that I draw heavily from the medieval Jewish exegetes, whose insights have largely been neglected. Indeed, some of their names will draw a blank even from scholars. Having lived in a premodern age, they are *a priori* written off as precritical. In page after page of this commentary, however, it will be demonstrated that they frequently anticipate the moderns and at times even supersede them. One can readily learn of my indebtedness to them merely by scanning the many citations from their commentaries in chaps. 1–5, appended below. Note as well the equal weight given to the hitherto ignored commentaries of the Karaites. Unfortunately, except for Rashi, Ibn Ezra (partially), and Ramban, the commentaries of these medievalists, composed in Hebrew (Saadiah's in Arabic), still await translation into English. At the least their authors deserve some identification. A thumbnail biography follows in chronological order.

1. *Saadiah* (ben Joseph) Gaon (882–942). Arguably the greatest leader, philosopher, and halakhist of the gaonic period, he was born and raised in Egypt and settled in Babylonia, where he became the head *(gaon)* of the academy of Sura. His Arabic translation and partial commentary *(Tafsir)* of the Bible has remained standard for Arabic-speaking Jews. His translation is not literal, yet he strives for the plain meaning of the text. For examples of his exegesis see 1:1; 2:14; 3:9, 16; 4:2, 7, 14; etc.

2. *Ibn Janaḥ* (Jonah: first half of the eleventh century) of Spain; physician, grammarian, and lexicographer. He compiled the first complete book on Hebrew philology preserved in its entirety. Its second half, known as *Seper haš-šorāšîm* 'The Book of Roots', is a complete dictionary of BH, which also contains exegetical excursuses on difficult biblical passages. His influence on succeeding generations of exegetes is enormous. See his comment on 2:1 etc.

3. *Rashi* (Solomon ben Isaac, 1040–1105) of Troyes, France. His commentary on the Bible and the Babylonian Talmud is standard curriculum in all traditional Jewish schools to this day. His Bible commentary is a blend of the literal and midrashic. Its methodology is defined in his comment on Gen 3:8, "As for me, I am only concerned with the literal meaning of Scriptures and with such *'aggādôt* (i.e., *Midrashim*) as explain the biblical passages in a fitting manner." There exists an annotated English translation (Rosenbaum-Silverman). For examples of his exegesis, see 1:3; 2:7, 11; 3:3; 4:14; 5:3, 4, 15, 24; etc.

4. *Rashbam* (Samuel ben Meir; ca. 1080–ca. 1174). The grandson of Rashi and commentator on the Bible and Babylonian Talmud. Of the former, only his commentaries on the Torah and Ecclesiastes survive. A confirmed literalist, he states his position as follows: "I have not come to explain the *hălākôt.* . . . Derived as they are from textual redundancies, they can partly be found in the commentaries of Rabbi Solomon, my maternal grandfather. My aim is to interpret the literal meaning of Scripture" (Exod 21:1). See his exegesis of 1:1, 4, 5; 3:17, COMMENT; chap. 4, COMMENT J; 5:14–26, COMMENT A; etc.

5. *Ibn Ezra* (Abraham; 1089–1164), poet, grammarian, exegete, philosopher, astronomer, physician. Until 1140 he lived in Tudela, Spain; thereafter, he was an itinerant scholar, mainly in Italy and France. Etymology and grammar were his main concerns. In his introduction to the Torah, he states his intention to determine the literal meaning of the text while adhering to the decisions of the rabbis in interpreting the legal portions. An English translation is now available for Genesis (1988) and Leviticus (1986). For examples of his exegesis, see 1:1, 5, 8, COMMENT; 2:7, 14; 3:4, 9, 17, COMMENT; 4:6, 14, 27, 35, COMMENT F; 5:4, 5, 11, 15, 21; 5:14–26, COMMENT A; etc.

6. *Bekhor Shor* (Joseph ben Isaac, twelfth century) of Orléans, France. In his Torah commentary, he follows the literal approach of his French predeces-

sors, Rashi and Rashbam, stressing the rational basis of the commandments. See his comments on 1:1, 15, COMMENT; 5:14–26, COMMENTS A, F; etc.

7. *Radak* (David Kimḥi: 1160?–1235?) of Narbonne, France: grammarian and exegete. Following the methodology of Ibn Ezra, he concentrates on philological analysis. Relying on rabbinic literature, however, he also includes homiletic interpretations. He wrote commentaries on Genesis, all of the prophetic books, Psalms, and Chronicles. His collected comments on the rest of the Pentateuch and Proverbs were probably culled from his philological writings. For examples of his exegesis, see 2:1, 2; 5:14–26, COMMENT A; etc.

8. *Ramban* (Moses ben Naḥman, also called Naḥmanides; 1194–1270), philosopher, kabbalist, exegete, talmudist, poet, physician. He was born in Gerona, Spain and spent his final years in Palestine. His Torah commentary always gives the literal interpretation, but it also makes frequent use of the Talmud, Midrash, and Zohar in order to create a reason for each commandment. An annotated English translation is available (Chavel 1960). For examples of his exegesis see 1:1, 8, 9, 15, 17, COMMENT; 2:11; 3:9; chap. 4, COMMENT E; 5:5; 5:14–26, COMMENT F; etc.

9. *Ḥazzequni.* A commentary on the Torah and on Rashi's commentary by Hezekiah ben Manoah of France (thirteenth century). He bases himself largely on his predecessors—Rashi, Rashbam, and Bekhor Shor—but he also quotes many midrashim that are no longer extant. See 1:1 etc.

10. *Seper Hamibḥar,* a Torah commentary by Aaron ben Joseph Ha-rofe "the elder" (ca. 1250–1320), a Karaite scholar and physician. He lived in Sokhet, Crimea and in Constantinople. Though a strict literalist, he occasionally introduces a midrashic interpretation, taken as a rule from Rashi. For examples of his exegesis see 1:3; 2:11, 14; 3:1, 9; chap. 4, COMMENT E; 5:5; 5:14–26, COMMENT F; etc.

11. *Ralbag* (Levi ben Gershom; 1288–1344), mathematician, astronomer, philosopher, and exegete. Born and raised in France, he wrote commentaries on many biblical books. His commentary on the Pentateuch is characterized by philosophic and theological discourses, referring extensively to his major philosophic work *The Book of the Wars of the Lord,* and contains his own set of hermeneutical principles; see the COMMENT on chap. 2 etc.

12. *Keter Torah,* a Torah commentary authored by Aaron ben Elijah (1328?–1369), a Karaite scholar, philosopher, and jurist. He lived in Nicomedia (near Izmir, Turkey). He was called Aaron the Younger to distinguish him from Aaron the Elder, who lived a century earlier. His commitment to the literal interpretation of the text did not prevent him from introducing allegorical and metaphysical interpretations. For examples of his exegesis, see 1:3, 6; 2:3, 14; 3:1, 9, 11, 17; 4:3, 22; 5:1–13, COMMENT; 5:14–26, COMMENT F; etc.

13. *Abravanel* (Isaac ben Judah; 1437–1508), statesman, philosopher, and exegete. He served as treasurer to Alfonso V of Portugal and in 1484, entered the service of Ferdinand and Isabella of Castile. Expelled from Spain together

with its Jewish population, he made his home in Italy, where he wrote his Torah commentary. His exegesis is characterized by lengthy answers to questions, sometimes numbering more than forty, which he raises before each unit. Eschewing grammar and philology, he concentrates on the rationale for the commandments, stressing their moral significance. See his remarks on 1:8; 2:8, COMMENT; 3:1, 8; INTRODUCTION to 4:13, 20, COMMENTS H, J; 5:14–26, COMMENT F; etc.

14. *Sforno* (Obadiah ben Jacob; ca. 1470–ca. 1550), Italian exegete and physician. His brief Torah commentary focuses on the literal meaning of the text, avoiding philosophy and philology. See his comments on 1:1 etc.

15. Naphtali Herz *Wessely* (1725–1805), poet, linguist, banker, and exegete. He stands on the threshold of the modern age. Born in Hamburg and educated at the yeshiva of Rabbi Jonathan Eyebeschuetz, he came under the influence of Moses Mendelssohn and pioneered the revival of BH. In his commentary on Leviticus, he relies on the medieval commentators, especially Rashi, always striving for the plain meaning of the text. His collocation of relevant talmudic comments is invaluable. See 3:9; 4:23; 5:13, 21; etc.

16. *Shadal* (Samuel David Luzzatto; 1800–1865), Italian scholar, philosopher, exegete, and translator. In his Torah commentary he favors the views of Rashi and Rashbam but also offers his own novel interpretations. He frequently quotes his students, citing them by name. Although chronologically he belongs to the modern period, his faithful pursuit of the plain meaning of the text qualifies him for the company of the above-cited medievalists. See his comments on 1:3, COMMENT; 2:14; 4:14; 5:1–13, COMMENT; 5:14–26, COMMENT A.

B. Moderns

I have benefited from the following commentators, whose works were composed during the past 150 years: Kalisch (1867–72), Dillmann and Ryssel (1897), Driver and White (1894, 1898), Bertholet (1901), Baentsch (1903), Hoffmann (1905–6, 1953), Noth (1965), Elliger (1966), Snaith (1967), Wenham (1979), Harrison (1980), and Levine (1989). In this list the only verse-by-verse commentaries are those by Kalisch, Dillmann, Baentsch, Hoffmann, Elliger, and Levine—the first and last in English. On a popular level, the reader is referred to the recent English work of Wenham and the fuller one of Levine.

C. My Students and Colleagues

This work began more than a quarter of a century ago with my first publication on the diet laws (1963). Material from this and from ensuing publications is included in the commentary, updated and, where necessary, corrected.

Volume 1 of this work was forged on the anvil of my graduate seminar over a period of five years. To qualify for this seminar, students had to display competence in the requisite languages (only Hittite was optional) and medieval Jewish exegesis. Their feedback was indispensable in challenging and refining my ideas. How fortunate I am to have benefited from their acumen and their uncommon skills, such as taxidermy (S. Pfann) and animal husbandry (S. Rattray). Two of them (S. Rattray and D. P. Wright) have contributed COMMENTS. Names contained in parentheses consisting of a first initial and a surname refer to my students. This volume, truly a collective effort, is gratefully dedicated to them.

I am grateful to D. P. Wright, my erstwhile student and now my colleague, for his comments on the entire manuscript. Special thanks are due to my editor, D. N. Freedman, for his friendship, support, and counsel. Where is there another editor whose comments nearly always match the length of the manuscript before him? His contributions are strewn throughout the commentary and, herewith, gratefully acknowledged. I also wish to thank my students Christine Hayes, Michael Hildenbrand, and Roy Gane for their help in typing, proofreading, and preparing indexes.

Completed March 21 (Purim) 1989

Postscript. In the spring of 1990, as a fellow of the Institute for Advanced Studies at the Hebrew University, Jerusalem, I was privileged to examine unpublished fragments from Qumran's cave 4 relating to Leviticus, some of which are cited in the NOTES.

BIBLIOGRAPHY

♦

Aaron ben Elijah
  1866–67 *Keter Torah*, ed. J. Saruskan. 5 vols. in 1. Gozlow: Eupatoria.
Aaron ben Joseph
  1835 *Seper Hamibḥar.* Eupatoriya: Y. Finkleman.
Aartun, K.
  1976 Eine weitere Parallele aus Ugarit zur kultischen Praxis in Israels Religion. *BibOr* 33: 285–89.

  ———

  1980 Studien zum Gesetz über den grossen Versöhnungstag Lv 16 mit Varianten. Ein ritualgeschichtlicher Beitrag. *Studia theologica* 34: 73–109.
Abramsky, S.
  1973 "Rosh Hashana" and "Pesah" in. Ezekiel. *Beer-Sheva* 1: 56–78 (Hebrew).
Abravanel, I.
  1964 *Commentary on the Torah.* 3 vols. Jerusalem: Bnai Arbel.
Achelis, H.
  1904 *Die syrische Didascalia.* Leipzig: J. C. Hinrichs.
Adler, R.
  1976 *Tumah* and *Taharah:* Ends and Beginnings. In *The Jewish Woman, New Perspectives,* ed. E. Koltun. Pp. 63–71. New York: Schocken.
Aharoni, J.
  1938 On Some Animals Mentioned in the Bible. *Osiris* 5: 461–78.
Aharoni, Y.
  1968 Arad: Its Inscriptions and Temple. *BA* 31: 2–32.

  ———

  1973 The Solomonic Temple, the Tabernacle, and the Arad Sanctuary. *Beer-Sheva* 1: 79–86 (Hebrew).
Aḥiṭuv, S.
  1971a "Azazel." *EM* 6: 113–15 (Hebrew).

  ———

  1971b *"Ṣōʾn."* *EM* 6: 648 (Hebrew).

Aistleitner, J.
1954 *Untersuchungen zur Grammatik des Ugaritischen.* Berlin: Akademie Verlag.
Al-Qūmisī, D.
1952 Quoted pp. 30–41 in L. Nemoy, *Karaite Anthology,* New Haven: Yale University Press.
Albeck, H.
1952 *Seder Moʿed.* Jerusalem: Bialik Institute (Hebrew).

_____

1956 *Commentary to the Mishnah, Holy Things.* Jerusalem: Bialik Institute.
Albright, W. F.
1934 The North Canaanite Poems of Aleyan Baʿal. *JPOS* 14: 101–40.

_____

1941 New Light on the Early History of Phoenician Civilization. *BASOR* 83: 19.

_____

1941–43 *The Excavation of Tell Beit Mirsim III: The Iron Age.* AASOR 21–22.

_____

1942 *Archaeology and the Religion of Israel.* Baltimore: The Johns Hopkins Press.

_____

1947 The Phoenician Inscriptions of the Tenth Century, B.C. from Byblos. *JAOS* 77: 158 n. 42.

_____

1949 *The Archaeology of Palestine.* Harmondsworth: Penguin.

_____

1950a Review of C. H. Gordon, *Ugaritic Grammar. JBL* 69: 388–94.

_____

1950b The Judicial Reform of Jehoshaphat. *Alexander Marx Jubilee Volume.* English Section pp. 61–82. New York: Jewish Theological Seminary.

_____

1957 Recent Books on Assyriology and Related Subjects. *BASOR* 146: 34–35.

_____

1961 Abram the Hebrew: A New Archaeological Interpretation. *BASOR* 163: 36–54.

_____

1964 *History, Archaeology, and Christian Humanism.* New York: McGraw-Hill.

_____

1968 *Yahweh and the Gods of Canaan.* Garden City, N.Y.: Doubleday.

Aldred, C.
1971 *Jewels of the Pharaohs*. New York: Ballantine.
Alfrink, B.
1948 L'expression *ne'ēsap'el-'ammāyw*. *OTS* 5: 118–31.
Alon, G.
1957 *Studies in Jewish History in the Times of the Second Temple and the Talmud*, vol. 1. Tel Aviv: Hakibutz Hameuchad (Hebrew). (= *Jews, Judaism and the Classical World*, trans. I. Abrahams. Jerusalem: Magnes, 1977.)
Aloni, J.
1983–84 The Place of Worship and the Place of Slaughter According to Leviticus 17: 3–9. *Shnaton* 7/8: 21–50 (Hebrew).
Amiran, R.
1970 *The Ancient Pottery of Eretz Israel*. Jerusalem: Israel Exploration Society.
Andersen, F. I. and D. N. Freedman
1980 *Hosea* AB 24. Garden City, N.Y.: Doubleday.
Andersen, J. G.
1969 Studies in the Medieval Diagnosis of Leprosy in Denmark. *Danish Medical Bulletin* 16, suppl. 9: 6–142.
Anderson, G. A.
1987 *Sacrifices and Offerings in Ancient Israel*. Atlanta: Scholars Press.
Andre, G. and H. Ringgren.
1986 *ṭāmē*. *TDOT* 5: 330–42.
Aubrey, J.
1881 *Remains of Gentilisme and Judaisme*. London: W. Satchess, Peyton & Co.
Audet, J.-P.
1952 La Sagesse de ménandre l'Égyptien. *RB* 59: 55–81.
Avigad, N.
1954 *Monuments of the Kidron Valley*. Jerusalem: Bialik Institute (Hebrew).

_____

1970–72 Excavations in the Jewish Quarter of the Old City of Jerusalem. *IEJ* 20: 5–6, 8, 129–34, 22: 193–98, 200.

_____

1975–77 Jerusalem, The Jewish Quarter of the Old City. *IEJ* 25: 260–61; 27: 55–56.
Avitsur, S.
1976 *Man and His Work*. Jerusalem: Israel Exploration Society (Hebrew).
Baentsch, B.
1903 *Exodus, Leviticus und Numeri*. Göttingen: Vandenhoeck und Ruprecht.
Baillet, M.
1982 *Qumran Grotte 4 III (40482–40520)*. *DJD* 7. Oxford: Clarendon.

Bailey, J. W.
1951 The Usage in the Post-Restoration Period of the Terms Descriptive of the Priest and High Priest. *JBL* 70: 217–26.
Bar-Adon, P.
1971 Another Settlement of the Judean Desert Sect at ʿAin el-Ghuweir on the Dead Sea. *EI* 10: 72–89 (Hebrew).
Barkay, G.
1986 *Ketef Hinnom: A Treasure Facing Jerusalem's Walls.* Jerusalem: Israel Museum.
Barr, J.
1963 Sacrifice and Offering. In *Dictionary of the Bible,* ed. J. Hastings, revised ed. F. C. Grant and H. H. Rowley. Pp. 868–76. New York: Scribners.
Barrois, A.
1931 La Metrologie dans la Bible. *RB* 40: 185–213.
Barton, G.
1929 *Royal Inscriptions of Sumer and Akkad.* New Haven: Yale University Press.
Baudissin, W. W. von
1967 *Die Geschichte des alttestamentlichen Priesterthums.* Osnabrück: O. Zeller. Orig. ed. 1889.
Bauer, H.
1932 Ein aramäischen Staatsvertrag aus dem 8 Jahrhundert v. chr. Die Inschrift der Stele von Sudschen. *AfO* 8: 27ff.
Baumgarten, J. M.
1980 The Pharisaic-Sadducean Controversies about Purity and the Qumran Texts. *JJS* 31: 157–70.
——
1990 The 4Q Zadokite Fragments on Skin Disease *JJS* 41: 153–65.
Bean, S. S.
1981 Towards a Semiotics of "Purity" and "Pollution" in India. *American Ethnologist* 8: 575–95.
Beattie, J. H. M.
1980 On Understanding Sacrifice. In *Sacrifice,* ed. M. F. C. Bourdillon and M. Fortes. Pp. 29–44. London: Academic Press.
Beit-Arieh, I.
1983 A First Temple Period Census Document. *PEQ* 115: 105–8.
Bekhor Shor
See Gad 1956–60.
Belkin, S.
1940 *Philo and the Oral Law.* Cambridge, Mass.: Harvard University Press.
Bell, H. I.
1948 *Egypt from Alexander the Great to the Arab Conquest.* Oxford: Clarendon.

BIBLIOGRAPHY

Ben-Aryeh, Y.
1977 *Jerusalem in the Nineteenth Century: The Old City.* Jerusalem: Yad Ben-Zui (Hebrew).

———

1979 *The New Jerusalem at Its Inception.* Jerusalem: Yad Ben-Zvi (Hebrew).
Bendavid, A.
1972 *Parallels in the Bible.* Jerusalem: Carta.
Ben-Tuvia, A.
1966 Red Sea Fishes Recently Found in the Mediterranean. *Copeia* 2: 255–75.
Berk, G. W. van
1960 Frankincense and Myrrh. *BA* 23: 70–95.
Bertholet, A.
1901 *Leviticus.* Tübingen: J. C. B. Mohr (P. Siebeck).
Bewer, J. A.
1922 *The Literature of the Old Testament in Its Historical Development.* New York: Columbia University Press.
Bickerman, E. J.
1980 *God of the Maccabees.* Leiden: Brill. (Trans. by H. Moehring of *Der Gott der Makkabäer,* Berlin: Schocken, 1937.)
Binder, G.
1976 *Reallexikon für Antike und Christentum XIV.* Stuttgart: A. Hiersemann.
Biran, A.
1974 Tel Dan. *BA* 37: 26–51.
Blackman, A. M.
1925 Oracle in Ancient Egypt. *JEA* 11: 249–55.

———

1951 Purification: Egypt. *ERE* 10: 476–82.
Bleeker, C. J.
1966 Guilt and Purification in Ancient Egypt. *Numen* 13: 81–87.
Bodenheimer, F. S.
1935 *Animal Life in Palestine.* Jerusalem: n.p.
Boehmer, R. M.
1972–75 Hörnerkrone. *Reallexicon der Assyriologie* 4: 431–34.
Borger, R.
1956 *Die Inschriften Asarhaddons. AfO* Beiheft 9; plus Nachträge und Verbesserungen. *AfO* 18: 113–18.

———

1961 Zu den Asarhaddon-Verträgen aus Nimrud. *ZA* 20: 173–96.
Bottero, J.
1957 *Textes économiques et administratifs.* ARM 7: 347–51.

Botterweck, G. J.
1980 *"ḥăzîr." TDOT* 4. 291–300.
Bourdillon, M. F. C.
1980 Introduction. In *Sacrifice,* ed. M. F. C. Bourdillon and M. Fortes. Pp. 1–27. London: Academic Press.
Boyce, M.
1975 *A History of Zoroastrianism,* vol. 1. Leiden: Brill.
Breasted, J. H.
1959 *Development of Religion and Thought in Ancient Egypt.* New York: Harper, 1912; repr. 1959.
Brenk, F. E.
1984 Review of R. Parker, *Miasma* (Oxford: Clarendon, 1983). *Gnomen* 56: 673–78.
Brenner, A.
1982 *Colour Terms in the Old Testament. JSOT* suppl. 21. Wiltshire: Redwood Burn.
Brentjes, B.
1962 Das Schwein als Haustier des Alten Orients. *Ethnographisch-Archäologische Zeitschrift* 3: 125–38.
Brettler, M. Z.
1978–79 The Promise of the Land of Israel to the Patriarchs in the Pentateuch. *Shnaton* 5–6: VII–XXIV.
Brian, A.
1974 Tel Dan. *BA* 37: 40–41.
Brichto, H. C.
1963 *The Problem of "Curse" in the Hebrew Bible.* SBL Monograph Series 13. Philadelphia: SBL.

———

1976 On Slaughter and Sacrifice, Blood and Atonement. *HUCA* 47: 19–56.
Briggs, C. A.
1897 The Use of *nepeš* in the Old Testament. *JBL* 16: 17–30.
Bright, J.
1973 The Apodictic Prohibition: Some Observations. *JBL* 92: 195–204.
Brin, G.
1989–90 Concerning the Formula "This is what the Lord spoke/commanded" and Its Congeners. *Seper Gevaryahu,* pp. 35–42. Jerusalem: Association for Biblical Research in Israel (Hebrew).
Bromberg, A. I., ed.
1969 *Commentary of the Rashbam on the Torah.* Jerusalem: author's publication.
Broshi, M.
1974 The Expansion of Jerusalem in the Reigns of Hezekiah and Manasseh. *IEJ* 24: 21–26.

BIBLIOGRAPHY

Brown, J. P.
1969 The Mediterranean Vocabulary of the Vine. *VT* 19: 146–70.

——
1979 The Sacrificial Cult and Its Critique in Greek and Hebrew, I. *JSS* 24: 159–73.

——
1980 The Sacrificial Cult and Its Critique in Greek and Hebrew, II. *JSS* 25: 1–21.

Brown, R. E.
1966 *The Gospel According to John, I–XII.* AB 29. Garden City, N.Y.: Doubleday.

Brumfeld, A. C.
1981 *The Attic Festivals of Demeter and Their Relation to the Agricultural Year.* New York: Arno.

Büchler, A.
1928 *Studies in Sin and Atonement in the Rabbinic Literature of the First Century.* London: Oxford University Press.

Bühler, G.
1879 *The Sacred Laws of the Aryans: Part I.* Oxford: Clarendon.

Bull, R. and E. Campbell
1968a The Excavation of Tell er-Ras on Mt. Gerizim. *BA* 31: 58–72.

——
1968b The Sixth Campaign at Balâṭah (Schechem). *BASOR* 190: 2–41.

Bulmer, R.
1967 Why Is the Cassowary Not a Bird? A Problem of Zoological Taxonomy Among the Karam of the New Guinea Highlands. *Man* n.s. 2: 5–23.

Burkert, W.
1983 *Homo Necans: The Anthropology of Ancient Greek Sacrificial Ritual and Myth.* Berkeley: University of California Press.

——
1985 *Greek Religion.* Trans. by J. Raffan from German ed. of 1977. Cambridge, Mass.: Harvard University Press.

Burton, J. W.
1974 Some Nuer Notions of Purity and Danger. *Anthropos* 69: 517–36.

Canaan, T.
1926 Mohammedan Saints and Sanctuaries in Palestine (cont.). *JPOS* 6: 1–69, 117–58.

——
1935 The Curse in Palestinian Folklore. *JPOS* 15: 235–79.

Cansdale, G. S.
1970 *All the Animals of the Bible Lands.* Grand Rapids, Mich.: Zondervan.

Caplice, R.
1965–71 Namburbi Texts in the British Museum I, II, III. *Or* n.s. 34: 105–31; 36: 1–38, 273–98; 39: 118–51; 40: 133–83.

_____

1974 The Akkadian Namburbi Texts: An Introduction. In *Sources for the Ancient Near East.* Los Angeles: Undena.
Caquot, A.
1978 d^ebhash. *TDOT* 3.128–31.
_____ and M. Sznycer
1974 *Textes Ougaritiques,* vol. 1. Paris: Éditions du Cerf.
Carmichael, C. M.
1976 On Separating Life and Death: An Explanation of Some Biblical Laws. *HTR* 69: 1–7.
Carnoy, A. J.
1919 Purification. *ERE* 10.492.
Cassin, E.
1968 *La Splendeur divine.* Paris: Mouton.
Cassuto, U.
1943 Biblical Literature and Canaanite Literature (concl.). *Tarbiz* 14: 1–10 (Hebrew).

_____

1944 *From Adam to Noah.* Jerusalem: Magnus (Hebrew). English ed., 1964.

_____

1951a *A Commentary on the Book of Exodus.* Jerusalem: Magnes.

_____

1951b *The Goddess Anath.* Jerusalem: Bialik Institute (Hebrew).

_____

1954 Bet hahopšit. *EM* 2.75–76.

_____

1971 *The Goddess Anath: Canaanite Epics of the Patriarchal Age.* Trans. by I. Abrahams. Jerusalem: Magnes, Hebrew University.
Cazelles, H.
1949 La Question de *lamed auctoris. RB* 56: 93–101.

_____

1969 Review of *Ugaritica* V. *VT* 19: 499–505.
Chan, K.-K.
1985 You Shall Not Eat These Abominable Things: An Examination of Different Interpretations of Deuteronomy 14:3–20. *East Asian Journal of Theology* 3: 88–106.
Charbel, A.
1959 Virtus sanguinis non expiatoria in sacrificio Š^elāmîm. *Sacra pagina (Miscellanea biblica Congressus internationalis catholici de re biblica)* 1: 366–76.

1970 Il sacrificio di communione presso i Cartaginesi. *Bibbia e Oriente* 12: 132–37.

Charles, R. H.

1908 *The Testaments of the Twelve Patriarchs.* London: Oxford University Press.

Chavel, H. D., ed.

1960 *Comments of the Ramban on the Torah.* 2 vols. Jerusalem: Kook.

1981 *Comments of Ḥazzequni on the Torah.* Jerusalem: Kook.

Clifford, R. J.

1971 The Tent of El and the Israelite Tent of Meeting. *CBQ* 33: 221–27.

Cody, A.

1969 *A History of the Old Testament Priesthood.* Analecta Biblica 35. Rome: Pontifical Biblical Institute.

Cohen, C.

1969 Was the P Document Secret? *JANESCU* 1/2: 39–44.

Cohen, M. R.

1978 *Biblical Hapax Legomena in the Light of Akkadian and Ugaritic.* Missoula, Mont.: Scholars Press.

Cohn, R. L.

1983 Form and Perspective in 2 Kings V. *VT* 33: 171–84.

Conrad, D.

1968 Zu Jes. 65,3b. *ZAW* 80: 232–34.

Conybeare, F. C. et al.

1913 *The Story of Ahikar from the Syriac, Arabic, Armenian, Ethiopic, Greek and Slavonic Versions.* 2d ed. Cambridge: Cambridge University Press.

Cook, S. A.

1930 *The Religion of Ancient Palestine in the Light of Archaeology.* London: Oxford University Press.

Cooke, G. A.

1903 *A Text-Book of North-Semitic Inscriptions.* Oxford: Clarendon.

Coulanges, F. de

1882 *The Ancient City.* Trans. by W. Small. Boston: Lee and Shepard.

Countryman, L. W.

1988 *Dirt, Greed, and Sex.* Philadelphia: Fortress.

Cowley, A.

1923 *Aramaic Papyri of the Fifth Century B.C.* Oxford: Clarendon.

Cross, F. M.

1947 The Priestly Tabernacle. *BA* 10: 45–68. (Reprinted in *The Biblical Archaeologist Reader,* vol. 1 [1961]: 201–28.)

1973 *Canaanite Myth and Hebrew Epic.* Cambridge, Mass.: Harvard University Press.

1981 The Priestly Tabernacle in the Light of Recent Research. In *Temples and High Places in Biblical Times,* ed. A. Biran. Pp. 169–80. Jerusalem: Hebrew Union College.

Culpepper, E.
1974 Zoroastrian Menstrual Taboos. In *Women and Religion,* ed. J. Plaskow. Pp. 199–210. Missoula, Mont.: Scholars Press.

Daiches, D.
1941 *The King James Version of the Bible.* Chicago: University of Chicago Press.

Dalman, G.
1928–39 *Arbeit und Sitte in Palästina,* vols. 1.2, 3, 4, 6. Gütersloh: Bertelsmann.

Danzig, D.
1863 *Ḥokmat ʾādām.* Stettin: Strentzel.

Daube, D.
1947 *Studies in Biblical Law.* Cambridge: Cambridge University Press.

1949 Error and Accident in the Bible. *RIDA* 2: 189–213.

1956a Neglected Nuances of Exposition in Luke-Acts. In *Aufstieg und Niedergang der römischen Welt,* vol. 2: *Principat.* Pp. 232–35. Berlin: de Gruyter.

1956b *The New Testament and Rabbinic Judaism.* London: University of London and the Athlone Press. Pp. 224–46.

1963 *The Exodus Pattern in the Bible.* London: Faber and Faber.

Davies, D.
1977 An Interpretation of Sacrifice in Leviticus. *ZAW* 89: 387–98.

Davis, S.
1985 The Large Animal Bones. In *Excavations at Tell Qasīle,* ed. A. Mazar. *Qedem* 20: 248.

Dayagi-Mendeles and R. Hestrim
1978 *Seals of the First Temple Period.* Jerusalem: Israel Museum (Hebrew).

Deist, F. E.
1971 The Punishment of Disobedient Zedekiah. *JNSL* 1: 71–72.

Dhorme, E.
1984 *Job.* Trans. by H. Knight. Nashville, Tenn.: Thomas Nelson.

BIBLIOGRAPHY

Dietrich, M. O. Loretz, and J. Sanmartin
1975a Das Rituel *RS* 1.5 = *CTA* 33. *UF* 7: 525–28.

——

1975b Zu *šlm kll* im Opfertarif von Marseille. *UF* 7: 569–70.

Dillmann, A.
1886 *Die Bücher Numeri, Deuteronomium und Josua.* 2d ed. Leipzig: F. Hirzel.

—— and V. Ryssel
1897 *Die Bücher Exodus und Leviticus.* 3d ed. Leipzig: F. Hirzel.

Dinari, Y.
1979–80 Customs Relating to the Impurity of the Menstruant: Their Origin and Development. *Tarbiz* 49: 302–24.

——

1983 The Profanation of the Holy by the Menstruant Woman and "Takanot Ezra." *Te'uda* 3: 17–38.

Dion, P. E.
1987 Early Evidence for the Ritual Significance of the "Base of the Altar." *JBL* 106: 487–90.

Doeller, J.
1917 *Die Reinheits—und Speisegesetze des Alten Testaments.* Münster: Aschendorff.

Douglas, M.
1966 *Purity and Danger.* London: Routledge and Kegan Paul.

——

1975a Deciphering a Meal. In *Implicit Meanings.* Pp. 249–75. London: Routledge and Kegan Paul. Reprint of *Daedalus* Winter 1972a: 61–81.

——

1975b Self-Evidence. In *Implicit Meanings.* Pp. 276–317. London: Routledge and Kegan Paul. Reprint of *Proceedings of the Royal Anthropological Institute* 1972b–73: 27–44.

Driver, G. R.
1936 Confused Hebrew Roots. In *Occident and Orient: M. H. Gaster Anniversary Volume,* ed. B. Schindler and A. Marmorstein. Pp. 75–77. London: Taylor's Foreign Press.

——

1940 Ordeal by Oath at Nuzi. *Iraq.* 7: 132–38.

——

1955 Birds in the Old Testament. *PEQ* 20: 129–40.

——

1956a *Canaanite Myths and Legends.* Edinburgh: T. & T. Clark.

——

1956b Three Technical Terms in the Pentateuch. *JSS* 1: 97–105.

1963 Leprosy. In *Dictionary of the Bible*, ed. J. Hastings, 2d revised ed. F. C. Grant and H. H. Rowley. Pp. 575–78. New York: Scribners.

1969 Ugaritic and Hebrew Words. *Ugaritica* 6: 181–84.
—— and J. C. Miles
1935 *The Assyrian Laws*. Oxford: Oxford University Press.
Driver, S. R.
1892 *Hebrew Tenses*. 3d ed. Oxford: Clarendon.

1895 *Deuteronomy*. ICC. New York: Charles Scribner's Sons.

1900 Offer, Offering, Oblation. In *Dictionary of the Bible*, vol. 3, ed. J. Hastings. Pp. 587–89. New York: Charles Scribner's Sons.

1911 *The Book of Exodus*. Cambridge: Cambridge University Press.

1913a *Notes on the Hebrew Text of the Books of Samuel*. 2d ed. Oxford: Clarendon.

1913b *An Introduction to the Literature of the Old Testament*. New York: Charles Scribner's Sons; reprinted 1948.
—— and H. A. White
1894 *The Book of Leviticus* (edition). Leipzig: J. C. Hinrichs.

1898 *The Book of Leviticus* (translation). New York: Dodd, Mead.
Du Chaillu, P. B.
1868 *Explorations and Adventures in Equatorial Africa*. New York: Harper.
Duke, R. K.
1988 Punishment or Restoration? Another Look at the Levites of Ezekiel 44:6–16. *JSOT* 40: 61–81.
Dussaud, R.
1941 *Les Origines cananéennes du sacrifice israélite*. 2d ed. Paris: E. Leroux.
Ebeling, E.
1931 *Tod und Leben nach den Vorstellungen der Babylonier*. Berlin and Leipzig: de Gruyter.

1949 Beschwörungen gegen den Feind und den bösen Blick aus dem Zweistromlande. *AnOr* 17: 203–6.

1954 Beiträge zur Kenntnis der Beschwörungsserie Namburbi. *RA* 48: 178–91.

Edelman, D.
1985 The Meaning of qiṭṭēr. *VT* 35: 395–404.
Edwards, I. E. S.
1976 *Treasures of Tutankhamun.* New York: Ballantine.
Eerdmans, B. D.
1912 *Das Buch Leviticus.* Giessen: Topelmann.
Ehrlich, A.
1899–1900 *Hamiqra Kifshuto* (Hebrew). 3 vols. Berlin: Poppelauer.

1908–14 *Randglossen zur hebräischen Bibel.* 7 vols. Leipzig: J. Hinrichs.
Eichrodt, W.
1961 *Theology of the Old Testament.* 6th ed. 2 vols. Trans. from German by
    J. A. Baker. Philadelphia: Westminster. German original, Stuttgart, 1959.
Eilberg-Schwartz, M.
1986 *The Human Will in Judaism.* Atlanta: Scholars Press.

1988 Israel in the Mirror of Nature: Animal Metaphors in the Ritual and
    Narratives of Ancient Israel. *Journal of Ritual Studies* 2.1: 1–30.
Eising, H.
1980 *zākhan.* *TDOT* 4.64–81.
Eitram, S. and J. Fontenrose
1970 Sacrifice. In *The Oxford Classical Dictionary,* ed. N. G. L. Hammond
    and H. M. Scullard. Pp. 943–45. Oxford: Clarendon.
Eliade, M.
1959 *The Sacred and the Profane.* New York: Harcourt Brace Jovanovich.
Elliger, K.
1966 *Leviticus.* HAT 4. Tübingen: J. C. B. Mohr (P. Siebeck).
Elliot-Binns, L. E.
1955 Some Problems of the Holiness Code. *ZAW* 76: 26–40.
Ellison, R.
1981 Diet in Mesopotamia: The Evidence of the Barley Ration Texts (c.
    3000–1400 B.C.). *Iraq* 43: 35–45.
Elman, Y.
1976 The Akkadian Cognate of Hebrew šᵉḥîn. *JANESCU* 8: 33–36.
Emerton, J. A.
1980 Notes on the Text and Translation of Isaiah XXII 8–11 and LXV 5. *VT*
    30: 446–50.
Engelhard, D. H.
1970 *Hittite Magical Practices: An Analysis.* Ph.D., Brandeis University. Ann
    Arbor, Mich.: University Microfilms.
Epstein, A.
1950 *Kitbe Abraham Epstein,* vol. 1, ed. A. M. Haberman. Jerusalem: Mosad
    Harav Kook.

Eshkoli, A. Z.
  1936 Halakha and Customs Among the Falasha Jews in the Light of Rabbinic and Karaite Halakha. *Tarbiz* 7: 121–25 (Hebrew).
Evans-Pritchard, E. E.
  1951 *Kinship and Marriage Among the Nuer.* Oxford: Clarendon.

  1956 *Nuer Religion.* Oxford: Clarendon.
Ezra, Ibn
  See Krimsky 1691.
Falkenstein, A. and W. von Soden
  1953 *Sumerische und akkadische Hymnen und Gebeten,* vol. 1. Zurich: Artemis.
Fallaize, E. N.
  1951 Purification, Introductory and Primitive. *ERE* 10.455–66.
Farnell, L. R.
  1951 The Causes of Impurity. *ERE* 10.483–88.
Feldman, E.
  1977 *Biblical and Post-Biblical Defilement and Mourning.* New York: Ktav.
Feliks, J.
  1962 *Animals in the Bible.* Tel Aviv: Sinai (Hebrew).

  1968 *The Plant World of the Bible.* Ramat Gan: Masada (Hebrew).

  1971a Pig. *EJ* 13.506.

  1971b Animals in the Bible. *EJ* 3.7–19.

  1971c Locusts. *EJ* 11.422–24.

  1984 *Animals and Plants in the Torah.* Jerusalem: Young Israel (Hebrew).
Fensham, F. O.
  1979 Notes on Treaty Terminology in Ugaritic Epics. *UF* 11: 265–74.
Ferro-Luzzi, G. E.
  1974 Woman's Pollution Periods in Tamilnad (India). *Anthropos* 69: 114–61.
Feucht, C.
  1964 *Untersuchungen zum Heiligkeitgesetz.* Berlin: Evangelische Verlagsanstalt.
Finkelstein, I.
  1985 Excavations at Shilo 1981–1984. Summary and Conclusions: History of Shilo from Middle Bronze Age II to Iron Age II. *Tel Aviv* 12: 159–77.

  1988 *The Archaeology of the Israelite Settlement.* Jerusalem: Israel Exploration Society.

BIBLIOGRAPHY

Finkelstein, L.
1962 *The Pharisees.* 3d ed. 2 vols. Philadelphia: Jewish Publication Society.
Fischer, H. G.
1976 Milk in Everything Cooked (Sinuhe B91–92). In *Varia.* Pp. 97–99. New York: Metropolitan Museum.
Firmage, E.
1990 The Biblical Dietary Laws and the Concept of Holiness. In *Studies in the Pentateuch,* ed. J. A. Emerton. Pp. 177–208. Leiden: Brill.
Fishbane, M.
1980 Biblical Colophons, Textual Criticism and Legal Analogies. *CBQ* 42: 438–49.

―――
1985 *Biblical Interpretation in Ancient Israel.* Oxford: Clarendon.
Fisher, L. R.
1972 *Ras Shamra Parallels,* vol. 1. Rome: Pontifical Biblical Institute.
Fitzmeyer, J. A.
1978–79 The Targum of Leviticus from Qumran Cave 4. *Maarav* 1: 5–23.

―――
1981 *The Gospel According to Luke I–X.* AB 28. Garden City, N.Y.: Doubleday.
Flusser, D. and S. Safrai
1984 Nadab and Abihu in Midrash and in Philo. In *Millet: Studies of the Open University in the History of Israel and Its Culture.* Pp. 79–84. Tel Aviv: Open University (Hebrew).
Fohrer, G.
1968 Twofold Aspects of Hebrew Words. In *Words and Meanings: Festschrift D. Winton Thomas.* Pp. 91ff. Cambridge: Cambridge University Press.
Fokkelman, J. P.
1975 *Narrative Art in Genesis.* Assen: Van Gorcum.
Frazer, J. G.
1911–15 *The Golden Bough,* vol. 3. 3d ed. London: Macmillan.

―――
1919 *Folklore in the Old Testament.* 3 vols. London: Macmillan.
――― and T. H. Gaster
1959 *The New Golden Bough.* New York: S. G. Phillips.
Freedman, D. N.
1974 Variant Readings in the Leviticus Scroll from Qumran Cave 11. *CBQ* 36: 525–34.
――― and K. A. Matthews
1985 *The Paleo-Hebrew Leviticus Scroll (11Q paleo Lev).* Winona Lake, Ind.: Eisenbrauns.

Freedman, R.D.
1976 "Put Your Hand Under My Thigh"—the Patriarchal Oath. *BAR* 2.2: 3–4, 42.
Friedman, R. E.
1980 The Tabernacle in the Temple. *BA* 43: 241–48.
Friedrich, I.
1968 *Ephod und Choschen im Lichte des alten Orients.* Vienna: Herder.
Friedrich, J.
1925 Aus dem hethitischen Schriftum. In *Der Alte Orient* 24.3. Pp. 3–32. Leipzig: J. C. Hinrichs.
Fruchtman, M.
1976 Notes on Biblical Narrative Research. *Hasifrut* 22: 63–66.
Frymer-Kensky, T.
1977 The Atrahasis Epic and Its Significance for Our Understanding of Genesis 1–9. *BA* 40: 147–55.
Füglister, N.
1977 Sühne durch Blut. Zur Bedeutung von Leviticus 17,11. In *Studien zum Pentateuch: W. Kornfeld Festschrift,* ed. G. Braulik. Pp. 143–65. Salzburg: Herder.
Gad, J., ed.
1956–60 *The Commentary of Bekhor Shor.* 3 vols. London: author's publication.
Gadd, C. G.
1958 The Harran Inscriptions of Nabonidus. *Anatolian Studies* 8: 35–92.
Galling, K.
1925 *Der Altar in den Kulturen des alten Orients.* Berlin: K. Curtius.
Gardiner, A.
1950 The Baptism of Pharaoh. *JEA* 36: 3–12.
———
1957 *Egyptian Grammar.* 3d ed. Oxford: Griffith Institute, Ashmolean Museum.
Garfinkel, Y.
1986–87 The Meaning of the Word *MPQD* in the Tel 'Ira Ostracon. *PEQ* 118–19: 19–23.
Gaster, T. H.
1946 The Canaanite Epic of Keret. *JQR* 37: 285–93.
———
1961 *Thespis.* 2d ed. Garden City, N.Y.: Doubleday.
———
1962a Sacrifices and Offerings, OT. In *IDB* 4.147–59. Nashville: Abingdon.
———
1962b Demon. In *IDB* 1.817–24. Nashville, Tenn.: Abingdon.

1969 *Myth, Legend, and Customs in the Old Testament.* New York: Harper.

Geiger, A.

1857 *Urschrift und Übersetzungen der Bibel.* Breslau: Hainauer.

Gelb, I. J.

1948 A New Clay-Nail of Hammurabi. *JNES* 7: 267–71.

——, B. Landsberger, A. L. Oppenheim, E. Reiner, et al., eds.

1964– *The Assyrian Dictionary.* Chicago: Oriental Institute.

Geller, M. J.

1980 The Šurpu Incantations and Lev. V. 1–5. *JSS* 25: 181–92.

Gennep, A. van

1960 *The Rites of Passage.* London: Routledge and Kegan Paul.

Gerleman, G.

1973 Die Wurzel *šlm.* *ZAW* 85: 1–14.

1980 Die Wurzel *kpr* im Hebräischen. In *Studien zur alttestamentlichen The-
ologie.* Pp. 11–23. Heidelberg: L. Schneider.

Gertner, M.

1960 The Masorah and the Levites. Appendix on Hosea XII. *VT* 10: 241–84.

Geva, H.

1979 The Western Boundary of Jerusalem at the End of the Monarchy. *IES*
29: 84–91.

Gill, D.

1966 Thysia and Shelamim. *Biblica* 47: 255–62.

Gilula, M.

1974 *Ṣĕwî* in Isaiah 28,1—A Head Ornament. *Tel Aviv* 1: 128.

Ginsberg, H. L.

1935 Notes on "The Birth of the Gracious and Beautiful Gods." *JRAS* 1935:
45–72.

1936 *Kitvē Ugarit.* Jerusalem: Bialik Institute (Hebrew).

1973 Ugaritico-Phoenicia. *JANESCU* 5: 131–147.

1982 *The Israelian Heritage of Judaism.* New York: Jewish Theological Seminary.

Ginsburg, C. D.

1889 *The Third Book of Moses Called Leviticus.* Vol. 3 of *The Handy Commentary,* ed. C. J. Ellicott. London: Cassell.

Girard, R.

1977 *Violence and the Sacred.* Baltimore: The Johns Hopkins University
Press.

Gitin, S.
1989 Incense Altars from Ekron, Israel and Judah: Context and Typology. *EI* 20: 25–67.
Goetze, A.
1938a The Hittite Ritual of Tunnawi. *JAOS* 14: 4–102.

1938b *The Hittite Ritual of Tunnawi.* New Haven: American Oriental Society.

1947 *Old Babylonian Omen Texts.* YOS 10. New Haven: Yale University Press.

1955 An Incantation Against Diseases. *JCS* 9: 8–18.

1957 Reports on Acts of Extispicy from Old Babylonian and Kassite Times. *JCS* 11: 89–105.
——— and J. Pedersen
1934 *Mursilis Sprachlähmung.* Copenhagen: Levin and Munksgaard.
Goldstein, J. A.
1976 *I Maccabees.* AB 41. Garden City, N.Y.: Doubleday.

1983 *II Maccabees.* AB 41A. Garden City, N.Y.: Doubleday.
Goldstein, N.
1979–80 The "Crimson Ribbon" in the Yom Kippur Ritual. *Ta* 49: 237–45 (Hebrew).
Gonda, J.
1980 *Vedic Ritual: The Non-Solemn Rites.* Leiden: Brill.
Gordis, R.
1950 Democratic Origins in Ancient Israel—The Biblical ʿĒdāh. In *A. Marx Jubilee Volume.* ed. S. Lieberman. New York: Jewish Theological Seminary.

1968 *Koheleth—The Man and His World.* New York: Schocken.
Gordon, C. H.
1949 Azitawadd's Phoenician Inscription. *JNES* 8: 108–15.
Görg, M.
1976 Zur sogenannten priesterlichen Obergewand. *BZ* 20: 242–46.

1977a Die Kopfbedeckung des Hohenpriesters. *BN* 3: 24–26.

1977b Weiteres zu *nzr* ("Diadem"). *BN* 4: 7–8.

1977c Die Bildsprache in Jes 28:1. *BN* 3: 17–23.

1977d Eine neue Deutung für *kăppōret. ZAW* 89: 115–18.

1978 Nachtrag zu *kăppōret. BN* 5: 12.

1979 *Piggul* und *pilaegaeš:* Experimente zur Etymologie. *BN* 10: 7–11.

1980 *zāhar. TDOT* 4.41–45.

1981 Der Brustschmuck des Hohenpriesters. *BN* 15: 32–34.
Gottlieb, Z. and A. Darom
1980 *Commentary of Obadiah Sforno on the Torah.* Jerusalem: Mosad Harav Kook.
Gradwohl, R.
1963–64 Das "Fremde Feuer" von Nadab und Abihu. *ZAW* 75–76: 288–95.
Gray, G. B.
1903 *Numbers.* ICC. New York: Charles Scribner's Sons.

1925 *Sacrifice in the Old Testament.* Oxford: Clarendon.
Gray, J.
1965 Social Aspects of Canaanite Religion. *SVT* 15: 170–92.

1970 *I and II Kings: A Commentary.* 2d ed. Philadelphia: Westminster.
Greenberg, M.
1962 Crimes and Punishments. *IDB* 1.733–44.

1983 *Ezekiel 1–20.* AB 22A. Garden City, N.Y.: Doubleday.
Greenfield, J.
1977 *Našû-nadānu* and Its Congeners. In *Essays on the Ancient Near East in Memory of Jacob Joel Finkelstein,* ed. M. Ellis. Pp. 87–91. Hamden, Conn.: Archon.
Grelot, P.
1956 La Derrière Élappe de la rédaction sacerdotale. *VT* 6: 174–89.

1964 *Hofši* (Ps. LXXXVIII 6). *VT* 16: 256–63.
Grimm, K. J.
1902 The Form *tārōnnâ,* Prov I. 20, VIII, 3. *JBL* 21: 192–96.
Grintz, Y. M.
1966 Do not eat on the Blood. *Tsiyon* 31: 1–17 (Hebrew). Translated in *ASTI* 8 (1970–71): 78–105.

1972 Ephod. *Enc Jud* 6: 804–6.

1974–75 Archaic Terms in the Priestly Code. *Leshonenu* 39: 5–30, 163–81; 40: 5–32.

1975 Ancient Terms in the Torah of the Priests. *Leshonenu* 39: 374–78.
Gruber, M. I.
1987 Women in the Cult According to the Priestly Code. In *Judaic Perspectives on Ancient Israel*, ed. J. Neusner et al. Pp. 35–48. Philadelphia: Fortress.
Guenther, A. R.
1977 A Diachronic Study of Biblical Hebrew Prose Syntax: An Analysis of the Verbal Clause in Jeremiah 37–45 and Esther 1–10. Ph.D. diss., University of Toronto.
Gunkel, H.
1933 *Einleitung in die Psalmen.* Göttingen: Vandenhoeck and Ruprecht.
Gurewicz, S. B.
1963 Some Examples of Modern Hebrew Exegesis of the Old Testament. *Australian Biblical Reviews* 11: 15–23.
Gurney, O. R.
1935 Babylonian Prophylactic Figures and Their Rituals. *AAA* 22: 31–95.

1952 *The Hittites.* London: Penguin.

1977 *Some Aspects of Hittite Religion.* Schweich Lectures 1976. Oxford: Oxford University Press.
Güterbock, H. G.
1974 Appendix: Hittite Parallels. *JNES* 33: 323–27.
Haag, H.
1980 *Chāmās. TDOT* 4.478–86.
Haas, V. and G. Wilhelm
1974 *Hurritische und luwische Riten aus Kizzuwatna.* AOAT supplement 3.
Hackett, J. A.
1980 *The Balaam Text from Deir ʿAllā.* Chico, Calif.: Scholars Press.
Haderlie, E. C.
1973 Marine Biological Migration Through the Suez Canal. *European Scientific Notes* 27.3.
Hallo, W. W.
1983 Lugalbanda Excavated. *JAOS* 103: 165–80.

1987 The Origins of the Sacrificial Cult: New Evidence from Mesopotamia and Israel. In *Ancient Israelite Religion: Frank Moore Cross Festschrift*, ed. P. D. Miller et al. Pp. 3–13. Philadelphia: Fortress Press.

BIBLIOGRAPHY

Hannemann, G.
1975–76 On the Preposition *bêt* in the Mishna and the Bible. *Leshonenu* 40: 33–53 (Hebrew).

Haran, M.
1955 The Ephod According to the Biblical Sources. *Ta* 24: 380–91 (Hebrew).

———
1956 Some Problems Concerning the Canonization of Scripture. *Ta* 25: 245–71.

———
1960a The Nature of the *ʾOhel Môʿedh* in Pentateuchal Sources. *JSS* 5: 50–65.

———
1960b The Uses of Incense in Ancient Israelite Ritual. *VT* 10: 115–16.

———
1961 The Complex of Ritual Acts Performed Inside the Tabernacle. *Scripta Hierosolymitana* 8: 272–302.

———
1962a Food and Drink. *EM* 4.543–58 (Hebrew).

———
1962b Shilo and Jerusalem: The Origin of the Priestly Tradition in the Pentateuch. *JBL* 81: 14–24.

———
1962c Priestly Gifts. *EM* 4.39–45 (Hebrew).

———
1962d Priesthood. *EM* 4.14–39 (Hebrew).

———
1968a *Minḥâ. EM* 5.23–30 (Hebrew).

———
1968b The Holiness Document. *EM* 5.1093–98 (Hebrew).

———
1968c *Nāzîr. EM* 5.795–99 (Hebrew).

———
1978 *Temples and Temple Service in Ancient Israel.* Oxford: Clarendon.

———
1979 Seething a Kid in Its Mother's Milk. *JJS* 20: 24–35.

———
1981 Behind the Scenes of History: Determining the Date of the Priestly Source. *JBL* 100: 321–33.

Harper, E. B.
1964 Ritual Pollution, Caste, and Religion. In *Religion in South Asia,* ed. E. B. Harper. Seattle: University of Washington Press.

Harris, M.
1974 *Cows, Pigs, Wars, and Witches.* New York: Random House.

Harris, R.
1955 The Archive of the Sin Temple in Khafajah (Tutub). *JCS* 9: 101–2.
_____

1965 The Journey of the Divine Weapon. *Assyriological Studies* 16: 217–24.
Harrison, J.
1959 *Prolegomena to the Study of Greek Religion.* Cleveland: World. Reprint of 3d ed., Cambridge: Cambridge University Press, 1922.
Harrison, R. K.
1980 *Leviticus: An Introduction and Commentary.* Leicester: Inter-Varsity Press.
Hass, G.
1953 On the Occurrence of Hippopotamus in the Iron Age of the Coastal Area of Israel (Tell Qasîleh). *BASOR* 132: 30–34.
Hauret, C.
1959 Moïse était-il prêtre? *Biblica* 40: 375–87.
Hayley, A.
1980 A Commensural Relationship with God: The Nature of the Offering in Assamese Vaishnavism. In *Sacrifice,* ed. M. F. C. Bourdillon and M. Fortes. Pp. 107–25. London: Academic Press.
Ḥazzequni
See Chavel 1981.
Heimpel, W.
1981 The Nanshe Hymn. *JCS* 33: 65–139.
Heinemann, I.
1932 Philons griechische und jüdische Bildung. Hildesheim: G. Olms.
Heinisch, P.
1935 *Das Buch Leviticus.* Bonn: Hanstein.
Held, M.
1965 Studies in Comparative-Semitic Lexicography. In *Studies in Honor of Benno Landsberger.* Pp. 395–406. Chicago: University of Chicago Press.
Heltzer, M.
1983–84 The Ugaritic *lth* and the Biblical *issaron.* *Shnaton* 7–8: 159–61 (Hebrew).
Hendel, R. S.
1989 Sacrifice as a Cultural System: The Ritual Symbolism of Exodus 24, 3–8. *ZAW* 101: 366–90.
Henig, R. M.
1982 Dispelling Menstrual Myths. *New York Times Magazine,* Mar. 7, pp. 64–65, 68, 70–71, 74–75, 78–79.
Henninger, J.
1979 Pureté et impureté: L'Histoire des religions. Peuples sémitiques, animaux impurs; le sang. *SDB* 9: 399–430, 459–70, 473–91.

BIBLIOGRAPHY

Hermisson, H.-J.
1965 *Sprache und Ritus im Altisraelitischen Kult.* WMANT 19. Neukirchen-Vluyn: Neukirchener Verlag.
Hesse, B.
1988 Patterns of Palestinian Pork Production. Paper delivered at Society of Biblical Literature Conference, Nov. 20.
Hestrin, R.
1973 The First Temple and Persian Periods. In *Inscriptions Reveal.* Pp. 23–158. Jerusalem: Israel Museum (Hebrew).
—— and M. Daygi-Mandels
1978 *Seals from First Temple Times.* Jerusalem: Israel Museum (Hebrew).
Hicks, F. C. N.
1953 *The Fullness of Sacrifice* 3d ed. London: S.P.C.K.
Hillel
See Koleditzky 1961.
Hillers, D. R.
1964 *Treaty-Curses and the Old Testament Prophets.* Rome: Pontifical Biblical Institute.

1967 Delocative Verbs in Biblical Hebrew. *JBL* 86: 320–24.

1970 Ugaritic *ŠNPT* "Wave Offering". *BASOR* 198: 142.

1972 *MŠKN* "Temple" in Inscriptions from Hatra. *BASOR* 207: 54–56.
Hirschfeld, H., trans.
1907 Saadiah: The Arabic Portion of the Cairo Genizah at Cambridge, XXXII Commentary on Leviticus. *JQR* 19: 136–61.
Hoffman, Y.
1986 Concerning the Language of P and the Date of Its Composition. *Teʿudah* 4: 13–22 (Hebrew).
Hoffmann, D. Z.
1953 *Leviticus.* Vol. 1. Jerusalem: Mosad Harav Kook (Hebrew). Trans. of vol. 1 of *Das Buch Leviticus,* Berlin: M. Poppelauer, 1905–6.

1961 *Deuteronomy.* 2 vols. Jerusalem: Mosad Harav Kook (Hebrew). Trans. of *Das Buch Deuteronomium,* 2 vols., Berlin: M. Poppelauer, 1913–22.
Hoffner, H. A.
1965 The Elkuninsa Myth Reconsidered. *RHA* 23.6, fasc. 76.

1967a Second Millenium Antecedents to the Hebrew ʾob. *JBL* 86: 385–401.

1967b Review of E. von Schuler *Die Kaškäer. JAOS* 87: 183.

1968 Review of O. Carruba *Das Beschwörungsritual für die Göttin Wišuriyanza. JAOS* 88: 531–34.

1969 Some Contributions of Hittitology to Old Testament Study. *Tyndale Bulletin* 20: 27–55.

1973 The Hittites and Hurrians. In *Peoples of Old Testament Times,* ed. D. J. Wiseman. Pp. 197–228. Oxford: Clarendon.

Höfner, M.
1967 Eine altsüdarabische Sühne-Inschrift. *SVT* 16: 106–13.

Hoftijzer, J.
1967 Das Sogenannte Feueropfer. *SVT* 16: 114–34.

Holladay, W. L.
1958 *The Root* šûbh *in the Old Testament.* Leiden: Brill.

Holma, H.
1913 *Kleine Beiträge zum assyrischen Lexikon.* Helsinki: Suomalaisen Tiedeakatemian Kunstantama.

Hölscher, G.
1922 *Geschichte der israelitischen und jüdischen Religion.* Giessen: A. Topelmann.

Hönig, H. W.
1957 *Die Bekleidung des Hebräers.* Zurich: Brunna, Bodmer.

Horowitz, C. M.
1890 *Baraita Di-masseket Niddah. Tosfata 'Atiqata,* vol. 5. Frankfurt am Main: n. p.

Horowitz, W. and V. Hurowitz
1991 Urim and Thummim in the Light of a Psephomancy Ritual from Assur *(LKA* 137). *JANESCU* 21: forthcoming.

Hubert, H. and M. Mauss
1964 *Sacrifice: Its Nature and Function.* Chicago: University of Chicago Press. Reprint of Paris 1898 ed.

Hulse, E. V.
1975 The Nature of Biblical "Leprosy" and the Use of Alternative Medical Terms in Modern Translations of the Bible. *PEQ* 107: 87–105.

Hunt, T. F.
1904 *The Cereals in America.* New York: O. Judd.

Hurowitz, A.
1974 Building Consecration Ceremonies in the Bible. M. A. thesis, Hebrew University, Jerusalem (Hebrew).

1985 The Priestly Account of the Building of the Tabernacle. *JAOS* 105: 21–30.

BIBLIOGRAPHY

Hurowitz, V.

1987 Salted Incense—Exodus 30, 35; Maqlu VI 111–13; IX 118–20. *Biblica* 68: 178–94.

1990 The Etymology of Biblical Hebrew *ʿayin*, "appearance" in Light of Akkadian *šiknu. Zeitschrift für Althebräistik* 3: 101–4.

Hurvitz, A.

1967 The Usage of *šēš* and *bûṣ* in the Bible and Its Implication for the Date of P. *HTR* 60: 117–21.

1971–72 On the Priestly Term *ʿēdâ* in the Bible. *Tarbiz* 40: 261–67 (Hebrew).

1972 *The Transition Period in Biblical Hebrew.* Jerusalem: Bialik Institute (Hebrew).

1974 The Evidence of Language in Dating the Priestly Code. *RB* 81: 24–56.

1982 *A Linguistic Study of the Relationship Between the Priestly Source and the Book of Ezekiel.* Cahiers de la *Revue biblique* 20. Paris: J. Gabalda.

1983a Studies in the Language of the Priestly Source: The Usage of *šēʾēr* and *šēkār* in Leviticus and Numbers. *Teʿudah* 2: 299–303 (Hebrew).

1983b The Language of the Priestly Source and Its Historical Setting—the Case for an Early Date. In *Proceedings of the Eighth World Congress of Jewish Studies (1981)*, vol. 5. Pp. 83–94. Jerusalem: World Union of Jewish Studies.

1988 Dating the Priestly Source in Light of the Historical Study of Biblical Hebrew a Century after Wellhausen. *ZAW* 100 supplement: 88–99.

Ibn Ezra, Abraham

1988 *Commentary on the Pentateuch*, vol. 1: *Genesis.* Trans. H. N. Strickman and A. M. Silver. New York: Menorah.

Ibn Janaḥ, J.

1968 *The Book of Roots*, ed. A. Neubauer. Oxford: Clarendon. Reprint of 1875 ed.

Jackson, B. S.

1972 *Theft in Early Jewish Law.* Oxford: Clarendon.

Jacobsen, T.

1961 Toward the Image of Tammuz. *History of Religions* 1: 189–213. (=Pp. 73–103 in *Toward the Image of Tammuz*, ed. W. C. Moran, Cambridge, Mass.: Harvard University Press, 1970.)

James, E. O.
1933 *The Origins of Sacrifice.* London: John Murray.

——

1938–39 Aspects of Sacrifice in the OT. *ET* 50: 151–55.
Janowski, B.
1980 Sühne als Heilsgeschehen. Ph.D. diss., Universität Tübingen.

——

1982 *Sühne als Heilsgeschehen.* Neukirchen-Vluyn: Neukirchener Verlag.
Japhet, S.
1977 *The Ideology of the Book of Chronicles and Its Place in Biblical Thought.* Jerusalem: Mosad Bialik (Hebrew).
Jastrow, M.
1913–14 The So-Called "Leprosy" Laws. *JQR* 4: 357–418.
Jolley, J.
1880 *The Institutes of Vishnu.* Oxford: Clarendon.
Jones, J. W.
1956 *The Law and Legal Theory of the Greeks.* Oxford: Clarendon.
Joüon, P. P.
1938 Notes de lexicographie hébraïque, XV, Racine ʾšm. *Biblica* 19: 454–59.

——

1965 *Grammaire de l'hébreu biblique.* Corrected reprint of 1923 ed. Rome: Institut Biblique Pontifical.
Junker, H.
1959 Vorschriften für den Tempelkult in Philä. *Analecta Biblica* 12: 151–60.
Kalisch, M. M.
1867–72 *Leviticus.* 2 vols. London: Longmans.
Kamler, M.
1970 *Comments of R. David Kimhi (Radak) on the Torah.* Jerusalem: Kook.
Kane, P. V.
1973 *History of Dharmaśāstra,* vol. 4. 2d ed. Poona: Bhandarkar Oriental Research Institute.
Kapaḥ, J., ed.
1963 *Comments of R. Saadiah Gaon on the Torah.* Jerusalem: Kook.

——

1967 *Mishnah with Maimonides' Commentary.* 3 vols. Jerusalem: Kook.
Kapelrud, A. S.
1963 Temple Building, a Task for Gods and Kings. *Or* 32: 56–62.
Kasher, M. M.
1953 Suspension of Immersion. In *Torah Shelemah,* 1.148–54. New York: American Biblical Encyclopedia Society.
Kaufmann, Y.
1937–56 *The History of Israelite Religion.* 4 vols. Tel Aviv: Dvir (Hebrew).

1960 *The Religion of Israel.* Trans. and abridged by M. Greenberg. Chicago: University of Chicago Press.

Kautzsch, E.
1904 Religion of Israel. In *HDB*, extra vol. 5.612–734. New York: Scribner's.

Kearny, J.
1977 Creation and Liturgy: The P Redaction of Ex. 25–40. *ZAW* 89: 375–86.

Keel, O.
1975 Kanaanäische Sühneriten auf ägyptischen Tempelreliefs. *VT* 25: 413–69.

1980 *Das Böcklein in der Milch seiner Mutter und Verwandtes.* Freiburg: Universitätsverlag.

Kellermann, D.
1964 *'ĀŠĀM* in Ugarit? *ZAW* 76: 319–22.

1971 *'Asham.* In *ThWAT* 1.463–65 (*TDOT* 1.429–37).

1973 Bemerkungen zum Sündopfergesetz in Num 15, 22 ff. In *Wort und Geschichte: K. Elliger Festschrift.* Pp. 107–13. Kevelaer: Butzon and Bercker.

1975 *Gur.* TDOT 2.439–49.

1980 *Ḥmṣ.* TDOT 4.487–93. Trans. from German by D. E. Green. Grand Rapids, Mich.: Eerdmans.

Kelso, J. L.
1962 Pottery. *IDB* 3.846–53.

Kennett, R. H.
1933 *The Church of Israel,* ed. S. A. Cook. Cambridge: Cambridge University Press.

Keter Torah
See Aaron ben Elijah.

Kikawada, I. M.
1974 The Shape of Genesis 11:1–9. In *Rhetorical Criticism: Muilenberg Festschrift,* ed. J. J. Jackson and M. Kessler. Pp. 18–32. Pittsburgh, Penn.: Pickwick.

Kimhi, D.
1847 *The Book of Roots,* ed. J. H. R. Bresenthal and F. Lebrecht. Berlin: Friedlander. Reprinted Jerusalem, 1966–67.

King, L. W.
1912 *Babylonian Boundary Stones.* London: British Museum.

Kinnier-Wilson, J. V.
1966 Leprosy in Ancient Mesopotamia. *RA* 60: 47–58.

———

1982 Medicine in the Land and Times of the Old Testament. In *Studies in the Period of David and Solomon*, ed. T. Ishida. Pp. 337–65. Winona Lake, Ind.: Eisenbrauns.

Kirschner, R.
1983 The Rabbinic and Philonic Exegesis of the Nadab and Abihu Incident (Lev 10:1–6). *JQR* 73: 375–93.

Kister, M. J. and M. Kister
1979 On the Jews of Arabia. *Tarbiz* 48: 231–47.

Kiuchi, N.
1987 *The Purification Offering in the Priestly Literature. JSOT* suppl. 56. Sheffield: Sheffield Press.

Klein, I.
1979 *A Guide to Jewish Religious Practice*. New York: Jewish Theological Seminary of America.

Knight, J. E.
1978 *The Hunter's Game Cookbook*. New York: Winchester.

Knobel, A. W.
1857 *Die Bücher Exodus und Leviticus*. Leipzig: S. Hirzel.

Knohl, I.
1983–84 The Priestly Torah Versus the Holiness School: Sabbath and the Festivals. *Shnaton* 7–8: 109–46. (English trans. *HUCA* 58 (1987): 65–117.)

———

1988 The Conception of God and Cult in the Priestly Torah and in the Holiness School. Ph.D. diss., Hebrew University.

Knudsen, E. E.
1959 An Incantation Tablet from Nimrud. *Iraq* 21: 54–61.

Koch, K.
1959 *Die Priesterschrift von Exodus 25 bis Leviticus 16: Eine überlieferungs-geschichtliche und literarische Untersuchung.* FRLANT 71. Göttingen: Vandenhoeck and Ruprecht.

———

1962 Der Spruch "Sein Blut bleibe auf seinem Haupt." *VT* 12:396–416.

Koehler, L.
1956 *Hebrew Man*. London: SCM Press.

Koleditzky, S. ed.
1961 *R. Hillel on the Sipra*. 2 vols. Jerusalem: author's publication.

Kook, A. I.
1961 *The Vision of Vegetarianism and Peace*. Watercourses in the Negeb 28, ed. D. Hakoken. Jerusalem: n. p. (Hebrew).

Kornfeld, W.

1965 Reine und Unreine Tiere im Alten Testament. *Kairos* 7: 134–47.

———

1969 Die Unreinen Tiere im Alten Testament. In *Wissenschaft im Dienste des Glaubens,* ed. J. Kisser et al. Pp. 11–27. Vienna: Wiener Katholische Akademie.

Kosmala, H.

1962 The So-Called Ritual Decalogue. *ASTI* 1: 31–61.

Kraemer, J. L.

1966 A Proposed Solution for an Unexplained Hapax. *JNES* 25: 125–29.

Kramer, S. N.

1963 *The Sumerians.* Chicago: University of Chicago Press.

Kraus, H.-J.

1966 *Worship in Israel.* Richmond: John Knox Press. German original, Munich 1962.

Krimsky, J.

1961 *Yahel ʾOr.* Commentary on Ibn Ezra in *Torah, Meḥoqeqe Yehudah,* vol. 3: *Leviticus.* Tel Aviv: Horeb.

Krutch, J. W. and H. E. Anthony

1957 The Sportsman or the Predator. *Saturday Review of Literature* 40 (Aug. 17): 8–9, 39–40.

Kuenen, A.

1886 *An Historico-Critical Inquiry into the Origin and Composition of the Hexateuch.* Trans. P. H. Wicksteed. London: Macmillan.

Kümmel, H. M.

1967 *Ersatzrituale für den hethitischen König.* StBoT 3. Wiesbaden: Harrassowitz.

———

1968 Ersatzkönig und Sündenbock. *ZAW* 80: 289–318.

Kuper, H.

1947 *An African Aristocracy.* London: Oxford University Press.

LaBarbera, R.

1986 *Satire in the Elisha Cycle.* Ph.D. diss., University of California, Berkeley.

Laessøe, J.

1955 *Studies on the Assyrian Ritual and Series bît rimki.* Copenhagen: Munksgaard.

Lagercrantz, S.

1953 Forbidden Fish. *Orientalia Suecana* 2: 3–8.

Lambert, W. G.

1955–58 Morals in Ancient Mesopotamia. *Ex oriente lux* 5: 184 –96.

1959 Three Literary Prophets of the Babylonians: Prayer to Marduk, No. 1. *AfO* 19: 55–60.

1960 *Babylonian Wisdom Literature.* Oxford: Clarendon.

1974 *Dingir.šà.dib.ba Incantations. JNES* 33: 267–322.
Landersdorfer, S.
1924 *Studien zum biblischen Versöhnungstag.* Münster: Aschendorff.
Landsberger, B.
1967a Über Farben in Sumerisch-akkadischen. *JCS* 21: 139 –73.

1967b *The Date Palm and Its By-Products According to the Cuneiform Sources. AfO* Beiheft 17.30–34.
Lang, B.
1982 *kippoer. ThWAT* 4.303–18.
Langdon, S. H.
1910–11 The Hebrew Word for "Atone." *ET* 22: 232–81.

1912 *Die neubabylonischen Königsinschriften.* Leipzig: J. C. Hinrichs.

1927 *Babylonian Penitential Psalms,* OECT 1.
Lapp, P.
1964 The 1963 Excavation at Taʿanek. *BASOR* 173: 4–44.
Laroche, E.
1971 *Catalogue des textes hittites.* Paris: Éditions Klincksieck.
Laughlin, J. C. H.
1976 The "Strange Fire" of Nadab and Abihu. *JBL* 95: 559–65.
Lauterbach, J. Z.
1927 A Significant Controversy Between the Sadducees and the Pharisees. *HUCA* 4: 173–205.

1951 Jesus in the Talmud. In *Rabbinic Essays.* Pp. 473–570. Cincinnati: Hebrew Union College.
Leach, E.
1976 *Culture and Communication.* Cambridge: Cambridge University Press.
Leeser, I.
1907 *The Holy Scriptures.* New York: Bloch.
Leeuwen, W. G. van
1988 The Meaning of *tupin* in Lev. 6,14. *ZAW* 100:268–69.
Leibovitch, J.
1953 Une Scène de sacrifice rituel chez les anciens Égyptiens. *JNES* 12: 59–60.

Leibowitz, J.
  1977 *rĕpûʾâ. EM* 7.407–25.
Lemke, W. E.
  1981 The Near and Distant God: A Study of Jer 23:23–24 in Its Biblical
    Theological Context. *JBL* 100: 541–55.
Levine, B. A.
  1963 Ugaritic Descriptive Rituals. *JCS* 17: 105–11.

———
  1965 The Descriptive Tabernacle Texts of the Pentateuch. *JAOS*
    85: 307–18.

———
  1965–66 Notes on Some Technical Terms of the Biblical Cult. *Leshonenu* 30:
    3–11 (Hebrew).

———
  1969 *Kippûrîm. EI* 9:88–95 (Hebrew).

———
  1974 *In the Presence of the Lord.* Leiden: Brill.

———
  1982a Assyriology and Hebrew Philology: A Methodological Re-examination.
    In *Mesopotamien und seine Nachbaren. XXV Rencontre Assyriologique
    Internationale Berlin,* vol. 2, ed. H.-J. Nissen and J. Renger. Pp. 521–30.
    Berlin: D. Reimer.

———
  1982b Research in the Priestly Source: The Linguistic Factor. *EI* 16: 124–31.

———
  1983 Late Language in the Priestly Source: Some Literary and Historical
    Observations. In *Proceedings of the Eighth World Congress of Jewish Stud-
    ies (1981),* 5.69–82. Jerusalem: World Union of Jewish Studies.

———
  1987 The Language of Holiness: Perceptions of the Sacred in the Hebrew
    Bible. In *Backgrounds for the Bible,* ed. D. N. Freedman and M. P. O'Con-
    nor. Pp. 241–55. Winona Lake, Ind.: Eisenbrauns.

———
  1989 *Leviticus.* Philadelphia: Jewish Publication Society.
Levinger, Y. M.
  1969 A Pure Bird May Be Eaten If Approved by Tradition. *Sinai* 30: 258–81
    (Hebrew).
Levy-Bruhl, L.
  1935 *Primitives and the Supernatural.* New York: Dutton.
Lewy, H.
  1944 Assyro-Babylonian and Israelite Measures of Capacity and Rates of
    Seeding. *JAOS* 64: 65–73.

1949 The Origin and Development of the Sexagesimal System of Numeration. *JAOS* 69: 1–11.

Licht, J.
1965 *The Rule Scroll.* Jerusalem: Bialik Institute (Hebrew).

1968 *Sukkot. EM* 5.1037–43.

Lichtenstein, H.
1932 Die Fastenvolle, eine Untersuchung zur jüdisch-hellenistischen Geschichte. *HUCA* 8–9: 257–352.

Liddell, H. G. and R. Scott
1940 *A Greek–English Lexicon.* Oxford: Oxford University Press.

Lieberman, S.
1933 Addendum. In *Methiboth,* ed. B. M. Lewin. Pp. 115–17. Jerusalem: n. p. (Hebrew).

1950 *Hellenism in Jewish Palestine.* New York: Jewish Theological Seminary.

1962 *Tosefta Kifshutah,* vol. 4: *Mo'ed.* New York: Jewish Theological Seminary.

1970 *Yemenite Midrashim* 2d ed. Jerusalem: Wahrmann.

Lindblom, J.
1962 Lot-Casting in the Old Testament. *VT* 12: 164–78.

Lipinski, E.
1970 "'Ūrīm and Tummīm," *VT* 20: 495–96.

Liver, J.
1968 *Chapters in the History of the Priests and Levites.* Jerusalem: Magnes.

Loewenstamm, S. E.
1958 *yôm hakippûrîm. EM* 3.595–600 (Hebrew).

1965 *'ānōkî 'ăhattennā. Leshonenu* 29: 69–70 (Hebrew).

1967–68 Remarks on Stylistic Patterns in Biblical and Ugaritic Literatures. *Leshonenu* 32: 27–36 (Hebrew).

1972–73 The Relation of the Settlement of Gad and Reuben in Num. 32:1–38. *Ta* 42: 12–26 (Hebrew).

1973 Lexicographical Notes on 1. *ṭbḥ;* 2. *hnny/ḫlny. UF* 5: 208–11.

1980 *Biqqōret tihyeh. Shnaton* 4: 94–97 (Hebrew).

BIBLIOGRAPHY

Lohfink, N.
1982 *Ḥopši. ThWAT* 3.123–28. English trans. in *TDOT* 5.114–18.
Lohse, E.
1951 *Die Ordination in Spät judentum und im Neuen Testament.* Göttingen: Vandenhoeck and Ruprecht.
Lorenzen, E.
1966 *Technical Studies in Ancient Metrology.* Copenhagen: Nyt Nordisk Forlag.
Loretz, O.
1975 Der hebräische Opferterminus *KLJL* "Ganzopfer." *UF* 7: 569–70.

———
1976 Ugaritisch-Hebraisch *ḪB/PT̠, BT ḪPT̠T̠-ḪPŠL BJT HḪPŠJ/WT. UF* 8: 129–31.

———
1977 Die Hebraischen Termini *ḪPŠJ "Freigelassen, Freigelassener"* and *ḪPŠH "Freilassung". UF* 9: 163–67.
Lucas, A. and A. Rowe
1940 Ancient Egyptian Measures of Capacity. *Annales du science des antiquités de l'Égypte* 40: 69–92.
Lucian
1976 *De Dea Syria,* ed. H. W. Attridge and R. A. Oden. Missoula, Mont.: Scholars Press.
Luncz, A. M.
1897 *Kaptor Waperaḥ by Ishtori Haparḥi.* Jerusalem: printed privately.
Lund, N. W.
1942 *Chiasmus in the New Testament.* Chapel Hill: University of North Carolina Press.
Luria, D.
1970 *Commentary to Midrash Rabbah.* Jerusalem: Sepher.
Luzzatto, S. D.
1965 *Commentary to the Pentateuch and Hamishtadel.* Tel Aviv: Dvir (Hebrew).
Macht, D. I.
1933 A Scientific Appreciation of Leviticus 12:1–5. *JBL* 52: 253–60.
Maḥzor Vitry
1923 *Maḥzor Vitry,* ed. S. Hurwitz. Nuremberg: Y. Bulka (Hebrew).
Maimonides
On the Torah, see Chavel; on the Mishna, see Kapaḥ 1967.
Malamat, A.
1979 *Ummatum in Old Babylonian Texts and Its Ugaritic and Biblical Counterparts. UF* 11: 527–36.
Malbim
1891 *Hattorah Wehammiṣwah.* 2 vols. Vilna: Romm.

Margoliot, M.
1956 *Midrash Leviticus Rabbah.* Jerusalem: Ararat.
Martens, F.
1977 Diététhique ou la cuisine de Dieu. *Communications* 26: 16–45.
Marx, A.
1988 Sacrifice de réparation et rites de levée de sanction. *ZAW* 100: 183–98.
———
1989 Sacrifice pour les péchés ou rites de passage? Quelques réflexions sur la fonction du *ḥaṭṭāʾt. RB* 96: 27–48.
Matthews, K. A.
1986 The Leviticus Scroll (11QpaleoLev) and the Text of the Hebrew Bible. *CBQ* 48: 171–207.
Mauer, C.
1971 σύνοιδα, συνείδησισ. *TDNT* 7.898–919.
Mazar, B.
1958–61 *Views of the Biblical World.* Jerusalem: International.
———
1969 *The Excavations in the Old City of Jerusalem.* Jerusalem: Israel Exploration Society.
McCarter, P. K., Jr.
1980 *I Samuel.* AB8. Garden City, N.Y.: Doubleday.
McCarthy, D. J.
1969 The Symbolism of Blood and Sacrifice. *JBL* 88: 166–76.
McEvenue, S. E.
1969 A Source-Critical Problem in Num. 14, 26–38. *Biblica* 50: 453–65.
———
1971 *The Narrative Style of the Priestly Writer.* AnBib 50. Rome: Biblical Institute Press.
McKenzie, J. L.
1968 *Second Isaiah.* AB20. Garden City, N.Y.: Doubleday.
Meachem, T. Z.
1989 Mishna Tractate Nidda, with Introduction. Ph.D. dissertation, Hebrew University, Jerusalem (Hebrew).
Meeks, D.
1979 Pureté et purification en Égypte. *SDB* 9: 430–52.
Meier, G.
1937 *Die assyrische Beschwörungssammlung Maqlu. AfO* Beiheft 2.
Meier, S.
1989 House Fungus: Mesopotamia and Israel (Lev 14:33–53). *RB* 96: 184–92.
Meigs, A. S.
1978 A Papuan Perspective on Pollution. *Man* 13: 304–18.
Meiri, M.
1970 *Beth Habekirah to Niddah,* ed. R. Sofer. Jerusalem: Talmudic Institute.

BIBLIOGRAPHY

Melamed, E. Z.
1944–45 Hendiadys and the Bible. *Ta* 16: 173–89, 242 (Hebrew).

1959 *hakkappārâ bammiqrā*? *Sinai* 22: 426–36.
Mendenhall, G. E.
1973 *The Tenth Generation.* Baltimore, Md.: The Johns Hopkins University Press.
Merwe, B. J. van der
1962 The Laying on of the Hands in the O.T. *Die O.T. Werkgemeenskap in Suid-Afrika* 5: 34–43.
Metzinger, A.
1940 Die Substitutionstheorie und die alttestamentliche Opfer mit besonderer Berücksichtigung von Lev. 17:11. *Biblica* 21: 159–68, 247–72, 335–37.
Meyers, C. L.
1976 *The Tabernacle Menorah.* Missoula, Mont.: Scholars Press.

1983 Jachin and Boaz in Religious and Political Perspective. *CBQ* 45: 167–78.
Middleton, J.
1960 *Lugabara Religion.* Oxford: Clarendon.
Milgrom, J.
1963 The Biblical Diet Laws as an Ethical System. *Interpretation* 17: 288–301. Reprinted in *Studies in Cultic Theology and Terminology.* Pp. 104–18. Leiden: Brill, 1983.

1964 Did Isaiah Prophesy During the Reign of Uzziah? *VT* 14: 164–82.

1967 The Cultic *Šĕgāgâ* and Its Influence in Psalms and Job. *JQR* 58: 73–79.

1970a *Studies in Levitical Terminology: The Encroacher and the Levite. The Term ʿAboda.* Berkeley: University of California Press.

1970b *kipper ʿal/bᵉadh. Leshonenu* 35: 16–17 (Hebrew).

1970c The Function of the *ḥaṭṭāʾt* Sacrifice. *Tarbiz* 40: 1–8 (Hebrew).

1970d The Shared Custody of the Tabernacle. *JAOS* 90: 204–9.

1970e Did Josiah Ever Rule Megiddo? *BM* 41: 23–27 (Hebrew).

1971a Sin-Offering or Purification-Offering? *VT* 21: 237–39. Reprinted in 1983d, pp. 67–69.

1971b A Prolegomenon to Leviticus 17:11. *JBL* 90: 149–56.

1971c Anointing. In *Enc Jud* 3.28–29.

1971d Leprosy. In *Enc Jud* 11.33–36.

1971e Fasting. In *Enc Jud* 6.1189–91.

1972a The Alleged Wave-Offering in Israel and the Ancient Near East. *IEJ* 22: 33–38. Reprinted in 1983d, pp. 133–38.

1972b The *šôq hatterûmâ:* A Chapter in Cultic History. *Tarbiz* 42: 1–14 (Hebrew). Trans. in 1983d, pp. 159–70.

1973a The *těnûpâ*. In *Zer Ligevurot: President Z. Shazar Volume*. Pp. 38–55. Jerusalem: Kiryat Sepher (Hebrew). Trans. in 1983d, pp. 139–58.

1973b The Alleged "Demythologization and Secularization" in Deuteronomy. *IEJ* 23: 156–61.

1974a Akkadian Confirmation for the Meaning of the Term *těrûmâ*. *Tarbiz* 44: 189. Trans. in 1983d, pp. 171–72.

1974b On the Origins of Philo's Doctrine of Conscience. *Studia Philonica* 3: 41–45.

1975a The Priestly Doctrine of Repentance. *RB* 82: 186–205. Reprinted in 1983d, pp. 47–66.

1975b The Missing Thief in Leviticus 5:20ff. *RIDA* 3d ser. 22: 71–85.

1975c The Compass of Biblical Sancta. *JQR* 65: 205–16.

1976a Two Kinds of *ḥaṭṭāʾt*. *VT* 26: 333–37. Reprinted in 1983d, pp. 70–74.

1976b The Concept of *maʿal* in the Bible and the Ancient Near East. *JAOS* 96: 236–47.

1976c The Legal Terms *šlm* and *brʾšw* in the Bible. *JNES* 35: 236–47.

1976d Israel's Sanctuary: The Priestly "Picture of Dorian Gray." *RB* 83: 390–99. Reprinted in 1983d, pp. 75–84.

1976e Profane Slaughter and a Formulaic Key to the Composition of Deuter-onomy. *HUCA* 47: 1–17.

1976f *Cult and Conscience: The ASHAM and the Priestly Doctrine of Repen-tance.* Leiden: Brill.

1976g Sacrifice and Offerings. In *IDB Supplement:* 764–71. Nashville: Ab-ingdon.

1976h First Fruits. In *IDB Supplement:* 336–37. Nashville: Abingdon.

1976i Repentance. In *IDB Supplement:* 736–38. Nashville: Abingdon.

1977a The Betrothed Slave-Girl, Leviticus 19:20–22. *ZAW* 89: 43–49.

1977b A Shoulder for the Levites. In *The Temple Scroll,* ed. Y. Yadin. Pp. 1.131–36. Jerusalem: Israel Exploration Society (Hebrew). Trans. in *The Temple Scroll,* ed. Y. Yadin. Pp. 1.169–76. Jerusalem: Israel Exploration Society, 1983.

1977c Concerning Jeremiah's Repudiation of Sacrifice. *ZAW* 89: 273–75. Reprinted in 1983d, pp. 119–21.

1978a Priestly Terminology and the Political and Social Structure of Pre-Monarchic Israel. *JQR* 69: 65–81. Reprinted in 1983d, pp. 1–17.

1978b Studies in the Temple Scroll. *JBL* 97: 501–23.

1978c "Sabbath" and "Temple City" in the Temple Scroll. *BASOR* 232: 25–27.

1979a The Offering of Incense in Second Temple Times. In *Sepher B. Z. Luria.* Pp. 330–34. Jerusalem: Kiryat Sepher (Hebrew).

1979b *Qĕṭōret. EM* 7.112–20 (Hebrew).

1980a Further Studies in the Temple Scroll, Part I. *JQR* 81: 1–17.

1980b Further Studies in the Temple Scroll, Part II. *JQR* 81: 89–106.

1981a A Kid in Its Mother's Milk. *Direction* 12.3: 7–8.

1981b Sancta Contagion and Altar/City Asylum. *SVT* 32: 278–310.

1981c The Case of the Suspected Adulteress, Numbers 5:11–31. In *The Creation of Sacred Literature*, ed. R. F. Friedman. Pp. 69–75. Berkeley: University of California Press.

1981d The Rebellion of Korah, Numbers Chapter 16: A Study in Redaction. In *De la Tôrah au Messie: Mélanges Cazelles*, ed. J. Doré et al. Pp. 135–46. Paris: Desclée.

1981e The Tassel and the Tallit. The Fourth Annual Rabbi Louis Feinberg Memorial Lecture, University of Cincinnati.

1981f Two Biblical Midrashim on the 'Asham. In *Jewish Tradition in the Diaspora*, ed. M. H. Caspi. Pp. 51–54. Berkeley: Magnes Museum.

1981g When Durkheim Meets Leviticus. *Direction* 12.2: 4–6.

1981h The Paradox of the Red Cow (Num xix). *VT* 31: 62–72. Reprinted in 1983d, pp. 85–95.

1981i Vertical Retribution: Ruminations on Parashat Shelah. *Conservative Judaism* 34.3: 11–16.

1982a Religious Conversion and the Revolt Model for the Formation of Israel. *JBL* 101: 169–76.

1982b Review of O. Keel, *Das Böcklein in der Milch seiner Mutter und Verwandtes: Im Lichte eines altorientalischen Bildmotivs*. *CBQ* 44: 123–24.

1982c The Levitic Town: An Exercise in Realistic Planning. *JJS* 33: 185–88.

1983a *Hättenûpâ*. In *Studies in Cultic Theology and Terminology*. Pp. 139–58. Leiden: Brill. Trans. of Hebrew in *Zer Ligevurot: President Z. Shazar Volume*, ed. B. Z. Luria. Pp. 93–110. Jerusalem: Kiryat Sepher, 1973.

1983b Of Hems and Tassels. *BAR* 9: 361–65.

1983c Magic, Monotheism, and the Sin of Moses. In *The Quest for the Kingdom of God: G. E. Mendenhall Festschrift*, ed. H. H. Huffmon et al. Pp. 251–66. Winona Lake, Ind.: Eisenbrauns.

1983d *Studies in Cultic Theology and Terminology.* Leiden: Brill.

1983e The Graduated Purification Offering (Leviticus 5:1–13). *JAOS* 103: 249–54.

1983f The Two Pericopes on the Purification Offering. In *The Word of the Lord Shall Go Forth: D. N. Freedman Festschrift,* ed. C. L. Meyers and M. O'Connor. Pp. 211–15. Winona Lake, Ind.: Eisenbrauns.

1984 New Temple Festivals in the Temple Scroll. In *The Temple in Antiquity,* ed. T. G. Madsen. Pp. 125–33. Salt Lake City: Brigham Young University Press.

1985a "You Shall Not Boil a Kid in Its Mother's Milk." *Bible Review* 1.3: 48–55.

1985b Review of B. Janowski, *Sühne als Heilsgeschehen. JBL* 104: 302–4.

1986a The Priestly Impurity System. In *Proceedings of the Ninth World Congress of Jewish Studies.* Pp. 1.121–27. Jerusalem: World Union of Jewish Studies.

1986b The Chieftains' Gifts: Numbers, chapter 7. *HTR* 9: 221–26.

1987 The Literary Structure of Numbers 8:5–22 and the Levitic *kippûr.* In *Perspectives on Language and Text,* ed. E. W. Conrad and E. G. Newing. Pp. 205–10. Winona Lake, Ind.: Eisenbrauns.

1988 The Korah Rebellions, Numbers 16–18: A Study in Tradition History. In *SBL Seminar Papers.* Pp. 570–73. Atlanta: Scholars Press.

1989a Ethics and Ritual: The Foundations of the Biblical Dietary Laws. In *Religion and Law: Biblical, Jewish, and Islamic Perspectives,* ed. E. B. Firmage et al. Pp. 159–91. Winona Lake, Ind.: Eisenbrauns.

1989b Rationale for Cultic Law: The Case of Impurity. *Semeia* 45: 103–9.

1989c The Qumran Cult: Its Exegetical Principles. In *Temple Scroll Studies,* ed. G. J. Brooke. Pp. 165–80. Sheffield: Sheffield Academic Press.

1990a *The Book of Numbers.* Philadelphia: Jewish Publication Society.

1990b Ablutions. In *Die hebräische Bibel und ihre zweifache Nachgeschichte: R. Rendtorff Festschrift.* Pp. 87–96. Neukirchen-Vluyn: Neukirchener Verlag.

1990c Scriptural Foundations and Deviations in the Laws of Purity of the Temple Scroll. In *Archaeology and History in the Dead Sea Scrolls,* ed. L. H. Schiffman. Pp. 83–99. Sheffield: JSOT Press.

Forthcoming A Two Priestly Terms: *šeqeṣ* and *ṭameʾ.* *S. Gevirtz Memorial Volume. Maarav.*

forthcoming B 4QThrA₁: An Unpublished Qumran Text on Purities. In *Dead Sea Scrolls Studies* (tentative title). Jerusalem: Magnes.
—— and R. Gane
1988 *Paroket. ThWAT* 6.755–57.
—— and D. Levy
1986 *ʿEdah. ThWAT* 5.1079–92.
—— and D. P. Wright
1985a *Niddah. ThWAT* 5.250–54.

1985b *Nazah. ThWAT* 5.322–26.

1986 *Samak. ThWAT* 5.880–88.
Milgrom, Jo
1978 Moses Sweetens the "Bitter Waters" of the "Portable Well" : An Interpretation of a Panel at Dura-Europos Synagogue. *Journal of Jewish Art* 5: 45–47.
Milik, J. T.
1956 Prière de Nabonide. *RB* 63: 407–15.

1959 *Ten Years of Discovery in the Wilderness of Judea.* Trans. J. Strugnell. SBT 26. Naperville, Ill.: Allenson.

1966 Fragment d'une source du Psautier, et fragments des Jubilées, du Document de Damas, d'un phylactère dans la grotte 4 de Qumran. *RB* 73: 94–106.

1977 *Qumrân grotte 4,* part II: *Tefillin, Mezuzot et Targums (4Q128–4Q157).* DJD 6. Oxford: Clarendon.
Moffatt, J.
1922 *The Holy Bible. A New Translation.* Garden City, N.Y.: Doubleday, Doran.

BIBLIOGRAPHY

Montgomery, J. A. and H. S. Gehman
1951 *A Critical and Exegetical Commentary on the Book of Kings.* ICC. New York: Charles Scribner's Sons.

Moor, J. C. de
1970a Studies in the New Alphabetic Texts from Ras Shamra II. *UF* 2: 303–27.

1970b The Peace Offering in Israel and Ugarit. In *Schrift en Uitleg: Festschrift W. H. Gispen.* Pp. 112–17. Kampen: Kok.

Moore, G. F.
1906 *Orientalische Studien Th. Noldeke gewidnet,* ed. K. Bezold. 2.761ff. Gieszen: A. Topelmann.

Moraldi, L.
1956 *Espiazione sacrificale e riti espiatori nell'ambiente biblico e nell'Antico Testamento.* AnBib 5. Rome: Pontifical Biblical Institute.

Moran, W. L.
1966 The Literary Connection Between LV 11, 13–19 DT 14, 12–18. *CBQ* 28: 271–76.

Moret, A.
1902 *Le Rituel du culte divin journalien en Égypte.* Annales du Musée Guimet, Bibliothèque d'études 14. Paris: Ernest Leroux.

Morgenstern, J.
1926 On Leviticus 10,3. In *Oriental Studies: P. Haupt Volume,* ed. C. Adler, A. Ember, et al. Pp. 97–102. Baltimore: The Johns Hopkins University Press.

Morris, L.
1968 Asham. *EvQ* 30: 196–210.

Moyer, J. C.
1969 The Concept of Ritual Purity Among the Hittites. Doctoral diss., Brandeis Univ.

1983 Hittite and Israelite Cult Practices. In *Scripture in Context,* ed. W. W. Hallo et al., 2.19–38. Winona Lake, Ind.: Eisenbrauns.

Muffs, Y.
1969 *Studies in the Aramaic Legal Papyri from Elephantine.* Leiden: Brill.

Münderlein, G.
1980 *Chēlebh. TDOT* 4.391–97.

Munn-Rankin, J. M.
1965 Diplomacy in Western Asia in the Early Second Millenium B.C. *Iraq* 18: 68–110.

Negev, A.
1972 *Archaeological Encyclopedia of the Holy Land.* New York: Putnam.

Nelson, H. M.
1949 Certain Reliefs at Karnak and Medinat Habu and the Ritual of Ame-
nophis I. *JNES* 8: 201–32, 310–45.
Nemoy, L.
1952 *Karaite Anthology.* New Haven: Yale University Press.
Neugebauer, O. and A. Sachs
1945 *Mathematical Cuneiform Texts.* New Haven: Americal Oriental Society
and Americal Schools of Oriental Research.
Neusner, J.
1973 *The Idea of Purity in Ancient Judaism.* Leiden: Brill.

——— 1974 *A History of the Mishnaic Law of Purities.* Part 3: *Kelim.* Leiden: Brill.

——— 1975 *A History of the Mishnaic Law of Purities.* Part 8: *Negaim.* Leiden: Brill.

——— 1976 *A History of the Mishnaic Law of Purities.* Part 14: *Miqvaot.* Leiden:
Brill.

——— 1977a *A History of the Mishnaic Law of Purities.* Part 16: *Niddah.* Leiden:
Brill.

——— 1977b *A History of the Mishnaic Law of Purities.* Part 18: *Zabim.* Leiden:
Brill.

——— 1977c *A History of the Mishnaic Law of Purities.* Part 22: *The Mishnaic
System of Uncleanness.* Leiden: Brill.

——— 1979 *Method and Meaning in Ancient Judaism.* Missoula, Mont.: Scholars
Press.

——— 1979–80 Scripture and Mishnah: The Exegetical Origins of *MADDAF.*
PAAJR 46–47: 459–71.

——— 1980 *A History of the Mishnaic Law of Holy Things.* Part 6 of *The Mishnaic
System of Sacrifice and Sanctuary.* Leiden: Brill.

——— 1981a *Judaism: The Evidence of the Mishnah.* Chicago: University of Chicago Press.

——— 1981b *Method and Meaning in Ancient Judaism.* 2d ser. Ann Arbor, Mich.:
Edwards.

1981c *Method and Meaning in Ancient Judaism.* 3d ser. Chicago: Scholars Press.

1984 *From Mishnah to Scripture.* Chicago: Scholars Press.
Nilsson, M. P.
1940 *Greek Folk Religion.* New York: Harper.
Noth, M.
1962 *Exodus.* Trans. by J. S. Bowden from the German. Philadelphia: Westminster.

1965 *Leviticus.* Trans. by J. E. Anderson from the German. London: SCM Press.

1967 Office and Vocation. In *The Laws of the Pentateuch.* Trans. by D. R. Ap-Thomas. Philadelphia: Fortress Press.
Notscher, F.
1929 Die Omen-Serie *šumma âlu ina mêlê šakin* (CT 38–40). *Or* 39–42: 3–245.
Nougayrol, J.
1948 *Sirrimu* (no* purîmu) "âne Sauvage." *JCS* 2: 203–8.
Obadiah ben Jacob
1980 *The Commentary of Sforno,* ed. A. Darom and Z. Gottlieb. Jerusalem: Mossad Harav Kook (Hebrew).
Obbink, H. T.
1937 The Horns of the Altar in the Semitic World, Especially in Jahwism. *JBL* 56: 43–49.
Oesterly, W. O. E.
1937 *Sacrifices in Ancient Israel.* London: Hodder and Staughton.
Oppenheim, A. L.
1943 Akkadian *pul(u)ḫ(t)u* and *melammu. JAOS* 63–64: 31–34.

1956 The Interpretation of Dreams in the Ancient Near East. *Transactions of the American Philosophical Society* 46: 179–354.

1964 *Ancient Mesopotamia.* Chicago: University of Chicago Press.
Orlinsky, H. M.
1944 The Hebrew Root *škb. JBL* 63: 37–39.

1969 *Notes on the New Translation of the Torah.* Philadelphia: Jewish Publication Society.
Otten, H.
1942 Die Überlieferungen des Telepinus-Mythus. *MVÄG*46.1.

1953 Ein kanaanäischer Mythus aus Boğazköy. *MIOF* 1: 125–510.

1961 Eine Beschwörung der Unterirdischen aus Boğazköy. *ZA* 54: 114–57.
—— and V. Souček
1969 *Ein althethitisches Ritual für das Königspaar.* StBoT 8. Wiesbaden: Harrassowitz.
Otto, E.
1960 Das ägyptische Mundöftnungsritual, I–II. *Ägyptologische Abhandlungen,* vol. 3. Wiesbaden: Harrassowitz.
Otto, R.
1958 *The Idea of the Holy.* Trans. J. W. Harvey. London: Oxford University Press.
Paran, M.
1983 Literary Features of the Priestly Code: Stylistic Patterns, Idioms and Structures. Ph.D. diss., Hebrew University (Hebrew). Reprinted as *Forms of the Priestly Style in the Pentateuch.* Jerusalem: Magnes, 1989.

1985 Two Types of "Laying Hands Upon" in the Priestly Source. *Beer-Sheva* 2: 115–20.
Pardee, D.
1979 A New Ugaritic Letter. *BibOr* 34: 3–20.
Parhon, S. ibn
1969–70 *Maḥberet he-ʾArukh.* Jerusalem: Maqor.
Parker, R.
1983 *Miasma, Pollution and Purification in Early Greek Religion.* Oxford: Clarendon.
Parunak, H. van Dyke
1983 Transitional Techniques in the Bible. *JBL* 102: 525–48.
Paschen, W.
1970 *Rein und Unrein. Untersuchung zur biblischen Wortgeschichte.* SANT 24.
Patai, R.
1947 Hebrew Installation Rites. *HUCA* 20: 143–225.
Paton, L. B.
1897 The Original Form of Leviticus XVII–XIX. *JBL* 16: 31–77.
Pedersen, J.
1926 *Israel, Its Life and Culture.* Vols. 1 and 2. Copenhagen: P. Branner.

1940 *Israel, Its Life and Culture.* Vols. 3 and 4. London: Oxford University Press.

BIBLIOGRAPHY

Peet, T. E.
1923 *The Rhind Mathematical Papyrus.* Liverpool: Liverpool University Press.

———

1930 *The Great Tomb Robberies of the Twentieth Egyptian Dynasty,* vol. 1. Oxford: Clarendon.
Pellett, P. L. and S. Shadarevian
1970 *Food Composition Tables for Use in the Middle East.* 2d ed. Beirut: American University of Beirut.
Péter, R.
1975 *Par* et *shor. VT* 25: 486–96.

———

1977 L'Imposition des mains dans l'Ancien Testament. *VT* 27: 48–55.
Petrie, F.
1926 *Ancient Weights and Measures.* London: University of London Press.
Pettazzoni, R.
1939 La Confession des péchés in Syria aux époques préchrétiennes. In *Mélanges syriens offerts à Monsieur René Dussaud,* 1.197–202. Paris: P. Geuthner.
Phillips, A.
1985 The Undetectable Offender and the Priestly Legislators. *JTS* 36: 146–50.
Philo
1929–62 Loeb Classical Library. 10 vols. London: W. Heinemann.
Pines, R.
1971 *ṣebāʿîm. EM* 6.663–72.
Plato
1970 *The Laws.* Harmondsworth: Penguin.
Pliny
1945 *Natural History.* Trans. H. Rackham. Loeb Classical Library. London: W. Heinemann.
Polzin, R.
1976 *Late Biblical Hebrew: Toward an Historical Typology of Biblical Hebrew Prose.* Missoula, Mont.: Scholars Press.
Pope, M.
1962 Number. *IDB* 3.561–67.
Popko, M.
1960 GISZA.LAM.GAR in den hethitischen Texten. *Rocznik Orientalistyczny* 41: 101–4.
Por, F. D.
1971 One Hundred Years of Suez Canal—A Century of Lessepian Migration: Retrospect and Viewpoints. *Systematic Zoology* 20: 138–59.

Porten, B.

1968 *Archives from Elephantine.* Berkeley: University of California Press.

Postgate, J. N.

1978 An Inscribed Jar from Tell al Rimah. *Iraq* 40: 71–75.

Preuss, J.

1971 *Biblisch-talmüdische Medizin.* Trans. F. Rosner. New York: Ktav. Reprinted New York: Sanhedrin, 1978. Original ed. Berlin: S. Karger, 1911.

Qimron, E. and J. Strugnell

1985 An Unpublished Halakhic Letter from Qumran. In *Biblical Archaeology Today,* ed. J. Amitas. Pp. 400–407. Jerusalem: Israel Exploration Society.

Rabad

See Weiss 1946.

Rabin, C.

1954 *The Zadokite Documents.* Oxford: Clarendon.

———

1974–75 *Avneṭ* and *piṭdah. Leshonenu* 39: 182–86.

Rad, G. von

1962 *Old Testament Theology,* Vol. 1. New York: Harper & Row. German original. Munich: C. Kaiser, 1957.

Radak

See Kamler 1970.

Rainey, A.

1970 The Order of Sacrifices in Old Testament Ritual Texts. *Biblica* 51: 485–98.

———

1975 Sacrifices and Offerings. *The Zondervan Pictorial Encyclopedia of the Bible.* Grand Rapids, Mich.: Zondervan.

Ramban

See Chavel 1960.

Rankin, O. S.

1930 *The Origins of the Festival of Hanukkah.* Edinburgh: T. & T. Clark.

Rashbam

See Bromberg 1969.

Rashi

See Silbermann 1946.

Reif, S. C.

1972 Dedicated to *ḥnk. VT* 22: 495–501.

Reiner, E.

1956 *Lipšur* Litanies. *JNES* 15: 129–49.

———

1958 *Šurpu. AfO* Beiheft 11.

Rendsburg, G.
1980 Late Biblical Hebrew and the Date of "P." *JANESCU* 12: 65–80.
Rendtorff, R.
1954 *Die Gesetze in der Priesterschrift.* Göttingen: Vandenhoeck and Ruprecht.

_____
1956 Priesterliche Kulttheologie und prophetische Kultpolemik. *ThLZ* 5–6: 339–42.

_____
1967 *Studien zur Geschichte des Opfers im alten Israel.* WMANT 24. Neukirchen-Vluyn: Neukirchener Verlag.

_____
1985 *Leviticus.* Vol. 3.1. Neukirchen-Vluyn: Neukirchener Verlag.
Renger, J.
1967–69 Untersuchungen zum Priestentum in der altbabylonischen Zeit. *ZA* 24: 110–88; 26: 104–230.
Reymond, P.
1965 Sacrifice et "spiritualité," ou sacrifice et alliance? *TZ* 21: 314–17.
Rhode, E.
1925 *Psyche.* Trans. W. B. Hills. London: Kegan, Paul, Trench, Trubner.
Ridderbos, N. H.
1948 *ʿāpār* als "Staub des Totenortes." *OTS* 5: 174–78.
Rinaldi, G.
1954 Note ebraiche. *Aegyptus* 34: 50–55.
Ringgren, H.
1966 *Israelite Religion.* Philadelphia: Fortress.

_____
1986 *Ṭāhar. TDOT* 5.287–96.
Ritter, E. K.
1965 Magical-Expert and Physician. *Assyriological Studies* 16: 299–321.
Rivlin, J. J.
1959 *The Song of the Jews of the Targum.* Jerusalem: n.p. (Hebrew).
Robertson, E.
1964 The Urim and Tummim: What Are They? *VT* 14: 67–74.
Robinson, E.
1841 *Biblical Researches in Palestine, Mt. Sinai and Arabia Petraea.* Boston: Crocker and Brewster.
Robinson, H. W.
1942 Hebrew Sacrifice and Prophetic Symbolism. *JTS* 43: 129–39.
Rodriguez, A. M.
1979 *Substitution in the Hebrew Cultus.* Berrien Springs, Mich.: Andrews University Press.

Rogerson, J. W.
1980 Sacrifice in the Old Testament. In *Sacrifice,* ed. M. F. C. Bourdillon and M. Fortes. Pp. 45–59. London: Academic Press.
Rokeach, D.
1986 Philo the Alexandrian: The Midrash and the Early Halakha. *Ta* 55: 433–39 (Hebrew).
Rosenthal, J.
1970 *Sefer Yosef Ha-mekanne.* Jerusalem: Mekitze Nirdamim.
Rost, L.
1953 Ein hethitisches Ritual gegen Familienzwist. *MIOF* 1: 345–79.

_____

1958 Erwägungen zum israelitischen Brandopfer. In *Vom Ugarit nach Qumran: Festschrift O. Eissfeldt.* Pp. 177–83. Beihefte zur *ZAW* 77.
Rothenberg, B.
1970 Un Temple égyptien découvert dans la Arabah. *Bible et terre sainte* 123: 3, 8–9.

_____

1972 *Timna.* London: Thames and Hudson.

_____

1975 Teman. In *Encyclopaedia of Archaeological Excavations in the Holy Land,* ed. M. Avi-Yonah and E. Stern, 4.1184–1203. Jerusalem: Massada.
Roubos, K.
1956 *Profetis en cultus in Israel.* Wageningen: H. Veenman en Zonen.
Rowley, H. H.
1946–47 The Prophets and Sacrifice. *ET* 58: 305–7.

_____

1950–51 The Meaning of Sacrifice. *BJRL* 33: 76–78.
Rudolph, W.
1955 *Chronikbücher.* Tübingen: Mohr.

_____

1977 Ussias "Haus der Freiheit." *ZAW* 89: 418.
Rüger, H. P.
1973 "Dann entfernt in seinen Kopf samt dessen Federn" (zu Lev 1,16). In *Wort und Geschichte: K. Elliger Festschrift.* Pp. 163–72. AOAT 18. Kevelaer: Butzon and Bercker.
Rupprecht, K.
1975 Quisquilien zu der Wendung *"ML' (ʾet) yad plony"* (jemandem die Hand füllen) und zum Terminus *"miluʾim"* (Füllung). In *Dielheimer Blätter zum AT,* Beiheft 1 (= *Sefer Rendtorff*). Pp. 73–93.
Ryckmans, J.
1972 Les Confessions publiques sabéenes: Le code sud arabe de purité rituelle. *AION* 32: 1–15.

Saadiah
See Hirschfeld 1907; Kapaḥ 1963.
Safrai, S.
1965 *Pilgrimage at the Time of the Second Temple.* Tel Aviv: Am Hassefer (Hebrew).
Saggs, H. W. F.
1962 *The Greatness that Was Babylon.* New York: Hawthorne.

___

1984 *The Might that Was Assyria.* London: Sidgwick and Jackson.
Salonen, A.
1965 *Die Hausgeräte der Alten Mesopotamier.* Helsinki: Suomalaisen Tiedeakatemian Toimituksia Annales Academiae Scientiarum Fennicae.
Sansom, M. C.
1982–83 Laying on of Hands in the Old Testament. *ET* 94: 323–26.
Saporetti, C.
1969 Emaru, Sutu e Qa'u nei documenti economici medio-assiri. *Rivista degli studi orientali* 44: 273–83.
Sarna, N. M.
1959 The Interchange of the Prepositions *Beth* and *Min* in Biblical Hebrew. *JBL* 78: 310–16.
Sauer, A. von Rohr
1968 The Cultic Role of the Pig in Ancient Times. In *In Memoriam Paul Kahle,* ed. M. Black. Pp. 201–7. Berlin: A. Topelmann.
Sauneron, S.
1960 *The Priests of Ancient Egypt.* New York: Grove.

___

1962 *Esna,* vol. 5. Cairo: Publications de l'Institut Français d'Archéologie Orientale.
Sawyer, J. F. A.
1976 A Note on the Etymology of Ṣāra'at. *VT* 26: 241–45.
Schley, D.
1989 *Shilo: A Biblical City in Tradition and History. JSOT* supplement 63. Sheffield: Sheffield Academic Press.
Schmid, R.
1964 *Das Bundesopfer in Israel.* Munich: Kösel.
Schottroff, W.
1964 *"Gedenken" im Alten Orient und im Alten Testament.* WMANT 15. Neukirchen-Vluyn: Neukirchener Verlag.
Schwartz, B.
1938 The Ritual of Zarpiya of Kizzuwatna. *JAOS* 58: 334–53.
Scott, J. A.
1965 The Pattern of the Tabernacle. Ph.D. diss., University of Pennsylvania.

Scott, R. B. Y.
1958 The Hebrew Cubit. *JBL* 77: 205–14.

——
1959 Weights and Measures of the Bible. *BA* 22: 22–23.
Segal, P.
1983–84 Further Parallels Between the Priestly Literature in the Bible and the Hittite Instructions for Temple Servants. *Shnaton* 7–8: 265–73.

——
1989 The Divine Verdict of Leviticus X 3. *VT* 39: 91–95.
Seidel, J.
1984 Why the Pig? Seminar paper, University of California, Berkeley.
Seidl, T.
1982 *Tora für den "Aussatz" -Fall.* St. Ottilien: EOS.
Seper Hamibḥar
See Aaron ben Joseph 1835.
Sforno
See Obadiah ben Jacob 1980.
Shachter, J., trans.
1986 *The Commentary of Abraham ibn Ezra on the Pentateuch*, vol. 3: *Leviticus.* Hoboken, N.J.: Ktav.
Shadal
See Luzzatto 1965.
Shalem, N.
1932 Concerning the Names of Colors in Hebrew. *Leshonenu* 4: 16–66 (Hebrew).
Shama, A.
1986 Two Trends in the Dedication of the Tabernacle and Their Reflex in the Sacrificial Codex. *Megadim* 1–2: 132–42 (Hebrew).
Shinan, A.
1979 The Sins of Nadab and Abihu in Rabbinic Literature. *Ta* 48: 201–14.
Silbermann, A. H., ed.
1946 *Pentateuch with Rashi's Commentary.* 2 vols. London: Shapiro, Vallentine.
Simoons, F. J.
1961 *Eat Not This Flesh.* Madison: University of Wisconsin Press.
Singer, I.
1978 The Hittite KI. LAM Festival. Ph.D. diss., Tel Aviv University.

——
1983–84 *The Hittite KI. LAM Festival.* 2 vols. StBoT 27–28. Wiesbaden: Harrasowitz.
Sjöberg, A. and E. Bergman
1969 *The Collection of the Sumerian Temple Hymns.* New York: J. J. Augustin.

BIBLIOGRAPHY

Skinner, J.
1910 *Genesis.* ICC. New York: Charles Scribner's Sons.

———
1922 *Prophecy and Religion.* Cambridge: Cambridge University Press.
Smith, W. R.
1908 *The Old Testament in the Jewish Church.* 2d ed. London: A. & C. Black.

———
1927 *Lectures on the Religion of the Semites.* 3d ed. New York: Macmillan.
Snaith, N. H.
1947 *The Jewish New Year Festival.* London: SPCN.

———
1967 *Leviticus and Numbers.* London: Thomas Nelson.

———
1970–71 The Sprinkling of Blood. *ET* 82: 23–24.

———
1973 A Note on Numbers XVIII 9. *VT* 23: 373–75.

———
1975 *zābaḥ* and *šāḥaṭ. VT* 25: 242–46.
Soden, W. von
1956 Eine altassyrische Beschwörung gegen die Dämonen Lamaštum. *Or* 25: 141–48.

———
1970 Mirjam-marion (Gottes-) Geschenk. *VF* 2: 69–72.
Soler, J.
1973 Sémiotique de la nourriture dans la Bible. *Annales* 28: 943–55. Trans. as The Dietary Prohibitions of the Hebrews in *New York Review* 26.10: 24ff. (June 14, 1979).
Sollberger, E.
1967 Samsuiluna's Bilingual Inscription. *RA* 61: 39–44.

———
1972 (1975) The Temple in Babylonia. *CRAI* 20: 31–34.
——— and J. R. Kupper
1971 *Inscriptions royales sumeriennes et akkadiennes.* Paris: Éditions du Cerf. See esp. pp. 222–23.
Sommer, F. and H. Eheloff
1924 *Das hethitische Ritual des Papanikri von Komana. KBo* 6 = *Bibliotheca orientalis* 2001.
Speiser, E. A.
1960 Leviticus and the Critics. In *Y. Kaufmann Jubilee Volume,* ed. M. Haran. Pp. 29–45. Jerusalem: Magnes.

———
1964 *Genesis.* AB 1. New York: Doubleday.

Sperber, A.

1959 *The Bible in Aramaic.* Vol. 1: *The Pentateuch, Onqelos.* Leiden: Brill.

Spiro, A.

1959 The Law on the Sharing of Information. *PAAJR* 28: 95–101.

Srinivas, M. N.

1952 *Religion and Society Among the Coorgs of South India.* Bombay: Asia Publishing House.

Stager, L. E. and S. R. Wolff

1981 Production and Commerce in Temple Courtyards: An Olive Press in the Sacred Precinct at Tel Dor. *BASOR* 243: 95–102.

Stager, L. E.

1985 The Archaeology of the Family in Ancient Israel. *BASOR* 260: 1–36.

Stein, S.

1957 The Dietary Laws in Rabbinic and Patristic Literature. *Studia patristica* 2.2: 141–54.

Stendebach, F. J.

1976 Das Schweinopfer im Alten Orient. *BZ* 18: 263–71.

Stengel, P.

1920 *Die griechischen Kultusaltertümer.* 3d ed. Munich: C. H. Beck.

Stern, E.

1979 Craft and Industry. In *The World History of the Jewish People,* vol. 5: *The Age of the Monarchies: Culture and Society,* ed. A. Malamat. Pp. 237–78. Jerusalem: Masada.

Stern, M.

1974 *Greek and Latin Authors on Jews and Judaism.* Jerusalem: Israel Academy of Sciences and Humanities.

Stevenson, M.

1951 Purification, Jain. *ERE* 10: 493–95.

Streck, M.

1916 *Assurbanipal I–III.* Leipzig: J. C. Hinrichs.

Strugnell, J.

1990 Moses-Pseudepigrapha at Qumran: 4Q375, 4Q376, and Similar Works. In *Archaeology and History in the Dead Sea Scrolls,* ed. L. H. Schiffman. Pp. 221–56. Sheffield: JSOT Press.

——— and E. Qimron

forthcoming *A Halakhic Letter from Qumran, MMT (4Q394–99).* Tentative title.

Tadmor, H.

1968 "The People" and the Kingship in Ancient Israel. *Journal of World History* 11: 3–23.

———

1982 *Taḥaš. EM* 8.520–21.

BIBLIOGRAPHY

Tal, A.
1980 *The Samaritan Targum of the Pentateuch,* vol. 2. Tel-Aviv: Tel-Aviv University Press.

Tallquist, K.
1934 Sumerisch-Akkadische Hymnen der Totenwelt. *Studia orientalia* 4: 17–22.

Talmon, S.
1967 The Judean *ʿam haʾ areṣ* in Historical Perspective. In *Proceedings of the Fourth World Congress of Jewish Studies.* Pp. 71–76. Jerusalem: World Union of Jewish Studies.

Tambiah, S. J.
1969 Animals Are Good to Think and Good to Prohibit. *Ethnology* 7: 423–59.

Tarragon, J.-M. de
1980 *Le Culte à Ugarit.* Paris: J. Gabalda.

———
1981 La *Kapporet* est-elle une fiction ou un élément du culte tardif? *RB* 88: 5–12.

Tas, J.
1971 *Ṣāraʿat. EM* 6.776–78.

Tawil, H.
1980 Azazel the Prince of the Steepe *(sic):* A Comparative Study. *ZAW* 92: 43–59.

Thompson, R. C.
1903–14 *The Devils and Evil Spirits of Babylonia.* 2 vols. London: Luzac.

———
1949 *Dictionary of Assyrian Botany.* London: British Academy.

———
1971 *Semitic Magic.* New York: Ktav. Reprint of London 1908 ed.

Thompson, R. J.
1963 *Penitence and Sacrifice in Early Israel Outside the Levitical Law.* Leiden: Brill.

Thureau-Dangin, F.
1907 *Die sumerischen und akkadischen Königsinschriften.* Leipzig: J. C. Hinrichs.

———
1909 L'U, le Qa et la Mine. *JA* 10th ser. 13: 79–111.

———
1919 Une Acte de donation de Marduk-zakir-šumi. *RA* 16: 117–56.

———
1921 Numération et métrologie sumeriennes. *RA* 18: 123–38.

———
1937 La Mesure du *"Qa." RA* 34: 80–86.

1938 *Textes mathématiques babyloniens.* Leiden: Brill.
Toeg, A.
1974 Num 15:22–31: A Halakhic Midrash. *Ta* 43: 20 (Hebrew).
Toombs, L. E.
1962 Clean and Unclean. *IDB* 1.641–48.
Toorn, K. van der
1985 *Sin and Sanction in Israel and Mesopotamia.* Assen: Van Gorcum.
Tov, E.
1968 A Commentary on 4QDª, col. XVII. Unpublished paper.

1978–79 The Textual Character of the Leviticus Scroll from Qumran Cave
11. *Shnaton* 3: 238–44 (Hebrew).
Tristam, H. B.
1873 *Natural History of the Bible.* London: Society for Promoting Christian
Knowledge.
Tserat, M.
1970 ʿinyan šĕmiṭṭâ ʾēṣel har sînay. In *Sefer S. Yeivin.* Pp. 283–88. Jerusalem:
Kiryat-Sepher.
Tufnell, O., et al.
1940 *Lachish II.* Oxford: Oxford University Press.
Tur-Sinai, N. H.
1957 *The Book of Job.* Jerusalem: Kiryat Sepher.

1960a Šĕtî. Ben Yehuda Dictionary and Thesaurus of the Hebrew Language
8.7496–97.

1960b śāpām. Ben Yehuda Dictionary and Thesaurus of the Hebrew Language
8.7605–6.
Turner, V. W.
1967 *The Forest of Symbols.* Ithaca, N.Y.: Cornell University Press.

1969 *The Ritual Process.* Chicago: Aldine Press.
Tylor, E. B.
1873 *Primitive Culture.* 3d ed. New York: H. Holt.
Unger, E.
1916 Die Nippurelle. In *Zwei babylonische Antiken aus Nippur.* Constantinople: Kaiserlischen Osmanischen Museen.
United Bible Society
1972 *Fauna and Flora of the Bible.* London: United Bible Society.
Urbach, E. E.
1935 Études sur la littérature polémique au Moyen Âge. *REJ* 197–98: 70–71.

Ussishkin, D.
1988 The Date of the Judaean Shrine at Arad. *IEJ* 38: 142–57.

Van Beek, G. W.
1960 Frankincense and Myrrh. *BA* 23: 70–95.

Van Gennep, A.
1960 *The Rites of Passage.* Chicago: University of Chicago Press.

Vaux, R. de
1961a *Ancient Israel.* New York: McGraw-Hill.

———
1961b Arche d'alliance et tente de réunion. In *À la Rencontre de Dieu:
    Mémorial A. Gelin.* Pp. 55–70. Le Puy: X. Mappus.

———
1964 *Studies in Old Testament Sacrifice.* Cardiff: University of Wales Press.

———
1971a Ark of the Covenant and Tent of Reunion. In *The Bible and the
    Ancient Near East.* Pp. 136–51. Garden City, N.Y.: Doubleday.

———
1971b The Sacrifice of Pigs in Palestine and in the Ancient Near East. In *The
    Bible and the Ancient Near East.* Pp. 252–69. Garden City, N.Y.: Double-
    day. Trans. from Von Ugarit nach Qumran. Beihefte zur *ZAW* 77: 250–
    65.

——— and J. T. Milik
1977 Qumrân Grotte 4,II: I Archéologie; II Tefillin, Mezuzot et Targums
    (4Q128–4Q157). *DJD* 6.86–89 (= 4Q156). Oxford: Clarendon.

Veenhof, K. R.
1966 Review of E. Kutsch *Salbung als Rechtsakt im Alten Testament und im
    Alten Orient. Bibliotheca orientalis* 23: 308–13.

Vieyra, M.
1966 Le Sorcier hittite. In *Le Monde du sorcier.* Pp. 110–15. Paris: Editions
    du Seuil.

———
1981 À propos d'un oiseau hittite et de la lecture du nom d'un oiseau bib-
    lique. *RA* 75: 176–79.

Virolleaud, C.
1931 La Lutte de Mot, fils des dieux et d'Alein, fils de Baal. *Syria* 12: 195–
    224.

———
1933 La Naissance des dieux gracieux et beaux. *Syria* 14: 128–51.

Volz, P.
1901 Die Handauflegen beim Opfer. *ZAW* 21: 93–100.

———
1937 Die radikale Ablehnung der Kultreligion durch die alttestamentlichen
    Propheten. *ZSTh* 14: 63–85.

Vriezen, T. C.
1950 The Term *hizza:* Lustra'tion and Consecration. *OTS* 7: 201–35.
Walkenhorst, K.-H.
1969 *Der Sinai im liturgischen Verständnis der deuteronomischen und pries-terlichen Tradition.* Bonner biblische Beiträge 33. Bonn: P. Hanstein.
Wapnish, P.
1988 Why Not Pig? Paper delivered at the Society of Biblical Literature Conference, Nov. 20, 1988.
——— and B. Hesse
Faunal Remains from Tell Dan: Perspectives on Animal Production at a Village, Urban and Ritual Center. Typescript.
Wayne, A.
1960 Why We Do Not Mix Meat and Milk. *American Examiner* 13 (Thursday, March 30).
Weidner, E. F.
1932 Der Staatsvertrag Aššurnirâris VI von Assyrien mit Matiʾilu von Bêt-Agusi. *AfO* 8: 17–33.

1954–56 Hof- und Harems-Erlasse assyrischer Könige aus den 2. Jahrtausend v. Chr. *AfO* 17: 256–93.
Weinberg, Z.
1973 *Ḥaṭṭāʾt weʾāšām.* *BM* 55: 524–30 (Hebrew).
Weinfeld, M.
1963 The Conception of Law in and Outside of Israel. *BM* 17: 58–63 (Hebrew).

1970 The Covenant of Grant in the Old Testament and the Ancient Near East. *JAOS* 90: 184–203.

1972 The Worship of Molech and the Queen of Heaven and Its Background. *UF* 4: 133–54.

1980 Julius Wellhausen's Understanding of the Law of Ancient Israel and Its Fallacies. *Shnaton* 4: 62–93 (Hebrew).

1981 Sabbath, Temple and the Enthronement of the Lord—the Problem of the Sitz im Leben of Genesis 1:1–2:3. In *Mélanges bibliques et orientaux en l'honneur de M. Henri Cazelles,* ed. A. Caquot. Pp. 501–12. AOAT 212. Kevelaer: Butzon and Bercker.

1982a A Comparison of a Passage from the Šamaš Hymn (lines 65–78) with Psalm 107. Pp. 275–79. *AfO* Beiheft 19.

1982b The Counsel of the "Elders" to Rehoboam and Its Implications. *Maarav* 3: 27–53.

1983 Social and Cultic Institutions in the Priestly Source Against Their Ancient Near Eastern Background. In *Proceedings of the Eighth World Congress of Jewish Studies (1981)*, 5.95–129. Jerusalem: World Union of Jewish Studies.

1987 The Mincha Prayer—Its Meaning and Development. In *Gevurot Haromah, M. H. Weiler Festschrift*, ed. Z. Falk. Pp. 77–82. Jerusalem: Kiryat Sepher.

1990 Traces of a Hittite Cult in Shiloh and Jerusalem. *Shnaton* 10: 107–14 (Hebrew).

Weiss, I. M. ed.
1946 *Sipra with Rabad's commentary.* New York: OM.

Welch, A. C.
1936 *Prophet and Priest in Old Israel.* Oxford: Blackwell.

Wellhausen, J.
1885 *Prolegomena to the History of Israel.* English trans. Edinburgh: A. & C. Black. Reprinted New York: Meridian, 1957.

1897 *Reste arabischen Heidentums.* 2d ed. Berlin: G. Reimer.

1963 *Die Composition des Hexateuchs und der Historischen Bücher des Alten Testaments.* 4th ed. Berlin: W. de Gruyter. (1st ed. 1885.)

Wenham, G. J.
1979 *The Book of Leviticus.* Grand Rapids, Mich.: Eerdmans.

1981 The Theology of Unclean Food. *EvQ* 53: 6–14.

1983 Why Does Sexual Intercourse Defile (Lev. 15:18)? *ZAW* 95: 432–34.

Wertheimer, S. A.
1955 *Bātê Midrāšôt.* 2 vols. Jerusalem: Kook.

1984 *Bēʾûr Šēmôt Hannirdāpîm ŠebbaTNK.* 2d ed. Jerusalem: Ketar Ve-sefer.

Wessely, N. H.
1846 *Netivot Ha-shalom,* vol. 3: *Leviticus,* ed. M. Mendelssohn. Vienna: von Schmid and Busch.

Westbrook, R.
1988 *Studies in Biblical and Cuneiform Law.* Cahiers de la *Revue biblique* 26. Paris: J. Gabalda.

Westermann, C.

1974 Die Herrlichkeit Gottes in der Priesterschrift. In *Forschung am Alten Testament.* Pp. 115–37. Gesammelte Studien 2. Munich: C. Kaiser.

Westermarck, E.

1908–12 *The Origin and Development of the Moral Ideas.* 2 vols. London: Macmillan.

Wheeler, A. J.

1923 Gongs and Bells. *ERE* 6: 313–16.

Wiesenberg, E.

1956 Related Prohibitions: Swine Breeding and the Study of Greek. *HUCA* 27: 213–33.

Wilkinson, J.

1977 Leprosy and Leviticus: The Problem of Description and Identification. *Scottish Journal of Theology* 30: 153–69.

–––––––

1978 Leprosy and Leviticus: A Problem of Semantics and Translation. *Scottish Journal of Theology* 31: 153–66.

Williams, R. J.

1976 *Hebrew Syntax: An Outline.* 2d ed. Toronto: University of Toronto Press.

Wilson, J. A.

1945 The Assembly of a Phoenician City. *JNES* 4: 245.

Wilson, M.

1957 *Rituals of Kinship among the Nyakyusa.* Oxford: Clarendon.

Wiseman, D. J.

1953 *The Alalakh Tablets.* London: British Institute of Archaeology at Ankara.

–––––––

1958 *The Vassal-Treaties of Esarhaddon.* Reprint from *Iraq* 20. London: British School of Archaeology.

Wold, D. J.

1978 The Biblical Penalty of *Kareth.* Ph.D. diss., University of California, Berkeley.

Wolff, H. W.

1974 *Hosea.* Trans. by G. Stansell from the German. Hermoneia. Philadelphia: Fortress.

Wright, D. P.

1984 The Disposal of Impurity in the Priestly Writings of the Bible with Reference to Similar Phenomena in Hittite and Mesopotamian Cultures. Ph.D. diss., University of California, Berkeley.

–––––––

1986 The Gesture of Hand Placement in the Hebrew Bible and in Hittite Literature. *JAOS* 106: 433–46.

BIBLIOGRAPHY

1987 *The Disposal of Impurity.* Atlanta: Scholars Press.

1988 Two Types of Impurity in the Priestly Writings of the Bible. *Koroth* 9: 180–93.
——— and R. N. Jones
forthcoming A Discharge. *Anchor Bible Dictionary.* Vol. 2. Forthcoming.
——— and R. N. Jones
forthcoming B Leprosy. *Anchor Bible Dictionary.* Vol. 4. Forthcoming.
Wright, L. S.
1989 *mkr* in 2 Kings xx 5–17 and Deuteronomy XVIII 8. *VT* 39: 438–48.
Würthwein, E.
1963 Kultpolemik oder Kultbescheid? Beobachtungen zu dem Thema "Prophetie und Kult." In *Tradition und Situation: A. Weiser Festschrift,* ed. E. Würthwein and O. Kaiser. Pp. 115–31. Göttingen: Vandenhoeck and Ruprecht.
Wylie, C. C.
1949 On King Solomon's Molten Sea. *BA* 12: 86–90.
Yadin, Y.
1962 *The Scroll of the War of the Sons of Light Against the Sons of Darkness* English ed. Oxford: Oxford University Press. Original Hebrew ed., Jerusalem: Bialik Institute, 1955; 2d ed., 1956.

1963 *Finds from the Bar Kokhba Period in the Cave of Letters.* Jerusalem: Israel Exploration Society.

1967 The Temple Scroll. *BA* 30: 135–39.

1969 The Temple Scroll. In *Jerusalem Through the Ages,* ed. J. Aviram. Pp. 72–87. Jerusalem: Israel Exploration Society (Hebrew).

1971a The Temple Scroll. *Enc Jud* 15.996–98.

1971b The Temple Scroll. In *New Directions in Biblical Archaeology,* ed. D. N. Freedman and J. Greenfield. Pp. 139–48. Garden City, N.Y.: Doubleday.

1975 *Hazor.* New York: Random House.

1983 *The Temple Scroll.* English ed. 3 vols. Jerusalem: Israel Exploration Society Hebrew original, 1977.
Yeivin, S.
1971 Uzziah. *EM* 6.131.

1972 Note in *Ha'aretz Museum* 14: 39.
Yerkes, K. Y.
1923–24 The Unclean Animals of Leviticus 11 and Deuteronomy 14. *JQR* 14: 1–29.
Yerkes, R. K.
1952 *Sacrifice in Greek and Roman Religions and Early Judaism.* New York: Scribners.
Zadok, P.
1978 Phoenicians, Philistines, and Moabites in Mesopotamia. *BASOR* 230: 57–66.
Zevit, Z.
1982 Converging Lines of Evidence Bearing on the Date of P. *ZAW* 94: 481–511.
Ziderman, I. I.
1981–82 The Blue Thread of the Tzitzit. *Journal of the Society of Dyers and Colourists* 97: 362–64; 98: 247.

1987 First Identification of Authentic *Tĕkēlet.* *BASOR* 265: 25–34.
Zimmerli, W.
1954 Die Eigenast des prophetischen Rede des Ezechiel. *ZAW* 66: 9–19.
Zucker, M.
1963–64 Comments on "Essa Meshali" of R. Se'adya Gaon. *Tarbiz* 33: 40–57 (Hebrew).
Zuidhof, A.
1982 King Solomon's Molten Sea and "π." *BA* 45: 179–84.

LEVITICUS 1–16
TRANSLATION, NOTES, AND COMMENTS

♦

PART I

THE SACRIFICIAL SYSTEM
CHAPTERS 1–7

◆

SACRIFICIAL INSTRUCTIONS DIRECTED TO THE LAITY (1:1–5:26)

THE BURNT OFFERING (1:1–17)

Introduction

1 ¹The Lord summoned Moses and spoke to him from the Tent of Meeting, and said: ²Speak to the Israelites, and say to them: When any person among you presents an offering of livestock to the Lord, he shall choose his offering from the herd or from the flock.

The Burnt Offering: From the Herd

³If his offering is a burnt offering from the herd, he shall offer a male without blemish. He shall bring it to the entrance of the Tent of Meeting, for acceptance on his behalf before the Lord. ⁴He shall lean his hand on the head of the burnt offering, that it may be acceptable on his behalf, to expiate for him. ⁵The bull shall be slaughtered before the Lord, and Aaron's sons, the priests, shall present the blood and dash the blood against all sides of the altar that is at the entrance to the Tent of Meeting. ⁶The burnt offering shall be flayed and quartered. ⁷The sons of Aaron the priest shall stoke the fire on the altar and lay out wood upon the fire. ⁸Then Aaron's sons, the priests, shall lay out the quarters, with the head and suet, on the wood that is on the fire upon the altar. ⁹Its entrails and shins shall be washed with water, and the priest shall turn all of it into smoke on the altar as a burnt offering, a food gift of pleasing aroma to the Lord.

From the Flock

¹⁰If his offering for a burnt offering is from the flock, of sheep or of goats, he shall offer a male without blemish. ¹¹It shall be slaughtered on the north side of the altar before the Lord, and Aaron's sons, the priests, shall dash its blood against all sides of the altar. ¹²When it has been quartered, the priest shall lay out the quarters, with the head and suet, on the wood that is on the fire upon the altar. ¹³The entrails and the shins shall be washed with water, and the priest shall present all of it and turn it into smoke on the altar. It is a burnt offering, a food gift of pleasing aroma to the Lord.

From Birds

¹⁴If his offering to the Lord is a burnt offering of birds, he shall present a turtledove or a young pigeon as his offering. ¹⁵The priest shall present it to the altar, pinch off its head and turn it into smoke on the altar; and the blood shall

be drained out against the side of the altar. ¹⁶He shall remove its crissum by its feathers, and cast it into the place of the ashes, at the east side of the altar. ¹⁷The priest shall tear it open by its wings, without severing [them], and turn it into smoke on the altar, upon the wood that is on the fire. It is a burnt offering, a food gift of pleasing aroma to the Lord.

INTRODUCTION TO CHAPTERS 1–7

In these chapters, the sacrifices are listed from the point of view of the donor: chaps. 1–3, the spontaneously motivated sacrifices (burnt, cereal, and well-being) and chaps. 4–5, the sacrifices required for expiation (purification and reparation). Their common denominator is that they arise in answer to an unpredictable religious or emotional need, and are thereby set off from the sacrifices of the public feasts and fasts that are fixed by the calendar (chaps. 9, 16, 23; cf. Num 28–29). Chapters 6 and 7 also deal with the same sacrifices, albeit in a different order, but from the point of view of the priests. The sacrificial instructions of chaps. 1–7 constitute the first divine pronouncement from the newly erected sanctuary (Exod 40), a fact that underscores the paramount importance of the cult. From a more practical view, however, these prescriptive sacrificial procedures had to come first in order to make sense of the descriptive sacrificial procedures of the consecration that follow: the priesthood and the inauguration of the public cult (chaps. 8–9).

NOTES

1: 1. *The Lord summoned Moses.* The text literally reads, "And he called to Moses." It connects with Exod 40:35, "And Moses could not enter the Tent of Meeting because the cloud rested on it and the presence of the Lord filled the Tabernacle." Indeed, because Moses could not enter the Tent, which at its erection was filled with the Lord's presence *(kābôd),* the Lord had to speak from the Tent while Moses stood outside in the Tabernacle court (*Tgs. Ps.-J., Yer.,* and *Neof.; Midr. Tanḥ.* 1:8; 2:1; Saadiah, Ibn Ezra, Rashbam, Ramban on Exod 40:35; Abravanel, Bekhor Shor, Ḥazzequni, Sforno). The uniqueness of this occurrence is proved by the fact that only here God's voice issues from the Tent. Every other time it originates from the Ark, with Moses standing inside the Tent but separated from the Ark by the veil (Exod 25:22; 30:6, 36; Num 7:89; 17:19); in the Priestly tradition, Moses never passes through the veil to stand before the Ark (Sforno—versus the rest of the medieval exegetes). See fig. 1.

The idea that Moses never entered the Holy of Holies in view of the Ark and the Cherubim is ostensibly contradicted by the unequivocal affirmation in the early epic tradition that Moses spoke to God "face to face" (Exod 33:11; Deut 34:10), "mouth to mouth" (Num 12:8), and beheld "the likeness of the

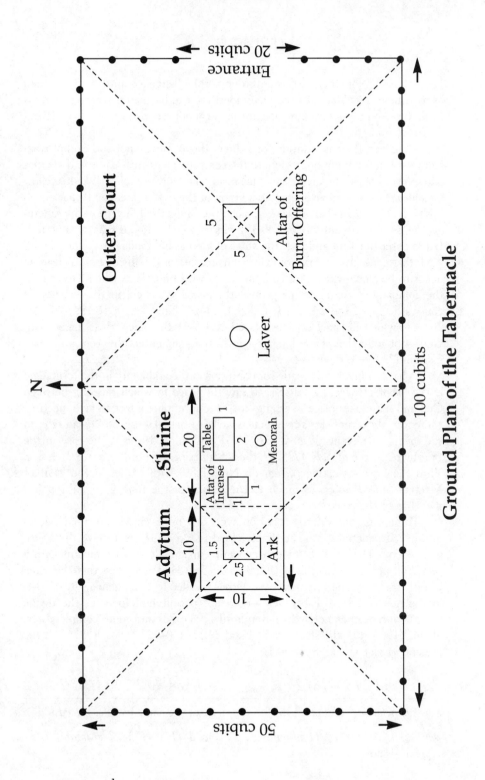

FIGURE 1

Ground Plan of the Tabernacle

Outer Court

Entrance 20 cubits

100 cubits

50 cubits

N

Shrine

Adytum

Altar of Burnt Offering

Laver

Table

Altar of Incense

Menorah

Ark

Lord" (ibid.). Nonetheless, this anthropomorphic language must be discounted as hyperbole. The "face" of the Deity must refer to his presence rather than his form, for "you cannot see my face, for man cannot see my face and live" (Exod 33:20; cf. Judg 6:22–23; 13:22).

Moreover, these attestations of a direct theophany do not and cannot stem from the Priestly tradition, which, to the contrary, takes great pains to deny that Moses ever beheld the divine presence inside the Holy of Holies. Like his fellow Israelites, Moses is only vouchsafed a vision of the kābôd (fire cloud) that envelops God (Num 9:15–16). Moreover, when the kābôd itself fills the entire sanctuary, he is unable to enter (Exod 40:35). His only distinction is that he is permitted to enter the Tent and hear the voice of God as he stands before the pārōket (veil) that conceals the Ark from view. The reason for this distinction is clear: he needs to be alone when God communicates with him. Thus when Moses is in the company of Aaron or his people, the kābôd is beheld in the Tabernacle courtyard (e.g., Exod 29:42–43; Lev 9:4, 23–24; Num 14:10; 16:19; 17:8, 15; 20:6), to which all Israel has access (see Lev 8:3–4). But when Moses meets with God—not for a theophany but for a revelation—he enters the Tent and takes his stand before the pārōket.

What has heretofore made for confusion is the ambiguity in the term ʾōhel môʿēd 'Tent of Meeting', that is to say, the place in which meeting between God and man takes place. Nothing in this term implies a face-to-face meeting. Moreover, the term bears a temporal as well as a spatial sense. môʿēd can refer to the time of a meeting (e.g., 2 Sam 20:5), and, indeed, this is the case in the Priestly texts, the môʿădê YHWH 'the set times of the Lord' (e.g., 23:1, 4, 37). Thus the Lord's meeting (nôʿad, cf. Num 7:89) with Moses in the Tent of Meeting (môʿēd) refers as much to the setting of the time, (i.e., an appointment) as to the place.

To be sure, one Priestly tradition avers that once, on Mount Sinai, Moses did indeed penetrate into the divine cloud (Exod 24:18) to receive the Decalogue (Exod 31:18; 34:28), which encounter made Moses' face radiant with a powerful, perhaps lethal, light (Exod 34:29–35). How is it then that the same Priestly tradition, the very next time Moses is called to an audience with God—in the newly erected Tabernacle—does not permit him to enter the divine cloud? Moreover, as noticed by Rendtorff (1985: 22) and more completely by Shama (1986: 40), the structure of Exod 24:15–18 + 25:1 closely parallels the present passage (Exod 40:35 + Lev 1:1).

Exod 24:15–18; 25:1	*Exod 40:34–38, Lev 1:1*
wayĕkas heʿānān ʾet-hāhār (15b)	*wayĕkas heʿānān ʾet-ʾōhel môʿēd* (34a)
wayyiškōn kĕbôd-YHWH ʿal-har sînay (16aα)	*ûkĕbôd YHWH mālēʾ ʾet-hammiškān* (34b)

wayyiqrā' 'el-mōšeh . . . mittôk
he'ānān (16b)

wayyiqrā' 'el-mōšeh mē'ōhel mô'ēd
(Lev 1:1)

kî 'ānan YHWH 'al-hammiškān
yômām
ûmar'eh kĕbôd YHWH kĕ'ēš 'ōkelet
wĕ'ēš tihyeh laylâ bô lĕ'ênê bĕnê
bĕrō'š hāhār lĕ'ênê bĕnê yiśrā'ēl (17)
yiśrā'ēl (38)

wĕlō'-yākōl mōšeh lābô' 'el-'ōhel
wayyābō' mōšeh bĕtôk he'ānān (18aα)
mô'ēd (35aα)

wayĕdabbēr YHWH 'ēlāyw (Lev
wayĕdabbēr YHWH 'el-mōšeh (25:1)
1:bα)

The congruence of these two passages is shattered by the opposition *wayyābō'/wĕlō'-yākōl lābô'* of the penultimate lines (Exod 24:18a/40:35a): in both passages the subject of *wayyiqrā' 'el-mōšeh* (Exod 24:16b; Lev 1:1) is *kĕbôd YHWH,* which also does not precede directly but is located in a previous sentence (Exod 24:16a; Exod 40:34b, 35b). At the Tent—in contradistinction to Sinai, where Moses is admitted into the divine cloud (Exod 24:18a)—he is expressly excluded from the Tent, which has been filled by the cloud (Exod 40:35aα), and he is constrained to remain in the courtyard and listen to the Lord's voice emerging "from" the Tent (Lev 1:1b). In this respect, Moses' initial experience of God at the Tent resembles his *initial* experience of God at Sinai, where God also called him, *wayyiqrā' 'ēlāyw,* before he spoke to him, *wayyōmer* (Exod 3:4), but then warned him not to proceed any closer (Exod 3:5; cf. *Sipra,* Nedaba par. 1:1–2).

The rabbis were clearly aware of the problem, for they explain that Moses entered the cloud atop Sinai only by divine dispensation and aid (*b. Yoma* 4b). At the newly erected Tabernacle, however, Moses reasoned differently: " 'To Mount Sinai, whose superiority was only temporary, and whose holiness was the holiness of three days, I could not ascend until the Word was spoken to me. But the superiority of this, the tabernacle of meeting, is an eternal superiority, and its holiness is an eternal holiness. It is certainly proper that I not enter therein until I am spoken to from before the Lord.' Then did the Word of the Lord call unto Moses" (*Tg. Ps.-J.;* cf. *Tg. Neof.; Midr. Exod. Rab.* 19:2). Thus, according to this rabbinic interpretation, this incident illustrates Moses' humility: he waited for God's invitation before entering. Be that as it may, the plain fact is that Moses did not enter the Tent at all: he had to learn the rules of the sacrificial cult (chaps. 1–5) while standing in the courtyard.

Despite the charm of the above-cited harmonization, the point made by the opening verses of Leviticus is altogether different. It implies that the Sinaitic theophany was unique in the history of the world; even a Moses was not vouchsafed this experience again. Thus when Moses hereafter will be permitted to enter the Tent it is to hear the voice of God, not to see him (note the verb *dibbēr* 'speak', Exod 25:22; 29:42; Lev 1:1; Num 7:89). Moses is barred from the Holy of Holies where the firecloud Presence has condescended upon the Cherubim-flanked Ark-throne. Moses must stand in the outer shrine, his view of the Ark blocked by the veil. And once the divine firecloud has in its first visitation to the newly erected Tabernacle spilled over to fill the entire Tent, Moses has no choice but to remain in the forecourt and await God's instructions.

What holds for Moses holds therefore for all other humans. When the priests dismantle the Tabernacle (ahead of its Levite porters), they must shield their eyes from the Ark by holding up in front of them the detached *pārōket*, with which they cover the Ark (Num 4:5). And even Aaron, who is commanded to enter the Holy of Holies annually to purge it of Israel's iniquities and impurities, is expressly warned that unless he blocks his vision by raising up a cloud of incense, his entry will prove fatal (16:2, 13). Perhaps, in this regard, P would claim Aaron's superiority over Moses. Whereas Moses is denied the privilege of ever entering the adytum and even of entering the divine cloud when it filled the entire Tabernacle (Exod 40:35), Aaron is granted the right to penetrate the incense cloud and enter the adytum each year on Yom Kippur (16:12–14). Thus the Priestly legislators downplayed the superhuman status that legend had attributed to the figure of Moses, not that they denied his greatness or, indeed, that he was the greatest of men. But, ever wary of subsequent veneration that might burgeon into a Moses cult, they took pains to underscore his mortal dimensions.

God's purpose in filling the Tent with his presence, clearly, is to sanctify it by contact (Sforno; cf. 1 Kgs 9:3, 7). Later, Israel's inaugural service within it will receive divine approbation by the emergence of the *kābôd* to incinerate the offerings on the altar (9:24; see 2 Chr 7:1). The same manifestation of divine approval is recorded at the dedication of Solomon's temple: "the priests were not able to remain and perform the service *(laʿămōd lěšārēt)* because of the cloud, for the Presence of the Lord filled the House of the Lord" (1 Kgs 8:11 [= 2 Chr 5:14]). Although Exodus and Kings are in agreement concerning the condensation of the Lord's cloud into the Tabernacle/Temple, the statement in Kings is factually in error. According to Priestly regulations, the high priest alone officiated within the Tabernacle/Temple (see on 24:3–4), whereas the priestly cadre officiated solely on the sacrificial altar. (Priests entered the shrine to assist the high priest and to look after its maintenance, but their officiating, *lěšārēt*, was restricted to the altar; see Exod 28:43; 30:20.) Thus when the Lord's presence filled Solomon's newly erected Temple, nothing prevented the priests from continuing to officiate at the sacrificial altar, which stood outside in the Temple court! Hence it may be concluded that the passage in Kings represents a deliberate attempt to attribute the same divine theophany in the Tabernacle to the Temple, despite the incongruous and illogical results. The secondary nature of the Kings account is thus betrayed.

THE SACRIFICES

A final remark on the immediately preceding words, the concluding verses of Exodus (Exod 40:36–38), is in order. By their content (Israel's guidance by the divine firecloud stated in full in Num 9:15–23) and by their language (the verbs are imperfects interrupting the narrative) these verses are clearly an interpolation. Furthermore, they only summarize Num 9:15–23. Why the need for this patent redundancy? The answer is crucial to an understanding of the redaction of Leviticus and its place within the Hexateuch. Exod 40:36–38 serves as a prolepsis of Num 9:15–23, thereby bracketing the intervening material (Lev 1–Num 9:14) as one giant parenthesis containing the laws given to Israel at Sinai following the revelation of the Decalogue and Book of the Covenant (Exod 20–24). Moreover, by occupying the very center of the Pentateuch it becomes the pivot in its palistrophic structure, thereby highlighting its supreme importance in Israel's formation as a covenant people. For details, see the introduction to vol. 2.

summoned. qārāʾ ʾel, an expression used in addressing a person who has shied away out of fear (e.g., Exod 34:31; Isa 40:2; Ehrlich 1908–14). By contrast, the rabbis, citing Exod 3:4 (where Moses is fearless!), conclude that Moses was always summoned before he was addressed (*Sipra,* Nedaba, par. 1).

and spoke. wayĕdabbēr YHWH, lit., "and the Lord spoke." Possibly, when Leviticus became a separate book, the Tetragrammaton was added (but in the wrong place) in order to provide a subject for this verse. As noted by M. Greenberg (1983: 176), however, Ezekiel 9:3–4 is precisely patterned after this passage. Not only is God's *kābôd* the distant subject of *wayyiqrāʾ* (cf. Exod 40:35b), but the subject switches to *YHWH,* just as in Lev 1:1. The Pesh. actually places the Tetragrammaton after the first word *wayyiqrāʾ* but, like the rendering adopted here, it is probably an interpretation of the MT and not a reflection of a variant Hebrew text.

Tent of Meeting. ʾōhel môʿēd, alternately called *miškān* 'tabernacle,' though the latter in P strictly refers to the innermost curtains that covered the Tent (see the NOTE at 8:10). As amply documented by Weinfeld (1983: 103–5), the tradition of the tent as a basic cult institution has its roots in the ancient Near East. A cultic tent ᏟⁱˢZA.LAM.GAR (= Akk. *kuštaru/kultaru*) is attested in Hittite texts (Popko 1960), where it is called DINGIRᴸᴵᴹ-*às* ᏟⁱˢZA.LAM.GAR 'the tent of the deity' (*KUB* XXXV 135, R.S. 20). In the myth of Elkunirsa, the Hittite version of the Ugaritic myth of El (*Elkunirsa = El qny ʾrs;* Otten 1953), Baal reaches the source of the Euphrates and enters the tent of Elkunirsa (Hoffner 1965). Similarly, we learn from the Ugaritic texts that El's tent *(qrš)* is also located at the source of the two rivers *UT* 51.4.20–26 = *CTA* 4.4.20–26 = *KTU* 1.4.4.20–26; Cross 1973: 36–39). It has also been suggested that the huge platform of the *bāmâ* at Tel Dan (Biran 1974: 40–41) and the platform uncovered at the Samaritan site of Tel-er-Ras on Mount Gerizim (Bull and Campbell 1968a, b) were originally the basis for tabernacles/tents (Cross 1981: 177–78).

That there are two traditions concerning the *ʾōhel môʿēd* 'Tent of Meeting' is clear from its two loci: according to the Priestly tradition it is located in the very center of the camp (e.g., Num 2:17; 3:38) and according to the epic tradition it is located outside the camp (e.g., Num 11:24–27; 12:4–5). Some scholars believe they are one and the same Tent. There is, however, a rabbinic source that speaks of two Tents, one inside the camp for cultic purposes, the other outside the camp for oracular purposes (*Midr. Exod. Rab.* 51:2; *Midr. Tanḥ.* Pekude 5; *Midr. Tanḥ. B.* Exod., 127; *Yal.* 1, 737; *Sipre Zuṭ* on Num 10:33). This rabbinic tradition is followed by most moderns (e.g., Haran 1960a).

The Priestly Tent also served an oracular function, for it was the focus of God's revelation. This can be inferred not only from the meaning of the name of the Tent, namely, "the Tent of Meeting between God and Israel," but also from the fact that the text frequently takes pains to explain it in that way (Num 7:89; 17:19; cf. Exod 25:22; 29:42–43; 30:6, 36). Thus LXX τοῦ μαρτυρίου and Vg *testimonii* are in error because they derive *mô'ēd* from the root *'wd* 'witness' and not *y'd* 'meet'. Because the outside Tent was clearly used for revelation (Num 11:16–30; cf. 12:4–10; Exod 33:7–11), then both Tent traditions agree that the basic purpose of the Tent was to provide a "meeting" between God and Israel (through the mediation of Moses).

They differ, however, concerning the mode of revelation. In the Priestly Tent only Moses can hear God's voice (and on occasion together with Aaron—but in the courtyard, not within the Tent, cf. Num 16:18–20; cf. 20:6); the outside Tent is available to anyone who seeks an oracle (Exod 33:7). In the latter instance, Moses or the petitioner stations himself inside, while the pillar of cloud descends upon the entrance (e.g., Num 12:5). This procedure is the prototype for the theophany to Moses and Elijah at Sinai/Horeb, when they enter the cleft of the rock and the cave, respectively (it may be the same place), as the presence of the Lord passes them by (Exod 33:22–23; 1 Kgs 19:9–14). Moreover, in the Priestly Tent, Moses is allowed to enter only the outer room, after the *kābôd* descends from the enveloping cloud onto the Ark-Cherubim throne located in the inner room of the Tent (see above). Thus Moses can only hear the voice of the Deity emanating from the inner side of the *pārōket*, but he cannot behold his presence; as noted, when God speaks to Aaron or allows Israel to behold his *kābôd*, the site of the revelation will not be inside the Tent at all but in the courtyard of the sacred enclosure. Nonetheless, despite these differences in the mode of revelation, the two Tent traditions concur that the Tent was the medium for revelation.

Another distinction is alleged: the outer Tent did not contain the Ark; in fact, it was empty. But R. de Vaux (1961a) has mustered compelling arguments to refute this allegation. First, the Ark is attested in other narratives as an oracular instrument (Judg 20:27–28; 1 Sam 3). Moreover, Joshua was stationed permanently within the Tent (Exod 33:11); the only possible reason would be to guard the Ark as Samuel did at Shiloh (1 Sam 3:3) and Eleazar at Kiriath-jearim (1 Sam 7:1). Then, too, if the Ark were not in the Tent of Meeting, where would it be? It would still require a shelter, a deduction that is confirmed by the tradition that God's presence was always inside a Tent (2 Sam 7:6); this must have been a hallowed tradition, else David could not have been prompted to erect a tent for the Ark as soon as he brought it to Jerusalem (2 Sam 6:17). And as for the objection that the Ark in the epic tradition was in the midst of the camp (Num 14:44), the term běqereb (Num 14:44) may only be a general reference without specifying any particular location (e.g., Deut 19:10; 23:15). Additionally, because the outside tent was used for oracular purposes (Exod 33:7–11), the probability is strong that it also contained the Ark.

Finally, the question needs to be asked whether this outside Tent also served a cultic function. Once again, the texts are silent. True, the epic tradition has Moses erecting altars and officiating on them (Exod 17:15; 24:3–8; cf. Ps 99:6) but, significantly, these acts take place before the Sinaitic revelation, in other words, before the cultic Tent of Meeting of the Priestly tradition was erected. Similarly, the Priestly tradition admits that during the consecration of the Aaronic priesthood, Moses himself officiated as a priest (Exod 29; Lev 8). After Sinai, however, the epic tradition says nothing concerning sacrifices or any other form of worship. Does this mean that the epic sources knew very well of a cultic Tent (a view that would be in consonance with the rabbinic tradition, cited above) but omitted any mention of it by sheer accident or that, conversely, the epic source had no such tradition and sacrifice continued to be offered upon improvised altars even after Sinai but references to them were edited out of the text because of their conflict with the Priestly Tent tradition? This question has yet to be resolved.

As shown by R. J. Clifford (1971: 211–27), the chances are that this term was borrowed from the Canaanites, where it meant "the tent of meeting (of the divine assembly under the presidency of the god El)." According to the Ugaritic texts, El lived in a *dd* 'tent' at the source of the cosmic waters (*KTU* 1.3.5.5–8 = *CTA* 3.5.13–16 = *UT* ʿnt 5.13–16; *KTU* 1.4.4.20–24 = *CTA* 4.4.20–24 = *UT* 51.4.20–24; *KTU* 1.6.1.32–36 = *CTA* 6.1.32–36 = *UT* 49.1.4–8; *KTU* 1.2.3.4–5 = *CTA* 2.3.4–5 = *UT* 129.3.4–5; *KTU* 1.17.6.46–48 = *CTA* 17.6.46–48 = *UT* 2 Aqht 6.46–48; cf. also the Hittite fragment of a Canaanite myth, Otten 1953: 125–30). The meeting of the divine assembly, the *puḫru môʿidi* (*KTU* 1.2.14–31 = *CTA* 2.1.14–31 = *UT* 137.14–31) presumably meets in the tent of El. The term *mʿd* also describes the assembly of eleventh-century Byblos (Wilson 1945: 245). From the fact that Moses is commanded to build the Tabernacle and its appurtenances according to the pattern that was shown to him on Mount Sinai (Exod 26:30; cf. Exod 25:9, 40; 27:8; Num 8:4), it is possible that he was shown the earthly sanctuary's heavenly counterpart. Other links between the Tent of Meeting and the Tent of El are that both are built with *qěrāšîm* 'wooden frames', are designed and constructed by divinely appointed craftsmen, and are staffed by a chief priest whose robes are trimmed with pomegranate decorations (Clifford 1971: 226). Thus the likelihood is strong that P reinterpreted a Canaanite term for the heavenly tent that brought the meetings of the divine assembly into the earthly shrine when God would meet with his people (Exod 29:42–43) through the agency of Moses. The Tent of Meeting as an oracular tent is attested not only in P (e.g., Exod 25:22; Num 7:89) but also in the older epic sources (e.g., Exod 33:7–11; Num 11:16–33; 12:4–10).

Another possible origin that merits consideration lies within the Hittite cult, where a tent, as the residence of the god, plays a significant role (Weinfeld 1983: 103–4). In view of the fact that David installed the Ark inside the tent he constructed in Jerusalem—one that may have been the model for the Tabernacle (Cross 1947)—and that Jerusalem had been occupied by Jebusites, a Hittite enclave, then the possibility exists that David constructed his Tent after the Hittite cultic prototype he found in Jerusalem.

Nevertheless, the immediate archetype for P's Tent of Meeting is not some mythic Canaanite model or hypothetical Hittite example but the ancient Israelite tradition of theophany at Sinai. P (Exod 24:15b–25:1) concurs with and, indeed, incorporates the epic tradition (Exod 19:20–20:1) that the Lord descended upon Sinai, but adds to it the notion that the Sinai summit was the site of only the initial "meeting" between Moses and God; when he transferred to the Tabernacle his earthly presence in the form of the fire *(kābôd)*-encased cloud, God thereby designated the Tabernacle as the site for all subsequent "meetings" between God and Moses, on the Sinaitic model—hence its name, the "Tent of Meeting" (cf. Westermann 1974: 120).

That the epic tradition concerning the Sinaitic theophany was compatible with P and, hence, incorporated by it (N.B., P forms the framework, Exod 19:1–2; 24:15–18, proving that, at least in this instance, P is not a source but a redaction!) was astutely recognized by Ramban, whose comment merits citation in full:

> Hereafter the Tabernacle in the Wilderness is zoned as Mount Sinai was zoned, since the Divine Glory was also thereon. And He commands: "the outsider *haqqārēb* shall be put to death" (Num 1:51) as He said there: "for he shall surely be stoned" (Exod 19:13); and He commands "let not (the Kohathites) go inside and witness the dismantling of the sanctuary" (Num 4:20) as He warned there: "lest they break through to the Lord to gaze" (Exod 19:21); and He commands: "you shall guard over the sanctuary and the altar" (Num 18:5) as He said there: "The priests also, who come near the Lord, must purify themselves . . . let not the priests or the people break through to come up to the Lord" (Exod 19:22, 24).

Ramban's parallels are striking, but they do not exhaust the comparison. For P, Mount Sinai is the archetype of the Tabernacle, and is similarly divided into three gradations of holiness. Its summit is the Holy of Holies; God's voice issues forth from there (Exod 19:20) as from the inner shrine (Exod 25:22; Num 7:89); the mountaintop is off limits to priest and layman alike (Exod 19:24b), and its very sight is punishable by death (Exod 19:21b), and so with its Tabernacle counterpart (cf. Lev 16:2 and Num 4:20); finally, Moses alone is privileged to ascend to the top (Exod 19:20b; see 34:2b) just as, later, the high priest is permitted entry to the inner shrine under special safeguards (Lev 16:2ff.).

The second division of Sinai is the equivalent of the outer shrine, marked off from the rest of the mountain by being enveloped in a cloud (Exod 20:21, 24:15bff.[P]). The entire mountain is not covered, however. Moses is able to ascend some distance with the priests and elders (24:1) and separately with Joshua (24:13) to the cloud perimeter, at which he probably leaves Joshua (32:17) when God calls him to enter the cloud. Thus, below the cloud is the third division, called "the bottom of the mountain" (19:17, 24:4), a technical term for the lowest portion of the mountain. This is where the altar and stelae are erected (24:4). It is equivalent to the courtyard, the sacred enclosure of the Tabernacle to which priests alone have access except for the forecourt "entrance," where the layman brings his sacrifice, provided he is in a pure state. This too is where the people witness the theophanies of the Tabernacle and Temple at their respective consecrations (Lev 9:4f., 24 and 2 Chr 7:3). Similarly, at Sinai: the nation is first purified (Exod 19:10–11, 14–15) and then brought out of the camp to the viewing stand at the foot of the mountain.

Thus the blazing summit, the cloud-covered slopes, and visible bottom rim correspond to Tabernacle divisions, and the analogous tripartite holiness of Mount Sinai and the Tabernacle is confirmed (for details, see Milgrom 1970a: 44–46).

2. *Speak to the Israelites.* The entire sacrificial system, though its operation is solely the job of the priests, should be revealed—and taught—to all Israelites. These opening words expose the gaping chasm that separates Israel from its neighbors. In ancient Mesopotamia, as A. L. Oppenheim informs us, "the common man was probably not permitted to enter the sanctuary" (1964: 186). A colophon to a Mesopotamian ritual text states that the commoner was barred not only from viewing the ritual but from viewing the text of the ritual: "This ritual which you perform, (only) the *qualified* person shall view. An outsider who has nothing to do with the ritual shall not view (it); if he does, may his remaining days be few! The informed person *(mudû)* may show (this tablet) to the informed person. The uninformed shall not see (it)—it is among the forbidden things of Anu, Enlil and Ea, the great gods" *(ANET*[3] 336). The *mudû,* rendered "informed person," is "the expert in a specific craft" *(CAD* M 2.165; Weinfeld 1963), in this case, the priest. In Egypt, as well, the people did not participate in any of the daily acts of the divine service: this was the affair of the priest-technicians (Sauneron 1960). Nor were they permitted access to the ritual

texts: "Do not show (the text) to anyone, not to your father, not to your son: it is for you alone" (Book of the Dead, 161.11f.).

Ancient Israel broke with this tradition: "the Torah commanded us by Moses is the heritage of the congregation of Jacob" (Deut 33:4). It is remarkable that the plethora of laws in Leviticus exclusively concerned with priestly duties are, in the main, taught to Israel and, with one exception (see below), mediated to the priests through Moses. The sacrificial rituals (chaps. 1–5), in which the commoner plays a significant role (see below), are commanded to the Israelites (1:2). The sacrificial laws that are the exclusive concern of the priests (chaps. 6–7) nonetheless conclude with "This is the ritual . . . when he commanded the Israelites to present their offerings to the Lord, in the wilderness of Sinai" (7:37–38), and even within this pericope, certain laws explicitly (7:22–27 and 28–34) and others implicitly (7:11–21) are directed to the Israelites. The service of the Day of Atonement, the sole prerogative of the high priest (16:1–28), nonetheless is followed with directions to the Israelites (vv 29–31). The priestly impurities and blemishes are, to be sure, addressed to the priests: "the Lord said to Moses: Speak to the priests, the sons of Aaron, and say to them" (21:1), yet they are concluded by the comment "Thus Moses spoke to Aaron and his sons and to all of the Israelites" (21:24). Another list of priestly impurities follows (22:1–16), only to lead into instructions addressed to both priests and commoners concerning blemished sacrifices (22:17–25). The diagnosis of contagious skin-diseases is left to the priests (13:1), but the ritual purification of their bearers—surely also the exclusive province of the priests—is revealed to Moses alone (14:1). Only one divine instruction is given solely to the priests— the prohibition to officiate in a state of intoxication (10:8–9)—and even here, the reason may be the very next verse, which neatly encapsules for the priest the essence of their service: "You must distinguish between the sacred and the common, and between the impure and pure" (10:10).

In any event, the "priests' manual," Israelite version, is not an esoteric doctrine, the zealously guarded secret of the priestly guild, but an open book or, more accurately, a school textbook for all Israel.

When. *kî,* the particle that heads up the main statement of a legal text; subdivisions are marked by *'im* (see vv 3, 10, 14; 3:1, 6, 12). The main statement declares that for a quadruped to qualify as a sacrifice it must be from the herd or the flock, in other words, a bovine, a sheep, or a goat (17:3). This statement also covers the well-being offerings of chap. 3 (see the COMMENT and at 3:1). The use of the relative conjunction *kî* also indicates the conditional and optional nature of the law that follows; the sacrifices discussed therein are not mandatory but voluntary.

any person (among you). 'ādām . . . (mikkem): this phrase is found again with *kî* in the laws of scale disease (13:2) and corpse contamination (Num 19:14), which, together with other impurity laws, are applicable not just to Israelites but to all humans (see also 5:3; Num 31:19). Here, however, the address is to the Israelites, *mikkem* 'of you'. The resident alien *(gēr)* is only required to bring mandatory sacrifices, brought for the violations of prohibitive commandments (Milgrom 1982a); hence he is exempt from the voluntary sacrifices mentioned in Lev 1–3. Why, then, it may be asked, is concern for the resident alien and foreigner included in later sacrificial laws (22:18b, 25), which are also voluntary? There the subject is sacrificial defects that invalidate the sacrifice and are offensive to the deity; here, however, the purely voluntary nature of the sacrifice eliminates any concern for the non-Israelite.

This being so, why does the text then address the Israelite as *ʾādām?* The answer must be that *ʾādām* includes both male and female and is the equivalent of *nepeš* 'person' (2:1; 4:2; etc.) or *ʾîš ʾô ʾiššâ* 'man or woman' (Exod 21:29; Lev 13:29, 38; 20:27; Num 5:6; 6:2). See Abravanel, who points to "He called them (Adam and Eve) *ʾādām*" (Gen 5:2). Nonetheless, the possibility must be entertained that originally the text read *ʾādām* 'anyone' (without *mikkem*) and, in consonance with 22:18–25, applied not only to the Israelite but to the resident alien and foreigner as well (as in 5:3; 7:21; 22:5; 24:17, 20, 21; but see the Note on 13:2).

presents. yaqrîb: the verb *hiqrîb (qrb, hiphʿil)* is capable of a wide range of meanings but has the specific sense of "offer, present" in a cultic setting. In this respect it is similar to Akk. *qerēbu* (D stem *qurrubu*) and Ug. *šqrb* (also a causative stem; *UT* 2.1.14, 18; 125.44). This meaning is unique to P. In other texts it either means "to come close, approach" (e.g., Gen 12:11; Exod 14:10) or "to present" tribute *(minḥâ),* gifts *(ʾeškār)* to a ruler (e.g., Judg 3:18; 1 Kgs 5:1 [*higgîš*]; Ps 72:10). It is this latter meaning, originating in the language of diplomacy, that may have been borrowed by the priests and applied to the divine rule, the king of kings (Paran 1983: 208–10). The reason the verb precedes *mikkem* instead of following it is unclear.

offering. qorbān, the nominal derivative of *qrb,* lit., "that which is brought near, presented, offered." This term is found exclusively in P and in Ezek 2:28; 40:43 and is not limited to offerings for the altar but applies to any sanctuary gift, such as draft animals and carts (Num 7:3) or spoils of war (Num 31:50). The LXX renders correctly δῶρον 'gift'. Archaeological excavations have turned up objects, inscribed with the word *qorbān,* for presenting or preparing offerings (Mazar 1969: plate 10, no. 5).

livestock (bĕhēmâ). According to the Masoretic accentuation, this term is part of the apodosis, to be read "When any of you presents an offering to the Lord, he shall choose his offering from livestock, from the herd or from the flock." The reason for this reading is to account for the inclusion of birds (vv 14–17) under this rubric, namely, that someone who wishes to bring a sacrifice can choose either livestock or a bird (see at vv 14–17, below). Then, too, this verse would correspond to 2:1: someone who wishes to bring a tribute offering, "his offering shall be . . ." (Dillmann and Ryssel 1897). The fault with this interpretation, however, is that *bĕhēmâ* embraces all quadrupeds (see 11:2), including impure ones, such as donkeys (Num 31:9, 28). Thus it could not be part of the apodosis, for no one would even conceive of bringing an impure animal to the altar. Moreover, this verse also heads the section of the well-being offering that is limited to animals from the herd and flock (see at 3:1) and thus fits v 2b as here rendered. Interestingly, Saadiah, Ramban, and Abravanel, without giving reasons, clearly understood the verse in this way.

he shall choose. taqrîbû, lit., "you shall present." The reason that there is a switch here to second-person plural, while in the rest of the chapter the offerer is in the third-person singular, is not altogether clear. Possibly, in contrast to the general tenor of the chapter, which speaks of a voluntary offering, the text here wishes to emphasize that the limitation of the animal to the herd and flock is obligatory; in other words, *all of you* make sure that this rule is observed *(Da'at Soferim).* The more likely reason, however, is that this verse is part of the general introduction (vv 1–2) to chaps. 1 and 3; hence, a discrete pericope and the second-person plural *taqrîbû* are but the logical transformation of the clause containing the same verb earlier in the verse *yaqrîb mikkem* 'any of you [plural] presents'.

from the herd or from the flock (min habbāqār ûmin haṣṣō'n). The use of the generic names indicates that this heading applies to more offerings than just the *'ōlâ;* the latter's animals, being all male, could have been expressed as *par, ben bāqār* 'bull' (v 5), and the like, or with the addition *zākār* 'male' (vv 3, 10). The well-being offering is also subsumed under this heading and is discussed in the NOTE on 3:1.

3. *burnt offering ('ōlâ).* This is the first sacrifice to be discussed. The rendering "burnt offering," as well as its antiquity, distribution, function, and purpose are discussed in the COMMENT below. A number of reasons combine to argue for awarding the *'ōlâ* pride of place: its hoary antiquity, popularity, versatility, and frequency (see the COMMENT). To these reasons, others can be added: as implied by the text, it is the first sacrifice (and last) each day (see at v 7); "Why is it called *'ōlâ?* Because it is superior *('elyônâ)* to all sacrifices . . . (because) no creature partakes of it but all of it ascends *('ōlâ)* to the Holy One who is superior *('elyôn)" (Midr. Tanḥ.* B *Zav,* a). Nevertheless, the most probable reason is neither historical nor ethical but simply and banally administrative: in every sacrificial series in prescriptive texts, the *'ōlâ* is listed first (see the COMMENT). Because the male herd or flock animal (but not the bird) may also be brought as a well-being offering (chap. 3), it is presumed by the text that the offerer himself will state its designation to the priest at the time of its presentation, most likely during the hand-leaning rite (see the NOTE on 1:4).

the herd. The generic term *habbāqār* includes all bovines and can also be rendered "cattle." Individual members of the species used in sacrifices and other rituals are the *par* 'bull' (4:4), also called *ben habbāqār* (1:5); *šôr* 'ox' (9:4); *pārâ* 'cow' (Num 19:2); *'ēgel* 'calf' (Lev 9:3); and *'eglâ* 'heifer' (Deut 21:3). Being the most valuable of the sacrificial animals, it is always listed first in the administrative, prescriptive texts (e.g., in Num 7:15–87 and 28:11–29:38), as it is here. The infelicitous *habbāqār zākār*, lit., "the herd, male," instead of the expected *ben habbāqār* 'bull' (cf. 1:5) is due to the stylistic need to strike a symmetrical balance with the prescription for a bovine in the *šĕlāmîm* offering (3:1), which can be either male or female (Rendtorff 1985: 28).

male. The male, *zākār*, is preferred because it is "more complete, more dominant than the female" (Philo, *Laws* 1. 200). Yet the more likely reason is that the male is economically the more expendable, the female being the one to supply milk and offspring.

without blemish. *tāmîm*, adjective from the verb *tāmam* 'be complete' (e.g., 23:15; Deut 31:24, 30). The same requirement prevailed in the Mesopotamian cult (Falkenstein and von Soden 1953: 275) and, presumably, in all others. The constant repetition of this requirement in the sacrificial laws (e.g., 3:1, 6, 9; 4:3, 23, 28, 32; 5:15, 18, 25; see esp. 22:17–25; Deut 17:1) is echoed in the prophet's charge that people were offering up defective animals (Mal 1:8–14). According to Philo, this requirement was scrupulously checked by the officiating priest (*Laws* 1. 166). In the priestly writings, *tāmîm* only refers to physical perfection of (sacrificial) animals (except for 23:15; 25:30, referring to time). Contrast D (and other sources), where it implies only spiritual perfection (Deut 18:13). Indeed, in the two pericopes that speak of the unblemished requirement of sacrifices, the word *tāmîm* is conspicuously missing (Deut 15:21; 17:1; noted by Paran 1983: 195).

bring it to (yaqrîbennû 'el). The same word is used here as in vv 2a, 2b, and 3b, but this time with *'el*, the preposition of motion. All instances of *hiqrîb (higîš) 'el* have as their object either God (Num 16:5, 9), the altar (Lev 1:15; 2:8 [= Num 5:25]; 6:7), the sanctuary entrance (Exod 29:4; 40:12; Lev 1:3), or the priest (Exod 28:1; Lev 2:8; 9:9), purposely chosen to express the notion of proximity (Milgrom 1970a: 37 n. 141). See further the NOTES on 2:8 and 9:9.

entrance of the Tent of Meeting. The expression *petaḥ 'ōhel mô'ēd* has been understood as a technical term for the narrow corridor within the sacred enclosure that extended between the entrance gate and the courtyard altar (see fig. 1), in other words, the forecourt (Haran 1978: 184). But the word *petaḥ* refers either to the opening of a structure or to the space outside and in front of it. Thus the *petaḥ* of the house (14:38; Gen 19:11; Deut 22:21; 2 Sam 11:9) and the *petaḥ* of the gate (1 Kgs 22:10; 2 Kgs 7:3; Ezek 46:3) designate—in these cited instances—the areas immediately in front of the opening (N.B. 1 Kgs 22:10, where the *petaḥ* of the gate is designated as the *gōren* 'the threshing floor'). Thus, the whole courtyard from the entrance of the courtyard to the entrance of the Tent was accessible to the layman (S. Rattray). It is there that he was directed to perform certain vital acts with his animal sacrifice, in preparation for the altar ritual of the priest: presentation, hand-leaning, slaughter, flaying (vv 3–6), and elevating (7:30). Also in the same area the people assembled both as spectators (8:3–4) and as participants (9:5).

The very fact that the sacrificial altar is located in "the entrance to the Tent of Meeting" (v 5) is clear evidence that the altar does not mark the boundary of the area but is, in its entirety, circumscribed by it. Moreover, that the lay offerer slaughters his flock animal "on the north side of the altar" (v 11)—rather than on its eastern side—indicates, with even greater certitude, that the layman was not barred from entering any part of the courtyard. Theoretically, he might even touch the altar with impunity (see chap. 7, COMMENT B); only encroachment, namely, officiating upon it, was forbidden to him (Milgrom 1981b: 282–87). Indeed, the tradition of lay processions around the altar of the Second Temple on the Feast of Tabernacles (*m. Sukk.* 4:5) also argues for the proposition that the entire Tabernacle courtyard was accessible to the laity (Milgrom 1970a: 54–55 n. 211). Furthermore, that the two curtains, both at the entrance to the Tent and at the entrance to the courtyard, are of identical materials and workmanship (Exod 26:36; 27:16) means that the entire courtyard bears the same degree of holiness (S. Rattray). That this is so is proved by the purgation of the entire sanctuary on Yom Kippur with the exception of the courtyard, an indication that the entire courtyard is homogeneous in its status, and that its sanctity is of a lesser quality than the rest of the Tabernacle and its sancta and, hence, accessible to the laity (see also the NOTE on 6:9). Finally, and conclusively, when the text wishes to distinguish between the entrance to the courtyard and the entrance to the Tent shrine, it calls the latter *petaḥ ʾōhel môʿēd* (Exod 38:30–31; Num 4:25–26; cf. Exod 26:36; 39:38). Thus its area must be coterminous with the entire courtyard.

In the Herodian Temple, the courtyard was preceded by an outer court called "The Court of Women," implying that women did not enter into the inner, sacrificial court. By contrast, rabbinic tradition affirms that women did enter it in order to perform their sacrifices (*t. ʿArak.* 2:1), a clear vestige of the pentateuchal rule (e.g., 12:6; 15:29; Num 5:16, 18, 25; 6:10, 13) that a woman had as much right as a man to be in "the entrance to the Tent of Meeting."

According to rabbinic tradition, the second, innermost half of the Tabernacle courtyard was of a higher grade of holiness (*m. Kelim* 1:9; *Sipre* Zuta on Num 5:2). The main difference was that laymen and disqualified priests had no access to it (*t. Kelim B. Qam.* 1:6) and that its defilement was of a more severe order than the defilement of the rest of the courtyard (*m. ʿErub.* 10:15). The rabbinic name for it, *bên hāʾûlām wĕlammizbēaḥ* 'between the porch [of the temple] and the altar', is biblical (Joel 2:17), but its holier status is not; the Bible contains not a single law concerning its special sanctity. But it does harbor a hint: King Joash raises money for needed temple repairs by installing a collection chest near the altar. The account reads: "The priestly guards of the threshold deposited there all the money" (2 Kgs 12:10). Thus laymen were permitted entry into the court, but there they transferred their monetary donation to threshold priests who, in turn, deposited it in the improvised chest. The latter, being at "the right side of the altar" (ibid.), was off limits to the laity, and only priests had access to it. The unanimity of the tannaitic sources—reflecting the historic reality at the end of the Second Temple period—reinforces the supposition that this dual division of the temple forecourt goes back to biblical times.

According to Y. Aharoni, the courtyard of the Israelite sanctuary at Arad "was divided by a step (a remnant of the ancient altar) into outer and main parts" (1968: 22). As the floor plans clearly indicate (ibid., figs. 12, 15, 16), the dividing step projects from the altar itself, from the side facing the shrine. This division conforms precisely with the biblical terminology *bên hāʾûlām wĕlammizbēaḥ* and provides graphic evidence of the subdivision of the temple courtyard in biblical days (Milgrom 1970a: n. 166). Still, caution should prevail in projecting what may have been the temple reality onto the Tabernacle (cf. also the NOTE on 6:9).

It is of interest to note that the equivalent space in the Sumerian temple, the *bar-kù* 'holy outside', was used by the gods for their private strolls. Enki "circles the Barku" in contemplation. Baʾ u and Ningirsu celebrate their anniversary on New Year's Day in the Barku (Gudea, Cyl B XVIII 1–3; cf. Heimpel 1981: 110, line 95).

for acceptance on his behalf. lirṣōnô, in other words, if the offering is unblemished *(tāmîm,* 3aβ) it will be acceptable on your behalf, but "if you present a lame or sick one—doesn't it matter? Just offer it to your governor: *hăyirṣĕkā,* will he accept you? *hăyiśśāʾ pānêkā,* will he show you favor?—said the Lord of Hosts" (Mal 1:8; see also Lev 22:19–20 and *Sipra,* Nedaba par. 3:13). From this citation two things can be derived. First, to be acceptable *(rāṣôn)* to God (and the governor), the sacrifice must be unblemished. This deduction is corroborated by the pericope on disqualifying blemishes (22:17–30), which contains no fewer than seven instances of the root *rṣh* (vv 19, 20, 21, 23, 25, 27, 29). Second, the terms *rāṣâ* and *nāśāʾ pānîm* are semantically equivalent, so the function of the *ʿōlâ* here is to elicit the favor of the deity. Thus it can hardly be an accident that the nominal derivative *rāṣôn* appears with the burnt offering (22:19–20; Jer 6:20; cf. Isa 60:7) and the well-being offering (19:5; 22:21, 29) but never with the purification and reparation offerings. These latter two sacrifices serve strictly expiatory functions (see the COMMENT below and chaps. 4–5). Their offerers approach God under the burden of sin; they seek his pardon, not his pleasure. That the prophet blames the priests for blemished oblations (Mal 1:7–8, 13) presumes that, at least in Temple times, each offering underwent priestly inspection before it was permitted near the altar. Here, however, it is the offerer himself who must assume the blame for a defective oblation. The *ṣîṣ* on the high priest's turban acts *lĕrāṣôn* for Israel in case their sacrifices are defective (Exod 28:38). The rabbis, perhaps correctly, limit its effect to their inadvertent defilement *(m. Zebaḥ.* 8:12; *m. Menaḥ.* 3:3). The subject of *lirṣōnô* is the sacrifice, the object, the offerer, and is so always (Lev 19:5; 22:19, 20). Its verbal form acts similarly (see v 4).

The verb *rāṣâ* and its nominal derivative *rāṣôn* bear two meanings in BH:

"be accepted"/"acceptance" and "desire"/"desire." The latter meaning, probably stemming from Aramaic *rĕʿâ*, is found only in the postexilic books of the Bible: Esther, Daniel, Ezra, Nehemiah, Chronicles, in some late Psalms (40:9; 103:21; 143:10; 145:16) and exclusively in postbiblical literature (e.g., Sir 15:15; 50:22; 1QS 9:22–24; CD 2.21.22; 3.11–12; *t. Pesaḥ.* 3:19; *m. ʾAbot* 5:20). The transition is detectable in Malachi, who adds the word *miyyedĕkem* (Mal 1:10, 13), which makes the expression *rāṣâ miyyad* equivalent to *biqqēš miyyad* 'desire' (2 Sam 4:11; Isa 1:12 [Paran 1983: 210–11]). The fact that there is no trace of this later meaning in the Priestly writings but that all attestations of *rāṣâ/rāṣôn* bear the older meaning of "be accepted"/"acceptance" is another bit of terminological evidence for the antiquity of P (see the Introduction, §B). This meaning is corroborated by those passages in which the parallel synonym is blessing (Deut 33:11, 23–24) and love (Prov 3:12) and the antonym is anger and abomination (Gen 49:6; Prov 11:1; 19:12).

before the Lord. lipnê YHWH, that is to say, within the sacred precincts. It can also refer, in a more limited sense, to the outer court area, "the entrance to the Tent of Meeting" (cf. 1:11 with 3:8). See at v 5.

4. *lean his hand (sāmak yādô).* As noted by Wessely (cf. also Daube 1956b: 224–25), *sāmak yad* must be distinguished from *šāt/śām yad* 'place the hand' (e.g., Gen 48:18). When the object is the head, the latter expression refers to the act of blessing (e.g., Gen 48:14); the hand may rest on the head lightly. By contrast, *sāmak* implies pressure. Thus *wĕsāmak yādô ʿal-haqqîr* 'he shall lean his hand on the wall' (Amos 5:19); *wayyilpōt šimšôn ʾet-šĕnê ʿammûdê hattāwek . . . wayyissāmēk ʿălêhem* 'Samson embraced the two middle pillars . . . and leaned against them' (Judg 16:29); *haqqāneh hārāṣûṣ hazzeh . . . ʾăšer yissāmēk ʾîš ʿālāw* 'this broken reed . . . which anyone who leans upon it' (2 Kgs 18:21 [= Isa 36:6]; cf. also Ps 81:6).

Philology is confirmed by practice. The Tannaites, many of whom lived during the time of the Temple (*m. Beṣa* 2:4; *m. Ḥag.* 2:2–3) dispute whether the rite of hand-leaning may be observed on festivals. The basis of this controversy is the fact that pressure on a live animal constitutes work and is, hence, forbidden on a holy day. Indeed, the Amoritic sages explicitly derive from this prohibition that the act of *sāmak* must be with "all one's strength" (*b. Ḥag.* 16b; cf. *b. Zebaḥ.* 33a), and *Tg. Ps.-J.* on this verse expressly renders this expression *wĕyismôk bĕtûqpāʾ yad yĕmînêh* 'he shall lean his right hand forcefully'. (That the right hand was used may also have been the accepted practice: cf. *b. Menaḥ.* 93b).

By contrast, the equivalent ritual among the Hittites not only does not require hand-leaning, but does not even call for hand-laying. Occasionally the subject *-šan tuwaz QATAM dal* 'places the hand from a distance over'. This implies that he need not come into direct contact with the object but merely places his hand over it or at a distance from it. "The king, for example, would not have to dirty his hand when performing the gesture with moist foods, such as a liver" (D. Wright, written communication; see now Wright 1986). Another significant difference in the Hittite rite is that it was rarely performed with live animals (Wright 1986: 442 n. 56).

The explanations of this rite fall into four categories: (a) *transference* of sin to the animal (Shadal; Volz 1901) or of ownership to God (Dillmann and Ryssel 1897); (b) *identification*, "intended to penetrate the animal with the soul of the offerer" (Dussaud 1941: 72), or the animal, turning into smoke, brings the offerer nearer to God (Hoffmann 1953); (c) *declaration*, to enable the offerer to declare its purpose (Büchler 1928: 418; Péter 1977) or his innocence (Philo, *Laws* 1. 202–4); (d) *ownership* (Pedersen 1940: 366; Robinson 1942; Lohse 1951; Eichrodt 1959: 164–66; de Vaux 1964: 28; Ringgren 1966: 169).

The key to understanding this rite is that only one hand is employed. So Ibn Ezra, who reasons as follows: that two hands are explicitly stipulated for the scapegoat (16:21) clearly implies that the latter differs from all other hand-leanings on animals, which, therefore, must involve only one hand (see also *Tg. Ps.-J.*, *Seper Hamibḥar*, and *Keter Torah*). This insight automatically eliminates the transference theory, which invariably requires two hands (Milgrom 1976g: 765b; Péter 1977; cf. Sansom 1982–83). Identification is alien to biblical thought both because it is magical and because it presupposes the belief that death brings one close to God. Declaration may have occurred but, as will be shown, was independent of hand-leaning.

First the question needs be asked: was hand-leaning required for all sacrifices? In the prescription for the *ʾāšām*, the reparation offering (7:1–7), hand-leaning is conspicuously absent. In the Priestly tradition, this is the only sacrifice commutable in money, which may be the reason that hand-leaning is not required. Alternatively, the absence of the rite may be due to the nature of the text itself: it is embedded in a section that deals exclusively with the duties of the priests (6:1–7:21), not those of the laity. Nonetheless, because the sacrificial procedure for the *ʾāšām* is missing in 5:14–26 (where it rightfully belongs) and because some of the provisions of 7:1–5 duplicate the previously mentioned laws (e.g., 7:3–5 parallels 3:3–5, 9, 11, 14–16; 4:8–10), even the repetition of the hand-leaning would have been expected and, hence, its absence from the *ʾāšām* can hardly be accidental. Moreover, there is a supportive rabbinic tradition that specifically exempts the *ʾāšām* from hand-leaning (Rashi on *b. Ned.* 70b; Tosafot on *b. Qidd.* 45b), especially for the *měṣōrāʿ* (*b. Zebaḥ.* 33a). Thus it is plausible to conclude that whenever the *ʾāšām* animal was brought, hand-leaning was practiced. But because the offerer was given the option of commuting the *ʾāšām* to money (except in case of the scale-diseased person; see at 14:21), hand-leaning could not be required (Milgrom 1976f: n. 48).

The absence of hand-leaning whenever the *ʾāšām* was presented in money supports the reason given above for the rite. Because the offerer holds the silver in his hands there is no further need for hand-leaning: clearly it is his. The same reason obtains for exempting the cereal offering from hand-leaning; it too is brought in the sacrificer's hands, and no further proof of ownership is required. (The appearance of protean *wĕhiqrîbâ* 'it shall be presented' following *wĕhēbē'tā* 'you shall bring' [2:8] implies a special ritual of presentation, which may be the equivalent of hand-leaning.) Finally, the absence of hand-leaning in the procedure for the *'ōlâ* of birds may also be due to the same circumstance: the bird is carried in the offerer's hands, so hand-leaning occurs automatically (see the COMMENT on vv 14–17).

Thus the hand-leaning rite seems not to be required whenever the offering could be carried by hand, as in the cases of the *'āšām* money, the cereal offering, and the burnt offering of birds. It is required for all quadrupeds because they would have to be dragged in by rope or bought from the sanctuary stock. In either case, ownership would have to be established. Without authenticated ownership, the sacrifice would be invalid. If a declaration accompanied the hand-leaning to specify the purpose of the sacrifice, it was a discrete, independent act (contra Péter 1977).

Recently, M. Paran (1985) has proposed that a distinction must be made between the expressions "lean the hand upon *('al)*" and "lean the hand upon the head *('al rō'š)*," the former denoting that the object becomes the substitute for the subject and the latter, that the sin of the subject is transferred to the object. His proposal fails on two counts: (1) not all sacrifices are for expiation. The experience of joy motivates sacrifice as much as sin. Even though, as will be argued (COMMENT on chap. 3), the *šĕlāmîm*, brought exclusively for joy, is accompanied by guilt feelings for having taken the life of the animal for the sake of its meat, the same guilt is not present in the *'ōlâ* of joy (22:18; Num 15:3), which is burned in its entirety on the altar. (2) There are two cases in which the hand-leaning is not expressly on the head: the Levites (Num 8:10) and Joshua (Num 27:18, 23; Deut 34:9). It is hardly an accident that the objects are persons and not animals. In other words, the placement upon the head is taken for granted. Proof that this is so is provided by a third case, in which the head is omitted in the hand-leaning rite for *ḥaṭṭā't* goats (2 Chr 2:23), and even Paran (1985: 119) must admit that it took place on the heads of the animals.

By the process of elimination, ownership is the only theory remaining. It receives striking support from Hittite ritual (Wright 1986). Although two rituals seem to indicate a transference motif (*KUB* 4.32ff.; Gurney 1977: 49, perhaps employing both hands?), all of the numerous others can be explained as rites of ownership. In them the king (or offerer) places his hand over the offering— bread, wine, liver, food tray, and so on. Strikingly, when the king himself continues to perform the ritual, there is no such rite (Wright 1986: 443 n. 62). The conclusion is inescapable that, in Hittite ritual at least, the placement of the hand is required so that regardless of who officiates, the offering will be credited to its owner. The same rationale may have obtained in Israel. Indeed, the Tannaites explicitly deny hand-leaning by proxy, and they insist that it be performed by the offerer (*Sipra*, Nedaba 4:2; *m. Menaḥ.* 9:8–9; *t. Menaḥ.* 10:9–10;

b. Menaḥ. 92b). Moreover, if the animal belongs to more than one person, all perform the rite together or, if there are too many, they perform it separately (Lev 4:15; 8:14; Num 8:12; 2 Chr 29:23; *t. Menaḥ.* 10:14–15). Finally, additional support may stem from the Akk. idiom *emēdu qātu* 'place the hand', the semantic equivalent of *sāmak yād*, which in legal texts clearly designates ownership *(CAD).*

The Tannaites exempt the public sacrifices from hand-leaning except for the bull brought by the *ʿēdâ* (4:15) and the scapegoat (16:21) (*m. Menaḥ.* 9:7). The latter, as noted above, falls into a different category of hand-leaning, and the former can hardly be called public: it is brought for the aggregate sins committed by the individual members of the community. The rabbinic tradition may, however, be perfectly right in connection with the fixed offerings of the calendar, which, representing no individual(s) in particular, would not have required hand-leaning. The Tannaites also exempt the *pesaḥ*, firstling, and animal tithe from this rite. Again, their tradition makes sense: all three are mandatory, not voluntary, offerings (Exod 12:3–6; 13:15; Lev 27:26, 32, 33); their sacrifice brings no special favor to their offerers.

Finally, notice should be taken of Philo's comment that hand-leaning was always preceded by hand-washing (*Laws* 1. 198; but see the NOTE on "all sides," v 5). Biblical texts provide indirect evidence to support his contention (e.g., Ps 26:6). The question of ablutions before sacrifice is discussed in chap. 15, COMMENT C. For further details on the hand-leaning rite, see Milgrom and Wright 1986; Wright 1986.

it may be acceptable on his behalf. wĕnirṣâ lô, the *niphʿal* denominative of *rāṣôn* (see at v 3). Again, the subject is the sacrifice (Tgs., Rashbam) and the dative object is the offerer (not the deity: Ramban). Their equivalence is made clear by their joint occurrence in the same pericope dealing with sacrificial blemishes: *lōʾ lĕrāṣôn yihyeh lākem* (22:20); *lōʾ yērāṣû lākem* (20:25), which in both cases means "will not be acceptable on your behalf." The "acceptance" here in v 4 differs from the "acceptance" in v 3. Whereas the latter is dependent on the unblemished condition of the animal, the "acceptance" in this verse relates to the hand-leaning rite. The two dative suffixes attached to this and the following verb, *kipper,* both mean "for, on behalf of," thereby emphasizing the indispensability of the hand-leaning by the offerer himself in his quest for "acceptance" and "expiation" (see below). Rabbinic tradition also insists that whereas the offerer may assign other lay rites, such as slaughtering, flaying, and washing, to others, he must perform the hand-leaning rite by himself *(Sipra,* Nedaba 4:2; *b. Menaḥ.* 92b).

to expiate (lekappēr). The burnt offering is here assigned an expiatory function that is attested in only a few cultic texts (9:7 [with the *ḥaṭṭāʾt*]; 14:20 [with the *minḥâ*]; 16:24 [the *ʿōlâ* alone, *pace* Janowski 1982: 190; Rendtorff 1985: 36]) and in one narrative (Job 1:5; 42:8). The possibility that this constitutes the original function of the *ʿōlâ,* which was in private offerings replaced by the exclusive expiatory sacrifices, the *ḥaṭṭāʾt* and *ʾāšām*, will be discussed in the COMMENT below. The analysis of the verb *kipper* is the subject of chap. 16, COMMENT F.

for him (ʿālāyw). For clear examples of this usage of *ʿal*, see Gen 19:7; Judg 9:17; 1 Kgs 2:18; Pss 44:23; 69:8; Job 42:8, always with the verb *kipper*.

5. *The bull. ben habbāqār*, lit., "a male bovine," equivalent to *par* 'bull' (Num 7:15; 15:24; 23:2; 29:36). The former term was chosen to be in keeping with the heading in v 3).

shall be slaughtered. wěšāḥaṭ, lit., "and he [the offerer] shall slaughter" (see 1 Sam 1:25 LXX, 4Q). Nevertheless, anyone was permitted to perform the immolation (see *Tg. Ps.-J.*; Jos., *Ant.* 3.226), even foreign slaves (Ezek 44:9). It is a mistake to claim that the rabbis restricted sacrificial slaughter only to priests; so Eilberg-Schwartz 1986: 164. That the slaughtering could be done by anyone is proved by the text of the priestly consecration service: although Aaron and his sons thrice perform the hand-leaning rite *(yismĕkû;* plural), the slaughtering is described each time as *wayyišḥaṭ*, singular, which can only be rendered as "and it was slaughtered" (8:14–15, 18–19, 22–23).

Ezekiel's demand that immolation should be the Levites' function (Ezek 44:10–11) was apparently ignored (Ezra 8:20). Philo's claim that it was done by priests (*Laws* 1. 199; see *Midr. Lev. Rab.* 22:7) is correct only in this sense: priests (and Levites) immolated their personal sacrifices (9:8, 12; 16:11) and those in the fixed public cult (9:15, 18; 16:5; Ezra 6:20; 2 Chr 29:24; 30:17; 35:6, 11). Certainly, the extrabiblical evidence also points in this direction. Among the pre-Islamic bedouins of northern Arabia, as among the patriarchs, sacrifice was performed on a simple stone by heads of families or clans but "on occasions of large bedouin assemblies, there was a more solemn form of sacrifice in which the immolation of the victim was performed by the *sâdin*" (Cody 1969: 15). Also Phoenician and Punic inscriptions indicate an immolator *(zbḥ)* who was distinct from the priest *(khn)* (*DISO, zbḥ* III, 71).

In P, *šāḥaṭ* is the technical term for ritual slaughter. It involves slitting the throat (see 2 Kgs 10:7). This is the exact meaning of the Arab. cognate *šḥt*, whose nominal form *mšḥt* means throat (Snaith 1975). Ugaritic has two terms for "slaughter": *zbḥ* 'sacred slaughter' and *ṭbḥ* 'profane slaughter' (*UT* 51.6.40 = *CTA* 4.6.40 = *KTU* 1.4.6.40; *UT* 62.1.18–28 = *CTA* 6.1.18–28 = *KTU* 1.6.1.18–28; *UT* 24.12 = *CTA* 22.2.12 = *KTU* 1.22.1.12; *UT* 127.17.20 = *CTA* 16.6.17, 20 = *KTU* 1.16.6.17, 20; *UT* 1153.3–5 = *CTA* 310.3–5; *UT* ʿnt pl.x.4.30 = *CTA* 1.4.30 = *KTU* 1.1.4.30; *UT* 2 Aqht 2.29 = *CTA* 17.2.29 = *KTU* 1.17.2.29). Hebrew also has these two terms plus a third, *šāḥaṭ*, which would be synonymous with *zābaḥ* as both refer to sacred slaughter. The former has a more restricted meaning, however. Rabbinic tradition affirms that that meaning is to slit the throat (see *b. Ḥul.* 27a). Moreover, the Mishna states anonymously, categorically, and without further explanation that "all may slaughter (ritually) at any time and with any implement" (*m. Ḥul.* 1:2), clear evidence that the method of sacrificial immolation was already fixed by tradition and stems from biblical times (Milgrom 1976e: 13–15).

Because the animal stands in the same position for the hand-leaning as for the slaughtering (*m. Yoma* 4:2–3), the following tannaitic information takes on special significance: "How does he (the offerer) perform the hand-leaning? The sacrifice stands to the north (of the altar; cf. the NOTE on v 11, below) with its face to the west. He who leans [his hands] stands to the east, with his face to the west" (*b. Yoma* 36a [bar.]; cf. *t. Menaḥ.* 10:12). "He (the high priest) came to his bull and his bull was standing between the porch (of the Temple) and the altar, its head to the south and its face to the west, and the priest stood in the east with his face to the west" (*m. Yoma* 3:8). Thus, the rabbis hold that both the animal (and its slaughterer) must face west, toward the sanctuary, even if the animal's head must be twisted ninety degrees! This tradition, I believe, has its roots in the Bible's protracted struggle against chthonic (and ancestral) worship. One of the indispensable requirements for the latter was that the victim's head was to be pointed to the earth. In Greek religion this practice contrasted sharply with Olympian worship, which mandated that the victim's head be pointed toward heaven. Thus, pointing the animal's face toward the sanctuary, despite the difficulties it may have involved, was the Priestly way of saying that the sacrifice must be directed to God. By contrast, when Saul's soldiers fell upon the animal spoil and *wayyišḥāṭû ʾārṣâ* 'and slaughtered toward the ground' (1 Sam 14:32), Saul cried out *bĕgadtem* 'You have acted treacherously' and instead commanded them to perform the slaughter on a large rock *wĕlōʾ-teḥetʾû laYHWH* 'that they would not sin against the Lord' (ibid., vv 33–34). Their treachery was idolatry, the worship of chthonic deities (cf. Ramban on 19:26; for details see the COMMENT on chap. 19 and the incisive, but flawed, study of Grintz 1970–71).

before the Lord. lipnê YHWH, equivalent to *petaḥ ʾōhel môʾēd* 'at the entrance of the Tent of Meeting', the outer half of the Tabernacle court between the entrance to the enclosure and the altar (see fig. 1 and at v 3).

present (wĕhiqrîbû) the blood. Beginning with the blood rite and thereafter, all other rites associated with the altar will be performed by the priests because only priests are permitted "to ascend my altar" (1 Sam 2:28). The manipulation with the blood (v 5b), however, is preceded by its presentation. This protean verb, whose subject is the priest, clearly refers to a specific rite (see also 1:13; 3:9, 14; 7:3; 8:18; cf. *b. Zebaḥ.* 13a). Perhaps it was executed with the priests carrying the blood, collected in special bowls (called *ʾaggānōt*, Exod 24:6; and in priestly texts, *mizrāqôt*, lit., "splashers," Exod 38:3; Num 4:14; cf. 11QT 34:7; *Tg. Ps.-J.*), in solemn, dignified procession. This ceremonial presentation of the oblation can also take the form of the *tĕnûpâ*, the "elevation offering" (see at 7:30).

and dash. wĕzārĕqû with *mizrāqôt (Tg. Ps.-J.).* Alternate forms of blood manipulation require *hizzâ*, aspersing (4:6; 8:30; 16:14) or *nātan*, daubing (4:7,

18, 25, 30, 34). The blood rite for the burnt offering is not as significant as it is for the other sacrifices. Whereas the sacrificial prebends are awarded to the priest who performs the blood rite for the purification offering (6:1a), reparation offering (7:7), and well-being offering (7:14, 33), the prebend of the burnt offering goes to the priest who *maqrîb* 'sacrifices' it (7:8), without specifying which, if any, rite is meant (see further the NOTES to 6:19; 7:14, chap. 4, COMMENT A; and chap. 11, COMMENT C).

against (ʿal). Not atop the altar but on its walls (*b. ʿErub.* 57a). The blood is not incinerated. It is not part of the offering but is the life of the animal (17:10–14), which must be returned to God via the altar lest the slayer-offerer be considered a murderer (17:3–4; Milgrom 1963).

all sides. sābîb, lit., "round about." Tannaitic sources claim that the blood manipulation was carried out in two throws, by splashing the opposite corners of the altar (*Sipra,* Nedaba par. 4:9; *m. Zebaḥ.* 5:4), thereby fulfilling the verse requirement in the most economical way. The rabbis also aver that in all sacrifices the blood rite for quadrupeds was performed on the lower half of the altar (*b. Zebaḥ.* 10b, 53a), with the exception of the blood of the purification offering, which was daubed on the altar's horns (4:25, 30, 34). Philo claims that the blood was "poured in a circle around the altar" (*Laws* 1. 205), but here he copies the text of his LXX, which renders κύκλῳ 'in a circle'. It is therefore doubtful that he ever saw the actual rite.

the altar. For its description and function, see the NOTES at 4:25.

that is at the entrance to the Tent of Meeting. Why this specification? Some say lest one think that the blood rite should be performed on the incense altar inside the Tent (Ibn Ezra; Rashbam). Elsewhere, the sacrificial altar is simply called "the altar" (e.g., 1:11, 12, 15–17; 2:2, 8, 12, 3:2, 5, 8, 11, etc.), except when there is a need to distinguish it from the inner altar, in which case it is called *mizbaḥ haʿōlâ* 'the altar of the burnt offering', as in the prescriptions of the purification offering, where the blood rite takes place on either altar (4:7, 18, 25, 30, 34). Why is this technical term for the outer altar not used here, instead of this lengthy circumlocution? Possibly because it would give the impression that only the burnt offering is sacrificed there (Ehrlich 1908–14). Most likely, "elaboration is needed here so that the reader can become knowledgeable of the elements and components in the account; after that the author will demand more of the reader and provide him with less" (Freedman; private communication). The same reasoning explains why the account of the first case of the purification offering (4:1–12) is fuller than the accounts of the cases that follow.

6. *shall be flayed. wěhipšîṭ,* lit., "and he (the offerer) shall flay." But the execution of this rite was permitted to anyone (*b. Yoma* 26b [bar.]; *m. Yoma* 2:7); thus the verb must be taken in a passive sense. Public sacrifices, though, were flayed and quartered by the priests and, under emergency circumstances, by the Levites (2 Chr 29:34; 35:11). For the meaning "flay," see Mic 3:3; 2 Chr 29:34; 35:11 and figuratively as "strip, remove (clothes)," see Gen 37:23; Num

20:26, 28. The flaying does not include the head and legs, which are removed first (Lev 8:20, 21). Otherwise, if the legs were skinned, why would it be necessary to wash them (1:9; *Keter Torah*)? Moreover, it would not be practical to skin the head, which—besides its difficulty—would have been damaged by the slit at the throat. The carcass is generally skinned down to the knees; this would support the view that the portion of the leg that was washed was below the knee (but see at v 9). The animal's skin was the prebend of the officiating priest (7:8).

quartered. wenittaḥ ʾōtâ linĕtāḥêhā, lit., "and he (the offerer) shall dismember it according to its members." But, the rite is permitted to anyone (*b. Yoma* 26b [bar.]; *m. Yoma* 2:7), the verb bearing a passive meaning. The animal had to be skinned before it was quartered in order to keep the skin intact as the emolument for the officiating priest (7:8). The evisceration of the entrails is assumed (see v 9). Flaying, quartering, and washing (the entrails) were not always required in other cultures, where the animal was burned whole on the altar. That such a practice may once have obtained in early Israel is echoed in the rabbinic tradition that on the open altar, *bāmâ,* neither flaying nor quartering was required (*b. Zebaḥ.* 120a; *b. Ḥag.* 6b). For a description of the quartering process, see S. Rattray's contribution in the Note on "the breast," 7:30.

The quartering followed the natural divisions of the animal's bone structure (see Judg 19:29). The process is described in detail in tannaitic sources *(m. Tamid* 4:2–3; see *m. Yoma* 2:3–7).

7. *the priest (hakkōhēn).* The LXX, Sam., and 4QLev^b read the plural, *hakkōhănîm,* as in the rest of this chapter (vv 5, 8, 11) and elsewhere in P (2:2; Num 3:3; 10:8). The term *hakkōhēn* by itself refers to the ordinary priest, not to the high priest (1:9, 12, 13, 15, etc.); yet "Aaron the priest" does occur (twelve times). The expression "the sons of Aaron the priest" is rarer, occurring once again, in Josh 21:4; however, in the equivalent passage in Chronicles (1 Chr 6:42), the word "priest" is deleted. Thus *bĕnê ʾahărōn hakkōhănîm* 'Aaron's sons the priests' is possibly the authentic reading. Either the name Aaron attracted the appellation "the priest" or *hakkōhēn* took the place of *hakkōhănîm,* influenced by the singular verbs in the previous verse. Alternatively, as normally a single priest is responsible for laying out the wood and stoking the fire (6:5), the sing. *hakkōhēn* may be the original to which *bĕnê ʾahărōn* was added and the verbs converted to the plural, in harmony with vv 5 and 8 (Rendtorff 1985).

stoke the fire. wĕnātĕnû ʾēš, lit., "put fire." For this expression see Lev 10:1; Num 16:7; 17:11, the contexts of which make it clear that the fire is transferred (from the altar), not kindled anew. Thus this rite is not speaking of starting a fire on the altar (*pace* Dillmann and Ryssel 1897; Rendtorff 1985)—a circumstance that would contradict the injunction to keep the altar fire burning continually (6:5–6)—but of stoking the existing fire by adding wood to it (1:7b). The text assumes that the original altar fire is of divine origin (9:24; *Sipra,* Nedaba 5:10); hence the injunction not to let the fire die out, even at night. For the implication of this passage for the sin of Nadab and Abihu, see the NOTES on 10:1–4 and chap. 10, COMMENT A.

lay out wood (wĕʿārĕkû ʿēṣîm). The wood must be arranged in a neat pile (Tgs.). The kind of wood permitted on the altar is unspecified. The Mishna declares all wood acceptable except the olive and the vine (*m. Tamid* 2:3). No reason is given, but two are surmised: they make poor fuel (*Tamid* 29b) and their fruit is needed for the altar libations (*Leqaḥ Ṭov* to 1:8; *Midr. Lev. Rab.* 7:1). The same Mishna also claims that the following woods were preferred: fig, nut, and pine. Rabbi Eleazar adds the carob, palm, and sycamore (*Sipra*, Nedaba 6:4). *Jubilees* provides another tradition: "Beware lest you bring wood for the altar in addition to these: cypress, bay, almond, fir, pine, cedar, svin, fig, olive, myrrh, laurel, aspalathus. And of these kinds of wood, lay upon the altar under the sacrifice such as have been tested as to their appearance, and do not lay [thereon] any split or dark wood, [but] hard and clean, without fault, a sound and new growth; and do not lay [thereon] old wood, [for its fragrance is gone] for there is no longer fragrance in it as before" (*Jub.* 21:12–14). Of the disqualifications mentioned here, the Mishna mentions only blemished and old wood (*m. Mid.* 2:5).

The source of the wood is not indicated by the text. The first reference to it stems from Second Temple times: "We have likewise cast lots, the priests, the Levites, and the people, for the wood offering, to bring it into the house of our God, according to our fathers' houses (LXX), at times appointed, year by year, to burn upon the altar of the Lord our God, as it is written in the Torah" (Neh 10:35; cf. 13:31). Thus it is clear that the wood for the altar was a voluntary offering made by several families ("fathers' houses") at various times during the year. This practice prevailed at the end of the Second Temple period, as attested by the following Mishna:

> The occasion for the wood offering of the priests and the people is nine (times in the year): on the first of Nisan, by the family of Arah of the tribe of Judah; on the fifth of Ab, by the family of Parosh of the tribe of Judah; on the seventh of the selfsame month, by the family of Jonadab the son of Rechab; on the tenth, by the family of Seenah of the tribe of Benjamin; on the fifteenth, by the family of Zattu of the tribe of Judah together with the priests and Levites and all whose ancestral descent was in doubt, and the family of the pestle-smugglers and the family of the fig-pressers; on the twentieth, by the family of Pahath Moab of the tribe of Judah; on the twentieth of Elul, by the family of Adin of the tribe of Judah; on first of Tebet, by the family of Parosh again. (*m. Taʿan.* 4:5)

Reliable manuscripts of this Mishna read *bĕtišʿâ* '*in the ninth*', that is, the ninth of Ab, making it clear (in conformity with other tannaitic evidence; *t. Bik.* 2:9; *Meg. Taʿan.*; cf. Jos., *Wars* 2.425) that the people as a whole brought the wood offering on the ninth and fifteenth of Ab, whereas on nine *other* times during the year the wood offering was contributed by families, listed by tribal affiliation. Thus it is most reasonable to presume that two traditions have been conflated in this Mishna: the older one, tracing back at least to Nehemiah, whereby the wood offering was volunteered by certain families; and a later one, which set aside two other dates for the nation at large (details in Safrai 1965: 22v–33).

It should therefore occasion no surprise that the calendar of the sectaries of Qumran also reflects this conflation, for it designates a six-day festival during which the wood offering is brought to the Temple by the whole nation, but, according to the individual tribes, two tribes per day. The festival is celebrated between the twenty-third and thirty-first of the sixth month (Elul), precisely fifty days after the preceding New Oil festival at the end of the dry season, the perfect time in terms of weather to collect wood for fuel (details in Yadin 1983: 122–31; cf. also the NOTE on "wood," 6:5).

8. *lay out (wĕʿārĕkû) the quarters.* The verb is in the plural because the weight of some of the bull's parts requires that they be carried by more than one priest. Contrast the descriptions of smaller animals of the flock, where the same verb appears in the singular (v 12; Ibn Ezra, Abravanel). It is assumed that prior to this rite the meat was salted (see the NOTE on 2:13).

with the head (ʾet-hārōʾš). ʾet has the force of "with" (e.g., 8:20). Clearly, the head, being listed separately, is not considered a *netaḥ* 'quarter'. In Egyptian culture, the head was also severed from the carcass but was neither sacrificed nor eaten (Herod. 2.39).

suet (peder). This term occurs again at 1:12 and 8:20. The LXX, Tg. Onq., and Mishna (*m. Tamid* 4:2) understood it to mean "suet." In that case there is no distinction between *peder* and *ḥēleb*, the term that predominates for suet (3:3, 4, 9, 14, 16, 17, etc.). Other opinions are that it is the suet that covers the internal organs *(Tg. Ps.-J.);* the suet of the diaphragm (Ramban); the internal organs (Ibn Janaḥ; Saadiah). Akk. *piṭru*, a possible cognate, denotes the suet on the liver *(AHw).* KB claims an Egyptian cognate *pdr*, which, however, occurs only in "The Story of Two Brothers" IV. 5 (*ANET*[3] 24), a composition of late Egyptian times, leaving open the possibility that it is a loanword from Hebrew. The exact meaning of *peder* remains a mystery.

9. *Its entrails (qirbô)* Akk *qerbu;* equivalent to *mēʿayim* (Isa 16:11). So frequently (Exod 12:9; 29:13, 22; Lev 3:3, 9, 14; 4:8; 7:3; 8:16; etc.). The term does not comprise the other internal organs, which would not be in need of washing. The purpose of washing the entrails (three times according to *m. Tamid* 4:2) is to remove the dung (see 4:11).

shins (kĕrāʿāyw). It is a dual noun, *kĕrāʿayim* (Lev 11:21; Amos 3:12). Its only other occurrences are in Exod 12:9; 29:17; Lev 1:13; 4:11; 8:21; 9:14. Some render it as "legs" (11QT 33:15; *Tg. Ps.-J.* on v 13) or "hindlegs" (because the back legs are soiled by the excreta; Snaith 1967). Yet all evidence points to the meaning "shins," that is to say, the legs below the knees: (1) this is the precise meaning of Akk. *kurītu* 'between the knee and the fetlock of the hind leg' *(CAD)* as well as of Arab. *kurāʿ*; (2) the denominative *kāraʿ* (also in Ug.) means "bend the knee, kneel down"; (3) it refers to the *Springbein*, the saltatory legs of the locust (Lev 11:21); (4) the shepherd brings "two *kĕrāʿayim*" as proof of his ravaged animal (Amos 3:12). Because the upper leg, containing ample meat, would have been eaten by the predator, only the shins would have been left behind; and because Amos specifies two shins, the term cannot be restricted to the hind legs but must include all four shins, as maintained by rabbinic tradition (*m. Tamid* 4:2; *y. Šeqal.* 5:13).

washed with water. yirḥaṣ bammayim, lit., "he shall wash with water," a rite assigned to the offerer but which can be performed by anyone, as is the case with slaughtering, flaying, and quartering the animal (vv 5–6). It has been noted (Paran 1983: 126–27) that this, the tenth and final ritual act, is expressed differently. Instead of a perfect preceded by a sequential *waw* beginning the sentence, here it is an imperfect in the middle of the sentence. For other examples of this Priestly style, to end a pericope by changing the verb form of the tenth and final discrete ritual act, see Exod 27:1–8; 38:1–7; Num 6:13–21; 19:2–7 (Paran 1983: 133–37).

Ramban feels that this rite is not in its proper sequence. He suggests that it immediately followed the quartering (v 6). In reply, it has been pointed out that Ramban had in mind the Temple ritual, where the quartered pieces were placed on the altar's ramp while the rite of washing took place. Thus this rite is at variance with Second Temple practice, a state of affairs that is noticeable quite frequently in Leviticus. Another distinction between the Tabernacle and the late Temple is that the latter contained ten lavers (1 Kgs 7:38; cf. Exod 30:17–21) in which the priests—not only the lay offerers—would wash the burnt-offering pieces (2 Chr 4:6). But this Temple practice may refer solely to the public sacrifices and not be in conflict with this chapter, which prescribes just for individual burnt offerings. Furthermore, the washing of the sacrifices in the Temple, at least by the time of Ezekiel, no longer employs *rāḥaṣ* but uses *hēdîaḥ* (Ezek 40:38; 2 Chr 4:6), a term that became exclusive for this operation in Mishnaic Hebrew (e.g., *m. Tamid* 4:2; *m. Mid.* 5:3 [Hurvitz 1982: 63–65]). These and other discrepancies between Leviticus and Second Temple practice are critical in determining the date of Leviticus; see the Introduction, §B.

turn . . . into smoke (wĕhiqṭîr). Akk. *quṭṭuru* also means "turn into smoke." Turning the offering into smoke was considered, originally, the only way of reaching the celestial gods: "rich sacrifice of bulls and goats . . . and savory odors, mixed with curling smoke, went up to the sky" (*Iliad* 1.317). This verb always carries as its object an offering to the deity on the altar, such as meat (8:20–21), cereal (6:8), suet (3:11), incense (Exod 30:7). Incense can also be offered on a pan (16:12–13; Num 16:6–7, 17–18), but in these cases other verbs are used. In non-Priestly texts, *hiqṭîr* is also used intransitively (e.g., 1 Kgs 3:3;

Jer 33:18), though for this purpose *qiṭṭēr* is generally employed (e.g., Jer 11:13; Hos 4:13 [Edelman 1985]). Above all, *hiqṭîr* is carefully distinguished from *śārap* 'burn', which is used for nonsacrificial incineration, especially in the cult (e.g., 4:12, 21; 10:16; 16:27–28; Num 19:5, 6, 8). The difference may lie in the fact that with *hiqṭîr* "the offering is not destroyed but transformed, sublimated, etherealized, so that it can ascend in smoke to the heaven above, the dwelling-place of God" (Hicks 1953: 13).

all of it. *'et-hakkōl*, that is, including the entrails and shins, the incineration of which has not been mentioned (Wessely 1846). The unique distinction of the burnt offering in the sacrificial system is that all of it, except for the skin (7:8), is consumed on the altar (cf. also v 13; contrast 2:9; 3:5; 4:26; 7:5).

on the altar (hammizbēḥâ). The locative *he* can also indicate the place where something happens (GKC §90.d), as in *šāmâ* 'there' (Jer 18:2); *maḥănāyĕmâ* 'in Mahanaim' (1 Kgs 4:14). This usage with the verb *hiqṭîr* occurs twenty-nine times in Exodus, Leviticus, and Numbers (Lev 4:10, the only exception) but never in Chronicles, which consistently uses *ʿal mizbēaḥ* (1 Chr 6:34; 2 Chr 26:16; 32:12; twice, however, *hammizbēḥâ* is found in Chronicles, but where a verb of motion is employed: 2 Chr 29:22, 24).

as a burnt offering (ʿōlâ). Possibly the pronoun *hûʾ* had accidentally fallen out (see the NOTE on "It is a burnt offering," v 13).

a food gift. The term *'iššeh* is usually rendered "fire offering" and is derived from *'ēš* 'fire'. This rendering, however, must be rejected not only because its derivation is dubious but because it does not meet the data. Certain offerings that never enter the altar fire are nevertheless called *'iššeh*, for example, the wine libation (Num 15:10; cf. *b. Sukk.* 48b), the priestly prebend from the well-being offering (7:30, 35–36), and the bread of display (24:7, 9). Conversely, certain offerings that are burned on the altar, at least in part, are never called *'iššeh*, such as the purification offering. Despite the fact that there is frequent mention of the burning of the suet and its related internal organs of the purification offering, not even once is the term *'iššeh* used (see Exod 29:13; Lev 8:16; 23:1, 19; Num 28:15; 29:38). In all of these contexts, all sacrifices are called *'iššeh* except the purification offering (Exod 29:18, 25; Lev 8:21, 28; 23:18; Num 28:15; 29:36). Indeed, in one case the purification offering is explicitly excluded from the *'iššeh:* "If this was done inadvertently, unnoticed by the community, the whole community shall present one bull of the herd as a burnt offering of pleasing odor to the Lord, with its proper cereal offering and libation, and one he-goat as a purification offering . . . and for their error they have brought their offering, an *'iššeh* to the Lord and their purification to the Lord" (Num 15:24–25). The conclusion is inescapable that in the last part of the citation (v 25b), *'iššeh* can only refer to the burnt offering and its accompaniments, the cereal offering and libation, from which the purification offering is purposely excluded (*Sipre* Num 111; cf. Maim., *Guide* 3.46.62–63).

Two ostensible exceptions only confirm the rule: the purification offering is burned on the altar "with the *ʾiššê* of the Lord" (4:35; 5:12), that is, again the purification offering is kept distinct from the *ʾiššeh;* and Num 28:24, where *ʾiššeh* refers to the previously mentioned burnt offerings and their accompaniments (vv 19–21) but not to the purification offering (v 22; cf. vv 11–13, 15).

Most likely, *ʾiššeh* is related to Ug. *itt* 'gift' (Hoftijzer 1967) or Arab. *ʾatâtu* 'possessions of every kind' (Ehrlich 1908–14; Driver 1969). Because the priests as well as the altar benefit from the *ʾiššeh* (7:35; 24:9; Deut 18:1; Josh 13:14; 1 Sam 2:28), I suggest "food gift," a shortened form of *leḥem ʾiššeh* (3:11, 16). This translation is in line with the rendering "a sacrifice that is willingly received by the Lord" (*Tgs. Ps.-J* and *Neof.*). It also suffices to explain why it cannot apply to the purification offering. A sacrifice that purges the sanctuary of the pollution caused by the accumulation of sin (see the discussion of chap. 4) can hardly be called a gift. Conversely, because the burnt offering functions primarily as a gift (see the COMMENT below), there is no better designation for it than *ʾiššeh.*

The absence of *ʾiššeh* from later biblical compositions, especially in similar contexts (cf. 23:37 with Ezek 45:17; Num 28:3–6 with Ezek 46:13–15; Num 28:12–13 with Ezek 46:7; Num 28:17–19 with Ezek 45:21–23), indicates that this term became obsolete by exilic times (Hurvitz 1982: 59–63)—a conclusion that strengthens the thesis that the provenience of the Priestly texts lies in the preexilic period (see Introduction, §B).

pleasing aroma. The term *rêaḥ nîḥōaḥ* is found in connection with the burnt offering (Exod 29:18, 41; Lev 1:9, 13, 17; 8:21, 28; 23:18; Num 28:6, 8, 27; 29:2, 8, 13, 26), the offering of well-being (Exod 29:25; Lev 3:5, 16; 17:6; Num 15:3; 18:17), the cereal offering (Lev 2:2, 9, 12; 6:8, 14; 23:13) and the libation (Num 15:7, 10, 13, 14; 28:24; 29:6) but is absent from the contexts dealing with the reparation offering and is found only in connection with the purification offering (see the NOTE on 4:31). The clear picture that emerges from this distribution is that, like its companion term *ʾiššeh* (see the NOTE above), it must connote something pleasurable to the deity. Contrariwise, a rendering like "appeasing, placating, soothing," favored by many commentators and translators, should be avoided. To be sure, such a meaning for the term may be present in passages like Gen 8:21 and Lev 26:31 (with the verb *hērîaḥ* 'smell'). And a case for it can be based on the root *nwḥ*, which in the *hiphʿil* can mean "appease" (e.g., Ezek 5:13), as well as on its Akk. cognate *nuḥḥu*, which similarly denotes "appease," especially in connection with the gods *(CAD nâḥu* A 4a, b). Further support might be sought from the Greek world: if Apollo "receives the aroma of lambs or goats, he may be willing to ward off the plague from us" (*Iliad* 1.66–67; cf. 1.316; 9.497–500). Yet, the rarity of this term in Israel's expiatory sacrifices can only signify that even if it had this meaning originally, it lost it in the cultic terminology of P. Maimonides was correct in his comment on the purification offering, "Its burning could not offer a *rêaḥ nîḥōaḥ* to the Lord, but the contrary, I mean there was detestable and abhorrent smoke" (*Guide* 3.46.67–68). Hence the LXX rendering "sweet savor" and the rabbinic explanation *naḥat rûaḥ* 'pleasure' (*Sipre* Num 143; see Tgs.) are right on target. Nonetheless, it is significant that Ezekiel (and later literature) avoids this term as well as the anthropomorphic verb *hērîaḥ* in describing the legitimate cult (Ezek 6:6; 45:21–24; 46:6–7; 46:13–15), whereas the corresponding P/H passages contain it (Lev 26:31–32; Num 28:16–24; Num 28:11–13; Num 28:3–6, respectively). Its occurrence in Ezekiel is confined to idolatrous worship (Ezek 6:1; 16:17–19; 2:28), except for Ezek 20:41, which bears a figurative meaning (Hurvitz 1982: 53–58), another indication of the preexilic provenience of P (see the Introduction, §B). For a fuller discussion of this term see Gray (1925: 77–81).

The ritual procedure with the burnt offering can be reconstructed as follows: After the offerer has performed the hand-leaning rite and slaughtered his animal, the officiating priest dashes the animal's blood—collected by his fellow priest(s)—upon all the sides of the altar, while the offerer skins and quarters the animal and washes its entrails and skins. Once the priests have stoked the altar fire, laid new wood upon it, upon which they then lay the animal parts, the officiating priest supervises the incineration of the sacrifice. The rabbis attest to a slightly different order (e.g., the preparation of the altar fire being first; *b. Yoma* 33a; cf. Ramban). But they are referring to the procedure for the required daily public burnt offering, the *tāmîd* (Exod 29:38–42), while Lev 1 deals with the voluntary private burnt offering (Wessely 1846; cf. also the NOTE on "washed with water," v 9a).

10–13. The sheep is the most frequent burnt offering in the cult. It figures in the daily, Sabbath, and festival sacrifices (9:3; 23:12, 18; Exod 29:38–41; Num 28–29; Ezek 46:13), in the chieftains' gifts for the inauguration ceremony of the altar, for impure persons (12:6; 14:10), and for the desanctification of the temporary Nazirite (Num 6:14). These sheep are one-year-old males. Goats, conversely, are never sacrificed as burnt offerings in the public cult but are brought as voluntary sacrifices of the individual (22:19; Num 15:11). The reference to the Flock Gate (Neh 3:1, 31–32) presumes the existence of a sheep market for purchasing this sacrificial animal. At the end of the Second Temple period such a market is attested for the Temple precincts (Matt 21:12–13).

The sacrificial procedure is repeated, but in an abbreviated form. The omissions are expendable or can be otherwise accounted for. The hand-leaning and flaying can be omitted because in the bovine pericope their prescriptions contain the word *'ōlâ* (vv 4a, 6a), thereby indicating that these rites apply to all burnt offerings and not just to the bull (Abravanel; cf. *Sipra*, Nedaba 4:6). The priest's presentation, *hiqrîb* (v 5), has been incorporated into a new clause that has been added to the text (see at v 13). Finally, v 7 is deleted in its entirety lest one conclude that each new animal required additional wood and stoking.

10. *for a burnt offering (lĕ'ōlâ).* The *lamed* indicates the type of offering, for example, *lišĕlāmîm* 'for an offering of well-being' (3:6).

of sheep or of goats. Their sacrificial procedure is the same for the burnt offering, but not for the offering of well-being (cf. 3:6–16) or the purification offering (4:27–35).

11. *side (yerek).* This word appears only in P (Exod 25:31; 37:17; 40:22, 24; Num 3:29, 35; 8:4) and in 2 Kgs 16:14, an attested old narrative source. Other sources employ derivatives of feminine *yarkâ** (Paran 1983: 183, 223).

north side of the altar. This place, *yerek hammizbēaḥ ṣāpônâ,* is clearly different from the place designated for the slaughter of the bull, "before the Lord" (v 5). A bovine is slaughtered anywhere in the forecourt east of the altar, whereas the slaughter of the sheep or goat must take place north of the altar. That such a distinction actually exists can be shown from the prescriptions dealing with the purification offering. For the purification bull, again the slaughter area is designated as "before the Lord" (4:4, 15); but for the flock animal, be it a he-goat, she-goat, or ewe, the text reads, "at the spot where the burnt offering is slaughtered (before the Lord)" (4:24, 29, 33). As the only "spot" for slaughtering the burnt offering is the one specified for flock animals, namely, "the north side of the altar," this must be the location wherever the expression is found.

The instruction to the priests concerning their perquisites from the purification offering declares that it should be slaughtered "at the spot where the burnt offering is slaughtered" (6:18). How could the text be so unspecific if the burnt offering could be immolated in two different spots? One must, however, be mindful of the fact that in the purification offering the priest may benefit only from the meat of the flock animal, whereas the bovine is always burned in its entirety (4:11–12, 21; 8:17; 16:27). Thus the *eaten* purification offering, that is, from the flock, is slaughtered, as is its burnt-offering counterpart, north of the altar. The immolation spot of the reparation offering is designated by the same phraseology (7:2). Elsewhere it is termed "in the sacred precinct where the purification offering and the burnt offering are slaughtered" (14:13). Again, the reference to the burnt offering becomes clear once it is realized that the reparation offering always consists of an ovine. Thus the slaughtering of the flock animals of the purification and reparation offerings takes place wherever the same animals are slaughtered as burnt offerings—north of the altar. Bovines, by contrast, can be slaughtered anywhere in the forecourt, "before the Lord" (Dillmann and Ryssel 1897, citing Knobel; Noth 1965).

The reason for the existence of two discrete slaughtering areas is not given and can only be surmised. It may stem from purely practical considerations: a bovine, especially a bull, is difficult to control; hence it may be slaughtered anywhere in the forecourt. Why was the north chosen for the flock animals? Again practical reasons may have come to the fore: the ash heap was located east of the altar (v 16), the laver to the west (Exod 40:30), and the stairs or ramp to the south (*m. Mid.* 3:3); the only area left with adequate space was the north.

The three sacrifices mentioned above are of the same holiness rank—*qōdeš qŏdāšim* 'most sacred'—and, hence, are afforded the same treatment. The well-being offering is of lower rank, *qōdeš* 'sacred,' and it is thus understandable why its slaughter area even for flock animals is termed "before the Lord" (3:7) in its limited sense of "at the entrance to the Tent of Meeting" (3:2, 13; see at v 8).

Is this distinction attested in the Jerusalem Temple? Ezekiel's futuristic temple plan hints that indeed it was. Ezekiel provides for eight tables inside the northern gate of the inner court for the slaughter of the burnt, purification, and reparation offerings (Ezek 40:39–42). The specification that the three "most-sacred" offerings are to be slaughtered at the *northern* gate of the inner court can hardly be accidental. First, the well-being offering clearly is to be slaughtered elsewhere. Moreover, that the slaughtering is to take place on "tables" is most instructive. Bovines cannot be slaughtered on tables! Thus Ezekiel's blueprint tacitly admits that only flock animals designated as most sacred offerings are slaughtered in a sacred spot north of the altar—precisely as can be deduced from the sacrificial prescriptions in Leviticus.

To be sure, rabbinic tradition holds no such distinction but avers that all sacrificial slaughter takes place north of the altar. It should be noted, however, that the Second Temple, at the end of its existence, boasted a separate slaughtering installation consisting of poles and attached iron rings with which to shackle the animals, a device that could be used equally for bovines and for smaller animals (*m. Tamid* 3:5; *m. Mid.* 3:5). Moreover, early rabbinic sources are aware of the fact that the introduction of the rings was a rather recent innovation, which they attributed to John Hyrcanus (*y. Soṭa* 9:11, 24a; cf. *m. Maʿaś.* S. 5:15; *m. Soṭa* 9:10; *t. Soṭa* 13:10).

It is of no small consequence that the sectaries of Qumran proposed a different installation called the house of slaughter, an unwalled roof supported by twelve columns to which was attached a complex of wheels, chains, and rings (11QT 34; Yadin 1977: 1.178–82). This mechanism is designated expressly and exclusively for shackling and slaughtering bovines! Presumably, sheep and goats are to be slaughtered by some other means located elsewhere.

In sum, the evidence from Ezekiel, the Temple Scroll, and tannaitic sources points to the conclusion that, initially, bovines were slaughtered in a different area and in a different manner (though with the same slaughtering technique; see v 5) from animals of the flock. But with the erection of a special abbatoir in the forecourt—initially for slaughtering bovines, as the Temple Scroll suggests—all immolation for the altar came to be performed there, as prescribed in the rabbinic sources.

shall dash. The verb *wězārěqû* is the only plural in the entire pericope of the flock animal (vv 10–13). Although most likely only one priest actually manipulated the blood, others assisted him (2 Chr 29:22) by constantly stirring the blood so that it would not congeal (*m. Yoma* 4:3; cf. Paran 1983: 131).

12. *lay out the quarters, with the head and suet. wĕʾet-rōʾšô wĕʾet-pidrô*

wĕʿărak . . . *ʾōtām*, lit., "with its head and with its suet he shall arrange them";
see v 8.

13. *shall be washed (yirḥaṣ).* Again this verb is expressed in the imperfect
(see v 9) to indicate that it is the final rite.

(the priest) shall present all of it. The clause *wĕhiqrîb ʾet-hakkōl* is not found
in the pericope on the bull. In a summary fashion, it states that all of the priest's
rites should be presentations, in other words, that they should be performed
with solemnity. Thus it obviates the need for repeating the blood presentation
rite prescribed for the bull (v 5b).

It is a burnt offering (ʿōlâ hûʾ). A declaratory formula used for all of the
sacrifices (cereal 2:6, 15; purification 4:21, 24; 5:9, 12; reparation 7:5; priestly
consecration 8:28) except the well-being offering. Implied is that a verbal statement is made by the officiating priest concerning the nature of the sacrifice
when he officiates on the altar (*Sipra*, Nedaba 6:9).

14–17. Because the introduction (vv 1–2) deals only with sacrifices from
quadrupeds (see the Note on v 2), this pericope on birds must have been added
subsequently. If it had been intended at the outset as another species of burnt
offering, in addition to the animal (so Abravanel), then it would have begun
with *kî* (see at v 2), eventuating in the following structure for this chapter:

1. quadrupeds
   a. from the herd
   b. from the flock
2. birds

Instead, the pericope on birds begins with *ʾim*, which means that it was subsumed together with the herd and the flock under the category "animal," giving
the structure 1.a, b, c. (Perhaps to compensate for this error, the Masoretes
made "animal" in v 2 part of the apodosis by placing the main disjunctive
accent on the previous word, the Tetragrammaton.) Another reason for considering this pericope an addition is that the introduction (vv 1–2) is the heading
for the offering of well-being (chap. 3), and the latter contains no provision for
birds.

Why was the bird pericope added? The Midrash provides a satisfactory
answer:

King Agrippa [probably Agrippa I, 41–44 c.e.] wished to offer up a
thousand burnt offerings in one day. He sent to tell the high priest, "Let
no man other than myself offer sacrifices today!" There came a poor man
with two turtledoves in his hand, and he said to the high priest, "Sacrifice these." Said he: "The king commanded me, saying, 'Let no man
other than myself offer sacrifices this day.'" Said he: "My Lord the high

priest, I catch four [doves] every day: two I offer up, and with the other two I sustain myself. If you do not offer them up, you cut off my means of sustenance." The priest took them and offered them up. In a dream it was revealed to Agrippa: "The sacrifice of a poor man preceded yours." So he went to the high priest saying: "Did I not command you thus: 'Let no one but me offer sacrifices this day'?" Said [the high priest] to him: "Your Majesty, a poor man came with two turtledoves in his hand, and said to me: 'I catch four birds every day; I sacrifice two, and from the other two I support myself. If you will not offer them up you will cut off my means of sustenance.' Should I not have offered them up?" Said [King Agrippa] to him: "You were right in doing as you did." (*Midr. Lev. Rab.* 3:5)

This Midrash, taken from real life, underscores the true purpose of this added pericope on birds—to provide the poor with the means to sacrifice the burnt offering. Such, indeed, is the explicit purpose of special allowances for birds in other sacrifices: the scaled purification offering (5:7–10) and the offerings of the parturient (12:8) and the healed *mĕṣōrāʿ* (14:21–22). The same motivation applies to the cereal offering (chap. 2; cf. esp. 5:11–13).

There is no requirement that the birds be males and unblemished. One cannot argue that these criteria are omitted for reasons of stylistic economy—to avoid repetition. They are much too basic to be taken for granted. Rather, it must be assumed that these requirements have been waived—again, for the sake of the poor. Another possible reason is that because the bird is covered with feathers, its sex and minor blemishes would be difficult to determine. Moreover, birds were relatively inexpensive, so that not even the poorest would conceive of bringing a blemished bird (Ehrlich 1908–14).

The hand-leaning rite is also absent, and rabbinic tradition holds that, indeed, it is not required (*Sipra*, Nedaba 4:7; Git 28b). If, as maintained (see at v 4), hand-leaning designates ownership, then waiving this rite with birds makes sense: it is brought in the owner's hands, so hand-leaning automatically occurs during the presentation of the birds (Dillmann and Ryssel 1897). A Hittite text offers corroboration. Mursillis II had a sickness that caused his mouth to "turn aside." He was told to send a GUD *puḫugari* (bull substitute) with some birds to be burned(!) in the temple at Kumanni. Mursillis performs the hand placement (not the hand-leaning) rite (see the NOTE on v 4) with the bull but not with the birds. Perhaps, then, in the Hittite cult as well, hand-leaning was not required for birds. Also, the prevalence of birds for the burnt offering in Hittite rituals and in Alalakh (see the COMMENT below) suggests the caveat not to confuse the age of a text with that of its contents; the bird pericope may be a late addition, but the antiquity of birds as burnt offerings is well attested in extrabiblical and prebiblical sources. Indeed, it should not be forgotten that the five kinds of animals specified for the burnt offering, bull, sheep, goat, turtledove, and pigeon, are precisely the five animals offered by Abraham in Gen 15:9 (Ginsburg 1889), a text that further specifies (v 10) that the birds differed from the other species in that they were not split (see the NOTE "without severing them," Lev 1:17).

14. *If his offering to the Lord is a burnt offering of birds (wĕ'im min hā'ôp 'ōlâ qorbānô laYHWH).* The structure of the protasis is fuller—and more awkward—than the protasis of v 3, *'im 'ōlâ qorbānô min habbāqār.* Whence the added Tetragrammaton and changed word order? The answer is to be found in chap. 3, which belongs to the same unit as vv 1–2 and, in particular, in 3:6, which reads as follows: *wĕ'im min haṣṣō'n qorbānô lĕzebaḥ šĕlāmîm laYHWH.* The word order in 3:6 is nearly the same as in 1:14. The only difference is that in 1:14 the name of the sacrifice precedes the word *qorbānô* and has no *lamed*—two phenomena found in 1:3. Thus the protasis here is a conflation—not notably successful—of two other extant forms in this text, 1:3 and 3:6.

a turtledove or a young pigeon (min hattōrîm 'ô min bĕnê hayyônâ). These birds were domesticated and plentiful in biblical times (Isa 60:8) and in later periods (Jos., *Wars* 5.4, 4; *Midr. Lev. Rab.* 27:6; cf. Matt 21:2; John 11:16). The partitive preposition *min* can also designate one of a species (e.g., Gen 28:11; Exod 6:25; Ibn Ezra; Abravanel). Both belong to the dove family. According to Cansdale (1970), there are four species of dove of the genus *Columba* that were given the designation *yônâ* (Gen 8:8). Of the four, the most important was *Columba livia palaestinae,* the Rock Pigeon and subsequent breeds (including homing pigeons), for it was easily domesticated. The designation *tôr* (Gen 15:9) was given to three species of the same genus *Streptopelia* (all of which have in some fashion the name "turtledove"). The two of most interest are the Eastern Turtledove *(S. turtur arenicola)* and the Collared Turtledove *(S. decaocto decaocto).* The only bird of the group that could be domesticated was the Collared Turtledove. The Eastern Turtledove (which is the most common turtledove known to most ancient writers) is migratory.

Because only *C. livia* and *S. decaocto* were domesticated, these may be the birds described in the sacrificial prescriptions of the Bible. If the others could be included, then pigeons and doves would be the only wild animals allowed for Temple sacrifice.

The word *bĕnê* preceding "pigeon" can designate the members of a class, like *bĕnê yiśrā'ēl* 'Israelites' (Snaith 1967). By contrast, the term *yônâ* is found by itself without any modifier (Gen 8:8; Isa 60:8, etc.), which can only mean that *bĕnê* here refers to the young (as clearly in 1 Sam 6:7, 10). The rabbis also hold to this distinction (*m. Ḥul.* 1:5; *Sipra,* Nedaba 8:3–4). The reason for it may be that pigeons are tough when old, whereas doves can be eaten at any age. J. E. Knight notes, "The trouble with pigeon is that when it gets beyond the squab stage—and a pigeon can live for a goodly number of years—it definitely is tough" (1978: 202). Doves, by contrast, are good to eat anytime. In captivity a Collared Dove can live at most five to six years. Knight further notes, "The life span of doves, as with most small birds, is short. Rarely do they live more than a year. Since this is a fact of their existence, it's unlikely that you will come across a tough dove" (S. Pfann).

15. *present it.* *wĕhiqrîbô,* as opposed to the offerer's presentation (v 14).

pinch off. *ûmālaq* is found only once again (5:8). The etymology is unknown. It must imply removal of the head, for it was burned separately, as in the case of every burnt offering (1:8, 12; 8:20; 9:13). Also the meaning could not be that the neck should be broken but not severed, because then the text would have said so explicitly, as in the law of the bird purification offering: *wĕlōʾ yabdîl* 'without severing it' (5:8; cf. *m. Zebaḥ.* 6:5). According to rabbinic tradition, the priest applied his fingernail close to the nape (5:8) to cut through the windpipe and gullet (*t. Zebaḥ.* 7:4). This is confirmed by my student, Steve Pfann, an experienced taxidermist, who reports that "to kill the bird the usual practice is to yank and twist the head, thus disjoining the head from the top vertebrae. After disjoining the head from the neck vertebrae, the head can be torn from the skin of the upper neck very easily with a thumb nail of any substance."

the blood. *dāmô,* lit., "its blood," not only of the head (v 15a) but also of the body, either together (*Sipra,* Nedaba par. 7:7) or separately (*m. Zebaḥ.* 6:5).

be drained (wĕnimṣâ). The same verb is used in squeezing a wet fleece (Judg 6:38) and in draining a cup (Isa 51:17; Ezek 23:34; Ps 75:9).

against the side of the altar, *ʿal qîr hammizbēaḥ.* The bird yields too little blood either to be collected in a vessel (Bekhor Shor) or to be wasted. Hence the entire operation takes place at the altar. The term *qîr* refers to the outer vertical surface, for example, of a city wall (Num 35:4; Josh 2:15) or of a fence (Num 22:25). The LXX reads instead "toward the base of the altar" (cf. 7:2 LXX; Deut 12:27 LXX; 11QT 34:8; 52:51), which probably reflects a rabbinic halakha (e.g., *m. Pesaḥ.* 5:8) based on the apprehension that blood tossed on the altar's side would impinge instead on the ramp, rendering the sacrifice invalid (*m. Zebaḥ.* 2:1 [Dion 1987]).

16. *its crissum by its feathers (murʾātô bĕnōṣātâ).* "Then he (the priest) came to the body, removed the crop, the feathers, and the entrails that came forth with it (i.e., the crop)" (*m. Zebaḥ.* 6:5). "Our rabbis taught *murʾātô,* that is, the *crop.* You might think that he cuts through with a knife and takes it (i.e., without the skin and feathers), therefore it states *bĕnōṣātâ;* hence he takes the plumage together with it. Abba Jose b. Ḥanan said: He takes it [*the crop*] together with the intestines. The school of R. Ishmael taught: *bĕnōṣātâ,* with its [very] own feathers (i.e., not more than the feathers opposite the crop); hence he cuts it [round] with a knife like a skylight (i.e., removing the crop, skin, and feathers)" (*b. Zebaḥ.* 65a [bar.]).

The LXX reads τὸν πρόλοβον σὺν τοῖ πτεροῖ, thus agreeing with the Mishna and Baraita, cited above, that *murʾâ* is "crop" and *nōṣâ* is "feathers." The only differing opinion is that of Abba Jose, who claims that *nōṣâ* means "intestines." But according to Ramban's commentary on this verse, Abba Jose actually holds that *nōṣâ* stands for "feathers," but he simply records his agreement with the Mishna, cited above, that the priest must also remove the intestines. The Tgs. concur that *murʾâ* means "crop" but render *nōṣâ* as "excrement," presumably relating the latter to *ṣôʾâ* 'excrement' (Isa 4:4; Prov 30:12) and assuming that the *ʾalep* was assimilated. Most interestingly, *Tg. Yer.* alone differs in maintaining that *murʾâ* means "intestines." The Sam. records a different reading, *mārātô* 'gall bladder' (cf. Rüger 1973).

There are six obstacles that must be cleared before reaching a solution: (1) the meaning of the hapax *murʾâ;* (2) why the crop is removed (it contains no excrement); (3) why "feathers" is in the sing.; (4) the meaning of the suffix "its"; what of the rest of the bird's feathers? (5) the force of the preposition *be;* and (6) are the entrails containing the excrement to remain? If not, why are they not mentioned in the text? (Note that the Mishna insists that they be removed.)

I begin with a presupposition: the bird must be cleaned out before it can be offered up. In distinction to quadrupeds (vv 9, 13), the bird's entrails are not worth the bother of washing and hence must be discarded. Thus *murʾātô* must comprise the lower digestive organs containing the excrement, and the rendering "its crop" must be rejected.

On the basis of Job 39:18, where *tamrîʾ* is rendered "she would soar," Tur-Sinai suggests that *murʾâ* stands for the bird's tail, which directs its flight. Yet, aside from the fact that *tamrîʾ* itself is a hapax, it is hard to credit the ancients with the discovery of the piloting function of the tail, known to us only since the development of aerodynamics. Tur-Sinai (1957: 547) aims for the right destination but has taken the wrong trail. The term *murʾâ*, contrary to the lexicons, is not a hapax. It occurs in Zeph 3:1, where it is next to and synonymous with *nigʾālâ* 'filthy'. Its meaning is underscored by the unique epithet given to Jerusalem, *hāʿîr hayyônâ* 'the oppressing city'. The prophet's choice of this epithet can only be understood on realizing the double entendre of *yônâ*, which can mean both "dove" and "oppressing" (E. Adler). (Thus Zeph 3:1 MT should be revocalized *môrâ* > mur'a, or, possibly, it is Lev 1:16 that should be revocalized *murʾātô* > *môrʾātô*.) *murʾâ* may be related to *rôʾî* (Nah 3:6), which in rabbinic Hebrew is a standard word for "excrement" (*m. Mak.* 6:7). In Lev 1:16, it would stand for the crissum, the area around the cloacal (anal) opening, lying beneath the bird's tail.

That the sing. *nōṣâ* is a collective meaning "plumage, feathers" is verified both by Scripture (Ezek 17:3, 7; Job 39:13) and Akk. *nāṣu* (which itself may be a West Semitic loanword, *CAD*). But to what can the suffix *â* in *nōṣātâ* refer? The antecedent cannot be the bird, *ʿôp* being masc., but can only be fem. *murʾâ*. In agreement with the rabbis, I understand the sense to be that the *murʾâ* (the entrails, not the crop) must be removed together with its adjoining feathers. It must, then, refer to the bird's tail wing.

170

Logic is corroborated by zoology. My student S. Pfann informs me that the crissum consists of loose, fatty material, which can be removed from the bird by cutting through its tail wing. "The anus is removed along with the tail. However, the anus separates from the intestines when it is removed. This leaves a portion of the intestines exposed. By pulling on these, the rest of the intestines can be pulled from the abdomen like a string attached to the gizzard." Thus the preposition *be* finds its most natural and, indeed, most obvious resolution: it is the *bet* of means. The text is, in fact, giving instructions on how the bird is to be cleaned.

That the *bet* of means is employed in this text is supported in the next verse, where *bikĕnāpâyw* means "by means of its wings," a term that also proves that the bird is not plucked; all of its feathers remain except for the tail. It is also possible (again S. Pfann) that the priest can perform this operation with his bare hands; the skin of doves and pigeons is so thin that it can be circumcised without a blade. If so, then this rite would compare with the bird's slaughter in that no death-dealing instrument would be brought to the altar, a prohibition explicitly stated in regard to the use of iron tools in building an altar (Exod 20:25), but which would have been relaxed at the end of the Second Temple period (Baraita, cited above).

To complete the picture, the supposition must be made that sometime during the Second Temple period, the decision was made to remove the bird's entire digestive tract. Thus arose the practice to excise the gizzard as well as the intestines, as recorded in rabbinic literature.

cast. wĕhišlîk, used in regard to something useless (e.g., Gen 21:14). The bird's entrails, in distinction to those of the quadruped (vv 9, 13), are puny and scarcely worth washing.

the ashes. (haddāšen). The literal meaning of *dešen* is "fatness," either of olives (Judg 9:9), food (Isa 55:2), or sacrifice (Sir 38:11). The ashes on the altar hearth derive primarily from the suet, because the suet of the sacrificial animal was always burned on the altar (3:3–5, 9–11, 14–16; 4:8–9; 7:3–5, 25; see the NOTE on 3:17). The denominative *diššēn* has the privative meaning "clean the altar of the suet ashes" (Exod 27:3; Num 4:13).

at the east side (qēdmâ). The reason for choosing the east side is not clear. Ibn Ezra suggested that it was the side farthest from the Tent shrine. In the Second Temple, the ash heap was located not east of the altar but east of its ramp, which was on its south side (*m. Mid.* 3:2; *m. Zebaḥ.* 5:3). The ashes were cleared off the altar and out of the sanctuary each morning (6:3–4).

17. *tear . . . open.* The verb *wĕšissaʿ* means "cut, split" (11:3), and when used with birds must be equivalent to the quartering required for quadrupeds (vv 6, 12). Note that all of the verbs in the bird pericope (vv 14–17) are in the singular because the entire sacrifice can be conducted by a single priest. The final verb, however, is expressed just like the other verbs as a perfect with a sequential *waw.* Thus it differs from the preceding two pericopes (see the NOTES

on vv 9 and 13) and adds to the suspicion that the bird pericope was added later by another hand (see Paran 1983: 133 and the introduction to vv 14–17 above).

by its wings (bikĕnāpāyw). For this use of the *bet,* see at *bĕnōṣātâ* (v 16). Thus there is no need to render it "at its wings" (Ramban) or "with its wings" (Rashi). This procedure, it has been suggested, allows the bird to burn better. Perhaps, more pragmatically, its purpose may be to increase its size and give the appearance of a more substantial gift (see below).

without severing [them] (lō' yabdîl). The Sam. and 4QLev^b (and presumably the LXX and Pesh.) read *wĕlō'*. Separation of the limbs is mandatory to correspond to the quartering of the animal (vv 6, 12). Nevertheless, the wings should still be attached. They are too fleshless and puny to comprise a befitting altar gift, and the wing spread will enlarge the size of the bird to many times the dimensions of its carcass.

turn it into smoke. This phrase refers to the body and attached wings, because the head was burned separately (v 15). For this reason the word *hakkōl* is missing here (contrast vv 9, 13).

upon the wood. No new wood need be added (also for the flock animal, v 12). Perhaps the assumption is that the wood pile has been arranged for the first sacrifice of the day, the *tāmîd.*

COMMENT
THE BURNT OFFERING:
NAME, ANTIQUITY, AND FUNCTION

'ōlâ literally means "that which ascends," which implies that the offering is entirely turned to smoke (Jos., *Ant.* 3.225; Ibn Ezra). Except for the skin that is given to the officiating priest as his emolument (7:8) this is true; the animal is completely incinerated on the altar. Two renderings for 'ōlâ are possible. The first, the usual one, is "burnt offering." It finds support in the Ug. *šrp* (Heb. *śrp* 'burn'), an offering that appears fifteen times in tandem with *šlmm*. Presuming that the latter stands for Heb. *šĕlāmîm* (de Tarragon 1980: 60–63; and see chap. 3), it is plausible to conclude that the Ug. *šrp w šlmm* is equivalent to Hebrew 'ōlâ wāzebaḥ/ ûšĕlāmîm (17:8; Num 15:8; Ezek 46:12). Interestingly, whereas Ug. *šlmm* differs from Heb. *šĕlāmîm* in that the offering can be a bird, grape cluster, or oil (see at chap. 3), the *šrp* corresponds to the 'ōlâ in being limited to an animal.

Alternatively, 'ōlâ can be rendered "whole offering." The support for this rendering is as follows: (1) The high priest's daily *minḥâ* differs from all other private *minḥâ* offerings in that it is completely burned on the altar: "every *minḥâ* of a priest shall be a *kālîl:* it shall not be eaten" (6:16). *kālîl,* usually met as an adjective/adverb meaning "entire(ly)" (e.g., 6:15; Exod 28:31; Judg 20:40), is, in this case, a noun and is justifiably rendered "whole offering"

(NJPS). (2) The Levites' job profile includes offering a *"kālîl* on your altar" (Deut 33:10); once again, *kālîl* is a noun and clearly refers to a sacrifice that is completely burned on the altar. (3) It is recorded of Samuel that he "took a suckling lamb and sacrificed it as a *kālîl* to the Lord" (1 Sam 7:9). To be sure, *kālîl* could be an adverb meaning "entirely," but the text clearly calls for the name of the sacrifice. Finally (4), Psalms contains the prayer, "Then you will want sacrifices offered in righteousness, *ʿōlâ wĕkālîl;* then bulls will be offered on your altar" (Ps 51:21). Here we may be confronting a hendiadys, "entirely burnt offerings" (Radak), but, more likely, it is evidence for an original *kālîl* glossed (correctly) by *ʿōlâ* (see below).

To complete the philological record it should be noted that the root *kll* occurs in Ugaritic and Punic. For example, *šlmm kll (UT* 611.9–10) is rendered *"šlmm* offered in connection with the *kll"* (Levine 1974: 10). Alternatively, it is just as possible, and perhaps preferable, to take *kll* as an adverb and translate the clause *"šlmm* [which the king eats] entirely" (Cazelles 1969: 504). The same phrase occurs in the Marseilles Tariff (*CIS* 1.165) as *šlm kll* (sing.) and in the same line (line 3) with *kll* (see also *kllm* in *CIS* 1.167.5; 3915.2). The meaning of all those terms is disputed to this day (Levine 1974: 118–22; Loretz 1975).

In any event, the biblical evidence decidedly points to the existence of an earlier term for the whole offering, *kālîl.* Why was it replaced by *ʿōlâ?* The answer can only be speculative. Perhaps originally the whole, unquartered animal was sacrificed on the altar. But after the skin was awarded to the officiating priest (7:8), the name *kālîl* was regarded as inaccurate and misleading, for it implied that all of it went up in smoke; hence the name *ʿōlâ* was adopted. An echo of this purported earlier practice of offering up the entire animal is still audible in rabbinic literature, which avers that one of the cultic deviations permitted Samuel at Mizpah (1 Sam 7:9) was to offer the *ʿōlâ* "skin and all" *(y. Meg.* 1:12; *Midr. Lev. Rab.* 22:9). Another rabbinic source adds that "the *ʿōlâ* sacrificed by the Israelites in the wilderness did not require flaying and quartering" *(b. Zebaḥ.* 120a [bar.]).

Thus it appears that the original name *kālîl* was changed to *ʿōlâ,* which *eo ipso* means that its new name denotes something other than "whole offering." But what? "Ascending offering," the name suggested by the root meaning of the verb *ʿālâ,* is meaningful only if it refers to the incineration of the sacrifice on the altar. Thus the noun *ʿōlâ* points to the burning of the sacrifice and should consequently be rendered "burnt offering." The verb *ʿālā* also means "disappear" (e.g., Gen 17:22; 35:13; Exod 16:14); this is also true of the Aram. verb *sālaq,* which denotes both "ascend" and "disappear" (Weinfeld 1983: 108 n. 68). What ultimately tips the scales in favor of this rendering, is that the *hiphʿîl heʿĕlâ* in the Priestly literature actually can mean "burn, kindle," e.g., "kindle *(heʿĕlâ)* the lamp(s)" (cf. Exod 25:37; 27:20; 40:25; Num 8:2 [cf. *Tgs.*]; see esp. Lev 24:2). Moreover, this same *hiphʿîl* is the verb used especially for sacrificing the *ʿōlâ* (e.g., Gen 8:20; 22:13; Exod 24:5; 32:6; 40:29; Num 23:2, 4, 14, 30;

Deut 12:12, 13). Even though the cultic usage of this verb is always rendered "offer up," what is meant is that the *ʿōlâ* is consigned to the altar's flames. Better, then, to render the verb as "burn" and to regard the *ʿōlâ* as the synonym for Ug. *šrp*, meaning "burnt offering."

The antiquity of the burnt offering is well established (contra Smith 1927: 236–39). First, there is the biblical evidence (Thompson 1963). The burnt offering is attested in the earliest sources (e.g., Gen 8:20; 22:2, 7, 8, 13; Exod 10:25; 18:12; Num 23:15; Judg 6:26; 13:16; 1 Sam 7:9; 1 Kgs 18:38; 2 Kgs 3:27; 10:24; Job 1:5; 42:8). Four groups of these citations deserve special mention. (1) In the story of the binding of Isaac (Gen 22), based on an old tradition, Isaac assumes that the sole sacrifice his father will offer is the *ʿōlâ* (vv 7–8). (2) The angel requesting the *ʿōlâ* from Manoah (Judg 13:16) indicates that such is God's preference in accordance with the rabbinic view that "the *ʿōlâ* is superior *(ʿel-yônâ)* to all sacrifices because no creature partakes of it" (*Midr. Tanḥ* Zav 1). (3) The sacrifice that Samuel offered up at Mizpah (1 Sam 7:9) shows, even as rabbinic tradition acknowledges, that he violated the sacrificial rules on three counts: "It [the burnt offering] was sacrificed with its skin (mentioned above); it was too young; and Samuel was a Levite" (*Midr. Lev. Rab.* 22:9); hence, that Samuel offered a "deviant" burnt offering must clearly be an old tradition. (4) The texts dealing with Canaanite and Moabite sacrifices (Num 23:15; 1 Kgs 18:38; 2 Kgs 3:27; 10:24) indicate that the burnt offering played an important role in the cult of Israel's immediate neighbors. Moreover, the burnt offering is never omitted on great occasions (e.g., Josh 8:31; 1 Kgs 3:4) and is instituted immediately as a regular rite in the newly built Temple (1 Kgs 9:25). Finally, it is of some importance that the burnt offering must be a male. This requirement would correspond to the socioeconomic reality that in all livestock-raising cultures the male animal is expendable; females are needed for their milk products and breeding. (The purification offering, requiring females for the commoners [see at chap. 4] would then be the later, more artificial construction.)

The biblical evidence is strongly supported by sources from anterior, contiguous cultures. The Ugaritic data—assuming that the *šrp* is the burnt offering—were presented above. A text from Alalakh in northern Syria reads "fire will consume the lambs and the birds" (126.15, 19), a clear allusion to the burnt offering. The Hittites of Anatolia make reference to the burnt offering in their rituals (examples supplied by D. Wright): "one sheep and four birds are to be completely burnt" (AOAT Supplement 3.212f. verso 1, 33); "They burn one bird (for the absolution) of wrath and one bird (for the absolution) of guilt" (AOAT Supplement 3.206f., IV.50'f.); "Before the gates he burns one bird to Alitapara and he burns one bird to the gods of the city" (Papanikri *KBo* V. 1.9–11); "They burn two birds for offense and sin, and they burn a lamb for ———" (Papanikri *KBo* V. 1.2–3); "They burn to the male cedar-gods a bird for offense and a bird for sin" (quoted in AOAT Supplement 3.54). These examples have a Kizzuwatnian (southeastern Anatolian) provenience. One text, however, suggests that the burning of animals was at home at Hattusa: "the offerer offers a bull and ram to the weather god of Zipalanta, they burn them up after the manner of Hattusa" (quoted in *StBoT* 3.24). Thus it is not possible, with Kümmel (1967) and before him Rost (1958), to conjecture that the *'ōlâ* originated south of the Taurus (northern Syria) because it is attested only in Greece, Phoenicia, and Canaan—but not in Mesopotamia, Egypt, or pre-Islamic Arabia. The Hittite evidence clearly points to the prevalence of the burnt offering all along the eastern Mediterranean littoral, beginning on the south in Canaan and arching north and then west over to Phoenicia, Anatolia, and Greece.

Moreover, the function of the burnt offering as exemplified by the Hittite sources, cited above, is clearly propitiatory and expiatory (for "wrath," "guilt," "offense," "sin"), a fact that accords with the purpose assigned to the burnt offering in this chapter: *lĕkappēr* 'to expiate' (v 4). Rabbi Akiba maintains that the burnt offering expiates, in the main, for neglected performative commandments (*t. Menah.* 10:2; *Sipra*, Nedaba 4:8). Other rabbinic sources add (on the basis of Job 1:5) the expiation of sinful thoughts (*Midr. Tanh.* B 3:9a; *Midr. Lev. Rab.* 7:3, 11). Some medieval commentators suggest the entire range of unwitting sins (Bekhor Shor; cf. Shadal) and even brazen sins, if their punishment is not specified (Ramban).

In truth, the rabbis applied the burnt offering to the wide range of sins that fall outside the scope of the purification offering (see at chap. 4). The Qumran sectaries also mentioned that the burnt offering served an expiatory function, for they assign such a role to the additional *(mûsāp)* ram required on Yom Kippur (Num 29:8), which implies that all the festival burnt offerings (Num 28–29) are for expiation (11QT 27:4). But does the biblical evidence warrant assigning an expiatory function to the burnt offering? Three cultic texts explicitly record such a function, twice on behalf of Israel (9:7 [with the *hattā't*]; 16:24) and once for the *mĕṣōrā'* (14:20 [with the *minhâ*]). Ezekiel too seems to attribute expiation to the burnt offering—again, for Israel (Ezek 45:15, 17 [with other sacrifices]). But when the cultic texts (outside of P) actually specify a motive for the burnt offering, it is an occasion of joy, such as the fulfillment of a vow or a freewill offering (22:17–19; Num 15:3).

The narrative texts prove more enlightening. In one instance, the purpose of the burnt offering is plainly specified. Saul explains to Samuel why he officiated at the sacrifice: *ûpĕnê YHWH lō' hillîtî wā'et'appaq wā'a'āleh hā'ōlâ* 'I had not entreated the Lord, so I force myself to sacrifice the burnt offering' (1 Sam 13:12). Entreaty, then, is the manifest purpose of the burnt offering. But entreaty covers a wide range of motives: homage, thanksgiving, appeasement, expiation (Thompson 1963). Appeasement was certainly the goal of Samuel's sacrifice at Mizpah, for the text dutifully records, "And the Lord answered him" (1 Sam 7:9); whereas Israel's entreaties during Jeremiah's time were rejected: "When they sacrifice burnt offering and cereal offering, I will not accept them"

175

(Jer 14:12). Other examples are as follows: David offers up an *ʿōlâ* to stop the plague (2 Sam 24:21–25); the Israelites offer up an *ʿōlâ* after their defeat at the hands of Benjamin at the end of a day-long fast (Judg 20:26). "The Tanna, R. Simeon, asks: why does the purification offering precede the burnt offering (in the sacrificial order)? It is comparable to an attorney who comes to appease. Having made his (plea of) appeasement, the gift (of appeasement) follows" (*t. Para* 1:1; *b. Zebaḥ.* 7b [Bar.]). The burnt offering then is a gift, with any number of goals in mind, one of which—the one singled out in this chapter—is expiation.

The fact that the burnt offering answers every conceivable emotional and psychological need leads to the inference that it may originally have been the only sacrifice offered except for the *šĕlāmîn*, which provided meat for the table (see the COMMENT on chap. 3). This would account for the widespread attestation in the early sources of the *ʿōlâ* (see above) and the tandem *ʿōlâ wāzebaḥ/ûšĕlāmîm* (Exod 10:25; 18:12; 24:5; 32:6; Num 10:10; 15:8; Deut 27:6–7; Ezek 46:12; etc.). With the advent of a tabernacle/temple, however, it became imperative to devise specific sacrifices to purge the sacred house and its sancta of their contamination and desecration. Thus the purification and reparation offerings, respectively, were devised. These two sacrifices, once introduced into the sacrificial system, became the expiatory sacrifices par excellence and ultimately usurped the expiatory function of the burnt offering for the individual. That these two sacrifices are later than the burnt, cereal, and well-being offerings is shown by the fact that the latter offerings are provided with no cases. The motivations for bringing them are taken for granted. Not so for the purification and reparation offerings: their cases are spelled out in detail precisely because knowledge of them is not widespread (Dillmann and Ryssel 1897). Thus the reference to expiation in the exposition of the burnt-offering procedure (1:4) may reflect as much an early stage in the history of this offering as its mention in the Job story (Job 1:5; 42:8).

Furthermore, evidence for the early provenience of the expiatory burnt offering is detectable in the requirement that all public animal sacrifices must be male. The only reasonable explanation of this fact is that the all-male *ʿōlâ* was at first the only expiatory sacrifice. When the purification and reparation offerings were incorporated into the public cult, the male requirement was still retained. Else how can one explain that the commoner will always bring a female of the flock for his *individual* purification offering (4:27–35; 14:10; Num 6:14; etc.), whereas the *public* purification offering is always a male (4:13–21; 9:3; 16:15; Num 28:15; etc.)? The exclusive maleness of all public sacrifices can only be attributed to the priority of the burnt offering, which then imposed its male requirement on the other sacrifices, which were incorporated later. Strikingly, rabbinic tradition affirms that on the *bāmâ*, the open altar, "all (sacrifices) were burnt offerings" (*t. Zebaḥ.* 13:1). It also harbors another view (based on Exod 24:5) that the *šĕlāmîn*, the well-being offering, was offered up on the *bāmâ* as well (*b. Zebaḥ.* 116a). In either case, the rabbis are in agreement that the purification and reparation offerings are post-Sinaitic; they do not come into existence until the open altar, the *bāmâ*, gives way to the Tabernacle, and until then—because the *šĕlāmîm* functions only for joyous occasions (see the COMMENT on chap. 3)—the burnt offering was the exclusive expiatory sacrifice. This conclusion would explain why the only notice for the *ʿōlâ* in P is expiation (1:4). H, by contrast, emphasizes solely its joyous nature (22:17–19; Num 15:3). The shift from sinfulness to rejoicing for the *ʿōlâ*, therefore, falls in the period (ninth–eighth centuries) that may also reflect the introduction of the *ḥaṭṭāʾt* and *ʾāšām* into the sacrificial system (see chap. 4, COMMENT N and the Introduction, §C).

Furthermore, the possibility must be raised that because the *ḥaṭṭāʾt* and *ʾāšām* were relatively late Priestly innovations, the sanctuary itself had to keep the required animals in stock for the benefit of worshipers who only found out when they arrived at the sanctuary that their sin or impurity was no longer expiable by an *ʿōlâ*. (Because the *ḥaṭṭāʾt* always requires a female animal, the male that might have been brought for an *ʿōlâ* would have to be sold or exchanged.) Support for this assumption stems from the indisputable evidence of a historical source: "Money brought as an *ʾāšām* or as *ḥaṭṭāʾôt* was not deposited in the House of the Lord; it went to the priests" (2 Kgs 12:17). The purchase of these sacrificial animals from the sanctuary would also explain their absence from both H, when it speaks of the necessity of bringing unblemished animals to the sanctuary (22:17–21), and D (e.g., Deut 12:6). Both sources were composed (eighth–seventh century), when the *ḥaṭṭāʾt* and *ʾāšām* sacrifices had just been introduced.

THE CEREAL OFFERING (2:1–16)

Raw Flour

2 ¹When a person presents an offering of cereal to the Lord, his offering shall be of semolina; he shall pour oil upon it, lay frankincense on it, ²and present it to Aaron's sons, the priests. [The priest]shall scoop out therefrom a handful of its semolina and oil, as well as all of its frankincense; and this token portion the priest shall turn into smoke on the altar, as a food gift of pleasing aroma to the Lord. ³And the remainder of the cereal offering shall be for Aaron and his sons, a most sacred portion from the Lord's food gifts.

Cooked: Baked, Toasted, Fried

⁴When you present an offering of cereal baked in an oven, [it shall be of] semolina: unleavened cakes mixed with oil, or unleavened wafers smeared with oil.

⁵If your offering is a cereal offering (toasted) on a griddle, it shall be a semolina mixed with oil, unleavened. ⁶Crumble it into bits and pour oil upon it; it is a cereal offering.

⁷If your offering is a cereal offering (fried) in a pan, it shall be made of semolina in oil.

⁸If you bring to the Lord a cereal offering prepared in any of these ways, it shall be presented to the priest who shall deliver it to the altar. ⁹The priest shall set aside the token portion from the cereal offering and turn it into smoke on the altar as a food gift of pleasing aroma to the Lord. ¹⁰And the remainder of the cereal offering shall be for Aaron and his sons, a most sacred portion from the Lord's food gifts.

Injunctions Concerning Leaven, Honey, and Salt

¹¹No cereal offering that you offer to the Lord shall be made leavened, for you must not turn into smoke any leaven or any honey as a food gift to the Lord. ¹²You may offer them to the Lord as a first-processed offering; but they shall not be offered up on the altar as a pleasing aroma. ¹³You shall season all your cereal offerings with salt; you shall not omit from your cereal offering the salt of your covenant with your God: on all your offerings you must offer salt.

Natural Grain

¹⁴If you bring a cereal offering of first-ripe fruits to the Lord, you shall bring milky grain parched with fire, groats of the fresh ear, as a cereal offering of your first-ripe fruits. ¹⁵You shall add oil to it and lay frankincense on it: it is a cereal offering. ¹⁶And the priest shall turn into smoke its token portion: some of its groats and oil, with all of its frankincense, as a food gift to the Lord.

NOTES

2:1. *When.* The conjunction *kî* indicates that this offering is voluntary (*Sipra,* Nedaba par. 8:3). The same holds true for the burnt and well-being offerings (see at 1:2).

a person (nepeš). This term is used whenever persons of either sex are intended (see Lev 4:2; 5:1, 15, 17, 21; 7:20; 20:6; Num 15:30–31). That *nepeš,* like *'ādām* (1:2), is neutral language is proved in the following law: "When a man or a woman commits any wrong toward an *'ādām* whereby he trespasses against the Lord, when that *nepeš* feels guilt, he *wĕhitwaddû . . . wĕhešîb . . . yôsēp . . . wĕnātān*" (Num 5:6–7; cf. the COMMENT on 5:14–26). Thus, not only are *nepeš* and *'ādām* synonyms, but each term also stands for "a man or a woman" and, though *nepeš* is feminine, it can take a third-person masculine verb, which refers to either sex. (Note that *taqrîb* [fem.] is followed by *yaṣāq, nātan* [masc.].) In its meaning "person, anyone," *nepeš* is found twice in Deuteronomy, four times in Ezekiel, and thirty-six times in P and H (Briggs 1897). The rabbis discern an egalitarian motivation: "Why is the *minḥâ* distinguished in that the expression *nepeš* is used therewith? Because the Holy One blessed be He said, 'Who is it that usually brings a *minḥâ*? It is the poor man. I account it as though he had offered his own soul *(nepeš)* to Me' " (b. *Menaḥ.* 104b).

an offering of cereal. *minḥâ*, lit., "tribute, gift" (see the COMMENT below); but in P, it always refers to a cereal offering in contrast to the other sacrifices, which are animals.

semolina. First, the term *sōlet* must refer to wheat (*Sipra*, Nedaba 10:1). So it is expressly identified *sōlet ḥiṭṭîm* 'semolina of wheat' the very first time it occurs in the Pentateuch (Exod 29:2), a clear indication of P's editorial hand. Moreover, *sōlet* is contrasted with barley in "A seah of *sōlet* sold for a shekel and two *seahs* of barley for a shekel" (2 Kgs 7:16; cf. vv 1, 18), from which can be derived that *sōlet*, not being barley, must be wheat (the only other common grain) and that it is ordinarily twice as expensive as barley. Rabbinic tradition confirms this identification: "[If one says] 'I pledge myself to offer a cereal offering of barley' he must offer one of wheat (because individual grain offerings must be from wheat)" (*m. Menaḥ.* 12:3). Second, *sōlet* is identified with grits or, more precisely, semolina, "The grain-like portions of wheat retained in the bolting-machine after the fine flour has been passed through" *(Webster)*. Again, this definition is confirmed by rabbinic tradition: "A sieve lets through the flour but retains the *sōlet*" (*m. 'Abot* 5:15); "When you sift, the flour is beneath (the sieve), the *sōlet* is above" (*y. Šabb.* 7, 10b, 17c; cf. *t. Menaḥ.* 8:14). Further confirmation stems from the cognates: Akk. *siltu* and Arab. *sult* also mean "grits" (see also Ibn Janaḥ, Parḥon, and Radak). In the Bible, *sōlet* is contrasted with ordinary flour, *qemaḥ* (1 Kgs 5:2).

The quantity is not specified, and probably none is intended. The rabbis fix it at one-tenth of an *ephah*, for such is the specification of the cereal offerings brought by the high priest (6:13), the suspected adulteress (Num 5:15), and the poor person for his purification offering (5:11). Clearly, it was choice flour, and it is listed with such luxury items as honey and oil (Ezek 16:13, 19; cf. Gen 18:6; 1 Kgs 5:2). Even in the royal household, twice as much *qemaḥ*, ordinary flour, was consumed as *sōlet* (1 Kgs 5:2); an even smaller proportion of *sōlet* could have been afforded by the ordinary Israelite family. Yet it was even less expensive than birds (see 5:11) and therefore considered the offering of the poor (see the COMMENT below).

he shall pour (wĕyāṣaq). Oil is required in all varieties of the cereal offering. It is applied in five different ways: pouring (v 1), mixing (v 4), smearing (v 4), "in," that is, frying (v 7), or adding (v 15). In this instance mixing is not required; it is assumed that the poured oil will be absorbed by the flour. By contrast, the public grain offering, which also requires uncooked semolina, calls for "semolina with oil mixed in" (Num 28:9, 12, 13, etc.).

oil (šemen). Olive oil was a primary ingredient of the cereal offering because of its combustible qualities. According to the Mishna (*m. Menaḥ.* 8:4–5), oil production took place in three stages, by (1) crushing, (2) pressing with beams and stones, and (3) grinding. Oil for the fuel of the candelabrum, requiring *šemen zak* 'pure oil', came from the first stage; burning "pure oil" inside the sanctuary would be less likely to darken the walls and curtains with soot (Stager and Wolf 1981: 97). Oil for the cereal offering was produced by stages 2 and 3.

Olive oil was used in place of butter in cooking vegetables (1 Kgs 17:12–16). It is associated with joy (Isa 61:3; Ps 45:8; Prov 21:17), especially at festive meals (Pss 23:5; 92:11; 104:15; etc.) but avoided in times of mourning (2 Sam 14:2; Dan 10:3) and solemnity, such as on the Day of Atonement (*m. Yoma* 8:1; *m. Šabb.* 9:4) and in the cereal offerings for the indigent's purification offering (5:11) and for the suspected adulteress (Num 5:15). In distinction from wine, which was offered as a discrete libation, oil could never constitute an independent offering (the *log* of oil for the healed *měṣōrāʿ* [14:10]is not a sacrifice).

frankincense. lěbōnâ, a fragrant gum-resin tapped from three species of the *Boswellia* tree native only to southern Arabia (see Jer 6:20) and Somaliland. The best information on its costliness is found in classical authors such as Pliny; its price in the year 1960 would vary between $87.50 and $175 per pound, depending on its quality (Van Beek 1960). As a result, southern Arabia became very prosperous during the first millennium B.C.E. The spice trade with the peoples of the fertile crescent and Mediterranean could not have been well developed much before then, for travel across Arabia would have been impossible without the use of the camel, the effective domestication of which took place in the thirteenth or twelfth century B.C.E. (Albright 1961: 38 n. 9; 1964: 158 n. 2). Although the main route of the spice trade followed the King's Highway in Transjordan, a secondary but significant route, to judge by the installations for spice manufacture at Arad (Aharoni 1968), cut through the Negeb and across the central mountain chain of Canaan. Ben Sira emphasizes its aromatic scent (Sir 39:14; 50:9). It was the main ingredient in the incense burned on the inner altar (Exod 30:7–8, 34–36).

Pliny relates that frankincense was burned at the obsequies for Nero's wife to mask the odor of burning flesh. Indeed, some commentators give this as the reason for its use in sacrifices (Abravanel, introduction to chap. 1; Maim., *Guide* 3.45). But frankincense was not required for the cereal offering that accompanied meat offerings (Num 15:1–9). Also, it cannot be presumed that its purpose was to provide "a pleasing aroma to the Lord" (Lev 2:2) because the flesh offerings by themselves fulfilled this purpose (1:9, 13, 17; 3:5, 16; Num 28:6, 24; 29:2, 8, 36). Moreover, the cooked cereal offerings also provided "a pleasing aroma to the Lord" (v 9) even though, it seems, they did not require frankincense as a special concession to the poor (see at vv 4–10 and the COMMENT below). The frankincense requirement for the uncooked cereal offerings brought by the individual (vv 1–3, 14–16) may have served the functional purpose of distinguishing them from the uncooked cereal offerings that accompanied the blood offerings.

The association of the cereal offering with frankincense (or incense, *qĕtōret*) is frequently attested in non-Priestly texts (Isa 1:13; 43:23; 66:3; Jer 17:26; 41:5; Ps 141:2; Neh 13:5, 9; cf. also Cowley 1923: 30.21, 25; 31.21; 32.9; 33.11), and the two continued to be offered privately between and even after the destruction of the First and Second Temples (see the COMMENT below).

on it. Whereas the oil was distributed over all of the semolina, the frankincense was placed upon it in a single lump so that it could all be scooped up in the priest's hand. The rabbis averred that the frankincense was not included in the portion of the cereal offering scooped up by the priest (*Sipra*, Nedaba 10:8; *b. Soṭa* 14b), an assertion that seems to contradict the plain implication of the text (see esp. 6:8).

2. [The priest]. Moved up from 2b for clarity.

scoop out . . . a handful (wĕqāmaṣ . . . mĕlō' qumṣô). The singular verb and noun indicate that the action is performed by one of the priests (see v 9; Num 5:26), though the subject *hakkōhănîm* is plural. The switch in number from plural to singular is not infrequent in these cultic texts (note the identical phenomenon in the cereal-offering passage, 6:7–8; see also 7:2). The execution of this rite is described by the rabbis as follows: "He should bend his three fingers over onto the palm of his hand" (*b. Menaḥ.* 11a; cf. *Sipra*, Nedaba par. 9:6; *b. Yoma* 47a). Nonetheless, the literal meaning of this text is "handful" (so Rabbi Pappa and Rabba in *b. Menaḥ.* 11a; Radak), corroborated by the explicit phrase "and he filled his palm with it" (9:17).

The priest's action, taking place at the altar, presumes a prior rite of presenting the cereal offering at the altar, akin to the presentation of the blood of the meat sacrifices (1:5, 15). This rite is explicitly demanded for the cereal offering in a subsequent passage (6:7). But why is it omitted here? Four kinds of cooked cereal offerings follow (vv 4–7); thus, to avoid repeating this rite for each offering, it is mentioned once in the summary (v 8) and, hence, must be presumed for each offering.

therefrom (miššām). One need not read *mimmennâ* (like the Sam.), for *miššām* can have the same meaning (see 2 Kgs 7:19; Ezek 5:3).

this token portion. Four renderings of *'azkārātâ* have been suggested: (1) "memorial," as in *zikkārôn* (*Sipra*, Nedaba par 9:12); (2) "the burnt portion" (see Ps 20:4, where *yizkōr* is paralleled by "reduce to ashes" (Saadiah); (3) "the fragrant portion" (Hos 14:8; see Isa 66:3; Ibn Ezra [2]); (4) "invocation portion" from *hizkîr* 'pronounce', in other words, the name of YHWH is pronounced when this portion is burned (Schottroff 1964); for evidence see the superscriptions to Pss 38 and 70 and Akk. *šumka azkur*, the pronunciation of the divine name in the cult (Eising 1980). Each of these theories is subject to serious question: theory 1, the purpose of such a "memorial" is unclear; theory 2, Ps 20:4 is frail proof because it most likely should be rendered "He will approve the token portion of your cereal offerings and approve the ashes of your burnt offering"; theory 3, token portions are taken from expiatory cereal offerings (5:12; Num 5:15), but these can hardly be intended to provide fragrance; theory 4, why should the name of the deity be invoked for a cereal offering, which in a sacrificial series is only an accompaniment of the meat offerings? And why should there be no invocation of the deity when the cereal offering is entirely consumed (as in the high priest's offering, 6:12–16 and the public cereal offering, Num 28–29) or when there is no cereal offering at all (e.g., with the expiatory sacrifices, Lev. 4–5)? No definitive answer can be given. Provisionally, it is best to understand *'azkārâ* as related to *zēker* 'remembrance', referring to the fact that the entire cereal offering should really go up in smoke and that the portion that does is *pars pro toto:* it stands for the remainder; in other words, it is a "token portion." Alternatively, it may derive from Akk. *zikru* 'image, counterpart, replica' *(CAD* 21.116) and hence yield "token" (Levine 1989).

as well as (ʿal). For this usage see Exod 12:8–9.

3. *And the remainder. wĕhannôteret,* a feminine abstract formed from the *niphʿal* participle like *nĕkônâ, neqallâ* (GKC §122.p, q). There is also a masculine form *nôtār* used in connection with the offering of well-being (7:17), the paschal sacrifice (Exod 12:10), the priestly consecration offering (8:32), and the oil used in the purification rites for the healed *mĕṣōrāʿ* (14:18). The suggestion has been made that the feminine form applies to large remainders and the masculine to small remainders (Abravanel), or that the remainder here is that of the *minḥâ,* a feminine noun, whereas *nôtār* is a masculine because its referents, *šĕlāmîm* 'offering of well-being' and *šemen* 'oil', are also masculine (E. Adler). Still, the possibility must be entertained that the Priestly legislation devised a new term, *nôteret,* to distinguish the remainder stemming from the *minḥâ,* a most sacred offering eaten solely by priests, from the remainders of less sacred offerings, called *nôtār.*

for Aaron and his sons. In none of the sacrificial prescriptions (chaps. 1–5) are priestly perquisites mentioned; the latter are the subject of the next section (chaps. 6–7). Why then are they mentioned here (and again in v 10)? The answer can only be that, contrary to expectations, the cereal offering is not burned on the altar in its entirety. The cereal offering is the poor man's surrogate for the burnt offering, which is entirely consumed (except for its skin) on the altar. Lest one think that the cereal offering is treated similarly, the text makes it clear that only a token portion is burned and the remainder is given to the priests (see further v 10 and the COMMENT below).

most sacred portion. The term *qōdeš qŏdāšîm* defines the burnt, cereal, purification, and reparation offerings (6:10, 18; 7:6), as distinct from the rest of the offerings, which are designated by the term *qōdeš* 'sacred', namely, the well-being offering, the *ḥērem,* and the first of animals, fruits, and processed foods (Num 18:12–19). *Ḥērem* is also termed "most sacred" (27:28), but only in regard to its irredeemability; otherwise it is treated as "sacred" (Milgrom 1976f:

51 n. 187, 66 n. 236). The designations "sacred" and "most sacred" are always applied to the portions of the offering that are eaten. For this reason the burnt offering (never eaten by man) is nowhere called "most sacred" but must be assumed to be so (see *m. Zebaḥ.* 5:1; 6:1). This bipartite division of offerings into "sacred" and "most sacred" is not the invention of Israel; clear traces of it are present in Egyptian and Hittite cultic texts (Milgrom 1976f: 41–43).

4–10. Four different preparations of the cereal offering are here included: oven-baked (two varieties), griddle-toasted, and pan-fried. Their common denominator is that they are all cooked, unleavened semolina. The directions for their preparation are not clear. Adding to the confusion is that these cereal offerings are mentioned elsewhere but are worded differently (see Exod 29:23; 1 Chr 23:29). The rabbis held that the basic procedures are the same, for example, all four preparations require three applications of oil: poured on the flour, mixed with the flour, and contained in the vessel (*m. Menaḥ.* 6:3).

No frankincense, it seems, is required for these cooked cereal offerings. Its presence cannot be assumed, for in the natural grain (vv 14–16) and the raw flour (vv 1–3) varieties frankincense is specified. Hence its absence in the cooked cereal offerings is deliberate *(Keter Torah)*. Frankincense is not required or expected in the high priest's cereal offering (6:12–16), for the latter is prepared on a griddle. (Frankincense is required for the display bread, a cooked cereal offering, 24:7. But there it is required for the token offering, because the bread in its entirety is eaten by the priests; see 24:5–9.) The omission of the frankincense requirement may be regarded as a deliberate concession to the poor. That is, if they cannot afford it (and it is expensive; see the NOTE on v 1), they have the option of bringing a cooked cereal offering for which it is not required. It has been argued that Jer 41:5 provides evidence to support the view that people did offer frankincense with other sacrifices. This verse reads as follows: "Eighty men came from Shechem, Shiloh, and Samaria, their beards shaved, their garments torn, and their bodies gashed, carrying cereal offerings and frankincense to present at the House of the Lord." The argument fails, however, for the following reasons: (1) their cereal offering was probably uncooked and, hence, required frankincense; (2) they were hardly poor, as they testify "we have stores hidden in a field—wheat, barley, oil, and honey" (v 8), and (3) their slovenly dress was a sign of mourning, not poverty.

Another distinction between the raw and cooked cereal offerings is that the former is distributed to the entire priestly corps, while the latter is assigned to the officiating priest (7:9–10). As in the case of the priestly perquisites from the well-being offering, the breast belongs to the priestly corps and the thigh to the officiating priest. The distinction in priestly recipients may stem from different sanctuary traditions: the officiating priest was recompensed at the small, local sanctuary, the priestly corps directed the perquisites equitably at the Jerusalem Temple. For details, see at 7:9–10, 31–33. "Another reason for the distinction in the distribution of raw and cooked offerings may be that raw offerings can be mixed together to make a larger pool or store of oiled-semolina from which portions can be drawn to make certain dishes whereas the cooked *mĕnāḥôt*, being already prepared, are a fixed dish or serving and suited to one or a few persons" (D. P. Wright, written communication).

4. *When.* *kî*, followed by *'im* twice (vv 5, 7), thereby structuring the three kinds of cooked cereal offering: oven-baked, griddle-toasted, and pan-fried.

you present (taqrîb). The subject may be *nepeš* (feminine) 'person' (v 1), which would result in the rendering "(a person) presents." This might explain the third-person verb *wĕhiqrîbāh* (v 8) (Ehrlich 1908–14), but would leave all of the intervening second-person verbs and nouns (vv 5, 6, 7, 8) unexplained.

oven (tannûr). A cylindrical mud or clay oven with a large opening at the top and, sometimes, a small hole at the base for air; it was constructed either fully above or partially embedded in the ground (Dalman 1935: 88–127; figs. 17–24). Lev 11:35 states that if the corpse of an impure reptile falls into a *tannûr*, it is rendered impure and must be broken. Thus it is clear that it did not represent a significant financial investment, that each family probably had its own, and that it could be replaced without too much difficulty. Witness the very different attitude displayed to the handmill in Deut 24:6, which indicates that for a family to be without its handmill was a very great hardship (S. Rudser).

semolina. The *sōlet* requirement applies to both kinds of baked cereal offerings.

cakes. These cakes, *ḥallôt*, are thick relative to the other kind of baked cereal offering, the wafers. The Sumerians distinguished between thick and thin breads, NINDA.KUR₄RA and NINDA.TUR.(TUR), also NINDA.SIG, where KUR₄ = *kabru* 'thick' and TUR = *ṣibru* 'thin' (Levine 1965–66). The Hittites, borrowing these Sumerian ideograms, distinguished punctiliously between the two thicknesses of bread. Outside of P, *ḥallâ* occurs only in 2 Sam 6:19. When this verse is cited by the Chronicler, however, *ḥallâ* is changed to *kikkār* (1 Chr 16:3). Perhaps, by then, *ḥallâ* had begun to designate the priestly prebend from the bread dough (cf. Num 15:20), as prevalent in Mishnaic Hebrew (Paran 1983: 199). In any event, the substitution of *ḥallâ* by *kikkār* in postexilic texts points to its early provenience.

The shape of the *ḥallôt* is not clear. Because the root *ḥll* means "pierce," some say that the bread was ring-shaped; others claim it was perforated, that is, pricked before or after baking.

wafers (rĕqîqîm). The root *rqq* means "thin" in biblical Hebrew (see Gen 41:19) as well as in Akk. *raqāqu; raqqaqu* (adj.). Arab. *ruqāqat* is a thin, round cake.

smeared (mĕšûḥîm). In the form of the letter X (Greek *chi*), according to the rabbis *(m. Menaḥ.* 6:3; *Sipra,* Nedaba, par. 10:6). The rabbis' claim that a cross made on the cereal offering indicates that their tradition antedates Christianity.

5. *griddle.* The *maḥăbat* is usually made of clay, like those found in archaeo-

logical excavations such as Gezer (*IDB* 1.462, fig. 48), or of iron (Ezek 4:3). This is the most frequently used form of the cooked cereal offering (see 6:14; 7:9; 1 Chr 23:29), giving rise to a special term for its production, *maʿăśeh haḥăbittîm* (1 Chr 9:31). The LXX renders it τήγανον, oil-fried, but probably the product was more like toast.

6. *Crumble . . . into bits. pātôt . . . pittîm* (with *Tg. Onq.*). After the cereal offering is toasted on the griddle, it is crumbled, and the hard bits are oiled to soften them and make them palatable. The verb is a hapax, but the noun *pat* is quite common (Gen 18:5; Judg 19:5; 1 Sam 2:36; 28:22; 2 Sam 12:3; 1 Kgs 17:11; etc.). Because the high priest's daily cereal offering was prepared on a griddle, it too required subsequent crumbling (6:14). The rabbis held that all cereal offerings prepared in a vessel, including the pan-fried, had to be crumbled (*m. Menaḥ.* 6:4); but see the NOTE on v 7.

it is a cereal offering. minḥâ hîʾ (hwʾ), in other words, it (prepared on a griddle) is an acceptable form for the cereal offering. This formula is used for the natural grain offering (v 15) but not for the baked and pan-fried varieties; the reason is obscure.

7. *pan (marḥešet)*. "What is the difference between a griddle and a pan? The pan has a lid to it but the griddle has no lid"; so Rabbi Jose the Galilean. Rabbi Hanina ben Gamaliel says, a pan is deep and what is prepared therein is spongy (*rôḥăšîn*, from *rḥš* 'move, vibrate': "The liquid contained in it appears as though it were creeping and moving" [Rashi]); a griddle is flat and what is prepared thereon is hard" (*m. Menaḥ.* 5:8; cf. *Sipra*, Nedaba 12:7). The relative difference in the depth of the two cooking vessels is emphasized by their respective propositions: the dough is placed *al* 'on' the griddle but *be* 'in' the oiled pan (7:9). Inserting the dough into boiling oil results in deep frying (Ibn Ezra).

8. *If you bring (wĕhēbēʾtā)*. The LXX and 4QLevᵇ read *wĕhēbîʾ* 'If he brings', the change in the MT being accounted for by a dittography of the following *ʾet;* the advantage of the LXX and the Qumran reading is that it eliminates the problem of the third-person *wĕhiqrîbāh* 'he shall present it' that occurs later in the verse. At the same time, the switch from second person (vv 4–7) to third person is unexplained.

prepared. yēʿāśeh, a masculine verb with a feminine subject *minḥâ* 'cereal offering'. The LXX reads *yaʿăśeh* 'which he (the offerer) prepares', thereby eliminating the problem of mixed gender. But the LXX may be guilty of harmonization (see above).

in any of these ways. mēʾēlleh, that is to say, prepared in an oven, griddle, or pan (vv 4–7), all subsumed under the initial *kî* 'when' (v 4).

it shall be presented. wĕhiqrîbāh, lit., "and he shall present it" (so the LXX). The subject is clearly the offerer *(Tg. Ps.-J.)*, but the third person is inexplicable unless the active verb is understood as having an impersonal subject and can, therefore, be rendered as a passive. It is also possible to repoint the MT and read the verb as an imperative second masc. sing. with the third fem. sing. suffix—

wĕhaqrēbāh 'present it', as in *haqrēb 'ōtâ* 'present it' (6:7)—or understand it as an impersonal verb with passive meaning, as here rendered.

shall deliver it. *wĕhiggîsāh,* a synonym of *hiqrîb* (see 6:7, also with the cereal offering). But Bekhor Shor observed perceptively that the term *higgîš* is used only with the baked cereal offerings but not with the raw ones (vv. 2, 14; 6:7), which he explains as an additional rite performed by the priest to show that the cereal offering was baked initially for the altar and not brought to the altar as an afterthought (see the NOTE on 6:7).

The presentation by the priest to the altar is an indispensable rite in the sacrificial procedure (see at 1:5); but whereas only the burnt parts of the other offerings are presented to the altar, the entire cereal offering undergoes presentation to the altar even though only its "token" is burned. This is done to indicate that the entire offering in reality belongs to God that he, by his grace, has bestowed most of it as a perquisite on the priesthood. This point is stated explicitly in the priestly instructions: "I have assigned it (the cereal offering) as their portion from my food gifts" (6:10; see 10:12–13; 24:9). Perhaps for this reason, as suggested by Abravanel, the priestly portion may not be eaten leavened (6:9–10) because, theoretically, all of it should be consumed on the altar on which leaven is prohibited (v 11). In rabbinic terminology, *haggāšâ* is the technical term for the priestly presentation to the altar (*m. Menaḥ.* 5:5, 6).

9. *set aside (wĕhērîm).* In P *hērîm* is a technical term meaning "set aside, dedicate" (Milgrom 1972b). It is equivalent here to *wĕqāmaṣ* 'scoop out' (v 2). The latter term, however, is inappropriate in this context because the cooked cereal offering is solid and cannot be scooped out but must be broken off. Nevertheless, *hērîm* may be used with raw flour, if the word *bĕqumṣô* 'a handful' is added (as in 6:8).

pleasing aroma. Even the lowly cereal offering gives off a pleasing aroma "to teach you that it is the same whether a man offers much or little, as long as he directs his heart to heaven" (*m. Menaḥ.* 13:11).

10. *for Aaron and his sons.* This is in flat contradiction to 7:9, which declares that these three cooked cereal offerings belong to the officiating priest and not to the entire priestly cadre. Abravanel's answer is that v 10 repeats v 3 to indicate that the cooked cereal offering is distributed differently from the uncooked one, the details of which are given in 7:9–10. Moderns hold that both v 3 and v 10 are glosses because they deal with the priestly perquisites, a topic that is discussed in chaps. 6–7 but not in chaps. 1–5 (Elliger 1966). Thus two problems need to be addressed: the contradiction with 7:9 and the propriety here of discussing the priests' share (vv 3, 10). First, it should be noted that vv 3–10 are addressed to the laity and not to the priests, and the fine distinction made by 7:9–10 would hardly be expected here. (The same vagueness characterizes the description of the display bread in another passage addressed to the laity, 24:5–9.) Moreover, there may be no contradiction between the two passages, for in 7:9 the officiating priest, if he so desires, may share his perquisite

with his fellow priests. That such a possibility is in fact presupposed by the text is shown by the distribution of the meat of the purification offering, which, though given to the officiant, may be eaten by any priest (6:19, 22). Thus vv 3 and 10 of this chapter refer not to the priestly owner of the cereal offering but to those who have the right to consume it, namely, the entire priestly cadre.

Alternatively, and preferably, vv 3 and 10 should be regarded as glosses. Their purpose is to state unequivocally that all priestly prebends from the cereal offering, be they raw or cooked, are to be distributed equitably among the priests. It should be borne in mind that most cereal offerings brought to the altar were cooked beforehand (1 Sam 10:3; 21:5; 22:13; Jer 7:18; 49:19) for the obvious reason that no frankincense was required and, thus, they were affordable by the masses. Thus, as the priestly corps of the Temple expanded, pressure began to build within the priesthood to declare all cereal offerings the perquisite of the priests.

Historic proof for this development can be found in the Josianic reform, which abolished local sanctuaries and centralized all worship in the Jerusalem Temple. Deuteronomy, whose centralization demand powered the reform, insisted that all (levitic) priests were entitled to officiate in the Temple (Deut 18:6–8), where *ḥēleq kĕḥēleq yōʾkēlû* 'they shall share the perquisites equally' (v 9a). In reality, however, "the priests of the *bāmôt* did not ascend the altar of the Lord in Jerusalem but *ate unleavened bread among their kinsmen (ʾākĕlû maṣṣôt bĕtôk ʾăḥêhem)*" (2 Kgs 23:9). That is, the Temple priests did not admit their country brethren into their corps but allowed them to eat the *maṣṣôt*, the unleavened bread, stemming from the offerings. Moreover, the term *ʾăḥêhem* 'kinsmen' must be understood literally. The jobless priests were from the southern kingdom of Judah (v 8); hence, they were Aaronids (cf. Josh 21:13–19; the cities apportioned to the Aaronids are located within the tribes of Judah and Benjamin). This, indeed, made them "kinsmen" of the Jerusalemite priesthood.

The rabbis (followed by Rashi and Ehrlich 1908–14) claim, on the basis of Lev 21:22, that the disqualified priests were permitted to share in all sacrificial prebends (*m. Menaḥ.* 13:10). Modern critics prefer to see in 2 Kgs 23:9 a reference to the unleavened bread of the Passover that Josiah instituted in the Temple (2 Kgs 23:21–23). Neither interpretation, in my opinion, is correct. The word *maṣṣôt* must also be understood literally. It refers to all cereal offerings, which had to be brought or consumed unleavened (even the raw cereal offering, 6:9). Here again, the Jerusalemite priesthood reneged on the deuteronomic injunction that their own high priest, Hilkiah, had endorsed. Not only did they not absorb their fellow priests into their order (versus Deut 18:6–7) but they limited their sacrificial prebends to the cereal offering (versus Deut 18:8a). Thus, this historical notice from Kings confirms that Lev 2:10 was put into operation. The text merely states—innocently and, hence, credibly—that it was observed. It may well have been the Temple practice even before the reform.

For the fuller discussion and implications, see the COMMENT to this chapter, below; chap. 7, COMMENT F; and the Introduction, §C.

Why is it so important to state here, not once but twice, that the priests receive the entire cereal offering as their perquisite except for a token portion? As mentioned above in the NOTE on v 3, the cereal offering as a subsidiary of and accompaniment to the burnt offering would be expected to be treated similarly—turned into smoke on the altar. Indeed, as noted on "shall deliver it" (v 8), the vocabulary of the cereal offering implies that in principle all of it should be burned on the altar (see 6:10; 10:12–13; 24:9). Moreover, the prophet Jeremiah testifies that pagan rites practiced in his country involved the use of the cereal offering: "The children gather sticks, the fathers build the fire and the mothers knead dough to make cakes for the Queen of Heaven" (Jer 7:18); "And when we make offerings (*meqaṭṭĕrîm*, lit., "turn into smoke") to the Queen of Heaven . . . have made cakes" (Jer 44:19; see vv 17–18). Thus it is clear that in the immediate ambience of ancient Israel, cereal offerings were offered up to the gods by burning them totally on improvised altars (see the COMMENT below). The twice-mentioned injunction to turn over the cereal offering to the priests except for a token portion may then spring from a polemic against contemporaneous pagan practice. The text of the cereal offering therefore inserts into its prescriptions a caveat that irrespective of what pagans do and, indeed, of what might be expected of the cereal offering as a surrogate burnt offering, Israel should not offer up the cereal offering—even though it belongs to God—but award it to the priests as their perquisite. (For further exposition, see the COMMENT below.)

11. *you offer (taqrîbû)*. The verbs in vv 11–12 are in the plural, and these injunctions concerning leaven and honey may therefore be addressed to the priests who have been mentioned in the previous verse (v 10) as the recipients of the cereal offering (Ramban). Certainly the subject of the next verb *taqṭîrû* 'turn into smoke' can only be the priests, for they are the sole legitimate officiants at the altar. Furthermore, because the lay offerers have already been instructed that their cereal offerings are to be unleavened (vv 4, 5), it would be sheer redundancy to repeat that their offering should not be leavened. Thus this injunction is addressed to the priests, reminding them that they should carefully inspect the cooked cereal offerings presented to the altar lest they be leavened.

leavened . . . leaven. ḥāmēṣ . . . śĕʾōr. The difference between the two is that "*śĕʾōr* leavens the dough and the leavened dough is called *ḥāmēṣ*" (*Yahel ʾOr*). Thus *ḥāmēṣ* is an elliptical term for bread that has been baked with a leavening agent, *śĕʾōr*, probably "sourdough," a leaven consisting of yeast and lactic acid, which itself is not eaten (Kellermann 1980). Similarly, Akk. *ēmēṣu* 'be sour' and *emṣu* 'sour' (adj.) are used in connection with wine, vinegar, beer, fruit, or leavened bread, in other words, with foods that have fermented and, in the case of bread, to which leaven has been added. Fermentation is equivalent to decay and corruption and for this reason is prohibited on the altar. The objection may be posed: how is it, then, that wine, the quintessence of fermentation, is offered up on the altar? It should be noted that the wine libation is not burned on the altar hearth but poured out at the altar base (Sir 50:20–21; Jos., *Ant* 3.234) and thus does not violate the prohibition to "turn into smoke" any fermented substance.

"Leaven in the dough" is a common rabbinic metaphor for man's evil propensities (e.g., *b. Ber.* 17a). The New Testament mentions "the leaven of malice and wickedness" (1 Cor 5:8) and "the leaven of the Pharisees," which is "hypocrisy" (Luke 12:1; cf. Mark 8:15). This view is shared by the ancients: "Leaven itself comes from corruption, and corrupts the dough with which it is mixed . . . and in general, fermentation seems to be a kind of putrefaction" (Plutarch, *Quaest. Rom.* 109). Plutarch records that the Roman high priest (Flamen Dialis) was forbidden even to touch leaven (ibid.). To be sure, all of the above-cited references stem from late antiquity (Christian, rabbinic, and Hellenistic sources), but they undoubtedly reflect an older and universal regard of leaven as the arch-symbol of fermentation, deterioration, and death and, hence, taboo on the altar of blessing and life.

honey. Opinion is divided about whether *děbaš* stands for bee honey or fruit honey. In favor of the former is that honey ferments easily (Pliny, *H. N.* 31.14[48]), and in rabbinic Hebrew *hidbîš* means "turn sour or corrupt" (e.g., *b. B. Meṣ.* 38a). Also, bee honey was regularly offered to nearly all of the Greek gods (Paus. 5.15.6) and was especially employed in offerings to the chthonic deities of the Hittites, Greeks, and Mesopotamians (Hoffner 1967a), thus providing a rationale for prohibiting its use in Israelite worship. Nonetheless, the view that *děbaš* is fruit honey is supported on scriptural and philological grounds. During the reign of Hezekiah, "The Israelites amassed the first-processed fruits of corn, wine, oil, *děbaš*, and all agricultural produce, and brought in a generous tithe of everything" (2 Chr 31:5; cf. Neh 10:36). Thus *děbaš* must be equivalent to the other products mentioned in this verse, for together with them it is subsumed under the rubric "all agricultural produce" *(Seper Hamibḥar).* Moreover, firstfruits, raw *(bikkûrîm)* or processed *(rēʾšît),* can only refer to agricultural produce (see below, vv 12, 14). Indeed, the stereotyped metaphor for Canaan, "a land flowing with milk and honey," must intend fruit honey, because Canaan from time immemorial was known for its abundant fruits, especially its dates, figs, and grapes (Deut 8:8). Also, bee honey is described by two other terms, *yaʿar* (1 Sam 14:26; Cant 5:1) and *nōpet* (Ps 19:11; Prov 5:3; 24:13; 27:7; Cant 4:11), the latter also being the cognate of the Ug. word *(nbt)* for bee honey. *děbaš* is too frequently associated with agricultural products (Gen 43:11; Deut 8:8; 2 Kgs 18:32; Ezek 16:13; 2 Chr 31:5) not to be regarded as a product of the soil. Furthermore, *děbaš* as fruit honey is supported by comparative philology: Arab. *dibs* is "grape syrup" and Akk. *dišip suluppi* is "date syrup"; that honey is processed from dates is verified by Josephus (*Wars* 4.468). In truth, only one scriptural passage clearly refers to *děbaš* as bee honey

(Judg 14:8). Jonathan's encounter with honey in the woods (1 Sam 14:26–29) mentions no bees and could actually refer to a sweet secretion of plant parasites. In any case, it is a wild product and definitely not produced by domesticated bees. A final argument for *dĕbaš* as fruit honey is that although the Hittites had domesticated the bee before the fourteenth century, there is no evidence that Israel practiced beekeeping during the biblical period (Caquot 1978).

The theory that honey was prohibited because of its widespread use in heathen worship (e.g., Maim., *Guide* 3.46) must be rejected because if that were so, the Torah would also have prohibited the use of flour, incense, oil salt—likewise the staples of idolatrous cults (Kalisch 1867–72: 141)—as well as blood, the main ingredient in chthonic worship. Moreover, in Jotham's parable the fig, in contrast to the olive and the grape, is not extolled as a fruit that honors God, that is to say, is offered on the altar (Judg 9:8–13). The association of leaven with fermentation, decay, and death remains the most plausible cause for the prohibition.

Abravanel asks why was it necessary to insert a blanket prohibition against honey when the only vegetable offering permitted was that of cereal (wheat or barley). His answer is attractive: because Canaan is blessed with seven species (Deut 8:8), four of which (wheat, barley, [olive] oil, and wine) are used on the altar, one might conclude that the remaining three (figs, pomegranates, and *dĕbaš* [date honey]) are also permitted. Hence, a prohibition concerning fruit honey was essential.

12. *them.* Refers not to leaven and honey per se but rather to the cereal offerings that are cooked with them (Dillmann and Ryssel 1897).

first-processed (rēʾšît). The gift of the firstfruits is due not only from the first-ripe crops of the soil but also from certain foods processed from these crops, namely, grain, new wine, new (olive) oil, fruit syrup, leavened food, and bread dough. The Priestly legislation preserves the terminological distinction between these two kinds: *bikkûrîm* 'the first-ripe' and *rēʾšît* 'the first-processed'. Thus, "All the best of the oil, and all the best of the wine and of the grain, the first-processed *(rēʾšît)* that they give to the Lord, I give to you. The first ripe *(bikkûrîm)* of all that is in their land, which they give to the Lord, shall be yours" (Num 18:12–13; cf. Ezek 44:30). Grain, wine, and oil as well as fruit syrup, leaven, and dough are clearly processed from plants and are termed *rēʾšît* in P (2:12; Num 18:12; cf. 2 Chr 31:5; Num 15:20–21; cf. Ezek 44:30; also wool in Deut 18:4). *ʿōmer rēʾšît qĕṣîrĕkem* 'the first sheaf of your harvest' (Lev 23:10) is not an exception. *rēʾšît* here is not a technical term for firstfruits, but simply the adjective "first." Its use emphasizes that the *ʿōmer* is not to be selected from among the many sheaves of the first-ripe harvest but must be the very first sheaf (Deut 16:9; cf. Exod 23:19; 34:26).

Proof that *rēʾšît* refers to the processed produce is found in the expression "as with the new grain from the threshing floor" (Num 18:27), referring to the Israelites' required *rēʾšît* contribution (Num 18:12), which is specified as coming not from the field but from the threshing floor, after the grain is fully separated from the chaff. Indeed, this corresponds with the view of the rabbis, who claim that the perquisite is removed from the produce only "when its work is completed" (cf. *m. Ter.* 1:10; Maim., Seeds; Tithe 3.13), that is, when it is fully processed. The time is specified in the case of the tithe as "grain, after the pile is smoothed off or stacked . . . wine, after it has been skimmed . . . oil, after it has dripped down into the trough" (*m. Maʿas.* 1:6–7; cf. *Sipre* Num 121). An offering of dough or bread (23:17; Num 15:19–21) would, of course, also qualify as a *rēʾšît*. The use of *rēʾšît* as first-processed fruits seemed to have continued at Qumran. Outside of P, *rēʾšît* has two other meanings: either it is equivalent to *bikkûrîm* 'first ripe' (e.g., Deut 26:2, 10; Jer 2:3) or it means "the best" (e.g., 1 Sam 2:29b; 15:21; possibly Exod 23:19; 34:26; but see above). That leavened bread and fruit honey were, in practice, permitted as a first-processed fruit offering is shown by 23:12 and 2 Chr 31:5, respectively.

be offered up. yaʿălû, lit., "they shall offer up," but this verb with an unspecified subject can be rendered as a passive (e.g., 1 Kgs 18:29, 36; Job 5:26).

13. *omit from.* Whereas salt should never be omitted *(hišbît min)* from your sacrifices, leaven should always be removed *(hišbît min)* from your homes before the Feast of Unleavened Bread (Exod 12:15). For other attestations of this idiom see Jer 7:34; 16:9; 36:29; 48:33; Ezek 34:10. All of the verbs in this verse are in the singular, a sign that the subject is once again the offerer. This means that the obligation to salt the offering falls not on the priest but on its owner. By contrast, in the public sacrifices the responsibility for salting fell to the priests (Ezek 43:24), and the salt came from Temple supplies (Jos., *Ant.* 12.140).

the salt of your covenant with your God. The idiom *melaḥ bĕrît ʾĕlōhêkā* is used again to refer to the binding character of the priestly perquisites (Num 18:19) and of the Davidic dynasty (2 Chr 13:5). Salt was the preservative par excellence in antiquity (see Philo, *Laws* 1. 289; Theophylact. in *Luc.* 14.34; Diog. Laert. *Pythag.* 19 [8.35]; Pliny *H.N.* 31.9 [45]). A figurative extension of its preservative properties is the reference to the apostles as "the salt of the earth" (Matt 5:17), in other words, teachers who guard the world against moral decay. Moreover, its preservative qualities made it the ideal symbol of the perdurability of a covenant *(Tg. Ps.-J.).* A neo-Babylonian letter speaks of "all who tasted the salt of the Jakin tribe" *(ABL* 747, r. 6), referring to the tribe's covenantal allies. Loyalty to the Persian monarch is described as having tasted "the salt of the palace" (Ezra 4:14). Arab. *milḥat,* a derivative of *malaḥa* 'to salt', means "a treaty" (G. B. Gray 1903: 232). "There is salt between us" implies among Arab bedouin a treaty stipulating mutual aid and defense (R. Smith 1927: 270). The Greeks likewise salted their covenant meals and referred to salt as "holy" *(Iliad* 9.214; Heliod. 4.16). Thus it is likely that in Israel as well salt played a central role at the solemn meal that sealed a covenant (e.g., Gen 26:30; 31:54; Exod 24:11). Salt was deemed so essential in Ezekiel's vision of the restoration that he makes room for marshes and swamps in his otherwise fertile land in order to provide salt (Ezek 47:11).

Why is this injunction to salt all sacrifices inserted here with the cereal offering rather than with any of the clearly more important blood sacrifices? Abravanel suggests that because bread normally contains flour, leaven, and salt, the question would naturally arise: if leaven is forbidden in the cereal offering, should not salt also be forbidden?

on all your offerings (ʿal kol-qorbānĕkā). Salt is added to all substances connected with sacrifice except wine, blood, and wood *(b. Menaḥ.* 20a, 21a). There is no biblical evidence for such a comprehensive application of this injunction; Ezek 43:24 speaks only of salting the burnt offering (cf. Jos., *Ant.* 3.227). Probably all offerings burned on the altar hearth required salting.

14. *If. (wĕʾim).* The third kind of cereal offering, of natural grain, is introduced by the subordinate particle *ʾim* (as in vv 5, 7) rather than the more expected *kî* (as in vv 1, 4); but see below.

first-ripe fruits. bikkûrîm, which in all biblical sources consistently refers to the first-ripe fruit (see Exod 23:16, 19; 34:22; Num 13:20; Neh 10:36). The use of *bikkûrîm* in tannaitic literature is also restricted to first-ripe (unprocessed) fruits (e.g., *m. Bik.* 3:1); but what precisely is the first-ripe cereal offering: barley, wheat, or both? To be sure, the term *bikkûrîm* is applied to either barley (2 Kgs 4:42) or wheat (Num 28:26), and it is certainly possible to argue that the cereal offering specified here should come from both (as do the Qumran sectaries, 11QT 19:7). The fact is, however, that to this day Arab peasants roast barley precisely as described in this verse, but not wheat because of the latter's flat taste (J. Feliks, oral communication; and cf. Dalman 1928: 457). Moreover, that barley is intended here is confirmed by the structure of this chapter. The previous cereal offerings are of *sōlet,* wheat groats, semolina; but that section (vv 1–10) is separated from the first-ripe cereal offering (vv 14–16) by a series of injunctions concerning leaven, honey, and salt (vv 11–13). Thus this chapter's structure makes it likely that the first-ripe cereal offering was deliberately severed from the other cereal offerings because it was of a different grain—not wheat but barley. (The argumentation is that of the Karaites; see *Seper Hamibḥar* and *Keter Torah.*)

The rabbis, who also maintain that this cereal offering is restricted to barley, identify it with the ʿōmer offering of barley *(m. Menaḥ.* 10:4; *Sipra,* Nedaba par. 13:4), which in their time was a public offering brought annually on behalf of the whole nation (see Jos., *Ant.* 3.250–51) on the sixteenth day of Nisan (see at 23:10–11). Yet the conditional construction of this verse indicates that it is a voluntary offering (Ibn Ezra), a conclusion underscored by the use of the particle *ʾim,* which continues the previous cases, all of which are voluntary (see Rabbi Hillel on *Sipra,* Nedaba par. 13:3); if it were the public ʿōmer offering, as claimed by the rabbis, this verse would have begun with *kî,* indicating an entirely new category of offering *(Yahel ʾOr; Shadal).* Thus this passage would seem to refer to the first-ripe barley offering brought by each individual Israelite farmer.

In the final analysis, however, the rabbis can be proved right, once it is established that *originally* the *ʿōmer* offering of barley was required of each Israelite barley grower (see at 23:10–11). Moreover, from the reference to the first-ripe wheat offering as "a new *minḥâ*" (23:16; Num 28:26), it can be inferred that the prior *ʿōmer* offering was also considered a *minḥâ*, further indentifying it with the *minḥâ* discussed here.

Also, the pericope on the *ʿōmer* offering (23:9–14) is totally silent concerning its disposition. All it tells us is that an armful *(ʿōmer)* of barley sheaves is brought to the priest, who then dedicates it to the Lord. What was done with it? There are only two possibilities: giving it to the priest or burning the flour prepared from its grains (cf. *m. Menaḥ.* 10:4) on the altar. If the former, then the text would have stated *qōdeš yihyeh laYHWH lakkōhēn* 'It shall be holy to the Lord, for the priest', as is stated in the case of the firstfruits of wheat (23:20b). But there is no need to declare in chap. 23 that the *ʿōmer* is burned on the altar, for that fact is already stated here in 2:14. That chap. 23 (H) bases itself on earlier P texts is made manifest by its repeated use of the generalization *wehiqrabtem ʾiššeh laYHWH* (23:8, 25, 27, 36), which refers to the sacrifices detailed in Num 28 and 29. (The reliance of chap. 23 [H] on chap. 2 [P] and Num 28–29 [P] is another indication of the chronological priority of P over H: see the Introduction §C.

Finally, if this barley offering were voluntary and was offered subsequent to the *ʿōmer* (Ibn Ezra, Karaites), there is no reason it could not be offered as bread (e.g., 2 Kgs 4:42) like the wheat offering. Hence, the passage does indeed refer to the *ʿōmer* offering of barley, and it is a compulsory and not a voluntary offering, incumbent on every Israelite farmer. In fact, the very term *bikkûrîm* 'first-ripe fruits offering' implies its compulsory nature, because all biblical sources mandate that firstfruits must be given to the sanctuary from every crop (Num 18:13; Neh 10:36).

Thus this offering is set apart from the previous cereal offerings not only because it is limited to barley while the others refer to wheat but also because it is not voluntary like the others but mandatory (Wessely 1846). That being the case, the initial clause may be rendered, "If you bring (this kind of) a cereal offering." Alternatively, the opening particle *wěʾîm* must be rendered "when" (*kî*, indeed, would have been preferable [see *Sipra*, Nedaba par. 13:1–3] but *ʾim* can also have the meaning "when," e.g., Gen 24:19; Num 36:4; Isa 4:4), that is, when you bring the first-ripe barley offering (= *ʿōmer*), it should be brought in the following manner (Milgrom 1983d: 148 n. 28, an opinion that is now reversed). For references to the roasted form of the *ʿōmer*, see 23:14 and Josh 5:11.

milky grain (ʾābîb). This rendering is that of H. L. Ginsberg, following the arguments of G. Dalman (1928–39: 1.2.416, 455–61; 3.8, 10) that (1) Saadiah translates *ʾābîb* (in Exod 9:31; Lev 2:14) and in the combination *ḥōdeš hāʾābîb*

(Exod 13:4; Deut 16:1) by Arab. *farīk* 'hulled by rubbing' (i.e., between the fingers); and (2) as rabbinic tradition makes clear *(m. Kil.* 5:7), *'ābîb* is an intermediate stage between mere stalks *('ăśābîm)* with no spikes or ears on them and fully ripe grain *(dāgān).* Ginsberg (1982: n. 60) writes as follows:

> In III, p. 1 Dalman notes that the change from soft-seeded ears to fully ripe ones is marked by a change in the color of the standing grain: barley turns from green to yellow; in wheat, the green fades to a shade that is so light as to be almost white. I have learned further from competent informants in Jerusalem that during the green phase of the standing grain the seeds in the hearts are likewise green and that if they are pressed liquid will ooze from them, for which reason this stage is called *havšalat halav,* literally 'milk ripening' in Ivrit. It is this term that has inspired my own coinage milky grain [anticipated by Dillmann—J.M.]. Of course milky grain, though it cannot be ground to flour, is not unusable for food. Christian Arabs in Jerusalem have informed me that wheat in this stage is cooked and eaten under the name *frike:* cf. Hans Wehr, Dictionary of Modern literary Arabic s.v. *farik.* Further, a combination of Lev 2:14 which speaks of a cereal offering of firstfruits, with Mishna *Menahot* 10:4, which speaks of the *'ōmer* of Lev 23:9ff. . . . suggests that milky grain of barley could also be rendered palatable by parching and grinding to grits.

parched with fire (qālûy bā'ēš). It cannot be prepared raw (as in vv 1–3) because it cannot be ground into flour (Elliger 1966). This is another reason the cereal must be barley and not wheat. Firstfruits of the latter are offered as bread loaves (23:17), whereas those of barley are offered up in sheaf (23:11), precisely as here (Dillmann and Ryssel 1897).

groats (gereś). So Arab. *ǧariš,* Syr. *gr(w)s',* and rabbinic *gĕrîsîn (b. 'Abod. Zar.* 65b). The related verb *gāras* means "crush" (Lam 3:16).

fresh ear (karmel; see 23:14; 2 Kgs 4:42). It is also the name of the mountain range that juts into the Mediterranean at Haifa, which is celebrated for its luxuriant vegetation, being the very last part of the country to suffer from drought (see Amos 1:2; 9:3), from which this term possibly derives its meaning. The sectaries of Qumran interpreted this word as *mĕlîlôt* 'parched grain' (11QT 19:7). But the preceding phrase *qālûy bā'ēš* would render this interpretation a redundancy. Indeed, the subsequent predicate, *tāqrîb 'ēt minhat bikkûrĕkā* (14bβ), repeats almost verbatim the initial predicate *wĕ'im-taqrîb minhat bikkûrîm*—a circular inclusion (Paran 1983: 38)—for the purpose of emphasizing that these firstfruits must be brought as groats of the fresh ear. The LXX and *Tgs. Onq.* and *Ps.-J.* render the expression *gereś karmel* as a hendiadys for "ground." The implausibility of this rendering is proved by the expression *karmel bĕṣiqlōnô* (2 Kgs 4:42), where *bĕṣiqlōnô* 'on the stalk' (1 Aqht 62 =

CTA 19.62 = *KTU* 1.19.2.13; Cassuto 1951b: 39; Albright 1950a: 392) assures that *karmel* must refer to the grain, namely, the fresh ear.

16. *some of its groats (miggirśāh)*. Note that this term replaces *missāltāh* in the otherwise identical formulas v 16a = v 2aβ, again showing that offering of wheat must be from flour whereas barley, if offered as firstfruits, must be from the sheaf.

COMMENT
THE CEREAL OFFERING: FUNCTION, NAME, TYPES, AND DEVELOPMENT

Rabbinic tradition clearly regards the cereal offering as the poor man's burnt offering.

> R. Joshua of Siknin said in the name of R. Levi: come and see how the Holy One, blessed be he, tried to spare the Israelites expense, for he said to them: "Whoever is obligated to bring a sacrifice, let him bring from the herd, as it is said, 'If his offering is a burnt offering from the herd' (Lev 1:3); if he cannot afford from the herd, let him bring a lamb, as it is written, 'If be brings a lamb' (Lev 4:32); if he cannot afford to bring an offering from the lambs, let him bring one from the goats, as it is said 'If his offering is a goat' (Lev 3:12); if he cannot afford to bring from the goats, let him bring from the birds, as it is said 'If his offering is . . . of the birds' (Lev 1:14); if he cannot afford to bring from the birds, let him bring semolina, as it is said 'His offering shall be of semolina' (Lev 2:1). Moreover, other offerings cannot be offered up in halves, but this one is to be offered up in halves, as it is said, 'half thereof in the morning, and half thereof in the evening' (Lev 6:13). Beyond that, one who offers it (the cereal offering) is accounted by Scripture as if he were offering a sacrifice from one end of the world unto the going down of the same. My name is great among the nations; and in every place offerings are presented unto My name, even a pure cereal offering" (Mal 1:11). (*Midr. Lev. Rab.* 8:4; cf. *m. Menaḥ.* 13:11; *b. Menaḥ.* 110a [bar.]; *b. Menaḥ.* 104b)

Philo echoes this rabbinic view: "God does not rejoice in sacrifices even if one offers hecatombs, for all things are His possession; yet though He possesses (all) He needs none of them, but He rejoices in the will to love Him and in men that practice holiness, and from these He accepts plain meal or barley (or "barley ground or unground") and things of least price, holding them most precious rather than those of highest cost" (*Laws* 1. 271 [Loeb 7.257]). Thus Philo also regarded the cereal offering as a surrogate blood offering, though his reference to barley is not in consonance with the Priestly insistence that the individual cereal offering is restricted to semolina wheat (see at v 2) except in the case of a firstfruit cereal offering, which may be composed of barley (vv 14–16). Stronger support for this position is the attested practice in the Mesopotamian cult, which explicitly labels cereal as the offering of the poor: "The widow brings you [šamaš] cheap flour, the poor woman [some] oil, the rich man from his riches brings a lamb" (Oppenheim 1956: 340); "The widow makes her offering to you (pl.) with cheap flour, the rich man with a lamb" (*CAD*, 10.331, s.v. *mashatu*).

The placement of the text on the cereal offering, right after that of the burnt offering, would also tend to support the view that the two are related. Their relationship would then be comparable to the graduated purification offerings, where too the cereal offering follows that of birds (5:7–10, 11–13) and where the reason for allowing both of them is explicitly stated: "if his means do not suffice (for an animal)" (vv. 7, 11). The juxtaposition of the cereal-offering prescriptions (chap. 2) after the burnt offering of birds (1:14–17) can be explained by the same rationale. To be sure, the burnt offering–cereal offering sequence has been afforded a different explanation: the cereal offering is the regular accompaniment to the burnt offering, and for that reason—not that it is a surrogate burnt offering for the poor—the two were conjoined in the sacrificial prescriptions (Ralbag; Elliger 1966, and most moderns). But Abravanel has effectively rebutted this explanation by pointing out that the cereal offering is also the required auxiliary of the well-being offering (Num 15:1–12) and, therefore, the cereal offering should logically have followed both the burnt offering and the well-being offering prescriptions, that is, after chap. 3.

Thus the cereal offering must be viewed as a discrete, independent sacrifice that functions to duplicate the manifold purposes of the burnt offering for the benefit of those who cannot afford a burnt offering of quadruped or bird. That the cereal offering is capable of the same wide range of applications as the burnt offering can be sustained on etymological grounds: *minḥâ* means "gift, tribute" for the purpose of showing reverence (1 Sam 10:27), homage (Gen 32:14, 19, 21), political friendship (2 Kgs 20:12), and political submission (Judg 3:15, 17). Arab. *manaḥa* means "to bestow a gift," and its nominal form, *minḥat*, means "gift, tribute." So does the Ug. noun *mnḥ* (*UT* 120.1, 4; 137.28) and the Akk. plural *manaḥātu* (*PRU* 1956: 4.293, no. 19.55), which probably entered into New Egyptian, *m(a)nḥîtu*, as a loanword (Albright 1957).

The most likely definition for biblical *minḥâ* is "a present made to secure or retain good will" (Driver 1900: 587). The emphasis, then, is clearly propitiatory and is best illustrated by the following two examples: David implores Saul, "If the Lord has incited you against me, let him be appeased by a *minḥâ*" (1 Sam 26:19). Jacob also, it should be recalled, attempted to appease Esau's wrath by sending on ahead several contingents, each bearing a *minḥâ* (Gen 32:14, 19, 21; 33:10). Indeed, in Babylonian religion as well, the function of the cereal offering, the *mašḥatu*, is to appease: "Did it bring its flour offering to appease the goddess's anger?" (Lambert 1960: 75, 1.51; cf. 39, 1.20).

On the basis of the fact that no *minḥâ* is prescribed for the new mother (12:6–8), the *zāb/zābâ* (15:14–15, 29–30), or on the Day of Atonement. (16:3, 5, 24), the conclusion has been drawn that the purpose of the *minḥâ* is essentially joyous and "perhaps sacrifices of a more somber nature were intentionally made without a cereal offering," in contrast to the joyous well-being offering, which was always accompanied by a cereal offering (Rainey 1975: 207). This conclusion is only partially correct. In P, there seems to be a clear attempt to modify the composition of the cereal offering in somber situations by deliberately eliminating the requirement of oil and frankincense from the offering, for example, in the cases of the poor man's purification offering (5:11) and the suspected adulteress (Num 5:15). It is these two ingredients, however, that determine the joyous nature of the cereal offering, not the offering per se. On the contrary, there are sacrifices whose somber purpose cannot be gainsaid, which nonetheless require a cereal offering, such as the purification rites of the *mĕṣōrāʿ*, which explicitly require the cereal offering for purposes of expiation (14:20); there is also the evidence of a text from a non-Priestly source that "The iniquity of the house of Eli will never be expiated by a flesh or cereal offering" (1 Sam 3:14). Thus the full evidence of Scripture, in both Priestly and non-Priestly texts, attests to the comprehensive, catchall function of the *minḥâ*, which matches the burnt offering in its range, and which corresponds to its etymological connotation of "gift" or "tribute." In the cult it serves as a discrete, autonomous offering, independent of and probably prior to its ancillary function as the auxiliary of the burnt and well-being offerings. Not surprisingly, this is precisely the role that the bread offerings occupy in the ancient Hittite cult. Ritual texts list offerings of loaves separately from animal offerings (e.g., five times in *ANET*³ 396–99), and, even more significantly, the bread offerings are mentioned first (e.g., *ANET*³ 399–400).

If the *minḥâ* means "gift, tribute," implying no limitation whatever on its specific form, how did it become restricted to P's cereal offerings? To be sure, in non-Priestly texts the *minḥâ* offered to God can consist of animals. Indeed, Abel's offering to God is so designated (Gen 4:3–4). The sons of Eli who seize their share of the meat offering illegitimately are said to have "treated the Lord's *minḥâ* impiously" (1 Sam 2:17), and, by expropriating their share of the meat even before the sacrifice upon the altar, they committed the ultimate offense of "fattening themselves on the best portions of every *minḥâ* of Israel before me" (1 Sam 2:29 LXX; cf. vv 15–16). Yet in P, the *minḥâ* exclusively refers to cereal offerings. The reason for this restriction cannot be ascertained with any assurance. A similar reduction will be noticed in the term *zebaḥ*, which originally embraced all blood offerings (lit., "slaughtered" offerings; e.g., 1 Sam 3:14, cited above), but in the Priestly literature was restricted to the thanksgiving and well-being offerings (see the COMMENT on chap. 3). This similar phenomenon for the *zebaḥ* suggests that as the number and types of sacrifices began to proliferate in the Priestly cult, the terms *minḥâ* and *zebaḥ* relinquished some of their original functions to the new offerings until they were contracted to the more limited compass now attested in P, the cereal offering and well-being offering, respectively. In the case of the cereal offering this process would have been aided by the fact that Israel, a grain-oriented society, would have brought its *minḥâ* mostly in grain (Anderson 1987).

The cereal offering in Scripture is of two types: an accompaniment to animal sacrifices and an independent, discrete offering. To begin with, it is the required auxiliary of the burnt offering and the well-being offering. "When the Hebrew ate flesh, he ate bread with it and drank wine and when he offered flesh on the table of his God, it was natural that he should add to it the same concomitants which were necessary to make up a comfortable and generous meal." This observation of R. Smith (1927: 222) was anticipated much earlier by Abravanel (on Num 15): "The four increases in proportion to the meat. This is akin to the human practice that the more the meat the more the need for bread." Thus, in Numbers, the bread auxiliary varies proportionally with the size and value of the animal. Ezekiel proposes a different scale. The following table projects the variations:

animal	cereal (Ezek 45)	cereal (Num 15)
lamb (regular)	optional	1/10 *ephah*
lamb *(tamid)*	1/6 *ephah*	1/10 *ephah*
ram	1 *ephah*	2/10 *ephah*
ox	1 *ephah*	3/10 *ephah*

In addition to these required cereal accompaniments, certain sacrificial situations also require cereal offerings, such as the *tôdâ*, the thanksgiving offering (7:12–14), the priestly consecration (8:26–27; cf. Exod 29:23–24), and the Nazirite on completion of his vow (Num 6:19–21). Outside P, the auxiliary cereal offering is amply attested in the early narratives and prophets, thereby underscoring its antiquity (see 1 Sam 1:24; 2:29; 3:14; 10:3; 1 Kgs 8:64; 2 Kgs 16:13, 15; Isa 19:21; 43:23; 66:3; Jer 14:12; 17:26; Amos 5:22, 25). Whereas the blood offering uses the verb *zibbaḥ*, the cereal offering prefers the verb *qiṭṭēr* 'go up in smoke' (e.g., 1 Kgs 22:44; 2 Kgs 12:4; 14:4; Isa 65:3; Hos 4:13; 11:2).

The cereal offering could also be offered by itself, in which case, according to the Priestly rules, it would be accompanied by oil and, if uncooked, by frankincense (2:1–3, 14–16). If it was cooked, the requirement of frankincense was waived (see at vv 4–10) as a special concession to the poor for whom even a few grains of this precious spice would have strained their means (see below). The elimination of the frankincense from the cooked cereal offering demonstrates that it was neither indispensable nor essential for providing a *rēaḥ nîḥōaḥ* (2:9; *pace* Weinfeld 1987). On the basis of the verse "Eighty men from Shechem, Shiloh, and Samaria, their beards shaved, their garments torn, and their bodies gashed, carrying cereal offerings and frankincense to present at the house of the Lord" (Jer 41:5), it is alleged that the indigent nonetheless did bring frankincense with their cereal offerings (Haran 1968a). But as these very men also disclosed, "We have stores hidden in a field—wheat, barley, oil, and honey" (v 8), it is clear that they were not poor. Furthermore, the reason they did not offer up animals was not their lack of means but the fact that the Temple was destroyed. The site of the Temple ruins continued to attract pilgrims who offered up cereal and incense offerings, but they drew the line at animal sacrifices for the lack of a legitimate altar and an officiating priesthood. Textual confirmation of this apparent distinction between blood and cereal offerings is provided by the book of Deuteronomy, which mandates that "You must bring everything that I command you to the site where the Lord your God will choose to establish his name: your burnt offerings and your offerings of well-being, your tithes and your contributions and all the choice votive offerings that you vow to the Lord" (Deut 12:11; cf. vv 6, 14, 27). That is, all Israel's blood offerings must be brought to the one legitimate altar, but the cereal offering (and incense) may be offered up anywhere. Indeed, even the Priestly legislation, which expressly forbids sacrifice outside of the Tent of Meeting, restricts this prohibition to "burnt offerings and offerings of well-being" (17:8; cf. Josh 22:23), apparently exempting the cereal offering (and incense—as long as it is not of the same composition as that prescribed for the authorized sanctuary—Exod 30:37–38).

At the end of the Second Temple period, the *Testament of Levi* records that the angels "offer to the Lord a sweet-smelling savor, a reasonable and bloodless offering" (*T. Levi* 3:6), again indicating that cereal offerings (and incense) could be offered outside the Temple. This background clarifies the correspondence of the Jews of Elephantine with the Bagohi, the Persian governor of Judea, and Johanan, the high priest at the end of the fifth century, requesting that they be permitted to rebuild their temple and offer there "the cereal offering, incense and burnt offering" (Cowley 1923: 113; 30.25). Their petition was granted with the exception of the burnt offering (Cowley 1923: 123; 32.9–10), and the Jews of Elephantine consented that "n[o] sheep, ox, or goat is offered there as a burnt offering, but only incense, cereal offering and [libation]" (Cowley 1923: 125; 33.10–11; Porten 1968: 289–93), proof that the authorities in Jerusalem, religious as well as civil, permitted bloodless sacrifices—expressly the cereal offering—to be offered outside the Temple. Finally, rabbinic literature, in both legal and midrashic contexts, confirms that the cereal offering was sacrificed in Second Temple times, and even after the Temple was destroyed: "If one offered outside (the Temple court) a cereal offering from which a handful had not been taken, he is not culpable. . . . R. Eleazar declares him not culpable (if he offered either the handful or the frankincense outside the Temple court) unless he offered the second also" (*m. Zebaḥ.* 13:5–6; cf. *t. Zebaḥ.* 12:4–5). Thus, the sages tolerated the de facto practice that cereal offerings and incense were being offered throughout the land (Finkelstein 1962: 654–60). Rabbi Ami interpreted the verse "everywhere incense and pure *minḥâ* are offered to My name" (Mal 1:11) as referring to Israel (*Midr. Tanḥ.* Aḥare 9; cf. *y. Meg.* 1:11; *y. ʿAbod. Zar.* 4:4). This means he knew full well that Jews were offering cereal offerings (and incense) outside of Jerusalem. Hence there is a persistent tradition beginning with the book of Deuteronomy and corroborated by later extrabiblical sources—the Elephantine papyri, the pseudepigraphal *Testament of Levi,* and rabbinic halakha and midrash—that the cereal offering continued to be offered privately and independently of the Temple cult by the people at large (Milgrom 1979a, b).

The independent cereal offering is attested in the following instances: the bread loaves of the thanksgiving offering (7:12–14), the priestly consecration (8:26–27), and the Nazirite (Num 6:19–21); the poor man's purification offering (5:11); the suspected adulteress (Num 5:15–26); the high priest's daily offering (6:12–16); the display bread (24:5–9); the firstfruits (*ʿōmer*) of the barley (2:14–16; 23:10–11) and the wheat (23:15–17); and the five forms of unleavened semolina prescribed in this chapter: raw flour (vv 1–3) and cooked flour, either baked cakes or wafers, griddle-toasted or pan-fried (vv 4–7).

When the cereal offering is part of a series of sacrifices, it is sometimes difficult to tell whether it is an adjunct to the burnt and sometimes the well-being offering or a discrete sacrifice. H. Albeck (1956: 364–65) has suggested this rule of thumb: the cereal offering listed before the blood offerings is clearly independent (e.g., Num 18:9–14; Ezek 44:29), but if listed after the blood offerings it is an adjunct (e.g., 14:10; Num 6:14–15; Ezek 45:17, 24, 25; 46:14). In some cases, however, this rule breaks down (see on 9:3–4, 17). Three of the independent cereal offerings are also involved in the *tĕnûpâ* (elevation) rite (see at 7:30), for the reason that they vary from the regular prescription for this offering. The *ʿōmer* (2:14–16; 23:10–11) and the cereal offering of the suspected adulteress (Num 5:15) are composed of barley; the firstfruits of the wheat (23:15–17) are leavened; and all three lack oil and frankincense—in contrast to the normal recipe for the cereal offering as found in this chapter: unleavened semolina plus oil and frankincense (Milgrom 1983d: 147–49). Also, the possibility must be reckoned with that during the period of the kingdom, the cereal offering was sacrificed daily at sunset by itself, unaccompanied by the burnt offering (1 Kgs 18:36; 2 Kgs 16:15; Ps 141:2 [Haran 1968a: 29]).

As noted by Haran (1968a), in all of the non-Priestly sources the cereal offering is burned in its entirety. The root *qṭr* 'go up in smoke' is the one most frequently met, either the *piʿel qiṭṭēr* when the illegitimate cult is intended (e.g., 2 Kgs 17:11; 18:4; 23:8; Jer 19:13; 32:29; 44:17–19, 25) or the *hiphʿil hiqṭîr* in the legitimate cult (e.g., 2 Kgs 16:13, 15; Jer 33:18). In the latter, the verb *heʿĕlâ* 'offer up' is also to be found (e.g., 14:20; Josh 22:23; Isa 57:6; 66:3; Jer 14:12). The recorded instances of the cereal offering in the narratives also indicate that it was totally incinerated, for example, Manoah (Judg 13:19–20), Gideon (Judg 6:19–21), and the dedication rites of Solomon's Temple, where we read: "He sacrificed the burnt offerings, the cereal offerings, and the suet of the well-being offerings (1 Kgs 8:64), implying that just as the suet and burnt offerings were burned in their entirety, so were the cereal offerings. Finally, P's language itself betrays the fact that originally the entire cereal offering was consigned to the altar: "I have assigned it (the cereal offering to the priests) as their portion from my food gifts" (6:10; see 10:12–13; 24:9). Thus all scriptural sources, both P and otherwise, give unanimous and incontrovertible testimony that in Israel the cereal offering was initially completely burned on the altar. Why then did the Priestly legislators alter this situation so radically that, but for the token portion, the cereal offering was given over to the priests?

The answer may lie in the immediate ambience of ancient Israel. The prophet Jeremiah testifies that in his country "The mothers knead dough to make cakes for the Queen of Heaven" (Jer 7:18) and that his fellow exiles in Egypt argued, "We will do everything which we have vowed—to make offerings to the Queen of Heaven and to pour libations to her, as we used to do, we and our fathers, our kings and our officials, in the towns of Judah and the streets of Jerusalem" (Jer 44:17; cf. vv 18–19). The Queen of Heaven is Ishtar, and the cakes, *kawwānîm*, are the familiar Akk. *kamānu/kamānātu*, the sweet baked cakes offered to the gods. The Judean masses, prior to the deuteronomic reform, were worshiping Ishtar, not in the Temple court but on the roofs of their homes (Jer 19:13) by offering up cereal offerings and libations on improvised incense altars. As noted by Weinfeld (1972: 153), these altars probably made their way into Israel from Assyria, where small portable incense altars, *niġnaqqu* and *garakku*, in contrast to the larger ones in the temples, were used in private home worship. The burning of cereal offerings and incense to the heavenly hosts was not limited to Assyria. A Hittite text reads, "When things get too much for a man and he approaches his gods in prayer, he sets up two altars . . . on the roof under the open sky . . . and on them loaves of barley . . . and wafers(?) with honey and oil . . . the king ascends to the roof . . . and says: Sun-god of heaven and Sun-goddess of Arinna, my lady, queen of the Hatti land . . ." (*ANET*[3] 397–98). Thus the Hittite cult actually prescribes the setting up of altars on the roofs of private homes for the purpose of offering up various cereal offerings to the celestial gods.

Therefore it can be surmised that a common, rampant form of idolatry practiced by the Israelite masses consisted of offering up cereal and incense offerings on private roof altars. Indeed, the requirement in Israel's cult that frankincense be added to the cereal offering and not to any of the blood offerings may be traced to this widespread older practice of burning both incense and cereal offerings on private altars. (For the tandem in non-Priestly texts see Jer

17:26; 41:5; Neh 13:5, 9.) In any event, that only a token of the cereal offering is burned on the altar may be evidence of a polemic against a popular folk practice of burning cereal offerings to the gods of the heavens. For this reason, the text on the cereal offering contains two similarly worded verses that the cereal offering, except for the token burned on the altar, is to be the perquisite of the priests (vv 3 and 10). The intrusion of these verses is accentuated by the knowledge that nowhere else in the prescriptions for the sacrificial procedure (chaps. 1–5) is there any mention of the priestly perquisites. Thus it may be deduced that this duplicate emphasis that priests must be the recipients of the cereal offering probably reflects a polemic against the prevailing practice of offering up the entire cereal offering to the deity. Hence, by insisting that the cereal offering belongs to the priesthood, the practice of private cereal offerings is declared invalid. Henceforth, whoever wishes to bring a cereal offering to the Lord must forego offering it up by himself on his own premises but must bring it to the Temple so that the priest can sacrifice a token on the altar and retain the rest as his perquisite.

The question, however, remains: why the insistence that both the raw and the cooked cereal offerings are the perquisites of the entire priestly corps, particularly when it flatly contradicts the unambiguous statement (7:9) that the cooked cereal offering belongs to the officiating priest? The answer, as suggested (NOTES on vv 3, 10) is that two traditions have been conflated in the cereal offering, that of the local sanctuary *(bāmâ)* and regional sanctuary (e.g., Shiloh), where only one priestly family officiated, and that of the Jerusalem Temple, which employed a whole cadre of priests. As for the contradiction in the disposition of the cooked cereal offering (2:10; 7:9) it can be explained as the result of a historic development. As the numbers of priests officiating in and dependent on the Jerusalem Temple continued to increase, pressure began to build within the priesthood for an egalitarian distribution of all cereal offerings (see the NOTE on v 10). The same cause may also be responsible for the transformation of the priestly perquisite of the right thigh from the property of the officiating priest (7:32–33) to that of the entire priestly cadre (9:21; 10:15). See the fuller discussion in chap. 7, COMMENT F, and the Introduction §C.

THE WELL-BEING OFFERING (3:1–17)

3 ¹If his offering is a sacrifice of well-being——

From the Herd

If he offers from the herd, whether male or female, he shall present it without blemish before the Lord ²and lean his hand upon the head of his offering. It shall be slaughtered at the entrance of the Tent of Meeting and

Aaron's sons, the priests, shall dash the blood against all sides of the altar. [3]He shall then present from the sacrifice of well-being a food gift to the Lord: the suet that covers the entrails and all the suet that is around the entrails; [4]the two kidneys and the suet that is around them, that is on the sinews; and the caudate lobe on the liver, which he shall remove with the kidneys. [5]Aaron's sons shall turn it (this food gift) into smoke on the altar, with the burnt offering that is upon the wood that is on the fire, as a food gift of pleasing aroma to the Lord.

From the Flock

[6]And if his offering for a sacrifice of well-being to the Lord is from the flock, whether male or female, he shall offer it without blemish. [7]If he offers a sheep as his offering, he shall present it before the Lord [8]and lean his hand upon the head of his offering. It shall be slaughtered before the Tent of Meeting, and Aaron's sons shall dash its blood against all sides of the altar. [9]He shall then present, as a food gift to the Lord from the sacrifice of well-being, its suet: the broad tail completely removed close to the sacrum; the suet that covers the entrails and all the suet that is around the entrails; [10]the two kidneys and the suet that is around them on the sinews; and the caudate lobe on the liver, which he shall remove with the kidneys. [11]The priest shall turn it into smoke on the altar as food, a food gift to the Lord.

[12]And if his offering is a goat, he shall present it before the Lord [13]and lean his hand upon its head. It shall be slaughtered before the Tent of Meeting, and Aaron's sons shall dash its blood against all sides of the altar. [14]He shall then present as his offering from it, as a food gift to the Lord, the suet that covers the entrails and all the suet that is around the entrails; [15]the two kidneys and the suet that is around them on the sinews; and the caudate lobe on the liver, which he shall remove with the kidneys. [16]The priest shall turn these into smoke on the altar as food, a food gift of pleasing aroma.

The Law of Suet and Blood

All suet is the Lord's. [17]It is a law for all time throughout your generations, in all your settlements: you must not eat any suet or any blood.

NOTES

3:1. *If.* *wĕʾim*, rather than *kî*, an indication that this chapter is subsumed under 1:1–2; that is to say, both the *šĕlāmîm* offering described in this chapter and the *ʿōlâ* offering of 1:3–17 are instances of the voluntary animal offerings set forth in 1:1–2.

his offering. All of chap. 3 is cast in the third person, as is chap. 1 (Dillmann and Ryssel 1897), another indication that chaps. 1 and 3 form a single literary unit. Thus the antecedent of "his" can only be *'ādām* 'any' (1:2). The LXX and 4QLev[b] append "to the Lord," a superfluous addition because it is already mentioned in the introduction (1:2) and is missing in the opening statement on the burnt offering (1:3), which parallels this verse.

sacrifice of well-being (zebaḥ šělāmîm). zebaḥ is the general term for animal sacrifice whose meat is eaten by its offerer; *šělāmîm* refers to the specific motivation that prompts the sacrifice, a feeling of "well-being." This rendering is argued in detail in the COMMENT below. The rendering of the Tgs., *qûdšayā'* 'holy things', reflects rabbinic terminology, which declares all other sacrifices in chaps. 1–5 as *qodšê qŏdāšîm* 'most holy', in contrast to this sacrifice, which is termed *qŏdāšîm qallîm* 'less holy'. This distinction is already anticipated in postexilic texts of the Bible, which categorize the *šělāmîm* as *qŏdāšîm* 'holy things' (Neh 10:33–34; 2 Chr 29:31–33). The distinction itself goes back to preexilic times (21:22; Num 18:9, 11, 19: cf. Lev 10:12–14). The reasons for this distinction will be discussed in the COMMENT below. Here the question of the order of the sacrifices must be raised: why was the *šělāmîm*, a less holy sacrifice, inserted here, thereby severing the most holy sacrifices from one another, the burnt and cereal offerings (chaps. 1–2) from the purification and reparation offerings (chaps. 4–5)? Clearly the criterion for this sequence was not the level of holiness. It turns out, instead, to be that the *šělāmîm*, like the previous burnt and cereal offerings, is voluntary, stemming solely from the offerer's initiative, whereas the purification and reparation offerings that follow are mandatory, to expiate for specified acts of wrongdoing (*Seper Hamibḥar; Keter Torah;* cf. Abravanel), a distinction that has induced the *Sipra* to separate chaps. 1–3 from chaps. 4–5, the former referred to as *nědābā* 'voluntary', the latter, *ḥôbâ* 'mandatory'. Also, the "lack of specifying situations for bringing the burnt, cereal and well-being offerings versus the specification of situations for the other offerings is the main textual or legislative difference in the two sections of chaps. 1–5" (D. P. Wright, written communication).

male or female. Whereas all other animal sacrifices are fixed regarding their sex, the well-being offering is not. This is due primarily to the fact that the latter's function is to provide meat for the offerer, a consideration that would vitiate any attempt to restrict either the animal's species or its sex.

present it (yaqrîbennû). This use of *hiqrîb* implies a rite of presentation performed by the offerer (see the NOTE on 1:3b).

without blemish. See the NOTE on 1:3. This qualification is given emphasis through the repetition of the verb *hiqrîb.*

2. *lean his hand.* see the NOTE on 1:4.

It shall be slaughtered. ûšěḥāṭô is to be taken impersonally, for anyone was qualified to perform the slaughter (cf. 1:5), in distinction from the hand-leaning, which had to be performed by the offerer himself (cf. 1:4). The LXX adds "before the Lord" (as in 1:5), but that qualification has already been stated in v 1b and the expression that follows, "at the entrance of the Tent of Meeting," is equivalent.

dash the blood. see the NOTE on 1:5b.

the altar (hammizbēaḥ). The LXX reads *mizbaḥ hāʿōlâ* 'the altar of burnt offering'; but the latter designation is used only to distinguish this altar from the incense altar inside the Tent (e.g., 4:7, 10, 18, 25, etc.). But when the text deals entirely with sacrifices—forbidden to be offered on the incense altar (Exod 30:9)—there can be no doubt that the outer, sacrificial altar is meant, and no further designation is needed.

3. *present (wĕhiqrîb).* Having first presented the whole animal to the priest, it is now incumbent on the offerer to make another ritual presentation—the portions of the animal that will be burned on the altar. The LXX presupposes an original Hebrew *wĕhiqrîbû*, plural, under the assumption that it is the priests who make this presentation to the altar. This is clearly wrong, as shown by a later description of this rite: "His (the offerer's) own hands shall bring the Lord's food gifts: he shall bring the suet together with the breast" (7:30). The suet (and breast) can only be presented after the animal has been flayed and quartered (see the NOTE on 1:6). Contrast the suet rite of the purification offering, which employs different verbs (*hērîm, hēsîr* 'remove', 4:8, 19, 31, 35), implying that in this case the suet is brought straight forward to the altar without an additional rite (Wessely 1846). The skin, along with most of the meat, is retained by the offerer, in distinction from the skin of the burnt offering, which becomes the property of the officiating priest (7:8).

food gift. See the NOTE on 1:9.

suet. ḥēleb, referring to the layers of fat beneath the surface of the animal's skin and around its organs, which can be peeled off, in contrast to the fat that is inextricably entwined in the musculature, called *šûmān* in rabbinic Hebrew (possibly reflected in Ps 109:24). Three kinds of suet are enumerated here: (1) "the suet that covers the entrails," known as the caul or greater omentum, referring to the fatty membrane, at times more than an inch thick, that surrounds the intestines and therefore secures for them a proper degree of warmth; (2) "the suet that is around the entrails," known as the mesentery, the fat that covers the individual organs and is often as thick as the caul fat and, like the latter, can be easily peeled off; and (3) "the suet that is about them (the kidneys), that is on the sinews" (v 4). These three varieties of suet are illustrated in fig. 2a, b, and c, below.

The use of suet in sacrifices is attested along the Mediterranean littoral but not in the interior, probably for the reason that in Mesopotamia the food offerings to the gods were not burned but were subsequently eaten by the priests (cf. Bel and the Dragon)—and the suet is inedible (see below). For example, the Greeks, Hittites, Canaanites, and Phoenicians burned sacrificial flesh in kidney fat (Yerkes 1952: 97–112; Gill 1966). It would be a mistake, however, to deduce from these parallels that in Israel the use of suet as a source of human food was

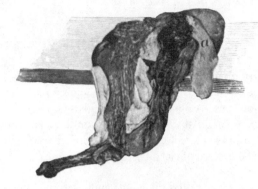

FIGURE 2a:
The Four Stomachs of an Ox
  Stomachs/Paunch
  Caul or Great Omentum
  Spleen

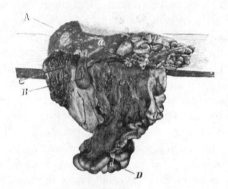

FIGURE 2b:
The Suet About the Entrails
  Suet/Mesentery
  Intestines
  Lesser Omentum
  Liver
  Gall-Bladder

FIGURE 2c:
The Suet About the Kidneys
  Kidneys
  Suet
  Paunch
  Omasum

interdicted because of its use in idolatry. The fact is that nowhere is Israel forbidden to use suet on the grounds that Israel is *qōdeš* 'holy' (cf. Exod 22:30), whereas suet is *ṭāmē'* 'impure' (cf. 11:8) or *šeqeṣ* 'an abomination' (cf. 11:42) (Hoffmann 1953). Besides, it is inconceivable that what is impure and abominable to Israel would be acceptable to the Lord on his altar. Equally to be rejected is the view that originally suet was used as food and only later, under the influence of the priestly legislation, was it banned (Münderlein 1980). Ostensible proof is found in Deut 32:14; Ps 63:6; and 1 Sam 9:24; but the first two texts are drawn from poetry, where *ḥēleb* can have either a metaphoric meaning or, more likely, another meaning altogether: "best" (see below at v 9). The latter verse (1 Sam 9:24) depends on an emendation, which, however, is disclaimed (v 9, below). But above all, this view must be rejected out of hand because all of the suet, enumerated above, is in fact inedible. Finally, the claim that *ḥēleb* at times refers to the entire sacrifice and not only to the suet (Münderlein 1980) must be denied. The supposed proof texts (6:5; 8:26; 9:24; 10:15; 16:25; 1 Sam 15:22; 1 Kgs 8:64; Isa 1:11) all refer to the suet of sacrificial animals and not to the animals themselves.

The reasons for reserving the suet for the deity, it must be admitted, are shrouded in mystery (not so for the blood; see the NOTE on v 17 and chap. 11, COMMENT C). The sacrificial procedure at the Shilonite sanctuary (1 Sam 2:15–16) takes for granted that the suet was burned on the altar (discussed in the COMMENT below). Thus sacrificial suet was forbidden for private use in premonarchic times, and there is no discernible change in regard to this taboo throughout Israel's history. Philology, however, shows that the *ḥēleb*, though inedible, was somehow associated with "the best," for example: "the *ḥēleb* of the land" (Gen 45:18); "the *ḥēleb* of wheat" (Deut 32:14). The process by which the suet became "the best" is still undetermined. Conjecturing that this meaning is due to the assignment of the suet to the deity only begs the question; it leaves unanswered the initial problem: why was the suet, to begin with, an exclusive reserve of the Lord?

entrails. qereb, meaning "entrails," is equivalent to Akk. *qerbu* (*AHw* 915a), but the root may be derivative in Semitic and is probably a loanword from Egyptian *q3b*.

around ('al). For this usage, see Exod 14:3; 27:21; 1 Sam 25:16; Ezek 13:5; Neh 2:8.

4. *kidneys.* kĕlāyôt; Akk. *kalītu* (*CAD* 8:74–76); Ug. *klyt* (*UT* 1001.3). They are embedded in the fattest parts of quadrupeds (see Deut 32:14), especially of rams (Isa 34:6), and are considered to be suet (v 10, below). Frequently they are associated with the heart as the seat of thoughts, emotions, and life (Jer 11:20; 17:10; 20:12; Pss 7:10; 16:7; 139:13).

sinews. kĕsālîm; sing. *kesel;* Akk. *kislu* 'the transverse process of the vertebra' (*CAD* 8.425); Ug. *ksl* (Aistl. 1352). The customary rendering "loins" has been definitively refuted by Held (1965: 401–3).

caudate lobe. yōteret, from *yeter* 'excess, protuberance', identified with the *lobus caudatus* or *processus pyramidalis,* a fingerlike projection from the liver, close to the right kidney, termed *ubānu* in Akkadian (*AHw* 1399a, no. 7), *ḥaṣrā*' in Aramaic (Tgs., ad loc.) and *'eṣbaʿ* in Rabbinic Hebrew (*m. Tamid* 4:3)—all meaning "finger (of the liver)." This lobe was significant in ancient hepatoscopy: its imperfections were a dire warning of forthcoming disaster (e.g., Goetze 1947, 1957). The identification was first made by G. F. Moore (1906: 761ff.). The caudate lobe protrudes conspicuously from the liver, as can be seen from the Babylonian clay model (fig. 3). Hepatoscopy was also practiced in Canaan, as evidenced by the finds at Gezer and Hazor of models of animal livers containing lines similar to a palmist's guide (see Cook 1930: pl. xxiii, fig. 2; *EM* 4.3). Why the caudate lobe was reserved for the deity is unknown. Nevertheless, the reason for this decision could not have been in order to prevent its use in divination; if so, then the rest of the liver—employed just as much as the long lobe in divination (hepatoscopy)—would also have been consigned to the altar.

which he shall remove (yĕsîrennâ). The subject is the offerer (see v 3a), and the sing. fem. object is the *yōteret,* the caudate lobe. Precisely because the lobe is attached to the liver and does not peel off as easily as the suet, a special verb is required to underscore that it must be removed surgically.

with. ʿal (so LXX, Pesh., and Ibn Ezra). For this usage, frequent in P, see 2:2, 16; 3:5; 4:11; 7:13, 30, etc. Strikingly, the sectaries of Qumran also adopted this interpretation, for their text explicitly states "the caudate lobe of the liver with (ʾim) the kidneys" (11Q Temple 23:15; see Milgrom 1980: 15). The rendering "at" (Hoffmann 1953; Elliger 1966), in other words, the place where the lobe is cut off, is inaccurate because the caudate lobe is close to the right kidney but not to both.

the kidneys. Situated near the back, the kidneys would be the last organs to be removed.

5. *Aaron's sons.* The LXX adds "the priests," as found in 1:5, 7 LXX, 8; 2:2; 3:2. But this appellation is missing in the rest of chap. 3 (vv 8, 13) and in 6:7; 7:10; 8:13, 24; 9:9, 12, 18—an indication that it is not essential. More than one priest is involved in the incineration of the bovine's suet, in contrast to the single priest who incinerates the suet of the flock animal (vv 11, 16), for the obvious reason that the suet of the larger bovine is too much for one priest to handle *(Keter Torah).*

it. The sing. object *'ōtô* has as its antecedent *'iššeh* 'the food gift' (v 3a, Kalisch 1867–72) or all of the previously named suet, taken collectively (but see at vv 11, 16).

with the burnt offering (ʿal hā'ōlâ). Others render ʿal here as "beside" (Rashi, Ḥazzequni) or "on" (Dillmann and Ryssel 1897, citing 9:14), but the use of ʿal meaning "with" is attested throughout the Priestly cultic texts (see at v 4). The burnt offering mentioned here clearly refers to the morning *Tāmîd* (Exod 29:38–39; Num 28:3–4), which is the first sacrifice each day. It is as-

THE SACRIFICES

FIGURE 3. Clay Model of a Liver (The Bialik Institute, Jerusalem)

sumed here that the *Tāmîd* burns all day long, just as it is said that the evening *Tāmîd* burns through the night (6:2). The assumption is quite plausible, for on an open-air altar the suet will take a long time to burn. Thus the text can be interpreted to mean that all subsequent sacrifices are added to the *Tāmîd*. The sequence, burnt offering (of the *Tāmîd*) followed by the suet of the well-being offering, is expressly stated in 6:5b.

on the fire. LXXAB and Sam. add *ʾăšer ʿal hammizbēaḥ* 'that is on the altar' (as in 1:8, 12). But the altar has already been mentioned at the beginning of this verse, and the addition here would constitute a redundancy, though it is possible that the missing phrase fell out by homeoarcton, that is to say, the scribe's eye jumped from *ʾš* at the beginning of *ʾăšer* to *ʾš* at the beginning of *ʾiššeh*, which is the next word (Freedman, personal communication).

8. *It shall be slaughtered.* See at v 2.

before the Tent of Meeting (lipnê ʾōhel môʿēd). Elsewhere this expression signifies before the Tabernacle enclosure (Num 3:7, 38) and is equivalent to *lipnê hammiškān* 'before the Tabernacle' (Num 3:38; 7:3). But the hand-leaning and slaughtering take place within the Tabernacle compound, in the forecourt, a location generally expressed either by *petaḥ ʾōhel môʿēd* 'the entrance of the Tent of Meeting' (e.g., v 2) or *lipnê YHWH* 'before the Lord' (e.g., 1:5, 11). The distinction between these two locations is clearly present in the induction rites of the levitic workforce: "you shall bring the Levites forward before the Tent of Meeting *(wĕhiqrabtā ʾet-halĕwiyyîm lipnê ʾōhel môʿēd).* Assemble the whole Israelite community *(wĕhiqrabtā ʾet-halĕwiyyîm lipnê YHWH)* and bring the Levites forward before the Lord" (Num 8:9–10a). This double "bring forward" of the Levites can only make sense if their first point of assembly was outside the sacred enclosure and the second point within. Similarly, the whole community, *haqqāhāl*, brings its purification offering *lipnê ʾōhel môʿēd*, that is, to the sacred enclosure (but not inside it); but the *ziqnê hāʿēdâ* 'the elders of the assembly'—the community's representatives—perform the hand-leaning rites *lipnê YHWH*, in other words, *within* the sacred enclosure (4:14b–15a).

Indeed, the LXX reads here "at the entrance (of the Tent of Meeting)," but this would require emending *lipnê* to *petaḥ*. The reading of the Pesh., which adds *YHWH petaḥ*, is preferable, yielding "before the Lord, at the entrance of the Tent of Meeting." This fuller expression for the cultic acts in the Tabernacle forecourt is found, for example, in 14:11, 23; 16:7; Josh 19:1; and in the LXX of v 13, below. An objection can be raised based on the one case in which *lipnê ʾōhel môʿēd* clearly refers to the forecourt, because the hand-leaning rite is performed there (Exod 29:10). Once again, however, the LXX reads *petaḥ* for *lipnê*, and this time Sam. reads the full formula, *lipnê YHWH petaḥ ʾōhel môʿēd*.

As remarked in the NOTE on "the north side of the altar" (1:11), the flock animal of the well-being offering, being of lesser sanctity than "most sacred" offerings, was not slaughtered in the same place as the latter, on the north side of the altar, but anywhere in the forecourt (cf. *b. Zebaḥ.* 107b).

its blood. dāmô, the term always used for flock animals in chaps. 1–7, implies all of its blood. With bovines the expression is invariably *haddām* 'the blood' (see at v 2), implying a portion of the blood, as there is too great a quantity to be contained in a single vessel (Abravanel).

9. *its suet: the broad tail (ḥelbô hāʾalyâ)*. Three resolutions of this crux are on record: (1) *ḥelbô* is rendered "its best part," a metaphoric meaning it has elsewhere (e.g., Gen 45:18; Num 18:12; Deut 32:14). This is *Tg. Ps.-J.*'s rendering: *ṭûb šumnēh* 'the best of the fat', followed by Rashi, Wessely 1846; and Ehrlich 1908–14; (2) reading, with the LXX and Saadiah, *ḥelbô wĕhāʾalyâ* 'its suet and the broad tail'. Both of these renderings dissociate the broad tail from the suet, and they conform to the view of Rabbi Akiba that the broad tail is not reckoned as suet *(Sipra*, Nedaba 19:2; cf. Ramban). Rabbi Judah (ibid.) holds that the broad tail, indeed, is suet, but only in sacrifices (see Maim., "Forbidden Foods" 7.5). In any event, the broad tail of nonsacrificial sheep would not be considered suet and would be permitted as food. The rabbis derive this concession from the verse: "you shall not eat the suet of any ox, sheep, or goat" (7:23), that is to say, only the suet that the aforementioned animals have in common, thus excluding the broad tail, which is generic only to sheep *(b. Ḥul.* 117a). Furthermore, they claim that Samuel fed Saul the broad tail from the sacrifice, reading *hāʾalyâ* for *heʿālêhā* in 1 Sam 9:24 *(b. ʿAbod. Zar.* 25a). Further strengthening the rabbis' view are the verses, cited by Ramban, that the suet is distinguished from the broad tail (Exod 29:22; Lev 8:25) and the kidneys and liver

lobe (4:31; 9:10), again dissociating the broad tail from the suet and thereby permitting it as food.

All of the argumentation given above can be parried. The rendering "its best" for *ḥelbô* would be *sui generis:* in all of its occurrences in sacrificial contexts it only means "suet." The insertion of the conjunctive *waw*, professed by Saadiah and found in the LXX, was countered by Ibn Ezra on grammatical grounds: the two terms should have the same morphology, either *ḥelbô wĕʾalyātô* 'its suet and broad tail' or *haḥēleb wĕhāʾalyâ* 'the suet and the broad tail'. The prooftexts cited by the rabbis are questionable: there is nothing in 7:23 that allows the suet of animals other than those encountered in the text. Although the rabbis initiated a (bold!) emendation of 1 Sam 9:24, followed to date by most moderns (e.g., Geiger 1857: 380, Wellhausen 1963, Driver 1913a), 4QSam[a] reads *[ḥ]ʿlynh*, which should be vocalized *(haššôq) hāʿelyōnâ* 'the upper thigh' (see McCarter 1980, ad loc.), thereby eliminating the broad tail from the text. As for the verses adduced by Ramban, none withstands scrutiny: Sam. omits the *waw* from Exod 29:22; 8:25, reading, "And you shall take (And he took) . . . the suet: the broad tail, etc."; 9:10 cannot be cited as evidence because it does not mention the broad tail; 4:31 actually proves the reverse: the suet removed from the purification offering "as it was removed from the well-being offering" must include the same internal organs removed from the latter, as expressly stated in the case of another purification offering (9:10).

This leaves the third explanation, adopted in my translation, that the suet includes the broad tail and the organs enumerated in the verse (Ibn Ezra). The following texts support this thesis: "He shall set aside all of the suet from the bull of the purification offering; the suet that covers . . . the two kidneys . . . and the caudate lobe" (4:8–9); "All of its suet shall be presented: the broad tail, the suet that covers the entrails; the two kidneys and the suet that is around them" (7:3–4); "and the suet pieces of the ox and the ram: the broad tail, the covering [suet], the kidneys, and the caudate lobes [of the livers]" (9:19); "They laid these suet pieces upon the breasts" (9:20); "he shall bring the suet together with the breast. . . . The priest shall turn the suet into smoke" (7:30–31); "He shall set aside all of its suet from it" (4:19). From all of the preceding citations, we may presume that suet, occasionally written in the plural, *ḥălābîm* 'suet pieces', is a general term for all the burned parts including the kidneys and caudate lobe of the liver. This is expressly the case in 7:3–4; 9:19, and by implication in 9:20 (see v 19), 7:30–31 (see chap. 3), and 4:19 (see vv 8–9). Thus there can be no doubt that the broad tail (as well as the kidneys and caudate lobe of the liver) is considered suet and that the Karaites, in opposition to the rabbis, who forbid its consumption *(Seper Hamibḥar, Keter Torah),* have seized on the plain meaning of the text. The sectaries of Qumran cut the Gordian knot: by deleting the terms *ḥelbô* and *yĕsîrennâ* from v 9 (1QT 20:4–9), they unambiguously state that the broad tail is part of the suet.

As early as Herodotus, the unusually broad tails of the sheep in the biblical lands have proved worthy of special notice: "There are also in Arabia two kinds of sheep worthy of admiration, the likes of which are nowhere else to be seen; the one kind has long tails, not less than four and one-half feet in length, which, if they were allowed to trail on the ground, would be bruised and break out with sores. As it is, all the shepherds know enough of carpentering to make little trucks for their sheep's tails. The trucks are placed under the tails, each sheep having one to himself, and the tails are then tied down upon them. The other kind has a broad tail, which is eighteen inches across sometimes" (Herod. 3.113). The celebrated geographer E. Robinson observed, "the sheep of Palestine are all of the broad-tailed species, the broad part being a mere excrescence of fat, with the proper tail hanging out of it" (1841: 477). The tail generally weighs about fifteen pounds, but some weigh as much as fifty pounds. Leo Africanus (apud Kalisch 1867–72: 1.489) claims to have seen one in Egypt weighing over eighty pounds. For a photo of a broad tail carried in a cart attached to a sheep, see fig. 4. The sheep's tail was sacrificed by the Egyptians (Herod. 2.47) and the Greeks (Schol. ad Aristoph. *Pac.* 1052; Clem. Alex. *Strom.* 7, p. 716 Col.).

completely. těmîmâ, in other words, at the sacrum (see below). Not having a definite article, this word does not modify the broad tail but should be taken as an adverb modifying the verb "remove." For the meaning "complete," see 23:15; 25:30; Josh 10:13.

FIGURE 4. Palestinian Sheep with Cart Supporting the Broadtail (The Jewish Encyclopedia)

removed. yĕsîrennâ, lit., "he [the offerer] will remove it [the broad tail]." The antecedent of the sing. suffix is clearly the broad tail (cf. vv 4, 10, where it is used with the caudate lobe). Both the caudate lobe and the broad tail require "removal," specifically by a cutting instrument, in contrast to the suet pieces and kidneys, which can be peeled or plucked off.

close to (lĕ'ummat). For this usage, see Exod 25:27; 28:27; 37:14; 39:20; 1 Kgs 7:20.

the sacrum. he'aṣeh refers to the lowest bone of the spine, closest to the broad tail (see *Tg. Onq.*). Perhaps related to Akk. *eṣettu, eṣemtu, eṣenṣēru* 'bone, backbone' and Arab. *'uṣ'uṣ* 'spine'.

11. *The priest. hakkōhēn;* sing. (as in v 16), for the suet of a flock animal can be handled by one priest, in contrast to that of the bovine (see v 5; *Keter Torah*). The same distinction obtains in the burnt offering (see 1:8, 11). It is assumed that the priest who burns the suet pieces is the one who lays them out on the altar (contrast the burnt offering, 1:8, 9).

(turn) it (into smoke) (wĕhiqtîrô). The antecedent of the sing. suffix is *ḥelbô* 'its suet' (v 9; *Keter Torah;* cf. vv 5 and 16).

food (leḥem). For this usage, see Jer 11:19; Dan 5:1 (Rashi). In the Semitic languages *leḥem* refers to the food of the country. In Arabic it means "flesh"; in seashore areas it can mean "fish"; in Judg 13:16 it refers to a kid; in 1 Sam 14:24–25, honey; and on the altar it stands for God's food (Snaith 1967). Clearly it harks back to earliest times, when sacrifices were intended to feed the gods (Deut 32:38; Isa 43:24; Ps 50:13). But Scripture rejects this notion (e.g., Ps 50:12–13), and in the cultic texts this term can be characterized as a linguistic fossil (21:6, 8, 17, 22; 22:25; 23:17; etc.).

12. *a goat ('ēz)*. Discrete sections are needed with respect to the sheep and the goat—in contrast to the burnt offering, which subsumes them under the heading of *ṣō'n* 'flock animals' (1:10–13)—because the sheep possesses the broad tail (v 9) but not the goat (*Sipra*, Nedaba 20:1; *b. Pesaḥ*. 96b). There is no need to state that a goat of either sex may be sacrificed, for that was already stipulated for both sheep and goats in v 6. That *keśéb* 'sheep' and *'ēz* 'goat' can refer to both the male and the female of the species is shown by the text of 1:10, which reads, "If his offering . . . is . . . of sheep or of goats, he shall offer a male" —so the requirement that it be a male must be specified.

13. *It shall be slaughtered. wĕšāḥaṭ*, lit., "he shall slaughter," but understood impersonally because the ritual slaughter need not be performed by the offerer himself. Textual proof for this reading is provided by 4:15; 8:18–19; etc., passages in which the subject of the slaughtering differs in number from the subject of the hand-leaning.

before. The LXX adds *YHWH petaḥ* 'the Lord, at the entrance of' (see at v 8).

14. *his offering. qorbānô*, namely, the suet pieces. The term *qorbān* refers to

whatever is donated to the sanctuary; it need not be burned on the altar (see at 1:2).

present (wĕhiqrîb). The LXX reads *wĕhiqtîr* 'turn to smoke' in order to be consistent in its erroneous view that not the offerer but the priest presents the suet pieces to the altar (see at v 3).

15. *which he shall remove (yĕsîrennâ).* The antecedent of the sing. suffix is the caudate lobe (see at v 4).

16. *(turn) these (into smoke) (wĕhiqtîrām).* The antecedent of the pl. suffix is all of the suet pieces (so too in 4:10, 35), in contrast to the sing. suffix (vv 5, 11), which treats the suet pieces as a collective.

of pleasing aroma. The principal disjunctive accent, the *'Athnaḥtā,* should be moved here (Dillmann and Ryssel 1897). The LXX and Sam. add "to the Lord," which provides the full formula attested throughout the sacrificial texts (v 5; 1:9, 13, 17; 2:2, 10; etc.). Moreover, this abbreviated form also occurs (Exod 29:18, 25, 41; Lev 2:12; 6:8; 8:21, 28; 23:13; Num 29:8).

All suet is the Lord's (kol ḥēleb laYHWH). This phrase begins a new paragraph, which, with v 17b, forms an inclusion, thereby indicating stylistically that 16b–17 is a self-contained unit. The phrase *kol-ḥēleb* 'all suet' is clearly a supplement of H. Verse 16b without this addition is the original P text, which conforms to the content and style of the other sectional endings in this chapter (vv 5b, 11a; Knohl 1987: 110; see further the NOTE on "any suet or any blood," v 17).

The full implication of this categorical statement cannot be overstated. It declares that all meat for the table must initially be brought as a sacrifice, so that its suet can be burned on the altar. Under no circumstances does it allow for nonsacrificial slaughter. As has been shown in the introduction (§B), H has no knowledge of D, whereas D is frequently cognizant of H (and P). Thus this fiat of H antedates the deuteronomic concession for nonsacrificial slaughter (Deut 12:15–16, 20–24) and carries much weight in dating the Priestly texts.

Not all suet on every animal is included in this injunction. Only the suet of sacrificial animals is intended (Saadiah). The suet of carrion, even of clean animals, and that of game may not be brought to the altar (see at 7:22–27). The indispensability of the sacrifice of blood and suet was not lost on the rabbis: "When R. Sheshet would conduct a fast, after his prayers he would say as follows: Master of the World, it is known to you that when the Temple existed, a person who sinned would bring a sacrifice and would receive expiation by offering up only its blood and fat. Now that I have conducted a fast my blood and fat have been reduced. May it be thy will that the blood and fat I have lost will be considered as if I offered them up to you upon the altar and you will accept me" *(b. Ber. 17a).*

17. *a law for all time (ḥuqqat 'ôlām).* P's *ḥuqqâ* derives from the root *ḥqq,* which means "inscribe, incise," reflecting the practice of inscribing laws on stone (Isa 22:16; 30:8; Ezek 4:1a; 23:14). It is thus fitting that this word is

combined with *ʿôlām* to emphasize that the law is permanent. In P, *ḥuqqâ* (fem.) 'law, statute' is scrupulously distinguished from *ḥōq* (masc.) 'due, portion' (cf. the NOTE on 10:13).

In all your settlements (bĕkōl môšĕbōtēkem). Including the Diaspora, according to the rabbis (*Sipra*, Nedaba 21:6) and most moderns (e.g., Grelot 1956: 79; Münderlein 1980). This expression occurs, however, in eight other laws: the unleavened bread on the Passover (Exod 12:20); prohibition against kindling a fire on the Sabbath (Exod 35:3); prohibition against consuming blood (7:26); prohibition against working on the Sabbath (23:3); prohibition against eating from the new grain crop prior to the *ʿōmer* offering (23:14); bringing the two first-fruit wheat loaves to the sanctuary (23:17); prohibition against work on the Day of Purgation (23:31); and the laws of homicide (Num 35:29). In none of these instances need the Babylonian exile be presupposed. On the contrary, they clearly refer to Israel's settlements in Canaan, as do the other nonlegal attestations of "your settlements" (Num 15:2; Ezek 6:6).

The prohibition against eating suet and blood "in all your settlements" can be explained in three ways: (1) it refers to sacrificial slaughter at local altars in or near one's settlement, hence to the pre-Josianic era; (2) it refers to nonsacrificial slaughter of animals fit for the altar (Rashbam, *Keter Torah*), permitted in the post-Josianic era (see Elliger 1966), in which case v 17 would be a post-Deuteronomic addition; or (3) it refers to the suet and blood of game and of sacrificial animals that were not killed ritually (e.g., they died or were killed by beasts; see 7:24), in which case this verse adds a new law to v 16b: (a) the suet of sacrificial animals is to be offered on the altar and (b) the suet and blood of nonsacrificial animals, ineligible for the altar, are forbidden as food.

This third explanation, however, is contradicted by 7:24–26, which clearly distinguishes between suet and blood: only the blood of game is forbidden as food, not its suet. Therefore, 3:16b–17 is addressing the issue of the blood and suet of sacrificial animals. Moreover, Deuteronomy prohibits solely the consumption of blood (Deut 12:16, 23) and, by its silence, thereby permits the suet of nonsacrificial animals to be eaten—in complete consonance with 7:24–26. Thus the second explanation, given above, must also be discounted (see further at 7:22–27).

The second and third explanations might still be maintained if one were willing to concede that this prohibition indeed conflicts with 7:24–26 and Deuteronomy, in other words, that originally suet of all animals, including game, was forbidden as food—the prohibition cited here—but later a concession was allowed to permit suet of game. But this logic, though impeccable, is purely theoretical; it has no grounding in either law or history. The prohibition of blood is absolute because it is equated with life and must be returned (symbolically) to God (see chap. 11, COMMENT C). Suet, by contrast, is forbidden to Israel only if it belongs to God, and this condition is only true for sacrificial animals. The suet of game is clearly exempt because there is no law comparable to that of blood (cf. 17:13; Deut 12:16, 24), which demands that the blood of game be discarded or buried. Hence, the equation of suet and blood in this prohibition can only apply to sacrificial animals. (Suet and blood of game are the subject of another passage: 7:22–27.)

Finally, the first explanation must also be eliminated on the grounds that it is hardly likely that any source in Leviticus, especially a subscript (H, see below) added later to its adjoining text, would posit the existence of multiple sanctuaries.

There remains, however, a fourth, simpler, and more plausible explanation. This verse (3:17, together with v 16b) was inserted by H (for the argumentation, see below), which bans common slaughter and insists that all meat must initially be a sacrifice *(šĕlāmîm)* and, hence, that its suet must be offered up on the altar (see Knohl 1987: 110–11 and the Introduction §C). The law of 7:24–26 ostensibly contradicts this verse. The two contexts, however, are different: there the subject is nonsacrificial animals, the blood of which is forbidden but not its suet; here the subject is sacrificial animals, the blood and suet of which are both forbidden.

you must not eat (lōʾ tōʾkēlû). The switch from impersonal third-person singular, prevalent in the entire chapter, to second-person plural in this final sentence can be explained as forming an inclusion with *taqrîbû* (1:2), thereby indicating that chaps. 1–3 are a discrete unit (Rendtorff 1985: 25), which implies the possibility that H not only supplemented but also redacted this chapter (see the Introduction, §§C and H).

any suet or any blood. Of sacrificial animals *(Tg. Ps.-J.;* Ibn Ezra), the same referent as v 16b and, hence, forming an inclusion with it. The blood prohibition, to be sure, is not mentioned there or in the entire chapter; its insertion here has a proleptic function, anticipating the material in 7:26–27. The suet and the blood are the exclusive preserve of the deity ("my food," Ezek 44:7).

That vv 16b–17, in part, form a supplement to this chapter can be seen from the structure of v 16b (Knohl 1987: 110–11; 1988: 43–45). One would expect the pericope on the goat to end as did the previous pericope on cattle and sheep, with the words *leḥem, ʾiššeh, rêaḥ nîḥōaḥ,* and *laYHWH* (vv 5b, 11b; cf. 1:9b, 13b, 17b). The MT of v 16b, however, reads *leḥem ʾiššeh lĕrēaḥ nîḥōaḥ kol-ḥēleb laYHWH.* Once *kol-ḥēleb* is removed, the full concluding formula appears intact. (The *lamed* of *lĕrēaḥ* is attested in the formula found in Num 18:17.) Thus, the supplementer who added v 17 to the chapter also inserted *kol-ḥēleb* into v 16b, thereby locking his addition into the chapter (for a similar locking stratagem, note the use of *rab lākem* and *hammĕʿaṭ* in Num 16:7, 9 [Milgrom 1981d]) and, at the same time, artistically creating an inclusion with the words *kol-ḥēleb* (vv 16b, 17b). That this supplement stems from H is betrayed by the reference to *môšĕbôtēkem* 'your settlements', of concern solely to H lest the land of Israel become polluted (see the NOTE on 7:26 and the Introduction §C).

COMMENT
THE WELL-BEING OFFERING: NAME,
MOTIVATION, RENDERING, AND FUNCTION

The term for the "well-being offering" comprises two words, *zebaḥ šĕ-lāmîm*, which has led R. Rendtorff (1967) to propose that two originally discrete sacrifices have been combined by the Priestly writers, the *zebaḥ* and the *šĕ-lāmîm*. He marshals an assortment of evidence that, he claims, points to the *šĕlāmîm* as a royal, festal, and public offering, marked by a distinctive blood ritual, which probably was not eaten, as opposed to the *zebaḥ*, a private family or clan offering, motivated by thanksgiving, freewill, or a vow. His evidence is subject to question on a number of grounds.

(1) To be sure, the *šĕlāmîm* figures together with the *ʿōlâ* in the regular, public cult, but the fact that different verbs are frequently employed with each sacrifice (e.g., Exod 32:6; Deut 27:7; Josh 8:31; 1 Kgs 3:15) indicates that the *šĕlāmîm* was regulated by an entirely different set of ritual requirements than the *ʿōlâ*. Besides, if the *šĕlāmîm* meat was burned on the altar just like the *ʿōlâ*, how could the two sacrifices be distinguished from each other?

(2) Not all *šĕlāmîm* were public. Rendtorff himself is aware of exceptions, for example, the Nazirite's ritual (Num 6:13–21); and the freewill and votive offerings in P (Num 15:8) and in Ezekiel (46:2, 12). Furthermore, the suet (6:5) and blood (7:14, 33) of P's *šĕlāmîm* also stem from the individual's sacrifices, and the king's *šĕlāmîm* is explicitly his personal offering (2 Kgs 16:13).

(3) The *šĕlāmîm*, like the *zebaḥ*, is eaten (explicitly, in Exod 32:6; 1 Kgs 3:15; and esp. Deut 27:7). To be sure, the *šĕlāmîm* was offered up on public fast days (e.g., Judg 20:26), but being offered up in the evening, at the end of the fast and as the final sacrifice can only mean that the fast was broken by partaking of the *šĕlāmîm*. Finally, the fact that Solomon "sacrificed the burnt offerings, the cereal offerings, and the suet pieces of the well-being offerings" (1 Kgs 8:64) indicates that the meat of the well-being offerings was not burned on the altar but eaten.

(4) The *zebaḥ* as much as the *šĕlāmîm* is characterized by a distinctive blood ritual (e.g., Exod 23:18; 34:25; Deut 12:27; 2 Kgs 16:15). And the term *šāpak dām* in Deut 12:27 does not signify that the blood of the *zebaḥ* was spilled on the ground instead of the altar (requiring Rendtorff to render *ʿal mizbaḥ YHWH* 'by the Lord's altar'!), but is simply D's peculiar idiom for the blood rite (Milgrom 1971).

(5) The non-P occurrences of *zebaḥ šĕlāmîm* (Exod 24:5; Josh 22:23; 1 Sam 10:8; 11:5; 1 Kgs 8:63; Prov 7:14) are either emended or explained away—dubious procedures, at best. Even so, there are also numerous instances within P of the three terms, the compound and the components, being interchanged in

the same pericope and even in the same verse (see 6:5; 7:11–21 [esp. vv 14, 16]; 17:5; 19:5–6; 23:37 [cf. v 19]; Num 29:39; cf. 2 Kgs 16:13, 15). The conclusion is inescapable: the *zebaḥ šĕlāmîm* is a discrete sacrifice that is synonymous with the *šĕlāmîm* and, on occasion, with the *zebaḥ* (see below).

There is no alternative but to understand the compound *zebaḥ šĕlāmîm*, like the term *ʿēṣ zayit* 'olive tree' (lit., "a tree of the olive variety"), to mean a *zebaḥ* of the *šĕlāmîm* variety or, to phrase it inversely, *šĕlāmîm* a variety of the genus *zebaḥ*. This implies that there must be other *zebaḥ* varieties, and outside of P, indeed, there are: *zebaḥ tôdâ* 'thanksgiving offering' (e.g., 22:29 [H, not P]; Pss 107:22; 116:17), *zebaḥ yāmîm* 'annual offering' (e.g., 1 Sam 1:21), *zebaḥ mišpāḥâ* 'clan offering' (e.g., 1 Sam 20:29), *zebaḥ pesaḥ* 'paschal offering' (Exod 12:23; 23:18; 34:25; cf. Deut 16:2–4), and D's firstling (treated like a *zebaḥ*, Deut 15:19–23). P's *zebaḥ šĕlāmîm*, however, is an all-inclusive term—embracing all of the above-mentioned *zebaḥ* offerings.

zebaḥ is generally rendered "slain offering" because the root *d/zbḥ/* in West Semitic means "slaughter." Akk. *zību* is defined as "food—probably meat —cooked and 'showed' [sic] to the gods" *(CAD)* and Ug. *dbḥ*, both verb and noun, refers to the slaughter of animals and fowl. Here, however, caution must be exercised because,·in one instance *(UT* 3.20–21 = *CTA* 35.20–21 = *KTU* 1.41.20–21, completed by its duplicate in *UT* 173.22 = *CTA* Appendix II (pp 136–38).22 = *KTU* 1.87.2), there is a reference to *dbḥ šmn mr šmn rqḥ* 'a *dbḥ* of oil myrrh; of oil mixed spices', a phrase that occurs partially in later Punic tariffs (*zbḥ šmn; KAI* 69.12; 74.9; cf. *zbḥ bmnḥ* 'cereal *zbḥ*', 74.10), suggesting the possibility that *d/zbḥ* should be rendered "food offering" (Levine 1974: 115–17).

In any event, biblical *zebaḥ* is limited to the meaning "slain offering whose meat is eaten by the worshiper." This is so not just because the verb *zābaḥ* in sacrificial contexts means "slaughter the *zebaḥ*" (with the sole exception of Exod 20:24) but because the frequently attested compound *ʿōlâ wĕzebaḥ* (e.g., Exod 10:12; 18:12; Lev 17:8; Num 15:8; Deut 12:6; Josh 22:26, 28; 1 Sam 15:22; 2 Kgs 5:17; Jer 7:22; Hos 6:6), found also at Elephantine (Cowley 1923: 31.27) and comparable to Ug. *šrp (w)šlmm* (*UT* 612.9–10; 613.15–16), can only mean the animal that is entirely burned *(ʿōlâ)* and the animal whose suet is burned but whose meat belongs to the offerer *(zebaḥ)*. Striking proof for this interpretation is provided by Jer 7:21b, "add your burnt offerings to *zibḥêkem* and eat meat." Thus the *ʿōlâ* was burned and the meat of the *zebaḥ* was eaten. In rabbinic Hebrew *zĕbāḥîm* refers to all slain offerings, a meaning that may have been anticipated by 2 Chr 7:12 (and possibly by Ezek 20:28).

The *šĕlāmîm* falls into three categories of motivation: *nĕdābâ* 'freewill'; *neder* 'vow'; and *tôdâ* 'thanksgiving' (7:11–16). The common denominator of these motivations is rejoicing (Wessely 1846): "You shall sacrifice the *šĕlāmîm* and eat them, rejoicing before the Lord your God" (Deut 27:7). The freewill offering *(nĕdābâ)* is, on logical grounds, the most frequently sacrificed, for it is the spontaneous by-product of one's happiness whatever its cause. *nĕdābâ* can even be found as a surrogate for *šĕlāmîm* (Num 15:3, 8). Ezekiel's *nāśîʾ* is expected, when offering a private sacrifice, to bring a freewill offering (Ezek 46:12). As illustrated by this citation from ancient Mesopotamia, "Present your freewill offerings to your god" (Lambert 1960: 105, line 137; cf. 109, line 12 and 316n.), it was a prominent factor in the sacrificial systems of all peoples.

The votive offering is brought following the successful fulfillment of a vow. Thus Absalom says to David: "Let me go to Hebron and fulfill *(waʾăšallēm)* the vow that I made to the Lord. For your servant made a vow when I lived in Geshur of Aram: If the Lord ever brings me back to Jerusalem, I will worship the Lord [in Hebron, LXX]" (2 Sam 15:7b–8). Or "I am obligated to sacrifice a well-being offering for today I fulfill my vows" (Prov 7:14).

The votive offering, however, must not be confused with the *tôdâ*, the thanksgiving offering (*pace* Rendtorff 1967: 135), for they are always differentiated in Scripture (e.g., Pss 50:14; 56:13; 116:17–19). The thanksgiving offering is based on a different motivation and is subject to a different procedure. The rabbis derive from Ps 107 that there are four occasions that require a thanksgiving offering: safe return from a sea voyage (vv 23–25), safe return from a desert journey (vv 4–8), recovery from illness (vv 17–22), and release from prison (vv 10–16; *b. Ber.* 54b; cf. Weinfeld 1982a on parallels to the Šamaš Hymn).

The rabbis also maintain that the thanksgiving offering is technically not a *šĕlāmîm* (*m. Zebaḥ.* 5:6–7; cf. 1 Macc 4:54–56). Their view is firmly anchored in Scripture (see 22:21, 29 [H, not P]; Jer 17:26; 2 Chr 29:31–33; 33:16). In the Bible, it is P, and only P, that subsumes the *tôdâ* under the *šĕlāmîm*, an indication that P reflects a later development in the history of this sacrifice (Levine 1974: 43). This position, apparently, was also maintained in later times by the Dead Sea sectaries (*MMT* B 9–13). Indeed, the *tôdâ* ritual procedure differs markedly from the other *šĕlāmîm*. It is coupled with a bread offering and must be eaten the same day it is offered (7:11–16), whereas the freewill and votive offerings are unaccompanied by bread offerings and may be eaten over a two-day period (19:5–6). Also, freewill and votive motivations inform the *ʿōlâ* as well as the *šĕlāmîm* (Num 15:8; Ezek 46:2, 12), but apparently the *ʿōlâ* is not brought for reasons of thanksgiving (see 2 Chr 29:31). In fact, the thanksgiving offering in many ways resembles both the ram offered in the priestly consecration and the paschal sacrifice (see the NOTES on 7:12). It is also possible that the psalms that stress a thanksgiving motif (e.g., Pss 30; 118:5–9; 138; Isa 38:10–20; Jonah 2:3–9) were composed (or adapted) for recitation during the offering of this sacrifice (Dussaud 1941: 104–7; Gunkel 1933).

The thanksgiving offering must be eaten during the same day it is offered, and what is left over is burned the following morning (7:15). In this respect, it resembles the *pesaḥ* (Exod 12:10), the priestly consecration offering (8:32; Exod 29:34), and the ram of the Nazirite (according to the rabbis, *m. Zebaḥ.* 5:6; cf. Num 6:19). These four sacrifices are also the only ones that must be eaten with bread (7:12–13; 8:31; Exod 12:8; Num 6:19; cf. the NOTE on 7:12). They fall into the general category of šĕlāmîm because they are consumed by the laity, in particular the offerer, his family, and his invited guests. Nevertheless, they differ from the šĕlāmîm in that the latter are consumed without bread and over a two-day period (7:16–17; 1:5–7). The difference between these two kinds of sacrifice can be explained on the basis of their respective motivations. The four one-day sacrifices are, in effect, mandatory; they must be eaten by their offerers. Furthermore, the three sacrifices offered by the laity—thanksgiving, pesaḥ, and Nazirite ram—share the same motivation: thanksgiving for deliverance, both national (pesaḥ) and individual. Conversely, the two-day sacrifices are, in effect, voluntary: the nĕdābâ 'freewill offering' a purely spontaneous offering and the neder 'votive offering' also a spontaneous offering, because it is dependent on the future fulfillment of a vow.

One should not be surprised that other cultures posit similar motivations for an individual's sacrifice. For example, it is said of the Greeks (the apposite Hebrew sacrifice is in parentheses): "Look what people usually do—all women in particular, invalids of every sort, men in danger or any kind of distress (tôdâ), or conversely when they have just won a property: they dedicate the first thing that comes to hand (nĕdābâ), they swear to offer sacrifice, and promise to found shrines for gods and spirits and children of gods (neder)" (Plato 1970: §909).

šĕlāmîm is a plural formation. The singular is found once in the Bible (Amos 5:22) but frequently in Ugaritic (e.g., UT 1.8 = CTA 34.8 = KTU 1.39.8; UT 3.17 = CTA 35.17 = KTU 1.41.17). Perhaps the plural originates from the fact that other sacrifices were offered with the šĕlāmîm (Levine 1974: 19–20), or it may refer to the multiple suet pieces, ḥălābîm, that were offered on the altar (Gerleman 1973). Others hold that šĕlāmîm is a pseudo-plural, the final mem due to mimation (de Vaux 1964: 50), a good example of which is tāmîm 'without blemish' (Freedman, personal communication).

šĕlāmîm has been translated here "well-being offering." This is but one of many suggested translations but all are, at best, educated guesses. Based on etymologies, they never leave the realm of conjecture (Janowski 1980), for example: (1) šālôm 'peace', because the offering "effects peace among the altar, the priests, and the offerer" (t. Zebaḥ. 11:1), for "the suet is for the altar, the thigh and breast for the priest (see 7:30–35), and the skin and meat for the offerer" (Sipra, Nedaba 16:2); (2) šālēm 'whole, sound, harmonious': "Rabbi Simeon says: he who feels wholesome brings šĕlāmîm but a mourner does not bring šĕlāmîm" (Sipra, Nedaba 16:3; cf. Philo Laws 1. 1.212)—thereby yielding the rendering "well-being offering" (NJPS); (3) W. R. Smith (1927: 265) maintains that the šĕlāmîm effected a mystic union between the offerer and the deity, citing the fact that the sacrifice was eaten "before the Lord" (e.g., Deut 27:7; cf. 1 Sam 1:18–19; 2:13–16) as a shared meal (Gen 31:50)—yielding "communion offering" (Jerusalem Bible; however, see below); (4) šillēm 'repay', that is to say, the sacrifice repays God for his blessings (Rashbam on 3:1; cf. Prov 7:14)—

yielding "recompense offering" (Moffatt 1922); the Akk. cognates (5) *salīmu* 'covenant' (Schmid 1964; Munn-Rankin 1965; Fensham 1979) or (6) *šulmānu* 'gift' (Levine 1974: 16–17); (7) the LXX provides three translations, two corresponding to (1) and (2), above, and *sōtērios* 'salvific'.

The main function of the well-being offering is to provide meat for the table. Assumed is that nonsacrificial slaughter is illegitimate (except for blemished animals and game; see the NOTES on 22:19–25 and the COMMENT on chap. 17) and that whenever an Israelite craved meat he would first have to offer his cattle, sheep, or goat (the only permitted domesticated species except birds, which, however, would be considered game, 17:13–14) as a sacrifice (see chap. 11, COMMENT C). Such an occasion perforce was rare, for only kings and aristocrats could afford the depletion of their flocks. For the commoner, the occasion had to be a celebration—and because the meat was probably too much for the nuclear family, it had to be a household or even a clan celebration—hence the joyous character of the sacrifice.

That this sacrifice implied a mystic union with the deity must be categorically rejected. First, the sacrifice is eaten "before the Lord" (e.g., Deut 27:7), not "with the Lord" (Ehrlich 1908–14). Then, Scripture takes pains to relate—indeed, in early narratives—that the angels who confronted Gideon and Manoah refused to eat their offering but insisted that it be offered up totally as an *ʿōlâ* (Judg 6:19–21; 13:15–16). Moreover, that the suet of expiatory offerings was burned on the altar surely does not imply that God partakes of them (Snaith 1967 on 4:8). Finally, in contrast to the Greek and Canaanite sacrifices, whose meat was burned on the altar, all of the meat of Israelite sacrifices was eaten by men, and the suet alone was assigned to the deity (de Vaux 1964: 80). Even for the Greeks, as J. Harrison cautions us, "In the Homeric sacrifice there is communion but not the mystical kind; there is no question of partaking of the life and body of the god, only of dining with him" (1922: 56). Furthermore, in Mesopotamia, the gods did not even participate in a shared meal; a king might serve a banquet and invite the gods to it, but he would prepare a separate banquet for himself and his nobles (Charbel 1970).

It has generally been denied that the well-being offering served an expiatory function (but see point 4 below). Maimonides is certainly correct when he wrote, "It appears to me that no confession is ever made over the well-being offering (since it is not brought for wrongdoing) but only words of praise" ("Sacrificial Procedure" 3.15). The key expiatory term *kipper* is missing from this sacrifice but is found in four ostensible exceptions: (1) Ezek 45:15, 17, where, however, *kipper* probably refers to the burnt, cereal, and purification offerings in the list and not to the well-being offering. The fact that the latter is last named is significant: it points to a feast at the end of the sacrificial ritual. So too, as Harrison observes, with Homer's Greeks: "Sacrifice and the flesh feast that followed were so intimately connected that one implied the other" (1922: 56; cf. *Ody.* 24.215); (2) 1 Sam 3:14, where, however, the term *zebaḥ ûminḥâ* is a synecdoche referring to all sacrifices (for *minḥâ* as a blood offering, see 1 Sam 2:17, 29); (3) Exod 29:32–33, but this expiation adverts to the priestly consecration offering, *milluʾîm*, which is not a *šĕlāmîm* (see at 8:34); and (4) in Lev 17:11, the *šĕlāmîm* is inherently expiatory; especially so, because it always ransoms the life of its offerer; yet paradoxically, it is brought on a joyous occasion (for the resolution of this paradox see chap. 11, COMMENT C).

The well-being offering is also present at covenant ratifications (e.g., Exod 24:5, 11), where both parties partake of it (Gen 26:30; 31:54). It is doubtful, however, whether the sacrifice was essential to the covenant ceremony (Levine 1974: 37–41). Rather, it may just have been the means of celebrating the covenant's successful conclusion (see Ps 50:5).

Because the primary purpose of the well-being offering is to provide meat—unique among the sacrifices—any sacrificial animal of either sex is eligible. Yet there is no provision for birds, and this occasions surprise. After all, birds qualify for the burnt offering (1:14–17) and certain purification offerings (5:11–13; 12:6–8; 14:22; 15:14–15, 29–30; Num 6:10–11). Why are they not allowed for the well-being offering? One cannot answer that birds are inadequate as food (Dillmann and Ryssel 1897), for the bird meat of the purification offering is assigned to the priests (6:19; 10:17) and birds as a source of food are taken for granted in Scripture (e.g., 7:26; 17:13; Num 11:31–32; Deut 14:11; 22:6–7). Besides, all ancient Near Eastern cultures include birds in their sacrificial lists and, in most cases, the birds are transferred from the table of the gods to the mouths of the priests. Alternatively, it has been suggested that birds were not domesticated by Israel until postexilic times (Haran 1962a: 552–53). But the fact that domesticated birds were available to the commoner for his sacrifices (see above) and to the king and the governor as their daily diet (1 Kgs 5:3; Neh 5:8) presumes the widespread cultivation of aviaries in ancient Israel (cf. also Isa 60:3).

There is, I believe, only one possible answer. All birds, even domesticated ones, even sacrificial pigeons and turtledoves, were treated as game, provided they were intended for the table. Indeed, the priesthood would have frowned on such an offering, as the infinitesimal blood and suet would have been an embarrassment for the altar. And precisely for this reason, the priestly prescriptions require a whole bird as an *ʿōlâ* (1:14–17) and to accompany the *ḥaṭṭāʾt* (5:7; 12:8; 14:22; 15:14–15, 29–30).

The blood rite is clearly the quintessential element in the well-being offering (the rabbis affirm the same, *b. Zebaḥ.* 13a). Its centrality is underscored by comparing the verbs used for assigning the perquisite to the officiating priest from each of the sacrifices: "the priest who sacrifices *(hammaqrîb)* a person's burnt offering" (7:8); the priest who offers it as a purification offering *(hammĕḥaṭṭēʾ)* shall enjoy it" (6:19); "the priest who performs expiation *(yĕkapper)* therewith [i.e., with the reparation offering]" (7:7). Only in the case of the well-being offering, however, is the rite with the blood singled out: "it shall belong to the priest who dashes the blood *(hazzōrēq 'et-dam)* of the well-being offering" (7:14; cf. v 33). So too it is said of King Ahaz: "He turned into smoke his burnt offering and cereal offering; he poured his libation and he dashed the blood *(wayyizrōq 'et-dam)* of his well-being offering against the altar" (2 Kgs 16:13; cf. Ezek 43:18). Thus the blood rite with the well-being offering must be of quintessential significance. Further discussion needs to be postponed until the COMMENT on chap. 17.

According to the Priestly texts, the meat of the well-being offering could be eaten anywhere and by anyone as long as the place and person were in a state of purity (7:19–21). Further information concerning the sacrificial meal can be derived from the narrative describing the Shilonite sanctuary: "This is how the priests used to deal with the people: when anyone offered a sacrifice *(zōbēaḥ zebaḥ)*, the priest's boy would come along with a three-pronged fork while the meat was boiling and he would thrust it into the cauldron, or the kettle, or the great pot or the small cooking pot; and whatever the fork brought up the priest would take away [for himself (LXX, Tg.)]" (1 Sam 2:13–14). Two bits of relevant data derive from this pregnant passage: the offerer's *zebaḥ* (i.e., the well-being offering) was boiled (and probably eaten) on the sanctuary premises, and the priests received their remuneration not from the raw but from the boiled meat. The latter practice is actually attested for the boiled shoulder, the priestly perquisite from the Nazirite's ram (Num 6:19), and the former—the tradition of cooking the meat of the well-being offering in the sanctuary courtyard—is attested in Ezekiel's blueprint for the temple (Ezek 46:26) and in the recorded practice of the Second Temple (*m. Mid.* 2:5) as well as in the rabbinic rule, "the Nazirite cooked (his offering) where he shaved" (*Midr. Num. Rab.* 10:21). That Jethro invited Moses, Aaron, and Israel's elders "to partake of the meal before God" (Exod 18:12) indicates that they ate near the altar. Similarly, the command to Israel to build an altar on Mount Ebal (cf. Deut 27:7, "and you shall sacrifice there well-being offerings and eat them, rejoicing before the Lord your God") also implies that the sacrificial meal took place in the altar's vicinity. Permanent sanctuaries probably provided special halls for the sacrificial meal (1 Sam 1:9 LXX; 9:22; Jer 35:2). There are Greek inscriptions that state that the requirement to eat sacrificial flesh within the holy precincts will be enforced (Eitram and Fontenrose 1970: 944). Indeed, the possibility exists that the sanctuaries of ancient Greece followed a similar practice, because the term for the sanctuary hall, *liškâ*, seems to be related to Greek *leschē*, where banquets were held (Brown 1969: 151–53). The Shilonite meal (1 Sam 2:13–17) is also reflected in the assignment of the thigh of the well-being offering to the officiating priest (7:33), a matter that will be developed in full in the COMMENT on chap. 7.

The earlier practice of eating the sacred meal within the sanctuary precincts is most likely responsible for the rules that both the sacrificial meat and its consumers be in a state of ritual purity (7:19–21) and that the meat not eaten within the set period of one or two days must be incinerated, lest the entire sacrifice be invalidated (7:15–18; 19:6–7) and its offerers incur the wrath of the deity (7:19b; 19:8; cf. Ezek 20:41; 43:27). The meal was probably preceded by a table blessing (1 Sam 9:13).

Many non-Priestly narratives speak of a public well-being offering (Exod 24:5; Judg 20:26; 21:4; 1 Sam 10:8; 11:5; 2 Sam 6:17–18; 24:25; 1 Kgs 3:15; 8:63–64; 9:25; Ezek 45:15, 17; 2 Chr 29:31–35; 30:22–27; 33:16). P itself posits the existence of a public well-being offering in the following verse: "On your joyous occasions, your fixed festivals and new moon days, you shall sound the trumpet over your burnt offerings and your well-being offerings" (Num 10:10a). The use of trumpets presupposes national, not private, events. But are there specific national occasions for which P prescribes well-being offerings? Two such are recorded: Pentecost (23:19) and the initiation of the public cult (9:4). On Pentecost two lambs are sacrificed as well-being offerings (23:18–20). It is likely, however, that originally this sacrifice was brought by each Israelite farmer together with the firstfruits of his wheat harvest, and only later was it incorporated into the public cult as a single festival offering and its meat assigned to the priests (for details see at 23:18–20). Thus it is hardly possible that this one public sacrifice, late in its development, is what is intended by the apparent prescription of the Numbers passage, cited above, that well-being offerings should mark the festival celebrations of the year. The second occasion (9:4) is more instructive. It calls for the sacrifice of a "well-being offering for the people" (9:18) during the institution of the public cult. It implies that the public sacrifice of well-being offerings took place not only on that occasion but on all joyous celebrations that would have been marked by the well-being offering, the joyous sacrifice par excellence. Surely, this is precisely what is meant by the Numbers passage: whereas the "fixed festivals and new moon days" require the burnt offerings (Num 28–29), the well-being offerings are reserved for "your joyous occasions *(ûběyôm śimḥatkem)."* Indeed, the emphasis on the martial use of the trumpets in this pericope (Num 10:1–9) implies that the "joyous occasions" include military triumphs (Ibn Ezra, ad loc.).

Moreover, other celebrations calling for well-being offerings are those on which the use of trumpets is attested, for example, coronations (2 Kgs 11:14; cf. Ps 98:6), the installation of the Ark in David's tent (1 Chr 16:6, 42; cf. v 2), the dedication of Solomon's temple (2 Chr 5:12–13; cf. 1 Kgs 8:64), the rededication of the altar and covenant under Asa (2 Chr 15:8–15; cf. v 11), the purification of Hezekiah's temple (2 Chr 29:27; cf. v 31), and the consecrations of the walls of Jerusalem (Neh 12:35, 41; cf. v 43). Other non-Priestly passages also attest to the sacrifice of well-being offerings on special public occasions, as follows: the ratification of the covenant (Exod 24:5), breaking a national fast (Judg 20:26), the dedication of an altar at Bethel (Judg 21:4), breaking a fast (probably) in preparation for battle (1 Sam 10:8; see 13:9–12), the dedication of the altar (2 Sam 24:25) at the site of the future temple (1 Chr 21:27–22:1),

Solomon's celebration after his dream-revelation at Gibeon (1 Kgs 8:63–64), the institution of the Passover rites in Hezekiah's temple (2 Chr 30:22–27), and the dedication of Manasseh's altar (2 Chr 33:16). All of these passages describing the public sacrifice of well-being offerings have in common that they are not fixed calendric days but are one-time-only, national occasions.

Who are the recipients of this public well-being offering? In the non-Priestly texts, it is clearly the people or their representatives—most often, the latter. Only in temple dedications, where the text takes pains to point out that hecatombs of animals were slain (e.g., 1 Kgs 8:63; 2 Chr 29:33; 30:24), can we assume that the assembled throngs partook of the sacrifice. In all other instances, the sacrificial meat was eaten by the people's representatives or those especially invited by the officiant. Thus, though the sacrifice at Ramah (probably a *zebaḥ yāmîm* or *zebaḥ mišpāḥâ*) is called "the people's sacrifice" (1 Sam 9:12) and, theoretically, should have been distributed to all of the town's inhabitants (see v 13), it is in fact eaten by approximately thirty invited guests, *qĕrû'îm* (v 22). In a similar fashion, it is Israel's elders who partake of the well-being offering sacrificed by Jethro (Exod 18:12). They also partook of the well-being offering by which the Sinaitic covenant was ratified (Exod 24:5, 11).

Ostensibly, P (rather, H) preserves a different tradition concerning the well-being offering at Pentecost. On that occasion the two lambs are assigned to the priests rather than to the people or their representatives (23:20). But the case of the inauguration of the public cult indicates otherwise. There the priests receive their normal perquisite, the breasts (9:21; on the problem of the thigh, see the COMMENT on chap. 7). This can only mean that the rest of the sacrificial meat was given to the people, or more likely their chieftains and elders. Further support is supplied by the text describing the priestly consecration. The meat of the consecration ram is eaten by its offerers who, in this case, are the priests (8:31–32; Exod 29:33–34); and this sacrifice, according to P's own acknowledgment, becomes the precedent for all well-being offerings (Exod 29:27–28). Thus P, no differently from the rest of Scripture, presumes that the meat of the public well-being offering, just as its private counterpart, is eaten by its offerers. Hence, the case of the Pentecostal lambs is an anomaly, for which the following hypothetical circumstances may have been responsible: when the local altars were abolished, the farmers no longer brought their two lambs and two wheat loaves each as a well-being offering. Because it became impractical, and in most cases impossible, for the Israelite farmer to make the pilgrimage to the single, central sanctuary during the busy harvest season, the offering was telescoped into a single set of two lambs and two loaves for the entire nation, and quite naturally, the priests officiating at the central sanctuary became the recipients of this offering (for further details, see the NOTES and COMMENT on 23:18–20).

THE PURIFICATION OFFERING (4:1–35)

Introduction

4 ¹The Lord spoke to Moses, saying: ²Speak to the Israelites thus:

When a person inadvertently does wrong in regard to any of the Lord's prohibitive commandments by violating any one of them——

Of the High Priest

³If it is the anointed priest who so does wrong to the detriment of the people, he shall offer for the wrong he has done a bull of the herd without blemish as a purification offering to the Lord. ⁴He shall bring the bull to the entrance of the Tent of Meeting before the Lord, lean his hand upon the head of the bull, and slaughter the bull before the Lord. ⁵The anointed priest shall take some of the bull's blood and bring it into the Tent of Meeting. ⁶The priest shall dip his finger in the blood, and sprinkle some of the blood seven times before the Lord against the veil of the shrine. ⁷The priest shall put some of the blood on the horns of the altar of perfumed incense, which is in the Tent of Meeting, before the Lord; and all the rest of the bull's blood he shall pour out at the base of the altar of burnt offering, which is at the entrance of the Tent of Meeting. ⁸He shall set aside all of the suet from the bull of the purification offering; the suet that covers the entrails and all of the suet that is around the entrails; ⁹the two kidneys and the suet that is around them, that is on the sinews; and the caudate lobe on the liver, which he shall remove with the kidneys—¹⁰just as it is set aside from the ox of the well-being offering. The priest shall turn them into smoke on the altar of burnt offering. ¹¹But the hide of the bull, and all its flesh, together with its head and shins, entrails and dung—¹²all the rest of the bull—shall be taken away to a pure place outside the camp, to the ash dump, and burned with wood; it shall be burned on the ash dump.

Of the Community

¹³If it is the whole community of Israel that has erred inadvertently and the matter escapes the notice of the congregation, so that they violate one of the Lord's prohibitive commandments, and they feel guilt ¹⁴when the wrong that they committed in regard to it becomes known, the congregation shall offer a bull of the herd as a purification offering and bring it before the Tent of Meeting. ¹⁵The elders of the community shall lean their hands upon the head of the bull before the Lord, and the bull shall be slaughtered before the Lord. ¹⁶The anointed priest shall bring some of the bull's blood into the Tent of Meeting, ¹⁷and the priest shall dip his finger in the blood and sprinkle of it seven times before the Lord, against the veil. ¹⁸Some of the blood he shall put on the horns

of the altar that is before the Lord in the Tent of Meeting, and all the rest of the blood he shall pour out at the base of the altar of burnt offering, which is at the entrance of the Tent of Meeting. 19He shall set aside all of its suet from it and turn it into smoke on the altar. 20He shall treat this bull as he treated the [first] bull of the purification offering; he shall treat it the same way. Thus the priest shall effect purgation for them that they may be forgiven. 21The bull shall be taken away outside the camp and it shall be burned as the first bull was burned: it is the purification offering of the congregation.

Of the Chieftain

22When the chieftain does wrong by violating any of the Lord's prohibitive commandments inadvertently, and he feels guilt 23or he is informed of the wrong he committed, he shall bring as his offering a male goat without blemish. 24He shall lean his hand upon the goat's head, and it shall be slaughtered at the spot where the burnt offering is slaughtered, before the Lord: it is a purification offering. 25The priest shall take some of the blood of the purification offering with his finger and put it on the horns of the altar of burnt offering; and (the rest of) its blood he shall pour out at the base of the altar of burnt offering. 26All of its suet he shall turn into smoke on the altar, like the suet of the well-being offering. Thus shall the priest effect purgation on his behalf for his wrong, that he may be forgiven.

Of the Commoner

27If any person from among the populace does wrong inadvertently by violating any of the Lord's prohibitive commandments and he feels guilt 28or he is informed of the wrong he committed, he shall bring as his offering a female goat without blemish for the wrong he committed. 29He shall lean his hand upon the head of the purification offering, and the purification offering shall be slaughtered at the spot (of the slaughter) of the burnt offering. 30The priest shall take some of its blood with his finger and put it on the horns of the altar of burnt offering; and all the rest of its blood he shall pour out at the base of the altar. 31All of its suet he shall remove, just as the suet was removed from the well-being offering; and the priest shall turn (it) into smoke on the altar as a pleasing aroma to the Lord. Thus the priest shall effect purgation on his behalf, that he may be forgiven.

32If the offering he brings is a sheep, he shall bring a female without blemish. 33He shall lean his hand upon the head of the purification offering, and it shall be slaughtered for purification purposes at the spot where the burnt offering is slaughtered. 34The priest shall take some of the blood of the purification offering with his finger and put it on the horns of the altar of burnt offering, and all the rest of its blood he shall pour out at the base of the altar. 35And all of its suet he shall remove just as the suet of the sheep of the well-being offering is removed; and the priest shall turn it (lit., them) into smoke on the altar, with the food gifts of the Lord. Thus the priest shall effect purgation on his behalf for the wrong he committed, that he may be forgiven.

NOTES

4:1. The heading (vv 1, 2a), like the opening of chapter 1, indicates that a new section is at hand. Although the subject is still the sacrifices, they are of a different kind: chaps. 1–3 dealt with voluntary sacrifices, a distinction recognized by the rabbis, who term the former *dinĕdābâ* 'voluntary' and the latter, *dĕḥôbâ* 'mandatory'. That the violation of prohibitive commandments will be the subject of this section (see at v 2) has been anticipated by the final statement of the previous chapter (3:17): it is a prohibition.

2. *When. kî*, the particle that begins the major casuistic statement in a legal case, whose subsections will be headed by *ʾim* (vv 3, 13, 32) and (very rarely) *ʾăšer* (v 22). See also on 1:2.

a person. As in 2:1, the term *nepeš* is used to indicate either sex (e.g., 5:2, 4, 15, 17, 21; 7:27; 22:11; Num 35:11, 15, 30); it is equivalent to *ʾādām* (Saadiah; see 1:2) and also includes the *gēr*, the resident alien, as well as the Israelite (Num 15:29; see also on 1:2).

inadvertently (bišĕgāgâ). Inadvertence is a key criterion in all expiatory sacrifice. A deliberate, brazen sinner is barred from the sanctuary (Num 15:30–31). Presumptuous sins are not expiable but are punished with *kārēt*—excision (see chap. 7, Comment D). Rodriguez (1979: 148) and Kiuchi (1987: 147) entirely miss the point in claiming that the Yom Kippur rite (16:16, 21) proves that the *ḥaṭṭāʾt* also atones for presumptuous sins. Of course it does. This is precisely the reason that such sinners are represented by the high priest: they themselves are barred from the sanctuary.

Inadvertent wrongdoing may result from two causes: negligence or ignorance. Either the offender knows the law but involuntarily violates it or he acts knowingly but is unaware he did wrong. The former situation underlies the examples of accidental homicide—Num 35:16–18, 22–23; Deut 19:5–6—and the latter is presumed by 1 Sam 14:32–34; Ezek 45:20; and such nonritual texts as 1 Sam 26:21; Prov 5:23; Job 6:24; 19:4. These two types of inadvertence have also been termed "error" and "accident" (Daube 1949). In either case, as the citations illustrate, unconsciousness of the sin and consciousness of the act are always presumed (contra Kiuchi 1987: 25–31), as recognized by the rabbis: "Scripture says *bišĕgāgâ* implying the existence of consciousness" (b. B. Qam. 26b). By contrast, an unconscious wrong, when the offender is unaware of both his act and his sin, when he only suspects that he has done wrong, is expiated by a different sacrifice, the *ʾāšām* (see the Notes on 5:17–19). This distinction throws light on the ideological and theological battle between Job and his friends (Milgrom 1967). The centrality of the concept "inadvertence" in this chapter is highlighted by the chiastic order of the opening statements of every case (Bendavid 1967: 1.21):

2	A + B	*tehĕṭāʾ*	*bišĕgāgâ*
3	A	*yehĕṭāʾ*	
13	B		*yišgû*
22	A	*yehĕṭāʾ*	
27	A + B	*tehĕṭāʾ*	*bišĕgāgâ*

does wrong (tehĕṭāʾ). Although the verb *ḥāṭāʾ* is found in Scripture referring to offenses against God and man (e.g., 1 Sam 2:25), in P it refers exclusively to sins against God, thus obviating the need to mention his name (e.g., 5:2, 5, 10, 13; Num 15:27, 28). Another difference lies in the fact that in Scripture this verb (like its Akk. cognate *ḥaṭû,* noun *ḥīṭu, ḥiṭītu*) refers to the entire range of offenses, from accidental misdemeanors to premeditated violence. P, conversely, reserves nouns like *ʿāwōn* and *pešaʿ* for premeditated offenses (b. *Yoma* 36b; see at 16:16, 21) but uses the verb *ḥāṭāʾ* and the noun *ḥāṭāʾt/ḥaṭṭāʾt* in categorizing involuntary offenses. A good example of this usage is the case of the Nazirite who accidently comes into contact with a corpse (Num 6:9); it is referred to as *ḥāṭāʾ ʿal hannepeš* 'erred in regard to the corpse'. That *ḥāṭāʾ* implies not sin but error or failure is shown by its noncultic usage, as in "sling a stone at a hair and not err" (Judg 20:16; Bekhor Shor; see also Isa 65:20; Prov 8:36; 19:2; Job 5:24).

in regard to any of. mikkōl, lit., "[with regard to] any of all." The preposition *min* is partitive (Kalisch 1867–72); compare *ʾaḥat mikkōl,* lit., "one of all" (v 13). Others (e.g., Shadal; Elliger 1966; recently Kiuchi 1987: 22–23) render *min* as "against," a meaning it does not have, because the alleged proof text, *wĕlōʾ rāšaʿtî mēʾĕlōhāy* (2 Sam 22:22 = Ps 18:22), should be rendered "I am not convicted by God."

prohibitive. ʾăšer lōʾ tēʿāśênâ, lit., "which are not done." God's commandments can be divided into two categories: performative and prohibitive ("dos" and "don'ts"). The performative commandments are violated by refraining from or neglecting to do them. The omission of a religious duty is a personal failing; but the sinner alone is affected. Because no act was performed, his sin carries no impact upon his environment. The violation of prohibitive commandments, by contrast, involves an act. It sets up reverberations that upset the divine ecology. Specifically, in the Priestly conceptual scheme, an act forbidden by God generates impurity, which impinges upon God's sanctuary and land. For example, sexual offenses and homicide pollute the land (18:27–28; Num 35:34–35), whereas Molech worship and corpse contamination pollute the sanctuary (20:3; Num 19:13, 20). It is of no minor importance that the verb *ṭimmēʾ* 'pollute' (and the related term *ḥillēl* 'desecrate') only appears in the context of prohibitive commandments but never with performative ones, and only in ritual but never in ethical contexts (see below). This is the significance of the qualification here: the violation of prohibitive commandments generates impurity, which can be lethal to the community of Israel unless it is purified—by the *ḥaṭṭāʾt*, the purification offering.

commandments. The term *miṣwôt* applies only to the religious command-ments *(fas)*, not to civil ones *(jus)*, to those enforceable solely by God, not by man. For example, inadvertent homicide (also characterized by the term *šĕgāgâ;* Num 35:12, 15) is expiable not by a purification offering but by banishment to a city asylum until the death of the high priest (Num 35:25). It is striking, how-ever, that the laws of homicide are called not *miṣwôt* but *mišpāṭîm* 'norms, procedures' (v 24) and *ḥuqqat mišpāṭ* 'law of procedure' (v 29), terms that designate civil laws (see Num 36:13 for the same distinction). Other legal tradi-tions designate religious law by other terms, for example, the Covenant Code, *dibĕrê YHWH* 'the words of the Lord' as opposed to *hammišpāṭîm* 'the norms' (Exod 24:3); also Moses declares, "I make known *ḥuqqê hāʾĕlōhîm wĕʾet-tôrātāyw* (the laws and teachings of God)," in contrast to "I arbitrate (*wĕšāpaṭtî,* i.e., decide the *mišpāṭ*) between a man and his neighbor" (Exod 18:16). Thus *miṣwôt* in P (and H) do not include the norms adjudicated and executed by the court but are restricted to those laws which fall solely under the jurisdiction of God (see 4:2, 13, 22; 5:17; 22:31; 26:3, 14, 15; 27:34; Num 15:22, 31, 39, 40; 36:13). This conclusion is corroborated in a second pericope dealing with the purification offering (Num 15:22–31; see COMMENT E below) where, again, the laws governed by this sacrifice are called *miṣwôt* (vv 22, 31; cf. *ṣiwwâ,* v 23) as well as *dĕbar YHWH,* cf. Exod 24:3, cited above) and the penalty for their flagrant violation is *kārēt,* a punishment meted out only by God (Zimmerli 1954). The term *miṣwâ* (and *tôrâ*) clearly refers to the Lord's covenantal revela-tion to Israel, in distinction to *ḥuqqîm/ḥuqqôt* and *mišpāṭîm,* which connote laws and legal procedures in general and, hence, can refer to the jurisprudence of all peoples (cf. 18:3, 30; 2 Kgs 17:40; Elliot-Binns 1955).

The limitation of the purification offering to laws punishable by God but not by man assumes central importance in evaluating the import of this super-scription. It extends beyond the bounds of ritual law to include ethics, an area that is also unenforceable in human courts. Thus it should occasion no surprise when later in Leviticus, in H, ethical and ritual prescriptions are intertwined, and both are stamped with the imprimatur of the Lord, *ʾănî YHWH* (19:3, 4, 10, 12, 14, 16, 18, etc.). The fusion of ethics and ritual is not an innovation of Israelite law. It is to be found in the earliest documents of the ancient Near East, for example, from Egypt, "The Protestation of Guiltlessness" (*ANET*[3] 34–36); from Mesopotamia, Šurpu II (Reiner 1958: 13–15); or from Hattia, Mastiggas (*ANET*[3] 350–51; cf. Moyer 1969: 143; Wright 1987: 262). Hence, in pagan cultures too the violation of ethical as well as ritual norms can enrage the gods. But it is in Israel alone that both norms are tied to the purification offering and its central message that the violation of ethics and/or ritual leads to the pollution of the sanctuary and its national consequence, the abandonment of the entire community of Israel by its God. Israel's neighbors also held to, indeed were obsessed by, a fear that their temples would be defiled and the concomitant need to purify them. But the source of this defilement, in their system, was not human beings but demons and the plethora of incantations, unctions, and rituals for the purification of the temple was directed toward eliminating or warding off this supernal evil (for details, see COMMENT C below). It was the genius of Israel's priesthood, as reflected in this sacrificial ritual, to give a national dimension to ethics, to make ethical behavior an indispensable factor in determining Israel's destiny. National destruction is predicted in the wake of the violation of *kol-hammiṣwôt* 'all the commandments' (26:14[H]). In this teaching (and in others, see COMMENT F on 5:14–26), Israel's priests are the precursors of its prophets.

any one of them (mēʾaḥat mēhēnnâ). The preposition *min* in the first word is partitive in meaning, giving the sense of "any" (GKC 119w n. 2).

3. *the anointed priest. hakkōhēn hammāšiaḥ,* the title of the high priest in preexilic times, for the sacred anointing oil (Exod 30:22–33) with which his head was anointed (21:10) was not reinstituted in the Second Temple (*t. Yoma* 2:15; *t. Soṭa* 13:1; *ʾAbot R. Nat.* A:41). In fact, this title or its paraphrase is found only in the Priestly writings (4:3, 5, 16; 6:15; 16:32; 21:10; Num 35:25). During the Second Temple period he was called *kōhēn hārōʾš* 'the head priest' (thirteen times in Ezra, fourteen times in Nehemiah, and ninety-one times in Chronicles). The term *hakkōhēn haggādôl* 'the high priest' was used in preexilic times (21:10; Num 35:25, 28; 2 Kgs 12:10; 22:4, 8; 23:4) and remained in currency during the restoration (Hag 1:1, 12, 14; Zech 3:1, 8). Later in the postexilic period, however, it was replaced by *kōhēn hārōʾš* (cf. 2 Chr 24:11 with 2 Kgs 12:11). Tannaitic literature refers to him as indefinite *kōhēn māšiaḥ* 'anointed priest' (e.g., *m. Hor.* 2:1; 3:1, 2), *hammāšiaḥ* 'the anointed one' (e.g., *m. Hor.* 2:6), and *kōhēn hammāšiaḥ* 'the anointed priest' (e.g. *m. Zebaḥ.* 10:8) but not *hakkōhēn hammāšiaḥ,* as in P; however, these rabbinic terms are archaistic and academic (Bailey 1951). Ordinary priests were also anointed by being aspersed with the sacred anointing oil, but only the high priest had the oil poured on his head (8:12, 30; cf. Num 3:3).

Why does the case of the high priest precede that of the community (vv 13–21)? The answer is supplied in the NOTE on vv 13–21, below.

to the detriment (of the people). lĕʾašmat is infinitival in form (see 5:26b). Biblical terms for good and bad behavior also connote their respective reward and punishment (Zimmerli 1954; Koch 1962; von Rad 1962: 262–72). The same can be shown for *ʾāšām;* it connotes both the wrong and the retribution (Milgrom 1976f: 3–12). The consequential *ʾāšām* is amply attested in the Bible (e.g., Gen 26:10; Jer 51:5b; Hos 5:15; Zech 11:5; Ps 34:22–23; 1 Chr 21:3) and in sacrificial texts as well (see the NOTE on 5:6). Thus the high priest's error has inflicted some penalty on the people. That priestly misconduct can harm the community is explicitly stated: "Do not dishevel your hair and do not rend your clothes, lest you die and *anger strike the whole community*" (10:6; cf. Gen 20:9, 17–18). What, then, is the high priest's error? Commentators differ. "He offers a purification offering for the people improperly" *(Tg. Ps.-J.).* Because all of his rites are on behalf of the people, any mistake in their execution will result in harm to the people (Dillmann and Ryssel 1897; Snaith 1967). The people are actually punished for his mistake (Shadal). The high priest's erroneous decision causes the people to sin *(m. Hor.* 2:2–3; cf. Ibn Ezra, Ramban). All of these answers are possible. There is no certainty but this: the nexus between cause and effect—the people suffer for the high priest's error.

The subsequent cases certify that remorse for *(ʾāšam)* and knowledge of *(yādaʿ)* one's error are prerequisites for the purification offering (see on vv 13–14, 22–23). Yet surprisingly, neither term is found in the case of the high priest. Moreover, the text does not even state that his error was committed inadvertently! The latter objection is removed once it is realized that the factor of inadvertence is expressly given in the previous verse, the heading for the entire chapter. But what of the missing remorse and knowledge? There is no choice but to infer that these things are taken for granted *(Keter Torah).* Because the high priest performs most of his rituals in the privacy of the tent-shrine, only he can inform himself of his error. And once discovered, it is inconceivable that he would not feel remorse.

bull of the herd. par ben-bāqār, lit., "bovine bull" (v 14; 16:3; 23:18). Scholarly opinion generally holds that this is an archaism that preserves the earlier meaning of *par* as an adult male animal (Elliger 1966; Péter 1975). But it is more likely that *bāqār* refers to domestic cattle, that is to say, "of the herd," and it has been purposefully inserted by the priestly legislator to indicate that sacrificial cattle must be domesticated (S. Rattray).

as a purification offering. lĕḥaṭṭāʾt is a *piʿel* formation derived from the verb *ḥiṭṭēʾ,* which is synonymous with *ṭihar* 'purify' (e.g., Ezek 43:23–26) and *kipper* 'purge' (Ezek 43:20, 26). The *ḥaṭṭāʾt,* therefore, is to be rendered "purification offering" (Milgrom 1970c, 1971a; see COMMENT A below). It should be noted that this translation had been given by Saadiah (tenth century) but has since been ignored.

4. *and slaughter (wĕšāḥaṭ).* Because the high priest is the offerer of the bull, he himself probably does the slaughtering (see at 1:5).

before the Lord. lipnê YHWH (see at 1:3).

5. It seems strange that the high priest is both the expiator and the expiated, that he officiates for his own sin. Yet who else? He alone is permitted to officiate within the tent-shrine, as indicated by the rites prescribed on all of the cult objects in the shrine—the incense altar (Exod 30:7–8), the lamps (Lev 24:2; on the anomaly of Exod 27:21, see Haran 1978: 209), the table of the bread of presence (Lev 24:8, implied)—and by the explicit statement "He among his

(Aaron's) sons who becomes priest in his stead, who enters the Tent of Meeting to officiate in the sanctuary . . ." (Exod 29:30).

6. *the priest.* hakkōhēn indicates the high priest himself (Ibn Ezra), not an ordinary priest (Philo, *Laws* 1. 231).

finger. Which? The rabbis opt for the index finger (*Sipra*, Ḥobah par. 3:8; *b. Zebaḥ.* 53a); but Egyptian anointment rites indicate that the priest used the small finger (Moret 1902: 190–200).

and sprinkle (wĕhizzâ). Sevenfold sprinkling is attested for the blood of the purification offering (4:6, 17; 16:14, 15, 19; Num 19:4), for the oil mixture of blood and water used in the purification of the mĕṣōrāʿ (14:7, 16, 27, 51), and for the anointing oil on the altar (8:11). It has been suggested (Vriezen 1950) that the purpose is consecratory: sprinkling on objects (altar, 8:11; 16:19) and people (mĕṣōrāʿ, fungous house, 14:7, 51) consecrates them, but sprinkling "before the Lord" (4:6, 17; 14:16, 27) or within the shrine (16:14, 15) or toward it (Num 19:4) consecrates the fluid. Thus, Vriezen argues, the purpose of the sevenfold sprinkling of the blood from the high priest's purification offering inside the shrine is to consecrate it so that it may effect purgation on the inner altar (v 7). The need for consecration could be explained by the fact that the high priest is a sinner, and his purgation rites with the blood cannot be efficacious unless he first consecrates the blood. Yet the objection can be raised that the blood of the community's purification offering is treated to a similar sprinkling rite, wherein the high priest is not implicated (see at vv 13–21). A second objection stems from the annual Day of Purgation, on which the same sprinkling rite is performed with the blood of the purification offerings of the high priest and community (see at 16:16b). Surely, after the high priest has expiated for himself and his household (16:11–14) there should be no reason for him to have to consecrate the blood of the community's purification offering. Finally, Vriezen's thesis breaks down completely over the purgation rites in the adytum, the inner shrine: the sevenfold sprinkling occurs *after* the Ark complex is aspersed (16:4). Thus the latter does not consecrate the blood but must be part of the purgation rites of the sanctuary. And, just as the sevenfold sprinkling of the purification blood purges the adytum on the annual Day of Purgation, so it purges the outer shrine, in this case, when the high priest performs it before the veil. Proof that the aspersion purges the entire area of the shrine is found in the wording that describes the same rite on the annual Day of Purgation: "he shall do likewise for the Tent of Meeting" (16:16). The text does not specify the veil or the incense altar, the objects that receive the blood, but the entire Tent, in other words, the shrine itself is purged. That the area of the shrine is as holy as the sancta it houses is further corroborated by the consistent distinctions made between the Tent (and not its sancta) and the sacrificial altar in regard to the priestly duties. Unqualified priests may not officiate at the altar, but they must not even enter the Tent (10:9; 21:23; Exod 28:43; 30:20 [Milgrom 1970a: 38–43]).

Is it an accident that the sevenfold sprinkling is the seventh rite in this pericope (vv 3–12) as well as in the purification of the scale-diseased person (14:24), as noted by Paran (1983: 139)?

of the blood. min haddām implies that the high priest dips his finger into the vessel containing the blood for each sprinkling (*Sipra*, Ḥobah par 3:8; *Sipre Zuṭa* on Num 19:4).

seven times. Ibn Ezra (on Num 23:1) points to the frequency of the number seven in the cultic calendar: the seventh day (Sabbath), the seventh week (Pentecost), the seventh month (Tishri), the seventh year (Sabbatical for land and remission of debts), seven burnt-offering lambs (on festivals, twice seven on Sukkot), seven sprinklings (in the sanctuary and for the purification of the *mĕṣōrāʿ).* He also points to the sacrificial requirement of seven bulls, seven rams, and seven altars for Balaam's divination (Num 23:1) and the same sacrifices for Job's friends (Job 42:8), as well as the astrological significance of seven. The magical use of seven is attested in the Bible: Naaman bathes seven times in the Jordan (2 Kgs 5:10, 14); Elijah orders his servant to scan the skies seven times for signs of rain (1 Kgs 18:43); Joshua's army circuits Jericho seven times on the seventh day. There are many other attestations of seven in the Bible (e.g., 25:8; Dan 9:24) and throughout the ancient Near East (Pope 1962). In the Talmud, a medical prescription requires seven twigs from seven trees, seven nails from seven bridges, and more (*b. Šabb.* 66b).

against. The expression *ʾet-pĕnê* can also mean "before" (Gen 19:13; 33:18; 1 Sam 2:11), but with a verb of motion such as "sprinkle" it denotes "toward" (so LXX, Vg., Pesh., Saadiah). But the blood does not touch the veil (*b. Yoma* 57a [bar.]; *y. Yoma* 5:4).

veil (pārōket). Akk. *parakku* means "shrine, the living quarters of the deity," and the verb *parāku* means "go across, block, bar," which can describe a curtain (*AHw* 829); thus *pārōket* is a fitting term for the veil that separates the adytum or Holy of Holies (Exod 26:33) containing the cherub-drawn chariot-throne of God (Ezek 10:15–19) from the rest of the shrine (Exod 26:31–35). See further Milgrom and Gane 1988.

the shrine. haqqōdeš (10:4, [also with *ʾet-pĕnê*] 18; Exod 26:33; 28:29, 35). Contrary to Kiuchi (1987: 170), it means "adytum" only in chap. 16 (vv 2, 3, 16, 20, 23), which originally belonged to another source (see at 16:2). Perhaps this added specification was considered essential to distinguish the veil from the other curtain *(māsāk),* which hung at the opposite end, at the entrance of the Tent (Exod 26:36).

7. *horns.* The altar's horns are right-angle tetrahedra projecting from the four corners. They are not added onto the altar but are of one piece with it (Exod 27:2; 30:2), as illustrated by an incense altar from Megiddo and the sacrificial altar (in an Israelite sanctuary) from Beer-sheba (see fig. 5a, b).

In the ancient Near East, the horns on the altar are emblems of the gods (Galling 1925). They are found on top of shrines (Obbink 1937) and the head-

FIGURE 5a. Incense altar from Megiddo (*Biblical Archaeologist*)

FIGURE 5b. The horned altar from Beer-sheba as reconstructed (*Biblical Archaeologist*)

dresses of the gods (Boehmer 1972–75). They signify the horns of a powerful animal (e.g., a bull or a ram) and are symbols of strength and force. Indeed, *qeren* in the Bible is invested with the same symbolism (1 Sam 2:1, 10; 2 Sam 22:3; Jer 48:25; Zech 2:4; Pss 75:5–6, 11; 89:18, 25; etc.). In Israel, the altar horns were clearly essential; to cut them off was to desecrate the altar (Amos 3:14). Their daubing with the purification blood meant the purgation of the entire altar, by the principle of *pars pro toto*. For details, see my discussion of the sacrificial altar (v 25).

the altar of perfumed incense (mizbaḥ qĕṭōret hassammîm). Described in detail in Exod 30:1–10; 37:25–28, its dimensions were $1 \times 1 \times 2$ cubits. Like the sacrificial altar (see v 25), it contained rings and staves for carrying and was made of acacia wood. It differed, however, in being plated with gold, not with bronze; also, the plating extended over the top, for it was solid and had a roof, in contrast to the sacrificial altar, which was hollow. Its place was directly in front of the veil, flanked by the two other golden cult objects, the candelabrum (Exod 25:31–40) and the display table (Exod 25:23–30). Incense was burned on it twice daily at the time of the *tāmîd*, but no other offering other than the prescribed incense was permitted (Exod 30:9b).

Reference to the incense altar of Solomon's temple is found in the construction account (1 Kgs 6:20–22; 7:48) and in the incense offering ascribed to King Uzziah (2 Chr 26:16). In Ezekiel's blueprint for the new temple (Ezek 40:42), he may have had in mind the incense altar he saw in the temple (as a priest, he had access to it). Since Wellhausen, the historicity of these accounts has been called into question, on the assumption that the burning of incense was not introduced into Israel until the time of the Second Temple (see 1 Macc 1:54). Nevertheless, many altars have been found in Canaan dating back to the Bronze Age that are too small for animal offerings. Some actually approximate the dimensions of the tabernacle incense altar and are even equipped with horns, for example, at Shechem and Megiddo (fig. 5a, above). Furthermore, these altars are circumscribed by a molding, recalling "a molding of gold around it" (Exod 30:3). Thus the incense altar was standard equipment for Canaanite temples. Moreover, several of these altars were found in Israelite sanctuaries (e.g., Arad, Lachish). Thus the use of incense in Israel during the First Temple period can hardly be denied.

As there is every reason to affirm the presence of an incense altar in Solomon's temple, there remains only the question of the incense altar attributed to the Tabernacle. Scholars have been nearly unanimous in declaring it an anachronistic insertion based on the Temple. They support their viewpoint by noting that the description of the incense altar is not joined to that of the other inner sancta (Exod 26), but rather is placed after the description of the entire Tabernacle and its paraphernalia (Exod 30:1–10)—an afterthought, as it were. The objection is fallacious. The fact that it is not found in its "logical" place is in itself reason to suspect that another kind of logic obtains here. It can be shown that the description of the Tabernacle is divided into two parts: Exodus 26:1–27:19, the Tabernacle in blueprint, and Exodus 27:20–30:38, the Tabernacle in operation. Because the incense altar is described functionally (Exod 30:7–8), it therefore belongs in the latter section. Furthermore, the use of the candelabrum (Exod 27:20–21), the investiture of those qualified to service the Tabernacle (Exod 28:1–29:37), the *tāmîd* offering (Exod 29:38–42), and the incense offering (Exod 30:1–10) are all part of *a single cultic activity to be conducted twice daily by the high priest.* Further evidence is that other cultic instruments, namely, the laver and anointment oil, are mentioned even later—again for the reason that their use is being described (Exod 30:17–21, 22–30). Therefore, there is no evidence, either textual or archaeological, to question the existence of an incense altar in the precinct of the Tabernacle (for new evidence from archaeological finds see Gitin 1989).

incense. qĕṭōret, a term that primarily denotes "that which goes up in smoke" (e.g., Ps 66:15; and see at 1:9) but whose restricted but more prevalent meaning is "incense" (e.g., Ezek 8:11; 16:18; 23:41). In Semitic languages *qtr(t)* means "smoke," as in *qtr* (Aram.) and *qutru, quturtu* (Akk.). In Arabic the verb *qaṭṭara* denotes the perfuming of garments with the smoke of aloe spice. In Hebrew the verb *qṭr (piʿel* and *hiphʿil)* means "burn incense"; the *piʿel* generally designates illicit worship, of idols or at bamot, whereas the *hiphʿil* is used of legitimate worship both in P and elsewhere (e.g., 1 Sam 2:28; 1 Kgs 12:33; 13:1). The incense burnt on the inner altar is designated as *qĕṭōret hassammîm* 'perfumed incense' (Exod 25:6; 30:7; 31:11), which consists of a mixture of powdered spices, specifically balsam, onycha, galbanum, and frankincense (Exod 30:34–38). It was also used in the Holy of Holies on the annual Day of Purgation (16:12–13). An ancient baraita dating from Temple times (*Ker.* 6a) claims that "eleven ingredients were mentioned to Moses at Sinai" and to the biblical four the following seven spices are added: myrrh, cassia-cinnamon, spikenard, saffron, costus, cinnamon, and cinnamon bark, some of which were components of the sacred anointing oil (Exod 30:23). Josephus avers that there were thirteen spices in the Temple's incense offering (*Wars* 5.218; for details, see note on 16:12).

Nonpriests were strictly forbidden to offer incense (Num 17:5). The daily offering of incense on the altar was restricted to the high priest (Exod 30:7–8), but in the Second Temple it could be performed by any priest. This conclusion can be deduced from the Bible itself and is confirmed by the rabbinic sources (e.g., *m. Tamid* 5:2, 4; 6:3). The Chronicler condemns King Uzziah for officiating at the incense offering in these words: "It is not for you, Uzziah, to offer incense to the Lord, but for Aaronite priests, who have been consecrated, to offer incense" (2 Chr 26:18; cf. also Num 17:5).

Incense rituals were extremely important in Egypt. Considerable effort was expended in procuring incense gums and resins required in the temple rituals. Egyptian priests burned incense in daily rituals at the temple. Following their purificatory bath they entered the temple gates at dawn. Once inside the temple proper the highest-ranking priest went into the sanctuary, prostrated himself before the effigy of the god, rose, chanted prayers, and infumed the air with incense. According to the Pyramid Texts, 376–78, incense burning was the "sympathetic agency by which, as the odorous vapor arises from earth to the gods, it bears aloft the fragrance of the king to mingle with that of the gods, and thus to draw them together in fellowship and association" (Breasted 1959: 126).

In Israel, the ascent of the smoke of incense became the visible manifestation of prayer: "Let my prayer be counted as incense before thee, and the lifting up of my hands as an evening sacrifice" (Ps 141:2)! The symbolism is even more explicitly stated in later periods: "And another angel came and stood before the altar. He had a golden censer and he was given abundant incense to add to the prayers of all the holy ones on the golden altar before the throne. And the smoke of the incense arose with the prayers of the holy ones from the hand of the Angel of the Presence. And the angel took the censer, and filled it from the coals on the altar and hurled them onto the earth. And there were claps of thunder, and loud voices and streaks of lightning, and an earthquake" (Rev 8:3–5). The burning of incense in the various cults presumably carried the same symbolic values. Burning of incense to the queen of heaven was accompanied by requests for fertility and well-being (Jer 44:17). The presence of incense altars and burners in the same archaeological context as fertility figurines attests the popularity of such cults in Israel.

The Priestly sources also attest that there was an incense offering on a fire pan (10:1–4; Num 16:16–18; 17:11–13), which, however, was not part of the fixed daily or festival cult. For details, see the NOTE on 10:1–4.

which is in the Tent of Meeting, before the Lord. This is the first time the inner altar is mentioned in Leviticus, hence the full data on its location, to make sure it is not confused with the sacrificial altar (v 26). That "before the Lord" can refer to the interior of the Tent is shown by Exod 27:21; 28:35; 30:8; 34:34; 40:23, 25.

the rest. kol- (so Saadiah), in other words, all that remains; cf. 5:9. For this usage, see Judg 16:17; 1 Sam 8:5.

shall pour out. yišpōk, that is to say, dispose of. The verb *šāpak* in P indicates a noncultic act (14:41; 17:13), in contrast to D (Deut 12:27). The question whether the discarded blood still retained its sanctity was debated by the rabbis (*m. Ḥul.* 8:6; *m. Me'il.* 3:3; cf. *Tiferet Israel* and *Tosfot Yom Tov* on *m. Yoma* 5:6), but they agreed that mishandling it would not invalidate the sacrifice (*m. Zebaḥ.* 5:1–2).

the base of (yĕsôd). To judge by the detailed description of the sacrificial altar in Ezekiel's visionary temple (Ezek 43:13–17), the base probably contained a trough, probably a trench dug around the base (1 Kgs 18:32; cf. Wright 1987: 158), that collected the sacrificial blood. Ezekiel's altar had two such troughs *(heq),* one at the base and the other in the middle (Ezek 43:14, 17), the latter to catch the purification blood daubed on its corners (Ezek 43:20). The altar in Solomon's Temple may also have contained a middle trough, for it was divided into an upper and a lower section (Ezek 16:24–25, 31, 39; cf. 43:13). So did the altar in the Second Temple, the bottom half also being called by this name, yĕsôd (m. Mid. 3:1; m. Kelim 17:10). The purification offering is the only sacrifice whose remaining blood is expressly to be disposed of at the altar's base (e.g., 4:7, 18, 25, 30, 34; 5:9; 8:15; 9:19); the blood of the other sacrifices is totally used in their respective blood rites; there is none left over requiring disposal.

8. *shall set aside (yārîm)*. Equivalent to *hiqrîb* (3:3, 9, 14; cf. 4:10) and *hēsîr* (4:31, 35; cf. 3:4, 9, 10, 15), that is, set aside as a dedication (Milgrom 1983g). For details see the NOTE on 7:32. This is the tenth and final rite in the sacrificial procedure of the high priest's *hattā't*. As in other similar constructs, the final verb is expressed differently from the preceding ones (in the imperfect, not as a perfect), to indicate stylistically that the pericope is about to close (see the NOTE on 1:9). In this case, however, the previous, ninth, verb is also in the imperfect, *yišpōk* (v 7b), perhaps for the purpose of contrasting the blood manipulations on the two altars, *wĕnātan* (v 7a) and *yišpōk* (v 7b) (Paran 1983: 138).

all of the suet (kol-ḥēleb). The specific suet pieces follow in vv 8–9; this expression is similar in function to *ḥelbô* (3:9).

(covers) the (entrails): 'al. Twenty-five manuscripts, LXX, Sam., Tg. Onq., and Tg. Ps.-J. read *'et-*, as in 3:3, 9, 14; and 7:3.

10. *it is set aside (yûrām)*. The antecedent is "all of the suet" (v 8).

ox. The term *šôr* can refer to either the male or the female of the species (e.g., 22:28).

shall turn them into smoke (wĕhiqtîrām). The antecedent of this plural suffix is the suet pieces, enumerated above (vv 8–9); see at 3:16.

11. *all its flesh (kol-bĕśārô)*. The flesh of the animal does not include the head and shins, which are enumerated separately (see at 1:9a).

and dung (ûpiršô). Akk. *paršu*, Syr. *pertā'*; Jewish Aram. *partā'*.

12. *all the rest (kol-)*. See the NOTE on v 7.

shall be taken away . . . burned (wĕhôṣî' . . . wĕśārap). The subject cannot be the high priest, for he would be rendered impure. For this reason, the LXX and Sam. read these verbs as plurals (and do so again in v 21). Instead, the subjects may be treated as impersonal and the verbs interpreted as equivalent to passive formations.

pure place (māqôm ṭāhôr). Why this specification; is it not obvious? Not at all. Among Israel's neighbors (e.g., Hittites, Mesopotamians), substances that absorb impurity are themselves lethally dangerous. In Israel, however, the only part of the purification offering that acts as the ritual detergent is the blood. The flesh of the ordinary purification offering is actually eaten by the officiating priest (6:19, 22), and the purification offering for severe impurities is incinerated outside the camp only because the fear of its lethal properties has survived (see COMMENT D below). Nevertheless, the latter is still treated like a sacrifice; its flesh is holy and must be burned in a pure place (Milgrom 1976a; 1978b: 511–12). The sectaries of Qumran, however, held that the ashes of the purification offering had to be separated from the ashes of other sacrifices (11QT 16:12).

it shall be burned (yiśśārēp). This ostensibly superfluous word is added to form a "circular inclusion" with *wĕśārap* (v 12a) so that it could emphasize, in an independent sentence, where the sacrificial carcass should be burned (Paran 1983: 29).

ash dump (šepek haddešen). That there actually existed a special dump for the sacrificial ashes outside Solomon's Temple is shown by Jer 31:39 (cf. 1:16; 6:3–4; Ezek 43:21). Furthermore, the sectaries of Qumran held that the ash dump must lie not just outside the Temple (cf. Ezek 43:21) but outside the boundaries of Jerusalem, because they maintained that the Temple city was equivalent in holiness to the Tabernacle camp (*MMT* B 29–33). Indeed, throughout the centuries a huge ash dump has been sited just north of Jerusalem (in agreement with *t. Pesaḥ.* 3:17; cf. *b. Yoma* 68a), "approximately the length of the course of a hippodrome" (*Kaptor Waperaḥ*, thirteenth century, Luncz 1897: 77), located at the Mandelbaum gate (the former passageway between East and West Jerusalem), which would put it beyond Herodian Jerusalem's third (outer) wall (Ben-Aryeh 1977: 54; 1979: 89). It is more than twelve meters high and, according to Luncz (1897: 77 n. 1), samples of it were chemically analyzed by a Professor Liebig of Munich, who found their contents to consist exclusively of the remains of animal flesh, bones, and teeth.

13–21. Because the sacrificial procedure for the community is identical to that of the high priest, there is no reason to repeat it verbatim. It is given in abbreviated form with the following omissions from the high priest's case: "for the wrong he has done . . . without blemish . . . to the Lord" (v 3); "entrance . . . Lord . . . before the Lord" (v 4); "shall take . . . it" (v 5); "in the blood . . . of the shrine" (v 6); "of perfumed incense . . . bull's" (v 7); "from the bull of the purification offering; the suet that covers the entrails and all of the suet that is around the entrails; the two kidneys and the suet that is around them, that is on the sinews; and the caudate lobe on the liver, which he shall remove with the kidneys" (vv 8–9); "just as it is set aside from the ox of the well-being offering. The priest . . . of burnt offering" (v 10); "But the hide of the bull, and all its flesh, together with its head and shins, its entrails and dung" (v 11) is reworded as "He shall treat this bull as he treated the [first] bull of the purification offering" (v 20); "all the rest of . . . to a pure place . . . to the ash dump" (v 12a); "with wood; it shall be burned on the ash dump" (v 12aβ, b) is reworded "as the first bull was burned" (v 21aβ).

There are certain phrases of the community's case (vv 13–21), however, that are missing in the case of the high priest, as follows: "erred inadvertently and the matter escapes the notice of the congregation . . . and they feel guilt" (v 13); "when the wrong that they committed in regard to it becomes known" (v 14a); "Thus the priest shall effect purgation for them that they may be forgiven" (v 20b); "it is the purification offering of the congregation" (v 21b). The first two omissions (vv 13–14a) have been accounted for (see the NOTE on v 3). The fourth omission (v 21b) is understandable: it is a summation. But how can we account for the third omission (v 20b); is it conceivable that the high priest fails to purge his own sin and so fails to gain divine forgiveness? Abravanel deduces from this anomaly that the notice of the community's purgation and forgiveness (v 20b) also covers the case of the high priest. He supports his conclusion by pointing out that because "as he treated the bull of purification offering" (v 20a) must refer back to the bull of the high priest, hence the plural suffixes *ʿălēhem* 'for them' and *lāhem* 'to them' must include both the high priest and the community. Abravanel finds additional support in the fact that the notice of purgation and forgiveness, which normally is found at the end of a case (see vv 26, 31, 35; 5:10, 13), is unexpectedly inserted before the procedure is completed, not at the end of v 21a but after v 20a. The reason, he concludes, is to indicate that the desideratum of purgation and forgiveness is effected for the purification offerings of both the high priest and the community.

I believe Abravanel is right, but the full implication is yet to be drawn. The logical conclusion of his thesis is that the purification offering of the high priest and the community comprise a single case. The high priest has erred in judgment, causing "harm to the people" (v 3) whereby, in following the high priest's ruling, the people also err. Because both their errors comprise inadvertent violations of prohibitive commandments (vv 2, 13) which pollute the Tabernacle shrine (see COMMENT C below), each party is responsible for purging the shrine with the blood of a similar sacrifice—a purification-offering bull. Abetting this thesis is the fact that in the two attested cases of public expiatory offerings, the high priest sacrifices his purification offering separately from and before the community (9:1–15; 16:3–19). The similitude of the prescriptive case of vv 1–21 with these two cited descriptive cases of purification offerings by the high priest and the community is tacitly acknowledged in this perceptive rabbinic statement: "Rabbi Hiyya taught: Because it is the anointed priest who effects purgation [for the community] and the community who is being purged, it is best that the [sacrifice of the] one who is to effect purgation should precede [the sacrifice of] those who are being purged, as it is written: 'And he shall effect purgation for himself and his household and for the community of Israel' (16:17)" (*Midr. Lev. Rab.* 5:6; cf. *t. Hor.* 2:4; *t. Zebaḥ.* 10:2).

13. *community of Israel* (*ʿădat yiśrāʾēl*). *ʿēdâ* is P's distinctive term for the entire Israelite nation—men, women, and children. In this usage, it occurs more than one hundred times in the early narratives (e.g., Exod 16:1; Num 17:11) and laws (e.g., Exod 12:19, 47; Num 1:53). It can also refer to all adult males (e.g., Num 14:1–4; 31:26, 28, 43), especially those bearing arms (e.g., Judg 20:1). Finally, *ʿēdâ* can be used of tribal leaders meeting as an executive body (e.g., Exod 12:3, 21; Josh 22:14–16; Judg 21:10, 13), acting on behalf of the entire community (Milgrom 1978a).

has erred inadvertently (yišgû). The root is *šgh* rather than *šgg* (vv 2, 22, 27). But biconsonantal roots that expanded into geminates and *lamed-he* are attested frequently (cf. GKC 319; Grimm 1902: 196; Milgrom 1967: 116 n. 5). These two roots have coalesced, as is evident in Job 12:16. The choice of the variant root here may not have been an accident. It holds the central, pivotal position in the chiasm that structures the entire chapter (see the NOTE on 1:2).

How is it possible for the entire people to err simultaneously? The thesis that vv 1–21 form a single case, propounded above, whereby the high priest's erroneous decision causes the whole community to err, makes this eventuality highly plausible. For example, if the high priest declares the new moon on the wrong day, festivals falling in the ensuing month will be observed by everyone on the wrong day. Indeed, the rabbis prescribe the rite of Lev 4:3–21 when the people (or most of them) follow the erroneous teaching of the Sanhedrin (*m. Hor.* 1:1–5), whereas Qumran prescribes it when a false prophet misleads the members of his own tribe (4Q375; cf. the corresponding view of Rabbi Judah in *m. Hor.* 1:5 [end]): my differences with Strugnell 1990 will be published separately.

escapes the notice. wĕneʿlam . . . mēʿênê, in other words, the community was conscious of its act (e.g., by following the high priest's decision), but they did not realize that it was wrong. For this usage, see Num 5:13; Job 28:21.

the congregation. Is there a difference between "congregation," *qāhāl*, and "community," *ʿēdâ*? None is ascertainable. If, then, they are synonymous, why are they used together? Perhaps the reason is literary: "The writer may wish to vary his style" (Gordis 1950: 380 n. 25). This may hold true in narratives (e.g., Exod 16:1–3; Num 16:3–33; 17:6–12; 20:1–6, 7–13) as it does in poetry, as an effort to avoid monotonous repetition. Yet the same alternation prevails in purely legal material (vv 13–21; 16:5, 17 [= *ʿam*, 15, 24]; Num 10:1–7), where, to judge by the confusion caused to exegetes, synonyms should have been avoided at all costs.

It can be shown that *ʿēdâ* is an ancient technical term for the sociopolitical body that was called into session by Israel's tribal chieftains whenever a national transtribal issue arose. Once the monarchy was firmly established, though, there was no further need for the *ʿēdâ* and, indeed, the term does not occur even once in writings that can be dated at the end of the monarchy, such as Deuteronomy or Ezekiel. Its absence from Ezekiel is astonishing, for the dependence of Ezekiel on P is a well-established fact (Hurvitz 1982). Instead, Ezekiel uses *qāhāl* (Ezek 16:40; 17:17; 23:3, 46, 47; 32:22, 23; 38:4, 7, 13, 16). Three of those verses are especially enlightening, for they deal with the judicial sentence of death by stoning (16:40; 23:46, 47) for adultery and murder (16:38; 23:44–45). Now, in P stoning as judicial punishment is carried out by the *ʿēdâ* (24:16; Num 15:35). Ezekiel, however, uses the term *qāhāl*—patently because *ʿēdâ* has disappeared from the linguistic currency of his day. And, indeed, this technical usage of *qāhāl* predominates in the postexilic literature (e.g., Ezra 10:12; Neh

8:2). Strikingly, the Chronicler always substitutes *qāhāl* for the older term (cf. 2 Chr 23:3 with 2 Kgs 11:17 and 2 Chr 24:6 with Exod 35:4, 20).

Thus it can be suggested that once *ʿēdâ* fell into desuetude, subsequent redactors of P had no choice but to substitute *qāhāl* for it, the very word that had usurped its place. Out of reverence for the text, however, they did not replace every *ʿēdâ* but only once or twice in each pericope, so that the reader would know that the term he knew as *qāhāl* originally read *ʿēdâ*. Thus the alternation of *ʿēdâ* and *qāhāl* in legal material may be due to editorial activity rather than stylistic criteria (Milgrom 1978a).

and they feel guilt (wĕʾāšēmû). The verb *ʾāšam* is stative. When followed by the preposition *l* and a personal object (e.g., 5:19b), it means "incur liability to"; without an object (so throughout this chapter), it refers to the inner experience of liability, that is, "to feel guilt." For additional details concerning the "consequential" *ʾāšam,* see the NOTE on v 3 and COMMENT A on 5:14–26.

14. *the wrong (haḥaṭṭāʾt).* It has been argued that the Masoretes erroneously vocalized this word as a *piʿel* formation, whereas only the *qal,* *ḥāṭāʾt,* means "wrong" (Levine 1974: 102). The latter term, however, is unattested (and the formation *ḥāṭāʾâ* is not attested in P). Moreover, Akk. *ḥaṭṭiʾu* 'sinner', a D formation (corresponding to Hebrew *piʿel*), also retains the LXX (corresponding to *qal)* meaning (Rodriguez 1979: 81).

in regard to it (ʿālêhā). The feminine suffix points to "one of the Lord's commandments" (v 13) as the antecedent (cf. 5:5). If the antecedent were "the wrong" (also feminine), then the preposition would have been *b* (cf. v 23; Dillmann and Ryssel 1897).

when . . . becomes known (wĕnôdĕʿâ). This verb is inchoative and inceptive in meaning (Orlinsky 1969: 34). The use of *waw* as "when" is amply attested; for example, *wĕšākabtî ʿim ʾăbōtay ûnĕśāʾtānî* 'when I rest with my fathers you will carry me' (Gen 42:30). Here the temporal sequence is reversed, *wĕʾāšēmû wĕnôdĕʿâ* 'and they feel guilt when [the wrong] becomes known': the second verb precedes the first in time. This phenomenon is also attested elsewhere in Scripture, for example, *kî yabʿer-ʾîš . . . wĕšillaḥ et-bĕʿîrōh,* lit., "if a man causes (a field or vineyard) to be grazed bare when he lets his livestock loose" (Exod 22:4).

The difference between the expression here and its formation in the subsequent cases must be noted: the *waw* is replaced by *ʾô* 'or' and the *niphʿal* passive by the *hiphʿil* active *hôdaʿ* (vv 23, 28). The change in the verb pattern is explained by the obvious fact that because everyone in the community erred, there is no uninvolved outsider (not even the high priest, who also has erred) who can objectively point out the error. That discovery must come from within their own ranks; hence, the passive (Shadal). This situation also explains the difference in the particles. The individual who errs either finds out the nature of his error on his own or *(ʾô)* someone else informs him of it. But as the community as a whole has erred there can be no "or"; the communal guilt results from the eventual discovery of the error by the community itself.

Alternatively, the temporal sequence wĕʾāšēmû wĕnôdĕʿâ need not be understood in reverse order if the meaning is that the community first "feels guilt" but does not know the reason for it and only later discovers the actual reason. Such a connotation for ʾāšam is, indeed, attested in one case (see the NOTES on 5:17). Yet the use of ʾāšam in the subsequent cases of the chieftain and commoner (vv 22, 27) clearly implies that the individual feels guilt only after discovering the nature of his error, and the same condition surely must prevail here. For other interpretations of this anomalous sequence, see Saadiah, Rashi, Ibn Ezra, and Shadal.

(the congregation) shall offer. The word wĕhiqrîbû marks the beginning of the apodosis (as in v 3b). The apodoses of the subsequent cases begin with hēbîʾ (vv 23b, 28b; cf. v 32b). The exceptional cases of the high priest and community (vv 1–21) require the additional notice that they must bring as their purification offering a bull, an animal that is attested as a ḥaṭṭāʾt only for priests (8:14; 16:11; cf. 9:8) and Levites (Num 8:12) but never for the community, which throughout P offers up a he-goat as a ḥaṭṭāʾt (9:3; 16:5; 23:19; Num 15:24; chaps. 28–29) —except here! (See COMMENT K below.)

bull of the herd. The LXX and Sam. add tāmîm 'without blemish' (cf. v 3). In view of the other omissions in this pericope, however, the MT is preferred (see the NOTE to vv 13–21).

before (lipnê). The LXX and Vg. add "the entrance of" (cf. v 4a). But the MT may be justified as original (see at 3:8).

15. *The elders of the community.* ziqnê hāʿēdâ, who act on behalf of the community (see 9:11; Exod 3:16; 4:29; 12:21; 17:6; 18:12; 24:9; Num 11:30; 16:25).

shall be slaughtered. wĕšāḥaṭ. This verb in the singular, following plural wĕsāmĕkû, shows that the former's subject is not the elders but anyone; hence, it must be rendered as an impersonal passive.

17. *in the blood.* min-haddam, lit., "from the blood"; in other words, he dips his finger into the vessel containing the blood for each sprinkling (see 14:16 and the NOTE on v 6). Verse 17a is a shortened form of *(wĕṭābal hakkōhēn ʾet-ʾeṣbāʿô) baddām wĕhizzâ min-haddām* (cf. v 6). The same phenomenon is attested in 14:16. In both instances baddām was omitted because of the following min-haddām (Paran 1983: 204 n. 36).

18. *the altar (hammizbēaḥ).* The LXX and Sam. read mizbaḥ qĕṭōret hassammîm (as in v 7). But this altar is adequately defined as being "in the Tent of Meeting" and the abridgment, attested throughout this pericope (see on vv 13–21), is justified.

19. *He shall set aside.* "He" is the high priest, proof that he too is one of the offerers (see v 31 and 3:3, 9, 14).

THE SACRIFICES

20. *the [first] bull of the purification offering. lĕpar haḥaṭṭāʾt,* namely, of the high priest.

effect purgation (wĕkipper). This verb is discussed in chap. 16., COM-MENT F.

that (they) may be forgiven (wĕnislaḥ). Whereas the high priest is the agent of purgation (the verb is *piᶜel,* active), the Lord alone is the agent of forgiveness —hence, the verb is *niphᶜal,* passive (contra Knohl 1988: 238 n. 42). The priest carries out the purgation rites but only God determines their efficacy. Contrast this with P's ruling on the woman who makes a vow but is thwarted in fulfilling it by her father or husband, in which case she is automatically forgiven by God (Num 30:6, 9, 13; *sālaḥ, qal*-active).

The rendering "forgive" for *sālaḥ* is, in reality, not accurate. When God grants *sālaḥ* to Moses' request for it (Num 14:19–20), it cannot connote forgiveness, considering that God qualifies it by declaring that all of adult Israel, with the exception of Caleb, will perish in the wilderness (vv 21–24). Furthermore, in the entire Bible only God dispenses *sālaḥ,* never humans. Thus, we confront a concept that must be set apart from anthropopathic notions: it does not convey the pardon or forgiveness that humans are capable of extending. Finally, because Moses invokes God's dreaded attribute of vertical retribution (v 18; cf. Exod 34:7), he clearly does not have forgiveness in mind. All he asks is that God be reconciled with his people: punish Israel, yes, but do not abandon it. Indeed, in the episode of the golden calf, God answers Moses' request for *sālaḥ* by renewing the covenant (Exod 34:9–10). For details see Milgrom 1981i.

By the same token, the offender who brings the *ḥaṭṭāʾt* does so because he knows that his wrong, though committed inadvertently, has polluted the altar and, hence, has alienated him from God. By his sacrifice he hopes to repair the broken relationship. He therefore seeks more than forgiveness. If God will accept his sacrifice he will be once again restored to grace, at one with his deity. Because I cannot offer a more accurate one-word rendering, I retain the translation "forgive"; but the reader should always keep the multivalent connotation of *sālaḥ* in mind.

they. lāhem includes the case of the high priest (Abravanel); see the NOTE on vv 13–21). The rabbis also interpret the community's purification offering as a case in which the high priest's error caused the community to err, but they regard the high priest's purification offering (vv 3–12) as an independent case in which the high priest alone has erred (*m. Hor.* 2:2)—disregarding the effect, "to the detriment of the people" (v 3).

21. *the first bull (happar hārīʾšôn).* The same ritual as that with the high priest's bull (spelled out in v 12b) is to be performed with the bull of the community. The similar expression *wayyĕḥaṭṭĕʾēhû kārīʾšôn* 'performed the purification rite with it as with the previous [one]' (9:15) provides further evidence that, just as the purification offerings of the high priest and community in the

latter passage form part of a single ritual (9:1–15), so do the purification offerings of the high priest and community in this chapter.

it is the purification offering of the congregation (ḥaṭṭāʾt haqqāhāl hûʾ). The reason for this addition, according to Ibn Ezra, is to distinguish it from the purification offering of the community brought for violating a *performative* commandment (Num 15:22–26). It is unlikely, however, that the Numbers pericope has a different purpose from this one (see COMMENT E below). Rather, it is a fitting close to this pericope, condensing and enveloping the opening statement of the apodosis (v 14b) as a summary inclusion.

The Sam. reads the pronoun as *hîʾ* (fem.) in agreement with *ḥaṭṭāʾt* 'the purification offering' (also in v 26). The MT's *hûʾ* (masc.) is in agreement with *happār* 'the bull'.

22. *When (ʾăšer).* Either the equivalent of *ʾim* 'if' (vv 3, 13, 27, 32; see Deut 11:27; cf. v 28 *ʾim;* 18:22; *Keter Torah*) or *kaʾăšer* 'when' (Josh 4:21; cf. v 6, *kî;* Isa 31:4, 11, *kaʾăšer*). Its use here is deliberate. First, it should be noted that it marks the midpoint and central case in this chapter:

Heading, *kî* (v 2)

Case 1, *ʾim* (v 3)

Case 2, *ʾim* (v 13)

Case 3, *ʾăšer* (v 22)

Case 4, *ʾim* (v 27)

Case 5, *ʾim* (v 32)

More important is that case 3, begun with *ʾăšer*, introduces a new kind of *ḥaṭṭāʾt.* The first two cases (vv 3–21) speak of the extraordinary *ḥaṭṭāʾt*, whose blood is sprinkled inside the Tent and whose carcass is incinerated outside the camp. The cases that now follow describe the ordinary *ḥaṭṭāʾt* (vv 22–35), whose blood is daubed on the horns of the courtyard altar and whose meat is consumed by the priests (cf. 6:22). The distinction between these two kinds of *ḥaṭṭāʾt* is crucial (see COMMENT D below and chap. 10, COMMENT C), and *ʾăšer* is the stylistic flag employed by the writer to catch the reader's attention to the transition from one kind to the other. For another example of the transitional *ʾăšer*, see the NOTE on 15:18.

the chieftain (nāśîʾ). He is the established leader of his clan, as is clear from his title, *nĕśîʾ bêt ʾāb* 'chieftain of the ancestral house', in connection with the clans that comprise the tribe of Levi (Num 3:24, 30, 35) and Simeon (Num 25:14). The term *nāśîʾ* is frequently equated with the title *rōʾš bêt ʾābôt* 'head of the ancestral house' (e.g., Num 7:2; 36:1). Indeed, whenever the phrase *rāʾšê ʾălāpîm/ʾābôt* 'heads of the clans/ancestral houses' occurs alone, it may safely be assumed that the chieftains are intended (e.g., Josh 14:1; 22:21). Because each

tribe comprised more than one clan, it follows that there was more than one
nāśîʾ per tribe. Thus we can understand Eleazar's title *nĕśîʾ nĕśîʾê hallēwî* 'the
head chieftain of the Levites' (Num 3:32). Also, there are three discrete lists of
the chieftains of the twelve tribes, none of which duplicates the other (Num
1:5–16; 13:1–15; 34:16–28). Most significantly, 250 chieftains of the *ʿēdâ* spear-
headed the rebellion of Korah against Moses and Aaron, and these men are also
designated "delegates of the assembly" (Num 16:2), showing that they represented only a portion of the chieftains.

That the *nāśîʾ* could hold national as well as clan or tribal office is clearly
indicated by Num 10:3–4. Here the chieftains are expressly defined as clan
leaders: yet they also act in an executive capacity on behalf of the *ʿēdâ*. It is
highly probable that in a national crisis the chieftains of each tribe would elect
one of their peers to be the tribal representative to a twelve-member, intertribal
ʿēdâ (e.g., Num 1:4–16, 44; 7:2; 17:17; 34:16–28). In the Mari archives, the title
for the clan head, *abu bītim*, lit., "father of the household," could also designate
the tribal chief.

The term *nāśîʾ* occurs more than one hundred times in the Bible in a
striking distribution. It clusters in the Tetrateuch and Joshua and again in
Ezekiel and the postexilic books. It is totally absent from Deuteronomy, Judges,
Samuel, and all of the prophets except Ezekiel. The term is densely concentrated in the wilderness and conquest traditions and does not resurface until the
exile, when it is resurrected in the futuristic visions of Ezekiel.

Further confirming the antiquity of the term *nāśîʾ* is its occurrence only
among those non-Israelite societies which are nomadic in character, namely,
Ishmaelites (Gen 17:20; 25:12) and Midianites (Num 25:8). Moreover, the institution of *nāśîʾ* persists in Israelite records only in the border tribes of Simeon
(1 Chr 4:38), Reuben (1 Chr 5:6), and Asher (1 Chr 7:40), where a sedentary
life-style was slow in developing (Loewenstamm 1965). Thus *nāśîʾ* joins the
other organizational units of Israel found in the opening chapters of Numbers,
ʿēdâ (see the NOTE on *qāhāl*, v 13), *maṭṭeh* 'tribe', and *ʾelep/bêt ʾābôt* 'clan', in
supporting the view that the Priestly account of the wilderness sojourn preserves
a number of traditions about ancient institutions that accurately reflect the
social and political realities of Israel's premonarchic age (Milgrom 1978a).

feels guilt (wĕʾāśam). The chieftain "learns on his own the nature of his
error" (Ibn Ezra; cf. Radak).

23. *or he is informed (ʾô hôdaʿ ʾēlāyw).* The MT is punctiliously correct.
Either the chieftain discovers his error (and regrets it) or someone else informs
him. "Rabbi Joshua said: 'he is informed of the wrong he committed' teaches
that he is not liable (for a purification offering) until he knows wherein he did
wrong" (*Sipra*, Ḥobah 7:7).

committed (ḥāṭāʾ bâ). The feminine suffix of the preposition *b* refers back to
ḥaṭṭāʾtô, lit., "his wrong" (see the NOTE on v 14). In contrast to the high priest,
the chieftain's wrongs have no effect on his community (v 3a). This is indirect

but supportive evidence that the prohibitive commandments he violates can only fall in the religious realm, that is, unenforceable by man and left solely to the jurisdiction of God (see the NOTE on v 2). This is also a clear indication that the chieftain was purely a secular official.

male goat. śĕʿîr ʿizzîm zākār, lit., "the hairy male of goats" (see Gen 27:11). It clearly refers to a mature specimen; a kid would be called *gĕdî ʿizzîm* (e.g., Gen 27:9). Because *śāʿîr* denotes the mature goat, pl. *ʿizzîm* 'goats' is not a redundancy; it adds the qualification that the goat must be domesticated. Thus it is equivalent to *min-haṣṣōʾn* 'from the flock' (5:15) and *ben-bāqār* 'of the herd' (4:3), terms that also specify domesticity in order to preclude wild members of the species from the altar. Indeed, *śāʿîr* by itself, without the modifier *ʿizzîm*, refers either to "wild goat" or to a goat demon (17:7; Isa 13:21; 34:14; 2 Chr 29:23; S. Rattray). The male goat is the standard purification offering only for the nation in the fixed public cult (16:9, 15; 23:19; Num 28–29) and in all special circumstances (e.g., 9:3, 5; 10:10; Num 15:12)—except here (see the NOTE on v 14 and COMMENT E below). The additional word *zākār* 'male' is superfluous. Perhaps it stresses the fact that a female goat is not acceptable for the chieftain (*Sipra*, Ḥobah par 6:6; Wessely 1846). More plausibly, *śāʿîr* (like *kebeś, ʿēz, śeh, gĕdî*) is neuter in gender, and the male attribute must be specified.

24. *the spot where the burnt offering is slaughtered*. This designation is missing for the purification bulls of the high priest and community, which are slaughtered "before the Lord" (vv 4, 15), that is, anywhere in the forecourt, in contrast to flock animals (vv 24, 29, 33), which are slaughtered at a designated spot north of the altar (see at 1:11).

slaughtered . . . slaughtered (wĕšāḥaṭ . . . wĕšāḥaṭ). The LXX and Sam. read both verbs as plurals (also in vv 29, 33) in order to indicate that anyone may perform the slaughter. No change, however, is required: the singular can be understood as a passive.

it is a purification offering (ḥaṭṭāʾt hûʾ). Elliger (1966), followed by Janowski (1982: 196), maintains that the pericopes on the lay purification offerings (vv 22–35) form a unified bloc to which the pericopes on the high priest and community (vv 3–21) were subsequently added. They provide three reasons: the references to (1) the outer altar in connection with the slaughtering and (2) the well-being offering as the model for the suet removal are present in the former pericopes (vv 24, 29, 33; vv 26, 31, 35) but are missing in the latter; and (3) the declaratory formula "it is a purification offering" is cited in the chieftains' pericope (v 26) but not in the opening pericopes of the chapter (vv 3–21), where it would have been expected.

All three reasons can be parried. (1) The outer altar is mentioned in reference to the slaughter of the lay purification offerings because the animals are from the flock and not the herd (see the NOTE at 1:11). (2) There is indeed a reference to the model of the well-being offering in the very first case, the high priest's purification offering, which moreover contains an itemization of the suet pieces (vv 8–10). To the contrary, the fact that the suet pieces of the lay offerings are not itemized (vv 26, 31, 35) is evidence that the author of these verses had vv 8–10 before him! (3) The declaratory formula indeed does appear in the earlier pericopes: *ḥaṭṭāʾt haqqāhāl hûʾ* 'it is the purification offering of the congregation' (v 21b), and it forms one of the proofs that vv 1–21 form an organic unity (see the introduction to vv 13–21). The declaratory formula is necessarily repeated for the chieftain not only because of the shift from the group to the individual but also because the very notion of the sacrifice changes: blood is not brought inside the tent, and its meat is not burned outside the camp.

25. *The priest. hakkōhēn,* that is to say, any priest.

the horns. The function of the altar horns is unknown. Because the name for the altar, *mizbēaḥ,* literally means "the place of slaughter," it is likely that originally sacrificial animals were slaughtered on the altar itself, a supposition that is supported by the ancient stories of the binding of Isaac (Gen 22) and the field altar erected by King Saul (1 Sam 14:34). If this be the case, then the altar's horns might have served as pegs to which the animal could be bound, and which would serve to explain the otherwise enigmatic verse: "Bind the festal offering to the horns of the altar with cords" (Ps 118:27; cf. W. R. Smith 1927: 341 n. 2). Unfortunately, this attractive suggestion becomes snagged on the horns of the incense altar, attested in many Bronze Age finds (see the NOTE at v 7), whose surface is too small to hold the tiniest sacrificial animal.

The daubing of the horns of the sacrificial altar with the blood of the purification offering implies that the entire altar is being purged, on the principle of *pars pro toto* (see at v 7). The choice of the horns to represent the altar is not arbitrary. The significance of this choice can be deduced through a series of analogies with other uses of sacrificial blood, such as the purification rite of a healed *měṣōrāʿ* (14:14–17, 25–28), the consecratory rite of new priests (8:23–24; Exod 29:20) and of the new altar (8:11; Exod 29:21), and the smearing of the lintel and doorposts with the blood of the paschal sacrifice (Exod 12:7, 22). The things that receive the blood are extremities, the very points of an object, which a hostile force would strike first in attacking it. In the ancient Near East, temples were periodically smeared with magical substances at precisely the same vulnerable points, such as entrances and corners, in order to expel the malefic force from those points and to protect them against future demonic incursion. In Israel, the monotheistic revolution had banished the world of demons, but the sancta were still vulnerable to the malefic power of man (see COMMENT C below). The physical and spiritual impurity of human beings is capable of polluting the sanctuary altar by attacking it at its extremities, namely, its horns. Support for this thesis stems from the purgation rite prescribed for the sacrificial altar in Ezekiel's visionary temple. It calls for daubing the purification blood not only on the altar's horns but also on the corners and rim of the ledge that circumscribed it in the middle (Ezek 43:20; cf. vv 13–17). Like the horns, it was an extremity and, hence, vulnerable to pollution. The indispensability of the altar horns is confirmed by the rabbinic rule that if even one of the altar's horns is missing, the sacrificial service is invalidated (*Sipra* Ḥobah, par. 4:12).

the altar of burnt offering (mizbaḥ hāʿōlâ). The sacrificial altar takes its name from its most frequent sacrifice, required twice daily (Exod 29:38–43) and at every festival (Num 28–29); it was the only sacrifice entirely consumed on the altar (see the COMMENT on chap. 1). It is also called *mizbaḥ hannĕḥōšet* 'the bronze altar' (Exod 38:30; Num 17:4; 2 Kgs 16:14, 15; Ezek 9:2) because it was plated with bronze (Exod 27:2). Actually, it was made of acacia wood, and its dimensions, in cubits, were 5 × 5 × 3. Its form is minutely described, though the meaning of all of the terms used is not certain (Exod 27:1–8; 38:1–7). Because this altar was part of a portable sanctuary, it was fitted with four rings and two staves. Moreover, it was hollow and hence not burdensome. The altar was only a portable frame because, in contrast to the incense altar (Exod 30:3), there is no mention of a roof, and at each encampment it would, therefore, be filled with earth and rocks (in conformity with Exod 20:24). The same system of hollowed altars is known from some Assyrian samples.

Although functionally the Israelite altar resembles its counterparts throughout the ancient Near East, it is important to note two fundamental limitations. Although pagan temple shrines clearly originate in the notion of caring for and feeding the resident deity, there is no trace of this notion in Israel. Only rare linguistic fossils survive, such as that the sacrifices are called "God's food" (22:25) and "pleasing aroma to the Lord" (1:17). The altar is also called "the Lord's table" (Ezek 41:22; 44:16; Mal 1:7, 12), but only in later texts, never in the early ones. Perhaps this is a result of the polemics waged in Israel's early history against the widespread pagan belief that the altar was the banquet table of the god; only a later generation could feel free to use pagan imagery so freely. The second limitation is that the altars of YHWH are legitimate only in the Promised Land. This is not because the power of Israel's God is spatially limited —he controls the destiny of all nations and can be addressed in prayer everywhere (e.g., 1 Kgs 8:33–53)—but because of the basic concept of the sanctity of Israel's territory: it is the Holy Land. This principle underlies the polemic against the erection of a Transjordanian altar (Josh 22:19), as well as the legal fiction of taking Israelite soil abroad, adopted by the Aramaean Naaman (2 Kgs 5:17) and, perhaps, by his Israelite townsmen (see 1 Kgs 20:34).

The sanctity of the altar is evidenced by the theophany that concludes the week-long consecration rites for the Tabernacle (9:23–24). It is an assumption common to biblical tradition that a sanctuary is not fully consecrated—or it is not divinely sanctioned—unless it has a tradition of a theophany upon its altar (1 Kgs 18:38; 2 Chr 7:1), or that its altar is built on the site of one (Gen 28:16–19). The sanctity of the altar is evidenced by the asylum it provided to anyone who "seized its horns" (e.g., 1 Kgs 1:50–51). An early law, however, stipulated that this privilege was not to be extended to murderers (Exod 21:14). On this basis, the altar provided no safety for Joab (1 Kgs 2:28–34); even then, Solomon tried at first to remove Joab, who "seized the altar horns" (v 34) before he had him killed. In order to prevent the pollution of the altar by such criminals, the priestly legislators nullified its sacred contagion to persons and, in order to provide justifiable asylum, specifically in the case of unintentional homicide, invented the scheme of asylum cities distributed throughout the land (Milgrom 1981b).

The altar is the only object outside the Tent to belong to the category of the "most sacred" (Exod 29:37), though to a lesser degree. For example, the nonpriest is prohibited from viewing the inner sancta (Num 4:20) but is only barred from encroaching on the altar (Num 17:5). Only the high priest may bless the people from the altar (9:22). Solomon, who performed this function, did so in front of the altar (1 Kgs 8:64–65). The composition of the sancta also reflects this sanctity differential: the inner sancta are plated with gold, the altar with bronze: in transit, the former are covered with a blue cloth, the latter with a purple cloth (Num 4:4–14).

Israel's altar may not bring God to earth but it enables man, through his worship, to reach heaven. This is nowhere more evident than in the dedicatory prayer for the Temple, attributed to Solomon, that even in a foreign land Israel's armies or exiles need but turn to the Temple and their prayer will travel to God along a trajectory that passes through their land, city, Temple, and then, at the altar, turns heavenward (1 Kgs 8:44, 48; cf. vv 31, 38). The altar, then, is the earthly terminus of a divine funnel for man's communion with God. It is significant that later Judaism carries the tradition that the air space above the altar is an extension of its sanctity.

Another significant function of the altar stems from the blood prohibition: persons—all persons, not Israel alone—are constrained from imbibing blood because it is the life of the animal (Gen 9:4). They must drain it and return it, as it were, to the Creator. For Israel, however, there is only one legitimate place in which this can be done: at the authorized altar. The altar, then, is the instrument by which a sacrificial animal's life is restored to God. Indeed, Leviticus contains the clear, unambiguous statement that whoever slaughters an ox, sheep, or goat anywhere except at the authorized sanctuary altar is guilty of murder (17:3–4). An Israelite may have meat for his food, he may kill to get it, but he may not tamper with its blood; he must return it to God at the altar if the animal can be sacrificed, and by means of the earth if he brings it down in the hunt (17:13–14). Thus the altar legitimizes animal slaughter: it is the divinely appointed instrument of ransoming the life of the person who has taken animal life (17:11 [Milgrom 1963, 1971]).

26. *for his wrong.* mēḥaṭṭāʾtô; see 5:6, 10; 14:19; 15:15; 16:34; Num 6:11; equivalent to ʿal ḥaṭṭāʾtô (v 35; 5:13, 18; 19:22).

27. *the populace.* ʿam hāʾāreṣ, namely, commoners who in this situation,

however, include Levites and ordinary priests (Ibn Ezra; cf. *Sipra,* Ḥobah par. 7:6). This term denotes those who are neither the ruler nor priests (Ezek 45:22; cf. 7:27; 45:16) and those who are neither king, nor officials, nor priests (Jer 1:18; Hag 2:4). It also has a specific, technical meaning, referring to a political group in the kingdom of Judah composed of loyal supporters of the Davidic dynasty (e.g., 2 Kgs 11; 21:24; 23:30 [Talmon 1967; Tadmor 1968]).

28. *female.* This word, *nĕqēbâ,* is superfluous because the specified animal, *śĕʿîrat ʿizzîm,* is clearly feminine (contrast v 32). Perhaps its purpose is to emphasize that the male of the species cannot be accepted, for it is assigned to the chieftain (see the NOTE on v 23). The question needs be asked: Why is the female, the more valuable animal, required of the commoner, whereas the male, of less worth, is required of the chieftain? The answer may be that a commoner, particularly a poor one, is likely to keep only female animals, which provide sustenance, and only if he could afford it would he retain a single male for breeding. The chieftain, by contrast, could well afford to keep several males in his flock (S. Rattray).

31. *he shall remove.* "He" refers to the offerer (see 3:3, 9, 14; 7:30).

as a pleasing aroma to the Lord (lērēaḥ nîḥōaḥ laYHWH). Some scholars regard this phrase as an intrusion (e.g., Gray 1925: 79). True, it never again occurs with the purification offering and not even once with the other exclusive expiatory sacrifice, the reparation offering. Nevertheless, it should be recalled that this phrase designates the burnt offering (1:9, 13, 17) particularly in an expiatory context (1:4). Also, there is nothing intrinsically jarring in a notice that the Lord is pleased with sacrificial expiation. On the contrary, because the sacrifice signifies a contrite heart intent on purging the pollution from the sanctuary, one would think that the God of Israel would be immensely pleased. Yet the studied absence of this phrase from the expiatory sacrifice indicates a conscious effort to distance Israel from the notion that these expiatory sacrifices possess the inherent power to appease God. On the problem of whether the purification offering is an *ʾiššeh,* see at v 35.

32. *a sheep (kebeś).* The Sam. reads *kibśâ,* feminine—an unnecessary emendation, for the attribute "female" follows in the verse. Yet the term *kebeś* is itself anomalous because it designates the male of the species, the immature ram. Perhaps, the metathesis *keśeb* should be read, which is the generic referring to any individual of the species *Ovis aries,* of any age or either sex. The order, goat following sheep, noted for the well-being offering (3:6–11, 12–17) is here reversed in order to juxtapose the goat of the commoner with the goat of the chieftain (vv 22–26, 27–31).

33. *(it shall be slaughtered) for purification purposes. lĕḥaṭṭāʾt,* in other words, to purify the sacrificial altar. Only here does the word *ḥaṭṭāʾt* designate the objective of the sacrifice and not its name.

35. *suet of the sheep. . . .* This clause needs be repeated because the suet of sheep includes the *ʾalyâ,* the broad tail, an organ absent in goats (Ibn Ezra).

it. 'ōtām, lit., "them," whose antecedent is the suet pieces enumerated in vv 8–9.

with (the food gifts). 'al, which proves that the purification offering itself is not considered an *'iššeh*, a food gift to the Lord. This conclusion is borne out by another pericope on the purification offering: "for their error they have brought their offering, an *'iššeh* to the Lord and their purification offering before the Lord" (Num 15:25b). This *'iššeh* refers to the burnt offering prescribed by the ritual (v 24) and, hence, excludes the purification offering (*Sipre* Num 111). The logic is clear: the Lord is surely pleased with the offering of the repentant wrongdoer (v 31), but it is not a gift; it is his humble expiation.

COMMENT:
THE PURIFICATION OFFERING

A. The Name

To my knowledge, all versions and translations, old and new, render the *ḥaṭṭā't* sacrifice as "sin offering." This translation is inaccurate on all grounds: contextually, morphologically, and etymologically.

The very range of the *ḥaṭṭā't* in the cult gainsays the notion of sin. For example, this offering is enjoined upon recovery from childbirth (chap. 12), the completion of the Nazirite vow (Num 6), and the dedication of the newly constructed altar (8:15; see Exod 29:36–37). In other words, the *ḥaṭṭā't* is prescribed for persons and objects who cannot have sinned.

Grammatical considerations buttress these contextual observations. Morphologically, it appears as a *pi'el* derivative. More importantly, its corresponding verbal form is not the *qal* "to sin, do wrong" but always the *pi'el* (e.g., 8:15), which carries no other meaning than "to cleanse, expurgate, decontaminate" (e.g., Ezek 43:22, 26; Ps 51:9). Finally, the "waters of *ḥaṭṭā't*" (Num 8:7) serve exclusively a purifying function (Num 19:19; see Ezek 26:25). "Purification offering" is certainly the more accurate translation. Indeed, the terse comment of Rashi (on Num 19:19) is all that needs to be said: "*ḥaṭṭā't* is literally the language of purification" (cf. also Barr 1963: 874).

It is not my intention to investigate the origin of this mistranslation. It can be traced as far back as the LXX, which consistently renders ἁμαρτία, followed by Philo (*Laws* 1. 226) and Josephus (*Ant.* 3.230). It is, however, important to note that if the rabbinic sources had been carefully read, the subsequent translations could have avoided this mistake. True, the sage Rabbi Eliezer states unequivocally that "the *ḥaṭṭā't* is brought on account of sin" (*m. Zebaḥ.* 1:1), but his generalization is directed only to chap. 4 (and its parallel, Num 15:22–31), where the *qal*, meaning "to sin, do wrong," indeed is found. All other *ḥaṭṭā't* sacrifices are prescribed for specific physical impurities, such as the new mother, the *mĕṣōrā'*, the contaminated Nazirite, and the like; and in these cases, not one sage claims that the afflicted brings this sacrifice because of his sins. Indeed, this idea is vigorously denied (*b. Šebu.* 8a; *Ker.* 26a). Moreover, not only is the *ḥaṭṭā't* unrelated to sin in rabbinic thought, but most authorities deny emphatically that the impurity itself was caused by sin. Even the minority who see a causal connection between sin and affliction argue that the affliction in itself suffices to expiate the sin (*'Arak.* 16a; *b. Nazir* 19a; *Nid.* 31b), and they concur with the majority that the purpose of the *ḥaṭṭā't* is for ritual purification.

The discussion on the parturient is decisive: "But according to R. Simeon son of Yahai who holds that a woman in confinement is a sinner, what can be said (concerning the purpose of her *ḥaṭṭā't*)? The sacrifice she brings is, nevertheless, for the purpose of permitting her to partake of consecrated food and *is not expiatory*" (*Ker.* 26a). Finally, the categorical statement of the talmudic commentators, the tosafists (on 12:8), leaves no doubt concerning the rabbinic view: "According to the literal meaning of the text her (the parturient's) sacrifice is not brought for sin."

The advantage of freeing the *ḥaṭṭā't* from the theologically foreign notion of sin and restoring to it its pristine meaning of purification is that now it is possible to see this sacrifice in its true ancient Near Eastern setting. Israel was part of a cultic continuum which abounded in purifications both of persons and of buildings, especially sanctuaries. The *ḥaṭṭā't*, I aver, is the key that opens the door to this world (for details see Milgrom 1971a).

B. The Function

The rendering of *ḥaṭṭā't* as a purification offering leads automatically to the question: Whom or what does it purge? Herein lies the first surprise: it is not the offerer of the sacrifice. It must be remembered that the *ḥaṭṭā't* is brought by an individual under two circumstances: severe physical impurity, such as that of the parturient, *mĕṣōrā'*, or *zāb* (chaps. 12–15), or because of the commission of certain inadvertent sins (e.g., chap. 4). Clearly, physical impurity is removed by ablution: "he shall launder his clothes [and] bathe in water" (15:8 inter alia). Spiritual impurity, conversely, which is caused by inadvertent violation of prohibitive commandments (4:2), requires no purificatory rite. The fact that his sin is inadvertent *(bišĕgāgâ)* and that he feels guilt *(wĕ'āšēm)* means that he has undergone inner purification.

The contention that the *ḥaṭṭā't* never purifies its offerer is supported by the use of its blood: "Moses took the *ḥaṭṭā't* blood and with his finger put [some] on the horns around the altar, decontaminating *(wayĕḥaṭṭē')* the altar" (Lev 8:15). The *ḥaṭṭā't* blood, then, is the purging element, the ritual detergent. Blood as a purgative is attested in Hittite ritual: "They smear with blood the golden god, the wall, the utensils of the entirely new god. The new god and the temple

254

become clean" (Ulippi 4.38–40, cited in Wright 1987: 36 n. 67). Still, the rationale for blood in Israel is *sui generis* (see chap. 11, COMMENT C).

Moreover, its use is confined to the sanctuary, but *it is never applied to a person* (Milgrom 1970c). For example, the rites for the healed *mĕṣōrāʿ* and the priests' consecration call for both the *ḥaṭṭāʾt* and the blood daubing, but the latter ritual stems from other sacrificial animals and not from the *ḥaṭṭāʾt* (14:14, 25; 8:22–24; Exod 29:20). Recently, Rodriguez has taken issue with this view. Conceding that the *ḥaṭṭāʾt* purges the sanctuary on Yom Kippur because the text says so explicitly (16:16–20), he therefore concludes that the absence of such a statement from all other attestations of this sacrifice means that in these cases it purifies not the sanctuary but the persons offering it (1979: 128–30). The only evidence he can muster is indirect: when the altar is purged, the *ḥaṭṭāʾt* blood is put on the altar's horns *sābîb* 'all around' (8:15; 16:18); whenever this latter term is missing, the blood is simply put on the horns and something else must be intended (1979: 136–38). If the designation *sābîb* were critically significant, however, it would not be missing from the prescriptive directive concerning the daubing of the altar in Exod 29:12. Furthermore, the latter chapter does not hesitate to use *sābîb* in describing the blood manipulation of the *ʿōlâ* (Exod 29:16) and *milluʾîm* (Exod 29:20), which clearly demonstrates that its absence in the *ḥaṭṭāʾt* pericope is of no consequence. Finally, the occurrence of *sābîb* in the procedures for the *ʿōlâ* (1:5, 11), *šĕlāmîm* (3:2, 8, 13), and *ʾāšām* (7:2) is meant simply to specify the four sides of the altar, and this is its meaning for the *ḥaṭṭāʾt* as well. The conclusion is inescapable that, just as the *ḥaṭṭāʾt* blood acts as a purgative on Yom Kippur, it acts likewise every time it is brought into contact with the sanctuary sancta.

Finally, a study of the *kipper* prepositions is decisive (Milgrom 1970b). In the context of the *ḥaṭṭāʾt*, *kipper* means "purge" and nothing else, as indicated by its synonyms *ḥiṭṭēʾ* and *ṭihar* (e.g., 14:51; cf. chap. 16, COMMENT F; Ezek 43:20, 26). When the object is nonhuman, *kipper* takes the preposition *ʿal* or *b* or a direct object. For example, all three usages are attested in the purging of the adytum on the Day of Purgation (16:16, 20), and they must be understood literally, for the *kipper* rite takes place on *(ʿal)* the *kappōret* and on the floor before it, in *(b)* the adytum, or it can be said that the entire room *(ʾet)* is purged *(kipper;* cf. also 6:23; 16:10, 33; Exod 30:10), (Janowski 1982: 185 n. 5, who claims that *kipper ʿal* always means "expiate for," must entertain the absurd idea that sancta [and the scapegoat, 16:10] are capable of sinning [see Milgrom 1985d: 302–4].) When the object of *kipper* is a person, however, it is never expressed as a direct object but requires the prepositions *ʿal* or *bĕʿad*. Both signify "on behalf of" (16:6, 24, 30, 33; Num 8:12, 21), but they are not entirely synonymous. The difference is that *ʿal* can only refer to persons other than the subject, but when the subject wishes to refer to himself he must use *bĕʿad* (e.g., 9:7; 16:6, 11, 24; Ezek 45:22). This distinction is confirmed by Job 42:8: "Offer a burnt offering for *yourselves (bĕʿadkem)* and Job, my servant, will intercede *on your behalf (ʿălêkem)"* (Milgrom 1970b). This means the purgation rite of the ḥaṭṭāʾt is not carried out on the offerer but only on his behalf.

If not the offerer, what then is the object of the ḥaṭṭāʾt purgation? The above considerations lead to only one answer: that which receives the purgative blood: the sanctuary and its sancta. By daubing the altar with the ḥaṭṭāʾt blood or by bringing it inside the sanctuary (e.g., 16:14–19), the priest purges the most sacred objects and areas of the sanctuary on behalf of the person who caused their contamination by his physical impurity or inadvertent offense.

This conclusion enables us to understand the distinction between the ḥaṭṭāʾt for impurities and that for inadvertencies. The inadvertent offender is never called "impure" and hence requires no ablutions. In his case the concluding formula reads, *wĕkippēr hakkōhēn . . . wĕnislaḥ lô* 'the priest shall perform the purgation rite . . . that he may be forgiven' (4:20, 26, 31, 35) whereas for the impure person the formula reads, *wĕkippēr hakkōhēn . . . wĕṭāhēr(āh)* 'the priest shall perform the purgation rite . . . and he (she) shall be clean' (12:6, 8; 14:9, 20). Thus the impure person needs purification and the sinner needs forgiveness. Ostensibly, this distinction breaks down in the case of the corpse-contaminated Nazirite who brings a purification offering because *ḥāṭāʾ ʿal-han-nāpeš* 'he erred in regard to the corpse' (Num 6:11). This leads a recent scholar to declare that "ritual impurity could be considered a sin" (Rodriguez 1979: 104); but he has overlooked the exceptional nature of the Nazirite. He is "holy" (Num 6:5, 8), and the contamination of holiness is a serious sin. Note the wording of the warning to priests in this regard: "Lest they incur *ḥēṭ*ʾ and die thereby" (Lev 22:9; cf. Kiuchi 1987: 72 and for details, see chap. 15, COMMENT E).

The inadvertent offender needs forgiveness not because of his act per se—as indicated above, his act is forgiven because of the offender's inadvertence and remorse—but because of the consequence of his act. His inadvertence has contaminated the sanctuary, and it is his responsibility to purge it with a ḥaṭṭāʾt. Confirmation of this thesis is provided by the Tannaites: "All of the *(ḥaṭṭāʾt)* goats purge the pollution of the Temple and its sancta" (*m. Šebu.* 1:4–5; cf. *t. Šebu.* 1:3). This rabbinic tradition has preserved the postulate that the ḥaṭṭāʾt blood is the ritual detergent employed by the priest to purge the sanctuary of the impurities inflicted upon it by the offerer of the sacrifice.

The ḥaṭṭāʾt as the authorized purgative of the sanctuary echoes with a familiar ring for students of ancient Near Eastern cults in which temple purifications play so dominant a role. Impurity was feared because it was considered demonic. It was an unending threat to the gods themselves and especially to their temples, as exemplified by the images of protector gods set before temple entrances (e.g., the *šēdu* and *lamassu* in Mesopotamia and the lion-gargoyles in Egypt) and, above all, by the elaborate cathartic and apotropaic rites to rid buildings of demons and prevent their return. Let examples from *ANET*[3] suffice: Egypt, 325, 329–30; Hattia, 346, 351–53, 357, 358; Mesopotamia, 331–34,

334–38, 338–39. Thus for both Israel and her neighbors impurity was a physical substance, an aerial miasma that possessed magnetic attraction for the realm of the sacred. As will be shown below, Israel thoroughly overhauled this concept of impurity in adapting it to its monotheistic system, but the notion of its dynamic and malefic power, especially in regard to the sancta, was not completely expunged from P. Thus Molech worship is forbidden because it contaminates "my sanctuary" (20:3). Whoever is contaminated by a corpse and fails to purify himself "has contaminated the Lord's sanctuary" (Num 19:20, 13). Those afflicted with pelvic discharges also need purification "lest they die through their impurity by contaminating my Tabernacle which is among them" (15:31). The two latter offenders are banished with the *měṣōrāʿ* "that they do not contaminate the camp in whose midst I dwell" (Num 5:2b). True, the rabbis interpreted each of these passages on the assumption that impurity came into direct contact with the holy, specifically that the offender while in an impure state entered the sanctuary or ate of sacred food (*t. Šebu.* 1:8; *Sipra,* Ḥobah 13:10). It is patently clear, however, that these texts are grounded in the axiom, common to all ancient Near Eastern culture, that impurity is the implacable foe of holiness wherever it exists; it assaults the sacred realm even from afar.

The dynamic, aerial quality of biblical impurity is best attested by its graded power. Impurity pollutes the sanctuary in three stages: (1) The individual's inadvertent misdemeanor or severe physical impurity pollutes the courtyard altar, which is purged by daubing its horns with the *ḥaṭṭāʾt* blood (4:25, 30; 9:9). (2) The inadvertent misdemeanor of the high priest or the entire community pollutes the shrine, which is purged by the high priest by placing the *ḥaṭṭāʾt* blood on the inner altar and before the *pārōket* (4:5–7, 16–18). (3) The wanton unrepented sin not only pollutes the outer altar and penetrates into the shrine but it pierces the veil and enters the adytum, housing the holy Ark and *kappōret,* the very throne of God (cf. Isa 37:16). Because the wanton sinner is barred from bringing his *ḥaṭṭāʾt* (Num 15:27–31), the pollution wrought by his offense must await the annual purgation of the sanctuary on the Day of Purgation, and it consists of two steps: the purging of the adytum of the wanton sins and the purging of the shrine and outer altar of the inadvertent sins (16:16–19). Thus the entire sacred area or, more precisely, all that is most sacred (Milgrom 1970a: n. 211) is purged on Purgation Day *(yôm hakkippūrîm)* with the *ḥaṭṭāʾt* blood.

In this way the graded purgations of the sanctuary lead to the conclusion that the severity of the sin or impurity varies in direct relation to the depth of its penetration into the sanctuary. This mathematical relationship between sin and sanctuary is best understood by the diagram in fig. 6. Moreover, this diagram provides graphic confirmation that P propounds a notion of impurity as a dynamic force, magnetic and malefic to the sphere of the sacred, attacking it not just by direct contact but from a distance. The outer altar is polluted though the wrongdoer is outside the sacred compound, the shrine is polluted though he, a nonpriest, may not even enter it and, finally, the adytum is polluted though no

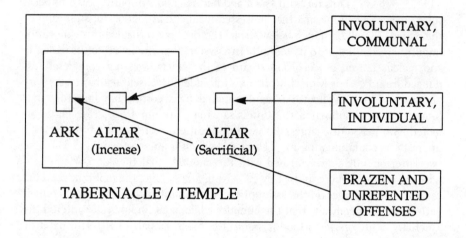

FIGURE 6

man, not even the priest, may enter (Milgrom 1970a: 38–43). Despite the fact that Israelites have had no access, the sancta must be purged "of the impurities of the Israelites" (16:16).

C. The Theology

Finally, why the urgency to purge the sanctuary? The answer lies in this postulate: the God of Israel will not abide in a polluted sanctuary. The merciful God will tolerate a modicum of pollution. But there is a point of no return. If the pollution continues to accumulate, the end is inexorable: "Then the cherubs raised their wings" (Ezek 11:22). The divine chariot flies heavenward, and the sanctuary is left to its doom. The book of Lamentations echoes this priestly theology: "The Lord has abandoned his altar, rejected his Sanctuary. He has handed over to the foe the walls of its citadels" (Lam 2:7). That the sancta can become polluted beyond repair is demonstrated by the measures taken by both Hezekiah and Josiah to invalidate the *bāmôt:* Hezekiah *hēsîr* 'removed' them (2 Kgs 18:4); presumably he razed them to the ground. This, however, did not stop Manasseh from rebuilding them and restoring them to their former use (2 Kgs 21:3). The lesson was not lost on Josiah. He not only destroyed them but polluted them by burning human bones on their altars (2 Kgs 23:16, 20), thereby invalidating them irremediably.

The abiding fear of temple pollution is demonstrated by the frequency of the purification offering in the public cult. As is keenly noted by Rabbi Simeon,

"More grievous is imparting pollution to the sanctuary and its sancta than all other transgressions in the Torah. All other transgressions that are listed in the Torah are atoned for with a single goat, but imparting pollution to the sanctuary and its sancta is atoned for through thirty-two goats (Lev 23:19; Num 28–29). All other transgressions in the Torah are atoned for one time in the year (Yom Kippur), but imparting pollution to the sanctuary and its sancta is atoned for every month (Num 28:15), as it is written: "Surely because you have polluted my sanctuary with all your detestable things and with all your abominations, therefore I will cut you down; my eye will not spare and I will have no pity" (Ezek 5:11). While grievous were the detestable things and abominations that you did, more grievous than all of them was imparting impurity to the sanctuary. (t. Šebu. 1:3)

The obsessive fear of polluting the sanctuary is graphically illustrated by the historical tradition reported by the Chronicler that the high priest Jehoiada "stationed the gatekeepers at the gates of the House of the Lord to prevent the entry of anyone impure for any reason *(wĕlōʾ-yābōʾ tāmēʾ lekol-dābār)"* (2 Chr 23:19). The sin of temple pollution is so great that not only must it be prevented at all cost but the negligent gatekeepers are guilty of a capital crime (Num 18:23), a proviso that, strikingly, is also found in the Hittite "Instructions for Temple Officials" (*ANET*[3] 209, III, lines 18–30; cf. Milgrom 1970a: 50–53).

On this point, Israel is in full accord with its neighbors' obsessive compulsion to purify their temples. They too, in their more sophisticated cultures, believed that human transgressions were responsible for the departure of the deity from his sanctuary. Thus in a Babylonian stele, dedicated to the mother of Nabonidus (dated 547 B.C.E.), we find, "Sin, the king of all the gods, became angry with his city (i.e., Harran) and his temple, and went up to heaven and the city and the people within it became desolate" (*ANET*[3] 560). Thus the sack of Harran (610 B.C.E.) is attributed not to the attacking forces but to the failings of its citizens. Nevertheless, this common ground is split by an unbridgeable chasm. One of Y. Kaufmann's keenest observations (1937–56: 1.350–416, 458–573; 2.111–37, 404–503; 1960: 21–121, 301–16) is that the ancients mainly feared impurity because it was demonic, even metadivine, capable of attacking the gods. Hence, men were summoned, indeed created, for the purpose of purifying temples to aid the benevolent resident gods in their battles with cosmic evil. In Israel, however, there are no traces of demonic impurity. Kaufmann would have us believe that biblical impurity has been completely devitalized.

Here B. A. Levine (1974: 79–91) is correct in criticizing Kaufmann, but he errs in claiming that impurity retains its demonic nature. "Anti-God forces" do not inhere in nature. Live animals do not pollute. Even animal carcasses, though impure, cannot contaminate the sanctuary; they threaten neither God nor man. The demons have been expunged from the world, but man has taken their place. This is one of the major contributions of the priestly theology: man is "demonized." True, man falls short of being a demon, but he is capable of the demonic. He alone is the cause of the world's ills. He alone can contaminate the sanctuary and force God out.

If this reconstruction of the priestly theology of the ḥaṭṭāʾt is correct, then we have succeeded in uncovering one of the ethical supports upon which the sacrificial system was reared. It constitutes the priestly theodicy. No intellectual circle of ancient Israel evaded the challenge of theodicy: the prophets agonized over it but came up with no solutions; Wisdom gives its superficial answer (e.g., Ps 92:8; Prov 24:19–20), and its refutation motivated the writing of Job. Thus we should be led to expect a priestly answer, but we search for it in vain. Is it possible that Israel's priests, who had as their prime function "to teach the Israelites" (10:10), had nothing to say concerning God's providence?

Now we know what the priestly theodicy is. It is found not in utterances but in rituals, not in legal statutes but in cultic procedures—specifically, in the rite with ḥaṭṭāʾt blood. I would call their response the Priestly *Picture of Dorian Gray*. On the analogy of Oscar Wilde's novel, the Priestly writers would claim that sin may not leave its mark on the face of the sinner, but it is certain to mark the face of the sanctuary; and unless it is quickly expunged, God's presence will depart. In truth, this teaching is not a startling innovation; it is only an extension of the doctrine of collective responsibility, a doctrine that, all concur, is basic to the Priestly theology. It is only natural that they would regard the sanctuary of which they were the stewards as the spiritual barometer to measure and explain God's behavior to his people. They knew full well that the prophet was justified in protesting "why does the way of the wicked prosper?" (Jer 12:1), and they provided their answer: the sinner may be unscarred by his evil, but the sanctuary bears the scars and, with its destruction, he too will meet his doom.

Levine's claim that Yahweh is not omnipotent in the Bible (1974: 79 n. 65) must therefore be rejected, the existence of the destroyer, mašḥît, notwithstanding. All of the sources make it emphatically clear that the destroyer acts only according to Yahweh's will (Exod 11:4 [JE]; 12:12–13 [P]; 12:23, 29 [JE]; Kaufmann 1937–56: 1.544). The rabbis' dictum, "Once leave has been granted to the mašḥît to do injury, it no longer discriminates between the righteous and the wicked" (Mekhilta on Exod 12:22b), adduced by Levine (1974: 86), is only a reaffirmation of the biblical postulate that God punishes collectively and even indiscriminately (Milgrom 1981f). That the righteous were engulfed in disaster (i.e., God's retribution) may have been protested by a few biblical voices (e.g., Gen 18:23; Ezek 18:1–32), but existential reality and the monotheistic premise made it impossible to conceive God otherwise. Perhaps for this reason some biblical and rabbinic theologians preferred to assign this disturbing attribute to God's agent rather than to God himself. But the priests of ancient Israel had no such qualms; they championed unqualifiedly the rule of collective retribution as epitomized by their conception of the sanctuary as *The Picture of Dorian Gray.*

The Priestly doctrine of collective responsibility yields yet another corollary. The "good" people who perish with the evildoers are not innocent. For allowing the evildoers to flourish, to pollute the sanctuary beyond repair, they share the blame. Indeed, they are the inadvertent sinners who contribute to the pollution of the sanctuary. Let a modern—hence, more vivid—example illustrate the point. World War II would have presented no theological quandary for Israel's priests of old. They would have rejected with scorn our contemporary theologians who have proclaimed that "God is dead." Instead of bewailing the silence of God, they would have pointed the accusing finger at the human culprits, the inadvertent sinners, the "silent majority"—the German people who voted the Nazis into power and the peoples of the free world who acquiesced to the annexation of the Saar, Austria, and Sudetenland while barring their own doors to the refugees who managed to escape. A worldwide cataclysm was thus inevitable. Indeed, Israel's priests would have asked: How long under these circumstances could God have been willing to abide in his earthly sanctuary?

To summarize: The *ḥaṭṭāʾt* is a vantage point from which to view Israel's cultic ties with its neighbors as well as the gulf that separates them. They hold in common that the impure and the holy are mutually antagonistic and irreconcilable. Thus the sanctuary needs constant purification lest the resident god abandon it together with his devotees. On one basic issue they differ: the pagan world is suffused with demonic impurity, whereas Israel has eviscerated impurity of its magical power. Only in its nexus with the sancta does it spring to life. This malefic impurity does not inhere in nature; it is the creation of man. Only man, even by inadvertence, can generate the impurity that will evict God from his earthly abode (for details see Milgrom 1976d).

D. The Two Kinds

Two discrete procedures are prescribed for the *ḥaṭṭāʾt.* They differ in that in one the blood is daubed on the outer, sacrificial altar and its meat becomes the perquisite of the officiating priest (4:30; 6:19), and in the other the blood is daubed on the inner, incense altar and sprinkled before the *pārōket,* but the animal, except for its suet, is burned on the ash heap outside the camp (4:6–7, 11–12). This distinction is to be maintained rigidly: "No *ḥaṭṭāʾt* may be eaten from which any blood is brought into the Tent of Meeting to effect purgation in the shrine; it shall be consumed in fire" (6:23; cf. 10:18). But how can it be explained?

Y. Kaufmann suggests that because both *ḥaṭṭāʾt* offerings are purificatory they are dangerous and must be eliminated either by eating or by burning (1937–56: 1.568–69). He correctly adduces 10:17b to prove that the *ḥaṭṭāʾt* is eaten by the priests who thereby destroy Israel's sins. (I have changed my mind concerning what I wrote in 1976a: 333–34; see the Note on 10:7 and chap. 10, Comment C.) Kaufmann further distinguishes between the two kinds of *ḥaṭṭāʾt* by the locus of the elimination procedure: one is eaten within the sacred precincts and the other is burned outside the camp. For Kaufmann, this distinction is crucial: "One of the dominant ideas in this source (P) is the distinction between the domain of holiness and the domain of impurity. . . . The camp is the sphere of holiness; outside the camp is the place of impurity" (1937–56: 1.542–43). Thus, the *ḥaṭṭāʾt* taken outside the camp cannot be eaten because it has become contaminated; it must be burned. This explanation, however, does not take into account that the burning of the *ḥaṭṭāʾt* must take place in a *māqôm ṭāhôr* 'a pure place' (4:12; cf. 6:4; Num 19:9); a priori, the area outside the camp cannot entirely be impure. Similarly, that the text must specify *ʾel-miḥûṣ lāʿîr ʾel-māqôm ṭāmēʾ* 'to an impure place outside the city' (14:40, 41, 45) indicates that not everywhere outside the city is impure. Lastly, Kaufmann's topographic distinction finds no support in the ancient Near East. On the contrary, there is evidence that the Israelite notion of "a pure place" outside the camp or city where ritual purifications are disposed is not its own invention, for example, *ana ṣeri ášri elli šuṣima* 'take it out to the plain, the pure place' (Reiner 1958: vii, 63). Thus the Mesopotamians also did not assume that the open field was automatically under demonic control.

It is, then, clear that "outside the camp/city" designates a neutral area, *ḥōl*, which is distinguished from the camp and which is also out of the range of sanctuary contamination. Only sins and impurities committed within the camp or city can pollute the sanctuary. For this reason, according to an old P law, the sufferers from scale disease, pelvic discharges, and corpse contamination are banished from the camp so that their impurity cannot harm the sanctuary (Num 5:2–3). True, those who handle the *ḥaṭṭāʾt* outside the camp are thereby contaminated (e.g., 16:27–28). Even so, not the place but the sacrifice is responsible. This can be established on several grounds: (1) Removing the altar ashes outside the camp does not cause contamination: the only exception is the ashes of the *ḥaṭṭāʾt* (6:4; cf. 16:28). (2) The initial purification rite of the *mĕṣōrāʿ* takes place outside the camp, but it does not contaminate (14:3). Yet this rite is typologically identical with the Azazel rite, which does contaminate its handlers (16:26). This disparity is due to the nature of the animals used: the scapegoat is a *ḥaṭṭāʾt* (16:5), while the birds are not. (3) The *ḥaṭṭāʾt* bull prescribed for the dedication of Ezekiel's altar is burned *bĕmipqad habbayit miḥûṣ lammiqdāš* 'in the *mipqād* of the temple area but outside the Temple precinct" (Ezek 43:21; cf. Milgrom 1970a: n. 78). Wherever the *mipqād* is to be located (see most recently Garfinkel 1986–87), it certainly must be a "pure place" because it falls within the sacred reserve assigned to the priests (Ezek 45:1–3). Again it is clear that the contamination caused by the burning of the *hattāʾt* is due not to the place but to the sacrifice itself.

Recently B. A. Levine has proposed that of the two kinds of *hattāʾt* only the burnt one is purificatory. It is provided by the priests "to safeguard the sanctuary and its ministering priesthood from contamination," whereas the eaten *hattāʾt* is provided by the people "to expiate certain offenses" of the individual and community and is given to the priests for their services (1974: 103–4). Several objections are in order: (1) The criterion for distinguishing the two kinds of *hattāʾt* by the donor is refuted by the sacrificed goat on the Day of Purgation: it is burned outside the camp though it is brought by the people (16:5, 27). Still, there is no need to regard it as an exceptional case (ibid. 113); it fits the rule concerning the *hattāʾt* whose blood is brought inside the sanctuary (6:23; 10:18, cited above), a rule that is alluded to in the text describing the sacrificial goat: "whose blood was brought into the sanctuary for purgation" (16:27). Furthermore, 4:13–21 (and perhaps Num 15:22–26) provides another instance in which the sanctuary is purged by a *hattāʾt* brought by the people. (2) The burnt *hattāʾt* is not for "safeguarding" because it has no apotropaic function. Moreover, it does not purify the priesthood, because the purgative element, the blood, is never placed on an individual, not even the priest (see above). (3) If the eaten *hattāʾt* is not purificatory but expiates for offenses, what offense has been committed by those who bring the same kind of *hattāʾt* for their physical impurity, for example, the new mother (chap. 12)?

Thus the eaten *hattāʾt* no less than the burnt one has a purificatory purpose. They differ not in kind but in degree, the degree of impurity that they purge. The eaten *hattāʾt* purges the outer altar. The altar is the first of the sancta met upon entering the sanctuary court and represents the minimal incursion of impurity caused by inadvertent sins of the individual. At this lowest level, the impurity transfered to the *hattāʾt* is slight and, hence, the latter is eaten by the priests for their services. The burnt *hattāʾt*, however, represents higher degrees of impurity caused by inadvertences of the high priest and community and, at its worst, by presumptuous sins. This impurity is powerful enough to penetrate into the shrine and adytum (see fig. 6 above) and is dangerously contagious. In being purged by the *hattāʾt* blood it is likely to infect the carcass itself, which therefore has to be burned.

The residual power of ritual detergents in ancient Near Eastern religions is emphasized by a provision in the Hittite Code: "If anyone has performed a rite of purification on a man he disposes of the remnants (of the offerings) at the place of burning. If he disposes of them in anyone's field or house, it is sorcery and (a case for the) court of the king" (HL 44b). The MÍŠU.GI ("old woman") wraps colored wools around a statue and offers incantations to remove the hex from a bewitched man and attach it to the statue (*KUB* 24.9 i 35–52). "She later buries the ritual tools and hammers nails into the ground to signify that the hex has been secured in the earth. . . . She breaks off a loaf of bread to the god

Marawayan and the god Aniya beside the hole where the tools are buried"
(Engelhard 1970: 18). "Her speech: '(He) who bewitched this (one), now I have
taken away the hex of that one and I have placed it in the earth' [lines 21–25].
She puts the tools of the ritual [now that they are polluted] in (the hole) and
pours mud over it. She smooths it over and nails in the pegs. Then she says the
following: '(He) who bewitched this (one), I have taken away the hex of that
one and I have placed it down in the earth. (Moreover), I have hammered it
down. Therefore let the hex and the evil dreams be hammered down! Let them
not come up (again) and let the dark earth hold them!' " (*KUB* 24.9 ii 19–25).

Similarly, equipment that had absorbed the sacrificer's impurity was discarded in a river so that the river current would carry it away (Tunnawi 3.12–16;
Goetze 1938b). The purpose of the river is clear, as explicitly stated in another
ritual: "Just as the river does not flow backward . . . let them not come back"
(*KUB* 29.7; *ANET*³ 346). In the Šurpu exorcism, cited above, the patient is
rubbed *(kupρuru)* and the impurity removed by the ritual detergent, called
kupiratu (Landsberger 1967b), is then taken out to a pure place in the plain
(7.59–63). The lexical congruence with Hebrew *kipper*, the exclusive term for
"purge" used in connection with the *ḥaṭṭāʾt*, need not be labored (see above and
chap. 16, COMMENT F). Thus there is firm precedent in ancient Near Eastern
praxis and vocabulary for explaining the burning of the *ḥaṭṭāʾt* because it absorbs
the malefic impurity of the object that it has purged (for details, see Milgrom
1976a).

One minor question remains. Why are the *ḥaṭṭāʾt* animals prescribed for
the priestly consecration (8:17; Exod 29:14) and the eighth day service of the
Tabernacle (9:11) burned outside the camp instead of eaten by the priests if
their blood purges only the altar? The answer lies in the datum that in both
cases the offerers of the *ḥaṭṭāʾt* are the priests and not the people, and here
another rule comes into play: priests are not to eat their own expiatory sacrifices
(cf. 6:16). They are not to benefit from their own offenses. Finally, my proposed
solution of the two kinds of *ḥaṭṭāʾt* may explain the anger attributed to Moses
over Aaron's violation of the rule of the burnt *ḥaṭṭāʾt* (see the NOTES on 10:16–
20 and chap. 10, COMMENT C).

E. The ḥaṭṭāʾt of Num 15:22–26

As shown (v 13), the *ḥaṭṭāʾt* laws are based on the assumption that the
inadvertent offender becomes aware of his act and feels remorse for it, expressed
by the verb *ʾāšam*. Repentance is thus a precondition for the *ḥaṭṭāʾt*. Moreover,
only the inadvertent *(šĕgāgâ)* violation of prohibitive commandments is subject
to this sacrifice (see at v 2), not the neglect or omission of performative commandments. This is so because impurity can result only from a violation, not an
act of omission (see at v 2).

The *ḥaṭṭāʾt* for inadvertences are graded according to the socioeconomic position of the offender: a bull for the high priest and community (vv 3–21), a he-goat for the tribal chieftain (vv 22–26), and a female of the flock for the commoner (vv 27–35). A variant in the procedure for communal inadvertences is found in Num 15:22–26, namely, an ʿōlâ bull and a ḥaṭṭāʾt he-goat. But the nature of the sin is not the same: in Lev 4 the sin is the inadvertent violation of a prohibitive commandment (v 13; cf. vv 2, 22, 27), whereas in Num 15 the sin is the inadvertent violation of any commandment (vv 22–23). These differences led Ibn Ezra (on Num 15:27) to postulate that these ostensibly similar laws are in reality dealing with two different sins: Lev 4 with violation of a prohibitive commandment *(lōʾ taʿăśeh)* and Num 15 with violation of a performative commandment *(ʿăśēh);* for this reason, different expiatory sacrifices are required. Thus if the community inadvertently violated the Passover by mistakenly celebrating it on the wrong day, they would have brought the purification offering of Lev 4 for violating the prohibition against eating leaven during the festival (Exod 12:15) for neglecting to perform the Passover sacrifice on the proper day (Num 9:13).

This solution, however, was faulted by Ramban (on Num 15:22), who noted that the Numbers passage cannot be limited to performative sins alone because the verb ʿāśâ 'to do, act' in "If this was done inadvertently" (v 24), "anyone who acts in error" (v 29), and "who acts defiantly" (v 30), predicates an active violation, one that involves actually doing rather than passively neglecting.

Indeed, as noted by *Seper Hamibḥar* (ad loc.), the language of Num 15— kol-hammiṣwôt . . . kol-ʾăšer ṣiwwâ 'any of the commandments . . . anything that [the Lord] has enjoined' (vv 22, 23)—must be understood literally: the word *kol-* embraces all of the commandments, positive and negative, performative and prohibitive. Supporting this insight is the recognition that not only this section but indeed the entire chapter emphasizes the totality of the commandments. First, it should be noted that v 22a–b, clearly an editorial interpolation, has been added to underscore the fact that all of the commandments are involved. It says in effect that sacrificial expiation is required for the violation not only of the prohibitive commandments of Lev 4 but of all commandments, including performative ones. Second, this section (vv 22–31) contains no heading, thus connecting it with the previous section on ḥallâ (vv 17–21). The intent is clear: ḥallâ and the sacrificial supplements (in the preceding section, vv 1–16) are positive, performative commandments and are therefore also subject to the prescribed penalties. Finally, the last unit in Num 15, on the ṣîṣīt (vv 37–41), contains the identical emphasis: "You will keep in mind all of the commandments" (v 40). Here we find the same usage of ʿāśâ and kol-miṣwôt as in vv 22 and 23. The reason for the inclusion of the ṣîṣīt ritual in this chapter is now clear: the wearing of the ṣîṣīt, itself a performative commandment, will be a constant reminder to its wearers of the totality of all commandments, performative as well as prohibitive, thus preventing or at least lessening the chance of inadvertent neglect or violation.

In sum, Num 15:22–31 emphasizes that all inadvertences are subject to sacrificial expiation, and the attachment of these verses to other performative commandments that make up this chapter, namely, sacrificial supplements (vv 1–16), *ḥallâ* (vv 17–21), and *ṣîṣît* (vv 37–41), points to a polemic against the position taken in Lev 4: not only prohibitive commandments require sacrificial expiation but also performative ones. Thus one cannot say that Lev 4 and Num 15 speak of discrete sins that warrant discrete sacrificial solutions. Both require sacrificial expiation for inadvertent violation of prohibitive commandments, and Num 15 also requires it for inadvertent violation of performative ones. Clearly, the solution suggesting that the two sections describe different sins does not work. There is an overlap: both speak of the violation of prohibitive commandments; hence, another solution must be sought.

Recently, A. Toeg (1974) has proposed that Num 15 is in reality a reworking of Lev 4. His position, briefly stated, is that the text of Lev 4 was shortened by eliminating the sacrificial procedure, then lengthened in order to emphasize elements of inadvertency (vv 25b, 26), the stranger (e.g., v 29), and presumptuousness (vv 30–31) while, at the same time, subjected to a major change: the purification-offering bull became the burnt-offering bull, to which the purification goat and the burnt-offering bull's supplementary meal and wine were added. Thus "a bull of the herd as a purification offering" (4:14) was expanded to "a bull of the herd [as a burnt offering of pleasing odor to the Lord, with its proper meal offering and libation, and one he-goat] as a purification offering" (Num 15:24).

An additional important bit of evidence supports his theory: the sacrificial requirement is governed by the verb *ʿāśâ* '[the community shall] sacrifice' (v 24). The verb *ʿāśâ* is a technical term in the cult that means "to sacrifice," in the sense of performing the entire sacrificial ritual (cf. 4:20; 9:7; 14:19, 30; 15:15, 30; 16:9, 24; 17:9; 23:19; Num 6:11, 16, 17; 8:12; 9:5; etc.). It is therefore a descriptive term; it tells exactly how and in what order the sacrificial ritual is to be performed. Now in all rituals calling for the use of both the burnt offering and the purification offering, the latter is invariably offered first (Milgrom 1976a, nn. 251, 295). As exemplified in the law of the Nazirite, even though the prescriptive ritual lists the burnt offering ahead of the purification offering (Num 6:10, 14), the descriptive ritual puts the latter offering first (vv 11, 16–17). It is important to realize that the descriptive ritual always uses the verb *ʿāśâ* and the prescriptive ritual uses a different verb. Thus in the induction of the Levites, the prescriptive text lists the burnt offering first (Num 8:8) but the descriptive text puts the purification offering first—and uses the verb *ʿāśâ* (v 12). Indeed, a descriptive ritual can be identified simply by its use of *ʿāśâ* and, conversely, a prescriptive ritual will be characterized by the use of some other verb. For example, the sacrificial order for the parturient (12:6, 8), which ostensibly violates the rule by listing the burnt offering before the purification offering, is in fact only a prescriptive text because it employs the verbs *hēbîʾ* and *lāqaḥ* but not the verb *ʿāśâ*. The passage 23:18–19 is also not an exception, even though, in this case, *ʿāśâ* is used and the burnt offering precedes the purification offering, for *ʿāśâ* refers solely to the purification offering whereas the burnt offering has its own different verb.

Thus Lev 4 must be a prescriptive ritual because it does not use the verb *ʿāśâ*, whereas Num 15 can only be descriptive because it does use the verb *ʿāśâ*. But here we encounter an exception to the rule: although the verb is *ʿāśâ*, the burnt offering is listed first! The solution therefore suggests itself that originally only one sacrifice was listed. And when one compares Num 15 with Lev 4, what that sacrifice was becomes clear: it was the purification offering. The writer of Num 15, not wanting to detail the complex procedure of Lev 4:15–20, changed the verb to *ʿāśâ*, thereby telescoping the entire ritual. Thus "the congregation shall offer *(wĕhiqrîbû)* a bull of the herd for a purification offering" became "the whole community shall sacrifice *(wĕʿāśû)* one bull of the herd for a purification offering." In other words, the verb *ʿāśâ* was correctly applied to one sacrifice. An interpolation was later inserted, however, adding the burnt offering and its accompaniments before the purification offering (above); the verb *ʿāśâ* was no longer correct, but it was not changed, thereby betraying the development of the text.

This solution, despite its virtues, is subject to two serious objections. (1) It does not explain why other cases of the purification offering found in Lev 4 are missing in Num 15. It might be suggested that the author of Num 15 had no interest in the cases of the high priest (4:1–12) or of the chieftain (4:22–26). But why would he have omitted the option of the individual's offering a ewe (4:32–35)? By selecting the she-goat as the exclusive offering for the individual (Num 15:27), he picked the animal that appears in no other specific case as a purification offering, whereas the ewe—the animal he rejected—is attested elsewhere as the individual's purification offering (e.g., the *mĕṣōrāʿ*, 14:10; the Nazirite, Num 6:14). (2) In the alleged reworking of the text of Lev 4 the author would have introduced yet another perplexing change. Instead of referring to the community as *qāhāl* (4:14–21), he consistently uses *ʿēdâ* (Num 15:24 [twice], 25, 26). It has already been shown that *ʿēdâ* is the old technical term for the Israelite community (Milgrom 1978a), and it is hardly likely that he would have replaced *qāhāl* by this more archaic term.

Thus the attempt to find literary dependency between the two pericopes dealing with the purification offering must be abandoned. There is no alternative but to assume that we are dealing with two independent traditions concerning the purification offering. But what of the term *ʿāśâ*, which strongly suggests that only one sacrifice was originally stipulated by Num 15:24?

The probability rests with R. Rendtorff (1967: 22) who, on other grounds, suggests that v 24 originally stipulated only the burnt offering and that the purification offering was added later. He correctly points to the burnt offering as initially being the sole expiatory sacrifice both for the nation (e.g., Judg 20:26;

21:2–4; 1 Sam 7:6, 9–10; 13:12; 2 Sam 24:25) and for individuals (Jer 7:21–22; 14:12; and esp. Job 1:15; 42:7–9). The evidence from this noncultic literature is confirmed by P, which continues to permit the use of the burnt offering as the individual's sole expiatory sacrifice (e.g., in 1:4). The rabbis express a similar view: originally "the open altars *(bāmôt)* were permitted and only the burnt offering was sacrificed" *(t. Zebaḥ.* 13:1). But Priestly legists made this alteration: they added the purification offering to the burnt for all fixed, public sacrifices. That even here the precedence of the burnt offering can still be detected is shown by the fact that all public sacrifices require male animals, even the purification offering, which, for the ordinary person, is limited to females (4:27–35). That the burnt offering must be a male, therefore, can only mean that originally it was the only public sacrifice; and when other sacrifices were added to the public cult, they were made to conform to the standard of the burnt offering. Parenthetically, it should be stated that other claims made by Rendtorff (1967: 83) must be rejected. Num 15:24a does not refer to an individual whose sin has harmed the community: such a case is only predicated of the high priest (4:3), not of the commoner. And the purification offering described in Num 15:25b is not a later interpolation: because the purification offering is not an *'iššeh*, it had to be listed separately.

Thus Num 15:22–31 represents a tradition of communal expiation independent of Lev 4. In its earlier stage it required only the bull of a burnt offering, but when the purification offering was added it was made to conform to the male requirement for sacrificial animals used in public, expiatory sacrifices; hence the sacrificial animals became a bull and a he-goat. The combination of a burnt-offering bovine and the purification offering he-goat is found in 9:3 and in the cultic calendar, 23:18–19 and Num 28–29. Regarding the individual's inadvertency, whereas Lev 4 allows either a female goat or a female sheep, Num 15 mandates only the female goat. Even in this common case of the female goat, the language is not the same: for example, *śĕ'irat 'izzîm*, 4:28; *'ēz bat šĕnātāh*, Num 15:27. Moreover, important innovations were added to the Numbers passage. Foremost among them is the ordinance, found nowhere else, that presumptuous, brazen sins are not eligible for sacrificial expiation but are punished by *kārēt* (vv 30–31 [Milgrom 1976f: 108–10]). Other important additions were the inclusion of the resident alien and the special emphasis on the factor of inadvertency (Milgrom 1982a). Of equal significance, as noted, is the inclusion of all of the commandments—performative as well as prohibitive—under the rule of sacrificial expiation and *kārēt.*

The formation of the Num 15 passage must have occurred early, for not only has its procedure become the rule for all public purification offerings (e.g., Num 28–29), but it is also incorporated into Ezekiel's rite for the consecration of the altar (Ezek 43:18–27). The latter passage is significant because it adopts both procedures, that of Lev 4 for the first day (vv 19–21) and that of Num 15 for the following seven days (vv 22–27). By contrast, the consecration of the

Tabernacle altar calls for the Lev 4 procedure only—during all seven days (Exod 29:36–37)! Thus the Num 15 rite must have crystallized into its present form after Lev 4—a deduction that concurs with the literary analysis presented above —and before Ezek 43. If it turns out that Num 15:22–31 is the product of H. as I. Knohl has strongly argued (1988: 149), then it provides further evidence of the preexilic provenience of all Priestly material (see Introduction, §§ B and C).

Finally, once it is accepted that we are dealing with two independent traditions, the possibility must be left open that Num 15, like Lev 4, speaks only of prohibitive commandments, that *ʿāśâ bišĕgāgâ* 'do . . . inadvertently' (v 29) implies an act of commission—in other words, that a prohibitive commandment has been violated—and it is the equivalent of the wording of Lev 4, "doing *(wĕʿāśâ)* inadvertently *(bišĕgāgâ)* . . . one of the commandments of . . . which should not be done" (4:22). If this be the case, then "these commandments" (Num 15:22) cannot refer to the previous performative commandments (vv 1–21) and the entire pericope (vv 22–31) may have to be considered as the displaced conclusion of another legal section. For other solutions, see K. Koch (1959: 57–58); D. Kellermann (1973). This problem cannot as yet be resolved (in details, see Milgrom 1983f).

F. Genital Discharges

Not all ritually impure persons bring a purification offering, only those whose impurity last more than seven days. The parturient and *zāb/zābâ* (one with an abnormal genital discharge) each bring a bird (12:6; 15:14–15, 29–30), and the *mĕṣōrāʿ* (one with scale disease) brings a female sheep or, if poor, a bird (see the COMMENT on 5:1–13). Whoever brings a bird (turtledove or pigeon) brings another of the same kind as an *ʿōlâ* to provide an adequate gift to the altar (Ibn Ezra on 5:7). The purification offering for impurity, like the one for inadvertences, purges sanctuary pollution (*b. Ker.* 26a). But it is not required for impurities that endure less than seven days. Thus the person who experiences a nocturnal emission or engages in sex need only bathe the following day and by evening his state of impurity is over (15:16–18; for the variant Qumran rule see the NOTE on this passage). The menstruant is a good case in point. If her periodic flow stops in a few days, as expected, her impurity lasts for seven days. On the seventh day she bathes and is pure in the evening (see the NOTE on 15:19). But "When a woman has a discharge of blood for many days, not at the time of her menstrual impurity, or when she has a discharge beyond the time of her menstrual impurity" (15:25), she requires a weeklong period of purification after her flow stops followed by a sacrificial rite on the eighth day (15:28–30). Her prolonged impurity is considered to have developed enough power not just to contaminate by contact but to pollute the sanctuary from afar. Hence, a purification offering is mandatory. Indeed, the prolongation of impurity is considered so dangerous that even a person who has contracted impurity secondarily

—that is, one who has come into contact with an impure person or animal and need but bathe (and sometimes launder) the same day in order to be rid of the impurity—will incur the capital punishment of *kārēt* if he wittingly neglects to purify himself (Num 19:13, 20; and see at 17:15–16), and must bring a graduated purification offering if his neglect to purify himself is not intentional (5:1–13). The implication here is clear: the contracted impurity, be it even so slight at the outset, will grow in force until it has the power to pollute the sanctuary from afar (see the COMMENT on 5:1–13). Let electromagnetism serve, mutatis mutandis, as an illustrative analogy. The minus charge of impurity is attracted to the plus charge of the sanctuary, and if the former builds up enough force to spark the gap, then lightninglike it will strike the sanctuary.

G. Corpse Contamination

The one ostensible anomaly in this purification system is the impurity of corpse contamination (Num 19). Even though one is only secondarily infected —contact is made with a corpse—the purificatory procedure must last seven days, as in the case of all severe impurities. Yet unlike the latter, a purification offering is not required on the eighth day. Instead, ashes of a burnt purification offering are sprinkled on the impure person on the third and seventh days. Moreover, while these ashes purify the contaminated, they contaminate their user (Num 19:21b). How can we account for this glaring, indeed bizarre, anomaly? The rabbis were equally perplexed, as the following anecdote illustrates:

A heathen questioned Rabban Yohanan ben Zakkai, saying: "The things you Jews do appear to be a kind of sorcery. A cow is brought, it is burned, is pounded into ash, and its ash is gathered up. Then when one of you gets defiled by contact with a corpse, two or three drops of the ash mixed with water are sprinkled upon him, and he is told, 'You are cleansed!' "

Rabban Yohanan asked the heathen: "Has the spirit of madness ever possessed you?" He replied, "No." "Have you ever seen a man whom the spirit of madness has possessed?" The heathen replied: "Yes." "And what do you do for such a man?" "Roots are brought, the smoke of their burning is made to rise about him, and water is sprinkled upon him until the spirit of madness flees."

Rabban Yohanan then said: "Do not your ears hear what your mouth is saying? It is the same with a man who is defiled by contact with a corpse—he, too, is possessed by a spirit, the spirit of uncleanness, and Scripture says, 'I will cause [false] prophets as well as the spirit of uncleanness to flee the land' " (Zech 13:2).

Now when the heathen left, Rabban Yohanan's disciples said: "Our master, you put off that heathen with a mere reed of an answer (lit., "you shoved aside that heathen with a reed"), but what answer will you give us?"

Rabban Yohanan answered: "By your lives, I swear: the corpse does not have the power by itself to defile, nor does the mixture of ash and water have the power by itself to cleanse. The truth is that the purifying power of the Red Cow is a decree of the Holy One. The Holy One said: "I have set it down as a statute, I have issued it as a decree. You are not permitted to transgress my decree. 'This is the statute of the Torah (Num 19:1).' " (*Pesiq. Rab Kah.* 4:7)

The discrepancy between the explanation given by the rabbi to the heathen and that given to his students reveals the great bewilderment among early Jewish scholars concerning the working and meaning of this ritual. What outwardly looks like an exorcism is flatly denied by Rabbi Yohanan. Yet he is at a loss to find a rationale. His perplexity is aggravated not just by the form of the rite, but by its paradoxical effect. Whereas the ashes of the Red Cow purify those whom they sprinkle, they defile those who do the sprinkling (vv 19, 21) and, indeed, anyone who handles them (v 21) and is involved in preparing them (vv 6–20). This paradox is neatly captured in the rabbinic apothegm: they purify the defiled and defile the pure (cf. *Pesiq. Rab Kah.* 4:6; *m. Para* 4:4; *Midr. Num. Rab.* 19:1, 5).

It is here proposed that the key to unlock the paradox of the Red Cow is that it is a *ḥaṭṭāʾt* sacrifice, as stated unambiguously by the text: "it is a *ḥaṭṭāʾt*" (v 9). The function of the *ḥaṭṭāʾt* sacrifice, as has been demonstrated, is to remove contamination (*ḥiṭṭēʾ* means "decontaminate"); hence, it should be rendered "purification offering." As the Red Cow is labeled a "burnt *ḥaṭṭāʾt*" (v 17), it falls into the category of the *ḥaṭṭāʾt* brought for severe impurities whose flesh may not be eaten but is burnt outside the camp (4:6–7, 11–12; cf. 6:23; 10:18). Yet the difference in the ritual procedure is glaring: the blood of the Red Cow is not offered up on the altar as is the blood of every *ḥaṭṭāʾt* and, indeed, of every other sacrifice, but the whole cow, together with its blood, is incinerated outside the camp (v 5). Thus it does not appear to be a sacrifice at all.

This discrepancy is a serious one but it can be resolved. The blood of the Red Cow is not offered on the altar for the simple reason that it is needed in the ashes as a continuing *ḥaṭṭāʾt*. It has been shown that the element of the *ḥaṭṭāʾt* that does the decontaminating is the blood. Its placement on the horns of the altars (4:4, 7, 18, 25, 30, 34), in the shrine (4:6, 17) or in the adytum (16:14) is what purges these sacred objects of their accumulated impurities. True, other traditional purgatives are contained in the ashes—cedar, hyssop, and crimson yarn—but these elements are clearly secondary to the blood. It is the blood that infuses the ashes with their lustral power.

The single postulate of the Red Cow as a *ḥaṭṭāʾt* suffices to break the back of the paradox. For the unique characteristic of the *ḥaṭṭāʾt* is that it defiles its handlers. Thus, the one who burns the ḥaṭṭāʾt outside the camp "shall launder his clothes and bathe his body in water; and after that he may reenter the camp" (16:28). Here we have a precise parallel to the defilement incurred by the one who burns the Red Cow outside the camp and who undergoes a similar purification (v 8). Furthermore, because the ḥaṭṭāʾt blood now bears the impurity it has absorbed, it contaminates anything it touches (6:20b). Hence the laws of impurities prevail in regard to objects touched by the ḥaṭṭāʾt: earthenware must be broken (cf. 6:21a with 11:33, 35; 15:12a) and metal ware scoured (cf. 6:21b with Num 31:22–23).

It is the very mechanism of the purgation that helps clarify the paradox. In effect, the ḥaṭṭāʾt absorbs the impurity it has purged and for that reason, it must be eliminated by incineration. This means that anyone involved in the incineration of the ḥaṭṭāʾt is infected by it and must undergo purification. As shown above, in the ancient Near East both praxis and vocabulary provide firm precedent for burning or otherwise eliminating the ḥaṭṭāʾt because it absorbs the malefic impurity of the object that it has purged. This, then, is the nature of the burnt ḥaṭṭāʾt: it transmits impurity from the purified to the purifier. Hence it purifies the defiled and defiles the pure.

The ḥaṭṭāʾt postulate commends itself for the additional reason that all by itself it can explain the main details in the preparation of the Red Cow's ashes, as follows:

1. *The cow* (Num 19:2). At first sight, the requirement of a cow clashes with the ḥaṭṭāʾt postulate, for everywhere else the ḥaṭṭāʾt for the individual is either a bull or a female of the flock. The discrepancy is chimerical. A bovine is required in order to provide the maximum quantity of ashes; yet the bull cannot be chosen because it represents the ḥaṭṭāʾt either of the high priest (4:1–12, 16:11) or of the community (4:13–21). The Red Cow, instead, is intended for the exclusive use of the individual Israelite and, according to P, the individual may bring only a female of the flock for a ḥaṭṭāʾt (4:22–35; Num 15:27–29). Thus because the ashes of the Red Cow must theoretically supply the purificatory needs of the entire population, the largest female animal is selected—a cow. Moreover, the Tannaites had a tradition that only very few Red Cows had been slaughtered even at the end of the Second Temple period, thus indicating that the ashes of a single cow had to last for a long time (*m. Para* 3:5).

2. *red* (Num 19:2). The association of red with blood is widely attested in primitive cultures. Thus the red hide of the cow symbolically adds to the quantity of blood in the ash mixture, as do the crimson yarn and the (red) cedar (v 7), and enhances its potency. The same phenomenon is attested in other cultures. For example, among the Ndembu, the celebrant reddens the river not only with the blood of a fowl; he also adds other red coloring matter such as powdered red clay and powdered red gum (Turner 1967: 62). The purpose of the remaining ingredient, the hyssop, is to provide ample ashes (*t. Para* 4:10).

3. *without blemish* (Num 19:2), the basic requirement for sacrificial animals (22:17–20).

4. *in his presence . . . in his sight* (Num 19:3–5). The cow is slaughtered and burned with Eleazar in attendance. The need for continuous priestly supervision betrays the inherent danger that the ritual may slip back into its pagan moorings, a point that will be developed subsequently. Incorporating the ritual into the sacrificial regime effectively places it under priestly control.

5. *Eleazar the priest shall take some of the blood with his finger and sprinkle (wĕhizzâ) it seven times toward the front of the Tent of Meeting* (Num 19:4). Sprinkling the blood toward the Tabernacle proves, in my opinion, that the rite is a sacrifice. Instead of sprinkling the blood on the altar—precluded by the need to add the blood to the ashes (see above)—the blood is sprinkled toward the altar. The effect is the same: the blood becomes consecrated. In a similar manner the priest sprinkles oil seven times "before the Lord" prior to the purification of the *mĕṣōrāʿ* (14:16). That is to say, he must consecrate it before he can use it.

An equally cogent parallel is provided by the *ḥaṭṭāʾt* blood on the Day of Purgation. It is first daubed on the outer altar's horns and then sprinkled on the altar seven times. The purpose of this double manipulation is supplied by the text: *wĕṭihărô wĕqiddĕšô miṭṭumĕʾōt bĕnê yiśrāʾēl* 'purify it [the altar] of the pollution of the Israelites and consecrate it' (16:19). After the altar is cleansed, it needs to be reconsecrated, an act accomplished by the sevenfold aspersion with the *ḥaṭṭāʾt* blood. By the same token, the sevenfold aspersion of the Red Cow's blood also consecrates the blood that it may always act as a purgative when, in the form of ashes, it is sprinkled upon the impure.

6. *The cow shall be burned in his sight—its hide, flesh, and blood shall be burned, its dung included* (Num 19:5). The parts of the cow that are burned duplicate those of the *ḥaṭṭāʾt* animal that are burned (4:11), with the notable exception of the blood. Indeed, it is the blood in the ashes that endows them with purificatory powers. According to the Tannaites, the Red Cow was slaughtered in the very pit in which it was burned (*m. Para* 3:9; *Sipre Zuṭa* to Num 19:9). Thus all its blood, except for the few drops used for sprinkling, was consumed in the fire. Moreover, after performing the sprinkling, the high priest would wipe his hands on the carcass so that not a single drop of blood would go to waste (*m. Para* 3:9; *Sipre* Num. 124).

7. *Cedar wood, hyssop, and crimson yarn* (Num 19:6). These ingredients, together with the blood, are added to the *mĕṣōrāʿ*'s lustral waters (14:6, 49–50). Thus the mixtures that purify the corpse-contaminated and the *mĕṣōrāʿ* are of the same composition. Yet their effect on their manipulators is not the same: the waters for corpse contamination defile, but the waters for scale disease do not. The obvious explanation is that the blood used for the scale-disease ritual is not a *ḥaṭṭāʾt*. In other words, the first-day ritual for purifying the *meṣōrāʿ* was not

incorporated into the *ḥaṭṭāʾt* system, and it still retains its pre-Israelite form. More on this below.

8. The priest who throws the cedar, hyssop, and crimson yarn into the fire (Num 19:6) is impure as well as the person who sets the cow in the fire (vv 5, 8) and the one who collects the ashes (v 10). But neither the slaughterer of the cow (v 3) nor the priest who consecrated its blood (v 4) is said to have become impure. The difference is one of time: only those who make contact with the Red Cow after the consecration of its blood become impure. This proves that the blood consecration transforms the Red Cow into a *ḥaṭṭāʾt*, a purification offering, for anyone handling the *ḥaṭṭāʾt* becomes impure (16:28; and see above).

9. *It is a ḥaṭṭāʾt* (Num 19:9). This is the attested formula by which a given sacrifice is declared a *ḥaṭṭāʾt* (cf. 4:24; 5:9, 11, 12; Exod 29:14). Yet this formula's use here bears greater significance. It follows upon the sentence stating that the ashes of the Red Cow are to be "preserved *(lĕmišmeret)* by the Israelite community for waters of lustration." "It" *(hwʾ, ketib)* is masculine and refers not to the cow but to *ʾēper*, the ashes. Thus the ashes of the Red Cow continue to operate as a *ḥaṭṭāʾt*.

In this manner, the *ḥaṭṭāʾt* postulate has unraveled the paradox: the ashes of the Red Cow are a burnt *ḥaṭṭāʾt* and, hence, they defile their handlers and purify their recipients. Moreover, this postulate has been shown to be the organizing principle throughout the Red Cow ritual. Indeed, as scientific method calls for seeking the simplest and most economical theory to explain any given set of data (parsimony), then the one postulate of the *ḥaṭṭāʾt* should be accepted as the explanation of the Red Cow ritual and the resolution of its paradox.

Still, there is one detail that the *ḥaṭṭāʾt* postulate does not explain, a detail that occurs not in the preparation of the ashes, but in their use. The ashes of the Red Cow are sprinkled not only on impure objects, but also, and primarily, on impure persons. This constitutes a break with the rule that the *ḥaṭṭāʾt* blood is applied solely to objects, indeed, solely to objects within the sanctuary precincts. These comprised sacred objects that have been polluted by the physical impurity or the inadvertent wrong of the one who offers the *ḥaṭṭāʾt*. He, the offerer, is cleansed of his physical impurity by his ablutions and cleansed of his wrongdoing by his remorse, but never by the *ḥaṭṭāʾt* blood (see above).

The uniqueness of the aspersion of *ḥaṭṭāʾt* ashes on the body of the corpse-contaminated person is significant. It constitutes a vestige of the ritual's pre-Israelite antecedents. In Mesopotamia, for example, an impure person might be purified by having him change or launder his garments, bathe with pure water, be aspersed with tamarisk and *tullal*-plant or fumigated with censer and torch, and, above all, be wiped with specially prepared detergents. Purification rituals, then, are performed on the body of the afflicted. No wonder then that Rabban Yohanan could put off the heathen with his rationale because exorcisms continued to be performed by aspersing the victim with magical substances, not only in ages gone by, but in his time as well.

THE SACRIFICES

The question needs to be asked: Why were the ashes retained? Why did not the Priestly legislators eliminate this "sore thumb" from the *ḥaṭṭāʾt* purification ritual it prescribed for corpse contamination? The answer must surely be that corpse contamination evoked an obsessive, irrational fear in individuals. In a Mesopotamian Namburbi ritual, the victim is in mortal fear that the evil he has seen has infected him with lethal impurity; he requires an exorcistic incantation in addition to sacrificing, bathing, changing his clothing, and remaining shut up in his house for *seven days* (Ebeling 1954: 178–81). That the fear of corpse contamination prevailed into rabbinic times is seen from the report of Josephus that King Herod had to use force to settle Jews in newly constructed Tiberias and to appease them even built them homes and gave them tracts of land (*Ant.* 18.36–38)—all because he had built Tiberias over a graveyard. Thus it stands to reason that the one who has been contaminated by contact with a corpse would demand an exorcism, the application of powerful countervailing forces to his body that would expunge the dreaded impurity. Thus, even had the Priestly legislators desired to eliminate the use of the ashes (a doubtful supposition), it is hard to believe that the people at large would have let them.

In truth, a rite of exorcism has been preserved in nearly pristine form in the Bible: the first-day purification of the healed *měṣōrāʿ* and fungous house (14:4–8, 49–53). As noted above, the same elements that comprise the ashes of the Red Cow are prescribed for the *měṣōrāʿ*'s purification: cedar, hyssop, crimson yarn, and above all blood. Once again, it is the blood that constitutes the chief detergent because each element must be dipped into it (vv 6, 51). Even the decisive verb *ḥiṭṭēʾ* 'decontaminate' is used (vv 49, 52), which indicates that an exorcism is called for—to remove the impurity from the stricken person or home. Yet the slain bird that has supplied the blood is not called a *ḥaṭṭāʾt*. Nor should we expect it, for the blood is not sprinkled in the direction of the Tabernacle as is the blood of the Red Cow. The aspersion of the *měṣōrāʿ*, then, must represent the more original rite and the Red Cow, transformed into a *ḥaṭṭāʾt*, constitutes a later, Israelite stage.

That the Red Cow rite represents a later stage than that of the *měṣōrāʿ* is also shown by the fact that it is the priest who performs the latter's aspersion rite (14:4–7; cf. vv 48–53). This is what we would expect on the basis of exorcistic practices in the ancient Near East, which were always performed by a cultic specialist. In Israel, however, the purification of the corpse-contaminated person breaks with the pattern: "A person who is pure *(ʾîš ṭāhôr)* shall . . . sprinkle . . . the pure person *(haṭṭāhôr)* shall sprinkle . . . ; Further, he who sprinkled *(ûmazzēh)* . . ." (Num 19:18, 19, 21). Clearly, the text reflects a deliberate attempt to declare that the aspersion is to be performed by *anyone*—not a priest, not a specialist, but any layman. The nexus between exorcism and purification is severed.

There is one additional requirement in the rite of the *měṣōrāʿ* that points to its antiquity. It also requires that a live bird be dipped into the blood of the slain bird and then dispatched to the open country (vv 6–7, 51–53). Thus it is not enough to exorcise the *měṣōrāʿ*'s impurity: it must be sent off to an uninhabited area where it can no longer do harm. There is no comparable requirement in the purification performed with the ashes of the Red Cow.

This double requirement of removing and dispatching the impurity is also found in the ritual for the Day of Purgation: the impurity of the sanctuary is purged (*kipper*, 16:16, 17, 18, 20) by the blood of a slain goat and bull. The impurity is then loaded upon the head of a live goat, which thereafter is dispatched to an inaccessible place in the wilderness (vv 21–22). Here too, the complete ritual, including exorcism and elimination, has been preserved for the reason that its locus is the sanctuary. The impurity of the sanctuary not only is purged, but must be banished to an inaccessible place whence it can harm the sanctuary no more. Yet despite the retention of the dispatch ritual, the Israelite transformation has been thoroughgoing: not only is the blood detergent taken from the *ḥaṭṭāʾt* (vv 11, 15), but the dispatch-goat is also called a *ḥaṭṭāʾt* (vv 5, 9), even though it is not sacrificed at all.

The ritual of the Red Cow falls between the two rituals of the *měṣōrāʿ* and of the Day of Purgation. Like the latter, the Red Cow is called a *ḥaṭṭāʾt* and follows, in nearly all respects, the procedure of a *ḥaṭṭāʾt*. Like the former, the blood and the same accompanying ingredients are used to asperse persons. Yet unlike either, the dispatch element is missing: there is no live animal to carry off the impurity. Thus the Israelite transformation of the presumed original ritual of exorcising and dispatching impurity is more thoroughgoing for corpse contamination than for scale disease or the sanctuary. Except for the use of the ashes, the Red Cow ritual conforms completely to the Israelite sacrificial system.

The metamorphosis of the Red Cow ritual is evident in yet another vital area: the power of corpse contamination has been vastly reduced. First, unlike the *měṣōrāʿ*, no ablutions are required of the corpse-contaminated person on the first day. (The Dead Sea sectaries reasoned differently [see the COMMENT on chap. 15].) The reason, I submit, is clear. Whereas the *měṣōrāʿ* is required to bathe before he enters the camp (14:8), the corpse-contaminated person need not bathe because he does not leave his community. True, another and probably older law requires the corpse-contaminated person (and the *zāb/zābâ* and the *měṣōrāʿ*) to leave the camp (Num 5:2), but Num 19 implies otherwise: (1) Nowhere does it state that the corpse-contaminated person leaves the camp. (2) The clause "and then he may return to the camp" found in the prescription for the priest who prepares the ashes (v 7) and for other bearers of impurity who are outside the camp (e.g., 14:8; 16:26, 28) is conspicuously absent from the otherwise detailed purification procedure of Num 19. (3) The ashes deposited outside the camp (v 9) are brought to the corpse-contaminated person (vv 17–18a), not the other way around, implying that he remains inside the camp. (4) Failure to undergo the water lustration "defiles the Lord's Tabernacle/sacred precincts" (vv 13, 20), a consequence that is possible only as long as he remains inside the camp. Thus that the corpse-contaminated person, unlike the *mĕṣōrāʿ*, is not required to bathe on the first day or be banished from the camp during the week of his purification is a clear indication that the priestly legislators eventually downgraded the degree of his impurity.

Further evidence for the diminution of an originally more powerful corpse contamination arises from another consideration: the corpse-contaminated person brings no sacrifice at the end of his purification. Unlike the parturient, the *mĕṣōrāʿ*, and the *zāb/zābâ*, who bring a *ḥaṭṭāʾt* no sooner than the eighth day of the purificatory period (12:6–8; 14:10, 21–23; 15:14, 29), the corpse-contaminated person completes his purification in seven days and brings no *ḥaṭṭāʾt*. This means that his impurity *ab initio* is not severe enough to pollute the sanctuary, as are the other impurities requiring a *ḥaṭṭāʾt*. Only if he delays his purification does his impurity, so to speak, gather force to impinge on the sanctuary, subjecting him to the *kārēt* penalty if his negligence is deliberate (Num 15:30–31) or to a *ḥaṭṭāʾt* if he has inadvertently forgotten (cf. 5:2–3). Lastly, that Num 19 reflects a reduction in the potency of corpse contamination is shown by the contrasting and more conservative view held by the priest-prophet Ezekiel that a corpse-contaminated priest must bring a *ḥaṭṭāʾt* at the end of his purificatory period (Ezek 44:27). The older taboos are still evident in the command to the high priest not to leave the sanctuary to follow a funeral bier (21:12), in other words, he may not even gaze upon a corpse. In effect, the Priestly legislators have reduced the degree of corpse contamination from the severest of the severe impurities to the least of them. That is to say, the severe impurities requiring a minimum of eight days of purification actually rank higher than corpse contamination, which requires seven days of purification and no sacrifice. The corpse-contaminated person is placed on a par with the menstruant, who also requires a seven-day purification without sacrifice. Just as she remains in the camp, so, it follows, does the corpse-contaminated person. There is, however, historical evidence that the menstruant was quarantined in the city during Second Temple times (cf. Jos. *Ant.* 3.261; *m. Mid.* 7:4; 11QT 48:16–17).

In sum, the lustral ashes of the Red Cow are the only vestige of a pre-Israelite rite of exorcism for the corpse-contaminated person. Otherwise the rite has been transformed by the Israelite values inherent in its sacrificial procedures. Above all, the hitherto demonic impurity of corpses has been devitalized, first by denying it the automatic power to contaminate the sanctuary (requiring a *ḥaṭṭāʾt*) and then by denying that the corpse-contaminated person need leave the camp or city during his purificatory period. Finally, the procedure for preparing the ashes has been restructured to conform to the *ḥaṭṭāʾt* requirements and integrated into Israel's sacrificial system. That the *ḥaṭṭāʾt* system was artificially imposed upon this ritual is betrayed by the fact that those who prepare the ashes become unclean even though the ashes have not yet been used. Because of these changes, the ritual of the Red Cow, as presently constituted in Num 19, is relatively later than the rituals for the severe impurities of Lev 12–15, which betray more primitive traces; and that, in the long run, is perhaps what accounts for its insertion in Numbers rather than Leviticus.

Thus Rabban Yohanan's answer to the heathen reflects the probable origin of the Red Cow ritual. But neither the rabbi nor his students believed it. For them, and for Judaism, it was inconceivable that any rite was inherently efficacious. In the absence of rational explanation there was, solely and sufficiently, the inscrutable will of God. The break with paganism was complete, but it was not the achievement of their age. More than half a millennium earlier the priestly legislators of this ritual severed its pagan roots and remodeled it to accord with their norms and praxis (for details, see Milgrom 1981h [= 1983d: 85–95]).

H. The Levites' Induction

The purification offering is prescribed for three additional individuals: the Levites upon their induction into the Tabernacle workforce (Num 8:5–22); the priests upon their consecration (chap. 8; Exod 29); and the Nazirite upon the abortion and completion of his/her Nazirite term (Num 6:1–21).

The Levites are involved twice with the purification offering. First, they are sprinkled with its ashes (Num 8:7; and see above) to cleanse them of corpse contamination. Then they lean their hands upon two bulls that Aaron, the high priest, sacrifices as purification and burnt offerings (Num 8:12). The purification bull is in keeping with the prescription of 4:13–21, the community's purification offering. As noted by Abravanel (on Num 8:12), because the Levites are inducted en masse they constitute "a community"; hence, a bull. The function of this purification offering is not stated. Nevertheless, it can be deduced both from its use elsewhere (above) and, especially, from its place in the threefold purificatory rites prescribed for the Levites. The Levites are bathed (laundering implies bathing, vv 7, 21), sprinkled with purificatory waters (containing the ashes of a red cow), and expiation is made for them by a purification bull. Bathing cleanses them of minor impurities; the purificatory water, of corpse contamination; the purification bull—of their severe impurities, which, according to the Priestly system described above, have impinged on the sanctuary and polluted its altar. Thus this induction rite purifies the Levites of their impurities and the altar of its contamination, a function that is aptly summed up in the concluding verse of this ritual: "The Levites purified themselves . . . and Aaron effected purgation for them to cleanse them" (Num 8:20, an inclusion with vv 6–7a; for details, see Milgrom 1987).

I. The Consecration of the Altar

The priests bring a bull as a purification offering each day during their consecration service (Exod 29:36–37) on behalf of the altar rather than for themselves. The text does not say *(bĕkapperĕkā) ʿălêhem* '(effect purgation) for them' (i.e., the priests) but *ʿālāyw* 'upon it' (i.e., the altar). Indeed, the entire text emphasizes this point: "Each day you shall sacrifice a bull as a purification offering, and you shall cleanse the altar by performing purgation upon it, and you shall anoint it to consecrate it. Seven days you shall perform purgation upon the altar and consecrate it" (Exod 29:36–37a). Thus the altar is being consecrated coevally with the priests, and the week-long blood rites with the purification bull are directed toward its consecration. The question, however, remains: the newly erected altar can hardly have become polluted; why then need it be purged? And why for seven days? The verb *kipper* here clearly ranges beyond the meaning "purge." This will be discussed in detail in chap. 16, COMMENT F. Here let it be noted that its meaning can be deduced through a series of analogies with other applications of sacrificial blood, such as in the consecration of new priests (8:23–24; Exod 29:20), the purification rite of a healed *mĕṣōrāʿ* (14:14–17, 25–28), the smearing of the lintel and doorposts with the blood of the paschal sacrifice (Exod 12:7, 22), and, the closest analogue of all, the reconsecration of the defiled altar (16:18–19). The common denominator of all of these rites is that the things that receive the blood are extremities, the particular points of the object that a hostile force would strike first. In the ancient Near East, temples were periodically smeared with magical substances at precisely the same vulnerable points, in order to expel the malefic power from the object and to protect it against future incursions. The blood rites therefore had both a purgative and an apotropaic function. It is not too difficult to conclude that in Israel these rituals *originally* had the same dual purpose: to purge the altar of pollution and to protect it from future pollution. It will be shown (NOTES on chap. 16) that the apotropaic function has been abandoned and, indeed, negated by Israel's monotheism. Ritual substances have no intrinsic force: they are powered by the will of God. Thus blood can act as a detergent. It cleanses but does not inoculate. Nonetheless, the week-long application of the blood of the purification offering to the newly built altar betrays the original purpose of this rite; it constitutes repeated coatings of prophylactic blood to protect it against ritual and moral pollutants (originally demonic).

J. The Nazirite

The Nazirite who has aborted his or her term by corpse contamination must bring a purification offering (Num 6:9–11). In this regard, he differs from any other corpse-contaminated person, even a priest, who needs only to be sprinkled with the ashes of the Red Cow (Num 19; see above). As noted above, however, Ezekiel preserves the clearly older tradition that the corpse-contaminated priest must bring a purification offering (Ezek 44:25–27). The resemblance between the Nazirite and Ezekiel's priest is hardly accidental. Like the priest, the Nazirite is "holy to the Lord" (21:6; Num 6:8; cf. Philo *Laws* 1. 249).

Actually, in his taboos (as noted in *Sipre* Naso 26, *Midr. Num. Rab.* 10:11), the Nazirite approximates the greater sanctity of the high priest: (1) he may not contaminate himself with the dead of his immediate family (21:11; Num 6:7; contrast the ordinary priest, 21:1–4); (2) for him, as for the high priest, his head is the focus of his sanctity (Exod 29:7; Num 6:11b; note the similar motive clauses, 21:12b; Num 6:7b; and contrast the consecration of the ordinary priest, Exod 29:21); and (3) he abstains from intoxicants during his term (Num 6:4), actually a more stringent requirement than that of the high priest, whose abstinence, like that of his fellow priests, is limited only to the time he spends inside the sacred precincts (10:9).

The purification offering makes sense for the Nazirite of the aborted term. Yet why is it required of the Nazirite who has successfully completed his vow (Num 6:14)? Had he contaminated the sanctuary by some severe impurity, his naziriteship would have been aborted, as in the previously mentioned case. Had he incurred some impurity or wrongdoing unknowingly, he could not have brought a purification offering, which requires awareness of the offense (see at 4:2). Indeed, the very fact that his vow ran full term is proof positive that he contracted neither impurity nor wrongdoing, the only causes allowed by the Priestly legislators for bringing a purification offering! It is Ramban (followed by Abravanel) who points to the most likely answer: the Nazirite's self-removal from the sacred to the profane realm requires sacrificial expiation (adumbrated by the rabbis; cf. *b. Ker.* 8b; *Midr. Num. Rab.* 10). He is depriving God of one of *qĕrōbay* 'my near ones' (cf. 10:4). True, as will be shown (see at 5:14–16), the Nazirite's desanctification transposes his action into the sphere of the reparation offering. But the latter sacrifice is imposed only for illegitimate desanctification, whereas the Nazirite's desanctification is perfectly legitimate. Nonetheless, the use of the purification offering for this purpose is unique. It may indicate that at one time, before the distinction between the purification and reparation offerings was sharply made, the purification offering was also used for purposes of desanctification.

What is striking about the above-mentioned cases is that they preserve old rituals whose original meanings have been abandoned as they were modified to conform to Israel's theology. Thus the priestly consecration contains a rite for the week-long application of the blood of a purification offering to the altar that corresponds to an apotropaic function observable in pagan temples but abandoned in Israel's Priestly system. The antiquity of this consecration service is attested by its very name, *millū˒îm* (see at 8:33), and by the fact that the *millū˒îm* ram serves as the archetype of the well-being offering (Exod 29:27–28; see the NOTE to 8:22). The Nazirite ritual, as shown, resembles the more conservative and probably older view of the priest's sanctity as found in Ezekiel and, moreover, prescribes a unique use of the purification offering, which can only hark back to an earlier period before the purification and reparation offerings became discrete sacrifices. The antiquity of the Nazirite rite is underscored by the prescription that the officiating priest receive the boiled shoulder of the well-being ram (Num 6:19), a priestly perquisite that is attested nowhere else in the Priestly legislation but is consonant with the practice of the ancient Shilonite sanctuary (1 Sam 2:13–14; Milgrom 1983a: 166–67).

K. The Public Cult

The remaining occasions for the purification offering in the Priestly texts are in the public, fixed cult: the inaugural service at the newly dedicated Tabernacle (9:2–3); the annual Day of Purgation (16:3, 5), the gift of the tribal chieftains to the newly consecrated altar (Num 7:16, 22, etc.), and the festival calendar (Num 28:15, 22, 30; 29:5, 11, 16, 19, 22, 25, 28, 31, 38). What they share in common is that the priestly purification offering is a bull, in consonance with 4:3–12, and the people's purification offering is a he-goat, as prescribed by Num 15:24 (but not by 4:13–21). Nevertheless, the requirement that the purification offering he-goat be coupled with a burnt-offering bull, mandated by Num 15:24 for the people's expiation, is not always followed: a heifer and sheep (9:3), a ram (16:5), a bull, ram, and sheep (Num 7:15, 21; etc.). In any case, the prescription for the people's purification-offering bull in 4:13–21 has been abandoned entirely in the public and festal sacrifices in favor of the he-goat requirement of Num 15:24, another indication that the Leviticus passage is older (see above). Certain other anomalies need but be noted and are discussed elsewhere. The purification he-goat offered for the people during the inaugural service is not eaten by the priests even though its blood is not brought inside the sanctuary (6:23), which leads to Moses' rebuke of Aaron (see the COMMENT on 10:16–20). The sacrificial prescriptions for the Day of Purgation in chap. 16 are in conflict with those of the festal calendar in Num 29:8–11 (see the NOTE on 16:24). The sacrificial gifts of the tribal chieftains were probably not offered up immediately but were contributions to the sanctuary's stock (Milgrom 1986); hence, they cannot be used as evidence for sacrificial procedure. Lastly, the purification offering is prescribed for all special days but not for the daily offering and the Sabbath (Num 28:3–10; cf. COMMENT O below).

L. Ezekiel's Temple and Priest

The text describing Ezekiel's visionary temple refers frequently to the purification offering (Ezek 40:39; 43:19–25; 44:29; 45:17, 18–20, 21–25; 46:20). Mention has already been made of the fusion of the two kinds of ḥaṭṭāʾt (Lev 4, Num 15) in Ezekiel's Passover observance (45:21–24). On the fourteenth of the first month (Pesaḥ) a purification bull is offered and, on each of the following seven days (of the Festival of Unleavened Bread), seven bulls and seven rams as burnt offerings with their cereal and oil accompaniments and one he-goat as a purification offering. The same sacrificial series is prescribed for the seven-day

Feast of Tabernacles (*bĕḥag*, v 25). The types and number of animals are at variance with P's prescriptions (Num 28:16–25). Moreover, the requirement that a purification bull be offered on the fourteenth, the same day and just before each Israelite family offers the paschal sacrifice (see Lev 23:5; Exod 12:1–14), is entirely novel. Still, it begins to make sense once it is realized that Ezekiel's sacrificial series for the Passover festival corresponds precisely to that prescribed for the altar dedication (43:18–27): a purification bull is offered on the first day (vv 18–20) and a purification he-goat and a burnt-offering bull and ram on each of the following seven days (vv 21–26). Yet the initiation of Ezekiel's altar is at variance with the altar initiation of the Tabernacle, which prescribes a purification bull for all seven days (Exod 29:36) together with a burnt-offering ram (8:18–21; Exod 29:15–18; that the altar was "initiated" and not "dedicated" is discussed in chap. 9's COMMENT). Also the length of the initiation service differs: the Tabernacle for seven days (8:33; Exod 29:35, 37) and Ezekiel's for eight. To be sure, the text states that the ceremony lasts for seven days (Ezek 43:25–26) and that the regular cult begins thereafter on the eighth day (v 27). But this seven-day period does not include the day on which the purification bull is offered; rather, it follows it. This can be deduced from the time specified for the beginning of this seven-day period, *ûbayyôm haššēnî* (v 22), which must be rendered "on the next day" (not "on the second day"), a usage clearly attested in a number of passages (e.g., Exod 2:13; Josh 10:32; Judg 20:24–25; Neh 8:13). Thus Ezekiel's altar initiation is prescribed for eight days precisely and with the same sacrificial ritual as his Passover celebration. And the one illuminates the other. Just as the altar initiation unambiguously serves the purpose of purging the altar, so Ezekiel's unique requirement that a purification bull be offered by the ruler *(nāśîʾ)* "on his own behalf and on behalf of the people of the land" (v 22) can only be understood as part of a total scheme to purge the temple in preparation for the Passover (for a vivid example of the concern for the temple's purity for the paschal sacrifice, see 2 Chr 30:15–20). To be sure, P is just as concerned with the purity of the sanctuary and for that reason mandates the presentation of a he-goat purification offering on every festival day (Num 28–29). The one exception is the day of the paschal sacrifice. It may be surmised that, in this matter, P reflects an earlier period—before the centralization efforts of Hezekiah and Josiah—when the paschal sacrifice was offered at local sanctuaries (see Introduction, §C). Be that as it may, Ezekiel's obsession with purifying the temple in preparation for the Passover is underscored by his instructions that on the first day of the first month the blood of a purification bull is to be applied to the doorposts of the temple building, the four corners of the altar's ledge (see at 4:25), and the doorposts of the (eastern, 46:1–5) gate (45:18–19). (For a comparison with P's purgation rites for the Tabernacle, see the NOTE to 16:19.)

The same purificatory ritual is enjoined "on the seventh day of the month [of the pollution caused] *mēʾîš šōgeh ûmippetî* by an inadvertent or ignorant person" (v 20). To be sure, the LXX reads the date as "in the seventh month, on the first of the month," implying that the second purgation of the temple is to fall six months later, a reading accepted by nearly every commentator since Wellhausen. Favoring the MT, however, is the added remark that the pollution has been caused by the inadvertent and ignorant. Inadvertence (for the verbal form *šāgâ* see the NOTE on 4:13) is familiar to us as an indispensable requirement of the purification offering (see at 4:2). But what does ignorance connote? Ezekiel is drawing a finer distinction. Accidental wrong can result from two causes: negligence or ignorance. Either the offender knows the law but violates it unintentionally or he acts intentionally but does not know that he has done wrong (Milgrom 1967). For Ezekiel, the *šōgeh* is characterized by lack of intention; the *petî*, by lack of knowledge. The former underlies the cases of involuntary homicide (Num 35:16–18, 22–23); the latter is presupposed in nonritual texts (e.g., 1 Sam 26:21; Prov 5:23; cf. Ps 19:15; Job 6:24; 19:4 [Milgrom 1967]).

It is assumed that after the temple is purged on the first of the month, all of Israel will make a concerted effort to avoid ritual impurity during the following two weeks so that the Passover will be observed in purity. One need but recall that P enjoins the safeguarding of the paschal sacrifice for four days (Exod 12:3–6). Indeed, the period leading up to the Passover is characterized by the ritual purification—the removal of leaven—from the home (Exod 12:15, 19–20; 13:7). Ezekiel also demands the simultaneous purification of the temple. He therefore institutes two temple purgation days, the second one on the seventh of the month for those who, despite their precautions, inadvertently or unwittingly contracted a temple-polluting impurity. Thus the LXX makes no sense whatever in scheduling the second temple purgation six months later. If the prophet really intended a semiannual cleansing of the temple, why would the second one be limited to cases of accidental pollution? P's annual Day of Purgation, as will be explained (NOTES on 16:16, 21), is expressly devised for Israel's presumptuous sins. By the same token, it must be assumed that Ezekiel's temple purgation on the first of the month effects a similar purpose: all impurity, caused by presumptuous and accidental acts, is cleansed. On the seventh, purgation is repeated lest pollution has recurred through inadvertence or ignorance. And, finally, on the fourteenth, before Israel offers its paschal sacrifices, a third purgation takes place, but this time on the altar alone, of the lesser impurities (above) that may have occurred during the preceding week. Thus Ezekiel prescribes, in all, three purgation bulls seven days apart, as the means of providing a ritually pure temple for the celebration of the Passover.

The *ḥaṭṭāʾt* prescribed for Ezekiel's priest occurs in the following passage: *wĕʾaḥărê ṭohŏrātô šibʿat yāmîm yispĕrû-lô ûbĕyôm bōʾô ʾel-haqqōdeš ʾel-heḥāṣēr happĕnîmît lĕšārēt baqqōdeš yaqrîb ḥaṭṭāʾtô nĕʾum ʾădōnāy YHWH* 'After his purification (from corpse contamination), seven days shall be counted off for him; and on the day he reenters the inner court of the Sanctuary to officiate in the Sanctuary, he shall present his purification offering—declares the Lord God' (Ezek 44:26–27).

Ezekiel's variance from our Priestly texts is striking. Whereas P (and H) makes no distinction between priests and laity regarding purification from corpse contamination—both require the ashes of the Red Cow and ablutions (Num 19 and see COMMENT G above)—Ezekiel extends the purification period an additional week, capped by a purification offering. Because this sacrifice is prescribed for severe cases of impurity such as the parturient (12:6, 8), the měṣōrāʿ (14:19, 31), and the zāb/zābâ (15:15, 30), Ezekiel obviously regards the impurity generated by the corpse to be greater for the priest than for the lay person. This is not surprising. In Ezekiel's system, the priest is subject to severer regulations: his marriage rules resemble those of the high priest (cf. Ezek 44:22 with Lev 21:14), and his priestly clothing is contagious not only to objects but to persons (Ezek 44:19; cf. chap. 7, COMMENT B).

Moreover, his stand is logical: if a Nazirite whose sanctity is temporary is required to bring a purification offering for corpse contamination, all the more so a priest whose sanctity is lifelong. In fact, the logic of Ezekiel's ruling leads one to suspect that he speaks for the older tradition, and that it was P or H that modified it. Indeed, the change is more likely the work of H, which, in opposition to P, enjoins holiness upon all Israel (1:2) and, without denying the intrinsic sanctity of the priest (21:8), does not hesitate to declare that the Lord sanctifies (měqaddēš) the people equally (20:8; 21:8, 15, 23; 22:9, 32; cf. the discussion in the Introduction, § E).

If, then, the equivalence of priests and laity was desired in this matter, why was the priest made to conform to the laity rather than the reverse: why not a purification offering for both? The answer may rest in the polemic generated by Israel's long struggle with ancestral worship (see the NOTES to 19:26–28, 31; 20:1–6): the fear that sacrifices *because* of the dead might turn into sacrifices *to* the dead (see COMMENT G above).

The text is silent concerning the animal required for the ḥaṭṭāʾt. On the analogy of the Nazirite (Num 6:10–11) we may assume that it was a bird (see further the chart and discussion in chap. 15, COMMENT F). The remaining references in Ezekiel to the purification offering (Ezek 40:39; 44:29; 46:20) throw no new light on the sacrifice.

M. The Remaining Instances

Outside of P and Ezekiel, the purification offering is mentioned in the following passages: Ezra 8:35; 2 Chr 29:21–24; Hos 4:8; 2 Kgs 12:17; Ps 40:7; and Jer 17:1. The first two refer to special occasions in the public cult. According to Ezra 8:35, the returnees from exile offer up twelve he-goats, clearly on behalf of Israel's twelve tribes (the other sacrificial animals are also multiples of twelve, if we adopt the reading "seventy-two" with 1 Esdr 7:63 [LXXA] instead of MT 77). Yet the text reads *hakkōl ʿōlâ laYHWH* 'all (the sacrifices) a burnt offering to the Lord" (Ezra 8:35b). The alternative to the blatant contradiction that the purification offering was offered up as a burnt offering is to postulate that in this case, possibly because of the severity of Israel's sins, the priests refrained from eating the sacrificial meat and, instead, consigned it to the altar *as if* it were a burnt offering. That is, the blood of the twelve he-goats was daubed on the altar's horns in conformity with the purification-offering requirements, but the priests relinquished their rights to the meat, and thus the entire animal was burned on the altar like a burnt offering (*b. Tem.* 15b).

At the dedication services of the purified Temple, King Hezekiah and the officials of Jerusalem "brought seven bulls and seven rams and seven lambs and seven he-goats as a purification offering for the royal house (Moran 1962) and for the sanctuary and for Judah" (2 Chr 29:21a). Subsequently, we are told, the king and the congregation performed the hand-leaning ceremony upon the he-goats "to expiate for all Israel, for the king had designated the burnt offering and the purification offering to be for all Israel" (v 24). Hezekiah had changed his mind concerning the beneficiaries of the sacrifice from the royal house, the sanctuary, and the people of Judah to "all Israel," a change that is underscored by "the congregation," which performs the hand-leaning rite.

Hezekiah's change of mind begs for investigation, but before we can determine the reason for it we must solve this verse's numerical conundrum. Two questions need to be answered: (1) How could each of the three original beneficiaries of the sacrifices be assigned the same number of animals—in other words, how can seven be divided by three? (2) How can, in Hezekiah's new calculation, such an incongruous number as twenty-one burnt offerings and seven purification offerings, a total of twenty-eight animals, stand for "all Israel"?

I submit that this twofold arithmetic problem can be solved by one presupposition: the four groups of seven animals were originally intended for *each* of the beneficiaries. That is to say, seven bulls, seven rams, seven lambs, and seven he-goats were to be offered up *three times*—first for the royal house, second for the sanctuary, and a third time for the people of Judah. Thus each beneficiary would have been assigned the same number of animals and sacrifices, and the total number of animals was therefore $3(7 + 7 + 7 + 7) = 84$. The solution to the second question is now obvious: $84 = 12 \times 7$. Twelve, of course, is symbolic of Israel's twelve tribes, and seven is the number of perfection, attested frequently in Scripture, especially in sacrificial rituals. To be sure, this configuration does not allow each tribe to be the recipient of the same animals. But this was not Hezekiah's intention. The dedication offerings are designated not for the tribes but for "all Israel," and the number eighty-four stands for the entire Israelite population irrespective of its tribal affiliation.

This proposed solution also unveils the motive behind Hezekiah's change of mind. He was not content to offer sacrifices on behalf of the inhabitants of his own kingdom of Judah. The rededicated Temple would henceforth serve "all

Israel" and embrace the inhabitants of northern Israel as well. Northern Israel had ceased to exist as a political entity, its territory absorbed into the Assyrian Empire. Hezekiah's ambition for Israel's political reunification might have to be suppressed, but it could be sublimated in the cultic realm, by making the Temple the central sanctuary for the entire people. Textual evidence of Hezekiah's cultic aspiration is contained in the following account of the first festival to be celebrated in the renovated Temple—the Passover or, more correctly, the delayed Passover (2 Chr 30:2–3; cf. Num 9:1–14). Messengers are dispatched to the inhabitants of northern Israel inviting them to join in the celebration of the Passover (v 1); in some tribal areas they are not received very kindly (v 10), but many do come (vv 11, 18 [Milgrom 1970e]).

Thus the text is justified in stating that "the Israelites present in Jerusalem celebrated the festival of unleavened bread for seven days with great joy" (v 21a). But this statement is pregnant with even more significant information. It is alluding to the masses of northern Israelites who settled in Jerusalem following the Assyrian invasions that razed their capital and put an end to their state.

What the text affirms, archaeology confirms. N. Avigad (1970, 1972; Geva 1979) has excavated in the Jewish Quarter of the old city a 130-foot stretch of a city wall, twenty-three feet thick, which dates to the end of the eighth century during the reign of Hezekiah (or, at the latest, in the reign of Mannasseh). Avigad's wall and his subsequent Iron Age finds (1975, 1977) make it certain that the city of Jerusalem about 700 B.C.E. had suddenly tripled or quadrupled in area compared to earlier times. According to one estimate (Broshi 1974), the 44 dunams of David's city and the 130–180 dunams of the eighth-century city had become the 500–600 dunams of the seventh-century city. Only one factor could cause a rapid territorial expansion of such magnitude: a population explosion. Although the subsequent ravaging of the Judean countryside by Sennacherib (701 B.C.E.) played a role, the major contributory factor must have been the successive waves of refugees who poured into Jerusalem from northern Israel after its fall in 721 B.C.E.

It was, then, the tide of northern Israelites who flooded Jerusalem, not as pilgrims but as permanent residents, that prompted Hezekiah to change the designees of his sacrifices for the Temple's rededication service from Judah to "all Israel" (for details, see Milgrom 1985e).

"They (the priests) feed on the ḥaṭṭāʾt of my people, so they desire its iniquity" (Hos 4:8). Scholars argue to this very day whether the rendering should be "sin" (Wolff 1974) or "purification offering" (Andersen and Freedman 1980). The former is supported by the coupling of ḥaṭṭāʾt and ʿāwōn elsewhere in Hosea (8:13; 9:9; 13:2), where the rendering can only be "sin." Even so, the expression ʾākal ḥaṭṭāʾt 'feed on sin' is an incongruous metaphor unless it means that the priests profit by the sacrifices brought by the people because of their sins. If this is so, the reference may well be the purification offerings brought, as demonstrated, for a whole range of sins, both ritual and moral, whose meat is assigned exclusively to the priests (6:19, 22). Furthermore, *wĕ'el 'ăwōnām yiśĕ'û napšô* 'so they desire its (the people's) iniquity' may be an ironic play of words on the duty of the priesthood *lāśē't 'et-'awōn hā'ēdâ* 'to bear the responsibility for the community' (10:17); in other words, instead of removing the people's sin they are promoting it. Of course, this interpretation would also suggest that the purification offering was a widely practiced sacrifice in northern Israel during the eighth century. Indeed, non-Priestly and, hence, more impartial evidence points to its practice in the Jerusalem Temple at an even earlier age, as follows.

In 2 Kgs 12:5–17 (Hebrew; the English is vv 4–16) there is an account of temple repairs in the twenty-third year of the reign of Joash (ca. 816 B.C.E.). This account is not from the temple's annals because it contains a stinging rebuke of the priests' negligence and dishonesty. Rather, it must be an excerpt from "the Annals of the Kings of Judah" (v 20). It tells parenthetically—and, hence, dispassionately—that by the order of the king the silver donated by the people went for temple repairs; however, "silver brought as a reparation offering or a purification offering was not deposited in the House of the Lord; it went to the priests" (v 17). The retention of these two offerings by the priests is totally in keeping with the Priestly legislation, which prescribes their meat as priestly perquisites (6:19; 7:7). This verse, however, speaks not of animals but of silver! For the reparation offering this is no problem; it is commutable in silver. Indeed, it is the latter that, in most cases, the text actually demands (see on 5:15). By contrast, nowhere is the purification offering commuted into silver. In some cases, permission is given on economic grounds to bring a cheaper animal (5:1–13; 14:21–23), and in one instance even a cereal offering is allowed (5:11–13); but silver is never sanctioned. There is yet another problem: if all of the silver went to the priests, what was left for God, that is to say, the Temple treasury? Does this then mean that the Temple practice of Joash's days is in conflict with the Priestly legislation? If so, it would imply that P, presumably reflecting the official Temple cult, must be later than the ninth century and that, conversely, the commutable purification offering represents an earlier stage in the development of this sacrifice. Neither conclusion is necessary, however. The text in Kings may merely be stating that the silver brought to the Temple for the purification and reparation offerings was retained by the priests in order to purchase the prescribed sacrificial animals and was not diverted to the fund for Temple repairs. Implied, therefore, is that the Temple complex contained a stockyard whose animals were available not only for the fixed daily and festal cult but for purchase by the laity for its private sacrifices. Such certainly is the implication of the commutable reparation offering: an individual would bring the equivalent in silver shekels, and the priests would provide the required animal (5:15). Moreover, the draft oxen donated by the tribal chieftains surely needed pasture and care, including both land and herdsmen (Num 7:6). Furthermore, P contains an entire chapter that speaks of the dedication of lands and animals to the sanctuary (chap. 27 [Milgrom 1976f. 51]). Deuteronomy explicitly allows the tithes and firstlings to be commuted into currency so that the far-off Israelite farmer could travel to the central sanctuary where he would commute them once more into oblations and libations (Deut 14:24–26). Finally, it can be shown that Babylonian sanctuaries of the sixth century controlled large landed estates abounding in crops and animals (Milgrom 1976f: 58–60). Thus the assumption that the Jerusalem Temple kept its own livestock is fully warranted. Of course, it is also possible that lay merchants rather than Temple clergy supplied the sacrificial animals. This seems to be the case at the end of the Second Temple period (m. Šeqal. 7:2). But even then we read of Temple officials who provided from Temple stores the libations, cereal offerings, and birds for the sacrifices of individuals (m. Šeqal. 5:1–5; cf. Matt 21:12). But it is hard to believe that the earlier Temple did not also breed its own livestock, particularly in view of the incessant sacrificial demands of the public cult (see Num 28–29). Thus this pregnant verse in 2 Kings affirms that the people of Judah in the late ninth century came to the Temple to purchase purification and reparation offerings to make expiation for their sins.

The purification offering also occurs in Ps 40:7 (under the variant name ḥăṭā'â) together with the well-being *(zebaḥ)*, cereal, and burnt offerings, but imparting no other information. Finally, Jeremiah plays on the dual meaning of ḥaṭṭā't as "sin" and "purification offering" in a telling way: "The ḥaṭṭā't of Judah is engraved . . . on the horns of their altars" (Jer 17:1). Judahites want to believe that their "purification offering," namely, its blood, is daubed on the altar, thereby effecting their expiation; but in truth, the prophet tells us, it is their "sin" condemning them before God.

N. The Provenience

It has already been suggested that the purification offering is an offshoot of the ʿōlâ and, hence, a late development in the history of Israelite sacrifices (COMMENT to chap. 1). Conversely, some of the texts adduced above make it clear that its origins are preexilic. Ezekiel takes the purification (and reparation) offering for granted (Ezek 40:39; 46:20). According to the Chronicler, Hezekiah (eighth century) switched the beneficiaries of the purification offering in the course of the Temple rededication (2 Chr 29:20–24). If the reference in Hos 4:8 is to the purification offering, it is also attested in eighth-century northern Israel. The attribution of a joyous purpose to the ʿōlâ in H (22:17–19; Num 15:3), in contrast to the exclusively expiatory function it manifests in P (1:4; 9:7; 14:20; 16:24) may indicate the period (before the eighth century) in which the ḥaṭṭā't usurped the expiatory role of the ʿōlâ (see the Introduction, § C). On much more solid ground is the annalistic reference to the purification offering in the Temple during the reign of Joash (ninth century; 2 Kgs 12:17).

The place and date of the *ḥaṭṭāʾt*'s origin may be moot, but it is probably the innovation of a temple and not of an open, countryside altar *(bāmâ)*. For this sacrifice predicates not just an altar but a building, a complex of sancta inside a shrine—in other words, a house or residence for the deity, which must be kept spotless if his presence is to be assured. As indicated above, this is precisely the view that was current in Israel's environment. And if Israel took its cue from the purificatory rites practiced in pagan temples, it is most likely that we owe its introduction into Israel to some Israelite temple. Another possible indication that the purification offering found its original setting in a temple is the fact that all of its meat is a priestly perquisite, which implies a fixed, permanent clergy, again a characteristic of a temple.

Regardless of when or where it took root in Israel, the purification offering was quickly modified to conform to the postulates undergirding Israel's sacrificial system. Man had replaced the demon as the sole threat to God's earthly presence. Hence, the sanctuary needed to be purged incessantly of its accumulation of man's moral and ritual pollution. But the ultimate teaching of this sacrifice is clear: the only effective way to eliminate or, at least, minimize the danger to the sanctuary is to purge its source—man himself.

O. The Function of the ḥaṭṭāʾt (and ʿōlâ): A New Proposal

A. Marx's new perspective on the *ḥaṭṭāʾt* and *ʿōlâ* (1989) appeared when my Leviticus manuscript was already in the hands of the publisher. A full discussion, therefore, which it richly merits, can no longer be undertaken on these pages. For the time being, let the main points of his thesis and some initial reaction suffice. I begin with Marx's own summary:

> The study of the different circumstances in which the *ḥaṭṭāʾt* appears and of its rôle in these contexts has brought to light a true system of rites de passage for the community, the function of which is to reintegrate the "sinner" and the unclean, to operate the transfer from the secular state to the sacred (or, in the case of the Nazirite, from the sacred state to the secular), to guarantee the regular alternation of times and seasons and, at the turn of the year, to regenerate the territory. The hub of the system is to be found in the *ḥaṭṭāʾt* and the holocaust, the former sacrifice being designed to operate the separation with the previous state, and the latter working the reintegration of the "sinner" and the unclean, or the aggregation to a new, or renewed, state. In the light of this function of the *ḥaṭṭāʾt*, it is suggested that the current translations of this term should be replaced by "sacrifice of separation". (p. 27)

The immediate advantage of Marx's proposal is that it satisfactorily resolves the enigma of the *ḥaṭṭāʾt* requirement for the Nazirite who has successfully completed his or her vow (Num. 6:14). I have also labeled it a rite of desanctification. But whereas I regard it as an anomaly, Marx declares it to be an archetypical example of the *ḥaṭṭā't* functioning in a rite of passage. Still, one is left to wonder why a *ḥaṭṭā't* was not also imposed upon the Nazirite when entering his or her holy status, as exemplified by the case of the newly consecrated priest (chap. 8). Thus, before jumping to the conclusion, with Marx, that the Nazirite is paradigmatic of all other *ḥaṭṭā't* cases, the patent weaknesses in his system need to be indicated.

The absence of philological justification is immediately apparent. If the main verbs employed with the *ḥaṭṭā't*—*kipper* and *ṭiḥēr* (and denominative *ḥiṭṭē'*)—mean, respectively and almost synonymously, "purge" and "purify" (COMMENT A; cf. chap. 16, COMMENT F), then the *ḥaṭṭā't* has to be more than an indication of a process; it *is* a process. And if it purges and purifies, a prior condition of impurity must be presupposed in all *ḥaṭṭā't* contexts, including wrongdoing, consecration, and festival observances. The notion of separation, however, can under no circumstances be supported philologically.

For evidence that the *ḥaṭṭā't* can signify consecration, the cases of the Levites, the priests, and the altar are cited. All three are found wanting. The objective of the Levites' induction is *lĕṭahărām* 'to purify them' (Num 8:6, 21); their prior impurity is therefore taken for granted. Moreover, the text states explicitly that *ḥaṭṭā't* waters are sprinkled on the Levites *lĕṭahărām* 'to purify them' (v 7). Evidently, then, the *ḥaṭṭā't* purifies, and the conclusion is therefore irrefutable that the *ḥaṭṭā't* blood daubed on the altar (v 8) *lekappēr ʿal-halĕwiyim* (v 12) purges the altar on the Levites' behalf.

The consecration of the priests and the altar (chap. 8) is not effected by the *ḥaṭṭā't* but by the anointment oil (Exod 29:36; 40:13; Lev 8:11, 12, 15, 30; see the NOTES on 8:11 and 12). To be sure, the priestly consecration is a rite of passage (see chap. 8, COMMENT G). But is the *ḥaṭṭā't* nothing more than an indication of a status change from profane to sacred? The fact that the *ḥaṭṭā't* is the first in the sacrificial series belies this assumption: the sanctuary altar must first be purified before it can effect expiation. More decisively, the text explicitly states that *wĕḥiṭṭē'tā ʿal-hammizbēaḥ bĕkapperĕkā ʿālāyw* 'You shall cleanse the altar (with the *ḥaṭṭā't)* by performing purgation upon it' (Exod 29:36). Thus the function of the *ḥaṭṭā't* is to remove impurity and has nothing to do with separation or with a rite of passage.

If the *ḥaṭṭā't* indeed were the element that separated the sinner from his sins and the impure person from his impurity, we should expect, following the model of the two other clearly attested rites of passage in Scripture—the *'āšām* blood daubed on the extremities of the healed *mĕṣōrāʿ* (14:14, 25) and the *millū'îm* blood on the same extremities of the consecrated priests (8:24)—that the *ḥaṭṭā't* blood would be placed directly on the offerer himself. That it is daubed on the altar can only mean that it operates solely on the altar—purging it, as has been demonstrated, on the offerer's behalf.

THE SACRIFICES

Because Marx maintains that the ḥaṭṭā't and 'ōlâ, in tandem, comprise a rite of passage, the former (using van Gennep's terminology, 1960 passim) an act of separation and the latter an act of aggregation (i.e., reintegration), he is hard pressed to account for the absence of the 'ōlâ in cases of wrongdoing (chaps. 4, 5, 6; Num 15:27–28). He is therefore forced to assume that in these cases the suet of the ḥaṭṭā't assumes the 'ōlâ function: it produces a rēaḥ nîḥōaḥ laYHWH 'a pleasing aroma to the Lord' (4:13), indicating that the offerer is now reconciled with his God. Not so. In each ḥaṭṭā't case, reconciliation (wěnislaḥ lô) is effected by the kipper action of the ḥaṭṭā't blood (e.g., 4:6–7, 17–18, 20, 25–26, 30–31, 34–35). In other words, it is the purgative action of the ḥaṭṭā't that effects reconciliation (Marx's reintegration), and there is no need for an 'ōlâ or a pseudo-'ōlâ in the form of the ḥaṭṭā't suet. Besides, 4:31 is the only instance of the ḥaṭṭā't producing a rēaḥ nîḥōaḥ (see the NOTE), an indication that the Lord does not derive much pleasure from this sacrifice. This conclusion is further warranted by the total absence of the term 'iššeh 'food gift' from the ḥaṭṭā't pericopes. If indeed this sacrifice celebrates the separation of the sinner from his sin and the impure person from his impurity, why should the Lord not be "pleased" with this sacrificial "gift"?

Marx claims further: "the fact that the wrongdoer who, in case of indigence, offers two doves, one as a ḥaṭṭā't and the other as an 'ōlâ, tends to suggest that the duality of this sacrifice is essential" (1989: 43). Not so. Indigence is a factor only in the marginal cases of 5:1–4 (and of the parturient and the měṣōrā') but not in the usual occurrences of the ḥaṭṭā't (see the COMMENT to 5:1–13). And as for the 'ōlâ bird, not only is it unessential to the rite but its presence is purely secondary, resulting from the need of additional substance for the altar (see the NOTE on 5:7).

Nonetheless, Marx's demonstration that the 'ōlâ is integrally connected with the ḥaṭṭā't and that together they form a coherent system deserves serious consideration. Furthermore, he correctly points to the quantity and value of the sacrificial animals as an index of the relative importance of each sacrifice. Thus, in rituals of purification and sanctification (or desanctification), the ḥaṭṭā't is clearly dominant because the 'ōlâ is limited to a single animal, whereas in the public cult (except on Yom Kippur) the 'ōlâ is dominant because it consists of numerous animals and is accompanied by cereal offerings and libations.

In truth, Marx's classification of the 'ōlâ as an aggregation or reintegration is practically identical with the one that I have proposed: the 'ōlâ integrates the offering with his God and community (chap. 7, COMMENT I). Where we differ is in regard to the ḥaṭṭā't. For Marx, the public ḥaṭṭā't signals the main transitions in the calendar year: the new moon, the equinoxes (1/15 and 7/15), the sacral poles (festivals of months 1 and 7), and the agricultural seasons (beginning and end of the grain harvest and the end of the agricultural year: maṣṣôt, šābūôt, and sukkôt). This scheme neatly accounts for the absence of the ḥaṭṭā't in the daily tāmîd and Sabbath rites, for these days are independent of the calendar.

I find this scheme artificial and forced, however. The *ḥaṭṭā't* is needed in these festival days because presumably the sanctuary is crowded with pilgrims and the consequent pollution of the altar is inevitable. The absence of the *ḥaṭṭā't* among the daily and Sabbath sacrifices, by contrast, is due not only to the relative paucity of laity on the sacred premises but to the principle derived from the Yom Kippur rites of chap. 16: as the entire sanctuary is purged of its accumulated impurities only once a year (though originally in emergency situations, see chap. 16, COMMENT A), the purgation of the most vulnerable of the sancta, the altar (COMMENT C above), need not be performed with the *ḥaṭṭā't* on a daily or weekly basis but once a month and more frequently when festivals occur.

I would also take issue with Marx over his contention that in the public cult the blood rite of the *'ōlâ* precedes the *ḥaṭṭā't* on the altar. First, the term *hiqrîb* in P usually means "offer, present" and less frequently "sacrifice" (see Num 7, where all of the offerings are gifts to the sanctuary treasury [Milgrom 1990a: Excursus 14] and see the NOTE on 1:2). To be sure, the verb *'āśâ* indicates the performance of the prescribed rite (see the NOTES on 9:6, 7), but in the festival calendar of Num 28–29, it occurs only in one *ḥaṭṭā't* case (28:15, in the passive *niph'al*). The other texts adduced by Marx are either attributable to H (23:18–19; Num 15:22–26) or influenced by H (Ezek 45:23–24), in which P terms repeatedly lose their precision (Introduction, § D). Thus the rabbinic rule that in a sacrificial series the *ḥaṭṭā't* blood always precedes that of the *'ōlâ* (m. *Zebaḥ.* 10:2; t. *Para* 1:1) must be upheld (see further chap. 7, COMMENT I). Admittedly, 2 Chr 29:21–24 is an exception. But because it deviates from P's norms in many other respects (e.g., the number and functions of both the animals and the officiant; see COMMENT M above), it cannot be used as a model for P's cultic system.

THE GRADUATED PURIFICATION OFFERING (5:1–13)

The Four Cases

5 ¹If a person does wrong:
When he has heard a public imprecation (against withholding testimony)—and although he was a witness, either having seen or known (the facts)—yet does not testify, then he must bear his punishment;
²Or when a person touches any impure thing—be it the carcass of an impure wild quadruped or the carcass of an impure domesticated quadruped or the carcass of an impure swarming creature—and, though he has become impure, the fact escapes him but (thereafter) he feels guilt;
³Or when he touches human impurity—any such impurity whereby one

becomes impure—and, though he has known it, the fact escapes him but (there-after) he feels guilt;

⁴Or when a person blurts out an oath to bad or good purpose—whatever anyone may utter in an oath—and, though he has known it, the fact escapes him but (thereafter) he feels guilt in any of these matters——

Resolution: Confession and Sacrifice

⁵When he feels guilt in any of these matters, he shall confess that wherein he did wrong. ⁶And he shall bring as his reparation to the Lord, for the wrong that he committed, a female from the flock, sheep or goat, as a purification offering; and the priest shall effect purgation on his behalf for his wrong.

⁷But if his means do not suffice for a sheep, he shall bring to the Lord as his reparation for what he has done wrong, two turtledoves or two pigeons, one for a purification offering and the other for a burnt offering. ⁸He shall bring them to the priest who shall offer first the one for the purification offering, pinching the head at its nape without severing it. ⁹He shall sprinkle some of the blood of the purification offering on the side of the altar, and what remains of the blood shall be drained at the base of the altar; it is a purification offering. ¹⁰And the second he shall sacrifice as a burnt offering, according to regulation. Thus the priest shall effect purgation on his behalf for the wrong that he committed so that he may be forgiven.

¹¹And if his means do not suffice for two turtledoves or two pigeons, he shall bring as his offering for what he has done wrong a tenth of an *ephah* of semolina for a purification offering; he shall not put oil upon it or place frankin-cense on it, for it is a purification offering. ¹²He shall bring it to the priest, and the priest shall scoop out a handful as a token portion of it and turn it into smoke on the altar, with the Lord's food gifts; it is a purification offering. ¹³Thus the priest shall effect purgation on his behalf for the wrong he commit-ted in any of these matters so that he may be forgiven. It shall belong to the priest, like the cereal offering.

NOTES

5:1. *When he has heard.* wĕšāmĕʿâ, but not when he "took [an oath]," that is to say, he was not adjured. For the significance of this fact, see the COMMENT.

public. qôl, lit., "voice"; for example, *(wayyaʿ ăbîrû) qôl*, '(had the) procla-mation (made)' (Exod 36:6 [Orlinsky 1969]); cf. Ezra 1:1 (= 2 Chr 36:22); 10:7; Neh 8:15; 2 Chr 24:9; 30:5. Notices of public proclamations are mandated in ancient Near Eastern legal documents in order to advertise or elicit informa-tion in regard to the status of property or the commission of crimes (Brichto 1963: 42–44). For example: *tuppi ina arki šudūti ina bab abullim ša Nuzi šaṭir* 'the tablet (describing a property transaction) was inscribed after proclamation in the city gate of Nuzi' (*CAD abullu* 1b, p. 84); there is a public proclamation (*šišit nagirim*, lit., "call of the herald") to elicit information concerning a fugitive slave (CH 16:45). Among the Arabs, the victim of stolen goods has a right to call out at any gathering, market or festival, "I adjure in the name of Allah each and every man who knows it that he tells it" (Wellhausen 1897: 192 n. 1). One should not assume, however, as do the rabbis (*m. Šebu.* 4:3), that the proclamation was issued in the court and that the witnesses were both present and adjured by responding "amen" (see the COMMENT below).

imprecation (ʾālâ). The proclamation is enforced by a contingent curse. Take, for example, the case of the suspected adulteress: "May the Lord make you a curse and imprecation among your people, as the Lord causes your thigh to sag and your belly to distend" (Num 5:21; cf. also *m. Šebu.* 4:13; *t. Šebu.* 2:15). The midrash also records a good example: "Reuben stole from Simeon, and Levi knew of it. Said Reuben to Levi: 'Do not show me up, and I will give you half.' The following day people enter the synagogue, and hear the overseer announce: 'Who has stolen from Simeon?' and Levi is present there" (*Midr. Lev. Rab.* 6:2). Other imprecations are attested in Scripture, though the curse formula is not cited. Thus Micah is induced by his mother's imprecation to confess that he had stolen her silver (Judg 17:1–5). A striking parallel to this case is cited in Proverbs: "He who shares with a thief (note the midrash, cited above) is his own enemy; (*ʾālâ yišmaʿ wĕlōʾ yaggîd*) he hears the imprecation and does not testify" (Prov 29:24). In Mesopotamia, the exorcist (*āšipu*) is called in to adjure a recalcitrant witness with an imprecation (MAL, A, 47; Driver and Miles 1935: 124). The pre-Islamic Arabs were wont to adjure witnesses by laying a curse on them (Wellhausen 1897: 192; cf. Canaan 1935: 240).

Some of the versions interpret *ʾālâ* as "a blasphemous oath" (*Tg. Neof.;* cf. the LXX), thus denying that there was an imprecatory proclamation at all. Rather, the witness had failed to report a blasphemous oath that he had heard. So also *Tg. Ps.-J.*, which adds, "sees that someone has violated the words of an oath, or knows that his companion has sworn or imprecated falsely" (cf. also Philo, *Laws* 2. 26). But the cases of a lying oath and blasphemy are taken up elsewhere (vv 21–26 and 24:10–23).

yet does not testify (wĕlōʾ yaggîd). Why not? There are any number of reasons, such as (a) complicity (Prov 29:24 and *Midr. Lev. Rab.* 6:2, cited above); (b) "influenced by friendship or shame or fear" (Philo, 2 *Laws* 26–28); (c) indifference: "Why should we bother with this mess?" (*m. Sanh.* 4:5). Indeed, the wisdom teachings of the ancient Near East are unanimous in actually advising witnesses *not* to testify: "Do not frequent a law court, / Do not loiter where there is a dispute, / For in the dispute they will have you as a *testifier*, / Then you will be made their witness. / And they will bring you to a law suit not your own to affirm. / When confronted with a dispute, go your own way; pay no attention to it" (Lambert 1960: 101, lines 31–36). The same motivation lies behind the advice of the Arabic *Ahiqar*: "And stand not betwixt persons quarreling . . . thou wilt be forced to bear witness; but run from thence and rest thyself: (Conybeare et al. 1913: 137, line 54). Meander the Egyptian records a similar passage: "If there is a quarrel in a street. . . . If you stand there and watch, you will be required to give witness before the court" (Audet 1952: 65, line 20). Implicit in all of these counsels is that the witness stand should be avoided even after hearing a public imprecation! With this widespread sapiential background, it is no wonder that the Priestly legislator feels it necessary to warn the reluctant witness that the imprecation is bound to take effect.

The witness's defiance of the imprecation is indisputably a deliberate, if not a brazen, misdemeanor. Ibn Ezra would add the element of a memory lapse, which plays a role in the following cases (vv 2–4), but its absence here is hardly accidental. Then, why is his sin expiable by sacrifice? The answer lies in his subsequent remorse, a factor that is not stated in the case itself but in the general protasis governing all four cases (vv 4b, 5a); it is his subsequent guilt feeling (ʾāšēm) that is responsible for converting his deliberate sin into an inadvertence, expiable by sacrifice. This principle is discussed in the COMMENT and, especially, in the analysis of the ʾāšām sacrifice (COMMENT F, vv 14–26). If so, why does not the offender bring an ʾāšām instead of the ḥaṭṭāʾt prescribed by the text (v 6)? The answer lies in the nature of the case. The ʾāšām, the reparation offering, is brought only when there is desecration. False oaths, the subject of the ʾāšām of vv 14–26, are a desecration of God's name (see 19:12). The reluctant witness of this case, however, is not guilty of perjury; his misdemeanor is that he did not respond to the oath imprecation, in that he did not testify. In this respect his case is similar to the fourth and last one in this series, wherein the misdemeanor is the nonfulfillment of an oath (v 4). In both cases, the offenders are not guilty of desecration and, hence, not liable for an ʾāšām, a reparation offering.

then he must bear his punishment. The expression wĕnāśāʾ ʿăwōnô always implies that the punishment will be meted out by God, not by man (*Tg. Ps.-J.; m. Sanh.* 4:5; *t. Šebu.* 3:1, 4; Philo, *Laws* 2. 26 [Zimmerli 1954]). "R. Joshua said: There are four acts for which the offender is exempt from the judgments of man but liable to the judgments of heaven . . . and to know evidence in favor of another and not to testify on his behalf" (*b. B. Qam.* 55b [bar.]; cf. *t. Šebu.* 3:2–4). ʿăwōn here bears its consequential meaning (e.g., Gen 4:13; Isa 53:11; cf. 1 Sam 25:24; 28:10; 2 Sam 14:9; 2 Kgs 7:9), namely, not "sin" but its consequence, "punishment" (Milgrom 1976t: 3–12; cf. 5:14–16, COMMENT A). The connotation of "forgive" for nāśāʾ ʿăwōn/ḥēṭʾ found in other sources (e.g., Gen 18:24; 50:17; Exod 23:21; 1 Sam 25:28) is never attested in P. Most moderns equate this phrase with wĕʾāšēm, which ends the subsequent verses (e.g., Hoffman 1953; Noth 1965; Rodriquez 1979: 90). Indeed, they were anticipated long ago by the sectaries of Qumran: "And everything that is lost without it being known who stole it from the property of the camp in which it has been stolen, let its owner charge with an imprecatory oath, and any one who hears (it), if he knows and does not tell *(wĕlō' yaggîd)*, is guilty *(wĕ'āšēm)"* (CD 9.10–12). This interpretation founders, however, on the assumption that *wĕ'āšēm* begins the apodosis and means "is guilty" (see at v 2 and esp. COMMENT A, vv 14–26). Indeed, this case (v 1) is not to be equated with any of the following cases (vv 2–4) in any of its particulars. As shown in the COMMENT, both its structure and its content differ from the verses that follow. Rather, it turns out to be an independent law that may have been part of another legal code, which the Priestly legislator incorporated into his pericope on the graduated purification offering.

This case, as it stands, without confusing it with the subsequent cases, simply and clearly states that the witness who defies the imprecation will be subject to its consequences.

It is of more than passing interest to note that in rabbinic times witnesses were not adjured but admonished, as follows:

Perhaps you will say what is but supposition or hearsay or at secondhand, or (you will say to yourselves) we heard it from a man who was trustworthy. Or perhaps you do not know that we shall prove you by examination and inquiry? Know you, moreover, that capital cases are not as noncapital cases: in noncapital cases a man may pay money and so make atonement, but in capital cases the witness is answerable for the blood of him (who is wrongfully condemned) and the blood of his posterity (who should have been born to him) to the end of the world. For so we have found it with Cain who slew his brother, for it is written, "the bloods of your brother cry" (Gen 4:10). It says not, "the blood of your brother," but "the bloods of your brother"—his blood and the blood of his posterity.

Therefore but a single man was created in the world, to teach that if any man has caused a single soul to perish Scripture imputes it to him as though he had caused a whole world to perish; and if any man saves alive a single soul Scripture imputes to him as though he has saved a whole world. . . . And if you should say: "Why should we bother with this mess?"—has it not been written "Although he was a witness, either having seen or known, yet does not testify, he must bear his punishment" (5:1)? And if you shall say: "Why should we be guilty of (taking) the blood of this man?"—has it not been written, "When the wicked perish there is rejoicing" (Prov 11:10)? (*m. Sanh.* 4:5)

This admonition proves that witnesses cannot be forced to testify; the punishment for their refusal or their prevarication rests with the deity. Moreover, the wording of the admonition possibly hints at the nature of the imprecation, which was pronounced in biblical times and abandoned by the time of the rabbis. The witness is informed that he is responsible for his inaccurate testimony, on the one hand, but is responsible for bringing the criminal to justice, on the other hand. And in capital cases, the saving or the destruction of an innocent life has lasting, worldwide repercussions.

Moreover, even while being taken to the place of execution, "a herald goes out before him (calling), 'Such-a-one, the son of such-a-one, is going forth to be stoned for he committed such or such an offense. Such-a-one and such-a-one are witnesses against him. If any man knows anything in favor of his acquittal let him come and plead it" (*m. Sanh.* 6:1). A baraita reports that forty days before Jesus' execution "a herald went out before him (calling) . . . if any man knows anything in favor of his acquittal let him come forth and plead it" (*b. Sanh.* 43a, b, in earlier printed editions and manuscripts; see its evaluation in Lauterbach 1951: 490–500).

2. *when.* '*ăšer*, equivalent to *kî* (vv 1, 3, 4). For this usage see 4:22.

touches (tigga' b). The case here and in the next verse is that of impurity contracted secondarily, by contact with the source of impurity. The source itself, if human, is expressed by *ṭum'ātô 'ālāyw*, lit., "the impurity is upon him" (7:20; cf. v 21).

impure (ṭamē'/ṭĕmē'â). Conspicuously missing in the animal list are clean cattle (see 11:39–40) and birds. The absence of pure cattle here and again in 7:21 can only mean that originally only carcasses of impure animals, those whose meat was not permitted (Ibn Ezra), could transmit impurity by contact, and that carcasses of pure animals (edible animals not legitimately slaughtered) did not transmit impurity: touching them did not render one impure. This matter will be discussed in greater detail at 11:39–40, which will be shown to be a later appendix to the diet laws. Indeed, that one may handle the carcasses of pure animals without incurring impurity is presumed by the law that, though forbidden as food, carcasses may be put to man's use (7:24). Birds, however, are totally absent from this list, implying that even the carcasses of their impure varieties do not transmit impurity. And, indeed, in the inventory of impure birds (11:13–23) there is no equivalent to the ban on touching the carcasses of impure quadrupeds (vv 8, 27), fish (v 11), or (certain species of) swarming creatures (v 31). Ancient rabbinic tradition and the LXX, however, reflect the view that all carcasses (except those of impure birds) transmit impurity (see the next NOTE).

the carcass of an impure wild quadruped ('ô bĕniblat ḥayyâ ṭĕmē'â). The LXX reads ἢ θνησιμαίου, ἢ θηριαλώτου ἀκαθάρτου, presuming the text '*ô binĕbēlâ 'ô bĕḥayya' ṭĕmē'â* 'or a carcass or an impure wild quadruped." Clearly, the purpose of breaking this construct chain into two is to maintain the view that touching any animal carcass renders one impure. But that the LXX is interpreting the MT and does not imply a different Hebrew text is shown by the implausibility of the second part: there is neither prohibition nor consequence in touching a *live* beast! Rabbinic tradition concurs with the first part of the LXX in regarding all carcasses as transmitters of impurity. This view is reflected in the rabbinic exegesis of this verse, which regards the adjective "impure" for all three listed species as superfluous (*Sipra*, Ḥobah 13:4–6), thus allowing the text to include all carcasses, pure and impure alike. The LXX adopts a different tack (see the next NOTE but one). That *ḥayyâ* is a wild quadruped, see the NOTES to 11:27 and 17:13.

domesticated quadruped (běhēmâ). If hoofed (11:26), then an impure example would be the pig (11:7).

or the carcass of an impure swarming creature (ʾô běniblat šereṣ ṭāmēʾ). The LXX reads ἢ τῶν θνησιμαίων κτηνῶν τῶνῆ ἀκαθάρτων, lit., "or the carcasses of swarming creatures, the impure ones," thereby allowing for the possibility that "impure" modifies "carcasses" rather than "swarming creatures," meaning that the carcasses of all swarming creatures are impure (the LXX adopts the same construction in rendering the previous phrase, *ʾô běniblat běhēmâ ṭěmēʾâ).* This interpretation is refuted by the adjective *ṭāmēʾ* 'impure', however. If it modified not "swarming creature" (masc.) but "carcass" (fem.), it would have to agree in gender and read *ṭěmēʾâ.* Rabbinic tradition reflects a similar exegesis (*Sipra*, Ḥobah 13:4–6; see above).

šereṣ 'swarming creatures', is divided into two categories: those on land, namely, insects and reptiles (11:20–23, 29–31) and those in water, namely, fish and other marine life (Gen 1:20; Lev 11:10). Certain swarming creatures, such as the locust and the grasshopper, are pure and, hence, excluded from this prohibition. Yet the possibility must be considered that the prohibition here applies only to the eight species enumerated in 11:29–30, which expressly transmit impurity by contact (vv 31–38; Ibn Ezra) and not to the rest of the species, whose incorporation into the taboo (11:41–44) may reflect a later development (see also at 22:5). See also the NOTE on "winged swarming creatures," 11:20.

and, though he has become impure (wěhûʾ ṭāmēʾ). A verb in the perfect between two perfects governed by *waw* consecutives has the force of a pluperfect, giving the reading that originally he knew that he had become impure but subsequently he forgot *(Tg. Ps.-J.).* This factor differs from the situation of the regular purification offering, wherein inadvertence *(šěgāgâ)* applies, that is to say, he had no idea initially that he had done wrong (see at 4:2, 13).

the fact escapes him (wěne ʿlam mimmennû). Some would render, "it was hidden by him." The preposition *min*, however, does not mean "by" (not even in Gen 9:11; Job 7:14; 14:9; 2 Sam 3:37, cited by Rodriguez 1979: 95 n. 3), and what is there to hide: contracting impurity is no sin! Moreover, if he had deliberately hidden the sin, the text would have used the active *hiphʿil* construction *heʿlîm et-ʿênāyw mimmenû*, lit., "he hid his eyes from it" (cf. 20:4). Besides, the clause "and though he has become impure" (as well as "and, though he has known it," vv 3–4) would be rendered superfluous. The sin rests only in his neglect to purify himself of his impurity (Dillmann and Ryssel 1897) within the prescribed one-day time limit (11:28, 31–40), thereby increasing the possibility that he will pollute the sanctuary and its sancta (see the COMMENT below). This limitation of impurity is significant. In Israel an impure animal can only transmit impurity when it is dead, and this impurity is harmless and of no consequence unless the affected person does not purify himself in time or, in the case of severe impurity, neglects to bring the prescribed purification offering.

but [thereafter] he feels guilt (wĕʾāšēm). For the discussion of this critical term, see the NOTES on 4:3, 13, and esp. COMMENT A on 5:14–26).

3. *touches (yiggaʿ b).* As in the previous case, the impurity is not primary (i.e., the source) but secondary (i.e., contracted). Such cases would be, for example, touching a gonorrheic or anything he or she sits or lies on (15:4–10, 26–27); touching a menstruant or anything she sits or lies on (15:19–24); touching a corpse or being in the same room with one (Num 19:14–16). By contrast, primary impurity bearers—such as the *zāb/zābâ* or menstruant (above), one experiencing sex or an emission of sperm (15:16–18), the *mĕṣōrāʿ* (chap. 13), the parturient (chap. 12)—would not qualify for the graduated purification offering because they would be fully conscious of their affliction and could not plead temporary amnesia (see below).

human impurity. ṭumʾat ʾādām, a subjective genitive, referring to impurity derived from a human source (see 7:21).

any such impurity whereby one becomes impure. lĕkōl ṭumʾātô ʾăšer yiṭmāʾ bāh, namely, impurity that results not only from touching human impurity bearers but from touching any of the objects that they may have contaminated (see 22:5b and the NOTE on "touches," above).

and, though he has known it (wĕhûʾ yādāʿ). A perfect with pluperfect force (Rashi; Zunz, apud Hoffman 1953). See v 2, above, on "and, though he has become impure."

the fact escapes him (wĕneʿlam mimmennû). During his memory lapse, he did not purify himself during the one-day or seven-day (corpse contamination) limit. See at v 2, above.

4. *blurts out an oath. tiššābaʿ lĕbaṭṭeʾ biśĕpātayim,* lit., "swears" (see v 4b). The verb *biṭṭēʾ* and the noun *mibṭāʾ* connote an impulsive statement (see Num 30:7; Prov 12:18; and esp. Ps 106:33). The implication here is that the oath was taken heedlessly. A righteous sufferer in ancient Babylonia complains, "(Like one who) has frivolously sworn a solemn oath by his god, do I appear" (Lambert 1960: 38, line 22; cf. 1974: 274, line 24). But it is the articulation of the oath, expressed with lips, that is the decisive factor. The exchange between Jephthah and his daughter is most instructive: " 'I have opened my mouth to the Lord (i.e., uttered a vow) and I cannot retract.' 'Father,' said she, 'you have opened your mouth to the Lord (i.e., uttered a vow): do to me according to what came forth from your mouth' " (Judg 11:35–36). Intention is binding only when it is expressed (Num 30:3), even when the expression does not correspond to the intention (see Isaac's blessing of Jacob, Gen 27:33–35).

Oaths are of two types: assertatory and promissory. Assertatory oaths are taken to clear oneself of a charge, for example, of misappropriating property (vv 20–26, below; cf. Exod 22:7). Here, however, we clearly deal with promissory oaths, the more prevalent type, which impose an obligation on the oath taker: for example, the oath repeatedly made by David that Solomon would reign after him (1 Kgs 1:13, 17, 30). A covenant, by definition, is a promissory oath (e.g., Gen 21:22–32; 31:44–53). So is an oath of abstention, as exemplified in the case of the married woman who denies to herself (and probably to her husband) a pleasurable or necessary act (Num 30:14). An oath of this kind is envisioned in the verse under consideration (see below). *Tg. Ps.-J.* presumes that the subject here is false oaths, but it is, in fact, the subject of vv 21–26, where both circumstances and consequences differ radically from those in this pericope. Vows are, by definition, promissory, but they differ from promissory oaths in that they are conditional (see further at 7:16).

to good or bad purpose. lĕhāraʿ ʾô lĕhêṭîb, lit., "to do harm or good," either (1) to oneself—as for instance "I shall eat" or "I shall not eat"; "I shall sleep" or "I shall not sleep" (Rashi, based on *b. Šebu.* 27a; cf. *b. Nazir* 62b) or (2) to another (Ibn Ezra). Nevertheless, this expression is probably a merism meaning "anything" (see Gen 24:5; 31:24; Num 24:18; 2 Sam 14:17, 20 [Cassuto 1964: 62]; Isa 41:23), confirmed by the following explanatory clause: "whatever a man may utter in an oath." In any event, Ibn Ezra's view must be rejected; the oath that harms another person is the subject of the *ʾāšām* offering of vv 21–26. With Rashi (and the Talmud), the oath must be restricted to anything that the oath taker promises to do or not do for himself.

and, though he has known it (wĕhûʾ yādaʿ). Of course, he was fully aware of the exact oath he took—even if he was heedless in stating it. For this expression, see at v 3, above.

the fact escapes him (wĕneʿlam mimmennû). The same factor as in vv 2 and 3. Here the context differs, however: he forgot to fulfill his oath. Presumably, it had a time limit and when he finally remembered it, it was too late (*b. Šabb.* 69a). Nonfulfillment of an oath is punishable by God (e.g., Ezek 17:13, 16, 18–19). Indeed, divine sanctions are implied in every oath formula (e.g., 1 Sam 3:17; 14:44; 2 Sam 3:35; 1 Kgs 2:23; Pss 7:46; 137:5–6; Ruth 1:17). But the punishment could also be meted out by man (Judg 21:5; cf. 20:1, 21 and Ibn Ezra on Exod 20:7).

he feels guilt in any of these matters. wĕʾāšēm lĕʾaḥat mēʾēlleh, that is, in any of these four cases. This clause will be repeated in the next verse (v 5a), where it rightfully belongs. Hence, retain *wĕʾāšēm,* to conform with the terminal word of vv 2 and 3, and delete *lĕʾaḥat mēʾēlleh* as a dittography of v 5a. For another case in which the first clause is probably a dittography of a similar clause that follows, see Ezek 18:10b, 11a which, strikingly, also summarizes a list of sins with the same phrase, *mēʾaḥad mēʾēlleh.*

5. *When he feels guilt in any of these matters.* That is to say, in any of these four matters *(Tg. Ps.-J.)* comprising three sins: withholding evidence, polluting the sanctuary, not fulfilling an oath (Rashbam on v 13). This is the general protasis embracing all four cases, and though it repeats the condition already

stated in vv 2, 3, and 4, it is essential because it is absent in v 1 (see the COMMENT below). By the same token, the ending of v 1 wĕnāśāʾ ʿăwōnô 'so that he must bear his punishment' must also be assumed as implied in the subsequent cases. That is to say, the prolongation of impurity (vv 2–3) and the nonfulfillment of an oath pollute the sanctuary and, hence, constitute a capital offense punishable by God (see the COMMENT below and the NOTES on 11:24–25, 39–40).

he shall confess (wĕhitwaddâ). This term begins the apodosis. The root ydh in the hiphʿil means "praise" but, in the Hithpaʿ el, "confess" (e.g., Dan 9:4, 20; Ezra 10:1; Neh 1:6; 9:2–3). In the Priestly writings the verb is always followed by an object (5:5; 16:21; 26:40; Num 5:7). In the postexilic book it either stands alone (Dan 9:4; Ezra 10:6; Neh 9:3) or is followed by the preposition ʿal (Neh 1:6; 9:2), an indication that the act of confession is independently important and is dissociated from sacrifice. The usage attested in P is therefore older (Paran 1983: 220–21).

The LXX correctly translates it ἐξαγορεύσει 'declare', in other words, articulate his confession (observed by Lieberman 1950: 140, and cf. Philo, Som. 2.296), in distinction to the contrition, which is the silent "confession" mandated for the inadvertent wrongdoer. Indeed, there are cases in which the hiphʿil means "confess" (e.g., Ps 32:5; Prov 28:13) and the Hithpaʿel means "praise" (2 Chr 30:22), indicating that both of these meanings derive from a single one, "declare" (Wessely 1846). Confession in P must be verbalized because it is the act that counts, not just its intention. Confession in thought (ballēb) would therefore be inadequate. By the same token, neither can mere thought bear evil consequences. For a curse to incur penalty, it must be pronounced and the name of God articulated (nāqab; see 24:16). To be sure, intention is a cardinal principle in priestly jurisprudence (e.g., Num 35:9ff. and see the COMMENT on 5:14–26), but only if the thought is carried out in deed (details in chap. 7, COMMENT G).

Confession is never required for inadvertences (Ibn Ezra, Ramban) but only for deliberate sins. Indeed, there are only four passages in P in which confession (hitwaddâ) is explicitly required, and each case deals exclusively with deliberate sin (5:1–4; 16:21; 26:40; Num 5:6–7). Moreover, these cases are the only ones in all of P wherein deliberate sins are expiable by sacrifice (26:40 finds Israel in exile, where sacrifice, obviously, is not possible). That this is no accident is clear from my rendering of the verb ʾāšam. For involuntary sin, ʾāšam or remorse alone suffices: it renders confession superfluous. For deliberate sin, however, confession is demanded over and above remorse. But what function does confession serve? Why must contrition of the heart be augmented by the confirmation of the lips? Confession must, then, play a vital role in the judicial process. Because it only occurs when deliberate sin is expiated by sacrifice, the conclusion is ineluctable: confession is the legal device fashioned by the Priestly legislators to convert deliberate sins into inadvertences, thereby qualifying them for sacrificial expiation. For the ramifications and implications of this thesis, see the COMMENT on vv 20–26.

The prescription that a crime must be confessed to qualify for sacrificial expiation is not an Israelite invention. It is amply attested in the literature of the ancient Near East, as the following Hittite text declares:

> Now, I have confessed before the Hattian Storm god, my Lord, and before the gods, my Lords (admitting): "It is true, we have done it." . . . If a servant has incurred guilt, but confesses his guilt to his lord, his lord may do with him whatever he pleases. But because (the servant) has confessed his guilt to his lord, his lord's soul is pacified, and his lord will not punish that servant. I have now confessed. (*ANET*³ 395, lines 9–10)

Confession, then, is a sine qua non in Hittite religion for attaining divine forgiveness. It figures no differently elsewhere in ancient Near East (*ANET*³ 391, lines 19–29; 340, lines 51–62; Reiner 1958: 13–16; Lambert 1959: 55–60, lines 136–40; 1960: 116; Langdon 1927: 72–74, lines 6–9; Blackman 1925: 249–55; Peet 1930: 49, 60; Pettazzoni 1939: 197–202).

It is uncertain, however, whether the confession was recited by the penitent himself or by the priest on his behalf. Whenever prayer is embedded in an incantation and expressed in the third person, there can be no question that the priest confesses for his client (e.g., Reiner 1958: 13–16). In fact, there are texts that expressly order the priest to recite the confession: *lubla pîšu ša la idi ma'duma annûa aḫtaṭi kalama* 'Let me (the priest) bring his confession (lit., mouth) of ignorance: "I have committed many trespasses indeed" . . .' (Lambert 1959: 58, lines 136–37). Conversely, other texts explicitly instruct the king to deliver the confession (e.g., *ANET*³ 339, A17; 340, A rev. 24), and still others seem to predicate that the layman express his penitence without a mediator (e.g., *ANET*³ 391, lines 18–29).

The Bible exhibits the same vacillation regarding the reciter of the confession. That the high priest was empowered to confess the sins of his people there can be no doubt (e.g., 16:21). Yet it is equally certain that a confession recited by the penitent himself was an integral part of the Temple ritual (1 Sam 7:6; 1 Kgs 8:33–43; Ezra 10:1; Neh 1:6; 9:2–3). Thus when P ascribes confession to the sinner, the likelihood is that it was actually performed by him and not by a surrogate. This probability becomes certainty when the question is posed: Where was the confession made? The biblical evidence is beyond doubt: because the confession has to precede the actual bringing of the sacrifice—note the word order: *wĕhitwaddâ* . . . *wĕhēbî'* 'he shall confess . . . he shall bring' (v 5); *wĕhitwaddâ* . . . *wĕhēšîb* 'he shall confess . . . he shall make (reparation)' (Num 5:7)—it was recited anywhere but at the sanctuary. Ostensibly, the annual Day of Purgation service reverses this rule, for the text specifies that the goat upon which the high priest makes confession is brought into the sanctuary first (16:5–10, 21). Even so, the exceptional nature of this ritual must be kept in mind. It is not an offering to God but an elimination of sin, the confession and hand-leaning serving as transfer agents. Also, as the high priest is robed in his special vestments (vv 3, 23), he may not leave the sanctuary, and there is no choice but that the goat be brought to him.

The only uncertainty is whether the confession was recited to God or to a person, that is, the one who was wronged. In the present cases (5:1–4), the confession was obviously made to God, because the offense was to him alone. But what happens when the tangible damage is done to man (COMMENT on vv 20–26)? On this question the postbiblical sources differ: the confession was made privately and inaudibly (*b. Soṭa* 32b; *y. Yebam.* 8:3); it was made to the injured party (*t. Taʿan.* 1:8; Philo, *Laws* 1. 235); it was made to the priest (CD 9.13; *Seper Hamibḥar*; *Midr. Tadshe*, quoted by Büchler 1928: 417 n. 2). Büchler's view that the penitent "goes to the court to confess to the judges" (p. 403) has no biblical foundation. Maimonides ruled that sins against God were confessed in private, those against man, in public (*Teshuvah*, chaps. 1–2). Nonetheless, confession solely to God became the Jewish norm (Urbach 1935: 70–71; Rosenthal 1970: 85–86, 104–5). The biblical postulate seems to have been that confession is made to the injured party—to God, to man, or to both (as in the case of vv 20–26). The purpose of confessing to man was that he might forgive the wrongdoer (*m. Yoma* 8:9). But what if forgiveness was not granted? On this the Bible is silent. The rabbis, however, decree that his confession should take place before a quorum of ten, and God would then forgive him (*Pesiq. R.* 38; *Midr. Tanḥ. B.*, Vayera 30). Why, then, verbalize to God who "tests the thoughts and mind" (Jer 11:20)? the social analogy is operative here. As one verbalizes to a person for his forgiveness, so to God for his forgiveness: for biblical persons God was a person.

6. *And he shall bring (wĕhēbî).* See also vv 6, 7, 11, 15, 18; 19:21; Num 6:12; 15:28. Chap. 4 uses *wĕheqrîb* 'he shall offer', another indication that the *ḥaṭṭāʾt* of chap. 4 must be distinguished from the graduated *ḥaṭṭāʾt* (and, of course, the *ʾāšām* offering) of chap. 5. Presumably, the offender will have performed his required ablutions corresponding to the type of impurity he has contracted before bringing his sacrifice (see chap. 15, COMMENTS C and F).

reparation (ʾăšāmô). Another instance of the consequential *ʾāšām*, denoting punishment or penalty (see the NOTE on 4:3). This precise usage is attested in vv 15, 25, and in 19:21, where it is equivalent and parallel to *qorbānô* 'his offering' (v 11) and must not be confused with *ʾāšām* 'the reparation offering'.

for the wrong. This expression occurs twice in this verse, first as *ʿal ḥaṭṭāʾtô* and then as *mēḥaṭṭāʾtô*. These two expressions are interchangeable (see vv 10, 13). The LXX and Sam. add at the end of the verse *ʾăšer ḥāṭāʾ wĕnislaḥ lô* 'which he committed that he may be forgiven', in consonance with vv 10, 13, and 4:35.

a female from the flock, sheep or goat. See 4:27–35. In this case, however, the word for sheep, *kiśbâ*, is a hapax, which should most likely be metathesized as *kibśâ*.

as a purification offering (lĕḥaṭṭāʾt). All cases of severe impurity require a purification offering on the assumption that the generated impurity is powerful enough to pollute the sanctuary from afar (chap. 4, COMMENT B). If, however, the offender willfully neglects to bring his sacrifice, he is punished by God with *kārēt* (Num 19:13, 20; cf. chap. 7, COMMENT D), and the purgation of the sanctuary must await the Yom Kippur rites of the high priest (chap. 16).

7. *But if his means do not suffice.* *wĕʾim lōʾ taggîaʿ yādô*, lit., "But if his hand cannot reach." The more frequent expression is *hiśśîgâ yādô*, lit., "his hand attains" (v 11; 14:21, 22, 30–32; 25:26, 47, 49; 27:8; Num 6:21) and only rarely *maṣesâ yādô*, lit., "his hand finds" (12:8; 25:28). From this idiom, the rabbis derive this rule: "One cannot compel the person to borrow (a sacrificial animal) or to work at his trade (until he can earn one)" (*Sipra*, Ḥobah 18:1). Sacrificial concessions to the indigent are recorded in the Punic Marseilles Tariff (third century B.C.E.): *bkl zbḥ ʾś yzbḥ dl mqnʾ ʾm dl ṣpr bl ykn lkhn [m mnm]* 'For every sacrifice which man may sacrifice who is poor in cattle or poor in birds, the priests shall have nothing [of them]' (*CIS* 165; Cooke 1903: 112–22; *ANET*[3] 656–57). Apparently, the concession was not a less costly animal but the waiving of the priestly prebend (cf. the NOTE on "whichever are within his means," 14:22).

his reparation. *ʾăśāmô*; cf. at v 6.

two turtledoves or two pigeons. See at 1:14.

one for a purification offering and the other for a burnt offering. "one (the burnt offering) is for suet, so the other for a purification offering is as required" (Ibn Ezra); in other words, the burnt offering is for God, and the purification offering is for the priest (Abravanel). Because the meat of the purification offering belongs to the officiating priest (6:19), there is very little that remains for God (i.e., the altar). Hence, a burnt offering is added so there will be a respectable sacrifice on the altar. The burnt offering, it should be recalled, also serves an expiatory function (see on 1:4) and the combination of *ʿōlâ* and *ḥaṭṭāʾt* in expiatory cases is attested frequently (Num 15:24–25; chaps. 28–29; Dillmann and Ryssel 1897).

8. *He shall bring them to the priest.* In the case of birds the offerer performs no preliminary rites (i.e., hand-leaning and slaughter) but brings them directly to the priest (see the NOTE on 1:14).

offer first the one for the purification offering. From this statement, the rabbis derive the rule that the blood ritual of the purification offering always precedes that of the burnt offering (*Sipra*, Ḥobah 18:5; *m. Zebaḥ.* 10:2; *b. Pesaḥ.* 59a; *b. Zebaḥ* 7b, 90a). The reason for the priority of the purification offering is best explained by the rabbis: "[Because it is] like an intercessor who enters [to appease the king]: when the intercessor has appeased [him], the gift [i.e., the burnt offering] follows" (*b. Zebaḥ* 7b).

pinching the head. For the expression *ûmālaq ʾet-rōʾšô*, see 1:15.

at its nape (mimûl ʿorpô). *ʿōrep* has to do with the neck because it can be gripped by the hand (Gen 49:8; Job 16:12). That it must be the back of the neck or nape is shown by such expressions as *hāpak, pānâ, herʾâ*, "turn" or "show" (the nape), in other words, to act in a cowardly way, in fear or flight (e.g., Josh 7:8, 12; Jer 18:17).

without severing it (wĕlōʾ yabdîl). The head need not be severed as in the case of the burnt-offering bird (1:15) because the entire bird belongs to the officiating priest (6:19; *m. Zebaḥ.* 6:4; Dillmann and Ryssel 1897).

9. *He shall sprinkle (wehizzâ).* The blood of the purification offering bird undergoes two manipulations, sprinkling and draining; the blood of the burnt-offering bird, only draining (1:15). The difference reflects the different blood rites of these two sacrifices: all burnt offerings undergo one blood rite (1:5, 11, 15), whereas all purification offerings undergo two blood rites, the main one being the daubing of the blood on the altar's horns. Because there is both too little blood and too little time for the priest to circumambulate the altar, however, from the very spot on which he breaks the bird's nape he sprinkles its blood on the side of the altar (*Sipra*, Ḥobah 18:8; *b. Zebaḥ.* 64b).

on (the side) [*ʿal(-qîr)*]. The Sam. reads *ʾel* "toward" (cf. 2 Kgs 9:33; Snaith 1970–71).

and what remains of the blood (wĕhannišʾār baddām). The preposition *b* can denote one or some "among" a multitude (e.g., Gen 8:17; 9:10; 23:18; Exod 14:8; and esp. 8:32; 14:18; 25:52; 1 Sam 11:11; Isa 10:2, where *nišʾār* and its synonym *nôtār* are used).

shall be drained (yimmāṣēh). "Said Raba: Is then *yĕmaṣṣēh* ['he shall drain' —*piʿel*] written? Surely, *yimmāṣēh* ['he shall be drained'—*niphʿal*] is written, which implies of its own accord" (*b. Zebaḥ.* 64b). Draining here corresponds to pouring in the regular purification offering (4:7, 18, 25, 30, 34). Both manipulations take place at the base of the altar and are not rituals per se but instead means of disposing of the unused blood (see the NOTE on 4:7).

it is a purification offering. Although the causal particle *kî* is missing (see v 11), this nominal sentence is an explanatory note, giving the reason that there are two discrete blood manipulations: such is the requirement of the purification offering.

10. *according to regulation. kammišpāṭ*, in other words, already detailed in the rite of the burnt offering bird (1:14). Thus the pericope on the graduated purification offering, like that of the regular purification offering (4:24, 29, 33), assumes the text of the burnt offering (chap. 1). The same formula appears in other ancient Near Eastern cultures, such as, Ugaritic: *dbḥ k sprt* 'the sacrifice according to the prescriptions' (RS 61/24.277.9; *Ugaritica* 6 [1968]: 168); Hittite: "they do it (the sacrifices) in exactly that manner" (Goetze and Pedersen 1934: 10–13).

11. *ephah (ʾēpâ).* An Egyptian measure, *ỉpt*, estimated as equivalent to 22.8

liters (Zuidhof 1982). One-tenth of an *ephah*, the most common amount of semolina for a cereal offering (6:13; 14:21; Num 5:15; 28:5, 9, 13, 21, 29; etc.), would amount to 2.3 liters, which suffices for a day's bread for one person (Ibn Ezra).

for it is a purification offering (kî ḥaṭṭāʾt hîʾ [hwʾ]). Again, this nominal sentence serves as an explanatory note (as in v 9); it tells why the semolina is not brought with oil and frankincense, both of which would be required in a cereal offering (2:1). Oil and frankincense are also deliberately omitted from the cereal offering of the suspected adulteress (Num 5:11). Thus it seems that both ingredients were considered signs of a joyous occasion, and their omission would accentuate the somber nature of the offerings.

12. *scoop out a handful. wĕqāmaṣ . . . mĕlôʾ qumṣô;* see at 2:2.

a token portion of it. ʾazkārātâ; see at 2:2. Because the token portion is burned on the altar, it is the equivalent to the suet of the purification-offering animal (4:8–10, 19, 26, 31, 35; *Keter Torah)* and, hence, the ingredient that effects the purgation (v 13). This law proves that the cereal offering can serve an expiatory function (see 14:20 and the COMMENT on chap. 2). That it can also purge the sanctuary as a purification offering is questionable, however (for details, see the COMMENT below).

with the Lord's food gifts. ʿal ʾissê YHWH; see the NOTE on 4:35.

it is a purification offering. The nominal sentence *ḥaṭṭāʾt hî ʾ (hwʾ)* is once again an explanatory note (as in vv 9, 11) that although the ritual does not differ from the regular cereal offering, it is a purification offering. Yet if the ritual does not differ, the statement describing it does: the cereal offering *is* an *ʾiššeh,* a "food gift" (2:2); the purification offering is not (see the NOTE on 4:35).

13. *Thus the priest shall effect purgation (wekippēr . . . hakkōhēn).* How can semolina effect purgation when it contains no blood, the ritual detergent of the purification offering (chap. 4, COMMENT B)? It may be no accident that in ancient Mesopotamia flour was indeed used in the *kuppuru* rituals (Geller 1980: 190–91). In the Šurpu ritual from Assur, the priest wipes off *(ukappar)* the patient with flour, which he throws into the fire, afterward sprinkling the patient with water. The priest then performs various acts of sympathetic magic, such as peeling an onion and ripping apart dates, matting, and wool, which are thrown into the fire; finally, the patient wipes himself off *(ukappar;* probably with the flour) and then throws it into the fire (Reiner 1958: 11, lines 11–23). As will be explained (chap. 16, (COMMENT F), the Semitic root *kpr* means "rub, wipe" and the pagans, as exemplified by the Šurpu ritual, above, literally wiped the magical detergent upon the body of the patient. The detergent purportedly absorbed his illness or impurity, necessitating its destruction (e.g., in the fire, as above). Similarly, the *ḥaṭṭāʾt* blood was daubed on the altar's horns (4:7, 18, 25, 30, 34) and, if the impurity was considered severe enough, the blood was aspersed inside the Tent (4:6, 17; 16:15–16), and the rest of the animal was burned outside the camp (4:11–12, 21; 16:27). The main distinction between

the pagan and biblical *kpr* rituals is that whereas in the former the detergent is smeared on the patient, in Israel the detergent is never applied to a person but only to the sanctuary and its sancta. The difference lies in the opposing theological postulates of these two systems (see chap. 4, COMMENT C). Nonetheless, the regular and frequently attested use of flour as a *kpr* agent may well account for its acceptance as a concession to the poor, in the borderline cases of the graduated purification offering, and the burning of its token portion on the altar effects the altar's purgation on behalf of the offerer.

for the wrong. ʿal-ḥaṭṭāʾtô, instead of the *mēḥaṭṭāʾtô* of the previous cases (vv 6, 10) because of its cacophonic clash with the subsequent *mēʾaḥat* (Wessely 1846).

in any of these matters. mēʾaḥat mēʾelleh, namely, the four cases or three sins (Rashbam) of vv 1–4 (see at v 5). This expression begins and ends vv 5–13, indicating its structural unity and certifying that the entire pericope, the cases (vv 1–4) and the procedural remedy (vv 5–13), deals with the graduated purification offering (see the COMMENT below).

so that he may be forgiven. The clause *wenislaḥ lô.* also covers the case of the flock animal, where it was missing (v 6), proving that this verse is a general statement (see the COMMENT below).

It shall belong to the priest, like the cereal offering. wĕhāyĕtâ lakkōhēn kamminḥâ; see 2:3, 10; 6:9; 10:12. This statement is necessary because one might think that the offerer, being so poor, should be entitled to it, or the offering, being so small, should be burned in its entirety to God (Ehrlich 1908–14). Thus this semolina offering is a purification offering also in respect to its disposal: the meat of the purification offering is awarded to the officiating priest (6:19).

COMMENT: THE GRADUATED PURIFICATION OFFERING: THE REDUCTION OF THE FORCE OF IMPURITY

The purification offering described in general terms in chap. 4 is also prescribed for the four specific cases of 5:1–13 but with one major distinction: in chap. 4 the sacrifice is scaled according to the socioreligious status of the offender and in 5:1–13, according to his means. In addition to the commoner's standard offering of a female of the flock (i.e., goat or sheep; cf. 5:6 with 4:28, 32), second and third alternatives are allowed: birds (two turtledoves or two pigeons, 5:8) or semolina (a tenth of an *ephah,* 5:11). A graduated purification offering is also prescribed on recovery from scale disease (14:10, 21–22), though there the flour option is eliminated. (It should also be noted that the parturient is allowed a graduated burnt offering, 12:8.) There can be no question that all of these instances represent an alleviation of the fixed *ḥaṭṭā't* ritual: birds and flour in comparison with livestock are cheap. Why has the *ḥaṭṭā't* been mitigated in these cases?

Modern critics tend to regard 5:1–13 as the "poor man's" purification offering ("die armseligen Verhältnisse der proletarisierten und verstäderten nachexilischen Gemeinde," Elliger 1966), the option given to the commoner of 4:27–35 who cannot afford the prescribed flock animal (e.g., de Vaux 1961a: 419–21; 1964: 92; Snaith 1967; Noth 1965; Elliger 1966; Rendtorff 1967: 207–10). This interpretation, however, is beset with stylistic and contextual difficulties: (1) The relative *kî* that begins chap. 5 is the sign of a new case and thus cannot continue 4:27–35, where *wĕ'im* is used twice (vv 27, 32). Thus 5:1 corresponds to the general introduction to the *ḥaṭṭā't* (4:2aβ, b). (2) A key condition of the *ḥaṭṭā't* is missing: the violation of a prohibitive commandment (4:2, 13, 22, 27, 32; correctly noted in *b. Hor.* 8b). (3) The sacrifice here is also called *'āšām* 'reparation' (vv 6, 7) and confession is required (v 5), terms not used in chap. 4 at all. (4) Most decisively, the antecedents of "any of these matters" (v 13; cf. vv 4b, 5a) can only be the specific and discrete cases of vv 1–4 and not chap. 4, which deals with only one general case. (5) The ideological objections are equally strong. In 5:1–4 the requirement of inadvertence *(šĕgāgâ)*, indispensable to the *ḥaṭṭā't* (4:2, 13, 22, 27), is absent. In vv 2–4, for example, it makes no difference whether the impurity contracted or the oath uttered was deliberate or not and v 1, whose subject is the withholding of evidence, allows for no inadvertence at all. Furthermore, the *ḥaṭṭā't* is directed at violations of prohibitive commandments (*miṣwōt YHWH 'ăšer lō' tē'āśênâ*, 4:2, 13, 22, 27). No such violation, however, occurs here. Contracting impurity is not prohibited, and the requirement to cleanse oneself of impurity, even when it stipulates sanctions (e.g., Num 19:13, 20), is not a prohibitive but a performative commandment, thus falling outside the purview of the *ḥaṭṭā't.* Clearly, this solution will not do.

To save this theory, some would regard vv 7–13 as the continuation of 4:27–35, whereas the intervening section (vv 1–6) would be transferred to the section on the reparation offering (vv 14–26; Rendtorff 1967: 207–10). This stratagem only compounds the difficulties: (1) vv 1–6 have no separate heading and, hence, are logically an extension of chap. 4, whereas the reparation offering has its own heading (5:14); (2) the sacrifice is explicitly called a *ḥaṭṭā't* (v 6), which Rendtorff is forced to emend to *'āšām;* (3) the *'āšām* sacrifice is always a male and is never a goat (see below).

Rabbinic tradition posits a different solution. It distinguishes between the sacrifices of chap. 4 and those of 5:1–13. It never even refers to the latter as *ḥaṭṭā't* but gives them an entirely separate title, *'ōleh wĕyōrēd* 'a graduated offering' (lit., "ascending and descending"), which ignores its *ḥaṭṭā't* status and concentrates on its scaled nature. The rabbis also interpolate the condition of *ṭûm'at miqdāš wĕqādāšāyw* 'the pollution of the sanctuary and its sancta', to wit:

having forgotten his state of impurity, the offender enters the sanctuary or comes into contact with sancta (*m. Šebu.* 1:4–6; *m. Hor.* 2:7; *m. Ker.* 2:4; cf. Philo, *Laws* 3. 205, where this interpretation is implied). While this solution correctly identifies the graduated *ḥaṭṭāʾt* as a discrete sacrificial category, the additional qualification that it is brought for "the pollution of the sanctuary and its sancta" by contact cannot be accepted for the following reasons: (1) The direct contact of impurity with sancta is banned elsewhere (e.g., 7:20–21; 12:4; 22:3–7), where the punishment is entirely different: *kārēt.* (2) Verse 3 speaks solely of those who are secondarily contaminated "when a person touches," implying that those who are primary sources, that is to say, bearers of impurity, are excluded (see on v 3); however, regarding contact with sancta no such distinction is made (cf. 7:20–21). (3) The condition of "the pollution of the sanctuary and its sancta" by contact is plainly eisegesis; it is nowhere expressed.

The recent treatment by A. Spiro (1959; independently, Noth 1965; anticipated by the Karaites; cf. *Seper Hamibḥar; Keter Torah)* calls for special mention. Spiro combines vv 1–4 into a single case. The witness (v 1) has observed the subjects of the following verses contaminate themselves (vv 2–3) or utter an oath (v 4) but he has failed to remind them of their condition. This negligent witness must then confess that he withheld his information and bring a sacrifice (v 5): "Since his offense is not a serious one—for a sin has not yet been committed by the forgetful person (cf. vss. 2–4)—provisions are made for the poor, permitting a less costly sacrifice" (Spiro 1959: 100).

This interpretation of vv 1–4 has the virtue of explaining why the final word of vv 2–4 *(wĕʾāšēm)* does not appear at the end of v 1, to wit: the cases of vv 2–4 are subsumed under v 1. Yet this gain is offset by the assumption that the antecedent of *wĕhûʾ* in each of the vv 2–4 is the witness of v 1. The use of this pronoun to indicate a change of subject cannot be countenanced because, first, the equivalent expression and syntax appear in 5:18 *(wĕhûʾ lōʾ yādaʿ),* where there is no change in subject; and, second, the pronoun rather reflects a change not in subject but in time, indicating that the perfect should be understood as a pluperfect, referring to the time in which the impurity was contracted. The Spiro solution fails on other counts as well: if vv 2–4 were in fact subsumed under v 1 their cases should be introduced by *ʾim,* not by *kî* (as in vv 7, 10, where subordination indeed exists); also, the setting of v 1 would be incomprehensible: why should the lax witness bring a purification offering, which is required solely for ritual impurity and not for moral negligence (see chap. 4, COMMENT B); moreover, as pointed out in *Keter Torah,* the imprecation to witnesses and the implied presence of a court in v 1 predicate a civil, not a religious case—a situation far removed from the domain of the purification offering.

Thus the conclusion is ineluctable that 5:1–13 deals with the *ḥaṭṭāʾt,* the purification offering. Even so, it is not a continuation of chap. 4 but comprises a discrete sacrificial category—a graduated *ḥaṭṭāʾt.* It is best understood as an appendix to the regular *ḥaṭṭāʾt* of chap. 4. Supporting this thesis is the fact that in the Priestly legislation, appendixes comprise borderline cases: whenever there is a case in which the data veer from the norm, the Priestly legislator will find it necessary to present the data in detail and then append it to the general category to which it belongs. Thus the reparation offering discussed below (vv 14–19) concludes (under a new heading, v 20) with the special case, spelled out in detail, of defrauding God (which requires the reparation offering) while, at the same time, defrauding man (vv 20–26). Similarly, the general classification of pure quadrupeds, which have cloven hoofs and which chew the cud (11:2–3), is followed by a list naming four animals that possess only one of the two qualifying criteria, followed by the assertion that they are impure. Israel, it seems, is not alone in following this classification procedure for its laws. It also holds for the Hittite laws, which "refer mostly to very peculiar cases, the presumption being that ordinary cases will be settled by single and generally accepted rules" (de Vaux 1961a: 145). So too in Greco-Roman jurisprudence where obvious laws are "taken for granted; it is the more complicated cases . . . which engage the lawgiver's attention" (Daube 1947: 257–58).

Here as well the general description of the purification offering (chap. 4) is followed by the detailed list of four cases that do not conform to all of the purification offering's criteria and yet qualify for that sacrifice. The differences are neatly summarized in *Keter Torah:* whereas in chap. 4 the offenders are distinguished by their social status and their offenses are inadvertent violations of prohibitions, in 5:1–13, the offenders differ in their economic status and their offenses can also consist in deliberate violations of performative commandments.

My hypothesis is that the graduated *ḥaṭṭāʾt* of 5:1–13 is a distinct sacrificial category, enjoined for failure or inability to cleanse impurity as soon as it occurs. Thus "the wrong that he committed" (vv 6, 10, 13) is not the contraction of the impurity but its *prolongation.* That this is the unifying postulate of this pericope can be deduced by focusing first on vv 2–3, the cases of impurity by contact. Here, it will be noticed, the impurity does not originate with the offender; he has acquired it. Such a person is asked to purify himself, but not to bring a sacrifice. Even corpse contamination, the most severe of the acquired impurities, necessitates a seven-day ritual of purification—but no sacrifice. Still, cadavers and fluxes become baneful not when their impurity is contracted by an Israelite but only if it remains on his person. Like contagious disease, it spreads and becomes more virulent unless it is cured and purified; for instance, "the priest shall pronounce the house pure, for the infection has healed" (14:48).

That prolonged impurity will increase in its vitality can be demonstrated by the quarantine periods imposed for *ṣāraʿat* 'scale disease' (13:1–12). Whoever is declared pure after one week's quarantine need not undergo purification: he is not impure. After a two-week quarantine he is required to launder and bathe: he has a minor, one-day impurity. If his scale disease is certified, however, his

310

purification—once he is declared to be healed—consists of a complex eight-day ritual (14:1–32): his impurity is major. (For details, see the NOTES on "he shall wash his clothes, 13:6 and 34.)

Prolonged impurity puts the offender into the category of the parturient, the *mĕṣōrāʿ*, and the *zāb/zābâ* (chaps. 12–15), who require the purification offering: "He has polluted the Lord's sanctuary" (Num 19:20; cf. v 13). For the willful neglect of purification the explicit penalty for the corpse-contaminated person is *kārēt* (ibid.), and for the carcass-contaminated person it is "he shall bear his responsibility" (*wĕnāśāʾ ʿăwōnô*, 17:15–16), which can be shown to mean the same (see the NOTE on v 1). If, then, those who contracted impurity in vv 2–3 may have done so deliberately, why is their willful act expiable by sacrifice? The answer is provided by the stipulation in the text, "the fact escapes him" (vv 2–4); it posits accidental neglect. His wrongdoing—not in contracting impurity but in prolonging it—is, in truth, an inadvertence. Nonetheless, the impurity that he acquired has now built up sufficient force to contaminate the sanctuary. It is henceforth no longer enough to purge himself by ritual washing. He must now assume the responsibility of purging the sanctuary by bringing the ritual detergent par excellence, the *ḥaṭṭāʾt*. But because the impurity did not arise from the violation of a prohibition (requiring a fixed animal, chap. 4), any *ḥaṭṭāʾt* will do—whatever the offender can afford.

That the ancients feared the prolongation of impurity is explicitly and forcefully stated in a Sabean (south Arabian) inscription: "Ḥarim, son of *T*awbân, avowed and did penance to *Dû*-Samâwî (a Sabean god) because he drew near a woman during a period illicit to him [or to her] and fondled a woman during her menses; and that he came together with a woman in child-bed; and that *he went without purification and wore his clothes without purification* (italics mine); and that he touched women during their menses and *did not wash himself* (italics mine); and that he moistened his clothes with ejections. And he humbled himself and abased himself and repented. And that he may be rewarded" (*ANET*³ 665a). The translator, A. Jamme, notes that another scholar, G. Ryckmans, would like to interpolate (like the rabbis) the notion that Ḥarim, the impure person, offended his god because he entered his temple, but this is nowhere stated. The wording of the text is unambiguous: *Ḥarim's sin was his neglect to purify himself.* Furthermore, the resemblance to the biblical text is even more striking because the Sabean impurity categories are completely congruent with the biblical ones: sex with a menstruant (15:24) and a parturient (12:2); prolonged impurity (5:3); touching a menstruant (15:19)—apparently not in itself a crime—and failing to wash himself; seminal emission (15:16–17). Finally, his expiation required repentance, the nature of which is not spelled out, but it obviously embraces biblical *ʾāšēm* 'feel guilt' and, possibly, *hitwaddâ* 'confess'.

The early rabbis also seem to have been well aware of the dangers of prolonged impurity: "If a creeping creature *(šereṣ)* was found in the Temple, a priest may remove it with his belt so that he suffer not the pollution to remain. So R. Johanan b. Beroka. R. Judah says: He should remove it with wooden tongs so that he suffer not the pollution to increase" (*m. 'Erub.* 10:15a). Thus Rabbi Johanan holds that it is better to allow the impurity to increase (by contaminating the priest's belt) than to have it *prolonged.* Rabbi Judah, by contrast, would rather risk the prolongation of impurity (during the interval it would take to get a pair of tongs) than have the pollution spread. In either case, impurity (inside the Temple, to be sure) is dangerous and cannot be allowed to remain.

The remaining peculiarities of the graduated purification offering, raised at the beginning of this COMMENT, can now be explained. (1) It is now obvious why vv 2–3 say nothing about inadvertence; because no prohibition was violated, it makes no difference whether the impurity was contracted deliberately or inadvertently. (2) The reason that only the secondarily infected ("he who touches") is allowed a graduated purification offering, not the primary carrier of human impurity (e.g., the *zāb*, 15:1–13), is that the latter cannot plead temporary amnesia ("the fact escapes him"); he is the bearer of the flux and is surely conscious of it. (3) That vv 2–3 were drawn up for nonprohibited occurrences of impurity is underscored by the use of the term *'āšām* (5:6) in its nonsacrificial civil connotation of "penalty" or "fine"; it could never be used in chap. 4, where the violation of a prohibition has given rise to severe impurity (see chap. 4, COMMENT B). (4) Confession is required because the impurity may have been contracted deliberately (see COMMENT F on vv 14–26), in contrast to the impurity created by the cases cited in chap. 4, which are all inadvertences. (5) Finally, the other two instances wherein graduated offerings are prescribed, the *mĕṣōrāʿ* (chaps. 13–14) and the parturient (chap. 12), turn out to be cases in which the onset of impurity cannot be prevented and its prolongation cannot be curtailed. This is the reason that, despite the severity of their impurity, a less costly sacrificial procedure is allowed. To be sure, it can be argued, the same privilege should be granted the *zāb/zābâ*, whose impurity also can be neither prevented nor curtailed. Here, however, it should be noted, the law already prescribes that he or she need only bring birds (15:14, 29)—the cheapest animal—so no alleviation is required. True, the option of bringing a cereal offering is not granted to the primary carriers of impurity, mentioned above, and in that respect they differ from the secondarily infected of vv 2–3, whose impurity has been prolonged. The reason for this distinction will be explored below. In the meantime, it should be borne in mind that those secondarily infected with impurity— provided they purify themselves within the prescribed time limits—bring no sacrifice at all: the corpse-contaminated person is sprinkled with purificatory waters, while those affected by touch, portage, or consumption as well as those who bear light, nonchronic impurity (see 15:16–18) need only submit to simple lustration. For all these aforementioned, there is no need to provide economic alleviation, for their purification involves little or no expense.

In sum, the analysis of the cases of vv 2–3 yields the following information:

someone has contracted impurity knowingly, even deliberately, but has forgotten to purify himself within the prescribed time limits. If he subsequently remembers and feels guilt, he must confess his wrong and expiate it by a purification offering (v 5), thereby purging the sanctuary of the pollution caused by his prolonged impurity. Yet because he has not violated a prohibitive commandment, the sine qua non of the *ḥaṭṭāʾt*, the latter is scaled according to his economic circumstances. This understanding of vv 2–3 provides the key to unlock the mystery of the other two cases in this pericope, vv 1 and 4.

Both v 1 and v 4 deal with oaths. We begin with the second case (v 4) because it is easier to explain. First, it should be noted, its form follows the preceding cases (vv 2, 3): someone, who has sworn an oath knowingly (*wĕhûʾ yādaʿ*, see v 3), even deliberately, has forgotten (*wĕneʿlam mimmennû*, see vv 2, 3) to fulfill it, but subsequently remembers and feels guilt *(weʾāšēm, see vv 2, 3)*. Moreover, just as there is no penalty in becoming impure, so there is no penalty in taking an oath. Just as there is a requirement to purify one's impurity, however, so there is a requirement to fulfill one's oath (Num 30:2). Also, both requirements are performative, not prohibitive, commandments and both wrongs—the prolongation of impurity and the non-fulfillment of the oath—are not deliberate acts but are caused by a memory lapse. Finally, if remorse is articulated by confession, the wrong is expiable by a graduated purification offering. Thus the impurity and oath cases are structurally similar. Still, there does exist one disparity: even if the oath case (v 4) is structured along similar lines, ostensibly impurity plays no role; and, if so, why is a purification offering required?

A brief survey of the nature of the oath, especially in its ancient Near Eastern setting, is mandated. The ancients regarded an oath as a risky undertaking: no telling when or what supernal forces would be offended. "Even oaths, sworn in good faith but conjuring up occult powers, are listed as actions from which the sufferer seeks a release, because the magical powers they arouse are potential sources of evil" (Reiner 1958: 3). Thus the Mesopotamian victim feels that he has fallen under a hex *(māmītu)* for "mentioning a god's name (i.e., swearing by a god) . . . taking an oath" (Laesse 1955: 64–65, lines 80, 84); "If he swore (many) oaths . . . if he swore by his god . . . if he swore true and false oaths, if he swore aware of what he was doing or swore inadvertently" (Reiner 1956: 137, lines 91–95). A Hittite text is more revealing: "Never have I sworn in thy name, my god, and then broken the oath afterward . . . I have not brought impurity upon my body" (*ANET*[3] 400, lines 12–14). Thus the Hittite ruler juxtaposes the sins of impurity with oath breaking precisely as in our pericope (vv 2–3, 4). In the Bible, to be sure, there is no fear of offending God as long as his name is used legitimately. Punishment follows in the wake of a false oath (see on vv 21–26, below) and an unfulfilled oath (or vow, Num 30:2; cf. Deut 23:22–24; Qoh 5:1–5). Still the fear and, hence, reluctance to take oaths persists into rabbinic times (*Midr. Tanḥ, Maṭṭot 1; y. Šebu. 6:5; Philo,*

Dec. 84). The Essenes, in fact, are reputed to have made it a principle not to take oaths (Jos. *Wars* 2.8.6; cf. *2 Enoch* 13:76).

Thus the evidence of Israel's ambience points to the fact that the neglect to cleanse impurity was equal in effect to the neglect to fulfill oaths: both aroused the same divine wrath and its dire consequences. In Israel, however, that equation produced other consequences as well: unfulfilled oaths, like impurities, pollute the sanctuary. At the same time, unfulfilled oaths are added to the violations of prohibitions (chap. 4), which, if mitigated by the factor of inadvertence, can be expiated by a purification offering. But because an unfulfilled oath is a violation of a performative and not a prohibitive commandment, it does not meet the criteria of a purification offering (4:2); hence leniency is granted by allowing the purification offering to be scaled in accordance with the economic means of the offender: a graduated *ḥaṭṭāʾt* is prescribed.

The first case (v 1) is more of a crux. First, it does not follow the structure of the subsequent cases (vv 2–4). Missing are the latter's commonalities: *bě/lĕkōl* 'any'; *wĕhûʾ ṭāmēʾ/yādaʿ* 'and though he has become impure/known it'; *wĕneʿlam mimmennû* 'the fact escapes him'; *wĕʾāšēm* 'he feels guilt'. Instead, we have a case stating that a witness who defies an imprecation (of the court) to testify will suffer its consequences (see at v 1). Thus, in contrast to the following cases, there is no lapse of memory or any other ameliorating factor. Moreover, there is no *ʾāšēm*, that is to say, no subsequent feeling of guilt. Hence, there can be no question that the witness has acted deliberately, brazenly. How then can his offense be expiated by sacrifice?

In answer, the first point to keep in mind is that the factor of *ʾāšēm* 'guilt' is explicitly stated—not in the case itself (v 1) but in the general protasis which governs all four cases (vv 4b, 5a). Indeed, as noted, this is the reason that the factor of "guilt" is repeated in vv 4b and 5a even though it had already been stated in vv 2, 3, and 4; it was essential to mention it in the all-inclusive protasis of vv 4b and 5a precisely because it was missing in the first case (v 1). The more telling objection (above) is the absence of inadvertence: there can be no doubt that the witness deliberately withheld his testimony. Yet the question must be asked: did he really commit a crime? First, let us notice that in defying the imprecation he did not commit perjury (as in vv 21–26 and 19:12, below). Second, he never actually accepted the imprecation by responding "amen" (see Num 5:22; Deut 27:11–26). All the text states is that he "heard" the imprecation. Had he answered "amen" the text would read not *wĕšāmeʿâ (qôl) ʾālâ* 'heard a (public) imprecation' but *bāʾâ bĕʾālâ*, lit., "entered an imprecation" (e.g., Ezek 17:13; Neh 10:30). Thus the text presumes that hearing suffices for the imprecation to take effect *(wĕnāśāʾ ʿăwōnô)*. Other biblical texts confirm this presumption (Tsevat 1970: 287): "When a person hears *(bĕšomʿ ô)* the words of this imprecation" (Deut 29:18) he certainly does not recite "amen" but, instead, tries to nullify the effect of the imprecation by thinking "I shall be safe" (ibid.). Nonetheless, "the Lord will never forgive him" (v 19). Also Micah confesses his theft to his mother for he fears "the imprecation which you uttered *in my hearing*" (Judg 17:2). Hearing, as much as touch and sight (see below), is contact. Moreover, the hearer's intention plays no role. The effect of hearing, even involuntarily, is graphically depicted in the requirement that those who heard the blasphemer must lay their hands on his head, thereby transferring to him the malefic force of his blasphemy (see at 24:14). Thus the witness need not have been adjured before the court (as claimed by the rabbis, *m. Šebu.* 4:10; cf. Shadal); it suffices that the imprecation entered his being via his ears for it to take effect. The factor of hearing also throws light on the crux of 1 Sam 14:24–45. The narrator exonerates Jonathan for violating Saul's imprecation because "Jonathan *had not heard* his father adjure his troops" (v 27) and, hence, it became possible for the troops to save Jonathan (v 45).

The present case states unambiguously that the witness who hears an imprecation is subject to its consequences. Apparently, this law did not satisfy the Priestly legislators. Of course, they could not overrule it, but they were able to mitigate it by incorporating it into their *'āšēm* rule: if the witness subsequently feels guilt, his willful disregard of the imprecation is reduced to an inadvertence, making it eligible for sacrificial expiation. Because a violated imprecation or oath (v 4, above) pollutes the sanctuary, a purification offering is required. But because one of the requirements for the purification offering was not met—the offense was deliberate, not inadvertent—a graduated purification offering is prescribed.

In sum, this first case (v 1) was originally an independent law stating that whoever defies a public imprecation by refusing to testify will be punished by the deity *(wĕnāśā' 'āwōnô)*. This law was amended by the Priestly legists, who incorporated it into the graduated purification-offering cases, which provided that if the offender subsequently felt remorseful and confessed his wrong, he could qualify for sacrificial expiation (v 5). The result of incorporating this law into the present text is to turn its apodosis, *wĕnāśā' 'āwōnô* 'then he must bear his punishment', virtually into part of the protasis (as recognized by Moses Mendelssohn in his editorial comment on Wessely [1846]), in parallel with the position of *'āšēm* that ends vv 2–4. Moreover, the resultant structure is not as awkward as it may seem. The idiom *wĕnāśā' 'āwōnô* is akin to *wĕ'āšēm* in that it does not imply that the punishment is irrevocable. Note that no punishment is specified. It leaves room for making amends: If the prescribed sacrificial rites are performed (vv 5–13), *wĕnislaḥ lô* "he may be forgiven" (vv 10, 13).

Here I permit myself a conjecture. The peculiar conditions of vv 1–4 that created the need for the discrete category of the graduated purification offering may throw light on the concession to allow the use of a cereal offering to substitute as a purification offering (vv 11–13). After all, if the sanctuary was in fact polluted, only the blood of a purification offering is empowered to purge it (chap. 4, COMMENT B). How can semolina produce the same effect? The semolina concession may therefore reflect the ambivalence in the mind of the legislator concerning the nature of the impurity in these cases. That impurity is produced by oath violation is only a deduction by analogy (with the impurity cases) and, hence, questionable. More important, it is also questionable whether the impurity produced in cases 2–3 is of sufficient force to pollute the sanctuary. That the prolongation of the secondary impurity can boost it to the force of a primary impurity capable of polluting the sanctuary is, after all, only a conjecture. Clearly, that is why the other two cases of graduated offerings, the mĕṣōrāʿ and the parturient, as well as the zāb, do not permit semolina: their impurity is primary and hence the ritual detergent of blood is necessary to purge the sanctuary. Thus it may be the anomalous nature of the impurity and its potency that have, in the long run, been responsible for creating the cultic fiction that semolina can purge the sanctuary.

Finally, having seen that the rabbis postulated the graduated purification offering as a discrete sacrificial category, it is well to ask how they could have insisted with equal unanimity that it applied only to cases of direct contact with sancta, a consideration that, as shown above, is in no way mandated by the text. The resolution of this question necessitates first a diachronic reordering of the data on impurity, though for the time being, it must be given in sketchy form (cf. also chap. 15, COMMENTS C–G). Three stages are reflected by the data:

(1) In the prebiblical stage all sancta communicate holiness to persons, the inner sancta directly by sight and indirectly (through a medium) by touch (e.g., Num 4:15, 18–20). This contagion is lethal even if the contact is accidental. The early biblical narratives exemplify the deadly power retained by the super-sancta: the Ark (1 Sam 6:19; 2 Sam 6:6–8), Mount Sinai (Exod 19:13), and the divine fire (10:1–5). True, there are no biblical texts that attribute an equivalent power to impurity. The possibility exists, however, that holiness and impurity were once both polaric and interchangeable: for example, the bones of the dead defile but those of Elisha resuscitate the dead (2 Kgs 13:21).

(2) In the Bible, impurity has been thoroughly eviscerated of any mythological or demonic content. Contracting impurity can bring no harm, per se: but it dare not be brought into contact with sancta or be allowed to persist in the community. The Priestly material, however, is not of one hue. Two substages come into view when considering three primary causes of human defilement: scale disease, pathological flux, and the corpse.

(A) The earlier stratum is reflected in Num 5:2–3, which calls for their banishment (also in Num 31:19, 24, for the corpse-contaminated person). Here God's presence is coextensive with the entire camp. This statute is in full accord with the deuteronomic imperative, "Let your camp be holy" (Deut 30:10–15).

(B) The remaining legislation dealing with these three human-impurity carriers reveals a later stratum. Banishment is decreed only for the mĕṣōrāʿ. The zāb/zābâ and the corpse-contaminated person, though they still jeopardize the community (15:31; Num 19:13, 20), are no longer excluded during their defilement (Milgrom 1981h; cf. Jos. Wars; CD 12.1–2; m. Kelim 1:8). The stringent demands of holiness for the entire camp are now confined to the sanctuary. Significantly, it is precisely the *zāb/zābâ* and the corpse-contaminated person, now permitted to remain in the community, who are warned about their danger to the sanctuary (15:31; Num 19:13, 20). Another passage, 17:15–16, stipulates punishment for the one who neglects to purify himself after he eats of what has died or has been torn by beasts. This law is unique to the Bible. It is the complement of 5:2 and also reflects the fear that procrastination in cleansing impurity may lead to its spread.

The two substages in human defilement, shown above, have their counterpart in animal impurities. Lev 17:15–16 (H) seems to reflect a later stage because it no longer distinguishes between the cadavers of pure and impure animals, as do 5:2 and 7:21 (see the NOTE on 5:2; also COMMENT A on 11:39–40).

(3) The third and final reduction in the power of impurity is the rabbinic stage, which limits its malefic effects to actual contact with sancta. Otherwise it is no longer sinful to remain impure. This stage is postbiblical, but it is clearly adumbrated by the following indications within P itself:

(A) The corpse-contaminated person and the *zāb/zābâ* have been permitted to remain at home (above).

(B) There is no longer any penalty for failing to undergo purification after eating or touching impure food as long as sancta are not contacted. In the case of touching cadavers of permitted animals (11:39–40), there is not even a prohibition. (This is only reasonable. The cadavers are probably of one's own livestock, and if their owner may not handle them, who else may?)

(C) The distinction between the sanctuary precinct and the rest of the camp is clearly made in 12:2–3. A second period of purification is enjoined for the parturient, during which only contact with sancta is proscribed.

(D) Nonetheless, as implied by the preceding and by 7:20–21; 22:3, dire consequences follow in the wake of contact between the holy and the impure.

Normative Judaism reflected in tannaitic legislation completes the skein:

(E) The last vestiges of airborne impurity (i.e., from a distance) can only be transmitted by contact. Moreover, such impure persons are punishable only if their contact is with sancta (*t. Šebu.* 1:5). Communicability of impurity without contact still remains the property of the human corpse through "overshadowing," explicitly demanded by Num 19:14, but its cases are severely restricted (*m. Ohol.* 3:2, 6). This change is manifest in the rabbinic interpretation of (a) the corpse-contaminated person (Num 19:13, 20), despite the text's clear statement to the contrary, and (b) the cadaver-contaminated person (17:15–16), where there is no mention whatever of sancta (details in Milgrom 1983e: 253–54 nn. 38, 39).

(F) One last step. There is complete agreement among the rabbis that the basic purpose of all of the purification offerings prescribed for the festivals is to expiate for "the pollution of the sanctuary and its sancta" (*m. Šebu.* 1:3–5). Herein lies corroboration that the common ground for all impurity taboos is the fear that impurity may impinge upon the realm of the holy. The rabbis, however, by their exegesis have reduced even the functional area of these public purification offerings to sancta contamination by direct contact.

Thus the analysis of ritual impurity presupposed by the graduated purification offering permits us to trace the development of a major religious concept over the entire lifespan of ancient Israel. The biblical and rabbinic ages are shown to be a single historical continuum in which the progressive reduction of the force of impurity leaves its traces at every stage. (The force of holiness is also subjected to diachronic reduction; see Milgrom 1981b and see chap. 7, COMMENT B.) The tannaitic legislation is only the end product of a process already at work in biblical days.

The motivating force behind this historical development is not difficult to discern. It is the working of the monotheistic idea. For the pagan, impurity is the domain of supernal evil that threatens the deities as well as man. But under the rule of one God, independent evil cannot exist. Pagan notions of impurity have to go. The baneful still inheres in things, but it spreads only under special conditions, such as carrion when consumed and discharges when contacted. These, however, are called impurities and are not confused with evils. But as long as impurity is conceived as miasma and allowed to spread invisibly, from afar as well as by touch, it is but a small step to its personification and autonomy. The danger ever persists that notions of demonic evil—affirmed by the surrounding religions during the same millennium—will be retained or reassimilated. The activity of impurity is then restricted to cases of contact, and the cases in which purification has been neglected (and a graduated purification sacrifice rather than ablution is enjoined) are further restricted to those in which contact with sancta has occurred.

Finally, the evolution of the graduated purification offering allows us to suggest an answer to the paradox of the rabbis' exegesis, which was initially raised: they recognized the graduated purification offering as a distinct sacrificial category and, at the same time, they qualified it by the criterion of "the pollution of the sanctuary and its sancta." Of course, the rabbis did not create the paradox; they only inherited it. The limitation of the concept of active impurity to cases of contact with sancta had taken place long before. It did not come about by the innovation of a reformer. It had no single originator, nor did it need one. It was the logical and irrevocable terminus for the monotheistic process, and it became oral tradition at an early age.

THE REPARATION OFFERING (5:14–26)

For Sacrilege Against Sancta

5 ¹⁴The Lord spoke to Moses, saying: ¹⁵When a person commits a sacrilege by being inadvertently remiss with any of the Lord's sancta, he shall bring as his penalty to the Lord a ram without blemish from the flock, convertible into payment in silver by sanctuary weight, as a reparation offering, ¹⁶and he shall make restitution for that item of the sancta wherein he was remiss and shall add one-fifth to it. When he gives it to the priest, the priest shall effect expiation on his behalf with the ram of the reparation offering so that he may be forgiven.

For Suspected Sacrilege Against Sancta

¹⁷If, however, a person errs by violating any of the Lord's prohibitive commandments without knowing it and he feels guilt, he shall bear his responsibility ¹⁸by bringing to the priest an unblemished ram from the flock, or its assessment, as a reparation offering. The priest shall effect expiation on his behalf for the error he committed without knowing it so that he may be forgiven. ¹⁹It is a reparation offering; he has incurred liability to the Lord.

For Sacrilege Against Oaths

²⁰The Lord spoke to Moses, saying: ²¹When a person sins by committing a sacrilege against the Lord in that he has dissembled to his fellow in the matter of a deposit or investment or robbery; or having withheld from his fellow ²²or having found a lost object he has dissembled about it; and he swears falsely about any one of the things that a person may do and sin thereby—²³when one has thus sinned and, feeling guilt, he shall return that which he robbed or that which he withheld, or the deposit that was entrusted to him, or the lost object he found, ²⁴or anything else about which he swore falsely; he shall restore it in its entirety and add one-fifth to it. He shall pay it to its owner as soon as he feels guilt. ²⁵Then he shall bring to the priest, as his reparation to the Lord, an unblemished ram from the flock, or its assessment, as a reparation offering. ²⁶The priest shall effect expiation on his behalf before the Lord so that he may be forgiven for whatever he has done to feel guilt thereby.

NOTES

5:14. *The Lord spoke to Moses, saying.* A new heading indicating a new topic (see at vv 17 and 20, below).

15. *When.* The particle *kî* begins the main case (1:2; 2:1, 4; 4:2; 5:1, 3, 4),

followed by *ʾim*, which introduces the secondary case (v 17; 1:3, 10, 14; 2:5, 7, 14; 3:1, 6, 12; 4:3, 13, 27, 32; 5:7, 11).

person. nepeš, which can be male or female (see on 2:1; 4:2), equivalent to *ʾādām* 'anyone' (see the NOTE on 1:2). The equivalence is proved by the replacement of *nepeš* (v 21) with *ʾîš ʾô ʾ iššâ* 'man or woman', in the rewording of the identical case (Num 5:6); see the NOTE on v 21.

commits a sacrilege (timʿōl maʿal). *maʿal* is the legal term for the wrong that is redressed by the *ʾāšām* offering (vv 15, 21; Num 5:6; cf. Ezra 10:10, 19). It is never defined in the Bible. Unfortunately, comparative philology is useless. Ibn Ezra (on this verse) suggests that because the nouns *meʿîl* and *beged* are synonyms for "cloak, covering," their respective verbs may be denominatives, originally meaning "cover one's deed" or "act deceitfully." As suggestive as this etymology is, it cannot be corroborated and, in particular, cannot shed light on the restricted, technical use of *maʿal* in the cultic laws. The answer will have to be sought in the *maʿal* contexts. From the synonymous use of *ḥillēl* 'desecrate' (19:12), the use of *maʿal* in the rabbinic texts, and similar contexts in ancient Near Eastern documents, it will be shown that the noun *maʿal* means "sacrilege," the verb *māʿal* means "commit sacrilege," and all cases of *maʿal* fall into two major categories: sacrilege against sancta and sacrilege involving oaths. These two categories are subsumed under the prescription for the *ʾāšām*: vv 14–19 deal with sacrilege against sancta and vv 20–26 with sacrilege involving oaths. Details are provided in the COMMENT below.

The object *bĕqodšê YHWH* was omitted because of the subsequent *miqqodšê YHWH* (Hoffmann 1953). A similar phenomenon is attested when *baddām* gives way to nearby *min-haddām* (see the NOTES on 4:17; 14:16).

inadvertently (bišĕgāgâ). See the NOTE on 4:2.

being . . . remiss (wĕḥāṭĕʾâ). That the verb *ḥāṭāʾ* can cover the entire range of sin from accidental misdemeanors, as in this case, to deliberate crimes, see the NOTES on 4:2 and 16:16.

with any. One of the possible usages of the partitive *min* (e.g., 5:13, 24; 11:34; and see the NOTE at 4:2).

the Lord's sancta (qodšê YHWH). The term is ambiguous. Does it denote every object dedicated to the Lord, whether *qōdeš qodāšîm* 'most sacred' or *qōdeš* 'sacred', and whether inside the sacred precincts or outside? First, an analysis of the two terms for "sacred" and "most sacred" is indicated.

The phrase *qōdeš qodāšîm* is an exact term in P. In the sacrificial system it embraces all sacrifices but the *šĕlāmîm* 'well-being offering'. These are the *ʿōlâ* (chap. 1), *minḥâ* (chap. 2), *ḥaṭṭāʾt* (chap. 4), and *ʾāšām* (5:14–26). They are alike as regards their place of slaughter (e.g., 4:24, 29; 7:2), consumers, and manner and place of consumption (e.g., 6:9, 22; 7:6), differing with the *šĕlāmîm* in all of these respects (3:2; 7:15–16; Num 18:18–19). This precision concerning "most sacred" sacrifices is also found in sources apart from but dependent on P, such as H (21:22), Ezekiel (42:13), and Ezra (2:63; cf. Neh 7:65). Snaith (1973) contends that *qōdeš qodāšîm* is limited to "the most holy gift" given to the priest, with the consequence that the *ʿōlâ,* being entirely consumed on the altar, would be excluded from this designation. But he loses sight of the partitive *mem* in *miqqōdeš haqqodāšîm* 'from the most sacred offerings' (Num 18:9), implying that there are other offerings of this type that are not the reserve of the priests (see also 21:22 and Ezra 2:63 [= Neh 7:65]).

For "most sacred" objects other than sacrifices, a greater plasticity is evident, but their range is confined to the Tabernacle sancta. The phrase *qōdeš qodāšîm* here generally refers to the entire Tabernacle complex (e.g., Exod 30:29; cf. v 26a), but it may also designate the cultic furniture (e.g., Num 4:4, 19) or the Tabernacle adytum (e.g., Exod 26:33–34). This variation, however, is not arbitrary. It should be noted that the two latter restricted meanings are employed for one purpose: to contrast the gradations within the "most sacred," namely, the adytum with the rest of the sanctuary (e.g., Exod 26:33) or the cultic furniture with the planks and curtains of the Tabernacle (e.g., Exod 29:30; Num 4:4, cf. v 15). Outside the sphere of P, a similar phenomenon is observable. The phrase *qōdeš qodāšîm* will also indicate gradations in holiness, but in a metaphoric rather than a strict legal sense. For example, the priests (Aaron and his sons) are called *qōdeš qodāšîm* (1 Chr 23:13), presumably to set them apart from the Levites, whom the Chronicler (but never P, see Milgrom 1970a: n. 46) calls *qōdeš* (e.g., 2 Chr 23:6; cf. Ezra 8:28). Similarly, Ezekiel uses *qōdeš qodāšîm,* unlike P, to distinguish the land assigned to the priests (45:3 LXX [also 48:12, where *sābîb sābîb* refers to the priests' land surrounding the Temple]) from the Levites' land, called *qōdeš* (48:14). The usage, again, is metaphoric and not legal because, even in Ezekiel's scheme, the Levites' land is indistinguishable in sanctity from the priests: both are *ḥērem* which may not be sold or exchanged (cf. 27:28).

The reverse, however, does not hold true: the "most sacred" are not always designated *qōdeš qodāšîm.* On occasion, P will resort to the general term *qōdeš* (e.g., the incense, Exod 30:37, cf. v 36; the altar, Exod 40:9, cf. v 10) or its plural *qodāšîm* (e.g., the sacrifices, Exod. 28:38; Num 18:18, cf. v 9). By the same token, the anointment oil, called "sacred" (Exod 30:32), must also rate as "most sacred" not only because incense exhibits the same terminological fluidity (vv 36, 37) but for two additional reasons: (1) because anointment confers a "most sacred" status the oil itself must be of similar status, and (2) by definition, the oil is holier than the "most sacred" incense because its manufacture and its use are both prohibited (cf. v 33 with v 37). Thus the term *qōdeš* can indicate not only less sacred sacrifices and objects (e.g., the *šĕlāmîm* and the Tabernacle court) but "most sacred" sancta as well. The generic use of *qōdeš* is especially characteristic of the sources other than of P and Ezekiel, such as Josh 6:19; 1 Kgs 7:51; 15:15 (= 2 Chr 5:1; 15:18); 2 Kgs 12:5, 19; 1 Chr 26:26–28 and 2 Chr 24:7.

In view of the plasticity of *qōdeš qodāšîm,* is it at all possible to determine the exact range of the *qodšê YHWH* subject to *maʿal* (5:15)? Mari is not of much help because there is only the barest warrant for associating *asakku*, roughly equivalent to "taboo," with sancta (Milgrom 1976f: 25–27). It is, however, of relevance that the range of *asakku* is unbounded: the god or the king can designate any object he wishes as *asakku* (e.g., spoils of war). This fact is matched by the Hittite text "Instructions for Temple Personnel" (*ANET*[3] 207–10), in which sacrilege is possible with all sancta, offerable and nonofferable alike, whether located inside or outside the sacred precincts or whether expropriated accidentally or intentionally. Indeed, there is no distinction among the sancta when it comes to Hittite *maʿal*. But the Hittites do distinguish among the sancta in other respects; see below for categories similar to biblical *qōdeš* and *qōdeš qodāšîm*.

How do the rabbis define *qodšê YHWH?* They too give it the broadest possible meaning, embracing all sancta, offerable and nonofferable alike, for example, in ornaments (necklaces, rings, bracelets, earrings); in implements (golden cups, sacred vesels); in dress (shirts, cloaks); in houses, land, produce, nonofferable animals, building material, moneys dedicated for most sacred offerings; and in property generally (*m. Meʿil.* 5:1; *t. Meʿil.* 2:1; *m. ʿArak.* 6:5; *b. Meʿil.* 20a [bar]; *m. Peʾa* 7:8; *m. Nazir* 6:6; *m. Meʿil.* 3:7–8; *m. Meʿil.* 4:1; *Sipra*, Ḥobah 20:3–5; *t. Meʿil.* 1:9; *m. Meʿil.* 6:6; *m. ʿArak.* 6:2). The Bible is not entirely silent on the nature of dedicated sancta. A glimpse is afforded us when it comes to spoils. In addition to the general categories of persons, oxen, asses, and sheep given to the sanctuary resulting from the war against Midian (Num 31:42–47), there is an itemized list of gold ornaments (v 50). Historical sources indeed attest that captured vessels were dedicated to the Temple (2 Sam 8:10–11; 1 Kgs 7:51 [= 2 Chr 5:1]; 1 Kgs 15:15 [= 2 Chr 15:18]; 1 Chr 26:27–28), including precious weapons (2 Sam 8:7; 1 Kgs 14:26–27; 2 Kgs 11:10). That they were subject to *maʿal* is expressly stated in the case of Ahaz (2 Chr 29:19). Most of the same categories are attested in the Hittite "Instructions" (2.32–58; 4.12, 17, 25). Nevertheless, the rabbis expressly exclude the *qodāšîm qallîm* 'minor sancta' (their term for biblical *qōdeš)* from being subject to *maʿal*. Thus, by rabbinic definition, *maʿal* only governs the *qōdeš qodāšîm*, the category of the "most sacred."

Are the rabbis correct in excluding minor sancta from the prohibition of *maʿal?* The text of 5:15 does not support such a deduction. In fact, there is another verse that contradicts it: "When you sacrifice an offering of well-being . . . he who eats of it (on the third day) shall bear his guilt, for he has desecrated the sanctum of the Lord" (19:5–8; cf. Exod 29:34). Thus the *šĕlāmîm*, one of the minor sancta, is called *qōdeš YHWH*, the same idiom as the subject of *maʿal* in 5:15, and moreover, the text of 19:8 expressly states that it is subject to *hillûl* 'desecration'. Thus the Priestly source, just like its Hittite counterpart, regards all sancta as subject to *maʿal*. Interestingly, the Karaites voice a similar objection to the rabbis' ruling: "The oral-traditionists (rabbis) say that 'the sancta of the Lord' are the most sacred . . . and not the less sacred whereas the Karaites have only exempted the Levitic tithe and the (third-year) tithe for the poor but have held all sancta liable to sacrilege" (*Keter Torah* on Lev 5:14).

The rabbis also define the time limits for *ma'al*. It operates from the moment that an object is dedicated *(hiqdîš)*, an act that may take place at the owner's home, and it ends as soon as the object becomes the property of the priest (*m. Qidd.* 1:6; *t. Qidd.* 119), for instance, the meat of the *ḥaṭṭā't* and *'āšām* after the blood offering and the *minḥâ* after the token offering *('azkārâ)* is consumed on the altar (*m. Me'il.* 1:1ff.; *t. Me'il.* 1:9). They derive this ruling from the expression *miqqodšê YHWH* (5:15), in other words, *ma'al* takes place with the Lord's sancta but not with those belonging to the priest. By the same token, they exempt all less sacred offerings (e.g., *šēlāmîm*) from the law of *ma'al* because the animal belongs to the owner both before and after the blood offering and never belongs to God, except for the suet.

What of the rabbis' opinion concerning the time span for *ma'al*? On the inception of *ma'al*, they stand on firm ground. The Hittite "Instructions" shows that even temple property outside the sacred precincts is taboo (4.1ff.). Moreover, the Hittite Code expressly states that if "the sacrificial loaf or wine destined for libation" is spoiled *in the home*, a trespass is committed and the home is defiled (HL 164). Thus there is good precedent for the rabbinic teaching that *ma'al* becomes operative when the object is dedicated, not when it is brought into the sanctuary. In the Bible the wording of the following dedications indicates that they were dedicated outside the sanctuary: the firstfruits (Num 18:12–13), the tithe (according to 27:30–33), most sacred offerings (6:18; 7:1–2), and other dedications (chap. 27). There is no warrant, however, for the rabbis' view that the sacrifice is no longer subject to *ma'al* once it is transferred from God to man (i.e., the owner or the priest). As was noted just above, 19:5–8 explicitly calls sacrificial meat—in the hands of its owner more than two days after the blood and suet offering—*qōdeš YHWH* and liable to *ḥillûl* 'desecration'. What holds for minor sancta, belonging to the owner, holds for "most sacred" meat after it becomes the property of the priests. It must be eaten under "most sacred" conditions (Num 18:10; cf. 1 Sam 21:5–6) and until then is actively contagious (6:11, 20; cf. Hag 2:12 [Milgrom 1981b]). The Hittite "Instructions" also elucidates a number of biblical concepts:

(1) Two items are related to the nature of the *'āšām*. A distinction is always made between apprehended and suspected sacrilege, the latter case requiring an ordeal. Also, in the one instance wherein a fine of one ox and ten sheep is imposed (D2 in the table in COMMENT B, below) the offender is guilty of delaying the sacrifice, in other words, he is suspected of sacrilege. The fixed fine recalls the *'āšām* prescription, and the distinction between actual and suspected *ma'al* will be crucial in distinguishing between the two *'āšām* pericopes, 5:14–16 and 5:17–19.

(2) The biblical concept that sacrificial meat must be eaten within a set

time is reflected in the Hittite provision, "If you *(wish)* to eat and drink . . .
on that day eat and drink. If you cannot finish it, keep on eating (and) drinking
[for] three days" (2.1–3). P differs in that the most sacred offerings and the *tôdâ*,
pesaḥ, and *millūʾîm* must be eaten the same day (7:15; cf. 22:30), whereas it
allows the votive and voluntary *šĕlāmîm* to be eaten on the second day (7:16;
19:8; Exod 12:10; 29:34), provided that on the third day the meat is incinerated
(7:17; 19:6–7).

(3) The Hittite text continues, "But your wives, your children (and) your
servants must in no circumstances (. . . cross) the threshold of the gods"
(2.4–5). The inference seems clear that the Hittites must have had a cultic law
that certain sacrificial portions could be eaten solely by male priests. So in Israel,
the most sacred meats are the prebend of the priests alone (6:11, 19; 7:6).
Furthermore, the sacred food in question consists of loaves, beer, and wine
(1.60–62), also described as "from thy divine loaves (or) from the libation bowl"
(1.64–65). The correspondence to the biblical "most sacred," in general, and
with *minḥâ* and *nesek*, in particular, should be obvious. Perhaps some sacrificial
portions were made available to the priest's family like the Israelite's *šĕlāmîm*,
but on this point the Hittite text is silent. (For a similar gradation in the
Egyptian sacrifices, see below.) Thus there is every reason to suspect that the
biblical distinction between "sacred" and "most sacred" is not original to Israel
but a legacy from the ancient Near East.

(4) The Hittite temple officials are enjoined not to "put (sacrifical animals)
under the yoke" (2.18). Similarly, the Israelite is cautioned: "You must not work
your firstling ox or shear your firstling sheep" (Deut 15:19), a prohibition that
probably applied not just to firstlings but to all sacrificial animals (So understood
by the Tannaites, e.g., *Sipre* and *Midrash Tannaim*, ad loc.).

(5) Finally, the Hittite text warns the temple officials lest "you appropriate
for yourselves either a fattened ox or a fattened sheep and substitute a lean one
which you had slaughtered" (2.13ff.); it stipulates that the herdsmen must take
care that "in the same condition in which they [the animals] are selected from
the pen (and) the fold, shall they bring them to the gods. In the road they must
not exchange them. But if any cowherd or shepherd does wrong on the road,
exchanges either a fattened ox or a fattened sheep, and puts in its place an
emaciated animal . . ." (4.58–66). This corresponds to the Priestly law concerning animals dedicated to the sanctuary: "One may not exchange or substitute another for it either good for bad, or bad for good" (27:10a). Both Hittite
and biblical law prohibit the exchange or substitution of the dedicated animal
(see the Note at 27:10).

The premises that underlie Hittite and biblical sancta trespass are not all
the same. Hittite sacrilege is deliberate; there is no equivalent to biblical *šĕgāgâ*.
Yet "Instructions" is only one text, and it may not be indicative of the entire
corpus of Hittite law. In Egypt, for example, this distinction is found, for example, "When a man has killed one of the sacred animals, if he did it with

malicious purpose, he is punished with death; if unwittingly, he has to pay such a fine as the priests choose to impose. When an ibis, however, or a hawk is killed, whether it was done by accident or on purpose, the man must die" (Herod. 2.65). The Egyptian parallel is even more striking because it imposes a fine for accidental trespass that corresponds to the biblical *ʾāšām* provisions (though the latter are fixed and not subject to the whim of the priests, as in Egypt). More importantly, the Egyptian law stipulates that there is no inadvertency in the realm of the most sacred. This postulate is still detectable in the early traditions concerning the superior sanctity of the Ark. Uzzah's touching the Ark (2 Sam 6:6) and the Beth Shemeshites' viewing of it (1 Sam 6:19) were not premeditated acts. P's laws also reflect this view, for the Kohathites are liable to be struck down for accidentally touching covered sancta (Num 4:15) or viewing uncovered ones (Num 4:20 [Milgrom 1970a: 20–21 n. 162]). Indeed, in positing inadvertency as a mitigating factor in sacrilege, P has broken with its own background in which intention is not a factor in trespass on the most sacred. But the glimmering of a tendency to alleviate the penalty for unintentional sacrilege is also detectable in older Egyptian law and perhaps in Hittite jurisprudence as well.

A clearer and more significant distinction is that biblical law authorizes the redemption of certain sancta; it legalizes desanctification (27:9–34). On this subject, to my knowledge, ancient Near Eastern law is silent. Indeed, the very categories of dedicated objects in the Bible—for example, impure animals, houses, *ḥērem*, and tithes—are missing in the Hittite "Instructions." By the same token, there are cultic laws of the Hittites that have no biblical counterparts. What would P say, for example, if a priest officiated at a ritual at an improper time (cf. 2.59–62) or if he were persuaded by the worshiper to delay his ritual (2.63–71)? The prohibition is implied for the layman in P's law of the delayed Pesach (Num 9:9–14), where being en route (*bĕderek*, v 13) is a legitimate reason for postponement (contrary to a similar excuse given in the Hittite "Instructions," 2.67). By implication, however, this excuse would be invalid for any other ritual. Still, the absence of an explicit prohibition, especially for the priesthood, is surprising. The possibility of *maʿal* with the cultic calendar must have been an ever-present reality in later times. In the Second Temple there was a special officer (one of fifteen) who was in charge of the temple calendar and protocol, without whose direction no rite could take place (m. *Šeqal.* 1:1; y. *Šeqal.* 5:1; b. *Yoma* 20b). Perhaps the answers still await the discovery of new texts. In the meantime, the more probable premise will have to be granted that some laws and the circumstances that motivated them may be sui generis (details in Milgrom 1976f: 16–35).

In sum, the Bible does not define the scope of the sancta subject to *maʿal*. Nevertheless, the detailed examples provided by both the anterior Hittite "Instructions" and the posterior tannaitic literature point to the widest possible meaning of *qodšê YHWH* (5:15), namely, all of the sancta, major and minor, from the time of their dedication until, if they be food, they are eaten or incinerated.

his penalty (ʾăšāmô). See the NOTES on 4:3 and 5:6.

from the flock (min-haṣṣōʾn). Because a ram has already been specified, is not this phrase superfluous? Not at all. Sacrificial animals must be domestic, not wild. The term *min-haṣṣōʾn* 'from the flock' is equivalent to *ben-bāqār* 'of the herd', which also implies domestication (see the NOTE on 4:3).

convertible. bĕʿerkĕkā, lit., "according to your valuation." The final *kap* is not to be understood as a pronominal suffix (LXX, *Tgs.*, Pesh, Rashi on 27:2), though it originally was "a pronominal suffix that became fossilized and thus absorbed in the nominal stem," that is, " 'your valuation' . . . became through common usage simply 'valuation' (by an outside party), with the pronoun inactivated and absorbed" (Speiser 1960: 30–31). That this term ultimately became a noun is shown by its assumption of the definite article *hāʿerkĕkā* (27:23). The rabbinic view that the valuation is minimally two shekels (Pesh., *b. Ker.* 10b) is followed by many moderns (e.g., Shadal; Ehrlich 1908–14; Elliger 1966). For evidence of the commutability of animal fines in the ancient Near East, see below.

Jackson (1972: 272), followed by Fishbane (1985: 222–23, 250–51), claims that the text originally read *bĕʿerkĕkā lĕʾāšām,* lit., "according to your assessment as a reparation offering," as in vv 18, 25, and that the intervening clause, *kesep-šĕqālîm bĕšeqel-haqqōdeš* 'payment in silver by sanctuary weight', is a later interpolation, borrowed from a similar phrase in 27:15, when monetary payment was permitted instead of the required animal. But originally in this case and still operative in the following two cases, "the ram required for expiation is established at a value equivalent to the guilt involved" (Fishbane 1985: 222). The objection to this interpretation is obvious: how could the priest always find a ram whose value was the precise equivalent of the desecrated sanctum? What if the latter—as is likely the case—would be more valuable than the most valuable ram? Moreover, why would only a desecrated sanctum be expiable by a monetary payment but not a desecrated oath (v 25)? Lastly, how could the priest find the ram to match the offerer's infraction in the next case, where the infraction is unknown (vv 17–19)?

The answer becomes clear once it is realized that every time the term *ʿerkĕkā* is used, a monetary payment is stipulated (Lev 27 [twenty-one times]; Num 18:16). Furthermore, the *ʾāšām* is the only sacrifice that takes the verb *hēsîb* 'restore' (Num 18:9), implying that the monetary compensation is envisioned (cf. Num 5:7–8; 1 Sam 6:3, 4, 8, 17). Finally, the mention of *ʾāšām* silver, to the exclusion of an *ʾāšām* animal, in 2 Kgs 12:17—admitted by all to be an ancient witness—proves that monetary payment for all cases of *ʾāšām* is based on ancient precedent. Indeed, the possibility must be reckoned with that *bĕʿer-kĕkā* does not connote a choice of animal or payment but, as indicated by the preposition *b*, it means payment only. Thus the priest, in the *ʾāšām* cases that follow, assesses both the equivalent value of the animal and the monetary equivalent of the involved desecration (v 16a). The priest charges the supplicant the amount of the desecrated sanctum (or arbitrarily sets a sum in the case in which sacrilege is suspected, vv 17–19) plus the amount needed to purchase the requisite 'āšām animal. The added clause here is not an interpolation singling out sanctuary desecration as eligible for monetary payment; rather, being the first 'āšām case, it functions as a standard for the cases that follow (cf. also Milgrom 1976f: 13 n. 42).

as a reparation offering (lĕ 'āšām). The 'āšām offering differs from all others by its unique use of the verb hēšîb 'return, restore' (Num 5:7–8; 18:9; cf. 1 Sam 6:3, 4, 8, 17 and CD 9.13–14). The inference may at once be drawn that the context of the 'āšām is a legal situation: damage has been done, and restitution is ordered. This initial inference is strengthened by the use of the same verb hēšîb in parallelism with šillēm 'repay', in one 'āšām case in which the restitution is itemized in detail: "when one has thus sinned and, feeling guilt, he shall return *(wĕhēšîb)* that which he robbed or that which he withheld, or the deposit that was entrusted to him, or the lost object he found, or anything else about which he swore falsely; he shall restore *(wĕšillēm)* it in its entirety and add one-fifth to it" (5:23–24). Moreover, in the Samuel passages cited above, the idiom hēšîb 'āšām refers to the golden mice and tumors (1 Sam 6:4–5; cf. 5:6; 6:1 LXX), to wit, a monetary payment. Thus this idiom and its synonym point to the conclusion that fundamentally the 'āšām sacrifice compensates for damages. Hence, its preferred translation is "reparation offering." This rendering is confirmed by another unique feature of the 'āšām offering. It is the only one in the entire roster of sacrifices that is commutable to currency (5:15, 18, 25; and 1 Sam 6:3–17).

The commutability of the reparation offering also speaks for its antiquity. It appears only twice in the early biblical narratives, and in both places it appears not as an animal sacrifice but as a monetary payment. The first has already been adduced: the golden mice and tumors for the plague that beset the Philistines because they possessed the holy Ark (1 Sam 6:3–17). It is also of no small importance that this practice is attested of a people residing in Canaan at the beginning of Israelite history. The other mention of 'āšām in the early narratives is in connection with King Joash's Temple repairs (2 Kgs 12:17). This account speaks of kesep 'āšām 'reparation silver', testifying that in First Temple days, 'asam offerers had the option of donating its monetary equivalent. The 'āšām silver is not confiscated by Joash but retained by the priests. This is in accordance with the rule of Num 5:8 (and Lev 7:7, which awards the 'āšām flesh to the officiating priest), indicating its grounding in ancient precedent. Elliger (1966) concludes from 1 Sam 6 that the 'āšām was originally a *Schadenersatz*. But 1 Sam 6 does not concern a civil crime and cannot be used as a basis for claiming a civil origin for the 'āšām .

An extrabiblical parallel from a civilization anterior to Israel also corroborates that the commutability unique to the *ʾāšām* is evidence for its antiquity. The Nuzi texts, as shown by Speiser (1960: 30–33), reflecting customary law that goes back at least to the middle of the second millennium, affirm that in certain cases fines were imposed in terms of fixed animal ratios that were commutable to stipulated amounts of currency, just as in the case of the biblical *ʾāšām* .

Moreover, the Nuzi parallel is even stronger than Speiser noticed. The animals specified in the fine remain the same in species and number regardless of the offense. So too in Israel, the reparation offering always calls for a fixed animal, a ram (or a lamb), regardless of the nature or the extent of the damage inflicted on the property of God or man (5:14–16; 19:19–21; Num 5:6–8; Ezra 10:19). The case of the *mĕṣōrāʿ* illustrates this point vividly. The indigent *mĕṣōrāʿ* will have all of his required offerings (i.e., the *ʿōlâ*, *ḥaṭṭāʾt*, and *minḥâ*) reduced to less expensive species; however, the requirement for the *ʾāšām* lamb remains unchanged (14:10–12, 21–22). Thus both the commutable and the fixed aspects of the Nuzi fines are duplicated in the reparation offering. The evidence points to the possibility that this Israelite sacrifice may have had an ancient history (details in Milgrom 1976f: 14–15 and nn.).

16. *make restitution (yĕšallem).* Not in kind (Daube 1947: 133–44) but in its monetary equivalent. This can be proved by its exact legal cognate, Akk. *šullumu*, which, similarly, is not limited to restitution in kind (Milgrom 1976f: 137–40). Implied also is that the desecrated sanctum must be replaced even if it is undamaged. The principle is: once desecrated it cannot be reconsecrated. This is confirmed by Josh 8:24; the desecrated *ḥērem*, which should have been devoted to the sanctuary (Josh 6:19–24), must now be destroyed. Perhaps ordinary sancta, being of lesser holiness than *ḥērem*, might be sold rather than destroyed.

one-fifth, hamîsitô, lit., "its fifth," that is to say, of its value. That the Priestly legislators imposed such a small fine for sacrilege is nothing short of astounding. Their leniency can only be appreciated by comparing this case with other kinds of theft found in the legal statutes of the Bible (see the table). The penalties are listed according to their severity in descending order.

PENALTIES FOR THEFT

The Theft	The Thief	Source	Penalty (% increase)
1. Property (destroyed)	apprehended	Exod 21:37 (JE)	300% or 400%
2. Property (undamaged)	apprehended	Exod 22:3 (cf. v 8 [JE])	100%

3. Property (undamaged) and false oath	unapprehended	Lev 5:20–26 (P); Num 5:6–8 (H)	20%
4. Property (undamaged)	unapprehended	———	0%

The table makes it clear that the decisive factor in penalties for theft is whether the thief (undamaged) was apprehended or surrendered voluntarily. In the former case, the required restitution is multiple; in the latter, it varies between 0 and 20 percent. True, the Bible is silent concerning the case of the voluntary return of theft. But the law can be extrapolated from one of the cases cited in Lev 5:20–26, *ʾăbēdâ*, the lost object. In ancient Near Eastern codes, the one who returns of a lost object is not subject to fine (e.g., HL 45, 66, 71), but if the finder denies it and is apprehended, he is considered a thief and is subject to heavy fines and even death (HL 45, later version; MAL Tablets C and G, 6a, 9; CH 9). The same law obtains in Israel (Exod 23:4 [JE]; Deut 22:1–3 [D]; cf. Lev 5:20–26 [P]). Rabbinic law is explicit that the voluntary surrender of theft is not subject to fine (e.g., *b. B. Qam.* 64b; 74b). The rabbis even generalize that "one who makes a voluntary confession in any penal law is exempt" (*b. B. Qam.* 74b; *b. Ketub.* 43a), a principle already assumed in the tannaitic laws on fines (e.g., *m. B. Qam.* 7:4; 9:7–8; *m. Šebu* 5:4–5).

The contrast stands out in bolder relief when it is realized that apprehended theft in Israel is dealt with more leniently than in the neighboring law codes (LE 6, 12–13; CH 6–13, 21–23, 259–60; MAL 3–5; HL 91–97, 101–13; cf. also "The Treaty Between Niqmepa of Alalakh and Ir-im of Tunip [*ANET*[3] 531, 6] "the Edict of Ammisaduqa" [*ANET*[3] 527, 7]). Yet even these reduced penalties for apprehended theft loom large against the negligible penalties for unapprehended theft. The answer was correctly noted by M. Greenberg: eliminating penalties for self-confessed theft encouraged "voluntary surrender in these cases, where, owing to the lack of evidence, or to the impotence of the victims—the victims of robbery and oppression are almost invariably poor and defenseless (Ps 35:6; Isa 3:14; Jer 7:6; Amos 4:1)—legal means of recovery were of little avail" (1962: 741b).

The following Hittite text shows that this motive is not original with the Bible:

You who are leatherworkers . . . take always oxhides and goatskins from the (royal) kitchen! Do not take any other! *If you take any other and tell the king about it, it is no crime for you.* I, the king, will send that abroad or give it to my servants. But if you conceal it and it becomes

known afterwards, they will put you to death together with your wives
(and) your children. (*ANET*³ 207; italics mine)

Furthermore, this motive is incorporated into the legal codes of Israel's anterior
environment as well as in subsequent tannaitic law. Indeed, the Tannaites convert this motive into a major postulate of their penal legislation, calling it *taqqānat haššābîm* 'a dispensation for the repentant', that is, eliminating the penalty in order to encourage repentance (e.g., *t. B. Qam.* 10:5; *b. Giṭ.* 55a (bar.);
m. Giṭ. 5:5; *m. ʿEd.* 7:9). There is a tendency in all ancient jurisprudence to
encourage the voluntary surrender of illegally aquired goods by reducing the
usual penalties. Jackson (1972: 174–78) propounds the astounding thesis that
5:20–26 represents no mitigation at all but, on the contrary, actually increases
the Covenant Code's *duplum* (Exod 22:3) by requiring a sacrifice "that is the
equivalent of the stolen property . . . (thus) restitution plus the *asham* plus a
fifth adds up to the double penalty of the Code plus a fifth" (175). Jackson can
achieve this tour de force by his exegesis of Lev 5:22–23 in general and the
ʾāšām in particular, whereby the passage deals only with secular offenses that
originally required neither oath nor confession (see below). What undermines
his thesis is the implied assumption that the offender could always find a ram
exactly "equivalent (in cost) to the stolen property." What if the amount turned
out to be less than the value of the most emaciated beast or more than the pride
of the Bashan? Besides, as indicated above, it was in the interest of ancient
courts to encourage the voluntary return of stolen goods by suspending penalties, and it is not without good biblical and extrabiblical precedent that the
Tannaites formulated the principle of *taqqānat haššābîm*.

   When he gives (wĕnātan). As will be developed below (on 5:25), a basic
legal and theological postulate of the Priestly legislators is that man can seek
reconciliation with God only after he has made the required restitution (to the
sanctuary or to man). Thus the apodosis begins here, requiring that the
ʾetnaḥtāʾ, the major disjunctive sign, be moved back to the previous word, *ʿālāyw.*
Yet the previous statement (vv 15–16a) prescribes the reverse, that sacrifice
precede the restitution. The ostensible discrepancy is due to a stylistic peculiarity of cultic texts. Prescriptive and descriptive statements differ in style. Prescriptive statements are unconcerned with sequence. Thus prescriptive vv 15–
16a (until *ʿālāyw*) call for bringing the sacrifice and restitution *together.* By
contrast, v 16aγb (beginning with *wĕnātān)* is descriptive, and the action is
sequential. Only after the payment of the restitution to the sanctuary does the
priest perform the expiatory ritual. A good example of the distinction between
prescriptive and descriptive texts is found in the sacrifices for the Nazirite who
has successfully fulfilled his or her vow. When the sacrifices are *prescribed,* the
whole offering appears first, but when the execution of the ritual is *described,*
the purification offering is listed first (Num 6:12–14; cf. *m. Nazir* 6:7; *m. Zebaḥ.*
10:12; *t. Para* 1:10).

to the priest. That is to say, to the sanctuary.

shall effect expiation (yĕkappēr). The root meaning of the verb *kippēr* is "rub, efface," and in contexts dealing in sin it connotes the sin's elimination. This broad-based meaning, however, is capable of more nuanced interpretation in specific sacrifices. Thus in the purification offering it means "purge." For a discussion of the full range of this crucial verb, see chap. 16, COMMENT F, where it will be shown that for the reparation offering, the general rendering "effect expiation, expiate" is best suited.

so that he may be forgiven (wĕnislaḥ lô). See the NOTE on 4:20.

17. *If, however (wĕʾ im).* The particle indicates that this case (vv 17–19) is integrally connected with and subsumed under the preceding case (vv 14–16; see at v 15). As succinctly stated by Rabbi Akiba, *"wĕʾim* supplements the previous passage by implying that cases of doubtful sacrilege (require) an *ʾāšām tālûy,* a suspended reparation offering" (*Sipra,* Ḥobah, par. 12:1). Some other Tannaites, Rabbi Tarfon, Rabbi Simeon, and Rabbi Yossi (though they differ in details) share this view (*m. Ker.* 5:2–8; *Ker.* 22b [bar.]). It is particularly noteworthy that because Rabbi Tarfon was a priest, who was born before the destruction of the Temple, he can testify as an expert eyewitness. The majority of the sages, however, hold that vv 17–19 do not apply to sancta desecration at all but to a larger spectrum of sins, which, if committed deliberately, are punishable with death by God *(kārēt);* and if committed inadvertently (but consciously), are expiated by a *ḥaṭṭāʾt,* and only here, if committed unconsciously, require an *ʾāšām.* Sancta desecration is ruled out because if committed inadvertently it requires an *ʾāšām,* not a *ḥa ṭṭāʾt* (vv 14–16), and if committed deliberately it is punishable (in the view of the majority) not with death but with flogging (see *t. Ker.* 1:6). It therefore follows that Rabbi Akiba would reason that deliberate sacrilege against sancta is deserving of death by God, which is the clear implication of the text. This weakness in the argumentation of the majority is augmented by their being forced into the untenable position of requiring no expiation whatsoever for suspected trespass on sancta, which, as noted below, was of obsessive concern to the ancients.

Nonetheless, the majority has textual criteria to back its view. There is no doubt that the language of v 17 is a precise replica of the *ḥaṭṭāʾt* laws (4:2, 13, 22, 27), and the Tannaites would maintain that ideologically speaking (but not textually, as many moderns claim, see below), 5:17–19 is a displaced *ḥaṭṭāʾt* passage. Additional support for their position is provided by the awkward phrase *wĕʾ im nepeš kî* (v 17aα). In the casuistic laws of P, main cases are introduced by *kî,* subordinate cases by *ʾim* (e.g., *ḥaṭṭāʾt:* 4:2, 3, 13, 23, 27, 32; graduated *ḥaṭṭāʾt:* 5:6, 7, 11; dedication of persons: 27:2, 4, 13; dedication of property: 27:14, 15–22). Note also the absence of the term *maʿal* in v 17, the telltale sign of an *ʾāšām* case (contrast vv 15, 21). Thus the possibility exists that *originally* the single verse, 5:17, was an independent law without the particle *weʾ im,* which stated simply that the unconscious violation of a divine taboo is subject to divine punishment, so only *wĕnāśāʾ ʿăwōnô* was the apodosis (for similarly constructed laws, see 5:1; 17:6; 24:15). The Priestly legists copied this law verbatim, prefixed it with *wĕʾim*, thereby connecting it to the law of inadvertent sancta desecration (vv 14–16), and affixed the penalty of the *ʾāšām* (vv 18, 19). It is of note that Rabbi Akiba and his colleagues do not discount the majority view that v 17 includes other kinds of suspected sin, but they are undoubtedly right in maintaining that basically the text predicates sancta desecration.

This lengthy note on the differences among the rabbinic sages has wide ramifications. First, it provides a glimpse into the redactional process and, in particular, into the penultimate state of the text, before it received its final form. Second, it lays the basis for the ultimate distinction between the *ḥaṭṭāʾt* and the *ʾāšām*. It has been shown separately that the *ḥaṭṭāʾt* is prescribed for every inadvertent violation of a prohibitive commandment once the sin becomes known (see the NOTE on 4:2), to which there is only one exception: the *ʾāšām* prescribed for the sin of desecration of the sancta or name of God, whether known or suspected (5:14–19). Third, it supports the postulate that the *ḥaṭṭāʾt* expiates for inadvertent ethical as well as cultic wrongs (cf. the NOTE on "commandments," 4:2) and for that reason the protasis formula of the *ḥaṭṭāʾt* laws (4:2a, 13b, 22, 27) was inserted here, albeit most awkwardly, and the term for desecration, *maʿal*, was deliberately excluded, in order to teach that the *ʾāšām* offering is prescribed not just for the desecration of sancta but also for the unconscious violation of all of the Lord's prohibitive commandments (Milgrom 1976f: 126).

Another obstacle encountered in this interpretation is a literary-stylistic one. The language of v 17, stating the case, follows not the wording of the protasis in v 15a—which should be expected if they were one law—but that of the *ḥaṭṭāʾt* offering (4:2, 13, 22, 27). This has led many moderns to postulate that vv 17–19 concern a *ḥaṭṭāʾt* offering for which commutation has been allowed (e.g., Noth 1965). Overlooked, however, is that the *ḥaṭṭāʾt* formula and this pericope differ in one fundamental criterion: the *ḥaṭṭāʾt* predicates subsequent knowledge of the sin (4:14, 23, 28), whereas the sin of 5:17–19 remains undiscovered (Milgrom 1967: 115–20). These additional words, *wĕ(hûʾ) lōʾ yādaʿ* 'without knowing it' (vv 17b, 18b), make all the difference. Their purpose is to create a category of sin dealt with nowhere else in biblical legislation, one that— as will be shown in COMMENT below—plagued the ancients more than any known sin. The Priestly legislation deliberately utilized the *ḥaṭṭāʾt* formula or an older law in order to suggest that any of the Lord's prohibitions could have been inadvertently violated (the assumption of the *ḥaṭṭāʾt*), but as the sin was not known but only suspected—the guilt feelings, however, being real—the possibility existed that the sin was in fact a *maʿal*, which unless expiated by an *ʾāšām* would arouse the wrath of God. Indeed, *wĕʾāšēm* in v 17 can serve as a showcase for the psychological component of the consequential *ʾāšām:* the subject is experiencing psychical (and perhaps even physical) suffering that, for lack of knowledge concerning its cause, he attributes to an unwitting offense against God (see COMMENT D below). The law of 5:17–19 is thus the legal formulation of the psychological truth that he who does not know the exact cause of his suffering imagines the worst: he has affronted the deity; he has committed sacrilege against the sancta and "incurred liability to the Lord" (v 19).

Moraldi (1956: 176) also recognizes that this passage speaks of guilt feelings over hidden sins, but he is hard put to explain why an 'āšām is required. He postulates that the 'āšām represents an alleviation of the ḥaṭṭā't for the benefit of both offender and officiating priest (citing the views of Baentsch, Dillmann, and Heinisch) because only the money equivalent and a simple blood manipulation are required. The facts are the reverse, however. The reparation ram is the most expensive of the flock animals and, even if commuted, would be more costly than the layman's ḥaṭṭā't goat or lamb (4:28, 32). And why is it important to alleviate the work of the priest? (The premise betrays a misconception of the function of the ḥaṭṭā't blood.) How much simpler, then, to postulate that 'āšām was prescribed precisely because it was expensive in order to expiate all possible taboo violations, including the most flagrant kind—sacrilege against sancta. For extrabiblical confirmation of the obsessive fear of unwitting sacrilege in the ancient world, see COMMENT D below.

without knowing it (wĕlō' yāda'). The key phrase in this case is pinpointed by Rabbi Jose the Galilean: "The text punishes one who does not know (his sin)" (*Sipra*, Ḥobah par. 12:7). Care must be taken not to confuse this term with D's *bibĕlî da'at* (Deut 4:42; 19:14), which is D's equivalent to P's *šĕgāgâ*, a conscious act. This ostensible contradiction is resolved once it is realized that the verb *yāda'* bears different connotations in P and D. In D it refers to wisdom, knowledge (e.g., Deut 1:13, 15), while in P it can also imply awareness (e.g., Exod 29:36; 31:13 [Milgrom 1967: n. 18]). This stipulation undermines L. S. Wright's contention that "the priest had to place a value on the ram to insure that the worth of the beast matched the seriousness of the offerer's infraction" (1989: 446). If the offerer's sin was unknown, how could the priest place a value on it?

One of the situations posited by the rabbis that incur the "suspended 'āšām" is that of the person who had before him two pieces of meat or fat, one sacred (e.g., of šĕlāmîm) and the other common, and he does not know which one he ate (*m Ker* 5.4–8). Proleptically, the same situation is posited by the Dead Sea Covenanters in a newly discovered document: [*'P '*]*l HSWM*[*Y*]*M ŠYNM RW'YM LHZHR MKL T'RW*[*BT*] *WT'RWBT* [*'*]*ŠM 'YNM RW'YM . . . KY ŠLW' R'H . . . LW'* [*Y*]*D' L'SWT* 'Also concerning the blind who cannot see so as to beware of any mixture, but the mixture incurring the reparation offering they cannot see . . . since he who has not seen . . . has no awareness of observing (the law)' (MMT B 49–54). Although the text specifies the blind (also the lame), it presumes, as did the rabbis some three centuries later, the same *Sitz im Leben*, namely, a mixture *(T'RBT)* of sacred and common causing a person to err unknowingly *(L W' YD').*

and he feels guilt (wĕ'āšēm). That this is the only logical rendering and that it must end the protasis (and not begin the apodosis), see COMMENT A below and the NOTE on 4:13.

he shall bear his responsibility (wĕnāśā' 'āwōnô). For this rendering and for the fact that it begins the apodosis, see the NOTE on 5:1.

18. *or its assessment.* For the morphology and meaning of the term *bĕ'er-kĕkā*, see the NOTE on v 15.

the error he committed without knowing it (šigĕgātô 'ăšer-šāgāg wĕhû' lō' yāda'). The term *šĕgāgâ*, normally rendered "inadvertence," implies consciousness, that is to say, awareness of the act (see the NOTE on 4:2). For this reason it is missing in the protasis, the statement of the case (v 17), which explicitly declares that it was an unconscious act, *wĕlō' yāda'* 'without knowing it' (a point missed by Kiuchi 1987: 30–31). How then are we to account for its appearance here in the apodosis? The answer, I believe, is that it is the object of the verb *kippēr* 'expiate'. There needs to be a term denoting an unconscious wrong that will be expiated by the reparation offering; but there is no such term in the Priestly vocabulary. This is all the more surprising because there is a plethora of words to describe deliberate sins (16:16; Num 15:30–31). Yet the regrettable fact is that P has only one term to describe an inadvertent sin, *šĕgāgâ*, but of a specific kind, a consciously committed inadvertence. Other scriptural sources are not so impaired, for example, *nistārôt* 'unperceived errors' (Ps 19:13); *ta'ălūmôt* 'hidden things' (Job 11:6). Thus P must resort to periphrasis, lit., "his inadvertence that he committed though he did not know," in other words, *šĕgāgâ* is expanded to mean an accidental wrong followed by the qualification that it was committed consciously. To be sure, a more unambiguous circumlocution could have been chosen, such as *'ăšer ḥāṭā' wĕhû' lō' yāda'* 'that which he sinned without knowing it'. It appears, however, that the framer of this law wanted to stress the organic unity of the two cases that comprise the topic of sacrilege against sancta: both are inadvertences *(šĕgāgâ)*, but whereas the first is committed consciously (vv 14–16), the second is committed unconsciously, *wĕ(hû') lō' yāda'* (vv 17–19).

19. *he has incurred liability to the Lord ('āšōm 'āšam laYHWH).* The verb *'āšam* followed by the preposition *l* and a personal object means "incur liability to" (see COMMENT A below); *'āšam l* has an inchoative function, namely, entering into a state of liability to someone (for reparation), as in *wĕnātan la'ăšer 'āšam lô* 'and give (it) to the one to whom he has liability' (Num 5:7b). The Chronicler uses *'āšam laYHWH* similarly: "Warn them not to incur liability to the Lord thereby bringing wrath upon you and your brethren" (2 Chr 19:10b; cf. 28:10, 13). This expression must be distinguished from *'āšam l* followed by an impersonal object, for example, *'āšēm lĕ' aḥat* 'feel guilt in regard to' (5:4, 5) or *lĕ'ašmâ bāh* 'feel guilt thereby' (5:26). The addition of the infinitive absolute

to the perfect may possibly be for emphasis: "He surely has incurred liability to the Lord." If so, then the meaning would be that even if a person merely suspects that he has desecrated a sanctum, he should take no chances but promptly bring a reparation offering to avert the wrath of the Lord in case he actually committed sacrilege. Because there is no certainty that sacrilege was committed, no restitution is required.

21. *by committing a sacrilege.* *ûmāʿálâ maʿal;* see the NOTE on v 15 and COMMENT B below.

against the Lord. *baYHWH,* by taking a false oath (see the NOTE on v 22). This qualification is not needed in the prior case of *maʿal* (v 15) because the desecration is explicitly *miqqodšê YHWH* 'with any of the Lord's sancta' (Wessely 1846).

dissembled. *kiḥēš,* i.e., "deny falsely" (e.g., Gen 18:4), especially in the context of oath taking (Hos 4:2; Ps 59:13 [Brichto 1963: 57–59]).

his fellow (ʿǎmîtô). In Akk., the *emūtu* is the husband's family, and originally this term may have been restricted to a clan member (synonymous with *ʾāḥ* 'brother', 19:17). But this derivative is doubtful (Hurvitz 1982: 74 n. 16). In all of its biblical attestations *ʿāmît* applies to any person, while the person directly addressed is one who is known and with whom there exists some relationship (e.g., 18:20; 19:11, 15, 17; 25:14, 15, 17).

This term is clearly old. It is found in Leviticus eleven times but is absent in corresponding passages in Ezekiel (cf. 5:21; 19:11–13 with Ezek 18:18; and 18:19–20 with Ezek 18:6), who ignores it altogether, as does all postbiblical literature—additional evidence for the early provenience of P's language (Hurvitz 1982: 74–78; and see the Introduction, § B).

deposit (piqqādôn). Akk. *puquddū.* The noun occurs only here and in Gen 41:36. The verbs *pāqad, hipqîd,* bearing the same meaning as Akk. *paqādu* are also attested (e.g., 2 Kgs 5:24; Isa 10:28).

investment. *tĕśûmet yād,* lit., "the placement of one's hand/power." Two explanations of this hapax are worthy of consideration: (1) "investment, loan," the translation adopted here (*Sipra,* Ḥobah 22:6) and (2) "partnership" (*Tg. Yer.; Tg. Ps.-J.;* LXX; Philo, *Laws* 1. 235). Both interpretations are cited in *Seper Hamibḥar.*

robbery (gāzēl). Tannaitic law distinguishes clearly: *gāzal* refers to robbery and *gānab* to theft, the difference being that robbery is committed openly by force ("openly and forcibly," Ibn Ezra on 19:13) whereas theft is by stealth (see *t. B. Qam.* 7:2; *Mek.* on Exod 22:6; *b. B. Qam.* 7ab; *Midr. Gen. Rab.* 54:3). Nevertheless, this distinction has to be adduced from their circumstances and penalties; it never appears in definitions (e.g., *m. B. Qam.* 7:9–10; *t. B. Qam.* 7:1). Thus it is not of rabbinic invention; indeed, it is already attested in Philo (4 *Laws* 2, though his penalties differ radically from those in biblical and postbiblical law; Jackson 1972: 181–85). Could it be biblical? A biblical provenience for the rabbinic definition of *gānab* and *gāzal* ostensibly runs aground on this pericope: although *gāzal* is included, *gānab* is conspicuously missing. Why is the thief omitted? Surely, it may be argued, the thief can also be subject to the acts that characterize the cases of vv 20–26, to wit: suspicion, denial, false oath.

The common denominator in all of the cases in vv 20–26 is that the claimant feels certain that he can identify the possessor of his object. Because he cannot produce witnesses or documents, however, the possessor needs but to assert his ownership under oath in order to retain the contested object. Thus it should be clear that ordinary theft *(gĕnēbâ)* has no place in this series. Theft, by definition, means that the object has been separated from its owner without his knowledge; hence, he has not seen the thief. As the point of this law is to list only those cases which culminate in the possessor's false oath, it would therefore be pointless to include the term "theft" whereby it is assumed that the possessor-thief is unknown.

Yet, it still may be argued, there are cases in which the thief can be tracked down or, at least, is under suspicion. Also, the object may be identified by its original owner so that its possessor (or seller) can be accused of thievery (the assumption of Exod 21:37; 22:3). Under these circumstances, would not the procedure of vv 20–26 obtain and, hence, should not theft of this nature appear among its cases? The answer is that it does. It appears in the final clauses of the protases: "(and he swears falsely) about any one of the things that a person may do and sin thereby" (v 22b) and "or anything else (about which he swore falsely)" (24a). As indicated, the general term *gānab* could not be used because of the assumption in this law that the claimant always points his finger at the possessor. In order to cover the limited cases of theft wherein the identification of the alleged thief does take place, however, the legislator has deliberately added appropriate generalizing clauses.

In sum, the understanding of the cases of vv 20–26 is based on the realization that they concern religious and not civil law, *fas* and not *jus*. All that matters to the Priestly legislator is to enumerate those situations wherein the defrauding of man leads, by a false oath, to the defrauding of God. The general category of theft in which the thief remains unidentifiable is therefore irrelevant to his purpose.

This analysis, I believe, is corroborated by the range of *šarāqu*, the Akk. equivalent of *gānab*. Jackson (1972: 181–85), following San Nicolo, correctly asserts that CH subsumes cases of misappropriation under *šarāqu* (see §§ 253, 255, 265). He also correctly points to the identification of lost property as theft in the Laws of Eshnunna (§ 50) and the Hittites (§§ 45, 66, 71). Thus generally throughout ancient Near Eastern law, theft embraced such items as *piqqādôn* and *'ăbēdâ*, deposited or lost property. This fact, then, supports my conclusion that vv 20–26 also deal with theft, not the general category in which the thief is unidentifiable but the special cases in which his identification leads to a false oath. For a discussion of the solutions proposed by A. Büchler (1928) and B. S. Jackson (1972), see Milgrom (1976f: 90–102).

withheld from (ʿāšaq). Gāzal and *ʿāšaq* are alike in one respect and differ in another. They are alike in that both are the product of open force (see Deut 28:29, 31; 1 Sam 12:3, 4; Ps 35:10; Job 35:9; Qoh 4:1). Perhaps the best illustration that open force is common to *ʿāšaq* and *gāzal* is Mic 2:1–2, where these two verbs describe the action of those who confiscate houses, lands, and persons: "By the light of morning they do it, because they have the power." But the two verbs differ from each other in this respect: in *ʿāšaq* the acquisition is legal whereas in *gāzal* it is illegal. There are two concrete cases of *ʿāšaq* in the Bible. One is withholding the wages of a hired laborer (Deut 24:14–15; cf. Mal 3:5). The other, heretofore unrecognized, is the confiscation, in cases of default, of property, which, however, must be returned (i.e., cannot be withheld) upon repayment of the loan (Deut 24:6–11; Ezek 18:7, 12, 16, 18; 22:29; 33:15; details in Milgrom 1976f: 94–104).

There can hardly be any cause for wonder that the terms *ʿāšaq* and *gāzal* are used synonymously by the prophets (e.g., Jer 21:12; 22:3), for the violation of life essentials is a violation of pentateuchal law and hence equivalent to robbery. Although the law only specifies garments and millstones in its prohibitions (Exod 22:25–26; Deut 24:6), they may serve as metonyms standing for all essentials such as land, farm animals, and persons (e.g., Mic 2:1–2; cf. 1 Sam 12:3–4). The outcry of the prophets can now be seen in its full dimension: Amos 2:8 (cf. Job 22:6) condemns the confiscation of clothing, which the old laws forbid one to keep overnight. The full bitterness in Amos's irony can now be tasted: in order to cohabit with hierodules, the creditors strip themselves of the garments they have stripped from the poor. Ezekiel condemns the withholding of all pledges (and in one verse, 18:16, even this particular seizure), thereby contesting the very legality of distraint. In this case, however, the Priestly legislator does not go that far. In view of the two instances cited above, this case deals either with a creditor who has illegally confiscated the life essential pledged by the debtor (Ezekiel's complaint), or, more likely, with an employer who has withheld the wages of his worker (see 19:13).

The legist was forced to employ a separate clause, *ʿāšaq ʾet-ʿămîtô,* instead of following the morphology of the preceding crimes (i.e., writing *bĕʿōšeq*) because the latter are the result of *kiḥēš* 'deny'. But the one who resorts to *ʿāšaq* openly admits his obligation; he just "withholds" it.

22. *and he swears falsely (wĕnišbaʿ ʿal šeqer).* This clause does not specify a discrete wrong. Rather, it applies to all of the preceding cases: not only has the offender wronged his fellow but he has denied it under oath. Assumed is that in the ancient Near East the plaintiff could always demand that the unapprehended but suspected criminal be put under oath (e.g., Gudea, Statue B 5.7–9; cf. Thureau-Dangin 1907).

The "sacrilege against the Lord" (v 21) is, therefore, fully clarified: the Lord has been made an accomplice to the defrauding of man. This understanding of the place of the false oath in this pericope is the basis for the mandated reparation offering: see COMMENT E below.

about any one of the things that a person may do and sin thereby (mikkōl ʾăšer yaʿăśeh hāʾādām laḥăṭōʾ bāhennâ). This clause is needed to teach that a false oath demands not only the prescribed reparation for the crimes specified above but reparation for all other sins (presumably also torts) accompanied by a false oath. The Masoretic verse division needs to be altered: the *ʾatnaḥ* currently under *šāqer* should be placed under *bāh.*

23. *feeling guilt (wĕʾ āšēm).* The end of the protasis, as in its previous attestations (4:13, 22, 27; 5:2, 3, 4, 5a, 17). For its meaning, see 4:13 and COMMENT A below. The usage here is fatal for the current rendering "realize guilt" (e.g., *NJPS;* Kiuchi 1987). The defrauder, embezzler, robber, and the like are quite aware of their guilt. It is their consciences that subsequently disturb them.

24. *or anything else (ʾô mikkōl).* For the view that *kōl* can also mean "the rest, the remainder," see the NOTE on 4:7. Thus *tĕśûmet yād,* missing in the apodosis (v 23), would be included.

he shall restore it (wĕšillam ʾōtô). The restitution does not have to be the same object or in kind (Daube 1947: 133–44) but can be its monetary equivalent. For details, see Milgrom (1976f: 137–40).

in its entirety. bĕrōʾ šô, lit., "its head." This technical term, as recognized by Rashi on this verse, on the basis of rabbinic sources (*Sipre* Naso 2), means "its principal." The rabbinic interpretation is strongly supported by Akkadian usage, where the exact semantic equivalent to *rōʾš* 'head' is *qaqqadu.* Wherever the latter is used in conjunction with interest, it can only mean "the principal" (*AHw* 9.900). Thus CH 65.0 (*BL* 2.41): "If a merchant has given corn or silver on loan (and) has not taken the principal *(qaqqadam la ilqi)* but has taken the interest . . . . . . or has then added the increments to the principal *(ṣibatim ana qaqqadim ut-ṭeq-ih-ḫi)."* Thus it is no accident that the two attested cases of biblical *bĕrōʾšô* (5:24; Num 5:7) occur in connection with an increment, namely, the one-fifth fine. It must therefore refer to the principal, the original value of the expropriated object.

add one-fifth to it. waḥamišîtāyw (pl.); but read *waḥămišîtô* (sing.) with many manuscripts, Sam., Pesh., *Tg. Ps.-J.,* Tg. (MS, Sperber). See Num 5:7 and the NOTE on v 16. The *ʾatnaḥ* is wrongly placed here and should be moved back to *laššeqer. as soon as. beyôm,* lit., "on the day." For this usage, see 6:13; 7:36, 38; Num 7:1, 84; cf. v 88b.

he feels guilt (ʾašmātô). Infinitive construct; see the NOTES on v 26 and 4:3.

25. *his reparation. ʾăšāmô;* see the NOTE on v 6.

or its assessment. bĕʿerkĕkā; see the NOTE on v 15.

26. *shall effect expiation. wĕkipper;* see chap. 16., COMMENT F.

to feel guilt thereby (lĕʾasmâ bāh). For this infinitival usage of *ʾāšam,* see the NOTE on 4:3.

Comments: The Reparation Offering

A. Etymology

The cognate languages are of no help in understanding the root *ʾšm*. The theory that Ug. *ʾṯm* is related to *ʾšm* (most recently Gray [1965: 177]; cf. *UT* no. 423) can no longer be maintained because the words in which this root is found are Hurrian and not Semitic (see Kellerman 1964). Our only resort is to the Bible. Not every occurrence of this root must be examined; see Joüon (1938: 454–59); Moraldi (1956: 159–80); Kellerman (1971). Only the cultic usage of *ʾšm* will interest us; other occurrences will be consulted only when they elucidate or reflect the cultic meaning. My conclusions will be stated from the outset to serve as a working hypothesis.

The cultic usages of the root *ʾšm* are as follows: the noun *ʾāšām* is the restitution for desecration by either composition or sacrifice and should be rendered "reparation" and "reparation offering," respectively. The verb *ʾāšam* is a stative. When it is followed by the preposition *l* and a personal object it means "to incur liability to" someone for reparation; without an object, it refers to the inner experience of this liability, meaning "to feel guilt."

It is universally accepted that the root *ʾšm* is associated with the concept of legal culpability or guilt, specifically that the noun *ʾāšām* means "guilt" and the verb *ʾāšam* means "is guilty." I submit that these meanings are not attested for the cultic *ʾāšām*. Instead, I would call the *ʾāšām* that prevails in the cultic texts the consequential *ʾāšām*. It has long been recognized that the biblical terms for good and bad behavior also connote their respective reward and punishment; see Zimmerli (1954); Koch (1962); von Rad (1962: 262–72). Thus *ḥēṭʾ* (Num 32:33; Isa 53:12; Zech 14:18–19; Prov 10:16; Lam 3:39; 4:6); *pešaʿ* (Isa 24:20; Ps 39:9); *ʿāwōn* (Gen 4:13; 1 Sam 25:24); *rāʿâ* (Jer 4:18; 18:8, 11; Lam 3:38), inter alia, stand not only for evil, but for its inherent punishment. The consequential meaning inheres in other roots (Gordis 1968: 418–19). The same can be shown for *ʾāšām*. It connotes both the wrong and the retribution. The principle was enunciated first by Ibn Ezra (on Gen 4:13). Among the moderns it was proposed for *ʾšm* by Joüon (1938), followed by Moraldi (1956) and L. Morris (1968). But I differ with them in the interpretation of many of their proof texts and postulates, as will be shown below. G. Fohrer (1968) applies this principle to many new roots, but, unfortunately, for *ʾšm* he only maintains the static notion "incur guilt" and the consequential expiation by sacrifice, but not the meanings adduced below. Consequential relationships are also attested in Akkadian. For example, not only can *arnu* mean both sin and punishment (*CAD*, s.v. *arnu*, 294–99) but also *ḫiṭītu*, the exact cognate of *ḥēṭʾ/ḥāṭāʾt;* cf. W. G. Lambert (1974: 286). The consequential *ʾāšām* is amply attested in the Bible, as follows:

A.   The verb *ʾāšam* outside the cult

1.   Evil shall slay the wicked and those who hate the righteous will be punished *(yeʾšāmû)*.

The Lord redeems the lives of his servants and none who take refuge in Him will suffer *(yeʾšĕmû)*. (Ps 34:22–23)

The synonymous parallelism in these two verses makes them a parade example of the consequential *ʾāšām*. It is stated in parallel both positively and negatively with verbs of retribution and salvation: *yeʾšāmû* || *t ĕmôtēt; wĕlōʾ yeʾšĕmû* || *pādâ*. *NEB* 's "brought into ruin" would seem to follow a similar interpretation, probably echoing G. R. Driver (1936: 75–77). Driver, however (followed with reservation by Joüon 1938 and Moraldi 1956, as well as by Loewenstamm and Blau in *TLB)*, opts for a meaning "be desolate" in Isa 24:6; Jer 2:3; Ezek 6:6; Hos 5:15; 10:2; 14:1; Joel 1:18; Zech 11:5; Ps 5:11; and this passage (Ps 34:22f.), considering *ʾšm* a dialectical variant of *šmm*. All of these verses, in my opinion, demonstrate the consequential meaning "is punished," as follows: Isa 24:6a *(ʾākĕlâ)* describes punishment; Joel 1:18 "even the flocks are punished"; Ps 5:11 *haddihēmô* || *yiplû* || *haʾăšîmēm*. The parallelism confirms the consequential *ʾāšām* (with Joüon). Ps 34:22–23; Hos 5:15; and Zech 11:5 are discussed in the text, Hos 10:2; 14:1 below, and Jer 2:3 will be treated separately.

2.   I will return again to my place until they are punished *(yeʾšĕmû)* and seek my face and in their distress they seek me. (Hos 5:15)

The retributive force of *yeʾšĕmû* is underscored by synonymous parallelism in the colon *baṣṣar lāhem* 'in their distress'. In Hosea, there is no meaning of *ʾšm* other than its consequential one, as its contexts will verify: "Since their heart deceived they must now be punished *(yeʾšāmû)*: he shall hack their altars" (10:2); "Samaria will be punished *(teʾšam)* because she has rebelled against her God: they shall fall by the sword" (14:1; the remaining occurrence, 13.1, is ambiguous because *wayyeʾšam* is capable of being rendered either "punished" or "incurred guilt").

3.   Those who buy them slaughter them and go unpunished *(wĕlōʾ yeʾšāmû)*. (Zech 11:5)

The consequential *ʾāšām* may also throw light on Gen 42:21 "We are being punished *(ʾăšēmîm)* on account of our brother" (with *NJPS*, which follows Bekhor Shor and Shadal; see Orlinsky 1969). Joseph's initial test of his brothers centers not on the bringing of Benjamin (the usual view) but on the incarceration of Simeon. Joseph reconstructs the circumstances of the brothers' crime against himself. The test is whether the brothers will abandon Simeon in prison as they abandoned Joseph in the pit. The brothers' remark indicates their acknowledgment of measure-for-measure retribution: they are being punished precisely the way they punished Joseph (so correctly Rashbam). The summoning of Benjamin allows Joseph to set up a second trial based on similar circumstances; only now it will be Benjamin—Rachel's remaining son, pampered by his father as was Joseph—who will be cast into the pit.

Prov 30:10 also contains the consequential *'āšām:* "Do not slander a servant to his master lest he curse you and you will be punished *(wĕ'āšāmt).*"

B.   The noun *'āšām, ' āšmâ* outside the cult

    1.   Abimelech said: See what you have done to us: One of the people might have lain with your wife and you would have brought upon us retribution *('āšām).* (Gen 26:10; Shadal)

    2.   For their land is filled with retribution *('āšām)* by the Holy One of Israel. (Jer 51:5b)

Mālĕ'â 'āšām m . . . is rendered by Moraldi as "full of crimes against" (so *RSV*); Joüon emends *m* > *l* and *NEB* translates "full of guilt, condemned by." But *min* never connotes "against." Moreover, the emendation of *m* and the addition of "condemned" are gratuitous (mālĕ'â is a stative perfect and not an adjective, cf. Gen 6:13; Jer 23:10; Ezek 7:23; Ps 119:64). If, however, *'āšām* is rendered by its consequential meaning "retribution," used elsewhere by Jeremiah (cf. 50:7), then neither emendation nor periphrasis is necessary.

    3.   Joab said. . . . It will only bring retribution *(yihyeh lĕ'ašmâ)* to Israel. (1 Chr 21:3)

C.   The cultic *'āšām.*

    1.   He shall bring his reparation *('āšāmô)* to the Lord . . . as a purification offering *(lĕḥaṭṭā't).* (5:6)

The sacrifice is clearly labeled *ḥaṭṭā't* (vv 6, 7, 11, 12), yet simultaneously it is called *'āšām.* The alleged contradiction is resolved by the previously enunciated principle: judgmental words may connote both behavior and its consequence. In this context, then, *'āšām* is not the wrong done but the punishment, the reparation of the offering as expressly stipulated in the context (see the Note on 5:6).

    2.   If it is the anointed priest who so does wrong to the detriment of the people *(lĕ'ašmat hā'ām).* (4:3)

Another possible rendering is "liable for an *'āšām* offering," the implication being that the high priest has inadvertently caused the people to desecrate sancta; cf. 22:16. The expression *lĕ'ašmat* is infinitival rather than nominal in form (see on 4:3).

3.　　He has incurred liability to the Lord *('āšōm 'āšam lĕYHWH)*. (5:19b)

This is the verbal form of the consequential *'āšām*, which always requires the preposition *l* and a personal object. *'āšam l* has an inchoative function, entering into a state of liability to someone (for reparation); see the NOTE on 5:19.

4.　　This shall be yours from the most sacred gifts from the fire: all of the most sacred offerings, namely, every cereal offering, every purification offering, and every reparation offering they bring me *(ûlĕkol 'āšāmām 'ăšer yāšîbû lî)* shall belong to you and your sons. (Num 18:9)

This text is overloaded and difficult (see the NOTE on 5:15). It was chosen to illustrate the peculiarity of the *'āšām* offering in its unique relation to the verb *hēšîb* 'restore'; even in a cultic catalog the author found it impossible to divorce it from its special verb (Cf. 1 Sam 6:3, 4, 8, 17; Num 5:7, 8). The other sacrifices never take the verb *hēšîb*, a point that was missed by the extant translations of Num 18:9; see further the NOTE on 5:15. This philological observation should suffice to indicate that the *'āšām* offering has to do with restitution or reparation; in some manner the property of the Lord (the sancta) has been damaged, and the *'āšām* is the cultic component of the required reparation—hence the rendering "reparation offering." Chiefly, the root *'šm* in the cultic material occurs as the *'āšām* offering, which will be treated below. Here it will suffice to note that the sacrifice must also be explained by the consequential *'āšām:* not the sin but its effect. Hence the usual translation, "guilt offering," is erroneous prima facie because it focuses on man's sinful condition and not on its punitive consequence. The discussion of the sacrifice must, however, await a more profound analysis into the nature of the retribution implied by the consequential *'āšām.*

The consequential *'āšām* also has a psychological component. The ancients did not distinguish between emotional and physical suffering; the same language describes pangs of conscience and physical pains (e.g., Jer 17:14; Pss 38:2–11, 18–19; 102:4–11; 149:3; cf. 34:19). That is why in the penitential psalms it is difficult to determine whether the speaker is suffering, on the one hand, from natural disease, economic want, or political persecution; or, on the other, from mental torment or guilt (Pss 6, 32, 38, 41, etc.). The same holds true in ancient

Mesopotamia, as in "A Semitic Prayer in Part-Song" (Langdon 1927: 61–65, esp. lines 22–24). The reason may well be that unexplainable suffering is held to be the result of sin, and the sufferer's efforts are therefore directed toward the discovery of the specific offense that gave rise to his plight. The result is predictable: wrongdoing creates guilt and fear of punishment, and, conversely, suffering reinforces the presence of guilt feelings because it is interpreted as punishment for sin. Thus it is logical to expect that a language that, as observed, will express the consequential syndrome of sin–punishment by a single word will also have at least one root in its lexicon to express another consequential relationship, that which exists between sin–punishment and guilt feelings. This root, I submit, is *ʾšm.*

Biblical persons were not reluctant to talk of guilt. This is evidenced in the nonlegal texts by idioms compounded with the emotion-centered organs of the body, for instance, *wayyak lēb dāwid ʾōtô* 'David's heart smote him' (1 Sam 24:5; 2 Sam 24:10); *mikšôl lēb* 'a stumbling [offense] of the heart' (1 Sam 25:31); or *yissĕrûnî kilyôtāy,* lit., "my kidneys have whipped me" (Ps 16:7). Often, metaphors will comprise a word picture of the penitent's guilt, for example, "Your indignation has left no part of my body unscarred: there is no health in my whole frame because of my sin. My iniquities have poured over my head; they are a load heavier than I can bear. My wounds fester and stink because of my folly. . . . I declare my iniquity and I am distressed over sin" (Ps 38:3–6, 19). With this compare "Sickness, headache, poison, misery, have rolled over him even grief and despair. Panting, terror, fright and fear, harass him, removing far his willpower. He has sinned and woefully he weeps before thee . . . 'many are my wrong-doings, I have sinned in all my ways' " (Langdon: 1927: 61–65, lines 6–10). In the cultic and legal texts, however, where metaphors are eschewed, a precise term would be essential to pinpoint the existence of guilt: it is the verb *ʾāšam.* Thus, contrary to usual translations, *ʾāšam* without an object does not refer to a state of guilt; rather, in keeping with its consequential meaning, it denotes the suffering brought on by guilt, expressed now by words such as qualms, pangs, remorse, and contrition. *ʾāšām* would then mean to be conscience-smitten or guilt-stricken, and henceforth it will be rendered as "feel guilt." The critical importance of this new rendering is that it necessitates an overhaul of every cultic passage in which the verb *ʾāšam* occurs without an object. Let a few illustrations suffice:

(1) *(wĕlōʾ yādaʿ) wĕʾāšēm wĕnāśāʾ ʿăwōnô* 'and he feels guilt, he shall bear his responsibility' (5:17). The meaning of *wĕʾāšēm* in this verse can hardly be "incurring guilt" *(NEB)* or "is guilty" *(RSV)* because the contiguous "he shall bear his responsibility" would render it a tautology. Other renderings, such as "realize guilt" *(NJPS;* Kiuchi 1987: 34) or "be conscious of his guilt" (Leeser 1907) cannot be correct: because the sinner's act is unconscious (note the preceding *wĕlōʾ yādaʿ*), how is he capable of realizing his guilt? The sole possible answer, I believe, is that he only suspects that he has done wrong, that is to say, he is

troubled by his conscience. *wĕʾāšēm*, therefore, belongs not to the apodosis but to the conclusion of the protasis; it is an indispensable precondition for his sacrificial fine.

(2) *wĕhāyâ kî-yeḥĕṭāʾ wĕʾāšēm* 'When one has thus sinned and, feeling guilt' (5:23a). The translations here err even more because they presuppose not just a tautology but a contradiction. The case is one of willful misappropriation. Even while planning his crime, the wrongdoer is fully aware of his guilt. It is a mistake in a legal text to state that after a deliberate crime, a person incurs guilt *(NEB)*, becomes guilty *(RSV)*, or realizes his guilt *(NJPS)*. Again, only the element of remorse fits *wĕʾāšēm* here. The sinner is stricken with pangs of conscience: he feels his guilt.

Although I came to this conclusion on my own (1967: 112 n. 11), I renounce all claims to originality. I have since discovered that I have been anticipated in hellenistic and rabbinic literature: see Philo, *Laws* 1. 23 (Loeb 7.236f.); Jos., *Ant.* 3.9.3 (which Belkin [1940: 155] wrongly attributes to Josephus's concept of *maʿal*); *Tg. Ps.-J.* on Lev 5:24d; *m. B. Qam.* 9:7; *m. Šebu.* 8:3; and *T. Gad* 6:3–4. Among the medieval exegetes, see Rashi and Radak on Lev 5:23; Ibn Ezra and Rashbam on v 24 and Rabad on *Sipra*, Ḥobah par. 13:1. Karaite exegesis also reflects this interpretation, for instance, *Seper Hamibḥar* on Lev 5:5, 23, 24 and Num 5:6. Finally, among the moderns, Shadal (in *Hamishtadel*), Ehrlich (1908–14), and Büchler (1928: 309 n. 1) have followed the Tannaites in this exegesis of Lev 5:23—the verse allows no alternative—but unfortunately neither they nor their predecessors applied this insight to all occurrences of the cultic *ʾāšām*.

(3) *wĕhāyâ kî yeʾšam lĕʾaḥat mēʾelleh wĕhitwaddâ* 'When he feels guilt in any of these matters, he shall confess' (5:5) and (4) *wĕʾāšmâ hannepeš hahîʾ wehitwaddû* 'When that person feels guilt, he shall confess' (Num 5:6b, 7). Both verses are similarly structured. As will be demonstrated below, both cases predicate deliberate crime. Again, as in example 2, it is both redundant and illogical to render "incur guilt" *(NEB)*, "is guilty" *(RSV)*, or "realizes his guilt" *(NJPS)*. Moreover, the requirement for confession that follows *ʾāšēm* makes better sense if it is motivated by genuine regret, in other words, if the sinner confesses because he "feels guilt." I now notice that my theory was partially anticipated by Rabad on *Sipra*, Ḥobah 7:3. He claims that *ʾāšam* implies a confession, in keeping with the tannaitic tradition that all expiatory sacrifices require confession (*Sipre Zuṭa* on Num 5:5; *t. Menaḥ.* 10:12).

(5) *wĕʾāšēm* 'and he feels guilt' (5:2, 3, 4). *wĕʾāšēm* in 5:2–4 is usually rendered "is guilty," that is to say, it is treated as an apodosis on the analogy of *wĕnāśāʾ ʿăwōnô* in v 1. Its usage is expressly explicated by vv 4 and 5, "and if he feels guilt in any of these matters" (see example 3, above) where *wĕʾāšēm* is clearly part of the protasis.

(6) *wĕʾāšēm ʾô hôdaʿ ʾēlāyw ḥaṭṭāʾtô ʾ ăšer ḥāṭāʾ wĕhēbîʾ* 'and he feels guilt or he is informed of the wrong he committed, he shall bring' (4:27–28). The rule

that *wĕʾāšēm* is always part of the protasis has its most radical implications for the *ḥaṭṭāʾt* pericope (chap. 4). All of the cases deal with the inadvertent violation of a prohibitive commandment wherein the wrongdoer becomes aware of his guilt on his own or is informed of his wrong by someone else. Then follows the apodosis, "he shall bring." If this interpretation is correct, then all of the cases in chap. 4 (vv 13–14, 22–23, 27–28) must be, and have been, reordered (for details see Milgrom 1976f: 1–12).

In sum, the cultic texts reveal four usages of the root *ʾšm*, as follows: the nouns "reparation" and "reparation offering," and the verbs "incur liability [to someone]" and "feel guilt" (without a personal object). These meanings derive from the consequential *ʾāšām*, the punishment or penalty incurred through wrongdoing. The fourth meaning, "feel guilt," involves the self-punishment of conscience, the torment of guilt. It is far removed from the hitherto accepted "be guilty." The latter connotes a legal guilt that, as shown, ill fits the contexts in which it is found. The new rendering "feel guilt" refers to psychological guilt. These findings are best summarized by citing two passages in which all four meanings appear (indicated in italics): "He shall pay it to its owner as soon as he feels guilt *(bĕyôm ʾašmātô).* Then he shall bring to the priest, as his reparation *(ʾāšāmô)* to the Lord, an unblemished ram from the flock, or its assessment, as a reparation offering *(leʾāšām)"* (5:24b–25); and "When that person feels guilt *(weʾāšĕmâ),* he [lit., "they"] shall confess the wrong he [lit., "they"] has done, make reparation *(ʾāšāmô)* in its entirety, add one-fifth to it, and give it to the one to whom he has incurred liability *(leʾāšer ʾāšam lô)"* (Num 5:6b–7).

These findings also bear theological implications. If the cause, the verb *ʾāšam* 'feel guilt', leads to the consequence, the noun *ʾāšām* 'reparation, reparation offering', then the feeling of guilt can only be the first step in seeking reconciliation with God. He also demands "reparation" both to him and to the defrauded person before his expiation can be won. In the Priestly demand for remorse and rectification we see the genesis of repentance, the doctrine that will flower into full bloom with Israel's prophets (see COMMENT G below).

B. Sacrilege

Although the study of the root *ʾšm* in the cultic texts stands completed, it is still premature to investigate the cases of the *ʾāšām* offering. One key word— found in the sacrificial texts only with the *ʾāšām*— has prior claims to investigation. This word is *maʿal.*

maʿal is the legal term for the wrong that is redressed by the *ʾāšām* (5:15, 21; Num 5:6; cf. Ezra 10:10, 19). Altogether it appears forty-four times in Scripture. That it refers to sacrilege is demonstrated by its antonym "sanctify," as in "you committed sacrilege *(mĕʿaltem)* against me . . . you did not sanctify *(qiddaštem)* me" (Deut 32:51). The common denominator in all occurrences is that *maʿal* constitutes a sin against God. This restriction to the deity is projected by the complex wording of Num 5:6, "When a man or woman commits any wrong against man (thereby) committing ma'al against the Lord." This verse makes it clear that ma'al against God must be distinguished from wrongs against man. The term ma'al, however, is not defined here or in any other cultic-legal text. The biblical narratives may prove more helpful because they, at least, incorporate actual cases of ma'al. These, it will be seen, fall into two major categories: the sacrilege against sancta and the violation of the covenant oath.

Cases of ma'al against Temple sancta are found only in Chronicles. Uzziah is charged with ma'al for offering incense inside the Temple (2 Chr 26:16–18). His offering is illicit in accordance with the Priestly tradition, for both place and rite—entering the sanctuary and officiating there—are forbidden to a nonpriest (Milgrom 1970a: 38–43). He is stricken with leprosy on the spot (see below). Ahaz is also charged with ma'al by Chronicles for tampering with the Temple sancta (2 Chr 28:19, 22–25; cf. 2 Kgs 16:14–17) and suspending their use (2 Chr 29:19). Finally, the Chronicler pinpoints ma'al as the cause of Judah's downfall because "they *contaminated the house of the Lord* which he had *sanctified* in Jerusalem" (2 Chr 36:14; italics mine).

That these instances of sacrilege against Temple sancta are limited to postexilic Chronicles must not be used as evidence for its late appearance in Israel. On the contrary, it is in the later books that one finds the more abstract, derivative notion of ma'al in regard to sins in general (e.g., Ezek 14:13; 18:24; 2 Chr 33:1a) or specific sins, which are the invention of the postexilic authors (e.g., intermarriage, Ezra 10:2, 10; Neh 13:27; see COMMENT C below). Moreover, extrabiblical parallels, adduced below, will demonstrate that the fear of the desecration of sancta was a formidable factor in molding the thought and legislation of ancient man. Indeed, early biblical tradition is preoccupied with the dangers of illicit contact with sancta to the point of obsession, as may be seen in the apodictic lay, "The stranger who encroaches shall be put to death" (Num 1:51; 3:10, 38; 18:7), and in the Korah episode (Num 16–18), which serves as a case study of this principle (Milgrom 1970a: 16–33).

An early tradition tells of Achan's ma'al against the ḥērem of Jericho (Josh 7:1ff.; 22:20; cf. 1 Chr 2:7). The taboo of ḥērem is adduced in other early narratives (e.g., Amalek: 1 Sam 15:3ff.; Ben Hadad: 1 Kgs 20:42) and laws (e.g., 27:21; 28–29; Num 18:14; Deut 7:25–26; Ezek 44:29). As construed by P, ḥērem is the ultimate in dedication: it is "most sacred to the Lord" in that it may never be redeemed (27:28), and if ḥērem is imposed on man, there is no alternative to his death (27:29; cf. 1 Sam 15:3, 33). Moreover, the case of Achan explicitly teaches that appropriation of sancta for whatever purpose constitutes ma'al. Note the verb lāqaḥ 'appropriate' (Josh 7:1, 11). Thus the principle of intention apparently plays no part in ma'al. It makes no difference if the ḥērem taboo was violated accidentally; if suffices that "ḥērem is in your midst, O Israel" (v 13). Verse 11b is particularly instructive: "They have taken from the ḥērem, they have stolen, they have dissembled, and they here put it among their posses-

346

sions." Here an attempt is made to distinguish among different degrees of *ma'al*: *gānĕbû* 'stole' is deliberate; *kiḥăšû* 'dissemble' adds the crime of denial; and *s'āmû bikĕlêhem* 'put among their possessions' is the final act of expropriation. The first verb in the series, *lāqaḥ*, then refers to the literal act of taking possession, even without intention. In this regard, the Bible is just as severe as the Mari texts, in which taking *(leqû)* sancta is as much a crime as stealing *(šarāqu)* and expropriating *(akālu)* sancta (see below). This parallel holds true only for *ḥērem*, however. In the Bible ordinary sancta are governed by the principle of intention (Lev 5:14–16; see below), and it constitutes a major distinction between Israel and its environment.

In another early tradition, which concerns the Transjordanian altar of the tribes of Gad and Reuben, the charge of *ma'al* is explicitly leveled (Josh 22:16, 22). That the *ma'al* involves sancta is apparent not only from the violation of the Priestly postulate that the only authorized altar is in the Tabernacle (vv 19, 29; cf. Lev 17:3–7) but from the comparison that the narrator makes with Achan, who committed sacrilege *(mā'al ma'al)* against the *ḥērem* of Jericho. Thus the suspected *ma'al* of the Transjordanian tribes and the actual *ma'al* of Achan constitute historic examples of this first category of *ma'al*, the sacrilege against sancta.

The second category of *ma'al*, oath violation, is integrally related to sacrilege against sancta, for the violated sanctum is none other than the deity himself. The Lord's name by which an oath is taken is called a sanctum, *šēm qōdeš* (e.g., 20:3; Isa 57:15; Ezek 36:20–22; Amos 2:7; Ps 111:9), and the oath itself is called *dĕbar qodšô* 'his sacred promise' (Ps 105:42, cf. vv 8–9) and is taken *bĕqodšô* 'by his holiness' (e.g., Amos 4:2; Ps 60:8). In the cultic laws, as will be shown below, the oath violation will be defined as "swearing falsely" or "desecrating the name of God." In the nonlegal texts, which are examined first, it appears in a variety of forms, all of which can be subsumed under one rubric: the violation of the covenant oath.

This notion of *ma'al* is already adumbrated in the admonitions of Lev 26, where the sin of "violating the covenant" (v 15) is also termed *ma'ălām 'ăšer mā'ălû bî* 'the sacrilege they committed against me' (v 40). That the violation of the covenant oath constitutes sacrilege is painstakingly underscored by Ezekiel: Zedekiah will be punished because *ûbāzâ 'ālâ lĕhāpēr bĕrît* 'he spurned the oath thereby violating the covenant' (Ezek 17:18; cf. vv 13, 16, 19), a sin that the prophet explicitly labels *ma'ălô 'ăšer mā'al-bî* 'the sacrilege that he committed against me' (v 20).

That the curse or oath is the quintessential element of the covenant is shown by passages in which *'ālâ* and *bĕrît* alternate (e.g., Gen 24:8, 41; Num 5:21). Note the rabbinic dictum, "Every *'ālâ* is an oath" (*Sipra*, Ḥobah par. 8:1). True, there is no direct evidence that all oaths were followed by a curse, even though this is what later Judaism taught (cf. *Sipre* on Num 5:21; Philo, *Laws* 4. 34, contra Belkin [1940: 146]; for a convincing evaluation of the development, see Jackson [1972: 218–23]). Yet divine punishment for nonfulfillment of oaths was implicit, if not actually verbalized, in a curse: examples include Jer 5:2–3; Zech 5:4; and Mal 3:5 (on false oaths). Although the halakha prescribes flagellation, there is ample witness to an ancient tradition that the penalty was death by God (cf. *Tg. Ps.-J.* on Lev 5:1; *m. Sanh.* 4:5; *t. Šebu.* 3:4; *t. Soṭa* 7:2–3; Philo, *Laws* 2. 26; CD 15.4).

The Ezekiel passage cited above is most illuminating: the condemnation of Zedekiah is based on the violation of the covenant with Nebuchadnezzar, not with God! Yet because the one involves a solemn oath as much as the other, its violation constitutes *maʿal*, a sacrilege against God. This view is shared by the Chronicler (2 Chr 36:13–14), the Qumranites (e.g., 1QH 4:34), and the rabbis (*Sipra*, Beḥuqotai, 26:1; cf. *Midr. Lev. Rab.* 6:5). The full force of Zedekiah's *maʿal* is felt in God's charge: "It is my oath *(ʾālātî)* he has despised and my covenant *(ûbĕrîtî)* he has violated" (Ezek 17:19; reading of D. Halperin). Indeed, it now can be shown that the severe measures taken by Nebuchadnezzar —razing Jerusalem, slaughtering Zedekiah's sons and nobles, and blinding Zedekiah—are precisely stipulated by the curses of 1 Sefire A 35–40 and, hence, most likely formed part of the written treaty between Nebuchadnezzar and Zedekiah; see Deist (1971: 71–72).

Because the swearing of fidelity is the root purpose of the Lord's covenant, it is hardly surprising that the *maʿal* of oath violation usually turns out to be idolatry (e.g., in general, 2 Chr 12:2; 33:19; Baal Peor, Num 31:16, Ahaz's foreign cult, 2 Chr 28:22–23).

Ahaz's additional *maʿal* consists of his alleged worship of Damascene gods (2 Chr 28:23), an indictment absent in Kings. Conversely, the Chronicler says nothing about Ahaz's architectural innovations in the Temple (2 Kgs 16:10–14), to which, however, he may allude in the earlier charge of *maʿal* (v 19). Saul is also charged with the *maʿal* of idolatry by the Chronicler (1 Chr 10:13), but it is unsubstantiated; the only specific fault he can pin on this most zealous Yahwist is that he once consulted a ghost (cf. 1 Sam 28). The midrash, however, labels Saul's annihilation of the priests at Nob (1 Sam 22:18–19) as *maʿal* because it is tantamount to sancta violation (*Midr. Lev. Rab.* 26:7). That Moses and Aaron committed (self-)idolatry at Meribah (Num 20:6–13), also called *maʿal* (Deut 32:51), requires separate treatment (Milgrom 1983c).

The two categories of *maʿal* are really one. Both acts of sacrilege are against the deity. Moreover, desecration of sancta is simultaneously desecration of the covenant, because reverence for sancta is presumed in the covenant relationship. Strikingly, it is P alone that makes this explicit; cf. Lev 19:30; 21:23; 26:2; Milgrom (1970a: 23 n. 78). In the incident of Achan's sacrilege—a case of sancta desecration—Israel is also accused of covenant violation (Josh 7:11, 15). Further underscoring their affinity is that both kinds of *maʿal* are termed *mered* 'rebellion' against God: for example, for sancta desecration, Josh 22:16, 18, esp. 22; and for oath violation, Ezek 17:15.

Finally, both *ma'al* categories share not only the nature of the sin—involving sacrilege against the divine property or name—but also call for a similar retribution. Both trespasses provoke God's consuming wrath against the family and community of the sinner. The doctrine of corporate culpability for sins against God informs not only P but all biblical literature. The tribes under Joshua are alarmed lest the sacrilege of Gad and Reuben bring down God's wrath on all Israel (Josh 22:18, 31), specifically citing Achan's sacrilege (v 20) as a case in point (cf. Josh 7). According to Chronicles, Ahaz's trespass led to the political subjugation of Judah (2 Chr 28:19). That destruction and exile on a national scale follow in the wake of the *ma'al* of oath violation is clear from the structure of the covenant itself (Lev 26:14–45; see explicitly Neh 1:5). Thus Ezekiel can pronounce exile for the entire nation because its king violated his solemn oath (Ezek 17:19–21). *ma'al*, then, means trespassing upon the divine realm either by poaching on his sancta or by breaking his covenant oath; it is a lethal sin that can destroy both the offender and his community.

There can be no question that Israel derived its notion of *ma'al* from its environment. The literature of the ancient Near East is replete with examples of divine punishment in the wake of sancta or oath violation. For examples of sancta trespass among the Mesopotamians, see "The Curse of Agade" (*ANET*[3] 647–51); "Prayer to Every God," lines 19f., 25f. (*ANET*[3] 391); Šurpu 2.5, 33f., 79 (Reiner 1958: 13–15; Lambert, 1974: 238); and among the Hittites, see "The Instructions for Temple Officials" (*ANET*[3] 207–11 and see below); "Prayer of Kantuzilis," lines 14f. (*ANET*[3] 400); cf. Güterbock (1974: 325). For examples of oath violation among the Assyrians, see E. F. Weidner (1932: 27ff.); R. Borger (1956: §11, Bab A–G 12–15); D. J. Wiseman (1958: 528–31, 419–30, 448–50); and especially D. R. Hillers (1964: 86f. n. 27); among the Hittites, see "The Soldiers' Oath," cols. 2.37ff.; 3.39ff.; 4.5ff. (*ANET*[3] 353f.); cf. "The Prayer of Kantuzilis" (*ANET*[3] 400); H. G. Güterbock (1974; 325; *ANET*[3] 353f.); among the Aramaeans, see Sefire 1, A.21–24, 32–33; B.30; 2, B.11, in H. Bauer (1932: 27ff.).

A Hittite text actually pinpoints both kinds of *ma'al* as responsible for the plague that has befallen the Hittite kingdom. The key passages follow:

> I made the anger of the gods the subject of an oracle. I learnt of two ancient tablets. The first tablet dealt with the offerings to the river Mala. The old king had regularly presented offerings to the river Mala. But now a plague has been rampant in the Hatti land since the days of my father, and we have never performed the offerings to the river Mala.
>
> The second tablet concerned Kurustama. When the Hattian Storm-god had brought the people of Kurustama to the country of Egypt and had made an agreement concerning them with the Hattians so that they were under oath to the Hattian Storm-god—although the Hattians as well as the Egyptians were under oath to the Hattian Storm-god, the

Hattians ignored their obligations; the Hattians promptly broke the oath of the gods. My father sent foot soldiers and charioteers who attacked the country of Amka, Egyptian territory. . . . The Hattian Storm-god, my lord, by his decision even then let my father prevail; he vanquished and smote the foot soldiers and charioteers of the country of Egypt. But when they brought back to the Hatti land the prisoners which they had taken a plague broke out among the prisoners and they began to die. When they moved the prisoners to the Hatti land, these prisoners carried the plague into the Hatti land . . . has this perhaps become the cause of the anger of the Hattian Storm-god, my lord? And (so) it was established. (*ANET*³ 395)

Thus the oracle reveals that the gods have sent a plague upon the Hittites for two reasons: they have violated their sancta and their treaty oath. It can be no accident that in the Bible both sins fall under the category of *ma'al.*

The parallel with sancta is not exact, for in the Hittite text the sin is one of neglect whereas in the Bible it consists of sacrilege. Yet because the *ma'al* in both cases is intentional, there is—at least in the Hittite mind—no distinction between one who misappropriates sancta and one who deprives them of their proper rites.

That the gods will severely punish sancta sacrilege is evidenced from many ancient Near Eastern texts. For example, Sennacherib's success in conquering Babylon is attributed to the city's wicked deeds, among which are the following: "They laid hands on the property of Esaggil, the temple of the gods, and sold silver, gold, and precious stones to the land of Elam" (Borger 1956: 13). Especially instructive is the tablet of Urukagina of Lagash (no. 27, translated in Kramer 1963: 322–23), which itemizes at length the sancta trespasses of Lugalzaggesi ruler of Umma and concludes, "It is not the sin of Urukagina, the king of Girsu. May Nidaba, the (personal) goddess of Lugalzaggesi, the *ensi* of Umma, make him (Lugalzaggesi) bear all (these) sins." The parallel with 2 Kgs 18:22, 25, where the Rabshakeh pinpoints Hezekiah's sancta trespass as the cause of his doom, cannot be missed. But the Sumerian text goes a step farther: one god will punish his devotee for violating the sancta of another god, a postulate that, of course, could not obtain in the Bible.

Another example is the Sumerian "Curse of Agade" (*ANET*³ 647–51). The gods decree the destruction of Agade when its king, Naram-Sin, pillages Ekur, the temple of Enlil (lines 59ff., 225f.; cf. also *T. Levi* 16:1–5; Jos., *Ant.* 20.166–67; *Wars* 6.93–111). Text 98 (Kh. 1935, 8), which records the donation of a field to a temple (Harris 1955: 101–2), reads, "[May the god x] and the god Daban not prevent (the evil consequences from befalling) me. Furthermore, if I gather (even) its (the field's) ŠE. BAL (barley?), may the god Shamash be (my) evil spirit." Thus, taking from the sanctuary's field, even if done by its former owner, is *ma'al* and punishable by the gods. The gods' sacred weapons were used for oath taking when litigants could not travel to the temple, in which case they rented a sacred weapon. But it was the "journey" they rented, not the weapon, a clear legal euphemism in order to avoid *ma'al*. For postbiblical times, compare the Psalms of Solomon, whose author considers the greatest sin of the priests and the temple officials—beyond their avarice and immorality—to be their pollution of the sancta (1:8b; 2:1–4; 8:12–14). As a result, Pompey profaned and despoiled the temple. The defilement of the temple by the Jerusalem priesthood, which they also label *ma'al* (CD 8.46), is cited by the Qumranites as a reason for their withdrawal (CD 6.11–14; 20.22–24; cf. 3.19–4.4; Psalms of Solomon 17:15–17).

Turning to the first category of *ma'al*, it is now germane to ask: what constitutes sacrilege against sancta? In the biblical codes it is never defined. Except for the ban on substituting for dedicated animals (Lev 27:9–14), the only law that alludes to sacrilege is "you must not work your firstling ox or shear your firstling sheep" (Deut 15:19). Even the law of Lev 5:14–16, which deals exclusively with this subject, adds not a single word of clarification. This is not surprising. As a rule, P resorts to the widest possible generalization in order to cover every future contingency. Only where doubtful cases make the application of the law uncertain will it resort to specification and precedent. The following examples illustrate this point: the doubtful *ḥaṭṭāʾt* cases (5:1–4); impure beasts that are borderline cases (11:5–7) and impure birds for which no generalization can be formed (11:13–20; contrast D, which lists the permitted birds despite the generalization, Deut 14:4–6); the doubtful application of the Law of blasphemy to the *gēr* 'resident alien' (see the COMMENT on 24:10–23); and the unclear penalty for gathering wood on the Sabbath (Num 15:32–36). The only exception to this principle is the *ma'al* of 5:20–26, where specific cases are cited (but not in its parallel, Num 5:6–8).

Thus because the Bible refrains from defining the *ma'al* of sancta, other aids must be sought. The most obvious are possible cognates in other Semitic tongues. Unfortunately, comparative philology is fruitless. Can rabbinic sources be of help? Their earliest statements are contemporaneous with the Second Temple, and as the cult is a most conservative institution, many of its practices and terms recorded in rabbinic literature may hark back to biblical times. Still, the antiquity of a ritual does not imply that it always carried the same meaning. On the contrary, as seen from the history of all religions, the same cultic act often undergoes reinterpretation in response to changing spiritual needs. Moreover, many rabbinic rulings were authored years and even centuries after sacrificial worship had ceased and are products of a hermeneutics that may not correspond to reality. With these precautions in mind, the rabbinic material can be mined for precious ore.

One tannaitic source offers a striking definition: "*ma'al* means (that the object undergoes) alteration" (*Sipra*, Ḥobah par. 11:1). The alteration is clearly in status. The sanctum has been desecrated; it is now profane. Although the qualifications added by the Tannaites must be rejected, their notion that *ma'al* means sancta desecration is substantially correct, as will be shown below.

The Dead Sea Scrolls contain a high incidence of the word *ma'al* and thereby warrant our attention. Of the fourteen certain occurrences, one clearly refers to sancta trespass (CD 8.46) and one to covenant violation (1QH 4:34), but they are couched in general terms and throw no light on our problem.

A more obvious resource for gleaning information to elucidate biblical *ma'al* is ancient Israel's environment. It is presumed that the ancient Near East was a cultural continuum in which forms and ideas were exchanged without resistance unless they clashed with the value system of the borrowing culture. In the area of cult, for example, Israel had no compunctions about imitating forms of architecture and administration and even modes of worship, because their alien religious content could be replaced by the norms and values of Israel's faith. Certainly in the matter of *ma'al*, Israel shared a concern with its neighbors, for all peoples believed that sacrilege against sancta threatened the commonweal. It is therefore reasonable to anticipate finding parallel laws, customs, and concepts in Israel's environment that deal with *ma'al*. The analogy to Mari *asakku akālu*, though attractive, must be rejected (cf. Milgrom 1976f: 25–27). Help stems from another quarter, however: the Hittite "Instructions for Temple Officials."

As the quest for semantic equivalents has proved inconsequential, it might be more fruitful to seek intercultural parallels in the realm of institutions and ideas. Certainly, in view of the universal concern to guard sancta against sacrilege, a codex or descriptive list of sancta desecrations—if it could be found—would have illuminating impact on the meaning of *ma'al*. Fortunately, at our disposal there are detailed provisions against sancta sacrilege in the Hittite "Instructions for Temple Officials" (*ANET*[3] 207–10). The text has already proved its worth in elucidating the division of guard duties between the priests and Levites according to P (Milgrom 1970a: 49–59). More relevant are its provisions dealing with encroachment upon sancta, which can be shown to correspond to the biblical injunction *hazzār haqqārēb yûmat* 'The stranger who encroaches shall be put to death' (Num 1:51; 3:10, 38; 18:7 [Milgrom 1970a: 5–53]). If this Hittite text elucidates one aspect of sacrilege—keeping the sancta out of reach of the encroacher—it is highly probable that it will yield information in other areas of sacrilege.

Even a cursory glance at the text in fact reveals that its sole concern is with sacrilege against sancta. In addition to the subject of guarding the temple against encroachment by the outsider (2.4–11; 2.80–3.4), the remaining provisions of the Hittite "Instructions" deal with the problem of sacrilege by those individuals most capable of committing it: the temple staff, specifically, the temple officials and their servants inside its precincts (1.46–66; 2.12–58) or the farmers and herdsmen employed on the temple fields (4.1ff.).

Sacrilege by the inner-temple personnel can take place through the misappropriation or expropriation of sacrificial portions (1.50–66) or animals (2.12–

31), or of nonsacrificial sancta such as garments and metal tools (2.23–58). Sacrilege occurs with sacrificial portions when they are eaten, given away, or offered to the god piecemeal ("He who divides it shall be killed," 1.59). Sacrilege is committed with sacrificial animals if they are slaughtered, eaten, expropriated, put under yoke, sold, or exchanged ("if you appropriate for yourselves either a fattened ox or a fattened sheep and substitute a lean one . . ." 2.13–14); also envisaged is the possibility of collusion with the worshiper (i.e., "make a deal with those who give," 1.46–49). As for nonsacrificial sancta such as gold and silver garments or bronze implements, the Hittite "Instructions" stipulates that they must not be expropriated, and, if gold or silver bullion, they may not be possessed or converted into ornaments for the wife and children (2.33–39). Temple officials who receive these objects as gifts from the palace must have the nature, weight, and date of the gift recorded and witnessed; the gift itself may not be kept but must be sold in court (2.40–58). A final form of sacrilege, limited to temple officials, is authorizing the celebration of public or private rites at the wrong time (2.60–79); cf. 4.1–10, 34–39). The penalty for all of these felonies is death. If the trespasser is apprehended, death is by man; if not, then by the gods. If the execution is left to the gods then they will see to it that the offender's household dies with him (1.64–66; 2.74–79).

The outside personnel of the temple are its farmers and herdsmen. The farmer commits sacrilege in delaying the delivery of grain, which results in an automatic fine of one ox and ten sheep in addition to whatever the oracle stipulates (4.3–11); in the theft of grain or the exchange of fields, for which sin all of the farmer's own grain is impounded (4.12–24); or in expropriating plow oxen, either by eating or by selling them, which, if apprehended, obligates the farmer to replace the missing animals or, if suspected, subjects the farmer to an ordeal. If the outcome is a verdict of guilty, then the sentence is death (4.25–33).

The herdsman commits sacrilege by delaying the delivery of a sacrificial animal, consuming or selling it, giving it away—even to his superiors (4.34–43) —or exchanging it or substituting for it an emaciated animal (4.56–68). If the crime becomes known, the penalty is death; if suspected, an ordeal is imposed; on conviction, the sentence is death for the offender and his family (4.56–77). For greater detail, see Milgrom (1976f: 27–35).

The Hittite "Instructions" thus sheds abundant light on the biblical categories of sancta desecration. One aspect of sacrilege, unauthorized entry or encroachment corresponding to biblical qārēb, has already been studied (Milgrom 1970a: 5–33). The Hittite text, however, covers the full range of biblical maʿal. As mentioned above, this entails the misappropriation of sancta by keeping, eating, using, selling, gifting, delaying, or exchanging the temple's animals, fields, or grain, by appropriating and using or wearing the temple's implements or garments, or by changing the time fixed for rites. Additional information on

Hierarchy of Penalties for Sancta Sacrilege Among the Hittites

Sentence	Text	Criminal	Crime	Place
A. Death by gods (collective)				
1. unapprehended	1.34–38	anyone	sins against gods	anywhere
2. unapprehended	1.39–66	official	expropriates sacrificial position	inside
3. unapprehended	2.59–79	official	changes time of rite	inside
B. Death by man (collective)				
1. convicted by ordeal	4.47–55	herdsman	expropriates firstling	outside
2. convicted by ordeal	4.56–77	herdsman	expropriates sacrificial animal	outside
3. apprehended	3.44–54	anyone	destructive fire from unquenched hearth	inside
C. Death by man (criminal only)				
1. apprehended	1.50–59	official	divides sacrificial portions	inside
2. apprehended	2.9–12, 2.80–3.20	outsider (and official/ keeper in charge)	encroaches	inside
3. apprehended	3.74–84	temple servant (and whoever knows)	"Approaches god's sacrificial loaves and libation bowl in unclean condition"	inside
4. convicted by ordeal	4.25–33	farmer	expropriates plow ox	outside
5. apprehended	4.34–36	herdsman	expropriates firstling	outside
6. apprehended	4.56–68	herdsman	expropriates sacrificial animal	outside
D. Less than death (all apprehended)				
1. repeats ritual at own cost	3.35–43	layman	quarrels, disrupts ritual	inside
2. fine (plus oracle's decision)	4.1–10	farmer	delays sacrifice	outside
3. confiscation of grain	4.11–24	farmer	expropriates fields/grain	outside
4. replace item	4.25–33	farmer	expropriates plow ox	outside

biblical *ma'al* can be derived from the range of penalties preserved in the Hittite text. They are listed in the following table in order of the severity.

The table shows that whereas temple officials are punished by the gods, their servants are punished by man. Even so, if an official is apprehended, say, dividing the gods' portion (C1) or on duty while encroachment takes place (C2), he is executed judicially. The reason for this distinction is obvious: the officials control the temple; they can only be apprehended by their peers, an occurrence that rarely takes place. Their apprehension and punishment, then, is usually left to the gods. In P, a different rule prevails. It affirms that sins against God are punishable only by God, and it makes no difference whether the criminal is a cleric or a layman, whether apprehended or not (Milgrom 1970a: table B; 22 n. 76; 26 table C; 56–57). To be sure, there is the ostensible exception of the lay encroacher who is put to death by the priestly and Levitic guards, but it can be shown that "the right to kill with which the sanctuary guards are empowered is not to be confused with the legal category of capital punishment whereby death is set as just payment for the crime . . . the formula *hazzār haqqārēb yûmat* (is) an illusory exception to the confirmed rule that God himself exacts the death penalty for cultic crime. In reality, it only reenforces the rule, since it states: unless the encroacher is slain, the deity is sure to exercise his wrath" (Milgrom 1970a: 21–22).

True, nowhere in the Bible is there a specific rule that sacrilege against sancta is punishable solely by God, but it can be safely inferred from the text. The Priestly account of Korah's rebellion assumes that the encroaching layman is struck down by divine wrath (Num 17:28; 18:22; *mwt, qal*). Num 18:32 also stipulates that the Levite must set aside a tithe of the tithe he receives from the Israelite: "You must not desecrate *(těhallělû)* the sacred portion of the Israelites lest you die," that is to say, at the hands of God. Here then is a clear reference in the law that the penalty for desecrating the sancta is death, but only the deity may exact it.

Although deliberate sacrilege against sancta is not explicitly handled in the biblical law-codes, there are cases of it in the narratives. The Priestly tradition itself adduces the examples of Nadab and Abihu (Lev 10:1–2) and Korah and the chieftains (Num 16:16ff.). The sin of deliberate sacrilege is held by the Chronicler to be the cause of Uzziah's leprosy (2 Chr 26:16–18) and the destruction of Judah (2 Chr 30:10). For the desecration of *ḥērem*—the worst sacrilege of all—the wrath of God consumes the nation (e.g., Achan, Josh 7; 22:20; 1 Chr 2:7; Amalek, 1 Sam 15:3–31; Ben Hadad, 1 Kgs 20:42). The *ma'al* of oath violation has already been discussed. In all of these cases the penalty is explicit: the trespasser is struck down by God.

A second lesson of the table is that the Hittite gods punish not only the offender but also his household. The juridical authorities, however, execute the criminal alone and will not include his family unless he is convicted by the gods (by ordeal or by oracle). The very prologue to the "Instructions" (1.34–37) confirms this: "If . . . anyone arouses the anger of the god, does this god take revenge on him alone? Does he not take revenge on his wife, his children, his descendants, his slaves, and slave-girls, his cattle (and) sheep together with his crop and will utterly destroy him?" Nonetheless, this rule is limited to the temple; it is not applied to all elements of Hittite society: "If a slave causes his master's anger, they will either kill him or they will injure him at his nose, his eyes (or) his ears; or [they will seize] him, his wife, his children, his mother, his sister, his in-laws, his kin whether it be a male slave or a slave girl, they may (either) *impose the extreme penalty,* (or) they may do to him nothing at all. If ever he is to die, he will not die alone; his kin will accompany him" (1.28–33). A similar postulate informs Israelite legislation, but it is applied consistently without class distinctions. For both cleric and layman, master and slave, the doctrine of collective culpability is reserved exclusively to divine justice; it never functions in the jurisprudence of humanity (Milgrom 1970a: 37–59).

Ostensibly, the case of Achan, who is killed for sacrilege together with his family, contradicts this principle, because this execution is performed by man (Josh 7:24–25). Yet the exception proves illusory. Achan's guilt is discovered by lot, in other words, God himself designates the culprit; and it is by his expressed command that collective punishment is carried out (v 15). Ehrlich surmises correctly: "If Achan were apprehended . . . he alone would have been burned" (1900: ad loc.). Moreover, Achan's case is supported by an exact Hittite precedent. The temple herdsmen convicted by oracle (i.e., by the gods) are put to death together with their families (B1, 2). Thus both in Hattia and in Israel, convictions by oracle are executed by the court.

In sum, every act of *ma'al* involves sacrilege against the sancta or name of God, an act that may cause the destruction of the community as well as the offender. The sacrilege against "the Name" is clear: it refers to oath violations and is amply attested. By contrast, the nature of sancta desecration in the Bible is neither defined nor clearly illustrated. The Hittite text, "Instructions for Temple Officials," answers this need. It deals exclusively with the subject of sancta desecration. Its motivating principle can be extrapolated from its penalties: when the trespasser is apprehended by man, he alone suffers death; but when he is convicted by the gods (i.e., by ordeal or oracle), he is executed together with his family. Israelite law, meanwhile, operates with two contrasting postulates: (1) sins against God are not punishable by man and (2) collective punishment is a divine right that may not be usurped by man (for details, see Milgrom 1976f: 16–35).

C. Additional Cases of Sancta Desecration

The first case to be discussed is the *'āšām* of the Nazirite. P (Num 6:1–21) contains a law dealing with one who vows that for a specific period he will abstain from: (1) drinking intoxicants, (2) cutting his hair, and (3) touching a corpse (vv 3–9). Such a person is called a Nazirite, from the root *nzr*, meaning "to dedicate or separate." The purpose of this law is to prescribe the proper ritual when the dedication period is terminated, either prematurely (vv 10–12) or as planned (vv 13–21).

In the person of the Nazirite, the layman is allowed entry into the sacred realm. Like the priest he becomes "holy to the Lord" (Num 6:8; cf. Lev 21:6). (So recognized by Philo, *Laws* 1. 249, and implied by *Midr. Num. Rab.*, Naso 10:11). If the Nazirite is to be compared to a sacred person, however, his taboos raise him to the level of the high priest. For one thing, both Nazirite and high priest are forbidden to contaminate themselves with the corpses of their immediate family (21:11–12; Num 6:6–7 and cf. *m. Nazir* 7:1; contrast the ordinary priest, 21:1–4). The rationale is almost identical in language and thought: compare "for the dedication of his God is upon his head" (Num 6:7b) and "for the dedication of the anointing (oil) of his God is upon him" (21:12b). For another, the focus of sanctity for both is the head: the high priest's is anointed (Exod 29:7; Lev 8:12; contrast the ordinary priest, Exod 29:21; Lev 8:30), while the Nazirite dedicates his hair (Num 6:11b). Also, both abstain from wine, but the high priest, like his fellow priests, is enjoined from intoxicants only while officiating (Lev 10:8); the Nazirite's prohibition is never suspended during his term of dedication (Num 6:4).

Land dedicated to the sanctuary (27:16–19) affords a more instructive parallel. Both result from a dedicative vow (Num 6:2; cf. Lev 27:2). Both periods are limited, the land reverting to its owner on the jubilee if not redeemed earlier (implied by 27:21; cf. Num 6:2). Both periods can be aborted, the Nazirite's by contamination (Num 6:9–12), the land by redemption (27:16–19). In the case of premature desanctification, a penalty is exacted from both: the Nazirite pays a reparation offering, the landowner adds one-fifth to the redemption price. In the case of the completion of the dedicated period, there is no desanctification penalty. True, the Nazirite offers up sacrifices on the altar together with his hair (Num 6:13–21), but the sacrifices are for thanksgiving and the hair, which cannot be desanctified, is shaved and burned on the altar. Similarly, dedicated land (so the text of 27:16–21 implies) reverts to the owner on the jubilee without cost.

The Nazirite's desanctification process warrants a closer look. In the case of the premature termination of his Nazirite period, the parallel with the redemption of dedicated land only holds true in that a penalty is exacted. But the penalty is not the same, nor can it be. Land redemption is legitimate and expected, whereas the Nazirite's contamination is sinful and is to be avoided. Moreover, the Nazirite's period must begin over again (Num 6:11b, 12). His ritual of purification, reparation, and reconsecration consists of the following steps: (1) He must undergo sprinkling with purificatory waters on the third and seventh days following corpse-contamination (inferred from Num 19:11–12). (2) On the seventh day he shaves his hair (Num 6:9b). (3) Three distinct ceremonies are prescribed for the eighth day. First he brings a purification offering because he came into contact with the dead. Then the Nazirite dedicates both his hair and his term for a second time (presumably by taking another vow, see v 2), for in keeping with 5:14–16, the desecrated sanctum must be restored. Finally, he brings a reparation lamb to make amends for the desecration. Indeed, that the Nazirite brings an ʾāšām when his term is interrupted and not when it is completed (Num 6:13–15), though both occasions mark his transit from sacred to profane status, demonstrates that the former constitutes illicit desanctification, requiring reparation to God, whereas the latter constitutes legitimate desanctification, and the šĕlāmîm of joy replaces the ʾāšām of reparation.

That the ʾāšām of the contaminated Nazirite expiates for the desecration of sancta is also shown by the required sacrificial order. Not only is the ʾāšām last in the series, following the ḥaṭṭāʾt and the ʿōlâ, but it is separated from the latter by a nonsacrificial ritual whereby the Nazirite reconsecrates his hair and vow (vv 11–12). This break is unprecedented, for in every other biblical ritual the prescribed sacrifices follow one another without interruption. The act of reconsecration could have been before or after the sacrificial service; why was it placed before the ʾāšām offering? The answer, I believe, is found in the procedure for the ʾāšām of sancta desecration, 5:14–16. The offender brings a reparation ram or its equivalent along with the restitution costs, including the penalty of one-fifth (vv 15–16aαβ). Still, before he may look for expiation through his sacrifice he must first give the priest the monetary restitution (16aγ, b). The purpose of the order is clear: the sanctum must be restored before God's forgiveness can be sought (see the NOTES on 5:20–26).

The same sacrificial priorities are invoked for the contaminated Nazirite. Before his ʾāšām is acceptable to God he must replace the desecrated sancta, namely, the consecrated hair that had been shaved and the preceding Nazirite period that had been canceled. Only after he reconsecrates his new hair and renews his Nazirite vow has total restitution been rendered, so that the priest can proceed with the ʾāšām sacrifice in the hope of divine forgiveness for the Nazirite. Thus the unique sacrificial order for the contaminated Nazirite reinforces the thesis that the ʾāšām is brought for sancta desecration. For details see Milgrom (1976f: 66–70).

A prophetic application of the law of sancta desecration is found in Jer 2:3, "Israel was holy (qōdeš) to the Lord, the best of his harvest. All who consumed it (ʾōkĕlāw) were punished (yeʾšāmû); evil came upon them." It is hardly accidental that Jeremiah resorts to the same vocabulary as Lev 22:14–16. Israel's enemies are guilty of consuming Israel (for ʾākal 'destroy', cf. Jer 30:16; Fishbane 1985: 302 n. 27, correcting Milgrom 1976f: 70) and must therefore suffer retribution (cf. ʾašmâ, 22:16). Their crime is the desecration of sancta; their punishment by God is therefore assured. Jeremiah, then, applies the law of trespass upon sancta metaphorically to Israel's enemies. It is ʾAggadic midrash.

Where, however, did the prophet derive the notion that all of Israel constituted a sanctum? The answer must await the analysis of a similar problem in the book of Ezra.

A unique application of sancta desecration is found in Ezra 10:19: "They agreed to put away their wives; their reparation offering was a ram from the flock for their sacrilege." The question is: How was Ezra able to persuade his people that intermarriage was a sacrilege that could only be expiated by divorcing the foreign wives and bringing an *'āšām* offering? There is no precedent for it in all of Scripture. The key to this puzzle is to be found at the beginning of the section on the intermarriages of the returned exiles: "Inasmuch as they and their sons have married some of their daughters, so that the holy seed *(zera' haqqōdeš)* has become mixed with the peoples of the lands; indeed the officials and chiefs were the leading offenders in this sacrilege *(ma'al)*" (Ezra 9:2). This verse reveals Ezra's line of reasoning. Israel is a "sacred seed" whose admixture with foreigners is a *ma'al*. The syllogism is clear: if Israel is holy then the adulteration of its blood constitutes *ma'al*. But whence his premise? What in Ezra's tradition allowed him to reckon his people as a sanctum? Certainly he could not have derived it from the P source; it does not even prohibit intermarriages! The most he could have deduced from D was that marriage with autochthonous Canaanites, or Moabites and Ammonites—from whom only some exiles selected their wives—was interdicted (Deut 7:1–3; 23:4). In no tradition whatever are all intermarriages prohibited or are they ever referred to as a cultic sin against God, a *ma'al*.

Two answers are possible. The first, I submit, is that Ezra spun a midrash. He began with D, which, alone among the traditions, regards Israel as an *'am gādôs* 'a holy people' (Deut 7:6; 14:2, 21; 26:19; 28:9). P, of course, also espouses the concept of ethnic sanctity. But it exists only for an elite, the priests (e.g., Lev 21:6–7) and the Nazirites (Num 6:5). The rest of Israel is not holy inherently but is called to *become* holy, as the dynamic, future-directed thrust of the root *qdš* in P indicates: "You shall sanctify yourselves and be holy"; "You shall be holy" (e.g., 11:44–45; 19:2; 20:7, 26). Indeed, the doctrine that holiness inheres in Israel constitutes in P the infamous heresy of Korah (Num 16:3). For P, holiness is a desideratum, not a fact; an ideal, not a status. Nor is this an innovation of P, for it is found in JE (Exod 19:6; 22:30). It is D alone that declares that the people as a whole bear the status of a sanctum.

D's doctrine of the ethnic sanctity of Israel is responsible for Jeremiah's 'Ag. midrash that the nations were punished for consuming Israel (Jer 2:3). Thus Ezra had already inherited from the deuteronomic school and one of its early disciples, Jeremiah, the notion that Israel was a sanctum and that punishment would follow its desecration. Ezra's innovation consists in taking a theological concept and a prophetic image and weaving them into a midrash (Milgrom 1981f). Note the process. D's limited prohibition on intermarriages (Deut 23:4; cf. Neh 13:1–3, 23–27) is extended to all exogamous unions. Next, Ezra derives from D that Israel is a sanctum and from P that sacrilege against sancta merits divine punishment. Yet unlike Jeremiah, who applies these two doctrines metaphorically to Israel's enemies, Ezra fuses them into a legal midrash directed against Israel itself for having allowed the "enemy" to infiltrate by means of intermarriage. Thus Israel, "the holy seed," has been adulterated. Because the intermarriages were contracted inadvertently—Israel being innocent of the law —their dissolution must be followed by an 'āšām offering, so that the desecration of the Lord's sancta may be expiated in accordance with the prescription of 5:14–16.

A second answer emerges once it is realized that Ezra may have forced the divorce of local non-Israelite wives only. This reading becomes possible once a distinction is made between two terms, 'ammê hā'āreṣ and 'ammê hā'ărāṣôt, the former referring to the non-Israelite inhabitants of Canaan (Ezra 10:2, 11; Neh 10:31, 32), the latter to those stemming from other lands (Ginsberg 1982: 8–16). Furthermore, if 'ammê hā'ărāṣôt in Ezra 9:1, 2, 11 can be regarded as an error for 'ammê hā'āreṣ (cogent reasons provided by Ginsberg 1982: 16), then it becomes clear that the texts of Ezra and Nehemiah are consistent in allowing outside wives to remain and autochthonous ones to be expelled.

This being the case, then Ezra's decree is hardly a midrash at all. He simply has applied Deuteronomy's ḥērem against the seven local peoples (Deut 7:1–3) to their latter-day progeny. Because tampering with ḥērem (literally, God's property) constitutes ma'al (note the case of Achan, above), it becomes evident that these women's Israelite husbands (who, presumably, were unaware of Deuteronomy's proscription) have inadvertently committed sacrilege and are liable for an 'āšām offering.

To be sure, Ezra's consternation is precipitated not only by being informed (Ezra 9:1) that his people have intermarried with Canaanites, Hittites, Perizzites, and Jebusites—four of the seven peoples forbidden in marriage to Israel (Deut 7:1)—but also with "Ammonites, Moabites, Egyptians, and Edomites (with LXX manuscripts and 1 Esd 8:68 for "Amorites"). It can hardly be an accident that these four nations are precisely the ones that are expressly prohibited by Deuteronomy from being admitted into the peoplehood of Israel (Deut 23:4–9), presumably via intermarriage (Milgrom 1982a). Thus the possibility exists that these four peoples were subsequently added to the list in order to justify the expulsion of Tobiah, the Ammonite, and other Ammonites who did their best to frustrate the building of Jerusalem's walls (Neh 3:33–4:2), whereas the original list only banned local aliens (Fishbane 1985: 124 n. 5, who deduces from Neh 13:23 with v 24 that " 'Ammorites, Moabites' is a tendentious addition—as in Ezra 9:1"). Herein possibly lies the midrashic innovation. Ezra (or a later tradent) added the four excluded nations of Deut 23 to the ḥērem list of Deut 7. In any event, according to this reading of the expulsion of the alien wives in Ezra and Nehemiah, Israel became liable for an 'āšām offering once it realized that it had committed sacrilege *(ma'al)* against *ḥērem* (for details, see Milgrom 1976f: 71–73).

To recapitulate, the inadvertent desecration *(ma'al)* of sancta imposes the following penalty: payment for the desecrated sanctum plus one-fifth and a reparation ram or its assessed value (5:14–16). Additional cases of sancta desecration are found in (1) 22:14–16 (see the COMMENT thereon) where, however, it is not certain that an Israelite who inadvertently eats sacred food (of lesser sanctity because it is available to the priest's household) must bring an *'āšām* in addition to his one-fifth fine; (2) The Nazirite's *'āšām* (Num 6:1–12), which expiates for the desecration of his hair and the premature termination of his Nazirite vow; (3) Jeremiah's 'Ag. midrash (Jer 2:3) on D's concept of the holiness of all Israel to justify the punishment of Israel's enemies for their desecration; and (4) the legal midrash of Ezra 10:19, wherein the returnees from the Babylonian Exile are required to bring an *'āšām* to atone for this desecration of the "holy seed" of Israel by their intermarriages or committing sacrilege by intermarrying with descendants of the Canaanites whom Deuteronomy had placed under *ḥērem* (Deut 7:1–3).

D. Unwitting Sin in the Ancient Near East

Unwitting sin as the cause of disaster is widely attested in the ancient world. The sin of unwitting sacrilege against the deity is especially feared. For example, in the Babylonian "Prayer to Every God," we find, "The sin which I have done, indeed I do not know. The forbidden thing which I have eaten, indeed I do not know. The prohibited (place) on which I have set foot, indeed I do not know" (*ANET*³ 391–92, lines 27–29). This text clearly underscores the fear of unconscious sin. The possibilities of wrongdoing are not enumerated (as in the rituals, e.g., Šurpu; see below). Only one sin is specified, clearly the one that was feared the most: sacrilege against sancta. In the confessional literature of the ancient Near East, the fear of sancta desecration dominates the sins: see, for example, the Egyptian "Protestation of Guiltlessness" (the Negative Confession); cf. A3, 17, 18, 29, 35, 36; B8, 13 (suspected sacrilege against the gods' person or property) with A8; B38, 42 (blasphemy) and A21; B20 (impurity) (*ANET*³ 34–36); the Babylonian "Prayer to Every God," lines 17, 19, 20, 28, 29 (*ANET*³ 391). Note its reflex in talmudic dictum: the fear of sacrilege aborts any conspiracy against sancta (*Šebu.* 42b). Indeed, many ancient and complex rituals have as their sole purpose the expiation for unknown sins. For example, Babylonian "Shurpu is performed when the patient does not know why or by what act of omission he has offended the gods or the existing order" (Reiner 1958: 3).

For the Hittites, it has been observed that

the offender may be unconscious that any sin has been committed . . . the god must inform the sufferer of the nature of the offense before penance could be rendered . . . through the mouth of an ecstatic or by means of a dream . . . (or) through divination . . . (extispicy, augury, or lottery. Through the latter) . . . an enormously lengthy process of elimination was possible to determine without fail the precise offense which required expiation. . . . The records of these acts of consultation of the "oracle" are among the largest and most numerous . . . tablets of the Hittite archives. (Gurney 1952: 158–60).

The ancient Greeks were equally obsessed by the trauma of unconscious taboo violation. For example: "the moral suffering of Oedipus was . . . called forth by the fact . . . that he has unintentionally and unwittingly done something which was objectively terrible. Here then the cause of the most terrible sin is *'amartía"* (Fritz apud von Rad 1962: 267). Indeed, at every turn the literature of the ancients reveals the pervasive fear that unconscious sin is responsible for misfortune.

Concern over unconscious sin also permeates the Bible (e.g., Deut 29:28; 1 Sam 26:19; Ps 19:13; Job 1:5). It is reasonable to suppose that this concern had greater theological significance for Israel than for any of its neighbors. The polytheist, acknowledging evil as an autonomous, supernatural force, could posit that it could be requisitioned by any man—through the agency of a sorcerer—to inflict harm upon his mortal enemy. This is why in many conjuration rituals the evil is not only exorcised from the victim but is also hurled back upon its enemy/sorcerer originator. Israel's monotheism, conversely, having vitiated the premise of autonomous, supernatural evil, had no choice but to attribute its existence to the one God. Natural evil, then, could be compromised by the pagan, but to the Israelite it was a scandal, a blatant contradiction of God's goodness and justice. Indeed, a case can be made that Job's polemic against his friends rests on their disagreement over the role of unconscious sin in theodicy: Job's friends champion the traditional view of Israel and its environment that Job is suffering for his unconscious sin; Job, by contrast, emphatically denies this doctrine and insists that his suffering is unjustified until he knows wherein he has sinned: "Let Shaddai answer me. Let my opponent write a document" (Job 31:35b; Milgrom 1967: 121–25). This, then, is one of the most significant contributions of Israel's expiatory sacrifices, the *ḥaṭṭāʾt* and *ʾāšām:* all accidental sins are expiable by sacrifice. Intention, therefore, does play a role in the divine judgment. This constitutes a major break with the theology of the ancient Near East and of old Israel.

In the early rabbinic period, the "suspended *ʾāšām"* (5:17–19) played a more central role. It was brought frequently by the pious, who were certain that they could deter conscious sins but were in dread over the possibility of committing sins unconsciously. "Rabbi Eliezer says: a man may donate a suspended

ʾāšām (tālûy) any day and any hour he desires and it is called 'the ʾāšām of the pious.' It was related of Baba ben Buti that he used to donate a suspended ʾāšām (tālûy) every day except the day after the Day of Atonement. He said: (I swear by) this Temple: if they would only permit me I would bring (one even on this day)" (m. Ker. 6:3; cf. t. Ker. 4:4).

The increased importance of the ʾāšām at the end of Second Temple days bespeaks a development whose significance cannot be underestimated. Heretofore, man tended to dichotomize the world into the sacred and the profane, the discrete realms of the gods and man. He believed that as long as he did not infringe on the sacred, the gods would not molest him; he might even thrive under this beneficence if he regularly rendered them their due. With the promulgation of 5:17–19 (and the complementary ḥaṭṭāʾt law of chap. 4), whereby the unwitting violation of any "of the Lord's commandments" requires expiation for sancta desecration, the boundaries between the sacred and the profane are obliterated forever. Henceforth, the sacred is unbounded; it is coextensive with the will of God. It embraces ethics as well as ritual, the relations between men and not just those between man and God. In short, the violation of any of the Torah's prohibitions constitutes sacrilege, maʿal, the expiation of which is essential if Israel is to remain in divine grace (details in Milgrom 1976f: 74–82).

E. The ʾāšām of the mĕṣōrāʿ

A case has been made for the ʾāšām requirement of the corpse-contaminated Nazirite on the basis of his actual maʿal, the desecration of his sacred status (see above). But how can the ʾāšām brought by the purified mĕṣōrāʿ (14:12, 21) be justified? His disease is not traceable to sancta desecration or for that matter to any other cause. The ʾāšām of 5:17–19 opens a door to the answer: he may have desecrated sancta. Because other sins may have been responsible for his affliction, he brings an array of sacrifices for his expiation, but the ʾāšām is ordained to expiate for the possibility of maʿal.

My hypothesis would rank as sheer conjecture were it not for the corroboration offered from an unexpected source. The Chronicler relates that Uzziah was stricken with scale disease precisely at the moment that, and because, he encroached upon sancta. The language of the text is most instructive: "When he grew powerful his pride led to his undoing. He committed sacrilege (māʿal) against the Lord his God by entering the Lord's Temple to burn incense on the altar of incense. . . . 'Leave the Sanctuary for you have committed sacrilege (māʿaltā).' . . . Scale disease broke out on his forehead in the presence of the priests in the Lord's house, beside the altar of incense" (2 Chr 26:16–19). It is no accident that Uzziah's sin is twice labeled maʿal. True, the tendentiousness of the story is transparent: it is part of the Chronicler's polemic against the royal prerogative to officiate as priests. Even though the story itself may be questioned, however, it rests upon the unchallenged premise that sacrilege against sancta is punishable by scale disease and, conversely, that the incidence of scale disease may be traceable to the sin of sacrilege against sancta. Thus it was imperative for the purified *mĕṣōrāʿ*, as part of his ritual of rehabilitation with his community and his God, to bring an *ʾāšām* to cover the contingency that his unwitting desecration of sancta was responsible for his disease.

The attribution of scale disease to sancta desecration is not limited to Israel. According to the Aramaic "Prayer of Nabonidus" found at Qumran (Milik 1956: 405–11), Nabonidus was stricken with *shnʾ bʾyšʾ* (=Heb. *šĕḥîn raʿ*) 'a serious inflammation'. Nabonidus's defection from Marduk in favor of Sin may have constituted sancta desecration. More likely, it would have been viewed by Marduk's priests as a violation of a loyalty oath to Marduk.

That oath violation was punished by scale disease is shown by many treaty curses, for example, "May Sin, the luminary of heaven and earth, clothe you in leprosy and (thus) not permit you to enter the presence of god and king" (*ANET*[3] 538). Scale disease is labeled in Akk. *erretum/šertu rabitum/lemuttum* 'the great/terrible curse/punishment', as in "Whoever desecrates this temple . . . Sin, the elder brother among the gods, his brothers, should curse him with the 'Great Curse' " (*ANET*[3] 550). For the demonstration that oath violation also constitutes *maʿal*, see below; and for the discussion of the diagnosis and causes of scale disease, see the COMMENT on chap. 13.

Finally, it must be posited that the *mĕṣōrāʿ* brings the "suspended *ʾāšām*" not just for the possibility of sancta desecration but for the contingency that he unconsciously violated one of the other prohibitive commandments (see the NOTE on 5:17). This wider range of wrongdoing allotted to the *ʾāšām* would then bring into sharper focus the equally distributive function of all required sacrifices: the *ʿōlâ* and *minḥâ* (14:20) for the neglect of the performative commandments (see the COMMENT on chap. 1), the *ʾāšām* for the unconscious violation of the prohibitive commandments (14:12–14), and the *ḥaṭṭāʾt* for the purgation of the polluted sanctuary (14:19).

That the *ʾāšām* is the key sacrifice in the ritual complex for the purification of the *mĕṣōrāʿ* is indicated by the following evidence: (1) The *ʾāšām* animal is never replaced by a less expensive offering for the sake of the indigent, as is the case with the other prescribed sacrifices (14:21–22; cf. vv 10–13). (2) The *ʾāšām* of the *mĕṣōrāʿ* is not commutable to silver, as is the case with the ordinary *ʾāšām*. The reason is obvious: its blood is needed for the prescribed ritual (vv 14, 25; cf. *m. Zebaḥ.* 10:5). (3) Contrary to all other rituals, the *ʾāšām* takes precedence over the other sacrifices and is the first to be offered during the ritual for the eighth day. (4) It is the only sacrifice requiring the *tĕnûpâ* ritual, which certifies that it is endowed with a higher dedicatory status (Milgrom 1973: 102–3; cf. chap. 7, COMMENT E). (5) The *mĕṣōrāʿ* is daubed with the blood of the *ʾāšām* rather than with the blood of any other sacrificial animal. (For details see Milgrom 1976f: 80–82.)

THE SACRIFICES

F. Sacrilege Against Oaths

The justification for the translation of vv 20–26, which differs from all extant ones, depends on answering the paradox raised by this pericope. As rendered, it flies in the face of the fundamental premise of P, that there can be no sacrificial expiation for the presumptuous sinner; he is barred from the sanctuary because "he acts defiantly . . . reviles the Lord . . . has spurned the word of the Lord and violated the commandment" (Num 15:30–31; contrast vv 24–29). Indeed, the ʾāšām cases thus far presume that their respective offenses were committed unintentionally. This ʾāšām passage, however, confronts us with the one who defrauds both God and his fellow willfully and yet is forgiven if he brings the proper sacrifice. To resolve this paradox we must identify the two basic postulates informing this legislation.

I submit that the clauses that speak of a false oath (vv 22aβ, b; 24aα) apply to all of the cases that precede them: not only does the offender deny he has wronged his fellow, he denies it under oath. If so, then the "sacrilege against the Lord" that heads the pericope (v 21) is fully clarified: the Lord has been made an accomplice to the defrauding of man. The reparation offering, which in vv 15–19 was enjoined for real or suspected desecration of God's property, is now imposed for the desecration of God's name. This postulate differs, to my knowledge, from all extant translations, both ancient and modern. Although I came to it on my own, I soon discovered that I had been anticipated by Philo and by some of the Tannaites and medieval exegetes (see Philo, *Laws* 1. 225; *Laws* 4. 31–32; *m. B. Meṣ.* 4:8; *Sipra*, Ḥobah par. 13:8 and chap. 23). The required sacrifice is even termed in some talmudic sources ʾāšam šĕbûʿâ ʾāšām of oath (e.g., *b. Ketub.* 42a); see also Bekhor Shor on Lev 4:3: "He who dissembles to his fellow regarding a deposit commits two (sins): he derives benefit and has sworn falsely"; cf. also Ramban (on Num 5:6); Abravanel (on vv 20–26); Maim., *Introduction to Seder Qodoshim*. This interpretation is also found among the Karaites; see *Keter Torah* (on 5:11ff.) and *Seper Hamibḥar* (on Num 5:6). Among the moderns who follow it, see Elliger (1966, ad loc.). Most of the ancients, however, maintain that the maʿal occurs by denial (so interpreting *Wĕkiḥeš*) and not by oath (e.g., Rabbi Akiba in *Sipra*, Ḥobah 22:4; *Sipre* on Num 2:2; *Midr. Num. Rab.* 9:2).

That the "sacrilege against the Lord" consists of the false oath can be demonstrated by comparing the malfeasances of vv 20–26 with a similar list in 19:11–13a:

lōʾ tignōbû wĕlōʾ-tĕkaḥăšû wĕlōʾ-tĕšaqqĕrû ʾîš baʿămîtô ¹²wĕlō-tiššābĕʿû bišmî laššāqer wĕḥillaltā ʾet-šēm ʾĕlōhêkā ʾănî YHWH ¹³lōʾ-taʿăšōq ʾet-rēʿăkā wĕlōʾ tigzōl. . . .

You shall not steal; you shall not dissemble or lie to one another; [12]you shall not swear falsely by my name, thereby desecrating the name of your God. I am the Lord. [13]You shall not withhold from your neighbor nor rob him. . . .

It is immediately obvious that both passages contain common terms: *kiḥēš, ʿāšaq, gāzal,* and *nišbaʿ laššeqer.* There are also terms that occur in only one of the lists: *piqqādôn, tĕśûmet yād,* and *ʾăbēdâ* in chap. 5 and *šeqer* and *gānab* in chap. 19. These peculiarities will be readily understandable once the terms themselves and the distinctive nature of each list are clarified. Before we turn to this task, however, let us see how chap. 19 supports my first postulate. It will be noted that it lists only one sin qualified by a motive clause—the false oath: "you shall not swear falsely by my name, thereby desecrating the name of your God" (v 12). The rabbis took the same view: " 'Thereby desecrating the name of your God' (19:12) teaches that a false oath is a desecration of the Name" (*Sipra,* Qedoshim par. 2:7). This view is also held by the Dead Sea sectaries (cf. CD 15.3). The proposition is herewith submitted that *wĕḥillaltā ʾet-šēm ʾĕlōhekā = māʿal bĕYHWH,* that is to say, desecrating God's name (19:12) is synonymous with committing sacrilege against God (5:21).

The root *hillēl* 'desecrate' implies a priori that we are dealing with sancta. It is therefore no accident that the name of God is often called *šēm qodš(î),* "(my) holy name." It is striking, however, that this divine epithet is used mainly in cases of desecration (20:3; 22:2, 32: Ezek 20:39; 36:20, 21, 22; 39:7; 43:7, 8; Amos 2:7), of which all but one occur in H and Ezekiel. The implication for 19:12 is clear: anyone who uses the name of God in a false oath has trespassed on a sanctum; hence he has committed *maʿal.*

How can we account for two distinct terms for the sacrilege of the false oath? A perusal of some vital statistics will provide us with an answer. Of the seventy-five loci of the root *hll* in the Bible, fifty are concentrated in P (including H) and Ezekiel. Yet, of those fifty, forty-seven are found in H and Ezekiel and only three are in P. *Ab initio,* it is clear that the root *hll* is not favored by P, despite its obvious concern with sancta desecration. P prefers *maʿal,* as seen in the *ʾāšām* pericope. By the same token, of the fifty-nine loci of the root *mʿl* only one occurs in H (26:40), significantly, not in its laws but in a paraenetic passage. The notion of trespass is expressed in H by *hll.* The statistics reveal more: the term *hillēl šēm* 'desecrate the name (of God)' occurs six times in H (18:21; 19:12; 20:3; 21:6; 22:2, 32), nine times in Ezekiel (20:9, 14, 22, 39; 36:20, 21, 22, 23; 39:7), and four times elsewhere, *but not once in P.* This fact is all the more astonishing because the false oath is labeled as sin only because it is a desecration of God's name, and for no other reason. Yet, in P, where the matter of a false oath is of major concern, it is never called a desecration of God's name! Oath or imprecation violations in P occur as a result of refusing to testify

(Lev 5:1), amnesia (5:4), conviction by ordeal (Num 5:19–21), and unfulfilled vows (Num 30:1ff.). Only the last-mentioned case uses the term *ḥll* and that, tellingly, not with the name of God, but with the vow itself (Num 30:3).

The anomaly can be resolved in the following manner: chaps. 5 and 19 stem originally from discrete sources, identified in biblical research as P and H. Indeed, investigation reveals that not only the false oath but other categories of desecration common to P and H exhibit the same terminological discrepancy: H alone labels them as desecrations of God's name. The conclusion is inescapable: *ḥillēl šēm YHWH* is an idiom of H, and it is totally foreign to P. Moreover, it becomes an unassailable criterion by which the H source can be disengaged from P (see Milgrom 1976f: 88 n. 309). Yet the question remains: How then does P express the notion of the desecration of God? As we have seen, the text of 5:20–26 implies that the equivalent term is *maʿal bĕ YHWH*, and the clincher is provided by the parallel passage just adduced: whereas 5:20–26 labels the sin *māʿal bĕ YHWH*, 19:11–12 calls it *wĕḥillaltā ʾet-šēm ʾĕlōhêkā*. Thus the comparative analysis of 5:20–26 and 19:11–13a provides confirmation of the first postulate. The "sacrilege against the Lord" (5:21) cannot refer to the enumerated cases but must be linked to the final clause in the series, "he swears falsely" (5:22aβ; cf. 24aα), thereby establishing that it is the false oath that makes the fraud a "sacrilege against the Lord." The question remains: If the *ʾāšām* expiates for oath violation, why only in the narrow circumstances of 5:20–26; why does not the Bible prescribe it for all cases of a false oath? The answer is provided by the Bible itself: no other case of a juridical false oath is attested or is possible! The bailee laws of Exod 22:6–12 are subsumed under *piqqādôn* and represent no new category. The imprecation of the suspected adulteress (Num 5:11–31) is not exculpatory but is to guarantee the efficacy of the ordeal (contrast CH 131; MAL 47). One might expect false oaths from witnesses, but Israelite witnesses did not testify under oath (contrast CH 9; Driver 1940). They might be convicted of lying (Exod 20:16; cf. v 7; Deut 19:16–21), but they were not guilty of *maʿal*.

Ancient Near Eastern legal practice knew of three kinds of oaths: promissory, declaratory, and exculpatory *(Reinigungseide)*. Promissory oaths are found in contracts but not in the laws (*BL* 1.466–69; cf. also LE 22, 37; HL 75; Cowley 1923: 6–8, 14, 44f.). Thus biblical law (as opposed to nonlegal texts) knows only of exculpatory oaths. The only time one is called upon in litigation to take an oath is to clear oneself of the charge of misappropriating property— precisely the setting of Lev 5:20–26.

This last conclusion, instead of simplifying the paradox, has only compounded it. Identifying the sacrilege against God with the false oath has now made it certain that the fraud was intentional. Moreover, it has aggravated the crime. In biblical jurisprudence, the defrauding of man is a civil offense and is punishable only by monetary composition. Conversely, defrauding God by a false oath, like all willful sins against the deity, is punishable by divine execution.

The penalty for swearing falsely is nowhere stipulated in biblical law. That one exists is the premise of biblical and rabbinic law (see COMMENT B above). Indeed, some tannaitic texts mandate that God will even execute the family of the oath violator, for example, "for the transgression of all of the other commandments in the Torah he alone will be punished, but for this (transgression, i.e., a false oath) he and his family," *t. Soṭa* 7:2 (= *b. Šebu.* 38b [bar.]). That oath violations are punished by the gods is an axiom of all ancient Near Eastern literature. For Mesopotamia, see the *māmītu* of Šurpu, 3.19–26, 8.35–44, and its discussion in Brichto (1963: 71–76), also the text and ritual of the fifth "house" in Laesse (1955: 52–67). For the Greeks, see Jones (1956: 136–39) and the remarks of Heinemann (1932: 92–96).

Here is the crux: because the axiom of all biblical jurisprudence—not only P —is that capital crime can never be commuted, how can it be expiated by sacrifice? The answer is provided by the psychological component of the consequential *'āšām*. The verb *'āšam* without an object, as demonstrated (COMMENT A above), has but one meaning in the cultic texts, "feel guilt." (Indeed, one of the proof texts was actually selected from this pericope, v 23.) This is the second postulate. It has been stated and proved; it need only be applied.

First, however, we turn to the parallel passage Num 5:6–8, which was also cited, in part, as evidence for the meaning of *'āšam* as "feel guilt" (COMMENT A above). Because it elucidates the basic question of sacrificial expiation for deliberate sins, it is quoted in full (for exegetical details, see Milgrom 1976f: 105–6):

> [6]If a man or woman commits any wrong against man whereby he commits sacrilege against the Lord, when that person feels guilt [7]he shall confess the wrong he has done, make reparation in its entirety, and add one-fifth to it, giving it to the one to whom he has incurred liability. [8]If he has no kinsman to whom reparation can be made, the reparation shall go to the Lord for the priest—in addition to the ram of expiation with which expiation is made on his behalf.

This passage from Numbers supplements Lev 5:20–26 in three important ways. First, it generalizes whereas Leviticus also cites specific cases, thus confirming that *ma'al* applies to all cases of defrauding man by means of an oath. Second, it adds the stipulation that in the case wherein the defrauded man dies and leaves no kin, the reparation belongs to the officiating priest. The third innovation is most crucial: restitution must be preceded by confession.

Knohl (1988: 153–55) argues for a fourth innovation: The omission of the false oath from the facts of this case is deliberate and, hence, points to the radical teaching that all violations of the commandment, civil and cultic alike, require remorse and sacrifice as expiation. This reading of the text is without foundation. The Numbers version is patently a digest of its Levitic counterpart. Just as "commits any wrong against man" generalizes the specific crimes of Lev

5:21–22aα, so "commits sacrilege against the Lord" repeats verbatim the generalization of Lev 5:21a, specified in the following verse as taking a false oath (22aβ, b). Moreover, it is inconceivable that any priestly legist would demand a reparation offering for a purely civil violation. What specific damage has he inflicted on the deity, on either his name or his sancta—the indispensable prerequisite of the reparation offering—that would warrant this sacrifice? Surely, the purification offering or, more suitably, the burnt offering, which expiates for a wide range of wrongdoing (COMMENT on chap. 1), would have served this purpose better.

Knohl adds a literary observation that, however, merits serious consideration. Noting that the vocabulary of this pericope veers sharply from the Leviticus original—to wit, its use of both *'îš 'ô-'iššâ* and *nepeš* (v 6), whereas P distinguishes between the two, the former for impurities (e.g., 15:2) and the latter for sacrifices (e.g., 4:2; cf. Knohl 1988: 76–77); its use of *'āšām* to refer to the monetary reparation instead of the sacrifice, calling the latter by the unique term *'êl hakkippûrîm* (ibid. 219 n. 83); and its use of *těrûmâ* (v 9) to designate all of the priestly gifts, as in 22:12 and Num 18:8 (ibid. 219 n. 84)—Knohl concludes that this pericope stems from the hand of H. (For details on this and other H passages heretofore attributed to P, see ibid., 53–100). If he proves correct, then the confessional requirement, absent in Lev 5 but inserted into Num 5, must be ascribed to the innovation of H.

The nature of biblical confession has been investigated in the NOTE on 5:5. Here the question must be asked: Was it a precondition for all expiatory sacrifice? As the confession in the literature of the ancient Near East includes every conceivable sin, especially those committed unwittingly (COMMENT D above), one would assume that the same held true for the Bible. Yet a review of the four passages in P wherein confession is explicitly required *(wěhitwaddâ)* reveals that each case deals exclusively with deliberate sin (5:1–4; 16:21; 26:40; Num 5:6). That this is no accident is clear from our new understanding of the verb *'āšam*. For involuntary sin, *'āšam*, remorse alone suffices; it renders confession superfluous. But for deliberate sin there is the added requirement that remorse be verbalized; the sin must be articulated and responsibility assumed. This conclusion can also be deduced from the wording of the basic postulate of the sacrificial system that atonement is denied to the individual who brazenly violates God's law (Num 15:30b). It should not be taken to mean, as many critics aver, that only involuntary wrongdoers are eligible for sacrificial atonement. For, as we have seen from the *'āšam* case under discussion, the defrauding of God by a false oath is manifestly intentional, yet atonement is achieved through sacrifice (even called *'êl hakkippûrîm* 'the ram of expiation', Num 5:8). A more correct understanding of this Priestly postulate would be that sacrificial atonement is barred to the wanton sinner, to the one who "acts flauntingly" (*běyad rāmâ; Tg. Onq., bryš gly* 'publicly', *byd rmh 'w brmyh* 'brazenly or deceitfully', 1QS 8:23), "reviles *(měgaddēp)* the Lord" (Num 15:30), but not to the deliberate sinner who, as in this case, is the only one who knows of his fradulent oath and is seized by remorse. This view is also shared by the Qumranites, as in the passages "No man who turns aside . . . *BYD RMH* shall touch the pure Meal . . . until his deeds are purified from all falsehood (1QS 8:17–18), or "Let no man . . . who violates any commandment *(BYD RMH)* be declared a reliable witness against his neighbor until he is purified" (CD 10.2–3).

The Tannaites confirm and amplify this teaching: "The *ḥaṭṭāʾt*, the *ʾāšām*, and death do not atone except with repentance" (*t. Yoma* 4:9; cf. *m. Yoma* 8:8), except that they also restrict its power: for example, (1) repentance atones for willful transgressions against positive precepts, but those against negative precepts require the Day of Atonement in addition to repentance to effect atonement (*t. Yoma* 4:7; cf. Maim., Commentary on *m. Yoma* 8:6); (2) the desecration of God's name is the one willful transgression for which the sinner must die in order that his atonement be complete (*t. Yoma* 4:8; cf. the remarks of Lieberman 1962: 824–25). To confess *(hitwaddâ)*, then, is a prerequisite for the ultimate expiation of deliberate sin; it means to "acknowledge" the sin by identifying it and accepting blame. The import of requiring confession for deliberate sin will be discussed presently.

A final point regarding both pentateuchal passages concerns the priority of the restitution: only after the rectification has been made with man can it be sought with God. This is the explicit stipulation of 5:24b–25: "He shall pay it (the restitution) to its owner as soon as he feels guilt. Then he shall bring to the priest. . . ." This inference is corroborated by the practice of the Second Temple, as reflected in both tannaitic law and the New Testament. For example, The Day of Atonement atones for the sins between man and God. But the Day of Atonement does not atone for the sins between man and his fellow until he has made restitution to his fellow (*m. Yoma* 8:9); "He who robs his fellow a penny's worth and swears (falsely and confesses) must bring it to him even unto the land of the Medes" (*m. B. Qam.* 9:5; cf. *Abot R. Nat.* B 21 and its modification in the baraita, *b. B. Qam.* 103b; cf. also *m. B. Qam.* 9:12; *t. Pesaḥ.* 3:1). "If when you bring your gift to the altar, you suddenly remember that your brother has a grievance against you, leave your gift where it is before the altar. First go make your peace with your brother, and only then come back and offer your gift" (Matt 5:23f. [*NEB*], and cf. *t. Pesaḥ.* 3:1). It marks a startling innovation in jurisprudence: in matters of justice man takes priority over God. That this postulate constitutes a radical change can best be appreciated from the vantage point of the sacrificial system, one of whose axioms is that God must receive his due from the altar before man. The violation of this axiom constitutes the sacrilege of the priest Eli and his sons: "You honor your sons above me by fattening yourselves upon the choicest parts of every offering of Israel ahead of me" *(lĕpānay*, LXX; 1 Sam 2:29b; cf. also the Notes on 7:30–32 and Milgrom 1983d: 159–70).

The exegesis of the *ʾāšām* of 5:20–26 and Num 5:6–8 receives unexpected corroboration from Philo. Despite his typical periphrasis, his statement merits quoting in full (italics mine):

> These and similar regulations for involuntary offences are followed by his ordinances for such as are voluntary. If, he says, a man lies about a partnership or a deposit or a robbery or as to finding the lost property of someone else, and *being suspected and put upon his oath, swears to the falsehood* —if then after having *apparently escaped conviction* (ἐλεγχον) *by his accusers, he becomes convicted inwardly by his conscience* (ἐνδον ὑπο τον συνειδοτο ἐλεγχθεις), *his own accuser, reproaches himself for his disavowals and perjuries, makes a plain confession of the wrong he has committed and asks for pardon*—then the lawgiver orders that forgiveness be extended to such a person on condition that he verifies his repentance not by a mere promise but by his actions, by restoring the deposit or the property which he has seized or found or in any way usurped from his neighbor, and further has paid an additional fifth as a solatium for the offence. And when he has thus propitiated the injured person, he must follow it up, says the lawgiver, by proceeding to the temple to ask for remission of his sins, taking with him as his irreproachable advocate, the soul-felt conviction (τὸν κατα ψυχην ἐλεγχον) which has saved him from a fatal disaster, allayed a deadly disease, and brought him round to complete health. For him, too, the sacrifice prescribed is a ram, as also for the offender in sacred matters. For *the lawgiver rated the involuntary sin in the sacred sphere as equal to the voluntary sin in the human, though indeed this last also is perhaps a desecration, since it is supplemented by an oath sworn under dishonest conditions, though rectified by the man's conversion to the better course.* (*Laws* 1. 235–38)

The following points of agreement will be noted: (1) The oath follows upon each fraudulent act. As pointed out to me by S. E. Loewenstamm (written communication), the absence in the LXX of the particle ʾô (v 24) enabled Philo to deduce that the oath was an integral sequel to the fraudulent act. Nevertheless, Masoretic ʾô can be retained, if *mikkōl* is rendered "anything else" (see the NOTE on v 24). (2) The criminal is not apprehended. (3) He is consciencestricken. (4) He confesses his crime voluntarily. (5) Violation of an oath is a desecration (Philo's alternate explanation). (6) The crime against God is mitigated by repentance (see below). (7) Restitution to the defrauded person precedes restitution to God. Thus Philo serves as an early witness to the interpretation of this *ʾāšam* that I have proposed. The sequence of sin followed by false oath is also predicated by the *Testament of Gad*: "Love ye one another from the heart; and if a man sins against thee, speak peaceably to him, and in thy soul hold not guile, and if he repent and confess, forgive him. But if he deny it, do not get into a passion with him lest catching the poison from thee he take to swearing and so thou sin doubly" (6:3–4; for details, see Milgrom 1976f: 111–14).

Whence did Philo derive his interpretation? All investigators have come to the conclusion, to a greater or lesser degree, that Philo's concept of conscience goes far beyond his Greek sources. His innovations are assigned either to his originality or to his Jewish tradition. For the latter, metaphors taken mainly from the penitential passages of the Bible and intertestamental literature are cited (Maurer, in *TDNT* 7.898). These, however, are vague and imprecise and hardly vary from the penitential literature of the rest of the ancient Near East. Hence, the Jewish origins of Philo's notions of the conscience have thus far remained conjectural.

In one respect, I believe, Philo's dependence on his Jewish sources can be traced. I refer to 5:20–26 and Philo's interpretation of it, cited above. Let us note the case. A person first defrauds his fellow and then compounds his crime by denying it under oath. If he confesses his act voluntarily he is allowed to expiate his crime against his fellow through a modest monetary fine and his crime against God by means of a sacrifice. The radical nature of the latter expiation needs to be underscored. Although he has deliberately taken a false oath—lying to God's face as it were—his sin is absolved through sacrifice, an absolution that elsewhere is permitted only for involuntary sins. Thus conscience is the source of a legal force that can convert a deliberate sin against God, always punishable by death, into an involuntary sin, now expiable by sacrifice.

My rendering of 5:20–26 provides a plausible source for the power that Philo ascribes to conscience. But until proved, it remains a theory. Still, there is one piece of evidence that points to the conclusion that my rendering may indeed be the tradition that Philo had before him.

The phrase *běyôm ʾašmātô* (5:24d) is rendered in the LXX by ᾗ ἡμέρᾳ ἐλεγχθῇ. The LXX uses ἐλέγχω sixty-eight times, sixty-four times for the Hebrew root *ykḥ* 'reprove, convict', three times for its near synonyms (*hiršîʿa*, Job 5:6; *ḥāqar*, Prov 18:17; and *niggaʿ* [*piʿel*], 2 Chr 26:20), and once, as indicated, in v 24 for the root *ʾšm*. The latter passage in the LXX must Therefore be rendered "on the day he is convicted." The context makes it clear, however, that the sinner is not convicted by an outside source but only from within, by his self-conviction. The force of conscience is at work. Furthermore, this rendering is corroborated by the *Tg. Ps.-J.*, which reads *bywmʾ dthʾ ʿl ḥwbtyh*, lit., "on the day he regrets his sin." The affinity of the LXX for the Palestinian traditions represented by Pseudo-Jonathan is well attested (Alon 1957: 83–114). Thus there is no need to turn to hellenistic sources for Philo's use of ἔλεγχος as conscience or, alternately, to claim it as his original contribution. On the basis of the LXX and *Tg. Ps.-J.* on 5:24d, it is apparent that this usage was already known within the Alexandrian Jewry in whose midst Philo was raised.

In sum, Philo derived from his own Jewish tradition a concept of conscience endowed with the legal power to reduce willful sins to inadvertencies and commute death sentences into fines. No wonder, then, that conscience plays such a dominant role in Philo as the teacher and healer of man.

Thus the paradox raised at the outset confronts us again: how can deliberate crime be expiated by sacrifice? The paradox, it will be recalled, was enhanced by the first postulate, which established that each case of fraud was aggravated by a false oath, thus compounding a civil crime against man with a capital crime against God. Yet from the prescribed punishment one is forced to deduce that a death sentence has been commuted to sacrificial expiation! Rephrasing the paradox exposes its audacity to the full. By what right did the Priestly legislators presume to mitigate God's penalty? That they could reduce the fine paid to the injured owner is readily explicable: the crime was a civil one, falling under the jurisdiction of the human court (see the NOTE on v 16). But when they legislate that a false oath is expiable not by death but by sacrifice, they, the priests, *qĕrōbay* 'my intimates' (10:3), have encroached upon the divine sphere. They have arrogated to themselves the power to alter God's decree. The paradox, then, is not the reduction of the monetary fine, for which ample precedent is available, but the unprecedented right of man to commute the death sentence imposed by the heavenly court. Indeed, the crime of desecrating God's name, instead of being expiated by sacrifice, would seem to be aggravated by it—for man has overruled the will of God! For details, see Milgrom 1976f: 84–117).

G. The Priestly Doctrine of Repentance

A resolution of this question is now possible. I submit that the repentance of the sinner, through his remorse *('āšam)* and confession *(hitwaddâ)*, reduces his intentional sin to an inadvertence, thereby rendering it eligible for sacrificial expiation.

I now have discovered that this principle was already known by the rabbis. "R. Simeon b. Lakish said: Great is repentance, which converts intentional sins into unintentional ones" (*b. Yoma* 86b). The early rabbis show awareness of this principle in another context: the ritual of the Day of Atonement. They raise the question of how the high priest's bull is capable of atoning for his deliberate sins, and they reply, "Because he has confessed his brazen and rebellious deeds it is as if they become as unintentional ones before him" (*Sipra*, Aḥare par. 2:4, 6; cf. *t. Yoma* 2:1). Thus it is clear that the Tannaites attribute to repentance—strikingly, in a sacrificial ritual—the power to transform a presumptuous sin against God, punishable by death, into an act of inadvertence, expiable by sacrifice. Whence do these rabbis derive this radically new doctrine? They do not tell us, but their precedent, I believe, is our *'āšām* case of Lev 5:20–26/Num 5:6–8, in which repentance has transmuted the double defrauding of God and man into an unintentional offense.

Yet the modus operandi of this doctrine is baffling. How is it possible for a post hoc confession to ameliorate a crime that perforce has already been committed? The crime, it must be remembered, is no ordinary one: it is the desecration of God's name. Now, all commitments taken in the name of God are irrevocable (for the laws, see Exod 20:7; Lev 19:12; Num 30:3; Deut 23:22–24; for the scriptural cases, Josh 9:19; Judg 11:35–36). Likewise, the sin of blasphemy can never be annulled or ameliorated (Exod 22:27; Lev 24:10–23; 1 Kgs 21:10, 13; Job 2:9). Yet, although oaths or vows may be triggered by rashness (unintentional), God's name is still violated when they are not fulfilled, and retribution is inexorable. "In desecrating the Name it is the same whether done unintentionally or wantonly" (*m. 'Abot* 4:4), in other words, the principle of intention is not operative in the desecration of God's name. All the more so in the case of a false oath (deliberate), a calculated act of lying to God's face. The question, worded in this way, reveals the magnitude of the submitted answer: repentance neutralizes the sting of a false oath by reducing its status to that of an involuntary sin.

My thesis would rank as mere conjecture were it not for the requirement of confession for deliberate sin. All told, five deliberate sins in P are expiated by sacrifice: the present case, the sin of the individual who withholds evidence under an imprecation (see at 5:1), the sin of the individual who forgets to purify himself within the prescribed time limits (see at 5:2–3), the sin of the individual who forgets to fulfill his oath (see at 5:4), and the sins of the community carried off by the scapegoat (see at 16:21). Strikingly, these five legal cases, *and only these*, explicitly demand a confession from the sinner over and above his remorse. But what function does the confession serve? Why must the contrition of the heart be augmented by the confirmation of the lips? Confession must thus be a vital link in the judicial process. Because it only occurs in the cases wherein deliberate sin is expiated by sacrifice, the conclusion is ineluctable: confession is the legal device fashioned by the Priestly legislators to convert deliberate sins into inadvertencies, thereby qualifying them for sacrificial expiation.

What is it about the confession that endows it with such power? Is it only a legal fiction invented by the Priestly legislators to ameliorate the crime, or does it possess some innate force that, as the Priestly legislators intuited, can generate a behavioral change? The answer must lie in the psychological realm. It can be elucidated by an analogous phenomenon in the contemporary world. I cite from "The Twelve Steps of Alcoholics Anonymous":

1. We admitted that we were powerless over alcohol—that our lives had become unmanageable.

2. Came to believe that a Power greater than ourselves could restore us to sanity.

3. Made a decision to turn our will and our lives over to the care of God as we understood Him.

4. Made a searching and fearless moral inventory of ourselves.

5. Admitted to God, to ourselves and to another human being the exact nature of our wrongs.

6. Were entirely ready to have God remove all these defects of character.

7. Humbly asked Him to remove our shortcomings.

8. Made a list of all persons we had harmed, and became willing to make amends to them all.

9. Made direct amends to such people wherever possible, except when to do so would injure them or others.

At first glance, the case of the alcoholic seems unbridgeably remote from Leviticus. Ostensibly he has sinned only against himself, hurting neither his God nor his fellow. Yet his cure lies precisely in his recognition that he has in fact offended God and man, and until rectification is made to both he cannot be cured. First he must experience remorse before God: *wĕʾāšēm* 'feel guilt' (nos. 1–4). Then he must confess his wrong: *wĕhitwaddâ*, to God and "another human being" (nos. 5–7). Finally, he must make full restitution: *wĕšillēm bĕrōʾšô*, to those he has wronged (nos. 8–9). Thus his chances of regaining control of his life depend on being reconciled with God and man. Only when he is at peace with the external world can he attain peace in his inner world.

And the confession plays a critical role. It assumes that it takes greater courage to verbalize one's faults to others than just to understand them oneself and that, correspondingly, the ability to confess bespeaks a more resolute desire to alter the status quo. Furthermore, the act of confession assumes the response of forgiveness, human and divine. Thereby the erstwhile isolation (self-imposed) of the alcoholic is by the single stroke of the confession converted to a supportive relationship: the universe, which has ostracized him (or so he felt), now takes him to its embrace. By the same token, Leviticus also presumes, mutatis mutandis, that the greater effort to articulate one's contrition and, if necessary, to make proper amends will effect one's reconciliation with God and man "so that he may be forgiven" (5:26).

P postulates a new category of jurisprudence: repentance as a factor in the mitigation of divine retribution. To be sure, the doctrine of repentance also informs the teaching of all of the prophets. Yet it is not their innovation, for the first of the writing prophets uses this term without bothering to explain it (Amos 4:6–11). Moreover, the concept is also presupposed by the early narratives about Pharaoh and the sons of Eli, which speak of God deliberately blocking their repentance (Exod 7:3f.; 8:28; 10:1; 11:10; 1 Sam 2:25). In addition, the motif of repentance turns up in the tales of Israel's early leaders: David (2 Sam 12:13–14; 24:10ff.), Ahab (1 Kgs 21:27ff.), and Josiah (2 Kgs 22:18ff.).

Nevertheless, it must be noted that the repentance in these early narratives is not the same repentance taught by the prophets. First, repentance in the early narratives is ineffectual. At best it mitigates retribution (e.g., David) or postpones it (Ahab, Josiah). And on occasion it is of no avail (e.g., for Moses himself, Deut 3:23–26). Repentance, it is true, is found in the admonitions of P and D (26:40; Deut 4:29–30; 30:1–10); but here, contrary to the prophets, repentance can only terminate the punishment but cannot prevent its onset (Milgrom 1964: 169–71). The limited scope of repentance in these stories can best be appraised by contrasting it with the success of the people of Nineveh in averting their doom (Jonah 3:1ff.) through the operation of prophetic repentance.

Second, wherever repentance occurs in the early narratives it is a human virtue, not a divine imperative. God calls neither upon man to repent nor upon his prophet to rouse him to repentance. The role of Moses is to intercede for Israel so that God will annul his evil decree (e.g., Exod 32:11–13; 31f.; 33:12–16; 34:9; Num 12:11–13; 14:13–19; Deut 9:16–29), but not once is he expected to bring his people to repentance so that they might merit divine forgiveness. Other intercessors are also recorded in the early narratives, such as Abraham (Gen 18:23ff.; 20:7), Samuel (1 Sam 7:5–9; 12:19ff.; 15:11; cf. Jer 15:1; Ps 99:6), Elijah (1 Kgs 17:20ff.; 18:24), Elisha (2 Kgs 4:33; 5:11; 6:15–20), and Job (Job 42:6–9). These righteous leaders, just like Moses, turn to God for pardon but not to man for his repentance.

It is against the backdrop of embryonic repentance that the innovation of the Priestly legislators can be measured. The analysis of the Priestly terms *ʾāšam* and *hitwaddâ* has shown that the principle of repentance is operative in sacrificial expiation. That this principle is also adumbrated in P's hortatory admonitions, Lev 26, becomes evident by comparing its idiom with Isaiah: *wěhanniśʾārîm . . . wěhitwaddû* (26:39–40) ‖ *šěʾār yāšûb* (Isa 10:21–22; cf. 7:3). Furthermore, if *yimmaqqû* (26:39) means "shall be heartsick" *(NJPS)*, then the theology of chap. 26 is precisely equivalent to Isaiah's, for like the prophet it predicts that Israel will repent *after* it is exiled. Thus, as both texts are saying the same thing—that a remnant (of Israel) will repent—Isaiah's *šûb* approximates P's *hitwaddâ*. Last, a third penitential term in the Leviticus passage, *yikkānaʿ* 'humble itself' (v 41), appears in the later narratives as a synonym for repentance (1 Kgs 21:29; 2 Kgs 22:19 [= 2 Chr 34:27]; 2 Chr 7:14 ‖ *šûb]*; 30:11; 32:26).

The fact that the Priestly lexicon contains three and possibly four terms for repentance *(ʾāšam, hitwaddâ, niknaʿ, nāmaq)*, but does not include *šûb*, hardly permits any inference concerning a sequential relationship between P and the prophets, for each genre may have developed its own terminology independently and coevally. Nevertheless, the distribution of the verb *šûb* in the Bible illuminates this question anew.

šûb in its covenantal meaning, "repent," is not found in the Tetrateuch and early narratives at all. In this literature, the root *šub* occurs in four passages but in the opposite sense of apostasy, "turning away from God," *šûb mēʾaḥărê YHWH* (Num 14:43 [JE]; 32:15 [JE, P]; Josh 22:16, 18, 23, 28 [P]; 1 Sam 15:11). This is in accord with our finding that in the early sources Israel is guilty of apostasy but is never expected to repent. Even in D, it has been noted, where covenantal *šûb* occurs (Deut 4:30; 30:1–10) repentance is still not full-fledged in the prophetic sense. It only follows punishment but cannot avert it, and in the case of Moses himself it has no effect at all (Deut 3:26).

šûb as "repent" exhibits the following pattern of distribution in the Bible: twenty-three times in three prophets of the eighth century; fifty times in Jeremiah (twenty-seven) and Ezekiel (twenty-three); and twenty-eight times in the postexilic books (Holladay 1958). The occurrences peak in Jeremiah and Ezekiel, whence it is dispersed evenly in nine of the later books. The implications of this pattern for the relative dating of P are clear. If P were postexilic, how could it have avoided using the verb *šûb*, which by then had become the accepted term for repentance? Conversely, the verb *ʾāšam*, which without an object means "feel guilt" (COMMENT A above) and thus approximates the notion "repent," is only found in P and *nowhere else*. Is it possible that when P allegedly rejected the established root *šûb* in the postexilic age, it created in its place a new term, *ʾāšam*, which thereafter disappeared, never again to surface in later biblical or postbiblical literature? The respective distribution of covenantal *šûb* and *ʾāšam* can lead to only one conclusion: P devised its terminology before *šûb* had not become the standard idiom for repentance. Under the influence of the prophets, however—especially Jeremiah and Ezekiel—the verb *šûb* overwhelmed all of its competitors, including *ʾāšam*. The inference is clear: the Priestly legislation on sacrificial expiation is preexilic.

This conclusion is supported by yet another consideration. As demonstrated, P's doctrine of repentance is of a piece with that found in early literature: repentance cannot erase sin or its consequences. True, P maintains that repentance can mitigate the force of a deliberate sin, converting it to an unintentional offense. For the complete annulment of the sin, however, for the assurance of divine forgiveness *(sālaḥ)*, sacrificial expiation *(kipper)* is *always* required. The question may be asked: if the prophetic teaching that repentance can "wipe out" sin *(māḥâ;* cf. Jer 18:23; Isa 43:25) had taken hold, as it did in exilic times, why does it only reduce the gravity of the sin in Priestly law? On the contrary, the catharsis of conscience that characterizes Priestly remorse and confession should have sufficed to expunge the sin altogether. Nor can it be maintained that in postexilic times prophetic and cultic repentance operated independently, because the postexilic prophets attest that prophetic *and* cultic repentance combine to nullify sin and its retribution (e.g., Joel 2:12–17; Mal 3:7–18). Thus the Priestly laws predicate a time before the prophetic teaching that repentance nullifies sin had penetrated the cultic institutions. Again P's sacrificial system of expiation must be of preexilic provenience.

Nonetheless, the magnitude of the Priestly innovation concerning the legal force of repentance should not be underestimated. The Priestly authors took a postulate of their own tradition, that God mitigates punishment for unintentional sins, and empowered it with a new doctrine, that the voluntary repentance of a deliberate crime transforms the crime itself into an involuntary act. True, P could go only as far as its theological premises would allow: repentance reduces the penalty but cannot nullify it. But it stands as a major step in the development of the prophetic doctrine of repentance. For the first time in history, perhaps, man is assured that his repentance is both desired and required by God. In truth, how far is this doctrine from the prophetic teaching that repentance leads to the remission of all sin? The difference is one of degree, but in substance the principle is the same: man's repentance is a prerequisite for divine forgiveness.

One additional conclusion derives from the Priestly doctrine of repentance: if *'āšēm* 'feel guilt' is the scarlet thread that courses through the texts on expiatory sacrifices, then every case of expiation by sacrifice must presuppose the repentance of the worshiper, a postulate that also informs rabbinic tradition (e.g., *m. Yoma* 8:8; *b. Šebu.* 13a (bar.); *t. Yoma* 8:9). The result is that the root purpose underlying the expiatory sacrifices is now seen in its true significance. Often the Priestly system of sacrificial expiation (exemplified by chaps. 4 and 5) was construed as a legalized witch hunt, hounding the conscience of man and damning him with guilt for his every accidental, presumed, or unapprehended crime. Now it is clear that the reverse is true. All of the cases stipulated or implied by the expiatory sacrifices present us with the existential situation of man in torment, racked by conscience over his actual or suspected sin. No man can help him, for his pain is known only to himself. Not even God can come to his aid, for he will not disclose his burden to heaven. It is to this silent sufferer that the Priestly law brings its therapeutic balm: if the prescribed restitution is inspired by his repentance, his sin can be absolved; he need suffer no more (details in Milgrom 1976f: 114–24).

SACRIFICES: THE ADMINISTRATIVE ORDER (6:1–7:38)

Introduction

6 ¹The Lord spoke to Moses, saying: ²Command Aaron and his sons thus:

The Burnt Offering

This is the ritual for the burnt offering—that is, the burnt offering that stays on the altar hearth all night until morning, while the altar fire is kept burning on it. [3]The priest having put on linen raiment, with linen breeches next to his body, shall remove the ashes to which the fire has reduced the burnt offering on the altar and put them beside the altar. [4]He shall then remove his vestments and put on other vestments, and take the ashes outside the camp to a pure place. [5]The fire on the altar shall be kept burning on it [the hearth]; it shall not go out. Every morning the priest shall feed wood to it, lay out the burnt offering upon it, and on top turn into smoke the fat parts of the well-being offerings. [6]A perpetual fire shall be kept burning on the altar; it shall not go out.

The Cereal Offering

[7]This is the ritual for the cereal offering. Aaron's sons shall present it before the Lord, in front of the altar. [8]A handful of the semolina and oil of the cereal offering shall be set aside from it, with all of the frankincense that is on the cereal offering, and this token of it shall be turned into smoke on the altar as a pleasing aroma to the Lord. [9]The remainder Aaron and his sons shall eat; it shall be eaten unleavened in a holy place; they shall eat it in the court of the Tent of Meeting. [10]It shall not be baked with leaven; I have assigned it as their portion from my food gifts; it is most sacred like the purification offering and the reparation offering. [11]Any male of Aaron's descendants may eat of it, as a due for all time throughout your generations from the Lord's food gifts. Whatever touches them shall become holy.

The High Priest's Daily Cereal Offering

[12]The Lord spoke to Moses, saying: [13]This is the offering that Aaron and his sons shall present to the Lord from the time of his anointment: a tenth of an *ephah* of semolina as a regular cereal offering, half of it in the morning and half of it in the evening. [14]It shall be prepared with oil on a griddle. You shall bring it well soaked, and present it as *tūpînê*, a cereal offering of crumbled bits, of pleasing aroma to the Lord. [15]And so shall the priest, anointed from among his sons to succeed him, sacrifice it; it is the Lord's due for all time; it shall entirely go up in smoke. [16]So every cereal offering of a priest shall be a total offering; it shall not be eaten.

The Purification Offering

[17]The Lord spoke to Moses, saying: [18]Speak to Aaron and his sons thus: this is the ritual for the purification offering. The purification offering shall be slaughtered before the Lord, at the spot where the burnt offering is slaughtered; it is most sacred. [19]The priest who offers it as a purification offering shall enjoy it; it shall be eaten in a holy place, in the court of the Tent of Meeting. [20]Whatever touches its flesh shall become holy; and if any of its blood is spattered upon a garment, the bespattered part shall be laundered in a holy place.

21An earthen vessel in which it is boiled shall be broken; if it has been boiled in a copper vessel, that shall be scoured and flushed with water. 22Any male among the priests may eat of it: it is most sacred. 23No purification offering, however, may be eaten from which any blood is brought into the Tent of Meeting to effect purgation in the shrine; it shall be consumed in fire.

The Reparation Offering

7 1This is the ritual for the reparation offering: it is most sacred. 2The reparation offering shall be slaughtered at the spot where the burnt offering is slaughtered, and he [the priest] shall dash its blood against all sides of the altar. 3All of its suet shall be presented: the broad tail, the suet that covers the entrails; 4the two kidneys and the suet that is around them on the sinews; and the caudate lobe on the liver, which shall be removed with the kidneys. 5The priest shall turn them into smoke on the altar as a food gift to the Lord; it is a reparation offering. 6Any male among the priests may eat of it; it shall be eaten in a holy place, it is most sacred.

The Priestly Prebends from the Most Holy Offerings

7The reparation offering is like the purification offering. There is a single rule for both: it shall belong to the priest who performs expiation therewith. 8The priest who sacrifices a person's burnt offering shall keep the hide of the burnt offering that he sacrificed. 9Any cereal offering that is baked in an oven, and any that is prepared in a pan or on a griddle shall belong to the priest who offers it. 10Any cereal offering, whether mixed with oil or dry, shall belong to all the sons of Aaron alike.

The Well-Being Offering

11This is the ritual for the sacrifice of well-being that one may offer to the Lord.

12If he offers it for thanksgiving, he shall offer together with the sacrifice of thanksgiving unleavened cakes mixed with oil, unleavened wafers smeared with oil, and well-soaked cakes of semolina mixed with oil. 13This offering, with cakes of leavened bread added, he shall offer together with his thanksgiving sacrifice of well-being. 14Out of this he shall present one of each [kind of] offering as a contribution to the Lord; it shall belong to the priest who dashes the blood of the well-being offering. 15And the flesh of his thanksgiving sacrifice of well-being shall be eaten on the day that it is offered; none of it shall be put aside until morning.

16If the sacrifice he offers is a votive or freewill offering, it shall be eaten on the day he offers his sacrifice, and what is left of it shall be eaten on the morrow. 17What is then left of the sacrificial flesh shall be consumed in fire on the third day. ¹⁸If any of the flesh of his sacrifice of well-being is eaten on the third day, it shall not be acceptable; it shall not be accredited to him who offered it. It is desecrated meat, and the person who eats of it shall bear his punishment.

¹⁹Flesh that touches anything impure shall not be eaten; it shall be consumed in fire. As for other flesh, anyone who is pure may eat such flesh. ²⁰But the person who, while impure, eats flesh from the Lord's sacrifice of well-being, that person shall be cut off from his kin. ²¹When a person touches anything impure, be it human impurity or an impure quadruped or any impure detestable creature, and eats flesh from the Lord's sacrifice of well-being, that person shall be cut off from his kin.

No Suet or Blood May Be Eaten

²²And the Lord spoke to Moses, saying: ²³Speak to the Israelites thus: you shall not eat the suet of any ox, sheep, or goat. ²⁴The suet of an animal that died or was mauled by beasts may be put to any use, but you must not eat it. ²⁵If anyone eats the suet of an animal from which a food gift is presented to the Lord, that person shall be cut off from his kin. ²⁶And you must not ingest any blood, whether of bird or animal, in any of your settlements. ²⁷Any person who ingests any blood shall be cut off from his kin.

The Priestly Prebends from the Well-Being Offering

²⁸And the Lord spoke to Moses, saying: ²⁹Speak to the Israelites thus: the one who presents his sacrifice of well-being to the Lord shall bring his offering to the Lord from his sacrifice of well-being. ³⁰His own hands shall bring the Lord's food gifts: he shall bring the suet together with the breast, the breast to be elevated as an elevation offering before the Lord. ³¹The priest shall turn the suet into smoke at the altar, but the breast shall belong to Aaron and his sons. ³²And the right thigh from your sacrifices of well-being you shall give to the priest as a gift; ³³the one from among Aaron's sons who offers the blood of the well-being offering and the suet shall receive the right thigh as his prebend. ³⁴For I have taken the breast of the elevation offering and the thigh of the contribution from the Israelites, from their sacrifices of well-being, and have assigned them to Aaron the priest and to his sons as a due from the Israelites for all time. ³⁵This shall be the perquisite of Aaron and the perquisite of his sons from the Lord's food gifts once they have been inducted to serve the Lord as priests, ³⁶which the Lord commanded to be assigned to them, once they had been anointed, as a due from the Israelites for all time throughout their generations.

Summary

³⁷This is the ritual for the burnt offering, the cereal offering, the purification offering, the reparation offering, the ordination offering, and the sacrifice of

well-being, [38]which the Lord commanded Moses on Mount Sinai, when he commanded the Israelites to present their offerings to the Lord, in the Wilderness of Sinai.

NOTES

6:2. *Command Aaron and his sons.* Chaps. 6–7 can be subdivided into nine sections: the burnt offering (6:1–6), the cereal offering (6:7–11), the high priest's daily cereal offering (6:12–16), the purification offering (6:17–23), the reparation offering and the priestly prebends from the most holy offerings (7:1–10), the well-being offering (7:11–21), the prohibition against eating suet or blood (7:22–27), the priestly prebends from the well-being offering (7:28–36), and the summary (7:37–38). Each section begins with "The Lord spoke to Moses" (6:12; 7:22, 28) or "This is the ritual for" (6:7; 7:1, 11, 37); in two instances both opening formulas occur together (6:1–2, 17–18).

That chaps. 6–7 are addressed to the priests sets off these two chapters from chaps. 1–5, which are addressed to the laity (Ramban). Yet this distinction is not quite correct, for three sections (7:11–21, 22–27, 28–36) unambiguously address the laity. The change in addressee is reflected in the style. In chaps. 1–5 the anonymous subject is the layman, and whenever the subject is the priest he is named. In chap. 6 the situation is reversed: the anonymous subject is the priest (6:3, 4, 5, 8, 20). By contrast, 7:1–7 reveals a mixed style (see the NOTES) and 7:11–36, addressed to Israel, once again makes the anonymous subject the layman. A more helpful division of these first seven chapters of Leviticus was proposed by the rabbis: chaps. 1–5, being addressed to the laity, focus on their needs; hence, the sacrifices are divided into those which are voluntary (*nĕdābā;* chaps. 1–3) and those which are mandatory (*ḥôbâ;* chaps. 4–5; *Sipra*). Chaps. 6–7, conversely, focus on the concerns of the priesthood; hence, the sacrifices are arranged in a different order: most holy (*qodšê qŏdāšîm;* 6:1–7:10) and holy (*qŏdāšîm;* 7:11–36; see Ramban on 6:18). This division helps explain why this latter category, the "holy" sacrifices, are addressed to the laity: the priestly prebends from these sacrifices must be set aside in advance by the laity (7:29–30) instead of being taken by the priests from the altar (cf. 6:9, 19; 7:7–10). In view of this division, chaps. 1–5 can be called "didactic," informing the laity of its role in the sacrificial service, whereas chaps. 6–7 are "administrative," stressing matters of interest to the priests (Rainey 1970).

ritual for (tôrat). Other Priestly texts are not limited to sacrificial rituals. Hence the term *tôrâ* in those texts (e.g., 11:46; 15:32) is better rendered "instructions" (cf. Hag 2:11). The book of Leviticus contains ten *tôrôt*, comprising a decalogue of ritual life (Hoffmann 1953: 297), as follows: five *tôrôt* of sacrifice —6:2 (the burnt offering); 6:7 (the cereal offering); 6:18 (the purification offering); 7:1 (the reparation offering); and 7:11 (the well-being offering)—and five *tôrôt* of impurity—11:46 (animals); 12:7 (the parturient); 13:59 and 14:54–57 (scale disease); 14:2, 32 (the purification of the *měṣōrāʿ*); and 15:32 (genital discharges). Four more *tôrôt* are found in the book of Numbers: Num 5:29–30 (the suspected adulteress); Num 6:21 (the Nazirite); Num 19:2, 14 (the corpse-contaminated person); and Num 31:21 (the purification rites for booty—a supplement to chap. 19). That these latter few *tôrôt* were not incorporated into Leviticus says a great deal concerning the redaction of the book of Numbers (Milgrom 1990a: excursus 48, pp. 438–43). More puzzling, however, is the fact that chaps. 1–5, dealing in sacrifices and, hence, falling under priestly jurisdiction, are not a collection of *tôrôt*. Perhaps the term *tôrâ* in P implies that the text in question derives from the priestly (temple) archives. This hypothesis surely accords with the fact that chaps. 6–7 and 13–14 are addressed to the priests or center on priestly concerns. Chaps. 12 and 15, though directed to the laity, also involve sacrificial rites—again the domain of the priests. The only *tôrâ* in Leviticus unaccounted for is 11:46 (impure animals); however, the opening clause of the following verse "to distinguish between the impure and pure" (11:47a) reminds one of the nearest thing we have in the Bible to a definition of the function of the priesthood: to *"distinguish* between the sacred and the common, and *between the impure and the pure;* and . . . *teach (lěhôrōt)* the Israelites all of the laws that the Lord has imparted to them through Moses" (10:10–11; cf. 14:57; Ezek 44:23). Thus the priests are charged with the responsibility for instructing the Israelites so that they will not desecrate or pollute that which is sacred or pure. For this reason the distinction between pure and impure animals is a priestly responsibility. In this way, the absence of the designation *tôrâ* from chaps. 1–5 may also be explained. Because sacrifices enter their sacred status only after their blood manipulation on the altar (or, in the case of the cereal offering, when its token portion is burned on the altar), the layman's role in the preliminary sacrificial rites (chaps. 1–5) does not fall under the purview of priestly *tôrâ*, whereas what happens to the sacrificial meat, endowed with a sacred status, most definitely falls into the category of *tôrâ*, that is to say, priestly responsibility. In keeping with this distinction, chaps. 1–5 are addressed to the Israelites (1:2), whereas most of chaps. 6–7 are addressed to the priests (6:1–7:21). For further discussion of this issue, see the INTRODUCTION, §F.

that is, the burnt offering. hîʾ (hwʾ) hāʿōlâ, in other words, the *Tāmîd* offering, which is the final sacrifice of the day and which lies smoldering on the altar all through the night (*Leqaḥ Ṭov*, Abravanel). Its requirements (Exod 29:38–41) and mode of preparation (Lev 1:10–13) are presumed. Alternatively, the referent is all burnt offerings (chap. 1), whose incineration may continue through the night (Wessely 1846). The third-person pronouns can be used for emphasis (e.g., Exod 21:4; Num 35:19; Jer 6:6).

hearth (môqědâ). Read *môqědāh* (*mappiq* in the *heh*), "its hearth" (with many manuscripts; cf. LXX and Zeb 83b [Rashi]), namely, the altar's. The *mappiq* is frequently missing from the MT (e.g., Exod 9:18; Lev 13:4; Num

15:31; 32:42). For the singular *môqēd*, see Isa 33:14; Ps 102:4; in rabbinic times, the hearth was called *bêt hammôqēd* (*m. Tāmîd* 1:1; *m. Šabb.* 1:11). Perhaps the term *môqēd* was reserved exclusively for the hearth of the sacrificial altar; the ordinary fireplace would have been called *yāqûd* (Isa 30:14).

all night until morning. "Out of respect to the Lord the altar was in continuous use" (Bekhor Shor). The rabbis derive from this fact the plausible rule that although sacrifices could only be offered during daylight, their incineration on the altar could continue through the night (*m. Ber.* 1:1; *t. Meg.* 2:10; *b. Meg.* 21a).

while the altar fire is kept burning (wĕʾēš hammizbēaḥ tûqad). This instruction is clearly directed to the priests (Ramban). Its importance is indicated by the fact that in this short pericope it is mentioned three times (vv 2, 5, 6), each for a different purpose. This first occurrence implies that in order for the sacrifices to burn through the night the altar fire must be kept burning. The verb *yāqad* means "kindle, burn" (Deut 32:22; Isa 10:16; 65:5; Jer 15:14; 17:4); note the Akk. cognate *qâdu* 'kindle'.

on it (bô). The referent is the hearth. If it were the altar, the preposition *ʿal* would have been used (e.g., v 6; Dillmann and Ryssel 1897; cf. *Midr. Lev. Rab.* 7:5, the first to note this peculiarity).

3. *linen raiment. middô bad*, lit., "his raiment, linen." Some commentators, indeed, give this phrase an appositional rendering (e.g., Dillmann and Ryssel 1897): his raiment, the linen one (e.g., Exod 28:17; 39:17; Zech 4:10; GKC §127.h). Moreover, the grammatical difficulty is compounded by a factual one: the priest wore four special garments (three, if the underpants are excluded; see below) and not one (Exod 28:39–42). Ḥazzequni justifies the singular usage on the grounds that all four priestly garments were made from the same material (though the belt included dyed wool, Exod 39:29). All problems are erased, however, by reading with the Sam. and Tgs. *middê* 'raiments of' (for the plural form, see Judg 3:16; 1 Sam 4:12; 17:38; 18:4; the singular occurs once, Ps 109:18, and in Ug., *md*). The purpose of this limitation to linen garments is made explicit by Ezekiel: "they shall not gird themselves with anything that causes sweat" (Ezek 44:18), that is, "they shall have nothing woollen upon them when they minister inside the gates of the inner court" (ibid., v 17). In the Ptolemaic period, Egyptian priests were expressly forbidden to wear woolen clothing (Bell 1948: 49).

linen (bad). The etymology of this word is unknown. For the exclusive use of this material in the high priest's vestments on Yom Kippur and in the garments of angels, see the NOTE on 16:4. In the meaning "linen," this term is attested ten times in P and once each in 1 Sam 2:18 and 2 Sam 6:14 (= 2 Chr 15:27). The plural *baddîm* is found in Ezekiel and Daniel (e.g., Ezek 9:2; Dan 1:5). It has, however, no association with the priestly garments. On the contrary, when Ezekiel refers to the latter, he uses *pištîm* (Ezek 44:17–18), an indication that *bad*, P's term, fell from use before the exile (Paran 1983: 197).

linen breeches. The priest's breeches are listed separately from his other garments also in Exod 28:42 (Ḥazzequni). In the itemization of the high priest's special vestments on Yom Kippur, the text seems to indicate that the high priest is already wearing his breeches before he dons his other garments (see the NOTE on 16:4). Similarly, both the prescriptive and the descriptive accounts of the priestly consecration specifically list all of the priestly garments except the breeches (Exod 29:8–9; Lev 8:13). Thus the impression conveyed by all these texts is that the breeches were not considered part of the sacred priestly garments, support for which stems from the fact that the consecratory blood and oil sprinkled on the clothing (Exod 29:21; Lev 8:30) obviously did not impinge on the unexposed breeches.

body. *běśārô*, lit., "his flesh," abbreviated from *běśar ʿerwâ*, lit., "naked flesh," a euphemism for the genitals (see 15:2, 19; Ibn Ezra). The breeches were required to "cover their nakedness" (Exod 28:42). An altar ascendable by steps is therefore implied (Ezek 43:17; cf. Lev 9:22; 2 Kgs 16:12). Steps on private altars attended by breechless laity, however, were expressly forbidden (Exod 20:26).

he shall remove (wěhērîm). The elimination of the altar ashes takes place in two stages, their removal to the side of the altar and, afterward, their removal outside the camp. Consequently, the rabbis declare that the first stage constitutes a ritual; it is performed by a priest who removes one panful of ashes from the altar while dressed in his sacred garments. They deem this act a ritual by interpreting the verb *hērîm* in its ritual sense "set aside, dedicate" (see the NOTE on 2:9), a denominative of *těrûmâ* 'dedicated gift' (see COMMENT F below), terming the entire ritual *těrûmat haddešen* 'the removal-dedication of the ashes' (*b. Yoma* 23b).

But the two-stage removal stems not from ritualistic considerations but from more pragmatic ones. All acts involving the altar are *eo ipso* rituals and require the priests to wear their sacred vestments. Conversely, all acts taking place outside the sanctuary are profane and, hence, bar the wearing of the sacred vestments. Thus it is simply the priest's need to change his clothes that has resulted in separating the ash removal into two parts, its removal from the altar and its removal outside the camp. The verb *hērîm* here has its normal, noncultic meaning of "remove," equivalent to *hēsîr* (as in 4:8, 10, 19).

According to the rabbis, the first lot cast by the priests each morning was to select the one to perform the ash-removal ritual (*m. Tāmîd* 1:2). It was performed at dawn in the following manner:

He whose lot it was to clear *(litrôm)* the altar of ashes went to clear the altar of ashes, while they said to him, "Take heed that you do not touch the vessel (i.e., the silver firepan) before you sanctify your hands and feet in the laver, and lo, the firepan lies in the corner between the ramp and the altar, on the western side of the ramp." None entered with him and he carried no lamp, but he walked in the light of the altar fire. They neither saw him nor heard the sound of him until they heard the noise of the wooden device that Ben Katin had made for the laver; and then they said, "The time has come." He sanctified his hands and feet at the laver, took the silver firepan, and went up to the top of the altar and cleared away the cinders to this side and to that, and scooped up the innermost burnt ones and came down again. When he reached the pavement he turned his face to the north and went some ten cubits to the east of the ramp. He heaped the cinders together on the pavement three hand-breadths away from the ramp at the place where they throw the crops of the birds (see 1:16) and the ashes of the inner altar and the lampstand. When his brethren saw that he was come down, they came running and hastened and sanctified their hands and feet at the laver, and they took the shovels and the rakes and mounted to the top of the altar. Any members (of the animal offerings) and fat pieces that had not been consumed during the evening they raked to the sides of the altar, and if the sides could not contain them they put them in order on the circuit [or] by the ramp. They began to heap up the ashes above the ash pile, and the ash pile was in the middle of the altar; sometimes there were about three hundred *kors* (of ashes, about 360 liters) upon it; and at the festivals, the priests did not clear away the ashes because they were an adornment to the altar: (whenever the ashes remained) it was never through the negligence of the priest to clear away the ashes. (*m. Tāmîd* 1:4–2:2)

the ashes (haddešen). The literal meaning of *dešen* is "fatness," either of olives (Judg 9:9), of food (Isa 55:2), or of sacrifice (Sir 38:11). The ashes on the altar hearth derive primarily from the suet because the suet of the sacrificial animal was always burned on the altar (3:3–5, 9–11, 14–16; 4:8–9; 7:3–5, 25; see the NOTE on 3:17). The denominative *diššen* bears the privative meaning "clear away (the altar of) the suet ashes" (Exod 27:3; Num 4:13).

to which (the fire has reduced) 'āšer (tō'kal hā'ēš): perhaps equivalent to *la'āšer* (Ehrlich 1908–14; Hoffmann 1953), though a double accusative for *'ākal* is nowhere attested.

beside the altar. At its eastern side (1:16).

4. *put on other vestments (wĕlābaš bĕgādîm 'ăḥērîm).* These must be non-sacral, profane vestments (*b. Yoma* 223b; Ramban; Bekhor Shor, citing *b. Yoma* 69a), as the priest was forbidden to wear his priestly garments outside the sanctuary. Ezekiel makes this prohibition explicit, and because he uses the same terminology of this verse, *yipšĕṭû 'et bigdêhem . . . wĕlābĕsû bĕgādîm 'ăḥērîm* 'they shall remove their vestments . . . and put on other vestments' (Ezek 44:19; cf. 42:14), it seems probable that this verse formed the basis for Ezekiel's ruling, to which he appends a rationale, *wĕlō'-yĕqaddĕšû 'et-hā'ām bĕbigdêhem*

'lest they sanctify the people with their vestments' (Ezek 44:19). The Qumranites apparently held a similar view because, like Ezekiel, they forbade the priests to leave the inner court in their priestly vestments (11QT 40:1–4, fragmentary). See COMMENT B below.

a pure place (māqôm ṭāhôr). Why this specification; is it not obvious? Not at all. Among Israel's neighbors (e.g., Hittites, Mesopotamians), substances that absorb impurity are themselves lethally dangerous and must be *ana ṣeri ašri elli šuṣima* 'taken out to the plain, the pure place' (Reiner 1958: 7.63). Yet the similarity to Israel's praxis ends here. In Israel, only the blood of the purification offering acts as a ritual detergent, and even in the instance of this sacrifice, the flesh is normally eaten by the priest (6:19, 22) and only purification offerings brought for severe impurities are incinerated "in a pure place" outside the camp (4:12; chap. 4, COMMENT D; Milgrom 1976a; 1978b: 511–12). All other sacrifices such as the burnt offering, discussed here, are incinerated on the altar, and their ashes are simply disposed of. They have no inherent powers; their holiness is not contagious (see the NOTES on 6:11, 20 and COMMENT B below). Bearing a holy status, though of a static nature, only one precaution is applicable to them: to be buried "in a pure place."

5. *on it. bô,* namely, the hearth (see the NOTE on v 2). Why is the admonition to keep the fire burning repeated here? Its juxtaposition to the instructions for the removal of the ashes provides the answer: while removing the ashes the priest must be careful not to extinguish the fire!

Every morning (babbōqer babbōqer). Repetition to express distribution (e.g., Gen 39:10; Exod 16:21; 36:4, 6, 30; Deut 14:22; cf. GKC §123.c, d).

shall feed. ûbi'ēr; bi'ēr (pi'el) usually means "kindle" (e.g., Exod 35:3; Jer 7:18; Ezek 21:4, 9–10). By extension, it also denotes "feed a burning fire" (e.g., Isa 44:15; Neh 10:35).

wood ('ēṣîm). According to the rabbis, wood could be brought to the altar up to the fourth hour of the day (*m. 'Ed.* 6:1; *Tg. Ps.-J.*). An offering of wood for the altar is well attested in various sources pertaining to the Second Temple period. The earliest reference is in Nehemiah (10:35; 13:31), which relates that lots were drawn to determine which families would supply wood for the Temple at various times during the year. The Mishna assigns nine dates for the wood offering, eight of them reserved for specific families and the ninth (the fifteenth of Av) for the public at large (*m. Ta'an.* 4:5; cf. Jos., *Wars* 2.430). Additionally, preferred manuscripts of the Mishna (e.g., Kaufmann, Parma, Geniza fragments) as well as other tannaitic sources (e.g., *t. Bik.* 2:9) include a tenth occasion—also for the public offering (the ninth of Av; see Safrai 1965: 221–22). According to tannaitic opinion the wood offering was instituted because the returning exiles in Nehemiah's time did not find wood in the wood chamber (*t. Ta'an.* 4:5; *b. Ta'an.* 28a). All woods except the grapevine and olive wood were valid for the offering (*m. Tāmîd* 2:3). This rule is explained by the Midrash as a sign of respect for the trees whose fruit (grapes and olives) are used for libations on the altar (*Midr. Lev. Rab.* 7:6; *Midr. 'Ag.* and *Leqaḥ Ṭov* on 1:8). The Talmud offers the more probable reason, however: both of these aforementioned woods do not burn well and produce too much smoke (*b. Taʿan.* 29b). Another tradition is preserved in the pseudepigraphical literature, which restricts the types of offerable wood to twelve (*T. Levi* 9:12; *Jub.* 21:12–14).

The wood was brought to the Temple with great ceremony. Bearers of the wood were forbidden to work on that day and were required to spend the night in Jerusalem, returning to their homes the following morning. 'Aggadic tradition tells of the courage and perseverance of those bringing the wood even in the face of danger to their lives (*t. Taʿan.* 4:7–8).

Six of the ten fixed occasions for bringing the wood offering fell in Av. This was a good time for cutting and collecting wood. An even better time was the end of the following month, Elul, the date chosen by the Qumran sectaries, because it fell at the very end of the dry season. Because of the fragmentary nature of the Temple Scroll, the date and observance of the Wood Offering festival are not fully certain. Sometime during the last week of Elul—perhaps beginning on Monday, Elul 23—a six-day festival took place during which the twelve tribes of Israel would bring their wood offerings, two tribes each day (11QT 23–25). The wood was accompanied by animal offerings, each tribe bringing one bull, one ram, and one lamb as burnt offerings and one he-goat as a purification offering. The doubling up of the tribes instead of spacing them out over twelve days probably was arranged so as not to conflict with the Day of Remembrance, set for the first of Tishri (see 23:24). Clearly, Qumran was engaged in a polemic with the Pharisaic tradition: instead of allotting the privilege of the wood offering mainly to a few aristocratic families, the Temple Scroll ordained that this offering, like all other festival offerings, must be financed from the public treasury. This rule of Qumran is in keeping with its quintessential democratic tradition (Milgrom 1984: 131). The wood offering is also mentioned in CD 11.18–19. Strikingly, Qumran's unpublished biblical text 4Q365 frag. 25 adds the prescription of the wood offering at the end of the festival list in Lev 23 (discussion is reserved for my second volume on Leviticus).

the burnt offering. *hāʿōlâ,* that is, the morning *tāmîd* (Exod 29:39–41), from which the rabbis derive the rule that the morning *tāmîd* must be the first sacrifice of the day (*b. Pesaḥ* 58b; *b. Yoma* 34a; *Zeb* 103b).

on top. *ʿālêhā,* as in the previous clause. But whereas in the latter case the referent is the fire, here the referent is the burnt offering, which is laid over the wood (1:8, 12) and which burns through the night (v 2). Alternately, this word may be rendered "with it" (see the discussion on 3:5).

the fat parts of the well-being offerings. *ḥelbê haššĕlāmîm* must refer to offerings brought voluntarily by individuals (Rashi). Assumed is that private well-being offerings would unfailingly be offered each morning; this is also the assumption of 3:5.

6. *A perpetual fire (ʾēš tāmîd).* This is the third mention of the admonition

to keep the altar fire burning; it differs from the other two (vv 2b, 5a) by the addition of the adverb *tāmîd*, which in this case means "always, continually" (so too 24:3; Exod 25:30; Deut 11:12; 1 Kgs 10:8). The term may have been borrowed from royal vocabulary. Just as a loyal retainer could be awarded the privilege of living off the king's "table perpetually" (e.g., 2 Sam 9:7, 10, 13; 2 Kgs 25:29, 30), so a number of cultic acts, such as the *Tāmîd* offering (Exod 29:42), the bread of presence (Exod 25:29), and the lighting of the menora (Lev 24:2, 3), were to be performed "perpetually" (Paran 1983: 209 n. 68).

Here the word *tāmîd* stresses the importance of maintaining the fire even if the sacrifices are totally consumed. This prescription, found in other cultures as well (e.g., among the ancient Greeks), may stem from the mundane necessity of keeping the fire burning during days on which kindling one was difficult (Yerkes 1952: 158). But a more likely explanation is indigenous to Israel's priestly circles. The sacrifices offered up at the inauguration of the public cult were consumed miraculously by a divine fire (9:24), and it is *this* fire which is not allowed to die out so that all subsequent sacrifices might claim divine acceptance (see Philo, *Laws* 1. 286, and the NOTE on "Fire came forth," 9:24).

This verse repeats v 5aα, thereby framing vv 5–6 in an inclusion that accentuates the significance of the intervening statement, thereby emphasizing the sequence of wood, burnt offering, and well-being offering which must begin each day's sacrificial rites.

7. *This is the ritual for the cereal offering.* Which cereal offering? Because this pericope (vv 7–11) deals solely with the raw type (2:1–3) and omits the baked type (2:4–10), it can hardly be claimed as a generalization for all cereal offerings. Hence, it has been suggested that it refers to the cereal offering that accompanies the *Tāmîd*, composed of raw semolina (Exod 29:40). Supporting this view is the fact that the previous pericope (vv 1–6) deals with the *Tāmîd* burnt offering (see the NOTE on v 2) and the following pericope (vv 12–16) deals with the daily offering of the high priest (see the NOTE on v 13; Kalisch 1867–72). Furthermore, this pericope is not headed by a special introduction (cf. 6:1, 12, 17–18; 7:22, 28), which further implies that this cereal offering is structurally tied to the previously mentioned burnt offering and that, therefore, both pericopes together (vv 1–11) concern themselves with the daily *Tāmîd*.

This theory is open to one objection, however, and it is a serious one. The cereal offering here is explicitly a priestly prebend (vv 9–11). This does not seem to be the case with the *Tāmîd* cereal offering. Three separate notices concerning the cereal offering that accompanies the burnt offering indicate that the former is treated like the latter, in other words, it is totally burned on the altar and none of it goes to the priests. The first instance is the sacrificial procedure for the healed leper: "the priest shall offer up *(wĕheʿĕlâ)* the burnt offering and the cereal offering on the altar" (14:20), which clearly points to the total incineration of not only the whole offering—which would be expected (see 1:9, 13)— but also the cereal offering. The second instance concerns the sacrificial accompaniment to the sheaf (barley) offering, which includes a burnt offering and a cereal offering, and the latter is expressly declared to be an *'iššeh laYHWH rêaḥ nîḥōaḥ* 'a food gift of pleasing aroma to the Lord' (23:13), again a reference to its total incineration on the altar. To be sure, it is nowhere explicitly stated that the *Tāmîd* cereal offering is similarly treated. But one verse—the third instance —makes this virtually certain: *wayyaʿal ʿālāyw 'et-hāʿōlâ weʾ et-hamminḥâ kaʾăšer ṣiwwâ YHWH 'et-mōšeh* 'he (Moses) burned upon it (the altar) the burnt offering and the cereal offering as the Lord commanded Moses' (Exod 40:29). Both the use of one verb "burn" (see the COMMENT on chap. 1) for the two sacrifices, implying that the cereal offering was not an independent sacrifice, and the reference to God's command, which can only mean Exod 29:38–43, unmistakably point to the *Tāmîd*. Thus one can always assume that whenever the cereal offering is not an independent sacrifice but is an adjunct of the burnt offering both are treated as a single offering and are burned together on the altar. This certainly is the opinion of later times, for example, Josephus (*Ant.* 3.233–34) and the Tannaites (*t. Zebaḥ.* 5:3; *m. Menaḥ.* 6:2). Moreover, the rabbis are probably right in maintaining that the adjunct cereal offering contained no frankincense (*m. Menaḥ.* 5:3). Their tradition is clearly supported by biblical evidence: the stipulations for the adjunct cereal offering scrupulously spell out the ingredients for this offering and their amounts (Num 15:4–9). It can hardly be accidental that the quantity of oil is stated for each type of adjunct cereal offering but not a word is said about frankincense. The reason for this omission is obvious: frankincense is required from the *'azkārâ* token of the independent raw cereal offering (2:2), the *'azkārâ* assigned to the altar, and the remainder to the priest (2:3). The absence of frankincense in the adjunct, raw cereal offering can only mean that the latter has no *'azkārâ* token and, therefore, the entire offering is burned on the altar. Thus the presence of frankincense in this cereal offering implies that the latter is not an adjunct of some other sacrifice but a discrete, private offering.

Nonetheless, it must be recorded that despite the evidence of Scripture and the concurring views of Josephus and the rabbis, the Sadducees consistently and vehemently maintained that the adjunct cereal offering (except for its *'azkārâ* token) was a priestly prebend, and only in Hasmonean times was the issue finally settled in favor of the Pharisees (*Meg. Taʿan.* 5:8; Lichtenstein 1932: 320). True, it can be argued that the Sadducees, who represented priestly interests, were merely attempting to maximize the priestly prebends. It is hardly conceivable, however, that their view was not based on old tradition and current practice.

The issue would have to be left as an insoluble draw were it not for an additional consideration. It is entirely possible to explain why this pericope is limited to the raw cereal offering on other grounds: the raw semolina type is the most common, and the disposition of the baked type is relegated to a single verse in a summation of the priestly prebends (7:9); also, because we have been previously informed that the baked cereal offering must be unleavened (2:4–5), there is special need to state this fact also for the raw cereal offering (v 9). In any event, the cereal offering of this pericope is not the adjunct to the *Tāmîd* or to any other sacrifice. It is the independent, private cereal offering of chap. 2. Implied, therefore, is that the author of this pericope had the fuller instructions concerning the cereal offering (chap. 2) before him, which ultimately determined how he worded this supplementary notice concerning the priestly share in the cereal offering. That chaps. 6–7 comprise a supplement to chaps. 1–5 is argued in the NOTE on 7:38b. For details on the name, function, types, and development of the cereal offering, see the COMMENT on chap. 2.

Aaron's sons. běnê 'ahărōn; in fact, one of the sons of Aaron, to judge by the verbs used in the execution of this rite (v 8).

shall present (haqrēb). The infinitive absolute has the force of an imperative; it is equivalent to *haqrēb yaqrîbû* (Ibn Ezra). The rabbis hold that this "presentation" is a rite that is also termed *higgîš* (*Sipra,* Ṣaw par. 2:4, 5). But the latter verb is only used in connection with the baked cereal offering (2:8) and not with the raw cereal offering. Its purpose probably was to demonstrate that the baking *ab initio* was intended for the altar lest "the offerer appear as one who initially prepares for himself and only subsequently distributes to others" (Bekhor Shor). Nonetheless, the rabbis require that all cereal offerings are subject to the *haggāšâ* rite (*m. Menah.* 5:5; see the NOTE on 2:2). Their view can be validated by the fact that meat sacrifices require a discrete presentation of their blood (see the NOTE on 1:5), and one should expect a similar rite for the presentation of the *'azkārâ,* the token portion of the cereal offering. The omission of this requirement in the prescription for the raw cereal offering can be explained on stylistic grounds: to avoid repeating this rite in each of the five cereal offerings described in 2:1–7, *higgîš* is mentioned only once, in the summation, 2:8.

in front of. The compound preposition *'el pěnê* expresses motion better than *lipnê* 'before'. Thus the priest must bring the cereal offering to the altar before he separates the offerable part from it (cf. 2:8–9).

8. *A handful. běqumṣô,* lit., "with his handful"; for more details on the term *qōmeṣ,* see the NOTE on 2:2.

semolina. For the meaning of *sōlet,* see the NOTE on 2:1.

set aside. wěhērîm, lit., "he shall set aside," referring to the priest. The anonymous subject throughout this chapter is always the priest (see the NOTE on v 2). For the cultic meaning of *hērîm,* see the NOTES on 2:9 and 6:3.

from it (mimmennû). The suffix is masculine, though the antecedent *hamminhâ* 'the cereal offering' (v 7) is feminine. The Masora reckons six instances of *mimmennû,* where *mimmennâ* would be expected (Exod 25:15; Lev 6:8; 7:18; 27:9; Josh 1:7; Judg 11:34), though all of these passages can be explained in different ways. Some would attribute a neuter force to the suffix, citing *mimmennû* of 27:9, whose referent is *běhēmâ* (Hazzequni). The existence of any sort of neuter in Hebrew is highly doubtful, however, and as for the cited proof text, the referent could just as well be *qorban* (see the NOTE on 27:9). In this verse, the grammatical problem can be easily resolved because the suffix can refer just as well to the ingredients of the cereal offering, the semolina and oil (*šemen* is masculine), even though they follow *mimmennû* (Kalisch 1867–72).

frankincense (lĕbōnâ). For a description, see the NOTE on 2:2.

9. According to Ramban (on v 7), this verse contains most of the innovations of this pericope, namely: (1) the cereal offering, but for its token, is eaten by the priests; (2) unleavened, (3) in a holy place, and (4) its holiness is contagious (v 11). This list is correct, except for the first item, for the assignment of the cereal offering to the priest has already been stated (2:3, 10).

unleavened (maṣṣôt). This requirement follows logically from the fact that "I have assigned it as their portion from my food gifts" (v 10). Thus, because the cereal offering stems from God—leaven being forbidden on the altar (2:11) —it follows that the priests should also eat it unleavened. This requirement is not found in the prescription for the raw cereal offering (2:1–3), and it may account for the omission of the baked offering in this pericope, for we have already been informed that the baked cereal offering must be unleavened (2:4– 5; see the NOTE on v 7). The repetition of the ostensibly superfluous verb *tēʾākēl* 'shall be eaten' (cf. *yōʾkēlû* in v 9a) throws emphasis on the state of the consumed *minḥâ:* it must be unleavened. The third mention of this verb in the verse (abβ, *yōʾkēl-ûhā*) is also for emphasis: it must be eaten in the sanctuary court (Paran 1983: 53).

(it shall be eaten unleavened) in a holy place; (they shall eat it) in the court of the Tent of Meeting (. . . bĕmāqôm qādōš . . . baḥāṣar ʾōhel-môʿēd). Clearly, the "holy place" is here identified as the Tabernacle court (Rashi). That is, because theoretically the entire Tent-shrine as "a holy place" would also qualify as the priests' dining room, the text then delimits the dining area to the court. This instance and the following (v 19) being the first two to mention and define the dining area of the priests, all subsequent attestations need but state *bĕmāqôm qādōš* 'in a holy place' or its equivalent, *bimqôm haqqōdeš*, lit., 'in the place of holiness' (6:20; 7:6; 10:17, 18; 14:13; 16:24) and the locus of the court must be understood. (Wright's attempt to distinguish between the two expressions [1987: 232–35] is not convincing.)

There is even stronger scriptural evidence for this identification. The place in which the priestly consecrands are to cook their sacrificial meat is called in Exodus *bĕmāqôm qādōš* 'in a holy place' (Exod 29:31), but in Leviticus *petaḥ ʾōhel môʿēd* 'the entrance to the Tent of Meeting' (8:31). Thus the priestly dining area must be located in the Tabernacle court. The cereal offering is eaten by the priests *ʾēṣel hammizbēaḥ* 'beside the altar' (10:12). Because the sacrificial altar is situated in the very center of the court, the expression "beside the altar" must designate the area within the altar's circumference, that is to say, anywhere inside the court. Finally, the reparation offering of lamb brought by the healed *mĕṣōrāʿ* is slaughtered *bimqôm ʾāšer yišḥaṭ ʾet-haḥaṭṭāʾt wĕʾet-hāʿōlâ bim-*

qôm haqqōdeš 'at the spot in the sacred precinct where the purification offering and the burnt offering are slaughtered' (14:13). Because the offerer or any other lay person performs the sacrificial slaughter (see the NOTE on 1:5), it is clear that the slaughtering takes place in the Tabernacle court, which elsewhere is expressly identified as *lipnê YHWH petaḥ ʾōhel môʿēd* 'before the Lord, at the entrance to the Tent of Meeting' (e.g., Exod 29:11) or, more restrictively, *yerek hammizbēaḥ ṣāpōnâ* 'on the north side of the altar before the Lord' (Lev 1:11).

P's system permitted the laymen to have access to the *petaḥ ʾōhel môʿēd* 'the entrance to the Tent of Meeting', in other words, to any part of the Tabernacle court. The latter did not have "most sacred" status, as did the Tent and the outer altar. In P's terms it was just "sacred"—*māqôm qādōš/mĕqôm haqqōdeš* 'a holy place/place of holiness'. On Yom Kippur only the "most sacred" areas are purged: the adytum, the shrine, and the outer altar (16:14–19), but not one drop of purgatorial blood is spilled upon the curtains of the court or its floor. Furthermore, during rites of consecration for the priests and the Tabernacle all of the priestly consecrands are anointed as well as all of the sancta, with the sole exception of the court and its curtains (8:10–11; Exod 30:26–30; 40:9–16). That is why some later rabbinic sources could argue on behalf of lay access to the inner court (of the permanent Temple). For example, processions around the altar took place on the Feast of Tabernacles (*m. Sukk.* 4:5; *m. Mid.* 2:6; cf. Albeck's note, 1952: p. 476). As a consequence, then, it is safe to assume that the entire court was available to the priests for their dining needs.

At the same time, there is good reason to believe that *in practice* the priests actually dined on their prebends in the inner court, called by the rabbis by the biblical expression *bên hāʾûlām wĕlammizbēaḥ* 'between the porch (of the Temple) and the altar' (Joel 2:17), which, in rabbinic sources, has a higher degree of sanctity than the forecourt (*m. Kelim* 1:9; *Sipre Zuṭa* on Num 5:2). Moreover, there is evidence that even in biblical times the priests' private activities were confined to the inner court. First, it is difficult to believe that the high priest, commanded on Yom Kippur to bathe "in a holy place" (16:24), would do so in the forecourt, in view of the worshiping Israelites (16:17). In the Herodian Temple, the place in which the high priest immersed himself was indeed a room in the inner court (*m. Mid.* 5:3; *m. Yoma* 3:3). Furthermore, Ezekiel locates the priests' chambers for cooking and eating the most sacred offerings to the rear (i.e., west) of the temple building, on the north and south sides of the inner court (Ezek 42:1–14; 46:19–20). Even though, in Ezekiel's system, the entirety of the inner court is the private preserve of the priests, nonetheless he does not locate their dining area in the eastern part of the court, presumably in keeping with the established custom within the Jerusalem Temple that the priests do not dine in the area accessible to the laity. Finally, mention should be made of the archaeological findings in Arad that the courtyard of its sanctuary (datable to the First Temple period) was clearly divided into two parts on either side of the sacrificial altar, thus suggesting the possibility that the bipartite division of the sanctuary court extends back into biblical times. Hence, this adduced evidence may indicate the existence of two priestly traditions: the theory, which allowed them to dine anywhere within the sacred precinct, and their practice, which confined their eating and, indeed, all of their private activities to the inner part of the court. Indeed, is the specification that the priests eat their prebends from the most sacred offerings in the *ḥāṣar ʾōhel môʿēd* (6:9, 19 only) and not in the *petaḥ ʾōhel môʿēd*, where lay persons perform their sacrificial duties (cf. the NOTE on 1:3), an attempt by the text to distinguish between the two (cf. also the NOTE on 8:31)?

Of certainty, theory—embodied in the canonized Torah—prevailed in the Herodian Temple, where chambers for dining were provided for the priests all along the wall of the sacrificial court (*b. Zebaḥ.* 56a [bar.]; *Sipra*, Ṣaw par 2:12; *Sipre*, Deut. 36). The sectaries of Qumran also ordained that the priests could eat anywhere within the sacrificial court, for which purpose tables and chairs were to be set up within the stoa surrounding the entire court wall. Furthermore, their temple blueprint prescribed two cooking installations flanking each of the four gates leading into this court as well as stoves in all of its four corners (11QT 37:8–15). In fact, the Temple Scroll explicitly equates "the court of the Tent of Meeting" with the entire area of the sacrificial court (20:11–12).

10. *baked (tēʾāpeh)*. Because the baking and cooking vessels for the priestly prebends from the most sacred offerings are located inside the sacred precincts (v 21), it must be assumed that the baking or cooking took place there as well. Such indeed is the provision of Ezekiel's temple (Ezek 42:13; 46:19–20) and of Qumran's Temple Scroll (11QT 37:8–15).

leaven (ḥāmēṣ). For its definition and distinction from *śeʾōr*, see the NOTE on 2:11.

I have assigned (nātattî). For this usage of the verb *nātan*, see the NOTE on 17:11 (and cf. 18:8, 21, 26). The unexpected use of the first person here and in the next word, below, suggests a later editor who reworked this passage (Dillmann and Ryssel 1897), identified as a tradent of H (Knohl 1988: 234 n. 7). One may ask, however, why only this verse and not the rest of the pericope? Perhaps, then, P might also have countenanced God's speaking in the first person (see the Introduction, §C).

from my food gifts (mēʾiššāy). For *ʾiššeh* meaning "food gift" and not "fire offering," as commonly rendered, see the NOTE on 1:9. This sentence, uniquely in this chapter, is set in the first person, most likely to underscore the reason that the priests must bake their cereal offering prebend unleavened: it stems from the Lord; in other words, it should theoretically go up in smoke on the altar but, by his grace, he has assigned it to the priests (see the COMMENT on chap. 2).

most sacred. The term *qōdeš qŏdāšîm* defines the burnt, cereal, purification, and reparation offerings (2:3; 6:10, 18; 7:6), as distinct from the rest of the offerings, which are designated by the term *qōdeš* 'sacred': the well-being offering, the *ḥērem*, and the first of animals, produce, and processed foods (Num 18:12–19). *ḥērem* is also termed "most sacred" (27:29), but only in regard to its irredeemability; otherwise it is treated as "sacred" (Milgrom 1976f: 53 n. 187, 66 n. 236). The designations "sacred" and "most sacred" are always applied to the portions of the offering that are eaten. For this reason the burnt offering (never eaten by man) is nowhere called "most sacred" but must be assumed to be so (see *m. Zebaḥ.* 5:1; 6:1). This bipartite division of offerings into "sacred" and "most sacred" is not the invention of Israel; clear traces of it are present in Egyptian and Hittite cultic texts (Milgrom 1976f: 41–43).

like the purification offering and the reparation offering (kaḥaṭṭāʾt wěkāʾāšām). The similitude is only in the manner of eating, not in other aspects of their common "most sacred" status. The data on the purification and reparation offerings are taken for granted: hence, the author of this text had before him chaps. 4 and 5.

11. *Any male of Aaron's descendants.* This statement agrees with 2:3 and 7:10 that the raw cereal offering belongs to the entire priestly cadre, even the blemished priests who are not permitted to officiate (21:21–22; cf. *m. Zebaḥ.* 12:1).

a due for all time (ḥoq-ʿôlām). For this meaning of *ḥōq* see 6:15; 7:34; 10:15; 24:9; Gen 47:22; Exod 29:28; Num 18:8, 11, 19. It should be distinguished from the term *ḥuqqâ* 'law', especially as found in the same construct, *ḥuqqat ʿôlām* 'a law for all time' (e.g., 3:17; 10:9; 23:14, 31; 24:3). See further the NOTE on 10:13.

throughout your generations (lĕdōrōtêkem). The second-person plural suffix is strange. Normally, its referent would be the Israelites. Instead, it is Aaron and the priests who are addressed here (v 2), and even they are consistently referred to in the third person (e.g., vv 3–5, 7–9)—indeed, in this very verse. Thus, there is no choice but to regard it as an unconscious imitation of the oft-repeated phrase *ḥuqqat ʿôlām lĕdōrōtêkem* 'a law for all time throughout your [i.e., the Israelites'] generations' (e.g., Exod 12:14, 17; Lev 3:17; 10:9; 23:14, 31, 41; 24:3; Num 15:15; 18:23). Alternately, one may wish to read *lĕdōrōtām* 'throughout their generations', referring to the priests (as in Exod 27:21).

Whatever touches them shall become holy (kōl ʾăšer-yiggaʿ bāhem yiqdāš). For the derivation, explanation, and implications of this formula, see COMMENT B below.

them (bāhem). The plural suffix cannot claim as its antecedent the cereal offering, which is found only in the singular throughout this pericope (vv 7–11). The antecedent cannot be anything else than *ʾiššê* 'food gifts of', a plural noun that refers not only to the cereal offering but also to the purification and reparation offerings mentioned in the verse (v 10b). Thus the formula cited here is clearly an attempt to generalize all of the sacrifices subject to the formula's jurisdiction. This deduction is confirmed by a verse in Ezekiel: "This is the place where the priests shall boil the reparation offering and the purification offering and where they shall bake the cereal offering in order not to bring *them* out into the outer court and so communicate holiness to the people" (Ezek 46:20). It is no accident that these three sacrifices comprise the *qodšê qodāšîm* 'the most sacred offerings' that are assigned to the priests as their prebends, implying that the meat of the well-being offering that is not subsumed under the category of "the most sacred" is not affected by this formula (for details, see COMMENT B below).

12. *The Lord spoke to Moses.* Because this pericope is not labeled a *tôrâ* (cf. 6:2, 7, 18; 7:1, 11), it purports to be a continuation of the previous pericope, a most logical association because it too deals with the same kind of sacrifice, the cereal offering. Why then does it begin with a discrete and lengthy introduction (vv 12–13aαβ)? The possibility must therefore be entertained that this pericope is an interpolation and that the function of the introduction was to set it off from its context. For this very reason—to continue the surmise—an introduction was affixed to the pericope on the purification offering (vv 17–23), instead of allowing it to begin with the words "this is the ritual for the purification offering" (v 18aβ; cf. 6:7; 7:1, 11), in order to distinguish it from the inserted interpolation (vv 12–16).

The same history may lie behind the evolution of chap. 7. The pericope on the suet and blood (7:22–27) contains an introduction but, like 6:12–17, is not a *tôrâ;* hence, both passages must be interpolations. The insertion of 7:22–27 therefore would have motivated the writing of an introduction (7:28–29a) to the subsequent pericope (7:29b–36), which, originally, did not have one because it was a continuation of the discussion of the well-being offering (7:11–21) and was part of latter's *tôrâ* (7:11).

Thus the original text of chaps. 6–7 probably had only one introduction (6:1–2aα) followed by a series of *tôrâ* pericopes (6:2aβ–6; 7–11; 18aβ–23; 7:1–10; 11–21, 29b–36; 37–38). After the insertion of two interpolations (6:12–16; 7:22–27), however, introductions were affixed to the passages that followed them (6:17–18aα; 7:28–29a). Because the second interpolation (7:22–27) and the subsequent connective (7:28–29a) stem from H (see the NOTE on 7:22–23a and the Introduction, §H), the insertion of 6:12–16 (and the composition of 6:17–18aα) should also be attributed to H.

13. *Aaron and his sons (ʾahărōn ûbānāyw).* Because this sacrifice, according to the explicit statement of this pericope, will be offered solely by the high priest (see esp. v 15), it would seem that the term "his sons" does not refer to all of Aaron's descendants—the entire priestly cadre—but only to those of his descendants who will succeed him, namely, the future high priests (Sir 45:14; Heb 7:27; *Tg. Ps.-J.*). But Philo preserves the tradition that this daily cereal offering is incumbent on every priest (*Laws* 1. 255–56). Josephus also seems to follow Philo's view: "The priest at his own expense, and that twice a day, offers meal soaked in oil and hardened by a little cooking" (*Ant.* 3.257), unless "the priest" (sing.) stands for the high priest. A third view is held by the rabbis: whereas they

agree that this pericope deals with the daily offering of the high priest, they interpret the conjunction *waw* in *ûbānāyw* 'and his sons' as implying that all of Aaron's sons, to wit, every priest, must sacrifice a cereal offering on the day of his consecration (*t. Šeqal.* 3:25; *Sipra*, Ṣaw par. 3:3; *b. Menaḥ.* 51b).

It seems to be the high priest's daily offering that is alluded to in the expression * maʿăśēh haḥăbittîm* 'the making of the flat cakes' (1 Chr 9:31), lit., "that which is made on griddles" (see v 14, below), which anticipates the rabbinic term for this offering, *minḥat haḥăbittîm* 'the cereal offering of the flat cakes' (*m. Menaḥ.* 6:5; *m. Tāmîd* 3:1). A special official and chamber were appointed for its preparation (*t. Šeqal.* 2:14; *m. Mid.* 1:3), a precedent for which was established in biblical times, for Scripture attests to the fact that at least as early as the Second Temple, a Levite family was assigned to the duty of preparing this offering (1 Chr 9:31). Thus the high priest had only the duty of sacrificing this offering but not of preparing it (further proof is supplied in v 15). Who bore the cost of this offering? Josephus unequivocally points to the high priest (*Ant.* 3.257, cited above). Yet the answer is not certain if *minḥat hattāmîd* 'the regular cereal offering', supplied from public funds (Neh 10:34), refers to the high priest's daily cereal offering (see the discussion at v 15, below).

Which of the preceding interpretations is correct? Philo's has to be ruled out, particularly if the priest himself had to bear the cost of the offering. This offering, requiring one-tenth of an *ephah* (approximately 2.3 liters) of the finest flour, *sōlet* 'semolina', would be economically burdensome for the average priest; only the high priest could afford it (see below). Furthermore, considering the large cadre of priests who serviced the First and Second Temples, the cost would be prohibitive for the temple treasury if it had to cover the costs of this daily offering for each and every priest. Thus this pericope most likely deals with the daily cereal offering of the high priest. Note should also be taken of the rabbis' apparent reluctance to give the meaning of "successors" to the word *ûbānāyw*, a meaning that admittedly is unattested in Scripture, claiming instead that it refers to a discrete offering of Aaron's sons, that is to say, every priest, made on the day of his consecration.

from the time (bĕyôm). Clearly, the usual translation of the word, "on the day," cannot be right because this offering is not for a one-time occasion but is to be offered *tāmîd* 'perpetually'. It has long been recognized, however, that *bĕyôm* can also mean *miyyôm* (*Sipra*, Ṣaw par. 2:4; Saadiah, Ibn Janaḥ, Ibn Ezra, Radak), and that it is not infrequent in biblical Hebrew (e.g., 8:32, cf. 7:32; 14:18, cf. 14:29; Josh 3:6 [K./Q.]; 2 Kgs 23:23 [K./Q.]), where *beth* possesses an ablative sense, equivalent to *mem* (Sarna 1959). This phenomenon is well attested in other Semitic languages, for example, Ug. *b* (*UT* 49.1.18, 38, 39; 51.3.15, 16; 52.6 [Ginsberg 1936]); Akk. *ina* (*CAD*, I–J, 141–42); and in early Northwest Semitic inscriptions (e.g., Abibaal [Albright 1947]; Nora [Albright 1941–43]; Karatepe, lines 13–14 [Gordon 1949]; Eshmunʾazar, lines 5–6 [Cooke 1903]).

Moreover, the word *yôm* has, beside its usual meaning "day," the abstract connotation "time," especially when affixed with the preposition *beth* (e.g., Ezek 38:18; 43:18), which gives *běyôm* the meaning "when, after, from the time." This usage is particularly clear in the text on the initiation ceremonies of the Tabernacle altar, where *běyôm* (Num 7:1, 10, 84) is replaced by *ʾaḥărê* 'after' (v 88).

ephah. *hāʾēpâ*, estimated as equivalent to 22.8 liters (Zuidhof 1982). Thus one-tenth of an *ephah*, the most frequently mentioned amount of semolina in a cereal offering (5:11; 14:21; Num 5:15; 28:9, 13, 21, 29; etc.), would amount to 2.3 liters.

regular. *tāmîd*, lit., "perpetually." This adverb ultimately developed into a noun when it referred to the daily sanctuary cult (see the NOTE on v 6 and COMMENT C below). As this cereal offering of the high priest was sacrificed twice daily, it was no doubt incorporated into the daily *Tāmîd*, and to distinguish it from other cereal offerings, it was probably called *minḥat hattāmîd* 'the regular cereal offering'. Surely, this is the meaning of the term as used in Num 4:16a, "The responsibility of Eleazar son of Aaron the priest: the lighting oil, the aromatic incense, *ûminḥat hattāmîd*, and the anointing oil." Of course, it is also possible that in this verse this term refers to the cereal offering that accompanies the *Tāmîd*, the daily burnt offering (Exod 29:40a; Num 28:5). If this were the case, however, then it would be inexplicable why Eleazar was not similarly responsible for the wine libation that also accompanies the daily burnt offering (Exod 29:40a; Num 28:7a). Furthermore, this "regular cereal offering" must correspond in its typology to the other ingredients placed in Eleazar's charge. Just as the lighting oil, the aromatic incense, and the anointing oil fall under the exclusive control of the high priest, so must the *minḥat hattāmîd*, a designation that, therefore, favors the high priest's daily cereal offering. That only the high priest could officiate with these other substances is proved by the fact that they were employed inside the Tent of Meeting, in which the high priest alone could officiate (for the incense, see Exod 30:7–8, and for the lighting oil, see Lev 24:3; Num 8:2–3); and, in the case of the anointing oil, it was used to anoint the head of Aaron and, presumably, of his successors (see chap. 8, COMMENT D), but not the heads of ordinary priests. Moreover, according to rabbinic tradition, the anointing oil was stored in the adytum (*t. Yoma* 3:7), to which only the high priest had access. Thus the regular cereal offering included in this list must also fall under the exclusive domain of the high priest.

Nevertheless, a third possibility must be reckoned with. The regular cereal offering in Num 4:16 also accurately describes the bread loaves on the table of presence, which are also termed a *Tāmîd* (24:3), a contention that is further supported by the fact that, like the other enumerated substances, these bread loaves are also employed inside the Tent of Meeting. It must be admitted that this claim would be nigh incontestable were it not for the fact that the bread of presence is already accounted for in the prescriptions for the Tabernacle transport: they are not removed from the table (Num 4:7b). Thus, by the process of elimination the regular cereal offering of Num 4:16 must refer to the high priest's daily offering.

There is one other attestation of the *minḥat Tāmîd*, in Neh 10:34, but its identification is not as unambiguous. Every Israelite family accepts the responsibility of contributing one-third of a shekel annually "for the rows of bread (of presence), for the *minḥat hattāmîd* and for the burnt offering of the *Tāmîd*, the sabbaths, the new moons, the festivals. . . ." Here the mention of the Tāmîd burnt offering might lead one to conclude that the *minḥat hattāmîd* refers to the cereal offering that accompanies the burnt offering. Yet in that case one would also expect that the cereal offerings for the sabbaths, new moons, and festivals would also be mentioned. That they are not can only mean that the *minḥat hattāmîd* must be a discrete offering, namely, the cereal offering of the high priest, the only other cereal offering sacrificed daily. Furthermore, the same argument used for Num 4:16 is applicable here: if *minḥat hattāmîd* were the adjunct cereal offering of the daily burnt offering, one would expect to see the adjunct wine libation also included.

The conclusion is, therefore, ineluctable: *minḥat hattāmîd* (Num 4:16; Neh 10:34) refers to the daily cereal offering of the high priest. Moreover, despite the evidence from Josephus (cited above) and what may have been the case in his time, at the very end of the Second Temple period, the cost of this offering originally was not charged to the high priest but was subsidized by communal funds.

half of it in the evening (ûmaḥăṣîtāh bāʿāreb). Because rabbinic tradition holds that the high priest's cereal offering was the final altar sacrifice of each day (*b. Yoma* 33a; Maim., *The Book of Temple Service*, Daily Offerings 6.5, 11), the possibility must be entertained that the term *minḥat hāʿereb* 'the evening cereal offering' (1 Kgs 18:29, 36; 2 Kgs 16:15; Ps 141:2; Dan 9:21; Ezra 9:4–5) refers to this sacrifice or, rather, to the time of this sacrifice—a convenient, if picturesque, way of saying: at day's end, just before evening sets in (Hoffmann 1953: 31–32). Alternately, because this expression presupposes a discrete offering, one would have to assume an earlier stage in the development of the *Tāmîd* when only the cereal offering (but no burnt offering) was sacrificed at the close of each day (see COMMENT C below).

14. *griddle (maḥăbat).* For the method of preparation, see 2:5–6.

well soaked. The term *murbeket* occurs again only at 7:12 and 1 Chr 23:29. Its meaning is disputed. Some claim that it means that the semolina must be prepared quickly (Ibn Ezra, second explanation) by deep frying it in oil (*Tg. Ps.-J.;* Maim. on *m. Menaḥ.* 9:3); however, frying takes place not on a griddle but in a pan (*marḥešet;* see the NOTE on 2:7). Others opt for the meaning "softened (in oil)" (Ibn Ezra, Rashbam), which, however, has no philological support. Most lexicons and translations render it "well mixed" on the basis of the Arab. cognate *rabaka;* but biblical Hebrew already possesses this verb, *bālal,* which is frequently found in cultic texts, especially in connection with the cereal offering (2:4; Exod 29:40; Num 28:5, 12, 20, 28; etc.), and, significantly, with the cereal offering prepared on a griddle (2:5). Thus the word *murbeket* must denote something else. A fourth explanation is cited by the rabbis: "thoroughly boiled in water" (*Sipra*, Ṣaw 4:6; cf. *Tg. Neof.*). But after the preparation is toasted on a griddle boiling it makes no sense. Perhaps the Akk. cognate *rabāku* sheds some light. It is chiefly found in pharmaceutical texts, where it refers to the preparation of a drug by boiling down its ingredients.

tūpînê. This hapax has been variously interpreted, for example: (1) "pastries" *(Tg. Neof.)*; (2) emended to *těputtênah* 'crumble it' (Dillmann and Ryssel 1897); (3) read as *tōʾpênāh* 'bake it' (*Sipra*, Ṣaw 4:6; *b. Menaḥ.* 50b; Jos., *Ant.* 3.257; cf. Rashi, Rashbam); (4) "folded" (LXX; van Leeuwen 1988). The word *tappinni* occurs in Akk. (*dabin* in Sumerian) and is rendered "a cereal preparation" *(AHw)*, and in Hittite it also designates "barley bread" (Hoffner 1968: 534). Because its exact meaning is not certain, it has been left untranslated here.

crumbled bits. pittîm; see 2:6. Notice should be taken of the absence of frankincense in this offering, a characteristic common to all baked cereal offerings (see the NOTE on 2:4 and the COMMENT on chap. 2). It might be argued, however, that the frankincense was omitted for the same reason that the *ʾazkārâ* was omitted: the high priest's cereal offering, being totally burned on the altar, requires no *ʾazkārâ* (contrast 2:9). So too the frankincense, which would entirely be removed with the *ʾazkārâ*, would also not be mentioned. The reply of *Tirat Kesep* is compelling: if the high priest's cereal offering were an exception to the rule, then the text would have said so, as it does in the cases of the cereal offerings for the poor person's graduated purification offering (5:11) and for the suspected adulteress (Num 5:15).

15. *anointed. hammāšîaḥ,* a past participle, equivalent to *hammāšûaḥ;* it is not a regular adjective.

sacrifice (yaʿăśeh). The extant renderings of this word are "bear its cost" (Jos., *Ant.* 3.257; cf. *m. Šeqal.* 7:6) and "prepare it" (most translations and commentaries). But in sacrificial texts the verb *ʿāśâ* has only one meaning, "sacrifice" (e.g., Exod 10:25; Lev 4:20; 5:10; 7:7, 22; 14:19, 30; 15:15, 30; 16:24; 17:9; 22:23). Thus, regardless of who bore its cost or who prepared it, it was the high priest's responsibility to offer it.

the Lord's due for all time (ḥoq-ʿôlām laYHWH). See v 11 for the same idiom (see also 7:34; 10:13, 15). Here, however, because the entire offering is burned on the altar, it is termed "the Lord's due."

entirely. kālîl, an old sacrificial term designating the burnt offering (Deut 33:10; cf. 1 Sam 7:9; Ps 51:21; see the COMMENT to chap. 1); here it bears instead its normal adverbial meaning, "entirely" (e.g., Exod 28:31; Deut 13:17; Isa 2:18).

16. *So every cereal offering of a priest (wěkol-minḥat kōhēn).* Because the priest, like the layman, is entitled to eat the meat of his well-being offering, one

might think that this verse only forbade the priest to benefit from his expiatory cereal offerings; but if they were offered for another reason, say, out of joy or thanksgiving (see the COMMENT on chap. 2), then, except for the *ʾazkārâ* token, the priest might eat his offering. This line of reasoning, logical in itself, is denied by the rule that *every* cereal offering of a priest, regardless of its motivation, must be consumed on the altar (*Sipra*, Ṣaw 8:4). "Indian-giving," retracting one's gift (or most of it) from the Lord, is unacceptable and is, more likely, reprehensible.

a total offering. kālîl, used nominally (see v 15). Alternately, the verb *toqṭār* 'shall go up in smoke' (v 15b) applies here as well, yielding "(shall go up in smoke) entirely" (see v 15b).

18. *this is the ritual for the purification offering (zōʾt tôrat haḥaṭṭāʾt).* For the theory that this pericope may originally have begun here and that the introduction (vv 17–18aα) would have been added following the insertion of vv 12–16, see the NOTE on v 12.

at the spot where the burnt offering is slaughtered. bimqôm ʾăšer tiššāḥēṭ hāʿōlâ, located at the northern side of the altar, the locus for slaughtering sacrificial animals from the flock (see the NOTE on 1:11). Yet cattle are also eligible as purification offerings (see, for example 4:1–21), and, hence, their slaughter should not be restricted to the area of the court north of the altar (see the NOTES on 1:5; 4:4)! The answer is that purification-offering cattle are never eaten by the priests but must be incinerated outside the camp (4:11–13, 21). Thus the purification animals referred to in this pericope are explicitly to be eaten by the priests (vv 19, 22; contrast v 23) and must, therefore, be restricted to flock animals.

Yet this specification for the slaughter of the purification flock animals has already been mentioned, and with precisely the same words, in 4:24, 29, and 33. Why repeat it here? Because this pericope is addressed to the priests (v 17aα), the purpose of the repetition can only be to place the responsibility for the proper slaughter of the purification offering specifically upon the priests. Although sacrificial slaughter is performed by the lay offerer (see the NOTES on 1:25a; 4:15b), it falls on the priests to supervise the slaughter, that it be done in the proper manner (see the NOTE on 1:5a) and place. The rabbis find an ethical motivation for this repetition: "not to publicize the sinners" (y. Yebam. 8:3; cf. y. Soṭa 8:9; y. Qidd. 4:1); that is to say, by locating the slaughter of the purification and burnt offerings in the same place, one cannot distinguish their owners and thereby identify the sinners. Unfortunately, this ethical desideratum cannot be met because the burnt-offering animals must be male whereas the commoner's purification animals are limited to females, which leads to an easy identification of the latter's owners.

most sacred. For the meaning of qōdeš qodāšîm see the NOTE on v 10. Why is it stated here? It must be an explanation of the previous statement. The purification offering is slaughtered at the same spot as the burnt offering because it is most sacred. Were it a well-being offering, which is "sacred" but not "most sacred," it could be slaughtered anywhere in the forecourt (see 3:2, 8).

19. *The priest who offers it as a purification offering. hakkōhēn haměḥaṭṭē 'ōtāh,* lit., "the priest who performs the decontamination rite," in other words, removes the impurity of the altar by means of the blood. For the privative function of the *pi'el ḥiṭṭē',* see 8:15; Exod 29:36; Num 19:19; and chap. 4, Comment A. Because the blood is the purifying agent (see Ibn Ezra and chap. 4, Comment B), the priest must be the one who performs the blood rites *(Tg. Onq.).* That such is the case is proved by the prescription for the prebends from the thanksgiving offering: "it shall belong to the priest who dashes the blood of the well-being offering" (7:14b). Presumed is that more than one priest officiates at each sacrifice. To be sure, at early, simple sanctuaries, a single priest would see the sacrifice through from beginning to end, and even in larger sanctuaries no more than a single priestly family would suffice to administer and perform the entire cult, such as the Aaronides at the Tabernacle and the Elides at Shiloh. It was only the Temple of Jerusalem that employed a large priestly cadre, which ultimately had to be broken into "divisions" and "fathers' houses" (1 Chr 24), though even here there were few vacancies, to judge by the refusal of the Temple hierarchy to absorb their unemployed rural colleagues (2 Kgs 23:9). The rabbinic tradition that "the priest" in this verse stands for his entire "father's house" *(Sipra,* Ṣaw 10:2) refers to the days of the Herodian Temple, when the sacrificial prebends would be distributed to the entire priestly cadre on duty that day. The same applies to large sanctuaries throughout the ancient world. For example, the Carthage and Marseilles tariffs state explicitly that the sacrificial prebends belong to the priests as a group *(ANET³ 502–3).*

shall enjoy it. yo'kělennâ, lit., "shall eat it." But the literal meaning cannot be maintained here because it is clearly impossible for a single priest to consume the entire animal in a single day (see below and the Note on v 22). For the figurative use of *'ākal* 'enjoy, benefit, possess', see Ps 128:2; Qoh 5:18 (Wessely 1846). The duration of the time in which the purification offering and, indeed, meat from any other most sacred offering may be eaten is nowhere stated. All ancient sources, however, agree that it must be eaten the same day (Philo, *Laws* 1. 240; Jos., *Ant.* 3.231; *b. Zebaḥ.* 36a [bar.]). This rule is presupposed in the story of Nadab and Abihu. If Aaron could have postponed eating the meat of the purification offering to the following day, he would not have responded to Moses, "Had I eaten the purification offering today, would the Lord have approved?" (10:19b; D. Wright). Furthermore, this story demonstrates that the flesh of the purification offering, at least partially, must be eaten by the officiating priest (Hoffmann 1953; for details see the Note on 10:17).

(in a holy place), in the court of the Tent of Meeting (baḥăṣar 'ōhel mô'ēd). The rabbis (and most moderns) claim that this clause explicates and is equivalent to "in a holy place" *(m. Zebaḥ.* 5:3). For evidence that the priests probably

ate their sacrificial portions in the innermost half of the court, between the altar and the Tent, see the NOTE on v 9.

20. *Whatever. kōl* refers to things and excludes persons (see COMMENT B below).

shall become holy. yiqdaš, meaning that it becomes the property of the sanctuary. For the derivation, explanation, and implications of this formula, see COMMENT B below.

and if (wa'ăšer). For this meaning, see 4:22, cf. vv 13, 27; 5:2, cf. vv 1, 3.

is spattered (yizzeh). The *qal* of *nāzâ* is intransitive (e.g., 2 Kgs 9:33; Isa 63:3).

upon a garment. The most likely garment is that of the priest who performs the blood rite. Yet the garment is treated as if it had become impure! For the explanation, see below.

the bespattered part. 'ăšer yizzeh 'ālêhā, lit., "that (i.e., the spot) upon which it is spattered" (Rashi, Ibn Ezra). The relative pronoun *'ăšer* can also denote the place in which a thing happens (e.g., Gen 30:38; Exod 32:34; [Judg 5:27;] Ruth 1:16). It is also possible to conceive of *'ăšer* as a noun on the basis of Akk. *ašru,* Ug. *'tr,* and Aram. *'atrā*. "What strengthens the view that the ordinary relative pronoun is not intended or understood here is that in the song of Deborah, the preferred relative pronoun is *ša-*, which is found in v 7, whereas *'ăšer* does not occur elsewhere in the poem, only in v 27" (Freedman, written communication).

'ālêhā is problematic because its antecedent, *beged* 'garment', is masculine. The Sam. reads *'ālāyw* (masculine), which, however, may be a conscious harmonization. Perhaps "the suffix of the third-person singular feminine sometimes refers in a general sense to the verbal idea contained in a preceding sentence (corresponding to our *it*)," for example, Gen 15:6; Num 23:19; 1 Sam 11:9 (GKC §135, p). A simpler alternative is to regard *beged* as feminine, with Ibn Ezra (e.g., Prov 6:27; cf. Ezek 42:14; Ps 45:9 [Freedman, privately]).

The blood spots alone need to be washed out, not the entire garment (*Sipra,* Ṣaw 6:5). The garment does not become holy by coming into contact with the blood of the purification offering. Instead of being confiscated by the sanctuary, as would any object that is rendered holy, it is restored to its former status by having its so-called holiness effaced through washing. Thus the garment is actually treated as if it were impure, for it is impure clothing that always requires laundering (e.g., 11:25, 28, 40; 15:5–8, 10–11). This ambivalence of the purification offering, which will be present in even sharper form in the following verse, should occasion no surprise. The ability of the purification offering to impart impurity has already been noted (chap. 4, COMMENT B). For its blood, having absorbed the impurity of the sanctum upon which it is sprinkled, now contaminates everything it touches. This characteristic of the purification-offering blood is the key that resolves the paradox of the Red Cow in Num 19 (chap. 4, COMMENT G), and it is vital to understanding the annual purgation of the sanctuary on Yom Kippur (chap. 4, COMMENT C). The rabbis were equally aware of the ambivalence of the purification offering, for they acknowledge that the severer burnt purification offering (but not the eaten one) transmits impurity to foods (t. Yoma 4:16; cf. m. Para 8:3).

shall be laundered. tĕkabbēs, lit., "you [the priest] shall launder" (Ibn Ezra). But the verbs in the following verse are all in the passive. So without changing the consonantal text, the word can be revocalized as *tĕkubbas (puʿal)* or *tukkabbas (hothpaʿal;* see 13:55–56), both meaning "shall be laundered" (Ehrlich 1908–14). The feminine form would correspond aptly with feminine *ʿālêhā,* thereby providing further evidence that the latter word is correct and should not be emended.

in a holy place. Namely, within the tabernacle courtyard (see vv 9, 10). This specification further emphasizes that although the purification offering is a source of impurity (see v 21), it itself is treated as sacred. This anomaly can only be explained by the theory that the Priestly legislators were responsible for the conversion of an impurity-laden ritual detergent into a most sacred offering (for details, see chap. 10, COMMENT C).

Strikingly, the rabbis hold the view that the requirement to wash a bespattered garment of its sacrificial blood and break earthenware that has come into contact with sacrificial meat (v 21) applies only to purification offerings, both burnt and eaten (m. Zebaḥ. 11:1; t. Zebaḥ. 10:9), but not to any other offering, even if it is most sacred (m. Zebaḥ. 11:4; cf. Maim., *Book of Temple Service,* Manner of Sacrifice 8.1). Still, they limit this contagious power of the blood of the purification offering to the short span between the time that the animal is slaughtered and the time that the blood is manipulated on the altar (m. Zebaḥ. 11:3). Thus they were clearly uncomfortable with Scripture's demand that the bespattered garment should be treated as if it were contaminated by some impurity instead of being sanctified by contact with a most sacred offering. The same discomfort is evidenced in the rabbis' treatment of the requirement to break earthenware that has come into contact with sacrificial flesh (see below, v 21).

21. *An earthen vessel in which it is boiled shall be broken (ûkĕlî ḥereś ʾăšer tĕbuššal-bô yiššābēr).* What happened to the sherds? According to the rabbis, they were buried in the sanctuary courtyard (b. Yoma 21a; b. Zebaḥ. 96a), presumably because they had become holy. A cogent question is posed in *Seper Hamibhar:* if the earthen vessel was now sanctified, why the need to break it? Rather, it should be added to the sanctuary's stock of holy vessels! Its answer, and that of other Karaite commentaries (e.g., *Keter Torah*), agrees with the rabbinic interpretation (b. ʿAbod. Zar. 76a): the remainder *(nōtār)* of the sacred food absorbed into the earthen vessel turns into a state of abomination *(piggûl,* v 18) one day later (v 19); it and its contents must be destroyed (v 17) lest the one who eats of or from it be punished by the deity (v 18b).

Yet this line of reasoning, adopted by the Karaites as well as the rabbis, is patently weak. Why should the requirement to break earthenware (and wash blood-spattered garments) be restricted to the purification offering? Should not garments and earthen vessels that come into contact with the blood or flesh of all other sacred offerings also be subject to the requirement of washing or breaking? Perhaps one might wish to argue that this rule, stated only in the purification pericope, is meant to act as a generalization for all most sacred offerings. But if this were so, then the rule should have been stated in the *previous* pericope of the cereal offering (vv 7–11). That it is found in the second of the three most sacred offerings whose substance is eaten—the purification offering follows the cereal offering (vv 7–11) and precedes the reparation offering (7:1–7) —is a certain sign that this rule is unique to the purification offering, a conclusion confirmed by both rabbinic and Karaitic tradition (above).

How, then, to explain this uniqueness of the purification offering? As observed above, in the case of the bespattered garment (v 20), we are dealing with matters of impurity, not holiness. Only impure earthenware needs to be broken (see 11:33, 35; 15:12) because its porous nature so totally absorbs the impurity that it can never again be purified. The sectaries of Qumran state this rationale explicitly: "All earthen vessels must be broken because they are impure and they cannot ever be purified" (11QT 50:18–19). This passage from the Temple Scroll is part of a larger context dealing with corpse contamination and vessels found in the house of a corpse. Strikingly, an ancient cemetery at Ain al-Ghuwair, some ten miles south of Qumran, contained much broken pottery (Bar-Adon 1971: 84–87). Most likely it was originally the deceased's earthen vessels that were smashed and buried with him (Yadin 1977: 251 n. 63 = 1983: 324 n. 64). The need to break earthenware that was present in the home of the deceased is nowhere stated in Scripture, but it is implied: whereas a corpse contaminates any person inside the house for seven days, it contaminates all open (earthen) vessels permanently (Num 19:14–15; see *Sipre* Num. 126, *Tgs.*).

Clearly we have here a case of ambivalence. On the one hand, Scripture states flatly that any object touching the flesh of the purification offering contracts holiness; on the other hand, the object is treated as if it were impure: blood-spattered garments must be washed, copper vessels scoured and rinsed, and earthen vessels broken. Only one answer suggests itself: the purification offering, uniquely among the sacrifices, originally contaminated objects, including persons, by direct contact. This stemmed from clearly pagan notions that substances used in exorcising impurity were themselves charged with the same dangerous power (see HL 44b and chap. 4, COMMENT D). In response, Scripture systematically reduced the contagious power of impurity by limiting its baneful effects to human contact with sancta and to its prolongation within the community (COMMENT to 5:1–13).

A further reduction occurred when the purification offering was made subject to the formula whereby it imparted holiness to all objects but not to persons. At the same time, the purification offering still retained its power to contaminate its handlers, but this power was limited to the burnt *ḥaṭṭāʾt*, the purification offering brought for severe impurities, such as the purging of the sanctuary on Yom Kippur (16:25, 28), the preparation and use of the ashes of the Red Cow (Num 19:7–10, 19), and, by inference, the sacrifice of the burnt purification offering on behalf of the high priest and community (4:1–21)—an ambivalence retained by and confirmed in rabbinic tradition (*t. Yoma* 4:16; cf. *m. Para* 8:3).

Thus Scripture was forced to tolerate the contradictory notion that the technique of purging the sanctuary of its impurities—the purification offering—could simultaneously be a most sacred offering and a source of impurity. This polemic and self-contradictory aspect of the purification offering gave rise to the paradox of the Red Cow (see chap. 4, COMMENT G). In the matter of objects contacted by the flesh of the purification offering, the subject of this pericope, a similar paradox ensued: although the objects that came into contact with the purification offering were treated as if they were impure they were nonetheless considered to be holy. That is to say, these objects became or remained the property of the sanctuary because they were rendered holy but were dealt with as impurities: bespattered garments were washed, copper vessels were scoured and rinsed, and earthen vessels smashed and discarded (or buried).

boiled (těbuššal, buššālâ). The boiling of the meat of the purification offering must take place within the Tabernacle compound because it is eaten there. This means that the courtyard is equipped with cooking implements. This is clearly the case in the blueprints for Ezekiel's temple (Ezek 42:13; 46:19–20) and that of Qumran (11QT 37:8–15); cf. the NOTE on v 10.

shall be scoured. ûmōraq, puʿal or *qal* passive (see below on *šuṭṭap*). In the *qal, māraq* means "polish" (Jer 46:4; 2 Chr 4:16), and the Akk. cognate *marāqu* means "grind, pulverize" *(CAD)*. Tg. Ps.-J. glosses "scoured with abrasive," which is what probably motivated Shadal to comment that the disjunctive *ṭipḥâ* should have been placed under this word and not under the following word, *wěšuṭṭap,* for the copper vessel was scoured with an abrasive and not with water. Nevertheless, the MT may be justified by pragmatics: in any scouring operation, the detergent/abrasive must be mixed with water (D. Mitchell). Purification of inorganic vessels in ancient India confirms this procedure: "(they) should first be scoured with salts (ashes) and water three times and should then be cast into fire so long as it can be borne (without the vessels being broken, melted or burnt up) and then they become pure" (*Visnusmṛti*, cited in Kane 1973: 326).

According to most texts of the Mishna, this prescribed treatment of copper vessels is also unique to the purification offering (*m. Zebaḥ.* 11:4). As pointed out by Rabad and *Mishne Kesep* (on Maim., *Book of Temple Service,* Manner of Sacrifice 8:14), however, the Tosefta explicitly states that copper vessels that have come into contact with the flesh of all most sacred offerings are subject to this procedure (*t. Zebaḥ.* 10:14). Nonetheless, better manuscripts of the Mishna omit this clause, ascribing scouring and rinsing to the purification offering alone

(Albeck 1956: 359–60). Indeed, because the procedure is also typical of those employed in the elimination of impurity (Num 31:22–23), it is more likely that once again we are dealing with a unique requirement of the purification offering. A newly edited text (*MMT* B 5–8) seems to imply (in a broken section) that the Qumran covenanters held, in opposition to their contemporaries (whose view is reflected in *Sipra*, Ṣaw par. 4 on 6:21), that the copper vessel must be scoured after each use and that once used for cooking the purification offering, it may not be used for other sacrifices.

and flushed (wĕšuṭṭap). *Qal* passive (not *puʿal*, for only the *qal* is attested [e.g., 15:11], never the *piʾel*).

22. *Any male among the priests may eat of it (kol-zākār bakkōhănîm yōʾkal ʾōtāh)*. Ostensibly, this statement contradicts the previous one that only the officiating priest shall eat it (v 19). The contradiction evaporates as soon as one realizes that although the officiating priest, who manipulates the blood, does indeed receive the prebend he may, if he so desires, distribute it among his fellow priests (see Shadal on 7:10 and the NOTE on 2:10). This interpretation is supported by the extended range of the verb *ʾākal*, which means not only "eat" but also "enjoy, benefit" (e.g., Ps 128:2; Qoh 5:18; Wessely 1846).

The alternative possibility must also be entertained that the conflicting verses represent two variant traditions: the small sanctuary with its single priest (v 19) and the Jerusalem Temple with its priestly cadre (v 22). This supposition also explains a similar difference between the priestly recipients of the raw and cooked cereal offerings (NOTE on 7:9) and the breast and right thigh of the well-being offering (NOTE on 7:32–33, and see the Introduction, §C).

Ibn Ezra claims that "any male" would only exclude a minor, one under thirteen years of age. But this age limit is rabbinic in origin (see *Sipre* Mattot 153; *ʾAbot R. Nat.* A 16; *m. ʾAbot* 5:24), not biblical. The qualification "of the priests" would seem to indicate that consecrated priests are being referred to, namely, those already officiating in the cult and, hence, present in the sanctuary court when the prebends from this and other most sacred offerings are distributed.

it is most sacred (qōdeš qodāšîm hîʾ [hwʾ]). This status for the purification offering has already been given (v 18). It needs be repeated here to explain why its consumption is limited to male priests (Ibn Ezra). The same rationale is provided for consigning the reparation offering to male priests (7:6).

23. *No purification offering, however, may be eaten from which any blood is brought into the Tent of Meeting (wĕkol-ḥaṭṭāʾt ʾăšer yûbāʾ middāmāh ʾel-ʾōhel môʿēd)*. These purification offerings are the bull of the high priest (4:1–12), the bull of the community (4:13–21), and the bull of the high priest and he-goat of the community on Yom Kippur (16:27). The rabbis add the he-goat of the community (Num 15:22–26), which, in their view, is brought for the sin of idolatry (*m. Hor.* 1:4; *Sipre* Shelaḥ 112; *Sipra*, Ḥobah 6:10). Some commentators feel that this rule applies only to the previously mentioned purification

offerings (4:1–21; Ibn Ezra, Ramban), but its generalized formulation argues for greater comprehensiveness.

This rule also explains Moses' rebuke of Aaron for not eating the purification-offering goat sacrificed on the day the regular Tabernacle cult was initiated (10:17): even though the goat was brought by the community—in a previously cited case the community's purification offering was not eaten but was incinerated (4:13–21)—because its blood was daubed on the outer altar and not taken inside the Tent (9:9 [see the NOTE], 15), it should have been eaten by the priests.

in the shrine (baqqōdeš). The protean term *qōdeš* means "holy place" and can thus refer to all or part of the Tabernacle compound. Ibn Ezra suggests that it is used in relative comparisons: the Tabernacle enclosure is sacred *(qōdeš)* in relation to the camp, the shrine in relation to the court, and the adytum in relation to the shrine. Yet the fluidity of this term is more apparent than real. In P, when *qōdeš* refers to a place, it stands for the shrine in contrast to the *qōdeš qodāšîm*, the adytum (e.g., Exod 26:33), or the area in the court between the altar and the Tent (10:4, 17, 18), or both (Exod 28:43; for details, see the NOTE on "from the front of the sacred area," 10:4). True, *qōdeš* in chap. 16 refers only to the adytum (16:2, 3, 16, 17, 20, 23, 27). It will be argued, however, that this chapter stems from a discrete source that was only subsequently incorporated into P (see the NOTE on 16:2 and chap. 16, COMMENT A). As for *bimqôm haqqōdeš* (10:17) and *baqqōdeš* (10:18), they are equivalent to *bĕmāqôm qādōš*, referring to a holy (adj.) place inside the Tabernacle court (see the NOTES on vv 9, 19). Alternatively, *baqqōdeš* (10:18) may be vocalized as *bĕqōdeš* 'in a sacred state', analogous to *bĕqōdeš qodāšîm* 'in a most sacred state' (Num 18:10; see the NOTE on 10:18). In any event, the place *qōdeš*, here and elsewhere in P, means "shrine" (see further the NOTE on 16:27).

7:1. *This is the ritual for the reparation offering (zō't tôrat hā'āšām)*. This introduction is original; so is that of the well-being offering (v 11), whereas the longer introductions in these two chapters (6:12, 17–18aα; 7:22, 28–29a) stem from the hands of a later editor (see the NOTE on 6:12).

it is most sacred. The designation *qōdeš qodāšîm hû'* appears twice in connection with the reparation offering, as it does in the pericope of the purification offering (6:18, 22), and the contexts of both occurrences are identical. The first occurrence is associated with the place of slaughter, whose word order, however, differs from that of the purification offering. Whereas in the latter, the status follows the slaughter (6:18), here it precedes. The reason for the switch may be in order to juxtapose the slaughter of the reparation animal and the dashing of its blood, precisely as is found with the burnt offering (1:5; *Seper Hamibḥar*).

2–5. The sacrificial procedure for the reparation offering is described in these four verses for the first time. Why was it omitted from the prescriptions for the reparation offering in 5:14–26? The reparation offering is "a ram without blemish from the flock, convertible *(bĕ'erkĕkā)* into payment in silver" (5:15).

The term *bĕ'erkĕkā* literally means "according to your valuation." The final *kap* is probably "a pronominal suffix that became fossilized and thus absorbed in the nominal stem," yielding the translation, " 'your valuation' . . . became through common usage simply 'valuation' (by an outside party), with the pronoun inactivated and absorbed" (Speiser 1960: 30–31). For the evidence of the commutability of animal fines in the ancient Near East, see the NOTE on 5:15. Even so, the possibility must be reckoned with that *bĕ'erkĕkā* implies not a choice of animal or payment (which would be denoted by an initial *kap, kĕ'er-kĕkā*, as in 27:12, 17) but, as indicated by the preposition *b*, it means only by payment. This certainly is its connotation in 27:2, 27 and Num 18:16, where money alone is acceptable. The absence of this term in the prescription for the reparation offering of the *mĕṣōrā'* (14:12–14, 24–25) would also be explained, for the *tĕnûpâ* ritual mandates the presence of the *'āšām* animal and precludes its monetary equivalent. Thus *bĕ'erkĕkā*, mentioned thrice in the reparation offering pericope (5:15, 18, 25) and the exclusive mention of *'āšām* silver in 2 Kgs 12:17 may very well imply that the offerer only brings to the sanctuary the monetary equivalent of the reparation offering. This provision, unique to the reparation offering, is readily understandable on the basis of the fact that the word *'āšām* quintessentially deals with payment for damages; it is a mulct imposed on the person for damage done to sancta (for greater detail, see 5:14–26, COMMENTS A and B). The omission of the hand-leaning requirement is further evidence that the offerer who, in every other case of an animal sacrifice, must perform this rite, in the case of the reparation offering does not bring an animal but instead its monetary equivalent (for details, see the NOTE on 1:4).

If it is indeed the case that the one liable for a reparation offering was expected to bring its monetary equivalent to the sanctuary, it should occasion no surprise that the procedure for the sacrifice of the reparation offering should be given here in the administrative unit addressed to the priests (chaps. 6–7) rather than in the didactic order addressed to the laity (chaps. 1–5; see the NOTE on 6:2). Once the lay offerer purchases the requisite *'āšām* animal from the priest, the latter makes certain that the proper sacrificial procedure is followed.

shall be slaughtered . . . is slaughtered. yišḥāṭû . . . yišḥāṭû, lit., "they shall slaughter . . . they shall slaughter." These plurals stand out in sharp contrast to the singular that follows, *yizrōq* 'he shall dash', whose subject can only be the priest. The anonymity of the subject of this latter verb contrasts with the subject in all of its previous occurrences, where the priest is always specified (1:5, 11; 3:2, 8, 13). By contrast, the verb for slaughtering, *šāḥaṭ*, is previously attested only in the singular, and its subject is always unnamed (1:5, 11; 3:2, 8, 13; 4:15, 24, 29, 33). Thus the differing forms of the verbs *zāraq* and *šāḥaṭ* in this verse by contrast to the forms found in chaps. 1–5 demonstrate in the clearest possible manner that chaps. 1–5 are directed to the laity whereas 6:1–7:7 (except for vv 3–4, see below) are intended for the priests.

3–4. Clearly, these two verses have been copied without change from the procedure for the well-being offering (see 3:3–4, 9–10, 14–15). That this section is secondary is proved by the inappropriateness of the singular verbs, which, because their subject is the layman, should have been voiced in the plural, as *yišḥāṭû* in v 2.

3. *shall be presented. yaqrîb* can also mean "offer, sacrifice" (where the subject is the priest (e.g., 1:5; 5:8; 6:14; 7:8). Here, however, context and form dictate that the subject is the layman (see above).

the broad tail (hāʾalyâ). Its inclusion as suet is proof that the *ʾāšām* animal is limited to sheep (see the NOTE on 3:9).

the entrails (haqqereb). The LXX and Sam. add *wĕʾet kol-haḥēleb ʾăšer ʿal-haqqereb* 'and all of the suet that is around the entrails', as in 3:9. The omission in the MT is a parade example of a homoioteleuton.

6. For the exegesis of this verse, see the NOTES on 6:22.

7. *The reparation offering is like the purification offering. There is a single rule for both (kaḥaṭṭāʾt kāʾāšām tôrâ ʾaḥat lāhem).* This statement applies to what follows: the priest who will receive the sacrificial portion (Rashi). The words *tôrâ ʾaḥat* 'there is a single rule' imply no generalization but refer to the immediate context (Milgrom 1976f: 15 n. 48). Alternatively, the entire ritual may be meant, with the exception of the blood manipulation (Rodriguez 1979: 60).

The mention of the purification offering presumes a knowledge of its pericope (6:17–23), another indication that chaps. 6–7, minus the long introductions and the two interpolations (6:12–16; 7:22–27) originally comprised a single, organic unit (see the NOTE on 6:2).

(it shall belong to the priest who) performs expiation (yĕkappēr). The meaning of "purge" for *kippēr* is limited to the purification offering (chap. 4, COMMENTS A and B); for the reparation, burnt, and cereal offerings, it takes on the general connotation "expiate" (see the NOTE on 1:4 and chap. 16, COMMENT F). According to Num 5:8, the officiating priest would also be entitled to the monetary reparation owed to the person from whom it was embezzled if the latter subsequently died, leaving no heirs. Perhaps for this reason the verses that follow (Num 5:9–10) stress the right of the offerer to give his dedicatory offerings to the priest of his choice.

8–10. The priestly perquisites from the burnt and cereal offerings need to be itemized because they were not mentioned in their respective pericopes. Nothing was stated concerning the disposition of the hide of the burnt offering in 6:1–6 or concerning the priestly portion of the cereal offering (limited to the raw form mixed with oil) in 6:8. This notice is appended here because of its contextual similarity with the previous verse (v 7), which speaks of the disposition of the reparation and purification offerings. It could also have been inserted in the prescriptions for the priestly prebends from the well-being offering (vv 28–34). That this was not done may be due to a deliberate decision by the redactor to keep the most sacred offerings (the burnt, cereal, purification, and reparation offerings) apart from the sacred ones (the well-being and ordination offerings).

8. *a person's burnt offering.* *ʿōlat ʾîš*, that is, the layman. This specification is needed to exclude the priest's own offering, in which case the entire animal would be burned, including the hide (Ehrlich 1908–14), just as in the case of the priest's cereal offering (6:15).

the hide (hāʿôr). It was a handsome prebend, considering the great number of private burnt offerings that were sacrificed each day (Philo, 1 *Laws* 151). What of the hides from other animal sacrifices? Clearly, the hide of the well-being offering belonged to the offerer, for the entire animal belonged to him. As for the hides of the purification and reparation offerings, Scripture is silent. The rabbis, however, deduce that they are given to the priests by *a fortiori* logic: "If in the burnt offering, to whose flesh they have no right, they yet have the right to the hide, how much more, therefore, in the most sacred offerings, to whose flesh they have right, have they the right to their hide!" (*m. Zebaḥ.* 12:3). Of interest is the insertion of this provision by the Qumran sectaries into their prescription for the *Tāmîd* (11QT 13:13–14; cf. Exod 29:38–42) for the logical reason that Exod 29 contains the first mention of the burnt offering in the Torah.

On the disposition of sacrificial hides in the ancient Near East, the evidence is scanty and inconsistent. Hides of Punic sacrifices were awarded at times to priests and offerers (*CIS* 167.2–5; 165; *ANET*[3] 502–3); at Sippar in Babylon, to priests (RS 435); also at Qaiyam, a Palestinian shrine (Canaan 1926: 43). Hides of Greek sacrifices belonged to the sanctuary or the priests (Burkert 1985: 57).

shall keep. lakkōhēn lô yihyeh, lit., "to that priest, to him it shall belong." The specification "to that priest" is required here because of the uncertainty of the referent "to him."

that he sacrificed. ʾăšer hiqrîb, in other words, offered up on the altar (1:9). The Sam. reads *hiqrîbû* (plural), implying that the subject is the laymen (cf. *yišḥăṭu*, v 2) and that its meaning is "present" (as in 1:2; 3:1). The MT is preferable, however; otherwise, the designation "to him" would be inexplicable (see above).

9. *baked in an oven. tēʾāpeh battannûr;* see 2:4.

in a pan. bammarḥešet; see 2:7.

or on a griddle. wĕʿal-maḥăbat; see 2:5–6.

shall belong to the priest who offers it (lakkōhēn hammaqrîb ʾōtāh lô tihyeh). This constitutes an innovation and an ostensible contradiction to 2:10, which assigns the cooked cereal offering to all of the priests. As already noted, a similar contradiction prevails in the purification-offering pericope: the meat of the sacrifice is eaten by both the officiant and the entire priestly cadre (6:19a, 22). All it means, however, is that the officiant has the right to distribute his prebend among his fellow priests. A similar problem and solution will again obtain in the

pericope on the well-being offering: its right thigh is awarded to both the officiant and all of the priests (vv 33–34). A practical consideration may be involved:
"It was in the interest of priests to share their prebends, since that way they
would reduce the extremes in which some might get a lot and others a little, or
some better portions and others worse portions . . . comparable to arrange-
ments among waiters to share their tips" (Freedman, written communication).

The reason for this distinction among the priestly recipients is nowhere
stated. I submit that the same historical development noted for the right thigh
and breast of the well-being offering (COMMENT F below; Milgrom 1983d: 167
n. 29) probably prevailed for the cooked and raw cereal offerings: the former is
the older tradition, stemming from the local sanctuary staffed by a single priest,
whereas the latter represents the later Temple, which housed a large priestly
staff. That the cooked cereal offering represents the more common form is
demonstrated by all attestations of the cereal offering except those of the Temple. The sanctuary at Bethel is the recipient of bread loaves (1 Sam 10:3). The
only sacred cereal offering in the sanctuary of Nob is the bread of Presence
(1 Sam 21:5, 7). Even cereal offerings prepared for a pagan deity (Ishtar) take
the form of kawwānîm cakes (Jer 7:18; 44:19). The latter should not surprise us;
the altar of the gods is a dining table, not a kitchen. Indeed, everywhere we turn
for the cultic practices of the ancient Near East we find cereal offerings in the
form of bread, not flour (e.g., Mesopotamia: ANET³ 335a, 343 [note: flour is
also offered, but only for incense, 338b; and magic, 336a]; Hattia: ANET³ 360–
61; Egypt: Sauneron 1960: 84). Only Jer 17:26 and 41:5, which speak of a
minḥâ, may refer to raw flour because it is accompanied by frankincense. Both,
however, were offered at the Temple site.

10. mixed with oil. Assumed is that this cereal offering is composed of sōlet,
raw semolina (2:3). The offering cannot refer to adjunct cereal offerings because
the latter were entirely consumed on the altar (see the NOTE on 6:7).

or dry (waḥărēbâ). A reference to the indigent's graduated purification offering (5:11–13). One other cereal offering is recorded as having been offered dry,
that of the suspected adulteress (Num 5:15). In both instances the absence of oil
(and frankincense) needs to be explained (see the NOTE on 5:11).

the sons of Aaron alike. In agreement with 2:3.

11. This is the ritual for (zōʾt tôrat). The section introduced by this formula
was part of the original form of chaps. 6–7; see the NOTE on 6:12.

the sacrifice of well-being. zebaḥ haššĕlāmîm, lit., "a slain offering of the
šĕlāmîm variety" (see the COMMENT to chap. 3). Three kinds of šĕlāmîm are
herewith prescribed. But why were they not cited in chap. 3? An obvious answer
is that the priestly prebends for the sacrifice are detailed here (vv 14, 31–35) in
like manner to the other sacrifices (6:9–11, 19, 22; 7:6–10). Another reason may
be the constant need for priestly supervision. For example, one type of bread
accompanying the thank offering is leavened (v 13). Heaven forbid that it become mixed with the unleavened bread and offered upon the altar (see 2:11)!

Furthermore, this is the only sacrifice whose meat is eaten by lay persons, and their negligence may lead to its desecration or contamination (vv 15–21). Hence, the priests must keep a watchful eye over the proceedings. But this pericope tacitly (vv 11–21), and the following ones expressly (vv 22–23, 28–29), are addressed to the laity, not the priests (see the NOTE on 6:2), an indication that the supervisory responsibility has shifted from the priests to the laity. The reasons for this development are explored in the NOTE on v 15. For the rendering "well-being" for šĕlāmîm, see the COMMENT on chap. 3.

that one may offer to the Lord. The phrase ʾăšer yaqrîb laYHWH is an admission that it is permitted to eat the meat of pure, nonsacrificial animals, for example, blemished animals (22:21–25) and game (17:13–14), as well as sacrificial animals slaughtered profanely for their meat. Note the absence of this phrase in sections dealing with the other sacrifices (6:2, 17, 18; 7:1). In 6:12 this phrase is modified by another factor: "from the time of his anointing." The fact that this phrase excludes pure, nonsacrificial animals is clear evidence that the purpose of this sacrifice is to provide meat for the table. This conclusion is confirmed by the similar expression below—"flesh from the *Lord's* sacrifice of well-being" (v 20), that is, meat is also permitted that is not assigned to the Lord —profanely slaughtered sacrificial animals (for details, see the Introduction, §C).

12. *for.* ʿal (with Rashi), that is to say, for the purpose of, a rare usage in P (e.g., Num 6:21; cf. Jer 4:28; Amos 1:14).

thanksgiving (tôdâ). The noun here is not the name of the sacrifice (contrast zebaḥ tôdâ, v 12aβ; 22:29) but an indication of its purpose. According to the rabbis (*b. Ber.* 54b) there are four occasions of escape from danger (based on Ps 107:22) that require this offering (for details, see the COMMENT on chap. 3). The fact that one pays *(šillēm)* a thanksgiving offering as one "pays" a votive offering (Ps 116:18; Prov 7:14) shows that it expresses gratitude for a concrete act of divine grace. Philo, however, suggests that this sacrifice is offered by one "who has never at all met with any untoward happening" (*Laws* 1. 224). In the Temple, the thanksgiving offering may have been accompanied by appropriate song (Pss 42:5; 95:2; 100:1; Jonah 2:10).

together. ʿal, a frequently attested meaning of this preposition in P (e.g., vv 13, 30; 2:2, 16; 3:4, 10, 15; 4:11).

the sacrifice of thanksgiving. The original name of this sacrifice before it was subsumed in P under the šĕlāmîm (see the NOTE on v 13). Yet the tradition that the zebaḥ tôdâ is an independent offering which must be distinguished from the zebaḥ šĕlāmîm is firmly anchored in all sources but P (e.g., 22:21, 29 [H, not P]; Jer 17:26; 2 Chr 29:31–33; 33:16) and even in rabbinic sources (*m. Zebaḥ.* 5:6–7; cf. 1 Macc 4:54–56). The uniqueness of the thanksgiving offering is extolled by the rabbis when they claim that it is "never brought for sin" (*Midr. Lev. Rab.* 9:1) and that "in the world to come all sacrifices will be annulled, but that of thanksgiving will not be annulled, and all prayers will be annulled, but (that of) thanksgiving will not be annulled" (*Midr. Lev. Rab.* 9:7).

cakes. Four types of breads are required. But their number is not given—nor need it be fixed—because they will be eaten by the offerer. The only stipulation is that one of each kind should be given to the officiating priest. The same holds true for the breads required for the Nazirite's well-being offering (NOTE on 6:19–20) and the priests' ordination offering (8:26–28), though in the latter case the breads are burned on the altar (see below). The rabbis, however, stipulate the number of loaves, ten of each kind for a total of forty (*m. Menaḥ.* 7:1), thereby providing the officiating priest with a tithe. The Karaites object to this stipulation on the grounds that no one could eat so much bread in a single meal. But they overlook the social parameters of the thanksgiving offering: it is the occasion for a feast that, in addition to family, most likely has many invited guests (Abravanel).

The resemblance of the thanksgiving offering to the offerings of the Nazirite and the priestly consecrands is hardly accidental. P itself declares the priestly ordination offering to be the archetype of all subsequent well-being offerings (Exod 29:25–28) in that the right thigh and breast are designated as priestly prebends (vv 3–35, below). But the thanksgiving offering bears an even closer parallel to the ordination offering in that both require three kinds of unleavened bread (Exod 29:2; Lev 8:1; the Nazirite's offering requires two kinds, Num 6:15), from which one of each kind is set aside for the officiating priest (v 14; Num 6:19–20) or, in the case of the ordination offering, for the altar (8:26–28). In the latter case, the consecrands are not yet priests; their status is that of laymen, ineligible for sacrificial prebends; hence the breads normally assigned to the priests are burned on the altar (see the NOTE on 8:33). Nonetheless, all three sacrifices are alike in prescribing that the remainder of the breads is eaten by the offerers (8:31) before the next morning (v 15; 8:32; *m. Zebaḥ.* 5:5). One major difference obtains in regard to the breads: the thanksgiving offering requires a fourth type: a leavened cake (v 13). Why this requirement is not imposed for the ordination offering is clear: being leavened, it may not be offered on the altar (2:11). Its omission from the Nazirite's offering is less clear. But one should take notice of this offering's inferior rating in comparison with the other two. It is not called by a special name: it is just a well-being offering (Num 6:14, 17, 18), and it requires two, not three, types of unleavened breads (Num 6:15). In fact, it probably represents the early form of the well-being offering (see the NOTE on v 15), whereas the ordination and thanksgiving offerings achieved a more elevated status.

13. *This offering.* qorbānô, lit., "his offering"; the referent is the unleavened breads (v 12).

cakes of leavened bread (leḥem ḥāmēṣ). Though not permitted on the altar, it is still considered an offering (cf. v 14a; 23:17–20; cf. Amos 4:5). "All cereal offerings were offered unleavened, excepting the leavened [cakes prescribed] for the thanksgiving offering and the two loaves (Lev 23:17) that were offered leavened" (m. Menaḥ. 5:1).

thanksgiving sacrifice of well-being. The hybrid construction *zebaḥ tôdat šĕlāmāyw* is a conflation of two sacrifices, the *zebaḥ tôdâ* (v 12) and the *zebaḥ šĕlāmîm* (v 11). P alone has subsumed the *tôdâ* under the *šĕlāmîm,* resulting in this artificial and awkward construction (see the NOTE on "cakes," v 12, above) whereas H treats them as discrete (22:21, 29).

14. *Out of this.* *mimmennû,* namely, the collection of breads.

offering (qorbān). Proof that the leavened bread, even though it is ineligible for the altar, is still considered an offering.

contribution (tĕrûmâ). The following things are called *tĕrûmâ:* the right hind thighs of the priestly ordination offering and well-being offering (Exod 29:27–28; Lev 7:32, 34; 10:14–15; Num 6:20), the materials for the building of the Tabernacle (Exod 25:2–3; 35:5, 21, 24; 36:3, 6), the census silver (Exod 30:13–15), the breads of the thanksgiving offering (7:12–14), the first yield of baked bread (Num 15:19–20), the tithe and its tithe (Num 18:24–29), the portion of the war spoils assigned to the sanctuary (Num 31:29, 41, 52), sacred gifts in general (Num 5:9; 18:8), and gifts of lesser sanctity in particular (22:12; Num 18:11–19). Ezekiel adds to this list land allotted to the priests and Levites (Ezek 45:1; 48:8–21) and the sacrificial ingredients levied on the people (Ezek 45:13, 16).

The tannaitic interpretation that *tĕrûmâ* is a ritual whereby the offering is subjected to a vertical motion (cf. *m. Menaḥ.* 5:6) is responsible for the accepted rendering "heave offering." This rendering, however, is questionable, for in the cultic texts of P, the verb *hērîm,* used exclusively with the preposition *min* and with the synonyms *hēsîr* 'remove' (e.g., 4:8–10, 31, 35) and *nibdāl* 'be separated' (Num 16:21; 17:10), never means "raise, lift," but only "set apart, dedicate." Consequently, the noun *tĕrûmâ* can refer only to that which is set apart or dedicated and, hence, must be rendered "dedication, contribution." This rendering is confirmed by *Tg. 'aprāšûtā',* LXX 'αφαιρεμα, Akk. *tarīmtu* (an exact cognate) and *rīmūtu* from the root *rêmu* 'give a gift' (details in Milgrom 1983d: 171–72), and Ug. (exact cognate) *trmt* (*CTA* 33[UTS].3; Dietrich et al. 1975a).

The function of the *tĕrûmâ* is to transfer the object from its owner to the deity. In this respect it is similar to the *tĕnûpâ* (v 30; see COMMENT E below), but with this crucial distinction: the *tĕnûpâ* is performed *lipnê YHWH* 'before the Lord', whereas the *tĕrûmâ* is never "before" but always "to the Lord," *laYHWH.* Thus the *tĕnûpâ* and *tĕrûmâ* comprise two means of dedication to the Lord: the former by a ritual in the sanctuary, and the latter by a ritualless dedication outside the sanctuary, either by the offerer's oral declaration (e.g., Judg 17:3), after which he brings the contribution to the sanctuary (e.g., Exod 35:24; Num 18:13), or by physically handing it directly to the priest (e.g., the right thigh, 7:32; the dough, Num 15:17–21; the tithe, Num 18:24; the tithe of the tithe, Num 18:26, 28; sacred gifts in general, 22:13, 18; Num 5:9–10). This distinction serves to resolve the alleged ambiguities resulting from the same object undergoing both *tĕnûpâ* and *tĕrûmâ* (e.g., Exod 29:22–24; 35:24; cf. 38:24), a distinction that can be formulated into this rule: every *tĕnûpâ* (ritual) is preceded by being set apart, dedicated as a contribution to the sanctuary (*tĕrûmâ;* details in Milgrom 1983d: 159–63). The *tĕrûmâ* of the right thigh (v 32) constitutes a special problem (see COMMENT F below).

The implication of this analysis of the *tĕrûmâ* for the contribution of the breads to the Lord is that their dedication or setting aside takes place outside the sanctuary, probably already in the home in which the cakes are prepared. The law here then states that the *tĕrûmâ*, the dedicated breads, are assigned to the officiating priest, one of whom, as another text explicates, will be chosen by the offerer (Num 5:9–10).

the priest who dashes the blood of the well-being offering (hakkōhēn hazzōrēq ʾet-dam haššĕlāmîm). The centrality of the blood ritual is clearly indicated by it being the rite that determines the recipient of the priestly prebends. Its uniqueness among the sacrifices is thrown into clear relief by comparing it with the priestly recipients of the other sacrificial prebends:

burnt offering	*wĕhakkōhēn hammaqrîb* (7:8)
cereal offering	*lakkōhēn hammaqrîb* (7:9)
purification and reparation offerings	*hakkōhēn ʾăšer yĕkappēr* (7:7)
well-being offering	*lakkōhēn hazzōrēq et-dam* (7:14)

The fact that the text here omits the *tôdâ* altogether and uses solely the expression *šĕlāmîm* is no accident; its intention is to apply this rule to every kind of well-being offering (see v 16). That the blood dashing of the *šĕlāmîm* constitutes its quintessential rite is also underscored in other passages: (1) "the one from among Aaron's sons who offers the blood of the well-being offering" (7:33) is a repetition and affirmation of this verse. (2) "He offered *(wayyaqṭēr)* his burnt offering and cereal offering: he poured *(wayyassēk)* his libation, and he dashed the blood *(wayyizrōq)* of his well-being offering against the altar" (2 Kgs 16:13) once again indicates that the quintessential rite in the well-being offering is its blood manipulation. (3) "These are the directions for the altar on the day it is erected, so that burnt offerings may be burnt *(lĕhaʿălōt)* on it and blood dashed against it" (Ezek 43:18). That the blood rite does not refer to the previously mentioned burnt offering but to the well-being offering is clarified by the final verse of this pericope: "from the eighth day onwards the priests shall offer your burnt offerings and your well-being offerings on the altar" (v 27). Indeed, that the text need but say *zāraq dam* 'dash blood', while the well-being offering is only implied, indicates the extent to which this expression became an accepted synecdoche for the sacrifice.

Yet the more basic question needs be asked: Why is the blood rite so essential to the well-being offering? The same rite is prescribed for the burnt offering: it too requires that its blood be dashed *(zāraq)* against the altar (e.g., 1:5, 11); yet not once is this fact singled out, as is the blood rite of the well-being offering. This question is partially dealt with in chap. 11, COMMENT C but will be discussed at length in the COMMENT to chap. 17. Only a summary of the argument can be given here.

The key to the answer resides in 17:11, which translates as follows: "for the life of the flesh is in the blood and I have assigned it to you upon the altar to ransom *(kpr)* your lives, for it is the blood that ransoms by means of life." It can be demonstrated that the context of this verse is concerned exclusively with the well-being offering. First of all, 17:10–14 constitutes a bipartite law, the second referring to game "that may be eaten" (v 13), the first to edible domesticated species (see 17:3). The same chapter rules that domesticated, pure animals must be sacrificed at the authorized altar before they may be eaten (vv 3–5). Also, the prohibition against *eating* blood (repeated five times in vv 10–14) implies that the blood is ingested while eating meat. This prohibition occurs elsewhere in connection with eating meat (Deut 12:15–16, 23–25; 15:23) and nowhere else. Thus 17:11 refers to the well-being offering, the only sacrifice eaten by the offerer. Yet this nonexpiatory sacrifice bears in this context a strictly expiatory *(kpr)* function! Moreover, the expression *lĕkappēr 'al nepeš* 'to ransom life' implies that a capital crime has been committed (see Exod 30:12–16; Num 31:50), yet it is expiated by sacrifice! This double paradox is resolved by 17:3–4: if one does not slaughter his animal at the altar, "bloodguilt shall be imputed to that man; he has shed blood." The animal slayer is a murderer unless he offers its blood on the altar to ransom his life (v 11). To be sure, chap. 17 stems from the pen of H; however, in the matter of the blood prohibition and its premise of the inviolability of life H has been anticipated by P (see the Introduction, §C).

This doctrine is related to the Priestly account of Creation, whereby the human race was meant to be vegetarian (Gen 1:29). Beginning with Noah, God concedes to man's carnivorous desires, providing he abstains from ingesting the blood (Gen 9:3–4). Thus all persons are enjoined to avoid the lifeblood of the animal by draining it and thereby returning it to its Creator (Gen 9:3–4; Lev 17:13–14). Israel, as part of its discipline to achieve holiness (19:2; 20:26), must observe an additional safeguard: the blood of sacrificial animals must be drained on the authorized altar, thereby ransoming the life of the animal's slayer (17:11).

No wonder, then, that the blood rite of the well-being offering is its main and indispensable element. The offerer has slain the animal for selfish reasons: he wants meat and will kill to get it. Absolution for this crime is available only if the non-Israelite abstains from the blood and if the Israelite, in addition, has the blood dashed on the altar as a ransom for his life.

15. *on the day that it is offered.* *bĕyôm qorbānô* is equivalent to *bĕyôm haqrîbô* (v 16), correctly rendered by *Tg. Neof.* as *bĕyômā' dĕyaqrîb qorbānēh* (cf. LXX). Thus *qorbān* here is a verbal noun. The fact that the day extends to the following morning indicates clearly that the biblical day began and ended

with sunrise (see the NOTE on v 17). The rabbis impose the restriction that the sacrifice should be eaten by midnight to prevent accidental transgression (*m. Ber.* 1:1; *m. Zebaḥ.* 6:1). The Dead Sea covenanters, however, insist that the Torah requires that the sacrifice be eaten earlier, by sundown (*MMT* B 9–13; 11QT 20:13). They base their ruling on the verse *bĕyôm . . . wĕlōʾ-tābôʾ ʿālāyw haššemeš* 'on the same day . . . before the sun sets' (Deut 25:15), presumably allowing a grace period until dawn to dispose of the remains.

none of it shall be put aside until morning (lōʾ-yanniaḥ mimmennû ʿad-bōqer). There are two forms for the *hiphʿil* of *nwḥ*, *hēniaḥ* 'satisfy, give rest' and *hinniaḥ* 'put down, deposit'. The development of the latter form is still unaccounted for. Another II-*waw/yod* verb that exhibits two *hiphʿil* forms is *hēsît/ hissît* 'incite'. The verb *swg* only exhibits the latter, *hiphʿil hissîg*. This anomalous form can be explained by the elongating tendency of sibilants. Thus I-*yod*, *ṣade* verbs experience a quantitative metathesis in *qal* (and *hophʿal*): the elongation of the *yod* passes on to the *ṣade*, **yîṣat > yiṣṣat*, a phenomenon that is passed on to other patterns such as the *niphʿal niṣṣat* and *hiphʿil yaṣṣîaʿ*. But this phenomenon will not explain the form *hinniaḥ*, whose initial radical is not a sibilant. Joüon (1923: §80p) suggests that it imitated the form of its synonym *nātan (yanniaḥ ‖ yittēn)*. Alternatively, it may be "due to the influence of *Pe-nun* verbs" (Freedman, privately).

Although this injunction is directed to the flesh of the thanksgiving offering, it undoubtedly also includes the accompanying breads. This can be deduced from the breads accompanying the priestly ordination offering, which are expressly to be burned with the sacrificial meat once the time limit has expired (8:32). Also, there is no explicit rule concerning the priestly prebends of the most sacred offerings (i.e., the cereal, purification, and reparation offerings) that they must be eliminated by the following morning. But it would follow *a fortiori* from the thanksgiving offering, which is of lesser sanctity (*m. Zebaḥ.* 5:3; Philo, *Laws* 1. 240; Jos., *Ant.* 3.231). It can also be deduced from 10:19: Aaron could not postpone eating the purification offering until the following day (Hoffmann 1953: 48).

The pericope on the thanksgiving offering makes an assumption that warrants some comment. The fact that it is addressed to the offerer and not to the priests (despite its inclusion in instructions to the priests; see the NOTE on 6:2) means that the offerer himself is responsible for seeing to it that the sacrificial meat does not remain beyond the following morning. This can only mean that the offerer ate (and probably cooked) the meat outside the sanctuary. This deduction is further strengthened by the subsequent section on the *šĕlāmîm*, which not only speaks of a two-day limit for eating its meat (vv 16–17), but also warns against its contact with impurity (v 19), an occurrence that would be precluded in the sanctuary. Yet it can be shown that originally, at least at the local *bāmâ*-sanctuary, the meat for the well-being offering was cooked and eaten inside the sanctuary precincts. This is preserved by the law of the Nazirite (Num

6:18-19), by the actual practice at the Shiloh sanctuary (1 Sam 2:13-14), by Ezekiel's blueprint for the future Temple (Ezek 46:24), and by archaeological findings (details in the NOTE on "in a pure place," 10:14). P opposes this practice and polemicizes against it: any "pure place" will do, though it is clear that the older practice survived, at least partially, in the later rabbinic insistence that the well-being offering be eaten inside the city walls of Jerusalem (m. Pesaḥ. 3:8; 7:8, 9; m. Meg. 1:11; m. Zebaḥ. 5:6-8; m. Kelim 1:8).

Still, the possibility must be entertained that the thanksgiving pericope, as preserved in the MT (vv 11-15), actually reflects the older practice. One cannot but notice that the prohibitions against piggûl and impurity, which are spelled out in detail for the two-day šĕlāmîm (vv 17-21), are absent in toto from the thanksgiving offering instructions. This omission would only make sense if the offering were eaten in the sacred precinct. The requirement that the meat would have to be consumed or otherwise eliminated by morning could be expeditiously supervised by the priests; they were wont to rise before dawn (cf. m. Tāmîd 1:2), and a brief inspection of the premises would quickly reveal potential violations. Besides, there was always a night watch of both priests and Levites (m. Tāmîd 1:1; m. Mid. 1:1; Milgrom 1970a: 8-16, 46-59). Perhaps, originally, the thanksgiving offering was treated in part like a most sacred offering, which was both eaten the same day *and* eaten within the sacred precinct. Its resemblance to the priestly ordination offering also suggests this conclusion (see the NOTE on "cakes," v 12). The wording of the pericope may, then, reflect this more ancient tradition (presumably, that of Shiloh: see the Introduction §C). But the fact that it was assimilated and subordinated to the šĕlāmîm (as shown by its awkwardly conflated title zebaḥ tôdat šĕlāmîm, vv 13, 15; cf. the NOTE on v 13), indicates that it was also made subject to its rules after being incorporated into the praxis of the Jerusalem Temple.

16. *he offers.* qorbānô is a verbal noun, as in the previous verse.

votive . . . offering (neder). The votive offering is brought following the successful fulfillment of a vow. That is, a well-being offering is vowed to God if a prayer is answered. The bringing of the sacrifice is termed šillēm neder 'pay/ fulfill a vow'. Thus Absalom says to David, "let me go to Hebron and fulfill the vow that I made (waʾăšallēm ʾet-nidrî ʾăšer-nādartî) to the Lord. For your servant made a vow when I lived in Geshur of Aram: if the Lord ever brings me back to Jerusalem, I will worship the Lord [in Hebron, LXX]" (2 Sam 15:7b-8). Or "I am obligated to sacrifice a well-being offering, for today I have fulfilled my vows (šillamtî nĕdārāy)" (Prov 7:14; cf. Isa 19:21; Nah 2:1; Pss 22:6; 50:14; 61:6, 9; 65:2; 66:13; 116:14, 18; Job 22:27).

freewill offering (nĕdābâ). The common denominator of all motivations in bringing a šĕlāmîm is rejoicing, for example, "you shall sacrifice the šĕlāmîm and eat them, rejoicing before the Lord your God" (Deut 27:7). Therefore, purely on logical grounds, the nĕdābâ, the freewill offering, would be the most frequently sacrificed, for it is the spontaneous by-product of one's happiness whatever its cause. It is thus not surprising to find *nĕdābâ* as a surrogate for *šĕlāmîm* (Num 15:3, 8). Ezekiel's *nāśî'* is expected, when making a private sacrifice, to bring a freewill offering (Ezek 46:12). It was also a prominent factor in the sacrificial systems of other peoples, to judge by this citation from ancient Mesopotamia: "present your freewill offerings (*šagigurû-ka*, lit., "your heart's desire") to your God" (Lambert 1960: 105, line 137; cf. 109, line 12 and 316n.). The rabbis distinguish between the two offerings as follows: "when are they votive offerings? When he says, 'I pledge myself to the . . . offering.' When are they freewill offerings? When he says, 'This shall be a . . . offering' " (*m. Qinnim* 1:1).

on the day he offers. bĕyôm haqrîbô; compare *bĕyôm zibḥăkem* (19:6). Whereas P prefers *hiqrîb* and H *zābaḥ*, both sources limit the use of *zābaḥ* to the offering of the *zābaḥ*, the well-being offering (see the NOTE on 9:4).

and what is left . . . on the morrow. ûmimmoḥŏrāt wĕhannôtār, lit., "and on the morrow and what is left." Rashi explains that the second *waw* is superfluous, citing Gen 36:24 and Dan 8:13 as examples. But it is simpler, with Ehrlich (1908–14), to move the "superfluous" *waw* to the preceding word, thereby reading *ûmimmoḥŏrātô hannôtār*, yielding the rendering "and on its morrow, what is left (of it shall be eaten)." For this usage, see 1 Sam 30:17. Alternatively, the last three words, *wĕhannôtār mimmennû yā'ākēl*, might be deleted, with the LXX and in agreement with the parallel text, 19:6–7, leaving the following: "it shall be eaten on the day he offers the sacrifice and on the morrow."

Persons would seek company to feast on the well-being offering, as is graphically illustrated by the ruse employed by the seductress: "I obligated myself to a well-being offering; today I fulfilled my vows. Therefore I have come out to you, seeking you, and have found you" (Prov 7:14–15; Wessely 1846).

17. *on the third day (bayyôm haššĕlîšî).* The equivalent injunction in 19:6 reads *'ad-yôm haššĕlîšî* 'by the third day', implying that once the third day begins, the remaining sacrificial flesh should have been incinerated. On the basis of this verse the rabbis maintain that it may be eaten only during daylight of the second day but not the following night (*m. Zebaḥ.* 5:7; *Sipra, Ṣaw* 12:13; *Zebaḥ.* 56b [bar.]; cf. Jub 21:10). This view is based on the assumption that the biblical day began with sunset. It is clear, however, from the earliest sources that the biblical day—and certainly so in P and in the sanctuary—began at sunrise (see the NOTE on 23:32; de Vaux 1961a: 181–83). Thus the votive and freewill offerings of well-being could be eaten for two days and two nights (with *Tg. Ps.-J.*).

18. *it shall not be acceptable (lō' yērāṣeh).* How is this possible, when the sacrifice has already been offered (asked by Rabbi Eliezer in *b. Zebaḥ.* 29a)? The equivalent law in 19:8 provides the answer: *kî-'et-qōdeš YHWH ḥillēl* 'for he has desecrated the sanctum of the Lord'. Implied is that the meat—and indeed all parts—of the sacrifice retains its holiness until the time of its elimination. A case in point is the Nazirite's hair. It is *qōdeš laYHWH* not only during his naziritic

period (Num 6:8) but afterward, even when he shaves it, for he must *burn* it (v 18). Even more to the point is the remainder of the ordination offering, which must be burned after its time limit has expired "because it is holy" (Exod 29:34). Thus by desecrating the sacrifice, in allowing it to remain beyond its prescribed time limit, the offerer has invalidated the entire sacrificial procedure retroactively. The rabbis, however, are reluctant to allow for the principle of retroactivity in the sacrificial system. They claim that if the offerer permitted the sacrifice to become desecrated by eating it beyond its time limit he must surely have intended to do so from the beginning. Thus they introduce a new principle: intentionality (*m. Zebaḥ.* 2:2–5; 3:6; see Eilberg-Schwartz 1986). Their support in Scripture is explained in the NOTE below (however, note the strictures of Rashbam). The Karaites, by contrast, reject the rabbinic notion of intention and opt here for the principle of retroactivity. A classic case of retroactivity in cultic law is the reparation offering brought for embezzlement, which is founded on the principle that voluntary repentance of a deliberate crime retroactively transforms the crime into an involuntary act (5:14–26, COMMENT F).

In passing, it should be noticed that most translations (following the *Tgs.* and, perhaps, relying on Mal 1:8), regard the next word, *hammaqrîb*, as the subject of this predicate, yielding "the man who offers it shall not be accepted." Certainly, this is not the understanding of the Masoretes, who place the major (and rare) disjunctive accent, the *sĕgôltā*, on *yērāṣeh*. Their interpretation is fully confirmed by the biblical evidence. The human object of the *niphʿal* of rṣh is always preceded by the dative *lamed*. Thus *wĕnirṣâ lô* 'and it shall be acceptable in his behalf' (1:4); *lōʾ yērāṣû lākem* 'it shall not be acceptable on your behalf' (22:25). If, however, the verb refers not to the offerer but to the offering, it can stand alone. For example, in the equivalent passage in 19:7, *lōʾ yērāṣeh* refers to the immediately preceding sacrifice, precisely as is the case here (cf. also 22:23). Thus *hammaqrîb*, beginning with a definite article, must be the subject of the next sentence (see below).

accredited (yēḥāšēb). The *niphʿal* of ḥšb is a legal term in P, implying that the heavenly court, as it were, is taking account of the act (e.g., 17:14; Num 18:27, 30; cf. Ps 106:31), as glossed by the rendering of *Tg. Ps.-J.*, "will not be reckoned to him for merit." Because the basic meaning of *ḥāšab(qal)* is "think," the word may have provided the ground for the rabbinic rule of intentionality: *lōʾ yēḥāšēb lô* could imply that the offerer actually planned to eat of the sacrifice after its time limit had expired. Hence, he did not think properly and his sacrifice was invalidated.

who offered it. hammaqrîb ʾōtô are the opening words of this verse and technically its subject. Literally, they should be rendered, "as for him who offered it." A similar (and clearer) construction is found in the next verse, *habbāśār* 'as for the [other] flesh'. This construction is amply attested in Scripture (e.g., Gen 34:8; 41:40; 1 Sam 9:20; cf. esp. Qoh 2:14 [Fruchtman 1976]). Its recognition resolves many a crux, for example, *haqqāhāl* (Num 15:15), which has baffled commentators, translators, and grammarians through the ages. Once Num 15:29a is brought in for comparison, it reveals a similar phraseology to v 15a, *ha-* . . . *wĕlaggēr haggār* . . . *ʾaḥat lākem*, thereby allowing for the equation of *haqqāhāl* (v 15) with *hāʾezraḥ*. Thus Num 15:15a should be rendered "as for the congregation (i.e., of Israelites) there shall be one law for you and for the resident stranger" (see Milgrom 1990a: *ad loc.*).

desecrated meat (piggûl). It is attested in just three other biblical passages (19:7; Isa 65:4; Ezek 4:14). The etymology is unknown. The attempt to supply it with an Akkadian or Egyptian derivative (Görg 1979) is unsatisfactory. The only resource is the Bible itself, especially the equivalent passage, 19:7–8, which reads as follows: "if it (the *šĕlāmîm*) is eaten on the third day, it is *piggûl;* it will not be acceptable. And he who eats it shall bear his punishment, for he has *desecrated (ḥillēl)* the sanctum of the Lord; that person shall be cut off from his kin." Thus *piggûl* is desecrated meat (Wright 1987: 140–43). This conclusion can also be derived from the rule concerning the priestly ordination offering whose time limit has expired: "it may not be eaten because it is holy" (Exod 29:34), implying that eating it desecrates it.

The remaining two *piggûl* passages conform to this interpretation. Ezekiel protests against the Lord's command to cook his food on human excrement: "My throat is undefiled *(mĕṭummāʾâ);* from my youth till now I have not eaten the flesh of a carcass *(nĕbēlâ)* or of an animal torn by wild beasts *(ṭĕrēpâ)*, nor has *piggûl* meat ever entered my mouth" (Ezek 4:14). A similar context is found in Isa 65:4, which describes renegade Israelites "who eat swine's flesh and broth *(mĕraq,* Q) of *piggûlîm.*" Thus *piggûl* falls into the same category as, and yet is different from, meat that is impure (like that of swine or a carcass, Isa 65:4; Ezek 4:14). It refers to sacred meat that has exceeded its prescribed time limit and thereby become desecrated (19:7–8). This specific kind of desecration is called *piggûl*. Hence, it is here rendered "desecrated meat" (see further Wright 1987: 140–43).

the person (wehannepeš). Perhaps *nepeš* was chosen instead of *ʾîš* because of its basic meaning "throat, appetite" (e.g., Isa 5:14; 58:11; Pss 63:6; 107:9) and its frequent association with the verb *ʾākal* 'eat' in this chapter (vv 18, 20, 27) and throughout Leviticus (16:29, 31; 17:10, 12, 14; 23:27, 29; B. Schwarz).

bear his punishment (ʿăwōnāh tiśśāʾ). For this idiom, see the NOTE on 5:1. (Because the subject *nepeš* is feminine so is its predicate.) *ʿăwôn* also means "sin, iniquity," but behavioral terms can also denote their consequences (5:14–26, COMMENT A). The rabbis claim that the exact nature of the punishment is defined in the following verse and in the equivalent law of 19:8 (*Sipra,* Ṣaw 13:9). Nevertheless, the possibility must be reckoned with that because 19:8 stems from a different Priestly school (H) it also prescribes a more specific penalty than this verse, which merely states that the offender will be punished by God (see the NOTE on 5:1). Besides, contaminating sacred meat (vv 19–20) should involve a severer punishment *(kārēt)* than desecrating it (see the Introduction, §D). In all passages containing the phrase *nāśā' 'āwôn/ḥēṭ'*, wherein man and not God is the subject, the crime is against God and is punishable only by God—lying outside the jurisdiction of the human court (e.g., 5:1, 17; 20:20; 22:16; 24:15; Num 5:31; 9:13; 14:12; 18:1, 23; 30:16).

19. *it shall be consumed in fire (bā'ēš yiśśārēp)*. This rule, that contaminated sacred meat must be burned, provides strong evidence that the burning of certain purification offerings (4:12, 21; 16:27; cf. 6:23) is due to the fact that they bear severe impurities (see chap. 4, COMMENT D); it also points to the possibility that originally all purification offerings were burned and only later, with the exception of those bearing severe impurities, they were eliminated by being ingested by the priests (see chap. 10, COMMENT C).

As for other flesh. wěhabbāśār, lit., "As for the flesh." It is similar in construction to *hammaqrîb*, lit., "as for the offerer" (v 18). For the attestation of this construction in biblical Hebrew, see the NOTE on v 18.

such flesh (bāśār). This word does not mean "any meat," for impure persons are not prohibited from eating meat, but must refer to the meat discussed in this context, namely, sacred meat.

20. *while impure (wěṭum'ātô 'ālāyw)*. The person is the source of the impurity (*Sipra*, Ṣaw 14:4), for instance, has gonorrhea or a nocturnal emission (15:1–17). The case of one who is secondarily infected is taken up in the next verse (see chap. 15, COMMENT B). A perfect case in point is David in the court of Saul, who is presumed to have had a nocturnal emission that prevented him from attending the sacred feast for the new month; but this could no longer be assumed when he was also absent for the second day of the feast (1 Sam 20:26–27). For the fuller implications of this incident, see the NOTE on 15:16 and chap. 16, COMMENT B. This same expression also describes the impure priest who makes contact with sacred food (22:3), but there his impurity stems from a variety of sources, as detailed in the text that follows (vv 4–5). The claim that the rabbis permitted an impure person to eat the flesh of a well-being offering (so Eilberg-Schwartz 1986: 154 221 n. 6, who misconstrues *m. Zebaḥ*. 5:7) is a flat contradiction of this verse.

The grammatical oddity should be noted: although the verse begins and ends in the feminine (the subject being *nepeš*), the middle clause is in the masculine. The same prevails in the following verse. But this phenomenon seems to occur where the subject is *nepeš*. It is a feminine noun, but when it denotes a person it is frequently treated as a masculine (e.g., 5:1–4).

eats (tō'kal). But not *tigga'*, touches? Surely touching sacred meat while in a state of impurity is also forbidden (see 12:4)! Yet the context of this entire pericope is the eating of the well-being offering (vv 16–21), and other forms of contact such as touching and carrying (e.g., 11:8, 27–28, 39–40) are taken for granted. But is the penalty the same? One cannot argue that because there is a difference in penalties for touching and eating impure common meat there should also be a difference if an impure person touches or eats sacred meat. In touch, the former case entails the same penalty: the impurity lasts until evening (e.g., 11:24–25, 39–40). The reason that the one who eats impure meat also has to launder his clothes is either because it is assumed that, while eating some of the food dropped or dripped on his clothes or because eating generates a more intensive impurity than touching (Wright 1987: 185–86 n. 39). Thus the case of impure common food leaves one to conclude that there is no distinction in penalty for contaminating sacred food either by touching it or by eating it.

The parallel case of impure priests contacting sacred food (22:3–9) further strengthens this conclusion. Again, the context deals with eating sacred food, not touching it (22:4–8; cf. vv 10–14). But the pericope begins with the general injunction "If any man among your offspring (Aaron's), while in a state of impurity, intentionally contacts *(yiqrab 'el)* any sacred gift that the Israelite people may consecrate to the Lord, that person shall be cut off from before me: I am the Lord" (22:3). This introductory generalization, then, clearly equates eating with all other forms of contact. If this holds true for the priest, it can safely be assumed that it also holds for the laity.

the Lord's. *'ăšer la YHWH,* lit., "[flesh from the sacrifice of well-being] that is the Lord's." Why this ostensibly superfluous clause? The implication is clear: meat that is not "the Lord's" is also permitted. That is, it is not brought to the altar as a sacrifice but is slaughtered profanely (Introduction, §C) or consists of game (17:13–14) and blemished animals (22:21–24). The same conclusion was drawn from the phrase *'ăšer yaqrîb la YHWH* in the opening verse of this pericope (see the NOTE on "that one may offer to the Lord," v 11). Once again, one can see that the focus of this pericope is sacred meat for the table.

that person shall be cut off from his kin. A penalty formula found in P, which declares that the person's line will be terminated by God and, possibly, that he will be denied life in the hereafter (see COMMENT D below). The question needs be addressed here whether such a drastic punishment is inflicted even if the wrongdoing proved accidental, for example, if he is unaware that he is impure or that the meat is sacred. The principle of intention is nowhere expressed in this pericope. Nonetheless, a sound deduction can be made from the sacrificial system in general, and the case of the impure priest in particular. The laws of the purification and reparation offerings make it clear that sacrificial expiation is possible only when the violation of a prohibitive commandment is committed inadvertently or unwittingly (4:2; 5:14, 17). Brazen sins against God are punished by God with excision (Num 15:30–31). As mentioned above, the parallel pericope dealing with the priest who eats sacred food is introduced by the generalization "If any man among your offspring (Aaron's), while in a state of impurity, intentionally contacts *(yiqrab 'el)* any sacred gift that the Israelite people may consecrate to the Lord, that person shall be cut off from before me: I am the Lord" (22:3). Yet the verb *qārab,* in cultic contexts, implies more than just contact; it connotes unlawful, unauthorized contact and, in most instances, it is better rendered by "encroach." Thus excision by divine agency is imposed on the impure priest only when he presumptuously comes into contact with holiness. The same must hold here; and we must assume, in consonance with the sacrificial system, which clearly recognizes the principle of intention (chaps. 4–5), that if any person inadvertently eats sacred food, his wrong will be expiated by a purification offering (4:22–35).

21. *anything impure. běkol-ṭāmēʾ*, itemized in the subsequent statement.

human impurity (běṭumʾat ʾādām). Assumed is that the impurity is contagious to people, a situation that can only occur if the human source bears a severe impurity lasting nominally for seven days, such as the gonorrheic or menstruant (chap. 15), the parturient (chap. 12), or the corpse-contaminated person (Num 19). But if the impurity is of one-day duration, for instance, resulting from sex or ejaculation (15:16–18), touching a severely impure person (15:19; Num 19:22), or entering a fungous house (14:46), then it cannot contaminate a person (for details see chap. 15, COMMENT B). It goes without saying that if a bearer of severe impurity eats the sacred meat he is punished with *kārēt*. This is an example of the practice of these Priestly laws to state the minor case and imply the major ones (D. Wright).

an impure quadruped (biběhēmâ ṭěmēʾâ). The case deals with a carcass, because a live impure animal does not contaminate. Nothing, however, is said about touching the carcass of a pure quadruped, which, according to 11:39–40, also contaminates. But this latter passage will be shown to be a later appendix to the diet laws (see chap. 11, COMMENT A). The similar expressions in 5:2, plus the fact that carcasses of pure animals may be put to man's use, imply that, originally, one might handle the carcass of pure animals without incurring impurity (see the NOTES on 5:2). The term *běhēmâ* implies a quadruped (LXX; see the NOTE on 11:2); other animal species are embraced by the next term.

any impure detestable creature. běkol-šeqeṣ ṭāmēʾ, lit., "any impure abomination." Several manuscripts, the Sam., *Tg. Onq.*, Pesh., and Saadiah read *šereṣ* '[any impure] swarming creature', which would seem preferable because it corresponds to the same animal chain in 5:2 and because *šeqeṣ ṭāmēʾ* 'impure abomination' is a tautology—indeed, it is a contradiction (see the NOTE on 11:10)—whereas the genus *šereṣ* 'swarming creatures' also possesses pure varieties (11:21; Ehrlich 1908–14). It is also possible to argue that *šeqeṣ* is equivalent to *šereṣ* because both terms are also found in connection with all nonquadrupeds (fish, 11:10; birds, 11:13, 23; and insects, 11:41). Then, for practical purposes, it would make no difference whether the correct reading were *šeqeṣ* or *šereṣ*.

Nevertheless, what of the alleged tautology *šeqeṣ/šereṣ ṭāmēʾ* 'impure abomination/swarming creature'? It can hardly be resolved by pointing to four kinds of locusts, which, uniquely among the vast varieties of *šeqeṣ/šereṣ*, are edible (11:21–22) and which would justify labeling all the rest as "impure." The answer is more likely found in the use of the verb *nāgaʿ* 'touch'. As will be discussed at length (see the NOTES on 11:10, 11), touching and eating a carcass must be strictly and uniformly differentiated. The eating of forbidden animals is

425

not defiling, while touching is defiling only if the carcass is that of a quadruped (11:8, 24–28) or one of the named eight nonquadrupeds (11:29–31). Hence the term *šeqeṣ ṭāmēʾ* here, or *šereṣ ṭāmēʾ* (5:2), both of which are used in the context of touching, must refer to the eight nonquadrupeds singled out in 11:29–31, whose contact is defiling.

eats. wĕʾākal, that is, deliberately (see the NOTE on "that person shall be cut off," v 20). If, however, the act is inadvertent, a purification offering suffices (4:23–35). As for the masculine form of the verb despite the feminine subject, *nepeš*, see the NOTE on "while impure," v 20.

the Lord's (ʾăšer laYHWH). See the NOTE on v 20.

that person shall be cut off from his kin (wĕnikrĕtâ hannepeš hahîʾ [hwʾ] mēʿammêhā). See the NOTE on v 20 and COMMENT D below. Thus, vv 19–21 deal with contact between impurity and sacrifices. It is important to note that, however, there is no penalty for eating an impure sacrifice; there is only a warning that it should be burned and not eaten (v 19). The reason is stated succinctly by the rabbis: "because one is culpable only on account of personal impurity" (*m. Zebaḥ.* 13:1). The implication is fundamental. Contrary to the rule in the pagan world, Israel holds that impure animals—even if they are brought into contact with sancta (e.g., by being sacrificed)—offer no threat to society. Danger resides in impurity only if it emanates from the human being (cf. chap. 4, COMMENT C).

22–23a. And the Lord spoke to Moses, saying: Speak to the Israelites thus (weyyĕdabbēr YHWH ʾel-Mōšeh lēʾmōr dabbēr ʾel-bĕnê yiśrāʾēl lēʾmōr). This long introduction is a sign of an insert that severed the original continuous passage on the thanksgiving and well-being offerings (vv 11–21, 29b–34). Besides, this passage (vv 22–27) differs from the rest of the chapter by employing the second-person plural (Bertholet 1901). The contextual rupture is particularly evident if we compare the content of the two offerings. Just as the passage on the thanksgiving offering (vv 11–15) includes the priestly prebends—the main objective of all of the sacrificial prescriptions in chaps. 6–7 (e.g., 6:9–11, 19, 22–23; 7:6–10) —so should the instructions on the well-being offering prescribe its priestly prebends, but these are located after the digression on the suet and blood (vv 22–27) in vv 31–34 (this same observation was made by Abravanel, question 22). This insert (vv 22–27) corresponds structurally to 6:12–16 in that both are intrusions within their respective chapters and are responsible for the long introductions in the pericopes that follow (6:17–18aα; 7:28–29b; see the NOTES on the introductions to 6:12 and 7:28). Because the content of this insert, the banning of the suet of all sacrificed animals (vv 23–25), represents the viewpoint of H (see the Introduction, §C), this insert and the prior one, together with their editorial linkages (6:17–18aα; 7:28–29b), must stem from the hand of H.

23. Speak to the Israelites thus. This introduction differs from all those of the previous pericopes in chaps. 6 and 7 in that it explicitly addresses the laity and not the priests (contrast 6:2, 13, 18). The reason is clear. Because the offerer is responsible for bringing the suet to the altar (vv 29–30), he may neglect to bring all of it and leave some behind to be eaten with the flesh, thereby incurring the *kārēt* penalty (v 25).

the suet of any (kol-ḥēleb). The suet of the subsequently named animals, even if blemished and ineligible for the altar (see the NOTE on v 25), may not be eaten. Conversely, the suet of other permitted animals, namely, game (see 17:13–14), may be eaten (Bekhor Shor on v 25). Support for this deduction stems from D's concession regarding the profane slaughter of these same animals (Deut 12:21). Strikingly, although the blood prohibition remains in force— with staccato emphasis (Deut 12:16, 23–25)—there is total silence regarding the suet. This can only mean that permitted domesticated animals now have the status of game (Deut 12:15b, 22a) and, henceforth, the suet of all permitted animals is allowed as food (Ibn Ezra, versus Ramban), except when they are offered as a sacrifice (Deut 12:11–14, 17–18, 26–28). Thus D adopts P's allowance of common slaughter (see the Introduction, §C) and overturns H's subsequent ban on common slaughter (17:3–7).

The objection may be raised that animal suet is inedible. Still, it must never be forgotten that biblical suet *(ḥēleb)* also comprises certain edible portions (cf. 3:9–10), and that suet was used in the preparation of food.

ox (šôr). Whereas *bāqār* stands for the collective species, *šôr* designates the single member regardless of sex or age (Péter 1975). For sex and age distinctions, *par/pārâ* and *ʿegel/ʿeglâ* would be used. "Ox" here denotes the bovine species and not the castrated male, its other meaning.

sheep (keśeb). The usual term for sheep is metathesized *kebeś*. Is there any difference between the two? It will be noted that the latter term, *kebeś*, only stands for the male, while the female is expressed by *kibśâ*. By contrast, *keśeb* can denote either sex (e.g., 3:7; 4:35; 22:27; Num 18:17), which is precisely what is intended here. True, the feminine *kiśbâ* is attested, but only once (5:6), and the suspicion cannot be dispelled that it may be a mistake for *kibśâ*.

goat (ʿēz). Of either sex, exactly as demanded by the context here. Sexual differentiation would be expressed by *śāʿîr/śeʿîrâ* (e.g., 4:23, 28; 5:6).

24. *an animal that died. něbēlâ,* in other words, the carcass of an animal that dies a natural death (see the NOTE on 5:2), from the verb *nābal* 'fade, wither'.

mauled by beasts. ṭěrēpâ (Gen 31:39; Nah 2:13), from the verb *ṭārap* 'tear [by wild beasts]' (e.g., Gen 37:33, 44:28, 49:27; Exod 22:12; Deut 33:20).

may be put to any use (yēʿāśeh lěkol-mělāʾkâ). Presumed is that the carcasses of these pure animals do not defile upon contact; else how could their suet be handled with impunity? Thus the law of 11:39–40 must be a later development (see chap. 11, COMMENT A). The same conclusion was derived from the expression "impure animal" (v 21 and 5:2).

Because v 24 interrupts the sense and symmetry of the two provisions of vv 23 and 25, it may constitute a subsequent economic concession (Fishbane

1985: 199), which the rabbis have expressed as "the Torah shows concern for a person's possessions" (*m. Neg.* 12:5; cf. the NOTE on 14:36).

but you must not eat it (wĕʾākōl lōʾ tōʾkĕlūhû). There is no prohibition (in P or H) against eating the meat of a *nĕbēlâ* or *ṭĕrēpâ* (but only a warning to cleanse oneself of the resultant impurity, 17:15–16), for if it were eligible for sacrifice as a well-being offering, it would be eaten by its owner. The suet of such a sacrificial animal, however, without exception belongs to God; and for this reason, if anyone eats the suet, even if the animal died naturally and can no longer be offered on the altar, it is as if he had encroached upon divine property and is subject to divine sanctions.

25. *an animal from which a food gift is presented to the Lord (habbĕhēmâ ʾăšer yaqrîb mimmennâ ʾiššeh laYHWH).* A circumlocution for sacrificial animals. Therefore, the suet of nonsacrificial animals—namely, game—may be eaten. The early critics err (e.g., Kuenen 1886; Wellhausen 1963: 151; cf. Paton 1897: 32–33) in claiming that this clause presumes that not all animals eligible for the altar were sacrificed and, hence, common slaughter was permitted. This clause is simply a generalization; it subsumes the ox, sheep, and goat under the category of sacrificial animals. Furthermore, this prohibition is not limited to eligible, that is to say, unblemished, animals. It is the species that is forbidden, not the individual animal. Thus the suet of a blemished pure animal may not be eaten, even though the animal itself is disqualified for the altar. For surely, if the suet of a sacrificial animal's carcass is forbidden as food (above) all the more so the suet of a healthy animal, which may not be sacrificed only because of some blemish (22:22–24).

that person shall be cut off from his kin. See the NOTE on v 20 and COMMENT D below.

26. *any blood. wĕkol-dām,* from any source, even from game, and in any place, even in your settlements. This prohibition has already been given in 3:17; why is it repeated here? The contrast with suet provides the answer. In 3:17 the two were equated because the context was that of sacrifice. Here they are differentiated because the focus has shifted to nonsacrificial animals: nonsacrificial suet may be eaten, but nonsacrificial blood is forbidden—hence, the addition of the word *ʿôp* 'bird', that is, game. Moreover, the term *bĕkōl môšĕbōtêkem* 'in any of your settlements' is attached only to the blood prohibition (but omitted in connection with the suet), emphasizing again that blood of game may not be ingested and implying that the suet of nonsacrificial animals (game) may be eaten anywhere.

of bird (lāʿôp). The omission of fish from this blood prohibition implies, according to the rabbis, that fish are exempt. Not so for the Karaites, who rely on Num 11:4, 22 to say that fish fall into the category of *bāśār* 'meat', hence their blood must be drained *(Seper Hamibḥar).*

in any of your settlements (bĕkōl môšĕbōtêkem). See the NOTE on 3:17, where it is shown that the referent is the Israelite settlements in Canaan and not in the diaspora. But the restriction of place, "settlements," to blood means that the background for this term has changed. In 3:17, the subject was sacrificial animals, which allowed for the possibility of ingesting suet and blood "in all your settlements." In this verse, however, the focus has shifted to game, and the distinction is therefore made between suet and blood; the former may be eaten but the latter is strictly forbidden. Thus the two passages that deal with the suet-and-blood prohibition do not contradict each other: 3:17 deals with sacrificial animals and, hence, prohibits the eating of suet, whereas 7:22–27 concentrates on the issue of game and legislates that whereas its suet may be eaten its blood is forbidden.

27. *ingests (tōʾkal)*. The verb *ʾākal*, lit., "eat" is invariably used in all occurrences of the blood prohibition (e.g., 3:17; 7:26, 27; 17:10[*bis*], 14[*bis*]; 19:26; Deut 12:16, 23[*bis*], 24, 25). It can only mean that the blood, instead of being drunk as a separate item, is ingested together with the meat of the animal, hence "eaten." One of the blood prohibitions in Deuteronomy makes this point explicitly: *wĕlōʾ-tōʾkal hannepeš ʿim-habbāśār* 'you shall not ingest [lit., "eat"] the life [i.e., the blood] with the meat' (Deut 12:23). The crucial importance of this point will be fully developed in the COMMENT to chap. 17 (tentatively, see chap. 11, COMMENT C).

any blood (kol-dām). No exceptions are allowed; see the NOTE on v 26.

shall be cut off from his kin. See the NOTE on v 20.

28–29. *And the Lord spoke to Moses, saying: Speak to the Israelites thus (wayyĕdabbēr YHWH ʾel-mōšeh lēʾmōr dabbēr ʾel-bĕnê yiśrāʾēl lēʾmōr)*. Because vv 29b–36 are a direct continuation of vv 16–21, this introduction was probably added because of the insertion of vv 22–27 (see the NOTE on 6:12). The Sam. and apparently the LXX invert v 29a, reading, *wĕʾel-bĕnê yiśrāʾēl tĕdabbēr lēʾmōr*, which Elliger (1966) regards as original on the grounds that what follow are instructions geared to the laity. As already noted, however, the previous section on the well-being offering (vv 16–21) was also addressed to the laity: priests could not possibly control *piggûl* or impurity violations once the sacrificial meat left the sanctuary.

29. *shall bring. yābîʾ*, that is, he himself (see v 30a; Saadiah). Thus the second half of v 29b is not a pointless repetition of the first half. It stresses the difference between the well-being offering and the most sacred offerings. Whereas the latter become the property of the deity as soon as they are dedicated, the well-being offering continues to remain the property of the owner even after it is brought to the sanctuary—indeed, even after its blood and suet are offered up on the altar (see the next NOTE).

his offering (qorbānô). Here *qorbān* does not refer to the sacrifice but denotes the portion of it, *mizzebaḥ* 'from [his]sacrifice', which is transferred to the deity. The latter word proves that not all of the *šĕlāmîm* belongs to God but only that which is offered up on the altar, namely, the blood and suet, and given to the priest, namely, the thigh and the breast. The meat remains the possession of the offerer. The LXX, correctly, renders *qorbānô* as "his gift," as shown by its synonymous term *ʾiššeh* 'food gifts' (v 30a). This word was most likely chosen in order to effect a symmetrical balance in the two halves of v 29b; thus *yābîʾ ʾet-qorbānô* parallels *hammaqrîb*.

30. *His own hands (yādāyw)*. This expression must be taken literally: it is the offerer's hands and no one else's that must present this gift to the sanctuary. This emphasis on the offerer's responsibility to bring the parts of the well-being offering dedicated to the Lord is repeated in the cases of the priestly ordination offering (8:27–28; Exod 29:24–25) and the Nazirite's well-being offering (Num 6:19). It is also the key factor in understanding the function of the *tĕnûpâ* (see COMMENT E below).

shall bring (tĕbîʾênâ). The repetition of the verb *hēbîʾ* (2a, ba) throws emphasis on *yādāyw*, the offerer himself.

the Lord's food gifts (ʾišše YHWH). The traditional rendering of *ʾiššeh* as "fire offering" is controverted here, for this term (plural) includes the breast, which is not burned on the altar but becomes the revenue of the priests (v 31). The term again appears in v 35, where its plural form refers to the breast and the right thigh. The latter portion not only is not burned on the altar but does not even come near it; it is given by the offerer directly to the priests—further and, indeed, better evidence that *ʾiššeh* cannot mean "fire offering." These priestly prebends are called "the Lord's" because through their dedication *(tĕrûmâ)* and the breast's elevation offering *(tĕnûpâ)*, they become the Lord's property before he transfers them to the priests (v 34). That they technically belong to the Lord is further supported by the concession granted the blemished priest that *leḥem ʾĕlōhāyw miqqodšê haqqodāšîm ûmin-haqqodāšîm yōʾkēl* 'he may eat of the food of his God, of the most holy as well as of the holy' (21:22). Thus even the prebends of the lesser holy offerings, such as the well-being offering, are called "the food of his God" (*pace* Haran 1962c: 40). On *ʾiššeh*, see the NOTE on 1:9.

together (ʿal). This meaning is verified by the parallel verse, 10:15a, where the order is reversed: "Together *(ʿal)* with the food gifts of suet, they must present the thigh of contribution and the breast of the elevation offering."

the breast (heḥāzeh). This vital information is provided by my student, Susan Rattray: "Our modern method of quartering an animal by dividing the carcass lengthwise into two halves would split the animal's breast (brisket) into two pieces—a right breast and a left breast—which does not fit the biblical prescription. However, my uncle (who keeps a small flock of sheep and does his own butchering) states that an animal can also be quartered by cutting through its loins and flank, thus separating the hind legs from the rib cage and forelegs (the hindquarters would then be split in two at the spine, to obtain the right thigh). The forelegs are easily removed as they are not attached to the spine or ribs in any way. That would leave the entire rib cage and attached vertebrae. The breast or brisket of the animal—namely, the area between the forelegs, from below the neck to the flank (corresponding more or less to the human breast) could then be cut away from the rest of the rib cage" (see fig. 7). This method of quartering would also explain how Abraham split the animals *bat-tawek* 'in the middle' (cf. also Jer 34:18).

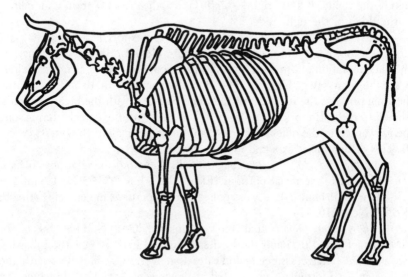

FIGURE 7

the breast to be elevated. But not the suet, because it (and the blood) inherently belong to God (Milgrom 1983d: 144 n. 19). The elevation rite follows the burning of the suet (9:21; R. Gane) because God (i.e., the altar) must precede man (i.e., the priests) in the receipt of prebends from the animal.

to be elevated (lěhānîp). For this rendering see COMMENT E below. Because this rite transfers the object from the offerer to the deity (represented by the priest), the hands of both the offerer and the priest are placed under the offering to perform this rite, as observed by the rabbis (*Sipra*, Ṣaw 11:3) and the Karaites (*Seper Hamibḥar*). That the priest is involved in the performance of the *těnûpâ* rite, see 8:29; 9:21; 14.12, hence the rendering of this verb is in the passive (see the NOTE on *hiqrîb*, v 35).

elevation offering (těnûpâ). The identification and function of this rite are discussed in detail in COMMENT E below.

31. *to Aaron and his sons.* As distinct from the right thigh, which is assigned to the officiating priest (v 33). The reason for this distinction is explained in COMMENT F below.

32. *the right thigh (šôq hayyāmîn).* Of the hind legs, not the shoulder of the

forelegs (so Philo, *Laws* 1. 145, perhaps confusing this prebend with that of Deut 18:3). It was choice meat, to judge by the fact that it was put aside by Samuel for Saul (1 Sam 9:24). The history of this offering is explored in COM-MENT F below. *hayyāmîn* is not the adjective of *šôq*, for the latter is neither masculine nor marked with the definite article. The term literally means "the thigh of the right," but as "right" *(yāmîn)* is an adjective, the term is an ellipsis of "the thigh of the right [side]."

a gift (tĕrûmâ). See the NOTE on v 14 and COMMENT F below.

33. *the one . . . who offers (hammaqrîb).* Here *hiqrîb* does not carry its general connotation of "present" but means "sacrifices," hence it means "offers up on the altar" (e.g., 7:8, 9). The staccato emphasis in this verse on the officiating priest as the recipient of the thigh contrasts with the breast, which is assigned to the entire priestly cadre (v 31). So too with the cereal offering: one type is awarded to the officiating priest, another type to all of the priests (vv 9–10). This distinction is explored in *Comment* F below.

as his prebend (lô . . . lĕmānâ). Initially the word *mānâ* seems to have been restricted to sacrificial portions (Exod 29:26; Lev 7:33; 8:23; 1 Sam 1:4; 9:23; 2 Chr 31:19) but later it was applied to food portions in general (Esth 2:9; 9:19, 22; Neh 8:10, 12).

34. *I have taken. lāqaḥtî,* that is to say, acquired, just as God has "taken" for himself Israel (Exod 6:7) and the Levites (Num 3:12; 18:6). But the following verb, *wāʾettēn* 'I have assigned', indicates that we are dealing here with the *lāqaḥ-nātan* legal formula, well attested in the ancient Near East, in which the king assigns a prebend to a loyal servant. For example, in an Akk. document from Ugarit, the king "takes" *(našû)* the city's tithe and "gives" *(nadānu)* it to the city ruler as a lifetime prebend (*PRU* 3.93; 16.244, lines 2–10; see Green-field 1977).

the breast of the elevation offering (ḥăzēh hattĕnûpâ). The stock expression for this prebend (Exod 29:27; Lev 7:34; 10:14, 15; Num 6:20; 18:18). The word *tĕnûpâ* indicates the rite by which the breast is transferred to the property of God (see COMMENT E below).

the thigh of the contribution (šôq hattĕrûmâ). The stock expression for this prebend (Exod 29:27; Lev 7:34; 10:14, 15; Num 6:20; 18:18). The word *tĕrûmâ* indicates that it was set aside *(hûram,* Exod 29:27), in other words, dedicated to God, an act by which he symbolically acquires it.

from the Israelites (mēʾēt bĕnê yiśrāʾēl). This phrase is mentioned twice in this verse and once again in v 36, stressing that the flesh of the well-being offering belongs to the offerer with the exception of the priestly prebends.

have assigned them to Aaron the priest and to his sons. wāʾettēn ʾōtām lĕʾahărōn hakkōhēn ûlĕbānāyw is a generalization. It does not contradict the detail in v 33 that the officiating priest alone is the recipient of the thigh. It merely states that God is the transfer agent for the priestly prebends. Similarly, the assignment of the baked cereal offering to the entire priestly cadre (2:10) is a generalization and not a contradiction of 7:9, which assigns it to the officiating priest.

a due . . . for all time (ḥoq-ʿôlām). P uses masc. *ḥōq* to designate "due" and fem. *ḥuqqâ* (from the same root, *ḥqq*) to designate "statute" (see the NOTE on 10:13). For the ostensible exception of *ḥuqqâ* in v 36, see below. The eternal due granted the priesthood by Israel's God is paralleled by the Babylonian gods Nana and Marbiti granting the priest Nabumutakki a daily portion "forever" (Thureau-Dangin 1919: 141–43).

35. *This (zōʾt).* What is its referent? Most exegetes aver that it refers to the contents of chaps. 6 and 7 (e.g., Rashbam) because it speaks of *ʾiššê* 'food gifts' in the plural (Dillmann and Ryssel 1897). The closing verses of chap. 7 would, then, contain a double summary of chaps. 6 and 7 consisting of the priestly prebends (vv 35–36) and the *tôrôt*, the sacrificial rituals (vv 37–38). Alternatively, the plural *ʾiššê* 'food gifts' could well apply to the two priestly perquisites from the well-being offering, the breast and right thigh. Indeed, even the combination of the suet and breast of the well-being offering are referred to in the plural as *ʾiššê YHWH* 'the Lord's food gifts' (v 30). Moreover, there is one incontrovertible argument why the plural *ʾiššê YHWH* cannot apply to all of the sacrifices in chaps. 6–7—the purification offering is not an *ʾiššeh*! Not once is it called by this term, and in one instance it is explicitly excluded from this designation: "for their inadvertence they have brought their offering, an *ʾiššeh* to the Lord and their purification offering before the Lord" (Num 15:25b). Indeed, in the one place in which all of the priestly prebends are enumerated (Num 18:8–20), the legist is forced to avoid the use of *ʾiššeh* and, instead, resorts to the expression *min hāʾēš* 'from the fire', precisely for the reason that he wishes to include the purification offering (Num 18:9). This, incidentally, is another strong argument against the possibility of rendering the term *ʾiššeh* 'fire offering', as heretofore (the other reasons are laid out in the NOTE on 1:9).

That vv 35–36 are a summary of only the well-being offering pericope (vv 11–34) is further supported by two statements in these verses: that these portions became priestly prebends at the time of the priestly ordination, and that they are gifts "from the Israelites," both being clear references to Exod 29:27–28, which declares that the priestly ordination offering set a precedent for all well-being offerings, in that the breast and right thigh are the priests' prebends from the Israelites as their eternal due (for details, see below).

perquisite. (so rendered by *Tg. Onq.*) The term *mišḥâ* is vocalized in its one other occurrence as *mošḥâ* (Num 18:8). The LXX renders it here "anointing" (but "portion" in Num 18:8), probably under the influence of the verbal form *mošḥô* in the following verse. These two homonyms probably stem from different roots, *māšaḥ* 'anoint' and *māšaḥ* 'measure, apportion'. Aram. and Syr. attest *mešḥâ* 'measure'; Arab. *masaḥa* also means "measure" and, most important, Akk. *mišiḥtu* and *mašāḥu* likewise denote "measure" (noun and verb). Although *mašāḥu* designating measures of quantity is only attested in the Neo-Babylonian and Achaemenid periods, whereas previously it had denoted the measurement of areas and distances, this is no basis for declaring this term a late entry into Hebrew, not before the exile or, at the earliest, at the end of the First Temple period (Levine 1982b: 125–27), because terms for volume and length were occasionally interchangeable. For example, it was customary in the ancient Near East to measure land by the amount of seed needed to plant it (27:6). To be sure, there is cause to wonder why the writer would employ this new and rare term instead of the previously attested and more common synonyms *mānâ* (v 33) or *ḥōq* (v 34). Before one can conclude that this term betrays the hand of a later writer (Levine 1982b), however, one should note that two of these synonymous terms are attested in a single, indisputably organic, verse: "I grant them to you and your sons as a perquisite *(lĕmošḥâ)*, a due for all time *(lĕḥoq-ʿôlām)*" (Num 18:8b). Because these synonyms appear again in v 34, the end of the pericope on the well-being offering and in v 35, the beginning of the summary statement, there can be no reason to deny that both the pericope and the summary on the well-being offering were written by the same hand.

once. bĕyôm (with Ibn Ezra, Abravanel), lit., "on the day" (for this rendering, see the NOTE on 6:13).

they have been inducted. hiqrîb ʾōtām, lit., "he brought them near." Because the pronoun has no antecedent, the verb must be understood passively. That *hiqrîb* is an allusion to the priestly ordination is indicated by its use in Exod 28:1 (cf. also Exod 29:4; Lev 8:6, 13). Admittedly, this allusion is remote. Nevertheless, it was necessitated by the writer's need to avoid the expected term *māšaḥ* 'anoint', lest it be confused with its homonym *mišḥâ* 'perquisite', which also explains why he is compelled to repeat this information in the next verse; see below.

36. *once they had been anointed (bĕyôm mošḥô ʾōtām).* The resemblance of this phrase to *bĕyôm hiqrîb ʾōtām* (v 35) cannot be missed. The equivalence of *hiqrîb* and *māšaḥ,* both denoting the priestly ordination, is therefore established. But why was this redundancy necessary? As indicated above, the writer was apprehensive lest the term *māšaḥ* 'anoint' be confused with its homonym "measure, apportion" in the same verse. He therefore substituted a synonym, albeit an uncommon one—*hiqrîb*—and postponed the precise term for the consecration of the priests, *māšaḥ,* to the following verse, where it would not be confused with its homonym, thereby creating the redundancy.

from the Israelites. The expression *mēʾēt bĕnê yiśrāʾēl* occurs twice in Exod 29:28, which sets forth the breast and right thigh as the priestly prebends from the well-being offering. The import of this expression is that these prebends are literally presented to the priests by their offerer: "his own hands shall bring the Lord's gifts" (v 30). This distinction, which sets apart the well-being offering from the other most holy offerings, is clearly demarcated in 10:13–14, where the latter's prebends are called *mēʾiššê YHWH* 'from the Lord's food gifts' and the former's *mizzibḥê šalmê bĕnê yiśrāʾēl* 'from the Israelites' sacrifices of well-being'. And so it is. The most holy offerings are the Lord's from the moment they are dedicated, but the well-being offering continues to remain the property of its offerer—as meat for his table—except for the suet and blood, which are offered on the altar, and the breast and right thigh, which are dedicated to the Lord (vv 30, 32) but are assigned to the priests. Thus, only with the well-being offering is it possible to say that its priestly prebends are a gift "from the Israelites."

a due . . . for all time (ḥuqqat ꜥōlām). This expression literally translates "a statute for all time," for P scrupulously distinguishes between ḥōq (masc.) 'due' and ḥuqqâ (fem.) 'statute' (see the NOTES on 10:13 and v 34, above). To be sure, the latter rendering is possible here, because the Lord's command to assign these prebends to the priests automatically becomes an everlasting statute. Still, because these prebends are called ḥoq-ꜥôlām 'a due for all time' (v 34), one would expect that the same thought is intended in this expression here. It is, therefore, not pure chance that the Sam. indeed reads ḥoq-ꜥôlām, and its reading should be adopted here. Its adoption would also remove the main prop supporting I. Knohl's claim (1988: 45) that v 36 (indeed, the entire pericope, vv 28–36) stems from the pen of a late H tradent. He makes this claim on the basis of ḥuqqat ꜥôlām lĕdōrōtām (v 30), ostensibly an H formula; the occurrence of mišḥâ (v 35), ostensibly a late term; and the use of the first person by God, wāʾttēn (v 34), ostensibly an H characteristic. That mišḥâ is late is refuted above, and the other two contentions are refuted in the Introduction (§C). Knohl tries to resolve the contradiction between this passage, which prescribes that the thigh prebend is given directly to the officiating priest (v 33), and the interpolated texts in 9:21 and 10:15, which ordain that the thigh undergoes the tĕnûpâ rite and belongs to the entire priestly cadre, by postulating that this pericope was inserted later by an H tradent who wanted to preserve the older custom practiced at the local altars of awarding the thigh to the priestly officiant (208 n. 11).

Knohl's thesis is illogical. Would an H tradent, a member of the priestly establishment of the Jerusalem Temple, have introduced a practice of the now banned local altars (17:3–4), thereby reinstituting the very abuses that the interpolations of 9:21 and 10:15 had intended to eliminate? Rather, it must be assumed that Lev 7:28–36 belongs to the older stratum of P together with 9:21 and 10:15, before the latter were interpolated. That is, all three passages represent the older (Shilonite) tradition, whereby the thigh is awarded to the priestly officiant. First the verses 9:21 and 10:15 were interpolated so that the thigh together with the breast would undergo the tĕnûpâ and be distributed equally to the entire priestly cadre. Then, however, this interpolation could not be introduced into the pericope of 7:28–36 because it would have contradicted the explicit statement there that the thigh belonged to the officiant (v 33).

Thus, it was left to the two interpolated texts (9:21; 10:15) to overrule the one uninterpolated one (7:28–36). Such a procedure is attested elsewhere in Priestly laws. The tithe, heretofore the perquisite of the priests (27:30), is transferred to the Levites (Num 18:21). Expiation for communal wrongdoing, heretofore demanding a ḥaṭṭāʾt bull, is altered to require an ʿōlâ bull (4:14) and a ḥaṭṭāʾt male goat (Num 15:24). Thus new cultic laws are introduced, but the ones they replace are not excised. A later generation is left to worry about their reconciliation. But because both were revealed by God, they are equally sacred and must be preserved.

37–38a. This is a summary and subscript to chaps. 6–7 for the following reasons: (1) the order of the sacrifices (which follows that of chaps. 6–7 but not that of chaps. 1–5), (2) its use of tôrâ 'ritual' (6:2, 7, 18; 7:1, 11; not found in chaps. 1–5), and (3) its mention of běhar sînāy 'Mount Sinai' (whereas chaps. 1–5 were revealed in the Tent of Meeting, 1:1). See the Notes on these terms, below.

37. ritual (tôrâ). See the Note on 6:2.

the ordination offering (wělammillûʾîm). This sacrificial rite is prescribed in Exod 29 and described in Lev 8. If so, why is it mentioned here? Hoffmann (1953) suggests that because this verse explicitly states that the tôrâ instructions concerning the sacrifices, that is to say, chaps. 6–7, were revealed to Moses on Mount Sinai, the ordination offering is therefore also included because it too was part of the instructions Moses received while he was on Sinai's summit (Exod 29; cf. Exod 25:40; 26:30; 27:8; 31:18; 34:32). Even so, the ordination offering does not fall into the same category as the other sacrifices for a fundamental reason: in its prescribed form (Exod 29) it was executed only once, at the ordination of Aaron and his sons (Lev 8), but was never repeated because their unction with the anointment oil (8:30; Exod 29:21) consecrated the Aaronid priests for all time (Exod 29:9; 40:15; see the Note on 10:7) and only each new high priest was inducted by this rite (Exod 29:29). (For the variant view of the Dead Sea sectaries, see chap. 8, Comment F.) Nonetheless, the place of the ordination offering in this series of sacrifices fits its rank in the order of holiness perfectly. It follows the most holy sacrifices and precedes the less holy well-being offering. Indeed, it is neither one nor the other, sharing some of the attributes of both. Its ambiguous state corresponds precisely to the ambiguous, liminal state of its priestly offerers (for details, see the Note on "eat it there," 8:31). For this reason one must reject out of hand the theory held by many scholars (beginning with Kuenen 1886: 84) that this term, millûʾîm, actually stands for the daily meal offering of the high priest (6:12–16). Beyond the fact that such an offering is not prescribed for the consecration of the priests (chap. 8) nor is it even adumbrated in this pericope (see the Note on "from the time," 6:12), the position of millûʾîm in this verse does not correspond to the position of the high priest's meal offering in these chapters. The possibility exists that because a knowledge of the tāmîd sacrifice (Exod 29:38–42) is presumed in chaps. 6–7 (see the Note on "that is, the burnt offering," 6:2) so too a knowledge of the millûʾîm sacrifice stemming from the same chapter immediately preceding the pericope of the tāmîd (Exod 29:1–37) is also presumed (Shama 1986). Alternatively, one must seriously reckon with the possibility that a special *tôrâ* for the ordination offering originally stood before the pericope on the well-being offering (vv 11ff.). If this conjecture be allowed, the *tôrâ* would have enumerated the prebends from this offering and their disposition (corresponding in content to 8:26–29, 31–33) but it was subsequently omitted when chaps. 1–7 were inserted between Exod 40 and Lev 8 because of the repetition of these same provisions in what became the next chapter. (For the evidence that originally chap. 8 followed Exod 40, see chap. 8, COMMENT A and the Introduction, §H.)

38. *on Mount Sinai (bĕhar sînay).* According to P, Moses not only received the Decalogue on Mount Sinai but also all laws concerning the construction of the Tabernacle and its sancta (Exod 31:18; 34:32). Moreover, there are other laws also attributed to the Sinaitic revelation (e.g., chaps. 25–26 [H]; cf. esp. the inclusion, 25:1; 26:46). One such attribution is singularly instructive (Num 3:1–14): the Levites are *designated* as the replacements of the firstborn on Mount Sinai (cf. v 1; *lāqaḥtî* 'I have taken', v 12) as a consequence of Israel's apostasy regarding the golden calf (Exod 32:26–29)—but they are mustered "in the Wilderness of Sinai" (v 14). This Num 3 passage also records that Nadab and Abihu were alive when God spoke to Moses at Mount Sinai (vv 1–2; cf. Exod 24:1), but they perished "in the Wilderness of Sinai" (v 4). Thus the terms *har sînay* 'Mount Sinai' and *midbar sînay* 'Wilderness of Sinai' are not identical. The former literally refers to the peak itself and—in the cited instances above—to its summit, where Moses spoke with God. The latter refers to Israel's encampment in the vicinity of Sinai (Exod 19:1, 2; Num 10:12), where God spoke to Moses only inside the Tent of Meeting (1:1; cf. Exod 25:22; 29:42; Num 7:89). Weinfeld, however, claims that there is no distinction between these two terms (1981: 505) because the Tent of Meeting was revealed to Moses on Mount Sinai (Exod 25:9; 25:40; 1 Chr 28:19; Wis 9:8). So too, the Esangil, the Babylonian temple, is seen as "the mirror *(maṭṭalātu)* of the Apsu, the image *(tamšil)* of Esana, the counterpart *(meḥret)* of Ea's dwelling, the image of the Eku constellation" (Borger 1956: 21, 47–48). Yet these Mesopotamian analogies only corroborate the biblical claim that Israel's Tabernacle was modeled after its heavenly counterpart, which was revealed to Moses on Mount Sinai. In no way do they imply that God speaking to Moses in the Wilderness of Sinai (i.e., in the Tabernacle) and on Mount Sinai are equivalent. The reference then to God's commands to Moses in the Wilderness of Sinai must perforce involve a different revelation, on which see below.

38b. *when. bĕyôm* (with Saadiah), equivalent in meaning to the same word in v 36 (see above).

offerings (qorbĕnêhem). This is the only attested plural for this word in Scripture, and it is masculine. There are also occurrences of the singular when a plural meaning is intended (e.g., 2:13; Num 7:3; 1:9); that is, the singular also serves as a collective. In postbiblical Hebrew, however, the plural is always

feminine in form, *qorbānôt* (e.g., *m. Šeqal.* 4:1; *m. Tem.* 1:6). Hence, P's usage
—masculine and collective—is clearly old (Paran 1983: 208–9).

in the Wilderness of Sinai (bĕmidbar sînāy). The specific area at the foot of
Mount Sinai where Israel was encamped from the third month of the first year
of the Exodus (Exod 19:1) till the twentieth day of the second month of the
second year (Num 10:11–12). According to the MT, the meaning might be that
the *tôrâ* series of sacrificial laws (i.e., chaps. 6–7 and Exod 29), which God
commanded Moses on Mount Sinai, Moses transmitted to Israel in the Wilderness of Sinai (Hoffmann 1953). But this interpretation is forced. Rather, vv 37–
38 distinguish between the *tôrâ* instructions imparted to Moses on Mount Sinai
(chaps. 6–7) and the commands given *to the Israelites* (not the priests, 6:2)
concerning *their* sacrificial duties—an unmistakable reference to chaps. 1–5, the
sacrificial laws directed to the Israelites (1:2; 4:2). Verse 38b is, then, an editorial
addition—and a most awkward one—which ties chaps. 1–5 to chaps. 6–7. The
purpose of this nexus is to state that, although chaps. 6–7 were commanded to
Moses on Sinai (vv 37–38a), they were taught to Israel, together with chaps.
1–5, in the Wilderness of Sinai (v 37b), that is, in the Tent of Meeting (1:1).
The attribution of chaps. 1–5 to the Wilderness of Sinai runs afoul of the claim
that the entire book of Leviticus was revealed to Moses on Mount Sinai (27:34).
The possibility must, therefore, be reckoned with that Leviticus bears the im-
print of two traditions: all of it was revealed to Moses on Mount Sinai (27:34)
and all of it, except where expressly noted (i.e., chaps. 6–7, 25–26) was revealed
to Moses in the Wilderness of Sinai once the Tabernacle was erected.

In any event, a later redactor added v 38b to the subscript of chaps. 6–7
(vv 37–38a) in the belief that chaps. 6–7 are a continuation of and supplement
to chaps. 1–5. That this was the conviction of the purported redactor can be
supported on internal grounds. First and foremost, it can be shown that chaps.
6–7 presume knowledge of chaps. 1–5. The place that the burnt offering from
the flock is slaughtered (6:18b; 7:2a) is cited only in chap. 1 (1:11). The summary statement concerning the baked cereal offering (7:9) presumes the knowledge of 2:4–7 and that of the dry cereal offering (7:10), the knowledge of 2:2–3
and 5:11–13. The mention of the suet of the well-being offering (6:5; 7:23, 31–
32) presumes a knowledge of its constitutive elements (3:3–4, 9–10, 14–15).

Furthermore, the supplementary nature of chaps. 6–7 is evident in each of
the sacrifices (Hoffmann 1953). The prescriptions for the burnt offering (6:1–6)
are entirely new; there is no duplication at all of chap. 1. The cereal-offering
procedure of 2:1–3 is encapsulated in 6:8, but only because it is needed as an
introduction to the new information—the manner and place of its consumption
(6:9b–11) and the high priest's daily cereal offering (6:12–16); similarly, 7:9–10,
the disposition of the cereal offering, supplements and qualifies 2:3, 10. Except
for the allusion to the place of slaughter (6:18b), the pericope on the purification
offering (6:17–23) supplements 4:1–5:13. The pericope on the reparation offering (7:1–6) supplements 5:14–26. The section on the suet and blood (7:22–28)

supplements and qualifies 3:17b. Finally, the pericope on the well-being offering (7:11–36) supplements chap. 3.

The exegetical principle of the school of Rabbi Ishmael is patently exemplified here: "Whenever a scriptural passage is repeated, it is only repeated because of the new point contained therein" (*b. Soṭa* 3a). Because chaps. 6–7 presume the knowledge of chaps. 1–5, there seems to be no alternative to the conclusion that a redactor is responsible for reworking and affixing the former to the latter, and either he or a later redactor added 7:38b in order to harmonize the discrepancy between two contiguous pericopes commanded by God from separate locations by stating that, although chaps. 6–7 were given to Moses on Mount Sinai, he did not transmit them to Israel until the Wilderness, in combination with chaps. 1–5.

The conjectured composition of chaps. 6–7, then, consists of two stages (possibly three; see the NOTE above on 7:38b), as follows:

Redaction I: Tôrôt (P₁)		*Redaction II: Supplements (P₂,H)*	
6:1–2aα	General Introduction		
6:2aβ–6	Burnt Offering		
6:7–11	Cereal Offering		
		6:12–16	High Priest's Cereal Offering
		6:17–18aα	Introduction, Purification Offering
6:18aβ–23	Purification Offering		
7:1–7	Reparation Offering		
		7:8–10	Burnt and Cereal Offering Prebends
[————	Ordination Offering]		
7:11–21	Well-Being Offering A		
		7:22–27	Suet and Blood
		7:28–29a	Introduction, Well-Being Offering B
7:29b–36	Well-Being Offering B		
7:37–38a	General Summary		
		7:38b	Summary

The supplements do not stem from the same hand: 7:8–10 is assigned to P₂; all of the others, 6:12–18aα; 7:22–29a, 38b(?), are assigned to the H redaction (details in the Introduction, especially §H).

COMMENTS: ON SACRIFICES

A. On the Theory of Sacrifice

"[The sacrifices]" may be compared to a king's son who was addicted to carcasses and forbidden meats. Said the king: Let him always eat at my table and he will get out of the habit" (*Midr. Lev. Rab.* 22:8). This midrash clearly implies that the sacrifices were not ends in themselves but were divinely ordained in order to wean Israel from idolatry. This approach was developed at length in a classic statement by Maimonides (*Guide* 3.32) and countered just as vigorously by Ramban (on 1:9), who maintained that the sacrifices were inherently and eternally efficacious. In truth, the Ramban's rationalizations (mainly mystical) and those offered by other rabbis (e.g., *b. Menaḥ.* 110a [bar.]; *b. Yoma* 86b; cf. Bekhor Shor on Exod 30:1; Lev 2:13; Abravanel, *Introduction*), no different from Maimonides', also betray uneasiness with this institution. Nonetheless we must begin with the assumption that Israel believed that the sacrifices had intrinsic value. It is therefore incumbent upon us to probe deeper, if at all possible, into the psyche of early humankind to see if any of its purported motivations for sacrifice also hold for Israel.

Researchers in primitive and comparative religions distinguish four possible purposes behind the institution of sacrifice: (1) to provide food for the god (cf. Eichrodt 1961: 1.141–44); (2) to assimilate the life force of the sacrificial animal (James 1933); (3) to effect union with the deity (Smith 1927); and (4) to induce the aid of the deity by means of a gift (Tylor 1873).

The first three purposes are not to be found in Israel. True, the first one is attested in Israel's environment, for example, in Egypt (Sauneron 1960: 84–85), in Mesopotamia (Oppenheim 1964: 187–93), and in some sacrificial idioms of the Bible: "my table" (Ezek 44:16), "the food of his God" (21:22; cf. v 17); "my food . . . my pleasant aroma" (Num 28:2), and the like. Moreover, the original aim of the sacred furniture of the Tabernacle-Temple—the table for the bread of presence, the candelabrum, and the incense altar—was to provide food, light, and pleasant aroma for the divine residence (Haran 1961: 286). Even the sacrificial procedure betrays this anthropomorphic background; for instance, God must receive his share of the sacrifice before man (cf. 1 Sam 2:29 [LXX]). Nonetheless, these words, objects, and mores are only fossilized vestiges from a dim past, which show no signs of life in the Bible.

The second purpose is found in animistic religions but not in the Bible. Nevertheless, its derivative—the animal lies on the altar instead of its offerer—continues to find adherents to this day. Originated in the field of general religions by Westermarck (1906: 65–66; 1908–12: 1.604–26) and championed most recently by Girard (1977), this motive was applied to Israel, among others, by

James (1938–39) and, most recently, by Rodriguez (1979) and Janowski (1982). Yet anthropologists have found primitive societies in which substitution plays no role (e.g., Middleton 1960: 100). And as for Israel, the main plank in the substitutionary platform, Lev 17:11, is capable of another interpretation (COMMENT on chap. 17; temporarily, see chap. 11, COMMENT C and Milgrom 1971b); the purification offering purges the sanctuary but not the wrongdoer, and certainly does not substitute for him on the altar (chap. 4, COMMENT B); and the scapegoat, which indeed carries off sin, does not even die or, for that matter, rate as a sacrifice (chap. 16, COMMENT E; cf. also the refutations by Metzinger 1940: 257–72; Moraldi 1956: 95–98; de Vaux 1964: 93–94).

The third purpose, union through commensality with the deity, has even less of a basis in Israel and elsewhere. For example, the shared meal that follows a Nuer sacrifice is purely a secular affair (Evans-Pritchard 1956: 215). In the Bible, union with the deity is expressly denied in sacrificial accounts (e.g., Judg 6:18–21; 13:16; cf. Ps 50:12–13). Moreover, as Ehrlich pointed out (1899–1900: 168), the sacrifice is eaten "before the Lord" not "with" him (e.g., Exod 18:12; Deut 27:7; cf. 1 Sam 2:13–16).

The fourth purpose, a gift to the deity to induce his aid, seems to be the only one that manifests validity in all sacrificial systems. To begin with, the word "sacrifice," in Latin, means "to make sacred" and existentially, not just etymologically, the asseveration can be made that "In every sacrifice, an object passes from the common to the religious domain; it is consecrated" (Hubert and Mauss 1964: 9). The quintessential sacrificial act, then, is the transference of property from the profane to the sacred realm, thus making a gift to the deity. That this notion is also basic to Israelite sacrifice is demonstrated by fundamental sacrificial terms that connote a gift, such as *mattānâ* (23:38; Deut 16:17), *qorbān* (see the NOTE on 1:2), *minḥâ* (see the COMMENT on chap. 2), and *ʾiššeh* (see the NOTE on 1:9). Moreover, it would explain why game and fish were unacceptable as sacrifices: "I cannot sacrifice to the Lord my God burnt offerings that have cost me nothing" (2 Sam 24:24; cf. Barr 1963: 871).

The motivation of seeking divine aid is attested in many texts, such as "Offer to God a thanksgiving offering and pay your vows to the Most High . . . I will deliver you, and you shall glorify me" (Ps 50:14–15). The help requested of God stems from two needs: (1) external aid, to secure fertility or victory, in other words, for blessing; and (2) internal aid, to ward off or forgive sin and impurity, that is, for expiation. Thus the *ʿōlâ* and *minḥâ* are gifts to God to obtain his blessing or forgiveness (see the COMMENTS on chaps. 1 and 2). The *šĕlāmîm* also reveals this two-faceted gift, for its blood ransoms the life of the slaughterer (chap. 11, COMMENT C), and its suet is a gift to God (*ʾiššeh*, 3:5, 11, 14) for the meat. The *ʾāšām*, though its purpose is solely expiatory, also labels its suet an *ʾiššeh* (7:6). Yet, though the *ḥaṭṭāʾt* falls under the same heading as the *ʾāšām* as an exclusive expiatory sacrifice, it is never called an *ʾiššeh*. Furthermore, it is explicitly distinguished from it: "For their error they had brought their

offering, an *'iššeh* to the Lord and their purification offering before the Lord"
(Num 15:25b). This *'iššeh* refers to the burnt offering prescribed by the ritual
(v 24) and, hence, excludes the purification offering (cf. *Sipre* Num 111). The
logic is clear: the Lord is surely pleased with the offering of the penitent wrongdoer, but it is not a gift: it is his humble expiation. Thus, even if the idea of gift
is the dominant motivation for Israelite sacrifice, it is not the only one, and in
the case of the *ḥaṭṭā't*, as demonstrated, it is not even present.

Recently, two studies on Greek religion have promulgated new theories on
the origin of sacrifice: (5) the animal served as a substitute for human victims of
aggression (Girard 1977) and (6) killing the animal evoked feelings of guilt that
could only be assuaged by dedicating the victim to the deity (Burkert 1983).
Whereas the former is remote from explaining biblical sacrifice, the latter rings
with clear associative echoes. The rationale invoked by the Priestly texts for a
mandatory sacrifice *(šĕlāmîm)* each time meat is desired for the diet (17:10–12)
is precisely the same: to expiate for the crime of taking the life of the animal
(chap. 11, COMMENT C). There is now evidence that the identical etiology
prevailed from earliest times in the ancient Near East. The Sumerian myth of
Lugalbanda relates that its hero, heretofore a vegetarian, receives divine approval in a dream to sacrifice whatever animals he can trap. He invites the four
principal deities of the Sumerian pantheon to partake of the ritual meal. "The
slaughtering itself is carried out according to divinely inspired prescriptions (see
chap. 11, COMMENT D), by a divinely chosen individual, with weapons of rare
metals. Presumably, then, we are to understand it as sacred, not profane, slaughter, indeed as the etiology of the sacrificial cult" (Hallo 1987: 9).

In the long run, this theory may prove to have penetrated deepest into the
mystery of sacrificial origins. At present, however, it leaves other essential aspects of sacrifice unexplained. For the Bible, it illumines the origins of the
šĕlāmîm but leaves in the dark the *ʿōlâ*, which, as shown (COMMENT on chap.
1), was comprehensive and more widely practiced than the *šĕlāmîm*. Nor does it
relate to the *minḥâ* (COMMENT on chap. 2), not to speak of other vegetable
offerings, such as the *bikkûrîm* and *rēʾšît* (Num 18:12–13; see the NOTE on
2:12). Finally, the recent attempt to base sacrifice on the anthropological distinction between roasted (allegedly illicit) and boiled meat (Hendel 1989) is
vitiated, among other things, by the fact that there is no prohibition against
roasting sacrificial meat in Scripture and that the "great sin" of Eli's sons (1
Sam 2:17) is not that they intended to roast the priestly portion but that they
took it before God received his portion, the suet, on the altar (vv 15aα,
29[LXX]).

In sum, no single theory can encompass the sacrificial system of any society,
even the most primitive. Evans-Pritchard, in fact, lists fourteen of the many
motivations that underlie the Nuer sacrifice: "communion, gift, apotropaic rite,
bargain, exchange, ransom, elimination, expulsion, purification, expiation, propitiation, substitution, abnegation, homage, and others" (1956: 281). Researchers

have been far more successful by premising multiple purposes for Israel's sacrificial system (e.g., Oesterly 1937; Rowley 1950–51; Eichrodt 1961; von Rad 1962; Gaster 1962; Thompson 1963; Kraus 1966). One cannot but agree with the general conclusion of the anthropologist Bourdillon: "Any general theory of sacrifice is bound to fail. The wide distribution of the institution of sacrifice among peoples of the world is not due to some fundamental trait which fulfills a fundamental human need. Sacrifice is a flexible symbol which can convey a rich variety of possible meanings" (1980: 23).

B. Sancta Contagion

The formula for sancta contagion is *kol-hannōgēaʿ b- yiqdāš*. It occurs four times in P, twice in connection with sacred furniture of the Tabernacle (Exod 29:37; 30:26–29) and twice with sacred offerings (Lev 6:11, 20). These objects of *nōgēaʿ b-* merit closer examination.

The first instance singles out the sacrificial altar (*hammizbēaḥ*, Exod 29:37). The singling out of the altar (Exod 29:37) should occasion no surprise. It was the most exposed of the sancta and within reach of the laity. In the second, the antecedent of *bāhem* (Exod 30:29) is all of the previously enumerated sancta: "With it (the sacred anointing oil) anoint the Tent of Meeting, the Ark of the Pact, the table and all its utensils, the lampstand and all its fittings, the altar of incense, the altar of whole offering and all its utensils, and the laver and its stand" (vv 26–28). Thus not just the outer altar but the Tabernacle and all its furniture—all anointed with the sacred oil—come under the jurisdiction of this formula.

The remaining two occurrences of the formula are found in the sections dealing with the priestly perquisites from two sacrifices, the *minḥâ* and *ḥaṭṭāʾt*. In the latter case, the object is specified as *bĕśārāh* (Lev 6:20). The context makes it clear that the reference is to the meat of the *ḥaṭṭāʾt* cooked by the priests (vv 19, 21). The same holds true for the *minḥâ;* the formula follows the notice that it has been baked by the priests (Lev 6:10). In both instances, the implication is that the contagious power of sacrifices is effective only after the altar (i.e., the deity) receives its due, that is to say, when the *ʾazkārâ* of the *minḥâ* is offered up (e.g., Lev 2:2, 9) and when the blood of the *ḥaṭṭāʾt* is daubed on the altar horns (e.g., Lev 4:7, 18, 25, 30, 34). It is no accident that the formula does not occur with the *ʿōlâ*, for all of the flesh is consumed on the altar with no opportunity for making contact with a profane object. One further implication: the sanctity of the animal is limited to its offerable parts, namely, the flesh, suet, and blood (cf. Lev 6:20) but not to its skin, which, in the *ʿōlâ*, is given to the officiating priest as his wages (Lev 7:8). Moreover, although the animal is "most sacred" from the time of its dedication (Milgrom 1973a: 41 n. 17 [=1983d: 142 n. 17]; 1976f: 39 n. 147; 1983d: 162 n. 16), its offerer, though a layman, may handle it and even perform preliminary rites with it inside the sacred precincts (e.g., hand-leaning and slaughtering, Lev 1:4–5; 4:29) without fear of contracting its sanctity. The reason seems to be that the power of contagion is not imparted to the sacrificial animal until its blood is sprinkled on the altar, thus charging it with the altar's sacred force. Similarly, the Red Cow—like every burnt ḥaṭṭā't—does not convey uncleanness to its handlers until its blood is sprinkled (Num 19:4).

The minḥâ citation is even more illuminating: bāhem, the object of nāgaʿ, is in the plural (Lev 6:11). At first glance this is surprising, for in the entire pericope (vv 7–11) the minḥâ is invariably in the singular. Nevertheless, closer inspection leaves no doubt that the antecedent is 'iššê, a plural noun, which refers not only to the minḥâ but also to the ḥaṭṭā't and 'āšām offerings mentioned in the immediately preceding verse (v 10b). The formula here is, then, an attempt to generalize all of the sacrifices subject to its ruling. This deduction is confirmed by a verse in Ezekiel: "This is the place where the priests shall boil the 'āšām and ḥaṭṭā't and where they bake the minḥâ in order not to bring them out into the outer court and so communicate holiness to the people" (Ezek 46:20). Without further ado, one may deduce that the formula applies only to qodšê qodāšîm 'most sacred offerings' (and so specified in each pericope, Lev 6:10, 18), implying that the meat of the šĕlāmîm, which does not fall into the category of "most sacred," would not be affected by the formula.

For the sake of completeness, it should be noted here that the book of Ezekiel applies the formula to a fifth case: the priestly garments (Ezek 44:19; cf. 42:14), which will be discussed below.

Two additional applications of the formula are alleged, for 1 Sam 21:6 and Isa 45:5. In Samuel the enigmatic phrase is 'ap kî hayyôm yiqdaš bakkelî. According to one interpretation, David argues that because men have remained holy by abstaining from women on ordinary campaigns, "how much more will they be holy today?" (NEB). But the claim that kĕlî can refer to the human body is unwarranted. The second interpretation, "how much more today will their vessels be holy?" (RSV), is open to the dual objection that the preposition b- is ignored and that yiqdaš must mean "to remain in a holy state." The third rendering, "All the more may consecrated food be put into their vessels today" (NJPS), has no basis in the text. The LXX's διὰ τα σκευη μου 'because of my weapons' requires the plural yiqdĕšû and kēlay. It leads S. R. Driver (1913) to conjecture "will they be consecrated with (their) gear?" In any case, at issue is the ancient doctrine of the holiness of the war camp (Deut 23:10–11), whose soldiers must refrain from all defilement including sexual congress (cf. 2 Sam 11:11). It has, however, nothing to do with the transfer of holiness.

kî qĕdaštîkā (Isa 45:5) is rendered "for I am set apart from you" (RSV); "for I am too sacred for you" (NEB); "for I am purer/holier than you" (Targum, Rashi, Ibn Ezra, Ibn Janaḥ, Abravanel). Common to all of these interpretations is the notion that the idolater, by dint of his ritual, feels holier than his fellows and keeps them at arm's length lest he defile him. In any case, this is no transfer of holiness, but, on the contrary, the fear of defilement. As far as I know, only J. Pedersen (1940: 281) and J. L. McKenzie (1968), preceded by Malbim, translate this phrase "I will sanctify you," requiring, however, that the verb be pointed as a *pi'el* (see now Emerton 1980). Our attention can now turn to the formula itself. Each term will be analyzed separately.

yiqdāš. The *qal* of *qādaš* means "become holy." This is its unquestioned meaning elsewhere in Scripture (e.g., Exod 29:21; Num 17:2, 3; Deut 22:9; 1 Sam 21:6). Yet in our formula this meaning has been disputed.

(1) The Targums consistently render it *yitqaddaš* 'will purify himself', as Pseudo-Jonathan (on Exod 29:37) makes clear: "whoever of the sons of Aaron touches the altar must purify himself; however, it is not possible for the rest of the people to touch (it) lest they be consumed by the flashing fire that emanates from the sancta." This interpretation of *yiqdāš*, however, cannot be correct because it is limited to the *pi'el* and *hithpa'el* stems (e.g., Exod 19:10, 14; Num 11:18; Josh 7:13; 1 Sam 16:5; 2 Sam 11:4; Isa 46:17) but is never found in the *qal*.

(2) The LXX consistently uses the future passive ἁγιασθήσεται 'shall be holy', which may also be rendered "shall be pure/purify oneself." The first rendering, "shall be holy," would mean that the person touching the sancta must himself be holy, in other words, he has to be a priest. But it is objectionable on philological grounds: only the adjective *qādōš* expresses the state of holiness, whereas the *qal* (and other verb forms) indicates the process of becoming holy. The second rendering, "shall be pure/purify oneself," is rejected for the reason given in (1), above.

Recently, B. A. Levine has taken up the cudgels for this interpretation, rendering *yiqdaš* as "must be in a holy state" (1987: 246). His view must be categorically rejected. First, the priests, the implied subject of *yiqdaš* (6:11, 20), are *already* in a holy state. Second, if the priests were the subject (an impossibility, as will be demonstrated below), then one would expect instead the verb *yiqrab*, yielding "all (priests) who contact (the sancta) must qualify" (for this meaning of permissive *qārab*, see Milgrom 1970a: 33–37). Third, as noted above, the *qal* imperfect of *qdš* only means "become holy" and cannot denote "must be holy." Finally, Levine's claim that Hag 2:11–13 "demonstrates that sanctity is *not* transferable through physical contact alone" is vitiated by the context of this passage. True, the priest denies that holiness is transmitted through a garment (i.e., at a second remove). Implied, however, is that holiness is contagious *by direct contact*.

(3) Of passing interest is A. B. Ehrlich's rendering, "absorb lethal taboo," in support of which he cites Num 4:15, where the Kohathites touching sancta are subject to death. The analogy, however, does not hold because the sancta alluded to in this verse are restricted to the most sacred furniture and exclude the most sacred offerings. Also, the death penalty is always indicated by the

roots *mwt* (Milgrom 1970a: 5–8) and *krt* (see COMMENT D below) but never by *qdš*.

The meaning of *(kol-hannōgēaʿ b-)yiqdāš* is clarified beyond doubt when it is compared to its antonymic formulation *(kol-hannōgēaʿ b-)yiṭmāʾ* (e.g., Lev 11:24, 26, 27, 31, 36, 39; 15:10, 11, 21, 23, 27; cf. Hag 2:12–13). Just as *yiṭmāʾ* can only mean "shall become impure," so *yiqdāš* must be rendered "shall become holy." The formula, then, must signify that contact with a most sacred object brings about the absorption of its holiness.

nōgēaʿ. There is almost no disputed that *nōgēaʿ b-* means "touch, come into contact with." Nonetheless, the nature of the contact is uncertain. Does it make a difference, for example, if the altar is touched deliberately or accidentally? It is of more than passing interest that the semantic equivalent in Akk., *lapātu*, carries not only the basic meaning "to touch" but also the extended connotations "to put hands on (a person, or object) with evil intentions" and "to commit a sacrilege" (*CAD* L, 85–86). Yet the question of intention, essential though it be, must await the analysis of the final term, *kōl*.

kōl. Surprisingly, it is the simple particle *kōl* rather than the other terms of the formula that is difficult to render. Does *kōl* include persons or is it restricted to inanimate objects: shall it be rendered "whoever" or "whatever"? As will be shown, the answer to this question will open a new chapter of Israel's cultic history.

The rabbis are unanimous in opting for "whatever" and eliminating the human factor completely. Indeed, they even reduce the compass of "whatever." The contagious sancta, as noted above, are of two kinds: the most sacred furniture and the most sacred offerings. Neither kind, aver the rabbis, is contagious to all objects. The most sacred furniture, such as the altar and its vessels (Exod 29:37; 30:29), *mĕqaddēš ʾet-hārāʾûy lô*, only "sanctifies that which befits it," for example, that which qualifies to be placed on the altar or into a sacred vessel. In other words, only whatever is eligible a priori as an offering is susceptible to sancta contagion. And as for the most sacred offerings (Lev 6:11, 20), their contagion is communicable only to articles of food *miššeyiblaʿ*, by absorption (*Sipra*, Ṣaw 3:6; par. 4:6; cf. *m. Zebaḥ.* 11:8).

Poles apart from the restricted contagion posited by the rabbis stands the cultic system of Ezekiel, who holds that most sacred offerings consecrate persons and not just food: "This is the place where the priests shall boil the *ʾāšām* and *ḥaṭṭāʾt* and where they shall bake the *minḥâ*, in order not to bring them into the outer court and so communicate holiness to the people" (Ezek 46:20). Moreover, Ezekiel adds a category of contagious sancta not included in the rabbis' system (or in the Pentateuch), namely, the priestly garments: "When they go out into the outer court (into the outer court) to the people, they shall take off the garments in which they have been officiating and lay them in the sanctuary's chambers; and they shall put on other garments, lest they communicate holiness to the people with their garments" (44:19; cf. 42:14).

THE SACRIFICES

It is germane to inquire whether Ezekiel's ruling is his own innovation or reflects an older law. An answer is at hand if we examine P's position on this matter. To be sure, P contains no explicit law concerning the contagion of the priestly garments; but its very omission from P's prescription on the contagion of sancta in Exod 30:26–30 betrays P's position in a striking way. These verses warrant close examination: "With it (the sacred anointing oil) anoint the Tent of Meeting, the Ark of the Pact, the table and all its utensils, the lampstand and all its fittings, the altar of incense, the altar of whole offering and all its utensils, and the laver and its stand. Thus you shall consecrate them so that they may be most sacred; kol-hannōgēaʿ bāhem yiqdāš. You shall anoint Aaron and his sons, consecrating them to serve me as priests."

That this principle ends with v 30 is shown by the next verse, which begins a new subject, the ways of misusing the anointing oil, and by its formulaic opening: "And speak to the Israelite people as follows." Moreover, the unity of vv 26–30 is proved by the other passages dealing with the anointing oil (prescriptive, Exod 29:1–37; 40:1–15; descriptive, Lev 8:1–30), in which both the priestly garments and the cult objects are anointed during the same ceremonial.

Now it should be noticed that in the pericope cited above, our formula comes not at its end but in its penultimate verse, after the roster of cult objects and before the anointing of the priests (v 29b). Thus the conclusion is unavoidable that the legislator intentionally excludes the priestly garments from the application of the formula because, in his system, the priestly garments do not communicate holiness. That the priestly garments are not subject to the law of sancta contagion is further underscored by a major omission. By itself, v 30 would lead to the deduction that only the persons of Aaron and his sons are anointed, despite the expressed inclusion of the priestly garments among the anointed articles in all other accounts (Exod 29:21; 40:13–15; Lev 8:30). Again, the reason for the omission here of the priestly garments must be attributed to an overt attempt to dissociate them from the notion of contagious holiness. This can mean only one thing: P is engaged in a polemic; it is deliberately opposing a variant tradition such as is found in the book of Ezekiel.

What is the basis for the polemic? It is to be found, I submit, in the taboo concerning clothing made of more than one material, šaʿaṭnēz (Lev 19:19). In the deuteronomic version of the taboo, the materials are specified as linen and wool (Deut 22:11), where it falls among several other taboos against mixtures, kilʾayim (vv 9–11), one of which is particularly instructive: "You shall not sow your vineyard with a second kind of seed, else the full crop will become consecrated, both the seed you have sown and all the yield of the vineyard" (v 9). The import of this verse is that mixed seed—again a sacred mixture—will transmit its holiness to the total yield. (The prohibition of mixed seeds is not unique to Israel. It is found in the Hittite code §§166–67, where the older law prescribes the death penalty for both men and women engaged in sowing "seeds upon seeds.") Thus this context allows us to conclude that a garment of mixed

447

fabrics is also taboo because it is contagiously sacred. Indeed, that the juxtaposition of the prohibitions against mixed seed and mixed fabrics (Deut 22:9, 11) implies that their common rationale is holiness is a principle explicitly stipulated by the Qumran sectaries: *W'L LBŠ[W KTWB ŠLW']* *YHYH Š'TNZ WŠL W' LZRW' ŚDW WK[RMW KL'YM B]GLL ŠHMH QDWŠYM* 'concerning his garment it is written that it should not be *ša'aṭnēz* (19:19) and he should not sow his field and vineyard with two kinds of seed because they (the mixed fabric and seed) are sacred' (4Q *MMT* B 77–79), generously supplied by its intended publishers, E. Qimron and L. Strugnell).

It is therefore hardly an accident that the inner Tabernacle curtains and the outer garments of the high priest—who alone among the priests is permitted to officiate inside the Tabernacle—also consist of a mixture of wool and linen (recognized by rabbinic tradition, cf. *m. Kil.* 9:1; *b. Yoma* 69a; cf. also Jos., *Ant.* 4.8, 11). These fabrics are sacred per se and their aspersion with sacred oil (Exod 29:21; 40:9) serves only to underscore their inherent sanctity. But is their sanctity also contagious? P's instructions concerning the transport of the Tabernacle point to the answer. Whereas the sacred furniture is dismantled and covered by the priests before it can be carried away by the Kohathite Levites (Num 4:3–15), it is the task of the Gershonite Levites to dismantle and cart away the Tabernacle curtains (with the exception of the *pārōket*, v 5) and to install them in the reassembled Tabernacle when camp is made (Num 4:24–28). Thus the Levites who, like the laity, are not holy and, hence, are theoretically ineligible to handle sancta, are explicitly charged with the responsibility of handling the sacred curtains. Clearly, these curtains, though of a sacred mixture and anointed with sacred oil, do not communicate holiness. By the same token, it is reasonable to conclude that the outer garments of the high priests, compounded of the same sacred mixture, also do not possess contagious holiness. Unfortunately, there is no comparable evidence to prove this point, but the fact that there is neither prohibition nor concern in P lest the high priest make contact with the people with his garments indicates that such contact is of no consequence and need not be avoided.

If, then, P allows lay contact with the officiating garments of the high priest and the Tabernacle curtains comprising a sacred mixture of materials, then it certainly would have no reservations about laity touching the garments of the ordinary priest made solely of linen and containing no sacred mixture. This reasoning is supported by an incident cited in P. When Nadab and Abihu are struck down at the sanctuary altar, Moses calls on their levitic cousins to carry them out "by their tunics" (Lev 10:5). One would have thought that the divine fire that had consumed their bodies would only have intensified the holiness of their garments, making it essential to drag them out by some other means. The only possible deduction from this case is that in P priestly garments neither are inherently holy nor do they transmit holiness.

In any event, this view is not shared by Ezekiel. Because the priestly garments have been aspersed with sacred oil he holds that they are imbued with sacred holiness. Now, Ezekiel can hardly have originated his ruling. The more likely prospect is that P is the innovator, restricting the power of sancta contagion to the most sacred furniture and offerings but denying it to sacred mixtures of fabrics, not to speak of ordinary priestly clothing. Indeed, as we shall now demonstrate, it even places limits on the degree of contagion it allots to the altar and to the other cult furniture.

We are now in a position to assault the question: does *kol* of our formula mean "whatever" or "whoever"? As has been shown, P denies Ezekiel's claim that the priestly garments transmit holiness to persons. But what is P's position on the contagious power of the other sancta? In particular, what is the extent of the contagious power of the sacrifices? Both P and Ezekiel expressly admit that most sacred offerings can transmit holiness (Lev 6:11, 20; Ezek 46:20); but does P agree with Ezekiel that sacrifices consecrate persons, or does P differ with Ezekiel on this issue even as it does concerning the priestly garments? Unfortunately, P is silent on this question; it is not even meaningfully silent, as in the case of the priestly garments. Nevertheless, four lines of indirect evidence can be brought to bear on this question, and they converge with telling force.

The first passage to be discussed is Lev 5:14–16: "The Lord spoke to Moses, saying: When a person commits a sacrilege by being inadvertently remiss with any of the Lord's sancta, he shall bring as his penalty to the Lord a ram without blemish from the flock, convertible into payment in silver by sanctuary weight, as a reparation offering, and he shall make restitution for that item of the sancta wherein he was remiss and shall add one-fifth to it. When he gives it to the priest, the priest shall effect expiation on his behalf with the ram of the reparation offering so that he may be forgiven." Is the trespasser upon the sancta affected by his sacrilege? This text states only that the trespasser must restore the sanctum 20 percent beyond its original value and bring an *ʾāšām* offering to atone for his desecration. Nothing in the ritual procedure indicates that by desecrating a sanctum the trespasser has absorbed any of its sanctity; otherwise he would be required to undergo a purification ritual to desanctify himself. Therefore, the absence of any desanctification ritual for the trespasses on sancta points to the probability that, in P's system, sancta are not contagious to persons and the formula does not apply.

The second text, Hag 2:12, reads, "If someone carries sacred meat in the corner of his garment, and with his corner touches bread, pottage, wine, oil, or any foodstuff, will any of these be sanctified? The priest replied, and said, 'No.' " That Haggai puts his question to priests indicates that his question is a cultic matter. Three inferences can be drawn from its formulation relevant to sancta contagion. The first is that the meat is "most sacred" (see above). Second, the meat has transferred its holiness to the garment but not to its bearer. Thus the question takes for granted that the person handling the sacred meat is not infected with its holiness. Here then is another indication that our formula applies to objects and not to persons. The third inference is that if the sacred meat had itself come into direct contact with the same objects touched by the garment they assuredly would have been sanctified. But what precisely are these objects? They are "bread, stew, wine, oil, or any other food." Thus only food-stuffs would have been affected. But is it not just as likely that the man's garment would have brushed by a table, a chair, or some other furniture? Thus the omission of household utensils and goods from Haggai's question can only imply that these objects cannot become sanctified by contact with sacred meat. In sum, the prophet's question indicated that the Jerusalemite priesthood at the end of the sixth century not only had limited the formula of sancta contagion to objects but had further narrowed its application just to articles of food.

The third relevant text is Exod 30:26–29, cited above. Our formula concluded the list of consecrated objects and, therefore, applies to all of them. If, however, the effect of touching not just the altar but also the inner sancta is to contract holiness, then it would clash with another basic formula in P's system, *hazzār haqqārēb yûmāt*, that is, death is meted out to the unauthorized encroacher. We would do well to ask how encroachers on sancta can simultaneously become holy and incur death. The reconciliation of these two formulas is obvious: encroachers are indeed put to death, and sancta contagion does not apply to persons.

The final text is Num 4:15: "When Aaron and his sons have finished covering the sacred objects and all the utensils of the sacred objects at the breaking of the camp, only then shall the Kohathites come and lift them so that they do not come in contact with the sacred objects and die."

Thus the sancta would appear to transmit both holiness and death to those who touch them. How can that be? Moreover, how is it possible for the Gershonite Levites to carry the inner curtains of the Tabernacle (Num 4:25) if according to P, they are most sacred (Exod 30:20) and hence lethal (Num 4:15)? Would not the Gershonites incur death? Haran (1978: 179) tries to resolve this problem by hypothesizing that P temporarily suspended the contagion of the Tabernacle structure in order to allow for the Levites to dismantle and transport it. Yet, as soon as we render *kol* as "whatever" and thereby deprive the sancta of the power to communicate holiness to persons, the paradox is resolved. The Tabernacle curtains, like the rest of the sancta, sanctify objects, not persons. The Levites, then, need have no fear in this regard. But is not the sanctity of the curtains lethal? Again, the answer is, No. Only the cult objects specified in the levitic labors (Num 4:4–14) are fatal to the unauthorized who touch them. The Tabernacle curtains are not in this list and, hence, may be carried by the Levites with impunity. In sum, the alleged paradox of the sancta is chimerical. The sancta transmit death only to persons and holiness only to objects.

In aggregate, the four texts cited above (Lev 5:14–16; Hag 2:10–12; Exod 30:26–29; Num 4:15) provide indirect but unanimous evidence that sancta are not contagious to persons. Thus the rabbis are probably right. *kol* in P's formula

450

means "whatever," not "whoever." Ezekiel, then, in insisting that sacred food is contagious to persons, harbors a variant tradition. Indeed, that Ezekiel is at odds with the prevailing opinion of his time can be extrapolated from the testimony of Haggai, who cannot have been removed from Ezekiel's time by more than one generation. From Haggai's question to the priests we have concluded that the Jerusalem priesthood that returned from the Babylonian exile maintained that the contagion of sacred food was restricted solely to other food and could on no account affect persons. How can we account for Ezekiel's polaric opposition to the priestly establishment of this time? That opposition, I submit, is thrown into clear relief by our formula.

Ezekiel—rather, the tradition he transmits—vehemently opposes the compromise with the laity proposed by P. His blueprint for the temple unequivocally excludes the laity from the inner court and even from the gates to that court (46:3). Sacrificial slaughter is, in his plan, to be performed within the northern gate (40:39–42)—but by the Levites, not the laity (44:11). Even the cooking of the šĕlāmîm, though it may be eaten by the lay offerer, is also to be done by the Levites in the outer court (46:24). Thus the blueprint of Ezekiel's temple reveals a different gradation of holiness from that of P's Tabernacle. Both hold in common that the shrine per se is the domain of the priest. They differ, however, in regard to the sanctity of the outer area. P holds that the layman has access to the forecourt up to the altar so that he can participate in the preparations of the sacrifice. Ezekiel instead bars the layman entirely from the inner court, even from the northern gate where, in his scheme, the slaughtering takes place, and even from touching the šĕlāmîm meat until it is cooked in the outer court. The slaughtering and cooking are, instead, to be performed by the Levites. The gradation of holiness in each scheme is illustrated in the diagrams of fig. 8.

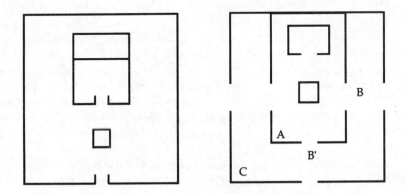

FIGURE 8: Ezekiel's temple is divided into three concentric domains of holiness, which correspond to the three classes in Israel: priests, Levites, and

laity. The geometric center of the temple complex is the altar. The innermost area, comprising the inner court (A) and its structures, the altar and the temple buildings, is the priestly domain. The northern gate of the inner court (B), where the sacrificial slaughter is performed, is accessible to the Levites. The eastern gate (B') is open to the *nāśîʾ*. The outer court (C) is the only area available to the laity. The Priestly Tabernacle is also constructed according to the notion of concentric domains of decreasing holiness, but the gradations are more subtle and the boundaries allow for blurring. The center is the adytum (in principle, the Ark). The domain of the priests comprises the Tabernacle tent, the sacrificial altar, and the courtyard between them. But this priestly area is not homogeneous; its sanctity is graded. The adytum is accessible to the high priest alone under limited circumstances (Lev 16); the high priest officiates in the Tent and priests on the altar; the altar marks the boundary line between the priestly and lay domains, but only the priests have access to it.

Is there an underlying principle that can account for the differences between the two sanctuary blueprints? I believe there is, and it finds expression in our formula. Ezekiel does not accept P's ruling that persons are not subject to the jurisdiction of the formula. According to this priest-prophet, *sancta are contagious to persons*. The proof is to be found, I submit, in the different centers of each sanctuary. It is no accident that Ezekiel has made the outer altar the exact geometric center of his temple complex. In P, the altar is the least holy of the sancta, as exemplified by its covering during transit, which is of material inferior to the coverings of the other sancta (Num 4:3–14). By moving the focus of holiness to the altar, Ezekiel takes the position that the altar is of equal sanctity to the inner sancta and hence qualifies for the same degree of contagion, which bars lay access. The rest of his plan is of a piece with this premise. It is so conceived that the priests never come into contact with the laity while they are officiating because the entire inner court, including its gates—in contradiction to that of P—is off limits to the laity. Moreover, because the sacrifices are as contagious to persons as the cult objects, all lay duties in connection with them, such as slaughtering, are transferred to the Levites. Thus, whereas in P's scheme Levites are indistinguishable from laymen in regard to their access to sancta, Ezekiel in effect *elevates* the Levites by granting them special functions (e.g., slaughtering) and space (the inner gates), which set them apart from the laity. Thus it is Ezekiel's postulate of sancta contagion to persons that accounts for the unique floor-plan of his temple and the distribution of the priests, Levites, and laymen within it.

Furthermore, Ezekiel's rule on sancta contagion is the key that explains his differences from P. For example, his list of prohibitions for the priesthood (44:17–27) is with only one exception in direct conflict with P, as follows: (1) priests may not wear wool (vv 17–18), while P's high priest wears woolen materials (see above), and the belts worn by ordinary priests probably contain wool (Exod 39:29; *b. Yoma* 12a); (2) the priestly garments are contagious to persons

452

(v 19), a view opposed by P (above); (3) priests are required to trim their hair (v 20), a rule unknown to P (cf. Lev 10:6); (4) the prohibition against entering the inner court while intoxicated (v 21) agrees with P (Lev 10:9); (5) the prohibition of marrying the widow of a nonpriest (v 22) is unknown to P, which only forbids a priest to marry a divorcee (Lev 21:7); (6) the purification rites for the corpse-contaminated priests are of two weeks duration with a purification offering as the climax (vv 25–27), while in P priests and laymen alike undergo the same week-long purification rite and require no sacrifice (Num 19:11–12, 16–19).

It should be noted that in each case Ezekiel takes the stricter point of view. This fact in itself should indicate that Ezekiel is no innovator but, on the contrary, a standard bearer of an older tradition, which has been rejected by P, but which he wishes to restore. As shown, Ezekiel invokes the viewpoint posited by the oldest biblical narratives that the sancta are contagious to persons. This simple postulate is all that is needed to explain Ezekiel's severer code for the priests whereby he both elevates their holy status and distances them more from the laity, even to the point of preventing the laity from direct contact with the priestly clothing and the sacrifices.

Another indication of the antiquity of Ezekiel's code is that he requires a purification sacrifice for the corpse-contaminated priest. The only other person who is subject to this same requirement is P's Nazirite (Num 6:9–11). It can be shown that the naziritic ritual reflected in P contains many ancient elements. For example, the requirements that the *šĕlāmîm* offering be cooked in the sanctuary premises and that the priest receive his portion from the boiled meat (v 19) are attested in the sanctuary of Shiloh (1 Sam 2:13–14). Also, the priestly portion is designated as the shoulder, a perquisite that is never again attested in P but which has hallowed precedents throughout the ancient Near East. Thus it can be safely concluded that the requirement that the corpse-contaminated Nazirite bring a purification offering also rests on ancient precedent and that there was a similar tradition for the priest, who, sharing with the Nazirite the designation "holy to the Lord" (Lev 21:7; Num 6:8), would also bring a purification offering as his decontamination ritual. Ezekiel's stringent provisions for the priesthood can reflect only an older tradition, which had been scuttled by the Jerusalem priesthood in favor of regulations now found in P. Thus Ezekiel is a religious conservative whose view represents a continuing polemic against the prevailing practice of the Jerusalem Temple.

The question of *kol* can now be answered. The answer, however, is not univocal. It is a coefficient of time and, hence, variable. In the earlier period, whenever the formula originated, the range of *kol* was unrestricted: even persons were included and intention was not a factor. Indeed, that the word *kol* was chosen for the formula probably indicates that initially no exceptions were intended. The early sources corroborate this assumption: the most sacred sancta are lethally contagious to persons even when their contact with them is respectful, for example, Uzzah's touching the Ark (2 Sam 6:6–7) and the Beth-Shemeshites' viewing it (1 Sam 6:19). The theophany at Sinai provides a particularly illuminating example. Whoever trespasses on the mountain must be slain, but his slayers must heed that "no hand shall touch him; he shall be either stoned or pierced through" (Exod 19:13). The implication is clear: the holiness communicated to the offender is of such power that it can be transmitted through a medium. Hence the instrument of death must not allow contact between the offender and his executioner. P also provides a telling example: the death of Nadab and Abihu (Lev 10:1–5). The divine fire has executed them for their cultic offense, but their bodies may not be touched directly; they must be wrapped in other garments before being removed from the sanctuary (v 5). Again, the holiness contracted by persons can be imparted to a third party with fatal results. This second-degree holiness is attributed to the sancta associated with the very presence of God (e.g., the Ark, Mount Sinai, the divine fire). The high voltage of the supersancta is also evidenced by their power to communicate not only by contact but by sight. This has already been noted in the story of the Ark at Beth-Shemesh (1 Sam 6:19). But even in P—which, as will be shown, strives for a reduction in the contagious power of the sancta—the sancta still possess the power to kill their viewers when they are being dismantled (Num 4:20). Thus even in the early sources a gradation may be detected in the most sacred sancta; the supersancta—those considered to be the earthly manifestations of the deity—are fatally contagious to those who view them directly and to those who contact them through a medium.

The salient point in P is that it has reduced the range and power of the sancta. First, as has already been demonstrated, P defuses the altar, rendering it noncontagious to persons. Furthermore, as can be shown (chap. 15, COMMENT E; cf. also Milgrom 1990a, Excursus 75, pp. 504–9), whereas in all early sources the altar proves its contagious power by providing asylum, in P this power is denied. Even so, P is not consistent in this respect. In the account of the Levites' labors in the Tabernacle (Num 4), all of the sancta bear a deadly contagion on contact (v 15) and, when dismantled, even on sight (v 20). By contrast, as demonstrated, the sancta list in Exod 30:26–29 allows no other inference but that the sancta are not contagious to persons.

It would seem that P preserves a *narrative* tradition that ascribed contagious power to the Tabernacle sancta, but this contagion was severely restricted in P's *legal* pronouncements. Further evidence of the devitalization of the sancta is the fact that in the conflict between impurity and holiness, impurity always wins (for the singular exception of the high priest, see the NOTE on 16:27). It is the holy object that requires cleansing; it can never purify the impure (S. Rattray). To be sure, this powerlessness stems, in part, from Israel's setting in the ancient Near East, where impurity and holiness were considered manifestations of supernal forces, which Israel transformed by coalescing all aspects of holiness under the aegis of the one God and transferring demonic power, if only in potential, to the human race (chap. 4, COMMENT C). In the Bible, holiness once again regains its dynamic force, but it is no longer inherent in sancta; it can only stem from the will and activity of man (see the Introduction to volume 2). In any event, the total elimination of persons from susceptibility to sancta contagion can only be ascribed to the legislative activity of Israel's priesthood.

Haggai attests a further reduction. Uncovered sacred food transmits its holiness to food only, not to other objects. Ezekiel, however, once again records a variant tradition. Holding that sacred food and garments communicate holiness to persons, he espouses the older view that sancta are contagious to persons and opposes the innovative view, championed by P and Haggai, which denies that persons can be infected by sancta. The final reduction in sancta contagion is posited in the tannaitic sources, wherein the altar and its vessels (but not the inner sancta) communicate holiness only to those foodstuffs which qualify as offerings.

The following stages in the reduction of *kol* in the formula *kol-hannōgēaʿ yiqdāš* can be discerned: (1) In the prebiblical stage all sancta communicate holiness to persons, the inner sancta directly by sight and indirectly by touch. This contagion is lethal even if the contact is accidental. The early biblical narratives exemplify this deadly power of the sancta in the Ark, Mount Sinai, and the divine fire. (2) The Priestly account of the Levites' work assignment in the Tabernacle (Num 4) reveals the sancta unchanged from the previous stage only for the brief and rare moment while they are being dismantled but otherwise, as shown by the list of the sancta to be anointed (Exod 30:26–29), the sancta have lost their power to infect persons even by touch. Ezekiel, however, opts for the older view that sancta are contagious to persons. (3) Haggai restricts the contagion of sancta to foodstuffs. (4) The Tannaites follow Haggai and reduce the contagion of the altar to those foods which qualify as offerings. This change, it should be noted, is minuscule. Both Haggai and the rabbis agree that the sancta transmit their holiness only to foods. Thus the rabbinic ruling on sancta contagion remains the same *all through the Second Commonwealth,* and the major innovation, first detected in Haggai, is traceable back, at the latest, to exilic times.

What was the motivating force behind the Priestly obsession to reduce the contagious power of the sancta? In particular, what lay behind their major radical innovation that the sancta are no longer contagious to persons? The texts are silent, but one sanctum provides the necessary clue—the altar. In ordaining that the formula *kol-hannōgēaʿ yiqdāš* 'all that touches [the sancta] becomes sanctified' (6:11, 20; Exod 29:37; 30:26–29) applies to objects but not persons, the priests had the altar chiefly in mind. They probably were deeply disturbed by the stream of murderers, thieves, and assorted criminals who flocked to the altar and resided on the sanctuary grounds on the basis of hoary, venerable traditions that the altar "sanctifies"; so they declared that those who entered the sacred precincts were no longer under divine protection. The priests therefore took the radical step of declaring that the altar was no longer contagious; those who touched it were no longer "sanctified," so they might be wrested from the altar by the authorities with impunity. In this cultic reform the priests would have won the support of the king and his bureaucracy, who would have earnestly wished to terminate the sanctuary's veto power over their jurisdiction.

Because the only attested case of altar asylum in the Bible—but surely not the first—is David's tent-shrine in Jerusalem (1 Kgs 1:51; 2:2–3), it is highly probable that this reform was enacted under Solomon, who used his royal power to introduce many administrative and cultic changes. The new altar in the new Temple was declared off limits to every nonpriest and never afforded asylum. There was still a need, however, to provide the accidental manslayer asylum from the *gōʾēl haddām* 'blood redeemer', and that need was answered by the asylum (but not the sanctuary) cities, also a Priestly innovation (details in Milgrom 1981b).

C. The Tāmîd

In outer form, the *Tāmîd* resembles the daily offering of Israel's neighbors, where—at least symbolically—it formed the daily diet of the gods. Thus in Egyptian temples there were three daily services, but only during the morning and evening were the gods served their meals (Sauneron 1960). In Mesopotamia the parallel is even more striking: "According to an explicit and detailed text of the Seleucid period, the images in the temple of Uruk were served two meals per day. The first and principal meal was brought in the morning when the temple opened, and the other was served at night, apparently immediately before the closing of the doors of the sanctuary. . . . Each repast consisted of two courses, called main and second" (Oppenheim 1964). Israel's *Tāmîd* also prescribed two offerings daily, a "main course" of a lamb with a meal offering and a libation as "side dishes." The menu for the Mesopotamian gods differed sharply: "The daily total, throughout the year, for the four meals per day: twenty-one first-class, fat, clean rams which had been fed barley for two years; two large bulls; one milk-fed bullock; eight lambs; thirty *marratu*-birds; thirty . . . -birds; three *cranes* which have been fed . . . -grain; five ducks which have been fed . . . -flour; two ducks of a lower quality than those just mentioned; four *wild* boars; three ostrich eggs; three duck eggs" (*ANET*[3] 344). The contrast is that of Nathan's parable: "The rich man had very large flocks and herds, but the poor man had only one little ewe lamb" (2 Sam 12:2–3). Indeed, as Abravanel has already observed, the *Tāmîd* was restricted to the essential staples of the Israelite diet: the flesh of lambs (the most inexpensive meat) and a portion of the three most abundant crops—from which firstfruits were prescribed (Num 18:12)—wheat, wine, and (olive) oil.

The biblical sources evidence different traditions concerning the *Tāmîd*. In the First Temple, the *Tāmîd* was indeed offered twice daily, but the burnt offering was only sacrificed in the morning and the meal offering, *minḥâ*, in the evening (2 Kgs 16:5; see 1 Kgs 18:29, 36). Ezekiel, though he also prescribes one burnt offering and one meal offering, specifies that both be offered up in the morning (Ezek 46:13–15). In the postexilic period mention is made of the regular burnt offering and regular meal offering (Neh 10:34), but their time is unspecified. Here the Torah's twice-daily offering is probably intended, but the meal offering seems to hold equal status with the burnt offering. In all of the aforementioned references, the wine libation is absent; but it is probably incorporated into one of the two offerings (as in Num 28:19–21; 29:14–15). An earlier association of the meal offering with the evening sacrifice is reflected in the terms "the evening *minḥâ*" (Ezra 9:4, 5) and "at the time of the evening *minḥâ*" (Dan 9:21), though undoubtedly the *Tāmîd* as prescribed in the Torah was scrupulously followed. The term persisted in post-Temple times, when the afternoon prayer that replaced the second *Tāmîd* offering was also called the *minḥâ* (*m. Ber.* 4:1; *m. Pesaḥ.* 10:1). Some scholars suggest that the text of the *Tāmîd* in the Torah also shows signs of developing from a single daily offering (Rendtorff 1967). But the term "the morning burnt offering" here (Num 28:23) and in the descriptive ritual of Lev 9:17 clearly implies that there was a regular evening offering as well.

The unbroken continuity of the *Tāmîd* in the Temple was reassuring to Israel, and its cessation a traumatic calamity (Dan 8:11–13; 11:31; 12:11). Legend has it that as long as the *Tāmîd* was uninterrupted the walls of Jerusalem were impregnable (*b. B. Qam.* 82b). One of the reasons for observing the fast of the seventeenth of Tammuz is that on this day the *Tāmîd* ceased (*Meg. Taʿan.* 4:6).

D. Kārēt

Jewish exegesis unanimously holds that *kārēt* is a divine penalty but is in disagreement concerning its exact nature. Among the major views are the following: (1) childlessness and premature death (Rashi on *b. Šabb.* 25a); (2) death before the age of sixty (*Moʿed Qat.* 28a); (3) death before the age of fifty-two (Rabad); (4) being "cut off" through the extirpation of descendants (Ibn Ezra on Gen 17:14); (5) at death, the soul too shall die and will not enjoy the spiritual life of the hereafter (Maim., *Teshuva* 8.1; cf. *Sipre* Num 112; Ramban on Lev 20:2). Most moderns, to the contrary, define *kārēt* either as excommunication or as death by man (e.g., von Rad 1962: 1.264 n. 182). Interestingly, so do the sectaries of the Dead Sea (1QS 8:22–24).

The latter theory can be discounted as soon as the loci of the *kārēt* are held up to view. All of them fall into the category of *fas*, not *jus*, in other words, they are deliberate sins against God, not against man. As the cardinal postulate of the Priestly legislation is that sins against God are punishable by God and not by man (Milgrom 1970a: 5–8), it follows that the punishment of *kārēt* is executed solely by the deity. There are nineteen cases of *kārēt* in the Torah, and they can be subsumed under the following categories:

A. Sacred time
    1. neglecting the *pesaḥ* sacrifice (Num 9:13)
    2. eating leaven during the *maṣṣôt* festival (Exod 12:15, 19)
    3. working on the Sabbath (Exod 31:14)
    4. working or not fasting on Yom Kippur (Lev 23:29, 30)
B. Sacred substance
    5. imbibing blood (Lev 7:27; 17:10, 14)
    6. eating suet (Lev 7:25)
    7. duplicating or misusing sanctuary incense (Exod 30:38)
    8. duplicating or misusing sanctuary anointment oil (Exod 30:33)
    9. eating of a sacrifice beyond the permitted period, *piggûl* (Lev 7:18; 19:8)
    10. eating of a sacrifice in the state of impurity (Lev 7:20–21)
    11. Levites encroaching upon sancta (Num 18:3; cf. 4:15, 19–20)
    12. blaspheming (flauntingly violating a prohibitive commandment, Num 15:30–31; cf. Lev 24:15)
C. Purification rituals
    13. neglecting circumcision (Gen 17:14; the purification is figurative, Josh 5:9)
    14. neglecting purification after contact with the dead (Num 19:13–20)
D. Illicit worship
    15. Molech and other forms of idolatry (Lev 20:2–5; Ezek 14:5)
    16. consulting the dead (Lev 20:6)
    17. slaughtering animals outside the authorized sanctuary (Lev 17:4)
    18. sacrificing animals outside the authorized sanctuary (Lev 17:9)
E. Illicit sex
    19. effecting forbidden consanguineous and incestuous marriages (Lev 18:27–29)

Thus the rabbinic view that *kārēt* is a divine penalty is upheld. As for the exact nature of *kārēt*, two of the five opinions registered above command attention. The first is that *kārēt* means extirpation (Ibn Ezra; cf. also Tosafot on *b. Šabb.* 25a), meaning that the offender's line is terminated. In contrast to the death penalty inflicted by man *(yûmat)* or God *(yāmût)*, *kārēt* is not necessarily directed against the person of the sinner. He may live a full life or an aborted one. His death need not be immediate, as would be the case if his execution were the responsibility of a human court. True, the rabbis of the Talmud opt for the definition of *kārēt* as signifying a premature death (no. 2, above). This view presumes the biblical postulate that each person is allotted a fixed number of years and that if he is worthy he "fulfills his years" (Exod 23:26; Isa 65:20;

Pss 39:5; 90:10–11). In the attested cases of premature death in the Torah (Nadab and Abihu, Lev 10; Dathan and Abiram and Korah, Num 16; the plagues in Egypt and in the wilderness, e.g., Exod 11; Num 11–14), however, the term *kārēt* never occurs. That *kārēt,* instead, refers to extirpation is supported by the following cases: (1) "May his posterity be cut off *(lĕhakrît); may* their name be blotted out in the next generation" (Ps 109:13)—this verse is significant because of its parallelism; it both equates *kārēt* with extirpation and states explicitly that *kārēt* need not be carried out upon the sinner himself but will affect his descendants. (2) "That the name of the deceased may not disappear *(yikkārēt)* from his kinsmen" (Ruth 4:10)—Boaz the levir redeems Ruth in order to perpetuate the line of her deceased husband. (3) "May the Lord cut off *(yakrēt)* from the one who does this all descendants from the tents of Jacob" (Mal 2:12)—there is some doubt that *ʿer wĕʿōneh* means "descendants," but the context clearly speaks of the extirpation of the line. (4) "(Dathan and Abiram and other families) vanished *(wayyōʾbĕdû)* from the midst of the congregation" (Num 16:33)—although the root *kārēt* does not occur, it is replaced by the attested synonym *ʾābad* (e.g., Lev 23:30; Deut 7:24). (5) "The Lord blots out *(ûmāḥâ)* his name from under heaven" (Deut 29:19)—the context is that of worshiping idols clandestinely. The root *kārēt* does not occur, but this is a D text and, instead, employs the synonym *māḥâ.* The crime can only be discerned by God (cf. v 28, Ibn Ezra), and the punishment is extirpation. Furthermore, *kārēt,* as extirpation, would be in consonance with the Priestly doctrine that God engages in collective responsibility: whereas man can only punish the sinner, God may also direct his wrath at the sinner's family and community.

Further illumination is provided by the context of the Malachi passage, cited above (no. 3). The priests are accused of scorning God's name by offering defiled food on the altar and preparing a blind, lame, or sick animal for sacrifice (Mal 1:6–8). As punishment, the Lord states, "I will strew dung upon your faces, the dung of your festal sacrifices, and you shall be carried out to its [heap]" (Mal 2:3). A Hittite text, "Instructions for Temple Officials," offers a striking parallel: "If . . . the kitchen servant . . . gives the god to eat from an unclean (vessel), to such a man the gods will give dung (and) urine to eat (and) to drink" (*ANET*[3] 209, lines 600–18). Furthermore, Malachi's *kārēt* penalty, which the Lord will impose on the offender and his descendants, is precisely matched in this Hittite text: "does the god take revenge on him alone? Does he not take revenge on his wife, his children, his descendants, his kin, his slaves, his slave-girls, his cattle (and) sheep together with his crop and will utterly destroy him?" (*ANET*[3] 208, lines 35–38). These resemblances (and others) between the two documents are so remarkable that the possibility must be entertained that this Hittite text lay before Malachi (Segal 1983–84). Be that as it may, the comparison between the two clarifies and defines the exact meaning of *kārēt:* extirpation of the offender's entire line.

The other possible meaning of *kārēt* is that the punishment is indeed executed upon the sinner but only after his death: he is not permitted to rejoin his ancestors in the afterlife (no. 5, above). This meaning for *kārēt* is supported by the idiom that is its antonym: *neʾĕsap ʾel* 'be gathered to one's [kin, fathers]' (e.g., Num 20:24; 27:13; 31:2; Gen 15:15; 47:30; Judg 2:10). Particularly in regard to the patriarchs, the language of the Bible presumes three stages concerning their death: they die, they are gathered to their kin, and they are buried (cf. Gen 25:8, 17; 35:29; 49:33). "It (the term "gathered") designates something which succeeds death and precedes sepulture, the kind of thing which may hardly be considered as other than reunion with the ancestors in Sheol" (Alfrink 1948: 128). This biblical term has its counterpart in the contiguous river civilizations of Egypt—for example, "going to one's Ka"—and of Mesopotamia—for instance, "joining the ghosts of one's ancestors" (Wold 1978)—all of which is evidence for a belief in the afterlife that permeated the ancient world and the concomitant fear that a wrathful deity might deprive man of this boon. This interpretation would be in keeping with *kārēt* as an individual, not a collective, retribution. Finally, that a person is cut off from *ʿammāyw* 'his kin' implies the family sepulcher in which his kin has been gathered.

It is difficult to determine which of these two meanings is correct. Because they are not mutually exclusive, it is possible that *kārēt* implies both of them, in other words, no descendants in this world and no life in the next.

Whether *kārēt* be defined as extirpation or denial of afterlife, or both, it illuminates two cruxes of *kārēt*. Lev 20:2–3 reads ". . . [whoever] gives any of his offspring to Molech shall be put to death; the people of the land shall pelt him with stones. And I will set my face against that man and will cut him off *(wĕhikrattî)* from among his people." The accepted interpretation is that if man does not put the Molech worshiper to death, God will (e.g., Abravanel). But the two sentences in the text are not alternatives; they are to be taken conjunctively: death plus *kārēt* awaits the criminal. This means that *kārēt* is not synonymous with death but is another form of punishment that only the deity can execute. Thus extirpation or premature death or both all fit the bill. The same conjunction of judicial death plus *kārēt* is prescribed for the Sabbath violator (Exod 31:14). Again, it implies that between them God and man will terminate the criminal: man will put him to death and God will extirpate his line and/or deny him life in the hereafter.

Furthermore, one can readily understand why the Molech and Sabbath violations are given the added punishment of death by human agency. Whereas the *kārēt* cases assume that the sin takes place in private so that only the deity is aware of the crime, the Molech and Sabbath violations are performed in public and, unless punished at once by judicial execution, they may demoralize the entire community.

THE SACRIFICES

E. The Tĕnûpâ

Several of the translators of the English Bible known as the King James's Version knew Hebrew and read the works of the Jewish commentators in the original (Daiches 1941). In this way speakers of English learned of the "wave offering" or "heave offering."

These translations for *tĕnûpâ* and *tĕrûmâ* are based on the view of the rabbis that the *tĕnûpâ* and *tĕrûmâ* constitute two cultic motions performed with an offering, the *tĕnûpâ* being a horizontal motion "extending and bringing back," and the *tĕrûmâ* being a vertical motion "raising and lowering" (cf. *m. Menaḥ.* 5:6; *t. Menaḥ.* 7:13–19; *Sipra*, Ṣaw 16:3; *b. Sukk.* 37b; *b. Menaḥ.* 61b–62a; *Midr. Lev. Rab.* 28:5). This interpretation found its way into most of the translations, commentaries, and dictionaries, and is accepted to this day.

· Only recently has a different conception of these terms developed in research. Some time ago, G. R. Driver (1956b) suggested that originally these terms referred to different rituals in the Temple, but as they appear in the Bible their original form is completely obscured. Their ritual character has disappeared, and both equally signify bringing gifts to the Temple. He was not the first to doubt the traditional interpretation. His father, S. R. Driver, and his colleagues in the *Lexicon of the Old Testament* (1907) also felt doubts about the rabbinic interpretation, even though they accepted it. And if we trace back these doubts, we find their origin in ancient times. The LXX, for example, is not at all consistent in its handling of these terms. It uses several renderings, whose general meaning is "dedication." The renderings alternate from term to term. For a clear example see the LXX on the uses of *tĕnûpâ* cited in one context, the *mĕṣōrāʿ* (Lev 14): ἀφόρισμα (v 12), ἀφαίρεμα (v 21), ἐπίθεμα (v 24). The situation is even worse, because ἀφαίρεμα is also utilized to translate *tĕrûma;* see for example on Lev 7:34 (v 24 in the LXX). Hence it is likely that the Alexandrian sages did not distinguish between *tĕnûpâ* and *tĕrûmâ* at all. These doubts that the rabbis' interpretation does not correspond to the plain meaning are also echoed by the medieval commentators—Bekhor Shor (on Exod 29:24), Ramban (on 7:30), and Abravanel (on Exod 32). As a result, up until now two interpretations have remained current, that of the rabbis, with *tĕnûpâ* and *tĕrûmâ* referring to a cultic ritual, and that of the moderns, who argue to the contrary, that these terms are totally devoid of any ritual character.

Nevertheless, a precise terminological distinction made by Scripture raises the suspicion that both the ancients and the moderns were wrong: *tĕnûpâ* is done "before the Lord" (Exod 29:24, 25; Lev 7:30; 8:27, 29; 9:21; 10:15; 14:12, 24; 23:20; Num 6:30; 8:11, 21; only in Exod 35:22 and Num 8:13 is *tĕnûpâ* "to the Lord"; all from P), whereas *tĕrûmâ* is always "to the Lord" (Exod 25:2; 29:28; 30:13; 35:5; Lev 7:14; Num 15:19, 21; 18:19, 24; 31:28, all from P; Ezek 45:1; 48:9); it never takes the preposition "before." This distinction, occurring

461

about one hundred times, shows that we are dealing with two discrete actions. The těnûpâ must be a cultic ritual because the expression "before the Lord" always refers to an action within the sanctuary. Conversely the těrûmâ, which is always "to the Lord," has no connection with either ritual or the sanctuary. In what follows I will discuss only the těnûpâ and its related aspects.

The following things require těnûpâ: the breast of the well-being offering (Exod 29:27–28; Lev 7:30; 9:21; 10:14–15; Num 6:20; 18:18), the suet and the right thigh of the priestly consecration ram together with a loaf of bread of every type (Exod 29:23; Lev 8:26–27), the breast of the priestly consecration ram (which is offered [hēnîp] alone, Exod 29:26; Lev 8:29), the gold and copper that was contributed to build the Tabernacle (Exod 35:22; 38:24, 29), the lamb of the reparation offering and the *log* of oil of the purified měṣōrāʿ (14:12, 21, 24), the ʿōmer offering (23:11, 15), the two loaves of bread and the two lambs on the festival of firstfruits (23:17, 20), the cereal offering of the suspected adulteress (Num 5:25), the boiled shoulder from the well-being offering ram of the Nazirite when he has completed his term, together with a loaf of bread of every type (Num 6:20), and the Levites at the time they begin their work in the Tent of Meeting (Num 8:11, 15, 21).

What is the common denominator in all of the offerings that undergo těnûpâ? Because this question is based on the assumption that there is no other těnûpâ besides those mentioned in Scripture (it is possible that there are rituals requiring těnûpâ that the Torah passes over in silence), our search for the common factor of the těnûpâs will be limited to only those specified above.

The common denominator of the těnûpâ may be clarified by two principles. The first is that *any offering that is still in its owner's possession before it is sacrificed on the altar requires a dedication ritual, which is called těnûpâ.* The first conclusion that follows from this principle is the exclusion of all of the most sacred gifts from the těnûpâ. It should be remembered that the most sacred gifts —burnt offering, cereal offering, purification offering, and reparation offering— are from the start a kind of "gift to the Lord *(ʾiššeh)*" (see 1:9; 2:3; 6:11; and esp. Num 18:9) and all enter the domain of the deity before they undergo těnûpâ. Obviously most of the lesser sacred gifts are excluded either because they are not brought to the sanctuary at all (e.g., the dough, Num 15:17–21) or because they also belong to the Lord from the start (e.g., the firstborn, 27:26). In fact, it can be shown that this principle refers in particular to the well-being offering and its accompaniments.

This principle can be inferred from the Torah. In the Priestly law there is a list that specifies the gifts by their categories (Num 18:9–19). In vv 9–10 the text lists the most sacred gifts "from the fire," but the word těnûpôt is not mentioned. The text, however, lists the lesser sacred gifts in v 11ff., and the word těnûpôt does appear at the beginning of the passage: "This, too, shall be yours: the těrûmâ of their gifts, all the těnûpôt of the Israelites." It seems clear from the evidence of the text itself that the *těnûpâ* falls outside the category of most sacred gifts and is associated with the lesser sacred gifts.

Are all items in this list (Num 18:9–19) subject to the *těnûpâ?* The firstborn (vv 14–18) certainly do not undergo *těnûpâ,* for they are sacred from birth, and the text even cautions that "no one may dedicate (them)" (Lev 27:27). An object is made *ḥerem* by declaration (as in Josh 6:17; 1 Sam 15:3), that is, before it is brought to the sanctuary (compare Josh 6:18 with the next verse). *těnûpâ* remains as a possibility only for firstfruits (first-ripe and first-processed; for the difference see Milgrom 1976h: 336–37), especially for the firstfruits about which the text says "that they bring to the Lord" (Num 18:13), in other words, the ones that must be brought to the sanctuary. If the firstfruits are sanctified by being set aside that means they do not need the sanctification of *těnûpâ;* but it can be argued otherwise. Because the firstfruits of barley (the *ʿōmer*) and the firstfruits of wheat (the two loaves) require *těnûpâ,* all of the other ones require it too. It is interesting that the rabbis were also divided on the question of *těnûpâ* for firstfruits. There are Tannaites such as Rabbi Eliezer ben Jacob (who lived when the Temple was in existence) who held that firstfruits require *těnûpâ* (*m. Bik.* 2:4; 3:6; *m. Menaḥ.* 5:6; cf. Rashbam on Lev 2:12), but from the wording of the Mishna (*m. Menaḥ.* 5:6, also the first Tanna in *m. Bik.* 3:6) and the Gemara (*b. Sukk.* 47b and see Tosafot, s.v. Bikkurim; *b. Mak.* 18b–19a) we infer that they disagreed about it.

It can be shown that the lesser sacred gifts not included in the list do not require *těnûpâ.* The tithe is considered a *těrûmâ* (Num 18:24) in spite of its not being considered sacred. Even the tithe of the tithe, called "the part thereof that is to be consecrated" (v 29), does not need *těnûpâ* because it is given directly to the priest and does not need to be brought to the sanctuary. The paschal sacrifice naturally does not require *těnûpâ* because it is eaten by the owners (Exod 12:8–10; Deut 16:7) outside the sanctuary (according to P, Num 9:10).

The Torah states explicitly that the well-being offerings initially belong to their offerers, whereas most sacred gifts belong to the Lord from the start—so, for example, we deduce from the text of 10:13–14, which labels the most sacred gifts as "the Lord's gifts" *(ʾiššê),* in contrast to the well-being offerings, which are labeled "from the well-being sacrifices of the Israelites." It is clear from this that the well-being offerings belong to the offerers even at the time they are sacrificed. So also logic dictates that if the well-being offering constitutes the only sacrifice that may be eaten by its offerers, then it is obvious that all of the meat of the sacrifice belongs to the offerers, and *těnûpâ* is performed—according to the principle I have adopted—for every part of it that is given to the Lord.

The text itself emphasizes that it is obligatory for the offerers to bring the parts of the well-being offering that are dedicated to the Lord *with their own hands.* Three examples will demonstrate this requirement: (1) The principal law on well-being offerings states, "the one who presents his sacrifice of well-being to the Lord shall bring his offering to the Lord from his sacrifice of well-being. His own hands shall bring the Lord's food gifts *('iššeh):* he shall bring the suet together with the breast" (7:29b–30a). The passage is likely to be considered inflated and awkward until it becomes clear that its purpose is to emphasize that the offerers are responsible for bringing the pieces of the well-being offering designated for the Lord. (2) This procedure is also underscored in the priestly consecration: "Place all of these on the palms of Aaron and his sons, and offer them as a *těnûpâ* before the Lord. Take them from their hands and turn them into smoke upon the altar" (Exod 29:24–25; cf. Lev 8:27–28). The priestly consecration ram was considered in the Torah to be the archetypal well-being offering (cf. Exod 29:27–28), and the text again emphasizes that the pieces designated for the Lord are delivered to him by the offerers themselves. Indeed, we will not understand the double action, which is to all appearances superfluous, wherein the officiating priest is first required to put the pieces to be offered as *těnûpâ* in the hands of the offerers and afterward to remove them, except in terms of the text's intention to stress that only the offerers, and not the officiating priest, are authorized to dedicate the offering to the Lord. (3) The description of the ritual for the Nazirite when he has completed his term reads, "The priest shall take the shoulder of the ram when it has been boiled, one unleavened cake from the basket, and one unleavened wafer, and place them on the hands of the Nazirite . . . the priest shall offer them as a *těnûpâ* before the Lord" (Num 6:19–20). Once again the text emphasizes, by putting the part of the well-being offering (the shoulder) that undergoes *těnûpâ* into the offerers' hands, that only they are authorized to dedicate the well-being offering to the Lord (cf. also *m. Qidd.* 1:6).

On the basis of all of these cases we may say that the offerings that require *těnûpâ* belong to the offerers until the moment the *těnûpâ* is done. It follows that the purpose of the *těnûpâ* is plain and simple: *těnûpâ* is a ritual of dedication that is performed in the sanctuary, with the result that the offering is removed from the domain of the owners and transferred to the domain of God.

The majority of the *těnûpâ* acts may be interpreted by this principle as follows:

(1) *The Levites:* God takes them from among the Israelites and gives them to the priests: "you shall place the Levites . . . *and designate them as a těnûpâ to the Lord. Thus you shall set the Levites apart from among the Israelites, and the Levites shall be mine.* Thereafter the Levites shall be qualified for the service of the Tent of Meeting" (Num 8:13–15). The purpose of the *těnûpâ* is clear: it separates the Levites from the Israelites and transfers them to the Lord's domain.

(2) *The gold and copper of the těnûpâ* are brought by the offerers themselves. If so, the role of the *těnûpâ* is clear beyond doubt—to dedicate these

metals to the Lord in order to qualify them for the construction of the Tent of Meeting.

(3) *The priestly consecration* is similar to the well-being offering. On the analogy of the well-being offering one might expect that the portions designated for the altar or given to the officiating priest would require *těnûpâ*, unlike the rest of the meat, which is eaten by the offerers and therefore does not require *těnûpâ*. This is in fact the case. The suet, the bread, and the thigh, which are offered on the altar, as well as the breast, which is delivered to the officiating priest, undergo *těnûpâ*, whereas the rest of the meat and bread are eaten by the offerers without *těnûpâ*. The difference between them is clear: *těnûpâ* transfers the offering from the domain of the offerers to the domain of the Lord.

(4) *The two lambs* for the Festival of Firstfruits are offered as a well-being offering. In accordance with the latter's procedure, the portions given to the Lord, and from the Lord to the priests, require *těnûpâ*. But, in contrast to the rest of the well-being offering, the lambs for Pentecost undergo *těnûpâ* in their entirety. The reason can only be explained by the principle I have adopted: because the animals are given completely to the priests, and not a single piece of the meat is eaten by the offerers, they undergo *těnûpâ;* they undergo *těnûpâ* in their entirety to indicate their transfer to the domain of God.

(5) *The měṣōrāʿ's log of oil* is analogous to the priestly consecration oil. The oil of the *měṣōrāʿ* is put on his extremities (Lev 14:17, 28), and the priestly consecration oil is poured on Aaron and sprinkled on his sons. There is a difference between the oils, however: that of the *měṣōrāʿ* undergoes *těnûpâ*, while that of the priestly consecration does not. Again the difference can be understood by my principle: the priestly consecration oil is taken from the anointing oil (Exod 29:7; Lev 8:12) and is sacred to begin with (Exod 30:25, 32), but the oil of the *měṣōrāʿ* is completely profane and therefore requires *těnûpâ* to sanctify it and transfer it to the Lord.

From the *těnûpâ* list enumerated above, there are four instances left that remain unexplained by the first principle: three cereal offerings (of the suspected adulteress, the *ʿōmer,* and the two loaves of bread) and the reparation offering of the *měṣōrāʿ.* The cereal offerings and the reparation offering are most sacred gifts (cf. Lev 6:10; 7:11) and, as said before, belong to the Lord even before they are offered. Yet even though they are already sanctified they require *těnûpâ.* How is this possible? In my opinion, these exceptions can be explained by means of a second principle: *most sacred gifts whose composition or mode of offering is different from the norm require additional sanctification by means of těnûpâ.*

First let us examine the cereal offerings that undergo *těnûpâ* and differ in their composition. It is a fact that these three cereal offerings are put together differently than the rest of the cereal offerings. According to the scheme of chap. 2, the cereal offering is composed of semolina (v 1), that is to say, of wheat, and oil and incense are added to it (v 1); if it is offered baked, it must be unleavened (v 11). But the cereal offerings here differ from the established recipe: the cereal offerings of the suspected adulteress and the ʿōmer are made of barley, not of semolina; the two loaves of bread are leavened, and all three lack oil and incense. Because all other cereal offerings are made in accordance with the scheme of chap. 2, we find that only the cereal offerings listed above deviate from the rule, and by the second principle they require tĕnûpâ.

The reparation offering of the mĕṣōrāʿ is different in the way it is offered, according to the scheme laid down for the reparation offering in 5:14ff. The reparation offering is the only offering for which money can substitute, "convertible into payment in silver" (5:15; cf. vv 18, 25). Nevertheless, it is impossible to substitute money for the reparation offering of the mĕṣōrāʿ, because its blood is indispensable for making atonement. The complex eighth-day ritual for purifying the mĕṣōrāʿ begins by putting the blood of the reparation offering on the mĕṣōrāʿ's extremities. Therefore this offering is in the "incommutable" category.

The reparation offering of the mĕṣōrāʿ is distinguished from the rest of the reparation offerings in yet another detail. The Mishna already recognized the uniqueness of the mĕṣōrāʿ 's reparation offering in its statement that "all of the purification offerings in the Torah precede the reparation offerings except the reparation offering of the mĕṣōrāʿ" (m. Zebaḥ. 10:5a). Indeed, in every ritual composed of several offerings, the purification offering always precedes (see m. Zebaḥ. 10:2; t. Zebaḥ. 10:4; b. Zebaḥ. 90b [bar.] [also Rainey 1970, based on Levine 1965]). If one argues, however, that the reparation offering is not included in other sacrificial services, the case of the impure Nazirite refutes it, for his atonement requires both a purification offering and a reparation offering, and the latter is the last to be offered on the altar (Num 6:10–12).

So we see that the most sacred gifts that undergo tĕnûpâ are distinguished from the rest of the most sacred gifts either in their composition or in the way they are offered, but it has not yet been explained why an offering that differs from the norm requires the further sanctification of tĕnûpâ. In my opinion, the answer will become clear by itself if we phrase the question differently: if the composition of all offerings is established in chaps. 1–5, how does it happen that there are exceptional offerings like the cereal offerings and the reparation offering mentioned above? This reformulation of the question compels us to return to the unique and special purpose of every one of the divergent offerings.

The meal offerings of the ʿōmer and the two loaves of bread comprise the firstfruits of the grain harvest in the land. They are brought not for their own sake but in order to bring added blessing to the rest of the produce waiting to be harvested. This purpose is emphasized in the passage "he shall offer (hēnîp) the ʿōmer before the Lord, for your favor" (23:11), that is, may the Lord derive pleasure from your offering so that he will continue to bless you. If so, not only do the cereal offerings of the ʿōmer and the two loaves function as a sign of thanks for the new crop, but their aim is that the crop be abundantly blessed (Ezek 44:16; Prov 3:9–10; cf. Lev 19:5; etc.). Therefore these cereal offerings, though they are most sacred gifts, require additional sanctification, which is exhibited by the ritual of *těnûpâ* so that the Lord's blessing shall come "for your favor."

The cereal offering of the suspected adulteress also differs from the rest of the cereal offerings in its purpose. This difference is explained in the text "The man shall bring his wife to the priest. And he shall bring as an offering for her one-tenth of an *ephah* of barley flour. No oil shall be poured upon it and no frankincense shall be laid on it, for it is a cereal offering of jealousy, a cereal offering of remembrance that recalls wrongdoing" (Num 5:15). This verse explains the change that has occurred in the composition of this cereal offering: barley is used instead of semolina and the oil and incense are omitted as a result of its special purpose, to be "a cereal offering of remembrance." But because the function of every other "remembrance before the Lord" in the Bible is that the offerer should be remembered for good, the text adds the explanatory phrase "that recalls wrongdoing." If so, the purpose of this cereal offering is to get God's attention, not to favor the offerer but the reverse: to treat the accused impartially and determine if in fact she is an adulteress. Sacrificing the cereal offering is the step that precedes making the woman drink the bitter waters (v 26), and the sequence is logical: after the meal offering of remembrance turns the Lord's attention to the woman he intervenes directly in her trial and activates the bitter waters in her stomach. It is precisely the insertion of the cereal offering of remembrance before giving her the bitter waters that enables the Priestly law to stress that the waters have no inherent power to reveal the truth; rather only the Lord, directed by the *těnûpâ* to the suspect standing before him, is capable of assuring that these waters will ascertain and verify whether the accused has sinned. Therefore the demonstrative ritual of *těnûpâ* is intended to focus the attention of the heavenly Judge on the judgment taking place in his sanctuary.

The reparation offering of the *měṣōrāʿ* supplies the blood that is put on his extremities. This ritual is the first step in his expiation on the eighth day. Thus, the priority of the blood brings about the change in the order of the sacrifices, and the reparation offering, which is usually last, becomes first. Why is it so vital to put the blood first and thus reverse the order of the sacrifices? The rabbis were also troubled by this problem, and their explanation in the Mishna paves the way to the answer. In their words, "All purification offerings in the Torah precede reparation offerings except the reparation offering of the *měṣōrāʿ* because it comes to render him fit (to come into contact with sancta)" (*m. Zebaḥ.* 10:5). Thus the function of the blood, in the opinion of the Tannaites, is to qualify him to enter the sanctuary and eat of the sacrifices. That is, his expiation until then merely qualified him to come into contact with profane things; the cultic ceremonies of the eighth day, beginning with smearing him with blood and oil, qualify him to come into contact with sacred things. This conclusion is confirmed by comparing the expiation of the scale-diseased man with that of the fungous house (14:48–57). The priest sprinkles blood on the house as he does on the person on the first day of his purification (cf. vv 4–7). But the purification of the house is finished on the same day, whereas the person's purification takes another seven days. The difference between them is plain. The house is attached to the ground and cannot approach sancta, but a man, because he moves, is capable of defiling the sanctuary and its sancta. Therefore the purification of the *měṣōrāʿ* requires the addition of the eighth day, to enable him to contact sancta, a transformation effected by his being smeared with the blood of the reparation offering and the *log* of oil.

I must admit that the nature of this ritual is still obscure, for we do not know how the blood functioned or why it was put just on the extremities in three particular places. Even so, there is much evidence about the use of oil in the ancient Near East, and from the oil we may also make inferences about the blood. There is an Egyptian rite that corresponds in a surprising fashion to the placing of oil on the *měṣōrāʿ*, namely, the daily anointing of the idol. I will cite the Egyptian rite as it is described by Sauneron (1960): the two rituals will be placed one after the other, and for greater clarity the parallels in the Egyptian rite will be underlined:

And the priest shall dip his right finger in the oil that is on his left palm. . . . The remainder of the oil on the priest's palm shall be put on the head of the one being purified" (14:16, 18).

A final ceremony ended the divine toilet (each morning): the anointment of the god with the cosmetic oil *medjet. Holding in his left hand* the little flacon of alabaster which contained the precious ointment, *the priest plunged in the little finger of his right hand,* then *touched the brow* of the divine statue with his finger, pronouncing the sacred formula. (Sauneron 1960: 87)

The correspondences are obvious: (1) the use of sacred oil; (2) holding the flacon of oil in the left hand and applying the oil with the little finger of the right hand; (3) the oil is rubbed on the head (brow) of the idol/*měṣōrāʿ*.

The reason for anointing the idol is explained by Sauneron as follows: "the god, washed, clothed, ornamented and smeared with the perfumed oil—satiated by excess—could brave anew the dark of the sanctuary: the divine forces were sustained, preserved from all injury, able to carry on, for another day, their cosmic role" (ibid.). This means that the oil serves an apotropaic purpose: to shield the anointed god from demons. The oil probably had a similar purpose in Israel as well, and the blood of the reparation offering certainly did. We cannot trace the process by which the ceremony shed its pagan form and took on a monotheistic form. But it is likely that the rabbis' explanation—that anointing with oil and blood constitutes the last stage of the expiation of the *měṣōrāʿ* (on the eighth day) and qualifies him to approach the sanctuary and its sancta—reflects the meaning of the ritual in P. Thus the function of *těnûpâ* with the oil and blood is clear: it constitutes a further sanctification of these materials, which enhanced their power to purge the *měṣōrāʿ* of his uncleanness vis-à-vis the sanctuary and its sancta. And because the use of blood and oil must take first priority among the rituals of the eighth day—because they all take place in the sanctuary—the order of the offering is reversed: the reparation offering and with it, the oil, undergo *těnûpâ* first.

Thus the common element in all four most sacred gifts that undergo *těnûpâ* is that each of them differs from others of its kind as they are defined in chaps. 1–5. The difference is found in the composition or the manner of offering the sacrifice, and is also recognizable in the special purpose assigned to each offering: the cereal offerings of the *ʿōmer* and the two loaves add blessing to the rest of the harvest, the cereal offering of the suspected adulteress influences God to judge the suspect by means of the cursed water, and the reparation offering whose blood is placed on the *měṣōrāʿ* enables him to approach the sancta. All of these goals require God's special attention, which is requested through *těnûpâ*.

To recapitulate, then, an offering requires *těnûpâ* under either of these two conditions: (1) it is still in its owner's domain when it is brought to the altar, or (2) it diverges from the established system in its composition, its way of being offered, or its aim. In these cases the offering needs the additional sanctification of *těnûpâ*.

I have explained the circumstances requiring the *těnûpâ* but have not yet determined its nature. What exactly is *těnûpâ*? Can it be a horizontal motion with the offering, "extending and bringing back," as the rabbis describe it? The Bible itself does not explain it. It is content with the one phrase, "offer *(hēnîp)* as *těnûpâ*," and that is all. One method is left to us—etymology.

Here a surprise awaits us. The Bible has no hint of the horizontal motion the rabbis describe. G. R. Driver (1956b), followed by G. Anderson (1987: 133–35), derives *těnûpâ* from Akk. *nūptu* 'additional payment' (verb *nâpu*). This term is found solely in monetary contexts, and payment is a far cry from dedication. Only one meaning is supported by the texts: *hēnîp* in the sense of "raising, lifting." As is known, biblical dictionaries admit to this interpretation and even substantiate it by comparing it with the Arab. root *nāfa*, which means "be high." But it is strange that although they relate this Arab. root to nouns such as *nôp* (Ps 48:3) and *nāpâ* (Josh 11:2; 12:2; 2 Kgs 4:11) not once do they apply it to the verb *hēnîp*.

In my opinion *hēnîp* too means "lift, raise," and many a *těnûpâ* in the Bible will become clearer if we drop the usual interpretation "wave" or "extend and bring back" and accept the meaning "raise." I will limit my examples to first Isaiah: (1) *kěhānîp šēbeṭ ʾet-měrîmâw kěhārîm maṭṭeh lōʾ-ʿēṣ* 'as though a rod raised him who lifted it, as though a staff lifted not-wood' (Isa 10:15). Note that the subject of *kěhānîp* is *měrîmâw*, and the verb corresponding to it is *kěhārîm*.

(2) ʿal har-nišpeh śěʾû-nēs hārîmû qôl lāhem hānîpû yād 'Hoist a standard upon a bare hill, raise a voice to them, lift a hand' (Isa 13:2). The parallel verbs are: śěʾû, hārîmû, hānîpû. (3) wěhēnîp yādô ʿal-hannāhār 'He will raise his hand over the Euphrates' (Isa 11:15). těnûpat yad-YHWH ṣěbāʾôt ʾăšer-hûʾ mēnîp ʿālāw 'the elevated hand of the Lord, which he will lift against them' (Isa 19:16).

Logic demands that a striking hand can only be a hand raised. There is no reason to explain the action as a swaying or shaking motion. This is true of any těnûpâ of a hand or instrument before a blow, for example, kî ḥarběkā hēnaptā ʿālêhā wattěḥalělehā 'because you raised your sword upon it, you have desecrated it' (Exod 20:25); lōʾ-tānîp ʿălêhem barzel 'do not lift an iron [tool] over them' (Deut 27:5; cf. Josh 8:31); wěhermēš loʾ tānîp ʿal qāmat rēʿeka 'do not lift a sickle over your neighbor's grain' (Deut 23:26). Thus the těnûpâ of a hand or instrument for a blow must be a lifting motion, and in all the cases discussed hēnîp means "to raise, lift."

Logic supports philology. First of all, I have already explained that těnûpâ is an act of dedication. It stands to reason that dedication would be carried out by means of lifting, whereby the offerer, as it were, delivers his offering to God. Second, it can be proved that cultic těnûpâ was done simultaneously to all of the materials requiring it. Take the priestly consecration as an example. The pieces undergoing těnûpâ are the tail, the fat covering the entrails, the lobe of the liver, the two kidneys, the fat on the kidneys, the right thigh, a flat loaf of bread, a cake of oil bread, and a wafer (Exod 29:22–23; Lev 8:25–26). And in order to remove all trace of doubt that these offerings undergo těnûpâ together, the text even emphasizes, "Place *all of these* on the palms of Aaron and his sons, and offer them as a těnûpâ before the Lord" (Exod 29:24; cf. Lev 8:27). Is it possible that ten items, some of them quite large, piled in a large heap on the hands of Aaron and his sons could be moved even slightly in a horizontal direction without toppling them?

Philology and logic are decisive: těnûpâ is a ritual of raising or lifting intended to dedicate the offering to God. (The *Tgs.* are praiseworthy, since both *Onq.* and the *Yer.* in the Torah and *Ps.-J.* in the Prophets and Hagiographa translate hēnîp in all of the cases mentioned above with the root rwm.) According to the principles I have established, this dedication indicates the transfer of the offering from the profane to the sacred, from the offerer's domain to God's, and with certain most sacred gifts it constitutes an act that underscores a request made of God.

Finally, Israel's environs provide an illuminating parallel to the těnûpâ, namely, the Egyptian rite for the elevation of offerings. The example chosen is depicted on a Karnak relief (Nelson 1949: 329–33), happily illuminating the text with its visual representation (see fig. 9). The translated text reads, "Come, O King, elevate offerings before the face (of the god). Elevate offerings to Amen-Raʿ, Lord of the Thrones of the Two Lands. All life emanates from him, all

FIGURE 9: Elevation rite on a relief from Karnak (University of Chicago Press)

health emanates from him, all stability emanates from him, all good future emanates from him, like Ra' forever."

The resemblances to the *těnûpâ* are apparent immediately: (1) Assuming for the sake of the argument that *hēnîp* means "elevate," the Egyptian formula "elevate . . . before the face of the god" is the exact equivalent of *hēnîp těnûpâ . . . lipnê YHWH.* (2) As depicted in the relief, the offering is an aggregate. It contains a sampling of all of the food placed on the god's table— bread, meat, cakes, fruit, and vegetables. Correspondingly in Israel, all of the objects subject to a *těnûpâ* during a single ritual must undergo the act together, never separately. (3) Like its counterpart in Egypt, the *těnûpâ* offering is placed on the palms of the hands. (4) The Egyptian rite is not limited to food but can be applied to any precious object dedicated to the sanctuary. In Medinet Habu, for example, the king dedicates gold to Amun (Nelson 1949: 331 n. 141). So, too, in Israel. Of the precious metals donated to the Tabernacle, the gold is consistently described as a *těnûpâ* (Exod 35:22; 38:24). (5) The purpose of the Egyptian rite is "that he (the god) may be content with what the king . . . does." In Israel's cultic lexicon there is a semantically equivalent word, *lir-ṣōnkem,* which appears with one of the *těnûpâ* offerings, the barley sheaf (23:11a).

On the basis of these parallels, the Egyptian elevation rite and the Israelite *těnûpâ* seem identical. Thus the findings of philology and typology point to the conclusion that the *těnûpâ* is an "elevation offering."

A methodological obstacle remains to be hurdled. If it is true, as is claimed, that a wave offering was used in the ancient Near East, then the possibility must be acknowledged that it also existed in Israel. Indeed, because Israel was particularly indebted to its neighbors for many of its sacrificial rites and terms, it would be surprising if it refrained from borrowing the *těnûpâ.* A closer look at the alleged non-Israelite wave offering is thus made essential.

A waving ceremonial is to be found in the Hittite cult, and Vieyra (1966) has, without hesitation, identified it with the biblical *těnûpâ.* Are the two rites identical, however? To judge by the texts available to me, the Hittite waving is not a sacrifice at all. It is a magical rite with a therapeutic aim, to rid the petitioner of his malady, be it his rage (Otten 1942), hostility (Rost 1953), sexual disability (Goetze 1938a), illness (Otten and Souček 1969), bloody deed (ibid.), or any other form of impurity or evil (ibid.). Moreover, it is generally not performed in a temple. Waving, in other words, is an integral component of the exorcist's art and is totally unrelated to the *těnûpâ* ritual in the sanctuary (see now Wright 1987: 33–34 n. 55). What indeed does sympathetic magic worked on humans have to do with dedicatory presentations to the gods?

A waving ritual is also attested in ancient Mesopotamia and, again, the correspondence to the biblical *těnûpâ* has been averred. The Akk. verb employed, *šubū'u,* is indeed defined "to move an object alongside a person or inside a room, etc., for ritual purposes" (*CAD,* s.v. *bâ'u* 3a 1 B. 181b 3. *šubū'u* a). Still, all of the cited texts deal with the use of three materials—incense, fire, and/or water—the use of which is strictly limited to the purification or exorcism of persons, figurines, or buildings. Thus Mesopotamian "waving" reveals the same *Sitz im Leben* as its Hittite counterpart and, consequently, it too is far removed from the frame of reference of the biblical *těnûpâ* (see now Wright 1987: 63 n. 136).

Finally, the claim has been advanced that the *těnûpâ* has been found at Ras Shamra (Hillers 1970). But the meaning of the purported Ugaritic cognate *šnpt* is still in doubt (de Moor 1970a: 324), and its contexts remain inscrutable. Thus for the time being, at least, the Ugaritic evidence must be ruled out.

To recapitulate: it is argued that neither Israel nor its environs exhibits a wave offering to the deity that bears any resemblance to the biblical *těnûpâ*. In the Hittite and Mesopotamian religions waving is a technique of exorcism practiced on animate and inanimate objects. This is far removed from the biblical *těnûpâ*, which, as philological and typological analyses demonstrate, refers to an actual or symbolic elevation rite in the sanctuary whereby an offering is dedicated to the Lord. Thus, it is submitted, the wave offering is a fiction that should be stricken from the cultic lexicon of the ancient Near East (for details see Milgrom 1972a; 1973a [= 1983d: 133–58]).

F. The Šôq Hattěrûmâ

The following things are called *těrûmâ:* the right thigh of the priestly consecration and the well-being offering (Exod 29:27–28; Lev 7:32, 34; 10:14–15; Num 6:20), the breast of the well-being offering (Exod 29:27), the materials for the construction of the Tabernacle (Exod 25:2–3; 35:5, 21, 24; 36:3, 6), the census silver (Exod 30:13–15), the bread of the thanksgiving offering (Lev 7:14), the first of the dough (Num 15:19–21), the tithe and the tithe of the tithe (Num 18:24–29), a percentage of the war spoils for the sanctuary (Num 31:29, 41, 52), sacred gifts in general (Num 5:9; 18:8), and the minor sacred gifts in particular (22:12, 15; Num 18:11–19). Ezekiel adds to the list the sacred land of the priests and Levites (45:1; 48:8–21) and parts of the offerings contributed to the prince by the people (45:13, 16).

In all of these occurrences *těrûmâ* means "gift" that is intended for the Lord or for his servant the priest. It is accepted that only the first *těrûmâ* in the list, the right thigh, is an exception to this definition. This *těrûmâ* is explained as a ceremony called "heave offering," an explanation that is based on the opinion of the rabbis, which states that the offering *(těrûmâ)* of the thigh is a vertical motion—a "raising and lowering" in their language (cf. *m. Menaḥ.* 5:6; *t. Menaḥ.* 7:17–19; *Sipra*, Ṣaw 16:3; *b. Sukk.* 37b; *b. Menaḥ.* 61b–62a; *Midr. Lev. Rab.* 28:5). Further, the thigh is unique in that it is in construct with the noun *těrûmâ* and is called "the thigh of the *těrûmâ*" (cf. Exod 29:27; Lev 7:34; 10:14, 15; Num 6:20), that is to say, the thigh is subject to the action called *tĕrûmâ.* Only recently have there been scholars who have objected to this view. They admit that the *tĕrûmâ* (and with it the *tĕnûpâ*) originally designated a particular ceremony in the sanctuary, but as it is reflected in the Bible, the *tĕrûmâ,* especially the *tĕrûmâ* of the thigh, is just a sacred gift (e.g., G. R. Driver 1956b).

If so, the thigh of the *tĕrûmâ* is somewhat puzzling. The solution, in my opinion, must begin with a linguistic observation that was somehow missed by scholars. As opposed to the *tĕnûpâ,* which is done "before the Lord," the *tĕrûmâ* is always "to the Lord." The text never uses the preposition "before" with regard to the *tĕrûmâ.* This distinction shows that the *tĕnûpâ* is a ceremony that takes place in the sanctuary (COMMENT E above), whereas the *tĕrûmâ* is not a ceremony at all, and in P has no connection with the sanctuary.

This conclusion is strengthened by looking at the way in which the verb *hērîm* is used. It is surprising that its usual meaning, "to carry, lift" never appears in a cultic context. Instead, two other meanings are indicated: (1) "donate, give a gift" (see 22:15; Num 15:19–21; 18:19); this sense, however, is secondary, a generalization and derivation from a more concrete and basic use, which is (2) "remove, set aside" (see Exod 35:24; Lev 2:9; 4:8, 10, 19; 6:3; Num 18:26–32; 31:28); and it is this usage that I will discuss.

There are several special characteristics typical of the verb *hērîm* in cultic usage. (1) Using the verb *hērîm* necessitates the use of the preposition *min;* that is, the *tĕrûmâ* is always removed from *(min)* something (Exod 29:27; Lev 2:9; 4:8, 10, 19; 6:8; Num 18:26, 28, 29, 30, 32; 31:28; cf. Ezek 45:1, 9; Dan 8:11). (2) If there is a verb parallel to *hērîm* in a cultic text, it is always *hēsîr* 'to remove' (e.g., 4:8–10, 31, 35; cf. Ezek 45:9). (3) *hērîm* in the sense of "set aside" is especially found in the narrative section of P; compare "remove yourselves *(hērōmmû)* from this community" (Num 17:10) with the parallel expression "stand back *(hibbādĕlû)* from this community" (Num 16:21). Levine's objection that "set aside" hardly implies "bestow a gift" (1982a: 527) is parried by the fact that in every *cultic* occurrence of this verb, the object is always "the Lord" and the context is always that of a gift.

This linguistic analysis, which proves that the cultic action *tĕrûmâ* is actually the dedication of things to the Lord, is confirmed by the fact that this dedication is performed outside the confines of the sanctuary, as may be derived from the following evidence. (1) As stated above, the *tĕrûmâ* is directed "to the Lord," as opposed to the *tĕnûpâ,* which is performed in the sanctuary "before the Lord." (2) At times, the Torah explicitly states that the offerer brings his gift only after he has dedicated it (e.g., Exod 35:24; Lev 10:15; Num 18:13). (3) In many cases the *tĕrûmâ* is not brought to the sanctuary at all; it is given directly to the priest (for example, the right thigh, 7:32–33; the dough, Num 15:17–21; the tithe, Num 18:24; the tithe of the tithe, Num 18:26, 28; sacred gifts in general, 22:13, 15; Num 5:9–10). (4) Even the use of the verb *nātan* 'give' in connection with the *tĕrûmâ* (a verb never found with *tĕnûpâ*) shows that it concerns the setting aside of something as a gift to the Lord (e.g., Exod 30:14–15; Lev 7:32; Num 15:21; 18:18; 31:29).

Corroboration comes from an extrabiblical source. In Akk., the root *râmu* III (Assyrian *riâmu*) means "to give a gift," and the nouns *rīmu* II, *rīmūtu*, *tarīmtu* mean "gift" (von Soden 1970). It is particularly instructive to trace the history of this Akk. root. According to von Soden, the root first appears in Middle Babylonian and Assyrian, but until the fourteenth century B.C.E. it is found only in personal names in Mari, Alalakh, and Ugarit. This fact leads him to suppose that the root's origin is not East Semitic but West Semitic, *alt-amoritisch*.

It seems that von Soden either did not know of or did not attach any importance to the book by Y. Muffs (1969), which treats the Akk. noun *rēmūtu;* unlike von Soden, Muffs derives *rēmūtu* from the root *rêmu* meaning "to be kind, charitable," a linguistic phenomenon equivalent to the noun *rḥmt* 'gift' in Aram., deriving from the root *rḥm*, which also means "to be kind." According to Muffs, one must distinguish between *irêm* 'he gives a gift', derived from *rêmu*, and *irâm* 'he loves', derived from *râmu*. By his method the root of *rīmūtu* 'gift' turns out to be *rêmu*, not *râmu*.

In any case, the discovery of the nouns *rīmu, rīmūtu*, and especially *tarīmtu* (equivalent in form to *tĕrûmâ*), which all mean "gift," and of the verb *râmu* (or *rêmu*), one of whose meanings is "to give a gift," clearly shows that the meanings "gift" for the noun *tĕrûmâ* and "set aside a gift" for the verb *hērîm*, proved by the internal evidence of the Bible, are strengthened and confirmed by the use in Akk. of the same root, whose origin is most likely in the West Semitic language closely related to Hebrew.

To recapitulate: in the cultic literature of P the verb *hērîm* means "dedicate" or "set aside," and the noun *tĕrûmâ* means "gift." Thus it follows that the usual explanation that the priest "raises and lowers" (heave offering) has no basis. Thus the act of *tĕrûmâ* is the setting aside of an object from its owner's domain to transfer it to God's domain. The setting aside is done by declaration (as in the dedication of the silver by Micah's mother, Judg 17:3) or by action (as with the tithe, according to Lev 27:30–33, and the firstfruits, according to Num 18:12–13). The rabbis declare that *'ămîyrātô laggābōah kimĕsîrātô lahedyôt* 'oral dedication is equivalent to transfer' (*m. Qidd.* 1:6; *t. Qidd.* 1:9), in agreement with Scripture; it is therefore not a rabbinic innovation (contra Eilberg-Schwartz 1986: 96).

Furthermore, the purpose of the *tĕrûmâ* is similar to that of the *tĕnûpâ:* both are dedications to the Lord, but they are distinguished from one another in this particular: the *tĕnûpâ* is a rite performed in the sanctuary, whereas the *tĕrûmâ* is carried out outside the sanctuary, without a rite (the Targums always read *'aprāšûtā'* 'setting aside', and even the words "thigh of the *tĕrûmâ*" are translated "thigh of the setting aside," which is the basic sense).

This new interpretation of *tĕrûmâ* may explain a crux of the biblical lexicon:

the supposed interchange between the terms *tĕrûmâ* and *tĕnûpâ*. Three examples will illustrate the problem: (1) the thigh of the priestly consecration undergoes *tĕnûpâ* (Exod 29:22–24), though it precedes the thigh of the *tĕrûmâ* (v 27); (2) the breast of the priestly consecration undergoes both *tĕrûmâ* and *tĕnûpâ* (v 26), though it is called a *tĕrûmâ* (v 27); (3) the copper contributed to the sanctuary is once called *tĕrûmâ* (Exod 35:24) and once *tĕnûpâ* (Exod 38:24).

Indeed, in accordance with what has been said about the indeterminacy of cultic terminology, it is possible to think, at first, that the *tĕrûmâ* and *tĕnûpâ*, judging by the examples above, are not univocal but are interchangeable. This is not so. The solution is simple and clear once we are convinced that the *tĕrûmâ* is not a ritual, and that its true sense is a dedication to God. *tĕrûmâ*, then, is a necessary step preceding *tĕnûpâ*. An offering requiring *tĕnûpâ* must undergo a previous stage of *tĕrûmâ*, that is to say, its separation from the profane to the sacred. This process can be formulated as a rule: *every tĕnûpâ requires tĕrûmâ* (cf. *Sipra*, Ṣaw 11:11). If so, *tĕrûmâ* and *tĕnûpâ*, so far from being identical, are completely different from each other. And throughout all of the citations, without exception, they retain their respective meanings and cannot be interchanged.

The basic text that defines the right thigh of the well-being offering is 7:32–33: "And the right thigh from your sacrifices of well-being you shall give to the priest as a *tĕrûmâ;* the one from among Aaron's sons who offers the blood of the well-being offering and the suet shall receive the right thigh as his prebend." This text makes it clear that the right thigh does not undergo *tĕnûpâ* (cf. v 30) but is given directly to the priest. Nevertheless, three verses stand in contradiction to this text. I will discuss them seriatim.

(1) In 8:26–27, we find, "and on the right thigh . . . *wayyānep* them as a *tĕnûpâ* before the Lord." This passage is not difficult, because it is talking about the thigh of the priestly consecration rather than the thigh of the well-being offering. The difference between them is that the thigh of the priestly consecration is not given to the priests but is burned on the altar. It requires *tĕnûpâ* for extra sanctification, to indicate that it has been transferred from its owner's domain to God's (see COMMENT E above). Indeed, it is this thigh's uniqueness, in that it is offered to the Lord on the altar, that necessitates the *tĕnûpâ*.

The two remaining instances are not so easily solved, but they provide a rare opportunity to penetrate the text and get a glimpse of the penultimate layer in the redaction of the Pentateuch.

(2) In 9:21, it is said, *"hēnîp* the breasts and the right thigh as a *tĕnûpâ* before the Lord—as Moses had commanded." Here the text deals with the cultic ritual of the eighth day, after the seven days of the priestly consecration. A ram and an ox were sacrificed as well-being offerings (vv 18–20), and according to this text Aaron *hēnîp* the thigh, in spite of Lev 7:32, which attests that the thigh does not require *tĕnûpâ*. But a look at the text reveals that all is not in order. For one thing, there were two right thighs, the ox's and the ram's, as with

the breasts. Why then does v 21 have "the right thigh" in the singular? For another, the preceding verse (20) reads peculiarly. As the thigh undergoes *tĕnûpâ*, it should have read, "they laid these fat parts over the breasts [and over the right thighs] and Aaron turned the fat parts into smoke on the altar." Why are the thighs missing?

Hence a doubt arises: are the words "and the right thigh" (v 21) really original, or were they added later? Indeed, when we remove them from the text the problems disappear. The ceremony with the thigh and the breast are performed in accordance with the rule of Lev 7:30–31: the breast is offered with the suet and undergoes the *tĕnûpâ* by itself, and there is no *tĕnûpâ* for the thigh.

One might ask why the thigh should not be mentioned. Is it not also a gift to the priests? The answer illuminates the aim of the text. Before us is a story about the revelation of the Lord in his Tabernacle in the form of fire eating the offerings on the altar (v 24). Hence, the main interest of the story is the altar and what takes place on it, and any outside event tending to distract the reader has no place in the story. Thus, for example, the ceremony of hand-leaning is missing. One cannot argue from silence and maintain that hand-leaning is not really needed in this instance, because the law that burnt offerings and well-being offerings require laying on of hands is unambiguous (see 1:4; 3:2, 8, 13). We must conclude, then, that the author wrote concisely and skipped the matter of gifts to the priests as he skipped other details that distracted from his main purpose of focusing on the revelation of the Lord in fire on the altar.

(3) My hypothesis is further strengthened by the last passage to be discussed (10:14–15): "But the breast of *tĕnûpâ* and the thigh of *tĕrûmâ* you, and your sons and daughters after you, may eat in any pure place, for they have been assigned as a due to you and your children from the Israelites' sacrifices of well-being. Together with the food gifts of suet, they must present the thigh of *tĕrûmâ* and the breast of *tĕnûpâ*, which are *lĕhānîp* as a *tĕnûpâ* before the Lord, and which shall be a due to you and to your children after you for all time—as the Lord has commanded." The first verse (14) is suited to its context: it completes the preceding topic on the *minḥâ* (vv 12–13), which establishes how the priests should eat it. This is not the place to bring up the problem of the continuity between the story of the eighth day (9:1–10:5) and the rules that are inferred from it (10:6ff.). But it is clear that because the absence of the priestly gifts from the story would have occasioned surprise, it was felt desirable to fill in the deficiency by adding what is mentioned in v 14 (see the NOTE on 10:14). By contrast, v 15 lacks any such purpose. First, its position is illogical. The *tĕnûpâ* of the gifts ought to precede eating them, but here the order is reversed. And, second, why is it mentioned here? The rule that the thigh and the breast belong to the priests was already given at the end of the previous verse. That the thigh requires *tĕnûpâ* along with the breast can be deduced from the story itself (9:21). The latter verse is the source of the trouble. Precisely because the words "the right thigh" (9:21) were probably added, it is therefore reasonable to sup-

pose that 10:15 was also added in order to derive the rule that the thigh requires *tĕnûpâ*. Thus the suspicion is strengthened that one editorial hand added both of them (see the NOTE on v 15). Consequently one may suppose that at first only the breast underwent *tĕnûpâ* and only in a later period was the thigh added to the *tĕnûpâ* ritual, and that this is what is reflected in the MT. This supposition will be confirmed by the historical data to be discussed below.

We can return now to the original rule about the breast and thigh of the well-being offering: "he shall bring the suet together with the breast, the breast to be elevated *(lĕhānîp)* as a *tĕnûpâ* before the Lord. The priest shall turn the suet into smoke at the altar, but the breast shall belong to Aaron and his sons. And the right thigh from your sacrifices of well-being you shall give to the priest as a *tĕrûmâ;* the one from among Aaron's sons who offers the blood of the well-being offering and the suet shall receive the right thigh as his prebend" (7:30–33).

This text establishes two important facts for us: the perquisite and the sequence. It is evident that the difference between the thigh and the breast is expressed not only in their dedication (the one a *tĕrûmâ*, the other a *tĕnûpâ*) but also in their disposition. The breast is given to all of the priests; it is divided among the priestly corps in the sanctuary. By contrast, the thigh is given only to the officiating priest, the one who offers the blood and suet on the altar. As shown above, the *tĕnûpâ* does not take place with the thigh, which lacks any ritual. The thigh is a perquisite for the officiating priest in return for his work. Also, according to the verse above the sequence of offering the thigh and the breast is clear. The steps are: (a) putting the suet on the breast; (b) the *tĕnûpâ* with the breast; (c) burning the suet; (d) giving the breast to the priests and the thigh to the officiating priest. It follows inexorably from this sequence that the burning of the suet must precede the distribution of the gifts to the priests. The descriptive texts in the Pentateuch confirm this sequence. For example, in the priestly consecration ritual (8:28–29) the breast is given to the officiating priest (Moses) only after he has burned the suet of the sacrifices and the thigh on the altar. In the cultic service for the eighth day, the burning of the suet again precedes the *tĕnûpâ* of the perquisites and their delivery to the priests (9:20–21). From these facts one can infer a basic principle of biblical cult: *God gets his portion before the priests do.*

Let us now turn to a historical event that testifies to these two facts: the sons of Eli in the sanctuary at Shiloh.

This is how the priests used to deal with the people: When anyone brought a sacrifice, the priest's boy would come along with a three-pronged fork while the meat was boiling, and he would thrust it into the cauldron, or the kettle, or the great pot, or the small cooking-pot; and whatever the fork brought up, the priest would take away on it. This was the practice at Shiloh with all the Israelites who came there. [But now] even before the suet was turned into smoke, the priest's boy would come and say to the man who was sacrificing, "Hand over some meat to roast for the priest; for he won't accept boiled meat from you, only raw." And if the man said to him, "Let them first turn the suet into smoke, and then take as much as you want," he would reply, "No, hand it over at once or I'll take it by force." The sin of the young men against the Lord was very great, for the men treated the Lord's offerings impiously. (1 Sam 2:13–17)

In this passage, the priest's perquisite is not fixed, but is "whatever the fork brought up." In this respect the Shilonite custom differed from that of P. Both agree, however, that only the officiating priest would receive his perquisite from the sacrifice, *and without any ritual.* Also, from the rebuking words of the narrator it is clear that even in his time it was customary to sacrifice the suet before the priests received their share. This is the "sin of the young men" (v 17), as is proved by the conclusion: "for the men treated the Lord's offerings impiously," namely, because Eli's sons were contemptuous of that part of the offering designated for the Lord: the suet. And if any doubts remain concerning this interpretation of the text, they are completely dispelled before the charge: "Why, then, do you maliciously trample upon the sacrifices and offerings which I have commanded? You have honored your sons more than me, feeding on the first portions of every offering of my people Israel [. . . offering of Israel before me: LXX]" (v 29). This verse clearly proves that Eli's sons' despising the offerings is related to the sin of their taking their share before God, namely, before sacrificing the suet.

By looking at the language and history we deduce that the passage on the right thigh in chap. 7 is the earlier, whereas in the passages in P that require the *tĕnûpâ* of the thigh in the manner of the breast, a later stage in the history of the cult is reflected.

When did the change take place in which the thigh of the *tĕrûmâ* began to undergo the *tĕnûpâ?* Assured historical facts are lacking, and any reconstruction can only be conjectural. One can only suggest some possible lines of development. Originally, the officiating priest received the wages for his work from the offering after the suet was burned on the altar, and without ritual. In the sanctuary at Shiloh the priest was the one who determined his wage, but in other sanctuaries it is likely that the custom reflected in 7:32–33 prevailed, in which the right thigh was fixed as the wage for the work of the officiating priest.

In contrast to the thigh, the breast was the portion for all of the priests. Such a practice was essential in the main sanctuary, where more than one priestly family served. As far as we know, only one sanctuary reflects this situation—the sanctuary at Jerusalem. From the beginning at least two families officiated there, the family of Abiathar and that of Zadok, plus a cadre of secondary priests. The breast, which was divided among the priests, also required *těnûpâ* before the Lord. This ceremony fulfilled three practical purposes: (a) It prevented quarreling among the priests, because no single one had a right to the whole breast. (b) It prevented favoritism on the part of the offerers. When there were several priests in the sanctuary, the offerers might wait until the priest they preferred came on duty at the altar, and then bring him their offering. Handing over the breast to the priests for *těnûpâ* transferred the ownership of the breast to the priests as a group. (c) The *těnûpâ* ritual added pomp and solemnity to the cult, and it was precisely the royal, national sanctuary at Jerusalem that was interested both in putting a stop to the arbitrariness of giving the thigh to the priest of one's choice, and in inserting it into a magnificent planned ritual.

It can thus be deduced that the ritual of 7:30–33 fuses two different customs: first, the thigh of the *těrûmâ* as the wage of the officiating priest reflects the practice of the small sanctuary with one priestly family; and second, the breast of the *těnûpâ* characterizes the sanctuary at Jerusalem; and it is the property of the whole body of priests in order to prevent quarreling by the priests, favoritism by the offerers, and for greater magnificence in the cult.

When was the next step added, the *těnûpâ* of the thigh? It is likely that the change occurred when the cult was centralized under Hezekiah or Josiah. Three factors operated at that time in the same direction. First, the end of the First Temple period is characterized by a trend toward collecting and consolidating ancient traditions. Probably P was also consolidated at that time. The tradition of the thigh of the *těrûmâ* in the ancient sanctuary was combined with the Jerusalem practice of the breast of the *těnûpâ*: the text of 7:30–33 was so edited. Second, it was impossible to preserve the custom of the thigh of the *těrûmâ* in the Jerusalem sanctuary. Giving it only to the officiating priest caused trouble, as was explained above. Thus it was established that the thigh should undergo *těnûpâ* with the breast and be given to all of the priests of that division. Finally, it is likely that all through the First Temple period the pressure mounted to add to the perquisites of the priests, especially from the well-being offering, because, as the importance of the Jerusalem sanctuary grew, so did the number of its priests. The same factors would have obtained in Solomon's time and thereafter: the need to provide an equitable distribution of the sacrificial portions to all members of the large priestly cadre. But the situation became critical under Hezekiah when levitic priests from northern Israel emigrated en masse to Judah and the high places were removed, so that the sanctuary became inundated by priests expelled from their high places. A further critical period would have been the aftermath of the Josianic reform, when the high places were destroyed and their priests became permanently unemployed. Indeed, according to Second Kings the priests of the high places were turned away by their colleagues in Jerusalem (2 Kgs 23:9), in spite of the deuteronomic injunction (Deut 18:6–7). But it is clear enough that King Josiah really tried to integrate all priests of the

Lord into Jerusalem: "he brought in all the priests from the cities of Judah" (2 Kgs 23:8).

If so, four historical factors operated at once: (1) the urge to clear up the blatant contradiction between the gift of the thigh and the gift of the breast; (2) the wish to prevent tension between the priests and the offerers and among the priests; (3) the wish to add pomp to the cult; and (4) the need to support the growing body of priests. For these reasons the těnûpâ of the thigh was probably initiated sometime in the seventh century, between the reigns of Hezekiah and Josiah, so that it was distributed to all of the priests as with the breast, which in turn led to the rule that the thigh of the těrûmâ required těnûpâ.

This history of the thigh is supported by a similar development with the cereal offering. Here also we have two contradictory recipients of the prebend: one text states that the cooked cereal offering belongs to all of the priests (2:10); the other states that it is the property of the officiating priest (7:9). Just as in the case of the thigh (8:32–33 versus 9:21; 10:15), we are probably faced with two traditions, that of the bāmâ/sanctuary, assigning the prebend to the (one) offici-ating priest, contested and superseded by that of the Temple, with its claim that the prebend must be shared by all priests. Here, too, an outside source provides corroborative evidence that the predicated transition took place. The abolition of the local altars in Judah under the Josianic reform brought its jobless priests to the Jerusalem Temple where 'ākělû maṣṣôt bĕtôk 'ăḥêhem 'they ate unleav-ened bread among their kinsmen' (2 Kgs 23:9b; for the exposition of this clause and its nonfulfillment in Deut 18, see the Note on 2:10). The maṣṣôt can only refer to the priestly prebend from the cereal offering, which may be brought raw or cooked (chap. 2) but must be eaten unleavened (6:9). Because it is shared by all of the priests it affirms that the prescription of 2:10 was in force. It stands to reason, then, that the cereal offering underwent a change in recipient at the same time as did the thigh.

A third step took place at the beginning of the Second Temple period, when attempts were made to clear up the differences and discrepancies in the laws of the Torah. The priests had two traditions regarding the right thigh: the text (and practice) according to which the thigh underwent těnûpâ (10:15), and another passage (7:32–33, and also the term "thigh of the těrûmâ") that desig-nated the thigh as a těrûmâ. Then, it seems to me, the těrûmâ and the těnûpâ were united to form one ritual comprising the two motions, support for which was found in the verse "you shall consecrate the breast of the těnûpâ and the thigh of the těrûmâ which undergoes the těnûpâ and the těrûmâ" (Exod 29:27; see Sipra, Ṣaw 11:11). The word těrûmâ was derived from the verb "to raise, lift," and joined to the těnûpâ, thereby yielding the ritual familiar to the rabbis at the end of the Second Temple period: "forward and backward, upward and downward" (e.g., m. Menaḥ. 5:6). For details, see Milgrom 1973ʾa (=1983d: 159–70).

G. The Prophets and the Cult

The thesis that the preexilic prophets repudiated the cult, espoused by the previous generation (e.g., Wellhausen 1885: 423; Kautzsch 1904: 723a; Hölscher 1922: 104; Bewer 1922: 267; Skinner 1922: 182; Kennett 1933: 120; Volz 1937), has been unanimously and convincingly rejected by its successor (Rowley 1946–47; Kaufmann 1937–56: 3.71–75, 443–46; Roubos 1956; Rendtorff 1956; de Vaux 1961a: 454–56; Reymond 1965; Hermisson 1965: 131–45; cf. also the earlier protestations of Welch 1936: 21; Oesterly 1937: 191–213). The latter have conclusively demonstrated that the prophets did not object to the cult per se but only to its abuse: those who leaned their hand on their sacrificial animals or raised their hands in prayer had blood on their hands (cf. Isa 1:15). To the contrary, the prophets uniformly affirmed the indispensability of the Temple (e.g., Isa 2:2–3; Jer 14:21; Ezek 43:1–12; Hag 1:9; Zech 2:14; 8:3); they only remonstrated against the blind belief in its efficacy without affecting the moral behavior of its adherents (forcefully: Jer 7:1–15; 26:1–15).

A much more difficult problem is the explicit statement uttered independently by two prophets, Jeremiah and Amos, that Israel neither offered sacrifices in the wilderness nor was commanded to do so:

Thus said the Lord of Hosts, the God of Israel: Add your burnt offerings (*'ōlôtêkem*) to your (well-being) sacrifices *(zibḥêkem)* and eat meat! For when I freed your fathers from the land of Egypt, I did not speak with them or command them concerning burnt offering *('ōlâ)* or (well-being) sacrifice *(zebaḥ)*. (Jer 7:21–22)

If you offer me burnt offerings *('ōlôt)* or your cereal offerings *(minḥōtêkem)* I will not accept them; I will pay no heed to your stall-fed well-being offering *(šelem)*. . . . Did you offer (well-being) sacrifices *(zĕbāḥîm)* or cereal offerings *(minḥâ)* to me those forty years in the wilderness, O House of Israel? (Amos 5:22, 25)

The prophets' claim is puzzling, for they surely were aware of the ancient tradition that Israel did indeed offer sacrifice in the wilderness (Exod 3:18; 5:3, 8, 17; 10:25; 18:12; 24:5; 32:6, 8). This quandary, in my opinion, was correctly resolved by Radak: "The Decalogue, which encapsules the entire Torah, contains no mention of burnt offerings or (well-being) offerings and even when it (the Torah) speaks of sacrifices it does not command them (the Israelites) to offer sacrifices, but (states) 'When any person among you presents an offering . . .' (Lev 1:2); that is, if he wishes to do it, the procedure is the following. As for the regular (daily) offerings *(tĕmîdîm)* that were commanded, they are for the honor of the Temple and are on behalf of the community, but individuals were not commanded to offer sacrifices" (Comment on Jer 7:22).

Radak's distinction between individual and communal sacrifices, namely, that only the latter were commanded, is right on target. Ostensibly, one might argue that the early covenanted codes attributed to Moses required the individual to offer sacrifices on the three pilgrimage festivals (Exod 23:18; 34:25). But these laws clearly presuppose the agrarian conditions of the settled land and could not have been carried out in the wilderness.

More to the point is the fact that the very sacrifices enumerated by Jeremiah and Amos in the preceding citations can apply only to individual sacrifices and not to those of the community. These sacrifices are the combination *ʿōlâ* and *zebaḥ* (Jeremiah), to which Amos adds the *šelem* and the *minḥâ*. The *zebaḥ* refers to what the P tradition calls *zebaḥ šĕlāmîm* 'well-being offering' (Lev 7:11–21), but which is broken down in other sources into *zebaḥ tôdâ* 'thanksgiving offering' (Lev 22:29[H]), *zebaḥ hayyāmîm* 'annual offering' (1 Sam 1:21), *zebaḥ mišpāḥâ* 'clan offering' (1 Sam 20:29), and *zebaḥ pesaḥ* 'paschal offering' (Exod 12:23; 23:18; 34:25; see the COMMENT on chap. 3). The common denominator of the *zebaḥ* in all of its varieties is that it is the only sacrifice whose meat is permitted to the worshiper. This point is underscored by Jeremiah's rebuke: henceforth, the *ʿōlâ* should be eaten just like the *zebaḥ* (Jer 7:21).

In P the combination of *ʿōlâ* and *zebaḥ* occurs only in the context of individual, voluntary sacrifices (Lev 17:8; 22:17–30; Num 15:1–16). The *zebaḥ* never appears in any cultic calendar dealing with communal, mandatory sacrifices. Indeed, the fact that the *zebaḥ* is not included in the cultic calendar of Num 28–29 but only in the subscript, Num 29:39, implies that the *zebaḥ* is one of the individual, voluntary sacrifices that stand outside the regimen of public sacrifice. To be sure, the *zebaḥ* in the subscript Lev 23:27 does refer to the pentecostal offering mentioned in the previous cultic calendar (Lev 23:19–20). Still, this sacrifice is brought by the individual worshiper and is not part of the cultic sacrifice prescribed for that day (see the NOTE on 23:19 in the next volume). In non-Priestly sources, the combination of *ʿōlâ* and *zebaḥ* also appears only as voluntary offerings of the individual and never as the required staple of the public cult (cf. Exod 18:12; Deut 12:11; Josh 22:26, 28; 1 Sam 15:22; 2 Kgs 5:17; 10:24; Isa 56:7). Ostensibly, the case for mandatory, public *ʿōlâ* and *zebaḥ* can be made for covenant-ratification ceremonies (e.g., Exod 24:5; Deut 27:6–7; Josh 8:31), but no specific numbers and kinds of animals are given, indicating that these are freewill offerings of the people. Especially instructive is the Chronicler's account of Hezekiah's purification of the Temple (2 Chr 29). Only after the prescribed *ḥaṭṭāʾt* and *ʿōlâ* are offered (vv 20–29) do the people bring *their* *ʿōlâ* and *zebaḥ* in unrestricted number (*nĕdîb lēb*, v 31). The inescapable conclusion is that the *ʿōlâ* paired with the *zebaḥ*, as found in Jer 7:21–22, never refers to the required public offering and certainly not to the daily *ʿōlâ* "instituted at Mount Sinai" (Num 28:6) but instead to the individual voluntary offerings brought by the people.

In P the *ʿōlâ*, like the *zebaḥ*, is generally a freewill offering brought on an occasion of happiness (see Lev 22:17–21; Num 15:1–8). Indeed, even when the *ʿōlâ* is offered for purposes of expiation, the text makes it amply clear (Lev 1:4), as Radak reminds us, that it is brought voluntarily and not as a requirement ("When a person among you presents an offering," Lev 1:2). In truth, P prescribes mandatory expiatory sacrifices, but these are the *ḥaṭṭāʾt* and *ʾāšām* (Lev 4–5), never the *ʿōlâ*. Even in non-Priestly sources the expiatory *ʿōlâ*, whether brought by an individual (e.g., Job 1:5; 42:8) or by the community (Judg 20:26; 2 Sam 24:25), is of a voluntary and not a compulsory nature. Only in rare cases of severe ritual contamination (see Lev 12–15) is an expiatory *ʿōlâ* enjoined upon the individual. Indeed, Ibn Ezra is surely right (see the NOTE on 5:7) that the *ḥaṭṭāʾt* is the main sacrifice of these impurity bearers and that the purpose of the *ʿōlâ* bird is to provide adequate substance for the altar, that is, for God. But is it conceivable that the throngs of ebullient Temple worshipers whom Jeremiah rebuked consisted solely of parturients, *zābîm*, and *mĕṣōrāʿîm?*

Furthermore, the fact that Jeremiah addresses the people at the Temple and not its officiating priests underscores that he speaks of the voluntary, individual sacrifices and not of those which are mandatory and communal. In the only other passage in which Jeremiah excoriates the sacrificial system (Jer 6:18–20), he again refers to the *ʿōlâ* and *zebaḥ*, and here he explicitly rebukes the people (*hāʿām*, vv 19, 21). Most significant of all is the language used by Jeremiah: *ʿōlôtêkem sĕpû* al-zibḥêkem wĕʾiklû bāśār (Jer 7:21). The words in roman type are those of Deut 12:15, *tizbaḥ wĕʾākaltā bāśār* (see Milgrom 1976e). Clearly, Jeremiah is alluding to the deuteronomic concession of profane slaughter: just as the *zebaḥ* need no longer be brought as a sacrifice in order to provide meat for the table, so the people would do better to eat their *ʿōlâ* offering rather than dedicate it to the altar. Amos pairs the *ʿōlâ* to the *minḥâ*, the cereal offering. The latter, by its nature, could not have been enforced in the wilderness. Indeed, when P specifies that the *minḥâ* must serve as an adjunct to the meat sacrifices, it explicitly states that this rule will take effect "when you enter the land" (Num 15:2). Amos also mentions the hapax *šelem* (found, however, in Ugaritic *UT* 1.8; 1131.5, 6, 7, 9), which clearly is the singular of *šĕlāmîm* and, therefore, equivalent to *zebaḥ*—again the voluntary offering of the individual.

In sum, Jeremiah and Amos have nothing whatever to say concerning the fixed Temple sacrifices such as the *tāmîd*. Rather, they turn to the people and urge them to renounce their individual offerings because this ritual piety is vitiated by their immoral behavior. They underscore this point with the claim that the wilderness covenant never enjoined upon the individual Israelite to honor God with sacrifices. Perhaps the Priestly legislators would have been offended by the prophets' abrasive tone, but as for this claim that the *ʿōlâ*, *zebaḥ,* and *minḥâ* were not commanded by the covenant, they would have no choice but to agree. (For greater detail, see Milgrom 1977c.)

H. Neusner on Holy Things

In 1981, I wrote, "J. Neusner, 'From Scripture to Mishna: the Origins of the Mishna's Fifth Division', *JBL* 98 (1979), pp. 269–83, claims that the fifth division of the Mishna contains two innovations: the principle of intention and the neutralization of the altar's power. However, both are rooted in Scripture. The reduction of the altar's power of sanctification to foodstuffs alone, as noted, took place as early as Haggai. Intention operates as the principle in a whole battery of cultic laws, e.g., (1) the repentant sinner is assumed to have been remorseful at the time of his crime (Lev 5:20–26; cf. 1976: 84–126). (2) Intention spells the difference between a purification offering and the *kārēt* penalty (Num 15:22–31). (3) The slaying of the encroacher presumes that his act is intentional (1970: 20–21). There are many other examples" (1981b: 298 n. 55). Because Neusner continues to make the same claim for the rabbis, I find it necessary to amplify my remarks.

In a masterful excursus, entitled "The Catalyst: Sanctification and Man's Will," Jacob Neusner demonstrates that the principle of intention is operative throughout rabbinic law, but this, he avers, verifies his opening claim: "The Mishna's principal message . . . that man is the center of creation . . . (is accomplished by imputing) power to man to inaugurate and initiate those corresponding processes, sanctification and uncleanness" (1981b: 270). It is my contention that this is not a rabbinic innovation but has its discernible and pervasive roots in Scripture. I shall cite two of Neusner's specific examples to prove my point.

"If a person sets aside an animal for a given sacrifice, the animal becomes holy. . . . When the householder wishes to separate the heave offering, he must both form the proper intention to do so and orally announce that intention, designating the portion of the crop to be deemed holy (M. Ter. 3:8). Without proper intention and proper deed, nothing has been done" (1981b: 277, 280). True, holiness in this world is created by man's will. But this is hardly a rabbinic innovation. One of the oldest narratives in Scripture relates that when Micah returns the money he stole from his mother, she says, "I herewith consecrate the silver to the Lord, transferring it to my son to make a sculptured image and a molten image" (Judg 17:3). Let us note: she consecrates the silver by oral declaration, precisely as prescribed by the rabbis. When we turn to the Priestly writings, we find that this method of consecration is taken for granted.

It is impossible to tell from the Bible when the status of "most sacred" begins, but there is no doubt that it has happened before the offering is brought to the sanctuary. The wording of the text shows this, for example, "this is the ritual for the purification offering. The purification offering shall be slaughtered before the Lord, at the spot where the burnt offering is slaughtered; it is most sacred" (6:18). That is to say, it is the prior status of the offering as most sacred that determines where it is to be slaughtered (cf. also 7:1–2 on the reparation offering). Indeed, this fact can be deduced, in particular, from the dedication of lesser sacred gifts in chap. 27, where it speaks of someone who dedicates his beast, his house, or his land, a dedication probably carried out by setting aside or by words (see Milgrom 1973a: 41 n. 17 [= 1983d: 142 n. 17]). Moreover, the precise Priestly term for a dedication to the sanctuary, tĕrûmâ, derives from the verb hērîm, whose basic meaning is "remove, set aside" (e.g., 2:9; 4:8, 10, 19; 6:3), as demonstrated by its parallel and synonymous verbs hēsîr 'remove, set aside' (e.g., 4:8–10, 31, 38) and hibbādēl 'remove oneself' (Num 16:21; 17:10). Finally, that the dedicating act (hērîm) takes place before the object is brought to the sanctuary (details in Milgrom 1972b: 2–4 [= 1983d: 160–62]) leads to the ineluctable conclusion that in ancient Israel, sanctification took place as a result of a person's intention, expressed by word and deed, by declaration and setting aside—in principle, not any differently from the method endorsed by the rabbis.

The principle of intention, however, is not restricted to sanctifications. It pervades the entire corpus of the Priestly literature. One could have deduced this a priori just by being familiar with the Priestly laws of homicide. It is this legislation that features the concept of šĕgāgâ 'inadvertence' (Num 35:11, 15), which signals a revolutionary break with criminal law in the ancient Near East by its categorical distinction between voluntary and involuntary homicide. Israel's priesthood endorses the postulate underlying the entire corpus of biblical law, that intention is the main criterion in determining the punishment of a murderer (cf. Exod 21:12–14; Deut 19:1–3).

Not unexpectedly, the notion of šĕgāgâ pervades the cultic texts as well. It is P that lays down the cardinal rule that expiatory sacrifices can be brought only in cases of inadvertence, while a presumptuous sinner is barred from the sanctuary (see the NOTE on "inadvertently," 4:2). For this reason both the ḥaṭṭāʾt and the ʾāšām, the two exclusive sacrifices of expiation, are predicated on the principle of the šĕgāgâ (4:2, 13, 22, 27; 5:15, 18). Moreover, even the two cases that ostensibly allow for a sacrifice to expiate a willful deed (5:1–4, 20–22) can only be resolved on the assumption that the offerer's amnesia or repentance have converted his intention from a deliberate to an inadvertent act (5:14–26, COMMENT F). Thus when Neusner proclaims that the rabbis have introduced the doctrine that "one who brings a sin offering must know precisely why he must do so, that is, for what sin or category of sin (M. Ker. 4:2–3)" (1981b: 275), he is, in fact, attributing to the rabbis a fundamental biblical postulate. The text of the sin (read: purification) offering specifies that the ḥaṭṭāʾt is enjoined only after the offender is fully apprised of his act (4:14, 23, 28; Milgrom 1967: 116 n. 6). Thus, if a person commits a wrong inadvertently (through ignorance or negligence), he is not liable for the sacrifice until he is cognizant of what he did, in other words, "for what sin or category of sin." Indeed, the rabbis themselves were fully aware that their doctrine was not of their own invention but was derived from the Bible: "Scripture says *bišĕgāgâ*, implying that he has knowledge (of the sin)" (*b. B. Qam.* 26b; see provisionally Eilberg-Schwartz 1986).

Neusner also counts among the rabbis' innovations their principle that "the altar sanctifies what is appropriate to it and does not sanctify what is not appropriate to it" (1981b: 206; cf. *m. Zebaḥ.* 9:1ff.; *t. Zebaḥ.* 9:4). He adds, "the neutralization of the altar's power to effect taboo through mere touch alone will have surprised the author of the pericope of Nadab and Abihu (Lev 10:1–3), as well as of Ex. 29:37 among the many Scriptural passages in which the intrinsic and uncontrolled sanctity of the cult, the altar, things offered on the altar, and cultic or holy objects, is taken for granted" (1981b: 206; cf. 1980: 28; 1981a: 162). First, it must be pointed out that the case of Nadab and Abihu is irrelevant. The altar is the source of their sin, not their punishment; they are struck down by a divine fire that emanates from within the Tent, not from the altar (see the NOTE on "from the Lord," 10:2). The second biblical citation, Exod 29:37, is quite relevant, but it proves Neusner wrong. This verse contains the Priestly formula *kol-hannōgēaʿ yiqdāš*, which, as has been shown (COMMENT B above), can only be rendered "whatever touches is sanctified"—whatever, but not whoever. The Priestly legislation has restricted the altar's contagion to objects and has completely eliminated its power to infect persons, even by touch.

Moreover, the reduction process did not stop with P. It takes another major step in the time of Haggai (if not before), when the altar's power to communicate its holiness becomes limited to "bread, stew, wine, oil, or any other food" (Hag 2:2; cf. COMMENT B above). Thus, the prophet is an unwitting witness (the most reliable kind) that the Jerusalemite priesthood at the end of the sixth century not only had restricted the altar's contagion to objects but had further reduced its potency to articles of food. If so, how different is Haggai's altar from the rabbis'? Both Haggai and the rabbis agree that the altar transmits its holiness solely to foods. The rabbis add: not all foods, but only those which qualify as offerings, to begin with. From Haggai's list bread, wine, and oil would qualify, but not the stew. Clearly, the difference is minuscule. One, then, would have to conclude that the rabbinic ruling on the altar's contagion had remained virtually the same from the time of Haggai. That is, for at least six hundred years, from the sixth century B.C.E. till the second century C.E. there is no appreciable change in the altar's sanctity. Thus, the most we can say about the rabbis' contribution to the reduction process is that they added nothing in kind but a trifle in degree. In contrast with the major changes that took place in biblical times, their contribution may be a refinement—but not an innovation.

I. The Order of Sacrifices in a Cultic Rite

The problem is succinctly and lucidly set in the rite of the Nazirite who has successfully completed his term. He brings sacrifices in the following order: *ʿōlâ, ḥaṭṭāʾt, šĕlāmîm, minḥâ, nesek.* They are sacrificed, however, in a different order: *ḥaṭṭāʾt, ʿōlâ, šĕlāmîm, minḥâ, nesek* (Num 6:13–17). This discrepancy has been explained by Anson Rainey as the difference between the administrative "book-keeping" order and the procedural, conducted order, the former *listing* the *ʿōlâ* before the *ḥaṭṭāʾt,* the latter *sacrificing* the *ḥaṭṭāʾt* before the *ʿōlâ* (1970). Rainey was obviously unaware that long ago the rabbis had reached a similar conclusion and, moreover, had provided a convincing rationale for the difference. The following is a sampling of their relevant statements.

(1) "The priest shall offer (the one designated) as the *ḥaṭṭāʾt* first (5:8). For what purpose is this stated? If to teach that it comes before the *ʿōlâ,* surely it is already stated 'And the second he shall sacrifice as an *ʿōlâ*' (5:10)? This, however, furnishes a general rule for all *ḥaṭṭāʾt* offerings, that they take precedence over all *ʿōlâ* offerings which accompany them" (*b. Zebaḥ.* 90a [bar.]).

(2) "The *ḥaṭṭāʾt* always takes priority" (*m. Nazir* 6:5; cf. *m. Zebaḥ.* 10:2; *t. Zebaḥ.* 10:4).

(3) "The blood of the *ḥaṭṭāʾt* precedes the blood of the *ʿōlâ* because it appeases" (*m. Zebaḥ.* 10:2).

(4) "R. Simeon said: To what may the *ḥaṭṭāʾt* be compared? To a paraclete, who enters in to appease [the judge]. Once the paraclete has accomplished appeasement, then the gift (i.e., the *ʿōlâ*) is brought in" (*t. Para* 1:1).

(5) "Raba said: Scripture accorded it (the *ʿōlâ*) precedence (in 12:8) in respect to designating it (*Zebaḥ.* 90a) or dedicating it" (tosafot on *Zebaḥ.* 90a, s.v. *lĕmiqrāʾâ*).

Transposing these statements into the idiom and interpretation in which I have cast these sacrifices, the *ḥaṭṭāʾt* of necessity comes first in any series because the sanctuary must be purged of the impurity caused it by the offerer (chap. 4, COMMENTS B and C) before the deity will consider his other sacrifices. Conversely, when the sacrifices are prescribed they are listed in order of their sanctity (i.e., importance), and therefore the ubiquitous and venerable *ʿōlâ,* burnt in its entirety as a total gift to God (COMMENT on chap. 1), comes first.

This basic distinction between the administrative and procedural orders will be found to be operative in all instances (for ostensible exceptions see below). It will even solve an exegetical crux. The alleged discrepancy in the order of the *ʾāšām* sacrifice and its monetary fine (5:15–16) can be resolved by the application of this distinction and by the transposition of the pausal notation (*ʾetnaḥ*) of the MT (see the NOTE on 5:16).

The one purported anomaly is the *mĕṣōrāʿ.* The procedural order of his sacrifices finds the *ʾāšām* first! The exceptional importance of the *ʾāšām* accounts for this peculiarity. It alone can neither be compromised (14:21–22) nor commuted, as proved by the indispensability of its blood (vv 14, 25) and its unique dedication by the *těnûpâ* (for details see the NOTE on 14:12). The rabbis were well aware of this exception: "All *ḥaṭṭā't* offerings enjoined in the Torah precede the *'āšām* offering, excepting the *'āšām* of the *měṣōrā'*, for this is offered *lěhakšîr*, to render him fit (to enter the sanctuary)" (*m. Zebaḥ.* 10:5).

I must also record the following disagreements with Rainey's article: (1) There is no evidence that "there must have been some observation or sign whereby the officiating priest announced to the offerer that his sacrifice had been accepted" (1970: 487). On the contrary, the presumption on the part of the priest to read the mind of God would have been considered blasphemous. (2) The pericope 6:12–16 deals not with the priests' ordination ceremony (1970: 489) but with the twice-daily cereal offering of the high priest (see the NOTES ad loc.). (3) The verse 1 Kgs 8:5 (= 2 Chr 5:6) hardly "alludes to the atonement stage of the ceremony in which sin *(ḥaṭṭā't)* and burnt *('ōlâ)* offerings were made" (1970: 498). The fact that they "were sacrificing sheep and oxen in such abundance that they could not be numbered or counted" points rather to *'ōlâ* and *šělāmîm* offerings, as stipulated in both the dedicatory rite of Hezekiah's Temple (2 Chr 29:31–33) and David's celebration of the installation of the Ark (2 Sam 6:13, 17–18). The latter ceremonies speak only of abundant *'ōlâ* and *šělāmîm* offerings but not of *ḥaṭṭā't* offerings, which would always be fixed in number. Besides, the likelihood exists that the *ḥaṭṭā't* (and *'āšām*) offering did not become an official part of the Jerusalem cult until later (see the COMMENT on chap. 1 and chap. 4, COMMENT N).

PART II

THE INAUGURATION
OF THE CULT
(CHAPTERS 8–10)

◆

THE CONSECRATION OF THE PRIESTS (8:1–36)

8 ¹The Lord spoke to Moses, saying: ²Take Aaron and his sons with him, the vestments, the anointing oil, the bull of purification offering, the two rams, and the basket of unleavened bread, ³and assemble the whole community at the entrance to the Tent of Meeting. ⁴Moses did as the Lord commanded him. And when the community was assembled at the entrance of the Tent of Meeting, ⁵Moses said to the community, "This is what the Lord has commanded to be done."

⁶Moses brought Aaron and his sons forward and had them washed with water. ⁷He put the tunic on him, girded him with the sash, clothed him with the robe, put the ephod on him, and girded him with the decorated band, which he tied to him. ⁸He put the breastpiece on him, and put into the breastpiece the Urim and Thummim. ⁹And he set the turban on his head; and on the turban, in front, he put the gold plate, the holy diadem—as the Lord had commanded Moses.

¹⁰Moses took the anointing oil and anointed the tabernacle and all that was in it, thus consecrating them. ¹¹He sprinkled some of it on the altar seven times, and he anointed the altar, all of its utensils, and the laver with its stand, to consecrate them. ¹²He poured some of the anointing oil upon Aaron's head, thereby anointing him to consecrate him. ¹³Then Moses brought Aaron's sons forward, clothed them in tunics, girded them with sashes, and tied caps on them —as the Lord had commanded Moses.

¹⁴He had the bull of purification offering brought forward. Aaron and his sons leaned their hands on the bull of purification offering, ¹⁵and it was slaughtered. Moses took the blood and with his finger put [some] on the horns around the altar, decontaminating the altar; then he poured out the blood at the base of the altar. Thus he consecrated it to effect atonement upon it. ¹⁶All of the suet that was about the entrails, and the caudate lobe of the liver, and the two kidneys and their suet, were then taken up and Moses turned [them] into smoke upon the altar; ¹⁷but the [rest of the] bull—its hide, its flesh, and its dung—was put to fire outside the camp—as the Lord had commanded Moses.

¹⁸Then the ram of burnt offering was brought forward. Aaron and his sons leaned their hands upon the ram's head, ¹⁹and it was slaughtered. Moses dashed the blood against all sides of the altar. ²⁰The ram was cut up into its quarters, and Moses turned the head, the quarters, and the suet into smoke. ²¹The entrails and shins were washed in water, and Moses turned all of the ram into smoke on the altar. This was a burnt offering for a pleasing aroma, a food gift to the Lord—as the Lord had commanded Moses.

²²Then the second ram, the ram of ordination, was brought forward. Aaron and his sons leaned their hands upon the ram's head, ²³and it was slaughtered. Moses took some of its blood and put [it] on the lobe of Aaron's right ear, and on the thumb of his right hand, and on the big toe of his right foot. ²⁴Then the

sons of Aaron were brought forward and Moses put some of the blood on the lobes of their right ears, and on the thumbs of their right hands, and on the big toes of their right feet; and Moses dashed the [rest of the] blood against all sides of the altar. 25He took the suet—the broad tail, all of the suet about the entrails, the caudate lobe of the liver, and the two kidneys and their suet—and the right thigh. 26From the basket of unleavened bread that was before the Lord, he took one cake of unleavened bread, one cake of oil bread, and one wafer, and placed [them] on the suet pieces and on the right thigh. 27He placed all of these on the palms of Aaron and on the palms of his sons, and presented them as an elevation offering before the Lord. 28Then Moses took them from their palms and turned [them] into smoke on the altar with the burnt offering. This was an ordination offering for a pleasing aroma, a food gift to the Lord. 29Moses took the breast and presented it as an elevation offering before the Lord; it was Moses' portion of the ram of ordination—as the Lord had commanded Moses.

30Then Moses took some of the anointing oil and some of the blood that was on the altar and sprinkled [it] upon Aaron's vestments, upon his sons, and upon his sons' vestments with him. Thus he consecrated Aaron's vestments, his sons, and his sons' vestments with him.

31And Moses said to Aaron and his sons: Boil the flesh at the entrance of the Tent of Meeting and eat it there with the bread that is in the basket of ordination—as I commanded: "Aaron and his sons shall eat it." 32The remainder of the flesh and the bread you shall destroy by fire. 33You shall not go outside the entrance of the Tent of Meeting for seven days, until the day that your period of ordination is completed; for your ordination will require seven days. 34Everything done today, the Lord has commanded to be done, to make atonement for you. 35You shall stay at the entrance of the Tent of Meeting day and night for seven days, observing the Lord's prohibitions, so that you do not die—for so I have been commanded.

36And Aaron and his sons did all of the things that the Lord had commanded through Moses.

INTRODUCTION

The eighth chapter of Leviticus provides the fulfillment of the command at Exod 29. Why are these two chapters so far apart? The answer is clarified by the context. Moses is commanded to consecrate Aaron and his sons into the priesthood by means of a series of sacrifices. Thus after Moses has the Tabernacle erected (Exod 35–40) he must first learn the sacrificial procedures (Lev 1–7) before he can proceed with the priestly consecration. He also will need to consecrate the Tabernacle (Lev 8:10–11) before he can consecrate the priests (see the NOTE on v 10), for when the Tabernacle and its sancta were assembled (Exod 40:17–33), they had not been consecrated.

The order (and even the nature) of the consecration is not the same in Exod 29 and Lev 8 (noted in *Sipra*, Millu'im Ṣaw 8). This in itself is not surprising because frequently the prescriptive (administrative) order will differ from the descriptive (procedural) order, as clearly recognized by the rabbis (e.g., *m. Zebaḥ.* 10:2; *t. Zebaḥ.* 10:4; *Zebaḥ.* 90a [bar.]). For details see COMMENTS B and C below.

NOTES

8:1. vv 1–2 are a resumptive repetition *(Wiederaufnahme)* of Exod 29:1–4, necessitated by the long intervening gap. It also enables the writer to introduce the *ʿēdâ* into the picture (vv 3–4), a factor that was omitted in Exod 29.

2. Take. *qaḥ* is the verb used in Exod 29:16, where, however, it is the predicate for the sacrificial animals (cf. 9:2, 3, 5). But it can also be used for persons (cf. Num 1:17, chieftains; 3:41, Levites; 11:16, elders; 27:18, Joshua; 21:25, Eleazar). Its sense here is that of "summon" (*Sipra*, Millu'im Ṣaw 2, recognizing the difficulty, renders *qāḥēm bidĕbārîm* 'take them with words', in other words, persuade him; Saadiah renders "present").

The priestly vestments are listed first as the priests will be dressed in them (vv 7–9, 13) before the sacrificial service begins (vv 14–29). The text is here concerned with the procedural order, whereas the comparable verses of Exod 29 are a random inventory of the materials required—without even describing their function. Thus even though these initial verses of Lev 8 are prescriptive they are influenced by the procedural order to be followed. Indeed, even the sacrificial items are listed in the order of their use: purification offering (vv 14–17), the two rams (vv 18–25), and the basket of unleavened bread (v 26). Strikingly, this trait is not the peculiarity of the Priestly writer, but is standard scribal style in the ancient Near East. Among the Hittites, for example, we find repeatedly that items in an inventory text are enumerated in an order that differs from that in the ritual text prescribing their use. Both Hittite texts, inventory and ritual, are prescriptive, thus fully comparable to Exod 29:1–4 and Lev 8:1–2. In the Tunnawi rite, for example (Goetze 1938a, b), the old woman is to take figures, tongues, oxen (figures), and *wawarkima* objects (1.43–44), but she holds over the patient tongues, figures, *wawarkima*, and oxen (1.63–2.2). In the greater ritual text, the fifty items listed in the inventory (1.11–52) are totally rearranged in the order of their use, as follows (compiled by D. Wright):

	Inventory			Performance	
	ram/ewe (1.11)	1	0	thin loaves (1.25)	⎫
	pig (1.12)	2	34?	jug of wine (1.25)	⎪
	dog (1.12)	3	33	"tallow cake and porridge" (1.25)	⎬ *
	black shirt (1.13)	4	0	thin loaf (1.27)	⎪
	black headband (1.13)	5	33	tallow cake and porridge (1.28)	⎪
	black hooded gown (1.14)	6	34?	libation (1.29)	⎭
female materials	black gaiters (1.14)	7	0	thin loaf (1.34)	
	black shoes (1.15)	8	33	scatters "tallow cake and porridge" (1.35)	
	girdle (1.15)	9	34?	libation (1.35)	
	TAḪAPŠU girdle (1.15)	10	39	acts with wool (1.54–56)	
	black wool in ears (1.16)	11	27?	black sheep (1.56)	
male materials	black shirt (1.17)	12	2	pig (1.60f.)	
	black gaiters (1.17)	13	3	dog (1.61f.)	
	ears stopped with wool (1.18)	14	36	clay tongue (1.63)	
	combs (1.18f.)	15	35	clay figures (2.1)	
	brush (1.19)	16	38	wawarkima (2.2)	
	TIYADU (1.19)	17	37	clay oxen (2.3)	
	NINDA.ZAB.MEŠ (1.19)	18	0?	string (2.4)	
	6 GIR₄ vessels (1.20)	19	40	wing (2.5)	
	black braziers (1.20)	20	17	TIYADU (2.8)	
	4 small black pots (1.20)	21	48	figures of wax (2.14)	
	4 large black pots (1.21)	22	49	figures of mutton tallow (2.14)	
	8 lids (1.21)	23	?	washes hands with wine (2.21)	
	3 black jugs (1.21)	24	20	brazier (2.23)	
	2 black pitchers (1.21)	25	26	wash with water (2.25)	
	2 black water vessels (1.21)	26	20	(other) brazier (2.26)	
	sheep (1.22)	27	39	wool (2.28, 2.40)	
	lamb (1.22)	28	12	black shirt torn (2.41f.)	
	3 hot loaves (1.22)	29	13	gaiters removed (2.43)	
	cheese (1.22)	30	14	ear-wool removed (2.44f.)	
	curd (1.22)	31	21/22?	pot (UTÚL) swung (2.52)	
	jug of beer (1.22)	32	15	combs (2.62)	

CONSECRATION

Inventory		Performance	
"tallow cake and porridge" •			
(1.23)	33	35	figure of clay (2.63f.)
ḫaniššar of wine (1.23)	34	16	brush (3.6)
figures of clay (1.43f.)	35	15, 16, 40, 12, 13	combs,
tongues of clay (1.43f.)	36		brush, wing, shirt, gaiters thrown in river (3:12–16)
oxen of clay (1.43f.)	37	2/3	dog and pig (3.17f.)
wawarkima of clay (1.43f.)	38	0	3 NINDA.KUR.RA and porridge set out by gates (3.23f.)
wools (1.45)	39		
eagle's wing (1.46)	40	0	throws thin bread (3.4; 3.5)
bone (1.46)	41	0	breaks thin loaf (3.56)
allin (1.46)	42	33	scatters "tallow cake and porridge" (3.58)
seeds (1.47)	43	34?	libation of wine (4.1)
zinakkiš (1.47)	44	0	breaks thin loaf (4.4)
heart & liver (1.48)	45	33	scatters tallow cake and porridge (4.4)
pig of dough (1.48)	46	50	cow [or bull] horn seized (4.7)
crumbs of various breads (1.49)	47	0	fruit tree analogy (4.15)
figure of wax (1.49)	48	27	[sheep] offered (4.24)
figure of mutton tallow (1.50)	49	28	[lamb]
cow/bull (1.52)	50	29	three hot loaves (4.29)
		30	cheese (4.29)
		31	[curd] (4.29)
		45/	liver and heart (4.30)
		32/34?	[beer] or wine libated (1.31)
		45?	liv[er and heart] (4.39)
		32/34?	[beer] or wine libated (4.40)

*The little section of 1.25–29 could be viewed as an inventory and performance section. The order of the elements does not coincide:

1.25	thin loaves		breaking loaves
	jug of wine	vs.	scattering "tallow cake and porridge"
	"tallow cake and porridge"		libation

the vestments. These are enumerated in Exod 29:5–6, 8–9 and described in Exod 28. Their importance is stated categorically by the rabbis: "When the priests are clothed in their vestments, their priesthood is upon them; when they are not clothed in their vestments, their priesthood is not upon them" (*b. Zebah.* 17b).

the anointing oil. This oil consists of two parts liquid myrrh, two parts cassia, one part each of cinnamon and aromatic cane, with olive oil added (Exod 30:23–24). The proportions work out to about 1 pint olive oil to 54 pounds of dry spices (Snaith 1967).

the . . . the . . . the . . . the . . . the. The five items listed by the definite article presume a prior knowledge of and dependency on Exod 29 (*Sipra,* Millu'im Ṣaw 3).

the bull of purification offering (par haḥaṭṭāʾt). The bull was identified as such in Exod 29:14, another clear indication of the dependency of this list on Exod 29.

the two rams. Following the language of Exod 29:1; the rams will be identified as burnt and ordination offerings below (vv 18, 22).

the basket of unleavened bread. The contents of the basket are only given below (v 26), an indication of the dependency of this phrase on Exod 29:2. Here the basket is listed last in accordance with the procedural order (v 26), but in Exod 29:3 it is listed first, another indication of the discrepancy between prescriptive inventories and prescriptive rituals (see above). A basket of unleavened bread is also prescribed in the ritual of the Nazirite (Num 6:15, 17, 19).

3. *the whole community (kol-hāʿēdâ).* The scope of ʿēdâ exhibits the following range: (a) the entire nation, including women and children; this is its chief meaning, occurring more than one hundred times in the early narratives (e.g., Exod 16:1; Num 17:11; 20:1, 7–8; 27:17; 31:16; 32:4; Josh 22:16, 17, 18, 20) and laws (e.g., Exod 12:19, 47; Lev 4:13; Num 1:53; 15:25); (b) all adult males (e.g., Num 8:9–10; Num 14:1–4, esp. v 2; 31:26, 28, 43), particularly those bearing arms (e.g., Judg 20:1); and (c) the tribal leaders meeting as an executive body (e.g. Exod 12:3, 21; Josh 22:13, 16; Judg 20:12, 27; 21:10, 13, 22). Thus ʿēdâ can be equivalent to all of the Israelites, to the adult males, or to their national representatives. The plasticity of ʿēdâ is not surprising in view of such other terms as ʿam, bĕnê yiśrāʾēl, ʾanšê yiśrāʾēl (yĕhûdâ), which can also refer either to the total population, or to the male adult population, or to the people's representatives. Moreover, this feature is not unique to Israel. Both the Amarna letters and the Ugaritic tablets testify to the existence of institutional bodies representing the city-states, alternately referred to as "the town of N (ᵃlN)," "the sons *(mārū)* of N," or "the men *(amīlū)* of N." In any event, ʿēdâ can never refer to a subdivision of the nation, be it tribe, clan, or city; it stands for the entire nation and not for any segment thereof (for the alleged exception of Korah's ʿēdâ, see Milgrom 1978a: 71–72).

It is not clear which of the three meanings of ʿēdâ is intended here. Ibn

Ezra opts for (c) the tribal leaders (as in 9:1) on the grounds that the theophany was witnessed by them (Exod 24:9–10). But this theory should be eliminated, if only for the reason that the writer would have used the term *něśî'ê hā'ēdâ* (Num 4:34) or, most likely, *ziqnê hā'ēdâ* (4:15)/*yiśrā'ēl* (9:1). Which of the two remaining alternatives should be used—all of the people or just the adult males—is not easy to determine, however. Elsewhere we find the *'ēdâ* also gathered at the entrance to the Tent of Meeting: (1) in the Korah episode (Num 16:19; contrasted with the chieftains, v 2); (2) at the call of the trumpets (Num 10:3; contrasted with the chieftains, v 4); and (3) for the case of Zelophehad's daughters (Num 27:2; contrasted with the chieftains, ibid.), where it is not ascertainable whether all of the people or its adult male population is intended. *Sipra*, Millu'im Ṣaw 4 suggests that all the people (a) were present as eyewitnesses of the priestly consecration, a contention Abravanel supports by referring to the case of Joshua's authorization as Moses' successor, which was similarly witnessed by all the people (Num 27:19–22). Further support can be adduced from the next chapter of Leviticus, where the elders bring the sacrifices (9:1, 3 LXX) but the people as a whole *(hā'ām)* witness the theophany (9:23). If, however, the objection is made that because this chapter is dealing not with a theophany but with the consecration of the priests, only the adult males or even their representatives would have sufficed as witnesses, then the dedication of Solomon's Temple can be brought forward as evidence that, for this kind of occasion, all of the people would have been summoned to be present (1 Kgs 8:1).

Indeed, the similarity to the dedication of the Solomonic Temple can be found not only in theme but also in vocabulary. Both accounts exhibit a double use of the root *qhl*, once in the *hiph'il* and once in the *niph'al* (vv 3–4; 1 Kgs 8:1–2). Furthermore, the two accounts contain other parallels: in both, the national leader blesses the assembled people (9:23; 1 Kgs 8:55); it is impossible to enter the sanctuary after it is filled with the divine presence (Exod 40:35; 1 Kgs 8:11); and the dedication is climaxed by a divine revelation—visual and auditory (9:23–24; Num 7:89; 1 Kgs 9:2–3; A. Hurowitz 1985). Which account is original and which derivative? When due consideration is taken of the fact that the assembling of the *'ēdâ* is not mentioned in the prescriptive account, Exod 29, but is the innovation of Lev 8, the possibility must be reckoned with that vv 3–5 are a later addition, by the same hand that inserted the brief notice of the sanctuary dedication (vv 10aβ–11; see the NOTE on v 10), in order to equate the story of the dedication of the Tabernacle and its priesthood with that of the dedication of Solomon's Temple.

4. *as the Lord commanded him.* The refrain *ka'ăšer ṣiwwâ YHWH* appears seven times in this chapter (vv 4, 9, 13, 17, 21, 29, 36) and seven times in the accounts that describe the manufacture of the priestly vestments (Exod 39:1–31) and the assembling of the Tabernacle (Exod 40:17–38). This refrain subdivides the chapter into seven coherent sections (see COMMENT A below) and constitutes the scaffolding upon which Lev 8 was constructed. A similar expres-

sion is attested in extrabiblical building accounts. For example, in the descriptive (as opposed to the prescriptive) text of the Samsuiluna B inscription, the scribe adds this final comment: *ša eli Šamaš Adad u Aya ṭābu epuš qibīt Šamaš u Marduk ana ašrum aškun* 'I did that which was good to Šamaš, Adad, and Aya; I fulfilled the command of Šamaš and Marduk' (for details see COMMENT B below). For a nearly identical phrase, see Gelb (1948: 270 Aii.27–29; Biii.18–20).

The significance of this refrain derives from the belief that "unless the Lord builds the house, its builders labor in vain on it" (Ps 127:1). This theme is echoed in a Hittite text: "Behold this temple we have built for you, the deity. . . . It is not we who have built it (but) all the gods who have built it" (*KBo* IV1.i.28–30; *ANET*[3] 356). The identical view was held by Israel.

entrance of the Tent of Meeting. This locus is here mentioned twice (vv 3–4); hence, it can be omitted below (vv 6, 14, 15; contrast Exod 29:4, 10, 11).

5. *This is what the Lord has commanded. zeh haddābār ʾăšer ṣiwwâ YHWH* is a typical idiom of P (Exod 16:16, 32; 35:4; Lev 9:6; 17:2; Num 30:2; 36:6). What is its referent? *Leqaḥ Tov* avers that it refers to the instructions of Exod 29. Perhaps the words *zeh haddābār* alone should be set off in quotes because they are the opening words of Exod 29 and should be rendered "This is the word/instruction." This interpretation implies that the writer merely cited the incipit of Exod 29 as a means of informing the readers that Moses actually recited the entire ritual of Exod 29 to the assembled community.

The use of incipits in Scripture is not unattested. One such example in P is Num 33:40, which is practically a literal quotation of Num 21:19, the beginning of the brief story of the victorious battle against the Canaanites (vv 1–3). Clearly, it is that victory which the writer of Num 33:40 had in mind, demonstrating that the entire account of Num 21:1–3 was before him and known to his readers and all he had to do was to quote the incipit in order to allude to the entire account.

Alternatively, this expression refers not to Moses' words but to his actions that immediately follow (vv 6ff.), in which case the entire sentence should be in quotes (so followed in my translation). This interpretation gathers strength in view of the possibility that vv 3–5 were added by the writer to equate the Tabernacle dedication with that of the Solomonic Temple (see COMMENT A below).

6. *(Moses) brought (Aaron and his sons) forward (wayyaqrēb).* Where? The object, the entrance to the Tent of Meeting, has already been twice stated (vv 3, 4) and need not be repeated. So again in vv 14, 15, the same object is missing but implicitly understood. Contrast Exod 29:4, 10, 11, where it is explicitly stated in the same contexts because it is not mentioned in the antecedent verses (see also COMMENT B below).

and had them washed with water (wayyirḥaṣ ʾōtām bammāyim). According to

Ibn Ezra, this verb should be understood impersonally. Ehrlich, however, holds that Moses, as the officiant, performed the ablutions, as they formed an integral part of the cultic service (see also Ramban's opinion, below). This issue is difficult to resolve. When the Levites were inducted into their service they too were washed, had their clothing laundered, and were sprinkled with purificatory waters (Num 8:7), but none of these operations was performed by Aaron, the officiating priest. Ibn Ezra, then, may be right. Moreover, one cannot argue that the waters came from the laver in the sanctuary court and were, therefore, accessible only to priests, for neither the laver nor the priests were yet sanctified. Washing with ordinary water is what the text suggests, and this could have been done by the priests themselves or with lay assistance. Ibn Ezra, though, is certainly wrong in claiming that the priests' washing was limited to their hands and feet. The latter act, as pointed out by Mizrahi, would have been expressed by *rāḥaṣ mayim*, without the preposition *beth* (e.g., Exod 30:20). The prefixed *beth, bammayim,* implies full immersion (*Sipra,* Rashi), as evidenced by 16:4, 24. A further question is where the washing was carried out. Because the priestly consecrands were still technically laymen, their washing took place in the forecourt. According to rabbinic tradition, an area of the court was curtained off for this purpose (*m. Yoma* 3:4). Indeed, the rabbis' insistence that the washing take place in an improvised space rather than in a permanent room (as the Qumranites prescribed for their temple, 11QT 31–33) shows that their tradition must be old, stemming back to the practice in the Tabernacle, as recorded here.

Ramban suggests that Moses first washed and dressed Aaron (vv 6–9) and then anointed the sanctuary and Aaron (vv 10–12) before he washed the latter's sons. This interpretation would overcome the difficulty of the present sequence in the MT, whereby Aaron's sons would be kept standing naked for a long time before Moses would get to dress them (see the NOTE on v 10).

7. *He.* Clearly the subject of all of the verbs in the dressing of Aaron is Moses. This fact can be derived from the transfer of the high priesthood from Aaron to Eleazar: Moses executes God's command to strip Aaron of his official vestments and to put them on Eleazar (Num 20:25–28). The priests' vestments are the outer symbols of their authority. Hence when Moses puts them on Aaron and his sons at the command of God, he thereby signifies that they are authorized to wear them.

The priestly vestments total eight in all, four undergarments worn by all of the priests and four outer garments worn by Aaron, the high priest, alone. They are described in Exod 28 and 39. Aaron's four outer garments are the *ephod*, the breastpiece, the robe, and the gold plate. Whereas the robe is fashioned out of one material, dyed wool, the ephod and breastpiece are of fine linen, dyed wool, and gold. The mixture of linen and wool was prohibited in nonsacred garments because it was considered holy (see COMMENT B below and the NOTE on the sash in v 13). The four undergarments are a tunic (the high priest's was more elaborate; see the NOTE below), a sash, a headdress (the high priest's again more elaborate; see below), and breeches. The breeches are omitted from the list of vestments donned by either Aaron or his sons (vv 7, 13) and only appear in an appendix to the inventory of the priestly vestments in Exod 28:42–43, which suggests that they were not considered sacred (cf. also the NOTE on 16:4 and 24). Sandals were forbidden on sacred ground (Exod 3:5; Josh 5:15).

A brief word on the materials of the vestments. Gold thread was made by hammering it into thin sheets and then cutting them into strands. Each of these strands was woven with one of the dyed woolen strands on a linen strand to make threads. Thus each thread was one-half gold (Exod 39:3; Haran 1978: 167 n. 41). Five types of materials for spinning and weaving were used; three were woolen and two were linen. The wool was dyed either blue-purple *(tĕkēlet)*, red-purple *('argāmān)*, or red *(tôla'at šānî)*. The dyes were extracted from animals: the *Murex trunculus*, the *Murex brandaris* (shellfish indigenous to the eastern Mediterranean), and the insect *Kermococcus vermilio*, respectively (Ziderman 1981–82; Milgrom 1983b). The linens were either fine *(šēš)* or plain *(bad)*. Three types of weaving are prescribed: elaborate workmanship containing designs *(ḥōšēb)* for the Tabernacle curtains, the veil, the ephod, and the breastpiece; less elaborate workmanship without designs *(rōqēm)* for the screens of the Tent and enclosures and the sash; and fabric made of one kind of material *('ōrēg)*. Precious stones were set aside for the ephod and the breastpiece. (Much of the information about the composition and manufacture of the priestly vestments stems from a class paper by S. Pfann; and see fig. 10.)

the tunic (hakkuttōnet). Made wholly of fine, embroidered linen (Exod 28:39; 39:27), it was worn by all priests (v 13). Aaron's tunic, in addition, is described as *tašbēṣ* (Exod 28:4; note the verb *šabaṣ,* v 39), etymology unknown, rendered either "fringed" (LXX) or "checkered" (Tgs., Rashi). As it was the first garment to be put on, it was worn next to the skin. *kuttōnet* (or *kĕtōnet*) is also "tunic" in Greek (χιτῶνα, LXX), Aramaic *(kytwn', ktwn')* and Akk. *(kitinnu,* a West Semitic loanword or a derivative from *kitû,* Sumerian *GADA*). Its other meaning, "linen, flax," is found in Aramaic *(kytn;* see Dan 7:9) and Phoenician *(ktn)*. For philological details, see Brown 1980: 7–15.

with the sash. bā'abnēṭ, a singular form with a collective meaning (see v 13). This article of Aaron's clothing is missing in the prescription (Exod 29:5), which the Sam. supplies. Nevertheless, the MT there is clearly the original, for it adds the clause "Aaron and his sons" in the prescription for the sons' sashes (Exod 29:9), in order to make up for its omission in the prescription for Aaron's clothing (see also *b. Yoma* 5b, 6a; *y. Yoma* 1:5).

Aaron's sash was woven of fine linen with blue-purple, red-purple, and red woolen threads and was of *rōqēm* embroidery (Exod 28:39). These constituents, with linen comprising the major part, correspond to the fabric of the Tabernacle's lower curtains, while the *rōqēm* weave is the same as that of the screens for the entrance to the Tent and the enclosure (Exod 26:36; 27:16). The word *'abnēṭ* is unique to P, save for one occurrence in Isa 22:21, where with

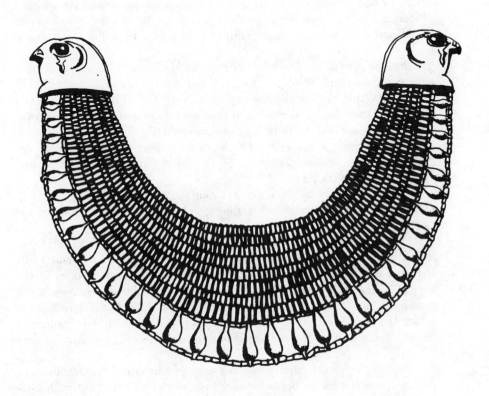

FIGURE 10

the tunic it is used to represent the transfer of authority and office from Shebna to Eliakim. The subsequent and exclusive attestation of its synonym *'ēzôr* (Jer 13:2, 4, 6, 7, 11; Ezek 23:15; Job 12:18) may indicate that *'abnēṭ* fell out of use by the seventh century (Paran 1983: 196). An etymology from Egyptian *'abnd* 'wrap or envelop, dress' has been proposed (Hönig 1957; Grintz 1974–76: 7, but denied by Rabin 1974–75). The length, width, and manner of weaving are open to speculation. The question of whether the sash for Aaron's sons was of similar or different composition is discussed in the NOTE on v 13 and in COMMENT B below.

the robe (hamměʿîl). Described in Exod 28:31–35 and 39:22–26, it is made entirely of blue-purple wool (to set off the multicolored ephod: Cassuto 1951a), as is the covering cloth of the Ark in transit (Num 4:6). It is apparently woven of *'ōrēg* workmanship as its reinforced neckline (of one piece with it, not separate and sewn on) is explicitly of *'ōrēg* workmanship (Exod 28:32). This garment is of a single piece of material with the neck opening in the middle. It was slipped on over the head, poncho-style, instead of having an open front and being donned like a coat.

The etymology of *měʿîl* is difficult. Hönig suggests *ʿly/ʿlh* 'over' (1957: 60). Görg recommends Egyptian *mʿr*, meaning "faultless, defectless," used of the clothing of the gods (1976: 245).

P uses *měʿîl* only of the high priest's "robe of the ephod" (Exod 29:5). But it is attested in a number of places outside of P, which lend insight to its character. Because it is worn over the tunic—the basic item of dress in the ancient Near East (Brown 1980: 7–15)—it would generally be worn only by the prominent and well-to-do (e.g., Samuel, in 1 Sam 2:19; 15:27; Jonathan, in 1 Sam 18:4; Saul, in 1 Sam 24:5, 12; Samuel's spirit, in 1 Sam 28:14; princes of the sea, in Ezek 26:16; Job and his friends, in Job 1:20; 2:12; and Ezra, in Ezra 9:3, 5).

Around the hem of Aaron's robe is a series of alternating representations of pomegranates and golden bells in wool. Pomegranates are a fruit especially associated with fertility and abundance. When the scouts return from reconnoitering the land, they bring with them pomegranates (Num 13:23), a fruit indigenous to Canaan but not found in Egypt (Edwards 1976: 165). The magical significance of bells in ancient culture is well attested (Wheeler 1923); they are generally interpreted as a means of scaring the demons away (Frazer 1919: 3.446–80). Interestingly, Ramban cites a similar reason, "that divine angels may not do him harm." Haran, however, takes exception to this interpretation because "the idea of demonic powers taking a hold inside the tabernacle is entirely foreign to P's conception" (1955: 295). Haran's objection is valid, but so is the Ramban–Frazer intuition. Transitions between the profane and sacred spheres are danger zones, judging by the week-long consecration rite of the priesthood (see COMMENT G below). To be sure, the high priest does not wear his blue-purple robe when he enters the shrine and adytum on Yom Kippur (16:4). But his function then is not *lĕšārēt* 'to officiate' (Exod 28:35) but *lĕkapper* 'to purge' these sacred areas (cf. chap. 16, COMMENT F and chap. 4, COMMENTS A–C).

ephod (ʾēpōd). This garment is made primarily of gold with blue-purple, red-purple, and red woolen threads and fine linen skillfully *(ḥōšēb)* woven into it. It is shaped like an apron that covers the loins (from waist to thigh?) and is suspended from two shoulder pieces (Exod 28:6–14). It must be distinguished from the linen ephod attributed, in sources other than P, to the ordinary priest (e.g., 1 Sam 2:18; 22:18; 2 Sam 6:14) and from the oracular ephod (1 Sam 23:6, 9; Hosea 3:4), though the same basic garment may be intended (Haran 1955).

The etymology is obscure. Perhaps it derives from Egyptian *yfd* (note: *yfd ntr* 'divine garment'), which denotes a type of material woven with four threads. This term entered Ug. as *ipd* and Akk. as *epattu/epadu* 'costly garment' (Friedrich 1968; Görg 1976; cf. Grintz 1974–76: 10–13). In Israel, however, its use was restricted exclusively to a type of cultic clothing. Some passages give the impression that the *ʾēpōd* was a statue (Judg 8:7; 18:18); most likely, however, they have identified the statue with its ornamental garments.

the decorated band. ḥēšeb hāʾēpōd (Exod 28:27, 28; 2:5; 39:20, 21). This phrase literally translates "the decorated work of the ephod," *ḥēšeb* being derived from *ḥāšab* 'devise, design' (e.g., Exod 31:4; 35:32, 35) and equivalent to *maʿăśēh ḥōšēb* 'designed or decorated work' (e.g., Exod 28:6, 15). But as the ephod itself is made of "decorated work" (Exod 28:6; 39:3), the *ḥēšeb* would be indistinguishable from it.

A way out of the impasse is to regard the word *ʾēpōd* here not as referring to the ephod but as a verbal noun meaning "that which binds/band." Supporting this rendering is that this expression occurs twice in a variant form, *ḥēšeb ʾăpuddātô* (Exod 28:8; 39:5), and that the word *ʾăpuddâ* also occurs separately in synonymous parallelism with *ṣippûy* 'cover, layer' (Isa 30:22).

which he tied to him. wayyeʾpōd lô bô, literally, "and tied it to him with it," that is, with the band (as explicitly stated in Exod 29:5). The verb *ʾāpad* is a denominative of *ʾēpōd* and used exclusively with it.

8. *the breastpiece. haḥōšen,* an item of apparel found solely in P (Exod 25:7; 28 [eleven times]; 29:5; 35:9, 27; 39 [eight times]). The etymology is moot. Arab. *ḥśn* 'be beautiful, excellent' and Aramaic *ḥsn* 'be strong, keep, protect' have been suggested and rejected (Noth 1965; Görg 1981: 32–34). It is possible, however, that the word is not Semitic but an Egyptian loanword. Görg suggests that Egyptian *ḥwy snʿ* 'protecting the breast' or *ḥw(n) snʿ* 'a cover for the breast' is directly applicable. But as *snʿ* is not widespread in Egyptian and final ʿ is a stumbling block for this derivation, Görg offers an alternate suggestion, that the second syllable of *ḥōšen* derives from Egyptian *šn* 'cartouche'. A look at Egyptian pectorals shows that *šn* symbols are a common motif (1981: 32–34). Nevertheless, Görg offers no evidence that the phrase *ḥw-šn* is attested in Egyptian.

Breastpieces or pectorals were a common royal accoutrement in the ancient Near East (see fig. 11). They were generally made of gold frames with precious

FIGURE 11

stones set in them. These pectorals were suspended by twisted gold cords or chains strung through gold rings on the edges or backs of the pectoral.

The high priest's *ḥōšen* was made primarily of gold (Exod 28:15). Unlike the other examples it was also woven (using *ḥōšēb* workmanship) with woolen and linen threads. Instead of being solid and flat, it was folded in half and formed a pouch about nine inches square (Exod 28:16). Like the Egyptian pectorals, it was set with precious stones. The twelve stones, however, were set in rows and formed no picture (Exod 28:17–20). The *ḥōšen* was firmly attached to the ephod from above by twisted gold cords, which passed through and attached to gold rings (Exod 28:22–27), and from below by a single blue-purple cord, which was drawn through two lower rings (Exod 28:28).

The *ḥōšen* served two purposes as part of the high priest's vestments. First, it served as a continual *(tāmîd)* reminder *(zikkārôn)* of the twelve tribes before the Lord. The names of the twelve tribes were engraved, each on a stone (Exod 28:21). Aaron bore these names upon his heart (*ʿal lēb*—hence we know that the *ḥōšen* was worn on the upper chest and not at the waist). Because the high priest officiated in silence (Kaufmann 1960: 303, 384) the engravings on the stones (both of the *ḥōšen* and of the ephod as well as the engraving on the *ṣîṣ*, see below) spoke to the Lord. Second, the *ḥōšen* served an oracular purpose; it became the receptacle for the Urim and Thummim (see below).

the Urim and Thummim (ʾet-hāʾûrîm wěʾet-hattummîm). The Urim and Thummim are mentioned in Scripture only seven times, as follows:

1. "Inside the breastpiece of decision you shall place the Urim and Thummim, so that they are over Aaron's heart when he comes before the Lord" (Exod 28:30).

2. "He put the breastpiece on him, and put into the breastpiece the Urim and Thummim" (Lev 8:8).

3. "But he shall present himself to Eleazar the priest, who shall on his behalf seek the decision of the Urim before the Lord" (Num 27:21).

4. "And of Levi he said: Your Thummim and Urim belong to your faithful man" (Deut 33:8).

5. "And Saul inquired of the Lord, but the Lord did not answer him, either by dreams or by Urim or by prophets" (1 Sam 28:6).

6, 7. "forbade them to eat sacred foods until a priest could be found for Urim and for Thummim" (Ezra 2:63; Neh 7:65).

From these citations, a few facts can be deduced. The Urim and Thummim were a form of oracle placed inside a pocket, "the breastpiece of decision," worn by the high priest on his chest. According to the Priestly tradition they were used exclusively by the high priest inside the Tabernacle, as stated explicitly in the Lord's charge to Moses: "he shall present himself to Eleazar, the priest, who shall on his behalf seek the decision of the Urim *before the Lord*" (Num 27:21a). Most likely, the high priest had to station himself inside the shrine so that he could be physically closer to the symbolic seat of the Godhead, the Ark. This may be inferred from Judg 2:27–28: "The Israelites inquired of the Lord (for the Ark of God's Covenant was there in those days, and Phineas son of Eleazar son of Aaron the priest ministered before him in those days), 'Shall we again take the field. . . .'" The interpolation, presumably by a Priestly editor, makes it clear that the use of the Urim and Thummim is associated with the Ark and they must be consulted in its proximity.

P's instructions concerning the Urim and Thummim merit quotation in full: "Inside the breastpiece of decision you shall place the Urim and Thummim, so that they are *over Aaron's heart* when he comes *before the Lord.* Thus Aaron shall carry the (instrument of) decision for the Israelites *over his heart before the Lord at all times*" (Exod 28:30).

This text clearly indicates, in conformance with Num 27:21 (above), that the high priest may only use the Urim and Thummim *lipnê-YHWH* 'before the Lord', in other words, inside the shrine (*haqqōdeš*, v 2a). As Kaufmann correctly notes (1937–56: 2.467), P is registering its opposition to their use outside the sanctuary as was the practice during the period of the Judges, Saul, and David (Judg 1:1–2; 18:20; 1 Sam 10:22; 14:41 LXX; 2 Sam 2:1; 5:23–24). The reason, however, is not the one given by Kaufmann (ibid.), that P desires to confine the priest to the sanctuary. The priest does not hesitate to inspect a suspected fungous house (14:35) and purify it (14:49) or even to leave the sanctuary's city (not to speak of the sanctuary itself) in order to certify whether the *měṣōrāʿ* is healed (14:3) and to initiate his purification (14:4–8). Rather, the text is expressing P's apprehension about the close resemblance of using the Urim and Thummim to the practice, current among Israelites, of using idolatrous materials for similar divinatory purposes (e.g., Hos 4:12; Hab 2:18–19; Zech 10:2). Their use was discontinued in postexilic times (see also *m. Soṭa* 9:12; *b. Soṭa* 48b), once again an indication of the early provenience of P's cultic vocabulary.

This is not much to go by, and it is hardly any wonder that speculation concerning their shape and function has been rife from earliest times. For example, the oldest interpretation is that of the LXX, which renders the two words as abstract plurals, "Revelation and Truth" from the words *ʾôr* 'light' and *tōm* 'perfection'. Another approach suggests that the words are antonyms: "curse" (from the root *ʾrr*) and "perfect, faultless," indicating that which was pleasing to God and that which was not (Wellhausen 1963: 110). In either case, the Urim and Thummim are conceived as two small objects (e.g., pebbles, sticks, arrows), which would be cast like dice; depending on the way they would turn up, a positive or negative answer would be given. This means that the Urim and Thummim could only respond to a question with yes or no. The only way an inconclusive answer (no. 5) might be obtained would be on the assumption that each die was capable of indicating yes or no (like flipping a coin, heads or tails), and if one came up yes and the other no, then the oracle would be considered inconclusive. This theory is supported by the Assyrian practice of fortune-telling called psephomancy, which utilized a white and a black stone, called "the desirable die" and "the undesirable die" (Lipinski 1970) or "the luminous die" and "the truthful die" (Horovitz and Hurowitz, forthcoming), respectively, and which might also point to the Urim and Thummim as being two stones that gave a yes-or-no answer.

To be sure, there is no evidence in the Bible that describes the procedure of using the Urim and Thummim—at least not in the MT. But the LXX has a lengthy expansion of 1 Sam 14:41 that merits quotation (the LXX addition is indicated by brackets): "Saul then said to the Lord, the God of Israel ['Why have you not responded to Your servant today? If this iniquity was due to my son Jonathan or to me, O Lord, God of Israel, show Urim, and if You say it was due to Your people Israel], show *tāmîm.'*" The LXX reading is made plausible by the homoioteleuton involved. The last word of the MT (before the LXX addition) and the last word of the LXX addition are the same—Israel. Thus the eye of the scribe may accidentally have skipped from the first "Israel" to the second, causing the long omission, a common error among ancient scribes and attested in other scriptural verses as well. Thus the LXX version of this text would corroborate the notion that the Urim and Thummim were two objects which could only give a yes-or-no answer.

Yet this theory, though attractive, is subject to three serious objections. For even if the LXX represents the correct Hebrew original, the theory would not allow for an inconclusive answer; also, it would not explain the plural forms of the names Urim and Thummim; and above all, it could not explain how the oracle was able to give more than a mere yes-or-no reply. That the oracle could indeed do so is shown by the following citations:

1. "After the death of Joshua, the Israelites inquired of the Lord, 'Which of us shall be the first to go up against the Canaanites and attack them?' The Lord replied, 'Let Judah go up. I now deliver the land into their hands'" (Judg 1:1–2).

2. "They proceeded to Bethel and inquired of God: the Israelites asked, 'Who of us shall advance first to fight the Benjaminites?' And the Lord replied, 'Judah first'" (Judg 18:20).

3. "They inquired of the Lord again, 'Has anyone else [the man (LXX)] come here?' And the Lord replied, 'Yes; he is hiding among the baggage'" (1 Sam 10:22).

4. "Sometime afterward, David inquired of the Lord, 'Shall I go up to one of the towns of Judah?' The Lord replied, 'Yes.' David further

asked, 'Which one shall I go up to?' And the Lord replied, 'To Hebron' " (2 Sam 2:1).

5.   "David inquired of the Lord, and He answered, 'Do not go up, but
circle around behind them and confront them at the *baca* trees. And
when you hear the sound of marching in the tops of the *baca* trees,
then go into action, for the Lord will be going in front of you to attack
the Philistine forces' " (2 Sam 5:23–24).

That the Urim and Thummim are being consulted can be deduced by the
occurrence, in each of these five sentences, of the technical term *šā'al b* 'inquire
of [the Lord]'. It is also clear that the Urim and Thummim had to be capable of
answering more than merely yes or no because, as these citations show, they
selected a tribe (1, 2) and a city (4), indicated the hiding place of Saul (3), and
detailed a complex military stratagem (5). Thus the LXX expansion of 1 Sam
14:41 may not be correct (Lindblom 1962); and even if it is, the procedure, as
indicated, is beset with difficulties and is therefore unclear.

D. N. Freedman (written communication) maintains that the LXX reading
in 1 Sam 14 is the right one, and that it reflects correctly the way in which the
system worked:

Let us suppose that there were two cubes (they might have been four-
sided pyramids, such as used in Egypt), each with six sides. On three of
the sides there would be an Aleph for Urim, while on the other three
there would be a Taw for Thummim. The use of Aleph and Taw is not
merismatic in my opinion but indicative of the original usage of these
stones, which was in judicial cases, and used for a single individual to
determine his/her fate. There were two possible judgments, innocent or
guilty, and this was a divine judgment, therefore using *'rr* for guilty, or
subject to divine ban and curse, and *tmm* for innocent, or the object of
divine approval and favor (like Noah and Job). If both stones turned up
Aleph then the person was guilty, and if both turned up Taw he was
innocent. If the dice came up mixed then the verdict was like the Scottish "Not Proven" one way or the other. Since that in fact was the
reason for appeal to Urim and Thummim, the way out of the impasse
was to throw the stones again. No doubt by increasing the number of
throws you increase the odds on securing a decision. But there could be a
limit on the number of times you could manipulate the stones at one
session, and so it would be possible to get a persistent "no answer."
Depending upon prior agreement or the nature and gravity of the situation, you might agree that you would try only once, or twice or however
many times, and if no answer was received during that specified number,
then you would conclude that was the answer. One can imagine that

when Saul tried to get an answer by U&T, they may have thrown the stones twenty times, and it always came up mixed. That would be pretty decisive, that Yahweh was not in a mood to respond. The point is that there are a lot of variables over which we have no control, but they certainly can cover your objections.

Another solution worthy of consideration is that the Urim and Thummim comprised the twenty-two letters of the alphabet. "As the basis of the Hebrew language is the triliteral root, it follows that any three letters could provide meaningful words from which the High Priest could extract a message" (Robertson 1964). By the same token, an undecipherable combination would connote God's silence. The names ʾ[ûrîm] and t[ummîm] would, then, stand for the first and last letters of the alphabet; they would form a merism, denoting all the letters. So with the Greek alphabet: "I am the alpha and omega, the first and the last, the beginning and the end" (Rev 22:13). And in common parlance we still say "from A to Z" when we wish to signify completeness. Strikingly, the Dead Sea Scrolls have disclosed a new Hebrew word ʾwrtwm (1QH 4:6, 23; 18:29), which, according to the context, means "perfect illumination." It is highly probable that it was formed by combining the singulars of ʾwr(m) 'light' and twm(m) 'perfect'. It would also explain why these words were chosen for the aleph and taw: God created ʾôr 'light' first (Gen 1:3) and tam, tāmîm means "complete, finished," corresponding to the rabbinic interpretation of this oracle: "Urim, because it illuminates their (the inquirers') words; Thummim, because it completes (i.e., fulfills) their words" (b. Yoma 73b; Sipre, Zuṭa to 27:21).

Nonetheless, this theory, like those just discussed, can at best be considered only an attractive speculation. The riddle of the Urim and Thummim still awaits resolution.

9. the turban. hammiṣnepet (Exod 28:4, 37, 39; 29:6; 39:28, 31; Lev 16:4; Ezek 21:31). This term derives from a common Semitic root ṣnp 'wind, bind' (cf. Akk. sanāp/bu). The high priest's miṣnepet thus appears to have been wound around the head like a turban (cf. Isa 28:18 and Lev 16:4—used of putting on the miṣnepet). The related word ṣĕnîp, also rendered "turban," is used of the high priest's headdress in Zech 3:5; of the headdress of women in Isa 3:23; of the royal headdress in Isa 62:3, and figuratively of justice in Job 29:14. Clearly, P devised its own special term so that it should not be confused with a secular headdress.

plate (ṣîṣ). This word means "flower, blossom" (Num 17:23; Isa 28:1; 40:6–8; Ps 103:15; Job 14:2). Akk. ṣiṣṣatu 'flower ornament' passed into Egyptian as ḏiḏi 'flower' (as a form of ornamentation; Görg 1977a). But there is another ancient tradition that it meant "plate" (LXX petalon; Vg lamina). The rabbis claim that the high priest's ṣîṣ was a gold plate, two fingers in breadth, reaching from ear to ear (b. Šabb. 63b). It is possible that the plate was called ṣîṣ because of its floral decoration, which it already had (Jos., *Ant.* 3.172–78), and that it continued to be called by this name even after the decoration had disappeared (Görg 1977a). The rendering "plate" has been adopted here.

The ṣîṣ was suspended from the high priest's turban by a violet cord. Because of its inscription "holy to the Lord" (Exod 28:36), it had the power "to remove the sin of the holy things that the Israelites consecrate, from any of their sacred donations" (Exod 28:38). In other words, any inadvertent impurity or imperfection in the offerings to the sanctuary would be expiated by the ṣîṣ. The rabbis extend its powers even further: "The ṣîṣ expiates for all sacrifices, both public and private, and for all (sacrificial) blood and bodily impurity" (*t. Pesaḥ.* 6:5; cf. *m. Pesaḥ.* 7:7). That is, the rabbis include the impurity of the offerers as well as their offerings within the expiatory scope of the ṣîṣ (but not if the officiating priest is impure, *t. Menaḥ.* 1:6; cf. Lieberman 1962: 584–85).

The ancients were certainly conscious of the deleterious effects of flawed rituals, for example, "If the aedile made a mistake in the formula or in the handling of the sacred vessels, then the games have not been duly performed. Expiation is offered for the mistake, and the feelings of the immortal gods are appeased by a recommencement of the games" (Cicero, *De haruspicum responso* 11.23; cf. Servius on *Aeneid* 4.696). In Assamese Vaishnavism a prayer is offered for errors in ritual performance, and Krishna is expected to accept the offering in spite of its imperfections: "Make these faults faultless, wipe away the hindrance of shortcomings, be pleased to take this offering and say it is your own" (quoted in Hayley 1980: 116).

diadem. The term *nēzer* means "dedication, consecration" (21:12; Num 6:4, 5, 7, 8, 12–13), from the verb *nāzar* 'keep apart [for sacred purposes]' (15:31; 22:2). Related to it is the term *nāzîr* 'Nazirite, one who is consecrated, set apart' either by his abstentions (Num 6:2; Judg 13:5; Amos 2:11) or by his high rank (Gen 49:26; Deut 33:16); the king wore a *nēzer* on his head as a sign of his consecration (2 Sam 1:10; 2 Kgs 11:12; Pss 89:40; 132:18).

The precise meaning of *nēzer* is difficult to determine. What one can say for certain is that it is a synonym of the previously mentioned ṣîṣ. This can be ascertained by its four attestations as part of the high priest's vestments:

ṣîṣ zāhāb ṭāhôr (Exod 28:36)

nēzer haqqōdeš (Exod 29:6)

ṣîṣ nēzer haqqōdeš zāhāb ṭāhôr (Exod 39:30)

ṣîṣ hazzāhāb nēzer haqqōdeš (Lev 8:9)

The first two citations (Exod 28:36; 29:6) make it clear that the high priest's *nēzer* and ṣîṣ refer to the same object. The latter two citations (Exod 39:30; Lev 8:9) contain both expressions and demonstrate incidentally, but significantly, that Lev 8 has conflated Exod 28 and 29 and, hence, must be of later composition (see COMMENT B below).

The fact that *nēzer* and *ṣîṣ* are synonymous has led scholars to suggest that *nēzer* must be rendered "flower" (e.g., de Vaux 1961a: 399). "Just as the Egyptian pharaohs used to wear on their foreheads the prophylactic primitive serpent, the kings of Israel wore a 'flower' as 'consecration'" (Noth 1962: 226). Following Noth, Görg suggests an Egyptian etymology *nzr.t* 'the snake goddess' (1977a, b: 3, 26) or *nśr.t* 'flame' (1977a, b: 4, 7), both of which describe the Uraeus projecting from the front of Pharaoh's crown (see fig. 11). Because the Uraeus acted as an apotropaic device, driving away demonic and pernicious forces, its association with the *nēzer/ṣîṣ* of the high priest, to which apotropaic powers are also attributed (see above), is particularly suggestive. Even so, the snake is not the only animal appearing on crowns. For example, the Canaanite god Resheph is seen in an Egyptian relief wearing a gazelle on his crown (see the illustration in Görg 1977a: 21), and such an ornamented headdress may have been worn in Israel (Isa 28:1; cf. Gilula 1974: 128). Finally, it may be suggested that just as the *ṣîṣ*, whatever its original meaning, became identified with the object that bore it on the high priest's head, so did the *nēzer*. Although it originally referred to some emblem that projected from the object that fastened it to the head, it eventually became identified with the object itself. Hence, the rendering "diadem" has been adopted here.

as the Lord had commanded Moses. Compare Exod 29:5–6 and COMMENT B below.

10. *Moses took (wayyiqqaḥ mōšeh).* Ibn Ezra renders this phrase as a pluperfect, "Moses had taken," in order to harmonize the sequence of events with Exod 40:9–15, namely, anointing the Tabernacle (vv 10–11), washing Aaron and his sons (v 6), dressing and anointing Aaron (vv 7–9, 12), and dressing his sons (v 13). In effect this would place vv 10–11 before v 6. Ramban, by contrast, justifies the MT sequence on the grounds that the anointment process should be continuous, first the Tabernacle (vv 10–11), then Aaron (v 12). Hence, Aaron is dressed first (vv 7–9) and later his sons (v 13). And as for Exod 40:9–15, which indicates that the washing and dressing of the priests follows the anointing of the Tabernacle, Ramban argues that this is a prescriptive text, which does not reflect the procedure actually followed.

Nevertheless, the sequence in the MT is subject to three serious objections. First, as Aaron's sons were washed together with their father (v 6), they would have had to stand naked until their father was dressed and the Tabernacle and he were anointed (vv 7–12). Second, the sanctification of the altar (vv 10–11) is made to precede its decontamination (v 15), a sequence that not only makes no sense but is the reverse of the expressed command of Exod 29:36–37 (for details, see the NOTE on v 15). Finally, the concluding phrase *kaʾăšer ṣiwwâ YHWH ʾet-mōšeh* 'as the Lord commanded Moses', found every time a rite prescribed in

Exod 29 is implemented (see COMMENT A below), is conspicuously missing after v 11, that is to say, after the Tabernacle is anointed. The suspicion is thus created that the passage on the anointing of the Tabernacle (vv 10–11)—and missing in Exod 29 (it is prescribed in Exod 30:26–29; 40:9–11)—may be a later interpolation. This suspicion is strengthened by examining the following comparative table:

Exod 29:7	Exod 40:9–13	Lev 8:10–12
wĕlāqaḥtā ʾet-šemen hammišḥâ	⁹wĕlāqaḥtā ʾet-šemen hammišḥâ ûmāšaḥtā ʾet-hammiškān wĕʾet-kol-ʾăšer-bô wĕqiddaštā ʾōtô wĕʾet-kol-kēlāyw wĕhāyâ qōdeš	¹⁰wayyiqqaḥ mōšeh ʾet-šemen hammišḥâ wayyimšaḥ ʾet-hammiškān wĕʾet-kol-ʾăšer-bô wayyĕqaddēš ʾōtām
	¹⁰ûmāšaḥtā ʾet-mizbaḥ hāʿōlâ wĕʾet-kol-kēlāyw	¹¹wayyaz mimmennû ʿal-hammizbēaḥ šebaʿ pĕʿāmîm
	wĕqiddaštā ʾet-hammizbēaḥ wĕhāyâ hammizbēaḥ qōdeš qŏdāšîm . . .	wayyimšaḥ ʾet-hammizbēaḥ wĕʾet-kol-kē-lāyw wĕʾet-hakkiyyōr wĕʾet-kannô lĕqad-dĕšām
	¹¹ûmāšaḥtā ʾet-hakkiy-yôr wĕʾet-kannô wĕqiddaštā ʾōtô	
	¹²wĕhiqrabtā ʾet-ʾahărōn wĕʾet-bānāyw ʾel-petaḥ ʾōhel môʿēd wĕ-rāḥaṣtā ʾōtām bam-māyim ¹³wĕhilbaštā ʾet-ʾahă-rōn ʾet bigdê haqqōdeš	
wĕyāṣaqtā ʿal-rōʾšô		¹²wayyiṣṣōq miššemen hammišḥâ ʿal rōʾš ʾahărōn wayyimšaḥ ʾōtô lĕqaddĕšô
ûmāšaḥtā ʾōtô	ûmāšaḥtā ʾōtô wĕqid-daštā ʾōtô wĕkihēn lî	

The interpolations are graphically clear. Lev 8 (and Exod 40) inserted the notice about the anointing of the Tabernacle between Exod 29:7aα and 7aβ. Moreover, Lev 8:11 and Exod 40:10, being in chiastic relationship, offer a clue to the puzzle of the mysterious sevenfold sprinkling of the anointment oil on the altar (Lev 8:11a). It corresponds to the statement (indicated by the broken arrow), literally, "[You shall consecrate the altar] so that the altar shall be most holy" (Exod 40:10b). This latter statement explicitly ranks the sacrificial altar as "most holy" in contrast to the Tabernacle and its other sancta, which are designated as qōdeš 'holy' (Exod 40:9). Moreover, whereas it is commanded that the altar and its vessels and the laver and its stand be anointed (Exod 40:10a, 11), it is only the altar (but neither its vessels nor the laver and its stand!) that is to achieve the status of "most holy." This "higher" status of the altar is attained, according to Lev 8:11, by an additional application of the anointment oil. Rather, it seems more likely that the author or redactor of Lev 8 so interpreted Exod 40:10b, to wit—for the altar, alone of all the Tabernacle sancta, to become "most holy" it required a second anointing. (Of course, all sancta enjoy the rank of "most holy" [Exod 30:25–29]. The actual reason for the sprinkling may have been to provide apotropaic power to the altar, as discussed in v 11, below.) But why should this second application take the form of a sevenfold sprinkling? This, I submit, would have been deduced from the Day of Purgation rites. Just as the sacrificial altar is both daubed and sprinkled seven times with the blood of the purification offerings, "to purify it and consecrate it" (16:19b), it stands to reason that the initial consecration of the altar, to achieve its "most holy" status, requires a similar application with its consecrating medium—a sevenfold sprinkling of the anointment oil. This proposed reconstruction rests on the assumption that Lev 8 was written later than both Exod 40 and Lev 16. The relative antiquity of the latter is discussed in chap. 16, COMMENT D; the date for Exod 40, however, falls outside the purview of this commentary.

In any case, this table provides strong evidence for the chronological priority of Exod 29 over Lev 8 (see COMMENT B below). It also provides an answer to another vexing problem: why didn't the author/redactor of Lev 8 insert the passage on the anointing of the Tabernacle before v 6 and, thereby, avoid the consequence of having the priests stand around naked while the Tabernacle was being anointed (vv 6, 13)? On the presumption that Lev 8 is modeled on Exod 29 and 40, the author/redactor of Lev 8 had no choice but to insert the pericope on the anointing of the Tabernacle after the statement, "And you shall take (Moses took) the anointing oil" (top line of the table, above). Neither could he have interpolated it after the anointing of Aaron and the dressing of the priests (vv 12–13), for it would have violated his fundamental premise: the anointing of Aaron should not take place in an unconsecrated sanctuary.

The question, however, remains: Why did Exod 29:36 mention the anointing of the altar and not that of the rest of the sanctuary? Hoffmann's explanation (1953) is that the altar was anointed in a manner similar to the anointing of the priests: both were sprinkled with the sacred oil (8:11, 30). A simpler answer is at hand. Exod 29 focuses only on the seven-day consecration service and therefore includes only those rites which were repeated each day, namely, those of the altar and the priestly consecration (vv 15, 39), omitting the anointing of the rest of the sanctuary, which took place on the first day alone. Lev 8, however, focuses on the ceremonies of the first day—it says nothing about the following days (except by implication, v 33)—and, hence, it enumerates all of the cult objects in the sanctuary.

the anointing oil. šemen hammishâ, consisting of "five hundred weight of solidified myrrh, half as much—two hundred and fifty—of fragrant cinnamon, two hundred and fifty of aromatic cane, five hundred—by sanctuary weight—of cassia, and a *hin* of olive oil" (cf. Exod 30:23–24). The function of anointing is discussed in COMMENT D below.

the tabernacle. The term *hammiškān* here means not the entire Tabernacle complex but its more restricted and more precise sense, the inner curtains of the Tent (e.g., Exod 26:7; 36:14). This usage may be compared with the Aramaic term *mškn²*, which stands for the innermost, forbidden portion of the Temple (Hillers 1972). Hence it is rendered "tabernacle," lowercased. It is this confusion that is probably responsible for the LXX's erroneous transposition of *wayyimšaḥ . . . ²ōtām* (v 10aβ, b) to the end of v 11, in the belief that *hammiškān* stands for the entire Tabernacle and must be a summary statement, belonging at the end of the description of the sanctuary's anointment. To the contrary, the anointing procedure follows the same pattern as the purgation procedure with the blood of the purificatory offerings (16:16–18)—commencing inside the Tent and working outward to the sacrificial altar. How precisely were the Tabernacle curtains anointed? It can only be surmised: most likely by sprinkling, according to the analogy of the priestly clothing (v 30) and the inner veil (4:6, 17).

and all that was in it (wĕ²et-kol-²ăšer-bô). For a compact list of the sancta involved, see Num 4:4–12.

thus consecrating them (wayyĕqaddēš ²ōtām). The *waw* is purposive.

11. *He sprinkled . . . seven times (wayyaz . . . šebaʿ pĕʿāmîm).* As discussed above (v 10), this additional application of the anointment oil on the altar may have been motivated by the exegesis of Exod 40:10b, to wit: for the altar to achieve a "most holy" status, it (but not its vessels) required additional consecration.

Another, more pragmatic, reason may have played its part. The altar, standing exposed in the Tabernacle court, is the most vulnerable of all sancta. It might have been considered advisable to inoculate the altar with additional sprinklings of consecrating oil to buttress it against incursions of impurity (the theology of the altar is discussed in chap. 4, COMMENT C). The prophylactic power of oil was acknowledged in the ancient Near East. It was believed to possess the intrinsic power to impart vitality to and repel evil from the statues of the gods: for example, "Oil, oil . . . you are on Horus' forehead. . . . You give him power over his body. You impose his fear on all who look at him and hear his name" (Otto 1960: 122, scene 95, line 11). Anointment oil was an important component of magical formularies. Thus the anointing of vassals was not mere ceremonial trapping: "As oil penetrates your flesh, so may they (the gods) make this curse enter your flesh" (Wiseman 1958: 78, lines 622–24). The magical power of oil was rejected by Israel (Judg 9:9). Still, the sevenfold sprinkling of the altar with anointment oil (and the daubing of the healed *měṣōrāʿ* with oil consecrated by its sevenfold sprinkling "before the Lord," 14:16) may betray an original apotropaic function (for the function of anointment in Israel, see COMMENT D below).

Another attractive explanation for the altar's sevenfold sprinkling stems from the work of A. Hurowitz (1974: 115–16). In Israel, the altar was always independent of the Temple. Before the centralization of the cult under Josiah, private altars abounded. Indeed the prevalent *bāmâ* probably designates an open cult area dominated by its altar (Haran 1978: 48–57). Even when the Temple was destroyed, sacrifices continued to be offered at its site on an improvised altar (Jer 41:5). The returning exiles built, consecrated, and sacrificed on an altar long before they constructed the Temple (Ezra 3:1–3). Thus, the autonomous existence of the altar allows for the possibility that it developed its own consecration ceremonial wholly independent of the consecratory rites performed in the Tabernacle/Temple, consisting of a sevenfold sprinkling with the anointment oil.

and he anointed the altar. The only other procedure for the inauguration of an altar is provided by Ezekiel (Ezek 43:18–27). It is at variance in many crucial respects with the altar rites described here. First, there is no anointment ceremonial. This accords with the rabbinic tradition that at the end of the First Temple period, the anointment oil disappeared and was never again reinstituted (*t. Yoma* 2:15; *t. Soṭa* 13:1; *ʾAbot R. Nat.* A.40). Ezekiel's rite prescribes a purification bull on the first day and a burnt-offering bull and ram on each of the following seven days; the Tabernacle altar is initiated with a purification bull and burnt-offering ram on each of seven days (8:18–21; Exod 29:15–18, 36). At stake here are two different traditions concerning the purgation of the altar on behalf of the community: Ezekiel follows Num 15:22–26, and the Tabernacle account is based on Lev 4:13–21 (details in chap. 4, COMMENT E). Finally, the length of the initiation service differs: the Tabernacle for seven days (8:33; Exod 29:35, 37) and Ezekiel's for eight (details in chap. 4, COMMENT J; and see the NOTE on 8:33). That the altar was "initiated" or "inaugurated," in other words, put into use, and not "dedicated," is discussed in chap. 4, COMMENT J.

How was the anointment of the altar performed? Again, on the analogy of the blood rites (16:18; cf. 4:25, 30, 34), one might presume that the altar's horns were daubed with the anointment oil. But one need be reminded that the daubing of the altar's horns is a rite peculiar to the purification offering alone. Indeed, were the anointing of the altar different in any respect from the anointing of the other sancta, the text would surely have made this difference explicit. One can only assume that the anointing of all sancta was accomplished by Moses dipping his finger into the oil and applying it with a single stroke to each sanctum. (The verb *māšaḥ*, however, is not limited to this technique; see v 12, below.)

the laver (hakkiyyôr). Also made of bronze, it stood "between the Tent of Meeting and the altar" (Exod 30:18). Solomon's Temple court contained ten lavers resting on wheeled bronze stands, five to the right of the Temple and five to the left (1 Kgs 7:27–39).

12. *He poured . . . upon Aaron's head. wayyiṣṣōq . . . ʿal rōʾš ʾahărōn*, so that it ran down his beard and his robes (Ps 133:2). The psalmist's image contains some hyperbole because Aaron's vestments were sprinkled (v 30), obviating the need for any other contact with the anointment oil.

thereby anointing (wayyimšaḥ). The *waw* is purposive, not conjunctive; there is no need for a double application of the oil (so too in Exod 29:7). Moreover, the verb *māšaḥ* is not restricted to the meaning "smear" but can denote other forms, as the following texts demonstrate:

1.   Jacob at Bethel:

    wayyiṣṣōq šemen ʿal-rōʾšâ (Gen 28:18)

    ʾăšer māšaḥtā (Gen 31:13)

2.   Samuel and Saul:

    wayyiṣṣoq ʿal-rōʾšô . . . kî-mĕšāḥăkā (1 Sam 10:1)

3.   Jehu and Elisha:

    wĕyāṣaqtā ʿal-rōʾšô . . . mĕšaḥtîkā (2 Kgs 9:3; cf. v 6)

In all three cases, the person/object is anointed *(māšaḥ)* by dousing *(yāṣaq).* Moreover, the anointing of the king is always performed with a horn *(qeren)* of oil (e.g., 1 Sam 16:13; 1 Kgs 1:39), an implement whose use implies that its contents were poured over the head of the king. This indeed is what Thutmose III declares concerning his vassal: "(he) had oil poured on his head" *(EA* 51.4). On a Dura Europos panel this is precisely how the anointment of David by Samuel is depicted. Finally, the fact that the anointment of the high priest is elsewhere solely referred to as dousing (21:10; cf. Ps 133:2) indicates that no other means was employed.

Thus the verb *māšaḥ* implies anointing by any ceremonial, and for this reason even the ordinary priests can be designated as *mĕšûḥîm* 'anointed' (e.g., Exod 28:41; 29:21; 30:30; 40:15; Lev 7:36; 10:7; Num 3:3), even though their anointment took the form of sprinkling (v 30). That the same verb, *māšaḥ*, is employed for both Aaron and the sancta is significant: Aaron is brought into metonymic association with the sacred cult objects (Levine 1965; Leach 1976:

89). Also of interest is the fact that among the Hittites both kings and priests were anointed, just as in Israel. The priestly class, *tazzelli* (= Sumerian *GUDU*, = Akk. *pašišu*), was by its very name "the anointed one." The Hittite king (and his substitute) was anointed "with the fine oil of kingship" (Hoffner 1973: 218).

to consecrate him (lĕqaddĕšô). As the oil is inherently holy (Exod 30:32), it can be applied directly; contrast the sacrificial blood, which must first be made holy by its contact with the altar (v 30). This term is missing in the corresponding verse, Exod 29:7. Its absence is no accident but stems from Exod 29's premise that the consecration of Aaron is incomplete until he is sprinkled with the sacrificial blood and anointment oil (see the NOTE on v 30 and COMMENT B below). This provides a more sensible sequence, for it insists that the daubing of the priests, a purgative procedure, must precede Aaron's sanctification (Exod 29:20–21). Lev 8, however, reverses the order by allowing the daubing of Aaron to follow his consecration (see the NOTES on vv 15, 23).

Sanctification *(qiddēš)* by man is always with oil. The use of consecrated blood provides the only exception (see the NOTE on v 30). Ugaritic texts have been cited to the effect that the king-priest must be pure, that is, consecrated, before he officiates; for instance, *yrthṣ mlk brr* (*UT 3.3, 6–7, 44, 46* = *CTA 35.3, 6–7, 44, 46* = *KTU 1.41.3, 6–7, 44, 46*; *UT 9.10* = *CTA 36.10* = *KTU 1.46.10*; *UT 173.4, 7, 49, 51, 55*). But this phrase speaks of washing, not consecration, and *brr* may be rendered as an active and not a passive participle, that is, "the king, the purifier." The other cited Ug. phrase, *mlk ytb brr* (*UT 3.7, 46; 173.7; KTU 1.109.2; 119.5*) is even less auspicious because it can be rendered "the purified king sits/responds" or "the king/the purifier sits/responds" (Tarragon 1980: 80–82).

It is important to emphasize that the purpose of the priestly investiture is sanctification *(qdš, vv 12, 30)*, in contrast to the purpose of the levitic investiture, which is purification *(ṭhr, Num 8:6, 7, 21)*. Indeed, the Priestly texts never use the root *qdš* in connection with the Levites; in matters of holiness they rank no higher than the laity (Milgrom 1970a: 29 n. 103).

13. *Then Moses brought Aaron's sons forward.* A repetitive resumption *(Wiederaufnahme)* of v 6a, necessitated by the digression on the anointment of the Tabernacle and of Aaron (vv 10–12). Alternatively, it could also be rendered, "When Moses brought Aaron's sons forward" (Ibn Ezra) or "Having brought Aaron's sons forward."

tunics. kuttanot; see the NOTE on v 7.

sashes ('abnēt). The Versions and Sam. render this word as a plural. In fact, it is a collective noun, to be understood distributively (cf. Exod 29:9). This fact suffices to refute Haran (1978: 170 n. 47), who claims that *'abnēṭ,* the only one of Aaron's vestments in Exod 39:27–29 expressed in the singular, proves that Aaron's sash was distinctive and distinguishable from the sashes of the ordinary priest. Rather, the sash was the only garment made of wool and linen *(ša'aṭnēz)* worn in common by the entire priestly cadre, including the high priest (*b. Yoma*

5b, 6a; Cassuto 1951a: 385–86). The right of the ordinary priests to wear *šaʿaṭ-nēz* and the relationship of this verse and its counterparts, Exod 29:9; 39:29 are discussed in COMMENT B below.

and tied (wayyaḥăbōš). The verb *ḥābaš* means "saddle" (e.g., Num 22:21; Judg 19:10) and "bandage" (Isa 3:7; Ezek 30:21), implying that the headdress was not just set on the head but strapped around the chin.

caps (migbāʿôt). Josephus (*Ant.* 3.157–58) claims that the ordinary priest wore a *pilos* (a skullcap shaped like half an egg) and not a *petasos* (hat). The word is related to *gābîaʿ* 'cup' (e.g., Exod 25:31–34; Jer 35:5), which gives us an image for its shape. For that reason, Görg maintains that it was bell-shaped (1977a: 24). It was made of fine linen (Exod 39:28).

as the Lord had commanded Moses. The phrase applies to the anointing of Aaron and the dressing of his sons (cf. Exod 29:7–9aα) but not to the anointing of the Tabernacle (vv 10–11), which has no counterpart in Exod 29 (see COMMENT A below). Exod 29 adds *wĕhāyĕtâ lāhem kĕhunnâ lĕḥuqqat ʿôlām* 'And they shall have priesthood as their right for all time' (Exod 29:9aβ), which the rabbis interpreted, correctly, as meaning that the consecration of Aaron's sons held good for their succeeding generations (*b. Sukk.* 43a) but which the Temple Scroll denies (see COMMENT E below).

14. *He had the bull of purification offering brought forward (wayyaggēš ʾet par haḥaṭṭāʾt)*. The use of *higgîš* for the purification offering is attested only in 2 Chr 29:23; in P, it is restricted to the cereal offering (2:8). The usual term is *hiqrîb*. Because this act was generally performed by the offerer (e.g., 1:2, 3; 3:1, 7) and not the officiant (in this case Moses), the verb (lit., "he brought forward") is rendered in the passive.

the bull of purification offering (par haḥaṭṭāʾt). The bull is the prescribed animal for the high priest and the priestly cadre (4:3). The reference is to Exod 29:10, but the identification of the animal as a *haṭṭāʾt* only comes at the conclusion of the prescription for its sacrifice (v 14).

leaned (wayyismōk). This verb is singular though the subject, Aaron and his sons, is plural. The LXX and Sam., however, read it as plural (as the MT in vv 18, 22). Exod 29:10, the corresponding verse, also has the singular, and this time only the LXX renders it as a plural. The text for the two subsequent sacrifices in Exod 29 shows one in plural (29:15) and the other in singular (29:19), which the Versions leave unchanged. The inconsistencies within the MT and between it and the Versions allow for no conclusions except to leave the MT unchanged. All of the priests perform the hand-leaning, not Aaron alone, for hand-leaning must be performed by the offerers, and this bull is offered by all of the priestly consecrands (*Sipra*, Milluʾim par. 1:13).

their hands. Their right hands (Tgs.; see the NOTE on 1:4).

15. *and it was slaughtered (wayyišḥāṭ)*. The slaughtering could be performed by anyone (see the NOTE on 1:5); hence this verb, which deliberately has no named subject, must be rendered in the passive (contra the LXX). Indeed, this

is a characteristic of the Priestly style. A verb that has no specified subject may not necessarily be attached to the subject of the previous verb but may represent an indefinite subject, in which case it should be rendered as a passive. Note this parade example: "You shall give it to Eleazar the priest. It shall be removed *(wĕhôṣîʾ ʾōtāh)* . . . and slaughtered in his presence *(wĕšāḥaṭ ʾōtāh lĕpānāyw)*. Eleazar the priest shall take . . . and sprinkle . . . ; The cow shall be burned in his sight *(wĕśārap ʾet-happārâ lĕʿênāyw)*" (Num 19:3–5).

took (wayyiqqaḥ). That the idiom here and in Exod 29:16 is *lāqaḥ dam*, in contrast to postbiblical *qibbēl dam* (2 Chr 29:22; *m. Yoma* 3:4; *m. Zebaḥ.* 2:3, 4; *m. Neg.* 14:8) is another sign that the language of P is preexilic (Hurvitz 1974: 43–44; see the Introduction, §B).

the blood (ʾet-haddām). Exod 29:12, the corresponding verse, reads *min haddām* 'some of the blood', which is the preferable reading.

around. sābîb, that is, on each horn of the altar, "around" modifying the altar. Ehrlich (1908–14; and recently Rodriguez 1979: 136–38) maintains that "around" modifies "horns," in other words, the blood is smeared around each horn. Yet why should the purgation of the altar in this instance differ from all others? For the refutation of this view, see chap. 4, COMMENT B. The use of "around" in connection with the daubing of the altar horns occurs just once again (16:18).

P's *sābîb* is replaced in Ezekiel, in identical contexts, by *sābîb sābîb* (cf. Exod 27:17; 38:16; 40:8, 33 with Ezek 40:17; Exod 30:3; 37:26 with Ezek 8:10; 41:17; Lev 25:31 with Ezek 40:5; 42:20; Gen 23:17 with Ezek 43:12). The latter occurs only once more, in 2 Chr 4:3, where it again replaces *sābîb* in the corresponding passage in Kings (1 Kgs 7:24), another indication of the early provenience of P's language (Hurvitz 1982: 85–87).

decontaminating the altar (wayyĕḥaṭṭēʾ ʾet-hammizbēaḥ). That *ḥiṭṭēʾ (piʿel)* means "decontaminate, purify" is shown in the NOTE on 6:19 and chap. 4, COMMENT A. The altar's decontamination by means of the blood of the purification-offering bull was repeated for seven days (expressly, Exod 29:37), as were all elements of the priestly investiture (see the NOTE on v 33). That it was crucially indispensable to their investiture is underscored in Exod 29, for it is the only rite in the entire ordination complex whose seven-day performance is explicitly commanded (Exod 29:36–37). Why is it singled out, and what is its purpose? It has been suggested that the Tabernacle may have been polluted by its builders (*Tirat Kesep* on *Seper Hamibḥar*). In that case, though, the requisite purification offering should have been brought by the builders (see 4:27–38) not the priests (v 14). This same criticism can be leveled against the opinion of the rabbis, who hold, "he (Moses) anointed the altar against any possible violence and force, for he said, 'Lest any of the chieftains have taken any of his gifts by violence and brought it for the construction of the Tabernacle. Or lest any of the Israelites unwillingly donate to the construction (of the Tabernacle), but having heard the voice of the announcer (Exod 25:2), was constrained, and did it reluctantly' " (*Tg. Ps.-J.;* cf. *Yal.* 1.515). Again, the purification offering should have been brought by the people, not the priests. The basic postulate of the *ḥaṭṭāʾt* offering is that it is required of the one who inadvertently violates a prohibition (4:2), and it is he who must perform the hand-leaning rite (cf. 4:4, 15, 24, 29, 33); the sole exception is the presumptuous sin that bars its doer from the sanctuary, in which case the high priest on the Day of Purgation performs the hand-leaning (see the NOTE on 16:11). Thus, as it is Aaron and his sons who perform the hand-leaning for the purification offering (v 14) and the two subsequently sacrificed animals (v 18, 22), the only possible inference is that they themselves are at fault (cf. Philo, *Vit. Mos.* 2.147). Living day and night for an entire week in the proximity of the altar, it is not difficult to contemplate the incidence of unavoidable physical impurities (e.g., a nocturnal emission, 15:16–17), which, because of their occurrence within the sacred precincts, would necessitate a purification offering. This would explain why the purification blood was not brought inside the Tent, as required of the high priest's bull (4:3–12). The sins were clearly minor (cf. Sforno on 8:2), and their effect was limited to the pollution of the altar. In any event, the repeated, seven-day decontamination of the altar is a quintessential prerequisite for the following consecratory rites.

A more difficult problem concerns the place of this purification offering in the procedural order. It follows the altar's sanctification (vv 10–11). Exod 29 expressly states, however, not just once but twice, that the sequence is reversed: "You shall decontaminate the altar by performing purgation upon it, and you shall anoint it to consecrate it. Seven days you shall perform purgation upon it and consecrate it" (Exod 29:36–37a). Thus decontamination precedes sanctification, clearly a more logical sequence. The same order is followed on the Day of Purgation: first the altar is daubed to purify it and then sprinkled to sanctify it (Lev 16:18–19). The priestly consecrands are similarly daubed and then sprinkled (vv 23, 30; Exod 29:20–21). The purpose of the sprinkling is expressly for sanctification (v 30; Exod 29:21), and though no purpose is stated for the daubing of the priests, the analogous daubing of the healed *mĕṣōrāʿ* is expressly termed "purgation" (14:18b, 29b; see the NOTE on 8:23). Thus we may presume that the blood daubing is a purgation rite. (A prophylactic function is also presumed; see the NOTE on v 23.) Once again, the logical order is maintained: before the priests are sanctified they must be purged (this principle speaks in favor of Exod 29 over Lev 8 concerning the sanctification process for Aaron: Exod 29:21 states that his sanctification is complete only after he is daubed and sprinkled, v 20; Lev 8:12, however, declares him sanctified after he is doused with anointment oil, even before he is daubed, v 23—an order that makes no sense).

The problem of the altar's decontamination with the purification offering is resolved once we regard the passage on the Tabernacle's sanctification (vv 10aβ–11) as an interpolation. For then the decontamination of the altar takes place first (v 15) and its sanctification, in consonance with Exod 29:36–37, is assumed to follow, presumably after the complete sacrifice of the purification offering (v 17) and before the burnt offering (v 18) and ordination offering (v 22), as the latter sacrifices could not be efficacious if offered on an unconsecrated altar. Besides, their blood must be rendered holy by contact with the altar in order to consecrate the priests (v 30). Perhaps the phrase at the end of this verse, *wayyĕqaddĕšēhû* 'then he consecrated it' (v 15), which otherwise would be difficult to interpret (see the NOTE below), may be a vestige of the original reference to the altar (and sanctuary's) consecration, which followed immediately upon the decontamination of the altar.

An alternative solution is proposed by the sectaries of Qumran. They prescribe two purification bulls, one for the priests and the other for the people (11QT 15:16–18). To be sure, the two bulls are sacrificed one after the other without allowing the altar's sanctification to intervene. Yet the prescription for an additional purification bull may preserve another exegesis of Exod 29:36–37, namely: the purification-offering bull whose purpose is to decontaminate the altar is not the same as the purification-offering bull that initiates the sacrificial series prescribed in our text (vv 15–17), and perhaps the sanctification of the altar followed the sacrifice of the first bull (in agreement with Exod 29:36–37) and preceded the second. This reconstruction, however, employs a number of unsubstantiated hypotheses and must be regarded as highly speculative.

In sum, the discrepancy between Lev 8 and Exod 29 is resolved by regarding the latter's order as authentic: the sanctification of the altar followed its decontamination. Hence, another reason is hereby provided for regarding the former's insertion into the order of the service at 8:10–11 as an erroneous interpolation.

then he poured out. *yāṣaq* is used again in 9:9, instead of the usual term *šāpak* (e.g., 4:7, 18, 25, 30, 34). Although the author of Lev 8 modeled his account on Exod 29:12, which employs *šāpak*, he felt free to introduce changes in vocabulary and style, a practice also attested in Hittite ritual texts (see COMMENTS B and C below for details). Of greater significance is the fact that this verb deviates from the preceding ones in being a simple perfect and forms the seventh in the list of rites describing the purification bull (vv 14–17). The purpose may well be to place emphasis on the blood rite as the key element of the *ḥaṭṭāʾt* sacrifice (Paran 1983: 143, and see chap. 4, COMMENTS A–C). It should also be noted that the verb describing the blood rite in the prescriptive order *tišpōk* (Exod 29:12b) also deviates from the form of the other verbs (Exod 29:10–14).

the blood (wĕʾet-haddām). This verse's counterpart, Exod 29:12, reads more precisely *wĕʾet-kol-haddām*, which means "the remaining blood" (e.g., 4:7, 18).

Thus he consecrated it (wayyĕqaddĕšēhû). This is a summary statement recalling vv 10–11, concerning the consecration of the altar. (See Exod 29:41 where this verb again performs a summarizing function). Still, the need to bring up the altar's consecration here is hard to justify. First, it interrupts the sacrificial series. As the altar's consecration was also essential for the burnt and ordination offerings that follow, one would have expected to find this summary notice after v 28. Furthermore, the account of the purification offering (vv 14–15) does not follow immediately upon the consecration of the altar (vv 10–11) but is preceded by the anointing of Aaron and the dressing of the priests (vv 12–13), to which there is no allusion in this purported summary. Thus the suspicion is aroused that *wayyĕqaddĕšēhû* does not refer to the account of the altar's consecration, given five verses back, but may be the original text of a statement that the consecration of the altar took place at this point in the procedure—after the altar was decontaminated with the blood of the purification offering (vv 14–15) and before the rest of the sacrificial service (vv 16–28). In light of this interpretation, the rendering of this word should be *"Then* he consecrated it."

   to effect atonement upon it (lĕkappēr ʿālāyw). Three extant renderings of this phrase need be considered: (1) *NJPS,* following the Vg., has "and purged it." But the parallel statement in Exod 29 reads, "And you shall decontaminate the altar by performing purgation upon it *(bĕkapperkā ʿālāyw)* and you shall anoint it to consecrate it *(lĕqaddĕšô)"* (Exod 29:36). Thus, as in its Exod 29 counterpart, *lĕkappēr* has to be understood literally as an infinitive and not as a disguised perfect. Besides, as demonstrated above, purging must precede consecration, not follow it. (2) *NEB* gives "by making expiation for it" (cf. *RSV, JB,* etc.): in other words, the consecration of the altar was accomplished by the blood of the purification offering. If this interpretation were true, it would eliminate the problem mentioned above: the consecration spoken of would refer back not to the altar's anointing but to the blood rite described in the immediate context. Yet one is hard put to justify the existence of an instrumental *lamed; lĕkappēr,* as indicated by its Exod 29:36 counterpart, cited above, is intended to be understood infinitively. Moreover, the notion that the same application of the blood of the purification offering can simultaneously decontaminate and consecrate is intrinsically wrong. The realms of impurity and holiness are incompatible with each other and their admixture is lethal (e.g., 15:31; chap. 4, COMMENT C). Impurity and holiness must be kept apart at all costs (chap. 15, COMMENT E). Thus an object must first be emptied of its impurities before it may be sanctified. This necessitates two discrete processes: first decontamination and then consecration. Decontamination takes place with the blood of the purification offering and consecration with the anointment oil (and, in special cases, with consecrated blood; see the NOTE on v 30). (3) Rashi and Ibn Ezra suggest "to effect purgation upon it," that is to say, in the future. In other words, the term *lĕkappēr* is totally unrelated to the purification offering just sacrificed. It refers to the permanent function of the newly consecrated altar: its effect is forevermore. Its use is not limited just to the purification offering and its exclusive purgative function but embraces all of the sacrifices in their expiatory roles: the burnt offering, the cereal offering, the reparation offering (COMMENTS on chaps. 1, 2,

5:14–26) and even the well-being offering (COMMENT on chap. 17). Hence the general, comprehensive rendering "atonement" is employed here. This distinctive use of *kippēr* as "atone," bespeaking the future function of the altar, is another point of divergence from Exod 29, where its use is limited to the immediate function of the consecratory sacrifices (29:33, 36, 37).

The preposition *ʿal* is rendered "upon" (with LXX) and is consonant with its use in cases wherein the purification blood purges other objects, such as the altar of incense (Exod 30:10), the leprous house (14:53), the adytum (16:16), the sacrificial altar (16:18).

16. *All of the suet that was about the entrails (kol-haḥēleb ʾăšer ʿal-haq-qereb).* The suet that covers the entrails (3:3; 7:3) is omitted here but is subsumed because the suet that "covers" *(hammĕkasseh)* is also "about" *(ʿal)* (Ibn Ezra).

were then taken up (wayyiqqaḥ). The subject is not specified, and like similar verbs, such as *wayyaggēš* (v 14), *wayyišḥaṭ* (v 15), the action could have been taken not just by the officiant, namely, Moses, but by anyone. Hence it must be understood as a passive. Nevertheless, when the suet is burned on the altar, an act that must be performed by the officiant (3:5, 11, 16; 7:5), Moses is identified as the subject.

17. *put to fire (śārap).* Again we find an active form of the verb with an impersonal subject that must be understood passively (see the NOTE on 4:12). It is placed in the middle of its sentence after a series of objects, in distinction to the previous verbs, which are imperfects (except the seventh in the list, *yāṣaq;* see the NOTE on v 15b) in order to indicate that this is the final rite in the *ḥaṭṭāʾt* series (Paran 1983: 143, and see the NOTE on 1:9). Why must this purification offering be incinerated? Because its blood was not brought into the Tent but emptied out on the altar's base (v 15), it should have been eaten by the officiant as his prebend (6:22–23; cf. 10:18). To be sure, Aaron and his sons had no right to it, for priests may never benefit from their personal expiatory sacrifices (Ḥazzequni on Exod 29:14) and, in this case, they are not priests but only the lay offerers (Dillmann and Ryssel 1897). But why then was it not assigned to the officiant, Moses? The answer can only be that although Moses officiates he is not a priest and, hence, he is not entitled to the priestly prebends from the most holy offerings. Indeed, even in the case of the ordination offering, which is of lesser holiness (see the NOTE on v 31), Moses does not receive all of the priestly prebends. He receives the breast (v 29) but not the right thigh, which, instead, is burned on the altar (vv 25, 28; contrast 7:31). Moses' reduced portion can only be understood as a means of underscoring his nonpriestly status (see the NOTE on v 29, below). Alternatively, the possibility must be considered that this purification offering represents an earlier stage in the history of this sacrifice when it was always incinerated outside the camp after its blood and suet were offered on the altar. This possibility is discussed in chap. 10, COMMENT C.

as the Lord had commanded Moses. In Exod 29:14.

18. *burnt offering.* The *ʿōlâ* functions as a gift (Philo, *Vit. Mos.* 2.148; see the COMMENT on chap. 1).

was brought forward (wayyaqrēb). Once again, an active form of a subjectless verb that must be understood as a passive whose subject is impersonal, analogous to *wayyaggēš* (v 14), *wayyišḥaṭ* (v 15), *wayyiqqaḥ* (v 16), and *śārap* (v 17). Like these aforementioned verbs, the action need not be performed by the officiant.

19. *and it was slaughtered (wayyišḥaṭ).* The situation is identical to that of v 15. The absence of an object as well as a subject proves that the subject is not Moses but anyone.

20. *The ram was cut up into its quarters (wěʾet-hāʾayil nittaḥ linětāḥāyw).* The word order of Exod 29:17 is followed precisely, indicating that it served as the model. The (active) verb with an impersonal subject must be treated as a passive, because the sectioning of the animal may be performed by anyone (see the NOTE on 1:6). The verb is a simple passive, in distinction to the previous verbs in this pericope (vv 18–19), and the word order is altered to accommodate it, indicating that it is the final rite in the procedure. It is followed by a summary verb, *wayyaqṭēr* (v 20b; Paran 1983: 145).

the suet (happāder). This term is missing in Exod 29:17. It is supplied from Lev 1:8 and represents an attempt to have the burnt-offering ritual conform with its prescription in chap. 1 (see the NOTE on v 21). The etymology of *peder* and its distinction from the usual term for suet, *ḥēleb,* are unknown (see the NOTE on 1:8).

21. That the writer of this verse has chap. 1 before him is not only evident from the word order, which follows 1:9 with complete fidelity, but also from the ritual procedure itself. The quartered animal, its head and its suet, are placed on the altar fire (v 20), to which the entrails and shins are added after they are washed (v 21). This accounts for the twofold occurrence of *wayyaqṭēr* 'turned into smoke' (vv 20, 21). Interestingly, the Aramaic and Greek additions (vv 25–30) to *T. Levi* (Charles 1908: Appendix III, p. 250) prescribe that the salted head (covered with suet) must be offered first—most likely in compliance with vv 20–21. This two-stage operation cannot be deduced from its Exod 29 counterpart (29:17–18), but it is clearly implied by 1:6–9 (and followed again in 9:13–14), again an indication that the writer of Lev 8 used Lev 1 as a corrective for his disagreements with his Exod 29 model. Verse 21bα repeats 29:18 in a slightly abbreviated form.

were washed (rāḥaṣ). Once again the subject of the (active) verb is impersonal and the verb must be rendered as a passive. The principle laid down in chap. 1 that the officiant is always specified whereas the lay participant is not (see the NOTES on 1:5, 6, 9) is scrupulously followed in this chapter. The verb again is a simple passive, a sign that a summary is about to follow *(wayyaqṭēr)* that will close the pericope (see the NOTE on v 20).

22. *was brought forward.* See the NOTE on v 18.

ordination (milluʾîm). Literally it means "filling" or, more precisely, "[hand]-filling," for it is an abstract plural stemming from the expression *millē'* *yad*, literally, "fill the hand of," discussed in detail in the NOTE on "your ordination will require," v 33.

This sacrifice has already made its appearance in Leviticus in the summation to chaps. 1–7: "This is the ritual for the burnt offering, the cereal offering, the purification offering, the reparation offering, the ordination offering, and the sacrifice of well-being," and in the NOTE to 7:37 it has been suggested that its prescriptive text, currently in Exod 29, originally stood after 7:10, between the prescription for the reparation offering (7:1–7) and the well-being offering (7:11–36), precisely in the order it occurs in this verse. Its place in this order is significant. It stands between the most holy offerings (burnt, cereal, purification, and reparation) and the holy offerings (well-being). The major difference between these two sacrificial categories is that the meat of most holy offerings may only be eaten by the priests (6:22; 7:6, 9–10), whereas the well-being offering is eaten by anyone in a pure state (7:15–21). The ordination offering in its median position shares the attributes of its adjoining neighbors. Like the most holy offerings it is eaten only by male priests in the sanctuary court (8:31; cf. 6:9, 19; 7:6), whereas the priestly prebends of the well-being offering may be eaten by members of the priest's family at any pure place. Of the three kinds of well-being offerings it resembles most the thanksgiving offering in that it is also accompanied by bread offerings (v 2; Exod 29:2; cf. 7:12) and is consumed on the same day. But here too a distinction is noticeable: the bread offerings of the ordination offering are entirely unleavened, but those of the thanksgiving offering are in part leavened. Moreover, even the prebends are not the same: whereas the breast and right thigh of the well-being offering are assigned to the priests (7:32–34; 10:14–15), only the breast of the ordination offering is assigned to Moses (as the officiant) while the thigh is burned on the altar together with the suet and one of each of the breads (vv 25–29). In effect, the ordination offering stands at the highest rung of the well-being offerings. Indeed, according to Exod 29:27–28, it served as the archetype for the priestly prebends from the well-being offering. Yet, as shown above, it also partakes of some characteristics of the most holy offerings. Hence it is a transitional offering, and it corresponds to the transitional nature of its offerers, the priestly consecrands, who are passing from the realm of the profane to the realm of the sacred. Thus the status of the sacrifice corresponds to the status of its offerers, a point that will be developed in the NOTES on vv 31 and 33 and in COMMENT G below.

23. *and it was slaughtered (wayyišḥāṭ)*. See the NOTE on the same word in v 19.

took . . . put (wayyiqqaḥ . . . wayittēn). These constitute two discrete ritual acts. For other examples, see vv 23–24, 25–27; 14:14; 16:12–13, 18; Num 6:18–19.

lobe (tĕnûk). So the LXX and Saadiah. But *Tg. Onq.* renders *rûm* 'the top' and *Tg. Ps.-J., ḥashûm*, which apparently corresponds to the *gādēr hā' emṣā'î*

527

'the middle ridge' (*Sipra*, Millu'im Ṣaw 21), whose scientific name is the *antihelix*, the hard, raised cartilage between the rim and opening of the ear (cf. Maim. on *m. Neg.* 14:9).

thumb/big toe (bōhen). Although its cognates in Akk., *ubānu* and Arab. *'ibhām* mean "finger, toe," in Hebrew the term is restricted to the thumb and the big toe.

right (yāmîn). In the Bible, the right side is the preferred side. Let these examples suffice: in court (1 Kgs 2:19; Pss 45:9; 80:16, 18; 110:1), in blessing (Gen 48:17–19), in wisdom (Qoh 10:2), in sight (Zech 11:17), in an oath (Isa 62:8), in power (Exod 15:6; Pss 118:15–16; 137:5), and in ritual (Lev 7:32; 8:23–24; 14:17, 25). This holds true in the entire ancient Near East, for example, Mesopotamia (Saggs 1962: 322), Egypt (*ANET*³ 7a), Ugarit (1 Krt 68, 161). Not surprisingly, it persists in rabbinic tradition: in the Temple, for example, every turn must be made to the right (*b. Yoma* 15b), priestly manipulations are performed with the right hand (*m. Zebaḥ.* 2:1, 32; *Menaḥ.* 1:2), and left-handedness disqualifies a priest (cf. Maimonides, *Temple Service*, "Entry to the Temple," 5.18).

The meaning of the rite is much debated. Some hold that the daubed organs represent the entire body, *partes pro toto* (Ehrlich 1908–14 on Exod 29:20; Snaith 1967). Others prefer a spiritual, allegorical explanation: "The organs of hearing, handling and walking are touched by the blood, imply that the priest is to have hallowed ears to listen to God's command, hallowed hands to perform his sacred offices, and hallowed feet to tread rightly the sacred places as also to walk generally in holy ways" (Driver 1911 on Exod 29:20). To be sure, the daubed organs of the priest represent his entire person, just as the daubed horns of the altar stand for its entirety and the aspersed veil and Ark denote the adytum in which they reside (4:6–7, 25; 16:14–15). Still, the objects selected for these metonymic rites are not chosen at random; *partes pro toto* does not tell the whole story.

There is abundant attestation of ritual daubing in the ancient Near East. The incantations recited during the ritual smearing of persons, the statues of gods, and buildings testify that their purpose is purificatory and apotropaic: to wipe off and ward off the incursions of menacing demonic forces. Always it is the *vulnerable* parts of bodies (extremities) and structures (corners, entrances) that are smeared with magical substances (e.g., *ANET*³ 338; Wright 1987: 34–36). Thus it can be seen that the blood-daubing of the altar's extremities—its horns—closely resembles the blood-daubing of the extremities of the priests. But it is the dedicatory rite of Ezekiel's altar that most closely corresponds to the daubing of the priests, for the purificatory blood is daubed not only on the altar's horns but also on the corners of its two gutters, located at its middle and bottom (Ezek 43:20). These points correspond to a person's earlobe, thumb, and big toe. It is safe then to conclude that these two congruent rites share the same purpose, which in the case of Ezekiel's altar is made explicit: *wĕḥiṭṭē'tā 'ôtô* *wĕkippartāhû* 'and you shall decontaminate it and thus purge it' (Ezek 43:20; note the same phraseology in Exod 29:36); *yĕkappĕrû ʾet-hammizbēaḥ wĕṭihărû ʾōtô* 'they shall purge the altar and thus purify it' (Ezek 43:26). Therefore, the daubing of the priest at points of his body and the daubing of comparable points on the altar must possess a similar goal: *kippûr*. One might object to this equation on the ground that the source for the blood is not the same in each rite: the blood for the daubing of the altar stems from a purification offering, whereas the blood for the priests' daubing comes from the ordination offering. One should keep in mind, however, a basic postulate of Israel's sacrificial system: the blood of the purification offering is only applied to objects, never to persons (chap. 4, COMMENT B). The purification of persons, *ipso facto*, must require the blood of other sacrifices. And, indeed, it does. The healed *mĕṣōrāʿ*, like the priestly consecrand, has his body daubed with sacrificial blood precisely at the same junctures: earlobes, thumbs, and big toes, and the blood is drawn from a reparation offering. Moreover, the purpose of this rite is expressly stated: *wĕkipper ʿālāyw hakkōhēn* 'the priest shall make expiation for him' (Lev 14:18; cf. v 29). Furthermore, the similarity between these two ceremonies is demonstrated by the fact that they serve the same function. They are rites of passage (see COMMENT G below and chap. 14, COMMENT B). Finally, it must be noted that the ordination offering itself is identified by an expiatory label. The priestly consecrands are ordered to eat the flesh of the ordination ram and its accompanying breads *wĕʾākĕlû ʾōtām ʾăšer kuppar bāhem* 'those who were expiated by them shall eat them' (Exod 29:33; cf. the NOTE on 8:34). In sum, there can be no doubt that the function of the blood-daubing of the priests is for *kippûr*, and that the nature of this *kippûr* is purgative and apotropaic.

An added bonus to this conclusion is that it places the two blood rites performed on the priestly consecrands, daubing and sprinkling, in proper perspective: the daubing is for *kippûr*—purgation—and the sprinkling is for *qiddûš* —sanctification (v 30). Thus the analogy to the blood rite on the sacrificial altar on the Day of Purgation is complete: the altar is also first daubed and then sprinkled, and the purpose of each blood manipulation is clarified by the text: *wĕṭihărô wĕqiddĕšô miṭṭumʾōt bĕnê yiśrāʾēl* 'Thus he shall purify it of the pollution of the Israelites and consecrate it' (16:19b). As for the reason why the blood (of the same sacrifice) when sprinkled upon the priests sanctifies, rather than purges, them, see the NOTE on v 30. Daubing of the priests, then, corresponds to the daubing of the altar. The blood is applied to the vulnerable extremities, and its function is purgative and prophylactic. Strikingly, the same reason is given by Frazer for the widespread practice among primitive peoples of mutilating the ear and fingers in magical rites—to guard these outlying parts against evil powers during rites of passage (1911–15: 3.165–269, esp. 261; cf. COMMENT G below).

24. *were brought forward. wayyaqrēb;* cf. the NOTE on v 18.

the sons of Aaron. Aaron is daubed separately from his sons, but the text of

Exod 29:20 implies they are daubed together. How can this difference be explained? The answer lies in the differing view in each account of Aaron's status at this point. Exod 29 presumes that Aaron continues to have the same profane status as his sons; all of them will become consecrated together by their joint aspersion with the sacrificial blood and anointment oil (Exod 29:21). Lev 8, conversely, presumes that Aaron has already been consecrated by his preliminary dousing with the anointing oil, *wayyimšaḥ 'ōtô lĕqaddĕšô* 'anointing him to consecrate him' (v 12b). Hence Aaron, now bearing a holy status, must be segregated from his sons, who are still profane. To "distinguish between the sacred and the common" (10:10a): what the priests are enjoined to teach to others, they must certainly practice themselves. Proof that Lev 8 presumes Aaron's holy status at this point is found in its variant version of the aspersion: Aaron himself is not sprinkled with the consecrating blood and oil (v 30). He does not need it; he is already consecrated (details in the NOTE on v 30). A judgment can even be made as to which of the two versions is more logical. The nod must be given to Exod 29, for the pouring of the ram's blood on the altar and its aspersion on the priests form a continuous rite (Exod 29:20–21), whereas in Lev 8 the two blood manipulations are separated—unnecessarily—by the lengthy elevation rite (vv 25–29).

25. *the suet—the broad tail (haḥēleb wĕ'et-hā'alyâ).* The Sam. reads *haḥēleb 'et-hā'alyâ.* Also in Exod 29:22, the Sam. reads *haḥēleb hā'alyâ* instead of MT's *haḥēleb wĕhā'alyâ.* The Sam. is correct because *haḥēleb* is the all-encompassing term that precedes the enumeration of its components (see 3:9; 9:19).

26. *that was before the Lord ('ăšer lipnê YHWH).* That the basket of unleavened bread was brought, and probably placed, before the altar is not mentioned in this chapter but in Exod 29:3, another indication of the dependent and derivative status of Lev 8 (see COMMENT B below).

one cake of unleavened bread (ḥallat maṣṣâ 'aḥat). The corresponding phrase in Exod 29:23 is *kikkar leḥem 'aḥat* 'one flat loaf of bread'. *kikkār,* like *ḥallâ* (see the NOTE on 2:4), denotes a thick but flat, round loaf—unlike the modern loaf. The freedom to use synonyms is the hallmark of the biblical and ancient Near Eastern writer (see COMMENTS B and C below). The analogy with the breads of the thanksgiving offering (7:12), with which the ordination offering is compared (see the NOTE on v 22), and with the baked cereal offering (2:4–5) leads to the conclusion that this (and every other) bread offering was mixed with oil.

one cake of oil bread (ḥallat leḥem šemen 'aḥat). Again on the analogy of the thanksgiving-offering breads, this bread is probably the equivalent of the *murbeket* (7:12), the cake whose dough is well soaked in oil (see the NOTE on 6:14). This also is the view of the rabbis (*t. Menaḥ.* 7:13; 8:17).

wafer (rāqîq). A thin, round cake as opposed to a thick, round cake (*ḥallâ, kikkār;* see above and the NOTES on 2:4).

the suet pieces (haḥălābîm). This general designation also includes the caudate lobe and the kidneys (v 25; see the Note on 3:9).

the right thigh (šôq hayyāmîn). This prebend was consigned to the altar and not to the officiant, Moses, as would have been the case had the officiant been a priest (see 7:32). Perhaps this is the very reason that Moses is granted the breast, one of the two priestly prebends (7:31), but denied the other one, the thigh— that he not be taken to be a priest, that his office was only temporarily valid until the permanent priesthood would be chosen. Indeed, withholding the right thigh from Moses while bestowing the breast may also be significant: whereas the breast is apportioned to the entire priestly cadre (7:31), the thigh, explicitly and emphatically, belongs solely to the officiant (7:33; see chap. 7, COMMENT F). Thus in receiving the breast Moses is granted quasi-priestly status, but in being denied the thigh he is not recognized as the officiant. The ambivalent status of Moses in P is explored in COMMENT E below.

27. *all of these. hakkōl,* namely, the suet, the breads, and the right thigh. The meat is subjected to the *tĕnûpâ,* the elevation rite, as a sign that it is transferred from the property of the offerer to the property of God (see below). The breads, as adjuncts of the meat and also destined for the altar, thus require a similar rite of transfer. (The Nazirite's loaves also undergo *tĕnûpâ* together with their accompanying meat, Num 6:20–21.) The suet, however, is unique in that only here is it subject to *tĕnûpâ,* whereas in the procedure for the well-being offering it is expressly excluded from this rite (7:30b; cf. 9:20–21). The solution eludes me.

on the palms of Aaron and on the palms of his sons ('al kappê 'ahărōn wĕ'al kappê bānāyw). In this double action the officiant (Moses) first places the sacrificial pieces in the hands of the offerers (the priests) and then transfers them to the altar. This can only be seen as an attempt by the author of this text to emphasize that only the offerers, and not the officiant, are authorized to dedicate the offering to the Lord. This act underscores the function of the elevation rite as a transfer of the elevated objects from the domain of the owners to the domain of God (see the Note on 7:29 and chap. 7, COMMENT E).

elevation offering (tĕnûpâ). Precisely because the right thigh of every well-being offering is given directly by its offerer to the officiating priest without the benefit of a ritual (7:32–33), it is imperative that in this instance it should undergo the rite of elevation to indicate that it no longer belongs to the offerer but now belongs to God and must be offered up on the altar. For a detailed analysis of the function of the elevation rite, see chap. 7, COMMENT E.

29. *took the breast and presented it (wayyiqqaḥ 'et-haḥāzeh wayyĕnîpēhû).* Why did Moses not put the breast in the offerers' (priests') hands together with the other pieces requiring the elevation rite? The breast was elevated separately to distinguish it from the other pieces, which were assigned to the altar. Moreover, it was not even placed in the offerers' hands but was taken directly by Moses to distinguish it from the breast of the well-being offering, which is

assigned to the priestly staff after it undergoes the elevation rite (7:31). The breast in this instance is comparable to the right thigh of the well-being offering, which is given only to the officiating priest without being subject to the elevation rite (7:32–33).

it was Moses' portion (lĕmōšeh hāyâ lĕmānâ). According to P, Moses should have received nothing: he is not a priest. Indeed, he gets nothing from the offerers. The right thigh, which normally would have been given directly to the officiant by the offerers, is instead given over to God and burned on the altar. Instead, Moses receives a prebend, not from the offerers, but from God: the breast is subjected to the elevation rite, that is, it is transferred to the authority of the divine so that God might award it to him. This is yet another reason why the breast rather than the thigh is assigned to Moses; the latter prebend, normally given to the officiating priest, would, if awarded to Moses, make him in the people's eyes a priest.

of the ram of ordination (mēʾêl hammillūʾîm). A smoother reading is obtained if this phrase is inserted after *heḥāzeh.* The verse would then read, "Moses took the breast from the ram of ordination and presented it as an elevation offering before the Lord. It was Moses' portion—as the Lord had commanded Moses."

as the Lord had commanded Moses. All of the instructions concerning the ordination ram (vv 22–29) were commanded in Exod 29:19–20, 22–26.

30. *some of the anointing oil and some of the blood (miššemen hammišḥâ umin-haddām).* In Exod 29:21, the order is reversed; Moses takes first the blood and then the oil. But the order is immaterial because the two liquids are mixed before they are aspersed (see below). The reason for mentioning the blood first in Exod 29 is contextual: it has just been dashed on the altar (Exod 29:20; cf. also COMMENT B below).

and sprinkled (wayyaz). The singular form of the verb (also in Exod 29:21, *wĕhizzêtā)* denotes a single, simultaneous toss of the oil and the blood, implying that they had been mixed.

upon Aaron's vestments . . . Aaron's vestments (ʿal-ʾahărōn ʿal-bĕgādāyw . . . ʾet-ʾahărōn ʾet-bĕgādāyw). Two hendiadys expressions, which contrast with their equivalents in Exod 29:21, *ʿal-ʾahărōn wĕ ʿal bĕgādāyw . . . hûʾ ûbĕgādāyw,* where the addition of the conjunctive *waw* on *bĕgādāyw* forces the rendering "upon Aaron and his vestments . . . he and his vestments." True, in Lev 8:30 seventy-four MSS, Sam., and Versions read *wĕ ʿal* and fifty-two MSS, Sam., LXX, Pesh., and *Tg. Ps.-J.* read *wĕ ʾet,* but just on the principle of *lectio difficilior,* the MT should be preferred (Wessely 1846). But this verdict rests on stronger, ideological grounds. On the one hand, in Lev 8 Aaron has already been consecrated by his being doused with the anointment oil *lĕqaddĕšô* 'to consecrate him' (v 12); there is no further need of anointing him for a second time. Exod 29, on the other hand, does not designate the dousing of his head with anointment oil as consecration (29:7), but delays the usage of the root *qdš* 'consecrate' until his aspersion with the anointment oil together with his sons (29:21).

The fact that Lev 8 has to resort to a pair of hendiadys structures instead of simply stating *ʿal-/ʾet-bigdê ʾahǎrōn* is strong evidence for the secondary and dependent relationship of Lev 8 to Exod 29. Is it, however, possible that the tradition of Lev 8, though later, is just as valid as that of Exod 29? Let us examine the matter. First, there is the difference between the two traditions concerning the place of the aspersion in the ritual procedure: Exod 29 places it after the extremities of the priests are daubed with the blood of the ordination ram (Exod 29:20–21); Lev 8 has the aspersion follow the elevation offering (vv 25–29). Exod 29, it would seem, is more logical, for it keeps all of the blood manipulations together (interestingly, 11QT 16:2–3 also prefers the procedure of Exod 29 to that of Lev 8; see COMMENT F below). Furthermore, v 30 seems to be out of place. It follows the concluding refrain, "as the Lord commanded Moses" (v 29bβ), and it is divorced contextually from the next pericope (vv 31–35). Because these aspersions were also commanded by God (Exod 29:21), perhaps they should be inserted into the previous pericope (e.g., before v 26). This argument is not decisive, however, for we find in the account of the assembling of the Tabernacle that the erection of the enclosure (Exod 40:33a) also falls outside the concluding refrain "as the Lord commanded Moses" (v 32b), though it too was clearly specified in the divine instructions (Exod 27:9–19). It can be shown, however, that the placement of the aspersions here (v 30) serves an aesthetic and literary purpose within the chapter: it forms an inclusion with vv 12–13, thereby framing and accentuating the consecratory service (BB' in Scheme II, COMMENT A below). Nonetheless, such a literary device, devoid of compelling ideological grounds, diminishes its positional claim and gives clear priority to the version of Exod 29:21, which has the aspersion of the priests follow their daubing and precede the elevation rite.

In regard to the nature of the aspersion, there is no way, to my knowledge, of deciding which of the two traditions, Exod 29 or Lev 8, is correct. Exod 29 claims that the aspersion sanctifies and, hence, Aaron too must be aspersed. Lev 8, however, claims that Aaron has already been consecrated by the anointment oil (v 12) and need not be anointed a second time. Both traditions are consistent, each within its respective text, and there seems no way to decide between them. Perhaps it is best, until further evidence can be adduced, to accept the position that Exod 29 and Lev 8 reflect two independent traditions; that Aaron was consecrated by the anointment oil when his head was anointed (Lev 8) or when he was aspersed with his sons (Exod 29).

Thus he consecrated (wayyĕqaddēš). That the anointment oil consecrated the priests and their clothing is obvious; such is the exclusive power and function of the anointment oil (Exod 30:22–30). But how is it possible for the blood to possess consecratory power? Its expiatory role *(kippûr)* in the sacrificial system is emphasized over and over again. Indeed, the very daubing of the priests with the blood of the ordination ram (vv 23–24) is for expiation (see the NOTE on v 23). How then can the same blood—from the ordination ram—suddenly have a consecratory role? The answer is provided by the text itself; it informs us that, as opposed to the daubing of the priests, wherein the blood was applied directly from the animal to the priests, the aspersion of the priests must be done with blood taken from the altar. Thus in keeping with the basic Priestly rule *kōl-hannōgēaʿ bammizbēaḥ yiqdāš* 'Whatever touches the altar is sanctified' (Exod 29:37b), as soon as the blood impinges upon the altar it partakes of its holiness and is then able to impart holiness to others (Ḥazzequni on Exod 29:21). Similarly, the blood of the purification offering, which has been sanctified by being aspersed inside the adytum and shrine of the Tent, is now qualified to consecrate the sacrificial altar when sprinkled upon it (16:14–19). In these two instances, and only these, the sacrificial blood is sanctified; only consecrated blood can consecrate. For the exposition of the way that the altar sanctifies objects (but not persons), see chaps. 6–7, COMMENT B.

31. *Boil (baššĕlû).* This imperative, clearly directed to the priestly consecrands, proves that the command *ûbiššaltā* (Exod 29:31), ostensibly directed to Moses, should be taken impersonally and rendered as a passive, "[the flesh] shall be boiled." This verse begins the concluding pericope (vv 31–36), which possesses the same structure as the opening pericope (vv 1–5), thereby enveloping this chapter in an inclusio (see COMMENT A below).

at the entrance of the Tent of Meeting (petaḥ ʾōhel môʿēd). Exod 29:31 reads instead *bĕmāqôm qādōš* 'in a holy place', which the LXX and Sam. add here. The corresponding section in Exod 29 also differs in this regard: whereas the meat is cooked "in a holy place," it is eaten "at the entrance to the Tent of Meeting" (29:31–32), in consonance with the prescription of this verse. These two terms are not synonymous but complementary: the holy place is specified as the courtyard (see the NOTE on 6:9).

and eat it there (wĕšām tōʾkĕlû ʾōtô). The meat of the ordination offering is treated like most sacrifices (i.e., cereal, purification, and reparation offerings), which are eaten within the sacred precincts by male priests on the same day (v 32). Yet it is also treated like the well-being offering, which is of lesser holiness because its meat is eaten by the offerers (in this case, the priestly consecrands), and the officiant (here Moses) receives as his prebend the breast (but not the right thigh; see the NOTE on v 26). Indeed, it most closely resembles the thanksgiving offering, which is also eaten the same day together with its accompanying breads (7:14). The ambiguous state of the ordination offering is reflected by its position in the sacrificial series: it follows the most holy sacrifices and precedes the less holy well-being offering (7:37). Indeed, the status of the sacrifice is congruent with the status of the offerers. The ambiguity that characterizes the ordination ram corresponds to the ambiguity of those ordained. And indeed this sacrifice may have been chosen for this very reason. A sacrifice that is neither holy nor most holy but lies somewhere between is a reflection of the consecrands who are in a liminal state: they are no longer of this common world but have not yet been admitted into the realm of the divine; they are in transit. Furthermore, because this liminal period is one of extreme danger, they remain inside the Tent; they may not appear outside (vv 33, 35). Indeed it is even doubtful that they are allowed to leave for their needs; toilet facilities may have been available within the Tabernacle court (see the NOTE on v 33).

with the bread (wĕ'et-hallehem). The bread, though an adjunct to the meat, is indispensable because it performs the same expiatory function: *wĕ'ākĕlû 'ōtām 'ăšer kuppar bāhem* 'they (the consecrands) who were expiated by them (the meat and bread) shall eat them' (Exod 29:33a). The bread has the status of a *minḥâ*, a cereal offering; it is most holy (6:10) and must, therefore, be consumed the same day it is offered (v 32).

I commanded (ṣiwwêtî). Read *ṣuwwêtî* 'I was commanded' with the LXX, Pesh., and *Tg. Onq.* and as found in v 35 and in 10:13 (cf. also the NOTE on 10:18). The command itself is located in Exod 29:31–32.

"Aaron and his sons shall eat it" (lē'mōr 'ahărōn ûbānāyw yō'kĕlūhû). This is not a direct quote, as the command reads, *wĕ'ākal 'ahărōn ûbānāyw* 'and Aaron and his sons shall eat'. The perfect with the sequential *waw* in Exodus has been transformed into an imperfect in order to conform grammatically with the other imperfects in its immediate context, *tō'kĕlû* (v 31), *tiśrōpû* (v 32), and *yĕmallē'* (v 33).

32. *The remainder (wĕhannôtār)*. Exod 29:34 adds the essential datum *'ad bōqer* 'until morning', a primary consideration with most holy offerings, which must be either eaten or incinerated by the following day. This criterion also holds for the thanksgiving offering (7:15), even though it is technically a well-being offering whose time limit is two days (7:16–17). The ordination offering, partaking of some of the characteristics of both the thanksgiving offering and the most holy offerings (cf. the NOTE on v 31), and in fact standing between them in rank (7:37), must therefore also follow their common rule—consumption or incineration by the next morning. Incidentally, this rule provides strong evidence for the theory that the biblical day, in Priestly circles at least, began in the morning.

of the flesh and the bread (babbāśār ûballehem). The medieval exegetes were fully aware of the interchangeability of the *beth* and *mem* (e.g., Ibn Ezra on Exod 38:8; Ramban, citing Judg 10:8; Ezek 43:27). This exchange has already been demonstrated with a synonym of *nôtar: wĕhanniš'ār baddām* 'what remains of the blood' (5:9).

33. *You shall not go outside (lō' tēṣĕ'û)*. How inclusive is this prohibition? The rabbis would limit it to the time of the consecration service (*Sipra*, Millu'im 42; cf. Ramban). The Karaites regard it as absolute, forbidding all exit except for bodily needs *(Seper Hamibḥar; Keter Torah)*. That there is room for debate is apparent from the ambiguity that is inherent in the Hebrew. The commandment "you shall dwell in booths seven days" (23:42) does not mean that the

entire week must be spent in booths. Nor does the statement "the Israelites bewailed Moses for thirty days" (Deut 34:8) imply that for one month the Israelites did not stop crying (Ḥazzequni). As will be shown below (and in COMMENT G), however, it is likely that Aaron and his sons did not budge from the sanctuary at all during the week of their consecration—perhaps not even to relieve themselves. The latter possibility would definitely be ruled out according to the view of Ezekiel that human feces are a source of defilement (Ezek 4:10–15)—a view shared by the sectaries of Qumran (11QT 46:13–16). By contrast, nowhere does P mention that human excrement defiles, a position emphatically endorsed by the rabbis, for example, "Rabbi Yose said: Is excrement (a source of) impurity? Why it is nothing but (a source of) purity" (y. Pesaḥ. 7:11; 35b). True, Deuteronomy's law of the war camp states that "there shall be an area outside the camp where you shall relieve yourself. . . . Because the Lord your God moves about in your camp . . . let your camp be holy: let him not find anything unseemly among you and turn away from you" (Deut 23:13–14). Still, "anything unseemly" (ʿerwat dābār) is not the same as impurity (ṭumʾâ). Thus there is a possibility that somewhere within the courtyard enclosure there was a space reserved for toilet facilities. Two bits of evidence point in this direction. The first is the fact, already discussed, that the place in which the priests eat their prebends from the most holy offerings not only is designated as "the enclosure of the Tent of Meeting" but is further qualified as "in a holy place" (6:9, 19). The implication is clear that not everywhere inside the enclosure was considered holy, thus raising the possibility that a toilet area was included. More significant information is provided by a passage about the Herodian Temple, which speaks of lit tunnels underneath the Temple leading to an immersion pool and toilet (m. Tamid 1:1). Thus the priests were able to get to a toilet without exiting the Temple court. One well might ask why, indeed, it was necessary to construct a tunnel instead of allowing the priest the simple expedient of relieving himself somewhere off the Temple mount. Moreover, what was the procedure in the Temple before the tunnel was built? And what was the procedure at other sanctuaries—Shiloh, Bethel, Dan, and so on and the Tabernacle—where there were no natural springs underneath? Thus the possibility must be reckoned with that Aaron and his sons never left the sacred premises during the entire week of their consecration: they ate there, slept there, and relieved themselves there—a situation that is entirely congruous with the picture presented by liminal rites of passage attested in many cultures throughout the world; see below and COMMENT G.

not. A prohibition introduced by lōʾ is stronger than one with ʾal, indicating long duration (Bright 1973: 192)—in this case, seven days.

seven days (šibʿat yāmîm). For the first time in this chapter we learn here that the priestly consecration is to last for seven days. There is only one good reason for the delay of this information. This chapter is modeled after Exod 29, which also mentions the seven-day duration of the consecration only at the end of the prescriptions for the service (29:30, 35–37; see COMMENT G below). The ritual significance of the number seven in Israel and the ancient Near East is discussed in the NOTE on 4:6 (see also Snaith 1947: 115–16). Of special interest is the dedication of Eninnu, the temple of Ningirsu, which also lasted seven days (Gudea II, 16–18; see Falkenstein and von Soden 1953: 137–82). But it is the initiation of Ezekiel's altar that affords the nearest parallel. The text reads, "Every day, for seven days, you shall present a goat of purification offering, as well as a bull of the herd and a ram of the flock; they shall present unblemished ones. Seven days they shall purge the altar and purify it; thus they shall ordain it" (Ezek 43:25–26). There can be no question that Ezekiel's demand that the new altar be purged with a purification offering each day for seven days is based on a passage contained in the account of the consecration of the Tabernacle and its priesthood: "You shall ordain them (Aaron and his sons) through seven days, and each day you sacrifice a bull of purification offering for purgation; you shall decontaminate the altar by performing purgation upon it, and you shall anoint it to consecrate it. Seven days you shall purge the altar and consecrate it" (Exod 29:35b–37a). Both rites are in accord in stating that the altar's initiation lasts for seven days. They differ, however, in three significant details. First, Ezekiel's altar is not consecrated because it is not anointed. But this is not surprising because after the destruction of the First Temple, the anointment oil was not reconstituted (see the NOTE on v 11). Then, the sacrificial animals differ. It can be shown, however, that this difference rests on two variant traditions concerning the purging of the altar on behalf of the community: Ezekiel relies on Num 15:22–26 and the Tabernacle account relies on Lev 4:13–21. More precisely, Ezekiel has fused the two traditions, for he calls for a purification bull (as Lev 4) for the first day (Ezek 43:21) and a purification goat (as Num 15) for the following seven days (details in chap. 4, COMMENT E). Finally, the length of the initiation, in fact, also differs: Ezekiel's actually runs for eight days (details in chap. 4, COMMENT J). Yet this deviation is not traceable to a variant tradition concerning the number of days but is due to Ezekiel's attempt both to conflate the two purification offering traditions (cited above) and to equate the altar initiation to his eight-day spring festival (Ezek 45:21–23; details in chap. 4, COMMENT E). The initiation of Solomon's altar *(ḥănukkat hammizbēaḥ)* also lasted seven days (2 Chr 7:9; cf. 1 Kgs 8:65 LXX, 66), a clear attempt by the Chronicler to equate the Solomonic Temple with the Tabernacle (Japhet 1977: 69)—as demonstrated by his attribution of a theophany on the Solomonic altar (2 Chr 7:1a) similar to that on the Tabernacle altar (see the NOTE on 9:24).

Two questions need to be asked: Were all seven days similarly observed; and were all of the rites on the first day repeated for the remainder of the week? Noth (1965) suggests that the consecrating ceremonial took place only on the first day (regarding vv 33b–34 as a secondary interpolation), and for the rest of the week the consecrands were only prohibited from leaving the sanctuary. Interestingly, the Karaites entertained a similar view, holding that only the purification bull was offered up for seven days (Exod 29:36–37; Yefet ben Ali, cited by *Seper Hamibḥar* on v 34). A. Hurowitz agrees (1974: 90), citing the case of the healed *mĕṣōrāʿ* whose purificatory rite ostensibly takes place the first day, after which he enters the camp but remains outside his tent for seven days (14:4–8). But the analogy of the *mĕṣōrāʿ* is wholly inappropriate. He undergoes a graded purification involving rites for the first, seventh, and eighth days that can only be compared with other purificatory rites, and his purification has nothing in common with an entirely different and, indeed, opposing field of activity—consecration, the passage from the profane to the holy (the Karaite contention is rebutted in the NOTE to v 34). Rather, it is preferable to regard the expression rendered "ordain" (see below) as implying that all seven days were alike. All rites described in this chapter were repeated every day for the entire week. The text, however, does indicate some ambiguity concerning the ongoing anointing of the priests, especially of Aaron, on which see below.

If the first-day rites were to be repeated each day, their purpose could well have been that of reinforcement (Baentsch 1903). But the text is silent concerning purpose and concerns itself with prohibitions: the consecrands are forbidden to leave the sanctuary for seven days on pain of death (v 35). We are dealing here with a rite of passage, such as the seven days of birth (circumcision on the eighth day marks the first day of the child's life (Gen 17:12), the seven days of marriage (Gen 29:27), and the seven days of mourning (Gen 50:10). "All these are 'passage times' when a person moved from one house of life to another, dangerous occasions when the demons were most active" (Snaith 1967 on 4:6). Thus the fact that Aaron and his sons are constrained to remain in the sanctuary for seven days can only mean that rites are being performed on them during this period by which they can pass from the house of commoners to the house of priests. They are consecrated as priests only at the end of the week, and during this liminal period they are highly vulnerable, not to demonic assault—the world of demons has been expunged from Priestly notions—but to human sin and impurity (see chap. 4, COMMENT C). The peril that attends all liminal periods is attested in cultures throughout the world, discussion of which is reserved for COMMENT G below. Here let it only be noted that the status of the ordination sacrifice is a perfect match for the status of the consecrands. The sacrifice is itself transitional and anomalous. It ranks lower than the most holy offerings and higher than the lesser holy offering (7:38), and shares the characteristics of both (details in the NOTE on v 22). So too with Aaron and his sons: they participate in the sacrificial services as offerers, not as priests; at the same time they are consecrated with holy oil. Theirs is a seven-day passage. It is inconceivable that after the first day they merely wait out the week at the Tabernacle door. Each day's rites will remove them farther from their former profane state and advance them to the ranks of the sacred, until they emerge as full-fledged priests.

your ordination will require. yĕmallēʾ ʾet-yedkem, literally, "he will fill your hands." This idiom occurs not only in P (Exod 28:41; 29:9, 29, 35; 32:29; Lev

8:33; 16:32; 21:10; Num 3:3) but elsewhere in Scripture (Judg 17:5, 12; 1 Kgs 13:33; Ezek 43:26 LXX; 1 Chr 29:5; 2 Chr 13:9; 29:31, where it usually refers to persons being installed in priestly functions). Especially instructive is the case of Micah: "he had ordained *(wayyĕmallē' 'et-yad)* one of his sons to be his priest. . . . Micah ordained *(wayyĕmallē'* . . . *'et-yad)* the Levite, and the young man became his priest and remained in Micah's shrine" (Judg 17:5, 12). Once it is found in connection with the initiation of Ezekiel's altar: *ûmillē'û yādāw (ydw)* 'and dedicated it' (Ezek 43:26b), but the LXX and Pesh. read *yādām* 'them' (lit., "their hand"), thus referring again to the consecration of the priests. It is, however, the exact cognate phrase in Akk., *mullû qātam*, literally, "fill the hands," that provides supportive evidence for this rendering, for instance, *barûtu umallû qātā'a* '(Šamaš and Adad) have inducted me into the priesthood' (Streck 1916: 254, 1.9); *uddušu ešrēti umallû qātūa* '(Marduk my lord) ordained me to renovate temples' (Langdon 1912: 110, 3.30; 142, 2.10). Even the origin of this phrase may be discernible in the Akk., for example, *ḫaṭṭa murtē'āt nišē ana qātiya ú-me-el-lu-ú* 'they handed over to me the scepter which shepherds all peoples' *(KAH* 2.84.8), referring to Adad-Nirari II *(CAD, malû* 9c, p. 187). Thus, into Adad-Nirari's hands was placed the scepter of authority, a ceremonial by which he was inducted into the kingship. One should not, however, point to the use in Mari of the idiom *ana mil kātišunu šumūdum* 'in order to increase their handful' (ARM 2.13), in other words, to fill their hands with spoil (Noth 1967: 232 n. 9). This meaning may perhaps pertain to Exod 32:29 (Cody 1969: 153 n. 22) but not here (Rupprecht 1975). Both in the cited Akkadian and in biblical passages, adduced above, *mullû qātam/millē' yad* means "ordain, authorize (through a ceremony)."

It now needs to be asked: What is the ceremony to which this phrase refers? According to *Tg. Onq.,* the phrase refers solely to the sacrificial service (cf. also *Midr. 'Ag.* to Exod 29:35), including most likely the purification and burnt offerings as well as the ordination offering (vv 14–28). Ezekiel, too, it should be remembered, identifies the purification and burnt offerings as the ordination agencies for the altar (Ezek 43:25–26). Nevertheless, the purification offering seems to have been excluded by the writer of Exod 29:35–36 (details in the NOTE on v 34). The rabbis adopt a broader definition. They extend this idiom to include the anointing of the priests. In other words, they claim that all rites performed on the first day were repeated each following day (*Sipra,* Millu'im Ṣaw 14; *Midr. Lev. Rab.* 10:8). A number of objections to this view come to mind: (1) *lĕmošḥâ bāhem ûlĕmallē' bām 'et-yādām* 'to anoint them and ordain them' (Exod 29:29b). Thus "ordain" does not include "anoint." (2) *ûmillē'tā yad-'ahărōn wĕyad-bānāyw* 'You shall ordain Aaron and his sons' (Exod 29:9b) heads up the sacrificial service (ibid., vv 10–26). Thus the prior anointing of Aaron (ibid., v 7) is excluded. (3) The purpose of the ordination (8:23) is *lĕkappēr 'ălêkem* 'to make expiation for you' (v 34b), a purpose fulfilled by the sacrifices (cf. Exod 29:33b), not the anointing. Still, the anointment by sprinkling (v 30) is clearly contingent on the sacrifices (the blood comes from the altar!) and cannot be separated from it. Moreover, the function of the priests' daubing with the sacrificial blood is clearly for *kippûr*—expiation (see the NOTE on v 23). This leaves the dousing of Aaron's head with the anointment oil (no. 2, above) as the only rite possibly excluded. But because *millē' yād* means "authorize, ordain," it is inconceivable that Aaron's private anointing rite by which he qualifies as high priest is not also intended. This idiom would still exclude the anointing of the sanctuary, for in P it is always attested with a human object, namely, the priests. Only Ezekiel extends this phrase to include the altar (Ezek 43:25; but cf. the LXX, Pesh., cited above), a matter that will be explained in the NOTES on v 34, below. Thus it can be assumed that all rites of the first day were repeated during the entire week of consecration, with the possible exception of the consecration of the sanctuary.

Two morphological observations concerning the idiom: though active in form it is rendered as a passive, a frequent occurrence in this chapter (vv 15a, 16a, 17a, 19a, 20a, 21a, 34a); and *yād* remains singular even when the subject is plural (Exod 29:29, 33, 35; Num 3:3; Ehrlich 1908–14).

34. *Everything done (ka'ăšer 'āśâ)*. Although the verb is active it must be understood as a passive. Either way, however, the subject is not impersonal; it refers to God—not Moses. For this reason we do not find the verb in the first person, *'āśîtî* 'I (Moses) have done', inasmuch as the verb in the previous verse is also not in the first person, *'ămallē'* 'I (Moses) shall ordain'. It is God who is the author and executor of the priestly ordination. Indeed, in the entire chapter, Moses is referred to in the third person with but one exception—and it is a telling one—*ṣuwwêtî* 'I was commanded' (v 35b; cf. the NOTE on v 33b).

the Lord has commanded to be done. ṣiwwâ YHWH la'ăśōt, that is, for seven days (Rashi, Ibn Ezra), as specified by the corresponding command in Exod 29; note the similar vocabulary: *wĕ'āśîtā . . . kākâ kĕkōl 'ăšer-ṣiwwîtî 'ōtākā šib'at yāmîm* 'Thus you shall do according to all I commanded you, seven days . . .' (Exod 29:35). Because the latter verse is followed by the command "you shall sacrifice a purification bull each day . . . you shall purge the altar seven days" (Exod 29:36–37), the Karaites hold that only the purification offering was to be continued for seven days, not the other sacrifices (Yefet ben Ali, cited by *Seper Hamibḥar*), which Ibn Ezra rebuts by pointing out that the purging of the altar is being singled out here, a function solely of the purification offering. Rashi (on Exod 29:36) responds more incisively: "Because it is stated 'you shall ordain them seven days' (Exod 29:35b) one may deduce that it refers only to that which is brought on their (the consecrands') behalf, namely, the rams (for the whole and ordination offerings) and the breads; but that which is brought for the altar, namely, the bull for decontaminating the altar, is not to be deduced (from this command). Therefore this verse (on the purification offering, v 36) is essential." Rashi is correct. The ordination *(millū'îm)* of the *priests* refers to all of the sacrifices except the purification offering, which is exclusively reserved for the altar. That is why Ezekiel can speak of the purging of the new altar with the purification offering *ûmillĕ'û yādāw (ydw)* also as its ordination (Ezek 43:26b). It is not an unwarranted application of the idiom. On the contrary, it refers to the induction of the altar by its special sacrifice in the same manner as the priests are inducted into their service by their sacrifices. And certainly, the attempt of the LXX and Pesh. to render Ezekiel's phrase in such a way that it refers to the priests' ordination, that is to say, *ûmillĕ'û yĕdêhem*, 'ordained them', must be vigorously rejected. In any event, it is the clear implication of both Exod 29 and Lev 8 that all of the sacrifices are to be continued for the seven days.

to make atonement for you (lĕkappēr ʿălêkem). The general term "atone" instead of "purge" renders the verb *kippēr* here because we are speaking of those sacrifices which ordain the priests, from which the purification offering, the exclusive purgative sacrifice, is excluded (see above). Purgation remains one of the objectives of the ordination offering because its blood daubed on the extremities of the priests performs a purgative function (see the NOTE on v 23). But the burnt offering and the bread also play a *kippûr* role, expressly the latter: *wĕ'ākĕlû 'ōtām 'ăšer kuppar bāhem* 'they (the consecrands) shall eat them (the ordination offering and the breads) who were expiated by them' (Exod 29:33), and sacrifices other than the purification offering are expiatory in a wider sense (see chap. 16, COMMENT F). See 14:20 for a discussion of why the burnt offering and breads (i.e., the cereal offering) perform expiation. Expiation in this general sense means being cleansed of all impurities and sins so that the offerer is reconciled and "at one" with God (cf. Milgrom 1983d: 155 n. 52).

35. *You shall stay . . . day and night (tēšĕbû yômām wālaylâ).* This datum is an innovation, not to be inferred from v 33a (Ehrlich 1908–14). It is a merism, meaning that during their consecratory week they are not to leave the sanctuary premises at all—not even to relieve themselves (see the NOTE on v 33a).

observing the Lord's prohibitions (ûšĕmartem 'et-mišmeret YHWH). The idiom *šāmar mišmeret* in connection with the Tabernacle means "perform guard duty" (Milgrom 1970a: 8–10). When its object is the Lord, however, the context always involves prohibitions so that "guarding" against violations is always meant. To cite examples only from P: Lev 18:30 (sexual violations); 22:9 (defiled priest and his food); Num 9:19, 23 (Israel is not to march except at God's command); Num 18:7a (priestly taboos concerning the altar and the shrine). In this verse too, several taboos are implied: the consecrands may not enter the Tent because Moses alone is the priest *(Seper Hamibḥar);* they may not officiate at the altar, for the same reason; and they may not leave the sacred precinct (v 33a). The same meaning is attested for this phrase in non-P sources as well (Milgrom 1970a: 11 and nn. 40, 41).

so that you do not die (wĕlō' tāmûtû). This comprises another innovation, which cannot be inferred from v 33a (Ibn Ezra). Death here is by divine agency (Milgrom 1970a: 5–8).

for so I have been commanded (kî-kēn ṣuwwêtî). But this command is not to be found in Exod 29, which may account for its wording, instead of the expected *ka'ăšer ṣiwwâ YHWH* (vv 9, 13, 17, 21, 29), the implication perhaps being: this *too* I was commanded (cf. Hoffmann 1953).

36. [*And Aaron and his sons*] *did. wayyaʿaś* refers only to vv 31–35, not to the entire chapter. In the previous verses Aaron and his sons did nothing; things were done to them. Only in this final pericope are they given direct orders. This final pericope—prescription (vv 31–35)–fulfillment (v 36)—forms a structural inclusion with vv 1–5 (see COMMENT A below).

all of the things that the Lord had commanded through Moses (kol-had-děbarîm 'ăšer-ṣiwwâ YHWH běyad-mōšeh). This is the seventh and enlarged repetition of the structural motif of this chapter (COMMENT A below). It uses *'ăšer* instead of *ka'ăšer* in order to allow the insertion of *kol-hadděbarîm* as its immediate antecedent. Now this verse echoes *zeh haddābār 'ăšer-ṣiwwâ YHWH laʿăśôt* 'This is what the Lord has commanded to be done' (v 5). Thus, vv 5 and 6 form an inclusio with v 36 that effectively envelops and, thereby, unifies this chapter.

COMMENTS: THE CONSECRATION OF THE PRIESTS

A. The Structure of Chapter 8

The consecration service comprises a double series of three acts: washing, clothing, and anointing the priests and three kinds of sacrifices. The text of the service, moreover, reveals an organizational phrase-motif of its own: the seven-fold repetition of *ka'ăšer ṣiwwâ YHWH* 'as the Lord commanded' (vv 4, 9, 13, 17, 21, 29, and 36 [enlarged]). This phrase subdivides the chapter into the following seven sections:

Scheme I

A.   *Assembling Materials and Persons*
   1.   vv 1–3   Command
        4a   Fulfillment
   B.   *Anointing Aaron*
        2.   4b–9   Washing the priests, dressing Aaron
        3.   10–11   Anointing the sanctuary
                12–13   Anointing Aaron, dressing his sons

B'. *The Sacrificial Service*

4.	14–17	The purification offering
5.	18–21	The burnt offering
6.	22–29	The ordination offering
	30	Anointing the sons and the priestly vestments

A'. *Admonitions for the Seven Days*

7.	31–35	Command
	36	Fulfillment

The opening and closing sections (AA') are neatly balanced because they both comprise in the main a prescriptive text with a brief, summary statement concerning its fulfillment. But neither section is germane to the actual ritual procedure for the consecration service, hence they serve as an introduction and conclusion, respectively, to the chapter. The middle sections (BB') comprise the two main elements in the consecration service: the anointing (and consecration) of Aaron and the sanctuary and the sacrificial rites. The septenary occurrence of this formula cannot be regarded as a matter of chance for it is used twice more, in the Priestly accounts of the manufacture of the priestly garments (Exod 39:1, 5, 7, 21, 26, 29, 31) and of the assembling of the Tabernacle (Exod 40:19, 21, 23, 25, 27, 29, 32) (Kearny 1977). Thus Lev 8 is a product of the same editorial hand, and it provides further support to the theory that Lev 8 is a direct continuation of Exod 40:17–33, with Exod 40:34–38 and Lev 1–7 as later insertions. In other words, the three pericopes containing this sevenfold formula (Exod 39; 40:17–33; Lev 8) may at one time have been consecutive (for details see the INTRODUCTION ʃH).

In Scheme I, two bulging units disturb the structural symmetry. Verses 10–11, the anointing of the sanctuary, clearly form a discrete unit, which does not conclude with the formula. Moreover, as shown in the NOTES on this unit, it disrupts the flow of the narrative, is logically incongruous with its context, and is better regarded as a subsequent interpolation. The other protruding unit is v 30, which is also discrete and bereft of the formula and, furthermore, at variance with its position in Exod 29. Yet it should by no means be regarded as a displaced verse. Its extrusion outside the last formula unit (vv 22–29) corresponds to Exod 40:33a, which similarly lies outside the formula scheme (ibid., vv 30–32). Thus the writer/editor divided each of these two chapters (Exod 40 and Lev 8) into eight units, but being committed to a septenary scheme, he had no choice but to leave the last unit (Exod 40:33a; Lev 8:30) outside the scheme. Moreover, v 30 in its present position forms an inclusio with vv 6–9, 12–13 (minus the sanctuary anointing), thereby highlighting the intervening sacrificial section. This new datum alters the structural scheme in the following way:

Scheme II

A.   *Assembling Materials and Persons*

    1.   vv 1–[3]   Command

        [vv 4–5]   Fulfillment

B.   *Anointing of the Priests*

    2.   vv 6–9   Washing the priests, dressing Aaron

        [vv 10–11]   Anointing the sanctuary

    3.   vv 12–13   Anointing Aaron, dressing his sons

    X.   *The Sacrificial Service*

        4.   vv 14–17   The purification offering

        5.   vv 18–21   The burnt offering

        6.   vv 22–29   The ordination offering

B'.   *Anointing of the Priests*

    v 30   Anointing the priestly vestments

A'.   *Admonitions for the Seven Days*

    7.   vv 31–35   Command

        v 36   Fulfillment

The advantage of this scheme is that it points to the actual consecration rites (X) as the center and pivot of the chapter and that whereas the beginning and conclusion (AA') continue to maintain the identical structure as in Scheme I, the middle sections (BB') now possess the same content—the anointing of the priests. Thus the placement of v 30 after the sacrificial service may not only reflect the ideological position that Moses must first complete all of the altar rites before he can turn to the task of anointing the priests but also may be due to aesthetic, literary reasons—to create an introverted, chiastic pattern. Moreover, this scheme also shows graphically why the units on the assembling of the *ʿēdâ* and the anointing of the sanctuary, presuming them to be later additions (of P₂), had to be inserted in their present positions, the former, in vv 3–5, to perfect the inclusio with vv 31–36 (A') and the latter, in vv 10–11, before the anointing of Aaron, to allow the consecration of the priests to take place in a consecrated sanctuary. The original structure, as here proposed, would still possess the heptad of *kaʾăšer ṣiwwâ YHWH* (vv 9, 13, 17, 21, 19) by adding *kāʾăšer ṣuwwêtî* (vv 31 LXX, 35).

CONSECRATION

B. Leviticus 8 and Exodus 29

The dependence of Lev 8 on Exod 29 (until v 37) has been pointed out in the NOTES. By themselves, singly and scattered, the pieces of evidence may not seem so weighty. They are herewith reenumerated and supplemented by additional evidence so that their cumulative effect will be felt.

1. The definite articles on all of the objects in v 2 can only refer to their counterparts in Exod 29. Particularly striking is the expression *sal hammaṣṣôt* 'the basket of unleavened bread', which clearly implies that the reader already knows its contents; these, however, are previously given only in Exod 29:2.

2. *zeh haddābār* (v 5) may be the incipit of Exod 29 and should be rendered "This is the instruction" (but the alternate interpretation given in the NOTE may be preferable).

3. *ṣîṣ hazzāhāb nēzer haqqōdeš* 'the gold plate, the holy diadem' (v 9) is a conflation of *ṣîṣ hazzāhāb* (Exod 28:36) and *nēzer haqqōdeš* (Exod 29:6).

4. The formula *ka'ăšer ṣiwwâ YHWH* 'as the Lord commanded' (v 4, etc.), repeated seven times, refers to specific commands of Exod 29.

5. The consecration of the sanctuary (vv 10aβ–11), absent in Exod 29, has been interpolated here from Exod 40:9–11, as the comparative table (NOTE on v 10) graphically demonstrates. Thus Lev 8 in its final form is subsequent not only to Exod 29 but also to Exod 40.

6. Aaron is daubed with the blood of the ordination ram separately from his sons (vv 23–24) because at this point he has already achieved a holy status by virtue of his anointing (v 12). In Exod 29, however, he and his sons are daubed together (v 20) because they still belong to the same profane order: they will become holy coevally but only after they are sprinkled with the altar blood and anointment oil (v 21). Lev 8 is clearly rewriting Exod 29; we find the same verb sequence—*šāḥaṭ, lāqaḥ, nātan*—to which Lev 8 adds *qārab* and *nātan* for the sons (vv 23–24). This change is particularly striking because here alone Lev 8 expands rather than condenses Exod 29.

7. *'ăšer lipnê YHWH* 'that was before the Lord' (v 26) assumes the prior knowledge that the basket of unleavened bread had been placed before the altar, a datum derivable solely from Exod 29:3.

8. Aaron is not sprinkled together with his vestments, his sons, and their vestments (v 30) because he has already been sanctified by the anointment oil (v 12). Yet Exod 29 insists that he be sprinkled together with his vestments, his sons, and their vestments (v 21) for it is this aspersion with blood and oil that simultaneously sanctifies Aaron and his sons. Surprisingly, the wording of both passages is precisely the same except for the missing *waw* in Lev 8. If Lev 8 were original it would have formulated its view in a less cumbersome way, such as *ʿal bigdê 'ahărōn*, instead of slavishly copying Exodus and resorting to a hendiadys (for details see the NOTE on v 30). Moreover, the double occurrence of *'ittô*

'with him' (v 30) makes no sense in its present context because Aaron himself was not sprinkled with the blood and oil. In Exod 29, however, he is sprinkled (v 21), and there the text states correctly that his sons together with their garments were sprinkled "with him."

9. The sprinkling rite (v 30) follows the *těnûpâ* (vv 25–29), whereas in Exodus the order is reversed (Exod 29:21–26). Exod 29 is more logical because it calls for manipulating the blood of the ordination ram in a continuous act, namely, daubing the priests followed by their sprinkling. Lev 8, by contrast, seems to be governed by literary considerations, specifically its commitment to an introverted structure (details in COMMENT A above).

10. Moses takes the oil before he takes the blood (v 30), but in Exod 29:21 he takes the blood first, then the oil. This distinction, however, is inconsequential because the sing. *wayyaz (wěhizzêtā)* betokens a single act of sprinkling, implying that the two liquids were mixed (for details see the NOTE on v 30).

11. The supplementary admonition that Aaron and his sons dare not leave the sanctuary premises for seven days at pain of death (v 35) is not found in Exod 29. The author of Lev 8 may have been aware of this fact; hence, he changed his regular "cf." notation, *ka'ăšer ṣiwwâ YHWH*, to *kî kēn ṣuwwêtî* 'for so I have been commanded', in other words, this too was commanded me by the Lord.

12. Nothing in the description of the consecration rite implies that it is of seven-day duration; it is the supplement alone that apprizes us of this fact (vv 33–35). That it was not introduced earlier in the text where it logically belongs can only be due to the author's attempt to follow the text of Exod 29 (except where he differs with its order), where the extension of the consecration to seven days also occurs in the appendix (vv 30, 35–37).

Those who maintain that Lev 8, at least in its core, is older than Exod 29 (Levine 1965; Elliger 1966; Walkenhorst 1969) point to two kinds of inequalities between the two chapters: items in Exod 29 missing in Lev 8, which, in their view, indicate that Exod 29 is the expanded and hence later text, and items solely in Lev 8, which, they claim, are original to Lev 8 but have been deleted in Exod 29. At face value, this methodological presupposition can be faulted as being weighted in favor of the theory. Moreover, the evidence that has been adduced is also subject to the following objections: the phrases and clauses of Exod 29 omitted in Lev 8 can be subsumed under three categories: (1) redundancies, (2) motives, and (3) precedents.

(1) Some phrases of Exod 29 would have been redundant in Lev 8, as follows: (a) "The Tent of Meeting" (Exod 29:4, 10, 11) is missing in Lev 8:6, 14, 15, respectively. But because the writer of Lev 8 has taken pains to mention twice at the beginning of the chapter that all of the participants were gathered at the entrance to the Tent of Meeting (8:3–4), there was no need to mention this fact again. (b) The purification offering section in Exod 29 ends with the

phrase *ḥaṭṭāʾt hûʾ* (29:14). It is omitted in Lev 8 for the obvious reason that the bull has already been labeled a *ḥaṭṭāʾt* (8:2, 14 [bis]).

(2) Motive clauses missing in Lev 8 are (a) the expiatory function of the ordination-offering portions eaten by the priests (29:33a), and (b) that its left-overs must be burned "because they are holy" (29:34b). But motive clauses that are fully justifiable in prescriptive texts are out of place in descriptive rituals, which are solely concerned with procedure.

(3) The rites for Aaron's sons (Exod 29:9aγ) and the priestly prebends from the ordination/well-being offering (Exod 27–28) are in the nature of precedents, most apt in prescriptions laid down for all time, but are irrelevant in a descriptive text, which purports to describe what took place at the very first occasion—the initial investiture of Israel's priesthood.

As for the reverse situation, the items in Lev 8 missing in Exod 29 can be shown to be secondary to the text of Lev 8 and clearly additions to or deliberate changes of Exod 29, as follows:

(1) The presence of the *ʿēdâ* (vv 3–5) to witness the priestly consecration has been influenced by the account of the theophany of the eighth day (9:5) or, more likely, by the account of the dedication of Solomon's Temple (1 Kgs 8:1–2; cf. the NOTE on v 3).

(2) The sanctification of Aaron *(lĕqaddĕšô,* v 12) as a result of his anointment is part of the polemic that Lev 8 wages against Exod 29 (see also the NOTE on v 30).

(3) It is true that Lev 8 does not slavishly imitate Exod 29 but resorts to synonyms. In the purification-offering pericope, for example, *yāṣaq* 'poured [the sacrificial blood]' (v 15) replaces the usual term *šāpak* (e.g., 4:7, 18, 25, 30, 34); *ʿal-qarnôt hammizbēaḥ sābîb* 'on the horns around the altar' (v 15), found again only in 16:18, replaces the customary *ʿal qarnôt hammizbēaḥ/mizbaḥ hāʿōlâ,* 'on the horns of the altar'/'the altar of burnt offering' (e.g., 4:18, 25, 30, 34; Exod 29:12); and *wayyaggēš* 'he had brought forward' (v 14), a term hitherto reserved solely for the cereal offering (2:8), substitutes for *wayyaqrēb* (e.g., vv 6, 13, 18, 22; 9:15, 16, 17; cf. Exod 29:3, 4, 8, 10). Yet instead of regarding these peculiarities as signs of an original core in Lev 8, which a purportedly later Exod 29 altered in vocabulary, we can more reasonably assume that the writer of Lev 8 felt free to introduce his own synonymous expressions even while following the text of Exod 29. This explanation finds strong support in Hittite Temple dedication texts, such as the Samsuiluna B inscription, adduced in COMMENT C below. The four parallel sentences of the prescriptive and descriptive text cited there show that although two of the sentences are replicas of each other, the other two show marked variations in vocabulary and style. Thus there is good ancient Near Eastern precedent for the Israelite writer to have inserted his own choice of words and idioms when he described the fulfillment of a command. Indeed, were it not for the other deviations adduced here, which show that Lev 8 represents a viewpoint different from that of Exod 29, it would even be possible

to argue, on the basis of the Hittite precedents, that Exod 29 and Lev 8 could have been written by the same author.

(4) Whereas Lev 8 relates that Aaron was girded *bāʾabnēṭ* 'with a sash' (v 7) and his sons were separately girded with *ʾabnēṭ* 'sashes' (v 13), the text of Exod 29 contains but one command: *wĕḥāgartā ʾōtām ʾabnēṭ ʾahărōn ûbānāyw*, literally, "you shall gird them with sashes, Aaron and his sons" (Exod 29:9). The appositional phrase "Aaron and his sons" is missing in the LXX. If it is an MT gloss, it is a correct one. As nothing has been said about Aaron's sash (see 29:5–6), it is clear that the suffix *ʾōtām* refers back to both Aaron and his sons. Still, the questions remain: Why is not Aaron's sash enumerated with his other vestments, and why must it, separately from the rest of his clothing, be included with his sons' sashes? Indeed, the text of Exod 29 actually gives the impression that Aaron is anointed when he is without his sash (29:7, 9)! The answer, I submit, lies in the unique composition of the sash. Whereas the priests' other vestments are made solely of linen (Exod 28:39), their sashes comprise colored wools and fine linen (Exod 39:29), precisely the same composition as the material worn by the high priest (Exod 28:6, 15) and sewn into the *miškān*, the inner curtain and veil of the Tent of Meeting (Exod 26:1, 31). Thus Exod 29, which does not regard Aaron as holy after he is anointed (see the NOTES on vv 12, 30), is stressing the fact that Aaron and his sons are at this point in their ordination of equal status and that each is entitled to wear the same most holy garment: the multicolored and multifibered sash. Lev 8, instead, which regards Aaron in his postanointment state as holy (v 12), is intent on emphasizing that Aaron is to be dressed with his sash separately from his sons and before his anointment. That it is Lev 8 which has reacted to and altered the text of Exod 29 is supported by the wording: Moses girds *ʾōtām ʾabnēṭ*, literally, "them [with] sashes" (v 13), precisely the same wording as Exod 29:9. By contrast, the girding of Aaron is described as *bāʾabnēṭ*, literally, "with the sash" (v 7). The addition of the preposition would seem to betray the hand of the author of Lev 8, who copied out Exod 29:9 regarding the sons' sashes but added the sash in the description of the dressing of Aaron (v 7).

A word on the composition of the priests' sashes is in order. As remarked above, the sash alone of all the ordinary priests' vestments is composed of wool and linen, the very same materials that comprise the outer garments of the high priest and the inner curtain in the Tent of Meeting. Yet the very mixture of wool and linen, called *šaʿaṭnēz*, is forbidden to the Israelite (Lev 19:19). That this prohibition stems from its holy nature can be derived from the injunction: "you shall not sow your vineyard with a second kind of seed, lest the crop—that from the seed you have sown and the yield of the vineyard—become sanctified *(yiqdaš)*" (Deut 22:9), that is to say, it will be confiscated by the sanctuary. Another biblical injunction commands the Israelite to attach a *pĕtîl tĕkēlet*, a violet cord, to the tassels suspended from his outer garment (Num 15:38). Because garments, unless otherwise specified, were made of linen, the attachment of a cord of violet—in ancient times only wool could successfully be dyed—automatically converted the garment into *ša'aṭnēz*. The Israelite was therefore commanded to weave a single woolen thread into each tassel so that "you shall be reminded to observe all my commandments and to be holy to your God" (Num 15:40).

The requirement that the priest wear a sash of *ša'aṭnēz* completes the picture of graded holiness within the ranks of Israel. The high priest alone wears outer garments of *ša'aṭnēz*, which match the inner Tabernacle curtains. Thus the high priest is sartorially of the same degree of holiness ("most holy") as the area—inside the Tent—in which he officiates. The ordinary priest is of lesser holiness than the high priest. He may not officiate inside the Tent but only on the altar; he is not "most holy" but "holy," and the symbol of his reduced degree of holiness is his *ša'aṭnēz* sash. Finally, the Israelite who may not officiate at all is neither "most holy" nor "holy." Nonetheless he is enjoined to wear *ša'aṭnēz* at the fringes of his outer garment as a reminder that he should aspire to a life of holiness (for details, see Milgrom 1981e; 1983b).

(5) Lev 8 includes the Urim and Thummim among the items donned by the high priest (v 8). The reason for their absence in Exod 29 is not difficult to discover. Exod 29 heads the list of the high priest's vestments with the words *wĕlāqaḥtā 'et-habbĕgādîm* 'You (Moses) shall take the vestments' (29:5). The definite article on *habbĕgādîm* 'the vestments' clearly refers back to the inventory cited in the previous chapter, which reads, "These are the vestments they are to make: a breastpiece, an ephod, a robe, a fringed tunic, a turban, and a sash" (Exod 28:4). Obviously, as the Urim and Thummim are not articles of clothing they are not included in this list. By contrast, when the manufacture, function, and operation of the vestments are detailed, it is only to be expected to find *wĕnātattā 'el-ḥōšen hammišpāṭ 'et-hā'ûrîm wĕ'et-hattummîm* 'You shall place inside the breastpiece of decision the Urim and Thummim' (Exod 28:30aα). Clearly it is this sentence that served as the model for Lev 8:8b: *wayyittēn 'el-haḥōšen 'et-ha'ûrîm wĕ'et-hattummîm* 'he put into the breastpiece the Urim and Thummim'. It should be noted that the articles donned by the high priest in Lev 8:7–9 are not qualified by the word *bĕgādîm* 'vestments'. The author of Lev 8 was solely interested in describing how the high priest was dressed before he was anointed and before he began to officiate. He therefore had to mention the Urim and Thummim because the high priest could not function without them.

C. The Samsuiluna B Inscription

There are many extant texts dealing with the dedication of temples in ancient Mesopotamia. None, however, is more illuminating for the understanding of Lev 8 and its relationship to Exod 29 than the bilingual (Sumerian–Akkadian) Samsuiluna B inscription (Sollberger 1967; French translation in

Sollberger and Kupper 1971). It relates how Samsuiluna, at the command of Šamaš, built the wall of Sippar and restored Šamaš's temple, Ebabbar. The translation of the Akkadian version follows:

1–7   When Enlil, the king of the gods, the great lord of the lands, looked upon Šamaš with his favorable countenance, and

8–24   with his immutable mouth commanded (him) to build the wall of Sippar, the ancient city, his holy city, to restore Ebabbar to its (original) site, to raise the top of its ziggurat, his lofty *gigunû* (as high) as the heavens, that Šamaš and Aya may enter their pure abode in happiness and joy;

25   at that time,

26–32   the heroic youth Šamaš was commissioned to (fulfill) the destiny which Enlil had decreed for Sippar and for Ebabbar as if for a festival.

33–38   Samsuiluna, the king made by his own hands, me, he happily appointed and (he) instructed me of that command.

39   At that time,

40–54   the entire land of Sumer and Akkad which had been hostile toward me, within the course of a single year I defeated by arms eight times. The cities of my enemies I turned into rubble heaps and ruins. I eradicated from the land the root of my enemies and of evil (doers). The entire land I brought under my command.

55–62   Since from days of yore, since the time the brick(work) of Ebabbar had been built, Šamaš had not been favorable to any king among the previous kings and (no one among them) had built the wall of Sippar;

63–78   Samsuiluna, the beloved of Šamaš and Aya, the mighty king, the king of Babylon, the king of the four regions of the earth, the king whose word is acceptable to Šamaš and Aya, I, at the command of Šamaš and Marduk, with the enlisted work force of my land, molded bricks during that year.

79–95   The wall of Sippar I raised like a great mountain. I renewed Ebabbar. I raised (as high) as the heavens the top of the ziggurat, its lofty *gigunû*. Šamaš, Adad, and Aya I brought into their pure abodes amid happiness and joy. I restored to Ebabbar its favorable protective genius/vigorous look.

96–101   I did that which was favorable to Šamaš, Adad, and Aya. I fulfilled the command of Šamaš and Marduk.

102–6 The name of that wall is "Šamaš has granted Samsuiluna excel-
       lent strength and good health."

107–23 In return for this, Šamaš, who raises the head of his kingship,
        has given him as a gift a long life of health and happiness,
        an unrivaled kingship, a righteous scepter that stabilizes the
        land, a mighty weapon that slays the enemy, and eternal
        mastery of the four regions of the earth.

Most significant for the present purpose is the fact that the buildings are
described twice, first by the divine instigation of the project in his initial command and later by the narrator, speaking on behalf of the king, in his description
of the fulfillment. This is precisely the situation in the Tabernacle story in
which the priestly consecration is first described by God, the instigator, in his
command to his messenger Moses, and subsequently by the narrator in his
description of how Moses implemented the divine command.

The command (prescription) and implementation (description) sections of
the Samsuiluna B inscription will now be compared:

The Command (lines 8–21)

1. to build the wall of Sippar, the ancient city, his holy city
    (UD.KIB.NUN^{ki} URU și-a-tim ma-ha-su BÀD-šu e-pé-ša-am)

2. to restore Ebabbar to its site
    (é-babbar a-na aš-ri-šu tu-ur-ra-am)

3. to raise the top of its ziggurat, his lofty *gigunû* as the heavens
    (U$_6$.NIR gi-gu-na-šu și-ra-am re-ši-ša ki-ma ša-me-e ul-la-a-am)

4. that Šamaš and Aya may enter their pure abode in happiness and joy
    (^{d}UTU ù ^{d}a'ya a-na šu-ub-ti-šu-nu el-le-tim in re-ša-tim ù ḫi-di-a-tim
    e-re-ba)

The Implementation (lines 79–92)

1'. The wall of Sippar I raised like a great mountain
     (BÀD UD.KIB.NUN^{ki} ki-ma SA.TU^{im} ra-bi-im ú-ul-li)

2'. I renewed Ebabbar
     (é-babbar ú-ud-di-iš)

3'. I raised as the heavens the top of the ziggurat, its lofty *gigunû*
     (U$_6$.NIR gi-gu-na-šu și-ra-am re-ši-ša ki-ma ša-me-e ú-ul-li)

4'.   Šamaš, Adad, and Aya I brought into their pure abodes amid happiness and joy

(ᵈUTU ᵈIM ù ᵈAya a-na šu-ub-ti-šu-nu el-le-tim in re-ša-tim ù ḫi-da-
tim ú-še-ri-ib)

The tenses of the verbs in the command differ from those in the implementation. The verbs in the command are infinitives, objects of the verb *iqbiu* 'he
commanded' (lines 2–4), while in the implementation section they are simple
preterites. So too in the biblical consecration account: in the command (Exod
29) the verbs are either in the imperfect or in the perfect tense with the sequential *waw*, while the corresponding verbs in the implementation (Lev 8) are in the
simple perfect tense or in the imperfect with the sequential *waw*.

Of greater significance is the fact that whereas the last two statements in
the command and fulfillment pericopes (3, 3' and 4, 4') are nearly identical in
language, the first two (1, 1' and 2, 2') differ sharply from each other. "To build
the wall of Sippar, the ancient city, his holy city" is replaced by "The wall of
Sippar I raised like a great mountain." And "to restore Ebabbar to its site"
becomes "I renewed Ebabbar." Thus the Babylonian scribe allowed himself the
privilege of changing all of the verbs; from "build" to "raise" and "restore" to
"renew" and to substitute for the epithets of Sippar, "the ancient city, his holy
city," the simile "like a great mountain." Should we then wonder that the
author of Lev 8 felt free to curtail the account of Exod 29 (particularly when
much was irrelevant to his purposes; see COMMENT B above) and to resort to
synonymous expressions (e.g., *šāpak* and *yāṣaq* 'pour'; *higgîš* and *hiqrîb* 'brought
forward'; see COMMENT B).

The Babylonian scribe actually added elements to the implementation section not found in the command. Although he writes that Šamaš had been
commanded by Enlil that just Šamaš and Aya should be seated in their abodes,
he states in the implementation section that Samsuiluna seated Šamaš, Aya, and
Adad as well. This additional god is further mentioned in the concluding refrain
(line 96), where it is stated that the king did that which was good before Šamaš,
Adad, and Aya. The scribe also adds (lines 93–94) that the king restored to
Ebabbar ᵈLAMA-šu da-mi-iq-tam (literally, "the good protecting divinity," figuratively as the vigorous or bright look of the temple [A. Hurowitz]), a datum
wholly absent in the command section. The author of Lev 8 thus need not have
had any compunctions about adding items concerning the *ʿēdâ* (vv 3–5), the
Urim and Thummim (v 8), the *peder* (v 20), and the supplement concerning the
seven-day prohibitions (vv 33–35). Unless one is willing to argue that the alternatives and additions in the Samsuiluna B implementation section are due to
another scribal hand, it is entirely gratuitous to presume that the changes in
Lev 8 do not stem from the same author.

Finally, note should be taken of the scribe's additional remark in the implementation section: qí-bi-it ᵈUTU ù ᵈAMAR.UD a-na aš-ri-im aš-ku-un 'I ful-filled the command of Šamaš and Marduk' (lines 99–101). This closing remark is obviously analogous to the sevenfold refrain that appears in the implementation account of Lev 8.

Therefore it may be concluded that the Samsuiluna B inscription demonstrates that (1) a prescriptive text may be expected to be followed by a descriptive text that repeats, at times verbatim, all of the essential information; (2) the repetition need not be literal; ample latitude is given to the scribe in the implementation section to alter the vocabulary and curtail or add to his account; and (3) the implementation section records that the command was fulfilled.

Because the Samsuiluna B inscription deals with the construction of a temple it has even more relevance for the relation between the command to build the Tabernacle (Exod 25–30) and the account of its implementation (Exod 35–40), as discussed by A. Hurowitz (1985).

D. The Purpose of Anointing

The main role of symbolic anointment in the ancient Near East, aside from its cosmetic, therapeutic, and magical functions, was to ceremonialize an elevation in legal status: the manumission of a slave woman, the transfer of property, the betrothal of a bride, and the deputation of a vassal, and—in Israel—the inauguration of a king, the ordination of a priest, and the rehabilitation of a meṣōrāᶜ. These cases indicate that in Israel symbolic unction took place in the cult but not in legal proceedings. This sharp distinction between the sacred and the profane is further illustrated by the discrete Hebrew roots employed in each realm: "the oil of sacred anointing *(mšḥ)* . . . shall not be rubbed *(swk)* on a person's body" (Exod 30:31–32); similarly throughout the Bible, *mšḥ* implies that the anointment stems from God (2 Sam 1:21; Jer 22:14 [cf. Isa 21:5] are the possible exceptions). The attribute *māšîaḥ* ('anointed') came to designate the king and the high priest and, by extension, other divinely appointed functionaries who were not anointed at all, such as the prophets (1 Kgs 19:16b; Isa 61:1), the patriarchs (Ps 105:15), and even foreign kings (1 Kgs 19:15; Isa 45:1; cf. 2 Kgs 8:7). This figurative use of *mšḥ* is not a later development, for it is already attested in Ugaritic (*UT* 76.2.22–23; cf. Ps 89:21 and 25). The implication of anointing as a sacred rite is that the anointed one receives divine sanction and that his person is inviolable (1 Sam 24.7, 8, 26.9, 11, 16, 23, 2 Sam 1:14, 16; 19:22).

Outside of Israel royal unction is thus far unknown except among the Hittites, where its meaning is unclear. In Israel anointment conferred upon the king the *rûaḥ YHWH* ('the spirit of the Lord'), that is to say, his support (1 Sam 16:13–14; 18:12), strength (Ps 89:21–25), and wisdom (Isa 11:1–4). The anointment of the high priest, however, served an entirely different function. It conferred neither *rûaḥ* nor any other divine attribute. Moses, for example, transferred his powers (by hand-leaning) to a *rûaḥ*-endowed Joshua (Num 27:18–20), but when he transferred the high priest's authority from Aaron to his son Eleazar, these spiritual features are conspicuously absent (Num 20:25–29). In the story of Joshua's investiture—told by P—Eleazar is declared the indispensable medium to ascertain the Divine will, but, tellingly, not by virtue of any innate spiritual powers, rather by his authority to work the oracle (Num 27:21). This instance is a vivid illustration of the function of the high priest's anointment, which is otherwise designated by the verb *qiddēš* ('to sanctify'). Indeed, the anointment "sanctifies" the high priest by removing him from the realm of the profane and empowering him to operate in the realm of the sacred, namely, to handle the sancta.

Critics have long postulated that the high priesthood is a late, postexilic phenomenon, modeled after the office of the king (e.g., Noth 1965). The respective functions of their anointment render this unlikely. The high priest undergoes the ubiquitous legal change of status, albeit in the sacred sphere, not the secular one. Conversely, the king incorporates divine attributes through unction, a phenomenon attested nowhere else. Thus, if anything, royal unction is derivative. History also leans toward this conclusion: sacred anointing ceased at the end of the Second Temple period and, according to rabbinic tradition, by the end of the First Temple period (*t. Soṭa* 13:1). Scripture makes the reason clear: the sacred oil was compounded only once and, having been lost or destroyed, it could not be reproduced (Exod 30:31–33; contrast the incense, v 34). Moreover, the high priest was anointed in conjunction with the cult objects (Exod 40:9–15), and the latter practice is found in the oldest portions of the Bible (anointment of pillars, Gen 28:18; 31:13; 35:14). Finally, the story of Solomon's anointment by the high priest Zadok (1 Kgs 1:39) could not be an interpolation of the Priestly editors, for the latter would by their own law have condemned Zadok to death (by God) for the crime of anointing a *zār*, a nonpriest (Exod 30:33). To the contrary, this incident complements the image of the king in the historical narratives: because he may officiate at the sacred altar like a priest (e.g., 1 Kgs 3:4; 8:63–64), why should he not be similarly anointed with the sacred oil? The most telling evidence, however, is extrabiblical. In Assyria and Babylonia not the kings, but a certain class of priests bore the name *pašīšu* 'anointed', attesting to the custom of anointing religious functionaries. Among the Hittites both kings and priests were anointed. The priestly class *tazzelli* (= Sum. GUDU. = Akk. *pašīšu*) was by its very name the class of "anointed ones" (Hoffner 1973: 218). Thus in civilizations anterior to Israel, the anointing of the king was, at least, optional but the anointing of a certain class of priests was required.

According to P, the sons of Aaron were anointed with him. Although the word *māšaḥ* is used (e.g., Exod 40:15a), it means only that they received the sacred oil and implies nothing about the manner of its application. Indeed, the respective ceremonies differ sharply: the sons were sprinkled *(hizzâ)* after the sacrifice (8:30; Exod 29:21), whereas Aaron's head was doused *(yāṣaq)* separately, before the entire service (8:12; Exod 2:7). Furthermore, whereas each succeeding high priest was anointed (6:15), the anointing of the first priests was never repeated; it was to be valid for their posterity (Exod 29:9b; 40:15b). This concept has proved to be ancient, for it is found in the Tel-el-Amarna letters, where a vassal stakes his authority on his grandfather's anointment (*EA* 51.4–9). The difference between the status of the high priest and that of the ordinary priests explains the difference between their consecratory rites. The high priest was born a priest, a status that is inherited and requires no special sanctification. The high priest, however, would require a special inaugural rite to elevate him to this position.

The *mĕṣōrāᶜ* was anointed on the eighth and concluding day of his purification ritual, but the oil was not sacred. The sevenfold sprinkling of the oil "before the Lord" (14:16) even before it could be used on the *mĕṣōrāᶜ* is clearly a rite of consecration; moreover, the indispensable verb *māšaḥ* is tellingly absent. Once again, the "change of status" is operative: the banishment of the erstwhile *mĕṣōrāᶜ* has ended and he is free to reenter society.

Whether the anointment rite was originally operative in Israel's legal procedures in the manner of her neighbors can no longer be ascertained. A clue that Israelite brides may once have been anointed lies in the surviving term for betrothal, *qiddûšîn* ('consecration'), and in the present-day betrothal formula, "Behold you are consecrated [*mĕquddešet*] to me" (cf. *t. Qidd.* 2b), which, though found only in rabbinic sources, are undoubtedly older (see further Milgrom 1971c).

E. Moses as Priest

R. Yudan citing R. Joseph ben R. Judah and R. Berechiah citing R. Joshua ben Qorḥa, said: During all the forty years that Israel was in the wilderness, Moses did not hesitate to perform the functions of the high priest, for Scripture says, "Moses and Aaron among his priests" (Ps 99:6). . . . R. Eliezer bar R. Joseph taught: (There is no need to seek out the inference from Scripture). We have a tradition that Moses, wearing a priestly white linen garment, served as high priest in the wilderness. However, said R. Tanḥum bar R. Yudan, a baraita (*Sipra, Shemini Milluʾim* 14) tells us that during the seven days of the priests' ordination when Moses was serving as high priest, the Presence did not, through Moses' agency, come down to dwell in the world. It was (only on the eighth day) when Aaron also began to serve as high priest that, through Aaron's agency, it came down to dwell in the world. (*Pesiq. Rab Kah.* 4.5)

According to this rabbinic midrash, the psalmist's claim that Moses was as much a priest as Aaron leads one group of rabbis to aver that Moses 'indeed served as a high priest during the entire wilderness sojourn. But another sage not only limits Moses' priesthood to the seven-day consecration of Aaron and his sons but even belittles its importance because the theophany was postponed to the eighth day, when Aaron began to officiate (9:24).

Actually there is no substantive evidence in the early biblical narratives that would support the psalmist's claim. The text adduced most often, the covenant ceremonial at Sinai (Exod 24:4–8), explicitly states that others, not Moses, offered up the sacrificial animals on the altar. True, Moses manipulates the blood, casting some on the altar and the rest on the people. But here he acts not as a priest but as a covenant maker. And it has been firmly established that blood rites in covenant sacrifices were generally "performed not by priests but by kings and chieftains" (Cody 1969: 43; e.g., *ANET* ³ 532–33). The claim that Moses learned his priestly craft from Jethro (Exod 18:22) carries no weight. The reason that Jethro, the guest, officiates and not Moses, the host, is not that Moses wanted to be instructed by Jethro (Gray 1925: 208) but, more obviously, that Jethro was a priest and Moses was not. A stronger bit of evidence is the claim of the Danite priesthood to be of Mosaic lineage (Judg 18:30; cf. *b. B. Bat.* 109b), but it may rest on the tradition that Moses was a Levite—that is, entitled to be a priest—not that he actually served as one.

Yet P states unequivocally that Moses officiated at the priestly consecration and that, moreover, he even received in part the priestly prebends from the sacrifices (8:29b). What can be the basis of this Priestly tradition?

The immediate answer is obvious: who else but Moses! Someone had to install the priests and someone had to officiate in the sanctuary before the priests were installed (Exod 40:22–27). Because, according to P, Israel as yet did not have a legitimate, divinely ordained priesthood, the installer *ipso facto* had to be a nonpriest. Moreover, as it was Moses alone to whom the proper sacrificial procedure was revealed (Lev 1–7), he would have been the only person sufficiently qualified both to impart the divine instructions to Aaron and his sons and to demonstrate the proper procedures by his personal example (*Sipra*, Millu'im Ṣaw 14).

This indirect reasoning finds substantive support from the direct evidence contained in Mesopotamian documents. The ample texts describing temple dedications also, on occasion, speak of the investiture of the temple's priesthood. And the same person who dedicates the temple also invests its priesthood—the king. LUGAL ÍL-*ut* EN.NA (= *našūt ēni) ippuš tillēšu ebbūti illabšu* 'the king performs the ceremony of the installation of the high priest, he puts on his clear apparel' (*R. Acc.* 73.16; cited in *CAD*, E 1799, 3'). Esarhaddon boasts LÚ *i-šip-pí āšipī kalê nārē . . . ušziz maḫaršun* 'I assigned (lit., 'installed') to them (the rituals of Esagila) purification priests, *āšipu* priests, exorcisers, and temple singers' (Borger, Esarhaddon 24 vi 24; cited in *CAD*, I/J 242–43). In other words,

Moses officiates at the dedication of the Tabernacle and the investiture of the priests in his capacity as leader of his people—as their king.

To be sure, Moses is no ordinary king. "After all we don't know of [Israel's] kings investing and consecrating priests. It is the other way around, and it is most significant that no one consecrates or invests Moses. His authority comes directly from God and is not mediated as is the power of both priests and kings" (D. N. Freedman, written communication). These strictures are well founded. Moses' prophetic role, indeed, as the founder of the prophetic movement, over-shadows all his other roles, even those of legislator, administrator, and warrior—not to mention king. As indicated above, however, there is ancient precedent in Israel's environment for kings investing priests. Even more significant is that Moses himself acts as priest—indeed, as Israel's first priest, the one who not only established Israel's cult but also officiated alone during the first week of its existence.

It should not surprise us that Moses' regal role entitles him to act as priest. The historical texts of the Bible clearly show that Israel's kings offered sacrifices: for instance, Saul at Gilgal (1 Sam 13:9–10), David at Jerusalem (2 Sam 6:13, 17–18; 24:25), Solomon at Gibeon (1 Kgs 3:4, 15) and at Jerusalem (1 Kgs 8:5, 62–64; 9:25). As de Vaux points out (1961a: 113–14), although some of these texts can be taken in the factitive sense, that the king "had sacrifice offered," other texts unambiguously assign the cultic action to the king. For example, Jeroboam "ascended the altar to sacrifice" (1 Kgs 12:32–33; cf. 1 Kgs 13:1); "the king (Ahaz) drew near the altar, ascended it, and offered his burnt offering and cereal offering; he poured his libation, and he dashed the blood of his offering of well-being against the altar" (2 Kgs 16:12–13). The latter account is most in-structive, for it continues, "and King Ahaz commanded the priest Uriah: 'On the great altar you shall offer the morning burnt offering and the evening cereal offering and the king's burnt offering and his cereal offering, with the burnt offerings of all the people of the land, their cereal offerings and their libations. And against it you shall dash the blood of all the burnt offerings and all the blood of the sacrifices' " (v 15). Thus it is clear that Ahaz only initiated the sacrificial service on the new, "great" altar but thereafter turned over these duties to the high priest. Possibly, Solomon himself officiated at the altar on the day he dedicated the Temple (1 Kgs 8:63–64). In other words, there is ample precedent both in Israel and in its environment that the king had the right to officiate in the cult and indeed exercised it, especially on the occasion of the dedication of the Temple and the installation of its priesthood.

Yet it is also true that P is uneasy about Moses' priestly role. The *Sipra*, cited above, is certainly correct that the postponement of the theophany to the eighth day (Lev 9:23–24) intentionally bypasses Moses in his capacity as priest in order to confer divine sanction upon Aaron and his sons. Moreover, even during his week-long ministry, Moses is not accorded the full privileges of the priesthood. His prebends from the ordination ram are limited to the breast

(8:29), while he is expressly denied the right thigh (vv 26–28), the very portion that automatically and exclusively belongs to the officiating priest (7:32–33). Moses, then, according to P, was the interim priest only by necessity and divine dispensation.

F. The Priestly Consecration According to the Temple Scroll

The relevant text and translation of 11QT 15:3–16:4 (Yadin 1983: 61–72) follow:

3 כמשפט הזה [?] יולמלואים איל איל לכול' [יום ריום]

3א [ו]סלי לחם לכול אי]לי המלואים סל אחד לא]יל

4 [ה]אחד וחצו את כו[ו]יל האילים והסלים לשבע'[ת ימי המלואים לכול]

5 [יום] רום כמחלקו[תיהמה] י'היו מקריבים ליהוה את שוק הימין'

6 עולה מן האי'ל ו[את החלב המכסה את הקרב ואת] ישתי'

7 הכליות ואת [ה]חלב [יאשר עלי'[הנה ואת החלב אשר על]

8 הכסלים ואת האלי'ה תמימה [ילעומת עציהה ואת יותרת הכבד'

9 ומנחתו ונסכו כמ[שפט ולקחו חלת מצה אחת מן ה]יסל וחלת'

10 לחם שמן אחת ורקיק' [אחד ושמו הכול על החלבים]

11 עם שוק התרומה אשיר לימין ריניפו ה.מקריבים את'

12 האלים ואת סלי הלחם ת[נופה ל]'פני יהוה עולה היא'

13 אשה ריח ניחוח לפני יהוֹה] והקסירו הכול המזבחה על]

14 העולה למלא על נפשותמה שבי'ע'ת ימי'[ן המלואים]]]

15 ואם הכוהן הג[דול יהיה עוֹמ[ד] לשרת לפני יהוה אשר] מלא

16 י'ד'ו' לל[ו]כו[ל]ש את ה]בנדים תחת אב]י'יהו ריקרי[ב פר]

17 [אחד ע[ל כול העם] ואחד על ה]כ[ו]הנים ריקרב את אשר'

18 [לכוה]'נ'ו'ם בריאש'ינה' וסמכו זקני הכוהנ[ים את ידיהמה]

CONSECRATION

01 ‫[על ראו]ישו ואחריהמה ה[י]כו[ו]יהֹן הגֹדֹול וכול הֹ[י]כוהנים ושחטו את] יהפרֹ׳‬

02 ‫[לפני יהוה]יולקחו זקני הכוהֹנֹים מדם הפר ו[נתנו]ימן הד[י]ם באצבעם על קרנות]‬

03 ‫[המזבח ואת הדם]יישפוכו סביב על אֹ[י]ר[ב]בֹ פנות עזרת הֹ[י]מזבח‬ ‫[‬

04 ‫[‬ ‫]‬

1 ‫[‬ ‫].שֹ[‬ ‫]‬

2 ‫[ולקחו מדמו ונֹ[תנו מן הדם [על תנוך אוזנו הימנית ועל בוהן ידו]‬

3 ‫[הימנית ורגלו]הימנית ריזו] מן הדם אשר על המזבח עליו ועל בגדיו]‬

4 ‫[ ] קדש יֹ[ה]יה כול ימֹיו] ועל כול נפשות מת לוא יבוא]‬

5 ‫[לאביו ולאמו לוא]יֹסמא כי קדֹ[ו]ֹש הוא ליהוה אלוהֹיו‬ ‫[‬

6 ‫[והקריב על המזֹ[בח והקסיר אֹ[ת חלב הפר הראישֹן‬ ‫[‬

7 ‫[את כול] החלב אשֹר על הקרב ואֹ[ת יותרת הכבד ואת שתי]‬

8 ‫[הכל]יֹזת ואת החלב אשר עליהֹ[נה] יוֹאֹ[י]ֹת החלב אשר על]‬

9 ‫[הכסלים ואת מנחתו ואת נֹס[וכו כמשפסמה] יירקסי[רמה המזבחה]‬

10 ‫[עו]לֹלה הוא אשה ריח ניחוח ל[ו]פני יהוה]   [ואת בשר הפר]‬

11 ‫[ואת עורו עם פרשו ישרופו מחוֹין ל[י]עיר המקדש(?) על עצים באש(?)]]‬

12 ‫[במקום מובדל לחסאות שמה ישֹרֹ[ופו אותו על ראושו וכרעיו]‬

13 ‫[עם כול קרביו ושרפו כולו שמה לבד מחלבו חֹטֹ[אֹת]‬

14 ‫[הֹוא ויקח הפר השני אשר לעם ויכפר בֹוֹ[ן] על כול עם]‬

15 ‫[הקהל בדמו ובחלבו כאשר עשה לפר הראֹישֹו[ֹן כן יעשה]‬

16 ‫[לפר הקהל ויתן מדמו באצבעו על קרנות הֹ[מזבח ואת כול]‬

17 ‫[דמו יזרוק ע[ל אר]בֹע פנות המזבח ואתֹ[] חלבו ואת]‬

18 ‫[מנֹ]חֹתו ואת נֹ[וסכ]ו יקסֹי[ו]ֹר המזבח חסאת קהל הֹא‬

3   according to this ordinance. ⟦ ? ⟧ ⌐And for the ordination, one ram for every⌐ [day,]

3a   [and] baskets of bread for all the ra[ms of the ordination, one basket for the] one

4   [ram.] And they shall divide a[l]⌐l the rams and the baskets for the seve⌐[n days of ordination for every]

5   day, according to [their] divisions ⌐they shall offer to the Lord the right thigh⌐

6   of the ram, a burnt offering, and [the fat that covers the entrails, and the] ⌐two⌐

7   kidneys and [the] fat ⌐that is on the⌐[m, and the fat that is on]

8 the loins, and the [entire] fat tai[l] ⌐near its backbone, and the appendage of the liver,¬

9 and its cereal offering and its drink offering, according to the ord[i-
nance. And they shall take one unleavened cake from the] ⌐basket
and one cake¬

10 of bread with oil and [one] wa⌐fer,¬ [and they shall put it all on the
fats]

11 with the offering o⌐f the right¬ thigh; ⌐and those that sacrifice shall
wave the¬

12 r{a}ms and the bread baskets, a wa[ve offering be]⌐fore the Lord; it is a
burnt offering,¬

13 an offering by fire, a pleasing odour before the Lord. [And they shall
burn everything on the altar over]

14 the burnt offering, to complete their own ordination, (throughout) the
sev⌐en days of¬ [ordination. ⟦   ⟧]

15 And if the high priest will be about [to serve the Lord, (the priest) who]
has been or-

16 d⌐ained¬ to w[ea]r the garments in place of ⌐his¬ father, ⌐he shall
offe¬r [one bull]

17 [fo]r all the peo[ple] and one for the pries⌐ts; he shall offer the one of
the¬

18 [prie]⌐st¬s fir⌐st.¬ And the elders of the priest[s] shall lay [their hands]

01 [upon] ⌐its¬ [hea]⌐d, and after them the high¬[pr]⌐iest and all the¬
[priests. And they shall kill] ⌐the bull¬

02 [before the Lord.] ⌐And the elders of the priests shall take some of the
blood of the bull, and¬ [shall put] ⌐some of the bloo¬[d with their
finger on the horns of the]

03 [altar, and the (rest of) the blood] ⌐they shall pour around on the
f¬[ou]¬r corners of the ledge of the¬ [altar   ]

04 [   ]

1 [   ]⊗∞[   ]

2 [And they shall take some of its blood and p]ut some of the blood [on
the tip of his right ear and on the thumb of his right]

3 [hand and on the great toe of his] right [foot.] And they shall sprinkle
[some of the blood that was on the altar upon him and his garments]

4 [he] shall be [holy] all his days. [And he shall not go near
any dead body,]

5 [nor] defile himself, [even for his father or for his mother;] for [he is]
   hol[y to the Lord his God   ]
6 [And he shall sacrifice upon the al]tar and burn th[e fat of the first
   bull   ]
7 [all] the fat that is on the entrails and th[e appendage of the liver and
   the two]
8 [kid]neys and the fat that is on the[m] ⌐and th⌐[e fat that is on]

9 the loins, and its cereal offering and [its] drink [offering, according to
   their ordinance,] ⌐and he shall bur⌐[n them on the altar,]
10 a burnt [offering] it shall be, an offering by fire, a pleasing odour be[fore
   the Lord. ⟦   ⟧ But the flesh of the bull]
11 and its skin with its dung they shall burn out⌐side the⌐ [temple city(?)
   on a fire of wood(?),]
12 in a place set apart for the sin offerings; there th[ey] shall bur[n it with
   its head and its legs,]
13 with all its entrails. And they shall burn all of it there, except its fat; it
   is a sin [offering.]

14 And he shall take the second bull, which is for the people, and shall
   make with it atonement [for all the people of]
15 the assembly, with its blood and with its fat; as he did with the fir[st]
   bull, [so he shall do]
16 with the bull for the assembly; he shall put some of its blood with his
   finger on the horns of the [altar, and all the rest of]
17 its blood he shall sprinkle o[n the f]our corners of the ledge of the altar,
   and [its fat and]
18 its [cereal] offering and its [drink] offering he shall b[u]rn upon the altar;
   it is the sin offering for the assembly.

According to Yadin (1977: 1.76–79; 1983: 91–96), the Scroll's innovations
are as follows:

1. The priestly consecration takes place yearly (cf. Lev 7:37; Ezek 43:26
    LXX versus *b. Sukk.* 43a; *Menaḥ.* 45a);

2. The seven-day consecration service begins on the first of Nisan (Exod
    40:1, 17; Rabbi Akiba, *Sipra*, Num 68 versus *Sipra*, Milluʾim Ṣaw 36);

3. The sacrificial items, the same for each of the seven days, are prepared
    in advance and distributed among the seven priestly divisions (11QT
    15:4–5);

4. The *tĕnûpâ* (elevation rite) is performed solely by the priestly consec-
    rands (15:11, and see below);

5. Two purification bulls and not one are sacrificed at the high priest's consecration (11QT 15:6–8; Exod 29:36; cf. Num 8:8); and

6. The high priest replaces the elders of the priests as the officiant after he is daubed and sprinkled with the blood of the ordination ram (16:2, 14–18; see below).

First it should be noted that the Scroll's account of the consecration of the ordinary priests, in contrast to that of the high priest, is severely truncated. Nothing is said about the purification bull (Lev 8:14–17; Exod 29:10–14), the burnt-offering ram (Lev 8:18–21; Exod 29:16–18), and—its most striking omission—the blood ceremonial: the daubing of the blood of the ordination ram upon the extremities of the priests and the sprinkling of the altar blood upon their persons and clothing (Lev 8:22–24; Exod 29:19–21). The Scroll only deals with the sacrifice of the priests' ordination ram (15:5–14; cf. Lev 8:25–28; Exod 29:22–25). The reason for these wholesale omissions is not too difficult to discern. It seems that the author of the Scroll wrote down only the parts of the consecration ceremonial in which he differed with the interpretation endorsed by the mainstream. In other words, his text is a polemic. This is strikingly evident in the prescription for the high priest's consecration, which deals exclusively with the sacrifice of two purification bulls, a matter that is absent from the biblical text, and may only with difficulty be inferred from it (Exod 29:36). The reason that the Scroll introduced a second purification bull can be surmised: it allows the altar to be decontaminated and sanctified by a discrete purification bull before the sacrificial series for the priestly consecration commenced (details in the NOTE on v 15).

According to the Temple Scroll, the first bull is sacrificed on behalf of the priests, the second bull on behalf of the people (15:16–18). The former is commanded by Scripture (Exod 29:10; Lev 8:14); the latter is totally the Scroll's initiative. Its innovation can be inferred from the existential difference between the Scroll and the Bible. Whereas the consecration of Aaron and his sons takes place in a brand new sanctuary, the consecration service of the Scroll takes place in a sanctuary that has presumably been polluted during the preceding year by all of Israel. Therefore the altar must be purged of Israel's sins as well as of those of the priests.

Where, however, did Qumran find a scriptural warrant for so radical an innovation? I submit that it was found in the book of Ezekiel, which ordains that each year on the first day of the first month the Temple is to be purged by a purification bull (Ezek 45:18–19). It surely did not go unnoticed by Qumran that Ezekiel's date corresponds to the annual priestly consecration rite. Although it did not go as far as the prophet and prescribe that the entire sacred compound be purged by the purification bull—in effect a minor Yom Kippur—it nonetheless added Ezekiel's bull to the one brought by the priests in order to ensure that the altar would be totally purged of the pollution caused it by the people.

The prescription for the consecration of the regular priests, as sparse as it is, only underscores its innovations: the advance preparation of all required sacrificial material and its distribution among the priestly divisions (15:3–5) and the execution of the elevation rite solely by the priestly consecrands (15:11–12)—all at variance with the received tradition. Thus the entire text of the priestly consecration in the Temple Scroll can be viewed as a polemic against prevailing practice in the Jerusalem Temple. The following refinements need also be added:

(1) Yadin points to the innovation of the Scroll in prescribing that the offerers of the sacrificial ram, the priestly consecrands, execute the *tĕnûpâ*, the elevation rite (15:11), whereas in the biblical text, this rite is performed by the officiant, Moses (Exod 29:24; Lev 8:27). First let it be noted that, on this point, the Scroll is truly an exception. In all attested cases of the *tĕnûpâ*, the officiating priest performs the rite (Milgrom 1973a: 41–45). True, the objects undergoing *tĕnûpâ* must be brought by the offerers and, in some cases, the text insists that the priest perform the rite while the objects are still in their hands (e.g., the priestly consecration, Exod 29:24–25; Lev 8:27–28; the Nazirite who has completed his term, Num 6:19–20). Even in these cases, however, the priest places his hands under those of the offerer and initiates the elevation. Ostensibly, the breast of the well-being offering is elevated by the offerer himself without the assistance of the priest. But in the text dealing with this ritual, *yādāyw tĕbî'ennâ . . . 'et hehāzeh lĕhānîp 'ōtô tĕnûpâ lipnê YHWH* 'His own hands shall bring . . . the breast to be elevated as an elevation offering before the Lord' (Lev 7:30), the verb must be rendered as a passive (*pace* Yadin). And the early rabbis and the later Karaites were certainly correct in assuming that in this case too the priest placed his hands under those of the offerer and thereafter executed the elevation (*Sipra*, Ṣaw par. 11:3; *Seper Hamibḥar*, ad loc.). Thus the Scroll's demand that the offerers—who in this case are priests—perform the elevation by themselves is truly an exception to the rule. How can it be explained?

I would suggest that the key to the solution is found in the fact (noted by Yadin) that in the consecration of the high priest the latter begins to officiate as soon as he is consecrated by the blood of the consecration ram (16:6, 14–18). What basis did the author of the Scroll find for it in Scripture? As noted, the high priest takes over the officiating from the elders of the priests as soon as he is sanctified by the blood of the consecration ram, though in the middle of the ritual. By the same token it can be assumed that the priestly consecrands officiate as priests as soon as they are consecrated by the sacrificial blood. Because the Scroll follows the text of Exodus in stating that the blood ceremonial takes place before the elevation rite (cf. Exod 29:20–21, 23–24; contrast Lev 8:24, 27, 30), then the priests execute the elevation rite not just as offerers but also as officiants, in agreement with all other cases of *těnûpâ*, which show that the rite is performed by the officiating priest.

It must therefore be presumed that, in disagreement with his contemporaries, the author of the Scroll read the biblical prescription for the elevation ritual as follows: *wěśamtā [wayittēn ʾet-] hakkōl ʿal kappê ʾahărōn wěʿal kappê bānāyw wěhēnaptā [wayyānep] ʾōtām těnûpâ lipnê YHWH* 'And you shall place (and he placed) all of these on the palms of Aaron and on the palms of his sons and designate them (he designated them) as an elevation offering' (Exod 29:24; Lev 8:27). And he would have had irrefutable biblical support for his rendering. In the induction service for the Levites, Moses again is the subject of *wěhēnaptā ʾōtām těnûpâ* (Num 8:11, 21). Moses, then, merely serves to order the elevation of the Levites. For the author of the Temple Scroll a similar procedure is invoked for the consecration of the priests: Moses ordered the elevation rite, but it is the priests themselves who execute the ritual.

(2) If the reconstruction *[qādôš yi]hyeh kôl yāmâw* '[holy sh]all [he] be all his days' (16:4) is correct, then it implies that the prohibitions of Lev 21:10–15 are in force for the entire lifetime of the high priest and not just the seven days of his consecration. This is also the plain meaning of the biblical text: the high priest may not leave the sacred precincts to attend the burial rites even of his parents.

The prohibition stipulating that a high priest may not even view a corpse is not unique to Israel. It is attested ubiquitously in antiquity. The alarm is sounded when Dumuzi returns from the land of the dead: "O temple of Ur! Lock your house, city lock your house! Your *entu*-priestess must not go out of her house . . ." (translation of T. Jacobsen, 1961: 208). The dead must be kept away from the city and temple, but the chief priestess may not even expose herself to the open air of the street. The vulnerability of the most sacred realm reaches down to the end of pagan times: the Roman high priest sins, as did his ancient Babylonian counterpart, if he but glances at a corpse. In pagan Syria of the common era, a priest who looks at a corpse is unclean for the day and is banned from the temple until the following day, and he must purify himself in the interim (Lucian, *De Syria Dea* 2.682). This view is also attested in rabbinic teaching. *m. Sanh.* 2:1 merits quotation in full: "If any of his (the high priest's) near of kin die, he may not follow after the bier, but he may go forth with the bearers as far as the city gate, *if he and they come not within sight of one another*. So Rabbi Meir [italics mine]. But Rabbi Judah says: He may not go forth from the temple, for it is written, 'neither shall he go out of the sanctuary (Lev 21:12).' " Rabbi Meir and Rabbi Judah do not differ at all. As the Roman and Babylonian parallels teach us, Rabbi Meir is citing the correct reason for the biblical prohibition.

Thus the Temple Scroll was only observing an ancient and universal obsession to prevent the high priest from being contaminated by a corpse—even by sight.

CONSECRATION

(3) The prescription to burn the purification offering *bĕmāqôm mûbdāl laḥaṭṭāʾôt šāmmāh yiśrĕ*[*pû* ʾ*ôtô* 'in the place set aside for purification offerings; there th[ey] shall bu[rn it' (16:12) is by its redundancy clearly intended as a polemic. The polemic is not difficult to determine. According to the biblical text, the purification offering was burned outside the camp at the *šepek haddešen* 'ash heap' (Lev 4:12), clearly where the ashes from the altar were deposited. In other words, the ashes of the purification offering were to be mixed with the ashes of the other altar sacrifices (cf. Rashi, ad loc.). This is also the view of the Tannaites, who call this place *bêt haddešen* (*m. Zebaḥ.* 12:5) or *bêt haddešen haggādôl* 'the great ash heap' (*t. Yoma* 3:17). Yet the opposing viewpoint is also registered in rabbinic sources, that the ashes of the purification offering were to be kept apart (*b. Zebaḥ.* 104b). Thus the controversy among the rabbinic sages clearly had ancient precedents, as now proved by the Temple Scroll (cf. also *MMT* B 29–33). Indeed, the controversy may reach back to the days of the Bible and beyond it, for it can be shown that the ashes of the purification offering had to be isolated because they were believed to possess residual power that, in the pagan world, was held to be black magic but which, in the Bible—eviscerated of demonic content—was held to be ritually defiling (Milgrom 1976a).

(4) *lĕmallĕʾ ʿal napšôtemāh* 'to ordain for their lives' (15:14; *pace* Yadin). This expression is a conflation of *lĕmallĕʾ yād* (Exod 29:35) and *lĕkapper ʿal nepeš* (e.g., Lev 17:11). Both terms occur in the priestly consecration (Exod 29:33b; cf. Lev 8:33b–34). The point of the conflation—a new coinage of the Scroll—is to show that the consecration ram and basket of breads fulfill both an expiatory and a consecratory function.

(5) *wĕsāmĕku ziqnê hakkôhăn*[*îm* ʾ*et-yĕdêhemāh ʿal rôʾ*]*šô wĕʾahărêhemāh ha*[*kkô*]*hēn haggādôl wekôl ha*[*kkôhănîm* 'and the elders of the priests shall lean their hands on its head and after them the high priest and all the priests' (15:18–16:1). Why do the priestly elders also perform the hand-leaning ceremonial? That the priestly consecrands perform it is understandable, for the purification bull is their sacrifice. Similarly in the biblical consecration service it is the consecrands, Aaron and his sons, who perform the hand-leaning (Exod 29:10; Lev 8:14). But why do the already consecrated priestly elders join in this ceremonial?

The answer is that this purification bull performs a different function. For the elders merely begin the hand-leaning ceremonial; they are followed by the high priest and, if the reconstruction is correct, the entire priestly corps. Thus the purification bull is intended not only for the consecrands but also for all of the priests, as is shown by the preceding sentence, *wayyaqrî*[*b par* ʾ*eḥād ʿa*]*l kôl hāʿā*[*m*] *wĕʾeḥād ʿal hakkôhănîm wayyaqrēb* ʾ*et-ăšer* [*lakkôhă*]*nîm bārîʾšônāh* 'a bull for all of the people and one for the priests were offered, that for the priests being offered first' (15:16–18). Hence, just as all of the people are expiated by a purification bull, so, we must assume, all of the priests are expiated by their purification bull. Now, however, a new question must be faced: just as the people's elders perform the hand-leaning on their behalf (Lev 4:15), should not the priestly elders act on behalf of the rest of the priests? The answer is that the two groups of elders are not alike in their powers. The people's elders are indeed empowered to represent the people, but the priestly elders hold only temporary powers; indeed, as soon as the priestly elders consecrate the high priest with the blood of the consecration ram, then the high priest immediately begins to officiate on behalf of his fellow priests and the people.

(6) *wĕśarĕpû kûllô šāmmāh* 'and all of it shall be burned there' (16:13). The plural verb shows that the burning of the purification bull is not done by the high priest. Is it then done by the elders of the priests? Probably not. Rather, the model is Lev 16:27–28, *wĕśārĕpû bā'ēš . . . wĕhaśśōrēp 'ōtām*, where the plural must be rendered as a passive, "[the bull] . . . shall be consumed by fire." Hence the burning is performed by an unnamed third party (see further Milgrom 1978b: 509–12).

G. The Priestly Consecration: A Rite of Passage

A. van Gennep (1960) has defined rites of passage as "rites which accompany every change of place, state, social position and age." They are marked by three phases: separation, margin (or *limen*, signifying "threshold" in Latin), and aggregation, as illustrated by the diagram in fig. 12 (Leach 1976: 78).

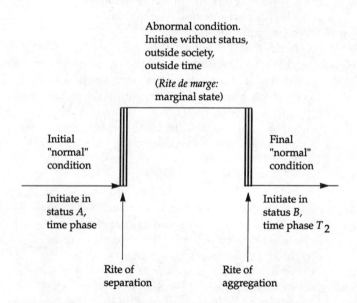

Abnormal condition.
Initiate without status,
outside society,
outside time

(*Rite de marge*:
marginal state)

Initial
"normal"
condition

Final
"normal"
condition

Initiate in
status *A*,
time phase

Initiate in
status *B*,
time phase *T*₂

Rite of
separation

Rite of
aggregation

FIGURE 12

"During the intervening liminal period, the characteristics of the subject (the passenger) are ambiguous: he passes through a cultural realm that has few or none of the attributes of the past or coming state . . . as liminal beings, they have no status, property, insignia, secular clothing indicating rank or rule, position in a kinship system—in short, nothing that may distinguish them from their fellow neophytes or initiands. Their behavior is normally passive or humble; they must obey their instructions implicitly, and accept arbitrary punishment without complaint" (Turner 1969: 94–95).

This description of the liminal state already bears many similarities to the biblical rite of priestly consecration. First, however, let a specific example throw these similarities into clear relief. During the installation rites of the Kanongesh (senior chief) or the Ndembu, the chief-elect is isolated in a hut called *kafwi*, a term Ndembu derive from *ku-fwa* 'to die', where he dies from his commoner state. He is clad in nothing but a ragged waist-cloth and sits crouched in a posture of shame or modesty. The officiant conducts the rite of *Kumukindyila*, which literally means "to speak evil or insulting words against him." His homily begins with these words: "Be silent! You are a mean and selfish fool, one who is bad-tempered! You do not love your fellows, you are only angry with them! Meanness and theft are all you have! Yet we have called you and we say that you must succeed to the chieftainship." After this harangue, any person who considers that he has been wronged by the chief-elect in the past is entitled to revile him, while the latter has to sit silently with head downcast. In the meantime, the officiant strikes his buttocks insultingly. The night before the rite, the chief-elect is prevented from sleeping, partly as an ordeal, partly because he may doze off and have bad dreams about the shades of dead chiefs. For the duration of the rite, he is submissive, silent, and sexually continent (Turner 1969: 100–9).

The above-cited taboos relating to the liminal state accompanying the elevation of a chief characterize many other primitive cultures as well. The chief-elect of the Swazi "remains secluded; . . . all day he sits naked on a lion skin in the ritual hut of the harem or in the sacred enclosure in the royal cattle byre. Men of his inner circle see that he breaks none of the taboos" (Kuper 1947: 219–20, cited by Turner 1967: 109). During the installation rite for the king of Gaboon, the people "surrounded him in a dense crowd, and then began to heap upon him every manner of abuse that the worst of mobs could imagine. Some spat in his face; some beat him with their fists; some kicked him; others threw disgusting objects at him; while those unlucky ones who stood on the outside, and could reach the poor fellow only with their voices, assiduously cursed him, his father, his mother, his sisters and brothers, and all his ancestors to the remotest generation. A stranger would not have given a cent for the life of him who was presently to be crowned" (Du Chaillu 1868: 43–44, cited by Turner 1969: 171).

Rites of passage are attested throughout the world, in every culture and age. The examples adduced above have been selected only because they have a bearing on Israel and the ancient Near East (cf. also Patai 1947: 183–84). The similarities to the biblical rite of priestly consecration are quickly recognizable: the seclusion of the consecrands (in the sanctuary court), their silence and submissiveness (they are commanded but do not respond), their sexual continence (they are isolated within the sacred premises), and their mortal fear lest they break any of the taboos. Regarding the latter, the biblical text is frustratingly brief. If specifies only one taboo, that of leaving the sanctuary. Clearly there were others. For example, because their status was still that of laymen, they were forbidden to officiate on the altar or enter the shrine (cf. Num 18:3; cf. the NOTE on v 35); they cooked and ate the sacrificial portions reserved for the laity in the area reserved for the laity (v 31) instead of eating the priestly prebends (vv 26–29) in the inner court (see the NOTE on "in front of the sacred area," 10:4)—the exclusive preserve of the priests (see the NOTE on "beside the altar," 10:12). Moreover, being in the sanctuary, they would have taken precautions against the occurrence of ritual impurity. The chief-elect of the Ndembu was prevented from sleeping the night before his installation because of the fear of a polluting dream. The high priest of Israel was kept awake on Yom Kippur night for fear of a polluting emission. "If he sought to slumber, young members of the priesthood would snap their middle finger before him and say to him, 'My lord, high priest, get up and drive away [sleep] this once [by walking] on the [cold] pavement.' And they used to divert him until the time of slaughtering drew near" (*m. Yoma* 1:7). One must presuppose that equally effective measures were enjoined for the priestly consecration.

It is the Babylonian New Year Festival that provides the most illuminating parallels to the cases cited above. For the Babylonians, New Year was a momentous rite of passage. The fate of the nation was decreed during this period: "He (the *šešgallu*-priest) shall strike the king's cheek. If, when [he strikes] the king's cheek, the tears flow, (it means that) the god Bel is friendly: if no tears appear, the god Bel is angry: the enemy will rise up and bring about his downfall" (*ANET*[3] 334). Moreover, the studied humiliation of the king is a prominent feature of the festival: "When he (the king) reaches [the presence of the god Bel], the *šešgallu*-priest shall leave (the sanctuary) and take away the scepter, the circle, and the sword [from the king]. He shall bring them [before the god Bel] and place them [on] a chair. He shall leave (the sanctuary) and strike the king's cheek. . . . He shall accompany him (the king) into the presence of the god Bel . . . he shall drag (him by) the ears and make him bow to the ground" (*ANET*[3] 334).

The similarities and, more important, the differences between the Babylonian New Year Festival and Israel's Yom Kippur are educed in chap. 16, COMMENT C. But the parallels between the Babylonian king and the Ndembu chief in their respective liminal states needs to be underscored here. Both are stripped of their clothing—their symbols of authority—and are subjected to rites of humiliation. Nothing of this sort obtains in the consecration ceremonies for

Aaron and his sons. To the contrary, Aaron is explicitly anointed while wearing his ornate robes; so too his sons after they don their official garments. Yet this may be the biblical method of accentuating their liminal state: dressed as priests, they may not serve as priests; they are in effect laymen and their priesthood still lies ahead. They are truly in passage. During the seven-day dedication of the temple built by Gudea of Lagash, all ranks were abolished (Falkenstein and von Soden 1953: 180; Gudea Cylinder B xvii; Barton 1929: 187, Statue B vii, 26–43). One can only recall that on Yom Kippur the high priest is indeed divested of his princely garments and dressed in simple linen vestments. This requirement has been variously interpreted (see the NOTE on 16:4). But on this annual day, when the welfare of the nation hangs upon the efficacy of his ritual, he is literally engaged in a rite of passage, entering and exiting the Holy of Holies, into which no man—not even a Moses—may enter. Yet no act of self-deprecation was instituted for the priestly investiture. Did a ritual of verbal humiliation perhaps obtain? The Bible is silent.

Thus anthropology helps illuminate the priestly consecration ceremony. The virtual quarantining of the consecrands within the sanctuary court and the admonition that they must observe the restrictions imposed upon them (as laymen) give the unshakable impression that we have to do here with a rite of passage wherein the priestly consecrands and their ordination offering share a transitional, liminal status. The priestly consecration, therefore, begs anthropological analysis. (An attempt was recently made by Leach [1976], but it is flawed by a multitude of exegetical errors.)

Why the liminal state is always a perilous one is difficult to answer. Perhaps the establishment, entrenched outside, regards the anarchical, amorphous status of the consecrands as a danger to societal law and order (Turner 1969: 108–9). M. Douglas's investigation (1966) would, rather, point to the anomalous position of the consecrands, which, by the very fact that it defies classification, is feared as dangerous. In either case, there would be complete agreement that Aaron and his sons underwent a transformation during their rite of passage. Henceforth they are priests; however, their acquired privileges and prestige are matched by greater responsibilities and restrictions.

THE INAUGURAL SERVICE (9:1–24)

The Sacrificial Procedure

9 ¹On the eighth day Moses summoned Aaron and his sons and the elders of Israel. ²He said to Aaron, "Take a calf of the herd for a purification offering and a ram for a burnt offering, both without blemish, and bring [them] before the Lord. ³And speak to the Israelites, saying, 'Take a he-goat for a purification offering; a calf and a lamb, both yearlings without blemish, for a burnt offering;

⁴and an ox and a ram for a well-being offering to sacrifice before the Lord; and a cereal offering mixed with oil. For today the Lord will appear to you.'"

⁵They brought what Moses had commanded to the front of the Tent of Meeting, and the whole community came forward and stood before the Lord. ⁶Moses said, "This is what the Lord commanded that you do, that the Glory of the Lord may appear to you." ⁷Then Moses said to Aaron, "Come forward to the altar and sacrifice your purification offering and your burnt offering and make atonement for yourself and for the people; and sacrifice the people's offering and make atonement for them—as the Lord has commanded."

⁸Aaron came forward to the altar and slaughtered his calf of purification offering. ⁹Aaron's sons presented the blood to him; he dipped his finger in the blood and put [it] on the horns of the altar; and he poured out [the rest of] the blood at the base of the altar. ¹⁰The suet, the kidneys, and the caudate lobe of the liver from the purification offering he turned into smoke on the altar—as the Lord had commanded Moses; ¹¹and the flesh and the skin were consumed in fire outside the camp. ¹²Then he slaughtered the burnt offering. Aaron's sons passed the blood to him, and he dashed it against all sides of the altar. ¹³They passed the burnt offering to him in sections, and the head, and he turned [them] into smoke on the altar. ¹⁴He washed the entrails and the legs, and turned [them] into smoke on the altar with the burnt offering.

¹⁵Then he brought forward the people's offering. He took the he-goat for the people's purification offering, and slaughtered it, and performed the purification rite with it as with the previous [purification offering]. ¹⁶He brought forward the burnt offering and sacrificed it in the prescribed manner. ¹⁷He then brought forward the cereal offering and, taking a handful of it, he turned [it] into smoke on the altar—in addition to the burnt offering of the morning. ¹⁸He slaughtered the ox and the ram, the people's sacrifice of well-being. Aaron's sons passed the blood to him—which he dashed against all sides of the altar—¹⁹and the suet pieces of the ox and the ram: the broad tail, the covering [suet], the kidneys, and the caudate lobes. ²⁰They laid these suet pieces upon the breasts; and he turned the suet pieces into smoke upon the altar. ²¹Aaron presented the breasts and the right thigh as an elevation offering before the Lord—as Moses had commanded.

Blessing and Theophany

²²Then Aaron lifted his hands toward the people and blessed them; and he came down after sacrificing the purification offering, the burnt offering, and the well-being offering. ²³Moses and Aaron then entered the Tent of Meeting. When they came out, they blessed the people; and the Glory of the Lord appeared to all of the people. ²⁴Fire came forth from before the Lord and consumed the burnt offering and the suet pieces on the altar. And the people saw, and shouted for joy, and fell on their faces.

NOTES

9:1. On the eighth day (wayyĕhî bayyôm haššĕmînî). "At the end of the seven days of initiation" (*Tg. Neof.;* cf. *Tg. Ps.-J.;* Philo, *Vit. Mos.* 2.153), which would have fallen on the eighth day of Nisan (cf. Exod 40:17; Rabbi Akiba in *Sipre* Num 68; *b. Pesah.* 90b, versus the main rabbinic position, *Sipre* Num 44; Seder Olam 7, that the Tabernacle was erected on the twenty-third of Adar and inaugurated on the first of Nisan). The Tabernacle took nearly one year in construction, the same period ascribed to the building of Eninnu, Ningirsu's temple in Lagash (Gudea A xxiii, B iii); strikingly, its dedication ceremonies also lasted seven days (B xvii).

The eighth day is integrally connected with the previous seven. This holds true throughout the cult, for example, circumcision (12:2–3), the firstling (Exod 22:20), eligibility for being sacrificed (22:26–27), the purification of the sanctuary (16:14–15, 18–19), of the *mĕṣōrāʿ* (14:8–10, 23), of the *zāb* (15:13–14), and of the Nazirite (Num 6:9–10), the dedication of Solomon's Temple (1 Kgs 8:65 LXX) and of Ezekiel's altar (Ezek 43:18–27; see chap. 4, COMMENT J and the NOTE on 8:33), the duration of Sukkot (23:34–36, 39; Num 29:35) and of the Jubilee cycle, $7 \times 7 + 1$ (25:8–10). In the noncultic arena, the sequence of $7 + 1$ is also attested (e.g., 1 Sam 16:10–11; 17:2; Mic 5:4; Qoh 11:2). It also occurs in the Ugaritic literature (*UT* 67, 5.8–9; 75, 2.45–46; 1 Aqhat 1.42–43; *UT* 128, 4.6–7).

The eighth day is not like the previous seven. The latter serves as *millūʾîm,* the investiture of the priesthood (chap. 8), and the consecration of the sanctuary (8:10–12) whereas the eighth day serves an entirely different purpose—the inauguration of the public cult conducted by its newly invested priesthood. The technical name for this inauguration is *ḥănukkâ* 'initiation' or, more precisely, *ḥănukkat hammizbēaḥ* 'the initiation of the altar'. The concentration of the entire chapter is upon the altar, as demonstrated by the curtailed description of the sacrificial procedure, which omits nearly every rite that is unrelated to the altar (e.g., the hand-leaning) but includes every rite involving the altar, even the most minute (e.g., the disposition of the suet pieces, vv 19–20), climaxed by the unique theophany upon the altar (vv 23–24). The etymology of this term *ḥănukkâ,* its relationship with the gifts of the chieftains (Num 7), and the paradigm of this eight-day celebration for subsequent Temple initiation are discussed in the COMMENT below. For the differences between the theophany in Israel's Tabernacle/Temple and those in ancient Mesopotamia, see the NOTE on "will appear," v 4.

Moses summoned Aaron. As in the previous seven days, Moses continues to act like a king; see chap. 8, COMMENT E.

the elders of Israel (ziqnê yiśrāʾēl). The elders are summoned in order to honor Aaron by their presence (*Midr. Tanḥ.* B. 5); to represent the people at the sacrificial service (Bekhor Shor; Ḥazzequni). Most likely both motivations were operative.

2. *calf* (*ʿēgel*). Elsewhere the priests bring a bull, *par*, as their purification offering (4:3; 8:2; 16:3). Because the people's calf is specified as a yearling (v 3), this calf is probably older, perhaps even equivalent to a bull (Ibn Ezra). This view would correspond to the opinion of the rabbis (*m. Para* 1:1) who hold, versus Rabbi Eliezer, that a calf may be as much as two years old (cf. *t. Para* 1:5). Indeed, there is even an attestation of a three-year-old calf (Gen 15:9).

ram (*ʾayil*). It is also the priests' burnt offering in 8:18; 16:3. Koch (1959: 70) wonders why Aaron must now bring a purification and a burnt offering after having already done so for the seven previous days. The answer lies in the contrasting function of the two periods. The week-long ceremonies focused on the investiture of the priests, but the eighth-day service marks the inauguration of the public cult in which all sacrifices play a role. That is, all sacrifices but the *ʾāšām*, the reparation offering, are prescribed for the eighth day, and its absence proves the case: the reparation offering is always a private offering; it is never required in the public cult. A comparable situation prevails when the chieftains bring their gifts for the newly consecrated altar: again, all sacrifices are accounted for but the reparation offering (Num 7:12–17, etc.; see the COMMENT below). Thus the sole absence of the reparation offering from the prescribed sacrifices for the eighth day implies the inauguration of the public cult.

3. *And speak to the Israelites* (*wĕ-ʾel-bĕnê yiśrāʾēl tĕdabbēr*). Instead of *bĕnê*, the LXX and Sam. read *ziqnê*, yielding "And speak to the elders of Israel." Supporting this reading is the fact that the term *bĕnê yiśrāʾēl* in P is inclusive of all Israelites, the priests as well. A good case in point is chap. 16: whenever the priests are included with their fellow Israelites, the term employed is *bĕnê yiś-rāʾēl* (16:16, 19, 21, 24). But whenever the priests are listed separately, the Israelites are called by different terms (16:5, 15, 17, 24, 33; see the NOTE on 16:21). Because Aaron is addressing the nonpriestly Israelites, MT's *bĕnê* may not be correct. Nonetheless, the reading *ziqnê* also faces a logical incongruity. The elders had been summoned by Moses (v 1) and were presumably standing before him. What need did Moses then have for the mediation of Aaron? He could have spoken to them directly! Ehrlich tries to support this emendation by making another one, reading *dibber* for *tĕdabbēr*, thereby yielding "And he spoke to the elders of Israel," on the grounds that the elders fulfilled Moses' command (v 5). Yet the anonymous subject in v 5, "they brought," could just as well refer to the Israelites as to the elders. It is best, then, to conclude with the MT that the Israelites brought their sacrifices (v 5) at the command of Moses but through the agency of Aaron (v 3). The presence of the elders is not superfluous but is explicable on other grounds (see the NOTE on v 1).

a he-goat for a purification offering. In accordance with Num 15:24 but not Lev 4:14 (see chap. 4, COMMENT E). The presupposition behind the requirement of the purification offering in all public sacrifices (chap. 4, COMMENT C) is that the ongoing occurrences of sin and impurity continuously pollute the altar (contra Kiuchi 1987: 58).

a calf and a lamb . . . for a burnt offering. With a he-goat for a purification offering one would expect for the burnt offering either a ram (e.g., 16:5) or a bull (e.g., Num 15:24). Here, however, both species (albeit of a younger variety) are enjoined, a situation that is found only in the public offerings prescribed for the festivals (e.g., Num 28:11, 15; 28:19, 22; 28:27, 30, etc.)—an indication that this eighth day is indeed a festive occasion for all Israel.

both yearlings (běnê-šānâ). That the two burnt offerings consist of young animals cannot be an accident, but the rationale escapes me.

4. *a well-being offering.* The *šělāmîm* is listed prior to the *minḥâ*, the cereal offering, even though it follows in the actual sacrificial procedure (vv 17–18). Here is another example of the difference in the order of the sacrifices between prescriptive and descriptive texts (see the introduction to chap. 8, and the NOTE to 7:38b). The reason for putting the *šělāmîm* ahead of the *minḥâ* may well be in order to keep all of the animal sacrifices together *(Seper Hamibḥar).*

The function of the well-being offering is clarified by the announcement of the forthcoming theophany (v 4b). The joy and privilege of witnessing the theophany are celebrated by a feast, as for instance in "They beheld God, and they ate and drank" (Exod 24:11b; cf. v 5), which in this case was projected (10:14–15) but aborted (10:16–20).

to sacrifice (lizbōaḥ). The verb *zābaḥ* is found only here in P, but it also occurs in H (17:5, 7; 19:5; 22:29). To be sure, it is found in all of the other pentateuchal sources (e.g., Exod 8:21, 25; 20:24; 34:15; Num 22:40; Deut 12:15, 21; 15:21), but whereas in the latter passages *zābaḥ* means "slaughter" either for a sacrifice or (in D) for profane purposes, in P and H *zābaḥ* is restricted to the technical meaning "sacrifice the *zebaḥ,*" in other words, to conduct the entire sacrificial procedure not for all offerings but only for the offering of well-being (see Exod 24:6; Deut 27:6–7 [= Josh 8:31] for a similar tendency in the other sources). When, however, the specific meaning of "slaughter" is desired, P and H resort to the term *šāḥaṭ* (cf. v 4 with v 18). For details see Milgrom (1976e: 13–15 and chap. 11, COMMENT D).

and a cereal offering (ûminḥâ). Ibn Ezra claims that this cereal offering is the adjunct to the burnt and well-being offerings prescribed in Num 15:1–16. But besides the fact that this sacrificial adjunct is enjoined only for the postconquest period (Num 15:2) and is not relevant here, there is the additional discrepancy that it is also burned entirely on the altar whereas the cereal offering prescribed here is eaten by the priests (10:12) with only a token (*'azkārâ,* cf. 2:2) burned on the altar (v 17; Wessely 1846). Furthermore, if the *minḥâ* were a sacrificial adjunct, its procedure would have been described as *kammišpāṭ* 'in the prescribed manner' (e.g., Num 15:24; 29:6; Malbim). Hence, both the manner and wording of its procedure demonstrate that it must be an independent offering (in agreement with *Sipra*, Millu'im Shemini 12).

The cereal offering is listed after the well-being offering even though it will be offered before it, in keeping with the former's higher rank as a most-holy offering (note the sacrificial series in Ezek 45:15, 17; the well-being offering is listed last). The prescriptive order never determines the actual procedure (see the NOTES to 5:16; 7:38b; and the introduction to chap. 8), a stylistic and archival peculiarity that obtains elsewhere in the ancient Near East (e.g., Hittite Tunnawi; cf. the NOTE to 8:2).

For today . . . (kî hayyôm . . .). An intimation that the sacrifices will be consumed miraculously during the theophany.

the Lord (YHWH). This is the only place in all of P in which the direct revelation of the deity is not mediated by his *kābôd.* The Targums, as is their wont, resort to euphemisms: "honor" (*Tg. Onq.,* as in v 6); "the glory of the Presence of the Lord" *(Tg. Ps.-J.);* "the Word of the Lord" *(Tg. Neof.).*

will appear (nir'â). The vocalization renders this word as a perfect. All of the Versions interpret or read it as a participle, *nir'eh.* Perhaps the Masoretic vocalization was deliberate, to avoid the anthropomorphism: not God but his fire (vv 23b, 24a) will appear, and as fire, *'ēš,* is feminine they vocalized the verb accordingly (Shadad).

The importance of the theophany in the newly consecrated Tabernacle cannot be exaggerated. It renders the Tabernacle the equivalent of Mount Sinai. God's presence was made manifest at both places. But whereas the people experienced *(rā'â)* God's voice at Sinai (Exod 20:18, JE), only an elite saw him *(wayyir'û . . . wayyeḥĕzû;* Exod 24:10–11, JE). In contrast, all of the people were privileged to see him sanction the inauguration of the regular cult in the Tabernacle. Thus P, in effect, regards the theophany at the Tabernacle as more important than JE's theophany at Sinai. Nonetheless, P has equalized the two theophanies in its supplement to the Sinaitic account, which relates that God's *kābôd* made itself visible at Sinai (Exod 24:17) just as it subsequently did at the Tabernacle inauguration (vv 6b, 23b, 24a). Still, according to this P verse it is not God's *kābôd* but he, himself, who will be seen by all of Israel. Therefore the possibility must be entertained—presuming the accuracy of the MT—that P deliberately allowed this description of the theophany to be unqualified by God's *kābôd,* or any other metonym. In this way it certifies the absolute equivalence of the Tabernacle theophany with that of Sinai when, according to the JE tradition, the leaders of Israel "saw the God of Israel. . . . Yet he did not raise his hand against the leaders *('ăṣîlê)* of the Israelites; they beheld God, and they ate and drank" (Exod 24:10–11).

The equivalence of the Tabernacle to Sinai is an essential, indeed indispensable, axiom of P. The Tabernacle, in effect, becomes a portable Sinai, an assurance of the permanent presence of the deity in Israel's midst.

The theophany at the Tabernacle must be sharply differentiated from theophanies reported at temple dedications outside of Israel. The latter are characterized by the entry of the god into the temple. For example, in the Kes Temple Hymn, the ceremony reaches its climax when the goddess Ninhursag takes her seat in the temple (Sjöberg and Bergman 1969: 155–58, lines 120–21). Indeed, every hymn in the Sjöberg and Bergman collection ends with the same refrain: "He/She (deity) has placed his house on your MÙŠ, he has taken his seat on your dais" (see also the Harran inscriptions of Nabonidus 3.21–25 [Gadd 1958: 65]; Gudea B 2.21–6.10 [Falkenstein and von Soden 1953: 167–70]; Esarhaddon A 6.28–36 [Borger 1956: 5]). In Israel, however, the Ark, the symbolic seat of the Godhead, is installed—the first among all of the sancta (Exod 40:20–21)—before God's presence in the firecloud descends upon the Tabernacle (Exod 40:34–35). In the Solomonic Temple, although the Ark is the last of the sancta to be installed (1 Kgs 8:3–5), it still precedes—following the Tabernacle model —the divine firecloud (1 Kgs 8:10–11). Israel's experience of the theophany is also precisely the opposite of Mesopotamia's. Whereas in the latter, the people behold their deity as his or her image *enters* the temple, the Israelites behold their God as he *emerges* from the Tabernacle in the form of fire (vv 23–24). Thus, in Israel, according to P, the severance of God from the Ark is unambiguous: even if the firecloud emerges from the Ark room, it has arrived there separately from and subsequent to the Ark's installation.

The *kābôd* presumably brightens in intensity as a signal to Moses whenever God desires an audience with him (Num 17:7–8) or when Moses (with Aaron) seeks divine counsel (Num 20:6–7) before it condenses between the outspread wings of the cherubim in the adytum. Otherwise, the *kābôd*, encased in cloud, remains suspended above the Tabernacle so that it is visible to all of Israel at night (Exod 40:38; Num 9:15). Here, uniquely at the inauguration of the public cult in the Tabernacle, the *kābôd* separates itself from its nebulous encasement in order to consume the sacrifices in the sight of all of Israel (see further the NOTE on "and the Glory of the Lord," v 23).

5. *They brought.* wayyiqḥû, including Aaron and the Israelites (see the NOTE on "And speak," v 3).

the whole community. kol-hā'ēdâ, comprising the priests and the Israelites (see the previous NOTE), but distinct from the 'am 'people' (vv 7, 15, 18, 22, 23, 24), a term that refers to the Israelites but excludes the priests.

to the front of . . . before ('el-pĕnê . . . lipnê). The two prepositions are identical in meaning, but the former follows the verb of motion "brought" (cf. 6:7) and the latter follows the intransitive verb "stood." In either case, the meaning is unambiguous: the people and their offerings were now in the forecourt of the sacred precinct, before the altar (see the NOTE on "in front of the holy place," 10:4).

6. *This is what the Lord commanded that you do* (zeh haddābār 'ăšer-ṣiwwâ YHWH ta'ăśû). "That," 'ăšer (before ta'ăśû), is missing; it may have fallen out because of the previously mentioned 'ăšer (Kalisch 1867–72) or it may be ex-

plained as the subordination of the complementary verbal idea in the imperfect (e.g., Isa 42:21; Hos 1:6; Job 32:22; Lam 1:10; GKC 120c).

What is the referent? None seems to exist. This situation is entirely unlike that of the previous chapter, where the same expression, *zeh haddābār* (8:5), clearly referred to the prescriptive text of Exod 29. Ibn Ezra eliminates the need for a referent by regarding the first word of this verse, *wayyōʾmer*, as a pluperfect, yielding "[Moses] had said," which in effect transposes this verse before v 2. That is, *zeh haddābār* 'this is what . . .' would now refer to the command to Aaron and the Israelites to bring the requisite sacrifices (vv 3–4). That an imperfect attached to a sequential *waw* can ever be a pluperfect is unlikely, however; and even more unlikely is the idea that its referent is the immediately preceding command. Ramban, by contrast, proposes that "this is what" has nothing to do with the preceding sacrificial inventory but serves as an introduction to the forthcoming sacrificial procedure (v 7). Because this is the first time that Aaron and his sons will officiate, Moses' instructions and supervision are still needed. Indeed, even though the ritual instructions for each sacrifice have already been given (chaps. 1–7), their procedural order has not. Hence, Moses now proclaims their order (v 7) as a new revelation: "This is what the Lord has commanded." Yet an objection may be raised against this interpretation, namely, that it implies that Moses directed his remarks solely to the priests, in which case there would be no need for a separate introduction to Aaron in the next verse. Also the Lord's theophany *ʾălêkem* 'to you' is surely not confined to the priests (see v 23b).

The most likely solution is that this entire verse is an editorial note explaining that Moses did not command these sacrifices on his own initiative (as v 2 implies) but was so commanded by God. (This solution is hinted at by *Seper Hamibḥar*: "What was undisclosed there [i.e., v 2] is disclosed here that this statement was ordered by God.") A special command by God is needed because the two prescribed purification offerings will vary in their procedure from the norm; see the NOTE below.

you do (taʿăśû). The verb *ʿāśâ*, as frequently used in P (e.g., Exod 29:39; Lev 5:10; 14:19, 30), is a technical term for "perform the sacrificial rite" (cf. the NOTE on *ʿāśâ*, v 7). This interpretation clarifies why the verse is an editorial note: the procedure adopted for the sacrifice of the priests' and people's purification offering will vary from the norm. The offerings will be burned outside the camp even though their blood has not been admitted inside the Tent (see 6:23), hence requiring an additional divine command.

Glory [of the Lord] (kābôd [YHWH]). The earthly manifestation of God is termed *kābôd*, and it takes the form of fire. It may be compared to Akk. *puluḫtu*, the garment of fire that surrounds the gods (see the NOTE "and the glory of the Lord," v 23, for details). The *kābôd* is not an earthly fire. In P's description of it, the *kaph* is used, for example, *kĕʾēš ʾōkelet* 'like a consuming fire' (Exod 24:17). Although *kābôd* is a favorite term of P it is not unknown to the other early traditions (e.g., Exod 33:18, 22; Num 14:21–22; 1 Sam 4:20–21). D, however, prefers the more abstract *šēm* 'name', designation for the deity (e.g., Deut 12:5, 11, 21; 14:23, 24; 16:2).

7. *Come forward to (qĕrab ʾel).* This is the only occasion on which such a command is given to Aaron. The reason is obvious: he officiates for the first time. Indeed, this is the deeper meaning of the idiom *qĕrab ʾel.* It can connote more than "approach" or "come forward." Where *qārab* is forbidden, it means "encroach" (e.g., 22:3; Num 18:22; see Milgrom 1970a: 16–33); where permitted, *qārab ʾel* can imply the reverse: "have access to" or "be qualified to."

The uses of *qārab* in the Korah pericope are illustrative of both the positive and the negative renderings of this term. For example: "An unauthorized person should not presume (may not qualify) to offer incense" (Num 17:5); the Levites "shall have no access to (may not encroach upon) the sacred vessels or the altar" (Num 18:3); "An unauthorized person shall not be associated with (shall not intrude upon) you" (Num 18:4); "Henceforth, Israelites shall have no access to (not encroach upon) the Tent of Meeting [so as not] to incur mortal punishment" (Num 18:22). In an apodictic prohibition only the negative sense applies: "The unauthorized person who encroaches shall be slain" (Num 18:7). Where there is no negation the permissive sense alone obtains: "But you shall associate with yourself your kinsmen the tribe of Levi" (Num 18:2). The same semantic range prevails for the synonym *nāgaš* and for the Akk. cognate *qerēbu* (Milgrom 1970a: 34–36).

Ezekiel is a particularly rich source of permissive *qārab ʾel.* Only after the priests change to street clothing "may they have access to the people" (Ezek 42:14); "they are the Zadokites who, [alone] of the Levites, have access to the Lord to serve him" (Ezek 40:46); "they (the Zadokites) shall have access to my table to serve me" (Ezek 44:16). The latter citation is particularly apt, for it speaks of *qārab ʾel* in regard to the priests and the altar.

The positive sense of *qārab* is also recorded with the laity. The resident alien who wishes to offer the *pesaḥ* must undergo circumcision, "and then he shall qualify to offer it" (Exod 12:48). In sexual prohibitions *qārab ʾel* obviously means more than "approach" and must be rendered "have intercourse" (e.g., 18:6, 14, 19; 20:16; Ezek 18:6).

The rabbis play on the sexual overtones of Moses' command to Aaron: "It may be compared to a king of flesh of blood who married a woman who was bashful in his presence. Her sister came to her and said, 'Why did you enter into this state (of marriage) if not to have intercourse with the king? Be bold and make love to the king.' In a similar manner Moses spoke to Aaron: 'Aaron, my brother, why were you chosen to be the high priest if not to officiate before the Holy One Blessed Be He? Be bold and render your service' " (*Sipra*, Milluʾim Shemini 8). The rabbis cannot be faulted for either their daring or their accuracy (see also the NOTE on "Aaron came forward," v 8).

Thus when Moses commands Aaron *qĕrab ʾel-hammizbēaḥ*, he intends more than that Aaron should step forward. He is telling Aaron to begin the sacrificial service, and his command must therefore be rendered "officiate."

sacrifice (bis) *('ăśēh)*. In P, the verb *'ăśâ* can bear the technical meaning of "perform, sacrifice" (see the NOTE on *ta'ăśû*, v 6). The semantic equivalent in Akk., *epēšu* 'make', is also capable of the more restricted meaning "perform [in ritual]" (cf. *CAD, epēšu,* 2f).

make atonement (wĕkappēr). The verb *kippēr* in the context of the purification offering denotes "purge" (chap. 4, COMMENT B), but with the burnt offering (and, indeed, with every other sacrifice) it bears the general meaning of "atone," in other words, to reconcile the individual (or community) with God so that they become "at-one" (chap. 16, COMMENT F). The more inclusive rendering is clearly implied here.

for yourself and for (ba'adkā ûbĕ'ad). When the object of *kippēr* is a person, it requires either the preposition *'al* or *bĕ'ad*, both signifying "on behalf of" (16:6, 24, 30, 33; Num 8:12, 21). These two prepositions, however, are not entirely synonymous. *'al* can refer only to persons other than the subject, but when the subject wishes to refer to himself *bĕ'ad* must be used (e.g., 16:6, 11, 24; Ezek 45:22). This distinction is confirmed by Job 42:28: "Offer a burnt offering for yourselves *(bĕ'adkem)* and Job, my servant, will intercede on your behalf *('ălêkem)"* (Milgrom 1970b). Thus, in this instance only *bĕ'ad* can be used.

the people (hā'ām). With the LXX, read *bêtĕkā* 'your household', on the analogy of 16:6, 11, 17, 24 LXX, where two sets of sacrificial animals are required, one to effect *kippûr* for the high priest and his household and the other for the people. The scribe's error may have been caused by the *hā'ām* that appears four words later.

the people's offering. qorban hā'ām; compare v 15a, referring to the purification, burnt, and cereal offerings (vv 3–4, 15–17), which clearly have expiatory functions, but also to the well-being offering (vv 18–21), whose flesh may be eaten (7:16–17, 31–34) provided its blood serves as a *kippûr* ransom on the altar (17:11; see chap. 11, COMMENT C). It is possible, however, that this language was chosen instead of enumerating the sacrifices, as was done in the case of the priests (v 7a), in order to prevent the attribution of expiation to the well-being offering (Janowski 1982: 191 n. 30).

and make atonement for them (wĕkappēr ba'ădām). This sequence is essential. The priests cannot atone for others until they have atoned first for themselves (*b. Yoma* 43b; cf. Heb 5:1–4; 7:23–28; 8:1–7).

as the Lord has commanded. The phrase *ka'ăšer ṣiwwâ YHWH* appears three times in this chapter (vv 7, 10, 21). What is its referent here? Perhaps the reference is to the animals chosen for the sacrifices, which are unprecedented, this being the first public service, and, hence, in need of a special divine order. But the plain meaning of the text suggests that the Lord's command has to do with the exceptional nature of the *kippûr* performed by these animals. Would it, then, refer to the high priest's purification offering because it is burned outside the camp even though its blood has not been admitted inside the Tent (see 6:23), an exceptional situation? But as this anomaly can easily be explained (see v 11), the choice must fall on the people's purification offering, which should have been eaten by the priests (in conformance with 6:19, 22) but which, instead, is burned outside the camp (10:16). Thus the emphasis on the divine origin of the command to carry out the purification offering underscores the subsequent deviation from this command practiced by Aaron and his sons, thereby provoking the wrath of Moses.

8. *Aaron came forward to the altar (wayyiqrab 'ahărōn 'el-hammizbēaḥ).* That *qārab 'el* means "had access to, qualified for" rather than "approach, come forward" is clearly indicated here. Aaron did not have to "approach" the altar in order to slaughter the sacrificial animal. The slaughter of ovines was specified to the north of the altar (see the NOTE on 1:11), but bovines (the text here specifies a calf) were slaughtered "before the Lord" (see the NOTE on 1:5), in other words, anywhere within the Tabernacle court, even at a remove from the altar. Thus Aaron's "coming forward" to the altar can only mean that he began to officiate (see also the NOTE on "come forward" in v 7, above).

and slaughtered. As Aaron was the offerer as well as the officiant, he performed the slaughtering instead of delegating it to others (so too on Yom Kippur, 16:11). It was customary for the offerer to slaughter his animal (see the NOTE on 1:5), but sacrifices for the public cult were generally executed by the priests (see v 18). On this day, in particular, it being the inaugural service of the public cult, it was only fitting that Aaron himself, in his capacity as high priest, should perform all of the main rites in the sacrificial service (see also the NOTE on "Aaron's sons presented," v 9).

One cannot help noticing the absence of any mention of the hand-leaning rite, not only here but for all of the following blood sacrifices (vv 12, 15, 18). Of course, the rite was not omitted; it was indispensable to any animal offering (see the NOTE on 1:4). Its omission from the text as well as the omission of all other rites unrelated to the altar are due to the deliberate intention of the writer to focus attention solely on the rites of the altar ending, with the climactic theophany upon it (see the NOTE "On the eighth day," v 1). Aaron himself would have performed the hand-leaning on his own animals, but the likelihood is that the elders (v 1), as the people's representatives, would have performed it on the people's animals (see the NOTE on "and slaughtered it," v 15). The hand-leaning rite is also missing from the Yom Kippur ceremonies (see 16:11, 15) and must be similarly taken for granted. Perhaps its absence there is to accentuate the special and different function of the hand-leaning performed on the live goat (see the NOTE on "he shall slaughter," 16:11).

9. *Aaron's sons presented the blood to him (wayyaqrîbû bĕnê 'ahărōn 'et-haddām 'ēlāyw).* It is difficult for one who slaughters also to collect the blood (Hoffmann 1953), as demonstrated by Second Temple practice (*m. Yoma* 4:3).

This is another indication that Aaron performed the slaughtering; otherwise, he could have collected the blood by himself. Moreover, the use of *hiqrîb ʾel*, literally, "brought near to" (see the NOTE on 1:3), indicates that Aaron did not even touch the bowl containing the blood but, as explicitly stated in the text, "dipped his finger in the blood."

poured out (yāṣaq). This verb instead of the usual one, *šāpak*, here and in 8:15 comprises one important piece of evidence that chaps. 8 and 9 were written by the same hand, in contrast to Exod 29 (see the NOTE on "poured out," 8:15 and chap. 8, COMMENT B). Notice once again the altered word order and the verb as a simple passive to indicate that this is the final rite in the sacrificial procedure (vv 8–15).

10. *The suet (haḥēleb).* This term comprises all of the suet pieces, specifically those that cover the entrails and surround the entrails and the kidneys (see 3:3–4).

turned into smoke (hiqṭîr). Tg. Neof. renders *sidder* as "set in order" to resolve the possible contradiction emerging from the subsequent statement that the suet pieces were also consumed by the divine fire (v 24). See the NOTES on "turned [them] into smoke," vv 13, 14 and "consumed," v 24.

[the caudate lobe] of [the liver]. min, only here. Elsewhere the preposition *ʿal* is employed (3:4, 10, 15; 4:9; 7:4) or there is no preposition at all (8:16, 25).

as the Lord had commanded Moses. See 4:8–9, which itself is based on 3:3–4. One would have expected this execution statement to come at the end of the next verse (v 11), which concludes the purification-offering pericope. Instead, the conclusion of the rite, namely, the incineration of the animal's flesh outside the camp, actually violates God's command (6:23; M. Hildenbrand) and must be accounted for separately (see chap. 10, COMMENT C).

11. *were consumed in fire (śārap bāʾēš).* The subject here is not Aaron (see the NOTE on "it shall be burnt," 4:12). Only this purification offering and that of the priestly consecration (8:17) were burned outside the camp, though their blood did not enter the Tent (see 6:23). In this case the reason is obvious: priests do not benefit from their own expiatory sacrifices *(Seper Hamibḥar);* hence, the only resort is to incinerate them. The question remains: why is this verse mentioned at all? It has nothing to do with the altar, the main focus of this chapter (see the NOTES on "On the eighth day," v 1 and "and slaughtered," v 8). Also it is out of sequence: Aaron does not perform the burning but remains at the altar to proceed with the burnt offering (v 12). The answer must be that it deviates from the norm. As the blood of this purification offering was not admitted into the Tent of Meeting it should have been eaten by the priests (in accordance with 6:19, 22). Proof of its anomalous nature is the fact that the words "as the Lord had commanded" are found in the previous verse instead of in their expected position here (see the preceding NOTE). The content of this verse, then, cannot be taken for granted and, therefore, needs to be mentioned.

A further question remains: as the purification offering was Aaron's why, indeed, wasn't its blood taken into the Tent? The blood of the high priest's purification offering, according to 4:3–12, must be brought into the Tent where it is aspersed before the veil and daubed on the horns of the incense altar! Here the answer is not so certain. One possibility is suggested by the differing natures of each purification offering. The one brought by the high priest in chap. 4 is for his own inadvertent violation of a prohibitive commandment (4:3) whose malefic pollution penetrates into the shrine (chap. 4, COMMENT B). Aaron's purification offering on this inaugural day is for no known sin of his own; it is comparable to the purification offering brought by the priestly consecrands during each of the seven days of their investiture—to purge the altar of the pollution they *may* have inadvertently caused (see the NOTE on "decontaminating the altar," 8:15). This answer cannot stand, however. According to the Priestly sacrificial system, the purification offering is brought for known sins, not for suspected ones (see the NOTE on "when . . . becomes known," 4:14); the latter require the *'āšām*, the reparation offering, not the purification offering (see the NOTE on "If, however," 5:17). The greater likelihood, then, is that the purification offering depicted here represents an earlier phase in the development of this sacrifice, possibly at open-air altars *(bāmôt)* where the blood of purification offerings purged the only available sanctum, the altar, and the carcasses were incinerated outside the community. In larger sanctuaries containing building installations (e.g., Shiloh), the interior sancta were also purged by the blood. Finally, a later reform was enacted to combat the magical powers associated with the sacrifice by decreeing that whenever its blood was not taken into the shrine but daubed on the outside altar, it was to be eaten by priests (details in chap. 10, COMMENT C).

12. *Then he slaughtered (wayyišḥaṭ).* Once again the subject is Aaron (see the NOTE on "and slaughtered," v 8).

passed (wayyamṣi'û). Aaron's sons passed the bowl containing the blood of the burnt offering to Aaron so that he could toss all of the blood on the altar while holding the bowl, whereas in the case of the purification offering they "presented" *(wayyaqrîbû,* v 9) the bowl of blood, that is to say, they continued to hold it while Aaron dipped his finger in the blood to perform the rite of daubing the altar horns (Wessely 1846).

Ibn Ezra suggests that this usage derives from the root meaning of *māṣā'* 'find', so that the *hiph'il* form *himṣi'û* means "they caused (Aaron) to find (the blood)." Rashi, however, states that it simply connotes "handing over and presenting," a meaning that is attested in other contexts (e.g., 2 Sam 3:8; Zach 11:6).

The fact that the blood was collected in a bowl, *mizrāq* (Exod 27:3; Num 4:14), literally, "tossing bowl" *(NEB),* is an indication that the verb *šāḥaṭ* 'slaughter' (vv 15, 19, 23) means "slit the throat," for only by cutting the main vessels in the throat can the blood be drained in a bowl (D. Wright). The significance of this slaughtering method for understanding the ethical import of the biblical diet laws is developed in chap. 11, COMMENT D.

13. *They passed (himṣî'û;* see the preceding NOTE). The altered word order and verb (a simple passive) are a sign that a closing verb, *wayyaqṭēr,* is about to follow (Paran 1983: 146).

in sections (linĕtāḥêhā). So the LXX, in other words, piece by piece.

and he turned [them] into smoke (wayyaqṭēr). The LXX renders ἐπέφηκεν 'placed' and *Tg. Neof.,* *siddēr* 'set in order' in order to avoid the ostensible contradiction that if Moses did indeed cause the burnt offering to go up into smoke there was nothing left for the divine fire (but see the NOTE on "consumed," v 24). Interestingly, Rashbam follows this same interpretation. *Tg. Neof.,* more consistently than the LXX, gives the same rendering to the *wayyaqṭēr* mentioned twice for the suet (vv 10, 20) because the suet is also reported to have been consumed by the divine fire (v 24).

14. *He washed (wayyirḥaṣ).* Aaron performed the washing rite because it was his own offering (see the NOTE on "he washed," 1:9). P's term *rāḥaṣ* (Exod 29:17; Lev 1:9, 13; 8:21) is replaced by *hēdîaḥ,* beginning with Ezekiel (40:38; also in connection with the burnt offering) and into Mishnaic Hebrew (e.g., *m. Tamid* 4:2; *m. Mid.* 5:3). The only other biblical occurrence of *hēdîaḥ* in a cultic context is in 2 Chr 4:6, where it is an addition to its counterpart in Kings (1 Kgs 7:38–39), thus providing another instance of the relative antiquity of P (Hurvitz 1982: 63–65).

In distinction to the description of the burnt-offering procedure in 8:21, the verb begins the sentence and is in the imperfect despite the fact that it is followed by the closing verb, *wayyaqṭēr* (cf. also v 13). I cannot fathom the reason for this change. Perhaps the writer wishes to say here that despite the double *wayyaqṭēr,* the *ʿōlâ* procedure is a single rite and the same altar fire consumed the entire sacrifice.

with the burnt offering (ʿal hāʿōlâ). For the expression, see 3:5. Here, however, it refers to the main parts of the burnt offering (enumerated in v 13), exclusive of the entrails and legs. There is no adjunct cereal offering, a requirement that is mandated, according to P, only after the settlement in Canaan (Num 15:1–16).

15. *the people's offering.* *qorban hāʿām,* enumerated in vv 3–4.

and slaughtered it (wayyišḥāṭēhû). It was performed by Aaron (Hoffmann 1953). Indeed, all of the sacrificial rites (with the exception of the hand-leaning; see below) were performed by Aaron on this day with the assistance of his sons. This does not contradict the sacrificial laws that permit the laity to perform the slaughter (1:5, 11; 3:2, 8, 13, etc.; see the NOTE on 1:5). This concession applies solely to the individual's sacrifice, but in the formal, public cult the slaughtering was performed by the professional staff, that is to say, the priests (e.g., 2 Chr 29:24) or the Levites (cf. Ezek 44:11; 2 Chr 35:6). It must not be forgotten: this is a public service—the inaugural one.

INAUGURAL

The hand-leaning rite, missing here and in the texts describing all of the blood sacrifices (see the NOTE on "and slaughtered," v 8), was probably performed by the elders (v 1) on behalf of the people, in conformance with the sacrificial laws (see 4:15 and the NOTE on "He shall lean his hand," 1:4). There is no reason to deduce from the fact that Aaron presented and slaughtered the people's sacrifices (vv 15–18) that he also performed the hand-leaning rite (so Koch 1959: 70 n. 1). Elsewhere, the elders perform the hand-leaning for the people's purification offering, though it is slaughtered by others (see the NOTE on "shall be slaughtered," 4:15) and even more explicitly in the account of the rededication of the Temple under Hezekiah, the people's representatives perform the hand-leaning on its purification offering but the slaughtering is done by the priests (2 Chr 29:21–24).

and performed the purification rite with it. wayyĕḥaṭṭĕᵓēhû, that is, daubing the blood on the horns of the sacrificial altar *(Tg. Onq.; Tg. Ps.-J.),* the same meaning that the *piᶜel ḥiṭṭēᵓ* has elsewhere (Exod 29:36; Lev 6:19; Ezek 43:22; and esp. 2 Chr 29:24). This verb, *ḥiṭṭēᵓ,* cannot refer to the disposition of the carcass (Koch 1959: 73; Fishbane 1985: 227) because its sole object is the altar (note the above-cited verses).

as with the previous [purification offering] (kārīᵓšôn). Contrast the procedure with the burnt offering, which is *kammišpāṭ* 'in the prescribed manner' (v 16). Both purification offerings, for Aaron and for the people, are exceptional in that their blood is not taken into the Tent (Dillmann and Ryssel 1897). For according to the Priestly sacrificial system, the sins of the whole community, whether inadvertent (4:13–21) or presumptuous (16:19; see the NOTE on "transgressions"), pollute the interior of the shrine, and the latter must be purged with the blood of the purification offering. The variance recorded here, however, cannot be explained except by assuming that it is a vestige of an older form of the purification offering, whose blood was employed solely upon the sacrificial altar (perhaps because most sanctuaries were *bāmôt,* open-air altars devoid of any structures) and whose carcass was totally incinerated outside the settlement. Only subsequently, a Priestly reform altered this rite and ordained that purification offerings whose blood was solely employed on the altar but not inside the shrine were to be eaten by the priests (see the NOTE on v 11 and details in chap. 10, COMMENT C).

16. *and sacrificed it (wayyaᶜăśehā).* For the technical usage of the verb *ᶜāśâ* see the NOTES on "you do," v 6 and "sacrifice," v 7.

in the prescribed manner (kammišpāṭ). For this usage, see 5:10. The procedure for the burnt offering is described in chap. 1.

17. *and, taking a handful of it (wayyĕmallēᵓ kappô mimmennâ).* In the prescription for the cereal offering, a different terminology is employed: this action is expressed as *wĕqāmaṣ mi . . . mĕlōᵓ qumṣô* (2:2) and the handful is called *ᵓazkārâ* (2:2, 9, 16). Undoubtedly, the same rite is described here *(Sipra,* Milluᵓim Shemini 11; *b. Menaḥ.* 9b). Hence, the changed vocabulary is a sign of

the freedom the writer allowed himself to employ synonyms and equivalent expressions, a practice widely attested in the ancient Near East (see the NOTE on 8:2).

Oil and frankincense, a requirement of the independent cereal offering (2:2), are assumed. So is the eventual consumption of the cereal offering by the priests (10:12–13; cf. 2:3; 7:10), which, however, will be aborted by the events described in 10:16–20.

in addition to the burnt offering of the morning (millĕbad ʿōlat habbōqer). The reference here is to the *Tāmîd,* in accordance with the view that it was offered at Sinai (Num 28:6), that is to say, as soon as the Tabernacle was erected. For this reason, the instructions for the *Tāmîd* were attached to the prescriptions for the priestly consecration (Exod 29:38–40) and its execution was inserted into the account of the erection of the Tabernacle (Exod 40:29). Why is it mentioned here, in association with the cereal offering, instead of with the burnt offering (v 16)? The writer presumes that the burnt offering and cereal offering are an inseparable pair and are sacrificed together. Ibn Ezra (on v 4) holds this to be the case on the assumption that the cereal offering is the adjunct to the burnt offering rather than an independent sacrifice—a suggestion, however, that has to be rejected in view of the disposition of the offering (see the NOTE on v 4). A further difficulty encountered by this phrase is that it presumes that Moses officiated at the *Tāmîd (Seper Hamibḥar),* even though Aaron had already been consecrated, for according to Moses' command to Aaron—"Come forward to the altar" (v 7)—Aaron is officiating for the first time (see the NOTE on v 7). All of the above point to the probability that this clause is a later interpolation by a glossator who assumed that the *Tāmîd* had been offered up and had to be accounted for. Another indication of its interpolative nature is its use of *millĕbad* instead of the older Priestly synonym, *ʿal* (for details see the NOTE on 23:35 and Knohl 1987 [1983–84]: 115–17).

18. *He slaughtered (wayyišḥaṭ).* Aaron also slaughtered the well-being offering of the people, in conformance with the attested practice that sacrifices in the public cult were slaughtered by the Temple clergy (2 Chr 29:24; and see the NOTE on "and slaughtered it," v 15). The rite of hand-leaning on these animals was probably performed by the elders (v 1) on behalf of the people (see the NOTE on "and slaughtered it," v 15).

passed (wayyamṣîʾû). See the NOTE on v 12.

which he dashed against all sides of the altar (wayyizrĕqēhû ʿal-hammizbēaḥ sābîb). A parenthetical statement, for the following verse continues as the direct object of "Aaron's sons passed"; hence it is construed as a dependent clause with the opening *waw* serving as a relative conjunction. It had to be mentioned because it concerned the altar—the central focus of the entire chapter (see the NOTE "On the eighth day," v 1).

19. *—and the suet pieces . . . (wĕʾet-haḥălābîm . . .).* This entire verse is the object of "Aaron's sons passed" (v 18b).

of the ox (min-haššôr). The Masoretes place the *ʾatnaḥ* here probably to avoid the impression that the ox also possesses a broad tail. As the MT reads now, the suet pieces of the ox are not listed—they are assumed to be known—whereas those of the ram are enumerated. It is preferable, however, to move the *ʾatnaḥ* to the ram so that the suet pieces that follow are possessed by both animals but not necessarily in common.

the covering [*suet*] *(wĕhamĕkasseh)*. An ellipsis for all of the suet pieces (Ramban). Their enumeration in the LXX is superfluous.

the kidneys (wĕhakkĕlāyōt). The omission of the usual *štê* 'two' (e.g., 3:4, 9, 15) is essential because we are dealing with the kidneys of two animals, in other words, four of them.

and the caudate lobes (wĕyōteret hakkābēd). Though singular in form it is a collective, standing for the caudate lobes of both animals.

20. *They laid (wayyāśîmû)*. The subject is Aaron's sons. As they have assisted in the blood rite (v 18) they now assist in the suet rite. These duties would normally devolve upon the lay offerer as part of his private sacrifice; compare 7:30, which explicitly instructs the offerer to lay the suet pieces on the animal's breast. This is another indication that we are dealing with the regular public cult in which all rites (except the hand-leaning, see the NOTE on "and slaughtered it," v 15) are performed by the clergy. The LXX, Sam., and Pesh. read this verb as a singular, apparently attributing this act to Aaron, a reading that must be rejected.

these suet pieces (ʾet-haḥălābîm). This object has already been mentioned in the previous verse (v 19). It is repeated here (a repetitive resumption) because of the enumeration of the individual pieces (v 19b). For a similar construction see 4:11–12 (Ehrlich 1908–14).

upon (ʿal). "Although most of the ribs do not meet under the animal's belly, the first several ribs (between the forelegs) do have a gristly sternum connecting them. This part could make a sort of basket which would be big enough to hold the suet, kidneys, etc. of the animal" (S. Rattray). Details on the quartering of the animal are discussed in the NOTE on 7:30.

21. *and the right thigh (wĕʾēt šôq hayyāmîn)*. According to this verse, Aaron performs the elevation rite with the right thigh in spite of 7:32, which attests that the right thigh does not require it! But a look at the MT here reveals that all is not in order. For one thing, there were two right thighs, one of the ox and one of the ram, as there were two breasts. Why then does this verse express the breasts in the plural but the right thigh in the singular? One can argue that *šôq hayyāmîn* may be a collective, singular in form but plural or dual in meaning, but this argument is countered by the attestations of the right thigh in dual form (e.g., Deut 28:35; Ps 147:10; Prov 26:7; Cant 5:15). For another, v 20a reads peculiarly. Because the thigh undergoes the elevation rite, it should have read, "They laid these suet pieces upon the breasts [and upon the right thighs]." Why are the thighs missing? Hoffmann (1953) tries to resolve the discrepancy

by declaring that *hēnîp* (v 21) is pluperfect, so Aaron had already performed the elevation rite with the thigh before he laid the suet on the breasts, and for this reason the thigh is not mentioned with them. But he did not pay attention to the literary style of this account. *hēnîp* is simple past tense, like *śārap* (v 11) and *himṣi'û* (v 13). The text here does not express *hēnîp* as an imperfect prefixed with the sequential *waw* because the verb is preceded by the object, which mandates the use of the perfect. Moreover, one should notice that *hēnîp* is the final rite in the people's sacrifices (vv 15–21), and, to indicate that it is the final rite, the verb is expressed in the simple perfect (Paran 1983: 142, and see the NOTE on 1:9).

Hence, doubt arises over the question whether the words "and the right thigh" are really original. Indeed, when they are removed from the text all problems disappear. The ceremony with the thigh and breast are then performed in conformance with the rule of 7:30–31: the breast is offered upon the suet and undergoes the elevation rite, but there is no elevation rite for the thigh. Thus the reason for interpolating the right thigh here is to endow it with an elevation rite; a change in ritual has occurred and its historical background is discussed in chap. 7, COMMENT F.

One might ask: Even if the right thigh is not subject to the elevation rite, should it not at least have been mentioned as a prebend for the officiating priest? The answer has already been given in connection with the omission of the hand-leaning rite even though its performance is mandatory (e.g., 1:4; 3:2, 8, 13): the writer skipped the matter of priestly prebends as he skipped other details that deviated from his intent to focus solely on the altar rites, climaxed by the fire theophany on the altar (see the NOTES on "On the eighth day," v 1, and "and slaughtered," v 8). The consumption of these priestly prebends is taken up in 10:14–15, but it never took place because of the tragedy described in 10:16–20.

elevation offering (tĕnûpâ). See the discussion in chap. 7, COMMENT E.

before the Lord (lipnê YHWH). Indispensable to the *tĕnûpâ*, this phrase is what distinguishes it from the *tĕrûmâ* (see the discussion in chap. 7, COMMENT E).

as Moses had commanded (ka'ăšer ṣiwwâ mōšeh). Thirty-four MSS, the LXX, and Sam. read *ka'ăšer ṣiwwâ YHWH 'et-mōšeh* 'as the Lord had commanded Moses', as in v 10; cf. v 7. Pesh. reads *ṣuwwâ* 'was commanded', but this *(pu'al)* passive would only make sense if Moses himself were the speaker (see the NOTE on "I was commanded," 8:35). Perhaps the MT is correct. The change from the attested formula might well be deliberate, a hint that Moses' command for the right thigh to undergo the elevation rite was of his own initiative and did not stem from God, who had commanded otherwise (7:32–33).

22. *Then Aaron lifted his hands (wayyiśśā' 'ahărōn 'et-yādāw; K./Q. ydyw)*. A posture of prayer (Pss 28:2; 134:2), which must be carefully differentiated from

nāśā' yād 'lift the hand' (singular) for the purpose of taking an oath (e.g., Exod 6:8; Num 14:30; Ezek 20:5). The position of the uplifted hands is more graphically conveyed by the synonymous expression *pāraś kappayim* (Exod 9:5, 29, 33; 1 Kgs 8:22, 54; Pss 44:21; 143:6; Job 11:13; Dan 6:10; Ezra 9:5; Luke 22:41; Acts 7:59). Good pictorial examples of this posture are visible on the panel of Miriam's well at the Dura-Europos synagogue (Jo Milgrom 1978). That it was not limited to Israel is demonstrated by cognate expressions in other Semitic languages, such as Ug. *ša ydk šmm* 'lift your hands to heaven' (Krt 75–76); Akk. *našû qata* 'pray with uplifted hands' (*CAD*, N 106–7). It was also practiced by the Greeks but with the following nuanced variations: "The suppliant stood with face and hands upraised to heaven when he called upon the dwellers therein. In addressing the deities of the sea, he might merely stretch his arms towards the waters. And when beings addressed were those of the nether world, the suppliant would stretch his hands downwards" (Gardner and Jevons, cited by Gray 1912: 23).

toward the people ('el-ha'am). The meaning here is that Aaron faced the people. His hands, of course, were raised toward heaven (Exod 9:29, 33).

and blessed them (wayĕbārĕkēm). The content of the blessing is not given. Most commentators opt for the priestly blessing of Num 6:24–26 (*Sipra*, Millu'im Shemini 30; *b. Soṭa* 38a; *y. Ta'an.* 4:1); others claim that a closing prayer like that of Solomon (1 Kgs 8:22) was employed (Ramban).

and he came down (wayyēred). From where? Theoretically, he need not have ascended the altar, for its top could have been reached from the ground; it was only three cubits (approx. 4½ ft.) high. But its length and width were five by five cubits (approx. 7½ × 7½ ft.). Thus the priest would have no choice but to ascend it in order to reach every part of its upper surface. Either steps or a ramp would be required. The prohibition of Exod 20:26 mandates the latter, and a ramp was built into the altar of the Second Temple (e.g., *m. Mid.* 3:4) but probably not in Ahaz's altar of the First Temple (2 Kgs 16:10–13), which may have served as the model for Ezekiel (Ezek 43:13–17).

Some authorities, however, deny that the blessing was recited from the top of the altar by rendering *wayyēred* as a pluperfect, "after he had come down" (*Sipra*, Millu'im Shemini 29; Saadiah, Ibn Janaḥ, Ibn Ezra, Hazzequni), in other words, Aaron offered his blessing after he had completed the sacrificial rites and descended from the altar (*b. Meg.* 18a). In support of this interpretation one can point to Solomon's blessing, which he delivered while standing in front of the altar (1 Kgs 8:54–55) or, in the Chronicler's version, while he was standing on a bronze *kiyyôr* platform (2 Chr 6:13). Nevertheless, the Solomonic example is not decisive. He most likely did not officiate at the dedication sacrifices and thus had no reason to ascend the altar. The Chronicler's tradition that he stood on a platform, presumably in order to be visible to the assembled throngs, has much to commend it. For the same reason one can also presume that this is the intention of the MT's notice here: Aaron offered his blessing on the altar, where he could be seen by everyone in the Tabernacle courtyard. (For other views, see *y. Ta'an.* 4:1 and Abravanel.)

after sacrificing (mēʿǎśôt). For the meaning of this technical Priestly term see the NOTES on "that you do," v 6 and "sacrifice," v 7.

The cereal offering is omitted from the list of sacrifices, presumably because there was no activity at the altar using the cereal except for the handful (v 17), which would have been consumed as soon as it came into contact with the altar's coals.

23. *then entered the Tent of Meeting (wayyābōʾ . . . ʾel-ʾōhel môʿēd).* For what purpose did Moses and Aaron enter the Tent? None is cited, and it can only be conjectured: (1) so that the divine presence might descend (*Sipra*, Millu'im Shemini 19) though, according to P, the divine presence was already there (Exod 40:34–35); (2) to pray for the emergence of the *kābôd* from the adytum (Ibn Ezra, Rashbam, Hazzequni, *Keter Torah*). Despite Moses' promise of the forthcoming theophany (vv 4b, 6b), he had no guarantee that it would take place. Hence, his prayer; (3) this latter explanation receives additional support from the fact that Moses' entry into the Tent takes place between the two blessings of the people. This Tabernacle pattern is duplicated by Solomon, who also blesses the people twice while facing them (1 Kgs 8:14–21, 54–61), and between these two blessings bows down at the foot of the altar (or on a platform, 2 Chr 6:13) and offers his personal prayer (1 Kgs 8:22–54). The Solomonic example, then, allows us to conclude that the entry of Moses and Aaron into the Tent between their blessings was also for purposes of prayer—that the Lord would establish the work of their hands in the building of the Tabernacle and the investiture of the priesthood by the appearance of his presence in the *kābôd* (A. Hurowitz).

Although Moses always prays to God in private (e.g., Exod 5:22; 8:8, 25–26)—in order that he not be taken for a pagan magician (Milgrom 1983f: 260) —Aaron is sometimes at his side (Num 2:6). God's reply, however, is reserved for Moses alone (Num 17:8–9).

they blessed the people (wayĕbārăkû ʾet-hāʿām). The content of their prayer is the subject of wide speculation, for example: "May the Memra of the Lord receive your sacrifices favorably, and remit and forgive your sins" *(Tg. Ps.-J.);* "May it be the divine will that his Presence will rest on all the work of your hands" (*t. Menaḥ.* 7:8). By contrast, the prayers that Mesopotamian monarchs recite after building or repairing a temple amount to a quid-pro-quo declaration: for example, "May Shamash who resides in this temple grant forever to Yahdun-Lim who built his temple, his beloved king, a mighty weapon (able) to defeat the enemies, a long and happy rule and everlasting years of abundance and happiness" (*ANET*[3] 556; cf. also Gudea B 2.21–3; Ur-Nammu Hymn, 39–51).

and the Glory of the Lord appeared to all of the people (wayyērāʾ kĕbôd-YHWH ʾel-kol-hāʿām). The presence reveals itself in the form of fire (v 24a; Ramban). Israel will be guided in the wilderness not by God's voiced commands but by his visible presence, a cloud-encased fire (Exod 40:38). During the day only the cloud is visible, for presumably the fire is dimmed by the sunlight. But the night renders the cloud invisible and only the luminous fire can be seen. It is the fire that is identified with the *kābôd* (Exod 24:17; Ezek 1:27–28; 2 Chr 7:3). The Lord's cloud and fire can be compared to Akk. *melammu* and *puluḫtu*, which describe, respectively, the refulgent areola and garment of fire that surround the gods and their sancta. The *melammu* stands for the gods' vital force, which takes the form of pulsating light (Cassin 1968); alternatively, it can also refer to the mask that hides the natural body of gods and demons (Oppenheim 1943). The winged sun disk of Egypt is also associated with fire and clouds (Mendenhall 1973: 32–66). Thus the Lord's *kābôd* is enveloped by a cloud but is visible, especially at night, *kĕmarʾēh-ʾēš*, 'as the likeness of fire' (Num 9:15). It needs to be emphasized that this is a simile, not an identity. Again, "And the likeness *(ûmarʾēh)* of the Lord's *kābôd* was *like* a consuming fire" (Exod 24:17a); "All the Israelites witnessed the descent of the fire *and* the *kābôd* of the Lord" (2 Chr 7:3a).

The first time the Lord's firecloud was seen by Israel was when it descended atop Mount Sinai (Exod 24:15b–18a). This passage reveals by its structure, not once but twice, that the "cloud" envelops the *kābôd* (Janowski 1982: 304), as follows:

> The *cloud* covered the mountain
> The *kābôd* of the Lord abode on Mount Sinai
> and the *cloud* hid it for six days

> On the seventh day he called to Moses from the midst of the *cloud*
> Now the *kābôd* of the Lord appeared in the sight of the Israelites as a
>   consuming fire on the top of the mountain
> Moses went inside the *cloud* and ascended the mountain.

It is the ascending and descending firecloud that determines whether Israel moves or encamps (Num 9:18). As soon as the Tabernacle is reassembled it is enveloped by the cloud. Thus, according to P, the Lord does not reside in the adytum of the Tabernacle but only enters it from the suspended cloud whenever he wishes to address Moses (e.g., Num 17:7; 20:6). Even when Moses seeks an audience on his own initiative, the *kābôd* must first become visible before he can be sure that his request for an audience is granted. Presumably, this visibility is effected when the *kābôd* becomes luminous enough to be seen in daylight by all of Israel (Exod 24:17; Num 20:6; 2 Chr 7:3).

Thus it was of no unusual significance that the Israelites could behold the Lord's *kābôd;* it was "a pillar of fire by night" (Exod 40:38; Num 14:14). What was unusual, indeed unprecedented, in the theophany was that the fire emerged from the adytum without its cloud cover and consumed the sacrifices upon the altar.

24. *Fire came forth from before the Lord (wattēṣēʾ ʾēš millipnê YHWH).* The sacrifices on the altar were slowly burning (vv 13, 14, 17, 24), a process normally taking many hours (6:2b), but the divine fire consumed them in a flash (Hoffmann 1953).

God appears as fire (Deut 4:21; 9:3) and his *kābôd* is expressly identified with fire (Exod 24:17; see the NOTE on "and the Glory of the Lord," v 23). On four other occasions God sends his divine fire to consume the burnt offering: the annunciation to Manoah and his wife of the birth of Samson (Judg 13:15–20); David's sacrifice to stop the plague (1 Chr 21:26; but contrast 2 Sam 24:25); the dedication of Solomon's Temple (2 Chr 7:1–3; but contrast 1 Kgs 8:62–63); and the contest between Elijah and the prophets of Baal (1 Kgs 18:22–39). The significance of the fire theophany on the inaugural day of the public cult is that it legitimizes the Aaronic priesthood—Aaron and his sons are officiating for the first time—and the following rabbinic observation hits the mark: "Rabbi Tanhum son of Rabbi Yudan said: . . . On every one of the seven days of the investiture of the priests Moses served as high priest, but it was not through his agency that the Presence came down to dwell in the world. When Aaron came and ministered, however, the Presence came down through his agency" (*Pesiq. R.* 14:11; cf. *Sipra*, Milluʾim Shemini 14; *p. Yoma* 1:1; *Midr. Tanḥ.* Ḥuqqat 58). By the same token, the Chronicler's tradition attributes a similar theophany to Solomon's Temple (but not Kings: verses cited above) in order to provide divine sanction for Solomon's reign (see Meyers 1983: 176).

Whence the fire? The silence of the text allows for ample speculation: (1) it came of itself (Jos., *Ant.* 3.207); (2) it descended from heaven (2 Chr 7:1; *Sipre Zuṭa* on Num 11:1; *Sipra*, Milluʾim Shemini 20; *Pirqe R. El.* 53); (3) it originated in the adytum (*Sipra*, Milluʾim Shemini 34; Philo, *Vit. Mos.* 2.154); (4) from the adytum it passed through the shrine, where it kindled the incense on the inner altar (the incense being burned before the *Tāmîd, b. Yoma* 33b), incinerated Nadab and Abihu, and then exited into the court and consumed the sacrifices on the altar (Rashbam; cf. *Sipre Zuṭa* on Num 11:1). But on the other occasions on which the divine fire consumes the sacrifice (cited above), it is explicitly stated or assumed that it descends from heaven: "the fire of the Lord fell *(wattippōl)*" (1 Kgs 18:38); "He (the Lord) answered him in fire from heaven" (1 Chr 21:26); "as the fire descended *(bĕredet)*" (2 Chr 7:3). Here, however, the verb employed is *yāṣāʾ* 'come out, emerge'. Thus there can be no doubt that the fire emerged from the adytum, in conformance with the Priestly theology that the Lord's *kābôd*, encased in cloud, would descend upon the Tabernacle and rest between the outspread wings of the cherubim flanking the Ark.

Anthropologists see the altar fire as a gateway to the other world through which offerings are transmitted to God and through which the power of God is directly manifested to man (e.g., Leach 1976: 88). The correctness of this observation is accentuated by a Priestly rule concerning the altar fire: it may never be allowed to die out. This admonition is given twice in two consecutive verses (6:5–6). The reason is now apparent. Because the altar fire is of divine origin it must be perpetuated (*Sipra*, Nedaba 5:10). Furthermore, a more pragmatic purpose underlies this injunction. Just as the initial appearance of the divine fire signified God's approval, so every sacrifice offered on the same altar will, with God's grace, also merit his acceptance.

the burnt offering (hā'ōlâ). The singular is generic for all of the burnt offerings sacrificed on this day: the priests', the people's, and the *Tāmîd*. Alternatively, it has been suggested that the sing. *'ōlâ* may refer to the people's burnt offering (v 16), which had not yet been consumed (Snaith 1967). This view, however, must be rejected on the grounds that animal sacrifices took a long time to burn on the altar, judging by the evening *Tāmîd*, which burned all night (6:2).

the suet pieces. hahălābîm, namely, from Aaron's calf (v 2) and the people's he-goat, ox, and ram (vv 3–4). Again, there is no mention of the cereal offering (see the NOTE on "after sacrificing," v 22), for the obvious reason that it was only a handful (v 17) and, therefore, was consumed by the altar coals before the onset of the divine fire.

And the people saw. God himself and not just his *kābôd* (see the NOTE on "will appear," v 4).

and shouted for joy (wayyārōnnû). The root *rnn* and its noun *rinnâ* mean "shout" (e.g., 1 Kgs 22:36; Ibn Ezra): ancient Israel did not worship God in silence. In this instance, the shouting surely stemmed from joy, a meaning for *rnn* that is amply attested (e.g., Isa 49:13; Jer 31:6; Pss 33:1; 35:27; 95:1; the paraphrase of 2 Chr 7:3; cf. *Tgs.*; *Sipra*, Millu'im Shemini 31). Philo, however, claims they shouted out of "great agitation and terrible consternation" (*Her.* 251; cf. Ibn Ezra and 1 Kgs 22:36).

and fell on their faces (wayyipplû 'al-pĕnêhem). "The root *npl* is normally used of a sudden swift descent" (Snaith 1967), for example, Gen 24:64. The idiom "fall on the face" connotes full abasement, often in prayer. It is not synonymous with *hištāḥāwâ* 'prostrate oneself' for the two terms occur in sequence (e.g., Josh 5:14; 1 Sam 20:41; 2 Sam 9:2; 14:22; Job 1:20; Ruth 2:10); the fact that "fall on the face" always precedes "prostrate oneself" implies a preliminary posture such as resting on the knees with the head arched over and touching the ground. This interpretation is supported by the synonymous expression *wayyikrĕ'û 'appayim 'arṣâ* 'they knelt with their faces to the ground', also followed by *wayyištaḥāwû* 'and they prostrated themselves' (2 Chr 7:3; cf. Esth 3:2, 5; 2 Chr 29:29). Strikingly, three out of the four other occurrences of the divine fire consuming the sacrifice also record the same response: the worshipers fall to the ground and praise God (Judg 13:20; 1 Kgs 18:39; 2 Chr 7:3).

COMMENT: THE EIGHTH DAY, MEANING AND PARADIGM

The eighth day marks the inauguration of the regular, public cult. During the previous week, the Tabernacle was consecrated and the priests were invested, all in preparation for this day. The eighth day is thus the climax of the foregoing seven, as in so many other rituals and events (see the NOTE "On the eighth day," v 1). Aaron is the exclusive officiant (assisted by his sons), and he offers up every kind of sacrifice with the exception of the 'āšām, the reparation offering, the only sacrifice that is wholly private and never incorporated into the public cult. The provision for well-being offerings guarantees the festive nature of this day (see the NOTE on v 4). Indeed, the promised theophany (vv 4b, 6b) is a happy prognostication that the consecration of the sanctuary and its priesthood will merit divine sanction.

The account of the rites that celebrate completion of Solomon's Temple supplies us with the technical name for this day. Solomon offers a series of sacrifices: burnt, cereal, and well-being offerings (1 Kgs 8:64). This last sacrifice is described in detail (vv 62–63), followed by the statement "wayyaḥnĕkû the House of the Lord." The verb ḥānak has been wrongly translated as "dedicate." S. C. Reif (1972), building on the pioneer study of O. S. Rankin (1930), has shown that the proper translation is "initiate." In fact, as noted by Reif, it is Rashi (on Gen 14:14) who must be credited as the first to have provided the correct meaning: "The word ḥnk signifies introducing a person or thing, for the first time, to some particular occupation in which it is intended that he (or it) should remain; similarly Prov 22:6; Num 7:84 and Ps 30:1; in old French *enseigner.*" Thus Deut 20:5 should be rendered, with Rashi: "Whoever has built a house and not started to live in it *(ḥănākô).*" Prov 22:6, *ḥănōk lanna'ar 'al-pî darkô,* is no longer an enigma when rendered "Start a boy on the right road" *(NEB).* Nehemiah's festivities after the wall is completed now should translate "At the inauguration *(ûbaḥănukkat)* of the wall of Jerusalem . . . to conduct initiation festivities *(ḥănukkâ)* with rejoicing" (Neh 12:27).

Returning to 1 Kgs 8:63, we can now render it "Solomon sacrificed 22,000 oxen and 120,000 sheep as well-being offerings to the Lord. Thus the king and the Israelites *initiated the use* of the House of the Lord." That Solomon's initiation offerings for the Temple were preceded by some ceremony of consecration can be deduced from the verse that follows: "On that day the king consecrated *(qiddēš)* the center of the court that was in front of the House of the Lord. For it was there that he sacrificed the burnt offerings, the cereal offerings, and the suet pieces of the well-being offerings, because the bronze altar that was before the Lord was too small to hold the burnt offerings, the cereal offerings, and the suet pieces of the well-being offerings" (1 Kgs 8:64).

Thus before Solomon could make the area around the altar an extension of it he had to consecrate it. By the same token one can assume that before Solomon could initiate the use *(ḥnk)* of the Temple, he first had to consecrate it *(qdš)*, precisely as demanded by the Tabernacle paradigm.

Additional evidence on the nature of this eighth-day initiation ceremony is supplied by the Chronicler, who adds to the Kings passage on Solomon's Temple the following comment: "They sacrificed the initiation offering for the altar *(ḥănukkat hammizbēaḥ)* seven days." Thus the Chronicler makes it clear that what is meant by *ḥănukkat habbayit* (Ps 30:1; cf. 1 Kgs 8:63; 2 Chr 7:5) is *ḥănukkat hammizbēaḥ*, the initiatory offerings on the altar. Still, it is to Josephus that we must turn for the most accurate (and graphic) interpretation of these rites: "This was the first time that he (Solomon) gave the Temple a taste of sacrifices" *(Ant.* 8.123).

This new rendering for *ḥnk* enables us to understand the purpose of the special contributions made by the Israelite chieftains to the Tabernacle altar (Num 7). The twelve tribal chieftains jointly contribute expensive gifts to the completed and consecrated Tabernacle consisting of six draught carts and twelve bulls so that the Gershonite and Merarite Levites can haul the dismantled Tabernacle. Then, individually and on successive days, each chieftain contributes to the consecrated altar the identical gift, as follows: one silver bowl and one silver basin, each filled with choice flour and oil for cereal offerings, one gold ladle filled with incense, and the same number and species of sacrificial animals. These altar gifts are called *ḥănukkat hammizbēaḥ*, which now can be rendered "initiation offerings for the altar" (Num 7:10, 11, 84, 88). What the chieftains did was to contribute an initial supply of vessels and animals so that the altar could begin to be used for all requisite ceremonies of the public cult. Thus it was not enough to purify and consecrate the altar by appropriate sacrifices and anointings during the week of the priestly investiture, and it was not enough for Aaron and the people to contribute the necessary flour and animals for the eighth day's initiation rites. The chieftains continue the altar's initiation rite for an additional twelve days, thereby extending its dedicatory period to a total of twenty days—a fitting inauguration for the Tabernacle. Moreover, it has been shown that the eighth day's rites focus on the altar (see the NOTES on "and slaughtered it," v 15; also cf. vv 1, 21). All that is unrelated to the altar, though indispensable, is unmentioned: the hand-leaning, the disposition of the right thigh, and the consumption of the sacrifices. The slaughtering rite is noted only because, exceptionally, it is performed by Aaron. Thus there is no room for doubt in subtitling this eighth day *ḥănukkat hammizbēaḥ* 'the initiation offerings for the altar' (see further Milgrom 1986b).

The eight days celebrating the inauguration of the Tabernacle became a paradigm for subsequent Temple inaugurations. Solomon had the ceremonies for his Temple coincide with the Feast of Tabernacles *(heḥag* 'The Festival') so as to assure attendance (1 Kgs 8:2, 65). On the eighth day, Solomon dismissed the people (v 66a). But this statement follows the notice in the MT that the celebration lasted fourteen days, ostensibly seven days for the Festival and seven days for the inauguration (v 65b), thus making the eighth day, presumably of the inauguration, fall on the thirtieth of the month. The LXX omits the phrase *wešibʿat yāmîm ʾarbāʿâ ʿāśār yôm,* thus restricting the initiatory rites to the seven-day festival and resulting in a smoother text, in that *bayyôm haššĕmînî* 'on the eighth day' now follows *šibʿat yāmîm* 'seven days'. The glossator's motivation in extending the seven days to fourteen is not clear, unless it was to avoid the coincidence of the two celebrations.

The matter becomes even more complex when we turn to the Chronicler's version. It seems that he had the full MT of 1 Kgs 8:65 before him, for he too ascribes a fourteen-day period to the celebration. But because he has the additional desire to avoid a conflict with the Festival of the Eighth Day of Assembly, ordained in P (Lev 23:36; Num 29:35) but not in D (cf. Deut 16:15), he switches around the two seven-day periods, making the Temple inauguration precede the Festival and Eighth Day of Assembly, and he has Solomon dismiss the people on the twenty-third of the month (2 Chr 7:9–10; see Radak on the conflict with Yom Kippur). In either version, however, the calculation rests upon a common assumption: the initiatory rites involve an eighth day.

A Temple purification is attributed by the Chronicler to Hezekiah (2 Chr 29:17). Here the basic number is not seven but eight, eight days for purifying the courts and eight days for purifying the Temple (*qiddēš* here means "purify").

The initiation of Ezekiel's altar (Ezek 43:18–27) has already been discussed (see chap. 4, COMMENT K and the NOTE on 8:33). What is relevant here is that following the altar rites, which continue for eight days (one plus seven), the text concludes, "And when these days are over, then from the eighth day onward the priests shall sacrifice your burnt offerings and your well-being offerings on the altar; and I will extend my favor to you—declares the Lord God" (Ezek 43:27). Thus, even though the regular, daily cult actually begins on the ninth day— having been preceded by eight days of initiation—Ezekiel uses the language *wĕhāyâ bayyôm haššĕmînî,* patently because he is influenced by the opening words of this chapter, *wayyĕhî bayyôm haššĕmînî* (v 1), thereby corroborating the conclusion that the eighth day represents the inauguration of the regular, public cult (as well as being another bit of evidence that Ezekiel is influenced by the text of P; see the Introduction §B).

A final word is needed on the festival of Hanukkah initiated by the Hasmoneans. The fact that it was ordained for eight days may rest ultimately upon the Tabernacle tradition. Undoubtedly, its earliest name "The Days of Tabernacles in the Month of Kislev" (2 Macc 1:9), which may indicate that it celebrated a postponed Feast of Tabernacles (Goldstein 1976: 273–84), also provided an impetus for the eight-day observance. In either case, the true meaning of its name, *ḥănukkâ,* is preserved: "They celebrated the dedication of the altar for eight days, joyfully bringing burnt offerings and sacrificing well-being offerings and thank offerings" (1 Macc 4:56). But the altar was "dedicated" through its use. Indeed, when Josephus describes the festival he "nowhere uses the Greek word 'dedicate' (enkainizein). Even in his paraphrases of our passage, he uses only Greek words connoting resumption or restoration or renewal, and he speaks not of the consecration of the new altar but of the resumption of the temple cult and the restoration of the temple. . . . It would appear that his abstention from the word 'dedication' here is deliberate, whatever the reason for it" (Goldstein 1976: 282). The reason is not too difficult to discern. "Consecrate" would be altogether wrong, for the rite of anointing was never reintroduced in the Second Temple, and "Dedication" would be wrong because ḥănukkâ means "Initiation [of the altar]," precisely that which happened in Maccabean times and on all of the preceding occasions.

THE TRAGIC AFTERMATH OF THE
INAUGURAL SERVICE (10:1–20)

Nadab and Abihu

10 ¹Now Aaron's sons, Nadab and Abihu, each took his pan, put coals in it, and laid incense on it; and they offered before the Lord unauthorized coals, which he had not commanded them. ²And fire came forth from the Lord and consumed them; thus they died before the Lord. ³Then Moses said to Aaron, "This is what the Lord meant when he said: 'Through those near to me I shall sanctify myself, and before all of the people I shall glorify myself.' " And Aaron was silent.

⁴Moses called Mishael and Elzaphan, sons of Uzziel the uncle of Aaron, and said to them, "Come forward and carry your kinsmen away from the front of the sacred precinct [to a place] outside the camp." ⁵They came forward and carried them out of the camp by their tunics, as Moses had ordered. ⁶And Moses said to Aaron and to his sons, Eleazar and Ithamar, "Do not dishevel your hair and do not rend your clothes, lest you die and anger strike the whole community. But your kinsmen, all the house of Israel, shall bewail the burning that the Lord has wrought. ⁷You must not go outside the entrance of the Tent of Meeting, lest you die, for the Lord's anointing oil is upon you." And they did as Moses had ordered.

The Conduct and Function of the Priests

⁸And the Lord spoke to Aaron, saying: ⁹Drink no wine or ale, you or your sons after you, when you enter the Tent of Meeting, that you may not die; it is a law for all time throughout your generations. ¹⁰You must distinguish between the sacred and the common, and between the impure and the pure. ¹¹And you

must teach the Israelites all of the laws that the Lord has imparted to them through Moses.

On Eating the Priestly Portions

12Moses spoke to Aaron and to his remaining sons, Eleazar and Ithamar: "Take the cereal offering that remains from the Lord's food gifts and eat it unleavened beside the altar, for it is most holy. 13You shall eat it in the sacred precinct, inasmuch as it is your due and your sons' due from the Lord's food gifts; for so I have been commanded. 14But the breast of the elevation offering and the thigh of contribution you, and your sons and daughters after you, may eat in any pure place, for they have been assigned as a due to you and your children from the Israelites' sacrifices of well-being. 15Together with the food gifts of suet, they must present the thigh of contribution and the breast of the elevation offering, which shall be elevated as an elevation offering before the Lord, and which shall be a due to you and to your children after you for all time —as the Lord has commanded."

16Then Moses insistently inquired about the goat of the purification offering, and it had already been burned! He was angry with Eleazar and Ithamar, Aaron's remaining sons, and said, 17"Why did you not eat the purification offering in the sacred precinct? For it is most holy and he has assigned it to you to remove the iniquity of the community to effect purgation on their behalf before the Lord. 18Because its blood was not brought into the interior of the sacred precinct, you certainly ought to have eaten it in the sacred precinct, as I commanded." 19And Aaron spoke to Moses, "See, this day they brought their purification offering and burnt offering before the Lord, and such things have befallen me! Had I eaten the purification offering today, would the Lord have approved?" 20And when Moses heard this, he approved.

NOTES

10:1. *Now.* It was still the eighth day (see "this day," v 19). The sacrifices had been offered (9:8–21) but had not yet been eaten by the priests (vv 12–20).

Nadab and Abihu. They were Aaron's eldest sons who, according to the Epic tradition (Exod 24:1, 9–11), were next in importance after Moses and Aaron, ranking even higher than the seventy elders.

took (wayyiqḥû). This is the opening word of this chapter and the opening word in the commands given to Moses (8:2) and Aaron (9:2). The contrast is striking: Nadab and Abihu also took but without authorization.

his pan (maḥtātô). Derived from the verb ḥātâ 'rake' (coals from the hearth, Isa 30:14; Prov 6:27; 25:22). Hence it is "any utensil which can be used for carrying what is too hot to be held in the hand" (Snaith 1967). The shape of the pan is not precisely known, but ancient Near Eastern iconography offers a number of possibilities (see the NOTE on "pan," 16:12). Pans are included among the sancta (Exod 25:38; 27:3; 37:23; 38:3; Num 4:9), but in all of these instances the pans are associated with either the menora or the sacrificial altar, and presumably their use is for the sole purpose of removing ashes and not for offering incense (the same deduction holds for the non-P occurrences of this object: 2 Kgs 25:15; Jer 52:19; 2 Chr 4:22). Pans for incense offering are mentioned in the Priestly account (see below), but in the case of Nadab and Abihu, as well as of Korah and his cohort, the text also specifies *ʾîš maḥtātô* 'each his pan' (Num 16:17–18); in other words, it was their private possession and not that of the sanctuary (note also the expressions "the pans of these sinners" [Num 17:3] and *wayyiqdāšû* 'they became sanctified' [ibid.], implying that previously they were not holy). Still, one should not conclude that an incense offering on a pan was unacceptable in the official cult (so Elliger 1966). There must have been pans for this purpose, as can be inferred from the command to Aaron on two occasions to burn incense on *hammaḥtâ* 'the pan' (16:12; Num 17:11). Moreover, a number of other (non-P) verses clearly imply a discrete incense offering (cf. Deut 33:10; 1 Sam 2:28; Isa 1:13), apart from the incense burned twice daily on the inner altar (Exod 30:7).

Ezekiel also speaks of an (illicit) incense offering in a vessel called *miqṭeret* (Ezek 8:11). It is hardly a different vessel from the *maḥtâ* (e.g., an upright censer, Haran 1978: 239); more likely it is a synonym that replaced *maḥtâ* in postexilic times. Uzziah, according to the Chronicler, offered incense on a *miqṭeret*, not a *maḥtâ* (2 Chr 26:19). Thus it is possible that *maḥtâ*, meaning censer, may be strictly a preexilic term, another instance of the early provenience of the Priestly terminology.

coals (ʾēš). The reference here could not be to the divine fire that consumed the sacrifices on the altar (9:24; so Ibn Ezra); it would have required the expression *min hāʾēš* 'from the fire'. The only possibility is that Nadab and Abihu took live coals from another source, support for which is its designation *ʾēš zārâ* 'unauthorized coals' (see below). That *ʾēš* can refer to its source, in this case coals, rather than to flames, see *wĕʾet-hāʾēš zĕrê-hālʾâ* 'scatter the coals abroad' (Num 17:2).

incense. Its components are not certain. The twice-daily incense offering on the inner altar is called by the special name *qĕṭōret sammîm* 'perfumed incense' (Exod 30:7) and, in the special case of the high priest's rite on Yom Kippur, it is referred to as *qĕṭōret sammîm daqqâ* 'finely ground perfumed incense' (16:12), a blend of various specified spices (Exod 30:34–36). Because the latter incense was also offered up on a pan (16:12), one must therefore infer that the incense offered up by Nadab and Abihu, called simply *qĕṭōret*, was of different composition. It had to be more than frankincense (the major ingredient of the incense on the inner altar, Exod 30:34–38, and the sole ingredient of the incense on the outer altar, 2:1) because, in that case, it would have been called by its name *lĕbōnâ* (e.g., 2:2, 15; 24:7).

unauthorized coals (*ʾēš zārâ*). The nature of Nadab and Abihu's sin is contained in these words. The adjective *zārâ* 'unauthorized' provides the clue. In contrast to Korah's incense offering, which was rejected because he was an *ʾîš zār* 'an unauthorized person' (Num 17:5), Nadab and Abihu's incense offering was rejected because they utilized *ʾēš zārâ* 'unauthorized coals'. Moreover, just as *qĕṭōret zārâ* 'unauthorized incense' (Exod 30:9, 37) means a composition other than that prescribed (Exod 30:34–36), so *ʾēš zārâ* 'unauthorized coals' implies that they were not the right kind. This can only mean that instead of deriving from the outer altar (e.g., 16:12; Num 17:11), the coals came from a source that was "profane" (*Tg. Onq.* on 16:1) or "outside" (*Tg. Yer.*), such as an oven (*Sipra*, Milluʾim Shemini 32; *Tg. Ps.-J.*; cf. *b.* ʿ*Erub.* 63a; *b. Yoma* 53a; *Midr. Num. Rab.* 2:23). The three other attestations of Nadab and Abihu's sin also pinpoint this cause, "when they offered unauthorized coals before the Lord" (Lev 16:1 LXX; Num 3:4; 26:61; see COMMENT A below). The LXX of Lev 16:1 is preferred over the MT *bĕqorbātām lipnê YHWH* 'when they encroached upon the Lord' chiefly because the term "encroach" is expressed by *qārab ʾel* and not by *qārab lipnê* (for details see the NOTE on 16:1; that *ʾēš* must be rendered "coals," see the NOTE above). The possibility must also be recognized that the coals were invalidated because they may have been placed on the personal pans of Nadab and Abihu instead of on those of the sanctuary (see the preceding NOTE on "his pan"); still, that in all four attestations the sin is specified as "unauthorized coals" and not "unauthorized pans" makes this alternative less likely.

In passing, one should also record the possibility that Korah and his cohorts were also guilty of using unauthorized coals. Gradwohl (1963–64) holds this to be the case because Moses says nothing about the coals in his instructions to them (Num 16:17–18). But Moses' command appears as a doublet, and in its earlier appearance (ibid., v 7) the coals are indeed specified. A stronger argument, though, can be made from the fact that the coals are discarded (Num 17:2) rather than returned to the altar, indicating that they were initially profane (Haran 1960b: 115–16). Thus the LXX on Num 17:2 may be correct when instead of *wĕ-ʾet-hāʾēš zĕrēh* 'scatter the fire' (Num 17:2) it reads *wĕ-ʾet-hāʾēš hazzārâ zĕrēh* 'scatter the unauthorized fire', which suggests that *hazzārâ* may have accidentally been omitted in the MT because of the haplography with contiguous *zĕrēh*. Alternatively, "the scribe may have thought that the two words constituted a dittography and he arbitrarily left out the first word" (D. N. Freedman, written communication). In either case, this verse would constitute a fifth occurrence of the term "unauthorized fire." The nature of the violation and the possible polemic that lurks behind it are explored in COMMENT A below.

which he had not commanded them (*ʾăšer lōʾ ṣiwwâ ʾōtām*). The subject is obviously the Lord, a fact made unambiguously clear in the LXX by its insertion of the Tetragrammaton. The possibility must be reckoned with, however, that it also occurred in the Hebrew *Vorlage* and fell out by haplography, as follows: *ṣ[wh] yh[wh] > ṣwh.*

2. *And fire came forth (wattēṣēʾ ʾēš).* Some commentators propose that the same divine fire that consumed the sacrifices (9:24), also struck down Nadab and Abihu in its path (Rashbam, Hazzequni). In that case, however, it should have been termed *hāʾēš* 'the fire' (Shadal). Hence, it refers to a different fire but one that also originated in the adytum (see the NOTE on "Fire came forth," 9:24 and the NOTE below). A measure-for-measure principle, attested often enough in divine punishments, is present here as well: those who sinned by fire are punished by fire (Hazzequni, *Seper Hamibḥar, Keter Torah*) with, however, a nuance of change: whereas the sinners' fire was impure, God's fire was pure (*Sipra*, Milluʾim Shemini 22).

The Lord appears as *ʾēš ʾōkelet* 'a devouring fire' (Exod 24:17; Deut 5:22) that incinerates indiscriminately everyone in its path (Num 11:1; 16:35; 2 Kgs 1:10, 12). The midrash enumerates twelve instances in Scripture in which the divine fire descended from heaven, six times beneficially (the eighth day, 9:24; Gideon, Judg 6:24; Manoah, Judg 13:20; David, 1 Chr 21:26; Solomon, 2 Chr 7:2; Elijah, 1 Kgs 18:38) and six times detrimentally (Nadab and Abihu, 10:1; the complainers, Num 11:1; Korah, Num 16:35; Job, Job 1:16; Ahaziah's emissaries, 2 Kgs 1:10, 12 [twice]) (*Sipre Zuṭa* on Num 11:1).

from the Lord (millipnê YHWH). The same expression as in 9:24, equivalent to *mēʾēt YHWH* (Num 16:35). It could not have been lightning or else its heavenly origin would have been mentioned, such as *wattippōl ʾēš YHWH* 'the fire of the Lord fell' (1 Kgs 18:38) or *min haššāmayim* 'from the sky' (1 Chr 21:26), or *yārĕdâ mēhaššāmayim* 'descended from the sky' (2 Chr 7:1). Neither could it have originated from the altar (so Laughlin 1976), either the inner altar, which had no fire except for the brief incense offering burned twice daily (Exod 30:7–8), or the outer altar, for which the verb *wattēṣēʾ* 'came forth', that is, exited, would have been inappropriate. The only remaining answer is that the fire stemmed from the adytum, in keeping with the Priestly *kābôd* theology, that the divine firecloud rests on the Ark whence it emerged twice on the same day, to consume the sacrifices and to incinerate Nadab and Abihu (see the NOTE on "Fire came forth").

thus they died (wayyāmūtû). Where were Nadab and Abihu when they were struck down? A comparison of their case with that of Korah and his band will provide the answer. Their respective tests follow, juxtaposed:

Lev 10:1   *wayyiqḥû . . . ʾîš maḥtātô wayyitĕnû bāhen ʾēš wayyāśîmû ʿālêhā qĕṭōret*

Num 16:18   *wayyiqḥû ʾîš maḥtātô wayyitĕnû ʿălēhem ʾēš wayyāśîmû ʿălēhem qĕṭōret*

Lev 10:1   *wayyaqrîbû* **lipnê YHWH**

Num 16:18   *wayyaʿamdû* **petaḥ ʾōhel môʿed**

Lev 10:2   *wattēṣēʾ ʾēš millipnê YHWH wattōʾkal*
Num 16:35a   *wĕʾēš yāṣĕʾâ mēʾēt YHWH wattōʾkal*

The nearly precise correspondence of these passages is striking. The conclusion is inescapable that Nadab and Abihu's offering *lipnê YHWH* 'before the Lord' took place while they were standing *petaḥ ʾōhel môʿēd* 'at the entrance of the Tent of Meeting', namely, in the Tabernacle court. The equivalence of these two expressions has already been demonstrated (1:3; 3:1, 2 and cf. 1:11 with 3:8).

Supporting this conclusion is the following evidence: (1) the fire "came forth," that is, exited, from the Tent, implying that Nadab and Abihu were standing outside; (2) Moses commands Mishael and Elzaphan *qirbû* 'come forward' (v 4), not *bōʾû*, 'enter' *(Keter Torah)*, the verb we would expect had Nadab and Abihu fallen inside the Tent; (3) their deaths took place "before all of the people" (v 3), in the only place they could assemble—the Tabernacle court; (4) in the Korah episode the *kābôd* theophany (Num 16:19) is followed by the emergence of the destructive fire (v 35). Here too the *kābôd* appears first in a theophany (9:23b) and then as a destructive fire (10:1). As the Israelites witnessed the *kābôd* while standing in the court so they witnessed fire emanating from the same divine source felling Nadab and Abihu in the Tabernacle court (for the rabbis' view that Nadab and Abihu were struck down inside the Tent, see the NOTE on "from the front of the sacred precinct," v 4).

[they died] before the Lord. This third mention of *lipnê YHWH* in vv 2–3 is essential because it provides the reason for the complex procedure in removing their corpses (vv 4–5)—they were struck down in the sanctuary (revising my rendering of Num 3:4 in 1990a: 15).

3. *This is what the Lord meant when he said (hûʾ ʾăšer-dibbēr YHWH lēʾmōr).* But where did he say it? Rashi, following *b. Zebaḥ.* 115b, points to Exod 29:43 (as if *kĕbôdî* 'my presence' should be read *mĕkubbāday* 'my honored ones'); Baḥya suggests Exod 19:22; Abravanel, Lev 8:33–35; Bekhor Shor, Lev 21:11—none of which even approximates the citation (see Brin 1989–90). A more acceptable approach is that of *Seper Hamibḥar,* followed by Shadal and Ehrlich 1908–14, that *dibbēr,* like prophetic *kōh ʾāmar YHWH,* refers to the immediate present. That is, it is the incident with Nadab and Abihu that prompts God's remark. The verb *dibbēr,* then, would have the connotation of "decree," a good example of which is *kaʾăšer dibbēr YHWH* 'as the Lord has decreed' (Gen 24:51). The rendering of the phrase would then be, "This is what the Lord has decreed, saying."

Through those near to me (biqĕrōbay). *qārôb* is a technical term, designating an official who can have access to *(qārab)* his sovereign directly, without resorting to an intermediary (Ezek 23:12; Esth 1:14). So too the Akk. cognate *qurbūtu,* in the expression *ša qurbūti,* is the title of an official. The noun *qurubtu* (collective) stands for a group of officials, and the verb *qerēbu* has among its meanings "to be close to, in intimacy with someone" (*CAD*, Q lb, p. 229). So too, biblical *qārab* describes the inner circle of the royal court (e.g., 1 Kgs 2:7; 5:7; Weinfeld 1982b: 52 n. 123). In particular, Israel's priests are specifically called *'ăšer-qĕrôbîm laYHWH* 'who are close to the Lord' (Ezek 42:13; cf. 43:19) and *hanniggāšîm 'el YHWH*, 'who approach the Lord' (Exod 19:22) (for the synonymity of *qārab/nāgaš 'el* see Milgrom 1970a: 34–35). The emendation *biqrēbay* (*ḥolam* to *ṣere*), yielding "those who trespass upon me" (Segal 1989; see Milgrom 1970a: 16–33) has to be rejected on the grounds that the verb *qārab* (*qal*) never takes a direct object but generally requires the preposition *'el* (e.g., 22:3; Num 18:3).

Some scholars claim that this statement is a poetic fragment and that the mention of "the people" indicates that originally the referent was not the priests but all of Israel, as in Ps 148:14, where Israel is called *'am qĕrōbô* 'the people close to him' (Elliger 1966; Lemke 1981: 548). But this one psalmodic metaphor does not negate the fact that only priests are permanent *qĕrôbîm*. This stems from the fact that the root meaning of *qārab 'el* in P is "have access to" or "be admitted to" (Milgrom 1970a: 33), a sense that is only applicable to Israel's priesthood (for a fuller treatment, see the NOTE on 9:7). Thus the application of the title *qārôb* to Israel in Ps 148:14 is a singular metaphoric extension and, hence, secondary.

I shall sanctify myself ('eqqādēš). Rashbam suggests that this clause refers to Aaron. That is, God will become sanctified by Aaron's abstinence from the rites of mourning. Ramban would rather point to Israel at Sinai as the closest analogy, for out of respect for the sanctity of the Lord neither the priests nor the people "broke through" to ascend to the Lord (Exod 19:24). For either exegete, the meaning of *'eqqādēš* is "I shall be treated as holy."

A different approach is exemplified by Ibn Ezra, who cites Amos: "You alone have I singled out of all the families on earth. That is why I will call you to account for all your iniquities" (Amos 3:2). Here, Israel's chosenness implies its greater responsibility; it is more culpable for its defection precisely because of its favored status. This interpretation clearly corresponds to the usage of the idiom *niqdaš be-*, which, whenever God is the subject, needs to be taken as a reflexive, "sanctify himself through." Thus *wayyiqqādēš bām* '[the Lord] sanctified himself through them' (Num 20:13), in other words, through the punishment inflicted upon Moses and Aaron (perhaps, also, on Israel); *wĕniqdaštî bākem lĕʿênê haggôyīm* 'I will sanctify myself through you (Israel) in the sight of all the nations' (Ezek 20:41), that is, when he restores Israel to its land; *bĕhiqqādĕšî bĕkā lĕʿênêhem gôg* 'when I sanctify myself through you, Gog, before their (the nations') eyes' (Ezek 38:16). Clearly, Moses and Aaron, Israel and Gog serve as instruments for the sanctification of God's name—in the cases of Moses, Aaron, and Gog through their punishment. Thus here, too, the deaths of God's intimate priests, Nadab and Abihu, perform the function of sanctifying God—

providing awe and respect for his power to all who witness the incident or who will subsequently learn of it.

Recently, it has been noticed (Segal 1989) that Ezekiel offers a striking parallel to this passage: *hinĕnî ʿālayik ṣîdôn* **wĕnikbadtî** *bĕtôkēk wĕyādĕʿû kî-ʾănî YHWH baʿăśôtî bāh* **šĕpāṭim wĕniqdaštî** *bāh* 'I am going to deal with you, O Sidon. *I will gain glory* in your midst; and they shall know that I am the Lord, when I wreak *punishment* upon her and *show myself holy through* her' (Ezek 28:22). Just as in Lev 10:3, we find in one statement the roots *kbd* and *qdš*, both in the *niphʿal* and in the adversative sense: the Lord becomes glorified and sanctified through punishment.

The greater responsibility of the priests is also evidenced in the rules dealing with the punishment for the crime of encroachment upon the sancta. The sacral responsibility in regard to the sancta is given in Num 18 and can be tabulated as follows:

Verse	*Clergy*	*Responsible for*	*The Encroach-ment of*
1b, 7a	priests	sancta	disqualified priests
3	priests and Levites	sancta at rest	Levites
1a	Kohathite Levites	sancta in transit	Israelites
22, 23	all Levites	sanctuary, as a whole	Israelites

Priests and Levites share the custody of the sanctuary, the priests guarding within (and at the entrance, Num 3:38) and the Levites guarding without (Num 3:23, 29, 35). All priests and Levites are responsible if disqualified priests or Levites encroach upon the sancta; Kohathite Levites are responsible for encroachment by Israelites while they carry the sancta (Num 3:31; 4:1–15); and all Levites whose cordons ring the encamped sanctuary (Num 3:23, 29, 35) are responsible for any Israelite encroachment (details in Milgrom 1970a: 16–33; 1990a: Excursus 40). The penalty priests and Levites pay for failure to prevent encroachment is that of Nadab and Abihu—death by divine agency (Num 18:3).

This *niphʿal niqdaš* is replaced by the *hithpaʿel hitqaddēš* beginning with Ezek 38:33 and into LBH (e.g., *Sipra*, Nedaba 2:5), proof that *niqdaš* (with God as the subject) must be understood as a reflexive. Especially striking is 1QM 17:2 and its rewording of the Nadab and Abihu incident: "But ye, remember ye the judgment [of Nadab and Abi]hu, the sons of Aaron, through whose judgment *(bĕmišpāṭām)*, God sanctified himself *(hitqaddēš)* in the sight [of all of the people]," thus providing another case of an older terminology that undergoes a change in the time and writing of Ezekiel (Hurvitz 1982: 339–42). Strengthening this conclusion is the fact that *hitqaddēš* indeed occurs in BH, but in non-Priestly sources (Exod 19:22; Num 11:18; Josh 3:5; 7:13; 1 Sam 16:5; 2 Sam

11:4; Isa 66:17; 1 Chr 15:14; 2 Chr 5:11; 29:5, 18, 34; 30:3, 15, 24; 31:18; 35:6), where it never means "sanctify oneself" (contra Hurvitz) but "purify oneself." This distinction between BH and LBH is further underscored by the term's subject in its attestations in P: the *niph'al* is reserved for God (e.g., 10:3; 22:32; Num 20:13) whereas the *hithpa'el* is reserved for Israel (11:44; 20:7); however, in LBH the *hithpa'el* refers only to Israel, and it no longer means "sanctify oneself" (as in P) but "purify oneself" (see the citations above).

The implication of the first half of this statement was fully comprehended by the medieval exegetes: "those who serve God more endanger themselves more. Just as those who are closest *(qĕrôbîm)* to the battlefront are more likely to die so those closest *(qĕrôbîm)* in the service of the sanctuary are more prone to err" (Abravanel).

before. wĕ'al-pĕnê, literally, "before the face of," that is to say, "in the sight of" (e.g., Jer 6:7; 13:26; Job 1:11; 6:28). This wording offers further support for the theory that Nadab and Abihu were felled in the Tabernacle court because their demise was witnessed by the people (see the NOTE on "thus they died," v 2).

I shall glorify myself. 'ikkābēd, in other words, by sanctifying myself through my intimates I thereby glorify myself before all of the people. "So by a single action, YHWH affirms his total sanctity . . . and also establishes his glory among the onlookers" (D. N. Freedman, written communication). The implication of the second half of this statement was not overlooked by the medieval exegetes, for instance, "they (the people) will apply *a fortiori* reasoning to themselves: if such [things happen] to his intimates, others will all the more so have cause to fear" (Bekhor Shor; cf. *b. Zebaḥ.* 115b). Ehrlich (1908–14, on Exod 14:4, followed by *NJPS;* cf. Orlinsky 1969: 168) translates "I will assert my authority"; and where *nikbad (niph'al)* is followed by the preposition *be*, he translates "assert my authority against" (e.g., Exod 14:4, 17, 18; Ezek 28:22). Yet he interprets the preposition as the *beth* of hostility, and it does not correspond to the usage of the *beth* in the corresponding and parallel phrase *'eqqādēš be* 'I will sanctify myself through'. Better, it would seem, to regard the *beth* in both phrases as the *beth* of means and to render here "I shall glorify myself."

Support for this rendering stems from the New Testament, which offers, in my opinion, a remarkable reflex of this verse. As noted by Brown (1966: 476), "Father, glorify your name" (John 12:28) is equivalent to the phrase in Jesus' prayer "May your name be hallowed" (Matt 6:9; Luke 11:2). The fact that these two statements are none other than the two halves of the Lord's words in this verse has been overlooked. The divine response to Jesus' request, "I have glorified it and will glorify it again" (ibid.), is explained in three ways by Brown (ibid.), all of which refer to Jesus' past ministry. Still, a fourth referent is possible. Indeed, the Lord had been glorified through the death of his intimates in only one documented case in Scripture—through the death of Nadab and Abihu. That this death was conceived as a prelude to their resurrection and, hence, may have been a model for Jesus becomes clear by examining the contemporary view of this incident held by Philo: "It is thus that the priests Nadab and Abihu die in order that they may live, receiving an incorruptible life in exchange for mortal existence, and being translated from the created to the uncreated. Over them a proclamation is uttered betokening immortality, 'They died before the Lord' (Lev 10:2), that is, 'They came to life,' for a corpse may not come into God's presence" (*Fug.* 59; cf. *Laws* 2. 57–58; *Som.* 267; *Her.* 309). This positive view of Nadab and Abihu's death is also reflected in later rabbinic literature, as a means of either consecrating the Tabernacle or sanctifying the name of God (*Sipra*, Millu'im Shemini 22, 36; cf. COMMENT B below). Thus John 12:28 provides strong evidence that the Philonic view of the death of Nadab and Abihu was current in first-century Palestine (details in COMMENT B below). Moreover, as D. N. Freedman reminds me, many scholars believe that the Fourth Gospel reflects the influence of Alexandrian Judaism and especially Philo. John's Jesus, then, would have interpreted Nadab and Abihu's death in the same positive light, and it became for him the model as well as the rationale for his own imminent death.

And Aaron was silent (wayyiddōm 'ahărōn). The LXX renders "was stupefied," based perhaps on the meaning of the root *dmm* in *yiddĕmû kā'āben* 'they became petrified as stone' (Exod 15:16), implying that Aaron was paralyzed, rather than resigned (Snaith 1967). But Ezekiel provides a more instructive parallel, *hē'ānēq dōm mētîm 'ēbel lō'-ta'ăśeh* 'Groan in silence. Do not mourn for the dead' (Ezek 24:17; cf. v 16). Thus Aaron, on his own initiative, did not mourn (Rashbam). Aaron's silence contrasts starkly with the people's shouting, only a few moments earlier (9:24; Wenham 1979).

4. *Mishael and Elzaphan, sons of Uzziel.* Why were they chosen? Uzziel was Amram's youngest brother (Exod 6:18). Why not the sons of Yizhar or Hebron, who were Uzziel's seniors? A possible explanation might follow this line of reasoning: Yizhar's eldest was Korah (Exod 6:21); hence, his entire line was disqualified (see Num 16). Hebron's children, by contrast, are unknown (1 Chr 23:19 lists Hebron's descendants, not his sons; cf. 1 Chr 26:30–31 and Liver 1968: 11–32). Uzziel alone remains, whose two oldest sons were chosen as the closest Levite relatives to Nadab and Abihu. Thus the choice of Uzziel's sons may simply rest on the implications of genealogy, an artificial construct rather than a reflection of historic causes. The notion that this episode reflects an internal dispute between two priestly groups, Nadab and Abihu versus Mishael and Elzaphan (Noth 1965; Elliger 1966), is sheer speculation.

Elzaphan ('elṣāpān). This name occurs with this spelling in Exod 6:22, where he and Mishael are added to the genealogical list as Levi's great-grandsons, a proleptic device alluding to this incident (as Korah [v 21] anticipates Num 16). The spelling *'elîṣāpān* (with the LXX, Sam., Pesh.), however, seems preferable, in agreement with its spelling in Num 3:30, where he is identified as the chieftain of the Kohathites. The MT, however, which originally was probably pronounced the same way as the fuller form, does preserve the older orthography. In either case, the meaning is the same, "[the god] Zaphon is my God" (D. N. Freedman, written communication).

Come forward. qirbû, implying, you need not fear to handle the corpses (Ehrlich 1908–14). The fact that Moses says "come forward" and not *bōʾû* 'enter' implies that Nadab and Abihu were struck down in the courtyard (*Keter Torah;* cf. the NOTE on "Thus they died," v 2).

kinsmen (ʾăḥêkem). As Uzziel was Aaron's uncle, Mishael and Elzaphan were great-cousins of Nadab and Abihu, or first cousins once removed.

from the front of the sacred precinct. mēʾēt pĕnê-haqqōdeš, in other words, from the *petaḥ ʾōhel môʿēd* 'the entrance to the Tent of Meeting' (see the NOTES on "thus they died," v 2, on "before," v 3, and on "Come forward," above). But the expression *mēʾēt pĕnê* means "from the front of"; see 2 Kgs 16:14. An equivalent expression to *pĕnê-haqqōdeš* is *pĕnê ʾōhel môʿēd* 'in front of the Tent of Meeting' (e.g., 9:5; Num 17:8; 19:4), which clearly stands for the forecourt. Thus, it is implied that Nadab and Abihu fell in the forecourt, near the entrance. The term *qōdeš,* however, is not as clear. Its protean range is reflected by its multivalent meanings. In general, it refers either to sacred objects (e.g., Num 4:15, 16, 20; 8:19; 18:5) or to sacred space. But in the latter instance, the space can be restricted to the adytum, the inner room of the Tent (a meaning found only in chap. 16; see the NOTES on 16:2, 23); the shrine, the outer room of the Tent (e.g., Exod 28:29, 35; 29:30; 31:4; Lev 6:23; Num 4:12; 28:7); or the Tabernacle court (10:4, 18 [bis]), alternately called *māqôm qādōš* 'a holy place' (6:9, 19, 20; 7:6; 10:13; 16:24), the equivalent of *ḥăṣar hammiškān/ ʾōhel môʿēd* (6:9, 19; Exod 27:9).

In the Solomonic (and Second?) Temple, *qōdeš* also refers to the sacrificial court, as explicitly stated by the Chronicler, *wěʿōlâ lōʾ-heʿĕlû baqqōdeš* 'They did not sacrifice burnt offerings in the sacred precinct' (2 Chr 29:7; cf. Ps 63:3). Again, in Ezekiel's visionary temple, *qōdeš* adverts to the sacrificial court, for example, "On the day he (the priest) enters the sacred area *(haqqōdeš),* the inner court, to officiate in the sacred precinct *(baqqōdeš)*" (Ezek 44:27; cf. 42:14). See further details in the NOTE on "in the shrine," 6:23). Thus the specification in this verse that the corpses of Nadab and Abihu were to be removed "from the front of the sacred precinct" means that they were struck down when they entered the forecourt.

Confusion over the meaning of *qōdeš* has led to some bizarre interpretations. The rabbis, for example, who held that *qōdeš* refers to the Tent, were trapped by the apparent contradiction that Mishael and Elzaphan, who were Levites, entered into an area forbidden to nonpriests (cf. Num 18:4–5). Rabbi Akiba speculates that they dragged out the corpses by thrusting spears into them while they were standing outside the Tent, and Rabbi Eliezer is forced to the conclusion that their corpses rolled out of the Tent through divine intervention (*Sipra,* Milluʾim Shemini 35). Ramban cites the rabbinic rule that priests are permitted to enter the Tent/Temple to make repairs and that, if priests are unavailable, Levites are permitted (*Sipra*, Emor 3:11), especially if a dire emergency exists, for the fallen corpses are polluting the sanctuary. By contrast, Dillmann, who correctly interprets *qōdeš* as coextensive with the entire Tabernacle enclosure, interprets "in front of the sacred area" to mean that Nadab and Abihu were felled *outside* the sacred compound, in which case, however, there would be prohibition for either priests (of the immediate family, 21:1–3) or Levites to come into contact with the corpses. Nevertheless, it makes no sense that Nadab and Abihu were offering incense *outside* the Tabernacle when, to the contrary, the text explicitly states that their offering was made "before the Lord" (v 1), that is, within the sacred compound. Moreover, if Nadab and Abihu died in front of the sacred compound, the site would have been designated as *pĕnê ʾōhel môʿēd* 'in front of the Tent of Meeting' (e.g., 9:5; Num 17:8; 19:4). Thus *qōdeš* here, and in the rest of the chapter (vv 17–18; cf. vv 12–13), refers to the Tabernacle court.

outside the camp (ʾel-miḥûṣ lammǎhaneh). An admission that burying a corpse anywhere inside the camp—even if the grave were declared off-limits to passersby—would ritually pollute the sanctuary (see chap. 4, COMMENT G).

5. *by their tunics (bĕkuttŏnōtām).* Whose tunics, those of the dead or those of the Levites? Clearly, this term must refer to the clothing of the dead (Rashi; cf. LXX), for the *kuttōnet* is the garment of priests (see the NOTE on 8:7) and never of Levites (*Sipra*, Milluʾim 34; Bekhor Shor). But why mention it at all? The midrash replies that the divine fire consumed only their souls but left their bodies and clothes intact (*Midr. Tanḥ.* 12). Instead, a more pragmatic motivation is probably at work. It has already been observed that P polemicizes against the more conservative priestly tradition, championed by Ezekiel, that maintains that the priestly clothing possesses contagious sanctity. This view is staunchly rebutted by P, which holds that the formula of contagion, *kol-hannōgēaʿ yiqdaš* 'whatever touches [sancta] is sanctified', excludes priestly vestments, even though they are sacred (Exod 30:29–30; details in chaps. 6–7, COMMENT B). Here, I submit, lies an additional contribution to this ongoing polemic. Despite the fact that Nadab and Abihu were dressed in tunics that had become consecrated by their week-long aspersion with the sacred anointment oil (8:30) and despite the additional consecration they achieved by their contact with the divine fire, still they did not gain the same degree of holiness as the other sancta. Indeed, whereas the latter transmit holiness to objects (but not to persons), the priestly garments affect neither persons nor objects: their sanctity is not contagious (cf. the complete documentation of this thesis in chaps. 6–7, COMMENT B).

An equally significant question is why the slain's Levitic relatives were involved and not their brothers, Eleazar and Ithamar? After all, only the high priest (Aaron) is forbidden under all circumstances to come into contact with the dead (21:12), but ordinary priests (i.e., Eleazar and Ithamar) are expressly permitted to engage in mourning rites for their brother (21:1–3)! Ramban (on v 6) suggests that because this, the eighth day, was their initial service, there was a divine decree *(hôrāʾat šāʿâ)* that on this day, the priests' inaugural service, they could not mourn. Haran proposes that Eleazar and Ithamar were still within their consecratory period so that the taboo of mourning incumbent on the high priest, which, in Haran's view, falls solely during the period of consecration, applied to his sons as well (1962d: 30; 1968c: 796). But his proposal founders on a number of shoals: the eighth day is not part of the consecration service; the statement "the Lord's anointing oil is upon you" (v 7) is a description of the priests' permanent status, not of their seven-day consecration; and the taboos incumbent upon the high priest (21:11–12) apply to his entire incumbency, not just to the initial week of consecration. A more plausible ground for banning the participation of Eleazar and Ithamar is that they were on duty. They had assisted their father in the performance of the sacrifices (9:9, 12, 18) and they had yet to eat the sacred meat (cf. v 17, below). Still, the text gives no indication that after they ate the sacred meat they might begin to mourn. To the contrary, they are explicitly warned not to leave the sacred precincts on pain of death (v 7)! The classic parallels of Minos (cited by Kalisch 1867–72) who, though learning of the death of his son Androgeus, continued to complete the sacrifice in which he was engaged, and of Horatius Pulvillus who continued to officiate while receiving news of his son's death, are not germane to our case, for in both instances the fathers merely delayed their expressions of grief until their sacred acts were completed, whereas Ithamar and Eleazar were absolutely and permanently forbidden to mourn.

The most acceptable explanation is the simplest. Aaron's sons were anointed, in contrast to their successors who were not (Exod 40:15b). For this reason, and for this reason alone, Aaron's sons are called *mĕšûḥîm* 'anointed' (Num 3:3) and Moses is commanded to anoint them "as you anointed their father" (Exod 40:15a; cf. Exod 29:29; 30:30). Thus their unique unction gave them the same status as their father: they were forbidden to mourn just as their father was (21:12) because "the Lord's anointing oil is upon you" (v 7).

A final problem presented by this incident is that the text passes over in silence the necessity to purge the sanctuary of the impurity imparted to it by the corpses of Nadab and Abihu. Ehrlich (1908–14 on v 2) suggests that no pollution was incurred on the supposition that death by divine agency does not affect divine property. If this were the case, however, the command to Mishael and Elzaphan to remove the bodies and their execution of this command (vv 4–5) would make no sense and Jehoiada's command to remove Athaliah's corpse from the Temple precincts (2 Kgs 11:15), as Ehrlich himself acknowledges, undermines this theory. Moreover, the Lord himself bids his appointed executioners to pollute the Temple by filling its courts with corpses and thereby making his own departure from it inevitable (Ezek 9:7). Thus, the problem of the Tabernacle's pollution by the corpses of Nadab and Abihu is real and cannot be rationalized away. This lacuna is surely responsible for the statement in the opening of chap. 16, which, as will be argued there (see the NOTE on v 1), was originally connected to chap. 10 and which explained that, indeed, it was the death of Nadab and Abihu within the sanctuary precincts that was responsible for the emergency purgation rites prescribed in chap. 16.

6. *his sons (bānāyw)*. The LXX and Pesh. add *hannôtārîm* '[his] remaining [sons]'; cf. v 12.

Do not (ʾal). The Sam. and LXX read *lōʾ*, the negative particle that implies a permanent prohibition (Bright 1973: 196), indicating that the priests may not mourn whenever they are on duty in their sacred vestments. If, however, the MT is correct, then the referent is to the immediate situation: the prohibition to mourn applies only to Aaron and his two remaining sons. The MT is to be preferred because, as explained above (in the NOTE on v 5), Eleazar and Ithamar are subject to the absolute prohibition against mourning, as if they were high priests (cf. 21:12), by dint of their unction with the sacred oil (v 7), a rite that was repeated only for each succeeding high priest (Exod 29:29), but not for ordinary priests (Exod 40:15b). Hence, subsequent generations of priests, not being aspersed with the sacred anointment oil (cf. 8:30), were permitted to participate in mourning rites for their close blood relations (21:1–4).

dishevel (tiprāʿû). The root *prʿ* has something to do with the hair of the head. Akk. *pērtu* actually denotes "the hair of the head." Still, the exact meaning of the verb *pāraʿ* is in dispute. Some hold that it means "let the hair grow" (*Sipra*, Milluʾim Shemini 40). Biblical support could be mustered from the case of the Nazirite, *gaddēl peraʿ śēʿar rōʾšô* 'the hair of his head shall be allowed to grow untrimmed' (Num 6:5). Indeed, according to the rabbis, priests whose hair is untrimmed *(pĕrûʿê rōʾš)* are not permitted to enter the sacred area between the altar and the Temple porch (*m. Kelim* 1:9); in other words, their status is reduced to that of laymen, thus providing a fitting reason that Aaron and his sons are subject to this prohibition. Yet this interpretation cannot apply in this instance, for obviously it would take many days before a haircut became necessary, whereas the prohibition pronounced on Aaron and his sons takes effect on that same day. Hoffmann (1953) supports this rabbinic hypothesis by referring to Ezek 44:20. True, *ûperaʿ lōʾ yĕšallēḥû* unambiguously means that priests "may not let their hair go untrimmed," but this is a general regulation for the priesthood and has nothing to do with their state of mourning and, certainly, is inapplicable to the situation of Aaron and his sons.

A second rendering for *pāraʿ* is "bare the head" (*Tg. Neof.;* Rabbi Akiba in *Sipra*, Tazriaʿ 12:6; cf. LXX), indicating that in mourning the head covering is removed. Biblical texts adduced in support are the *mĕṣōrāʿ, wĕrōʾšô yihyeh pārûaʿ* 'his head shall be *pārûaʿ*' (Lev 13:45) and the suspected adulteress whose rite includes the step *ûpāraʿ ʾet-rōʾš hāʾiššâ* 'and he (the priest) shall *pāraʿ* her head' (Num 5:18). Now this interpretation could apply to the priests whose heads, while on duty, were always turbaned (cf. 8:9, 13). There is, however, no evidence that the ordinary person normally wore a head covering, and the more likely rendering for the citations concerning the *mĕṣōrāᶜ* and suspected adulteress, adduced above, is that they were commanded to loosen their hair and let it be unkempt. Indeed, the rabbis themselves declare that the priest unbraids *(sôtēr)* the hair of the suspected adulteress *(t. Soṭa* 1:7; cf. *Tg. Ps.-J.* to Num 5:18) and that the hair of the *mĕṣōrāᶜ* has to be allowed to grow wild *(Sipre* Naso 25). Strikingly, this rendering is confirmed by the cognate idiom in Akk. *perasà wašarat* 'her hair is unloosened' (von Soden 1956). Further buttressing this view is the use of the verb *pāraᶜ* in figurative contexts. For example, "Moses saw that the people were out of control *(pārūaᶜ)* because Aaron had let them get out of control *(pĕrāᶜōh)*" (Exod 32:25). And (to cite one rendering) during time of war soldiers would "let their locks go untrimmed *(biprōaᶜ pĕrāᶜōt)*" (Judg 5:2).

your hair rā'šêkem, literally "your heads." For this usage, see 13:40, 41, 45.

and do not (lō'). This time the negative particle implying permanence is entirely plausible: the priests may never rend their garments, whether for mourning or for any other reason.

rend. tiprōmû; cf. 13:45; 21:10. A mourner tears his clothes (Gen 37:29, 34; 2 Sam 3:31; 13:3; Job 1:20; cf. *b. Moᶜed Qaṭ.* 15a). But these adduced verses use the verb *qāraᶜ,* and the rabbis aver that there is a difference between *pāram* and *qāraᶜ (m. Soṭa* 1:5; cf. *t. Soṭa* 1:7). Radak *(Sēper Haššorāšîm)* maintains that *qāraᶜ* refers to tearing any part of a garment, whereas *pāram* takes place only at the seam. Bartinoro, instead, holds that *qāraᶜ* implies multiple tears (note Arab. *qaraᶜa* 'shred'). The distinction between these two forms, if any, cannot be determined. At any rate, other rabbinic sources have no compunctions about glossing the verb *pāram* with *qāraᶜ (Sipra,* Milluʾim Shemini 41).

lest (wĕlō'). The negative particle applies to the following two clauses, "you die" and "anger strike the whole community" (Ibn Ezra). But a question needs to be addressed: Why is the threat of divine wrath upon the community found, in this incident, only here? Why was there not collective retribution following the death of Nadab and Abihu? The answer is that the presence of Aaron here makes the difference, for only the sins of the high priest are visited upon the people (4:3), whereas the sins of ordinary priests, such as Nadab and Abihu, affect only themselves (Hoffmann 1953).

you die (tāmūtû). It can be demonstrated that death by divine agency *(mût)* is imposed for desecration *(ḥillēl),* whereas the severer penalty of excision of the line *(kārēt;* cf. chap. 7, COMMENT D) is imposed for the severer crime against the deity—pollution *(ṭāmēʾ)* of sancta (see the NOTE on "from their impurity," 15:31). Hence the penalty of death in this case is imposed not for participating in the funerary rites (a *ṭāmēʾ* act) but for merely leaving the sacred precinct during the week of consecration, regardless of the reason (a *ḥillēl* act).

anger strike (yiqṣōp). The verb *qāṣap* is characteristic of BH (Gen 40:2; 41:10; Exod 16:20; Num 16:22; 31:14; Deut 1:34; 9:19; Josh 22:18; etc.), but it is replaced in LBH by *kāᶜas* (Ps 112:10; Qoh 5:16; 7:9; Neh 3:33; 2 Chr 16:10), beginning with Ezekiel (Ezek 16:42), another indication of the preexilic provenience of P's terminology (Hurvitz 1982: 135–36).

shall bewail (yibkû). For *bākâ*, meaning "mourn," cf. Gen 23:2; Num 20:25; Deut 21:3; 2 Sam 15:30; 19:2.

the burning (haśśĕrēpâ). This word is used instead of *haśśĕrūpîm* 'the burned ones' (Num 17:4) or a personal noun, which one would expect as the object of *bākâ* (cf. Num 2:29; Deut 34:8), an indication that the people's mourning would be not for the sinners, Nadab and Abihu, but for the tragedy that befell the sanctuary on its inauguration day (Ehrlich 1908–14).

7. *You must not go outside. lō᾽ tēṣĕ᾽û,* that is, to follow the bier (cf. 2 Sam 3:31; Rabbi Judah in *m. Sanh.* 2:1; *Sipra,* Millu᾽im Shemini 28; Saadiah). The negative particle *lō᾽* implies that this law has permanent validity. But it can be interpreted in two ways. (1) Priests may not interrupt their sanctuary duties in order to indulge in rites of mourning (Maimonides, "Entry to the Sanctuary" 2.5, following Saadiah). Rabad (on the *Sipra*) further maintains that this prohibition is limited to the inaugural day; afterward, priests may interrupt their duties and leave the sanctuary to mourn their immediate blood relations. (2) This prohibition is restricted solely to Aaron's remaining sons, but not just when they are on duty, rather throughout their lifetimes. The reason is that by virtue of their unction with the sacred oil (8:30) they are subject to the same restrictions as the high priest, who may never leave the sanctuary to mourn—even for his closest relatives (21:12). It is no accident that *Tg. Ps.-J.* (on 16:1) refers to Nadab and Abihu as *trên kahănā᾽ rabrĕbayā᾽* 'the two high priests' (followed by Ibn Ezra, Ramban, and Sforno on Num 3:3). By contrast, subsequent generations of priests are not anointed (Exod 29:9aγ; 40:15b) except for the high priest (Exod 29:29). Hence it is not only not contradictory but even completely consistent that this prohibition should fall on Eleazar and Ithamar, while all subsequent priests (but not the high priests) are permitted to defile themselves by engaging in the funerary rites for close blood relatives (21:1–4). Ezekiel, to be sure, converts the mourning prohibition into a blanket rule covering all priests (Ezek 44:20), but he takes a much severer stand than P in regard to almost all of the priestly prohibitions (see chap. 4, COMMENT J and chap. 7, COMMENT B). Finally, of no small importance is the absence in this verse of the formula *ḥuqqat ῾ôlām lĕdōrōtêkem* 'a law for all time throughout your generations', found in the contiguous prohibition of imbibing alcoholic drinks (v 9), which can only mean that this prohibition to mourn was limited to the generation of Aaron and his sons.

for the Lord's anointing oil is upon you (kî-šemen mišḥat YHWH ῾ălêkem). This is the rationale for the prohibition against mourning. It can be used to justify either of the two explanations cited in the NOTE above: (1) because the oil has anointed your priestly garments, you may not interrupt your duties while you are wearing them, or (2) because you yourselves are anointed you are subject to the same restrictions as the high priest, who may not mourn—thus defiling himself by contact with a corpse—under any circumstance. As the wording here states explicitly that the oil is "upon you"—not upon "your vestments"—the second explanation is preferable, in agreement with the conclusion reached in the NOTE above. The expression "the Lord's anointing oil" (cf. 21:12), also called *šemen mišḥat qōdeš* 'the sacred anointing oil' (Exod 30:25, 31) only emphasizes its sanctifying power and helps explain why the anointing of Aaron's sons elevated them to a holier status than the priests of subsequent generations who no longer were anointed.

8. *And the Lord spoke to Aaron (wayyĕdabbēr YHWH ʾel-ʾahărōn).* The implied meaning is "directly" (*Sipra*, Milluʾim Shemini 36). The only other two instances of this wording are recorded in Num 18:1, 8. Hoffmann (1953) suggests that the disjunctive accent, the *zāqēp parvum*, over the Tetragrammaton (also in Num 18:1) may be an indication of Masoretic abbreviation for *wayyĕdabbēr YHWH [ʾel-mōšeh dabbēr] ʾel-ʾahărōn* 'And the Lord spoke [to Moses: Speak] to Aaron'. Other commentators also hold that God spoke only through the agency of Moses and the prophets, as in *wayyōsep YHWH dabbēr ʾel-ʾāḥāz* 'And the Lord continued to speak to Ahaz' (Isa 7:10), a communication surely mediated by Isaiah (cf. v 3; Ibn Ezra, and cf. Rabbi Ishmael in *Sipra*, Ahare, par 1:5). Yet Aaron (and Miriam) claims to have possessed prophetic powers (Num 12:2). This claim must be based on some text. The MT, therefore, is correct (D. N. Freedman).

9. *Drink no wine . . . (yayin . . . ʾal-tēšt).* The relation between this prohibition and the preceding pericope is unclear. Midrash claims that Nadab and Abihu may have been inebriated (*Pesiq. Rab Kah.* 26:9; *Midr. Lev. Rab.* 20:9); others suggest that this prohibition reflects the concern lest Aaron and his surviving sons drown their sorrow in drink (Bekhor Shor). But the entire section, vv 8–11, is a heterogeneous piece, which was probably added at a later date (see further the NOTES on "that you may not die," below, and on "you must distinguish" v 10).

The negative particle *ʾal* is inexplicable because this prohibition is permanent. The corresponding prohibition in Ezekiel (Ezek 44:21) uses *lōʾ*. Perhaps, then, *lōʾ* should also be read here, with the LXX (Bright 1979: 196).

ale (šēkār). Some claim that it is a synonym for wine and that, therefore, *yayin wĕšēkār* form a hendiadys (Melamed 1944–45; Hurvitz 1982: 117). But *šēkār* occurs in two other P passages in which it is clearly not to be identified with wine. First, the prohibition of intoxicants to Nazirites includes *ḥōmeṣ yayin wĕḥōmeṣ šēkār* 'vinegar of wine or of *šēkār*' (Num 6:3), where wine and *šēkār* must be taken as discrete substances and, second, the use of *šēkār* in the cult, *baqqōdeš hassēk nesek šēkār laYHWH* 'to be poured in the shrine as a *šēkār* libation to the Lord' (Num 28:7b) clearly indicates that *šēkār* can stand alone, independent of wine. In fact, the case can be made that the latter verse reflects a more ancient cultic practice of offering a libation of ale (see below), not on the outer altar where subsequent libations were exclusively offered, but inside the sanctuary, probably on the inner altar. Relics of this practice are the *golden* libation vessels stored on the Table of Presence (Exod 25:29; 37:16; Num 4:7) and the prohibition against libations on the inner altar (Exod 30:9b) (for the complete argument see Milgrom 1990a: at Num 28:7). *Šēkār* is attested elsewhere in Scripture: in poetry (e.g., Isa 5:22), prose (e.g., 1 Sam 1:15), exhortation (e.g., Deut 29:4–5), and in the cult (e.g., Deut 14:26).

The identification of *šēkār* is not completely certain. *Tg. Ps.-J.* renders "anything intoxicating" and, in the same vein, Ibn Ezra suggests intoxicants from substances other than grapes, which he specifies as wheat, dates, or honey. Nevertheless, the most likely candidate is beer or ale because of the Akk. cognate *šikāru* and its prevalent use in the cult throughout the ancient Near East.

The effects of wine and *šēkār* are graphically depicted and condemned in Scripture (e.g., Isa 28:7; Hos 4:11; 7:5; Prov 20:1). Isa 28:7, in particular, is worth quoting in full: "But these are also muddled by wine and dazed by *šēkār:* priest and prophet are muddled by *šēkār;* they are confused by wine, they are dazed by *šēkār;* they are muddled in vision, they stumble in judgment." The intoxication of priests (and prophets), then, was not a hypothetical matter; the priestly injunction recorded here can only attest to the reality that evoked it. It is also possible that cultic intoxication may have been a pagan practice (e.g., Babylonia: *ANET*[3] 66; Enuma Elish 3.134–38), and this prohibition may, in part, also be a polemic against it. It is clear from Eli's rebuke of Hannah and her defense (1 Sam 1:13–15) that it was forbidden for anyone, not just for priests, to be intoxicated inside the sacred precincts. The existence of a beer industry in Israel is attested by the prevalence of the beer jug in archaeological excavations. This vessel was equipped with a strainer spout, obviously "to strain out the beer without swallowing the barley husks" (Albright 1949: 115). The fact that this vessel is Philistine in origin throws light on the story of Samson, in which the Philistines engage in drinking bouts (Judg 14:10) whereas Samson abstains from wine and beer (Judg 13:14).

when you enter the Tent of Meeting (bĕbōʾăkem ʾel-ʾōhel môʿēd). With the LXX add *ʾô bĕgištĕkem ʾel-hammizbēaḥ* 'or when you make contact with the altar' (cf. Exod 28:43; 30:20; for *nāgaš ʾel* denoting "make contact with [for the purpose of officiating]" see below). The rabbis infer this addition from the analogy to Exod 30:20 (*Sipra,* Shemini, par. 1:4). Indeed, it is inconceivable that inebriation would be forbidden only on entry into the Tent but not while officiating at the altar!

But is it true that an intoxicated priest is liable to death merely for entering the Tent? The rabbis (followed by Ramban) asseverate that this prohibition is strictly limited to the case of an inebriated priest who officiates in the Tent (*Sipra,* Shemini, par. 1:4). Maimonides, by contrast, interprets the prohibition literally: it applies to an inebriated priest who enters the Tent for any reason whatsoever (*Sēper Hammiṣwôt,* Prohibition 73), but his penalty is lashes, not death ("Entry to the Sanctuary" 1.15–16). Among the moderns, Haran agrees with the rabbis that this prohibition deals with officiating inside the Tent, but it applies only to the high priest, for he alone may officiate there (1978: 206).

There is a way out of this impasse, and it will become evident once this prohibition is compared with the other prohibitions falling on the priests. In Scripture there are four disqualifications that forbid priests to come into contact with the sanctuary and outer altar on pain of death: improper washing, a physical blemish, improper dress, and drunkenness. The texts follow in order:

1. *běbō'ām 'el-'ōhel mô'ēd yirḥāṣû-mayim wělō' yāmūtû 'ô běgištām 'el-hammizbēaḥ lěšārēt lěhaqṭîr 'iššeh laYHWH* 'When they enter the Tent of Meeting they shall wash with water, that they may not die; or when they make contact with the altar to officiate, to turn into smoke a food gift to the Lord' (Exod 30:20; cf. 40:32).

2. *'ak 'el-happārōket lō' yābō' wě'el-hammizbēaḥ lō' yiggaš kî-mûm bô* 'But he shall not enter to the veil or make contact with [to officiate on] the altar, for he has a blemish' (Lev 21:23; cf. vv 17, 18, 21).

3. *wěhāyû 'al-'ahărōn wě'al-bānāyw běbō'ām 'el-'ōhel mô'ēd 'ô běgištām 'el-hammizbēaḥ lěšārēt baqqōdeš* 'They (the breeches) shall be worn by Aaron and his sons when they enter the Tent of Meeting or when they make contact with the altar to officiate in the sacred precinct' (Exod 28:43; cf. v 35).

4. *yayin wěšēkār 'al-tēšt 'attâ ûbānêkā 'ittāk běbō'ākem 'el-'ōhel mô'ēd* 'Drink no wine or ale, you or your sons after you, when you enter the Tent of Meeting' (Lev 10:9); *wěyayin lō'-yištû kol-kōhēn běbō'ām 'el-heḥāṣēr happěnîmît* 'No priest shall drink wine when he enters the inner court' (Ezek 44:21).

Two preliminary observations must be made: (1) the expression *nāgaš 'el* 'approach' (10:9 LXX; 21:23) and its synonym *qārab 'el* (e.g., Exod 40:32) are auxiliaries to verbs denoting ministration, such as *lěšārēt* 'to officiate' (Exod 28:43; 30:20), *lěhaqṭîr* 'to turn into smoke' (Exod 30:20), or *lěhaqrîb* 'to sacrifice' (21:17, 21 [bis]), and hence should be rendered "make contact with [for purposes of officiating]" in positive cultic statements and "encroach" in negative, prohibitive statements (details in Milgrom 1970a: 33–43); (2) *qōdeš* (Exod 28:43) denotes the Tabernacle court (for details, see the NOTES on v 4 and on 6:9; 9:7).

That these verses invariably and unambiguously point to the conclusion that the disqualified may not enter the Tent under any circumstance is demonstrated by three pieces of evidence. First, the prohibition to minister is limited to the altar. Never do we find the verbs *qārab/nāgaš* or the specific ministerial acts *lěhaqṭîr, lěšārēt, lěhaqrîb* (see above) in connection with the Tent (the unique expression *'el-happārōket* and its implications will be discussed in the

NOTE on 21:23. Provisionally, see Milgrom 1970a: 40 n. 154). Second, Ezekiel does not mention the altar in connection with his prohibition directed against the inebriated priest, but for an obvious reason. He has extended the prohibition of entering the Tent (Temple) to the entire sacrificial court. For in Ezekiel's system, the inner court containing the altar is the private preserve of the priest. Because he prohibits "entry" to the court and not just to the altar, the conclusion is inescapable that physical entry by the drunken priest into the court is strictly forbidden. And third, despite the rabbinic statement (cited above), older, tannaitic texts unambiguously concur that "entry" must be understood literally. For example: "Between the porch and the altar is still more holy (than the forecourt) for none (of the priests) that has a blemish or whose hair is untrimmed may enter there. The shrine is still more holy, for none (of the priests) may enter therein with hands and feet unwashed. . . . R. Jose said: In five things is the space between the porch and the altar equal to the shrine: for they (the priests) may not enter there that have a blemish, or that have drunk wine, or that have hands and feet unwashed" (*m. Kelim* 1:9; cf. *t. Kelim B. Qam.* 1:6–8; *Sipre* Zuṭa on Num 5:2). There is controversy over whether the prohibitions within the space between the porch and the altar are in origin rabbinic or biblical (*b. Yoma* 44b), but all are in agreement that the prohibition for a disqualified priest to enter the shrine (Tent) for any reason whatsoever is biblical. While the biblical prohibition pertaining to the blemished priest may lend itself to the interpretation that he may be allowed to enter the Tent to perform a noncultic task, such as to clean or repair the sancta, under no circumstances may he officiate (see the NOTE on 21:23).

after you ('ittĕkā). In the patriarchal promises *'ittĕkā* (Gen 28:4) is equivalent to *'aḥarêkā* 'after you' (Gen 17:8; 35:12; Brettler 1978–79: IX n. 9). This surely is its meaning in the Priestly texts describing the progeny of Aaron (not the usual rendering "with you"), for his daughters are entitled to the priestly perquisites from the sacred (but not most sacred) offerings (v 15; Num 18:19). Because Aaron had no daughters *'ittĕkā* must denote subsequent generations.

that you may not die (wĕlō' tāmūtû). This threat may be the link that ties this pericope to the preceding: both vv 1–7 and vv 8–9 deal with prohibitions imposed on priests, the penalty for the violations of which is death (Elliger 1966).

throughout your generations (lĕdōrōtêkem). This term is absent in the corresponding prohibition in Ezek 44:21 and in all other passages in Ezekiel modeled on P (cf. Exod 31:13 with Ezek 20:12, 20; Num 15:21 with Ezek 44:30; Num 15:23 with Ezek 39:22). The plural form corresponds to the cognate Akk. expression *ana dāriātim* (Weinfeld 1970: 199; Grintz 1974–76: 29), though the addition of the suffix may be a peculiar Israelite innovation (Loewenstamm 1967–68: 31; Hurvitz 1982: 100 n. 145). Thus, the term *lĕdōrōtêkem* fell out of currency in LBH (cf. Exod 30:7–8 with 2 Chr 2:3) and is a sign of the antiquity of P (Hurvitz 1982: 98–101).

10. *You must distinguish (ûlăhabdîl).* The infinitive can convey the sense of obligation (GKC §114, l). The prefixed *waw* could then be understood conjunctively, the preceding prohibition and penalty being cause for requiring the priest to make the specified distinctions (Rashi). Or the *waw* can be taken as an emphatic (GKC §114, p), in other words, "and that . . ." (e.g., Exod 32:29). The LXX and Pesh. omit the *waw;* and so, apparently, does Ezekiel. For his definition of the priestly role (clearly based on this verse and the next), *wĕ'et-'ammî yôrû bên qōdeš lĕḥōl ûbên-ṭāme' lĕṭāhôr yôdî'um* 'They shall teach my people [the differences] between the sacred and the common and inform them [of the differences] between the impure and the pure' (Ezek 44:23) is separated from the wine prohibition (v 21) by yet another prohibition (v 22). Thus, Ezekiel knew this verse and the next (vv 10–11) as a discrete injunction, unconnected with the previous wine prohibition. In fact, what Ezekiel actually does is to fuse the priestly roles of P and D. The rest of his definition, *wĕ'al-rîb hēmmâ ya'ămdû lĕmišpāṭ* (K./Q.) *bĕmišpāṭay yišpĕṭûhû* (K./Q.) 'In lawsuits, too, they shall act as judges; they shall decide them in accordance with my rules' (Ezek 44:24a), is based on Deuteronomy, which—in contrast to P—assigns judicial functions to the priests: "If a case is too baffling for you to decide *(lammišpāṭ)* . . . matters of dispute *(rîbōt)* in your courts . . . appear before the levitical priests" (Deut 17:7–9); "every case of dispute *(rîb)* and assault is subject to their ruling" (Deut 21:5b).

The making of distinctions *(lĕhabdîl)* is the essence of the priestly function. Ezekiel scores the priests of his time precisely on this point: "Her priests have violated *(ḥāmĕsû)* my teaching: they have desecrated what is sacred to me, they have not distinguished *(hibdîlû)* between the sacred and common, they have not taught the difference between the unclean and the clean . . . I am desecrated in their midst" (Ezek 22:26). The failure of the priests to distinguish between the sacred and common has resulted in the desecration of God's name. It constitutes *ḥāmās* 'violence', the very sin for which God brought a flood on mankind (Gen 6:11, 13) and for which Ezekiel's countrymen face destruction (Ezek 7:23; 9:9). Israel too is charged with the task of making distinctions, particularly in the animal food it eats (11:47; 20:25) as a sign and reminder of its own differentiation from the nations (20:24, 26; see chap. 11, COMMENT E).

the sacred (haqqōdeš). Holiness implies separation to God as well as separation from the common (Snaith 1967). Thus God sanctifies his day, the Sabbath (Gen 2:3; Exod 20:10–11), his priesthood (22:9), and his people (22:32).

the common (haḥōl). In the Pentateuch this term occurs only here (elsewhere in 1 Sam 21:5–6; Ezek 22:26; 42:20; 44:23; 48:15).

between . . . and between (bên . . . ûbên). This idiom changes in LBH to *bên . . . lĕ* (Hannemann 1975–76), beginning with Ezekiel (Ezek 22:26; 42:20) and, most significantly, in Ezekiel's corresponding text: *wĕ'et-'ammî yôrû bên qōdeš lĕḥōl ûbên-ṭāme' lĕṭāhôr yôdî'um* (Ezek 44:23), another indication of the preexilic provenience of P's terminology (Hurvitz 1982: 113–14).

and between the impure and the pure (ûbên haṭṭāmēʾ ûbên haṭṭāhôr). One would have expected the reverse order in view of the preceding clause (D. Wright). Instead, this chiastic arrangement is probably intentional, if we judge by the repetitions of this formula in Ezekiel, which preserve the same chiastic scheme (cf. Ezek 22:26; 44:23; cf. also 11:47; 20:25; and the NOTE on 11:47). For Ibn Ezra, this clause serves as an introduction to chaps. 11–15, which, indeed, distinguish between the impure and pure. Yet it is more likely that chaps. 11–15 were inserted between chaps. 10 and 16 in order to exemplify the sanctuary pollutions that require thoroughgoing purgation rites, and only subsequently were vv 10–11 inserted in their present place in chap. 10 to act as their introduction. In either case, this clause can justly be claimed as a proleptic introduction to chaps. 11–15.

The relations among the four categories mentioned here can be better understood by examining the following diagram:

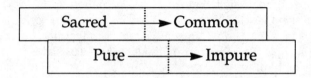

Persons and objects are subject to four possible states: sacred, common, pure, and impure, two of which can exist simultaneously—either sacred or common and either pure or impure. Nevertheless, one combination is excluded in the priestly system: whereas the common may be either pure or impure the sacred may not be impure. For example, the layman (common) is in a state of purity unless polluted by some impurity, such as forbidden meat (chap. 11), a sexual flow (chap. 15), or a corpse (Num 19), for which purification procedures are prescribed. Still, there is neither danger nor liability for the layman who contracts impurity as long as he does not allow it to be prolonged (see the COMMENT on 5:1–13). Not so for the sacred. The sanctuary, for example, must at all times remain pure; impurity befalling it must immediately be purged, lest the whole community be blighted (chap. 4, COMMENT C). These relationships are depicted in the diagram. The common is contiguous with the realms of the pure and impure, but the sacred is contiguous only with the pure; it may not contact the impure. The broken line separating each of the two polarities indicates that these relationships are not static. In particular, it is incumbent upon the priests, through their constant instruction (v 11), to enlarge the realms of the sacred and the pure by reducing the areas of the common and the impure. Israel is to be instructed by the priests how to reduce the incidence of impurity by purifying (and avoiding) it—for instance, by eschewing forbidden meats (11:4–8), contacting sancta in a state of impurity (12:4), and following the prescribed purification procedures (chaps. 12–15)—and how to reduce the realm of the common by sanctifying it—for example, by faithfully observing sacred time (the Sabbath and festivals) and frequenting holy space (the sanctuary). Hence, the goal is that the categories of common and impure shall largely disappear, by their respective conversion into the sacred and pure. The priestly task is, therefore, a dynamic one. It is to make all of Israel into "a royalty of priests and a holy nation" (Exod 19:6). This objective is the hallmark of H, a fact that raises the possibility that vv 10–11 stem from the hand of H.

11. *And you must teach (ûlĕhôrōt).* The teaching of God's commandments is one of the main functions of the priesthood (Deut 24:8). In one statement it is mentioned exclusively: "For the lips of a priest guard knowledge, and rulings are sought from his mouth" (Mal 2:7a). In another it is mentioned first, ahead of the priests' cultic duties: "They shall teach your norms to Jacob and your instructions to Israel. They shall offer you incense to savor and whole offerings on your altar" (Deut 33:11; cf. 17:8–13; 21:5; 24:8).

Ezekiel clearly knew vv 10–11 as a single unit because he uses the verb *yôrû* 'teach' (v 11), with the categories sacred and common (v 10), even though in his text (Ezek 44:21–23) it is dissociated from the previous alcohol prohibitions (vv 8–9; see the NOTE on "you must distinguish," v 10). Philo also treats vv 10–11 as a single unit. He adds to his citation of v 10 the words "lawful and unlawful" (*Laws* 1. 100), implying that the priests' pedagogic function is not only to distinguish among the four categories (v 10) but to teach the laws (v 11).

the laws (hahuqqîm). In P the term for law is *ḥuqqâ,* pl. *ḥuqqōt* (see the NOTE on v 13). The masc. pl. is attested only twice more (26:46; Num 30:17), whereas it is used exclusively by E and D (e.g., Exod 15:26; 18:16, 20; Deut [19 times]). It is hardly an accident that all three occurrences are part of subscripts to their respective contexts. They probably betray the hand of the final redactor of the Priestly texts (if not of the entire Pentateuch), who was not aware of this grammatical nuance. Thus, vv 10–11 comprise a late interpolation (see the NOTE on "and between the impure and the pure," v 10).

to them. ʾălêhem, but not *ʾălêkem* 'to you', namely, the priests. The priests are not the recipients of the divine teachings. These teachings are imparted to Israel through the mediation of Moses. The priests, then, carry no new instruction; they transmit the old. In this respect, Israel broke sharply with its environment, where the divine instruction was the jealously and zealously guarded secret of the priesthood (for details, see the NOTE "Speak to the Israelites," 1:2). It is no wonder, then, that the corpus of laws in Leviticus exclusively concerned with priestly duties is, in nearly its entirety, to be taught to Israel and, with one exception (vv 8–9), mediated to the priests through Moses. The sacrificial rituals (chaps. 1–5) are commanded to the Israelites (1:2). Those sacrificial laws which are the exclusive concern of the priests (chaps. 6–7) nonetheless conclude with "[these are the rituals . . .] when he commanded the Israelites to present their offerings to the Lord, in the Wilderness of Sinai" (7:38). The section on impurities (chaps. 11–15), many of which require sacrificial remedies, ends with the injunction, "You shall set apart the Israelites from their impurity" (15:31). The service of the Day of Purgation, though the sole prerogative of the high priest (16:1–28), is nevertheless followed by directions to the Israelites (vv 29–31). The discussion of priestly impurities and blemishes is, to be sure, addressed to the priests (21:1), yet it is concluded by the comment, "thus Moses spoke to Aaron and his sons and to all of the Israelites" (21:24). There can be no esoteric doctrine hidden away in priestly archives: "the Torah commanded us by Moses is the heritage of the congregation of Jacob" (Deut 33:4).

12. *Moses spoke.* Moses, not God, is the speaker, a sign that the following instructions are not new but have been given before (Koch 1959: 73). Why are they then repeated here? To let us know that the ritual for the eighth day is not yet complete: the sacrifices have been offered but their priestly portions have yet to be eaten.

cereal offering. It is assumed that although its token portion had been offered (9:17), the remainder had not been eaten before Nadab and Abihu were struck down. Moses thus reminds the priests to complete the ritual first by eating the cereal offering, and he recites the procedure already given in 2:3; 6:9; and 7:10.

that remains (hannôteret). In *"bānāyw hannôtārîm,* as opposed to *hamminḥâ hannôteret,* lies an expression of indescribable sadness" (Ehrlich 1908–14).

the Lord's food gifts (mēʾiššê YHWH). For the basis of this rendering, see the NOTE on 1:9.

beside the altar (ʾēṣel hammizbēaḥ). This phrase, unique in its description of the place in which the priests eat their prebends from the most sacred offerings, is clearly synonymous with its designation *bĕmāqôm qādōš* 'in the sacred precinct' the phrase used in the next verse (v 13). As has been shown, "in a holy place" (and, hence, "beside the altar") is defined as "in the court of the Tent of Meeting" (see the NOTE on "in a holy place," 6:9). To be sure, it could hardly be expected that the priests would dine at the sacrificial ash dump, which was located—note the identical phrase—*ʾēṣel hammizbēaḥ* 'beside the altar' (6:3). But here we are confronted by a matter of aesthetics, not of cultic law. Theoretically, the priestly prebends could be eaten there for the ashes derive from the altar and, hence, are "most sacred," a similar degree of sanctity to the cereal offering and other most sacred offerings eaten by the priests. Thus Aaron and his sons may eat the cereal offering anywhere within the Tabernacle court.

13. *in the sacred precinct. bĕmāqôm qādōš,* that is to say, inside the Tabernacle court (see the preceding NOTE and the NOTE on "in the holy place," 6:9).

your due (ḥoqkā). In distinguishing between "law" and "due, assigned portion," though both derive from the same root *ḥqq,* P prefers (as does H) the masculine form *ḥōq* for "due" (6:11, 15; 7:34; 10:13, 14, 15; 24:9; Exod 29:28;

Num 18:8, 11, 19) and the feminine form *ḥuqqâ* for "law" (3:17; 7:36; 10:9; 16:29, 31, 34; 17:7; 18:3, 4, 5, 26; 19:37; 20:8, 22; 23:14, 21, 31, 41; 24:3; 25:18; 26:3, 15, 43; Exod 12:14, 17, 43; 27:21; 28:43; 29:9; Num 9:3, 12; 10:8; 15:15; 18:23; 19:2, 10, 21; 27:11; 31:21; 35:29). The only exceptions to this rule are Exod 30:21, where "eternal statute" is expressed by *ḥoq ʿôlām;* and Lev 7:36, where "eternal due" is expressed by *ḥuqqat ʿôlām.* Instead, the Sam. reads, in my opinion correctly, *ḥuqqat ʿôlām* and *ḥoq ʿôlām* (overlooked in BH³), respectively. See also the NOTES on 6:11 and 7:34, 36.

for so I have been commanded (kî-kēn ṣuwwêtî). The reference is to 2:3, 9–10; 6:9. For the expression, see 8:35b.

14. The text presumes that the people through their representatives, the elders (9:1), will consume the meat of the well-being offering (cf. Exod 18:12; 24:5, 11). Instead, the focus here on the priestly prebends from the sacrifice is intended to lay the basis for the climactic confrontation between Moses and Aaron over the prebends from the purification offering (vv 16–20).

But [the breast]. wĕ-ʾēt, with *Tg. Neof.* The object heads the sentence and is introduced by the adversative *waw* to indicate that the priestly prebends from the well-being offering, a lesser holy sacrifice, are to be treated differently from the previously mentioned prebends from the cereal offering, a most holy sacrifice.

the breast of elevation offering (ḥăzēh hattĕnûpâ). See the NOTE on 7:34, and chap. 7, COMMENT E.

the thigh of contribution (šôq hattĕrûmâ). See the NOTE on 7:34 and chap. 7, COMMENT F.

you may eat (tōʾkĕlû). This verb forms an inclusio with *waʾăkaltem* (v 13), indicating that vv 13–14 form an integral unit and suggesting that v 15 is (at least partially) a later addition (see below).

in any pure place (bĕmāqôm ṭāhôr). This phrase must indicate a place outside the sacred precincts because it stands in contrast to *ʾēṣel hammizbēaḥ* 'beside the altar' (v 12) and *bĕmāqôm qādōš* 'in the sacred precinct', which, as determined above, locate the eating of the most holy offerings inside the sanctuary court. But is this "pure place" limited to a specific locale? The rabbis claim that the lesser holy offerings are to be eaten within the camp (*b. Zebaḥ.* 55a) and, subsequently, within Jerusalem (*m. Zebaḥ.* 5:7). Yet because there are also pure areas outside the camp (see the NOTE on 4:12), the plain meaning of the text can only be any place that is not impure. As the entire priestly household is eligible to eat from these prebends, including his slaves (22:11), the most obvious "pure place" is the priest's home.

The emphasis here on the purity of the place instead of the purity of the persons eating the sacrifice (contrast 7:19; Num 18:11) may possibly betray a polemic against a concurrent but older and, hence, more hallowed practice of cooking and eating the well-being offerings within the sanctuary court. Near the altar of the Lachish temple, dating from pre-Israelite Canaan, bones from the right foreleg of a number of animals were found. Significantly, these bones were not burned, indicating that these portions were not consumed on the altar but cooked nearby and eaten (Tufnell 1940: Appendix B, 93–94). Clearer and more striking witness is provided by the Bible itself. At Shiloh and other contemporary sanctuaries during the days of Samuel, the following was the practice: "The custom of the priests in their dealings with the people was this: when a man offered a sacrifice, the priest's servant would come while the flesh was stewing and would thrust a three-pronged fork into the cauldron or pan or kettle or pot; and the priest would take whatever the fork brought out" (1 Sam 2:13–14). Two bits of relevant information can be derived from this pregnant text: the offerer's sacrifice of well-being was boiled at the sanctuary premises, and the priests received their due not from the raw but from the boiled meat. That the offerer's sacrificial meat was cooked and eaten at the sanctuary is also attested in other early sources (e.g., 1 Sam 1:4, 7, 8, 9, 18; 9:12–13, 22–25).

This practice is strikingly confirmed in P's law of the Nazirite: the officiating priest receives as his prebend the boiled shoulder of the well-being ram cooked in the Tabernacle court (Num 6:18–19). Indeed, P is so unambiguous about where the Nazirite's well-being offering was cooked that the rabbis could not but ordain that "the Nazirite cooked when he shaved" (*Midr. Num. Rab.* 10:21), a rule that was manifestly observed in the Second Temple (*m. Mid.* 2:5).

An even more telling case is Ezekiel's blueprint for the Temple, which prescribes that the people's well-being offering be cooked and, presumably, eaten in the outer court (Ezek 46:24). The Temple Scroll of the Dead Sea sectaries also prescribes that lay persons must eat the lesser holy offerings within the confines of the outer court (11QT 17:8–9; 21:3; 22:11–14; etc.). Indeed, the possibility also exists that when Deuteronomy ordains that the people's sacrifices be eaten "before the Lord" (Deut 12:12, 18; 16:11; 27:7) it has in mind the sanctuary court. Because "at the place *(māqôm)* where the Lord your God will choose to establish his name, there alone shall you slaughter the passover sacrifice" (Deut 12:6) clearly refers to the sanctuary precincts, then "you shall cook it and eat it at the place that the Lord your God shall choose" (v 7) must also take place in the sanctuary precincts. By contrast, when D's place *(māqôm)* was identified with the Jerusalem Temple, the impossibility of containing the pilgrims, let alone the population of expanding Jerusalem, inside the Temple area made it imperative to limit the cooking of the passover and auxiliary sacrifices to the sanctuary precincts (2 Chr 35:13) while allowing their consumption in the city. It is certain that in Second Temple times, when Jerusalem received the attribute "the holy city" (Isa 52:1; cf. Jer 31:39), the eating of the lesser holy offerings within the city walls became legitimized (cf. *m. Pesaḥ.* 3:8; 7:8, 9; *m. Meg.* 1:11; *m. Zebaḥ.* 5:6–8; *m. Kelim* 1:8).

The groundwork for this legitimization, however, had already been laid by P. Its silence about where lay persons may eat their offerings, in contrast to the specific directives about where the priests must eat their most holy offerings can only mean, as noted above, that any place is permitted as long as it is not impure. Moreover, the warning that impurity should not come into contact with the meat of the well-being offering (7:19–21) implies that the meat is taken outside the sanctuary, where impurities are allowed to exist. Furthermore, the bipartite prohibition that the parturient not contact any holy thing or enter the sanctuary (12:4) presumes that holy things exist in both the community and the sanctuary (D. Wright). Thus P takes issue with the practice that obtained in the older sanctuaries and that continued to be championed by conservative priestly circles (to which Ezekiel clearly belonged; see chap. 7, COMMENT B). It ordains that the lay portions of the well-being offering need not be eaten in the sanctuary court; any pure place will do. For the argument that P's rule applied to all sacred food of lesser holy rank, see the NOTE on *qōdeš* (22:10).

assigned (nittĕnû). The plural refers to the breast and thigh, not the word "due."

your children (bānêkā). This term includes *bĕnōtêkā* 'your daughters' (cf. Gen 3:16; Job 1:5). The rabbis, however, draw from the omission of "your daughters" in this phrase the inference that these priestly prebends are the sons' by right, but the daughters' by sufferance (*Sipra*, Shemini 1:10).

15. *Together with. 'al (Keter Torah)*; cf. the NOTE on 7:30.

the thigh of contribution and the breast of the elevation offering, which shall be elevated as an elevation offering (šôq hattĕrûmâ waḥăzēh hattĕnûpâ . . . lĕhānîp tĕnûpâ). Rashi confesses, "We cannot fathom why the text assigns (the terms) *tĕrûmâ* to the thigh and *tĕnûpâ* to the breast because both (portions) are subject to raising and waving." His question is valid. Because, according to rabbinic definition, both portions undergo raising and waving (see chap. 7, COMMENT F) and, even according to this biblical text, both portions undergo *tĕnûpâ*, it makes no sense that one portion should be termed *tĕrûmâ* and the other *tĕnûpâ*. First, it should be noted that the terms are reversed from their normal order; elsewhere the breast is always mentioned before the thigh (Exod 29:27; Lev 7:34; 10:14; Num 6:20; cf. Lev 7:30–33; 9:21; Num 18:18). Then, it is always the breast and never the thigh that is subject to the *tĕnûpâ* (for the alleged exception of 9:21, see the NOTE ad loc.). Thus either this entire verse was added by a later editorial hand, for after v 14 this verse is superfluous (Milgrom 1983d: 165) or, more likely (I have changed my mind), only the opening words, *šôq hattĕrûmâ* 'the thigh of contribution', were inserted at the head of this verse once the thigh was added to the *tĕnûpâ* ritual. The deletion of this phrase reveals a clear and essential bit of information: although both the breast and the thigh are prebends for the priestly households, the breast must initially undergo an elevation rite before it can become the property of the priests.

and to your children (ûlĕbānêkā). The LXX and Sam. add *ûlibĕnōtêkā* 'and to your daughters', but see the NOTE on v 14.

as the Lord has commanded. ka'ăšer ṣiwwâ YHWH; see Exod 29:27–28;

Lev 7:30. These verses speak only of the breast as subject of the *těnûpâ*, which supports the supposition that only the phrase *šôq hattěrûmâ* was interpolated by a later editor, not the entire verse (see the NOTE above).

16. *Then Moses insistently inquired (dārōš dāraš mōšeh).* Why did Moses need to inquire? He must have known what happened, for he had supervised Aaron and his sons during the entire sacrificial ritual (Dillmann and Ryssel 1897)! The answer might be that Moses had left the sanctuary to summon Mishael and Elzaphan, during which time the purification carcass was burnt (Hoffmann 1953), or that it was not the function of the high priest (or any priest) to burn the purification carcass (see the NOTE on 4:12), a task that could be performed by any layman (Elliger 1966).

about the goat of the purification offering (wĕʾēt śĕʿîr haḥaṭṭāʾt). This clause, though the object of the sentence, stands first—an indication of its importance (see also the NOTE on v 14). No complaint is registered regarding the burning of the priests' purification offering (9:11): the priests may not benefit from their personal expiatory sacrifices (see the NOTE on 8:17 and COMMENT B below). The question, however, concerns the disposition of the people's purification offering (9:3). The text has only informed us that its blood was daubed on the horns of the outer altar (see the NOTE on 9:15), but the text tells us nothing about its disposition.

had already been burned (śōrāp). If this verbal form is a *puʿal* (a hapax), the Masoretic vocalization is no accident (Shadal). Perhaps its intention would be to indicate that nothing of the carcass was retrievable; it had been completely burned. It is more likely, however, that this verbal form is a *qal* passive (GKC 52, e).

He was angry with Eleazar and Ithamar (wayyiqṣōp ʿal-ʾelʿāzār wĕʿal-ʾîtāmār). "Out of respect for Aaron, he (Moses) turned toward the sons and then vented his anger" (Rashi; cf. Kalisch 1867–72; Dillmann and Ryssel 1897).

remaining (hannôtārîm). The purpose of this adjective here is not clear (contrast v 12). Perhaps it underscores the frightening possibility that if Eleazar and Ithamar are punished the same way as their late brothers, Nadab and Abihu, the entire priestly line would be wiped out.

17. *"Why did you not eat the purification offering.* The *ḥaṭṭāʾt*, whose blood is daubed on the horns of the outer altar (4:25, 30, 34) but not brought inside the Tent (6:23; and see the NOTE on the next verse), must be eaten by the officiating priest (6:19), namely, Aaron, and what he cannot finish must be eaten by the rest of the priestly cadre (6:22), his sons. The reasons for such stringency in the case of the eaten *ḥaṭṭāʾt* are explored in COMMENT C below.

in the sacred precinct (bimqôm haqqōdeš). An equivalent expression to *běmāqôm qādōš* (v 13; see the NOTE on 6:9).

assigned it to you. The LXX adds "to eat."

to remove the iniquity of the community (lāśēʾt ʾet-ʿāwōn hāʿēdâ). The idiom *nāśāʾ ʿāwōn* has two meanings, depending on its subject. If the subject is man, then the idiom denotes "bear responsibility/punishment" (e.g., 5:1, 17; 17:16; Exod 28:43; Num 18:1, 23). If the subject is God, then it denotes "remove iniquity" (e.g., Exod 20:5; 34:7; Num 14:18; Isa 33:24; Hos 14:3). As the subject here is the priest (not God), then the first meaning would seem to apply. The prebends from the purification offering would then be assigned to the priests as their reward for effecting purgation on behalf of the community (Knobel 1857; Ehrlich 1908–14; Milgrom 1976a: 333; but see below). Because this process involves purging the sanctuary altar of its accumulated impurity, a process possibly fraught with danger to themselves lest they become contaminated, they are awarded the meat of the purificatory animal. Analogically, the priests would resemble the Levites who are rewarded with the tithe for assuming the responsibility *(nāśāʾ ʿāwōn)* of guarding the sanctuary against lay encroachment at the peril of their lives (Num 18:22–23; Milgrom 1970a: 22–33). As will be pointed out (COMMENT B below), however, the officiating priest who purges the sanctuary of its impurities is immune to its contagion (see also the NOTE on 16:24), and besides, in the Priestly system impurity has been eviscerated of its demonic content: it is baneful only to sancta but not to man (see chap. 4, COMMENT C). Thus it is hardly likely that this text would single out the purification offering as a special bonus for the priests when, in essence, it differs not a whit from any other prebend assigned to the priests from the most sacred offerings.

The second meaning, "remove iniquity," must now be considered. True, the subject is man, not God, but in this case it is the priest who serves as the divine surrogate on earth and exclusively so in the sanctuary. Moreover, there are three instances in the Bible wherein *nāśāʾ ḥaṭṭāʾt* (= ʿāwōn) in the sense of "remove iniquity" has as its subject man: Joseph (Gen 50:17), Moses (Exod 10:17), and Samuel (1 Sam 15:23). In each case a superior, but one who is assumed to be favored by God, is implored by an inferior (Joseph's brothers, Pharaoh, Saul, respectively) for forgiveness. If so, then the power to remove iniquity can certainly reside in the cult as operated by God's confidants *(qĕrōbay,* v 3), his priests. Moreover, their authority and ability to remove the iniquity of the congregation is expressly attributed to the high priest: "It (the gold plate) shall be on Aaron's forehead, that Aaron may remove any iniquity arising from the sacred things that the Israelites consecrate, from any of their sacred donations *(wĕnāśāʾ ʾahărōn ʾet-ʿāwōn haqqŏdāšîm ʾăšer yaqdîšû bĕnê yiśrāʾēl lĕkol-mattĕnōt qodšêhem);* it shall be on his forehead at all times, to win acceptance for them before the Lord" (Exod 28:38). The function of the high priest's *ṣîṣ* (for the rendering "plate," see the NOTE on 8:9) is clear. Any inadvertent impurity or imperfection in the offerings brought by the Israelites to the Tabernacle would be expiated by the *ṣîṣ*. The rabbis aver that even the impurity of the offerers—not just of their offerings—was expiated by the high priest's *ṣîṣ* *(t. Pesaḥ.* 6:5). In any event, Aaron's permanent powers, which enable him to remove the iniquity *(nāśāʾ ʿāwōn)* of Israel's donations to the sanctuary, are completely compatible with the priests' function, which requires them to remove the iniquity *(nāśāʾ ʿāwōn)* of the community by effecting purgation on its behalf with the purification offering. Furthermore, just as the *ʿāwōn* of Israel's sacred donations (Exod 28:38) refers to their impurity, so *ʿāwōn* here (though rendered "iniquity") refers to impurity, specifically, the impurity arising from Israel's ritual and moral failings that has polluted the sanctuary. The choice of the term *ʿāwōn* was not by chance. Although it refers to cultic violations (e.g., Exod 28:38, 43; Lev 7:18), it extends beyond this limited area to embrace ethical violations as well. Note its ethical import in the following Priestly contexts: the person who withholds testimony (5:1), the person who is unaware of his sin (see the NOTE on 5:17), the suspected adulteress and her accuser husband (Num 5:15, 31), and the husband who belatedly cancels his wife's vow (Num 30:16). This choice of *ʿāwōn* also reinforces the supposition that the *ḥaṭṭāʾt* expiates for the inadvertent violation of *all* prohibitive commandments, ritual and ethical alike (see the NOTE on 4:2).

How does the priest effect the removal of the community's iniquity? What is his modus operandi? The text is unambiguous in its response: by ingesting the purification offering. As succinctly stated by the rabbinic aphorism, *hakkōhănîm ʾōkĕlîm wĕhabbĕʿālîm mitkappĕrîm* 'When the priests eat (the purification offering) the offerers are expiated' *(Sipra, Shemini 2:4)*. Indeed, that ingestion is an indispensable element of the purification rite is underscored in the LXX, which adds the phrase "[I have assigned it to you] to eat" (see above).

Thus the *ḥaṭṭāʾt* is the analogic counterpart to the high priest's *ṣîṣ*. As the latter symbolically draws to itself all of the impurities of Israel's sacred offerings, so the former, by the blood manipulation, draws out the pollution of the sanctuary caused by Israel's impurities and iniquities. Through the media of the *ṣîṣ* and *ḥaṭṭāʾt*, the priests, then, perform the identical function. Just as the high priest absorbs the impurities of Israel's offerings by means of the *ṣîṣ*, so the officiating priest absorbs the impurities of the Israelites by means of the *ḥaṭṭāʾt*.

Ingestion of impurity as a means of eliminating it is not unknown in other cultures. In some forms of Hinduism, "when mechanistic transfer is unavoidable, recourse is made to the Brahmin who in a literal sense is believed to digest the impurity without himself becoming impure" (Hayley 1980: 123). In more recent times, one can cite the old English custom of hiring a "sin-eater" at funerals, who was given sixpence together with a loaf of bread and a bowl of beer to consume over the corpse, "in consideration whereof he tooke upon himself (ipso facto) all the Sinnes of the Defunct" (Aubrey 1881: 35). Did the removal of impurity by ingestion obtain in Israel's contemporary world? No such process is attested in ancient Greece (Parker 1983: 283 n. 11). By contrast, an incantation tablet from Nimrud reads as follows:

> Purify the man, the son of his god
> The dough with which you have purified his body
> . . . he shall eat and it will remove his illness

   . . . he shall eat and it will tear out his illness
   . . . he shall eat and a bird will take his *namtaru* up to heaven
   . . . he shall eat and a fish will carry his *asakku* down to Apsu
                             (Knudsen 1959: 54–61, lines 32–41)

The cited lines of the tablet are unfortunately broken. Nevertheless, enough remains to deduce that the sick person himself consumes the dough, a process that absorbs his illness and thereby eliminates it.

In sum, it may be concluded that the function of the priest is to remove Israel's iniquity. The only doubt that remains concerns his method. Is it by purging the sanctuary with the blood of the purification offering, in reward for which he receives its meat (Milgrom 1976a), or by ingesting the purification offering, which has symbolically absorbed the purged impurity (as I now maintain; cf. also Rodriguez 1979: 134 n. 2)? The latter answer, at face value, seems more logical. Once the blood has removed the impurities they are transferred to the carcass, which must now be disposed of. Because a carcass bearing severe impurities is burned (4:12; 16:27), it must therefore follow that the carcass bearing lesser impurities is eliminated by ingestion. If this proves to be the answer, a larger question surfaces in its place: if the impurity-laden carcass must be eliminated, why cannot the purification offerings for severer impurities be eaten instead of being burned and, conversely, what is so terribly wrong about eliminating the lesser impurities by burning the purification offering, as did Aaron and his sons, instead of eating it? This larger question will be the subject of COMMENT C below.

18. *Because its blood was not brought into the interior of the sacred precinct.* *hēn lō'-hûbā' 'et-dāmāh 'el-haqqōdeš pĕnîmâ,* that is to say, inside the Tent. The rule that purification offerings whose blood was brought into the Tent are burned and not eaten is found in 6:23, which, however, reads *baqqōdeš* instead of *'el-haqqōdeš pĕnîmâ,* proving that the term *qōdeš* is used differently in each formula: in 6:23 it means "the sanctuary," that is, the Tent; here it means "the sacred precinct," namely, the court (see also the NOTE below). The semantic range of this pleonastic term *qōdeš* is discussed in the NOTES on 6:9 and 23.

you certainly ought to have eaten it ('ākôl tō'kĕlû 'ōtāh). The infinitive absolute is added for emphasis (GKC §113, l–n). For the use of the following imperfect describing a past event, see *hayādôaʿ nēdaʿ* 'How could we have known' (Gen 43:7, Ehrlich 1908–14). Curiously enough, this latter example is also preceded by an infinitive absolute construction, *šā'ôl šā'al* 'kept asking' (Gen 43:7, *NJPS*), just as Moses' comment here also begins with a similar construction, *dārōš dāraš* (see the NOTE on "then Moses insistently inquired," v 16). These two examples explain and justify each other. Precisely because the man (Joseph) asked such penetrating questions, the brothers were thrown off guard. And Moses was so persistent in inquiring about the sacrifice because of the importance of the priests' obligation to eat it (Freedman, orally).

in the sacred precinct (baqqōdeš). By contrast, *baqqōdeš* used in the same rule in 6:23 denotes "in the sanctuary," that is to say, inside the Tent. The term *qōdeš* can refer either to holy objects (sancta, e.g., Exod 28:43; 29:20; Num 3:32, 4:15–16) or to holy space (the adytum, 16:7, 27; the shrine, Exod 28:29, 35; or the Tabernacle court, 10:4, 17, 18; cf. v 13). The latter citation shows that the *qōdeš* in all four instances in this chapter consistently denotes the court (see also the NOTE above and the NOTE on 6:23).

The fact that the blood of the purification offering was not brought into the Tent means that the death of Nadab and Abihu occurred subsequently (see also the NOTE on v 14). Otherwise, the severe pollution resulting from their corpses would have necessitated the purging of the entire sanctuary, even of the adytum, with the purification-offering blood. Indeed, according to the redactor of Leviticus, it is the death of Nadab and Abihu inside the sacred precincts that necessitates the emergency purgation rite prescribed in chap. 16 (see the NOTE on 16:1).

as I commanded (kaʾăšer ṣiwwêtî). Tg. Ps.-J. and the Pesh. read (or interpret) *kaʾăšer ṣuwwêtî* 'as I was commanded' (cf. 8:31a); the LXX retains the active verb but reads (or interprets) *kaʾăšer ṣiwwâ YHWH ʾōtî* 'as the Lord commanded me'. The reference is to 6:23.

19. *See (hēn).* Moses' argument began with the word *hēn* (v 18). Hence Aaron also begins his counterargument with *hēn.*

they brought hiqrîbû, in other words, all his sons, including Nadab and Abihu.

their purification offering and burnt offering (ʾet-ḥaṭṭāʾtām wěʾet-ʿōlātām). Refers to the sacrifices that the priestly household brought on its own behalf (9:2, 8–14). Although Aaron alone officiated, his sons assisted him (9:9a, 12b). Aaron omits any mention of himself in order to emphasize the dimensions of the tragedy: his four newly consecrated sons had ministered for the first time and two had died in the effort.

befallen (wattiqreʾnâ). For this usage, see Exod 1:10. The equivalence of and interchange between III-aleph and III-heh verbs is frequently attested (GKC 75, rr).

Had I eaten (wěʾākaltî). The *waw* is conditional and has the force of *ʾim* 'if' (Rashi). The tense is pluperfect.

the purification offering today (ḥaṭṭāʾt hayyôm). This incidental remark serves as the only proof that the most holy offerings must be eaten on the same day they are offered (Hoffmann 1953). This fact is assumed, without proof, by Second Temple sources (m. Zebaḥ. 5:3, 5; 6:1; Philo, 1 *Laws* 240; Jos., *Ant.* 3.231–32).

have approved. hayyîtab běʿênê, literally, "would it have been proper in the eyes of [the Lord]?" The definite article followed by the *dageš forte* has puzzled grammarians and commentators alike (e.g., Rashi, Ibn Ezra). All but the Karaites (e.g., *Seper Hamibḥar, Keter Torah*) recognize that an interrogative *heh* is required. A way out of this impasse (without resorting to emendation) has been suggested by Ehrlich (1908–14, on Gen 17:17 [H]): when the question is one of wonderment, the interrogative *heh* is treated as a definite article, for instance, *hallĕben* (Gen 17:17), *hā'eḥād* (Gen 19:9), *hā'ādām* (Deut 20:19). Ehrlich, in my opinion, is on the right track, but his statement needs refinement. The interrogative *heh* is vocalized as a definite article only when the question is rhetorical and the answer is certain. Thus when Abraham asks, "Can a child be born to a man a hundred years old?" (Gen 17:17a), he is making a positive statement concerning his virility (but he does have doubts concerning Sarah, v 17b). The other two cited instances: "The fellow came here as an alien, and already he acts the ruler!" (Gen 19:9) and "Are the trees of the field human?" (Deut 20:19) are unequivocally rhetorical. Thus the Masoretic vocalization in *hayyîṭab* is of the same order: the answer is obvious, and it is so acknowledged by Moses (v 20) and, presumably, by God (v 19b).

20. *When Moses heard this (wayyišmaʿ mōšeh).* Fishbane (1985: 227) suggests, on the basis of *wĕ'ešmĕ'â* (Num 9:8b), that Moses put Aaron's question to the Lord and "heard" an oracular response. But Aaron's question is merely rhetorical and, moreover, the antecedent of the subsequent "he approved" is Moses, not the Lord. For the text to state that Moses approved the divine decision would be effrontery if not heresy.

he approved (wayyîṭab bĕʿênāyw). This entire pericope ends as mysteriously as it began. Moses' ire is aroused because the priests alter the procedure with one of the sacrifices, the purification offering. One suspects that more is involved than just a slight deviation in sacrificial ritual, and the deeper possibilities will be explored in COMMENT C below. Equally enigmatic is the ultimate approval of this deviation both by Moses and, by implication, God (v 19b). The rabbis suggest two answers: the priests were in mourning and/or the corpses of Nadab and Abihu had defiled the meat of the purification offering (*b. Zebaḥ.* 101a, b). Yet neither answer will do. The priests were forbidden to mourn (v 6) and, hence, qualified—indeed, required—to eat sacred meat (Shadal), and if the death of Nadab and Abihu had indeed defiled the purification offering, the remaining sacrifices—the cereal and well-being offerings—would also have been defiled and should not have been eaten (cf. Ehrlich 1899–1900). This problem will be explored and a solution offered in COMMENT C below.

There is, however, one deduction from this pericope that can be made here. Although Aaron gets the better of Moses on a legal point (discussed in COMMENT C), the fact that the ministration of Aaron and his sons required the approval not only of God but of Moses is striking proof that the superiority of the prophet (Moses) over the priest (Aaron) is acknowledged by P!

COMMENTS: THE TRAGIC AFTERMATH OF THE INAUGURAL SERVICE

A. What Lies Behind the Nadab and Abihu Incident?

The deeper but more problematic question concerns the historical circumstances that lie behind this incident. Gradwohl (1963–64) has proposed that Nadab and Abihu are in reality Nadab and Abijah, sons of Jeroboam I, who died prematurely for their father's apostasy (1 Kgs 14:1–17; 15:27–28), and this Priestly version alludes to the sin of Jeroboam at Bethel and Dan (1 Kgs 12:28, 32; 13:1–10) by making Nadab and Abihu die for Aaron's sin of the golden calf at Sinai. Snaith (1967), instead, sees in this incident a conflict between the Zadokites of Jerusalem and non-Zadokites of other shrines. Finally, Laughlin finds in this pericope a polemic against Zoroastrianism, which prescribed "the enthronement of the fire in the temple by two priests who carried the holy flame into the sanctuary on a censer" (1976: 564). It must be admitted that the hypotheses thus far proposed are unadulterated speculation and that the historical background remains a mystery.

Still, the possibility exists that the background to this incident lies in the religious, not the political, sphere. Just as the squabble with the purification offering (vv 16–20) will be found to be grounded in an attempt to eviscerate a deeply ingrained pagan belief that holds that impurity has the inherent power to harm those persons who contract it (see COMMENT C below), so the Nadab and Abihu account may also prove a polemic against paganism—the offering of incense in private idolatrous cults.

A number of biblical sources testify that toward the end of the First Temple period, Assyrian astral worship penetrated into Judah in the form of incense offerings on the rooftops of private homes (e.g., Jer 19:3; 32:29; Zeph 1:5; cf. 2 Kgs 23:5, 12; Jer 44:17–19, 25). In Assyrian rituals dedicated to Šamaš, Sin, Adad, and Ishtar—all astral deities—it was customary to clean the roof, *šabāṭu ūra*, set up an altar, *kānu paṭīra*, and offer incense, *šakānu qutrinna* (examples in Weinfeld 1972: 152). What distinguishes this cult is its private character. The incense altars were of a small, portable type, *nignakku*, in contrast to the large ones in the temple. Small altars made of bricks, *garakku*, were also used, a practice that may be reflected in Isa 65:3, "and burn incense on bricks" (Conrad 1968). The Hittites also offered incense on their roofs to the gods of heaven, for example, "When things get too much for a man and he approaches his gods in prayer, he sets up two altars . . . on the roof . . . and on them loaves of barley . . . and wafers [?] with honey and oil" (*ANET*³ 397–98). According to Weinfeld (1972: 153–54), this cult is Aramaean-Phoenician in origin, and the Assyrian conquests of the eighth century helped bring it into the land of Israel.

Archaeology confirms what the Bible affirms. Many small incense altars and censers were discovered in excavations conducted in all parts of Israel, including Gezer, Gerar, Samaria, Tel-el-Faraᶜ, Tel Kadesh, Makmish, Tel-es-Saᶜidiyeh, and Lachish, dating mainly between the sixth and fourth centuries. Many of these implements were found in private homes. They hardly served a cosmetic function (Yeivin 1972) but, more likely, were intended for the offering of incense on roofs of houses.

All biblical attestations of this private cultic practice refer to idolatry. But it is only logical to assume that it was also functional in the worship of the Lord. Certainly, the plethora of incense vessels found in Israelite levels of archaeological excavations in all parts of the land would support this deduction. Moreover, the fact that these objects date to Second Temple times is further evidence of the prevalence and persistence of private incense offerings in Israel.

It must be borne in mind that the book of Deuteronomy forbids only *blood* sacrifices outside the central sanctuary: "you must bring everything I command you to the site that the Lord your God will choose to establish his name: your burnt offerings and other slain offerings, your tithes and contributions, and all choice votive offerings that you vow to the Lord" (Deut 12:11; cf. vv 6, 14, 27). Even H, which prohibits all worship outside the Tabernacle, in effect, also limits itself to blood sacrifices: "If any person of the house of Israel or of the aliens who reside among them sacrifices a burnt offering or another slain offering, and does not bring it to the entrance of the Tent of Meeting to offer it to the Lord, that person shall be cut off from his people" (17:8–9). Thus, all cultic laws in the Bible that prescribe that legitimate worship is possible only on one authorized altar (cf. Josh 22:23) limit this prescription to blood sacrifices without even mentioning incense.

Positive evidence of an independent incense offering can be derived from the fact that "eighty men came from Shechem, Shiloh, and Samaria, their beards shaved, their garments torn, and their bodies gashed, carrying cereal offerings and frankincense to present at the House of the Lord" (Jer 41:5)— after the Temple had been destroyed! This event gave rise to the later ruling, "R. Gidel said in the name of Rab: (even) after an altar is destroyed, it is permitted to offer incense at its site" (b. Zebaḥ. 59a). T. Levi, composed at the end of the Second Temple period, speaks of "archangels, who serve and offer propitiatory sacrifices to the Lord (in the heavenly sanctuary) on behalf of all the sins of ignorance of the righteous ones. They present to the Lord a pleasing odor, a rational and bloodless oblation" (T. Levi 3:5–6). Thus, at all times, regardless of whether the Temple was standing or destroyed, it was not uncommon for the people to worship the Lord at that site or anywhere else by means of incense offerings.

Only against this customary background is it possible to explain the request made by Elephantine Jewry of Bagohi, the governor of Judah, Johanan the high priest, and his colleagues, the priests, to rebuild their temple: "they shall offer the cereal offering, incense and burnt offering on the altar of God" (Cowley 1923: 30.25; cf. 30.18–21; 31.21, 25, 27). From Bagohi's response, it follows that permission was granted except for the burnt offering (Cowley 1923: 32.9–10). The Jews of Elephantine accepted his terms: "n[o] sheep, ox, or goat is offered there as a burnt offering, but only incense, cereal offering and [libations]" (Cowley 1923: 33.10–11; cf. Porten 1968: 291–92). Thus both the religious and civil authorities, Jews and non-Jews alike, permitted bloodless sacrifices outside Jerusalem, including incense.

If the objection is raised that a concession was allowed for the diaspora, as was later done for the Temple of Onias (m. Menaḥ. 13:10), while in Judah itself incense offerings were prohibited outside the Temple, then evidence can be cited from rabbinic literature that private incense offerings were permitted in Judah. Note the following: "If he offered outside [the Temple] a cereal offering from which the handful (i.e., token portion, cf. 2:2) had not been taken, he is not culpable. . . . R. Eleazar declares him (who offers the handful, or the frankincense or one of the two bowls of incense [cf. 24:7; m. Menaḥ. 11:5] outside the Temple) not culpable unless he offers the second (bowl) also" (m. Zebaḥ. 13:5–6; cf. t. Zebaḥ. 12:4–5). Finkelstein's observation (1962: 654–60) is surely correct that the rabbis were deliberately lenient in the matter of incense offerings because they knew full well that because they were widely practiced their prohibition would only be ignored. That the rabbis gained knowledge of this practice at first hand is confirmed by the following ruling: "The rabbis taught: if one strolls outside the city and detects an aroma, if the majority of the inhabitants are heathens then he should not recite a blessing, but if the majority is Israelite he should recite a blessing. R. Jose says that even if the majority is Israelite he also should not recite a blessing because Israelite women offer incense for magical ends" (b. Ber. 53a). Thus in rabbinic times women in the countryside were accustomed to offer incense, and the rabbis feared that their practice was heathen in nature. Finally, because Rabbi Ami explicates the verse, "Everywhere incense and pure cereal offering are offered to my name" (Mal 1:11) as referring to Jews in the diaspora, he thus affirms that Jews did offer incense (and cereal offering) outside the Temple (Midr. Tanḥ., Aḥare 9; Midr. Tanḥ. B. 14; cf. also y. Meg. 1:11; p. ʿAbod. Zar. 4:4). The conclusion is inescapable that the rabbis were well aware of the fact that Jews in Palestine indulged in private incense offerings and did not try to stop them. In fact, the practice continued at least into the ninth century, according to the Karaite Daniel Al-Qumisi, who claimed that Jews offered incense "on the tenth of Tevet and at other times" (Lieberman 1970: 9–10; for a broader treatment of this subject see Milgrom 1979a: 330–34).

This brief survey of private Israelite incense offerings over the span of two millennia yields a twofold conclusion: the authorities feared, correctly, that it was or could lead to a heathen practice and that try as they might—H, D, Persian governors, outstanding rabbis notwithstanding—they could not stamp it out. Against this backdrop of ingrained practice and failed protest, it is possible to view the Nadab and Abihu incident afresh. I submit that it is but another attempt—this time in P—to polemicize against private offerings of incense. First, let it be noted that P prohibits the manufacture and use of the authorized incense outside the cult under pain of death—even just for "sniffing," that is, for noncultic purposes (Exod 30:37–38). Such a pointed prohibition can only mean that its violation was rampant. Surely, if any Israelite authority was zealous over the possibility of pagan practices infiltrating into Israelite cult, it would have been the priests. But they were not just content with a legal pronouncement banning the duplication and use of the authorized incense. They also told the story of priests, not laity, Aaron's sons, not ordinary priests, who offered legitimate incense, not an illicit compound, inside the sanctuary, not outside it —and yet were struck down by God. Their crime: they offered incense on coals not taken from the altar but on ʾēš zārâ 'unauthorized coals'. Thus this story invalidates by a single stroke all incense offerings outside the sanctuary, for perforce their coals cannot possibly be taken from the altar. Moreover, the Priests resort to a case in point to score illicit incense offerings. They tell how King Uzziah was struck with leprosy for usurping the role of the priesthood by offering incense in the Temple (2 Chr 26:16–21). Similarly, by citing the case of Nadab and Abihu, they also championed their own interests, not against royalty, as in the case of Uzziah, but against the populace at large, who were wont to offer incense freely, either on their rooftops in brazen worship of astral deities or, in most instances, in pious worship of the God of Israel. The death of Nadab and Abihu—legitimate priests, offering legitimate incense, in the legitimate sanctuary but using ʾēš zārâ, illegitimate coals, not from the altar—was held up as a perpetual reminder and threat to anyone else who would use ʾēš zārâ, all the more so because he or she would not be a priest, not with the proper incense, and not in the sanctuary.

Thus the Nadab and Abihu incident must be understood exactly as it reads. Its background is not political but religious. It is based not on some single event but on an ongoing rite. To be sure, the story's motivation is to protect the vested interests of its Priestly authors and tradents. They saw only too well that offering incense was an easily accomplished ritual, requiring no sanctuary, no elaborate apparatus, and, above all, no priests. But we would sell the priests short by attributing to them this one, selfish motive. They also saw, as the case of Jeremiah and the exiles in Egypt verifies, that offering incense was a widespread idolatrous practice and that in time of despair Israel, especially its women, might be seduced by other gods. If my understanding of the Nadab and Abihu incident is correct, then the priests are to be added to the company of Israel's other spiritual leaders—the Deuteronomists, civil authorities, and rabbis—who disapproved and remonstrated against private incense offering, but to no avail. Against the backdrop of the wilderness narratives, the story of Nadab and Abihu is the Priestly counterpart to the episode of the golden calf. Just as the latter followed upon the theophany of God at Sinai, so the former took place as the aftermath of the divine theophany at the Tabernacle. Clearly, Nadab and Abihu's heresy (and hence, the heresy of those who followed their example) was deliberately equated in the mind of the Priestly writer with the heresy of Israel at Sinai.

Finally, the question should be raised: if all the priests intended was to teach that private incense offerings are forbidden, why did they not simply say so in the form of a law instead of resorting to a story (the same question would apply to the case of Uzziah, 2 Chr 26:16–21)? My student, D. Wright, contributes an illuminating answer, which I cite in full:

> Leviticus 10:1–7 is a good example of law in story form. While P regularly uses more patent forms of legal writing it also includes many examples of story law (e.g., Korah's rebellion, the transfer of the priesthood to Eleazar, the blasphemer, the Sabbath stick-gatherer). Law in story form generally has a greater effect upon hearers and readers than apodictic, casuistic or other legal forms: it allows for ready recall of the principles taught and makes principles concrete and easily understandable.
>
> The didactic effect of story over other legal forms is hinted at in Anton Chekhov's short story "Home." When a father found out that his seven-year-old son had been smoking, he fumbled around to find a way to convince his son not to smoke. As the father spoke, the child paid little attention, going on thinking about his own concerns and often changing the subject. Finally the father laid down the law: "Give me your word of honour that you won't smoke again." The son answered inattentively and insincerely as he was drawing a picture: "Word of honour!" The father, after wondering about his ineffectiveness as a moral teacher and giving up the fight, told the child to go to bed. The boy asked for a story first and the father consented. The father improvised. After wandering a bit, he began to tell of an emperor who had a son that smoked.
>
> > The emperor's son fell ill with consumption through smoking, and died when he was twenty. His infirm and sick old father was left without anyone to help him. There was no one to govern the kingdom and defend the palace. Enemies came, killed the old man, and destroyed the palace, and now there are neither cherries, nor birds, nor little bells in the garden. . . . That's what happened.
>
> While the story was "absurd and naïve" to the father, it wrought a change in the boy. His "eyes were clouded by mournfulness and something like fear; for a minute he looked pensively at the dark window, shuddered, and said, in a sinking voice: 'I am not going to smoke any

more. . . .'" The father's story had effect where his blunt command did not.

Of course the point of Chekhov's labor is not simply to show the heart-changing effect of story. After telling the tale the father wonders, "Why must morality and truth never be offered in their crude form, but only with embellishments, sweetened and gilded like pills? It's not normal. . . . It's falsification . . . deception . . . tricks. . . ." Maybe stories are not really *good* teachers after all. But, paradoxically and perhaps in order to make his point, Chekhov has raised this question *through story*. Just as the jurymen and even the lawyer father of whom the story says "absorb history only from legends and historical novels" and not from "sermons and laws," we who read Chekhov's story and think about the rightness of teaching through story are taught and quizzed about it in story form. Interestingly, should we decide that story is not a good mode of moral instruction, we shall have come to that conclusion, which is necessarily moral and good from our perspective, by means of story.

At any rate, for the biblical legislators there was no moral question about the use of story. It was a proper and acceptable mode of legal discourse and teaching. By it they augmented their more abstract teachings to show how in "real life" the principles apply and their breach brings deleterious effects (Anton Chekhov, *The Cook's Wedding and Other Stories* [The Tales of Chekhov, 12; New York: Ecco Press, (1920) 1984] 65–78; cf. also Wayne Booth, *The Company We Keep: An Ethics of Fiction* [Berkeley: University of California Press, 1988] 483–84).

B. Nadab and Abihu in the History of Exegesis

The death of Nadab and Abihu is a prominent theme in biblical literature (16:1; Num 3:4; 17:2 LXX [see the NOTE on "unauthorized coals," v 1]; 26:61; 2 Macc 2:11 [see COMMENT C below], John 12:28 [see the NOTE on "I shall be glorified," v 3]), but especially among the rabbis and, in a bizarre way, in Philo.

The rabbis propose twelve theories to justify their deaths (*Pesiq. Rab. Kah.* 26; *Midr. Lev. Rab.* 20), six of which are ritual in nature and are grounded in the biblical text. Rabbi Jeremiah is the author of the three that follow:

1. They entered the adytum, based on rendering *běqorbātām lipnê YHWH wayyāmūtû* (16:1) as "because they *came near* before the Lord they died." For this reason the high priest is thereupon instructed how to enter the adytum properly (16:2–28).

2. Their incense offering was illicit because it was unessential and wrongly timed, based on rendering *bĕhaqrîbām 'ēš zārâ lipnê YHWH* 'because they *offered* unauthorized coals before the Lord' (Num 3:4; 26:61), and supported by Rabbi Ishmael (*Sipra*, Millu'im Shemini 32) and *Tg. Neof.* and the Pesh. to 16:1.

3. They offered incense on unauthorized coals, *'ēš zārâ* (10:1), the reason advocated in this commentary (see the NOTE on v 1).

Rabbi Levi (ibid.) also finds three possible sins to account for Nadab and Abihu's death, each having to do with a priestly prohibition whose violation incurs death:

4. They officiated while drunk, based on the contiguous passage (v 9).

5. They neglected to wash their hands and feet (Exod 30:21).

6. They lacked one of the required priestly garments, i.e., the robe (so interpreting Exod 28:43).

The remaining six justifications, unanchored in the biblical text, are pure flights of fancy (for details, see Shinan 1979). Five of the six, cited above, are also disposed of easily. Rabbi Levi's choices (4, 5, and 6) are merely attempts to attribute the death of Nadab and Abihu to the violation of priestly prohibitions entailing the death penalty, which, however, have no foundation in the text. That Nadab and Abihu may have ventured inside the Holy of Holies (no. 1) is rebutted by the statement *wattēṣē' 'ēš millipnê YHWH* 'And fire came forth from the Lord' (v 2), which indicates that Nadab and Abihu were outside not only the adytum but even the Tent (see the NOTE on "from the front of the sacred precinct," v 4). Nor can much weight be assigned to the suggestion that Nadab and Abihu offered illicit incense (no. 2), for their sin would have been pinpointed as *qĕṭōret zārâ* 'unauthorized incense' (e.g., Exod 30:9, 37), not *'ēš zārâ* 'unauthorized coals'. The elimination of the reasons analyzed above leaves the field clear for no. 3: Nadab and Abihu offered incense on *'ēš zārâ* 'unauthorized coals', in other words, not from the sacrificial altar but from a profane source (*Tg. Yer.; Tg. Onq.* on 16:1; *Sipra*, Millu'im Shemini 32; followed among the moderns by Baudissin [1967: 22], Morgenstern [1926], Haran [1960b: 115–16], Laughlin [1976]).

This incident takes a fascinating, if bizarre, exegetical turn in the writings of Philo. In all four passages in which he mentions it (*Laws* 2. 57–58; *Som.* 2.6–7; *Fug.* 59; *Her.* 309), Nadab and Abihu are singled out for praise! Their garments were not consumed because they had stripped themselves and "offered their nakedness to God" (*Laws* 2. 57–58). The fire of v 2 was a sign of divine favor, as in the contiguous passage, 9:24. The fire that consumed them was termed *'ēš zārâ, pur allotrion* (LXX), implying that it was "alien to creation, but akin to God" (*Som.* 2.6–7). Philo's exegesis is analyzed by Kirschner, who concludes that his "praise for Nadab and Abihu derives from the text and not from a preconceived philosophical notion" (1983: 390; also Rokeach 1986; contra Flusser and Safrai 1984).

The motivations behind Philo's positive view of Nadab and Abihu's act are unclear, but they are worth mentioning not only because of their intrinsic interest but because of their manifest influence on subsequent exegesis. The possibility exists that, in the view of John (12:28), the glorification of the Lord through the death of Nadab and Abihu (v 3) may have served as a model for the crucifixion and resurrection of Jesus (for details, see the NOTE on "I shall be glorified," v 3). That the Philonic view of the death of Nadab and Abihu was current in first-century Palestine would explain the presence of a positive evaluation of this incident, albeit as a minor tradition, in rabbinic literature. Thus, Nadab and Abihu consecrated the Tabernacle by their deaths and thereby sanctified the divine name (*Sipra*, Millu'im Shemini 36). For their zeal in attempting to hasten the theophany by offering incense to God with impure fire, God rewarded them by consuming them with his pure fire (*Sipra*, Millu'im Shemini 22). They responded to the divine fire (9:24) with fire of their own, thereby "adding (their) love to (God's) love" (*Sipra*, Millu'im Shemini 32).

C. What Lies Behind the Squabble over the Purification Offering?

The enigmatic pericope on the purification offering (vv 16–20) has puzzled translators and commentators through the ages. Its enigma is recalled in 2 Macc 2:11, itself an abstruse passage, which by a slight emendation of *to* to *ti* reads, "For what reason did you not eat the purification offering but it was consumed [by fire]?" (Goldstein 1983: 184–86). The overall problem of this pericope is twofold: why was Moses angered by the priests, and why was he assuaged by their answer? The text makes it clear that Moses took the priests to task for burning the purification offering instead of eating it (vv 18–19) and Aaron responded that, considering his situation, he could not be expected to eat it (v 19). Yet, it is hard to conceive that Moses would fly into a rage over this slight deviation from the prescribed ritual. And the vagueness of Aaron's answer, "Such things have befallen me" (v 19) does not even offer a clue as to the exact reason that prompted him to alter the mode of disposition of the sacrifice. Besides, one may well ask, why was this episode considered so important that it concludes the long account of the sanctification of the Tabernacle and its priesthood?

That Aaron and his sons deviated from the prescribed rite is certified by Moses' accusation (v 18; cf. 6:23). Yet nothing is said or implied concerning the priests' motivation for altering the rite. It is apparent from Aaron's enigmatic response (v 19) that he did not change the rite inadvertently. He acted deliberately, but his reasons remain hidden. The rabbis offer two answers: the priests were in mourning, hence forbidden to partake of sacred food (see Deut 26:14), and/or the death of Nadab and Abihu in the Tabernacle court had defiled the purification offering. Both answers miss the mark. First, as the priests were forbidden to mourn they should have eaten their prescribed offerings (Shadal) and, second, if the purification offering was defiled so were the cereal and well-being offerings, which, however, were permitted to the priests (vv 12–15; Ehrlich). The solution offered by Ehrlich (1908–14) is also flawed. He suggests that Nadab and Abihu offered incense only after they had assisted in the sacrifice of the people's purification offering, which led Aaron to deduce that they died because God had rejected their sacrifice. But the patent defect in their ministration lay in the *ʾēš zārâ* 'unauthorized coals' of their incense offering (v 1) and not in the purification offering. Besides, as the purification offering was the first of the people's sacrifices (9:15), their cereal and well-being offerings, which would have followed the tragedy (9:17–21), should not have been eaten either; indeed, they should not even have been sacrificed!

Thus the answer must reside in the specific and exclusive nature of the *ḥaṭṭāʾt*. There is something inherent in its function that made it *mandatory* for the priests to eat it and, correspondingly, that made Aaron absolutely certain that he and his sons were unqualified to eat it.

The investigation begins with the *ḥaṭṭāʾt* offered on behalf of the priests (9:2). Anomalously, its blood is daubed on the outer altar while its carcass is burned outside the camp (9:8–11). One can understand the latter rite: priests may not benefit from their personal expiatory sacrifices (see the NOTES on 8:17 and 9:11). But why was the *ḥaṭṭāʾt* blood only applied to the outer altar? Why was it not brought into the Tent, as prescribed for the *ḥaṭṭāʾt* of the high priest (4:1–12)? Furthermore, the same anomalous situation prevails with the *ḥaṭṭāʾt* brought by the priestly consecrands: its blood was daubed on the outer altar and its carcass was burned (8:14–17), again without a hint concerning the moral or ritual lapse that necessitated its sacrifice. To be sure, in this case the function of the *ḥaṭṭāʾt* is to decontaminate the altar (8:15). Still, the problem here is not the manipulation of its blood but the disposition of its carcass: Why was it burned instead of eaten by the officiant who, in this instance, was Moses? It was suggested, in the case of the priestly consecration, that Moses was deprived of the *ḥaṭṭāʾt* as well as the thigh (8:26–29), also a priestly prebend (7:32), in order to deny him the title and due of a priest (see the NOTE on 9:17). But a more plausible answer is at hand. The precise similarity in the ritual for the *ḥaṭṭāʾt* in both the priestly consecration service (chap. 8) and the inaugural service (chap. 9) leads one to suspect that this block of Priestly material (and the corresponding prescriptive text, Exod 29:10–14) preserves an older form of the *ḥaṭṭāʾt* ritual (in partial agreement with Janowski 1982: 227–47). The reason that these texts (Exod 29; Lev 8 and 9) were allowed to remain, though their procedure contradicts the normative one (cf. Lev 6:23), is this: the anomalous rituals are those of the priestly consecration and the inaugural service. They took place once, *never to be repeated again*. It thus seems plausible to conclude that originally, every *ḥaṭṭāʾt*, regardless of where its blood was applied, was burned outside the camp and only subsequently did the Priestly legislators introduce an innovation: the *ḥaṭṭāʾt* whose blood was daubed on the outer altar had to be eaten by the priests.

The dimensions of this innovation can be assessed when the question is asked: How often was the *ḥaṭṭāʾt* burned? Aside from the anomalous cases of the priestly consecration and inaugural services (chaps. 8–9), the surprising answer is that there were just two occasions for burning the *ḥaṭṭāʾt*: the rare, and probably hypothetical, case of the anointed priest committing some sin that endangers both him and the whole community (4:3–21) and the annual purgation of the sanctuary on Yom Kippur (16:27). Thus in nearly all instances the *ḥaṭṭāʾt* would be eaten by the priests. Now it has been shown that in the ancient Near East, ritual detergents were always destroyed after they were used lest their potent remains be exploited for purposes of black magic (see chap. 4, COMMENT D). By requiring that the *ḥaṭṭāʾt* be eaten, Israel's priests were able to affirm that the power to purge the sanctuary does not inhere in a ritual but is solely dependent on the will of God. Moreover, they backed up their conviction by their act: they ate the *ḥaṭṭāʾt* and were willing to suffer the consequences if their conviction proved wrong. Yet their faith was not without its limits: the *ḥaṭṭāʾt* prescribed for the deep pollution of the sanctuary, when its blood was brought into the shrine, continued to be burned. The pollution incurred by Israel's brazen sins and impurities, which had infested the very seat of the Godhead in the Holy of Holies (see the NOTE on 16:16a), was just too lethal to be ingested. As mentioned, however, this problem was rarely faced, initially only in emergencies and, subsequently, once a year on Yom Kippur, when—and only then—the Holy of Holies was purged (for details, see chap. 16, COMMENT D).

One cannot claim that the eating of the *ḥaṭṭāʾt* was a Priestly innovation. Ingesting edible ritual detergents was practiced elsewhere (see the NOTE on v 17) and, hence, was probably known in Israel. Rather, the Priestly innovation lay in the requirement that the ordinary *ḥaṭṭāʾt* *must* be eaten and not burned or disposed of in any other way. In this respect, the *ḥaṭṭāʾt* (and probably the other expiatory sacrifices; see below) differed from the well-being offering. The latter is eaten by lay persons or priests, and whatever remains is burned (e.g., 7:17; 8:32; 19:6; Exod 12:10; 29:33–34), but there is no requirement that it be eaten. Theoretically, all of the meat may be burned. Eating from these sacrifices, then, is a privilege, not a requirement. This is not the case, I submit, with the *ḥaṭṭāʾt*: it must be eaten—if not entirely, at least partially—by the priests. Strikingly, the rabbis hold the same opinion in their dictum *hakkōhănîm ʾōkĕlîm wĕhabbĕʿālîm mitkappĕrîm* 'the priests eat and [thereby] the offerers are expiated' (*Sipra*, Shemini 2:4; *b. Pesaḥ*. 59b; *b. Yoma* 68b; *b. Yebam*. 40a, 90a). To be sure, they apply this rule to all expiatory *(kippēr)* sacrifices. They may be right (even though their biblical support, Exod 29:33, hardly provides such warrant). It can hardly be an accident that lay persons are expressly commanded to burn what they cannot eat of their sacrifices, namely, the Passover (Exod 12:10a, 12b; 23:18; 34:25; Num 9:12; Deut 16:4), the thanksgiving offering (7:15; 22:30), the well-being offering (7:17; 19:6), the ordination offering (8:32; Exod 29:34—the priestly consecrands are still laymen at this point). By contrast, the absence of this rule in the case of the priests and the expressed command that they should "eat" their prebends from the most sacred offerings, namely, the cereal, purification, and reparation offerings (6:9, 11, 19, 22; 7:6; 10:12–13, 17–18), implies that the priests have no choice: these prebends must be eaten, if not by the officiating priest, then by his fellow priests (see Maim., "Manner of Sacrifice" 10.1). Because the purification and reparation offerings are exclusively expiatory and the cereal offering, partially so (see the COMMENT on chap. 2), there is a strong possibility that they had to be eaten by the priests in order to complete the expiatory process. But the purification offering, uniquely among the piacular sacrifices, absorbs the impurities of the sanctuary and hence presents a potential danger to its priestly handlers, not to speak of its priestly consumers. This is especially true in this case, when it had to absorb the severe pollution of the sanctuary by the corpses of Nadab and Abihu.

Moreover, it is precisely because the purification offering is associated with impurity that its ingestion by the priest becomes so crucial. The priest is the personification of holiness; the ḥaṭṭāʾt is the embodiment of impurity. In the Priestly symbolic system (fully developed in H), holiness (qĕdûšâ) stands for life whereas impurity (ṭumʾâ) stands for death (chap. 11, COMMENT E; chap. 12, COMMENT B; chap. 15, COMMENT G). When the priest consumes the ḥaṭṭāʾt he is making a profound theological statement: holiness has swallowed impurity; life can defeat death. This symbolism carries through all of the rites with the purification offering. The priest is unaffected by daubing blood on the altar, though the blood is absorbing impurity (4:13–21, 22–35; chap. 4, COMMENTS B and C). The trepidation the high priest feels when entering the adytum on Yom Kippur is not due to the virulent impurity that has been implanted there but, to the contrary, because of the virulent holiness of the Ark (16:2, 13). Indeed, not only does he effect the removal of all of the sanctuary's impurities, he also transfers them (together with Israel's sins) onto the head of a live goat by means of a hand-leaning ritual—yet he emerges unscathed (see the NOTES on 16:21, 24).

The priest's immunity stands in stark contrast to the sanctuary's vulnerability. As demonstrated (chap. 4, COMMENTS B and C), the sanctuary is polluted by every physical and moral aberration, even those inadvertently committed. But within that same sanctuary the priest is impervious to impurity. Once he leaves it his immunity is canceled; hence, his Levite cousins have to remove the corpses of Nadab and Abihu (10:4), and the priest who prepares the ashes of the Red Cow *outside the sanctuary* is rendered impure (Num 19:6–7). Herein lies an ancillary teaching of the Priestly impurity system. Impurity pollutes the sanctuary, but it does not pollute the priest *as long as he serves God in the sanctuary.* H applies this teaching to the people at large. As long as they live a life of holiness and serve God by obeying his commandments, they can overcome the forces of impurity-death.

Finally, it is hardly an accident that the story of Nadab and Abihu is followed by the laws of impurity (chaps. 11–15). To be sure, this story adds the impurity of corpse contamination to those in the subsequent impurity collection which must be purged on Yom Kippur (see 16:1). But its significance lies deeper. Through their uninterrupted service, the remaining priests exemplify the principle that holiness is more powerful than impurity, that life can conquer death. The Holiness school carries the meaning farther: the priest must teach this truth to the people (10:10–11 [H]) so that they too will aspire to a life of holiness (11:43–45; 19:2; 20:7–8, 26, etc.—all H).

If this theory proves correct, it solves all of the questions raised above at a single stroke. Aaron and his sons could eat the sacrificial prebends of the cereal and well-being offerings because they were forbidden to mourn. Yet they refrained from eating the *ḥaṭṭāʾt* because they apparently felt that the deaths of Nadab and Abihu in the very midst of the sacred precincts had polluted the entire sanctuary and, though the *ḥaṭṭāʾt* blood had been applied only to the outer altar, its carcass was too laden with impurity to be safely ingested. Moses, by contrast, became enraged when he learned that Aaron and his sons had burned an ordinary *ḥaṭṭāʾt*—its blood had not been brought into the shrine— instead of eating it. He was afraid that the priests would thereby engender the suspicion that they were indeed afraid of the harm that might befall them if they ate the impurity-laden meat of the purification offering, a belief that was current in Israel's contemporary world but which P assiduously attempted to eradicate. Aaron, however, answered Moses that "after such things have befallen me" (v 19), he could not be expected to eat the *ḥaṭṭāʾt*. It was not, he protested, that he was afraid to eat it. Rather, he felt that he was not permitted to eat it. The deaths of his sons and the consequent pollution of the sanctuary by their corpses had changed the status of the sacrifice from an eaten *ḥaṭṭāʾt* to a burned *ḥaṭṭāʾt*. And subsequent events, according to the Priestly redactor (16:1), prove him correct. This incident is followed by the complete purgation of the sanctuary with two *burnt* purification offerings, one on behalf of the priests and the other on behalf of the people (16:1–28; NOTE v 27).

In sum, we are dealing with a borderline case. As the *ḥaṭṭāʾt* blood was offered on the altar, it should have been eaten, according to Moses. But because Nadab and Abihu died before the *ḥaṭṭāʾt* meat was eaten, their corpses contaminated the sacrifice. That is, in Aaron's view, the impurities absorbed by the *ḥaṭṭāʾt* by dint of its blood manipulation were now increased by corpse contamination, thereby making it subject to the law of the burnt *ḥaṭṭāʾt* and not the eaten *ḥaṭṭāʾt*. Thus their disagreement turned on a point of cultic law. But behind it, as shown above, lurked the fear of magical, pagan beliefs that Israel's priests assiduously fought to extirpate. Interestingly, the rabbis also intuit that Aaron corrected Moses on a point of law, though the grounds they cite (see above) are not acceptable. They interpret the phrase *wayyišmaʿ mōšeh* (v 20) as "Moses now understood," that is, he was taught by Aaron (for this usage of *šāmaʿ*, see 1 Kgs 3:9), on which they comment "he confessed (his mistake) at once and said 'I had not understood' " (*Sipra*, Shemini 2:12). After all, it is not surprising that it is P that preserves the tradition that it was their founder, Aaron, who taught Moses a lesson in cultic law.

PART III

THE IMPURITY SYSTEM (CHAPTERS 11–16)

◆

DIET LAWS (11:1–47)

Introduction

11 21The Lord spoke to Moses and Aaron, saying to them: 22Speak to the Israelites thus:

Quadrupeds

These are the creatures that you may eat from among all of the quadrupeds on the land: 23any quadruped that has hoofs, with clefts through the hoofs, and that chews the cud—such you may eat. 24The following, however, of those that chew the cud or have hoofs, you shall not eat: the camel—although it chews the cud, it has no hoofs: it is impure for you; 25the rock badger—although it chews the cud, it has no hoofs: it is impure for you; 26the hare—although it chews the cud, it has no hoofs: it is impure for you; 27and the pig—although it has hoofs, with the hoofs cleft through, it does not chew the cud: it is impure for you. 28You shall not eat of their flesh or touch their carcasses; they are impure for you.

Fish

29These you may eat of all that live in water: anything in water, whether in the seas or in the streams, that has fins or scales—these you may eat. 30But anything in the seas or in the streams that has no fins and scales, among all of the swarming creatures of the water and among all of the [other] living creatures that are in the water—they are an abomination for you 31and an abomination for you they shall remain: you shall not eat of their flesh and you shall abominate their carcasses. 32Everything in water that has no fins and scales shall be an abomination for you.

Birds

33The followinga you shall abominate among the birds; they shall not be eaten, they are an abomination: the eagle, the black vulture, the bearded vulture, 34the kite, and falcons of every variety; 35all varieties of raven; 36the eagle owl, the short-eared owl, and the long-eared owl; hawks of every variety; 37the tawny owl, the fisher owl, the screech owl, 38the white owl, and the scops owl; the osprey, 39the stork, and herons of every variety; the hoopoe, and the bat.

a Some of the animals listed throughout this chapter cannot be identified with certainty, as indicated by alternative renderings in the NOTES.

Flying Insects

⁴⁰All winged swarming creatures, that walk on all fours, shall be an abomination for you. ⁴¹But these you may eat among all the winged swarming creatures that walk on all fours: all that have, above their feet, jointed legs to leap with on the ground. ⁴²Of these you may eat the following: locusts of every variety; all varieties of bald locust; crickets of every variety; and all varieties of grasshopper. ⁴³But all other winged swarming creatures that have four legs shall be an abomination for you.

Purification Procedures

⁴⁴And you shall make yourselves impure with the following—whoever touches their carcasses shall be impure until evening, ⁴⁵and whoever carries any part of their carcasses shall wash his clothes and be impure until evening—⁴⁶every quadruped that has hoofs but without clefts through the hoofs, or does not chew the cud. They are impure for you; whoever touches them shall be impure. ⁴⁷Also all animals that walk on flat paws, among those that walk on all fours, are impure for you; whoever touches their carcasses shall be impure until evening. ⁴⁸And anyone who carries their carcasses shall wash his clothes and remain impure until evening. They are impure for you.

⁴⁹The following shall be impure for you from among the creatures that swarm on the earth: the rat, the mouse, and large lizards of every variety; ⁵⁰the gecko, the spotted lizard, the lizard, the skink, and the chameleon. ⁵¹Those are for you the impure among all the swarming creatures; whoever touches them when they are dead shall be impure until evening. ⁵²And anything on which one of them falls when they are dead shall be impure: be it any article of wood, or fabric, or skin, or sackcloth—any such article that can be put to use shall be immersed in water, and it shall remain impure until evening; then it shall be pure. ⁵³And if any of those falls into any earthen vessel, everything inside it shall be impure and [the vessel] itself you shall break. ⁵⁴Any food that might be eaten shall become impure when it comes into contact with water; and any liquid that might be drunk shall become impure if it was inside any vessel. ⁵⁵Everything else on which the carcass of any of them falls shall be impure. An oven or stove shall be smashed; they are impure and impure they shall remain for you. ⁵⁶A spring or cistern in which water is collected shall remain pure, however, but whoever touches such a carcass [in it] shall be impure. ⁵⁷If such a carcass falls upon seed grain that is to be sown, it remains pure; ⁵⁸but if water is put on the seed and such a carcass falls upon it, it shall be impure for you.

⁵⁹If a quadruped that you may eat has died, anyone who touches it shall be impure until evening; ⁶⁰and anyone who eats of its carcass shall launder his

clothes and remain impure until evening; and anyone who carries its carcass shall launder his clothes and remain impure until evening.

Land Swarmers

61All creatures that swarm upon the earth are an abomination; they shall not be eaten. 62You shall not eat anything that crawls on its belly, or anything that walks on all fours, or anything that has many legs, comprising all creatures that swarm on the earth, for they are an abomination. 63You shall not defile your throats with any creature that swarms. You shall not make yourselves impure therewith and thus become impure, 64for I the Lord am your God. You shall sanctify yourselves and be holy, for I am holy. You shall not contaminate your throats with any swarming creature that moves upon the earth. 65For I the Lord am he who brought you up from the land of Egypt to be your God; you shall be holy, for I am holy.

Summary

66These are the instructions concerning quadrupeds, birds, all living creatures that move in the water, and all creatures that swarm on the earth, 67for discriminating between the impure and the pure, between creatures that may be eaten and creatures that may not be eaten.

NOTES

11:1. *Aaron.* He is included in the divine address because it is the priests' function to teach the difference between the pure and the impure (v 47; 10:10–11; Ibn Ezra, Ramban, Abravanel, *Keter Torah*). So too is Aaron the addressee in other ritual instructions (e.g., 13:1; 14:33; 15:1; Num 2:1; 4:1,17; 26:1), but a few are reserved—inexplicably—just for Moses (e.g., 12:1; 14:1).

to them (ʾălēhem). It is exceptional to find this prepositional phrase after *lēʾmōr* 'saying'. Perhaps its purpose is to emphasize Aaron's parity with Moses (Ehrlich 1908–14).

2. *the creatures (hahayyâ).* The generic term for animals: "which teaches that quadrupeds *(běhēmâ)* are subsumed under *hayyâ*" (*Sipra*, Shemini par. 2:8). A similar connotation is ascribed to *hayyâ* in vv 27, 47. *hayyâ,* and more frequently the expression *hayyat hāʾāreṣ,* refer to wild beasts (Gen 1:24–26); however, in the same chapter of Genesis, the word also carries the wider notion of animals, creatures (Gen 1:28, 30; cf. Gen 8:17, 19).

the quadrupeds on the land (habběhēmâ ʾăšer ʿal-hāʾāreṣ). The phrase "on the land" is tacked on in order to contrast these animals with those in the seas (vv 9–12) and in the air (vv 13–23). *běhēmâ* by itself means "quadruped" (v 26 [contrast v 27]; Deut 4:17; 1 Kgs 5:13). This verse "teaches that impure animals are more numerous than pure animals [because] everywhere Scripture only enumerates the lesser quantity" (*Sipre* Deut. 100).

3. *any quadruped (kōl . . . babběhēmâ)*. The latter term has been added at the end of v 3b to make clear that the referent of *kōl* in v 2 is *habběhēmâ* 'the quadrupeds', not *haḥayyâ* 'the creatures'. The textual counterpart in Deuteronomy adds *běhēmâ* to *wěkol-*, while retaining *babběhēmâ* at the end of the clause (Deut 14:6b). But because *běhēmâ* is the only referent there (v 4; *ḥayyâ* does not appear in the deuteronomic text), its addition is unnecessary—an indication that Deut 14:6 was modeled on the MT of Lev 11:3 (see COMMENT B below).

that has hoofs. mapreset parsâ, literally, "that grows a hoof." The *hiphʿil* is a denominative, analogous to *maqrīn* 'has (i.e., grows) a horn' (Ps 69:32). The Tgs., followed by Rashi, render this phrase as "that has cloven hoofs," support for which may be adduced from Akk. *parāsu* 'divide'. Still, there is no evidence that BH *pāras/pāraś* means "divide." Furthermore, the horse, which has no cloven hoof, still possesses a *parsâ* (Isa 5:28; Jer 47:3; Ezek 26:11), as do other animals that also do not have cloven hoofs (e.g., Ezek 32:13; Zech 11:16). True, the pig is characterized in Deut 14:8 as a *maprîs parsâ*, though its hoofs are clearly cloven. Nonetheless, the Sam. adds the words *wešōsēaʿ šesaʿ* 'and has cleft hoofs' (as in the Leviticus counterpart, v 7) and, more significantly, the general rule under which the pig is itemized also adds *šěsûaʿ* 'cloven' (Deut 14:7a). Thus, with Ibn Ezra and Rashbam, it is preferable to render *parsâ* as "hoof," and all of the ostensible problem cases are resolved. The rock badger and hare are ineligible as food (vv 5–6) because they have no hoofs at all, not because they lack cloven hoofs. Stronger proof for this rendering is provided by the camel: its feet are indeed cloven, but it walks on paws and what passes as a hoof above the paw is only hardened skin (see the NOTE on v 4b). Thus, the characterization of the camel as *ûparsâ ʾênennû maprîs* cannot mean "it has no cloven hoofs," for its feet are clearly cloven, but must instead be rendered "it has no hoofs," which, indeed, is the indisputable fact. Additional proof for this rendering is contained in the other mention of this criterion in this chapter. The impure quadrupeds are defined as *mapreset parsâ wěšesaʿ ʾênennâ šōsaʿat* 'that [have] hoofs but without clefts through the hoofs' (v 26). If *parsâ* itself meant "cloven hoofs," we would be confronted with a blatant contradiction. Finally, the deuteronomic counterpart of this criterion adds the word *štê* 'two' before *pěrāsōt* in the next phrase (Deut 14:6), as do a number of MSS and Versions in this verse (see below). Thus the cleft *(šesaʿ)* creates "two *pěrāsōt*," which can only be rendered "two hoofs." *parsâ*, then, must mean "hoof," and it can be qualified as with or without a *šesaʿ* 'cleft' (see also the NOTE below).

with clefts through the hoofs (wěšōsaʿat šesaʿ pěrāsōt). The LXX, Sam., Pesh., and nine MSS add *štê* 'two' before *pěrāsōt* 'hoofs', as does the corresponding text, Deut 14:6. Because this entire verse is expressed in the singular, where the sing. *parsâ* stands for the pl. "hoofs," the pl. *pěrāsōt* can only refer to the result of splitting the *parsâ* into two hoofs. Thus not only is the adjective *štê* 'two' essential or, at least, to be assumed, but the term *pĕrāsôt* must be rendered "hoofs," not "cloven hoofs" (see above).

and that chews (maʿălat). The word literally means "brings up" and refers to the constant regurgitation of the fodder from the animal's stomachs to its mouth and back again. The conjunction "and" must be understood (LXX, Pesh., Saadiah), but as this word is asyndetic in the parallel deuteronomic passage (Deut 14:6), the MT must be considered correct as it stands.

cud (gērâ). Some commentators relate the noun to *gārôn* 'throat' (e.g., Ibn Ezra). As the *qāmēṣ* in *gārôn* changes to a *šĕwâ* in its declined forms (e.g., *gĕrônî*), the root would be *grh (Keter Torah),* and the nominal form *gērâ* would be similar to that of *gēʾâ* (from *gʾh*) and the verb *yiggār* (v 7) would follow the pattern of *yimmaḥ* (Ps 109:13), whose root is *mḥḥ.* It is more likely, however, that the root is *grr,* a geminate, meaning "drag" (e.g., 2 Sam 14:14), referring to the cud being dragged back and forth from the stomachs to the mouth (Rashi), with the specific connotation of "drag up" in this instance, a meaning attested by *yĕgōrēhû* || *hēʿălâ* (Hab 1:15; Dillmann and Ryssel 1897).

The question arises: Why were not the permitted quadrupeds listed, as they are in the parallel list, Deut 14:4–5? The answer is that the legislator takes the sacrificial quadrupeds for granted, namely, cattle, sheep, and goats. His only concern is to classify the nonsacrificial animals, which, in the main, are wild. This supposition is corroborated by the list of birds (vv 13–19), which only contains the prohibited species because, once again, it is taken for granted that everyone knows that only two birds are permitted for the altar: the turtledove and the pigeon. In fact, the deuteronomic list admits that such is the case when it simply states "you may eat every pure bird" (Deut 14:11) without specifying them. Thus, the common denominator of all of the animals listed in chap. 11 is that they are not eligible for the altar and, hence, if permitted as food, they are slaughtered profanely, as game, with the only restriction (mandated by H) that their blood must receive burial (17:13–14). Conversely, because Deuteronomy permits sacrificial animals to be treated as game (Deut 12:15, 21–22), it is compelled to list the sacrificial quadrupeds so that it will be clear that they may be slaughtered for food without being sacrificed (B. Schwartz).

such you may eat (ʾōtāh tōʾkēlû). The predicate is repeated *(tōʾkēlû),* enveloping vv 2b–3 in a "circular inclusio" (Paran 1983: 33) for the purpose of emphasizing the general criteria of quadrupeds permitted to be eaten.

4. *The following, however (ʾak ʾet zeh).* The subsequent four animals are named because there are no others (b. Ḥul. 59a [Rashi]; Ramban). For the truth and implications of this assertion, see COMMENT E below.

or (û). Clearly, the *waw* is not a conjunctive, because the four anomalous quadrupeds, named below, possess only one of the two required criteria.

have hoofs (ûmimmaprīsê happarsâ). The actual criterion is cloven *(šsʿ)* hoofs (v 3). Yet the three enumerated quadrupeds that follow—the camel, rock badger, and hare (vv 4b–6)—possess no hoofs whatever, and for that reason the qualification of cloven hoofs is omitted here. But no sooner is the cloven-hoofed pig mentioned than the qualification "with the hoofs cleft through" (v 7) reappears. To be sure, Deuteronomy adds this qualification to its parallel version of this generalization, *haššĕsûʿâ* 'cloven' (Deut 14:7a), which, however, does not apply to the three animals that follow (v 7b), thereby betraying the later, and illogical, addition of Deuteronomy. This is one of the many indications that the deuteronomic account of the prohibited animal foods is based on Leviticus; see COMMENT B below. For the same reason, the reading *ûmiššōsĕʿê šesaʿ* in the LXX cannot be original; it is influenced by Deuteronomy.

the camel (haggāmāl). The camel has a three-chambered stomach, and it chews the cud. The feet have cushionlike soles enveloped in hardened skin. Each foot is cleft into two toes, but it has no hoof. The camel of the Bible was probably the single-humped dromedary.

it is impure for you (ṭāmēʾ hûʾ lākem). The impurity mentioned here and for the other enumerated animals (vv 5–7) applies only to their carcasses (v 8). Not only do these four animals impart impurity by ingestion, however, but also by touch (v 8), in distinction to the carcasses of fish, birds, insects, and vermin (except those named in vv 29–30 and generalized in vv 24–28), which contaminate by ingestion but not by touch (see the NOTES on "abomination" [*šeqeṣ*], v 10, and "you shall abominate," v 11).

"What does Scripture mean by *ṭāmēʾ*? [It means] *ṭāmēʾ lĕʿōlām,* impure forever" (*Sipre* Num 126). The declaration *ṭāmēʾ hûʾ* 'it is impure' is found only in cases of impurity that are indefinite and irreversible by man: for instance, various forms of scale disease (13:11, 15, 31, 44, 46) and moldy fabrics or a fungous house, which, after being declared impure, must be destroyed (13:51, 55; 14:44). Thus, certain animals and objects are declared impure irrevocably (vv 4, 5, 6, 7, 8, 26, 27, 28, 35, 38).

5. *the rock badger (haššāpān).* It has no hoofs but has broad nails. It is not a true ruminant, but only resembles one because in chewing it moves its jaws from side to side. Thus the attribution of cud-chewing to this animal was made by observing its chewing habits rather than by dissecting it to determine whether it has multiple stomachs, the characteristic anatomical feature of the ruminant. Moreover, the fact that this animal is wild, living in the craggy regions from the Dead Sea to Mount Hermon (cf. Ps 104:18; Prov 30:26), indicates that the criteria of chewing the cud and of cloven hoofs came first and that at a later period the environment was scoured to find the animals that bore one of the two criteria. For the significance of the chronological priority of the criteria, see COMMENT E below.

6. *the hare (hāʾarnebet).* Akk. *arnabu.* There are two varieties of this animal in Israel: *Lepus syriacus* and *Lepus judea.* The first lives in wooded and inhabited areas, the second in barren areas. It is not to be confused with the common rabbit, which belongs to a different genus. Like the rock badger, it is not a true ruminant, but the sideward movement of its jaws gives it the appearance of one.

Its habit of regurgitating the food it eats and returning to it later also creates the impression that it is incessantly chewing its food.

7. *the pig (haḥăzîr).* The pig is the only one of the four named quadrupeds that has cloven hoofs but is not a ruminant. Thus it is clear that these criteria for edible quadrupeds were deliberately formulated in order to exclude the pig. Otherwise, Scripture could have stipulated one criterion—cloven hoofs—and it would have eliminated the other three quadrupeds. It must, therefore, have added cud-chewing as a second criterion for the sole purpose of eliminating the pig. This conclusion is also drawn by the rabbis: "For a Tanna of the school of R. Ishmael taught . . . The Ruler of the Universe knows that there is no other beast that has cloven hoofs and is impure except the pig" (*b. Ḥul.* 59a).

It is of no small significance that Mary Douglas, who had initially argued that the pig, like the other forbidden animals of Lev 11, was declared impure because it was a taxonomic anomaly (1966) in that it did not chew the cud—one of the requisite criteria (for details, see COMMENT E below)—subsequently recanted her views on the pig when it was demonstrated to her, on anthropological grounds (Bulmer 1967), that it was equally logical, if not more so, to argue the reverse: the pig was declared anomalous because it was inherently repugnant. "It carries the odium of multiple pollution. First it pollutes because it defies the classification of ungulates. Second, it pollutes because it eats carrion. Third it pollutes because it is reared by non-Israelites. An Israelite who betrothed a foreigner might have been liable to be offered a feast of pork. By these stages it comes plausibly to represent the utterly disapproved form of sexual mating and to carry all the odium that this implies" (1972a: 79 = 1975a: 272). Douglas's subsequent admission that the pig indeed was anomalous because it was abhorred is, as I shall demonstrate, correct. But it has nothing to do with forbidden marriages (1972b: 38–39 = 1975b: 306).

Two other modern anthropological theories concerning the abhorrence of the pig need to be mentioned. The first (Simoons 1961) argues that the pig is incompatible with the nomadic/pastoral way of life and, compounded with the pastoralists' contempt for settled agricultural populations that raised and ate swine, the pig became the symbol of the revulsion of the pastoralist for the farmer. Simoons is supported by Henninger (1979: 479–82), who points to the fact that there is hardly any prejudice against pigs in regions in which pastoralists had little influence (e.g., western Europe, the coast of Guinea, the Congo basin, Southeast and East Asia, and the Pacific islands). A complementary hypothesis is offered by Harris (1974: 28–50), who suggests that because the pig is a creature of forests and shaded river banks, its most efficient sources of energy and body fat are nuts, fruits, tubers, and grains, putting it into direct competition with humans for food. In addition, Harris argues, the pig is not a good animal for pastoralists like the Hebrews (Simoons's argument, above); it is not a good source of milk and is not thermodynamically well adapted to the hot, dry climate of Palestine; and with extensive deforestation and the commensurate rise in population in the ancient Near East, eating pork became more and more an ecological and economic luxury (ibid. 37). These hypotheses, based on scanty evidence, may have some validity but, as will be shown below, ignore the unique and more salient reason that underlies the pig's proscription in the Bible and within the Israelite community, its association with chthonic deities.

First it should be noted that there was widespread revulsion for the pig throughout the ancient Near East. For example, an Assyrian tablet (VAT 8807), dated in the sixth year of Sargon II (716 B.C.E.) reads, *šaḫû la qa-šid* [. . . *mu-bal-l*]*il ar-ki mu-ba-ḫi-iš su-qa-ni* x [*mu*]-*ta-an-ni-pu bītāti*[meš] *šaḫû la si-mat ēkurri la amēl* [*ṭ*]*è-me la ka-bi-is a-gur-ri ik-kib ilāni*[meš] *kāl-a-ma taḫ-da-a*[*t il*]*i ni-zir-ti* [d]*šamaš* 'The pig is unholy [. . .] bespattering his backside, making the streets smell, polluting the houses. The pig is not fit for a temple, lacks sense, is not allowed to tread on pavements, an abomination to all the gods, an abhorrence [to (his) god,] accursed by Šamaš' (Lambert 1960: 215, lines 13–16). E. Ebeling (MAOG 2.3.40–50, quoted by Lambert 1959: 189) suggests that this tablet bears strong Aramaic, that is to say, West Semitic, influence. But the abhorrence of the pig is not limited to the Semitic sphere (*pace* Lambert, ibid.). Among the Hittites, pigs and dogs were considered impure animals. The term "swineherd" applied to the Kaskeans was probably an opprobrious designation (Hoffner 1967b). Temple servants were warned to exclude dogs and pigs from the sanctuary premises: "Furthermore, let a pig or a dog not stay at the door of the place where the loaves are broken. Are the minds of men and of the gods generally different? No! With regard to the matter with which we are dealing? No! Their minds are exactly alike" (*ANET*[3] 207–8, I, lines 20–22; cf. III, lines 60–61). The rejection of the pig (and dog) here stems not from aesthetic but from cultic reasons: it contaminates porous vessels: "If a pig [or] a dog somehow approaches the implements of wood or bitumen (now understood as "[fired-] clay") which you have, and the kitchen servant does not discard it, but gives the god to eat from an unclean [vessel], to such a man the gods will give dung [and] urine to eat [and] to drink" (ibid., III, lines 65–69).

Nonetheless, the pig and dog were used not in the Hittite cult but in magical rites dedicated to chthonic deities (Moyer 1983). In the ritual of Tunnawi one small black pig and one small black dog were waved over the worshipers while proper incantations were intoned. These animals were then burned. Thus the evil or impurity of the worshipers was transferred to the animals and then, in turn, probably returned to the dark underworld via the sacrifice of the black animals, black being the appropriate color for chthonic deities (Goetze 1938a, b). In the ritual to resolve domestic quarrels "the Old Woman takes a small pig, she presents it to them (the quarrelers), and speaks as follows: 'See! It has been fattened with grass (and) grain. Just as this one shall not see the sky and shall not see the (other) small pigs again, even so let the evil curses not see the sacrificers either!' She waves the small pig over them, and then they kill it. They dig a hole in the ground and put it down with it, she also pours out a libation of wine and they level the ground" (*ANET*³ 351). Similarly, in a ritual for producing a fertile vine, nine holes are dug in the vineyard and bread and the genitals of a female pig are thrown into them secretly (Engelhard 1970: 169–70). Hence the reproductive organs of a fertile sow are offered to the chthonic deities who, in turn, are expected to allow the sow's fertility to be transmitted to the earth.

Thus one may conclude that whenever pigs were used in worship among the Hittites they were offered up to underworld deities (Hoffner 1967a: 400). This was also the practice among the Greeks. The pig was considered sacred to certain gods of the underworld, especially Demeter and Dionysus. Live piglets were thrown into ditches called *megara* (Semitic *mĕ'ārâ* 'cave'?) by the women of Athens at the Thesmophoria, "the great feast of Demeter and Persephone, and their decomposed remains were later taken out and offered on the altar" (de Vaux 1971b: 263; Brumfeld 1981: 73–74). Xenophon "sacrificed and offered a holocaust of pigs (to Meilichios, the underworld aspect of Zeus [Harrison 1959: 12–28]) in accordance with ancestral custom and the omens were favorable" (*Anabasis* 7.8.4).

These textual inferences are supported by archaeological findings. The onset of the Iron Age in Canaan is marked by a precipitous drop in pig production; Israel had entered the scene. Three excavated sites, however, turn out to be exceptions: Tel Migne, Tel Batash, and Ashkelon (Hesse 1988). They prove the rule, for to judge by the Philistine ware found at these sites, they were probably settled by Philistine invaders who stemmed from the Greek orbit. To be sure, there is as yet no evidence that the pig featured in the Philistine cult—of which we know next to nothing—but the stark contrast between the proliferation of pig at these Philistine sites and its near total absence everywhere else in contemporaneous Israelite sites raises the possibility that Israel's aversion to the pig stemmed from two sources that in effect were one: the dietary habits and the cultic practice of the hated Philistines.

Finally, one should note that in Egypt, as well, the pig was regarded as a chthonic animal abominable to Horus but sacred to Seth, the force of evil (de Vaux 1971: 258). Indeed, Seth changed himself into a black pig during his fight with Horus (*Book of the Dead*, chap. 112). The same holds true for Mesopotamia, where the pig was offered up to evil demons, such as the *lamaštu* (Engelhard 1970: n. 555).

In Israel, the pig was also regarded as repulsive, as is apparent from the following apothegm: "Like a gold ring in the snout of a pig is a beautiful woman bereft of sense" (Prov 11:22). Moreover, the pig was associated with idolatrous worship (Isa 66:3) and with those "who eat pig's flesh, and the *šeqeṣ* (see the NOTE on v 11), and the mouse" (Isa 66:17), apparently in a cultic rite. Here too the cult seems to be directed to chthonic deities, for the worshipers "sit inside tombs and pass the night in secret places (perhaps *ûbannĕṣûrîm* > *ûbên ṣûrîm* 'among the rock fissures' [Ehrlich 1908–14]); eat the flesh of swine, with broth

(K./Q. *mĕraq*) of unclean things in their bowels; and say 'Keep your distance! Don't come closer! For I would render you consecrated' " (Isa 65:4b–5a). Furthermore, there is archaeological evidence to support the textual evidence: underground sanctuaries at Tel-el-Far'ah (north) and Gezer disclosed pig bones; an alabaster statuette (ca. 2000 B.C.E.) shows a naked man holding a young pig to his chest and grasping its genitals in his hand while one of the pig's feet is standing on the man's phallus—possibly a libation vessel for fertility rites (de Vaux 1971); there are also the statuette of a swine from the megaron temple at Jericho (fourth millennium), a cultic pedestal with the head of a swine from the holy of holies of the temple at Beth-Shan, a rhyton with a swine's head from Jericho (Brentjes 1962), and the 140 pig astragali (knuckle bones) found at Taanach, dated to the tenth century and found next to a well-cut block of flint but virtually absent elsewhere on this site, which may also have served a cultic purpose (Lapp 1964; von Rohr Sauer 1968; but note the reservations of Stager and Wolff 1981: 100 n. 7).

Thus it is clear from the evidence of the ancient Near East that the pig was not only universally reviled but, at the same time, revered in chthonic cults, which penetrated into Israel as late as the sixth century, arousing the wrath of prophet and priest alike. The former expressed himself in denunciatory orations, the latter in ritual taboos. By adding the criterion of cud chewing, the priests deliberately excluded the pig from the list of permitted animals, which proves that they were rejecting the pig because it was an abomination both aesthetically and culturally. The stipulation of the other criterion, cleft hoofs, however, was based on other grounds: to limit the Israelite's access to the main domestic species of the animal kingdom—cattle, sheep, and goats (plus several wild but virtually inaccessible animals, Deut 14:4). For details, see COMMENT E below.

Nonetheless, one must also record that although the pig was singled out as especially abhorrent, it did not become the reviled animal par excellence until the eating of its flesh became a test of the Jews' loyalty to Judaism in Hellenistic times (2 Macc 6:18). It is even possible (but as yet unproved) that when Antiochus offered up swine on the Temple's altar (Diodorus the Silician, Stern 1974: 267) he was attempting to introduce a new syncretistic form of Dionysiac ritual as the proper worship of the "God of Heaven" (Goldstein 1976: 158; Bickerman 1980; Seidel 1984). Finally, following the incident (which probably took place during the Romans' siege of Jerusalem, 70 C.E.; Wiesenberg 1956: 213–33), when a pig was hoisted up the walls of Jerusalem instead of an animal fit for sacrifice it was decreed, "Cursed be he who breeds pigs" (b. *Sota* 49b; y. *Ta'an.* 4:8, 68c), a prohibition that was subsequently incorporated into the Mishna (m. *B. Qam.* 7:7).

The domestic pig, *Sus scrofa domestica*, is descended from the wild boar, *Sus scrofa*. The latter was also known in biblical times (*ḥăzîr miyya'ar*, lit., "the pig of the forest," Ps 80:14), and is also subject to this prohibition (Feliks 1971a: 506).

It is interesting to note that in the Hittite religion the dog was as much abominated as the pig. For example, the "Instructions to the Temple Officials" reads "Let a pig or dog not stay at the door of the place where the loaves are broken" (1.21; *ANET*³ 207). Moreover, as noted above, the dog and the pig were both sacrificed to chthonic deities (cf. also Kümmel 1967: 152; *HBR* 379 n. 75). Indian religion also eschewed the dog (but not the pig), for example, "If implements are licked by dogs, etc., wooden ones are to be burnt, earthenware is to be thrown into the water, metal ones are to be cleansed with ashes" (Gonda 1980: 171). The impurity of dogs and pigs in Hittite culture and of dogs in Indian culture stands in sharp contrast to the impurity of animals in the Bible. In nonbiblical cultures, the animals may pollute while alive; in the Bible, animals can only pollute when dead (see the NOTE at vv 24–28). Thus it comes as quite a surprise to find that the Dead Sea sectaries, according to "An Unpublished Halakhic Letter from Qumran" (Qimron and Strugnell 1985), forbade the bringing of dogs into Jerusalem—a prohibition for which there is not even the faintest echo in all rabbinic literature. But the complete text of this prohibition states the reason: lest they eat the bones of sacrifices "and the meat attached to them" (*MMT* B 58–62). Thus, the Qumranites were apprehensive over *nôtār* 'unconsumed sacrificial flesh' turning into *piggûl* 'desecrated meat' (see the NOTE on 7:18), though it is not clear to me, at this juncture, what danger this meat holds for Jerusalem once it has been eaten by a still-living dog.

chew. yiggār, qal of *grr*. The Sam. (here and in Deut 14:8) reads *yāgôr*. See the NOTE on *gērâ*, v 3.

8. *You shall not eat (lōʾ tōʾkēlû).* It forms an inclusio with *lōʾ tōʾkēlû* (4aα), emphasizing by repetition that these four specified animals should not be eaten.

of their flesh. mibbĕśārām, namely, of the four above-mentioned quadrupeds that possess one of the two required criteria (vv 4–7). But what of quadrupeds that have neither criterion? Their interdiction can be deduced a fortiori (*Sipra*, Shemini 4:9) as well as from the fact that touching their carcasses imparts impurity (vv 26–27). In this sense, v 8 is proleptic of vv 24–28. The fact that "flesh" *(bāśār)* is distinguished from "carcass" *(nĕbēlâ)* in this verse means that the animal did not die naturally but was slaughtered (see the next NOTE).

touch (tiggāʿû). The prohibition against touching the carcass of any of the four above-mentioned quadrupeds may be a "fence" to prevent their consumption (analogous to Gen 2:17, 3:3). Perhaps this word should be rendered "or even touch" (E. Firmage). But eating or touching the carcass of a quadruped is not subject to any penalties unless the purificatory ablutions are neglected (cf. 17:15–16 and the COMMENT on 4:14–26).

their carcasses. nĕbēlâ is generally defined as the carcass of an animal that was neither killed nor slaughtered but died naturally (Bekhor Shor). But this definition only applies to pure animals; hence, the fact that they become *nĕbēlâ* as a result of natural death must be spelled out, *kî yāmût* (v 39). Indeed, if they die an unnatural death, for instance, at the hands of another animal, they are called *ṭĕrēpâ* (7:24; 17:15; 22:8). Conversely, carcasses of impure animals are always termed *nĕbēlâ* no matter how they died—even if they were slaughtered ritually (Hoffmann 1953).

they are impure for you (ṭĕmē'îm hēm lākem). The antecedent subject is the four above-named animals (vv 4–7). This verse gives the reason that each of them is called "impure." The other impure animals are covered by the general rule, given below (vv 24–28). The term *ṭāmē'* 'impure' connotes impurity transmitted by touch and not by ingestion (see the NOTES on vv 10, 11), in contrast to the use of this term in H and D in their reference to the diet prohibitions (e.g., 20:25; Deut 14:7, 10, 19), where it refers solely to ingestion (see the NOTE on v 43 and COMMENTS A and B below).

No sanctions are invoked for eating or touching animal carcasses except if done by priests (22:8–9; cf. Ezek 44:31). This conclusion can be deduced a fortiori from corpse contamination, forbidden only to priests (21:1). Thus if the Israelite is not penalized for coming into contact with a human corpse, he certainly should not be penalized for touching an animal carcass. P, however, enjoins against touching a carcass of a quadruped for the same reason it is opposed to eating its flesh: both acts cause impurity. To be sure, Deuteronomy permits the Israelite to "give" (i.e., hand) the carcass to the resident alien (Deut 14:8), implying that there is no prohibition against touching it (Bekhor Shor). But this is the view of D, not P.

The only penalty—and it is a severe one—is incurred when coming into contact with the sanctuary or its sancta while in a state of impurity (7:20–21) or if the impurity is not cleansed but allowed to be prolonged (5:2; 17:15–16). That is why the rabbis infer that touching a carcass is forbidden only during a pilgrimage (*b. Roš. Haš.* 16b [bar.]; *Sipra*, Shemini 4:9), namely, when there is bound to be direct contact with the sanctuary and the sancta; otherwise there is no prohibition (*Sipra*, Shemini 4:8). One can readily understand the radical leniency of the rabbis, for by their time the Temple and its cult were no longer in existence, and the whole problem of the defilement of sancta was purely academic. The impurity deriving from a carcass may account for the practice of removing one's sandals before entering a sacred precinct (Exod 3:5; Josh 5:15); sandals, being fashioned of animal skins, are eo ipso impure, but only in regard to the sacred. This rule is to this day strictly enforced in Islam. It is also recorded in ancient Greece; for example, at Eresos neither shoes nor any other leather garment were brought into the temple, and women participating in the mysteries at Andania were required to wear nonleather sandals and garments made of wool (Farnell 1951: 486).

9. *in water (bammayim).* The second occurrence of this word in this verse is marked by a *rĕbîa',* a disjunctive accent, indicating that what follows is a subdivision.

whether in the seas or in the streams. bayyammîm ûbannĕhālîm, that is to say, both in salt and in fresh waters (*Sipra*, Shemini par. 3:2). Ponds, marshes, and reservoirs would also be included (*b. Ḥul.* 66b–67a; Ibn Ezra), and these may have been subsumed under the term *yammîm*, which would then connote self-contained bodies of water as contrasted with *nĕḥālîm*, flowing waters. But see the Note on v 12.

fins (sĕnappîr). Etymology unknown; perhaps related to Akk. *s/šappartu* 'shaggy skin'; Arab. *sufr* 'eyelashes'. Not all marine animals have fins; for example, crustaceans propel themselves by their legs.

scales (qaśqeśet). Etymology unknown; however, in addition to meaning fish scales (e.g., Ezek 29:4), it is also found in Scripture in reference to a warrior's armor (1 Sam 17:5), which is built like and looks like fish scales. *Tg. Onq.* renders *qalpîn* (from the root *qālap* 'peel'), which implies the rabbinic definition of scales as that which can be peeled off. Fish that lose their scales during their maturation (e.g., swordfish) or when they are brought to land are therefore permissible (*Sipra,* Shemini par. 3:11). Because "all fish that have scales also have fins" (*m. Nid.* 6:9), one need but look for scales to determine if the fish is permissible (*t. Ḥul.* 3:9). Thus, the rabbis admit that the criterion of fins is superfluous (*b. Nid.* 51b). Nevertheless, it is possible that the criteria for fish and, indeed, for all other animal species contained in this chapter are so worded as to emphasize the means of locomotion, on the assumption that those animals which are permitted move in a way that is natural to their environment: land animals walk (on feet, not paws), water animals swim (not crawl), and air animals fly (Douglas 1966; details in Comment E below). Other explanations given for these criteria are hygiene (Ramban, Abravanel); influence on character (Saadiah, Abravanel); aesthetics (Kalisch 1867–72; Lagercrantz 1953); a secondary analogy to land animals (Firmage 1990: 189–90). Shadal, who vehemently opposes the hygienic theory (in *Hamishtadel*), gives three other motivations: separation, obedience (to God), and teaching self-control. In any event, these criteria effectively reduce edible marine life for the ancient Israelite to a handful of fish; see the Note on v 12.

10. *in the seas or in the streams. bayyammîm ûbannĕḥālîm* (with *Sipra,* Shemini par. 3:2). *bammayim* 'in the water' (v 9) is omitted here because it occurs twice in the rest of this verse (Ehrlich 1908–14).

swarming creatures (šereṣ). This collective noun "includes all small creatures that go about in shoals and swarms, insects that fly in clouds, such as gnats and flies generally (cf. Ethiopic, germinate), and small creatures such as weasels, mice, and lizards that are low on the ground (cf. Aramaic, crawl)" (Snaith 1967; and see the Note on "an impure swarming creature," 5:2).

among all of the swarming creatures of the water and among all of the [other] living creatures that are in the water (mikkōl šereṣ hammayim ûmikkōl nepeš hahayyâ ʾăšer bammāyim). The former refers to fish, the latter to nonswimming but creeping, walking marine life (Ramban). Other opinions are: all marine life and amphibians (Mendelssohn, in Wessely 1846); asexual and sexual marine creatures (Ibn Ezra); creeping and moving (i.e., swimming and walking) marine creatures *(Seper Hamibḥar)*. Yet marine life, created on the fifth day, is called *šereṣ nepeš ḥayyâ* 'swarms of living creatures' (Gen 1:20; cf. v 21). Thus the term *šereṣ bammayim* refers to marine life that moves in swarms (see the NOTE above), and *ûmikkōl nepeš ḥayyâ* denotes "all of the other living creatures." For the discussion of *kōl* meaning not only "each" or "all" but also meaning "other, remaining," see 4:7, 12 (= 5:9); Judg 16:17; 1 Sam 8:5. Note that in the Priestly view, animals share with man the possession of *nepeš* 'life' (cf. v 46; Gen 1:20, 21, 24, 30; 9:10, 12, 15, 16—all P), hence their lifeblood may not be abused; see COMMENT C below.

   an abomination (šeqeṣ). Akk. *šakāṣu* 'menace, give the evil eye'; *šakṣu* 'menacing, evil-eyed'; and *šikṣu* 'ulcer' are clearly related cognates. In Scripture, the verb *šiqqēṣ* is paralleled by *ṭi'ēb* 'abominate' (Deut 7:26) and *bāzâ* 'despise' (Ps 22:25), and the noun *šiqqûṣ* stands for a detested idol or thing (Deut 29:16; 1 Kgs 11:5, 7; 2 Kgs 23:24; Hos 9:10; Nah 3:6; Zech 9:7; etc.). Thus the term *šeqeṣ* connotes something reprehensible. Yet in this chapter it bears a more precise, technical meaning. It should be noted that *šeqeṣ* is not attributed to all species of forbidden animals. It is reserved for marine animals (v 10), birds (v 13), flying insects (v 23), and reptiles (vv 41–44), but it is missing in the passages that deal with the quadrupeds (vv 2–8, 24–28, 39–40) and the eight exceptional vermin (vv 29–38), where instead the term *ṭāmē'* 'impure' is employed (see the NOTES on "impure," vv 8, 24–28, 31). There is a legal and ritual distinction between these two terms: *šeqeṣ* refers to animals whose ingestion is forbidden but which do not pollute, whereas *ṭāmē'* refers to animals that, in addition, pollute by contact (for details, see the NOTE "you shall abominate," v 11).

   11. *and an abomination for you they shall remain (wěšeqeṣ yihyû lākem)*. Vv 10b and 11a form a complete sentence as *ṭěmē'îm hēm ûṭěmē'îm yihyû lākem* 'they are impure for you and impure they shall remain for you' (v 35b; cf. 43b, 44a). Thus the repetition is not unfelicitous redundancy but, on the contrary, a stylistic device that underscores the urgency to heed the prohibition.

   and you shall abominate their carcasses (wě'et-niblātām těšaqqēṣû). In contrast to quadrupeds whose flesh may not be eaten and whose carcasses may not be touched because they are *ṭěmē'îm* 'impure' (vv 4–8; cf. vv 24–28, 39–40), the flesh of fish may not be eaten, but their carcasses should be "abominated." Nothing, however, is stated about any prohibition to touch them. It is striking that there is no prohibition specified against contact with the other forbidden animal species whose carcasses are "abominated"—birds (v 13), the flying insects (vv 20, 23), the reptiles (vv 41–42). By contrast, in regard to the carcasses of the eight reptiles singled out by name and which defile by contact (vv 29–38), the term *šeqeṣ* 'abomination' and its denominative *šiqqēṣ* 'to abominate' are omitted. There is but one possible conclusion: those animals whose carcasses are to be "abominated" defile not by contact but only by ingestion. Paradoxically, *šeqeṣ* animals are cultically pure! (For details see Milgrom, forthcoming A.)

Unexpected corroboration stems from a verse outside P: *'ōkĕlê bĕśar haḥăzîr wĕhaššeqeṣ wĕhā'akbār* 'eating the flesh of the pig, the *šeqeṣ*, and the mouse' (Isa 66:17a). Why did the prophet choose among his three items two specific creatures and one nonspecific category? (The LXX reading, the equivalent of *šereṣ*, makes no sense because it would overlap the mouse, which is also a *šereṣ*, v 29.) If, however, this Isianic verse is understood as completely harmonious with Lev 11, then the prophet's itemization makes perfect sense. He is denouncing his fellow countrymen for eating indiscriminately from the animal world, including all that is forbidden. The pig and the mouse are synechdochic of the two categories of *ṭame'* (non-*šeqeṣ*) animals that defile not only by ingestion but also by contact ([vv 1–8], 24–28; 29–40), whereas *šeqeṣ* covers all other forbidden animals, which defile only by ingestion (vv 9–23, 41–42). The anomalous nature of the eight named rodents and reptiles is underscored by the terminology: they are *haṭṭāmē' baššereṣ* 'impure *from among* the swarming creatures' (v 29a); *'ēlleh haṭṭĕmē'îm lāhem bĕkol-haššāreṣ* 'those are for you impure *among* all the swarming creatures' (v 31); *kol-hannōgēa' bāhem bĕmôtām yiṭmā' 'ad-hā'āreb* 'whoever touches *them* (but not others) when they are dead shall be impure until evening" (ibid.). Implied, therefore, is that all other reptiles—referred to as *šeqeṣ* (vv 41–42)—do not defile even by ingestion. This general category of reptile is singled out in Isaiah by the term *šeqeṣ* in distinction to the pig and the mouse, which, as in Leviticus, are not called *šeqeṣ* and differ from all animals subsumed under *šeqeṣ* by the fact that they defile by touch.

The distinction between the *ṭāmē'* and *šeqeṣ* classifications in this chapter is clearly made in the chapter's subscript: *lĕhabdîl bên haṭṭāmē' ûbên haṭṭāhōr ûbên haḥayyâ hanne'ĕkelet ûbên haḥayyâ 'ăšer lō' tē'ākēl* 'for discriminating between the impure and the pure, between creatures that may be eaten and creatures that may not be eaten' (v 47). Both classifications are present here. In addition to creatures that may not be eaten there are those (the quadrupeds and the eight named rodents and reptiles) which are "impure," meaning that their carcasses may not be eaten and that they must also not be touched.

One may ask, however, what is the rationale behind the distinction between *ṭāmē'* and *šeqeṣ?* Why should larger quadrupeds fall entirely under the category of *ṭāmē'* and thereby contaminate by touch as well as by ingestion, but fish and birds, falling under the category of *šeqeṣ*, do not contaminate, whereas rodents and reptiles are partially *ṭāmē'*, contaminating by touch (the eight specified species) and, in the main, *šeqeṣ*, which do not contaminate?

The key to the solution, I submit, is found in v 36: "A spring or cistern in which water is collected shall remain pure, however, but whoever touches [in it] such a carcass [of the specified eight, vv 29–30] shall be impure." This verse informs us that in spite of the fact that water is the prime conveyer of impurity (vv 34, 38), the sources of water themselves always remain pure. The intrinsic purity of the water source thus stands in total contrast to water removed from its source, which becomes the conveyer of impurity. This principle gives rise to the mishnaic ruling: "all (utensils made from the skin of creatures) that are in the sea are pure" (*m. Kelim* 17:13; cf. *t. Kelim B. Meṣ.* 7:4; *Sipra*, Shemini par. 6:9), that is to say, they do not contaminate by contact.

Now, it can hardly be an accident that the very species that are *šeqeṣ* and, hence, according to our interpretation, do not contaminate by contact have, according to the Priestly creation story, their origin in water: "God said, 'Let the waters bring forth *(yišrĕṣû)* swarms *(šereṣ)* of living creatures, and birds that fly above the earth across the expanse of the sky' " (Gen 1:20). Thus both fish and birds were created from (and by) the waters and, therefore, like the waters, they do not contaminate by touch (cf. Ḥazzequni on v 23). Yet reptiles *(šereṣ)*, which are creatures of both water (Gen 1:20) and land *(remeś,* Gen 1:25, 26) do not contaminate in the main *(šeqeṣ,* vv 41–43), but some do *(ṭāmēʾ,* vv 29–38).

That this distinction between animal carcasses that do and do not contaminate stems from the creation story, it seems to me, may have been known to the rabbis. How else can one explain the very next mishna: "In that which was created on the first day there is impurity; on the second (day) there is no impurity; on the third (day) there is impurity; on the fourth and fifth (days) there is no impurity. . . . All that was created on the sixth is impure" (*m. Kelim* 17:14). Thus fish and birds, the total creations of the fifth day, are declared pure, so they do not contaminate by touch. The Mishna's enumeration of the days of creation can hardly have been a mnemonic for remembering which elements do and do not contaminate (so *The Mishna Aḥaronah*). Rather —so it is clear to me—it was the rabbis' way of grounding the distinctions between animals that do and do not contaminate by touch on the principle of whether they were created on land or on water. On the first day the earth itself was created (out of which stems earthenware—the most vulnerable of all materials to impurity, cf. vv 33, 35). On the third day, trees (i.e., wooden vessels, also permeable to impurity, v 32) were created. And all that was created on the sixth day, quadrupeds, reptiles, and man—all of the defiling creatures—were created on the land. Conversely, on the second, fourth, and fifth days the heavenly bodies and the sea creatures were created—and these, according to the rabbis, do not impart impurity by touch.

Thus the Priestly distinction between animal carcasses that are *ṭāmēʾ* and those which are *šeqeṣ*—traces of which are detectable in tannaitic sources—is rooted in the Priestly scheme of creation (see Eilberg-Schwartz 1986: 106–7 for other examples). But what presuppositions undergird this creation scheme? Here we enter the realm of speculation. Is it somehow connected with the fact that waters—in distinction to land—preexisted creation (Gen 1:2)? Or is it based on more pragmatic grounds: water is indispensable to life and, hence, sources of water could not be allowed to be defiled by impure objects within them? Or do both reasons—mythological and practical—lie behind this distinction?

This two-tiered classification of carcass impurity has wider implications.

First, it elucidates other contexts of contact impurity. The *niblat šereṣ ṭāmēʾ* 'the carcass of an impure swarming creature', forbidden to touch (5:2), can only refer to the eight specified rodents and reptiles (vv 29–30). The priest *ʾăšer yiggaʿ běkol-šereṣ ʾăšer yiṭmāʾ-lô* 'who touches any swarming creature *by which he is made impure*' (22:5) has obviously touched one of the eight touch-defiling creatures. Indeed, the extra phraseology employed in this verse "by which he is made impure" implies—and further corroborates—the conclusion deduced from Leviticus 11 that there must be two kinds of *šereṣ:* those which defile by touch and those which do not.

Finally, it must be noted that this classification among impure animal carcasses reveals a gradation that hitherto has not been noticed in any previous attempt to account for and systematize the biblical impurities. Clearly, there are animals whose carcasses defile by touch and those whose carcasses do not. It has already been demonstrated that originally it was only forbidden to touch the carcasses of prohibited quadrupeds (see the NOTE on 5:2) and only at a later date were the carcasses of permitted animals added to this list (see the NOTE on vv 39–40, below). Now it becomes clear that this prohibition against touch was never extended beyond the quadrupeds and the eight exceptional rodents and reptiles. The rest of the animal kingdom did not transmit impurity even when ingested. For further implications of this classification, see the NOTES on vv 29–38 below and chap. 15, COMMENT B.

12. *in water (bammāyim).* This verse is an abridgment of v 10. What is the need for this repetition? The rabbis claim that v 10 is limited to *yammîm* and *něhālîm* 'seas' and 'rivers'; other bodies of water such as ponds, marshes, and reservoirs are covered in this verse by the designation "in water" (*Sipra*, Shemini par. 3:2; Ibn Ezra). The striving for comprehensive coverage, characteristic of this chapter, is responsible for duplication. Thus vv 20 and 23 also seem redundant; both prohibit flying insects that walk on four feet. But because certain flying insects are permitted for the table (vv 21–22), the pericope then repeats the prohibition, in the form of an inclusion, which stresses that all *other* flying insects are prohibited. Here, lest it be thought that the criteria for fish are limited to seas and rivers (vv 9, 10), another verse is added (v 12) to include all bodies of water.

Because criteria are stipulated for fish there is no need to name the fish, just as in the case of the quadrupeds (vv 2–8), where the criteria obviate the need to name the individual animals, except the four whose possession of one of the two criteria is likely to lead the observer astray. Yet it is of more than passing interest that the deuteronomic pericope on the prohibited animals, which takes pains to enumerate the permitted quadrupeds (Deut 14:4–5; cf. vv 11, 20), is also silent concerning the permitted fish. One commentator attributes the omission to the fact that fish "are hidden from human sight" (Ḥazzequni). More to the point is the observation that Adam did not name the fish and, hence, their species were unknown (*Moshab Zeqenim* on v 10).

The reality is that ancient Israel had little acquaintance with marine life. This is proved not only by the fact that Adam names the whole animal kingdom with the exception of the fish (Gen 2:19–20), but also by the fact that in the entire Hebrew Bible not a single fish is named except the *tannînîm* (Gen 1:21; Isa 51:9; Ps 74:13) and the *liwyātān* (Pss 74:14; 104:26; Job 3:8; 40:25)—and both are mythical! To be sure, the city of Jerusalem could be entered via "the fish gate" (Neh 3:3; 12:39; 2 Chr 33:14), implying a fish market nearby, but it is no accident that the fish trade in Jerusalem was controlled by Tyrian merchants (Neh 13:16; cf. Job 40:30). Israelites simply were not fishermen—at least, not until the end of Second Temple times (e.g., Matt 4:18, 21; Mark 1:16; Luke 5:1–10). Finally, it should not be overlooked that when the other Priestly source, called H, summarizes the forbidden foods, it lists all of the generic categories of chap. 11—beasts, birds, and swarmers—but omits the fish (20:25)!

The exigencies of geography are responsible. There were few streams under the control of ancient Israel. The largest body of fresh water, the Sea of Galilee, was for most of the time the contested border between Aram and Israel and, subsequently, annexed by Assyria during the collapse of northern Israel. Even then, to judge by the small variety present today in its waters—and this, after the artificial breeding of new species—ancient Israel would, at best, have known a few species of freshwater fish. The Israelite access to the Mediterranean was also blocked during many periods of its history and, to judge by the silence of the Bible on this matter, there were no Israelites who earned their livelihood by fishing the sea. Yet would not the rich variety of fish contained in their waters have been known to Israel—if not by their own fishermen, at least through the agency of foreign merchants (e.g., Neh 13:16)? On the answer to this question hangs my personal tale.

On July 11, 1973, I chanced upon a lecture on the Berkeley campus given by Eugene C. Haderlie of the Naval Post-graduate School at Monterey, California on ecological changes in the marine life of the Suez Canal, the substance of which was soon afterward published (1973). It was fascinating to hear that with the opening of the Suez Canal in 1869 the rich marine life of the Red Sea began to migrate successfully to the Mediterranean. He explained that the eastern Mediterranean had a very low nutritive capacity due to the fact that the rich silt of the Nile flowed counterclockwise along the coasts of Israel and Lebanon but in currents that were too deep for most fauna to reach it until it surfaced in the Aegean Sea. The import of his statement did not strike me until I left the lecture hall. This means, I realized, that before the Canal, before the Red Sea fauna had penetrated the Mediterranean, the eastern Mediterranean littoral was an impoverished area for marine life. The scientific studies on this phenomenon, subsequently supplied me by Dr. Haderlie, fully confirmed his point. "It can be said that the Eastern Mediterranean is a zoogeographical 'cul de sac,' a tropical sea, undersaturated with an Atlantic-temperature fauna. By reopening artificially the contact with the Red Sea—a typical tropical sea—Lesseps helped unknowingly to reestablish a zoogeographical equilibrium and to fill this peculiar ecological vacuum in the Eastern Mediterranean" (Por 1971: 156). The success of the Red Sea migration can be measured by the fact that of the twenty-four species of immigrant fish along the Levant coast, thirteen are extremely common and eleven are of commercial value (Ben-Tuvia 1966).

The implications of this scientific finding for the present pericope are unambiguous and decisive. The Israelites were unacquainted with fish not because they had no contact with the sea but, to the contrary, the sea with which they had contact was virtually devoid of fish. The fish brought to Jerusalem by Tyrians (Neh 13:16) came from fishing fleets that plied the far-off waters of the Aegean but were beyond the reach of the Israelites. Hence, it is this piscatorial dearth in the immediate vicinity of ancient Israel that accounts for the fact that denominations for the fish are lacking.

There is a concomitant conclusion that is germane to the subject. The fact that the fish species are few to begin with means that imposing the fish-scales criterion severely restricts the edible varieties. Surely only a few species passed muster. By contrast, as the criteria excluded crustaceans and other burrowers that thrived on the coast, just to judge by the heaps of murex shells all along the Lebanese coasts (Milgrom 1983b), it seems reasonable to surmise that the very purpose of the criteria for fish, just like the criteria for quadrupeds, had the singular purpose in mind—to limit Israel's access to the animal world. This thesis will be developed and substantiated in COMMENT E below.

13. *The following (wĕ'et-'ēlleh)*. This expression corresponds to *'et-zeh* (vv 4, 9, 21). But because no criteria are stated for birds, what follows is a list of impure birds, twenty in all, which will be numbered consecutively. The fact that only the impure birds are enumerated implies that "the species of pure birds are innumerable" (*b. Ḥul.* 63b; cf. *Sipre* Deut 103; Feliks 1971: 27, 30). The Karaites claim that only the pigeon and turtledove are pure (Al-Qumisi); but their contention is refuted by Saadiah (1907: 159), who points out that the exclusiveness of these two birds is only in regard to eligibility for sacrifice. Still, just as there are quadrupeds unfit for sacrifice but permitted for the table (Deut 14:5) so there must be birds that are unfit for sacrifice but permitted for the table.

The common denominator of all impure birds, according to the rabbis, is that they are *dôrēs* (*m. Ḥul.* 3.6). This term means to "tread or attack with the claws." A more specific meaning has been suggested: (1) to hold down the prey with the claws while it is eaten (Rashi, Maimonides); (2) to eat the prey while it is still alive (Rabbi Tam, *b. Ḥul.* 61a, s.v. *haddôrēs*); (3) to seize the prey in flight without alighting on the ground (Rabbi Gershom). In general, one can say that the forbidden birds are all predatory carnivores, a notion that is as old as the Letter of Aristeas (146). The rabbis, however, admit that there is one exception to this rule, either the *peres* or the *'ozniyyâ* (v 13b; *b. Ḥul.* 61b), whose flesh is harmful but is not found in inhabited regions (Ramban). Some scholars point to additional nonpredatory carnivores in this list (e.g., *bat hayyaʿānâ*, v 7; *šaḥap*, v 9; *ʿōrēb*, v 15; *ʾănāpâ*, v 17; *ḥăsîdâ*, v 18; *dûkîpat*, v 19; *ʿăṭalēp*, v 20; Feliks 1962). The most exhaustive study of these birds (Driver 1955) also concludes that their common characteristic is that they are raptors, consumers of either carrion (1–3, 6), live prey (4–5, 7–18), or both, except for the last two in the list (19–20), the hoopoe and the bat, which, however, are tabooed because of their dirty habits and inedibility.

In addition, the rabbis prohibit any bird that "divides its feet" (*m. Ḥul.* 3:6), in other words, whenever it perches on a bar or rope it divides its toes evenly, two toes on each side. They also stipulate three criteria for pure birds (*m. Ḥul.* 3:6; *Tg. Ps.-J.* on v 13): they have (1) a toe in the back, the hallux, (2) a crop, and (3) a gizzard that can easily be separated from the outside muscular portion (see the NOTE on "crissum," 1:16). Saadiah (1907: 157) offers this rationale: "God has ordained the offering of animals of tame habits, and only these are clean to be eaten; but those with canine teeth, claws, ferocity, and tearing habits have been denied this privilege, not for any fault of their own, such being their nature, but in order to teach us that modest men are preferable to sinful ones." Ramban adds that their flesh will influence their consumers' nature by making them cruel. The rabbis never compiled a list of the pure birds, relying instead on oral tradition (these birds are enumerated by Levinger 1969).

they shall not be eaten, they are an abomination (lōʾ yēʾākĕlû šeqeṣ hēm). The text here is explicit that *šeqeṣ* implies the prohibition against ingestion but not touch (see the NOTE on "you shall abominate their carcasses," v 11). The same phrase, but in inverted order, occurs in v 41b.

The birds are numbered consecutively: 1–15 are land birds; 16–18, sea birds (Driver 1955). The identifications are, in many cases, educated guesses, as the many alternate suggestions readily indicate.

(1) *eagle. nešer* or griffon-vulture of the desert (Exod 19:4; Deut 32:11), which feeds on carrion (Prov 30:17; Job 39:38) and is bald-headed (Mic 1:16). Birds 1–4 are accipiters, one of the hawk families (Driver 1955).

(2) *black vulture (peres)*. Or "bearded vulture" or "lamb vulture." It breaks the bones of its prey, derived perhaps from Akk. *parāsu* 'break [bones]'; cf. *Tg. Onq.; Tg. Ps.-J.*

(3) *bearded vulture (ʿozniyyâ)*. Or "black vulture" or "falcon" *(Tg. Ps.-J.)*.

14. (4) *kite (dāʾâ)*. Probably related to the verb *dāʾâ* 'pounce, swoop' (Deut 28:49; Jer 48:40; 49:22). The deuteronomic list reads instead *rāʾâ* (Deut 14:13), which is clearly equivalent (*b. Ḥul.* 63b) but, on semantic grounds alone, is inferior to Leviticus (see COMMENT B below). The interchange of *dalet* and *resh*, especially in names, is frequently attested (e.g., Gen 10:4 and 1 Chr 1:7; Gen 10:3 and 1 Chr 1:6; Num 1:14 and 2:14; 2 Sam 22:11 and Ps 18:11). The deuteronomic list of accipiters (Deut 14:13) contains the additional name *dayyâ* (cf. Isa 34:15), which, however, is omitted in the LXX and Sam.

(5) *falcons of every variety (hā'ayyâ lĕmînāh)*. The first of four generic names (also nos. 6, 10, 18). This name may be onomatopoeic (Job 28:7).

15. (6) *all varieties of raven (kol-'ōrēb lĕmînô)*. Literally, "the black one"; it includes all kinds of ravens and crows (Gen 8:7; 1 Kgs 17:4; Ps 147:9; Prov 30:17). These birds belong to the corvids, characterized by a stout, moderately long, cultrate beak.

16. Birds 7–9 are large striges—of the owl family.

(7) *eagle owl. (bat hayya'ănâ;* Isa 13:21; 34:13; Jer 1:39; Mic 1:8). Literally, "daughter of the desert" (Arab.). The usual rendering, "ostrich" (LXX, Pesh., *Tgs.*), must be abandoned because ostriches do not haunt ruins, as do owls.

(8) *short-eared owl (taḥmās)*. Or "barn owl" or "screech owl" or "kestrel." The LXX renders "owl." Perhaps the name is derived from *ḥāmās* 'violence' (Ibn Ezra). *Tg. Ps.-J.* renders *ḥaṭpîtā'* 'snatcher'.

(9) *long-eared owl (šāḥap)*. So identified by Aharoni (1938). The accepted rendering "gull" (LXX) would place it among the water birds (nos. 16–18).

(10) *hawks of every variety. hannēṣ lĕmînēhû (b. Ḥul.* 63). Or "vulture" (LXX, *Tgs.*), "sparrow hawk," or "kestrel." It technically belongs to the accipiter family (nos. 1–4), but this grouping represents a smaller species (Driver 1955) and, hence, is inserted at the head of the list of the smaller owls (nos. 11–15).

17. Birds 11–15 are smaller striges (owls). They are nocturnal birds of prey found in ruins, tombs, rocks, and thickets. They feed on mice and serpents.

(11) *tawny owl. kôs* (Ps 102:7). Or "little owl." Perhaps an onomatopoeic word.

(12) *fisher owl. šālāk (b. Ḥul.* 63a; cf. *Tgs. Onq., Ps.-J.*). Or "cormorant" (LXX) or "pelican." Perhaps related to the root *šlk* 'dart [on prey]'; cf. *hiph'îl hišlîk* (Judg 9:17; Jonah 1:14). In Deuteronomy, it occurs as no. 16, before the stork and heron; hence, it too may be a water bird but of the owl family (Aharoni 1938: 470).

(13) *screech owl. yanšûp* (Isa 34:11). Perhaps derived from *nāšap* 'blow' (sound made by owls) or *nešep* 'twilight' (Isa 5:11; 22:4; cf. *Tgs.*, Pesh.).

18. (14) *white owl (tinšemet)*. Or "barn owl" or "little owl" or "screech owl." Perhaps derived from *nāšam* 'snort'. It is not to be confused with its homograph meaning "chameleon" (v 30).

(15) *scops owl (qā'āt)*. Or "horned owl" (Isa 34:11; Zeph 2:14; Ps 102:7). It may be onomatopoeic, imitative of the owl's hoot (Aharoni 1938: 471).

(16) *osprey (rāḥām)*. A sea bird, also sometimes called an ossifrage; or it could be a lammergeier (Driver 1955). It is otherwise identified with the Egyptian vulture, *Neophron percnopterus* (Arab. *rahm*); *yĕraqrêqā'*, 'greenish' vulture (*Tg. Onq.;* Pesh.); *šăraqrăqā' (Tg. Ps.-J.; b. Ḥul.* 63a), clearly an onomatopoeic attempt to produce its sound (Arab. *širiqriq*). Its juxtaposition to the eagle and eagle owl in the Deir 'Alla inscription (Hackett 1980: 25, line 8) favors the vulture identification.

19. Birds 17–18 are lake or river birds.

(17) *stork. ḥăsîdâ* (Isa 38:14; Jer 8:7). Or "heron" (LXX). Possibly derived from *ḥesed* 'loving kindness', because the stork has a reputation for affectionately caring for its young (cf. *b. Ḥul.* 63a).

(18) *herons of every variety. hā'ănāpâ lěmînāh* (*Ḥul.* 63a). Or "black hawk" *(Tg. Ps.-J.)* or "white hawk" (*Tg. Ps.-J.* at Deut 14:18).

(19) *hoopoe. dûkîpat* (LXX), which feeds on dunghills, has a filthy nest, and the smell of its flesh is rank. Or "wild cock" (Pesh.); "mountain pecker" *(Tg. Onq.; Tg. Ps.-J.).* M. Vieyra (1981) suggests that *dûkîpat* should be read as *kûkûpat*, which would make it equivalent to Demotic *ququpd-t*, Greek εποψ, Latin *upupa epos*, and Hittite *ḥapupuᴹᵁˢᴱᴺ (var. ḥapupa-, ḥapupi-)*, all of which stand for the hoopoe and onomatopoeically represent its sound.

(20) *bat. ᶜăṭālēp* (Isa 2:20), a mammal. The wings of bats are membranes connecting the hind- and forelegs.

20. *winged swarming creatures. šereṣ hāᶜôp*, in other words, flying insects (Rashi, Ibn Ezra, Ramban); but whereas Rashi defines them by their small size, Ramban does so by the number of their legs: two-legged winged creatures mostly fly, hence they are called birds (vv 13–19), but four-legged creatures mostly walk and for this reason constitute a discrete group. This pericope (vv 20–23) constitutes the second category of *šereṣ*, those of the air, the first being of the water (vv 9–12), and the third of the land (vv 41–42).

The rendering "swarming creatures" is justified by the denominative *šāraṣ* 'teem, swarm' (Gen 1:20–21; 7:21; 8:17; 9:7; Exod 1:7; 7:28; Ezek 47:9; Ps 15:30). "It is an indeterminate form of movement, since the main animal categories are defined by their typical movement; 'swarming' which is not a mode of propulsion proper to any particular element, cuts across the basic classification. Swarming things are neither fish, flesh nor fowl" (Douglas 1966: 56). Even so, many swarmers among the fish (v 9) and fowl (v 21) are permitted!

that walk on all fours (hahōlēk ᶜal-'arbaᶜ). The number four would seem to constitute a minimum. It designates all creatures that do not walk upright (Hoffmann 1953; Wenham 1979). *Tg. Ps.-J.* cites examples: flies, hornets, and bees.

abomination (šeqeṣ). See the NOTE on v 11.

21. *that have. 'ăšer-lō'* (*lô*, K./Q.). For other examples of this *ketib-qere'*, see Exod 21:8; Lev 25:30.

above their feet, jointed legs (kěrāᶜayim mimmaᶜal lěraglāyw). Members of the locust-grasshopper family actually have a third pair of long, jointed legs that are attached close to the neck, appear to be above the other legs, and are bent when the insect is in a squat position (Wessely 1846). The Priestly term *kěrāᶜayim* means "shins" in connection with a quadruped, that is, the lower part of the leg below the knee (see the NOTE on "shin," 1:9) and, by extension, refers here to the saltatory legs of this creature (illustrations in *VBW* on Joel 1:4 or in

EncJud, s.v. "locust"). *Tg. Neof.* renders accurately "leaping legs above their legs."

The rabbis specify criteria for these edible flying insects: four legs, four wings that cover the body, and knees (*m. Ḥul.* 3:7; cf. Maimonides, *Holiness*, "Forbidden Foods" 1.22). Ostensibly, Deuteronomy, which forbids all winged swarming creatures and does not exempt any species (Deut 14:19), would contradict Leviticus (Kalisch 1867-72: 126). Nevertheless, Deuteronomy follows this prohibition with its own supplement: "You may eat only pure winged creatures" (Deut 14:20), which clearly refers to flying insects (*ʿôp* not *ṣippôr*, Deut 14:11), certainly an allusion to Leviticus's exemptions (for details, see COMMENT B below).

to leap. lĕnattēr (lĕqappāṣāʾ, Tg. Onq.). A hapax in the *piʿel*, but it occurs in the *qal* (Job 37:1) and, indeed, this is how the sectaries of the Dead Sea read this word: *lntwr* (11QT 48:5).

with. bāhen, literally, "with them," referring to the *kĕrāʿayim*, 'the jointed legs', a feminine noun (cf. Amos 3:12). But the reading *bāhem* (ca. fifty MSS, Sam.) must be considered, for all other plural pronominal suffixes in this chapter are masculine, even when their antecedents are feminine (see the NOTE on "them," v 26).

The Temple Scroll adds the criterion *wĕlāʿûp bikĕnāpāyw* 'and fly with its wings' (11QT 48:5), which, however, may reflect the rabbinic "ban on eating various kinds of locusts before they sprout wings, lest one err in differentiating between them" (Yadin 1983: 1.320).

22. *locusts. hāʾarbeh*, Akk. *erbu/aribu.* This word translates as *gôbāʾ* (*Tg. Onq.; Sipra*, Shemini 5:9), equivalent to BH *gôbay* (Amos 7:1; Nah 3:16), which may be related to Arab. *jabāʾ* 'collect' and hence mean "swarm [of locusts]." Indeed, *ʾarbeh* itself may stem from *rābâ* 'be many', and in Scripture the *ʾarbeh* is a favorite metaphor for a multitude (e.g., Judg 6:5; 7:12; Jer 46:23; Nah 3:15, 17).

of every variety (lĕmînô). In Akkadian there are eighteen names for locusts. Scripture itself uses ten (*gēb*, Isa 33:4; *gôbay*, Amos 7:1; *gāzām*, Joel 1:4; *ḥāgāb*, Num 13:31; *ḥāsîl*, 1 Kgs 8:37; *ḥargōl*, v 22; *yeleq*, Ps 105:34; *sōlʿām*, v 22; *sĕlāṣal*, Deut 28:42). Maimonides reduces them to eight (*Holiness*, "Forbidden Foods" 1.21).

Some scientists regard four of these names—*ʾarbeh, yeleq, ḥāsîl*, and *gāzām*, listed in this sequence in Joel 2:25—not as four different species of locust but as stages in its development, from the larva to its fully grown form.

After being fertilized, the female lays a cluster of eggs in a hole which it makes in the ground. From the eggs, dark wingless larvae, the size of tiny ants, are hatched, these being the *yeleq*, a word apparently connected with *lāqaq*, "to lap, lick up." Eating the tender vegetation of the field, the *yeleq* grows rapidly, and since (as with all insects) its epidermis does not become bigger, it sheds it at various stages of its growth, during which it changes the color of its skin. The next stage, during which its skin is pink, is the *ḥāsîl*, which word, from the root *ḥsl*, refers to its total destruction of the vegetation of the field, for at this stage it consumes enormous quantities; hence *ḥāsîl* is used as a synonym of *'arbeh*. Thus in Solomon's prayer at the dedication of the Temple he declared that during a plague of *'arbeh ḥāsîl* people would come there to pray for its riddance (1 Kgs 8:37; cf. Ps 8:46). It now casts its skin twice, grows short wings, and becomes the *gāzām*. At this juncture, when no more vegetation is left in the field, it "cuts off" (this being the meaning of *gāzām*) and chews the bark of trees with its powerful jaws; as Joel (1:7) says: "he hath made it (the fig-tree) clean bare . . . the branches thereof are made white"; and Amos (4:9): it devours "your gardens and your vineyards and your fig-trees and your olive-trees." Finally, after casting a further epidermis, it becomes the fully grown, long-winged *'arbeh*, the yellow-colored female which is fit to lay its eggs. This cycle of the locust's development extends from spring until June (Feliks 1971c; cf. Aharoni 1938: 475–77; the pictures of these stages are depicted in *EM* 1, pl. 9, s.v. *'arbeh*).

These four names occur in a different order in Joel 1:4, but the sequence is the same (beginning with *gāzām* rather than with *'arbeh*), thus pointing to the developmental stages (Aharoni 1938: 476). But as only one of the four—*'arbeh* —is listed here, and as each name stands for a type, it is clear that different species are intended, not the development of a single species (Dillmann and Ryssel 1897).

The reason for exempting the locusts is not clear. Douglas's explanation (1966: 56) is unsatisfactory (see COMMENT E below). It may be related to Israel's pastoral life in its presettlement period, when the community subsisted on its herds as well as on the sporadic visits of locusts, just as bedouin do to this day (for the implications, see COMMENT E). Indeed, it should be remembered that one inhabitant of the wilderness, John the Baptist, made "locusts and wild honey" his exclusive fare (Matt 3:4; Mark 1:6) and that Yemenite Jews still eat fried locusts.

bald locust (ḥassal'ām). Or "long-headed locust"; a hapax. In Aramaic, this word means "swallow" (cf. Tg. of *billēa'*, Job 10:8) or "destroy" (cf. Tg. of *'ăbalēa'*, Isa 19:3).

crickets (haḥargōl). A hapax; similar to Akk. *ergilu (AHw)*. Perhaps related to Arab. *ḥarjala* 'leap in going' (for a surmised identification, see Bodenheimer 1935: 319).

grasshopper. heḥāgāb (Num 33:11; Isa 40:22; 2 Chr 7:13). It was so common that it became for the rabbis the generic term for all locusts (*m. 'Ed.* 7:2; 8:4; *m. Ḥul.* 3:7; 8:1; *m. Ter.* 10:10).

23. *But all other. wĕkōl* (Abravanel). This verse is not a mere repetition (and inclusion) of v 20; it emphasizes that only the four named species of winged swarming creatures are pure—and none other.

that have four legs. Even if it does not walk but flies (Ibn Ezra). But then it would not belong to the category of winged swarming creatures, rather to the category of birds (Ramban; cf. Douglas 1966 on v 20).

vv 24-28. *The impurity conveyed by impure quadrupeds.* Thus far, only the four named quadrupeds have been declared as *ṭāmēʾ* (vv 4-7) and as conveyers of impurity by contact (v 8). This rule also holds for all quadrupeds that do not possess the requisite criteria, as is made clear by vv 24-28. That vv 24-40 constitute an insertion is discussed in COMMENT A below. Vv 24-25 begin a new section and are not to be attached to vv 20-23 (contra Ibn Ezra); see the NOTES on "with the following," v 24 and on v 28. It should be emphasized that a live animal never imparts impurity; only a carcass does (*m. Ohol.* 1:6; *Sipre*, Num 125).

24. *you shall make yourselves impure. tiṭṭammāʾû (hithpaʿel).* As noted above ("they are impure for you," v 8), the use of *ṭāmēʾ* in this chapter implies contracting impurity by touch as well as by ingestion, as is confirmed by the statement that immediately follows: "whoever touches."

with the following. ûlĕʾēlleh, referring to vv 24-28 (*Sipra*, Shemini 4:1ff.; Saadiah [1907: 160-61], Rashi, Rashbam, Ramban), versus Ibn Ezra who renders this word as "with the above," namely, the winged swarming creatures (vv 20-23), on the grounds that the impurity conveyed by quadrupeds is discussed further on (vv 26-28). But winged swarming creatures are termed *šeqeṣ* (vv 20, 23), not *ṭāmēʾ*; in other words, their ingestion is forbidden but they do not defile. The only swarming creatures *(šereṣ)* that defile are the eight expressly called *ṭāmēʾ*, whose contagious impurity is minutely described (vv 29-38; cf. Ramban).

shall be impure until evening (yiṭmāʾ ʿad-hāʿāreb). That the impure person must undergo ablutions is implied, not only here but throughout the chapter. Ablutions are explicitly called for in Lev 11 only in the case of impure vessels: if ablutions are required for vessels contaminated by touch, all the more so for persons. Furthermore, one who eats the carcass of a pure animal ostensibly is only "impure until evening" (v 40), but other texts inform us that he also requires ablutions (17:15; 22:6). Finally, as all who carry a carcass must launder their clothes (vv 25, 28, 40b), it is inconceivable that they are not also obliged to undergo ablutions (15:5, 6, 7, 8, 10, 11, 13, etc.; and see below, the NOTE on v 25, as well as chap. 15, COMMENT B). The rabbis derive this same rule from Exod 19:10 (see *Mek.* Yitro 3). The Dead Sea sectaries adopt an even stricter view, requiring laundering as well as ablutions for touching carcasses (11QT 51:2-3), which, however, has no basis in the text.

25. *any part of their carcasses (minniblātām).* The Pesh. and four MSS read *ʾet-niblātām* (v 28). But the MT is justified, for part of the carcass conveys

impurity the same way as does its entirety (cf. Num 19:16). The same construction is present in *mibbĕśārām* 'of their flesh' (v 11). The rabbis limit the term "carcass" to the animal's flesh but "not any part of their bones, nor of their teeth, nor of their nails, nor of their hair shall be unclean" (*Sipra*, Shemini 10:2). The Dead Sea sectaries thought otherwise (11QT 51:4–5; *MMT* B 21–22), as did the Sadducees (*m. Yad.* 4:6).

shall wash his clothes (yĕkabbēs bĕgādāyw). Because the carcass most likely came into contact with his clothes (Ramban). Or the reason may be the greater intensity of the contact. Whereas touching presumes light contact, carrying implies that the pressure of the carcass on the clothes, even when indirectly (e.g., when the carcass is wrapped), suffices to transmit the impurity. An illustrative case is the purification rite for one who handles the lustral waters: *ûmazzēh mê-hanniddâ yĕkabbēs bĕgādāyw wĕhannōgēaʿ bĕmê hanniddâ yiṭmāʾ ʿad-hāʿāreb* 'Further, he who sprinkle the lustral waters shall launder his clothes; and whoever touches the lustral waters shall be impure until evening' (Num 19:21b). Both the one who sprinkles and the one who touches must bathe, but only the one who sprinkles launders as well, clearly because his contact with the lustral waters is more intense. This factor is called by the rabbis *midrās* 'pressure' (cf. *m. Hag.* 2:7; *m. Nid.* 6:3; cf. also the Notes on 14:47; 15:5; and chap. 15, Comment B). A person whose impurity lasts more than one day also requires laundering (e.g., 14:8, 9; 15:13; Num 19:19).

Tg. Onq. and *Tg. Ps.-J.* translate the verb as *yĕṣabbaʿ* 'immerse' rather than the expected *yĕhawwēr* 'wash' *(Tg. Neof.),* indicating that complete ablutions for the person and his clothing are mandated. The Sam. actually adds the words *wĕrāhaṣ bammayim* 'and he shall wash himself in water' but, as noted above (v 24), this chapter assiduously avoids stating the fact because it is presumed in the expression *yiṭmaʿ ʿad-hāʿāreb* 'he shall be impure until evening'.

26. *every quadruped (lĕkol-habbĕhēmâ).* Refers back to *ûlēʾelleh* 'with the following' (v 24; Shadal). The *lamed* that prefixes *lekol* has the force of generality and total inclusion (vv 42, 46; 5:3, 4; 16:16; 22:5; Num 31:4; see Milgrom 1970a: nn. 237, 279). The *lamed* may also be understood as an emphatic particle (Arab. *la*, Akk. *lu*, Ugaritic *l*), as in v 46 (D. Levy).

The possibility must be entertained that *bĕhēmâ* here must be rendered "domesticated quadruped" as distinguished from *hayyâ* 'wild quadruped' (v 27), in consonance with the same differentiation found in 5:2. If so, then the usage of *bĕhēmâ* here differs from that in v 2, where it clearly refers to all quadrupeds, and it would explain why vv 24–40, dealing with impurity by contact, form a later insert written by another hand (see Comment A below).

has hoofs but without clefts through the hoofs. For example, the horse, donkey, and mule. The three animals specified in vv 4–6 are not subsumed under this criterion because they are not even hoofed. These and other nonhoofed (and nonruminant) quadrupeds are covered in vv 27–28.

Ramban asks (on v 24) why the passage on pure animals (vv 39–40) is not included here, if their carcasses are subject to the same law. He replies that in their case, the term *něbēlâ* 'carcass' is defined differently: only as a result of *wěkî yāmût*, a natural death. If it is properly slaughtered, it is not a "carcass." This distinction holds good (see the NOTE on v 39), but it begs the question. It does not resolve the problem of why vv 39–40 did not immediately follow vv 24–28 so that the impurity conveyed by quadrupeds would form a unified pericope. This fact, among others (see COMMENT A below), leads to the conclusion that vv 39–40 are a subsequent insertion.

or (wě[gērâ]). This usage of *waw* is frequently attested in P (e.g., v 4; 21:14; 22:23, 24; cf. Exod 21:17, 37).

whoever touches them shall be impure (kol-hannōgēaʿ bāhem yiṭmāʾ). A superfluous sentence in view of v 24b and its bulge in the structure of vv 24–28; see the NOTE on "they are impure for you," v 28. It may be an ellipsis for vv 24–25 forming an inclusio with them, thereby indicating that the following verses (27–28), dealing with the unhoofed quadrupeds, form a separate subunit.

them (bahem). Ibn Ezra comments that "there are some Sadducean sectarians who said that (this meant) everyone who touches them while they are alive shall be impure. Such nonsense does not require refutation, for the biblical text forbade only their flesh by saying not to touch their carcass." Indeed, six MSS and the LXX read *běniblātām* (as in v 27b). The MT, however, is preferred. This pronominal suffix and the previous pronoun "they" refer to the antecedent *běniblātām* of v 24, proving that vv 24–26 are a cohesive unit. The masculine pronoun is used throughout this pericope even when the referent is feminine, for example, *běhēmâ* (v 26), *něbēlâ* (v 24), *hayyâ* (v 27).

27. *animals (hahayyâ).* See the NOTE on v 2.

flat paws (kappāyw). The *kap* is the hollow or flat of the hand or foot, that is, the palm or sole. (For the latter see Deut 2:5; 11:24; 28:56, 65.) For the importance of this precision, see COMMENT E below.

among those that walk on all fours (běkol -[hahayyâ]haḥōleket ʿal-ʾarbaʿ). This qualification is essential because *hayyâ* embraces all animals, not just quadrupeds (see the NOTE on v 2).

whoever touches. Why is purification ordained for touching (also in v 28) and not for eating? The latter can be deduced a fortiori from the former.

their carcasses (běniblātām). Because a new category of quadrupeds is mentioned here, the unhoofed ones, the word for "carcass" must be mentioned. Contrast "them," v 26, above, again demonstrating that vv 24–26 and 27–28 form discrete units.

28. This verse's ostensible repetition of v 25 prompts Ibn Ezra to regard vv 24–25 as part of the pericope on the winged swarming creatures (vv 20–23; see the NOTE on v 24). But this verse refers to the unhoofed quadrupeds (v 27) and has nothing to do with the rule on the hoofed quadrupeds (vv 24–26), as proved by the similarly worded endings to each of these subunits (vv 26aγ, 28b) and their common linkage (v 26b). The introverted structure of vv 24–28 is

diagrammed below. Hence, some statement is needed concerning carrying the carcass of a hoofed animal; this is supplied by v 25. Besides, vv 24–25 use the word *ṭāmēʾ*, as do the following verses dealing with the impure quadrupeds (vv 26–27), whereas the previous pericope on the flying insects uses the word *šeqeṣ* (vv 20, 23). Because these terms are mutually exclusive (see the NOTE on v 11), vv 24–25 must belong to the following verses and not to the preceding.

They are impure for you (ṭĕmēʾ îm hēmmâ lākem). A repetition of vv 26aγ and 27aβ. But whereas the latter serve as endings for the two specified cases, the hoofed and unhoofed quadrupeds, the repetition here fulfills a stylistic function, together with vv 27b–28a, as the chiastic repetition of vv 24–25, thereby framing the two cases with an inclusion. Indeed (with Lund 1942: 51) vv 24–28 reveal a palistrophic, introverted structure (A B X B′ A′), which can be represented diagrammatically as follows:

A. *vv 24–25*

    a. 24a   *ûlĕʾēleh tiṭṭammāʾû*

    b. 24b–25   *kol-hannōgēaʿ bĕniblātām yiṭmāʾ ʿad-hāʿ āreb*
                     wĕkol-hannōśēʾ minniblātām yĕkabbēs bĕgādâw
                     wĕṭāmēʾ
                     ʿad-hāʾāreb

    B.   *v 26a*

        a. 26aαβ   *lĕkol-habbĕhēmâ ʾăšer hîʾ(hwʾ) mapreset parsâ*
                     wĕšesaʿ ʾênennâ šōsaʿat wĕgērâ ʾênennâ maʿălâ

        b. 26aγ   *ṭĕmēʾ îm hēm lākem*

        X.   *v 26b kol-hannōgēaʿ bāhem yiṭmāʾ*

    B′. *v 27a*

        a′. 27aα   *wĕkōl hōlēk ʿal-kappâw bĕkol-haḥayyâ hahōleket*
                     ʿal-ʾarbaʿ

        b′. 27aβ   *ṭĕmēʾîm hēm lākem*

A′. *vv27b–28*

    b′. 27b–28a   *kol-hannōgēaʿ bĕniblātām yiṭmaʾ ʿad-hāʿāreb wĕhan-*
                     nōśēʾʾet-niblātām yĕkabbēs bĕgādâw wĕṭāmēʾ ʿad-
                     hāʿāreb

    a′. 28b   *ṭĕmēʾîm hēmmâ lākem*

The inclusion (AA′) stands in chiastic order (ab b′a′). Chiasm and inclusion are stylistic devices found in other parts of this chapter (e.g., vv 43–44, 47), which, significantly, are later additions to the chapter (see COMMENT A below). Because A′a′, for obvious reasons, cannot duplicate Aa, it adopts the wording of

Bb and B'b'. The pivotal position of X is revealed by the structure. It is located in the very center not only by its locus but also by its wording: it repeats the beginning of the inclusion (Ab, A'b'). Its purpose is thereby made clear: to emphasize that the quadrupeds, in distinction to the creatures of the water and the air (vv 9–23), defile by contact.

29. *impure (haṭṭāmēʾ)*. This term automatically implies that the subsequently listed creatures convey impurity not only by ingestion but also by touch, as spelled out in vv 31–38 (see the discussion in the NOTE on v 11). This characteristic applies only to the eight itemized reptiles and rodents that follow (vv 29–30; Rashi, Ibn Ezra), whereas the rest of the swarming creatures do not defile even by ingestion (vv 41–43).

from among [the creatures that swarm on the earth] (ba[ššereṣ haššōrēṣ ʿal-hāʾāreṣ]). Contrast *wĕkol-/lĕkol-(haššereṣ haššōrēṣ ʿal-hāʾāreṣ)*, 'all/comprising all [the creatures that swarm on the earth]' (vv 41, 42) thus distinguishing between the enumerated eight and the rest of their kind. See also *bĕkol-(haššereṣ)* 'among all' (v 31). These eight would commonly be found in the kitchen and, being small, might be found inside vessels, a frequent occurrence in cases cited by the rabbis (e.g., *m. Kelim* 8:18; 9:3; 10:9).

on the earth (ʿal-hāʾāreṣ). This constitutes the third and final category of swarming creatures: in the water (v 10), in the air (vv 20, 23), and now on land (vv 29–43).

the rat (haḥōled). Or "weasel" (LXX, *m. Pesaḥ.* 1:2; *Tg. Ps.-J.)* or "mole" *(y. Ḥag.* 1, 80c).

the mouse (hāʿakbār). A collective for all small rodents of the family *Muridae*.

large lizards (haṣṣāb). Or "the dab lizard" (Feliks 1971b), or "thorn-tailed lizard" (Bodenheimer 1935: 196), or "large Libyan lizard" *(Tg. Ps.-J.)*, or "toad" (Rashi; cf. *m. Ṭohar.* 5:6), or "crocodile" (LXX). Because of the subsequent phrase "of every variety," however, the term must be generic for a wide range of lizards and should not be identified with a particular one.

30. *the gecko (hāʾănāqâ)*. An onomatopoeic term related to this creature's plaintive cry. Or "ferret" (LXX) or "hedgehog" *(Tg. Ps.-J.,* Rashi).

the spotted lizard. hakkōaḥ (Tg. Ps.-J.). Or "chameleon" (LXX). Feliks and others prefer the monitor lizard which, however, is large, reaching more than four feet in length, hardly a creature that would inhabit the kitchen or be held in the hand (see the NOTES on "whoever touches," v 31, and "into," v 33).

the lizard. hallĕṭāʾâ, a generic name for lizards. Or "gecko" (KB), or "newt" (LXX) or "salamander" (Pesh.).

the skink (haḥōmeṭ). A lizard found in desert country with protective yellow coloring. Unlike a true lizard it does not climb, but hides under stones or in holes. Or "snail" (Rashi), or "newt" (LXX) or "sand lizard" *(Tg. Ps.-J.)*. Akk. *ḥulmittu* (perhaps from *ḥamātu* 'hasten') stands for all small reptiles that are not identified.

the chameleon (hattinšāmet). Perhaps derived from *nāšam* 'snort'. Or "white owl" (KB) or "salamander" *(Tg. Ps.-J.).*

31. *Those are for you the impure (ʾelleh haṭṭĕmēʾîm lākem).* Repeated (see v 29) for emphasis, that is to say, *only* these eight (Ibn Ezra).

among all. bĕkol, indicating that the rule that follows applies only to some of the swarming reptiles (cf. also the NOTE on "from among," v 29).

the swarming creatures (haššōreṣ). The modifier *ʿal-hāʾāreṣ* 'on the land' is missing (contrast v 29a). Nonetheless no emendation is necessary. In truth, these eight named swarmers are the only ones that are *ṭāmēʾ;* the others are *šeqeṣ,* namely, fish (v 10), birds (vv 13, 19), and insects (v 41).

whoever touches (kol-hannōgēaʿ). Nothing is said about *carrying* the forbidden carcass, as in the case of quadrupeds (vv 25, 40). The rabbis infer from this omission that carrying indeed is permitted provided there is no direct contact *(m. Kelim* 1:1). Yet carrying is also omitted where its prohibition is clearly in force (e.g., contamination from a corpse, Num 19:16). Thus the omission is self-understood. Also, as these are small creatures, it is most likely that they would be carried in the hand and not come into contact with clothing (see the NOTE on v 40b). Ingestion is also omitted, but it will be explicitly (and emphatically) mentioned in connection with the rest of the land-swarming creatures (vv 41–42). This is but one indication that vv 29–38, the section dealing with the land-swarming creatures, are a later insert (see COMMENT A below).

them when they are dead (bāhem bĕmōtām). These eight creatures are so repulsive that one might think that touching them when alive might be contaminating: hence, the text stresses only "when they are dead" (Wessely 1846). Also, the use of *bāhem bĕmōtām* instead of *bĕniblātām* 'their carcasses' (see v 24b) may be influenced by *bĕmōtām* in the next verse.

shall be impure until evening (yiṭmāʾ ʿad-hāʿāreb). Ablution for the contaminated person is not mentioned but is implied; rather, it is taken for granted. Mention is also omitted but taken for granted for many other impure persons and things, such as utensils (v 32); touching the carcass of an impure quadruped (vv 25–28) and a pure quadruped (v 40; cf. 17:15); touching an impure person or reptile (22:6a; cf. v 6b); the *zābâ* (15:28; cf. v 13); the menstruant (15:19–20) and parturient (chap. 12, whose defilement is as severe as that of the *zāb/zābâ);* the one who gathers the ashes of the Red Cow (Num 19:10; cf. vv 7–8).

The reason for the omission of ablution in so many cases, however, is not just due to its being self-understood. As will be shown (chap. 15, COMMENT C), ablution constitutes the stage in the purification process by which the contaminated person is permitted to come into contact with the common, but not with the sacred (which requires the last stage—the arrival of the evening). It is no crime, let us say, to eat ordinary food while impure, in contrast to the severe penalties imposed for eating sacred food in a state of impurity (7:20). Hence it is more important to stress the terminal state of purification, instead of the penultimate stage, the ablution (Ramban).

32. *And anything on which one of them falls (wĕkōl ʾăšer-yippōl ʿālāyw mēhem)*. Literally, "And anything that will fall upon it of one of them." This generalization includes everything, even those unmentioned in this verse, such as metal vessels. Furthermore, the preposition ʿal 'on' (contrast *ʾel-tôk* 'into', v 33) signifies that the carcass need not fall inside the vessel in order to contaminate it.

when they are dead (bĕmōtām). By contrast, they need not be dead when they fall into the vessel (Dillmann and Ryssel 1897; Wenham 1979). For this reason the text avoids the term *minniblātām* 'of their carcass' (see also the NOTE on "them when they are dead," v 31).

article of wood (kĕlî-ʿēṣ). Biblical *kĕlî* is not limited to a vessel or receptacle. It is used of weapons (Gen 27:3; Judg 18:11), tools (Num 35:16, 18, 22), ornaments (Isa 61:10; Hos 6:17), clothing (Deut 22:5), and musical instruments (Amos 6:5; 1 Chr 15:16). Therefore, *kĕlî-ʿēṣ* connotes much more than just a wooden bowl or tray (D. Wright).

Wood absorbs like earthenware except if it is highly polished; and yet it can be purified (cf. also 15:11; Num 31:20)! The Hittites, in contrast, regard wooden utensils as highly susceptible to impurity: "If a pig (or) a dog somehow approaches the implements of wood or bitumen [rather, "clay"—D. Wright; see the NOTE on "any earthen vessel," v 33] which you have, and the kitchen servant does not discard it, but gives the god to eat from an unclean (vessel), to such a man the gods will give dung (and) urine to eat (and) to drink" (*ANET*³ 209).

To be sure, Hindu religion also permits the purification of wooden vessels, but by planing them (e.g., Manu 5.115), not by washing them. Still, Hindu practice is not consistent in this regard: "(Impure) vessels of wood or earthenware must be thrown away" (*Visnusmṛti* 23.1–5; Jolley 1880: 98). The principle behind the disposal of impure items seems to have been that "(objects) that have been defiled very much may be thrown away" (*Gautama—Dharmaśāstra* 1.34; Bühler 1879).

What, then, accounts for the fact that impure wooden vessels are discarded by the Hittites, purified by the Israelites, and either discarded or purified by the Hindus? The answer may rest on economic grounds. Wooden utensils would rarely be found in the Israelite kitchen. Rather, this concession would have been intended for more costly items, such as the handles of tools and weapons, the beams of roofs and looms, and the like. The same reason that exempted the outside of sealed crockery from being permeable to impurity (see the NOTE at "into," v 33) may have prevailed here as well: to spare the Israelites severe economic loss. Perhaps the same motivation obtains among those Indians who permit the reuse of contaminated wooden vessels. Also, one could surmise that the reason that Hittite religion demanded their destruction was that wood in Anatolia was relatively inexpensive. This, however, is but a conjecture and awaits investigation. (For greater details on Indian practice, see Wright 1984: 107–9; 1987: 107–10.)

The limitation to *kělî*, literally, "instrument," would eliminate decks or floors, which, by their omission, could not be contaminated *(Keter Torah)*. For the same reason articles of stone are not susceptible to contamination (Rashbam), though the Dead Sea sectaries held that stone implements were permeable to impurity (CD 12:15–18; 11QT 49:13–16; 50:16–17).

fabric (beged). This term includes more than clothing (see the NOTE on 13:47). This point can also be inferred from the qualification "that can be put to use," for example, furniture covers (Num 4:6–9), bedcovers (1 Sam 19:13; 1 Kgs 1:1), saddle cloth (Ezek 27:20).

sackcloth. śaq, an international word. "It was the coarse cloth which slaves wore as a loin cloth, and later was a sign of mourning" (Snaith 1967). On the basis of Num 31:20, where the same list of articles subject to contamination is enumerated and *śaq* is replaced by *ma'ăśeh 'izzîm,* literally, "goat product," some would render *śaq* as "cloth of goat feathers *(sic)*" (Rashbam), or "cloth of goat skins" *(Keter Torah,* Hoffmann 1953). But most likely it translates as "cloth of goat hair" because *'izzîm* means "goat hair" as well as "goats" (Exod 25:4; 1 Sam 19:13, 16). To this day the black tents, so characteristic of the bedouin, are made of goat hair, and sacks of goat hair transport and protect the grain (Dalman 1933: 3.198).

It is not surprising that metal implements are omitted from this list. Metal articles were not to be found in the ordinary home (Finkelstein 1962: 129). Even so, the more likely reason is that, being nonporous, there was no question about whether they could be purified (Wright 1987: 111 n. 69). The enumerated vessels, by contrast, are all organic and their porosity would have made it doubtful whether they could be purified. Metal vessels were, of course, used in the cult and in armaments, hence they are listed among the items requiring purification (6:21; Num 31:22). The question of whether articles of metal (and glass) required purification was the subject of a Sadducean controversy *(t. Ḥag.* 3:35; cf. Finkelstein 1962: 128–30).

that can be put to use. 'ăšer-yē'āśeh mělā'kâ bāhem, that is to say, once again. For this meaning of *mělā'kâ,* see 7:24. The rabbis derive from this stipulation, correctly, that the vessel must be a finished product in order to be susceptible to impurity *(m. Kelim* 4:4; 12:8; 13:2; 16:1). Although wood, cloth, and leather are porous and, hence, permeable to impurity, they can be purified if they are usable. Presumably, the cost of replacing them would be prohibitive for the poor, in contrast to earthenware. (See the NOTE on "article of wood," n. 32.)

shall be immersed in water (bammayim yûbā'). Literally, "shall be brought through water." That immersion is meant is made clear by Jer 13:1; Ps 66:12. Also note its synonym, *he'ĕbîr bammayim* 'pass through water' (Num 31:23; Ezek 47:3, 4). Ablution, the penultimate step in the purification process, needs to be mentioned here lest one conclude that only persons require it. Objects are also impure in regard to sancta even after the ablution and only shed this last vestige of impurity at sundown (cf. *b. Yebam.* 75a).

then it shall be pure (wĕṭāhēr). This added word is needed lest one reason that objects, unlike persons, may be made pure by washing alone without having to wait till evening.

33. *into. ʾel-tôkô,* literally, "into its midst." But not if the carcass only makes contact with the vessel's outer surface *(m. Kelim* 2:1; *b. Ḥul.* 24b [bar.]; *Sipra,* Shemini 7:6), as can be derived from the rule that an earthen vessel in the same tent as a corpse is contaminated only if it is not tightly sealed (Num 19:15; *Sipre* Num 126). The reason for this leniency may be economic, for all contaminated earthenware must be destroyed (Ḥazzequni). The question still remains, however: Why is the inside of earthenware susceptible to impurity but not its outside? Here, the answer may well be the fear that earthenware, the impurity of which can never be removed, may by accident become the receptacle for sacred food, the penalty for the eating of which is of the severest—excision by God (see the Notes to 7:19–21). This distinction between the inside and the outside of earthenware may throw light on the following New Testament passage: "But the Lord said to him, 'You Pharisees usually clean the outside of the cup and the platter; but the inside of you is full of greed and wickedness' " (Luke 11:39; cf. Matt 23:5–6). (For the possibility that Jesus' homily was coined at a time in which debate over the priority of inside versus outside was a live issue, see the discussion in Neusner 1974: 374–81.)

It is questionable, however, whether this rabbinic interpretation is correct. The outside of closed earthenware may have been declared insusceptible to impurity only when it was located inside a tent containing a corpse (Num 19:15), that is, corpse contamination was indirect, impinging on the vessel by being reflected from the ceiling of the dwelling (see chap. 15, Comment F); but had the corpse or corpse-contaminated person come into direct contact with the vessel, the vessel would have been rendered impure. Similarly, if the carcass of one of these eight specified animals had touched the outside of earthenware, even if it were closed, it would be impure (Wright 1987: 98).

These animals must be small in size because they can fall *into* earthenware vessels (cf. also the Note "whoever touches," v 31). Flat earthenware was apparently rare: "the thin plate such as we use today was a difficult ceramic form to manufacture, and it was little used until NT times" (Kelso 1962: 3.851a). See the various pottery types in Amiran (1970), where the flattest ware is still bowl-shaped (D. Wright).

any earthen vessel (wĕkol-kĕlî-ḥeres). This rule would probably not apply either to glazed clay, which would not absorb, or to unfired clay, which would maintain its status as soil/earth and not be susceptible to contamination (Hoffmann 1953). Not surprisingly, Hindu purity laws also distinguish between objects with hard exteriors like iron or brass, which can be purified by washing or burning, and clay vessels, which must be discarded (Hayley 1980: 123). Earthen vessels that have been contaminated by lesser impurities can be purified by two burnings (Manu 5.122–23), but "an earthen vessel if polluted by the contact of wines, urine, excrement, phlegm, tears, pus, and blood is not purified even by being burnt [sic] in fire" (*Vas.* 3.59, cited in Kane 1973: 327). The likelihood that the Hittites also discarded defiled earthenware is supported by David Wright's communication on the disputed term GIR$_4$, which I quote in full:

> Let us now turn to a question which concerns GIR$_4$ implements, that is, those apparently made of fired clay, and the Hittite and Biblical cults. There are two Hittite texts which reveal a distinction in the reusability of various implements which have become ritually impure, much like the distinction in Biblical texts between clay objects and other objects which have become impure:
>
> A. *Temple Officials' Instructions* (KUB XIII, 4, iii, 64–68; cf. *ANET,* p. 209d)

> 64. *ma-a-an* U-NU-[*TE*]. MEŠ*IṢ-Ṣ* I Ú-*NU-TE*.MEŠ GIR$_4$ *ku-e ḫar-te-ni*

> 65. *na-aš-ša ma-a-a*n ŠAḪ-*aš* UR.GI$_7$-*aš ku-wa-pí-ik-ki an-da ša-a-li-qa*

> 66. EN UTÚL-*ma-at ar-ḫa* UL *pí-eš-še-ya-zi nu a-pa-a-aš* DINGIR.MEŠ-*aš pa-ap-ra-an-da-za*

> 67. *a-da-an-na pa-a* ⌈*-i*⌉ *a-pí-e-da-ni-m*a DINGIR.MEŠ-*eš za-ak-kar: du-ú-úr*

> 68. *a-da-an-na a-ku-*⌈*wa*⌉ *-an-na pí-an-z*i

> "If the implements of wood and implements of fired clay (GIR$_4$) which you hold, if a pig or a dog ever approach [possibly a euphemism for "touch, contact," similar to biblical *qārab*—JM] them, but the kitchen official does not throw them (the vessels) away, (and) he gives to the god to eat from an unclean (implement), then to him the gods will give excrement and urine to eat and drink."

Here implements of wood and fired clay (GIR$_4$) must be thrown away when they are polluted. The text does not indicate that they can be purified. Compare KUB, V, 7, obv. 34: UR.GI$_7$-*ša-an ku-it* ^{GIŠ}BAN-ŠUR-*i ša-li-ik-ta nu* NINDA.KUR$_4$.RA *U$_f$-MI ka-ri-pa-aš* ^{GIŠ}BANŠUR *ka-ri-pa-an-zi,* "since a dog approached the table and consumed the daily bread, they 'consume' the table." Goetze (*ANET*^{3}, p. 497d) interprets the consuming of the table as "they will *discard* the table." If this is correct, then we have a further example of pollution of a wooden(?) item which cannot be reused.

B. *Birth Ritual "When a Woman Conceives"* (CTH 489; KBo XVII, 65, obv. 24–25, paralleled in the text by rev. 28f.; edited by Beckman, *HBR*, pp. 163ff.)

24.   [Ú-NU-U(T GIŠ-*ya* Ú-NU-UT GIR₄-*ya* ᴳᴵˢ*ḫa-a*)]*š-ša-al-li* ᴳᴵˢ-NÁᴴᴵᴬ-*ya bu-u-ma-an* GIBIL-*TIM*

25.   [da-an-na-ra-an-da) . . . (d)a-an-z]i Ú-NU-UT ZABAR-*ma ku-e na-aš-ta an-da wa-ar-nu-wa-an-zi*

> "[Implemen]ts of wood, implements of GIR₄, the stool and the bed, all new, empty [. . . they ta]ke, but implements which are of bronze, they burn therein."

Apparently here only items of wood and fired clay (GIR₄) which are new can be used (cf. Papanikri KBO 5.1i6 where the broken birthstool is no longer clean, hence a new one must be made). Yet items of bronze (ZABAR) are to be "burnt in," probably to purify them (for reuse?; Beckman suggests that "the metal utensils are to be purified through burning [of aromatics?]," p. 198).

Even if one does not take GIR₄ as "fired clay" (as Moyer, Diss., p. 106, who saw the parallel between text A and the Biblical material), a parallel still exists in a general way between Hittite and Biblical texts. Both cultures distinguish between impure items which are not reusable and impure items which may be reused after purification. All impure clay vessels must be destroyed according to Biblical prescription (Lev 6:21 [Eng. 28]; 11:32f.; 15:12). Other items may be purified for reuse (see the same references). Especially interesting in connection with text B is Num 31:19–24, which prescribes that metal items be purified in fire, while other items should be purified in water. Thus, this parallel between Biblical and Hittite materials gives support to GIR₄ as "fired clay."

See now Wright 1984: 100–6; 1987: 100–7.

you shall break (tišbōrû). Contaminated earthenware must be broken because its absorbed impurity cannot be removed (*Sipra*, Shemini par. 7:13). This law is consistently maintained (6:21; 15:12). The Mishna reveals the relative cheapness of clay vessels in discussing the evacuation of a fungous house (14:36): "Rabbi Meir said: Which of his goods would it render impure? If you say his articles of wood, cloth, or metal, he may immerse these and they become pure. What does the Torah really have in mind? His earthen vessels, his cruse, and his ewer. If the Torah thus show compassion for his abject *(bāzûy)* property, how much more for the property precious to him" (*m. Neg.* 12:5). For a detailed discussion of the disposal of earthenware in Israel and the ancient Near East, see Wright 1984: 95–112; 1987: 93–113).

34. *that might be eaten.* *ʾăšer yēʾ ākēl,* in other words, edible for man; animal fodder would not be affected (cf. the NOTE on v 37 and *Sipra,* Shemini 9:1). The rabbis interpret this phrase as meaning all that can be eaten with one swallow (approximately the size of an egg); but anything less than that is not subject to contamination (*b. Yoma* 80a). It seems more likely, however, that this phrase connotes permitted food (e.g., 17:13; cf. Eilberg-Schwartz 1986: 216 n. 9), which elsewhere will be described as *ṭāhôr* 'pure', a term that in this chapter is reserved for carcasses whose contact does not defile (see the NOTE on v 37b).

shall become impure (yiṭmāʾ). If it comes into contact with the carcass of one of the enumerated eight species (vv 29–30).

when it comes into contact with water (ʾăšer yābôʾ ʿālāyw mayim). Once wetted by any liquid (*Sipra,* Shemini par. 8:1), food becomes susceptible to impurity—even after it has dried (*b.Ḥul.* 36a). Rashi, however (followed by Noth 1965; Elliger 1966; and others) takes the verse to be a continuation of the preceding one, in other words, that a contaminated earthen vessel defiles the food it contains if water is added to it. This interpretation ostensibly fits better with these words, which literally translate, "that water comes from it," implying that food is contained in a vessel. In fact, this seems to be the way the Dead Sea sectaries interpret this phrase, as they substitute for *yābôʾ* the word *yûṣaq* 'is poured' (11QT 49:7). Nevertheless, *bāʾ ʿal* is equivalent to *nātan ʿal* 'put on' in a later verse (v 39) in which the same item is involved—water contacting an object. Besides, Rashi's interpretation implies that dry food inside a contaminated bowl remains pure, an implication contradicted by v 33. The objection may be raised that this verse cannot be independent of vv 32–33 because it depends on the latter for the information that the defiling carcass fell on the food. But that fact is clearly assumed, in view of v 35a: "Everything else on which the carcass of any of them falls," that is, in addition to the ones mentioned. Thus, this verse comprises the generalization, the susceptibility of water, and v 39, the particular, the wetted seed.

and any liquid that might be drunk. *wĕkol-mašqeh ʾăšer yiššāteh,* in other words, potable liquid. The rabbis limit these liquids to seven: wine, blood, oil, milk, dew, honey, and water (*t. Šabb.* 8:24–28; *m. Mak.* 6:4).

inside any vessel (bĕkol-kĕlî). Conversely, if the liquid is not in a portable container but is embedded in the ground (e.g., an oil or wine vat), it is not a carrier of impurity (v 36; Rashbam). Rashi (followed by Dillmann and Ryssel 1897) continues to interpret this verse as an extension of the previous one, claiming that the liquid stems from a vessel contaminated by the carcass of one of the eight enumerated animals (vv 29–30). Perhaps the disjunctive accent on *yiššāteh* would support him (Kalisch 1867–72). But his interpretation would constitute a redundancy in view of v 33b. Besides, this phrase, "inside any vessel," should logically have been placed at the beginning of the verse, so that the verse would be stating that the contaminated vessel defiles food as well as drink. But as the text stands, Rashi's interpretation implies that only earthen vessels can defile wetted food, whereas all vessels (including earthen ones) can defile only liquids. These inconcinnities are removed once this verse is allowed to stand by itself: wetted food and potable drink are alike susceptible to impurity.

The rabbis ascribe even greater impurity susceptibility to liquids by declaring that their impurity is always of the first remove, even if the contaminating is of a lesser (i.e., second) remove (*t. Yom* 1:6; *m. Para* 8:7). This distinction is even more apparent in the purity rules of Qumran, which declare that a novitiate may partake of the community's dry food after the initial year of probation but of its liquids only after the second year (1QS 6:16–21). For the sectaries of Qumran and the Sadducees, the power of water to transmit impurity was so great that if poured in an unbroken stream from a pure vessel into an impure one, the water would transmit the receiving vessel's impurity "upstream" to the pure vessel (*MMT* B 55–58)—a position that the rabbis categorically rejected (*m. Yad.* 4:7).

Thus, water constitutes an anomalous, indeed, paradoxical status. It is the purifying agent par excellence (v 32b); yet it is most vulnerable to impurity. The only logical answer seems to be that water used for purification (ablution) does indeed become contaminated by the object it is purifying. Hence, it most probably must be drained off without allowing it to come into contact with any person or object.

35. *Everything else. wĕkōl* (with Dillmann and Ryssel 1897), for example, metal vessels not mentioned in v 32. For this usage of *wĕkōl*, see v 23. Otherwise if it were rendered literally as "And all," v 35aα would be a mere repetition of v 32aα. These latter verse segments form an inclusion, a stylistic device also attested in the rest of the chapter (e.g., vv 20, 23; 41aβ, b), which also explains the absence of the datum, contact with the eight carcasses, from v 34 (see above). Thus vv 35aβ–38 constitute a discrete subunit.

oven (tannûr). For baking (Ibn Ezra). On the structure and operation of biblical ovens, see the NOTE on 2:4.

stove (kîrayim). For cooking (Ibn Ezra). A hapax, but frequently used by the rabbis, who claim that this stove contains openings for two pots (*m.Šabb.* 3:1) (hence, the dual formation). Such a stove was indeed discovered at Masada (Avitsur 1976: 116 fig. 307).

shall be smashed (yuttāṣ). A *qal* passive, first recognized by Rabbi Moses the Priest, mentioned by Ibn Ezra (according to Hoffmann 1953). The antonym of the verb *nātaṣ* is *bānâ* 'build' (e.g., Jer 1:10). Hence, *nātaṣ* refers to the destruction of something built (e.g., 14:45; Isa 22:10; Saadiah, Ramban).

Although the oven and stove are also made of earthenware their destruction must be specified lest one reason that because they are embedded in the ground they are not susceptible to impurity (Ramban; and see the NOTES on the next verse) or that because they might not be easily replaceable, they have been conceded as an exception to the rule that contaminated earthenware must be broken (Ehrlich 1908–14).

and impure they shall remain for you (ûṭĕmēʾîm yihyû lākem). The pausal *ʾatnaḥ* precedes this phrase, thereby declaring it a discrete statement. It implies that after the oven or stove is smashed it may not be rebuilt (cf. Jer 18:4; *Keter Torah*). For the form of v 35aβ, b, see vv 10b–11a, 43b, 44a.

36. *spring (maʿyān).* Natural (e.g., Gen 7:11; Josh 15:9; Pss 74:15; 104:10; 114:8).

cistern (bôr). Manmade (e.g., Exod 21:33; Deut 6:11; Jer 2:13; Ps 7:16).

in which water is collected (miqwēh-mayim). As the absence of the copulative indicates, this term is not a discrete container of water (contra LXX, Saadiah, and Ibn Ezra [second opinion]) but is a generalizing apposition to the preceding phrase, necessitated by the fact that *bôr* can also mean a (waterless) "pit" (e.g., Gen 37:20) or "prison" (e.g., Jer 38:6).

shall remain pure (yihyeh ṭāhôr). Because they are embedded in the ground (*b. Šabb.* 81a [bar.]). The use of the adjective *ṭāhôr* instead of the verb *yiṭhar* (cf. v 32b) indicates that the status quo continues unchanged (see the NOTE on "it remains pure," v 37).

however. ʾak denotes the restriction, contrast, or qualification of a preceding idea (Snaith 1964); cf. v 4; 21:23; 23:39; 27:26, 28. The referent is clearly v 34.

such a carcass (bĕniblātām). When one of the eight carcasses is in the water, though the water remains pure, the carcass defiles whatever contacts it (*Sipra,* Shemini par. 9:5).

37. *seed grain (zeraʿ zērûaʿ).* Inedible grain, in contrast to *hāʾōkel ʾăšer yēʾākēl* 'edible food' (v 34; Ramban). *zērûaʿ* is not an adjective but a noun, as in *zērûʿêhā* 'its seed' (Isa 61:11; cf. also *zērōʿîm, zērʿōnîm* 'seeds', Dan 1:12, 16, cited by Rashi, Ibn Ezra, Rashbam).

that is to be sown (ʾăšer yizzārēaʿ). That is, the grain is loose, but once it is in the ground, it cannot be rendered impure (*Sipra,* Shemini 11:3).

it remains pure (ṭāhôr hûʾ). As long as it is dry (*Tg. Ps.-J.*). The use of the adjective instead of a verbal form (cf. v 32b) indicates that its condition remains unchanged (see the NOTE on "shall remain pure," v 36).

38. *is put (yuttan).* Another *qal* passive (cf. *yuttaṣ,* v 35; *śōrāp,* 10:16; *zōraq,* Num 19:13; *šuppak,* Num 35:33). *mayim* 'water' is treated as a collective and, hence, takes a singular verb (e.g., Num 19:13).

on the seed (ʿal-zeraʿ). That is, the loose and inedible seed of v 37. "For if you claim that there is susceptibility to impurity for things embedded (in the soil), you will never find a seed that has not become susceptible" (Rashi). "Else there would be no pure plant whatever, for there is none, near or upon which some impure swarming creature is not found" (Rashi on v 34; cf. *Sipra,* Shemini 11:3; *b. Ḥul.* 118b).

The basic principle is that the earth and everything that is embedded in it, such as cisterns (v 36) and planted seeds (v 37), are not susceptible to impurity. But objects unattached to the land such as vessels (vv 32–33), solid food (v 34a), potable drink (v 34b), and loose seed (v 38) are susceptible. The sole exceptions are earthenware ovens or stoves, even if they are embedded in the ground (v 35b). Strikingly, in various Hindu sects (e.g., Assamese), the soaking of grain also renders it permeable to impurity (Hayley 1980: 115).

39. *has died. yāmût*, that is, naturally. But if it has been slaughtered properly as a sacrifice (17:3–7) or if it was brought down as game (17:13–14), it is not considered a *nĕbēlâ* and does not convey impurity. This verse proves indirectly that this interpolation (see below) does not permit profane slaughter and, hence, cannot stem from P, which does not hold that all animals eligible for the altar had to be offered on the altar (see the Introduction, §C). Note that in Zoroastrianism and Hinduism, carcasses killed for sacrifice do not defile (Boyce 1975: 302; Manu 5.39).

anyone who touches it shall be impure until evening (hannōgēaʿ bĕniblātāh yiṭmāʾ ʿad-hāʿāreb). On the verse "For in respect of the fate of man and the fate of beast, they have one and the same fate: as the one dies so dies the other . . . man has no superiority over beast" (Qoh 3:19), the rabbis comment wryly, "Just as man defiles by touch when he dies (Num 19:11) so a beast defiles by touch when it dies. Moreover, the beast is in reality superior to man since one who touches a human corpse is impure for seven days but one who touches the beast's carcass is only impure until evening" (*Letters of R. Akiba* in Wertheimer 1955: 2.381; cf. *Midr. Tanḥ.* Emor 21).

40. *and anyone who eats of its carcass.* Why need this be mentioned when it is obvious that if a person who touches or carries a carcass is rendered impure (see the NOTE on v 27), all the more so if he eats of it? Furthermore, as eating was omitted in the case of an impure animal carcass (vv 24–28), why was the case of the pure animal included here? The answer is obvious: whereas a person would hardly be expected to eat the carcass of an impure quadruped, he might not hesitate to eat the carcass of a pure quadruped on the assumption that it was properly slaughtered. Hence, there was a need to specify that the required purification was equivalent to (but not severer than) that required of one who carried the carcass (Ramban).

and anyone who carries its carcass (wĕhannōśēʾ ʾet-niblātāh). The midrash plays on the verb *nōśēʾ*, reading it as *nōśēʾ* 'forget' (cf. Jer 23:39) and deriving from it that this impurity is contracted "regardless if it took place deliberately or accidentally" (Wertheimer 1955: 266)—a reminder that intention is not a coefficient of impurity (see chap. 4, COMMENT B).

It has already been observed (NOTES on 5:2 and 7:21, 24) that originally the carcass of a pure animal did not defile by touch. At this juncture, it would be apt to summarize the evidence: (1) 5:2 deals with impurity arising from contact *bĕniblat ḥayyâ ṭĕmēʾâ ʾô bĕniblat bĕhēmâ ṭĕmēʾâ ʾô bĕniblat šereṣ ṭāmēʾ* '[with] the carcass of an impure wild quadruped or the carcass of an impure domesticated quadruped or the carcass of an impure swarming creature'. Thus this verse implies, by omission, that the carcasses of pure wild quadrupeds (e.g., 17:13–14; Deut 14:5), pure domesticated quadrupeds (e.g., Deut 14:4), and pure swarming creatures (e.g., 11:21–22) do not defile by touch. (2) The same conclusion must be derived from 7:21, dealing with one who "touches anything impure, be it human impurity or an impure quadruped or any impure detestable creature." Once again pure quadrupeds are omitted from this list, the implication being that their carcasses do not defile by touch. (3) If the suet from the carcass of a pure quadruped may be utilized in man's service (7:24), clearly it does not defile. (4) The only creatures in chap. 11 whose carcasses expressly defile by touch are the impure quadrupeds (vv 4–8, 24–28), the eight named rodents and reptiles (vv 29–38), and the pure quadrupeds (vv 39–40). But the first two categories are distinguishable by being called *ṭāmēʾ*, whereas all others in the chapter are referred to as *šeqeṣ*, the latter term implying only that their ingestion is forbidden but they do not defile. The pericope on pure quadrupeds that defile by touch (vv 39–40), however, does not contain the adjective *ṭāmēʾ* and, moreover, is out of place (belonging logically after v 28 instead of interrupting the section on the *šereṣ*, 29–38, 41–42). (5) Impurity is contracted by a priest if he touches *bĕkol-šereṣ ʾăšer yiṭmāʾ-lô* 'any swarming creature by which he is made impure' (22:5). As there are swarming creatures whose touch does not defile (all but the eight rodents and reptiles, 11:29–30), it stands to reason that a similar distinction exists among the other animal species, namely, that some of their carcasses do not defile by touch. Moreover, as the priest is only forbidden to eat a carcass (22:8) it can be deduced that touching is not forbidden. Otherwise, the prohibition would have been against touching, and eating would have been deduced a fortiori. As will be shown (COMMENT A below), the original kernel of this chapter dealt solely with an enumeration of the prohibited animals as food (quadrupeds, vv 1–8; fish, vv 9–12; birds, vv 13–23, and reptiles, vv 41–43) and the section on purification procedures imposed for *handling* the carcasses of impure quadrupeds and eight creatures (vv 24–38) was a later insertion. It therefore follows that vv 39–40, which declare that the carcasses of pure animals defile by touch (and portage) as well as by ingestion (plus the final section, vv 43–47, see below) belong to the last stage in the development of this chapter. For details, see COMMENT A below.

The Dead Sea covenanters and the Sadducees held that the skins and bones of a pure carcass (not to speak of an impure one; see the NOTE on v 24) as well as its flesh transmit impurity (11QT 51:4–5; *MMT* B 22–23; cf. *m. Yad.* 4:6). The rabbis, however, restricted impurity contagion exclusively to the flesh (*m. Ḥul.* 9:12).

shall launder his clothes (yĕkabbēs bĕgādāyw). The LXX (Old Greek) adds the equivalent of *wĕrāḥaṣ bammayim* 'and he shall bathe in water'—a superfluous addition because it must be assumed. "In the Torah, there is no laundering that does not require [bodily] immersion" (*Mek.* Yitro 3).

41. *All creatures that swarm upon the earth (wĕkol-haššereṣ haššōrēṣ ʿal-hāʾāreṣ).* The third and final category of "swarmers" (the first being the fish, *šereṣ hammayim,* vv 9–12, and the second, the flying insects, *šereṣ hāʿôp,* vv 20–23) is divided into three subcategories: the creeping, the four-footed, and the many-footed (v 42a). The eight named rodents and reptiles (vv 29–30) are theoretically included in this category (Ibn Ezra, Ramban), but not being *šeqes* clearly do not belong. Besides, it is anomalous to find the exceptions (vv 29–30) listed ahead of the main category (see COMMENT A below).

are an abomination; they shall not be eaten (šeqeṣ hû lōʾ yēʾākēl). The use of *šeqeṣ,* as explained (NOTE on v 11), means that ingestion is forbidden but not defiling. This is again demonstrated by the following epexegetical comment: "they shall not be eaten" (see also v 42b).

42. *belly.* gāḥôn (Gen 3:14). In most MSS the *waw* is written large; it is the middle letter of the Pentateuch (*b. Qidd.* 30a; Sopherim 9:2).

comprising (lĕkol). See the NOTE on "every quadruped," v 26.

comprising all creatures that swarm on the earth, for they are an abomination (lĕkol-haššereṣ haššōrēṣ ʿal-hāʾāreṣ lōʾ tōʾkĕlûm kî-šeqeṣ hēm). A chiastic reprise of v 41, thus indicating stylistically that vv 41–42 form an organic unit: the three species of land swarmers framed by an inclusio structure in chiastic form, whose most significant consequence is that the following verse (v 43) heads up a new unit. The purpose of the repetition is not just literary but ideological. It stresses that in contradistinction to the other animal categories (quadrupeds, birds, and fish), which have permissible species, all of the swarming creatures are forbidden as food. Note that the word *kōl* 'every, all' occurs six times in vv 41–43. This distinction is carried out in exactly the same manner in 20:25, where again only the land swarmers are defined by the particle *kōl.*

43–44. These two verses reveal a symmetric, introverted structure, which aids significantly in their exegesis, as follows:

43   A   *ʾal-tĕšaqqĕṣû ʾet-napšōtêkem bĕkol-haššereṣ haššōrēṣ [ʿal-hāʾāreṣ]*
          B$_1$ *wĕlōʾ tiṭṭammĕʾû bāhem wĕniṭmētem bām*
44   B$_2$ *kî ʾănî YHWH ʾĕlōhêkem*
          B′$_1$ *wĕhitqaddištem wihĕyîtem qĕdōšîm*
          B′$_2$ *kî qādôs ʾănî [ʾĕlōhêkem]*
       A′   *wĕlōʾ tĕṭammĕʾû ʾet-napšōtêkem bĕkol-haššereṣ hārōmēś ʿal-hāʾāreṣ*

43   A   You shall not defile your throats with any creature that swarms [upon the earth].
          B$_1$ You shall not make yourselves impure therewith and thus become impure,
44   B$_2$ for I the Lord am your God.
          B′$_1$ You shall sanctify yourselves and be holy,
          B′$_2$ for I [your God] am holy.

A' You shall not contaminate your throats with any swarming creature that moves upon the earth.

The chiastic arrangement leads to the following main observations: (1) The inclusion (AA') is identical in meaning; hence the different verbs *šiqqēṣ* and *ṭimmēʾ* are synonymous. Their synonymity contrasts sharply with their discrete meanings in the previous verses, an indication that another source is operative here. (2) The *kî* clauses (B₂B'₂) are rationales for the immediately preceding statements, indicating a need for reversification: v 43 should end with v 44aα and v 44 should begin with v 44aβ. (3) The injunction to Israel to refrain from impurity is justified by its imperative to attain holiness (B₁B'₁). These injunctions are similarly structured, leading to the firm conclusion that MT's hapax *wĕniṭmētem* should be read *wĕniṭmēʾtem* 'and become impure'. (4) The reconstructed words, in brackets, are explained in the NOTES, below.

43. *You shall not defile (ʾal-tĕšaqqĕṣû).* The denominative of *šeqeṣ* 'abomination' appeared earlier (vv 11, 13) but with the impure carcass as its object. Here, however, it appears with the object *nepeš*, which clearly refers to the person and not his food. It corresponds and, hence, is synonymous with *wĕlōʾ tĕtammĕʾû* 'you shall not contaminate' (v 44b), for the latter also has the same object, *nepeš*. The fact that this verb, *šiqqēṣ*, has a different connotation than that found earlier in the chapter (where it means "abominate") and that, moreover, its use is identical to that found in 20:25b, is an indication that these two verses (vv 43–44)—most likely part of the same source as 20:25b—were added later to the chapter (see the NOTES below and COMMENT A). *šiqqēṣ/šeqeṣ* always concerns ingestion, as recognized by the rabbis (*b. Meʿil.* 16b; Rashi); see the NOTES on vv 10, 11.

your throats (ʾet-napšōtêkem). Earlier it was established that the noun *šeqeṣ* and its denominative verb *šiqqēṣ* refer to the abomination resulting from eating (but not touching) impure animal food (see the NOTE on vv 10, 11). This conclusion is supported in this verse by the word *nepeš*. Although it can, and often does, refer to a person (e.g., 2:1; 4:2; 5:1, 4; 7:20, 27; 15:17; 17:11; 22:11) and, hence, could in this instance be rendered "your own persons, yourselves," the context of ingestion of impure food favors the more limited notion of *nepeš* as referring to the digestive system, more specifically, the throat. This meaning is amply attested in Scripture (e.g., Num 21:5; Isa 5:14; 29:8; 32:6; 55:2; 58:11; Jer 2:12; 3:12, 14, 25; Jonah 2:6; Hab 2:5; Pss 63:6; 69:2; 124:4–5). Particularly impressive is Ezekiel's comment: "my throat is undefiled *(napšî lōʾ mĕṭummāʾâ);* from my youth till now I have not eaten the flesh of a carcass *(nĕbēlâ)* or of an animal torn by wild beasts, nor has fouled meat entered my mouth" (Ezek 4:14). Not only is the context identical—the ingestion of forbidden meat—but the idiom is precisely the same, *ṭimmēʾ (= šiqqēṣ) ʾet-hannepeš* (cf. v 44b) 'contaminate the throat'. That the identical phrase also occurs in 20:25b is an indication of the possibility that these two verses (vv 43–44) belong to H; see the NOTES below and COMMENT A.

any creature that swarms (bĕkol-haššereṣ haššōrēṣ). The LXX and Pesh. add *ʿal-hāʾāreṣ* 'on the land', which would then allow v 43a to form an inclusio with v 44b. In support of this view are the previous context, the expressed statement of v 44b, and the fact that the subject matter here is not all swarming creatures (which would include the fish and the flying insects, some of which are pure, vv 9, 21–22) but only those which swarm on the land (none of which are pure; see below).

[you shall not] make yourselves impure [therewith]([wĕlōʾ] tiṭṭammĕʾû [bāhem]). A *hithpaʿel* (cf. v 24; 18:24, 30; 21:1, 3, 4, 11; Num 6:7). In distinction to the earlier verses, *ṭāmēʾ/ṭimmēʾ* here connotes defiling not by touch (e.g., v 24), but by ingestion (Rashi, correctly)—a concept conveyed in the previous verses by *šeqeṣ/šiqqēṣ* (see the NOTE on vv 10, 11)—further evidence that this verse (and the following) belong to a different source; see below.

and thus become impure (wĕnitmētem bām). Or "lest you become impure"; the particle *loʾ* in the previous sentence (v 43bα) does double duty and applies here as well (e.g., 19:29; 22:9; Driver 1892: §115, p. 133). The *aleph* missing in the verb is supplied by the Sam. (for similar omissions, see Gen 20:6; Deut 1:12; Isa 13:20; Ps 18:40). Some exegetes, however, would regard the MT correct as it stands, either deriving it from the root *ṭmh* (e.g., Job 18:3—a hapax) or deriving it from *ṭmm* (reading *nĕṭammōnû*), the equivalent of rabbinic *ṭmṭm* 'stupid, dumb' (so interpreted in *b. Yoma* 39a, and by Saadiah, Ibn Ezra [second explanation], and Radak), the idea being that the consumption of forbidden meat leads to mental obtuseness (an idea promulgated by Philo and later interpreters; see COMMENT E below).

The very structure of this verse, however, favors the former interpretation: *wĕlōʾ tiṭṭammĕʾû bāhem wĕniṭmē[ʾ]tem bām* contrasts in meaning with but is parallel in structure to *wĕhitqaddištem wihĕyîtem qĕdōšîm* 'you shall sanctify yourselves and be holy' (v 44b). Both phrases employ roots that occur twice, the first in the *hithpaʿel* and the second in a passive formation (Hoffmann 1953). A more exact parallel lies in *ʾal-tiṭṭammĕʾû . . . niṭmĕʾû* 'do not make yourselves impure . . . became impure' (18:24), where the same root, *ṭmʾ,* recurs and in the same verb patterns, *hithpaʿel* and *niphʿal.* Thus the rendering "became impure" is mandated here, which also allows the added inference that this verse belongs to the same source as that of 18:24.

The question remains, why the emphasis on the repulsiveness of the land-swarming creatures, which far exceeds that of the previously mentioned creatures? That these verses (43–44) stem from another source really begs the question, for it still could be asked: Why did this source single out the swarming creatures? The answer (Eerdmans 1912: 65) probably lies in the unique nature of the *šereṣ hāʾāreṣ.* In contradistinction to all other categories, which can boast of at least several permitted creatures (quadrupeds, v 3; Deut 14:4; fish, v 9;

birds, Deut 11:11; flying insects, vv 21–22), the land swarmers allow for no exceptions—all (*běkol;* six times in vv 41–43) are forbidden. Hence they are decisively abhorred. Furthermore, the land swarmers are ubiquitous, especially in the kitchens or wherever food is stored (see the NOTES on v 32). Yet these reasons still do not explain why all land swarmers were eschewed and none were allowed.

For a possible answer one must resort to the speculative but cogent explanation proffered by Paschen (1970: 58). Earth (*'ereṣ*) can denote *šě'ōl* 'the underworld', the abode of the dead (e.g., Exod 15:12; Jer 17:13; Jonah 2:7; Pss 22:30; 71:20), also Ugaritic *arṣ* (e.g., *KTU* 1.10, 2.24) and Akk. *erṣetu* (*CAD*, E 310). Even more to the point is that *'āpār,* usually rendered "dust," at times denotes "the grave" or "the underworld" (e.g., Isa 26:19; Ps 22:16, 30; Job 7:21; 10:9; 17:16; 20:11; Dan 12:2; cf. Ridderbos 1948). Thus, it is the association with the earth, the sphere of death, that led to the exclusion of all land swarmers from Israel's diet. This explanation, admittedly speculative for the present, will take on added force once it is demonstrated that all ritual impurity, embedded and legislated in chaps. 11–15, has this as its common denominator: the association with death. Perhaps for this reason, the call to holiness is attached to the blanket prohibition of all land swarmers. As will be shown (COMMENT E below), because the antonym of *ṭāmē'* 'impure' is *qādōš* 'holy', then if the former stands for the forces of death, the latter symbolizes the forces of life. Israel, then, is commanded here to desist from land swarmers, the denizens of the sphere of death, by keeping in mind that its task is to be holy, to seek life, for its God is holy: he is the source of life. For a fuller substantiation of this thesis, see chap. 12, COMMENT B and chap. 15, COMMENT G.

44. *for I the Lord am your God (kî 'ănî YHWH 'ělōhêkem).* YHWH is part of the subject, as shown by v 45a (Hoffmann 1953). This is a phrase that is typical of H and its dependencies: without *kî* (18:2, 4, 30; 19:3, 4, 10, 25, 31, 34, 36; 20:24; 23:22, 43; 25:38, 55; 26:13; Exod 29:46b; Num 10:10; 15:41 *bis;* Ezek 20:5, 7, 19); with *kî* (20:7; 24:22; 25:17; 26:1, 44); with *kî* and as object of the verb *yāda'* 'know' (Exod 6:7; 16:12; 29:46a; Ezek 20:20; 28:26; 34:30; 39:22, 28). As indicated by these citations from H (with *kî*), this phrase always provides the rationale for the previous statement. Thus it must be connected with 43b, a fact further supported by the structure of vv 43–44 (see above). It declares that the reason Israel must abstain from eating land swarmers is that its God has forbidden it. A second reason—holiness—follows.

You shall sanctify yourselves and be holy. wěhitqaddištem wihyîtem qědōšîm, literally, "you shall make yourselves holy so that you will be holy" (see 20:7). This statement is parallel in structure and opposite in meaning to v 43b: Israel must not contaminate itself by ingesting land swarmers because holiness, the goal it must seek, cannot coexist with impurity. That Israel is commanded to be holy is the main thrust of H (chaps. 17–26; cf. Num 15:40). Israel can become holy (which it is not at present, the position of D) by obedience to God's moral and ritual commandments (cf. chap. 19 and the Introduction to vol. 2). This objective is adumbrated in earlier sources (Exod 19:6; 22:30) but is assiduously avoided—and, by implication, denied—by P, which holds that only the priests (and temporary Nazirites) are holy. On the significance of these additions from H, see COMMENT A below.

for I am holy (kî qādôš 'ănî). The reason that Israel must aspire to holiness is *imitatio dei.* This rationale is applied to these diet laws once again (20:26; cf. v 25) and is discussed in COMMENT E below. Note that in Leviticus, *qādôš* (full) always refers to God but *qādōš* (defective) always refers to man (cf. 11:44–45; 19:2; 20:7, 26; 21:6–8; Hoffmann 1953). The LXX adds *YHWH 'ĕlōhêkem*, which gives the complete formula as found elsewhere (e.g., 19:2) but which, more importantly, balances its counterpart (B'_2 of the scheme above). The fact that this truncated form also appears in v 45b may have influenced its formation here. Even there, however, reconstruction may be required; see below.

You shall not contaminate your throats (wĕlō' tĕṭammĕ'û 'et-napšōtêkem). The counterpart to v 43aα with two slight variations: the negative particle is *lō'* rather than *'al,* and the verb is *ṭimmē'* instead of *šiqqēṣ.* The switch to *lō'* is significant in that it indicates that the prohibition is permanently binding (see the NOTES on 10:6, 7, 9). The use of *ṭimmē'* as a synonym of *šiqqēṣ* indicates a different source from the previous verses of this chapter, in which these two terms differed radically in meaning (see the NOTE on "make yourselves impure," v 43, above).

that moves (hārōmēś). The counterpart to and synonym of *haššōrēṣ* 'that swarms' (v 43aβ). It is found frequently with the object *'al-hā'āreṣ* (cf. Gen 1:26, 28, 30; 7:14, 21; 8:17, 19) and also with *'al-hā'ădāmâ* (cf. Gen 7:8; Ezek 38:20) or in construct with *'ădāmâ* (cf. 20:25; Gen 9:2). That the verb *rāmaś* can mean "move, stir" and, hence, apply to all animals and not just to creepers; see Gen 7:21; 9:3 for land animals and Gen 1:21; Ps 69:35 for sea creatures; see also the NOTE on this word in v 46.

45. *For I the Lord (kî 'ănî YHWH).* A favorite expression (with or without *kî*) in H (18:5, 6, 21; 19:12, 14, 16, 18, 28, 30, 32, 37; 21:12; 22:2, 3, 8, 30, 31, 33; 26:2, 45; cf. Exod 6:2, 6, 8, 29; 12:12; Num 3:15, 45). The Sam. and Pesh. add *'ĕlōhêkem* (see v 44aα). Nevertheless, the lack of this word at the end of this verse militates against adding it here. The MT reveals that this phrase forms an inclusio with the end of the verse, as follows:

A   *kî 'ănî YHWH*

    X *hamma'ăleh 'etkem mē'ereṣ miṣrayim lihyôt lākem lē'lōhîm. wihyîtem qĕdōšîm*

A'   *kî qādôš 'ănî [YHWH]*

am he who brought you up (hammaʿăleh). This is the only place in P or H that uses this verb in this context. Elsewhere we find the verb *hôṣîʾ*, both in the perfect (25:38, 42; Exod 29:46; Num 15:41) and as a participle, *môṣîʾ* (22:33; Exod 6:7). The use of the participle with God as the subject is typical of H (e.g., 21:8, 15, 23; 22:33).

from the land of Egypt. This motif is linked with the Passover (Exod 12; Deut 16:1), the pilgrimage festivals (23:43; Deut 16:3, 12), the return from Babylon (Isa 51:10), the obligation to obey the Lord's commandments (19:36; 26:13), the injunction to attain holiness (11:45; 22:33; Num 15:41), and laws concerning the redemption of slaves (25:38, 42, 45). Above all, the Lord's redemption of Israel from the land of Egypt means, in legal terms, that the ownership of Israel is transferred from Pharaoh to God (26:12–13; Exod 20:2) and Israel now must serve him (25:42, 55) and, hence, obey all his commands (Daube 1963: 442–46). For further details, especially on its legal background in the ancient Near East, see the COMMENT on chap. 25.

you shall be holy, for I am holy (wihyîtem qĕdōšîm kî qādôš ʾănî). The LXX adds "the Lord," needed to make this statement an inclusio with v 45a. It would also be precisely equivalent to 20:26a, which, strikingly, is also attached to and is the rationale for the animal-food prohibitions (20:25)—another indication that vv 43–44 belong to H.

46. *These are the instructions (zōʾt tôrat)*. There are a total of twelve Priestly *tôrôt*: eight in Leviticus and four in Numbers. This *tôrâ* is the only one not directly involved with priestly concerns; but the function of the priest is to teach the *tôrâ* to Israel, in this case, the distinctions between pure and impure animals (v 47). Hence, what the priests teach, the laity observe (see also the NOTE on 6:2). This expression, *zōʾt tôrat*, is found in 6:2, 7, 18; 7:1, 11; 14:2; Num 6:13; in the absolute in 7:37; 14:54; Num 19:14; and as a subscript, as here, in 12:7; 13:59; 14:32, 57; and 15:32. The subscripts frequently resume the title lines, as can be seen by comparing v 2 with v 46; 15:2 with 15:33; 13:2 with 14:56; Num 5:12, 14 with 5:29–30; Josh 20:2 with 20:9 (Fishbane 1980: 441–42). The resumptive subscript is also characteristic of Hittite texts. The Papanikra text begins "thus speaks the priest of the land Kummanni: 'If a woman sits on the birth stool . . . and the dish broke . . .' " (1.1–3) and it ends "If a woman sits on the birth stool and the dish broke. This is the word of Papanikri, the priest from Kummanni" (4.37–40; Sommer and Eheloff 1924). The ritual of Zarpiya of Kizzuwatna against pestilence opens "Thus [said] Zarpiya. . . . If the year is bad and there is constant dying . . ." and concludes "Word of Zarpiya: if the year is bad and there is constant dying" (Schwartz 1938).

birds, all living creatures that move in the water. The order of fish and birds (vv 9–12, 13–19) is here reversed, probably for aesthetic, literary reasons. In this way v 46b is composed of two symmetrically balanced parts: creatures of the water and creatures of the earth. The absence of the generic *dāgâ* 'fish', attested in the creation story (Gen 1:26, 28), clearly indicates that the latter was not the model for this subscript's author who, instead, followed the language of v 10b—with the exception of *hārōmeśet* (see below).

move (hārōmeśet). For this rendering see the NOTE on v 44. Here it is clearly the semantic equivalent of *haššōreṣet* 'swarm'. Again, literary grounds mandated the use of a synonym to avoid duplicating both the subject and the verb. To be sure, the writer might have avoided the repetition by writing *wĕkol nepeš haḥayyâ haššōreṣet bammayim wĕʿal-hāʾāres* 'all living creatures that swarm in the water and on the land', but that would have broken the symmetrical balance he wanted to attain. The use of *rōmēś* for fish is attested in Gen 1:21.

and all creatures (ûlĕkol-nepeš). Here the *lamed* is emphatic (see the NOTE on "every quadruped," v 26). The *lamed* coming at the end of a series is conjunctive in force, but stronger than the *waw* and, thus, may also be rendered "including" (Milgrom 1970a: nn. 237, 262, 279).

47. *for discriminating (lĕhabdîl).* Creation, according to P, was the product of God making distinctions (Gen 1:4, 6, 7, 14, 18). This divine function is to be continued by Israel: the priests to teach it (10:10–11) and the people to practice it (cf. Ezek 22:26). The purpose of the discriminations that Israel must impose on the animal world is not explained here. But the rationale is stated unambiguously in 20:25–26, "You shall distinguish *(wĕhibdaltem)* the pure quadruped from the impure, the impure bird from the pure. You shall not defile your throats with a quadruped or bird or anything that moves [on] the earth, which I have set apart *(hibdaltî)* for you to treat as impure . . . and I have set you apart *(wāʾabdāl)* from all other peoples to be mine." The animal world mirrors the human. The separation of the animals into the pure and the impure is both a model and a lesson for Israel to separate itself from the nations. The latter have defiled themselves by their idolatry and immorality. Israel must, therefore, refrain from partaking of their practices and, thereby, become eligible for a life of holiness—the way and nature of its God (see further COMMENT E below).

For H, which enjoins the attainment of holiness upon all Israel, the diet laws are indispensable, not just as a heuristic and disciplinary regimen but as a constitutive and integral element of holiness itself. As impurity and holiness are antithetical states, Israel can *eo ipso* not be holy if it defiles itself with impure forces. The result of such defilement is also spelled out: expulsion from the land (20:22–23), a national form of *kārēt* (18:29). This notion that Israel's land tenure is dependent on its collective practice of separation and holiness is solely the teaching of H. It is not to be found in this verse, the product of a P tradent (see COMMENT A below) who, in consonance with P's ideology, implicitly denies that holiness is a desirable goal for Israel or that its land tenure is dependent on its abstention from impure forces. Rather, P inculcates that holiness is confined to the sanctuary, its sancta, and its officiants. Only within this sacred sphere is the one defiled by a carcass subject to *kārēt*, a penalty that befalls the individual sinner but not the nation. Everywhere else, however, this impurity is of no great consequence, and by evening it is gone. Further discussion of this seminal verb, *hibdîl*, is reserved for the NOTE on 20:24.

between the impure and the pure (bên haṭṭāmēʾ ûbên haṭṭāhôr). If the reference here is to the ingestion of animal flesh, then v 47b becomes sheer redundancy. The deduction is ineluctable that the subject here is the only other one specified in this chapter—contact with animal carcasses. Corroboration is supplied by the fact that the word *ṭāmēʾ* 'impure' is used exclusively with regard to the carcasses that defile by touch, namely, the quadrupeds (vv 4–8, 24–28, 39–40) and the eight named rodents and reptiles (vv 29–38). Further supporting this deduction is this verse's chiastic structure (see the NOTE below). Another deduction from this phrase is that the subscript is the work of the final editor of this chapter, for it presumes the presence of vv 29–38 (and 39–40?), which were inserted at a secondary stage in the development of this chapter; for details, see COMMENT A below. That this subscript is the work of the P school and not of H is underscored by the use of *ṭāmēʾ* and *ṭāhôr* to describe defilement by contact and not by ingestion (see below and COMMENT A).

between creatures that may be eaten and creatures that may not be eaten (ûbên haḥayyâ hanneʾĕkelet ûbên haḥayyâ ʾăšer lōʾ tēʾākēl). The permitted and prohibited animals here stand in chiastic relation to the terms "impure" and "pure" in the beginning verse. This technique is more graphically evident in the one other subscript referring to the animal-food prohibitions: *wĕhibdaltem bên habbĕhēmâ haṭṭĕhōrâ laṭṭĕmēʾâ ûbên-hāʿôp haṭṭāmēʾ laṭṭāhōr* 'you shall discriminate between the pure and impure quadruped and between the impure and pure bird' (20:25a). One should also note that the chiasm can be explained on logical as well as stylistic grounds. In both attestations of this chiasm (11:47; 20:25), *ṭāmēʾ* precedes *ṭāhôr* when the impure species are less numerous, and *ṭāhôr* (or its equivalent, as in this verse) precedes when the pure species are less numerous. The reason is that one always sets aside the lesser quantity from the larger one (Ḥazzequni on 20:25). Thus the permitted creatures are fewer than the forbidden ones, whereas the impure creatures (by touch, not by ingestion!) are fewer than the pure ones. Similarly, in 20:25 pure quadrupeds are fewer than impure ones (Deut 14:4–5), whereas impure birds are fewer than pure ones (see the NOTE on Lev 11:13). Ḥazzequni's insight is corroborated by another chiastic structure involving *ṭāmēʾ* and *ṭāhôr*, that with *qōdeš* and *ḥōl* (10:10; Ezek 22:26; 44:23): the smaller quantities of *qōdeš* and *ṭāmēʾ* precede the larger quantities of *ḥōl* and *ṭāhôr*, respectively.

The conclusion of 20:25 is illuminating: *ʾăšer-hibdaltî lākem lĕṭammēʾ* 'which I have set apart for you to treat as impure'. In this verse and, indeed, in H to which this verse belongs, the distinction preserved in P that *ṭāmēʾ* refers to defilement by contact (cf. also 5:2) and not by eating (for which *šeqeṣ/šiqqēṣ* is used; see the NOTE on v 11), is no longer upheld: *šeqeṣ/šiqqēṣ* and *ṭāmēʾ/ṭimmēʾ* are indistinguishable, both referring to ingestion (cf. 20:25; 22:8) as in v 44. The same holds true for the terminological distinction between the permitted animals: edible ones are *hanneʾĕkelet* 'that may be eaten', and those whose contact does not defile are *haṭṭāhōr* 'pure'. This distinction is consistently preserved in the P sections: *ʾākal* (vv 2, 3, 4, 9, 21, 22; see esp. 34 and 39); *ṭāhōr* (vv 32, vessels; 36, water; 37, seed). Later, this differentiation is effaced in H (and in D; see COMMENT B below), where *ṭāhōr* describes edible animals (20:25).

COMMENTS: DIET LAWS

A. The Composition of Lev 11

Chapter 11 exhibits the following sequence of animal categories: quadrupeds (vv 2–8), fish (vv 9–12), birds (vv 13–19), flying insects (vv 20–23), quadrupeds (vv 24–28), land swarmers (vv 29–38), quadrupeds (vv 39–40), land swarmers (vv 41–45), all animals (vv 46–47). The offending category here is the quadrupeds. Had they been grouped together, then each category would have been a discrete unit: quadrupeds (vv 2–8, 24–28, 39–40), fish (vv 9–12), birds (vv 13–19), flying insects (vv 20–23), land swarmers (vv 29–38, 41–45), all animals (vv 46–47). Nevertheless, there is logic to the MT if subject matter is taken into consideration: whereas vv 2–23, 41–45 define or declare which animals are impure, vv 29–40 ordain purification procedures in case of defilement. Thus the ordering of chap. 11, taking into account both subject and content, actually looks like this:

Impure Animals	Purification Procedures
quadrupeds (vv 2–8)	
fish (vv 9–12)	
birds (vv 13–19)	
flying insects (vv 20–23)	
	forbidden quadrupeds (vv 24–28)
	eight land swarmers (vv 29–38)
	permitted quadrupeds (vv 39–40)
land swarmers (vv 41–45)	

Clearly, the repeated animal categories comprise a unified bloc (vv 24–40) and are informed by a different subject matter—purification. Moreover, once they are excised from the chapter, an orderly sequence of animal categories is revealed: quadrupeds (vv 2–8), fish (vv 9–12), birds (vv 13–19), flying insects (vv 20–23), and land swarmers (vv 41–45). Thus a traditionalist like Hoffmann (1953) is forced to admit that the passage on land swarmers (vv 41–45) should logically belong after flying insects (vv 20–23). The bloc on purification (vv 24–40) also manifests inconcinnity, and Ramban (on v 24) cannot but question why its two sections on quadrupeds (vv 24–28, 39–40) were not grouped together. Thus, a priori, the conclusion can be drawn, however tentatively, that the purification bloc (vv 24–40) constitutes a later insert into the chapter. Furthermore, as its two passages on quadrupeds are not contiguous, the second one (vv 39–40) may itself be a later supplement to the bloc.

One might be tempted to justify the order in the MT on the following grounds: just as birds (vv 13–19) and flying insects (vv 20–23) are grouped together because they are winged creatures, so are quadrupeds (vv 24–28) and swarmers (vv 29–38) because they are land animals. Yet this reasoning only adds fuel to the insert hypothesis. Precisely because the author of vv 24–38 found this sequence in the existing text (vv 13–23), he gave a similar form to his own material before he inserted it. Besides, this observation only underscores why vv 39–40 must have been added subsequently to the purification bloc: they fit into no sequence, either in the bloc or in the rest of the chapter.

Bible critics have long been aware of the disorder present in Lev 11. Wellhausen (1885; 4th ed. 1963: 148) deduces that vv 24–40 were a later insert on the ground that this bloc dealt with impure animals that were ṭāmēʾ and not šeqeṣ, the term used in the rest of the chapter. He was rebutted by Eerdmans (1912: 60), who pointed out that the four named quadrupeds (vv 4–8), belonging to the main part of the chapter, are also called ṭāmēʾ. Nevertheless, it turns out that Wellhausen was correct even if he gave the wrong reason. The bloc, vv 24–40, is an insert because it deals with a different topic, purification from defilement by contact, and because it interrupts the sequence of prohibited animal foods (vv 2–23, 41–42).

The demonstration that vv 24–40 are an insert must begin with a glance at the comparable inventory of forbidden animals in Deut 14. Its detailed examination is the subject of COMMENT B below. It suffices here solely to note that its sequence of animal categories is precisely the same: quadrupeds (vv 4–8), fish (vv 9–10), birds (vv 11–18), flying insects (vv 19–20), and carcasses of pure animals (v 21). A word of explanation on the last two categories is needed (for more comprehensive treatment see COMMENT B). The flying insects, ʿôp—in distinction to ṣippôr 'birds'—are neatly capsuled into two verses: the first rules out impure kinds (v 19; cf. vv 20, 23) and the second permits pure kinds (v 20; cf. vv 21–22). The verse on carcasses (v 21) begins with the proscription lōʾ tōʾkĕlû kol-nĕbēlâ 'do not eat any carcass'. The wording is significant: "any carcass" must include the carcasses of pure animals. It is thus a reference to vv 39–40, which, as will be demonstrated below, belong to the last stages in the composition of Lev 11. As will be shown in COMMENT B below, D eliminated two subjects, defilement by contact and the purification process, and focused solely on the subject of diet. D also found it unnecessary to include the section on land swarmers (details in COMMENT B). Otherwise D has the entire inventory of Lev 11 and in the same order. Thus, as D probably had the final form of

Lev 11 to draw from, it cannot serve as a means of penetrating the earlier stages in the formation of Lev 11.

Let us now zero in on the intrusive bloc, vv 24–40. As indicated above, it is composed of two units, vv 24–38 and 39–40. The first, vv 24–38, can be shown to be an insert for several reasons.

1. In the passage on impure quadrupeds (vv 24–28), *bĕhēmâ* is contrasted with *ḥayyâ* 'wild quadrupeds', implying that *bĕhēmâ* can only mean "domesticated quadrupeds." But this usage stands in opposition to its function in v 2, where it embraces all quadrupeds, wild species as well (e.g., the rock badger, v 5). Different terminology implies different sources.

2. Verses 29–38, on the eight impure rodents and reptiles, exhibit their intrusive character by limiting defilement to contact. The omission of the consequence of defilement by eating, however, was no accident; it is discussed farther on, in vv 41–42. Thus the fact that the author of vv 29–38 took into consideration a subsequent passage (vv 41–42) can only mean that the latter stood before him and, hence, his own passage is a later insertion.

3. The most decisive reason, already mentioned, is that the entire bloc on purification (vv 24–40) sticks out like a sore thumb from the midst of organically related material, namely, laws dealing solely with diet.

Thus, the conclusion is ineluctable that vv 24–38 (and its supplement, vv 39–40; see below) comprise a subsequent layer to the diet laws represented in vv 1–23, 41–42, 46. To which source can they be ascribed? Their terminology and content leave no room for doubt. Their concern with contact impurity and its purification are of a piece with the theme and vocabulary of the subsequent chapters, 12–15, especially chaps. 12 and 15. As will be demonstrated below (see the NOTE to 16:1 and chap. 16, COMMENT A), chaps. 11–15 comprise a bloc of material that was inserted between chaps. 10 and 16. Hence the conclusion suggests itself, however tentatively, that whoever composed chaps. 12–15 linked them to 11:1–23, 41–42, 46 by inserting vv 24–38, thereby presenting a fuller spectrum of communicable impurity not just by humans (chaps. 12–15) but also by animals (chap. 11).

Of course, the tableau of communicable impurity is incomplete. The list of purification procedures for impurity transmitted by animal carcasses should be supplemented by a similar tabulation for communicable impurity stemming from human corpses. Instead, chaps. 12–15 deal solely with the impure fluxes and skin eruptions of live persons, not dead ones. The answer has already been suggested (chap. 4, COMMENT G) that the original severity of corpse contamination was subsequently attenuated as a result of a long battle with the pagan notion that contact with the dead meant exposure to malevolent, demonic forces. And for this reason a later version of corpse contamination, its potency reduced and adapted to settled life in Canaan, was incorporated into Scripture —not in the book of Leviticus but in the book of Numbers (chap. 19).

A specific reason has already been given for regarding vv 39–40 as an appendix to the purification bloc: the cumulative evidence (presented in summary form in the NOTE on v 40) that originally the carcass of a pure animal did not carry impurity by contact. Thus vv 39–40, which prescribe purificatory remedies for such impurity, must reflect a subsequent development. In addition, this passage shares with the preceding verses on purification (vv 24–38) their intrusive character within the homogeneous diet laws (vv 2–23, 41–42). Still, it is clearly an appendix to the purification bloc (vv 24–38) because it logically belongs with the other quadrupeds (vv 24–28). Its placement at the end, after the long section on land swarmers (vv 29–38), betrays its supplemental nature. Also, another indication of its discreteness is that it alone prescribes purification for eating a carcass as well as handling it (but see Ramban's explanation in the NOTE on v 40). It was clearly composed by a P tradent, for its vocabulary, *ṭāmēʾ* 'be defiled [by touch]' and *ʾăšer-hîʾ lākem lĕʾoklâ* 'that you may eat', corresponds to P usage (see below and the NOTE on v 47b). It could not be part of H, which holds that a priest is only forbidden to eat of a pure animal carcass (22:8) but is not forbidden to touch it. Otherwise the prohibition enjoined upon the priest to refrain from touching the carcass of (any of the eight, 11:29–31) swarming things (22:5) would also have included the wording *bĕkol-bĕhēmâ ʾăšer-hîʾ lĕʾoklâ* 'any edible quadruped' (as in 11:39). And if contact with such a carcass is not forbidden to a priest, all the more so to a lay person. Thus H agrees with P that touching a carcass of a pure animal does not impart impurity (see the NOTE on v 40). Hence vv 39–40 must be later than the two Priestly strata described above, as well as H (see below).

In addition to the intrusive purification bloc (vv 24–40), this chapter contains an appendix (vv 43–45) that also betrays signs of supplementation. Suspicion rests on the altered use of the verb *šiqqēṣ;* throughout the chapter it denotes "abominate" but here it means "defile" (see the NOTE on v 43). The verb *ṭimmēʾ* also exhibits a change in meaning; it continues to mean "defile," but whereas in the rest of the chapter it connotes defilement by contact here it is limited to defilement by ingestion (see the NOTE on "make yourselves impure," v 43b), a characteristic of H (20:25bβ: see the NOTE on "that may not be eaten," v 47). Furthermore, the expression *šiqqēṣ ʾet-hannepeš* 'defile the throat' is not a P idiom but is attested in H (20:25). This dependency on H is strongly corroborated by the imperative to Israel to make itself holy (v 44), which is the most distinctive characteristic of H (hence its name) but which stands in flat contradiction to the opposing doctrine of P, that holiness of persons is reserved exclusively for priests and Nazirites (see the NOTE on "you shall sanctify yourselves," v 44). Even the Levites, the lifelong servants of the Tabernacle, are scrupulously denied by P the attribute of holiness (Milgrom 1970a: n. 103). Finally, this passage's dependence on H is evidenced by the fact that the call to holiness serves as a specific rationale for the diet laws both here (v 44aβ) and in H (20:26a).

The chapter's subscript (vv 46–47) is composed of two parts. The first (v 46) sums up the animal categories but says nothing of purification. It probably was the work of P_1 and serves as a balance to the introduction (vv 1–2a). The second subscript is probably the work of P_2, who had to make sure that the resumptive subscript would also summarize the two polarities, edible/inedible, and the one he introduced, impure/pure, corresponding respectively to the laws of ingestion and contact (see the NOTE "between the impure and the pure," v 47). To be sure, it cannot be the work of H. It is punctilious in preserving the use of *ṭāmēʾ* for defilement by contact, in concert with the rest of P. Moreover, its use of the polaric term *ṭāhôr* for carcasses whose contact does not defile (see also vv 32, 36, 37) clashes with its use in H, where it designates edible animals (20:25a). P, by contrast, refers to the latter as "animal(s) that may be eaten" (v 39; cf. v 34).

The implications of this analysis for the development of chap. 11 are as follows: first, P experiences inner growth; the dietary prohibitions (vv 2–23, 41–42) are supplemented by a bloc dealing with purification procedures for handling carcasses of impure animals (vv 24–38). That it is the work of a P tradent is assured by the continued use of *ṭāmēʾ* to designate defilement by contact (see the NOTE on v 8) in distinction from *šeqeṣ*, the term reserved for the prohibition against ingestion (see the NOTE on v 11). It should be recalled that chaps. 9–10 also exhibit P accretions. Thus the possibility exists that P_1 and P_2 discerned there continue their course in this chapter as well. If this holds true, then P_2 here, as in the prior chapters, is a redaction and not a source, that is to say, the author of vv 24–38 also inserted them. Theoretically, he might also have inserted the supplements, vv 39–40, 43–45, and 47. But the first of these passages (vv 39–40) must be ruled out because of its position as an appendix, as indicated above. The second passage (vv 43–45) is automatically eliminated by its content and vocabulary, which place it in the sphere of H. The third supplement (v 47), however—clearly the work of the P school (see above)—remains a possibility. Because it neatly capsules the animals that defile either by contact or by ingestion, the likelihood is that its author is indeed P_2, the one who inserted vv 24–38, thereby providing a fitting summary for the augmented chapter. By the process of elimination, vv 39–40 must therefore be attributed to a later interpolator. Indeed, as the doctrine expressed in vv 39–40 is alien to P_1, P_2, and H, it follows that these verses comprise the last stage in the composition of Lev 11, a deduction that has significant implications for the redaction of the book of Leviticus; see the Introduction, §H.

What of the remaining passage, vv 43–45? Clearly, as the product of H it is alien to the chapter. Moreover, it is found at the end of the chapter and is neither adumbrated in the resumptive subscripts (vv 46–47) nor in harmony with them. As indicated above, the verbs *šiqqēṣ* and *ṭimmēʾ* clash with their usage in the rest of the chapter and, more significantly, they clash with the second subscript (v 47) in the usage of *ṭāmēʾ*. The question must be asked: Why did the H redactor find it necessary to supplement the dietary code? His leitmotif "holiness" provides the answer. The Priestly school, as evidenced by this chapter, is concerned with Israel's ritual purity, but only in regard to the sanctuary and its sancta. For H this is not enough. Israel has to strive for holiness, a higher rung on the ladder of virtue (cf. *m. Sota* 9:15). Holiness implies moral as well as ritual perfection; it is *imitatio dei* (19:2; see the COMMENT on chap. 19 and, tentatively, COMMENT E below).

Thus the conclusion is inescapable that the insertion of vv 43–45 occurred after the P material was in place. The implications are extraordinarily significant. Instead of assuming, with the scholarly consensus, that H is prior to and assimilated into P, I believe that Lev 11 indicates that the reverse may be true: H is the redactor of P, not just of earlier P_1, but also of subsequent P_2. This conclusion will be supported by the cumulative evidence that H passages frequently occur outside the main H bloc (chaps. 17–26), where they appear, as here, as inserts that supplement and even interrupt the flow of the text (e.g., the Sabbath, Exod 31:12–17; 35:1–3; the tassels, Num 15:37–41; the laws concerning the *gēr*, Exod 12:47–49; Lev 16:29–34; Num 9:14; 15:13–16, 22–31; 19:10b; 35:15). See the brief remarks in chap. 16, COMMENT A, and in the Introduction. The question, however, remains: Is H the last stratum of this chapter, or, perhaps, is P_3 (vv 39–40) still later? This question is not without significance. If the latter alternative proves correct, then H is not the final hand in this chapter or, presumably, in Leviticus as a whole; a P tradent subsequent to the H redaction then updated the material. Or if it turns out that P_3 was already in place before H inserted his interpolation, then the possibility clearly exists that H is the redactor of all of P and, perhaps, of the entire Torah. The full investigation of this question is reserved for the introduction to the Holiness source, in the second volume of this study.

These findings may be summarized and tabulated as follows:

The Composition of Lev 11

Verses	Stage I: Diet Rules (P_1)	Stage II: Purification (P_2)	Stage III: H Redaction	Stage IV: Interpolation (P_3)
1–2a	Introduction			
2b–8	Forbidden quadrupeds			
9–12	Fish			
13–19	Birds			
20–23	Flying insects			
24–28		Forbidden quadrupeds		
29–38		Eight land swarmers		
39–40				Permitted quadrupeds
41–42	Land swarmers			
43–45			Call to holiness	
46	Subscript			
47		Subscript		

697

Postscript: David Wright proposes (in a written communication) that H's interpolation consisted not only of vv 43–45 but also of vv 41–42. His reasons are as follows: (1) If vv 41–42 were part of the original stage I (vv 2b–23), stage II (vv 24–38) should follow them instead of preceding them. (2) The addition of vv 41–42 to the H interpolation explains why the holiness rationale is limited only to the land swarmers *(šereṣ hāʾāreṣ):* their addition to the prohibited animals is now justified. (3) The absence of land swarmers in the prohibited-animal list of Deut 14:4–21 is now explained: the author of D had before him only stage I (11:2b–23), a list in which the land swarmers were absent.

Wright's arguments are cogent but not decisive. Answering them seriatim: (1) the list of vv 24–38 (stage II) consists of more than land swarmers; it begins with the general category of quadrupeds (vv 24–28). It would therefore have made no sense to append it to the land swarmers. P_2 was therefore inserted before the land swarmers (vv 41–42) so that its laws on land swarmers (vv 29–38) would immediately precede vv 41–42, thereby forming the section on land swarmers into one continuous bloc. (2) The limitation of the holiness motif to land swarmers can be explained on other grounds (see the note on "and thus become impure," v 43). (3) The inclusion of land swarmers (and, indeed, the carcasses of all animals) in Deut 14 is indicated by its general prohibition: "Do not eat any carcass *(kol-nĕbēlâ)"* (v 21a; details in COMMENT B below).

Besides, how can one justify a list of diet rules (stage I) that details the forbidden swarmers of the water (vv 9–12), skies (vv 13–19)—even including the anomalies (vv 20–23)—and yet would omit the swarmers of the land? As an independent list, it would have led to the conclusion that all land swarmers are permitted!

B. Deut 14:4–21, An Abridgment of Lev 11

The relation between Lev 11 and Deut 14:4–21 has occupied scholars for the past century—without their reaching a consensus. Most have agreed with Kuenen (1886: 266) that Leviticus is an expansion of Deuteronomy. A few have suggested that they derived from a common source (Driver 1895: 163–64). To my knowledge, only two scholars (Eerdmans 1912: 61–62; Rendtorff 1954: 45 n. 34) have surmised that Deuteronomy is dependent on Leviticus, but without offering proof. The problem deserves a fresh appraisal.

COMMENT A has already provided a working hypothesis. It was noted there that D manifests the same sequence as P: quadrupeds, Deut 14:4–8 and Lev 11:2–8; fish, Deut 14:9–10 and Lev 11:9–12; birds, Deut 14:11–18 and Lev 11:13–19; and flying insects, Deut 14:19–20 and Lev 11:20–23. (The absence of land swarmers from D and the function of 14:21aα will be discussed below.) The last correspondence requires a word of explanation. Because D designates birds by *ṣippôr* (14:11), its shift to the synonym *ʿôp* (14:19–20) means that it is describing a different species of flying creatures, which can only be the *šereṣ hāʿôp* 'the flying insects' of Lev 11:20–23. Moreover, the relation between the two passages is confirmed by D's statement: "you may eat pure *ʿôp*" (14:20), a clear reference to the permitted flying insects that P itemizes by name (Lev 11:21–22; see *Sipre* Deut 103). Theoretically, the influence could have gone either way: D abridging P or P expanding D; but logic favors abridgment. It can hardly be maintained that D permitted some flying insects without having some specific ones in mind. And conversely, P lays down a criterion for identifying pure flying insects: they must possess saltatory legs (Lev 11:21). P, therefore, has no need—nor any basis—for deriving either its criterion or the enumerated species from D's cryptic generalization. The case of the flying insects, then, presents us with a working hypothesis: D is an abridgment of P. Corroboration will be provided by a studied comparison of the two texts, verse by verse, which follows forthwith:

Deut 14:3: lōʾ tōʾkal kol-tôʿēbâ 'you shall not eat any abominable thing'. D is clearly the author of this introduction. It is set off from the subsequent diet laws by its verb, which is couched in the singular; the same verb will henceforth appear as *tōʾkĕlû*, plural. Even more significant is the word *tôʿēbâ* 'abomination'. It is found in H (but not in P), where it refers only to forms of incest (Lev 18:22, 26, 27, 29, 30; 20:13). D, conversely, employs it over a broad range: idolatry, sorcery, sodomy, adultery, sacred prostitution, blemished sacrifices, false weights, and forbidden foods (Deut 7:25, 26; 12:13; 13:15; 14:3; 17:1, 4; 18:12; 20:18; 22:5; 23:19; 24:4; 25:16; 27:15; 32:16). There is no common denominator for these abominations. Idolatry, in the broadest sense, would cover most of them, but deceit in sacrifices (Deut 17:1) and in business (Deut 25:16) would not be included. A more likely candidate is deceit *(DDS* 267–69), but here too there is at least one exception, the diet prohibitions (14:3; omitted in Weinfeld's list). What is striking is the absence of *tôʿēbâ* in all of P—a sure sign that P was not influenced by wisdom teachings. In any event, D has placed *tôʿēbâ*, one of its favorite terms, at the head of its list of prohibited foods. D, however, avoids P's synonym *šeqeṣ*, a matter that will be discussed in the Com-MENT on 14:10b, below.

Deut 14:4a: zōʾt habbĕhēmâ abridges Lev 11:2b and *bĕhēmâ* continues to mean "quadruped." The plural *tōʾkĕlû* continues consistently to the end (vv 4–21aα), just as in Lev 11. D's diet pericope contrasts sharply with its contiguous passages, whose verbs are in the singular (vv 3, 21aβ, b). If the diet prohibitions were indigenous to D, one would have expected an unchanging, consistent usage.

Deut 14:4b–5a: The enumeration of the permitted animals argues strongly for D's dependence on P. The specification of criteria (v 6) is superfluous unless they were present in D's source. Furthermore, if it holds true that the criteria for quadrupeds preceded and determined the four animal anomalies (Lev 11:4–8, demonstrated in COMMENT E below), then D's attempt to name all of the qualifying animals makes sense, but again only on the assumption that D is based on P.

Deut 14:6–7a: These verses are identical to Lev 11:3–4a, except for three additions: (1) superfluous *běhēmâ,* probably added to balance *zō't habběhēmâ* (v 4); (2) *štê,* which should be restored in Lev 11:3 (see the Note); (3) *haššěsû'â,* probably borrowed by D from P's statement on the pig (11:7a), where it belongs, and put at the head of the list of anomalous quadrupeds so as to balance v 7a with *šōsa'at šesa'* (v 6). The result is that the criteria are now misleading: the camel, rock badger, and hare lack cleft hoofs (but they aren't even hoofed!) and the pig (v 8) is hoofed (but its hoofs are also cleft!). Moreover, D's additions break the rhythm and symmetry of the corresponding P passage (Paran 1989: 349–52). Thus the text of Lev 11 makes perfect sense and that of D turns out to be a poor derivative (see the next paragraph).

Deut 14:7b–8a: An abridgment of Lev 11:4–7, but now vv 7b–8a (hoofs) do not match the criteria of v 7a (cleft hoofs). *těmē'îm hēm lākem* has been copied from Lev 11:8b (see the next paragraph) in order to declare all four anomalies impure. *wělō' gērâ* is corrupt (see the Note on 11:7). The secondary nature of D is clear (corroborated by the next paragraph).

Deut 14:8b: Identical to Lev 11:8a. There can be no more certain proof that D is derivative. D is concerned solely with food prohibitions, namely, ingestion. Why does it suddenly, and uniquely, mention touch? The only possibility is that the author of D copied it from his source, Lev 11:8a. He did eliminate *těmē'îm hēm lākem* (Lev 11:7b), which was for him superfluous (but not for P, where it indicated the result of contact; see the Note), but his failure to eliminate *ûběniblātām lō' tiggā'û* betrays his source.

Deut 14:9a: Identical to Lev 11:9a.

Deut 14:9b: Identical to Lev 11:9b, minus *bammayim bayyammîm ûbanněhālîm;* an abridgment (see the next paragraph). Also, the repetition of *tō'kēlû* in this verse and in v 6 (cf. v 4), a style foreign to D but typical of P (Paran 1989: 53–72), is further evidence that D copied from P (ibid., 352–53).

Deut 14:10a: Identical to Lev 11:10–12a, minus *mibběśārām . . . bayyammîm* (11:10ab–11a) and *wě'et-niblātām . . . bammayim* (11:bβ–12a). That D is an abridgment of P is shown by the word *tō'kēlû* (end of Deut 14:9), which is superfluous. D must have copied it from Lev 11:9 (end) where it was stylistically required after the elongated enumeration of the bodies of water. The latter was dropped by D (paragraph above) as well as the word *'ōtām.* Why did he not also drop *tō'kēlû?* He needed it to balance *lō' tō'kēlû* in 14:10.

Deut 14:10b: Identical to Lev 11:12b, except that P's *šeqeṣ* is replaced by *ṭāmē'.* Two reasons may be offered for this change. The first is that D discarded *šeqeṣ* because it uses this root in its condemnation of idolatry (Deut 7:26; 29:16). But this reason is insufficient, for D also uses *tô'ēbâ* to denigrate idolatry (comment on v 3, above) and it has no qualms in applying it to the diet laws. A more plausible reason is that D knew that in P *šeqeṣ* had the restricted technical meaning of animals that may not be eaten. To be sure, *ṭāmēʾ* in P also had a technical connotation—defilement from touch. But D has freed *ṭāmēʾ* from its ritual bounds and has added to it a moral dimension. In D, *ṭāmēʾ* is opposed to *ʿam qādôš* 'a holy people' (14:21), a designation that Israel can maintain if it observes all of God's commandments (Deut 28:9), ethical as well as ritual ones (also the view of H; cf. Lev 19). Hence, D suppressed P's *šeqeṣ* everywhere in this pericope and replaced it with *ṭāmēʾ*.

Deut 14:11: "You may eat any pure bird *(ṣippôr).*" This verse is in keeping with D's tendency to specify the species that may be eaten (cf. vv 4–5, 20). It adds to Lev 11 what the latter only implies: any bird not expressly prohibited is permitted. D chooses the term *ṣippôr* over P's *ʿôp* (Lev 11:13) because it reserves the latter term for the flying insects (v 20; see above). P, however, uses both terms for birds but distinguishes between them by employing *ʿôp* as the generic (e.g., 1:14; 7:26; cf. Gen 1:20, 21, 22, 26, 28, 30; 9:2) and *ṣippôr* for the individual (e.g., 14:4–7, 49–53).

ṭĕhôrâ 'pure' in D signifies edible (also in v 20). But in Lev 11, *ṭāhôr/ṭāhēr* is the antonym of *ṭāmēʾ* in the sense that it does not defile by contact (11:32, 36, 37, 47; see the NOTE on v 47). Edible animal foods are expressed in P literally, by means of the verb *ʾākal* 'eat': *ʾăšer yēʾākēl/tōʾkĕlû/lĕʾoklâ* (11:2, 3, 4, 8, 21, 22, 34, 39, 47).

Thus Deut 14:11 is a distinctive addition of D in order to conform the text of Lev 11 to its terminology.

Deut 14:12a: Parallel to Lev 11:13a. *šeqeṣ/šiqqēṣ* is eschewed for reasons given above (on v 10a), and *mēhem* is inserted because of v 11 (Koch 1959: 76 n. 5).

Deut 14:12b–18: Parallel to Lev 11:13b–19. The following are the changes in D: (1) *wĕhaddayyâ* (v 13) is added (see the NOTE on 11:13); (2) *hārāʾâ* (v 13) replaces *haddāʾâ* (11:14; see the NOTE); (3) *hārāḥāmâ* (v 17) replaces *hārāḥām* (11:17); (4) the position of *haššālāk* (v 17) has been altered (11:17); (5) *wĕhāʾănāpâ* (v 18) replaces *hāʾănāpâ* (11:19; see below); and (6) ten birds have *ʾet* and ten do not, in contrast with Lev 11, where all birds except *hāʾănāpâ* have *ʾet*.

D's list of ten birds with *ʾet* and the four forms with *mîn* were copied from Lev 11 (Koch 1959: 76 n. 6). Moran (1966) offers this compelling proof: in both lists three of the *mîn* birds occur with *ʾet* but one, *hāʾănāpâ*, does not (14:18; Lev 11:19). Furthermore, all scholars are in agreement that as *mîn* is not a D term, D must have borrowed it from some other source. It follows that if Lev 11 has the same four *mîn* birds—one of which, the same bird, *hāʾănāpâ*, is not introduced by *ʾet*—then Lev 11 must be that source. To be sure, Moran also argues that not all of D's list was copied from Lev 11. He reaches this conclusion by observing that D lists ten edible quadrupeds without the *ʾet* particle (14:4b–5), which leads him to the inference that D's original list of impure birds, like the quadrupeds, consisted of ten birds without *ʾet* and that, subsequently, the additional ten birds with *'et* and the forms of *mîn* were borrowed directly from the parallel passage in Lev 11. It is hard to conceive, however, that D's purportedly original lists would have omitted the following well-known and widespread *'et* birds: *'ōrēb* 'raven' (Gen 8:7; 1 Kgs 17:4; Isa 34:11; Ps 147:9; Prov 30:17; Job 38:41; Cant 5:11), *bat ya'ǎnâ* 'eagle owl' (Isa 13:21; 34:13; 43:20; Jer 50:39; Mic 1:8; Job 30:29), *nēṣ* 'hawk' (Job 39:26), and *yanšûp* 'screech owl' (Isa 34:11). Rather, it would seem preferable to assume that D borrowed the entirety of Lev 11 and then allowed his decimal preferences to break up the list into ten with *'et* and ten without.

Deut 14:19: Parallel to Lev 11:20. D makes the following changes: (1) "that walk on all fours" is omitted because some winged insects have more than four legs; (2) *šeqeṣ* is again replaced by *ṭāmē'* (see the COMMENT on 14:10a, above); (3) *lō' yē'ākēlû* is added to balance *tō'kēlû* (v 20). In Lev 11:20 "eating" is implied by *šeqeṣ* (see the NOTE on Lev 11:11). Thus all three changes favor the hypothesis that D borrowed from P.

Deut 14:21aα: lō' tō'kēlû kol-nĕbēlâ 'Do not eat any carcass'. The fact that the verb—for the last time—is in the plural indicates that D is borrowing from Lev 11. But what could that be? D has stopped at the flying insects (Lev 11:20–23) and still has the large purification bloc (vv 24–40) and the land swarmers (vv 41–42) before him. He is not interested in the matter of impurity caused by handling their carcasses (in fact, he opposes it; see below) or in purification procedures; his focus is narrowed to one concern—diet. He therefore sums up the remaining verses in Leviticus by banning all carcasses. The common denominator of all of the animals enumerated in the purification bloc (11:29–40) is that their carcasses defile. D therefore encapsulates them in the blanket prohibition against eating any carcass (correctly surmised by Rendtorff 1954: 45 n. 34).

Nevertheless, there remains the problem of the land swarmers (11:41–42), missing in D. Not only may their carcasses *(nĕbēlâ)* not be eaten (by implication) but they may not even have been killed for food. Nevertheless, the definition of *nĕbēlâ* must be recalled: carcasses of *impure* animals are always *nĕbēlâ* even if they were slaughtered properly (see the NOTE on 11:8). The same definition probably obtained for D (cf. Deut 21:23). Thus all land swarmers are *nĕbēlâ*, no matter how they die. Furthermore, the unique status of land swarmers offers a clue as to why D so cavalierly dismissed them. Land swarmers are the only animal category without a single permitted species (contrast quadrupeds, 14:4–5; fish, 14:9; birds, 14:11; flying insects, 14:20). Because D's additions to Lev 11 (the preceding citations) reveal his interest in specifying what may be eaten, it is easy to understand why he sweeps all land swarmers under the rubric of *nĕbēlâ*.

The *nĕbēlâ* prohibition solves another problem. That D's list consists solely of food prohibitions could have led to the conclusion that D only had P₁ before him—which also is limited to the forbidden animal foods (see COMMENT A above). Yet the fact that this prohibition forbids the consumption of "any carcass" means that even the carcasses of permitted quadrupeds are included in the prohibition. Moreover, as demonstrated in COMMENT A, the corresponding verses in Lev 11 (vv 39–40) represent the last stage in the composition of the chapter. Thus, there can be no doubt that D had the entirety of Lev 11 before him (including the H passages; see below). Also, the fact that D specifies *nĕbēlâ* to the exclusion of *ṭĕrēpâ* 'torn by beasts' (17:14; 22:8; cf. Exod 22:30) further corroborates the conclusion that D had all of Lev 11, for the latter also limits itself to the *nĕbēlâ*.

"Give it to the resident alien in your community" (Deut 14:21aβ). This statement is important, for it provides concrete evidence that D not only is unconcerned with defilement by handling—P's obsession (11:29–40; cf. chap. 15)—but is at odds with it. Otherwise, how could he advise his people that God wants them to "give," that is, hand, all carcasses to the resident alien? That this advice is solely D's contribution is strikingly demonstrated by the sudden shift of the verb number—*tittĕnennâ* 'you [sing.] give it'. Moreover, *laggēr ʾăšer bišĕʿārêkā* 'to the resident alien in your community', literally, "in your gates," is a typical D phrase (Deut 5:14; 14:21, 29; 16:14; 24:14; 31:12). By contrast, P and H employ the expression *haggār bĕtôkām/bĕtôkĕkem* 'who resides in their/ your midst' (e.g., Lev 16:29; 17:8, 10, 12, 13; 18:26; 19:33, 34; Num 15:29; 19:10; 35:15).

"Or you may sell it to a foreigner" (Deut 14:21aγ). *nokrî* is also a D term (Deut 14:21; 15:3; 7:5; 23:21; 29:21); H expresses the notion of foreigner by *ben-nēkār* (Lev 22:25).

"For you are a holy people to the Lord your God" (Deut 14:21aδ). D's attachment of the notion of holiness to the diet laws parallels the holiness prescriptions in Leviticus, which are also appended to its diet laws (11:43–45). Thus H's contribution to Lev 11, representing one of the last stages in its composition (see COMMENT A above), demonstrates once again that D must have had all of Lev 11 before him. Note, however, the difference: P aspires but D asseverates. For D the holiness of Israel is a fact, not a desideratum. Israel inherently, by dint of its election, is an *ʿam qādôš* 'a holy people' (Deut 7:6; 14:2, 21; 26:19; 28:9). Indeed, precisely because D has nuanced P's notion of Israel's holiness, he changes it from the plural, *wihyîtem* 'you [shall be]', to the singular, *ʾattâ*, literally, "thou."

Deut 14:21b: "Do not boil a kid in its mother's milk." This prohibition initially occurs in a cultic context (Exod 23:19; 34:26; cf. the Sam. on 23:19), but D includes it among the dietary prohibitions. The fact that Lev 11 makes no mention of it is an indication that for P this prohibition still belonged to the sphere of the cult and had no place in dietary instructions for the people. Thus, once again, P is shown to be earlier than D. But how can we account for the change? How did a cultic prohibition restricted to the sanctuary become a dietary prohibition applicable everywhere? The answer is clear: as long as this prohibition remained cultic, all animals were slaughtered and cooked in the sanctuary (see COMMENT C below) and, hence, were under the supervisory jurisdiction of the priests. But in D, the right to slaughter anywhere is conceded to the laity. Therefore, this prohibition becomes a dietary law, of concern to all Israel (this prohibition is discussed in detail in COMMENT F below). That P breathes the atmosphere of the old Epic tradition (Exod 23:19; 34:26) has a great deal to say concerning its date; see the Introduction.

The cumulative evidence of this investigation points, witout exception, in one direction. All of the additions, omissions, protuberances, inconcinnities, and inconsistencies that mark off Deut 14:4–21 from Lev 11 can be explained by the one premise: D had the entire MT of Lev 11 before him, which he copied, altered, and above all abridged to suit his ideological stance and literary style.

C. The Ethical Foundations of the Dietary System: 1. The Blood Prohibition

The diet laws of Lev 11 cannot be comprehended in isolation. They form part of a larger dietary system whose rules are dispersed over much of P. Only when the system is viewed in its totality does the significance of Lev 11 become clear. COMMENTS C, D, E, and F address different aspects of the ethical foundations of this dietary system.

Primacy of place in the dietary system, however, belongs not to Lev 11 but to the blood prohibition. It has already been encountered twice in the sacrificial laws. The first (3:17) prohibits the ingestion of sacrificial blood (and suet) everywhere (see the NOTE on "in all your settlements," 3:17), and the second (7:26) extends the prohibition to game (see the NOTE on "any blood," 7:26). It is the major theme of an entire chapter, Lev 17 (H), where its centrality is certified not only by its length but by its unique wording:

> If any individual of the house of Israel or any alien who resides among them *ingests* (lit., "eats") *any blood,* I will set my face against the person who *ingests blood,* and I will cut him off from his kin. . . . Therefore I say to the Israelite people: No person among you shall *ingest blood,* nor shall any alien that resides among you *ingest blood.* . . . And I say to the Israelite people: you shall not *ingest the blood* of any flesh, for the life of all flesh is its blood. Anyone who *ingests it* shall be cut off. (17:10, 12, 14)

The detailed exegesis of these pregnant verses is reserved for the COMMENT on chap. 17. Here it suffices to notice that within five verses (17:10–14), the prohibition occurs five times. Such staccato repetition is unprecedented in law; it betrays the strident alarm of the legislator lest this fundamental principle be violated. The book of Deuteronomy also repeats the blood prohibition with a shrill voice: "But you must not *ingest blood.* . . . But make sure that you do not *ingest blood:* for the blood is the life, and you must not *ingest life with flesh. You must not ingest it* . . . *you must not ingest it"* (Deut 12:16, 23–25). The blood prohibition in Deuteronomy is all the more remarkable. Despite its revolutionary change in allowing profane slaughter (details in Lev 17), it keeps the blood prohibition intact—testimony to the latter's basic importance.

But why is it important? It is P that discloses its rationale: "Every creature that lives shall be yours to eat. . . . You must not, however, eat flesh with its life-blood. For your life-blood, too, I will require a reckoning. Whoever sheds the blood of man, for that man shall his blood be shed. For in the image of God was man created" (Gen 9:3–6). God's command to Noah and his sons takes the form of a law—the first in the Bible, the first for humanity. And the blood prohibition is the quintessential component of this law. It is the divine remedy for human sinfulness, which hitherto has polluted the earth and necessitated its purgation by flood (Frymer-Kensky 1977). Because "all flesh *(kol-bāśār)* had corrupted its ways," God decided "to put an end to all flesh *(kol-bāśār)"* (Gen 6:12–13), an allusion to the violence committed by both man and beast in spilling blood and eating *bāśār* 'flesh'. Man's nature will not change; he shall continue sinful (Gen 8:22), but his violence need no longer pollute the earth if he will but heed one law: abstain from blood. According to the customary exegesis of this passage, man is given the responsibility of punishing homicide *bā'ādām* (Gen 9:6), being rendered "by man," in other words, by human jurisdiction. But the chiastic structure of this verse, *šōpēk dam hā'ādām bā'ādām dāmô yiššāpēk* (ABC C'B'A'), makes it certain that both *'ādām* words (CC') refer to the same man, namely, the victim, and the prefixed *beth* must therefore be the *beth pretii,* meaning "in exchange, for" (Pedersen 1926: 533–34). The context bears this out. Because man is created in the divine image it is God's responsibility, not man's, to requite the murder, and the text says so explicitly: "Of every beast will I require it: of man, too, will I require a reckoning for human life, of every man for that of his fellow!" (Gen 9:5ab, b). This exegetical note isolates and, thereby, accentuates the blood prohibition. Man must abstain from blood: human blood must not be shed and animal blood must not be ingested. In the Priestly scale of values, this prohibition actually stands higher than the Ten Commandments. The Decalogue was given solely to Israel, but the blood prohibition was enjoined upon all mankind; it alone is the basis for a viable human society.

Moreover, the position of the blood prohibition in the primeval history discloses another aspect of its significance. *'ak* 'however' (Gen 9:4) is the language of concession. Originally, according to the Priestly account, man was a vegetarian. He ruled the animal kingdom (Gen 1:26), but it was not the source of his food. For God said, "See, I give you every seed-bearing plant . . . and every tree . . . ; they shall be yours for food" (Gen 1:29). But after eating the forbidden fruit, he is no longer satisfied with his role as the steward of paradise. He wants to be the active agent of his own destiny. And this new man is also carnivorously inclined. No longer Adam, the ideal, but Noah, the real, he insists on bringing death to living things to gratify his appetite and need. This concession is granted him, reluctantly, but not without reservation: he is to refrain from ingesting the blood.

The import of this prohibition is projected in even clearer relief against the backdrop of the ancient Near East. First, it must be noted that blood plays no significant role whatever in the cults of Israel's neighbors, with the sole exception of the pre-Islamic Arabs (Henninger 1979: 486). Second, nowhere else do we find Israel's postulate of the life force residing in the blood, even among the early Arabs (Noldeke, Dalman, cited by Henninger 1979: 487–88). Third, there is no attestation anywhere else of an absolute prohibition against ingesting blood (McCarthy 1969; Fischer 1976: 92 n. 14); even the Arabs, down to the age of Muḥammad, partook of blood (Smith 1927: 234). Thus, Israel's blood prohibition cannot be passed off as an outlandish vestige of some primitive taboo but must be adjudged as the product of a rational, deliberate opposition to the prevailing practice of its environment. Moreover, as shown above, the blood prohibition is intended to be not only absolute but universal: it is incumbent on all mankind. Post-Noah man may have meat for food and may kill to get it, but he must eschew the blood. Although he is conceded animal flesh he must abstain from its lifeblood: it must be drained, returned to its source, to God (cf. G. Klameth 1923, cited by Henninger 1979: 489–90).

Whereas humanity is enjoined to abstain from animal blood by draining it, Israel is to do so only for game (17:13–14) but must offer the blood of sacrificial animals on the altar (17:11). This crucial verse reads: "As for the life of the flesh it is in the blood. It is I who have assigned it to you upon the altar to ransom your lives. For it is the blood that ransoms by means of life." Because this latter verse not only prescribes a rite but provides its own rationale, it merits a close reading on the chance that it will also throw light on the rationale for the blood prohibition.

17:11aα, b: kî-nepeš habbāsār baddām hî' [*hw'*] . . . *kî-haddām hû' bannepeš yĕkappēr*. The use of the two *beth* prepositions requires comment. The first obviously means "in with"; the second is the *beth instrumentii* 'by means of' (correcting Milgrom 1971b: 149; Levine 1974: 67; Brichto 1976: 28), because, as pointed out by many scholars, most recently by B. Schwartz (orally), this is the only attested meaning of the *beth* in the verbal expression *kipper b* (Exod 29:33; Num 5:8; 35:33; 1 Sam 3:14; Isa 27:9; Prov 16:6; except for the two instances in which the *beth* indicates place, 6:23; 16:17, 27). The two clauses translate, literally, "As for the life of the flesh it is in the blood . . . for it is the blood that ransoms (chap. 16, COMMENT F) by means of life." The repeated nouns *dām* and *nepeš* form a chiasm (Janowski 1982: 245). Thus the *nepeš* 'life' of 11b must be the same as in 11a—the life of the animal. This point is crucial: the object of the *kippēr* action must be the slain animal. Furthermore, the clauses form an inclusio, endowing the verse with an ABA' structure and thereby highlighting the middle section, B.

17:11aβ: wa᾽ănî nĕtattîyw lākem ʿal-hammizbēaḥ. The meaning is clear except for the term *nĕtattîyw.* A survey of P shows that wherever the subject of *nātan* is God, it means "bestow, appoint, assign" (e.g., Num 8:19 [N.B. *wā᾽ettĕnâ . . . nĕtūnîm*]; 18:8, 19; cf. also Gen 1:29; 9:3; Lev 6:10; 7:34; 10:17; Num 35:6). This usage, however, is not to be confused with *nātan dām* when the subject is the priest, in which case the meaning is "place the blood" (e.g., on a person, Exod 29:20; Lev 14:14, 25; on doorposts, Exod 12:7; Ezek 45:19; on the altar, Lev 4:7, 25; Ezek 43:20). This clause is therefore rendered, "and it is I who have assigned it to you upon the altar" (with *NJPS* and *NEB;* this distinction is important to prevent the association of Lev 17:11 with the *ḥaṭṭā᾽t* offering, the blood of which is indeed "placed" on the horns of the altar, Lev 4:7 et passim).

17:11aγ: lĕkappēr ʿal-napšōtêkem. The final clause constitutes the crux of the verse and requires that each word be analyzed separately. There is general agreement about *nepeš.* It refers to the life essence of both man and beast as distinct from the body. It does not disintegrate into dust but departs from the body (Gen 35:18; Jer 15:9) and enters Sheol (Pss 16:10; 30:4; Job 33:22). The translation "life" is therefore warranted. In a legal context, moreover, *nepeš* specifically connotes capital crime or punishment (e.g., Exod 21:23; Lev 24:15; Deut 19:21), and expressions compounded with it often imply that life is at stake (e.g., Judg 5:18; 12:3; 1 Sam 19:5). Especially relevant is the condemnation of Korah and his cohorts, those who have sinned "at the cost of their lives" (*bĕnapšōtām,* Num 17:3 [P]). Thus Lev 17:11 implies that human life is in jeopardy unless the stipulated ritual is carried out. The nature of both the crime and its atonement will follow from the explanation of the full phrase *lĕkappēr ʿal-napšōtêkem.*

First, however, a word on *lĕkappēr ʿal.* The key to the meaning of the *piʿel* of *kpr* is in its adjunct prepositions. It can be shown that whenever the object of *kippēr* is a person, a preposition must follow, either *ʿal* or *bĕʿad,* both signifying "on behalf of, for" (see chap. 4, COMMENT B). This verse, therefore, denotes that the blood is the means of carrying out the *kippūr* rite on behalf of the persons offering the sacrifice. As for the root *kpr,* nothing less than a monograph would do it justice (see Janowski 1982 and, provisionally, chap. 16, COMMENT F). For the purpose of this comment, however, it will be rendered "ransom" (Milgrom 1971b: 151 n. 15).

The full idiom *kippēr ʿal-nepeš* occurs again in only two pericopes: Exod 30:11–16 and Num 31:48. As noted by Rashbam (on Num 31:49), in the name of his father, Rabbi Meir, son-in-law of Rashi, they are strikingly similar in (a) *context,* for both deal with censuses (Exod 30:12; Num 31:49); (b) *procedure,* for precious metal is brought in both to the Tent of Meeting, "as a remembrance before the Lord" (Exod 30:16; Num 31:54); and (c) *purpose,* for both are intended *lĕkappēr ʿal-napšōtêkem* (Exod 30:15–16; Num 31:50). More importantly, the purpose is explicated by the clause "that no plague shall come upon them in their being counted" (Exod 30:12b). Here is an explicit statement that the purpose of the *kippūr* money is to prevent destruction at the hands of God. Implied, therefore, is that a census is a capital offense in the sight of God and that the silver half-shekel and the gold vessels are the necessary ransom for the life of the polled persons.

Moreover, the verb *kippēr* must be related to the expression found in the same pericope *kōper napšô* 'a ransom for his life' (Exod 30:12). The same combination of the idiom *kōper nepeš* and the verb *kippēr* is found in the law of homicide (Num 35:31–33). Thus in these two cases, *kippēr* is a denominative from *kōper,* whose meaning is undisputed: "ransom" (cf. Exod 21:30). Therefore, there exists a strong possibility that all texts that assign to *kippēr* the function of averting God's wrath have *kōper* in mind: innocent life spared by substituting for it the guilty parties or their ransom. Thus the above-mentioned homicide law is elucidated as follows: although no substitute is allowed for a deliberate murderer, the accidental homicide is ransomed by the natural death of the high priest (Num 35:25). Similarly, the census money ransoms each counted soldier. A ransom function can also be assigned to the Levite guards who siphon off God's wrath upon themselves when an Israelite encroaches upon the sancta (Num 1:53; 8:19; 18:22–23; Milgrom 1970a: 28–31) as well as to Phineas (the chief of the Levite guards, Num 3:32) who ransoms Israel from God's imminent wrath (Num 25:10). Other examples of the ransom function of *kippēr* are the slaying of Saul's sons as a ransom for his violation of the Gibeonite covenant (2 Sam 21:3–6); the inability of Babylon to ransom itself, that is, to avert its fate (Isa 47:11); and Moses' attempt to ransom Israel by his intercession (Exod 32:30–34). Thus, the meaning of *nepeš* in legal contexts and the meaning of *kippēr ʿal-nepeš* in census contexts both point to the conclusion that in Lev 17:11, Israelites have become liable to death before God and the purpose of the sacrificial blood is *lĕkappēr ʿal-napšōtêkem* 'to ransom your lives' (details in Milgrom 1971b).

The Sacrifice. The assignment of the blood to the altar makes it clear that sacrificial blood is meant. Unclear, however, is the kind of sacrifice. Does this verse refer to all sacrifices or does it concern a particular sacrifice? The answer lies in another idiom, which by its fourfold repetition forms a theme in the pericope in which it is found: *lōʾ tōʾkal dām,* the prohibition of eating blood. The notion that blood, a liquid, would be eaten rather than drunk points to the meaning. Had the prohibition been directed against imbibing the blood itself, the text would have resorted to the verb *šātâ* 'drink' (e.g., Num 23:24; Ezek 39:17–19), *ʿilla* 'sip' (= *lāʿâ;* Job 39:30), or *lāqaq* 'lick' (1 Kgs 21:19). The idiom is explicable by assuming that the blood is consumed in the course of eating meat. The objection has been raised that in Akkadian, the cognate *ākil dami* occurs in a context in which eating it (blood) with flesh is not required (Rodriguez 1979: 241). Not so. On the contrary, this text speaks of demons who are *ākil šīrī* 'flesh eaters' who, when consuming the blood separately from the flesh, *šātū ušlāti* 'drink [the blood of] the arteries' (*CT* 14 26f. 34f., cited in *CAD* A1, 246). Thus, the Akkadian distinguishes very well between drinking blood (alone) and eating blood (with its flesh). Indeed, in the Bible, wherever *ʾākal dām* is met, the context invariably shows that the blood is not being drunk for its own sake but as a consequence of eating meat. Thus, Deuteronomy repeatedly warns about the danger of consuming blood as a result of allowing profane slaughter (Deut 12:15–16, 23–25) and of permitting the eating of the flesh of firstlings by the laity (Deut 15:23). So in P the blood prohibition occurs exclusively in the discussion of the *šĕlāmîm*, the offering of well-being, the only sacrifice whose flesh is eaten by the lay worshiper (3:17; 7:26; 17:1–7; cf. Gen 9:4).

Furthermore, this conclusion is demanded by the context of this pericope. It comprises two laws (vv 10–12, 13–14), which together form a logical unity (see the COMMENT on chap. 17). Because the second deals with wild animals— hunted, obviously, for their meat and not for sport *(ʾăšer yēʾākēl)*—the first law undoubtedly also speaks of the flesh of edible animals; these, however, are not game but domestic animals, which, according to H, must be sacrificed at the altar. Thus vv 10–14 constitute a bipartite law for disposing of the blood of all victims killed for their flesh: the blood of game must be covered, and the blood of sacrificial animals must be drained upon the altar. Moreover, it implies that just as the uncovered blood of game will cry out for vengeance, so the improperly disposed blood of a sacrificial animal will also condemn the life of its slaughterer. For the moment we may conclude that Lev 17:11 does not concern itself with all sacrifices, but refers only to the one sacrifice whose flesh is permitted to be eaten by the laity, the *šĕlāmîm*. It is the blood of the *šĕlāmîm* that would serve as the *kippūr* agent for the lives of the Israelites.

The Contradiction. This conclusion, however, lays bare a glaring contradiction, for the *šĕlāmîm* never functions as a *kippūr*! Of the four categories of animal sacrifices, three are for *kippūr:* the *ḥaṭṭāʾt* ('purification offering') and *ʾāšām* ('reparation offering') exclusively (e.g., Lev 4:20, 26, 31, 35; 5:16, 18, 26), and the *ʿōlâ* ('burnt offering') partially (e.g., Lev 1:14; 16:24). Conversely, the *šĕlāmîm* ('offering of well-being') is the only sacrifice that never serves in a *kippūr* role. To be sure, there are three cases in which *šĕlāmîm* is coupled with *kippēr*, but they do not stand up under scrutiny. (1) In Ezek 45:15, 17 the *šĕlāmîm* is the last in a series of sacrifices, and the *kippūr* function is probably that of the preceding *ʿōlâ* and *ḥaṭṭāʾt*. (2) Exod 29:32–33 refers to the priestly consecration offering, *milluʾîm*, which, however, is not a *šĕlāmîm* (see the NOTE on 8:34). (3) 1 Sam 3:14 assigns a *kippūr* role to *bĕzebaḥ ûbĕminḥâ*. That not specific sacrifices but sacrifices in general is meant, is shown in the same pericope by 1 Sam 2:17, where *minḥâ* is clearly not the cereal offering of P but, as is correctly understood by Rendtorff (1967: 142), stands for flesh offerings. For this generic usage, see 1 Sam 2:29; Isa 19:21. The uses of the *šĕlāmîm* are carefully detailed in P and abundantly attested in the biblical literature; both law and practice unanimously testify that the offerings of well-being are joyous in character and not expiatory. The law ordains it as an expression of thanks *(tôdâ)*, as the completion of a vow *(neder)*, or as a freewill offering *(nĕdābâ,* Lev 7:11–12, 16). Furthermore, wherever it is found in narrative or liturgical literature, it occurs in precisely such contexts (e.g., Num 15:3; Deut 16:10–11; 27:7; 1 Sam 11:15; Pss 107:21; 116:17–19). The case of the Nazirite illustrates the point vividly. The *šĕlāmîm* is one of the sacrifices ordained at the completion of his vow. Yet if he contracts severe impurity during his Nazirite period, he brings the same sacrifices, except that an *'āšām* is substituted for the *šĕlāmîm*. The reason is clear: his sacrifices are now for expiation, not for thanksgiving (note also the choice of verbs in Lev 7:7–9, 14; 14:18–20; for details, see the COMMENT on chap. 3).

The exposed contradiction is brought into sharper relief by yet another consideration. Expiation of ordinary sin is not the subject of Lev 17:11. As noted, *lĕkappēr 'al-nepeš* must mean that the Israelite is guilty of a capital offense against God, and unless he brings sacrificial blood to the altar, he is subject to the death penalty. In the Priestly laws, however, there is no sacrificial expiation for capital crime or, for that matter, for any deliberate violation. The presumptuous sinner is banned from the sanctuary because he "acts defiantly *(bĕyād rāmâ)* . . . reviles the Lord . . . has spurned the word of the Lord and violated his commandment" (Num 15:30–31; contrast vv 24–29).

Thus the contradiction is reinforced. The *šĕlāmîm* cannot be used for expiation purposes, and the sin implied in Lev 17:11 cannot be expiated by any sacrifice at all. Indeed, the nonexpiatory *šĕlāmîm* is presumed to expiate that which is nonexpiable!

The Resolution. The answer is to be found in the opening law of the chapter (17:3–4). It ordains that any Israelite who slaughters a sacrificial animal (for its meat) without bringing it to the Tabernacle altar as an offering of well-being, *dām yēḥašēb lā'îš hahû' dām šāpāk* 'blood guilt shall be reckoned to that man: he has shed blood' (v 4ba). To take these two formulas as mere figures of speech is to misconstrue them. They are precise legal terms, which define and categorize the guilt. The idiom *šāpak dām* is the well-attested accusation of murder (in P, Gen 9:6; Num 35:33; so in all sources: e.g., narrative, Gen 37:22; 1 Sam 25:31; 1 Kgs 2:31; 2 Kgs 21:16; 24:4; legal, Deut 19:10; 21:7; wisdom, Prov 1:16; 6:17; prophetic, Isa 59:7; Jer 22:3, 17; esp. Ezek 16:38; 18:10; 22:3, 4, 6, 9, 12) and the *niph'al* of *ḥšb* 'be reckoned', is the declaratory statement in P and H for designating a cultic act as either acceptable or unacceptable to God (Lev 7:18; Num 18:27, 30; cf. Ps 106:31). Indeed, the coupling of these two legal formulas only underscores the enormity of the crime: he who commits profane slaughter is reckoned to be a murderer because he has shed blood.

That the law of 17:3–4 is inextricably connected with 17:11 is demonstrated by the distribution of the term *gēr* in this chapter. The *gēr* and the

Israelite are equated in all laws of Lev 17 dealing with legitimate means of permitting meat for the table (vv 8–9, 10–12, 13–14, 15–16) except in two of them: the prohibition of profane slaughter (vv 3–7) and the requirement to bring the blood of the slain animal to the altar (v 11). The *gēr* is conspicuously absent in the first of these two laws (vv 3, 5). The second law (v 11) implies the same by its pronominal suffixes. In vv 10–14, the larger context of which v 11 is part, the Israelite is addressed in the second person; the *gēr* is always in the third person. Thus "to you" and "your lives" (v 11) can only refer to the Israelites ("to you" but not to others, *Sipra,* Ahare par. 8). These two laws complement each other perfectly. The first states that an Israelite who slaughters the animal for its meat without offering it as a sacrifice is a murderer. The second provides the rationale that the purpose of this sacrifice—indeed, of dousing the animal's blood on the altar—is to atone for killing it. The omission of the *gēr* from this law now becomes understandable. The *gēr* is permitted nonsacrificial slaughter because (like the non-Israelite, Gen 9:3–4) he need only drain the blood (the animal being treated like game, vv 13–14). Conversely, he need not bring his animal as a sacrifice because its slaughter is not sinful for him and requires no sacrificial expiation (see Milgrom 1982a). Thus, the interdependence of vv 3–4 and v 11—one cannot be fully explained without the other—argues for the conclusion that both passages stem from the same legislative hand. (Indeed, the presence of the *gēr* in the other laws of this chapter points to the same conclusion; see the COMMENT on chap. 17.)

The law of Lev 17:3–4, then, provides an eminently satisfactory basis for explaining the crux of v 11. (The underlying redactional unity of Lev 17 is assumed. This is not to say that the materials that comprise this chapter are of a single hue, as source analysis and form-critical studies have demonstrated. For the details, see the COMMENT on chap. 17. It already has been shown that v 11 and its context (vv 10–14) relate exclusively to the problem of how to eat meat without ingesting its blood, a problem that concerns only the offering of well-being. It has also been indirectly deduced from the language of the pericope that the improper disposal of the animal's blood is a capital violation. Verses 3–4 now make this explicit: animal slaughter constitutes murder except at the authorized altar. Verse 11 complements the indictment with the remedy and its rationale: the blood must be brought to the altar to ransom the murder of the animal because "as for the life of the flesh, it is in the blood . . . for it is the blood that ransoms by means of life" (the inclusion: 11aα, b).

Finally, the identification of blood with life clarifies its function in the sacrificial system. It has been established that the animal's blood is the ritual detergent in the *ḥaṭṭāʾt* sacrifice (chap. 4, COMMENT B). The blood daubed on the altars or aspersed inside the shrine purges *(kippēr)* the sanctuary of its accumulated impurities (chap. 4, COMMENT E). Now we are in a position to grasp its rationale. Impurity *(ṭumʾâ)* is the realm of death (see COMMENT E below). Only its antonym, life, can be its antidote. Blood, then, as life is what purges the sanctuary. It nullifies, overpowers, and absorbs the Israelites' impurities that adhere to the sanctuary, thereby allowing the divine presence to remain and Israel to survive. (For greater details, see chap. 15, COMMENT G.)

The doctrine that unauthorized animal slaughter constitutes murder is found nowhere else in Scripture. It is, however, stated emphatically in Jub 7:32–33 on the basis of its midrash on Gen 9:4–5. (Another instance may be the blood of the heifer whose neck is broken. Deut 21:1–9.) And it accords well with the general view of the animal in biblical literature, especially in the Priestly tradition. An animal also has a *nepeš* (Gen 9:10; Lev 11:10, 46; 24:18; Num 31:28). *nepeš ḥayyâ* refers to man in J (Gen 2:7), but only to animals in P (Gen 1:20, 21, 24, 30; 9:10, 12, 15, 16; Lev 11:10, 46; cf. Ezek 47:9; Gen 2:19, attributed to J, also refers to animals as *nepeš ḥayyâ;* it, however, is considered to be an explanatory gloss by Skinner 1910 and Speiser 1964). The vengeance sought by its blood is to be feared as much as man's; hence its blood must be covered (Lev 17:13; cf. Gen 4:10; Isa 26:21; Job 16:18; Qoh 3:18–19 and esp. Ezek 24:6–8); it is responsible under the law (Gen 9:5; Lev 20:15–16; cf. Exod 21:28–32) and is a party to God's covenant (Gen 9:9–10; Lev 26:6, 22; cf. Hos 2:20).

Above all, it must be recalled that according to the Priestly account of creation, man was initially meant to be a vegetarian. Later, God concedes to man's carnivorous desires: his craving for meat is to be indulged, but he is to abstain from consuming the blood. Thus P's theory of anthropogenesis reveals its reservation and, indeed, its uneasiness regarding man's uncontrolled power over animal life. Through its law code, of which Lev 17:11 can now be seen as an integral part, it seeks to curb that power. All men must eschew the lifeblood of the animal by draining it, thereby returning it to its creator (Gen 9:3–4; Lev 17:13–14). Israel, as part of its striving toward holiness (e.g., Lev 19:2; 20:26), is enjoined to observe an additional safeguard: the blood of sacrificial animals must be drained upon the authorized altar, for "it is I who have assigned it to you upon the altar to ransom your lives," when you take the animal life for its flesh. Thus, the law of Lev 17:11 informs the Israelite that slaughtering a sacrificial animal for its flesh constitutes murder unless he offers its blood upon the altar to ransom his life (details in Milgrom 1971b).

The ethical sensitivity displayed by this rationale need not surprise us when we consider its likely background. Anthropological and comparative evidence indicates that the reluctance to kill an animal harks back to a much earlier period, when it was believed that the disembodied spirit of the animal, unless ritually appeased, would take revenge upon the hunter and his community (for examples see Frazer and Gaster 1959: 471–79).

The survival of this belief is attested among the sacrificial rites of the ancient Greeks: "A procession escorts the animal to the altar. Everyone hopes as a rule that the animal will go to the altar complaisantly, or rather voluntarily. . . . The animal is sprinkled with water, causing it to jerk its head, which is interpreted as the animal nodding its assent. The god at Delphi pronounced through the oracle: 'That which willingly nods . . . I say you may justly sacrifice'" (Burkert 1985: 56; 1983: 12–22). A similar belief apparently lies behind the rabbinic rule: "If the (Red) Cow refuses to go forth they may not send out with her" (*m. Para* 3:7), which clearly implies that the Red Cow (Num 19) could not be dragged by force (Lieberman 1950: 159–60).

It is in ancient Mesopotamia, however, that we find the closest prototype to our rationale. As demonstrated by Hallo (1987; 1983) the Sumerian myth of Lugalbanda relates that he is the first(?) human to make the transition from vegetarian to carnivore. He is only able to assuage his reservations about killing the animal he has captured by means of a revealed ritual and a sacred meal to which he invites the high gods of the Sumerian pantheon, presumably to sanction the slaughter and consumption of the animal. Thus the guilt engendered by the slaying of animals is embedded deep in the psyche of the human race. It was, however, the innovation of the Priestly legists that converted this guilt into an ethical imperative.

In sum, we see that the Bible decrees that blood is life; human blood may not be spilled and animal blood may not be ingested. Israel is enjoined to observe an additional safeguard: Blood of sacrificial animals must be drained on the authorized altar. But to complete the biblical record of the blood prohibition we must take note of the far-reaching amendment introduced by Deuteronomy. This book desacralizes the blood requirement: henceforth Israel may slaughter its meat profanely (Deut 12:15–16, 22–24). Thus, in effect, Israelite and non-Israelite are equated. Jew and non-Jew are bound by a single prohibition, to abstain from blood. The rationale is now clear. The human being must never lose sight of the fundamental tenet for a viable human society. Life is inviolable; it may not be treated lightly. Mankind has a right to nourishment, not to life. Hence the blood, the symbol of life, must be drained, returned to the universe, to God (see further Milgrom 1963; 1989a).

D. The Ethical Foundations of the Dietary System: 2. Ritual Slaughter

The technique for animal slaughter is nowhere prescribed in Scripture. Nevertheless, it may be implied by the terminology. Our investigation begins with Deuteronomy. Twice in the same pericope it concedes the right of profane slaughter: "But whenever you desire, you may slaughter *(tizbaḥ)* and eat meat . . . in all your settlements" (Deut 12:15); "you may slaughter *(wĕzābaḥtā)* any of your cattle or sheep . . . as I commanded you and you may eat in your settlements" (Deut 12:21). In both citations, the key verb "slaughter" is rendered by *zābaḥ*. Its use here occasions surprise because elsewhere in biblical Hebrew and cognate languages it bears a sacral connotation.

Of the 129 times *zābaḥ* occurs in Scripture it most often denotes sacrificial slaughter (e.g., Exod 23:18 [||šāḥaṭ, Exod 34:25]; Isa 66:13 [||šāḥaṭ]; Hos 8:13). This is also the dominant meaning of all its cognates. The case of Ugaritic is most illuminating. Ug. *dbḥ* chiefly designates sacrificial slaughter (e.g., *UT* 121.1.1, 10 = *CTA* 20.1.1, 10 = *KTU* 1.20.1.1, 10; *UT* 2.24, 32 = *CTA* 32.24, 32 = *KTU* 1.40.24, 32). As in Hebrew, the cultic context is corroborated by the nominal forms: *zebaḥ/dbḥ* and *mizbēaḥ/mdbḥ(t)*, "sacrificial meal" and "altar." Again in both languages, the verb carries with it a secondary meaning "offer the *zebaḥ/dbḥ* sacrifice" (e.g., compare the offering of the *zebaḥ: lizbōaḥ lipnê YHWH* [Lev 9:4; cf. Deut 18:3; 1 Sam 2:15; Zech 14:21] with that of the *ʿōlâ* and *ḥaṭṭāʾt: wĕhaqrēb lipnê YHWH* [Lev 9:2; cf. 1:3, 10, 14; 4:3, 14, 23]).

zebaḥ also describes illegitimate sacrifices to the Lord (e.g., Isa 65:3; Ezek 20:25) and worship of other gods (e.g., Exod 34:15; Deut 32:17; Judg 16:23). Its scope also includes a metaphoric usage, the *zebaḥ* of corpses that the Lord arrays for the wild beasts and birds (e.g., Isa 34:6; Jer 46:10; Ezek 39:17–19; Zeph 1:7–8), but even here the sacrificial context is evident from the use of cultic vocabulary: *hiqdîš qĕrūʾāyw, ḥēleb wĕdām*, and the like. Finally, *piʿel zibbēaḥ* is found twice with the iterative connotation of performing numerous sacrifices (1 Kgs 8:5 [2 Chr 5:6]; 2 Chr 30:32) and in the remaining instances with regard to illegitimate or idolatrous worship (1 Kgs 3:2–3; 11:8; 24:44; 2 Kgs 12:4, 32; 14:4; 15:4, 35; 16:4 [2 Chr 28:4]; Hos 4:13–14; 11:2; 12:2; Hab 1:16; Ps 136:38; 2 Chr 28:23; 33:22). Thus the *piʿel* also verifies that the root *zbḥ* is exclusively a cultic term, referring to ritual slaughter and sacrifice.

According to the Lexicons, there are seven alleged exceptions. Five of them seem to deal with nonsacrificial feasts (Num 22:40; 1 Sam 28:24; 1 Kgs 19:16, 21; Ezek 34:3; 2 Chr 18:2). Yet a closer examination of their respective contexts will not support this claim. Neither Balak nor Ahab would have invited Balaam or Jehoshaphat, respectively, to a profane feast (Num 22:40; 2 Chr 18:2) whose purpose was to implore the help of the Lord against the enemy. It is hardly conceivable that Elisha would have slaughtered the team of oxen for a profane meal in celebration of his anointment as Elijah's successor (1 Kgs 19:16, 21). Nor is it likely that the witch of Endor would have prepared a profane meal (1 Sam 28:24) before the very king who troubled himself to improvise an altar on the battlefield so that his troops would not be guilty of profane or illicit slaughter (1 Sam 14:32–35). It is possible that the last of these alleged exceptions (Ezek 34:3) deals with common slaughter—though the text is obscure—because its setting is in the Babylonian exile when sacrifice was impossible and after the deuteronomic concession had gone into effect. Indeed, according to the accepted view that common slaughter was permitted for the first time with the promulgation of Deuteronomy under Josiah (cf. Rabbi Ishmael in *Sipre* on Deut 12:20; *b. Ḥul.* 16b [bar.]), a legal sanction for profane slaughter is simply out of the question for early Israel.

The two instances that remain (Deut 12:15, 21) are indeed exceptions to the rule. Their context leaves no room for doubt: Deuteronomy's demand for cult centralization has made profane slaughter imperative. Why then does it use the verb *zābaḥ*, which, as shown, never refers to profane slaughter but only to the slaughter and preparation of sacrifices?

The key to this puzzle, I submit, lies in a clause in the second citation: "you may slaughter . . . *ka'ăšer ṣiwwîtīkā* as I commanded you" (v 21). What is the antecedent; to what command does it refer? Modern scholars, without exception, hold that this phrase in v 21 refers to the similar instruction of v 15, namely, that Israelites may now obtain meat by common slaughter (v 21) as indicated earlier in the same pericope (v 15). This interpretation cannot stand for three reasons: (1) *ṣiwwîtīkā* 'I commanded you' implies an obligation. Conversely, the tone of the pericope—"whenever you desire" (vv 15, 20, 21); "if you have the desire" (v 20)—implies volition. Profane slaughter, just like eating meat, is a matter of choice, not a requirement. (2) D. Z. Hoffmann correctly observed (1961 *ad loc.*) that whenever Deuteronomy refers to its own statements it invariably resorts to the expression *'ăšer 'ānōkî mĕṣawweh* 'that I command' (4:2, 40; 6:2, 5; 7:11; 8:1, 11; 10:13; 11:8, 13, 22, 27, 28; 12:14, 28 [N.B. in the same chapter!]; 13:11, 19; 15:5; 19:9; 27:1, 4, 10; 28:1, 13, 14, 15; 30:2, 8, 11, 16). Thus when Deuteronomy cites itself it always uses the participle and never the perfect. (3) More importantly, the clause *ka'ăšer ṣiwwâ* or *ka'ăšer nišbaʿ* or *ka'ăšer dibber* serves a specific literary function in Deuteronomy: it is D's "cf.," its unique formula by which it indicates its sources (for details, see Milgrom 1976e). Thus *wĕzābaḥtā . . . ka'ăšer ṣiwwîtīkā* 'you may slaughter . . . as I commanded you' (Deut 12:21) signifies that common slaughter must follow the same method practiced in sacrificial slaughter. Indeed, this is precisely how the Tannaites interpret this verse (*Sipre* on Deut 12:21). But if it indicates that D relied on a source, we search for it in vain. The plethora and minutiae of P's sacrificial laws contain not one hint concerning a proper technique for slaughtering. This glaring omission compels D. Z. Hoffmann to endorse the view of Rabbi Judah (*Sipre* on Deut 12:21; *b. Ḥul.* 28a [bar.]) that it was an oral tradition. I believe instead that there is textual evidence that has been overlooked—the verb *šāḥaṭ*.

The most significant fact about *šāḥaṭ* is that it is P's *exclusive term* for animal slaughter. *šāḥaṭ* is found seventy-nine times in Scripture, forty of which are in P and thirteen more in writings dependent on P, to wit: four times in Ezekiel, chaps. 40–48 (40:39, 41, 42; 44:1) and nine times in Second Chronicles (29:22[3], 24; 30:15, 17; 35:1, 6, 11). Outside P it is found three times in connection with the paschal sacrifice (Exod 12:21; 34:25; Ezra 6:20); seven times in a cultic context (Gen 22:10; 1 Sam 1:25; 14:32, 34[2]; 22:13; Isa 66:3; Hos 5:2); three times in regard to human sacrifice (Isa 57:5; Ezek 16:21; 23:39) and ten times in regard to mass human slaughter (Num 14:16; Judg 12:6; 1 Kgs 18:40; 2 Kgs 10:7, 14; Jer 39:6[2]; 41:7; 52:10[2]). Thus the spectrum of *šāḥaṭ* is congruent with that of *zābaḥ* in that both designate sacrificial slaughter and, in metaphoric usage, the mass slaughter of persons.

The lexicographical question is obvious: why does P refrain from using *zābaḥ*, employing exclusively *šāḥaṭ*? The answer lies in the restricted application of *zābaḥ* in P: it is found only in connection with the *zebaḥ* sacrifice; hence, it cannot denote the slaughter of *other* sacrifices. Indeed, P is reluctant to use the verb *zābaḥ* even with the *zebaḥ* (the sole exception is Lev 9:4; contrast v 18) but prefers *hiqrîb* (Lev 3:1, 3; 7:11–18, 29, 33; etc.). To be sure, H, entwined with P material in Lev 17–26, prefers the verb *zābaḥ* (Lev 17:5[2], 7; 19:5[2]; 22:29). Even so, the specific meaning of *zābaḥ* in H is not "slaughter" but "offer the *zebaḥ*," in other words, it refers to the entire sacrificial procedure, including slaughter (this also holds true for P; contrast *zābaḥ*, Lev 9:4, with *šāḥaṭ* v 18). Indeed, when H wishes to specify "slaughter," it also resorts to *šāḥaṭ* (Lev 22:28, and cf. v 29). Thus in all of P (H included) *zābaḥ* means "offer the *zebaḥ*," leaving *šāḥaṭ* as the exclusive term for slaughter.

Is *šāḥaṭ* capable of greater precision? I believe it means "slit the throat." Such is the meaning of Arab. *śaḥaṭa;* more importantly, the noun *maśḥaṭ* means "throat" (Snaith 1975). Moreover, because the sacrificial blood was collected in bowls, *mizrāqôt* (e.g., Exod 27:3; Num 4:14), literally, "tossing bowls" *(NEB)*, it seems that the only way this could happen was to slit the animal's throat so that the blood from the major blood vessels would quickly drain from the cut into a vessel (D. Wright: see the Note on 9:12). Indirect evidence is also supplied by cognate languages. Akkadian for animal slaughter is *ṭabāḫu*, but "cut the throat" can only be expressed literally, as *nakāsu napištam*. Akkadian, then, has no single word for this concept. Ugaritic has two verbs for slaughter, *dbḥ* and *ṭbḥ;* the former, as shown above, denotes sacred slaughter and the latter, it can be shown, denotes common slaughter: *UT* 51.6.40 = *CTA* 4.6.40 = *KTU* 1.4.6.40; *UT* 62.18–28 = *CTA* 6.1.18–28 = *KTU* 1.6.1.18–28; *UT* 124.12 = *CTA* 22.2.12 = *KTU* 1.22.2.12; *UT* 127.17, 20 = *CTA* 16.6.17, 20 = *KTU* 1.16.6.17, 20; *UT* 'nt pl.x.iv.30 = *CTA* 1.4.30 = *KTU* 1.1.4.30; *UT* 2 Aqht 2.29 = *CTA* 17.2.29 = *KTU* 1.17.2.29; *UT* 1153.3–5. Neither term, however, is limited to the meaning "cut the throat." In Hebrew, likewise, *zābaḥ* and *ṭābaḥ* denote, respectively, sacred and common slaughter: *zābaḥ*, as demonstrated above, and *ṭābaḥ*, by the following: Gen 43:16; Exod 21:32; Deut 28:31; 1 Sam 25:11; Isa 53:7; Jer 11:19; 12:3; 50:27, 40; Ps 44:23; Prov 7:22; 9:2. Significantly, only Hebrew has a third term for slaughter, *šāḥaṭ*. Thus Hebrew would seem to contain two identical words for sacred slaughter, *zābaḥ* and *šāḥaṭ*, unless the latter had a more restricted, technical meaning, which may be slaughtering by cutting the throat.

Rabbinic evidence, also by indirect inference, points to the same conclusion. Jewish tradition has always interpreted *šāḥaṭ* in this manner (cf. *b. Ḥul.* 27a; Ramban on Deut 12:21). Moreover, that the Mishna states anonymously and categorically "all may slaughter (ritually) at any time and with any implement" (*m. Ḥul.* 1:2), foregoing any discussion concerning the method of slaughter, is clear evidence that the slaughtering method was already fixed by tradition and may stem from biblical times. Our verse now adds greater force to this argument: *wĕzābaḥtā . . . ka'ăšer ṣiwwîtīkā* 'you may slaughter . . . as I commanded you' (Deut 12:21). D therefore implies that there *is* a specific method of slaughtering sacrificial animals, which is to be followed in common slaughter, a method that, I suggest, may be implied by *šāḥaṭ* 'slit the throat'. (There is no proof, however, that the rabbinic technique of ritual slaughter, i.e., a clean, transverse cut of both the esophagus and the trachea so that all the main blood vessels are severed [cf. *Sipre* on Deut 12:22; *m. Ḥul.* 2:4], stems from biblical times. The absence of *šāḥaṭ* in Deut 12:15, 21 and indeed, in all of D, is probably due to D's ignorance of its technical meaning as developed by P.)

But what is the authorized slaughtering technique of the sanctuary? The Bible gives no answer, but the Talmud does, and with many details. All of these clearly demonstrate the perfection of a slaughtering technique whose purpose is to render the animal unconscious with a minimum of suffering. To be sure, these regulations are postbiblical, but they are only the refinements of the ethical impulse that generated the initial method developed by Israel's priests for the sanctuary. Moreover, there is extrabiblical evidence for the antiquity of supervised ritual slaughter. Scenes from the period of the Old Kingdom in Egypt testify to the importance of certifying the purity of slaughtered animals, which was done by a "doctor and a *wʿb*-priest" (Fischer 1976: 98 n. 14), who have rightly been compared to the *šôḥēṭ*, the authorized ritual slaughterer of rabbinic law (Leibovitch 1953: 59–60). It thus would be germane to cite some of the talmudic rules concerning the slaughtering knife (cited for convenience from the law code, the *Shulḥan ʿAruk*):

> The slaughtering knife must be razor sharp and perfectly smooth, and must have no dents or nicks, since these would tear the flesh and cause unnecessary pain. The knife must be examined before and after the slaughtering to make sure it is without blemish during the actual slaughtering (*Yoreh Deʿah* 18:3, 12). The three sides of the knife, i.e. the sharp edge and its sides, must be examined (*b. Ḥul.* 17b; *ʿAruk Hashulḥan, Yoreh Deʿah* 18:12). If the slightest dent or nick is felt, the knife is invalidated (*Yoreh Deʿah* 18:10).

Of germane interest are the five cutting processes that invalidate the slaughter (cited from Klein 1979: 311):

1. *Šĕhîyâ*—pausing or delaying. The knife must be drawn quickly across the neck of the animal, beast, or bird without a stop. The smallest delay or pause renders the slaughter defective and the animal not kosher (*Yoreh Deʿah* 23:2, in Rama).

2. *Děrāsâ*—pressing. The blade must be applied with a to-and-fro motion, not with a chopping or striking motion (*Yoreh De'ah* 24:1).

3. *Ḥălādâ*—burrowing. The blade must not be inserted under the skin and used with an upward thrust (*Yoreh De'ah* 24:7, 8).

4. *Hagrāmâ*—cutting outside the specified zone, or deflecting (*Yoreh De'ah* 24:12).

5. *'Ăqîrâ*—tearing out. The trachea and esophagus must be cut with the blade and not torn out or lacerated in any way (*Yoreh De'ah* 24:15).

Could this concern for humaneness be the invention of the talmudic rabbis instead of their legacy from the past? Hardly so. The rabbis themselves are ignorant of the humane rationale for their method and resort only to Deut 12:21 as proof that the same technique was employed by the biblical priests. To be sure, they refined the technique and added safeguards. But in effect, they preserved and enhanced its original ethical motivation—that the death of the animal should be effected in such a way (by painless slaughter and the immediate drainage of the blood) that the slaughterer's sense of reverence for life will never be blunted (see further Milgrom 1976e).

E. The Ethical Foundations of the Dietary System:
3. The Prohibited Animals

The literature on Lev 11 is vast. There are as many theories as theorists. The traditionalist view is that the list of prohibited animals is simply arbitrary, the unalterable and inscrutable will of God: "A man should not say 'I do not desire to eat the flesh of swine.' . . . On the contrary, he should say 'I desire it but must abstain because my father in heaven has so ordered'" (*Sipra*, Qedoshim 11:22; cf. *Sipra*, Aḥare 13:10). This position will not be discussed because, as we shall see, there are definite and ascertainable reasons that lie behind the food taboos of Leviticus. Some widely held theories can be dismissed out of hand. For example, the cultic theory holds that forbidden animals either represent deities (i.e., totems) or were used in pagan worship (e.g., Smith 1927: 269–310, 596–600). This position, however, founders on its own premises: Canaanites sacrificed the same animals prescribed in Israel's cult and, consequently, they should have been prohibited by Scripture. A recent proposal theorizes that all of the prohibited animals are life-threatening because either they are chthonic, inhabiting locations that are inimical to life, or they are predators and carcass eaters (Kornfeld 1965). This theory, however, cannot explain the exclusion of such domesticated herbivorous animals as the camel, donkey, rabbit, and horse. Similar obvious objections springing from the biblical data can be mustered to refute many of the other proposals (see Kornfeld 1965: 134–36).

There are, however, two theories that merit serious consideration. The first is the hygienic hypothesis: the forbidden animals are carriers of disease. The ancients discovered the harmful animals empirically, and modern science has verified their findings: the pig is a bearer of trichinosis, the hare of tularemia; carrion-eating birds harbor disease and fish without fins and scales attract disease because they are mud burrowers. The hygienic hypothesis is an honored one. It counts among its proponents Maimonides (*Guide* 3.48), Ramban (on 11:9), and Rashbam (on 11:3), and it is probably no accident that the former two were physicians. And in our own day, William Foxwell Albright, in his last work, became its partisan (1968: 175–81). Even so, there are weighty objections to this theory. For example, the camel, a prohibited animal, is a succulent delicacy for the Arabs to this day, and there is no evidence that they suffer gastronomically. Also, if hygiene were the sole reason for the diet laws, why were they restricted to the animal kingdom? Why were poisonous plants not prohibited?

A different approach is taken by the symbolic theory. It avers that the behavior of animals corresponds to and informs the behavior of man. The tabooed animals are those whose ways do not exemplify proper conduct. Conversely, if they remind man of virtue they are adjudged to be edible. Thus the Letter of Aristeas, probably of the second century b.c.e., explains that cud-chewing is the sign of a permitted animal because it teaches the importance of meditation: man should have thoughts as well as food to chew on (153–54; cf. Philo, *Laws* 4. 116–18). Nonetheless, this theory too is riddled by objections. It is highly subjective and capricious: animal behavior will mean whatever its beholder wants it to mean, and no independent verification is possible.

Yet there is one modern offshoot of the symbolic theory that meets the canons of scientific method. It was advanced by the social anthropologist Mary Douglas (1966). Douglas adheres to the basic teaching of Emile Durkheim that the customs and rituals of any society are reflections of its values. So too a society's taxonomy of the animal world will mirror its value system. Douglas has applied this Durkheimian insight to Lev 11 by means of her theory of dirt. She defines dirt as matter out of place. Dirt, then, is a by-product of the classification of nature found in each society: what it considers "order" is fine; whatever is "disorder" is dirt.

Douglas came to Lev 11 via the Lele tribe of Africa, which, she discovered to her surprise, has complex dietary regulations. What did it mean, she asks, that a primitive society could develop a sophisticated system of food taboos? Her conclusion is that it is fundamental to human nature to order and classify nature. When earliest man had to make his way through an unknown universe, he had need of categories that would enable him to distinguish between what was beneficent and what was harmful. He had to know how to relate to any new phenomenon that confronted him. Therefore, he created criteria by which he could discern whether the phenomenon was going to be helpful or prove a danger.

This taxonomic characteristic of the mind developed at the inception of humanity, but it continues unabated in modern man. We too classify, and whatever we reject we call "dirt." Nor are our categories always rational or logical. Douglas cites some personal examples. Allow me to do the same. My wife brings cups of tea into her study. Occasionally, I find a half-filled cup in the bathroom. Anything wrong hygienically? No, but I am invariably annoyed. Conversely, I recall bringing home a new pair of shoes and setting them on the kitchen table. A sweep of the hand tumbled them to the floor. "But," I protested, "they are new, never worn." "I don't care," she replied, "they don't belong on the kitchen table." Indeed, the tea cups and shoes become dirt if, in Douglas's definition, they are matter out of place. (The association of pollution with disorder has recently been verified for India [Bean 1981]). This insight is the key to unlocking the enigma of Lev 11.

First, the Durkheimian thesis that animal taxonomy is a mirror of human society is fully corroborated by the Bible, especially P. Animals, like humans, possess a *nepeš* (Gen 9:9–10; Lev 11:10, 46; 24:18; Num 31:28). Hence, their blood must also be buried (Lev 17:13). Animals are responsible under the law. If they kill a human being they must die (Gen 9:5), and their meat may not be eaten nor may their carcasses be sold (Exod 21:28–32). Bestiality incurs the death penalty for the animal as well as for the human participant (Lev 20:15–16). As animals were also a party to God's covenant (Gen 9:9–10) they must keep the Sabbath (Exod 20:10), and once again in the Messianic age they will renew their covenant with God (Hos 2:20) and will be predators no more (Isa 11:7).

Douglas divides the animal world into three spheres. The classification is that of Gen 1, corresponding to the three elements of creation: water, air, and earth. Each sphere has a peculiar mode of motion associated with it. For the skies, birds need two wings to fly and two legs to walk. On the land, animals have four legs and hoofs to walk on (actually split hoofs, 11:3; Deut 14:6, a crucial point overlooked by Douglas; see below). And in the seas, fish have fins and scales to swim with (in which case scales are superfluous—another point overlooked by Douglas; see the NOTE on "scales," v 9). Creatures that cross boundaries are anomalies. Insects that fly but have four or more legs (11:20) are an abomination, but if they have two legs to hop with (11:21–22) they are edible. (Here Douglas confuses *šereṣ* and *remeś* [1966: 56] and mistakenly assumes that because frogs hop they are permitted as food. True, frogs do not defile, *m. Ṭohar.* 5:1—not being among the eight named rodents and reptiles of 11:29–30—but they may not be eaten!) Birds that are carnivores (*m. Ḥul.* 3:6) are tabooed because carrion contains blood (Letter of Aristeas 146). And creepers *(remeś)* engage in an indeterminate form of locomotion. They are neither fish, flesh, nor fowl. Rather, they belong to the underworld—an abomination. Strikingly, Douglas reminds us, the serpent was cursed by the removal of its feet (Gen 3:14).

The parenthetical remarks, above, are a caveat to the reader of Douglas that her biblical comments, especially in her early writings, are replete with errors. A constellation of them appears in the compass of three pages of one essay (1972a [1975a]: 73–75), where she not only cites a host of wrong or nonexistent verses but commits the following mistakes, in consecutive order: (1) *běhēmâ* (1:2) is a quadruped, not a domestic animal (cf. 11:2). (2) The sparrow may be permitted for the table but absolutely not for the altar. (3) Firstlings are eaten by their owners, not by the priests, according to Deuteronomy. (4) Anomalous creatures are not to be touched only when dead *(něbēlâ)*. (5) Only bearers of impurity are banned from the Temple (12:3), not bearers of blemishes! (This last error vitiates fig. 7 and, hence, its analogy with fig. 8.) (6) Priests not Levites "judge the cleanness and purify the uncleanness of Israelites." (7) Neither Levites nor priests, even unblemished ones, may enter the Holy of Holies; only the high priest may do so, under special safeguards (chap. 16). Besides, blemishes disqualify a priest from officiating at the altar but not from entering the sanctuary court or partaking of sacred food (21:17–23). A far more serious error is her conclusion that "the dietary laws . . . inspired meditations on the oneness, purity, and completeness of God" (1966: 57). To be sure, her definition of the term "Holy as wholeness and completeness" (ibid. 51) is justified, but in the Priestly system the realm of the holy is restricted to the sanctuary, the sacrifice, and the priest. But a blemished (pure) animal may be eaten, and a blemished Israelite may enter the sacred precincts. The altar, by contrast, is served only by whole (unblemished) animals and priests (cf. 21:16–23; 22:17–25). Douglas has confused the binary opposites of *qōdeš* 'holy' and *ḥōl* 'common'. Her error, unfortunately, has been followed by others (e.g., Countryman 1988: 25–27).

Furthermore, Douglas's theory of dirt as matter out of place has been trenchantly criticized by Meigs (1978), who correctly argues that though many phenomena are out of place only a few are pollutants. To illustrate, let me use the example I cited. Shoes on the table are polluting because they may carry feces, spit, etc., that litter the streets, but a dress laid on the table would not evoke revulsion. I objected to the cup of tea in the bathroom because I instinctively feared its contamination by bathroom odors. But had the cup been empty or had I found clothing hanging there, again, it would be matter out of place but I would not have reacted viscerally. The reason, Meigs suggests, is that things pollute only when they threaten to gain access to one's body: the dirt on the shoes may get into our food; the polluted tea may be ingested. Meigs's own theory of pollution is closer to the mark and will be discussed in chap. 15, COMMENT G. In any event, Douglas's theory of dirt has proved helpful but inadequate; it throws light on the animal classification of Lev 11, but does not explain it.

Far more useful, however, is Douglas's utilization of the Durkheimian hypothesis that the classification of animals reflects society's values. The correspondences between the human and animal worlds come into clearer view once it is noticed that each comprises three identical divisions that can be depicted as

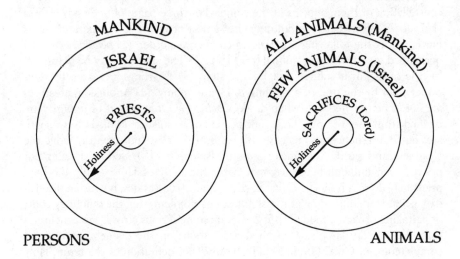

PERSONS   ANIMALS

FIGURE 13

concentric circles, as depicted in fig. 13. In the priestly view (P and H), the tripartite division of the human race corresponds to three of its covenants with God: mankind (Gen 9:1–11, including the animals), Israel (i.e., the patriarchs, Gen 17:2; Lev 26:42), and the priesthood (Num 25:12–15; Jer 33:17–22).* The three human divisions are matched by the three animal divisions: all animals are permitted to mankind, except their blood (Gen 9:3–5); the edible few to Israel (Lev 11); and of the edible, the domesticated and unblemished qualify as sacrifices to the Lord (Lev 22:17–25).

The congruence of the two sets of concentric circles begs for cross-comparison. First, the innermost circles: priests–sacrifices. Both priests and sacrifices fit to serve the altar must be unblemished (21:17, 21; 22:17–20). Moreover, it is no accident that two consecutive chapters of Leviticus (chaps. 21–22[H]) specify

* A word on the scriptural support for the Priestly covenant is also in order. Num 25:12–13 promises Phineas *běrît kěhunnat ʿôlām* 'a covenant of priesthood for all time'—not the high priesthood (the prevalent interpretation) but the priesthood! Only one *Sitz im Leben* suggests itself: the banishment of Abiathar *and his entire family* from the Jerusalem Temple (1 Kgs 2:26–27; cf. 1 Sam 2:27–36), with the result that the Zadokites (the line of Phineas) became its sole officiants. To be sure, non-Zadokites continued to serve on the Temple staff but not as officiants (Ezek 40:45–46; 43:19; 44:15–16). Jeremiah, by contrast, probably of the house of Ithamar, rejects the Zadokite monopoly and, hence, employs the deuteronomic term "levitical priests" (Jer 33:17–22).

the imperfections that disqualify priests and animals for the altar—and by and large they prove identical! These are the priestly blemishes: *ʿiwwēr* 'blind'; *pissēaḥ* 'lame'; *ḥārum* 'split nose' *(Sipra)*/'stunted limb' (Ibn Ezra); *śārûaʿ* 'overgrown limb'; *šeber regel* 'broken leg'; *šeber yād* 'broken arm'; *gibbēn* 'hunchback'; *daq* 'dwarf'(?); *tĕballul bĕʿênô* 'a growth in his eye'; *gārāb* 'sores'; *yallepet* 'scabs'; *mĕrôaḥ ʾāšek* 'crushed testes' (21:18–20). The disqualifying animal blemishes are: *ʿawweret* 'blind'; *šābûr* 'broken bones'; *ḥārûṣ* 'maimed' (Ibn Ezra)/'sty' (*Tg. Ps.-J.*, Rashi); *yabbelet* 'wart'(?); *gārāb* 'sores'; *yallepet* 'scabs'; *śārûaʿ* 'overgrown limb'; *qālûṭ* 'stunted limb'; *māʿûk, kātût, nātûq, kārût* 'bruised, crushed, torn, cut [testes]' (22:22–24). Each list contains twelve items, probably to achieve parity in the totals. Certain additions were made to the originally shorter animal list, namely, the minutiae of injuries to the testes. Indeed, the patent artificiality of the lists underscores my main point: human and animal defects are equated. Yet, despite this artificial extension, the correspondences are manifestly clear. There are five identical items: blind, overgrown limb, broken bones (comprising two items in the priestly list), sores, and scabs. The remaining items are difficult to match because they are mainly unidentifiable. But the following are possibly semantic equivalents: *ḥārūm* 'stunted limb'(?) or *pissēaḥ* 'lame' || *qālûṭ* 'stunted limb'; *tĕballul bĕʿênô* 'a growth in his eye' || *ḥārûṣ* 'sty'(?); *mĕrôaḥ ʾāšek* 'crushed testes' || *māʿûk, kātût, nātûq, kārût* 'bruised, crushed, torn, cut [testes]'. The difference in terminology may be ascribed to the special circumstances of each species. Obviously, the exposed testes of the animal would be subject to a greater variety of injuries than those of man, and a hunchback would only be considered a defect in the upright human but not in the animal. Nonetheless, *mutatis mutandis,* the same blemishes that invalidate officiating priests also invalidate animal sacrifices.

The innermost circles, it should be borne in mind, are deliberately set apart from the middle ones, implying that the realms of priest and laity, on the one hand, and sanctuary and land, on the other, must remain distinct entities. The list of edible quadrupeds in Deuteronomy points to this goal. Of the list's seven wild animals (Deut 14:5) the first three are identifiable. They are the *ʾayyāl* 'roe deer' (Ginsberg 1973: 131 n. 3), *ṣĕbî* 'gazelle', and *yaḥmûr* 'fallow deer' (Feliks 1984). It should be noted, however, that two of them, the *ʾayyāl* and *yaḥmûr,* were sacrificial animals in Ugarit (*CTA* 61.18–29; Ginsberg 1973: 131–32). Furthermore, faunal remains in the altar room and in the chamber immediately to the north of it at Tel Dor, dating from the eleventh to the eighth century B.C.E., contain bone fragments of twenty-eight deer (Wapnish and Hesse, table 4). Thus it is clear that deer were acceptable as sacrifices in Canaanite and even in (north) Israelite sanctuaries. The fact that they were excluded from the Priestly system must therefore be ascribed to a conscious effort to restrict the sacrificial quadrupeds to a narrower range of edible animals, namely, the domesticated species, as a model for the differentiation between priests and ordinary Israelites. Just as not all edible animals but only domesticated ones qualify for the altar, so not all Israelites but only descendents of Aaron qualify for the priesthood.

Another correspondence offers greater precision: the firstborn males of both humans and animals are the Lord's property (Exod 13:2). That is why the Levites who replace the firstborn also belong to God (Num 3:11–13) and why the remaining firstborn (Num 3:44–51) and those of subsequent generations must be redeemed from the sanctuary (Num 18:15–16).

The innermost circles, however, are not fixed and static. For both man and beast there is a centrifugal movement to the middle circles. According to H, although priests are inherently holy, all of Israel is enjoined to achieve holiness (e.g., 19:2; see the NOTE on 11:44). Not that Israel is to observe the regimen of the priests or to attain their status in the sanctuary. Rather, by scrupulously observing God's commandments, moral and ritual alike, Israel can achieve holiness. Signs of this mobility are reflected in the animal sphere. Sacrificial animals are slaughtered by their lay owners, not by priests (NOTE on 1:5). Thus it is hardly surprising that when the layman is permitted to slaughter his animals at home (Deut 12:15, 21), he is enjoined to employ the same slaughtering technique practiced in the sanctuary (see COMMENT D above).

This dynamic quality of the innermost circle is evident in yet another realm, space. It also comprises the same tripartite divisions: mankind, Israel, and priests, as demonstrated schematically in fig. 14.

P harbors an old tradition that the entire camp of Israel in the wilderness cannot tolerate severe impurity (Num 5:1–4; cf. 31:19). This tradition is echoed in D, which states explicitly that the camp must remain holy (Deut 23:10–15). It is H, however, that extends this view logically and consistently to the future residence of Israel—the Promised Land. Hence, impurities produced by Israel by violating the Lord's prohibitions—both moral and ritual (see the NOTE on "commandments," 4:2)—pollute not only the sanctuary but the entire land. Because God dwells in the land as well as in the sanctuary (e.g., 25:23; 26:11; cf. Josh 22:19; Hos 9:3–4), the land cannot abide pollution (e.g., 18:25–30; cf. Num 35:33–34). It is, therefore, no accident that H enjoins upon both the Israelite and the resident alien *(gēr)*, that is to say, all those who live on the land, to keep the land holy by guarding against impurity and following the prescribed purificatory procedures (e.g., Num 15:27–29; 19:10b–13, in which *gēr* is an H addition) so that the Lord will continue to reside in it and bless the land and its inhabitants with fertility and security (26:3–11).

Comparison of the two middle circles of the human and animal realms yields the following unambiguous relationship: as God has restricted his choice of the nations to Israel, so must Israel restrict its choice of edible animals to the few sanctioned by God. The bond between the choice of Israel and the dietary restrictions is intimated in the deuteronomic code when it heads its list of prohibited animals with a notice concerning Israel's election: "For you are a holy *(qādôš)* people to the Lord; the Lord your God chose you from among all the

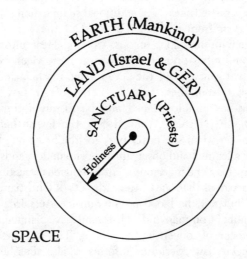

FIGURE 14

peoples on earth to be his treasured people" (Deut 14:2). Furthermore, Israel's designation as "a holy *(qādôš)* people" concludes the deuteronomic diet list, thereby framing it as an inclusion (14:21; see COMMENT A above). What is merely implicit in D, however, is forcefully explicit in Lev 20 (H): "I am the Lord your God who set you apart *(hibdaltî)* from other peoples. So you shall set apart *(wĕhibdaltem)* the pure quadrupeds from the impure, the impure birds from the pure . . . which I have set apart *(hibdaltî)* for you to treat as impure. You shall be holy *(qĕdōšîm)* to me, for I the Lord am holy *(qādôš)* and I have set you apart *(wā'abdîl)* from other peoples to be mine" (20:24b–26). What could be clearer! Israel's attainment of holiness is dependent on setting itself apart from the nations and the prohibited animal foods. The dietary system is thus a reflection and reinforcement of Israel's election.

This motif of separation in Lev 20 (note that *hibdîl* occurs four times in these two and a half verses) is further extended and underscored by its context. It is the peroration to the pericope on forbidden sexual unions (20:7–21), which are attributed to the Canaanites, Israel's predecessors in the land, and to her Egyptian neighbor (18:3; 20:23). The implied nexus between sex and food, on the one hand, and apostasy, on the other, is expressly stated elsewhere in Scripture, for example, "you must not make a covenant with the inhabitants of the land, for they will lust after their gods and sacrifice to their gods and invite you, and you will eat of their sacrifices. And when you take wives from among their daughters for your sons, their daughters will lust after their gods and will cause your sons to lust after their gods" (Exod 34:15–16). This message was very well understood in Hellenistic times: "An additional signification (of the diet laws) is that we are *set apart* from all men. For most of the rest of mankind defile themselves by their promiscuous unions, working great unrighteousness, and whole countries and cities pride themselves on these vices. Not only do they have intercourse with males, but they even defile mothers and daughters. But we have kept apart from these things" (Letter of Aristeas 151–52; cf. also Jub 22:16). Thus sex and food, bed and board, are intimately related. In *Marjorie Morningstar* (Herman Wouk, 1955), the Jewish heroine finally succumbs to her seducer when she tastes pork for the first time. It is no accident that the author is a learned and observant Jew who understands that a breach in the dietary system may endanger one's entire religious structure.

It is also no accident that one of the early acts of Christianity was to abolish the dietary laws (but not the blood prohibition [cf. Acts 15:20]—significantly, because it is incumbent on mankind). Historians have claimed that the purpose was to ease the process of converting the gentiles. This is, at best, a partial truth. Abolishing the dietary laws, Scripture informs us, also abolishes the distinction between gentile and Jew. And that is exactly what the founders of Christianity intended to accomplish, to end once and for all the notion that God had covenanted himself with a certain people who would keep itself apart from all of the other nations. And it is these distinguishing criteria, the dietary laws (and circumcision), that were done away with. Christianity's intuition was correct: Israel's restrictive diet is a daily reminder to be apart from the nations (cf. Acts 10:9–16, 27–28; 11:4–12).

To recapitulate at this juncture, the insights of the Durkheimian school, especially as exemplified in the work of Mary Douglas, have led to the disclosure of the intricate connections between Israel's animal taxonomy and aspects of its value system, specifically, the requirement to separate itself from the nations by refraining from their meat and women and to separate itself to God by following his commandments along the road to holiness. In particular, Douglas has uncovered the basic postulate that underlies the criteria for permitted animals: each species must exhibit the locomotion that fits its medium. Still, this postulate does not completely satisfy. Regarding the quadrupeds, Douglas writes, "Any creature which has two legs and two hands and which goes on all fours like a quadruped is unclean (xi, 27). . . . This feature of this list is lost in the New Revised Standard Translation which uses the word 'paws' instead of hands" (1966: 55–56). Douglas is wrong. The word *kap* does not mean "hand" but its hollow, its palm. The foot, too, possesses a *kap*, namely, its sole (e.g., Gen 8:9; Deut 2:5; 28:56; Josh 3:13; 2 Kgs 19:24; Isa 1:6; 60:14). The *NEB*'s translation of *hōlēk ʿal-kappayim* as "go on flat paws" is precise. Thus, it is erroneous to say that animals with paws are excluded because they walk on hands. Moreover, even assuming hypothetically that Douglas were correct to contend that the only natural way for a quadruped to walk would be on hoofed feet, why then would the hoofs have to be split? A ruminant with a solid hoof should also be permitted!

Thus a new rationale for the criteria of quadrupeds must be sought. But in order to discover it, a prior question needs to be answered: which came first, the criteria or their application? Were the animals first tabooed and criteria were later devised to justify the taboos or, the reverse, criteria were drawn up first which then were used in classifying the animals? We are back to the contest between the hygienist and the anthropologist. Who is correct, Albright or Douglas? If Albright is right, criteria were devised to exclude certain animals because they were reputed disease-carriers. If Douglas is right then certain animals were excluded as a consequence of not meeting the criteria.

I submit that the four anomalous quadrupeds—the camel, the hare, the rock badger, and the pig—can serve as a decisive test. Let us first set the terms. If the hygienic theory holds, then these animals were tabooed because they were injurious to health. Only much later a classification was devised to justify their exclusion: chewing the cud and having split hoofs. The fact that there were just four anomalous quadrupeds bearing one of the two qualifying criteria can only mean that ancient Israel had a negative culinary experience only with those four anomalies. In fact, the chances are that Israel's environment possessed other such anomalies, but they were not entered into the list of prohibited animals either because, being wild, they were unattainable or because they were digestible. But if, in accordance with Douglas, the criteria came first, then it would have fallen upon Israelite zoologists to scour their environment to find all anomalous creatures possessing one of the two qualifying criteria.

This then is the test: If the four anomalies were listed because they were unfit for the table (the hygienist's theory), then Israel's zoological ambience probably numbers other quadrupeds with the same anomaly. But if they are listed because, as the text states, they do not fit the criteria, then the list is complete: there are no other such quadrupeds in Israel's environs. Thus if it turns out that even one more animal known to Israel is akin to the specified four, bearing one criterion but not the other, then it is a fatal blow to Douglas, for she cannot explain why the animal was omitted.

The results are in. There are six animals that bear this anomaly: the biblical four plus the llama and hippopotamus. The llama is indeed a ruminant whose hoofs are not cloven. But it (and its relatives, the alpaca, the guanaco, etc.) are indigenous to South America and clearly were unknown to ancient Israel. The hippopotamus, conversely, cloven-hoofed, herbivorous, but nonruminant, existed in the marshy (Philistine) coastal areas (Hass 1953; perhaps alluded to in Job 40:15–24) and probably was eaten (Davis 1985). Yet the cleft in its hoofs is so slight that it was missed by the ancients and even omitted by Aristotle in his *Historia animalis* (for other mistakes made by biblical zoologists, see the NOTES on the rock badger and hare, vv 5–6). Thus the verdict is clear and decisive: the criteria came first and only afterward four anomalies were found.

The Bible itself corroborates our findings. It is significant that the Deuteronomist is not satisfied merely to cite the criteria for quadrupeds; he takes pains to enumerate all of the permitted animals (Deut 14:4–5): three domestic and seven wild, mostly unidentifiable. This list is then followed by the criteria, as follows: *wĕkol-ʿbĕhēmâ mapreset parsâ* . . . , which must be rendered, "And any *other* quadruped that has hoofs . . ." (Deut 14:6). Therefore, this passage is saying that these ten quadrupeds are permitted plus all others that fit these criteria but as yet have not been found. The Deuteronomist lists the domestic animals because they need no longer be brought to the altar as a sacrifice but may be slaughtered profanely, that is, they are treated as game (see the NOTE on 11:3). He is induced, however, to include the seven wild species only for the reason that the criteria were before him and they impelled him to sponsor an investigation of all fauna of the land, even in wild, inaccessible places, in order to find all quadrupeds that matched the criteria. That the Deuteronomist has indeed done so is also supported by the conclusion, reached above (COMMENT B), that the deuteronomic list of prohibited animals (Deut 14:4–21) is based on Lev 11. What then is true for Deut 14 holds for Lev 11. The text of the latter must be accepted at face value. The camel, rock badger, hare, and pig were excluded only for the reason stated by the text: they do not fit the criteria.

It has been shown that of these four anomalies, the pig was abominated to begin with, and the criterion of chewing the cud was deliberately created in order to eliminate it from Israel's diet (for details see the NOTE on v 8). It seems that the unique circumstances of the pig can account for Douglas's subsequent change of mind. Succumbing to the critiques of fellow anthropologists (Bulmer 1967; Tambiah 1969), she has abandoned her original conclusion that the rejected animals are those that did not meet the criteria (1966) and she now maintains that these four animals reflect and reinforce important societal rules. Let us admit, though reluctantly, the case for the pig as a symbol of intermarriage on the grounds that dining with a Canaanite girl and her family, where pig is likely to be served (?), ultimately leads to intermarriage (Douglas 1975b), though the argument for idolatry—that is, the pig in chthonic worship—musters much more evidential support (NOTE on v 8). But what particular social values are symbolized by the camel, the rock badger, and the hare—not to speak of the legion of prohibited animals that cannot boast of either criteria? No, Douglas's initial insight stands, confirmed both by the test for the anomalous quadrupeds and by the textual evidence of Deuteronomy, adduced above.

One final question remains regarding quadruped criteria. If their intent was to confine Israel's meat diet to only the three domesticated species—cattle, sheep, and goats—why the need for criteria to begin with? Could not the Priestly legislator have simply stated *zōʾt habbĕhēmâ ʾăšer tōʾkēlû šôr śēh kĕśābîm wĕśēh ʿizzîm* 'These are the quadrupeds that you may eat: the ox, the sheep, and the goat' (cf. Deut 14:4)? Reference to the concentric-circle diagram (fig. 13) provides the answer. These three domesticated quadrupeds are eligible for the altar; they belong to the innermost circle: the domain of God. Yet Israel occupies the middle circle. It is under fewer constraints than the altar and, hence, is entitled to additional animals for its diet. These are provided by wild game. Israel's privilege to hunt down game is acknowledged by Leviticus (17:13-14) and confirmed by Deuteronomy, which explicitly adds seven wild quadrupeds—most of which are still unidentifiable (Deut 14:5). Thus, criteria had to be in place in order to extend Israel's approved list to animals of the hunt. This means that the diet laws of Lev 11 only deal with the nonsacrificial animals (with the exception of vv 39-40) and the sacrificial animals are taken for granted. This conclusion also vitiates the rationale for the dietary laws that the Israelites were "concerned that the animals they raise for food and those that they hunt be like those that God 'eats' (in the form of sacrifices)" (Firmage 1990: 97). If so, then the Israelites—or their priests—should have had their meat diet restricted solely to the sacrificial animals, which could simply have been named (as in Deut 14:4) without the need for criteria at all! (See further the NOTE on vv 3, 39-40.)

The chronological priority of the criteria implies a concomitant conclusion: they were not drawn up arbitrarily—to serve as generalizations for the already existent taboos, as erroneously maintained by the hygienists—but were formulated rationally, deliberately, with a conscious purpose in mind. And we have every right to ask: What was this purpose; what, indeed, could have been the intention behind the formulation of such bizarre criteria: cud-chewing and split-hoofed ungulates?

Because outside analogies do not seem to help, we are forced once again to return to the biblical text. A rationale, it turns out, is not at all absent from Lev 11. It is found in one concept—holiness. To the casual reader of the Bible it comes as a great surprise that this exalted concept of holiness is given as the reason in all four sources in which the prohibited foods are enumerated (Exod 22:30; Lev 11:44-45; 20:22-26; Deut 14:4-21). Moreover, one whose ear is sensitive to the sound of repeated words will react to these verses as a geiger counter to a lode of uranium. Listen to Lev 11:44: ". . . make yourselves holy . . . that you be holy . . . for I am holy." Of the six Hebrew words here, three contain the root *qādôs* 'holy'. And twice more it occurs in the succeeding verse. Relatively few individual statutes of the Bible are coupled with the demand for holiness. And none of these present the demand with the same staccato emphasis and repetition as do the food prohibitions.

Thus the Bible takes greater pains to offer a rationale for these laws than for any other commandment. Yet, because the rationale, holiness, has been so variously interpreted, we are at a loss to understand its exact meaning. (This task will be taken up in the Introduction to H in the second volume of this study.) Because both the blood prohibition and the ritual slaughtering, as we have seen (COMMENTS C and D), are invested with the same ethical principle, we might surmise that the food prohibitions, too, as a part of the same dietary system, would be similarly rooted in ethics. But surmises and guesswork are not sufficient; an investigation of the biblical concept of holiness, however brief, must be essayed.

Again we must resort to the heathen environment of ancient Israel to understand both their common cultural legacy and the unique distinctiveness of Israel's religion. An examination of Semitic polytheism (and indeed of any primitive religion) shows that the realm of the gods is never wholly separate from and transcendent to the world of man. Natural objects such as specific trees, rivers, stones, and the like are invested with supernal force. But this earthbound power is independent of the gods and can be an unpredictable danger to the latter as well as to man. "Holy" is thus aptly defined, in any context, as "that which is unapproachable except through divinely imposed restrictions," or "that which is withdrawn from common use."

In opposition to this widespread animism we notice its marked absence from the Bible. Holiness there is not innate. The source of holiness is assigned to God alone. Holiness is the extension of his nature; it is the agency of his will. If certain things are termed holy—such as the land (Canaan), person (priest), place (sanctuary), or time (holy day)—they are so by virtue of divine dispensation. Moreover, this designation is always subject to recall. Thus the Bible exorcises the demoniac from nature; it makes all supernatural force coextensive with God. True, just as in the idolatrous religions, the sancta of the Bible can cause death to the unwary and the impure who approach them without regard for the regulations that govern their usage. Indeed, the sense of withdrawal and separation that inheres in qādôš is verified by the Bible. If we but scan the Pentateuchal codes for instances of Israel being enjoined to holiness, we find them, outside of the dietary laws, in just two other connections: the priesthood and idolatry. As to the former, it cannot be missed that the root qdš occurs seven times in three verses (21:6–8). As shown above, the priesthood, Israel, and man, respectively, form three concentric circles of decreasing holiness. The biblical ideal, however, is that all Israel shall be "a royalty of priests and a holy (qādôš) nation" (Exod 19:6). If Israel is to move to a higher level of holiness, then it must bind itself to a more rigid code of behavior. And just as the priest lives by severer standards than his fellow Israelite, so the Israelite is expected to follow stricter standards than his fellowman. Here, again, holiness implies separation. As for idolatry, because the quintessence of immorality, not to speak of impurity, is imputed to the cult of idolators, it is not startling to find the third grouping of qādôš words in the context of a stern admonition to Israel to separate itself from idolatry (20:6–7; Deut 7:4–6; 14:1–2). Thus, the biblical laws that limit Israel's diet to only a few of the animals permitted to other peoples constitute a reminder—confronted daily at the dining table—that Israel must separate itself from the nations.

But as for Israel the holy is the extension of God's will, it means more than that which is "unapproachable" and "withdrawn." Holiness means not only "separation from" but "separation to." It is a positive concept, an inspiration and a goal associated with God's nature and his desire for man. "You shall be holy, for I am holy." That which man is not, nor can ever fully be, but that which man is commanded to emulate and approximate, is what the Bible calls *qādôš* 'holy'. Holiness means *imitatio Dei*—the life of godliness.

What is God, that men may imitate him? We have to remember that the Godhead for Israel is the seat of ethics. True, the ethical is bound up with and inseparable from the ritual, and the Pentateuchal codes make no distinction between them. But it is surely significant that wherever Israel is commanded to be holy, ethical precepts are also involved. Thus, Israel is consecrated to attain the ideal of a "holy people" when it is given the Decalogue (Exod 19:6). Again, the demand for holiness, as phrased in the text of the dietary laws, is found at the head of Lev 19; here ritual commandments are inextricably interwoven with ethical commands such as "Love your neighbor as yourself" (v 18). The book of Psalms, moreover, which contains the prayers of the Temple service, speaks of striving after God's holiness exclusively in ethical terms: "Who shall stand in His holy place? He that hath clean hands and a pure heart" (Ps 24:3-4). And as for the prophets, their main burden is to teach the supremacy of ethics as the will of God. For Isaiah, "the holy God becomes sanctified in justice" (Isa 5:16); and when he hears the heavenly adoration of God as *qādôš, qādôš, qādôš* (Isa 6:3), he is smitten with the awareness that he and his people are morally inadequate.

Thus, the emulation of God's holiness demands following the ethics associated with his nature. But because the demand for holiness occurs with greater frequency and emphasis in the food prohibitions than in any other commandment, we can only conclude that they are Torah's personal recommendation as the best way of achieving this higher ethical life.

But what could be the specific ethical teaching of the diet laws implied by the concept of holiness? Although our examination of the term *qādôš* is complete, our search need not come to an end. If we find its exact antonym and are able to determine its contextual range, we will be able to declare what *qādôš* is unlike, what it negates and, hence, being the semantic opposite, what it affirms. There can be no doubt that the antonym of *qādôš* 'holy' is *ṭāmē* 'impure'.

Doubts concerning this relationship may be raised on the grounds that Scripture ostensibly chooses *ḥōl* 'common' (or "profane") as the antonym of *qādôš* 'holy'. The Priestly legislators themselves define the relationship in terms of their pedagogic rule, to "distinguish between the sacred and the common, and between the impure and the pure" (10:10; cf. Ezek 44:23). The relations among these four categories can be shown by referring to the diagram that accompanies the NOTE to 10:10, repeated here for convenience:

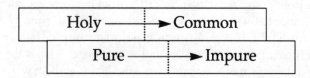

Persons and objects are subject to four possible states: holy, common, pure, and impure. Two of them can exist simultaneously, either holy or common and either pure or impure. Still, one combination is excluded in the Priestly system: whereas the common may be either pure or impure, the sacred may never be impure (for the anomaly of the ḥaṭṭāʾt carcass, see chap. 4, COMMENT D and chap. 10, COMMENT C). For example, the layman (common) is assumed to be pure unless polluted by some impurity, such as a carcass (chap. 11), scale disease (chaps. 13–14), genital flow (chaps. 12–15), or a corpse (Num 19), for which purification procedures are prescribed. There is neither danger nor liability for the layman who contracts impurity as long as he does not allow it to be prolonged (COMMENT on 5:1–13). Not so for the sacred. The sanctuary, for example, must at all times remain pure; impurity befalling it must immediately be purged, lest the whole community become blighted (chap. 4, COMMENT C).

These relationships are depicted in the diagram. The common is contiguous to the realms of the pure and the impure, but the sacred is contiguous only to the pure; it may not contact the impure. Furthermore, the conversion of the holy into the common need not always be illegitimate (desecration), requiring a reparation offering and a fine (5:14–26, COMMENT B). It can be perfectly legitimate (desanctification), requiring only a 20-percent surcharge (COMMENT on chap. 27). Conversely, the holy may never become impure. These two categories are antagonistic, totally opposite. They are antonyms. Moreover, they are dynamic: they seek to extend their influence and control over the other two categories, the common and the pure. In contrast to the former, the latter two categories are static. They cannot transfer their state; there is no contagious purity or contagious commonness. Indeed, they are, in effect, secondary categories. They take their identity from their antonyms. Purity is the absence of impurity; commonness is the absence of holiness (cf. Paschen 1970: 64). Hence, the boundaries between the holy and common and between the pure and the impure are represented by a broken line. There is no fixed boundary. Israel by its behavior can move the boundaries—either way. But it is enjoined to move in one direction only: to *advance the holy* into the realm of the common and to *diminish the impure* and thereby enlarge the realm of the pure.

Now it can be shown that ritual impurity stems from the three sources mentioned above: carcasses/corpses (chap. 11; Num 19), genital discharges (chaps. 12, 15), and scale disease (*ṣāraʿat*, chaps 13–14). The common denominator of these impurities is that they symbolize the forces of death: carcasses/corpses obviously so; the emission of blood or semen means the loss of life; and the wasting of flesh characteristic of scale disease is explicitly compared to a corpse (Num 12:12). Further substantiation is supplied in chap. 15, COMMENT G. But for the purposes of this discussion, the conclusion is manifestly clear: if *ṭāmēʾ* 'impure' stands for the forces of death, then *qādôš* 'holy' stands for the forces of life. This is the same conclusion derived from the blood prohibition (COMMENT C) and prescribed slaughtering technique (COMMENT D)! Therefore, there can be no doubt that the list of prohibited animals (Lev 11, Deut 14) must be part of the same unified and coherent dietary system whose undergirding rationale is reverence for life.

Once this conclusion is granted, the enigma of the quadrupeds is resolved. Their purpose is to limit the Israelite's access to the animal kingdom. The reconstruction of the process by which these criteria were formulated might go as follows: a deliberate attempt was made to limit the edible species to those quadrupeds which were bred for their flesh: cattle, sheep, and goats. Split hoofs sufficed to do the job. When, however, this criterion was found to admit the pig —an abominated creature—the criterion of chewing the cud was added.

My student, Edwin Firmage, Jr. (1990), has proposed an alternative theory to explain the origin of the quadruped criteria. The cloven hoof, he claims, was chosen in order to limit Israel only to those animals permitted on the altar; rumination was added (here he agrees with me) solely to exclude the abominated pig. Furthermore, these two externally visible criteria could easily be inspected by the sanctuary priest. His theory is flawed on two counts. It does not explain the admission of game (see above), which neither qualify for the altar nor are inspected by the priest (nor, as I contend, are all sacrificial animals inspected by the priest because, according to P, they may be slaughtered profanely). Nor does Firmage's sacrificial paradigm explain why Israel was not also commanded to restrict its vegetable diet to grain, wine, and oil—the only nonmeat products permitted on the altar.

Lev 17 (H) may also be the repository of evidence that the Priestly diet laws have been designed to limit access to animal life. This chapter mandates that all animals intended for the table must be slaughtered at the sanctuary (17:3–7). If a single, central sanctuary is presupposed, as most scholars aver, then a sharp diminution in meat consumption must have been its aim. For it would only be that rare pilgrimage to the central sanctuary which would have provided an opportunity for a meat meal. To begin with, meat was a rare item on the Israelite table. To provide it, the householder would have to be willing to deplete his stock. Hence, there had to be a special occasion, such as the annual clan celebration, *zebaḥ mišpāḥâ/yāmîm* (e.g., 1 Sam 20:6, 29), or some joyous event, such as the fulfillment of a vow (e.g., 2 Sam 15:7, 12), to warrant the reduction of his capital. Of course, such occasions would have to be occasions of thanksgiving to the Lord, when a journey to and sacrifice at the sanctuary would be expected.

When altars abounded throughout the land the Israelite need not have traveled far to offer his sacrifice. By contrast, once worship was centralized the pilgrimage for most Israelites became a major undertaking. Yet the Priestly legists of Lev 17 may not have thought that their edict was unworkable. On the premise that H is related to Hezekiah's reform (see the Introduction, §C), then the Holiness laws were legislated for a people who lived in rather circumscribed borders, that is, the country of Judah. If we assume that its dimensions were about the same as at the beginning of Josiah's reign, then it extended from Geba (in Benjamin) to Beer-Sheba (2 Kgs 23:8a), a distance of about fifty miles. Still, for someone living in the Negeb of Beer-Sheba, a journey to the Jerusalem Temple, located near the northern border, would have been an arduous task.

Under Josiah, the borders of Judah expanded to embrace most of the erstwhile territory of northern Israel. The ban on profane slaughter, as impractical as it may have been during the days of Hezekiah, was now totally unworkable. Profane slaughter therefore became an indispensable component of centralization. Perhaps this historical reality forms the background of D's concession to profane slaughter, which, strikingly begins with the clause, "When the Lord enlarges your territory, as he had promised you, and you say, 'I shall eat some meat' . . ." (Deut 12:20). Indeed, this is the second statement concerning profane slaughter (cf. vv 15–16). It seems reasonable to suggest that the first statement applies to the land of Judah and the second ("When the Lord enlarges your territory") refers to the historical reality of Judah's northward expansion. In any case, the deuteronomic concession to profane slaughter must be regarded as a polemic against its total ban, as promulgated by the school of H.

In sum, the earlier Priestly stratum, P, maintains that meat is strictly God's fare. If Israel wishes to partake of it, it can only do so from God's table, that is, *any* legitimate altar. In enjoining only one legitimate altar, H certifies that the only possibility of its occurrence is the rare pilgrimage to the central sanctuary. Therein lies H's distinctive contribution to the overall Priestly aim to limit access to animal life.

What of the other animal categories—fish, birds, flying insects, land swarmers? Criteria for edible animals are specified only for flying insects (11:21–22) and fish (11:9). Douglas suggests that "the case of the locusts is interesting and consistent. The test of whether it is a clean and therefore edible kind is how it moves on the earth. If it crawls it is unclean. If it hops it is clean" (1966: 56). Yet locusts are distinguished not from creepers (vv 29–42) but from "winged creatures that walk on all fours" (v 20). As locusts do not exclusively hop but also "walk on all fours," their saltatory ability does not comprise their total means of locomotion. Here it would seem that an exception was made because allowing locusts as food was a hallowed practice stemming back to the wilderness period when, as pastoralists, they lived off their herds and feasted on locusts, a delicacy among the bedouin of the Sinai and Arabian peninsulas to this day. By contrast, the criteria for fish—fins and scales—fit my conclusion neatly. As demonstrated (NOTE on v 12), ancient Israel was unacquainted with marine life for the main reason that there were few varieties of fish in its waters. In effect, these criteria effectively eliminated, with a single stroke, shellfish (mollusks do abound on the Mediterranean shores) and fish without scales, thereby reducing the eligible species to a handful. Thus access to marine life was severely restricted, just as it was with quadrupeds.

Hence, if a count is taken of the permitted animals, excluding game, which was available only to hunters, the inventory reads as follows: cattle, sheep, goats, several kinds of fish, pigeons, turtledoves, several other nonraptorial birds, and locusts. The net result is self-evident: the Israelite's choice of animal food was severely circumscribed. To be sure, certain animals may have been eschewed (e.g., the pig) or allowed (e.g., the locust) on independent grounds (see the NOTES on vv 7 and 21). But aside from these few, the animal kingdom is governed by the criteria set forth in Lev 11. This conclusion provides the needed piece to complete the reconstruction of the rationale for the dietary system. Its purpose is to teach the Israelite reverence for life by (1) reducing his choice of flesh to a few animals; (2) limiting the slaughter of even these few permitted animals to the most humane way (COMMENT D); and (3) prohibiting the ingestion of blood and mandating its disposal upon the altar or by burial (COMMENT C) as acknowledgment that bringing death to living things is a concession of God's grace and not a privilege of man's whim. (For further implications of this rationale see Milgrom 1989a.)

Two related questions intrude themselves at this point. The criteria of Lev 11 only block access to the forbidden animals but not to the permitted ones. Limits are placed on the animal species (variety), but not on their numbers (quantity). How then can these criteria keep the Israelites from wholesale butchery (raised by Firmage 1990: 195 n. 24)? The answer is rooted in the economic realities of biblical times. The average Israelite could not afford to deplete his livestock. Eating meat was therefore reserved for special occasions, as evidenced by the three stipulations of the šĕlāmîm, the sacrifice required whenever meat was sought for the table: thanksgiving, spontaneous joy, and fulfillment of a vow (COMMENT on chap. 3). Animal slaughter was thus an infrequent event in the Israelite household. But what of the Sanctuary? It is subject to no economic constraints. The fixed, public cult (Num 28–29), not to speak of private offerings, voluntary (chaps. 1–3) and mandatory (chaps. 4–5), assured it of an undiminishable torrent of animal blood. How then could God have circumscribed Israel's access to the animal world but permitted, indeed mandated, interminable holocausts of animals for himself? The answer to this second question resides in the postulate of Priestly legislation: the supernal realm runs by different rules than the earthly realm. For example, the deity punishes collectively—the child, the family, even the tribe and nation for the sin of the individual (chap. 4, COMMENT C)—but the guilty party alone may be punished by man (cf. Exod 21:31; Deut 24:16; Lev 20:4–5; contrast vv 2–3). Moreover, in this instance, logic reinforces the postulate that what God has created he has a right to recall.

In all sacrifices except the burnt offering, the animal is returned to God, who then allocates it to the officiating priests: "I have assigned it as their portion from my food gifts" (6:10aβ). Thus, the offerer experiences no qualms of conscience in killing an animal if by means of the authorized altar he restores it to God. In the well-being sacrifice, however, he does not relinquish the animal to God; he keeps it for himself. He is, therefore, faced with a moral and psychological dilemma: he wants meat and he has to kill to get it. The well-being sacrifice, therefore, assuages his conscience. Man is a criminal only if he appropriates the animal's lifeblood. But if he returns it to its divine source via the altar he commits no crime.

One final demur intrudes itself. Why a ritual? Could not the Bible have acted in a more ideological way, defined its concept of reverence for life and then left each individual free to live by it without the encumbering restrictions? The answer implied by the Priestly legislation is that ideals are just abstractions, which humans may pay lip service to yet rarely actualize. All religions urge reverence for life though few adherents live by it. Albert Schweitzer, who made this principle the core of his life and work, wrote, "The universal effort of Reverence for Life shows the sympathy with animals, which is often represented as sentimentality, to be a duty which no thinking man can escape."

But Schweitzer's influence on humanity is a result of his life commitments, not his preachments. In fact, the latter can be conveniently subverted by tendentious reasoning. Thus as noted by Joseph Wood Krutch and H. E. Anthony (1957), Schweitzer's rule—that life may be destroyed only in the service of some higher life—can justify the decimation of plumed birds in the year 1914 to gratify the millinery fancies of the ladies of London. The Bible, to the contrary, takes no chances with the variables of human nature and insists on being rudely pragmatic. It allows the slaughtering of animals only for human food. A ritual, then? Yes, if it is to discipline. So frequent? Yes, if it is to sanctify the home. So tedious? Persistent rain makes holes in rocks.

The Priestly legislators were so sensitive to the ethical primacy of the dietary system that they enjoined one of its tenets, the blood prohibition, on all humankind. As noted at the beginning of this COMMENT, the Ten Commandments were originally intended for Israel alone. Only one biblical statute, the blood prohibition, is enjoined upon all humanity. In the biblical view the Decalogue would fail were it not rooted in a regularly observed ritual, central to the home and table, and impinging on both senses and intellect, thus conditioning the reflexes into patterns of ethical behavior.

F. The Ethical Foundations of the Dietary System: 4. The Kid Prohibition

The prohibition *lōʾ-tĕbaššēl gĕdî bahălēb ʾimmô* 'you shall not boil a kid in its mother's milk' does not appear in Leviticus but is thrice found elsewhere (Exod 23:19; 34:26; Deut 14:21). In Exodus it concludes an appendage to the cultic calendar, but in Deuteronomy it concludes an appendage to the dietary prohibitions. The change that has occurred between the time of Exodus and that of Deuteronomy bears investigation, as does the absence of this prohibition from Leviticus. But what does this prohibition mean? The rabbis claim that it mandates an absolute ban on mixing dairy and meat dishes, and they interpret its threefold occurrence as prohibiting the eating, cooking, or profiting from such a mixture (*m. Ḥul.* 8:4; *Mek.* Mishpatim, par. 20; *b. Ḥul.* 115b [bar.]). The rabbinic solution seems so removed from the plain meaning of the text that we shall, for the present, pass it by without further comment.

As we scan the legion of interpretations put forth through the ages, there are four that merit consideration. One firmly established view is that this prohibition is directed against Canaanite cultic practice. That it was a common culinary practice is attested by the Egyptian Sinuhe, who reports during the twentieth century B.C.E. that in Syro-Palestine he feasted on "milk in every (kind) of cooking" (*ANET*[3] 20a). To this day, moreover, a popular combination of milk and meat in this region is called *laban ummu* 'the milk of his mother' (Fischer 1976: 98). This cultic theory was first proposed by Maimonides:

> As for the prohibition against eating meat [boiled] in milk, it is in my opinion not improbable that—in addition to this being undoubtedly very gross food and very filling—*idolatry* had something to do with it. Perhaps such food was eaten at one of the ceremonies of their cult or at one of their festivals. A confirmation of this may, in my opinion, be found in the fact that the prohibition against eating "meat [boiled] in milk," when it is mentioned for the first two times, occurs near the commandment concerning pilgrimage: "Three times a year, etc." (Exod 23:17; 34:23). It is as if it said: When you go on pilgrimage and enter "the house of the Lord your God" (Exod 23:19aβ; 34:26aβ), do not cook there in the way they used to do. According to me this is the strongest view regarding the reason for this prohibition; but I have not seen this set down in any of the books of the Sabians [idolaters] that I have read. (*Guide* 3.48)

Maimonides' opinion that eating a kid boiled in its mother's milk was an idolatrous rite has been championed by commentators down to the present day who, however, have glossed over Maimonides' admission that he had no evidence for it.

Nonetheless, a powerful impetus was given to the view, some fifty years ago, with the unearthing of the second-millennium Ugaritic texts at Ras Shamra, a site on the Mediterranean coast of Syria. In one of its mythological tablets, the following line appears: *ṭb[ḫ g]d bḥlb annḫ bḥmat* (*UT* 52.14 = *CTA* 23.14 = *KTU* 1.23.18), which was translated as "Coo[k a ki]d in milk, a lamb (?) in butter" (Ginsberg 1935; cf. Virolleaud 1933: 140). This text, it should be noted, being broken, requires reconstruction. The reconstruction is, at best, an educated guess—undoubtedly influenced by the biblical prohibition. Nonetheless, this reconstruction was accepted at once by virtually every interpreter (e.g., Cassuto 1943; 1951b: 5; Driver 1956a: 121; Gaster 1961: 407–9, 422–23; Kosmala 1962: 52–53; Fisher 1972: 29; a notable early skeptic was Gordon 1947: 221), and it became a dogma of scholarship that Maimonides' intuition concerning the practice as a pagan rite was correct.

But objections posed initially by Loewenstamm (1973) and reinforced by Haran (1979) have once and for all vitiated the reconstruction. The objections are as follows: (1) The broken passage must now be read differently: *ṭb.* (?) *[g]d* (*CTA* p. 98), which indicates that the dividing mark between the two words follows *ṭb*, thereby leaving no room for adding the letter *ḫ*. Thus the reconstruction *ṭb[ḫ]* 'coo[k]' must be rejected. (2) Moreover, even were the reconstruction correct, *ṭbḫ* means not "cook" but "slaughter" (Milgrom 1976e). (3) The probability is that the term *annḫ*, contained in the next clause, corresponding to Akk. *ananiḫu* (cf. *CAD*), refers not to an animal but to a herb (Aistleitner 1954: 41; Driver 1956a: 121; Caquot and Sznycer 1974: 371 n. q.). (4) It therefore follows that *[g]d*—presuming the correctness of the reconstruction—cannot mean "kid" but, as it must correspond in meaning to the parallel word *annḫ*, also connotes a plant. Hence, *ṭb[ḫ]*— keeping in mind that the reading is speculative —cannot mean "slaughter," a term hardly appropriate for a plant. (5) Finally, there is nothing in the text that states that the kid(?) was cooked(?) in the milk of *its mother*, in which case it has absolutely nothing to do with the biblical prohibition!

In sum, the Ugaritic text in question is a broken one, its suggested reconstruction is palpably wrong, its clearer portion has been misconstrued, and a key word of the biblical prohibition, "mother," is not there. In recent memory, nothing matches this example of the hazards of interpreting broken texts on the basis of a purported biblical echo. Thus the cultic theory cannot be grounded in Ugaritic practice and without any support, biblical or extrabiblical, it must be abandoned.

The second theory, also a respected one, espouses a humanitarian interpretation. It originates with Philo of Alexandria, who writes as follows: "He has forbidden any lamb or kid or other like kind of livestock to be snatched away from its mother before it was weaned (cf. Exod 22:29; Lev 22:27). . . . . If anyone thinks it good to boil flesh in milk let him do so without cruelty and keeping clear of impiety. . . . The person who boils the flesh of lambs or kids or any other young animal in their mother's milk, shows himself cruelly brutal in character and gelded of compassion" (*Virt.* 143–44). Philo's focus on cruelty as the basis for the prohibition is echoed by Clement of Alexandria (cited by Haran 1979: 29) and, independently, by Ibn Ezra and Rashbam (who surely were unaware of both Philo and Clement). Among moderns, this view is championed by Haran (1979) and Ginsberg (1982: 52 n. 69) who, in agreement with Philo (above), argue that the kid law is cut of the same cloth as the prohibition against slaughtering the dam and its offspring on the same day (22:28), sacrificing the newborn during the first week of its life (22:27; Exod 22:29), or taking the mother bird together with its young (Deut 22:6–7). If humanitarianism is the motivation, should not the prohibition embrace all animals instead of being restricted to a kid? Ginsberg suggests, citing Dalman (1939: 6.189), that he-goats, unlike rams, are expendable because they provide neither wool nor palatable meat, hence it must have been a common practice to dispose of one's superfluous male kids during the Sukkot festival (1982: 53; cf. also Abravanel). The attribution of this prohibition to Sukkot would appear to be justified both from its position in the biblical text, where it occurs after injunctions concerning the other two pilgrimage festivals, Pesach and Shabuot (Exod 23:18–19a; 34:25–26a), and from its zoological basis, because goats drop their young in the rainy season, which begins in autumn. "Therefore, the Israelite is warned that during the feast of ingathering, the most exuberant and joyful of the annual pilgrim-feasts, celebrated with much food and drink and the choicest delicacies —he must remember not to seethe a kid in its mother's milk . . . a deliberate reminder of humane behavior even in the midst of general jollity" (Haran 1979: 35).

The main argument against the humanitarian theory challenges its very use as the rationale for the kid law and the other cited animal prohibitions. It may be true that one may not slaughter the dam and its young on the same day (22:28) but it surely is permitted on successive days. The newborn must be permitted to suckle for seven days (22:27; Exod 22:29), but on the eighth day it may be brought to the altar—even though it is still suckling. The mother bird and her fledglings or eggs may not be taken together (Deut 22:6), but surely they may be taken separately. By the same token, the mother goat can in no way be aware that her kid is boiling in her milk. Incidentally, there is genuine doubt whether this prohibition can be tied to the Sukkot festival. Yeaning time for goats begins in December (Aḥiṭuv 1971b: 648)—at least two months after Sukkot! Thus, it is more likely that this prohibition was intended to be enforced at all pilgrimage festivals or, for that matter, whenever a sacrifice was offered at the sanctuary. In any event, the humanitarian theory must give way to another.

Recently, under the influence of the French school of structural anthropology, which has proved so helpful in understanding Lev 11 (see COMMENT E above), a third theory has been propounded. Starting with the Durkheimian hypothesis that a customary or legal prohibition reflects some societal taboo, J. Soler interprets the kid law as meaning, "You shall not put a mother and her son in the same pot any more than in the same bed" (1973). That is to say, it is an injunction against incest (fully developed by Martens 1977). This theory is fascinating, but it is undermined by one glaring fault: the word *gĕdî* 'kid', is asexual. Indeed, in BH animal names that are masculine in form and have no female counterpart denote both sexes. Thus, in Isaiah's vision of messianic bliss (Isa 11:6), the *zĕʾēb* 'wolf', *kebeś* 'lamb', *nāmēr* 'leopard', and *gĕdî* 'kid' are generic names, applying to both male and female of each species. A more instructive proof text is the one cited above: "You shall not slaughter a cow *(śôr)* or ewe *(śeh)* and its young *(bĕnô)* on the same day" (22:28). Despite the use of the masculine forms *śôr* and *śeh* for the parent and *bēn* for the child, the mother and her offspring of either sex are clearly intended. To be sure, as indicated above, the economically unviable male kids were slaughtered for their meat. Still, the prohibition as it stands applies to the female as well. Had it been restricted to the male it would have been so worded, for instance, *gĕdî zākār* 'a male kid' (cf. *śeh zākār* 'a male sheep', Exod 12:3) or *zākār bāʿizzîm* 'male of the goats' (cf. *zākār babbāqār* 'male of the herd', 22:19). Just as it is forbidden to slaughter the mother on the same day as her young—of either sex—so it is forbidden to cook the young—of either sex—in its mother's milk. The social anthropologists, I believe, are correct: society's values are mirrored in its laws and mores, especially in its food taboos (COMMENT E above). In this case, however, they picked the wrong one.

A fourth, and more fruitful, approach has recently been broached by O. Keel (1980; Milgrom 1981a, 1985a). His iconographic studies in ancient Near Eastern art have led him to the plethora of seals and ceramic and rock tomb-paintings that feature the motif of a mother animal suckling her young. The symbolism takes on cosmic dimensions as soon as it is realized that the portrayed animals can stand for divinities; and in Egypt the human (or animal) nursing at the udders of the cow-goddess Hathor (or another animal divinity) is the young Pharaoh himself. The suckling mother, according to Keel, is thus the symbol of the love and tenderness that is sustained by the divine order of the universe. Because this image, as it appears in the art of Syro-Palestine, is not attributable to any particular deity, it would have encountered no difficulty in being incorporated into the monotheism of ancient Israel. There it would have resulted in a taboo against cooking a kid in its mother's milk, a culinary practice that in effect would have opposed and vitiated the life-sustaining and divinely ordained nurture inherent in all living beings.

Keel, I submit, is on the right track. His explanation, more so than the humanitarian theory, throws clearer light on the prohibition to slay the mother and its young simultaneously (22:28). Here he is in accord with Philo, whom he quotes, that "it is the height of savagery to slay on the same day the generating cause and the living creature generated" (*Virt.* 134). Yet when applied to the kid prohibition, Keel's theory does not fully satisfy. The mother has been separated from her young. Thus the image of the suckling mother, which represents the transmission of the life-sustaining force proceeding from generation to generation, is not present. More to the point is another of Philo's comments: "[It is] grossly improper that the substance which fed the living animal should be used to season and flavor the same after its death . . . the license of man should rise to such a height as to misuse what has sustained its life to destroy also the body which remains in existence" (*Virt.* 143; see also Bekhor Shor on Exod 23:19). This citation is used by C. M. Carmichael (1976) to propose that the root rationale behind the kid prohibition is in opposing the commingling of life and death (cf. Wayne 1960). A substance that sustains the life of a creature (milk) should not be fused or confused with a process associated with its death (cooking). This would be but another instance of the binary opposition characteristic of biblical ritual and praxis: to separate life from death, holy from common, pure from impure, Israel from the nations. Both ideas inhering in the kid prohibition —the reverence for life and Israel's separation from the nations—are also present in the dietary laws, the former in the blood prohibition (COMMENT C above) and the latter in the animal prohibitions (COMMENT E above). Thus the kid prohibition automatically locks into Israel's dietary system. Therefore, it should occasion no surprise that the kid prohibition, which in Exodus is related to the cult, is transformed in Deuteronomy into a dietary law. D, it should be recalled, has transferred the act of slaughtering an animal for its flesh from the sanctuary to the home. With the centralization of worship at the Temple, D has had to enact a concomitant law permitting common slaughter to obviate the necessity of journeying to the Temple each time a family desires meat for the table (COMMENT D above). The result is that the taboo of cooking a kid in its mother's milk, which needed but to be observed within the sanctuary compound while under priestly supervision, must henceforth be heeded by every Israelite family, without outside supervision, in every kitchen.

The life-versus-death theory, I submit, completely and neatly elucidates the other prohibitions, which, heretofore, have been explained as humane. The common denominator of all of these prohibitions is the fusion and confusion of life and death *simultaneously*. Thus, the life-giving process of the mother bird hatching or feeding her young (Deut 22:6) should not be the occasion of their joint death. The sacrifice of the newborn may be inevitable, but not for the first week while it is constantly at its mother's breast (22:27), and never should both the mother and its young be slain at the same time (22:28). By the same token, the mother's milk, the life-sustaining food for her kid, should never become associated with its death.

Is it, then, so farfetched for the rabbis to have deduced that all meat, not just of the kid, and all milk, not only of the mother, may not be served together? Their interpretation is clearly an old one. It is already adumbrated in the third century B.C.E. LXX, which translates the word *gĕdî* in all three occurrences of the prohibition, but only there, not as "kid" but as "sheep." By the first century C.E. the tradition is recorded by Philo (cited above) that the prohibition applies to "the flesh of lambs or kids or any other young animals" (*Virt.* 144). One cannot say that Philo is dependent on the Palestinian rabbis for his teaching because he holds, contrary to their view, that the prohibited milk is only that of the animal's mother (a view also held subsequently by the Karaites; Nemoy 1952: 267). Alexandria, then, the home of the LXX and Philo, must have harbored a tradition that had extended the biblical prohibition to embrace all animals. It is, therefore, not too difficult to foresee that the next logical step would have been to forbid the use of any milk with any meat. For milk, the life-sustaining force of the animal, should not commingle with meat, the animal that has met its death.

The binary opposition of life and death, we shall discover, is also at the root of the severe impurities that are the subject of the following chapters, Lev 12–15. It is therefore fitting and logical that Lev 11, the chapter that ensconces the life–death principle in the laws dealing with animal impurities, be the prelude to the same principle in the laws dealing with human impurities.

Is it, therefore, not puzzling that the kid prohibition, which also embodies this principle, does not occur in Lev 11? Only one answer, I submit, is possible. The deuteronomic transformation has not yet taken place. Leviticus still breathes the atmosphere of Exodus. Cooking a kid in its mother's milk is still a cultic act, a sacrifice that takes place in the sanctuary under the control of the priests. It is still not the concern of the home, a radical change that only Deuteronomy engineered. Here, once more, is another indication of the preexilic and predeuteronomic provenience of P's laws in Lev 11.

CHILDBIRTH (12:1–8)

12 ¹The Lord spoke to Moses, saying: ²Speak to the Israelites thus: when a woman at childbirth bears a male, she shall be impure for seven days; she shall be impure as during the period of her menstrual infirmity. —³On the eighth day the foreskin of his member shall be circumcised. —⁴She shall remain in [a state of] blood purity for thirty-three days; she shall not touch any consecrated thing, nor enter the sacred precinct until the period of her purification is complete. ⁵If she bears a female, she shall be impure for two weeks as at her menstruation, and she shall remain in [a state of] blood purity for sixty-six days.

⁶On the completion of her period of purification, for either son or daughter, she shall bring a yearling lamb for a burnt offering, and a pigeon or turtledove for a purification offering to the priest, at the entrance of the Tent of Meeting. ⁷He shall offer it before the Lord and effect expiation on her behalf, and then she shall be pure from her source of blood. This is the ritual for the woman who

bears a child, male or female. ⁸If, however, her means do not suffice for a sheep, she shall take two turtledoves or two pigeons, one for a burnt offering and the other for a purification offering. The priest shall effect expiation on her behalf, and she shall be pure.

NOTES

12:1. Why do the rules of animal impurities (chap. 11) precede those of human impurities? Rabbi Simlai offers this explanation: as man was created after the animals (Gen 1:24–27) so the *tôrâ* of persons (chaps. 12–15) follows the *tôrâ* of animals (*Midr. Lev. Rab.* 14:1), and in the *tôrâ* of persons, it is logical to begin with birth (chap. 12; *Keter Torah*). Yet the various impurities of persons in chaps. 12–15 may have been ordered according to the decreasing length of their purification: birth (forty to eighty days), scale disease (eight days), genital discharges of male (eight days, one day), of female (seven days, eight days).

to Moses. The absence of Aaron (also in 14:1), though the priestly officiation is essential (vv 6–8), seems inexplicable. Contrast the diet laws revealed also to Aaron (11:1), though the priest plays no role whatever (but cf. the NOTE on "These are the instructions," 11:46). Still, the minutiae of rules regarding the contamination of vessels and persons from carcasses and the doubtful classification of many animals would, indeed, require priestly consultation. Contrast the unambiguous nature of the parturient's impurity; see below.

2. *Speak to the Israelites.* The active agent in this chapter is solely the new mother. It is she who must scrupulously keep count of the days of her purification period and, at its termination, bring its requisite offerings. The priest is merely the passive recipient, awaiting her and her offerings in the sanctuary.

at childbirth. tazrîaʿ, literally, "produces seed." The Sam., followed by the Versions, reads *tizzāraʿ (niphʿal)* 'becomes pregnant, conceives'. But the emendation is unnecessary. *zeraʿ,* normally "seed," can also stand for the fully grown fruit (Gen 1:11, 12; Wessely 1846), which, in the case of human seed, means "offspring" (e.g., Gen 3:15). The *hiphʿil tazrîaʿ* would then denote "produces offspring." Furthermore, the womb of the woman is associated with the womb of the earth. Human offspring, like the earth's vegetation, can reproduce (cf. Ibn Ezra). Alternatively, the *hiphʿil* may be considered to be a stative, but in the elative mode, otherwise known as an internal *hiphʿil* (GKC §53d), connoting the completion of an action, as in *hiqrîb tābôʾ* 'he was about to enter' (Gen 12:11), in other words, he had reached the border: *yaʾărikûn yāmêkā* 'that your days may be very long' (Exod 20:12), in other words, permanent, forever. The rendering here would, then, be "when a woman comes to term (i.e., at the completion of her pregnancy) and delivers a male" (D. N. Freedman). In either case, the verb *tazrîaʿ* is apt. Yet the probability rests with the literal translation, "produces seed." The rabbis held that conception occurred when the woman's blood united with the male sperm. Moreover, many of the ancients (e.g., Galen; cf. Preuss 1978: 387–88) assumed that menstrual blood contains the seed (i.e., ovum) that unites with the male seed (i.e., semen) to produce the human being. And the Aramaic translation *ta'ădê* (*Tgs. Onq., Ps.-J.)* is semantically related to words for youth, pubescence, and menstrual clothing (cf. Isa 64:5; Jer 2:32; esp. Ezek 16:7), thus creating a semantic field around the basic meaning "[genital] seed."

a male. *zākār*, rather than *bēn* 'son'. The rabbis suggest that the reason *bēn* is not used is that it would imply that the child is alive, whereas this law holds even if the child is stillborn (*Sipra*, Tazriaʿ par. 1:5). Nevertheless, this explanation would not account for the use of *bēn* (and *bat*) later in this chapter (v 6). A more likely explanation is that at birth the only way to tell the gender is by the sexual organ (Wessely 1846; cf. Gen 17:10). The etymology is unknown.

seven days. Rabbi Simeon ben Yohai (*b. Nid.* 31b) believes that originally the mother of a male was impure for fourteen days, just as in the case of a female, but the term was reduced to seven to allow the circumcision (on the eighth day, v 3) to take place in a state of purity. Hoffmann (1953) further suggests that the circumcision actually curtails her impurity, and Shadal proposes that because the foreskin, *'orlâ*, renders the infant impure (cf. Isa 52:1), it is fitting that mother and child be purified together. But these conjectures are rendered invalid by the evidence that elsewhere, such as among the Hittites, the mother's impurity following the birth of a male was also shorter than for a female (see the NOTE on "thirty-three," v 4). Furthermore, it is hardly conceivable that the rite performed on the boy could in any way affect the ritual status of the mother. And besides, the newborn child is not considered impure (in distinction to other cultures, see COMMENT A below); otherwise the female would be in a state of perpetual impurity, for no rite comparable to circumcision was performed on her!

A seventh-day ritual for the newborn is also attested among the Hittites (*HBR*[2] 157). And in the *amphidromia* ceremony of the ancient Greeks, on the seventh day the child was repeatedly carried around the house of his parents, after which he or she could no longer be disposed of through exposure (see further COMMENT A below).

as during the period. *kîmê*, literally, "as the days," equivalent to *kĕbîmê* 'as during the days' (Hoffmann 1953). The force of the particle *kĕ* is to stress that the quality of the impurity and not just its length is equivalent to that of the menstruant (see 15:19–24). The same holds true for the equivalent expression in the case of the *zābâ* (15:25).

menstrual (niddat). *niddâ* occurs twenty-nine times in Scripture and is capable of three meanings: (1) "menstrual impurity" (here and chap. 15); (2) "impurity [in general]; abomination" (e.g., 2 Chr 29:5; cf. v 16); and (3) "lustration" (Num 19:9; Zech 13:1).

The etymology of *niddâ* is not readily apparent. It has been derived from the root *ndd* (Ibn Janaḥ, Rashi, Ibn Ezra), *qal* "depart, flee, wander" (e.g., Isa 21:15; Hos 9:17), *hiphᶜil* "cause to flee, chase away" (Job 18:18; cf. Ug. *ndd* 'to wander, go'), or from *ndh* (KB², p. 596), *piᶜel* "chase away, put aside" (Isa 65:5; Amos 6:3; cf. Ug. *ndy*[?] 'drive out'; Akk. *nadû* 'throw, cast down'). Morphologically, the word appears to follow the nominal formation of a double-ᶜ*ayin* root, like *gizzâ* (Judg 6:37), *zimmâ* (Jer 13:27), and the like (Joüon 1923: §88Bh). It should be remembered, however, that *lāmed-hē* and double-ᶜ*ayin* verbs with corresponding radicals often have similar if not synonymous meanings (e.g., *šgg*/ *šgh*, *qṣṣ*/*qṣh*, *ḥṣṣ*/*ḥṣh*, *gzz*/*gzh*).

Common to the roots *ndd* and *ndh* is the meaning "chase away, expel." By assigning to *niddâ* the putatively original meaning "expulsion, elimination," then the relation of the opposite meanings of the word becomes clear. In the case of the menstruant, the word originally referred to the *discharge* or *elimination* of menstrual blood, which came to denote menstrual impurity and impurity in general. In addition, *niddâ* came to refer not just to the menstrual discharge but to the menstruant herself, for she too was "discharged" and "excluded" from her society not by being kept at arm's length from others but, in many communities, by being banished to and quarantined in separate quarters (for details, see COMMENT A below and *Thwat*, S.V. "niddah").

In the phrase *mê niddâ* (Num 19:9), the word carries on the meaning of expulsion: "water of expulsion [of impurity]" or simply "water of lustration." A similar linguistic phenomenon is attested in Egyptian, where the word for "menstruate," *ir ḥsnn*, means "make a purification with natron" (Blackman 1951: 477). Further support for this understanding of *mê niddâ* is provided by the word *ḥaṭṭāʾt* in Zech 13:1. It has been shown that *ḥaṭṭāʾt* is a privative *piᶜel* noun with the meaning "purification," corresponding to the *piᶜel* verb *ḥiṭṭēʾ* 'purify' (Milgrom 1971a: 237ff.). Consequently, *ḥaṭṭāʾt* and *niddâ* in Zech 13:1 are synonyms, and the phrase there should be construed as "for purification and for lustration." (Thus there is no need to derive *niddâ* from a putative *piᶜel* privative denoting "remove impurity," as I originally conjectured, 1990a: 160, on Num 19:9.) Further evidence for this meaning of *niddâ* is found in the synonymous appellation of the water used to cleanse the Levites, *mê ḥaṭṭāʾt* 'water of purification' (Num 8:7).

The reference to the *niddâ* presumes a knowledge of 15:19–24, which led Wellhausen to conclude (1963) that originally chap. 12 followed chap. 15. As pointed out by Dillmann, however, no displacement whatever need be presumed because the laws of *niddâ* were well known and taken for granted (Dillmann and Ryssel 1897).

her . . . infirmity (dĕwōtāh). An infinitive construct—not a plural noun— of the verb *dāwâ* (Lam 5:17; *Keter Torah*), which also appears as an adjective, *dāweh* (15:33; 20:18), *dawwāy* (Isa 1:5; Jer 8:18) and as a noun, *dĕwāy* (Ps 41:4), *dāwâ* (Isa 30:22), a menstruous garment (cf. *b. Nid.* 9a), and *madweh* (Deut 7:15; 28:60). The cognates, Akk. *dawû* 'be sick, stagger' *(AHw)* and Ug. *dwy* 'sickness' (*KTU* 1.16 = *CTA* 16.6 [127] 35, 51) conform to and confirm the contextual connotation of the biblical root "be sick, infirm." Interestingly, in Hittite, "the linguistic form of the word for moon, *arma-* is not only associated with conception, pregnancy, and menstruation but also with weakness and sickness" (Moyer 1969: 70). Thus philology confirms experience: menstruation is associated with sickness. Hence, *niddâ* and *dāwâ* are related.

The question may be asked: Why is the compound "her menstrual infirmity" used instead of the simpler *niddātāh* 'her menstruation', employed in v 5? The answer may well be that there was a need to distinguish her menstrual infirmity from the other genital infirmities she experiences, as a parturient (chap. 12) and as a *zābâ* (chap. 15).

she shall be impure (tiṭmā'). The impurity of the parturient is common to many cultures (see COMMENT A below). The overlap, attested in this verse, of the parturient and menstruant is also an observable cross-cultural phenomenon, for example, "water into which no menstruant *(harištu)* has descended, no parturient *(musukkatu)* has washed her hands" (*CAD*, M 239). Indeed, the latter term for a parturient can also stand for a menstruant (ibid., 240). In Israel, however, despite the overlap in the degree of impurity, the two laws are ritually and legally distinct.

In other cultures, the newborn child is also impure, for instance, among the Hittites (COMMENT A). What of the Israelite child? Is he (or she) rendered impure by contact with the mother? The text is silent. Nor is there even a hint of an answer in Scripture. Does its silence mean that the newborn is exempt from the laws of *niddâ*, or must we assume that the child's impurity is taken for granted, that the child is isolated with the mother during the seven (or fourteen) days, and that at the termination of this period it undergoes immersion with her? There is no clear answer.

That this severe "menstrual" impurity is terminated by immersion is nowhere stated either for the parturient or for the menstruant. But as all statements regarding the duration of impurity automatically imply, if they do not explicitly affirm, that it must terminate with ablutions (see the NOTE on "he shall be impure until evening," 11:24b), the mere statement that the period of the parturient's severer impurity lasts seven (or fourteen, v 5) days assumes that this period is terminated by ablutions. The same holds true for the menstruant (see the NOTE on *bĕniddātāh*, 15:19). Besides, if a minor impurity such as seminal discharge requires ablution (15:16), all the more so the major genital discharges. By the same token, the ablution permits her contact with the common, including sexual congress with her husband (Jub 3:6), though this latter point is disputed by the sectarians (see the NOTE on "she shall remain," v 4).

3. This verse, which switches from the mother to the boy, is clearly an editorial parenthesis that interrupts the prescriptive ritual for the mother. Nor can it be claimed that the circumcision is a purificatory rite for the boy and thus comparable to the purificatory rites enjoined upon his mother, for there is no

equivalent rite for a newly born girl (Dillmann and Ryssel 1897). The purpose of this interpolation is to emphasize the uniqueness of this rite; not the rite itself, which was practiced ubiquitously by Israel's Semitic neighbors, but the timing of the rite, which in Israel alone was performed in infancy and, precisely, on the eighth day.

The rite of circumcision is attested throughout the world. According to Jer 9:25, it was practiced by the Egyptians, Edomites, Ammonites, Moabites, and Arabs as well as by Israel. In Egypt, however, it seems—at least in the Hellenistic period—to have been limited to the priests. Everywhere it is a puberty rite that fits a man for marriage. In Israel alone is it associated with infancy, though originally it also may have been a premarital rite. Such an earlier practice may be reflected in Ishmael's circumcision at the age of thirteen (Gen 17:25). Philology provides even stronger evidence (Snaith 1967). Hebrew *ḥātān* 'daughter's husband' is etymologically "the one who undergoes circumcision," and *ḥōtēn* 'wife's father' is the circumciser (cf. Arab. *ḥātin*, from *ḥatana* 'circumcise'). In Ug., *ḥtn* connotes son-in-law and marriage (CTA 24 [UT 77], 25, 32) and Akk. *ḥatnūtu* 'marriage' means literally "become a son-in-law," from *ḥatanu* 'a relative by marriage', such as a son-in-law, brother-in-law, bridegroom. Perhaps the bizarre incident of Moses' vicarious circumcision and his designation as *ḥātan dāmîm lammûlōt* 'a bridegroom of blood because of the circumcision' (Exod 4:26) reflects the older practice of circumcision as a premarital prerequisite.

With the transfer of circumcision to infancy, it became a sign of the covenant, an initiation rite into the religious bond between Israel and its God (Gen 17:1–27). The fact that the uncircumcised may not participate in the paschal sacrifice (Exod 12:43–49; Josh 5:2–10) and that, in the oldest narrative stratum, circumcision was required of the non-Israelite bridegroom (Gen 34:14–17, 22) indicates that the covenant idea was associated with circumcision from earliest times.

Israel's ancient custom of taking an oath while holding the circumcised membrum (Gen 24:2–9; 47:29–31) may be related to the Babylonian practice, attested as early as 1700 B.C.E., of settling matters by means of an oath in the presence of a symbol of the god (e.g., the saw of the sun god, the spear of Ishtar, the mace of Ninurta). As no image of Israel's God was permitted, the circumcision, the sign of the covenant, was employed instead. The circumcised membrum indicates the presence of God as a divine witness who, by implication, will punish the violation of the oath (Freedman 1976).

the foreskin (ʿorlâ). Akk. *urullu* (middle and late Babylonian). The etymology is unknown. The uncircumcised person was metaphorically, but not ritually, impure (Isa 52:1). He was barred from the paschal sacrifice only because it was a covenantal rite, but he could partake of other sacred food. In Egypt, however, the uncircumcised were in some respects regarded as impure (Blackman 1951: 442). This expression is found only in P (Gen 17:11, 14, 23, 24, 25) and in Ezekiel (44:7, 9) where, however, it is combined with *ʿerel/ʿarlê leb* (Lev 26:41;

Deut 10:16; Jer 4:4; 9:25), an indication that Ezekiel borrowed the two terms from P and H/D, respectively, and combined them (Paran 1983: 197).

the foreskin of his member. bĕśar ʿorlātô; cf. Gen 17:11, 14, 23–25. Most translations render "the flesh of his foreskin" (e.g., *NJPS*), which, however, is senseless—the foreskin and, indeed, any skin are not flesh, either in Hebrew or in any other language. Rather, *baśar* here refers to the penis, a usage not infrequently found in Scripture (e.g., 15:2, 3; Ezek 16:26; 23:20), and the construct form, known as *genit. explicativus* (GKC §128 k–o), would be akin to *ʿēṣ haz-zayit* 'the olive tree' (Hag 2:19), where the *nomens regum* would be a larger category than the *nomens rectum*.

shall be circumcised (yimmôl). Niphʿal of *mwl* (cf. Josh 5:5), which can also be followed by an accusative (e.g., Gen 17:11, 25; GKC §121c, d[d]).

4. *She shall remain (tēšēb).* For this meaning of *yāšab,* see Gen 13:18; 24:55; Exod 16:29; Deut 1:46; Judg 6:18; 1 Sam 1:23; Saadiah; Rashi. Ramban adds the nuance "remain apart, isolated," a usage found in the case of the *mĕṣōrāʿ:* "*yēšēb* isolated outside the camp" (13:46). He thus draws close to the Karaites' interpretation that *yāšab* here denotes—in disagreement with the rabbis (see the Note below)—"abstain [from her husband]," which they support by a different verse from the pericope on the *mĕṣōrāʿ:* "*wĕyāšab* outside of his tent" (14:8), which, they argue—this time in agreement with the rabbis—clearly implies sexual abstinence (see the Note on 14:8). As further evidence the Karaites point to the phrase *wĕṭāhărâ mimmĕqôr dāmêhā* (v 7aβ), which they render literally as "she shall be purified of the source of her blood [flow]" on the analogy of *gillĕtâ ʾet-mĕqôr dāmêhā* 'she has exposed the source of her blood [flow]' (20:18), implying that only now after forty days for a boy or eighty days for a girl may she resume sexual intercourse with her husband *(Keter Torah).* Indeed, the Samaritans and Falashas also bar sexual relations with the parturient during her entire purificatory period (Eshkoli 1936: 122; note the vehement protestations of Maim., "Conjugal Prohibitions" 11.15). Moreover, there is clear evidence that parturients indeed behaved in this manner during Talmudic times (*b. Šabb.* 55b; *Sipre* Nas. 8; *y. Ketub.* 13:1; cf. Lieberman 1933).

Philological support for this interpretation can be mustered from one of the attested meanings of *yāšab,* 'be inactive' (e.g., Jer 8:14; Ruth 3:18), which in describing a woman in relation to her husband clearly connotes abstention from sex (Hos 3:3; Ehrlich 1908–14). This usage is also found in rabbinic sources, for example, in the phrase *šēb wĕʾal taʿăśeh,* literally, "be inactive and do not act" (cf. *b. Ber.* 20a; *b. ʿErub.* 100a; *b. Qidd.* 3a). Indeed, *yĕtab* in rabbinic Aramaic unquestionably can refer to sexual abstention (e.g., *Midr. Gen. Rab.* 9:8).

If this interpretation holds, then one would have to posit that the purpose of the parturient's ablution on the thirty-third (and sixty-sixth) day following her severe menstruallike impurity would be to allow her conjugal intercourse with her husband, whereas that evening's sunset would permit her to partake of sacred food (see chap. 15, COMMENT F). Unfortunately for this interpretation, no such ablution is mentioned in the text, though the matter is disputed by the rabbis (see the Note on "she shall bring," v 6). The absence of any mention of ablution at the end of her purificatory period would then imply that none was necessary: the ablution after the initial seven (or fourteen) days would allow her contact with the common, including intercourse with her husband, but not with the sacred; and the completion of her full purificatory period, with the setting of the sun, would give her access to things sacred. Thus the rendering "remain" for *tēšēb* is preferred.

in [a state of] blood. bidĕmê, literally, "in bloods of." The plural *dāmîm* most often connotes "blood guilt" (e.g., 20:9, 11; Exod 22:1, 2) or "[illicit] bloodshed" (e.g., Gen 4:10, 11; 2 Kgs 2:5, 31; 9:7, 26). But it can also refer simply to blood without a pejorative connotation (e.g., 20:18; Ezek 16:6). Blood never defiles, except if spilled illicitly (Num 35:33–34); otherwise it only purifies and sanctifies (e.g., 16:19).

The parturient's blood discharge (lochia) is mentioned here three times (vv 4, 5, 7), emphasizing its long duration beyond the initial seven/fourteen-day impurity. The first discharge is bright red, then turns brown and increasingly paler. The total discharge lasts from two to six weeks. Hence the round figure of forty days is quite accurate. Moreover, the bright red of the initial discharge resembles the menstrual flow and is therefore treated as such (Wenham 1979).

[blood] purity (ṭohŏrâ). A nominal formation like *ḥokmâ* 'wisdom' and *ʿormâ* 'guile'. It is not an infinitive construct that would require, in this form, a modifier, for instance, *lĕʾahăbâ* 'to love' (Deut 10:15); *ḥumṣātô* 'its leavening' (Hos 7:4). Such, indeed, is the case with this verb too: *ṭohŏrātô* 'his purification/healing' (14:2; Num 6:9; Ezek 44:26); *lĕṭohŏrātô* 'for his purification' (13:7; 14:23; 15:13). Thus we have here an abstract noun, "purity" (cf. Neh 12:45). The first vowel is therefore a *qāmeṣ ḥāṭûp* (being derived from *ṭohar;* cf. GKC §84b). It seems, however, that this word was pronounced *ṭahărâ* at Qumran, for it is written there as *ṭhrh* and not *ṭwhrh*, which would have been the case for a *qāmeṣ ḥāṭûp*. There is no need to follow Rinaldi (1954), who opts for an otherwise unattested ellipsis "blood (by whose flow the woman recovers) purity."

Thus, the expression *dĕmê ṭohŏrâ* 'blood purity', found twice in this chapter (vv 4a, 5b), is probably a frozen idiom that refers exclusively to the parturient's state following her initial seven- (or fourteen-)day impurity. The LXX, attempting to resolve the paradox that she continues impure during her "purity," renders *dĕmê ṭohŏrâ* as "her unclean blood." But the use of *ṭohŏrâ* here makes sense. It implies that her previous impurity no longer exists, a fact that the following verse makes explicit by stating that she remains impure only in regard to sancta. Thus she now has unrestricted access to the common sphere, including her husband (*b. Ḥul.* 31a; cf. *Tg. Ps.-J.*). Indeed, the fact that the abstract noun *ṭohŏrâ* 'purity' is used twice in reference to her blood flow strongly suggests that sexual contact with this blood does not defile. At least, so the Masoretes want us to conclude, to judge by their insertion of a *mappiq* in the final *hēh* of this same word whenever the context speaks of the woman's purificatory period, *yĕmê ṭohŏrāh* 'the period of her purification' (vv 4b, 6b). Nor can one say that the *mappiq* here was omitted by mistake, for its omission follows a fixed rule: it will only happen before a soft or *begadkepat* letter, but is unlikely in a pausal form, as in this case (GKC §91e). One should also note that *Tg. Onq.* preserves this distinctive rendering *dĕkû*, without suffix, here (and in 5b) in contrast to *dĕkûtāh* in vv 4b, 6b. The LXX, by contrast, consistently renders "her unclean blood."

thirty-three days. Thereby a total of forty days is given for the purification period following the birth of a boy. This number is well attested throughout the Bible, but what is unexpected is that this forty-day period for the postpartem purification of the mother is prevalent in many other cultures as well. For example, in exact conformance with this verse, the parturient was not allowed to enter a Greek temple for forty days (Preuss 1971: 464) and, according to a number of Greek sources, a parturient undergoes purification forty days after giving birth (cf. Stengel 1920: 66; Binder 1976: 87ff.). The same holds true among peoples as diverse and widespread as the California Indians (Doeller 1917: 23), Persians (Boyce 1975: 308), Jainists (Stevenson 1951: 493), Malaysians (forty-four days; Fallaize 1951: 457), and Bulgars (ibid. 458).

Comparative material also duplicates the disparity in the purificatory periods following the birth of a boy and that of a girl, with the period following a girl's birth nearly always being longer. Thus in India a new mother is barred from religious rites for thirty days if the child is male and forty days, if female (Kane 1973: 270–71). In southern India, however, the seclusion of mother and child is reversed: nine days for boys and five for girls (Bean 1981: 582). The Hittites who lived within Israel's cultural continuum exhibit an even more striking parallel: "If a male child is born . . . when the third month arrives . . . they cleanse . . . and if a female child is born . . . when the fourth month arrives they cleanse" (*KBo* 17.65.32–36; Beckman 1978: 18). Nonetheless, the Hittite ritual must be sharply distinguished from its Israelite counterpart not only by its length and content but by the fact that purificatory rites are applied to the child as well as to the mother. Among the Hittites and among other cultures the newborn is impure (i.e., of potential danger) just like the mother (see COMMENT A below).

The reason for this disparity between the sexes is unknown. Some have conjectured that the postnatal discharge for a female lasts longer (Dillmann and Ryssel 1897; Macht 1933). Others suggest that, judging by Israelite law and practice, the disparity reflects the relative status of the sexes: the redemption price of the woman is about half that of a man (27:2–7; Abravanel on chap. 27, p. 176b; Wenham 1979). An old legend offers the etiology that whereas Adam was created at the end of the first week and was brought into "sacred" Eden on the forty-first day, Eve was created at the end of the second week and admitted into Eden on the eighty-first day (Jub 3:8–14; *Midr. Tadshe* 15; see chap. 15,

COMMENT F). A biological distinction is proposed by Rabbi Ishmael: the male embryo is completely formed in forty-one days and the female in eighty-one days (*m. Nid.* 3:7). That this view was current in the ancient Near East is supported by Greek sources: Aristotle holds that the male is formed in forty days and the female in three months (*Hist. anim.* 7.3), and Hippocrates opts for thirty days for the male and forty-two days for the female (*De natura pueri,* chap. 17, cited in Preuss 1971: 452).

Many would agree with the view that "the cultic inferiority of the female sex is expressed in giving the female birth a double 'uncleanness' effect" (Noth 1965), which M. Gruber (1987: 43 n. 13) has correctly rebutted: "greater defilement is not necessarily an indication of less social worth. Hence, a corpse defiles more than a dead pig, the latter more than a dead frog." This point is explicitly made by the rabbis:

> The Sadducees say, we cry out against you, O you Pharisees, for you say, "the Holy Scriptures render the hands impure," [and] "the writings of Hamiram (Homer?) do not render the hands impure." Rabban Yohanan B. Zakkai said, Have we naught against the Pharisees save this!—For lo, they say, "the bones of an ass are pure, and the bones of Yohanan the high priest are impure." They said to him, As is our love for them, so is their impurity—that no man make spoons of the bones of his father or mother. He said to them, Even so the Holy Scriptures: As is our love for them, so is their impurity; [whereas] the writings of Hamiram which are held in no account do not render the hands impure. (*m. Yad.* 4:6)

touch (*tigga*ʿ). The majority of the rabbis render *nāga*ʿ in this instance as "eat" (*b. Yebam.* 75a; *b. Mak.* 14b; etc.), for the likelihood is that the only sancta she will chance to touch will be sacred food for her table (see the NOTE below). But the minority view of Rabbi Yohanan (ibid.), that it is touching that is proscribed, is undoubtedly correct. This can already be deduced from the many prohibitions against touching, in addition to those of eating, found in the previous chapter on the diet laws. The taboo against contact with sancta by an impure person is not limited to the Priestly tradition. Narrative relates how Ahimelek, the priest of Nob, was reluctant to provide sacred bread to David's soldiers until he was assured that they had abstained from sexual intercourse (1 Sam 21:5–6). And Josephus understood the episode of Rachel and the teraphim very well (Gen 31:34–35) when he remarks that Laban did not search Rachel because he was sure that in her condition she would not have touched the idols (*Ant.* 1.323). That any kind of contact between impurity and sancta was dreaded, even indirectly through the air, can be derived from the Priestly system of sacrificial expiation (see chap. 4, COMMENT C and chap. 16, COMMENT F) and from the Hittite instructions (see below).

consecrated thing (*qōdeš*). The chances are that the only opportunity for the parturient and, indeed, for any lay person to contaminate sancta would be in connection with eating sacred food. For that reason all of the laws warning about contact with sancta deal solely with this problem: eating the well-being offering (7:19–20), the paschal offering (Num 9:6), and the priestly prebends (22:3–9; Num 18:11, 13). Yet it is assumed that any form of contact between impurity and sancta is strictly forbidden. For example, in the matter of tithes, the Israelite farmer must be able to declare, "I have not cleared away any of it while impure" (Deut 26:14), which clearly implies that touching the tithes in a state of impurity is forbidden (see also the NOTE on "eats," 7:20). The same taboo would apply to all other objects that inherently belong or have been dedicated to the sanctuary, such as precious weapons and booty (2 Sam 8:7–11; 1 Kgs 7:51; 14:26–27; 15:15), animals, land, houses, firstlings, and animal and crop tithes (27:9–33).

That v 4 covers not just sacred food but a wider range of sancta is evident from the Hittite instructions, "You, all the kitchen personnel . . . will have to swear an oath of loyalty to the king every month. Fill a bitumen cup with water and pour it toward the Sun-god and speak as follows: 'Whoever does something in an unclean way and offers to the king polluted water, pour you, O gods, that man's soul out like water!' " (ANET³ 207a). "If the implements of wood and the implements of fired clay which you hold (in the temple), if a pig or a dog ever approach (i.e., contact; J.M.) them, but the kitchen official does not throw them (the vessels) away, (and) he gives to the god to eat from an unclean (implement), then to him the gods will give excrement and urine to eat and drink" (ANET³ 209b; D. P. Wright's translation; cf. the NOTE on 11:33). "Whoever sleeps with a woman . . . and without having bathed approaches (i.e., contacts; J.M.) the god's sacrificial loaves (and) libation bowl in an unclean condition . . . shall be killed" (ANET³ 209b). These examples from the Hittite sphere illustrate, first, the great fear of impurity invading the palace and temple and thereby defiling the king and the gods (the king was a sacred person because he officiated at major temple rites), and, second, the contamination of the king or the gods' food need not be necessarily direct but could be through the medium of an implement such as the kitchen table or the libation bowl, that is to say, any object that could convey its impurity to the food.

Thus the probability exists that the qōdeš that the parturient (or any impure person) may not touch refers to any consecrated thing, in other words, an object that has been transferred and now belongs to the divine sphere.

enter (tābōʾ). Similarly worded prohibitions in regard to the entry of priests into the sanctuary provide an instructive contrast between the status of the priests and that of the laity. There are four disqualifications that bar priests from contact with the sanctuary on pain of death: improper washing, a physical blemish, drunkenness, and improper dress. The texts follow in order:

When they enter *(bĕbōʾām)* the Tent of Meeting they shall wash with water, that they may not die; or when they seek access *(bĕgištām)* to the altar to serve, to turn into smoke a food gift to the Lord. (Exod 30:20; cf. 40:32)

But he (the high priest; Milgrom 1970a: 40) shall not enter *(yābōʾ)* to the veil or have access *(yiggaš)* to the altar, for he has a blemish. (Lev 21:23; cf. vv 17, 18, 21)

Drink no wine or ale, you or your sons after you, when you enter *(bĕbōʾăkem)* the Tent of Meeting [or when you seek access to the altar, LXX], that you may not die. (Lev 10:9)

They (the priestly garments; Milgrom 1970a: n. 148) shall be worn by Aaron and his sons when they enter *(bĕbōʾām)* the Tent of Meeting or when they seek access *(bĕgištām)* to the altar to officiate in the sacred precinct *(baq-qōdeš)* so that they do not incur guilt and die. (Exod 28:43; cf. v 35)

These four disqualifications are not impurities *(ṭumʾōt);* they are desecrations and fall into the category of the profane *(ḥōl).* Yet what they illustrate is that the disqualifications for the priests in the realm of the profane correspond to the disqualifications of the laity in the realm of impurity. Note also the other correspondences and distinctions. A profane priest may not enter the Tent (except if he is blemished; Milgrom 1970a: 40–41) but, by implication, he may enter the Tabernacle court. The impure lay person is barred from the Tabernacle court and so, of course, if he is a priest (that the verb *bāʾ* 'enter' must be taken literally, see the NOTE on 10:9). Conversely, a lay person who is in a pure state may enter the court with his sacrifice (see the NOTE on "entrance to the Tent of Meeting, 1:3). Thus a disqualified priest and a pure lay person are on the same level: both have access to the Tabernacle court. Their equalization is perfectly logical: the disqualified priest is reduced to the status of a layman.

Ostensibly, they differ in regard to the second area of the prohibition, the altar: the disqualified priest may not *officiate* on the altar but, otherwise, he may make contact with it (for the demonstration that *nāgaš* and its synonym *qārab,* when used in a positive sense, must be rendered "seek access [for the purpose of officiating]"; see Milgrom 1970a: 38–43). Nevertheless, this distinction is, in reality, nonexistent. For it has been demonstrated that the pure lay person may also touch the altar with impunity (see chaps. 6–7, COMMENT B). Thus, in effect, the disqualified priest assumes lay status with regard to the altar. To be sure, the former is not deprived of his right to eat sacred food (21:22). Nonetheless, even this allowance is a major exception. First, let it be noted that this verse is couched in the language of concession *(ʾak).* Second, as the layman is entitled to his sacred food (from the well-being offering), so the disqualified priest is entitled to his (from all the sacrifices). That the priest is not also restricted to the meat of the well-being offering is explicable on the most pragmatic and logical of grounds: he has no animals of his own and, indeed, his income derives entirely from the sacrifices brought by others; deprived of it he would starve! (For other reasons for this leniency, see Milgrom 1970a: n. 156.)

The distinction in the verbs used in regard to the priest's access to the altar and the parturient's access to consecrated things can readily be explained. We are dealing with a disqualified priest, not an impure one; the latter would be under even greater constraints (and sanctions) to distance himself from all things sacred (cf. 22:2–9). By contrast, although there is genuine concern that a layman may encroach on the altar (*hazzār haqqārēb yûmat;* Num 1:51; 3:10, 38; 18:2; Milgrom 1970a: 1–37), it is beyond imagination to conceive of such a possibility for a woman, not to speak of an impure woman. The only concern in her case is that she may unwittingly enter the sacred precincts or, while at home, touch sacred food.

Historical sources indicate that this fear of entering the sanctuary in an impure state was deeply ingrained in the Jewish woman's psyche. A Christian preacher from Syria rebukes Jewish converts for not entering the church during their menstrual periods (Achelis 1904: 114). And all through the Middle Ages there are recorded instances of menstruants refusing to enter synagogues (Horowitz 1970: 30–33; Zucker 1963–64; Maim., "Forbidden Entry" 11.5; *Midr. Leqaḥ Ṭov,* Tazria᷅ on 12:8; Maḥzor Vitry: 606) despite the explicit permission and urging of the rabbis to do so (*b. Bek.* 27b; *t. Ber.* 2:12; *y. Ber.* 3:4). The Eastern church has a long tradition of barring menstruants from worship, and even the Roman church records bans of this type (Doeller 1917: 49–50).

the sacred precinct (hammiqdāš). In P (and H) this term can either mean "the sacred objects, sancta" (21:23; 26:31; Num 3:38; 10:21; 18:1) or "the sacred area, precinct" (12:4; 16:33; 19:30; 20:3; 21:12; 26:2; Num 19:20). Of the former group, especially compelling are Num 18:1, where "your father's house" clearly refers to the Kohathites who alone are responsible for the sancta in transit (cf. Num 10:21), and Lev 26:31, where the verb "desolate" implies concrete objects, in other words, "your sancta" and not an area, so that the plural *miqdēšêkem* no longer has to be taken as evidence of multiple sanctuaries! (The term *qōdeš* also admits of these two meanings: cf. Milgrom 1970a: 39 n. 149.)

What is significant about this term is that in the entire Bible it never stands for the sanctuary or Temple building (despite the LXX, Pesh., *Tgs. Ps.-J.* and *Neof.* on this passage). The one ostensible exception, "make me a *miqdāš*" (Exod 25:8), is rebutted on the grounds that this term is defined in the following verse as "the Tabernacle . . . and all its furnishings," in other words, all objects contained in the sacred precincts of which the Tabernacle is but one. Indeed, the full name for the Second Temple confirms it: *bêt hammiqdāš* (2 Chr 36:17; *t. Šabb.* 1:13; *b. Sukk.* 51b; etc.), which, to judge by the two possibilities mentioned above, could mean either "the house of the sacred objects" or "the house of the sacred area." That the latter is the probable meaning is strongly indicated by the statement the Chronicler attributes to David: "See then the

Lord chose you (Solomon) to build *bayit lammiqdāš*, a house for the sacred area" (1 Chr 28:10), a rendering that makes sense in view of the fact that David had already purchased the sacred area (1 Chr 21:18–27; 2 Sam 25:18–25).

Indeed, it seems that the connotation of sacred objects for *miqdāš* is limited to P and H (and possibly Jer 51:51). Everywhere else it refers to the sacred area or compound in which the Temple *(habbayit)* is the chief component but only one among others. It is striking that in Ezekiel, despite its dependency on the P and H traditions, all twenty-seven occurrences of *miqdāš* refer to "the sacred precincts," an indication that the connotation of "sacred objects" had by then fallen out of use. It can also be shown that this understanding of *miqdāš* illumines the entire pericope of Ezekiel's visionary temple (Ezek 40–48) in a new light (see Milgrom 1970a: n. 78).

[the period of] her purification ([yĕmê] ṭohŏrāh). Probably an infinitive construct of the verb *ṭāhēr* 'be pure', on the order of *mokrāh* 'to sell her' (Exod 21:8). Theoretically, this term could also be construed as a noun with a pronominal suffix. Yet the noun *ṭōhar* occurs only once (Exod 24:10), outside P, where its meaning is entirely different, "clarity(?)." Prefixed by *yĕmê* 'period of' here, and again in v 6a, it clearly refers to the purificatory process that the parturient undergoes, and it must be carefully distinguished from the same consonantal and vocal construction, but without the *mappiq-hēh*, which bears an entirely different connotation (see the NOTE on v 4a, above).

is complete. mĕlōʾt, literally, "the completion of" (for the meaning, cf. Gen 29:21; Lam 4:18). This infinitive construct is treated like a *lamed-hēh* verb *(Keter Torah)*, for instance, *qĕrōʾt* (Judg 8:1); *śĕnōʾt* (Prov 8:13). It occurs again in v 6 and earlier in 8:33.

5. *If. wĕʾim* introduces the second case; "when *(kî)* . . . a male . . ." is the first.

a female. nĕqēbâ, from the verb *nāqab* 'bore [a hole]' (2 Kgs 12:10); 'pierce' (2 Kgs 18:2); cf. *nāqûb* 'riddled' (Hag 1:6); *hnqbh* 'the piercing through' (Siloam inscription). The probable reason that the legislator chose this word, which clearly refers to the sexual organ of the female is that it is the only indication of gender at the time of birth (Wessely 1846; see the NOTE on "a male," v 2).

two weeks. Double that of a male (v 2b; for the possible reasons for this doubling, see the NOTE on "thirty-three days," v 4a). Just as in the case of a male child, it is assumed that the end of this period is marked by immersion (see the NOTE on 15:19 and *m. Neg.* 4:3; *Tg. Ps.-J.*).

as at her menstruation. kĕniddātāh, literally, "as her menstruation," but its sense is that of *kibĕniddātāh* 'as at her menstruation'. Its meaning is similar to the parallel expression for the boy, *kîmê* (= *kĕbîmê*; cf. the NOTE on "as during the period," v 2b). Still, the two expressions are not identical, for *kîmê* is missing here, and for an obvious reason. The seven-day impurity for the birth of a boy is indeed identical to the length of the menstrual period (15:19). For the birth of a girl, however, the mother's "menstrual" impurity is double that of menstruation. Probably for the same reason, the other term used in the case of the birth of a boy, děwōtāh 'her infirmity', is also omitted here, for this weakened condition is associated just with menstruation (15:33; 20:18).

in. ʿal-(děmê), literally, "upon," but equivalent here to *biděmê* (v 4a).

blood purity (děmê ṭohŏrâ). See the NOTES on "in [a state of] blood" and "[blood] purity," v 4a.

sixty-six days. Double the second period for the birth of a boy, giving a total of eighty days before the parturient may enter the sanctuary. The reasons for this doubling are cited in the NOTE on "thirty-three days," v 4a.

6. *On the completion (ûbimlōʾt).* See the NOTE on "is completed," v 4b. Implied is the forty-first and the eighty-first day.

her period of purification (yěmê ṭohŏrāh). See the NOTE on the same phrase in v 4b for an explanation of the *mappiq* in the final *hēh* and its significance.

for either son or daughter (lěbēn ʾô lěbat). Because the gender of the child has been determined at birth, now that its fortieth or eightieth day has been reached, the designation "son" or "daughter" can be employed (see the NOTE on "a male," v 2a).

she shall bring (tābîʾ). This verb is the key to understanding why the *ʿōlâ,* the burnt offering, precedes the *ḥaṭṭāʾt,* the purification offering, in this verse: it signifies that here is a prescriptive (and administrative) sacrificial list in which the burnt offering is always listed first. In a descriptive text, conversely, where the actual rite is described, the purification offering comes first because it is always the first to be sacrificed. This principle was succinctly enunciated by Raba in his comment on this verse: "Scripture accords it (the burnt offering) precedence in regard to its designation" (b. Zebaḥ. 90a). A good example of this distinction between prescriptive and descriptive sacrificial series is found in the text dealing with the Nazirite who has successfully completed his or her vow. When the sacrifices are prescribed, the burnt offering appears first; but when the execution of the ritual is described, the purification offering is first (Num 6:14–16; cf. Lev 5:8; m. Nazir 6:7; m. Zebaḥ. 10:2; t. Para 1:1; b. Zebaḥ. 90a [bar.]; cf. also the NOTE on "when he gives," 5:16b).

That these sacrifices are brought after the impurity has totally disappeared is irrefutable proof that their function is not apotropaic or medicinal. In Israel, the puerperal period is not feared as governed by the demonic (in polemical opposition to other cultures; see COMMENT B below). Only ritual impurity adheres, which time and ablutions remove (see chap. 15, COMMENT F). To be sure, no ablutions whatever are mandated by the text for the parturient; but it has already been pointed out that the ablution requirement is always omitted for the simple reason that it is taken for granted except in cases in which it is not self-understood (see the NOTE on "shall be impure until evening," 11:24). Such will clearly be the case with the menstruant (see the NOTE on 15:19) and a fortiori for the parturient.

That the parturient must undergo immersion at the end of her first, "menstrual," period of seven or fourteen days is assumed by the rabbis (*m. Neg.* 4:3; cf. *Tg. Ps.-J.* on v 5). But they dispute the necessity for the second ablution at the end of the forty or eighty days, the school of Shammai demanding it and the school of Hillel forgoing it (*m. Nid.* 10:7). The grounds for the dispute are not given, but they can be extrapolated from the chart in chap. 15, COMMENT F: "The Effect of the Purification Procedures." Hillelites would argue that the ablutions of the seventh or fourteenth day suffice to remove the last vestige of impurity and thereby qualify the parturient to enter the sanctuary (but not to partake of sacred food; cf. *m. Ḥag.* 3:3 and chap. 15, COMMENT F), but instead of having to wait till the following day—as is the case with all other severe impurities—her waiting period is prolonged thirty-three or sixty-six days. Indeed, the Amoraic sages who follow the Hillelite ruling refer to the parturient during this period as *ṭĕbûlat yôm ʾārôk* 'immersed for a long day' (*b. Nid.* 30a). That is, her ablutions on the seventh or fourteenth day give her access to the common, but her access to the holy is postponed not to the following day but until she brings her sacrifices, a month or two later. The Shammaites apparently argue instead that as long as she is emitting blood, even of "her purity," her contact with sancta might be misconstrued by the public (*y. Ḥag.* 3:3). Furthermore, as in the case of all other impurities, access to the holy is always preceded by an ablution on the previous day, so here too it is the ablution on the fortieth (or eightieth) day that matters (cf. *m. Nid.* 4:3 and Albeck 1956 on *m. Nid.* 10:7). The comprehensive discussion of this question is reserved for chap. 15, COMMENT C.

yearling (ben-šĕnātô). The usual expression is *ben-šānâ.* With the pronominal suffix it occurs only in 13:6; 14:10; 23:12; Num 6:12, 14; 7 (twelve times); 15:27; Ezek 46:13. Is there any distinction in meaning between these two forms? Rabbi David the Prince (cited by *Seper Hamibḥar*) proposes that the suffixed expression in this verse should be rendered "within its year," that is to say, the animal is less than one year old. Independently, Ehrlich (1908–14; followed by Joüon 1923: 129j) comes to the same conclusion on the basis of rabbinic usage: a *ben yômô* infant (*b. Šabb.* 151b), a *bat yômāh* cheese (*b. Šabb.* 134a), and *bĕnê yômān* fruits (*b. Pesaḥ.* 4b) are all items that are less than one day old.

Ṭirat Kesef (on *Seper Hamibḥar)* counters Rabbi David's proposal with evidence from Num 7: whereas the lamb offered each day is called *ben-šĕnātô* (e.g., Num 7:15), in the totals the lambs are described as *bĕnê šānâ* (v 82), without the suffix! *Ṭirat Kesef* thus presents us with a clue to the solution. The suffixed form only occurs in the singular—indeed, in every attestation with the exception of Exod 12:5. The plural, conversely, never occurs with the suffix; it always appears as *bĕnê šānâ* (9:3; 23:18, 19; Num 7 [fourteen times]; 28–29 [fifteen times]; Mic 6:6). Hence the only legitimate conclusion is that this orthographic distinction is simply a matter of style.

for a burnt offering (lĕ'ōlâ). Why the need for a burnt offering? There is a good reason for it whenever the purification offering is a bird. For then another bird is sacrificed as a burnt offering to provide an adequate contribution to the altar (Ibn Ezra; see the NOTE on 5:7). But why the need, as in this case, for a lamb? Perhaps it is offered in thanksgiving for the new child (Koch 1959: 79 n. 5; cf. v 8. That the ʿōlâ can function as a thanksgiving offering is seen at 22:18; Num 15:3; and in the COMMENT on chap. 1). Nevertheless, the fact that the parturient is purified by the action of *both* sacrifices (vv 7a, 8b) indicates that the purpose of the burnt offering, like that of the purification offering, is expiatory (see the NOTE on "effect expiation," v 7), but it addresses other matters than pollution. These matters are alluded to by the rabbinic statement, "The Tana, R. Simeon asks: Why does the purification offering precede the burnt offering (in the sacrificial order)? It is comparable to an attorney who comes to appease. Having made his (plea of appeasement), the gift (of appeasement) follows" (*t. Para* 1:1; *Zebaḥ.* 7b [bar.]). The burnt offering, then, is a gift with any number of goals in mind, one of which—the one singled out here (and in 1:4)—is expiation. Why, then, a lamb and not a bird, to begin with? A precious boon, the birth of a child, is deserving of a decent gift, and only in the case of indigence is the cost reduced (v 8).

a pigeon or turtledove (ûben-yōnâ ʾô-tōr). For their identification, see the NOTE on 1:14. The order of the two birds is everywhere else reversed. For the significance see the NOTE on these two birds in v 8. In Ugaritic sacrificial lists two birds *(ʿṣrm)* are offered and specific mention is made of pigeons *(ynt* or *ynt qrt;* e.g., *KTU* 1.41 [= 1.87]; 5.10, 21, 36, 43) as well as turtledoves *(tr; KTU* 1.115; 5.13; cited by Weinfeld 1983: 109). Even more striking, however, is the text of the corresponding Hittite rite of Papanikri for the purification of a childbearing woman, which records the following: "they bring two birds for offense and sin. They burn one lamb for appeasement(?)" (Sommer and Eheloff 1924: 2.2–3; translation by D. Wright). Not only are the same animals offered— bird and lamb—but the birds, as in Israel, are expiatory. And if the Hurrian term *enumašši* means "appeasement" (see Haas and Wilhelm 1974: 75–76), then the lamb may also be expiatory but covering a different range of wrongs than the birds, just as in Israel, where both the burnt offering and the purification offering are expiatory, but they are complementary in function and not identical. For the significance of the Hittites' two birds, see the NOTE on v 8.

for a purification offering (lĕḥaṭṭāʾt).

R. Simeon b. Yohai was asked by his disciples: Why did the Torah ordain that a woman after childbirth should bring a sacrifice? He replied: When she kneels in bearing she swears impetuously that she will have no inter- course with her husband. The Torah, therefore, ordained that she should bring a sacrifice. R. Joseph demurred: Does she not act presumptuously in which case the absolution of the oath depends on her rejecting it?

Furthermore, she should have brought a sacrifice prescribed for an oath (5:5–6)! (*b. Nid.* 31b)

Rabbi Simeon is the only sage who attributes the parturient's need to bring a purification offering to her sin but, significantly, he dissociates her sin from the procreative act and assumes that her labor pains led her to utter a rash oath, which she never intended to keep. Another comment on Rabbi Simeon's explanation is more to the point: "But according to Rabbi Simeon ben Yohai, who holds that a woman in confinement is a sinner, what can be said (concerning the purpose of her *ḥaṭṭāʾt*)? The sacrifice she brings is nevertheless for the purpose of permitting her to partake of consecrated food and is not expiatory" (*b. Ker.* 26a). This statement is significant on two counts: (1) it severs all connection between the *ḥaṭṭāʾt* (a *piʿel* formation) and the similar term for sin (*ḥăṭāʾt*, a *qal* formation) and thus leads to a new rendering of this sacrifice as a "purification offering" (details in chap. 4, COMMENT A); (2) it avers that the sacrifice, the last stage of the purificatory rite, gives the parturient access to sacred food. In the discussion of the subject (chap. 15, COMMENT F) it will be shown that this insight is correct, not just for the parturient but for all impurity bearers who are required to bring a sacrifice.

to the priest (ʾel-hakkōhēn). "(This) teaches that she (and not her husband or some surrogate) attends to them (the offerings) and brings them to the entrance of the Tent of Meeting to the Priest" (*Sipra*, Tazriaʿ 3:4). This rabbinic deduction is verified by the case of the suspected adulteress, where the text states explicitly that the husband brings the sacrifice on her behalf. Thus, if it were the responsibility of the parturient's husband to bring the sacrifices, the text would have so stated. Note that the same language prevails in the case of the *Zābâ* (15:29) and the contaminated Nazirite (Num 6:10), who might also be a woman (ibid. v 2).

To be sure, Hannah does not reappear at the Shiloh sanctuary until her son Samuel is weaned (1 Sam 1:22). This discrepancy can be resolved in either of two ways: either Leviticus does not reflect the practice of Shiloh, or Hannah brought her required purificatory sacrifices to a local *bāmâ.*

7. *He shall offer it (wĕhiqrîbô).* "It" refers to both sacrifices. All that one offers to the sanctuary at one time, even if some of it is not for the altar, can collectively be termed by the singular, *qorbān,* as in "His offering *(wĕqorbānô)*: one silver bowl . . . one silver basin . . . one gold ladle . . . one bull of the herd, one ram," etc. (Num 7:13–17; Shadal). Thus the LXX's reading *wĕhiqrîbāh* 'He shall offer it' (sing., i.e., the *ḥaṭṭāʾt*) must be rejected. Besides, the burnt offering also serves an expiatory role (v 8), and see below. The Sam. and one MS as well as LXX, Pesh., and *Tg. Ps.-J.* add the word *hakkōhēn,* thereby rendering "The priest shall effect purgation." This addition is superfluous because it occurs as the final word in the previous verse and is the obvious subject to this verb.

and effect expiation on her behalf (wĕkippēr ʿ̄alêhā). The verb *kippēr* bears the specific meaning "purge" when its subject is the purification offering. The parturient has polluted the altar, albeit unintentionally, by her severe and prolonged discharge (lochia) and, hence, must bring a purification offering to purge it (cf. chap. 4, COMMENT B and chap. 16, COMMENT F). The burnt offering plays a greater expiatory role (see the NOTE on "burnt offering," v 6), though its exact nature can only be conjectured (cf. the NOTE on "burnt offering," v 6 and the COMMENT on chap. 1). Because this verb must cover both sacrifices, it is rendered by the broader of its two meanings, "expiate."

and then she shall be pure. wĕṭāhărâ, to eat sacred food (*b. Yebam.* 74b [bar.]). This root appeared earlier as a noun, *ṭohŏrâ* (vv 4a, 5b), and as an infinitive construct, *ṭohŏrāh* (vv 4b, 6a), both of which referred to the initial purification that set in following the initial seven or (fourteen) days that allowed the woman to contact profane objects but not sacred ones. Now that forty (or eighty) days have elapsed and she has brought her requisite sacrifices to the sanctuary, she is purified completely and is eligible to make contact with sacred objects. The demarcation of these stages of impurity diminution by the verb *ṭāhar* is best exemplified in the case of the *mĕṣōrāʿ:* its threefold occurrence (14:8, 9, 20) corresponds to the three stages through which the *mĕṣōrāʿ* passes in his purificatory process, as recognized by the rabbis (*m. Neg.* 14:2–3; cf. the discussion in chap. 15, COMMENT F). To be sure, the rabbis also distinguish three stages in the purification of the parturient (ibid.), but that is because they add an additional stage at the evening following the fortieth (or eightieth) day (discussed in chap. 15, COMMENT C).

It is important to note that the result of *kippēr* in the case of the parturient and other bearers of physical impurity (chaps. 13–15) is radically different from the *kippēr* used in the previously discussed cases: the former are followed by the verb *ṭāhēr* (e.g., 12:7, 8; 14:20, 53), the latter by the verb *nislaḥ* (e.g., 4:20, 26, 31, 35). This distinction in terminology makes it crystal clear that the parturient and all others who suffer *physical* impurity have committed no moral wrong that requires divine forgiveness. Their impurity is cleansed by means of water; and if it is severe enough (or prolonged, see 5:1–5) to have polluted the altar, the latter must be cleansed by a purification offering.

Furthermore, the verb patterns should be carefully noted. *Moral* impurity can only be forgiven by God and not by the action of the priest. Hence, the verb for forgiveness is couched in the *niphʿal,* "be forgiven," but *physical* impurity is eliminated mechanically: the effect of the ablution and the sacrifice is automatic. Hence the verb for purification is given in the *qal,* "is pure," another indication that there is no stigma attached to physical impurity because there is no judgment by God of the offerer.

The importance of this distinction is illustrated by the ceremonial of the induction of the Levites into the labor force for the sanctuary (Num 8). To be sure, they offer up a bull for a purification offering (v 8). Lest one think that it purges the sanctuary of their moral wrongdoing, however, the text makes it explicit that "Aaron effected purgation on their behalf to purify them *(lĕṭahărām)*" b and (v 21), a point further corroborated by the additional detail in their induction rite that they were sprinkled with "purificatory waters" (v 7), lest they had become impure through corpse contamination (Num 19). Thus the Levites were cleansed of ritual, not moral, impurity.

from [her] source [of blood]. mimmĕqōr [dāmêhā], with *Tg. Ps.-J.*, *Tg. Neof.*, *b. Nid.* 35b. "This teaches us that all the blood she sees issues from the source" *(Sipra*, Tazria' 3:6). That *māqôr* here stands for the female pudenda is shown by the other occurrence of this phrase: "If a man lies with a woman in her infirmity and uncovers her nakedness, he has laid bare her source *(mĕqōrāh)* and she has exposed her blood source *(mĕqōr dāmêhā)*" (20:18). The same context for the male, of necessity, requires a different term: "When a man with a discharge is healed *(yiṭhar)* of his discharge *(mizzôbô)*" (15:13). It is thus not surprising that *māqôr* is also a metaphor for a wife (Prov 5:18). The basic meaning of *māqôr* (root *qwr*) is a fountain, well, or source (Hos 13:15 || *ma'yān;* Jer 2:13; 17:13), in other words, a source of flowing liquid (e.g., *mĕqôr dim'â* 'a fount of tears', Jer 8:23). So too Ug. *mqr (KTU* 1.14: 5.217) and *qr (KTU* 1.19: 3.152).

This is the ritual for (zō't tôrat). For the occurrences and function of this subscript, see the NOTE on 6:2b and v 8, below.

male or female. lazzākār 'ô lannĕqēbâ, literally, "in the case of the male or the female" (Ehrlich 1908–14). The preposition *lamed* can mean "in reference to, regarding" (cf. Joüon 1923: §133c). The repeated *lamed* signifies "or" (e.g., 22:18; Num 18:9), equivalent to Akk. *lu . . . lu.*

8. This verse is clearly a later supplement, as shown not only by its placement after the true end of the chapter, the subscript v 7b, but—more importantly—by its altered vocabulary. Note these changes from the terminology of v 6: *śeh* instead of *kebeś* and *lāqaḥ* in place of *hēbî'.* Furthermore, the order of turtledoves and pigeons is reversed, to conform with the usual sequence (1:14; 5:7, 11; 14:22, 30; 15:24, 29; Num 6:10). This phenomenon of a supplement following a concluding subscript is attested elsewhere: 23:38–44 after subscript v 37 and Num 5:31 after subscript vv 29–30.

her means do [not] suffice for ([lō'] timṣā' yādāh dê). For the identical idiom, see 25:28 (H). P's idiom is slightly different, *hiśśîg yād dê* (5:7). The possibility thus exists that this verse is an H supplement; see the Introduction, §H.

two turtledoves or two pigeons. Two birds occur in sacrificial texts in Ugaritic (see the NOTE on v 6) and in Hittite in the Papanikri ritual (see the NOTE on v 6); the latter involves a similar context: the purification of a childbearing woman (Sommer and Eheloff 1924: 2.1–3). Moreover, the function of these sacrificial birds is strikingly similar: "two birds for offense and sin" (2.2), in other words, they are expiatory. Even so, the difference between the two cultures should not be overlooked. Israel's purification offering has moved away from the general realm of sin and has been restricted to one area: the pollution of the sanctuary and its sancta through the inadvertent violation of prohibitions or through the creation of severe physical impurity.

The Torah's option that the indigent parturient may bring this less costly sacrifice is attested historically: "When the days of their purification according to the Mosaic law had passed (lit., "were fulfilled"), they brought him up to Jerusalem to present him to the Lord—as it is written in the law of the Lord, *'Every male that opens the womb* is to be considered *sacred* (Exod 13:2) to the Lord'—and to offer a sacrifice as is prescribed in the Law of the Lord: *'a pair of turtledoves or two young pigeons'* (Lev 12:8)" (Luke 2:22–24; J. A. Fitzmeyer's translation). The only discrepancy between this NT text and its Leviticus counterpart is the phrase "their purification." Leviticus leaves no room for doubt that only one person needs be purified: the new mother. Perhaps identifying the referent of "their" will provide the answer. Assuming the text is correct, and it is verified by the best textual witnesses, there are two possibilities: Mary and Joseph or Mary and Jesus. Most commentators opt for the former because of the main verb, *anēgagon* 'they (the parents) brought him up'. The deviation from Leviticus has been best accounted for by the fact "that Luke, not being a Palestinian Jewish Christian, is not accurately informed about this custom of the purification of a woman after childbirth" (Fitzmeyer 1981: 424). Nevertheless, I would like to suggest that the second alternative—Mary and Jesus—despite the change in subject, is more acceptable as the referent to "their." Luke probably was not a Greek but "a non-Jewish Semite, a native of Antioch, where he was well educated in a Hellenistic atmosphere and culture" (Fitzmeyer 1981: 42). Now in Greek religion, and earlier in Anatolia and Egypt (see COMMENT A below), both mother and child had to be purified from the pollution of birth (Rhode 1925: 318 n. 72). Both underwent a ritual bath (Parker 1983: 50), and the purpose of carrying the child at a run around the hearth during the *amphidromia* rite on the fifth day may well have been to purify the child by fire (de Coulanges 1882: 53). Thus Luke may have deduced that the purificatory sacrifices offered by Joseph and Mary in Jerusalem on the forty-first day following Jesus' birth were on behalf of both the mother and the child.

burnt offering . . . purification offering. The Sam. and Pesh. reverse the order of these sacrifices, most likely to correspond to the actual procedure (cf. the NOTE on v 6). But the verb *wĕlāqĕḥâ* 'she shall take' testifies that this statement of the sacrifices—like the previous one (v 6, verb *tābîʾ* 'she shall bring')—expresses the prescriptive order, which always lists the burnt offering first.

It must be asked why there is no further concession to the indigent mother to allow her to bring a cereal offering, as in the case of the graduated purification offering (5:11–13). The explanation that what is required here is "life for life" (Kalisch 1867–72) cannot be accepted, for that principle applies solely to homicide, the replacement of one human life for another (see the COMMENT on chap. 3). Besides, the měṣōrāᶜ is also permitted to lower his sacrificial costs by bringing birds (14:21–32) but not a cereal offering, and in his case no life, either lost or gained, is involved. But the case of the měṣōrāᶜ provides a valuable clue. The cereal offering is permitted to substitute for an animal only in the special, marginal case in which there is only a suspicion that the prolonged impurity generated sufficient pollution to defile the sanctuary (COMMENT on 5:1–13). But both the parturient and the měṣōrāᶜ are cases of severe impurity—actually, the most severe possible (chap. 15, COMMENT F). The sanctuary altar has definitely been polluted and blood—the only authorized ritual detergent—is essential for the altar's purgation. Thus the further concession of a cereal offering could not be granted.

effect expiation (wěkippēr). Both sacrifices are expiatory in function (see the NOTE on v 6). But why two birds? If this concession is on behalf of the indigent, because both birds perform an expiatory role one bird should suffice. Ibn Ezra's astute observation (on 5:7) applies here: as the priest benefits from the meat of the purification offering, the burnt offering is added to provide a decent contribution to the altar, that is, to God.

she shall be pure (wětāhērâ). The purpose of this final stage of the parturient's purification is explained in the NOTE on this word, v 7a.

COMMENTS: CHILDBIRTH

A. The Impurity of Genital Discharges: A Comparative Survey

The most striking fact about genital discharges is that they are regarded as a source of impurity virtually throughout the world. If we focus for a moment just on the woman's genital discharges, the following examples will illustrate the universality of this belief. Ancient Egypt deemed both the menstruant and parturient (and her child) to be impure (Blackman 1951: 444). In Babylonia, the menstruant was not only impure herself; she also contaminated others, even those in her proximity (see chap. 15, COMMENT A). Hence, "the woman in labor I caused to go forth from the city" (Gudea, Statue B IV.4). In a Sabean inscription, a man confesses that "he fondled a woman during her menses and that he came together with a woman in childbed" (*ANET*³ 665). Pre-Islamic Arabian menstruants were quarantined in a hut outside the encampment (Smith 1927: 477 n. 1). In ancient Persia, parturients and menstruants were routinely quarantined (Boyce 1975: 306–7). In ancient Greece, the Cyrene cathartic law (*LSC* 115A 16–20) decreed that for three days the new mother pollutes all who enter under her roof (Parker 1983: 336), and Thucydides records that for the purification of the island of Delos, a decree was passed that no one should either die or be born there (3.104).

Thus far the greatest resemblances are with the birth rituals of the Hittites (examples culled by D. Wright). In one text (*HBR*[2], text "K"), the woman is kept in isolation for the last two months of her pregnancy. On the seventh day after the birth a sacrifice is offered. Three months after the birth, the child is pure if it is a male, four months if it is female. The similarities to the biblical rite are obvious: there is postpartem purification on the seventh day (v 2), and the waiting period of three or four months depending on the sex of the child approximates the forty/eighty days prescribed in the Bible. Differences, however, should not be overlooked. The Hittite rite speaks of the purification of the child, not of the mother, and it is not limited to the postparturition period, as in Israel, but embraces the preparturition period as well. Nonetheless, the Hittite mother is also purified. In *HBR*[2] "B," a ewe is "waved" over the mother. The midwife speaks: "Whatever [evils? afflict?] the woman . . . may [they (some purificatory objects)] release the woman" (1, 2'–27").

The Papanikri ritual (Sommer and Eheloff 1924) prescribes that a lamb—washed, anointed, and dressed in clusters of red wool—be placed on the lap of a *katra* woman and then removed. *HBR*[2] 122–23 suggests that the lamb represents the child as a substitute for removing evil. The animal is dressed as the child. Placing the lamb in the hands of the *katra* woman and removing it represents the birth of the child. The washing of the lamb represents the normal purificatory rites performed on a child. This interpretation, if correct, has no Israelite analogues. It is a typical Hittite example of sympathetic, substitutionary magic (see also *HBR*[2], text C), the likes of which had been thoroughly extirpated in Israel.

In sum, both biblical and Hittite cultures affirm the impurity that exists at the time of birth, but both express their concern differently. The Bible's rite is simple, covering only the period of postparturition, and it regards only the mother as impure. The Hittites prescribe varied and complicated rites for the purification of both mother and child during the time before and after the delivery. The purificatory methods of the Hittites are of a purely magical nature (e.g., the incantation, the waving) whose absence in Israel is meaningfully conspicuous. These differences notwithstanding, the similarities are more significant. The sex of the child in both cultures makes a difference in exactly the same way: the purificatory period for the female is longer than for the male. Moreover, the impurity arising from birth is greater than that arising from intercourse (see chap. 15, COMMENT F).

When we move outside Israel's cultural continuum, the most attested and remarkable parallels are located in ancient India. If the sample is again limited to the discharging woman, the following rites are worthy of notice: all relatives of a newborn child and the house itself are rendered impure (Manu 5.58); Hindu women are barred from temples and quarantined inside the house during their menses (Ferro-Luzzi 1974); birth pollution is treated like death pollution in most *smṛtis* and made to last ten days (Kane 1973: 270; cf. also the NOTE on "thirty-three days," v 4a). To round out the picture, a survey of primitive societies reveals that the parturient was quarantined in many diverse societies, such as Tahitian, Maori, Kodiak (Alaska) Indian, Sinaugolo of British New Guinea, Bribri Indian of Costa Rica, Advi or forest Golla of Southern India, Ba-Pedi and Ba-Thonga of South Africa (Frazer and Gaster 1959: 167–68).

Of special relevance is the virtually uniform practice of exotic and sectarian Jewish communities, particularly in regard to the quarantine imposed on parturients and menstruants. They comprise the following: Arabians (Kister and Kister 1979: 241), Kurdistanis (Rivlin 1959: 55), Samaritans and Karaites (Eshkoli 1936: 124), Falashas (Epstein 1950: 173), the sect reflected in *Baraita De masseket Niddah* (Horowitz 1890: 13, 17; cf. Ramban on Gen 31:35), and the sectaries of Qumran. The Qumranites' actual practice is not known, but they project a clear vision of the future: "And in every city you shall allot places . . . for women during their menstrual impurity and after giving birth, so that they may not defile in their midst with their menstrual impurity" (11Q Temple 48:14–17; cf. Yadin 1983: 1.305–7). There is also ample evidence that the rabbinic authorities were fully aware that in their own communities parturients and menstruants were quarantined (*Sipra*, Měṣōrāʿ 2:2; ARM A2; B42; *Tg. Ps.-J.* on 12:2, 5; 15:19; Rabad on *Sipra*, Nedaba 12:8; and Meiri 1970: 279, who cites a lost tosefta). Indeed, the Mishna itself records the existence of "a House for Impure Women" (*m. Nid.* 7:4; *b. Nid.* 56b [Rashi]), which the Tosefta identifies as "washing places for women" (*t. Nid.* 6:15), and Josephus testifies that menstruants were quarantined for seven days (*Ant.* 3.261). In fact, historical records show that the custom of isolating parturients and menstruants persisted among Jews to the end of the first millennium (Dinari 1979–80: 306; 1983: 17–37). The menstruant is discussed in greater detail in chap. 15, COMMENT A.

What is true for menstruation and lochia also holds for other sources of human impurity: chronic genital discharges, semen, and corpses (see chap. 15, COMMENTS E and F). These impurities too, like a woman's discharge, can be exemplified throughout the world, not just in the Bible (chaps. 12–15; Num 19). Of course, there are significant differences between one culture and another. Moreover, one should never forget that the parallels—even when exact—stem from different, and often conflicting, values; thus it is perilous and sometimes dangerously wrong to conclude that similar rules imply similar motivations. Nevertheless, when over and over again the same phenomena are documented as generators of impurity, it becomes reasonable and, indeed, necessary to raise the inquiry whether they may be linked by a common cause.

Certainly one corollary can be drawn from this comparative survey: all attempts to explain these common impurity sources in terms of the customs or values of any particular culture are bound to fail. Thus their origin cannot be traced to a creed or a ritual but must reside in some universal human condition that has evoked the same response all over the globe. In a word, we have to do with the human psyche.

B. The Impurity of Bodily Discharges: A Rationale

A spate of reasons offered to explain the bodily impurities in chaps. 12–15, conveniently collected and rejected by Dillmann and Ryssel (1897: 520–22), are as follows: sin, aesthetics, fear of demons, holiness of the sanctuary, separation of Israel, health, enhancing priestly power. To be sure, as shown above (COM-MENT A), because the phenomena are attested universally, those reasons which only apply to Israel can summarily be dismissed. Other rationales have also been proposed. Henninger (1979: 399–430), citing Fallaize, ties the causes of impu-rity to moments of crisis such as birth, initiation, puberty, marriage, and death. Israel, it would seem, was highly selective of this scheme, for it imputed no impurity to initiation, puberty, and marriage and restricted the impurity of birth to the mother, exempting the child. A more recent theory argues the notion of wholeness as the solution: "A bleeding or discharging body lacks wholeness" (Douglas 1966: 51). But physical perfection is required only for sacrifices and priests (chap. 11, COMMENT E), not for edible animals or the laity, even when the latter enter the sacred compound. More to the mark, I submit, is Dillmann's own suggestion that bodily discharges result in the weakening of one's strength and that the scale-diseased person, in particular, exhibits a polarity between life and death. It is this insight that I now wish to explore.

Members of primitive societies (Henninger 1979) have testified to their researchers that menstrual and lochial blood is dangerous to persons. Written sources give testimony that this view was also held by the ancients, for instance, the Romans and the pre-Islamic Arabs (Smith 1927: 448). It is also recorded as a folk belief in the Talmud: "If a menstruant woman passes between two [men], if it is at the beginning of her menses, she will slay one of them, and if it is at the end of her menses, she will cause strife between them" (b. Pesaḥ. 111a). More-over, menstrual blood was regarded as a powerful charm among the Arabs (Smith, ibid.), and here too we find an echo in rabbinic writings: "If a woman sees a snake . . . she should take some of her hair and fingernails and throw them at it and say, 'I am menstruous' " (b. Šabb. 110a; cf. further examples in Dinari 1979–80: 310–11). Thus it was the worldwide fear of menstrual blood as the repository of demonic forces that is most likely the cause of the isolation of the menstruant.

Yet Israel's monotheism had exorcised the demons (see chap. 4, COMMENT C). What dangers, then, continued to lurk in impurity? And why was not impurity per se eliminated from the Bible? To be sure, the demons disappeared from the official religion, but not the demonic—it continued in man. Impurity was now given an added component: moral failing as well as physical infirmity. The former represented Israel's disobedience—their violation of God's prohibi-tive commandments (chap. 4, COMMENT B). In physical impurity too, the de-monic continued to reside. It was no longer an autonomous force but was inherent in the very nature of the impurity. The loss of vaginal blood and semen, both containing seed, meant the diminution of life and, if unchecked, destruction and death. And it was a process unalterably opposed by Israel's God, the source of its life: "you shall keep my laws and my norms, by the pursuit of which men shall live: I am the Lord" (18:5).

Moreover, in the Israelite mind, blood was the archsymbol of life (17:10–14; Deut 12:23; cf. chap. 11, COMMENT C). Its oozing from the body was no longer the work of demons, but it was certainly the sign of death. In particular, the loss of seed in vaginal blood (see the NOTE on "at childbirth," v 2) was associated with the loss of life. Thus it was that Israel—alone among the peoples —restricted impurity solely to those physical conditions involving the loss of vaginal blood and semen, the forces of life, and to scale disease, which visually manifested the approach of death (see chaps. 13, COMMENT A and 15, COMMENT G). All other bodily issues and excrescences were not tabooed, despite their impure status among Israel's contemporaries, such as cut hair or nails in Persia and India and the newborn child as well as its mother in Greece and Egypt. Human feces were also not declared impure (despite Deut 23:10–12; Ezek 4:12). Why, wonders Dillmann, does not the Bible label human feces impure, as do the Indians (Manu 5.138ff.), Persians (Vend. 17.11ff.), and Essenes (Jos., *Wars* 2.8, 9; cf. 11QT 46:15)? The answer is clear. The elimination of waste has nothing to do with death; on the contrary, it is essential to life. That is why it was decreed from early on that the act of excretion should be accompanied by this blessing: "Blessed is he who has formed man in his wisdom and created in him many orifices and many cavities. It is fully known before the throne of thy glory that if one of them should be (improperly) opened or one of them closed it would be impossible for a man to stand before you. [Blessed are you] who heals all flesh and performs wondrously" (*b. Ber.* 60a).

The association of blood with life and its loss with death is fully comprehended in the rabbinic law that a quarter of a log (about two-thirds of a pint) of human blood can cause defilement (*b. B. Qam.* 101b; cf. *b. Sanh.* 4a). Thus the rabbis go beyond Leviticus in ruling that not only does vaginal blood defile but if blood issues in large enough quantities from any part of the body it also defiles. The equation of sperm and life is, of course, self-evident: "It (impurity) is the same with lost sperm (e.g., sex, nocturnal emissions, chronic genital discharges), because it has been endowed with living power, capable of engendering a human being" (Halevi 2.60). This view was echoed by Shadal (on 12:2): "the discharge of blood or seed (involuntarily) is the beginning of death" (Shadal's parenthetical insertion is in error, for voluntary emissions, such as during intercourse, are equally defiling).

Some of Israel's neighbors also associated impurities with the forces of death. Mary Boyce is probably right when she deduces from her study of Zoroastrianism that "Apart from the corpse, the chief cause of pollution is all that leaves the living body, whether in sickness or in health, the bodily functions and malfunctions being alike regarded, it seems, as *daevic* (demonic) in origin, perhaps since they are associated with change and mortality rather than with the static state of perfection" (1975: 306). Of course, as she acknowledges (307), this sweeping generalization would also include excrement, dead skin, cut nails, and hair among the polluting substances, which Israel categorically denied. Egypt too regarded all forms of decay as falling into the category of impurity, with one notable exception—the corpse. Quite the contrary, tombs enjoyed essentially the same holy status as the cult centers; in fact, the tombs were themselves centers of cultic activity (Meeks 1979: 430–52).

Finally, it should be recorded that the equation of bodily discharges with death in the Bible did not escape the notice of some recent observers. Its most precise formulation is by Adler (1976): "Begetting and birth are the nexus points at which life and death are coupled. . . . The nexus points are those in which there appears to be a departure or a transfer of vital force." Kornfeld (1969) has also recognized that the rationale for impurity in chaps. 11–15 is its threat to life. Paschen (1970: 60–64) and Wenham (1983: 188) also maintain this view. This position holds true for the blood prohibition and slaughtering technique (chap. 11, COMMENTS C and D) but not the prohibited-animal criteria (11:1–23; 41–42), which are founded on other principles (chap. 11, COMMENT E). The explicit sources of impurity detailed in chaps. 11–15—carcasses, scale disease, genital discharges—together with corpses (Numbers 19) are all founded on this postulate: they symbolize the forces of death, as will be demonstrated in chap. 15, COMMENT G.

SCALE DISEASE (13:1–59)

Introduction

13 ¹The Lord spoke to Moses and Aaron, saying:

Shiny Marks

²When a person has on the skin of his body a discoloration, a scab, or a shiny mark, and it develops into a scaly affection on the skin of his body, it shall be reported to Aaron the priest or to one of his sons, the priests. ³The priest shall examine the affection on the skin of his body: if hair in the affection has turned white and the affection appears to be deeper than the skin of his body, it is scale disease; when the priest sees it, he shall pronounce him impure. ⁴But if it is a white shiny mark on the skin of his body which does not appear deeper than the skin and its hair has not turned white, the priest shall quarantine [the person with] the affection for seven days. ⁵On the seventh day the priest shall examine him, and if the affection has retained its color and the affection has not spread on the skin, the priest shall quarantine him for another seven days. ⁶On the

seventh day the priest shall examine him again: if the affection has faded and has not spread on the skin, the priest shall pronounce him pure. It is a scab; he shall wash his clothes, and he shall be pure. [7]But if the scab should spread on the skin after he has presented himself to the priest and been pronounced pure, he shall present himself again to the priest. [8]And if the priest sees that the scab has spread on the skin, the priest shall pronounce him impure; it is scale disease.

Discolorations

[9]When a person has a scaly affection, it shall be reported to the priest. [10]If the priest, on examining [him], finds on the skin a white discoloration and it has turned some hair white, with a patch of raw flesh in the discoloration, [11]it is chronic scale disease on the skin of his body, and the priest shall pronounce him impure; he shall not quarantine him, for he is impure. [12]But if the scales break out over the skin so that they cover all of the skin of the affected person from head to foot, wherever the priest can see—[13]if the priest sees that the scales have covered the whole body—he shall pronounce the affected person pure; because he has turned all white, he is pure. [14]But as soon as raw flesh appears in it, he shall be impure; [15]when the priest sees the raw flesh, he shall pronounce him impure. The raw flesh is impure; it is scale disease. [16]If the raw flesh again turns white, however, he shall come to the priest, [17]and the priest shall examine him: if the affection has turned white, the priest shall pronounce the affected person pure; he is pure.

Boils

[18]When a boil appears on the skin of one's body and it heals, [19]and a white discoloration or a reddish-white shiny mark develops where the boil was, he shall present himself to the priest. [20]The priest shall examine [it]; if it appears lower than his skin and the hair in it has turned white, the priest shall pronounce him impure; it is scale disease that has broken out in the [site of the] boil. [21]But if the priest on examining it finds that there is no white hair in it and it is not lower than his skin, and it is faded, the priest shall quarantine him for seven days. [22]If it has spread on the skin, the priest shall pronounce him impure; it is an affection. [23]But if the shiny mark remains stationary, not having spread, it is the scar of the boil; the priest shall pronounce him pure.

Burns

[24]When the skin of one's body sustains a burn by fire, and the patch of the burn becomes a reddish-white or white shiny mark, [25]the priest shall examine it. If some hairs in the shiny mark have turned white and it appears deeper than the skin, it is scale disease that has broken out in the burn. The priest shall pronounce him impure; it is scale disease. [26]But if the priest on examining it

finds that there is no white hair in the shiny mark, and it is not lower than the skin, and it is faded, the priest shall quarantine him for seven days. 27On the seventh day the priest shall examine him: if it has spread on the skin, the priest shall pronounce him impure; it is scale disease. 28But if the shiny mark has remained stationary, not having spread on the skin, and it is faded, it is the discoloration from the burn. The priest shall pronounce him pure, for it is the scar of the burn.

Scalls

29If a man or a woman has an affection on the head or in the beard, 30the priest shall examine the affection. If it appears deeper than the skin and the hair in it is yellow and sparse, the priest shall pronounce him impure; it is a scall, scale disease of the head or jaw. 31But when the priest examines the scall affection and finds that it does not appear to go deeper than the skin, yet there is no black hair in it, the priest shall quarantine [the person with] the scall affection for seven days. 32On the seventh day the priest shall examine the affection. If the scall has not spread, and there is no yellow hair in it, and the scall does not appear deeper than the skin, 33the person [with the scall] shall shave himself, without shaving the scall; the priest shall quarantine him for another seven days. 34On the seventh day the priest shall examine the scall. If the scall has not spread on the skin, and does not appear deeper than the skin, the priest shall pronounce him pure; he shall wash his clothes, and he shall be pure. 35If, however, the scall should spread on the skin after he has been pronounced pure, 36the priest shall examine him. If the scall has spread on the skin, the priest need not look for yellow hair; he is impure. 37But if [subsequently] the scall has retained its color, and black hair has grown in it, the scall has healed; he is pure. The priest shall pronounce him pure.

Tetters

38When a man or woman has numerous shiny marks on the skin of the body and they are white, 39the priest shall examine [them]. If the shiny marks on the skin of the body are dull white, it is a tetter that has broken out on the skin; he is pure.

Baldness

40When a man's hair falls out from his head, he is bald [on the crown] but pure. 41If the hair falls out from the front of his head, he is bald on the forehead but pure. 42But if a reddish-white affection appears on the bald crown or forehead, it is scale disease that is breaking out on his bald crown or forehead. 43The priest shall examine him: if the discolored affection on his bald crown or forehead is reddish white, like scale disease of fleshy skin in appearance, 44the man has scale disease; he is impure. The priest shall not fail to pronounce him impure; he has an affected head.

The Comportment of a Certified Carrier

[45]As for the person stricken with scale disease, his clothes shall be rent, his hair shall be disheveled, he shall cover his moustache, and he shall call out, "Impure! Impure!" [46]He shall be impure as long as the affection is on him. He is impure: he shall dwell apart; his dwelling shall be outside the camp.

Fabrics

[47]When mold disease occurs in a fabric, either a wool or linen fabric, [48]or in the warp or woof of the linen or the wool, or in a skin or in anything made of skin: [49]if the affection in the fabric or the skin, in the warp or the woof, or in any article of skin, is bright green or bright red, it is mold disease. It shall be shown to the priest. [50]The priest shall examine the affection and shall quarantine the [article with the] affection for seven days. [51]On the seventh day he shall examine the affection: if the affection has spread in the fabric, or in the warp, or in the woof, or in the skin, for whatever function the skin serves, the affection is malignant mold disease; it is impure. [52]The fabric, or the warp, or the woof, whether in wool or linen, or any article of skin that contains the affection, shall be burned, for it is a malignant mold; it shall be destroyed by fire. [53]But if the priest sees that the affection in the fabric, or in the warp, or in the woof, or in any article of skin, has not spread, [54]the priest shall order the affected material to be washed, and he shall quarantine it for another seven days. [55]And if, after the affected material has been washed, the priest sees that the affection has not changed its color and that it has not spread, it is impure. You shall destroy it by fire; it is a fret, whether on its inner side or on its outer side. [56]But if the priest examines [it] and finds the affection faded after it has been washed, he shall cut it out from the fabric, or from the skin, or from the warp, or from the woof; [57]and if it reappears in the fabric, or in the warp, or in the woof, or in any article of skin, it is breaking out afresh; you shall destroy the affected material by fire. [58]If, however, the affection disappears from the fabric, or warp, or woof, or any article of skin that has been washed, it shall be washed once more, and it shall be pure. [59]This is the procedure for mold disease of fabric, woolen or linen, or of warp, or of woof, or of any article of skin, for pronouncing it pure or impure.

NOTES

13:1. *Aaron.* His name is deleted in *Targ. Ps.-J.*, but it is clearly essential for the priest alone diagnoses the ailment described in this chapter. Moreover, this is not only a requirement of the Priestly legislation but is inculcated by other sources as well (e.g., Deut. 17:8; 21:5; and esp. 24:8). Why, then, were Moses and Aaron not commanded to teach this chapter to the Israelites, as is the case with nearly all other divine laws? The answer clearly must rest in the apprehension lest the Israelites themselves, armed with this information, would make their own diagnoses—and misdiagnoses—instead of calling in the experts, the priests. The reverse, however, holds for discharges from the genital organs, where the instructions are explicitly commanded to be taught to the Israelites (15:2). Whereas skin diseases are visible and soon become public knowledge, genital flows are a private matter. Only the affected person is aware of his or her condition and, hence, must be given full information about the way to proceed (cf. Ramban).

2–17. Shiny Marks and Discolorations. Discolorations, scabs, and shiny marks are the main criteria for diagnosing scale disease. If they have turned the hair white and appear deeper than the skin, the priest declares them impure. In the case of white shiny marks, if the scaliness only appears superficial and the hair has not turned white, the patient is quarantined by the examining priest for one week. If the scaliness has not spread, he is quarantined for another week. If the affection has faded and not spread it is considered a scab, and the priest pronounces him pure. In the case of white discolorations, if a patch of raw flesh appears in them that has turned the hair white, it is immediately diagnosed as scale disease. But if the white scales have covered the entire body, the person is pronounced pure.

2. *When. kî*, the particle denoting the beginning of a new subject. It does not reappear until v 18, a literary indication that the first subject comprises vv 2–17. The use of *kî* as a relative conjunction in P differs from its use in other sources in that it will always follow the subject (1:2; 2:1; 4:2; 5:1, 4, 15, 17, 21; 12:2; 13:2, 9, 18, 29, 38, 40, 47; 15:2, 16, 19, 25). The same is true of H (19:20; 21:9; 22:2, 13, 14, 27; 24:15, 17, 19; 25:26, 29; 27:2) (Hoffmann 1953: 79 n. 7, citing J. L. Shapira; cf. Malbim, *Leviticus,* 12). Contrast JE (Exod 21:2, 33, 37; 22:4, 5, 6, 9; 23:4, 5) and D (Deut 12:20, 21, 29; 13:2, 7, 13; 14:24; 15:12; 17:2, 8, 14).

a person (ʾādām). This term includes women, children (*m. Nid.* 5:3), and *gērîm* (*Sipra,* Neg. Tazriaʿ 1:1). But because the rabbis rendered *gērîm* as "proselytes," they excluded resident aliens and all other non-Israelites from this prescription (*m. Neg.* 3:1). That they are probably right is demonstrated by the fact that the same term, *ʾādām,* is expressly restricted to Israelites in the opening instruction of chaps. 1–6 dealing with sacrifices (1:2; see the NOTE on "any [of you]"). The absence of the resident aliens from these instructions is, at first blush, surprising for they are required to observe a host of prohibitions (e.g., 17:8, 10, 13, 15; 20:2) and to bring purification offerings for accidental violations (Num 15:27–29) and to incur the *kārēt* penalty for presumptuous violations (Num 15:30–31). This ostensible discrepancy is resolved, however, once it is realized that the latter passages are all part of the H source, which extends the domain of holiness to the entire land and, hence, requires all its inhabitants, aliens included, to obey all prohibitions. Chapter 13, however, belongs entirely to P, a source that restricts holiness to the sanctuary and its priests, thereby excluding the resident alien from all commandments except the Noachide prohibition against murder and consuming blood (Gen 9:1–5; cf. chap. 11, COM-MENT C).

on the skin of his body (bĕʿôr-bĕśārô). As opposed to the hair-covered parts of the body (v 29; Rashbam). Hence the added specification *bĕśārô,* literally, "his flesh," that is, the skin attached to flesh but not with hair *(Seper Hamibḥar).* Or, as more precisely put by Wessely (1846 on vv 27–29) here the skin is separated from bone by flesh but the scalp and jaw are just beneath the skin without intermediary flesh and therefore listed separately.

a discoloration (śĕʾēt). This is the first of several obscure technical terms in the chapter. It is found only here (13:2, 10, 19, 28, 43; 14:56). Most of the rabbis interpret it as "swelling," deriving it from the verb *nāśāʾ* 'raise, lift' *(Sipra,* Neg. Tazriaʿ 1:4; *b. Šebu.* 6b; Rashbam; cf. *NJPS).* The Tgs., however, render it as "deep spot" *(Tg. Onq.),* "prominent mark" *(Tg. Ps.-J.),* or "mark" *(Tg. Neof.).* Their renderings are certainly preferable to the notion of "swelling" championed by the previously cited rabbinic sources, because the very next verse (v 3) states explicitly that this sore appears lower than the surrounding skin. The idea of "mark" is supported by Arab. *šiʾatu* (G. R. Driver 1963: 575b). Still, as the two terms that follow are also "marks," each of them must bear some different distinguishing trait. Note that the LXX, in despair, melds all three terms into a single hendiadys, "bright clear spot." Ibn Ezra, presumably with equal consternation, renders "inflammation" on the basis of *masʾet* 'fire signal' (Jer. 6:1); but the latter term is probably an abbreviation of *maśʾat ʿāšān* 'pillar of smoke' (e.g., Judg 20:38, 40), referring to the formations of the rising *(nāśāʾ)* smoke for purposes of signaling.

The rabbinic sages are on record with the following definitions: "The colors of leprosy signs (of the body skin) are two, which are, indeed, four: *baheret,* which is white, bright like snow—and the secondary shade of it (i.e., *sappaḥat,* as white) as the lime used in the Temple (cf. *m. Mid.* 3:4); and *śĕʾēt,* which is (as white) as the skin of an egg—and the secondary shade of it (i.e., *sappaḥat,* as white) as white wool; so R. Meir. But the Sages say: *śĕʾēt* is (as white) as white wool and the secondary shade of it (i.e., *sappaḥat,* as white) as the skin of an egg" (*m. Neg.* 1:1; cf. Maim., "Impurity of Scale Disease" 1.2). Thus, according to the rabbis, the *ṣāraʿat* described in vv 2–17 is white in four shades: the whitest is snow, the next lime, the next white wool, and the dullest, the skin membrane of an egg. This interpretation of *sappaḥat,* as a shade secondary to the other two terms, is discussed below. For want of a better translation, *śĕʾēt* will be rendered "discoloration," implying, with the rabbis, that the initial sign of skin disease is a change in color, though precisely what that color change is can no longer be determined.

scab (sappaḥat). The term occurs only here, in 14:56, and in the variant *mispaḥat* in vv 6, 7, 8. As it is declared pure if it does not spread (v 6b), it is clearly less potent than the *śĕʾēt* and *baheret* sores mentioned in this verse. Moreover, the rabbis declare it as being secondary to and derivative from the other two sores (*m. Neg.* 1:1, translated above). Etymology supports them in view of the meaning of the root *sapaḥ* 'attach, add' (e.g., 1 Sam 2:36; 26:19; Isa 14:1; note the rendering in *Tg. Onq.,* "added thing"; cf. *Sipra,* Neg. Tazriaᶜ 1:4; *b. Šebu.* 6b). Further support derives from the structure of this chapter: there is no separate law for the *sappaḥat* as there is for the *śĕʾēt* (vv 9–17) and the *baheret* (vv 3–8; Bekhor Shor)! But what exactly is it? On the basis of the term *sāpîaḥ* 'aftergrowth' (e.g., 25:5), Jastrow renders "growth" (1913–14: 360); Abravanel, however, interprets it as something "glued." He is undoubtedly influenced by the rendering of the Pesh. and most of the Tgs., "scab" (*Tg. Ps.-J.; Tg. Yer.; Tg. Neof.*). Indeed, because scab formation is essential to the healing process, this rendering for a clearly benign condition may be correct. Hulse, however, who also commends the translation "scab," suggests that it refers to a plague of scales produced in psoriasis (1975: 97; see COMMENT A below). The sectaries of Qumran posit an entirely different cause: the result of a blow delivered by a wooden or stone implement (4QDᵈ1; D⁹2).

shiny mark. baheret appears only in this context (vv 2, 4, 19, 23, 24, 25, 26, 28, 38, 39; 14:56). Clearly it is related to Akk. *biʾāru,* which, however, is as yet undetermined except for being a "spot on the skin" *(AHw).* Nonetheless, the unambiguous meaning of Hebrew *bāhîr* 'bright' (Job 37:21) gives credence to the rabbis' view that it is as bright as snow (*m. Neg.* 1:1; cf. the NOTE on "discoloration," above) and that there is nothing whiter (Maim., "The Impurity of Scale Disease" 1.2). They may be right in view of Hulse's remark (1975: 98) that all three sores mentioned in this verse bear a shiny appearance and once it becomes faded, *kēheh,* it is no longer *ṣāraʿat* 'scale disease' (vv 6, 21, 26, 39). Thus the likelihood is great that these three sores manifest varying degrees of shininess with *baheret,* as indicated by its adjective, *bāhîr* 'bright' (Job 37:21), the brightest of the three. *Tgs. Ps.-J.* and *Yer.* render *bahaqê,* thereby equating *baheret* with *bōhaq* 'tetter', which is pure (v 39). Indeed, whiteness by itself is not a pathological symptom (see the NOTE on v 13), but as this verse goes on to state, it may develop into scale disease.

develops (wĕhāyâ . . . l ĕ[negaᶜ]). Initially there is just a skin eruption, but the spots must grow to a certain size before it qualifies as scale disease. This fact is not specified in this text. But the rabbis determine, in the case of the *baheret,* that its minimum space is that of a square with sides the length of a Cilician split bean, or the equal of thirty-six hairs (*m. Neg.* 6:1).

scaly. ṣāraʿat, literally, "of scales." In P it occurs only here (chaps. 13–14). As a verb it appears as a past-participle *qal* (vv 44, 45; 14:3; 22:4; Num 5:2—all P) and as a *puʿal* participle (14:2 [P]; Exod 4:6 [Moses' hand]; Num 12:10 [Miriam]; 2 Sam 3:29 [Joab's descendants]; 2 Kgs 5:1, 11 [Naaman], 27

SCALE DISEASE (13:1–59)

[Gehazi]; 7:3, 8 [*mĕṣōrāʿîm*]; 15:5; 2 Chr 26:20, 21, 23 [Uzziah]). It is perhaps related to Akk. *ṣennîtum/ṣennittum*, as first proposed by Holma (1913), having undergone the following development: **ṣarraʿatu* > **ṣarraʿtu* > **ṣanna ʿtu* > *ṣanneʿtu* > *ṣennētu/ṣennetu* (Goetze 1955: 12). In support, Ethiopic *ṣĕrnĕʿĕt* is attested (Dillmann, cited in KB 998).

The etymology is obscure. The following suggestions have been proposed: (1) *ṣrʿ* in Old South Arabic, meaning "throw down" (G. R. Driver 1963: 575); hence it denotes "a stroke" (Koehler 1956: 56), that is, stricken by God. (2) If related to *ṣārûaʿ* 'elongated' (21:18; 22:23) and *hiśtārēaʿ* 'stretch oneself, spread' (Isa 28:20)—for the *ṣ* > *ś* shift, see *ṣāhaq/śāhaq* 'laugh' (e.g., Ps 2:4; Prov 29:9; Qoh 3:4) and *yiṣḥāq/yiśḥāq* (Jer 33:26; Amos 7:9, 16)—then it may connote a "rash." (3) Perhaps it is related to biblical *ṣirʿâ* 'wasp' (Exod 23:28; Deut 7:20; Josh 24:12). "A victim looked or felt as though he had been stung by a wasp or swarms of wasps" (Sawyer 1976: 244), which yields the rendering "swelling." There are serious objections to each of these proposals. (1) The full, and prevalent, term *negaʿ ṣāraʿat* argues against the "stroke" theory; because "stroke" is also the meaning of *negaʿ*, the full term would be tautologous. (2) The *ṣ* > *ś* shift is speculative; even if acceptable, "elongation" is a far cry from "rash." (3) The rendering "wasp" for *ṣirʿâ* is itself moot; Ibn Ezra (on v 19) reverses the direction of the derivation, suggesting that *ṣirʿâ* means "skin disease."

What can be asserted with some assurance is that the morphology of *ṣāraʿat* is akin to *dalleqet* 'inflammation' (Deut 28:22) and *qāraḥat* 'baldness' (v 42), thus a medical term (Sawyer 1976: 245). What disease is indicated by this term has not yet been determined. Indeed, there is strong suspicion that none was actually intended (see COMMENT A below). To be sure, it can in no way be identified with leprosy, if for no other reason than that even the LXX calls it by a distinctive term, *lepra* 'scaly condition', not by *elephantiasis* 'leprosy'. Besides, leprosy is not attested in the ancient Near East until Hellenistic times (for details, see COMMENT A). According to the most recent investigation, the disease that fulfills most of the characteristics of this chapter is psoriasis, with the exception of *neteq* (v 31), which describes *favus* (Hulse 1975: 99–101). But to judge by the quarantine procedures prescribed in this chapter, even this identification is in doubt (see COMMENT A). Nevertheless, we must have a translation. Hulse suggests "a repulsive scaly skin disease" (1975: 103). Moreover, this rendering is supported by the Akk. term for *ṣāraʿat*, *saharšuppû*, which literally means "covered with dust [i.e., with dustlike, whitish scales]," Sumerian *SAHAR* being the equivalent of Akk. *eperu* 'dust' (Oppenheim 1956: 273 n. 54; Kinnier-Wilson 1966: 49). Thus, as scaling is clearly the common denominator in all of the sores described in this chapter, it is safe to admit this definition into the translation. Still, the adjective "repulsive" must be rejected: *ṣāraʿat* is a medical term (see above) and hence neutral, without an aesthetic component. Henceforth, *ṣāraʿat* will be rendered as "scale disease" (the equivalent of the LXX's *lepra*). In the Bible *ṣāraʿat* is a ritually impure affection *(negaʿ)*, which implies that there are other affections. Rabbinic Hebrew actually eschews the term *ṣāraʿat* in favor of *negaʿ* (e.g., *m. Neg.* 1:1), which suggests their full awareness that *ṣāraʿat* cannot be identified with any one particular malady but comprises multiple diseases (Wilkinson 1977, 1978).

affection (negaʿ). This word appears sixty-one times in chaps. 13 and 14, either as an absolute or in construct with *ṣaraʿat* or *neteq.* To judge by its verb, *nāgaʿ* 'touch', it literally means "becoming touched" and probably, in its origins, relates to attacks (*Befall:* Elliger 1966) from the demonic sphere. Significantly, Akk. *lapātu* 'touch' also denotes "attack by demons" (*CAD*, L 88), and the noun *liptu* 'touch' also denotes "affliction, plague, disease, discolored spot" (*CAD*, L 201–2). Thus the resultant impurity may actually have connoted a contact with the pagan sphere that aroused God's wrath (Elliger 1966).

In the Bible, God is always the author of *negaʿ* (cf. 14:34). It is invariably a divine punishment (e.g., Gen 12:17; Exod 11:1; 2 Sam 7:14; 1 Kgs 8:37, 38 [= 2 Chr 6:28, 29]; 2 Kgs 15:5; Isa 53:4; Pss 38:1; 89:33; 91:10 [Prov 6:33 provides an ostensible exception, but cf. Rashi, Ibn Ezra, and *Meṣudat David* ad loc.]). In P *negaʿ* always refers to *ṣāraʿat.* The same holds for D (Deut 17:8; 21:5; 24:8; cf. Hoffmann's detailed note in his commentary on Deut 17:8 (1961: 302–10). Instead, the rabbis apparently distinguish between the two, referring to all of the skin diseases described in this chapter as *negaʿim* (cf. *m. Neg.* 1:1) while using *ṣāraʿat* in a more limited sense (see Ramban and the NOTE on "affection," v 22).

negaʿ is also a metonym for the affected person (e.g., vv 4, 12, 13) or garment (v 50). Similarly, *neteq* means both a scab (v 30) and a scabby person (v 33).

on the skin of his body (bĕʿôr-bĕśārô). Is this phrase not superfluous, having once appeared in this verse? Not at all. The text is emphasizing the fact that these sores must appear on the fleshy part of the body *(bāśār)* and not on the head.

it shall be reported. *wĕhûbāʾ,* with Shadal and Ehrlich 1908–14 (see the NOTE on 14:2; cf. also Exod 18:16; 22:8; 2 Sam 14:10; Isa 1:23). The reluctance of persons stricken with a skin eruption to report it to a priest and face quarantine and possible banishment is quite understandable. It is also implied by Jesus' instruction to the ten lepers: "Go and show yourselves to the priests" (Luke 17:13).

or to one of his sons, the priests. In other words, to any priest. There is no need to travel to a main sanctuary. To be sure, the text could simply have stated *ʾel-hakkōhēn* 'to the priest' (vv 3, 4, 5, 6, 7, etc.). But that expression might have been misinterpreted as referring to Aaron. Hence the opening reference to the priest carefully specifies Aaron or his sons, that is, any priest, and later references resort to the single word "priest." Similarly, the opening references to the priest in each pericope of the block on sacrifices also specifies "the sons of Aaron the priest" (e.g., 1:5, 6, 7, 8, 11; 2:1; 3:2, 5, 8, 13), but the references that follow merely state "the priest" (e.g., 1:9, 12, 15, 17; 2:2b, 9, 16; 3:11, 16).

one (ʾaḥad). "The numeral here cannot be in the construct state, but is merely a rhythmical shortening of the usual (tone-lengthened) form" (GKC §130g; cf. Gen 3:28; 48:22; 1 Sam 9:3).

3. *shall examine (wĕrāʾâ)*. For this meaning, see, for instance, 14:36 *(bis)*; Exod 2:25; 1 Kgs 9:12. It is also attested in rabbinic Hebrew (e.g., *m. B. Meṣ.* 10:6; *m. Ohol.* 11:7). The text, however, says nothing about how and when this examination takes place. The precise information is provided by the rabbis: "They (the priests) may not inspect skin disease in the early morning or in the evening or within the house or on a cloudy day, for then the dull white would appear bright white; or at midday, for then the bright white would appear dull white. When should they inspect, then? At the third, fourth, fifth, seventh, eighth, or ninth hour. So R. Meir. R. Judah says: At the fourth, fifth, eighth, or ninth hour" (*m. Neg.* 2:2; cf. *Sipra*, Neg. Tazriaʿ 2:3). Of course, inspections are precluded on Sabbaths and festivals and on those days which would force subsequent inspections to fall on Sabbath or festival days (*m. Neg.* 1:4). As to the procedure, the Mishna records the following: "A man is inspected (while he stands) like one who hoes, and like one who gathers olives, and the woman (while she stands) like one who rolls out bread, and like one who gives suck to her child, and like one who weaves an upright loom if the sign is within the right armpit. R. Judah says: Also like one who spins flax if the sign is within the left (armpit)" (*m. Neg.* 2:4).

[if] hair. wĕśēʿār is a collective (e.g., Cant 4:1; 6:5) meaning "some hairs."

has turned (hāpak). An intransitive use of the *qal* (vv 4, 10, 13, 20, 25), equivalent to the *niphʿal, nehĕpak le* (vv 16, 17; Ibn Ezra). The object is either the hair (vv 3, 4, 10, 20, 25) or the affection (vv 13, 16, 17, 55).

white (lābān). The identification of *ṣāraʿat* with the color white is nowhere better illustrated than the philological evidence from Akkadian, where the verb *peṣû* 'be white' yields the noun *pūṣu* 'white spot, lesion'. Indeed, one text explicitly equates *qummāl/nu* 'scale disease, fungus' with *pūṣu* (*CT* 41, 27, 21; *AHw*, 927)! This would accord with the rabbinic view that all forms of *ṣāraʿat* are white in color, varying only in shade (see the NOTES on "discoloration," v 2, and "shall examine," v 3). Nevertheless, medical authorities claim that skin disease does not turn the hair white. Perhaps the scales, loosened from the skin, adhere to the adjacent hair, as in cases of severe dandruff, so that the hair appears flecked with white—a condition common to psoriasis (Hulse 1975: 98). Perhaps also this is what the rabbis also intended when they aver that the hair must turn white at the roots for the diagnosis to be confirmed (*m. Neg.* 4:4).

[the affection] appears to be. ûmarʾēh, literally, "and the appearance of [the affection]." The sense of this noun (a *hiphʿil* participle) is passive throughout this chapter, except in v 12, where it is active. Elsewhere in P it is also passive (Exod 24:17; Num 8:4; 9:15, 16).

deeper than the skin (ʿāmōq mēʿôr). The rabbis understand the text literally: the lesion only appears deeper, but is not in reality (*Sipra*, Neg. Tazriaʿ 2:5), on the basis that the color white always appears deeper than its surroundings (*b. B. Bat.* 84a), "as the reflection of the sun which is deeper than the shade" (*b. Šebu* 6b). Some medical authorities suggest that this phenomenon is due to the involvement of the dermis, the deeper part of the skin; in effect, a thickening of the skin has occurred—a characteristic of psoriasis (and *favus*, cf. the NOTE on v 30; Hulse 1975: 98). Wall fungus also has a sunken appearance (cf. 14:37).

when the priest sees it (wĕrā²āhû hakkōhēn). A resumptive repetition after a long predicate. It also serves to emphasize the indispensability of the priest in the diagnosis. The rabbis aver that the decision must be given by the priest even if he is an imbecile and must be instructed by the sages (*m. Neg.* 3:1). In Qumran, this stipulation is made quite explicit: "If there be a judgment regarding the law of scale disease, then the priest shall come and stand in the camp, and the overseer shall instruct him in the exact meaning of the law. Even if he (the priest) be an imbecile, he alone shall quarantine him; for theirs is the judgment" (CD 13.4–7).

he shall pronounce (wĕṭimmē²). A declarative *piʿel* (*Sipra*, Neg. Tazriaʿ 2:10; Rashi; Ibn Ezra; cf. GKC 52g; Joüon 1923: §52), also called delocative (Hillers 1967) or factitive (Williams 1976: 141). This implies that the person suspected of scale disease is in a state of impurity while he is quarantined, analogous to the quarantined house, which contaminates everything within it and all who enter it (vv 46–47). The rabbis, however, claim that suspected impurity is not as severe as certified impurity, contaminating by touch but not by (indirect) carrying (*m. Kelim* 1:1); so too the inside of the suspected house is contagious but not its outside (*m. Neg.* 13:4).

4. *white.* The color white is a sine qua non for the positive diagnosis of scale disease (see the NOTE on "discolorations," v 2). It is emphasized here because it is the only criterion that is observable at this stage (see the NOTE on "which does not appear deeper," below). Wright and Jones, however, claim that whiteness here refers to flakiness of the skin because, according to vv 38–39, whiteness is a pure condition.

shiny mark. Although *baheret* is listed last in the heading (v 2) it is discussed first (Bekhor Shor; *Seper Hamibhar*). Indeed, a chiastic order emerges: *baheret* (v 4), *mispahat* (v 6), *śĕ²ēt* (v 10); cf. the NOTE on v 24.

which does not appear deeper. wĕ²amōq ²ēn-marehâ, literally, "and deeper its appearance is not." Because the adjective is emphasized it is placed first; as the negative particle ²ēn cannot modify an adjective, it is placed before the substantive (Ehrlich 1908–14). Rashi's admission, "I do not understand its meaning," is based on the ostensible contradiction with the explicit statement of the previous verse that whiteness appears lower than the surrounding skin. Other exegetes attempt to explain: for example, the lesion is not deeper because in this case it is not actually whiter (Abravanel); the whiteness must be extremely bright to appear lower than the skin (Wessely 1846). The truth, however, is that neither of the two criteria of v 3 is present here. The lesion does not appear deeper, nor has it turned the hair white. The only suspicious symptom is its whiteness, and for this reason the diagnosis cannot be made, so a quarantined waiting period is imposed.

and its hair (ûśēʿārâ). A *mappiq* in the final *he* would normally be expected. Yet there are many instances wherein it is omitted, especially before a *běgadkěpat* and other soft consonants (GKC §91e). Because of this word's vocalization it cannot be the feminine noun, which takes the spelling *śāʿārâ* (Hoffmann 1953).

shall quarantine (wěhisgîr). Some medieval exegetes claim that this verb implies that the lesion is enclosed with a mark in order to determine if in the course of the quarantine it has spread (Tur in the name of his father, Jacob ben Asher; Meir on *b. Neg.* 8b in the name of some Geonim; and *Moshav Zeqenim* citing a lost tosefta). Further support for the theory is adduced from the object of this verb: it is the *negaʿ*, the affliction, that is "enclosed," not its bearer (but cf. the NOTE below). This interpretation, however, is countered by Bekhor Shor, who argues logically that if the lesion does overgrow the mark, the afflicted person may then draw a new circle around it in order to be declared pure by the priest. If, indeed, such a test were intended it would have followed the procedure for a *neteq*, which calls for shaving the hair around the lesion (vv 32–34). The decisive evidence against this interpretation rests in the use of this verb with "house" as its object (14:38). It is, then, the person who is enclosed, not the lesion; in other words, he is quarantined. *hisgîr* in the meaning "quarantine" is only found in chaps. 13–14 (P) and with the following objects: afflictions on persons (vv 4, 5, 31, 33) and on fabrics (vv 50, 54), persons (vv 11, 21, 26), and houses (14:38, 46). Elsewhere it means "surrender, extradite" (e.g., Deut 23:16; 32:30; Josh 20:5; 1 Sam 23:11, 12; Amos 1:6; 6:8). It does occur once outside P with the meaning of "quarantine" (Num 12:14–15), but in the *niphʿal*, not in the *hiphʿil*, as here.

The question must be asked: Where is he quarantined? Obviously, he does not remain at home, else all of its contents will be contaminated retroactively once his affliction is confirmed (cf. the NOTES on 14:36). The rabbis claim that he or she is banished outside the camp/city (*b. Neg.* 8b), just as happened to Miriam (Num 12:14–15), and treated as if the affection were confirmed, with the exception that no clothes-rending or mouth-veiling is imposed (v 45; cf. *m. Neg.* 8:8). Rashi, however, suggests that the afflicted person is isolated in special quarters, as was King Uzziah (1 Kgs 15:5; 2 Chr 26:21). The root meaning of the verb *sāgar, hisgîr* 'close, enclose' favors this interpretation, but even if correct, the possibility remains that such quarters were erected outside the camp/city.

One final question asserts itself: If the impurity is not certain, why the need for quarantine? Indeed, banishment is prescribed only after the diagnosis is certified! The answer can only be that even a suspected disease-carrier is ritually impure. Proof can be adduced from the case of a house suspected of being afflicted: the priest has all of its contents removed before he quarantines it (14:36). Hence it becomes impure not on the day he condemns it, but retroactively, to the day that he imposed the quarantine (cf. *m. Neg.* 8:8). Even if the priest declares the person or house pure, it is likely that there still exists retroactive impurity, but of a minor character (cf. the NOTES on "he shall wash his clothes," vv 6 and 34).

[*the person with*] *the affection (ʾet-hannegaʿ).* A metonym for the person (vv 31, 33, 50; 14:38;. cf. the NOTE on "affection," v 2).

for seven days. The seven-day ritual period predominates in the Priestly writings: for example, priestly consecration (8:33, 35); severe impurity (12:2; chap. 13; 15:13, 19, 24); purificatory periods (14:8, 9; 15:28); festivals (23:6, 18, 34); sabbaticals (23:3; 25:4, 8). Medical reasons are also adduced: a week's confinement is needed to detect a change (Bekhor Shor); for nature to take its course (Abravanel). Even so, it is precisely this seven-day quarantine that raises the suspicion that no identifiable skin disease is here being described (see COMMENT A below).

5. *if (wĕhinnēh).* The notion of "if" is conveyed by the *waw* beginning the protasis clause followed by the *waw* beginning the apodosis clause *wĕhisgîr* 'shall quarantine', with the particle *hinnēh* acting as a buffer (e.g., 1 Sam 9:7; 2 Sam 8:11; Joüon 1923: §1671N). *hinnēh* is frequently employed after *rāʾâ* 'see' and other verbs of discovery (e.g., vv 6, 7, 8, 9; Gen 1:31; Deut 13:15; 17:4; 19:18; 1 Sam 20:12; Joüon 1923: §177iN).

has retained (ʿāmad). This verb is found with this sense only in this chapter (vv 5, 37 with *bĕʿênāyw;* vv 23, 28 with *ṭaḥtāyw*).

its color (bĕʿênāyw). This word is capable of two interpretations: (1) "In his (the priest's) opinion," literally, "in his eyes" (LXX; *Sipra,* Neg. Tazriaʿ 9:14; *Tg. Neof.;* Ramban; Bekhor Shor; *Seper Hamibḥar;* Shadal; Ehrlich 1899–1900; cf. Gen 19:14; 2 Kgs 1:13). In this case, there exists only one criterion for a positive diagnosis: the sore has spread. (2) "In its appearance." This sense is probably intended by *Tg. Onq.* and *Tg. Ps.-J.* in their rendering "as it was" (cf. "in its place," LXX, Pesh.), probably equating this word with *ṭaḥtāyw* 'stationary' (vv 23, 28; cf. *Midr. Num. Rab.* 6:2). "Appearance" would refer to color or hue; in other words, it has not become brighter, an interpretation that would find support in the following verse, which describes the characteristics of the sore if a change for the better is detected: it does not spread and it fades. This evidence would appear to be conclusive. But objections can be made to the plural form: *ʿayin* meaning "appearance, color" should be a singular (e.g., 21:20; Num 11:7; Mizrachi). This objection can be rebutted by pointing to the occurrence of the singular *ʿênô* in the same contextual frame within the chapter (v 55). Moreover, V. Hurowitz has convincingly shown (1990) that *ʿayin* in this verse (and in vv 37, 55) is derived from the stem *ʿwn* 'dwell' and its metamorphosis into "appearance" is paralleled in Akk., where *šiknu* 'appearance' is derived from *šakānu* 'dwell'. Thus, with the LXX and Pesh. and in conformance with v 55, read the sing. *ʿênô* and render "its color," that is, its appearance. A further objection might stem from the fact that the priest condemns the sore at the end of the quarantine period only on the basis of its spread and that nothing at all is stated regarding its appearance (vv 7–8). This objection too may be parried on the grounds that only the sore's spread matters. Its change in color is insufficient in itself to condemn it, hence this criterion is omitted, whereas in order to declare the sore healed both criteria, fading and the absence of spreading, are required. (See the NOTE on "But if the scab should spread," v 7.) Indeed, had the color faded by the end of the first week as it does by the end of the second, it would have been declared pure (see the NOTE on "quarantine for seven days," v 33). Thus, this interpretation mandates two criteria for a positive diagnosis: the sore has changed color and has spread (see also the NOTE on v 37).

and. The Hebrew word is omitted here, but implied, on the basis of its presence in *wĕlōʾ-pāśâ*, the same phrase and context in the following verse.

spread (pāśâ). This verb appears twenty-two times in chaps. 13–14. Its etymology is uncertain. A possible candidate is Arab. *faśâ* 'I spread' and esp. South Arabic *fś²m*, which appears in the context of a skin disease (Höfner 1967).

6. *again. šēnît,* literally, "a second time." In fact, the priest is now examining the person for the third time (cf. vv 3a, 5a). What is meant is a "second heptad of days" (BDB; cf. v 5b).

has faded (kēhâ). This root appears in the chapter both as a *piʿel* verb (vv 6, 56) and as an adjective (vv 21, 26, 28, 39). Objection has been raised that were it a verb here a *ḥîreq* would have been expected, namely, *kihâ* (e.g.), hence it should be taken as an adjective (Radak, *Keter Torah*). This objection is effectively rebutted on the grounds that were it an adjective then the second radical would have been vocalized with a *sĕgōl* and not a *qāmeṣ*, for *negaʿ* is masculine (Ibn Janaḥ). As for the argument offered by Radak that the term *negaʿ ṣāraʿat* is treated as a feminine (v 9), in that case it is the *nomen rectum, ṣāraʿat,* which determines the gender (see the NOTE on v 9). The *ḥireq* is lengthened to a *ṣere* because the following consonant, *he,* cannot be doubled (e.g., Exod 15:13; *Seper Hamibḥar*), though usually with strong gutturals such as *ʿayin* and *he* this lengthening does not occur.

There is some difference of opinion regarding the meaning of this verb here; whereas the connotation of "fade, be pale, be dim" is clearly attested (e.g., 1 Sam 3:2; Isa 42:4), there are those who would render it "contained," believing it to be the antonym to the following verb *pāśâ* 'spread', citing 1 Sam 3:13 for support (Ibn Ezra). Others would render "weakened," citing 1 Sam 3:2; Isa 42:4 (cf. Radak); Ezek 21:12 (Wessely 1846). But in the present context the "weakening" of the sore could only be detected by its fading.

shall pronounce him pure (wĕṭihārô). A declarative *piʿel* (Ibn Ezra), comparable to *wĕṭimmēʾ* 'shall pronounce him impure' (v 3). In chaps. 13–14, this sense predominates (vv 6, 13, 17, 23, 28, 34, 37, 59; 14:7, 48); otherwise it denotes "purify" (e.g., 14:11; 16:19), especially in the *hithpaʿel* (twelve times in chap. 14). The subject is always the priest. The fact that the person is now pronounced pure means that during his quarantine he was considered impure (*y. Naz.* 9:4; see further the NOTES on "he shall wash his clothes," below and on v 34).

scab (mispaḥat). Is this term to be distinguished from *sappaḥat* (v 2)? One commentator suggests that it refers to the area of the *sappaḥat* (Dillmann and Ryssel 1897). Whereas *Tg. Neof.* renders them both by the same term *qalpa* 'scab', *Tg. Onq.* translates the first by *ʿadyaʾ* and the second *ʿădîtāʾ*, and *Tg. Ps.-J.* offers *qĕlôpê* for the first and *qēlûpê mitaplāʾ* for the second—"a minor scab"— in order to explain why it is pronounced pure (Rashi). Indeed, perhaps this was the very intent of the priestly writer: by changing the morphology of the noun he was saying that *mispaḥat* is the pure form of *sappaḥat*. Nevertheless, the possibility exists that *mispaḥat* may just be a stylistic variant of *sappaḥat*, in keeping with the writer's penchant for synonyms, for instance, *ʿāmōq* and *sāpāl* for "deep" (vv 20, 25).

he shall wash his clothes (wĕkibbes bĕgādāyw). Bathing (implied; cf. the NOTE on 11:25) and laundering are signs that the impurity was minor—the equivalent of one-day impurity imposed for eating or carrying forbidden meat (11:25, 28, 40). Thus, though the person ends up pure, he was not so to begin with and requires quarantine (Rashi). During the quarantine period the presumable impurity is communicable, contaminating not only his clothes but everything under the same roof (*m. Neg.* 8:8; cf. also chap. 15, COMMENT F). Indeed, according to the rabbis there is little difference between the quarantine and certified scale disease except that the latter requires "shaving and birds" (14:4, 8; *m. Meg.* 1:7; *m. Neg.* 8:8).

Yet the duration of the quarantine does make a difference. Laundering (and bathing) is required only when a second week of quarantine is imposed (vv 6, 34), in contrast to a one-week quarantine, which requires no purification at all (cf. vv 23, 28)—an indication that the longer period creates a severer impurity (D. Wright). This deduction is completely consistent with the basic postulate, drawn from the study of the graduated purification offering, that impurity allowed to remain will increase in intensity (see the COMMENT on 5:1–13 and the NOTE on 15:31). Tentatively, this observation gives us a gauge by which to measure the relative strength of various degrees of scale disease impurity:

one-week quarantine—no impurity;

two-week quarantine—minor impurity (= one day, requiring bathing and laundering);

certified scale disease—major impurity (= eight days, described in 14:1–32).

7. *But if the scab should spread* The only criterion for declaring the scab impure is if it spreads. Appearance is immaterial: even if it should fade the scab is impure. As noted above (NOTE on "unchanged," v 5), however, fading is a necessary criterion for declaring the lesion healed.

and been pronounced pure (lĕṭāhŏrātô). Some would render this more literally "for his cleansing" (*Tg. Neof.*, Ibn Janaḥ). But the context demands that it be understood as modifying the previous clause, that is, after showing himself to the priest at the end of the second week so that the latter would pronounce him pure *(Keter Torah).*

he shall present himself again (wĕnirā' šēnît). Those who render *šēnît* literally as "twice" might explain the discrepancy that the priest now actually sees him for the third time by arguing that the priest did indeed see him twice, after the first and again after the second week, as indicated by the *qal* verb *wĕrā'â* (vv 5, 6). But this time the *niph'al* is employed to indicate not that the priest came to him but that he was brought to the priest; because this happened once before when the priest first inspected him (v 2b), it is now the second time (Wessely 1846). This ingenious interpretation, however, founders on its involuted reasoning and is countered by the fact that even when he was brought to the priest the first time he did so at the priest's initiative (see the NOTE on "reported," v 2). Besides, all falls into place once *šēnît* is rendered "again, once more, next." For the ample attestation for this rendering, see Exod 2:13; Josh 10:32; Judg 20:24–25; Ezek 43:22; Neh 8:13; cf. chap. 4, COMMENT J and the NOTE on "again," v 5).

8. *And if [the priest] sees (wĕrā'â).* Continues v 7 as the protasis. The symptom of v 7 is repeated to emphasize that only the priest's validation of the symptom determines if the disease has returned (Paran 1983:86).

pronounce him impure (wĕṭimmĕ'ô). Some would claim that the pronominal suffix stands for the affection (Hoffmann 1953), analogous to the explicit object of the verb "quarantine" (v 4) and to the implicit object of *wĕhisgîrô* (v 5). As noted above, however (in the NOTE on "affection," v 4), *nega'* 'affection' can also serve as a metonym for the person (Rashi; cf. vv 11, 15, 20, 22). If, indeed, the object were the affection, it would have been specified in the verse (as in v 27) and not be located two verses back; see also the NOTE below.

it. hî' (hw'), namely, the *mispaḥat* 'scab', a feminine noun (Rashi). Once declared impure, it becomes a *sappaḥat* (see the NOTE on "scab," v 6). The fact that the Masoretes vocalize the pronoun as a feminine supports the view that they regard the masculine suffix of *wĕṭimmĕ'ô* as referring to the person.

9. *When a person has (kî tihyeh bĕ'ādām).* This verse, which repeats the words of the introduction to this chapter (v 2), is needed lest the following verse be considered a continuation of the previous case, in other words, that after the shiny spot *(baheret)* is healed (v 6), a white discoloration occurs (v 10; Hoffmann 1953). Feminine *tihyeh* modifies the *nom. rect.* (cf. Gen 4:10; Exod 25:5; 26:12; GKC §146a; Joüon 1923: §150n). Because *bĕ'ādām,* literally, "in a person" is

elliptical for *bĕʿôr-bĕśārô,* the "skin of one's body" (v 2a), hence the first pericope (vv 1–8) must have lain before the composer of the second (vv 9–17).

a scaly affection (negaʿ ṣāraʿat). The LXX, Sam., and Pesh. prefix this phrase with a *waw,* a likely reading for it opens a new case, the second in a series (cf. vv 18, 29, 38, etc.). Because this term here describes not the actual disease but only its symptoms, the rendering "scaly infection" is preferred, as in v 2.

10. *a white discoloration (śĕʾēt-lĕbānâ).* In order for the discoloration to become scale disease, it must first appear white, just as in the case of the *baheret* 'shiny mark' (v 4). For *śĕʾēt* as "discoloration," see the Note on v 2.

and it has turned (wĕhîʾ hāpĕkâ). In contrast to v 2, where *hāpak* is intransitive, implying that when the priest examines the shiny mark the hair in it has already turned white, the verb in this case is transitive and the preceding pronoun, *wĕhîʾ,* is there to emphasize that the discoloration has already taken place and is the cause of the hair turning white (cf. *m. Neg.* 4:11).

some hair. śĕʿār; cf. the Note on "hair," v 3.

white (lābān). An abbreviation for *lĕlābān (Tg. Onq.;* Saadiah).

with (û[mihyat]). Some commentators follow the rabbis in rendering "or" (*Sipra,* Neg. Tazriaʿ par. 3:8; Saadiah; Rashi; Maim., "Impurity of Scale Disease" 3.4), contending that only one criterion is required for a positive diagnosis, either white hair or raw flesh within the white discoloration. As evidence they cite (1) the *ʾatnaḥ* under *lābān,* which implies a choice, instead of under *bāʿôr,* which would have implied that the following two conditions were both mandatory (Wessely 1846); (2) the appearance of white hair by itself is sufficient cause to certify that it is scale disease (v 3; *Seper Hamibḥar*); and (3) if the white discoloration covers the entire body it is pure (vv 12–13), implying that only the existence of the patch, one of the criteria, is required (Wessely 1846). But the white covering over the *entire* body automatically means that the raw flesh has disappeared and the latter need not be mentioned (eliminating arguments 2 and 3, above), and the Masoretic punctuation (argument 1) is hardly critical. More decisive is the statement that raw flesh is the essential criterion if the once-healed lesion is again to be declared impure (vv 14–15), thereby favoring the rendering "and, with."

with a patch of. ûmihyat, literally, "place of life." The Tgs. and Pesh. render this noun "sign, trace," probably deriving it from the root *ḥwh* (Arab. *ḥwy*) 'gather', related to *ḥawwa* 'encampment'. It is more likely, however, to be a denominative of *ḥaya* 'be alive'. Some would associate it with its other attested meanings—"life preservation" (Gen 45:5), "sustenance" (Judg 6:4; 17:10)—and render it "growth, formation" (Kalisch 1867–72). Preferably, its meaning should be drawn from its context: *"ûmihyat* a place of life for *bāśār ḥay* flesh of life" (Wessely 1846; Hoffmann 1953), that is to say, a patch *(NJPS).*

raw flesh (bāśār ḥay). It is called *ḥay* 'living' (so rendered by Saadiah) because it looks like healthy flesh, but its redness is due to the inflammation of the skin (Rashi). Rashi's interpretation was anticipated by the Qumran sectaries, who state explicitly *WR'H HKHN 'WTW KMR'Y HBŚR HHY* 'and the priest sees it as *the appearance* (italics mine) of healthy flesh' (4QDᵃ2). On the assumption that the disease is psoriasis, this refers to the tiny areas of bleeding where the psoriasis scales are rubbed off. The rendering "raw" for *hay* in regard to flesh is attested elsewhere (1 Sam 2:15). Thus the *śě'ēt* 'discoloration' is given a third criterion in addition to white hair and spread, the two already prescribed for the *baheret* 'shiny mark' (cf. vv 3, 7, 10, 12)—a patch of raw flesh within the discoloration (cf. *m. Neg.* 1:5).

11. *it hi' (hw')*. Refers to the discoloration (*śě'ēt* is feminine).

chronic. nôšenet, a *niph'al* participle from *yāšan* 'be old', and figuratively "be resident for a long time" (Deut 4:25). In this instance, however, the sore is not old because it has just erupted (Ehrlich 1908–14). Hence this adjective addresses the future; it is bound to recur and remain, so it is "chronic."

he shall not quarantine him (lo' yasgīrennû). This warning is essential, for one might argue that if a white shiny spot warrants quarantine (v 4), so a white discoloration, despite the clear evidence of white hair and raw flesh, should also be quarantined (Jastrow 1913–14; 362 n. 12).

for he is impure (tāmē' hû'). The adjective *tāmē'* connotes indefinite impurity, which is irreversible by man (cf. vv 11, 15, 36, 44, 46; 15:2, 25; and the NOTE on 11:4).

12. *break out. pārôah tiprah;* faster than *pāśâ* 'spread' (vv 5–8). This verb is particularly apt in describing a skin eruption (Exod 9:9, 10).

all of the skin of the affected. kol-'ôr hannega', literally, "all of the skin of the affection," which leads Ramban to interpret this phrase as the skin plus the affection (as if a *waw* preceded *hannega'*). But as noted above (v 4), "affection" is a metonym for the body (Wessely 1846) or, stated differently, *nega'* 'affection' is equivalent to *nāgûa'* 'afflicted' (Saadiah, Shadal).

from head to foot. mērō'šô wĕ'ad-raglāyw (cf. Isa 1:6). Akkadian has an equivalent expression, *ištu qaqqādišu adi šēpēšu* 'from his head to his feet'.

wherever the priest can see (lĕkol-mar'ēh 'ênê hakkōhēn). The rabbis take this clause as a stipulation: the priest must see the discolored patch at a glance. On this basis they exempt twenty-four points in the convex areas of the body that are not totally visible at once (*m. Neg.* 6:7), in addition to one's private parts (*Sipra*, Neg. Tazria' 4:3). This underscores the rabbis' insistence that only the inspection of the priests, not the testimony of the victim or anyone else, is decisive (see the NOTE on "when the priest sees it," v 3; Jastrow 1913–14: 362 n. 13).

13. *because he has turned all white, he is pure.* Healing has occurred by desquamation; the scaly crust peels off, leaving white beneath (G. R. Driver 1963: 576a). It is a sign of exfoliative dermatitis (Hulse 1975: 95). Older commentaries offer a different natural explanation: the spreading of the scales indicates that the affliction has surfaced and healing has commenced (Ibn Ezra), but if scales do not spread, the affliction deepens into the skin *(Baal Haturim)*.

Ostensibly, this statement that complete whiteness is a symptom of purity flies in the face of various scriptural attestations that ṣāraʿat is kaššeleg 'like snow' (Moses' hand, Exod 4:6; Miriam, Num 12:9; Gehazi, 2 Kgs 5:27). The answer may well be that the comparison with snow is not because of the latter's whiteness but because of its flakiness (Hulse 1975: 92–93). Indeed, the common denominator for all of the skin eruptions called ṣāraʿat in this chapter is that they appear as scales (see the NOTE on "scaly," v 2). The Talmud, however, rejects this phenomenon as an insoluble paradox: "If it breaks out (and covers his skin, beginning) from (a sign that was certified) impure, he is pure. . . . (If it breaks out) from (a sign that was certified) pure, he is impure" (m. Neg. 8:1; indeed, they view it as a parable for the messianic age (b. Sanh. 97a).

14. But as soon as. ûbĕyôm, literally, "on the day"; for the attestations of this idiom, see 14:2, 57; Num 7:1, 84; 9:15. It indicates a continuation of the preceding case; otherwise the verse would have begun with wĕʾim rāʾōh yērāʾeh 'if [raw flesh] appears' (Ehrlich 1908–14).

he shall be impure (yiṭmāʾ). But when the priest decides it is impure, the imperfect switches to the adjective, ṭāmeʾ (v 15). This distinction is consistently observed in P: the imperfect yiṭmāʾ designates brief, temporary impurity; the adjective ṭāmēʾ refers to a more permanent state (see the NOTE on v 46). Even though the appearance of raw flesh is impurity, this fact must be certified by the priest (Wessely 1846).

16. if (kî). One would have expected ʾim, for this is not a new case but a continuation (cf. v 12a). Was it the possible phonetic blurring or scribal haplography with preceding ʾô that motivated the change?

again turns (yāšûb . . . wĕnehpak). For this idiomatic use of šûb, see Gen 30:31; Judg 19:7; 1 Kgs 13:33; 2 Kgs 19:9; 21:3. It might also be rendered literally "turn back, withdraw, retract" (e.g., 2 Kgs 20:29), signifying that if the raw flesh contracts and new skin has grown over the area, it is a sign that healing is taking place (Ibn Ezra; cf. Sipra, Neg. Tazriaʿ 6:1).

however (ʾô). For this usage, see Exod 21:31, 36 (Wessely 1846).

he shall come (ûbāʾ). It carries the sense of "he himself will come." He need not be brought to the priest, nor need the priest learn of his condition from others (wĕhûbāʾ; cf. vv 2, 9). Because he sees that his sores are healing, he will come to the priest of his own accord that he may be declared pure and be eligible to return to his community.

18–28. Boils and Burns. Scale disease occurring in the site of healed boils and a burn caused by hot coals or ashes, manifesting themselves in white discolorations or reddish-white shiny marks, are to be treated more leniently than the preceding cases. If the hair has not turned white and the lesion appears no deeper than the surrounding skin—the two critical symptoms—the patient is quarantined for one week only, not for two. If after the quarantine the sore has not spread, it is considered a scab resulting from the boil or burn, and the victim is pronounced pure.

18. *boil (šěḥîn)*. Its occurrences in Scripture attest to its being a highly visible and dreaded disease sent by the divinity (e.g., Exod 9:9, 10, 11; 2 Kgs 20:7; Isa 38:21; Job 2:7) for the violation of the covenant (Deut 28:27, 35). Rashi explains it as a sore that develops "when the flesh grows hot." The Targum to Isa 44:16 renders *ḥammôtî* with *šaḥênît* 'I grew hot'. Support also stems from Ug. *šḥn* 'burn' and Akk. *šaḥānu* 'grow hot'. The rabbis comment, "What is a *šěḥîn?* If a person suffered hurt from wood or stone or olive-peat or Tiberias water; any hurt that is not caused by fire is a *šěḥîn*" (*m. Neg.* 9:1). Finally, according to a recent researcher, Akk. *šeḥḥānu*, the cognate of Hebrew *šěḥîn*, must be rendered as "one afflicted with boils" (Elman 1976).

on the skin. bô-běʿōrô, literally, "in it, in its skin." S. R. Driver and M. A. White (1898) comment,

> Although examples of the anticipation of a substantive by a pronoun occur in the Old Testament, especially in its later parts (cf. as here, after a preposition, Num 32:33; Josh 1:2b [the substantive omitted by LXX]; Judg 21:7; Jer 48:44; 51:56; Ezek 41:25; 42:5; 1 Chr 4:42; 2 Chr 26:14; Dan 11:11), yet the idiom, except where some special emphasis is intended, is more Aramaic than Hebrew (Dan 5:12, 30, etc.); and there is no apparent reason for its adoption here, especially as the ordinary *běʿōrô* (alone) occurs in v 24. It can hardly be doubted that *bô* is merely a corrupt transcriptional anticipation of *bʿ* in *bʿrw*.

It should also be noted that the Sam. reads *bô* (alone), whereas the LXX and Pesh. have *běʿōrô* (alone).

one's body. ûbāśār, literally, "as for a body," in other words, a person, short for "man or woman" (v 38; Saadiah), as in *yābōʾ kol-bāśār* 'every person will come' (Isa 66:23; Abravanel). The text chooses *bāśār* 'body, flesh' over *ʾādām* 'person' (vv 2, 9) or *ʾîš ʾo-ʾiššâ* 'man or woman' (v 38) because *šěḥîn* 'boils' also afflicts animals (e.g., Exod 9:9, 10), and only *bāśār* comprises both (Malbim).

and it heals (wěnirpāʾ). That is, it only begins to heal; otherwise the statement that the new sore within it has "broken out" (v 20b) makes no sense (Hoffmann 1953). Still, the text can be taken at face value: the boil did indeed heal, but a new sore has erupted within it (*Sipra*, Neg. Tazriaʿ par. 4:1).

19. *discoloration or . . . shiny mark (śěʾēt . . . ʾô baheret)*. But not a *suppaḥat* 'scab', again proving that the latter is a benign symptom declared pure by the examining priest (see the NOTES on "scab," vv 2 and 6).

reddish-white (lěbānâ ʾădamdāmet). The rabbis explain, "Where there is a (reddish) mixture in the snowlike whiteness (of shiny marks, the color) is like wine mingled with snow; in the limelike whiteness (of the derivative of shiny marks [see the NOTE on "scab," v 2], the color) is like blood mingled with milk. So R. Ishmael. R. Akiba says: In either of them the reddishness is like wine mingled with water, save only that in snowlike whiteness (the color) is bright, and in limelike whiteness (the color) is duller" (*m. Neg.* 1:2). Ostensibly, both sages agree that there is a diminution in brightness in this mixture. As pointed out by A. Brenner (1982: 107), however, the debate here is over the hue of the reddish-white mixture and of the redness indicated by the word *'ǎdamdemet.* Otherwise both rabbis would be differing with the prevailing rabbinic opinion (cf. below).

Illumination is provided by focusing on the meaning of the term *'ǎdamdemet* in contrast to the ordinary word for red, *'ādôm.* Whereas the view has been registered that *'ǎdamdemet* means "light red" (e.g., GKC §131i), rabbinic opinion is virtually unanimous in rendering it "bright red" (*t. Neg.* 1:5; *Sipra,* Neg. Tazria' 6:5; *y. Sukk.* 3:6; cf. Rashi on v 49; Wessely 1846). Unexpected support derives from the *Sam. Tg.* on Exod 28:17–20 (MS E; Tal 1980), which translates the twelve stones on the high priest's breastpiece as follows:

smwq	smq	sk/mqmq	(red)
ḥkwm	ḥkm	ḥkmkm	(blue)
yrwq	yrq	yrqrq	(green)
'w'r	w'br	'brbr	(gray)

The colors in each horizontal row are ordered according to their increase in intensity. Thus the second and third vertical columns register the comparative and superlative of each color, for example, row 1: red, redder, reddest. In the Bible the superlative is formed by doubling the word, as in *sābîb sābîb* 'completely around' (Ezek 8:10; 37:2); *mě'ōd mě'ōd* 'very much' (Gen 7:19; 17:2; Exod 1:7). Thus a form like *'dmdm* can be regarded as an ellipsis of the two words *'dm 'dm* that connotes the maximum intensity of redness (Shalem 1932). Therefore, *'ǎdamdāmet* can only mean "bright red" and *yěraqraq* (v 49) can only mean "bright green." Medical evidence supports this finding, for skin inflammations and eruptions are characterized by their brightness, and in the course of healing this color progressively fades, in complete agreement with this text (vv 6, 21, 2, 28, 56). For a fuller discussion, see Brenner (1982: 106–10, 124).

20. *it appears (mar'ehā).* The referent for the feminine suffix is the *śě'ēt* 'discoloration' or the *baheret* 'shiny mark' (v 19). The Sam.'s reading, *mar'ēhû* (masc.), would have to refer to *haśśěḥîn* 'the boil' (v 19) but is contradicted by the consistent use of the feminine in what follows.

lower (śāpāl). Previously the synonym *'āmōq* was used (vv 3, 4). Is there a difference? Some claim that *'āmōq* is deeper (Ramban on v 3; Wessely 1846) because reddish white would not appear as deep as all white (vv 3, 4). But both terms alternate later in the chapter with no apparent distinction in meaning (e.g., vv 25–26). Note as well that the order of the symptoms here—lower–turned white—stands in chiastic relation with their order in vv 3, 25, presenting the form ABA (Ben-David).

21. *white hair . . . lower than his skin.* A chiasm with v 4 (Ben-David).

faded (kēheh). A sign that the illness has peaked and healing has begun (see the NOTE on v 6).

22. *If it has spread.* That is, at the end of the week (cf. v 27).

it [is] (hî²[hw²]). "It" refers to the discoloration or the shiny mark (v 19); both are feminine nouns. (See the NOTE on "it appears," v 20).

an affection (nega²). Ehrlich (1908–14) would add *ṣāraʿat* 'scale disease', as elsewhere in this chapter (vv 2, 25, 27, 49), for the term "affection" needs to be defined. But there is no support for this addition from the Versions. The answer may rest on stylistic rather than logical grounds; the addition would supply an eighth *ṣāraʿat hûʾ/hîʿ* in this chapter (vv 3, 8, 15, 25 [bis], 27, 49).

The anomalous appearance of *negaʿ* within the chapter may throw light on one of the cruxes of the Dead Sea Temple Scroll, in which *negaʿ* appears along-side and independent of *ṣāraʿat: ṣarûʿa ûměnûgaʿ* 'bearing scale disease and affec-tion' (45:18); *měnûgāʿîm běṣāraʿat ûběnegaʿ ûběneteq* 'afflicted with scale dis-ease, affection, and scall' (48:15). Both of these citations, especially the latter, make it certain that a hendiadys for *negaʿ ṣāraʿat* is ruled out. The answer may very well lie in this verse. The author of the Temple Scroll noticed that one form of skin disease was termed not *ṣāraʿat* but *negaʿ*, and he thus felt con-strained to list it separately. The same exegesis may lie behind the later rabbinic distinction between the two (see the NOTE on "affection," v 2), regarding *negaʿ* as the more inclusive term (e.g., *m. Neg.* 1:1). J. Neusner, in an extensive discussion (1975: 221–58), attributes the distinction to Rabbi Akiba. But the evidence of Qumran proves that it is the product of an earlier tradition, which may ultimately originate in an early exegesis of this verse.

23. *the shiny mark (baheret).* But what happened to the *śěʾēt* 'discoloration' (v 19)? Its omission is explicable on stylistic grounds. The order *śěʾēt* (v 19), *pāsōh tipseh* (v 22), and *baheret* (v 23) will occur in reverse order in the next pericope: *baheret* (v 24), *pāsōh tipseh* (v 27), *śěʾēt* (v 28; Fishbane 1980: 443; cf. the NOTE on "shiny mark," v 24).

stationary. taḥtêhā, literally, "under itself" (For this idiom, see 1 Sam 14:9). *Tg. Onq.* renders *běʾatrāʾâ* 'its place' on the basis of *bimqôm* (v 19), literally, "in the place of" *(baʾătar, Tg. Onq.).*

scar. ṣārebet is found only here and in v 28. Rashi renders it "retrecisse-ment"—that is, retrenchment, contraction—citing Ezek 21:3; Prov 16:27. But the verb *ṣārab* in these verses probably means "scorch" (akin to Hebrew *ṣārap/ śārap;* Akk. *ṣarāpu).* The LXX and *Tg. Ps.-J.* render "scar," to wit, that which results from the burn/boil, and the rabbis explain that the wound is covered with a crust, the thickness of a garlic shell (*m. Neg.* 9:2). Snaith (1967) renders "puckered scar," combining both interpretations.

24. *one's body. bāśār;* cf. the NOTE on v 18.

burn by fire (mikwat-²ēš). As opposed to the *šěḥîn* 'boil', which stems from a burn from another source (*m. Neg.* 9:1; cf. the NOTE on "boil," v 18). But a *mikwâ* is defined by the rabbis as follows: "What is a *mikwâ?* If a person was burnt by burning coal or by embers: any hurt that is caused by fire is a *mikwâ"* (*m. Neg.* 9:1). A baraita qualifies this distinction, as follows: "What is a boil and what is a burn? A wound caused by wood, or stone, or olive-peat, or the hot springs of Tiberias, or any wound caused by lead just taken from the mine, is a boil. And what is a burn? A burn caused by a live coal, or hot ashes, or boiling lime, or boiling gypsum, or any burn that is caused by fire, including a burn caused by water heated by fire, is a burn" (*b. Ḥul.* 8a [bar.]). The rabbis also ask: If the symptoms and the treatment of the boil and the burn are identical, why are they treated separately? Their answer is that the boil and the burn cannot be combined to comprise the minimum size for scale disease (*t. Neg.* 3:13). Instead, the obvious answer is that it is the nature of priestly style not to coalesce different categories even if their content is the same. (For a parade example, see Num 7:12–83.) Besides, there are slight differences in the symptoms (see the NOTE on "patch," below).

The rendering "burn" is corroborated by the verbal form of this root, *kwh* (Isa 43:2; Jer 23:29; Prov 6:28), its other nominal forms, *kĕwiyyâ* (Exod 21:25) and *kî* (< **kĕwî;* Isa 3:24), and the Akk. cognate *kawu (AHw)*—all of which mean "burn, brand."

the patch of (miḥyat). Rashi renders "sainement," that is to say, the healing of the burn (from *ḥayâ* 'live, revive'), probably on the basis of the parallel statement in the similarly structured pericope on the boil that had healed, *wĕnirpāʾ* (v 19). But there is no indication here that the burn had healed. To the contrary, the *miḥyâ* in the *śĕʾēt* is the bearer of raw flesh and is unhesitatingly labeled as chronic scale disease (vv 10–11). In fact, a comparison of these contiguous pericopes on the boil and burn shows that the analogue to *miḥyat* is *bimqôm* 'in the place of'. Nevertheless, the change in terminology should not be understood as a quest for synonyms. The reverse is probably true: the term *miḥyâ* is employed to connote that the burn, unlike the boil, does not heal but is covered by a shiny mark. For the translation "patch" see the NOTE on v 10.

shiny mark (baheret). The *śĕʾēt* occurs in v 28 but not here. As explained in the NOTE on v 23, the two adjoining pericopes (vv 18–23 and 24–28) are in chiastic relation. The order of the first is *śĕʾēt* (v 19), *pāsōh tipseh* (v 22), *baheret* (v 23) and of the second, *baheret* (v 24), *pāsōh tipseh* (v 27), *śĕʾēt* (v 28; Fishbane 1980: 443). Still, the two sores are implied throughout each pericope.

28. *and it is faded (wĕhîʾ [whwʾ] kēhâ).* That is, it remains as faded as it appeared to the priest in his first examination (v 26). It is not necessary for it to have faded more, which would have required the verb *kihătâ*, not the adjective *kēhâ.* This criterion of fading is missing in the description of the *baheret* resulting from a boil (v 23). Its lack there leads Ibn Ezra to deduce that spreading (v 22) is the only criterion. But fading is mentioned in the priest's initial examination (v 21), and its continuation as a faded lesion must be taken for granted in the second examination.

the discoloration (śĕʾēt). If the *baheret* neither spreads nor fades, what can it mean that it becomes a *śě'ēt?* First, as noted above (NOTES on "shiny mark," vv 23, 24), the *baheret* is not transformed into a *śě'ēt* but both lesions are presumed in the text to be the possible result of a boil or burn. As for the fact that the *śě'ēt* in this pericope is pronounced pure, as is the *baheret* in the previous pericope (v 23), one should keep in mind that these sores are in themselves neutral; they do not become impure until additional symptoms show themselves, namely, whiteness, deepness, raw flesh, and the sine qua non—spread. Indeed the very opening of this chapter implies this fact: "a discoloration, a scab, or a shiny mark, and *it develops* into a scaly affection" (v 2). See also the NOTE below.

it is the discoloration from the burn . . . it is the scar of the burn (śě'ēt hammikwâ hî ' [hw'] . . . ṣārebet hammikwâ hî' [hw']). In view of the preceding NOTE, the need for the repetition should be apparent. Even though all that remains of the burn is a *śě'ēt,* a "discoloration," it is not of the impure variety; it is only a scar and, hence, pure (v 23).

This verse ends the first section of this chapter, dealing with skin disease of the fleshy parts of the body. Its symptoms are neatly summarized in the Mishna, as follows:

> The skin of the flesh (13:2–17) may be certified impure within two weeks by three symptoms: by white hair (v 3), or by raw flesh (vv 10, 14), or by spreading (vv 7, 8). "By white hair or by raw flesh"—in the beginning, or by the end of the first week, or by end of the second week, or even after it had been pronounced pure. "Or by spreading"—by the end of the first week, or by the end of the second week, or even after it had been pronounced pure. It may be certified impure within two weeks that are thirteen days. A boil (vv 19–23) or burn (vv 24–28) may be certified impure within one week and by two symptoms: by white hair (vv 20, 25) or by spreading (vv 22, 27). "By white hair"—in the beginning, or by the end of the week, or even after it had been pronounced pure. "Or by spreading"—by the end of the week, or even after it had been pronounced pure. They may be certified impure within one week, that is, seven days. (*m. Neg.* 3:3–4)

it is faded (wěhî' [whw'] kēhâ). The color is faint from the outset, as in the case of the boil (v 21), and for this reason neither lesion requires a second quarantine if there is also no further spread (see the NOTE on "quarantine him for another seven days," v 33).

29–37. Scalls. These verses deal with the infections of the scalp and the beard, to wit, the hairy parts of the head. The treatment is the same as for the scale disease described in vv 2–8, though the priest is told to look out for yellow hair rather than white hair. The yellowing of the hair favors the diagnosis of *favus* rather than psoriasis (Hulse 1975: 99). The rabbis summarize this pericope as follows:

Scalls may be certified impure within two weeks and by two symptoms: yellow sparse hair (v 30) or by spreading. "By yellow sparse hair"—in the beginning, or by the end of the first week, or by the end of the second week, or even after they have been pronounced pure. "By a spreading"—by the end of the first week, by the end of the second week, or even after they have been pronounced pure. They may be certified impure within two weeks that are but thirteen days. (*m. Neg.* 3:5)

29. *If a man or a woman (wĕ'îš 'ô 'iššâ).* The sexes are here differentiated instead of using the inclusive form *'ādām* (vv 2, 9) because the beard applies only to the man (Ibn Ezra).
    on the head or in the beard (bĕrō'š 'ô bĕzāqān).

What is the head and what is the beard? From the cheekbone and upward, this is the head. From the cheekbone and downward, this is the beard. From the front, one stretches the thread from ear to ear: for from the thread and upward, this is the head; from the thread and downward, this is the beard. As to the back of the head: from the protruding cartilage of the neck and upward, this is the head; from the protruding cartilage and downward, even though it produces hair, lo, this is like the skin of the flesh in every respect. In front of him: from the knob of the windpipe upward, this is the beard; from the knob of the windpipe downward, even though it produces hair, lo, this is the skin of the flesh in every respect. (*t. Neg.* 4:12; cf. *m. Neg.* 10:9)

In actuality, *bĕzāqān* should be rendered "on the jaw," the area in which the beard grows and the disease takes root (cf. the NOTE on "jaw," v 30 below).
    30. *the hair in it (ûbô śē'ār).* The fact that a nominal sentence is found here that avoids the verb *ṣāmaḥ* 'grow' implies that the yellow hair does not represent a new growth but a change of color in the existing hair (Wessely 1846; cf. the NOTE on "has grown," v 37).
    yellow (ṣāhōb). Black hair has turned yellow, but not white or any other color (*Sipra*, Neg. Tazria' par. 5:5; Ramban). It is this distinction in hair color that necessitated listing the scall *(neteq)* as a separate category: scale disease in the fleshy parts of the skin turns hair white; in scalls, yellow (*Sipra*, ibid.; Rashi). The color *ṣāhōb* appears only in this chapter (vv 30, 32, 36). Its identification is moot. Some rabbis render it "golden" (*Sipra*, ibid.) or "pale gold" (*pale*, Rashi on v 37) or describe it: "like the plumage of young pigeons after they have lost their first feathers" (Radak in his *Book of Roots:* cf. *b. Ḥul.* 22b). By contrast, Saadiah, on the basis of the Arab. cognate *ṣahiba* 'gold-shining', renders it "chestnut, reddish brown." Indeed, *Tg. Onq.* actually gives "red," whereas *Tg. Ps.-J.* and the Pesh. offer "shiny" (Pines 1971: 670). Thus, the range would allow for "pale to [golden, or reddish] yellow, shiny" (Brenner 1982: 105). The

translation adopted here is, for want of a definitive study, the traditional one, "yellow," bearing in mind that the ancients did not distinguish between yellow and green (Landsberger 1967; cf. the NOTE on "green," v 49). Yellow, moreover, is favored because it is characteristic of *favus*, the disease associated with scall (see the NOTE below), "the crusts being yellow the hair itself takes on the colour of hay" (Hulse 1975: 99). The Qumran sectaries take the yellow color as a sign of decay: *KY KʿŠB HWʾ ʾŠR [Y]Š HRḤŠ TḤTW WYQYṢ ŠRŠW WYBŠ PRḤW* 'for it is like a plant, which has a worm under it that severs its root and makes its blossom wither' (4QDᵃ 7–8).

sparse (dāq). Rabbi Yohanan ben Nuri claims it means "thin," that is, emaciated (Gen 41:6). Rabbi Akiba claims it means "defectively thin and short."

> R. Yohanan b. Nuri says even if it is long. R. Yohanan b. Nuri said: what does the expression mean when they say "this stick is *daq*," or "this reed is *daq*"?—does it mean that it is defectively thin and short or defectively thin and long? R. Akiba said to him: Before we learn from the reed let us learn from the hair—[for if we say,] "the hair of such-a-one is *daq*" *daq* means that it is defectively thin and short, not that it is defectively thin and long. (*m. Neg.* 10:1; *Sipra*, Neg. Tazriaᶜ par. 5:6)

Medical science would reject both interpretations, however, in favor of the evidence that the fibrous tissue destroys hair follicles so that the hair has thinned out, in other words, it has become "sparse" (Hulse 1975: 99).

scall (neteq). It is so called because the hair is *nittaq* 'torn off', as one whose testes are *nātûq* (22:24; Ramban). The hair weakens and snaps, as a strand of tow or rope is torn apart (*yinnātēq*, Judg 16:9; Qoh 4:12 [Wessely 1846]). Thus the term *neteq* is appropriate for hair disease (*Sipra*, Neg. Tazriaᶜ par. 5:9); the hair becomes detached or is torn from the follicles or the scalp. The yellowing of the hair is characteristic of *favus* rather than psoriasis (Hulse 1975: 99), *favus* being defined as "a severe fungus infection of the skin" (Hulse 1975: 103).

> The yellow cup-shaped crust of favus is certainly very different from the plaque of scales of psoriasis and the crusting of severe seborrhoeic dermatitis. Thus it is not inappropriate that a different word should be used for the two types of lesion. The way this passage is written and the reference to *neṯeḵ* in Lev. 14:54 both suggest that although favus came within the priests' concept of *ṣāraᶜat* it was recognized that there was a difference between *neṯeḵ* and what we might call the "psoriasis-like form of *ṣāraᶜat*." (Hulse 1975: 99)

Yet another explanation holds that "inadequate nutrition must always be considered a significant etiology for disease. For example, Kwashiakor, a protein deficiency syndrome, seen in Arab children, is associated with copper-red to yellow colored fine hair and scaling of the skin" (Wright and Jones forthcoming B).

The question can be raised: Why is the disease not labeled *neteq* from the start, instead of *nega*ᶜ 'affection' (v 29)? This verse gives the answer: The hair must first fall out and be replaced by yellow hair before the verdict of *neteq* can be given (Ramban). But if yellow hair precedes the fallen hair, then it is not *neteq* and is considered pure (*Sipra*, Neg. Tazriaᶜ 8:6). Scientific opinion disagrees: the hair falls out after turning yellow (Hulse 1975: 99).

scale disease (ṣāraᶜat). After the identification has been made that the *neteq* is a form of *ṣāraᶜat,* the latter term does not occur again in this pericope (vv 29–37).

jaw. *zāqān,* literally, "beard." But because the disease actually attacks the skin to which the hairs of the beard are attached, "jaw" is the more accurate rendering. It also complements the term *rōʾš* 'head', that is, its hairy area.

31. Seidl (1982: 38) correctly points to the semantic and structural parallelism between vv 31–36 and vv 4–8. Note the verbal equivalents that follow in the same sequential order: *ʾēn-marʾēhû ᶜāmōq min-hāᶜōr* (v 31aβ ‖ v 4aβ); *wĕhisgîr hakkōhēn ʾet-negaᶜ . . . šibᶜat yāmîm* 'the priest shall quarantine [the person with] the . . . affection for seven days' (v 31b ‖ v 4b); *lōʾ-pāśâ* 'has not spread' (v 32aβ ‖ v 5aγ); *wĕhisgîr hakkōhēn . . . šibᶜat yāmîm šēnît* 'The priest shall quarantine . . . for another seven days' (v 33b ‖ v 5b); *wĕrāʾâ hakkōhēn . . . bayyôm haššĕbîᶜî* 'On the seventh day the priest shall examine' (v 34aα ‖ v 6aα); *lōʾ-pāśâ* 'has not spread' (v 34aβ ‖ v 6aα); *wĕṭihar ʾōtô hakkōhēn wĕkibbes bĕgadāyw wĕṭāhēr* 'the priest shall pronounce him pure; he shall wash his clothes, and he shall be pure' (v 34b ‖ v 6b); *wĕʾim pāsōh yipseh . . . bāᶜōr ʾaḥărê tohŏrātô wĕrāʾāhû hakkōhēn wĕhinnēh pāśâ . . . bāᶜōr . . . ṭāmēʾ hûʾ* 'If, however, the . . . should spread on the skin after he has been pronounced pure, the priest shall examine him. If the . . . has spread on the skin . . . he is impure' (vv 35, 36a ‖ vv 7a, 8). Clearly, both pericopes were composed by the same hand.

But when (wĕkî). Because this verse is a continuation of vv 29–30, the particle *wĕʾim* should have been expected, as in the parallel (v 4). But the sense of *kî* here is not the conditional "if," rather the temporal "when."

it does not appear to go deeper than the skin. But if it did, it would be pronounced impure (cf. vv 32b, 34a).

yet there is no black hair in it. If there were, it would have been pronounced pure (cf. v 37; *Sipra*, Neg. Tazriaᶜ 8:9). According to the rabbis, the hair need not be black in order to be pure; any color but yellow would do (*Sipra*, Neg. Tazriaᶜ 8:5). But if the text only mentions black, does it mean that there were no blonds or redheads among the Israelites? This may be the case, for Semites always appear in Egyptian wall-paintings as blackheads. Moreover, the Sumerians refer to non-Sumerians, presumably Semites, as blackheads. Unfortunately, this deduction cannot be definitively derived from this verse, because the very reading "black" is in doubt. For "black" the LXX reads "yellow." Support for the latter reading can be mustered from the facts that yellow hair is the key symptom for *neteq* (v 30) and that the appearance of yellow hair is what the priest looks for after the quarantine (v 32). Once this reading is accepted, then the conclusion follows that any hair but yellow will qualify for a diagnosis of purity, hence there is no need to assume that Israelites are just blackhaired. But because regrowth of black hair is a sine qua non for healing (v 37), the MT must be adjudged correct, and the question of the absence of nonbrunettes in Israel still stands.

the priest shall quarantine. On the basis of MT's "black," the priest would impose the quarantine to see whether there would be a regrowth of black hair in order to purify him (v 37). But on the basis of the reading "yellow" (LXX), the quarantine would be imposed to see whether the scall generates yellow hair, which would render him impure.

32. *and there is no yellow hair in it.* wĕlōʾ-hāyâ bô śēʿār ṣāhōb, literally, "and there was no yellow hair in it," in other words, none grew in the scall during the quarantine. Neither did black hair grow in it; otherwise, the person would have to be pronounced pure (v 37). This verse states three negative criteria for the continuation of quarantine: the scall has not spread, it has not generated yellow hair, and does not appear deeper than the skin. Apparently, the positive indication of any one of these criteria suffices for impurity. This is expressly true for the scall's spread (v 36) and must be presumed for the others. Thus, if the situation remains static, quarantine is mandated. If there is a change then a verdict is handed down: spread, yellow hair, or deepness for impurity, black hair for purity.

Qumran mandates the following diagnosis: WŜR̊[Ḥ HRḤŠ MTḤT HŚ]ʿR WHPḤ MRʾ {Y}Hᵂ LDQ ṢWHB KYKŚB HWʾ ʾŠR [Y]Š ḤRḤŠ THTW WYQYṢ ŠWRŠW WYBŠ PRḤW 'Then will flour[ish the "worm" under the ha]ir and its appearance will become thin, yellow, for it is like grass that has a worm underneath it, and it will cut off its root and its flower will wither' (4QDᵃ 17:7-8; Milik 1966: 105). Qumran's misdiagnosis on the worm is balanced by its correct observation concerning the circulation of the blood (see the NOTE on v 34).

not [appear] deeper (ʾēn ʿāmōq). Ehrlich (1908-14) would read ʾēnennû for the negative particle, as in v 34, because ʾēn can only be used with a noun (v 4), but in construct with an adjective it requires a suffix.

33. *shall shave himself.* wĕhitgallāḥ; that is, round about the scall (*Tg. Onq.*; *Tg. Neof.*; *Sipra*, Neg. Tazriaʿ 9:7). Had the text meant that he should shave all his hair it would have added kol-śēʿārô, as in 14:8, 9. The area to be shaven is specified by the rabbis: "How is he shaven that has a scall? They shave the space outside it but leave (a circle) two hairs (deep) next to it so that it shall be manifest if it spreads" (*m. Neg.* 10:5; cf. *Sipra*, Neg. Tazriaʿ 9:7). The fact that the verb is a *hithpaʿel* is interpreted by the rabbis as indicating that the shaving may be performed by anyone (*t. Neg.* 4:1; *Sipra*, Neg. Tazriaʿ 9:4) in contrast to

the shaving that takes place during the purificatory period, which, expressed as a *piᶜel* (14:8, 9), is performed by a priest (*t. Neg.* 8:6). The rabbis are surely right in claiming that the *hithpaᶜel* here does not preclude anyone else's performing the shaving. (The *piᶜel*, however, does; see the NOTES on 14:8, 9.) Strikingly, the Qumran sectaries adopt a similar position by interpreting (or altering) this verse, as follows: *WᵓŠR ᵓMR WSᵚWH HKWHN WGLHW ᵓT H{B}R ᵂŠ{R}* 'Concerning that which was said: The priest shall command that they shall shave the head' (4QDᵃ 17:19; Milik 1966: 105). This wording makes it clear that the priest orders others to shave (*piᶜel* of *glḥ*) his head. Another difference is that the shaving of the hair takes place at the initial inspection before the seven-day quarantine. The enlarged *gimel* found in most MSS indicates, according to one rabbinic source (*b. Qidd.* 30a), the middle verse of the Pentateuch. But the Masoretes fix it on 8:7 (cf. also *Sop.* 9:3).

without shaving the scall. If the scall is disturbed, the test is apparently invalidated.

quarantine him for another seven days. Why is there a need for a second quarantine if no change has taken place—no spread, no yellow hair, no sunken appearance—particularly when the absence of these symptoms suffices for a purity verdict at the end of the second quarantine (v 34)? The answer begins to surface once it is realized that the scall (vv 29–37) follows the pattern of the *baheret* 'shiny mark' (vv 4–8; see the NOTE on v 31), for in that case too a static condition suffices to warrant a second quarantine (v 5). Conversely, there is only one week of quarantine prescribed for a boil or a burn (vv 19–28). Why then should two quarantines be imposed for a shiny mark or a scall but only one quarantine for a boil or a burn? To be sure, the latter, like the former, manifest a static condition at the end of the first week, to wit, the lesion has not spread (vv 23, 28). In the cases of the boil and the burn, however, the lesion appears faded from the start (vv 21, 26). The case is otherwise with the shiny mark and the scall. The shiny mark is bright at the outset (see the NOTE on "shiny mark," v 2) and is not required to fade by the end of the first quarantine (v 5); it only must have faded by the end of the second quarantine to qualify for a verdict of purity (v 6). It must, therefore, be assumed that had it faded by the end of the first quarantine, in addition to fulfilling the other criterion of not spreading, it would at that point have been declared pure. The situation is otherwise with the scall: fading is no criterion at all, either at the beginning or at the end (vv 29–37). Spread, yellow hair, and depth are the only symptoms, but as there is no diminution in color (i.e., the condition remains static) a second quarantine needs to be imposed. The argument presented here is corroborated by the case of the fabric (vv 47–58). There, too, if there is no change in its condition after the first quarantine (v 53) a second quarantine is prescribed (v 54), but only if the color becomes faded (*kēhâ*, the verbal form, the same as in v 6) is the fabric declared pure (v 56).

34. *spread . . . deeper.* Lack of spread and depth are the only criteria for

purity, not the appearance of black hair (cf. v 37). Is it perhaps too soon to expect it? But what if a yellow hair reappears? Hoffmann (1953) says that the lesion is still adjudged pure because it answers the criteria of this verse. But one must assume, with v 30, that yellow hair within a scall is always an inexorable sign of impurity (cf. the NOTE on "spread," v 35).

Qumran's diagnosis continues as follows: *WR'H 'M YW{Š}SP MN {K} HHY 'L HMT BŠB'T HYMYM ṬM' HW'H W'M LW L̊YWSP MN HH̊[YWT] 'L HMYTWT WHGYD NML' [D]M̊ W̊R̊[W]H HHYYM 'WLH WYWRDT BW* 'And the priest will examine if there will be added from the live to the dead (hairs) during the seven days, it is impure. But if there will not be added from the l[ive] to the dead (hairs) and if the artery will be filled with [bl]ood and the sp[i]rit of life will ascend and descend in it' (4QD^a 17:10–12; Milik 1966: 105, cf. also 4QD^9 1:3, 7; 2:1). Two remarkable things highlight this text: the recognition that the onset of scale disease is symbolic of the approach of death (see chap. 11, COMMENT B and chap. 15, COMMENT G) and that the blood circulates ("ascend and descend") in the arteries (cf. also 4QD^9 2:1), a medical fact that was first observed by Asaph the Physician in the sixth century C.E. and not fully understood until the seventeenth century by William Harvey (Baumgarten 1990). The difference between the Bible and Qumran should also be noted: Qumran's diagnosis take place during the first week; unlike the Bible it does not mention a second week.

he shall wash his clothes. In addition, he must undergo ablutions (see the NOTE on 11:28). Its purpose is to exempt him from the purificatory rite he would have had to undergo had the priest declared him impure (14:1–32; *Sipra,* Neg. Tazria^c 9:8). Still, the fact that he must bathe at all indicates that he has contracted some form of impurity, a lesser one to be sure, one that does not require external purifications and sacrifices, but one that will be eliminated when he immerses himself in water (cf. the NOTES on vv 6 and 58).

35. *spread.* In view of the statement in v 36 that the priest need not look for a yellow hair, it should be obvious that its discovery, even without any sign that the lesion had spread, should suffice for the priest to declare him impure (Abravanel).

36. *look. yĕbaqqēr,* in other words, inquire, investigate. This interpretation of *biqqēr* seems clear from this context as well as from that of 27:33, and is adopted by *Tg. Ps.-J., Tg. Neof.,* Rashi, Ibn Ezra, and Rashbam (cf. Ezek 34:11, 12; Prov 20:25). It becomes problematical with its nominal form, a hapax, *biqqoret* (cf. the detailed NOTE on 19:20 and, in the interim, Milgrom 1976f: 129 n. 460; Loewenstamm 1980).

he is impure (ṭāmē' hû'). It is assumed that the priest pronounced him impure, that is, his scall was certified as scale disease and he was banished from the camp (cf. the NOTE on "he is pure. The priest shall pronounce him pure," v 37).

37. This verse has no counterpart in the similarly structured pericope, vv 2–8 (cf. the NOTE on v 31). It speaks of a second certification by the priest that the scall is pure if it spreads again following the priest's first certification of its purity.

has retained its color (bě'ēnāyw 'āmad). The meaning of this expression has been discussed at length in the NOTE on v 5. Note the three different renderings: "appearance, color" (Radak); priest's opinion, literally, "in his eyes" (*Tg. Neof.; Sipra*, Neg. Tazria' 9:14); "as it was" (*Tg. Onq., Tg. Ps.-J.)*; and the proof for the first reading.

and (wě[šě'ār]). Does the *waw* here mean "and" or "or"? Are two symptoms or one needed to declare him pure? A debate rages across the pages of the Talmud between Rabbi Josiah and Rabbi Jonathan (e.g., *b. Yoma* 57b; *b. B. Meṣ.* 94b; *b. Menaḥ.* 90b) about whether the *waw* can mean "or." Now there is no doubt that *waw* can be equivalent to 'ô (e.g., Exod 12:5; 21:15, 17; Ḥazzequni), and some claim that to be its meaning here (Hoffmann 1953). This is doubtful, though, for the criterion of spread is sufficient in itself to declare the lesion impure (vv 35–36). Thus, even if a black hair appears while the scall continues to spread, the scall cannot be pronounced pure. Both criteria are essential, requiring the *waw* to be rendered "and."

has grown (ṣāmaḥ). This verb stands for new growth (e.g., Judg 16:22). Its absence in v 30 implies that in that case the hair is not new, rather, the existing black hair has turned yellow (Wessely 1846). The rabbis claim that any color but yellow also qualifies (*Sipra*, Neg. Tazria' 8:5) but, as noted above (NOTE on "yet there is no black hair in it," v 31), the chances are that redheads or blonds were rare or nonexistent in ancient Israel and its environs.

The Qumran sectaries specify, *Y{Š}PWR HKWHN 'T HŚ'WRT HMYTWT WHḤYWT WR'H 'M YW{Š}SP MN {K}HḤY 'L HMT BŠB'T HYMYM ṬM' HW'H W'M LW LYWSP MN HḤYWT 'L HMYTWT . . . [NRP'] HNG'* 'the priest may count the dead and live hair and see whether any has been added from the live to the dead; while if none has been added from the live to the dead . . . the affliction [is healed]' (4QDª 10–13).

he is pure. The priest shall pronounce him pure (ṭāhôr hû' wěṭihărô hakkōhēn). Some claim that just as he requires immersion and laundering after his quarantine (v 34), so too he must bathe and launder after his scall has erupted again and then healed (e.g., Hoffmann 1953). The rabbis, noting the peculiar order of these sentences, interpret them as follows: only if the scall is truly pure may the priest pronounce it pure (*Sipra*, Neg. Tazria' 9:16; *y. Pesaḥ.* 6:1), and they further record that this is one of the three scriptural difficulties that motivated Rabbi Hillel to leave Babylonia to study with the masters Shemaiah and Abtalim in the land of Israel (*t. Neg.* 1:15). Nevertheless, it is precisely in the peculiar order of the sentences that the solution lies (contrast vv 13, 17, 34). Its import is that because he has become pure, the priest imposes upon him the rite of purification (Wessely 1846). Indeed, following the scall's initial healing (v 34), it began to spread again, whereupon it was declared impure (v 36). Presumably, the person was banished from the camp (vv 45–46) until the affection was certified as healed by the priest (14:2–3a), who then prescribed the necessary purificatory rites (14:3b–32). This interpretation requires that these verses be understood as they appear—in sequence. Verse 37 cannot follow v 34 chronologically, which would imply that the priest must issue two consecutive verdicts of purity. Rather, after a period during which the scall had reappeared and its bearer has been declared impure and banished from the camp, the scall heals; the priest certifies this and enjoins upon him the requisite purificatory rites.

38–39. *Tetters.* A white skin eruption that is faded, is not sunken, and does not have white hair is considered pure and requires no quarantine. The question needs to be asked: Why did not the editor first complete his description of impure cases (vv 42–44) before describing pure cases? Apparently, he ordered his material according to the subject: men and women together first (vv 38–39), then men alone (vv 40–44; *Keter Torah*).

38. *When a man or woman (wĕʾîš ʾô ʾiššâ).* The neutral *ʾādām* 'person' could have been used (as in vv 2, 9), but probably the opening of the previous pericope (v 29) influenced this opening as well.

has (yihyeh). The verb is singular despite its plural subject, "shiny marks." The verb *hāyâ* in the singular frequently takes a plural subject (e.g., Gen 1:14). The possibility also exists that the writer wished to preserve a uniform style in opening each pericope with *kî-yihyeh* (vv 2, 18, 24, 29; Paran 1989).

numerous shiny marks (bĕhārōt bĕhārōt). The *ʾatnaḥ* under the first *beharot* should be disregarded. Repetition at times expresses hyperbole, for instance, *beʾĕrōt beʾĕrōt ḥēmār* 'all asphalt pits' (Gen 14:10); *gēbîm gēbîm* 'nothing but trenches' (2 Kgs 3:16; GKC §123e). The emendation of the second *beharot* to *kēhôt* 'fading', as in v 39, must be rejected, for the evaluation of the affection can only be made by the priest.

39. *dull (kēhôt).* It must be assumed that not only are the marks not shiny but also they are not sunken and do not have white hair; any one of these symptoms would place the eruptions under suspicion of scale disease (v 3).

white (lĕbānôt). This dull white appearance is basically what distinguishes the *bōhaq* 'tetter' from the previous *ṣāraʿat* 'scale disease' group (Radak). The white is that of the white spaces between freckles (Rashi) or the white spots on young boys' faces (Rashi on *b. Nid.* 19a). According to *Keter Torah*, dark *bōhaq* spots are impure; hence white had to be specified lest the conclusion be incorrectly drawn that just as white condemns a lesion in the previous cases, so it does here. Medical authorities are of the opinion that *bōhaq* diagnoses as leukoderma or vitiligo and *ṣāraʿat* as psoriasis and its congeners (Hulse 1975: 99–100; cf. the NOTE below).

a tetter (bōhaq). A hapax but found in rabbinic Hebrew (e.g., *b. Ber.* 58b; *b. Meg.* 24b). It may be related to Akk. *epqu* 'scale disease', as in

LU.SAHAR.SUB.BA = *e-ep-qa-am ma-lu-u;* (Sumerian) "covered with scales" = (Akkadian) "full of scale disease" (*CAD* E, 246). The LXX renders *alphos,* which is defined as "dull white leprosy" (Liddell and Scott 1940: 1.74). Most scientists identify it with either vitiligo or leukoderma (Driver 1963: 575; Hulse 1975: 95; cf. Leibowitz 1976: 422). It is noncontagious, common in tropical and semitropical countries. It is unsightly, but no danger to health (Snaith 1967).

40–44. **Baldness.** Ordinary baldness, whether it starts from the forehead or the crown, is not impure unless it is marked by reddish-white patches.

When a man's hair. But not a woman's, for she is rarely affected by baldness (Ibn Ezra on v 41). The word "hair" is not in the text but must be understood from the use of the root *mrt;* cf. below.

falls out (yimmārēṭ). The verb *mārat* means "pluck, tear out hair" (Isa 50:6; Ezek 29:18; Ezra 9:3; Neh 13:25), though others relate it to the *puʿal môrāṭ,* that is, *mĕmôraṭ* 'polished' (1 Kgs 7:45; Ezek 21:16; cf. also Akk. *marāṭu* 'rub') on the grounds that a bald head looks shiny (Ramban). Ordinary baldness differs from a scall, which also causes baldness, in that in the latter case, the hair first turns yellow before it falls out (v 30) but in baldness, the hairs that fall out are black and healthy (Wessely 1846). Also the scall remains surrounded by hair (v 33; Ramban), and the hair of the scall will regenerate (v 37), whereas baldness is permanent (Rashi on *m. Neg.* 10:10; Ramban).

bald [on the crown] (qērēaḥ). For this meaning, see 2 Kgs 2:23. Akk. *qarruḫu* also has this meaning, but is a loanword from Aramaic *(AHw* 905b). It is clearly related to the noun *qeraḥ* 'ice' (Ps 147:17; Job 6:10; 37:10; 38:29). That the baldness here refers only to that which begins on the crown but not on the forehead, see *m. Neg.* 10:10; *Sipra,* Neg. Tazriaʿ 10:7, and the Notes below.

41. *from the front of his head.* *mippĕ'at pānāyw,* literally, "from the rim of his face," that is, the front slope of the head (Rashi).

bald on the forehead. gibbeaḥ; in other words, the baldness starts from the forehead and not from the crown. According to the rabbis, the temples are also included (*Sipra,* Neg. Tazriaʿ 10:7) in this condition, which they define as follows: "What counts as (i.e., what is the area covered by) forehead-baldness *(gabbahat).* [Lack of hair] from the crown sloping forward over against the hair above [the face]" (*m. Neg.* 10:10). Thus when King Uzziah was struck with scale disease and his forehead shone (2 Chr 26:19), he was technically a *gibbeah,* but one whose affection was impure (v 43). The Akk. cognate *gubbuḫu* also means "bald," but not in the narrower, technical sense of the Hebrew. The word *gbh* occurs in a recently excavated inscription from Tel Ira (Beit-Arieh 1983). It is one of four personal names in a census list *(mpqd),* and it may be the individual's nickname based on his defect, namely, "baldy."

42. *reddish-white (lābān 'ădamdam).* See the Note on v 19. Hulse (1975: 98) identifies it as a form of psoriasis. It is the brightness of this color that renders it impure. For the meaning of *'ădamdam* as "bright red," see the Note on v 19.

on the bald crown (baqqārahat). "What counts as (i.e., what is the area covered by) crown-baldness? [Lack of hair] from the crown sloping backward to the protruding bone of the neck" (*m. Neg.* 10:10). This noun should not be confused with the noun *qorhâ* (21:5; Deut 14:1; Amos 8:10; Isa 3:24), which refers to manmade, self-imposed baldness. *qārahat* is a nominal formation that connotes diseases (cf. Deut 28:22 for some examples). By the same token, scale disease of the forehead is therefore called *gabbahat.*

on his bald crown or forehead (bĕgārahtô 'ô bĕgabbahtô). These two terms are repeated in order to emphasize that the reddish-white patches are not on the fleshy parts of his body and hence boils (v 19) or burns (v 24), but are on the hairy parts of the head.

43. *him ('ōtô).* The antecedent is probably the *nega'* (v 42) 'affection', as in vv 3, 30, 31, 32. The Sam. reads *'ōtāh,* that is, the *ṣāra'at* (v 42). In either case the disease stands for the person (see the NOTE on "affection," v 3).

discolored affection (śĕ'ēt hannega'). The discoloration by itself is neutral (v 2). It is not impure unless it generates raw flesh and turns the hair white (v 10) or, as in this case, it is characterized by reddish-white streaks (Wessely 1846). Perhaps the term *śĕ'ēt* is chosen for stylistic reasons—to balance the *bĕharōt* at the beginning of this pericope (v 38). It has already been observed that the two terms are used synonymously but chiastically in the pericopes on boils (vv 18–23) and on burns (vv 24–28; see the NOTES on "shiny mark," vv 23, 24). The chiastic alternation of the two was also detected in the first pericope on skin affections (vv 2–18). Note the order *śĕ'ēt, baheret* (v 2), *baheret* (v 4), *śĕ'ēt* (v 10). Thus their alternation in this pericope may also have been deliberate.

like scale disease of fleshy skin in appearance (kĕmar'eh ṣāra'at 'ôr bāśār). One way of interpreting the clause is to link it to the opening words of this verse: the priest will examine him as if he had a skin- and not a hair-affection. But the use of *hinnēh* indicates the beginning of a new sentence (see the NOTE on v 6) and the clause in question merely indicates that the appearance—or rather the color—of the affection has to be like the reddish white of boils (v 19) and burns (v 24) in order to require the priest to condemn it. This clause is what differentiates v 43 from v 42: first, the person notices the reddish-white patches on his scalp, but the priest's examination is more precise—the patches must resemble the reddish-white appearance of fleshy-skin scale disease.

44. *has scale disease. ṣārû'a',* literally, "is scale-diseased." The passive participle is used for the first time. It serves as an introduction to the instructions concerning his comportment (vv 45–46). This term is found in the Priestly writings (13:44, 45; 14:3; 22:4; Num 5:2); but it should be noticed that in P (13:44, 45; 14:3) it is used participially, referring to the one who is stricken with scale disease, while in H (22:14; Num 5:2) it is a noun, the technical term for the one who has been so certified. Yet he still is not called a *mĕṣōrā',* P's technical term for a certified bearer of scale disease (14:2), because the priest's certification has not yet taken place (see the NOTES on v 45 and 14:2, 3).

he is impure. The priest shall not fail to pronounce him impure (*ṭāmēʾ hûʾ ṭammēʾ yĕṭammēʾennû hakkōhēn*). The threefold mention of the root *tmʾ* is for staccato emphasis. Lest the priest confuse his condition with baldness, he should be particularly punctilious in examining his patient.

he has an affected head. bĕrōʾšô nigʿô, literally, "the affection is on his head." The sense is, because he has an affected head (Saadiah). The purpose of this added sentence may be to stress the fact that although his affection is treated like fleshy-skin scale disease (v 43b), it is technically a *negaʿ rōʾš* 'a head affection' and should be classified with the *neteq* 'scall' (vv 29–33), which is also labeled "a head affection" (v 29). Thus it is logical that this pericope is placed here, after the *neteq.* Hence, this chapter so far divides into two main sections: *negaʿ ʿôr* 'fleshy skin affections' (vv 1–28) and *negaʿ rōʾš* 'head affections' (vv 29–44). To be sure, vv 38–39, dealing with pure tetters on the body, are, in this classification, out of place. But, as observed already (see the NOTE on vv 38–39), the editor desired to list first all skin diseases affecting both men and women (vv 1–39) before the ones concerning only men (vv 40–44).

45–46. The Comportment of a Certified Carrier of Scale Disease. He must rend his clothes, dishevel his hair, veil his mouth, warn persons in his ambience that he is impure, and isolate himself outside the camp. These and salient features of his purification are striking reminders of his similitude to the corpse-contaminated person. Both rend their clothes, dishevel their hair (10:4), contaminate by overhang (see the NOTE on 14:47; Num 19:14), and are sprinkled (14:7, Num 19:19) with spring water (14:6; Num 19:17) containing cedar, hyssop, and crimson yarn (14:6; Num 19:6). These differences should not be overlooked: The corpse-contaminated person does not veil his mouth, warn others of his presence, or offer sacrifices for his purification (contrast 14:1–32), but uniquely requires the ashes of a red cow (Num 19:1–12). The quantitative (purificatory) and qualitative (theological) comparison will be made in chap. 15, COMMENTS F and G.

45. *As for the person stricken with scale disease. wĕhaṣṣārûaʿ ʾăšer bô han-negaʿ,* literally, "As for the scale-diseased person in whom there is an affection." This lengthy circumlocution is necessary because the *ṣārûaʿ* here is no longer the same as the one in the previous verse. For now he has been certified as a bearer of scale disease. Hence, the clause needs to be added "in him there is an affection." That is, the *ṣārûaʿ* of v 44 is now the certified *ṣārûaʿ* of v 45. To be sure, the circumlocution could have been avoided by using the technical term *mĕṣōrāʿ.* But this term is reserved for the purificatory period (chap. 14). Besides, it was important to qualify the *ṣārûaʿ* of v 44 by the additional clause "in whom there is an affection" to indicate that henceforth we are dealing not with the case of an affected scalp but with every incidence of scale disease. As his scale disease is now confirmed, his appearance changes, as follows: "The *mĕṣōrāʿ* who is quarantined differs from the *mĕṣōrāʿ* who is certified impure only in disheveled hair and rent garments" (*m. Meg.* 1:7; cf. *m. Neg.* 8:8). The rabbis also define the difference in this way: "one whose scale disease requires healing (14:3) and excludes one whose scale disease is such in virtue not of [requiring] healing but seven days [of isolation]" (*b. Meg.* 8b).

rent (pĕrûmîm). The purpose is for mourning *(Tg. Ps.-J.; Tg. Neof.).* There exists the possibility that this term means "rent [at the seams]," in contrast with *qĕrûʿîm* "rent [anywhere]" *(Keter Torah).* Yet the rabbis equate the two terms *(Sipra,* Neg. Tazriaʿ 12:6). Cf. the discussion of this term in the NOTE on 10:6; cf. also 21:10.

disheveled (pārûaʿ). This word is given a detailed discussion in the NOTE on 10:6 (cf. also the NOTE on 21:10), where the three most accepted translations— "untrimmed," "uncovered," and "disheveled"—are evaluated. The last rendering, justified in the NOTE on 10:6 and accepted here, is affirmed by the rabbis (Rabbi Eliezer in *Sipra,* Neg. Tazriaʿ 12:6; the Tgs. to 10:6; Ezek 34:6), by analogy to the unbraiding of the hair of the suspected adulteress (*t. Sota.* 1:7; *Tg. Ps.-J.* to Num 5:15) and to the Nazirite who had to let his hair grow wild *(Sipra,* Nasoʾ 25).

he shall cover (yaʿteh). With his clothes, according to Ibn Ezra, probably basing himself on the rabbinic claim that he lowers the mantle over his head like a mourner "in the manner of the Arabs" (*b. Moʿed Qat.* 24a; cf. *Sipra,* Neg. Tazriaʿ 12:7; *Tg. Onq.; Tg. Ps.-J.*). Elsewhere in Scripture the verb *ʿātâ* 'cover' is found with the following objects: cloak (1 Sam 28:14), clothing (Ps 109:19), light (Ps 104:2), passion (Isa 59:17), and shame (Ps 71:13).

moustache (śāpām). On the basis of the term *śĕpāmô* (2 Sam 15:25), Ibn Ezra claims that the *mem* is part of the root. This is disputed by Tur-Sinai (1960b: 7605b n. 2), who argues that the *mem* is affixed like *pidyôm* (Num 3:49) and the proper nouns *gēršōm* and *milkōm* (cf. GKC §85t), hence a form of *śāpâ* 'lip' or 'moustache' (so rendered by the LXX in 2 Sam 19:25). *Tg. Ps.-J.* translates "His mouth will be covered." But the idiom *ʿāśâ ʾet-śĕpāmô* (2 Sam 19:25) can only mean "trim his moustache" (for *ʿāśâ* 'trim' cf. Deut 21:12).

The expression *ʿātâ śāpām* is found again in Ezek 24:17, 22, where it refers to a rite of mourning (a rite still practiced by Babylonian Jews and their Arab neighbors during the rabbinic period, *b. Moʿed Qat.* 24a; see the NOTE above) and in Mic 3:7, where it is used metaphorically for the time in which people will be speechless from humiliation (cf. Saadiah).

The reason for this covering rite is explained as "probably to make himself unrecognizable to the mysterious powers that hover round him even as they do round those who mourn" (Noth 1965). But the prescription speaks of covering the upper lip (or mouth). That he also covers his eyes and a good part of his face is clearly incidental. More to the point is Ibn Ezra's comment that his breath should not contaminate. This too is what the rabbis must have had in mind: "R. Yohanan said: It is prohibited to go four cubits to the east of a leper. R. Simeon b. Laqish said: Even a hundred cubits. They did not really differ: the one who said four cubits referred to a time when there is no wind blowing, whereas the one who said a hundred cubits referred to a time when a wind is blowing" (*Midr. Lev. Rab.* 16:3). The Qumran sectaries go farther by specifying *WRḤWQ MN HṬHRH ŠTYM ʿSRH ʾMH BDBRW ʾLYW* 'He shall be [at least] twelve cubits distant from [food of] purity when speaking with him [any person]' (4QThr A1:1–2; Milgrom forthcoming B). "R. Mana would walk with people affixed with boils. R. Abaye said to him: Do not walk to the east of him but to the west of him" (*y. B. Bat.* 3:9). As the prevailing winds came from the west, the rabbis were obviously concerned to prevent the breath of one who was in mourning or afflicted with scale disease from impinging on anyone. We are dealing here once again with ritual impurity powerful enough to be airborne and to affect persons and objects (but not sancta) without coming into direct contact with them. But the Priestly system of impurity limits airborne impurity to persons only when they find themselves under the same roof (see chap. 4, COMMENT C and chap. 15, COMMENT F). Contamination by breath is not incorporated into the Priestly system and, hence, must represent folk belief.

The rabbis' warning about distancing oneself greatly to the east of a scale-diseased person was anticipated by the sectaries of Qumran, who prescribed that the dwellings of such persons should not only be placed outside the community, in conformance with Scripture (v 40), but to the east (11QT 46:16–18). Yadin adds the suggestion that such a practice explains why the house of Simeon the leper, where Jesus stayed, was located in Bethany (Mark 14:3), located to the southeast of Jerusalem (1983: 1.305). It is certainly not out of place to point to the comparative evidence from ancient Persia: the Zoroastrian priest wore a piece of gauze before his mouth when he came near the sacred fire lest he soil it by his breath (Carnoy, *ERE* 10.492; Boyce 1975: 309). Finally, one should note that the rites prescribed for the scale-diseased person are precisely the same as for the corpse-contaminated one. The association of scale disease and, indeed, all severe impurity with death is discussed in detail in COMMENT A below and in chap. 15, COMMENT G.

and he shall call out, "Impure! Impure!" (wĕṭāmēʾ ṭāmēʾ yiqrāʾ). So that people will withdraw from him (*Sipra*, Neg. Tazriaʿ 12:7; *b. Moʿed Qaṭ.* 5b), lest he contaminate them by touch or by overhang, according to the Priestly system (see chap. 15, COMMENT F), or by his breath, according to popular belief (see the NOTE on "moustache," above). *Tg. Neof.* paraphrases: "He calls out, 'Withdraw from the impure lest you become impure.'" The practice of certified scale-diseased persons to ward off oncomers by pointing to their impurity is paralleled by this poignant picture of the Jerusalemites after their city was destroyed: "They wandered blindly through the streets, defiled with blood, so that no one was able to touch their garments. 'Away! Unclean!' people shouted at them, 'Away! Away! Touch not!'" (Lam 4:15a). Here, however, the call has been reversed: instead of the warning being issued by the self-diseased persons it originated from bypassers—emphasizing the extent to which the Jerusalemites had become repugnant. Later commentators softened the harshness of the ostracism, for example, "He thereby informs others of his sorrow so that they implore mercy on his behalf" (b. Nid. 66a); he must call out because being garbed like a mourner others may approach him to offer consolation (Wessely 1846). The fear of being in the proximity of one who has scale disease is apparent from the statements in the Avesta that a prayer should be recited upon sighting such a person (Dillmann and Ryssel 1897).

46. *as long as (kol-yĕmê ʾăšer)*. A relative conjunction preceded by a noun in construct is treated as a preposition (Gen 39:20; Num 9:19; Deut 23:5; Joüon 1923: §129q; GKC §130c).

He shall be impure. . . . He is impure (yiṭmāʾ . . . ṭāmēʾ hûʾ). The imperfect is used because it is modified by the statement that the complaint is limited. It is followed by a repetition of the same word, but as an adjective, without qualifications: the impurity is indefinite; there is no telling how long it will last (see the NOTE on v 14).

It is significant that the text does not describe the effect of the scale-diseased person on other persons and things as it does in the cases of the *zāb/zābâ* and the menstruant (chap. 15). This is clearly attributable to his exclusion from the community; he will be in total isolation (D. Wright). The rabbis, however, equate him with the *zāb/zābâ*, menstruant, and parturient in the effect of his impurity when one touches him (m. Zabim 5:6; cf. t. Zabim 5:3).

he shall dwell apart (bādād yēšēb). His banishment is described graphically (and realistically) in a Babylonian *kudurru* (boundary) inscription: "As a prisoner driven out of the gate of the city, forced to dwell outside its walls . . . so that its citizens do not approach him" (Nougayrol 1948: 207). The rabbis go farther, interpreting *bādād* as *bilĕbād* 'alone'; in other words, he must dwell apart even from bearers of other impurities (Tgs.; *Sipra*, Neg. Tazriaʿ 12:13; *Sipre* Num. 1; *Midr. Lev. Rab.* 16:3), but not from other bearers of the same impurity, to judge from the evidence of the narratives (2 Kgs 7:3–10; Luke 17:11–19). The sectaries of Qumran affirm this view explicitly: *BDD LKWL ḤṬMʾYM YŠB* 'Of all of the impurity bearers he shall dwell apart' (4QThr A1:1; Milgrom forthcoming B). That scale disease requires total isolation is not due to its ostensible physical contagion, which must be emphatically denied (see COMMENT A below), but for the ritual—but not medical—reason that its impurity is contagious under the same roof, a postulate not only explicit in the rabbinic system (m. Kelim 1:4; m. Neg. 13:7; cf. Jos., Con Ap. 1.281) but implicit in the Priestly biblical system (see chap. 15, COMMENT F). In this regard the scale-diseased person bears the same degree of impurity as the corpse (Jos., Ant. 3.264; Sipre Num. 105; b. Yebam. 103b).

The question needs to be addressed: Why banish the *mĕṣōrāʿ* if his disease is not contagious; what difference does it make if he is ritually contagious and even contaminates his whole community? The answer rests upon the distinctive virulence of his impurity to contaminate by overhang. If he were to remain in the community, people might be with him under the same roof and be unaware of it and then enter the sanctuary or eat sacred food. And it is this fatal contact between the impure and sacred that had to be avoided at all costs. Hence the Priestly legislators banished the *mĕṣōrā*ᶜ. But they had no such fear concerning the *zāb/zābâ* (chap. 15), for he or she could not contaminate by overhang (see chap. 15, COMMENT F).

The rabbis remark homiletically that the total isolation of the scale-diseased person is the terminal result of his refusal to repent: "The Omnipresent judges the person with compassion. Lo, they (plagues) come on his house: if he repents it requires dismantling; and if not, it requires demolishing (14:33–53). Lo, they appear on his clothing: [if] he repents, it requires tearing; and if not, it requires burning (vv 47–58). Lo, they appear on his body: [if] he repents, he repents; and if not 'he shall dwell apart; his dwelling shall be outside the camp' (v 46b)" (*t. Neg.* 6:7). Because the rabbis attribute his disease to his slanderous tongue (see COMMENT B below), they moralize further: "He separated man from his wife, a man from his neighbor, therefore said the Torah: 'He shall dwell apart'" (*b. ʿArak.* 16b). Qumran's sectaries take it for granted that the scale-diseased person has sinned and that he must repent: *YḤL LHPYL ʾT TḤ[NW]NW* 'He shall begin to lay his plea' (4QThr A1:1; Milgrom forthcoming B).

his dwelling shall be outside the camp. mihûṣ lammaḥăneh môšābô (see Num 5:2–5; 12:10); and outside the city (2 Kgs 7:3). Yet, as the later citation indicates and as the rabbis affirm, he could roam the country freely (*Sipre* Zuṭa to Num 5:2). Nonetheless, the Qumran sectaries planned to confine him to separate dwellings outside the city (11QT 46:16–18; 48:14–15; 4QThr A₁:2).

When King Uzziah was stricken with scale disease, he was confined to the *bêt haḥopšît* (2 Kgs 15:5; 2 Chr 26:21). On the meaning of this term, D. P. Wright supplies the following comment:

The interpretation of the term *byt hḥpšyt* enjoys no general consensus. For over fifty years (since Virolleaud 1931: 224) scholars have usually drawn upon the parallel Ugaritic term *bthptt* (*VT* 51.vii.7; 67.v.15) to help clarify the Hebrew. Unfortunately, the Ugaritic term (generally divided *bt hptt*) due to the Hebrew, but cf. Gaster 1946f: 292, who divides it *b-thptt*) is just as obscure as the Hebrew term. All that can be said with certainty is that it is the term for the netherworld. The attempts at interpreting the Hebrew term can be sorted out into six categories: (1) *hpšyt* is an abstract nominal formation related to the adjective *ḥopšî* "free". Radak (ad loc.) understands it to be a place where the king stayed having been released or freed from his royal service (similarly Lohfink 1982: 125). Montgomery (1941: 321; cf. Montgomery and Gehman 1951: 448) perceives it more abstractly as "'house (= state?) of exemption', i.e., from royal duties". (2) *byt hḥpšyt*, still connected with *ḥopšî* or other related Semitic words, is a special place for lepers. Ralbag (on 2 Kgs 15:5) says the place was called such because lepers were secluded and thus free from contact with other people. Loretz (1976: 129–31; cf. 1977: 165), connecting it with Akkadian *ḫupšu*, a member of one of the lesser social orders' (*CAD*, H, p. 2419), interprets both the Ugaritic and Hebrew terms as '*Haus der Ḥupšu-Mannschaft*'. The place where these lower classes of society lived is applied to the underworld in the Ugaritic texts. In the Bible, according to him, a *ḫupšu* house continued to exist where lepers stayed after the *ḫupšu* class died out. Cassuto (1971: 23; 1954: cols. 75f.) refers to Ps 88:6 and Job 3:19 to show that there was a tradition that the dead were considered 'free'. Hence the Ugaritic and Hebrew terms designate the underworld 'house of freedom' meaning 'house of the dead'. The Hebrew term was applied to the place lepers lived since they were considered as dead (cf. *b. Nid.* 64b; *b. Sanh.* 47a; Num 12:13; Feldman 1977: 37f.; for this view see Gurewicz (1963: 22). W. Rudolph (1955: 284; 1977: 418) treats the term in Hebrew and Ugaritic as euphemisms for 'house of isolation' (cf. Morgenstern 1937–38: 1 n. 1). (3) Klostermann, with J. Gray following (1970: 618 n. b; 619f.; Gray does not connect the Hebrew term with the Ugaritic, see 1952: 53; 1957: 46), emends the text to *bêtōh ḥopšît* 'his house freely' (i.e., released from obligations). (4) Albright (1934: 131, and n. 162) connects the Hebrew with Arabic *ḫbt* 'below, base' and interprets it as 'subterranean house, basement'. (5) Grelot (1964) seeks to establish two separate Hebrew roots, *ḥpš* I ('free') and *ḥpš* II. For *ḥpš* II (attested for him in *byt hḥpšyt* and in Ps 88:6) he proposes two possible meanings. The first is derived from Arabic *ḫabata/ḫabutu* which denotes the idea of corruption or impurity. Both the Hebrew and Ugaritic terms connected with this second root mean 'place of putrefaction, rottenness'. (6) Grelot alternately connects the Hebrew term with *ḥbš* 'bind, tie up, incarcerate'. Thus Hebrew *byt hḥpšyt* means 'place of confinement'. He admits that the Ugaritic *bthptt* cannot be adapted to this interpretation for phonological reasons. (We note in passing that popular Jewish tradition called the burial cave of the Bene Hazir in the Kidron Valley the *bêt haḥopšît*, see Avigad 1956: 4.) (1984: 368 n. 25; cf. 1987: 174–76 n. 25)

Unfortunately, no etymology can be made to determine the location of this house, in particular, whether it was located inside or outside the city. One suspects that it was the former case. First, Chronicles specifies that Uzziah was cut off from the house of the Lord (2 Chr 26:21). Because the Temple was the royal chapel (see Amos 7:13) and adjoined the royal palace (Ezek 43:7–8), then what is implied is that Uzziah was banished from the royal compound but not from the the city of Jerusalem. Furthermore, we are told that he was buried "with his fathers in the city of David" (2 Kgs 15:7). According to Chronicles, he was interred "in the burial field of the kings, because, they said, he was a scale-diseased person" (2 Chr 26:23). These verses are not in contradiction, for "the burial of the kings" was most likely adjacent to the royal sepulcher and, hence, also inside the old city (Yeivin 1971), a precedent for which would have been established by Uzziah's predecessors Jehoram and Joash, who were buried "in the city of David but not in the Tombs of the Kings" (2 Chr 21:20; 24:25; cf. 28:27, Ahaz). If, then, Uzziah was allowed to remain in the city in his death, all the more would one expect that there would have been no objection had he remained in the city during his life—isolated, yes, but not banished beyond the city walls. Strikingly, Uzziah's fate, that he had to abdicate his throne (with Jotham as coregent) and leave the palace, was anticipated in a *kudurru*, a Babylonian boundary inscription "may (Sin) cause them to lose their position in the temple or palace" (Nougayrol 1948: 207).

47–58. Fabrics. In semitropical climates dampness gives rise to mold or fungus, which affects and destroys fabrics (Ralbag; Snaith 1967). These infections resemble those on humans and are treated similarly. Two seven-day periods of quarantine are prescribed. If the fungus or mold has not spread after the first seven days, the garment is washed and quarantined for another seven days. If it still has not spread, the affected part is torn out and the fabric may be reused. If, however, the affection has spread or it has failed to fade, the fabric must be burned.

The question needs to be asked: Why was the pericope on fabric affections attached to those of the body? Indeed, its very structure, bearing a separate summation (v 59), and the fact that it interrupts and jars the flow of chaps. 13 and 14 (see the NOTE on v 59) indicate that it is clearly an editorial interpolation. Why, then, was it included at all? The medieval commentators conjecture that there is a likelihood that scale disease of the body will spread to the clothing (Abravanel) or that "scale disease" of fabrics is an unnatural phenomenon; it occurs only in the land of Israel as a warning to the owners of the garments to mend their ways (Maim., "The Impurity of Scale Disease" 16.10; cf. *t. Neg.* 6:7, cited above). Nevertheless, the juxtaposition of the two pericopes on affections of persons and fabrics is most likely due to their strikingly similar symptoms. Both "are abnormal surface conditions that disfigure the outside of the skin or garment. Both cause the surface to flake or peel" (Wenham 1979).

Another presupposition of this pericope is that a moldy garment in no way reflects on the character of its bearer; otherwise sacrifices or some other rite would have been prescribed for the owner of the garment, so that he could make expiation for his suspected wrong. The nexus between malady and sin has been severed. The malady is diagnosed objectively—scientifically, if you will. The extension of scale disease from persons to garments (and to house, 14:33–53) is artificially drawn, far removed from its original basis in which the law, that every natural disorder is the result of man's willful disobedience, inexorably reigns (see also the NOTE on "and I inflict," 14:34).

The rabbis, to be sure, maintain the sin–punishment syndrome here, claiming that all forms of ṣāraʿat are but a concatenation of plagues visited upon the unrepentant sinner: "He would come to the priest, and the priest says to him, 'My son, go and examine yourself and return [from your evil ways]'. For affections come only because of gossip, and scale disease comes only to those who are arrogant" (*t. Neg.* 6:7; cf. *Pesiq. R.* 17; the question is fully treated in the NOTE on "he shall dwell apart," v 46).

47. *mold disease (nega* ṣāra'at). The term denoting scale disease is now applied to fabrics. Because, however, the affection is due to mold (or fungus), it is here and throughout this pericope rendered "mold disease."

a fabric (beged). This word undeniably refers to clothing, but is also generic for fabrics (e.g., covers for the sancta: Num 4:6–9, 11–13; bedcovers: 1 Sam 19:13; 1 Kgs 1:1; saddle cloth: Ezek 27:20). The rabbis also include curtains and sails (*m. Neg.* 11:11).

wool or linen (ṣemer 'ô . . . pištîm). What about other materials? As Ibn Ezra answers (at v 52), "Scripture speaks [of fabrics] that are in contemporaneous use," and for corroboration he cites "when you see the ass of your enemy prostrate . . ." (Exod 23:5), which would also apply to other beasts of burden such as the mule or horse. In support of his observation it could be added that in the similar law in Deuteronomy, written for a later age when more animals were in domestic use, the text makes sure to include the ass, ox, sheep—and even garments (Deut 22:1–4). That nearly all fabrics in biblical days were made of wool or linen is attested by the frequent reference to them as a generic for all fabrics (e.g., Deut 22:11; Hos 2:7, 11; Prov 31:3). This also holds in Israel's environs: Greek authors know only of wool and linen fabrics (Voss, cited by Dillmann and Ryssel 1897) and the same appears to be the case in Egypt (cf. Herod. 2.81).

48. *in the warp (bišětî).* For this rendering, see the LXX. This is also its meaning in rabbinic Hebrew (*m. 'Erub.* 1:10; *m. Ketub.* 5:9; *m. Kelim* 17:2; *m. Ohol.* 13:6; *m. Neg.* 11:4, 8). Its extended connotations are "vertical" (e.g., *m. Miqw.* 6:9) and "length" (*t. Ţohar.* 10:4). Its Semitic cognates, Akk. *šatû* III *(AHw)*, Ug. *stt* (from *sty*), and Aramaic *šětā', sětê,* carry the more general meaning "weave." Its etymology is unknown, but Ibn Ezra conjectures (on Isa 20:4) that it it is related to the word for "foundations, buttocks," *šēt* (Isa 20:4); *šātôt,* pl. (2 Sam 10:4; Ps 11:3). It is most likely a technical term that spread over the ancient world, for example, Greek *histis;* Latin *sto,* referring to the standing weaver's beam (Tur-Sinai 1960a: 7496a n. 2).

[in the] woof (be'ēreb). So rendered by the LXX and the rabbis (citations noted above). It refers to the horizontal action of the shuttle by which the thread weaves in and out of the threads of the warp. Perhaps it is related to Akk. *erēbu,* Ug. *ʕrb* 'enter' (Levine 1987). Ibn Ezra suggests that it is associated with the noun *'ēreb* 'mixture' (e.g., Exod 12:38; Neh 13:3) because it "mixes," that is, entwines itself with the warp.

or [in the warp or woof] ('ô). The "or" at the beginning of the verse makes it clear that the warp and woof must be distinguished from the fabric discussed in the previous verse. This distinction is sustained throughout the pericope (vv 49, 50, 52, 53, 57, 58). Most commentators agree. They add that the warp and woof threads could not be in the loom else they would contaminate each other. Hence, they claim, the reference must be to the yarns that are of different texture and thickness for the warp and woof and which await being placed on the loom. Indeed, support for this view can be mustered from the rabbinic notion that the coils of thread for the warp and woof are capable of contracting mold disease (*m. Neg.* 11:8). Driver and White take an alternative view, that "it is a very common thing for the woof of cloth to be so thick, that a spot on it would not touch the warp-thread at all, and *vice versa*" (1898: 77). They are right. Their observation is fully confirmed by Lillian Elliot of Berkeley, a noted weaver and authority on weaving, who specifies even further that the warp and woof can vary in three ways—in thickness, dye, and spin—so that the mold on the one will most likely run along similar threads and not transfer to the others. Thus, the warp and woof in this pericope refer to their respective threads on the loom.

of the linen or the wool (lappištîm wĕlaṣṣāmer). The order is reversed to create a chiasm with the previous verse. Ḥazzequni suggests that its purpose is to indicate that here linen is listed first because in yarn linen is more expensive, but in v 47 and thereafter in the pericope wool is first because we are dealing with garments, and those of wool are more expensive than linen. Nevertheless, the likelihood is that the chiastic arrangement is due to purely literary, stylistic considerations. Rashi points out that the prefixed *waw* must be translated "or" else the text might imply a fabric woven of linen *and* wool, a forbidden mixture (19:19; Deut 22:11; cf. chap. 7, COMMENT B).

in a skin (bĕʿôr). The rabbis would exclude raw skins from this category because, in their system, a substance must be usable to become susceptible to impurity (see the NOTE on "that can be put to use," 11:32). Thus, in order to be functional, the skins must be treated. Presumably, they would distinguish this term from the one that follows, "anything made in skin" (and from "any article of skin," v 49) by claiming that the latter would refer to manufactured items requiring cutting and shaping, such as water skins, in contrast to the former, which would apply to tanned and stretched but uncut and unshaped hides used for tent skins, rugs, or bedding (cf. *Sipra*, Neg. Tazriaʿ 13:12). One wonders, however, whether susceptibility to impurity is of the same order as susceptibility to mold. Impurity is invisible to the eye and a product of the postulates of an abstract ritualistic system. By contrast, mold is highly visible and attacks substances without regard for theoretical postulates. What, indeed, is the law if mold breaks out in raw skins? Would it not create as much concern as an infected tent skin? Thus, the likelihood is that "skin" here refers to untreated skins, those which are perhaps stored on a person's property awaiting treatment.

anything made of skin. bĕkol-mĕleʾket ʿôr, namely, any functional skin, such as one for containing liquids (cf. Judg 4:19; 2 Kgs 8:15). In this pericope, *mĕlāʾkâ* is synonymous with *kĕlî* 'article' (see below, v 49). The technical usage of *mĕlāʾkâ* has been discussed (see the NOTE on "that can be put to use," 11:32).

49. *or [in] the skin . . . or in any article of skin (ʾô bāʿôr ʾô bĕkol-kĕlî-ʿôr).* A distinction is made between skins and articles of skin. In the rest of the pericope only one term will occur, the word "skin" by itself (v 56) or skin modified by either *mĕlāʾkâ* (v 51) or *kĕlî* (vv 52, 53, 57, 58, 59)—in keeping with the stylistic tendency of the Priestly texts to state the full terms at the outset and to telescope them in the rest of the pericope.

article. kĕlî, meaning a manufactured implement (cf. the NOTE on 11:32).

bright green (yĕraqraq). It has been demonstrated that this adjectival form bespeaks intensification (cf. the NOTE on "reddish-white," v 19). So too maintain the rabbis: "Garments contract impurity by the greenest of green and by the reddest of red" (*m. Neg.* 11:4); cf. *Sipra*, Neg. Tazriaʿ 14:2). The exact shade is disputed: "R. Eliezer says: 'Like wax and like a gourd'. Sumkhos says: 'Like the wing of a peacock and like the branches of a palm tree' " (*t. Neg.* 1:5). It has been doubted whether the ancient Near East distinguished between yellow and green. In fact, B. Landsberger prefers that *yārôq* be translated "yellowish" rather than "green" (1967: 139–73). More likely, the fact that the word derives from *yereq* 'vegetation' probably means that it is associated with all of the chromatic qualities that can be observed in the world of vegetation, which, indeed, varies between yellow and green (Pines 1971). Nonetheless, I have rendered it "green/ bright green" here not because it is more accurate but in order to distinguish it from *ṣāhôb*, which has arbitrarily has been assigned the color "yellow" (see the NOTE on v 30).

bright red (ʾădamdam). "Sumkhos says: . . . what is the reddest of the red? Like the finest crimson that is in the sea" (*t. Neg.* 1:6). For the demonstration that the word means "bright red," see the NOTE on v 19.

It shall be shown (wĕhorʾâ ʾet). The *nota accusativi*, *ʾet*, meaning "to," is found in exceptional situations, and in those the *ʾet* appears before the second object of a doubly transitive verb that is allowed to take the accusative when the verb is in the passive (Job 7:3; cf. Exod 25:40; 26:30; Joüon 1923: §128c; GKC §121c).

51. *malignant (mamʾeret).* The etymology is obscure. Arab. *maʾira* means "break open" (of a wound): (BDB). Rashi, recognizing that the root is *mʾr* (see also Ibn Ezra), finds its meaning in *sillôn mamʾir* (Ezek 28:24), which he regards as synonymous with the following phrase: *wĕqôṣ makʾib* 'lacerating thorns', thus leading to the translation "poignant" (i.e., "prickly, piercing"). Here he follows the rendering of *Tg. Onq.*, *mĕḥazrāʾ*, from *ḥîzrāʾ* 'thorn' (*b. Ber.* 8a; *b. B. Meṣ.* 103b; cf. Ramban) (But the better texts read *mĕḥasrāʾ* 'defective'; see Sperber 1959). The LXX and *Tg. Neof.* (margin) render "persistent, incurable," whereas Saadiah speaks for "destructive." The rabbis relate it to the noun *mĕʾērâ* 'curse' (*Sipra*, Tazriaʿ 14:11), though as the latter stems from a different root (*ʾrr*), the rabbinic comment is intended as a midrash. The word must clearly be associated

with *nôšenet* 'chronic' (v 11) because it occupies the same place in the diagnosis of those respective affections. The rendering of the LXX and *Tg. Neof.* is, therefore, preferable. It should be noted that this term is used only for fabrics and houses (14:44), but never for persons. The reason may be that the former must be destroyed whereas the latter, by the grace of God, may be healed (Paran 1989). The Qumran sectaries, however, apply the term to persons (4QDᵃ 5).

it is impure (ṭāmēʾ hûʾ). Because the same term is used for scale disease, the conclusion must be drawn that affected garments pollute in the same manner as affected persons (*m. Neg.* 13:8; *t. Neg.* 7:6; *b. Yebam.* 103b).

52. *whether in wool or linen (baṣṣemer ʾô bappištîm).* The *bet* means "of," that is, made of (Rashi), equivalent to *mem.*

shall be burned. wĕśārap, literally, "And he shall burn." Elliger (1966) favors the active, literal rendering on the grounds that if it were impersonal, it would have been written as a plural, for example, *wĕkibbĕsû* 'be washed' (v 54). But the latter word is translated by the LXX as a singular (i.e., *wĕkibbes*), and it may well be original (see the Note on v 54). Besides, the change of number is quite frequent in P (e.g., 14:41, 42), and no semantic distinction should be attributed to this fluctuation. Finally, the end of the verse explicitly uses the passive, *bāʾēš tiśśārēp* 'it shall be destroyed by fire', which clearly indicates that the burning may be performed by anyone.

The fabric is burned in the camp instead of being dumped outside because, being organic, it can be totally destroyed and, hence, will not continue to contaminate like condemned but indestructible building materials (D. Wright).

53. This verse is the exact reverse of v 51a, which underscores the equivalence of *lĕkōl ʾăšer-yēʿăśeh hāʿôr limĕlāʾkâ* 'for whatever function the skin serves' (v 51) and *kol-kĕlî-ʿôr* 'any article of skin' (v 53), namely, worked, manufactured skins. The absence of unqualified *ʿôr* 'skin' in these two verses as opposed to vv 48 and 49 is due to telescoping (see the Note on "or [in] the skin," v 49).

54. *the affected material (ʾăšer-bô hannegaʿ).* According to the rabbis only the affected area and its immediate surroundings needs to be washed *(Tg. Ps.-J.; Sipra,* Neg. Tazriaʿ 15:5). Yet the equivalent phrase, *ʾăšer-yihyeh bô hannegaʿ* 'which contains the affection' (v 52), surely pertains to the entire skin because it is nearly impossible to burn out just the affected spot. Then, too, if only the affected area were intended the text would have resorted to the simple *hannegaʿ* 'the affection'. Finally, the suffix of the verb that follows, *wĕhisgîrô* 'and he shall quarantine', can only refer to the entire fabric.

shall . . . be washed. wĕkibbĕsû, literally, "And they shall wash." The verb clearly has to be understood as an impersonal passive, to wit, anyone may perform the washing (*Sipra,* Neg. Tazriaʿ 15:5). This washing is not a ritual, it is a physical cleansing; the residue of the affection must be completely eradicated. This distinction is neatly acknowledged by *Tg. Onq.,* which renders *wîhawrûn* here but *wĕyiṣṭabba* in v 58, where the washing is clearly a ritual (for details, see the Note on v 58). According to the rabbis, the detergent comprises seven ingredients (*m. Nid.* 9:6; *b. Sanh.* 49b; *b. Zebaḥ.* 95a). The LXX reads this verb as a singular, *wĕkibbes*, which is what should be expected in view of *wĕśārap* (v 52) as well as the verbs in the singular farther on (e.g., 16:4, 5). If so, then the error can be easily accounted for: the next verb, *wĕhisgîrô*, was misread as a plural, *wĕhisgîrû*. But because, in the next chapter, active verbs frequently alternate between singular and plural, yet are understood as impersonal passives (14:4, 5, 30, 40, 41, 42), no decision can be given.

55. *after the affected material has been washed.* *'aḥărê hukkabbēs 'et-han-nega'*, that is, after the second quarantine at the end of the second week. The usual vocalization *hukkabbēs* is generally accepted as a *hothpa'al* passive of the *hithpa'el* (e.g., *hotpāqdû*, Num 1:47; *huṭṭammā'*, Deut 24:14; *huddašnâ*, Isa 34:6; GKC §54h), but if so, then the *taw* has anomalously been assimilated into the *kap*. Wessely (1846) takes it as a combination of *hoph'al* and *hithpa'el*. The *nota accusativa*, *'et*, following a passive has been noted earlier (see the NOTE on "It shall be shown," v 49) and will be repeated in the next verse (for examples of this phenomenon, see GKC §121a, b).

its color ('ênô). The Sam. has *'ênāyw* but it is clearly wrong, for in its other occurrences (vv 5, 37) it is the object of *'āmad* and its referent is probably the priest (see the NOTES on vv 5, 37). Here, however, it is the object of *hāpak* 'turn, change' (cf. vv 4, 10, 13, 16, 17, 20, 25), and the only rendering that makes sense is "color," which in the Hebrew is always singular (e.g., Exod 10:5; Num 11:7; Ezek 1:4, 7).

has not changed its color and . . . has not spread. It is all the more impure if it either spreads (v 51) or changes its color, unless the color fades (v 56). Thus fabrics are subject to a severer law than persons. Symptoms in persons that do not change are signs of purity (vv 4, 6, 21, 23, 28, 32, 37), but in fabrics they are condemned as impure. The reason may be that infections in fabric may spread inward without spreading on the surface (Malbim).

You shall destroy it [by fire] (tiśrĕpennû). The second-person singular appears here unexpectedly (and again in vv 57, 58). But who is the subject? The priest is the most logical person; it is inconceivable that he would leave the scene before the affected article is burned. But the priest is addressed in the third person (vv 55c, 56a)! Nor can it be the owner of the garment, for the chapter itself is addressed to Moses and Aaron but not to the Israelites (v 1). Besides, the owner cannot be depended on to destroy his garment without priestly supervision. The antecedent of the pronominal suffix is clearly the entire article, which in case it contains a malignant mold (v 52) is totally burned (see also the NOTE on the word in v 57).

a fret (pĕḥetet). This hapax has been variously interpreted. Deriving it from *paḥat* 'pit' (2 Sam 17:9; 18:17; cf. Rashi), some claim that "it appears sunken" (*Sipra*, Neg. Tazria' 15:5; cf. *Tg. Neof.*), that it is "a deeply ingrained mark" (LXX). Others rely on rabbinic Hebrew *paḥat*, which means either "hollow out, dig" (e.g., *m. Beṣa* 4:3; *m. Miqw.* 4:5), yielding "perforated, eaten out" or "diminish, lessen" (e.g., m. Pesah. 10:1; m. Meg. 4:1), yielding "diminished, reduced" (Ibn Ezra). The exact meaning has yet to be determined.

on its inner side or on its outer side. bĕqāraḥtô 'ô bĕgabbaḥtô, literally, "on its crown or on its forehead." Clearly an extended use of the terms for scalp disease (cf. v 42). But what do these terms mean when applied to fabrics? The following are some of the suggestions: "on the beaten, rough side or on the hairy, smooth side" (Tg. Ps.-J.); "on the threadbare part or the new part" (Tg. Onq.; Sipra, Tazria' 15:9); "on the inner ('kidney') part or on the worn part" (Tg. Neof.). Maimonides (on m. Neg. 11:11) explains, "bĕqāraḥtô refers to old clothes on which the tufts have been smoothed out (niqrĕḥû), whereas bĕgabbaḥtô refers to new clothes on which the tufts are still elevated (gĕbōhîm [gbh = gbḥ])." Saadiah adds that it refers to "the reverse side, which is smooth and has no embroidery; and the obverse of the garment, which has the embroidery." In any case, these two terms refer to the front and back of the garment.

56. he shall cut (wĕqāra'). Although the normal meaning of qāra' is "tear," it also denotes "cut [with an instrument]," as in yiqrā'ehā bĕta'ar hassōpēr 'he would cut it with a scribe's knife' (Jer 36:23). This is also its meaning in rabbinic Hebrew (t. Yebam. 11:1; m. Ḥul. 4:5; t. Nid. 2:17). Clearly, the subject here is the priest: he would cut it himself or order it to be done. Of course, excision of the affected part is essential because only bodies heal, not fabrics. Yet it should be noted that the garment itself is not condemned; again, economic considerations have entered the picture (see 5:1–13; 12:6–8; 14:21–32, and esp. 14:36). It may be "his only garment, the sole covering of his skin" (Exod 22:26; cf. "A Letter from the Time of Josiah," ANET³ 568). Incinerating the part that has been cut out is not mentioned, but it must be deduced from vv 55, 57 (Elliger 1966).

The same rule prevails in Hindu religion, probably motivated by the same economic concerns: "Of a garment which has been defiled in the highest degree, let him cut off that part which, having been washed, is changed in color" (Visnusmṛti 23:6; Jolley 1880: 98).

57. and if it reappears. wĕ'im tērā'eh; "it" refers to the fret (Ibn Ezra).

it is breaking out afresh. pōraḥat hi' (hw'), namely, the fret (Ibn Ezra). It is not a new outbreak but a continuation of the old.

you shall destroy (bā'ēš tiśrĕpennû). Again Ibn Ezra claims that the fret is the referent. But this time it must be the entire fabric (Sipra, Neg. Tazria' 16:6) because "fret" (pĕḥetet) is feminine but the suffix of tiśrĕpennû is masculine (Hoffmann 1953), and a second accusative object, 'et 'ăšer-bô hannāga' 'the affected material', is added in order to indicate that the entire material has to be burned (see the NOTE on the latter plural, v 54). It is not unusual to find a verbal pronominal suffix together with a nominal object in apposition (e.g., Exod 35:5; 1 Kgs 21:13; 2 Kgs 16:15[K]; Joüon 1923: §146e). Still, the subject of this verb —anomalously in the second person—cannot be explained (see the NOTE on this word, v 55).

58. *[the affection] disappears. wĕsār*, that is, by the end of the second week. This verse offers a third option in addition to those of vv 55 and 56: during the second quarantine the affection remains the same (v 55), fades (v 56), or disappears (v 58) (Rashi, Wessely 1846). Elliger (1966), by contrast, claims that this verse is a continuation of the preceding. That is, the portion that remains after the affected part is removed needs to be washed again. This interpretation, however, founders on the word *wĕsār:* because the remaining part never showed signs of the affection, what sense does it make to state: "If, however, the affection disappears" (cf. Wright 1987: 91 n. 15)?

that has been washed. 'ăšer tĕkabbēs, literally, "that you will wash," that is, at the end of the first week (v 54). The subject is clearly impersonal (cf. the NOTE on *wĕkibbĕsû* 'shall be washed', v 54; note also the passives *hukkabbēs*, vv 55, 56, and *wĕkubbas*, v 58), though the use of the second person is here anomalous (cf. the NOTE on "you shall destroy it," v 55).

it shall be washed (wĕkubbas). The first washing (v 54) served to quarantine the fabric; this, the second, serves to purify it (*Sipra*, Neg. Tazria᷃ 16:11). Thus the first is a physical act, to cleanse the fabric, whereas the second is a ritual act, which declares it pure. This distinction is clearly preserved by *Tg. Onq.*, which renders the first washing by *wiḥawrûn* (v 54) and here by *wĕyiṣṭabba᷃*, and by the rabbis, who prescribed a detergent comprising seven ingredients for the first washing (*b. Zebaḥ.* 95a), whereas the second is performed just with water. In this respect, the fabric is analogous to the person suspected of scale disease, who, being declared pure after his quarantine, needs but to wash (v 6; Bekhor Shor).

59. *This is the procedure (zō᷃t tôrat).* Because the entire topic of scale disease (chaps. 13–14) will be concluded by a subscript that enumerates all of its components, including fabrics (14:54–56), why is there a need for this repetitious and, ostensibly, superfluous subscript for fabrics? A number of cogent reasons can be offered. (1) It sets off the pericope from chap. 14, which returns to the subject matter of persons (Abravanel). (2) There is no subscript in v 46, at the end of the discussion of human scale disease, because its purificatory rites continue in chap. 14 whereas this pericope on fabrics is complete unto itself: there is no purificatory rite beyond the burning or washing of the fabric (Wessely 1846). An additional reason suggests itself: (3) without this subscript, the impression might be gained that the purificatory rites (chap. 14) also apply to fabrics.

procedure for mold disease of fabric, woolen (tôrat nega᷃-ṣāra᷃at beged haṣṣemer). Four consecutive constructs, topped only by 1 Chr 9:13, which has five (Ibn Ezra). Saadiah, however, suggests that *beged* is an ellipsis for *bebeged*, which would yield the reading "that occurs in fabric (of wool and linen . . .)."

It might seem strange that in this long chapter dealing with scale disease nothing at all is said about the transmission of its impurity to those who come into contact with its bearers. Contrast the pericope on genital fluxes, chap. 15; and even the short passage on the parturient makes a point of referring to the section on the menstruant (15:19–24), where similar impurity rules prevail. Moreover, the transmission of impurity from a fungous (i.e., scale-diseased) house is discussed by Scripture (14:46–47). Why, then, the total silence on this subject in connection with scale-diseased persons? The answer can only be that because scale disease is the severest of all physical impurities (see chap. 15, COMMENT F), its contagious force can be derived a fortiori from the other impurities; even its unique property of overhang (chap. 15, COMMENT F) can be derived from the fungous house (see the NOTE on 14:47).

Interestingly, even the Qumran texts, which are wont to fill the gaps in the biblical laws, are also silent on the topic of contagion except for one innovative statement, which cannot be derived from Scripture: 'YŠ MKWL ḤṬMᵓYM [ᵓŠ]Ř Ŷ[Gᶜ] ẞW WRḤṢ BMYM WYKBS BGDYW WᵓḤR YWᵓKL BW 'Any of the impure persons who touches him shall bathe in water and launder his clothes and thereafter may eat of it (pure food)' (4QThr A1:3; Milgrom forthcoming B). Thus, according to Qumran—assuming the reconstructed text is correct—even an impure person receives an added layer of impurity by contacting the scale-diseased person and requires an immediate ablution, just like any pure person who contacts a severe impurity-bearer (e.g., 15:7, 19b). The only concession allowed him is that he may eat before sunset, while he is still, in rabbinic terminology, a těbûl yôm. This concession, however, does not contravene the Priestly impurity system, which also implies that after the ablution he who is secondarily infected no longer transmits impurity (see the table in chap. 15, COMMENT F).

COMMENTS: SCALE DISEASE

A. The Nature of Ṣaraᶜat and Its Rationale

Biblical ṣāraᶜat is difficult to identify. One thing, however, is certain: it is not leprosy (Hansen's disease), despite Preuss 1978: 324–26). This was well known in Hellenistic times, for the LXX translates ṣāraᶜat consistently by lepra, not by the Greek term for leprosy, elephas or elephantiasis. Furthermore, the New Testament also uses the term lepra but never elephas/elephantiasis. Indeed, it is most probable that true leprosy was totally unknown in the Near East before the Hellenistic period, and it is surmised that it was first brought into the area by Alexander's armies when they returned from India (Andersen 1969). Apparently, the two diseases were not confused until the ninth century C.E., when the Arab physician John of Damascus referred to leprosy by the term lepra (Andersen 1969), and his mistake persists till this day.

Hippocrates (fifth century B.C.E.) uses lepra as a generic for multiple skin diseases. His descriptions correspond, in the main, to psoriasis and fungal infections (Hulse 1975: 88). Subsequent observers, Galen (second century C.E.),

Oribasius (fourth century C.E.), and Paulus of Aegina (seventh century C.E.) conform to the Hippocratic diagnosis. (On the one ostensible exception in Galen, see Andersen 1969.)

If the nonidentification of *ṣāra'at* with leprosy is certain, one can say with equal assurance that the identification of *ṣāra'at* is uncertain (Tas 1971). Münch in 1893, cited by Preuss (1978: 325), identified *ṣāra'at* with vitiligo (called *pisj* by the Sarts of Turkestan). The most recent, comprehensive medical analysis of *ṣāra'at* reaches the following conclusion: psoriasis is the disease that fulfills most of the characteristics of *ṣāra'at*, with two exceptions: *neteq* (13:30–39) resembles *favus*, a fungus infection of the skin, and the pure skin-condition called *bōhaq* (13:39) resembles vitiligo (Hulse 1975). Yet even these identifications are hedged with reservations. Let me add a personal demur. I invited a respected San Francisco Bay Area dermatologist, Marvin Engel, to address my graduate seminar on this subject, and, after carefully studying the biblical text and its derivative medical literature, he stated his conclusion without any hesitations, that the symptoms described in Lev 13 do not correspond to any known skin disease. His main difficulty, surprisingly, was not the diagnosis but the treatment. Chronic skin diseases, he claimed, such as psoriasis, *favus*, and vitiligo, will not disappear or even change appreciably within one or two weeks. Thus, if these are the diseases described in Lev 13, the prescribed quarantine period is ineffectual and, indeed, can be misleading. The safest statement that can be made about these diseases is that they share one feature in common: they produce scales. Hence their designation as *ṣāra'at* has been rendered "scale disease" (see the discussion with the NOTE on "scaly," v 2).

The enigma of *ṣāra'at* cannot be resolved by medical science but it can, at least, be illumined once the medical approach is abandoned and attention is directed to the text itself. The text does not purport to be a diagnosis of disease; it is part of the Priestly system of impurity. In Israel, "it is the prophet who prescribes the healing rite, not the priest. This bifurcation of duties fits into the larger OT picture where prophets heal and priests diagnose" (cf. 1 Kgs 17:13–24; 2 Kgs 4:17–37; 20:7 = Isa 38:2; Wright and Jones forthcoming B). In chaps. 13–14, the verbal statistics underscore this point: *ṭāhēr* 'be pure' occurs thirty-six times; *ṭāmē'* 'be impure' thirty times, and *nirpā'* 'be healed' only four times. Nothing could be clearer: we are dealing with ritual, not medicine. Moreover, the text stresses that it is not the disease per se but its appearance that is the source of its impurity. Indeed, it is the focus on appearance that has resulted in condemning clothes infected by mold and houses by fungus, surely not because they are stricken with *ṣāra'at* but because they bear the appearance of *ṣāra'at*. The suspicion that we are not dealing with the disease aspect of this phenomenon can be buttressed by yet another consideration. The ancient world was familiar with a wide variety of diseases. In Mesopotamia, for example, a large percentage of its surviving cuneiform tables treat of the diagnosis and treatment of disease (Oppenheim 1964: 289–305). In Israel, these diseases were probably known as well. Yet Scripture concerns itself with just a minute portion.

Furthermore, these skin diseases—if their tentative identification be granted—are mainly not contagious. This medical fact is confirmed by Scripture itself. The Aramaean general Namaan, though afflicted with ṣāraʿat, was not prevented from leading an army, living with his family, confronting the prophet's servants, and, above all, entering the temple of Rimmon with his king leaning on his arm (2 Kgs 5). To be sure, had he been an Israelite he would have been banished like Miriam (Num 12:14–16), the four outcasts (2 Kgs 7:3–10), and Uzziah (2 Kgs 15:5). But this only proves that Israelites bearing ṣāraʿat were not banished for hygenic reasons. In fact, Leviticus confirms the impression that ṣāraʿat was not considered a disease: furniture removed from the house before the priest's examination cannot be declared impure (14:36). The rabbis also presume that ṣāraʿat is not disease, for they declare that its rules are not applicable to non-Jews and their homes in the Holy Land (m. Neg. 3:1) and to all houses outside the Holy Land (m. Neg. 12:1). In short, we are dealing with ritual, not pathology. It is significant to compare Israel's ṣāraʿat with one of its Mesopotamian counterparts. A Mari letter relates that when the king learns that a harem wife has contracted skin disease (simmam), he orders, "Let no one drink from her cup, sit in her chair, lie in her bed. . . . This skin disease (simmum) is contagious" (ARM 10.129; cf. the NOTE on 15:5a). If, indeed, the concern of the Priestly legislators was to quarantine and banish those stricken with virulent and contagious diseases, why were those not inserted in their list? Again the conclusion is inescapable: these rules are grounded not in medicine but in ritual.

Finally, "it is possible, knowing the systematic propensities of P, that this source has described a disease which does not reflect medical reality, perhaps by conflating symptoms of separate diseases thought to be impure. The latter possibility is attractive since elsewhere in these regulations we find clear evidence of ideological systematization: (a) the term ṣāraʿat is applied not only to human skin diseases, but to phenomenologically discrete defects in fabrics and houses. (b) The literary and prescriptive structure of the ṣāraʿat rules for persons, fabrics, and house is very similar. (c) Seven day quarantine periods are prescribed for each of these three cases though the conditions are discrete. (d) The three cases focus on the color of the lesions as the main or initial criterion for diagnosis" (D. Wright, written communication).

ṣāraʿat is cut from the same cloth as other ritual impurities: carcasses (chap. 11), parturition (chap. 12), and genital discharges (chap. 15). The fact that ṣāraʿat (chaps. 13–14) is ensconced within these subjects is in itself sufficient warrant for realizing that ritual impurity is its motivating postulate. The question, then, is not what is ṣāraʿat, but what is ritual impurity? This question will be dealt with at length in chap. 15, COMMENTS F and G. Here the main outlines will be sketched, with specific reference to ṣāraʿat.

The main clue for understanding the place of *ṣāraʿat* in the impurity system is the fact that it is an aspect of death: its bearer is treated like a corpse. This equation is expressly stated by Aaron in his prayer on behalf of Miriam when she is stricken with *ṣāraʿat:* "Let her not be like a corpse" (Num 12:12). In addition, both *ṣāraʿat* and the corpse contaminate not only by direct contact but, unlike all other impurity bearers, also by overhang, that is to say, by being under the same roof (see the NOTE on "he shall dwell apart," v 46). Furthermore, the purification rites of the corpse-contaminated person and the one afflicted with *ṣāraʿat* are strikingly similar: both require aspersion with animal blood that has made contact with cedar, hyssop, and scarlet thread and been diluted in fresh water (14:4–7; Num 19:1–13). Finally, the explicit identification of scale diseases with death is found in a verse from Job, *yōʾkal baddê ʿ ôrô / yōʾkal baddāyw bĕkôr māwet* (Job 18:13), the first stich being rendered "His skin is eaten away by a disease" (reading *yēʾākēl bidway;* G. H. B. Wright, cited by Dhorme 1984) or "the tendons under his skin are consumed" *(NJPS),* and the second, about which there is no disagreement, "Death's firstborn consumes his limbs." Because Job was stricken by *šĕhîn raʿ* 'malignant boils', a verified form of *ṣāraʿat* (vv 18–23), his disease is here called metaphorically "death's firstborn" (Paschen 1970: 56).

The association of *ṣāraʿat* with death is fully affirmed and legalized by the rabbis. "Four are similar to a dead man: a pauper, a leper, a blind man, and he who has no children" (*b. Nid.* 64b; *Midr. Gen. Rab.* 1:29); like the corpse, the scale-diseased person contaminates by overhang (*Sipre*, Num 105; cf. Jos., *Ant.* 3.264) by as much as the size of an olive (*b. Yebam.* 103b); neither the corpse-contaminated person nor the scale-diseased person may cut his hair, wash his clothes, engage in sex, extend greetings, or send sacrifices to the temple (for other comparisons, see *b. Moʿed Qat.* 14a–16a; cf. Paschen 1970: 55–64; Feldman 1977: 35–41). The sectaries of Qumran actually use the word "death" in their diagnosis of scale disease. The latter's spread is described as "the addition of the living part [of the body] to the dead part" (4QDᵃ 4–5, 10–11, 11–12; Milik 1966: 105) and the healing force, in contrast, is termed "the spirit of life" (ibid., line 12; cf. also 4QDᵍ1, 2:1). Tov (1968: n. 21), noting that this Qumran fragment covers the topics treated in 13:24–15:5, has plausibly proposed that it belongs in the lacuna between CD, cols. 11 and 12, because col. 12 begins with the law of 15:18 (see now Baumgarten 1990).

Thus, the common denominator of all the skin ailments described in Lev 13 is that the body is wasting away. As the continuation of Aaron's prayer expressed it: "Let her not be like a corpse that emerges from its mother's womb with half its flesh eaten away" (Num 12:12). As pointed out by medical authorities, "The most striking external feature of such a stillborn child is the way the superficial layers of the skin peel off" (Hulse 1975: 93). Thus it is the visible "peeling off," the striking characteristic of the scale diseases listed in Lev 13—reminders of the disintegration of the corpse and the onset of death—that has led to their impure status and to the banishment of their carriers from the community. This criterion is also the governing postulate of all of the other impurities discussed in chaps. 11–15, and its elucidation and confirmation in these impurities as well will serve to support its existence here.

B. The Causes of Ṣaraʿat

Throughout the ancient Near East, disease is considered the work of supernal, malevolent forces. Scale disease, in particular, stands out as a prime means of divine punishment. In Mesopotamia, it is called *šērtu rabītu* 'great punishment', as can be inferred from the statement: "May Sin, the lord of the crown. . . . The father of the great gods make him bear scale disease (which cannot be healed), his *great punishment (šērtašu rabīta)*" (Nougayrol 1948: 207 n. 12). It is also called *erretu rabītu* 'a great curse'; *erretu lemuttu* 'evil curse'; *erretu maruštu* 'a baleful curse'; *arrat la napšuri maruštu* 'a terrible, irreversible curse'; and *arrat la pašāri* 'a curse that cannot be dispelled' (*CAD*, A 234–35). These citations are part of curse formulas that are generally appended to treaties: the offender risks divine retribution in the form of scale disease. Scale disease *(saharšubbû)* is explicitly mentioned in curses inscribed on boundary stones, for example, *Sin . . .* SAHAR.ŠUB.BA-*a la tēbâ gimir lānišu lilabbišma* 'May Sin clothe his whole body in scale disease which will never lift' (King 1912: 41 no. 7.II.16; cf. no. 8 IV 8, no. 11.III.2). The same formula occurs at the end of Esarhaddon's vassal treaty, [ᵈxxx n]*a-an-ar* [AN-*e u KI-ti*] *sahar* (?)-*šub* (?)-*bu* [*li-h*]*al-lip-ku-nu* '[May Sin], the brightness [of heaven and earth], clothe you with [sca]le disease' (Wiseman 1958: 59 line 415; cf. Borger 1961: 187). The graphic description of a curse that is appended to Hammurabi's Code clearly refers to scale disease: "May Ninkarrak, the daughter of Anum, my advocate in Ekur, inflict upon him in his body a grievous malady, an evil disease, a serious wound that never heals, whose nature no physician knows, which he cannot allay with bandages, which like a deadly bite cannot be rooted out" (CH 44.50–69; and *CAD*, S 277; *ANET*³ 179b, 180a). Ostracism from the human community, the expected consequence of scale disease (see vv 45–46), is originally spelled out in a curse, such as "May Sin, the light of the bright heavens, clothe his whole body with scale disease that never departs, so that he may not be pure till the day of his death. May he roam outside his city like a wild ass" (King 1912: 41 lines 16–18; cited in Hillers 1964: 15–16); or "May he be excluded from his house, may he roam the desert like a desert animal and may he not tread the square of his city" (MDP 2.109, vi. 41–vii.4, cited in Hillers 1964: 16).

The attribution of scale disease to the punitive action of the deity is not limited to Babylonia. According to the Greeks, the population of Delos incurred scale disease when they permitted a burial on their sacred island and thereby committed sacrilege against the gods (Parker 1983: 218). Herodotus reports that in Persia anyone stricken with scale disease *(lepra)* has "sinned against the sun" (1.139).

The sin and scale-disease syndrome is not limited to the ancient Near East but is a universal phenomenon that cannot be confined to cultural bounds; rather, it stems from the concerns of the human psyche. One can point to the Nuer of Africa, who "believe that incest brings misfortune in the form of skin disease which can be averted by sacrifice" (Douglas 1966: 130; cf. Evans-Prichard 1956: 183–97).

Certainly, many of the biblical narratives concerning *ṣāraʿat* confirm its origin in divine wrath (Miriam, Num 12:9; Gehazi, 2 Kgs 5:27; Uzziah, 2 Chr 26:18–21). Thus, analogous to its Mesopotamian counterpart, it is attested in biblical curse formulas, such as "May the house of Joab never be without someone suffering from discharge or scale disease" (2 Sam 3:25; cf. 7:14). And, probably under the influence of treaty formulations in Imperial Assyria, the curse of scale disease is expressly included in the admonitions that concluded the book of Deuteronomy: "The Lord will smite you with Egyptian boils *(šĕḥin miṣrayim)* . . . and with scabs *(gārāb)* and itches from which you shall never recover" (Deut 28:27: for *šĕḥin* as a form of scale disease, see the NOTE on 13:18; and for *gārāb*, see *DDS* 117 n. 5; Kinnier-Wilson 1966: 55–58). It is also not surprising that among those falling under the curse is he "who moves his neighbor's landmark *(massîg gĕbŭl)*" (Deut 27:17), in other words, his boundary stone. The sectaries of Qumran were emphatic in their conviction that scale disease and, indeed, all illnesses were the signs of divine punishment (e.g., 1Q Hab 9:9–12; 11:12–16; Baillet 1982: 265.vii, fragment 30.8–9; Dª1, 2.5).

It can be seen from all of the foregoing examples that scale disease as a divine punishment falls into the category of *fas*, not *jus*, religious and not civil crimes: the sins have been committed against the deity, not against man. The violation of a treaty, though outwardly a hostile act of a vassal to his suzerain, is punishable by the deity because of the broken vows taken in his or her name. Oath violation is sacrilege, a trespass against the deity commensurately culpable with pilfering a sacred object from the temple. The biblical term for it is *maʿal* 'sacrilege' (see the COMMENT on 5:14–26; cf. Milgrom 1976b). King Uzziah's encroachment upon the Temple illustrates this beautifully. Chronicles relates that Uzziah was stricken with scale disease precisely when, and because, he committed sacrilege *(maʿal)* against the Lord: "When he grew powerful his pride led to his undoing, he committed sacrilege *(maʿal)* against the Lord his God by entering the Lord's Temple to burn incense on the altar of incense. . . . 'Leave the sanctuary for you have committed sacrilege *(maʿaltā)*' . . . scale disease broke out on his forehead (see the NOTE on 13:41) in the presence of the priest in the Lord's house, beside the altar of incense" (2 Chr 26:16–19).

Nonetheless, the other attestations of scale disease in Scripture, whether in narration, law, or the cult, testify to the fact that scale disease is also a punishment for moral failings. That is, the sin is still committed against God but only because Israel's moral behavior has been subsumed under divine law. It has been cogently argued that Gehazi is afflicted with Naaman's scale disease because in accepting the latter's gift, he tacitly acknowledges that Naaman has been cured by Elisha rather than by the God of Israel (van der Toorn 1985: 74)—a clear case of sacrilege. It is just as likely, however, that Gehazi is punished because his greed leads him to prevarication: by lying first to Naaman and then to Elisha, he seeks to reap the reward that his master has rejected (2 Kgs 5:20–27). The quid pro quo is precise: having illicitly expropriated Naaman's possession he now inherits his disease as well (see Cohn 1983). It has already been noted that scale disease is one of the many punishments held out in the curses of Deut 28 for disobeying the Lord. One must only recall that this disobedience comprises "all of the commandments and laws that I command you this day" (Deut 28:15), the referent for which can only be the Deuteronomic Code, containing many moral injunctions of the highest order (*DDS* 282–97). Even cultic law alludes strongly to the possibility that scale disease may be a product of moral misdemeanor. A whole array of sacrifices is prescribed for the person healed of scale disease. To be sure, *ʾāšām*, the reparation offering, covers the possibility that the person has committed a sacrilege against the Lord by trespassing on one of the sancta (NOTE on 14:12; cf. Milgrom 1976f: 80–82). Still, the healed person is required to offer three other sacrifices: the *ḥaṭṭāʾt* 'purification offering', the *ʿōlâ* 'burnt offering', and the *minḥâ* 'cereal offering', all of which serve an expiatory function (14:19–20). It already has been proposed that the introduction to the *ḥaṭṭāʾt* law, "When a person inadvertently does wrong in regard to any of the Lord's prohibitive commandments" (4:2), embraces the moral as a well as the ritual law, in other words, that the violation of God's ethical prohibitions, like the violation of ritual prohibitions, is capable of polluting the sanctuary (see the NOTE "commandments," 4:2). Also the *ʿōlâ* (and possibly the *minḥâ*) serves to expiate for the violation of performative laws, which embrace many moral injunctions (see the COMMENT on chap. 1).

Finally, one should point to the punishment of Miriam. She was afflicted with scale disease for defaming Moses. She (and Aaron) "had spoken against Moses *(bĕmōšeh)* because of the Cushite woman: 'he married a Cushite woman'" (Num 12:1). Nevertheless, as can be garnered from their complaint "Has the Lord spoken only through Moses? Has he not spoken through us as well?" (v 2) and from the Lord's subsequent accusation, "With him I speak mouth to mouth. . . . How then did you not shrink from speaking against my servant Moses!" (v 8), it becomes clear that this complaint about Moses' marriage was only a pretext. What they were really after was a share in Moses' leadership. Yet it is the ethnic slur against Moses' wife that maligns him in public and is responsible, according to the rabbis, for Miriam's punishment (*Sipra*, Neg. Meṣoraʿ par. 5:7; *Sipre* Zuta on Num 12:1; *ʾAbot R. Nat.* A, 40). Indeed, the rabbis' insistence that scale disease results from slander is the basis of the wordplay that *mĕṣōraʿ* is an abbreviation of *môṣîʾ (šēm) raʿ* 'defame, slander' (*b. ʿArak.* 15b).

Alternatively, Maimonides attributes Miriam's scale disease to her refusal to accept Moses' unique prophetic status:

> Now on this matter there is a warning, in Scripture, which says, "Take heed in regard to scale disease . . . remember what the Lord thy God did to Miriam along the way" (Deut 24:8–9). That is to say, consider what befell Miriam the prophetess, who spoke against her brother, even though she was older than he and had nurtured him on her knees and had put herself in jeopardy to save him from the sea. Now she did not speak despitefully of him but erred only in that she put him on a level with other prophets; nor was he resentful about all these things for it is said, "Now the man Moses was very meek" (Num 12:3). Nevertheless, she was forthwith punished with scale disease. How much more then does this apply to wicked and foolish people who are profuse in speaking great and boastful things! (*Book of Cleanness,* "Uncleanness of Scale Disease" 16.10)

Thus, except for the Bible, the attribution of scale disease to moral offenses is not attested in the ancient Near East. It does, however, surface in classical Greece. In Aeschylus's *Choephoroe,* Orestes remarks that the Furies will inflict scale disease on anyone who refuses to avenge the murder of a kinsman, and a goatherd in one of Theocritus's *Idylls* compliments his beloved by exclaiming that he runs no risk of scale disease in singing her praises (cited by Gaster 1969: 300). According to J. Baumgarten, in a new Qumran fragment "Ms. E (4Q 270) of the *Damascus Document* (CD) 'one affected with the plague of *ṣaraʿat*' is listed in a catalogue of transgressors" (1990: 162). Finally, the moral direction initiated in Scripture blossoms into full flower in rabbinic literature. "For ten things does scale disease come upon the world: (1) idol worship, (2) gross unchastity, (3) bloodshed, (4) the desecration of the Divine Name, (5) blasphemy of the Divine Name, (6) robbing the public, (7) usurping [a dignity] to which one has no right, (8) overweening pride, (9) evil speech (slander), and (10) an evil eye (greed)" (*Midr. Lev. Rab.* 17:3). Other rabbinic treatises cite only moral causes: "R. Samuel b. Nahman said in the name of R. Yochanan: Because of seven things the plague of scale disease is incurred: slander, the shedding of blood, vain oaths, incest, arrogance, robbery, and envy" (*b. ʿArak.* 16a; cf. *b. Šebu.* 8a; *Midr. Lev. Rab.* 18:4).

The negative associations engendered by biblical *ṣāraʿat* and especially by its identification with leprosy have induced my student, D. P. Wright, to supply the following relevant note:

Several writers have been concerned about the ethical propriety of translating *ṣāraʿat* as "leprosy" when in fact the two are not to be equated. It may lead some to view those with Hansen's Disease as morally deficient and objects of supernatural punishment. Other writers have warned against the effect of equating other diseases, such as psoriasis, with *ṣāraʿat.* (E.g., F. C. Lendrum, "The Name 'Leprosy,'" *American Journal of Tropical Medicine and Hygiene* I (1952) 999–1008; L. Goldman, R. S. Moraites, K. W. Kitzmiller, "White Spots in Biblical Times," *Archives of Dermatology* 93 (1966) 744–53.) History has made it undeniably clear that those with Hansen's Disease have in fact been the object of scorn and seclusion partly due to the identification of this disease with *ṣāraʿat.* And those with psoriasis, to learn from John Updike's case, for example, hardly need any more humiliation by identifying that disease with *ṣāraʿat* (cf. John Updike, *Self-Consciousness: Memoirs* [New York: Knopf, 1989] 42–78; a beautifully drafted insider's view of the ugliness and metamorphoses of the disease and an individual's accommodation to it). What is historical and medical science to do? Certainly it cannot hide from the attempt to identify the biblical diseases. Nevertheless, it should probably strive in some way to make its audience aware of the ethical implications of its conclusions. While the ethical issues here are certainly not of the same degree as those surrounding more prominent and pressing medical issues such as genetic screening, genetic engineering, invitro-fertilization and the like, they are worthy of thought. Apart from the effect of a particular translation or the identification of the disease, the case of biblical *ṣāraʿat* provides a springboard for ethical thought about other diseases which are more in the public mind today, such as cancer or AIDS. There are many parallels between the Bible's view about those suffering from *ṣāraʿat* and unscientific popular views about those suffering from the serious diseases of modern concern. These popular views grow out of society's fears and attempts to explain evil, and out of its social context. These explanations, while turning chaos to order for some, are sometimes injurious, psychologically if not physically, to the sick (cf. Susan Sontag, *Illness as Metaphor* [New York: Farrar, Straus, and Giroux, 1977], *AIDS and Its Metaphors* [New York: Farrar, Straus, and Giroux, 1988]). Knowledge about the ancients' symbolic understanding of biblical *ṣāraʿat* and the effects it had upon sufferers in antiquity can serve as an avenue for critiquing our own thinking (or misthinking) about modern disease.

SCALE DISEASE (1 3 : 1 – 5 9)

C. Symptomatology and Diagnosis of Ṣāraʿat in Humans, by David P. Wright

	verses	lesion type	color of lesion	hair/depth and other conditions	Q1	result of Q1	Q2	result of Q2	further change	pure	impure
	2–3	śēʾēt, sappahat baheret	any(?)	+W, +D							X
	4–5	baheret	white	−W, −D	X	[spread]					[X]
A	4–5	"	"	" "	"	[faded]				[X]	
	4–6	"	"	" "	"	same	X	[spread]			[X]
	4–6	"	"	" "	"	"	"	[same]		[X?]	[X]
	4–6	"	"	" "	"	"	"	faded		X	
	4–8	"	"	" "	"	"	"	"	spread		X
	9–11	śēʾēt	white	+W, +R							X
B	12–13, 16–17	"	"	" [−R], covers skin						X	
	14–15	"	"	" +R, " "							X
	18–20	śēʾēt -------- baheret after a	white ---------- red-white	+W, +D							X
C	18–22	"	"	−W, −D [not faint]							X
	18–22	"	"	" " faint	X	spread					X
	18–23	"	"	" " "	X	same				X	
	18–23	"	"	" " "	X	[faded]				[X]	
	24–25	baheret (after a burn)	red-white, white	+W, +D							X
D	24–27	"	"	−W, −D [not faint]							X
	24–27	"	"	" " faint	X	spread					X
	24–27	"	"	" " "	"	[same]				[X?]	
	24–28	"	"	" " "	"	faded				X	
	29–30	neqaʿ (head, beard)	any(?)	+Y, +D							X
	31–32	"	"	−B, −D [−Y]	X	[spread, +Y]					[X]

825

	verses	lesion type	color of lesion	hair/depth and other conditions	Q1	result of Q1	Q2	result of Q2	further change	pure	impure
	31–32	"	"	" " "	"	[faded]				X	
E	31–32, 37	"	"	" " "	"	same, +B				X	
	31–34	"	"	" " "	"	same, −Y, −D	X+S	[spread, +Y, +D]			[X]
	31–34	"	"	" " "	"	"	"	[faded, −D, +B]		[X]	
	31–34	"	"	" " "	"	"		same, −D		X	
	31–35	"	"	" " "	"	"	"	"	spread, even −Y	X	
	38–39	multiple *behārōt*	white	faint						X	
F	38–39	"	"	[not faint]					[further examination according to 2– 8 would probably be needed]		
	40–41	baldness								X	
G	42–44	*negaʿ/śeʾēt hannegaʿ* in baldness	red-white like *ṣāraʿat*								X

Explanation of Sigla:

B = black hair
D = deepness
Q = quarantine period (Q1 = first quarantine period; Q2 = second quarantine period)
R = raw flesh
S = shaving (in connection with quarantine)
W = white hair
Y = yellow hair
+ = condition present
− = condition lacking
[ ] = a deduction

This chart summarizes the various conditions in humans discussed by Lev 13:2–44, which may or may not be diagnosed as *ṣāraʿat*. These verses generally present the symptoms in a developmental or chronological fashion. This chart follows the order of presentation found in these verses. Each horizontal section describes the symptoms at a particular stage in the presentation and indicates whether the symptoms at that stage are considered impure (i..e, they are *ṣāraʿat*) or pure. Deductions for cases not found explicitly in the verses are included.

PURIFICATION AFTER SCALE DISEASE (14:1–57)

Rite of Passage

14 ¹The Lord spoke to Moses, saying: ²This shall be the ritual for a scale-diseased person at the time of his purification. When it is reported to the priest, ³the priest shall go outside the camp. If the priest sees that the scale-diseased person has been healed of scale disease, ⁴the priest shall order two wild pure birds, cedar wood, crimson yarn, and hyssop to be brought for the one to be purified. ⁵The priest shall order one bird slaughtered into an earthen vessel over spring water; ⁶and he shall take the live bird, along with the cedar wood, the crimson yarn, and the hyssop, and dip them together with the live bird in the blood of the bird that was slaughtered over the spring water. ⁷He shall then sprinkle [the blood] seven times on the one to be purified of the scale disease. When he has thus purified him, he shall release the live bird over the open country. ⁸The one to be purified shall launder his clothes, shave off all of his hair, and bathe in water; then he shall be pure. After that he may enter the camp, but must remain outside his tent for seven days. ⁹On the seventh day he shall shave off all of his hair—of his head, chin, and eyebrows—indeed, he shall shave off all of his hair. He shall launder his clothes and bathe in water; then he shall be pure.

Purification Sacrifices

¹⁰On the eighth day he shall take two male lambs without blemish, one yearling ewe without blemish, three-tenths [of an *ephah*] of semolina mixed with oil for a cereal offering, and one *log* of oil. ¹¹The priest who performs the purification shall place the one to be purified, together with these [offerings], before the Lord at the entrance to the Tent of Meeting. ¹²The priest shall take one of the male lambs and present it as a reparation offering, together with the *log* of oil, and offer it as an elevation offering before the Lord. ¹³The lamb shall be slaughtered at the spot in the sacred precinct where the purification offering and the burnt offering are slaughtered. For the reparation offering is like the purification offering; it [goes] to the priest; it is most holy. ¹⁴The priest shall take some of the blood of the reparation offering, and the priest shall put [it] on the lobe of the right ear of the one who is being purified, and on the thumb of his right hand, and on the big toe of his right foot. ¹⁵The priest shall then take some of the *log* of oil and pour [it] into the palm of his own left hand. ¹⁶And the priest shall dip his right finger in the oil that is on his left palm and sprinkle some of the oil with his finger seven times before the Lord. ¹⁷And some of the oil left on his palm the priest shall put on the lobe of the right ear of the one being purified, on the thumb of his right hand, and on the big toe of his right

foot—on top of the blood of the reparation offering. ¹⁸The remainder of the oil on the priest's palm shall be put on the head of the one being purified. Thus the priest shall make expiation for him before the Lord. ¹⁹The priest shall then offer the purification offering and effect purgation for the one being purified for his impurity. After this, the burnt offering shall be slaughtered, ²⁰and the priest shall offer up the burnt offering and the cereal offering on the altar. And the priest shall make expiation for him. Then he shall be pure.

Purification Sacrifices for the Poor

²¹If, however, he is poor and his means are insufficient, he shall take a reparation offering of one male lamb for an elevation offering to make expiation for him, one-tenth [of an *ephah*] of semolina mixed with oil for a cereal offering, a *log* of oil; ²²and two turtledoves or two pigeons, whichever are within his means, the one to be the purification offering and the other the burnt offering. ²³On the eighth day of his purification he shall bring them to the priest at the entrance of the Tent of Meeting, before the Lord. ²⁴The priest shall take the lamb of reparation offering and the *log* of oil, and elevate them as an elevation offering before the Lord. ²⁵When the lamb of reparation offering has been slaughtered, the priest shall take some of the blood of the reparation offering and put it on the right ear of the one being purified, on the thumb of his right hand, and on the big toe of his right foot. ²⁶The priest shall then pour some of the oil on the palm of his own left hand, ²⁷and with the finger of his right hand the priest shall sprinkle some of the oil that is on the palm of his left hand seven times before the Lord. ²⁸The priest shall put some of the oil on his palm on the lobe of the right ear of the one being purified, on the thumb of his right hand, and on the big toe of his right foot, on top of the blood spots of the reparation offering; ²⁹and the remainder of the oil on the priest's palm shall be put on the head of the one being purified, to make expiation for him before the Lord. ³⁰He shall then offer one of the turtledoves or pigeons that are within his means— ³¹whichever he can afford—the one as a purification offering and the other as a burnt offering together with the cereal offering. Thus shall the priest make expiation before the Lord for the one being purified. ³²This is the ritual for the one who has scale disease [and] whose means are insufficient at [the time of] his purification.

Fungous Houses: Diagnosis and Purification

³³The Lord spoke to Moses and Aaron, saying: ³⁴When you enter the land of Canaan, which I give you as a possession, and I inflict a fungous infection upon a house in the land you possess, ³⁵the owner of the house shall come and tell the priest, saying, "It appears to me that there is something like an infection in my house." ³⁶The priest shall order the house cleared before the priest enters

to examine the infection, so that nothing in the house may become impure; after that the priest shall enter to examine the house. [37]If, when he examines the infection, the infection in the walls of the house is found to consist of bright green or bright red eruptions, which appear deeper than the wall, [38]the priest shall come out of the house to the entrance of the house, and quarantine the house for seven days. [39]On the seventh day the priest shall return. If he sees that the infection has spread on the walls of the house, [40]the priest shall order the stones with the infection in them to be pulled out and cast outside the city into an impure place. [41]The house shall be scraped inside all around, and the mortar that is scraped off shall be dumped outside the city in an impure place. [42]They shall take other stones and replace those stones [with them], and take other coating and plaster the house.

[43]If the infection breaks out again in the house, after the stones have been pulled out and after the house has been scraped and replastered, [44]the priest shall come and examine: if the infection has spread in the house, it is a malignant fungus in the house: it [the house] is impure. [45]The house shall be demolished—its stones and timber and all of the mortar of the house—and taken to an impure place outside the city.

[46]Whoever enters the house during the whole time it is quarantined shall be impure until evening. [47]Whoever lies down in the house must launder his clothes, and whoever eats in the house must launder his clothes.

[48]If, however, the priest comes and sees that the infection has not spread in the house after the house was replastered, the priest shall pronounce the house pure, for the infection has healed. [49]To decontaminate the house, he shall take two birds, cedar wood, crimson thread, and hyssop. [50]One bird shall be slaughtered over spring water in an earthen vessel. [51]He shall take the cedar wood, the hyssop, the crimson yarn, and the live bird, and dip them in the blood of the slaughtered bird and the spring water, and sprinkle on the house seven times. [52]Having decontaminated the house with the blood of the bird, the spring water, the live bird, the cedar wood, the hyssop, and the crimson thread, [53]he shall release the live bird over the open country outside the city. Thus he shall perform purgation upon the house, and it shall be pure.

Summary of Chapters 13–14

[54]This is the procedure for all [fleshy] scale diseases, for scalls, [55]for mold in fabrics and houses, [56]for discolorations, for scabs, or for shiny marks—[57]to determine when they are impure and when they are pure. This is the procedure for scale disease.

NOTES

14:1–32. The Purification for a Cured Scale-Diseased Person. Three separate ceremonies are required: for the first day (vv 2–8; also invoked for houses, vv 48–53), for the seventh (v 9), and for the eighth (vv 10–32). The first-day ritual is performed by the priest outside the camp (or city) from which the stricken person has been banished. Cedar wood, crimson yarn, and a live bird are dipped into an earthen vessel containing a mixture of spring water and the blood of a second bird. The cured person (or house) is sprinkled with this mixture seven times, after which the live bird is set free. He is admitted into the camp (or city) after he launders his clothes, shaves all his hair, and bathes, but he is not allowed to enter his residence. That is permitted him on the seventh day, after shaving, laundering, and bathing again. On the eighth day he brings to the sanctuary oil, semolina, and sheep for various sacrifices, which are offered up in the following order—reparation, purification, burnt, and cereal offerings. The animals for the burnt and purification offerings may be commuted to birds if the offerer is poor. By contrast, the reparation lamb and the *log* of oil may not be changed, as the blood of the lamb and the oil are needed to daub the person's right earlobe, right thumb, and right big toe.

1. *The Lord spoke to Moses.* The omission of Aaron is puzzling because the conduct of the purification rite is entirely in the hands of the priest. That the Israelites are also omitted, however, should occasion no surprise. The diagnosis of scale disease is not only an intricate body of knowledge that requires expertise, but its consequences for the sanctuary and welfare of Israel are too severe to be left to the decisions of the laity. Indeed, the possibility must be entertained that originally chaps. 13–14 were an archival document of the priests, stored in the Temple, and only during the long course of redaction of the Pentateuch was it inserted in its present place. Perhaps the deuteronomic injunction, "In cases of scale disease be most careful to do exactly as the levitical priests instruct you" (Deut 24:8), is responsible for their inclusion.

2. *This shall be the ritual for (zō'>t tihyeh tôrat).* This formula is used for subjects *previously* described (chap. 13). Thus 6:2, 7, 18; 7:1, 11; and 13:59 also advert to subjects previously discussed (chaps. 1–5; Hoffmann 1953).

shall be (tihyeh). This verb is missing in all other occurrences of this formula (see above). Ehrlich (1908–14) suggests its deletion. But, in contrast to the immediately previous mention of this formula (13:59), which is the summary subscript to the *preceding* verses, the formula here introduces the verses that *follow.* The change is from treatment of symptoms to a description of the ritual that will take place once the scale disease is cured *(Seper Hamibḥar; Keter Torah).* This transition is also marked by the introduction of the scale-diseased person as *mĕṣōrāʿ* (see below).

a scale-diseased person. hamměṣōrāʿ is the technical name for one afflicted with scale disease (cf. 2 Kgs 5:1, 27; 7:3, 8; 15:5). Just as the *piʿel ṭimmēʾ* and ṭihēr refer to the priest's declaration that one is *ṭāmēʾ* 'impure' and *ṭāhôr* 'pure', respectively, so does the *puʿal* participle *měṣōraʿ* refer to the one whom the priest has certified as *ṣārûaʿ* (*qal* passive participle, 13:44, 45; Ehrlich 1908–14). The technical term in rabbinic Hebrew for such a person is *mûḥlāt* 'certified' (e.g., *m. Meg.* 1:7). For the rabbinic homily that *měṣōraʿ* is an acronym based on *mōṣîʾ šēm raʿ* 'slander', see chap. 13, COMMENT B.

at the time of. běyôm, literally, "in the day of." For this idiomatic meaning, see v 57; 7:38; Num 3:1.

purification. ṭohŏrātô, that is, after he has healed. Here, however, the root *ṭhr* may denote physical healing. If so, it would be the only time in P (see chap. 15, COMMENT C); contrast 2 Kgs 5:10. The significance should not be overlooked. The avoidance of the connotation of healing (as well as the verb "heal," *rāpāʾ;* see chap. 13, COMMENT A) is clearly deliberate, in order to divorce ritual purification from theurgic rites.

When it is reported to the priest. wěhûbāʾ ʾel-hakkōhēn (with Saadiah; cf. the NOTES on 13:26, 9). The alternate rendering for this clause—"When he is brought to the priest"—must be rejected in view of the subsequent statement, that "the priest shall go outside the camp" (v 3a). Until the priest verifies that he is actually cured he remains a *měṣōraʿ* and may not enter the camp.

3. *outside the camp* (ʾel-miḥûṣ lammaḥăneh). Following a verb of motion, the preposition ʾel is used (e.g., 4:12, 21; 6:4; 10:4, 5), which demonstrates that the prepositional phrase miḥûṣ lammaḥăneh/lāʿîr (cf. vv 40, 41, 45, 53) is treated as a compound noun.

If the priest sees that (wěrāʾâ hakkōhēn wěhinnēh). Alternatively (and literally), "the priest shall examine (him): if" (see the NOTE on "if," 13:5; and contrast v 8). wěhinnēh always introduces a new fact (Rashbam on Gen 25:24).

the scale-diseased person has been healed of scale disease. nirpāʾ negaʿ-haṣ-ṣāraʿat min-haṣṣārûaʿ, literally, "the scale disease has been healed of the scale-diseased person," which prompts Ibn Janaḥ (cited by Ibn Ezra) to remark that the text should have read *nirpāʾ haṣṣārûaʿ minnegaʿ-haṣṣāraʿat,* thereby yielding the translation adopted here. Nevertheless, this reversal of subject and object may not be necessary in view of the biblical notion that it is the affliction that is healed rather than the afflicted (e.g., v 48; 13:37; Ibn Ezra) Still, the phrase *min-haṣṣārûaʿ* 'of the scale-diseased person' is exceptional and awkward; after all, the person is not a sickness (Malbim)! Kalisch (1867–72) suggests that the phrase means "[and disappeared from] the afflicted." He is on the right track. But this interpretation is not only implied (hence, put into parentheses); it is explicit: *min* continues to be rendered "from" but *nirpāʾ* is semantically equivalent to *sār* 'depart, disappear', a word that is regularly (and logically) followed by *min* 'from' (e.g., 13:58). Thus this clause, in effect, could be translated, "the scale disease has disappeared from the scale-diseased person."

It should also be noted that this is the last time that either *mĕṣōrāʿ* or *ṣārûaʿ* appears. Henceforth, the erstwhile scale-diseased person will be referred to as *hammiṭṭahēr* 'the one being purified' (vv 4, 7, 11, 17, 18, 19, etc.).

4. *The priest shall order . . . to be brought. wĕṣiwwâ hakkōhēn wĕlāqaḥ,* literally, "the priest shall order and he shall take." Some commentators suggest that in view of the active verb *wĕlāqaḥ* (and *wĕśāḥaṭ,* v 5), the preceding words *wĕṣiwwâ hakkōhēn* (here and in v 5) are editorial additions; originally, the priest would have been responsible for bringing the birds and performing the slaughter (v 5) and only later was the law altered to transfer these duties to the offerer (Rendtorff 1954: 52; Koch 1959: 84). Perhaps, in support of this view, one could point to the Hittite "Ritual Against Domestic Quarrel" (*ANET*³ 350–51), where the sacrificer brings the two sheep but the officiant (old woman) brings the small pig as well as the other sacrificial ingredients. In BH, however, the active verb frequently implies an impersonal subject, which in these two chapters appears both as a singular (e.g., 13:52, 54b, 56; 14:42) and as a plural (13:54a) and, strikingly, following the same expression, *wĕṣiwwâ hakkōhēn* (vv 36a, 40a). Thus this expression is not an editor's addition but is intrinsic to the original intent of the text, declaring that the priest is not liable for the sacrificial expenses *(Seper Hamibḥar; Keter Torah)* but should charge them to the patient (Abravanel) or, more accurately, instruct the patient as to what sacrifices to bring (Saadiah). Perhaps to avoid this confusion, some Versions read the plural, *wĕlāqĕḥû* (Sam., LXX, Pesh.), thereby clarifying that the priest is not the subject. Nevertheless, in view of the many alterations in these two chapters of the singular verb with an impersonal subject, the emendation is unwarranted.

wild. ḥayyôt (with *Seper Hamibḥar*). For this usage, see 11:27; contrast v 26). Alternatively, this word can be rendered "live" or "healthy." The former designation is superfluous, however: all animals are assumed alive unless otherwise specified. The latter connotation is also attested in Scripture (e.g., Exod 1:19; Josh 5:8), but it too is superfluous here: because the remaining live bird will have to distance itself from the patient, a healthy specimen must be taken for granted. As will be explained in the NOTE that immediately follows, a wild bird is essential so that it does not return to the community.

Nonetheless, the notion of "live" must also be denoted here, on thematic grounds. It is also the preferable rendering in the occurrences that follow, vv 6, 7, 51, 53. Life is the theme, the *Leitwort,* of the ritual: "live" waters (v 5) are employed; blood, the symbol of life (chap. 11, COMMENT C), is added to the waters; so too the red yarn and the (red) cedar, which, again symbolically, supplement the blood or life-giving qualities of this potion. In fact, this emphasis on blood and red substances concerns the basic intent of this ritual; because the scale-diseased person is akin to the dead (cf. Num 12:12; chap. 13, COMMENT A), this rite effects his restoration to life (cf. Dillmann and Ryssel 1897 and the NOTE on "cedar" below).

pure (ṭĕhōrôt). Purity is a ritual requirement for birds either for the altar or for the table. One might argue that in this case altar birds are intended, in view of the analogy to the scapegoat of the Yom Kippur rite, which is also dispatched from the community and which is expressly called a *ḥaṭṭāʾt*, a "purification offering" (16:5). Yet sacrificial birds are restricted to pigeons and turtledoves (e.g., 5:11; 12:8): if these were intended they would have been named. Moreover, there is reason to believe that these birds were not domesticated but wild (see below). Hence they could only qualify as food (see the NOTE to 11:13).

Yet the question remains. If the scapegoat rite was incorporated into the sacrificial system—though its origins are indubitably pagan (see chap. 16, COMMENT E)—why could not the birds have undergone the same transition; why, indeed, were they not restricted to the turtledove and pigeon and given a sacrificial designation? First, it should be noted that in other respects as well, the bird rite represents a more pristine, "undoctored" pagan practice than the scapegoat, for example, the blood of the slain bird is sprinkled on the patient, whereas the blood of the slain goat on Yom Kippur, in conformance with the *ḥaṭṭāʾt* regulations, is daubed or sprinkled on the sanctuary and its sancta but not on persons (see chap. 4, COMMENT E). The bird rite resembles more the rite with the ashes of the Red Cow (containing its blood), which calls for their aspersion on the impure persons (Num 19:12, 19). Yet the question remains and, indeed, is reinforced. The ashes of the Red Cow are, in fact, called a *ḥaṭṭāʾt* (Num 19:9, 17). This means that they have been incorporated into Israel's sacrificial system (for other evidence, see chap. 4, COMMENT G). Why then was not the same procedure applied to the birds? Indeed, because these birds, like the ashes of the Red Cow, also serve a purificatory function, why could they not also have been designated a *ḥaṭṭāʾt*?

The answer, I submit, is that the birds had to be wild, else there would remain the ever-present fear that the live bird dispatched to the open country would return to the settlement and bring back the very impurity it was supposed to eliminate (for details, see the NOTE below). A *ḥaṭṭāʾt* bird, or for that matter any sacrificial animal, perforce had to be domesticated, and a turtledove or pigeon most likely would have returned "home," in other words, to the community. Therefore, the birds were made to conform to Israel's monotheistic system not as sacrifices but as "pure" birds, eligible not for the altar but for the table.

two . . . birds (*štê-ṣippŏrîm*). The birds are not specified. This clearly implies that they are not turtledoves or pigeons, the exclusive sacrificial birds, else they would have been named. But could they be included among the birds eligible for the rite? Theoretically, the answer is yes, for they obviously merit the designation "pure." But the text has added another qualification, *ḥayyôt*, which must be rendered "wild" (for the substantiation, see above). Supporting this view is the opinion of the rabbis that the birds in question are sparrows (*m. Neg.* 14:1, 5; cf. Feliks 1984: 75), which, as indicated by their name *dĕrôr* 'freedom' (cf. 25:10; Isa 61:1; Jer 34:8, 15, 17), never allow themselves to be tamed (*Sipra*, Neg. Mĕṣōrāʿ 5:14; *b. Šabb.* 106b; *b. Beṣa* 24a).

Why were birds and not some other creatures chosen for this ceremony? On the basis of a Hurrian rite that calls for the sacrifice of three birds to the chthonic deities (Otten 1961: 130), one might argue that the live bird carries the impurity of the erstwhile scale-diseased person back to its source, the underworld (cf. Weinfeld 1980: 84). But the birds in Mesopotamian and Hittite rituals are sent heavenward, directed apparently toward the celestial deities. Thus in one *Namburbi* ritual, a male bird is released "to the east, before Šamaš" (Caplice 1965–71: 36.34–38 r. 6'); in another, an incantation is recited before the Sun god, Šamaš: "May the evil of this bird cross over [the mountain]," and then a male bird is again released to the east, before him (Caplice 1965–71: 36.273–78, obv. 11' and r. 28'f.). Even in rituals in which the released-bird motif is only mentioned, but not acted out, we find the following specifications: "May a bird take my sin up to the sky, may a fish take my sin down to the abyss" (Reiner 1956: 140–41, 1.22'; cf. 142, 1.37'); "May my headache fly like a dove to the west, like a raven to the . . . of heaven, like a bird to the wide-place" (cf. Thompson 1903–4: 2.76; translation corrected by D. Wright); "Let me cast off my evil that the bird may fly up to heaven with it" (Thompson 1971: 186). Similarly, birds in Hittite purificatory rituals are released heavenward or, as the magician states, "I released them into the branches" (Otten and Souček 1969: 4.37–39; cf. Engelhard 1970: 157–58; and for additional examples see Wright 1987: 75–86).

Thus, birds are chosen not because they are favored by chthonic deities or even by celestial deities. They are chosen because they transport the assumed freight of impurity upward and outward, to far-off distances whence the impurity cannot return. That the function of the birds is to carry off the impurity as far as possible is graphically depicted by the two women who "had wings like those of a stork" (Zech 5:9) for the purpose of carrying the tub of wickedness to far-off Babylonia (ibid., vv 5–11). To be sure, there is a significant contrast between the function of the birds in the biblical and in the nonbiblical rites. In the latter, the impurity removed by the birds covers the entire gamut of evil— sin, curse, headache, fate-demon, sickness, anger, and more (see Wright 1984: 87)—whereas the biblical rite does not purport to cure at all—the patient is already healed—but only removes residual ritual impurity, and only the first layer of it at that (see the COMMENT below and chap. 15, COMMENT F).

Nonetheless, this bird rite would seem to have undergone little or no change from its purported pagan model. Contrast the scapegoat in the Yom Kippur rite, which serves the same function but has undergone a transformation that has tailored it to fit into the Israelite sacrificial system as a *ḥaṭṭāʾt* (see the NOTES on "and it shall be pure," v 43 and on 16:5, 8; and see chap. 4, COMMENT G). The question, of course, remains: Why did not the Priestly legislators also convert the two birds into a *ḥaṭṭāʾt?* The superficial answer would be that birds do not qualify as *ḥaṭṭāʾt* offerings (chap. 4) except under special circumstances (5:1–3). A deeper, and probably more accurate answer would focus on the relative rarity of scale-disease rites in comparison with rites of corpse contamination (Num 19) and the annual purging of the sanctuary (chap. 16). Only the latter, of necessity involving every Israelite at one time or other in his or her life, had to be weaned completely from its pagan origins.

cedar wood ('ēṣ 'erez). Probably a stick (*t. Neg.* 8:2; *Sipra*, Měṣōrāʿ Neg. par. 1:2). For *'ēṣ*, normally "tree," meaning "stick, twig," see Exod 15:25; Ezek 37:16, 19. The identification of the *'erez* was not certain among the rabbis, who felt that it was a generic name for ten different trees (*b. B. Bat.* 80b). In fact, one opinion identified this *'erez* with the cypress (*Sipra*, Měṣōrāʿ Neg. par. 1:3). But there seems no doubt today that it is the Cedar of Lebanon.

Wood was frequently added to water in Mesopotamian purification rites (Laessøe 1955: 65 n. 148), especially the tamarisk (Reiner 1958: 45, 9.1.1, cf. *CAD*, B 240), but also the cedar (cf. *CAD*, E 277–78). For example, in the "Ritual for Covering the Temple Kettle-Drum," the bull (whose hide becomes the drumskin) would be sprinkled with cedar balsam, burned with cedar wood, and buried in a red cloth (2.12, 18, 19; cf. *ANET*[3] 335). Yet of all woods with magical powers, cedar might have been selected because of its color, red. As indicated in the previous NOTE on "live," the power of the blood, the symbol of life, was abetted by the addition of two red ingredients, the crimson yarn (see below) and the cedar wood, in order to counter and reverse the death process vividly and visually represented by the deterioration of the body stricken with scale disease. To be sure, in the Israelite system the patient had to be cured before this purificatory rite could be applied. But the rite itself was not created by Israel. Indubitably, it was—as was most of the sacrificial system—a legacy from Israel's pagan past. A similar verdict must be accorded to the use of these same ingredients in the purification rite for corpse-contaminated persons (Milgrom 1981a). Indeed, the fact that the same life-enhancing ingredients are used in purificatory rites for those contaminated by a corpse or by scale disease further supports the theory that the scale-diseased person is regarded as a corpse (chap. 13, COMMENT B) and that impurity, in general, is associated with death (see chap. 15, COMMENT G).

crimson yarn. šěnî tôlaʿat, literally, "the red of the worm." That *šānî* is "red" is shown by other scriptural contexts (e.g., Isa 1:18; Cant 4:3) and the Versions (cf. LXX). It may be an Egyptian loanword (Grintz 1975: 174–78). The red worm in question is the *Kermes biblicus,* cochmial, biblical *karmîl* (2 Chr 2:6, 13; 3:14), and the red coloring-matter extracted from the female is used to dye wool (*Sipra*, Měsōrāʿ Neg. par. 1:14; cf. Rashi).

hyssop ('ēzōb). Aramaic *zūpā, zōpā* with a prosthetic *'aleph.* Akk. *zūpu* is a loanword from Aramaic *(AHw).* The rabbis are unsure of its identification and cite three possible plants: *Artemisia abrotanum, Origanum maru,* and *Origanum majorana* (*b. Šabb.* 109b). The last-named is the identification accepted today (more specifically, the *O. majorana syriaca;* Feliks 1984: 176), which was correctly identified by Saadiah as *ṣaʿtr,* a popular spice and herb in the Near East.

In this case, however, and throughout the Bible, the plant is used as an instrument for sprinkling (Exod 12:22; Num 19:6, 18; Ps 51:9); the liquid into which it is dipped adheres to it in the form of droplets.

5. *The priest shall order.* See the NOTE on v 4.

one bird slaughtered. wĕšāḥaṭ, literally, "and he shall slaughter," another example of an active verb with an impersonal subject (cf. the NOTE on "the priest shall order . . . to be brought," v 4). *Tg. Ps.-J.* renders accurately, if inelegantly, "The priest shall order to slaughter." Some of the versions (Sam., LXX, Pesh.) read this verb as a plural, wĕšāḥăṭû, as they did for wĕlāqaḥ (v 4a), so that the priest will not be taken as the subject.

That the bird was killed by slaughtering and not by pinching off its head (1:15) is firm proof that it was not treated as a sacrifice. Indeed, the fact that this rite was performed after the Temple was destroyed (*t. Neg.* 8:2) is further proof of its nonsacrificial character. šāḥaṭ 'slaughter' probably means cutting the throat (cf. chap. 11, COMMENT D). Rabbinic tradition avers that the slaughtered bird was buried on the spot, in full view of the participants (*m. Tem.* 7:4; *m. Neg.* 14:1). It makes sense; assurance is needed that the slaughtered bird, which has symbolically absorbed the impurity/disease of the victim, will not contaminate others. The same rationale holds for the probable destruction of the bowl holding the purificatory ingredients (see the NOTE on "an earthen vessel," below) and the release of the live bird (v 7).

into (ʾel). The rabbis interpret ʾel as ʿal 'over' (*m. Neg.* 14:1), followed by Ibn Ezra, who finds scriptural support in ʾel-hannaʿr hazzeh hitpallāltî 'It was for this boy that I prayed' (1 Sam 1:27), where ʾel clearly stands for ʿal. Yet the MT's ʾel must be understood in its primary meaning, "into," thereby specifying that the blood of the slaughtered bird must be drained *into* the bowl *(Yahel ʾOr).*

an earthen vessel (kĕlî-ḥereś). The rabbis' insistence that the bowl be a new one (*m. Neg.* 14:1; *b. Soṭa* 2:2) makes sense, for earthenware, once contaminated, cannot be purified (see the NOTE on 11:33). The latter regulation also certifies that after the rite is completed the bowl is smashed (cf. 6:21; 11:33), not because it becomes sanctified (Elliger 1966) but, to the contrary, because it becomes contaminated by receiving and absorbing the victim's scale disease (cf. also the NOTE on 6:21). The use of an earthen bowl is also prescribed for the suspected adulteress (Num 5:17) because it is contaminated by the priest's curse rubbed into its waters (ibid., v 23). The rite for corpse contamination surprisingly does not specify the composition of the vessel holding the waters and the Red Cow's ashes (Num 19:17), which led the rabbis to postulate that this vessel may be of any material (*m. Para* 5:5). Nevertheless, *Tg. Ps.-J.* (ad loc.) specifies paḥar 'earthenware'.

over (ʿal). When the same context reappears (v 51), however, the preposition bĕ 'in' is used.

spring water. mayim ḥayyîm, literally, "living waters." The Tgs. render accurately "flowing water." *Yahel ʾOr*'s explanation is also on target: "the waters are called 'living' because they flow perpetually and do not cease like the living being whose movements never cease." Thus water from a cistern would be invalid. That the biblical writer distinguished between those two sources of water can be derived from the expression *maʿyān ûbôr miqwēh-mayim* 'a spring or cistern in which water is collected' (11:36). By contrast, a cistern in which water is not collected, by rain or by drawn water, but into which water flows from an underground source—that is, an Artesian well—would certainly pass muster. This can be derived from the explicit statement that "Isaac's servants, digging in the wadi, found there *bēʾēr mayim ḥayyîm* 'a well of spring water' (Gen 26:19). Further evidence will be added in the NOTE on 15:13.

Water (or some other liquid) was obviously needed because the blood of the bird would have been insufficient for dipping the required materials plus the live bird into it (Ḥazzequni). But why the necessity for spring water? Spring water is required in two other purificatory rituals: for genital discharges (15:13) and corpse contamination (Num 19:17). The latter case has already been discussed regarding three other similar ingredients required for the rite: cedar wood, crimson yarn, and hyssop (see the NOTES on v 4). That spring water is also a common element leads to the suspicion that, like the other ingredients mentioned, spring water was an essential element of the original purification rite prior to its incorporation into the Priestly system, and that its function in its pagan setting was, together with the other ingredients, to exorcise the disease from the patient. To be sure, things are no longer the same in this Priestly text: the patient is already cured. What, then, is the function of these same ingredients here? Although it is subsequently stated that the ritual has purified him (v 7b), it will turn out that nothing of the sort has happened (see the NOTE on "When he has thus purified him," v 7). Nonetheless, the explicit wording of the text is an incontrovertible admission that originally, at one time, purification did indeed occur.

Support for this hypothesis can be adduced from the Bible itself. Scale-diseased Naaman is told by Elisha, God's prophet, "Go and bathe seven times in the Jordan, and your flesh shall be restored, and you shall be pure" (2 Kgs 5:10). Now, it should be borne in mind that because the Jordan flows, its waters qualify as *mayim ḥayyîm.* Yet the text states unambiguously that these waters will heal Naaman. Thus we see that the folk tradition, ensconced in the book of Kings, is at variance with the official, Priestly tradition, embodied in this levitical ritual. Nevertheless, each tradition is aware of the other, to judge by the slight concession each accords the other. The folk tradition concerning Naaman's cure repeatedly states that not only will his flesh be healed but that, in addition, he will become *ṭāhôr* 'pure' (2 Kgs 5:10, 12, 13, 14; La Barbera 1986).

The Priestly tradition, as we now see, has incorporated an older exorcistic rite, and though it serves no practical function at all—the patient has already been healed and the residual impurity is eliminated by the subsequent ablutions (see the NOTES on vv 8, 9, 20)—it stands as the indispensable beginning of an eight-day purificatory rite, because the people, not the priests, have demanded it. Presumably, this rite would fall into the same category as the ashes of the Red Cow, which, together with its ingredients—the same as the ones mentioned here—are sprinkled on the corpse-contaminated person despite the fact that as a *ḥaṭṭāʾt* (Num 19:9, 17) they should be applied only to objects, never to persons. Here too is a Priestly concession to a popular demand for a widely practiced exorcistic rite (details in chap. 4, COMMENT G). Thus, just as the exorcism for corpse contamination was eviscerated of its pagan content and incorporated into the Priestly sacrificial system, so the exorcism for scale disease was allowed to remain at the head of week-long purification rites, but deprived of its originally inherent magical powers. Israelite monotheism, in its Priestly version, had clearly been at work.

6. *and [he shall take the live bird,] along with (ʾet . . . ʾōtāh wĕʾet).* All of the Versions read the first *ʾet* as *wĕʾet*. The function of this triple *ʾet* is to indicate that the bird is not bound together with the other ingredients but is held separately (*Sipra,* Mĕṣōrāʿ Neg. 1:5), which is also demonstrated in the following *ʾōtām wĕʾēt* 'them together with'. The rabbis explain how this is done: "He took cedarwood and hyssop and crimson yarn and bound them together with the ends of the strip [of the yarn] and brought near to them the tips of the wings and the tip of the tail of the second [bird held in the other hand]" (*m. Neg.* 14:1).

The purpose of dipping the live bird is rationalized in later times as an attempt to mark it with blood so that other birds will kill it or that no other scale-diseased person will use it (Ḥazzequni). The symbolism, however, in view of other purification rituals, is crystal clear. The blood of the slain bird absorbs the disease from the patient and transfers it to the water. The live bird reabsorbs the disease when it is dipped into the water and transports it into the open country. Without doubt, in its pagan antecedents, this exorcistic rite was accompanied by incantations, which were subsequently excised by Israel's priesthood (see chap. 16, COMMENT E on the original form and function of the scapegoat and its congeners in the ancient Near East). In addition, the rite was thoroughly transformed so that it was no longer a cure for disease but a ritual for purification after the disease was cured. In truth, however, the bird rite plays no role whatsoever in the actual purification of the healed *mĕṣōrāʿ.* His purification is effected by his immersion into water following the bird rite (v 8) and, again, on the seventh day (v 9). Indeed, the fact that the bird rite turns out to be extraneous to the rest of the Priestly ceremony proves that it has been borrowed from Israel's anterior cultures and it was retained not because Israel's priests wanted it but probably because the people at large demanded it, practiced it, and would not have tolerated its deletion. For them, this rite of exorcism was indispensable. The same rationale probably lies behind the purification of corpse-contaminated persons with the ashes of the Red Cow (chap. 4, COMMENT G). The use of spring water also supports this hypothesis (see the NOTE on v 5). For a comprehensive discussion, see COMMENT B below and chap. 15, COMMENT F.

dip (ṭābal). In P, the subject is the priest (contrast Exod 12:22). In the corpse-contamination ritual (Num 19:18), by contrast, the purificatory waters paradoxically contaminate those who employ them (chap. 4, COMMENT G). The direct object of the verb "dip" is hyssop, either by itself (Num 19:18; cf. Exod 12:22) or, as in this case, together with a bird, cedar wood, and crimson yarn (14:6, 51). The indirect object is blood (4:6, 17; 9:9), oil (14:16), or purificatory waters (14:6, 51; Num 19:18).

over the spring water (ʿal hammayim haḥayyîm). The definite articles prove that this prepositional phrase modifies the past participle, *haššĕḥūṭâ* 'slaughtered', and that the latter is not an adjective modifying *haṣṣippōr* 'the bird'.

7. *He shall then sprinkle (wĕhizzâ).* Where? On what part of the body? Rabbinic tradition differs: on the back of the hand or on the forehead (*m. Neg.* 14:1), or on the face *(Tg. Ps.-J.),* or on any part (*t. Neg.* 8:3). The nonspecificity of the text here and in that of the purificatory rite for corpse contamination (cf. Num 19:19) is an indication that the last answer is correct: no specific part of the body is the object of the sprinkling (this also holds for the sprinkling of the novitiate priests, 8:30). As observed above (NOTE on "spring water," v 5), the aspersion with the bloody springwater had no effect either on the scale disease (which had already been eliminated) or on the ritual impurity (see also COMMENT A below and chap. 15, COMMENT F). In Israel's environs, however, purificatory water had both medicinal and apotropaic (i.e., magical) powers, for example, "may they (the daughters of Anu) sprinkle purifying water and extinguish the *sikkatu* disease" (*CAD,* S 86a).

seven times. For the significance of seven sprinklings in priestly rites, see the NOTES on "seven times," 4:6 and 8:11 (cf. also the NOTE on "he shall sprinkle," 16:19). Sevenfold sprinkling also played a role in the Mesopotamian cult: "and sprinkle it seven and seven times over the door and the handle of the door wedge" (*CAD,* S 86a).

When he has thus purified him (wĕṭihărô). The LXX presumes *wĕṭāhēr* 'and he is pure', in conformance with (and probably influenced by) the form of this verb in vv 8 and 9. Other commentators render "and he (the priest) declares him pure" (Ḥazzequni; Sforno). That these interpretations are wrong is shown by the fact that this first day of purification is not complete until he launders his clothes and bathes himself (see the NOTE on "then he shall be pure," v 8). Indeed, the Masoretes must have been clearly aware that this word does not mark the completion of the purificatory rite when they placed the pausal *'athnaḥ* on the preceding word, thereby indicating that *wĕṭihărô* is not the conclusion of the previous sentence but the beginning of the following one (Wessely 1846). Thus, the meaning of the word is not that the erstwhile scale-diseased person has been partially purified, namely, that some of his ritual impurity has been removed, but that only part of the first-day rite is over. Now he must proceed to the ritual of laundering, shaving, and bathing before this first stage of his purification is complete.

he shall release (wĕšillaḥ). piʿel of *šlḥ* means "free, release" (e.g., Gen 8:7; Exod 6:11; 7:26). Like the scapegoat (16:23), the bird is not killed. Therefore to be certain that the bird will not return, symbolically laden with impurity (or the disease, *Tg. Ps.-J.* on v 53), the bird must not be domesticated (see the NOTE on "wild," v 4). And if it chances to return it must be sent out again (*t. Neg.* 8:4). The analogy with the scapegoat is even more significant because both share the same goal: elimination of impurity (Ramban), a common purpose that was recognized as early as Origen (*Lev. Hom.* 8.10, cited by Kalisch 1867–72).

It may seem surprising that whereas those who handle the scapegoat are rendered impure (16:26, 28) the same does not hold for the handler of the birds. It should be noted, however, that the bird handler is a priest and that the high priest who leans his hands on the scapegoat (16:21) is also unaffected. The answer can only be this: the officiating priest is immune to the impurity that he removes (see the NOTE to "and leave them there," 16:23), provided he does not leave the sanctuary (cf. Num 19:7 and the NOTE on v 46). This priestly immunity would also explain why the priests' daubing of the altar horns to remove its impurity would not result in their contamination (4:7, 18, 25, 30, 34), whereas those who handle the scapegoat (16:26, 28) and the one who sprinkles the ashes of the Red Cow (Num 19:21) are contaminated because they are laymen.

over the open country (ʿal-pĕnê haśśādeh). śadeh 'field' can also denote "open, wild country" (e.g., 2 Kgs 4:39), a meaning particularly evident in its compounds: *ḥayyat haśśādeh* 'the wild beasts' (Gen 2:19); *gepen śādeh* 'wild vine', and *paqquʿōt śādēh* 'wild gourds' (2 Kgs 4:39). The equivalent term in Akk., *ṣēru*, exhibits the same semantic range: "timberland, back country, open country, fields, plain, steppeland" (*CAD*, S 138a). The parallel prescription in the ritual for the purification of houses adds the stipulation that the bird should be released *ʾel-miḥûṣ lāʿîr* 'outside the city' (v 53). Yet here it would have been redundant to add the equivalent phrase, *ʾel-miḥûṣ lammaḥāneh* 'outside the camp', for the bird rite must take place outside the camp; the healed person may not return to the camp until the very end of his first-day purificatory rites (v 8).

8. *launder . . . shave . . . bathe (wĕkibbes . . . wĕgillaḥ . . . wĕrāḥaṣ).* The order is determined by priestly considerations. Self-ablution comes last, lest the person become reinfected by his impure clothes or hair. Is any part of the rite performed by someone other than the healed person? One rabbinic opinion claims that the shaving is done by the priest (*t. Neg.* 8:6). But on the analogy of the ritual for the induction of the Levites (Num 8:7) the shaving is done by the person undergoing the rite. One problem remains regarding the priority of laundering: Will not the washed clothes be reinfected by the as yet impure person? Yet there is no doubt that laundering precedes bathing in all of P's purificatory rites (cf. 15:5, 6, 7, 8, 10, 11, 13, 21, 22, 27; 16:26, 28; 17:15; Num 19:7, 8, 19; 31:24; contrast Gen 35:2; Exod 19:10, 14 JE). Would laundering,

then, have been performed by another party? Not necessarily. On the analogy of the man with a chronic discharge, who does not transmit impurity by touch if he first washes his hands (15:11), one may argue that while the scale-diseased person has his hands in the water washing his clothes, he too does not transmit impurity. By contrast, the reverse process, bathing before laundering, would not work. Before the purified person could put his clothes into the water, they would have defiled him and his ablutions would have been in vain. The Jewish practice, reflected in *Baraita di Masseket niddah* (Horowitz 1890: 18) calls for a different procedure, but the passage there is unclear.

It is interesting to see that Hindu religion solves the problem along similar lines:

> To become pure a person must have a complete bath, including pouring water over the hair. . . . If cotton clothing is worn it must have been washed by someone in *madi* [purity], and to remain in a state of madi the wearer must not touch any cloth which is not madi. . . . [For example] A man bathes in his *panche*, a piece of cloth around his waist. *He then changes to another panche while bathing so that he can remove and wash the one he has been wearing. While wet both panches are madi* (italics mine). He dries himself using the panche he has just washed (to use a dry towel which was not madi would remove his own madi), rewashes the panche he has just used as a towel, and then leaves the bathing area to go to the clothesline in the attic of the house. Madi clothes are generally dried and kept here to insure that no one not in a state of madi accidentally touches them. He then changes to the panche he had washed the previous day and hangs up to dry that which he has just washed and is wearing. (Harper 1964: 154)

Thus Hindu practice raises the possibility that those required by biblical law to launder and bathe might do both at the same time (E. Firmage).

all of his hair (kol-śě ʿārô). This should be understood literally. The rabbis, however, exempt the hair not visible to the eye (*m. Neg.* 2:4), an exemption, they claim, that also prevails during the priest's inspection (see the NOTE on "shall examine," 13:3).

and bathe in water (wěrāḥaṣ bammayim). The full formula is *rāḥaṣ (ʾet-) běśārô bammayim* 'bathe his body in water' (e.g., v 9; 15:13, 16; 16:4, 24, 26, 28; 22:6; Num 19:7, 8). Purificatory ablutions among the Hittites also mandated the bathing of the entire body (Moyer 1969: 104). Indeed, their temple personnel not only had to bathe before entering the sacred precincts but, like their Egyptian counterparts, they had to remove their body hair and pare their nails ("Instructions for Temple Officials" 1.15, 3.63–64, *ANET*[3] 207b, 209b).

In rabbinic Hebrew, *ṭābal* becomes the exclusive word for ritual immersion (e.g., *m. Neg.* 14:2, 3), except when citing Scripture. Apparently, biblical *rāḥaṣ* was felt to be imprecise, connoting both ordinary and cultic washing. But *ṭābal* is also a biblical term, meaning "dip" (e.g., v 16). And on one occasion it occurs with the sense of immersion (2 Kgs 5:14)—strikingly, in a classic case (Naaman) of scale disease. The Qumranites, though, taking their cue from Scripture, never use *ṭābal* to mean "immerse."

then he shall be pure. wĕṭāhēr; in other words, he no longer has to dwell outside the camp (Sforno). This is the first of three mentions of *wĕṭāhēr* (vv 8, 9, 20). Each *wĕṭāhēr* indicates that another layer of impurity has been removed. Before this purification, his impurity is that of a corpse (*Sipre*, Num 105: Jos., *Ant.* 3.264). Now, after his first-day ablution, he reenters his community. No one need be concerned about being under the same roof. By the elimination of the initial layer, this first-day purification rite renders the healed scale-diseased person incapable any longer of contaminating persons and vessels by overhang (cf. *m. Kelim* 1:4; *m. Neg.* 13:17). For details see the chart and explanatory notes in chap. 15, COMMENT F. The rabbis hold that henceforth the person contaminates persons and vessels by direct contact but not by carrying (indirectly, without touching) (*m. Kelim* 1:1). Thus, although their system operates on different postulates than mine, it should be noted that they too maintain that *wĕṭāhēr* always implies a diminution of impurity and that the person continues to contaminate directly but not indirectly.

Ibn Ezra claims that the decrease of impurity commences in the evening. His view must be rejected. The person may reenter the camp as soon as he bathes. Clearly, he does not make his way into the camp after dark. This fact also refutes the theory proposed by J. Neusner (1976: 197–205) that only fresh water purifies but bathing in any other water necessitates waiting till evening for purification. This verse and the next (the first- and seventh-day rites) state explicitly that bathing in any water suffices for purification (see also 16:26, 28).

After that he may enter the camp. To mingle freely with members of the community, but he may not touch them or their vessels (see below).

but must remain outside his tent (wĕyāšab mihûṣ lĕʾohŏlô). According to the rabbis, this means he is barred from sexual intercourse (*m. Neg.* 14:2; *t. Neg.* 8:6; *Tg. Ps.-J.; Sipra,* Mĕṣōrāʿ Neg. par. 2:11), but the exclusion applies only to a male, not a female (*b. Ker.* 8b). Instead, the plain meaning seems to be that the person (male or female) must camp in the open so as not to come into direct contact with other persons and objects. But why not allow the person to be admitted into the house and be given special utensils and quarters, as clearly was done for the parturient and the *zāb/zābâ* (see chaps. 12 and 15)? The answer will become apparent by referring to the table in chap. 15, COMMENT F. The healed scale-diseased person possesses a higher degree of impurity than either the parturient or the *zāb/zābâ,* and he contaminates the profane by overhang and the sacred from afar. When the initial impurity layer has been removed by the rites of the first day, he or she still contaminates the profane by direct contact but the sacred by overhang. It is the latter condition—unique to the bearer of scale disease—that necessitates banishment from the home, lest any sacred food (e.g., meat from the well-being offering) or sacred object (e.g., donations to the sanctuary) be contaminated by overhang. My view is confirmed by a new Qumran document (*MMT* B 66–68): [*Y*]*ŠB MḤWṢ* [*L'WHL W ŠB'T Y*]*MYM W'TH BHYWT ṬM'TM 'MHM* [*HṢRW'YM B'YM '*]*M ṬHRT HQWDŠ LBYT* '[The scale-diseased person] shall dwell outside his tent seven d]ays. But now [i.e., outside Qumran] because their impurity is [still] with them [the scale-diseased persons are entering] into the house cont[aining] the purity of sacred [food].' See also chap. 15, COMMENT F. This view is not markedly different from that of the rabbis who hold that the person contaminates like a carcass of a reptile (*m. Neg.* 14:2) and transmits a one-day impurity to persons and vessels (*m. Kelim* 1:1). The effect is the same, but it does not explain the person's exclusion from the tent unless the principle of overhang is invoked.

seven days. At this stage the healed scale-diseased person is equivalent to the new mother (of a male), the *zāb/zābâ*, the menstruant, and the corpse-contaminated person at the commencement of their purificatory periods, who contaminate by direct contact and who must wait seven days for the next stage of their purification (see the chart and explanatory notes, chap. 15, COMMENT F).

9. *(shave off) all of his hair—of his head ('et-kol-śe'ārô 'et-rō'šô).* All modern translations (except *NJPS*) render "all the hair of his head," regarding the two apposite nouns as a hendiadys, in order to avoid the patent redundancy in this verse of the twice-stated "shave off all of his hair." The redundancy, however, is deliberate; see below.

chin (zĕqānô). For this rendering, see the discussion in the NOTE on 13:29.

eyebrows (gabbōt 'ēnāyw). Arab. *jubbatum* denotes the bone surrounding the cavity of the eye (KB). In BH, it denotes the rim of a wheel (1 Kgs 7:33; Ezek 1:18). Here, however, it clearly refers to the brows.

—indeed, he shall shave off all of his hair (wĕ'et-kol-śĕ'ārô yĕgallaḥ). The rabbis explain that this redundancy is for the purpose of qualifying the generalization, that is, all of his hair but not that of his private parts (*Sipra*, Mĕṣōrā' Neg. 2:2). They are right, but the reason is just the opposite: the repetition is indeed a euphemism for the private parts, but its purpose is to make certain that they are included; so Ehrlich (1899–1900), who drops the *waw* of *wĕ'et* as a dittography of the final letter of the previous word. This emendation, though, is hardly necessary for the *waw* is frequently attested as having emphatic force (*GKC* §154aN). *NJPS* ingeniously attempts to avoid the difficulty by making this phrase the apodosis of a new sentence: "When he has shaved off all his hair." Nevertheless, this construction, beginning with the object—particularly if the object begins with a *waw*—will not admit of such a translation. On the contrary, this sentence stands in chiastic relation with *yĕgallaḥ 'et-kol-śĕ'ārô* (v 9α), forming a circular inclusio with it (Paran 1983: 33), thereby emphasizing that the entire body should be shaved, including the pubic hair.

This expression must be distinguished from the one used to describe a similar rite for the induction of the levitic labor force: *wĕheˁĕbîrû taˁar ˁal-kol-bĕśārām* 'Go over their bodies with a razor' (Num 8:7), that is, shave their bodies lightly, not as meticulously as the bodies of scale-diseased persons.

then he shall be pure (wĕṭāhēr). The second of three occurrences of *wĕṭāhēr* (vv 8, 9, 20). This declaration of purity again follows an ablution (cf. v 8), proving that the ablution always reduces the impurity by one degree. The person need no longer remain outside his tent but can now enter it (Sforno) for he no longer contaminates sancta by overhang, only by touch (see the table in chap. 15, COMMENT F). To eliminate the last vestige of impurity he needs to bring the appropriate sacrifices to the sanctuary on the following day. Again, there is no mention of the evening, as in the case of minor impurities (e.g., 11:24–40), presumably because for major impurities sacrifices and not sundown terminate the impurity (for the possibility that sundown terminates impurity both for major and for minor impurities, however, see chap. 15, COMMENT F). In the rabbinic system, however, consecrated food *(tĕrûmâ)*—but not sacrificial food— may be handled by the laity and eaten by the priests after sundown (*Sipra*, Emor. 4:8; *b. Yebam.* 74b–85a). The evening before the sacrifice as a separate stage in the diminution of impurity (called *ṭĕbûl yôm*) is purely a rabbinic invention (see *m. Zabim* 5:12; Rashi on *b. Ḥul.* 128a, s.v. *mĕhaddēr*). Yet in minor impurities this notion can be shown to exist (see chap. 15, COMMENT F and the NOTES on 22:4–8).

10. *On the eighth day.* The biblical day begins at sunrise. This can certainly be verified in P. God made the world only during daylight, allowing nighttime to intervene between one creative day and the next (Gen 1). Sacrifices may be eaten through the night but on the following morning—the start of a new day— they must be incinerated (see the NOTES on 7:15, 17). The case in this verse is even more obvious: sacrifices are never offered at night. Technically, nightfall should end all impurities as it does for all minor impurities. It is, then, the need to await daylight before entering the sanctuary that accounts for the additional, eighth day. Because the Dead Sea sectaries hold that Jerusalem possesses the same degree of holiness as the Temple, one can presume that they would have barred bearers of scale disease and other major impurities from even entering Jerusalem until the eighth day (cf. 11QT 45:17–18)—and not before evening (see the NOTE on v 11).

two male lambs (šnê-kĕbāśîm). The LXX and Sam. add *bĕnê šānâ* 'yearlings', a correct interpretation to judge by 12:6 and Num 6:12–14.

[and] one [yearling] ewe (wĕkabśâ ʾaḥat). A knowledge of the laws of sacrifice (chaps. 1–5) is presumed (Ramban); they make it clear that the ewe was destined to be a purification offering: only that offering is exclusively female when brought by a commoner (4:27–35), whereas the other expiation sacrifices are exclusively male (1:2–13; 5:14–19). Note too that in this prescriptive order the purification offering is listed last, whereas in the descriptive order of the

actual ritual it precedes the burnt offering (vv 19–20). In all other sacrificial series it is offered first; on the exception in this case that the reparation offering is sacrificed first, see the NOTE on v 12.

yearling (bat-sĕnātāh). This qualification for the ewe furnishes strong support that a similar qualification described the male lambs, as preserved in the LXX and Sam. (see above).

three-tenths [of an ephah]. The measure is not cited, but it must be assumed to be an *ephah* (cf. Num 28:5; 15:4 LXX). A tenth of an *ephah*, according to the calculations of my student S. Rattray, is slightly more than one quart (see COMMENT C below). Each person was permitted to gather this amount of manna (Exod 16:16, 36). Ruth gleaned a full *ephah* of barley (Ruth 2:17).

But why were three-tenths needed? The division of the semolina into adjunct cereal offerings for each of the blood sacrifices is not mentioned. Yet because the latter are only three in number and because all are sheep, each of which requires one-tenth (cf. Num 15:3–4), the conclusion is ineluctable that every sacrificial animal was accompanied by one-tenth of an *ephah* of semolina (cf. also v 21). This too is the conclusion of the rabbis (*b. Menaḥ.* 91a [bar.]), though it confronts them with a serious problem. For it means that the *ḥaṭṭāʾt* and *ʾāšām* sacrifices are also accompanied by a *minḥâ*, a possibility that the rabbis categorically reject but which they must concede here (cf. *m. Menaḥ.* 9:6). The lengthy argumentation on this matter in the Talmud (cf. *b. Menaḥ.* 90b–91b) reflects a long and extended controversy.

Now we know that the opposing view that all blood sacrifices, including the *ḥaṭṭāʾt* and *ʾāšām*, require cereal adjuncts was adopted and vigorously championed by the Dead Sea sectaries (11QT 18:4–6; 25:5–6, 12–15). They even alter the wording of the public sacrifices in the calendar of Num 28–29 to reflect this view (e.g., cf. Num 29:20–22 with 11QT 28:6–9; and see Yadin 1983: 143–46). Yet the exact scriptural (MT) foundation for their ruling is not cited in their writings. Perhaps they derived it from Num 28:15. This verse reads, *ûśĕʿîr ʿizzîm ʾeḥād lĕḥaṭṭāʾt laYHWH ʿal-ʿōlat haṭṭāmîd yēʿāśeh wĕniskô* 'And there shall be one goat as a purification offering to the Lord, to be sacrificed in addition to the regular burnt offering and its libation'. The problem is that the suffix on the final word, *wĕniskô* 'its libation', is masculine, whereas its antecedent, "burnt offering," is feminine (the Sam. reads *wĕniskêhen* (pl.) which may presuppose MT *wĕniskāh*, i.e., as feminine). Thus the Qumranites could have deduced that the antecedent of the masculine suffix must be the "goat" and, hence, the purification offering must be accompanied by libation (and its requisite cereal offering; Num 15:4–5). Nonetheless, it must be recorded that the MT's masculine suffix need not advert to the goat nor be amended to refer to the burnt offering; rather, its referent is the word *tāmîd*, which, in this verse, is used as a noun, literally, "the burnt offering of the *tāmîd*."

In any event, the implicit deduction from this verse in Leviticus, that the *ḥaṭṭāʾt* and *ʾāšām* were accompanied by a cereal offering, would have provided sufficient justification for Qumranites, Karaites, and their followers to deduce that all blood sacrifices must have cereal adjuncts. As for the rabbis, who admit that this verse is an anomaly, the requirement of the adjunct cereal offerings presents an enigma. To be sure, they offer the explanation that this *ḥaṭṭāʾt* exceptionally does not expiate for sin but permits the person to eat sacred food (*b. Soṭa* 15a) and enter the sanctuary (*t. Neg.* 8:120). But this is the function of every purification offering (see chap. 4, COMMENTS A and B). They also suggest that the cereal offering (and the libation) was denied to other *ḥaṭṭāʾt* and *ʾāšām* offerings in order not to glorify the sacrifice of a sinner; but in this case, because the scale-diseased person has already atoned by his suffering, he is now permitted these joyous adjuncts (*y. Soṭa* 2:1). The problem remains unresolved.

semolina mixed. sōlet . . . bĕlûlâ; cf. the NOTES on 2:1, 4.

for a cereal offering (minḥâ). Although the three-tenths of semolina are split up among the three blood sacrifices, they are considered to be an independent offering (*b. Menaḥ.* 91a).

one (ʾeḥād). This word seems superfluous in that the notion of "one" need not be expressed and it is, indeed, omitted in v 21. Besides, it ungrammatically breaks the construct *lōg ʾeḥād šemen,* which the LXX and Sam. rectify by reading *lōg šemen ʾeḥād.* Yet the MT can be justified on a number of grounds: (1) the word for "one" is inserted to contrast with *šĕlōšâ,* the "three"-tenths of semolina; (2) *ʾeḥād* in its present place as an adjective immediately following *lōg* signifies more than the number "one"; it means "special" (Ehrlich 1908–14); (3) each *minḥâ* contains one-quarter *hin* of oil (= three *logs*). Hence, the three cereal offerings comprise nine *logs* of oil, which, together with this freestanding *log,* give a total of nine plus one or ten *logs* of oil. Thus *ʾeḥād* also implies the notion of "additional."

log. This measure is the smallest unit of capacity in the Bible. It occurs only in this chapter and as a measure of oil. It is also attested in a Ugaritic text as *lg šmn* 'a log of oil' (*KTU* 1.148.21) within a ritual context (Cohen 1978: 36) and in an Aramaic inscription (*DISO* 135). One *log* = one-twelfth *hin* = six eggs, slightly less than one pint in rabbinic times (*b. Menaḥ.* 89a). The biblical *log,* however, seems to have been half that size, according to the calculations of my student, S. Rattray (see COMMENT C below).

11–20. The ritual for the eighth day is laid out in introverted fashion, as recognized by Lund (1942: 53–55). It is diagrammed below, with Lund's plan modified in a few instances. Discussion of the italicized words follows.

A.   The *priest* who performs the *purification* shall place *the one* to be *purified,*

                                                         11

    together with these (offerings), before the Lord at the entrance to the Tent of Meeting.

The priest shall take one of the male lambs   12

and present it as a reparation offering,

B.   together with the log of *oil,*

      and offer it as an elevation offering *before the Lord.*

      The lamb shall be slaughtered at the spot in the sacred precinct13

      where the *purification offering* and the *burnt offering* are slaughtered.

      (13b is a gloss)

    C.   The priest shall take some of *the blood of the reparation offering,*   14

        D.   *and the priest shall put [it] on the lobe of the right ear*

            of the one who is being purified, and on the thumb of

            his right hand, and on the big toe of his right foot.

            E.   The priest shall then take some of the log of *oil*   15

               and pour [it] into the *palm* of his own left hand.

                X.   And the priest shall dip his right finger   16

                    in the *oil* that is on his left *palm* and sprinkle

                    some of the oil with his finger seven times *before the Lord.*

               E'.   And some of the *oil* left on his *palm*   17

        D'.   *the priest shall put on the lobe of the right ear of the*

            one being purified, on the thumb of his right hand,

            and on the big toe of his right foot—

    C'.   on top of *the blood of the reparation offering.*

B'.   The remainder of the *oil* on the priest's palm   18

      shall be put on the head of the one being purified.

      Thus the priest shall make expiation for him *before the Lord.*

      The priest shall then offer the *purification offering*   19

      and effect purgation for the one being purified

      for his impurity. After this, *the burnt offering shall be slaughtered,*

      and the priest shall offer up the burnt offering and   20

      the cereal offering on the altar.

A'.   And the *priest* shall make expiation for *him.*

    Then he shall be *pure.*

The italicized words indicate the symmetries. The purifying priest and the purified person are stressed in the beginning (A) because complete purification is the end result of the rite (A'). Particularly striking is the ostensible redundancy of the spot in which both the purification and burnt offering are slaughtered (B), in that every other mention of this spot refers solely to the burnt offering (4:24, 29, 33; 7:2). Nevertheless, a glance at its corresponding section (B') provides the answer: the execution (including the slaughtering) of both sacrifices. The exact congruence of the blood and oil rites on the healed mĕṣōrāʿ (DD') is obvious; nonetheless, the positioning of the phrase "the blood of the reparation offering" in order to maintain the chiastic structure (CC') is noteworthy. Similarly, the ostensibly awkward use of a direct object instead of subject or verb to begin v 17 (E') can also be explained as an attempt to match its corresponding member in the introverted structure (E). Finally, the added dedication of the oil in order to enhance its powers of purification (see the NOTE on v 17) is highlighted as the center of the introversion (X). It repeats three items from both halves of the structure—oil, palm (EE'), and before the Lord (BB')—thereby locking in the entire unit (see a similar craftsmanship in the designing of vv 21–32 and 51–52).

Nonetheless, this introversion (and that of vv 21–32; see below) glosses over some jarring elements: for example, "before the Lord" appears not only in B, X, B' but also in A, and the priest's palm occurs not only in E, X, E', but also in B' (D. Wright). This passage is a clear indication that the large-scale chiastic structure was not perfected by the P school. Contrast the intricate structures developed by H (exemplified in the Introduction, §D). Thus the degree of sophistication in introverted structures becomes a criterion for distinguishing P from H.

11. *The priest who performs the purification (hakkōhēn hammĕṭahēr).* This phrase has been compared to Ug. *mlk brr*, which has led to rendering the latter "the king, the purifier" (Levine 1963: 106). Yet because the complete formulaic expression, *yrtḥṣ mlk brr*, describes the first act in a ritual day (e.g., *KTU* 1.46.10 = *CTA* 36.10 = *UT* 9.10; *KTU* 1.106.27; 1.112.11, 16–17; 119.5), it seems more reasonable to presume that *brr* describes the status of the king when he begins his sacral role in the temple. Thus *brr* must either be understood as a passive participle, *bārûr* 'purified/the purified one', or as an infinitive absolute bearing an additional connotation, *bārōr* 'in a purified way' (for this biblical usage, see *GKC* §113h–k). An altered form of this expression fits either interpretation: *mlk ytb brr* 'the king sits purified' or 'the purified king sits' (*KTU* 1.41.6–7 = *CTA* 35.6–7 = *UT* 3.6–7), though two other occurrences clearly favor the passive participle: *wmlk brr rgm yttb* 'the purified king responds with a recitation' (*KTU* 1.41.44–45 = *CTA* 35.44–45 = *UT* 3.44–45); *rgm yttb mlk brr* 'with a recitation the purified king responds' (*KTU* 1.41.46 = *CTA* 35.46 = *UT* 3.46). In any event, the king is not a purifier. Besides, nowhere in Ugaritic rituals does he officiate at purifications. Thus the alleged Ugaritic analogy must be rejected (cf. also the NOTE on 8:12).

shall place (wĕheʿĕmîd). When the placement occurs inside the Tabernacle court it is indicated, as in this verse, by the expression "before the Lord" (16:7, 10; Num 5:16, 18, 30) or "before the priest" (27:8, 11; Num 3:6; 18:13; 27:19, 22). The parallel text uses the verb *wĕhēbîʾ* 'shall bring' (v 23) and utilizes both prepositional objects.

together with these [offerings]. wĕʾōtām, namely, the sacrifices enumerated in v 10.

at the entrance to the Tent of Meeting (petaḥ ʾōhel môʿēd). According to the rabbis, this location must be understood literally: at the very entrance and not inside. In their system the person is still contagious to the realm of the sacred (*b. Menaḥ.* 61a) and hence is required to remain "at the entrance," which in the Second Temple meant the Nicanor gate (*m. Neg.* 14:8; *t. Neg.* 8:9; *m. Kelim* 1:8; *Sipra,* Meṣōrāʿ Neg. par. 3:6). Nonetheless, their construction of this term need not be endorsed if we assume that the last vestige of impurity to holy things has disappeared the previous evening, just as is the case with minor impurities (see the table, chap. 15, COMMENT F). The person brings his purification offering because he has polluted the sanctuary; but, like any other bearer of the *ḥaṭṭāʾt,* he has a perfect right to enter the Tabernacle court and perform his required rites inside the court. At the same time, the rabbis are surely right that he may not partake of sacred food until he has offered his sacrifices. Of a certainty, he must atone to the Lord before he may enjoy the Lord's food. For the wide range of sins he may possibly have committed, see below.

In the Herodian Temple there was an open-air enclosure in the northwest corner of the outer court known as "the chamber of *mĕṣōrāʿîm*" (*m. Mid.* 2:5) in which scale-diseased persons would bathe before presenting their sacrifices for the eighth day (*m. Neg.* 14:8). This immersion is not required by Scripture, but the rabbis ordained it for fear they had defiled themselves subsequent to the time of this bath the previous day (*b. Yoma* 30b). The opinion is also recorded that this immersion was required of all bearers of severe impurity who had to enter the inner court to present their sacrifice (*t. Neg.* 8:2). This too has no scriptural foundation but reflects a sensitivity of the Temple authorities, which was amplified by the rabbis, to prevent the pollution of the sanctuary at all costs.

Indeed, the rabbis go even farther and mandate that "He whose atonement is yet incomplete (on the eighth day before bringing the sacrifices) needs to immerse himself (after the sacrifices) for sacred things" (*m. Ḥag.* 3:3). Thus, the rabbis have added another proviso to the Torah that the last vestige of impurity that prevents contact with the sacred (e.g., eating sacrificial meat) cannot be lifted by the requisite sacrifices alone but only by a subsequent ablution. The upshot is that carriers of severe impurity have to add to their eighth-day requirements two ablutions, one before and one after the sacrifices.

The sectaries of Qumran, in fact, go even beyond the rabbis. According to a new Qumran document (4Q 394–99), the contents of which were recently reported (Qimron and Strugnell 1985), a scale-diseased person must wait until sundown at the end of the eighth day before he or she may partake of sacred food. The relevant text (lines 71–72), graciously supplied by the authors, reads, *ʾYN LHPKYLM MHQW[D]ŠYM ʿD BWʾ HŠMŠ BYWM HŠMYNY*, literally, "they are not to be fed from the sacred [food]until sunset on the eighth day." Thus Qumran avers that the impurity is not finally terminated with the ablution after the sacrifices—the rabbis' view—but only by the subsequent evening. Apparently, Qumran has reached this ruling by inventing a hermeneutical technique, which may be called exegetical homogenization (Milgrom 1989b, 1990b). The reasoning is that if ablutions and sunset are required as the final stage of the purificatory process for minor impurities (e.g., 11:24–40; 15:5–27), all the more so should ablutions and sunset be required as the final stage for major impurities. Qumran may also have found biblical support for this homogenizing exegesis in the wording of the purificatory rite for priests: a major impurity bearer "shall not eat sacred food *ʿad ʾăšer yiṭhar*" (22:4), whereas a minor impurity bearer "shall not eat the sacred gifts unless he has washed his body in water. As soon as the sun sets then he is pure *(wĕṭāhēr); and afterward he may eat of the sacred gifts*" (ibid., vv 6–7). The indeterminate *yiṭhar* for major impurities—so Qumran may have argued—is explicated by the *wĕṭāhēr* specified for minor impurities: ablution and sunset.

Strikingly, this radical Qumranite ruling is actually reflected in some tannaitic sources (e.g., *t. Šeqal.* 3:3, 20; *b. Zebaḥ.* 99a [bar.]), collected and discussed in the tosafot to *b. Ḥag.* 21a. Thus despite the prevailing view—the most harmonious with Scripture—that sacred food was permitted after the sacrifices on the eighth day, there were other voices among the rabbis that insisted on a subsequent ablution and others who even added the requirement of a subsequent sunset. Qumran clearly sided with the latter.

12. *present it (wĕhiqrîb ʾōtô).* Does this presentation constitute a rite? One commentator answers in the affirmative, suggesting that it takes the form of the *tĕnûpâ* (Mendelssohn, in Wessely 1846). Yet previous instances of this verb in sacrificial contexts (e.g., 9:16, 17) suggest that this act precedes the rite, that is, the offering is brought into position for a rite. In this case, the presentation is for the purpose of performing the *tĕnûpâ*.

as a reparation offering (lĕʾāšām). That the reparation offering is the key sacrifice in the ritual complex for the purification of scale-diseased persons is demonstrated by the following evidence:

(1) The reparation animal may not be replaced by a less expensive offering for the sake of the indigent, as is the case with the other prescribed sacrifices (vv 21–22; cf. vv 10–13).

(2) This animal is not commutable to silver, as are other reparation animals. The reason is obvious: its blood is needed for the ritual (vv 14, 25). The rabbis also preclude the Nazirite's *ʾāšām* from commutation (*m. Zebaḥ.* 10:5). They are forced to this conclusion because only the *mĕṣōrāʿ* and the Nazirite bring a lamb for their *ʾāšām*, and the rabbis hold that a ram alone is subject to commutation

(see *Sipra*, Ḥoba par. 12:21; Rashi and tosafot on *b. Zebaḥ.* 48a; and my remarks in 1983d: 150 n. 33).

(3) Contrary to all other rituals, the *ʾāšām* takes precedence over all other sacrifices and is the first to be offered up during the rites of the eighth day (tosafot on the Mishna, *b. Zebaḥ.* 90b). Everywhere else the *ḥaṭṭāʾt* precedes the *ʾāšām* (cf. *m. Zebaḥ.* 10:2; *t. Zebaḥ.* 10:4; *b. Zebaḥ.* 90a [bar.]). If one would argue that the reparation offering is not included in other sacrificial series the case of the impure Nazirite refutes it, for his expiation requires both a purification and a reparation offering, and the latter is the last in its series to be offered on the altar (Num 6:10–12). The exception of this *ʾāšām* was not ignored by the Tannaites, and they even provided a rationale for it: "Every *ḥaṭṭāʾt* in the Torah precedes the *ʾāšām* except for the *ʾāšām* of the scale-diseased person because it renders [him] fit *(mipĕnê šehûʾ bāʾ ʿal hāhekšēr)*" (*m. Zebaḥ.* 10:5a; cf. tosafot to *b. Zebaḥ.* 90b, s.v. *ḥûṣ*). That is, his daubing with the *ʾāšām* blood renders him henceforth fit to enter the sanctuary and partake of sacred food.

(4) The reparation offering of the scale-diseased person is unique in this respect: it is the only blood sacrifice in which the entire animal is required to undergo the *tĕnûpâ* rite. When the *tĕnûpâ* is prescribed for other sacrifices it only applies to certain organs, namely, the breast of the well-being offering (7:30; 9:21); the suet, breast, and right thigh of the priestly consecration ram (8:26–27, 29); and the boiled shoulder of the Nazirite's well-being offering when he has completed his term (Num 6:20). This distinction means that the entire *ʾāšām* animal has been endowed with a higher dedicatory status (see chap. 7, COMMENT E, and the NOTE on "elevation offering," below).

(5) The scale-diseased person is daubed with the blood of the *ʾāšām* instead of blood from any of the other sacrificial animals.

together with the log *of oil (weʾet-lōg haššāmen).* The oil of the scale-diseased person is applied in a manner somewhat similar to the oil of the consecrated priest. The former is daubed on the person's extremities (vv 17, 18) and the latter is poured on Aaron and sprinkled on his sons (8:12, 30). Yet there is a difference in the status of the oils: the priestly consecration oil is taken from the anointing oil (8:12) and is therefore sacred to begin with (Exod 30:25, 32), but the oil prescribed for the scale-diseased person is completely profane and therefore requires the *tĕnûpâ* rite to sanctify it and dedicate it to the Lord (see chap. 7, COMMENT E).

elevation offering (tĕnûpâ). The etymology, rendering, origin, and significance of this rite are discussed in chap. 7, COMMENT E. As indicated there, the rabbinic understanding of the *tĕnûpâ* is entirely different. Yet, clearly, their view is based on authentic tradition, not on hypothetical reconstruction. The rite had radically changed during the period of the two Temples. This is how it was performed for the scale-diseased person in the last decades of the Second Temple: "He would bring his reparation offering and its *log* [of oil] in his hand and set it up by Nicanor's gate. And the priest stands on the inside and the scale-diseased person places his hand under the hoof of the beast. And the priest places his hand on the hand of the scale-diseased person and brings it from one side to the other and up and down" (*t. Neg.* 8:9). Noteworthy in this description are the rabbinic presuppositions that the scale-diseased person still bears impurity that can contaminate sancta, for which reason he must stand at the threshold but may not enter the inner court; and that the *těnûpâ* consists of a horizontal and vertical motion with the object, and as such a motion obviously cannot be performed with the beast itself it is done with its hoof.

13. *shall be slaughtered . . . are slaughtered (wěšāḥaṭ . . . yišḥaṭ).* This verb must be translated as an impersonal passive (with *Tg. Ps.-J.*) because the slaughtering rite may be performed by anyone (see the NOTE on 1:5). Indeed, the LXX and Sam. actually read the second verb as a plural, *yišḥāṭû* 'they will slaughter', clearly indicating its passive intention. This and the previous *těnûpâ* are the only rites mentioned in connection with the reparation lamb; the rest of the sacrificial ritual must be presumed on the basis of 7:1–7.

at the spot in the sacred precinct. bimĕqôm haqqōdeš, in other words, inside the Tabernacle court (cf. 10:17). This expression is equivalent to *bĕmāqôm qādōš* 'in a holy place' (see the NOTE on 6:9).

where the purification offering and the burnt offering are slaughtered. Why was this information necessary? We have already been given it in the instructions on the way to sacrifice the reparation offering (7:2). It is necessary lest one think that the slaughtering rite takes place where the *těnûpâ* rite was performed —at the Nicanor gate (*Sipra*, Meṣōrāʿ Neg. par. 3:8). This rabbinic observation is well taken, but it can be challenged in two respects; the *těnûpâ* rite is performed "before the Lord," that is, anywhere in the Tabernacle court (see the NOTE on "before the Lord," 1:5), and the lamb is slaughtered at a spot north of the altar, a requirement incumbent on all most-sacred animals of the flock (i.e., for the burnt, purification, and reparation offerings: see the NOTE on "the north side of the altar," 1:11), but not on flock animals for well-being offerings (see the NOTE on "before the Tent of Meeting," 3:8). The answer, however, lies not in ideology but in aesthetics—to provide symmetry to the literary structure (see the NOTE on vv 11–20).

it [goes] to the priest. lakkōhēn, that is, to the officiating priest (6:19; 7:7), though other priests may partake of it (7:6).

it is most holy (qōdeš qŏdāšîm hûʾ). This is the rationale (7:6; cf. 21:22).

14. *and the priest (hakkōhēn).* This second mention of the priest as the subject in the verse seems superfluous, and it is omitted in the Sam. and in four MSS. The rabbis, however, seize on this apparent redundancy and infer that two priests are involved, one to dash the blood on the altar, the other to dash it on the person (*m. Neg.* 14:8).

the lobe (těnûk). So the LXX and Saadiah. Rabbinic sources, however, light upon different areas of the ear: the top (*Tgs. Onq.* and *Neof.*) and the middle

PURIFICATION (14:1-57)

ridge (*Tg. Ps.-J.; Sipra,* Měṣōrāʿ Neg. 3:5), that is, the antihelix (see the NOTE on 8:23).

right (hayĕmānît). The *qāmas* is used instead of the expected *ḥireq* (NOTE masc. *yāmîn*) in order to distinguish it from *yĕmînît* 'Benjaminite woman' (Ibn Janaḥ; cf. Radak). See *m. Para* 1:1 for a rabbinic example. The significance of the right limb is discussed in the NOTE on 8:23.

thumb . . . big toe. Compare the NOTE on 8:23. The purpose of the blood rite is both purificatory (note the verb *kipper* 'expiate', v 20) and apotropaic (cf. the NOTE on 8:23). And, like the priestly consecration, it is also a rite of passage (Davies 1977: 396–97; Rogerson 1980: 55). The blood on the extremities protects the person as it protects the priestly novitiates during their transition from one status to another: the consecrands from the profane realm to the sacred, the scale-diseased persons from being outcasts to full members of their community (see the NOTE on "right," 8:23; and chap. 8, COMMENT G). Most significantly, the process in each case takes seven days (see COMMENT A below; and cf. chap. 8, COMMENT G).

15. *the palm of his own left hand. kap hakkōhēn haśśĕmā'lît,* literally, "the palm of the priest's left hand." This expression gives the rabbis further reason to assume that two priests are engaged in the ritual (*m. Neg.* 14:10). Nevertheless, the parallel text makes it clear that the left hand of the same officiating priest is involved (v 16; Ibn Ezra). Why then does not the text say simply *kappô* 'his palm'? This word, however, would create an ambiguity: the antecedent of the suffix might be taken to refer to the scale-diseased person (Hoffmann 1953). Also, if the text had another priest in mind, what difference would it make if he received the oil in his right or left hand (Wessely 1846)?

16. *finger.* The index finger, according to the rabbis (*Sipra,* Ḥabah par. 3:8; *b. Zebaḥ.* 53a); the small finger, according to the Egyptians (Moret 1902: 190–200; Sauneron 1960: 87; and see below).

in (min). Equivalent to the preposition *b* (Ḥazzequni), as in 4:17 (Wessely 1846); see v 18, where *baśśemen = min haśśemen.* For the interchange of the prepositions *mem* and *bet,* see Sarna 1959. It is also possible that *min haśśemen* here was influenced by its appearance in the second half of the verse (see the NOTE on 4:17).

sprinkle. The priest dips each time he sprinkles (*Sipra,* Měṣōrāʿ Neg 3·9).

before the Lord. The priest faces the adytum (*m. Neg.* 14:10) and flings the drops on the courtyard floor. The purpose of this rite is to dedicate the oil to the Lord (Vriezen 1950). Unlike the oil used for the priestly consecration, which is taken from the holy anointment oil (see above), this oil requires dedication to the Lord. The same meaning applies to the sevenfold sprinkling of the blood of the Red Cow "toward the front of the Tent of Meeting" (Num 19:4), which is also a dedicatory rite (see chap. 4, COMMENT G). But a similar rite with the blood of the *ḥaṭṭā't* offering (4:6, 17) is purificatory in function; it requires no prior dedication because its source, the purification offering, has already been dedicated to the Lord. Yet the question arises: the oil has already been dedicated by the *těnûpâ* rite; why the need for a second dedication? And if it be argued that the purpose of the *těnûpâ* is to provide additional dedication in cases of most-sacred gifts whose composition or mode is different from the norm (Milgrom 1983d: 147–50), the situation here is that the *těnûpâ* comes first, not second, and it therefore cannot be a reinforcement of a prior dedication. The answer well may be that the sprinkling rite should have been the first to provide for the initial dedication of the oil and that the "booster" *těnûpâ* should have followed. But because the oil had to undergo the *těnûpâ* together with the *ʾāšām* lamb, and the latter had to be the very first rite of the day to provide sacrificial blood for the requisite daubing, there was no choice but to have the sevenfold sprinkling follow the *těnûpâ* as its dedicatory reinforcement (see further Milgrom 1983a: 147 n. 25).

17. *And some of the oil left on his palm* (*ûmiyyeter haššemen ʾăšer ʿal-kappô*). This verse is begun with the direct object in order to maintain the chiastic arrangement of this reaction (see the Note on vv 11–20).

on top (*ʿal*). The LXX, Pesh., and *Tg. Ps.-J.* add *měqôm*, as in v 28, thereby yielding the more precise "on top of the spots of [the blood]." There is an Egyptian rite that corresponds in a surprising fashion to the placing of oil on the scale-diseased person, and it is the daily anointment of the idol. We will cite the Egyptian rite as it is described by Sauneron. The two rituals will be placed one after the other, and for greater clarity the parallels in the Egyptian rite will be italicized:

And the priest shall dip his right finger in the oil that is on his left palm. . . . The remainder of the oil on the priest's palm shall be put on the head of the one being purified. (14:16, 18).

A final ceremony ended the divine toilet (each morning): the anointment of the god with the cosmetic oil *medjet*. *Holding in his left hand the little flacon of alabaster which contained* the precious ointment, *the priest plunged in the little finger of his right hand*, then *touched the brow* of the divine statue with his finger, pronouncing the sacred formula. (Sauneron 1960: 87)

The correspondences are obvious: (1) the use of sacred oil; (2) holding the flacon of oil in the left hand and applying the oil with the little finger of the right hand; (3) the oil being rubbed on the head (brow) of the idol/*měṣōrāʿ*.

The reason for anointing the idol is explained by Sauneron as follows: "the god, washed, clothed, ornamented and smeared with the perfumed oil—satiated by excess—could brave anew the dark of the sanctuary: the divine forces were sustained, preserved from all injury, able to carry on, for another day, their cosmic role" (ibid.). This means that the oil serves an apotropaic purpose: to shield the anointed god from demons. The oil probably had a similar purpose in Israel as well, and the blood of the reparation offering certainly did. We cannot trace the process by which the ceremony shed its pagan form and took on a monotheistic form. But it is likely that the rabbis' explanation, that anointing with oil and blood constitutes the last stage of the expiation of the scale-diseased person (on the eighth day) and qualifies him to approach the sanctuary and its sancta, reflects the meaning of the ritual in P. Thus the function of *těnûpâ* with the oil and blood is clear: it constitutes a further sanctification of these materials, which enhanced their power to purge the scale-diseased person from his uncleanness vis-à-vis the sanctuary and its sancta. And because the use of blood and oil must take first priority among the rituals of the eighth day—because they all take place in the sanctuary—the order of the offering is reversed: the reparation offering, and with it the oil, undergo *těnûpâ* first.

18. [*The remainder*] *of the oil (baššemen).* As in 8:32; cf. 5:9. The *bet* is equivalent to *min* (see the NOTES on "in," v 16, and "of the flesh and bread," 8:32).

shall be put. yittēn, literally, "he (the priest) shall put." Note that the oil is placed (*nātan*, vv 14, 17) not poured *(yāṣaq)*, as with the consecration of the high priest (8:12); mere contact is all that is required.

head (rō'š). In fact, the forehead is clearly intended. This is the part of the body that is the focus of oil rituals elsewhere in the ancient Near East. A description of the Egyptian rite was cited above. The following is a sample of another text: "Recitation: 'Oil; oil! You are that which is on the brow of Horus; you are on the brow of Horus'" (Otto, cited by Veenhof 1966: 309). Whereas the Egyptian rite is reserved for the consecration of the god's statue, in Mesopotamia and Ugarit we find it applied to persons. For example: "(PN2) has freed PN1, the slave of PN2, before Šamaš, and gave him a clean forehead" (*CAD*, E 105a). *Pūt PN ullulum* 'to clean someone's forehead' is a technical term for the manumission of slaves (Veenhof 1966: 310). Ugarit records the following: *wlqḥ. hw / šmn. b. qrnh / w.yṣq. hw. l. r'iš / bt. mlk. 'amr / mnm. ḥt ['u. d. ḥt 'at] / ky. 'umy [.td'. ky] / [kp]r* 'He also took oil in his horn and poured it on the head of the daughter of the King of A[murru]. Whatever si[n she has committed against] me, [you should know that it has been ato]ned' (RS 32.124.26'–32'). The common denominator in all of these anointing ceremonials is that they symbolize an elevation in status. The divine statue is consecrated; the slave is freed; the status of the divorced queen is restored (Pardee 1979: 14–20). The Ugaritic text is significant in that the queen's atonement is expressed by the verb *kpr* (presuming the restoration is correct), precisely what we find in this verse concerning the effect of the unction of the scale-diseased person (see below). Pardee now casts doubt on his interpretation on the basis of his recent reading of the original text, which shows that *ḥt* ['u 'sin' (line 30') and *kpr* 'stone' (line 34', not shown here) are not separated by four lines but by eleven, rendering any connection between them out of the question and, hence, rendering the restoration [kp]r (line 32') unlikely (private communication). For a fuller discussion of the manifold functions of anointing, see chap. 8, COMMENT D.

make expiation (wĕkipper). Thus the oil is definitely an agency of expiation (cf. v 29). Still, this phrase should probably be understood as a summary for the total unction ceremonial, that is, the blood plus the oil (Ramban). That the *'āšām*, in fact, is the main expiatory agent is stated explicitly in v 21. The use of the oil on the consecrated priests (chap. 8) and in ceremonial rites in Egypt, Mesopotamia, and Ugarit (above) narrows the wide range of this verb (see chap. 16, COMMENT F) to a precise meaning. Indeed, the very attestation of the root *kpr* in the clear context of the Ugaritic letter cited above provides an illuminating parallel to the action of the oil here on the scale-diseased person. Just as the oil effects a reconciliation between the king and his divorced queen, so does the anointing of the erstwhile scale-diseased person complete his reconciliation with his Lord. He may freely enter the sanctuary, partake of sacred food, and participate in all of the rituals and festivals incumbent upon the Israelites. The indispensable nature of this rite was clearly grasped by Rabbi Akiba (*Sipra,* Mĕṣōrā' Neg. 3:12).

A more fundamental question needs be asked: Why, in the first place, was he asked to bring the *'āšām?* This sacrifice is brought for cases of sancta trespass (COMMENTS on 5:14–26), but his disease is not traceable to sancta or for that matter to any other cause. The *'āšām* of 5:17–19 opens a door to the answer: He *may* have desecrated sancta (see 5:14–26, COMMENT D). Because other sins may have been responsible for his affliction, he brings an array of sacrifices for his expiation (see the NOTES on "the burnt offering" and "the cereal offering," v 20), but the *'āšām* is ordained to expiate for the possibility of *ma'al* 'sacrilege' (5:14–26, COMMENT B).

This hypothesis would rank as sheer conjecture were it not for the confirmation offered by an unexpected source. Chronicles relates that King Uzziah was stricken with scale disease precisely when, and because, he encroached upon sancta. The language of the text is most instructive: "When he grew powerful his pride led to his undoing. He transgressed *(mā'al)* against the Lord his God by entering the Lord's Temple to burn incense on the altar of incense. . . . 'Leave the Sanctuary for you have trespassed *(mā'altā).*' . . . Scale disease broke out on his forehead in the presence of the priests in the Lord's house, beside the altar of incense" (2 Chr 26:16–19). It is no accident that Uzziah's sin is twice labeled *ma'al.* True, the tendentiousness of the story is transparent: it is part of the Chronicler's polemic against the royal prerogative to officiate as priests (cf. Milgrom 1976f: 81 n. 289). Still, though the story itself may be questioned, it rests upon the accepted premise that trespass against sancta is punishable by scale disease and, conversely, that the incidence of scale disease may be traceable to the sin of trespass against sancta. Thus, it is imperative for the person who has been healed of his scale disease, as part of his ritual of rehabilitation with his community and his God, to bring an *ʾāšām* to cover the contingency that his disease has been caused by some unwitting sacrilege.

before the Lord. The addition is a reminder of its occurrence in v 11, and this phrase is meant to indicate that all of the rites performed on the scale-diseased person share in his expiation, including the blood rite.

Only the oil contained in the priest's palm (v 17) has been utilized for the ritual. Nothing, however, is mentioned concerning the remainder of the *log* (v 15). The rabbis aver that it is consumed by the priests (*t. Neg.* 9:5). They are clearly right: the oil having been doubly dedicated to the Lord—by *tĕnûpâ* and sevenfold aspersion "before the Lord" (vv 12, 16)—most assuredly remains in the sacred realm, as a prebend for the priests.

19. *then offer.* *wĕ'āśâ*, to wit, perform the entire sacrificial ritual.

the purification offering. As required, the *ḥaṭṭāʾt* precedes the *'ōlâ* and, indeed, all other sacrifices (*m. Nazir* 6:7): "The purification offering resembles the advocate who enters [the court] to appease [the king]; after he has appeased the gift (i.e., the burnt offering) enters" (*Sipra,* Mĕṣōrāʿ Neg. 3:14; *t. Para* 1:1; *b. Zebaḥ.* 7b [bar.]).

effect purgation (wĕkipper). There are three expiatory acts in this eighth-day rite, all signified by the expiatory verb par excellence, *kipper* (vv 18, 19, 20). Note, however, that only with the purification offering does the text specify that the expiation is directed at impurity. Here, then, is incontrovertible proof that the *ḥaṭṭāʾt* decontaminates, purifies, and must be rendered "purification offering," that and the verb *kipper* in this context has the specific meaning of "purge" (see chap. 4, COMMENT A and chap. 16, COMMENT F). A similar instance of this sacrifice's operation is recorded in the rite for Yom Kippur: "Thus he (the high priest) shall purge *(wĕkipper)* the adytum of the pollution *(miṭṭum'ōt)* and transgressions of the Israelites" (16:16). As noted earlier, the purification offering also purges the sanctuary of Israel's moral impurity: "Thus shall the priest effect purgation *(wĕkipper)* . . . for his wrong *(mēḥaṭṭāʾtô),* that he may be forgiven *(wĕnislaḥ lô)"* (4:26; see the NOTE on "commandments," 4:2). The distinction between moral and physical impurity is indicated not only by the terms for the causes of the sanctuary's pollution (*ṭumʾâ* versus *ḥēṭʾ)* but by the consistent use of two different verbs that describe the effect of the purgation: physical impurity is purified *(ṭāhēr);* moral impurity is forgiven *(nislaḥ).* Indeed, Yom Kippur, which effects the total cleansing of the sanctuary and of Israel, prescribes two distinctive rites in order to encompass all of Israel's sins, physical and moral alike: the sacrifice *ḥaṭṭāʾt* purges the sanctuary of its impurities *(ṭumʾōt,* 16:16; see above) and the live *ḥaṭṭāʾt* (16:4) purges Israel of its sins *('āwōnōt,* 16:21; see the full discussion in the NOTES on 16:16, 21). The conclusion is therefore inescapable that the scale-diseased person brings a *ḥaṭṭāʾt* because his physical impurity has polluted the sanctuary. Moral impurity also enters the picture but via other sacrifices; see below.

for his impurity. *miṭṭumʾātô,* in other words, which he inflicted on the sanctuary. The *mem* here is causative (e.g., Gen 16:10; 1 Kgs 8:5; Jer 24:2; Prov 20:4; Paran 1989; cf. GKC §1192). See especially *měhaṭṭāʾtô* 'for his wrong' (4:26; 5:6, 10; 16:34; Num 6:11); *mizzôbô* 'for his discharge' (15:15).

20. *offer up (wěheʿělâ)*. This verb with the burnt offering must be contrasted with *ʿāśâ*, the verb with the purification offering. The latter is all-inclusive; no other verb is necessary. Conversely, this verb is preceded by *šāḥaṭ* 'slaughter'. Thus *heʿělâ* is also inclusive but only for the action that takes place on the altar. As mentioned earlier, *heʿělâ*, which normally carries the meaning "cause to rise, raise" in sacrificial contexts, has the special, technical meaning "cause to disappear," namely, by being incinerated on the altar. Hence the *ʿōlâ* translates as "burnt offering" (see the COMMENT on chap. 1).

the burnt offering. There is nothing in the text to indicate the function of the burnt offering except its expiatory goal, *wěkipper*. But what does it expiate? It has been suggested that originally the burnt offering was the exclusive expiatory sacrifice, but once the purification and reparation offerings were assigned their specific expiatory functions, the burnt offering retained the remainder of the wrongs requiring expiation. Because the former sacrifices expiated for violations of prohibitive commandments (4:2) and known or suspected desecrations (5:14–26), the burnt offering retained the power to expiate for neglected performative commandments or for sinful thoughts (for other possibilities, see the COMMENT on chap. 1). The battery of all four expiatory sacrifices—reparation, purification, burnt, and cereal offerings—thereby assures the scale-diseased person that all possible inadvertent misdemeanors have been covered. His wrong is expiated; his disease will not return.

the cereal offering. hamminḥâ, comprising the total (three-tenths of an *ephah*) semolina, the accompaniment to all three blood sacrifices. Two points can be derived from this fact: first, an adjunct cereal offering need not be offered up together with its blood sacrifice but, as here, may be combined with other cereal adjuncts to constitute a substantial *minḥâ;* and, second, the adjunct *minḥâ*, being governed by *heʿělâ*, the same verb as the *ʿōlâ*, is disposed of the same way as the *ʿōlâ*—by total incineration. This procedure contrasts with the individual's independent *minḥâ*, which is awarded to the priests, except for the *ʾazkārâ* (token; 2:1–3; 7:10). Because this cereal offering is an adjunct, it bears no independent function but takes on the function of its respective blood offerings.

shall make expiation. Ramban holds that this *wěkipper* is a summary of all of the sacrificial rites for the eighth day. Perhaps he had v 31 in mind, where this verb indicates a summation. But there are three mentions of *kipper*, one for each sacrifice (vv 18, 19, 20). Hence, this *kipper* must apply to the sacrifices listed in this verse: the burnt and adjunct cereal offerings. That the cereal offering is capable of an expiatory function is discussed in the COMMENT on chap. 2.

Then he shall be pure (wěṭāhēr). As *kipper* appears three times in this pericope (above), so does *ṭāhēr* (vv 8, 9, 20). Its placement is crucial. It occurs at the end of the three rites that mark the stages through which the scale-diseased person passes in his rehabilitation to society and his reconciliation with his God. The initial *ṭāhēr* at the end of the first day admits him to the camp (v 8); the second, to his tent (v 9); and the third, to his God (v 20). The first two are preceded by ablutions that, as pointed out (vv 8, 9), execute the rites of passage. This third *ṭāhēr*, however, is not preceded by an ablution. It signifies the completion of the process: the healed and now purified person is henceforth a full-fledged participant in his community and its worship. Note its absence in v 31 and especially in the eighth-day sacrificial rites for the *zāb/zābâ* (15:15, 30). It is not essential for it only refers to the effect of the sacrifices, an effect that has been adequately described by *kipper:* the sacrifices have effected expiation for him before the Lord.

21–32. As noted by Lund (1942: 55–56; again with modifications), the pericope on the indigent *mĕṣōrāʿ* is constructed on the same introverted pattern as vv 11–20, as follows:

A. If, however, he is poor and his *means are insufficient,* 21

 B. he shall take a reparation offering of one male lamb for an elevation to *make expiation* for him, one-tenth [of an ephah] of semolina mixed with oil

 for a *cereal offering,* a log of oil;

 and two *turtledoves* or two *pigeons,* whichever are *within his means,* 22

 the one to be *the purification* offering and the other *the burnt offering.*

 On the eighth day of his purification he shall bring them to the *priest* 23

 at the entrance of the Tent of Meeting, *before the Lord.*

 C. The *priest* shall take the lamb of reparation offering 24

 and the log of *oil,*

 and elevate them as an elevation offering *before the Lord,*

  D. When the lamb of reparation offering has been slaughtered, 25

  the priest shall take some of the *blood of the reparation offering*

   E. and put it on *the right ear of the one being purified,*

   on the thumb of his right hand, and on the big toe of his right foot.

F.   The *priest* shall then pour *some of the oil*   26
       on the palm of his own left hand,

      X.   and with the finger of his right hand *the priest*   27

        shall sprinkle *some of the oil* that is *on the palm*

        of his left hand seven times *before the Lord.*

  F′.   The *priest* shall put *some of the oil on his palm*   28

 E′.   *on the lobe of the right ear* of the one being purified,
      on the thumb of his right hand,
      and on the big toe of his right foot,

D′.   on top of the *blood* spots *of the reparation offering;*

C′.   and the remainder of the *oil* on the *priest's* palm   29
   shall be put on the head of the one being purified,
   to make expiation for him *before the Lord.*

B′.   He shall then offer one of the *turtledoves* or *pigeons*   30
   that are *within his means*—whichever he can afford—
   the one as a *purification offering* and the other as a *burnt offering*   31
   together with the *cereal offering.*
   Thus the *priest* shall *make expiation before the Lord*
   for the one being purified.

A′.   This is the ritual for the one who has scale disease   32
   [and] whose *means are insufficient* at [the time of] his purification.

The indigence of the offerer begins and closes this pericope (AA′). His indigence is again stressed in the next corresponding pair (BB′) as well as in the enumeration of the sacrifices and the expression "make expiation." The oil (CC′), blood of the reparation offering (DD′), and their placement (EE′) follow. The phrase "some of the oil on the palm" (FF′) encloses the pivotal center, which (as in v 16) stresses the added dedication of the oil (X). Key elements of both halves of the introversion are repeated in the center: "the priest" (BCFF′C′B′), "some of the oil on the palm" (FF′), and "before the Lord" (BCC′B′).

21. *poor (dal).* The meaning is clear from its cognates: Ug. *dl* 'poor'; Akk. *dallu* 'small, inferior', *dullulu* 'oppressed'.

and his means are insufficient (wĕ'ên yādô maśśeget; cf. 5:11; 25:26, 49), literally, "beyond his reach." The qualification that he is destitute is necessary for as pointed out by Ibn Ezra, *dal* admits of many other meanings, among them "emaciated" (Gen 41:19), "powerless" (Exod 23:3), "insignificant" (Judg 6:15), "dejected" (2 Sam 13:4), "lowly" (Jer 5:4).

a reparation offering. The *ʾāšām* always calls for a fixed animal, a ram or a lamb, regardless of the nature or extent of the damage inflicted on the property of God (5:14–26; 19:20–22; Num 5:6–8; Ezra 10:19). The indigent has his required offering reduced to less expensive species, but the requirement for the *ʾāšām* lamb remains the same. One cannot argue that no change can be made for the *ʾāšām* because its blood is needed for daubing the extremities of the *mĕṣōrāʿ* (v 14). The small amount needed could just as well have been drawn from a bird (cf. 5:7–9). This unchangeable feature is also attested in Nuzi texts, reflecting customary law that goes back at least to the middle of the second millennium, which affirms that in certain cases fines were imposed in terms of fixed animal ratios that were commutable to stipulated amounts of currency (Speiser 1960: 30–33). The animals specified in the fine remain the same in species and number regardless of the offense. The fact that the *ʾāšām* always calls for a fixed animal and that it too is commutable (5:15, 18, 25) points to the possibility that this Israelite sacrifice is based on an ancient practice (Milgrom 1976f: 16 n. 50).

one [lamb] (ʾeḥād). In Hebrew this numeral is superfluous. Here it serves to contrast this prescription with the previous one, where two lambs are required (v 10).

to make expiation for him. By the blood rite on the altar (7:7) and on him (v 14).

one-tenth (wĕʿiśśārôn . . . ʾeḥād). Again the numeral is needed to contrast this prescription with its counterpart in the previous pericope, where three-tenths were required (v 10). Also the fact that one-tenth of an *ephah* of semolina is prescribed (in accordance with the tariff of Num 15:4–5) proves that the three-tenths previously prescribed were intended for the three blood sacrifices, one-tenth for each.

a log (wĕlōg). The numeral *ʾeḥād* is omitted because there is no change in the quantity (cf. v 10)—proof that its mention previously in this verse indicated that a change had occurred.

22. *whichever are within his means.* ʾăšer taśśîg yādô (correctly in the *NEB*). The assumption is that he should bring the dearer birds (cf. v 30). It would seem that the turtledoves are costlier, for the pigeons are stipulated young, *bĕnê yônâ* (see the NOTES on 1:14 and on 12:6). Also the more expensive animal generally precedes in a series (e.g., 7:23; 17:3; 22:27). Thus the switch from earlier *kesep wĕzāhāb* 'silver and gold' (e.g., Gen 24:35; Num 22:18; 24:13) to later *zāhāb wĕkesep* 'gold and silver' (1 Kgs 10:22; Ezek 16:13; 28:4) betrays a diachronic change in the relative value of these two precious metals (Ehrlich 1908–14). Sacrificial concessions to the indigent are also recorded in Israel's ambience, for

instance, Mesopotamia: "The widow makes her offering to you (pl.) with cheap flour, the rich man with a lamb" (*CAD*, 10.331, s.v. *maṣḥatu*); the Marseilles Tariff (third century B.C.E.): "For every sacrifice that a man may sacrifice who is poor in cattle or poor in birds, the priests shall have nothing [of them]" (*CIS* 1.165; Cooke 1903: 112–22; *ANET*³ 656–57; and see the NOTE on 5:7).

the one . . . and the other (ʾeḥād . . . wĕḥāʾeḥād). After the first bird is designated, the second is automatically determined, hence the definite article; similarly in 15:15 (Ehrlich 1908–14).

28–29. *shall put . . . shall be put (wĕnātan . . . yittēn).* The last acts with the oil (vv 26–29) are indicated by the same verb; the final one is a simple imperfect, a distinct characteristic of the Priestly style (Paran 1983: 31, and see v 42 and 10:13–14).

29. *to make expiation (lĕkapper).* This *kipper* corresponds exactly to that of v 18, referring to all of the rites performed with the ʾāšām and the oil (vv 24–29). It should be noted that those rites are precisely the same as in the previous pericope. They are repeated in order to emphasize that they are not to be compromised; they are the quintessential element in the final stage of purification.

30. *one (ʾet-hāʾeḥād).* In view of the occurrence of this phrase twice in the next verse, Ehrlich (1908–14) suggests its deletion here.

that (mēʾăšer). The *mem* is carried over from the twice-mentioned *min*.

31. *whichever he can afford (ʾēt ʾăšer-taśśîg yādô).* Delete, with the LXX, Pesh., and Vg, as a variant of v 30b (Driver and White 1898). Even Hoffmann (1953) admits its redundancy. The *NEB* tries to justify its retention by rendering "whichever it may be," in other words, either the turtledove or the pigeon (cf. v 22), but the idiom cannot be stretched to encompass this meaning.

together with the cereal offering (ʿal-hamminḥâ). The preposition ʿal 'together' occurs with the *minḥâ* to emphasize that it is not an independent offering but, in this case, the adjunct of the ʾāšām. The adhesion of the cereal offering to the other sacrifices is further emphasized by the fact that it has no independent verb but is dependent on ʿāśâ 'offer', the verb used for the ḥaṭṭāʾt and ʿōlâ, just as the *minḥâ* shared the same verb heʿĕlâ 'offer' with the ʿōlâ in v 20. The latter verb, which implies incineration (see the NOTE in v 20), could not be used here because the meat of the ḥaṭṭāʾt becomes the prebend of the officiating priest (6:19).

Nothing is said in either pericope concerning the sacrifice of the ʾāšām. It is clear that the legislator wished to focus on the ʾāšām blood rite in the person. He therefore mentions only the essential prerequisites, the elevation rite and the slaughtering (vv 12–13, 24–25), but presumes a knowledge of the altar rites (7:1–5) that follow. The hand-leaning rite is also omitted because in the case of the ʾāšām the offerer has the option of bringing its monetary equivalent (see the NOTE on "lean his hand," 1:4).

Thus shall [the priest] make expiation (wĕkipper). This *kipper* varies from its counterpart in the previous pericope (v 20): whereas the previous *kipper* refers to the expiatory action of the *ʿōlâ* and *minḥâ*, this one clearly summarizes the entire eighth-day rite. This impression is reinforced by the addition of the phrase *ʿal hammiṭṭahēr lipnê YHWH* 'before the Lord for the one being purified', absent in v 20.

32. *This is the ritual for the one who has scale disease (zōʾt tôrat ʾăšer-bô negaʿ ṣārāʿat).* A subscript for vv 2–20 forming an inclusion with *zōʾt tihyeh tôrat hammĕṣōrāʿ* 'this shall be the ritual for a scale-diseased person' (v 2a). The future orientation of the opening is explicable (see the NOTE on "shall be," v 2). But why the change from the technical term *mĕṣōrāʿ* to the cumbersome phrase *ʾăšer-bô negaʿ ṣārāʿat*, which becomes even more awkward as the *nomen rectum* of a construct with *tôrat?* The answer is, paradoxically, one of style: to match the similar construction in the second half of the verse; see below.

[*and*] *whose means are insufficient (ʾăšer lōʾ-taśśîg yādô).* The double appearance of the relative conjunction *ʾăšer* is admittedly awkward (Rendtorff 1954: 54), but the awkwardness disappears as soon as one follows the LXX in reading for its second occurrence *waʾăšer* (following Hoffmann 1953 and Ehrlich 1908–14), thereby making v 32b a subscript for vv 21–31 and also explaining why the two *ʾăšer* clauses were constructed—despite the alleged awkwardness. Now this verse forms a perfect inclusio with v 2a on behalf of all of vv 2–32, taking into account the two inner pericopes, vv 2–20 and 21–31, by juxtaposing them with perfectly balanced symmetry, v 32a and 32b.

at [*the time of*] *his purification. bĕṭohŏrātô* (with Saadiah). Thus a perfect balance is created with *bĕyôm ṭohŏrātô* 'at the time of his purification' (v 2a), thereby completing the inclusion (vv 2a, 32).

33–53. The Diagnosis for a Fungous House and Its Rite of Purification. Bright green or bright red eruptions on the walls of the house warrant a seven-day quarantine. If the infection has not subsided, the infected stones are removed and replaced, the interior plaster is removed and recoated, and a second quarantine is imposed. If the infection persists, the house is demolished. If it has healed, the priest performs a ceremonial that is a duplicate of the first-day rite for the purification of cured scale-diseased persons. Springwater containing the blood of a bird, cedar wood, hyssop, and crimson yarn is sprinkled on the house seven times and a live bird is released into the open country.

It would seem more logical that the pericope on houses would have preceded the purificatory rites for persons (vv 1–32) and be included with the differential diagnosis of persons and fabrics (chap. 13). But this pericope combines the diagnosis with the purification (Koch 1959: 87), the latter modeled on and presuming the purificatory rite for persons (vv 1–32). As pointed out by Jastrow (1913–14: 397), the diagnosis follows the *ṣāraʿat* legislation in the following manner: (1) the emphasis is on the change of color; (2) the mark(s) must be beneath the surface; (3) the quarantine lasts for seven days; (4) the decision hinges on the spread of the mark(s). The new point is the removal of the stones containing the suspicious marks, which, however, corresponds to (5) the tearing out of the mark(s) from the fabric. Moreover, the purificatory rite follows precisely the first-day rite for persons (vv 4–8). It is the latter fact, then, that makes it imperative that this pericope follow the purificatory rite for persons. Another reason, a chronological one, mandated this order. The purificatory rite for persons (and garments), given at Sinai, is therefore operative in the wilderness. Were the pericope on houses to precede it, then it would take effect only upon entry into Canaan. This was not in the mind of the legislator. It is of interest to note that based on the construction of this chapter, the author of Qumran's Temple Scroll added the term "cities" to his quotation of Num 18:14 in order to update it from the wilderness to the settled land (11QT 49:5–7; cf. Yadin 1983: 1.325).

Although this pericope is clearly modeled on the diagnosis and purification of persons, this does not mean that it is purely an artificial construct. Elsewhere in the ancient Near East, fungous growths on houses were considered to be omens, divine signs, most of which portended evil for the occupants. Most striking is the Mesopotamian series dealing with *katarru* fungus. Black-colored fungus is a sign of health and prosperity but white, red, and green fungi are invariably omens of ill fortune (Nötscher 1929: 56–65). It cannot escape notice that in Israel precisely red and green fungi are condemnatory signs. Equally impressive is the Namburbi rite from Mesopotamia prescribed for discovering *katarru* fungus in a house. First, its appearance portends death for one of the occupants: the master if it appears on the outer north wall; the wife, if on the southeast wall; the son, if on the outer west wall. To avert the evil, the intended victim or a surrogate, in case of the wife, is either aspersed with holy water or immerses himself in a river seven times facing upstream and seven times facing downstream while releasing gifts to Ea, the god of the river, that he may both purify the person and receive his evil (Caplice 1965–71: 40.140–47; 1974: 18). A letter of Nergal-Šarrani to Esarhaddon states, "This *kamunu*-fungus was seen in the inner courtyard of the temple of Nabû, and *katarru*-lichen (was seen) on the wall of the central stonehouse; there are Namburbi-texts for them" (*ABL* 367.8). Namburbi are not exorcisms but apotropaics. Like their Israelite counterparts, the persons asperse and/or bathe (they also change their clothing), but the goal is to ward off evil. In a ritual for the purification of a house (Gurney 1935), the entrances and openings to the house are anointed with various substances that act as detergents *(takpiratu)*, and figures of wood and clay are buried there as protectors of the house against evil spirits (for the close association of this rite with the purgation of the sanctuary on Yom Kippur, see chap. 16, COMMENT C; and for the relationship of *takpirtu/kuppuru* with its Hebrew cognate, *kipper*, see chap. 16, COMMENT F).

The Hurrians supply an even more striking parallel. A ritual for purging a house of evil prescribes two birds for the Annunaku (infernal deities) and one for the Api deity, which the officiant takes to the desert, where he burns cedar

(Otten 1961: 130, cited by Weinfeld 1983: 101). The parallels with the birds and cedar rites, with one bird dispatched to the wilderness (vv 49–53; cf. vv 4–7), are obvious. The Hittite ᴸᵘHal (= Akk. *bārû*) purifies homes of the following impurities: sickness, blood, unfulfilled oaths, slander. Chthonic deities are invoked to take the impurities with them into the earth by digging a ritual pit (Hebrew *'ôb;* see the NOTE on 19:31 and Hoffner 1967a). The officiant pours several liquids into the pit and throws in a shekel of silver. The pit *(A-a-bi)* is implored to examine the materials of purification by means of a scale (Hoffner 1967a: 391). It is hoped that a verdict of purity for the worshiper would be forthcoming (Engelhard 1970: 27–28). In general, holes dug in the floor send impurity into the netherworld. The sun goddess is requested to release the evils from the floor, bedroom, hearth, four corners, courtyard, and gateway. And appeal is made to the water sources to cleanse the evil and purify the doorway. According to Engelhard (1970: 76–78), Hittite rituals for purifying a house differ from Mesopotamian ones in a significant way: in Mesopotamia impurity derives from demons, but in the Hittite texts it derives solely from humans, a concept totally congruent with the Bible (see below and Wright 1987: 261–63). The common denominator in nonbiblical rites is the belief that the eruptions of malignant affections on the bodies of persons and their possessions, such as clothing and houses, are a sign of divine disfavor, and remedies are prescribed both to rid the object of the affection and to placate the divinity so that it may not reappear (for Israel, see the NOTE on v 36).

In a recent publication (1989), S. Meier has cataloged the differences between the biblical and the Mesopotamian rites for the fungous house. The main points are: (1) in Leviticus the material on which the fungus has grown is discarded together with the fungus, whereas in Mesopotamia only the fungus is eliminated. (2) In Leviticus only the fungus is destructive: there is no hint of it being a portent of calamity, as in Mesopotamia. (3) In Mesopotamia the very presence of fungus is threatening, whereas in Leviticus it is threatening only if it spreads. Indeed, once it has been determined that the fungus has not spread, there is no requirement that it has to be removed. (4) In Leviticus only the house is perceived as afflicted, as proved by the purification rite: the house alone is aspersed, not its owner. In Mesopotamia, however, the recipient of the aspersion is the owner, not the house.

In short, Israel's priesthood has eviscerated the magical and demonic from the rites of the fungous house prevalent in the contiguous cultures and, as in the case of the scale-diseased person, has incorporated them into its overarching symbolic system that proclaims the victory of the forces of life over the forces of death (details in COMMENT B below; see also chap. 11, COMMENT C and chap. 15, COMMENT G).

References to "camp" and "tent" point to early stages and are not "a deliberate invention to uphold a tradition of the Mosaic origins of the Pentateuchal legislation. If such had been the deliberate intention of the compilers they would not have committed the inconsistency of introducing the word 'city' in the same chapter (Lev 14:40, 41, 45)" (Jastrow 1913–14: 413).

33. *The Lord spoke to Moses and Aaron.* Ramban questions this heading: why to them? They were not going to enter the Land! Besides, priests were not going to be recipients of land. Would it not have been more appropriate for the heading to read, "Speak to the Israelites (as 11:2; 12:2)? The context clarifies the answer. The diagnosis of scale disease is totally in the hands of the priests. This heading is structured precisely like that of 13:2; *ṣāraʿat* in all its forms is the exclusive concern of the priests. And as for the inclusion of Moses, it has been established that God does not address Aaron directly (with the exception of 10:8; see the NOTE *ad loc.*), but only in Moses' presence. Ramban's other stricture is chronologically irrelevant: this is Leviticus, not Numbers, so Moses and Aaron are as yet unaware of their fate and the distribution of land has not yet taken place.

34. *When you enter the Land of Canaan.* Entry into the land is a condition in several Priestly (H?) laws: fruit of trees (19:23); firstfruit of a grain (23:10; the Sabbatical and Jubilee (25:2); the sacrificial adjuncts (Num 15:2); division of the land (Num 33:51; 34:2); the cities of refuge (Num 35:10). This regulation, however, is unique. The others take effect in the land; this one attempts to update a current law to newer conditions. The same approach to diagnosis and purification (for the first day) that prevails for the scale-diseased person is now applied to houses.

This law of scale-diseased houses, according to the rabbis, does not apply to Transjordan (*Sipra*, Mĕṣōrāʿ Neg. par. 5:1). The Karaites, however, include Transjordan because it is also called Israel's *ʾăḥuzzâ* 'possession' (Num 32:22, 29; *Keter Torah*). In this case, the rabbis are clearly in the right because in the Priestly tradition the Jordan River is the eastern boundary of Canaan (Num 34:12). According to another view, this law could not have taken effect in the wilderness in the absence of stone houses (*Midr. Tadshe* 17). The question then is: Does this law apply everywhere (the Karaites), though in this particular case it applies to Canaan, because that is where Israel will first confront stone houses; or does it strictly apply to the boundaries of Canaan (the rabbis)? Ibn Ezra clearly sides with the rabbis by remarking that the rationale for the law is the presence of the future Temple.

which I give you . . . and I inflict (ʾăšer ʾănî nōtēn . . . wĕnātattî). The change in style between this pericope and the previous is readily apparent in this verse. Its expansiveness here contrasts sharply with the terseness of chap. 13. The same verb *nātan* is employed here for both a blessing and a curse. Above all, God speaks in the first person. All of these factors are characteristics of the redactor or author of H, who may have reworked an older (P) passage.

as a possession. laʾăḥuzzâ, literally, "as seized [property]." ʾăḥuzzâ is a technical term denoting inalienable property received from a sovereign, in distinction to naḥălâ, inalienable property transmitted by inheritance—that is, patrimony (S. Rattray). *'ăḥuzzâ* is most appropriate here because the land has to be seized. The distinction between the two terms seems to have been blurred in some texts. The two are even conflated: *'ăḥuzzat naḥălâ* 'inherited holding' (Num 27:7; 32:35) and *naḥălat 'ăḥuzzātām* 'holdings apportioned to them' (Num 35:2). Even so, the terms are not necessarily interchangeable. The land seized by the Israelites *('ăḥuzzâ)* became their inheritance *(naḥălâ)*. Moreover, some sources prefer one term over the other. D uses *naḥălâ* exclusively (Deut 32:49 is patently from another source [H?]), whereas H uses *'ăḥuzzâ* exclusively (Lev 25:10, 13, 24, 25, 32, 33, 34, 41, 45; 27:16, 21, 22, 28).

and I inflict. *wĕnātattî,* literally, "I place." The verb *nātan* is neutral. With God as its subject, the object can be either blessing or curse (Deut 30:1, 19), a point driven home by the exhortations that conclude H (e.g., blessing (26:4, 6, 11) and curse (26:19, 30, 31). The remarkable thing about this pericope is that although God is explicitly included as the author of the injunction, nowhere is it stated or even intimated that the infection comes as punishment for sin. The owner is enjoined, under the guidance of a priest, to subject his house to an elaborate test to see whether the infection spreads and, if the examination is positive, to dismantle the house or, if negative, to purify the house. But the owner does nothing to or for himself.. He does not bring sacrifices, as does the certified scale-diseased person, a rite that surely would have been prescribed if he were suspected of having sinned. And if he launders and bathes it will only be for the reason that he, or anyone else, entered the house *after* it was condemned by the priest (vv 45–46). Thus the disparity between Israel and its neighbors could not be any wider than in this ritual they observed in common. The Mesopotamians attribute the fungous house to demons, the Hittites to its occupants, but Israel to neither. YHWH, as the one and only God, must be the source of all that happens in nature. Yet whereas calamitous events are elsewhere in Scripture ascribed to human disobedience of divine law, in this case there is no such attribution. The infection has been diagnosed and treated objectively— in a real sense, scientifically. Human causality has been dismissed. (For a similar conclusion deriving from the pericope on fabrics, see the NOTE on 13:47–58.)

Nevertheless, it is clear that 14:34 bears the hallmarks of H. Knohl (1988: 22 n. 122) suggests that originally the verse may have read *wĕhabbayit kî-yihyeh bô nega' ṣāra'at* 'when scale disease occurs in a house' (cf. 13:47) and that H replaced it with the present verse "in order to resolve the difficulty inherent in a command concerning fungous houses (given) during the wilderness sojourn" *(ibid.).* His reconstruction is plausible, but his rationale must be rejected. P no less than H projects Israel's settlement in its land. Otherwise—to cite one of many examples—how could it obtain cereal offerings, both voluntary and required (8:26; 9:17; 14:10, 21; etc.), including the firstfruits of the grain harvest (2:14–16), while Israel was still in the wilderness? The verse, however, speaks for itself. As mentioned above, by attributing the fungous house to an act of God it implies that it is the result of the sins of its owner, thereby canceling the impression given by the following text that the owner is blameless. Such a change would be in keeping with the nature and purpose of H to attribute all natural calamities befalling Israel to its rebellion against God (e.g., 26:14–22). It is striking that it is P, the older Priestly tradition reworked by H, that adopts a neutral, objective—one might say scientific—point of view, motivated perhaps by its sustained struggle to exorcise the demonic from erstwhile pagan rites. H, instead, betrays in this instance its roots in the popular religion, a topic reserved for the second volume of this study (in the meantime, see Knohl 1988: 146–71).

To be sure, the rabbis also betray no hesitation whatever in attributing house infection to the sins of the owner. *Tg. Ps.-J.* adds before v 34b the following: "[possession], and a man be found who builds his house through violence [I shall inflict . . .]." Moreover, the rabbis tie all forms of *ṣāraʿat* described in chaps. 13–14 into a sequence of punishments that God inflicts on the unrepentant sinner:

> God begins first with a man's house. If a man repents, the requirement is no more than that the stones discolored by the infection be taken out (v 40). If a man does not repent, the requirement is that the stones [and the house itself] be broken down (v 45). Next, God begins on the man's garments. If the man repents, the requirement is no more than that the part of the garment spotted by this infection be torn out (13:56). But if the man does not repent, the requirement is that the garment be burned (13:52). Then God begins on the man's body. If the man repents [he will be cured of his leprouslike scalls]; but if he does not repent, [stricken with scale disease] "he shall dwell apart: his dwelling shall be outside the camp." (*Pesiq. R.* 17; cf. *t. Neg.* 6:7)

Rabbinic tradition also records the view: "A stricken house has never come into existence and is never going to come into existence" (*t. Neg.* 6:1), an indication that this law was not practiced in tannaitic times. But testimonies about a place in Gaza that was called "a quarantined ruin" and a place in Galilee of which they said "infected stones were in it" (ibid.) point to an earlier period.

upon a house in the land you possess. běbêt ʾereṣ ʾăhuzzatkem, literally, "in a house of the land of your possession," in other words, in one of the houses in your land (Joüon 1923: §166). The rabbis, intent upon their premise that house infections are inflicted upon sinful Israelites, derive from this expression that these regulations do not apply to the houses of non-Jews (*m. Neg.* 12:1).

35. *the owner of the house shall come (ûbāʾ ʾăšer-lô habbayit).* The avoidance of the verb *wěhûbāʾ* 'is reported' (13:2; 14:2) is an indication that no one else knows. This can only mean that the infection occurs inside the house (see the NOTE on "in my house," below).

something like an infection (kěnegaʿ). "Even a disciple of a sage, knowing that it certainly is a plague, will not decisively state 'An infection has appeared to me in the house,' but 'Something like a plague has appeared to me in the house'" (*m. Neg.* 12:5). The rabbis correctly deduce from the text that the decision rests with the priest alone.

in my house (babbayit). But not outside (*Sipra,* Měṣōrāʿ Neg. par. 5:11). Besides, in Canaan's climate, the nearly year-round sunshine would probably have burned up any outside growth (see the NOTE on "inside," v 41).

36. *the house cleared (ûpinnû ʾet-habbayit).* Literally this reads, "and they shall clear the house." Ibn Ezra deduces from the plural form of the verb that the owner probably needs help. For this meaning of *pinnâ* see Gen 24:31; Ps 80:10.

before the priest enters. Therefore, this impurity does not officially exist until so declared by the priest (Rashi).

so that nothing in the house may become impure (wělōʾ yiṭmāʾ kol-ʾăšer babbāyit). There are a number of significant presuppositions ensconced in this clause. (1) Impurity of "scale-diseased" houses, like that of scale-diseased persons, contaminates by overhang, for if even a single stone be certified by the priest as ṣāraʿat, then everything within that house is contaminated. (2) The impurity is not retroactive. Only those objects found in the house when the priest condemns it are declared impure, but if these same objects are removed before the priest arrives they are considered pure. (3) Those persons who were in the house before the priest declares the quarantine are also pure, including the investigating priest! Thus there can be no lingering doubt that this impurity is wholly symbolic. To be sure, the formal laws and procedures must be followed: the impurity is transmitted by overhang and it must be eliminated by the same bird rite employed for persons. But, in reality, the impurity of the infected stone has not been transmitted to the persons and objects in the house. Transmission occurs only if and when the priest so declares.

The rabbis stress the point that the impurity is transmitted to all objects in the house. Rabbi Judah adds, "even bundles of wood, and even bundles of reed," ordinarily unsusceptible to impurity. Rabbi Meir, however, objects: "And what of his property does it render impure? If you say, his wooden objects, and his clothing, and his metal objects—he immerses them and they are pure. For what has the Torah shown concern? For his clay utensils, his cruse, and his ewer (always susceptible to impurity). If thus the Torah has shown concern for his humble possessions, all the more so for cherished possessions" (*m. Neg.* 12:5; cf. *Sipra,* Měṣōrāʿ Neg. par. 5:12).

after that the priest shall enter to examine the house (wěʾaḥar kēn yābōʾ hakkōhēn lirʾōt ʾet-habbāyit). The point of v 36b is to emphasize that the priest may not enter the suspected house until its owner has had a chance to clear out his possessions. But this is exactly what v 36a has stated! The discursiveness of this pericope once again contrasts sharply with the clipped style of its predecessor and furnishes another bit of evidence for the case that this pericope was written or rewritten by another hand.

37. *If. wĕhinnēh* (cf. v 3a). Equivalent to *wĕ'im* (vv 43, 48).

bright green or bright red (yĕraqraqqōt 'ô ădamdammōt). See the NOTE on 13:19.

eruptions (šĕqa'ărûrōt). The interpretations of the word are legion. The ancients and medievalists provide the following: (1) "streaks" (Saadiah, Ibn Ezra); (2) "depressions, cavities" (LXX; *Tg. Onq., paḥtān; Tg. Ps.-J., mĕšaq'ān; Tg. Neof., šaq'ān; Sipra,* Mĕṣōrā' Neg. par. 6:5, *šôqĕ'ôt bĕmar'êhen* 'sunk in appearance'; Ibn Janaḥ 1968: 539), deriving it from the root *šq'* 'sink'. Shadal, by contrast (followed by BDB and KB), derives it from *q'r* (note: *qĕ'ārâ* 'bowl'), a *qetalul* formation with a *š* prefix. But the objection has rightly been raised that this meaning would duplicate the next phrase, "which appear deeper (than the wall)" *(Keter Torah).* (3) Kimḥi (1847: 815) renders "black/ugly depression, the word taken as a conflation of two roots, *šq'* + *š'r.* If this were a new color, however, then one would have expected it to be preceded by the particle *'ô* *(Keter Torah).*

Among postmedieval interpreters, (1) Wessely also maintains it to be a conflation of two roots, *šq'* and *'rh,* rendering "removable sunken [stones]," and adding that it is a feminine because it modifies *'ăbānîm* 'stones' (v 42). (2) Recently, Kraemer (1966) has related this word to Arab. *iqša'arra (qš'r* iv) 'be coarse to the touch, rough, mangy, scrabby', yielding "coarse, crusty, scaly, spots," claiming that the first two metathesized in Hebrew as *šq'r.* (3) Görg (1981) has objected to this reading on the grounds that the consonantal shift of Arabic *š* to Hebrew *š* is exceptional, a metathesis is required, and as Arabic possibilities are inexhaustible, an Arabic etymology is of necessity imprecise. Görg instead proposes a loanword from Egyptian *sqr r rwtj* 'eruption, rash', an internal corrosion of the wall that manifests itself on the outer surface as discoloration and depression. Thus the etymology is moot; the rendering "eruption" is adopted not because of Görg's etymology but because it corresponds to the general appearance of all form of *ṣāra'at.*

The nature of the eruption has been described by Snaith (1967): "this may be the fungus of dry rot which sometimes forms a layer of greenish or reddish material between lath and plaster, or it may be a deposit of calcium nitrate which can form by the action of the gases of decaying matter on the lime of the plaster, sometimes called mural salt." But the color of the eruption indicates that it is a type of mold or fungus, not a deterioration by the formation of saltpeter (Driver and White 1898). Supporting the notion that we are dealing with wall fungus is the fact that the Mesopotamian omen and Namburbi texts, cited above, focus on *kamunu* and *katarru* appearing on walls and in inner courtyards, and both growths are identified as fungi (*CAD*, K 133, 303). Even more significant is that the *katarru* appears as red and green, precisely like its biblical counterpart, and that the term for red, *miqtu*, also stands for a fungus (*CAD*, M 105, no. 8).

the wall (haqqîr). qîr and *hômâ* are not synonyms: the former refers only to the outer surface of the latter. This distinction is crucial in the measurement of the *migraš* surrounding the levitic city (Num 35:4; cf. Milgrom 1982b).

38. *the priest shall come out of the house.* He must first leave the house, not because he has to bar the entrance (see below), but because he cannot impose a quarantine as long as he is inside it.

and quarantine the house (wĕhisgîr 'et-habbayit). The fact that he leaves the house implies that he closes off the entrance (Rashi); otherwise, the text would have read *wĕhisgîr 'et-hannegaʿ* 'and quarantine (the person with) the affliction', that is, by pronouncement (13:4, 50; Wessely 1846). As Ehrlich has pointed out, however (1908-14), if this were so then the prior phrase, "the priest shall come out of the house," would be redundant and, more decisive, the possibility of chance entry, entertained by the legislation (v 46), could not have been envisaged. Thus the only alternative is that the quarantine is imposed, as in previous cases (13:4, 5, 21, 26, 31, 33, 50, 54), by declaration. This too is the opinion of the rabbis, as can be derived from their statement: "He (the priest) does not go into his own house and (from there) quarantine [the other house], nor into the house in which the infection is located and quarantine it" (*m. Neg.* 12:6).

39. *the priest shall return (wĕšāb hakkōhēn).* Another indication of the expansive style of this pericope, in contrast to the previous (cf. 13:4b, 5b, etc.). The same discursiveness will continue in the following verses (cf. 41bβ, 43aβb, 44a, 45aβγ; Jastrow 1913-14: 395; Elliger 1966).

the infection has spread (pāśâ hannegaʿ). What if it does not spread (ʿāmad, cf. 13:5, 37)? Are houses analogues to persons who, in the same circumstances, are quarantined for a second week (e.g., 13:6, 33) and only then, if there is no change, are declared pure (13:6, 34)? Or shall we say that because persons are required to bathe and wait till sunset, whereas houses are exempt from this requirement, the analogy breaks down and, hence, houses in which the infection remains static do not require an additional quarantine but are declared pure (Bekhor Shor)? Or shall we say that houses cannot be compared to persons: whereas a static condition for the latter indicates healing, for the former, it implies an incurable infection? The answer must await the NOTE on "the infection has not spread in the house," v 48.

40. *the stones (hāʾăbānîm).* Care must be taken not to assume that the ordinary Israelite home was built of stone. Only the most imposing structures were wholly of stone. According to Stern (1979: 269), "the great majority of Israelite buildings, irrespective of their plan, were built on stone foundations topped with mud brick."

to be pulled out. (wĕhillĕṣû), literally, "and they shall pull out." The plural, having no antecedent, clearly indicates that the verb should be treated as a passive. Its meaning is attested by the Tgs.—*wĕyišlĕpûn* (Tg. Onq.); *wĕyišmĕṭûn*

(Tg. Ps.-J.; Tg. Neof.)—and in other biblical passages (e.g., Deut 25:9–10; Isa 20:2, *qal*, 'remove, withdraw'; Pss 81:8, 40:2, *pi'el*, 'remove from danger, rescue'). See also Akk. *ḥalāṣu* 'press, squeeze out'. The use of the *pi'el* in preference to the *qal* is explained by the assumption that the removal of the stones requires great effort by more than one person, which accounts for the plural (Wessely 1846).

outside the city ('el-miḥûṣ la'îr). The stones are contagiously impure. They transmit their impurity to objects and persons, to judge by the fact that the priest must clear out the house before inspecting it (v 36) and that persons entering it thereafter contract impurity (vv 46–47). Thus the infected stones must be removed from human habitation lest persons and objects around them become contaminated.

into an impure place ('el-māqôm ṭāmē'). This pericope contains the only attestation (with vv 41, 45) of such a designation in all of Scripture. The impression is thus given that it must have been a definite place, known and recognized by everyone, so that it would be avoided and people would not use the discarded materials in other building projects (D. Wright). This phrase contrasts with *māqôm ṭāhôr* 'a pure place', the site for dumping sacrificial refuse (e.g., 4:12; 6:4). The latter clearly was a definite site because it is called "the [sacrificial] ash heap" (4:12). Thus the text gives no hint concerning the site for dumping the infected stones. That there was such a site is assumed by the rabbis, for they gloss the phrase with *šeyĕhē' mĕqômô ṭāmē'* 'its place is already impure' (*Sipra*, Mĕṣôrā' Neg. 4:4). Because the ground itself is not susceptible to impurity, the rabbis must be referring to a place with impure materials, that is, a dump. Some suggest it was the camp graveyard (*Tiferet Israel* on *m. Neg.* 13:1); others that it was a dump for carcasses (*Mid. Haḥefeṣ* MS, cited in *Torah Shelemah*). In any case, it must also have been the depository for discarded potsherds, which, once contaminated, could no longer be purified (11:3).

Whereas the diagnosis follows scale disease of persons—(1) color changes, (2) which appear below the surface, (3) quarantined for seven days, and (4) whose spread is the decisive factor in the priest's decision—the remedy follows that of moldy garments—the removal of the infected area (13:56). "Here, evidently, we have a piece of legislation specifically devised for the case in question, and not based upon an attempt to provide in the case of a mark in the house something analogous to an unclean mark on an individual" (Jastrow 1913–14: 397).

41. *shall be scraped (yaqṣīa').* Most of the Versions read *yaqṣî'û*, plural, in keeping with the verbs in vv 40–42 (but note *yiqqaḥ wĕṭāḥ*, v 42b). Yet the singular here (and in the "exceptions" of v 42b) can be explained on Wessely's principle (see the Note on "to be pulled out," v 40) that the plural is used only when more than one person is needed. The scraping can certainly be done by a single individual. In the Bible this verb is found only here (vv 41–43), though most commentators connect it with the noun *maqṣū'ôt* 'planes' (Isa 44:13; Ibn

Janaḥ, Rashi, Ibn Ezra). The verb is also attested in rabbinic literature (e.g., *m. Kelim* 27:4). The purpose of removing the plaster of the inner wall is to ascertain whether the fungus has penetrated to the stones.

inside. mibbayit; but not outside. Therefore the infection, to begin with, was in the house (see the NOTE on "in my house," v 35).

all around (sābîb). According to the rabbis, the scraping is done all around the infection (*Sipra*, Měṣōrā' Neg. 4:5). But as the infection has already been removed together with the attached stones (v 40), "all around" must refer to the house (see the Versions).

the mortar. he'āpār, to wit, the wall plastering. The Akk. cognate *eperu* also manifests the same range: the basic meaning is "dust, loose earth" and one of its extended meanings is "mortar" (*CAD*, E 189).

is scraped off (hiqṣû). The root *qṣh* is considered equivalent to *qṣ'* (above), according to the Tgs., which render both verbs by the root *qlp* 'peel, scrape' (cf. also Saadiah, Rashi). Most commentators read *hiqṣî'û*, assuming that the *'ayin* dropped out, as in *wnšqh* for *wnšq'h* (Amos 8:8; K./Q.; many MSS; cf. Amos 9:5; W. R. Smith, cited by Driver and White 1898); cf. the NOTE on v 43. As noted by Seidl (1982: 22 n. 150), however, the root *qṣh* denoting "scrape" is attested both in the Bible (2 Kgs 10:32) and in rabbinic Hebrew, for instance, "Seventh-year figs may not be cut off *(qôṣîn)* with the fig knife *(bammuqṣeh)*" (*m. Šebu.* 8:6). Moreover, both roots can occur in the same passage with the same meaning: "If a man hired a laborer to help him harvest (*liqṣôt*, literally, "cut") figs . . . during the fig harvest *(qěṣî'â)*" (*m. Ma'aś.* 2:7).

42. *They shall take . . . and replace (wělāqěḥû . . . wěhēbî'û).* The plural is used to indicate that many persons are needed to speed the job (Ibn Ezra; cf. his comment on "the house is cleared," v 36). The rabbis suggest that the plural refers to the owner and his neighbor who share a common wall (*m. Neg.* 12:6; see below).

take . . . and plaster (yiqqaḥ wěṭāḥ). The Sam., LXX, and Pesh. read the plural, but the changes of number are characteristic of this chapter's style (Seidl 1982: 60). The rabbis, on the assumption that the case here refers to two neighbors sharing an infected wall, explain the shift in number as follows: "On this basis have they said 'woe to the wicked, woe to his neighbor.' The two of them remove *(ḥôlěṣîn)* the stones, the two of them scrape the walls *(qôṣě'în)*, the two of them bring *(měbî'în)* stones. But he alone brings the coating *(hě'āpār)*, as it is said 'and he shall take other coating and plaster the house' (v 42); his fellow does not join with him in the plastering *(haṭṭîḥâ)*" (*m. Neg.* 12:6). The rabbinic view must be given serious consideration. Recent archaeological studies have demonstrated that Iron Age (Israelite) dwellings frequently clustered in "multiple-family compounds . . . comprised of two or three individual houses, each one either completely independent or linked to another unit by one or two *common walls*" (Stager 1985: 18; italics mine). The verb *ṭāḥ* means "cover" (Isa 44:18) and its technical meaning is "plaster" (Ezek 13:10).

43. *If the infection breaks out again (wĕʾim-yāšûb hannegaʿ ûpāraḥ).* There is an implicit waiting period that ensues, presumably seven days (*m. Neg.* 12:7; 13:1). The infection may reappear anywhere in the house (cf. v 44: Ramban).

after . . . have been pulled out (ʾaḥar hillēṣ). The Tgs. and most commentators treat this verb as a perfect, the equivalent of *ʾăšer hillēṣ* (Rashi, Ibn Ezra), *ʾaḥar hikkâ* 'after he had murdered' (Jer 41:16) serving as a precise example. Yet the singular here would conflict with and be secondary to the plural form in v 40. The Sam.'s *ḥlysw*, presuming *hilēṣû*, is a patent harmonization. Ehrlich (1908–14; followed by Joüon 1923: §56, bN) repoints to *ḥullaṣ*, presumably to conform with the ostensibly passive infinitives in the rest of the verse (but see below). But this form, a *puʿal* infinitive, does not exist; *gunnōb* (Gen 40:15), mistakenly offered as proof by GKC §52, is not a *puʿal* infinitive but a *qal* passive infinitive. A third and more acceptable alternative is to repoint it *hallēṣ* (with the LXX), a *piʿel* infinitive, which would correspond to the active *(hiphʿîl)* infinitive *hiqṣôt*, the next verb; see below.

has been scraped (hiqṣôt). There are a number of ways to treat this anomalous form: (1) as a *niphʿal* (Rashi), which Ehrlich (1908–14) repoints *hiqqāṣôt*, analogous to the vocalization of the following verb, *hiṭṭôaḥ*, a *niphʿal* infinitive; (2) read *hiqṣîaʿ* (W. R. Smith, cited by Driver and White 1898), a radical emendation without textual warrant; (3) read *haqṣôt* (with the LXX), a *hiphʿîl* infinitive; and (4) leave as is: this form of the *hiphʿîl* infinitive is attested elsewhere, for instance, *hišmîdekā* (Deut 7:24; Shadal; GKC §531).

replastered (hiṭṭôaḥ). Perhaps the use of the *niphʿal* accounts for the absence of the normally expected object, *ʾōtô*. A *niphʿal* infinitive does occur with the *nota accusativa,* but rarely (Gen 21:5a; Num 7:10).

44. *the priest shall come.* That is, at the end of the second week (see the NOTE on "If the infection breaks out again," v 43).

the infection has spread in the house (pāśâ hannegaʿ babbāyit). Even if it occurs in another part of the house, it is not adjudged to be a new oubreak requiring quarantine (v 38), rather a continuation of the old, requiring the demolition of the house (Ramban, *Seper Hamibḥar*). The rabbis also hold that if the infection does not spread but only reappears in one of the same spots in the new stones, the house is also condemned (*Sipra,* Mĕṣōrāʿ Neg. par. 7:1). Instead of *pāśâ* 'has spread', the Sam. reads *pārah* 'has broken out'. Technically, the Sam. is correct (see the NOTE on "the infection has not spread in the house," v 48).

a malignant fungus (ṣāraʿat mamʾeret). The expression is borrowed from the pericope on fabrics (vv 51–52), but whereas the infected fabric is burned, the infected house is razed.

it is impure (ṭāmēʾ hûʾ). According to the rabbis, the certified impure house communicates impurity on the outside as well as the inside, but a quarantined house only conveys impurity on the inside (*m. Neg.* 13:4; *t. Neg.* 7:4; cf. *Sipra,* Mĕṣōrāʿ Neg. par. 7:13). This distinction between the inside and the outside of the house prevails for the sectaries of the Dead Sea in the case of corpse contamination. Entering a house together with a woman with a dead fetus causes a seven-day impurity, but touching her house while she is within is a one-day impurity (11QT 50:12–13). The rabbis actually attribute severer impurity to the scale-diseased person in this regard.

45. *shall be demolished . . . and taken (wĕnātaṣ . . . wĕhôṣîʾ).* Active verbs understood as impersonal passives. The Sam., LXX, and Pesh. read them as plurals, in conformance with v 41. Clearly, the demolition takes place from the outside and instruments are used lest the workmen be contaminated by overhang from within or by direct contact from without.

its stones and timber and all of the mortar. The enumeration is essential to emphasize that the house is totally razed and it and all its contents removed.

46–47. A passage dealing with the extraordinary power of the fungous house to contaminate by overhang. Nothing is said about contamination by direct contact, for it is self-evident. Also the case is restricted to a quarantined house, the assumption being that a certified house will contaminate similarly a fortiori. Had this passage been placed after v 38 or v 42, in the section dealing with the quarantine of the house, the impression might have been given that the specified impurity-contagion would only apply to the quarantined house but not to one certified as impure.

46. *Whoever enters the house (wĕhabāʾ ʾel-habbayit).* Contrast the same situation in the case of a person who enters a house containing a corpse: *kol-habbāʾ ʾel-hāʾōhel . . . yiṭmāʾ šibʿat yāmîm* 'Anyone who enters the tent . . . becomes impure for seven days' (Num 19:14). Both residences contaminate by overhang, but not in the same degree: the corpse house for seven days, the fungous house for one day. Also, the former contaminates clothing as well as persons (Num 19:19b); the latter, only persons (see below). The rabbis are not even certain whether objects are contaminated to the same degree (*m. Neg.* 13:12; *t. Neg.* 7:13). The question arises: Is the examining priest himself rendered impure because he has entered the house? If all who enter it during the quarantine become impure, does not that hold equally for the priest when he examines the house at the end of the quarantine period? One must presuppose either priestly immunity or that the priest, just like a layman, must bathe and abstain from contact with the sacred until evening. The latter possibility is the more likely. The priest's performance on the first day and the high priest's on Yom Kippur cannot be cited as instances of immunity. The priest asperses the person with blood from the bird (v 7) but does not touch him. To be sure, the high priest puts Israel's sins on the head of the scapegoat (16:21), but these are Israel's *ʿăwōnōt* (moral sins), not its *ṭumʾōt* (ritual sins; 16:16).

during the whole time it is quarantined. kol-yĕmê hisgîr ʾōtô; that is to say, during the two-week quarantine (Ibn Ezra). The construct state is used when independent sentences stand in genitive relation (e.g., 1 Sam 25:15; Ps 90:15;

GKC §130d; Joüon 1923: §129p), short for *kol-yĕmê-*ʾăšer* (GKC §130c; Joüon 1923; §298; see the Note on "as long as," 13:46).

shall be impure until evening (yiṭmaʾ ʿad-hāʿāreb). Of course, bathing is presumed (Ibn Ezra; see the Note on 11:24). That the quarantined house suspected of ṣāraʿat contaminates teaches that the quarantined person suspected of ṣāraʿat also contaminates (see the Note on "shall quarantine," 13:4).

47. *Whoever lies down . . . and whoever eats (wĕhaššōkēb . . . wĕhāʾōkēl)*. Why is reclining or eating more severe, requiring laundering, than entering? The rabbis claim that the difference is in the time spent inside the quarantined house. On this view, reclining and eating are not to be taken literally, but, rather, during the time needed to recline, his clothes would become contaminated and their laundering would be required (*m. Neg.* 13:9–10; *Sipra*, Mĕṣōrāʿ Neg. 5:5–11). For the rabbis, then, duration of exposure determines the severity of impurity. A second criterion, they would concede, is the nature of the impurity source. A person entering a house containing a corpse is impure for seven days, at the end of which he must launder (Num 19:14, 19). Thus, as pointed out above (v 46), the house with a corpse possesses severer impurity than a fungous house. The third criterion would be the pressure exerted on or by the impure source (*Midrās;* cf. *m. Ḥag.* 2:7; *m. Nid.* 6:3; cf. also the Note on "launder his clothes," 15:5). The rabbis, then, would posit three criteria for impurity contagion: the duration of the exposure, the intensity of the impurity source, and the intensity of the contact.

All three criteria are surely operative in the transmission of impurity. But is any of them responsible for the difference between entering a house and reclining or eating in it? The second, the impurity source, is ruled out because it remains constant: the quarantined house. The third, pressure, also remains constant: the impurity is radiated from the infected stones by overhang (neither the mat he lies on nor the chair he sits on—presuming they were not removed (v 36)—communicate impurity; the matter is otherwise for the *zāb/zābâ* 15:5–6). By the same token, one must also be careful not to think solely in terms of direct contact with the impurity source: that is, in reclining, the person touches the floor and in eating, he leans or crouches against the wall. After all, merely standing in the house provides contact with the floor; and in eating he need not touch the walls. Besides, "if the requirement to launder was based purely on the contact of the clothing with the impurity, then the clothing on the person who merely enters the house should be impure by overhang as the person does when he enters and should, consequently, require laundering" (Wright 1987: 186, n. 39).

This leaves only the first criterion—duration. Yet this too may be questioned. After all, the text does not say the person entered for a moment, only that he entered. It does not specify the time it takes to recline or eat, only the action itself—reclining and eating. Nonetheless, it must be assumed that duration is what the text has in mind. First, it should be recalled that duration is the factor responsible for turning what would normally be a one-day impurity into the severer one requiring sacrificial expiation (5:1–5; see the COMMENT on 5:1–13). On this basis, it is then difficult to presume that a person entering the house for a lengthy period is contaminated no differently from one who enters it for a fleeting moment. And that duration in this instance makes a difference is demonstrable. Consider the following instance. The owner of the house removes all of his possessions prior to the priest's examination lest they be declared impure (v 36). This must mean that everything in the house is liable to become contaminated by overhang—including clothing. Yet we are told that a person who enters the house must bathe—that is, he personally is impure—but he does not launder, clearly because his clothes are not contaminated! The only possible explanation for this discrepancy is time: the one who enters does so fleetingly; he who enters to recline or to eat stays longer.

launder his clothes. The requirements of bathing and sunset are presumed (see the NOTE on 11:25).

48. *If, however, the priest comes (wĕ'im-bō' yābō' hakkōhēn).* We have come to the alternative situation at the end of the second week (Rashi). Thus vv 43–47 deal with the case that the trouble has recurred and vv 48–53 specify the purificatory rite if there is no further trouble.

the infection has not spread in the house. lō'-pāśâ hannega' babbayit, that is, in the other, remaining stones. Implied, therefore, is that there is no trace of infection anywhere in the house. Thus the question implicitly raised by v 39 is answered. The question was: What if the priest found at the end of the first week that the infection remained the same (*'āmad;* cf. 13:5, 37)? The answer, implied by this verse, is that a second week of quarantine is imposed, and if the infection reappears, even infinitesimally, the house is declared impure (cf. Wessely 1846). This house cannot be compared with persons for whom a static affection can be an indication of healing (13:5–6, 37).

The Sam. here, as in v 44, reads *pārah* 'broken out' instead of *pāśâ* 'spread'. This reading makes sense. Because the original infection has been removed with the afflicted stones, there can be no spreading, no continuous extension of the infection. The fungus reappears in broken patterns; in other words, it breaks out, *pārah.* Nevertheless, the use of *pāśâ* can be justified and preferred once it is realized that the legislator wanted to equate this law of quarantine with that of persons, and the verb consistently used for the latter is *pāśâ* (cf. vv 5, 6, 7, 22, 27, 32, 34, 35, 36). Moreover, the verb *pārah* is used only when the person's condition is declared pure (vv 12–13, 39)! And the legislator did not want to leave any room for suspecting that if the infection did indeed break out *(pārah),* the house would be declared pure.

the priest shall pronounce the house pure (wĕṭihar hakkōhēn). For the expression, see the NOTE on 13:6.

for the infection has healed (kî nirpā' hannāga'). See the NOTE on v 3. The rabbis summarize this pericope on houses as follows:

There are ten [conditions which develop concerning plagues in] houses:
1. that which grows dim in the first [week] and that which disappears—
one scrapes it and it is pure. 2. That which grows dim in the second
[week], and that which goes away—one scrapes it, and it requires [a pair
of] birds. 3. That which spreads in the first [week]—one removes [the
stones] and scrapes, [and another stone is put in its place], and one
plasters [it], and one gives it a week. 4. [If] it returned, it (the house) is
torn down. [If] it did not return—it requires birds. 5. It stood [in place]
in the first week and spread in the second—one removes [the stones] and
scrapes [it], and [another stone is put in its place, and] one plasters [it]
and one gives it a week. 6. [If] it returned, it is torn down. [If] it did not
return, it requires birds. 7. It stood [in one place] in this [week] and in
this [week]—one removes [the stone] and scrapes [it] and [another stone
is put in its place, and] one plasters [it], and one gives it a week. 8. [If] it
returned, it is torn down. [If] it did not return, it requires birds. 9. If
before one completed its purification with birds, a plague appeared in it,
lo, this is to be torn down. 10. And if, after one completed its purification with birds, a plague appeared in it, it is examined afresh. (*m. Neg.*
13:1; translation by Neusner 1975: 69–70; cf. also *Sipra*, Měṣōrāʿ Neg.
par. 7:7)

Hoffmann (1953, on vv 49–53) tabulates the results after the first week of
quarantine as follows:

First Week	Second Week	Third Week
faded—scrapes and is pure		
goes away—scrapes and is pure		
	faded—scrapes and birds goes away—scrapes and birds	
stood in one place— second quarantine	spread—removes and third quarantine stood in one place— removes and third quar- antine	returned—tears down didn't return—birds
spread—removes and second quarantine	returned—tears down did not return—birds	

The rabbis also order the diagnosis of the infection according to its signs:

The houses are made impure in three weeks and with three signs: with a bright green color, and with a bright red color, and with spreading. With bright green and with bright red—in the beginning, at the end of the first week, at the end of the second week, at the end of the third week, after the clearance. And with spreading—at the end of the first week, at the end of the second week, at the end of the third week, after the clearance. And they are made impure within three weeks—which are nineteen days. Among affections none [is quarantined] less than one week and none more than three weeks. (*m. Neg.* 3:8)

These tannaitic statements highlight the two rabbinic expansions of the biblical text. The first is the criterion of *ʿāmad* 'stood in one place', which, missing in this pericope, is clearly borrowed from the pericope on scale disease of persons (13:5, 37). The second is the additional third-week quarantine (for its derivation from Scripture, see *Sipra*, Měṣōrāʿ Neg. par. 7:8; tosafot Yom Tov on *m. Neg.* 13:1). But the diagnosis for houses does not differ from that of persons and fabrics, namely, a maximum of two quarantines and a static condition *(ʿāmad)* as well as spread *(pāśâ)* by the end of the second week suffices to condemn the house.

49. *To decontaminate (lĕḥaṭṭēʾ).* So the LXX, Pesh.; *lĕdakkāʾâ* in *Tg. Onq.* and *Tg. Ps.-J.*; *lĕmidkê* in *Tg. Neof.* For the meaning and implications of the verb *ḥiṭṭēʾ* 'decontaminate', see the NOTES on 6:19; 10:15; and chap. 4, COMMENT A. Z. Weinberg (1973) wonders why this verb appears here in the bird rite for purifying a house but not in the same rite for purifying a person (vv 4–7). The answer rests in the verbs. The pericope on houses used *ḥiṭṭēʾ ʾet* (vv 49, 52) and *kipper ʿal* 'purge, perform purgation upon' because the house is completely purified by the sprinkling rite, whereas sprinkling is only the first stage in a seven-day purificatory rite for the person. Similarly, when the corpse-contaminated person is sprinkled by the purificatory water (*mê ḥaṭṭāʾt,* Num 8:7) on the seventh and final day of his purification, the text also resorts to the verb *wĕḥiṭṭĕʾô* (Num 19:19).

he shall take (wĕlāqaḥ). Assumed is that the subject is the owner of the house, a fact made explicit by the longer version on persons, of which this is an abridgment, which adds the words *wĕṣiwwâ hakkōhēn* 'the priest shall order' (v 4). The costs of this ritual are to be borne by the beneficiary, not by the officiating priest. The Sam. clarifies this point by reading *wĕlāqĕḥû*, that is, 'they', but not the priest. Nevertheless, the singular can be justified as the act following upon the order of the priest (Strade, cited by Seidl 1982: 23).

two birds. The LXX adds "pure living [birds]," that is, *ḥayyôt ṭĕhōrôt,* another clear instance of an abridgment of the MT (see v 4). That the ritual for purifying the house is equivalent to the ritual for the initial purification of the person is indicated by the rabbinic ruling that the birds designated for the one may be used for the other (Maim., "Impurity of Scale Disease" 11.8). For the use of birds in exorcistic rituals of the ancient Near East, see the NOTES on "two . . . birds" (v 4) and on the introduction to vv 33–53.

50. *shall be slaughtered (wĕšāḥaṭ).* Rendered impersonally because it too is an abridgment of v 5, which adds *wĕṣiwwâ hakkōhēn* 'the priest shall order' (see the NOTE above on "he shall take," v 49).

51–52. As recognized by Boys (cited by and more correct than Lund 1942: 52), these two verses are structured chiastically, as follows:

A.　*wĕlāqaḥ ʾet-ʿēṣ-hāʾerez wĕʾet-hāʾēzōb wĕʾet šĕnî hattôlaʿat*

　　B.　*weʾet haṣṣipōr hahayyâ*

　　　　C.　*wĕṭābal ʾōtām bĕdam haṣṣipōr haššĕḥûṭâ ûbammayim hahayyîm*

　　　　　　D.　*wĕhizzâ ʾel-habbayit*

　　　　　　　　X.　*šebaʿ pĕʿāmîm*

　　　　　　D'.　*wĕhiṭṭeʾ ʾet-habbayit*

　　　　C'.　*bĕdam haṣṣipôr ûbammayim hahayyîm*

　　B'.　*ûbaṣṣipōr hahayyâ*

A'.　*ûbĕʿēṣ hāʾerez ûbāʾēzōb ûbišĕnî hattôlaʿat*

The near-perfect symmetry of the corresponding parts shows up best in the italicized words of the translation:

A.　He shall take *the cedar wood, the hyssop, the crimson thread,*　　　　51

　　B.　and *the live bird,*

　　　　C.　and dip them in *the blood of the* slaughtered *bird*
　　　　　　　and the spring water,

　　　　　　D.　and sprinkle on *the house*

　　　　　　　　X.　seven times.

　　　　　　D'.　Having decontaminated *the house*　　　　52

　　　　C'.　with *the blood of the bird, the spring water,*

　　B'.　*the live bird,*

A'.　*the cedar wood, the hyssop, and the crimson thread*

As in the two introverted structures regarding the purification of the *mĕṣōrāʿ* on the eighth day (vv 11–20, 21–32), the sevenfold sprinkling again occupies the pivotal position (cf. vv 16b, 27). This time, however, it is not to dedicate the oil but to cleanse with the bird's blood, as also prescribed for the first day of the purification of the mĕṣōrā' (v 7a). The writer's deliberate attempt to develop this introversion is revealed in its second half when he reverses the list of the materials utilized in the purification (ABCC'B'A').

The tightness, precision, and lack of extraneous elements in this introversion contrasts sharply with those of vv 11–20 and 21–32 and furnish additional support for the conclusion derived from v 34 (see the NOTES) that vv 34–57, though they also stem from the hand of P, have been reworked by another hand, probably that of H (see the Introduction, §H).

51. *and the live bird (we'ēt haṣṣippōr haḥayyâ).* Assumed is that the bird is taken separately (v 6).

and the [spring] water. ûbammayim, literally, "and in the water." Yet two dippings are not intended. The original text (v 6) makes this clear by reading *'al hammayim* '[blood of the bird slaughtered] over the [spring] water."

[and sprinkle] on the house. 'el-habbayit, literally, "toward the house." The preposition *'el* 'toward' may not be a synonym or a mistake for *'al* 'upon' because its intention may be to indicate that any part of the house will do. Indeed, the rabbis debate this very issue: one tradition opts for the whole house (*Sipra,* Mĕṣōrā' Neg. 5:14) and another just for the door lintel (*m. Neg.* 14:1), in other words, where it could be seen *(Tiferet Israel).*

52. *Having decontaminated (wĕḥiṭṭē').* "What is the proof that ḥēṭ' (Ps 51:7) bears the meaning of purifying? Because it is written 'wĕḥiṭṭē' the house' (14:52), which is translated *wîdakkê* and he shall purify *(Tg. Onq.).* And if you prefer I might reply: the proof is derived from the following: 'Purify me *(tĕḥaṭṭĕ-'ēnî)* with hyssop and I shall be pure' (Ps 51:9)" *(b. Nid.* 31b).

with the blood of the bird, the spring water, the live bird, the cedar wood, the hyssop, and the crimson thread. These items are repeated, though they were already mentioned twice (vv 49, 51), to emphasize that each one is indispensable in the purificatory rite: the blood as the purgative; the spring water to give the blood volume; the live blood to carry off the impurity; the cedar wood as additional blood; the hyssop as the sprinkling instrument; and the crimson thread as additional blood (see the discussion in the NOTES on v 6).

53. *over the open country ('el-pĕnê haśśādeh).* In a corresponding Hurrian ritual, the birds are sent to the underworld; in the Mesopotamian and Hittite equivalents, the birds are dispatched to the heavens (see the introduction to vv 33–53). Common to all of these texts is that the birds are intended as gifts to the appropriate celestial or chthonic gods. This motif is still evident in the text of the scapegoat rite on Yom Kippur (see the NOTE on "Azazel," 16:8), but it is totally absent in this rite. The open country is uninhabited; the ritual impurity borne by the bird therefore cannot contaminate persons and possessions. Nonetheless, the latent power of the impurity is fully acknowledged by *Tg. Ps.-J.:* "But if it is destined for the house to be stricken again with ṣāra'at, the bird will return on that day."

outside the city ('el-miḥûṣ la'îr). These words are added to the text of v 7b because the scene has shifted from the wilderness camp to the urbanized settlements of Canaan (v 34). Both this clause and the previous one are preceded by the preposition *'el* 'to, toward', in contrast *'al*, literally, "on, over" in v 7, for the action in the latter case takes place outside the camp whereas the former occurs at the house, within the camp.

perform purgation (wĕkipper). The rendering "purge" for *kipper* in this verse was recognized by Bekhor Shor, who also cites Exod 29:36. For a complete discussion of this term, see chap. 16, COMMENT F. The question needs to be asked: Why did not the legislator use the verb *wĕṭāhēr*, which he found in his model, the bird rite for persons (v 7)? An obvious answer is that the bird ritual for houses should close the same way as its counterpart for persons: *wĕkipper 'ālāyw . . . wĕṭāhēr* (v 20b) = *wekipper 'al . . . wĕṭāhēr* (v 53b). Another reason may be that this bird rite, being so close in form to its analogues in Mesopotamia and Hittite, uses the common verb *kipper* (= Akk. *kuppuru*) in the sense of "wipe, purge" (see chap. 16, COMMENT F). But the choice of this term was not just dictated by stylistic or lexical concerns. Its semantic function in the text is more significant. *ṭihar* is used in designating the grades of purification by ablutions and by sacrifice (vv 7, 9, 21). *kipper*, by contrast, marks the conclusion of a rite. So, indeed, is it used for the person on the occasion of his final sacrificial rites on the eighth day (vv 18, 19, 20; cf. v 31). It is used here, therefore, because no further ritual is necessary: "Buildings simply have to be clean, not in communion with God" (Wenham 1979). This also explains why no *ḥaṭṭā't* sacrifice is required. The impurity generated by the house is not strong enough to contaminate the sanctuary from afar, as proved by the fact that all who contact it contract a one-day impurity (vv 46–47).

upon ('al). Whereas this preposition following the verb *kipper* always means "on behalf of, for" when the object is a person, it can take the meaning "on" when the object is a thing (e.g., 8:15, 16:16, 18; see chap. 4, COMMENT B; chap. 16, COMMENT F).

and it shall be pure (wĕṭāhēr). A comparison with the scapegoat rite on Yom Kippur (16:21–22) is indicated. The mechanics of impurity transfer are the same. When the blood of the *ḥaṭṭā't* animal is daubed on the altars or aspersed inside the Tent, it absorbs this impurity; and when the live *ḥaṭṭā't* animal is dispatched into the wilderness, it symbolically carries the sanctuary's impurities with it. (This seems to have been the original meaning of the scapegoat rite; see the NOTE on "of the Israelites," 16:21.) Similarly, the aspersion of the scale-diseased person or house with the blood symbolically absorbs the latter's impurity, and the live bird carries it off into the open country. Thus both bipartite rites employ slaughtered and live animals, the former for supplying blood as a ritual detergent and the latter for transporting the impurity from human habitation.

There are, notwithstanding, fundamental differences between the two rites, and they must not be overlooked. For one thing, in the Yom Kippur rite, the animals are called *ḥaṭṭāʾt;* not so the birds in the scale-disease rite. Also, a second animal has been added to the Yom Kippur rite, a bull to purge the sanctuary on behalf of the priests. Finally, in the Yom Kippur rite the dispatched animal, the scapegoat, carries off not Israel's impurities but its sins, which the high priest has confessed as he leaned his hands on the scapegoat. Thus, the bird rite for scale disease represents a more pristine ritual than the Yom Kippur rite, which has been fully incorporated into Israel's sacrificial system (for details, see chap. 4, COMMENT G; chap. 16, COMMENTS C and E). Of course, the biblical rite has distanced itself from its pagan analogues. Whereas the latter proposes to cure the patient of his ills, the biblical rite is performed only after the patient is healed (for other similarities and differences, see Wright 1987: 78–80).

54. *This is the procedure for (zōʾt hattôrâ lĕ).* This formula is used for the purpose of summarizing previously mentioned laws (e.g., 7:37). The term *tôrâ,* in Priestly literature, denotes "ritual, procedure" (e.g., 6:2, 7, 18; 7:1, 11; 13:59; Num 6:13; 19:14; 31:21).

for all scale diseases (lĕkol-negaʿ haṣṣārāʿat). In view of the fact that certain types of scale disease are specified in the list that follows (vv 54–56), there is disagreement over what types are subsumed under this heading. One commentator claims it refers to boils (13:18–23) and burns (13:24–28) on the grounds that, being the most common sores, they are therefore listed first (Ramban). Another opinion is that this heading embraces both tetters (13:38–39) and baldness (13:40–44) because these sores are omitted in this subscript (Hoffmann 1953).

The answer, however, can become more precise if we focus on the distinction of the term *negaʿ ṣāraʿat* in these two chapters. Thus it is found to be attested for discolorations, scabs, and shiny marks (13:2, 9), and for boils (13:20) and burns (v 25). Scalls, instead, are described as *ṣāraʿat hārōʾš ʾô hazzāqān* 'scale disease of the head or the chin' (v 30), and baldness is termed *ṣāraʿat pōraḥat* 'scale disease that has broken out' (v 42). Hence, *negaʿ ṣāraʿat* may be the technical term adopted in these chapters just for scale diseases of the (fleshy) *skin,* and it is mentioned first in the subscript simply because it occupies first place in the legislation (13:1–28). The particle *kōl* can be explained as being necessitated by the fact that three kinds of scale disease are subsumed under this title: discolorations, scabs, and shiny marks (vv 2–17). Thus the heading, rightfully, is all-inclusive. The sores that follow in the text—scalls (13:29–37) and baldness (13:40–44)—are called "scale disease of the head or chin" (v 30; cf. v 44), which, in case of malignancy, is described as *kĕmarʾeh ṣāraʿat ʿōr bāśār* 'like scale disease of fleshy skin in appearance' (v 43).

Thus, the conclusion is inescapable that v 56—"discolorations, . . . scabs, . . . shiny marks," which technically have already been subsumed under *negaʿ ṣāraʿat*—must be an addition supplied by an editor for stylistic reasons, to supply an inclusion for chaps. 13–14 (see further the NOTE on 14:56 below). Finally, it should be noted that, according to this explanation, *bōhaq* 'tetters' (vv 38–39) have been deliberately omitted from the subscript, but for a cogent reason: they are always pure (in contradistinction to baldness, cf. vv 42–44), hence they can never fall under the rubric ṣāraʿat.

scalls (netek). Once it is accepted that "every scale disease" adverts to the skin sores of 13:1–28, scalls (13:29–37) follow in the correct order.

55. *for mold in fabrics and houses (ûlĕṣāraʿat habbeged wĕlabbāyit).* These sores, which close the list, are also in perfect sequence (13:47–58; 14:33–53). Their pericopes are separated from each other by the purificatory process for persons (14:1–32) and by the subscript for chap. 13 (v 59), necessitated by the intrusion of the purificatory rite for persons (see the NOTE on "this is the procedure," 13:59).

56. *for discolorations, for scabs, or for shiny marks (wĕlaśʾēt wĕlassappaḥat wĕlabbehāret).* These three sores, being the very first to be discussed in the legislation (13:1–17), are manifestly out of sequence in this subscript. One scholar's verdict is that this verse, together with v 54, comprised the original subscript to 13:1–46 and was moved to its present position when 13:47–58 and 14:33–53 were added (Fishbane 1980: 440–42). Unfortunately, this complex theory explains nothing about the present sequential disorder of the subscript. Another opinion holds that this verse is simply an itemization of "every scale disease" (v 54; Hoffmann 1953). This solution would be perfect if this verse had followed the words "for every scale disease" (v 54), and the *waw* of *wĕlaśʾēt* did not appear. Then the order of chap. 13 would have followed perfectly: "This is the ritual for every scale disease: for discoloration, for scabs, for shiny marks, or for scalls." Even granted this major transposition, however, the order would still remain defective: scalls are not *negaʿ* ṣāraʿat, scale disease of the skin (see the NOTE on v 54).

The problem is solved once it is granted that v 56 is an addition—not a careless, arbitrary editorial interpolation but a deliberate, logical addition—attributable to the author of this subscript who wanted to close chaps. 13–14 by enveloping them in an inclusion. The proof that this, indeed, is what happened rests in the fact that the order of the skin diseases is not that of the legislation (13:2b–17) but of its introduction (13:2a). Thus, just as chaps. 13–14 open with discolorations, scabs, and shiny marks, it now closes with the same diseases and in the same sequence.

57. *to determine (lĕhôrōt).* This verb, normally rendered "teach" (cf. 10:11), here carries the nuance "determine, decide" (Ehrlich 1908–14), as in rabbinic Hebrew (e.g., *m. Sanh.* 11:2). This meaning follows from the verb being a denominative of *tôrâ*, which, in these texts, means not "teaching" but "procedure." The verb, then, would describe the act of applying the procedure, in other words, determining whether the affection is pure or impure.

when . . . and when they are pure. bĕyôm . . . ûbĕyôm haṭṭāhōr (with Saadiah). For this usage see 7:38; Num 3:1. It also occurs with this sense in *běyôm tohŏrātô* (14:2a). Thus a neat mini-inclusion is created for chap. 14 (see below).

This is the procedure for scale disease (zōʾt tôrat haṣṣārāʿat). This sentence frames the subscript in an inclusio (vv 54–57), a technique followed in other Priestly laws (e.g., Num 7:84a, 88b). The net effect of this subscript is that it encapsulates three inclusios: "for discoloration, for scabs, or for shiny marks" (v 56 and 13:2a); "when it is pure" (v 57aβ and v 2aβ); and "This is the procedure for scale disease" (v 57b and v 54a) in descending order: chaps. 13–14; chap. 14; subscript to chap. 14.

The aesthetics of this subscript is further enhanced by its artfully crafted design: "The classification is arranged so that there are two examples of each of the first two, exactly parallel, with the first in each group a construct chain, while the second is attached through a preposition. Then in v 56 we have individual items all preceded by the preposition *l* as is true of the first two sets. The total of all the cases is seven, probably deliberate" (D. N. Freedman, written communication).

The net result is that these concluding verses form the following structure:

A. *Summation*

    54a   *zōʾt hattôrâ*

    54b   *lěkol-negaʿ haṣṣāraʿat wělannātek* (13:2–17, 18–23, 24–28; 13:29–37, 42–44)

    55   *ûlěṣāraʿat habbeged wělabbāyit* (13:47–58; 14:33–53)

B. *Inclusions*

    56   *wělaśěʾēt wělassappaḥat wělabbehāret* (13:2a)

    57a   *lěhôrōt běyôm haṭṭāmēʾ ûběyôm haṭṭāhōr* (14:2aβ)

    57a   *zōʾt tôrat haṣṣāraʿat* (14:54a)

Thus the first two of the final four verses of this chapter sum up all varieties of malignant scale disease discussed in chaps. 13–14. The last two verses comprise inclusions—with the beginning of chap. 13, with the beginning of chap. 14, and with the summation (vv 54–55). Thereby, the subscript has skillfully and effectively locked in and enveloped chaps. 13–14, the entire unit on scale disease. Because H is the last stratum detectable in these two chapters (14:34–53), this artful subscript, which also summarizes H's contribution, must be attributed to the same hand.

COMMENTS: PURIFICATION AFTER SCALE DISEASE

A. The Composition of Chapters 13–14

When the evidence adduced in sporadic observations in the NOTES is assembled, a describable picture emerges regarding the composition of chaps. 13–14.

The chapters' core is easily isolated. It consists solely of the prescriptions for scale disease of persons (13:1–46; 14:1–32). This first unit can be broken down into the following sections: diagnosis (13:1–44), consequence (13:45–46), and purification (14:1–32). The cohesion of this unit is amply demonstrated by its logical sequence.

A second hand is responsible for the insertion of the unit on fabrics (13:47–59). It interrupts the smooth flow of the unit on persons, and it supplies its own subscript (v 59)—in contradistinction to the other units—in order to prevent the misunderstanding that the purificatory rite for persons (14:1–32) also applies to fabrics (see the NOTE on 13:59).

The unit on houses, based on the language and style of the units on both persons and fabrics (see the NOTE on "into an impure place," 14:40) has been composed (or reworked) and interpolated by a third hand. It could not have stemmed from the author of the unit on fabrics because of the irreconcilable differences in style: God suddenly speaks in the first person (14:34) and the unit is marked by a discursiveness that contrasts sharply with the terse style of its predecessors. In particular, mark the following: vv 36b, 39a, 41bβ, 43aβb, 44a, 45aβγ (see Elliger 1966 and the NOTES *ad loc.*). When this stylistic peculiarity is supplemented by the fact that the unit also introduces two new concepts, "entry into Canaan" and *ʾăḥuzzâ* '[land] holdings, possession,' both of which are characteristic of H (Canaan, 19:23; 23:10; 25:2; and possession, throughout chaps. 25 and 27), then the suspicion arises that the author (or editor) of this unit may be from the school of H. The subscript (14:54–57) would then also be a product of H, for it includes the pericope on the house. Furthermore, the love and concern for literary devices such as chiasm and, in this case, inclusion has already been spotted in a similarly compact unit (11:43–44), which betrays the major hallmarks of H.

These tentative conclusions can be tabulated as follows:

THE COMPOSITION OF LEVITICUS, CHAPTERS 13–14

P_1	P_2	H
13:1–46		
	13:47–59	
14:1–32		
		14:33–53
		14:54–57

B. The Priest and the Ritual

In contrast to his pagan counterpart, the Israelite priest is not involved in epidemics or illnesses (except in emergencies, when he intercedes through sacrifices, Num 17:9–15; 2 Sam 24:25—David officiating as a priest) but only in scale disease. This limitation is clearly implied in the deuteronomic exhortation: "In cases of scale disease be most careful to do exactly as the levitical priests instruct you. Take care to do as I have commanded them" (Deut 24:8). Moreover, as part of the priest's judicial function, he is charged with the responsibility to decide *bên negaʿ lĕnegaʿ* 'between affection and affection' (Deut 17:8; cf. vv 9a, 11a), in other words, to determine which skin eruptions should be quarantined, declared pure, or declared impure. Thus, the Deuteronomist brings the priest out of the sanctuary only for scale disease, clear evidence that in the case of every other disease the priest has nothing to do with diagnosis and therapy. The legislation for genital discharges, the very next case taken up in the MT (15:1–15, 25–30), underscores the anomaly. Genital discharges also generate impurity, severe enough to pollute the sanctuary from afar (15:31). Hence the afflicted person, like the sufferer from scale disease, must bring appropriate sacrifices to the sanctuary after healing has taken place (15:13–15, 28–30). Yet the priest has no function whatever in the diagnosis of the malady. He remains confined to his sanctuary, ready to receive the supplicant and his or her sacrifices on the eighth day of recovery, but nothing more. One cannot even equate the priest with a "quarantine officer, an ecclesiastical public health official" (Milgrom 1971d: 35, a statement I now revoke), for it is now clear that the scale disease diagnosed in chap. 13, as much as it corresponds with known skin diseases, is generally not of the contagious variety (see chap. 13, COMMENT A), thereby rendering the presence of a *quarantine* public-health officer entirely superfluous.

Above all, the priest does nothing to promote the cure; his rituals commence only after the disease has passed. It is the responsibility of the afflicted to pray (1 Kgs 8:37–38; 2 Kgs 20:2–3) and to fast (2 Sam 12:16) in order to win God's healing. As mentioned, Deuteronomy (24:8) charges the priest with the diagnosis and containment of scale disease (but no other malady), citing the case of Miriam (Deut 24:9). It is noteworthy that in Miriam's case healing comes from God, not through any priestly intervention but through Moses' prayer

(Num 12:11–16). Thus Israel's priest is a far cry from the pagan physician or magician. Healing comes from God alone, either directly (Exod 15:26) or through his surrogate, the prophet (e.g., Moses, Exod 15:25; Elijah, 1 Kgs 17:22; Elisha, 2 Kgs 2:21; Isaiah, 2 Kgs 20:7–8). The disease is not a demonic entity independent of God, nor is the ritual an intrinsically effective agency of healing. Both disease and healing stem from the one God. The ritual, bereft of its inherent power, is transformed into a symbolic purification; it becomes a religious, and not a therapeutic act (contrast Mesopotamian and Hittite ritual, Wright 1987: 83–86).

What is this symbolism, and why does it call for the intervention of the priest? As will be explained in chap. 15, COMMENT F, the root cause of the priest's intervention in cases of scale disease is the anomalous nature of the impurity. It alone, among the impurities generated by live persons, contaminates by overhang (the corpse also shares this power), necessitating the banishment of its carrier from the community. The enforcement of the banishment and the comportment of the carrier are matters that are delegated to the priest (13:45–46). Moreover, the bird rite, though it is extraneous to the *Priestly* system of impurity (see the NOTE on "he . . . along with," v 6) and is a residual of a pagan exorcistic rite (see the NOTE on "two . . . birds," v 4), is performed under the supervision of the priest (vv 4–7). Indeed, it is most likely the pagan origins of this rite that motivated Israel's priesthood to take charge of the execution of the rite. In large measure, the priests succeeded in excising, and failing that in blunting, the most blatant pagan elements of the rite. The live bird was not offered as a gift to some chthonic deity (see the NOTE on "two birds," v 4). In this respect, the transformation of the bird rite into a practice compatible with Israel's monotheism was more successful than the similarly structured scapegoat rite for the purging of the sanctuary, where the name of the original divine recipient of the animal, Azazel, was preserved (16:8, 10). To be sure, the birds were not recast as a *ḥaṭṭāʾt*, as was the scapegoat (16:5). Nevertheless, it must be remembered that such a conversion was not possible by the very rules of this sacrifice. First, the purpose of the *ḥaṭṭāʾt* is to purge the sanctuary. This, indeed, the scale-diseased person does as the final stage of his purification. On his eighth day he brings a ewe for this purpose (vv 10, 19), and if he cannot afford the ewe he brings a bird (v 22). But on the first day, how can he bring a sacrifice to the sanctuary if he still must reside outside the camp limits? This restriction also accounts for the fact that the slain bird as well cannot be converted into a *ḥaṭṭāʾt;* it too must remain outside the camp. Moreover, as pointed out (see the NOTE on "pure," v 4), a *ḥaṭṭāʾt* bird is limited to two species, the turtledove and pigeon, both proverbial for their homing instincts. And the last thing desired of the live bird is to return to the community bearing the scale disease it has symbolically carried off to the open country. Thus, although the Priestly legislators could not incorporate the bird into their sacrificial system, they were able to box in and, in effect, eliminate its potency by ordaining that the actual purification of the scale-diseased person take place by laundering and bathing on the first day, immediately following the bird rite (v 8). Thus the bird rite was denied any role whatsoever in the purification process. It was stripped of all inherent powers; it was reduced to a symbolic function.

The same transmutation and evisceration are evident in the bird rite for fungous houses (vv 49–53), but to an even greater degree. Whereas scale disease is indirectly attributed to the sins of the bearer by dint of the wider range of sacrifices that he brings to the sanctuary (vv 10–20), there is only the barest hint (the work of H; see the NOTE on "upon a house in the land you possess," v 34) that fungous houses are due to the malfeasance of their owners (see the NOTE on v 34). Moreover, the affection itself is not only denied a demonic source, it is drained of any inherent power. At most it communicates a minor impurity to person and objects, which is eliminated by bathing and sunset on the very day the impurity is contracted. But even more significant is the fact that the impurity does not begin to exist until it is "discovered" by the priest. Of course, the same holds true for the scale-diseased person (e.g., 13:3, 11, 20, 25, 30), but the legislation on houses takes pains to warn the owner to remove all of his possessions before the arrival of the priest and thereby save them from possible condemnation (v 36). In short, we are dealing with an impurity that has been eviscerated of its principal potency.

What then is the meaning of this Priestly impurity and, if there was the ever-present danger of confusing it with demonic impurity, why was it retained? A major clue, provided by the text, is that the scale-diseased person must bring a *ḥaṭṭāʾt*, implying that he has polluted the sanctuary. Thus, in this case, as in all cases of ritual impurity, we are confronted with the binary opposition between holiness and impurity, which, as demonstrated earlier (chap. 11, COMMENT C), symbolizes the forces of life and death, respectively, (see the fuller discussion at chap. 15, COMMENT G). Thus the bird rite was retained not only for the negative reason that the masses insisted on it (see the NOTE on "spring water," v 5), but because from the Priestly point of view it presented vividly and forcefully the very battle and victory of life over death. All elements employed in the rite were connotative of life: the "live" birds *(ḥayyôt)*, the "live" waters *(ḥayyîm)*, the "life" blood (chap. 11, COMMENT C), and the bloodlike ingredients: the red cedar and the crimson yarn. As to the opponent, there could be nothing clearer than the fact that scale disease was illustrative of the forces of death (for details, see chap. 13, COMMENT A).

Thus the entire purification process is nothing but a ritual, a rite of passage, marking the transition from death to life. As the celebrant moves from the realm of impurity outside the camp, restored first to his community, then to his home, and finally to his sanctuary, he has passed from impurity to holiness, from death to life, is reinstated with his family, and is reconciled with his God.

C. The Biblical Measures of Capacity, by Susan Rattray

The metric system will be used throughout the following discussion, for metrological arguments are complicated enough without having to cope with gallons, quarts, bushels, and the like—not to mention the distinction between the dry quart and the liquid quart. Not only does the metric system make the relationships of the various measures readily apparent, but conversion between cubic centimeters and liters is straightforward: 1 liter = 1,000 cubic centimeters. The modern equivalents proposed here for the biblical measures will be converted to U.S. measures at the end.

The Bible mentions the following measures of capacity: *bath, cor, ephah, hin, homer, issaron, kab, lethech, log, omer,* and *seah.* The *bath, hin,* and *log* are liquid measures; the *ephah, homer, issaron, kab, lethech, omer,* and *seah* are dry measures; and the *cor* is used as both a liquid and a dry measure. Estimates of the sizes of these measures vary widely, for no complete measuring vessels have yet been discovered that can be measured directly.

Two shards that apparently were once parts of measuring vessels have been discovered. Unfortunately, the pieces are not large enough to enable us to determine the capacity of the jars. One of the fragments, labeled *bt lmlk,* which probably means "royal *bath,*" has been compared to similar, complete jars (which, however, lack any designation of capacity). The original volume of this "royal *bath*" jar has thus been estimated to be 22 liters (Albright 1941–43: 3.58–59). The volumes of the other measures of capacity are usually derived from this estimate on the assumption that the biblical measures had the same proportions to one another that they have in the Talmud (Barrois 1931; Scott 1959). As we shall see in the case of the *bath* itself, however, this was not true.

The *bath* Measure in the Bible and the Talmud. The texts relating to King Solomon's bronze "sea," or tank, provide insight into the ratio between cubic cubits and the *bath,* which was used in the Bible. From 1 Kgs 7:23, 26, we learn that the dimensions of the tank were 10 cubits in diameter, 5 cubits in height, and 30 cubits in circumference, and that the tank had a capacity of 2,000 *baths.* The fact that the radius, 5 cubits, was equal to the height, suggests that the tank may have been hemispherical. Calculating its volume as a hemisphere, the writer would have obtained a capacity of 250 cubic cubits, in which case there would be 8 *baths* per cubic cubit. If, instead, the tank was cylindrical, he would have arrived at a volume of 375 cubic cubits, and there would be 5.33 *baths* per cubic cubit. (The writer of Kings was plainly using an approximate value for pi [3], for he gives the ratio of circumference to diameter as 3 to 1.)

This text is repeated in 2 Chr 4:2–5, but there the volume is reported as 3,000 *baths* rather than 2,000. If 3,000 is the correct figure, there would be either 8 *baths* per cubic cubit for a cylindrical tank, or 12 *baths* per cubic cubit for a hemispherical one. Interestingly, the two texts agree, as Wylie (1949: 89–

90) noted, if the writer of Chronicles calculated for a cylinder while the writer of Kings calculated for a hemisphere. This means that both writers were using the same dimensions for the tank, and the same number of *baths* per cubic cubit —eight—and that they only differed as to the shape of the tank.

The shape of the tank was also important in rabbinic calculations. In fact, Solomon's tank caused serious problems for the rabbis. According to their system of measurements, in which there were 40/9 *baths* per cubic cubit, 2,000 *baths* would have a volume of 450 cubic cubits, rather than 250 or 375. In order to achieve this total, they proposed that the bottom three cubits of the tank must have been square (giving 300 cubic cubits), while the upper two cubits were cylindrical (giving 150 cubic cubits) (*b. ʿErub.* 14a–b). Such an implausible shape for a tank shows clearly that the rabbinic system of measurements differs substantially from the biblical system—at least for the volume of the *bath*. Plainly we must reckon with the possibility that other measures have also changed.

The Biblical Cubit: The Standard for the *bath.* Actually, we need only determine the size of the cubit in modern terms to calculate the size of the biblical *bath* directly from the data given above. Scott (1958) presents archaeological evidence showing that the Israelite cubit was probably equal to about 44.5 cm. This cubit is almost identical to the Egyptian common cubit of 45 cm (Scott 1958: 208). The Egyptians also used a "royal" cubit, equal to 7/6 of the common cubit, which measured about 52.5 cm (Scott 1958: 207).

In all likelihood, the cubit of Kings and Chronicles was the common cubit of 44.5 cm. Because there were 8 *baths* per cubic cubit, the *bath* must have been equal to 11 liters. If, however, the cubit used was the "royal" one of 52.5 cm, the *bath* would have been equal to 18 liters. This suggests the possibility that the jar mentioned above, estimated to contain 22 liters, was actually a *bath* based on the royal cubit, and was accordingly labeled "royal *bath.*"

Two Systems of Measurement. In addition to assuming that the biblical measures were identical to the Talmudic ones, previous approaches have also treated all measures as if they belonged to a single metrological system. In fact, the measures are by no means evenly distributed in the Bible. Priestly texts mention only the *ephah, hin, homer, issaron, log,* and *omer;* Kings and Chronicles use only the *bath, cor, kab,* and *seah.* Moreover, two of the measures found in P, the *ephah* and the *hin,* are of Egyptian origin, while three of the measures of Kings and Chronicles seem to be borrowed from Mesopotamia, the *cor* corresponding to the Mesopotamian *kurru,* the *seah* to the *sutu,* and the *kab* to the *qa.* These facts suggests the existence of two distinct sets of measures in the Bible: a "Priestly" set and a "monarchic" set.

The Talmud itself presents two separate systems of measurement. On the one hand there was the system in everyday use, which included the *cor, lethech, seah,* and *kab* as dry measures (*b. B. Bat.* 89b) and the *hin* and *log* as liquid measures (*b. B. Bat.* 90b). On the other hand there were the measures used in the Temple—the *ephah* and *issaron* as dry measures, and the *hin* and *log* for liquids (*b. Menah.* 87a–b). Both systems used the same liquid measures, but the dry measures differed. In addition, the dry measures in everyday use were those derived from Mesopotamian measures and had the same proportions to one another as the neo-Babylonian *kurru, sutu,* and *qa*—1 : 30 : 180.

Thus it appears that for both the Bible and the Talmud there were two sets of measures: a "temple" or "Priestly" set, consisting of the *homer, ephah, issaron, omer, hin,* and *log;* and a "Mesopotamian" or "monarchic" set, consisting of the *cor, lethech, seah, kab, hin,* and *log.* Neither the term "Priestly" nor the term "monarchic" should be taken to mean that those measures were used only in the temple or in the monarchic period, respectively. The terms simply refer to the texts in which each set of measures predominates.

There is necessarily some uncertainty regarding the members of the biblical sets, for the Bible nowhere provides a complete list of measures. The *lethech* is grouped with the Mesopotamian set because it was part of that system in the Talmud. Likewise the *hin* and *log* are included with both sets on the basis of the Talmud, even though they are not mentioned in Kings or Chronicles. The *homer,* which Hosea mentions alongside the *lethech* (Hos 3:2), may have belonged to both sets in the biblical times, for it has an Assyrian cognate, the *imeru,* which was equal to 10 *sutus* (i.e., 10 *seahs*). Judging by Isa 5:10 and Ezek 45:11, which mention the *bath* alongside the *ephah* and *homer,* the *bath,* too, may have belonged to both sets. Alternatively, the terms in these passages may result from the mixing of two systems of measurement. Ezekiel's statement, in particular, which asks that "the *ephah* and the *bath* should be one measurement" (Ezek 45:11), can be viewed as an attempt to reconcile two systems that were similar but not identical, and whose slight differences were causing confusion and dishonest dealing (cf. the preceding verse, Ezek 45:10).

The Monarchic Dry Measures: The *kab, seah, cor,* and *lethech.* As noted above, three of the monarchic measures are of Mesopotamian origin: the *cor* is derived from the *kurru,* the *seah* from the *sutu,* and the *kab* from the *qa.* In Mesopotamia, the *qa* was a fundamental measure indicating a day's supply of grain (Lewy 1949: 6–8, Ellison 1981: 37–38). In the absence of evidence to the contrary, we shall assume that the biblical *kab* also supplied a day's ration of grain, and use this hypothesis as a basis for calculating the volume of the *kab.*

The average healthy adult consumes about 2,500 to 3,000 calories per day. The two major grains in the ancient Near East were barley and wheat. Barley contains 3,600 calories per kg, and wheat 3,540 calories (Pellett and Shadarevian 1970). Thus a person would need either .83 kg of barley or .85 kg of wheat to obtain 3,000 calories. (Such a diet, incidentally, would be deficient only in vitamins A and C [Ellison 1981].)

As grain was measured by volume rather than weight in the Bible, we must determine what volume of wheat or barley would supply 3,000 calories. Although grain varies in volume for any given weight, let us for the moment use the current legal weights of barley and wheat in the U.S. as a starting point, which set barley at 48 lbs. per bushel (or .62 kg per liter), and wheat at 60 lbs. per bushel (or .77 kg per liter; Hunt 1904: 321–22). Using these figures, one would need to eat 1.3 liters of barley or 1.1 liters of wheat to obtain 3,000 calories.

On this basis, one may provisionally set the *kab* at 1.2 liters (about 4 cups). But as the weight of barley can range from .54 to .875 kg per liter, and wheat may range between .69 and .84 kg per liter, and as it is not certain how many calories were to be supplied, the volume of the *kab* might actually have been anywhere between about .8 liter and 1.5 liters.

The Mesopotamian *qa* (the cognate to the biblical *kab*) has also been estimated to be about 1 liter on the basis of Babylonian mathematical texts, which make it equal to 216 cubic fingers (Thureau-Dangin 1937). As the Babylonian cubit was equal to about 50 cm and contained 30 fingers (Unger 1916; Neugebauer and Sachs 1945: 4), a *qa* equal to 216 cubic fingers amounts to about 1 liter (Thureau-Dangin 1937).

Unlike the Babylonian texts, the Bible does not provide any information regarding the number of *kabs* per cubic cubit. Nevertheless, the Talmud does provide this information indirectly. As there were 40/3 *seahs* per cubic cubit (*b. 'Erub.* 14b) and 6 *kabs* per *seah*, there were 80 *kabs* per cubic cubit. That this ratio probably applied to the biblical *kab* as well can be demonstrated by calculating the size of the *kab* from the biblical common cubit of 44.5 cm. The result is a *kab* of 1.1 liters, which fits perfectly with a *kab* that supplied a day's worth of grain.

In Mesopotamia, the *sutu (seah)* and *kurru (cor)* derived their sizes from the *qa (kab);* that is, the *sutu* was defined by the number of *qas* it contained. This number varied from 3 to 12 (*CAD*, s.v. *sutu*); in mathematical texts the *sutu* contained 10 *qas* in the Old Babylonian period and 6 in the neo-Babylonian period (Neugebauer and Sachs 1945: 6). In Assyria, the *sutu* typically contained 10 *qas* (Lewy 1944: 69; Saporetti 1969).

The *kurru* usually contained 30 *sutus* (Neugebauer and Sachs 1945: 6, Lewy 1944: 66), but other *kurrus* existed, such as the *kurru* of 12 *sutus* used in Mari (Bottero 1957: 349). The size of the *kurru* also varied according to the size of the *sutu;* thus the Old Babylonian *kurru* of 30 *sutus* contained 300 *qas* (because this *sutu* held 10 *qas*), while the neo-Babylonian *kurru* of 30 *sutus* contained 180 *qas* (because its *sutu* held 6 *qas*). The Mari *kurru* of 12 *sutus* held 120 *qas*; that is, the Mari *sutu*, like the Old Babylonian *sutu*, contained 10 *qas* (Bottero 1957: 348).

As was mentioned above, the Talmudic *cor* contained 30 *seahs* of 6 *kabs* each, just as the neo-Babylonian *kurru* contained 30 *sutus* of 6 *qas* each. It seems likely that this ratio was not adopted until the Exile, or shortly before, when Judah was under Babylonian rule. Prior to that time, it is possible that the *seah* had the Assyrian (and Old Babylonian) value of 10 *kabs*. If this conjecture is admitted, then it follows that there were 8 *seahs* per cubic cubit, for there were 80 *kabs* per cubic cubit. As there were also 8 *baths* per cubic cubit, the *seah* would have been equal to the *bath*, which would also have contained 10 *kabs*.

In the Talmud, the *lethech* was equal to half a *cor*, or 90 *kabs*. Possibly the *lethech* was equal to 90 *kabs* in the Bible as well. It is equally possible that the ratio of 2 *lethechs* per *cor* was the one used in the Bible. In the latter case the size of the *lethech* would have varied according to the size of the *cor*. If the *cor* were equal to 300 *kabs*, the *lethech* would have been equal to 150 *kabs*. More interestingly, if the *cor* were equal to 120 *kabs*, the *lethech* would have contained 60 *kabs* and would thus have been equivalent to a Babylonian measure called the *parsiktu*, which also contained 60 *kabs*. This measure was in fact equal to one-half of the Mari *kurru (cor)*, which was equal to 120 *qas* (Bottero 1957: 349).

In the only passage in which the *lethech* occurs (Hos 3:2), it is mentioned alongside the *homer*. The text reads "a *homer* of barley and a *lethech* of barley." If the text is not corrupt (the LXX has "a *nebel* of wine" instead of "a *lethech* of barley"), there are several ways to interpret this phrase. (1) The *homer* and the *lethech* are part of the same system of measures and have the same relationship as in the Talmud, where the *lethech* is one-half of a *homer* because the *homer* is equal to the *cor*. In that case, however, one would have expected the text to say simply "a *homer* and a half." (2) The *homer* and the *lethech* are from different systems of measures; therefore their relationship is not a simple one such as 1 to 2, and the phrasing "a *homer* and a *lethech*" is much more appropriate. In modern terms, it would be like saying "a gallon and a liter." (3) The *homer* and the *lethech* are from the same system of measures, but their relationship is not the Talmudic one of 1 to 2. This interpretation is made more likely when we compare the *homer* to its Assyrian cognate, the *imeru*, which typically contained 100 *qas* (Salonen 1965: 291–92; Lewy 1944: 69). If the *homer* intended by Hosea was a *homer* of 100 *kabs*, then the *lethech* whether equal to 90, 150, or 60 *kabs*, was not half a *homer*, but 9/10 or 3/2 or 3/5 of a *homer*. In this case, too, the phrase "a *homer* and a *lethech*" is more meaningful.

The arguments presented above are admittedly highly conjectural, but the evidence available at this time does not permit more definitive conclusions. The following chart, summarizing the monarchic system of measures as outlined above, is therefore only tentative. I have opted for a *cor* of 120 *kabs* and *lethech* of 60 *kabs*. The metrical equivalents are based on a cubit equal to 44.5 cm.

cor	1 = 132 liters (about 4 bushels)				
cubic cubit	1.5	1 = 88.12 liters or 88121.125 cc (about 3 cubic feet)			
lethech	2	4/3	1 = 66 liters (about 2 bushels)		
bath/seah	12	8	6	1 = 11 liters (about a peck)	
kab	120	80	60	10	1 = 1.1 liters (about 4 cups)

The Priestly Dry Measures: The *omer, issaron, ephah,* and *homer.* From Exod 16:16ff. we learn that an *omer* of manna is one day's supply of food for one person. It is not necessary to know the caloric content of manna to calculate the size of an *omer,* for it is unlikely that the *omer* was developed specifically for measuring rations of manna. It is much more plausible to assume that it was originally intended to measure a day's supply of a common staple, such as wheat or barley. The *omer* is therefore equivalent to the *kab,* and should have been approximately the same size (i.e., 1 to 1.2 liters).

The *omer* is also said to be one-tenth of an *ephah* (Exod 16:36). One-tenth of an *ephah* of semolina is the required grain offering accompanying the daily sacrifice (Num 28:5); this amount is given as one *issaron* in a parallel passage (Exod 29:40). We can therefore affirm that the *issaron* is equal to the *omer,* and therefore approximately 1 to 1.2 liters. As *issaron* is the more common term, I shall use it for the rest of this discussion.

The *ephah,* then, being 10 *issarons,* ought to be equal to 10 to 12 liters. Yet its Egyptian counterpart, the *ipt,* held about 18 to 20 liters (Gardiner 1957: 198). But the Egyptian *ipt* was apparently based on the royal cubit, while the biblical *ephah* was based on the common cubit. Egyptian mathematical texts (Peet 1923: 24–26) use a ratio of 7.5 *ipts* per cubic cubit, and a royal cubit of 52.5 cm produces an *ipt* of about 19 liters. If the biblical *ephah* had the same proportion, namely, 7.5 *ephahs* per cubic cubit, but was based on a common cubit rather than a royal one, it would be equal to 11.75 liters—or 10 *issarons* of 1.175 liters each.

The *homer* is probably derived from *hamor* 'donkey', and apparently means "donkey load." The corresponding Assyrian measure, *imeru,* which was discussed above in connection with the *lethech,* actually does mean "donkey." Whether the *homer* is part of the monarchic system of measures or the Priestly system, or both, it should be an amount appropriate for a donkey load.

Lewy (1944: 69) states that a donkey can carry about 90 kg, which would be between 103 and 166 liters for barley, or between 107 and 130 liters for wheat. If the *homer* were equal to ten *ephahs,* as it was for Ezekiel and the Talmud, then the *homer* would be about 117.5 liters; if it was equal to 100 *kabs,* like the Assyrian *imeru* of 100 *qas,* it would be about 110 liters. Both figures are consistent with a donkey load. Possibly there were two *homers* of slightly different sizes, a monarchic *homer* and a Priestly *homer.*

Thus we arrive at the following sizes for the Priestly dry measures. Note that the *ephah* is almost the same size as the *bath,* leading to the confusion that Ezekiel tried to alleviate by making them equal (Ezek 45:11). I shall use the same cubit length for the Priestly measures as I did for the monarchic measures, in order to facilitate comparisons.

homer   1 = 117.5 liters (about 3.5 bushels)
cubit   4/3   1 = 88.12 liters or 88121.125 cc (about 3 cubic feet)

| *ephah* | 10 | 7.5 | 1 = 11.75 liters (about a peck) |
| *issaron* | 100 | 75 | 10 | 1 = 1.17 liters (about 4 cups) |

The *hin* and *log:* The Liquid Measures. As was shown above, the *hin* and *log* were apparently used by both the Priestly and the monarchic systems, though they were not necessarily the same size in both systems. In the Talmud, there were 6 *hins* per *bath* (also 6 *hins* per *ephah*), a ratio that appears to be related to the *kab*-to-*seah* ratio (also 6). Yet I suggested above that in the Bible the ratio of *kabs* to *seahs* may have been 10 to 1 rather than 6 to 1. If the ratio of *baths* to *hins* was indeed connected to the ratio between *seahs* and *kabs*, this raises the possibility that there were once 10 *hins* per *bath* just as there may have been 10 *kabs* per *seah*.

This decimal ratio is also more suited to the Priestly system of measures, which is entirely decimal (apart from the ratio to the cubit, which we would expect to be different). Furthermore, if the *seah* and the *bath* were alike in containing 10 *kabs*, then the *hin*, if it was one-tenth of a *bath*, was equal to the *kab;* and as the *bath* and *ephah* were equivalent, there could also have been 10 *hins* per *ephah*, with the *hin* and *issaron* alike in the Priestly measures. All of this would only be idle speculation were it not for the fact that the *issaron* and *hin* are mentioned in specific amounts in Priestly texts. These amounts may provide a clue to the ratio between the measures.

In Num 15 we are given recipes for the grain offerings that must accompany sacrifices: .25 *hin* oil to 1 *issaron* flour for a lamb, .33 *hin* oil to 2 *issarons* flour for a ram, and .5 *hin* oil to 3 *issarons* flour for a bull.

Moreover, the oil and flour must be mixed together; hence the amounts of oil specified must be great enough to blend with the flour. A little experimentation will show that the proportion of flour to oil must be at least 8 to 1, and can be as much as 2 to 1. (The grain offering is actually quite similar to a modern pie crust, which contains the same ingredients—flour, shortening, water, and salt— and uses a proportion of about 4 to 1.)

This suggests that there must be between 5 and 13.33 *hins* per *ephah*. A ratio of 5 *hins* per *ephah* (i.e., the *hin* equals 2 *issarons*), in the preceding recipes, would produce a flour-to-oil mix of 2 to 1 for lambs and 3 to 1 for rams and bulls, while a ratio of 13.33 *hins* per *ephah* (i.e., the *hin* equals .75 *issaron*) would produce a mix of 5.33 to 1 for lambs and 8 to 1 for rams and bulls.

Ezekiel has different recipes. He calls for .33 *hin* oil to .165 *ephah* flour for the daily offering (Ezek 46:14), and otherwise 1 *hin* per *ephah* (Ezek 46:5, 7). Ezekiel's *hin*-to-*ephah* ratio, then, must be between 4 to 1 and 8 to 1.

Ezekiel also mentions the *hin* in connection with the water rations. In Ezek 4:11, Ezekiel is allotted .165 *hin* of water per day. Now if Ezekiel's *hin* was in fact equivalent to the *kab* or *issaron*, as suggested above, his water ration would have been less than .2 liter—less than a cup. If, instead, Ezekiel's *hin* were the Talmudic *hin* equal to .165 *bath* or 3 *kabs* (because the *bath* was .1 *cor* and the *cor* contained 180 *kabs*), his water ration would have been about .55 liter, or a little over a pint. As the latter is much more likely, Ezekiel was probably using the Talmudic *hin.*

Obviously, both Numbers and Ezekiel could be using the Talmudic proportion of 6 *hins* per *ephah.* But it is curious that the Numbers recipes can be reconciled with Ezekiel's recipes—for rams and bulls—if we suppose that Numbers used a decimal ratio of 10 *hins* per *ephah* (with the *hin* equal to the *issaron*), while Ezekiel used the rabbinic ratio of 6 *hins* per *ephah.* If this is so, the proportion of flour to oil for both Numbers and Ezekiel would be 6 to 1.

Thus it is somewhat more plausible to suppose that the Priestly measures did in fact use a ratio of 10 *hins* per *ephah,* and that the *hin* was therefore equal to the *issaron.* Likewise, it becomes more plausible to posit a ratio of 10 *hins* per *bath* for the monarchic measures, with the monarchic *hin* equal to the *kab.*

The other liquid measure, the *log,* is only mentioned in Lev 14, where it is presumably a small measure, as only a small quantity of oil was used in the ritual. In the Talmud, the *log* was equal to one-fourth of a *kab,* a small size that suits the biblical passage well enough.

Furthermore, if the *hin* were equal to the *kab,* as suggested above, there would be 4 *logs* per *hin.* And in the Priestly system, the same ratio of *logs* per *hin* could be applied, resulting in a proportion of 4 *logs* per *issaron.*

The Biblical Measures: Summary. The two systems, monarchic and Priestly, can now be presented in full. Again, I shall use a cubit of 44.5 cm for both. Modern U.S. equivalents are also given, rounded to the nearest whole unit where appropriate; these would represent approximate translations of the biblical measures. It must be emphasized that both the ratios between the measures and the modern equivalents are often highly conjectural.

Monarchic:

cor	1 = 132 liters, about 4 bushels or 35 gallons					
homer	1.2	1 = 110 liters, about 3 bushels				
cubit	1.5	(⁵/4)	1 = 88.12 liters or 88121.125 cc, about 3 cubic feet			
lethech	2	(⁵/3)	4/3	1 = 66 liters, about 2 bushels		
bath/seah	12	(10)	8	6	1 = 11 liters, about 3 gallons or a peck	
kab/hin	120	(100)	80	60	10	1 = 1.1 liters, about a quart
log	480	(400)	320	240	40	4	1 = .275 liters, about a cup

Priestly:

homer	1 = 117.5 liters, about 3.5 bushels	
cubit	4/3	1 = 88.12 liters or 88121.125 cc, about 3 cubic feet

ephah	10	7.5		1 = 11.75 liters, about a peck
hin/issaron	100	75	10	1 = 1.17 liters, about a quart
log	400	300	40	4 1 = .3 liters, about a cup

The Development of the Biblical Systems into the Talmudic Systems. Because the biblical measures, according to my hypotheses, differed from the Talmudic measures in many instances, it seems appropriate to suggest how the two systems of biblical measures might have developed into the system known in the Talmud.

The first step may have been the development of a set of "royal" measures, that is, measures based on the royal cubit of 52.5 cm instead of on the shorter common cubit. Such a move may have produced the "royal *bath*" jar mentioned above. This step is here presumed to have applied to all of the Priestly measures. The use of the royal cubit as the basis for a new set of temple measures may also be reflected in Ezekiel's use of this cubit to describe his visionary temple (Ezek 40:5). In the monarchic system this step is presumed to have produced two new measures, the royal *bath* and royal *hin*, in addition to the standard *bath* and *hin*. Moreover, as there were about 4.8 new royal *baths* in each cubic common cubit, I shall assume that this ratio was adopted in order to simplify calculations. These changes are illustrated in the following charts:

Priestly measures:

homer	1 = 193 liters (5.5 bushels)			
royal cubit	4/3	1 = 144.7 liters (5 cubic feet)		
ephah	10	7.5	1 = 19.3 liters (2 pecks)	
hin/issaron	100	75	10	1 = 1.93 liters (2 quarts)
log	400	300	40	4 1 = .48 liters (a pint)

Monarchic measures:

royal cubit	1 = 146.9 liters (from a cubit of about 52.7 cm)							
cor	—	1 = 132 liters (4 bushels or 35 gallons)						
cubit	—	1.5	1 = 88.12 liters (3 cubic feet)					
lethech	—	2	4/3	1 = 66 liters (2 bushels)				
royal *bath*	8	7.2	4.8	3.6	1 = 18.4 liters (5 gallons)			
bath/seah	—	12	8	6	5/3	1 = 11 liters (a peck, or 3 gallons)		
royal *hin*	80	72	48	36	10	6	1 = 1.84 liters (2 quarts)	
kab/hin	—	120	80	60	50/3	10	5/3	1 = 1.1 liters (a quart)
log	—	480	320	240	200/3	40	20/3	4 1 = .275 liters (a cup)

The next step was possibly the adoption of the neo-Babylonian ratios among the *cor, seah,* and *kab.* It is assumed that this change also affected the *bath*-to-*hin* ratios, for both the common and the royal measures. Furthermore, the *cor* and the *seah* were adjusted using the *kab* as the standard, but the *bath* and *hin* were adjusted using the *bath* as the standard. The *lethech* continued to be half a *cor* and the *log* remained one-fourth of a *kab.* Thus the monarchic system would have changed as follows:

cor	1 = 198 liters (6 bushels, or 52 gallons)							
lethech	2	1 = 99 liters (3 bushels)						
cubit	9/4	9/8	1 = 88.12 liters (about 3 cubic feet)					
royal *bath*	10.8	5.4	4.8	1 = 18.4 liters (5 gallons)				
bath/seah	30	15	40/3	25/9	1 = 6.6 liters (6 quarts, almost a peck)			
royal *hin*	64.8	32.4	28.8	6	2.16	1 = 3.1 liters (3 quarts)		
kab/hin	180	90	80	50/3	6	25/9	1 = 1.1 liters (a quart)	
log	720	360	320	200/3	24	100/9	4	1 = .275 liters (a cup)

The next step would probably have been the elimination of the common *bath* and *hin.* In addition, the royal *bath* and *hin* might have been altered slightly to produce ratios to the other measures that were easier to work with. One possible way of doing so might have been to round the ratio between the royal *hin* and *seah* to 2, thus increasing the size of the *bath* and the *hin.*

cor	1 = 198 liters (6 bushels, or 52 gallons)							
lethech	2	1 = 99 liters (3 bushels)						
cubit	9/4	9/8	1 = 88.12 liters (about 3 cubic feet)					
royal *bath*	10	5	40/9	1 = 19.8 liters (5 gallons)				
seah	30	15	40/3	3	1 = 6.6 liters (6 quarts, almost a peck)			
royal *hin*	60	30	80/3	6	2	1 = 3.3 liters (a gallon)		
kab	180	90	80	18	6	3	1 = 1.1 liters (a quart)	
log	720	360	320	72	24	12	4	1 = .275 liters (a cup)

In addition, the Priestly measures might have adopted the monarchic *hin* and *log,* thereby eliminating the confusion arising from the existence of slightly different measures having the same name. If they incorporated these measures by identifying the *ephah* with the *bath,* they would obtain a ratio of 6 *hins* per *ephah.*

homer	1 = 193 liters (5 1/2 bushels)	
royal cubit	4/3	1 = 144.7 liters (about 5 cubic feet)

ephah	10	7.5	1 = 19.3 liters (2 pecks)					
hin	60	45	6	1 = 3.2 liters (a gallon)				
issaron	100	75	10	5/3	1 = 1.93 liters (2 quarts)			
log	720	540	72	12	7.2	1 = .27 liters (a cup)		

Note that at this point the *bath* and the *ephah* differ by only about .5 liter, that is, by about 2 *logs*, and the *cor* and the *homer* differ by only 5 liters, or about 5 *kabs*. When the *ephah* is equated with the *bath*, the result is the system used in Ezekiel and in the Talmud:

cor/homer	1 = 198 liters (6 bushels, or 52 gallons)								
lethech	2	1 = 99 liters (3 bushels)							
cubit	2.25	9/8	1 = 88.12 liters (about 3 cubic feet)						
bath/ephah	10	5	40/9	1 = 19.8 liters (2 pecks, or 5 gallons)					
seah	30	15	40/3	3	1 = 6.6 liters (6 quarts, almost a peck)				
hin	60	30	80/3	6	2	1 = 3.3 liters (a gallon)			
issaron	100	50	400/9	10	10/3	5/3	1 = 1.98 liters (2 quarts)		
kab	180	90	80	18	6	3	1.8	1 = 1.1 liters (a quart)	
log	720	360	320	72	24	12	7.2	4	1 = .275 liters (a cup)

Heltzer raises two points in an article (1983–84) that touch on the biblical systems of measurement. (1) In footnote 2, Heltzer argues on etymological grounds that Ug. *ltḥ* should not be equated with the Hebrew *lethech*. I am inclined to agree, and therefore any conclusions about the capacity of the Ug. *ltḥ* are simply irrelevant for the Hebrew *lethech* (and vice versa). (2) Heltzer tries to equate Ug. *ltḥ* with the Hebrew *issaron,* which he takes to be equal to 2.2 liters, following other scholars (this figure is based on Albright's "royal *bath*" jar and the assumption that Ezekiel's equation of the *ephah* and the *bath* was true for all periods and all sources). He has no evidence from the Ugaritic texts regarding the absolute size of the *ltḥ;* in fact, he is trying to discover the size of the Ugaritic measure from the Hebrew one, which he takes to be already established. His argument would not be affected if the *issaron* should turn out to be only half that size, as I am arguing, or twice or even ten times that size.

Moreover, I am not even sure that Heltzer is justified in equating Ug. *ltḥ* with the biblical *issaron.* His sole support for this correspondence is the Ugaritic text *šᵓhd ltḥ qmḥ* 'one sheep/goat, a *ltḥ* of flour' listed as provision for a feast. Because this resembles the biblical ratio of one *issaron* per sheep/goat (e.g., Num 29:9–10), Heltzer equates the two measures, and as he accepts the view that the *issaron* held about two liters, he believes that the *ltḥ* also held that amount. But he does not ask whether two liters of flour is actually enough for a feast! In fact, two liters of flour (approximately eight cups) is about enough for two, maybe three loaves of bread. I do not know how many men could be fed on one sheep (or goat), but is it likely that only two or three loaves of bread would satisfy them for a feast? When Abraham entertains three visitors at Mamre, he has Sarah take three *seah*s of flour to go with one young bull (Gen 18:6–7). Three *seah*s is equivalent to at least 10 *issaron*s using the Talmudic system, or as many as 30 *issaron*s using my system. Moreover, the *issaron* that accompanies a sacrifice is not for the offerers to feast on, but for the altar—similar to the *ʾazkarah* of the grain offering. Hence it does not need to be very large, and may actually represent a "tithe" of the amount required for a feast: if Sarah bakes three *seah*s for one bull, and a *seah* is equal to 10 *issaron*s as I have argued, then one-tenth would be 3 *issaron*s per bull, which is exactly the ratio we find (cf. Num 15:9).

Heltzer's only Ugaritic evidence for the size of the *ltḥ* comes from a text that reads *bn slˤn prs* 'for Ben [son of] Slˤn a *parīsu*', followed by a list of six men receiving one *ltḥ* each. From this Heltzer suggests that the *ltḥ* was smaller than the *parīsu* (which is equal to half a *cor*), probably a subdivision of it. Nevertheless, the *parīsu* is still a relatively large measure; the *ltḥ* could just as well be equivalent to the *seah* or *ephah* instead of the *issaron*. In fact, if it were equal to my monarchic *seah*, there would be exactly 6 *ltḥ*s per *parīsu*. Is it possible that this text should be read "for the Bene [sons of] Slˤn a *parīsu*," followed by the names of the men to whom the *parīsu* will be distributed in equal amounts?

There is necessarily some uncertainty regarding the members of the biblical sets, for the Bible nowhere provides a complete list of measures. The *lethech* is grouped with the Mesopotamian set because it was part of that system in the Talmud. Likewise, the *hin* and *log* are included with both sets on the basis of the Talmud, even though they are not mentioned in Kings or Chronicles. The *homer*, which Hosea mentions alongside the *lethech* (Hos 3:2), may have belonged to both sets in the biblical times, for it has an Assyrian cognate, the *imeru*, which was equal to 10 *sutus* (i.e., 10 *seah*s). Judging by Isa 5:10 and Ezek 45:11, which mention the *bath* alongside the *ephah* and *homer*, the *bath*, too, may have belonged to both sets. Alternatively, the terms in these passages may result from the mixing of two systems of measurement. Ezekiel's statement, in particular, which asks that "the *ephah* and the *bath* should be one measurement" (Ezek 45:11), can be viewed as an attempt to reconcile two systems, which were similar but not identical, and whose slight differences were causing confusion and dishonest dealing (cf. the preceding verse, Ezek 45:10).

GENITAL DISCHARGES (15:1–33)

Introduction

15 ¹The Lord spoke to Moses and Aaron, saying: ²Speak to the Israelites and say to them:

Abnormal Male Discharges

When any man has a discharge, his discharge being from his member, he is impure. ³This shall be his impurity in his discharge—whether his member runs with his discharge or his member is blocked by his discharge, this is his impurity. ⁴Any bedding on which the man with a discharge lies shall be impure; and every object on which he sits shall be impure. ⁵Anyone who touches his bedding shall launder his clothes, bathe in water, and remain impure until evening. ⁶Whoever sits on an object on which the man with a discharge has sat shall launder his clothes, bathe in water, and remain impure until evening. ⁷Whoever touches the body of the man with a discharge shall launder his clothes, bathe in water, and remain impure until evening. ⁸If the man with a discharge spits on one who is pure, the latter shall launder his clothes, bathe in water, and remain impure until evening. ⁹Any means for riding that the man with a discharge has mounted shall be impure. ¹⁰Whoever touches anything that was under him shall be impure until evening; and whoever carries such things shall launder his clothes, bathe in water, and remain impure until evening. ¹¹Anyone whom a man with a discharge touches without having rinsed his hands in water shall launder his clothes, bathe in water, and remain impure until evening. ¹²An earthen vessel that a man with a discharge touches shall be broken; and any wooden implement shall be rinsed with water.

¹³When a man with a discharge is healed of his discharge, he shall count off seven days for his purification, launder his clothes, and bathe his body in spring water; then he shall be pure. ¹⁴On the eighth day he shall obtain two turtledoves or two pigeons and come before the Lord at the entrance of the Tent of Meeting and give them to the priest. ¹⁵The priest shall offer them up, the one as a purification offering and the other as a burnt offering. Thus the priest shall effect purgation on his behalf, for his discharge, before the Lord.

Normal Male Discharges

¹⁶When a man has an emission of semen, he shall bathe his whole body in water and remain impure until evening. ¹⁷All fabric or leather on which semen falls shall be laundered in water and remain impure until evening.

GENITAL DISCHARGES (15:1-33)

Marital Intercourse

18[This applies to] a woman, with whom a man has sexual relations; they shall bathe in water and remain impure until evening.

Normal Female Discharges

19When a woman has a discharge, her discharge being blood from her body, she remains in her menstrual impurity seven days; whoever touches her shall be impure until evening. 20Anything she lies on during her menstrual impurity shall be impure; and anything she sits on shall be impure. 21Anyone who touches her bedding shall launder his clothes, bathe in water, and remain impure until evening; 22and anyone who touches any object on which she has sat shall launder his clothes, bathe in water, and remain impure until evening. 23If it [the object] is on the bedding or on the seat on which she is sitting when he touches it [the object], he shall be impure until evening. 24And if a man proceeds to lie with her, her menstrual impurity is transmitted to him, and he shall be impure seven days; any bedding on which he lies shall become impure.

Abnormal Female Discharges

25When a woman has a discharge of blood for many days, not at the time of her menstrual impurity, or when she has a discharge beyond the time of her menstrual impurity, as long as her impure discharge lasts, she shall be impure, just as during her menstrual period. 26Any bedding on which she lies while her discharge lasts shall be for her like bedding during her menstrual impurity; and any object on which she sits shall be impure, as during her menstrual impurity: 27whoever touches them shall be impure; he shall launder his clothes, bathe in water, and remain impure until the evening.

28When she is healed of her discharge, she shall count off seven days, and after that she shall be pure. 29On the eighth day she shall obtain two turtledoves or two pigeons, and bring them to the priest at the entrance of the Tent of Meeting. 30The priest shall offer up the one as a purification offering and the other as a burnt offering; and the priest shall effect purgation on her behalf, for her impure discharge, before the Lord.

Consequences for the Sanctuary and for Israel

31You shall set apart the Israelites from their impurity, lest they die through their impurity by polluting my Tabernacle which is among them.

Summary

[32]This is the procedure for the one who has a discharge: for the one who has an emission of semen and becomes impure thereby, [33]and for the one who is in her menstrual infirmity, and for anyone, male or female, who has a discharge, and for a man who lies with an impure woman.

NOTES

This chapter comprises four main cases of genital discharges, each introduced by the particle *kî* (vv 2, 16, 19, 25). Each case is defined, its consequences described, and its purification prescribed. This chapter is structured chiastically, in an ABC–C'B'A' pattern, equally divided between men and women, where BB' stands for long-term discharges and CC', for short-term discharges (cf. Wenham 1979). The symmetry and balance of the structure can be presented diagrammatically, as follows:

A. Introduction (vv 1–2a)
    B. Male discharges, long-term (vv 2b–15)
        1. definition (vv 2b–3)
        2. consequences (vv 4–12)
        3. purification by sacrifice (vv 13–15)
        C. Male discharges, short-term (vv 16–18)
            1. semen emission (vv 16–17)
            2. intercourse (v 18)
        C'. Female discharges, short-term (vv 19–24)
            1. menstruation (vv 19–23)
            2. intercourse (v 24)
    B'. Female discharges, long-term (vv 25–30)
        1. definition (v 25)
        2. consequences (vv 26–27)
        3. purification by sacrifice (vv 28–30)
        [Consequences for the Sanctuary and for Israel (v 31)]
A'. Summary (vv 32–33)

A more meaningful division of this chapter is the following:

904

GENITAL DISCHARGES (15:1–33)

A. Introduction (vv 1–2a)
  B. Abnormal male discharges (vv 2b–15)
    C. Normal male discharges (vv 16–17)
      X. Marital intercourse (v 18)
    C'. Normal female discharges (vv 19–24)
  B'. Abnormal female discharges (vv 25–30)
[motive (v 31)]
A'. Summary (vv 32–33)

The main difference between this scheme and the prior one is the recognition that X (v 18) is the center and pivot of the introverted structure. As demonstrated by my student, James Randolph (in a term paper), the syntactic construction and vocabulary of this verse qualify it as an "inverted hinge" (Parunak 1983), which both designates it as a separate case and as an interlocking device that effectively binds the male (BC) and female (C'B') cases together. See the NOTE on v 18 for details.

With the possible exception of vv 31 and 33aβ (see the NOTES), this chapter was composed by a single hand. Its unity is not only demonstrated by its artistic arrangement but by the fact that the second half of the chapter, dealing with female discharges, is wholly dependent on the language and content of the first half (see, in particular, the NOTES on vv 24b, 27a, 28b, 29b).

A remark on the place of chap. 15 is also called for. One would have expected this chapter to have been joined to chap. 12 because both deal with genital discharges. As noted there (see the NOTE to 12:1), however, the sequence of chaps. 12–15 seems to have been determined according to the duration and complexity of the purification process, in descending order: parturients (chap. 12), forty or eighty days; scale-diseased person (chaps. 13–14), eight days, four sacrifices, and anointing; persons with genital discharges (chap. 15), eight days and two sacrifices for long-term discharges, seven days for menstruation, and one day for seminal emission.

15:1. *Aaron.* Aaron is included because sacrifices are required *(Keter Torah).* If so, how are we to account for the omission of Aaron as the addressee in chaps. 12–14? Ibn Ezra opines that only the priest has the knowledge to distinguish between short-term (menstrual) and long-term female discharges, as confirmed by Scripture, *bên dām lĕdām* 'between blood and blood' (Deut 17:8; cf. *b. Sanh.* 87a). But this phrase refers to bloodshed, not genital discharges. (The priest does play a role in Deuteronomy's judicial system—to diagnose scale disease— see chap. 14, COMMENT B.) Moreover, the absence of the priest from the diagnosis and his confinement to the sanctuary to officiate at the sacrifices (vv 13–15, 28–30) confirm the fact that the diagnosis of genital discharges is left

905

entirely to the skill and honesty of the affected person (see below). The omission of Aaron in chaps. 12 and 14 remains a mystery.

2. *Speak to the Israelites.* Being a disease of the private parts, only the person can determine if he or she has a flow. Thus, because scale disease is exposed and can be reported by others to the priest, the instruction in 14:1–2 is not addressed to the Israelites; by contrast, the rules of genital discharges must be taught to the Israelites, who are responsible for their own diagnosis; hence these instructions are addressed to them (cf. also 12:2).

This explicit injunction to the Israelites implies that non-Israelites, according to Scripture, are not susceptible to the impurity of genital discharges. This is acknowledged by the rabbis (*t. Zabim* 2:1, *m. Zabim* 2:3), but they decreed that non-Israelite males above the age of nine are susceptible (*b. Nid.* 34a) as a deterrent to sodomy (*b. ʿAbod. Zar.* 36b). The fact that the resident alien *(gēr)* is also not addressed is an indication that this chapter is from P and not from H (see the Introduction, §C).

any man (ʾîš ʾîš). Ehrlich (1908–14) claims that this expression requires the addition of *mibbêt yiśrāʾēl* 'from the house of Israel', or *mibbĕnê yiśrāʾēl* 'from the Israelites', or *mizzeraʿ ʾahărōn* 'of the seed of Aaron' (e.g., 17:3, 8, 10, 13; 20:2; 22:4, 18), in other words, any person from a larger grouping and, therefore, one ʾîš should be deleted as a dittography. Further support might be adduced from the fact that the cited attestations of the phrase all stem from H, whereas this chapter is P (see above). Nevertheless, Ehrlich's evidence is not precise. There are at least three occurrences of ʾîš ʾîš that are not followed by a larger grouping (18:6; 24:15; Num 9:10). Conversely, one can argue that just as the three latter citations are injunctions to all Israelites (cf. 18:2; 24:15a; Num 9:10a), so the fact that this instruction to the individual is also addressed to all Israelites (v 2a) certifies that all of these verses are not exceptions to the rule and, hence, no emendation is necessary.

has a discharge. yihyeh *zāb*, literally, "becomes discharging." The imperfect of *hāyâ* is added to a participle "to emphasize an action continuing in the future" (GKC §116r). It is clear from this chapter that *zāb/zābâ*, literally, "the discharging one," is a technical term for "the one with a discharge." The meaning of the root *zûb* is clear from scriptural and wider Semitic usage; thus, Akk. *zâbu* 'ooze', as in *damī iz-zu-[ba]* 'my blood has oozed away' (*CAD*, Z 10a). In the Bible, the verb is used for flowing water (Isa 48:21; Pss 78:20; 105:41) and in the expression "a land flowing *(zābat)* with milk and honey" (20:24; Num 13:27; etc.).

his discharge being from his member (mibbĕśārô zôbô). An explanatory clause, parallel to, and verified by, the same construction for the female: *dām* yihyeh *zōbāh bibĕśārāh* 'her discharge being blood from her genitals'. If so, then the Masoretic cantillation should be altered so that the *zāqēp* should be on the word *zāb* as on *zābâ* (v 19). Alternately, one could, with the LXX, connect *mibbĕśārô* with the previous phrase, yielding "when any man has a discharge from his member," but the rest of the verse, *zôbô ṭāmē᾽ hû᾽* can only with great difficulty be rendered "his discharge (it) is impure."

his discharge (zôbô). A nominal formation (Ibn Ezra). What is the nature of this discharge? What is clear is that it is not seminal; the term *zeraʿ* 'seed' is never attached to the *zāb* (contrast vv 16–18), and where the two occur in the same verse they are carefully distinguished (22:4; Kalisch 1867–72). The rabbis provide an anatomical and analogic distinction: "Discharge comes from a limp penis, and semen from an erection. Discharge is watery like the white of a crushed egg, and semen is viscous like the white of an egg which is not crushed" (*t. Zabim* 2:4). Or "the discharge of a *zāb* resembles the dough water of barley" (*b. Nid.* 35b). Even the urine of a *zāb* is considered impure for fear that it has been contaminated (*Sipra*, Zab. par. 1:12–13); so too his semen (*b. Nazir* 66a).

Scientific opinion is nearly unanimous "that the only illness we know of that can be referred to here is gonorrhea" (Preuss 1978: 410), an identification already made by the LXX and Josephus (*Ant.* 3.261; *Wars* 5.273; 6.426), but it should be clear that this disease is not *Gonorrhoea virulenta*, unknown before the fifteenth century, but *Blennorrhea urethrae* (Kalisch 1867–72) or *Gonorrhoea benigna*, urinary Bilharzia (related to Akk. *mûṣu;* Kinnier-Wilson 1982: 358), which solely refers to an inordinate secretion of mucus. The rabbis further state that three emissions in one day or on three consecutive days qualify the man as a *zāb* (*m. Zabim* 1:1–3). But they exclude discharges that might reasonably be attributed to external causes: diet, physical activity, and sexual fantasies (*m. Zabim* 2:2). In effect, the rabbis identify the discharge as something due to disease. Because gonorrhea is the major but not the only cause of abnormal urethral discharge, the translation of *zāb* as "gonorrheic" is avoided.

from his member. mibbĕśārô, literally, "from his flesh," a euphemism for the penis (v 19; 6:3; 16:4; Ezek 16:26; 23:20; cf. the NOTE on 12:3). When this chapter uses the term in the sense of body it resorts to the expression *kol-bĕśārō* 'his whole body' (v 16; but cf. v 7a). The rabbis derive the meaning here by reasoning analogically from the *zābâ:* the same part of her body that is the source of a woman's lesser impurity of the *niddâ* (vv 19–23) is also the source of the greater impurity of the *zābâ* (vv 25–30); hence, the part of the body that is the source of a man's lesser impurity of *qerî* (i.e., seminal emission: cf. Deut 23:11) is also the same source of his greater impurity of *zāb*, namely, his genitals (*Sipra*, Mĕṣōrāʿ Zab. par. 1:4).

he is impure (ṭāmē᾽ hû᾽). The adjective is used for indefinite periods of impurity. Conversely, the impurity of persons and objects that contact the *zāb* is temporary, and it will be expressed by the imperfect *yiṭmā᾽* (see the NOTES on v 4 and on 11:4).

3. *This shall be his impurity in his discharge (wĕzō᾽ t tihyeh ṭum᾽ātô bĕzôbô).* The LXX reads as if the text were *wĕzō᾽t tôrat ṭum᾽ātô* 'this is the procedure concerning his impurity', which would then envelop chap. 15 in an inclusio (vv 3a, 32), comparable to the inclusio of the previous chapter, the rite for scale-

diseased persons and houses (14:2a, 54). To be sure, chap. 14 also incorporates the imperfect *tihyeh* (v 2a), which is in order there because the rest of the verse reads *běyôm ṭohŏrātô* 'at the time of his purification', in other words, the rite is set in the future, *after* he is healed. Here, however, where the text speaks of the impurity of the *zāb*, not his ritual purification, the use of *tihyeh* is suspicious. The LXX may be correct.

In any event, v 3b is parenthetical, as indicated by the perfect tense of the verbs (Hoffmann 1953). The impurity is itemized beginning with v 4. The point of v 3b is to define the parameters of a *zāb* diagnosis—either leakage or blockage (Ibn Ezra). It is clearly an insertion.

runs (rār). A hapax, a denominative from *rîr* 'juice' (Job 6:6), meaning "saliva" (1 Sam 21:14; Rashi on *b. Nid.* 56a; Ibn Ezra). That *rār* bears the meaning of "run, drip, drain" here is supported by *heḥtîm* 'is blocked', clearly its antonym. *rār* is transitive in meaning, equivalent to *hiphʿîl mērîr*, "that is, his member causes his discharge to drip and run" (Rashbam; cf. Elliger 1966). Another suggestion is to render *ʾet-zôbô* 'from his discharge', which then allows *rār* to retain its intransitive meaning "run, drip" (*Tg. Neof.;* Ḥazzequni); however, the equivalence of *ʾet* and *min* is unattested, despite *kěṣēʾtî ʾet-hāʿîr* 'as I go out of the city' (Exod 9:29). Nonetheless, it is possible to retain the intransitive meaning of the *qal, rur,* by rendering *ʾet-zôbô* as "with his discharge." Perhaps it is this condition that is described in a Mesopotamian text: "If a man constantly has ejaculations, this man is impure, he carries a weighty sin" (*CAD*, E 104b).

is blocked. heḥtîm, a *hiphʿîl* stative, like *běhaqšôtāh* 'be at its (the labor's) hardest', *yaʿăśîr* 'become rich' (Ps 49:17), or *yalbînû* 'become white' (Isa 1:18). The Sam. has an addition before the word; see the Note on "this is his impurity," below.

by his discharge. mizzôbô, literally, "from his discharge." For the equivalence of the prepositions *mem* and *bet* (of means), see the Notes on 5:9; 8:32; and Sarna 1959. The rendering "so that there is no discharge" *(NJPS; cf. NEB)* is incorrect because at least some flow is needed as a prerequisite for impurity. Besides, if the blocked flow includes his urine, he could not survive. And if only the urine was able to pass, why would his condition be considered pathological? Most likely, in this situation the flow emerges thickly viscous, causing blockage (Abravanel; Wessely 1846). This view is supported by Preuss (1978: 354), "That diminution of the secretion occurs, for example, in epididymitis." Thus the difference between these two conditions is one of consistency: *rār* implies free, uncontrollable flow; *heḥtîm,* sluggish, thick, and equally uncontrollable.

this is his impurity (ṭumʾātô hîʾ [hwʾ]). Before and after this sentence, other texts include additions. For comparison, they are listed in a single column:

LXX: *mizzôbô] ṭāmēʾ hûʾ kol-yěmê zôb běśārô ʾô heḥtîm běśārō mizzôbô [ṭumʾātô hîʾ*

Sam.: *'ô]* *ḥātûm bĕśārō mizzôbô ṭāme' hû' kol-yĕmê zāb bĕśārō 'ô [heḥtîm bĕśārō*

11Q: *ṭum'ātô hî']* *bô kol-yĕmê zā[b bĕśārō 'ô heḥtîm bĕśārō mizzôbô ṭum'ātô hî'*

LXX: blocked by his discharge] he remains impure during the entire period his member runs or his member is blocked in discharging; [this is his impurity

Sam.: runs with his discharge or] his member is blocked by his discharge. He is impure during the entire period his member discharges or [his member is blocked

11Q: it is his impurity] in him during the entire period [his member]ru[ns or his member is blocked by his discharge; it is his impurity

"11Q Lev., while fragmentary, agrees with Sam. and LXX against MT in having the addition . . . the occurrence of *bw* shows that as between Sam. and LXX, 11Q Lev. agrees with LXX . . . and not with Sam." (Freedman 1974: 529). All three of the above-cited texts clearly illustrate that the additions to the MT could have fallen out by homoioteleuton. Thus it is reasonable to assume that the addition is required (Freedman 1974; Tov 1978–79). It is, however, difficult to choose among the texts. Each is plausible: each stresses the fact that the impurity lasts as long as the discharge. For the publication and analysis of the Qumran fragment, see Freedman and Matthews 1985.

4. *Any bedding (kol-hammiškāb).* *kol* plus the definite article can mean "any, every" (Exod 18:22; Num 15:13; GKC §127b, c, e). Alternatively, render "the entire bedding" (J. Randolph), that is to say, not just the part touched by his body. The average bed consisted of a mat, a quilt to lie upon, and a covering: "For the bed *(maṣṣā')* is too short for stretching out, and the cover *(massēkâ)* too narrow for curling up" (Isa 28:20). In wealthier homes, of course, the framework and trappings of the bed were ornamental (cf. Amos 6:4; Prov 7:16–17; Esth 1:6) and were raised above the floor (Gen 49:4). Among the poorer classes, however, beds were probably light, portable frames for keeping the bedding off the ground and, in their simplest form, consisted only of mats of wickerwork and the owners' day clothes: "If you take your neighbor's garment in distraint, you must return it to him before the sun sets; it is his only clothing, the sole covering of his skin. In what else shall he sleep?" (Exod 22:25–26; cf. Judg 4:18).

lies (yiškab). The use of the imperfect, here and throughout this chapter, implies that the bearers of impurity are not banished from the community or even isolated within the community (see COMMENT A below) but remain at home. This fact differentiates the chapter from the rules of the wilderness camp, which expel the *zāb* (Num 5:2–4) and of the war camp, which even exclude the emitter of semen (Deut 23:10–12). This chapter is primarily concerned with the communicability of impurity, whereas the previous pericope, on scale disease (chaps. 13–14), says nothing on this matter. This difference can only be explained by the premise that the scale-diseased person is banished from the community and, hence, has no contact with persons or objects, whereas those experiencing sexual fluxes continue to reside at home.

The imperfect also leads the rabbis to rule that the object the man lies on must have been manufactured for that purpose, rendering *yiškab* as "wont to lie on" (*Sipra*, Měṣōrāʿ Zab. 2:1–6). It seems more likely, however, that this applies to anything he lies on (see the NOTE on v 4b, below).

shall be impure (yiṭmāʾ). The imperfect is used instead of the adjective *ṭāmēʾ* (as in v 2) to indicate temporary impurity. The bedding will require dismantling and immersion and waiting till evening. For proof that such a practice was actually followed, see *m. Kelim* 19:1. But why is this purificatory procedure not mentioned? The answer is that he is still sleeping on it. The impurity becomes temporary only if he refrains from contacting the bedding after it has been washed. It is of interest that in ancient southern Arabia the impurity of persons could be transmitted to other persons and objects by direct contact, whereas in Islamic law such transference does not exist (Ryckmans 1972: 9–10; see other comparative evidence, at chap. 12, COMMENT A).

and every object on which he sits (wĕkol-kĕlî ʾăšer-yēšēb ʿālāyw). The rabbinic term is *môšāb*, which in biblical Hebrew mainly denotes "dwelling, dwelling place, sojourning" but also "seat" (1 Sam 20:18, 25; Ps 1:1; Job 29:7). Why was it, or the usual term *kisseʾ*, avoided here? The answer can only be, contra the rabbis (see the NOTE on "lies," above), that anything sat on by the *zāb* is rendered impure, including objects not made for sitting.

5. *Anyone who touches (wĕʾîš ʾăšer yiggaʿ).* The text uses the term *ʾîš*, literally, "man" instead of *nepeš* 'person' (cf. 7:21) because of the exclusive use of man and woman in the impurity bloc (chaps. 12–15). Clearly "anyone" is intended. Still, it is puzzling why the text did not simply state *hannōgēaʿ*, as in vv 7, 10, 21, 22, 27. Moreover, not only persons but objects that make contact with the *zāb*'s bedding will require washing and waiting for evening (*m. Ḥul.* 1:6; *m. Kelim* 1:1; *b. B. Qam.* 2b; cf. COMMENT B below).

This is the first time we learn about the transmission force of impurity: it can affect persons and objects indirectly, at a second and even a third remove (cf. v 23). This extrastrength impurity is limited to objects directly underneath the *zāb* and his congeners: males incurring seminal emission and females in their menses or discharging abnormally. Their common denominator is that they are discharging from their genitals and hence, the objects beneath them are directly contaminated by their genital flow. That is why only the bedding, seat, and saddle are singled out as their defilable objects. There is no mention of the table or cup or any other object that is likely to be touched being able to pass on its impurity. To be sure, earthenware and wooden implements can be contaminated by the *zāb* (v 12), but nothing is said about their ability to contaminate others. Indeed, the only generalization in this pericope is "Whoever touches anything that was *under him* shall be impure" (v 10a). The difference, again, is that his discharge is assumed to make direct contact with the objects beneath. The likelihood for this to happen is strong, seeing that underpants were not worn (except by priests while officiating, Exod 28:43), hence there was nothing to stop or impede the flow of genital discharge to the furniture underneath. That direct contact with the discharge is contemplated by the text can be derived from the law of seminal emission: the contaminated objects are "all fabric or leather on which semen falls" (v 17a). To be sure, the *zāb* contaminates by his touch, but not if he has first washed his hands (v 11). The assumption surely must be that his hands have touched his genitals during micturation and that washing cleanses them of any adhering discharge.

It is of inestimable value to compare the biblical system with its counterparts in the ancient Near East. Unfortunately there is nothing precisely parallel, but a passage from the Šurpu incantations more than compensates for this lack:

> He slept on the bed of an accursed person,
> he sat in the chair of an accursed person,
> he a[te] at the table of an accursed person,
> he dran[k] from the cup of an accursed person.
> (*Šurpu* 2.100–103; Reiner 1958: 16)

The relationship of this passage with the pericope on the *zāb* is immediately apparent (also noted by Geller 1980). Both speak of contact with a bed and a chair, but Šurpu adds the table and the cup. A more significant difference is that Šurpu is concerned with demonic contagion, a concept totally absent from P. There is also the minor difference that in Šurpu the bed is slept in while the bed of the *zāb* is touched; cf. the NOTE on "anything that was under him," v 10a. These differences not only demonstrate the disparity between the two systems but enable us to grasp the magnitude of the change wrought by Israel's priesthood from its Mesopotamian antecedents. The demonic has been excised from impurity. It is not the accursed, demon-possessed person who contaminates, but his genital discharge. Hence his table and cup cannot be contaminated unless he touches them with unwashed hands. A letter from Mari also attests to the transmission of impurity, but in this case as well, we are dealing with demonic contagion. When the king learns that one of his wives has contracted a skin disease he issues the order, "Let no one drink from her cup, sit in her chair, lie in her bed. . . . This skin disease (*ṣimmum;* CAD, S 277) is contagious (*muštaḫḫiz;* CAD, MII 283)." We would be mistaken, however, to regard the imposed quarantine simply as the consequence of a clinical diagnosis of contagion. "The common notion in these contexts was that the sinner, or defiled, or diseased individual was liable to demonic attack, and it is the demons themselves who are the contagious agents" (Geller 1980: 188; but we differ fundamentally on the interpretations of Lev 5:1–5). In this case, however, the correspondences with Israel are much greater. Scale disease *(ṣāraʿat)*, defiling by overhang, is of greater impurity than the *zāb*. And though the transmission force of impurity is not made explicit, it can be derived from the fungous house, which contaminates everything within. As it were, the entire house becomes a single impurity source. Yet nothing is said concerning the transmission of the impurity to a second or third remove. Is the person contaminated by entering the house capable of contaminating others? The text is silent, perhaps deliberately. It takes issue with the Mesopotamian view: the chain of impurity is broken. As argued before (chap. 14, COMMENT A), biblical *ṣāraʿat* is not even contagious. We are dealing with a symbolic system, whose meaning will be given separate treatment (COMMENT G below).

shall launder his clothes (yĕkabbēs bĕgādāyw). The question that must be addressed is: Why does touching the bedding of a *zāb* require laundering and bathing while touching his seat or saddle requires only bathing (see the NOTES on vv 6, 9, 10)? A similar problem was confronted in the pericope on fungous houses, where entering the house required bathing but reclining or eating in it required, in addition, laundering (14:45–46). Three possible causes for the distinction were put forth: the intensity of the impurity source, the intensity of the contact, and the duration of the exposure. Because the first two factors remained constant, it was decided—by the process of elimination—that only the third factor, the duration of the exposure, was responsible (for details, see the NOTE on "Whoever lies down . . . and whoever eats," 14:47). Here the matter is not so simple. In the previous case, the impurity source was the fungous part of the house, not its furniture. In this case, however, the impurity source is not only the *zāb* but also his furniture. One can account for the difference between his bedding and his seat or saddle on the basis of all three possible factors enumerated above. Because he lies on his bedding longer and with more of his body than in sitting or riding on the object beneath him, the bedding has become a source of more intensive impurity. Thus it makes sense that a person touching it becomes impure to a greater degree than a person touching the seat or saddle; the impurity is intense enough to communicate to his clothes even if they are not in direct contact with the bedding. The intensity of the contact (i.e., touching versus sitting and riding), the second factor, also differs—but not in the way we would expect. Clearly, sitting or riding is a more intensive contact than touching. Yet, paradoxically, it is the latter (i.e., touching the bed) that generates greater impurity. Thus it may be concluded that the intensity of the contact is not a factor in the transmission of impurity. But the same considerations are operative in the third factor, the duration of the exposure. Certainly, one sits or rides longer than one touches and, again, it is the touching that conveys greater impurity. Thus by the process of elimination we are left with one factor responsible for the distinction between the *zāb*'s bedding and his seat or saddle: his bedding is a more intensive impurity source. Of course, this distinction breaks down once we deal not with touching the impure object but with carrying it, where the other two factors, intensity and duration of the contact, must be presumed (see the NOTE on v 10b). That the impurity can be conveyed without direct contact should not surprise us in view of the airborne quality of major impurity sources (see chap. 4, COMMENT C) and the overhanging nature of the scale-diseased person and house (chap. 14). Here, then, is another residue of the original impurity, which has been eviscerated of its demonic quality but is still dynamic. The rabbis, who essentially reduce the factors to the second one, intensity of the contact (in their terms *midras* 'pressure'), arrive at a different conclusion on both the distinctions (see the NOTE on v 10a) and their rationale (cf. *m. Zabim* 2:4; cf. also Wright 1984: 376–78 n. 39).

The various rationales for impurity transmission must at this point be summarized. So far three sources of communicable impurity have been encountered: carcasses (chap. 11), fungous houses (chap. 14), and the *zāb* along with the objects he contacts (chap. 15). Carrying a carcass requires laundering because the clothes have been contacted directly or because of the intensity of the contact (see the NOTE on 11:25). Reclining or eating in a fungous house requires laundering because of the long duration of the contact (see the NOTE on 11:47). Touching the bedding of a *zāb* requires laundering because of the intensity of its impurity. Thus all three possible factors have come into play, but in each case one will dominate.

In any event, the impurity generated by the *zāb* is clearly different from any encountered so far: the objects contaminated by the *zāb* bear the same degree of impurity as he has possessed. Consequently, just as he imparts one-day impurity requiring laundering to those he touches or who touch him (v 7), so his contaminated bedding imparts a one-day impurity requiring laundering to those who touch it (v 5). For other such examples, see the charts in COMMENT B below.

bathe in water (wĕrāḥaṣ bammayim). Considering that the sequence laundering–bathing is operative in all purification rites, would not the just laundered clothes be reinfected by the impure person? While this question is relevant for a person who is the primary impurity source, such as the scale-diseased person (see the NOTE on 14:8), it does not apply to person or objects contaminated by him. Thus the person and his clothing, being at a second remove—they have been contaminated by the *zāb*'s bedding—cannot reinfect each other (see the charts in COMMENT B below).

remain impure (yiṭmāʾ). The imperfect implies a temporary, one-day impurity requiring bathing and waiting till evening (see the NOTES on v 4 and 11:24).

6. *Whoever sits (wĕhayyōšēb).* Implied is that the *zāb* lives at home and is not banished like the *mĕṣōrāʿ.* Because the former's impurity is not strong enough to contaminate by overhang, persons have no fear of entering his home as long as they do not touch him directly (vv 8, 11) or the furniture upon which he can rest his body (vv 5–6, 9–10).

It is crucial to note that there is no mention of *touching (yigga^c)* the seat, parallel to touching the bedding (v 5). Because touching generates lesser impurity than sitting, one should be led to expect that the purification measures are also less severe. The exegetical principle to be borne in mind is that the law presents the minimal act that will generate a specified penalty/purification, and leaves the more severe acts to be derived a fortiori. Thus, if touching the *zāb*'s bed requires laundering (v 5), all the more so the acts of sitting, standing, and lying on it (cf. *m. Zabim* 2:4). By the same token, if sitting on the *zāb*'s seat requires laundering, all the more so lying on it—but not touching it, which involves a lesser contact. We shall have to look elsewhere for the rule on touching the *zāb*'s seat, and we shall find it—or rather, derive it—from v 10a.

on an object upon which the man with a discharge has sat (^cal-hakkĕlî 'ăšer-yēšēb ^cālāyw hazzāb). This circumlocution is deliberate in order to teach that not only does the *zāb*'s seat (*môšāb*, 1 Sam 20:18, 25; *kissē'*, 1 Sam 1:9) contaminate but anything he sits on (see the NOTE on v 4b).

7. *the body of (bibĕśar [hazzāb]).* Some claim that the *bāśar* here refers to the genitals, as in vv 2 and 19, on two grounds: otherwise v 11 is redundant and, if the body were meant, one would have expected the text to read *bazzāb* '[touch] the *zāb*' (Ehrlich 1908–14; Elliger 1966). Yet the immediate question arises: What if the rest of the body is touched? Therefore, it is preferable to render *bāśar* as "body" (Saadiah; Ibn Ezra). The rabbis reach the same conclusion on logical grounds: if touching any part of a menstruant's body is contaminating (v 19b), all the more so touching any part of the *zāb*'s body, which is of a greater impurity (*Sipra*, Mĕṣōrā^c Zab. 3:5, 6). As for the objection raised above: (1) v 11 is not redundant because it speaks of the reverse process, the *zāb* touching others, *with unwashed hands;* and (2) the inclusion of the word *bāśar* emphasizes that one making direct contact with the *zāb*'s body is subject to laundering, but not if he only touches the *zāb*'s clothes (contra Wright 1987: 183 n. 34). The latter impurity, it must be presumed, is of lesser intensity than contact with the *zāb*'s bedding (Wessely 1846), unless the *zāb* lies on his clothes (see the NOTE on "Any bedding," v 4).

launder his clothes. The reason for the severer impurity, implied by the need to launder, cannot be that the clothing of the *zāb* was touched—the text specifies "the body" (see above). Nor can it be the rabbinic rationale of *midras* 'pressure'—for touching implies the lightest possible contact. We are left with the conclusion derived above (the NOTE on "shall launder his clothes," v 5): the intensity of the impurity source—the body of the *zāb!*

Of all impurity bearers discussed in chaps. 11–15, the case of the *zāb* is the only one that deals with the consequences of the impurity bearer touching someone else. This provided an opening for the Qumran sectaries to investigate the consequences of a menstruant touching the *zāb*: WHZBH DM LŠB^cT HYMYM 'L TG^c BZB WBKWL KLY [']ŠR YG^c BW HZB WŠ[KB] ^cLYW^{)w} 'ŠR YŠB ^cLYW [W'M] NG^cH TKBS BGDYH WRḤṢ W'ḤR

TWKL 'A woman whose blood flows for seven days should not touch either a *zāb* or any object [wh]ich he has touched, la[in] upon, or sat on. [If] she has touched (any of them) she shall launder her clothes and bathe; afterward she may eat' (4QThr A1:4–5). Thus the rule of a menstruant touching a *zāb* is the same as that of a pure person touching a *zāb*, with one difference: the menstruant need not wait till evening until she may eat. What looks ostensibly like a lenient concession is, in fact, a severer restriction. The evening provision of the Torah guarantees that thereupon *sacred* food may be eaten; during the impurity period, however, ordinary food may be eaten. Qumran also did not require any impure person to fast. Still, it did insist that additionally acquired impurity, such as the menstruant touching a *zāb*, must be eliminated by ablutions before any food may be eaten (further details in Milgrom forthcoming B).

Qumran attributes the *zāb*'s ailment to sin, which is specified as [M] *ḤŠBT* [Z]*MH* 'lewd thoughts' (4QDᵃ 15; Milik 1966: 105). Another Qumran fragment, as yet unpublished, reads, *M]ḤŠBT ZMH . . . MGʿW KMGʿ YHW[H]* 'lewd thoughts . . . his affliction is like an affliction from the Lord' (D⁹1 2:4, 5). Assuming that this text deals with the *zāb*, it confirms that the cause is lewd thoughts and adds that the punishment stems from God (see 2 Sam 3:29). The "affliction from the Lord" to which the punishment is compared is clearly scale disease (see chap. 14, COMMENT B), lending further plausibility to the reading that the subject of the text is the *zāb*. Moreover, only a *zāb* would fit the "measure-for-measure" principle that generally describes divine punishments: the *zāb* is afflicted on the very organ with which he planned to sin.

8. *If (wĕkî)*. Because we are still dealing with the *zāb*, why is this verse introduced by *kî*, implying a new unit, rather than *'im*, normally used for a subunit? The answer is that the subject has shifted to the *zāb* himself; he now initiates the action. Also, it may not be an accident that the chapter contains seven occurrences of *kî* (vv 2, 8, 13, 16, 19, 25 bis).

spits (yārōq). The root is *rqq*, as indicated by its nominal form, *ruqqî* (Job 7:19; Ibn Ezra). Elsewhere the root *yrq* is used (e.g., Num 12:14; Deut 25:9). Biconsonantal roots that have expanded into *lamed-heh* and double-*ʿayin* are well attested (GKC §77C; cf. the NOTE on "menstrual," 12:2). Elsewhere saliva was considered a source of impurity, for instance, among the Hittites (Moyer 1969: 66–67). In Mesopotamia, it was a symptom of certain diseases and, in the form of foam, was considered poisonous (*CAD*, I 139–41). In Israel, however, spitting was just an expression of disdain (Num 12:14; Deut 25:9; cf. 1QS 7:13; Jos., *Wars* 2.147; *b. Ber.* 24b), but it never was considered inherently impure (cf. *m. Šeqal.* 8:1). Similarly, excrement (despite Ezek 4:12–14), urine, and sweat were excluded as sources of impurity in the Priestly system. Nevertheless, folk tradition transferred the laws of a *zāb*'s spittle to other impurity bearers. Thus, in the sectarian *Baraita diMasseket Niddāh* (Horowitz 1890: 10), the spittle of a menstruant contaminates clothes and bedding. The latter in turn contaminate those who contact them (similar to the *zāb*, v 5), and they must immerse themselves before entering the synagogue (ibid.: 36). From this verse one can deduce that not only genital discharges but any fluids exuding from the *zāb* contaminate. The rabbis, in fact, add phlegm (*m. Nid.* 7:1), even of the nose (*Sipra*, Měṣōrāʿ Zab. 3:8). Some sectarians also include sweat (Horowitz 1889: 26), which, however, is expressly exempted by the rabbis (b. *Nid.* 55b).

9. *Any means for riding (wěkol-hammerkāb).* Not only a saddle is intended by *merkāb* but anything that a person sits on so that his or her feet do not touch the ground (Ehrlich 1908–14). The question needs to be asked: Why is the riding seat (v 9) separated from the bedding (v 5) and the seat (v 6) by laws about the person of the *zāb* (vv 7–8)? The answer is that the laws in this pericope are grouped not by subject but by predicate. Bedding and seat are followed by the touch of the *zāb* and his saliva (vv 5–8) because they all involve laundering, while touching the riding seat (v 10a) does not. An ancillary reason is that contact with bedding and seat is unavoidable, but riding can be avoided; for this reason riding is omitted in the pericopes on the women (vv 19–30; cf. *Keter Torah*). Yet the latter explanation will not hold: there is nothing inevitable about contact with the *zāb*'s body (v 7), and the omission of riding may be due to stylistic reasons (see the NOTE on v 10).

mounted (yirkab). But not *yěšēb* 'sits', for then it would be equivalent to v 6. Hence Ehrlich (above) must be correct: the feet must not be touching the ground.

shall be impure (yiṭmāʾ). The LXX adds the equivalent of *ʿad hāʿāreb* 'until evening'. As indicated in the NOTE on this word (v 4), the impurity terminates in the evening only if the *zāb* refrains from mounting it after it has been washed.

10. *Whoever touches (wěkol-hannōgēaʿ).* Sitting, however, is omitted because it was covered in v 6.

anything that was under him (běkōl ʾǎšer yihyeh taḥtāyw). There are four possible interpretations concerning the antecedent of the pronominal suffix of *taḥtāyw.* (1) Some render *taḥtāyw* 'under it', with the riding-seat (*merkāb*, v 9) as the referent. Because the riding seat does not need to be laundered, neither does anything under it (Ibn Ezra). But this interpretation fails to meet the logical objection posed by the rabbis: if the *zāb* defiles vessels only by direct contact, how can the riding seat defile anything under it that has not been touched by the *zāb* (cf. *Sipra*, Měṣōrāʿ Zab. 4:1)?

(2) The rabbis render *taḥtāyw* 'under him', namely, the *zāb*, but interpret the three previous words, *běkōl ʾǎšer yihyeh*, as referring to the riding seat (*Sipra*, Měṣōrāʿ Zab. 4:1), in other words, "Whoever touches that thing under him." The rabbis presume that the pressure of the *zāb* is so great that his impurity passes through the riding seat to anything under it, "even ten saddles" (*Sipra*, Měṣōrāʿ Zab. 3:12). Therefore, as the riding seat requires no laundering, neither

does anything under it. Clearly, the interpretation of *kōl* as referring to one thing, the riding seat, is difficult.

(3) Some Versions render simply "anything that was under him" (LXX, Pesh., *Tg. Neof.*), but the meaning of "anything" is unclear. If understood literally it surely cannot include the bedding, which requires laundering (v 5). Or does "anything" mean anything other than the objects previously mentioned (the bedding, the seat, and the riding seat)?

(4) The answer surfaces as soon as one takes into account the organization of this pericope and notices that vv 9–10 are structured like vv 4–6, with v 9 corresponding to v 4a; v 10a to v 5 and v 10 to vv 5–6. Setting these verses in parallel columns will throw the similarities into clear relief.

4a. *kol-hammiškāb ʾăšer yiškab* *ʿālāyw hazzāb yiṭmāʾ*	9. *wĕkol-hammerkāb ʾăšer yirkab* *ʿālāyw hazzāb yiṭmāʾ*
b. *wĕkol-hakkĕlî ʾăšer yēšēb ʿālāyw* *yiṭmāʾ*	
5a. *weʾîš ʾăšer yiggaʿ bemiškābô* b. *yĕkabbēs bĕgādāyw wĕrāḥaṣ* *bammayim wĕṭāmēʾ ʿad-hāʿāreb*	10a. *wĕkol-hannōgēaʿ bĕkōl ʾăšer* *yihyeh taḥtāyw yiṭmāʾ ʿad-* *hāʿāreb* b. *wĕhannōśēʾ ʾōtām*
6a. *wĕhayyōšēb ʿal-hakkĕlî ʾăšer* *yēšēb ʿālāyw hazzāb* b. *yĕkabbēs bĕgādāyw wĕrāḥaṣ* *bammayim wĕṭāmēʾ ʿad-hāʿāreb*	*yĕkabbēs bĕgādāyw wĕrāḥaṣ* *bammayim wĕṭāmēʾ ʿad-hāʿāreb*

Just as v 4 presents the case of the *zāb* contaminating his furniture, so does v 9. And just as vv 5–6 present the case of the same furniture contaminating others, so we should expect v 10 to name the furniture of v 9. But mark the change. Whereas vv 5–6 specify that it is the same furniture (bedding and seat), v 10 says nothing about the riding seat (v 9) but uses the generalization "anything that was under him" (v 10a) and then refers to it by *ʾōtām* 'them, such things', in the plural. Thus v 10 clearly refers not only to the riding seat (v 9) but also to other things, which of necessity have not yet been legislated. Because such things must be of the same category as *merkāb*, the riding seat, and must fit the description *taḥtāyw* 'under him', the sought-for objects must be seats.

A glance at vv 5–6 confirms this hypothesis. Verse 5 cites the law for one who *touches* the bedding of the *zāb*, but v 6 cites the law for one who *sits* in his seat. But nothing is said about one who *touches the seat!* As indicated (NOTE on "whoever sits," v 6), if the law mentions sitting on the seat it refers to the minimal contact that will require a specified action, namely, laundering as well as bathing (v 6b). But touching, which involves a lighter contact, clearly must generate lesser impurity and, hence, requires a reduced purification. This can be surmised as bathing without laundering. But where is it so stated? There can be no doubt about the answer: It is made explicit in v 10a, which specifies that whoever *touches* anything under the *zāb* remains impure till the evening, that is, must bathe, but not launder.

Thus we can now understand why v 10 avoided specifying the riding seat, though the structure of the pericope would have led one to expect it. Its author wanted to pick up the item that he had until now neglected—the matter of touching the seat—and he therefore generalized his language to include it: everything *taḥtāyw* 'under him', in other words, that he might sit on, and *'ôtām* 'them', that is to say, not only the riding seat but all seats. The significance of this interpretation also rests in the fact that it differs fundamentally from the rabbinic differentiation between these objects. The rabbis claim unequivocally that the laws of *miškāb* 'bedding' and *môšāb* 'seat' are identical and only that of *merkāb* 'riding seat' is different. Touching the bedding and seat of the *zāb* requires laundering and bathing, whereas touching his riding seat requires only bathing (cf. *m. Kelim* 23:3). My findings result in a different distinction: bedding incurs the severer impurity and purification, while seat and riding seat show a lesser impurity and purification. Logic too supports this conclusion. After all, a seat is a seat. Whether one rides or sits, the contact is the same. But reclining with one's entire body and for a much longer time is manifestly a more intensive contact.

Wright, who accepts my solution (1987: 188), remains troubled by three problems: (1) touching a *zāb*'s bed results in severer impurity than touching his other objects; (2) there is no corresponding distinction for the menstruant (vv 19–24) or the *zābâ* (vv 25–30); (3) logically, this law should follow vv 5–6. Wright, therefore, regards vv 9–10 as an editorial addition (1987: 188 n. 41). I shall answer his points seriatim. (1) One lies on a bed longer and with more of the body than in sitting or riding; intensity and duration of contact are factors in determining the degree of impurity (NOTE on "shall launder his clothes," v 5). (2) The menstruant and the *zābâ* are not analogous to the *zāb:* the former exude genital blood, a severer instrument of impurity than genital mucus. Hence, those persons contacting any object that bears their vaginal blood require laundering (NOTES on "shall launder his clothes," v 22 and "it," v 23). (3) The *zāb*'s laws are listed not according to the contraction of the impurity but according to the purification procedure: first, all cases requiring laundering (vv 5–8), followed by the one exception (vv 9–10). The *zāb* pericope is, therefore, logical, orderly, and free of problems.

A final remark is necessary concerning the emphasis only on those objects under the *zāb*, *taḥtāyw*. Its significance is borne out by the injunction to the priests that they must wear breeches during their ministration in the sanctuary (Exod 28:42–43; Lev 16:4), implying that outside the sanctuary, they—and the ordinary Israelite—did not wear them. The probability of any genital flux contacting anything *under* the *zāb* was therefore enhanced immeasurably.

shall be impure until evening (yiṭmā' 'ad-hā'āreb). Bathing is always assumed by this expression, for it is a basic requisite for all purifications. The evidence is herewith reviewed. (1) Lev 11:40 states that one who eats the carcass of pure animals must "launder his clothes and remain impure until evening." A parallel passage states that whoever eats such carcasses must "launder his clothes, *bathe in water,* and remain impure until evening" (17:15). (2) If washing of a utensil contaminated by a swarming creature is necessary (11:32), the same should be necessary for people who touch the swarming creature (11:31). (3) A priest who touches certain impurities "becomes impure until evening" (22:6a). Lest there be any mistake, Scripture adds the explanation: "He shall not eat of the holy things unless he has bathed his body in water" (v 6b). (4) Num 31:24 omits bathing, but Num 19:19 clearly requires it. (5) Bathing is lacking for the gatherer of the ashes of the Red Cow (Num 19:10), but it is explicitly required for the priest and the burner who participated in this rite (vv 7, 8). (6) Ablution is often assumed and is thus omitted in the cases of the menstruant (see the NOTE on "seven days," v 19), the parturient (see the NOTE on "she shall bring," 12:6), and the corpse-contaminated Nazirite (Num 6:9).

and whoever carries (wĕhannôśē'). Carrying invites greater intensity of contact, including pressure and, probably, direct contact with the clothes (cf. the NOTE on 11:25).

such things ('ôtām). According to the rabbis, the antecedent of this plural suffix refers to all of the preceding objects: the bedding, seat, and riding seat (*Sipra*, Mĕṣōrā' Zab. 4:3). But because v 10a refers to seats and riding seats but excludes bedding (see above), it could hardly be expected that v 10b would do otherwise. Thus, '*ôtām* probably refers, as well, only to seats; and the law of carrying bedding need not be stated because it can be derived a fortiori: if carrying seats, a lesser impurity, requires laundering, all the more so carrying bedding, a severer impurity.

This verse, with its broader general terms such as *taḥtāyw* and '*ôtām*, provides the rabbis with a golden opportunity for fanciful exegesis, which, however, has a clear purpose in mind. On the basis of this verse, the rabbis introduce the principle of *maddāp*, an article not used for reclining or sitting but that can, nonetheless, incur impurity (cf. *m. Zabim* 5:2). By a process of analogic-contrastive exegesis (Neusner's term, 1977b: 187–96), the rabbis make the following deductions. (1) Verse 10 continues v 9 and, therefore, deals with the riding seat, but disjunctively: it refers to objects under the *zāb* but not in contact with him. (2) These objects fall into the foregoing categories: bedding, seats, and riding seats. Hence, contrastively, if these same objects are not below him, but above, then they are pure. (3) Those objects other than his bedding, seat, and riding seat (called *maddāp*), which are under him, are pure. (4) Hence these same objects above him are impure.

By this exegesis, the rabbis have restricted the realm of impurity in relation to the *zāb.* To be sure, in order to be consistent in their logic they must grant that *maddāp* articles above the *zāb* are susceptible to his impurity, but they succeed in confining his impurity to those objects beneath him—the more likely situation—which falls strictly under the mentioned rubrics, and they even deny that these objects can be contaminated if they are above him.

11. *without having rinsed his hands (wěyādāyw lōʾ -šāṭap bammāyim).* The verb *šāṭap* connotes using water with force, in other words, "flush, rinse" (6:21; 1 Kgs 22:38; Ezek 13:11; 16:9; Ps 32:7). The Sam. and four MSS read *wěyādô* 'his hand' (sing.), which may be correct because only the hand that touches needs to be washed.

What if he does rinse his hands? Ibn Ezra opines that in that case, the person he touches would be rendered impure but not his clothing. It is implied that cleansed hands reduce the impurity. But the likelihood is that neither the person nor his clothing would be rendered impure. That is, cleansing the hands eliminates the communicability of the *zāb*'s impurity by touch, temporarily. It is presumed that the *zāb*'s hands have been contaminated by contact with his genitals during micturition, and washing them removes their impurity momentarily (Wessely 1846). The specification of bedding, chair, and riding seat as the defilable objects implies that other contacted objects are not susceptible to impurity or, more likely, that these objects cannot convey their impurity to others, and if touched with washed hands, cannot even be defiled. Thus it is the objects directly underneath the *zāb* that can be endowed with contagious impurity.

The implications of this leniency are far-reaching. For if the *zāb* takes the precaution of rinsing his hands he can touch persons, vessels, utensils—anything (unless it is underneath him). Thus he can live at home! This conclusion can indirectly be deduced from the fact that the text details the laws regarding the contamination of his household, a matter that is totally absent in the laws of the scale-diseased person, for the obvious reason that he is banished from his home and community. Here, however, we find the legal device by which the Priestly legists allowed the *zāb* to remain at home. That they were required to devise such a legal mechanism is apparent from the coexistence in Scripture of another, probably older, law stating that the *zāb* should be banished from the camp (Num 5:2). This severer consequence continued to be practiced, as demonstrated by Josephus's testimony that in his day the *zāb* was treated like the scale-diseased person: both were banished from the city (*Wars* 5.227; *Ant.* 3.261). Although the rabbis, fully aware of the implications of this chapter, allowed the *zāb* to remain in the city, they nonetheless barred him not just from the Temple but even from the Temple Mount (*m. Kelim* 1:8; *b. Taʿan.* 21b). And much later Hai ben Sherira Gaon (938–1038) ruled that the *zāb* would have to be seated apart from the others in the synagogue (Alon 1957: 172 n. 102 [= 1977: 228]).

It is interesting to note that the rabbis refused to accept the implications of this Priestly concession that the *zāb* can continuously and expeditiously remove the communicability of the impurity on his hands simply by rinsing them. Instead they interpret this verse as referring to his purificatory process on the seventh day after he bathes (b. Ḥul. 106a; cf. Ramban). Thus the leniency of the Torah becomes the stringency of the rabbis. According to them, not only does the *zāb* have to bathe but, in addition, he must lave his hands.

Finally, the interesting but bizarre interpretion of Rashbam should be mentioned. He suggests that *yādāyw* 'his hands' is a euphemism for the genitals, and he points to mouth (Prov 30:20) and legs (Judg 3:24) as other body organs that are employed as euphemisms. Of course, one could support his claim philologically, for *yād* as a euphemism is attested in the Bible (e.g., Isa 57:8, 10) and in Ugaritic (e.g., *KTU* 1.23.33, 34, 35).

12. *An earthen vessel . . . shall be broken (ûkělî-ḥereś . . . yiššābēr)*. The irredeemability of contaminated earthenware has been legislated and explained in 6:21; 11:33, 35.

and any wooden implement shall be rinsed with water. Why? The porosity of wood is as pronounced as that of earthenware! It would seem that economic considerations entered here: wooden implements were too expensive to replace (for details see the NOTE on 11:32). Indeed, it is probably the case that a special concession was made with wood, which accounts for its mention here.

But what of metalware? Why was it omitted here? The distribution of this item in the Priestly texts dealing with the laws of utensils is most instructive. It is missing in the home (11:32−33; 15:2) but found in the sanctuary (6:21) and among war spoils (Num 31:22). The latter attestation is significant. Its context is not part of Moses' instructions (v 15) but an amendment attributed to high priest Eleazar (v 21). It is thus clear that metalware was not found in the ordinary Israelite home, hence there was no need to be concerned about its contamination there. By contrast, in dealing with the Temple and war spoils, precious items such as metalware were clearly prized, so their contamination would be of importance. As in 6:21 and Num 31:22, it must be assumed that metalware, like wooden utensils, would be thoroughly rinsed (cf. also Mark 7:4). To be sure, metalware that has been corpse contaminated must first be passed through fire (Num 31:23). Still, this would not apply to their contamination by a *zāb*.

13. *is healed (yiṭhar)*. Here the verb *ṭāhar* denotes physical, not ritual, purification (13:35; see the NOTE on 14:2; cf. 2 Kgs 5:10), for it modifies *mizzôbô* 'of his discharge' (*Tg. Ps.-J.: Sipra*, Měṣōrāʿ Zab. 5:1).

count off. wěsāpar lô, literally, "count for himself" (cf. *Sipra*, Měṣōrāʿ Zab. 5:4). Implied is that this counting is private; after all, no one else is aware of his condition (cf. also 23:11). Ehrlich (1908−14, on Gen 15:5) claims that *sāpar* here is a denominative of *sōpēr* 'scribe, writer' (Jer 8:8; 36:23; cf. Akk. *šāpiru*) bearing the sense of "write down" (Ps 87:6), claiming that whenever the number was large the counting had to be marked off lest the count fall into error, as in the fifty-day count between the firstfruit festivals of the grain (23:15), the fifty-year count for the Jubilee (25:8), and the seven-day count of the corpse-contaminated priest (Ezek 44:26). However attractive, his suggestion is not essential and, in a seven-day count, unconvincing.

seven days. Thus his impurity must be of the same major category as that of the scale-diseased person. Moreover, as he does not undergo ablutions on the first day of his purificatory period, like the scale-diseased person (14:8), his impurity remains the same; he continues to contaminate objects and persons by direct contact (see COMMENTS B and F below). Rabbinic halakha, however, allows him to cohabit with his wife, though there is ample testimony of rabbis who prohibited it (*Sipre* Naso 8; *y. Ketub.* 13:1; cf. Lieberman 1933).

launder his clothes (wĕkibbes bĕgādāyw). Uniquely here, but not in any other occurrence of this expression (e.g., vv 5, 6, 7, 8), the *'atnaḥ* was placed under *bĕgādāyw* so that the impression should not be given that the laundering need be done with spring water (*Shem Olam*, cited by Hoffmann 1953).

The sectaries of Qumran add the following concern: *WHSWPR 'M ZKR W'M NQBH 'L YG[⟨ . . .]B̊W BDWH BNDTH KY 'M ṬHRH M[ND]TH KY HNH D[M] HNDH KZWB W'Š[R] NWG⟨ BW* 'One who is counting off (the seven days), whether male or female, may not tou[ch . . .] . . . a woman in her menstrual infirmity unless she has been purified from her m[en]ses. For, behold, menstrual blo[od] is equivalent to genital discharge, as well as one who touches it (the blood)' (4QThr A1:7–8). This passage implies that a residue of impurity still remains during the purificatory period, which will become amplified by touching a menstruant (see the NOTE on "laundering clothes," v 7). They exemplify this further by stating *W'M [ṬṢ' MWNW Š]KBT HZR⟨ MG⟨W YṬM'* 'If he (the *zāb*) has a seminal emission (during his purificatory period), his touch defiles' (4QThr A1:8). Qumran is more stringent than Scripture. Whereas the latter ascribes contagion to the semen (v 17), the former adds that its emitter also defiles.

This Qumran text concludes with a generalization: *[WKW]L̊ N̊WG⟨ B'DM MKWL HṬM'YM H'LH BŠB⟨T YMY ṬH[RTM ']L YWKL K'ŠR YṬM' LNP[Š WRḤṢ] YKBS W'H̊[R YKL* '[Anyo]ne who touches any of these impure persons during the seven days of [their] purif[ication may n]ot eat. As in the case of (touching) a corpse-contaminated person, [he shall bathe], launder, and afterwa[rd he may eat' (4QThr A1:8–9). Thus Qumran declares that the seven-day purificatory period required for all severe impurities (scale disease, parturition, abnormal genital discharge, and corpse contamination) is also impure, so that contact with anyone during this period is defiling, necessitating ablutions before partaking of food. Strikingly, this rule corresponds to the Priestly system of the Bible, as I have reconstructed it, but only in cases of contact with sancta (COMMENT F below, Table, D-1). This, indeed, is precisely what we would expect from the Qumran sectaries, who ate their food in a state of purity, namely, after performing ablutions to eliminate any residual impurity (details in Milgrom forthcoming B).

his body (bĕśārô). bāśār must mean "body" here (as in v 10) and not genitalia (vv 2, 19), on logical grounds: if the lesser (one-day) impurity of seminal emission requires bodily immersion (v 16), all the more so the severer (seven-day) impurity of the *zāb*. To avoid the misinterpretation, the Temple Scroll reads *wĕrāḥaṣ ʾēt kôl bĕśārô* 'he shall wash his entire body' (11QT 45:16), clearly modeled on v 16.

in spring water] bĕmayim ḥayyîm. The attestation of this expression in Scripture demonstrates that the water is found in an artesian well (Gen 26:29; Cant 4:15) and in running water (see the NOTE on Lev 14:5). Thus spring water either above the ground *(maʿyān,* Lev 11:36) or below *(bĕʾēr,* an artesian well) is what is meant, but stored water *(bôr,* cistern) or drawn water (cf. *m. Para* 6:5; see below) is excluded. The *maʿyān* is spring water (Ibn Janaḥ), while the *bôr* is a manmade pit: *ûbōr ōtḥăṣûbîm* 'hewn cisterns' (Deut 6:11), into which rain and snow water are gathered (Radak). Therefore, the verb that is used with *bôr* is *ḥāṣab* 'hew', for it is artificial (Malbim). This philological distinction between *maʿyān* and *bôr* is confirmed in a single verse: *maʿyān ûb ôr miqwēh-mayim yihyeḥṭāhôr* 'A spring or cistern in which water is collected shall remain pure' (Lev 11:36a). Thus fresh water, even rain, as long as it is collected, is no longer *mayim ḥayyîm,* and the rabbinic distinction between drawn and natural water is unknown (Wertheimer 1984: 221).

Spring water is required in the first-day purification of scale-diseased persons and houses (14:5–6, 50–52) and corpse-contaminated persons (Num 19:17). The reason for the stringency, it was surmised (cf. the NOTE on 14:8), is that these rites are basically exorcisms that were borrowed from non-Israelite cultures where the use of spring water was mandatory. But why the requirement of spring water for the purification of the *zāb?* Neusner (1976: 197–202) hypothesizes that because the word that follows here is *wĕṭāhēr* 'then he shall be pure', the *zāb* is uniquely purified by his ablutions, whereas other impurity bearers are not purified by their ablutions because it need not be spring water and the impurity is only terminated at the onset of the evening. Neusner's hypothesis founders on two shoals. The scale-diseased person is also purified *(wĕṭāhēr)* by his ablution on the seventh day of his purification without the benefit of spring water (14:9), and the omission of the evening factor occurs not only here with the *zāb* but with all major impurity bearers, who offer up sacrifices on the following day (e.g., the parturient, 12:6; the scale diseased person, 14:9; the corpse-contaminated Nazirite, Num 6:9, and priest, Ezek 4:26). As will be argued in COMMENT F below, the function of evening for minor impurities is replaced by sacrifices for major impurities; hence the arrival of the evening is of no meaning for the latter. Thus we are left to question why the ablution of the *zāb* necessitates spring water (it is missing in LXXAB).

I believe I have the answer. The three cases which require spring water—corpse contamination, scale disease, and the *zāb*—comprise all the sources of severe impurity (lasting seven days or more) except for the parturient, the menstruant, and the *zābâ*. It should be noted, however, that these latter three, ostensibly, do not require ablutions at all (12:2; 15:19, 28)! Surely, this cannot be true. The problem resolves itself once it is realized that the *zāb* stands first in the list of genital discharges in chap. 15. The cases that follow, the menstruant and the *zābâ* (see the NOTES to vv 20–21, 26–27), abbreviate their contamination rules because they are derivable from the *zāb*. The same must hold true for the ablution; it is not mentioned because it is assumed; and as spring water is mandated for the *zāb*, it must also be mandated for the others. The same logic holds for the parturient, for she is likened to the menstruant and, hence, is subject to the same rules (see the NOTE on 12:26). It can hardly be an accident that the term for spring water is *mayim ḥayyim*, lit. 'life-water'. Since impurity is symbolic of death (see COMMENT G), its antidote, appropriately, is that which gives life. One-day impurities, however, being of minor strength, do not require spring water; any water—drawn or collected—will do.

Support for my thesis can be found in the rabbinic tradition that also distinguishes gradations in purificatory waters. According to the rabbis there are six grades of ritual baths, in ascending order of superiority. (1) Lowest in quality is water in cavities for collecting water, such as cisterns or ponds. (2) Better is the rainwater flowing down the hill slope into a cavity before the flow of water has ceased. (3) Better yet is the ritual bath that contains forty *seahs* (about twenty-four cubic feet). In this water people may immerse themselves and impure objects. (4) "Superior is a well whose water is small in quantity and is increased by a large quantity of drawn water. It is the equal to the ritual bath for rendering pure, as is a cavity for collecting water, and is the equal of the well for immersion therein, however small the quantity of the water." (5) Still superior are "smitten waters," that is, warm or saline water, or spring, or the like, formed by some upheaval. This type of water cleanses while creeping along, even if it does not collect in a cavity. (6) "Best of all are *mayim ḥayyîm*, for with them are performed the functions of the ritual immersion of those suffering from a discharge, and of the sprinkling of the scale-diseased, and they are valid for mingling with the ashes of the Red Cow purification-offering" (*m. Miqw.* 1:1–8).

then he shall be pure (wĕṭāhēr). What is the meaning of this purification, if another day has to elapse before purificatory sacrifices are brought to the sanctuary? As demonstrated by the chart and explanation in COMMENT B below, the *zāb* is no longer impure in relation to common objects and persons. This implies that during the seven preceding days he was impure, just as he was when he was discharging. The Dead Sea sectaries rule that at this point the *zāb* may enter the Temple city (but not the Temple precincts). Clearly they have homogenized the law of the *zāb* with that of the scale-diseased person and menstruant, who are also forbidden to enter the city (cf. 14:8) until their ablution (11QT 45:15–17). Of interest is the occurrence in a Dead Sea Scroll of immersion in a rock pool, the lowest grade of static water (no. 1, above), which is made impure when touched by an impure person (CD 10:10–14).

14. *On the eighth day.* Eerdmans (1912, *ad loc.*) makes the intriguing comment that because the sanctuary had to be reached a good while before sundown the same day, the sacrifice was brought not to a main sanctuary but to the local altar. His suggestion has to be considered seriously. The *zāb* could not have undertaken the journey on the previous (seventh) day for he was still directly impure to the common (by touch) and indirectly to sancta (by overhang) until he bathed (see the chart, COMMENT F below). This consideration adds weight to the hypothesis that P conceived of a central but not a single sanctuary (see the Introduction, §C).

and come (ûbā²). The LXX presupposes *wĕhēbî²âm* 'and he shall bring them' (cf. the Pesh.; *Tg. Ps.-J.*), a clear attempt at harmonization with v 29. There, however, this reading is fine. But here *ûbā²* is followed by the verb *ûnĕtānām*, yielding "and come . . . and give them," whereas in v 29 and elsewhere (e.g., 12:6; 14:23; Num 6:10), there is no intermediate verb between *wĕhēbî²â . . . ²el-hakkōhēn* 'and he shall bring . . . to the priest'.

before the Lord. lipnê YHWH, an expression that always means "in the divine domain," in other words, inside the sacred precincts, which for the Tabernacle means the Tabernacle court before the altar. By contrast, the rabbis, who forbid *mĕḥussārê kappārâ* 'those who lack sacrificial expiation', that is, severely impure persons who are required to bring sacrifices at the termination of their purificatory period (e.g., parturients and persons with scale disease and abnormal discharges) from entering the sacrificial court, can still claim that they are "before the Lord" because both the First and Second Temples expanded the sacred precincts to include a second court into which such persons could enter. The rite describing the entry of the scale-diseased person into the sanctuary with his sacrifices (*t. Neg.* 8:9; cf. the NOTE on "elevation offering," 14:12) applies here as well.

at the entrance of the Tent of Meeting and give them to the priest. Thus it is clear that the supplicant entered the court and gave over his sacrifice to the waiting priest. In the Herodian Temple, however, the supplicant entered into the outer court and placed his sacrifices on the threshold of the Nicanor inner gate. The priest, standing in the inner court, received the sacrifices and, with the threshold separating him from the offerer, performed the required preliminary rites (see the NOTE on "elevation offering," 14:12). It is of interest to note that the Qumran sectaries permitted the *zāb* to enter the Temple city after he bathed on the seventh day (11QT 45:15–16) but, presumably, he was not allowed to enter the Temple with his sacrifice until the following day. Thus the Temple Scroll implicitly endows the Temple with a higher holiness than its city, a distinction that is not apparent anywhere else in the scroll.

15. *offer . . . up (wĕˁāsâ).* This verb in cultic contexts connotes the entire sacrificial ritual (e.g., v 30; 9:7; 14:30).

a purification offering. An apotropaic rite so that the illness will not return, according to Ramban. Rather, it is a purificatory offering—as the name implies —because severe impurity contaminates the sanctuary wherever in the camp it occurs (see chap. 4, COMMENTS A, B, C).

the cther (hā'eḥād). A definite article is appropriate, for after the first bird is chosen as the *ḥaṭṭā't,* the remaining one is *definitely* an *'ōlâ* (Ehrlich 1899– 1900).

a burnt offering ('ōlâ). A thanksgiving offering for recovery, according to Ramban. Rather, because the meat of the *ḥaṭṭā't* bird is a priestly prebend (6:19; 10:17), the *'ōlâ* is added merely to supply a respectable gift for the altar (Ibn Ezra on 5:7). The thanksgiving motif is ruled out by the sacrifice's expiatory function (see below).

The question must be asked: Why birds, the least expensive animal? The reason surely must be economic, not for the sake of the male—gonorrhea being infrequent—but for the sake of the female suffering from an equivalent affliction (v 2). Because of hormonal imbalances, a woman is prone to abnormal discharges (S. Rattray) and, hence, requires an inexpensive sacrificial procedure.

effect purgation on his behalf, for his discharge (wĕkipper 'ālāyw . . . mizzōbô). To my knowledge there are only four cases in which the expression *kipper 'al* is followed by *min: mēḥaṭṭā'tô* 'for his wrong' (4:26; 5:6, 10); *miṭṭum'ātô* 'for his impurity' (14:19); *mizzôbô* 'for his discharge' (15:15; cf. v 30b); and *miṭṭum'ōt bĕnê yiśrā'ēl ûmippiš'êhem* 'of the impurities of the Israelites and their transgressions' (16:16). The *mem* is causative (see the NOTE on 14:19). The fact that all four cases deal with the *ḥaṭṭā't* rather than the other expiatory sacrifices *('āšām, 'ōlâ,* and *minḥâ)* is significant. They explain that the *ḥaṭṭā't* is required because it has adversely affected the sanctuary. The individual's ethical "wrong" (see the NOTES on 4:2), the impurity of the person with scale disease (chap. 14) or abnormal discharge (chap. 15), and the physical impurities and moral iniquities of collective Israel (chap. 16) have this in common: they are responsible for the pollution of the sanctuary (see chap. 14, COMMENTS A, B, C; chap. 16, COMMENT F).

The fact that the text pinpoints the reason for the sacrifice as *mizzôbô* (and in the case of scale disease, *miṭṭum'ātô,* 14:19) merits notice. One bearing physical impurities, even the most severe kind, is not accused of sin; his sacrifice is not *mēḥaṭṭā'tô* 'for his wrong' (4:26). Above all, the purpose of the sacrifice is not *wĕnislaḥ lô* 'that he may be forgiven' (4:31, 35). It is true that chronic discharges were popularly regarded as a divine curse (cf. 2 Sam 3:29). But nowhere is this reflected in this Priestly, ritual text. Contrast the Mesopotamian fiat: *šumma amēlu ginâ igdalanalut* NA. BI NU *el ḫīta magal irašši* (TUK) 'If a man constantly has ejaculations, this man is impure, he carries a weighty sin' (*CAD,* E 104b).

16. *has an emission. tēṣē' mimmennû,* literally, "exits from him." The verb is not *yôṣî'* 'produces'. It is *qal* intransitive, and the construction is deliberate,

meaning even if the act is involuntary (cf. *Tg. Ps.-J.*). Thus any discharge of semen, regardless of the circumstances, generates impurity. It must be emphasized, however, that the impurity is solely of a ritual nature: it disqualifies the person from contact with sancta. Contrast the Hittite belief that a nocturnal emission of semen is a sign that the man has cohabited with a spirit *(succuba)*, involving even an incestuous union with a deceased family member (HL 190; Hoffner 1969: 42).

semen. šikbat-zeraʿ, literally, "an outpouring of seed" (vv 16, 17, 18, 32; 19:20; 22:4; Num 5:13). The noun *šĕkābâ* means "discharge, ejaculation, fall," as in *šikbat haṭṭāl* 'the fall of dew' (Exod 16:13, 14; for the verb, see Job 38:37; Saadiah, Ibn Janaḥ, Ibn Ezra; cf. Orlinsky 1944). It is the standard idiom for "semen" (v 17). The noun *šĕkābâ* must be distinguished from *šĕkōbet*, which also appears in P in construct form with a suffix *(šĕkobt-)* preceded by the verb *nātan b/ʾel*, denoting "penis" (18:20, 23; 20:15; Num 5:20; Orlinsky 1944).

To be sure, the only requirement for the man who has a seminal emission is to bathe and wait until evening before partaking of sacred food (see COMMENT F below). Indeed, this is the only danger (7:20). A classic case in point may be that of David, whose absence from the court of Saul for the sacred feast of the New Month is rationalized as *miqreh hûʾ biltî ṭāhôr hû kî-lōʾ ṭāhôr* 'It is an accident; he is not pure, because he has not purified himself' (1 Sam 20:26, reading the second *ṭāhôr* as *ṭōhar*, with the LXX). The resort to the word *miqreh* may be an allusion to the euphemism *miqreh-lāylâ* 'nocturnal emission' (Deut 23:11), in which case Saul's excuse for David is that even if David has bathed he must still wait for evening, for he is still impure and therefore cannot attend the feast. On the morrow, however, when David still does not appear, this excuse evaporates (1 Sam 20:27). The fear of defilement by an involuntary "nocturnal" emission forced the high priest to be kept awake all through the night preceding the Yom Kippur service: "If he sought to slumber, you members of the priesthood would snap your middle finger before him and say to him, 'My lord High Priest, get up and drive away [sleep] this once [by walking] on the [cold] pavement'" (*m. Yoma* 1:7).

The rules governing the sanctuary were extended to the synagogue, even while the Temple was standing. Thus the sectaries of Qumran ordained *wĕkolhabbāʾ ʾel bêt hištaḥăwôt ʾal yābôʾ ṭĕmēʾ kibbûs* 'Everyone who enters the house of [meeting in order to] pray (lit., make obeisance), let him not come in a state of uncleanness requiring (lit., of) washing' (CD 11:21–22; Rabin's translation, 1954: 58). That is, after seminal emission one should not pray until after washing. The rabbis agree with Qumran (*m. Ber.* 3:4–5), but they are more lenient in allowing less than a full bath (*b. Ber.* 22b). There were, however, among them those who insisted on a full bath every morning before engaging in prayer: "Those who immerse at dawn *(ṭôbĕlê šaḥărît)* say, 'We complain against you, Pharisees, for you mention the divine name at dawn without first immersing'" (*t. Yad.* 2:20). The rationale for semen impurity is discussed in COMMENT G below.

bathe (wĕrāḥaṣ). This verb can imply total immersion, the equivalent to *ṭābal:* "Go and bathe *(wĕrāḥaṣtā)* seven times in the Jordan. . . . So he went down and immersed himself *(wayyiṭbōl)* in the Jordan seven times" (2 Kgs 5:10, 14). Because of the ambiguity in *rāḥaṣ,* rabbinic Hebrew employs *ṭābal* exclusively to denote immersion.

his whole body (ʾet-kol-bĕśārô). The addition of *kol* 'whole' is necessary lest one suspect that only the genitals are meant (as in vv 2, 19). Elsewhere only *bāśār* is used for body (e.g., 14:9; 16:4, 26, 28; 22:6) because the euphemism does not occur there (Ehrlich 1908–14).

impure until evening. Until then, he may not enter the sanctuary or partake of sacred food (see COMMENT E below).

17. *All fabric or leather (wĕkol-beged wĕkol-ʿôr).* Why are persons omitted here? Could it be that if semen touches another person it is not defiling? Hardly. A person is included, the only one imaginable—the sexual partner (v 18). A nocturnal emission is presumed here (*migrēh-laylâ,* Deut 23:11), and the enumerated materials are his bedding. It is also presumed that he is sleeping nude; otherwise laundering *(kibbes)* would surely have been mentioned in v 16.

on which [semen] falls shall be laundered (ʾăšer-yihyeh ʿālāyw . . . wĕkubbas). The assumption is that the material was directly contaminated. What happens if the laundering is neglected? Obviously, the impurity persists and, moreover, it intensifies so that—presuming the delay is unintentional—the sanctuary is also polluted and a purification sacrifice must be brought (5:3, 5). If, however, the delay is intentional, it becomes a capital crime punishable by the deity (see the NOTE on v 31).

Delay in purification in a similar situation is confessed by a penitent according to a Sabean (southern Arabian) inscription: "he moistened his clothes with ejaculations" (*CIH* 523.8; *ANET*[3] 665). That he neglected to launder his clothes can be deduced from the previous statement, "he touched women during their menses and did not wash himself" (lines 6–7).

For the rabbis, however, who limited transmission of impurity to cases only of direct contact and overhang, the only way a man who had a seminal emission could contaminate sancta was by touch. Yet while they reduced the possibility of the transmission of impurity, they broadened the concept of sancta after the destruction of the Temple to include prayer and study of Torah. Thus "the pentateuchal requirement [for immersion] referred to *tĕrûmâ* and sacrifices and he (Ezra) came along and claimed that even for [the study of] the words of Torah [immersion is needed]" (*b. B. Qam.* 82b). That immersion after sex was routinely practiced is attested both by Philo (*Laws* 3.63) and by Josephus (*Con. Ap.* 2.202–3, 203, citing a Platonic rationale). It continued to be practiced by Jews who lived among Muslims, for the latter also practiced it, as attested in a responsum by Maimonides (cited by Kasher 1953: 152).

The Dead Sea sectaries, who lived by the literal interpretation of Scripture, of course fulfilled this requirement too. With regard to the Temple city, however, they imposed the law of Sinai (Yadin 1983: 1.287–89), which mandated a two-day purificatory period (Exod 19:10–15). Even more strictly, they prescribed not two but three full days of purification (cf. 1QSa 1:25–26), with laundering and bathing for seminal emission on the first and third days (11QT 45:7–10) before entry into the Temple city was allowed (see Milgrom 1978b: 512–18). It is imperative to examine the biblical text to see if there is any basis for 11QT's interpretation.

First, one is struck by the unusual wording of the command given by Moses to the people: *hĕyû nĕkōnîm lišĕlōšet yāmîm* (Exod 19:15), which literally translates "Be ready for three days" (it should have read *layyôm haššĕlîšî*, as in v 11). This meaning is paradoxically buttressed by the view of Rabbi Jose that because God commanded Moses "sanctify (i.e., purify) them today and tomorrow," Moses could not possibly have begun doing so that selfsame day. He needed two complete days, hence the first ablution took place on the following day (*'Abot R. Nat.* A2; *b. Šabb.* 87a; *b. Yebam.* 62a; cf. *Pirqe R. El.* 41). Thus Rabbi Jose agrees with 11QT that Israel spent three days preparing for the revelation and differs with it only in the timing of the two ablutions, holding that they occurred on the second and third days, whereas 11QT opts for the first and third. The scroll's position is easily defensible. After all, the Bible expressly prescribes ablutions for seminal emissions on the first day (Lev 15:16–18). Hence, 11QT engaged in an analogic comparison, or what I prefer to call the homogenization (see below) of two different biblical texts, and prescribes that entry into the Temple city requires three days of purification, consisting of two ablutions, just as Israel did at Mount Sinai, except that the first ablution occurs on the first day.

Moreover, it is my impression that 11QT was not just indulging in exegesis. More likely, it was following an ancient tradition. Philo informs us that after sex, the husband and wife "are not allowed to leave the bed, to touch anything until they have had their ablution" (*Laws* 3. 63, 205). His view that before the ablution they contaminate objects and persons may fly in the face of rabbinic halakha but makes perfect sense in view of the impurity-removing function of the ablution. When the impure male wishes to enter the Temple city he must make two transitions, from impure *(ṭāmēʾ)* to common *(ḥōl)* and then to holy *(qādôš)*. Or, to put it differently, he must eliminate two degrees of impurity. Thus two ablutions are required, precisely at the two points of transition: on the first day, when he washes off his initial impurity and is free to associate with the common; and on the third day, when he washes off his residual impurity and is qualified to be in the presence of the holy. The graded power of the ablutions can be represented diagrammatically as follows:

PURIFICATION FOR SEMINAL EMISSION

Stage	The Effect upon the common	The Effect upon the sacred
Before ablution	direct	airborne
First-day ablution	none	direct
Third-day ablution and sunset	none	none

11QT, in agreement with Philo, would maintain that prior to his initial ablution, the impure male contaminates persons and objects by direct contact but that afterward he may contact them freely. A further postulate of the Priestly impurity system in Scripture is that the sacred is more vulnerable to contamination by one degree (see COMMENT E below). Thus before the first ablution, the impurity is powerful enough to contaminate the sanctuary from afar (hence he must leave the Temple city). Even after his first ablution, though he is pure in respect to the common, he is still impure to the sacred; he can still contaminate it by direct contact. Thus he is not free to enter the sanctuary or partake of sacred food until he has bathed a second time. To be sure, P has reduced this three-stage purification by eliminating one ablution, in conformance with its goal to demythologize impurity (see chap. 4, COMMENT G; and the COMMENT on 5:1–13). Nonetheless, 11QT and Philo (in part) preserve the older view (for details concerning Qumran's exegetical hermeneutics, see Milgrom (1989c, 1990c).

18. [*This applies to*] *a woman, with whom a man has sexual relations* (*wĕʾiššâ ʾăšer yiškab ʾiš ʾōtāh šikbat-zāraʿ*). The second half of the chapter dealing with discharges from women begins not here but in the next verse. The proof is found in the absence of the relative conjunction *kî*, which would be expected if the verse began a new law. Thus v 18 is a continuation of vv 16–17 and still deals with semen. Further proof is supplied by the subscript, v 32b, which summarizes vv 16–18 as a single unit with semen as its subject (Dillmann and Ryssel 1897).

At the same time, the construction of this sentence has baffled the commentaries. Why is the woman the subject if her case does not begin until the next verse? Would not this sentence flow more smoothly if it had read *wĕʾiš ʾăšer yiškab ʾiššâ šikbat-zāraʿ* 'If a man has sexual relations with a woman'? A convincing explanation has been proposed by my student, J. Randolph (in a term paper). Randolph recognizes v 18 as an "inverted hinge," which is defined as "a transitional unit of text, independent to some degree from the larger units on either side, which has affinities with each of them and does not add significant information to that presented by its neighbors. . . . The inserted hinge . . .

offers the pattern A/ba/B and reverses the order of the joining elements of the larger blocks of text" (Parunak 1983: 541). Thus *wĕʾiššâ* 'a woman' begins the sentence (b) because it anticipates the succeeding topic (B), whereas *ʾîš* 'man' follows in the sentence (a) because it refers back to the preceding topic (A). Furthermore, the use of the relative *ʾăšer* rather than *kî* calls attention to this chapter as an introverted structure.

A.   *kî* (v 2)
    B.   *kî* (v 16)
        X.   *ʾăšer* (v 18)
    B'.   *kî* (v 19)
A'.   *kî* (v 25)

That *ʾăšer* will be used by an author/redactor as both a pivot and a marker to indicate the transition to a new category within the same unit has already been demonstrated by its placement in the *ḥaṭṭāʾt* pericope (chap. 4), where it marks the change from the severe, burnt *ḥaṭṭāʾt* (4:1–21) to the lesser, eaten *ḥaṭṭāʾt* (4:22–35). For details see the NOTE on 4:22, and for other examples of the inverted hinge see Gen 11:5 (Kikawada 1974); Isa 53:4; Ezek 16:59–63; Ps 19:12; Prov 3:16 (discussed in Parunak 1983). Thus v 18 is indeed a separate law case (contra Dillmann and Ryssel, above) whose distinctiveness, Randolph suggests, is based on the equality of the responsibility in the sexual act, on being the only case of impurity that is under the complete control of the individuals involved (but see the NOTE on v 24), and on representing in literary form the unification of man and wife as "one flesh" (Gen 2:24).

   a woman (wĕʾiššâ . . . ʾōtāh). The original vocalization should be *ʾittāh,* literally, "with her," equivalent to *ʿimmāh* (v 33; Deut 22:23, 25, 28, 29; Driver and White 1898). The emendation is unnecessary, however. The notion of "with" can be understood if "woman" is taken as an adverbial accusative (GKC §118m). Moreover, *šākab* in the connotation of sexual intercourse, in P and H takes *ʾet* of a person (15:18, 24; 18:22; 19:20; 20:11, 12, 13, 18, 20; Num 5:13, 19) and *ʾim* 'with' only in v 33. Finally, even in the connotation of "with" no emendation is required. There is ample attestation for this spelling of the preposition (e.g., Josh 10:25; 14:12; 2 Sam 24:24).

   The evening before worship at the sanctuary, cohabitation was strictly prohibited—a taboo not just limited to Priestly texts (cf. Exod 19:15; 1 Sam 21:6). Indeed, Josephus (*Ant.* 6.235) interprets David's impurity, which allegedly kept him from Saul's New Moon feast, as the result of not having completed his ablutions following sexual intercourse. These ablutions are emphasized by Philo to an extreme: "So careful is the law to provide against the introduction of violent change in the institution of marriage that a husband and wife, who have intercourse in accordance with the legitimate usages of married life, are not allowed, when they leave their bed, to touch anything until they have made their ablutions and purged themselves with water" (*Laws* 3. 63; the significance of Philo's extreme position is explained in Comment F below).

The Qumran sectaries, as indicated above (NOTE on v 17), banished those with seminal emissions from the Temple city. It is obvious then that they would impose the same restriction on sexual intercourse, except that seminal emission, being accidental, would lead to the banishment of its bearer, whereas sexual intercourse, a deliberate act, is forbidden within the city to begin with. This might account for the slight variation in the language between these two laws. The sex-defiled are forbidden to "the entire Temple city" (45:11–12), whereas those having seminal emissions are barred from "the entire Temple" (45:7–10). The difference may be a matter of logistics: seminal emission can take place within the city; sexual intercourse, forbidden in the city, can only take place outside. The author of the scroll, therefore, had to distinguish between the two cases by this point of origin: the one who has an emission in the city may not enter the Temple, and the one who has sexual intercourse outside the city may not enter the city (Milgrom 1978a; 1978b).

In Egypt, a person who wished to enter a sacred precinct had to abstain from sex for at least a whole day and temple personnel, for nine days (Sauneron 1962: 340, 345). "The Egyptians first made it a point of religion to have no intercourse with women in sacred places, and not to enter them without washing, after such intercourse" (Herodotus 2.64). Egyptian men in modern times, and probably in ancient times, "are very scrupulous about purifying themselves after sexual intercourse or after a nocturnal emission, sometimes having a bath, and always washing the genital organs" (Blackman 1951: 477).

Among the Arabs, sexual intercourse was forbidden to pilgrims to Mecca (Smith 1927: 454). Among the Sabeans of southern Arabia, a penitent confesses "that he went (i.e., had sexual intercourse; Ryckmans 1972: 7) without purification" (*ANET*[3] 665), that is to say, the sexual act should have been followed by a bath (cf. Henninger 1978: 469). For the ancient Persians, the emission of semen, whether in sex or otherwise, was polluting; hence, the husband and wife bathed after intercourse (Boyce 1975: 306). In Hindu religion, bathing is required for the male after sexual intercourse (Manu 5.63, 144) because semen is considered impure (Manu 2.181; 11.121–23). In ancient Greece, as well, sexual activity was incompatible with sacred activity. "Apart from Egyptians and Greeks, almost the whole of the rest of mankind copulate in sacred places and go into shrines without washing after sleeping with a woman" (Herodotus 2.64). Herodotus was wrong about others, but he certainly can be trusted regarding his own people. There is ample attestation of this fact in Greek drama and sanctuary regulations (Parker 1983: 74–79; Burkert 1985: 87).

The Hittites were no less scrupulous in demanding ablutions following sexual intercourse before engaging in cultic activity. Sharing the same cultural continuum as Israel, their regulations merit quotation and comment. The "Instructions to Temple Officials" (*ANET*[3] 207–10) is a treasure trove of such information. Temple officials are permitted to go into town to eat, drink, and sleep with a woman, but they must spend the rest of the night at the temple (2.82ff.). It is not said at this point that the "partying" officials need to purify themselves. Later, however, the text states explicitly that bathing after intercourse is necessary. The text allows kitchen workers and other officials to have intercourse, but only in a pure condition: "as he executes the god's rite (and) gives to the god to eat and drink, in that way let him go with the woman." But after his recreation he is to purify himself immediately in the morning by bathing (3.71–72).

The "Instructions" further stipulate (3.74–80) that if an official has had intercourse, but does not report it to his leader, he is still to purify himself by bathing. If he does not bathe and a companion knows of his lapse and allows him to remain impure, then both of them are to be put to death; his sexual impurity has defiled the bread and the libation vessel of the gods (3.79–80).

One final Hittite example of the impurity of sexual intercourse is found in the account of Mursili's speech impediment (Goetze and Pedersen 1934). The text describes the ritual acts that Mursili undertook to correct a speech defect he had suffered from earlier in life. The affliction was understood to be a divine punishment. He sought an oracle to determine the offense and how he could placate the god. He was told to send a substitute bull, birds, and other materials to the temple in Kumanni. The morning he sent these items to the temple, he bathed (v 19). Mursili is very insistent on this point. He repeats it more fully by saying that he had spent the previous night with his wife, but in the early morning he had bathed before performing the various rites. "On which day they decorated the substitute ox, on that (same) day my majesty bathed. (It is true that) the previous night he had slept with a woman, but (only) when he bathed in the morning, he placed his hand on the substitute ox" (vv 18–21). The rite was performed in a pure condition and was thus efficacious. Moreover, bathing following cohabitation seems to have been practiced, if not required, even under ordinary circumstances. A bath ritual prescribes, "In the morning the woman washes and when the woman is pure from sexual intercourse . . ." (*KUB* 9.22.3.29–32; Moyer 1969: 51), and "Mursili's Speech Loss" reports, "throughout the night there was sleep (intercourse) with a woman. But when the morning came he washed" (1.19–20). Thus, for the Hittites, "sexual intercourse produced defilement for both the man and the woman and necessitated a ritual bath early the next morning to restore a state of purity" (Moyer 1969: 61).

Thus the entire ancient world is unanimous in its concern for cultic purity. In all cultures sexual intercourse disqualifies a person from participating in the cult, and the same rite is prescribed for purification from sexual impurity— bathing. The Bible uniquely adds one stipulation: for the impurity to be completely eliminated one must wait until evening. The question however, remains:

Why is the sexual act defiling? One can understand that seminal emissions, being a total loss of life-giving fluid, were regarded as impure. But in conjugal union, the act of procreation? Ramban's reply merits consideration: "The reason for the defilement of seminal emissions, even though it is part of the process of procreation, is like the reason for the defilement of death . . . the individual does not know if his seed will be wasted, or if a child will result." Ramban's insight will be developed in COMMENT G below. The ubiquity of the menstruant taboo and its purification are discussed in COMMENT A below.

a man (ʾîš). The Sam. reads *ʾîšāh* 'her husband'. But the law is not concerned with legitimate or moral relationships.

they shall bathe in water (wĕrāḥăṣû bammayim). Theoretically, their clothing would also be contaminated. The text assumes that they were naked. The bedding, however, might have to be laundered (v 17).

19. *When a woman has a discharge (wĕʾiššâ kî-tihyeh zābâ).* This clause parallels the opening clause of the pericope on the *zāb: ʾîš ʾîš kî yihyeh zāb.* Why is the menstruant called a *zābâ?* And why is this term *zāb* denied to the male with a seminal emission? The answer rests in the nature of the exudation. The man's results from an ejaculation, the woman's from a flow, and the latter is the root meaning of *zāb*—one who has a flow. Thus this pericope on discharges of women is divided into two kinds of flows: regular *(niddâ)* and irregular *(zābâ).*

her discharge being blood from her body (dām yihyeh zōbāh bibĕśārāh). This clause is parallel to and explanatory of the similarly constructed clause for the male, *mibbĕśārô zôbô* (v 2). It is an explanatory asyndeton, requiring the addition of the term *dām* 'blood' to distinguish the nature of her discharge from that of the male *(Keter Torah).*

from her body (bibĕśārāh). A euphemism for her genitals (cf. the NOTE on v 2). The preposition *b* is equivalent to *min* 'from' (Ḥazzequni). The rabbis, however, take the *bet* in its usual sense, namely, "in her body," arguing that because her organ is internal the flow originates inside the body; and even if it does not emerge, as long as the woman senses it (it will be accompanied by cramps—S. Rattray), she is impure (*Sipra,* Mĕṣōrāʿ Zab. par. 4:4; *Tg. Neof.;* cf. *Keter Torah*).

in her menstrual impurity (bĕniddātāh). A compression of *bĕṭumʾat niddātāh* 'in her menstrual impurity' (cf. v 26b). For the etymology and meaning of the term *niddâ* see the discussion in the NOTE on 12:2. For the comparative evidence concerning the menstrual taboo, see the discussion in COMMENT A below.

seven days. There is no mention of ablutions for the menstruant or for the woman with chronic discharges (v 28). Still, all statements regarding the duration of impurity automatically imply that it is terminated by ablutions (see the NOTE on "he shall be impure until evening," 11:24b). They can also be deduced from corpse contamination, also a seven-day impurity terminated by ablutions (Num 19:19; *Keter Torah*). Besides, if a minor impurity such as a seminal discharge requires ablutions (15:16), all the more so the major genital discharges. Indeed, Maimonides regards the case of seminal emission (vv 16–18) as a *binyan* *ʾāb* 'archetype' for all impurity bearers ("Forbidden Sexual Unions" 4.3; cf. also the Geonim, cited by Bahya: tosafot on *b. Yoma* 78; and *ʾOṣar Geonim, Ḥag.* 11). The same deductions must be made from the absence of ablutions in the prescriptions for the parturient (see the NOTE on "she shall be impure," 12:2b). Thus ablutions must be omitted from these three major impurity cases *for women*—the parturient, the one discharging chronically, and the menstruant— because they are taken for granted. Note that when their performance is essential to the narrative, the writer mentions them (2 Sam 11:4). Furthermore, because laundering is also prescribed for severe impurities (seven days or longer; cf. 14:8, 9; 15:13; Num 19:18) it must also be assumed for the menstruant.

Nor is there any mention of sacrifices. Here, however, none is to be expected. First, menstruation is a normal condition and is, therefore, not to be compared with abnormal genital discharges (vv 13–15, 28–30). More important, however, is a practical consideration: are we to expect a woman to bring a sacrifice to the sanctuary every month?

The seven-day period, it would seem, corresponds to the normal limit of the menstrual flow. "R. Meir used to say, why did the Torah ordain that the impurity of menstruation should continue for seven days? Being in constant contact with his wife [a husband might] develop a loathing for her. The Torah, therefore, ordained: let her be impure for seven days in order that she be beloved by her husband as at the time of her first entry into the bridal chamber" (*b. Nid.* 31a). The rabbis contend that "seven days" means pure days, in other words, that the counting begins after the discharge has stopped, in effect equating the menstruant with the *zābâ* (v 28; cf. *b. Nid.* 57b, 69a). Strikingly, so do the Falashas (Ethiopian Jews), who never had contact with rabbinic traditions (Eshkoli 1936), in contrast to the Karaites, who contend that the impurity does not extend beyond the seven-day period.

whoever touches her shall be impure until evening (wĕkol-hannōgēaʿ bāh yiṭmāʾ ʿad-hāʿāreb). The communicability of the menstruant's impurity is attested everywhere, for instance, the Hindus (Manu 5.66, 85). The Sabean penitent confesses "that he touched women during their menses and did not wash himself" (*CIH* 523, lines 6–7; *ANET*[3] 665; cf. Ryckmans 1972). As with the menstruant herself, ablutions are assumed here and in all of the following cases (vv 20–27; cf. the NOTE on 11:24). "Touches her" implies contact with her body, not with her clothes, just as in the case of the *zāb* (v 7; contra Wright 1987: 183 n. 34).

This clause also implies that touching a menstruant generates less impurity than touching a *zāb*, which requires laundering (v 7; also touching a *zābâ*, according to v 27 LXX). But this flatly contradicts the following verses (vv 21– 22), where laundering is required. For how could touching the menstruant's bedding or seat, a second remove from the menstruant, be more contaminating than touching her directly?

One cannot answer by saying that laundering, like ablutions, must be assumed. The phrase *yiṭmāʾ ʿad-hāʿāreb* only implies ablutions, never laundering; the latter must always be specified (see the NOTES on 11:24–25). The rabbis who are fully aware of the contradiction are forced, first, to deduce that laundering takes place by reasoning a fortiori from the laundering required for touching her bedding (v 21) and, then, to interpret this sentence midrashically (*Sipra*, Mĕṣōrāʿ Zab. par. 4:9). Nevertheless, there is no textual warrant to insert the required words, *yĕkabbēs bĕgādāyw*, and emend *yiṭmāʾ* to *wĕṭāmēʾ* (cf. 11:40b). A less drastic proposal would be to delete *ʿad-hāʿāreb*. The resulting shortened sentence, *wĕkol-hannōgēaʿ bāh yiṭmāʾ* 'whoever touches her would be impure', would be explicated by the following verses where, indeed, laundering is required. A similar structure has twice been encountered in chap. 11. Touching the carcass of an impure quadruped is forbidden in 11:24–26, where *kol-hannōgēaʿ bāhem yiṭmāʾ* (v 26b) forms an inclusio with v 24. The function of the inclusio is to summarize vv 24–26, which includes a prescription for laundering. Similarly, *wĕnōgēaʿ bĕniblātām yiṭmāʾ* (11:36b) is shorthand, indeed an *incipit*, for the assumed rules regarding touching and carrying the carcass. Thus by deleting *ʿad-hāʿāreb* here, the new shortened sentence would correspond to the structure of the two sentences that make up the following verse (v 20). The implication would be clear: just as the menstruant's bedding and seat require laundering (see the NOTE on "shall be impure," v 4a), so would anyone who touches the menstruant. Must we, however, resort to such a speculative emendation?

One other solution comes to mind. There is a qualitative difference between the impurity of the menstruant herself (i.e., her body) and that of her bedding and seat. The latter, it is assumed, has been generated by direct contact with her menstrual flow. But her body, especially its exposed parts that another person might touch, will not come into contact with her flow. Note that there is no prohibition barring the menstruant from touching anyone. This can only mean that in fact her hands do not transmit impurity (see the NOTE on "during her menses," below). The consequence is that she is not banished but remains at home. Neither is she isolated from her family. She is free to prepare their meals and perform her household chores. They, in turn, merely have to avoid lying in her bed, sitting in her chair, and touching her. Thus human physiology may have resolved the exegetical enigma. The key factor is the difference in the intensity of the impurity source (see the NOTE on "he shall launder his clothes," v 5). Therefore, anyone who touches her (v 19b) contracts a lesser impurity than one who touches anything beneath her (vv 21–22). This leniency contrasts markedly with the fear of the menstruant's touch and even of her breath that prevailed elsewhere and is attested in rabbinic folklore (see COMMENT A below).

It clearly represents the concerted efforts of the Priestly legists to eviscerate the notion of the demonic that was universally attributed to the menstruant.

The one-day impurity prescribed for touching a menstruant is more lenient than the penalty for a similar act in Mesopotamia: "A man who has touched a *musukkatu* woman who is passing by, for six days he will not [be pure]" (*CAD,* 10.239; the *musukkatu* denotes both the menstruant and the parturient; ibid., 240).

20. *lies . . . sits (tiškab . . . tēšēb).* What about *tirkab* 'rides' (cf. v 9)? The suggestion offered by commentators that women were not wont to ride is refuted by the narratives: Rebecca (Gen 24:64); Rachel (Gen 31:34); Achsah (Josh 15:18; Judg 1:15); Abigail (1 Sam 25:20); the Shunamite (2 Kgs 4:24). The answer probably is that riding is subsumed under sitting, precisely as in v 10. The story of Rachel and the teraphim raises a tantalizing possibility. According to these menstrual laws, Rachel would have defiled her riding seat, which in turn would have defiled anything beneath it (Lev 15:27), namely, her idols! Thus the story may have a hidden agenda: it is a polemic against idolatry.

during her menstrual impurity (běniddātāh). But after her menses she would purify her bedding and chairs as well as herself. If, however, she purified only herself, her furniture would continue to defile.

The limitation of the defilable objects to bedding and chairs implies that anything else she touches would not be defiled. This would mean that if she touches any bedding or chair that she did not use during her menses it would not be rendered impure. But those same objects (including her riding seat, inferred from v 10), if beneath her, are presumed to have been defiled because they may have been touched by her menstrual flow (see the NOTE on v 11) and must undergo purification (see below). Alternatively, one might argue that the menstruant is subject to the preceding laws of the *zāb* and, hence, her hands will defile unless she first washes them. Yet menstruation, a blood flux, is a different category from the mucous secretion of the *zāb,* thereby vitiating any deduction by analogy. Moreover, the condition of the menstruant (also of the parturient) is natural, and the Priestly legists may have deliberately restricted her impurity to just her flow and exempted her touch in order to permit her to remain at home (contrast Isa 30:22 and later practice; see COMMENT A below).

shall be impure (yiṭmāʾ). The imperfect implies that the impurity is temporary. The period of impurity is not specified because it lasts as long as the menstruant reclines on her bedding or sits in her chair. Obviously, she will purify these objects at the time she purifies herself; otherwise, they would recontaminate her (vv 21–22). Of course, someone else can assume the responsibility of purifying her furniture, but the possibility exists that if she and her contaminated fabrics are purified simultaneously there is no recontamination (see the NOTE on "launder . . . shave . . . bathe," 14:8). That the contaminated fabrics need to be purified, that is to say, laundered, can be deduced from the explicit prescription that semen-defiled fabrics must be laundered (v 16).

21. *shall launder his clothes (yĕkabbēs bĕgādāyw)*. There is no need to assume that his clothes came into contact with the bedding when he touched it. Rather, it is the intensive impurity imparted to the bedding by sleeping on it (i.e., with the whole body for a long period) that possesses enough force to be conveyed via the body to the clothing (see the NOTE on "shall launder his clothes," v 5). The dynamic quality of impurity, a residue of its original demonic nature, is manifest here (see chap. 4, COMMENT C).

22. *and anyone who touches (wĕkol-hannōgēaʿ)*. The reason an added verse is needed for the case of touching the menstruant's chair, though the consequences are the same as touching her bedding, is that it is an entirely new law. The comparable law for the *zāb* (v 6) speaks only of *sitting* on his chair (see the NOTES on vv 5 and 10a).

shall launder his clothes (yĕkabbēs bĕgādāyw). Here the analogy with the *zāb* breaks down. Touching his seat mandates only bathing, not laundering (see the NOTE on v 10a)! The answer is that the impurity of blood is greater than the impurity of semen. For example, menstrual blood, exuded during sexual intercourse, contaminates for seven days (v 24), whereas semen contaminates for only one day (v 18). Blood also has greater transmitting power, as will be derived from v 23.

23. *it (hûʾ)*. What is the antecedent of this pronoun? There are five possibilities.

(1) *hûʾ* is to be rendered "he," in other words, the person who touches either the bedding or chair (vv 21–22). Wessely (1846) connects this verse with the following and explains, "If he is on the bed or on the object on which she is sitting when he makes contact with it, he is impure until evening. But if a man has intercourse with her, her menstrual impurity shall be on him; he shall be impure for seven days." But this interpretation would contradict vv 21 and 22: if touching her bedding or seat, even when she is not on it, mandates laundering (vv 21–22), all the more so when she is on it; yet no laundering is required (v 23b)!

(2) *hûʾ* is to be read *hîʾ* (of the LXX), yielding the translation "And if *she* is on the bed or on the object upon which she sits when he touches *her* (reading *bô* as *bâ*), he shall be impure until evening." It seems that the LXX also interprets v 23 as a contrast to v 24: that is, whereas touching her involves a one-day impurity, having sex with her mandates a seven-day impurity. This interpretation is totally superfluous, however. We already know that touching her generates a one-day impurity (v 19b). Furthermore, if he only touches her, what difference does it make whether she is on her bed or on her seat? Finally, the same objection raised in discussing v 19b recurs here: if touching her bed or seat requires laundering, should not touching her directly also require laundering?

(3) *hûʾ* read as *hîʾ* (*hyʾ* in the Sam), but without the LXX's emendation of *bô*, yielding "If she is on the bed or on the object upon which she sits when he touches *it* (i.e., the object), he shall be impure until evening." This rendering

however, creates the same logical impasse encountered by the previous interpretations: touching the bedding or seat while she is on it results in a lighter impurity requiring bathing (v 23), while touching the same object when she is not on it results in a severer impurity, also requiring laundering (vv 21-22).

(4) *hû'* is to be rendered "it," and its antecedent is the "object on which she sat," namely, her seat (v 22; Ibn Ezra). As Wessely (1846) rightly protests, if one who touches the seat has to launder (v 22), why should he only have to bathe if he touches the seat while it is on her bed? Furthermore, what sense does it make that the seat she sat on (v 22) can be on the seat she is currently sitting on (v 23)?

(5) The correct answer is indeed that *hû'* means "it," but its antecedent is not the seat she was sitting on but the term *kol-kĕlî* 'any object' (v 22), that is to say, any *uncontaminated* object (*Leqaḥ Tov;* Dillmann and Ryssel 1897). The sense of this verse is as follows: if an object that the person touches (v 22) is either on the bedding on which she is reclining or on the chair on which she is sitting, he is rendered impure. Thus the law deals with the case of touching an object that is on the same furniture as the menstruant. It is a case of tertiary transmission of impurity: menstruant → bedding or seat → object → person. This tertiary contact, however, requires a medium. It is still not as severe as the case of a corpse-contaminated or scale-diseased person, who can transmit his impurity to nonsacred objects without a medium, that is, by overhang.

Note, also, that this transmission can occur only when all of the objects and persons form a chain and are in *simultaneous* contact. The clue is the unique use in this pericope of the participle *yōšebet* 'sitting': she must be on the bedding or seat when he touches the object. If she is not, its impurity is only strong enough to transmit itself once, to a person or object, but not beyond that. And it is precisely because the impurity has been attenuated as it has moved from the menstruant to the furniture, to the object, and then to the person that the latter need only bathe and not launder. The greater power of simultaneous contact is patently recognized by the rabbis, who distinguish between the impurity of simultaneous contact and *pērēš,* the lesser impurity if separation ensues and the chain is broken (e.g., *m. Zabim* 5:2, 7).

Because tertiary transmission is attested for the lesser impurity of the menstruant, who requires no sacrifice, shall it be assumed for the greater impurity of the *zāb, zābâ,* and parturient, who require sacrifices? It is doubtful that it exists for the *zāb.* Because he is mentioned first, ahead of the menstruant, one would have expected to find the rule included among his regulations. And if it does not exist for the *zāb,* there is a good reason for it, the same reason that motivates the rule that there is a severer consequence in touching the chair of a menstruant than in touching the chair of a *zāb* (see the NOTE on v 22): semen impurity is less severe than blood impurity. By contrast, as the *zābâ* and the parturient exude blood, it would follow that tertiary transmission applies to them. As to why this fact is not mentioned in their respective pericopes, the answer is obvious: the *zābâ* section follows that of the menstruant and takes its cue from it (cf. vv 25b, 26ab, 27a); and the parturient laws, though they precede (chap. 12), are also modeled on and assume the knowledge of the menstrual laws (see the NOTE on 12:2b).

[she] is sitting (yōšebet). The participle, in contrast to the imperfect verbs that describe the other contacts with furniture in this chapter (cf. vv 4a, 4b, 5a, 6a, 9a, 20a, 20b, 22a, 24b, 26a, 26b), emphasizes that simultaneous contact is taking place among the impure person, the functioning object, and the person touching (see above).

it (bô). The antecedent is *kol-kĕlî* 'any object' (v 22), also referred to as *hû'* (v 23a).

he shall be impure until evening (yiṭmā' 'ad-hā'āreb). This formula implies ablutions but not laundering (see the NOTE on v 19b). The reason for this reduced consequence is the weakening of the impurity as it undergoes tertiary transmission (see the NOTE on "it," v 23a).

24. *And if a man proceeds to lie with her (wĕ'im šākōb yiškab 'îš 'ōtāh).* There are two possibilities in this case. (1) He was contaminated by her menstrual blood by accident, that is, her menstruation began during intercourse. Thus, this clause and the next would be rendered "If a man lies with her *so that* her menstrual impurity is conveyed to him" (Ibn Ezra; *Seper Hamibḥar; Keter Torah*). If, however, he had intercourse knowing that she was menstruating, both of them would be subject to the capital punishment of *kārēt* (20:18). According to this interpretation, this case would be an inadvertent violation of a prohibitive commandment, expiable by a purification offering (cf. *m. Nid.* 2:2 and cf. the NOTE on "prohibitive," 4:2). (2) It is also possible to posit that copulating with the menstruant was a deliberate act (such is the force of the inf. obs. [D. N. Freedman]), and the omission of the *kārēt* penalty is explicable on the grounds that Scripture here is only concerned with the nature of impurity and not with its penalties (Abravanel). These two possibilities were envisioned by the rabbis (*y. Hor.* 2:5). (3) Finally, the possibility must be considered that P did not envisage any penalty at all for the violation of impurity rules. This possibility is ostensibly enhanced after realizing that v 31, which mandates death by divine agency for violators, was interpolated by the school of H (see the NOTE on v 31). This supposition, however, must be dismissed out of hand. P is much concerned, indeed obsessed, with the potential contamination of the sanctuary by Israel's impurities (see the COMMENT on 5:1–3 and the NOTE on 16:16), and its silence concerning penalties is explicable, on the grounds supplied by Abravanel (above), that P concentrates on the effect of impurity on persons and objects and not on divine sanctions for its bearers.

her menstrual impurity is transmitted to him (ûtĕhî niddātāh 'ālāyw). Again there are two possible interpretations. (1) This clause is part of the protasis: that is to say, during intercourse her menstrual blood is transmitted to him, an accidental act (Ibn Ezra and the Karaites; see above). S. R. Driver (1892: 213), who posits that the jussive *ûtĕhî* is equivalent to the infinitive *lihyôt,* and Joüon (1923: §167e), who emends the jussive to imperfect *wattihyeh,* clearly also hold that this clause is part of the protasis. But as part of the protasis this clause should begin *wĕhāyĕtâ;* MT's *ûtĕhî* rather indicates a consequence, hence it belongs with the apodosis (Ehrlich 1899–1900). Also, the antecedent of *'ōtāh* is the menstruant (v 19); therefore, her menses began prior to intercourse. Finally, the structure of the pericope—v 24 is a collapsed version of vv 19b–20a; because v 24b parallels v 20a, v 24a must correspond to v 19b—shows that this clause deals with the *consequence* of intercourse with a menstruant. The conclusion is therefore inescapable: (2) this clause is part of the apodosis (Saadiah).

Scrupulousness in avoiding sexual intercourse with a menstruant is one of the attributes of righteousness (Ezek 18:6) and its disregard, one of the sins of Israel's leaders (Ezek 22:10; cf. Cant 8:12). It is a cardinal accusation that Qumran levies against the Jerusalemite priesthood: "Also they pollute the Temple inasmuch as they do not keep separate according to the Torah, but lie with her who sees the blood of her discharge" (CD 5:6–7; *dām zōbāh* 'the blood of her discharge' refers not to the abnormal discharge of v 25 [Rabin 1954: 19] but to *dām yihyeh zōbāh* of v 19, her menses).

It may be questioned, of course, why this taboo is so severe; all other contacts with the menstruant result only in a one-day impurity, whereas in this case it involves the identical degree of impurity as borne by the menstruant herself: seven days plus contagion to other things and persons upon contact. J. W. Burton, in his study of the Nuer of Africa, provides the needed illumination: "The necessity (among the Nuer) of maintaining the distance between bleeding youths (undergoing initiation) and pregnant women, and between bleeding women (menstruants) and potential life (intercourse) is thus a symbolic statement of the necessity for keeping life-creating processes from potentially life-destructive forces" (1974: 530). Thus it may be the loss of both life-giving semen and genital blood that evokes the utmost horror of the legislator (see further COMMENT G below).

he shall be impure seven days. And all of the regulations concerning the menstruant (vv 19–23) now apply to him (see below).

any bedding on which he lies shall become impure (wĕkol-hammiškāb 'ăšer-yiškab 'ālāyw yiṭmā'). This sentence refers to v 20a, which heads the series of consequences resulting from contact with the menstruant (vv 20a–23), implying that all of them also apply to the man who copulated with her. This is a perfect example of an *incipit* (for another example in this chapter see the NOTE on v 19b). The Karaites, however, being literalists, claim that he defiles only bedding but not other furniture, and they deny that the person who touches them is contaminated *(Keter Torah).* The rabbis also hold that one who cohabits with a menstruant causes a lesser impurity than the menstruant herself, namely, his bedding or seat cannot contaminate persons *(m. Zabim* 5:11; cf. 5:6; *m. Kelim* 1:3; *b. Nid.* 33a).

25. *When a woman has a discharge of blood. wĕʾiššâ kî-yāzûb zôb dāmāh,* literally, "Regarding a woman when her blood discharge flows." Why this circumlocution? Could not the text simply have read *wĕʾiššâ kî tihyeh zābâ* 'When a woman has a discharge', corresponding in form to the formula for the male, *ʾîš ʾîš kî tihyeh zāb* 'When any man has a discharge'? There are two reasons that motivate the change: her discharge is blood, and that factor had to be mentioned; and the *zāb* formula has already been preempted by the menstruant, *wĕʾiššâ kî-tihyeh zābâ.*

for many days (yāmîm rabbîm). The time is not specified. The disorder can last for years (e.g., Matt 9:20; Mark 5:25; Luke 8:43). The rabbis opt for a minimum of three days beyond her normal menstrual seven (*Sipra,* Mĕṣōrāʿ Zabim par. 5:9).

not at the time of her menstrual impurity. bĕlōʾ ʿet-niddātāh, in other words, separated from and not continuous with her normal catamenial period (cf. *Sipra,* Mĕṣōrāʿ Zab. 8:2).

beyond the time of her menstrual impurity. ʿal-niddātāh, to wit, continuous with and extending beyond her normal catamenial period.

as long as her impure discharge lasts. kol-yĕmê zôb ṭumʾātāh, literally, "all the days of the discharge of her impurity." This expression distinguishes the abnormal discharge of the *zābâ* from the normal discharge of the menstruant (see the Note on 30b).

she shall be impure (ṭĕmēʾâ hîʾ [hwʾ]). This wording corresponds to the verdict for the *zāb: ṭāmēʾ hûʾ* (v 2bβ). The rabbis maintain that all who live in the Promised Land are susceptible to the impurity of discharge, even proselytes, slaves, and the like (*m. Zabim* 2:1), proof of a long, continuous tradition that discharges from non-Israelites contaminate the sanctuary (P) or land (H).

26. Her bedding and seat are mentioned, but not her riding seat (cf. v 9). It is subsumed under the category of her seat, just as in the case of the menstruant (v 20b) and in the summary statement for the *zāb* (v 10).

like bedding during her menstrual impurity (kĕmiškab niddātāh). A reference to vv 20, 21 and v 23. That is to say, she contaminates her bedding, anyone or anything touching the bedding, and anyone touching an object that is on her bedding while she is on it. Thus her law follows that of the menstruant, not that of the *zāb.* The reason is obvious: both women are alike because this discharge is that of blood, whereas the discharge of the *zāb* is slightly less severe (see the Note on "it," v 23).

as during her menstrual impurity (kĕṭumʾat niddātāh). A reference to vv 20b, 22. Her seat also resembles that of the menstruant: it contaminates persons, objects, and anyone touching an object that is on the chair while she is sitting on it. The menstruant's seat differs from the seat of the *zāb* in another respect: touching the latter results in a lesser impurity requiring ablutions (v 10a), whereas touching the seat of the menstruant or of the *zābâ* also requires laundering (v 21a). The rabbis astutely note that the text does not state *kîmê nid-*

dātāh 'as during her menstrual period': her bedding or seat is impure only as long as she is upon it, but once she leaves it, it is impure not for seven days but only for one day: ablutions and evening terminate the impurity (cf. *Sipra*, Měṣōrāʿ Zab. 8:10).

27. *them (bām)*. With two MSS and the LXX, read *bāh* 'her'. Which is preferable? The MT's *bām* implies that the structure of the pericope on the *zābâ* follows that of the menstruant: v 26 ‖ v 20; v 27 ‖ vv 21–22, thus the case for touching her bedding and seat is complete. But what about impurity incurred in touching her? If it is to be derived a fortiori from v 19b, we would have to conclude that touching the *zābâ* requires no laundering! But surely this is impossible: if touching the *zāb* necessitates laundering, then touching the *zābâ*, an equal if not greater source of impurity (see the NOTES on "it," v 23 and "like bedding," v 26), should certainly require laundering! If, however, we follow the reading *bāh* 'her', then the structure of the pericope on the *zābâ* is modeled on that of the *zāb:* v 26 ‖ v 4; v 27 ‖ v 7. What about the impurity incurred in touching her bedding and seat (‖ vv 5–6)? It can logically be derived a fortiori from the menstruant (vv 21–22). Moreover, it has already been alluded to in v 26. As pointed out (see the NOTES on v 26), the reference to the menstruant's bedding and seat implies that all of their regulations apply equally to the bedding and seat of the *zābâ*. Thus the reading *bāh* is preferable.

he shall launder his clothes (wěkibbes běgādāyw). Again, there are two possibilities. (1) If the MT's *bām* is retained, then this verse deals with the impurity incurred in touching her bedding or seat. The law here would be equivalent to that of the menstruant but different from the law of the *zāb:* touching the latter's seat does not require laundering. The reason (as explained in the NOTE on "it," v 10) is that the discharge from the female (blood) generates a severer impurity than the discharge from the male. (2) If, instead, we follow the reading *bāh*, then the verse deals with the consequences of touching the *zābâ*. But now the *zābâ* and the menstruant are not alike: touching the menstruant (v 19b) does not require laundering. This difference also makes sense: the abnormal discharge of the *zābâ* is surely a severer impurity than the natural discharge of the menstruant, by analogy to the more complex purification rite incumbent upon the *zābâ* (vv 28–30). Thus, just as the *zābâ*'s purification requirement is severer than that of the menstruant, we should expect some indication that her impurity is also severer. This might be it—one who touches her also launders. Also, whereas the menstruant does not communicate impurity by touch (see the NOTE or "whoever touches her," v 19), the *zābâ*, bearing a severer impurity, does. Furthermore, we must also assume that one who copulates with the *zābâ* fully incurs impurity of the same degree as hers, an a fortiori deduction from the case of the menstruant (v 24).

28. *When (wěʾim)*. The purificatory rite of the *zāb* begins with *kî* (v 13). Why not here as well? Perhaps, as the rites are identical, they are not considered

a new item. And the possibility is that the author of this chapter wishes to allow only seven mentions of *kî* (see the NOTE on "If," v 8).

she is healed (ṭāhărâ). This use of *ṭāhar* implies physical, not ritual, purification (cf. *Sipra*, Mĕṣōrāʿ Zab. 9:1; and see the NOTE on "is healed," v 13).

and after that she shall be pure. *wĕʾahar tiṭhār*, that is, after the seven days and implicitly after she has laundered her clothes and bathed her body in spring water (v 13). Alternatively, this clause might be rendered "and after that she shall purify herself," in other words, after the seven days have elapsed she shall launder and bathe. For this usage in the *qal*, see Num 31:24. Or, the *qal* here might be equivalent to the *niphʿal*, having a reflexive meaning as in *wĕhiṭṭehārû* 'purify yourselves' (Num 8:7). In either case, the verb *ṭāhar* connotes ritual purification.

29. *and bring them (wĕhēbîʾâ ʾōtām)*. A shortened form for *ûbāʾ lipnê YHWH . . . ûnĕtānām* 'he shall come before the Lord . . . and give them' (v 14), and the indication that the pericope on the *zābâ* is structured on that of the *zāb* but in a condensed form.

The accent on the affirmative *a* in the *hiphʿil* perfect preceded by a sequential *waw* is unusual (Ibn Ezra). It is attested only once more, in *wĕhibdîlâ happārōket* 'the veil shall divide' (Exod 26:33; Radak). The reason seems to be that the Masoretes attempted to avoid a hiatus with the first syllable of the following word (GKC §53r; Joüon 1923: §33).

30. *for her impure discharge (mizzôb ṭumʾātāh)*. The comparable phrase for the *zāb* reads *mizzôbô* 'for his discharge' (v 15b). Why the addition of *ṭumʾātāh* here, particularly when the tendency of this pericope is to abbreviate the pericope on the *zāb*? The answer may well be that its purpose is to distinguish the *zābâ* from the menstruant, who is also defined by the term *zābâ* (v 19), to wit: although the menstruant also discharges blood, the severer impurity *(ṭumʾâ)* of the *zābâ* necessitates sacrificial expiation (Wessely 1846).

The sectaries of Qumran mandate a more stringent rule: *WHYʾH ʾL TWKL QWDŠ WʾL [TBWʾ] ʾL HMQDŠ ʿD BW HŠMŠ BYWM HŠMYNY* 'She (the *zābâ*) may neither eat sacred food nor [enter] into the sanctuary until the sun sets on the eighth day' (4QDᵇ9 2:3–4). From this as yet unpublished text two significant points can be derived. First, couched in the language used for the parturient during her purificatory period (12:4b), we learn that the *zābâ* may not come into contact with sancta. This rule corresponds precisely to the Priestly system regarding all severe impurity bearers (COMMENT F, Table D-2). Second, her impurity to sancta ends not with her sacrifices on the morning of the eighth day, as stated in this verse, but later, with sunset. Precisely the same situation, as I have noted, holds for the scale-diseased person at Qumran (see the NOTE on "the entrance to the Tent of Meeting," 14:11). Qumran's principle of homogenization is again at work. It was found operating in the case of scale disease to equate its termination with that of minor impurity bearers who terminate their impurity at sunset. Predictably, what Qumran ordained for scale disease would apply equally to other major impurity bearers. This new text supplies the proof.

31. *You shall set apart . . . from (wĕhizzartem . . . mi-).* The root is *nzr*, and in the *niphʿal* and *niphʿil*, followed by the preposition *min*, it carries the connotation "to separate, withdraw from." The rabbis pinpoint its meaning accurately: *ʾēn nĕzîrâ ʾellaʾ haprāšâ* 'every *nzr* implies separation' (*Sipra*, Mĕṣōrāʿ Zab. 9:6; *Tgs. Ps.-J.* and *Onq.*). Thus the priests are enjoined *wĕyinnāzĕrû miqqodšê* 'separate themselves from the sacred donations of [the Israelites]' (Lev 22:2). The Israelite is warned lest *wĕyinnāzēr mēʾaḥăray* 'he separate himself from me [the Lord]' (Ezek 14:7; cf. v 5). Followed by the preposition *lĕ*, the verb takes on the meaning of "separate to, dedicate." For example, while the Nazirite is enjoined *miyyayin wĕšēkār yazzîr* 'He shall abstain from wine and beer' (Num 6:3a), he is also defined as one who *wĕhizzîr laYHWH* 'separates/ dedicates to the Lord' (Num 6:12; cf. vv 2, 5, 6). Thus the Nazirite *(nāzîr)* is so called because of both "separating" abstentions from impure practices on the one hand, and dedicated service to the Lord, on the other. Conversely, backsliding Israel is condemned because *wayinnāzĕrû labbōšet* 'they separated/dedicated themselves to shamefulness (i.e., the Baal)' (Hos 9:10). Returning to the passage in Leviticus, we find that the imperative *(dabbĕrû)* in the plural, ostensibly addressed to Moses and Aaron (v 2), is actually aimed at the priests whose perpetual function is to separate Israel from impurity (10:10; Saadiah), that is, to teach the Israelites (10:11; Ezek 44:23) to abstain from impurity and to purify them when it occurs lest they bring about the pollution of the Sanctuary (see below).

Alternatively, one might emend this word, with the LXX and Sam., to read *wĕhizhartem* 'you shall warn', a *hiphʿil* from the root *zhr* (a rendering also considered by the rabbis (*Sipra*, Mĕṣōrāʿ Zab. 9:7; cf. Philo, *Laws* 3. 15). It is also possible to support the MT, regarding the omitted *he* as a suppressed weak guttural (Görg 1980). This interpretation, however, is less satisfying. What is the purpose of "warning," if the impurities listed in this chapter are mostly unavoidable (Driver and White 1898)? Moreover, it is Israel's prophet who warns (Ezek 33:7–9), while the priest teaches.

from their impurity (miṭṭumʾātām). Which impurity? There are three possibilities. (1) This verse is a summation of all impurities mentioned in chaps. 11–15 (cf. *Sipra*, Tazriaʿ par. 1:3; Bekhor Shor), and the mention of the sanctuary's pollution connects it with chap. 16. If so, perhaps the subscript (vv 32–33) is an addition (Koch 1959: 9). (2) This verse may come from the hand of H (see the Note on "my Tabernacle," below) and hence be an insertion into the chapter. If so, it would still be a summation of chaps. 11–15. (3) The impurity is only that of genital discharges (chap. 15) and is where it belongs, a peroration to the regulations and before the subscript. A definitive answer eludes me.

lest they die (wĕlōʾ yāmūtû). Because the punishment for willfully polluting the sanctuary is *kārēt* (cf. Num 19:13, 20), this verse is proof that *mût (qal)* is equivalent to *kārēt* (*Sipre* Num 125). There can be no doubt that *mût* *(qal;* in distinction to *hēmît, hiphꜥil)* denotes death by divine agency (Milgrom 1970a: 5–8). But is it equivalent to *kārēt?* A glance at the *mût* penalties in P will help clarify the problem. For convenience, they are tabulated below:

Violator	*Violation*	*Source*
1. High Priest	Improper entry to the shrine	Lev 16:2, 13
2. Priests	Improper officiation	Exod 28:43; 30:20–21; Lev 10:9
3. Priests	Prohibited mourning	Lev 10:6
4. Priests	Delinquent "guarding"	Lev 22:9
5. Levites	Touching the sancta	Num 4:15
6. Levites	Viewing (the dismantling of) the sancta	Num 4:19–20
7. Levites	encroachment	Num 18:3
8. Laity	encroachment	Num 17:28; 18:22

All eight violations whose penalty is death by divine agency deal with desecration *(ḥll),* not pollution *(ṭmʾ).* Still, the clash of the sacred with the impure is subject to *kārēt,* as explicitly specified for the lay person or priest who eats sacred food in a state of impurity (7:20–21; 22:3). Does this, then, mean that in the present verse, which speaks of the pollution of the sanctuary, *mût* is equivalent to *kārēt?* Not necessarily. We have already determined that *kārēt* means "extirpation": it not only signifies the death of the sinner but also the end of his line (chap. 7, COMMENT D). The *kārēt* would be inappropriate here. Our verse is concerned not with the individual but with the nation, *běnê yiśrāʾel.* All Israelites are addressed (hence the plurals), and the pollution of the sanctuary means the total destruction of Israel: all will die. Thus, instead of using *kārēt,* which addresses the individual (e.g., *hannepeš hahîʾ,* 7:20, 21, 27; *hannepeš hāʾōkelet,* 7:18, 25), the verse employs *mût* and focuses on the death of the nation. Finally, it should not escape notice that the divine quid pro quo is at work here: if Israel produces impurity and thereby adds to the realm of death, it too will die. The association of impurity with death is described in COMMENT G below.

through their impurity (beṭumʾātām). The impurity can be incurred anywhere in the camp; it need not be brought into the sanctuary. If this verse refers to all of the pericopes in chaps. 11–15, it includes not only the major impurities whose sacrificial requirements imply that the sanctuary has been polluted, but even the minor impurities, such as eating carcasses (chap. 11), which, however, turn into major impurities if their purification is neglected (see the COMMENT on 5:1–13).

my Tabernacle (miškānî). The use of the first person and of the root *nzr* (22:4) raises the suspicion that the verse may be an interpolation from the hand of H (see the Introduction, §H). The objection may be raised that this verse is concerned with the purity of the sanctuary rather than of the land (18:25–28). But the purity of the sanctuary is still not far from the mind of H: not only must the sanctuary be revered (19:30; 26:2), it must not be polluted (20:3).

32. *This is the procedure for (zōʾt tôrat).* There are five *tôrôt* dealing with impurity (11:46; 12:7; 14:2, 32; 14:54–57; 15:32) which correspond to the five *tôrôt* on sacrifices (6:2, 7, 18; 7:1, 11) (Hoffmann 1953). If this balance was intentional, then it would point to a sixth *tôrâ* (13:59) as being a subsequent interpolation (see the NOTE on 13:59). If v 3 also reads *zōʾt tôrat* (with the LXX), the count would not change, for vv 3, 32 would serve as an inclusio for the single unit on genital discharges, just as 14:2, 32 encloses the unit on scale disease.

the one who has a discharge (hazzāb). Is this term the first in the series of subjects summarized in the subscript, or is it the title of the subscript? This question must be asked because the *zāb* occurs again in v 33aβ. The answer will have to wait until the latter citation is discussed.

for the one who has an emission of semen (waʾăšer tēṣēʾ mimmennû šikbat-zeraʿ). A résumé of vv 16–18 that deals with seminal discharge.

and becomes impure thereby (lĕṭomʾâ-bāh). As rendered, this clause seems superfluous. After all, the other enumerated cases also cause impurity without having to say so. Perhaps the verb should be vocalized as a *piʿel: lĕṭamměʾah-bāh* 'to contaminate her with it (the semen)'. This clause would then comprise two parts: semen emission (vv 16–17) and sexual intercourse (v 18).

33. *and for the one who is in her menstrual infirmity (wĕhaddāwâ bĕnid-dātāh).* A résumé of vv 19–23. The idiom is borrowed from 12:2 (cf. 20:18). The word *tôrat* forms a multiple construct chain with several nouns in the absolute state: *hazzāb . . . wĕhaddāwă . . . wehazzāb* (vv 32–33; Ehrlich 1908–14).

and for anyone, male or female, who has a discharge (wĕhazzāb ʾet-zôbô lazzākar wĕlannĕqēbâ). A résumé of vv 2–15, 25–30 (note *ʾet-zôbô,* v 3b). This clause is suspect on two counts: it repeats one of the terms, *zāb,* and breaks the ordered sequence of this chapter's units: male discharges (vv 2–15), seminal emission (vv 16–18), menstruation (vv 19–23), [male and female discharges (vv 2–15, 25–30)], sex with a menstruant (v 24). Thus this clause, v 33aβ, is an insertion. It is probably the work of a later editor who thought that the initial phrase in the series, *zōʾt tôrat hazzāb,* was the title for the entire chapter "this is the procedure for the one who has a discharge" (the present rendering)—and he felt it necessary to insert this clause, which would also distinguish between the *zāb* (vv 2–15) and the *zābâ* (vv 25–30). Instead, the original order may have been as follows: *zāb,* male and female (vv 2–15, 25–30), seminal emission (vv 16–18), menstruation (vv 19–23), sex with the menstruant (v 24). Does this hypothetical reconstruction also imply that originally the unit on the *zābâ* was joined to that of the *zāb?* Hardly! The structure and wording of the *zābâ* unit is dependent on that of the menstruant (e.g., 25b, 26aβ, bβ) and must therefore follow it. Rather, as the conjectured order implies, the term *zāb* is inclusive of male and female. It must not be forgotten that *zābâ* is a technical term in rabbinic Hebrew for the woman with a chronic flux. It is not the biblical term. On the contrary, *zābâ* describes the menstruant (v 19a). Thus in the absence of a technical term for the woman, her condition is subsumed under the term *zāb*. Indeed, even the interpolator had to resort to the circumlocution *"hazzāb*, male or female" in order to include the female.

and for a man who lies with an impure woman *(ûlĕʾîš ʾăšer yiškab ʿim-ṭĕmēʾâ)*. A résumé of v 24.

Comments: Genital Discharges

A. The Menstruant

Ramban writes as follows:

In ancient days menstruants kept very isolated, for they ever were referred to as *niddôt* on account of their isolation, because they did not approach people and did not speak with them. For the ancients in their wisdom knew that their breath is harmful, their gaze is detrimental and makes a bad impression, as the philosophers have explained. . . . And the menstruants dwelled isolated in tents where no one entered, just as our rabbis have mentioned in the *Baraita de Massekat Niddah:* "A learned man is forbidden to greet a menstruant." Rabbi Nehemiah says, "Even the utterance of her mouth is impure." Said Rabbi Yochanan: "One is forbidden to walk after a menstruant and tread her footsteps, which are as impure as a corpse; so is the dust upon which the menstruant stepped impure, and it is forbidden to derive any benefit from her work." (on Gen 31:35)

Today it is recognized that the work cited by Ramban is a sectarian document, composed in Palestine probably in Gaonic times (end of the first millennium c.e.), which does not reflect rabbinic halakha (*EncJud* 4.4, 194; 12.1145–46). A survey of the former's rules will confirm the disparity. The menstruant is forbidden to boil, bake, or sift in the preparation of food for her husband. She may not pour water for him from an earthen vessel or strip the bed. She may not sit with the members of her household around the table or place her hand in the dish with them. It is forbidden to fill a cup of wine to give her a drink. It is forbidden to greet her or look at her. It is forbidden to recite a blessing in her presence lest she respond with Amen and desecrate the name of God. She may not enter a house full of sacred books, or a house prepared for prayer. She may not comb her hair or pare her nails by her bed, lest they fall on the floor and are trod upon by her husband or children. A man is forbidden to walk after a menstruant or to tread her dust because it is impure.

These regulations for the menstruant are refuted by the Babylonian Talmud, which states categorically that a menstruant may attend to all of the needs of her household, with the exception of filling her husband's cup of wine, making his bed, and washing him (*b. Ketub.* 61a). In the homeland, however, severer restrictions were imposed. The biblical doctrine that the land of Canaan was holy (H) led to the principle, adopted by many of the pious, that the laws of purity observed in the sanctuary should prevail in the Land (tentatively, see the INTRODUCTION, §E). Moreover, after the destruction of the Temple and, indeed, with the encouragement of the rabbis, the same purity rules were transferred into the home and its occupants were urged to come to the dining table in a state of purity. Hence, it is no wonder that in the rabbinic statements stemming from the Holy Land, a harsher attitude toward the menstruant prevailed. She was quarantined in a special house known as "a house for impurities (or impurity bearers)" (*m. Nid.* 7:4); indeed, Josephus affirms that she was isolated (*Ant.* 3.261); she was called *galmûdâ* 'segregated' (Rabbi Akiba, *Roš. Haš.* 26a); it was forbidden to eat with a menstruant (*t. Šabb.* 1:14), nor was she permitted to attend to her household duties even before she was totally segregated (*'Abot. R. Nat.* I, 1:4). A Qumran text, as yet unpublished, warns the menstruant *WBKWL MWDH* [*'L*] *TT'RB BŠB'T YMYH B'BWR 'ŠR L[W]' TG'L 'T M[Ḥ]NY QD[WŠY] YŚR'L* 'During her seven days (impurity) she should (strive) with all her might [not] to intermingle lest she defile the c[amps] of the hol[y ones] of Israel" (4QThr A1:5-6). If my reconstruction of this text is correct, it confirms my interpretation of 11QT 48:14-17, that the Qumran sectaries did not banish the menstruant—an extreme they applied only to the scale-diseased person—but quarantined her within their community (details in Milgrom 1978b: 512-18). Thus, in this respect, they advocated the severer procedure that obtained among their Jewish brethren in the Holy Land.

Be that as it may, ideological differences between Babylonia and Palestine do not explain the severities of the latter. In fact, Babylonia was not exempt from the morbid terror of being in the presence of a menstruant. For example: "If a menstruant woman passes between two [men], if it is at the beginning of her menses, she will slay one of them, and if it is at the end of her menses, she will cause strife between them" (*b. Pesaḥ.* 111a). Moreover, menstrual blood was regarded as a powerful charm: "If a woman sees a snake . . . she should take some of her hair and fingernails and throw them at it and say, 'I am menstruous' " (*b. Šabb.* 110a; further examples in Dinari 1979–80: 310–11). Thus it was the fear of menstrual blood as the repository of demonic forces that, most likely, caused the ostracism of the menstruant. In other words, we are dealing with a worldwide male psychological phenomenon.

The abhorrence of the menstruant is a cardinal rule among all primitive societies. The impurity extends to things she touches such as eating and cooking utensils, weapons, food, and even footpaths. The effects can be deleterious: crop failures, disease, military defeat, hunting failures (Frazer 1911–15: 3.145–47). The result is that she is isolated. Each Ndembu and Nuer village has at least one grass hut near the edge of the bush for menstruants (Turner 1967: 78; Evans-Pritchard 1951: 125; for the Coorg of India, see Srinivas 1952). Primitives do not confuse catamenial flow with other blood loss. "The menstrual discharge, before it leaves the woman's body is an embryonic human being, which is alive and which, were it not expelled, would assume a human form . . . but what terrifies the Maoris is that it nevertheless continues to live, but as the dead live, as a spirit" (Levy-Bruhl 1935: 313). Perhaps Monica Wilson's description of the menstrual taboos of the Nyakyusa best conveys the obsessive fears that motivate them:

> Contact with menstrual blood or a menstruating woman is held to be dangerous to a man, more particularly to a warrior, hence there is an absolute taboo on intercourse during menstruation (for five to eight days) and restrictions on cooking for a man. A menstruating woman does not blow up the fire on which her husband's food is cooking, or squeeze the food to test whether it is ready, or scrape ash off bananas or sweet potatoes she has roasted, or serve food, for "her breath comes from her belly and it is dirty; her belly is dirty on account of the menstrual blood. All her body is dirty. She does not wash. When she washes, you, the husband, think that the flow has dried up and catch hold of her!" So a woman who is menstruating fans the fire instead of blowing it, and calls a co-wife or a child to serve the food she has cooked. She does not even crouch over the fire to warm herself, lest she contaminate it; and she neither uses the common calabash cup for drinking nor scoops water from the household water jar with her hand, but fashions a cup for herself from a leaf, or has her own little water-pot. She avoids passing behind or shaking hands with a man; she avoids a new-born infant; she keeps well away from cattle, neither passing behind them when they are in the homestead nor clearing out dung from the byre; she avoids touching medicines or entering the house of a doctor; and she avoids eating pumpkin or pumpkin leaves, or picking them. These taboos are enforced lest she injure men or infants or cattle or medicines, for "she is dirty" and her "dirt" is thought to cause purging and to rot medicines, and she, for her part, fears lest the medicines with which men protect themselves and their cattle may injure her, causing her menstrual flow to "last a whole month." (1957: 131–32)

Israel's neighbors were similarly obsessed, if in more sophisticated ways. In Egypt, there is no evidence that the menstruant was regarded as dangerously impure except in contact with the sacred. An inscription of the Ptolemaic period (*RA* 2 [1883]: 181; *RA* 13 [1889]: 70ff.) states that "people who had become impure through sexual intercourse (Herod. 2.64), birth, miscarriage, menstruation, etc. had to pay dues before being admitted into the temple at Ptolemais. These were apparently paid into a money-box at the entrance to the temple" (Blackman 1951: 481). Possibly, the money box was a "slot machine"; the inserted coin would release water for purification (ibid.). The temple at Esna laid down a rule that those who wished to enter were required to be washed, purified, properly dressed, and to have abstained from sex for at least one day (Sauneron 1962: 480). The washing, however, was generally not in the form of a bath. Reliefs of the Pharaoh or the priests taking their ablutions show water being poured over them through a spout (Bleeker 1966).

In Mesopotamia, the terms *musukkatu* and possibly *ḫarištu* can refer either to a parturient or to a menstruant. Despite the paucity of evidence, it is clear that the menstruant was considered defiled and defiling: "If a man touches a *musukkatu* woman who is passing by, for six days he will not [be pure]"; "Water into which no *ḫarištu* has descended, no *musukatta* has washed her hands" (*CAD*, 10.239); "As for a woman of the harem for whom intercourse is forbidden *(ša lā qarabšani)*, she may not come into the presence of the king" (Weidner 1954–56: 276, lines 46–47; cf. *CAD*, Q 233b). The kind of ablutions required for worship is not clear. Both verbs, *mesû* 'wash [the hands]' and *ramāku* 'bathe', are attested. For example: "If you enter the temple of Ishtar with your hands unwashed, you (invalidate what you have done)" (Wiseman 1953: 63, lines 38–40). Yet officiants would bathe before offering the sacrifice (*ANET*³ 33a; 331b; 332a; 339a) and for certain ceremonies a ritual bath house, the *bît rimki*, was set up for this purpose (Laessøe 1955). There is even less evidence for the impurity of the menstruant in Hittite society, for the texts as yet have not revealed a word for menstruation. It is, however, significant that *arma-* 'moon' is associated with sickness and weakness as well as with pregnancy and menstruation (Moyer 1969: 70).

The impurity of menstruation was also accepted by the Arabs (*Koran* 2:222; cf. Smith 1927: 447–48). There is more precise information from southern Arabia that not only is the menstruant considered impure but anyone who cohabited with her or even touched her was required to bathe (*ANET*³ 665; see the NOTE on v 17). There is more information on the menstruant from the Hellenistic world. Beliefs concerning her malevolent power abound. Even an Aristotle affirms that the menstruant dims the mirror in front of which she stares, and Pliny claims that she blights agriculture and rusts tools (details in Parker 1983: 102–3). Purification, however, is required of her only as a condition for entering a temple, and then it is found exclusively in late texts. Earlier ones, surprisingly, while banishing the parturient from the temple, say nothing about a menstruant (e.g., the Cyrene cathartic law, Parker 1983: 336, lines 16–20). This fact has led one authority to write, "In the *hieroi nomoi* of the Greek temples we might have expected to find under this head (pollution) some rule of tabu concerning menstruous women, about whom the code of Leviticus is anxiously severe; but no direct evidence touching this matter has yet been found, and probably none will be; for the Greek religious mind was more easy and tolerant than the Hebrew, and the vast number of priestesses would make the application of any such rule very different" (Farnell 1951: 486). Farnell may be right concerning the Greek position, but on Leviticus he is dead wrong; see below.

Rabbinic tradition asserts that the Zoroastrians were chaste in sexual matters (*b. Ber.* 8b), and centuries later Maimonides writes that "the (Zoroastrian) menstruating woman remains isolated in her house; the places upon which she treads are burned; whoever speaks with her becomes impure; and if a wind that blows passes over a menstruating woman and a pure individual, the latter becomes impure" (Guide 3.47). Maimonides' information is confirmed by Zoroastrian texts. The menstruant is isolated during her period plus an extra day. She must avoid touching or even looking at others. She is not allowed to touch food with her bare hands, thereby contaminating it, but must eat wearing gloves. When she goes to her chamber, which is apparently located outside the home, dust is spread on the ground along her path, so that she will not directly touch the ground. She must not walk out in the rain, and thus contaminate it. Her look can even defile the sun, moon, and stars (Culpepper 1974). Hindu taboos are just as strict. Whoever cohabits with a menstruant loses his vitality and wisdom (Manu 4.40–41). Touching or even seeing a menstruant is defiling (Manu 5.85–86). Of course, menstruants are barred from temples (Ferro-Luzzi 1974).

In Israel, the attitude to the menstruant may not have been very much different. There is very little evidence, but some non-Priestly biblical verses point in that direction: "You will treat as impure the silver overlay of your images and the golden plating of your idols. You will cast them out like a menstrous woman (*dāwâ;* cf. Lev 12:2; 15:33). 'Out!' you will call to them" (Isa 30:22). "They shall throw their silver into the streets, and their gold shall be treated as a *niddâ* . . . therefore I will make them (the adornments) into a *niddâ* (Ezek 7:19–20). Thus the menstruant *(niddâ)* not only was isolated; she was ostracized and abhorred. "The Lord has summoned against Jacob his enemies all about him; Jerusalem has become among them a *niddâ*" (Lam 1:17). "The land that you are about to possess is *niddâ* through (the) *niddat* (of) the peoples of the land, through their abhorrent practices with which they, in their impurity, have filled it from one end to the other" (Ezra 9:11). The menstruant, therefore, is a metaphor for extreme pollution, ultimate revulsion.

Against this backdrop of Israel's immediate and remote contemporaries and what was probably the dominant practice within Israel itself (see above), the Priestly legislation on the menstruant is all the more remarkable. First and foremost, she is neither banished from the community nor even isolated within her home. The implicit assumption of the pericope on the menstruant is that she lives at home, communicating with her family and performing her household chores. How is this possible, considering the severity of her impurity: even more than the *zāb*, she can contaminate an object she does not even touch if her bed or seat connect them (v 23)! The answer, the ingenious answer of the legislators, was to restrict her impurity to that which was underneath her, in effect, whatever might receive a drop of menstrual blood. Of course, she herself was rendered impure and, in turn, could render persons and objects impure. Thus anyone touching her is contaminated (v 19b). But what if she touches someone? The text is silent. It was not silent on this matter in the case of the *zāb*. It stated explicitly that anyone he touches becomes impure but only if he does so with unrinsed hands (v 11). The conclusion is inescapable: the menstruant may touch (though Qumran thought otherwise: see the NOTE on "launder his clothes," v 7). As long as she is scrupulous about rinsing her hands, she may clean the house, cook and serve the food, and perform whatever other chores she desires. All she needs is a separate bed, a separate chair, and the discretion to stay out of her family's reach. Thus the lenient rulings recorded in the Babylonian Talmud, cited above, are in complete agreement with the biblical text. Technically, even the rabbis' few restrictions—filling her husband's cup of wine, making his bed, and even washing him—could be performed without contaminating him. But the evidence from other texts, rabbinic and nonrabbinic alike, indicates that the people at large and many of their spiritual leaders, particularly in Palestine, rejected these leniencies, even though they were rooted in the Torah. The attitude to the menstruant continued to be dominated by fear.

Finally, it should be noted that in ancient times (and, indeed, until the present age) women did not menstruate frequently during their childbearing years: "Menstruation as we know it today is largely a product of contraception and of an increase in the number of childbearing years. Until this century, most women spent the years between their first menses around the age of 14 and their menopause at age 35 or 40 either pregnant or breastfeeding. Today, improved nutrition and health care have pushed the onset of first menses earlier, to about age 12, and delayed menopause until about age 50" (Henig 1982: 65). Furthermore, it is clear from biblical passages (cf. 1 Sam 1:22–24; Isa 7:15; 28:9–10; 2 Macc 7:27) that mothers nursed their children up to three years, resulting in the suppression of the menses (evidence collected in Gruber 1987. n. 40). The implication of this evidence is that the biblical woman, who was generally in a state of pregnancy or nursing, was rarely excluded from participating in the cult.

B. The Communicability of Impurity, by David P. Wright

The following diagrams and an explanatory preface are taken from Wright's doctoral dissertation, which ingeniously employs a "trees" device to illustrate the complexities of impurity transmission. I have indicated the relevant biblical verses on the branches. Also appended are my comments on the first three diagrams: the *zāb*, the menstruant, and the *zābâ*. Wright's says,

> I have devised "trees" to illustrate the communicability of impurity so that it may be comprehended in a glance. Each tree consists of the "father" of uncleanness, to use rabbinic terminology, with branches showing "offspring" of impurities. Certain sigla are used to denote whether an offspring is human or inanimate, in what way the person or object was contacted, the manner in which they are purified and the duration of the impurity. Deductions are bracketed and deduced branches occur with dashed lines.

For greater detail (particularly in the rabbinic system) and extensive explanatory notes, see Wright 1987: 179–219).

Key to sigla in the charts of figs. 15–30:

a	denotes the "father" contacting the "offspring" in the described manner
b	denotes the "offspring" contacting the "father" in the described manner
B	a bed (Heb. *miškāb*)
br	breaking, of earthenware vessels
c	contact by carrying
e	contact by eating
F	purification of metal utensils by fire
i	contact by sexual intercourse
l	contact by lying on something
L	laundering one's clothes *(kibbēs)*
o	overhang, contracting impurity by being in the same enclosure with an impurity
P	a person
r	contact by riding
s	contact by sitting
sp	contact by spitting
spr	contact by sprinkling
S	a saddle *(merkāb)*
T	a thing, object
t	contact by touch
u	contact by something being under someone
W	washing, bathing for people, rinsing or immersing for utensils
wp	purification by the water of purgation
x	indefinite length of impurity

()   in parentheses are the requirements for purification and the duration of the impurity

(1)   a one-day impurity

(7)   a seven-day impurity

[]   brackets indicate a deduction

....   a dotted line indicates a deduced branch

The following impurities are not diagrammed in the charts:

The parturient in her first stage of impurity. Source: Lev 12. The tree of this impurity would be drawn like the menstruant's.

A person suspected of ṣāraʿat. Source: Lev 13, esp. vv 4, 5, 6, 21, 26, 31, 33, 34. This impurity would be no more severe than one diagnosed as having ṣāraʿat.

Fabrics with ṣāraʿat. Source: Lev 13:47–59. Probably polluted on the analogy of a house with ṣāraʿat.

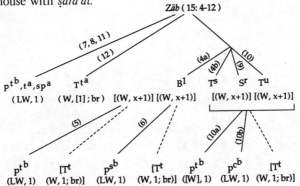

Sources: Lev 15: 2-25; f. 22: 4-6; Num 5; 2-3

FIGURE 15

    The zāb. (1) The impurity period for the zāb's bedding, seat, saddle, or anything under him should be x, not x + 1. Unlike the scale-diseased person, the zāb does not bathe on the first day of his purificatory period, so the objects under him retain their impurity until he bathes on the seventh day. Then these objects also are washed and are ready for use by evening.

    (2) According to my interpretation of v 10a, the seat and saddle share the same degree of impurity, in that anyone who touches them need only bathe. Therefore the bracket under Sʳ and Tᵘ should be extended to Tˢ and the branches extending from them should appear as in fig. 16.

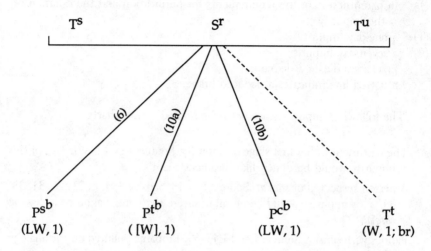

FIGURE 16

See now Wright (1987: 188), who revises his *zāb* diagram in accordance with correction (2). (But his diagram for the person touching the *zāb*'s bed should read LW, not [W].)

The menstruant. (1) The bracketed tᵃ and Tᵗᵃ (branches 1 and 2 for the menstruant and Pⁱ) should be stricken; the menstruant does not impart impurity by touch if she first washes her hands. Also, the person who touches her need not launder (see the NOTE on "whosoever touches her," v 19). Even if the menstruant were subject to the law of the *zāb* (v 11), her touch would still not contaminate if she first washed her hands (see the NOTE on "during her menses," v 20).

(2) Every $(x + 1)$ should read (x); see remark (1) on the *zāb*, above.

(3) According to the interpretation of v 23 (see the NOTE on "it"), the end of the fourth branch should be redrawn (see now Wright 1987: 192) as in fig. 18.

The zābâ. (1) Every $(x + 1)$ should read (x); see remark (1) on the *zāb*, above.

(2) Following v 27 LXX (the preferred reading; see the NOTE on "them," v 27), the tree remains the same but three branches have to be redrawn: branch 1, *zābâ* to Pᵗᵇ, becomes a solid line and the sigla should now read Pᵗᵇ, [ta, spᵃ], and the solid lines B¹–Pᵗᵇ and Tˢ–Pᵗᵇ (branch 4) should now be broken.

(3) The lines from B¹ and Tˢ should accord with the revised diagram of the menstruant (see now Wright 1987: 194–95).

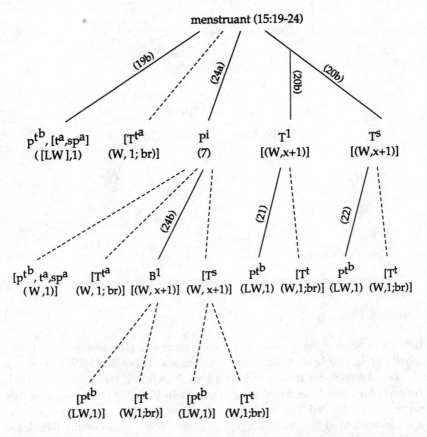

FIGURE 17

C. Ablutions

The religious valorization of ablutions has been neatly capsuled by Eliade: "Emersion repeats the cosmogonic act of formal manifestation; *immersion* is equivalent to a dissolution of forms. This is why the symbolism of the water implies both death and rebirth. Contact with water always brings a regeneration —on the one hand because dissolution is followed by a new birth, on the other because immersion fertilizes and multiplies the potential for life" (1959: 130). Eliade's definition certainly holds true for primitive societies. For example, "Nearly everywhere they (the Euahlayi aborigines) 'cleanse themselves' from

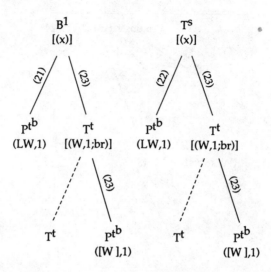

[provided T and menstruants of these bottom legs are simultaneously on B¹Tˢ]

FIGURE 18

defilement (such as being present at funeral ceremonies, for instance), by taking a bath, preferably in running water or in the sea" (Levy-Bruhl 1935: 345).

It also obtains for the ancient Near East. Nowhere is this double, ostensibly contradictory effect, of water so apparent as in Egypt: "Thus the same Nile waters both cleansed and vivified—a phenomenon that seems to have profoundly influenced the ancient Egyptian's ideas about purification" (Blackman 1951: 476). One can safely say that the Egyptians were obsessed with ablutions. "Morning ablutions were so much a matter of course that a 'wash' (ꜥiꜥw) is not an uncommon term for a light morning repast—a *petit déjeuner* doubtless being served directly [after] the morning toilet had been completed" (ibid.). Washing of the hands and feet was performed during the day. Meals were also preceded by handwashing: "Even before drinking a cup of beer, a man would have his hands washed by his wife" (ibid. 477).

The religious function of water in ancient Egypt is best exemplified in the life of the Pharaoh. In infancy he underwent a ceremony of being sprinkled with water. "This rite was intended to transfer to the Pharaoh a goodly portion of the power of the divinities who presided over the four quarters of the globe" (Gardiner 1950: 12). At his coronation, this ceremony was renewed. The priest, impersonating the god, thus addressed the king: "I purify thee with the water of all life and good fortune, all stability, all health and happiness" (ibid. 478). In scenes of both ceremonies the water issues from the vessels as strings of beads, each in the form of the *ankh,* the symbol of life (Gardiner 1950; Ringgren

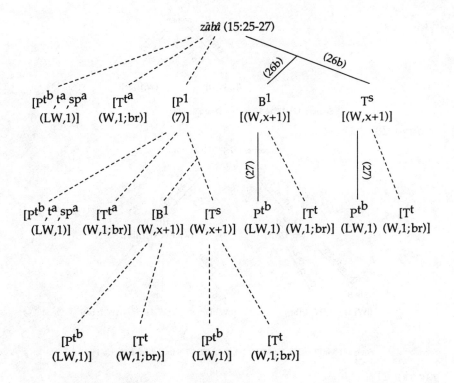

Sources: Lev 15:25-30, 33

FIGURE 19

1986). Washing was mandatory in every temple rite: the sacrifice, the altar, the temple, the priest, and the worshiper were sprinkled with water. Every temple possessed a sacred pond for this purpose: "the sacred water, like the primordial sea from which the world came in the beginning, is regenerative: whoever is sprinkled with it feels himself invaded by a new power, raised from this life below to the eternal world where the gods reside" (Sauneron 1960: 79). Nowhere is this purificatory and regenerative power of water so powerfully demonstrated as in the multiple ablutions performed upon the dead to assure them of the afterlife (see Blackman 1951: 478–79).

The realization that v 23 deals with a case of a person touching an object on the menstruant's bedding or seat at the same time she is on it is responsible for the addition of two new branches, P^{tb} to T^t, and for correcting broken lines B^1 to T^t and T^s to T^t into unbroken ones. The same changes are also indicated for the branches stemming from P^i because the force of his impurity duplicates that of the menstruant (v 24).

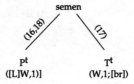

Sources: Lev 15: 16-18; cf. 22:4; Deut 23:10-12.

FIGURE 20

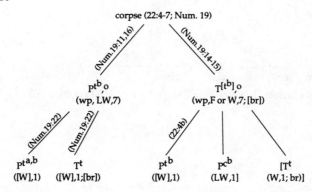

Sources: Num19: cf. Lev 10: 4-5; 21: 1-4, 10-12; 22: 4-7 Num 5: 2-3;6: 6-12; 9: 6-14; 31: 13-24.

FIGURE 21

Water's polaric powers to purify and regenerate are also attested in Mesopotamian religion. The righteous sufferer "was sprinkled with water for purification" (Lambert 1960: 60, line 88). The *bārû* priest (diviner) prays "while purifying his mouth and hands with water" (*BBR* 212, nos. 96.3; 96.7). As in Egypt, the sacrifice, temple, altar, and worshiper are all sprinkled, while the worshipers either bathe or wash their hands with water (*ANET*[3] 331–41): "Quickly, fetch me water for my hands, and give it to me so that I can sacrifice to my God" (Lambert 1960: 147, lines 54–55). Indeed, the gods themselves bathe in sea water or fresh water for their purification (Reiner 1958: 47, ix, lines 63, 74). A bewitched person prays: "I present water to the gods of the heavens. As I purify you, yes you, so purify me, yes me!" (Meier 1937: 9, Ia, lines 47–49; cf. the Šurpu incantation below).

The magical component of purification is especially apparent in exorcisms: "Cast the water of the incantation *(mê šipti)* over him"; "Put water upon the man and pour forth the water of the incantation. . . . As the water trickleth away from his body so may the pestilence in his body trickle away" (Thompson 1903–14: 2.73, ix, lines 36–90; 109, rev. 4–9; cf. 95, lines 65–69).

Water is not inherently a cathartic of evil except when it is taken from the proper source and charged with the proper incantations; for example:

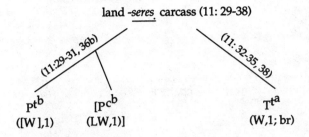

land *-seres* carcass (11: 29-38)

Sources: Lev 11:29-38; cf. Lev 5:2; 7:21; 22:5-6

FIGURE 22

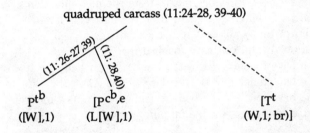

quadruped carcass (11:24-28, 39-40)

Sources: Lev 11:4-8, 24-26, 27-28, 39-40; 17:15-16

FIGURE 23

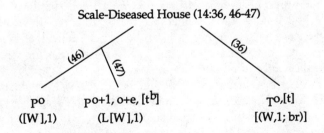

Scale-Diseased House (14:36, 46-47)

Sources: Lev 14:36, 46-47

FIGURE 24

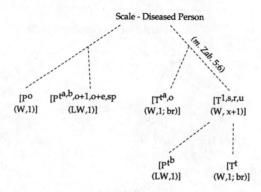

Sources: Cf. Lev 13,14; 22: 4; Num 5: 2-3

FIGURE 25

High waters! Flowing straight from the high mountains,
waters, flowing out straight from the pure Euphrates,
born of the Apsû, dealing out everything,
born of Eridu, you have touched the . . . ,
you have touched the cedar, you have [touched] the tree of Ḫašur,
you have touched Enki, the king of the Apsû, the pure one,
you have touched the body of (this) man, son of his god,
made him clean, made him pure; / may the evil tongue [stand] aside!"
(Reiner 1958: 49, ix, lines 119–28)

Where an image of the sorcerer is improvised, water will wash off the hex impurity from the victim on to the image (Meier 1937: 49–51; vii; lines 81–82, 119–37; 63, ix, lines 153–92; Laessøe 1955: 37–47).

The resuscitative powers of water are also in evidence: "he (Namtar) sprinkled the waters of life upon Ishtar" (*ANET*³ 1955: 108, line 38; cf. 102, line 62). And it is not without significance that in Akk. *mû*, the word for water, is also the word for semen. Above all, it should be recalled that in Mesopotamian cosmogony, primordial matter is Apsû and Tiamat, fresh and salt water; that is, water, the source of all life.

The Hittite religious experience duplicates the Mesopotamian. Temple personnel, from priests to servants, must bathe before engaging in ritual preparations: "When a servant is to stand before his master, he is bathed and clothed in clean (garments)" (*ANET*³ 207, I, line 24; cf. 209, III, line 63). If the bath is neglected, and the person is in a state of impurity (e.g., he had sexual intercourse the night before), it is a capital crime (ibid. 209, III, lines 69–85). Before the king officiates, he bathes (ibid.: 355, lines 27, 31). When the king and queen enter the temple and periodically during the ritual, they rinse their hands (ibid. 359–60, II, lines 11–12, 16–18; IV, lines 1–2; VI, lines 18–22).

Purifying Scale-Diseased Person

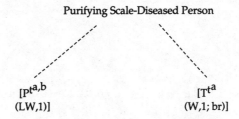

[P^{ta,b}\
(LW,1)]

[T^{ta}\
(W,1; br)]

Sources: Lev 14:8-10; cf. Comment F

FIGURE 26

In ancient Greece, hands were washed before libation and sacrifice. Everyone entering a temple would dip his hands in a vessel set up at the entrance and sprinkle himself with water (Burkert 1985: 77). At the altar, a second washing takes place; water is poured over the hands of each participant in turn. The animal too is sprinkled with water (ibid. 56). The images of the gods were also bathed, either carried to the sea in an annual procession or in emergencies when the temple was defiled (ibid. 75). Ritual washing is attested as early as Homer, before prayer (*Iliad* 6.266–68; 9.171–72; 24.305) and before sacrifices, not just by washing the hands (*Odyssey* 3.440) but by bathing (*Iliad* 1.449) and changing clothes (*Iliad* 4.750–52).

Eliade's understanding of the ritual power of water is totally absent in the Bible. Water is not regenerative, only purificatory, and even in the latter aspect it is devoid of any magical component. That is, water purifies not inherently but only by the will of God.

This radical difference between Israel and its neighbors was accomplished by some major changes in the function and meaning of the ablution. First of all, the ablution is a wordless ceremony; it is unaccompanied by prayer. Second, water for the bath is never qualified by *ṭāhôr* 'pure'. In fact, of the thirty-six times that P calls for bathing with water, only once does the attribute *ḥayyîm* 'spring, running [water]' appear (15:13). Nonetheless, it is always present when the waters convey the purifying agent (the compound of blood, hyssop, cedar, and scarlet for purifying the scale-diseased person, the fungous house, and the corpse-contaminated person (14:5–6, 50–53; Num 19:6, 12). Here, however, *mayim ḥayyîm* is an ingredient in an ancient theurgic recipe, a vestige of and a link to pre-Israelite rituals, shown to be originally exorcistic rites (see chap. 4, COMMENT G). Above all, whereas Israel's contemporaries employ purifications as a prerequisite for healing, Israelite law and practice indicate that purification always follows healing. The result: impurity has been eviscerated of any innate— that is, magical—power. In the Priestly system, as we have observed, purificatory rites are enjoined upon parturients and persons with scale disease and genital discharges only after they are healed.

This rule also holds true for the rest of Scripture. There are two ostensible

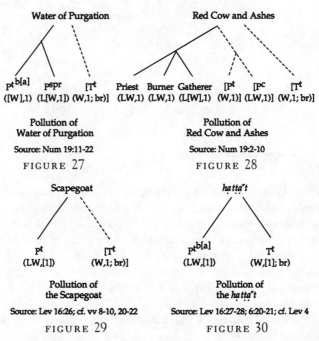

Pollution of
Water of Purgation

Source: Num 19:11-22

FIGURE 27

Pollution of
Red Cow and Ashes

Source: Num 19:2-10

FIGURE 28

Pollution of
the Scapegoat

Source: Lev 16:26; cf. vv 8-10, 20-22

FIGURE 29

Pollution of
the *ḥaṭṭāʾt*

Source: Lev 16:27-28; 6:20-21; cf. Lev 4

FIGURE 30

exceptions, but they evaporate on examination. The Aramaean general, Naaman, is cured of scale disease by immersing himself seven times in the Jordan. Here the verb *ṭāhar* means "cure" (2 Kgs 5:10–14), in contrast to the Priestly writings (see the NOTE on "healing," 14:2; and chap. 13, COMMENT A). Yet the main point of the narration is entirely missed unless it is realized that we are dealing here with a polemic against idolatry. After all, Naaman is sent into the Jordan by the Lord's prophet, advice that both disappoints and entraps Naaman because "I thought," he said, "he (the prophet) would surely come out to me, and would stand and invoke the Lord his God by name, and would wave his hand toward the spot, and cure the affected part" (2 Kgs 5:11). Herein lies the thrust of the story. Elisha wanted to demonstrate that Israel's God operates not through incantations and gesticulations, which would render him dependent on the metadivine realm of magic—an axiomatic principle in all polytheistic systems (Kaufmann 1960: 21–24). To the contrary, Israel's God is superior to all other gods in that the universe, his creation, responds to his will. The humble Jordan—not the mightier "Amanah and Pharpar, the rivers of Damascus" (2 Kgs 5:12) will heal Naaman, not by magic but only by the Lord's word as mediated through his prophet. The proof that this is the intent of Naaman's cure is demonstrated by the sequel—Naaman converts. More than just admitting the Lord to his pantheon—what a polytheist would be expected to do—Naaman declares his exclusive loyalty to the Lord: "For your servant will never again offer up burnt offering or well-being offering to any god, except the Lord" (ibid., v 17). A simple dip in the Jordan, minus incantation and gesticulation, has convinced Naaman that the Lord is superior to all other gods (for further theological implications of this story, see Milgrom 1983f).

The second ostensible exception is contained in the Priestly writings: the ordeal of the suspected adulteress (Num 5:1–31). Here there can be no denying that the waters she is forced to drink work magically: if she is guilty they will cause her thigh to sag and belly to distend (i.e., become barren), and if innocent, she will be fertile. Yet once it is realized that the point of the ordeal is to provide a "cooling off" period and thereby prevent her being lynched by her husband and community, then the ordeal makes complete sense within the Priestly system (details in Milgrom 1981g). Even here the legists made sure that the waters would not be credited with innate powers by interpolating a verse—patently rupturing the sequence—that ascribes these powers solely to the Lord (v 21).

Turning our attention to ritual ablution in Scripture, it can be shown that there is no difference whatever between Priestly and non-Priestly texts regarding its modus operandi. Focusing first on the non-Priestly texts, we note that the key word is *hitqaddēš*, literally, "sanctify oneself," which is the non-Priestly technical term for purification through bathing in preparation for receiving the presence of the Lord the following day, either in the sanctuary or in a theophany.

The locus classicus for this phenomenon is the theophany at Sinai. In preparation for this event Moses is commanded, "Go to the people and sanctify them *(wĕqiddaštām)* today and tomorrow. Let them launder their clothes; for on the third day the Lord will come down in the sight of all the people on Mount Sinai. . . . Moses came down from the mountain to the people and sanctified *(wayyĕqaddēš)* the people and they laundered their clothes . . . and he said to the people: 'Be ready for the third day: do not go near a woman' " (Exod 19:10–15). This text certifies that the sanctification is accompanied by laundering and that sexual congress (causing impurity, cf. 15:18; 1 Sam 21:5–6) is forbidden. The Priestly texts that consistently conjoin bathing and laundering (e.g., 15:5–11, 21–22, 27) lead one to suspect that the term *hitqaddēš* in the epic narratives refers to the ritual bath of purification, a supposition that is supported by the story of David and Bathsheba: "He saw from the roof a woman bathing . . . she was sanctifying herself *(mitqaddešet)* from her (menstrual) impurity" (2 Sam 11:2, 4).

The time element involved in this "sanctification" can be clarified by a few examples: (1) Before crossing the Jordan, "Joshua said to the people: 'Sanctify yourselves *(hitqaddāšû)*, for *tomorrow* the Lord will do wonders among you' " (Josh 3:5). Thus for the waters of the Jordan to rise up miraculously "in a heap" (Josh 3:16; cf. Exod 15:8)—that is, for God's presence to be operative in the sight of all Israel—the entire people have to sanctify themselves on the preceding day. (2) Later, during the crisis at Ai, the command is issued: "Sanctify yourselves *(hitqaddĕšû)* for *tomorrow*. . . . *In the morning* you will come forward tribe by tribe, and the tribe that the Lord marks out with the lot . . ."

(Josh 7:13–14). The casting of lots no less than the miracle of the crossing requires the immediacy of God—but on condition that Israel is sufficiently holy to receive him. Again, their purification takes place the day preceding the revelation. (3) One of the oldest sources speaks of Jacob's pilgrimage to Bethel in similar terms: "Rid youselves of the alien gods in your midst, purify yourselves *(wĕhiṭṭahărû),* and change your clothes. Let us promptly go up to Bethel and I will build an altar there to God" (Gen 35:2–3). Thus the arrival at the sacred site of Bethel—obviously on the next day (vv 5–6)—must be preceded by bathing *(hithpaʿel* of *ṭāhēr* means "bathe"; cf. Num 8:7) and by new garments (the equivalent of laundering). (4) God commands Moses: "Say to the people 'sanctify yourselves *(hitqaddĕšû) for tomorrow,* and you shall eat meat.' . . . And a wind from the Lord started up, swept quail from the sea" (Num 11:18, 31). Thus the miracle of the quail is a theophany, requiring purification the day before. (5) "When a round of feast days was over, Job would send word to them (his children) to sanctify themselves *(wayyĕqaddĕšēm),* and rising early in *the morning,* he would sacrifice burnt offerings" (Job 1:5). Again, sacrifice requires sanctification, via ablutions, on the preceding day.

Thus, the common denominator in all of these examples is that bathing (and laundering) must take place on the day before one is admitted into the presence of the Lord. It can therefore be assumed that when Korah and his cohorts are commanded to appear before the Lord *in the morning* (Num 16:5, 7, 16), they must undergo ablutions before nightfall. And conversely, when the elders of Bethlehem together with Jesse and his sons are commanded by Samuel to sanctify themselves *(hitqaddĕšû)* before participating with him in the sacrifice, and then Samuel personally sanctifies *(wayĕqaddēš)* Jesse and his sons so that they will be eligible for the sacrifice (1 Sam 16:5), we can be certain that the sacrifice indeed took place the following morning. Finally, when God commands Moses "Be ready *(nākôn) by morning,* and *in the morning* come up to Mount Sinai and present yourself to me" (Exod 34:2), the reason Moses is not permitted to ascend at once is that he must first purify himself through ablutions the day before (cf. also 1 Chr 15:12, 14; 2 Chr 29:5, 15, 30; 30:3, 17).

It occasions no surprise, therefore, that the command to gather in the Temple for solemn fasts contains the imperative *qaddĕšû* (Joel 1:14; 2:15–17). When the same imperative *(qaddĕšû)* is used in regard to the worship of the Canaanite god, Baal, we must assume that it is a call to prior purification (2 Kgs 10:20). Certainly, the surreptitious cults involving the consumption of forbidden animals required their devotees initially to "sanctify and purify themselves" (Isa 66:17). The same rules obtained in the war camp. If a soldier "has been rendered impure by a nocturnal emission, he must leave the camp, and he must not reenter the camp. Toward evening he shall bathe in water, and at sundown he may reenter the camp. . . . Because YHWH your God moves about in your camp . . . let your camp be holy" (Deut 23:11–15). Thus bathing is a prerequisite for purification. But in this case it is not enough. The war camp is holy;

additional time is needed for the residual impurity to wear off—the day must end—before the soldier can regain admittance. This deuteronomic prescription is entirely consonant with the Priestly system, which also enjoins waiting until nightfall for the impurity of nocturnal emissions to cease (15:16) and, as will be shown in COMMENT E below, the purpose is precisely that of the deuteronomic war camp: to allow access to the holy. Of course, sexual congress in the war camp is strictly forbidden (1 Sam 21:5–6; cf. 2 Sam 11:11). Thus, it is entirely logical that the expression to prepare for battle employs the verb *qiddēš* (e.g., Jer 6:4; Joel 4:9; Mic 3:5).

Finally, it should be noted that P and H never use the verb *qiddēš (piʿel)* or *hitqaddēš (hithpaʿel)* for ritual bathing. This is because P and H reserve the root *qdš* for sacred objects or persons and will only use it when a regimen of conduct is enjoined upon Israel that will endow all the people with a holy status (e.g., 11:44; 19:2; 20:26; Num 15:40). Hence they eschew the verb *qiddēš* 'sanctify' and employs the unambiguous verb *rāḥaṣ* 'wash' (e.g., 14:8–9; 15:5–13; 16:25, 28) or, in two cases, the verb *ṭāhēr* 'purify' (Num 8:7; 31:24).

Thus we find that the Priestly rule that the termination of impurity by sacrifice or nightfall must be preceded by a penultimate ablution is not of its own making. It is a hoary practice followed by all of the people. Moreover, the non-Priestly texts make it amply clear that the ablution by itself does not suffice to warrant admission to the sphere of the holy, but hinges upon the subsequent arrival of nightfall or the following day's sacrifice. One might suppose that if the ablution is insufficient to remove communicable impurity in relation to the holy, perhaps it is sufficient in relation to the profane. This speculation can be buttressed by some data.

The scale-diseased person undergoes two ablutions, on the first and seventh days. Moreover, they are vital to his rehabilitation to his community. Both ablutions are followed by the critical word *wĕṭāhēr* 'and he becomes pure' (14:8, 9). And the meaning of the term is clarified by the action that follows; after the first ablution he is admitted to the camp, and after the second, to his home. Thus, the ablutions function to remove layers of impurity to the profane world. As already intimated in the NOTES on these verses and as will be more fully developed in COMMENT F below, the first ablution eliminates his airborne impurity to the sanctuary so that he can thereafter reside in the camp. But he can still contaminate persons and objects by direct contact and, hence, must reside outside his tent until his second ablutions on the seventh day. The same factors are responsible for the regulation concerning the *zāb*. According to one tradition he is banished (Num 5:2–3), but according to another, he is permitted to remain in community and home on the condition that his touch does not transmit impurity if his hands are washed (see the NOTES on Lev 15:11). This leniency would apply to those with other genital discharges, the parturient, menstruant, and *zābâ*, enabling them as well to live at home (see the NOTES on vv 19, 20).

That the rabbis were aware of the efficacy of ablutions to eliminate successive layers or degrees of impurity can be deduced from some of their statements: for example, "Said Raba . . . on the view of the rabbis, *kêwān dĕṭābal qālšā ṭum'ātô* since he has immersed, his impurity has weakened" (*b. Me'il.* 8b on *m. Me'il.* 2:1). Is this notion an Israelite innovation attributable to Israel's priests? There is no direct evidence for it outside Israel. Yet as ablutions abound in the ancient Near East it is hard not to believe that wherever multiple ablutions were prescribed, their purpose was precisely the same—to eliminate impurity by degrees. Commenting on the Mesopotamian rite of *bît rimki* (lit., "bath house"), J. Laessøe writes, "It is suggested that by passing from chamber to chamber, terminating his stay in each with a ritual ablution of the hands . . . and in various ways transferring the evil influences threatening him to images of sorcerers, witches, etc., the king would gradually liquidate the power of witchcraft which had afflicted him, until when leaving the seventh chamber he would emerge freed from all obsessions" (1955: 85).

The probability is therefore strong that Israel's priests incorporated the ablution into their system—as they did with so many of their rites—by purging it of its magical puissance so that it no longer healed the sick or exorcised the bewitchment but instead progressively reduced ritual impurity so that its bearer could be rehabilitated with his community and reconciled with his God.

The rationale for impurity is discussed in COMMENT G below, and the impurity system in COMMENT F.

D. First-Day Ablutions in Qumran

In 1978, just after the publication of the Temple Scroll, I offered a solution to one of its perplexing innovations: ablutions for all impurity bearers on the first day of their purification. This is what I wrote:

A. Nocturnal Emission
If a m[an] has a nocturnal emission he shall not enter into the entire sacred area until he completes three days. He shall launder his clothes and bathe on the first day. On the third day he shall launder his clothes and bathe and after sunset he may enter the temple. They shall not enter my temple to pollute it with their impure flow (45:7–10).
B. Sexual Intercourse
If a man has sexual intercourse with his wife he shall not enter the entire Temple city, on which I shall cause my name to dwell, for three days (45:11–12; cf. CD 12:1–2).
C. Corpse Contamination
As for persons: whoever was in the house and whoever enters the house shall bathe in water and launder his clothes on the first day (49:16–17).

D. Corpse Contamination

If a woman is pregnant and her child dies in her womb . . . whoever enters the house with her shall be impure for seven days. He shall launder his clothes and bathe on the first day (50:10–14).

E. Corpse Contamination

After they have withdrawn from the slain toward the encampment. . . . In the morning they shall launder their garments, wash themselves of the blood of the guilty cadavers (1QM 14:2–3).

F. The Temple City

You shall set up three quarters east of the city at a distance from each other to receive those with scale disease and discharges, and men who have a seminal emission (46:16–18).

G. Other Cities

In every city you shall set up quarters for those afflicted with scale-disease affections and scalls so that they shall not enter your cities and pollute them. The same (should be done) for persons with discharges and for women in their menstrual impurity and in their parturition that they not pollute their surroundings with their impure flow (48:14–17).

The distinction between the ritual status of the Temple city and other cities is fundamental to the understanding of the purification system of the Temple Scroll. The most glaring distinction, one that ostensibly differs with Scripture, is that the Temple city requires a three-day purification rite for those who experience nocturnal emissions and have sexual intercourse (quotes A, B), whereas, according to the Torah, their impurity lasts only one day (Lev 15:16–18). However, as Yadin has correctly noted (1983: 1.223), the three-day purification imposed for the Temple city is modeled after the Sinaitic purification consisting of ablutions, laundering, and sexual abstinence (Exod 19:10–15). Thus, not only the mountain but also the camp, situated in its proximity, is endowed with a sacred status. Once the tabernacle is built it virtually becomes a portable Sinai, endowing the wilderness camp with Sinaitic sanctity (e.g., "Remove from the camp the scale diseased, discharging, and the corpse-contaminated person . . . so that they do not defile the camp of those in whose midst I dwell," Num 5:2–3). It is therefore only logical that in the land the city that houses the Temple will be endowed with an equal degree of holiness and will require the same ritual purification.

The above-cited passages from the Temple Scroll, however, reveal another aberration from the Torah that is not as easily resolved. Specifically, why does seminal emission in the Temple city require two ablutions, on the first and third days (A), and why does corpse contamination in any other city require ablutions on the first day (C, D, E)?

The answer I suggest is that each ablution serves a specific function: to remove a layer (or degree) of impurity. This, I submit, is the key to the ablution regimen in the Priestly Code of the Torah, a subject which, however, requires monographic treatment. Let it suffice for this paper to apply the hypothesis to the Temple Scroll.

Since the Temple city is holy it cannot tolerate impurity even of the slightest degree and all its residents who incur impurity of any kind are banished to special installations built for them east of the city (F). However, one ablution is not enough. It would suffice to reestablish non-sacred contacts with persons and objects (i.e., in the ordinary city), but to be admitted to the higher level of holiness of the Temple city an extra ablution is required.

The fact that the Temple Scroll increases the severity of the Torah's purificatory procedure regarding nocturnal emissions from one to three days is matched by its procedure for the purification of the scale-diseased person. According to the Torah, he performs ablutions (and other rituals) on the first and seventh days. After the first day he is permitted to enter the camp/city but not his home (Lev 14:8). However, the Scroll mandates that he spend all seven days of his purification outside the Temple city: "Anyone with scale disease or (other) afflictions shall not enter it (i.e. the Temple city) until they are purified. And when he is pure he shall sacrifice . . ." (45:17–18). Thus, whereas the scroll presumably will follow the Torah in allowing the healed leper to enter the camp/city after the first day ablutions, it does not permit him to enter the Temple city until the second set of ablutions on the seventh day. Since the scroll also requires two ablutions for someone incurring a nocturnal emission to enter the Temple city, it follows that two ablutions are a minimal requirement for admission into the Temple city.

For the sectaries of Qumran, the war camp also bears the same holy status as the Temple city. Its holiness can be deduced from the War Scroll which speaks of "holy angels" in the midst of the camp (1QM 7:5–6, modeled on Deut 23:15) and which prohibits those possessing physical defects from entering the camp (ibid., 4–5) just as the Temple Scroll prohibits the same persons from entering the Temple city (45:12–14). It is no less significant that the Qumran sectaries enjoin the same prohibition as an entrance requirement into the assembly of the sect in the messianic age (1QSa 2:4–11). The purification ceremony for soldiers returning from battle is also prescribed in the War Scroll (1QM 14:2–3) but, unfortunately, it is only partially preserved. Ablutions are required for the first day (E) and it must be assumed, with Yadin, that the sect also followed the Torah's injunction that the soldiers remain outside the camp for seven days until their purification is complete (Num 31:24). Again, this latter requirement would have given the author of the Temple Scroll an adequate reason for imposing it upon the analogue of the war camp, the Temple city.

When we turn to the ordinary city, we note that the ablutions function in the same way but because the city enjoys a different status—profane rather than holy—the consequences are different. First, two facts must be established: (1) nocturnal emission and corpse contamination are missing from the list of those impurity bearers who are expelled from the city (G), and (2) those incurring seminal emission or corpse contamination wash on the first day, as specified in the Torah (Lev 15:16–17) and in the Temple Scroll (C, D). These two facts are related and lead to but one conclusion: the purpose of the first-day ablution is to allow the impurity bearer to remain in the city. The implications of this conclusion need to be elaborated. The absence of the corpse-contaminated from the list of those quarantined or expelled (G) corresponds with the historical reality at the end of the Second Commonwealth. We know from Josephus (*Ant.* 3.261) and the Mishnah (*Nid.* 7:4) that those incurring severe impurity were quarantined or banished from the city. They are the scale-diseased, the gonorrheic *[zāb/ zābâ]*, and the parturient. Josephus claims that the corpse-contaminated required isolation (ibid., 262) but, as we have seen, it is not required by the Temple Scroll. How could the sectaries of Qumran have envisaged the corpse-contaminated to have free mobility within the city during the seven days of his impurity? The Temple Scroll has an answer: ablutions on the first day. These ablutions defuse the impurity of its contagious power and allow its bearers to remain in the city. (Milgrom 1978b: 512–18).

My solution has been confirmed (as first realized by Baumgarten 1980: 160) by the publication of a new Qumran fragment, 4QOrd^c (Baillet 1982: 295–98). It deals with the purification of the man with a genital discharge, the *zāb*. The text, translation, relevant notes, and conclusions follow:

1

Col. II   **Col. I**

[   ]‫ אשה‬‫[   ]ת‬

[   ]‫כב לכל·הס]פ[אים‬   ‫אל יאכל]‬

‫ואל]‬ ‫לספר ל]ו שבעת ימי ר]חץ ורחץ וכבס בי]ו[ם סהרת]ו‬

[‫יאכל] איש]אשר לא החל לסהור·ממק]ר]ו [וגם אל יאכל עד‬

5 ‫בסמאתו הרישתה וכל סמאי הימים ביום] ס]הרתם ירחצו‬

‫וכבסו במים וסהרו ≈≈≈ ואחר יאכלו את לחמם כמשפß ה]ס]הרה‬ [‫פ‬

‫ואל יאכל חõד בסמאתö הרישנהö אשר לא החל לסהור ממקרו‬

‫תם אל יאכל עד במסאתו הרישה וכל] ס]מֿאי הימם ביום‬ [‫פ‬

‫ס]הרת]ם ירחצו וכבסו במים וסהרו ואחר יאכלו את לחמם‬ [‫לק‬

10 ‫כמ]שפ וחל יאכ]אל איש ואל י]ש]תה עמכול אי]ש]אשר י̇עֿרוך‬ ‫מ‬

]   ‫ור ב]מצ]פֿד אא]‬ [‫ור‬

2. Let him not eat . . . including all the im[pu]re ones

3. To count off [seven days of ba]thing, and he shall bathe and launder on the [da]y of [his] healing. [And

4. a man shall not] eat who has not begun to become pure from his sour[c]e. [He indeed shall not continue to eat while]

5. in his initial impurity. And all those "impure of days" shall, on the day of their [he]aling, bathe

6. and launder in water, and become pure. And afterward they may eat their food according to the purity regulations.

7. And he shall not eat while in his initial impurity who has not begun to become pure from his source.

8. He indeed shall not eat while in his initial impurity. And all those "[im]pure of days" on the day of

9. their he[aling] shall bathe, and launder in water, and become pure. And afterward they may eat their food

10. according to the reg[ulations]. And a man [shall not ea]t nor d[r]ink with any ma[n] who prepares

1:3. *to count off [seven days of ba]thing.* Baillet's reconstruction of "seven days" is undoubtedly correct, for the idiom *lispôr le* only appears where there is a long count (e.g., Lev 23:15; 25:8) and, in particular, for seven-day purifications (Lev 15:13, 28; Ezek 44:26). If the reconstruction *[yĕmê ra]ḥaṣ* 'days of bathing' proves correct, it discloses a new technical term for the purificatory period. It would have been devised at Qumran to emphasize that ablutions are required on the first and the last of the seven days. The corresponding rabbinic phrase is *yĕmê sopr(ô)* 'the days of [his] counting' (e.g., *m. Kelim* 1:1) or *sĕpîrâ* 'counting' (e.g., *m. Zabim* 1:2). The term is clearly rooted in Scripture (Lev 15:13, 28).

the [da]y of [his] healing. This expression is repeated in lines 5, 8–9. The rendering is based on Lev 14:2, the only instance in P of the root *ṭhr* meaning "heal" (contrast 2 Kgs 5:10–14).

4. *has . . . begun to become pure. hēḥēl liṭhôr* (also in line 7). Baillet points to Gen 6:1; 10:8 as attestations of this usage. Alternatively, render "has begun to purify himself," treating the stative *liṭhôr* as a reflexive. In any event, the use of *hēḥēl* calls attention to the beginning of the purificatory process, in other words, the first day.

from his sour[c]e. MMQ[R]W (also line 7). A euphemism for the genitals, verified by Lev 12:7; 20:18. The same idiom, *ṭāhôr mimqôrô*, appears in 1QM 7:6, where it unmistakably means "pure in regard to his sexual organs" (Yadin 1962). This identification further proves that 4QOrd^c deals exclusively with the *zāb*. Only genital discharges that are abnormal are subject to a seven-day purification.

5. *[while] in his initial impurity.* Referring to his condition prior to the start of his purification. For the idiom, see Num 19:13.

impure of days. ṭĕmē'ê hayyāmîm (also in line 8). Probably a technical term for those whose impurity and hence, whose purification last more than one day.

5–6. *bathe and launder in water.* The addition of "in water" distinguishes the first day from the seventh, which requires *mayim ḥayyîm* 'spring water' (Lev 15:13). Furthermore, that the first day is intended is demonstrated by the absence of sunset as the time that eating is permitted. Also, the order is the reverse of that found in Scripture, which consistently lists laundering ahead of bathing (see the NOTE on 14:8).

6. *And afterward they may eat (wĕ'aḥar yō'kelû).* The language of Lev 22:7 (noted by Baillet).

according to the purity regulations. kĕmišpaṭ haṭṭāhărâ (cf. also line 10). The term *kĕmišpaṭ* 'according to the regulations' is frequently attested in Qumran's halakhic texts (e.g., 11QT 15:3; 18:5; 22:10; 28:5, 8; 50:7, 17). The term *ṭāhărâ* 'purity' can refer to all of the sect's purity rules but, in particular, to the rule that all food at the common table must be eaten in a state of purity. It is patently the latter meaning that prevails here. See, in particular, the Qumran idioms *ṭaharat hārabbîm* 'the pure (food) of the many' (1QS 6:16–17, 25; 7:3) and *ṭaharat 'anšê haqqôdeš* 'the pure (food) of the holy persons' (1QS 5:13; 8:17), and the discussion in Licht 1965: 294–303. This term must be distinguished from *tahărat haqqôdeš* 'the pure sacred (food)', which requires stricter purification—and in the case of the *zāb*, the ablutions and sacrifices of the seventh and eighth days.

7. *while in his initial impurity.* These words, added in the repetition of lines 4–6, comprise the sect's rationale for requiring first-day ablutions: whoever has not undergone ablutions on the first day of his purificatory period retains the same degree of impurity he possessed during his affliction.

The number of repetitions in the short document of nine partially preserved lines is astounding: not to eat (six times, lines 2, 3–4, 4, 7, 8, 10) except after ablutions (twice, lines 6, 9) on the first day (thrice, lines 3, 5, 8–9). In fact, lines 7–9 are almost a verbatim copy of lines 4–6.

Repetition is for emphasis, and emphasis implies a polemic. 4QOrd^c is championing first-day ablutions. Neither the biblical section on impurities (chaps. 11–15) nor rabbinic halakha ordains first-day ablutions except for the scale-diseased person. The only other exception, a one-time occasion, was the encampment at Mount Sinai, when two successive ablutions were ordained (Exod 19:10). Because Qumran transferred Mount Sinai to the Temple, it prescribed double ablutions for those who resided in the Temple city (A, B). If Qumran were the Temple city the purificatory rites would have to take place outside (F). But Qumran fitted the category of "other cities," where these rites were performed within (G). In this respect, they followed Scripture faithfully. Even for scale disease, a severer impurity than genital discharge, readmission to the community is permitted on the first day (14:8). But this biblical warrant confronted Qumran with a difficult and, from its point of view, dangerous situation. The erstwhile *zāb* would contaminate the pure food of Qumran, the community of the *'anšê qôdeš* 'holy persons' (1QS 5:13; 8:17). Qumran's answer was, as expected, derived from Scripture: to emulate the scale-diseased person who laundered and bathed on the first day, and then was permitted to reenter the camp (14:8). By his ablutions he would no longer be impure to the profane realm. Of course, he would still retain his impurity to the sacred realm (nonexistent at Qumran), which required a second set of ablutions on the seventh day and expiatory sacrifices on the following day (15:13–15).

What emerges from the document is that Qumran must have distinguished between the concepts of *tăhără* 'purity' and *qĕdûšâ* 'holiness'. Note that they allowed their pure food to be eaten before the purificatory rites were complete. Thus Qumran knew and practiced some precursory form of the later rabbinic distinction between *tĕrûmôt* and *qodōšîm*. *tĕrûmôt* is the rabbinic term for agricultural produce owed to the Temple and its priesthood (e.g., firstfruits), whereas *qodōšîm*, in its alimentary aspect, refers to sacrificial food (e.g., the meat of the well-being offering). The rabbis ruled that although *qodōšîm* may be eaten only after the requisite sacrifices are offered, the *těrûmôt* may be eaten (by a priest) the evening before, provided he has bathed (*Sipra*, Emor. 4:8; and the laity may eat of their redeemed tithe immediately after the ablution; *m. Kelim* 1:5; *m. Neg.* 14:3; *m. Nid.* 10:7).

It is now apparent from 4QOrd^c that Qumran also distinguished between two grades of sanctity, corresponding approximately to rabbinic *qodōšîm* and *těrûmôt*, except that instead of *těrûmôt* Qumran employed the term *ṭāhărâ*, by which they meant that their food should be maintained in a state of purity. That Qumran did not invent this category but based it on a biblical precedent becomes manifest upon examining Lev 22:1–15. This passage deals with the prohibitions imposed on impure priests and nonpriests against eating sacred foods. Although it uses the term *qōdeš, qodōšîm* 'sacred thing(s)' (vv 2, 3, 4, 6, 7, 12, 14, 15, 16), it does not have sacrificial food in mind. These terms are qualified by *ʾăšer hēm maqdîšîm* 'which they dedicate' (v 2), and—note the verb —*ʾăšer-yārîmû* 'which they contribute' (v 15) and—note the noun—*těrûmat haqqŏdāšîm* 'the sacred gifts' (v 12). Furthermore, these sacred gifts are called *qodšê běnê-yiśrāʾēl* 'the sacred things (i.e., contributions) of the Israelites' (vv 2, 15), not *qodšê YHWH* 'the sacred things of the Lord' (e.g., 5:15). Thus, the terminology of this pericope clearly indicates that it is treating of food gifts donated by the Israelites that the text itself labels *těrûmâ* 'gift, contribution' (for the etymology, see Milgrom 1983d: 171–72).

The key passage, however, is the following: "He shall not eat of the sacred donations unless he has bathed his body in water. When the sun has set, he shall be pure; and afterward he may eat *(wěʾaḥar yōʾkal)* of the sacred donations, for they are his food *(laḥmô)*" (vv 6b–7). The bracketed terms in the Hebrew will at once indicate that this text lay before the author of 4QOrd^c (cf. lines 6, 9). Moreover, this text employs the language of concession, *kî laḥmô hûʾ* 'for they are his food'. As this is the priests' only subsistence, they need not wait till the following day after they bring their sacrifices in order to eat. They may do so the evening before, provided they have bathed (the rabbis were fully aware of the biblical basis for this priestly concession; cf. *b. Yebam.* 74b). This is not the plain meaning of this text, which refers only to minor impurities where no sacrifices are involved (major impurities are confined to v 4a). Nevertheless, Qumran and the rabbis interpreted it in this way, but Qumran added its own nuance: the ablution permitting pure food takes place on the first day (see further Milgrom 1978b: 512–18).

The surprising element in this document may be that it contravenes other Qumranic rules, which explicitly prohibit an impure person from having access to pure food until the *completion* of the purificatory period (e.g., 11QT 49:19–21). However, in view of 4QTmA₁ (Milgrom forthcoming B), a different inter-

pretation is now possible (forthcoming in the proceedings of the Dead Sea
Scrolls Madrid Congress, March 1991): An impure person is forbidden to eat
any food (i.e., he must fast) until he undergoes initial ablutions. If so, then
4QOnd^c does not contravene Qumranic halakha.

E. The Priestly Laws of Sancta Contamination

The ancients feared impurity because they imputed to it malignant power
of supernatural origin. They conceived it as demonic, aggressively alive, contagious not just to touch, but reaching out through air and solid matter to assail its
victims:

> The highest walls, the thickest walls
> like a flood they pass
> from house to house they break through
> no door can shut them out
> no bolt can turn them back
> through the door like a snake they glide
> through the hinge like a wind they blow.
> (Thompson 1903–14: 1.53, V, lines 25–31)

That impurity is dangerous from a distance is a commonplace in Mesopotamian ritual texts like the one cited above. One is contaminated "if he talked to
an accursed man" (Reiner 1956: 137, line 85; cf. 1958: 22, III, line 130), or
"[Namburbi] for the evil of a dove or strange bird which . . . has hovered (lit.
stood) [over a m]an" (Caplice 1965–71: 36.34, lines 1–2), or "When a man
looketh upon a corpse" (Thompson 1971: 26), or "The roving Evil Eye hath
looked on the neighborhood, and vanished afar, hath looked on the vicinity, and
vanished afar, it hath looked on the chamber of the land, and vanished afar, it
hath looked on the wanderer, and like wood cut for kindling(?), it hath bent his
neck" (Thompson 1903–14: 2.112, lines 6–11; cf. Ebeling 1949: 203–6, lines 5–
15). B. Landsberger could without hesitation speak of "the circumambient
danger" of Mesopotamian impurity (cited by Ritter 1965: 302 n. 13).

The airborne quality of impurity was amplified many times over in the
presence of the sacred: "An impure person has come near the sacrifice" (*CAD*,
4.106); "An impure man or woman must not see (the ritual proceedings)"
(*CAD*, 1.2.8). Moreover, impurity as the embodiment of divine evil was even a
threat to the gods themselves, particularly to their sanctuaries. One recalls the
images of the protector gods, the *šēdu* and *lamassu*, set before the entrances of
Mesopotamian temples and palaces, and, above all, the elaborate purification
rituals for both temples and homes to rid them of demons and prevent their
future incursions (Saggs 1962: 315–16). Indeed, to say that impurity attacks
from a distance is to admit that it is demonically alive (see now Wright 1987:
247–61).

Turning to Israel, we find that animate impurity has completely disappeared. Its devitalized traces, however, are still detectable in the rules for the scale-diseased person (14:46–47) and the corpse (Num 19:14–16): everything under the same roof is contaminated except the contents of tightly sealed vessels (Num 19:15). Here we can still discern impurity as a gaseous substance, a volatile force, a miasma exuded by the source of impurity. To be sure, this impurity is no longer of pagan dimensions; it has "clipped wings," being airborne only within an enclosure. Above all, it has lost its malignancy; contaminated objects and persons need merely undergo ritual purification.

In the sacred sphere, however, an entirely different situation exists. The very power that has been stripped from impurity in contact with the common is now revealed in all of its primeval force. This fact can be demonstrated by examining the system of scaled sancta taboos upon which the Priestly legislation is structured. First, however, the nomenclature must be clarified. I begin by noting two sets of opposites: holy *(qōdeš)* and common *(hōl);* pure *(ṭāhôr)* and impure *(ṭāmēʾ)*. The common and the holy are presumed pure, their normal status, unless we are told that they have been contaminated. The holy is divided into two classes: sacred *(qōdeš)* and most sacred *(qōdeš qodāšîm;* cf. the NOTE on 5:15). The latter, found exclusively in the sanctuary, are further subdivided by their location, depending on whether they are in the outer courtyard, the sanctuary building, or the inner shrine (Milgrom 1976f: 35–37).

As the common and the holy are presumed to be pure—their normal and acceptable condition—three of the four categories listed above can interact: the holy, the common, and the impure. They can interact in five different pairs: (1) most sacred and common; (2) sacred and impure; (3) sacred and common; (4) most sacred and impure; and (5) common and impure.

Contact 1 (most sacred and common) yields the following correlations. The common object (but not person) is rendered "holy" on touching all "most sacred" objects—even those in the sanctuary courtyard such as the altar (Exod 29:37) or the sacrifices (6:11, 20; Ezek 46:20; cf. chap. 7, COMMENT B). A common person, that is, a nonpriest, will pay with his life if he encroaches upon them (Num 1:51; 3:10, 38; 4:19 17:5, 28; 18:3, 7; cf. Milgrom 1970a: 16–33). Moreover, if he but gazes upon the sancta while they are being dismantled—even if he does so through inadvertence—the consequences are fatal (Num 4:20; Neh 6:11). Only the priest may handle the most sacred because he is like them: both have been anointed to sacred status (Exod 28; Lev 8). But even he is barred from the adytum except under severe restrictions (chap. 16). The Levite is like the layman in all respects (Num 18:3) except that, if he is a Kohathite, he carries the most sacred sancta when the camp is in transit and when they have been covered by the priests (Num 4:5–20). It must be borne in mind that in these examples the sancta are not being contaminated because their contact is with the common, not with the impure. The common is an inert category, devoid of active power. The activity is on the part of the "most sacred," which "sanctifies" the common person (and thing) or can kill him on sight if he is inside the shrine. Thus, the superholiness with which the most sacred is charged exhibits the same airborne quality that obtains in severe impurity. Although the rabbis subsequently deny that the Temple has the power to sanctify areally (see chap. 7, COMMENT B), their writings bear witness to such a belief. For example, a sacrifice does not lose its sanctity if it has not been carried beyond Mount Scopus, that is, the Temple can still be seen (*t. Pesaḥ.* 3:12–13) or that the lesser sacred sacrifices (e.g., the *šĕlāmîm*) may be eaten anywhere the Temple is in sight (*t. Zebaḥ.* 12:4; cf. also *t. Maʿas. Šeni* 2:12–16; *t. Nid.* 9:18).

Contact 2 (sacred and impure) is illumined by the contrast with contact 1, above. The prescribed penalty is not death by divine agency *(mût)* but excision *(kārēt):* for example, "the person who, while impure, eats flesh from the Lord's sacrifice of well-being, that person shall be cut off *(wĕnikrĕtâ)* from his kin" (7:20; cf. chap. 7, COMMENT D).

Contact 3 (sacred and common) has no effect whatsoever as long as the common remains uncontaminated. So indeed reads the rule of eating the flesh of the well-being offering (7:19b; 10:14). Conversely, the illegitimate contact of the sacred and the common (desecration) is subject to severe penalties: if inadvertent, a fine of 20 percent and a reparation offering (5:14–26); if deliberate, death at the hands of God (5:14–26, COMMENT B). Even the legitimate contact of the sacred and common is subject to the 20-percent penalty (chap. 27; see the NOTE on 5:15).

As for contact 4 (most sacred and impure) our texts are silent, but only because the death penalty is obvious, a deduction a fortiori from the capital punishment prescribed for the contact 1 cases discussed above. We also have the precedent of Nadab and Abihu, whose immediate death was caused by "a strange fire" (10:1), which, whatever its nature, resulted in the contamination of the sanctuary. Perhaps the clash between most sacred and impure results in even greater calamity if we note the frequent reference to the wrath of God punishing not only the offending priest but his community as well (e.g., 4:3; 10:6; Num 18:5). These relationships are also integrated into a dynamic theology that is described and represented diagrammatically in the NOTE on "and between the pure and impure," 10:10.

Having discussed the penalties for bringing sancta into contact with the common and the impure, we can now focus exclusively on sancta–impure contacts (2 and 4, above) to study the processes involved, to wit, how a sacred object is contaminated and then purified. Contact 5 (impure and common) need not be discussed here because it has been the subject of all of the impurity laws in chaps. 11–15. It is rarely prohibited (e.g., 11:8) and never penalized, unless the prescribed purification is not observed. When this occurs, even minor impurities become major ones, polluting the sanctuary from afar (5:2–3; COMMENT on 5:1–13). But then we are dealing with the contact of the sacred and the impure. The pollution of the sanctuary by airborne impurity has already been discussed in connection with its purification by the blood of the purification offering (chap. 4,

COMMENT C). It remains to discuss the impact of impurity on Israel's other dominant sanctum, the priest.

It comes as no surprise to find airborne and deadly impurity in texts dealing with the pagan priests of the ancient Near East. The Babylonian *mašmašu* is contaminated if he even glances at dirty water (Meier 1937: 11, I, lines 105, 107) or a person with "unwashed hands" (Thompson 1903–14: 2.139–40). The *šešgallu*, the head priest of Babylon's Esagila, "shall not view the (New Year's) purification of the temple. If he does view (it), he is no (longer) pure" (*ANET*³ 333, lines 364–65; see chap. 16, COMMENT C). The "loosening" of the impurity from the temple walls and its transfer to the scape-ram has, in effect, made it airborne once again and doubly dangerous to the holiest of the priests. The human corpse, in particular, can contaminate from afar, but the priest is its special target. Note the alarm sounded in Ur warning of the approach of Dumuzi from the land of the dead:

> O city of Ur! At my loud cry
> lock your house, lock your house! city lock your house!
> O temple of Ur! Lock your house, city lock your house!
> Your *entu* priestess must not go out of her house,
> O Giparu city lock your house!
> (translation of Jacobsen 1961: 208)

The dead must be kept away from the city and temple, but the chief priestess *(entu)* may not even expose herself to the open air of the street. The susceptibility of the priesthood reaches down to the end of pagan times: the Roman high priest, the Flamen Dialis, sins as did his ancient Babylonian counterpart if he but glances at a corpse (Servius, *ad Aeneid* 6.176). So too in Hellenistic Syria: "Those priests who bore the corpse of a Galloi priest of Syria were not allowed to enter the temple for seven days; if any priest looked at a corpse he was impure for that day and could only enter the temple the following day if he was cleansed" (Luc. 2.62).

In these essentials, the priest of Israel is not different from his pagan colleague. His sensitivity to impurity is greater than the layman's, and the high priest, by virtue of his supreme holiness, is the most vulnerable of all. Accordingly, the ordinary priest is permitted to attend the burial of his immediate blood relatives only (21:1–4); the high priest, not even for his parents (21:11). In Ezekiel's system, the priest is further set apart from the layman in that his purification from corpse contamination lasts two weeks, climaxed by a *ḥaṭṭāʾt* sacrifice (44:26–27), whereas the layman needs only sprinkling with *ḥaṭṭāʾt* waters on the third and seventh days (Num 19:9). Thus, of the three bearers of corpse contamination—the Nazirite, Ezekiel's priest, and the layman—the two consecrated classes require sacrifices for their purification but not the layman. This contrast is dramatically projected by the table in COMMENT F below (C.4,

5, 7), and it demonstrates the distinction between the contamination of the sacred (contact 2) and the contamination of the common (contact 5). Finally, the prohibition issued to Israel's high priest that "he may not leave the sanctuary" to follow after the bier is strikingly reminiscent of the Babylonian high priestess, who "must not go out of her house" (above). In this instance, Babylonian and Israelite ritual law coincide exactly.

The susceptibility of the high priest to airborne impurity persists into rabbinic times: "If any of his (the high priest's) near of kin die he may not follow after the bier, but he may go forth with the bearers as far as the city gate, *if he and they come not within sight of one another*" (my emphasis). So Rabbi Meir. But Rabbi Judah says: "He may not go forth from the Temple, for it is written 'neither shall he go out of the sanctuary' (Lev 21:12)" (*m. Sanh.* 2:1). Rabbi Meir and Rabbi Judah do not differ at all. As the Roman and Babylonian parallels teach us, Rabbi Meir is correctly citing the reason for the biblical prohibition. Moreover, just as the Flamen Dialis was not allowed to spend a single night outside Rome, so Israel's high priest was never allowed to lodge outside the Temple (Lieberman 1950: 165 n. 12). A residue of the notion of the areal contamination of sancta in rabbinic times is further evident from the provisions that one who witnesses the burning of the Yom Kippur *ḥaṭṭāʾt* bull and he-goat (16–27)—laden with the total impurity of the sanctuary and people (see the NOTE on "iniquities," 16:21)—should not be able to see the high priest while he is officiating (*m. Yoma* 7:2) and that one who defecates or urinates may not face in the direction of the sanctuary if he can see it (*t. Meg.* 5:25–26). Perhaps this is what the Dead Sea sectaries had in mind when they prohibit the slaughter and consumption of a maimed animal at any distance less than thirty *stadia* (four miles) from the Temple (11QT 52:17–19).

The contamination of Israel's sanctuary, discussed in detail in chap. 4, COMMENTS B and C, needs only to be summarized here: (1) the accidental sins or impurities of the individual contaminate the outer altar, requiring purification blood on its horns (4:22–35); (2) the accidental sins or impurities of the community invade and contaminate the shrine, requiring purification blood on the horns of the inner altar and before the veil (4:1–21); and (3) the deliberate sins penetrate the veil into the adytum, requiring purification blood on and before the Ark cover (16:14–15). Thus, the contamination of the sanctuary varies directly with the intensity of the impurity charge. This law will hold true for all sancta. The sanctuary, however, is set apart from other sancta in that it is, first of all, capable of different levels or degrees of contamination, and, second, automatically contaminated by impurity no matter where it occurs in Israel's camp (P) or land (H). This property is not shared by other sancta. Instead, as we have already observed, the latter are governed by another correlation, that the closer the impurity source to the sanctum and the greater the holiness charge of the sanctum, the more readily contamination takes place. More precisely, the comprehensive law reads, *sancta contamination varies directly with the charge (holiness) of the sanctuary and the charge of the impurity, and inversely with the distance between them.* If we resort to the vocabulary of electromagnetism (but not to equate the phenomena), we could describe the workings of the law as follows: opposites attract, and in the Priestly system holiness is opposite in charge to the impure. If either the holiness or the impurity source is strong enough or the distance between them small enough, impurity will become airborne, spark the gap, and impinge on the sanctum (see the mathematical formulation below).

The fixed levels of penetration observed for the contamination of the sanctuary yield a second law: impurity displaces an equal amount of sanctuary holiness. This correlation is adumbrated, outside P, in the ancient regulation of the holy war camp: "let him not find anything unseemly among you and turn away from you" (Deut 23:15b; cf. contact 4). Thus, God withdraws from the contaminated camp. In P, this general principle becomes mathematical law. Holiness and impurity are finite, quantitative categories; impurity displaces sanctuary holiness in fixed amounts until a saturation point is reached beyond which the sanctuary cannot endure. It might be termed Archimedes' law of holiness displacement. It certifies that holiness can abide with a limited but fixed amount of impurity, and it accounts for the repeated admonitions not to pollute the sanctuary (e.g., 12:4; 15:31; 20:1–4; Num 19:13, 20).

In P's own terms this law can be understood as follows: God will tolerate inadvertent wrongs that contaminate the outside altar (4:22ff.) and the shrine (4:1–21), for they can be purged through purification offerings. Conversely, as for the perpetrator of *pešaʿ* 'rebellious acts' (16:16), "who acts defiantly, reviles the Lord" (Num 15:30), personal sacrifice will not avail him. The nation as a whole must expiate for him and others like him at the annual Purgation rite of the sanctuary (chap. 16), cleansing the contaminated adytum with the purification blood and transferring the released impurities to "the goat for Azazel" (16:10, 20b–22). Even then, only a limited amount of deliberate sin will be tolerated. There is a point of no return. One day, purgation will no longer avail; the impurities, especially the accumulated *pešaʿ* in the adytum, will go beyond the set limit; God's endurance of his people's impurities will end; he will forsake his abode and abandon it and his people to destruction (details in chap. 4, COMMENT C).

In essence, this Priestly theology of sanctuary contamination is structured on the lines of pagan analogues. Indeed, all three laws controlling Israel's system operate with equal validity in the polytheistic world, but with one crucial distinction. The pagans, who gave highest priority to protecting their sanctuary from impurity, believed the latter to be personified demonic forces intent on driving out their patron god from his sanctuary, and they sought magical apotropaic rituals, mediated by the priesthood, to enhance the life force of the deity and shield the sanctuary from invasion. In Israel these universal laws are recast in terms of its monotheism: impurity is the outcome not of demonic force but of the people's sin. The cause of impurity has radically changed. Man has replaced the demon. Rather, the demon is in man. Man has the unique power to obey or resist God. If he chooses to rebel—to use the Priestly idiom—he will pollute the sanctuary to the point that God will no longer abide in it. But whether the cause is the demon or the man, the net effect is still the same: God is evicted from his earthly abode.

Only a theological structure such as the one just outlined can explain the thought and imagery of Ezekiel, prophet-priest par excellence. The first section of his book (chaps. 1–11) is a vivid description of Jerusalem's forthcoming destruction, dramatized by P's conceptual imagery of God's departure from his Temple. Equally characteristic of P is Ezekiel's indictment, solely stressing the presumptuous, rebellious sin, the *pešaʿ* and its semantic equivalents, as having contaminated the adytum and forced God's departure (note the similar vocabulary of Ezek 39:24a and Lev 16:16). Six times he explicitly labels the contamination of the Temple as the end result of Israel's sin (5:11; 8:6; 23:38; 23:39; 24:21; 44:7), and seven times he prophesies its ultimate purification (11:16; 37:26, 27, 28; 48:8; 48:10, 21). Indeed, only by recognizing that the Priestly laws of sancta contamination inform Ezekiel's thought are we able to explain the ideological framework of his book. God's abandonment of his contaminated Temple is complemented by his return to an uncontaminable Temple, so assured because Israel will never be less than pure. Ezekiel is his own best witness:

> Son of man, do you see what they are doing, the great abominations that the house of Israel are committing here, to drive me from my sanctuary? (Ezek 8:6)
> They shall not contaminate themselves any more with their idols and their detestable things, or with any of their transgressions *(pešaʿ);* . . . but I will purify them . . . and I will set my sanctuary in the midst of them for evermore. (Ezek 37:23a, bβ, 26bβ)

Thus, the blueprint of the new Temple is not a chance appendix to the book; it is a logical, fitting climax to all that has preceded it. First comes the reunification, restoration, and purification of Israel, ending with a promise of a Davidic ruler and a new Temple (chaps. 36–37). Then follows the purification of the land after the slaughter of Israel's enemies therein (chaps. 38–39, esp. 39:12–16). With purging of people and land complete, the new Temple can be built (chaps. 40–48).

Having described the process and effect of impurity impinging on the sacred and the common both following and preceding the ablution (COMMENT C above), we are now ready to extrapolate a third and final law. So far it has been ascertained that the ablution removes impurity to the extent that it can no longer contaminate the common, but it may contaminate the sacred until evening or, in severer cases of impurity, till sacrificial purification on the following day (see also columns D-1 and D-2 of the Table of Purification Procedures and Effects, COMMENT F below). Prior to the ablution, however, both the common and the sacred are subject to contamination, which can take place from a distance.

Thus, the periods before and after ablution offer two new criteria for comparing the realms of the sacred and the common: (1) *The sacred is of greater sensitivity than the common to contamination by one degree*, and (2) *each purification stage reduces contagion to both the sacred and the common by one degree*. There are three possibilities for the contamination of an object: from afar, by direct contact, or by overhang. Specifically, a severely impure person contaminates a common object by direct contact and a sacred object from afar. After the ablution, he is no longer contagious to the common object but can contaminate a sacred object by direct contact (but not from afar). Finally, after the last stage of purification (by that evening or after sacrifices on the following day) he is no longer contagious even to sancta. If these two correlations are correct, then a reconstruction of the entire system of ritual impurities contained in the Priestly source is now feasible. Despite the large gaps in our biblical data we would only need to know either the number of ablutions required or the final purification procedure (evening or sacrifices) to deduce the missing stages. This reconstruction is tabulated in columns D-1 and D-2 of the table in COMMENT F, where the impurities are listed in order of severity (determined by the length and procedure of purification, cols. B and C).

Occasionally, lacunae are also filled by the rabbinic evidence, accepted whenever it proves an ancient and uncontested tradition. To our delight it also corroborates our general laws, which nearly always independently predict the same results. For example, tannaitic sources and Josephus affirm that the scale-diseased person has the impurity status of a corpse and analogously contaminates everything under the same roof (*m. Kelim* 1:4; *m. Neg.* 13:7, 11; Jos., *Con. Ap.* 1.31; *Ant.* 3.264). This "overhang" principle creates an extra stage in the contamination scale (see box 1D of the table in COMMENT F). An additional stage for the scale-diseased person is also predictable, for he alone among the contaminated requires not one but two ablutions for his purification, and the third law states that each ablution reduces contagion by one degree. A third, converging line of evidence stems from the analogy of the "scale-diseased" house, which also contaminates by overhang (14:46–47).

Other correlations with rabbinic tradition will be found in the notes on the table in COMMENT F. Differences will also appear. Still, because the biblical assumption of postablution sensitivity of sancta also informs the rabbinic system, the differences are in details rather than in principle. Herein, we maintain, lies the greater harvest of our study. The discovery of the biblical laws of sancta contamination will lead to the isolation of the rabbinic laws that veer from their biblical predecessors. These can now be studied for the concrete, historical situations that brought about their change (e.g., Milgrom 1983e).

The laws of sancta contamination, derived in this paper, are summarized as follows:

1.   The contamination of a sanctum varies directly with the intensity of the impurity source, directly with the holiness intensity of the sanctum and inversely with the distance between them. Also, contamination has a threshold, a fixed value, below which it cannot be activated.

2.   The sanctuary is a special case of the general law (1), whereby

    a.   Contamination is a function of the intensity of the impurity source alone, i.e., impurities of a severe amount and from any distance (in the camp) will contaminate the sanctuary.

    b.   Contamination takes place at three ascending thresholds: the outer altar, the shrine, or the adytum.

    c.   Contamination displaces an equal volume of the sanctuary holiness (the Archimedean principle) until a saturation point is reached.

3.   Sancta are related to common things in regard to their contamination and purification, as follows:

    a.   Sancta are more vulnerable to contamination by one degree.

    b.   Each purification stage reduces the communicability of the impurity source to both sancta and common things by one degree.

These laws can be expressed mathematically, as follows:

Contamination occurs in accordance with the equation:

$$c = f\,[p + (i - n) + k - 4]$$

where

c is the degree of contamination;

f is an increasing, discretely valued function of one discrete variable satisfying $x \leq 0 \Rightarrow f(x) \equiv 0$;

$p \equiv$ contagion factor of the contaminating process (airborne $= 1$, overhang $= 2$, direct $= 3$);

$i \equiv$ initial impurity of source (0, 1, 2, or 3);

n≡ number of relevant purification
    rituals;
k≡ holiness constant of sanctum
    (holy $= 1$, common $= 0$)

In the case of the sanctuary there exists a critical level of contamination, C_s, such that

(1) $C \leqq C_s$;
(2) if $C < C_s$, purification is possi-
    ble; and
(3) if ever $C = C_s$, then this condi-
    tion becomes permanent.

I gratefully acknowledge the assistance of Randy Wohl, graduate student in mathematics at the University of California, Berkeley, in formulating these equations.

F. The Table of Purification Procedures and Effects
Part I

	A. Impurity Bearer	B. Duration	C. Purification Stage (days)	C. Purification Procedures
			X	
M	1. *mĕṣōrāʿ*, scale-		1st	sp, l, sh, b
A	diseased person	x + 7 (8)	7th	sh, l, b
J	(Lev 14)			*ḥaṭṭāʾt* ewe/bird + 3
O			8th or [eve]	sacrifices + 2 daubings
R				
	2. Parturient		7 (14)	
	(Lev 12)	7 (14)	7th (14th)	[l, b]
		+ 33 (66)	41st (81st) or [eve]	*ḥaṭṭāʾt* bird + lamb/bird
S				
A	3. *zāb*, person with		x	
C	genital discharges	x + 7 (8)	7	
R	(Lev 15:3–15, 28–30)		7th	l, b
I			8th or [eve]	*ḥaṭṭāʾt* bird + bird
F				
I	4. Corpse-		7	[sp on 3rd, 7th]
C	contaminated priest	7 + 7 (8)	7th	[l, b]
E	(Ezek 44:26–27)		15th or [eve]	*ḥaṭṭāʾt* (bird?)
S	5. Corpse-contaminated	7 (8)	7	[sp on 3rd, 7th]
	Nazirite		7th	sh, [l, b]
	(Num 6:9–12)		8th or [eve]	*ḥaṭṭāʾt* + bird + bird + lamb
	6. Person whose impurity is accidentally		x	
	prolonged	x + 1	xth	[b]
	(Lev 5:1–13)			*ḥaṭṭāʾt* ewe/bird/
			(x + 1)st or [eve]	semolina

M	7. Corpse-contaminated lay person (Num 5: 2–4:19)	7	7 7th 7th	sp on 3rd, 7th l, b eve
I N O R	8. Menstruant (Lev 15:19–24)	7	7 7th 7th	 [l, b] eve
E V E N I N G	9. Handler of Red Cow, scapegoat or burnt *ḥaṭṭāʾt* (Num 19:7–10; Lev 16: 27, 28)	1	P-A ablution eve	 l, b [eve]
	10. Emits semen (Lev 15:16–18)	1	P-A ablution eve	 l, b eve
	11. Carcass-contaminated (Lev 11:24–40; 22:5)	1	P-A ablution eve	 (l), b eve
	12. Secondarily contaminated (Lev 15; 22:4b–7; Num 19)	1	P-A ablution eve	 (l), b eve

Sigla: [ ] reconstructed   eve evening   sh shaving
      x indefinite   l laundering   sp sprinkling
      b bathing   P-A pre-ablution

Part II

	D-1. THE EFFECT ON THE COMMON		
	P₁	P₂/H	
	[overhang.] Those under same roof may not enter sanctuary		
M	direct. Stays outside tent		1. *mĕṣōrāʿ*
A	none		
J			
O	none		
R			
	direct. At home [wash hands]	[direct] isolated, no leniency	2. part.
	none, sex permitted	none	
	none	none	
S			
A	direct. At home. Wash hands	direct. Banished (Num 5)	3. *zāb*
C	ditto	ditto	
R	none	none	
I	none	none	
F			
I	direct. At home (Num 19)	direct. Banished (Num 5)	4. c-c. p.
C	[none]	[none]	
E	none	none	
S			
	direct. At home (Num 19)	direct. Banished (Num 5)	5. c-c. N.
	[none]	[none]	
	none	none	
	direct. At home	direct. At home	6. prolonged
	[none]	[none]	
	none	none	

M	direct. At home (Num 19) but isolation assumed	direct. Banished (Num 5)	**7. c-c.l.p.**
	none	none	
	none	none	
I **N** **O** **R**	direct. At home (touch with washed hands)	direct. Isolated at home	**8. mens.**
	none	none	
	none	none	
	none	[direct.] Remains outside	**9. handler**
	none	none	
E	none	none	
V	none	direct. Philo	**10. sem.**
E	none	none	
N	none	none	
I **N**	none	[direct] for priest?	**11. carcass**
G	none	none	
	none	none	
	none	[direct] for priest?	**12. second**
	none	none	
	none	none	

Sigla: [ ] reconstructed eve evening   sh shaving
x indefinite   l laundering sp sprinkling
b bathing   P-A pre-ablution

Part III

	D-2. THE EFFECT ON THE SACRED		
P_1	P_1	P_2/H	
1. měṣōrāᶜ	Airborne. Must sacrifice [overhang] to sacred food. Hence, outside tent		M
	[direct.] Hence, no sancta contact		A
			J
	none		O
	Airborne. Must sacrifice.	Airborne. Must sacrifice.	R
2. part.	Concession: at nome	Isolated in community (Jos.)	
	Direct (Lev 12:4)	Direct	
	none	none	
3. zāb	Airborne. Must sacrifice. Concession: at home	Airborne. Banished (Num 5)	S
			A
	ditto	ditto	C
	[direct] No sancta contact	[direct] No sancta contact	R
	none	none	I
4. c-c. p.	Airborne. Must sacrifice.	Airborne. Must sacrifice	F
	At home (Num 19)	Banished (Num 5)	I
	[direct] No sancta contact	[direct] Returns home. No sancta contact	C
	none	none	E
5. c-c. N.	Airborne. Must sacrifice. At home (Num 19)	Airborne. Must sacrifice. Banished (Num 5)	S
	[direct] No sancta contact	[direct] Returns home. No sancta contact	
	none	none	
6. prolonged	Airborne. Must sacrifice. At home	Airborne. Must sacrifice. At home	
	[direct] No sancta contact	[direct] No sancta contact	
	none	none	

	Direct	Airborne	
7. c-c.l.p.	Direct. At home (Num 19) Isolation assumed	Airborne. Banished (Num 5)	
	none	Direct. Returns home after l, b (Num 31:24)	
	none	none—after eve	M
8. mens.	Direct. At home. No sancta. Touch with washed hands	[airborne] At home. Isolated	I N
	none	[direct] after l, b	O
	none	none	R
9. handler	Direct. Remains outside	[airborne] Remains ouside	
	none	[direct] after l, b—returns home	
	none	none—after eve	E
10. sem.	Direct. No sancta	[airborne] at home	V
	none	[direct] after l, b	E
	none	none	N
11. carcass	Direct. No sancta	[airborne] at home	I N
	none, even for priests (Lev 22:4b–6)	[direct] after l, b	G
	none	none—after eve	
12. second	Direct. No sancta	[airborne] for priests?	
	none	[direct] after l, b	
	none	none—after eve (sacrifice for priest?)	

Sigla: [ ] reconstructed eve evening sh shaving x indefinite
l laundering sp sprinkling b bathing P-A pre-ablution

The impurity bearers (and their biblical sources) are listed in order of their severity. Severity is determined by the duration and complexity of the purification procedure. Thus, the scale-diseased person *(mĕṣōrāʿ)*, whose period of impurity is indeterminate and who must undergo a seven-day purificatory rite involving two ablutions, followed by an eighth-day sanctuary rite comprising four sacrifices and two daubings, qualifies for first place in this scheme.

The impurity bearers, twelve in number, fall into two divisions, determined by the way the impurity is terminated. The first six end by sacrifice; the second group of six, by evening. Focusing first on the sacrificial group, the most prominent fact to be noted is that each purification rite features primarily the *ḥaṭṭāʾt*, the purification offering. The implications of this fact are clear. We are dealing with the phenomenon of the indirect, airborne pollution of the sanctuary. That is, whenever such impurity occurs in the Israelite camp it is powerful enough to convey itself to the sanctuary and it can only be eliminated by the purgative action of the blood of the purification offering (COMMENT E above; chap. 4, COMMENTS A, B, C). A corollary implication is that until this sacrifice is offered (and for the lesser impurities, until the prescribed evening), one may not partake of sacred food or enter the sanctuary. Thus the elimination of sancta pollution must be the final stage in the purification process, a conclusion corroborated by the explicit statement on the parturient who, following the initial period of severe impurity of seven or fourteen days, is now permitted to contact common things but "may not touch any consecrated thing, nor enter the sacred precinct" (Lev 12:4). Additional proof is provided by Ezekiel, who prescribes that a corpse-contaminated priest must first complete his purificatory rites and only then "on the day he reenters the inner court of the Sanctuary to minister in the Sanctuary, he shall present his purification offering" (Ezek 44:22). On the měṣōrāʿ, see below.

A further assumption of this table is that the ablution required in every purification procedure functions to reduce the level of impurity (shown in COMMENT C above). Thus, as the měṣōrāʿ must undergo two ablutions, we must assume that there are four stages in his purification of which the ablutions constitute the intermediate stages (1C). This, however, creates a problem. Ordinarily, there are only three stages in the reduction of impurity to the sanctuary; it can be polluted by air, by touch, or not at all. Now, however, a fourth stage is required. This new category is supplied by the rabbis, who aver that the měṣōrāʿ also contaminates by overhang (see COMMENT E above). This category can be deduced from the biblical case of the fungous house, which explicitly contaminates by overhang (Lev 14:46–47). Strikingly, the independent testimony of the rabbis that there is a fourth level in the impurity range of the měṣōrāʿ jibes perfectly with the four stages in his purification, as required in this table (1D). Also, the rabbis' concept of overhang illustrates their awareness that impurity is a gaseous substance that needs to be dissipated in the open air but, if confined in an enclosed space, will contaminate everything within it. Note their graphic descriptions of impurity's dynamic, airborne power: it "penetrates upward and downward" (e.g., m. Ohol. 7:1–2); "its nature is to expand, not to contract" (e.g., m. Ohol. 4:1–3).

The function of the ablution to reduce impurity is further supported by the case of the zāb. His purification, like that of the měṣōrāʿ, also proceeds in four stages. But unlike the měṣōrāʿ, he undergoes just one ablution (3C). The ostensible discrepancy is resolved once it is noticed that the zāb's impurity remains the same in both the first and the second stages; during his seven-day purification he continues to contaminate in exactly the same way (3D). Thus only one ablution is required, on the seventh day, after which he can no longer contaminate common things.

Perhaps the most significant assumption of the table stems from the last column, to wit: each purification stage reduces impurity by one degree, but the sacred is more vulnerable to pollution than the common by one degree. It is the third law of sancta contamination (COMMENT E above). The case of the měṣōrāʿ will exemplify this relationship. The měṣōrāʿ is banished from the camp not because he is contagious, but because he pollutes common things by overhang. Thus he is not allowed to remain in the camp lest he contaminate all persons and objects that are with him under the same roof. The danger becomes lethal if someone unknowingly contaminated by him enters the sanctuary or eats sacred food. This factor of overhang, however, is not present for other impurity bearers, such as the parturient and zāb, which accounts for the fact that, though this impurity is severe, they do not leave the camp. Because they do not contaminate by overhang, they may remain at home. The table also informs us that the měṣōrāʿ's impurity is more contagious with respect to the sacred sphere, polluting it from afar (1D-2). Thus, no sooner has he been declared impure than his impurity ipso facto pollutes the sanctuary and, as a consequence, he will have to bring a purification offering to the sanctuary to purge it of the impurity that he has imparted to it.

On the first day of his purificatory rites, the měṣōrāʿ enters the camp but still may not enter his tent (Lev 14:8). The reason cannot be that he contaminates the common sphere by direct contact (cf. m. Neg. 14:2; contra Wright 1987: 213). Note that the zāb contaminates all that he or she touches (Lev 15:4-12, 25-27), yet is allowed to stay at home (3 D-1 P). The reason for the měṣōrāʿ's stricter rule is his overhang effect upon the sacred. Sacrificial food may be present in the home, to become polluted as soon as he enters. It is this contact between the impure and the sacred that is most dreaded, subjecting the violator to the penalty of kārēt (Lev 7:20) and the nation as a whole to destruction (Lev 15:31; cf. Ezek 9:7). On the seventh day of his purification, after his second ablution, he is pure in regard to common objects and persons. Because he no longer contaminates the sacred by overhang, he may enter his tent. Yet as the sacred is still vulnerable to his touch, he may neither eat sacred food nor enter the sanctuary. This last barrier is lifted the following day, when he purifies the sanctuary of the impurity he has caused. The rabbis were fully aware of the susceptibility of the měṣōrāʿ to the sacred, as shown by their tradition of his sacrificial rite: "He would bring his reparation offering and its log [of oil] in his hand and set it up by Nicanor's gate (the entrance to the inner court). And the priest stands on the inside and the měṣōrāʿ on the outside . . . for he cannot enter the court until some of the blood of the reparation offering and the purification offering (sic!) is sprinkled upon him" (t. Neg. 8:9).

What pertains to the měṣōrāʿ also holds for the other impurity bearers: at every stage of their purification, the sacred is more susceptible to impurity than the common by one degree. The final stage of the purificatory process always finds the erstwhile impurity bearer pure in regard to the common but still impure in regard to the sacred. If his impurity is major, he has polluted the sanctuary from afar and must purge it with his ḥaṭṭāʾt offering. If his impurity is minor, it is incapable of generating airborne pollution to the sanctuary but still defiles by direct contact (e.g., sacred food) until it fades away by evening.

The sectaries of Qumran, it seems, held to a similar system. From two as yet unpublished fragments dealing with the *mĕṣōrāʿ*, the following procedures can be ascertained: During his affliction he dwells alone, northwest of the camp, at least twelve cubits from any settlement, persons, or (food) purity while he prays for his recovery. He must warn anyone approaching him that he is impure, for whoever touches him must bathe and launder before he may again eat (pure) food. (4QThr A1:1–4). During his seven-day purification, however, he enters camp but may not enter any house lest he contaminate sacred food, in contrast to the Priestly authorities (of Jerusalem) who permit his entry (*MMT* B 65–68).

Thus we see that Qumran distinguishes between impurity's power to defile pure food and its power to defile sacred food. During the period of his affliction the *mĕṣōrāʿ* defiles all food, but when he is undergoing purification—that is, after his initial ablutions have removed one layer of impurity—he is no longer impure to pure food but only to sacred food. The rabbis, as was observed (NOTE on "must remain outside his tent," v 8), are more lenient, permitting entry but forbidding sexual congress. Interestingly, the sect's Jerusalem opponents also allow him unrestricted entrance to the house. Perhaps they too, with the rabbis, would also prohibit cohabitation with his wife. If so, then MMT will have provided another piece of evidence that the priestly establishment of its time anticipated by two or more centuries the viewpoint that was espoused by the Pharisaic rabbis, as opposed to Qumran, which championed the viewpoint later attributed to the Sadducees (details in Strugnell and Qimron forthcoming).

Qumran's rule corresponds precisely to the Priestly system, as I have reconstructed it. Both ordain that the healed *mĕṣōrāʿ* must initially remain outside his (or any other) house lest he defile the sacred food within, presumably in accordance with the principle of overhang, which, as I have postulated, operates in case of the *mĕṣōrāʿ*. Thus Qumran confirms, at least in this detail, the correctness of the reconstructed Priestly system of impurities and, conversely, proves that Qumran thought biblically, carrying the implications of the scriptural data to their logical conclusion (for a similar deduction from Qumran's prescriptions concerning the *zāb*, see the NOTE on 15:13). Coevally, the dominant priestly establishment of Jerusalem had begun to liberalize some of the scriptural restrictions, a process continued and amplified by the rabbis.

All sources agree, not just the Priestly legislation but also the narratives (e.g., Num 12; 2 Kgs 7:3–10), that the *mĕṣōrāʿ* is banished. By contrast, the treatment of the other impurity bearers in the table is subject to two differing traditions (col. D). The one that unmistakably stems from P is labeled P_1; the other, which also manifests Priestly style and vocabulary, either stems from the school of P (P_2) or from the Holiness source (H; see the Introduction, §H). Therefore column D is split in two, reflecting the data either stated in or inferred from each.

Beginning with the parturient (2D), we note that according to P₁ (chap. 12), she is likened to the menstruant during her initial impurity of seven or fourteen days, which can only mean that like the menstruant she remains at home. This is possible because she most likely only contaminates the objects immediately beneath her but not those she touches with washed hands (see the NOTE on "without having rinsed his hands," v 11). Again like the menstruant, she is assumed to undergo ablutions at the end of this first stage (see the NOTE on "she shall be impure," 12:2), but it is uncertain whether a second ablution was required at the end of the next stage (thirty-three or sixty-six days; see the NOTE on "she shall bring," 12:6). Num 5:2-3 (P₂ or H), however, suggests that there was a coeval tradition concerning the parturient. To be sure, this passage does not mention her; yet the fact that the menstruant is also absent implies that the text only mandates the banishment of erratic impurities, not normal ones. Furthermore, that she is required to bring a ḥaṭṭāʾt offering implies that her impurity was considered by the Priestly legislators to be powerful enough to pollute the sanctuary. Theoretically, this should have led to her banishment (like the zāb, Num 5:2-3). That she was not is attributable to the normality of her condition, which would correspondingly evoke less apprehension even from extremists. It is not without significance that the Qumranites also did not banish the parturient and menstruant from their cities (11QT 48:14-17), and Josephus records that only the mĕṣōrāʿ and zāb—in other words, those with abnormal impurities—were expelled while the others were quarantined (Ant. 3.261-62). Nevertheless, if the parturient was not banished she may have been quarantined, if not in her own house then in separate quarters, but within her community. The latter expedient was endorsed by many who regarded the parturient (and menstruant) as a grave source of impurity (see COMMENT A above; chap. 12, COMMENT A; and cf. Jos., Ant. 3.261). That the sacred realm remains vulnerable to her impurity during the intermediate stage is made explicit in 12:4.

Because severe genital discharges require only one ablution (v 13), only three stages of purification should have been anticipated for the zāb. But, as noted above, the fact that the zāb's impurity continues undiminished during his week of purification renders his four stages equivalent to three (3C). Furthermore, the very absence of an ablution between those first two stages is further corroboration of the thesis that it is the ablution that is responsible for the reduction of the impurity (COMMENT C above). Despite the fact that severe impurity polluting the sanctuary (indicated by the ḥaṭṭāʾt requirement) would normally banish its bearer, as demanded by Num 5:2-3 (P₂/H), the legislators of chap. 15 (P₁) have conceded the zāb the right to remain at home and have enabled him to function, first, by limiting the impurity contagion to objects directly beneath him (v 10) and, second, by allowing him to handle anything with washed hands (v 11). The third law of sancta contamination (COMMENT E above) necessitates that after the ablution on the seventh day, the zāb remain impure to sancta by direct contact until he brings his purification offering to the sanctuary on the following day. Naturally the purification of the *zābâ* (vv 28–30) follows the procedure of the *zāb*.

The information on the purification of the corpse-contaminated priest (4C) comes from Ezek 44:26–27. That the Priestly writings do not register such a distinction between the priesthood and the laity is not to be explained as a contradiction of sources. Ezekiel may just have chosen to be stricter than his fellow priests. Note that his marriage rules for priests resemble those of the high priest (cf. Ezek 44:22 with Lev 21:14). Thus it may have been as much a matter of predilection as one of tradition. His general outlook was severe, to judge from his book, and he would be expected to eschew lenient observances. In any event, one cannot deny the logic of Ezekiel's ruling: if a layman of temporary sanctity (the Nazirite) is required to bring a *ḥaṭṭā'ṭ* for corpse contamination (Num 6:11), a priest of lifelong sanctity all the more so. The adjoining boxes of the *zāb* and the Nazirite (3C, 5C) induce us to infer that the *ḥaṭṭā'ṭ* of Ezekiel's priest also consisted of a bird. We should also assume that he follows the ritual of the corpse-contaminated lay person in requiring sprinkling with *ḥaṭṭā'ṭ* waters on the third and seventh days and laundering and bathing on the seventh (7C; Num 19:19). That his postablution contagion to sancta (by direct contact) lasts a whole week (till the fifteenth day) likens him to the parturient's "extended day of ablution" (see the NOTE on "she shall bring," 12:6). By the third law of sancta contamination (COMMENT E above), he could mingle freely with his friends and family but could not return to his priestly duties.

The Nazirite who, by definition, is a holy person (Num 6:5, 8) elevates himself into the sacred sphere, the domain of the priest. It is therefore not surprising that the stages of his (or her) purification are an exact copy of those of Ezekiel's priest (5D and 4D). Nor should one wonder that the Nazirite (after all, a lay person) is required to bring an additional sacrifice for corpse contamination: the *'āšām* (Num 6:12a). Precisely because his impurity cancels out his prior Nazirite service (Num 6:12b), he is guilty of desecration, the penalty for which is the *'āšām* (see 5:14–26, COMMENT C). Procedures mandated for the purification of the contaminated Nazirite and priest (Ezekiel's) were probably originally followed by all priests. Subsequently, P denied them to the priesthood but conceded them to the Nazirite, possibly because the laity demanded or, in any event, practiced them. Perhaps, as sacrificing *because* of the dead could easily become sacrificing *to* the dead, sacrifices were abolished altogether for the laity and priesthood alike. The net result is that, in P, there is no difference between lay persons and priests in regard to purification for corpse contamination.

The last of the major impurity bearers is the one whose minor impurity, incurred by touching a communicable animal or human impurity (5:2–3), has accidentally been prolonged (details in the COMMENT on 5:1–13). His requirement to offer a *ḥaṭṭā'ṭ* implies that he has polluted the sanctuary, that is to say, his impurity became airborne. Also implied is that during this period he has contaminated persons and objects by direct contact (6D-1) and that even after he bathes, his contagion to sancta persists until his sacrifice the following day.

So far we have seen that the Priestly laws of impurity are not univocal. Discrepancies and outright contradictions (except for the *měṣōrāʿ*) necessitate the supposition of more than one Priestly tradition. When we turn to the minor impurity bearers grouped in the bottom half of the table (7–12), the problem becomes more complex. The corpse-contaminated lay person, to begin with, is an anomaly; he is purified uniquely by being sprinkled with the ashes of a Red Cow on the third and seventh days (7C). Although these ashes derive from a *ḥaṭṭāʾt* (Num 19:9, 17), it has been shown that originally this rite was an exorcism, which was only subsequently adapted to Israel's sacrificial system (chap. 4, COMMENT G). That originally corpse contamination was considered a major impurity is shown by the law of Num 5:2–3, which links it with the major impurities of scale disease and genital discharges. That the banishment of the corpse-contaminated person was actually practiced or that, at least, there was a tradition to this effect, is shown by the account of the campaign against Midian, where the returning soldiers had to remain outside the camp until their purificatory rites were completed (Num 31:19, 24). Moreover, the latter passage records another anomaly: the soldiers reenter the camp not in the evening of the seventh day, as would be required by the law of Num 19:19b, but earlier after their ablutions on that day (Num 31:24). This aberration might be dismissed as inconsequential or even erroneous were it not for the fact that it is also attested for three other minor impurity bearers: the priest who supervises the incineration of the Red Cow (Num 19:7; and, presumably, the one who incinerates it, v 8), the one who dispatches the scapegoat (16:26), and the one who incinerates the *ḥaṭṭāʾt* animals (16:28; see the NOTE on this verse); all three are permitted to return to the camp after their ablutions even though their impurity lasts until evening (Num 19:7; see the NOTE on 16:26).

The implications are clear. These impure persons are not permitted to return to the camp because their impurity, being airborne, would pollute the sanctuary. But according to the third law of sancta contamination (COMMENT E above), airborne impurity must undergo two stages of purification, the first to reduce its force to direct contact and the second to eliminate it altogether. This, indeed, is what the above-cited cases provide: the ablution that allows the impurity bearer to return to camp, where, however, his impurity can still be transmitted to sancta by direct contact until the evening, after which his impurity is gone. Thus three, not just two, stages of purification must be presupposed: preablution, postablution, and evening. Strikingly, this newly introduced intermediate stage, postablution, is present in the rabbinic system, where its bearer goes by the name *ṭěbûl yôm*, literally, "immersed for a day," who, likewise, is free to associate with the common but it still barred from the sacred until the evening or, if his impurity is major, until the prescribed sacrifices the following day (*m. Kelim* 1:5; *Sipra*, Emor. 4:8; *b. Šabb.* 14b).

Ostensibly, this three-tiered purification does not apply to the other minor impurity bearers (8, 10, 11, 12) who are not banished from the camp but stay at home, implying that in the preablution stage their impurity is not airborne. Nonetheless, there is ample evidence outside Scripture that, as late as the end of the Second Temple period, these same impurity bearers were quarantined. Regarding the corpse-contaminated person (7) and the menstruant (8), Josephus avers that they were quarantined (*Ant.* 3.261–62), and as for the emitter of semen (10), Philo declares that husband and wife, after sex, "are not allowed when they leave the bed, to touch anything until they have made their ablutions" (*Laws* 3. 63), implying that before their ablutions they contaminated common things directly (10D). Note that, according to the sancta contamination law (2a, COMMENT E above), impurity bearers who contaminate the common directly contaminate the sacred from afar. Why then does not this severer ruling (attributed to P_2/H) demand their expulsion from the camp? The answer may well be one of logistics. The corpse-contaminated soldiers (Num 31:19, 24) and the handlers of the Red Cow, scapegoat, and burnt *ḥaṭṭā't* (9) have this in common: they incur impurity *outside* the camp. The other minor impurity bearers incur impurity *within* the camp. Those already outside perform their ablutions outside; those within also bathe within, but in the meantime *they are isolated*, perhaps in separate quarters (for the menstruant, see *m. Nid.* 7:4; *t. Nid.* 6:15; Jos., *Ant.* 3.261; and chap. 12, COMMENT A). Thus, in this tradition, it is the locus of the impurity that determines the locus of the quarantine. But the result is the same: until the ablution, the impurity bearer is considered dangerous to the common and sacred alike; after the ablution and until the evening (or the sacrifices), the impurity has been reduced to allow contact with the common but not with the sacred. Of course, common sense dictates that the ablution would take place as soon as possible (as recorded by Philo, above) so that the person could go about his or her business and need only take care not to enter the sanctuary or partake of sacred food for the rest of the day.

The purificatory process described above is at odds with the system developed in the main Priestly texts. This process consists of components that do not fit, indeed, that clash with these texts but, in aggregate, presuppose a system of their own, corroborated by the operative laws of sancta contamination. I have tentatively designated this secondary Priestly tradition as P_2/H. The double sigla bespeak the ambiguity that exists in identifying this tradition. If it is the case that all Priestly texts are from the P school, then the two traditions surviving in the Pentateuch are diachronically related: one P source replaced by another. Because P_2 clearly comprises older material—for instance, the law of the wilderness camp—whereas P_1 reflects the settled, urbanized Israelite society (e.g., contrast Lev 15 and Num 19 with Num 5:2–3), it is clear that the historic development was from P_2 to P_1. If, however, H proves to be the source of this secondary tradition, then we have to speak of a synchronic relationship for the texts: two variant traditions concerning impurity (P and H) circulating within Priestly circles.

Regardless of whether P_1 succeeded or was contemporaneous with P_2/H, the question still remains: Why did the former reject the latter? Specifically, why did P_1 refuse to banish the *zāb* and the corpse-contaminated person but allow him to stay at home? Why did P_1 not accept the older tradition, which probably required the corpse-contaminated person to sacrifice (as did the corpse-contaminated Nazirite and [Ezekiel's] priest) and, instead, reduce corpse-contamination to a minor impurity, requiring solely ablution and sunset but no sacrifice? Finally, why, according to the preceding reconstruction, did P_1 reduce the purificatory process of minor impurity bearers from three stages to two?

A glance at column D of the table provides the answer: P_1 initiates the long historic process whereby the power of impurity is progressively reduced. From the beginning, Israel eviscerated impurity of its demonic content but allowed traces of its original virulent force in the presence of sancta. Still, airborne impurity could not remain. It too closely resembled demonic impurity, and the danger persisted that the masses would not be able to distinguish the two. Slowly, then, almost imperceptibly, airborne impurity was progressively eliminated: all impurity bearers, with the exception of the *mĕṣōrāʿ*, were allowed to remain at home. Impurity to sancta was restricted to contact, and contact with the common, even in cases of severe impurity, became possible with washed hands. Ultimately, by the time the rabbinic age was reached, airborne impurity had totally disappeared from the scene. And when the Temple was destroyed and contamination of the sacred (except for agricultural gifts to the priests) was no longer possible, then the very ground for virulent impurity was removed. Except for the menstruant (cf. 18:19; 20:18), it was no longer a sin to remain impure. The full development of the historic process in the reduction of impurity is chronicled in the COMMENT on 5:1–13.

One presupposition of the table can be called into question, that sacrifices, the final stage for major impurities, are equivalent to evening, the final stage for minor impurities. Implied by this equation is that for minor impurities, evening combines with laundering and bathing to eliminate the last traces of impurity whereas for major impurities, the evening prior to the sacrifices performs no function at all. This anomaly can be justified by the fact that whenever sacrifices are prescribed, the previous evening is never mentioned. Moreover, in the case of two major impurity bearers, the *mĕṣōrāʿ* and the *zāb*, the text explicitly states that the person is purified *(wĕṭāhēr)* after laundering and bathing on the day prior to the sacrifice (14:8; 15:13), thus demonstrating that the intervening evening does not count in the purificatory process. Furthermore, the text also specifies for the parturient and *mĕṣōrāʿ* that they achieve complete purification *wĕṭāhēr(â)* only after the prescribed sacrificial rites (12:7, 8; 14:20). This can only mean that the last stage for major impurity is indeed the sacrifice, hence it is equivalent to the evening, the last stage for minor impurity.

Corroboration for this thesis is provided by the rabbis' description of the *mĕṣōrāʿ* standing outside the sacrificial court until the purificatory sacrifice is completed (*m. Neg.* 14:8–9) and by their categorical statement that the major impurity bearers—specifically the *mĕṣōrāʿ*, parturient, *zāb, zābâ,* and corpse-contaminated Nazirite—are forbidden to enter the sacrificial court until their sacrifices are offered (*m. Ker.* 2:1; cf. Maim., "Those Lacking Expiation" 1.1).

This thesis, however, is subject to a major question. The text expressly states, in contradiction to the rabbis, that the *mĕṣōrāʿ* and the *zāb* bring their prescribed sacrifices *lipnê YHWH petaḥ ʾōhel môʿēd* 'before the Lord, at the entrance to the Tent of Meeting' (14:11, 23; 15:14; cf. v 29), in other words, into the sacrificial court (see the NOTE on 1:3). And if the Hebrew is considered ambiguous enough to allow the interpretation that the sacrifices are admitted but not the person, the specificity of the language in the prescription for Ezekiel's corpse-contamination priest removes any lingering doubt: *ûbĕyôm bōʾô ʾel-haqqōdeš ʾel-heḥāṣēr happĕnîmît lĕšār ēt baqqōdeš yaqrîb ḥaṭṭāʾtô* 'On the day he reenters the sacred compound—the inner court—to officiate in the sacred compound, he shall offer his purification offering' (Ezek 44:27). In other words, the offerer *together* with his offering may enter the court. And as for the "purification" that is accredited to the parturient and the *mĕṣōrāʿ after* the sacrifices (12:7, 8; 14:20), this may refer to the sanctuary. That is, although the person is completely pure and may enter the sanctuary, he or she in effect is not considered pure until the sanctuary is also purified (D. Wright). Alternatively, this final purification, *wĕṭāhēr(â),* may be understood as a clause of summary, not of result; that is, having gone through the prescribed previous stages, the person shall have become completely pure (B. Schwartz).

As I have no explanation for the unambiguous and incontrovertible evidence of the text that the sacrifices are brought into the sanctuary court together with their offerers, I have therefore inserted into the final stage (c) of the major impurity bearers the alternative "or [eve]," thereby allowing for the possibility that the evening before the sacrifice, though never mentioned in the text, suffices—just as with minor impurity bearers—to eliminate the last vestige of impurity, which then permits the person to enter the sanctuary with the prescribed sacrifices the following morning. According to this construction, the residual impurity would last only for the few hours between laundering/bathing and evening, and would correspond to the rabbinic category of *tĕbûl yôm,* noted above, for some of the minor impurity bearers. The net effect would be total congruence between major and minor impurities: both would cease to pollute the common by the ablution and the sacred by the evening.

G. The Rationale for Biblical Impurity (Continued)

In this COMMENT, I continue the discussion begun in chap. 12, COMMENT B. Studies in the concept of impurity have generally identified its underlying cause as the fear of the unknown or of demonic possession (e.g., Levy-Bruhl 1935; Kornfeld 1965; Elliger 1966). Aside from the total inapplicability of this definition to biblical impurity, it has been challenged on its own grounds by Douglas (and others, e.g., Paschen 1970: 62), who points out that from earliest times human beings reacted to the mysteries of nature as much with awe as with fear (1966: 1).

Douglas's theory is not without its own defects. As discussed earlier (chap. 11, COMMENT E), she has equated impurity with what we call dirt, which she defines as matter out of place. Applying this definition to Lev 11, she declares that the forbidden animals are "out of place" in their media, as determined by their means of locomotion. This insight, as I have indicated, proved helpful but inadequate to explain why only certain animals were permitted and not others. More valuable is her utilization of the Durkheimian hypothesis that the animal world is a mirror of human society (ibid.).

The opposite of "dirt out of place" is, of course, order, which in the Bible would correspond to the sphere of the holy. This accounts for Douglas's definition of the holy as "wholeness and completeness" (ibid.: 51), and she correctly points to the biblical injunctions that priests and sacrificial animals must be unblemished. That wholeness (Hebrew tāmîm) is a significant ingredient of holiness cannot be gainsaid. Indeed, it is precisely for this reason that the Qumran sectaries ban blemished persons from residing in the Temple city (11QT 45:12–14).

Nevertheless, this definition falls short because it fails to take into account the two pairs of antonyms laid down by the Priestly legislators: holy–common and impure–pure (10:10). A blemished animal or priest is not impure but common (ḥōl). As for the prohibition against the blemished in the sanctuary, it only applies to priests officiating in the sanctuary and to animals offered on the altar. By contrast, any blemished Israelite—priest and lay person alike—may enter the sacred precincts and offer his sacrifices. If the holy and the impure are lethal antagonists, and they certainly are, then they clash not in the matter of "wholeness" but on an entirely different plane.

It is best to begin again with some comparative data. Meigs, who critiqued Douglas so trenchantly on her "dirt" hypothesis (chap. 11, COMMENT E), comes close to the mark in defining impurity as "(1) substances which are perceived as decaying, carriers of such substances and symbols of them; (2) in those contexts in which the substances, their carriers, or symbols are threatening to gain access to the body; (3) where that access is not desired" (1978: 313). Meigs's conclusions are founded on her investigations of the Hua of New Guinea, and they are congruent with those reached in Culpepper's study of Zoroastrian practices: "all sickness and body excretions were understood to participate in death-impurity" (1974: 205) and Burton's evaluation of Nuer impurity: "The necessity of maintaining the distance between bleeding youth (undergoing initiation) and pregnant women, and between bleeding women (menstruants) and potential life (intercourse) is thus a symbolic statement of the necessity for keeping life-creating processes from potentially life-destructive forces" (1974: 530). The common denominator of these conclusions is that impurity is associated with the sphere of death. This line of approach has been taken by some biblical researchers (Dillmann and Ryssel 1897: 523; von Rad 1962: 1.272; Kornfeld 1965; Paschen 1970: 63; Feldman 1977: 35–37; Füglister 1977). Their suggestion merits consideration.

A mere glance at the list of impurity bearers in the impurity table (column A, COMMENT F above) suffices to reveal that this list is arbitrary and artificial. It does not focus on disease or even on disorders, if by that is meant unnatural disruptions of bodily functions; the inclusion of the parturient, menstruant, and emitter of semen contravenes such a notion. Furthermore, to judge by the high percentage of medical texts in the cuneiform documents of ancient Mesopotamia (Oppenheim 1964: 288–305), there can be no doubt that many diseases were also diagnosed, cataloged, and treated in ancient Israel. Thus, the conclusion is inescapable that the impurities entered into this list have no intrinsic meaning in themselves but were selected because they serve a larger, overarching purpose. It is of no small significance that the diet laws of the Priestly system (chap. 11), which are contiguous to and inseparable from the bodily impurities in this list (covering chaps. 12–15) are also governed by criteria, such as cud chewing and hoof splitting, which are equally arbitrary and meaningless in themselves but serve a larger, extrinsic purpose. This purpose can be deduced both from the explicit rationale of holiness (11:43–45; chap. 11, COMMENT E) and from the implications of relevant texts (e.g., Gen 9:4; Lev 17:3–5, 10–14; cf. chap. 11, COMMENT C), to wit: to treat animal life as inviolable except for a few animals that may be eaten provided they are slaughtered properly (chap. 11, COMMENT D) and their blood is drained (chap. 11, COMMENT C).

I submit that the same rationale or, more precisely, its complement obtains here. The bodily impurities enumerated in the impurity table (COMMENT F above) focus on four phenomena: death (4, 5, 7, 11), blood (2, 3, 8), semen (3, 10), and scale disease (1). Their common denominator is death. Vaginal blood and semen represent the forces of life; their loss—death (see chap. 12, COMMENT B). In the case of scale disease, this symbolism is made explicit: Aaron prays for his stricken sister, "Let her not be like a corpse" (Num 12:12). Furthermore, scale disease is powerful enough to contaminate by overhang, and it is no accident that it shares this feature with the corpse (Num 19:14). The wasting of the body, the common characteristic of all biblically impure skin diseases, symbolizes the death process as much as the loss of blood and semen.

Thus *ṭum²â* and *qĕdûšâ*, biblical impurity and holiness, are semantic opposites. And as the quintessence and source of *qĕdûšâ* resides with God, it is imperative for Israel to control the occurrence of impurity lest it impinge upon the realm of the holy God. The forces pitted against each other in the cosmic struggle are no longer the benevolent and demonic deities who populate the mythologies of Israel's neighbors but the forces of life and death set loose by man himself through his obedience to or defiance of God's commandments. Among all of the diachronic changes that occur in the development of Israel's impurity laws (see COMMENT F), this clearly is the most significant: the total severance of impurity from the demonic and its reinterpretation as a symbolic system reminding Israel of its imperative to cleave to life and reject death.

I have been asked three questions (Eilberg-Schwartz 1988: 26 n. 21). The first is: "If the distinction between life and death was so crucial for the biblical writers why did they continue the institution of sacrifice, which requires the slaughter of animals?" The obvious retort is: What choice did they have? As perceptively observed by Maimonides, "man, according to his nature, is not capable of abandoning suddenly all to which he was accustomed" and Israel's God, therefore, "suffered the above-mentioned kinds of (sacrificial) worship to remain, but transferred them from created or imaginary and unreal things to His own name" (*Guide* 3.32). Besides, this alleged discrepancy would have been categorically dismissed by the Priestly legists. Sacrifice, in their view, means returning life to its creator. This is the underlying postulate of the blood prohibitions as well (chap. 11, COMMENT C). Herein lies the link between the two major corpora in P's Leviticus, sacrifices (chaps. 1–10) and impurities (chaps. 11–16). Because the concept of holiness represents the forces of life (chap. 11, COMMENT E), the sacrificial system enables Israel to enter the sanctuary—the realm of holiness—and receive, via the sacrifices, the divine blessing (cf. Exod 20:24) of life-giving procreation and life-sustaining produce (19:25; 23:11; Ezek 44:30; Prov 3:9–10). Simultaneously, Israel must guard against the occurrence and incursion of impurity, the symbol of death. Thus, it is this eternal struggle between the forces of good and evil, life and death—removed by Israel from polytheistic theomachy to the inner life of man—that is represented by the tandem, P's sacrificial and impurity systems (for details see the Introduction, §E).

The second query states that "one would expect purification (from corpse contamination) to occur via a substance that symbolizes life" rather than by means of the ashes of a cow. Here, in keeping with Maimonides' dictum (above), Israel adopted an exorcistic rite and eviscerated it of its pagan content (chap. 4, COMMENT G). Moreover, the purificatory waters do in fact symbolize life: the Cow is *red*, *red* substances are included, and so the association with the blood, that is, life, is clear!

As for the final objection, that on the basis of the life–death opposition Israel should have been forbidden to cook a kid in the milk of any animal, not just that of its mother, I need only cite my conclusions that the prohibition originally was directed against a specific cultic act before it was incorporated (by D) as a dietary law, that iconography emphasizes the mother suckling its young, and the rabbis indeed draw the logical inference that all milk (and all animals) is intended (chap. 11, COMMENTS B and F).

As an afterthought, I would mention this rationale for biblical impurity may lie behind the enigmatic dictum of the tannaitic sages that "all sacred writings defile the hands" (*m. Yad.* 3:5). That something sacred can transmit impurity is unprecedented, illogical, and ostensibly inexplicable. Frequently cited is this subsequent rabbinic explanation: It was customary to store the Torah Scroll alongside *terûmâ*, the portion of the produce set aside for the priests (cf. Num 18:11–12; Deut 12:6; Neh 10:38, 40). Because the *terûmâ* attracted mice that damaged the scrolls, the rabbis forced the separation of the scrolls from the *terûmâ* by imposing an impure status on the scrolls. Nevertheless, even if it can be proved that sacred scrolls were indeed stored with sacred produce (a Roman practice, according to an oral communication by S. Lieberman to N. Sarna) it is difficult to accept that "mice are responsible for this ruling" (Ish-Shalom). Moreover, there is good reason to believe that this ruling is pretannaitic in origin (details in Haran 1956: 259–62). How then are we to account for it, particularly in view of the following exception made to this rule: "All [sacred] scrolls defile the hands except the scroll of the Temple Court" (*m. Kelim* 15:6)?

P. Kyle McCarter has proposed a solution (lecture, April 1988, the full text of which he kindly sent me) that makes sense and merits serious consideration. He writes: "A Torah Scroll . . . is sacred. For this very reason, then, it is a potential source of defilement. If it is blemished or corrupted, it transmits uncleanness. The Books of the Temple Court were protected from corruption by 'The Correctors of the Book' (*y. Šeqal.* iv, 48a; cf. *b. Ketub.* 106a). Other sacred books, however, could not be counted upon to be unblemished and were regarded as sources of defilement. . . . They are copies of the scroll of the Temple Court, imitations. The copies are not subject to the vigilance of the correctors, so they are apt to be corrupt."

If McCarter's theory proves correct, then the biblical postulate of the sanctity of human life as the repository of the divine image was subsequently extended to the sacred book, the repository of the divine word.

H. Neusner on Purities

Jacob Neusner has rendered a unique and lasting contribution to scholarship by his translations, commentaries, and studies of the classic literature of the talmudic period. As a historian of religion, he has focused on tracing the diachronic development of this literature, beginning with its roots in Scripture. It is the latter aspect of his work that concerns us here. Because he is the first to have undertaken this important task, it is inevitable that mistakes will be made. Neusner himself is fully aware of this hazard, as he frequently reminds his readers. He is to be congratulated for dauntlessly pursuing this task. He is fulfilling the dictum laid down by the rabbis themselves: "It is not your duty to complete the work, but neither are you free to desist from it" (*m. ʾAbot* 2:21).

Neusner's greatest mistake is his unawareness that much of what he attributes to the rabbis as their innovation has its roots in Scripture. Thus he concludes his work on the tractate *Niddah "Because the tabernacle is in their midst, Israel must be clean, even when not in the tabernacle,* which is exactly what Lev 15:31 says—to a Pharisee" (1977a: 221; cf. 1981b: 227; 1981c: 21–22). But this is precisely what this verse says to biblical Israel. Neusner has seized upon a seminal verse in Priestly theology and has misconstrued it. Severer impurity can impinge on sancta from wherever it occurs (COMMENT E above; chap. 4, COMMENTS B and C). Thus the priests are commanded, "You shall set apart the Israelites from their impurity" (15:31a), not in the sanctuary but in the house, in the marketplace, in the daily routine—wherever corpse and carcass contamination, scale disease, genital discharge (chaps. 11–15) can occur. Lev 15:31 does not confine "the observance of menstrual and related taboos to the sanctuary" (1977a: 202) but, to the contrary, emphatically states that the sanctuary is endangered by impurity arising from any source. Neusner asseverates, "What would have surprised the priestly authors was the requirement of purity outside the Jerusalem Temple and for a purpose other than the conduct of the Temple cult" (1973: 53); it is we who are surprised.

Another of Neusner's axiomatic mistakes is in lumping all of the Priestly material together, forgetting that the difference between P and H is not one of semantics or style but one of ideology. Hence, a doctrine missing in one source may very well be ensconced in another. Thus the notion that illicit sex is sinful is not only found outside the Priestly text (Gen 34:5–13; Ezek 22:11 [incorrectly cited as 24:11]; 1973: 14) but is a cardinal doctrine of H (Lev 18, 20), the very source of the verse cited from Ezekiel (cf. Ezek 22:11 with Lev 18:15; 20:12). Moreover, that impurity defiles the land as well as the sanctuary (1973: 15 n. 1) is the very rock upon which H's theology rests (18:24–30; 20:22–24), again a model for Ezekiel (e.g., Ezek 22:24).

Neusner's repeated claim that it is the signal contribution of the Mishna to transfer the locus of holiness (and concern for impurity) from the sanctuary to the bed and the table (e.g., 1977c: 298–99) completely ignores the fact that the Priestly source H is the Mishna's source for this doctrine (for the table, 11:43–45; for the bed, 20:7–8, 26). Indeed, the Mishna and Qumran can focus on these loci (1977c: 38–39, 52, 76) precisely because the Priestly legislators have constructed a system based on the postulate that severe impurity pollutes the sanctuary (P) and the land (H). Neusner is certain that no one "except the *yaḥad* (i.e., Qumran) in the period of the Second Temple (did) claim that sin causes impurity" (1973: 81; cf. 54). But the claim is biblical. It is Israel's priest who proclaimed that sacrificial expiation was required for violating any prohibitive commandment (see the NOTE on 4:2) and for this reason, *pace* Neusner. This notion became a prophetic doctrine, especially for the priest-prophet Ezekiel.

Neusner also maintains that the rabbis innovated, particularly during the period 70–140 C.E., both the relation between intentions and action and the conception of levels of sanctification and corresponding removes of cleanness (1977c: 182; 1984: 71). The former has been shown to be anchored in Scripture (chap. 7, COMMENT H), the latter in the "Table of Purification Procedures and Their Effects" (COMMENT F above). Thus it is patently wrong to assert that the "destruction of the Temple, the primary locus of the sacred, is the motivation for the establishment of the peripheral levels of sanctity" (1977c: 192; cf. 1977b: 176). These levels—with the exception of *tĕrûmâ*—were established long before, in biblical times (COMMENT F above). And the converse is equally wrong: "But in the dim past of the tractate (Tebul Yom) is the conception, which Scripture certainly does not know, that the person is unclean in a *diminished* (emphasis mine) state of uncleanness" (1981b: 213). To counter this claim, it should suffice merely to recall the graduated reduction in the impurity of the scale-diseased person, explicitly stipulated by the telltale verb *wĕṭāhēr* (14:8, 9, 19; details in COMMENT F above).

Furthermore, it is unwarranted to aver that "In the (rabbinic) system of uncleanness, it is man who inaugurates the processes by which food and utensils become subject to uncleanness" (1977c: 186). The innovation, once again, is biblical. Man is charged with the responsibility to avoid impurity (15:31) and to eliminate it, if avoidance proves impossible (chaps. 11–15; Num 19). Impurity can strike man's objects but only if they are manufactured, usable (see the NOTE on 11:32), and—with the exception of earthenware—can be purified. The conclusion that "the mysterious, supernatural force of contamination therefore is subjected to human manipulation, specifically to human will" (1977c: 186) is equally true for the Bible. To state categorically that "Kelim begins in the original conception that utensils not in the Temple and not for use in the cult are subject to uncleanness. Neither Scripture nor exegesis of Scripture generates that revolutionary conception" (1981a: 182) is not only hyperbole but, in view of Lev. 11, dead wrong (see above). Finally, to proclaim that "Mishnah in its most basic conceptual stratum certainly does assume *what Scripture nowhere recognizes* (emphasis mine), which is that immersion in the still waters of a pool, collected naturally on the ground and without human intervention effects purification" (1977c: 85) is not only unsupported by evidence but contravened by the fact that nowhere (except for the *zāb;* see the NOTE on 15:13) is there any qualification for the water used in ablutions; moreover, the explicit statement that pure, unpollutable water can be collected (see the NOTE on 11:36) implies that the use of rain (collected) water is not a rabbinic innovation but a commonplace biblical practice.

Perhaps the clearest way of demonstrating how Neusner has failed to recognize the biblical foundations of the Mishnaic order of Purities is to quote his summation of those positions which he attributes to the founding of the Mishnaic system, which, he claims, "originates, in the century or so before 70" (1981a: 210):

First, cleanness with special reference to food and drink, pots and pans, is possible outside the cult. Second, cleanness is required outside the cult. Third, the cultic taboos governing the protection and disposition of parts of the sacrificial meat which are to be given to the priests apply to other sorts of food as well. They apply, specifically, to ordinary food, not food deriving from, or related to, the altar; that is, not food directed to the priesthood. Fourth, the levitical taboos on sources of uncleanness therefore apply to ordinary food, and, it follows, fifth, one must be careful to avoid these sources of uncleanness or to undergo a rite of purification if one has had contact with said contaminating sources. Finally, the direction and purpose of the system as a whole, in its earliest formulation, clearly are to preserve the cleanness of the people of Israel, of the product of the land of Israel, of the sexual life of Israel, of the hearth and home of Israel. (1981a: 211)

The present examination of the Priestly laws of impurity (chaps. 11–15) and their implied system has demonstrated that they rest on the postulate that impurity incurred anywhere is potentially dangerous to the sanctuary. One who has touched, carried, or eaten a carcass *anywhere* must purify himself and his contaminated vessels even if he or the vessels never come near the sanctuary (11:24–40). Persons with genital discharges must purify themselves and the furniture they have lain or sat on *anywhere* they live (chaps. 12, 15). If moldy garments and fungous houses, located *anywhere*, cannot be purified, they must be destroyed (13:47–58; 14:33–53). Indeed, this last-mentioned item is deserving of special emphasis: what threat does an immovable, inert house offer to the sanctuary that it should be subject to the same law of impurity as a scale-diseased person and must undergo the same initial rite of purification (14:4–7)? Thus, the Priestly legislators are very much concerned with the need to eliminate or, at least, control the occurrence of impurity *anywhere in the land*— whether in the home, on the table, or in the bed. Had they been asked whether their goal was "to preserve the cleanness of the people of Israel, of the product of the land of Israel, of the sexual life of Israel, of the hearth and home of Israel," they would have responded with a resounding "Amen!"

Neusner's discussion of Mishna's biblical foundations is also replete with errors, which, unfortunately, grate on the reader because he is wont to repeat himself, often verbatim. The following is a sample. It is erroneous to claim that live animals and moldy fabrics are sources of impurity (1977c: 27–28); see chap. 11; 13:47–59. It is not true that it is a sin to become unclean (ibid. 33); it is only a sin to forego purification (5:2–3; 17:15, 16; COMMENT on 5:1–13). It is further not true that "When . . . people not involved in priestly activities are declared unclean, the consequence is not specified" (1977c: 34); see Num 15:31; Num 19:13, 20; etc. Qumran is hardly a "SYSTEM WITHOUT (EXTANT) RULES" (1977c: 37); Yadin's preliminary reports on 11QT (1967, 1971a,

1971b) should have sufficed to prove that Qumranites were even more obsessed by priestly rules than their fellow Jews (see COMMENT D above). Both halves of the verse, Lev 15:10a and 15:10b, are mistranslated and misunderstood (1977c: 67–68; see the NOTES). The theory that the new house (tent) takes the place of the old (the corpse) (1977c: 74–75) is wrong; corpse impurity acts like a gas (the term "viscous gas" is an oxymoron); it simply fills its container. Purification is *not* attained through the application of blood (1977c: 30; 1976: 199–203; 1981b: 216); see chap. 4, COMMENTS A and B. Thus Qumran could not have substituted water for blood in their purifications (ibid.). Nor is sunset by itself a means of purification (ibid.) without prior ablution (see the NOTE on 11:24). Further, the rabbis could ignore the sunset requirement (1977c: 87) for the single reason that without the Temple there was no longer any fear of contaminating the realm of the sacred. Also, "to be unclean is abnormal and is the result of unnatural processes" (1977c: 95) is belied by the natural, normal impurities of menstruation, birth, and sex. That the menstrual taboo functions "through extended spatial affects, by pressure on beds and chairs" and that corpse contamination, by contrast, functions "through extended temporal affects, for a week" (ibid.) is misleading; both impurities function spatially and temporally because each is communicable and lasts a week; indeed, the menstruant defiles to an even severer degree because her impurity can be transmitted to a second remove (NOTE on "it," 15:23). The supposition that there is conflict between removes of uncleanness and susceptibility to sancta (1977c: 160) is groundless; both conceptions are rooted in a single coherent system in Scripture (COMMENT F above).

For Neusner, all biblical objects and loci subject to impurity are confined to the cult and only subsequently "someone opened the pertinent Scriptures and decided to apply them to utensils not involved in the cult" (1974: 383; cf. 1981a: 182). In this regard, the rabbis invented nothing; Lev 11 deals with carcasses that contaminate persons and utensils outside the cult. Neusner believes that the burning of the Red Cow (Num 19) is "conducted in a state of uncleanness" (1981a: 183, 203–4; 1981b: 217, 221) because "the rite takes place outside of the camp, which is to say, in an unclean place" (1981a: 56; 1984: 66), an assertion explicitly contradicted by Scripture itself (e.g., 4:12; 6:4; Num 19:9). His contention that only spring water purifies (1976: 197–200) has already been refuted (in the NOTE on 15:13). Corpse contamination is *not* primarily "the concern of the priesthood" (1973: 21–22); see Num 19 and esp. Num 31:19–20. For the Nazirite, "the primary matter of uncleanness is that of a corpse" (1973: 23) for the simple reason that the contact occurred accidentally (Num 6:9a) whereas other impurities are deemed avoidable. The claim that the doctrine that scale disease is caused by sin is "the innovation of earlier rabbinic Judaism" (1973: 88) and "a startling innovation" (1973: 106) is refuted by Num 12 and 2 Chr 26:16, by the purpose of the enjoined sacrifices (see the NOTES on

14:12–13, 19–20), and by the prevalence of this doctrine throughout the ancient Near East in cultures anterior to Israel (chap. 13, COMMENT B).

In sum, Neusner's comprehension of Scripture is wanting. The result is not only the errors that crop up in his writings but his frequently wrong conclusions concerning the relationship of rabbinic impurity to Scripture. Specifically, many of the innovations ascribed to the rabbis turn out to have biblical precedents. We can all be grateful to Neusner for initiating the long-needed project of explaining the biblical roots of the rabbinic ideas on impurity. The task, however, must begin anew.

THE DAY OF PURGATION (YÔM KIPPÛR) (16:1–34)

Introduction

16 ¹The Lord spoke to Moses after the death of the two sons of Aaron who died when they encroached upon the presence of the Lord.

Precautions and Provisions

²The Lord spoke to Moses: Tell your brother Aaron that he is not to come whenever he chooses into the adytum, inside the veil, in front of the kappōret that is upon the Ark, lest he die; for by means of the cloud I shall appear on the kappōret. ³This is how Aaron shall enter the adytum: with a bull of the herd as a purification offering and a ram for a burnt offering; ⁴he shall put on a sacral linen tunic, linen breeches shall be on his body, and he shall gird himself with a linen sash, and he shall don a linen turban. These are the sacral vestments he shall put on after bathing his body in water. ⁵And from the Israelite community he shall take two he-goats for a purification offering and a ram for a burnt offering.

The Purgation Ritual

⁶Aaron shall bring forward his own bull of purification offering to effect purgation for himself and for his household; ⁷and he shall take the two he-goats and set them before the Lord at the entrance of the Tent of Meeting. ⁸Aaron shall place lots upon the two goats, one marked "for the Lord" and the other "for Azazel." ⁹Aaron shall bring forward the goat designated by lot "for the Lord" to sacrifice it as a purification offering; ¹⁰while the goat designated by lot "for Azazel" shall be stationed alive before the Lord to perform expiation upon it by sending it off into the wilderness to Azazel.

¹¹When Aaron shall bring forward his bull of purification offering to effect purgation for himself and his household, he shall slaughter his bull of purification offering. ¹²He shall take a panful of fiery coals from atop the altar before

the Lord, and two handfuls of finely ground perfumed incense, and bring [these] inside the veil. ¹³He shall put the incense on the fire before the Lord so that the cloud from the incense covers the *kappōret* that is over [the Ark of] the Pact, lest he die. ¹⁴He shall take some of the blood of the bull and sprinkle it with his finger on the *kappōret* on its east side; and in front of the *kappōret* he shall sprinkle some of the blood with his finger seven times.

¹⁵He shall then slaughter the people's goat of purification offering, bring its blood inside the veil, and manipulate its blood as he did with the blood of the bull; he shall sprinkle it upon the *kappōret* and before the *kappōret*. ¹⁶Thus he shall purge the adytum of the pollution and transgressions of the Israelites, including all of their sins; and he shall do likewise for the Tent of Meeting, which abides with them in the midst of their pollution. ¹⁷No one shall be in the Tent of Meeting when he goes in to effect purgation in the adytum until he comes out. Thus he shall effect purgation for himself and his household and for the entire congregation of Israel. ¹⁸He shall then come out to the altar that is before the Lord and effect purgation upon it. He shall take some of the blood of the bull and of the goat and put it upon the horns around the altar; ¹⁹and he shall sprinkle some of the blood upon it with his finger seven times. Thus he shall purify it of the pollution of the Israelites and consecrate it.

The Scapegoat Ritual

²⁰When he has finished purging the adytum, the Tent of Meeting, and the altar, he shall bring forward the live goat. ²¹Aaron shall lean both of his hands upon the head of the live goat and confess over it all of the iniquities and transgressions of the Israelites, including all of their sins, and put them on the head of the goat; and it shall be sent off to the wilderness by a man in waiting. ²²Thus the goat shall carry upon it all of their iniquities to an inaccessible region.

The Altar Sacrifices

When the goat is set free in the wilderness, ²³Aaron shall go into the Tent of Meeting, take off the linen vestments that he put on when he entered the adytum, and leave them there. ²⁴He shall bathe his body in water in a holy place and put on his vestments; then he shall go out and sacrifice his burnt offering and the burnt offering of the people, effecting atonement for himself and for the people. ²⁵The suet of the purification offering he shall turn into smoke on the altar.

The Purification of the High Priest's Assistants

²⁶He who sets free the goat for Azazel shall launder his clothes and bathe his body in water; after that he may reenter the camp. ²⁷The purification-

offering bull and the purification-offering goat whose blood was brought in to effect purgation in the adytum shall be taken outside the camp; and their hides, their flesh, and their dung shall be burned in fire. ²⁸He who burned them shall launder his clothes and bathe his body in water; and after that he may reenter the camp.

The Date: An Appendix

²⁹And this shall be for you a law for all time: In the seventh month, on the tenth day of the month, you shall practice self-denial; and you shall do no manner of work, neither the native-born nor the alien who resides among you. ³⁰For on this day shall purgation be effected on your behalf to purify you of all your sins; you shall become pure before the Lord. ³¹It shall be a sabbath of complete rest for you, and you shall practice self-denial; it is a law for all time. ³²The priest who has been anointed and ordained to serve as priest in place of his father shall effect purgation. He shall put on the linen vestments, the sacral vestments. ³³He shall purge the holiest part of the sanctuary, and he shall purge the Tent of Meeting and the altar; he shall effect purgation for the priests and for all the people of the congregation. ³⁴This shall be for you a law for all time: to effect purgation on behalf of the Israelites for all their sins once a year.

Summary

And he [Aaron] did as the Lord had commanded Moses.

NOTES

16: 1. *after the death of the two sons of Aaron.* According to this initial verse, chap. 16 follows upon chap. 10. Thus chaps. 11–15 are an insert specifying the impurities that can pollute the sanctuary (15:31), for which the purgation rite of chap. 16 is mandated. From the point of view of the redactor, the connection of chap. 16 to chap. 10 makes sense. Nadab and Abihu had polluted the sanctuary doubly, in life by their sin and in death by their corpses (see chap. 4, COMMENT G). Yet chap. 10 has said nothing about the procedure for purging the sanctuary, which in such a case of severe pollution—the sin and subsequent death of Nadab and Abihu occurred in the sacred precincts—the entire sanctuary, including the adytum, would need to be purged. This procedure is detailed in chap. 16. Indeed, the fact that the rite described here could be regarded as an emergency measure originally (vv 2–3, and see COMMENT A below) fits the case of Nadab and Abihu perfectly.

when they enroached upon (bĕqorbātām). An infinitival construction, *lĕqorbâ* (Exod 36:2), found with other verbs as well, such as *ʾoklâ* (Jer 12:9), *ʾahăbâ* (Deut 10:2); *mošḥâ* (Exod 29:29). Three interpretations have been proffered. (1) It means "enter," that is, the adytum (Ibn Ezra). But the textual support he gives, *lĕqorbâ ʾel-hammĕl āʾkâ* (Exod 36:2), can only be rendered "to qualify for the project" (Milgrom 1970a: 77–80, and see below). (2) Ramban reads it as "seek access," citing *bĕqorbātām ʾel-hammizbēaḥ* 'in seeking access to the altar' (Exod 40:32). This meaning is correct for legitimate access (Milgrom 1970a: 33–42), but Nadab and Abihu were guilty of illegitimate access. (3) In such a situation the rendering must be "encroach" (Milgrom 1970a: 16–32). The nature of this encroachment is discussed in the NOTE on 10:1. The Versions presume *bĕhaqrîbām ʾ ēš zārâ* 'when they offered alien fire', the precise wording found in Num 3:4; 26:61 (see the NOTE on 10:1). This reading is more appropriate when the preposition *lipnê* follows (see below).

upon the presence (lipnê). The usual preposition with *qārab* is *ʾel*, 'to' (e.g., 9:7, 8; 22:3; Num 17:28; 18:3, 22). But with the Lord as object, the implied anthropomorphism is softened by the use of *lipnê* 'before', in other words, not in direct contact with divinity but in his presence (e.g., Exod 16:9[P]; Ps 119:169; esp. in the *hiphʿîl*, 3:1, 7; 6:7; 10:1; Num 3:4; 6:16; 17:3), a nicety not observed in the other sources (e.g., Exod 22:7; 1 Sam 14:36; Isa 48:16; Ezek 44:15; Zeph 3:2). If the reading of the Versions is accepted (see above), this preposition offers no difficulties (cf. 10:1; Num 3:4; 26:61).

2. *The Lord spoke to Moses.* These words begin the long unit of vv 2–28, which had an independent existence before it was linked to v 1 and given an appendix, vv 29–34 (see COMMENT A below). If this verse were really the continuation of v 1, it would have begun with the words *wayyōʾmer ʾēlāyw* 'and spoke to him' (e.g., Exod 7:26; 8:16; 9:13; Lev 1:2; 15:2; 17:2).

Tell your brother Aaron. It has already been noted (cf. 10:8) that the divine instructions concerning the sacrificial system and, indeed, the entire description of the priestly duties are communicated to Aaron through the mediation of Moses (see also the NOTE on 21:1). The rare exceptions (10:8; Num 18:1, 8, 20) only accentuate this fact. It is all the more astounding here, where the entire ritual complex is conducted solely by Aaron. Moses' name does not appear again until the final verse, where we are informed that Aaron "did as the Lord had commanded Moses" (v 34b). Again, we are confronted with P's tacit assumption that the prophet is superior to the priest (for details see the COMMENT on 10:16–20).

that he is not to come (wĕʾal yābōʾ). A warning, not an apodictic prohibition (Bright 1973).

whenever he chooses. bĕkol-ʿēt, literally, "at all times" (e.g., Exod 18:22, 26; Ps 34:2). It should be noted that nothing is said concerning a fixed time. This fact is observed by the midrash, which makes this striking comment: *bĕkol šāʿâ šehûʾ rôṣeh likkānēs yikkānēs ûbilbad šeyĕhēʾ niknās kassēder hazzeh* 'He (Aaron) may enter any time he chooses as long as he follows this procedure' (*Midr. Lev. Rab.* 21:7; cf. *Midr. Exod. Rab.* 38:8), from which Elijah of Vilna (cited by David Luria, ad loc. and Abraham Danzig 1863: 461–62) concludes that Aaron could enter the adytum whenever he chose but his successors could do so only on the annual Day of Purgation. His observation, I believe, is correct, for it points to the possibility that initially the purgation rite for the sanctuary was an emergency measure, a thesis that fits the theory that originally this chapter followed upon the deaths of Nadab and Abihu (see the NOTE on v 1) and which can be supported on many additional counts (see COMMENT A below). M. Margoliot (1956: 484) objects to this interpretation of the midrash because the midrash continues with this statement: "Rabbi Judah ben Rabbi Eleazar said he (Aaron) must, when entering, wear thirty-six bells and thirty-six pomegranates; our Rabbis say: seventy-two bells and seventy-two pomegranates." Margoliot comments that this action by the high priest must have taken place daily in the outer shrine when he wore his full regalia (see Exod 28:33-34) in the performance of the *Tāmîd* (see Exod 30:6-8; Lev 24:1-4). Thus, concludes Margoliot, the midrash is interpreting the term *qōdeš* (in this verse) as the outer shrine (see also *b. Menoḥ.* 27b). As pointed out by Samuel Strashun (on *Midr. Lev. Rab.* 21:7), however, this second statement of the midrash can also refer to the sanctuary purgation rite, for the high priest does indeed don his full regalia at its conclusion when he sacrifices the burnt offering (see v 24). As for *qōdeš*, whereas it can mean the outer shrine elsewhere in P, in this chapter, uniquely, it stands for the adytum (v 2, above). Thus the insight of the midrash stands; for its implications, see COMMENT A below.

the adytum (haqqōdeš). This term means "adytum," the inner shrine containing the Ark, only here in chap. 16 (vv 2, 3, 16, 17, 20, 23, 27), whereas elsewhere in P it stands for the outer shrine and the adytum is called *qōdeš haqqŏdāšîm* 'the holy of holies' (e.g., Exod 26:33). This terminological anomaly is one of the many reasons for regarding vv 2–28 as comprising a discrete literary unit that was not originally composed by the author or redactor of P (see COMMENT A).

inside the veil (mibbêt lappārōket). An alternate expression for the adytum (vv 12, 15; Exod 26:33; Num 18:7). The redundancy here can only be explained as an editorial gloss, underscoring the fact that *haqqōdeš* should be understood as the adytum, not as the outer shrine, as elsewhere in P (see above).

Strangely, the Masoretes have placed the major disjunctive accent, the *'etnaḥtā'*, here instead of at *yāmût* 'he will die', the logical end of this statement. This accentuation may reflect either of two rabbinic views: (1) that of the Pharisees versus the Sadducees (*b. Yoma* 19b, 53a; *y. Yoma* 39a), that entering the adytum (with the unlit censer) and proceeding to the Ark (with lit censer) comprise two discrete actions (cf. v 13), or (2) that the high priest must be careful upon entry into the adytum even when there is no Ark inside, as in the Second Temple, and all the more so when there was an Ark (v 2b; Rabbi Judah in *b. Menaḥ.* 27b; see Shadal).

in front of ('el pĕnê). Distinguished from *lipnê* 'in front of' in that it is used with verbs of motion, such as "they brought (wayyiqḥû) what Moses had commanded to the front of *(ʾel pĕnê)* the Tent of Meeting . . . and stood *(wayyaʿamdû)* before *(lipnê)* the Lord" (9:5).

the kappōret. Untranslatable, so far. This term refers to the solid gold slab (3.75 feet by 2.25 feet) atop the Ark, at the edges of which were two cherubim, of one piece with it and made of hammered gold, kneeling and facing each other with bowed heads and outstretched wings so as to touch in the middle. It can hardly be rendered "mercy seat/throne" *(RSV, JB;* cf. the LXX) or "cover" *(NJPS, NEB,* LXX on Exod 25:17)—even though the targum fragments from Qumran (4QtgLev) renders it *ksyʾ* 'cover' (Milik 1959: 31; 1977: 86–89; Fitzmeyer 1978–79)—either on etymological or on semantic grounds: the verb *kippēr* never implies mercy or cover (see COMMENT F below), and the *kappōret* never served an expiatory or covering function. Furthermore, in the Temple of Solomon the cherubim did not rest on the Ark but stood apart from it (1 Kgs 6:27; Paran 1989). But as the *kappōret* (rather than the cherubim or the Ark) is the focal point of the purgation rite *(kipper),* perhaps it took its name from its function on the Day of Purgation (D. Wright). Recently M. Görg (1977d; 1978) has suggested that it is a loanword from Egyptian *kp(n)rdwy* 'sole of the foot', current in the New Kingdom and probably pronounced *kappuri(e)t* at that time, and whose meaning could have been extended to denote "the place where the feet rest." The image of the Ark as the Lord's footstool is familiar from Scripture (Ps 132:7; 1 Chr 28:2).

for by means of the cloud I shall appear (kî beʿānān ʾērāʾeh). There is a venerable tradition that the sight of the uncovered Ark is fatal (1 Sam 6:19, cf. Num 4:20). Thus when camp was broken and the Tabernacle dismantled, the priests, who alone were permitted to cover the sancta (Num 4:15), took special pains to cover the Ark without viewing it; they would first remove the veil and, while holding it up before them, would march forward toward the Ark and cover it, thus accounting for the fact that whereas all of the other Tabernacle sancta were covered with specially made cloths (Num 4:7–14), the Ark had to be covered initially with the Tabernacle veil (Milgrom 1990a: 25–26).

Which cloud is meant, the cloud of incense the high priest raises in the adytum (v 13) or the divine firecloud that, according to P, descends upon the Tabernacle as a sign that Israel is to make camp (Num 9:15–23; cf. Exod 40:34–35) and rests upon the Ark whenever God speaks to Moses (Exod 25:22; Num 7:89)? Rabbinic exegesis splits on this question, the former view advocated by the majority: *Sipra,* Aḥare par. 1:13; *b. Yoma* 53a; cf. Ibn Ezra, and the latter by *Tg. Ps.-J.; Tg. Neof.;* Rabba in *b. Yoma* 53a; Rabbi Eleazar in *Sipra,* Aḥare par. 1:13; cf. Saadiah, Rashi, Rashbam. Both views are possible, for the preposition *b* can be rendered either as "by means of" (instrumental) or "as" (essential). The difference is not inconsequential. The incense-cloud interpretation implies that the high priest may only see the Ark *(kî* 'for', here being equivalent to *kî ʾim* 'except, only' [Rashi]) if his view is blocked by a screen—in conformance with the teaching of the Sadducees (above). The firecloud interpretation instead says nothing on this score but merely states why the high priest may not come at will into the adytum: the divine presence in the form of the firecloud rests upon the Ark.

The firecloud interpretation, however, is subject to the following objection: there is no prohibition against seeing the divine firecloud; every Israelite could testify that he or she witnessed its guiding presence (Exod 40:38; Deut 1:31–33). Neither can it be argued that the firecloud within the Tabernacle possessed more lethal power, for the Lord's *kābôd* (see Exod 16:10) was seen by all of Israel when it was inside the Tabernacle at the time of its dedication (9:23b). The cloud-of-incense interpretation, however, is not free of objection either, for it is only ten verses later that we are told that "the cloud" means the cloud of incense produced by the high priest after he has entered the adytum and has ostensibly seen the Ark. Yet this objection can be parried if it can be shown that "the cloud" is produced not by the incense but by a separate ingredient placed on the coals before the high priest enters the adytum, in which case the screen interpretation holds (see the NOTE on v 13). Finally, the screen interpretation is preferable, for vv 2a–5 are an inventory of the materials the high priest needs to perform his rites and the screen, this verse tells us, is indispensable (see COMMENT A below). Indeed, the fact that the verb appears in the first person, in contradistinction to the rest of this chapter, is an indication that this clause was inserted by a later hand (most likely that of H—see the Introduction, §H) precisely for the purpose of emphasizing the indispensability of the shield.

3. *This is how (bĕzōʾt).* For this usage, see Gen 34:15, 22; 42:15, 33; Exod 7:17; Num 16:28. The materials needed for the purgation of the sanctuary now follow (vv 3–5).

Aaron shall enter the adytum. Aaron enters the adytum three times during the course of the ritual: to create the cloud of incense (vv 12–13), to asperse the adytum with the blood of his purification bull (v 14), and then to asperse it with the blood of the people's purification goat (v 15). The rabbis add a fourth entry, to remove the censer and firepan (*m. Yoma* 7:4), which, presumably, the high priest left behind (*m. Yoma* 5:1), but which has no biblical warrant. But the placement and removal of the censer constitute a discrete ceremonial in the Babylonian temple-purifications (see COMMENT C below).

Perhaps one should not always infer from the silences of the text that there were no additional precautions. For example, is it conceivable that the high priest undertook the awesome responsibility of entering the adytum without intensive spiritual preparation? Here rabbinic tradition, stemming from the end of the Second Temple period, comes to our aid. It informs us that seven days before the festival, the high priest was separated from his wife and isolated in a special cell, effectively quarantining him from outside sources of impurity. During the week he rehearsed the several manipulations required by the rite, coached by the elders, who read and interpreted to him the ordinances of this chapter. On the eve of the festival it was deemed necessary to keep him awake the entire night lest he have a nocturnal emission and thereby become polluted (see 15:16). To ward off sleep he would expound the rituals, if he were a scholar; if not, they were expounded to him by the elders; or he would read, and, if illiterate, others would read to him, from biblical books such as Job, Daniel, Ezra, and Chronicles. If in spite of these measures, he would doze off, the priests would keep him awake by snapping their fingers (but avoiding any contact with him) or making him walk on the cold pavement of the Temple courtyard. When the ashes had been removed from the sacrificial altar (see 6:2–4) and it was certified that the day had dawned, the high priest was conducted to his ritual bath and the day's rites began. For details, see *m. Yoma* 1:1–3:2.

4. *linen (bad).* The etymology of this word is unknown. Why these simple linen vestments? Three answers are given in the early sources. (1) "Like the ministration on high so was the ministration below" (*y. Yoma* 7:2; cf. Ramban). For biblical evidence that the angels were dressed in linen, see Ezek 9:2–3, 11; 10:2; Dan 10:6; cf. Mal 2:7. (2) The clothing should indicate that the high priest is humble, stripped of all pretense (*y. Yoma* 7:3); he therefore dons the vestments of the ordinary priest (Abravanel); thus, as befits a person in the liminal state during a rite of passage, he is stripped of all emblems of his former status (chap. 8, COMMENT G). (3) "The accuser cannot act as defender. It was in order that no opportunity might be given to Satan to bring accusations and say: 'The other day they made for themselves a god of gold (Exod 32:4) and today they seek to officiate in garments of gold (Exod 28:6)!' " (*Tg. Ps.-J.; Midr. Lev. Rab.* 21:10). Hence the high priest wears the garments of an ordinary priest (Rashi).

Be that as it may, the high priest's vestments were not identical to those of the ordinary priest. The latter's sash was not made of pure linen but was a mixture of linen and dyed wool (Exod 39:29; cf. 29:9; *b. Yoma* 12b). Moreover, the high priest's head covering for this ritual was a turban *(miṣnepet)* and not a *migbāʿâ,* the simpler headdress of the ordinary priest (Exod 28:40). Thus the first explanation, that entry into the adytum is equivalent to admission to the heavenly council, seems the most plausible. Two further explanations are grounded in practical considerations. (4) The high priest had to remove these linen garments once he completed his purgation rites with both purification offering goats, wash his entire body, and change to his ornate garments (vv 23–24). His rites of purgation required clothes different from those required by his rites on the altar (see the NOTE on v 24). Had he worn his ornate garments in the adytum he would not have been able to complete the rites that required him to wear them during the execution of the burnt offerings (v 24). Because he had to wear different clothes in the adytum, it was therefore logical that he be fitted with garments of the same material worn by the angels; like them he was being given access to the divine presence. (5) "The simple clothes worn in the text on the Day of Atonement may have been to prevent soiling the regular high priestly clothing with blood which is sprinkled in abundance in the ceremony.

The reason for the change of clothes may simply be to remove the soiled clothes and put on the clean, regular high priestly clothing. The soiling of the clothing could furthermore be connected with 6:20. Certainly the laundering in a holy place and Lev 16's requirement for bathing in a holy place are a suggestive parallel" (D. P. Wright, written communication).

The priests of Egypt wore white linen garments. The Hittite king also officiated in the cult wearing a simple white garment (Singer 1983–84).

linen breeches shall be. Why is there no transitive verb in connection with the breeches, as in the prescriptions for the three other linen garments? This may be an indication that the high priest had already officiated at the *Tāmîd* (Exod 29:38–42) and had offered incense and trimmed the lamps (Exod 30:7) as he did in Second Temple times (*m. Yoma* 3:4), in which case he would already be wearing linen breeches. Indeed, the mention of the breeches as an appendix to the inventory of the priestly clothing (Exod 28:42–43)—and with the same verb, *hāyâ* (v 43)—as well as their absence from the descriptive text on the priestly ordination (8:7, 13) would indicate that breeches were not considered an article of the ordinary priest's sacral clothing. Here, however, the high priest's breeches are expressly called "sacral vestments," and they had to be removed together with his other linen garments at the close of his service in the adytum (v 23) and probably exchanged for new ones (cf. v 24).

his body (běśārô). Euphemism for the genitals (6:3; 15:2, 19).

These are sacral vestments (bigdê-qōdeš hēm). These words needed to be added because these linen garments could be and were worn by laymen. Indeed, after they were removed they probably could not be used again except, possibly, by the high priest in performing the same function (cf. v 23).

bathing his body in water. Normally, a priest was required to wash his hands and feet before entering the Tent or officiating at the altar (Exod 30:19). Nothing is said in Scripture of the priest washing them at the conclusion of his service or of bathing his whole body. Some change must have taken place in Second Temple times, for Jubilees also requires the priest to wash his hands and feet after he has officiated at the sacrifice (Jub 21:16). The anomaly of the high priest bathing his entire body at the beginning of his ministration is matched by the requirement that he bathe his body again when he completes the purgation rite with the purification offerings (v 24). The reason is not difficult to discern; entry into the adytum requires more thoroughgoing purification. It is not amiss here to recall that when Isaiah was admitted into the adytum of the heavenly temple he required special purification (Isa 6:5–6).

How many times did the high priest wash during the day? He bathed his body twice, before and after he officiated in his special linen garments (vv 4, 26). He would have washed his hands and feet each time he entered the Tent or officiated at the altar (Exod 30:19), that is to say, the three times he entered the Tent to minister in the adytum (see the NOTE on v 3) and a fourth time when he officiated on the altar (v 24b). If he also officiated at the morning and evening *Tāmîd* (see above) he would have washed two more times. Thus, in sum, he would have bathed his body twice and washed his hands and feet six times.

The sectaries of Qumran surprisingly require the high priest to wash his hands and feet before he offers his confession upon the Azazel goat (11QT 26:10; see COMMENT A below). Unfortunately, the fragmentary state of the Temple Scroll prevents us from knowing if there were additional ablutions not mandated by the biblical text. The rabbinic system, which may well reflect the actual practice of the Herodian temple, calls for fifteen ablutions: five immersions and ten washings of the hands and feet (*m. Yoma* 3:3). For details, see the NOTE on v 24.

his body (ʾet-bĕśārô). The LXX and Sam. read *ʾet kol bĕśārô* 'his entire body', which, if not the original text, is certainly its intention.

5. *community (ʿadat).* The people are alternately referred to as *ʿēdâ* (v 5), *qāh āl* (v 17), *ʿam* (vv 15, 24), and *ʿam haqqāhāl* (v 33). For the discussion of *ʿēdâ* and its synonyms see the NOTE on 4:13; for the unique expression *ʿam haqqāhāl*, see the NOTE on v 33.

he shall take (yiqqaḥ). Usually, the offerer himself brings his sacrifice to the sanctuary. Wanton, presumptuous sinners are barred, however. This is the reason that the high priest "takes" their offerings and brings them to the altar himself (see vv 9, 26). Strikingly, the Babylonian Nashe Hymn also bars those who willfully did not fulfill the temple's moral and ritual requirements from participating in the annual sacred meal held on New Year's Day (Heimpel 1981: 67–68).

two he-goats for a purification offering (šĕnê-śĕʿîrê ʿizzîm lĕhattāʾt). The prescription for the people, a *hattāʾt* he-goat and an *ʿōlâ* ram, follows more closely that of 9:3 (cf. Num 15:24) than 4:14. The he-goat for Azazel was not a sacrifice. Here, then, the term *hattāʾt* may have been chosen for its philological sense "that which removes sin," which precisely defines the function of the scapegoat (see v 22 and COMMENT E below). Alternatively, like the ashes of the Red Cow, also termed a *hattāʾt* (Num 19:9, 17), this sacrificial label may represent the attempt of the Priestly legislators to incorporate what originally was a pagan rite into Israel's sacrificial system (Milgrom 1981h; and see v 8, below).

6. *shall bring forward (wĕhiqrîb).* This verse is identical to v 11a. The verb must be rendered "bring forward," a meaning frequently attested in ritual (e.g., 8:6; Exod 28:1; 29:8; Num 8:9, 10). Support for this rendering here is provided by the subsequent verse, where its parallel verb is *lāqaḥ* 'take'. (These two verbs alternate regularly in other sacrificial passages and are clearly synonymous, e.g., 8:2, 6; Exod 29:1, 8; Num 8:5, 8, 9, 10, 18); see further the NOTE on v 7.

to effect purgation (wĕkipper). The purposive *waw* is equivalent to *lamed* (Ibn Janaḥ; Abravanel) and means "in order to." Thus the action is thrown forward to the blood manipulations (vv 14–19; *Sipra*, Aḥare par. 2:3; Ibn Ezra; Rashbam). Why is it necessary to state the purpose at all, when we have been clearly told (v 3) that the animal will be a purification offering whose sole purpose is for purgation (chap. 4, COMMENT A)? The answer must be that otherwise we would not know that the rest of the priests will be the beneficiaries of the sacrifice.

for himself (baʿădô). bĕʿad is synonymous with *ʿal* followed by a human object (e.g., 4:20, 26, 31, 35), but when the pronominal object refers to the subject, only *bĕʿad* can be used (see 9:7; chap. 4, COMMENT B; Milgrom 1970b).

his household. bêtô, in other words, all of the priests (see v 33). The high priest is considered the chieftain of the priestly clan and, hence, all his personal sacrifices are also on behalf of his fellow priests (see 9:7) unless he alone has erred (4:3-12). His "household," however, does not include the Levites, even though Aaron is acknowledged to be the head of *bêt lēwî* 'the household of Levi' (Num 17:23) because, in the latter case, *bayit* or *bêt ʾāb* denotes "tribe" (see Num 17:17, 21). Indeed, when P wishes to relate Aaron to his Kohathite clan, it calls the latter *bêt-ʾābîkā* 'your ancestral house', literally, "the household of your father" (Num 18:1)—a fitting designation for, according to the levitic geneal-ogy, Kohath was Aaron's grandfather (see Exod 6:16-20). Thus Aaron's "house" must refer to his own family and the "house" of subsequent high priests, to the Aaronid priests. The Levites, however, must be included among the commu-nity/people (vv 5, 15) and expiation is made for them as for the others by the purification goat. Corroboration for this conclusion is found in the summary of the ritual contained in this chapter's appendix, "he shall effect purgation for the priests and for all the people of the congregation" (v 33). Thus the high priest's "household" embraces solely the Aaronid priests. The sectaries of Qumran made sure that there would be no doubts on this matter by expanding this term to *bêt ʾabîhû* 'his father's household' (11QT 25:16).

7. *and he shall take (wĕlāqaḥ).* The subject is Aaron (v 6), thus proving that both vv 6 *(wĕhiqrîb)* and 7 *(wĕlāqaḥ)* deal with bringing the sacrificial animals (specified in vv 3 and 5) to the sanctuary.

before the Lord at the entrance of the Tent of Meeting (lipnê YHWH petaḥ ʾōhel môʿēd). Because "before the Lord" can designate anywhere in the sacred precincts, even within the Tent (e.g., 4:6, 17), it was necessary to specify further —in the forecourt. As to why there was need for the initial phrase "before the Lord," see below.

8. *shall place lots upon (wĕnātan . . . ʿal . . . gōrālôt).* Elsewhere we find the use of the following verbs with lots: *hippîl* (Isa 34:17), *hišlîk* (Josh 18:10), *hiddû* (Joel 4:3), *yārâ* (Josh 18:6)—all meaning "cast, thrown down." The use of the verb *nātan* here is unique. Thus the text may not be speaking of the deter-mination of the lots but of their disposition. This interpretation is confirmed by the preposition *ʿal.* The lots, once determined, are to be placed literally on the heads of the goats so that they will not be confused. In other words, the lots serve as their identification markers. This, in fact, is the tradition preserved by the Tannaites. The lots consisted of small tablets made of boxwood (and, later,

of gold); on one was written *laššēm* 'for the Name', and on the other *laʿăzāʾzēl* 'for Azazel'. The prefixed *lamed* as a sign of proprietorship is frequently attested in early Hebrew inscriptions (e.g., nos. 2, 15, 17, 19, 20, 22, 23, 24, 25, 26–31 [Lachish], 34–38 [Samaria], 42; Hestrin 1973), seals (e.g., nos. 2–13, 15–19, 21, 25–29, 32–34, 36–82; Dayagi-Mendeles and Hestrin 1978), and the Bible (e.g., Isa 8:1). The wooden chest in which the lots were kept was shaken by the high priest while he was flanked by his chief assistant *(sĕgan)* and the chief of the priestly division serving that week *(nōʾš bêt ʾāb)*. Then the high priest took out one lot with each hand, and put that which he held in his right hand upon the goat that was standing on his right side, and that in his left hand upon the goat on his left side, exclaiming each time, *laYHWH ḥaṭṭāʾt* 'a purification offering for the Lord' *(m. Yoma* 3:9; 4:1). That we are dealing here with the destination of the lot and not its execution is shown by the verb *ʿālâ* in the verses that follow (see vv 9, 10).

The purpose of the lots is clearly to leave the selection of the animals to the Lord. Otherwise, if the high priest chose the animals, it would appear that he and the people he represented were offering an animal to Azazel. Thus the text takes pains to state that both animals were placed "before the Lord" (v 7; Ramban; *Zohar*, Aḥare 63:1), that both were designated a purification offering (v 5), and that the goat of Azazel will be placed alone "before the Lord" (v 10). Here is clear evidence of the Priestly efforts to alter what was most likely in its original form a pagan rite (see below and COMMENT E).

"for Azazel" (laʿăzāʾzēl). The *lamed auctoris* indicates the name of the owner (Cazelles 1949). There are three main views concerning the meaning of Azazel. The first is that it means "scapegoat," following the LXX's τω αποπομπαιω 'for the one carrying away the evil' (v 8) or τον χιμαρον ταν διεσταλμενον ʾειαφεσιν 'the goat determined for dismissal' (v 26); cf. the Vg's *caper emissarius*, probably reading the word as *ʿēz ʾāzal* 'the goat that departs' (though *ʾāzal* is Aramaic, it occurs in BH, e.g., Prov 20:14; Job 14:11). The second view is that it means "a rough and difficult place" *(Tg. Ps.-J.; b. Yoma* 67b; *Sipra*, Aḥare 2:8), referring to the goat's destination. This view is based on a midrashic interpretation of *ʾereṣ gĕzērâ* (v 22) as "a rough and rocky terrain" and for its etymology relies either on Arab. *ʿzʿz* 'rough ground' (Saadiah: Ibn Janaḥ) or regards the *aleph* unessential and the *lamed* a formative addition, as in *kerem/karmel* (Driver 1956b: 97–98). Finally, it could be the name of a demon. This is the dominant view in midrashic literature, dating back to the early postbiblical period (3 *Enoch* 4:6; *Pirqe R. El.* 46; cf. Ibn Ezra, Ramban). It is supported by (1) the parallel syntactic structures of this verse by which one goat is designated "for the Lord," the other "for Azazel," which imply that Azazel is the personal name of a divine being. (2) The wilderness to which the goat is dispatched (vv 10, 22) is the habitation of demons (e.g., Isa 13:21; 34:14; Bar 4:35; Tob 8:3; Matt 12:34; Luke 11:24; Rev 18:2). (3) 1 *Enoch* 10:4–5 relates that the angel Raphael is commanded to bind the rebellious demon ʿAzel hand

and foot and banish him to a wilderness called Dudel (=*Ḥadûdû, m. Yoma* 6:8) and cover him with sharp rocks (reminiscent of the cliff from which the goat is thrown, according to *m. Yoma* 6:6; cf. v 22). The reference to Azazel is obvious. (4) Perhaps *ʿzʾzl* is a metathesis of *ʿzzʾl* 'fierce god' (cf. *Tg. Ps.-J.* to v 10; *b. Yoma* 67b; Zadok 1978: 58) on the analogy of the personal name *ʿzzyhw* (1 Chr 15:23; Levine 1969: 94 n. 42), on the basis of Cant 8:6, where *qšh* || *ʿzh* 'fierce, overbearing' refers to *šʾwl* || *mwt* 'netherworld death [personified]', and on the basis of the theophoric name *ʿzmwt* (e.g., 2 Sam 23:21) and the place-name *byt ʿzmwt* (Neh 7:28; 12:29), meaning "Mot is fierce." Indeed, the sectaries of Qumran actually read the name as *ʿzzʾl* (11QT 26:13; *DJD* 5.180, line 7). If so, then Azazel may be identified with the Canaanite god Mot, who would have been reduced to the status of a demon in the Bible and his name deliberately metathesized "to conceal the true demonic nature of this supernatural being" (Tawil 1980: 58).

The most plausible explanation is that Azazel is the name of a demon (no. 3, above) who has been eviscerated of his erstwhile demonic powers by the Priestly legislators. First, the goat sent him is not an offering (so Elliger 1966; Kümmel 1968); it is not treated as a sacrifice, requiring slaughter, blood manipulation, and the like, nor does it have the effect of a sacrifice, namely, propitiation, expiation, and so on. Moreover, an animal laden with impurities would not be acceptable as an offering either to God or to a demon (cf. v 26). Second, the goat is not the vicarious substitute for Israel (Hoffmann 1953) because there is no indication that it was punished (e.g., put to death) or demonically attacked in Israel's place. Instead of being an offering or a substitute, the goat is simply the vehicle to dispatch Israel's impurities and sins to the wilderness/netherworld (see the NOTE on v 21). The banishment of evil to an inaccessible place is a form of elimination amply attested in the ancient Near East (see COMMENT E below).

Azazel himself is deprived of any active role: he neither receives the goat nor attacks it. Regardless of his origins—in pre-Israelite practice he surely was a true demon, perhaps a satyr (cf. Ibn Ezra on 16:8), who ruled in the wilderness—in the Priestly ritual he is no longer a personality but just a name, designating the place to which impurities and sins are banished. As for the survival of the name Azazel, "demons often survive as figures of speech (e.g., "gremlins") long after they have ceased to be figures of belief. Accordingly, the mention of a demon's name in a scriptural text is not automatic testimony to living belief in him" (Gaster 1962b: 818). Azazel suffers the fate of all angels and spirits in Scripture. They can represent the powers of the physical world (e.g., Pss 104:4; 148:8) but they are not deified (Deut 4:19; 17:3; Job 5:1) and their worship is prohibited (Exod 20:4-5; 22:19; Deut 5:7-8).

9. *shall bring forward (wěhiqrîb)*. As the high priest's next action is "to sacrifice," the verb here must mean "bring forward." It therefore corresponds in meaning to its usage in v 6, indicating an action similar to that with the high

priest's bull. Normally, the offerer himself "brings forward" his sacrifice. In this case, the offerers are the people or their representatives (v 5). But as the people are guilty of "iniquities and transgressions" (vv 16, 21) they fall into the category of brazen, presumptuous sinners and are therefore barred from the sanctuary (Num 15:30–31; see chap. 4, COMMENT B). Hence the high priest must act on their behalf (see also the NOTES on vv 5, 21).

designated by lot. ʾăšer ʿālâ ʿālāyw haggôrāl, literally, "upon whom the lot was raised." This expression might indicate the method of the lottery, that is, the lots being drawn out of an urn (see the NOTE on v 8), particularly because the same verb ʿālâ 'come up' is actually used elsewhere in the drawing of lots (e.g., Josh 18:11; 19:10), where it alternates with the verb yāṣāʾ 'come out, emerge' (Josh 19:1, 17; Dillmann and Ryssel 1897). Yet here alone is ʿālâ followed by the preposition ʿal, which favors the rendering "upon which the lot was placed" (Ehrlich 1908–14). For other instances of ʿālâ ʿal also meaning "place upon," see 19:19; Judg 16:17; and esp. Num 19:2.

to sacrifice it (wěʿāśāhû). The waw is purposive, like that in wěkipper (vv 6, 11). For ʿāśâ as a technical cultic term, indicating the execution of the entire sacrificial procedure, see 9:7, 22; 14:19; 16:24; Exod 29:38.

as a purification offering (ḥaṭṭāʾt). Why does not the text add wěkipper běʿad hāʿām 'to effect purgation for the people', as it did in the cases of the high priest's bull (vv 6, 11) and, later, the Azazel goat (v 10) and the people's ram (v 24)? The answer can only be that in declaring the animal a purification offering it is taken for granted that its purpose is purgation (chap. 4, COMMENT B). Also, as the text has already specified that the goat is for the people (v 5), it need not repeat this fact. Conversely, it was necessary to state the purpose of the high priest's bull (vv 6, 11); otherwise it could not have been deduced that its beneficiary included the entire priestly house (cf. the NOTE on v 6).

10. stationed alive (yoʿŏmad-ḥay). In contrast to the bull and other goat, which are about to be slaughtered (vv 11, 15), the Azazel goat is "stationed alive." The early rabbinic tradition holds that a red ribbon was tied to the horns of the live goat (m. Yoma 4:2). This practice has confirmed ancient precedents. For example, in the Hittite rituals for the elimination of a plague, the bull driven to the land of the enemy (Pulisa, line 25; see the text cited in COMMENT E below), the ram driven to the open country (Ashella, line 8; text in COMMENT E), and the ram driven to the land of the enemy (Uhhamuwa, lines 4–5; text in COMMENT E) are all decorated with colored ribbons (see Gurney 1976: 49; Singer 1983–84: 1.59 n. 26). Nevertheless, their symbolism in Hittite religion has yet to be clarified (see provisionally Wright 1987: 52, 56). In Israel, the significance of the ribbon was practical: to distinguish the scapegoat from the goat to be slaughtered (b. Yoma 41b), for the goats had to be alike in appearance (m. Yoma 6:1). The use of red ribbons as marks of identification is attested in the Bible (Gen 38:28; Josh 2:18; cf. Goldstein 1979–80: 238 n. 5), and one

wonders whether the equivalent rite in Hittite religion did not serve a similar purpose.

The possibility must be entertained that the verb originally read *ya'ămîd* 'he [Aaron] shall station', in conformance with *wĕhe'ĕmîd* 'he [Aaron] set' (v 7b), and that the first word in this verse, *wĕhaśśā'îr*, originally read *wĕ'et-haśśā'îr*, the *'et* falling out due to a haplography with the last two letters of the previous word, *ḥṭ't* (Paran 1983: 147). The reconstructed sentence would then conform to P's pattern of altering the word order in the final act in ritual procedures (for examples, see 1:9, 13; 3:4, 10, 15; 4:8, 19, 25, 31; 8:17, 20; 9:9, 13, 21).

before the Lord. This fact has already been stated (v 7)! The legislators' obsession to make it perfectly understood that the goat is offered to the Lord and not to Azazel is again clearly revealed (see the NOTES on vv 5, 7).

to perform expiation upon it (lĕkapper 'ālāyw). The preposition *'al* following the verb *kippēr* always means "for, on behalf of" when the object is human (see chap. 4, COMMENT B), but when the object is inanimate it can also mean "upon" (e.g., the altar, 8:15; 16:18; Exod 30:10; the adytum, 16:16). There is no warrant whatever to read *'al* as "in proximity to" (Levine 1974: 80). Here, uniquely, the object is an animal, but it is treated as an inanimate object; hence *kippûr* (purgation) takes place upon it. Its meaning is not that the goat itself is purged but that the purgation of the sanctuary is completed when the goat, laden with the sanctuary's impurities, is dispatched to the wilderness. The need to effect this transfer is what accounts for the fact that the goat must be brought into the sanctuary itself. Yet there remains another route that *kippēr* can take. As will be shown in the NOTE on vv 21–22, the expressed purpose of the scapegoat is to carry off the sins of the Israelites transferred to it by the high priest's confession. Here, then, *kippēr* takes on the more abstract notion "to expiate." In effect, the original purpose of the scapegoat, to eliminate the impurities removed from the sanctuary, has been altered to accommodate a new theological notion—once a year, on the tenth of Tishri, the purgation rites of the sanctuary also remove Israel's sins, provided the people show their remorse through acts of self-denial and cessation from labor. Kiuchi's proposal that "v 10 refers to Aaron in *'ālāyw*" (1987: 209) must be rejected on many counts, not the least of which is that, in view of the following *'ōtô* (referring to the goat), *'ālāyw* should have read *'al 'ahărōn* 'on Aaron'. For details, see the NOTES on vv 21, 29; and on the various meanings of *kippēr*, see COMMENT F below.

sending it off (lĕśallaḥ). The *pi'el* can bear the connotation of "send away, release, let loose" without the possibility of return (e.g., birds, 14:7, 53; Hagar, Gen 21:14; Tamar, 2 Sam 13:17; a wife, Deut 22:19, 29; Israel, Exod 5:2). The absence of the conjunction *waw* indicates that this word is the object of the previous verb, *kippēr*. This implies that the dispatch of the goat was (the final) part of the purgation rite of the sanctuary. Accordingly, the translation of the verb *lĕkapper* should be "to effect purgation," as in the rest of the ritual (vv 6, 11, 16, 17, 18, 20, 24). But the function of the Azazel goat has been altered from the purgation of the sanctuary to the expiation of the people's sins (cf. v 21), which is reflected in the rendering for *lĕkapper* given here (cf. also COMMENTS A and F below).

into the wilderness. See the NOTE on v 21.

11. *when [Aaron] shall bring forward (wĕhiqrîb).* Verse 11a is identical to v 6. It can be explained as a repetitive resumption; in other words, after the digression on the goats, the text now returns to the procedure with the bull (Ibn Ezra and the Karaites). This stylistic device is frequently attested (e.g., Num 5:16b, 18a; 7:1; 13:3a, 17a; 21:25b, 31; 22:21a, 35b; 33:3a, 5a). Alternatively, the two statements need not be understood as identical, for the word *hiqrîb* here probably means "offer" (as in 3:1a, 7a, 9), whereas earlier it meant "bring forward" (v 6). The explanation that it is an example of repetitive resumption is preferred here for another reason, the repetition of *'et-par hahattā't 'ăšer-lô*, literally, "the purification offering bull which is his," in both halves of the verse. Thus v 11a was attached to v 11b in spite of the resulting redundancy, in order to effect the resumptive repetition.

to effect purgation (wĕkipper). The *waw* is purposive, as in v 6; see the NOTE on v 6 for the reason for this clause. The rabbis explain this apparent redundancy as the need for the high priest to lay his hands twice over the bull and recite a short confession, first for himself and his family and then for the rest of the priests, as follows:

> O Lord, I have committed iniquity, transgressed, and sinned before you, I and my house and the descendants of Aaron, your holy people. O Lord, grant atonement *(kappēr nā')* for the iniquities *('ăwônôt)*, the transgressions *(pĕšā'îm)* and sins *(hātā'îm)* that I have committed and transgressed and sinned before you, I and my house, as it is written in the Torah of your servant Moses: "From this day shall atonement be made for you to purify you of all your sins; thus shall you become pure before the Lord." (v 30; *m. Yoma* 3:8; 4:2; the recital of the sins follows the order of v 21)

he shall slaughter (wĕsāhat) The blood was collected in a bowl (*m. Yoma* 4:3; of v 14). In connection with neither the bull nor the goat (v 15) do we learn of the hand-leaning ritual, though it was certainly performed (4:4, 15, 24, 29, 33). Because it is indispensable, it is at times taken for granted (e.g., in the inaugural service, 9:8–11). Here, however, another motivation may be detected: to accentuate the unique hand-leaning that will take place on the goat for Azazel (v 21).

12. *panful (mahtâ).* Incense can legitimately be burned on the altar of incense (see the NOTE on 4:7) or in a portable censer, either a long-handled pan *(mahtâ, 10:1; Num 16:6; 17:11)* or an upright vessel *(miqteret, Ezek 8:11).* The former was used twice daily by the high priest (Exod 30:7–8), the latter, by any

priest in the Tabernacle court (see the NOTE on 10:1) and, under exceptional circumstances, even outside the sacred precincts (Num 17:11–12). What the *maḥtâ* of the biblical period looked like is unknown. If the pans that serviced the candelabrum were made of pure gold (Exod 25:38), it is all the more likely that the pan that the high priest brought into the Holy of Holies was as well (cf. also 1 Kgs 7:50). Beyond that we know little. It is said to be a kind of shovel; it may be what is depicted in the mosaic of the synagogue at Beth Shean (illustration in Negev 1972: 84). Similar censers were found in the Cave of Letters in the Judean wilderness, dating to the second century C.E. Yet because they resemble the censers found at Pompeii, they may be of non-Jewish origin (Yadin 1963: 48–58).

To judge from the many representations of incense offerings in portable censers found on Egyptian reliefs, their primary purpose was to offer homage to the Pharaoh/god (Keel 1975), though in depictions of sieges in Canaan and Syria, their purpose may also have been apotropaic, to ward off the demonic powers of the enemy (Haran 1960b), precisely as in the case of Aaron, who stops a plague with such an offering (Num 17:11–12).

the altar (hammizbēaḥ). There can be no question that the reference must be to the sacrificial altar in the Tabernacle court and not the incense altar in the shrine, for only the former had a perpetual fire (6:5–6).

before the Lord (millipnê YHWH). Both altars are so specified (e.g., 1:5; 4:6), though here the sacrificial altar is intended (see above). The preposition *min*, literally, "from [before the Lord]" is difficult, though it might be understood as a complementary apposition to the previous double preposition, *mēʿal*, literally, *"from* atop the altar, *from* before the Lord," which would have the force of a hendiadys, in other words, "from atop the altar which is before the Lord." Also, had the text read *lipnê*, the clauses might have been misread "from atop the altar to the presence of the Lord."

two handfuls (mĕlōʾ ḥopnāyw). Probably related to Akk. *upnu* 'hand, fist'; it is a dual formation (see Qoh 4:6). A question of logistics: how did the high priest manage to carry two handfuls of incense and the pan simultaneously? The rabbis maintain that the incense was emptied into a ladle *(kap)* and the high priest carried the pan of coals in one hand and the ladle of incense in the other (*m. Yoma* 5:1). This rabbinic tradition is based on verifiable ancient precedents: for example, incense in Egyptian temples was offered in a long-handled ladle shaped like the palm of a hand (= *kap)*, as shown in a tomb painting of Amenemhat (Twelfth Dynasty) at Beni Hasan (*VBW* 1.191). See also similarly shaped incense ladles found at Hazor and Ein Gev, dating to the Israelite period (*EM* 3, pl. 6; 7.115).

finely ground (daqqâ). Because the perfumed incense designated for the altar of incense had to be ground quite finely (*hādēq*, Exod 30:36), this incense had to be *daqqâ min haddaqqâ* 'extra fine' (*m. Yoma* 4:4; cf. *Sipra*, Aḥare 3:8). The tripartite gradation should be noted: on the sacrificial altar ordinary incense (frankincense) was offered (2:2, 15–16); on the inner altar, perfumed incense (Exod 30:7); and in the adytum, finely ground perfumed incense. The refinement of the incense as it is burned in areas of increasing holiness is best seen in the Hebrew: *qĕṭōret/qĕṭōret sammîm/qĕṭōret sammîm daqqâ.* The purgation ritual will also follow this tripartite division (vv 16–19, and see the NOTE on v 19).

perfumed incense (qĕṭōret sammîm). Its composition is specified in the Torah: "The Lord said to Moses, Take the herbs *nāṭāp, šĕḥēlet,* and *ḥelbĕnâ*—these herbs with pure frankincense; they shall be of equal measure—and make them into incense—perfume, a compound expertly blended, refined, pure, sacred" (Exod 30:34–35).

Such is the recipe for the sacred incense, burned on the incense altar in the Tabernacle twice a day, and on a censer in the adytum once a year on the Day of Atonement. It is called *qĕṭōret sammîm* to distinguish it from ordinary incense *(qĕṭōret).* It consists of four ingredients, of which only one is mentioned elsewhere in the Bible: *lĕbōnâ* 'frankincense' (see the NOTE on 2:1). The other three—*nāṭāp, šĕḥēlet,* and *ḥelbĕnâ*—are more difficult to identify. What follows is the result of the research of my student S. Rattray.

There is common accord in regard to *ḥelbĕnâ.* The Versions are all agreed: *Tgs. ḥelbĕnātāʾ* or *ḥelbānayyāʾ*, the LXX *chalbanē,* Vg *galbanum.* The Talmud also has *ḥelbĕnâ* (b. Ker. 6a). This substance is known to us from Greek and Roman sources as well, under the same name: *chalbanē* or *galbanum* (Dioscorides, *De materia medica* 3.97; Pliny, *H.N.* 12.61, 126). Both describe it as derived from a type of *Ferula* (giant fennel) that grows in Syria. It is a gum-resin "like frankincense" (Diosc.). According to Pliny it will drive away snakes by its smell when burned. It has an unpleasant odor. Nowadays galbanum is derived from *Ferula galbaniflua,* which grows in Persia. It was also known in ancient Mesopotamia: Sumerian ḪAL, Akk. *baluḫḫa* (Thompson 1949: 342–43).

The usual equivalent of *šĕḥēlet* is "nail": *Tg. Onq. ṭûpraʾ*, LXX *onyx,* Vg *onycha,* Talmud *ṣippôren* (b. Ker. 6a). According to Ramban, *šĕḥēlet* comes from the ocean. Indeed, the *onyx*—as a seashell—was known to Dioscorides (*De materia medica* 2.10), who describes it as the covering *(operculum)* of a shellfish like the murex, coming from India or the Red Sea. He also says that, when laid on coals, it has a sweet smell rather like castor. It has been identified as a shellfish of the genus *Strombus* (United Bible Society 1972) or *Unguis odoratus* (*EM* 7.621–22). Tristam (1873: 297) says the following about it: "When burnt it has a strong, pungent smell, and is still used in the composition of some kind of frankincense in the East. . . . Onycha was formerly employed in medicine under the name of *Blatta Byzantina.*"

There is no ancient consensus on the meaning of *nāṭāp.* The verb means "to drip," and the noun could conceivably mean "resin, gum," used as a generic term for any substance dripping from trees; but in the present context it must refer to a specific item. The LXX's equivalent is *staktē,* Vg *stacte. Tg. Onq.* has simply *nĕṭopā'*, while the other *Tgs.* have *qĕṭap* (*Tg. Yer.* has *qĕṭab*). The Talmud equates it with *ṣŏrî* 'the juice that drips from *qĕṭap* trees' (*b. Ker.* 6a). Medieval and modern suggestions include "mastic" (e.g., *Keter Torah*), "theriac" (e.g., Rashi) and "storax" (most moderns). To add to the confusion, Greek *staktē* and Latin *stacte* are used to translate other terms, notably *lōṭ* (Gen 37:25; 43:11), while separate terms are used for *ṣŏrî* (namely, *rhētinē* and *resina*). The *Tgs.* are a bit more consistent, rendering *ṣŏrî* in Gen 37:25 and 43:11 as *qĕṭap* or *śĕrap qĕṭap*; but as *šĕ'îp* in Jer 46:11; 51:8; Ezek 27:17. A related term, *šĕ'ap* (*Tg. Onq.*) is used to translate *nĕkō't* in Gen 37:25; 43:11; for the latter the Vg has *styrax* (cf. the modern suggested equivalent for *nāṭāp!*). In the LXX, an adjectival form of the word *styrax* is found in Gen 30:37 as the equivalent of *libneh* —a tree thought by some moderns to be the *Styrax officinalis* from which storax was supposed to be derived (but others equate the *libneh* with the poplar). This confusing array of equivalents is set out in the following chart for greater clarity:

	nāṭāp	*ṣŏrî*	*lōṭ*	*nĕkō't*	*libneh*
LXX	staktē	rhetine	staktē	thymiama	styrakinos < styrax
Vg •	stacte	resina	stacte	aroma/styrax	populeas < populus
Tg. Onq.	nĕtôpā'	qĕṭap	lĕṭôm	šĕ'ap	lĕban
Tg. Ps.-J.	qetap	śĕrap qĕṭap	lĕṭôm	ša'āwâ	lĕban
Tg. Yer.	—	šĕ'îp	—	—	lĕban

Thymiama and *aroma* are general terms for spices or things that can be burned as incense; *rhetine* and *resina* mean simply "resin." *Stacte* in Greek and Latin sources refers to oil of myrrh (Dioscorides, *De materia medica* 1.73; Pliny, *H.N.* 12.25, 68). According to Pliny this is the juice that the myrrh tree exudes naturally, before it is tapped. It has a sweet smell. In view of the loose usage of the word as discussed above, however, the term *staktē* is probably being used here in its etymological sense, as anything that drips (cf. *stazein* 'to drip', *staktos* 'oozing out in drops'), thus agreeing with the etymology of *nāṭāp* (*nāṭap* 'to drip'). The Greek and Latin may therefore be left out of consideration as being too loosely used or too general to be of any help.

Turning to the *Tgs.*, we note that (1) *lōṭ* is clearly distinguished by the equivalent *lĕṭôm*, so it may be omitted from consideration; (2) likewise the *libneh* has its own rendering, *lĕban*, so it is not the source of *ṣŏrî/nāṭāp*, which is called *qĕṭap*; (3) only *Tg. Ps.-J.* uses *šĕ'îp* to translate *ṣŏrî*, and in those verses the word *nĕkō't* (rendered *šĕ'ap* or *ša'āwâ* by the other *Tgs.*) does not occur (the rendering *šĕ'ap* may also be simply a peculiarity of *Tg. Ps.-J.*). Thus the equation *nāṭāp* = (*ś ĕrap*) *qĕṭap* = *ṣŏrî* appears quite tenable. Indeed, Y. Feliks (1968:

246–48), following I. Löw, approaches the problem in this way, and so makes use of rabbinic descriptions of ṣŏrî (or qĕṭap) as well as biblical descriptions (which are meager), comparing them to Greek and Latin descriptions of resin- or gum-producing plants growing in the Near East. This leads him to identify ṣŏrî/nāṭāp with storax. Also, other equivalents of ṣŏrî or nāṭāp are excluded as not having the desired characteristics: *Commiphora opobalsamum,* given by the United Bible Society (1972) as the identification of nāṭāp, is not native to the Syria-Palestine area, whereas ṣŏrî is a product of Gilead in particular (Gen 37:25; Jer 8:22; 46:11); and *Balanites aegyptiaca* (ibid., for ṣŏrî) is common in Egypt, whereas Gen 37:25 and 43:11 imply a product imported into Egypt.

Storax is described by Dioscorides (*De materia medica* 1.79) and Pliny (*H.N.* 12.40, 81; 55, 124) as the product of a tree resembling quince, found in Syria, Judea, Cyprus, and parts of Asia Minor. Modern storax is derived from *Liquidambar orientalis;* but some scholars report that storax has also been derived from *Styrax officinalis.* It was also known in Mesopotamia, where it was called BAL or MUK in Sumerian and *ballukku* in Akk. (Thompson 1949: 340ff.). Some scholars identify the *libneh* as *Styrax officinalis;* others (cf. Feliks 1968) as *Populus alba.* Because ṣŏrî was not, in fact, derived from the *libneh* (as evidenced by the *Tgs.*), then, if the *libneh* is *Styrax officinalis,* ancient storax must have been derived from *Liquidambar orientalis* just like modern storax. If, however, the *libneh* is *Populus alba,* then storax could have been derived from either *L. orientalis* or *S. officinalis.* The identity of the qĕṭap tree thus depends on what we determine for the *libneh.*

To sum up: the most likely modern equivalents of nāṭāp, šĕḥēlet, and ḥelbĕnâ are storax, *Unguis odoratus* (or *Strombus* or *Blatta byzantina*), and galbanum. They are evidently to be combined as "spices" *(sammîm)* and mixed with an equal quantity of frankincense. For the additional ingredients to the incense, according to the traditions held by Josephus and the rabbis, see the NOTE on 4:7.

inside the veil. See the NOTE on v 2.

13. *He shall put [the incense . . .] (wĕnātan . . .).* Clearly this verse favors the Pharisaic interpretation: the high priest lights the incense only after he enters the adytum (*t. Yoma* 1:8; *Sipra,* Aḥare 3:11). How then did the Sadducees, who insisted that the high priest must light the incense before he enters the adytum (cf. also Philo, *Laws* 1. 72), interpret this verse? Possibly they interpreted wĕnātan as a pluperfect, "after he had put [the incense . . .]," so that first the high priest lights the incense "before the Lord," that is, in the shrine (or at the sacrificial altar) and then he enters the adytum with it (Lauterbach 1927: 198–99). But if this is their exegesis, it is hardly admissible: the sequential *waw* in wĕnātan implies consecutive action; a pluperfect should take the form wĕhû᾿ nātan (see, for example, wĕhû᾿ yādaᶜ, 5:3, 4). Alternatively, the Sadducees might have interpreted the phrase ᶜal-hā᾿ēš appositionally: "(He shall put the incense) that is on the coals (before the Lord)," in other words, the high

priest added the incense to the coals before he entered the adytum (Lieberman 1962: 730). This rendering, however, is equally unacceptable: the previous verse described the high priest holding the incense and coals in separate hands.

If, then, the Pharisees are correct, it would mean that they harbored no fear of viewing the Ark! To be sure, one can rationalize such a fear as purely academic, for the adytum of the Second Temple was bare except for the outcropping of natural rock, known as 'eben haššĕtîyâ 'the foundation stone' (m. Yoma 5:2; t. Yoma 2:14). It is clear, however, that they grappled with the logistics of this text, for they declare emphatically "when he (the high priest) reached the Ark he placed the pan between the two staves (of the Ark; see Exod 25:13–15), heaped the incense (from the ladle) on top of the coals so that the entire house was filled with smoke" (m. Yoma 5:1). Thus it is certain that the high priest, even according to the rabbis, had, be it for a moment, an unobstructed view of the Ark!

Four explanations are in order. (1) As the adytum was windowless, it was pitch black inside, and the Ark could not be seen. The function of the incense would then have been to guarantee its invisibility or to fulfill another purpose. This view is hardly likely for in parting the veil while entering, light would have penetrated. (2) The incense was not intended to be a screen (a function unattested elsewhere), rather, a means of propitiating God, to assuage the wrath of the deity for the presumption of coming into his presence (Levine 1969: 93). In this respect, Aaron would be duplicating the incense offering he made at the behest of Moses: "Take the pan and put on it fire from the altar. Add incense and take it quickly to the community and make expiation (kappēr) for them. For wrath has gone forth from the Lord: the plague has begun!" (Num 17:11). Ancient Egyptian pictorial and documentary evidence points to the use of incense offerings in portable censers that have precisely this purpose in mind—to placate the deity (Keel 1975). The weakness of this interpretation lies in the wording of the verse under discussion: if the incense were propitiatory, why is it necessary that, literally, "the cloud of incense cover the kappōret that is over the Pact lest he die"? The need to "cover" (wĕkîssâ) can only be to screen the Ark from the high priest's sight. (3) The high priest, indeed, was allowed to view the Ark as a means of weaning the people away from the superstition that God's presence is restricted to the Ark (Lauterbach 1927: 173–205). As will be seen below, however, the rabbis maintained that the high priest's view of the Ark should be blocked. Besides, the scriptural demand that the cloud of incense should cover the Ark would still be left unexplained.

(4) The purpose of "the cloud" in the adytum was to screen the Ark, the unambiguous meaning of this verse. Nevertheless, the cloud must be differentiated from the incense, which fulfills a different function. As suggested by Albeck (1952: 215 n. 2), the Pharisaic interpretation of this text must be understood differently. "For what purpose is it stated 'by means of the cloud I shall appear' (v 2)? It comes to teach us that a smoke raiser is put into it (the

incense). Whence do we know that a smoke raiser is put into it? Because it is said: 'so that the cloud of incense covers the *kappōret'* (v 13)" (*b. Yoma* 53a [bar.]: cf. *t. Yoma* 1:8; *Midr. Cant. Rab.* 3:7). Thus the rabbis hold that the cloud was created not by the incense but by means of an added ingredient whose sole purpose was to be a *ma'ălēh 'āšān* 'smoke raiser'. The "cloud" (v 2), then, stands for the screen created by the "smoke-raiser" substance, also referred to as "the cloud of incense" (v 13). According to Albeck, therefore, the Pharisees, in agreement with the Sadducees, maintained that the purpose of the incense was to shield the Ark from the view of the high priest. They both agreed that the smoke screen had to be raised outside the adytum and before the entry of the high priest. They differed only concerning the composition of the screen. On the one hand, the Pharisees held that the "cloud" was to be created from the added smoke-raising ingredient but, in keeping with vv 12–13, the incense should be kindled only when the high priest was inside the adytum. The Sadducees, on the other hand, maintained that the incense plus the smoke raiser should be ignited prior to the high priest's entry. In effect, the Pharisees and Sadducees were in complete agreement concerning the exegesis of the biblical instructions concerning the *'ānān* 'cloud'. It stands for the smoke screen that the Lord requires in order to manifest himself to the high priest (v 2), and it is this same *'ānān* that must cover the Ark (v 13). The cloud, however, must be distinguished from the *qĕţōret* (incense), whose function is not to act as a screen but, as suggested above, to placate God for the high priest's presumption in entering before his presence.

The controversy thus rages over a single detail: is the incense (but not the cloud) kindled inside the adytum or outside? It may seem picayune and, perhaps, incredible that this long-enduring and bitter controversy could have revolved about such a trifling matter. Yet it should never be forgotten that Israel, like its contemporaries, was of the opinion that the slightest deviation from the prescribed ritual would not only nullify the ritual but arouse the wrath of the deity. The Hittites, for example, warned the king that he must carry out the rites of the KILAM festival *šakuwaššaran* 'punctiliously' (Singer 1978: 178). And Israel's Priestly theology dealt with still higher stakes. If the ritual were marred in the slightest detail, the sanctuary would not be purged, leaving the prospect that the Lord would abandon it and his people to their doom (see chap. 4, COMMENT C).

This interpretation is supported by a piece of realia. The perfumed incense offered in the sanctuary consisted of four ingredients: *nāţāp* (stacte: either *Styrax officinalis* or myrrh), *šĕḥēlet* (*Ungusis odoratus*, a mollusk), *ḥelbĕnâ* (galbanum), and an equal measure of *lĕbōnâ* (frankincense; Exod 30:34; for their identification see the NOTE on v 12). An experiment conducted by my student, S. Rattray, with three of the four ingredients of the sanctuary incense (the *šĕḥēlet* mollusk being unavailable) proved that the smoke they generated was woefully insufficient to produce a screen. Indeed, the rabbis state explicitly that the incense compound offered in the Herodian Temple consisted of eleven aromatic spices (thirteen, according to Jos., *Wars* 5.5.5) plus a number of additives, including a *maʿăleh ʿāšān* 'smoke raiser' (*b. Ker.* 6a; *y. Yoma* 4:5 [bar.]). Moreover, the rabbis' contention that the incense was supplemented by nonaromatic ingredients is buttressed by Scripture itself, which mandates that the incense must be salted (Exod 30:35), a view shared by the ancient Mesopotamian (Maqlu 6.111–13; 9.118–20; cf. Hurowitz 1987).

Thus, the rabbis' exegesis of v 13 must be correct: the Ark is covered by "the cloud" and not by "the incense." Moreover, the procedure they prescribe fits the data the best. Because the Lord insists that the high priest may only enter the adytum if the Ark is shielded by a cloud (v 2), the high priest produces this cloud by igniting a "smoke-raising" substance just before he enters the adytum; and once inside, in keeping with the sequence of vv 12–13, he ignites the incense.

before the Lord (lipnê YHWH). Because this designation applies anywhere within the sacred precincts, it was possible for the Sadducees to use this phrase to buttress their contention that the incense should be ignited outside the adytum (see above and *b. Yoma* 58b).

the cloud from the incense. *ʿănan haqqĕṭōret,* literally, "the cloud of incense." But it was shown above that what covered the Ark was the *ʿānān* (cloud), not the *qĕṭōret* (incense). The rabbinic tradition that the cloud stemmed from the incense but was not produced by the incense is adopted here.

the kappōret. For its description, see the NOTE on v 2. The fact that the smoke screen is to cover the *kappōret* rather than the Ark is further corroboration that its purpose is to shield the divine presence that rests on the *kappōret,* between the cherubim (Exod 25:22; Num 7:89).

the Pact. *hāʿēdût,* synonymous with the Covenant (Exod 31:18) and an ellipsis for *ʾărôn hā ʿēdût* 'the Ark of the Pact' (Exod 25:22), which is frequently attested (e.g., Exod 16:34; 27:21; 30:6, 36).

After the high priest offered the incense, he clearly had to return to the court in order to get the blood of the slaughtered purification offerings. According to the rabbis, he withdrew from the adytum walking backward, lest he turn his back on the divine presence, and when he reached the shrine he would offer a short prayer (see *Midr. Lev. Rab.* 20:4 for the extant versions), "but he would not prolong his prayer lest he terrify Israel (who might think he died)" (*m. Yoma* 5:1).

14. *take some of the blood.* From the priest who, according to the rabbis, was assigned the task of continually mixing the blood to prevent it from congealing (*m. Yoma* 4:3; 5:3). Instead, the blood of the slain goat may have been brought into the adytum in its entirety (see the NOTE on v 15).

on. al pēnê, literally, "on the surface of." The rabbis interpreted this phrase as meaning *kĕneged* 'over against', that is, in the direction of the Ark but not touching it (*b. Yoma* 55a [bar.]). But in the next verse the same manipulation

with the blood of the goat employs the preposition *'al* 'on' (v 15), as does 4
QtgLev. Nonetheless, both prepositions are correct: the darkness of the adytum,
abetted by the smoke screen, makes it impossible to determine whether the
blood actually makes contact with the *kappōret*. 4QtgLev renders *['ʾl ksyʾ* 'on
the lid', omitting the word *pĕnê* (see below).

on its east side. *qēdōmâ*, literally, "eastward," which leads one scholar to
suggest that the high priest had to circle around the Ark to its western side in
order to be able to sprinkle the blood in an easterly direction (Loewenstamm
1958). But the locative *he* in compass directions can refer to the orientation of
the object as well as the subject, for example, *wĕhišlîk . . . hammizbēaḥ
qēdĕmâ* 'he shall cast . . . the east side of the altar' (1:16).

It is striking that 4QtgLev reads *ʿL KSYʾ WQDM KSYʾ LMDNḤʾ* '[sprin-
kle it with his finger] on the cover and in front of the cover on the east side [he
shall sprinkle . . .]', which presumes that the Hebrew *Vorlage* at Qumran read
wĕqēdmâ lipnê instead of the MT's *qēdmâ wĕlipnê*. The transposition of the
conjunctive *waw* from *lipnê* to *qēdmâ* effectively attaches the adverb *qēdmâ* to
the subsequent clause, thus asserting that the high priest first sprinkles the
kappōret and then sprinkles seven times before the *kappōret*, on its eastern side.
This reading clarifies—rather, it gives Qumran's solution to—two ambiguities:
the high priest sprinkles the *kappōret* itself (as clearly stated in v 15) and then he
sprinkles the eastern part of the adytum, namely, the portion of its floor between
its entrance and the *kappōret*, but not the eastern part of the *kappōret* (as
implied by the MT). This variant reading can hardly be termed "minimal"
(Fitzmeyer 1978–79: 9). Nonetheless, one need not conclude that Qumran's
Hebrew *Vorlage* read any differently from the MT: 4QtgLev, as is the case with
most targumic variants, may only be an interpretation. On Qumran's rendering
of *kappōret* as "cover," see the NOTE on v 2.

How many times does the high priest sprinkle the blood on the *kappōret?*
The Karaites opt for seven, interpreting the expression "seven times" as the
object of both sprinklings, on and before the *kappōret (Seper Hamibḥar; Keter
Torah)*. Josephus also maintains the same interpretation (*Ant.* 3.243), indicating
that the Karaites' view was based on an old tradition. In that case, however, the
second occurrence of the verb "sprinkle" *(yazzeh)* would be superfluous. Moreover, the Karaites arc shown to be wrong because of the symmetry demanded by
the blood manipulations, which calls for the configuration 1 + 7 in the three
areas of the Tabernacle where the purgation takes place (details in v 19). Thus,
with rabbinic tradition, it must be concluded that the high priest sprinkles the
kappōret only once (*m. Yoma* 5:3, 4).

sprinkle. The purpose of the blood sprinkling is to purge the adytum of its
impurities (v 16; cf. also the NOTE on 4:6). The text is silent concerning the
manipulating technique. The rabbis claim it was done *kĕmaṣlîp* 'with a whip-
ping motion', by the flick of the wrist, once upward and seven times downward
(*m. Yoma* 5:3; cf. Meiri on *b. Yoma* 54b). Josephus asserts that the sprinklings

were aimed for the ceiling and floor, respectively (*Ant.* 3.243), thus avoiding the place of the Ark completely; so too the rabbis (*m. Yoma* 5:3).

sprinkle . . . sprinkle (wĕhizzâ . . . yazzeh). These two verbs are the ninth and tenth active verbs in this pericope (vv 11–14), the final one being a simple imperfect and requiring an altered word order (Paran 1983: 157). The "circular inclusio" (Paran's term, 1983: 31) employing the same verb in chiastic order is also demonstrated in 10:13–14; 14:28–29, 42; cf. also Exod 29:44; Num 30:5; 31:7–8; 33:52; 35:3.

15. *[bring] its blood. [wĕhēbî']* '*et-dāmô,* implying that all of it should be brought inside the adytum where it becomes consecrated and is thereby empowered to sanctify the altar (v 19). Functionally, this act is equivalent to sanctifying the priestly consecrands by sprinkling them with blood that has been taken from the altar (8:30). The LXX's reading of *middāmô* must therefore be discounted as a harmonization with v 14.

and manipulate its blood. wĕ'ā śâ 'et-dāmô, literally, "he treats its blood," in referring to its manipulation. The particle *'ēt* is not the preposition, meaning "with," but the sign of the accusative. The LXX presumes *middāmô* 'some of its blood', probably on the basis of *middam happār* 'some of the blood of the bull' (v 14). Nevertheless, after the verb *'āśâ* this construction is unhebraic.

he did with the blood ('āśâ lĕdam). Here the preposition is in order, referring to the procedure that had just been followed.

16. *Thus he shall purge (wĕkipper).* The rite inside the adytum concludes with a statement of its purpose. The same is true for the rites inside the shrine and upon the altar (vv 17b, 19b).

of the pollution (miṭṭum'ōt). Here, this term refers to the ritual impurities described in chaps. 11–15 and the moral impurities generated by the violation of the prohibitive commandments (see the NOTE on 4:2). Of the three Israelite malfeasances listed in this verse, the focus is clearly on the term "pollution." This is shown by its repetition in the second half of this verse and its sole mention in the purging of the altar (v 19). Its predominance is only logical, for the result of Israel's wrongdoing is the creation of impurity, which then attaches itself to the sanctuary and pollutes it (chap. 4, COMMENT C). Furthermore, once it is determined that the verb *kippēr* literally means "purge," that is, to expunge impurity (COMMENT F below), then the function of all of the blood manipulations becomes clear: to purge the sanctuary of its accumulated pollution. Finally, this function is underscored by contrast with the wording of the rite with the Azazel goat (v 21). There too three malfeasances of Israel are enumerated. Two of them, "transgressions" and "sins," correspond to ones purged here by the blood. Only "pollution" is not repeated; instead we find "iniquities" *('ăwōnôt).* Thus the ritual in the sanctuary concerns itself with removing its pollution (also caused by Israel's wrongs; see below); the rite with the Azazel goat, by contrast, focuses not on pollution, the effects of Israel's wrongs, but exclusively on the wrongs themselves. This distinction was clearly understood by the rabbis: "For *pollution* that befalls the Temple and its sancta through wantonness, atonement is made by the goat whose blood is sprinkled within the adytum and by the Day of Atonement; for *all other wrongs* specified in the Torah—minor or grave, wanton or inadvertent, conscious or unconscious, through commission or omission . . . the scapegoat makes atonement" (*m. Šebu.* 1:6; cf. *Sipra,* Aḥare 5:8; italics mine). See further v 21.

transgressions. The noun *pešaʿ* means "rebellion" and its verb, *pāšaʿ,* "rebel." Its usage originates in the political sphere, where it denotes the rebellion of a vassal against his overlord (e.g., 1 Kgs 12:19; 2 Kgs 1:1; 3:5, 7; 8:20, 22); by extension, it is transferred to the divine realm, where it denotes Israel's rebellion against its God (e.g., Isa 1:2; 43:27; Jer 2:8; 33:8). Thus it is the term that characterizes the worst possible sin: open and wanton defiance of the Lord. According to the Priestly scheme, it is this sin that generates the impurity that not only attacks the sanctuary but penetrates into the adytum and pollutes the *kappōret,* the very seat of the godhead (see the diagram and discussion, chap. 4, Comment B). It should also be noted that this term occurs nowhere in P except here, another indication that this text originates in a different provenience and was subsequently adopted and adapted by P (see Comment A below). The fact that all of Israel's sins, including the brazen *pešāʿîm,* are responsible for the pollution of the sanctuary and are now purged by the blood of the two purification offerings makes it highly probable that *originally* the high priest's confession over the live goat referred only to those purged impurities and that the purpose of the rite was to dispatch these impurities into the wilderness (see the Note on "iniquities," v 21 and Comment A below). It should further be noted that as intention plays no part in the creation of physical impurity (indeed, a nocturnal emission [Lev 15:16; Deut 23:11] is purely accidental whereas impurities such as sex and motherhood are exclusively deliberate), the term *pešāʿîm* must be directed solely to the pollution generated by Israel's moral violations.

of the Israelites. The priests are included, for this clause sums up the purpose of the purgative blood from both the priests' bull and people's goat (see also vv 19, 21).

including all of their sins (lĕkol-ḥaṭṭōʾtām). A catchall phrase that incorporates all of the wrongs except for the *pešāʿîm,* the brazen sins, as correctly understood by the Mishna, cited above. The importance of this phrase is that it emphasizes that not only do physical impurities pollute the sanctuary but so do Israel's sins—all of them. For this usage of *lĕkōl,* see 11:26 and Milgrom (1970a: nn. 232, 279).

he shall do likewise [for the Tent of Meeting] (wĕkēn yaʿăśeh). In other words, the shrine should be purged in the same manner as the adytum. Specifically, one object (the incense altar) is to be purged by direct contact with the purgation blood, and the rest of the shrine is to be purged by a sevenfold sprinkling of the purgation blood on the shrine floor. Thus, "likewise" refers to the 1 + 7 sequence (but in reverse order, versus *b. Yoma* 56b) employed in the adytum (see further the NOTE on v 19). There is, however, no need to specify how the purgation of the incense altar takes place, for the procedure was already given in 4:6–7, 17–18. True, the rabbis (*m. Yoma* 5:4), the Karaites *(Seper Hamibḥar)* and Josephus *(Ant.* 3.243) claim that "likewise" means that the blood is sprinkled once above (seven times according to Josephus and the Karaites; see the NOTE on v 14) and seven times below, in the direction of the veil, but not on the incense altar itself. They are forced to adopt this interpretation because they identify the altar, which, according to the text (v 18), is the next sanctum purged by the high priest, as the altar of incense. But the symmetrical patterning of the purgation rite militates against their position (see the NOTE on v 19). Moreover, once it can be shown that the purged altar is the sacrificial altar standing in the courtyard (see the NOTE on v 18), then there is no choice but to conclude that the purging of the shrine must include the daubing of the blood on the altar of incense, in conformance with the explicit requirement of Exod 30:10. The purging of the shrine took place with the blood of the bull and goat separately, just as in the adytum (see *m. Yoma* 5:4).

It should also be noted that uniquely in this chapter the term *ʾōhel môʿēd* does not refer to the entire Tent of Meeting, as everywhere else in P, but only to the outer room, the shrine. P's term for the shrine, *haqqōdeš* (e.g., Exod 25:33), could not be used in chap. 16 because it was already usurped for the adytum—again, another indication of a different provenience for this text.

abides (haššōkēn). The participle requires a definite article because Tent of Meeting is a proper noun (Ehrlich 1908–14). It is a denominative of *miškān,* the Tabernacle; hence its subject is always the Lord who, in his grace, has "tabernacled" himself in Israel.

[in the midst of] their pollution (ṭumʾōtām). The effect of Israel's wrongdoing—brazen sins *(pěšāʿîm)* plus other sins *(ḥaṭṭāʾōt)*—produces pollution *(ṭumʾōt).* Hence this latter term focuses on the effect and not the cause. In the first half of the verse, however, where this term is one of three different kinds of wrongdoing, its meaning is restricted to ritual impurity, as described in chaps. 11–15.

17. *No one. wěkol-ʾādām,* literally, "every man." This warning is, in practice, directed solely to the priests and not to the Israelites, who have no access to the shrine.

until he comes out. From the adytum or the shrine? As there is no one in the shrine, no one would know when the high priest exited from the adytum. Therefore, the only logical answer is that no one may enter the shrine until the high priest emerges from the Tent into the courtyard. Still, it is clear why the high priest must enter the inner room, the adytum, alone, but the question remains: Why may no priest be with him as he purges the outer room, the shrine? The answer may be that just as severer precautions are invoked when the Tabernacle is dismantled—even the sacrificial altar, normally seen by everyone, may not be viewed by a nonpriest (Num 4:20)—so special precautions are taken when the purgation is in process. For the static picture of the sancta at rest now turns turbulent: their impurities are being absorbed by the blood detergent. The shrine is just too dangerous a place for anyone but the high priest. The high priest's mission is fraught with peril. He is engaged in a rite of passage. Daring to enter the holy of holies, the adytum, the symbolic realm of the wearers of linen, the divine assembly (see the NOTE on v 4), he must emerge from it unscathed. No wonder that, according to a later tradition, "he made a feast for his friends for having come forth safely from the adytum" (*m. Yoma* 7:4).

Thus he shall effect purgation (wĕkippēr). The *waw* introduces the purpose of the high priest's rites in the shrine, thereby making it similar in function to *wĕkippēr* in v 16, which stated the purpose of the high priest's rites in the adytum. Alternatively, the *waw* may introduce a protasis whose apodosis is in v 18 (so *NJPS*). But as a statement of purpose concludes the description of the rites in the adytum (v 16a) and on the altar (v 19b), one should also be expected in the text dealing with the shrine (see COMMENT A below).

for himself and his household. The wording in this verse implies that there were two blood rites in the shrine, one for the priestly house and the other for the rest of the Israelites—called "community" (v 5) and "congregation" (v 17) —the same discrete rites as in the adytum (vv 14–15).

congregation of Israel. qĕhal yiśrā'ēl, a synonym of *'ădat bĕnê yiśrā'ēl* 'the community of the Israelites' (see the NOTE on v 5); in both cases the priests are excluded, for they are enumerated separately (vv 3, 17).

18. *He shall then come out. wĕyāṣā',* that is, of the Tent.

the altar that is before the Lord (hammizbēaḥ 'ăšer lipnê-YHWH). This must be the sacrificial altar (Ibn Ezra, Jos., *Ant.* 3.243) and not the incense altar (*m. Yoma* 5:5; *Sipra,* Aḥare 4:8), because the verb "come out" (above) implies that he emerges from the Tent. That the sacrificial altar is also considered to be "before the Lord" is discussed at v 12.

and effect purgation upon it (wĕkippēr 'ālāyw). Whereas the preposition *'al* after *kippēr* always means "for, on behalf of" if the object is human, it can literally mean "on, upon" if the object is nonhuman (see vv 10, 16 and chap. 4, COMMENT B). For the identical usage in connection with the altar, see Exod 29:36.

It should be noted that, in contrast to the previous purgations in which the entire Tent, comprising the total area of the adytum and shrine, is purged and not just its sancta, in this instance only the altar receives the blood, but not one drop of purgatorial blood is sprinkled on the courtyard floor or its surrounding curtains. This is no accident but follows inexorably from P's own system. Whereas the Tent and its sancta and the sacrificial altar are "most sacred," the Tabernacle enclosure is only "sacred." The inferior holiness of the latter is proved by the fact that, during the consecration rites, it alone was not anointed (Exod 30:26–30; 40:9–16). Furthermore, whereas lay persons were strictly forbidden to enter the Tent or officiate on the altar, they had unqualified access to the Tabernacle courtyard. To be sure, the inner portion of the enclosure, between the altar and the Tent, was regarded by the priests as their exclusive reserve in rabbinic times (*m. Kelim* 1:9; *Sipre Zuṭa* on Num 5:2); however, this distinction is not recognized by P or any other pentateuchal source (see Milgrom 1970a: nn. 166, 211). Indeed, rabbinic sources speak of lay processions around the altar on the Feast of Tabernacles (*m. Sukk.* 4:5), a custom that may go back to biblical times (cf. Ps 26:6). In any event, the conclusion must be drawn that only the "most sacred" requires purgation, not the "sacred." In effect, this means that impurity is dangerous only when it comes into contact with holiness of a superior nature, namely, those objects or spaces to which the priests alone have access.

some of the blood of the bull and of the goat (middam happār ûmiddam haśśā'îr). It is implied here that a single application of the blood is made to the altar—in other words, that the blood of the bull and goat is mixed—whereas the blood of each animal was applied separately inside the Tent (vv 14–15; see 17b). This fact is acknowledged by the rabbis (*m. Yoma* 5:4). For the significance, see the NOTE on v 19.

around. sābîb (see 8:15 and chap. 4, COMMENT B).

19. *and he shall sprinkle (wěhizzâ).* This constitutes a second manipulation with the blood purgative: first, the altar horns were daubed (*nātan,* v 18), followed by the sevenfold aspersion of the altar (*hizzâ,* v 19). The reason for these two discrete acts is explicitly given in this verse: to "purify it" and "consecrate it." The order of the verbs is crucial, for it corresponds to the sequence of the manipulations. The daubing of the altar horns purifies the altar, and the sevenfold sprinkling of the altar consecrates it.

Support for this sequence is found in the prescriptions for the altar's consecration (Exod 29:36–37): first it is purged *(ḥiṭṭē', kipper)* and then it is consecrated *(māšaḥ, qiddēš).* Further corroboration is supplied in the text of the priestly consecration, where not only are the identical verbs used but even the objects to which the sacrificial blood is applied also correspond. The extremities of the priests, namely, their right ear lobes, thumbs, and big toes, are daubed (*nātan;* 8:24), whereas they and their clothing are sprinkled (*hizzâ;* 8:30). The only distinction is the nature of the sacrificial blood: the blood for the altar stems from the purification offering, which, by definition, is applied solely to objects (see chap. 4, COMMENT B) whereas the blood used on the priests stems from *'ēl hammillu'îm,* the consecration ram (8:22–44). Another distinction is that the blood used for consecrating the priest is taken from the altar. The consecrating power of the blood is generated by its contact with the sacred altar. The priests are then consecrated with the anointing oil, which, holy from its inception, transmits its consecrating power directly. (For details, see the NOTES on 8:15, 23 and chap. 8, COMMENT D). Those minor differences apart, there are striking similarities between these two rites, not just in form but in purpose; priests and altar require purgation and consecration.

Yet a number of questions remain regarding the altar blood rite: (1) Why does the blood sprinkled in the adytum and shrine have a purgative effect, but on the altar its function is consecratory? It can be answered that the sprinkling on the altar was preceded by its daubing. The purpose of the second application cannot be the same as the first. The text tells us: it is for consecration. (2) If the altar needs to be sanctified, why not use the anointment oil, whose very purpose is to consecrate and indeed was so used on the altar for its consecration (8:15)? The answer may be that this time the altar is not consecrated but reconsecrated. It first needs to be purged of "the pollution of the Israelites" (v 19). The blood that purges is available again, this time for sanctification. Its sanctifying power derives from being brought inside the Tent—indeed, inside the adytum itself (so the explicit statement concerning the blood of the goat, v 15). (3) Why is the altar the only sanctum that requires purgation and consecration whereas the Ark and incense altar need only to be purged? Here the answer points to the singular function of the altar: it is the medium of God's salvific expiation of the sins of Israel. Therefore, not only does it have to be purged of Israel's sins; it must be a fit instrument for effecting expiation for Israel when sacrifices are offered upon it. This is precisely what the text states when the purification offering is sacrificed upon the newly consecrated altar: *wayĕqaddĕšēhû lĕkappēr ʿālāyw* 'and he (Moses) consecrated it to effect atonement upon it" (8:15). (4) Why is the blood of the bull and the goat mixed together in purging the altar but used separately in purging the adytum and shrine? Here the numerical symmetry of the Priestly scheme comes into play. First, it should be noted that the tripartite purgation rite falls into the following symmetrical arrangement:

adytum	shrine	altar
1 + 7	7 + 1	1 + 7

In each sacred space, an object is purged once (Ark, incense altar, sacrificial altar), followed by a sevenfold aspersion (adytum, shrine, sacrificial altar). The one variation in this scheme takes place in the shrine, where the seven aspersions precede the purging of the object instead of following it. This is no random aberration but, on the contrary, creates a classic symmetrical introversion, the pattern ABA'. Furthermore, when the number of manipulations is actually tabulated, the following is the result:

	adytum	shrine	altar
bull	1 + 7	7 + 4	4 + 7
goat	1 + 7	7 + 4	

The difference between this table and the preceding one is twofold; now the manipulations with the blood of the bull and goat are counted separately, and one must figure four blood manipulations on the altar corresponding to its four horns. The total number of manipulations adds up to forty-nine, or seven times seven. Seven, the number that stands for completion and perfection, is multiplied by itself.

The significance of the number forty-nine is evident from the pentecontad calendar of chap. 23 (see the discussion there). It is of even greater significance in determining the structure of Num 19 on the preparation and use of the ashes of the Red Cow. As noted by the rabbis (*Pesiq. Rab Kah.* 58), this chapter contains seven different subjects, each mentioned seven times, as follows: (1) the cow and its ashes (vv 2, 5, 6, 9 [twice], 10, 17); (2) burned items, including skin, flesh, blood, dung, cedar, hyssop, and crimson (vv 5–6); (3) sprinkling (v 4); (4) persons who wash (vv 7 [referring to three priests, vv 4, 6, 7], 8, 10, 19, 21); (5) items in a tent contaminated by a corpse—occupants, those who enter, open vessels—and, in an open field, those who touch someone slain, someone who died naturally, a human bone, a grave (vv 14–16); (6) those that are purified: tent, vessels, persons in the tent, persons who touched a bone, or the corpse of one who was slain, or one who died naturally, or a grave (v 18); (7) priests (vv 1 [Moses and Aaron], 3, 4, 6, 7 [twice]). (For other aspects of the structure of Num 19, see Milgrom 1990a: 437–38, Excursus 47.)

Thus the septenary system operates in the rites of the Red Cow and Yom Kippur. Both are purgative rites involving the blood of the purification offering, or, rather, blood rites that have been incorporated into the purification offering. They therefore stem from the same Priestly school, P.

Alternatively or, perhaps, complementarily, because the altar is exposed to the air and to contact by the laity, it is the most vulnerable of the sancta to pollution and, hence, it must be reconsecrated annually. Thus the added "inoculation" of the sevenfold aspersion of the blood supplies it with extra protection (see the NOTE on 8:33).

some of the blood (min-haddām). The rest of the blood is poured at the base of the altar (4:10b, 18b, 25b, 30b, 34b; *m. Yoma* 5:6).

purify it (wĕṭihărô). A synonym of *kippēr* (Ezek 43:20, 26), which may have been chosen here because of its indirect object *miṭṭum'ōt* 'of the pollution'. The juxtaposition of *ṭihēr* and *ṭum'â* is pervasive (e.g., Jer 33:8; Ezek 36:25, 33; Ps 51:4; Neh 13:30).

of the Israelites. Priests are included in this case (see the NOTE on v 21).

and consecrate it (wĕqiddĕšô). The purpose of the dual blood application is neatly caught by the rabbis: "Purify it of the past (impurities) and consecrate it for the future (sacrificial uses)" (*Sipra,* Aḥare 4:13). Of course, it is not consecration but reconsecration that is effected here. The sanctuary and its sancta were consecrated at the time of their completion and installation (8:10–11).

It should also be noted that ancient Mesopotamia uses the exact cognate, Akk. *quddušu* 'to consecrate' with precisely the same objects as found in the Bible: persons, buildings, sites, and ritual objects. (Mesopotamia also adds divine images to their list, which, patently, would be taboo in aniconic Israel.) Although most of the translated texts render it "to purify" (cf. *CAD*, Q 46), it is clear that sanctification is what is intended. An object or sacrifice dedicated to the deity is not just purified, for which the verbs *ḫubbu* or *ullulu* would generally be used (cf. *CAD*, E 81–82; H 20–21), but consecrated. Thus a Namburbi ritual records, "When you dig a well, at sunset *[t]uqaddaš* the site. You surround it with flour . . ." (Caplice 1965–71: 39.150–51, lines 27'–28'). Because the site is being prepared for a sacrificial rite to Šamaš, the great gods (Anunnaki), and the ancestral spirits (lines 33'–35'), it is clear that the site is not just purified but sanctified. In Mesopotamia as well as in Israel, the transfer from the profane to the sacred domain mandates ritual that goes beyond the act of cleansing or purifying that abounds in normative, communal life. More is involved than the removal of impurity. An inner change takes place that transforms the identity of the entire object. It becomes permeated by divine energy. In a word, it is consecrated.

The Babylonian New Year's festival is the occasion for the annual purgation of the temple (discussed in COMMENT C below). The above-mentioned terms for purification abound as well as *kuppuru*, the precise cognate of biblical *kippēr*, with the same meaning, "purge." Unfortunately, the surviving text breaks off on the fifth of the eleven- or twelve-day festival and we do not know whether its annually purified altar was also reconsecrated, just as was done in Israel.

This latter point is significant. In Israel only the altar was reconsecrated, to the exclusion of the other sancta. Manifestly, the altar, the most vulnerable target of the unending impurities generated by Israel (see chap. 4, COMMENT B), would become so polluted that its very holiness was endangered. Hence, a periodic rite of consecration was prescribed.

20. *purging the adytum (mikkappēr 'et-haqqōdeš)*. Things but not persons can be the direct object of the verb *kippēr* (chap. 4, COMMENT B). The purpose of v 20a is to stress the fact that the purging of the sanctuary must be complete before beginning the Azazel rite. This precaution is well advised: all of the sanctuary's impurities must first be released by the blood rite before the high priest can transfer them onto the head of the live goat. Most likely, it is this special warning that prompted the author of the Temple Scroll to prescribe that the entire sacrificial ritual of the purification offerings must be completed, including the burning of their suet (v 20) and carcasses (v 27), before the rite with the Azazel goat can begin (see COMMENT A below).

he shall bring forward (wĕhiqrîb). While the sacrificial goat had been "brought forward" to be offered on the altar (v 9), the Azazel goat had been "stationed alive before the Lord" (v 10). Now it is the latter's turn to be "brought forward" for its peculiar ritual. Ordinarily, it is the offerer himself who "brings forward" his sacrifice (e.g., 1:2, 3, 10, 14). In this case the offerer is the people or their representatives (v 5), whose iniquities and transgressions—that is to say, whose brazen and presumptuous sins—are to be carried away by the goat. But as the brazen, presumptuous sinner is barred from the sanctuary, there is no other alternative but that the high priest should act on behalf of the people (see the NOTES on vv 5, 9 and chap. 4, COMMENT B).

21. *both of his hands (štê yādāw)*. The fact that the text stresses that the hand-leaning rite is executed with both hands is the key to understanding the function of the Azazel goat. It is not a sacrifice, else the hand-leaning would have been performed with one hand (see the NOTE on 1:4). The two-handed ceremonial instead serves a transference function: to convey, by confession, the sins of Israel onto the head of the goat (see the NOTE on "iniquities" below and COMMENT E).

Recently, D. P. Wright has argued that the two-handed rite is "the means of designating the focus of the ritual action" and that "in the case of the scapegoat it signifies: 'This goat is the recipient of the sins of the people'" (1986: 436). He admits in this case and in the two-handed rite performed by Moses on Joshua (Num 27:18, 23; Deut 34:9) that transference also takes place (cf. *Sipre* Num. 141). In the two other attestations of this rite (Lev 24:14; Sus 34), however, nothing at all is transferred, leaving as the only possible explanation that those performing the hand-leaning are declaring, "This one is guilty; he/she is worthy of death."

The case of Susanna is particularly cogent; by contrast, that of the blasphemer (Lev 24) is not. If those who heard the blasphemy performed the rite in order to convict the culprit, why did they have to wait until the oracle specified the penalty (vv 12–16)? They should have performed it as soon as he was apprehended and charged! It therefore seems more plausible to posit that those who heard the blasphemy were contaminated by it and, via the hand-leaning, they effectively transferred the pollution back to the blasphemer and eliminated it by executing him outside the camp. To be sure, as Wright correctly argues, "there is no indication elsewhere in the Bible that blasphemy cause pollution" (1986: 435). Yet it must be remembered that Lev 24 is not P but H, a source that extends the generating source of impurity to such as as Molech worship (20:3) and incest (18:24–28). Moreover, in the similar case of the wood gatherer (Num 15:32–36), why are not those who discover him violating the Sabbath required to "testify" by leaning their hands on him?

And consider this further analogy. He who hears an imprecation to testify and withholds his testimony, *wĕnāśā' 'ăwōnô* 'he must bear his punishment' (Lev 5:1; cf. 1 Sam 14:43–45), a formula implying capital punishment that, in the case of remorse and confession, is commuted to a graduated purification offering (see the COMMENT on 5:1–13). The fact that a purification offering is prescribed means that merely to ignore an authorized curse containing the name of God creates a pollution. How much more so, then, would a blasphemy, not just ignoring God but cursing him, give rise to a pollution that must be returned to the blasphemer and then eliminated with him outside the community! (I would also presume that if he could not be apprehended, those who heard the blasphemy would be required to bring a purification offering.)

Nevertheless, I concede that the case of Susanna and the Elders baffles me. Perhaps it is a late, postexilic development, as reflected in the rabbinic comment on 24:4 that the witnesses and the judges lean their hands on the blasphemer and say "your blood be on your head for you have caused this" (*Sipra,* Emor. 19:2). Thus hand-leaning for the rabbis, in the case of capital punishment, is a rite that removes blood guilt from those responsible for the death sentence (cf. the NOTE on 20:9). Presumably, the elders may have said or implied the same by their hand-leaning rite on Susanna. Note that Daniel responds, "I am innocent of this woman's death" (Sus 46). If this interpretation is correct, then transference still takes place, not of pollution but of blood guilt. This rite is the same even if its content has changed. For now, I shall suspend judgment on Susanna and accept the possibility of Wright's interpretation, noting again, however, that in the case of the scapegoat (and Joshua), even if the hand-leaning designates the recipient of the rite, transference nonetheless has occurred.

confess over it (wĕhitwaddâ ʿālāyw). Confession is only required of brazen, presumptuous sins (see the NOTE on 5:5 and the COMMENT on 5:20–26). The Azazel rite, according to Levine (1974: 82), epitomizes the demonic character of the Day of Atonement. The high priest compels the demon Azazel to admit the goat into his domain by entering the adytum to be "invested with its numinous power" and infusing the goat with it by leaning his hands on it. The purpose of the confession is "to trap the sins by exposing them, by calling them by their name, and thus preventing their escape or concealment." Three comments are in order. First of all, confession would release sins, not entrap them, to judge by the operation of any utterance containing the divine Name, be it a vow, blessing, or curse. Its function, moreover, is judicial and not magical: to reduce the gravity of a nonexpiable wanton sin to an inadvertency expiable by sacrifice (see the NOTE on 5:5). Second, instead of fulfilling the magical objective of infusing the scapegoat with the adytum's sacred power, the hand-leaning rite simply transfers the sins of the people onto the goat, as expressly indicated by the text (v 21). Finally, and more significantly, the requirement of two *ḥaṭṭāʾt* goats for the people reveals how Israel transformed an ancient exorcism. Demonic impurity was exorcised in three ways: curse, destruction, or banishment. The last was often used; instead of evil being annihilated by curse of fire, it was banished to its place of origin (e.g., netherworld, wilderness) or to some other place where its malefic powers could either work in the interests of the sender (e.g., enemy territory) or do no harm at all (e.g., mountains, wilderness). Thus the scapegoat was sent to the wilderness, which was considered to be uninhabited except by the satyr-demon Azazel. The best-known example of this type of temple purgation is the Babylonian New Year festival, when the officiant literally wipes the sanctuary walls with the carcass of a ram and then throws it in the river. Thus the same animal that purges the temple impurities carries them off (see COMMENTS C and E below).

The hand-leaning, according to Levine, serves a different function: "perhaps one may see in the hand-leaning the activation of divine power. The priest is girded with divine power when he stands in the Deity's chamber, and with this power, he compels the goat and arouses it to action against the second goat-demon Azazel" (1969: 94). Besides the unsupportable notion that entering the adytum invests the high priest with divine power, this interpretation is unacceptable because it attributes discrete functions to the hand-leaning and confession, whereas they clearly complement and reinforce one another: the imposition of the hands simply designates the destination of the confessed sins. The hand-leaning, so to speak, is the vehicle that conveys the verbal pronouncement of the people's sins onto the head of the goat. A transfer thus takes place—not from the high priest, who is personally immune from the contamination produced by the sins he confesses—but from Israel itself; its sins, exorcised by the high priest's confession, are transferred to the body of the goat, just as the sanctuary's impurities, absorbed by the purgation blood, are (originally) conveyed to the goat (see COMMENT A below for details).

What was recited in the confession? Scripture is silent. Yet the Mishna records the following: "O Lord, your people, the house of Israel, have committed iniquity, transgressed, and sinned before you. O, by the Lord (see Exod 33:19; 34:5), grant atonement, I pray, for the iniquities *(ʿăwônôt)*, and transgressions *(pĕšāʿîm)* and sins *(ḥăṭāʾîm)* that your people the house of Israel have committed and transgressed and sinned before you; as it is written in the Torah of your servant Moses: 'For on this day shall atonement be made for you to purify you of all your sins; thus you shall become pure before the Lord' (v 30)" *(m. Yoma* 6:2; the sequence of the sins follows their order in v 21; for the high priest's confession on behalf of the priests, see the NOTE on v 11). The crucial significance of the confession is accurately pinpointed by this rabbinic comment: "By confessing the iniquities and transgressions, they turn them into inadvertences" *(Sipra,* Aḥare par. 2:6), thus qualifying them for sacrificial expiation (see the NOTE on 5:5).

iniquities (ʿăwōnōt). This is the key term in the confession because it is the only category of sin repeated in the summation (v 22). Thus it parallels and corresponds in importance to *ṭumʾōt* 'impurities', the term selected in summing up the purpose of the sanctuary purgation (see the NOTE on v 16). Indeed, the only difference between the inventory of wrongs purged by the blood of the bull and goat and that purged by the scapegoat is that "impurities" is replaced by "iniquities." Thus it is clear that the blood purges the impurities of the sanctuary and the scapegoat purges the sins of the people (see the NOTE on v 16). This distinction was neatly caught by the rabbis *(m. Šebu.* 1:6, cited in the NOTE on "of the pollution," v 16). The rabbis define "iniquities" as *zĕdônôt,* deliberate wrongdoing *(Sipra,* Aḥare par. 2:4; *t. Yoma* 2:1), whose gravity is one notch below that of "transgressions" (see below).

The rabbis are surely correct in their conviction that the sacrificial *ḥaṭṭāʾt* animals purge the sanctuary of Israel's impurities whereas the live goat atones for Israel's sins. Two bits of evidence confirm their conviction. (1) In the purgation rite of the shrine in Lev 4:3–21, the sacrificial *ḥaṭṭāʾt* suffices; an additional live animal is not required (answering Rodriguez 1979: 117). Thus, from the standpoint of P, the sacrificial animals of Lev 16 also suffice to purge the sanctuary. This leaves the live goats to function in an entirely different sphere: the elimination of Israel's sins. (2) Two animals are required to purge the sanctuary of its impurities: a *ḥaṭṭāʾt* bull for the priests and a *ḥaṭṭāʾt* goat for the people. Two animals are needed because the high priest must first purge the sanctuary of his and his fellow priests' impurities before he can act on behalf of the people. But only one live goat suffices to atone for both the priests and the people. If its purpose was to carry off the sanctuary's impurities, should not the high priest have first confessed his sins and those of the priests over a live goat of their own before he could officiate with the live goat of the people? Again, the only answer can be that the live goat has nothing to do with the sanctuary's impurities but, as the text emphatically and unambiguously states, it deals with *ʿăwōnōt* 'iniquities'—the causes of the sanctuary's impurities, all of Israel's sins, ritual and moral alike, of priests and laity alike.

Nevertheless, the possibility must be considered that *originally* the purgation rites of the sanctuary resembled those of the scale-diseased person and house (14:4–7, 49–52). Just as in the latter case, two birds were prescribed, one to remove the iniquities and the other to dispatch them to the wilderness, so in the purgation rites for the sanctuary, the goat would have removed the impurities and the live goat would have carried them off to the wilderness. The creative contribution of the Priestly legists consisted of first adding a purification-offering bull for the priestly house and, more importantly, confining the sanctuary's purgation to the action of the purification-offering blood (on the model of 4:3–21), thereby freeing the live goat, as demonstrated by the high priest's confession, for focusing exclusively on the elimination of Israel's *ʿăwōnōt*, its sins. The wording of v 21 would be the precipitate of the Priestly innovation.

transgressions. *pĕšāʿîm*, correctly defined by the rabbis as *mĕrādîm* 'rebellions' (*t. Yoma* 2:5, *Sipra*, Aḥare par. 2:4), for which they cite scriptural proof, 2 Kgs 8:22 (*Sipra*, Aḥare 4:3) and 2 Kgs 3:7 (*b. Šebu.* 12b; see the NOTE on v 16).

of the Israelites. In this chapter, whenever the priests are included with their fellow Israelites, the term for Israelites is *bĕnê yiśrāʾēl* (vv 16, 19, 21, 24). But whenever the priests are listed separately, the Israelites are called by the terms *ʿădat bĕnê yiśrāʾēl* (v 5), *qĕhal yiśrāʾēl* (v 17), *hāʿām* (v 15, 24), and *ʿam haqqāhāl* (v 33).

including all of their sins. See the NOTE on v 16.

sent off to the wilderness (wĕšillaḥ . . . hammidbārâ). Purgation and elimination rites go together in the ancient world. Exorcism of impurity is not enough; its power must be removed. An attested method is to banish it to its place of origin (e.g., the wilderness of the netherworld; see below) or to some place where its malefic powers could work in the interest of the sender (e.g., enemy territory; see COMMENT E below). Thus the scapegoat was sent off to the wilderness, which was considered inhabited by the satyr-demon Azazel (see COMMENT C below). This dispatch of the scapegoat into the wilderness is as integrally tied to the purgation of the sanctuary as the release (also *šillaḥ*) of the bird into the wilderness is tied to the purification rite of the healed scale-diseased person and house (14:4–7, 49–53). The analogy with the purificatory rite for scale disease is instructive in another respect. Just as the former requires two birds, one to provide the blood to asperse the impure *mĕṣōrā'* and the other to dispatch the released impurities to an uninhabited place, so the latter requires two goats, one to provide blood for aspersion of the contaminated sanctuary and the other to dispatch Israel's sins to an uninhabited place. Thus even though the goat, according to the present text, transports Israel's sins, not its impurities, it still forms an integral part of the ritual, whose original purpose was to transport the released iniquities of the sanctuary but at a later stage was reinterpreted to effect symbolically the elimination of Israel's sins.

According to the rabbis, the goat was pushed off a cliff (*m. Yoma* 6:6; for the description, see below). Philo, however, presumes that the goat was allowed to live (*Plant.* 61). Killing the goat was not essential, for the high priest would resume the service as soon as he was notified that the goat had reached the wilderness (*m. Yoma* 6:8; see COMMENT C below).

to the wilderness (hammidbārâ). The *midbār* is an "infertile land [literally, salty land] without inhabitant" (Jer 17:6), a place "in which there is no man" (Job 38:26; cf. Jer 22:6; 51:43). Thus the purpose of dispatching the goat to the wilderness is to remove it from human habitation (see the NOTE on "inaccessible region," v 22).

a man in waiting (ʾîš ʿittî). For the rendering, see the LXX, Tgs., *y. Yoma* 6:3; *b. Yoma* 66b. Still, the etymology of this hapax remains unsolved. Perhaps it implies someone who could find his very way in and out of the wilderness so that he, but not the goat, would be able to return (Rashbam). The rabbis admit that this job could be handled by a layman, but the high priests insisted that it be executed by a priest (*m. Yoma* 6:3).

22. *Thus the goat shall carry upon it (wĕnāśāʾ haśśāʿîr ʿālāyw).* This literal meaning of the idiom *nāśāʾ ʿal* 'carry upon' was met in 10:17 (see also Exod 28:38). The function of the scapegoat was clearly understood in rabbinic times, as the following statements illustrate: "They made a causeway for him (the scapegoat) because of the Babylonians (or Alexandrians, *b. Yoma* 66b) who pull its hair, shouting to it, 'Take (our sins) and go forth; take our sins and go forth'" (*m. Yoma* 6:4); "Why does the goat tarry here, seeing that the sins of this generation are so many?" (*b. Yoma* 66b).

all their iniquities (kol-ʿăwōnōtām). See the NOTE on v 21.

an inaccessible region. ʾereṣ gĕzērâ, literally, "a cutoff land," in other words, from which the goat cannot return. Akkadian rituals also speak of an *ašru parsu,* which also means "a cutoff place." The Versions interpret *gĕzērâ* as "uninhabitable" *(Tg. Onq.),* "desolate" (LXX), and "uncultivated" (Pesh.). The verb *gāzar* can mean "cut off [from the living]," that is, to die (e.g., Isa 53:8; Ezek 37:11; Ps 88:6; Lam 3:54). It has been observed that in Akkadian, the terms for wilderness, such as *ṣēru,* also connote the netherworld and that demons who are denizens of the underworld are prone to take residence in the wilderness (Tallquist 1934; Tawil 1980). Thus it is possible that the satyr-demon Azazel is being driven to its natural home in the wilderness/netherworld (but see Wright 1987: 25–30). The rabbis, however, are the bearers of the tradition that the scapegoat was not just banished but also killed by pushing it off a cliff (*m. Yoma* 6:6). Could it be that the change was made after a scapegoat was once able to make its way back to civilization, still laden with Israel's sins?

When the goat is set free in the wilderness (wĕšillaḥ et-haśśāʿîr bammidbār). This clause need not be a redundancy of v 21b if it is taken as the protasis of v 23, and it is so rendered. Support for it is the slight but significant change from *hammidbārâ* 'to the wilderness' (v 21) to *bammidbār* 'in the wilderness' (v 22), in other words, only after the scapegoat actually enters the wilderness can the high priest continue with the ritual. Further support is furnished by the rabbis: "They said to the high priest, 'the he-goat has reached the wilderness' " (*m. Yoma* 6:8). This statement implies that before the high priest could proceed with his ritual (ibid., 7:1–4), he had to be notified of the scapegoat's arrival in the wilderness—a literal fulfillment of the biblical prescription once vv 22b, 23 are read as a single statement. Note that this mishna also implies that the high priest waited to be informed of the scapegoat's arrival in the wilderness and not of its slaying. This can only mean that the death of the scapegoat was not an integral part of the original ritual but must have been added later.

23. The sequence of acts in vv 23–24 raises many questions. It seems that the high priest enters the Tent, undresses, leaves his linen clothes there (polluted?), bathes himself either in the Tent (where?) or in the courtyard (naked?), and then emerges (whence?) to officiate on the altar (see Ramban). The rabbis assert flatly, "The whole ritual is recited in the correct order with the exception of this passage (v 23)" (*b. Yoma* 32a, 71a; cf. *y. Yoma* 7:2). Instead, the rabbis place v 23 after v 25 and reconstruct the following sequence: after his ablutions, the high priest changes to his ornate garments, sacrifices the burnt offering (v 24) and purification offering (v 25), changes back to his linen garments in which he reenters the Tent (v 23a) to remove the censer and pan from the adytum, and then dons his ornate garments, leaving the linen garments in the courtyard (never to be reused), in order to offer the remaining sacrifices, the festival supplement (Num 29:9–11) and the *Tāmîd* (*Sipra,* Aḥare 6:2–5; *y. Yoma* 7:2; *b. Yoma* 32a, 71a). Nevertheless, the rabbis explain, the reason for the present arrangement of the text is to keep all of the rites performed in the linen garments in one unit (see Ramban).

The rabbis' proposed reconstruction raises as many questions as it answers. They are constrained to adopt the complex order just cited because of the tradition they had, which undoubtedly reflects the actual practice of the Herodian Temple, that the high priest bathed five times and washed his hands and feet ten times in the course of the day (m. Yoma 3:3). They obtain these requisite ablutions in the following manner:

A.　*Immersion* (1)

　　Hands and feet (1)

　　　　Ornate garments—morning *Tāmîd*

　　Hands and feet (2)

B.　*Immersion* (2)

　　Hands and feet (3)

　　　　Linen garments—purgation rites (vv 6–22)

　　Hands and feet (4)

C.　*Immersion* (3)

　　Hands and feet (5)

　　　　Ornate garments—burnt offerings and suet of purification offerings (vv 24–25)

　　Hands and feet (6)

D.　*Immersion* (4)

　　Hands and feet (7)

　　　　Linen garments—removal of censer and pan (v 23)

　　Hands and feet (8)

E.　*Immersion* (5)

　　Hands and feet (9)

　　　　Ornate garments—festival supplement and evening *Tāmîd*

　　Hands and feet (10)

The ablutions in this scheme are based on two principles: (1) hands and feet are washed after as well as before each rite (see the NOTE on v 4), and (2) complete immersion is required before engaging in a new rite (*Sipra*, Aḥare 6:3; b. Yoma 32a). That there once was a great controversy over the correct order of the Temple service on Yom Kippur is mirrored in the Temple Scroll of the Dead Sea sectaries, composed not later than the second century B.C.E., which prescribes an entirely different sequence (details in COMMENT A below).

Strikingly, there is one great rabbinic authority who champions the order of the MT. Elijah of Vilna (eighteenth century), basing himself on the midrash (*Midr. Lev. Rab.* 21:7), proposed that the text of vv 6–28 deals not with the annual Day of Purgation but with an emergency rite that the high priest could employ whenever he felt that the sanctuary was dangerously polluted (see the NOTE on v 2). Hence, he claims, there is no need to read into this text five immersions and ten washings. The latter is required only on Yom Kippur, but for an emergency three immersions and six washings suffice (*'Anap Hillel* on *Sipra*, Aḥare 6:3; David Luria on *Midr. Lev. Rab.* 21:7), as implied by the MT (see the NOTE on v 2).

that he put on when he entered the adytum (*'ăšer lābaš běbō'ô 'el-haqqōdeš*). A reminder that the high priest donned the linen garments solely for the purpose of entering the adytum (see v 4), hence the garments have contracted its superior holiness (see below). It may be that for the same reason the Hittite king removed his white (priestly) garments when he finished officiating at the sacred rites (Singer 1983–84: 1.73; cf. Weinfeld 1990).

and leave them there. wĕhinnîḥām šām, after which they will be washed and rinsed. But why must Aaron reenter the Tent; could he not divest himself of the linen garments while in the court? Sforno's comment is worth quoting: "For in bringing them to the presence of the Lord they became sanctified to an exceptional degree." Thus the objection posed by the rabbis (and Ramban, on this verse) that the high priest could not have left his linen garments in the shrine because they were polluted is based on a wrong assumption. Neither the high priest nor his clothing is polluted by the purgation rites. The immunity of the priest to the impurity that he removes by means of his ritual is demonstrated by the cases of the scale-diseased person and house. The priest who performs the bird rite is himself not contaminated, even though the rite removes a level of impurity (14:4–8, 49–53; see the NOTE on "he shall release," 14:7). To the contrary, the garments are endowed with greater sanctity because the high priest entered the adytum. Thus they must remain in a place of comparable sanctity, inside the "most sacred" Tent and not in the courtyard, which, as noted above (on v 18), possesses an inferior degree of sanctity (see also the NOTE on v 26).

24. *He shall bathe his body in water (wĕrāḥas 'et-běśārô bammayim).* This is the only time that immersion after sacrifice is mentioned. In the Mesopotamian cult, the officiant frequently bathed after performing the ritual (Laessøe 1955: 11). In Israel, however, only the washing of hands and feet before the ritual is mandated (Exod 30:17–21; see the NOTE on "bathing his body in water," v 4).

The purpose of the ablution cannot be the removal of impurity that the high priest purportedly removed from the scapegoat; he is immune to the impurity that he removes (see the NOTE above). Only one plausible reason remains: to remove the superholiness that he contracted by entering the adytum. This premise would account both for the discarding of his supercharged garments inside the Tent (see the NOTE above) and for the need to wash when he resumes his usual operations on the lower level of holiness within the shrine.

in a holy place (bĕmāgôm qādôš). Where? It could not be inside the Tent, for the entire space is not just *qādôš* 'holy', but "most sacred." Hence the place must be in the courtyard. This deduction is supported by the explicit statement that the cereal and purification offerings are eaten by the priests "in a holy place, in the court of the Tent of Meeting" (6:9, 19; cf. 7:6). Unfortunately, the location of this "holy place" cannot be identified. The Herodian Temple court contained a special bathhouse for the priestly ablutions (*m. Yoma* 3:3; cf. *m. Mid.* 5:3). The Temple Scroll describes, in lavish detail, a "House of the Laver" located in the southeastern portion of the Temple court, fifty cubits from the sacrificial altar, boasting three gates and gold-plated cubicles where the priestly garments were deposited while the priests performed their ablutions (11QT 31–33). Thus later theory and practice alike indicate the probability that the place for the priestly ablutions in the Tabernacle was in its courtyard.

One further question concerning the high priest's immersion still remains: Did the high priest really streak naked from the Tent to the place of the bath? Two answers are possible: either his path was curtained off, or he emerged wearing his breeches. The plausibility of the latter is supported by the fact that the high priest (and all priests) always wore breeches while officiating (Exod 28:43), hence he must have had them on while he moved about in the sanctuary during his Yom Kippur rites (see the NOTE on v 4). Rabbinic tradition, however (*m. Yoma* 3:4, 6) and the evidence of the Hittite KI.LAM festival (Singer 1983–84) testify that the high priest/Hittite king was separated from his viewers by an improvised curtain.

his vestments (bĕgādāyw). These cannot be a new set of linen garments (Ibn Ezra) but instead his ornate ones, which he always wore while officiating at the altar.

and sacrifice. wĕʿāśâ; see chap. 4, COMMENT E.

effecting atonement. The burnt offering is also an expiatory sacrifice; indeed, originally it was the exclusive expiatory sacrifice (see the NOTE on 1:4 and the COMMENT on chap. 1). While it atones, however, it does not purge (see COMMENT F below). How many burnt offerings were sacrificed on that day? According to Num 29:8–11 there were nine: one bull, one ram, and seven lambs. If the burnt-offering ram of Lev 16:24 is the same as that of Num 29:8, then a total of ten burnt offerings were sacrificed (Philo, *Laws* 1. 188). Or if the two rams are discrete, then eleven burnt offerings were sacrificed (Jos., *Ant.* 3.240–42; 11QT 25:12–16. The controversy is recorded in *Sipra*, Aḥare par. 2:2; *b. Yoma* 70b).

for himself (bāʿădô). The LXX and two MSS add *ûbĕʿal bêtô* 'and for his household' (as in vv 6 and 17).

25. *the purification offering (ḥaṭṭāʾt).* Of course, both purification offerings are intended, the high priest's (v 3) and the people's (v 5). The object coming first in the sentence (also in v 27) yields the sense of "As for the suet. . . ."

This construction was deemed necessary because the last reference to the purification offering occurred in v 15. The sectaries of the Dead Sea reasoned otherwise (see COMMENT A below).

turn into smoke (yaqṭîr). Note that the sequence of vv 24–25 implies that the suet of the purification offering is burned only after the burnt offering, in accordance with the rabbinic rule: "The blood [rite] of the purification offering precedes the blood [rite] of the burnt offering because it appeases; the members of the burnt offering precede the suet of the purification offering because they are entirely given over to the [altar] fire" (*m. Zebah.* 10:2).

The high priest's rites are now completed. "He would throw a party for his friends when he emerged safely from the sanctuary" (*m. Yoma* 7:4).

26. *launder his clothes and bathe. yĕkabbēs bĕgādāyw wĕrāḥaṣ;* see the NOTE on 11:25. According to one view, because he has handled the sin-laden goat he is contaminated. For the same reason (though there are others; see the NOTE on v 4) the high priest wears a set of simple linen garments for the purgation rites: they become sullied and must be discarded (v 23) and, presumably, laundered for subsequent use. Alternatively, and more probably, the high priest, in purging the sanctuary and in transferring the sins of Israel to the goat, does not contaminate himself at all, and the reason for his change of clothes is the opposite one—they become "most holy" once they have been in the adytum and, hence, have to be left in the shrine, together with the other "most holy" sancta (see below and the NOTE on v 23). In any event, if the high priest were to wear his regal garments in the adytum, he would require a second set of regal garments in order to complete the ritual at the outer altar (v 24b). There is no provision for two sets of clothing in the text (Exod 28) for the probable reason that they were too costly and, comprising gold threads and colored wools, are difficult to launder without causing the threads to break and the colors to run.

after that he may reenter the camp. This may be taken as implying that the person has been completely purified by the ablution. How is that possible? Even one who has contracted the slightest impurity must, in addition to bathing, wait until evening (e.g., 11:25, 40; 15:5–11). One cannot argue that the case of the scapegoat is *sui generis,* for the same concession is granted to the one who burns the carcass of the purification offering (v 28) even though, in an analogous situation (Num 19:8), that individual may not return to camp until the evening! Nor can one side with the Karaites who claim that the dispatcher of the Azazel goat and the burner of the purification offering carcasses need not wait till the evening because the text does not expressly state that they are impure *(Seper Hamibḥar; Keter Torah).* L. Finkelstein (1962: 668–71) has made the plausible suggestion that as the impurity involved relates only to sancta, that is, the bearer of a one-day impurity is only forbidden to enter the sanctuary or partake of sacred food (see chap. 15, COMMENT E), then the dispatcher of the scapegoat and the burner of the purification offering, though they remain impure until evening, may return to camp after they have washed; it being Yom Kippur, they will neither enter the sanctuary (off limits to the laity; see the NOTE on v 5) nor partake of sacred food (as they are fasting). Indeed, this legislative situation can be clarified by comparing the purification procedures on Yom Kippur (Lev 16) with those of corpse contamination (Num 19). Because the sanctuary and sacred food are off limits, so to speak, on Yom Kippur, the Lev 16 text does not need to mention that the dispatcher and *ḥaṭṭāʾt* burner are impure until evening; but in Num 19, as the sanctuary is open and food may be eaten, the text needs to state explicitly for each of the three participants that they are impure until evening. It should be recalled that only severe impurities, those of at least a week's duration, threaten the sanctuary from afar (see the COMMENT on 5:1–13). By contrast, impurities of a one-day duration are dangerous only in direct contact with sancta.

The question remains: Why is not the high priest also rendered impure when he purges the sanctuary with the purification offering blood and, especially, when he lays his hands upon the Azazel goat and, as the text states explicitly, transfers Israel's sins to it? One cannot aver that he, in fact, does become impure because he is required to undergo ablutions after he completes the purgation rites (v 24). If he truly were contaminated then he would not be able to continue the ritual but would have, at least, to wait for nightfall to restore him to a state of purity. Moreover, his ablutions need not be explained as the result of contamination but, on the contrary, they may stem from the need to change garments because he moves from the area of highest sanctity (the adytum) to an area of lesser sanctity (the sacrificial altar). In other words, his ablutions are a mark of desanctification rather than contamination; note that for that very reason his linen garments are deposited in the shrine (see the NOTE on v 23).

It may therefore be presumed that the high priest, exceptionally, is never contaminated by officiating at purgation rites. This is certainly the case for the purification offering (4:1–21), where he requires no ablutions following his rites and, more instructively, when he prepares the *ḥaṭṭāʾt* ashes of the Red Cow. In the latter instance, it will be noted, the one who burns the cow and the one who gathers its ashes are rendered impure, but not the high priest who sprinkles its blood (Num 19:1–12; cf. chap. 4, COMMENT G). Thus it seems likely that, in the Priestly scheme, the high priest is immune to the effects of the purgation rites.

Thus the high priest is contaminated neither when he purges the sanctuary with the purification offering blood nor when he transmits, by confession, Israel's sins onto the Azazel goat. Both the purification offering and the Azazel goat contaminate their handlers after the high priest's ritual, specifically, after the carcasses and goat become contaminated with Israel's impurities/sins, but not before. The reason for this special concession to the high priest is not clear; that it may stem from a pragmatic concern to guarantee the completion of the ritual is addressed in the NOTE on v 28. It is also possible, as indicated above, that the animals are not rendered impure until after the high priest completes his purgation rites. Analogously, the Red Cow does not begin to transmit impurity until the high priest completes the blood rite (Num 19:4; chap. 4, Comment G). The rabbis resolve this problem by declaring that the scapegoat does not contaminate until it leaves Jerusalem (*m. Yoma* 6:6) and that the *ḥaṭṭāʾt* carcass does not contaminate until it leaves the sanctuary court (*m. Yoma* 6:7; *m. Zebaḥ.* 12:6).

The implication is that the holiness of the sanctuary is powerful enough to suppress the impurity-laden *ḥaṭṭāʾt* carcass until it leaves the sanctuary precincts. The principle is enunciated but, I believe, is wrongly applied. The sanctuary itself is not immune to impurity. On the contrary, it is the continuous pollution of the sanctuary by Israel's moral and physical impurity that mandates its indispensable purgation by means of the *ḥaṭṭāʾt* offering. Rather, it is the holiness of the priest that renders him immune to impurity while he serves in the sanctuary. That is why he is unaffected by the impurity he dislodges from the altar (4:22–35), why the high priest is unscathed by the more potent impurity he removes from the shrine (4:13), why, on Yom Kippur, he can not only remove the virulent impurity caused by Israel's presumptuous sins that has collected in the adytum but even transfer it with his hands onto the head of a live goat, and why the priest who prepares the ashes of the Red Cow (Num 19:6–7) is defiled by the process—he is outside the sanctuary. (For the deeper significance of this priestly immunity, see chap. 10, Comment C.) Conversely, the ones charged with handling the scapegoat (16:21bβ), burning the sacrificial remains (16:28), and burning the Red Cow (Num 19:5, 8) and sprinkling its ashes (Num 19:21) are all laymen. Bearing no sacral antidote to impurity, they succumb to it quickly.

The possibility that this verse and v 28 presume that the handlers of the purification-offering carcass and the Azazel goat are fasting can only mean that the prescription of vv 29–34, which mandates a public fast, underlies vv 25–28 as well.

27. *The purification-offering bull and the purification-offering goat (wĕʾēt par hahaṭṭāʾt wĕʾēt śĕʿîr hahaṭṭāʾt).* The direct object is first, giving the sense of "As for . . . ," a construction necessitated by the fact that the pericope of the scapegoat has intervened, so the reader has to be reminded of the purification offerings, last heard from in v 15 (see also the Note on v 25).

whose blood was brought in to effect purgation in the adytum (ʾăšer hûbāʾ ʾet-dāmām lĕkappēr baqqōdeš). This clause also occurs in 6:23 and almost in the same language in 10:18. In both of these places, however, *qōdeš*, as everywhere else in P, denotes "the shrine" and only in this chapter (as noted in v 2) does it designate "the adytum." The legislator may, then, have employed this clause creatively by applying it to the unique situation of this rite, which, indeed, requires the purging of the adytum.

shall be burned. wĕśārpû, literally, "and they shall burn." Ibn Ezra thinks that a priest handles the burning (as in the case of the dispatcher of the goat, according to the rabbis, m. Yoma 6:3; see on v 21). But the lack of a subject in the text and, especially, the plural form of the verb indicate that the operation is carried out by a layman.

The purpose of burning the carcass of the purification offering is to eliminate the impurities absorbed by the blood and carcass of this offering (see chap. 4, COMMENT B). This is precisely the rite prescribed for the purgation of the Babylonian temple: the body of the ram used in purging the temple is eliminated; the Babylonians do it by throwing it into the river (ANET³ 333; for the text, see COMMENT C below).

28. *He who burned them (wĕhaśśōrēp ʾōtām).* The one who burns the Red Cow is also rendered impure (Num 19:8), and one can deduce that the burnt purification offering (see chap. 4, COMMENT B) always contaminates the one who handles it; this, indeed, is the tradition of the rabbis (m. Para 8:3; t. Yoma 3:16). They also transmit another tradition that neither the scapegoat nor the carcasses of burnt purification offerings transmit impurity while they are still inside the sacred precincts (m. Yoma 6:6–7; t. Yoma 3:15–16). Clearly, this rule guarantees that the high priest and the priestly cadre can handle these sacrifices without fear of contracting impurity (see the NOTE on v 26). But whence this rule? That it may have been devised because of pragmatic considerations instead of being integral to the Priestly theology may be indicated by the following evidence: (1) The Passover of Hezekiah is observed in the Temple, though many of the participants are impure (2 Chr 30:17–20). (2) The rabbis generalize this event into a rule: "If the majority of the congregation has become impure (through corpse contamination) or if the priests were impure but the congregation pure, it (the Passover sacrifice) shall be performed in a state of impurity" (m. Pesaḥ. 7:6; cf. 7:4), which a baraita supplements: "If the Israelites are impure while the priests and service-vessels (used with the sacrifice) are pure, or the Israelites are pure while the priests and service-vessels are impure, and even if the Israelites and the priests are pure while the service-vessels are impure, they must sacrifice in impurity" (b. Pesaḥ. 79a). (3) According to the rabbis, the suspicion that unobservant Israelites may be in a state of impurity was suspended during the pilgrimage festivals in all of Jerusalem (m. Ḥag. 3:4–8; y. Ḥag. 79d). Thus it seems clear that there were a number of occasions in Second Temple days on which the laws of impurity were curtailed or even suspended whenever there was a danger that an entire observance would be invalidated. It is therefore possible, on these same pragmatic grounds, that the impurity of the scapegoat and the burnt purification offering were decreed as not taking effect within the sacred precincts (and in the case of the scapegoat, until it left Jerusalem—patently so that the people who lined the streets as it was paraded out of the city would not become impure upon touching it: m. Yoma 6:4, 6; and see the NOTE on v 22).

29. *for you (lākem).* The people are addressed for the first time. Heretofore,

they were referred to in the third person. Moreover, they played no part whatever in the sanctuary ritual. Even their offerings were brought not by them but by Aaron (see v 5). Additionally, the entire ritual was addressed to Moses who, in turn, is to impart it to Aaron but not directly to Israel (vv 1–2). Thus this switch to second-person, direct address to Israel is the first of several signs that this and the following verses comprise an appendix to the text.

a law for all time (lĕḥuqqat ʿōlām). Referring to what follows (Wessely 1846), not to what precedes (Ibn Ezra).

In the seventh month. Strangely and uniquely, the date for these rites is given at the end. For the implications, see COMMENT A below.

practice self-denial (tĕʿannû ʾ et-napšōtêkem). The *piʿel* of the root ʿnh is used to express the humbling or mishandling of an individual (Gen 16:6), of a nation by war or bondage (Gen 15:13), of a woman by cohabitation (Gen 34:2), or it connotes affliction by God as a discipline (Deut 8:2–3). The verb does not specify by itself the mode, subject, or object of affliction; these must be determined from the context. The entire phrase is usually interpreted as referring to fasting. Ibn Ezra declares categorically that ʿinnâ nepeš always denotes fasting (cf. also Ramban, *Keter Torah*). There are, however, several reasons why the limitation to fasting does not do justice to the range of the idiom. (1) The words themselves imply more than hunger. To be sure, *nepeš*, like its Akk. cognate *napištu*, can have the restricted notion of appetite (Ps 107:9) or throat (Isa 5:14). In P, however, it only denotes the individual (2:1) or the body (21:1). Moreover, that *nepeš* here refers to the self, the entire person, is evident from the use of the root ʿnh in the *hithpaʿel*, where *nepeš* does not appear (Ezra 8:21; Dan 10:12; cf. Ps 107:17) and need not appear, because the *hithpaʿel* is reflexive. Surely, there are more ways to "afflict" the body than just by starving it. (2) *wĕkol-šĕbuʿat ʾissār lĕʿannōt nāpeš* 'every sworn obligation of self-denial' of the wife can be annulled by her husband (Num 30:14). Of a certainty, her absentions are not limited to fasting. (3) *ʿinnêtî baṣṣôm napšî* 'I afflicted myself with a fast' (Ps 35:13) clearly implies that there are other means of self-affliction than fasting. (4) Daniel's attempt *lĕhitʿannôt* (Dan 10:12) consisted of three weeks of mourning during which he "refrained from all choice food, no meat or wine passed my lips and I did not anoint myself" (ibid., v 3). Thus his self-denial consisted of a partial fast and, in addition, he abstained from anointing his body. The latter deprivation is included among the items enumerated in the rabbinic definition: "Afflict yourselves, from food, drink, and from enjoying bathing, and from anointing, and from sexual intercourse" (*Tg. Ps.-J.*; cf. *m. Yoma* 8:1). (5) King David not only fasts, but sleeps on the ground, does not change his clothes, and refrains from sex, anointing, and bathing (2 Sam 12:16–20), a striking confirmation of the rabbinic definition.

and you shall do no manner of work (wĕkol-mĕlāʾkâ lōʾtaʿăśû). The prohibition of labor on the Sabbath and the Day of Purgation is described by the phrase *kol-mĕlāʾkâ* (23:3, 28; Num 29:7), whereas on the festivals it is described as *mĕle'ket 'ăbōdâ* 'laborious work' (23:7, 8, 21, 25, 35, 36; Num 28:18, 25, 26; 29:1, 12, 35). The implication is that on the festivals, light work, unrelated to one's livelihood, would be permitted, whereas on the Sabbath and Day of Purgation even the slightest exertion would be forbidden (Milgrom 1970a: 77–81). This distinction is confirmed by the designation conferred on this day as a "Sabbath of complete rest" (see v 31).

neither the native-born nor the alien (hā'ezrāḥ wĕhaggēr). The prohibition directed to the resident alien only concerns his work. He is not required to practice self-denial (see Ibn Ezra). This view may be justified on the grounds that the *gēr* is bound by the prohibitive commandments and not by the performative ones. The violation of a prohibitive commandment requires an act. According to P, an act forbidden by God generates impurity that impinges upon God's sanctuary and land. For example, sexual offenses and homicide pollute the land (18:27–28; Num 35:34–35), whereas Molech worship and corpse contamination pollute the sanctuary (20:3; Num 19:13, 20). It therefore makes no difference whether the polluter is Israelite or non-Israelite. Anyone in residence in the Lord's land is capable of polluting it or his sanctuary. Thus the individual, *gēr* as well as citizen, is required to bring a purification offering for the inadvertent violation of a prohibitive commandment (Num 15:27–29; chap. 4, COMMENT E) and is subject to the *kārēt* penalty if the violation was presumptuous (Num 15:30–31). Moreover, a purification offering must be brought by the entire community to expiate not only for the Israelites but for the resident aliens as well (Num 15:22–26, esp. v 26).

Performative commandments, by contrast, are violated by refraining or neglecting to do them. (Note the apt rabbinic term: *šēb wĕ'al tā'ăšeh* 'stay put and do nothing,' cf. *b. Ber.* 20a; *b. 'Erub.* 100a; *b. Yebam.* 90a.) Such violations are sins not of commission but of omission. They too can lead to dire consequences, but only for the Israelite who is enjoined to observe them. The *gēr*, however, is not so obligated. Sins of omission, of nonobservance, generate no pollution either to the land or sanctuary. Thus the *gēr*, the resident non-Israelite, does not jeopardize the welfare of his Israelite neighbor by not complying with the performative commandments. Consequently, he need not, for example, observe the *pesaḥ* (a performative commandment), but if he so desires he must be circumcised (Exod 12:48) and be in a state of ritual purity (Num 9:6–7, 13–14). Conversely, under no circumstances may he possess leaven during the festival, a prohibitive commandment (Exod 12:19; 13:7). The Day of Purgation is characterized by the same distinction: the resident alien is required to refrain from all work on this day (a prohibitive commandment) but he need not afflict himself (a performative commandment); for details see Milgrom 1982a.

And if it be argued that the *gēr* who does not fast indeed violates the prohibition against eating, one can counter with the rabbinic principle: *la'w habbā' mittôk 'ăšēh 'ăšēh* 'a negative commandment derived from a positive commandment has the force of the positive commandment' (cf. *b. Pesaḥ.* 41b;

b. Yebam. 54b, 56b, 68a; *b. Zebaḥ.* 34b; *b. Ḥul.* 81a). Thus, as the positive commandment to fast is explicit it takes precedence over the derived negative commandment not to eat, and is hence not incumbent on the *gēr.*

Nonetheless, there is an equally cogent line of reasoning that effectively counters this position. The principle of *šēb wĕʾal taʿăśeh* applies only in such positive commandments as *pesaḥ* (above) and *sukkâ* (23:42), where one violates them by abstention, that is, by inactivity. But one violates the fasting rule by eating. Similarly, one violates the positive commandment to rest on the Sabbath (Exod 23:12) by working. The difference between fasting and Sabbath, on the one hand, and *pesaḥ* and *sukkâ*, on the other, is that the latter are activities violated by abstention, whereas the former are abstentions violated by activity, namely, eating and working. Thus eating on Yom Kippur (and the Sabbath rest) is not "a negative commandment derived from a positive commandment" of fasting, but the reverse. Fasting on Yom Kippur as much as not working on Yom Kippur is, in effect, a negative commandment. Its violation (by eating) as much as working generates impurity that pollutes Israel's land and sanctuary and, hence, is incumbent on all residents of the land, the *gēr* included.

That the inclusion of the *gēr* demonstrates that this passage (vv 29–34a) stems from H is discussed in COMMENT A below.

30. *For on this day (kî-bayyôm hazzeh).* A repetition of the notice in the previous verse (and for the third time in v 34), emphasizing that the changeover from an emergency rite to an annual one is the main innovation of this supplement. This emphasis is further augmented by the chiastic structure of these verses, of which this one (v 30) is the pivot (see the v 31).

shall purgation be effected. *yĕkappēr,* literally, "he will effect purgation." There is, however, no antecedent subject. Hence the sense is passive and impersonal, and will be explicated in the words that follow.

to purify you (lĕṭahēr ʾetkem). The purgation rites in the sanctuary purify the sanctuary, not the people. Yet as the sanctuary is polluted by the people's impurities, their elimination, in effect, also purifies the people. The reference to purification could also be to the scapegoat, which expressly carries off the people's sins into the wilderness (v 24). To be sure, purity is effected by the elimination of impurity (12:8; 14:7, 9, 20, 31; 15:13; 28). Instead, it is the people's participation in this day through their self-purgation that is probably meant; see the NOTE on v 31. This metaphoric use of *ṭiher* is another sign of the authorship of H (see the Introduction, §D).

of all your sins (mikkōl ḥaṭṭōʾtêkem). This is the all-inclusive term for wrongdoing (found in vv 16, 21), which therefore combines both the pollution of the sanctuary and the iniquities of the people.

you shall become pure before the Lord (lipnê YHWH tiṭhārû). The reference is not to the high priest's rites "before the Lord," that is, in the sanctuary. Rather, if Israel practices the prescribed cessation from labor (v 29) and self-denial (v 30), then it will become purified "before the Lord," in other words, will be reconciled to him. The correctness of this interpretation will be demonstrated in v 31. It was also expounded by Rabbi Eleazar ben Azariah: " 'You shall become pure before the Lord'—for transgressions that are between man and God, the Day of Atonement effects atonement; but for transgressions that are between man and his fellow, the Day of Atonement effects atonement only if he has appeased his fellow" (*m. Yoma* 9:9). Even so, transgressions of the former type, between man and God, demand another prerequisite for atonement—repentance (*t. Yoma* 4:9; *m. Yoma* 9:8).

31. *a sabbath of complete rest (šabbat šabbātôn).* An idiom used to describe the Sabbath (23:3; Exod 35:2), the Day of Purgation (16:31; 23:32), and the sabbatical year for the land (25:4). In each case the context is the prohibition against labor. Work on the Sabbath and Day of Purgation is defined as *kol-mĕlā'kâ* 'any manner of work' (23:3; 16:31; 23:31; see on v 29) and on the sabbatical year, this prohibition is spelled out in detail: "You shall not sow your field or prune your vineyard. You shall not reap the aftergrowth of your harvest or gather the grapes of your untrimmed vines" (25:4–5), thereby making it clear that the land is not to be tampered with, but given absolute rest. Thus "a sabbath of complete rest" is synonymous with the expression "you shall do no manner of work" (v 29). For the reason of this apparent redundancy, see the NOTE below.

and you shall practice self-denial; it is a law for all time (we'innîtem 'et-napšōtēkem ḥuqqat 'ôlām). A repetition of the same words in v 29 without resorting to synonyms. This blatant redundancy is not due to editorial sloppiness but is part of a carefully constructed chiasm (D. Wright):

A. *wĕhāyĕtâ lākem l ĕḥuqqat 'ôlām* (29)

 B. *tĕ'annû . . . 'et-napšōtêkem* (29)

  C. *wĕkol-mĕlā'kâ ō' ta'ăśû . . .* (29)

   X. *kî bayyôm hazzeh yĕkappēr 'ălêkem lĕṭahēr 'etkem mikkōl ḥaṭṭō't êkem lipnê YHWH tiṭhārû* (30)

  C'. *šabbat šabbātôn hî' lākem* (31)

 B'. *wĕ'innîtem 'et-napšōtêkem* (31)

A'. *ḥuqqat 'ôlām* (31)

AA' and BB' are terminologically equivalent. CC' are semantically equivalent, providing firm support, adduced above, that *šabbat šabbātôn* denotes the complete cessation of labor. X, the center and pivot of this chiasm, is also the main point of the construction: this day of purgation *(kippēr)* provides purification for all Israel if the prescriptions contained in the body of the chiasm—self-denial and cessation of labor—are faithfully followed. Yet the repetition of the command to practice self-denial serves a more utilitarian function: in abrogating the emergency rites for the purgation of the sanctuary and restricting them to the fixed, annual rite on the tenth of Tishri, the day lost its original joyous character and became, instead, a day of self-denial. The call for self-denial on this day is its true innovation, hence the need for its repetition (for details, see COMMENT D below). The purgation of the sanctuary is the subject of the verses that follow.

32. *The priest who has been anointed and ordained (hakkōhēn ʾăšer-yimšaḥ ʾōtô waʾăšer yĕmalleʾ"et-yādô).* The description of the high priest is virtually identical with that found in 21:10 (H) and contrasts sharply with *hakkōhēn hammāšîaḥ* (P; Elliger 1966), further evidence that vv 29–34a belong to the Holiness stratum (see COMMENT H below). For an explanation of these terms, see the NOTES on 8:12 and 33.

to serve as priest in place of his father (lĕkahēn taḥat ʾābîw). In distinction from vv 2–28, which speak solely of Aaron, this verse focuses on his successors, a hint from the author of this appendix that the original rite has changed. Elijah of Vilna (see the NOTE on v 3) came to the same conclusion while at the same time avoiding the necessity of positing two different sources, to wit: Aaron was permitted to purge the sanctuary whenever he believed there was an emergency; his successors, however, were restricted to performing this rite only on the prescribed Day of Purgation (see COMMENT A below).

the sacral vestments (bigdê haqqōdeš). The purpose of this gloss on the linen vestments is not clear. Does it possibly connote that the high priest is not to don the same linen items, which, with the exception of the turban (see at v 4), are the standard apparel of the ordinary priest? If so, does it mean that these vestments were set aside for him in advance or, possibly, that they were the same vestments he wore the previous year (see the NOTE on v 23)?

33. *the holiest part of the sanctuary (miqdaš haqqōdeš).* This expression for the adytum is a hapax. Because *qōdeš* here means "sanctuary" and not "adytum" (vv 2–28) or "shrine" (P; see the NOTE on v 2), the writer was forced to eschew the terminology of both this chapter and P and to devise his own. He chose *miqdaš* (construct), whose absolute form is probably *miqdēš*, on the analogy of *mispēd* 'mourning' (construct *mispad;* Ehrlich 1908–14). It occurs once again *miqdĕšô* 'its holiest portion' (Num 18:29), where the vocalization leads to the inference that the absolute form is probably *miqdēš* and certainly not *miqdāš* (which would have yielded *miqdāšô*). In any event, this term for adytum is strong evidence that the author of vv 29–34a is not the same as that of vv 2–28. The objects of the purging are all direct (indicated by *ʾet),* as in v 20.

the people of the congregation (ʿam haqqāhāl). Another invention of this legislator, who conflates two of the terms for "people" found in vv 2–28, *ʿam* (vv 15, 24) and *qāhāl* (v 17). He refrains from using *ʿēdâ* (v 5), possibly because, by this time, the term *ʿēdâ* had fallen out of use and was replaced by *qāhāl* (see the NOTE on 4:13; Milgrom 1978a).

34. *This (zōʾt).* Refers back to *bĕzōʾt* (v 3; Hoffmann 1953), forming an

inclusio with it. Its purpose is clear: only by observing all of the procedures detailed in this chapter can Israel be purged of its sins. Perhaps it even implies a subtle polemic: *kippûr* is achieved no longer by purging the sanctuary whenever there is an emergency (vv 2–28) but only at the fixed annual date, when it is accompanied by the people's abstention from work and self-denial (vv 29–33); see below.

the Israelites (bĕnê yiśrā'ēl). See the NOTE on v 21.

once a year ('aḥat baššānâ). This wording implies that heretofore the sanctuary was purged more than "once a year," an inference that confirms the conclusion derived from vv 2–3. This phrase occurs once more (two times in Exod 30:10), where it again refers to the annual Day of Purgation, for this verse also mentions the use of *ḥaṭṭā't hakkippūrîm* 'the purification offering of purgation' (see also Num 29:11), hinting that the purification offering no longer will purge the incense altar whenever the high priest declares an emergency but only on the fixed date, "once a year" (see COMMENT A below).

And he [Aaron] did (wayya'aś). The subject is not Aaron's successors, the nearest antecedent (v 32), but Aaron himself, who followed Moses' instructions immediately following the death of his sons, Nadab and Abihu (v 1). Thus v 34b originally followed v 28. A fulfillment passage is frequently found at the end of a prescriptive text (e.g., 8:4, 36; 10:7; Num 1:54; 2:34; 5:4; 8:20; 9:5).

as the Lord had commanded Moses (ka'ăšer ṣiwwâ YHWH 'et-mōšeh). The inference is unambiguous: although Aaron alone may enter the adytum, his instructions come to him only through the mediation of Moses. Thus the supremacy of prophet over priest is an uncontested axiom of P: for details, see the NOTES on v 2 and, especially, on 10:16–20.

COMMENTS: THE DAY OF PURGATION

A. The Structure of Chapter 16

A. *Introduction, v 1*

—following the death of Nadab and Abihu (1)

B. *Materials Required, vv 2–5*

   1. high priest's screen (2b)

   2. his sacrificial animals (3)

   3. his special vestments (4)

   4. the people's sacrificial animals (5)

C. *Preliminaries, vv 6–10*

   1. brings forward his bull for priestly house (6)

    2. stations the two goats (7)

    3. lots on goats (8)

    4. brings forward goat for purification offering (9)

    5. Azazel goat held back (10)

D. *Procedure I: Purging the Sanctuary, vv 11–19*

    1. resumptive repetition of v 6 (11a)

    2. bull slaughtered (11b)

    3. the adytum

        a. incense (12–13)

        b. bull's blood (14)

        c. goat's blood (15)

        d. purpose (16a)

    4. the shrine

        a. its purgation (16b)

        b. no one else in shrine (17a)

        c. purpose (17b)

    5. the sacrificial altar

        a. daubed (18)

        b. sprinkled (19a)

        c. purpose (19b)

E. *Procedure II: Purging the People, vv 20–22*

    1. bring forward Azazel goat (20)

    2. confession and dispatch to Azazel (21–22)

F. *Altar Sacrifices, vv 23–25*

    1. bathe, change clothes (23–24a)

    2. the burnt offerings (24b)

    3. the suet of the purification offerings (25)

G. *Purification of Assistants, vv 26–28*

    1. dispatcher of goat to Azazel (26)

    2. burner of purification-offering carcasses (27–28)

H. *Appendix: Israel's Self-Purgation, vv 29–34a*

    1. date (29a, bα)

    2. self-denial and work cessation (29bβγ)

    3. purpose (30)

4. complete sabbath and self-denial (31)
5. purging of sanctuary by Aaron's successors (32–33)
6. purpose (34a)

I. *Execution, v 34b*

by Aaron

The details concerning this chapter's structure are discussed in the verse-by-verse commentary. The remainder of COMMENT A summarizes the main points.

1. The MT strongly indicates that the original form of the purgation rite described in vv 2–28 was an emergency measure invoked by the high priest whenever he felt that the entire sanctuary had to be purged.

a. Verse 1 is an editorial link between chaps. 10 and 16. Thus the likelihood is that originally chap. 16 immediately followed chap. 10, which recounts the death of Nadab and Abihu in the sanctuary, and chaps. 11–15 were inserted later, as an inventory of the impurities that could pollute the sanctuary. The purification procedure for corpse contamination is not found in chaps. 11–15 but in Num 19; for the reason, see chap. 4, COMMENT G and chap. 11, COMMENT A.

b. *běkol-ʿēt* (v 2) 'whenever he chooses', literally, "at any time" clearly implies, with *Midr. Lev. Rab.* 2:7, that Aaron, indeed, can enter whenever he chooses, provided he acts *bězōʾt* 'in this manner' (v 3).

c. The symmetry of the tripartite purgation of the sanctuary (see the NOTE on v 19) suggests that the same rules that prevail for the outer altar and shrine should prevail for the adytum. Because the former's sancta are always purged immediately upon their pollution (chap. 4), there is no reason for delaying the purgation of the adytum until the annual Day of Purgation. To the contrary, as the pollution of the adytum is caused by Israel's presumptuous, wanton sins, whose consequence is the deity's abandonment of his sanctuary (see chap. 4, COMMENT C), there would be, by the sheer logic of the situation, an urgent need to purge the sanctuary at once.

d. All of the scapegoat rituals extant in the ancient Near East are emergency rites (see COMMENT E below). They are not fixed calendric occasions but are prescribed whenever a catastrophe threatens or has struck. By the same token, the ceremonial with the Azazel goat originally must have been employed for similar emergencies.

e. That the sanctuary's purgation is fixed as "once a year" (v 34) implies that, heretofore, it occurred more than once a year. This deduction is buttressed by the only other verse in which the phrase occurs, appearing there not once but twice: "*Once a year* Aaron shall perform purgation on its horns with blood of the purification offering of purgation; purgation shall be performed upon it *once a year* throughout the generations. It is most sacred to the Lord" (Exod 30:10). What is striking in this wording is not only the double mention of "once a year," implying that this rite should not be performed more than once a year, but that this annual day is clearly identified with the one fixed in chap. 16 by its reference to the "purification offering of purgation" *(ḥaṭṭaʾt hakkippūrîm)*, that is, the purification offering whose blood performs *kippūrîm* (an abstract plural noun), which at once identifies the rite with the annual *yôm hakkippūrîm* 'Day of Purgation' (23:27, 28; 25:29) on which a *ḥaṭṭaʾt hakkippūrîm* 'a purification offering of purgation' (Num 29:11) is employed—all the work of the Holiness source. I. Knohl (1987 [1983–84]: 87) claims that v 34 and Exod 38:10, both containing the same phrase, "once a year," stem from the pen of P. Hence, P mandates that the high priest had to purge the sanctuary annually at a date that he alone determined. This view must be rejected for the following reasons. (1) It makes no sense that P would permit the high priest to choose the date— presumably whenever he felt it was urgent to purge the sanctuary—and then limit him to once a year. What if the sanctuary were severely polluted a second time that year? (2) If "once a year" were the coinage of P we would expect to find it at the beginning of the chapter: the high priest may not enter the adytum "whenever he chooses" (v 2) but only "once a year." (3) The language of v 34, *lĕkappēr ʿal-bĕnê yiśrāʾēl mikkol-ḥaṭṭōʾtām,* is not found in vv 1–28 (P) but only in v 30 (H). It emphasizes the purification of the people; note the metaphoric use of *ṭāhēr,* a hallmark of H. Thus it is H that introduced the term "once a year" as an outright polemic against P—not "whenever he [the high priest] chooses" but only "once a year."

The fact that the object of the purgation in Exod 30:10 is the incense altar (see vv 1–9) gives rise to two questions: (a) Why was it necessary at all to state that the incense altar needs to be purged, when the prescriptive texts dealing with other sancta ignore this necessity (see Exod 25:10–40; 27:1–8)? (b) The incense altar was purged not just annually but every time the sanctuary was seriously polluted by the inadvertent sins of the high priest or the entire community (4:1–21). Why, then, does this text insist (twice) that the incense altar was purged only "once a year"? A solution suggests itself that though conjectural, fits all of the preceding data. The possibility exists that the purging of the incense altar and, indeed, of the entire sanctuary became a frequent phenomenon. One must bear in mind that the purging of the sanctuary was occasioned only by an impending or existing catastrophe of national dimensions. Even the purging of the incense altar would be mandated only if the community as a whole (or the high priest himself) was found to be in error (4:3–21). Moreover, the probability exists, as will be shown below, that the purging of the sanctuary was accompanied by a nationwide call to observe a public fast in addition to other abstentions (see COMMENT B below). Thus if the high priests' declarations of "emergency" occurred too often, they may have proved annoyingly troublesome to priests and people alike. And a movement to reform this abuse may have led to an edict that henceforth the sanctuary was not to be purged *bĕkol-ʿēt,* whenever "he (the high priest) chooses" but only "once a year." The possible date of enactment of this change from emergency rite to annual rite (rather, the time span in which it could not have occurred) will be discussed below.

In any event, Exod 30:10, the last verse in the prescription for the incense altar, is clearly an addition. This can be proved by comparing it with the closing verses of the prescriptions for the making of the anointment oil and incense, found in the same chapter (Exod 30:22–33, 34–38). Whereas in the latter two pericopes, the closing sentences (vv 31, 36) are followed by warnings (vv 32–33, 37–38), the closing of the incense altar pericope (v 8) is followed not only by a warning (v 9) but by the anomalous statement that it should be purged annually (v 10). Exod 30:10 is therefore an editorial addition. Its staccato emphasis on "once a year" (twice stated) identifies it with the appendix to chap. 16, vv 29–34a (see below), and is probably from the same hand (H). It marks the transition of the Day of Purgation from an emergency rite to an annual rite.

f. Verses 2–28 contain unique terms that differentiate them from P: (1) pĕšāʿîm 'transgressions' (vv 16, 21), in other words, wanton, brazen sins (contrast Num 15:30–31); (2) ʾōhel môʿēd 'shrine' (vv 16, 17, 20, 23), whereas in P, this term stands for the entire Tent; (3) P's term for the shrine, qōdeš (e.g., Exod 28:29, 35) here designates "the adytum" (vv 2, 3, 16, 17, 20, 23, 27), which P labels exclusively by the term qōdeš haqqŏdāšîm 'the holy of holies' (e.g., Exod 26:33, 34). Hence, vv 2–28 must stem from an earlier source, which was only subsequently incorporated into P.

2. The function of vv 6–10 is not to provide an outline of the subsequent ritual, vv 11–28 (Wenham 1979), but to emphasize that the selection of the goats by lot must precede the sacrifice of the bull, a fact that could not be derived from the verses that follow. And it is precisely this long but necessary digression on the goats (vv 7–10) that necessitates the resumptive repetition of v 6 in v 11a in order to remind the reader that the high priest's bull should be readied for sacrifice.

3. The purgation of the sanctuary takes place in the adytum (vv 12–16a), the shrine (vv 16b–17b), and on the outer altar (vv 18–19b), but not in the courtyard because it does not have the "most sacred" status of the rest of the Sanctuary (see the NOTE on v 18). The symmetry of the purgation rites is set forth not only in the type and number of blood manipulations (see the NOTE on v 19), but also textually, in that each purgation prescription concludes with a statement of its purpose (vv 16a, 17b, and 19b, respectively).

4. The preceding point only underscores the question: What is the function of v 20a, "When he has finished (wĕkillâ) purging the adytum, the Tent of Meeting, and the altar"? As is suggested in the notes, the legislation thereby stresses the importance of completing the entire purgation ritual before transferring the released impurities onto the head of the Azazel goat (v 21). It seems that the author of Qumran's Temple Scroll followed the same reasoning but came to a different conclusion: wĕkillâ 'when he has finished' means that the high priest must "finish" the entire sacrificial ritual prescribed for the purifica-

tion offering. Thus not only should the high priest perform the blood manipulations (vv 14–19) before turning to the Azazel goat (v 21) but he also must "finish" with the purification offering by offering up its suet (v 25) and burning its carcass (v 27). Thus for the Dead Sea sectaries, the latter verses (25–27) are not in sequence: they chronologically belong before v 20 (11QT 26:7–10). Supporting their interpretation is the fact that both prescriptions (vv 25, 27) list the object first: "[As for] the suet of the purgation offering" (v 25a) and "[As for] the purification-offering bull and the purification-offering goat" (v 27a), thereby giving the impression that they are addenda, an appendix of omitted items and, hence, out of their chronological order. The rabbis, however, justify the sequence of the MT because it conforms to their rule (*m. Zebaḥ.* 10:2) that on the altar, the burnt offering (v 24) precedes the suet of the purification offering (see the NOTE on v 25).

Another interesting innovation of the Temple Scroll is its prescription that after the high priest completes the entire sacrificial ritual of the purification offering, *wĕrāḥaṣ ʾet yādāyw wĕʾet raglāyw middam haḥaṭṭāʾt* 'He shall wash his hands and feet of the blood of the purification offering' (26:10). The MT prescribes no ablutions whatever between the rites with the blood and with the Azazel goat. And even the rabbis who prescribe ablutions before and after each rite, for a total of fifteen discrete washings, do not require an ablution at this point, for the high priest is still wearing his linen garments, a sign that his purgation rite is not yet completed (see the table, v 23). On what basis, then, does the Temple Scroll require it? The answer is embedded in the wording of its text: *middam haḥaṭṭāʾt* '[he shall wash his hands and feet] of the blood of the purification offering'. Here is corroboration that the blood of the purification offering, uniquely among all of the sacrifices, causes defilement (see the NOTES on 6:20–21). Whereas the rabbis rule, correctly, that the blood of the purification offering contaminates only inanimate objects (chap. 7, COMMENT B), the sectaries of Qumran apparently ordain that persons also are infected. The high priest on Yom Kippur, then, is certainly infected because he actually dips his finger into the blood in order to perform the rites of aspersion (vv 14, 19).

5. The original function of the Azazel goat was to carry off the impurities of the Israelites *(ṭumʾōt bĕn ê yiśrāʾēl)*, which had contaminated the sanctuary (cf. v 16). Only at a later stage was the rite reinterpreted so that the goat bore the sins of the Israelites that the high priest confessed over it (see the NOTES on v 21).

6. Verses 29–34a comprise an appendix that was tacked onto chap. 16, as can be inferred from the following evidence.

a. The entire pericope is couched in a second-person, direct address to Israel, whereas the purgation rites (vv 2–28) are transmitted to Aaron via Moses (vv 1–2), Israel being referred to in the third person (cf. v 5). The counterargument might be proposed that the appendix truly concerns the duties of the people, whereas the purgation rites are the sole concern of the high priest. In that case, however, one would have expected a totally new heading for this pericope, such as "The Lord spoke to Moses, saying: Speak to the Israelite people . . ." (e.g., 12:1). In the absence of a heading, this pericope's status as an addendum is revealed.

b. Not Aaron but his descendants are officiating (v 32), a clear indication of a later date than vv 2–28.

c. The terminology has been altered. The adytum is now *miqdaš haqqōdeš* instead of *haqqōdeš*, the people are called *ʿam haqqāhāl* instead of either *ʿam* or *qāhāl* (see the NOTE on v 33), and the high priest's description is that of H (21:10) and not P (4:3; see the NOTE on v 32). The purgation rites *(kipper)* purify *(ṭihēr)* the people, whereas heretofore they purify only the sanctuary (see the NOTE on v 30 and cf. Num 8:21).

d. Significantly, this observance is the only one whose date is specified at the end of its prescription (vv 29, 34), whereas all other festival prescriptions begin with the date (e.g., 23:5, 6, 15, 24, 27, 34, 39).

e. The unexpected mention of the *gēr* (v 29) is an unmistakable indication that we are dealing with H, a different literary source. The fact that the *gēr* as well as the native-born Israelite is bound by the prohibition against performing work on the Day of Purgation can only be explained on the assumption that the violation of this prohibition adversely affects the land (see the NOTE on "neither the native-born nor the alien," v 29). This doctrine, however, is found only in H. It is hardly an accident that this is the first time that *gēr* occurs in Leviticus. All of its subsequent attestations in this book (17:8, 10, 12, 13, 15; 18:26; 19:10, 33, 34; 20:2; 22:18; 23:22; 24:16, 22; 25:23, 35, 47) are, by common scholarly consent, attributed to H. The implication of this fact as well as the few other identifiable H passages in chaps. 1–16 for the composition of Leviticus is discussed in the introduction, §H.

Thus vv 29–34a must be considered to be an appendix whose purpose is to abolish the privilege heretofore vested in the high priest to decide to purge the sanctuary "whenever he chooses" (v 2) and to establish the purgation of the sanctuary only "once a year" (v 34) on the tenth of Tishri (v 29). Are the other prescriptions imposed upon the people, to desist from work and to practice self-denial, also the innovations of this pericope? This matter will now be discussed.

B. The Public Fast

Although the prescription *tĕʿannû ʾet-napšōtêkem* 'you shall practice self-denial' (v 29; cf. v 31) is here interpreted to emphasize abstention rather than fasting (see the NOTE on v 29), there can be no doubt that the fast was central and indispensable to the observance. Although individuals would fast for sundry private reasons (Milgrom 1971e), a common denominator runs through all attestations of the public fast: the community is struck or threatened by a calamity that stems either from man (e.g., 1 Sam 7:6; Jer 36:9; Esth 4:16) or from God (1 Kgs 21:9; Joel 2:12ff.; Jonah 3).

The Tannaites specify the forms of direct divine punishment as pestilence, blasting or mildew, locust or caterpillar (*m. Taʿan.* 3:4–5; see Joel 2:12ff.) and, above all, the delay of the autumnal rains (*m. Taʿan.* 1:3–7). It stands to reason that such a national disaster would be attributed to an egregious sin that the people had committed against the deity. The Hittite king, Mursilis, for example, attributes the plague that ravaged his country to the fact that "we have never performed the offerings to the river Mala" (*ANET*³ 395; for the full text, see 5:14–26, COMMENT B). By the same token, Israel's priesthood, in conformance with its own theology, would point to the pollution of the sanctuary by Israel's sins as the source of the divine displeasure. Under such circumstances, the high priest would declare an emergency and take the prescribed measures to purge the sanctuary. At the same time, he would call on the people to observe a public fast, in addition to the other abstinences implied by the term *ʿinnûy nepeš* 'self-denial'. Thus, despite the fact that the demand of self-denial is contained solely in the appendix (vv 29, 31), it is hard to believe that it is a later feature, added to the purgation rite for the sanctuary only after it became an annual rite (e.g., Loewenstamm 1958). On the contrary, the chances are that the threat or the actuality of divine retribution evoked a response that rippled through the entire community, not just its priesthood. Thus while the latter purged the sanctuary, the former purged themselves so that God might revoke his evil decree. The words of the king of Nineveh surely hold true for Israel as well: "By the decree of the king and his nobles: No man or beast—of flock or herd—shall taste anything! They shall not graze, and they shall not drink water! They shall be covered with sackcloth—man and beast—and shall cry mightily to God. Let everyone turn back from his evil ways and from the injustice of which he is guilty. Who knows but that God may turn and relent? He may turn back from his wrath, so that we do not perish" (Jonah 3:7–9).

A strong argument can be marshaled to demonstrate that the annual Day of Purgation for Israel's sanctuary, the tenth of Tishri, was, at first, entirely disassociated from the notion of public fast. Precisely because it was probably the climax of the New Year's festival, it must have been altogether joyous in nature. The original joyousness of the tenth of Tishri is, to be sure, suppressed in the prescriptions for the day (16:29–34; 23:26–32; Num 29:7–11). Still, it can be adduced from Scripture itself, from the fact that the Jubilee year was proclaimed on this day (25:9). The Shofar blast proclaimed each fiftieth year as the occasion on which ancestral lands reverted to their owners (25:10–34) and Israelites who, because of indebtedness, had been sold into slavery were given their freedom (25:35–59). Surely, the day that heralded this "year of liberty" (Ezek 46:17; cf. Lev 25:10) was a day of unbridled joy and in no way reflected the sober character of the later Day of Atonement. It is, in fact, a later rabbinic source that preserves the best evidence of the original nature of this day: "Rabban Simeon b. Gamliel said: there were no happier days for Israel than the fifteenth of Ab and the Day of Atonement, for on them the daughters of Jerusalem used to go forth in white raiments. . . . And the daughters of Jerusalem went forth to dance in the vineyards. And what did they say? 'Young man, lift up your eyes and see what you would choose for yourself: set not your eyes on beauty, but set your eyes on family'" (m. Ta'an. 4:8). The image of nubile maidens dancing in the vineyards recalls when Shilonite maidens dancing in the vineyards on the annual "Feast of the Lord" were snatched as brides by the surviving Benjaminites (Judg 21:19–24).

Thus it can be surmised that on the tenth of Tishri, the culmination of Israel's ancient New Year Festival (for further details, see the NOTE on 23:23–25), the people rejoiced that the new year was successfully launched and that the high priest had emerged safely from his purgations in the innermost shrine (note that the high priest was wont to throw a party for his friends, m. Yoma 7:4; see the NOTE on v 25). This day, then, was marked by feasting, merriment, and the dancing of the maidens in the vineyards, which, no doubt, resulted in many marriages throughout the land—a far cry from the 'innûy nepeš, the practice of "self-denial," which characterized this day's successor. The transformation may have occurred when the emergency contingency for purging the sanctuary was abolished and its somber, mournful aspect was transferred to the "once a year," annual purgation of the sanctuary on the tenth of Tishri, whose original jubilant character was replaced by fasting and penitence.

C. Temple Purgation in Babylon

It has been averred that the New Year's festival in Babylon was marked by rites of penitence and, hence, there is no basis for presuming that the penitential rites prescribed for the tenth of Tishri are late. The text of the Babylonian New Year festival is unfortunately fragmentary, but it describes the events from the second to the fifth of Nisan in great detail. Because the similarities to Yom Kippur are striking, the pertinent sections, dealing with the rites on the fifth day, are cited herewith in full (my student, D. Wright, has suggested a number of corrections of ANET³ 332–34, initialed in brackets):

On the fifth day of the month Nisannu, four hours of the night (remaining?), the šešgallu [D.W.]-priest shall arise and wash . . . he shall [put on (i-de-qu)] a linen robe in front of the god Bel and the goddess Beltiya. . . . When the purification of the temple (of Bel and Beltiya) is completed, he (the šešgallu [D.W.]-priest) shall enter the temple Ezida, into the cella [D.W.] of the god Nabu, with censer, torch, and egubbū-vessel to purify the temple, and he shall sprinkle water (from) the Tigris and Euphrates cisterns on the sanctuary. He shall smear all the doors of the sanctuary with cedar oil [D.W.]. In the court of the cella [D.W.], he shall place a silver censer, upon which he shall scatter aromatic ingredients and cypress. He shall call a slaughterer to decapitate a ram, the body of which the *mašmašu*-priest shall use in performing the purgation *(kuppuru)* ritual for the temple. He shall recite the incantations for exorcising the temple. He shall purify the whole cella [D.W.], including its environs, and shall remove the censer. The *mašmašu*-priest shall lift up the body of the aforementioned ram and proceed to the river. Facing west, he shall throw the body of the ram into the river. He shall (then) go out into the open country. The slaughterer shall do the same with the ram's head. The *mašmašu*-priest and the slaughterer shall go out into the open country. As long as the god Nabu is in Babylon, they shall not enter Babylon, but stay in the open country from the fifth to the twelfth day (of *Nisannu)*. The *šešgallu* [D.W.]-priest of the temple Ekua shall not view the purification of the temple. If he does view (it), he is no (longer) pure. . . .

When he (the king) reaches [the presence of the god Bel], the *šešgallu* [D.W.]-priest shall leave (the sanctuary) and take away the scepter, the circle, and the sword [from the king]. He shall bring them [before the god Bel] and place them [on] a chair. He shall leave (the sanctuary) and strike the king's cheek. . . . He shall accompany him (the king) into the presence of the god Bel . . . he shall drag (him by) the ears and make him bow to the ground. . . . The king shall speak the following (only) once: "I did [not] sin, lord of the countries. I was not neglectful (of the requirements) of your godship. [I did not] destroy Babylon; I did not command its overthrow . . . the temple Esagil, I did not forget its rites. [I did not] rain blows on the cheek of a *kidinnu*. . . . I did not humiliate them. [I watched out] for Babylon; I did not smash its walls. ". . . After (the *šešgallu* [D.W.]-priest) says (this), the king shall regain his *composure*. . . . The scepter, circle, and sword [shall be restored] to the king. He shall strike the king's cheek. If, when [he strikes] the king's cheek, the tears flow, (it means that) the god Bel is friendly; if no tears appear, the god Bel is angry: the enemy will rise up and bring about his downfall.

The similarities between the Babylonian New Year's festival and Israel's Yom Kippur are immediately apparent. On both occasions, (1) the temple is purged by rites that demand that the high priest rise before dawn (*m. Yoma* 1:7), bathe and dress in linen, employ a censer, and perform a sprinkling rite on the sanctuary; (2) the impurity is eliminated by means of slaughtered animals; (3) the participants are rendered impure; and (4) the king/high priest submits to a ritual of confession and penitence.

In each of these categories there are also significant differences. (1) Whereas in Babylon, the demon-intruder is exorcised, in Israel, it is the sin and iniquity generated by man that must be expurged. Moreover, whereas the purgation of the temple is the predominant aim of all of the rituals during the Day of Purgation, the Babylonian purgation rite is relatively minor, preparing one of the many cellas in Marduk's temple, Esagila, for the brief stay of a visiting god, Nabu. (2) In Babylon, the detergent itself (the carcass of the ram) is eliminated; In Israel elimination is achieved by dispatching a goat onto which Israel's sins have been loaded. To be sure, Israel's detergent, the carcass of the purification offering, is burned, thereby paralleling the Babylonian elimination procedure (see chap. 4, COMMENT D). Hence it can be inferred that the Azazel goat was originally a discrete elimination technique that was artificially attached to the sanctuary purgation in order to focus on Israel's moral failings rather than on the sins and impurities that polluted the sanctuary. (3) In Babylon, the impurity of the slaughterer and officiating priest lasts seven days—the remainder of the festival—whereas in Israel, the impurity of the dispatcher of the goat and the burner of the purification offering carcasses lasts one day. Furthermore, the exact Israelite counterparts, the officiating priest and the slaughterer, are not rendered impure. And in Babylon, because the high priest becomes impure merely by viewing the purgation, the ritual is conducted by lower temple officials. In Israel, by contrast, the entire ritual is conducted by the high priest. (4) In Babylon, the king undergoes a ritual of humiliation: the high priest strikes his cheek, drags him by the ears, and makes him bow to the ground; tears indicate the king's penitence and the god's favor. His confession is within a political context; he has been a faithful custodian of the god's temple and city and has not violated the political rights of the *kidinnu* (a specially protected group). The major difference lies in the self-righteousness of the Babylonian king and in the fact that he focuses on his own conduct, whereas in Israel the high priest confesses the failings of his people. In other words, in Babylon the viability of the society depends solely on the worthiness of the king; in Israel, the determinant of the national destiny is the moral condition of the people. (5) The two ceremonies differ in that the Babylonian lasted eleven or twelve days, whereas the Israelite counterpart was of one day's duration. Still, if the tenth of Tishri can be seen as the culmination of Israel's New Year festival, then it was the tenth and climactic day of Israel's ten-day New Year festival. The first ten days of Tishri are, in Jewish tradition, a penitential period during which man, through his repentance, can alter the divine decree (b. Roš. Haš. 18a). Its roots could, then, be traced back to a putative ten-day New Year festival ending in the joyous celebration of the sanctuary's purgation on the tenth and last day.

In sum, there is no reason to doubt the antiquity of an annual purgation rite for the sanctuary on the tenth and final day of the New Year festival, which, in accordance with Israel's ancient agricultural calendar, began in the autumn (see Exod 23:16b; 34:22b). Because this day was a national holiday, it was marked by complete cessation from labor. The vestiges of jubilation and merriment that survived in its observance even into rabbinic times make it doubtful that the element of "self-denial" is original. Most likely it played an integral and indispensable role during the emergency situations declared by the high priest when he felt that divine punishment was imminent because the people's sins had polluted the sanctuary. When the high priest's prerogative to declare an emergency "whenever he chooses" (v 2) was abrogated and the sanctuary's purgation was restricted to an annual observance "once a year" (v 34) on the tenth of Tishri, then the penitential characteristics of the emergency days were transferred to the annual day, thereby altering its nature from one of unrestrained joy to one of subdued optimism—that the purgation of the sanctuary, coupled with the people's repentance, as reflected in their acts of self-denial, would result in a blessed new year.

D. The Date of Yom Kippur

It has been put forth, above, that when the purgation of the sanctuary became an annual observance rather than an emergency rite, its nature changed from joy and happiness to abstinence and penitence. When and why did this change take place? This question cannot be answered; the data are lacking. All that can be said with some degree of certainty is that it did not occur in the postexilic period. To be sure, most critical scholars, even to this day, presume that Yom Kippur on the tenth of Tishri was not observed by the returnees from the Babylonian exile. Their arguments will be marshaled and rebutted in the following paragraphs.

(1) Because the First Temple had no veil but doors that separated the adytum from the shrine (1 Kgs 6:31–32), the rite of Lev 16, which requires a veil (vv 2, 12, 15) could only be performed in the Second Temple, which, indeed, was equipped with a veil (Jos., *Wars* 5.5.5). Answer: P reflects the ancient Tabernacle, not the First Temple. When the first Zionists rebuilt the Temple they rejected the Solomonic heresies and followed P.

(2) Ezek 45:18–20 predicates an annual purgation of the Temple on the first and, again, on the seventh of Nisan and is oblivious of the tenth of Tishri. Answer: Ezekiel's temple-purgation prescriptions for Nisan are motivated by a special reason—that all Israelites since the time of Josiah and the deuteronomic reform must purify themselves and the Temple so that they may offer the paschal sacrifice on the fourteenth of Nisan in purity. The throne's concern that this centralized Passover be observed in purity is illustrated by the account of Hezekiah's Passover (2 Chr 30; for details, see chap. 4, COMMENT J). Ezekiel accomplishes this end by converting the consecration rite of the altar (43:20, 26; cf. Exod 29:36–38) into an annual event (Abramski 1973: 75–77). Because Ezekiel makes drastic changes in the ritual calendar—for example, he omits the Feast of Pentecost though its observance is clearly ancient (e.g., Exod 23:16a; 36:22a)—one cannot draw any conclusions from Ezekiel's silence about whether Yom Kippur was observed on the tenth of Tishri.

(3) The returnees from the exile observed the Feast of Tabernacles but omitted Yom Kippur (Ezra 3:1–6). Answer: The text states unambiguously, "However, the foundations of the Temple of the Lord had not yet been laid (ibid., v 6). Without a temple there is no need for temple purgation.

(4) Ezra instructs his community regarding the Feast of Tabernacles but says not a word on Yom Kippur (Neh 8:2, 13–18). Answer: The Torah's prescriptions on the building of booths on the Feast of Tabernacles and the use of the four species of vegetation are unclear (23:39–43). Indeed, Ezra's interpretation (Neh 8:15) is in total opposition to that of normative Judaism (see *m. Sukk.* chaps. 3, 4). The observance of Yom Kippur is a problem only for the priests, who must fulfill the prescriptions of Lev 16 scrupulously. The people, however, need no further instruction; they have enough experience in the way to observe a public fast (see below).

(5) The people hold a public fast on the twenty-fourth of Tishri (Neh 9:1), a sign that the fast of Yom Kippur, ostensibly scheduled two weeks earlier, was not observed. Answer: Yom Kippur, a *šabbat šabbātôn*, a day of total cessation from labor, is wholly inappropriate for the sealing and signing of the *ʾămānâ*-covenant (Neh 10:1–30).

(6) Solomon's two-week-long dedication of the Temple ending on the twenty-second of Tishri (2 Chr 7:8–10; cf. 1 Kgs 8:65–66) precludes the observance of Yom Kippur. The Chronicler would not record a conflict with Yom Kippur, which surely was observed in his day, unless his sources clearly said so. Moreover, Rabbi Yohanan preserves the tradition that Solomon actually omitted its observance that year (*Moʿed Qat.* 9a; *Midr. Gen. Rab.* 35:4). Answer: The dedication services need not suspend the observance of Yom Kippur. On the contrary, they require the purgation of the altar (2 Chr 7:9) each day during the dedication rites (Exod 29:36; Ezek 43:26). As for the rabbinic citation, Rabbi Yohanan alone opines that Yom Kippur was suspended that year; the rest of the rabbis hold that only the fast was suspended. They are clearly right. Dedication is the time for rejoicing and feasting; yet the purgation rites of the temple need not be abated. In fact, the Yom Kippur that fell during the dedication of Solomon's Temple may not have varied from the norm at all—it was probably observed in its pristine nonfasting form, as conjectured above.

In sum, the tenth of Tishri, as the annual event for the purgation of the Temple, was observed in preexilic times. Even so, the date on which it changed its character from a day of joy to a day of penitence for the people can no longer be determined.

E. Azazel and Elimination Rites in the Ancient Near East

The antiquity and ubiquity of the Azazel rite are immediately apparent. Purgation and elimination rites go together in the ancient world. Exorcism of impurity is not enough (COMMENT C, above); its power must be nullified. This was accomplished in one of three ways: curse, destruction, or banishment. The last mentioned, as the examples below will demonstrate, was used frequently: evil was banished to its place of origin (e.g., netherworld, wilderness) or to some place in which its malefic powers could work to benefit its sender (e.g., to enemy territory) or in which it could do no harm at all (mountains, wilderness).

In the Mesopotamian world, the wilderness *(ṣēru)* is one of the symbolic designations of the netherworld. Moreover, *ḫurbū (ḫurbātu)/namû (namûtu)/ kīdi/tillanu/karmu,* which usually denote "ruins/waste/desolation," can also refer to the netherworld (Tallquist 1934: 17–22). Demons were believed to come out of the netherworld through a hole in the ground (Tawil 1980: 48–50), for example, "As soon as the hero Nergal opened a hole in the netherworld, the ghost of Enbidu came forth from the netherworld, like a breath of wind" (Gilgamesh 12.78–80 [=82–84]; cf. *ANET*[3] 98). Elimination rites are therefore employed to drive the demons from human habitations and back to the wilderness, which is another way of saying that the demons are driven back to their point of origin, the underworld, for instance, "May the spell go out (from the patient) and vanish in the wilderness; may it meet a strong ghost and may they roam the desolated places" (BRM 4.18.22–24, cited by Tawil 1980: 48–50). Thus, in Israel, the goat for Azazel bearing the sins of Israel, though it is bound for the wilderness, is in reality returning evil to its source, the netherworld.

In the Hittite world, evils are returned to enemy lands or to uninhabited mountain regions; the detergent materials are burned, dumped in the open country, or thrown into the river or seas. As in Mesopotamia, these places are connected with the underworld.

Methods of impurity removal among the Hittites can be classified under these categories (following Wright 1987: 32–45): (1) *transfer,* by waving (an object over a person), spitting on contact; (2) *detergents,* natural elements like water, clay, plants, wools, blood, fire, and the like that are used ritually to remove impurity; (3) *substitution,* whereby the consequences of the evil will fall on another animate being instead of the patient; (4) *entreaty and appeasement,* by offerings that will appease the invoked deity and enlist his aid; (5) *analogy,* that is, sympathetic magic, by the use of an item present in the ritual materials or environment, such as breaking pots or untwining threads; (6) *concretizing,* by placing materials that represent the evil on the patient's body and then removing them; (7) *reversal* (called "annulment" by Wright), a ritual that puts the evil back on the sorcerer who caused it; (8) *disposal,* rituals that discard the materials symbolizing or infected by the evil; (9) *prevention,* rituals that seek to keep an evil from returning after it has been dispelled; and (10) *invigoration,* rites and prayers for health and well-being after the removal of the evil.

Of the five texts studied by Wright (1987: 45–60), the rituals dealing with pestilence in the army or land of Hatti (Pulisa, Ashella, and Uhhamua) contain the motifs of appeasement and substitution, motifs that Lev 16 does not have.

Only the Ambazzi and Hurwali rituals, which exhibit the idea of transfer, are satisfying parallels. Wright's translations follow:

The Ritual of Pulisa (*CTH* 407; cf. Kümmel 1967: 111ff.): [Th]us (says) Pulisa [. . . if the king] smites the [la]nd of an enemy an[d he from the border of the land of the enemy] marches [away . . . of the land of the enemy] [ei]ther some [male]-god [or a female god . . .]the people a plague occur[s. . . .] When he [marches a]way from the border of the land of the enemy, they take one prisoner and one woman of the land. The ki[ng on which road] he came from the land of the enemy, the king on that road m[oves]. All the leaders move down to him. One prisoner and one woman they bring forth to him. He removes the clothes from himself. They put them on the man. But on the woman [they p]ut clothes of a woman. The king speaks thus to the man—bu[t] if it is [not] convenient to the king, then he sen[ds] another person. That one takes care of the rite. That one [spe]aks [to the] man thus: "If some male-god of the enemy land has caused this plague, b[ehol]d, to him I have given the decorated man as a substitute man. At his head this o[ne is gre]at, at the heart this one is great, at the member this o[ne is gre]at. You, male-god, be appeased with t[his de]corated man. But to the king, the [leaders], the ar[my and the] land of Hatti, tur[n yourself fa]ithfully.[. . .] But let this prisoner b[ear] the plague, and carry (it) ba[ck into the land of the enemy."]

And [t]o the woman he speak[s . . . l]ikewise, regarding the fema[le-go]d.

Afterward, [they drive up] one bull and one e[we . . .] of the la[nd] of the enemy. Him his ears, earrin[gs? . . .] red wool, green wool, bla[ck] wool, [white wool . . .] from the king's mouth he dra[ws] forth. [He speaks the following:] "In regard to the king becoming blood[-red, green,] [d]ark and [white . . .] [th]is back to the land of the en[emy . . .] and [to the king] himself, the leaders, the ar[my,] the [ho]rse[s . . .] [do not] pay attention, (but) take note of it for the land of the enemy." [. . .][. . .] takes. It on *emmer* [. . . .] [The bull with e]arrings. He spe[aks] thus: "The god of the en[emy who caused this plague] if he is a male-god, to you I have gi[ven] the deco[rated,][ear]ringed, approved(??) [bull.] You, male-god, be appeased. Let [th]is bull carry [this plague] back into the land of the enemy. [To the king, the] king'[s sons,] the leaders, the army and the la[nd of Hatti turn yourself faithfully."]

Afterward, the deco[rated] ewe [. . .] he speaks likewise, regarding the
female-god [. . . .]

Then th[ey se]nd forth the decorated bull [and the ewe to the prisoner]
and the woman.
[the rest is broken]

The Pulisa ritual resembles the biblical Azazel rite in that humans and
animals are chosen to bear the plague back to the enemy land. Nevertheless,
instead of being a transfer it is a *diversion* of the evil from the patient to
substitutes. The animals and persons, chosen by their stature, dress, and decoration, are intended to be pleasing gifts to the angry deity. By contrast, there is no
appeasement motif associated with Azazel (see the NOTE on v 8). Moreover,
they act as substitutes (LÚ *PU-ḤI-* ŠU), that is, they are more enticing targets
for the wrath of the deity. As substitutes, they absorb the plague and bear it to
the enemy land. Because the biblical rite has naught to do with the notions of
offering or substitution, we should avoid associating this ritual piece too closely
with the scapegoat rite in Lev 16 (for details, see Wright 1987: 45–50).

The Ritual of Ashella (*CTH* 394; cf. Friedrich 1925: 11–13): Thus (says)
Ashella, the man of Happalla: If in the land or in the army a plague
occurs, I perform this ritual:

I take the following: When day becomes night, all whoever are the
leaders of the army, each one prepares a ram. But if the ram(s) are white
or black, it does not matter. A cord of white wool, red wool (and) green
wool I wind together. He weaves them (into) one(?). I bring together
one *erimmatu*-stone and one ring of iron and lead. I bind them on the
necks and horns of the rams. They bind them (i.e., the rams) before the
tents at night. They say the following at that time: "Whatever god is
moving about, whatever god has caused this plague, for you, behold,
these rams I have tied up. Be herewith appeased!"

At morning, I drive them to the open country. With each ram they take
a jug of beer, one thick bread (and) one cup of milk(?). But before the
tent of the king he has a decorated woman sit. He places with the
woman one *ḫuppar*-vessel of beer and three thick breads.

Then, the leaders of the army place their hands over the rams. Thereupon, they say the following: "Whatever god has caused this plague,
now, behold, the rams are standing, they are very fat in liver, heart, and
member. Let the flesh of humans be hateful to him. Moreover, be appeased with these rams." The leaders of the army show reverence to the

rams, and the king shows reverence to the decorated woman. Then, they bring the rams and the woman, the bread and the beer out through the army. They drive them to the open country. They go and make them run inside the border of the enemy (so that) they do not arrive at any place of ours. Thereupon, in this way they say: "Behold, whatever evil of this army was among men, cattle, sheep, horses, mules and donkeys, now, behold, these rams and woman have taken it out from the camp. Whoever finds them, may that land receive this evil plague."

Despite the formal similarities with the Azazel rite (hand placement, driving the bearers of the evil away), the dissimilarities should not be overlooked. Again we see the theory of appeasement and substitution in operation. Furthermore, the hand-leaning reflects the establishment of identification between the animals and the humans, meaning in effect, "These are our rams of appeasement, these are our substitutes, these are better objects of attack than we are." Indeed, other cases of hand placement in Hittite texts lead to the conclusion that there are no examples of transfer of impurity or the like, only examples of identification (for details see Wright 1987: 50–55; cf. also the NOTE on 1:4).

The Ritual of Uhhamuwa (*CTH* 410; cf. *ANET*³ 347b): Thus (says) Uhhamuwa, the man of Arzawa: If in the land they keep dying, and if some god of the enemy has caused it, I perform the following:

They drive up one ram. Blue wool, red wool, green wool, black wool and white wool they twine together. They make it as a wool-crown. They put it on the head of the ram. The ram they drive forth to the road of the enemy. They say the following to him: "Whatever god of the enemy land has caused this plague, behold, this crowned ram, to you, O god, we have driven up for peaceful relations. As the herd is strong, and it is peaceful toward this ram, so may you, whatever god, who has caused this plague, be likewise peaceful toward Hatti-land. Turn faithfully toward Hatti-land. The crowned ram they drive away into the enemy land.

The god of an enemy is appeased by sending him a decorated ram. Because it is an offering of appeasement and (implicitly) a substitute, it is unlike the biblical scapegoat rite, which exclusively symbolizes the idea of transfer.

The following two texts, however, do embody the idea of transfer without the admixture of appeasement and substitution:

The Ritual of Ambazzi (*CTH* 391, II, lines 34–52; cf. *ANET*³ 348a): She wraps a little tin on the bowstring. She puts it on the right hand (and) feet of the offerers. Then she takes it away and puts it on a mouse (saying): "I have taken away from you evil and I have put it on the mouse. Let this mouse take it to the high mountains, the deep valleys (and) the distant ways." She lets the mouse go (saying): "Alawaimi, drive this (mouse) forth, and I will give to you a goat to eat."

This text deals with the transfer of evil to an animal, which is sent away to distant and apparently uninhabited places. The mouse is not an offering to a god. Alawaimi's service is requested to drive the mouse out, in return for which he is promised an offering. The only uncertainty is in the function of the bowstring: does it absorb the evil and become a vehicle of transfer itself or does it represent the evil, and the removal of it magically imitate the removal of the evil?

The Ritual of Huwarlu (*CTH* 398, II, lines 5–14): . . . They take a live small dog. They wa[ve] it over the king and queen and they wave it inside the palace. The ol[d woman thus] speaks: "Whatever [magical] word is in the king and queen, in his(!) body and in the palace, behold, (his) member (is) great, his heart (is) great. He, the "ass," will bear (it). He has overcome it. Let him take away the evil, the ma[gical word]. Wherever the gods have designated it, there let him carry it." When they take away the live dog. . . .

This text also deals with a rite of transfer. The dog is waved over the patient, thereby removing his evil. By being called an "ass" the dog's powers are aggrandized, enabling it to be more effective in removing the evil. The end of the ritual is broken so that, unfortunately, we have no idea what was done to the dog. In the Tunnawi rite a pig and a dog are burned after they have been "held over" the patient (*CTH* 409, III, lines 17–42; cf. Goetze 1938a: 16–20). In the Mastigga rite a dog is killed and buried after the patients have spat into its mouth, thereby transferring the evil (*CTH* 404, III, lines 14–16; cf. Rost 1953: 358f.). A similar rite of disposal may be assumed to have been carried out on the dog in the Ritual of Huwarlu.

The major difference between the Hittite and biblical rituals rests in the dissimilarity in the evils that are eliminated. In the Hittite texts evils such as plague, witchcraft, and the evil tongue are being removed. In the Bible it is "the iniquities and transgressions of the Israelites, including all their sins" (v 21). Moreover, the Hittite plague-rituals presuppose that the offended deity must be appeased by an attractive offering, which also acts as a substitute to siphon off the plague onto itself. In the Bible, by contrast, though Azazel is a demon, he is totally devitalized. Neither is Azazel thought to be discharging his work on Israel nor has Israel offended Azazel: "There is no prayer to Azazel to make him act in a beneficent manner or to receive the goat as a substitute. The only active supernatural being in Lev 16 is Israel's God. The appearance of the motif of transfer alone, without appeasement and substitution, serves to underscore the centrality of God in this rite" (Wright).

The Mesopotamian corpus of ritual texts also yields many examples of the elimination of evils by transfer and disposal (contra Kümmel 1968: 313) that relate conceptually to the Azazel rite. In such rites, the demonic illness of the affected patient or building is transferred to another object (a slaughtered animal, bread, dough, figurine, etc.), which is then disposed of in an appropriate place. The examples that follow will focus on the conceptual and systemic differences between the Mesopotamian and biblical rites instead of on the purely formal similarities and dissimilarities. Once again, I am indebted to the paper of my student, D. Wright, for his analysis of these examples (see now Wright 1987: 60–72).

1. The first text is one that has to be discounted, though it invariably crops up in any discussion of the scapegoat rite (e.g., Tawil 1980: 54; Aḥituv 1971a: 113–15). In this ritual (*KAR* 33; Ebeling 1931: 73–75), the patient has a sickness that does not allow him to eat or drink. A goat is tied up at the head of his bed. A stick with twined wools, a cup of water, and an almond branch are obtained. The next morning the goat and other objects are taken to the wilderness *(mu-da-bi-ri)*. The stick and cup are left in one place, while the almond branch and goat are put in another place. The goat is slaughtered. The legs are put in the skin, the head is cut off, and the flesh is cooked. Bronze bowls with honey and oil in them are brought. The skin is wrapped around the almond branch. The front legs are tied with snares. A hole is dug, into which the honey and oil are inserted. A foreleg is cut off and put in the hole. The almond branch follows, and on top of it the other foreleg. From here on the text is broken and obscure.

The rite is not concerned with transfer and disposal. Rather, the goat is a substitute for the man. The deposit of honey, oil, and flesh parts seems to be an offering, not a disposal of an impure scapegoat. Yet even this interpretation is in doubt, for the patient ultimately eats the meat. Surely, the patient does not eat meat that he is offering to placate a deity! And he certainly would not eat meat that is now purportedly bearing his illness! In view of these lacunae and obscurities, this text cannot be profitably compared to the biblical rite.

2. The Fifth Day of the *akītu*-Festival: The Babylonian New Year.

This text has been cited and analyzed in COMMENT C above.

3. *Utukkē Limnūtī* (lines 115–38; Gurney 1935: 84–95):

Ea instructs his son, Marduk, how to purify a patient beset by demons. Among the many rites performed, a *mašḥultuppû*-goat is brought to the patient's body and his head is bound with the animal's headband. The demons are exorcised by incantations: "From the body of the disturbed man, arise . . . whatever evil, [arise, set out] to Ereshkigal's place (i.e., the underworld)." The incantations are followed by the removal of the *mašḥultuppû*'s skin from the patient's body and its disposal in the street, symbolic of the hope that all "evil will return to the underworld."

The rite is clearly one of transfer in which the skin serves as the instrument whereby the evil is removed. Becoming thus impure, the skin is discarded. The dissimilarities, however, are more significant. This rite, like the *akītu*-Festival, seeks to remove a demonic impurity that infects an individual, whereas the biblical rite only seeks to remove the impurity from the area of human habitation.

4. *Asakkī Marṣūti* (*CT* 17, 10–11, lines 68–87; cf. Thompson 1903–14: 2.33–37): A man beset by demons cannot sleep or rest. Marduk's help is summoned by taking a white goat and placing it near the patient. Its heart is removed and placed near the man's head. After an incantation, the goat, along with bread and dough, are used to wipe *(kuppuru)* the man. Then the wiping materials, censer, and torch are dumped in the street.

This rite is similar to the one in the *Utukkē Limnūti* series, discussed above. The contrasts with the biblical rite are much the same.

5. *Šurpu* (VII, 45–70; Reiner 1958: 36–38):
[Go my son, Mar]duk! Take seven loaves of bread made of pure *tappinni*-flour, string (them) on a bronze (skewer), set a carnelian bead (on it). Wipe *(kuppuru)* (with it) the man, son of his god, whom the hex has seized. Cast his spit on the wiping material *(kupiratu)*. Cast the incantation of Eridu (upon it). Take (it) out to the open country, the pure place. Place (it) at the base of an *ašāgu*-bush. Remove from his body [the disease(?) that be]set him. Deliver his hex [to the] Lady of the Open Country and Plain. May Ninkilim, lord of animals, transfer his serious illness to the vermin of the ground.

"Though no animal is used as the vehicle of transfer, the rite is extraordinarily similar to the biblical rite since, like the scapegoat, the impurity laden material is disposed of in the wilderness. Even more striking is the mention of deities of the steppe and animals to whom the impurity is delivered. The phrase 'deliver his curse [to the] Lady of the Open Country and Plain' is amazingly similar to the biblical requirement of sending the goat to Azazel in the wilderness (Lev 16:10). Yet it is in this very similarity that the greatest contrast is found. The desert deities in Šurpu are very prominent and active. Ninkilim is called upon to act in transferring the evil to the vermin. The ensuing portion of the ritual calls upon other deities to revive, purify, and bless the patient (lines 71ff.). In contrast, Azazel does not act; he has no personality. The name refers more to a locale than to a supernatural figure" (Wright 1987: 69).

6. A Namburbi Ritual (Caplice 1965–71: 36.1–8): A person receives an omen of evil portended by a howling dog. He makes a figurine of a dog. Offerings and an incantation are made to Šamaš to enlist his help to avert the evil.

The offerer then declares, while standing over the figurine, that he has ripped out the evil from his person and put it on the figurine, which he terms his substitute *(dinānu)*. He goes to the river and recites an incantation: "Transport that dog to the *apsû*, do not release it!" Take it down to your *apsû!* Remove the dog's evil from my body!" After this he throws the figurine into the river.

Here is a mixture of the motifs of substitution and transfer. The nature of Namburbi rituals is to avert portended evil; it is preventive medicine (Caplice 1965–71: 34.105; 1974: 7–9). Just as the substitute king is installed to suffer for the real king the evil portended by adverse astronomical phenomena, so here the figurine of the dog is created to suffer the coming evil by serving as the person's substitute. Furthermore, even though the evil has not yet arrived, the person is inchoately affected by the omen. He has already been singled out by the forces of evil as the target of their attack. Thus the figurine acts both as a transfer agent receiving his incipient impurity and as a substitute that will bear any evil that might yet come. Finally, it is to be noted that the figurine itself, in the form of a dog, also substitutes for the howling dog that bore the evil omen. Thus, when the figurine is disposed of, the evil omen is likewise eliminated. One is reminded of the golden tumors and mice sent by the Philistines not only as a reparation *('āšām)* to the Lord but also as a means of reconveying the plague back to its divine source (1 Sam 6:3–8). Nevertheless, the dissimilarities between the Namburbi ritual and the Azazel rite should not be overlooked. The motif of substitution and the notion of undoing a portended evil are alien to the scapegoat rite.

The foregoing examples of Mesopotamian elimination rites resemble the biblical scapegoat rite in that an object that is selected to draw the evil from the affected person is consequently disposed of. The differences between them are more significant: (1) In Mesopotamia, the evil removed by such rites is demonic and very real; in the Bible, while the impurity is real, it does not possess the vitality and independence of demonic evil. (2) There are no group transfer rites in Mesopotamia: the biblical scapegoat, in contrast, removes the sins of the entire nation. (3) The Mesopotamian rites seek the aid of the deities of the wilderness to accept the evils; in the Bible, the entire rite is done under the aegis of its one God. (4) The Bible rejects the idea of substitution, which presupposes demonic attack and the appeasement of threatening demons (see now Wright 1987: 60–74).

F. Kippēr

"Atone" or "expiate" is the customary translation for *kippēr*, but in most cases this is incorrect. In biblical poetry its parallel synonym is usually *māḥâ* 'wipe' (Jer 18:23) or *hēsîr* 'remove' (Isa 27:9), suggesting that *kippēr* means "purge." Ritual texts also support this meaning, for they regularly couple *kippēr* with *ṭihar* 'purify' and *ḥiṭṭē'* 'decontaminate' (Lev 14:48, 52, 58). Other poetic passages will use in parallel *kissâ* 'cover' (Neh 3:37 [Eng. 4:5]), giving the contrary notion that *kippēr* connotes smearing on a new substance instead of effacing an existent one. Philologists have been divided on the etymology, because evidence from Semitic cognates can be cited in support of either connotation, mainly from Arabic ("cover") and Akkadian ("wipe"). Yet both meanings may go back to a common notion: "rub." Because a substance may either be "rubbed on" or "rubbed off," the derived meanings, "wipe" and "cover," may be complementary and not contradictory. This is true especially in Akkadian, where both usages are attested in medical/magical texts and where "the step between *auswischen* and *ausschmieren* is so short we cannot distinguish between cleaning and treatment" (Landsberger 1967: 32a).

Examples of each type will prove enlightening. First, the meaning "rub on": (1) *ṭābti amānim burāša ištēniš tasâk muḫḫi šinnīšu tukappar* 'You take . . . salt and resin of juniper, pulverize them into one drug and rub it on the front of his teeth' (*BAM* 30 = *LKA* 136, lines 12–13); (2) *ina dišpi ḫimēti pâšu tukappar*, 'You daub his mouth with honey and ghee' (*AMT* 79, line 15). Akkadian *kapāru* corresponds to Hebrew *kāpar (qal)*, whose one attestation means "rub on, smear" (Gen 6:14). But Akk. *kuppuru* (D stem), whose equivalent is Hebrew *kippēr (pi'el)*, is only attested for the meaning "rub" or "rub off, wipe" but never "rub on, smear"; for instance, (1) *šumma panīšu ú-kap-pir* 'if he rubs his face' (*CT* 28, 29:8; *CAD*, K 179b); (2) BE ZA ŠU! MEŠ-*šú uk-ta-na-pár* 'if a man constantly rubs his hands' (*KUB* 37, 210.8; *CAD*, K 179a); (3) *ina tiši . . . šēpšu tu-kap-par* 'you wipe his foot with dough' (*CT* 23, 1.4; *CAD*, K 179a); (4) NÍG. SILAG. GÁ . . . *zumur amēli tu-kap-par-ma* 'you wipe the man's body [with] dough' (*KAR* 92.10; *CAD*, K 179a).

Certain instances of *kuppuru*, however, reveal an abstraction of the literal meaning, yielding "purify, purge" without indication of actual wiping: (1) *mātkunu ugārkunu ka-pi-ra* 'purify your land and field' (Landsberger 1967: 32–33 n. 103; *CAD*, K 179b); (2) LÚ. MAŠ. MAŠ *u* LÚ. GALA URU. BI *u-kap-ru-'* 'The *mašmaššu* and the *kalû* purify that city' (Thureau-Dangin 1921: 38, r. 12; *CAD*, K 179b). It is difficult to conceive of an entire field, let alone a city, being wiped. Thus the abstract meaning "purify" without reference to actual wiping recommends itself. Nevertheless, in another text in which a city and house are objects of the verb, the rite that follows the *kuppuru* indicates that an actual act of wiping was performed: *7-ta- àm* NINDA. MEŠ KI GI. IZI. LÁ KI [. . .] URU *u* É *tu-kap-par ina na-mi-e na-[du-ti . . .]lu-u ana* ÍD SUB-*di* '[you obtain?] seven breads with a reed-torch, a place [. . .] you wipe the city and house, you throw (it) in either the unin[habited] steppe or in the river' (*KAR* 72.3–5; Ebeling 1954: 182). The disposal of the wiping material indicates that a wiping rite was in fact performed on the city and house. A hint of the way that such wiping rites were performed on these larger objects is contained in a passage describing a building's purification: "the corners (of?) the rooms *(bītāti)*, the gateway-wings, the court, the roof, the beams, and the windows(?)" are touched *(lapātu)* with bitumen, gypsum, oils, honey, holy water, seven censers, torches, etc." (Gurney 1935: 58–59, lines 49–52). Following this the *kuppuru* rite occurs: 7 MÁŠ. ḪUL. DUB. MEŠ 7 MÁŠ. GI. IZI. LA. MFŠ 7 UDU. TI. LA. MEŠ 7 ŠAḪ. TUR. MEŠ 7 ᵘʳᵘᵈᵘNÍG. KALA. GA-e 7 SU. GUD. GAL. MFŠ TFR(?) KA(?) LILIZ ZABAR TÚG SA₅ ᵏᵘˢUSAN₃ ᵈᵘᵍSILA₃. GAZ. MEŠ SE. FŠTUB ŠE. MUŠ₅ ŠE. IN. NU. ḪA ŠE. GIG ZÍD. ÀM GÚ. GAL GÚ. TUR GÚ. NIG. HAR. RA *zi-dub-dub-bi-e* É *tu-kap-par-ma,* '(with) seven *mašḫultuppi*-goats, seven *mašgizillû*-goats, seven 'sheep-of-life'(?), seven piglets, seven *nigkaagû*-drums, seven great bull hides, TER KA(?), a bronze kettledrum, red cloth, a whip, a *sil(a)guzu*-vessel, *arsuppu* meal, *šegušu* meal, *inninu* barley, wheat, emmer, chick peas, lentils, *kiššanu,* and flour heaps you wipe the house' (ibid., lines 53–60 = *BBR* 41–42, lines 21–28; the foregoing three examples and translations were provided by D. Wright). The actual performance of wiping is underscored by the ensuing direction to "[remove] the wiping material of the house *(takpirāt bīti)* through the door (ibid., lines 60–61; *CAD,* K 179b). It is most likely that the wiping rite was carried out, like the "touching" rite, by wiping various key locales such as corners, entrances, windows, beams, and the like on the building (Milgrom 1976d: 394–95). If so, it illuminates the parallel rite in the Israelite sanctuary in which aspersing the horns of the altar and the floors of shrine and adytum suffices to purge the sacrificial altar and the Tent (16:14–19). Thus it is possible that the aforementioned cases of the *kuppuru* of the field and city may also involve wiping in a *pars pro toto* manner and that the abstraction "purify" for *kuppuru* does not exist (D. Wright). In Israel, however, the abstraction for *kippēr* abounds, as we shall see.

Certainly in the ritual texts the meaning "rub off, wipe" predominates. As has been demonstrated, *kippēr* in all instances of the *ḥaṭṭāʾt* offering bears this meaning exclusively. The blood of the sacrifices is literally daubed or aspersed on the sancta, thereby "rubbing off" their impurities (see chap. 4, COMMENT B). Does *kippēr* in the sense of "rub on" occur in the Israelite cult? It might, if it could be shown that blood was an apotropaic as well as a cathartic. There are two possible instances; the first is the paschal blood upon the doorposts. Indeed, the term *pesaḥ* itself probably means "protection" (cf. Exod 12:27 with Isa 31:5), and the rite is parallel in Babylonian Namburbi rituals in which blood and other apotropaics are smeared on doors and keyholes that the "evil [plague] shall not enter the house." But the verb *kippēr* is not used in the texts on the paschal observance, and its sacrifice is not a *ḥaṭṭāʾt.* The second possible instance is the blood-and-oil rite for the purified *mĕṣōrāʿ,* in which the term *kippēr* does indeed occur (14:18, 20, 29, 31). The blood, however, stems from the *ʾāšām* offering, whose *kippēr* function is best rendered by the abstract notion "expiate" (see below). As this is the only instance in which *kippēr* is used with oil, there is no way to determine its precise meaning. Thus the connotation of "rubbing on, smearing" for *kippēr* cannot be definitely ascertained from the cultic texts.

The agents of ritual *kippēr,* exclusive of the *ḥaṭṭāʾt* blood, not yet discussed are the consecration of the priests (Exod 29:33), the scapegoat (Lev 16:10, 21–22), the induction of the Levites (Num 8:19), the incense offering (Num 17:11–12), the execution of idolators (Num 25:1–15) and homicides (Num 35:32–36), the broken-necked heifer (Deut 21:1–9), and the blood of sacrifices other than the *ḥaṭṭāʾt*.

In Mesopotamian rites, the purgative or wiping material (called *takpertu* or *kupīrātu)* is always assiduously disposed of, for example, *tak-pir-ta-šú a-na su-uq ir-bit-ti* Š[UB²-*di²*] '[You thr]ow its wiping material into the square' (*CT* 17, 1.5; cf. Thompson 1903–14: 2.3); *kupiratišú ana* ÍDŠU[B-*di*] 'You throw his wiping material into the river' (*LKA* 42.17; examples provided by D. Wright; see further Janowski 1982: 29–60; Wright 1987: 291–99). Thus the purgation of the impurities from a person or a building requires the elimination of the wiping material, which, having absorbed the impurities, is now lethal (for an example from the Hittite laws, see chap. 4, COMMENT D).

This leads to the phenomenon of the "substitute" or "ransom," the substance to which the evil is transferred and thereupon eliminated. This notion of the *kippēr* carrier is clearly represented in the Bible in the cases of the scapegoat (16:10, 21–22) and the broken-necked heifer (Deut 21:1–9). There can be no doubt that the scapegoat rite is an integral part of the sanctuary's purgation and that initially its purpose was to carry off the impurities removed from the sancta to the wilderness. According to the MT, however, a new purpose has been attached to this rite—to expiate for the sins of the Israelites (see below). The rite with the broken-necked heifer preserves its pristine function. In cases in which the murderer is unknown, the community closest to the corpus delicti must disavow complicity by breaking a heifer's neck over a perennial stream so that its blood is washed away. In this case the heifer serves as the substitute for the slain and a ransom for the suspected community.

There are other cases in which the ransom principle is clearly operative. (1) The function of the census money (Exod 30:12–16) is *lĕkappēr ʿal-napšōtêkem* 'to ransom your lives' (Exod 30:16; cf. Num 31:50): here the verb *kippēr* must be related to the expression found in the same pericope *kōper napšô* 'a ransom for his life' (Exod 30:12). (2) The same combination of the idiom *kōper nepeš* and the verb *kippēr* is found in the law of homicide (Num 35:31–33). Thus in these two cases, *kippēr* is a denominative from *kōper*, whose meaning is undisputed: "ransom" (cf. Exod 21:30). Therefore, there exists a strong possibility that all texts that assign to *kippēr* the function of averting God's wrath have *kōper* in mind: innocent life spared by substituting for it the guilty parties or their ransom. Thus the above-mentioned homicide law is elucidated as follows: though no substitute is allowed for a deliberate murderer, the accidental homicide is ransomed by the natural death of the high priest (Num 35:25). Similarly, the census money ransoms each counted soldier. (3) A ransom function can also be assigned to the Levite guards, who siphon off God's wrath upon themselves when an Israelite encroaches upon the sancta (Num 1:53; 8:19; 18:22–23; Milgrom 1970a: 28–31), as well as to Phineas (the chief of the Levite guards, Num 3:32), who ransoms Israel from God's imminent wrath (Num 25:10). Other examples of the ransom function of *kippēr* are: (4) the slaying of Saul's sons as a ransom for his violation of the Gibeonite covenant (2 Sam 21:3–6); (5) the inability of Babylon to ransom, in other words, to avert its fate (Isa 47:11); and (6) Moses' attempt to ransom Israel by his intercession (Exod 32:30–34). This *kippēr* must be sharply distinguished from that of the sanctuary. In the latter instance, the impurities are purged to keep them from provoking the indwelling God to leave. In the ransom cases, however, *kippēr* has the immediate goal of preventing the divine anger from incinerating innocent and guilty alike.

(7) The remaining occurrence of the phrase *lĕkappēr ʿal-napšōtêkem* 'to ransom your lives' occurs in 17:11, where the blood of the *šĕlāmîm* sacrifice must be drained on the altar to ransom the life of the offerer for slaughtering the animal for food (see the COMMENTS on chaps. 3, 11 [C], and 17). (8) A fascinating extension of the "ransom" connotation of *kippēr* is found in the Dead Sea scrolls. The firstfruits of the newly processed wine and (olive) oil are assigned the function *ykprw ʿl htyrwš/[kw]l yṣhr hʾrṣ* 'ransom the wine crop/the enti[re] oil crop of the land' (11QT 21:7–9; 22:15–16). The firstfruits serve the purpose of releasing the rest of the crop for common use (Milgrom 1976h: 336–37). This usage of *kippēr* is not attested in the Bible. Its equivalent is the non-Priestly term *ḥillēl* 'desanctify' (see Deut 20:6). This application of *kippēr* to ransoming or releasing the rest of the crop must be accounted as an innovation of the Dead Sea sectaries.

The final stage in the evolution of the verb *kippēr* yields the abstract, figurative notion "atone" or "expiate." This development in the history of a term corresponds to the conclusion of the anthropologist Victor Turner that "the general direction is from the concrete to the increasingly abstract" (1967: 53–54). Having begun as an action that eliminates dangerous impurity by absorbing it through direct contact (rubbing off) or indirectly (as a ransom/substitute), *kippēr* develops into the process of expiation in general. As shown (COMMENT E above), it is found in the scapegoat rite, which, according to its text (16:10, 21), atones for all of Israel's sins. This is probably its meaning in the incense offering by which Aaron stops the plague, thus expiating on Israel's behalf (Num 17:11). Such is also the *kippēr* role of all other sacrifices whose blood is not daubed on the altar's horns like the *ḥaṭṭāʾt*. Atonement is also one of the functions of the *ʿōlâ* (1:4; COMMENT on chap. 1), the minḥa (14:20, COMMENT on chap. 2), and the sole function of the *milluʾîm*, the priestly consecration ram (Exod 29:33) and the *ʾāšām* (5:16, 18, 26). The meaning here is that the offerer is cleansed of his impurities/sins and becomes reconciled, "at one," with God.

Outside the cult, *kippēr* undergoes a vast change, which is immediately apparent from its new grammatical syntax. Whereas in rituals the subject of *kippēr* is usually a priest and the direct object is a contaminated thing, in nonritual literature the subject is usually the deity and the direct object is a sin (e.g., Isa 6:7; 22:14; 27:9; Jer 18:23; Ezek 16:63; Pss 65:4; 78:38; 79:9). Actually, this represents no rupture with cultic *kippēr;* on the contrary, it gives voice to its implicit meaning. Although the cult concentrates heavily on the purging of sanctuary impurity, it too recognizes that the ultimate source of impurity is human sin. The subject registers even less of a change: though the priest performs the rituals, it is only by the grace of God that they are efficacious. Thus nonritual exhortations, requiring no priestly mediation, uncompromisingly turn to God, the sole dispenser of expiation. An instructive example of this transition from cultic to moral *kippēr* is found in the temple vision of Isaiah (it does not inaugurate his career; Milgrom 1964). Isaiah's sins are removed when the seraph touches his lips with a hot coal from the altar (Isa 6:6–7). Here we have an amalgam of both the early and the late stages of *kippēr.* Isaiah is purged by contact with a sacred detergent (the altar coal), and at the same time his sins are *expiated.*

The enigmatic *ʾăkappĕrâ pānāyw* (Gen 32:21) may embody the literal meaning of *kippēr* 'wipe', for it may derive from the Akk. cognate *kuppuru panê* 'wipe the face', which gives the sense of "appease," hence, "wipe [the anger from] the face" (Prov 16:14). Finally, the crux *ʾăhaṭennâ* (Gen 31:39) is best explained as related to Akk. *ḫâṭu* (from *ḫiāṭu*) 'weigh [out], pay' (*CAD*, H 161) instead of from *ḫaṭû* 'miss, neglect', and it should be vocalized *ʾăhiṭennâ* (from the root *hyṭ, qal*), thus having nothing to do with the verb *hiṭṭēʾ*) (Loewenstamm 1965).

For a summary of other views concerning the meaning of *kippēr,* see Lang 1982.

INDEX OF SUBJECTS

Aaron   34–35, 604, 626–27, 639–40, 771–72, 905–6
abomination
   birds   662
   fish   656–59
   flying insects   664
   and impurity   656–59
   land swarmers   683–86
Alcoholics Anonymous   374–75
altar
   consecration   278–79
   horns   234–36, 249–50
   incense   235–36
   north side   164–65
   sanctification   30
altar sacrificial   250–51
   anointment   517–18
   ashes   385–86
   atonement upon   524–25
   consecration   523–24
   decontamination   521–23
   fire   383–89
   initiation   592–95
   wood offering   387–88
amnesia   298–99, 300
anointed priest   231. See also high priest
anointing   11, 513–19, 553–55, 852–58
   Egypt   854–55
   Mesopotamia   855–56
   Ugarit   855–56
Arabah   30
Arad   see archaeology
archaeology
   Arad   30, 149, 236, 393–94
   deer   723

Dor   723
   incense altars   629
   Jerusalem   286
   Lachish   11, 236
   pig   651–52
   Shilo   31–34. See also Shilo
   Timnah   30
archaizing   6–8. See also P
ash dump   240
asylum   45
Azazel   44, 1020–21, 1022–23

Baal-peor   12
Balaam   12
birds   661–69, 701–2, 838–40
blood,   215–16, 251, 222–23, 273, 279, 403–04, 704–13
   anointing   852–53
   consecratory   533–34, 1037–39
   discharge   749–50
   prohibition   47–48, 426–29
   purgative   233–38, 249–51, 254–58, 1031–35. See also sacrifices
booths   27–28
burnt offering   133–77, 267–68, 290–91, 382–89, 526, 581–82, 757–58, 858
   antiquity   174–75
   birds   166–72, 304–5
   function   175–77
   name   172–74
   private   10
   see also sacrifices

camp, shape   11
Canaan, boundaries   11

INDEX OF SUBJECTS

carcass/corpse 46
census 12
cereal offering 11, 177–202, 389–401, 465–
    67, 573–74, 583–84, 858
    development 200–2
    function 195–96
    name 196–97
    token portion 181–82
    types 198–201
    see also sacrifices
chieftain 246–47
chthonic worship, pig 650–52
circumcision 746–48
collective responsibility 260–61
commentators
    medieval 63–66
    modern 66
community 241–43, 489–99
confession 24–25, 301–3, 369–73, 374–75,
    1042–43
congregation 242–43
conscience 369–73
    Philo 370–73
consequential *see* reparation offering
    'āšām 231–32, 303, 339–42
    'āwōn 295–96, 422–23
contagion *see* sancta contagion
crissum 169–71
covenant 9

D and P *see* P
Day of Purgation *see* Yom Kippur
Deir ʿAlla 12
demons 42–45, 249–50, 256–57, 259–60, 318,
    766–67, 1021
deposit 335
desecration 366–67
diet laws 10, 46, 643–742
    ethics 704–42
    hygenic theory 718–19, 727–28
    symbolic theory 719–26
dissembling 335
divine fire *see* fire
Dorian Gray 260–61
due 518, 519

eighth day 571, 592–95, 925–26
Eleazar 606–7
Elephantine 629–30
elevation offering 431, 461–73, 476–78, 479–
    81, 621, 851–52
Egyptian 468, 470–72
etymology 469–70
ethics 21–26. *See also* diet laws
exorcism 270–78

fire
    divine 590–91, 599–600
    unauthorized 598

first fruits 18
fish 654–61
    Suez Canal 660–67
flying insects 664–67
    locusts 665–66
forgive/reconciliate 245
frankincense 180–81
fungous houses 863–83
    causes 867–68
    eruptions 870–71
    Hittite 865
    impurity of 869
    Mesopotamia 864–65
    overhang 875–77
    quarantine 871
    stones 871–74
    structure 880–81
    summary 878–79

genital discharges 46, 902–56
    abnormal female 942–45
    abnormal male 32, 34, 44, 906–26
    comparative 763–65
    menstruant 744–45, 934–41, 948–53
    normal male 926–30
    semen 927–28
    sexual relations 930–34, 940–41
    structure 904–5
    summary 947–48
gēr 1055–56
guard duty 7
guilt 243, 300–1, 343–45

H 1, 13–25, 26–30, 28–29, 34, 216, 268–69,
    366–67, 439, 686–90, 694–98, 734, 885,
    886–87, 1054–56, 1064–65
    composition 61–63
    Sabbath 19–21
    structure 39–42
    style 15
    terminology 16–21, 35–38
    theology 48–49
hand-leaning 150–53, 520, 1041–43
herd animals 232
hērîm "set aside" 239, 474–75
Hezekiah's reform 27, 29–34
high priest 54–55, 232–33
    ablutions 1017–18, 1047–49
    anointment 518–19
    consecration 519
    corpse contamination 564
    daily offering 396–401
    garments 501–13, 1016–17, 1046, 1048
    immunity 1051–52
    precautions 1012–18
    successor 1058
holiness 46, 48, 686–87, 688, 689, 703, 729–
    32

INDEX OF SUBJECTS

holy place 392–94

imprecation 294–97, 314–15
impurity
ablutions 992–93, 995–96
and abomination 656–59
airborne 257–58, 978–82, 991–92, 1007
animal 425–26
bedding 909
carcasses 297–99
by carrying 667–71
by contact 297–99, 423–24, 653–54, 667–
71, 681–82
corpse 46, 270–78, 996
and death 46
diagrams 953–57
duration 876–77
dynamic 257–58
by eating 681–82
elimination 263–64, 276, 1044–46, 1052–
53, 1071–79
equations 983–85
hands 1004
high priest's assistants 1050–53
and holiness 46, 729–32
human 299, 423, 425, 742–1009
land swarmers 297–98, 425–26, 671–75
major 991–97
Mesopotamian 911–12
minor 996–98
Neusner 1004–8
overhang 875–77
prolonged 269–70, 310–12
quadrupeds 297–98, 425–26, 647–54, 681–
82
rationale 766–68, 1000–3
reduced 276–77, 307–18
by removes 910–12, 938–40
by riding 916
sancta 976–85
by sight 564
sitting 913–14
spitting 915–16
by touch 669, 672, 751–52, 910, 914–15,
935–37
underneath 916–18, 937, 942–43
by water 678–79, 680–81
inadvertent wrongs 25, 228–29, 256
communal 240–42
known 243–49
inaugural service 569–95
incense cloud 1014–15, 1024–31, 1025–28
incense rites 54, 237–38, 597, 629–32
incipits 500
intentional wrongs see wrongs, intentional
investment 335
Ithamar 606–7

Jerusalem
expansion 286
Temple see Temple

kābôd 58–59, 136, 575, 576–77, 588–90
kappōret 1014, 1031–33
kārēt 37–38, 424–25, 426, 457–60, 945–46
kid 703–04
kid prohibition 10, 732–42
kipper 279, 707–10, 760–61, 857, 882, 1023,
1079–84
prepositions 255–56
Korah 11

lampstand 10
land swarmers 671–81, 83–86, 683–86, 702
eight named 298, 425–26, 671–72
law and due 618–19
Levites
absence of 1
encroachment 602
induction 464
prebends 9
libation bowls 12
life and death 46, 50, 732–33, 740–42, 767–
68, 887–89, 924, 1002–3

measures of capacity 890–901
menstruant see genital discharges
methodology 2
Midianite
war 11
women 11
Mishael and Elzaphan 604–5
Molech 26
Moses
and Aaron 56–57, 622–27
as priest 555–58
prebend 532
music 19, 60–61

Nadab and Abihu 55, 596–600, 606–8, 628–
40, 1011–12
Name of Leviticus 1
Nazirite
boiled shoulder 11
see also purification offering
Neusner
holy things 485–87
Purities 1004–9
New Moon 20–21
Nineveh 26
Numbers commentary 3, 10–12

oath 299–300, 313–14, 337–38
ordination offering 436–37, 526–38
consecration 534–35
doubling 527–30
elevation rite 531

P   1, 366–67, 439, 734
    anthropomorphism   58–60, 134–36
    antiquity   3–13
    blessing   18
    composition   61–63
    and D   8–13, 29, 54, 698–704, 741
    date   26–27
    ethics   21–26, 704–42
    and grace of God   17–18
    impersonal God   17
    interpolations   34
    and Moses   56–57
    ostensibly archaizing   6–7
    ostensibly postexilic   5–6
    parameters   13–26
    performative commandments   265–66
    perquisite   433–37
    provenance   28–34
    structure   14–15, 542–44, 670–71, 846–48,
        859–60, 904–5, 931
    style   15
    terminology   3–8, 16–21, 35–38
    theology   42–51
parturient   742–68, 995
physical labor   7–8
pig   see quadrupeds
pollution   48–49, 258–59
populace   251–52
prayer   19, 60–61
priests   52–57, 157
    ablutions   500–1
    blessing   18, 586–88
    consecration   493–570
    encroachment   602
    function   615–18, 622–25
    garments   384–85, 403–4, 447–49, 519–20,
        548–49, 606
    immunity   47, 638–39, 840
    inebriation   611–14
    Josianic reform   187
    and laity   55–56
    and Moses   56–57
    mourning   608–11
    ordination   538–40
    prebends   33, 182–84, 186–88, 402–3, 407,
        410–12, 416–17, 429–36, 478–81, 531–
        32, 619–22
    rarely exclusive   1
    rite of passage   534–42, 566–69, 610
prohibitive commandments   229–31
promised land, boundaries   11
prophets and cult   482–85
punishment   295–96, 315, 422–23
pure place   239–40, 262, 387, 619–21
purification
    ablutions   667, 672, 674–75, 746, 756–57,
        840–41, 929–30, 935–36, 957–76, 992–93
    birds   879–80
    laundering   668, 682

    rinsing   920–21
    carcass   667–82
    eighth day   844–59
    laundering   840–41, 912–13, 1050
    priest   996
    rite of passage   889
    shaving   840–41
    spring water   836–38, 923–24
    sprinkling   839
    tables   986–1000
    vessels   404–7, 673–82, 836, 921
purification offering   49–50, 226–318, 401–8,
        520–25, 577–81, 582–83, 622–27, 926,
        1018. See also sacrifices
    altar consecration   278–79
    ashes   274–75
    birds   304–5
    burnt   239–40, 261–64, 407–8, 525, 580–81
    cereal   305–7
    consumption   622–27, 635–40
    corpse contamination   270–78, 283–84
    date   288–89
    desanctification   280
    decontamination   521–23
    eaten   261–64, 402
    Ezekiel's   281–84
    Ezra's   284–85
    function   254–58
    genital discharges   269–70
    graduated   292–318
    Hezekiah's   285–87
    and impurity   404–7
    Joash's   287–88
    Levites'   278
    name   253–54
    Nazirite's   10, 179–81, 996
    Num 15:22–26   264–69
    origin   177
    priest   996
    public   281
    rite of passage   289–92
    theology   258–61
    two kinds   261–64

quadrupeds   297–98, 425, 645–54, 667–71,
        681–82, 727–29
    camel   648
    dog   650, 653
    hare   648–49
    hoofed   646–48, 668–69
    pawed   669
    pig   649–53
    rock badger   648
    ruminant   647
    test   727–28
Qumran   see Temple Scroll; Index of Sources

red   272, 835
Red Cow   270–78

reparation offering   11, 50, 319–78, 339–42,
    408–10, 466–68, 850–51, 856–57, 861
  commutability   326–28, 408–9
  conscience   342–45
  Numbers 5:6–8   368–79
  origin   177
  psychology   342–45
  scale disease   363–64
  see also sacrifices
repentance   5, 373–78
restitution   328–30, 370
right thigh   see well-being offering
rite of passage   see priests, scale disease,
    purification offering
robbery   335–37

Sabbath   19–21, 27–28
sackcloth   674
sacrifices
  acceptable   420–21, 149–50
  acceptance   153
  administrative order   439
  barley   192–93
  birds   758–59, 761–62
  blood rite   155–56, 222–23, 292, 416–17,
    1037–39
  broad tail   210–12
  burnt offering   757–58, 858
  cakes   184, 414–15
  cereal offering   858
  and confession   1042–43
  desecration   422
  first-processed   190–91
  first-ripe   192–93
  flaying   156–57
  flock animals   163–68
  food gift   161–62, 430
  frankincense   183
  gift   415–16, 473–75
  herd animals   146–47
  hides   411
  honey   189–90
  incense offerings   201–2
  indigent   195–96, 304–7, 761–63, 859–63
  and laity   52–53, 143–44
  leaven   188–89
  most sacred   182–83, 320–22, 394–95
  offerable   304–7
  and offerings   133–489
  order   488–89
  pleasing aroma   162–63, 252
  quarter   157
  salt   191–92
  set aside   186
  slaughter   154–55, 248, 520–21, 579, 584,
    713–18
  sprinkling   233–34, 273, 516–17, 1031–33,
    1037–39
  suet   159, 205–7, 214–15

tāmîd   388–89, 398–99, 456–57, 584
thanksgiving   32–33
theory   440–43
turn into smoke   160–61, 200–1
washing   160
wood offering   158–59
see also burnt offering, purification offering,
    reparation offering, well-being offering
sacrilege   36, 319–30, 345–56
  Achan   346–47, 356
  Ahaz   348
  in Ezra   359–61
  Hittite   323–26, 349–50, 352–56
  in Jeremiah   358
  Mesopotamian   350–51
  Nazirite   356–58
  oath(s)   347–48, 365–73
  sancta   319–31, 346–49, 351–52, 449–50
  suspected   331–34
  Transjordanian altar   347
  Uzziah   346, 821
  Zedekiah   348
Samsuiluma   549–53
sancta
  contagion   45, 51, 443–56
  contamination   254–64, 976–85, 1033–37
  reduction   453–56
sanctification
  altar   see altar
  God   601–3
  Israel   686–70, 729–32
scale disease   9, 43, 46, 768–889
  affection   776, 789
  anointing oil   465
  baldness   800–2
  banishment   802–9
  bird rite   832–35, 879–83, 889
  boils   786–89
  bright green   811
  bright red   787–88
  burns   789–91
  causes   820–24
  color change   780–81
  comportment   802–9
  definition   774–76, 816–18
  discoloration   773, 783–86, 790–91, 801
  examinations   777
  exorcism   275
  fabrics   808–15
  fading   781
  houses   863–83
  malignant   811–12, 874
  Miriam   822–23
  Naaman   822, 964
  priest   887–89
  purification   782, 827–63, 967, 993
  quarantine   779–80, 782, 795–96
  rationale   819–20
  rite of passage   830–44

scale disease (*cont.*)
  scab 774, 782
  scalls 791–99
  shaving 843–44
  shiny mark 774, 778–83, 790, 799
  structure 846–47, 859–60, 880–81
  summary 825–26, 883–85
  symbolism 887–89
  tetters 799–800
  Uzziah 806–8, 856–57
  white 777, 784, 785–86
  yellow 792–93
  see also fungous houses
semolina 179
seven 234, 273, 279, 282, 283–84, 285, 536–
  38, 744, 780, 839, 843, 922, 934–35,
  1038–39
Shilo 11, 17, 29–34, 223, 419, 478–80
shoulder *see* Nazirite
shrine 408
Sinai 136–38
  Mount 437
  wilderness 438
slaughter 9, 28–29, 409, 713–18
sociopolitical terms 5
sprinkling *see* sacrifices
  priest's garments 532–33
statute 16–17, 435–36
Sukkot *see* booths
suet 28, 426–29
synonyms 4

Tabernacle 30–34, 36–37
  custody of 10
  Sinai prototype 142–43
  see also Tent of Meeting
tāmîd see sacrifices
Temple 29–34
  entering impure 751–55
  Ezekiel's 393, 451–52
  Jerusalem 187–88, 287–88, 393, 480–81,
    499, 620
Temple Scroll 165, 194, 394, 405, 620, 789,
    969–71, 1064
  priestly consecration 558–66
Tent of Meeting 134–43, 177
  adytum 1015–16, 1024–35
  anthropomorphism 59–61
  entrance 147–79, 156, 209–10, 393, 605–6,
    849–50, 925
  guarding 602
  holy place 1049
  silence 59–60
  see also Tabernacle
terminology controls 3–8
testimony 294–95
text of Leviticus 2
theft 328–30, 335–37
theophany 574–75, 588–90

throat 684, 687
Timnah 30
tithe 12, 17
tôrâ ritual 382–83
tôrâ, tôrôt 2, 688
trespass *see* sacrilege
trumpets 55

unblemished 147
unwitting *see* wrongs
Urim and Thummim 11, 507–11, 549

vegetarianism 712–13
veil 234
vessels
  leather 675–78, 679–80
  scouring 406–7
  wood 673–74

well-being offering 49, 202–20, 412–36, 573,
    708–10
  birds 222
  breast 430–31
  elimination 417–19, 420–22
  freewill 218–19, 419–20
  function 221–22
  name 220–21
  public 224–25
  right thigh 11, 431–32, 473–82, 585–86,
    621
  thanksgiving 219–20, 413–19
  votive 219, 419
  see also sacrifices
wilderness, itinerary 12
withholding 337
wrongs
  intentional 25, 295, 1034, 1043–44
  unintentional *see* inadvertent wrongs
  unwitting 333–34, 361–63

Yom Kippur 24–25, 51, 1009–84
  altar consecration 1039–40
  altar purgation 1036–39
  altar sacrifices 1046–50
  Babylonian festival 1067–70
  date 1053–59, 1070–71
  emergency rite 1012–13, 1061–64, 1065–67
  H appendix 1064–65
  impurities 1033–37
  iniquities 1043–44
  lots 1019–20
  public fast 1065–67
  purgation rite 1018–40
  scapegoat rite 882–83, 1040–46. *See also*
    Azazel
  self-denial 1054. *See also* confession
  structure 1059–61
  transgressions 1034
  work prohibition 1054–55

Index of Terms

Akkadian

abu bītim 247
akālu 347
ākil dami 708
ākil šīri 709
akītu 1078
amīlū 498
ana dāriātim 614
ana ṣeri ašri elli šuṣima 262, 387
ananiḫu 738
apsû 1079
arnabu 648
arnu 339
arrat la napšuri maruštu 820
arrat la pašāri 820
ašāgu 1078
asakku 322
āšipu 294
āšipu/mašmaššu 52
ašru 403
ašru parsu 1046
ballukku 1028
baluḫḫa 1026
barûtu umallû qata'a 539
bi'āru 774
bîl rimki 968
bītāti 1080
dāgil iṣṣūrē 52
dallu 860
dawû 745
dinanu 1079
dišip suluppi 189
dullu 7
dullulu 860
egubbu 1067
emēdu qātu 153

ēmēšu 188
emūtu 335
entu 979
epattu/epadu 505
eperu 775, 873
epēšu 578
epqu 799
erbu/aribu 665
erēbu 809
ergilu 666
ērīb bīti 52
erretu lemuttu 820
erretu maruštu 820
erretu rabītu 820
erretum/šertu rabitum/lemuttum 364
erṣetu 686
eṣettu, eṣemtu, eṣenṣēru 213
garakku 201, 628
gubbuḫu 800
ḫalāṣu 872
ḫamātu 671
ḫatnūtu 747
ḫarištu 746
ḫatanu 747
ḫaṭṭi'u 243
ḫaṭû 230, 1084
ḫiāṭu 1084
ḫiṭītu 339
ḫīṭu 230
ḫubbu 1040
ḫulmittu 671
ḫupšu 807
ḫurbātu 1072
idequ 1067
imeru 895, 901
ina 397
iqbiu 552

INDEX OF TERMS

irâm 475
irêm 475
istu qaqqādisu adî šēpēšu 785
kabru 184
kalītu 207
kalû 52
kamānu/kamānātu 201
kamunu 864, 870
kānu paṭīra 628
kapāru 1080
karmu 1072
katarru 864, 870
kawu 790
kīdi 1072
kidinnu 1069
kislu 207
kittinnu 502
kudurru 805
kupiratu 264, 1078
kuppuru 264, 1040, 1080, 1081
kuppuru panê 1084
kurītu 160
kurru 891, 892, 894
lamassu 976
lamaštu 651
lapātu 446, 776, 1081
leqû 347
liptu 776
lu 668
lu . . . lu 761
maḫḫu 52
māmītu 313, 368
manaḫātu 196
marāqu 406
marāṭu 800
marratu-birds 456
mārū 498
mašāḫu 5, 433
maṣḫatu 196, 197
mašḫultuppú-goat 1077
maṭṭalātu 437
meḫret 437
mišiḫtu 433
mû 962
mudû 143
mu-da-bi-ri 1077
mullû qātam 539
muskkatu 746
mūṣu 907
musukkatu 937
nadānu 432
nadû 745
nakāsu napištam 716
namû 1072
namūtu 1072
napištu 1054
nâpu 469
nâru/nârtu 52
nâṣu 170, 432

našû qata 587
niĝnaqqu 201, 628
nuḫḫu 162
nūptu 469
palāḫu 7
paqādu 335
purakku 234
parāku 234
parāsu 646, 662
parīsu 901
parsiktu 894
paršu 239
pašišu 519, 554
perasà wašarat 609
pērtu 608
peṣû 777
piṭru 159
puluḫtu 576
puquddū 335
pūṣu 777
qa 891, 892, 893
qâdu 384
qaqqadu 338
qarruḫu 800
qerbu 159, 207
qerēbu 577, 600
quddušu 1039
qummāl/nu 777
qurbūtu, qurubtu 600
qutru 237
qutturu 160
quturtu 237
rabāku 400
râmu 475
raqāqu 184
raqqaqu 184
rêmu 415, 475
rēmūtu 475
riāmu 475
rīmu 475
rīmūtu 475
s/šappartu 655
saharšuppû 775, 820
salīmu 221
sanāp/bu 511
sikkatu 839
siltu 179
sutu 891, 892, 893
ṣarāpu 789
ṣennītum/ṣennittum 775
ṣēru 840, 1072
ṣibru 184
ṣimmum 911
ṣiṣṣatu 511
ša qurbūti 600
šā'ilu/šā'iltu 52
šabāṭu ūra 628
saḫānu 787
šakānu 781

INDEX OF TERMS

šakānu qutrinna 628
šakāṣu 656
šakṣu 656
šangu 52
šāpiru 921
šarāqu 336, 347
šatû 809
šātū ušlāti 709
šēdu 976
seḫḫānu 787
šēratašu rabīta 820
šērtu rabītu 820
šešgallu 52, 568, 979
šikāru 612
šiknu 781
šikṣu 656
šišit nagirim 294
šubū'u 472
šullumu 328
šulmānu 221
šumka azkur 181
taḫḫiz 911
takpirāt biti 1081
takpiratu, takpirtu 864
tamšil 437
tappinni 400
tarīmtu 415, 475
tillanu 1072
ṭabāḫu 716
ubānu 208, 528
uddušu ešrēti umallû qātūa 539
ukappar 306
ullulu 1040
upnuh 1025
urullu 747
zābu 906
zību 218
zikru 182
zūpu 835

Arabic

ᵓatâtu 162
ᵓibhām 528
ᶜuṣᶜuṣ 213
ᶜzᶜz 1020
dibṣ 189
farik 194
faŝâ 781
ǧariš 194
habaṭa/ḥabuṭu 807
ḥatana 747
ḫātin 747
ḥbṭ 807
ḥarjala 666
ḥśn 505
ḥwy 784
iqšaᶜarra 870

jabāᵓ 665
jubbatum 843
kurāᶜ 160
la 668
maᵓira 811
manaḥa 196
masaḥa 433
milḥat 191
nāfa 469
qaraᶜa 609
qaṭṭara 237
qšᶜr 870
rabaka 399
raḥm 663
ruqāqat 184
sufr 655
sult 179
ṣaḥiba 792
ŝaḥaṭa 716
šiᵓatu 773
širiqriq 663

Aramaic

ᵓaprāšûtāᵓ 475
ᵓatrāᵓ 403
ᶜadîtāᵓ 782
ᶜadyāᵓ 782
baᵓătar 789
ḥashûm 527
ḥaṣraᵓ 208
ḥsn 505
ktwnᵓ 502
kytn 502
kytwnᵓ 502
mĕḥasrāᵓ 811
mĕḥazrāᵓ 811
meṣḥā 433
mŝknᵓ 516
partāᵓ 239
pĕlaḥ 7
qēlôpê 782
qēlûpê mitaplāᵓ 782
qlp 873
qṭr 237
qûdšaya 204
rḥm 475
rḥmt 475
rûm 527
šaḥênît 787
sālaq 173
šētāᵓ 809
sĕte 809
ṭûb šumnêh 210
yĕṣabbaᶜ 668
yĕtab 748
yitqaddaš 445
zōpā 835
zūpā 835

INDEX OF TERMS

Demotic

ququpd-t   664

Egyptian

ʾabnd   504
ʾiˤw   958
ankh   958
didi   511
ḥw(n) snˤ   505
ḥw-sn   505
ḥwy snˤ   505
ipt   895
ir ḥsnn   745
kappuri(e)t   1014
kp(n)rdwy   1014
mˤr   504
m(a)nḫītu   196
nśr.t   513
nzr.t   513
pdr   159
pt   305
q3b   207
snˤ   505
sqr r rwtj   870
šn   505
wˤb-priest   717
yfd   505
yfd nṯr   505

Ethiopic

ṣ̌ernĕˤĕt   775

Greek

alphos   800
anĕgagon   762
aphairema   415, 461
aphorisma   461
chalbanĕ   1026
dōron   145
elephantiasis   816
elephas   816
enkainizein   595
epephĕken   582
epithema   461
epops   664
hagiasthĕsetai   445
hamartia   253
histis   809
kuklō   156
lepra   775, 816, 821
leschĕ   223
megara   651
nebel   894
onyx   1026
petalon   511

petasos   520
pilos   520
pur allotrion   634
rhetine   1027
sōtĕrios   221
staktĕ   1026, 1027
staktos   1027
stazein   1027
styrakinos   1027
tĕganon   185
thymiama   1027
tou marturiou   140
xitōna   502

Hebrew

Azazel   1020–21
ʾābîb   193–94
ʾabnēṭ   502–4, 519–20
ʾādām   144–45
ʾădamdam   787–88
ʾaḥuzzâ   4, 866–67
ʾākal dam   428–29
ʾālâ   294, 314–15
ʾalyâ   210–12
ʾănāpâ   664
ʾănāqâ   671
ʾarbeh   665–66
ʾarnebet   648–49
ʾāšam   231–32, 243, 295–96, 300–1, 339–45,
   372
ʾāšam lĕ   334–35
ʾāšām   50, 295, 303, 339–42, 356–61, 363–64,
   365–73, 368–69, 850–51, 856–57, 860
ʾăser lōʾ tēˤāśênâ   229–31
ʾazkārâ   181–82
ʾēpōd   505
ʾereṣ   686
ʾereṣ gĕzērâ   1045–46
ʾēš zārâ   598
ʾēzōb   835–36
ʾiššeh   161–62, 430
ʾōhel môˤēd   139–43
ʾûrîm wĕtummîm   507–11
bāʾādām   705
bubbōqer babboqer   387
bad   348, 1016–17
bādād   805–6
baheret   775, 799
bannepeš   706–7
bāqār   146–47
bāśār   907, 934
bat hayyaˤānâ   663
bath   890–91
bĕˤad   578
bĕˤerkĕkā   326–28, 408–9
beged   809
bĕhēmâ   145–46, 645–46
bĕkōl môšĕbōtĕkem   215, 428–29

INDEX OF TERMS

běkol-ʿēt 1012–13
bēn . . . ûbēn 615
ben-šānâ/sĕnātô 757
bĕnê yônâ 168–69
bĕrōʾšô 338
bĕśar ʿörlâ 748
bêt haḥopšît 806–7
bĕyôm 397
biˤēr 387
bikkûrîm 192–93
biqqēr 797
bišĕgāgâ 228–29, 334
biṭṭēʾ 299–300
bōhaq 799–800
bōhen 528
gānab 335–37
gāzal 335–37
gēr 710–11, 1055–56
gereś 194
gibēaḥ 800
gillaḥ 795, 843–44
gôrāl 1019–20
dāʾâ 662
dal 860
daq 1025–26
dāwâ 743–46
dĕbaš 189–90
degel 4
dĕrāsâ 718
dešen 171
dôrēs 661–62
dûkîpat 664
ephah 305–6, 398, 895
hagrāmâ 718
hāpak 777
har sînay 437–39
heˤēlâ 173–74
heḥtîm 908
hērîm 186, 339, 385, 474–75
hēšîb ʾāšām 327
hibdîl 615, 689–90, 725–26
higgîd 294–95
higgîś 186
himṣîʾ 581–82
hin 896–97
hipšîṭ 156–57
hiqrîb 155, 188, 205, 391
hiqṣâ 873
hiqsîaˤ 872–73
hiqṭîr 160–61
hisgîr 779–80
hiśśîg/higgîaˤ yad 304, 861–62
hitaqaddēš 686, 965–67
hitwaddâ 301–3, 367–70, 1042–43
hizrîaˤ 743–44
hizzâ 232–34, 516–17, 839, 1032–33, 1037
hizzîr 945
homer 895
hôrâ 617, 884

huʾ ʾăšer-dibbēr 600
hûbāʾ 776, 831
zāb 906–7, 942
zābâ 934
zābaḥ 573, 713–15
zāqān 794
zebaḥ 205–7, 214, 427
zeraˤ zērûaˤ 680
ḥāgāb 666
ḥălādâ 718
ḥallâ 184
ḥāmās 48
ḥāmēṣ 188–89
ḥānak 592–95
ḥargōl 666
ḥăsîdâ 664
ḥaṭṭāʾt 253–56, 261–64, 271–74, 279–81, 291, 306, 309–12, 525, 580–81, 583, 635–40
ḥay 784–85, 832
ḥayyâ 645
ḥāzeh 430–31
ḥăzîr 649–53
ḥēšeb 505
ḥillēl 366–67
ḥillēṣ 874
ḥiṭṭēʾ 512–23, 879, 881
ḥōl 977–78
ḥōled 671
ḥōmet 671
ḥōpen 1025
ḥōq 395, 433, 618–19
ḥōšen 505–7
ḥuqqâ 16–17, 124–25, 435–36, 618–20
ṭāḥ 873
ṭāhar 760–61, 882–83, 924–25, 964, 967
ṭāhôr 963
ṭāmēˤ ˤad hāˤereb 667, 672, 876, 919, 936
ṭāmēʾ, ṭumʾâ 297, 423, 425–26, 648, 654, 657–59, 682, 690, 804–5, 907, 910, 937, 1002–3, 1033–34
ṭihar 781–82
ṭimmēʾ 778
ṭohŏrâ/ṭāhărâ 749–50, 973–74
yāmîn 528
yanšûp 663
yāraq 915–16
yāšab 748–49, 913–14
yāṣaq 518, 523–24
yāṭab 626–27
yĕraqraq 811
yerek hammizbēaḥ ṣāpônâ 164–65
yĕsôd hammizbēaḥ 238–39
yōteret 208
kaʾăšer ṣiwwâ/nišbaˤ/dibbēr 9, 16–17, 435, 618–19
kab 893
kābôd 58–59, 136, 575–77, 588–90
kāhâ 781
kālîl 173

INDEX OF TERMS

kammišpāṭ 305, 973–74
kap 669, 726–27
kappōret 1014
kārēt 424–25, 426, 457–60, 945–46
karmel 194–95
kĕlāyôt 207
kĕlî 673–74, 675–77, 678–79
kĕrāʿayim 159–60, 664–65
kĕsālîm 207
keseb 427
kibbēs 668, 912–13, 943, 1050
kiḥēš 335
kipper 255–56, 306–7, 524–25, 541, 707–8, 857, 1023, 1079–84
kîrayim 679
kōaḥ 671
kōhēn 52–57, 157, 887–88
kôs 663
kuttōnet 502
lābān 777
lĕbōnâ 180–81
lĕhāraʿ ᵓô lĕhēṭîb 300
leḥem ḥāmēṣ 414–15
lĕrāṣôn 149
lēṭāᵓâ 671
lethech 894, 900–1
lipnê ᵓōhel môʿēd 209
lōᵓ yādaʿ 333–34
log 846, 896–97
maʿal maʿal 320, 322–23, 345–49, 351–52, 356
mad 384
maḥăbat 184–85
mamᵓîr 811–12
mānâ 432
maprîs parsâ 646, 727–28
māqôm ṭahor 387
māqôm ṭāmēᵓ 872
māqôm ṭāhôr 239–40, 619–20
māqôm qādōš 392–94, 1049
māqôr 761, 973
māraq, mōraq 406–7
marḥešet 185
māšaḥ 517–19, 553–55
mayim ḥayyim 836–38, 923–24, 963
mĕʿil 504–5
mĕlāᵓkâ 674
melaḥ (bĕrît) 191–92
merkāb 916
mĕṭahēr 848
midbar sînay 438–39
miḥyâ 784
mikwâ 789–90
milleᵓ yād 538–40
millūᵓîm 436–37, 526–27
minḥâ 196–201, 858
miqdāš 754–55
miqdaš haqqōdeš 1058
miqrāᵓ qōdeš 21
mišḥâ 433–34

miškāb 909
miškān 516
mišmeret 7
miṣnepet 511
mispaḥat 782
mizbaḥ hāʿōlâ 156, 250–51
mizbaḥ haqqĕṭōret 235–36
môʿēd 20–21, 27–28, 136
môqēd 383–84
murᵓâ 169–71
murbeket 397–400
mût 609, 945–46
nāgaʿ bĕ 297, 299, 446, 751, 936
nāśāᵓ ʿāwōn/ḥēṭᵓ 295–96, 422–23, 622–25
nāśāᵓ yād 586–87
nāśîᵓ 246–47
nātan 867
nātan ʿēš 157–58
neʿlam mi 298–99, 300
nĕbēlâ 653–54, 667–68, 702–3
nĕdābâ 218–19, 419–20
neder 218–19, 419
negaʿ 776, 789
neḥšāb 421
nepeš 178–79, 684–85
nĕqēbâ 755
nēṣ 663
nešer 662
neteq 793–94
nēzer 512–13
niddâ 744–45, 937, 940–41, 942
nikbād 603–4
niqdaš 601–3
nislaḥ 17–18, 245
nittēr 665
nôdaʿ 243–44
nôṣâ 169–71
nôṣān 785
nôṭār/nôteret 182, 420–535
sābîb 156
sālʿām 666
sāmak yād 150–53, 167, 520, 1041–43
sāpar 920–21
sappaḥat 773–74
sĕnappîr 655
sōlet 179
ʿăbōdâ 7–8
ʿakbār 671
ʿam hāᵓāreṣ 251–52
ʿāmôq 778–79
ʿăqîrâ 718
ʿārak ʿēṣîm 158–59
ʿāśâ 266–67, 400, 578
ʿāṣeh 213
ʿāṭâ 803
ʿăṭālēp 664
ʿāwōn 25, 1043–44
ʿayin 780–81
ʿēdâ 241, 242–43, 498–99

1096

INDEX OF TERMS

ʿēdut 1031
ʿēgel 572
ʿereb 809
ʿēṣ ʾerez 835
ʿinnâ 1054, 1065–67
ʿōlâ 146, 172–77, 482–84, 858
ʿōmer 192–93, 895
ʿōrēb 663
ʿōrlâ 747–48
ʿozniyyâ 662
par ben-bāqār 146, 232
pāraʿ 608–9
pāram 609
pārōket 234
parsâ 877
peder 159
pěḥetet 813–14
peres 662
pešaʿ 1034
petaḥ ʾōhel môʿēd 147–49
piggûl 442
piqqādôn 335
ṣāb 671
ṣāhōb 792–93
ṣāraʿat 775–76, 816–18
ṣārebet 789
ṣārûaʿ 701–802
ṣîṣ 511–13
qaʾāt 663
qādaš 944–46
qādôš 48, 729–31
qāhāl 243–43
qāmaṣ/qōmeṣ 181
qārāʾ ʾel 139
qārab ʾel 577–78
qārab/nēgaš ʾel 613–14, 1011–12
qarnê hammizbēaḥ 234–36, 249–50
qārôb 600–1
qaśqeśet 655
qědûšâ 1002–3
qērēaḥ 800
qereb 159
qěṭōret 237–38, 597
qěṭōret sammim 1026–28
qiddēš 519, 523–24, 533–34, 966–67, 1039–40
qîr 169
qōdeš 320–22, 408, 605–6, 751–52, 975, 1013
qōdeš qodāšîm 182–83, 320–22, 394–95
rāʾâ 777
raḥam 663
rāḥaṣ 16, 500–1, 582, 841–42, 1017–18
rāmaś 687
rār 908
rāṣâ 149–50, 153, 420–21
rēʾšît 190–91
rēaḥ niḥōaḥ 162–63, 252
rōʾš 855–56
śāʿîr 248
śādeh 840–81

śāpām 803–4
śaq 674
śěʾēt 773, 790–91, 801
śěʾōr 188–89
šaʿatnēz 548–49
šabbat sabbātôn 1057
šāgâ 242
šaḥap 663
šāḥaṭ 154–55, 520–21, 715–17
šākab 876–77, 909–10, 940
šālāk 663
šāpān 648
šāṭap 920–21
šebaʿ 234, 282–85, 536–38, 744, 839, 935–36,
    1038–39
šěbûʿâ 313–14, 368–73
šěḥîn 787
šěḥiyâ 717
šěkābâ/šěkōbet 927
šēkār 611–12
šěnî tōlaʿat 835
šepek haddešen 240
šěqaʿărûr 870
šeqeṣ 47, 656–69, 682
šeres 298, 425–26, 655–56
šereṣ hěʿôp 664
šětî 809
šillaḥ 1044–45
šillēm 328, 370
šiqqēṣ 684
šissaʿ 171–72
šōgeh 282–83
šôq hayyāmîn 431–32, 476–81, 531, 585–86
šōšēaʿ šesaʿ 646–48, 728
šûb 376–78
taḥmās 663
tāmîd 388–89, 398–99, 456–57, 584
tāmîm 147
tannûr 184
taqqānat haššābîm 330
tēnûk 527–28
těnûpâ 461–73, 476–78, 531–32, 850–52
těrûmâ 415–16, 473–75, 975
těšumet yād 335
tinšemet 663, 672
tôdâ 219–20, 413
tôr 168–69
tôrâ 382–83, 688, 830, 883, 947
tūpînê 400

Hittite

arma- 951
GIR₄ 676, 677
ḫapupa- 664
ḫapupi- 664
ḫapupuᵐᵘšᵉⁿ 664
katra 764
KILAM 1030, 1049

INDEX OF TERMS

ᴸᵁHal 865
MÍŠU.GI 263
puḫugari 167
šakuwaššaran 1030
-šan tuwaz QATAM dal 150
tazzelli 519, 554
wawarkima 495
ZABAR 677

Hurrian

enumašši 758

Kanongesh

kafwi 567
ku-fwa 567
kumukindyila 567

Latin

aroma 1027
galbanum 1026
lamina 511
Levitikon 1
onycha 1026
populeas 1027
populus 1027
resina 1027
stacte 1026, 1027
sto 809
styrax 1027
testimonii 140
upupa epos 664

Old French

enseigner 592

Old South Arabic

fṣ²m 781
ṣrᶜ 775

Phoenician

khn 154
ktn 502
zbḥ 154

Punic

zbḥ² 218
zbḥ bmnḥ 218
zbḥ šmn 218

General Semitic

mᵉᶜārâ 651

Sumerian

BAL 1028
DABIN 400
GADA 502
GUDU 519, 554
HAL 1026
KUR₄ 184
LU.SAHAR.SUB.BA 800
MUK 1028
NINDA.KUR₄ RA 184
NINDA.SIG 184
NINDA.TUR.(TUR) 184
SAHAR 775
TUR 184

Syriac

gr(w)s² 194
mešḥâ 433
pertā² 239
siprā² dĕkāhanā² 1

Ugaritic

²tm 339
²tr 403
ᶜrb 809
ᶜṣrm 758
annḥ 738
arṣ 686
b (preposition) 397
bt hptt 806
dbḥ 218, 714, 716
dbḥ ksprt 305
dl 860
dwy 745
dd 141
ḥ ṭ²u 855
ḥtn 747
ipd 505
iṭṭ 162
klyt 207
kpr 855, 856
ksl 207
l 668
lg šmn 846
ltḥ 900, 901
md 384
mlk brr 848
mlk ytb brr 520, 848
mnḥ 196
mqr 761

INDEX OF TERMS

ndd   745
ndy   745
puḫru môᶜidi   141
qr   761
rgm yttb mlk brr   848
stt   809
sty   809
ša ydk šmm   587
šḥn   787
šlmm   172
šlmm kll   173

šqrb   145
šrp   172, 174
šrp (w)šlmm   218
trmt   415
ṭb   738
ṭbḥ   154, 716, 738
wmlk brr rgm yttm   848
ynt   758
ynt qrt   758
yrtḥṣ mik brr   519, 848
zbḥ   154

INDEX OF AUTHORS

Aaron ben Elijah (*Keter Torah*)   65, 151, 157, 183, 192, 204, 208, 211, 213, 215, 232, 246, 306, 309, 310, 323, 365, 404, 535, 588, 599, 600, 605, 621, 626, 645, 647, 674, 680, 743, 745, 748, 755, 781, 783, 799, 803, 830, 832, 866, 870, 905, 916, 934, 940, 941, 1027, 1032, 1050, 1054

Aaron ben Joseph (*Seper Hamibḥar*)   65, 151, 189, 192, 204, 211, 265, 303, 309, 335, 344, 365, 404, 408, 428, 431, 535, 538, 540, 541, 563, 576, 580, 584, 599, 600, 626, 656, 757, 773, 780, 781, 784, 830, 832, 874, 940, 1032, 1035, 1050

Abravanel, I.   7, 134, 145, 146, 159, 163, 166, 168, 182, 190, 196, 198, 204, 210, 241, 245, 278, 280, 304, 365, 383, 414, 426, 434, 440, 444, 456, 460, 461, 588, 600, 603, 645, 655, 667, 739, 750, 774, 778, 780, 787, 808, 815, 908, 1016, 1018

Achelis, H.   754
Abramski, S.   1070
Adler, E.   170, 182, 768
Aharoni, J.   663, 666
Aharoni, Y.   30, 149, 180
Ahituv, S.   739, 1077
Aistleitner, J.   207, 738
Al-Qumisi, D.   630, 661
Albeck, H.   200, 393, 407, 757, 1029, 1030
Albright, W. F.   54, 60, 180, 195, 196, 397, 612, 719, 807, 890, 900
Alfrink, B.   460
Alon, G.   372, 920
Aloni, J.   29
Andersen, J.   286, 816, 817
Anderson, G.   198, 469
Anthony, H. E.   736

Aubrey, J.   624
Audet, J.-P.   295
Avigad, N.   286, 807
Avitsur, S.   679

Baentsch, B.   65, 333, 538
Bailey, J. W.   231
Baillet, M.   821, 971, 973
Bar-Adon, P.   405
Barr, J.   253, 441
Barrois, A.   890
Bartinoro   609
Barton, G.   569
Baudissin, W. W.   634
Bauer, H.   349
Baumgarten, J. M.   797, 819, 823, 971
Bean, S.   720, 750
Beckman, G. M.   677, 750
Beit-Arieh, I.   800
Bekhor Shor (Joseph ben Isaac)   64, 134, 169, 175, 186, 229, 340, 365, 384, 386, 391, 427, 440, 461, 600, 603, 606, 611, 653, 654, 741, 774, 779, 780, 815, 871, 882, 945
Belkin, S.   344, 347
Bell, H.   384
Ben-Aryeh, Y.   240
Bendavid, A.   788
Ben-Tuvia, A.   661
Bergman, E.   575
Bertholet, A.   65, 426
Bewer, J. A.   482
Bickerman, E. J.   652
Binder, G.   750
Biran, A.   139
Blackman, A. M.   302, 745, 747, 763, 932, 951, 958, 959

INDEX OF AUTHORS

Blau, J. 340
Bleeker, C. J. 951
Bodenheimer, F. S. 666, 671
Boehmer, R. M. 236
Booth, W. 633
Borger, R. 349, 350, 437, 556, 575, 820
Bottero, J. 893, 894
Bourdillon, M. F. C. 443
Boyce, M. 681, 750, 763, 767, 768, 804, 932
Breasted, J. H. 238
Brenner, A. 788, 792
Brentjes, B. 652
Brettler, M. Z. 614
Brichto, H. C. 29, 293, 335, 368, 706
Briggs, C. A. 179
Bright, J. 536, 608, 611, 1012
Brin, G. 600
Broshi, M. 286
Brown, J. P. 223, 502, 504, 603
Brumfeld, A. C 651
Büchler, A. 151, 303, 336, 344
Bühler, G. 674
Bull, R. 139
Bulmer, R. 649, 728
Burkert, W. 411, 442, 713, 932, 963
Burton, J. W. 941, 1001

Campbell, E. 139
Canaan, T. 294, 411, 886
Cansdale, G. S. 168
Caplice, R., 834, 864, 976, 1040, 1078, 1079
Caquot, A. 190, 738
Carmichael, C. M. 741
Carnoy, A. J. 804
Cassin, E. 589
Cassuto, U. 195, 300, 504, 738, 807
Cazelles, H. 173, 1020
Charbel, A. 221
Charles, R. H. 526
Chekhov, A. 633
Clifford, R. J. 141
Cody, A. 154, 539, 556
Cohen, M. 846
Cohn, R. L. 822
Conrad, D 628
Conybeare, F. C. 295
Cooke, G. A. 304, 397, 862
Coulanges, F. de 762
Countryman, L. W. 721
Cowley, A. 181, 199, 218, 367, 630
Cross, F. M 7, 31, 59, 139, 142
Culpepper, E. 952

Daiches, D. 461
Dalman, G. 184, 192, 193, 194, 674, 706, 739
Danzig, A. 1012
Daube, D. 150, 228, 310, 328, 338, 688
Davies, D. 853
Davis, S. 727

Dayagi-Mendeles 1020
Deist, F. E. 348
Dhorme, E. 819
Dietrich, M. 415
Dillmann, A. 3, 17, 20, 65, 145, 151, 157,
  164, 167, 176, 190, 194, 203, 208, 214, 222,
  232, 243, 298, 304, 305, 333, 384, 394, 400,
  433, 525, 583, 606, 622, 647, 666, 673, 678,
  679, 745, 747, 750, 766, 767, 775, 782, 805,
  809, 832, 930, 931, 939, 1002, 1022
Dinari, Y. 765, 766, 949
Dion, P. E. 169
Doeller, J. 750, 754
Douglas, M. 569, 649, 655, 664, 666, 667,
  719, 720, 721, 726, 727, 728, 734, 766, 821,
  1001
Driver, G. R. 162, 294, 340, 367, 461, 469,
  474, 662, 663, 738, 773, 775, 785, 787, 800,
  1020
Driver, S. R. 35, 196, 211, 444, 461, 528, 685,
  698, 810, 862, 870, 873, 874, 931, 940, 945
Du Chaillu, P. G. 567
Duke, R. K. 8
Durkheim, E. 719, 720, 721, 726, 740
Dussaud, R. 151, 219

Ebeling, E. 275, 650, 976, 1077, 1080
Edelman, D. 161
Edwards, I. E. S. 504
Eerdmans, B. D. 26, 32, 685, 698, 925
Eheloff, H. 688, 758, 761, 764
Ehrlich, A. 27, 139, 156, 162, 167, 184, 187,
  210, 221, 307, 326, 344, 356, 386, 404, 411,
  420, 425, 441, 445, 501, 521, 528, 540, 541,
  585, 600, 603, 605, 607, 610, 618, 623, 625,
  627, 636, 645, 651, 655, 680, 748, 757, 761,
  776, 778, 780, 785, 786, 789, 795, 830, 831,
  843, 846, 861, 862, 863, 871, 874, 906, 914,
  916, 921, 926, 928, 941, 947, 1022, 1035,
  1058
Eichrodt, W. 151, 440, 443
Eilberg-Schwartz, M. 56, 154, 421, 423, 475,
  487, 658, 678, 1003
Eising, H. 181
Eitram, S. 223
Eliade, M. 957, 963
Elijah of Vilna 1048, 1058
Elliger, K. 65, 186, 194, 196, 208, 215, 229,
  232, 248, 308, 326, 365, 429, 546, 597, 601,
  604, 614, 622, 678, 776, 812, 814, 815, 836,
  871, 886, 908, 914, 1001, 1021, 1058
Elliot, L. 810
Elliot-Binns, L. E. 26, 230
Ellison, R. 892
Elman, Y. 787
Emerton, J. A. 445
Engelhard, D. H. 264, 651, 834, 865
Epstein, A. 765
Eshkoli, A. Z. 748, 765, 935

INDEX OF AUTHORS

Evans-Pritchard, E. E.   441, 821, 950, 442

Falkenstein, A.   147, 537, 569, 575
Fallaize, E. N.   750, 766
Farnell, L. R.   654, 952
Feldman, E.   807, 819, 1002
Feliks, J.   192, 652, 661, 662, 666, 671, 723, 833, 835, 1027, 1028
Fensham, F. O.   221
Ferro-Luzzi, G. E.   764, 952
Feucht, C.   26
Finkelstein, I.   31
Finkelstein, L.   200, 630, 674, 1050
Firmage, E.   655, 729, 733, 735, 841, 653
Fischer, H. G.   706, 717, 737
Fishbane, M.   326, 358, 360, 427, 583, 627, 688, 789, 790, 884
Fisher, L. R.   738
Fitzmeyer, J. A.   762, 1014, 1032
Flusser, D.   635
Fohrer, G.   339
Fontenrose, J.   223
Frazer, J. G.   504, 529, 712, 765, 950
Freedman, D. N.   209, 286, 403, 412, 418, 510, 557, 598, 603, 604, 605, 611, 625, 743, 885, 909, 940
Freedman, R. D.   747
Friedman, R. E.   31
Friedrich, J.   505, 1074
Fritz, V.   362
Fruchtman, M.   421
Frymer-Kensky, T.   48, 705
Füglister, N.   1002

Galling, K.   234
Gane, R.   234, 431
Gardiner, A.   895, 958
Garfinkel, Y.   262
Gaster, T. H.   443, 712, 738, 765, 806, 823, 1021
Gehman, H. S.   806
Geiger, A.   211
Gelb, I. J.   500
Geller, M. J.   306, 911, 912
Gerleman, G.   220
Gertner, M.   12
Geva, H.   286
Gill, D.   205
Ginsberg, H. L.   193, 194, 360, 397, 723, 738, 739
Ginsburg, C. D.   168
Girard, R.   440, 442
Goetze, A.   208, 305, 472, 495, 650, 775, 933, 1076
Goldman, L.   824
Goldstein, N.   594, 595, 635, 652, 1022
Gonda, J.   653
Gordis, R.   242, 339
Gordon, C. H.   397, 738

Görg, M.   422, 504, 505, 511, 512, 513, 520, 870, 945, 1014
Gradwohl, R.   598, 628
Gray, G. B.   59, 163, 191, 252, 556, 587
Gray, J.   339, 807
Greenberg, M.   139, 329
Greenfield, J.   432
Grelot, P.   215, 807
Grimm, K. J.   242
Grintz, Y. M.   8, 28, 155, 504, 505, 614, 835
Gruber, M.   751, 953
Guenther, A. R.   8
Gunkel, H.   219
Gurewicz, S. B.   807
Gurney, O. R.   19, 152, 362, 864, 1022, 1081
Güterbock H. G.   349

Haag, M.   48
Hackett, J. A.   663
Haderlie, E. C.   660
Hai ben Sherira Gaon   920
Hallo, W. W.   713
Halperin, D.   348
Haran, M.   3, 26, 29, 30, 59, 140, 147, 152, 199, 200, 222, 232, 430, 440, 450, 502, 504, 505, 517, 519, 597, 598, 607, 612, 634, 738, 739, 1004, 1025
Harper, E. B.   841
Harris, M.   350, 649, 650
Harrison, J.   221, 651
Harvey, W.   797
Hass, G.   758
Hayley, A.   624, 676, 681
Hazzequni (Hezekiah ben Manoah)   65, 134, 208, 384, 385, 391, 525, 534, 572, 587, 588, 599, 658, 659, 675, 690, 798, 810, 837, 839, 853, 908, 934
Heimpel, W.   149, 1018
Heinemann, I.   368
Heinisch, P.   26, 333
Held, M.   207
Heltzer, M.   900, 901
Hendel, R. S.   442
Henig, R. M.   953
Henninger, J.   649, 706, 766, 932
Hermisson, H.-J.   482
Hesse, B.   651, 723
Hestrin, R.   1020
Hicks, F.   161
Hildenbrand, M.   580
Hillers, D. R.   349, 473, 516, 778, 820
Hoffman, Y.   4, 7
Hoffmann, D. Z.   65, 151, 207, 208, 295, 299, 320, 382, 386, 399, 402, 418, 436, 438, 515, 542, 579, 582, 585, 590, 608, 609, 611, 622, 626, 654, 664, 674, 675, 679, 685, 686, 687, 691, 715, 744, 772, 776, 779, 783, 784, 787, 797, 798, 814, 830, 853, 862, 863, 878, 883, 884, 908, 922, 947, 1021, 1058

Hoffner, H. A.   139, 189, 400, 519, 554, 650, 651, 865, 927
Höfner, M.   781
Hoftijzer, J.   162
Holliday, W. L.   377
Hölscher, G.   482
Hönig, H. W.   504
Horowitz, A.   754
Horovitz, C. M.   509, 765, 841, 915, 916
Hubert, H.   441
Hulse, E. V.   774, 775, 777, 778, 785, 786, 791, 793, 794, 799, 800, 816, 817, 819
Hunt, T. F.   893
Hurowitz, A. (V.)   37, 499, 509, 517, 553, 588, 1031
Hurvitz, A.   3, 4, 5, 7, 8, 27, 160, 162, 163, 242, 335, 521, 582, 602, 610, 611, 614, 615
Hurwitz, S.   754

Ibn Ezra, A.   18, 63, 64, 134, 151, 156, 159, 168, 172, 181, 185, 193, 208, 211, 216, 232, 233, 234, 244, 246, 247, 252, 265, 269, 295, 296, 298, 300, 301, 304, 306, 320, 335, 339, 344, 385, 391, 397, 399, 402, 403, 404, 407, 408, 427, 434, 444, 457, 458, 459, 484, 501, 513, 519, 524, 525, 540, 542, 572, 573, 576, 584, 587, 588, 591, 597, 601, 609, 610, 611, 616, 626, 645, 646, 647, 655, 659, 663, 664, 667, 669, 671, 672, 679, 680, 683, 685, 723, 739, 743, 745, 758, 763, 773, 775, 776, 777, 778, 781, 785, 786, 792, 797, 800, 803, 809, 811, 814, 815, 831, 836, 842, 853, 861, 866, 869, 870, 873, 874, 875, 876, 907, 908, 914, 915, 916, 920, 926, 927, 939, 940, 944, 1012, 1014, 1018, 1020, 1021, 1024, 1036, 1052, 1054, 1055
Ibn Janah, J.   64, 159, 179, 397, 444, 587, 745, 781, 783, 831, 853, 870, 873, 923, 927, 1018, 1020

Jackson, B. S.   326, 330, 335, 336, 348
Jacobsen, T.   564, 979
James, E. O.   440, 441
Jamme, A   311
Janowski, M.   153, 220, 248, 255, 441, 578, 589, 636, 706, 707, 1082
Japhet, S.   537
Jastrow, M.   774, 785, 866, 871, 872
Jolley, J.   674, 814
Jones, J. W.   368
Jones, R. N.   778, 794, 817
Joüon, P. P.   339, 340, 341, 418, 745, 757, 761, 778, 780, 783, 805, 811, 814, 868, 874, 876, 941, 944

Kalisch, M. M.   65, 190, 208, 212, 229, 389, 392, 575, 607, 622, 655, 665, 678, 762, 784, 831, 840, 907
Kane, P. V.   406, 676, 750, 764

Kaufmann, Y.   3, 9, 10, 18, 19, 26, 29, 42, 54, 59, 60, 61, 259, 260, 261, 262, 387, 482, 507, 508, 964
Kautzsch, E.   482
Kearny, J.   543
Keel, O.   740, 741, 1025, 1029
Kellermann, D.   188, 269, 339
Kelso, J. L.   675
Kennett, R. H.   482
Kikawada, I.   39, 931
Kimḥi, D.   870; see Radak
King, L. W.   820
Kinnier-Wilson, J. V.   775, 821, 907
Kirschner, R.   635
Kister, M. J.   765
Kitzmiller, K. W.   824
Kiuchi, N.   228, 229, 234, 256, 334, 338, 343, 573, 1023
Klameth, G.   706
Klein, I.   717
Klostermann   807
Knight, J. E.   168
Knobel, A. W.   164, 623
Knohl, I.   9, 13, 15, 16, 17, 18, 19, 20, 21, 26, 27, 28, 29, 30, 34, 35, 36, 38, 49, 56, 59, 60, 61, 214, 216, 245, 269, 368, 369, 394, 435, 584, 867, 868, 1062
Knudsen, E. E.   625
Koch, K.   231, 269, 339, 572, 583, 618, 701, 758, 832, 863, 945
Koehler, L.   775
Kook, A. I.   208
Kornfeld, W.   718, 768, 1001, 1002
Kosmala, H.   738
Kraemer, J. L.   870
Kramer, S. N.   350
Kraus, H.-J.   443
Krutch, J.   736
Kuenen, A.   29, 428, 436, 698
Kümmel, H. M.   175, 653, 1021, 1073, 1077

La Barbera, R.   837
Laessøe, J.   313, 368, 835, 951, 962, 968, 1048
Lagercrantz, S.   655
Lambert, W. G.   4, 24, 43, 197, 219, 294, 299, 302, 339, 349, 420, 650, 960
Landsberger, B.   264, 793, 976, 1080
Lang, B.   1084
Langdon, S. H   302, 343, 539
Lapp, P.   652
Laughlin, J.   599, 628, 634
Lauterbach, J. Z.   296, 1028, 1029
Leach, E.   518, 566, 569, 591
Leeser, I.   343
Leeuwen, W.   400
Leibig   240
Leibovitch, J.   717
Leibowitz, J.   800
Lemke, W. E.   601

INDEX OF AUTHORS

Lendrum, F. C.   824
Leqah Ṭov   383, 388, 500, 939
Levine, B. A.   5, 65, 173, 182, 184, 218, 219, 220, 221, 222, 243, 260, 263, 434, 445, 466, 474, 518, 546, 706, 809, 848, 1021, 1023, 1029, 1042, 1043
Levinger, Y. M.   662
Levy, D.   668
Levy-bruhl, L.   950, 958, 1001
Lewy, H.   892, 894, 895
Licht, J.   27, 974
Lichtenstein, H.   390
Liddel, H. G.   800
Lieberman, S.   301, 370, 512, 630, 713, 748, 922, 980, 1004, 1029
Lipinski, E.   509
Lindblom, J.   510
Loewenstamm, S. E.   10, 247, 340, 371, 614, 738, 797, 1032, 1066, 1084
Lohfink, N.   806
Lohse, E.   151
Loretz, O.   173, 807
Löw, I.   1028
Luncz, A. M.   240
Lund, N. W.   670, 846, 859, 880
Luria, D.   1012
Luzzatto, S. (Shadal)   65, 151, 175, 192, 229, 232, 243, 244, 315, 326, 340, 341, 344, 406, 407, 599, 600, 627, 636, 655, 668, 759, 767, 776, 780, 785, 870, 874, 1013

Macht, D. I.   750
Maimonides   161, 162, 163, 180, 190, 191, 210, 221, 303, 365, 370, 399, 404, 406
Malamat, A.   13
Malbim   445, 573, 772, 787, 813, 831, 923
Margoliot, M.   1013
Martens, F.   740
Marx, A.   289, 290, 291, 292
Matthews, K. A.   909
Maurer, C.   372
Mauss, M.   441
Mazar, B.   145
McCarter, P. K. Jr.   211, 1004
McCarthy, D. J.   706
McEvenue, S. E.   10, 38, 39
McKenzie, J. L.   445
Meeks, D.   768
Meier, G.   960, 962, 979
Meier, S.   865
Meigs, A. S.   721, 1001
Meiri, M.   765
Mendelssohn, I.   315, 655, 850
Mendenhall, G. E.   589
Meṣudat, David   776
Metzinger, A.   441
Meyers, C. L.   30, 590
Middleton, J.   441
Miles, J. C.   294

Milgrom, J.   3, 5, 7, 8, 9, 10, 13, 15, 27, 35, 42, 45, 47, 55, 56, 58, 59, 60, 143, 145, 147, 148, 149, 151, 153, 155, 156, 182, 183, 186, 193, 200, 216, 217, 229, 231, 232, 233, 234, 240, 241, 242, 243, 245, 247, 251, 254, 255, 256, 257, 258, 259, 261, 262, 264, 266, 267, 268, 269, 278, 281, 283, 286, 288, 292, 295, 316, 317, 318, 321, 322, 323, 325, 327, 328, 332, 333, 336, 337, 338, 344, 345, 346, 348, 352, 353, 355, 356, 358, 359, 360, 362, 363, 364, 367, 368, 370, 372, 373, 376, 378, 383, 387, 388, 395, 410, 412, 415, 416, 419, 422, 431, 441, 443, 445, 446, 454, 457, 463, 473, 481, 484, 485, 486, 498, 502, 519, 541, 542, 549, 555, 563, 566, 573, 577, 578, 588, 593, 600, 601, 602, 612, 613, 614, 621, 623, 625, 630, 661, 668, 689, 694, 706, 707, 708, 711, 712, 713, 715, 718, 735, 738, 740, 745, 752, 753, 754, 755, 797, 804, 805, 806, 816, 821, 822, 835, 850, 854, 856, 861, 871, 887, 922, 929, 930, 932, 946, 949, 965, 971, 975, 977, 984, 1012, 1014, 1018, 1019, 1034, 1037, 1039, 1055, 1058, 1065, 1081, 1082, 1083, 1084
Milgrom, Jo   587
Milik, J. T.   795, 796, 797, 819, 915, 1014
Mitchell, D.   406
Mizrachi   780
Moffatt, J.   221
Montgomery, J. A.   806
Moore, G. F.   208
Moraites, R. S.   824
Moraldi, L.   333, 339, 340, 341
Moran, W. L.   701
Morgenstern, J.   634, 807
Morris, L.   339
Moyer, J. C.   230, 650, 677, 746, 841, 915, 933, 951
Muffs, Y.   475
Münch, G. N.   817
Münderlein, G.   207, 215
Munn-Rankin, J. M.   221

Naḥman, Moses ben (Nahmanides); see Ramban.
Negev, A.   1025
Nelson, H. M.   470, 472
Nemoy, L.   742
Neugebauer, O.   893
Neusner, J.   485, 486, 487, 675, 789, 842, 878, 919, 923, 1004, 1005, 1006, 1007, 1008
Nilsson, M. P.   27
Nöldeke, J.   706
Noth, M.   35, 65, 164, 295, 308, 309, 332, 505, 513, 537, 554, 604, 678, 751, 803
Nötscher, F.   864
Nougayrol, J.   805, 808, 820

Obbink, H. T.   234

INDEX OF AUTHORS

Oesterly, W. O. E.   443, 482
Oppenheim, A. L.   52, 59, 143, 196, 440, 456, 589, 775, 818, 1002
Orlinsky, H. M.   243, 293, 340, 603, 927
Otten, H.   139, 141, 472, 834, 864
Otto, R.   60, 517, 855

Paran, M.   5, 7, 8, 12, 38, 39, 40, 145, 147, 150, 160, 164, 165, 172, 184, 194, 234, 239, 240, 244, 301, 384, 389, 392, 438, 504, 523, 525, 526, 582, 586, 609, 647, 700, 748, 783, 799, 843, 858, 862, 1014, 1023, 1033
Pardee, D.   855
Parḥon, S. ibn   179
Parker, R.   624, 762, 763, 820, 932, 951
Parunak, H.   905, 931
Paschen, W.   686, 732, 768, 819, 1001, 1002
Patai, R.   568
Paton, L. B.   29, 428
Pedersen, J.   151, 305, 445, 705, 933
Peet, T.   302, 895
Pellett, P. L.   892
Peter, R.   151, 152, 232, 427
Pettazzoni, R.   302
Pfann, S.   169, 171, 502
Pines, R.   792, 811
Polzin, R.   8
Pope, M.   234
Popko, M.   139
Porten, B.   630
Preuss, J.   744, 750, 751, 816, 817, 907, 908

Qimron, E.   448, 653, 849

Rabad (Abraham ben David, Ibn Daud)   344, 406, 457
Rabin, C.   504, 927, 941
Radak (David Kimḥi)   65, 173, 179, 181, 247, 344, 397, 482, 483, 484, 594, 609, 685, 781, 792, 798, 799, 806, 853, 870, 923, 944
Rad, G. von   160, 231, 339, 362, 443, 457, 841, 928, 967, 1002
Rainey, A.   197, 382, 466, 488, 489
Ralbag (Levi ben Gershom)   65, 196, 806, 808
Ramban (Moses ben Naḥman)   63, 65, 134, 142, 146, 153, 155, 159, 160, 163, 170, 172, 175, 188, 210, 211, 232, 265, 280, 301, 341, 365, 382, 384, 386, 392, 408, 427, 440, 457, 461, 501, 504, 513, 535, 576, 585, 587, 588, 604, 605, 607, 610, 612, 645, 647, 655, 661, 662, 664, 667, 668, 672, 679, 680, 681, 683, 691, 716, 719, 748, 765, 780, 785, 788, 792, 793, 794, 800, 811, 840, 844, 856, 858, 866, 874, 883, 921, 926, 934, 948, 1012, 1016, 1020, 1026, 1046, 1054
Randolph, J.   905, 909, 930, 931
Rankin, O. S.   592
Rashbam (Meir, Samuel ben)   64, 65, 134, 153, 156, 215, 220, 300, 307, 344, 399, 400, 421, 433, 463, 582, 588, 590, 599, 601, 646,

667, 674, 678, 680, 707, 719, 739, 773, 797, 831, 908, 1014, 1018, 1045
Rashi (Isaac, Solomon ben)   63, 64, 65, 151, 172, 185, 187, 208, 210, 213, 244, 253, 299, 300, 326, 338, 344, 383, 388, 392, 400, 403, 410, 413, 420, 444, 457, 501, 502, 524, 540, 565, 581, 592, 600, 606, 615, 621, 622, 626, 646, 647, 661, 664, 667, 671, 678, 679, 680, 684, 685, 707, 723, 745, 748, 765, 776, 778, 779, 782, 783, 784, 787, 788, 789, 790, 792, 797, 799, 800, 811, 812, 813, 815, 835, 844, 851, 869, 871, 873, 874, 877, 908, 1014, 1016, 1027
Rattray, S.   5, 147, 148, 157, 232, 248, 252, 430, 454, 585, 846, 867, 926, 934, 1026, 1030
Reif, S. C.   592
Reiner, E.   21, 23, 230, 262, 302, 306, 313, 349, 361, 387, 834, 835, 911, 960, 962, 976, 1078
Rendsburg, G.   8
Rendtorff, R.   136, 147, 153, 157, 216, 217, 219, 267, 268, 308, 457, 482, 698, 702, 709, 832, 863
Renger, J.   52
Reymond, P.   482
Rhode, E.   762
Ridderbos, N. H.   686
Rinaldi, G.   749
Ringgren, H.   151, 958
Ritter, E. K.   976
Rivlin, J. J.   765
Robertson, E.   511
Robinson, H. W.   151
Robinson, E.   212
Rodriguez, A. M.   228, 243, 255, 256, 295, 298, 410, 441, 521, 625, 708, 1044
Rogerson, J. W.   853
Rosenthal, J.   303
Rost, L.   175, 472, 1076
Rothenberg, B.   30
Roubos, K.   482
Rowley, H. H.   443, 482
Rudolph, W   807
Rüger, H. P.   170
Rupprecht, K.   539
Ryckmans, G.   311, 910, 932, 935
Ryssel, V.   20, 65, 145, 151, 157, 164, 167, 176, 190, 194, 203, 208, 214, 222, 232, 243, 298, 304, 305, 384, 391, 400, 433, 525, 583, 622, 647, 666, 673, 678, 679, 745, 747, 750, 766, 782, 805, 809, 832, 930, 931, 939, 1002

Saadiah ben Joseph   63, 64, 134, 146, 159, 181, 193, 210, 211, 214, 228, 232, 234, 238, 244, 397, 425, 429, 437, 495, 527, 587, 610, 647, 655, 661, 662, 667, 679, 680, 685, 748, 784, 785, 787, 792, 802, 803, 811, 814, 815, 831, 832, 835, 852, 863, 870, 873, 884, 914, 927, 941, 1014, 1020

INDEX OF AUTHORS

Sachs, A.   893
Safrai, S.   159, 387, 635
Saggs, H. W. F.   52, 528, 972
Salonen, A.   894
San Nicolo, M.   336
Sansom, M. C.   151
Sarna, N. M.   397, 853, 908, 1004
Sauenron, S., 19, 52, 53, 59, 143, 412, 440, 456, 468, 853, 854, 932, 951, 959
Sauer, A. von Rohr   652
Sawyer, J. F. A.   775
Schmid, R.   221
Schottroff, W.   181
Schwartz, B.   422, 688, 706, 1000
Schweitzer   736
Scott, R. B. Y.   800, 890, 891
Scott, J. A.   30
Segal, P.   601, 602
Seidel, J.   652
Seidl, T.   794, 873, 879
Sforno (Obadiah ben Jacob)   65, 134, 138, 522, 610, 839, 842, 844
Shadal; see Luzzatto
Shadarevian, S.   892
Shalem, N.   788
Shapira, J. L.   772
Shinan, A.   634
Simoons, F. J.   649
Singer, I.   1017, 1022, 1030, 1049
Sjöberg, A.   575
Skinner, J.   482, 712
Smith, W. R.   174, 191, 198, 220, 249, 440, 706, 718, 763, 766, 873, 874, 932, 951
Snaith, N. H.   65, 159, 168, 213, 232, 305, 308, 320, 498, 528, 537, 538, 591, 596, 604, 615, 628, 655, 674, 680, 716, 789, 800, 808, 870
Soden, W. von   147, 475, 537, 569, 575, 609
Soler, J.   740
Sollberger, E.   549, 550
Sommer, F.   688, 758, 761, 764
Sontag, S.   824
Soucek, V.   472, 834
Speiser, E. A.   326, 328, 409, 712, 861
Sperber, A.   338, 811
Spiro, A.   309
Stager, L. E.   180, 652, 873
Stengel, P.   750
Stern, E.   871
Stern, M.   652
Stevenson, M.   750
Strashun, S.   1013
Streck, M.   539
Strugnell, J.   242, 448, 653, 849
Sznycer, M.   738

Tadmor, H.   36, 252
Tal, A.   788
Tallquist, K.   1046, 1072

Talmon, S.   252
Tarragon, J.-M. de   172, 519
Tawil, H.   1021, 1046, 1072, 1077
Thompson, R. C.   834, 960, 976, 979, 1026, 1028, 1078, 1082
Thompson, R. J.   174, 175, 443
Thureau-Dangin, F.   337, 433, 893, 1080
Tiferet Israel   881
Toeg, A.   266
Toorn, K. van der   24, 822
Tov, E.   819
Tsevat, M.   314
Tufnell, O.   620
Tur-Sinai, N. H.   170, 803, 809
Turner, V. W.   42, 272, 567, 569, 950, 1083
Tylor, E. B.   440

Unger, E.   893
Updike, J.   824
Urbach, E. E.   303

Van Beek, G. W.   180
Van Gennep, A.   291, 566
Vaux, R. de   140, 151, 220, 221, 308, 310, 420, 441, 473, 482, 513, 557, 651, 652
Veenhof, K. R.   855
Vieyra, M.   472, 664
Virolleaud, C.   738, 806
Voltz, P.   151, 482
Vriezen, T. C.   233, 853

Walkenhorst, K. -H.   546
Wapnish, P.   723
Wayne, A.   741
Weidner, E. F.   349
Weinberg, Z.   879
Weinfeld, M.   3, 30, 139, 142, 143, 173, 199, 201, 219, 437, 601, 614, 628, 699, 758, 821, 822, 834, 865, 1048
Welch, A. C.   482
Welhausen, J.   5, 29, 211, 236, 283, 294, 428, 482, 508, 692, 745
Wenham, G.   65, 604, 664, 673, 749, 750, 768, 808, 882, 1063
Wertheimer, S. A.   681
Wessely, N. H.   65, 150, 161, 163, 193, 205, 210, 218, 248, 301, 307, 315, 335, 383, 402, 407, 420, 532, 573, 655, 664, 672, 743, 744, 755, 773, 779, 781, 784, 785, 786, 788, 792, 793, 798, 800, 801, 805, 813, 815, 839, 850, 853, 870, 871, 872, 908, 914, 920, 923, 938, 939, 944
Westermann, C.   142
Westermarck, E.   440
Wheeler, A. J.   504
White, H. A.   65, 787, 810, 862, 870, 873, 874, 931, 945
Wilhelm, G.   758
Wilkinson, J.   776

INDEX OF AUTHORS

Williams, R. J.   778
Wilson, J. A.   141
Wilson, M.   950
Wiseman, D. J.   349, 517, 820
Wohl, R.   985
Wold, D. J.   460
Wolff, H. W.   286, 652
Wolff, S. R.   180
Wouk, H.   726
Wright, D. P.   151, 152, 153, 174, 184, 204,
   230, 238, 255, 392, 402, 422, 424, 425, 472,
   473, 495, 528, 581, 616, 621, 674, 675, 677,
   678, 698, 716, 752, 758, 764, 778, 782, 794,
   805, 806, 812, 815, 817, 818, 823, 834, 848,
   865, 872, 876, 883, 888, 913, 914, 918, 935,
   953, 954, 956, 976, 993, 1000, 1014, 1017,
   1022, 1041, 1042, 1046, 1057, 1067, 1072,
   1073, 1074, 1075, 1077, 1078, 1079, 1081,
   1082

Wright, G. H. B.   819
Wright, L. S.   333
Wylie, C. C.   890

Yadin, Y.   159, 165, 405, 558, 563, 565, 665,
   765, 804, 845, 863, 929, 969, 973, 1007, 1025
Yahel 'Or   188, 192
Yefet ben Ali   538, 540
Yeivin, S.   629, 808

Zadok, P.   1021
Zevit, Z.   10
Ziderman, I. I.   502
Zimmerli, W.   230, 231, 295, 339
Zucker, M.   754
Zuidhof, A.   306, 398
Zunz, L.   299

INDEX OF SOURCES

Genesis

1:2–3 19	3:28 777	9:3–6 705
1:2 658	3:14 683	9:4–5 712
1:3 511	4:3–4 197	9:4–6 47
1:4 689	4:10 296, 712, 749, 783	9:4 26, 46, 49, 251, 705,
1:6–8 15	4:11 749	709, 1002
1:6 689	4:13 25, 295, 339	9:5 712, 720
1:7 689	5:1 4	9:5ab 705
1:11 743	5:2 145	9:5b 705
1:12 743	6:1 973	9:6 705, 710
1:14 689, 799	6:9 26	9:7 664
1:18 689	6:11 26, 48, 615	9:9–10 712, 720
1:20–23 15	6:12–13 705	9:10 305, 656, 712
1:20–21 664	6:13 341, 615	9:11 298
1:20 298, 656, 658, 701, 712	6:14 1080	9:12 16, 656, 712
1:21 656, 660, 687, 689,	6:19–22 47	9:13–14 711
701, 712	6:34 341	9:15 656, 712
1:22 701	7:8 687	9:16 656
1:24–27 743	7:10 788	9:17 712
1:24–26 645	7:11 680	10:3 662
1:24 656, 712	7:14 687	10:4 662
1:25 658	7:21 664, 687	10:8 973
1:26 658, 687, 688, 701, 705	8:7 663, 702, 840	11:5 931
1:28 645, 687, 688, 701	8:8 168	12:11 145, 743
1:29 417, 705, 707	8:9 726	12:17 776
1:30 645, 656, 687, 701, 712	8:17 305, 645, 664, 687	13:18 748
1:31 780	8:19 645, 687	14:10 799
2:3 19, 615	8:20 173, 174	14:12 538
2:7 712	8:21 162	14:14 592
2:17 653	8:22 705	15:5 921
2:19–20 660	9:1–11 722	15:6 403
2:19 712, 840	9:1–5 773	15:9 168, 572
2:24 931	9:2 687, 701	15:13 1054
2:33 653	9:3 687, 707	15:15 460
3:14 720	9:3–4 417, 711, 712	15:16 25
3:16 621	9:3–5 722	16:6 1054

1108

16:10 858
17:1–27 747
17:1 26
17:2 722, 788
17:7–8 8
17:8 614
17:9 16
17:10 744
17:11 747, 748
17:12 16
17:14 457, 458, 747, 748
17:17 627
17:17a 627
17:17b 627
17:20 247
17:22 173
17:23–25 748
17:23 747
17:24 747
17:25 747
18:4 335
18:5 185
18:6–7 901
18:6 179
18:23 260
18:23ff 376
18:24 295
19:7 154
19:9 627
19:11 147
19:13 234
19:14 780
19:15 25
19:19 627
20:6 685
20:7 376
20:9 232
20:11 26
20:17–18 232
21:5a 874
21:14 171, 1023
21:22–32 300
22 249
22:2 174
22:7 174
22:8 174
22:10 715
22:13 173, 174
23:2 610
23:10 341
23:17 521
23:18 305
24:2–9 747
24:5 300
24:8 347
24:12 247
24:19 193
24:31 869
24:35 861

24:41 347
24:51 600
24:55 748
24:64 591, 937
25:8 460
25:16 11
25:17 460
25:24 831
26:10 231, 341
26:19 837
26:29 922
26:30 191, 222
27:11 248
27:3 673
27:9 248
27:33–35 299
28:4 614
28:11 168
28:16–19 250
28:18 518, 554
29:21 755
29:27 538
30:31 786
30:38 403
31:13 554
31:24 300
31:34–35 751
31:34 937
31:35 765, 948
31:39 427, 1084
31:44–53 300
31:50 220
31:54 191, 222
32:14 196
32:19 196
32:21 196, 1084
33:10 196
33:18 234
34:2 1054
34:5–13 1005
34:8 421
34:14–17 747
34:15 1015
34:22 747, 1015
34:41–40 421
35:2 840
35:2–3 966
35:5–6 966
35:12 614
35:13 173
35:14 554
35:18 707
35:29 460
36:24 420
37:20 680
37:23 156
37:25 1027, 1028
37:29 609
37:33 427

37:34 609
38:28 1022
39:8–9 26
39:8 26
39:10 387
39:20 805
40:2 609
40:15 874
41:6 793
41:10 609
41:19 184, 861
41:36 335
42:15 1015
42:18 26
42:21 340
42:30 243
42:33 1015
43:7 625
43:11 189, 1027
43:16 716
44:28 427
45:5 784
45:18 207, 210
47:22 395
47:29–31 747
47:30 460
48:14 150
48:17–19 528
48:18 150
48:22 777
49:4 909
49:6 150
49:8 305
49:26 512
49:27 427
49:33 460
50:10 538
50:17 295, 623

Exodus

1:7 664, 788
1:10 626
1:19 832
2:5 506
2:7 555
2:13 282, 783
2:16–21 11
2:25 777
3:4 137, 139
3:5 137, 502, 654
3:16 244
3:18 482
4:6 774, 786
4:26 747
4:29 244
5:2 1023
5:3 482
5:8 482

INDEX OF SOURCES

5:17   482
5:22   60, 588
6:2   15, 687
6:6   687
6:7   8, 432, 686, 688
6:8   587, 687
6:11   840
6:16–20   1019
6:16   264
6:18   604
6:21   604
6:22   604
6:25   168
6:29   687
7:3f   375
7:8–13   47
7:17   1015
7:26   840, 1012
7:28   664
8:1–30   447
8:8   60, 588
8:12–15   47
8:16   1012
8:21   573
8:25–26   60, 588
8:25   211, 573
8:28   375
9:5   587
9:8–12   47
9:9   785, 787
9:10   785, 787
9:11   264
9:13   1012
9:18   383
9:29   60, 587, 908
9:31   193
9:33   60, 587
10:1   375
10:4   626
10:5   813
10:11   787
10:12   218
10:13   626
10:17   623, 626
10:18   60, 626
10:25   174, 176, 400, 482
11   225, 459
11:1   776
11:4   260
11:10   375
12   688
12:1–14   282
12:3   241, 498, 740
12:3–6   153, 283
12:5   757, 798
12:7   249, 279, 707
12:8–10   463
12:8–9   182
12:8   220

12:9   159
12:10   182, 219, 324, 637
12:10a   638
12:12–13   260
12:12   687
12:12b   638
12:14   395, 619
12:15   191, 265, 283, 458
12:16   21
12:17   395, 619
12:19–20   283
12:19   241, 458, 498, 1055
12:20   215
12:21   241, 244, 498, 715
12:22   249, 279, 836, 838
12:23   218, 260, 483
12:27   1081
12:29   260
12:38   809
12:43–49   747
12:43   619
12:47–49   696
12:47   241, 498
12:48   577, 1055
13:2   724
13:4   194
13:7   283, 1055
13:15   153
14:3   207
14:4   603
14:8   305
14:8–10   571
14:10   145
14:17   603
14:18   603
14:23   571
15:6   528
15:8   965
15:12   686
15:13   781
15:16   604
15:25   835, 888
15:26   617, 888
16:1–3   242
16:1   241, 498
16:2   4, 408
16:3   408
16:9   1012
16:10   1015
16:12   686
16:13   927
16:14–15   571
16:14   173, 927
16:16   408, 500, 845, 895, 1023
16:17   408
16:18–19   279, 571
16:20   408, 609
16:21   387

16:23   408, 840
16:27   408
16:29   748
16:31   1057
16:32   500
16:34   1031
16:36   845, 895
17:6   244
17:15   141
18:12   174, 176, 218, 223, 225, 244, 441, 482, 483, 619
18:16   230, 617
18:20   617
18:22   556, 909, 1012
18:26   1012
19:1–2   142
19:1   437, 438
19:2   437
19:4   662
19:6   359, 617, 687, 730, 731
19:10–15   929, 965, 969
19:10–11   143
19:10   445, 667, 840, 974
19:12–13   45
19:13   314, 454
19:14–15   143
19:14   445, 840
19:15   929, 931
19:17   143
19:20–20:1   142
19:20   143
19:20b   143
19:21b   143
19:22   142, 600, 601, 602
19:24   142, 143, 601
20:2   688
20:4–5   1021
20:5   25, 623
20:7   300, 367, 374
20:8–11   40
20:10–11   615
20:10   19, 720
20:11   21
20:12   743
20:16   367
20:18   574
20:21   143
20:24   218, 250, 573
20:25   171, 470
20:26   385, 587
21:2   772
21:4   383
21:8   664, 755
21:12–14   486
21:14   251
21:15   798
21:17   669, 798
21:23   707

21:25 790
21:28–32 712
21:28 720
21:29 145
21:30 708, 1082
21:31 736, 786
21:32 716, 720
21:33 680, 772
21:37 328, 336, 669, 772
22:1 749
22:2 749
22:3 328, 330, 336
22:4 243, 772
22:5 772
22:6–12 367
22:6 335, 772
22:7 299, 1012
22:9 772
22:12 427
22:19 1021
22:20 571
22:25–26 337, 909
22:26–27 571
22:26 814
22:27 374
22:29 738, 739
22:30 207, 359, 687, 703, 729
23:3 861
23:4 329, 772
23:5 772
23:5 809
23:10 40
23:12 1056
23:16 192
23:16a 1070
23:16b 1069
23:17 737
23:18–19a 739
23:18 217, 218, 483, 638, 714
23:19 10, 190, 191, 192, 703, 704, 737, 741
23:19aβ 737
23:21 295
23:26 458
23:28 775
23:32 1057
24:1 143, 437, 596
24:3–8 141
24:3 230
24:4–8 556
24:4 143, 437
24:5 173, 176, 217, 222, 224, 225, 473, 482, 483, 619
24:6 155, 573
24:9–10 499
24:9–11 596

24:9 244
24:10–11 574
24:10 755
24:11 191, 222, 619
24:11b 573
24:13 143
24:15b–25:1 142
24:15–18 136, 142
24:15b–18a 589
24:15bff 143
24:16–17 58
24:16 59
24:16a 137
24:16b 137
24:17 574, 576, 589, 590, 599, 777
24:17a 58, 589
24:18 136
24:18a 58, 137
25:1 136
25:2 461, 521
25:2–3 415, 473
25:4 674, 1057
25:5 461, 783
25:6 237
25:7 506
25:8 754
25:9 141, 437
25:10–40 1062
25:13–15 1029
25:15 391
25:17–21 53
25:17 1014
25:19 4
25:22 58, 134, 138, 140, 142, 143, 437, 1014, 1031
25:23–30 236
25:27 213
25:28 506
25:29 59, 389, 612
25:30 389
25:31–40 236
25:31–37 39
25:31–34 520
25:31 164
25:33 1035
25:37 173
25:38 597, 1025
25:40 141, 436, 437, 811
26 236
26:1 548
26:7–14 36
26:7 36, 516
26:12–13 4
26:12 783
26:23 36
26:30 36, 141, 436, 811
26:31–35 234
26:31 548

26:33 36, 234, 321, 408, 944, 1013, 1063
26:36 234, 502
27:1–8 160, 250, 1062
27:1 4
27:2 234, 250
27:3 171, 386, 581, 597, 716
27:8 141, 436
27:9–19 533
27:9 36, 605
27:16 502
27:17 4, 521
27:20–30:38 237
27:20–21 237
27:20 173
27:21 207, 232, 238, 395, 619, 1031
28 977
28:1–29:37 237
28:1 147, 434, 1018
28:4 502, 511, 549
28:6–12 39
28:6–4 506
28:6 506, 548, 1016
28:8 506
28:15–16 4
28:15 506, 507, 548
28:16 507
28:17–20 507, 788
28:17 384
28:21 507
28:22–27 507
28:27 213, 506
28:28 506, 507
28:29 54, 234, 548, 605, 626, 1063
28:30 54, 507, 508
28:30a 549
28:31–35 504
28:31 400
28:32 504
28:33–34 1013
28:35 234, 238, 506, 605, 613, 626, 753, 1063
28:36 512, 545
28:37 511
28:38 25, 55, 321, 512, 623, 624, 1045
28:39–42 384
28:39 502, 511, 548
28:40 1016
28:41 518, 538
28:42–43 502, 918, 1017
28:42 385
28:43 8, 16, 25, 138, 233, 408, 612, 613, 619, 623, 624, 626, 634, 753, 911, 946, 1048
29 141, 278, 436, 438, 576

29:1–37 436, 447
29:1–4 495
29:1 498, 1018
29:2 179, 414, 498, 527, 545
29:3 498, 530, 545, 547
29:4 147, 434, 500, 546, 547
29:5–6 498, 513, 548
29:5 502, 504, 506, 549
29:6 511, 512, 545
29:7–9a 520
29:7 280, 357, 464, 514,
  518, 520, 532, 548
29:7a 515
29:7aβ 515
29:8–9 385, 498
29:8 547, 1018
29:9 436, 502, 520, 538,
  548, 619, 1016
29:9a 547, 610
29:9b 539, 555
29:10–26 539
29:10–14 523, 562, 636
29:10 210, 500, 520, 546,
  547, 562, 565
29:11 393, 500, 546
29:12 255, 521, 523, 547
29:12b 523
29:13 159, 161
29:14 264, 274, 498, 520,
  525, 547
29:15–18 282, 517
29:15 520, 533
29:16–18 562
29:16 255, 495, 521
29:17–18 526
29:17 159, 526, 582
29:18 161, 162, 526
29:19–21 562
29:19–20 532
29:19 520
29:20–21 520, 522, 530,
  533, 563
29:20 249, 255, 279, 522,
  528, 530, 532, 626, 707
29:21–26 546
29:21 249, 280, 357, 385,
  436, 445, 447, 448, 518,
  522, 530, 532, 533, 546,
  555
29:22–26 504, 532
29:22–25 56
29:22–24 416, 476
29:22–23 470
29:22 159, 210, 530
29:23–24 198, 563
29:23 183, 462, 530
29:24–25 430, 464, 563
29:24 461, 470, 563, 564
29:25 161, 162, 461

29:25–29 533
29:25–28 414
29:26 432, 462, 476
29:27–28 225, 280, 415,
  433, 462, 464, 527, 621
29:27 432, 473, 474, 476,
  481, 621
29:28 395, 434, 461, 618
29:29 436, 538, 540, 607,
  608, 610, 1011
29:29b 539
29:30 233, 321, 434, 537,
  605
29:31–36 533
29:31–32 533, 535
29:31 392, 533
29:32–33 222, 709
29:32 36
29:33–34 225, 637
29:33 211, 525, 529, 535,
  540, 541, 587, 637, 706,
  1082, 1083
29:33a 547
29:33b 539, 565
29:34 219, 322, 324, 421,
  422, 535, 638
29:34b 547
29:35–37 517, 537
29:35–36 539
29:35 282, 538, 540, 565
29:35b 540
29:35b–37a 537
29:36–38 1070
29:36–37 253, 269, 278,
  513, 521, 523, 538, 540,
  1036
29:36–37a 279, 522
29:36 282, 290, 333, 402,
  515, 517, 524, 525, 529,
  540, 562, 583, 882, 1036,
  1071
29:37–28 473
29:37 251, 282, 443, 445,
  446, 455, 487, 521, 525,
  977
29:37b 533
29:38–43 250, 390
29:38–42 163, 237, 411,
  436, 1017
29:38–41 163, 383
29:38–40 584
29:38–39 208
29:38 1022
29:39–41 388
29:39 516, 576
29:40 389, 400, 895
29:40a 398
29:41 162, 523
29:42–43 136, 140, 142

29:42 138, 389, 437
29:43 600
29:44 1033
29:45 8
29:46 688
29:46a 686
29:46b 686
30:1 440
30:1–10 236, 237
30:1–2 4
30:2 234
30:3 4, 236, 250, 521
30:6–8 1013
30:6 58, 134, 140, 1031
30:7–8 54, 180, 232, 237,
  398, 599, 614, 1024
30:7 160, 237, 597, 1017,
  1026
30:8 238
30:9 59, 205, 598, 634, 1063
30:9b 236
30:10 255, 525, 1023, 1035,
  1059, 1062, 1063
30:11–16 707
30:12–16 417, 1082
30:12–15 39
30:12 707, 708, 1082
30:13–15 415, 473
30:13 461
30:14–15 475
30:15–16 708
30:16 1082
30:17–21 160, 237, 1048
30:18 518
30:19 1017
30:20–21 946
30:20 138, 233, 450, 501,
  612, 613, 753
30:21 16, 612, 619, 634
30:22–30 237, 533
30:22–33 231, 1063
30:23–24 498, 516
30:23 237
30:25–29 515
30:25 464, 611, 851
30:26–30 393, 447, 1036
30:26–29 443, 450, 454,
  455, 514
30:26–28 443
30:26a 321
30:29–30 606
30:29 321, 443, 446
30:30 518, 607
30:31–32 553, 554
30:31 611, 1063
30:32–33 1063
30:32 21, 321, 464, 520, 851
30:33 321, 458, 554, 1030
30:34–38 237, 1063

30:34–35 1026
30:34–36 180, 597, 598
30:35 1031
30:36 134, 140, 321, 1025,
  1031, 1063
30:37–38 199, 631
30:37 21, 321, 598, 634
30:38 458
31:4 506, 605
31:11 237
31:12–17 11, 696
31:13–17 39, 40
31:13 4, 333, 614
31:14 21, 38, 458, 460
31:18 136, 436, 437, 1031
32 461
32:4 1016
32:6 173, 176, 217, 482
32:8 482
32:11–13 60, 376
32:14 437
32:17 143
32:25 609
32:26–29 437
32:29 538, 539, 615
32:30–34 708, 1083
32:30–31 60
32:31f: 376
32:34 403
33:7–11 60, 140, 141, 142
33:7 140
33:11 134, 140
33:12–16 376
33:18 577
33:19 1043
33:20 136
33:22–23 140
33:22 577
34:2 966
34:2b 143
34:5 1043
34:7 245, 623
34:9–10 245
34:9 25, 376
34:15–16 726
34:15 573, 714
34:22 192
34:22b 1069
34:23 737
34:25–26 739
34:25 217, 218, 483, 638,
  714, 715
34:26 10, 190, 191, 703,
  704, 737
34:26aB 737
34:28 136
34:29–35 136
34:31 139
34:32 436, 437

34:34 238
35:1–3 696
35:2 21, 1057
35:3 215, 387
35:4 5, 243, 500
35:5 415, 814
35:8–9 4
35:9 506
35:11 36
35:20 5, 243
35:21 415, 473
35:22 461, 462, 472
35:24 415, 416, 473, 474,
  476
35:27 505
35:32 505
35:35 505
36:2–3 53
36:2 1011, 1012
36:3 415, 473
36:4 387
36:6 293, 387, 415, 473
36:14 36, 516
36:22a 1070
36:30 387
36:35 4
37:14 213
37:16 59, 612
37:17 164
37:23 597
37:25–28 236
37:26 521
38:1–7 160, 250
38:3 155, 597
38:8 535
38:10 1062
38:14–15 4
38:16 521
38:24 416, 462, 472, 476
38:29 462
38:30 250
39 61
39:1–31 499
39:1 543
39:3 502, 506
39:5 506, 543
39:7 543
39:17 384
39:20 213, 506
39:21 506, 543
39:26 543
39:27–29 520
39:27 502
39:28 511, 520
39:29 384, 452, 520, 543,
  1016
39:30 512
39:31 511, 543
40:1–15 447

40:1 36, 561
40:2 36
40:6 36
40:8–9 4
40:8 521
40:9–16 393, 1036
40:9–15 513, 554
40:9–13 514
40:9–11 514, 545
40:9 321, 448, 515
40:10 321, 515
40:10a 515
40:10b 515, 516
40:11 515
40:12 147
40:13–15 447
40:13 290
40:15 436, 518
40:15a 554, 607
40:15b 555, 607, 608, 610
40:17–38 499
40:17–33 61, 494, 543
40:17 561, 571
40:19 543
40:20–21 575
40:21 543
40:22–27 556
40:22 36, 164
40:23 238, 543
40:24 36, 164
40:25 173, 238, 543
40:27 543
40:29 36, 173, 390, 543, 584
40:30 164
40:32 543, 613, 753, 1012
40:32b 533
40:33 521
40:33a 533, 543
40:34–38 543
40:34–35 58, 59, 575, 588,
  1014
40:34b 137
40:35 134, 136, 138, 499
40:35a 137
40:35b 137, 139
40:36–38 61, 139
40:36 58
40:38 137, 575, 589, 1015

Leviticus

1:1–2 53, 203
1:1 36, 58, 59, 136, 138,
  139, 436, 437, 438
1:1b 137
1:2–13 844
1:2 56, 144, 178, 204, 216,
  228, 284, 319, 383, 388,
  411, 438, 482, 484, 520,

617, 721, 772, 1012, 1040
1:3–17 203
1:3 26, 144, 147, 168, 195,
    204, 209, 320, 520, 600,
    714, 1040
1:4–5 444
1:4 177, 204, 252, 268, 288,
    477, 484, 586, 758, 862
1:4a 163
1:5–7 220, 255, 305, 408,
1:5 146, 147, 157, 181, 204,
    208, 209, 409, 410, 417,
    582, 777, 852, 1025, 1040
1:6–9 526
1:6 777
1:6a 163
1:7 208, 777
1:7b 157
1:8 157, 169, 208, 213, 388,
    526, 777
1:8b 351
1:9 4, 157, 162, 180, 213,
    237, 252, 389, 411, 440,
    462, 526, 582, 777, 1023
1:9b 216
1:10–13 213, 383
1:10 26, 144, 213, 320, 714,
    1040
1:11 53, 150, 156, 157, 209,
    210, 213, 248, 255, 305,
    393, 409, 417, 438, 582,
    600, 777, 852
1:12 156, 157, 169, 209,
    388, 777
1:13 157, 159, 162, 180,
    252, 389, 582, 1023
1:13b 216
1:14–17 62, 63, 145, 196,
    222
1:14 144, 168, 195, 305,
    320, 701, 709, 714, 761,
    1040
1:15–17 156
1:15 147, 157, 181, 305,
    777, 836
1:16 170, 240, 386, 1032
1:16b 216
1:17 162, 168, 180, 250,
    252, 777
1:17b 216
2:1–5:13 438
2:1–7 391
2:1–4 351
2:1–3 198, 389, 392, 438,
    858
2:1 38, 59, 145, 228, 306,
    319, 464, 597, 772, 777,
    684, 1054
2:2–3 438

2:2 156, 157, 162, 180, 186,
    208, 306, 390, 413, 443,
    573, 583, 584, 597, 630,
    1026
2:2b 777
2:3 33, 63, 307, 390, 392,
    394, 395, 412, 438, 462,
    584, 618
2:4–10 11, 198, 389
2:4–7 438, 530
2:4–5 390, 392
2:4 319, 400
2:5 320, 400
2:6 166
2:7 320
2:8–9 391
2:8 147, 152, 156, 391, 520,
    547
2:9–10 619
2:9 161, 162, 199, 391, 400,
    443, 474, 486, 583, 777
2:10 33, 63, 187, 202, 307,
    392, 432, 438, 481
2:11 392, 412, 414, 464
2:12 156, 162, 190, 463
2:13 437, 440
2:14–26 867
2:14–16 62, 63, 198, 200
2:14 186, 193, 194, 320
2:15–16 1026
2:15 59, 166, 597
2:16 208, 413, 583, 777
3:1ff 29
3:1 26, 144, 147, 220, 320,
    411, 520, 600, 1012, 716
3:1a 1024
3:2 49, 156, 165, 208, 255,
    320, 409, 477, 582, 586,
    600, 777
3:3–5 151, 171, 386
3:3–4 410, 438, 580
3:3 159, 239, 244, 252, 525,
    716
3:4 159, 239, 413, 580, 585,
    1023
3:5 156, 161, 162, 180, 208,
    388, 525, 582, 777
3:5b 216
3:6–16 164
3:6–11 252
3:6 26, 144, 147, 163, 168,
    320
3:7 165, 427, 520, 1012
3:7a 1024
3:8 49, 150, 156, 255, 409,
    477, 582, 586, 600, 777
3:9–11 171, 386
3:9–10 410, 427, 438
3:9 147, 151, 159, 239, 244,

252, 410, 530, 585, 1024
3:10 239, 413, 580, 1023
3:11 151, 156, 160, 525, 777
3:11b 216
3:12–17 252
3:12 144, 195, 320
3:13 49, 165, 255, 409, 477,
    582, 586, 777
3:14–16 151, 171, 386
3:14–15 410, 438
3:14 15, 159, 239, 244, 252
3:15 239, 413, 580, 585,
    1023
3:16 159, 162, 180, 525, 777
3:16b–17 28, 29, 62, 63, 215
3:16b 10, 28
3:17 159, 216, 228, 395,
    428, 429, 619, 704, 709
3:17b 439
4 17, 265, 267, 268, 269,
    281, 291
4:1–21 401, 406, 408, 980,
    981, 1051, 1062
4:1–12 156, 267, 272, 407,
    636
4:1 53
4:2–4 295
4:2 21, 24, 26, 38, 145, 178,
    230, 298, 308, 312, 319,
    331, 332, 369, 424, 438,
    486, 522, 772, 822, 857,
    858, 684
4:2a 332
4:2b 308
4:2aβ 308
4:3–21 242, 637, 1044, 1062
4:3–12 281, 522, 581, 1019
4:3 11, 50, 147, 228, 231,
    248, 268, 320, 331, 365,
    520, 572, 581, 609, 978,
    1065, 714
4:4 146, 164, 270, 522, 1024
4:4b 295
4:5–7 257
4:5 231
4:5a 295
4:6–7 261, 270, 291, 528,
    1035
4:6 155, 233, 270, 306, 516,
    537, 838, 853, 1019, 1025
4:7 156, 205, 239, 270, 305,
    306, 443, 523, 547, 656,
    707, 840
4:8–10 151, 306, 415, 474
4:8–9 171, 211, 386, 580
4:8 159, 205, 385, 474, 486,
    1023
4:9 50, 580
4:10 161, 205, 214, 239,

385, 474, 486
4:10b   1039
4:11–13   401
4:11–12   164, 261, 270, 306,
   585
4:11   159, 208, 273, 413
4:12   161, 262, 387, 423,
   565, 580, 625, 656, 831,
   872, 1008
4:13–21   11, 55, 176, 263,
   272, 278, 281, 407, 408,
   517, 537, 583, 638
4:13–14   345
4:13   21, 50, 228, 230, 291,
   298, 308, 320, 331, 332,
   338, 403, 486, 1052
4:13b   332
4:14–26   295
4:14–21   267
4:14   232, 266, 332, 436,
   486, 572, 581, 714, 1018
4:14b–15a   210
4:15–20   267
4:15   153, 164, 213, 409,
   499, 522, 547, 565, 583,
   1024
4:16–18   257
4:16   161, 231
4:17–18   291, 1035
4:17   233, 270, 306, 516,
   838, 853, 1019
4:17a   401
4:18   156, 205, 239, 270,
   305, 306, 443, 523, 547,
   840
4:18b   1039
4:19–21   268
4:19   205, 211, 306, 385,
   474, 486
4:20   37, 256, 291, 400, 709,
   760, 1019
4:21   161, 164, 166, 306,
   401, 423, 831, 1044
4:22–35   55, 272, 425, 426,
   638, 931, 980, 1052
4:22–26   56, 267
4:22–23   345
4:22ff   981
4:22   21, 50, 228, 230, 269,
   296, 308, 331, 332, 338,
   403, 486
4:23   50, 147, 230, 331, 332,
   427, 486, 714
4:24   164, 166, 230, 239,
   274, 305, 320, 401, 409,
   522, 848, 1024
4:25–26   291
4:25   156, 205, 257, 270,
   305, 306, 443, 517, 523,

528, 547, 622, 707, 840,
   1023
4:25b   1039
4:26   37, 256, 306, 709, 760,
   857, 858, 926, 1019
4:27–38   521
4:27–35   164, 176, 268, 303,
   308, 844
4:27–28   344, 345
4:27   38, 50, 308, 320, 331,
   332, 338, 403, 486
4:28   147, 268, 307, 333,
   427, 486
4:29   164, 230, 305, 320,
   401, 409, 444, 522, 848,
   1024
4:30–31   291
4:30   156, 239, 257, 261,
   270, 305, 306, 443, 517,
   523, 547, 622, 840
4:30b   1039
4:31   37, 205, 211, 230, 239,
   256, 291, 306, 415, 474,
   709, 760, 926, 1019, 1023
4:32–35   267
4:32   147, 195, 228, 307,
   308, 320, 331, 333
4:33   164, 305, 401, 409,
   522, 848, 1024
4:34–35   291
4:34   156, 239, 270, 305,
   306, 443, 517, 523, 547,
   622, 840
4:34b   1039
4:35   37, 162, 205, 214, 239,
   256, 303, 306, 415, 427,
   474, 709, 760, 926, 1019
5   291
5:1–13   270, 286, 292, 307,
   308, 309, 310, 814, 978,
   986
5:1–5   303, 760, 877, 912
5:1–4   291, 307, 308, 351,
   369, 423, 486
5:1–3   834
5:1   25, 38, 178, 296, 301,
   308, 319, 332, 344, 348,
   367, 403, 423, 623, 624,
   684, 772, 1041
5:2–4   308, 344
5:2–3   277, 301, 310, 978,
   996, 1007
5:2   38, 228, 229, 300, 301,
   317, 338, 344, 403, 425,
   427, 654, 659, 668, 681,
   144
5:3–4   298
5:3   145, 296, 300, 301, 311,
   319, 338, 344, 403, 668,

1028
5:4   38, 50, 228, 296, 299,
   301, 319, 334, 338, 344,
   367, 668, 684, 772, 1028
5:4b   308
5:5–13   307
5:5–6   759
5:5   50, 229, 301, 302, 308,
   334, 344
5:5a   300, 308, 338
5:6–13   51
5:6   251, 303, 307, 308, 310,
   312, 331, 341, 369, 427,
   858, 926
5:7–13   308
5:7–10   167, 196
5:7   222, 269, 303, 308, 309,
   320, 331, 341, 761, 763,
   926
5:7–9   861
5:8   169, 307, 410, 488, 756
5:9   166, 238, 239, 274, 306,
   369, 535, 656, 855
5:10   37, 229, 251, 303, 307,
   309, 310, 400, 488, 576,
   583, 858, 926
5:11–13   167, 196, 222, 286,
   412, 438, 762
5:11   179, 180, 197, 200,
   274, 303, 304, 305, 306,
   307, 320, 331, 341, 365,
   398, 400, 761, 833, 860
5:12   162, 166, 182, 274, 341
5:13   37, 229, 251, 303, 306,
   308, 310, 320
5:14–26   50, 151, 308, 320,
   408, 409, 421, 422, 438,
   486, 732, 858, 861, 978
5:14–19   320, 332, 844
5:14–16   24, 323, 328, 331,
   332, 347, 351, 358, 360,
   361, 449, 450
5:14–16a   330
5:14ff   466
5:14   178, 301, 308, 320,
   323, 424, 623
5:15–19   365
5:15–16   488
5:15–16aab   358
5:15   36, 38, 147, 228, 248,
   286, 303, 320, 322, 323,
   325, 327, 331, 345, 408,
   409, 466, 486, 772, 861,
   975
5:15a   332
5:16   37, 709, 1083
5:16a   327
5:16ab   330
5:16b   358

5:16a 358
5:17–19 24, 323, 326, 327, 331, 332, 333, 334, 361, 363, 856
5:17 24, 25, 38, 50, 178, 228, 230, 331, 332, 338, 343, 423, 424, 772
5:17a 331
5:18 37, 147, 251, 303, 309, 326, 327, 332, 409, 466, 486, 709, 861, 1083
5:19 332
5:19b 243, 342
5:20–26 11, 50, 302, 320, 329, 330, 336, 351, 365, 367, 368, 370, 372, 373, 485
5:20–22 486
5:21–26 299, 300
5:21–22aa 369
5:21 4, 38, 178, 228, 320, 335, 345, 365, 366, 367, 772
5:21a 369
5:21–26 300
5:22–23 330
5:22ab 336, 365, 367, 369
5:23–24 327
5:23 4, 50, 344
5:23a 344
5:24 11, 320, 338, 344, 371
5:24a 336, 365, 367
5:24b–25 51, 345, 370
5:24d 372
5:25 147, 303, 326, 327, 409, 466, 861
5:26 11, 37, 334, 375, 709, 1083
5:26b 231
6 291
6:1–7:21 1, 151, 383
6:1–7:10 382
6:1–7:7 409
6:1–6 382, 410, 438
6:1–2 382
6:1–2a 396, 439
6:1 389
6:2–6 2
6:2–4 1016
6:2aβ–6 396, 439
6:2 209, 382, 384, 395, 396, 413, 426, 436, 438, 591, 688, 830, 883, 947
6:2b 389, 590
6:3–5 395
6:3–4 171, 240
6:3 5, 382, 474, 486, 618, 907, 1017

6:4 262, 382, 831, 872, 1008
6:5–6 157, 591, 1025
6:5 207, 217, 218, 382, 384, 438
6:5b 209, 389
6:6 384
6:7–16 2
6:7–11 382, 396, 405, 439
6:7–8 181, 395
6:7 147, 181, 186, 208, 382, 396, 436, 575, 688, 830, 883, 947, 1012
6:8 59, 160, 162, 181, 186, 382, 391, 410, 438, 474
6:9–11 412, 426
6:9b–11 438
6:9–10 186
6:9 187, 307, 320, 382, 394, 481, 527, 536, 605, 618, 619, 638, 1048
6:9a 392
6:10–12 188
6:10–11 15
6:10 17, 182, 186, 188, 201, 307, 392, 394, 443, 444, 464, 535, 707
6:10aβ 736
6:11 17, 186, 323, 324, 387, 400, 443, 444, 445, 446, 449, 455, 462, 618, 638, 977
6:12–18a 63, 439
6:12–17 396
6:12–16 183, 200, 382, 396, 401, 410, 426, 436, 438, 489
6:12–13aβ 396
6:12 382, 389, 408, 426
6:13 188, 195, 306, 338, 426
6:14 162, 185, 410, 530
6:15 231, 395, 396, 401, 411, 555, 618
6:17–23 2
6:17–18 382, 389
6:17–18a 62, 396, 401, 408
6:17 404, 413
6:18aβ–23 396, 439
6:18 17, 164, 182, 323, 382, 394, 396, 404, 408, 413, 423, 426, 436, 444, 486, 688, 830, 883, 947
6:18aβ 396
6:18b 404, 438
6:19–20 414
6:19 33, 47, 187, 222, 239, 261, 286, 304, 305, 324, 382, 387, 392, 394, 401, 404, 407, 412, 426, 443,

527, 536, 579, 580, 583, 605, 622, 638, 852, 862, 879, 926, 1048
6:19a 411
6:20 323, 382, 387, 392, 443, 445, 446, 449, 455, 605, 977, 1017
6:20b 272
6:21 394, 443, 673, 674, 677, 836, 920, 921
6:21a 272
6:21b 272
6:22–23 426, 525
6:22 17, 47, 187, 239, 246, 286, 320, 387, 401, 407, 408, 411, 412, 426, 527, 580, 622, 638
6:23 255, 261, 263, 270, 281, 401, 423, 427, 576, 579, 580, 605, 622, 625, 626, 635, 636, 706, 1052
7:1–10 382, 396
7:1–7 2, 151, 382, 405, 439, 527, 852
7:1–6 438
7:1–5 151, 862
7:1–2 323, 437, 486
7:1 17, 382, 396, 413, 436, 437, 688, 830, 883, 947
7:2 164, 169, 181, 255, 320, 848, 852
7:2a 438
7:3–35 414
7:3–5 151, 171, 386
7:3–4 211
7:3 159, 239, 525
7:4 11, 580
7:5 161, 166, 525
7:6–10 412, 426
7:6 17, 182, 320, 324, 392, 394, 527, 605, 638, 852, 1048
7:7–11 444
7:7–10 382
7:7–9 33, 710
7:7 156, 222, 286, 327, 400, 410, 416, 852, 861
7:8–10 63, 439
7:8 156, 157, 172, 205, 222, 410, 416, 432, 443
7:9–10 183, 186, 432, 438, 527
7:9 33, 157, 185, 186, 202, 390, 416, 432, 433, 438, 481
7:10 33, 208, 395, 438, 527, 584, 618, 858
7:11–36 29, 382, 439, 527
7:11–34 433

7:11–21 56, 144, 382, 396, 413, 439, 483
7:11–18 716
7:11–17 49
7:11–16 218, 219
7:11–15 11, 32, 33, 419
7:11–12 710
7:11 218, 382, 396, 415, 436, 437, 464, 688, 830, 883, 947
7:12–14 198, 200, 415
7:12–13 220
7:12 415
7:12aβ 413
7:12 399, 437, 527, 530
7:13–15 33
7:13 208, 412, 413, 414, 419, 498, 830
7:14 156, 217, 218, 223, 412, 414, 416, 461, 473, 533, 710
7:14b 402
7:15–21 413, 527
7:15–18 224
7:15–16 320
7:15 32, 219, 324, 414, 419, 535, 638
7:16–21 423, 429
7:16–17 14, 220, 418, 535, 578
7:16 218, 300, 324, 416, 417, 710
7:17–21 419
7:17 14, 182, 324, 637, 638
7:18 14, 25, 37, 38, 391, 422, 458, 624, 710, 946
7:19–21 223, 621
7:19–20 422, 752
7:19 418, 619
7:19b 224, 978
7:20–21 309, 317, 458, 654, 946
7:20 37, 38, 178, 296, 422, 427, 672, 684, 752, 927, 946, 978, 993
7:21–36 16
7:21 38, 145, 218, 296, 299, 317, 427, 682, 910, 946
7:22–36 15, 56
7:22–29a 63, 439
7:22–28 438
7:22–27 29, 62, 144, 216, 382, 396, 410, 429
7:22–23 413
7:22 53, 382, 389, 400, 408
7:23–34 527
7:23–25 426
7:23 10, 211, 438, 861
7:24–26 216

7:24 296, 427, 442, 461, 654, 673, 674, 682
7:25 171, 386, 427, 458, 946
7:26–30 447
7:26–27 216
7:26 215, 222, 429, 701, 704, 709
7:27 228, 416, 422, 429, 458, 684, 946
7:28–34 144, 410
7:28–29 396, 413
7:28–29a 396, 408
7:28–29b 426
7:28–36 16, 17, 382, 435
7:28 382, 389, 426
7:29–30 382, 427
7:29b 429, 430
7:29b–31a 464
7:29b–34 426
7:29b–36 396, 429, 439
7:29 716
7:30–33 478, 480, 621
7:30–31 211, 477, 586
7:30 147, 161, 205, 208, 252, 413, 435, 447, 461, 462, 476, 563, 585, 622, 851
7:30a 429, 430
7:30b 531
7:31–35 412
7:31–34 426, 578
7:31–32 438
7:31 33, 430, 432, 525, 531, 532
7:32–33 11, 202, 474, 476, 481, 531, 532, 558, 586
7:32 397, 415, 435, 473, 475, 476, 479, 528, 531, 585, 636
7:33–34 412
7:33 6, 16, 17, 33, 156, 217, 223, 416, 431, 432, 434, 435, 479, 531, 716
7:34 6, 16, 395, 400, 415, 430, 432, 434, 435, 461, 473, 618, 621, 707
7:35–36 161, 433
7:35 6, 16, 162, 430, 431, 434, 435
7:36 16, 338, 382, 432, 433, 435, 518, 619
7:37–38 144, 382, 396, 433, 438
7:37–38a 438, 439
7:37 533, 535, 561, 688, 883
7:37b 438
7:38 338, 538, 618, 831, 884
7:38b 62, 63, 438, 439, 573
8 61, 141, 278, 290, 436, 977

8:1–21 517
8:1–5 542
8:1–2 495
8:1 414
8:2 522, 527, 545, 547, 572, 596, 1018
8:2a 508
8:3–5 62, 63, 500, 544, 547
8:3–4 136, 147, 499, 500, 546
8:3 500
8:4 499, 500, 542, 545, 1059
8:5–22 48
8:5 545, 576
8:6–9 501, 543
8:7–12 513
8:7–9 495, 513, 549
8:6 434, 500, 513, 515, 546, 547, 549, 1018
8:6a 520
8:7 5, 502, 548, 796, 1017
8:8 54, 499, 507, 512, 542, 544, 545, 608
8:10–12 501, 514, 520, 571
8:10–11 63, 393, 494, 513, 520, 522, 523, 524, 544, 1039
8:10ab–11 499, 522, 545
8:10 36, 516, 545
8:10ab 516
8:10b 516
8:11 233, 249, 290, 514, 515, 516, 231, 290, 357, 464
8:11a 515
8:12–14 351
8:12–13 515, 524, 533, 543
8:12 513, 518, 520, 522, 530, 532, 533, 542, 545, 547, 548, 555, 851, 855
8:13–21 282
8:13 208, 385, 434, 495, 499, 502, 513, 515, 542, 544, 547, 548, 608, 1017
8:14–29 61, 495
8:14–28 539
8:14–17 495, 523, 562, 636
8:14–15 154, 524
8:14 153, 244, 500, 521, 522, 525, 526, 546, 547, 562, 565
8:15–28 562
8:15–17 523
8:15 5, 239, 253, 255, 290, 402, 500, 513, 516, 523, 525, 526, 546, 547, 580, 636, 882, 1023, 1036, 1038
8:15a 540
8:16–28 524

8:16   159, 161, 526, 580
8:16a   540
8:17   164, 264, 499, 523, 526, 542, 544, 580, 636, 1023
8:17a   540
8:18–25   495
8:18–21   562
8:18–19   154, 213, 526
8:18   498, 520, 522, 523, 547, 572
8:19   544
8:19a   540
8:20–21   160, 526
8:20   157, 169, 526, 545, 1023
8:20b   526, 540
8:21   157, 159, 161, 162, 499, 526, 542, 544, 545, 546, 582
8:21a   540
8:21b   526
8:22–44   1036
8:22–29   532, 543
8:22–24   255, 562
8:22–23   154
8:22   431, 432, 498, 520, 522, 523, 530, 539, 547, 1036
8:23–24   249, 279, 527, 528, 533, 545
8:24   208, 290, 563, 1036
8:25–30   526
8:25–29   527, 530, 546
8:25–27   527
8:25–26   470
8:25   210, 525, 580
8:26–31   32
8:26–29   437, 636
8:26–28   414, 558
8:26–27   198, 200, 462, 476
8:26   207, 461, 470, 495, 498, 533, 545, 563, 564, 867
8:26bβ   62, 63
8:27–28   430, 464, 563
8:28–29   478
8:28   161, 162, 166, 524, 525
8:29   461, 462, 499, 525, 542
8:29b   447, 556
8:29bβ   533
8:30–32   543
8:30   155, 231, 290, 357, 385, 436, 447, 516, 518, 520, 522, 523, 529, 530, 532, 533, 540, 543, 545, 546, 555, 563, 606, 608, 610, 838, 851, 1033, 1036
8:31–36   544

8:31–35   533, 542
8:31–33   437
8:31–32   225
8:31   220, 392, 414, 527, 535, 544
8:31a   626
8:32–33   481
8:32   182, 219, 305, 397, 414, 418, 533, 535, 637, 638, 855
8:33   282, 517, 527, 535, 539, 755, 780
8:33b–34   537, 565
8:33a   541, 542
8:34b   539
8:34a   540
8:35–37   546
8:33–35   546, 600
8:35   516, 535, 538, 544, 546, 780
8:35b   540, 619
8:36   499, 540, 542, 1059
9:1–10:5   477
9:1–21   61
9:1–15   241, 246
9:1   499, 572, 579, 583, 584, 592, 593, 619
9:2–3   281
9:2   495, 576, 591, 596, 626, 636, 714
9:3–4   576, 578, 582, 591
9:3   146, 163, 176, 244, 248, 268, 281, 495, 499, 572, 588, 622, 757, 1018
9:4f   143
9:4   136, 146, 224, 571, 573, 584, 714, 716
9:4b   573, 588, 592
9:5   147, 248, 495, 572, 573, 605, 606, 1014
9:6   500
9:6b   58, 588, 592
9:7   153, 175, 255, 266, 288, 575, 576, 578, 579, 584, 586, 925, 1012, 1019, 1022
9:7a   578
9:8–21   596
9:8–15   580
9:8–14   626
9:8–11   636, 1024
9:8   154, 244, 547, 1012
9:9   147, 208, 257, 408, 523, 581, 607, 838, 1023
9:9a   626
9:10   211, 578, 582, 586
9:11   244, 579, 580, 586, 622, 636
9:12   36, 154, 208, 579, 580, 607

9:12b   626
9:13–14   526
9:13   169, 580, 582, 586, 590, 1023
9:14   159, 580, 590
9:15–21   586
9:15–17   578
9:15   154, 245, 547, 575, 579, 581, 585, 593, 622, 636
9:15a   578
9:16   547, 583, 584, 591, 850
9:17–21   636
9:17–18   573
9:17   181, 457, 547, 573, 588, 590, 591, 850, 867
9:17b   15, 63
9:18–21   578
9:18–20   476
9:18   154, 208, 224, 573, 575, 579, 585, 607, 716
9:18b   584
9:19–20   571
9:19   211, 239, 530, 581, 585
9:20–21   478, 531
9:20   211, 477, 582
9:20a   585
9:21   16, 17, 33, 202, 225, 431, 435, 461, 462, 476, 477, 481, 578, 586, 593, 621, 851, 1023
9:21aβ   62, 63
9:22   251, 385, 575, 591, 1022
9:23–24   58, 136, 250, 499, 557, 571
9:23b–24a   15
9:23   18, 54, 61, 499, 575, 576, 581, 590
9:23b   58, 574, 576, 600, 1015
9:24   138, 143, 157, 207, 389, 477, 556, 575, 580, 582, 590, 597, 599, 604, 634, 635, 558
9:24a   58, 574, 588
10   62, 459
10:1–20   595
10:1–7   614, 632
10:1–5   314, 454
10:1–4   238
10:1–3   487
10:1–2   45, 55, 355
10:1   599, 600, 606, 634, 636, 978, 1012, 1024
10:2–3   600
10:2   600, 603, 604, 634
10:3   373, 602, 603, 623, 635
10:4–5   600, 607

10:4   234, 280, 408, 568,
  600, 605, 634, 638, 802,
  831
10:5   144, 448, 454, 831
10:6–11   15
10:6ff   477
10:6   4, 50, 232, 453, 627,
  946, 978
10:7   518, 598, 607, 608,
  1059
10:8–15   1
10:8–11   57, 611
10:8–9   144, 614, 617
10:8   357, 863
10:9   4, 233, 280, 395, 453,
  610, 613, 619, 634, 753,
  946
10:10–11   62, 383, 617, 639,
  645, 689
10:10   4, 144, 248, 260, 611,
  617, 690, 731, 978, 1001
10:10a   530
10:11   52, 617, 884, 945
10:12–20   596
10:12–15   636
10:12–14   204
10:12–13   186, 201, 477,
  606, 638
10:12   307, 392, 568, 573,
  584, 608, 619, 622
10:13–14   434, 463, 619,
  862, 1033
10:13   400, 535, 584, 605,
  618, 619, 622
10:14–15   415, 462, 473,
  477, 527, 573, 586
10:14   33, 56, 419, 432, 473,
  477, 618, 621, 978
10:15   16, 17, 33, 202, 207,
  395, 400, 432, 435, 461,
  473, 474, 477, 478, 481,
  614, 618, 619, 879
10:15a   62, 430
10:15aβ   63
10:16–20   573, 584, 586,
  628, 635
10:16–11   619
10:16   161, 579, 625, 680
10:17–18   606, 638
10:17   25, 47, 222, 286, 392,
  408, 607, 707, 852, 926,
  1045
10:17b   262
10:18–19   635
10:18   234, 261, 263, 270,
  392, 408, 525, 605, 626,
  635, 1052
10:19   418, 596, 635, 639
10:19b   627

10:20   57, 640
11   10, 11, 47
11:1–38   62
11:1–23   2, 62, 693
11:1–20   17
11:1–15   662
11:1–8   657, 682
11:1–4   662
11:1–3   662
11:1–2a   695
11:1   53, 743
11:2–8   656, 659, 691, 697
11:2–23   691, 692, 694, 695
11:2–3   310
11:2   646, 668, 688, 691,
  693, 701, 721, 863
11:2b–23   697
11:2b–3   647
11:2b   699
11:3–4a   700
11:3   171, 646, 647, 680,
  685, 691, 700, 701, 719,
  720, 872
11:3b   646
11:4–8   617, 656, 682, 690,
  692, 699
11:4–7   653, 654, 667, 700
11:4–6   668
11:4–5   662
11:4   646, 648, 661, 669,
  680, 691, 700, 701
11:4a   653
11:4b–6   647
11:5–7   351, 648
11:5–6   646
11:5   648, 693
11:6   171, 648, 662, 700
11:7–18   662
11:7   298, 646, 647, 648, 662
11:7a   700
11:7b–8a   700
11:7b   700
11:8   207, 296, 423, 426,
  648, 653, 667, 701, 978
11:8a   700
11:8b   700
11:9–23   657, 671
11:9–12   645, 664, 682, 683,
  688, 691, 697
11:9–10   695
11:9   655, 659, 661, 662,
  664, 685, 691, 700, 719,
  734
11:9a   700
11:9b   700
11:10–12a   700
11:10   298, 425, 648, 656,
  659, 671, 712, 720
11:10a   701

11:10b   656, 689
11:10b–11a   680
11:11–15   663
11:11   37, 296, 648, 656,
  659, 662, 668, 684, 701
11:11a   656
11:12   171, 659
11:12b   700
11:13–23   296, 645, 682, 692
11:13–20   351
11:13–19   647, 664, 688,
  691, 692, 697
11:13   425, 656, 672, 684,
  701
11:13a   701
11:13b   661
11:13b–19   701
11:14–17   171
11:14   701
11:15   662
11:16–18   662
11:17   662, 701
11:18   662, 701
11:19–20   662
11:19   662, 672, 692, 701
11:20–23   298, 664, 667,
  669, 683, 691, 692, 697,
  699
11:20   656, 659, 662, 667,
  671, 679, 692, 701, 702,
  720, 734
11:21–22   425, 659, 682,
  685, 686, 692, 699, 720,
  734
11:21   159, 160, 425, 661,
  664, 691, 692, 699, 701
11:21a   697
11:22   665, 691, 701
11:23   425, 656, 658, 659,
  667, 671, 679, 692
11:24–40   667, 668, 691,
  692, 693, 694, 702, 844,
  850, 987, 1007
11:24–38   1, 62, 63, 682,
  693, 694, 695, 697
11:24–28   426, 648, 653,
  654, 656, 657, 667, 669,
  670, 681, 682, 690, 691,
  692, 693, 694, 697
11:24–26   669, 936
11:24–25   424, 667, 669, 670
11:24   446, 667, 668, 669,
  685, 691, 936
11:24b   669, 672, 746
11:25–28   672
11:25   403, 669, 670, 672,
  687, 782, 1050
11:26–28   667
11:26–27   653, 670

11:26   298, 446, 645, 646, 648, 669, 689, 832, 1034
11:26a   669, 670
11:26b   669, 936
11:27–28   423, 668, 669
11:27   296, 446, 645, 648, 668, 669, 726, 832
11:27aβ   670
11:27b   669
11:27b–28a   670
11:28   298, 403, 648, 667, 669, 782
11:28b   669
11:29–43   671
11:29–42   734
11:29–40   657, 693, 703
11:29–38   656, 658, 659, 667, 672, 682, 690, 691, 692, 693, 694, 697
11:29–31   298, 426, 694
11:29–30   298, 648, 657, 659, 671, 678, 682, 683, 720
11:29   657, 672
11:29a   657, 672
11:30   663
11:31–40   298
11:31–38   298
11:31   296, 446, 657, 671, 919
11:32–33   678, 681, 921
11:32f   677
11:32   658, 672, 679, 691, 695, 701, 919
11:32a   679
11:32b   679, 680
11:33   272, 405, 671, 673, 674, 658, 678, 836, 921
11:33b   678
11:34–38   657
11:34   320, 679, 680, 691, 695
11:35   184, 272, 405, 648, 658
11:34a   681
11:35aβ–38   679
11:34b   681, 656
11:35   680
11:35a   678, 679
11:35aβ   680
11:35b   680, 681
11:36   446, 657, 681, 691, 695, 701, 837, 922
11:36a   922
11:36b   936
11:37   680, 681, 691, 695, 701
11:38   648, 681

11:39–40   62, 63, 296, 317, 423, 424, 425, 427, 656, 659, 668, 669, 682, 690, 691, 692, 693, 694, 695, 696, 703, 729
11:39   446, 653, 678, 691, 694, 695, 701
11:40   403, 667, 672, 694, 782, 919, 1050
11:40b   936
11:41–45   691
11:41–44   298, 656
11:41–43   658, 671, 682, 683, 686
11:41–42   2, 62, 656, 657, 664, 672, 682, 683, 692, 693, 694, 695, 697, 702
11:41   425, 671, 672, 683
11:41aβ   679
11:41b   679, 662
11:42   207, 668, 671
11:42a   683
11:43–45   11, 15, 46, 62, 63, 639, 694, 695, 696, 697, 703, 1002
11:43–44   39, 40, 683, 684, 685, 686, 688, 886
11:43   683, 684, 697, 1005
11:43a   685, 687
11:43aβ   687
11:43b   656, 680, 685, 686, 694
11:44–45   359, 687, 729
11:44   603, 684, 689, 690, 694, 729, 967
11:44a   656, 680
11:44aβ   684, 694
11:44a   687
11:44b   684, 685
11:45   8, 688, 1005
11:45b   687
11:46–47   62, 691, 694, 695
11:46   62, 382, 383, 656, 668, 687, 688, 693, 695, 712, 720, 743, 947
11:46b   688
11:47   1, 62, 63, 615, 616, 645, 657, 688, 690, 694, 695, 701
11:47a   383
11:47b   690
12   253, 299
12:1–8   2, 742
12:1   53, 1065
12:2–3   317, 571
12:2   38, 311, 579, 764, 767, 772, 780, 863, 924, 947, 952, 995

12:2b   755
12:3   721, 744, 749, 752, 754
12:4   21, 309, 423, 617, 621, 981, 990, 992, 995
12:4a   749, 755, 756, 760
12:4b   750, 760, 944
12:5   38, 746, 749
12:5b   749, 760
12:6–8   197, 222, 277, 743, 814
12:6   148, 163, 256, 266, 269, 284, 744, 755, 760, 761, 762, 844, 922, 925, 995
12:6a   755, 760
12:6b   750
12:7   383, 607, 688, 749, 758, 760, 763, 947, 973, 999, 1000
12:7a   758
12:7b   761
12:8   51, 63, 167, 222, 254, 256, 266, 284, 304, 308, 488, 758, 760, 762, 833, 999, 1000, 1056
12:8b   758
13   299, 814, 955
13:1–59   2
13:1–46   884, 886
13:1–28   802, 883, 884
13:1–17   884
13:1–12   310
13:1–8   784
13:1   144, 645, 813
13:2–44   825–26 824
13:2–18   801
13:2–17   772, 773, 791, 885
13:2b–17   884
13:2–8   798
13:2   144, 688, 772, 773, 774, 777, 778, 782, 783, 784, 786, 787, 788, 789, 791, 792, 796, 799, 801, 863, 868, 883
13:2b   783, 784, 884, 885
13:3–8   774
13:3   773, 776, 777, 779, 781, 784, 785, 788, 789, 791, 799, 801, 841, 889
13:3a   781
13:4–8   794, 796
13:4–7   888
13:4   383, 774, 776, 777, 778, 779, 783, 784, 785, 788, 794, 795, 801, 813, 871, 888, 955
13:4b   871
13:5–8   785
13:5–6   877

13:5 776, 779, 780, 783, 796, 813, 831, 871, 877, 879, 888, 955
13:5a 781
13:5b 871
13:6 757, 774, 776, 778, 780, 781, 782, 783, 788, 796, 813, 815, 871, 888, 955
13:6b 774
13:7–8 781
13:7 749, 774, 776, 780, 781, 783, 785, 791
13:8 774, 780, 789, 791, 831
13:9–17 774, 784
13:5–8 785
13:9 772, 780, 786, 787, 792, 799, 883
13:10–11 790
13:10 773, 777, 778, 783, 785, 791, 801, 813, 888
13:11 648, 779, 783, 785, 812, 889
13:12–13 784
13:12 776, 785
13:12a 786
13:13 776, 777, 782, 798, 813
13:14 791
13:15 648, 783, 785, 786, 789
13:16 777, 813
13:17 777, 782, 798, 813
13:18–28 786
13:18–23 790, 801, 883, 885
13:18 772, 784, 799
13:19–28 796
13:19–23 791
13:19 773, 774, 775, 788, 789, 790, 801, 870
13:20 777, 782, 783, 791, 792, 813, 883, 889
13:20b 787
13:21 774, 779, 781, 788, 790, 796, 813, 871, 955
13:22 776, 783, 789, 790, 791
13:23 774, 780, 782, 789, 790, 791, 796, 813
13:24–28 790, 791, 801, 883, 885
13:24 774, 789, 790, 791, 799, 801
13:25–26 788
13:25 774, 777, 782, 788, 789, 791, 813, 889
13:26 774, 779, 781, 790, 796, 871, 955
13:27 783, 789, 790, 791

13:28 773, 774, 780, 781, 782, 788, 789, 790, 796, 813
13:29–44 802
13:29–37 794, 796, 883, 884, 885
13:29–33 802
13:29–30 794
13:29 38, 145, 772, 773, 784, 794, 799, 802
13:30–39 817
13:30 776, 778, 792, 795, 797, 800, 801, 889
13:31–36 794
13:31 648, 775, 779, 780, 798, 801, 871, 955
13:32–34 779
13:32 792, 795, 801, 813
13:32b 794
13:33–53 885
13:33 776, 779, 780, 781, 800, 871, 955
13:34 780, 782, 795, 796, 798, 799, 871, 955
13:34a 794
13:35–36 798
13:35 797, 921
13:36 785, 792, 795, 797, 799, 889
13:37 780, 781, 782, 792, 794, 795, 797, 799, 800, 813, 831, 871, 877, 879
13:38–39 778, 799, 802, 883
13:38 38, 145, 772, 774, 784, 787, 801
13:39 774, 781, 799, 817
13:40–44 799, 802, 883
13:40 609, 772, 804
13:41 609
13:42–44 799, 885
13:42 775, 801, 814, 773, 800, 801
13:43b 802
13:44 648, 774, 785, 801, 802, 831
13:45–46 801, 820, 886, 888
13:45 608, 609, 774, 779, 801, 802, 831
13:46–47 778
13:46 44, 648, 748, 785, 815, 819, 876
13:47–59 62, 63, 886, 955, 1007
13:47–58 43, 46, 796, 884, 885, 1007
13:47 772, 810, 867
13:48 812
13:49 788, 789, 810, 812
13:50 776, 779, 780, 810,

871
13:51 648, 811
13:51a 812
13:51 813, 809, 810, 811, 812, 813, 832, 868
13:53 796, 810, 811, 812
13:54 779, 796, 815, 871
13:54a 832
13:54b 832
13:55–56 404
13:55 648, 777, 780, 781, 814, 815
13:55c 813
13:56 781, 788, 796, 811, 815, 832, 868, 872
13:56a 813
13:57 810, 811, 813, 814
13:58 810, 811, 812, 813, 815, 831
13:59 383, 688, 782, 808, 811, 830, 883, 884, 886, 947
14:1–57 2
14:1–32 311, 782, 797, 802, 884, 886
14:1–2 906
14:1 144, 743
14:2–27 883
14:2–20 863
14:2 383, 688, 749, 786, 801, 868, 947, 973
14:2a 885, 908
14:2aB 885
14:3b–32 799
14:3 262, 508, 774, 801, 803, 870
14:3a 831
14:4–8 275, 508, 538, 1048
14:4–7 275, 468, 701, 819, 879, 1007, 1044, 1045
14:4 46, 782, 813, 832, 879, 880
14:4a 836
14:4abβ 886
14:5–6 918, 922, 963
14:5 813, 832, 877, 880, 922
14:6–7 850
14:6 273, 275, 802, 832, 838, 877, 881
14:7 233, 782, 802, 832, 836, 837, 875, 877, 882, 1023, 1048, 1056
14:7a 881
14:7aβ 748
14:7b 837, 881
14:8–9 967
14:8 276, 668, 748, 760, 780, 782, 795, 796, 838, 842, 844, 859, 889, 922,

924, 935, 937, 970, 974, 993, 999, 1006
14:9–10 918
14:9 256, 668, 760, 780, 795, 796, 838, 841, 842, 844, 859, 882, 922, 928, 935, 967, 1006, 1056
14:9a 843
14:10–20 889
14:10–13 364, 850
14:10–12 328
14:10–11 32
14:10 163, 176, 180, 200, 267, 277, 307, 757, 849, 861, 867
14:10b 699
14:11–20 39, 859, 880, 881
14:11 210, 407, 782, 832, 857, 1000
14:12–14 364, 409
14:12–13 862, 877, 1009
14:12 363, 431, 461, 462, 489, 857, 925
14:13 164, 392, 393
14:14–17 249, 279
14:14 255, 290, 364, 489, 527, 707, 850, 855, 861
14:15 857
14:16 233, 244, 273, 468, 517, 555, 838, 842, 853, 854, 855, 857, 937
14:16b 880
14:17 464, 528, 832, 848, 851, 855, 857
14:18–20 710
14:18 182, 397, 468, 529, 832, 851, 853, 854, 857, 858, 882, 1081
14:18b 522
14:19–20 822, 845, 1009
14:19 251, 266, 284, 364, 400, 576, 832, 857, 858, 882, 926, 1006, 1022
14:20 153, 175, 201, 256, 288, 306, 364, 389, 760, 842, 844, 853, 856, 857, 858, 859, 862, 863, 882, 999, 1000, 1056, 1081, 1083
14:20b 882
14:21–32 51, 763, 814, 880, 881
14:21–31 863
14:21–23 277, 286
14:21–22 32, 167, 307, 328, 364, 489, 850
14:21 39, 304, 306, 363, 398, 462, 846, 856, 867, 882

14:22 222, 304, 761, 862, 877, 888
14:23 210, 749, 849, 925, 1000
14:23a 799
14:24–29 862
14:24–25 409, 862
14:24 234, 461, 462
14:25–30 918
14:25–28 249, 279
14:25 255, 290, 364, 489, 528, 707, 850, 883
14:26–29 862
14:27 233, 877, 880
14:28–29 1033
14:28 464, 854
14:29 397, 529, 856, 1081
14:29b 522
14:30–32 304
14:30 266, 400, 576, 761, 813, 861, 883, 925
14:31 284, 858, 859, 882, 1056, 1081
14:32 39, 383, 688, 877, 947,645
14:32b 863
14:33–53 43, 62, 806, 808, 880, 881, 884, 1007
14:34–57 881
14:34–53 885
14:34 15, 808, 867, 877, 881, 882, 886, 889
14:34b 868
14:35–53 46, 63
14:35 508, 777, 780, 814, 877
14:36 872, 873, 876, 877
14:36a 832, 869
14:36b 869, 886
14:37 778
14:38–39 883
14:38 147, 779, 780, 874, 875
14:39 877
14:39a 886
14:40–42 872
14:40 813, 831, 863, 868, 872, 873, 874
14:40a 832
14:41–43 872
14:41 238, 812, 813, 831, 863, 872, 875
14:41bβ 871
14:42–44 884
14:42 812, 813, 832, 862, 870, 873, 875, 883, 1033
14:42b 872
14:43–47 877
14:43 834, 870, 874, 883

14:43aβb 871, 886
14:44 648, 812, 874, 877, 883
14:44a 871, 886
14:45–46 867, 912
14:45 679, 831, 863, 868, 872
14:45aβ 871, 886
14:46–47 816, 872, 882, 977, 983, 992
14:46 425, 779, 871, 876
14:46b 806
14:47–58 806
14:47 912
14:48–57 468
14:48–53 275, 877
14:48 310, 782, 831, 870, 871, 874, 1079
14:49–53 275, 701, 878, 889, 1045, 1048
14:49–52 1044
14:49–50 273
14:49 508, 879, 880, 881
14:50–53 963
14:50–52 922
14:51–52 874, 880
14:51 233, 255, 275, 832, 836, 838, 881, 879, 881, 1079
14:53 525, 760, 831, 832, 840, 1023
14:54–57 62, 63, 383, 885, 886, 947
14:54–56 815, 883
14:54–55 885
14:54 688, 793, 884, 908
14:54a 885
14:53b 882, 885
14:55 885
14:56 688, 773, 774, 883, 885
14:57 383, 688, 786, 831
14:57a 885
14:57aB 885
14:57b 885
14:58 1079
15 233
15:1–32 2
15:1–17 423
15:1–15 44, 887
15:1–13 312
15:1–5 887
15:1–2a 17
15:1 53, 645
15:2–15 947
15:2 369, 385, 688, 748, 772, 785, 904, 910, 914, 915, 921, 922, 926, 928, 934, 945, 975, 1012, 1017

15:2a 906
15:2bβ 942
15:3–15 986
15:3 2, 748, 947, 975
15:3a 907
15:3b 908
15:4–6 917
15:4 908, 917, 975
15:4–12 993
15:4–10 299
15:4a 917, 936, 940, 975
15:4b 940
15:5–27 850
15:5–13 967
15:5–11 965, 1050
15:5–8 403, 916
15:5–6 876, 913, 917, 943
15:5 38, 667, 840, 876, 913, 914, 916, 917, 922, 936, 938
15:5a 940
15:6 667, 840, 916, 922, 938, 975
15:6a 940
15:6b–7 975
15:7–8 916
15:7 667, 816, 840, 910, 913, 916, 922, 935, 953, 975
15:8 254, 667, 840, 913, 915, 922
15:9–10 913, 917
15:9 916, 917, 937, 942
15:9a 940
15:10–11 403
15:10 446, 667, 840, 910, 917, 918, 922, 942
15:10a 911, 916, 917, 918, 919, 955, 1008
15:10b 919, 1008
15:11 446, 667, 673, 674, 840, 841, 911, 913, 914, 929, 953, 956, 995
15:12 405, 677, 911, 975
15:12a 272
15:13–15 32, 887, 905, 935, 974
15:13–14 571
15:13 667, 668, 672, 749, 761, 780, 837, 840, 841, 915, 935, 943, 944, 963, 973, 995, 999, 1056
15:14–15 197, 222, 269
15:14 33, 34, 51, 277, 312, 944, 975, 1000
15:15 251, 266, 284, 400, 858, 859, 862, 921, 926, 975
15:15b 944

15:16–18 269, 299, 312, 425, 907, 929, 930, 935, 947, 969, 987
15:16–17 311, 522, 930, 947, 971
15:16 746, 772, 841, 904, 915, 922, 927, 928, 935, 967, 975, 1016, 1034, 1056
15:17 684, 922, 927, 934
15:17a 911
15:18 819, 927, 928, 930, 931, 938, 947, 965
15:19–32 947
15:19–30 916
15:19–24 299, 744, 745, 816, 918, 987
15:19–23 907, 941, 947
15:19–20 672
15:19 38, 311, 385, 425, 755, 772, 780, 904, 906, 907, 914, 915, 919, 922, 924, 928, 941, 943, 944, 956, 1017
15:19a 948
15:19b 44, 816, 914, 936, 938, 941, 943, 953
15:19b–20a 941
15:20–27 935
15:20 936, 942, 943, 956
15:20a 940, 941
15:20a–23 941
15:20b 940, 942
15:21–22 44, 935, 936, 937, 938, 939, 943, 965
15:21 446, 840, 910, 921, 936, 942, 965, 1056
15:22 840, 910, 939, 940, 942, 446, 910, 938
15:22a 940
15:23 939, 942, 953, 959
15:23a 940
15:23b 938
15:24 38, 311, 761, 780, 931, 938, 941, 943, 947, 948, 960
15:24a 941
15:24b 905, 940, 941
15:25–30 44, 887, 907, 947
15:25–27 993
15:25 38, 269, 744, 772, 785, 904, 915, 941
15:25b 940, 947
15:26–27 299
15:26 38, 943
15:26a 940
15:26ab 940
15:26aβ 947
15:26b 934, 940
15:26bβ 947

15:27 446, 840, 910, 935, 937, 943, 956, 965
15:27a 905, 940
15:28–30 269, 887, 905, 935, 943, 986
15:28 672, 780, 924, 934, 935, 973, 1056
15:28b 905
15:29–31 269
15:29–30 197, 222
15:29 148, 277, 312, 759, 761, 925, 1000, 1056
15:29b 905
15:30 266, 284, 400, 859, 925, 1056
15:30b 926
15:31 15, 37, 38, 62, 63, 257, 314, 317, 512, 524, 609, 618, 887, 905, 940, 981, 993, 1005, 1006, 1011
15:31a 1005
15:32–33 945, 947
15:32 382, 383, 688, 907, 927, 947
15:32b 930
15:33 38, 688, 745, 756, 931, 952, 1018
15:33aβ 63, 905, 947
16 62, 292
16:1–28 36, 144, 618, 639, 1062
16:1–2 1054, 1064
16:1 57, 63, 598, 610, 633, 639, 1012, 1039
16:2–28 1, 62, 633, 1012, 1013, 1058, 1059, 1063, 1064, 1065
16:2–3 1011, 1059
16:2a–5 1015
16:2ff 143
16:2 143, 234, 638, 946, 1013, 1029, 1030, 1031, 1039, 1052, 1059, 1062, 1063, 1070
16:2b 1013
16:2bβ 63
16:3–22 48
16:3–19 241
16:3–5 1015
16:3 36, 197, 232, 234, 281, 303, 572, 1013, 1019, 1036, 1039, 1048, 1058, 1059, 1063
16:4 233, 501, 504, 511, 813, 841, 857, 907, 918, 928, 1017, 1039
16:5–10 303
16:5–6 1039
16:5 154, 197, 244, 262,

263, 276, 281, 572, 573, 813, 833, 834, 1018, 1019, 1020, 1022, 1036, 1039, 1044, 1048, 1054, 1058, 1064
16:6–22   1047
16:6–10   1063
16:6   255, 578, 1019, 1021, 1022, 1023, 1024, 1039, 1048, 1063
16:7–10   1063
16:7   210, 626, 849, 1019, 1020, 1039
16:8   834, 1018, 1020, 1021, 1039
16:9   248, 266, 276, 1018, 1020, 1023, 1039, 1040
16:10   44, 255, 849, 981, 1020, 1022, 1023, 1036, 1039, 1040, 1078, 1082, 1083
16:11–28   1063
16:11–14   233, 1033
16:11   154, 244, 255, 272, 276, 578, 579, 1022, 1023
16:11a   1018, 1024, 1063
16:11b   1024
16:12–16a   1063
16:12–14   138
16:12–13   160, 237, 527, 1015, 1030, 1031
16:12   597, 598, 1013, 1036, 1070
16:13   638, 946, 1013, 1014, 1030, 1031
16:14–19   256, 393, 533, 1064, 1081
16:14–16   1039
16:14–15   528, 980, 1036
16:14   155, 270, 393, 1015, 1024, 1064
16:15–16   53, 306
16:15   176, 233, 242, 248, 276, 572, 579, 1013, 1015, 1018, 1019, 1022, 1024, 1032, 1038, 1044, 1050, 1052, 1058, 1070
16:16–20   255
16:16–19   257, 1026
16:16–18   516
16:16b–17b   1063
16:16   24, 36, 55, 59, 228, 229, 233, 234, 255, 258, 276, 334, 525, 572, 668, 857, 875, 882, 926, 981, 982, 1013, 1022, 1023, 1032, 1036, 1043, 1044, 1063, 1064

16:16a   24, 1063
16:16b   233
16:17   36, 276, 572, 578, 706, 1013, 1018, 1023, 1036, 1039, 1044, 1048, 1058, 1063
16:17b   1033, 1036
16:18–19   522
16:18–19b   1063
16:18   255, 276, 517, 525, 527, 547, 882, 1023, 1035, 1036, 1039, 1048
16:19   233, 273, 529, 572, 583, 619, 749, 782, 1032, 1034, 1035, 1036, 1038, 1039, 1044, 1064
16:19b   515, 1033, 1036, 1063
16:20b–22   981
16:20   234, 255, 276, 1013, 1023, 1063, 1064
16:20a   1040, 1063
16:21–22   44, 276, 882, 1082
16:21   24, 37, 47, 55, 151, 153, 228, 229, 301, 302, 303, 369, 572, 840, 857, 875, 1022, 1024, 1034, 1039, 1042, 1043, 1044, 1046, 1052, 1063, 1064, 1076, 1083
16:21a   24
16:21b   1046
16:21bβ   1052
16:22   1018, 1020, 1021, 1043, 1045, 1046
16:23–24   1016, 1046
16:23   234, 303, 840, 1013, 1017, 1046, 1047, 1050, 1063, 1064
16:23a   1046
16:24–25   1047, 1050
16:24   25, 153, 175, 197, 242, 255, 266, 288, 392, 393, 400, 501, 572, 578, 605, 709, 841, 1013, 1016, 1017, 1018, 1022, 1023, 1044, 1046, 1048, 1050, 1051, 1056, 1058, 1064
16:25–28   1052
16:25–27   1064
16:25   207, 406, 967, 1046, 1064
16:25a   1064
16:26–40   301
16:26   262, 276, 840, 841, 842, 928, 1017, 1018, 1020
16:27–28   53, 161, 262, 565
16:27   36, 164, 263, 306,

407, 423, 625, 626, 637, 706, 987, 1013, 1040, 1063, 1064
16:27a   1064
16:28   262, 272, 274, 276, 406, 840, 841, 842, 928, 967, 987, 997, 1050, 1052, 1059
16:29–34   63, 696, 1012, 1052, 1066
16:29–34a   37, 62, 63, 1056, 1058, 1064
16:29–33   15, 1059
16:29–31   39, 40, 144
16:29   25, 51, 422, 703, 1057, 1065, 1066
16:30   255, 578, 1024, 1043, 1056
16:31   422, 619, 1055, 1056, 1057, 1066
16:32   231, 539, 1059, 1065
16:33   255, 572, 578, 754, 1019, 1044
16:34   251, 619, 858, 1056, 1059, 1062, 1065, 1070
16:34b   57, 1012, 1059
17:1–7   709
17:2   500, 1012
17:3–7   8, 28, 29, 49, 347, 681, 711, 733
17:3–5   46, 417, 1002
17:3–4   16, 49, 156, 251, 417, 435, 710, 711
17:3   38, 144, 417, 711, 861, 906
17:4   59, 458
17:4b   710
17:5   28, 218, 573, 711, 716
17:6   162, 332
17:7   248, 573, 619, 716
17:7a   28
17:8–13   617
17:8–9   629, 711
17:8   38, 172, 199, 218, 483, 703, 772, 906, 1065
17:9   266, 400, 458
17:10–14   39, 46, 156, 417, 704, 709, 711, 767, 1002
17:10–12   442, 709, 711
17:10   422, 429, 458, 703, 704, 772, 906, 1065
17:11   49, 222, 251, 417, 565, 578, 684, 705, 706, 708, 709, 710, 711, 712, 1083
17:11a   706
17:11aβ   707
17:11a   707

17:11b 706
17:12 422, 703, 704, 1065
17:13–14 221, 251, 413, 417, 424, 427, 647, 681, 682, 706, 709, 711, 712, 729
17:13 216, 222, 238, 417, 678, 703, 712, 720, 772, 906, 1065
17:14 421, 422, 429, 458, 703, 704
17:15–16 311, 317, 428, 653, 654, 711
17:15 654, 667, 672, 772, 840, 919, 1007, 1065
17:16 623
18:2 686, 906
18:3 230, 619, 725
18:4 619, 686
18:5 619, 687, 767
18:6 577, 687, 906
18:8 394
18:10 1065
18:14 577
18:15 254, 1005
18:16 776
18:19–20 4
18:19 577, 999, 1065
18:20 37, 335, 927
18:21 49, 366, 394, 687
18:22 246, 699, 931
18:23 927
18:24–30 1005
18:24–29 49
18:24–28 1041
18:24 37, 49, 685
18:25–39 724
18:25–28 37, 947
18:26 48, 394, 619, 699, 703, 1065
18:27–29 458
18:27–28 229, 1055
18:27 699
18:29 689, 699
18:30 230, 541, 685, 686, 699
19 32
19:2–4 14
19:2 359, 417, 639, 687, 696, 712, 724, 967
19:3 230, 600, 686
19:4 230, 686
19:5–8 322, 323
19:5–6 218, 219
19:5 14, 149, 466, 573, 716
19:6–7 14, 224, 324, 420
19:6 14, 420, 637, 638
19:7–8 14, 422

19:7 421, 422
19:8 37, 224, 322, 324, 420, 422, 458, 1012
19:9–11 447
19:9 447
19:10 230, 686
19:11–13 4, 335
19:11–13a 365, 367
19:11–12 367
19:11 335
19:12 230, 295, 320, 366, 374, 687
19:13 14
19:14 230, 687
19:15 335
19:16 4, 230, 687
19:17 335
19:18 230, 687, 731
19:19–21 328
19:19 447, 448, 548, 810, 1022
19:20–22 861
19:20 14, 772, 927, 931
19:21 303
19:22 251
19:23 863, 886
19:24 686
19:25 686, 1003
19:26 429
19:28 687
19:29 685
19:30 348, 687, 754, 947
19:31 37, 49, 686
19:32 687
19:33 703, 1065
19:34 703, 1065
19:36 686, 688
19:37 619, 687
20:1–6 48
20:1–4 981
20:2–5 458
20:2–3 38, 460, 736
20:2 49, 457, 772, 906, 1065
20:3 59, 229, 257, 347, 366, 754, 947, 1041, 1055
20:4–5 38, 736
20:4 298
20:5 15
20:6–7 730
20:6 178, 458
20:7–21 725
20:7–8 639, 1005
20:7 359, 603, 686, 687
20:8 284, 619
20:9 749
20:11–24 48
20:11–12 394
20:11 749, 931

20:12 931, 1005
20:13 699, 931
20:15–16 712, 720
20:15 927
20:16 577
20:18 745, 748, 749, 756, 761, 931, 940, 947, 973, 999
20:20 423, 931
20:21 38, 145
20:22–26 729
20:22–24 1005
20:22–23 689
20:22 619
20:23 725
20:24 686, 906
20:24b–26 725
20:25–26 689
20:25 11, 153, 615, 616, 654, 660, 683, 687, 688, 690, 691, 694
20:25a 690, 695
20:25b 36, 684
20:25bβ 694
20:26 359, 417, 639, 687, 712, 967, 1005
20:26a 688, 694
20:27 145
21:1–4 4, 280, 357, 608, 610, 979
21:1–3 4, 606, 607
21:1 144, 618, 654, 685, 1054
21:3 685
21:4 685
21:5 617, 801
21:6–8 687, 730
21:6–7 359
21:6 213, 279, 357, 366
21:7 48, 453
21:8 48, 213, 284, 688, 772
21:10–15 564
21:10 231, 518, 539, 609, 803, 1058, 1065
21:11–12 357, 607
21:11 280, 600, 685, 979
21:12 37, 277, 512, 564, 606, 608, 610, 611, 687, 754, 980
21:12b 357
21:14 4, 284, 669, 996
21:15 48, 284, 688
21:16–23 721
21:17–23 721
21:17 213, 440, 613, 722, 753
21:17b–21 40
21:18–20 723

21:18   613, 753, 775
21:20   780
21:21–22   395
21:21   613, 722, 753
21:22   187, 204, 213, 320,
   321, 430, 440, 753, 852
21:23   48, 233, 284, 348,
   613, 688, 753, 754
21:24   144, 618
22:1–16   144
22:1–15   975
22:2–9   754
22:2   366, 512, 687, 772, 945
22:3–9   424, 752
22:3–7   309
22:3   38, 317, 424, 577, 601,
   687, 946, 1012
22:4–8   424
22:4b–7   987
22:4–6   38
22:4b–6   991
22:4   11, 774, 801, 850, 906,
   907, 927, 946
22:5   145, 659, 668, 682,
   694, 987
22:5b   299
22:6   667, 841, 928
22:6a   672, 919
22:6b   672
22:7   973
22:8–9   654
22:8   654, 682, 687, 690,
   694, 703, 776
22:9   37, 38, 48, 256, 284,
   541, 615, 685, 946
22:10–14   424
22:10   621
22:11   228, 619, 684
22:12   369, 473
22:13   474, 772
22:14–16   358, 361
22:14   772, 801
22:15   473, 474
22:16   11, 48, 342, 358, 423
22:17–30   149, 483
22:17–25   144, 147, 721, 722
22:17–21   177, 484
22:17–20   273, 722
22:17–19   175, 177, 288
22:18–25   145
22:18   152, 758, 761, 906,
   1065
22:18b   145
22:19–29   149
22:19–20   149
22:19   149, 163, 740
22:20   149, 153
22:21–25   413

22:21–24   424
22:21   149, 219, 413, 415
22:22–24   428, 723
22:23   149, 400, 421, 603,
   669, 775
22:24   669, 793
22:25   145, 149, 213, 250,
   421, 703
22:27   149, 427, 738, 739,
   772, 861
22:28   239, 716, 739, 740
22:29   149, 218, 219, 413,
   415, 483, 573, 716
22:30   324, 638, 687
22:31   230, 687
22:32   48, 284, 366, 615
22:33   8, 687, 688
23   11
23:1–3   20
23:1   136, 161, 213
23:2aβ–3   1, 19, 26, 28
23:2   5
23:2a   26
23:2aβ   20
23:2b   20
23:3   21, 26, 215, 780, 1054,
   1057
23:4–38   26
23:4   20, 136
23:4a   26
23:5   282, 1065
23:6   780, 1065
23:7   1055
23:8   21, 26, 193, 1055
23:9–14   193
23:9ff   194
23:10–22   200
23:10–11   192, 193, 200
23:10   18, 190, 863, 886
23:11   19, 462, 466, 921,
   1003
23:11a   472
23:12–13   26
23:12   163, 191, 757
23:13   162, 390
23:14   193, 194, 215, 395,
   619
23:15–17   200
23:15   147, 212, 462, 921,
   973, 1065
23:16   193
23:17   191, 194, 215, 415,
   462
23:18–20   224
23:18–19   26, 267, 268, 292
23:18   161, 162, 163, 232,
   757, 780
23:19–20   483

23:19   161, 218, 224, 244,
   248, 259, 266, 483, 703,
   757
23:20   225, 461, 462
23:20b   193
23:21   21, 619, 1055
23:22   686, 1065
23:24–25   21
23:24   388, 1065
23:25   26, 193, 1055
23:26–32   1066
23:27–32   39
23:27–28   21
23:27   26, 51, 193, 422, 483,
   1062, 1065
23:28   1054, 1062
23:29   51, 422, 458, 1065
23:30   458, 459
23:31   215, 395, 619, 1057
23:33–36   26
23:34–36   571
23:34   780, 1065
23:35   21, 1055
23:36   21, 26, 193, 594, 1055
23:37–38   20
23:37   4, 26, 136, 162, 218
23:38   441
23:39–44   26
23:39–43   1, 28, 1071
23:39   571, 680, 1065
23:41   395, 619
23:42   27, 535, 1056
23:43   686, 688
24:1–4   1013
24:2–15   707
24:2   173, 232, 389, 395, 398
24:4   1042
24:5–9   183, 186, 200
24:6–7   5
24:7   161, 597, 630
24:8   232, 617, 619
24:9   59, 161, 162, 186, 188,
   201, 395, 618
24:10–23   294, 374
24:12–16   1041
24:14–23   39, 40
24:14   1041
24:15   332, 423, 458, 772,
   906
24:15a   906
24:16   5, 242, 1065
24:17   145, 183, 772
24:18   712, 720
24:19   772
24:20a   40
24:22   686, 1065
25:1   437
25:2   863, 886, 1065

25:3 40
25:4–5 1057
25:4 780
25:5 774
25:8 234, 780, 922, 973
25:10 833, 867
25:10–34 1066
25:13 867
25:14 335
25:15 335
25:17 335, 686
25:23 724, 1065
25:24 867
25:25 867
25:26 304, 772, 860
25:28 8, 304, 619, 761
25:29–34a 1065
25:29 772, 1062, 1065
25:30 147, 212, 664
25:31 4, 521, 1065
25:32–34 1
25:32 867
25:33 867
25:34 867, 1065
25:35–39 1066
25:35 1065
25:38 686, 688
25:41 867
25:42 688
25:45 688, 867
25:47 304, 1065
25:49 304, 860
25:52 305
25:55 686, 688
26:1–12 4
26:1 686
26:2 348, 687, 754, 947
26:3–11 724
26:3 230, 619
26:4 867
26:6 712
26:9 4
26:11–12 4
26:11 37, 724
26:12–13 688
26:12 8
26:13 686, 688
26:14–45 349
26:14–22 868
26:14 230, 231
26:15 48, 230, 347, 619
26:18 48
26:19 867
26:22 712
26:30 4, 867
26:31–32 163
26:31 162, 754, 867
26:34–35 49

26:39–40 376
26:40 36, 301, 347, 366, 369, 376
26:41 376, 747
26:42 722
26:43 4, 619
26:44 686
26:45 8, 687
26:46 37, 437, 617
27:2–7 750
27:2 331, 357, 409, 772
27:4 331
27:6 6, 434
27:8 304
27:9–34 325
27:9–33 752
27:9–14 351
27:9 391
27:10a 324
27:12 409
27:13 331
27:14 331
27:15–22 331
27:15 326
27:16–24 6
27:16–21 357
27:16–19 357
27:16 867
27:17 409
27:21 346, 357, 867
27:22 867
27:23 326
27:26 153, 462, 680
27:27 409, 463
27:28 182, 321, 346, 680, 867
27:28–29 346
27:29 346, 395
27:30–33 323, 475
27:30 17, 435
27:32 5, 153, 797
27:34 230, 438

Numbers

1:2 12, 228
1:3 12
1:4–16 247
1:5–16 247
1:9 437
1:14 662
1:17 495
1:18 4
1:44 247
1:47 813
1:49 12
1:51 346, 352, 754, 977

1:53 1082, 241, 498, 708
1:54 1059
2:1 645
2:2 365
2:3 6
2:6 588
2:10 6
2:14 18, 662
2:17 140
2:18 6
2:25 6
2:29 610
2:34 1059
3:1–14 437
3:1 831, 884
3:3 157, 231, 518, 539, 540, 607, 610
3:4 598, 600, 633, 634, 1012
3:5 7
3:6 849
3:7 209
3:10 346, 352, 754, 977
3:11–13 724
3:12 432
3:15 4, 687
3:23 602
3:24 246
3:29 164, 602
3:30 246, 604
3:31 602
3:32 247, 626, 708, 1083
3:35 164, 246, 602
3:38 140, 209, 346, 352, 754, 977
3:41 495
3:44–51 724
3:45 687
3:49 803
4:1–15 602
4:1 645
4:3–15 448
4:3–14 452
4:4–14 251, 450
4:4–12 516
4:4 321
4:5–20 977
4:5 138, 448
4:6–9 674, 809
4:7 14 1014
4:7 612
4:7b 399
4:9 597
4:11–13 809
4:11a 12
4:12 605
4:13 171, 386
4:14 155, 581, 716
4:15–16 626

4:15   45, 321, 325, 445, 450,
   458, 605, 946, 1014
4:16   398, 399, 605
4:16a   398
4:17   645
4:19–20   458, 946
4:19   321, 977
4:20   45, 143, 251, 325, 454,
   605, 977, 1014, 1035
4:24–28   448
4:25   36, 450
4:27   12
4:32   12
4:34   499
4:49   12
5   988, 989, 990, 991
5:1–31   965
5:1–4   724
5:2–5   806
5:2–4   44, 909
5:2–3   262, 316, 967, 969,
   995, 997
5:2   276, 774, 801, 920
5:2b   257
5:4   1059
5:5–8   13
5:5   344
5:6–8   328, 351, 368, 373,
   861
5:6–7   178, 301, 329, 370
5:6b–7   345
5:6   145, 320, 344, 345, 346,
   365, 369, 427
5:6b   344
5:7–8   326, 327
5:7   301, 302, 338, 342, 344
5:7b   334
5:8   327, 342, 369, 410, 706
5:9–10   410, 415, 416, 474
5:9   415, 473
5:11–31   367
5:11   179, 306
5:12–31   2
5:12   36, 688
5:13   242, 927, 931
5:14   688
5:15–26   200
5:15   25, 179, 180, 182, 197,
   200, 306, 398, 400, 412,
   467, 624, 803
5:16   148, 849
5:16b   1024
5:17   836
5:18   148, 608, 609, 849
5:18a   1024
5:19–21   367
5:20   927
5:21   294, 347
5:22   314

5:23   836
5:25   147, 148, 462
5:26   181, 467
5:29–30   383, 688, 761
5:30   849
5:31   25, 423, 624, 761
6   253
6:1–21   2, 278, 356
6:1–12   361
6:1   145
6:2   357, 512, 759, 945
6:3–9   357
6:3   611
6:3a   945
6:4   280, 357, 512
6:5–8   48
6:5   256, 359, 512, 608, 945,
   996
6:6–7   357
6:7   280, 512, 685, 945
6:7b   280, 357
6:8   256, 279, 357, 421, 453,
   512, 996
6:9–12   32, 357, 986
6:9–11   279, 453
6:9–10   571
6:9   229, 749, 919, 922
6:9b   357, 1008
6:10–12   357, 466, 851
6:10–11   284
6:10   148, 266, 759, 761, 925
6:11–12   358
6:11   251, 256, 266, 858, 996
6:11b   280, 357
6:12–14   330, 844
6:12–13   512
6:12   303, 357, 414, 757, 945
6:12b   996
6:13–21   160, 217, 357
6:13–17   488
6:13–15   358
6:13   148, 688, 883
6:14–16   756
6:14–15   200
6:14   163, 176, 266, 267,
   280, 290, 414, 757
6:15   414, 498
6:16–17   266
6:16   266, 1012
6:17   266, 414, 421, 498
6:18–19   32, 419, 527, 620
6:19–21   198, 200
6:19–20   414, 464, 563
6:19   11, 219, 220, 223, 281,
   430, 453, 498
6:20–21   531
6:20   415, 432, 462, 473,
   621, 851
6:21   304, 383, 413

6:22–27   54
6:22–24   18
6:24   587
6:26   587
6:30   461
7   292, 593, 757
7:1   338, 398, 786, 1024
7:2   246, 247
7:3   145, 209, 437
7:6   287
7:10   398, 593, 874
7:11   593
7:12–83   790
7:12–17   572
7:13–17   759
7:13–14   15
7:15–87   147
7:15   154, 281, 757
7:16–17   15
7:16   15, 281
7:21   281
7:22   281
7:82   757
7:84   338, 398, 592, 593, 786
7:84a   885
7:88   398, 593
7:88b   338, 885
7:89   58, 134, 136, 138, 140,
   142, 143, 437, 499, 1014,
   1031
8:2–3   398
8:2   173
8:4   141, 164, 777
8:5–22   278
8:5   1018
8:6–7a   278
8:6   290, 519
8:7   253, 278, 501, 519, 745,
   761, 840, 844, 879, 944,
   966, 967
8:8   266, 562, 760, 1018
8:9–10   498
8:9–10a   210
8:9   1018
8:10   152, 1018
8:11   461, 462, 564
8:12   153, 244, 255, 266, 278
8:13–15   464
8:13   461
8:15   462
8:18   578, 1018
8:19   605, 707, 708, 1082
8:20   278, 1059
8:21   255, 290, 461, 462,
   519, 564, 578, 761, 1065
9:1–14   286
9:3   619
9:5   266, 1059
9:6–7   1055

9:6   752
9:8b   627
9:10   463, 906
9:10a   906
9:12   619, 638
9:13–14   1055
9:13   265, 423, 458
9:14   696
9:15–23   61, 139, 1014
9:15–16   136
9:15   58, 575, 589, 777, 786
9:16   777
9:17–23   59
9:18   58, 589
9:19   541, 805
9:23   18, 541
10:1–9   224
10:1–7   242
10:3–4   247
10:3   499
10:4   499
10:8   157, 619
10:9   55
10:10   2, 20, 176, 686
10:10a   224
10:11–12   438
10:12   59, 437
10:14   6
10:18   6
10:21   754
10:22   6
10:25   6
11:1   599
11:4   428
11:7   780, 813
11:16–33   142
11:16–30   140
11:16   495
11:18   445, 602, 966
11:22   428
11:24–27   140
11:30   244
11:31–32   222
11:31   966
12   994
12:1   645, 822
12:2   611, 822
12:4–10   140, 142
12:4–5   140
12:5   140
12:8   134, 822
12:9   786, 821
12:10   774, 806
12:11–16   888
12:11–13   376
12:12   46, 733, 819, 832, 1002
12:13   807
12:14–16   818

12:14–15   779
12:14   915
13:1–15   247
13:3a   1024
13:17a   1024
13:20   192
13:23   504
13:27   906
13:31   665
14:1–4   241, 498
14:1   414, 645
14:2   498, 774
14:10   136
14:12   423
14:13–19   376
14:14   589
14:16   715
14:18   623
14:19–20   245
14:20   197
14:21–22   577
14:30   587
14:34   25
14:43   377
14:44   141
15   267, 269, 281
15:1–21   269
15:1–16   266, 483, 573, 582
15:1–12   196
15:1–9   180
15:1–8   484
15:2   215, 484, 573, 863
15:3–4   845
15:3   152, 162, 175, 177, 219, 288, 420, 710, 758
15:4–9   390
15:4–5   845, 861
15:4   845
15:7   162
15:8   172, 176, 217, 218, 219, 420, 901
15:10   161, 162
15:11   163
15:12   248
15:13–16   696
15:13   162, 909
15:14   162
15:15   395, 421, 619
15:15a   422
15:17–21   266, 415, 462, 474
15:19–21   191, 473, 474
15:19–20   415
15:19   461
15:20–21   190
15:20   184
15:21   4, 461, 475, 614
15:22–31   253, 266, 268, 269, 485, 696
15:22–27   268

15:22–26   246, 263, 264, 265, 292, 407, 517, 537, 1055
15:22–25   13
15:22   230, 265, 269
15:23   4, 614
15:24–29   365, 710
15:24–25   161, 304
15:24   17, 154, 244, 266, 267, 281, 436, 572, 573, 1018
15:24a   268
15:25   498
15:25b   161, 253, 268, 433, 442, 1055
15:27–31   257
15:27–29   272, 724, 772, 1055
15:27–28   291
15:27   229, 265, 267, 268, 757
15:28   229, 303
15:29   228, 269, 422, 703
15:30–31   178, 228, 277, 334, 365, 424, 458, 710, 772, 1022, 1055, 1063
15:30   369, 981
15:30b   369
15:31   230, 384, 1007
15:32–36   351, 1041
15:35   5, 242
15:37–41   13, 266, 696
15:38   548
15:39   230
15:40   230, 549, 686, 967
15:41   8, 9, 686, 688
16   459
16:2   138, 247, 499
16:3–33   242
16:3   359
16:5   147, 242, 966
16:6–7   160
16:6   1024
16:7   966
16:8–9   4
16:9   8, 147
16:13   138
16:14   1033
16:15   57
16:16–18   238
16:16f   355
16:16   966
16:17–18   160, 597, 598
16:17   242
16:18–20   140
16:18   599
16:19   136, 499, 600
16:21   415, 474, 486
16:22   609

16:25   244
16:28   1015
16:33   459
16:35   45, 599, 600
16:35a   600
17:2   445, 597, 598, 633
17:3   445, 597, 707, 1012
17:4   250, 610
17:5   237, 251, 577, 598, 977
17:6–12   242
17:7–8   58, 575
17:7   589
17:8–9   588
17:8   136, 605, 606
17:9–15   887
17:10   415, 474, 486
17:11–13   238
17:11–12   1025, 1082
17:11   241, 498, 597, 598,
   1024, 1029, 1083
17:15   136
17:17   247, 1019
17:19   134, 140
17:21   1019
17:23   511, 1019
17:27–28   45
17:28   355, 946, 977, 1012
18:1–24   57
18:1   8, 423, 611, 623, 754,
   1012
18:1a   602
18:1b   602
18:2–3   55
18:2   577, 754, 1019
18:3   8, 45, 458, 568, 577,
   601, 602, 946, 977, 1012
18:3b   6, 7, 8
18:4–5   605
18:4   577
18:4a   8
18:4b–5   8
18:5   605, 978
18:6   432
18:7   346, 352, 577, 977,
   1013
18:7a   541, 602
18:8–20   433
18:8   369, 395, 415, 433,
   611, 619, 707, 1012
18:8b   434
18:9–19   462, 463
18:9–14   200
18:9–10   462
18:9   204, 321, 327, 342,
   433, 462, 761
18:10   323, 408
18:11–19   415, 473
18:11–12   1004
18:11   8, 204, 395, 619, 752

18:11a   8
18:12–19   182, 395
18:12–13   190, 323, 442, 475
18:12   190, 210, 456
18:13   193, 415, 463, 474,
   752, 849
18:13a   8
18:13aβ   8
18:14–18   463
18:14   8, 346, 864
18:15–16   724
18:16   326, 409
18:17   162, 427
18:18–19   320
18:18   321, 432, 462, 473,
   475, 621
18:19   191, 204, 395, 461,
   474, 614, 619, 707
18:20   8, 1012
18:21   17, 436
18:22–23   623, 708, 1082
18:22   355, 577, 602, 946,
   1012
18:23   8, 259, 395, 423, 602,
   619, 623
18:24–29   415, 473
18:24   415, 461, 463, 474
18:25–32   12
18:26–32   474
18:26–29   568
18:26   12, 415, 474
18:27   190, 421, 710
18:28   415, 474
18:29   463, 474, 1058
18:30   421, 710
18:31   474, 568
18:32   38, 355, 474
19   270, 276, 277, 279, 988,
   989, 990, 991
19:1–13   819
19:1–12   802, 1051
19:1   271
19:2–7   160
19:2   146, 272, 273, 383,
   619, 1022
19:3–5   273, 521
19:3   274
19:4   233, 273, 274, 444,
   605, 606, 853, 1052
19:5–6   15
19:5   15, 161, 273, 274, 1052
19:6–7   638, 1052
19:6   46, 161, 273, 274, 802,
   836, 963
19:7–10   406, 987
19:7–8   672
19:7   840, 841, 919, 997
19:8   161, 274, 840, 841,
   919, 997, 1050, 1053

19:9   262, 274, 276, 744,
   745, 833, 838, 979, 997,
   1008, 1018
19:10   16, 274, 619, 672,
   703, 919
19:10b–13   724
19:10b   696
19:11–12   357, 453
19:11   681
19:12   2, 833, 963
19:13–20   458
19:13   229, 257, 270, 276,
   304, 308, 311, 316, 317,
   680, 945, 973, 981, 1007,
   1055
19:14–16   299, 977
19:14–15   405
19:14   144, 317, 383, 688,
   802, 875, 876, 883, 1002
19:15   675, 977
19:15a   422
19:16–19   453
19:16   668, 672
19:17–18a   276
19:17   802, 833, 836, 837,
   838, 922, 997, 1018
19:18   275, 836, 839, 935
19:19   253, 275, 402, 406,
   668, 802, 833, 839, 840,
   876, 879, 919, 934, 996
19:19b   875, 997
19:20   229, 257, 270, 276,
   304, 308, 311, 314, 317,
   754, 945, 981, 1007, 1055
19:21   16, 275, 619, 840,
   1052
19:21b   270, 668
19:22   425
20:1–6   242
20:1   498
20:6–13   348
20:6–7   58, 575
20:6   136, 140, 589
20:7–13   15, 242
20:7–8   498
20:13   601, 603
20:24   460
20:25–29   554
20:25–28   501
20:25   610
20:26   157
20:28   157
21:1–3   500
21:1   234
21:5   684
21:6–9   15
21:8–9   30
21:12b   280
21:16–18   15

21:19　500
21:25　495
21:25b　1024
21:31　1024
22:3　424
22:12　415
22:13　415
22:18　415, 861
22:21　15, 520
22:21a　1024
22:25　169
22:29　15
22:35b　1024
22:40　573, 714
23　152
23:1　234
23:2　154
23:2　173
23:4　173
23:14　173
23:15–17　200
23:15　174
23:17–20　414
23:19　403
23:24　708
23:30　173
24:13　861
24:18　300
25:1–15　1082
25:8　247
25:8–10　571
25:9　1066
25:10　708, 1083
25:10–13　35
25:12–15　722
25:12–13　722
25:14　246
25:15　12
26:1　645
26　12
26:29–34　12
26:61　598, 633, 634, 1012
26:62–64　4
27:2　499
27:7　6, 867
27:8　849
27:11　619, 849
27:13　460
27:17　498
27:18–20　554
27:18　152, 495, 1041
27:19–22　499
27:19　849
27:21　54, 507, 508, 554
27:21a　508
27:22　849
27:23　1041
28　19, 21
28:2　20, 440

28:3–10　281
28:3–6　3, 4, 162, 163
28:3–4　208
28:5　306, 398, 400, 845, 895
28:6　162, 180, 484, 584
28:7–10　19, 27
28:7　605, 612
28:7a　398
28:7b　59, 611
28:8　162
28:9–10　21
28:9　179, 306, 398
28:11–15　20, 21
28:11–13　162, 163
28:11　573
28:12–13　4, 162
28:12　179, 400
28:13　179, 306, 398
28:15　161, 162, 176, 259,
　　281, 292, 573, 845
28:16–25　282
28:16–24　163
28:17–19　4, 162
28:18　21, 1055
28:19–21　162, 457
28:19　573
28:20　400
28:21　306, 398
28:22　162, 281, 573
28:23　457
28:24　162, 180
28:25　21, 1055
28:26　18, 21, 192, 193, 1055
28:27　162, 573
28:28　400
28:29　306, 398
28:30　281, 573
29:1　21, 1055
29:2　59, 162, 180
29:5　281
29:6　162, 573, 589
29:7–11　1066
29:7　21, 25, 51, 1054
29:8–11　281, 1049
29:8　162, 175, 180, 1049
29:9–10　900
29:9–11　1046
29:11　281, 1059, 1062
29:12–34　27
29:12　21, 1055
29:13　162
29:14–15　457
29:16　281
29:19　281
29:20–22　845
29:22　281
29:25　281
29:26　162
29:28　281

29:31　281
29:35　571, 594, 1055
29:36　154, 161, 180
29:38　161, 281
29:39　20, 27, 218, 483
30:1ff　367
30:2　313, 500
30:3　299, 367, 374
30:5　1033
30:6　17, 245
30:7　299
30:9　17, 245
30:12b　708
30:13　17, 245
30:14　300, 1054
30:16　25, 423, 624, 707
30:17　617
31:2　460
31:4　668
31:6　55
31:7–8　1033
31:9　146
31:14　609
31:16　12, 348, 498
31:18　11
31:19–24　677
31:19　144, 314, 724, 997,
　　998
31:20　674
31:21–24　2
31:21　383, 619, 883
31:22–23　272, 407
31:22　674, 921
31:23　674
31:24　314, 840, 919, 944,
　　967, 991, 997, 998
31:26　241, 498
31:28　146, 241, 461, 474,
　　498, 712, 720
31:29　415, 473, 475
31:41　415, 473
31:42–47　322
31:43　241, 498
31:48　707
31:49　707
31:50　145, 417, 708, 1082
31:52　415, 473
31:54　707
32:4　498
32:15　377
32:22　863
32:29　863
32:33　339, 787
32:35　6, 867
32:42　384
33　12
33:3a　1024
33:5a　1024
33:11　666

33:40 500
33:51 863
33:52 1033
34 11
34:2 863
34:12 863
34:16–28 247
35:1–15 12
35:2 6, 867
35:3 1033
35:4 169, 871
35:6 707
35:9ff 301
35:10 863
35:11 228, 486
35:12 230
35:15 228, 230, 486, 696, 703
35:16–18 228, 283
35:16 673
35:18 673
35:19 383
35:22–23 228, 283
35:22 673
35:25 230, 231, 708, 1082
35:28 231
35:29 215, 619
35:30 228
35:31–33 708, 1082
35:32–36 1082
35:33–34 724, 749
35:33 680, 706, 710
35:34–35 229, 1055
36:1 246
36:4 193
36:6 500
36:13 230

Deuteronomy

1:12 685
1:13 333
1:15 333
1:31 1015
1:33 1015
1:34 609
1:46 748
2:5 669, 726
3:23–26 376
3:26 377
4:2 715
4:17 645
4:19 1021
4:21 590
4:25 785
4:29–30 376
4:30 377
4:40 715

4:42 333
5:7–8 1021
5:14 703
5:15 21
5:22 599
6:2 715
6:5 715
6:11 680, 923
7:1–3 359, 360, 361
7:1 360
7:4–6 730
7:5 703
7:6 359, 703
7:11 715
7:15 745
7:20 775
7:22–27 215
7:24–26 215
7:24 459, 874
7:25–26 346
7:25 699
7:26 656, 699, 700
8:1 715
8:2–3 1054
8:8 189, 190
8:11 715
9:3 590
9:16–29 376
9:19 609
10:1–10 54
10:2 1011
10:5 54
10:9 8
10:13 715
10:14 715
10:15 715, 749
10:16 748
11:8 715
11:11 686
11:12 389
11:13 715
11:22 715
11:24 669
11:27 246, 715
11:28 715
12 32
12:5 577
12:6 177, 199, 218, 620, 629, 1004
12:7 33, 620
12:11–14 427
12:11 199, 483, 577, 629
12:12 33, 174, 620
12:13 174, 699
12:14 199, 629, 715
12:15–16 29, 214, 417, 709, 713, 734
12:15 8, 484, 573, 647, 713, 714, 715, 717, 724

12:16 8, 29, 215, 216, 427, 429, 705
12:17–18 427
12:18 620
12:20–24 214
12:20 734, 772
12:21–25 29
12:21–22 647
12:21 8, 427, 573, 577, 713, 714, 715, 716, 717, 718, 724, 772
12:22–24 713
12:22 717
12:23–25 8, 417, 427, 705, 709
12:23 29, 215, 429, 767
12:24 216, 429
12:25 429
12:26–28 427
12:27 169, 199, 217, 238, 629
12:28 715
12:29 772
13:2 772
13:7 772
13:11 715
13:13 772
13:15 699, 780
13:17 400
13:19 715
14:1–2 730
14:1 801
14:1a 700
14:2 359, 703, 725
14:3 699
14:4–5 10, 647, 659, 690, 701, 702, 728
14:4b–5a 699
14:4b–5 701
14:4–8 351, 692, 697
14:4–21 697, 704, 728, 729
14:4–21aa 699
14:4 652, 682, 685, 729
14:4a 699
14:5 661, 682, 723, 729
14:6–7a 700
14:6 646, 647, 699, 720
14:6b 646
14:7 654
14:7a 646, 648
14:7b 648
14:7b–8a 700
14:8 646, 653, 654
14:8b 700
14:9–10 692, 697
14:9 685, 700, 702
14:9b 700
14:10 654
14:10a 700

INDEX OF SOURCES

14:10b 700
14:11–18 692, 697
14:11 222, 647, 665, 697,
  701, 702
14:12a 701
14:12b–18 701
14:13 662
14:18 664, 701
14:19–20 692, 697
14:19 654, 665, 702
14:20 665, 699, 701, 702
14:21 10, 359, 692, 701,
  703, 725, 737
14:21aβ 699, 703
14:21a 702
14:21aδ 703
14:21a 703
14:21b 699, 703
14:22 387
14:23 577
14:24–26 288
14:24 577, 772
14:26 612
14:29 703
15:3 703
15:5 715
15:12 772
15:19–23 218
15:19 324, 351
15:21 147, 573
15:23 417, 709
16:1 194, 688
16:2–4 218
16:2 577
16:3 688
16:4 638
16:7 463
16:9 190
16:10–11 710
16:11 620
16:12 688
16:14 703
16:15 594
16:17 441
17:1 147, 699
17:2 772
17:3–7 427
17:3 1021
17:4 699, 780
17:7–9 615
17:8–13 54
17:8 772, 776, 887, 905
17:9a 887
17:11 54, 417
17:11a 887
17:14 772
18:1–2 8
18:1 8, 162
18:3 432, 714

18:4 190
18:6–7 187, 480
18:6–8 33, 187
18:8a 187
18:9a 187
18:12 699
18:13 147
19:1–3 486
19:5–6 228
19:9 715
19:10 141, 710
19:14 333
19:16–21 367
19:18 780
19:21 707
20:5 592
20:6 1083
20:10 627
20:18 699
20:19 627
20:19b 627
20:20 627
21:1–9 712, 1082
21:3 146, 610
21:5 54, 772, 776
21:5b 615
21:7 710
21:10–14 11
21:12 803
21:23 702
22:1–3 329
22:1–4 809
22:5 673, 699
22:6–7 222, 739
22:6 739, 741
22:9 445, 448, 548
22:11 447, 448, 809, 810,
  1023
22:21 147
22:23 931
22:25 931
22:27 741
22:28 741, 931
22:29 931, 1023
23:4–5 970
23:4–9 360
23:4 359
23:5 805
23:10–15 724
23:10–12 767, 910
23:10–11 444
23:11–15 966
23:11 907, 927, 928, 1034
23:13–14 536
23:15 141, 970
23:15b 981
23:16 779
23:19 699
23:21 703

23:22–24 313, 374
23:26 470
24:4 699
24:6–11 337
24:6 184, 337
24:8–9 823
24:8 8, 52, 617, 772, 776,
  830, 887
24:9 887
24:14–15 337
24:14 703, 813
24:16 736
25:9–10 872
25:9 915
25:15 418
25:16 699
26:2 191
26:10 191
26:14 636
26:19 359, 703
27:1 715
27:4 715
27:5 470
27:6–7 176, 483, 573
27:7 217, 218, 220, 221,
  223, 419, 441, 620, 710
27:10 715
27:11–26 314
27:15 699
27:17 821
28:1 715
28:9 359, 703
28:22 775, 801
28:27 787, 821
28:29 337
28:31 337, 716
28:35 585, 787
28:42 665
28:49 662
28:56 669, 726
28:60 745
28:65 669
29:4–5 612
29:12 9
29:16 656, 700
29:18 314
29:19 459
29:21 703
29:28 362
30:1–10 376, 377
30:1 867
30:2 715
30:8 715
30:10–15 316
30:11 715
30:16 715
30:19 867
31:6 54
31:12 703

31:24   147
31:30   147
32:11   662
32:14   207, 210
32:16   699
32:17   714
32:22   384
32:30   779
32:38   213
32:49   867
32:51   345, 348
33:4   144, 618
33:5   144
33:8   507
33:10   52, 173, 400, 597
33:11   150, 617
33:16   512
33:20   427
33:23–24   150
34:8   536, 610
34:9   152, 1041
34:10   134

Joshua

1:2b   787
1:7   391
2:15   169
2:18   1022
3:5   602, 965
3:6   397
3:13   726
3:16   965
4:21   246
5:2–10   747
5:5   748
5:8   832
5:9   458
5:11   193
5:14   591
5:15   340, 502, 654
6:17   463
6:19–24   328
6:19   321
7   355
7:1ff   346
7:1   346
7:8   305
7:11b   346
7:11   346, 348
7:12   305
7:13–14   966
7:13   346, 445, 602
7:15   348, 356
7:24–25   356
8:24   328
8:31   174, 217, 470, 483, 573
9:19   374
10:2   340

10:25   931
10:31   212
10:32   282, 783
11:2   469
12:2   469
13:14   162
14:1   246, 340
14:12   931
15:9   680
15:18   937
18:1a   31
18:6   1019
18:9b   31
18:10a   31
18:10   1019
18:11   1022
19:1   210, 1022
19:7–8   4
19:10   1022
19:17   1022
19:50–51   31
19:51a   31
20:2   688
20:5   779
20:9   688
21:2–4   31
21:4   157
21:13–19   187
22:12b   31
22:13   498
22:14–16   241
22:16   347, 348, 377, 498
22:18   348, 349, 377, 498,
   609
22:19   250, 724
22:20   346, 349, 355, 498
22:21   246
22:22   347, 348
22:23   199, 201, 217, 377,
   629
22:26   218, 483
22:28   218, 377, 483
22:31   349
24:12   775

Judges

1:1–2   508, 509
1:15   937
2:10   460
2:27–28   508
3:15   196
3:16   384
3:17   196
3:18   145
3:24   921
4:18   909
4:19   810
5:2   609

5:18   707
5:27   403
6:4   784
6:5   11, 665
6:15   861
6:18–21   441
6:18   748
6:19–21   201, 221
6:22–23   136
6:24   599
6:26   174
6:37   745
6:38   169
7:12   665
8:1   755
8:7   505
8:27   11
9:8–13   190
9:9   171, 386
9:17   154, 663
10:8   535
11:11   31
11:34   391
11:35–36   299, 374
12:3   707
12:6   715
13:5   512
13:14   612
13:15–16   221
13:15–20   590
13:16   174, 213, 441
13:19–20   201
13:20   591, 599
13:22   136
14:8   190
14:10   612
16:9   793
16:17   238, 656, 1022
16:22   798
16:23   714
16:29   150
16:30   798
17:1–5   294
17:2   315
17:3   415, 475, 485
17:5   54, 539
17:7–18:20   53
17:10   784
17:12   539
18:11   673
18:17–20   54
18:18   505
18:20   508, 509
18:30   556
18:31   31
19:5   185
19:7   786
19:10   520
19:29   157

20:1 31, 241, 300, 498
20:12 498
20:16 229
20:18 31
20:21 300
20:23 31
20:24–25 282, 783
20:26 31, 176, 217, 224, 484
20:27–28 140
20:27 31, 498
20:38 773
20:40 773
21:2–4 268
21:4 224
21:5 31, 300
21:7 787
21:8 31
21:10 241, 498
21:13 31, 241, 498
21:19–24 1067
21:19 32
21:22 498
29:26 267

1 Samuel

1–3 31, 32
1:1–3 31
1:4 49, 432
1:9 223, 914
1:12–17 61
1:13 155
1:18–19 220
1:21 218, 483
1:22–24 953
1:23 748
1:24 198
1:25 LXX 154
1:25 715
1:27 836
2:1 236
2:10 236
2:11 234
2:13–14 33, 223, 281, 419, 453
2:13–16 220, 441
2:13–17 223, 479
2:15–16 197
2:15 207, 714, 785
2:15a 442
2:17 197, 222, 442, 479, 709
2:18 384, 505
2:19 32, 504
2:22 53
2:25 229, 375
2:27–36 34, 722
2:27–28 34
2:28 155, 162, 237
2:28a 52

2:29 197, 198, 222, 440, 442, 479, 709
2:29b 191, 370
2:36 185, 774
3 140
3:2 781
3:3 140
3:9 155
3:11 162
3:13 33, 781
3:14 155, 197, 198, 221, 706, 709
3:16 162
3:17 300
4:3b 31
4:7 155
4:12 384
5:6 327
6 327
6:1 327
6:3–8 1079
6:3–17 327
6:3 326, 327, 342
6:4–5 327
6:4 326, 327, 342
6:7 168
6:8 326, 327, 342
6:17 326, 327, 342
6:19 45, 316, 325, 454, 1014
7:1 140
7:3 155
7:5–6 31
7:5–9 376
7:6 268, 302, 1066
7:9–10 268
7:9 173, 174, 175, 400
8:5 238
8:18 155
9:3 777, 780
9:12–13 57
9:13 224
9:20 421
9:21 49
9:22 223
9:23 432
9:24 207, 210, 211, 432
10 168
10:1 518
10:3 187, 198, 224, 412
10:8 217, 224
10:22 508, 509
10:27 196
11:5 217, 224
11:9 403
11:11 305
11:15 710
12:3–4 337
12:3 57, 337
12:4 337

12:19ff 376
13:9–14 57
13:9–12 224
13:12 175, 268
14:3 31
14:9 789
14:24–25 213, 315
14:26–29 190
14:26 189
14:27 315
14:31–35 28
14:32–34 228
14:32–35 49, 714
14:32 155, 715
14:33–34 155
14:34 249, 715
14:35 29
14:36 1012
14:41 (LXX) 55
14:41 508, 509, 510
14:43–45 1041
14:44 300
15:3–31 355
15:3ff 346
15:3 346, 463
15:11 376, 377
15:21 191
15:22 207, 218, 483
15:29 504
15:33 346
16:5 445, 966
16:13–14 553
16:13 518
17:38 384
18:4 384, 504
18:12 553
19:5 707
19:13 674, 809
19:16 674
20:6 733
20:12 780
20:18 910, 914
20:22 55
20:25 910, 914
20:26–17 423
20:26 927
20:29 218, 483, 733
21:5–6 323, 751, 965, 967
21:5 187, 412
21:6 444, 445, 931
21:7 412
21:14 908
22:3 423
22:13 187, 715
22:18–19 348
22:18 505
23:6 505
23:9 505
23:11 779

23:12 779
24 49
24:5 343, 504
24:7 553
24:8 553
24:12 504
25:11 716
25:15 875
25:16 207
25:20 937
25:24 295, 339
25:28 295
25:31 343, 710
26:9 553
26:11 553
26:16 553
26:19 196, 362, 774
26:21 228, 283
26:23 553
28:6 507
28:10 295
28:14 504, 803
28:22 185
28:24 714
30:17 420

2 Samuel

1:10 512
1:14 553
1:16 553
1:19a 553
1:21 553
1:22 759
2:1 55, 508, 510
3:25 821
3:29 774, 915, 926
3:35 300
3:37 298
4:11 150
5:23–24 55, 508, 510
6:6–7 45, 454
6:6–8 316
6:6 325
6:13 489
6:14 384, 505
6:17–18 224, 489
6:17 31, 141
6:19 5, 184
7 31
7:6–7 30
7:6 141
7:14 776, 821
8:7–11 752
8:7 322
8:10–11 322
8:11 780
9:7 389
9:10 389

9:12 225
9:13 225, 389
9:22 225
10:4 809
11:2 965
11:4 445, 935, 965
11:9 147
11:11 444, 967
12:2–3 456
12:3 185
12:13–14 376
12:16–20 1054
12:16 887
13:4 861
13:17 1023
14:2 180
14:9 295
14:10 776
14:17 300
14:20 300
15:7b–8 18, 219, 419
15:7 733
15:12 733
15:25 803
17:9 813
18:17 813
19:25 803
20:5 136
21:3–6 708
22:3 236
22:22 229
23:8a 734
23:21 1021
24:10 343
24:10ff 376
24:21–25 176
24:24 441, 931
24:25 224, 268, 484, 887
25:18–25 755

1 Kings

1:1 674, 809
1:13 300
1:17 300
1:30 300
1:39 518, 554
1:50–51 250
1:51 456
2:2–3 456
2:18 154
2:19 528
2:23 300
2:26–27 34, 722
2:28–34 251
2:31 710
3:2–3 714
3:3 160
3:4 174, 554

3:15 217, 224
4:14 161
5:1 145
5:2 179
5:3 222
6:20–22 236
6:27 1014
6:31–32 1070
7:20 213
7:23 890
7:24 521
7:26 890
7:27–39 518
7:33 843
7:38 160
7:45 800
7:48 236
7:50 1025
7:51 321, 322, 752
8:1–2 499, 547
8:1 499
8:5 489, 714, 858
8:11 138, 499
8:31 251
8:33–43 302
8:33–53 250
8:37–38 887
8:37 665, 666, 776
8:38 251, 776
8:44 251
8:48 251
8:55 499
8:63–64 224, 225, 554
8:63 217, 225
8:64–65 251
8:64 198, 201, 207, 217, 224
8:65–66 1071
8:65 537
9:2–3 499
9:3 138
9:7 138
9:12 777
9:25 174, 224
10:8 389
10:22 861
11:8 714
12:19 1034
12:33 237
13:1 237
13:33 539, 786
14:26–27 322, 752
15:5 779
15:15 321, 322, 752
17:4 702
17:11 185
17:12–16 180
17:13–24 817
17:20ff 376
17:22 888

18:24   376
18:29   191, 399, 457
18:32   238
18:36   191, 200, 399, 457
18:38   174, 250
18:40   715
18:43   234
19:9–14   140
19:15   553
19:16   714
19:16b   553
19:21   714
20:34   250
20:42   346, 355
21:9   1066
21:10   374
21:13   374, 814
21:19   708
21:27ff   376
21:29   376
22:10   147
22:38   920
22:44   198

2 Kings

1:1   1034
1:13   780
2:5   749
2:21   888
2:23   800
2:31   749
3:5   1034
3:7   1034, 1044
3:16   799
3:27   174
4:10   937
4:11   469
4:17–37   817
4:24   937
4:33   376, 840
4:42   192, 193, 194
5   818
5:1   774, 831
5:10–14   964, 973
5:10   234, 831, 837, 921, 928
5:11   376, 774, 964
5:12   837, 964
5:13   837
5:14   234, 837, 842, 928
5:17   218, 250, 965
5:20–27   822
5:24   335
5:27   483, 774, 786, 821, 831
6:15–20   376
7:1   179
7:3–10   805, 818, 994
7:3   147, 775, 806, 831
7:8   775, 831

7:9   295
7:16   179
7:18   179
7:19   181
8:7   553
8:15   810
8:20   1034
8:22   1034, 1044
9:3   518
9:6   518
9:7   749
9:26   749
9:33   305, 403
10:7   715
10:14   715
10:20   966
10:24   174, 483
10:32   873
11   252
11:8   8
11:10   322
11:12   512
11:14   224
11:17   243
12:4   198, 714
12:5–27   287
12:5   321
12:10   148, 231, 755
12:11   231
12:17   177, 284, 287, 288,
     326, 327, 409
12:19   321
12:20   287
12:32   714
13:21   316
14:4   198, 714
15:5   775, 776, 806, 807,
     818, 831
15:35   714
16:4   714
16:5   457
16:10–14   348
16:12   385
16:13   198, 200, 217, 218,
     223, 416
16:14–17   346
16:14   164, 250
16:15   200, 217, 218, 250,
     399, 814
16:19   348
17:11   200
17:27b   52
17:40   230
18:2   755
18:4   200, 258
18:5   32
18:21   150
18:22   350
18:25   350

18:32   189
19:9   786
19:24   726
20:2–3   887
20:7–8   888
20:7   787, 817
20:12   196
21:3   258, 786
21:16   710
21:24   252
22:4   231
22:8   231
22:18ff   376
22:19   376
23:4   231
23:8–9   33
23:8   200, 481
23:9   187, 402, 480
23:9b   481
23:20   259
23:21–23   187
23:23   397
23:26   259
23:30   252
24:4   710
25:29   389
25:30   389

Isaiah

1:2   1034
1:5   745
1:6   726, 785
1:11   207
1:12   150
1:13a   20
1:13   181, 597
1:14   20
1:15   482
1:18   835, 908
1:23   776
2:2–3   482
2:8   26
2:18   26, 400
2:20   664
2:21   26
3:7   520
3:14   329
3:23   511
3:24   790, 801
3:46   520
4:4   170, 193
5:10   892, 901
5:11   663
5:14   422, 684, 1054
5:16   731
5:22   612
5:28   646
6:3   731

6:5–6   1017
6:6–7   1084
6:7   1084
7:3   376, 611
7:10   611
7:15   953
8:1   1020
10:2   305
10:9   3
10:10   26
10:11   26
10:15   469
10:16   384
10:21   376
10:22   376
10:26   335
11:1–4   553
11:6   740
11:7   720
11:15   470
13:2   470
13:20   685
13:21   248, 663, 702, 1020
14:1   774
16:11   159
19:3   666
19:11   26
19:16   470
19:21   419, 709
20:2   872, 809
21:5   553
21:15   745
22:4   663
22:10   679
22:14   1084
22:16   214
22:21   502
24:6   340
24:6a   340
24:20   339
26:19   686
26:21   712
26:39   376
27:9   706, 1079, 1084
28:1   511
28:7   612
28:9–10   953
28:18   511
28:20   775, 909
29:8   684
30:8   214
30:14   384, 596
30:22   505, 745, 937, 952
31:4   246
31:5   1081
31:7   26
31:11   246
32:6   684
33:4   665

33:14   384
33:24   623
34:6   207, 714
34:11   663, 702
34:13   663, 702
34:14   248, 1020
34:15   662
34:17   1019
36:6   150
37:16   257
38:2   817
38:10–21   219
38:14   664
38:21   787
40:2   139
40:6–8   511
40:22   666
41:23   300
42:4   781
42:21   576
43:2   790
43:20   702
43:23   181
43:24   213
43:25   377
43:27   1034
44:13   872
44:15   387
44:16   787
44:18   873
45:1   553
45:5   444
46:17   445
47:11   708, 1083
48:16   1012
48:21   906
49:13   591
50:6   800
51:9   660
51:10   688
51:17   169
52:1   620, 744, 747
53:4   776, 931
53:7   716
53:8   1046
53:11   295
53:12   339
55:2   171, 386, 684
57:5   715
57:6   201
57:8   921
57:10   921
57:15   347
58:11   422, 684
59:7   710
59:17   803
60:3   222
60:7   149
60:8   168

60:14   726
61:1   553, 833
61:3   180
61:10   673
61:11   680
62:3   511
62:8   528
63:3   403
64:5   744
65:3   198, 628, 714
65:4b–5a   652
65:4   422
65:5   384, 745
65:20   229
66:3   181, 201, 651, 715
66:13   714
66:17   603, 651, 966
66:17a   657
66:23   787

Jeremiah

1:10   679
1:18   252
1:39   663
2:3   191, 340, 358, 359, 361
2:8   1034
2:12   684
2:13   680, 761
2:32   744
3:12   684
3:14   684
3:25   684
4:4   748
4:18   339
4:28   413
5:2–3   348
5:4   861
6:1   773
6:4   967
6:6   383
6:7   603
6:18–20   484
6:19   484
6:20   149, 180
6:21   484
7:1–15   482
7:6   329
7:18   187, 188, 201, 387, 412
7:21–22   268, 482, 483
7:21   483, 484
7:21b   218
7:22   218, 483
7:34   191
8:7   664
8:8   921
8:14   748
8:18   745
8:22   1028

8:23 761
9:25 747, 748
11:13 161
11:19 213, 716
11:20 207, 303
12:1 260
12:3 716, 1011
13 5
13:1 674
13:2 504
13:4 504
13:6 504
13:7 504
13:11 504
13:26 603
13:27 745
14:12 176, 201, 268
14:21 482
15:1 376
15:7 707
15:14 384
16:9 191
17:1 284, 288
17:4 384
17:6 1045
17:10 207
17:13 686, 761
17:14 342
17:26 181, 202, 219, 412,
   413
18:2 161
18:4 680
18:8 339
18:11 339
18:17 305
18:23 377, 1079, 1084
19:3 628
19:13 200, 201
20:12 207
21:12 337
22:3 337, 710
22:6 1045
22:14 553
22:17 710
23:29 790
23:39 681
24:2 858
26:1–15 482
30:16 358
31:6 591
31:39 240, 620
32:29 200, 628
33:8 1034, 1039
33:17–22 722
33:18 161, 200
33:26 775
34:8 833
34:15 833
34:17 833

34:18 431
35:2 223
35:5 520
36:9 1066
36:23 814, 921
36:29 191
38:6 680
39:6 715
41:5 181, 183, 199, 202,
   412, 517
41:7 715
41:16 874
44:17–18 188, 200, 628
44:17 201, 238
44:18–19 201
44:19 188, 412
44:25 200, 628
46:4 406
46:10 714
46:11 1027, 1028
46:23 665
47:3 646
48:25 236
48:33 191
48:40 662
48:44 787
49:19 187
49:22 662
50:7 341
50:27 716
50:39 702
50:40 716
51:5b 231, 341
51:8 1027
51:43 1045
51:51 755
51:56 787
52:10 715
52:19 597

Ezekiel

1:4 813
1:7 813
1:18 843
1:27–28 589
1:27 4
2:28 145, 163
4:1a 214
4:3 185
4:10–15 536
4:11 896
4:12–14 915
4:12 767
4:14 422, 684
4:26 923
5:3 181
5:6 4
5:11 259, 982

5:13 162
6:1 163
6:3–5 4
6:6 4, 163, 215, 340
6:13 4
7:19–20 952
7:19 38
7:20 38
7:23 48, 341, 615
7:27 252
8:6 4, 982
8:10 4, 521, 788
8:11 237, 597, 1024
8:67 982
9:1 8
9:2–3 1016
9:2 5, 250, 384
9:3–4 139
9:7 607, 993
9:9 615
9:11 1016
10:2 1016
10:15–19 234
11:16 982
11:22 258
13:5 207
13:6 4
13:10 873
13:11 920
14:5 458, 945
14:7 945
14:13 346
16:6 749
16:7 744
16:9 920
16:13 179, 189, 861
16:17–19 4, 163
16:18 237
16:19 179
16:21 715
16:24–25 239
16:26 748, 907
16:31 239
16:38 242, 710
16:39 239
16:40 5, 242
16:42 4, 610
16:59–63 931
16:63 1084
17:3 170
17:7 170
17:13 300, 314, 347
17:15 348
17:16 300, 347
17:17 242
17:18–19 300
17:18 347
17:19–21 349
17:19 347, 348

17:20 347
18:5 4
18:6 335, 577, 941
18:7 337
18:10 710
18:10b 300
18:12 4, 337
18:16 337
18:18 4, 335, 337
18:19–20 335
18:23 4
18:24 346
19:1–32 260
19:7a 907
19:16 907
20:2 4
20:5 686
20:7 686
20:9 366
20:12 614
20:13 4
20:14 366
20:19 686
20:20 614, 686
20:22 366
20:25 714
20:28 4, 218
20:39 366
20:41 4, 163, 224, 601
21:3 789
21:4 387
21:9–10 387
21:12 781
21:16 800
21:31 511
22:3 710
22:4 710
22:6 710
22:9 4, 710
22:10 941
22:11 1005
22:12 710
22:24 1005
22:26 4, 52, 53, 615, 616,
    689, 690
22:29 337
23:3 242
23:12 600
23:14 214
23:15 5, 504
23:20 748, 907
23:34 169
23:38 982
23:39 715, 982
23:41 237
23:46–47 5
23:46 242
23:47 242
24:6–8 712

24:16 604
24:17 604, 803
24:21 982
24:22 803
25:1 461
25:10 1066
26:11 646
26:16 504
26:25 253
26:31–32 3
27:17 1027
27:20 674, 809
28:4 861
28:22 602, 603
28:24 811
28:26 686
29:4 655
29:18 800
30:5 587
30:21 520
32:13 646
32:22 242
32:23 242
33:7–9 945
33:15 337
34:3 714
34:6 803
34:10 191
34:11 797
34:12 797
34:30 686
36:20–22 347
36:20 366
36:21 366
36:22 366
36:23 366
36:25 1039
36:33 1039
37:2 788
37:11 1046
37:16 835
37:19 835
37:23a 982
37:23bβ 982
37:26–27 4
37:26 982
37:26bβ 982
37:27 37, 982
37:28 982
38:4 242
38:13 242
38:16 242, 601
38:18 398
38:20 687
38:33 602
38:78 242
39:7 366
39:12–16 982
39:17–19 708, 714

39:22 4, 614, 686
39:24a 982
39:28 686
40:5 4, 521, 898
40:12 4
40:17 4, 521
40:38 4, 160, 582
40:39–42 165, 451
40:39 281, 284, 288, 715
40:41 715
40:42 236, 715
40:43 145
40:45–46 722
40:46 577
40:47 4
41:2 4
41:17 521
41:18–19 4
41:22 4, 250
41:25 787
41:31 4
42:1–14 393
42:5 787
42:12 521
42:13 320, 394, 406, 601
42:14 386, 403, 444, 446,
    577, 605
42:20 521, 615
43 269
43:1–12 482
43:1 594
43:7–8 807
43:7 366
43:8 366
43:11 4
43:13–17 238, 250, 587
43:13 239
43:14 238
43:17 238, 385
43:18–20 282
43:18–27 268, 282, 517,
    571, 594
43:18 223, 398, 416
43:19–25 281
43:19 601, 722
43:20 232, 239, 250, 255,
    528, 529, 707, 1039, 1070
43:21–26 282
43:21 240, 262
43:22 253, 583, 783
43:23–26 232
43:23 255
43:24 191, 192
43:25–26 282, 537, 539
43:25 540
43:26 232, 253, 255, 529,
    539, 561, 1039, 1070, 1071
43:26b 539, 541
43:27 224, 535, 594

44:1 715
44:7 216, 747, 982
44:8–16 8
44:9 154, 747
44:10–11 4, 154, 615
44:11 451, 582
44:14 7
44:15–16 722
44:15 1012
44:16 250, 440, 466, 577
44:17–18 452
44:17–27 452
44:17 384
44:18 384
44:19 45, 284, 386, 387,
  444, 446, 453
44:20 453, 608, 610
44:21–23 617
44:21 4, 453, 611, 613, 614,
  615
44:22 4, 284, 453, 615, 992,
  996
44:23 52, 383, 615, 616,
  731, 945
44:24 20, 54
44:24a 615
44:25 4
44:25–27 279, 453
44:26–27 284, 979, 986, 996
44:26 749, 922, 973
44:27 8, 277, 605, 1000
44:29 200, 281, 284, 346
44:30 4, 19, 190, 614, 1003
44:31 654
45:1–3 262
45:1–2 4
45:1 415, 473, 474
45:3 321
45:7 4
45:9 474
45:10 892, 901
45:11 892, 895, 901
45:13 415, 473
45:15 175, 221, 224, 574,
  709
45:16 252, 415, 473
45:17 162, 175, 200, 221,
  224, 281, 574, 709
45:18–19 282, 562
45:18–20 281, 1070
45:19 707
45:20 228
45:21–25 281
45:21–24 4, 281
45:21–23 162, 537
45:21 163
45:22 252, 255, 578
45:23–24 292
45:24 163, 200

45:25 200
46:1–9 20
46:1–5 282
46:2 217, 219
46:3 147, 451
46:5 896
46:6–7 4, 163
46:7 162, 896
46:12 172, 176, 217, 219,
  420
46:13–15 4, 162, 163, 457
46:13 163, 757
46:14 200, 896
46:17 1066
46:19–20 393, 394, 406
46:20 45, 281, 284, 288,
  396, 444, 446, 449, 977
46:24 32, 419, 451, 620
46:26–27 32
46:26 223
46:47 242
47:3 674
47:4 674
47:9 664, 712
47:11 192
48:8–21 415, 473
48:8 982
48:9 461
48:10 982
48:12 321
48:14 321
48:15 615
48:21 4, 982

Hosea

1:6 576
2:7 809
2:11 809
2:20 712, 720
3:2 892, 894, 901
3:3 748
3:4 505
4:2 335
4:6–8 53
4:8 284, 286, 288
4:11 612
4:12 55, 508
4:13–14 714
4:13 161, 198
5:2 715
5:15 231, 340
5:18 761
6:6 218
6:17 673
7:4 749
7:5 612
8:13 286, 714
9:3–4 724

9:9 286
9:10 656, 945
9:17 745
10:2 340
11:2 198, 714
12:2 714
13:1 340
13:2 286
13:15 761
14:1 340
14:3 623
14:8 181

Joel

1:4 664, 665, 666
1:7 666
1:14 966
1:18 340
2:12–17 377
2:12ff 1066
2:15 966
2:17 148, 393, 966
2:25 665
4:3 1019
4:9 967

Amos

1:2 194
1:6 779
1:14 413
2:7 347, 366
2:8 337
2:11 512
3:2 601
3:12 159, 160, 665
3:14 236
4:1 329
4:2 347
4:5 414
4:6–11 375
4:9 666
5:5 19
5:19 150
5:22 220, 482
5:23 19
5:25 482
6:2 745
6:4 909
6:5 673
6:8 779
7:1 665
7:9 775
7:13 807
7:16 775
8:10 801
9:3 194
9:5 873

Jonah

2:3–9 219
2:6 684
2:7 686
2:10 413
3 1066
3:1ff 376
3:7–9 1066
3:8–10 26

Micah

1:8 663, 702
1:16 662
2:1–2 337
3:3 156, 967
3:7 803
5:4 571
6:6 757

Nahum

2:1 419
2:13 427
3:6 170, 656
3:15 665
3:16 665
3:17 665

Habakuk

1:15 647
1:16 714
2:5 684
2:18–19 55, 508

Zephaniah

1:5 628
1:7–8 714
2:14 663
3:1 170
3:2 1012

Haggai

1:1 231
1:6 755
1:9 482
1:12 231
1:14 231
2:2 487
2:4 252
2:10–12 450
2:11–13 445
2:11 52, 382
2:12–13 446

2:12 323, 449
2:19 748

Zechariah

2:4 236
2:14 482
3:1 231
3:5 511
3:8 231
4:10 384
5:4 348
5:5–11 834
5:9 834
8:3 482
9:7 656
10:2 55, 508
11:5 231, 340
11:6 581
11:16 646
11:17 528
13:1 744, 745
13:2 270
14:21 714
14:18–19 339

Malachi

1:6–8 459
1:7–8 149
1:7 250
1:8–14 147
1:8 149, 421
1:10 12, 150
1:11 195, 200, 630
1:13 12, 149, 150
2:3 459
2:7 52, 1016
2:7a 617
2:12 459
3:5 337, 348
3:7–18 377

Psalms

1:1 910
2:4 775
5:11 340
6 342
7:10 207
7:16 680
7:46 300, 666
11:3 809
15:30 664
16:7 207, 343
16:10 707
18:11 662
18:22 229

18:40 685
19:11 189
19:12 931
19:13 334, 362
19:15 283
20:4 181
22:6 419
22:16 686
22:25 656
22:30 686
23:5 180
24:3–4 731
26:6 153, 1037
28:2 586
30 219
30:1 592, 593
30:4 707
32 342
32:5 301, 920
32:7 920
33:1 591
34:2 1012
34:19 342
34:22–23 231, 340
34:22f 340
35:6 329
35:10 337
35:13 1054
35:27 591
38 342
38:1 776
38:2–11 342
38:3–6 343
38:18–19 342
38:19 343
39:5 459
39:9 339
40:2 872
40:7 284, 288
40:9 150
41 342
41:4 745
42:5 413
44:21 587
44:23 154, 716
45:8 180
45:9 403, 528
48:3 469
49:17 908
50:5 222
50:12–13 213, 441
50:13 213
50:14–15 441
50:14 219, 419
51:4 1039
51:7 881
51:9 253, 836, 881
51:21 173, 400
56:13 219

59:13   335
60:8   347
61:6   419
61:9   419
63:3   605
63:6   207, 422, 684
65:2   419
65:4   1084
66:12   674
66:13   419
66:15   237
69:2   684
69:8   154
69:32   646
69:35   687
71:13   803
71:20   686
72:10   145
74:13   660
74:14   660
74:15   680
75:5–6   236
75:9   169
75:11   236
78:20   906
78:38   1084
78:60   31
78:67   31
79:9   1084
80:10   869
80:14   652
80:16   528
80:18   528
81:6   150
81:8   872
87:6   921
88:6   807, 1046
89:18   236
89:21–25   553
89:21   553
89:25   236, 553
89:33   776
89:40   512
90:10–11   459
90:15   875
91:10   776
92:8   260
92:11   180
95:1   591
95:2   413
98:6   224
99:6   141, 376, 555
100:1   413
102:4–11   342
102:4   384
102:7   663
103:15   511
103:21   150
104:2   803

104:4   1021
104:10   680
104:15   180
104:18   648
104:26   660
105:8–9   347
105:15   553
105:34   665
105:41   906
105:42   347
106:31   421, 710
106:33   299
107   18
107:4–8   219
107:9   422, 1054
107:10–16   219
107:17–22   219
107:17   1054
107:21   710
107:22   218, 413
107:23–25   219
109:13   459, 647
109:18   384
109:19   803
109:24   205
110:1   528
111:9   347
112:10   609
114:8   680
116:14   419
116:17–19   219, 710
116:17   218
116:18   413, 419
118:5–9   219
118:15–16   528
118:27   249
119:64   341
119:169   1012
124:4–5   684
127:1   500
128:2   402, 407
132:7   1014
132:18   512
133:2   518, 586
136:38   714
137:5–6   300
137:5   528
138   219
139:13   207
141:2   181, 200, 238, 399
143:6   587
143:10   150
145:16   150
147:9   663, 702
147:10   585
147:17   800
148:8   1021
148:14   601
149:3   342

Proverbs

1:16   710
3:9–10   466, 1003
3:10   19
3:12   150
3:16   931
5:3   189
5:18   761
5:23   228, 283
6:17   710
6:27   403, 596
6:28   790
6:33   776
7:14–15   420
7:14   217, 219, 220, 413, 419
7:16–17   909
7:22   716
8:13   755
8:36   229
9:2   716
10:16   339
11:1   150
11:10   296
11:22   651
12:18   299
16:6   706
16:14   1084
16:27   789
18:17   372
19:2   229
19:12   150
20:1   612
20:4   858
20:14   1020
20:25   797
21:17   180
22:6   592
24:13   189
24:19–20   260
25:22   596
26:7   585
27:7   189
28:13   301
29:9   775
29:24   294
30:10   341
30:12   170
30:17   662, 663, 702
30:20   921
30:26   648
31:3   809

Job

1:5   153, 174, 175, 176, 362,
    484, 621, 966
1:11   603
1:15   268

1:16 599
1:20 504, 591, 609
2:7 787
2:9 374
2:12 504
3:8 660
3:19 807
5:1 1021
5:6 372
5:24 229
5:26 191
6:6 908
6:10 800
6:24 228, 283
6:28 603
7:3 811
7:14 298
7:19 915
7:21 686
10:8 666
10:9 686
11:6 334
11:13 587
12:18 504
14:2 511
14:9 298
14:11 1020
16:12 305
16:13 46
16:18 712
17:16 686
18:3 685
18:13 819
18:18–23 819
18:18 745
19:4 228, 283
20:11 686
22:6 337
22:27 419
28:7 663
28:21 242
29:7 910
29:14 511
30:29 702
31:35b 362
32:22 576, 707
35:9 337
37:1 665
37:10 800
37:21 774
38:26 1045
38:29 800
38:37 927
38:41 702
39:13 170
39:18 170
39:26 702
39:30 708
39:38 662

40:15–24 727
40:25 660
40:30 660
42:6–9 376
42:7–9 268
42:8 153, 154, 174, 176,
      234, 255, 484
42:28 578

Canticles

4:1 777
4:3 835
4:5 923
4:11 189
5:1 189
5:11 702
5:15 585
6:5 777
8:6 1021
8:12 941

Ruth

1:16 403
1:17 300
2:10 591
2:17 845
3:18 748
4:10 459

Lamentations

1:8 38
1:10 576
1:17 38, 952
2:6 20
2:7 258
3:16 194
3:38 339
3:39 339
3:54 1046
4:6 339
4:15a 804
4:18 755
5:17 745

Qohelet

2:14 421
3:4 775
3:19 681
3:18–19 712
4:1 337
4:6 1025
4:12 793
5:1–5 313
5:16 609

5:18 402, 407
7:9 609
10:2 528
11:2 571

Esther

1:6 909
1:14 600
2:9 432
3:2 591
3:5 591
4:16 1066
9:19 432
9:22 432

Daniel

1:5 384
1:12 680
1:16 680
5:1 213
5:12 787
5:30 787
6:10 587
7:3 502
8:11–13 457
8:11 474
8:13 420
9:4 301
9:20 301
9:21 399, 457
9:24 234
10:3 180, 1054
10:6 1016
10:12 1054
11:11 787
11:31 457
12:2 686
12:11 457

Ezra

1:1 293
2:36–42 12
2:63 320, 321, 507
3:1–6 1071
3:1–3 517
3:5 5
3:6 1071
4:14 191
6:20 154, 715
8:15 12
8:20 154
8:21 1054
8:28 321
8:35 284
8:35b 285

9 11
9:1 360, 499
9:2 359, 360
9:3 504, 800
9:4–5 399
9:4 457
9:5 457, 504, 587
9:6 12
9:7 12
9:11 38, 360, 952
9:13 12
9:15 12
10:1 301, 302
10:2 346, 360
10:6 301
10:7 293
10:10 12, 320, 345, 346
10:11 360
10:12 5, 242
10:19 320, 328, 345, 359, 361, 861
10:32 360

Nehemiah

1:5 349, 788
1:6 301, 302
2:8 207
3:1 163
3:3 660
3:31–32 163
3:33–4:2 360
3:33 609
3:37 1080
5:8 222
6:11 977
7:5 4
7:28 1021
7:65 320, 321, 507
8:2 5, 242, 1071
8:10 432
8:12 432
8:13–18 28, 1071
8:13 282, 783
8:15 293, 1071
9:1 1071
9:2–3 301, 302
9:2 301
9:3 301
10:1–30 1071
10:30 314
10:31 360
10:33–34 204
10:34 20, 397, 399, 457
10:35 158, 387
10:36 189, 192, 193
10:38 1004
10:40 1004
11:3 6

12:9 7
12:24 7
12:27 592
12:29 1021
12:35 224
12:39 660
12:41 224
12:43 224
12:45 749
13:1–3 359
13:3 809
13:5 181, 202
13:9 181, 202
13:16 660, 661
13:23–27 359
13:25 800
13:27 346
13:30 7, 1039
13:31 158, 387

1 Chronicles

2:7 346, 355
4:32–33 4
4:38 247
4:42 787
5:6 247
6:34 161
6:42 157
7:6–7 4
7:40 247
9:2 6
9:13 815
9:31 185, 397
10:13 348
15:12 966
15:14 966
15:16 673
15:22 12
15:23 1021
16:2 224
16:3 184
16:6 224
16:42 224
17:5–6 30
21:3 231, 341
21:18–27 755
21:27–22:1 224
22:9 34
23:1 20
23:13 321
23:29 183, 185, 399
24 402
24:3 34
24:18 12
25:8 7
26:26–28 321
26:27–28 322

28:2 1014
28:10 755
28:19 437
29:5 539

2 Chronicles

2:3 5
2:6 835
2:13 835
2:23 152
3:14 4, 835
4:3 521
4:6 160
4:16 406
4:2–5 890
5:1 321, 322
5:6 489, 714
5:12–13 224
5:14 138
6:28 776
7:1 138, 250
7:1a 537
7:3 143
7:3a 58
7:8–10 1071
7:9 537, 1071
7:12 218
7:13 666
7:14 376
8:13 20
9:31 397
12:2 348
13:5 191
13:9 539
15:8–15 224
15:11 224
15:18 321, 322
15:27 384
16:3 5
18:2 714
19:8 54
19:10b 334
19:11 54
21:20 808
23:1–3 5
23:3 243
23:6 321
23:19 259
24:6 5, 243
24:7 321
24:9 293
24:11 231
24:25 808
26:14 787
26:16–19 363, 821, 856
26:16–18 346
26:16 161, 236, 1008
26:18–21 821

26:18 237
26:19 800
26:20 372, 775
26:21 775, 779, 806, 807
26:23 775, 807
26:24 372
28:4 714
28:10 334
28:13 334
28:19 346, 349
28:22–25 346
28:22–23 348
28:23 348, 714
28:27 808
29:5 744, 966
29:10 322
29:15 966
29:16 744
29:19 346
29:20–24 288
29:21–24 284, 292
29:21a 285
29:22–29 483
29:22 5, 161, 165, 521, 715
29:23 153, 248, 520
29:24 154, 161, 285, 715
29:27 224
29:30 966
29:31–35 224
29:31–33 204, 219, 413, 489
29:31 219, 224, 483, 539
29:33 225, 156
30:2–3 286
30:3 966
30:5 293
30:10 355
30:11 376
30:15–20 282
30:15 715
30:17–20 1053
30:17 154, 715, 966
30:22–27 224, 225
30:22 301
30:24 225
30:32 714
31:1 6
31:3 20
31:5 189, 190, 191
31:6 5
31:19 432
32:12 161
32:26 376
33:1a 346
33:16 219, 224, 225, 413
33:19 348
33:22 714
34:27 376
35:1 715
35:6 154, 715

35:11 154, 156, 715
36:13–14 348
36:14 346
36:17 754
36:22 293

New Testament

Matthew
3:4 666
4:18 660
4:21 660
5:17 191
5:23f 370
6:9 603
9:20 942
12:34 1020
21:2 168
21:12–13 163
21:12 288
23:5–6 675
Mark
1:6 666
1:16 660
5:25 942
7:4 921
8:15 189
14:3 804
Luke
2:22–24 762
5:1–10 660
8:43 942
11:2 603
11:24 1020
11:39 675
12:1 189
17:11–19 805
17:13 776
22:41 587
John
1:14 663
11:16 168
12:28 603, 604, 633, 635
Acts
7:59 587
10:9–16 726
10:27–28 726
11:4–12 726
15:20 726
1 Cor 5:8 189
Hebrews
5:1–4 578
7:23–28 578
7:27 396
8:1–7 578
Revelation
8:3–5 238
18:2 1020
22:13 511

Apocrypha and Pseudepigrapha

Bar 4:35 1020
1 Enoch 10:4–5 1020
2 Enoch 13:76 312
3 Enoch 4:6 1020
1 Esd
7:63 284
8:68 360
Jub
3:6 746
3:8–14 750
7:32–33 712
21:10 420
21:12–14 158, 388
21:16 1017
22:16 726
1 Macc
1:54 236
4:54–56 219
4:56 595
4:54–56 413
2 Macc
1:9 594
2:11 633, 635
6:18 652
7:27 953
Pss. Sol. 17:15–17 351
Sir
15:15 150
38:11 171, 386
39:14 180
45:14 396
50:22 150
50:9 180
50:20–21 189
Susanna 46 1042
Testament of Gad 6:3–
   4 344, 372
Testament of Levi
3:5–6 629
3:6 199
9:12 388
16:1–5 350
Tob 8:3 1020
Wis 9:8 437

Qumran Sources

CD
2:21.22 150
3:11–12 150
3:19–4:4 351
5:6–7 941
6:11–14 351
8:46 351, 352
9:10–12 296
9:13–14 327

9:13 303
10:2-3 370
10:10-14 925
11 819
11:18-19 388
11:21-22 927
12 819
12:1-2 314, 968
12:15-18 674
13:4-7 778
15:3 366
15:4 348
20:22-24 351
D⁹1
2:4 915
2:5 915
DJD 5.180, line 7 1021
4Q MMT B
5-8 407
9-13 219, 418
21-22 668
22-23 682
29-33 565, 240
49-54 333
55-58 679
58-62 653
65-68 994
66-68 843
77-79 448
1 QH 4:34 352
1QH
4:6 511
4:23 511
4:34 348
18:29 511
1QHab
9:9-12 821
11:12-16 821
1QM
7:5-6 970
7:6 973
14:2-3 969, 970
17:2 602
1QS
5:13 973, 974
6:16-21 679
6:16-17 973
6:25 973
7:3 973
7:13 915
8:17-18 370
8:17 973, 974
8:22-24 457
8:23 369
9:22-24 150
1QSa
1:25-26 929
2:4-11 970
4Q 394-99 849

4Q365 388
4Q375 242
4QD⁹
1:3 797
1:7 797
2 774
2:1 797
4QDᵃ
2 785
4-5 819
5 812
7-8 793
10-11 819
10-13 798
11-12 819
12 819
15 915
17:7-8 795
17:10-12 797
17:19 796
4QDᵇ9 2:3-4 944
4QDᵈ 1 774
4QDg1, 2:1 819
4QLeᵍvb 2
4QLevd 2
4Qordᶜ 971, 973, 974, 975
4Qtg Lev. 1014, 1032
4QThr
A1:1-4 994
A1:1-2 804
A1:1 805, 806
A1:2 806
A1:3 816
A1:4-5 915
A1:5-6 949
A1:7-8 922
A1:8-9 922
A1:8 922
11QLev 15:3 2
11QTemple
13:13-14 411
15:3-5 563
15:3 973
15:4-5 561
15:5-14 562
15:6-8 562
15:11-12 563
15:11 561, 563
15:14 565
15:16-18 523, 562, 565
15:18-16:1 565
16:2-3 533
16:2 562
16:4 564
16:6 563
16:12 240, 565
16:13 565
16:14-18 562, 563
17:8-9 620

18:4-6 845
18:5 973
19:7 192, 194
20:4-9 211
20:13 418
21:3 620
21:7-9 1083
22:10 973
22:11-14 620
22:15-16 1083
23:15 208
23:25 388
25:5-6 845
25:12-16 1048
25:12-15 845
25:16 1019
26:7-10 1064
26:10 1018, 1064
26:13 1021
27:4 175
28:5 973
28:6-9 845
28:8 973
31-33 501, 1048
33:15 159
34 165
34:7 155
34:8 169
37:8-15 394, 406
40:1-4 387
45:7-10 929, 932, 968
45:11-12 932, 968
45:12-14 970, 1001
45:15 789
45:15-17 924
45:15-16 925
45:16 922
45:17-18 844, 970
45:18 789
46:13-16 536
46:15 767
46:16-18 34, 804, 806, 969
48:5 665
48:14-17 765, 806, 949, 969, 995
48:16-17 277, 963
49:5-78 863
49:7 678
49:13 16 674
49:19-21 975
50:7 973
50:10-14 969
50:12-13 875
50:16-17 674
50:17 973
50:18-19 405
51:2-3 667
51:4-5 668, 682

52:17–19   980
52:51   169

Versions

Septuagint
Genesis 30:37   1027
Exodus
  25:17   1014
  28:4   502
  29:9   548
Leviticus
  1:5   204
  1:7   158, 159
  1:8   209
  1:9   163
  1:12   209
  1:15   169
  1:17   172
  2:5   185
  2:8   185
  3:1   204
  3:2   204, 205
  3:3   205
  3:4   208
  3:5   208
  3:7   209
  3:8   210
  3:9   211
  3:13   210, 213
  3:14   214
  3:16   214
  4:6   234
  4:10   239
  4:12   239
  4:14   243, 244
  4:24   248
  5:1   294
  5:2   297, 298
  5:15   326
  5:21   335
  5:24   371
  5:24d   372
  6:2   383
  6:14   400
  7:2   169
  7:3   410
  7:14   415
  7:15   414
  7:21   425
  7:24   461
  7:28–29   429
  7:30a   430
  7:35   433
  8:8   508
  8:9   511
  8:10   516

  8:11   516
  8:14   520
  8:15   520, 525
  8:23   527
  8:30   532
  8:31   535
  8:32   534
  8:35   544
  9:3   572
  9:7   578
  9:13   582
  9:20   585
  9:21   586
  9:24   634
  10:2   634
  10:3   604
  10:4   604
  10:5   606
  10:6   608
  10:9   611, 613
  10:10   615
  10:15   621
  11:16   663
  10:17   622, 624
  10:18   626
  11:19   664
  11:26   669
  11:27b   669
  11:29   661
  11:3   646, 647
  11:30   661
  11:36   680
  11:40   682
  11:43   685
  11:44   687
  11:45   688
  12:2   743
  12:4   749, 750, 754
  12:7   759
  13:2   772, 775
  13:23   789
  13:31   794, 795
  13:39   800
  13:47   809
  13:5   780, 781
  13:51   811, 812
  13:52   812
  13:54   813
  13:9   784
  14:4   832, 835
  14:5   836
  14:7   839
  14:10   844, 845, 846
  14:12   461
  14:13   852
  14:14   852
  14:17   854
  14:21   461
  14:24   461

  14:31   862
  14:32   863
  14:37   870
  14:42   873
  14:43   874
  14:45   874
  14:49   879
  15:2   906, 907
  15:3   2, 907, 908, 909, 947
  15:9   916
  15:10   917
  15:13   921
  15:14   925
  15:23   938
  15:27   935, 943, 956
  15:31   945
  16:1   598
  16:2   1014
  16:4   1018
  16:6   578
  16:8   1020
  16:11   578
  16:12   1026, 1027
  16:15   1033
  16:17   578
  16:21   1045
  16:22   1046
  16:24   578
  16:25   1049
Numbers
  9:1   499
  9:3   499
  14:4   845
  17:2   598, 633
Deuteronomy
  12:27   169
  14:13   662
  22:27   741–42
  22:28   741–42
  22:6   741–42
Joshua 1:2b   787
1 Kings 8:65   537, 594
1 Samuel
  1:9   223
  1:25   154
  2:13–14   223
  2:29   440, 442, 479
  2:29b   370
  6:1   327
  12:3   57
  14:14   55
  14:41   508, 509, 510
  20:26   927
  21:6   444
  30:17   420
2 Samuel
  15:7b–8   219, 419
  19:25   803
Isaiah 66:17a   657

Ezekiel
  43:25 540
  43:26 539, 541
  45:3 321
  48:12 321
Ezra 9:1 360
Hosea 3:2 894
1 Esdras 7:63 284

Targums

General references

Genesis
  37:25 1027
  43:11 1027
Exodus
  28:17–20 788
  28:4 502
Leviticus
  1:9 163
  1:15 170
  5:8 1027
  3:1 204
  3:4 208
  5:15 326
  6:21 405
  11:3 646
  11:16 663
  12:2 743
  13:10 784
  13:46 805
  14:40 871
  14:41 873
  16:12 1027
  16:21 1045
Numbers 8:2 173
1 Samuel 2:13–14 223
Isaiah
  19:3 665
  44:16 787
Jeremiah 46:11 1027
Ezekiel
  27:17 1027
  43:26 539
Job 10:8 665

Onkelos

Genesis 37:25 1027
Exodus
  24:15–18 137
  25:1 137
  40:34–38 137
Leviticus
  1:1 137
  1:8 159
  2:14 194

3:10 213
4:10 239
5:1–4 369
6:19 402
7:21 425
7:35 433
8:23 527
8:31 535
9:4 574
9:6 574
9:15 583
11:9 655
11:13 662
11:19 664
11:22 665
11:25 668
12:2 744
13:2 772
13:5 780
13:6 782
13:10 784
13:23 789
13:29 792
13:31 795
13:37 789
13:45 803
13:51 811
13:53 812
13:55 814
14:14 852
14:37 870
14:40 871
14:49 879
15:31 945
16:1 598, 634
16:12 1026, 1027
16:22 1046

Pseudo-Jonathan

Exodus
  24:15–18 137
  25:1 137
  25:2 522
  28:6 1016
  32:4 1016
  40:34–38 137
  40:35 134
Leviticus
  1:1 137
  1:3 153
  1:4 150
  1:5 154, 155
  1:8 159
  1:9 162
  1:13 159
  2:8 185
  2:13 191
  2:14 194

3:9 210
4:10 239
5:1 294, 295, 348
5:2 298
5:21 335
5:24 338
5:24d 344, 372
5:4 300
5:5 300
6:4 387
6:13 396
6:14 399
6:21 406
7:14 415
7:17 420
7:18 421
8:23 527
8:30 532
9:1 571
9:4 574
9:15 583
9:23 588
10:1 598
10:9 612
10:18 626
11:13 662
11:16 663
11:19 664
11:20 664
11:25 668
11:29 661
11:30 661
11:37 680
12:2 744
12:4 749, 754
12:5 755, 757
12:7 759, 761
13:1 771
13:2 772, 774
13:5 780
13:6 782
13:23 789
13:29 792
13:36 797
13:37 789
13:45 803
14:5 836
14:7 839, 840
14:8 842
14:13 852
14:14 853
14:17 854
14:34 868
14:37 870
14:40 872
14:49 879
15:13 921
15:16 927
15:31 945

16:1   610
16:8   1020
16:10   1021
16:12   1027
16:13   1014
16:21   151
16:29   1054
21:18–20   723
Deuteronomy 14:18   664

Neofiti

Exodus 40:35   134
Leviticus
1:3   153
1:9   162
5:1   294
6:14   400
7:15   414
9:1   571
9:4   574
9:10   580
9:13   582
10:14   619
11:25   668
12:4   754
12:7   761
13:2   772, 774
13:5   780
13:7   783
13:31   795
13:36   797
13:37   789
13:45   803, 804
13:51   811, 812
13:55   813, 814
14:14   852
14:37   870
14:40   872
14:49   879
15:3   908
15:10   917
15:19   934
16:13   1014

Yerushalmi

Exodus 40:35   134
Leviticus
5:21   335
5:24   338
10:1   598
13:2   774
16:1   634
16:12   1027

Samaritan Pentateuch

Exodus
28:17–20   788

29:5   502
Leviticus
1:8   209
3:7   209
3:8   210
3:16   214
4:10   239
4:12   239
4:14   244
4:24   248
5:24   338
6:20   403
7:3   410
7:8   411
7:21   425
7:28–29   429
8:14   520
8:25   530
8:30   532
8:31   534
9:3   572
9:20   585
9:21   586
10:4   604
10:6   608
10:7   653
10:15   621
11:3   646
11:21   665
12:2   743
12:7   759
13:9   784
13:55   813
14:4   832
14:5   836
14:10   844, 845, 846
14:13   852
14:42   873
14:43   874
14:45   874
15:3   2, 908, 909
15:18   934
15:23   938
15:31   945
16:4   1018
Deuteronomy
14:7a   646
14:8   646, 653
14:13   662

Peshitta

Leviticus
1:17   172
3:4   208
5:15   326
5:24   338
7:6   234
7:21   425

8:30   532
8:31   535
9:7   586
9:20   585
10:10   615
10:18   626
10:4   604
11:3   646, 647
11:16   663
11:25   667
11:30   661
11:43   685
12:4   754
12:7   759
13:10   784
13:29   792
13:5   780, 781
13:9   784
14:4   832
14:5   836
14:17   854
14:31   862
14:42   873
14:45   874
14:49   879
15:10   917
16:22   1046
Ezekiel
43:25   540
43:26   539, 541

Vulgate

Leviticus
4:6   234
4:14   244
8:9   511
14:31   862
16:12   1026, 1027

Rabbinic Sources

Mishna
ʾAbot
4:4   374
2:21   1004
5:15   179
5:20   150
5:24   407
ʿArakin
6:2   322
6:5   322
Baba Meṣiʿa
4:8   365
10:6   777
Baba Qamma
7:4   329
7:7   652

7:9–10   335
9:5   370
9:7   344
9:12   370
9:7–8   329
Berakot
1:1   384, 418
3:4–5   927
4:1   457
Beṣa
2:4   150
4:4   813
Bikkurim
2:4   463
3:1   192
3:6   463
ᶜEduyyot
6:1   387
7:2   666
7:9   330
8:4   666
ᶜErubin
1:10   809
10:15   148
10:15a   312
Gittin 5:5   330
Ḥagiga
2:7   668, 876
3:3   757, 849
2:2–3   150
3:4–8   1052
Horayot
1:1–5   242
1:4   407
1:5   242
2:1   231
2:2–3   232
2:6   231
2:7   309
3:1   231
3:2   231
Ḥullin
1:2   154, 716
1:5   168
1:6   910
2:4   717
3:6   661, 662, 720
3:7   665, 666
4:5   814
8:1   666
8:4   737
8:6   238
9:12   682
Kelim
1:1   672, 778, 842, 843,
         910, 973
1:3   941
1:4   805, 842, 983
1:5   975, 997

1:8   314, 419, 620, 849,
         920
1:9   148, 393, 608, 614,
         1036
2:1   675
4:4   674
8:18   671
9:3   671
10:1   910
10:9   671
12:8   674
13:2   674
15:6   1004
16:1   674
17:2   809
17:10   239
17:13   658
17:14   658
23:3   918
27:4   873
Keritot
2:1   1000
2:4   309
6:3   363
4:2–3   486
5:4–8   333
5:28   331
Ketubot 5:9   809
Kilʾayim
5:7   194
9:1   448
Maᶜaserot
1:6–7   191
2:7   873
5:15   165
Makkot
6:4   678
6:7   170
Meᶜila
1:1ff   323
2:1   968
3:3   238
3:7–8   322
4:1   322
5:1   322
6:6   322
Megilla
1:7   782, 802, 831
1:11   419, 620
4:1   814
14:10   853
Menaḥot
1:2   528
3:3   149
4:3   1
5:1   415
5:3   390
5:5   186, 391
5:6   186, 415, 461, 463,

473, 481
5:8   185
6:2   390
6:3   183, 184
6:4   185
6:5   397
7:1   414
8:4–5   180
9:6   845
9:7   153
9:8–9   152
10:4   192, 193, 194
11:5   630
12:3   179
13:10   187, 630
13:11   186, 195
Middot
1:1   419
1:3   397
2:5   158, 223, 620, 849
2:6   393
3:1   239
3:2   171
3:3   164
3:4   587, 773
3:5   165
5:3   160, 393, 582, 1048
7:4   277
Miqwaʾot
1:1–8   924
4:5   813
6:9   809
Nazir
6:5   488
6:6   322
6:7   330, 756, 857
7:1   357
Negaᶜim
1:1   773, 774, 776, 789
1:2   788
1:5   785
2:2   777
2:4   777, 841
3:1   772, 778, 818
3:3–4   791
3:5   792
3:8   879
4:3   755, 757
4:4   777
4.11   784
6:1   774
6:7   785
8:1   786
8:3   779
8:8   780, 782, 802
9:1   787, 789, 790
9:2   789
10:1   793
10:5   795

10:9   792
10:10   800, 801
11:4   809, 811
11:8   809, 810
11:11   809
12:1   818, 868
12:5   428, 677, 869
12:6   871, 873
12:7   874
13:1   874, 878, 879
13:4   778, 874
13:7   805, 983
13:8   812
13:9–10   876
13:11   983
13:12   875
13:17   842
14:1   833, 836, 838, 881
14:2–3   760
14:2   841, 842, 843, 993
14:3   841, 975
14:5   833
14:8–9   1000
14:8   521, 849, 852
14:10   853
Niddah
3:7   751
4:3   757
5:3   772
6:3   668, 876
6:9   655
7:1   916
7:4   765, 949, 971, 998
9:6   813
10:7   757, 975
ᵓOholot
1:6   667
3:2   317
3:6   317
4:1–3   992
7:1–2   992
11:7   777
13:6   809
Para
1:1   572, 853
3:7   713
3:9   273
3:55   272
4:4   271
5:5   836
6:5   923
8:3   404, 406, 1053
8:7   679
Peᵓa 7:8   322
Pesaḥim
1:2   671
3:8   33, 419, 620
5:8   169
7:4   1053

7:6   1053
7:7   512
7:8   33, 419, 620
7:9   33, 419, 620
10:1   457, 814
Qiddušin 1:6   323, 464, 475
Qinnim 1:1   420
Roš Haššana 1–2   21
Šabbat
1:11   384
2:1   610, 980
3:1   679
4:5   294, 295, 296, 348
6:1   296
9:4   180
11:2   884
Šebuᶜot
1:4–6   309
1:4–5   256
1:3–5   317
1:6   1034, 1043
4:3   294
4:10   314
4:13   294
5:4–5   329
8:3   344
8:6   873
Šeqalim
1:1   325
4:1   438
5:1–5   288
7:2   288
7:6   400
8:1   915
Soṭa
1:5   609
9:10   165
9:12   508
Sukka
4:5   148, 393, 1037
chap. 3   1071
chap. 4   1071
Taᶜanit
1:3–7   1066
3:4–5   1066
4:5   158, 387
4:8   1067
Tamid
1:4–2:2   386
1:1   384, 419, 536
1:2   385, 419
2:3   158, 387
3:1   397
3:5   165
4:2–3   157
4:2   159, 160, 582
4:3   208
5:2   237
5:4   237

6:3   237
Temura
1:6   438
7:4   836
Terumot
1:10   191
8:8   485
10:10   666
Ṭoharot
5:1   720
5:6   671
Yadayim
3:5   1004
4:6   668, 682, 751
4:7   679
Yoma
1:1–3:2   1016
1:7   568, 927, 1068
2:3–7   157
2:7   156, 157
3:3   393, 1018, 1047, 1049
3:4   501, 521, 1017, 1049
3:6   1049
3:8   155, 1024
3:9   1020
4:1   1020
4:2–3   155
4:2   1022, 1024
4:3   165, 579, 1024, 1031
4:4   1025
5:1   1015, 1025, 1029, 1031
5:2   1029
5:3   1031, 1032, 1033
5:4   1032, 1035, 1037
5:5   1036
5:6   1039
6:1   1022
6:2   1043
6:3   1045, 1052
6:4   1045, 1053
6:6   1021, 1045, 1046, 1053
6:8   1021, 1045, 1046
7:1–4   1046
7:2   980
7:4   1015, 1036, 1050
8:1   180, 1054
8:8   370, 378
8:9   303, 370
9:8   1057
9:9   1057
Zabim
1:1–3   907
1:2   973
2:1   942
2:2   907
2:3   906
2:4   913, 914

5:2   919, 939
5:6   805, 941
5:7   939
5:11   941
5:12   844
Zebaḥim
1:1   253
2:1   169, 528
2:2–5   421
2:3   521
2:4   521
2:32   528
3:6   421
5:1–2   238
5:1   183, 395
5:3   171, 402, 418, 626
5:4   156
5:5   414, 626
5:6–8   419, 620
5:6–7   219, 413
5:6   219
5:7   420, 423, 619
6:1   183, 395, 418, 626
6:4   305
6:5   169
8:12   149
9:1ff   487
10:2   292, 304, 466, 488,
       495, 756, 851, 1050,
       1064
10:5   364, 467, 489, 850
10:5a   466, 851
10:8   231
10:12   330
11:1   404
11:3   404
11:4   404, 406
11:8   446
12:1   395
12:3   411
12:5   565
12:6   1052
13:1   426
13:5–6   200, 630

Tosefta

ʿAboda Zara 4:4   630
ʿArakin 2.1   148
Baba Qamma
7:1   335
7:2   335
10:5   330
Berakot 2:12   754
Bikkurim 2:9   158, 387
Ḥagiga 3:35   674
Horayot 2:4   241
Ḥullin 3:9   655

Kelim Baba Qamma
1:6   148
1:6–8   614
Kelim Baba Mesiʿa 7:4   658
Keritot
1:6   331
4:4   363
Maʿaser Šeni 2:12–16   978
Meʿila
1:9   322, 323
2:1   322
Megilla
2:10   384
5:25–26   980
Menaḥot
1:6   512
7:8   588
7:17–19   473
7:13–19   461
7:13   530
8:14   179
8:17   530
10:2   175
10:9–10   152
10:12   155, 344
10:14–15   153
Negʿaim
1:5   811
1:6   811
1:15   798
3:13   790
4:1   795
4:12   792
6:1   868
6:7   806, 808, 809, 868
7:4   874
7:6   812
7:13   875
8:2   835, 836, 849
8:3   838
8:4   840
8:6   796, 840, 842
8:9   849, 852, 925, 993
8:10   846
9:5   857
Niddah
2:17   814
6:15   765, 998
9:18   978
Para
1:1   176, 292, 488, 756,
      758, 857
1:5   572
1:10   330
4:10   272
Pesaḥim
3:1   370
3:12–13   978
3:17   240

3:19   150
6:5   512, 623
7:11, 35b   536
Qiddušin 119   323
1:9   475
2b   555
Šabbat
1:13   754
1:14   949
8:24–28   678
Šebuʿot
1:3   256, 259
1:5   317
1:8   257
2:15   294
3:1   295
3:2–4   295
3:4   295, 348
Šeqalim
2:14   397
3:3   850
3:20   850
3:25   397
Soṭa
1:7   609, 803
7:2   368
7:3–4   348
13:1   231, 517, 554
13:10   165
Ṭebul Yom 1:6   679
Taʿanit
1:8   303
4:5   387
4:7–8   388
Ṭoharot 10:4   809
Yadayim 2:20   928
Yebamot 11:1   814
Yoma
1:1   590
1:8   1028, 1030
2:1   373, 1043
2:5   1044
2:14   1029
2:15   231, 517
3:7   398
3:16   1052
3:17   565
4:7   370
4:9   370, 1057
4:16   404, 406
8:9   378
Zabim
2:1   906
2:4   907
5:3   390, 805
7:4   169
9:4   487
10:2   241
10:4   466, 488, 495, 851

10:9   404
10.14   406
11:1   220
12:4–5   200, 630
12:4   978
13:1   176, 268

Other Tannaitic Sources

ʾAbot de Rabbi Nathan A
1:4   949
2   929
16   407
40   517, 822
41   231
ʾAbot de Rabbi Nathan B
21   370
Megillat Taʿanit   158
4:6   457
5:8   390
Mekhilta
On Exod 12:22b   260
Mishpatim, par. 20   737
Yitro 3   667, 682

Sipra

Aḥare
1:5par.   611
1:13par.   1014
2:2par.   1049
2:3par.   1018
2:4par.   373, 1043, 1044
2:6par.   373, 1043
2:8   1020, 1025
3:11   1028
4:3   1044
4:8   1036
4:13   1039
6:2–5   1046
6:3   1047
8par.   711
13:10   718
Beḥuqotai, 26:1   348
Emor
3:11   606
4:8   844, 975, 997
19:2   1042
Ḥoba
3:8par.   233, 234
3:8   853
4:12par.   250
6:6par.   248
6:10   407
7:3   344
7:6par.   252
7:7   247

8:1par.   347
10:1par.   331
11:1par.   351
12:7par.   333
12:21par.   851
13:1par.   344
13:8par.   365
13:4–6   298
13:10   257
18:1   304
18:5   304
18:8   305
20:3–5   322
22:4   365
22:6   335
Meṣoraʿ Zabim
4:4par.   934
4:9par.   936
9:6par.   945
Meṣoraʿ Negaʿim
1:2par.   835
1:3par.   835
1:4   907
1:5   838
1:14par.   835
2:1–6   910
2:2   843
2:11par.   842
3:5   853, 914
3:6par.   849, 914
3:8par.   852, 853, 916
3:9   853
3:12   856, 916
3:14   857
4:1   916
4:3   919
4:4   872, 934
4:5   873
5:1par.   863, 866, 921
5:4   921
5:5–11   876
5:7par.   822
5:11par.   869
5:12par.   869
5:14   881
6:5par.   870
7:1par.   874
7:7par.   878
7:8par.   879
7:13par.   874
8:2   942
8:10   943
9:1   944
9:7   945
Milluʾim Ṣaw
1:13par.   520
2   495
3   498
4   499

8   495
14   539, 556
21   528
36   561
42   535
Milluʾim Shemini
8   577
11   583
12   574
14   555, 590
19   588
20   590
22   599, 604, 635
28   610
29   587
30   587
31   591
32   598, 634, 635
34   590, 606
35   605
36   604, 611, 635
40   608
41   609
Nedaba
1:1–2par.   137
1par.   139
2:5   602
3:13   149
4:2   152, 153
4:6   163
4:7   167
4:8   175
4:9par.   156
5:10   157, 591
6:4   158
6:9   166
7:7par.   169
8:3–4   168
8:3par.   178
9:6par.   181
9:12par.   181
10:1   179
10:6par.   184
10:8   181
12:7   185
13:1–3par.   193
13:3par.   192
13:4par.   192
16:2   220
16:3   220
19:2   210
20:1   213
21:16   215
Qedoshim
2:7par.   366
11:22   718
Ṣaw
2:4par.   391, 397
2:5par.   391

2:12par.   394
3:3par.   397
3:6par.   446
4par.   407
4:6   400, 446
4:8   401
6:5   403
10:2   402
11:3par.   563
11:3   431
11:11   476, 481
12:13   420
13:9   422
14:4   423
16:3   461, 473
Shemini
1:4par.   612
1:10   621
2:4   624, 637
2:8par.   645
2:12   640
3:2par.   654, 655, 659
3:11par.   655
4:1f   667
4:8   654
4:9   653, 654
5:9   665
6:9par.   658
7:6   675
7:3par.   677
8:1par.   678
9:1   678
9:5par.   680
10:2   668
11:3   680
Tazria‹
1:3par.   945
1:5par.   744
3:4   759
3:6   761
12:6   608
14:11   811
15:9   814
Tazria‹ Nega‹im
1:1   772
1:4   773, 774
2:3   777
2:5   778
2:10   778
4:1par.   787
4:3   785
5:5par.   792
5:6par.   793
5:9par.   793
6:1   786
6:5   788
8:5   794, 798
8:6   794
8:9   794

9:4   795
9:7   795
9:8   797
9:14   780, 798
9:16   798
10:7   800
12:6   803
12:7   803, 804
12:13   805
13:12   810
14:2   811
15:5   812, 813
16:6   814
16:11   815
Zab
1:4par.   907
1:12–13par.   907

Sipre

Sipre Num (Horowitz)
1   805
2   338
8   748, 922
25   609
26   280
44   571
63   571
68   561
105   805, 819, 842
111   161, 253, 442
112   407, 457
121   191
124   273
125   667, 946
126   405, 648, 675
141   1041
143   163
153   407
Sipre Zuta
5:2   148, 393, 614, 806,
      1036
5:5   3
10:33   140
11:1   590, 599
12:1   822
19:4   234
19:9   273
27:21   511
Sipre Deut
12.20   714
12:21   715
36   394
100   646
103   661, 699

Babylonian Talmud

‹Aboda Zara
25a   210

36b   906
65b   194
76a   404
‹Arakin
15b   823
16a   254, 823
16b   806
Baba Batra
80b   835
84a   778
89b   891
90b   891
109b   556
Baba Meṣi‹a
38a   189
94b   798
103b   811
Baba Qamma
2b   910
7ab   335
26b   228, 487
55b [bar.]   295
64b   329
74b   329
82b   457, 928
101b   767
103b   370
Bekorot 27b   754
Berakot
8a   811
8b   952
17a   189, 214
20a   748, 1055
22b   927
24b   915
53a   630
54b   219
58b   799
60a   767
Beṣa 24a   833
‹Erubin
11a   748
14a–b   891
14b   893
57a   156
63a   598
100a   1055
Gittin
28b   167
55a   330
Ḥagiga
6b   157
16b   150
21a   850
Horayot 8b   308
Ḥullin
8a [bar.]   790
16b [bar.]   714
17b   717

22b 792
24b [bar.] 675
27a 154, 716
28b [bar.] 715
31a 749
36a 678
59a 647, 649
61a 661
61b 661
63 663
63a 663, 664
63b 661, 662
66b–67a 655
81a 1056
106a 921
115b [bar.] 737
117a 210
118b 680
128a 844
Keritot
6a 1026, 1027, 1031
8b 280, 842
10b 326
22b [bar.] 331
26a 254, 269, 759
Ketubot
42a 365
43a 329
61a 949
106a 1004
Makkot
14b 751
18b–19a 463
Meꜥila
8b 968
16b 684
20a [bar.] 322
Megilla
8b 803
18a 587
21a 384
24b 799
Menaḥot
9b 583
11a 181
20a 192
21a 192
27b 1013
45a 561
50b 400
51b 397
61a 849
87a–b 892
89a 846
90b 798
91a [bar.] 845
91a 846
92b 153
93b 150

104b 179, 195
110a [bar.] 195, 440
61b–62a 461, 473
90b–91b 845
Moꜥed Qatan
5b 804
9a 1071
15a 609
24a 803
28a 457
14a–16a 819
Nazir
19a 254
62b 300
66a 907
Nedarim 70b 151
Negaꜥim 8b 779
Niddah
9a 745
30a 757
31a 935
31b 254, 744, 759, 881
33a 941
34a 906
35b 761, 907
51b 655
55b 916
56a 908
56b 765
57b 935
64b 807, 819
66a 805
69a 935
Pesaḥim
4b 757
41b 1055
58b 388
59a 304
59b 637
79a 1052
90b 571
96b 213
111a 766, 949
Qiddušin
3a 748
30a 683, 796
45b 151
Roš Haššana
16b [bar.] 654
18a 1069
26a 949
Šabbat
14b 997
25a 457, 458
55b 748
63b 511
66b 234
69a 300
81a [bar.] 680

87a 929
106b 833
109b 835
110a 766, 949
134a 757
151b 757
Sanhedrin
4a 767
43a 296
43b 296
47a 807
49b 813
87a 905
97a 786
Šebuꜥot
6b 773, 774, 778
8a 254, 823
12b 1044
13a [bar.] 378
27a 300
38b [bar.] 368
42b 361
Soperim
9:2 683
9:3 796
Soṭa
3a 439
14b 181
15a 846
2:2 836
32b 303
38a 587
48b 508
49b 652
Sukka
37b 461, 473
43a 520, 561
47b 463
48b 161
51b 754
Taꜥanit
21b 920
28a 387
29b 388
Tamid 29b 158
Temura 15b 285
Yebamot
40a 637
54b 1056
62a 929
68a 1056
74b [bar.] 760
74b 975
75a 675, 751
90a 637, 1055
103b 805, 812, 819
74b–85a 844
Yoma
4b 137

5b   502
6a   502
12a   452
12b   1016
15b   528
19b   1013
20b   325
21a   404
23b   385
26b [bar.]   156, 157
30b   849
32a   1046, 1047
33a   163, 399
33b   590
34a   388
36b   229
39a   685
41b   1022
43b   578
44b   614
47a   181
53a   598, 1013, 1014
53a [bar.]   1030
55a [bar.]   1031
56b   1034
57a [bar.]   234
57b   798
58b   1031
63a   240
66b   1045
67b   1020, 1021
68b   637
69a   386, 448
70b   1048
71a   1046
73b   511
78   935
80a   678
86b   373, 440
223b   386
367a   155
Zebaḥim
  7b [bar.]   176, 758, 857
  7b   304
  10b   156
  13a   155, 222
  17b   498
  19a [bar.]   495
  29a   420
  33a   150, 151
  34b   1056
  36a [bar.]   402
  48a   851
  53a   156, 233, 853, 619
  56b [bar.]   394, 420
  59a   629
  64b   305
  65a [bar.]   169
  83b   383

90a [bar.]   488, 756, 851
90a   304, 488, 756
90b [bar.]   466
90b   851
95a   813, 815
96a   404
99a [bar.]   850
101a   627
101b   627
103b   388
104b   565
107b   210
115b   600, 603
116a   177
120a   157
120a [bar.]   173

Jerusalem Talmud

ʿAboda Zara 4:4   200
Baba Batra 3:9   804
Berakot 3:4   754
Ḥagiga
  80c   671
  3:3   757
  79d   1052
Horayot 2:5   940
Ketubot
  13:1   748
  13:8   922
Megilla
  1:11   200, 630
  1:12   173
Nazir 9:4   782
Pesaḥim 6:1   798
Qiddušin 4:1   401
Šabbat
  7   179
  17c   179
  10b   179
Šebuʿot 6.5   313
Šeqalim
  5:1   325
  5.13   160
  iv, 48a   1004
Soṭa
  2:1   846
  8:9   401
  9:11, 24a   165
Sukka
  3:6   788
  4.1   26
Taʿanit
  4:1   587, 588
  4:8   652
  4:68c   652
Yebamot 8:3   303, 401
Yoma
  1:5   502

4:5 [bar.]   1031
5:4   234
6:3   1045
7:2   1016, 1046
7:3   1016
39a   1013

Midrash

ʾAggadah on Lev 1:8   388
ʾAggadah on Exod
    29:35   539
Canticles Rabbah 3:7   1030
Exodus Rabbah
  19.2   137
  38:8   1012
  51:2   140
Genesis Rabbah
  9:8   748
  1:29   819
  35:4   1071
  54:3   335
Haḥefeṣ ms., cited in Torah
    Shelemah   872
Leviticus Rabbah
  2:7   1059
  3:5   167
  5:6   241
  6:2   294
  6:5   348
  7:1   158
  7:2   3
  7:3   175
  7:5   384
  7:6   388
  7:11   175
  8:4   195
  9:1   413
  9:7   414
  10:8   539
  12:7   1012
  14:1   743
  16:3   804, 805
  17:3   823
  18:4   823
  20   633
  20:4   1031
  20:9   611
  21:7   1013, 1048
  21:10   1016
  22:7   154, 440
  22:9   173, 174
  26:7   348
  27:6   168
  28:5   461, 473
Numbers Rabbah
  2:23   598
  6:2   780
  9:2   365

10 280
19:1 270
19:5 270
10:11 280, 357
10:21 223, 620
Tadshe 303
15 750
17 863
Tanḥuma
Ahare
5:8 1034
9 200, 630
Emor 21 681
Ḥuqat 58 590
Maṭṭot 1 313
1.8 134
2.1 134
12 606
Pequde 5 140
Zav 1 174
Tanḥuma (Buber)
3:9a 175
5 572
14 630
Exod., 127 140
Vayera 30 303
Zav a 146
Pesiqta Rabbati
14:11 590
17 809, 868
38 303
Pesiqta de Rab Kahana
4.5 555
4:7 270
26 633
26:9 611
58 1039
Pirqe Rab Eliezer
41 929
46 1020
53 590
Seder ʿOlam Rabbah 7 571
Yalqut
1,737 140
1,515 522

Post-Rabbinic Sources

Maimonides

Commentary on m. Yoma
8:6 370
"Daily offerings"
6.5 399
6.11 399
"Entry to the sanctuary"
1.15–16 612

2.5 610
5.18 528
"Forbidden foods"
1.21 665
1.22 665
7.5 210
11.5 754
"Forbidden sexual unions"
4.3 935
11.15 748
Guide
3.32 440, 1003
3.45 180
3.46.62–63 161
3.46.67–68 163
3.46 190
3.47 952
3.48 719, 737
"Impurity of scale disease"
1.2 773, 774
11.8 880
16.10 808, 823
Introduction to Seder
Qodoshim 365
"Manner of sacrifice"
3.15 221
8.1 404
8:14 406
10.1 638
On m. Menaḥ. 9:3 399
On m. Neg. 14:9 528
On m. neg. 11:11 814
"Tithe" 3.13 191
Seper Hammiṣwot, prohibi-
tion 73 612
Teshuvah, chaps 1–2 303
8.1 457
"Those lacking expiation"
1.1 1000

Codes

ʿAruk Hashulḥan, Yoreh
Deʿah 18:12 717
ʾOṣar Geonim, Hag.
11 935
Yoreh Deʿah
18:3 717
18:10 717
18:12 717
23.2 717
24:1 718
24:7 718
24:8 718
24:12 718
24:15 718

Other Post-Rabbinic Sources

Baraita Di Masseket
Niddah 915
13 765
17 765
David Luria on Leviticus
Rabbah 21:7 1048
Halevi 2.60 767
Hillel on Sipra, Aḥare
6:3 1048
Letters of R. Akiba in
Wertheimer
2.381 681
Maḥzor Vitry 606 754
Meiri on b. Yoma 54b 1032
Mishneh Kesep on Maim.,
"Manner of sacrifice"
8:14 406
Moshav Zeqenim 779
Tiferet Israel 238, 872
Ṭirat Kesef 757
Tosfot Yom Ṭov 238
Zohar, Aḥare 63:1 1020

Aramaic Sources

Cowley
30.18–21 630
30.21 181
30.25 181, 630
31.20 630
31.21 181
31.25 181, 630
31.27 218, 630
32.9–10 630
32.9 181
33.10–11 630
33.11 181
Sefire
1, A.32–33 349
1, A 35–40 348
1, A.21–24 349
1, B.2 349
1, B.11 349
1, B.30 349
Aḥiqar 137, line 54 294

Mesopotamian Sources

ABL
367.8 863
747, r. 6 191
Alalakh
126.15 174
126.19 174

AMT 79, line 15   1080
ARM
   2.13   539
   10.129   818
A2   765
B42   765
BAM 30 = LKA 136, lines
      12–13   1080
BBR 41–42, lines 21–
      28   1081
   212 nos. 96.3   960
   212 nos. 96.7   960
BL
   1.466–69   367
   2.41   338
BRM 4.18.22–24   1072
CH
   5.11–21, reverse 24.1–
      61   25
   6–13   329
   9   329, 367
   16:45   294
   21–23   329
   44.50–69   820
   65.0   338
   131   367
   253   336
   255   336
   259–60   329
   265   336
CT
   17, 1.5   1082
   17, 10–11, lines 68–
      87   1078
   21   777
   23, 1.4   1080
   27   777
   28, 29:8   1080
   41   777
EA
   51.4   518
   51.4–9   555
   280.25–29   57
Enuma Elish 3.134–38   612
Esarhaddon A 6.28–36   575
Eshnunna
   6   329
   12–13   329
   22   367
   37   367
   50   336
Gilgamesh 12.78–80   1072
Gudea Cyl
   A xxii   571
   B iii   571
   B vii, 26–43   569
   B xvii   569, 571
   B xvii 1–3   149
   B 2.21–6.10   575

B 2.21–3   588
II, 16–18   537
Statue B 5.7–9   337
Statue B IV.4   763
Harran Inscriptions of Na-
      bonidus 2.21–25   575
KAH 2.84.8   539
KAR
   33   1077
   72.3–5   1080
   92.10   1080
KUB 37, 210.8   1080
LKA 42.17   1082
MAL
   3–5   329
   47   367
   tablets C and G, 6a,
      9   329
Maqlu
   6.111–13   1031
   9.118–20   1031
MDP 2.109, vi. 41–
      vii.4   820
Šurpu
   2.5   349
   2.33   349
   2.79   349
Ur-Nammu Hymn, 39–
      51   588
VAT 8807 an assyrian
      tablet   650

Hittite Sources

KUB 4.32ff   152
"Instructions for Temple of-
      ficials"
   1.15   841
   1.21   653
   1.28–33   356
   1.34–37   355
   1.46–66   352
   1.46–49   353
   1.50–66   352
   1.59   353
   1.60–62   324
   1.64–66   353
   1.64–65   324
   2.1–3   324
   2.4–5   324
   2.4–11   352
   2.12   352
   2.12–58   352
   2.13–14   353
   2.13f   324
   2.18   324
   2.23–58   353
   2.31   352
   2.32–58   322

2.33–39   353
2.40–58   353
2.59–62   325
2.60–79   353
2.63–71   325
2.74–79   353
2.80–3.4   352
2.82ff   933
3.63–64   841
3.71–72   933
3.74–80   933
3.79–80   933
4.1f   323
4.1   352
4.1–10   353
4.3–11   353
4.12   322
4.12–24   353
4.17   322
4.25–33   353
4.25   322
4.34–43   353
4.34–39   353
4.56–77   353
4.56–68   353
4.58–66   324
KUB
   9.22.1.19–20   933
   9.22.3.29–32   933
   24.9 i 35–52   263
   24.9 i 21–25   264
   24.9 i 19–25   264
   29.7   264
   V, 7, obv. 34   676
   XIII, 4, iii, 64–68   676
AOAT supplement
   3.54   174
   3.206f., IV.50ʾf.   174
   3.212f. verso 1, 33   174
Ashella l. 8   1022
HBR²
   122–23   764
   157   744
   "B"   764
   "C"   764
   "K"   764
Hittite laws
   44b   263, 405
   45   329, 336
   66   329, 336
   71   329, 336
   75   367
   91–97   329
   101–12   329
   164   323
   166–67   447
   190   927
KBo
   17.65.32–36   750

IV1.i28–30 500
V. 1.9–11 174
V. 1.2–3 174
V. 5.6 677
XVII, 65, obv. 24–25 677
Papanikra
  1.1–3 688
  2.2–3 758
  4.37–40 688
Pulisa l. 25 1022
StBoT 3.24 175
Uhhamuwa ll. 4–5 1022
Ulippi 4.38–40 255

Greek Sources

Anabasis 7.8.4 651
Aristotle Hist. anim.
  7.3 751
Herodotus
  2.39 159
  2.47 212
  2.64 932, 951
  2.65 325
  2.81 809
  3.113 212
Iliad
  1.66–67 162
  1.316 162
  1.317 160
  1.449 963
  4.750–52 963
  6.266–68 963
  6.171–72 963
  9.214 191
  9.497–500 162
  24.305 963
Josephus
  Antiquities
    1.323 751
    3.9.3 344
    3.26a 920
    3.157–58 520
    3.172–78 512
    3.207 590
    3.225 172
    3.226 154
    3.227 192
    3.230 253
    3.231 402, 418
    3.231–32 626
    3.233–34 390
    3.234 189
    3.240–42 1048
    3.243 1032, 1033,
      1035, 1036
    3.250–51 192
    3.257 396, 397, 400
    3.261–62 995, 998

  3.261 34, 277, 765,
    907, 949, 971, 995,
    998
  3.262 971
  3.264 805, 819, 842,
    983
  4.8 448
  4.11 448
  6.235 931
  8.123 593
  12.140 191
  18.36–38 275
  20.166–67 350
Con. Ap.
  1.31 983
  1.281 805
  2.202–3 928
Wars
  2.8 767
  2.8.6 312
  2.9 767
  2.147 915
  2.425 158
  2.430 387
  4.468 189
  5.4, 4 168
  5.5.5 1031, 1070
  5.218 237
  5.227 34, 920
  5.273 907
  6.426 907
  6.93–111 350
Letter of Aristeas
  146 720
  151–52 726
  153–54 719
LSC 115A 16–20 763
Odyssey
  3.440 963
  24.215 221
Pausanias 5.15.6 189
Philo
  Dec. 84 312
  Fug. 59 604, 634
  Her. 251 591
    309 604, 634
  Laws
    1.23 344
    1.72 1028
    1.100 617
    1.145 432
    1.151 411
    1.166 147
    1.188 1048
    1.198 153
    1.199 154
    1.200 147
    1.205 156
    1.212 220

  1.224 413
  1.225 365
  1.226 253
  1.231 233
  1.235 303, 335
  1.240 402, 418, 626
  1.249 279, 357
  1.271 195
  1.286 389
  1.289 191
  1.202–4 151
  1.235–38 371
  1.255–56 396
  2.26 294, 295, 348
  2.26–28 294
  2.57–58 604, 634
  3.15 945
  3.63 928, 929, 932, 998
  3.205 309, 929
  4.2 335
  4.31–32 365
  4.34 347
  4.116–18 719
Plant. 61 1045
Som.
  2.6–7 634, 635
  2.67 604
  2.296 301
Virt.
  134 741
  143 741
  143–44 739
  144 742
Vit. Mos.
  2.147 522
  2.148 526
  2.153 571
  2.154 590
Plato 1970: Par. 909 220
Plutarch, Qaest. Rom
  109 189
Thucydides 3.104 763

Ugaritic Sources

1 Aqhat 1.42–43 571
1 Aqht 62 571
1 krt 68 528
1 krt 75–76 587
1 krt 161 528

CTA

Appendix II (pp. 136–
    38).22 218
  1.4.30 154, 716
  2.1.14–31 141
  2.3.4–5 141
  3.5.13–16 141

4.4.20–26 139, 141
4.6.40 154, 716
6.1.18–28 154, 716
6.1.32–36 141
16.6 [127] 35, 51   746
16.6.17 716
16.6.20 716
17.2.29 154, 716
17.6.46–48 141
19.62 195
20.1.1, 10 714
22.2.12 154, 716
23.14 738
32.24, 32 714
33.3 415
34.8 220
35.3 520
35.6–7 520, 848
35.17 220
35.20–21 218
35.44–45 848
35.44 520
35.46 520, 848
36.10 520, 848
61.18–29 723
167.6.17,20 154
310.3–5 154

CTH
391, II, lines 34–52   1075
394 1074
398, II, lines 5–14   1076
404, III, lines 14–16   1076
407 1073
409, III, lines 17–42   1076
410 1075
489 677

KTU
1.1.4.30 716
1.2.3.4–5 141
1.2.14–31 141
1.3.5.5–8 141
1.4.4.20–26 139
1.4.4.20–24 141
1.4.6.40 154, 716
1.6.1.32–36 141
1.6.1.18–28 154, 716
1.10 686
1.14.30 154
1.14 761
1.16 746
1.16.6.17 154, 716
1.16.6.20 154, 716
1.17.2.29 154, 716
1.17.6.46–48 141
1.19.2.13 195
1.19 761
1.20.1.1, 10 714
1.22.1.12 154
1.22.2.12 716

1.23.18 738
1.23.33 921
1.23.34 921
1.23.35 921
1.39.8 220
1.40.24, 32 714
1.41[= 1.87] 758
1.41.3 520
1.41.6–7 520, 848
1.41.17 220
1.41.44 520
1.41.46 520, 848
1.41.20–21 218
1.41.44–45 848
1.46.10 520, 848
1.87.2 218
1.106.27 848
1.112.11 848
1.112.16–17 848
1.115 758
1.119.5 848
1.148.21 846
2.24 686
3.152 761
5.10 758
5.13 758
5.21 758
5.36 758
5.43 758
5.217 761
PRU 3.93 432
PRU 1956:4.293, no.
        19.55 196
RS
  32.124.26ʾ–32ʾ 855
  61/24.277.9 305
  435 411
Ugaritica 6:168 305
UT
  ʿnt pl.x.iv.30 716
  ʿnt pl.x.4.30 154
  ʿnt 5.13–16 141
  1.8 220, 484
  2.24, 32 714
  2 Aqht 2.29 154, 716
  2 Aqht 6.4647 141
  2.1.14 145
  2.1.18 145
  3.3 520
  3.6–7 520
  3.17 220
  3.44 520
  3.46 520, 848
  3.6–7 848
  3.20–21 218
  3.44–45 848
  9.10 520, 848
  24.12 154
  49.1.18 397

49.1.38 397
49.1.39 397
49.1.4–8 141
51.3.15 397
51.3.16 397
51.4.20–24 141
51.4.20–26 139
51.6.40 154, 397, 716
52.14 738
62.1.18–28 154, 716
67, 5.8–9 571
75, 2.45–46 571
76.2.22–23 553
120.1 196
120.4 196
121.1.1, 10 714
124.12 716
125.44 145
127.17 154, 716
127.20 154, 716
128, 4.6–7 571
129.3.4–5 141
137.14–31 141
137.28 196
173.4 520
173.7 520
173.22 218
173.49 520
173.51 520
173.55 520
423 339
611.9–10 173
612.9–10 218
613.15–16 218
1001.3 207
1131.5 484
1131.6 484
1131.7 484
1131.9 484
1153.3–5 154, 716

Punic Sources

Marseilles Tariff 173, 304,
        802
Sabean
  CIH 523.8 928
  CIH 523; lines 6–7 935

Egyptian Sources

Book of the Dead
  chap. 112 651
  161.11f 144
Pyramid Texts, 376–78 238

Hindu Sources

Gautama Dharmasastra
    1.34 674
Manu
  2.181 932
  4.40–41 952
  5.39 681
  5.58 764
  5.63 932
  5.66 935
  5.85 935
  5.85–86 952
  5.115 674
  5.122–23 676
  5.138ff 767
  5.144 932
  11.121–23 932
Vas. 5.59 676
Visnusmṛti
  23.1–5 674
  23n6 814

Persian Sources

Vend. 17.11ff 767

Latin Sources

Cicero, De haruspicum responso 11.23 512
Clem. Alex. Strom. 7, p. 716 Col 212
Diog. Laert. Pythat. 19[8.35] 191
Dioscorides, De materia medica
  1.73 1027
  1.79 1028
  2.10 1026
  3.97 1026
Heliod. 4.16 191
Hippocrates, De natura pueri, chap 17 751
Lucian, De Syria Dea
  14.34 191
  2.62 979
  2.682 564
Origen Lev. Hom.
  8.10 840
Pliny, H. N.
  12.25 1027
  12.40 1028
  12.55 1028
  12.61 1026
  12.68 1027
  12.81 1028
  12.124 1028
  12.126 1026

31.9 [45] 191
31.14[48] 189
Schol. ad Aristoph. Pac
  1052 212
Servius ad Aeneid
  4.696 512
  6.176 979

Other Sources

Ancient Near Eastern Texts, ed. James Pritchard, 3d ed.
  6 329
  7 329
  7a 528
  20a 737
  24 159
  27–29 361
  33a 951
  33b l.41 19
  33b l.337 19
  34–36 230, 361
  66 612
  98 1072
  102 l.62 962
  108 l.38 962
  109b 841
  165 25
  168 25
  179b 820
  180a 820
  207–10 322, 352, 933
  207–11 349
  207 330, 653
  207a 752
  207b 841
  207 l.24 962
  207 III, l. 63 962
  207 III, ll. 69–85 962
  207–8, I, ll. 20–22 650
  207–8, III, ll. 65–69 650
  207–8, III, ll. 60–61 650
  208, ll. 35–38 459
  209 674, 962
  209, ll. 600–18 459
  209, III, ll. 21–24 52
  209, III, ll. 18–30 259
  209b 752
  209d 676
  325–41 19
  325 256
  331–41 960
  329–30 256
  331–34 256
  331–34 ll. 33–35 53
  331–34 ll. 190–95 53
  331–34 ll. 201–8 53
  331–34 ll. 353–63 53

331b 951
332–34 1067
332a 951
332b l 279 19
333 1052
333 ll. 364–65 979
334–38 257
334 25, 568
335 835
335a 412
335a ll. II, 14 19
336 143
336a 53, 412
338–39 257
338 528
338b 412
338b l 33 19
339, A17 302
339a 951
339b ll. 6, 13 19
340 ll. 51–62 302
340, A rev. 24 302
340b l 6 19
343 412
344 456
346 256, 264
347b 1075
348a 1075
350–51 230, 832
351–53 256
352a l 32 19
353f 349
356 500
357 256
358 256
358b ll. 39–44 19
359–60, II, ll. 11–12, 16–18 962
359–60, IV. ll. 1–2 962
359–60, VI, ll. 18–22 962
360–61 412
360a ll. 36–40 19
361b ll. 29–30 19
371b ll. 2–3 19
373a XIV.3 19
391–92 361
391 349, 361
391 ll. 18–29 302
391 ll. 19–29 302
395 350, 1066
395 ll. 9–10 302
396–99 197
397–98 201, 628
399–400 197
400 349
400, ll. 12–14 313
497d 676
527 329
531 329

INDEX OF SOURCES

532–33 556
538 364
550 364
556 588
560 259
568 814
502–3 402, 411
647–51 349, 350
656–57 304, 862
665a 311
665 763, 932, 935, 951
665 ll. 6–7 928
CIS
    1.165 173

1.167.5 173
165 304, 411
167.2–5 411
3915.2 173
DISO zbh III 154
KAI
    69.12 218
    74.10 218
    74.9 218
Koran 2:222 951
Lachish
    2 1020
    15 1020
    17 1020

19 1020
20 1020
22 1020
23 1020
24 1020
25 1020
26–31 1020
Samaria Ostrica 34–
    38 1020
The Twelve Steps of Alco-
    holics
        Anonymous 374